Peterson's Scholarships, Grants & Prizes 2014

About Peterson's

Peterson's provides the accurate, dependable, high-quality education content and guidance you need to succeed. No matter where you are on your academic or professional path, you can rely on Peterson's print and digital publications for the most up-to-date education exploration data, expert test-prep tools, and top-notch career success resources—everything you need to achieve your goals.

Visit us online at **www.petersonsbooks.com** and let Peterson's help you achieve your goals.

For more information, contact Peterson's, 3 Columbia Circle, Suite 205, Albany, NY 12203-5158; 800-338-3282 Ext. 54229; or find us on the World Wide Web at www.petersonsbooks.com.

By producing this book on recycled paper (40% post-consumer waste) 284 trees were saved.

Sustainability—Its Importance to Peterson's

What does sustainability mean to Peterson's? As a leading publisher, we are aware that our business has a direct impact on vital resources—most especially the trees that are used to make our books. Peterson's is proud that its products are certified by the Sustainable Forestry Initiative (SFI) chain-of-custody standard and that all of its books are printed on paper that is 40% post-consumer waste using vegetable-based ink.

Being a part of the Sustainable Forestry Initiative (SFI) means that all of our vendors—from paper suppliers to printers—have undergone rigorous audits to demonstrate that they are maintaining a sustainable environment.

Peterson's continuously strives to find new ways to incorporate sustainability throughout all aspects of its business.

OTHER RECOMMENDED TITLES

Peterson's The Best Scholarships for the Best Sudents
Peterson's The "C" Students Guide to Scholarships
Peterson's How to Get Money for College: Financing Your Future Beyond Federal Aid

Contents

CONTENTS

A Note from the Peterson's Editors

Billions of dollars in financial aid are made available by private donors and governmental agencies to students and their families every year to help pay for college. Yet, to the average person, the task of finding financial aid awards in this huge network of scholarships, grants, and prizes appears to be nearly impossible.

For nearly forty years, Peterson's has given students and parents the most comprehensive, up-to-date information on how to get their fair share of the financial aid pie. *Peterson's Scholarships, Grants & Prizes* was created to help students and their families pinpoint those specific private financial aid programs that best match students' backgrounds, interests, talents, or abilities.

In *Peterson's Scholarships, Grants & Prizes,* you will find more than 3,600 award programs and resources that are providing financial awards to undergraduates in the 2013–14 academic year. Foundations, fraternal and ethnic organizations, community service clubs, churches and religious groups, philanthropies, companies and industry groups, labor unions and public employees' associations, veterans' groups, and trusts and bequests are all possible sources.

For those seeking to enter college, *Peterson's Scholarships, Grants & Prizes* includes information needed to make financing a college education as seamless as possible.

The **How to Find an Award That's Right for You** section paints a complete picture of the financial aid landscape, discusses strategies for finding financial awards, provides important tips on how to avoid scholarship scams, and offers insight into how to make scholarship management organizations work for you.

Also found in **How to Find an Award That's Right for You** is the "How to Use This Guide" article, which describes how the more than 3,600 awards in the guide are profiled, along with information on how to search for an award in one of eleven categories.

If you would like to compare awards quickly, refer to the **Quick-Reference Chart.** Here you can search through the "Scholarships, Grants & Prizes At-a-Glance" chart and select awards by the highest dollar amount.

In the **Profiles of Scholarships, Grants & Prizes** section you'll find updated award programs, along with information about award sponsors. The profile section is divided into three categories: *Academic Fields/Career Goals, Nonacademic/Noncareer Criteria,* and *Miscellaneous Criteria.* Each profile provides all of the need-to-know information about available scholarships, grants, and prizes.

Finally, the back of the book features thirteen **Indexes** listing scholarships, grants, and prizes based on award name; sponsor; academic fields/career goals; civic, professional, social, or union affiliation; corporate affiliation; employment/volunteer experience; impairment; military service; nationality or ethnic background; religious affiliation; residence; location of study; and talent/interest area.

At the end of this book, don't miss the ads placed by Peterson's preferred clients. Their financial support helps make it possible for Peterson's Publishing to continue to provide you with the highest-quality test-prep, educational exploration, and career-preparation resources you need to succeed on your educational journey.

Peterson's publishes a full line of books—financial aid, career preparation, test prep, and education exploration. Peterson's publications can be found at high school guidance offices, college libraries and career centers, and your local bookstore and library. Peterson's books are now also available as eBooks and online at www.petersonsbooks.com.

We welcome any comments or suggestions you may have about this publication. Your feedback will help us make educational dreams possible for you—and others like you.

HOW TO FIND AN AWARD THAT'S RIGHT FOR YOU

All About Scholarships

Dr. Gary M. Bell
Academic Dean, Honors College, Texas Tech University

During the next four (or more) years you will spend earning your college baccalaureate degree, think of the learning task as your primary employment. It is helpful to think of a scholarship as part of the salary for undertaking your job of learning. One of your first inquiries as you examine a potential college setting is about the type of assistance it might provide given your interests, academic record, and personal history. Talk to a financial aid officer or a scholarship coordinator at the school. At most schools, these are special officers—people specifically employed to assist you in your quest for financial assistance. Virtually all schools also have brochures or publications that list scholarship opportunities at their institution. Get this literature and read it carefully.

Also, visit your local bookstore or public library for books that have several hundred scholarships listed in different categories. These books are inexpensive and can be found in the reference section.

Last, high school counselors often have keen insight into resources available at colleges, especially for the schools in your area. These people are the key points of contact between institutions of higher education and you.

In general, it is not a good idea to use a private company that promises to provide you with a list of scholarships for which you might be eligible. Such lists are often very broad, and you can secure the same results by using available high school, university, web-based, and published information. The scholarship search you perform online will probably be more fruitful than what any private company can do for you.

What do we mean by the word "scholarship," anyway? In the very broadest sense, scholarships consist of outright grants of monetary assistance to eligible students to help them attend college. The money is applied to tuition or the cost of living while in school. Scholarships do not need to be repaid. They do, however, often carry stringent criteria for maintaining them, such as the achievement of a certain grade point average, the carrying of a given number of class hours, matriculation in a specific program, or membership in a designated group. Scholarships at many schools may be combined with college work-study programs, in which some work is also required. Often, scholarships are combined with other forms of financial aid so that collectively they provide you with a truly attractive financial aid package. This may include low-interest loan programs to make the school of your choice financially feasible.

Scholarships generally fall into three major categories: *need-based scholarships*, predicated on income; *merit-based scholarships*, based on your academic and sometimes extracurricular achievements; and *association-based scholarships*, which are dependent on as many different associations as you can imagine (for instance, your home county, your identification with a particular group, fraternal and religious organizations, or the company for which a parent may work). The range of reasons for which scholarships are given is almost infinite.

Most schools accommodate students who have financial need. The largest and best grant programs are the U.S. government-sponsored Federal Pell Grants and the Federal Supplemental Educational Opportunity Grants, which you might want to explore with your financial aid counselor. Also inquire about state-sponsored scholarship and grant programs.

Merit-based scholarships come from a variety of sources—the university, individual departments or colleges within the university, state scholarship programs, or special donors who want to assist worthy students. Remember this as you meet with your financial aid officer, because he or she knows that different opportunities may be available for you as a petroleum engineering, agriculture, accounting, pre-veterinary, or performing arts major. Merit-based scholarships are typically designed to reward the highest performers on such precollege measures as standardized tests (the SAT or ACT) and high school grades. Because repeated performance on standardized tests often leads to higher scores, it may be financially advantageous for you to take these college admission tests several times.

Inquire about each of the three categories of scholarships. The association-based scholarships can sometimes be particularly helpful and quite surprising. Employers of parents, people from specific geographic locations, or organizations (churches, civic groups, unions, special interest clubs, and even family name associations) may provide assistance for college students. Campus scholarship literature is the key to unlocking the mysteries of association-based financial assistance (and the other two categories as well), but personal interviews with financial officers are also crucial.

There are several issues to keep in mind as you seek scholarship assistance. Probably the most important is to determine deadlines that apply to a scholarship for which you may be eligible. It's wise to begin your search early, so that your eligibility is not nullified by missing a published deadline. Most scholarship opportunities require that you complete an application form, and it is time well spent to make sure your answers are neat (if using a paper application), grammatically correct, and logical. Correct spelling is essential. Have someone proofread your application. Keep in mind that if applications require essays, fewer students typically take the time to complete these essays, and this gives those students who do so a better chance of winning that particular scholarship. Always be truthful in these applications, but at the same time provide the most positive self-portrayal to enhance your chances of being considered. Most merit-based and association-based scholarships are awarded competitively.

Finally, let the people who offer you assistance know whether you will accept their offer. Too many students simply assume that a scholarship offer means automatic acceptance. This is not the case! In most instances, you must send a letter of acknowledgement and acceptance.

Virtually all schools have agreed that students must make up their minds about scholarship acceptance no later than May 1, but earlier deadlines may apply.

As you probably know, tuition at private schools is typically higher than tuition at state colleges and universities. Scholarships can narrow this gap. Many private institutions have a great deal of money to spend on scholarship assistance, so you may find that with a scholarship, going to a private college will cost no more than attending a state-supported college or university. **Note:** A substantial scholarship from a private school may still leave you with a very large annual bill to cover the difference between the scholarship amount and the actual cost of tuition, fees, and living expenses.

When you evaluate a scholarship, take into account your final out-of-pocket costs. Also consider the length of time for which the school extends scholarship support. Be cautious about schools that promise substantial assistance for the first year to get you there, but then provide little or nothing in subsequent years. The most attractive and meaningful scholarships are offered for four to five years. Do not abandon the scholarship search once you are enrolled at the school of your choice. Often, a number of additional scholarship opportunities are available for you once you're enrolled, especially as you prove your ability and interest in a given field.

It's Never Too Early to Look for College Scholarships

Many high school students make the mistake of thinking that their race to the top of the scholarship mountain begins during their senior year. Some have the forethought to begin their hunt for college money in their junior year. But even that may be too late. Rising costs of college tuition, the increasing number of people attending college for the first time, and the reduction in federal, state, and local grants for college goers have made paying for college without student loan debt a competitive sport. And only those who are prepared are coming out unscathed and debt free.

The importance of securing scholarships and grants to help pay for college cannot be overestimated. The nation is currently in the midst of a student-loan debt crisis that is crippling the earning power of millions of college graduates. If you need any further convincing to get serious about finding money for college other than student loans, check out these sobering statistics:*

- In 2010, college students borrowed more than $100 billion to pay for college, the highest amount of student borrowing ever.

- In 2012, the outstanding balance of student loan debt reached nearly $1 trillion (yes, that's with a "T"), surpassing credit card debt of $693 billion.

- Nearly every student who earns a four-year degree graduates with student loan debt, which currently averages about $23,300.

- Americans age 60 or older collectively own more than $36 billion in student loan debt. (Senior citizen debt includes co-signing student loan debt as well as incurring their own debt while going to school later in life.)

Student loan debt may be inevitable, but it doesn't have to be crippling. And the more money you can get that doesn't require repayment, the better your financial future will be once you do get your college degree. Here are some tips on how to get ahead of the college money rat race and come out a winner:

1. **Make a Family College Payment Plan**. While 70 percent of parents surveyed by an investment group said their students are so brilliant that they will win enormous amounts of scholarships to pay for college, the reality is paying for college without student loans doesn't happen by chance. Paying for college takes planning, and the sooner you begin the better off you'll be. But a student cannot plan for college payments alone. Parents must meet with their children to develop a college payment plan. In their discussions, they need to discuss all family college payment plan options, including parental tax credits, college saving accounts, trusts, savings bonds, and even stock options. At the meeting, parents and their children should do the following:
   - Calculate the real costs of attending college.
   - Decide who is going to pay and how much.
   - Develop a strategy to meet those payment commitments.

   Making a family college payment plan is an essential first step. The outcome of this plan gives students a clear scholarship money goal and provides an excellent starting point for your scholarship sojourn.

2. **Start scholarship research on day one**. While most scholarships and grants require you to be a junior or senior in high school, this does not preclude you from creating an application strategy the day you enter high school—or even before! In truth, the minute you decide to go to college you should start researching the best ways to pay for it. Talk to guidance counselors, do research online, learn what the scholarship requirements are, and develop a plan to apply when ready. By searching for scholarships as early as possible, you will be able to zero in on the ones that match with your skills, abilities, characteristics, and passions. In addition to finding scholarships, use this preliminary time to learn the scholarship rules. Build a checklist of all the accompanying documents you're going to need to accompany your scholarship application. Save items

---

* All statistics are derived from the Federal Reserve Bank of New York as well as its report "Grading Student Loans." http://libertystreeteconomics.newyorkfed.org/2012/03/grading-student-loans.html

that you think would work well in your personal statement or essay. Develop a list of people who could be references or write letters of recommendations. Organize, organize, organize—the more organized you are, the easier it will be to apply for multiple scholarships.

3. **Be Your Guidance Counselor's Best Friend.** Long the butt of jokes, guidance counselors are the most maligned members of a high school system. But they can be your best ally when it comes to securing scholarships and grants for college. Get to know your guidance counselor well. Offer your counselor a proactive strategy for getting money for college. Your guidance counselor is more apt to help you with planning your high school career if he or she knows you are serious about going to college.

4. **Rack up scholarships as you go along.** College savings bonds may seem like a blast from the 1950s, but believe it or not there are still essay, speech, and music contests all over the nation that offer them to winners. You can earn these types of rewards as well as cold hard cash at anytime—even before you even get into high school. Check out contests such as the Ayn Rand Institute's Anthem and Atlas Shrugged Essay Contests, or the American Legion National High School Oratorical Contest. These are open to all high school-age students.

5. **Plan Your High School Years with College in Mind.** As you do your research on college scholarships, you will see that many have academic requirements. You need to start early on developing a course of study to help you hit those necessary academic marks. Few students wake up one day and score 31 on the ACT or start a charity out of the blue. So plan your classes, extracurricular events, and charity activities with college in mind. To be sure, you need to do what appeals to you, but keep in mind that every class you attend, every test you take, and every club you join can be an asset to your scholarship hunt. Be deliberate about your school choices, and start with the end goal in mind.

Filling out a scholarship application is the end, not the beginning of a long process to earn money for college. Fortunately, you can begin all the organization and planning necessary to secure scholarship money well before the scholarship is due. Do not wait. It's never too early to start your scholarship journey. The earlier you begin, the better your journey will be!

A Strategy for Finding Awards

Private scholarships and awards can be characterized by unpredictable, sometimes seemingly bizarre, criteria. Before you begin your award search, write a personal profile of yourself to help establish as many criteria as possible that might form a basis for your scholarship award. Here is a basic checklist of fifteen questions you should consider:

1. **What are your career goals?**

   Be both narrow and broad in your designations. If, for example, you aim to be a TV news reporter, you will find many awards specific to this field in the *TV/Radio Broadcasting* section. However, collegiate broadcasting courses are offered in departments or schools of communication. So, be sure that you consider *Communications* as a relevant section for your search. Consider *Journalism,* too, for the same reasons. Then look under other broadly inclusive but possibly relevant areas, such as *Trade/Technical Specialties.* Or check a related but different field, such as *Performing Arts.* Finally, look under marginally related basic academic fields, such as *Humanities, Social Sciences,* or *Political Science.* Peterson's makes every attempt to provide the best cross-reference aids, but the nuances of specific awards can be difficult to capture even with the most flexible cross-referencing systems. You will need to be broadly associative in your thinking to get the most out of this wealth of information.

   If you have no clear career goal, browsing the huge variety of academic/career awards may well spark new interest in a career path. Be open to imagining yourself filling different career roles that you previously may not have considered.

2. **In what academic fields might you major?**

   Your educational experiences or your sense about your personal talents or interests may have given you a good idea of what academic discipline you wish to pursue. Again, use both broad and narrow focuses in designing your search, and look at related subject fields. For example, if you want to major in history, check the *History* section, but be sure to check out *Social Sciences* and *Humanities* as well, and maybe *Area/Ethnic Studies. Education,* for example, could suggest the perfect scholarship for a future historian.

3. **In which jobs, industries, or occupations have your parents or other members of your immediate family been employed? What employment experiences do you have?**

   Individual companies, employee organizations, trade unions, government agencies, and industry associations frequently establish scholarships for workers, children of workers, or other relatives of workers from specific companies or industries. These awards might require that you stay in the same career field, but most are offered regardless of the field of study you wish to undertake. Also, if one of your parents is a public service employee, especially a firefighter or police officer, you have many relevant awards from which to choose.

4. **Do you have any hobbies or special interests? Have you ever been an officer or leader of a group? Do you possess special skills or talents? Have you won any competitions? Are you a good writer?**

   From gardening to clarinet playing, from caddying to playing basketball, your special interests can win awards for you from groups that wish to promote and/or reward these pursuits. Many scholarships are targeted to "student leaders," including sports team captains; yearbook or newspaper editors; student government officers; and club, organization, and community activists.

5. **Where do you live? Where have you lived? Where will you go to college?**

   Residence criteria are among the most common qualifications for scholarship aid. Local clubs and companies provide millions of dollars in scholarship aid to students who live in a particular state, province, region, or section of a state. This means that your residential identity puts you at the head of the line for these grants. State of residence can—depending on the sponsor's criteria—include the place of your official residence, the place you attend college, the place you were born, or anywhere you have lived for more than a year.

6. **What is your family's ethnic heritage?**

   Hundreds of scholarships have been endowed for students who can claim a particular nationality or racial or ethnic descent. Partial ethnic descent frequently qualifies, so don't be put off if you do not think of your identity as a specific "ethnic" entity. Awards are available for Colonial American,

English, Polish, Welsh, Scottish, European, and other backgrounds that students may not consider especially "ethnic." One is even available for descendants of the signers of the Declaration of Independence, whatever ethnicity that might have turned out to be some ten generations later.

7. **Do you have a physical disability?**
   Many awards are available to individuals with physical disabilities. Of course, commonly recognized impairments of mobility, sight, communication, and hearing are recognized, but learning disabilities and chronic diseases, such as asthma and epilepsy, are also criteria for some awards.

8. **Do you currently or have you ever served in the Armed Forces? Did one of your parents serve in a war? Was one of your parents lost or disabled while serving in the Armed Forces?**
   Hundreds of awards use these qualifications.

9. **Do you belong to a civic association, union, or religious organization? Do your parents belong to such groups?**
   Hundreds of clubs and religious groups provide scholarship assistance to members or children of members.

10. **Are you male or female?**

11. **What is your age?**

12. **Do you qualify for need-based aid?**

13. **Did you graduate in the upper one-half, upper one-third, or upper one-quarter of your class?**

14. **Do you plan to attend a two-year college, a four-year college, or a trade/technical school?**

15. **In what academic year will you be entering?**

Be expansive when considering your possible qualifications. Although some awards may be small, you may qualify for more than one award—and these can add up to significant amounts in the end.

Who Wants to Be a College Scholarship Millionaire?

There are high school seniors around the country who are becoming rich beyond their wildest dreams even before stepping inside the hallowed halls of higher education. These college upstarts are not start-up kings and queens, á la Mark Zuckerberg of Facebook fame. But they may be just as innovative. They're a part of small, but growing, elite—the College Scholarship Millionaire Club.

The concept of earning a million dollars for college sounds like the premise of a television game show. And to be honest, such a goal remains incredibly lofty for some and downright impossible for others. But what was once a fantasy of every would-be college student is now fast becoming a reality for those willing to work incredibly hard to make it happen.

So just what is the College Scholarship Millionaire Club? It's a group of students who have won $1 million or more in scholarship commitments from universities and colleges and private scholarship funds. The definition should clue you in on at least one prerequisite for joining this club—you have to apply for scholarships—A LOT OF THEM. Still, a quick analysis of some college scholarship millionaires and how they secured their awards can offer any pre-college student great advice on how to get the most out of their scholarship application season.

While there is no sure-fire way to ensure that you earn big bucks in the college scholarship process— anyone promising that is just running a scam—there are steps you can take to increase your odds of having a big scholarship haul. Here are some valuable tips:

Make High-Achieving a Group Sport

More than a decade ago James Ralph Sparks, a calculus teacher at Whitehaven High School (WHS), in Memphis, Tennessee, wanted to find a way to get more of his students into college. Back in 2002, the public school located on Elvis Presley Blvd., wasn't exactly known for its academic aptitude. Back then, graduating seniors were bringing in less than $5 million in scholarship offers for the entire school. But Sparks felt the school could do better. So he created a competition. The 30+ club was the first weapon in the battle to get students more money for

college there was only one criterion for membership: a score of 30 or higher on the ACT. By encouraging students to score high on the national standardize test, Sparks ensured that his students would be in the running for top scholarships. Students who achieved entrance into the club had their scholarship offer letters and scores posted on bulletin boards in the school.

But Sparks wasn't finished. He created the Fortune 500 club, providing exclusive membership only to students who could achieve more than $100,000 in scholarships. The combination of the 30+ club and the Fortune 500 club helped to spur students to achieve. The WHS graduating senior class brought in more than $30 million in scholarship offers in 2010–11.

Apply, Apply, and Apply Again

Another facet of the Whitehaven High School's scholarship program was playing the odds. Anyone who has guided students through a college scholarship application understands that the process can become a numbers game. The more applications you complete, the better your chances of securing a scholarship. While the average high school student applies for two to three scholarships, WHS' millionaire club members applied for ten times that number—about thirty or forty.

Become a Super College Candidate

By now everyone applying to college knows you have to do more than get good grades to stand out. If you want to rise to the top of the scholarship heap, you're going to have to be extraordinary. You can't just volunteer at your local soup kitchen—that's a given. You might have to start your *own* soup kitchen to be considered above your peers. To be a part of the million-dollar scholarship club, you're going to have to go above and beyond to pull down that six-figure college gift.

So let's break down what it takes to be a million-dollar scholar:

- **Start early.** It's never too early to research scholarship opportunities as well as plan your scholarship strategy. Practice writing your personal statement, essay, interviewing skills, and so on to get yourself acquainted with the scholarship process.

- **Make applying a group sport.** Everyone loves a good competition, and it seems earning scholarship money is no exception. At Whitehaven High School, teachers publicly list the scholarship earnings of students with more than $100,000. WHS also has a scoreboard in front of its school that highlights scholarship amounts, not just football scores.

- **Don't forget the academics.** Many scholarships have an academic threshold, so you want to make sure to get above that to open more opportunities. Generally, a 30 or higher on the ACT and a 1300 or more on the SAT are good baselines to put you in the scholarship category.

- **Keep Your Options Open.** There are critics who say that applying for scholarships you have no intention of using is not appropriate. But how do you know where you want to go until you figure out how to pay for it? Don't pigeon-hole yourself into one option. If you don't get your first-choice, you'll at least have something to fall back upon.

- **Be sincere.** You may think it's all about the numbers, but you become a million-dollar scholar through authenticity not fakery. Apply to scholarships that fit your passion, purpose, and educational prowess. And apply to schools you actually want to attend. Applying for scholarships and grants take time, and you don't want to waste it on pipe dreams.

Tweeting for Dollars: Use Your Fingertips and Social Media to Pay for College

Felecia Hatcher
Author of *The C Student's Guide to Scholarships*

The biggest question you may have right now is where do I find the money? What if I told you that you could find thousands of scholarship dollars and opportunities by using your cell phone and your thumbs!

It's said that over 1 billion dollars in scholarships goes un-awarded each year. You may think that this money is being hidden on purpose. I promise you that colleges and scholarship committees are not trying to hide the money from you; they are actually starting to use social media to get the information directly to you. Currently, there are thousands of social media sites on the Internet, and these sites could possibly bring you one step closer to paying for college. Keep reading to find out how you can use social media and crowd funding sites to get creative with your search—and not only think outside the box but also think outside the application.

TWITTER™

Twitter allows you to get short messages of 140 characters or less in real time. The one thing that is great about Twitter is that it has a search bar that allows you to search for tweets from anyone or any entity that belongs to the social network. By using special keywords in the search bar, you should be able to find scholarship information and direct links to scholarship applications, about which the scholarship organizations have tweeted.

Go to the search bar in Twitter and type in the following keywords:

"Scholarship Deadline"
"Scholarshi+[Your State]"
"Scholarship PDF"
"Scholarship Deadline http"

GOOGLE IT!

I jokingly tell people that I feel like I can rule the world with my iPhone and Google. Need a restaurant recommendation? Google it! Need to research the best place to get school supplies for a project? Google it! Need to find money for your college? Google it! Yes, believe it or not, it may be just that simple. But in order to not be bombarded with thousands of useless results, you must use the right keywords. Here is a short list of some keyword combinations that will yield some great results in your scholarship search.

You can use the same search terms previously used for your Twitter searches for Google as well as the following:

Scholarship+2013
Scholarship+2014
Scholarship+Deadline+Current Month
Scholarship+[Your City]
Scholarship+[your race/ethnicity/religion]
Scholarship+[Your Talent]

You can also replace the word "Scholarship" with grant or fellowship.

CROWD FUNDING

So, you applied but didn't win that big $25,000 scholarship. Don't despair—put the power of your network of family, friends, and social media follower to work, and create your own scholarship through crowd funding! With crowd funding, you can get 5,000 strangers to donate $5 each, which equals $25,000 … right? No, I'm not talking about standing on a busy corner and playing your guitar. Websites like Paypal.com, Indiegogo.com, YouCaring.com, and PeerBackers.com allow you to reach out to your friends and family or total strangers; pitch your need through a profile, pictures, and compelling video; and creatively fundraise your way to funding your college education.

TIPS TO HELP YOU MAXIMIZE YOUR CHANCES OF GETTING FUNDING

Tell a Compelling Story: Scholarship committees know that you need money, that's a given. But you want to captivate the committee with an exciting story that will keep them reading and opening up their wallets with each word. Tell them who you are and what makes you and your needs different from other students. Most importantly, tell them why they should care enough to part with their money. Get Creative!

Create an exciting profile: Photos and video go a long way when you are creating profiles on crowd funding sites or even on an application that asks for additional information. Take the time to capture great pictures that really let your personality shine. There are an increasing number of applications asking for video submissions. This is your time to shine, so take out your camera and start shooting testimonials from teachers, coaches, and guidance counselors raving about how fabulous you are instead of (or in addition to) submitting the traditional recommendation letter. Pictures and video paint the best picture and make the need *real*.

Don't be afraid to ask for help: Let me put it frankly, the truth is you only get what you ask for! Networks like Facebook®, Twitter, LinkedIn, and YouCaring.com allow you to amplify your message, so put the message out there. If you don't ask for the help and let everyone know, then you can't expect anyone to help you.

So, the next time your parents tell you to get off Facebook or Twitter or to put down your phone, tell them that you are tweeting or searching for scholarship dollars.

CLEAN UP YOUR ACT: SPRUCE UP YOUR INTERNET AND SOCIAL MEDIA PRESENCE

Social media is a huge part of today's social realm. There is a good chance that you probably communicate with your friends on Facebook and Twitter more then you do in person. While these social networks are great for connecting with friends and family, and even meeting new people, they can hurt your scholarship efforts if you are not careful. Having this information in mind, set aside some time before, or directly after, you mail out that first scholarship application to investigate and (if necessary) clean up your online presence.

Are you wondering why this is necessary? I bet you think that your Facebook page has nothing to do with your scholarship application. Well, if these are your thoughts, you are unfortunately very wrong. There's an excellent chance that a scholarship organization will spend time searching for you on the Internet. If you're shuddering at the thought of the scholarship committee members seeing anything on your page, I recommend you follow these tips for "scrubbing" your web reputation squeaky clean:

1. **Google yourself.**

   Search for every possible variation of your name on Google. If anything unbecoming pops up in the search results, do what you can to have it taken down.

2. **Check your social media sites.**

   This includes Facebook, LinkedIn, Twitter, Flickr, Tumblr, Wordpress, and so on. Make sure all the content on these sites is dignified and academic, meaning that it's serious and grammatically correct. It would be wise to include blog posts about social issues, quotes from famous people you admire, poetry you've written (not including dirty limericks), etc. Your social media pages need to present you as being "smart," "mature," and "hardworking." If it doesn't do those things, then clean up your page, and replace it with content that does. I am not saying that you have to be boring; just be cautious of how everything you post on the Internet *looks* because it's like a tattoo—once it is posted, it can not be erased.

3. **Web pages that can't be scrubbed should be hidden.**

   Try to use nicknames when creating your social profiles, and always use the highest privacy settings so that people must be approved in order to see the page. After doing these things, you should still log out and check what information appears on your default profile page. If a picture that depicts you partying or anything else that would be unflattering to a scholarship committee appears, log back in and replace it with something else.

4. **Take those videos off YouTube.**

   Do this right now. You know which ones I mean.

5. **Remain vigilant.**

   Just because you cleaned up your web presence today doesn't mean it will be clean as a whistle next week. Be aware of what others are posting and tagging with your name. Some search engines even allow you to set up "alerts" to warn you every time your name shows up on the web. I would recommend using this to your full extent.

6. **Check your voicemail.**

   This is of the utmost importance. If you have an inappropriate ring-back tone or voicemail greeting, you need to either replace it with something professional and appropriate, or kiss your scholarship chances goodbye.

ABOUT THE AUTHOR

Felecia Hatcher is a trailblazing social entrepreneur with an authentic voice for change. For the past decade, Felecia has dedicated her life to inspiring a new generation of leaders through her conversational talks on entrepreneurship, college funding, and personal branding.

Hatcher has been honored by the White House as one of the Top 100 Entrepreneurs under 30, was a TEDx presenter, and has been featured on NBC's *Today Show*'s "Young African Americans Making History," on the Food Network, Inc., and in the *Wall Street Journal, Entrepreneur, Essence Magazine,* and *Black Enterprise.*

As a "C" student in high school, Hatcher beat the odds and won over $100,000 in scholarships to attend college by getting creative. She used her experience and knack for personal marketability to start her first business called Urban Excellence as a freshman in college. She built and ran innovative college-prep programs for DeVry University and companies such as MECA, AMPS Institute, the YMCA, the TED Center, and the Urban League. Hatcher continued her successful career spearheading experiential marketing and social media campaigns around the country for Fortune 500 companies like Nintendo, Sony, Wells Fargo, Microsoft, and Little Debbie. She also worked for the NBA as the Front Office Marketing Manager for the Minnesota Lynx and spearheaded their 10th anniversary rebranding campaign.

In 2008, after falling flat on her face while attempting to chase an ice cream truck in heels, Hatcher started her own gourmet ice pops and ice cream catering company, Feverish Ice Cream. The company specializes in vegan-friendly ice cream and ice pops for events and retail. Tapping into her marketing acumen, Hatcher formed strategic partnerships with many companies, including Universal Music, Adidas, Whole Foods, Live Nation, JCrew, Capitol Records, The W Hotel, and Vitamin Water, helping them promote their new products through her trucks, carts, social media networks, and sponsored ice cream give-a-ways. Feverish Ice Cream is dedicated to sustainability and innovation and donates a portion of each popsicle sold to charity. Hatcher and her partner Derick Pearson also run a youth entrepreneurship program called PopPreneurs to teach youngsters in urban areas how to become entrepreneurs through ice cream carts.

Scholarship Management Organizations

Richard Woodland
Former Director of Financial Aid, Rutgers University–Camden

The search for private scholarships can be confusing and frustrating for parents and students. Many families feel that they just don't know how to go about the process, so they either hire a private scholarship search company or simply give up. The success rate of many scholarship search firms is not good, and college financial aid professionals always warn parents to be skeptical of exaggerated claims.

The process also confuses many donors. A corporation may want to help its employees or the children of its employees or may want to offer a national scholarship program to its customers or the general public. Unfortunately, the corporation may not want to devote valuable administrative time to managing a scholarship program. Similarly, many donors want to target their funds to a particular group of students but simply do not know how.

Stepping in to help are scholarship management organizations. Although many have been around for a long time, most people know very little about them because scholarship management organizations often do not administer scholarship funds directly to students. Rather, they serve as a clearinghouse for their member donor organizations. Today, savvy parents and students can go online to find these organizations and the scholarship programs they administer.

Two of the largest scholarship management programs are the National Merit Scholarship Corporation and Scholarship America. The National Merit Scholarship Corporation sponsors a competitive scholarship program that seeks to identify and reward the top students in the nation. High school students who meet published entry/participation requirements enter these competitions by taking the Preliminary SAT/National Merit Scholarship Qualifying Test (PSAT/NMSQT®), usually as juniors. A particular year's test is the entry vehicle to a specific annual competition. For example, the 2012 PSAT/NMSQT was the qualifying test for entry into competitions for scholarships to be awarded in 2014. For more information, you should visit http://www.nationalmerit.org.

Another major player is Scholarship America, which has distributed more than $2.5 billion dollars to more than 1.7 million students since its founding more than fifty years ago. Scholarship America has become the nation's largest private-sector scholarship and educational support organization by involving communities, corporations, organizations, and individuals in the support of students through its major programs, Dollars for Scholars and Scholarship Management Services. Working with national leaders in response to the September 11th tragedy and with corporations such as Kohl's and Best Buy, Scholarship America is an important organization that helps thousands of students every year. For more information, go online to http://scholarshipamerica.org.

In addition to the National Merit Scholarship Fund and Scholarship America, other organizations raise funds and administer scholarships for specific groups of students. These organizations include:

- American Indian College Fund **www.collegefund.org**
- Hispanic Scholarship Fund **www.hsf.net**
- United Negro College Fund **www.uncf.org**
- Organization of Chinese Americans **www.ocanational.org**
- National FFA Organization (Future Farmers of America) **www.ffa.org**
- Gates Millennium Scholars **www.gmsp.org**

In addition to using scholarship search engines, think broadly about your background, your interests, your family connections (work, religious, fraternal organizations), and your future career plans. Then spend some time browsing the Web. We hope that some of the sources mentioned here will help. Remember, the key is to start early (junior year in high school is best) and be persistent.

Winning the Scholarship with a Winning Essay

Who knew it was going to be this hard? You've already dealt with SO much: the SAT, doing community service, excelling in your AP class, etc. Convincing your parents that you will be fine 1,500 miles from home and that each and every one of those college application fees are, yes, absolutely necessary! You even learned calculus for goodness sake!

And now in front of you—yet, for right now, somehow out of reach—the golden ticket to make it all come true. Just 500 words (more or less) separate you from those hallowed halls: It's the scholarship essay.

IT HAS TO BE EASY, RIGHT?

Much as you may feel like, c'mon, I'm worth it, just give me the scholarship money, we all know it just doesn't work like that. Because you know what—lots of students are worth it! And lots of students are special, just like you! And where does that leave a scholarship selection committee in deciding to whom their money should be awarded? Yes, now you are catching on—they will pour over *everyone's* scholarship essay.

So, first and foremost, write your scholarship essay in a way that makes it EASY for the scholarship-awarding committees to do their job! It's almost like a partnership—you show them (in 500 words, more or less) why YOU ARE THE MOST WORTHY RECIPIENT, and they say, thank you, you're right, here is a scholarship for you, and everyone wins! Easy, right?

SORRY, IT REALLY ISN'T THAT EASY

What? You are still sitting there in front of a blank computer screen with nary a thought or sentence? Understood. It's really not that easy. That, too, is part of the point.

No doubt that your GPA, SAT scores, volunteer efforts, leadership roles, and community service are immensely important, but again, you must remember that, during the process of selecting an award recipient, pretty much all the applicants are going to be stellar on some level. And so the scholarship-awarding committee uses your essay to see what sets you apart from the crowd. They are looking for a reason to select you over everyone else.

Your scholarship essay serves many purposes. You have to convince the scholarship-awarding committee you are able to do the following:

- Effectively communicate through the written word
- Substantiate your merit and unique qualities
- Follow directions and adhere to guidelines

A winning scholarship essay can mean up to tens of thousands of dollars for your college education, so let's get started on putting that money in YOUR hands!

EFFECTIVE WRITTEN COMMUNICATION

Be Passionate

Let's face it—you have already written lots of essays. And, we won't tell, but most were probably about topics that were as interesting to you as watching paint dry, right? But you plowed through them and even managed to get some good grades along the way. You may think about just "plowing through" your scholarship essay the same way—mustering up the same amount of excitement you feel when you have to watch old videos of your Aunt Monica on her summer camping trips. But that would be a huge mistake!

An important feature of all winning essays is that they are written on subjects about which the author is truly passionate. Think about it—it actually takes a good bit of effort to fake passion for a subject. But when you are genuinely enthusiastic about something, the words and thoughts flow much more easily, and your passion and energy naturally shine through in your writing. Therefore, when you are choosing your scholarship essay topic, be sure it is something about which you truly care and for which you can show affinity—keeping both you and your reader interested and intrigued!

Be Positive

You've probably heard the expression: "If you don't have anything nice to say, don't say anything at all." Try to steer clear of essays that are too critical, pessimistic, or antagonistic. This doesn't mean that your essay shouldn't acknowledge a serious problem or that everything has to have a happy ending. But it does mean that you should not just write about the negative. If you are writing about a problem, present solutions. If your story doesn't have a happy ending, write about what you learned from the experience and how you would do things differently if faced with a similar situation in the future. Your optimism is what makes the scholarship-awarding committee excited about giving you money to pursue your dreams. Use positive language and be proud to share yourself and your accomplishments. Everyone likes an uplifting story, and even scholarship judges want to feel your enthusiasm and zest for life.

Be Clear and Concise

Don't fall into the common essay-writing trap of using general statements instead of specific ones. All scholarship judges read at least one essay that starts with "Education is the key to success." And that means nothing to them. What does mean something is writing about how your tenth-grade English teacher opened your eyes to the understated beauty and simplicity of haiku—how less can be more—and how that then translated into you donating some of your old video games to a homeless shelter where you now volunteer once a month. That's powerful stuff! It's a very real story, clearly correlating education to a successful outcome. Focusing on a specific and concise example from your life helps readers relate to you and your experiences. It also guarantees you bonus points for originality!

Edit and Proofread and Then Edit and Proofread

There is an old saying: "Behind every good writer is an even better editor." Find people (friends, siblings, coaches, teachers, guidance counselors) to read your essay, provide feedback on how to make it better, and edit it for silly, sloppy mistakes. Some people will read your essay and find issues with your grammar. Others will read your essay and point out how one paragraph doesn't make sense in relation to another paragraph. Some people will tell you how to give more examples to better make your point. All of those people are giving you great information, and you need to take it all in and use it to your advantage! However, don't be overwhelmed by it, and don't let it become all about what everyone else thinks. It's your essay and your thoughts—the goal of editing and proofreading is to clean up the rough edges and make the entire essay shine!

And when you do get to that magical point where you think "DONE!"—instead, just put the essay aside for a few days. Come back to it with an open mind and read, edit, and proofread it one last time. Check it one last time

for spelling and grammar fumbles. Check it one last time for clarity and readability (reading it out loud helps!). Check it one last time to ensure it effectively communicates why you are absolutely the winning scholarship candidate!

YOUR UNIQUE QUALITIES

It's one thing to help out at the local library a few hours a week; it's a completely different thing if you took it upon yourself to suggest, recruit, organize, and lead a fundraising campaign to buy 10 new laptops for kids to use at the library!

And don't simply rattle off all your different group memberships. Write about things you did that demonstrate leadership and initiative within those groups. Did you recruit new members or offer to head up a committee? Did you find a way for the local news station to cover your event or reach out to another organization and collaborate on an activity? Think about your unique qualities and how you have used them to bring about change.

A SLICE OF YOUR LIFE

While one goal of your essay is surely to explain why you should win the scholarship money, an equally important goal is to reveal something about you, something that makes it easy to see why you should win. Notice we said to reveal "something" about you and not "everything" about you. Most likely, the rest of the scholarship application gathers quite a bit of information about you. The essay is where you need to hone in on just one aspect of your unique talents, one aspect of an experience, one aspect of reaching a goal. It's not about listing all your accomplishments in your essay (again, you probably did that on the application). It's about sharing a slice of your life—telling your story and giving your details about what makes YOU memorable.

YOUR ACCOMPLISHMENTS, LOUD AND PROUD

Your extracurricular activities illustrate your personal priorities and let the scholarship selection committee know what's important to you. Being able to elaborate on your accomplishments and awards within those activities certainly bolsters your chances of winning the scholarship. Again, though, be careful to not just repeat what is already on the application itself. Use your essay to focus on a specific accomplishment (or activity or talent or award) of which you are most proud.

Did your community suffer through severe flooding last spring? And did you organize a clothing drive for neighbors who were in need? How did that make you feel? What feedback did you get? How did it inspire your desire to become a climatologist?

Were school budget cuts going to mean the disbanding of some afterschool clubs? Did you work with teachers and parents to write a proposal to present to the school board, addressing how new funds could be raised in order to save the clubs? How did that make you feel? What feedback did you get? How did it inspire you to start a writing lab for junior high kids?

You have done great things—think about that one special accomplishment and paint the picture of how it has made you wiser, stronger, or more compassionate to the world around you. Share the details!

But Don't Go Overboard

A five-hanky story may translate into an Oscar-worthy movie, but rarely does it translate into winning a scholarship. If your main reason for applying for the scholarship is that you feel you deserve the money because of how much suffering you have been through, you need a better reason. Scholarship selection committees are not really interested in awarding money to people with problems; they want to award money to people who solve problems. While it's just fine to write about why you need the scholarship money to continue your education, it's not fine for your essay to simply be a laundry list of family tragedies and hardships.

So, instead of presenting a sob story, present how you have succeeded and what you have accomplished despite the hardships and challenges you faced. Remember that everyone has faced difficulties. What's unique about you is how YOU faced your difficulties and overcame them. That is what makes your essay significant and memorable.

FOLLOWING DIRECTIONS

Does Your Essay Really Answer the Question?

Have you ever been asked one question but felt like there was another question that was really being asked? Maybe your dad said something like, "Tell me about your new friend Logan." But what he really meant to ask you was, "Tell me about your new friend Logan. Do his lip rings and tattoos mean he's involved in things I don't want you involved in?"

The goal of every scholarship judge is to determine the best applicant out of a pool of applicants who are all rather similar. Pay attention and you'll find that the essay question is an alternate way for you to answer the real question the scholarship-awarding committee wants to ask. For instance, an organization giving an award to students who plan to study business might ask, "Why do you want to study business?" But their real underlying question is, "Why are you the best future business person to whom we should give our money?" If there is a scholarship for students who want to become doctors, you can bet that 99 percent of the students applying want to become doctors. And if you apply for that scholarship with an essay simply delving into your lifelong desire to be a potter, well, that doesn't make you unique, it makes you pretty much unqualified for that opportunity. Be sure to connect your personal skills, characteristics, and experiences with the objectives of the scholarship and its awarding organization.

Does Your Essay Theme Tie In?

Let's say that you are applying for a community service-based award and, on the application, you go ahead and list all the community service groups you belong to and all the awards you have won. But in your essay, you write about how homeless people should find a job instead of sitting on street corners begging for money. Hey—everyone is entitled to their opinion, but would you agree that there is some sort of disconnect between your application and your essay? And no doubt you have made the scholarship-awarding committee wonder the same thing.

So how do you ensure your essay doesn't create a conflicting message? You need to examine the theme of your essay and how it relates both to your application and the reason the scholarship exists in the first place. If the scholarship-funding organization seeks to give money to someone who wants a career in public relations and your essay focuses on how you are not really a "people person," well, you can see how that sends a mixed message to your reader.

Think about it this way: The theme of your essay should naturally flow around the overarching purpose or goal of the organization awarding the scholarship money. Once you have clarified this nugget, you can easily see if and how your words tie in to the organization's vision of whom their scholarship winner is.

Three More Pieces of Advice

1. **Follow the essay length guidelines closely.** You certainly don't want your essay disqualified simply because it was too long or too short!

2. **The deadline is the deadline.** A day late and you could certainly be more than a dollar short in terms of the award money that isn't going to be awarded to you if your application is not received by the due date. Begin the essay writing process well in advance of the scholarship deadline. Writing and editing and rewriting takes time so you should probably allow yourself at least 2 weeks to write your scholarship essay.

3. **Tell the truth.** No need to say anything further on that, right? Right.

Getting in the Minority Scholarship Mix

Did you know that a great duck call can win you scholarship money in the Chick and Sophie Major Memorial Duck Calling Contest?

Website: http://www.stuttgartarkansas.org/index.php?fuseaction= p0004.&mod=45

Perhaps duck calling is not your calling but creativity with Duck brand duct tape is. If so, the "Stuck at Prom" scholarship may be just for you—design promware for you and your date and win some moola!

Website: http://duckbrand.com/Promotions/stuck-at-prom.aspx

How about this tall order? Tall Clubs International awards scholarships to men who are taller than 6'2" or women who are taller than 5'10".

Website: http://www.tall.org/scholarships.cfm

Oh, not necessarily the minority group you had in mind? That's OK because guess what? In this day and age, just about everyone is a minority of some sort. It all depends on a scholarship benefactor's definition of minority.

In the college realm, the word "minority" takes on myriad meanings. One definition of a minority that often springs to mind is of someone of an underrepresented ethnicity, such as Native Americans, African Americans, or Hispanic Americans. No question there. Similarly though, a minority can be someone pursuing an under-represented college major, such as paranormal research. Think that all scholarships for minorities target United States–specific groups? Think again. For example, Canadian students, whether they plan to study at home or abroad, can qualify for scholarships for aboriginals. Getting the picture? The key is to use your own unique qualities as you search for scholarships. Think about your gender, your family's economic status, your religious background, and your geographic locale just to start the ball rolling. Once you broadly frame your search along those lines, you'll quickly see how easily you can qualify for a scholarship!

AM I REALLY A MINORITY?

No matter the source—federal, state, professional organization, private endowment, corporate donor, college, or university—they all offer minority scholarships, looking to create diversity and inclusion in an increasingly global marketplace.

It's more than probable that you fit into at least one of the ever-expanding minority scholarship categories—nearly everyone does—by some broadly based definition of minority. Some of the niche scholarship "minorities" have already been mentioned. Now let's take a look at some of the broader categories—one of which likely fits you!

African American Students

While African Americans make up a large U.S. minority group, they are still met with one of the biggest barriers to college enrollment—money. To combat that challenge, scholarships for African American students have grown over the years, with some of the best sources of funding found within partnerships between minority organizations and corporate sponsors.

As the nation's largest minority education organization, the United Negro College Fund (UNCF) provides operating funds for 38-member historically black colleges and universities (HBCUs), along with scholarships and internships for students at about 900 institutions. The UNCF has helped more than 400,000 students attend and graduate college with the more than $3.3 billion it has raised—more funds helping minorities attend college than any other entity outside of the U.S. government.

United Negro College Fund
8260 Willow Oaks Corporate Drive
P.O. Box 10444
Fairfax, VA 22031-8044
Phone: 800-331-2244
Website: www.uncf.org

Hispanic American Students

Fortunately, over the years, the U.S. government has contributed millions of dollars toward startup costs for the development of Hispanic universities and colleges and toward already established Hispanic universities and colleges. The effort has been paying off with dramatic increases in college enrollment by Hispanic American students. Scholarship programs for Hispanic American students look to increase the number of Hispanic students studying in subject areas most underrepresented by them, for instance, the sciences, engineering, math, and technology.

As the nation's leading Hispanic higher-education fund, the Hispanic Scholarship Fund (HSF) works to remove the barriers keeping many Hispanic American students from earning a college degree. Over the past 35 years, HSF has awarded more than $360 million in scholarships and supported a wide range of outreach and education programs for both college students and their families.

Hispanic Scholarship Fund
55 Second Street, Suite 1500
San Francisco, CA 94105
Phone: 877-HSF-INFO (877-473-4636)
E-mail: scholar1@hsf.net
Website: www.hsf.net

Asian American Students

Identifying yourself as Asian American means you probably consider yourself Cambodian, Hmong, Laotian, Malaysian, Okinawan, Tahitian, or Thai—just to name a few possibilities. As a somewhat smaller, yet growing, minority group, Asian Americans attend college more than any other minority group and tend to stay in college once they have enrolled. Excellent merit-based aid sources for Asian American students include cultural organizations, university departments such as law and journalism, and professional organizations.

The Asian & Pacific Islander American Scholarship Fund (APIASF), founded in 2003, has provided more than $50 million in scholarships to Asian and Pacific Islander Americans with financial need.

The Asian & Pacific Islander American Scholarship Fund
2025 M Street NW, Suite 610
Washington, DC 20036
Phone: 202-986-6892

Phone (toll-free): 877-808-7032
Fax: 202-530-0643
E-mail: info@apiasf.org
Website: http://www.apiasf.org/

Native American Students

Native American (inclusive of American Indians and Native Alaskans) students make up the smallest minority population on college campuses. As you explore scholarship opportunities for Native Americans, you may find that you'll need proof of your Native American status, which means your Certificate of Indian Blood (CIB), as well as belonging to a well-recognized tribe. If you are like most Native American descendants, though, you will probably not have this proof, as many tribes change names and have nonexistent documentation records. If somehow you do have a CIB and belong to a tribe, you may have an upper hand in qualifying for some more esoteric scholarship and grant programs.

The American Indian College Fund puts its mark on Indian higher education through its funding and creation of awareness of the unique, community-based accredited Tribal Colleges and Universities. The Fund awards about 6,000 annual scholarships to American Indian students seeking to better their lives through education.

The American Indian College Fund
8333 Greenwood Boulevard
Denver, CO 80221
Phone: 303-426-8900
Phone (toll-free): 800-776-3863
Website: www.collegefund.org/

Interracial Students

There is an interesting trend in minority scholarships where scholarship-funding organizations seek to include students of mixed heritage, blended cultures, and students whose ethnic backgrounds don't fit neatly into one particular category. Search for prizes tagged as "interracial scholarships," "multicultural scholarships," or "multiethnic scholarships."

Lesbian, Gay, Bisexual, and Transgender Students

Lesbian, gay, bisexual, and transgender (LGBT) students are recognized as a legitimate minority, and many colleges and organizations offer scholarships to this group. As an LGBT student, also be on the lookout for scholarship opportunities for sons and daughters of gay and lesbian parents, as well as friends and allies of the LGBT community.

Since its inception in 2001, the Point Foundation has invested more than $3 million in outstanding gay, lesbian, bisexual, and transgender students. An average Point Scholarship is about $13,600 and covers tuition, books, supplies, room and board, transportation, and living expenses.

Point Foundation
5757 Wilshire Boulevard, Suite 370
Los Angeles, CA 90036
Phone: 323-933-1234
Fax: 866-397-6468
E-mail: info@pointfoundation.org
Website: www.pointfoundation.org

EVERYONE NEEDS A GOOD RESOURCE

From specialized databases to award programs serving as umbrella organizations for numerous other organizations and awards, many resources are out there for criteria-based scholarships, all with one goal—to help you find the money you need to get you on your college path.

CHCI

CHCI provides a free, comprehensive list of scholarships, internships, and fellowships for Hispanic students.

Website: www.chci.org/scholarships/

Gates Millennium Scholars

The Gates Millennium Scholars program was founded by a grant from the Bill and Melinda Gates Foundation with the intention of increasing the number of African Americans, Native Americans, Asian Americans, and Hispanic Americans enrolling in and completing undergraduate and graduate degree programs.

Gates Millennium Scholars
P.O. Box 10500
Fairfax, VA 22031-8044
Phone (toll-free): 877-690-4677
Website: www.gmsp.org

GETTING CREATIVE WITH MINORITY SCHOLARSHIPS

Now that you are really thinking outside of the box, you may consider one or more of your outstanding features as the conduit to classifying yourself as a minority.

And if you still need some more inspiration:

- Juniata College in Pennsylvania offers a scholarship for left-handed students.
- Little People of America offers a scholarship to adult students who are 4'10" or shorter.
- There are even scholarships for white males offered by The Former Majority Association for Equality, a nonprofit group in Texas.

Be creative and get in the mix! To which minority groups do *you* belong?

What to Do If You Don't Win a Scholarship, Grant, or Prize

More than 20 million students will enroll in the nation's colleges and universities this year, and you can bet nearly all of them will be vying for the more than $4 billion in private scholarship money that's available. In fact, 85 percent of all first-time undergraduate students attending a four-year college receive some type of financial aid—including scholarships, grants, awards, and student loans.

Yet, even though billions of dollars are out there for the grasping, the average scholarship award is just $2815. That's only going to put a minor dent in the $20,000 annual price tag for in-state tuition, room, and board at a public four-year institution ($39,800 for private). So, unless you started working as a toddler you're going to have to do something spectacular to avoid buckling under a mountain of student loan debt to get your degree.

Applying for grants and private scholarships is a given. But what if your living room table is filling up with denial letters? What do you do then? Well, the first thing is not to panic. There are plenty of ways to pay for college without going into an enormous amount of debt. Here are some tips and suggestions that will help you to formulate a back-up plan if, by some miracle, you miss out on the college scholarship lottery.

IF AT FIRST YOU DON'T SUCCEED

A rejection letter doesn't mean no, it really means, "Not right now." There is nothing wrong with applying for a private scholarship, fellowship or grant again, even if you've been rejected. Just think, you'll have a leg up on everyone who is coming to the competition cold, as you've been there before. Before you dust off your essay from last year and shove it into an envelope this year, be sure to contact the organization and ask for feedback.

Sure, some may not be willing to speak to you, but you won't lose any sleep by trying. Often the best advice comes from the unlikeliest places, and asking pointed, mature questions about why your first application failed can only serve you in your college money hunt. In addition, the counsel might help you to improve an application for another organization. So follow up on those who've said no—you never know what kind of great tips

and suggestions they will have for you. Here are some questions you may ask when you seek feedback:

- Did my application get rejected because of a procedural mistake? Did I mess up the application process? Did I meet the deadline? Were all my documents included?
- Was my personal statement/essay well done? How could it have been improved?
- Could you give me suggestions on how best to apply for your scholarship again?

Note: You, of course, can't do any of this if you waited until the last minute to fill out your scholarship application, so it pays to start your quest for college treasure early.

YOU CAN APPLY FOR SCHOLARSHIPS WHILE IN COLLEGE

Even if you've already started your college career with your scholarship coffers empty and your student loan debt toppling over, do not fret. You can still apply for grants, scholarships, and programs that do not require you go into debt while you're attending school. Many scholarships are not automatically renewed, and if students do not apply for them, there may be more cash for you. Create an application cycle for every year you attend school. You never know what opportunity you may be missing if you do not at least try to apply while attending school.

WORK NOW, NOT LATER

It used to be that flipping burgers at the local fast-food joint was the way most college students paid for college. And to be sure that option is still open. But the recent technology boom fueled by the monetization of the Internet has allowed even the youngest among us to become entrepreneurs. From teen-age search engine app maker Nick D'Alosio, who has raised capital from one of China's billionaires, to the pre-adolescent Mallory Kiveman, who invented a lollipop to cure the hiccups, the spirit of innovation runs deep among the young. Use technology to start your version of a lemonade stand, and you may make enough in your senior year to pay for college and beyond. Technology has allowed people to think better, smarter, and bigger than ever before. As you're working on that latest science project, think about ways to monetize it. It could be your ticket to a full-ride to college.

DON'T LEAVE MONEY ON THE TABLE

Did you know that only 1 in 10 undergraduate students receive a scholarship award? This isn't because there aren't enough scholarships available. On the contrary, millions of dollars in scholarship money go unclaimed because students do not apply for them. Instead, 9 out of 10 students borrowed an average of $63,400 to complete their degrees, according to the National Center for Education Statistics.

Yes, that's right. College students, desperate to incur massive amounts of debts forget to apply for grants, miss deadlines and sloppily fill out scholarship applications to ensure they get rejected and leave money on the table. You, of course, would never do that. But some people will.

Do not be one of those people. Make sure you are taking advantage of all your opportunities to gain debt-free money for college. In addition to applying for private scholarships, make sure you go beyond the Federal Pell Grant. Remember, there are state grants, local grants, need-based grants, merit grants, and college university grants that are available for students. Be sure to check with your admitting institution to make sure you haven't overlooked grants—many of which are automatically offered to students regardless of income.

PRACTICE SOME ALTRUISM

Though it may seem to have gone the way of milkshakes and quaint small-town post offices, there are still some programs that will help pay for your college education as long as you commit to do public service. From Ameri-Corps, which defrays college costs for students who work for nonprofits or in high-need areas to the newly minted Public Service Loan Forgiveness Program, which will wipe out federal loan debt for people who, after October 2007, work full-time in government or nonprofit jobs, there are dozens of programs that will lower your college costs in exchange for public service. Even top-tier universities such as Harvard and Princeton are offering free

tuition (Harvard for just one year) for students who choose to work in public service careers. There are loan forgiveness programs for virtually every public service profession from state-appointed prosecutors, teachers, primary care doctors, and law enforcement officers; members of the armed forces; nurses and health-care workers; and even Peace Corps volunteers. But beware—the programs have strict guidelines; one misstep and you could end up footing the bill for your entire college dream. And, as always, consult your tax advisor as current law categorizes the loan amount that is forgiven as income.

Here are some contacts for programs that pay down college costs for volunteerism or public service:

AmeriCorps

More than 75,000 adults work with thousands of non-profits around the country providing tutoring, mentoring, housing management, and a host of other services to the disadvantaged through AmeriCorps. In exchange they receive money to pay for college or graduate school, or they obtain forgiveness on student loans plus a pay check.

AmeriCorps

1201 New York Avenue, NW
Washington, DC 20525
Phone: 202-606-5000
TTY: 800-833-3722 (toll-free)
Website: www.americorps.gov

National Health Service Corps

The National Health Service Corps awards scholarships to students who are pursuing careers in primary care. Students must be pursuing degrees in medicine, dentistry, nursing, and physician assistant studies.

National Health Corps

Phone: 800-221-9393 (toll-free)
Website: http://nhsc.hrsa.gov

Public Service Loan Forgiveness

Congress created the Public Service Loan Forgiveness Program in 2007 as an incentive for people to enter fields that focused on public service. The beneficial program offers qualified borrowers the opportunity to have their federal loans forgiven if they work in certain public service areas.

Website: www.studentaid.gov.

How to Use This Guide

The more than 3,600 award programs described in this book are organized into eleven broad categories that represent the major factors used to determine eligibility for scholarships, awards, and prizes. To build a basic list of awards available to you, look under the broad category or categories that fit your particular academic goals, skills, personal characteristics, or background. The categories are:

- Academic Fields/Career Goals
- Civic, Professional, Social, or Union Affiliation
- Corporate Affiliation
- Employment/Volunteer Experience
- Impairment
- Military Service
- Nationality or Ethnic Heritage
- Religious Affiliation
- Residence/Location of Study
- Talent/Interest Area
- Miscellaneous Criteria

The **Academic Fields/Career Goals** category is subdivided into 131 subject areas that are organized alphabetically by award sponsor. The **Military Service** category is subdivided alphabetically by branch of service. All other categories are organized A to Z by the name of the award sponsor.

Full descriptive profiles appear in only one location in the book. Cross-references to the name and page number of the full descriptive profile appear at other locations under the other relevant categories for the award. The full description appears in the first relevant location in the book and cross-references later locations, so you will always be redirected toward the front of the book.

Your major field of study and career goals have central importance in college planning. As a result, we have combined these into a single category and have given this category precedence over the others. The **Academic Fields/Career Goals** section appears first in the book. If an academic major or career area is a criterion for a scholarship, the description of this award will appear in this section.

Within the **Academic Fields/Career Goals** section, cross-references are only from and to other academic fields or career areas. You will be able to locate relevant awards from nonacademic or noncareer criteria through the indexes in the back of this book.

For example, the full descriptive profile of a scholarship for any type of engineering student who resides in Ohio might appear under *Aviation/Aerospace*, which is the first engineering category heading in the **Academic Fields/Career Goals** section. Cross-references to this first listing may occur from any other relevant engineering or technological academic field subject area, such as *Chemical Engineering, Civil Engineering, Electrical Engineering/Electronics, Engineering-Related Technologies, Engineering/Technology, Mechanical Engineering,* or *Nuclear Science.* There would not be a cross-reference from the *Residence* category. However, the name of the award will appear in the Residence index under Ohio.

Within the major category sections, descriptive profiles are organized alphabetically by the name of the sponsoring organization. If more than one award from the same organization appears in a particular section, the awards are listed alphabetically under the sponsor name, which appears only once, by the name of the first award.

HOW THE PROFILES ARE ORGANIZED

Here are the elements of a full profile:

Name of Sponsoring Organization

These appear alphabetically under the appropriate category. In most instances, acronyms are given as full names. However, occasionally a sponsor will refer to itself by an acronym. In these instances, we present the sponsor's name as an acronym.

World Wide Web Address

Award Name

Brief Textual Description of the Award

Academic Fields/Career Goals (only in the Academic Fields/Career Goals section of the book)

This is a list of all academic or career subject terms that are assigned to this award.

Award

Is it a scholarship? A prize for winning a competition? A forgivable loan? For what type and for what years of college can it be used? Is it renewable or is it for only one year?

Eligibility Requirements

Application Requirements
What information do you need to supply to be considered? What are the deadlines?

Contact
If provided by the sponsor, this element includes the name, mailing address, phone and fax numbers, and e-mail address of the person to contact for information about a specific award.

USING THE INDEXES
The alphabetical indexes in the back of the book are designed to aid your search. Two are name indexes. One lists scholarships alphabetically by academic fields and career goals. The other ten indexes supply access by nonacademic and noncareer criteria. The indexes give you the page number of the descriptions of relevant awards regardless of the part of the book in which they appear.

These are the indexes:

> **Award Name**
> **Sponsor**
> **Academic Fields/Career Goals**
>> [131 subject areas, from Academic Advising to Women's Studies]
>
> **Civic, Professional, Social, or Union Affiliation**
> **Corporate Affiliation**
> **Employment/Volunteer Experience**
> **Impairment**
> **Military Service**
> **Nationality or Ethnic Heritage**
> **Religious Affiliation**
> **Residence**
> **Location of Study**
> **Talent/Interest Area**

In general, when using the indexes, writing down the names and page numbers of the awards that you are interested in is an effective technique.

DATA COLLECTION PROCEDURES
Peterson's takes its responsibility to its readers as a provider of trustworthy information very seriously. Peterson's administered an electronic survey between January and April 2013 in order to update information from all programs listed within this guide. All collected data was updated between January and April 2013. Additional award program data was obtained between January 2009 and April 2013. Peterson's research staff makes every effort to verify unusual figures and resolve discrepancies. Nonetheless, errors and omissions are possible in a data collection endeavor of this scope. Also, facts and figures, such as number and amount of awards, can suddenly change, or awards can be discontinued by a sponsoring organization. Therefore, readers should verify data with the specific sponsoring agency responsible for administering these awards before applying.

CRITERIA FOR INCLUSION IN THIS BOOK
The programs listed in this book have the primary characteristics of legitimate scholarships: verifiable sponsor addresses and phone numbers, appropriate descriptive materials, and fees that, if required, are not exorbitant. Peterson's assumes that these fees are used to defray administrative expenses and are not major sources of income.

QUICK REFERENCE CHART

Scholarships, Grants & Prizes At-a-Glance

This chart lists award programs that indicate that their largest award provides $2000 or more. The awards are ranked in descending order on the basis of the dollar amount of the largest award. Because the award criteria in the Academic Fields/Career Goals and Nonacademic/Noncareer Criteria column may represent only some of the criteria or limitations that affect eligibility for the award, you should refer to the full description in the award profiles to ascertain all relevant details.

Award Name	Page Number	Highest Dollar Amount	Lowest Dollar Amount	Number of Awards	Academic Fields/Career Goals and Nonacademic/Noncareer Criteria
Army ROTC Green to Gold Scholarship Program for Two-Year, Three-Year and Four-Year Scholarships, Active Duty Enlisted Personnel	586	$130,000	$10,000	200–400	Military Service: Army.
Indian Health Service Health Professions Scholarship Program	208	$106,110	$37,319	257–307	Construction Engineering/Management; Dental Health/Services; Engineering-Related Technologies; Environmental Health; Food Science/Nutrition; Health and Medical Sciences; Health Information Management/Technology; Nursing; Optometry; Pharmacy; Psychology; Therapy/Rehabilitation. Limited to American Indian/Alaska Native students.
Intel Science Talent Search	797	$100,000	$7500	40	Must be in high school.
J. Wood Platt Caddie Scholarship Trust	783	$100,000	$1000		Limited to caddies at a Golf Association of Philadelphia Member Club.
Careers Through Culinary Arts Program Cooking Competition for Scholarships	214	$90,000	$1000	50–70	Culinary Arts; Hospitality Management. Residence: Arizona; California; Illinois; Maryland; New York; Pennsylvania; Virginia. Must be in high school.
SME Family Scholarship	292	$80,000	$5000	1–10	Engineering/Technology.
Terry Foundation Scholarship	729	$76,000	$19,000	208–650	Residence: Texas. Studying in Texas. Talent/Interest Area: leadership. Must be in high school.
Intel International Science and Engineering Fair	797	$75,000	$500	1–600	Must be in high school.
UNCF/Merck Science Initiative	149	$70,000	$25,000		Biology; Chemical Engineering; Environmental Science; Health and Medical Sciences; Natural Sciences; Neurobiology; Physical Sciences. Limited to Black (non-Hispanic) students.
Elks National Foundation Most Valuable Student Scholarship Contest	749	$60,000	$4000	500	Talent/Interest Area: leadership. Must be in high school.
Davidson Fellows Scholarship Program	386	$50,000	$10,000	15–20	Literature/English/Writing; Mathematics; Music; Philosophy; Science, Technology, and Society.
Miss America Organization Competition Scholarships	752	$50,000	$2000	70	Talent/Interest Area: beauty pageant.

Award Name	Page Number	Highest Dollar Amount	Lowest Dollar Amount	Number of Awards	Academic Fields/Career Goals and Nonacademic/Noncareer Criteria
U.S. Army ROTC Four-Year Nursing Scholarship	430	$50,000	$5000	175	Nursing. Disability: physically disabled. Military Service: Army; Army National Guard.
Tuition Exchange Scholarships	565	$47,000	$4000	5,000–7,000	Employment/Volunteer Experience: teaching/education.
Kentucky Transportation Cabinet Civil Engineering Scholarship Program	183	$44,000	$10,600	15–25	Civil Engineering. Residence: Kentucky. Studying in Kentucky.
Army (ROTC) Reserve Officers Training Corps Two-, Three-, Four-Year Campus-Based Scholarships	569	$40,000	$10,000	1,200–2,500	Disability: physically disabled. Military Service: Army; Army National Guard.
Boettcher Foundation Scholarships	671	$40,000	$13,000	40	Residence: Colorado. Studying in Colorado. Talent/Interest Area: leadership. Must be in high school.
Mas Family Scholarship Award	156	$40,000	$8000	5–10	Business/Consumer Services; Chemical Engineering; Civil Engineering; Communications; Economics; Electrical Engineering/Electronics; Engineering-Related Technologies; International Studies; Journalism; Materials Science, Engineering, and Metallurgy; Mechanical Engineering. Limited to Hispanic students.
National Academy of Television Arts and Sciences John Cannon Memorial Scholarship	192	$40,000	$1000	1–10	Communications; TV/Radio Broadcasting. Must be in high school.
Ron Brown Scholar Program	637	$40,000	$10,000	10–20	Talent/Interest Area: leadership. Must be in high school. Limited to Black (non-Hispanic) students.
U.S. Army ROTC Four-Year College Scholarship	587	$40,000	$9000	1,000–2,000	Military Service: Army; Army National Guard.
U.S. Army ROTC Four-Year Historically Black College/University Scholarship	569	$40,000	$9000	20–200	Disability: physically disabled. Military Service: Army; Army National Guard.
Science, Mathematics, and Research for Transformation Defense Scholarship for Service Program	102	$39,000	$22,000	200	Applied Sciences; Engineering-Related Technologies; Engineering/Technology; Mathematics; Physical Sciences.
Indian Health Service Health Professions Pre-graduate Scholarships	105	$35,228	$28,823	57–107	Applied Sciences; Biology; Health and Medical Sciences. Limited to American Indian/Alaska Native students.
Health Professions Preparatory Scholarship Program	141	$32,237	$26,376	25–50	Behavioral Science; Health and Medical Sciences; Nursing; Pharmacy; Psychology; Social Sciences. Limited to American Indian/Alaska Native students.
Master's Scholarship Program	171	$32,000	$25,000	1–15	Chemical Engineering; Computer Science/Data Processing; Electrical Engineering/Electronics; Engineering/Technology; Materials Science, Engineering, and Metallurgy. Limited to American Indian/Alaska Native; Black (non-Hispanic); Hispanic students.
Environmental Protection Scholarship	145	$30,000	$15,000	1–2	Biology; Chemical Engineering; Civil Engineering; Earth Science; Environmental Science; Hydrology; Mechanical Engineering; Natural Sciences. Studying in Kentucky.

Award Name	Page Number	Highest Dollar Amount	Lowest Dollar Amount	Number of Awards	Academic Fields/Career Goals and Nonacademic/Noncareer Criteria
The Frank M. and Gertrude R. Doyle Foundation, Inc.	778	$30,000	$500		Limited to students age 17–99.
Los Alamos Employees' Scholarship	700	$30,000	$1000	50	Residence: New Mexico.
National Security Agency Stokes Educational Scholarship Program	203	$30,000	$1000	15–20	Computer Science/Data Processing; Electrical Engineering/Electronics. Must be in high school.
St. Andrews Scholarship	637	$30,000	$20,000	2	Limited to students of Scottish heritage.
South Carolina Police Corps Scholarship	379	$30,000	$7500	20	Law Enforcement/Police Administration.
Voice of Democracy Program	762	$30,000	$1000	54	Talent/Interest Area: public speaking; writing. Must be in high school.
National FFA Collegiate Scholarship Program	528	$26,000	$300	1,500–1,600	Civic Affiliation: Future Farmers of America.
Florida Space Research Program	132	$25,000	$12,500	13–15	Aviation/Aerospace; Earth Science; Materials Science, Engineering, and Metallurgy; Mathematics; Mechanical Engineering. Residence: Florida. Studying in Florida.
Ford Opportunity Program	688	$25,000	$1000	36	Residence: California; Oregon. Studying in California; Oregon.
Ford ReStart Program	688	$25,000	$1000	46	Residence: California; Oregon. Studying in California; Oregon.
Ford Scholars Program	688	$25,000	$1000	46	Residence: California; Oregon. Studying in California; Oregon.
Princess Grace Awards in Dance, Theater, and Film	309	$25,000	$5000	15–25	Filmmaking/Video; Performing Arts.
Safety Scholars Video Contest Scholarship	771	$25,000	$10,000	3	Limited to students age 16–21.
Sons of Italy Foundation's National Leadership Grant Competition	638	$25,000	$4000	8–14	Limited to students of Italian heritage.
U.S. Army ROTC Military Junior College (MJC) Scholarship	569	$25,000	$2705	110–150	Disability: physically disabled. Military Service: Army; Army National Guard.
Illinois Restaurant Association Educational Foundation Scholarships	215	$24,000	$750	50–70	Culinary Arts; Food Science/Nutrition; Food Service/Hospitality; Hospitality Management. Employment/Volunteer Experience: food service; hospitality/hotel administration/operations. Residence: Illinois.
Accenture American Indian Scholarship	616	$20,000	$2000	10	Must be in high school. Limited to American Indian/Alaska Native students.
1B USD Worldwide Venture Capital	107	$20,000	$2000	1–20	Applied Sciences; Aviation/Aerospace; Business/Consumer Services; Campus Activities; Communications; Computer Science/Data Processing; Fashion Design; Filmmaking/Video; Industrial Design; Marketing; Materials Science, Engineering, and Metallurgy; Science, Technology, and Society. Nationality: Chinese; Japanese; Korean. Talent/Interest Area: Asian language; entrepreneurship; foreign language; international exchange; public speaking.
Coca-Cola Scholars Program	773	$20,000	$10,000	250	Must be in high school.

Award Name	Page Number	Highest Dollar Amount	Lowest Dollar Amount	Number of Awards	Academic Fields/Career Goals and Nonacademic/Noncareer Criteria
Gates Millennium Scholars Program	616	$20,000	$500	150	Talent/Interest Area: leadership. Limited to American Indian/Alaska Native students.
GlaxoSmithKline Opportunity Scholarship	730	$20,000	$5000	1–10	Residence: North Carolina. Studying in North Carolina.
Horatio Alger Association Scholarship Programs	781	$20,000	$5000	965	Must be in high school.
Milton Fisher Scholarship for Innovation and Creativity	793	$20,000	$1000	5–8	Limited to students from the Connecticut and New York City Metropolitan area.
Pride Foundation Scholarship Program	721	$20,000	$1000	85–125	Residence: Alaska; Idaho; Montana; Oregon; Washington. Talent/Interest Area: LGBT issues.
Samsung American Legion Scholarship	598	$20,000	$1000	98	Military Service: General. Must be in high school.
Sweet Diggity Dawg Scholarship	803	$20,000	$500	30–41	Must be in high school.
Verizon Foundation Scholarship	549	$20,000	$5000	250	Corporate Affiliation: Verizon. Must be in high school.
Washington Crossing Foundation Scholarship	466	$20,000	$1000	5–10	Political Science; Public Policy and Administration. Must be in high school.
Maryland Association of Private Colleges and Career Schools Scholarship	157	$19,950	$500	50	Business/Consumer Services; Computer Science/Data Processing; Dental Health/Services; Engineering/Technology; Food Science/Nutrition; Home Economics; Trade/Technical Specialties; TV/Radio Broadcasting. Residence: Maryland. Studying in Maryland. Must be in high school.
American Legion Department of Kansas High School Oratorical Contest	740	$18,000	$150	4	Talent/Interest Area: public speaking. Must be in high school.
American Legion National High School Oratorical Contest	741	$18,000	$1500	54	Talent/Interest Area: public speaking. Must be in high school.
Air Force ROTC College Scholarship	580	$15,000	$9000	2,000–4,000	Military Service: Air Force.
Armenian Relief Society Undergraduate Scholarship	617	$15,000	$13,000		Limited to students of Armenian descent.
Blade Your Ride Scholarship Program	794	$15,000	$5000	3–5	Limited to students who have a 3.0 GPA or higher.
Center for Architecture, Women's Auxiliary Eleanor Allwork Scholarship	110	$15,000	$5000	1–3	Architecture. Residence: New York. Studying in New York.
Common Scholarship Application	793	$15,000	$500	95–110	Most scholarships require San Diego County residency
Community Foundation Scholarship Program	680	$15,000	$1000	100–150	Residence: Florida. Must be in high school.
First in Family Scholarship	697	$15,000	$12,500	10	Residence: Alabama. Studying in Alabama. Must be in high school.
GuildScholar Award	572	$15,000	$10,000	16	Disability: visually impaired. Must be in high school.
Jesse Brown Memorial Youth Scholarship Program	554	$15,000	$5000	12	Employment/Volunteer Experience: community service; helping handicapped.
LIFE Lessons Scholarships Program	784	$15,000	$2000	60	Limited to students who have experienced the death of a parent or legal guardian.

Award Name	Page Number	Highest Dollar Amount	Lowest Dollar Amount	Number of Awards	Academic Fields/Career Goals and Nonacademic/Noncareer Criteria
Lowe's Educational Scholarship	559	$15,000	$1000	375	Employment/Volunteer Experience: community service. Talent/Interest Area: leadership. Must be in high school.
National Beta Club Scholarship	527	$15,000	$1000	221	Civic Affiliation: National Beta Club. Must be in high school.
National Black MBA Association Graduate Scholarship Program	786	$15,000	$2500	10–25	Limited to Black (non-Hispanic). students.
Pennsylvania Institute of Certified Public Accountants Sophomore Scholarship	79	$15,000	$1000	60–85	Accounting. Residence: Pennsylvania. Studying in Pennsylvania.
Texas 4-H Opportunity Scholarship	729	$15,000	$1500	225	Residence: Texas. Studying in Texas. Talent/Interest Area: animal/agricultural competition.
Tribal Priority Award	626	$15,000	$2500	1–5	Limited to American Indian/Alaska Native students.
Howard P. Rawlings Educational Excellence Awards Guaranteed Access Grant	702	$14,800	$400	1,000	Residence: Maryland. Studying in Maryland.
American Angus Auxiliary Scholarship	786	$14,000	$1000	10	Must be in high school.
South Dakota Space Grant Consortium Undergraduate and Graduate Student Scholarships	134	$14,000	$1000	45–50	Aviation/Aerospace; Earth Science; Energy and Power Engineering; Engineering-Related Technologies; Engineering/Technology; Environmental Science; Materials Science, Engineering, and Metallurgy; Mathematics; Natural Sciences; Physical Sciences; Science, Technology, and Society. Studying in South Dakota.
Entitlement Cal Grant B	672	$13,665	$700	56,200	Residence: California. Studying in California.
Law Enforcement Personnel Dependents Scholarship	552	$13,665	$100		Employment/Volunteer Experience: police/firefighting. Residence: California. Studying in California.
DeVry Dean's Scholarships	775	$13,500	$1500		Must be in high school.
National Space Grant College and Fellowship Program	106	$13,333	$1250	1–50	Applied Sciences; Aviation/Aerospace; Chemical Engineering; Civil Engineering; Computer Science/Data Processing; Earth Science; Engineering/Technology; Mathematics; Mechanical Engineering; Natural Sciences; Physical Sciences. Residence: Nevada. Studying in Nevada.
National Honor Society Scholarships	527	$13,000	$1000	200	Civic Affiliation: National Honor Society. Must be in high school.
Legislative Scholarship	715	$12,995	$2000	300–350	Residence: Ohio. Studying in Ohio. Must be in high school.
Law Enforcement Officers/Firemen Scholarship	560	$12,707	$1705		Employment/Volunteer Experience: police/firefighting. Residence: Mississippi. Studying in Mississippi.
Competitive Cal Grant A	672	$12,192	$5472	1,000–2,000	Residence: California. Studying in California.
Airline Pilots Association Scholarship Program	502	$12,000	$1000	1–3	Civic Affiliation: Airline Pilots Association.

Award Name	Page Number	Highest Dollar Amount	Lowest Dollar Amount	Number of Awards	Academic Fields/Career Goals and Nonacademic/Noncareer Criteria
Humane Studies Fellowships	190	$12,000	$2000	140–180	Communications; Economics; History; Humanities; Law/Legal Services; Literature/English/Writing; Political Science; Social Sciences.
Kappa Alpha Theta Foundation Scholarship Program	523	$12,000	$1000	200–230	Civic Affiliation: Greek Organization.
Margaret McNamara Memorial Fund Fellowships	785	$12,000	$12,000	6–12	Residence: Must be from a developing country.
Massachusetts AFL-CIO Scholarship	703	$12,000	$250	100–150	Residence: Massachusetts. Studying in Massachusetts. Must be in high school.
National Italian American Foundation Category II Scholarship	115	$12,000	$2500		Area/Ethnic Studies. Talent/Interest Area: Italian language.
Police Officers and Firefighters Survivors Education Assistance Program-Alabama	654	$12,000	$1600	15–30	Residence: Alabama. Studying in Alabama.
Principal's Leadership Award	755	$12,000	$1000	100	Talent/Interest Area: leadership. Must be in high school.
U.S. Army ROTC Guaranteed Reserve Forces Duty (GRFD), (ARNG/USAR) and Dedicated ARNG Scholarships	569	$12,000	$10,000	800–1,000	Disability: physically disabled. Military Service: Army National Guard.
Seneca Nation Higher Education Program	638	$11,000	$6000		Limited to American Indian/Alaska Native students.
SPIE Educational Scholarships in Optical Science and Engineering	105	$11,000	$2000	100–150	Applied Sciences; Chemical Engineering; Electrical Engineering/Electronics; Engineering-Related Technologies; Engineering/Technology; Materials Science, Engineering, and Metallurgy; Mechanical Engineering.
Frank O'Bannon Grant Program	726	$10,992	$200	48,408–70,239	Residence: Indiana. Studying in Indiana.
Washington State Need Grant Program	735	$10,868	$176	74,000	Residence: Washington. Studying in Washington.
Vermont Incentive Grants	733	$10,800	$500		Residence: Vermont.
Academy of Television Arts and Sciences College Television Awards	765	$10,000	$500	20–25	Communications; TV/Radio Broadcasting.
AG Bell College Scholarship Program	566	$10,000	$1000	15–25	Disability: hearing impaired.
A Legacy of Hope Scholarships for Survivors of Childhood Cancer	726	$10,000	$500	1–6	Residence: Colorado; Montana. Must be in high school.
American Legion National Headquarters Eagle Scout of the Year	551	$10,000	$2500	4	Employment/Volunteer Experience: community service. Must be in high school.
Arkansas Governor's Scholars Program	666	$10,000	$4000	75–375	Residence: Arkansas. Studying in Arkansas. Must be in high school.
Atlas Shrugged Essay Contest	770	$10,000	$50	84	Talent/Interest Area: writing.
California Junior Miss Scholarship Program	671	$10,000	$500	25	Residence: California. Talent/Interest Area: beauty pageant; leadership; public speaking. Must be in high school.
Canadian Nurses Foundation Scholarships	429	$10,000	$1500	50–60	Nursing. Employment/Volunteer Experience: nursing. Nationality: Canadian.
Christianson Grant	782	$10,000	$2500	8	Limited to students age 18–28.

Award Name	Page Number	Highest Dollar Amount	Lowest Dollar Amount	Number of Awards	Academic Fields/Career Goals and Nonacademic/Noncareer Criteria
Cystic Fibrosis Scholarship	568	$10,000	$1000	40–50	Disability: physically disabled.
DC Tuition Assistance Grant Program (DCTAG)	683	$10,000	$2500	6,000	Residence: District of Columbia.
Director's Scholarship Award	291	$10,000	$1000	1–5	Engineering/Technology. Talent/Interest Area: leadership.
Eagle Scout of the Year Scholarship	511	$10,000	$1000	1	Civic Affiliation: Boy Scouts. Residence: Nebraska.
E. Wayne Kay Community College Scholarship Award	291	$10,000	$1000	1–20	Engineering/Technology; Trade/Technical Specialties.
Executive Women International Scholarship Program	776	$10,000	$1000	75–100	Must be in high school.
ExploraVision Science Competition	761	$10,000	$5000		Talent/Interest Area: science.
Federation of American Consumers and Travelers Graduating High School Senior Scholarship	519	$10,000	$2500	2	Civic Affiliation: Federation of American Consumers and Travelers. Must be in high school.
Federation of American Consumers and Travelers In-School Scholarship	777	$10,000	$2500	2	Civic Affiliation: Federation of American Consumers and Travelers.
Federation of American Consumers and Travelers Second Chance Scholarship	777	$10,000	$2500	2	Civic Affiliation: Federation of American Consumers and Travelers.
Fisher Broadcasting Inc. Scholarship for Minorities	154	$10,000	$1000	5	Business/Consumer Services; Journalism; TV/Radio Broadcasting. Limited to ethnic minority students.
The Fountainhead Essay Contest	770	$10,000	$50	236	Must be in high school.
Freetestprep.com Scholarship Contest	778	$10,000	$1000	1	Talent/Interest Area: writing.
Governor Guinn Millennium Scholarship	709	$10,000	$1	1	Residence: Nevada. Studying in Nevada.
Hellenic Times Scholarship Fund	624	$10,000	$500	30–40	Limited to students of Greek heritage.
Herman O. West Foundation Scholarship Program	546	$10,000	$2500	1–7	Corporate Affiliation: West Pharmaceuticals. Must be in high school.
The Hirsch Family Scholarship	775	$10,000	$2000		Limited to dependent children of active employees of Eagle Materials, Performance Chemicals and Ingredients, Martin Fletcher, Hadlock Plastics, Highlander Partners and any of their majority-owned subsidiaries.
Hispanic College Fund Scholarship Program	625	$10,000	$500	500–600	Limited to Hispanic students.
Holocaust Remembrance Project Essay Contest	751	$10,000	$300	30	Talent/Interest Area: writing. Must be in high school.
HORIZONS Scholarship	408	$10,000	$500	5–6	Military and Defense Studies.
HSF/General College Scholarship Program	625	$10,000	$1000	2,900–3,500	Limited to Hispanic students.
Illinois Future Teachers Corps Program	238	$10,000	$5000		Education. Residence: Illinois. Studying in Illinois.
James R. Hoffa Memorial Scholarship Fund	522	$10,000	$1000	1–100	Civic Affiliation: International Brotherhood of Teamsters. Must be in high school.

Award Name	Page Number	Highest Dollar Amount	Lowest Dollar Amount	Number of Awards	Academic Fields/Career Goals and Nonacademic/Noncareer Criteria
Janet L. Hoffmann Loan Assistance Repayment Program	240	$10,000	$1500	700	Education; Law/Legal Services; Nursing; Social Services; Therapy/Rehabilitation. Employment/Volunteer Experience: government/politics. Residence: Maryland. Studying in Maryland.
John Lennon Scholarship Program	409	$10,000	$5000	3	Music. Talent/Interest Area: music.
Lee-Jackson Educational Foundation Scholarship Competition	699	$10,000	$1000	27	Residence: Virginia. Talent/Interest Area: writing. Must be in high school.
Legislative Essay Scholarship	683	$10,000	$1000	62	Residence: Delaware. Must be in high school.
Marine Corps Scholarship Foundation	542	$10,000	$500	1,000–1,500	Civic Affiliation: American Legion or Auxiliary; Boy Scouts. Military Service: Marine Corps.
Medicus Student Exchange	639	$10,000	$2000	1–10	Talent/Interest Area: foreign language.
Miller Electric International World Skills Competition Scholarship	262	$10,000	$1000	1	Engineering-Related Technologies; Engineering/Technology; Materials Science, Engineering, and Metallurgy; Trade/Technical Specialties.
NAAS Awards	526	$10,000	$200	10–14	Civic Affiliation: National Academy of American Scholars. Must be in high school.
Nancy Lorraine Jensen Memorial Scholarship	176	$10,000	$2500	1–6	Chemical Engineering; Electrical Engineering/Electronics; Mechanical Engineering. Talent/Interest Area: science.
National Aviation Explorer Scholarships	128	$10,000	$3000	5	Aviation/Aerospace. Talent/Interest Area: aviation; leadership.
National Italian American Foundation Category I Scholarship	632	$10,000	$2500	40–45	Limited to students of Italian heritage.
National Peace Essay Contest	362	$10,000	$1000	50–53	International Studies; Peace and Conflict Studies. Talent/Interest Area: writing. Must be in high school.
National Society of Women Engineers Scholarships	205	$10,000	$1000		Computer Science/Data Processing; Engineering/Technology.
NBFAA Youth Scholarship Program	562	$10,000	$500		Employment/Volunteer Experience: police/firefighting. Residence: California; Connecticut; Georgia; Indiana; Kentucky; Louisiana; Maryland; Minnesota; New Jersey; New York; North Carolina; Pennsylvania; Tennessee; Virginia; Washington. Must be in high school.
Needham and Company September 11th Scholarship Fund	787	$10,000	$7000	8–15	Limited to children of the victims who lost their lives at the World Trade Center.
Nightingale Awards of Pennsylvania Nursing Scholarship	439	$10,000	$6000	6	Nursing. Studying in Pennsylvania.
NRA Youth Educational Summit (YES) Scholarships	786	$10,000	$1000	1–6	Must be in high school.
Oracle Community Impact Scholarship	646	$10,000	$5000		Residence: California. Limited to Black (non-Hispanic) students.
Phelan Art Award in Filmmaking	309	$10,000	$5000	3	Filmmaking/Video.
Phelan Art Award in Video	309	$10,000	$5000	3	Filmmaking/Video.
Sir John M. Templeton Fellowships Essay Contest	782	$10,000	$1000	6	Talent/Interest Area: writing.

Award Name	Page Number	Highest Dollar Amount	Lowest Dollar Amount	Number of Awards	Academic Fields/Career Goals and Nonacademic/Noncareer Criteria
Sons of Italy National Leadership Grants Competition Language Scholarship	322	$10,000	$4000	1	Foreign Language.
Spencer Educational Foundation Scholarship	360	$10,000	$5000	30–40	Insurance and Actuarial Science.
Stephen Phillips Memorial Scholarship Fund	726	$10,000	$3000	150–200	Residence: Connecticut; Maine; Massachusetts; New Hampshire; Rhode Island; Vermont.
Swanson Scholarship	734	$10,000	$1000	1–10	Residence: Nebraska.
Tailhook Educational Foundation Scholarship	590	$10,000	$2000	70	Military Service: Coast Guard; Marine Corps; Navy.
Talbots Women's Scholarship Fund	798	$10,000	$1000	5–50	Limited to female students.
Technical Minority Scholarship	177	$10,000	$1000	122	Chemical Engineering; Computer Science/Data Processing; Electrical Engineering/Electronics; Engineering-Related Technologies; Engineering/Technology; Materials Science, Engineering, and Metallurgy; Mechanical Engineering; Physical Sciences. Limited to ethnic minority students.
Teletoon Animation Scholarship	122	$10,000	$5000	9	Arts; Filmmaking/Video. Residence: Alberta; British Columbia; Manitoba; New Brunswick; Newfoundland; Northwest Territories; Nova Scotia; Ontario; Prince Edward Island; Quebec; Saskatchewan.
Theodore R. and Vivian M. Johnson Scholarship Program for Children of UPS Employees or UPS Retirees	549	$10,000	$1000	1–250	Corporate Affiliation: UPS-United Parcel Service. Residence: Florida. Studying in Florida.
Toshiba/NSTA ExploraVision Awards Program	203	$10,000	$5000	16–32	Computer Science/Data Processing; Engineering/Technology; Nuclear Science; Physical Sciences. Must be in high school.
United Realty Students Scholarship Program	800	$10,000	$5000	14–14	Limited to students age 16–22.
Washington State Achievers Program Scholarship	678	$10,000	$5000	600	Residence: Washington. Studying in Washington. Must be in high school.
Win Free College Tuition Giveaway	788	$10,000	$500	1	Limited to high school seniors and college undergraduates.
Worldfest Student Film Award	310	$10,000	$1000	10	Filmmaking/Video.
Young American Creative Patriotic Art Awards Program	753	$10,000	$500	8	Talent/Interest Area: art. Must be in high school.
YoungArts, National Foundation for Advancement in the Arts	765	$10,000	$100	700	Talent/Interest Area: art; music/singing; photography/photogrammetry/filmmaking; theater; writing.
Minnesota State Grant Program	706	$9620	$100	71,000–105,000	Residence: Minnesota. Studying in Minnesota.
DeVry High School Scholarship	776	$9000	$2000		Must be in high school.
DeVry University First Scholar Award	748	$9000	$3000		Talent/Interest Area: science. Must be in high school.
Edward T. Conroy Memorial Scholarship Program	560	$9000	$7200	121	Employment/Volunteer Experience: police/firefighting. Military Service: General. Residence: Maryland. Studying in Maryland.

Award Name	Page Number	Highest Dollar Amount	Lowest Dollar Amount	Number of Awards	Academic Fields/Career Goals and Nonacademic/Noncareer Criteria
New Jersey Society of Certified Public Accountants High School Scholarship Program	78	$9000	$7000	20–25	Accounting. Residence: New Jersey. Must be in high school.
Delegate Scholarship Program-Maryland	702	$8650	$200	3,500	Residence: Maryland. Studying in Maryland.
Critical Languages Scholarships for Intensive Summer Institute in Turkish Language	320	$8500	$8000	50–60	Foreign Language. Talent/Interest Area: Turkish language.
Undergraduate STEM Research Scholarships	106	$8500	$3000	1–35	Applied Sciences; Aviation/Aerospace; Biology; Chemical Engineering; Computer Science/Data Processing; Electrical Engineering/Electronics; Engineering-Related Technologies; Materials Science, Engineering, and Metallurgy; Mathematics; Mechanical Engineering; Physical Sciences; Science, Technology, and Society. Studying in Virginia.
Connecticut Independent College Student Grants	681	$8166	$250		Residence: Connecticut. Studying in Connecticut.
North Dakota Scholars Program	715	$8135	$4588	45–50	Residence: North Dakota. Studying in North Dakota. Must be in high school.
Vermont Part-Time Student Grants	733	$8100	$250		Residence: Vermont.
AACE International Competitive Scholarship	108	$8000	$2000	15–25	Architecture; Aviation/Aerospace; Business/Consumer Services; Chemical Engineering; Civil Engineering; Construction Engineering/Management; Electrical Engineering/Electronics; Engineering-Related Technologies; Engineering/Technology; Mechanical Engineering.
AIFS-HACU Scholarships	616	$8000	$6000		Talent/Interest Area: international exchange. Limited to Hispanic students.
AQHF Racing Scholarships	98	$8000	$4000	1–5	Animal/Veterinary Sciences. Civic Affiliation: American Quarter Horse Association.
California Wine Grape Growers Foundation Scholarship	672	$8000	$2000	6–6	Residence: California. Studying in California. Must be in high school.
Kapadia Scholarships	296	$8000	$1500		Engineering/Technology.
Liederkranz Foundation Scholarship Award for Voice	754	$8000	$1000	14–18	Talent/Interest Area: music/singing.
The Louis Stokes Health Scholars Program	144	$8000	$5000	10–12	Biology; Health and Medical Sciences; Nursing; Physical Sciences; Public Health; Science, Technology, and Society; Therapy/Rehabilitation.
Pat and Jim Host Scholarship	353	$8000	$2000	1	Hospitality Management; Travel/Tourism.
Vocational Nurse Scholarship Program	434	$8000	$4000		Nursing. Residence: California.
AGC Education and Research Foundation Undergraduate Scholarships	181	$7500	$2500	100	Civil Engineering; Construction Engineering/Management; Engineering/Technology.
American Legion Department of Pennsylvania High School Oratorical Contest	663	$7500	$4000	3	Residence: Pennsylvania. Talent/Interest Area: public speaking. Must be in high school.

Award Name	Page Number	Highest Dollar Amount	Lowest Dollar Amount	Number of Awards	Academic Fields/Career Goals and Nonacademic/Noncareer Criteria
Civil Air Patrol Academic Scholarships	517	$7500	$1000	40	Civic Affiliation: Civil Air Patrol.
Epsilon Sigma Alpha Foundation Scholarships	623	$7500	$350	125–175	Limited to ethnic minority students.
E. Wayne Kay Scholarship	292	$7500	$2500	10–30	Engineering/Technology; Trade/Technical Specialties.
International Violoncello Competition	763	$7500	$2500	3	Talent/Interest Area: music.
Life Technologies Scholarship	174	$7500	$2500	3	Chemical Engineering; Civil Engineering; Computer Science/Data Processing; Electrical Engineering/Electronics; Engineering/Technology; Materials Science, Engineering, and Metallurgy; Mechanical Engineering.
Palmetto Fellows Scholarship Program	724	$7500	$6700	4,846	Residence: South Carolina. Studying in South Carolina. Must be in high school.
Paraprofessional Teacher Preparation Grant	240	$7500	$250		Education. Residence: Massachusetts.
TELACU Education Foundation	684	$7500	$500	350–600	Residence: California; Illinois; New York; Texas.
William Faulkner-William Wisdom Creative Writing Competition	758	$7500	$250	8	Talent/Interest Area: English language; writing.
Teaching Assistant Program in France	97	$7280	$1040	1,120	American Studies; Art History; Education; European Studies; Foreign Language; History; Humanities; International Studies; Literature/English/Writing; Political Science; Social Sciences. Talent/Interest Area: English language; foreign language; French language; international exchange.
Tuition Aid Grant	711	$7272	$868		Residence: New Jersey. Studying in New Jersey.
Indiana National Guard Supplemental Grant	585	$7110	$20	503–925	Military Service: Air Force National Guard; Army National Guard. Residence: Indiana. Studying in Indiana.
Charles and Lucille King Family Foundation Scholarships	189	$7000	$3500	10–20	Communications; Filmmaking/Video; TV/Radio Broadcasting.
Myrtle and Earl Walker Scholarship Fund	270	$7000	$1000	1–25	Engineering-Related Technologies; Engineering/Technology; Mechanical Engineering.
Selby Scholar Program	736	$7000	$1000	40	Residence: Florida. Talent/Interest Area: leadership.
Senatorial Scholarships-Maryland	703	$7000	$400	7,000	Residence: Maryland. Studying in Maryland.
Twin Towers Orphan Fund	799	$7000	$5000		Limited to students age 16–22.
Pennsylvania Burglar and Fire Alarm Association Youth Scholarship Program	563	$6500	$500	6–8	Employment/Volunteer Experience: police/firefighting. Residence: Pennsylvania. Must be in high school.
Nissan Scholarship	706	$6306	$6292		Residence: Mississippi. Studying in Mississippi. Must be in high school.
Summer Developmental Program Grant	706	$6280	$656		Residence: Mississippi. Studying in Mississippi. Must be in high school.

Award Name	Page Number	Highest Dollar Amount	Lowest Dollar Amount	Number of Awards	Academic Fields/Career Goals and Nonacademic/Noncareer Criteria
Taylor Opportunity Program for Students Honors Level	700	$6131	$780	8,781	Residence: Louisiana. Studying in Louisiana.
Toward EXcellence Access and Success (TEXAS Grant)	729	$6080	$2680		Residence: Texas. Studying in Texas.
Air Traffic Control Association Scholarship	126	$6000	$2000	7–12	Aviation/Aerospace; Engineering/ Technology. Employment/Volunteer Experience: air traffic control. Talent/ Interest Area: aviation.
American Legion Department of New York High School Oratorical Contest	662	$6000	$2000		Residence: New York. Talent/Interest Area: public speaking. Must be in high school.
Buckingham Memorial Scholarship	550	$6000	$2000	15–20	Employment/Volunteer Experience: air traffic control.
Contemporary Record Society National Competition for Performing Artists	748	$6000	$2000	1	Talent/Interest Area: music/singing.
Foster Care to Success/Casey Family Scholars Scholarship Program	778	$6000	$1000	100	Limited to students under the age of 25.
Friends of 440 Scholarship Fund, Inc.	688	$6000	$500	1–60	Residence: Florida.
GCSAA Scholars Competition	349	$6000	$500		Horticulture/Floriculture. Civic Affiliation: Golf Course Superintendents Association of America.
Gilbane Scholarship Program	113	$6000	$5000	1	Architecture; Engineering/Technology; Mathematics. Residence: Delaware; New Jersey; Pennsylvania. Limited to Black (non-Hispanic) students.
Golden Gate Restaurant Association Scholarship Foundation	214	$6000	$1000	9–15	Culinary Arts; Food Service/Hospitality; Hospitality Management. Residence: California.
Higher Education Scholarship Program	634	$6000	$50	72	Limited to American Indian/Alaska Native students.
International Foodservice Editorial Council Communications Scholarship	83	$6000	$250	1–8	Advertising/Public Relations; Communications; Culinary Arts; Food Science/Nutrition; Food Service/ Hospitality; Graphics/Graphic Arts/ Printing; Home Economics; Hospitality Management; Journalism; Literature/ English/Writing; Marketing; Photojournalism/Photography. Talent/ Interest Area: photography/ photogrammetry/filmmaking; writing.
Jo Anne J. Trow Scholarships	766	$6000	$1000	35	Civic Affiliation: Greek Organization
Marion Huber Learning Through Listening Awards	525	$6000	$2000	6	Civic Affiliation: Learning Ally. Employment/Volunteer Experience: community service. Disability: learning disabled. Talent/Interest Area: leadership. Must be in high school.
Mary P. Oenslager Scholastic Achievement Awards	525	$6000	$1000	9	Civic Affiliation: Learning Ally. Employment/Volunteer Experience: community service. Disability: visually impaired. Talent/Interest Area: leadership.

Award Name	Page Number	Highest Dollar Amount	Lowest Dollar Amount	Number of Awards	Academic Fields/Career Goals and Nonacademic/Noncareer Criteria
Minority Scholarship Award	330	$6000	$2000	5–10	Health and Medical Sciences. Employment/Volunteer Experience: physical therapy/rehabilitation. Limited to ethnic minority students.
Montana University System Honor Scholarship	708	$6000	$4000	200	Residence: Montana. Studying in Montana. Must be in high school.
National Competition for Composers' Recordings	748	$6000	$2000	1	Talent/Interest Area: music/singing.
National Scholarship Program	567	$6000	$1000	10–40	Disability: hearing impaired; physically disabled; visually impaired.
Office and Professional Employees International Union Howard Coughlin Memorial Scholarship Fund	531	$6000	$2400	18	Civic Affiliation: Office and Professional Employees International Union.
Tennessee Education Lottery Scholarship Program Tennessee HOPE Scholarship	728	$6000	$2000		Residence: Tennessee. Studying in Tennessee.
Higher Education Legislative Plan (HELP)	706	$5835	$721		Residence: Mississippi. Studying in Mississippi.
Taylor Opportunity Program for Students Performance Level	700	$5731	$580	10,938	Residence: Louisiana. Studying in Louisiana.
Tuition Equalization Grant (TEG) Program	729	$5712	$3808		Residence: Texas. Studying in Texas.
Kansas Teacher Service Scholarship	239	$5514	$2206		Education.
Academic Scholars Program	788	$5500	$1800		Studying in Oklahoma. Must be in high school.
Oregon Veterans' Education Aid	606	$5400	$3600	1–200	Military Service: General. Residence: Oregon. Studying in Oregon.
Taylor Opportunity Program for Students Opportunity Level	700	$5331	$380	23,870	Residence: Louisiana. Studying in Louisiana.
Academy of Motion Picture Arts and Sciences Student Academy Awards	308	$5000	$2000	3–15	Filmmaking/Video.
AHETEMS Scholarships	289	$5000	$1000	100	Engineering/Technology; Mathematics; Science, Technology, and Society.
AIA New Jersey Scholarship Program	109	$5000	$2500	3–5	Architecture. Residence: New Jersey. Studying in New Jersey. Talent/Interest Area: art.
Alabama Student Assistance Program	653	$5000	$300		Residence: Alabama. Studying in Alabama.
Albert E. Wischmeyer Memorial Scholarship Award	289	$5000	$1000	1–10	Engineering/Technology. Residence: New York. Studying in New York.
All-Ink.com College Scholarship Program	766	$5000	$1000	5–10	Limited to students with 2.5 GPA or higher.
American Academy of Chefs College Scholarship	212	$5000	$1000	1–10	Culinary Arts; Food Service/Hospitality.
American Chemical Society Scholars Program	162	$5000	$1000	100–200	Chemical Engineering; Environmental Science; Materials Science, Engineering, and Metallurgy; Natural Sciences; Paper and Pulp Engineering. Limited to American Indian/Alaska Native; Black (non-Hispanic); Hispanic students.

Award Name	Page Number	Highest Dollar Amount	Lowest Dollar Amount	Number of Awards	Academic Fields/Career Goals and Nonacademic/Noncareer Criteria
American Legion Legacy Scholarship	597	$5000	$2000		Military Service: General.
American Occupational Therapy Foundation State Association Scholarships	330	$5000	$150		Health and Medical Sciences; Therapy/Rehabilitation.
Anchor Scholarship Foundation Program	610	$5000	$2000	35–43	Military Service: Navy.
Angus Foundation Scholarships	528	$5000	$250	75–90	Civic Affiliation: American Angus Association.
ARTBA-TDF Lanford Family Highway Workers Memorial Scholarship Program	551	$5000	$1000		Employment/Volunteer Experience: construction; roadway work.
Arthur and Gladys Cervenka Scholarship Award	289	$5000	$1000	1–10	Engineering/Technology.
Arthur J. Packard Memorial Scholarship	213	$5000	$2000	3	Culinary Arts; Food Service/Hospitality; Hospitality Management; Recreation, Parks, Leisure Studies; Travel/Tourism.
Ashby B. Carter Memorial Scholarship Fund Founders Award	526	$5000	$2000	3	Civic Affiliation: National Alliance of Postal and Federal Employees. Must be in high school.
Associated General Contractors NYS Scholarship Program	181	$5000	$1500	15–25	Civil Engineering; Construction Engineering/Management; Surveying, Surveying Technology, Cartography, or Geographic Information Science; Trade/Technical Specialties; Transportation. Residence: New York.
BMI Student Composer Awards	117	$5000	$500	10	Arts; Music. Talent/Interest Area: music/singing.
Boys and Girls Clubs of Chicago Scholarships	515	$5000	$3000		Civic Affiliation: Boys or Girls Club. Residence: Illinois. Must be in high school.
Bruce Lee Scholarship	801	$5000	$2000	1	Must be in high school.
Caterpillar Scholars Award Fund	289	$5000	$1000	1–15	Engineering/Technology.
Center for Architecture, Douglas Haskell Award for Student Journals	110	$5000	$2000	1–3	Architecture; Engineering/Technology; Landscape Architecture; Urban and Regional Planning. Talent/Interest Area: writing.
Central Scholarship Bureau Grants	673	$5000	$1000	20–30	Residence: Maryland.
Chapter 198-Downriver Detroit Scholarship	290	$5000	$1000	1–5	Engineering/Technology; Industrial Design; Mechanical Engineering; Trade/Technical Specialties. Studying in Michigan.
Chapter 23-Quad Cities Iowa/Illinois Scholarship	290	$5000	$1000	5	Engineering/Technology. Studying in Illinois; Iowa.
Chapter 31-Tri City Scholarship	290	$5000	$1000	5	Engineering/Technology. Studying in Michigan.
Chapter 3-Peoria Endowed Scholarship	290	$5000	$1000	5	Engineering/Technology. Residence: Illinois. Studying in Illinois.
Chapter 4-Lawrence A. Wacker Memorial Scholarship	290	$5000	$1000	1–10	Engineering/Technology; Mechanical Engineering. Studying in Wisconsin.
Chapter 63-Portland James E. Morrow Scholarship	290	$5000	$1000	5	Engineering/Technology. Residence: Oregon; Washington. Studying in Oregon; Washington.

Award Name	Page Number	Highest Dollar Amount	Lowest Dollar Amount	Number of Awards	Academic Fields/Career Goals and Nonacademic/Noncareer Criteria
Chapter 63-Portland Uncle Bud Smith Scholarship	290	$5000	$1000	5	Engineering/Technology. Residence: Oregon; Washington. Studying in Oregon; Washington.
Chapter 67-Phoenix Scholarship	290	$5000	$1000	1–5	Engineering/Technology; Industrial Design; Mechanical Engineering; Trade/Technical Specialties. Studying in Arizona.
Chapter 6-Fairfield County Scholarship	291	$5000	$1000	4	Engineering/Technology.
Chapter 93-Albuquerque Scholarship	291	$5000	$1000	1–5	Engineering/Technology. Studying in New Mexico.
Chesapeake Urology Associates Scholarship	334	$5000	$1500	3	Health and Medical Sciences; Nursing. Residence: Maryland.
CIF/FARMERS Scholar-Athlete of the Year	772	$5000	$2000	22	Must be in high school.
Clarence and Josephine Myers Scholarship	291	$5000	$1000	5	Engineering/Technology. Studying in Indiana.
Clinton J. Helton Manufacturing Scholarship Award Fund	291	$5000	$1000	1–5	Engineering/Technology; Trade/Technical Specialties. Studying in Colorado.
Colonel Hazel Elizabeth Benn U.S.M.C. Scholarship	519	$5000	$1000	1–10	Civic Affiliation: Fleet Reserve Association/Auxiliary. Military Service: Navy.
Colorado Student Grant	678	$5000	$850	69,602	Residence: Colorado. Studying in Colorado.
Congressional Black Caucus Spouses Education Scholarship	774	$5000	$500	250–400	Performing Arts.
Congressional Hispanic Caucus Institute Scholarship Awards	621	$5000	$1000	100–150	Limited to Hispanic students.
Connie and Robert T. Gunter Scholarship	291	$5000	$1000	1–5	Engineering/Technology. Studying in Georgia.
Continental Society, Daughters of Indian Wars Scholarship	236	$5000	$2500	3	Education; Social Services. Limited to American Indian/Alaska Native students.
Culinary Trust Scholarship Program for Culinary Study and Research	214	$5000	$1000	21	Culinary Arts; Food Science/Nutrition; Food Service/Hospitality.
Daughters of the Cincinnati Scholarship	581	$5000	$3000	4–5	Military Service: Air Force; Army; Coast Guard; Marine Corps; Navy. Must be in high school.
Donaldson D. Frizzell Scholarship	777	$5000	$2500	6	Limited to members of the U.S. uniformed services (active, reserve, and retired) and their spouses and dependents, First Command Financial Services' clients and their families, and dependent family members of First Command Advisors and field office staff members.
Doris and John Carpenter Scholarship	643	$5000	$2000		Limited to Black (non-Hispanic) students.
Drs. Poh Shien & Judy Young Scholarship	648	$5000	$2000		Must be in high school. Limited to Asian/Pacific Islander students.
Duke Energy Scholars Program	546	$5000	$1000	15	Corporate Affiliation: Duke Energy Corporation.

Award Name	Page Number	Highest Dollar Amount	Lowest Dollar Amount	Number of Awards	Academic Fields/Career Goals and Nonacademic/Noncareer Criteria
EDSF Board of Directors Scholarships	153	$5000	$1000		Business/Consumer Services; Computer Science/Data Processing; Graphics/Graphic Arts/Printing.
Education Exchange College Grant Program	750	$5000	$1000	34	Talent/Interest Area: leadership. Must be in high school.
Edward M. Nagel Foundation Scholarship	82	$5000	$2000		Accounting; Business/Consumer Services; Economics. Residence: California. Limited to Black (non-Hispanic) students.
Edward S. Roth Manufacturing Engineering Scholarship	291	$5000	$1000	1–10	Engineering/Technology. Studying in California; Florida; Illinois; Massachusetts; Minnesota; Ohio; Texas; Utah.
Elie Wiesel Prize in Ethics Essay Contest	749	$5000	$500	5	Talent/Interest Area: writing.
Emerging Texas Artist Scholarship	122	$5000	$500	8–12	Arts. Studying in Texas. Talent/Interest Area: art.
E. Wayne Kay Co-op Scholarship	292	$5000	$1000	1–10	Engineering/Technology.
Explosive Ordnance Disposal Memorial Scholarship	554	$5000	$1000	25–75	Employment/Volunteer Experience: explosive ordnance disposal. Military Service: General.
Federated Garden Clubs of Connecticut Inc. Scholarships	144	$5000	$1000	2–5	Biology; Horticulture/Floriculture; Landscape Architecture. Residence: Connecticut. Studying in Connecticut.
Federation of American Consumers and Travelers Trade/Technical School Scholarship	519	$5000	$1000	1–3	Civic Affiliation: Federation of American Consumers and Travelers.
Fleet Reserve Association Education Foundation Scholarships	589	$5000	$1000	1–15	Military Service: Coast Guard; Marine Corps; Navy.
Foreclosure.com Scholarship Program	777	$5000	$1000	5	Talent/Interest Area: writing.
Fort Wayne Chapter 56 Scholarship	292	$5000	$1000	1–10	Engineering/Technology; Industrial Design; Mechanical Engineering; Trade/Technical Specialties. Studying in Indiana.
Franz Stenzel M.D. and Kathryn Stenzel Scholarship Fund	338	$5000	$2000	70	Health and Medical Sciences; Nursing. Residence: Oregon.
Gene and John Athletic Fund Scholarship	760	$5000	$2500	1–3	Talent/Interest Area: athletics/sports; LGBT issues.
General John Ratay Educational Fund Grants	603	$5000	$4000	1–5	Military Service: General.
Georgia Engineering Foundation Scholarship Program	281	$5000	$1000	45	Engineering/Technology. Employment/Volunteer Experience: community service. Residence: Georgia.
Geraldo Rivera Scholarship	369	$5000	$1000		Journalism; TV/Radio Broadcasting.
Governors Scholarship Program	678	$5000	$1000	30	Residence: Washington. Studying in Washington. Must be in high school.
Graco Inc. Scholarship Program	546	$5000	$3500		Corporate Affiliation: Graco, Inc..
Graduate and Professional Scholarship Program-Maryland	224	$5000	$1000	584	Dental Health/Services; Health and Medical Sciences; Law/Legal Services; Nursing; Social Services. Residence: Maryland. Studying in Maryland.
Great Falls Broadcasters Association Scholarship	499	$5000	$2000	1	TV/Radio Broadcasting. Residence: Montana. Studying in Montana.

Award Name	Page Number	Highest Dollar Amount	Lowest Dollar Amount	Number of Awards	Academic Fields/Career Goals and Nonacademic/Noncareer Criteria
Greenhouse Scholars	555	$5000	$500	20–35	Employment/Volunteer Experience: community service. Residence: Colorado; Illinois. Talent/Interest Area: leadership. Must be in high school.
Guiliano Mazzetti Scholarship Award	292	$5000	$1000	1–10	Engineering/Technology.
Harry A. Applegate Scholarship	153	$5000	$1000	20–25	Business/Consumer Services; Education; Fashion Design; Finance; Hospitality Management; Marketing. Civic Affiliation: Distribution Ed Club or Future Business Leaders of America.
Harry C. Jaecker Scholarship	339	$5000	$2000		Health and Medical Sciences. Limited to Black (non-Hispanic) students.
Harry C. Jaecker Scholarship	340	$5000	$2000		Health and Medical Sciences. Limited to Black (non-Hispanic) students.
Harry Ludwig Scholarship Fund	576	$5000	$500	1–3	Disability: visually impaired.
Herbert Hoover Uncommon Student Award	693	$5000	$1000	15	Residence: Iowa. Must be in high school.
Hispanic Engineer National Achievement Awards Corporation Scholarship Program	130	$5000	$500	12–20	Aviation/Aerospace; Biology; Chemical Engineering; Civil Engineering; Computer Science/Data Processing; Electrical Engineering/Electronics; Engineering/Technology; Materials Science, Engineering, and Metallurgy; Mechanical Engineering; Nuclear Science. Limited to Hispanic students.
Hispanic Metropolitan Chamber Scholarships	625	$5000	$1000	40	Residence: Oregon; Washington. Limited to Hispanic students.
Houston Symphony Ima Hogg Competition	412	$5000	$300	5	Music. Talent/Interest Area: music.
Howard Rock Foundation Scholarship Program	620	$5000	$2500	3	Limited to American Indian/Alaska Native students.
IFMA Foundation Scholarships	112	$5000	$1500	25–35	Architecture; Construction Engineering/Management; Engineering-Related Technologies; Engineering/Technology; Interior Design; Urban and Regional Planning.
Indiana Health Care Policy Institute Nursing Scholarship	435	$5000	$750	1–5	Nursing. Residence: Indiana. Studying in Illinois; Indiana; Kentucky; Michigan; Ohio.
Indian American Scholarship Fund	626	$5000	$500	3	Residence: Georgia. Must be in high school. Limited to Asian/Pacific Islander students.
Indiana Nursing Scholarship Fund	441	$5000	$200	490–690	Nursing. Residence: Indiana. Studying in Indiana.
International Society of Automation Education Foundation Scholarships	131	$5000	$500	5–15	Aviation/Aerospace; Chemical Engineering; Electrical Engineering/Electronics; Energy and Power Engineering; Engineering-Related Technologies; Engineering/Technology; Heating, Air-Conditioning, and Refrigeration Mechanics; Materials Science, Engineering, and Metallurgy; Mechanical Engineering; Paper and Pulp Engineering; Pharmacy.

Award Name	Page Number	Highest Dollar Amount	Lowest Dollar Amount	Number of Awards	Academic Fields/Career Goals and Nonacademic/Noncareer Criteria
ISA Educational Foundation Scholarships	265	$5000	$500	15	Engineering-Related Technologies.
James L. and Genevieve H. Goodwin Memorial Scholarship	417	$5000	$1000	10	Natural Resources. Residence: Connecticut.
Jane M. Klausman Women in Business Scholarships	161	$5000	$4000	12	Business/Consumer Services.
Jerry McDowell Fund	265	$5000	$1000	1–3	Engineering-Related Technologies; Engineering/Technology.
Jesse Jones Jr. Scholarship	160	$5000	$2000		Business/Consumer Services. Limited to Black (non-Hispanic) students.
Jewish Vocational Service Scholarship Fund	627	$5000	$1000	125–200	Residence: California. Religion: Jewish.
Jimi Hendrix Endowment Fund Scholarship	415	$5000	$2000		Music. Limited to Black (non-Hispanic) students.
John Kimball Memorial Trust Scholarship Program for the Study of History	345	$5000	$300	3–10	History. Residence: Massachusetts.
John L. Dales Scholarship Program	796	$5000	$1000	1–16	Must be in high school.
John M. Azarian Memorial Armenian Youth Scholarship Fund	627	$5000	$500	1–5	Limited to students of Armenian descent.
Joseph Shinoda Memorial Scholarship	350	$5000	$1000	8–15	Horticulture/Floriculture.
Judith McManus Price Scholarship	501	$5000	$2000		Urban and Regional Planning. Limited to American Indian/Alaska Native; Black (non-Hispanic); Hispanic students.
Kappa Alpha Theta Foundation Non-Degree Educational Grant Program	523	$5000	$100	1–50	Civic Affiliation: Greek Organization.
Keck Foundation Scholarship	644	$5000	$2000		Limited to Black (non-Hispanic) students.
Kosciuszko Foundation Chopin Piano Competition	413	$5000	$1500	3	Music; Performing Arts. Talent/Interest Area: music/singing.
Lilly Reintegration Scholarship	573	$5000	$2500	70–100	Disability: physically disabled.
L. Ron Hubbard's Illustrators of the Future Contest	745	$5000	$500	12	Talent/Interest Area: art.
L. Ron Hubbard's Writers of the Future Contest	745	$5000	$500	12	Talent/Interest Area: writing.
Lucile B. Kaufman Women's Scholarship	292	$5000	$1000	1–5	Engineering/Technology.
Macy's Hallmark Scholarship	648	$3000	$2000	1	Must be in high school. Limited to Asian/Pacific Islander students.
Mae Maxey Memorial Scholarship	123	$5000	$1000		Arts; Literature/English/Writing. Limited to Black (non-Hispanic) students.
Maine Community Foundation Scholarship Programs	701	$5000	$500	150–700	Residence: Maine.
Mary Oenslager Scholarship	645	$5000	$2000		Limited to Black (non-Hispanic) students.
Math, Engineering, Science, Business, Education, Computers Scholarships	151	$5000	$500	180	Business/Consumer Services; Computer Science/Data Processing; Education; Engineering/Technology; Humanities; Physical Sciences; Science, Technology, and Society; Social Sciences. Limited to American Indian/Alaska Native students.

Award Name	Page Number	Highest Dollar Amount	Lowest Dollar Amount	Number of Awards	Academic Fields/Career Goals and Nonacademic/Noncareer Criteria
Michael & Donna Griffith Scholarship	645	$5000	$2500		Limited to Black (non-Hispanic) students.
Mary McMillan Scholarship Award	233	$5000	$3000	1–6	Education; Health and Medical Sciences; Therapy/Rehabilitation. Employment/Volunteer Experience: physical therapy/rehabilitation.
Minority Teacher Incentive Grant Program	236	$5000	$2500	71	Education. Studying in Connecticut. Limited to ethnic minority students.
MOAA American Patriot Scholarship	603	$5000	$2500	65	Military Service: General.
NADONA/LTC Stephanie Carroll Memorial Scholarship	437	$5000	$1000	1–20	Nursing.
National Asian-American Journalists Association Newhouse Scholarship	364	$5000	$1000	5	Journalism.
National Ground Water Research and Educational Foundation's Len Assante Scholarship	229	$5000	$1000	5–10	Earth Science; Environmental Science; Hydrology.
Native American Journalists Association Scholarships	370	$5000	$500	10	Journalism. Civic Affiliation: Native American Journalists Association. Talent/Interest Area: writing. Limited to American Indian/Alaska Native students.
Native American Leadership in Education (NALE)	151	$5000	$500	30	Business/Consumer Services; Education; Humanities; Physical Sciences; Science, Technology, and Society. Limited to American Indian/Alaska Native students.
Naval Reserve Association Scholarship Program	611	$5000	$1000		Military Service: Navy.
New England Employee Benefits Council Scholarship Program	77	$5000	$1000	1–3	Accounting; Business/Consumer Services; Economics; Health Administration; Human Resources; Insurance and Actuarial Science; Law/Legal Services; Public Health; Public Policy and Administration. Residence: Connecticut; Maine; Massachusetts; New Hampshire; Rhode Island; Vermont. Studying in Connecticut; Maine; Massachusetts; New Hampshire; Rhode Island; Vermont.
New York State Tuition Assistance Program	712	$5000	$500	350,000–360,000	Residence: New York. Studying in New York.
Norm Manly—YMTA Maritime Educational Scholarships	389	$5000	$500	6–7	Marine Biology; Marine/Ocean Engineering; Oceanography; Trade/Technical Specialties. Residence: Washington. Must be in high school.
North Carolina Association of CPAs Foundation Scholarships	77	$5000	$1000	50–60	Accounting. Residence: North Carolina. Studying in North Carolina.
North Central Region 9 Scholarship	292	$5000	$1000	1–10	Engineering/Technology; Industrial Design; Mechanical Engineering; Trade/Technical Specialties. Studying in Iowa; Michigan; Minnesota; Nebraska; North Dakota; South Dakota; Wisconsin.
NSCS Scholar Abroad Scholarship	529	$5000	$2500	3	Civic Affiliation: National Society of Collegiate Scholars.

Award Name	Page Number	Highest Dollar Amount	Lowest Dollar Amount	Number of Awards	Academic Fields/Career Goals and Nonacademic/Noncareer Criteria
Outdoor Writers Association of America - Bodie McDowell Scholarship Award	193	$5000	$1000	2–6	Communications; Filmmaking/Video; Journalism; Literature/English/Writing; Photojournalism/Photography; TV/Radio Broadcasting. Talent/Interest Area: amateur radio; art; athletics/sports; photography/ photogrammetry/filmmaking; writing.
Patrick Kerr Skateboard Scholarship	793	$5000	$1000	4	Must be in high school.
Patriot's Pen	762	$5000	$500	46	Talent/Interest Area: writing.
Paul Shearman Allen & Associates Scholarship	648	$5000	$2000	1	Must be in high school. Limited to Asian/ Pacific Islander students.
Pellegrini Scholarship Grants	639	$5000	$500	50	Residence: Connecticut; Delaware; New Jersey; New York; Pennsylvania.
PepsiCo Hallmark Scholarships	648	$5000	$2000	1	Must be in high school. Limited to Asian/ Pacific Islander students.
PFund Scholarship Award Program	720	$5000	$2000	18–20	Residence: Minnesota. Studying in Minnesota. Talent/Interest Area: LGBT issues.
PHCC Educational Foundation Scholarship Program	158	$5000	$2500	1–4	Business/Consumer Services; Engineering-Related Technologies; Engineering/ Technology; Heating, Air-Conditioning, and Refrigeration Mechanics; Mechanical Engineering; Trade/Technical Specialties.
Planned Systems International Scholarship	648	$5000	$2000		Must be in high school. Limited to Asian/ Pacific Islander students.
Print and Graphics Scholarships Foundation	193	$5000	$1500	150–200	Communications; Graphics/Graphic Arts/ Printing.
Promise of Nursing Scholarship	433	$5000	$1000		Nursing. Studying in California; Florida; Georgia; Illinois; Massachusetts; Michigan; New Jersey; Tennessee; Texas.
Raymond W. Cannon Memorial Scholarship	382	$5000	$2000		Law/Legal Services; Pharmacy. Limited to Black (non-Hispanic) students.
Regional and Restricted Scholarship Award Program	680	$5000	$250	200–300	Residence: Connecticut.
Samuel Robinson Award	652	$5000	$250	16	Religion: Presbyterian.
Scholarship Program for Sons & Daughters of Employees of Roseburg Forest Products Co.	777	$5000	$3000	100	Must be a dependent child or stepchild of an employee of Roseburg Forest Products Company.
Screen Actors Guild Foundation/ John L. Dales Scholarship Fund (Standard)	796	$5000	$1000	100–135	Must be a member of SAG AFTRA Union or the child of a member of SAG AFTRA Union.
Sergeant Major Douglas R. Drum Memorial Scholarship	598	$5000	$1000	1–24	Military Service: General.
SHRM Foundation Student Scholarships	355	$5000	$200	40	Human Resources. Civic Affiliation: Society for Human Resource Management.
Sigma Xi Grants-In-Aid of Research	95	$5000	$1000	400	Agriculture ; Animal/Veterinary Sciences; Biology; Chemical Engineering; Earth Science; Engineering/Technology; Health and Medical Sciences; Mechanical Engineering; Meteorology/Atmospheric Science; Physical Sciences; Science, Technology, and Society; Social Sciences.
Society of Physics Students Leadership Scholarships	464	$5000	$2000	17–22	Physical Sciences. Civic Affiliation: Society of Physics Students.

Award Name	Page Number	Highest Dollar Amount	Lowest Dollar Amount	Number of Awards	Academic Fields/Career Goals and Nonacademic/Noncareer Criteria
Society of Plastics Engineers Scholarship Program	171	$5000	$1000	25–30	Chemical Engineering; Electrical Engineering/Electronics; Engineering/Technology; Industrial Design; Materials Science, Engineering, and Metallurgy; Trade/Technical Specialties.
Specialty Equipment Market Association Memorial Scholarship Fund	80	$5000	$2000	60–90	Accounting; Advertising/Public Relations; Business/Consumer Services; Communications; Computer Science/Data Processing; Electrical Engineering/Electronics; Engineering/Technology; Finance; Marketing; Mechanical Engineering; Trade/Technical Specialties; Transportation. Talent/Interest Area: automotive.
SPENDonLIFE College Scholarship	797	$5000	$500	2–10	Based on financial need.
Stanley A. Doran Memorial Scholarship	519	$5000	$1000	1	Civic Affiliation: Fleet Reserve Association/Auxiliary. Military Service: Coast Guard; Marine Corps; Navy.
Sunday Supper Atlanta Scholarship	217	$5000	$2000	5	Culinary Arts.
Sun Student College Scholarship Program	563	$5000	$2000	1–16	Employment/Volunteer Experience: community service. Residence: Arizona. Must be in high school.
Taylor Michaels Scholarship Fund	559	$5000	$1000		Employment/Volunteer Experience: community service. Must be in high school. Limited to ethnic minority students.
Theta Delta Chi Educational Foundation Inc. Scholarship	799	$5000	$1000	15	Civic Affiliation: Greek Organization.
Tribal Business Management Program (TBM)	70	$5000	$500	35	Accounting; Business/Consumer Services; Computer Science/Data Processing; Economics; Electrical Engineering/Electronics; Engineering-Related Technologies. Limited to American Indian/Alaska Native students.
Truckload Carriers Association Scholarship Fund	159	$5000	$1500	18	Business/Consumer Services; Transportation. Employment/Volunteer Experience: transportation industry.
Underwood-Smith Teacher Scholarship Program	246	$5000	$2500	30–60	Education. Residence: West Virginia. Studying in West Virginia.
UPS Hallmark Scholarships	648	$5000	$2000		Must be in high school. Limited to Asian/Pacific Islander students.
Higher Education Success Stipend Program	732	$5000	$300	422–7,028	Residence: Utah. Studying in Utah.
Vertical Flight Foundation Scholarship	124	$5000	$1500	10–19	Aviation/Aerospace; Electrical Engineering/Electronics; Engineering-Related Technologies; Engineering/Technology; Mechanical Engineering. Talent/Interest Area: aviation.
Vincent L. Hawkinson Scholarship for Peace and Justice	733	$5000	$4000	1–6	Residence: Iowa; Minnesota; North Dakota; South Dakota; Wisconsin. Studying in Iowa; Minnesota; North Dakota; South Dakota; Wisconsin. Talent/Interest Area: leadership.

Award Name	Page Number	Highest Dollar Amount	Lowest Dollar Amount	Number of Awards	Academic Fields/Career Goals and Nonacademic/Noncareer Criteria
Warner Norcross and Judd LLP Scholarship for Minority Students	380	$5000	$1000	3	Law/Legal Services. Residence: Michigan. Studying in Michigan. Limited to ethnic minority students.
Watson-Brown Foundation Scholarship	735	$5000	$3000	200–200	Residence: Georgia; South Carolina.
William E. Weisel Scholarship Fund	255	$5000	$1000	1–10	Electrical Engineering/Electronics; Engineering/Technology; Mechanical Engineering; Trade/Technical Specialties.
WJA Scholarship Program	124	$5000	$500	1	Arts; Trade/Technical Specialties. Talent/Interest Area: art.
Women's Independence Scholarship Program	802	$5000	$250	500–600	Limited to female students.
Worldstudio AIGA Scholarships	124	$5000	$1000	10–25	Arts; Graphics/Graphic Arts/Printing.
W. Price Jr. Memorial Scholarship	564	$5000	$2000	4	Employment/Volunteer Experience: food service.
Young Artist Competition	455	$5000	$500	8	Performing Arts. Residence: Illinois; Indiana; Iowa; Kansas; Manitoba; Michigan; Minnesota; Missouri; Nebraska; North Dakota; Ontario; South Dakota; Wisconsin. Talent/Interest Area: music.
Youth Activity Fund	420	$5000	$500	10–30	Natural Sciences; Science, Technology, and Society.
Alaska Performance Scholarship	654	$4755	$500		Residence: Alaska. Studying in Alaska.
Arkansas Academic Challenge Scholarship Program	666	$4500	$1250	30,000–35,000	Residence: Arkansas. Studying in Arkansas.
Brook Hollow Golf Club Scholarship	775	$4500	$2000		Must be in high school.
DeVry/Keller Military Service Grant	600	$4500	$1000		Military Service: General.
Ernest Alan and Barbara Park Meyer Scholarship Fund	716	$4500	$1000	5	Residence: Oregon.
Glenn Miller Instrumental Scholarship	750	$4500	$1000	3	Talent/Interest Area: music/singing. Must be in high school.
Greater Washington Society of CPAs Scholarship	73	$4500	$2000	3–5	Accounting. Residence: District of Columbia. Studying in District of Columbia.
Hawaii Association of Broadcasters Scholarship	497	$4500	$500	20–30	TV/Radio Broadcasting.
Passport to College Promise Scholarship	734	$4500	$1	1–400	Residence: Washington. Studying in Washington.
Charley Wootan Grant Program	799	$4394	$1000		Must demonstrate financial need.
Pennsylvania State Grant	720	$4348	$200		Residence: Pennsylvania.
ASCSA Summer Sessions Scholarships	100	$4250	$500	10–11	Anthropology; Archaeology; Architecture; Art History; Arts; Classics; Historic Preservation and Conservation; History; Humanities; Museum Studies; Philosophy; Religion/Theology. Talent/Interest Area: international exchange.
American Legion Department of Indiana High School Oratorical Contest	660	$4200	$200	4–8	Residence: Indiana. Talent/Interest Area: public speaking. Must be in high school.
Alexander and Maude Hadden Scholarship	566	$4000	$2500		Employment/Volunteer Experience: community service.

Award Name	Page Number	Highest Dollar Amount	Lowest Dollar Amount	Number of Awards	Academic Fields/Career Goals and Nonacademic/Noncareer Criteria
American Legion Department of New Jersey High School Oratorical Contest	740	$4000	$1000	5	Talent/Interest Area: public speaking. Must be in high school.
American Legion Department of New Jersey Scholarship	511	$4000	$1000	8	Civic Affiliation: American Legion or Auxiliary. Military Service: Army. Must be in high school.
American Society for Enology and Viticulture Scholarships	90	$4000	$500	30	Agriculture ; Chemical Engineering; Food Science/Nutrition; Horticulture/Floriculture.
Armed Forces Communications and Electronics Association ROTC Scholarship Program	127	$4000	$2000	35–45	Aviation/Aerospace; Communications; Computer Science/Data Processing; Electrical Engineering/Electronics; Engineering-Related Technologies; Engineering/Technology; Foreign Language; International Studies; Mathematics; Physical Sciences. Military Service: Air Force; Army; Marine Corps; Navy.
BCIC Young Innovator Scholarship Competition (Idea Mash Up)	104	$4000	$2000		Applied Sciences; Biology; Business/Consumer Services; Earth Science; Engineering-Related Technologies; Engineering/Technology; Environmental Science; Graphics/Graphic Arts/Printing; Mathematics; Natural Sciences; Physical Sciences. Nationality: Canadian. Must be in high school.
Bridging Scholarship for Study Abroad in Japan	770	$4000	$2500	40–80	Limited for use in undergraduate junior or senior years.
C.A.R. Scholarship Foundation Award	469	$4000	$2000	20–30	Real Estate. Residence: California. Studying in California.
CIA Undergraduate Scholarships	97	$4000	$1000	15–30	American Studies; Aviation/Aerospace; Computer Science/Data Processing; Criminal Justice/Criminology; Foreign Language; History; Law Enforcement/Police Administration; Military and Defense Studies; Natural Sciences; Near and Middle East Studies; Peace and Conflict Studies; Political Science.
College Now Greater Cleveland Adult Learner Program Scholarship	678	$4000	$500	250–450	Residence: Ohio.
Community Bankers Assoc. of IL Annual Scholarship Program	679	$4000	$500	16	Residence: Illinois. Must be in high school.
Community Bankers Assoc of IL Child of a Banker Scholarship	517	$4000	$1000	2	Civic Affiliation: Community Banker Association of Illinois. Employment/Volunteer Experience: banking. Residence: Illinois. Must be in high school.
Elks Emergency Educational Grants	518	$4000	$1000		Civic Affiliation: Elks Club.
Engineering Scholarship	163	$4000	$1000	1–5	Chemical Engineering; Civil Engineering; Electrical Engineering/Electronics; Engineering-Related Technologies; Engineering/Technology; Materials Science, Engineering, and Metallurgy; Mechanical Engineering. Residence: Pennsylvania.

Award Name	Page Number	Highest Dollar Amount	Lowest Dollar Amount	Number of Awards	Academic Fields/Career Goals and Nonacademic/Noncareer Criteria
Federal Junior Duck Stamp Conservation and Design Competition	123	$4000	$1000	3	Arts. Talent/Interest Area: art. Must be in high school.
Gerald W. & Jean Purmal Endowed Scholarship	644	$4000	$1000		Limited to Black (non-Hispanic) students.
GMP Memorial Scholarship Program	520	$4000	$2000	10	Civic Affiliation: Glass, Molders, Pottery, Plastics and Allied Workers International Union. Must be in high school.
Illinois CPA Society Accounting Scholarship Program	74	$4000	$500	12–20	Accounting. Residence: Illinois. Studying in Illinois.
Iowa Tuition Grant Program	696	$4000	$100	16,500–19,000	Residence: Iowa. Studying in Iowa.
John F. and Anna Lee Stacey Scholarship Fund	120	$4000	$1000	3–5	Arts. Talent/Interest Area: art.
Kaiser Permanente Allied Healthcare Scholarship	336	$4000	$3000	40	Health and Medical Sciences; Social Services; Therapy/Rehabilitation. Residence: California. Studying in California.
Lois McMillen Memorial Scholarship Fund	118	$4000	$500	1–5	Arts. Residence: Connecticut. Talent/Interest Area: art.
Malcolm Baldrige Scholarship	152	$4000	$2000	1–3	Business/Consumer Services; International Studies. Residence: Connecticut. Studying in Connecticut.
Minority Student Summer Scholarship	108	$4000	$1500	2	Archaeology; Arts; Classics; Foreign Language; History. Limited to ethnic minority students.
Mississippi Press Association Education Foundation Scholarship	368	$4000	$1000	1	Journalism. Residence: Mississippi.
New Mexico Vietnam Veteran Scholarship	605	$4000	$3500	100	Military Service: General. Residence: New Mexico. Studying in New Mexico.
NGPA Education Fund, Inc.	136	$4000	$3000	3–4	Aviation/Aerospace. Employment/Volunteer Experience: community service. Talent/Interest Area: aviation; LGBT issues.
Part-Time Grant Program	726	$4000	$20	4,680–6,700	Residence: Indiana. Studying in Indiana.
Sikh Education Aid Fund	770	$4000	$400		Religion/Theology.
South Florida Fair College Scholarship	725	$4000	$1000	10	Residence: Florida.
SSPI International Scholarships	138	$4000	$2500	1–4	Aviation/Aerospace; Communications; Law/Legal Services; Meteorology/Atmospheric Science; Military and Defense Studies.
Student-View Scholarship program	798	$4000	$500	11	Must be in high school.
Tennessee Student Assistance Award	728	$4000	$100	30,000–35,000	Residence: Tennessee. Studying in Tennessee.
Texas Mutual Insurance Company Scholarship Program	799	$4000	$500	1–10	Limited to students that have 2.5 GPA or higher.
Union Plus Credit Card Scholarship Program	503	$4000	$500		Civic Affiliation: American Federation of State, County, and Municipal Employees.
Union Plus Education Foundation Scholarship Program	540	$4000	$500	100–120	Civic Affiliation: AFL-CIO.

Award Name	Page Number	Highest Dollar Amount	Lowest Dollar Amount	Number of Awards	Academic Fields/Career Goals and Nonacademic/Noncareer Criteria
Union Plus Scholarship Program	527	$4000	$500	3	Civic Affiliation: National Association of Letter Carriers. Must be in high school.
University Film and Video Association Carole Fielding Student Grants	309	$4000	$1000	5	Filmmaking/Video.
Wenderoth Undergraduate Scholarship	533	$4000	$1750	1–4	Civic Affiliation: Phi Sigma Kappa.
Weyerhaeuser Company Foundation Scholarships	549	$4000	$1000	50	Corporate Affiliation: Weyerhauser Company. Must be in high school.
William L. Cullison Scholarship	419	$4000	$2000	1–2	Natural Resources; Paper and Pulp Engineering.
Young Women in Public Affairs Award	803	$4000	$1000	5	Must be in high school.
Sallie Mae Fund Unmet Need Scholarship Program	794	$3800	$1000		Limited to students that have 2.5 GPA or higher.
Early Childhood Educators Scholarship Program	240	$3600	$150		Education.
Nebraska Opportunity Grant	709	$3600	$100		Residence: Nebraska. Studying in Nebraska.
Teacher Assistant Scholarship Fund	241	$3600	$600		Education. Employment/Volunteer Experience: teaching/education. Residence: North Carolina. Studying in North Carolina.
Taylor Opportunity Program for Students Tech Level	701	$3556	$380	1,242	Residence: Louisiana. Studying in Louisiana.
American Foreign Service Association (AFSA) Financial Aid Award Program	503	$3500	$1000	50–60	Civic Affiliation: American Foreign Service Association. Limited to Asian/Pacific Islander students.
American Legion Auxiliary National President's Scholarship	593	$3500	$2500	15	Military Service: General. Must be in high school.
American Legion Department of Arkansas High School Oratorical Contest	659	$3500	$1250	4	Residence: Arkansas. Talent/Interest Area: public speaking. Must be in high school.
American Society of Naval Engineers Scholarship	103	$3500	$2500	8–14	Applied Sciences; Aviation/Aerospace; Civil Engineering; Electrical Engineering/Electronics; Energy and Power Engineering; Engineering/Technology; Marine/Ocean Engineering; Materials Science, Engineering, and Metallurgy; Mechanical Engineering; Physical Sciences.
Annual Award Program	650	$3500	$800	20–45	Religion: Muslim faith.
Armenian Students Association of America Inc. Scholarships	617	$3500	$1000	30	Limited to students of Armenian descent.
BDSA Scholarships	746	$3500	$1000		Talent/Interest Area: golf. Must be in high school.
International Order Of The Golden Rule Awards of Excellence Scholarship	322	$3500	$2000	2	Funeral Services/Mortuary Science.
Kansas Nursing Service Scholarship Program	436	$3500	$2500		Nursing.

Award Name	Page Number	Highest Dollar Amount	Lowest Dollar Amount	Number of Awards	Academic Fields/Career Goals and Nonacademic/Noncareer Criteria
National Defense Transportation Association, Scott Air Force Base-St. Louis Area Chapter Scholarship	708	$3500	$2000	6	Residence: Illinois; Missouri. Studying in Colorado; Illinois; Indiana; Iowa; Kansas; Michigan; Minnesota; Missouri; Montana; Nebraska; North Dakota; South Dakota; Wisconsin; Wyoming.
OAB Foundation Scholarship	193	$3500	$2500	4	Communications; Journalism; TV/Radio Broadcasting. Residence: Oregon.
Robert Guthrie PKU Scholarship and Awards	575	$3500	$500	4–8	Disability: physically disabled.
Unmet NEED Grant Program	633	$3500	$1000	10–500	Residence: Pennsylvania. Limited to Black (non-Hispanic) students.
American Cancer Society, Florida Division R.O.C.K. College Scholarship Program	566	$3300	$300	200–225	Disability: physically disabled. Residence: Florida. Studying in Florida. Talent/Interest Area: leadership.
Cal Grant C	672	$3168	$576	7,761	Residence: California. Studying in California.
Actuarial Diversity Scholarship	359	$3000	$1000		Insurance and Actuarial Science; Mathematics. Limited to ethnic minority students.
Adelante Fund Scholarships	613	$3000	$1000	30–45	Studying in Arizona; California; Florida; Illinois; New Mexico; New York; Texas. Talent/Interest Area: leadership. Limited to Hispanic students.
Air Force Sergeants Association Scholarship	580	$3000	$500	30	Military Service: Air Force; Air Force National Guard.
AlaskAdvantage Education Grant	654	$3000	$500		Residence: Alaska. Studying in Alaska.
The Alexander Foundation Scholarship Program	655	$3000	$300	6–35	Residence: Colorado. Studying in Colorado. Talent/Interest Area: LGBT issues.
AMBUCS Scholars-Scholarships for Therapists	124	$3000	$500	275	Audiology; Therapy/Rehabilitation.
American Dietetic Association Foundation Scholarship Program	312	$3000	$500	200–225	Food Science/Nutrition. Civic Affiliation: American Dietetic Association.
American Hotel & Lodging Educational Foundation Pepsi Scholarship	212	$3000	$500		Culinary Arts; Food Service/Hospitality; Hospitality Management; Recreation, Parks, Leisure Studies; Travel/Tourism. Residence: District of Columbia.
American Legion Department of Tennessee High School Oratorical Contest	664	$3000	$1000	3	Residence: Tennessee. Talent/Interest Area: public speaking. Must be in high school.
American Montessori Society Teacher Education Scholarship Fund	233	$3000	$1000	10–20	Education
American Physical Society Corporate-Sponsored Scholarship for Minority Undergraduate Students Who Major in Physics	462	$3000	$2000		Physical Sciences. Limited to ethnic minority students.
American Physical Society Scholarship for Minority Undergraduate Physics Majors	460	$3000	$2000	30–40	Physical Sciences. Limited to American Indian/Alaska Native; Black (non-Hispanic); Hispanic students.
American Savings Foundation Scholarships	665	$3000	$500		Residence: Connecticut.
American Water Ski Educational Foundation Scholarship	515	$3000	$1500	5	Civic Affiliation: USA Water Ski.

Award Name	Page Number	Highest Dollar Amount	Lowest Dollar Amount	Number of Awards	Academic Fields/Career Goals and Nonacademic/Noncareer Criteria
Annual Scholarship Grant Program	213	$3000	$500		Culinary Arts; Food Service/Hospitality; Hospitality Management; Recreation, Parks, Leisure Studies; Travel/Tourism.
Arizona Nursery Association Foundation Scholarship	347	$3000	$500	12–16	Horticulture/Floriculture.
Arthur Ross Foundation Scholarship	641	$3000	$1000		Limited to Black (non-Hispanic) students.
Astrid G. Cates and Myrtle Beinhauer Scholarship Funds	537	$3000	$1000	2–7	Civic Affiliation: Mutual Benefit Society. Residence: Yukon.
A.T. Cross Scholarship	549	$3000	$1000		Corporate Affiliation: A.T. Cross. Residence: Rhode Island.
Blackfeet Nation Higher Education Grant	618	$3000	$2800	180	Limited to American Indian/Alaska Native students.
Central Indiana ASSE Jim Kriner Memorial Scholarship	446	$3000	$1000	3	Occupational Safety and Health.
Chief Master Sergeants of the Air Force Scholarship Program	580	$3000	$500	30	Military Service: Air Force; Air Force National Guard.
Clan MacBean Foundation Grant Program	114	$3000	$500	1	Area/Ethnic Studies; Child and Family Studies.
CollegeBound Foundation Last Dollar Grant	674	$3000	$500	45–60	Residence: Maryland. Studying in Maryland. Must be in high school.
College Tuition Assistance Program	630	$3000	$2000	25–30	Residence: New Jersey; New York. Must be in high school. Limited to Hispanic students.
Deerfield Plastics/Barker Family Scholarship	545	$3000	$1500	1	Corporate Affiliation: Deerfield Plastics. Residence: Kentucky; Massachusetts.
Delta Sigma Pi Undergraduate Scholarship	153	$3000	$250	1–40	Business/Consumer Services. Civic Affiliation: Greek Organization.
Distinguished Raven FAC Memorial Scholarship	622	$3000	$500	5–10	Limited to Asian/Pacific Islander students.
The Donaldson Company, Inc. Scholarship Program	545	$3000	$1000		Corporate Affiliation: Donaldson Company.
Don't Mess With Texas Scholarship Program	684	$3000	$1000	2–3	Residence: Texas. Studying in Texas. Must be in high school.
Duck Brand Duct Tape "Stuck at Prom" Scholarship Contest	780	$3000	$1000	3	Talent/Interest Area: art.
DuPont Challenge Science Essay Awards Program	749	$3000	$100	100	Talent/Interest Area: writing. Must be in high school.
Edna F. Blum Foundation Scholarship	643	$3000	$1000		Residence: New York. Limited to Black (non-Hispanic) students.
Edward J. and Virginia M. Routhier Nursing Scholarship	441	$3000	$500		Nursing. Studying in Rhode Island.
Francis D. Lyon Scholarship for Film Student	308	$3000	$2000	1	Filmmaking/Video.
Fresh Start Scholarship	736	$3000	$1000	10–15	Residence: Delaware. Studying in Delaware.
George and Pearl Strickland Scholarship	679	$3000	$1000	1–25	Residence: Georgia. Studying in Georgia.
Hilton Baltimore Convention Center Hotel Scholarship Fund	152	$3000	$1000	13–15	Business/Consumer Services; Hospitality Management. Residence: Maryland. Must be in high school.

Award Name	Page Number	Highest Dollar Amount	Lowest Dollar Amount	Number of Awards	Academic Fields/Career Goals and Nonacademic/Noncareer Criteria
Hubertus W.V. Wellems Scholarship for Male Students	169	$3000	$2000	1	Chemical Engineering; Engineering-Related Technologies; Engineering/Technology; Physical Sciences. Civic Affiliation: National Association for the Advancement of Colored People. Limited to ethnic minority students.
Humana Foundation Scholarship Program	781	$3000	$1500	75	Must be a dependent of a Humana Inc. employee.
One Million Degrees Signature Fund Scholarship	695	$3000	$500	1–80	Residence: Illinois. Studying in Illinois.
International Airlines Travel Agent Network Foundation Scholarship	353	$3000	$500	10–15	Hospitality Management; Travel/Tourism. Employment/Volunteer Experience: travel and tourism industry.
James Duval Phelan Literary Award	758	$3000	$2000	3	Talent/Interest Area: writing.
Joseph A. McAlinden Divers Scholarship	609	$3000	$500		Military Service: Marine Corps; Navy.
Joseph and Rebecca Meyerhoff Scholarship	675	$3000	$1000	3–5	Residence: Maryland. Studying in Maryland. Must be in high school.
Joseph H. Bearns Prize in Music	747	$3000	$2000	2	Talent/Interest Area: music.
Joseph Henry Jackson Literary Award	724	$3000	$2000	3	Residence: California; Nevada. Talent/Interest Area: writing.
Joseph S. Rumbaugh Historical Oration Contest	756	$3000	$1000	1–3	Talent/Interest Area: public speaking.
Kellogg Scholarship	174	$3000	$1000	3	Chemical Engineering; Mechanical Engineering. Civic Affiliation: Society of Women Engineers.
Kentucky Tuition Grant (KTG)	699	$3000	$200	11,500–12,500	Residence: Kentucky. Studying in Kentucky.
Kildee Scholarships	93	$3000	$2000	3	Agriculture ; Animal/Veterinary Sciences.
Marion A. and Eva S. Peeples Scholarships	240	$3000	$1000	30–35	Education; Engineering/Technology; Food Science/Nutrition; Nursing; Trade/Technical Specialties. Residence: Indiana. Studying in Indiana.
MasterCard Worldwide Special Support Program	645	$3000	$2000	1	Limited to Black (non-Hispanic) students.
Millie Brother Scholarship for Children of Deaf Adults	773	$3000	$1000	2–5	Must be a hearing child of deaf parents.
Minority Nurse Magazine Scholarship Program	437	$3000	$1000	3	Nursing. Limited to ethnic minority students.
Miss American Coed Pageant	754	$3000	$150	52	Talent/Interest Area: beauty pageant
Missouri Higher Education Academic Scholarship (Bright Flight)	707	$3000	$1000		Residence: Missouri. Studying in Missouri.
MRCA Foundation Scholarship Program	112	$3000	$500	40	Architecture; Civil Engineering; Construction Engineering/Management; Drafting; Engineering/Technology; Industrial Design; Materials Science, Engineering, and Metallurgy; Trade/Technical Specialties. Employment/Volunteer Experience: construction.

Award Name	Page Number	Highest Dollar Amount	Lowest Dollar Amount	Number of Awards	Academic Fields/Career Goals and Nonacademic/Noncareer Criteria
NAACP/Hubertus W.V. Willems Scholarship for Male Scholars	271	$3000	$2000		Engineering-Related Technologies; Mathematics; Natural Sciences. Limited to Black (non-Hispanic) students.
NAAS II National Awards	785	$3000	$500	1–5	Limited to students under the age of 25.
National Asphalt Pavement Association Research and Education Foundation Scholarship Program	183	$3000	$500	50–150	Civil Engineering; Construction Engineering/Management.
National Federation of Paralegal Associates Inc. Thomson Reuters Scholarship	381	$3000	$2000	2	Law/Legal Services.
National High School Essay Contest	761	$3000	$750	3	Talent/Interest Area: writing. Must be in high school.
National High School Journalist of the Year/Sister Rita Jeanne Scholarships	783	$3000	$1000	1–7	Must be in high school.
National Multiple Sclerosis Society Mid America Chapter Scholarship	575	$3000	$1000	100	Disability: physically disabled.
Ohio American Legion Scholarships	511	$3000	$2000	15–18	Civic Affiliation: American Legion or Auxiliary. Military Service: General.
OSCPA Educational Foundation Scholarship Program	79	$3000	$500	50–100	Accounting. Residence: Oregon. Studying in Oregon.
Overseas Press Club Foundation Scholarships	372	$3000	$2000	14	Journalism. Talent/Interest Area: writing.
Pennsylvania Masonic Youth Foundation Educational Endowment Fund Scholarships	533	$3000	$1000		Civic Affiliation: Freemasons.
Plastics Pioneers Scholarships	170	$3000	$1500	30–40	Chemical Engineering; Engineering-Related Technologies; Engineering/Technology; Materials Science, Engineering, and Metallurgy; Trade/Technical Specialties.
Profile in Courage Essay Contest	386	$3000	$500	7	Literature/English/Writing. Talent/Interest Area: writing. Must be in high school.
PSE&G Scholarship	82	$3000	$2500		Accounting; Business/Consumer Services; Computer Science/Data Processing; Economics; Engineering/Technology; Finance; Marketing. Residence: New Jersey. Limited to Black (non-Hispanic) students.
Rama Scholarship for the American Dream	213	$3000	$1000		Culinary Arts; Food Service/Hospitality; Hospitality Management; Recreation, Parks, Leisure Studies; Travel/Tourism. Limited to ethnic minority students.
Roadway Worker Memorial Scholarship Program	768	$3000	$2000	2–5	Limited to children of roadway workers.
Rockefeller State Wildlife Scholarship	146	$3000	$2000	20–30	Biology; Marine Biology; Marine/Ocean Engineering; Natural Resources; Oceanography. Residence: Louisiana. Studying in Louisiana.

Award Name	Page Number	Highest Dollar Amount	Lowest Dollar Amount	Number of Awards	Academic Fields/Career Goals and Nonacademic/Noncareer Criteria
Roothbert Fund Inc. Scholarship	794	$3000	$2000	20	Studying in Connecticut; Delaware; District of Columbia; Maryland; Massachusetts; New Hampshire; New Jersey; New York; Ohio; Pennsylvania; Rhode Island; Vermont; Virginia; West Virginia.
Scholarships for Education, Business and Religion	153	$3000	$500		Business/Consumer Services; Education; Religion/Theology. Residence: California.
Seol Bong Scholarship	577	$3000	$2000	21	Disability: learning disabled. Residence: Connecticut; Delaware; Maine; Massachusetts; New Hampshire; New Jersey; New York; Pennsylvania; Rhode Island; Vermont. Studying in Connecticut; Delaware; Maine; Massachusetts; New Hampshire; New Jersey; New York; Pennsylvania; Rhode Island; Vermont. Limited to Asian/Pacific Islander students.
Society of Louisiana CPAs Scholarships	79	$3000	$500		Accounting. Residence: Louisiana. Studying in Louisiana.
Sonne Scholarship	434	$3000	$1000	2–4	Nursing. Residence: Illinois. Studying in Illinois.
Sorantin Young Artist Award	415	$3000	$1000	5–12	Music; Performing Arts. Talent/Interest Area: music.
Spring Meadow Nursery Scholarship	350	$3000	$3000	3–3	Horticulture/Floriculture; Landscape Architecture.
Steven Hymans Extended Stay Scholarship	214	$3000	$1000		Culinary Arts; Food Service/Hospitality; Hospitality Management; Recreation, Parks, Leisure Studies; Travel/Tourism.
Texas History Essay Contest	98	$3000	$1000	3	American Studies; History. Talent/Interest Area: writing. Must be in high school.
Timothy and Palmer W. Bigelow Jr., Scholarship	86	$3000	$3000	1	Agribusiness; Entomology; Horticulture/Floriculture; Landscape Architecture. Residence: Connecticut; Maine; Massachusetts; New Hampshire; Rhode Island; Vermont.
Traub-Dicker Rainbow Scholarship	760	$3000	$1000	3–9	Talent/Interest Area: LGBT issues.
Two Ten Footwear Foundation Scholarship	565	$3000	$500	200–300	Employment/Volunteer Experience: leather/footwear industry.
Wal-Mart Higher Reach Scholarship	549	$3000	$250		Corporate Affiliation: Wal-Mart Foundation.
West Virginia Engineering, Science and Technology Scholarship Program	257	$3000	$1500	200–300	Electrical Engineering/Electronics; Engineering-Related Technologies; Engineering/Technology; Science, Technology, and Society. Residence: West Virginia. Studying in West Virginia.
We the Living Essay Contest	770	$3000	$25	116	Must be in high school.
William P. Willis Scholarship	716	$3000	$2000		Residence: Oklahoma. Studying in Oklahoma.
Wings Over America Scholarship	613	$3000	$1000	40	Military Service: Navy.
Wisconsin Higher Education Grants (WHEG)	737	$3000	$250		Residence: Wisconsin. Studying in Wisconsin.
WRI College Scholarship Program	186	$3000	$1500	2–5	Civil Engineering; Construction Engineering/Management.

Award Name	Page Number	Highest Dollar Amount	Lowest Dollar Amount	Number of Awards	Academic Fields/Career Goals and Nonacademic/Noncareer Criteria
Writer's Digest Annual Writing Competition	764	$3000	$25	100	Talent/Interest Area: writing.
Writer's Digest Self-Published Book Awards	764	$3000	$1000	10	Talent/Interest Area: writing.
WSTLA American Justice Essay Scholarship Contest	383	$3000	$2000	3	Law/Legal Services. Studying in Washington. Must be in high school.
Postsecondary Child Care Grant Program-Minnesota	706	$2800	$100	2,500–3,000	Residence: Minnesota. Studying in Minnesota.
Howard P. Rawlings Educational Excellence Awards Educational Assistance Grant	702	$2700	$400	15,000–30,000	Residence: Maryland. Studying in Maryland.
NJ Student Tuition Assistance Reward Scholarship	710	$2600	$500		Residence: New Jersey. Studying in New Jersey.
South Carolina Tuition Grants Program	725	$2600	$100		Residence: South Carolina. Studying in South Carolina.
Florida Postsecondary Student Assistance Grant	687	$2534	$200		Residence: Florida. Studying in Florida.
Florida Private Student Assistance Grant	687	$2534	$200		Residence: Florida. Studying in Florida.
Florida Public Student Assistance Grant	687	$2534	$200		Residence: Florida. Studying in Florida.
Florida Student Assistance Grant-Career Education	687	$2534	$200		Residence: Florida. Studying in Florida.
2013 Scholarship Essay Contest	776	$2500	$250	3	Talent/Interest Area: writing.
ACES Copy Editing Scholarship	363	$2500	$1000		Journalism. Talent/Interest Area: writing.
Adult Students in Scholastic Transition	776	$2500	$250	100–150	Must be an adult student.
Agnes Jones Jackson Scholarship	526	$2500	$1500	1	Civic Affiliation: National Association for the Advancement of Colored People. Limited to ethnic minority students.
AHIMA Foundation Student Merit Scholarship	340	$2500	$1000	1	Health Information Management/Technology. Civic Affiliation: American Health Information Management Association.
AIA/AAF Minority/Disadvantaged Scholarship	109	$2500	$500	20	Architecture. Limited to ethnic minority students.
AIAA Foundation Undergraduate Scholarship	102	$2500	$2000	30	Applied Sciences; Aviation/Aerospace; Electrical Engineering/Electronics; Engineering-Related Technologies; Engineering/Technology; Materials Science, Engineering, and Metallurgy; Mechanical Engineering; Physical Sciences; Science, Technology, and Society. Civic Affiliation: American Institute of Aeronautics and Astronautics.
Allen and Joan Bildner Scholarship	641	$2500	$2000		Residence: New Jersey. Limited to Black (non-Hispanic) students.
American Board of Funeral Service Education Scholarships	322	$2500	$500	5–15	Funeral Services/Mortuary Science.
American Council of the Blind Scholarships	566	$2500	$1000	16–20	Disability: visually impaired.

Award Name	Page Number	Highest Dollar Amount	Lowest Dollar Amount	Number of Awards	Academic Fields/Career Goals and Nonacademic/Noncareer Criteria
American Legion Auxiliary Department of Maine National President's Scholarship	550	$2500	$1000	3	Employment/Volunteer Experience: community service. Military Service: General. Residence: Maine. Must be in high school.
American Legion Auxiliary Department of North Dakota National President's Scholarship	550	$2500	$1000	3	Employment/Volunteer Experience: community service. Military Service: General. Residence: North Dakota. Studying in North Dakota. Must be in high school.
American Legion Auxiliary Department of Oregon National President's Scholarship	594	$2500	$1000	3	Military Service: General. Residence: Oregon. Must be in high school.
American Legion Auxiliary Department of Utah National President's Scholarship	506	$2500	$1000	15	Civic Affiliation: American Legion or Auxiliary. Military Service: General. Residence: Utah. Must be in high school.
American Legion Auxiliary National President's Scholarships	595	$2500	$1000	15	Military Service: General. Must be in high school.
American Legion Department of Washington Children and Youth Scholarships	512	$2500	$1500	2	Civic Affiliation: American Legion or Auxiliary. Military Service: General. Residence: Washington. Studying in Washington. Must be in high school.
American Welding Society District Scholarship Program	261	$2500	$100	150–200	Engineering-Related Technologies; Trade/Technical Specialties.
BIA Higher Education Grant	625	$2500	$50	1–150	Limited to American Indian/Alaska Native students.
Breakthrough to Nursing Scholarships for Racial/Ethnic Minorities	432	$2500	$1000		Nursing. Limited to ethnic minority students.
California Council of the Blind Scholarships	567	$2500	$375	20	Disability: visually impaired. Residence: California. Studying in California.
Carpe Diem Foundation of Illinois Scholarship Competition	772	$2500	$1500	15–20	Limited to undergraduate study only.
Clem Judd, Jr. Memorial Scholarship	352	$2500	$1000	2	Hospitality Management. Residence: Hawaii. Limited to Asian/Pacific Islander students.
Crohn's & Colitis Foundation of America Student Research Fellowship Awards	335	$2500	$2500		Health and Medical Sciences.
CrossLites Scholarship Award	748	$2500	$100	33	Talent/Interest Area: writing.
Deloras Jones RN Nursing as a Second Career Scholarship	435	$2500	$1000		Nursing. Residence: California. Studying in California.
Deloras Jones RN Scholarship Program	435	$2500	$1000		Nursing. Residence: California. Studying in California.
Deloras Jones RN Underrepresented Groups in Nursing Scholarship	436	$2500	$1000		Nursing. Residence: California. Studying in California. Limited to ethnic minority students.
Donna Jamison Lago Memorial Scholarship	633	$2500	$500	9	Talent/Interest Area: writing. Must be in high school. Limited to Black (non-Hispanic) students.
Education Foundation, Inc. National Guard Association of Colorado Scholarships	583	$2500	$500	20–30	Military Service: Air Force National Guard; Army National Guard. Residence: Colorado.

Award Name	Page Number	Highest Dollar Amount	Lowest Dollar Amount	Number of Awards	Academic Fields/Career Goals and Nonacademic/Noncareer Criteria
E. Wayne Kay High School Scholarship	292	$2500	$1000	1–20	Engineering/Technology.
Foundation for Accounting Education Scholarship	78	$2500	$500	1–60	Accounting. Residence: New York. Studying in New York.
Foundation for Surgical Technology Scholarship Fund	335	$2500	$500	10–20	Health and Medical Sciences.
Foundation of the National Student Nurses' Association Career Mobility Scholarship	432	$2500	$1000		Nursing.
Foundation of the National Student Nurses' Association General Scholarships	432	$2500	$1000		Nursing.
Foundation of the National Student Nurses' Association Specialty Scholarship	433	$2500	$1000		Nursing.
Friends of Bill Rutherford Education Fund	716	$2500	$1000	1–2	Residence: Oregon.
Fulfilling Our Dreams Scholarship Fund	637	$2500	$500	50–60	Residence: California. Studying in California. Limited to Hispanic students.
HANA Scholarship	623	$2500	$1000		Religion: Methodist. Talent/Interest Area: leadership. Limited to American Indian/Alaska Native; Asian/Pacific Islander; Hispanic students.
Harry and Rose Howell Scholarship	542	$2500	$2000	3	Civic Affiliation: Naval Sea Cadet Corps.
HBCUConnect.com Minority Scholarship Program	624	$2500	$1000	1–12	Limited to ethnic minority students.
High School Scholarship	280	$2500	$1500	6	Engineering/Technology. Residence: Florida. Must be in high school.
Hopi Education Award	626	$2500	$50	1–400	Limited to American Indian/Alaska Native students.
Institute of Management Accountants Memorial Education Fund Scholarships	74	$2500	$1000	6–15	Accounting; Business/Consumer Services.
International Association of Fire Chiefs Foundation Scholarship Award	311	$2500	$500	10–25	Fire Sciences.
Jack and Jill of America Foundation Scholarship	644	$2500	$1500		Must be in high school. Limited to Black (non-Hispanic) students.
Jackson-Stricks Scholarship	573	$2500	$1500	1–7	Disability: physically disabled. Residence: New York. Studying in New York.
Joseph S. Garske Collegiate Grant Program	521	$2500	$1500	1–4	Civic Affiliation: Golf Course Superintendents Association of America. Must be in high school.
Kentucky Educational Excellence Scholarship (KEES)	699	$2500	$125	65,000–70,000	Residence: Kentucky. Studying in Kentucky.
Kentucky Society of Certified Public Accountants College Scholarship	75	$2500	$1000	23	Accounting. Residence: Kentucky. Studying in Kentucky.
Koniag Education Foundation Academic/Graduate Scholarship	628	$2500	$500	130–170	Limited to American Indian/Alaska Native students.

Award Name	Page Number	Highest Dollar Amount	Lowest Dollar Amount	Number of Awards	Academic Fields/Career Goals and Nonacademic/Noncareer Criteria
Korean-American Scholarship Foundation Northeastern Region Scholarships	628	$2500	$1000	60	Studying in Connecticut; Maine; Massachusetts; New Hampshire; New Jersey; New York; Rhode Island; Vermont. Limited to Asian/Pacific Islander students.
Larry Fullerton Photojournalism Scholarship	458	$2500	$500	1–2	Photojournalism/Photography. Residence: Ohio. Studying in Ohio. Talent/Interest Area: photography/photogrammetry/filmmaking.
LEAGUE Foundation Academic Scholarship	753	$2500	$1500	4–8	Talent/Interest Area: LGBT issues. Must be in high school.
Legislative Endowment Scholarships	711	$2500	$1000	1	Residence: New Mexico. Studying in New Mexico.
Lessans Family Scholarship	619	$2500	$1000	12–20	Residence: Maryland. Religion: Jewish.
Leveraging Educational Assistance Partnership	666	$2500	$100		Residence: Arizona. Studying in Arizona.
Library Research Grants	116	$2500	$500		Art History; Arts. Studying in California. Talent/Interest Area: art.
Literacy Grant Competition	521	$2500	$300	18	Civic Affiliation: Phi Kappa Phi.
Moody Research Grants	344	$2500	$500	10–15	History; Political Science. Studying in Texas.
Maine State Society Foundation Scholarship	701	$2500	$1000	5–10	Residence: Maine. Studying in Maine.
Marshall E. McCullough-National Dairy Shrine Scholarships	93	$2500	$1000	2	Agriculture ; Journalism; TV/Radio Broadcasting. Must be in high school.
Mary Rubin and Benjamin M. Rubin Scholarship Fund	673	$2500	$1000	20–35	Residence: Maryland.
Massachusetts Gilbert Matching Student Grant Program	704	$2500	$200		Residence: Massachusetts. Studying in Massachusetts.
Minnesota Space Grant Consortium Scholarship Program	132	$2500	$500	25–50	Aviation/Aerospace; Earth Science; Engineering/Technology; Mathematics; Physical Sciences. Studying in Minnesota.
Minority Undergraduate Retention Grant-Wisconsin	649	$2500	$250		Residence: Wisconsin. Studying in Wisconsin. Limited to ethnic minority students.
Mississippi Eminent Scholars Grant	706	$2500	$392		Residence: Mississippi. Studying in Mississippi.
Missouri Broadcasters Association Scholarship	499	$2500	$1000	3	TV/Radio Broadcasting. Residence: Missouri. Studying in Missouri.
Missouri Insurance Education Foundation Scholarship	360	$2500	$2000	6	Insurance and Actuarial Science. Residence: Missouri. Studying in Missouri.
NAACP/Agnes Jones Jackson Scholarship	645	$2500	$1500		Limited to Black (non-Hispanic) students.
NASA Idaho Space Grant Consortium Scholarship Program	146	$2500	$1000	1–15	Biology; Chemical Engineering; Civil Engineering; Computer Science/Data Processing; Earth Science; Electrical Engineering/Electronics; Geography; Materials Science, Engineering, and Metallurgy; Mathematics; Mechanical Engineering; Natural Sciences; Physical Sciences. Studying in Idaho.

Award Name	Page Number	Highest Dollar Amount	Lowest Dollar Amount	Number of Awards	Academic Fields/Career Goals and Nonacademic/Noncareer Criteria
New Jersey Association of Realtors Educational Foundation Scholarship Program	470	$2500	$1000	20–32	Real Estate. Civic Affiliation: New Jersey Association of Realtors. Residence: New Jersey. Must be in high school.
New Mexico Student Incentive Grant	711	$2500	$200	1	Residence: New Mexico. Studying in New Mexico.
NMCRS Gold Star Scholarships for Children of Deceased Service Members	610	$2500	$500	1–100	Military Service: Marine Corps; Navy.
North Carolina 4-H Development Fund Scholarships	713	$2500	$500		Residence: North Carolina. Studying in North Carolina.
North Carolina Hispanic College Fund Scholarship	633	$2500	$500		Residence: North Carolina. Limited to Hispanic students.
Northwest Journalists of Color Scholarship	364	$2500	$500	1–4	Journalism. Residence: Washington. Limited to ethnic minority students.
Ohio Environmental Science & Engineering Scholarships	305	$2500	$1250	18	Environmental Science. Studying in Ohio.
Optimist International Oratorical Contest	757	$2500	$1000	90–115	Talent/Interest Area: public speaking.
Overseas Spouse Education Assistance Program	769	$2500	$500		Must be a spouse of military personnel.
Polish Heritage Scholarship	636	$2500	$1500	1–9	Residence: Maryland.
Raymond W. Miller, PE Scholarship	280	$2500	$1500	1	Engineering/Technology. Residence: Florida. Studying in Florida.
Richard B. Gassett, PE Scholarship	280	$2500	$1500	1	Engineering/Technology. Residence: Florida. Studying in Florida.
SCACPA Educational Fund Scholarships	80	$2500	$500	19–25	Accounting. Residence: South Carolina. Studying in South Carolina.
Scotts Company Scholars Program	349	$2500	$500	5	Horticulture/Floriculture.
Seventeen Magazine Fiction Contest	759	$2500	$100	8	Talent/Interest Area: writing.
Sidney B. Meadows Scholarship	351	$2500	$1500	10–15	Horticulture/Floriculture. Residence: Arkansas; Florida; Georgia; Kentucky; Louisiana; Maryland; Mississippi; Missouri; North Carolina; Oklahoma; South Carolina; Tennessee; Texas; Virginia.
Simon Youth Foundation Community Scholarship Program	797	$2500	$1400	100–200	Must be in high school.
Society of Physics Students Outstanding Student in Research	464	$2500	$500	1–2	Physical Sciences. Civic Affiliation: Society of Physics Students.
South Carolina Need-Based Grants Program	724	$2500	$1250	1–26,730	Residence: South Carolina. Studying in South Carolina.
Steve Dearduff Scholarship	334	$2500	$1000	1–3	Health and Medical Sciences; Social Services. Residence: Georgia.
Stockholm Scholarship Program	543	$2500	$2000	1	Civic Affiliation: Naval Sea Cadet Corps.
Sussman-Miller Educational Assistance Fund	655	$2500	$500	25–30	Residence: New Mexico.
Swiss Benevolent Society of Chicago Scholarships	639	$2500	$750	30	Residence: Illinois; Wisconsin.
Tennessee Society of CPA Scholarship	81	$2500	$250	120–130	Accounting. Residence: Tennessee.

Award Name	Page Number	Highest Dollar Amount	Lowest Dollar Amount	Number of Awards	Academic Fields/Career Goals and Nonacademic/Noncareer Criteria
Tilford Field Studies Scholarship	225	$2500	$500	4–5	Earth Science. Civic Affiliation: Association of Engineering Geologists.
Tortoise Young Entrepreneurs Scholarship	730	$2500	$1000	3–3	Residence: Kansas; Missouri. Studying in Kansas; Missouri.
Undergraduate Marketing Education Merit Scholarships	151	$2500	$500	3	Business/Consumer Services; Marketing.
Utah Leveraging Educational Assistance Partnership	732	$2500	$300		Residence: Utah. Studying in Utah.
West Virginia Higher Education Grant Program	735	$2500	$300	19,000– 21,152	Residence: West Virginia. Studying in Pennsylvania; West Virginia.
Writer's Digest Popular Fiction Awards	764	$2500	$500	6	Talent/Interest Area: writing.
Y.C. Yang Civil Engineering Scholarship	180	$2500	$2000	2	Civil Engineering.
Peter and Alice Koomruian Armenian Education Fund	635	$2300	$1000	4–20	Limited to students of Armenian descent.
David W. Self Scholarship	653	$2200	$100	1–5	Religion: Methodist. Must be in high school.
Menominee Indian Tribe Adult Vocational Training Program	630	$2200	$100	50–70	Limited to American Indian/Alaska Native students.
Menominee Indian Tribe of Wisconsin Higher Education Grants	630	$2200	$100	136	Limited to American Indian/Alaska Native students.
Richard S. Smith Scholarship	641	$2200	$100	1–5	Religion: Methodist. Must be in high school. Limited to ethnic minority students.
Scholarship Incentive Program (ScIP)	683	$2200	$700	1,000–1,253	Residence: Delaware. Studying in Delaware; Pennsylvania.
Osage Higher Education Scholarship	635	$2100	$1200	1,000	Limited to American Indian/Alaska Native students.

PROFILES OF SCHOLARSHIPS, GRANTS & PRIZES

ACCOUNTING

ALABAMA SOCIETY OF CERTIFIED PUBLIC ACCOUNTANTS

http://www.ascpa.org/

ASCPA EDUCATIONAL FOUNDATION SCHOLARSHIP

Scholarships available for students with a declared major in accounting. Must have completed intermediate accounting courses with a 3.0 GPA average in all accounting courses, and a 3.0 GPA average overall. Available for fourth or fifth year of study. Must be U.S. citizen or hold permanent resident status.

Academic Fields/Career Goals: Accounting.

Award: Scholarship for use in senior or graduate years; not renewable. *Number:* up to 30. *Amount:* up to $2500.

Eligibility Requirements: Applicant must be enrolled or expecting to enroll full-time at a four-year institution or university; resident of Alabama and studying in Alabama. Applicant must have 3.0 GPA or higher. Available to U.S. and non-Canadian citizens.

Application Requirements: Application form, essay, personal photograph, transcript. *Deadline:* March 15.

Contact: Ms. Diane Christy, Vice President of Communications
Alabama Society of Certified Public Accountants
1041 Longfield Court
Montgomery, AL 36117
Phone: 334-834-7650
E-mail: dchristy@ascpa.org

ALASKA SOCIETY OF CERTIFIED PUBLIC ACCOUNTANTS

http://www.akcpa.org/

PAUL HAGELBARGER MEMORIAL FUND SCHOLARSHIP

Scholarships open to all junior, senior, and graduate students who are majoring in accounting and attending institutions in Alaska.

Academic Fields/Career Goals: Accounting.

Award: Scholarship for use in junior, senior, or graduate years; not renewable. *Number:* 2–3. *Amount:* $2000.

Eligibility Requirements: Applicant must be enrolled or expecting to enroll full-time at a four-year institution or university and studying in Alaska. Available to U.S. citizens.

Application Requirements: Application form, recommendations or references, resume, transcript. *Deadline:* November 15.

Contact: Linda Plimpton, Executive Director
Alaska Society of Certified Public Accountants
341 West Tudor Road, Suite 105
Anchorage, AK 99503
Phone: 907-562-4334
Fax: 907-562-4025
E-mail: akcpa@ak.net

AMERICAN ASSOCIATION OF HISPANIC CERTIFIED PUBLIC ACCOUNTANTS (AAHCPA)

http://www.alpfa.org/

ALPFA ANNUAL SCHOLARSHIP PROGRAM

One-time award to undergraduate and graduate Hispanic/Latino students pursuing degrees in accounting, finance, and related majors. Awarded based on financial need and academic performance. Must be enrolled full-time at a U.S. college or university. Minimum 3.0 GPA required. Must be U.S. citizens or legal permanent residents.

Academic Fields/Career Goals: Accounting; Business/Consumer Services.

Award: Scholarship for use in freshman, sophomore, junior, or senior years; not renewable. *Amount:* $1250–$1500.

Eligibility Requirements: Applicant must be of Hispanic heritage and enrolled or expecting to enroll full-time at a two-year or four-year institution or university. Applicant must have 3.0 GPA or higher. Available to U.S. citizens.

Application Requirements: Application form, essay, financial need analysis, recommendations or references, transcript. *Deadline:* March 15.

Contact: Geraldine Contreras, Director of Student Affairs
American Association of Hispanic Certified Public
Accountants (AAHCPA)
801 South Grand Avenue, Suite 650
Los Angeles, CA 90017
E-mail: geraldine.contreras@national.alpfa.org

AMERICAN INSTITUTE OF CERTIFIED PUBLIC ACCOUNTANTS

http://www.aicpa.org/

AICPA/ACCOUNTEMPS STUDENT SCHOLARSHIP

The AICPA/Accountemps Student Scholarship program provides financial assistance to outstanding accounting students who demonstrate the potential to become leaders in the CPA profession. Students must have maintained a minimum GPA of 3.0 and have completed at least 30 semester credit hours (or equivalent) with at least 6 semester hours (or equivalent) in accounting coursework. Students must be enrolled full-time for the upcoming academic year. Additionally, award recipients are required to perform 16 community service hours to advocate on behalf of the CPA profession. More details and information is available on the program website: http://ThisWayToCPA.com/aicpascholarships.

Academic Fields/Career Goals: Accounting.

Award: Scholarship for use in sophomore, junior, senior, or graduate years; not renewable. *Number:* up to 10. *Amount:* up to $2500.

Eligibility Requirements: Applicant must be enrolled or expecting to enroll full-time at a four-year institution or university. Applicant must have 3.0 GPA or higher. Available to U.S. citizens.

Application Requirements: Application form, application form may be submitted online (http://www.ThisWayToCPA.com/Accountemps), essay, recommendations or references, test scores, transcript. *Deadline:* April 1.

Contact: Samantha Mithell, Scholarship Programs Manager
American Institute of Certified Public Accountants
American Institute of CPAs
220 Leigh Farm Road
Durham, NC 27707
Phone: 919-402-2161
Fax: 919-419-4705
E-mail: scholarships@aicpa.org

SCHOLARSHIP FOR MINORITY ACCOUNTING STUDENTS

The AICPA Minority Scholarship awards outstanding minority students to encourage their selection of accounting as a major and their ultimate entry into the profession. Funding is provided by the AICPA Foundation, with contributions from the New Jersey Society of CPAs and Robert Half International. For four decades, this program has provided over $14.6 million in scholarships to approximately 8,000 accounting scholars. Additionally, award recipients are required to perform 16 community service hours to advocate on behalf of the CPA profession. More details and information is available on the program website: http://ThisWayToCPA.com/aicpascholarships.

Academic Fields/Career Goals: Accounting.

Award: Scholarship for use in sophomore, junior, senior, or graduate years; not renewable. *Number:* 67–110. *Amount:* up to $5000.

Eligibility Requirements: Applicant must be American Indian/Alaska Native, Asian/Pacific Islander, Black (non-Hispanic), Hispanic and enrolled or expecting to enroll full-time at a four-year institution or university. Applicant must have 3.0 GPA or higher. Available to U.S. citizens.

Application Requirements: Application form, application form may be submitted online (http://www.ThisWayToCPA.com/MinorityScholarship), copy of acceptance letter, essay, recommendations or references, test scores, transcript. *Deadline:* April 1.

Contact: Samantha Mitchell, Scholarship Programs Manager
American Institute of Certified Public Accountants
220 Leigh Farm Road
Durham, NC 27707
Phone: 919-402-2161
Fax: 919-419-4705
E-mail: scholarships@aicpa.org

AMERICAN SOCIETY OF WOMEN ACCOUNTANTS

http://www.aswa.org/

AMERICAN SOCIETY OF WOMEN ACCOUNTANTS TWO-YEAR COLLEGE SCHOLARSHIP

Scholarship for students pursuing an accounting or finance degree in community, state, or two-year colleges. Must have a minimum cumulative college GPA of 3.0 and be a member of ASWA.

Academic Fields/Career Goals: Accounting.

Award: Scholarship for use in sophomore year; not renewable.

Eligibility Requirements: Applicant must be enrolled or expecting to enroll full-time at a two-year institution. Applicant or parent of applicant must be member of American Society of Women Accountants. Applicant must have 3.0 GPA or higher. Available to U.S. citizens.

Application Requirements: Application form, essay, financial need analysis, recommendations or references, transcript. *Deadline:* varies.

Contact: Kristin Edwards, Administrator
Phone: 703-506-3265
Fax: 703-506-3266
E-mail: kedwards@aswa.org

AMERICAN SOCIETY OF WOMEN ACCOUNTANTS UNDERGRADUATE SCHOLARSHIP

Scholarship awards are presented to students who have completed their sophomore year of college and are majoring in accounting or finance. Candidates will be reviewed on leadership, character, communication skills, scholastic average, and financial need.

Academic Fields/Career Goals: Accounting.

Award: Scholarship for use in junior, senior, or graduate years; not renewable.

Eligibility Requirements: Applicant must be enrolled or expecting to enroll full- or part-time at a four-year institution or university and must have an interest in leadership. Available to U.S. and non-U.S. citizens.

Application Requirements: Application form, essay, financial need analysis, recommendations or references, transcript. *Deadline:* varies.

Contact: Kristin Edwards, Administrator
Phone: 703-506-3265
Fax: 703-506-3266
E-mail: kedwards@aswa.org

ASSOCIATION OF CERTIFIED FRAUD EXAMINERS

http://www.acfe.com/

RITCHIE-JENNINGS MEMORIAL SCHOLARSHIP

Applicant must be an undergraduate or graduate student, currently enrolled full-time (12 semester hours undergraduate; 9 semester hours graduate, or equivalent) at an accredited four-year college or university (or equivalent) with a declared major or minor in accounting or criminal justice.

Academic Fields/Career Goals: Accounting; Criminal Justice/Criminology.

Award: Scholarship for use in freshman, sophomore, junior, or senior years; not renewable. *Number:* up to 30. *Amount:* $1000.

Eligibility Requirements: Applicant must be enrolled or expecting to enroll full-time at a four-year institution or university. Available to U.S. and non-U.S. citizens.

Application Requirements: Application form, essay, recommendations or references, transcript. *Deadline:* April 16.

Contact: Keely Miers, Scholarship Coordinator
Association of Certified Fraud Examiners
The Gregor Building, 716 West Avenue
Austin, TX 78701
Phone: 800-245-3321
Fax: 512-478-9297
E-mail: scholarships@acfe.com

CATCHING THE DREAM

http://www.catchingthedream.org/

TRIBAL BUSINESS MANAGEMENT PROGRAM (TBM)

Renewable scholarships available for Native American and Alaska Native students to study business administration, economic development, and related subjects, with the goal to provide experts in business management to Native American tribes in the U.S. Must be at least one-quarter Native American from a federally recognized, state recognized, or terminated tribe. Must demonstrate high academic achievement, depth of character, leadership, seriousness of purpose, and service orientation.

Academic Fields/Career Goals: Accounting; Business/Consumer Services; Computer Science/Data Processing; Economics; Electrical Engineering/Electronics; Engineering-Related Technologies.

Award: Scholarship for use in freshman, sophomore, junior, senior, graduate, or postgraduate years; renewable. *Number:* up to 35. *Amount:* $500–$5000.

Eligibility Requirements: Applicant must be American Indian/Alaska Native and enrolled or expecting to enroll full-time at a four-year institution or university. Applicant must have 3.0 GPA or higher. Available to U.S. citizens.

Application Requirements: Application form, certificate of Indian blood, essay, financial need analysis, personal photograph, recommendations or references, test scores, transcript. *Deadline:* varies.

Contact: Mary Frost, Recruiter
Catching the Dream
8200 Mountain Road, NE, Suite 203
Albuquerque, NM 87110
Phone: 505-262-2351
Fax: 505-262-0534
E-mail: nscholarsh@aol.com

CENTRAL INTELLIGENCE AGENCY

http://www.cia.gov/

CENTRAL INTELLIGENCE AGENCY UNDERGRADUATE SCHOLARSHIP PROGRAM

Need and merit-based award for students with minimum 3.0 GPA, who are interested in working for the Central Intelligence Agency upon graduation. Renewable for four years of undergraduate study. Must apply in senior year of high school or sophomore year in college. For further information refer to website http://www.cia.gov.

Academic Fields/Career Goals: Accounting; Business/Consumer Services; Computer Science/Data Processing; Economics; Electrical Engineering/Electronics; Foreign Language; Geography; Graphics/Graphic Arts/Printing; International Studies; Political Science; Surveying, Surveying Technology, Cartography, or Geographic Information Science.

Award: Scholarship for use in freshman, sophomore, junior, or senior years; renewable. *Amount:* up to $18,000.

Eligibility Requirements: Applicant must be enrolled or expecting to enroll full-time at a four-year institution or university. Applicant must have 3.0 GPA or higher. Available to U.S. citizens.

Application Requirements: Application form, financial need analysis, recommendations or references, resume, test scores, transcript. *Deadline:* November 1.

Contact: Van Patrick, Chief, College Relations
Phone: 703-613-8388
Fax: 703-613-7676
E-mail: ivanilp0@ucia.gov

COHEN & COMPANY CPAS

http://www.cohencpa.com/

COHEN AND COMPANY CPAS SCHOLARSHIP

Renewable scholarships for outstanding sophomores and juniors enrolled full-time at accredited Ohio colleges or universities. Must be majoring in accounting. Deadline varies.

Academic Fields/Career Goals: Accounting.

Award: Scholarship for use in sophomore or junior years; renewable. *Amount:* $500–$1000.

Eligibility Requirements: Applicant must be enrolled or expecting to enroll full-time at a four-year institution or university and studying in Ohio. Available to U.S. citizens.

Application Requirements: Application form, essay, recommendations or references. *Deadline:* varies.

Contact: Angela Ferenchka, Scholarship Coordinator
Cohen & Company CPAs
1350 Euclid Avenue, Suite 800
Cleveland, OH 44115
Phone: 216-579-1040
Fax: 216-579-0111

COLORADO SOCIETY OF CERTIFIED PUBLIC ACCOUNTANTS EDUCATIONAL FOUNDATION

http://www.cocpa.org/

COLORADO COLLEGE AND UNIVERSITY SCHOLARSHIPS

Award available to declared accounting majors at Colorado colleges and universities with accredited accounting programs. Must have completed at least 8 semester hours of accounting courses. Overall GPA and accounting GPA must be at least 3.0. Must be Colorado resident.

Academic Fields/Career Goals: Accounting.

Award: Scholarship for use in junior, senior, graduate, or postgraduate years; not renewable. *Number:* 15–20. *Amount:* $2500.

Eligibility Requirements: Applicant must be enrolled or expecting to enroll full- or part-time at a four-year institution or university; resident of Colorado and studying in Colorado. Applicant must have 3.0 GPA or higher. Available to U.S. citizens.

Application Requirements: Application form, recommendations or references, transcript. *Deadline:* June 1.

Contact: Gena Mantz, Membership Coordinator
Phone: 303-741-8613
Fax: 303-773-6344
E-mail: gmantz@cocpa.org

COMMUNITY FOUNDATION OF WESTERN MASSACHUSETTS

http://www.communityfoundation.org/

GREATER SPRINGFIELD ACCOUNTANTS SCHOLARSHIP

MA and Hartford County, CT residents who have completed their college sophomore year, pursuing accounting or finance.

Academic Fields/Career Goals: Accounting; Finance.

Award: Scholarship for use in junior or senior years; not renewable. *Number:* 3. *Amount:* $1000.

Eligibility Requirements: Applicant must be enrolled or expecting to enroll full-time at a two-year or four-year institution and resident of Connecticut, Massachusetts. Available to U.S. citizens.

Application Requirements: Application form, application form may be submitted online (http://www.communityfoundation.org), essay, financial need analysis, Student Aid Report (SAR), transcript. *Deadline:* March 29.

Contact: Dorothy Theriaque, Education Associate
Community Foundation of Western Massachusetts
1500 Main Street, PO Box 15769
Springfield, MA 01115
Phone: 413-732-2858
Fax: 413-733-8565
E-mail: scholar@communityfoundation.org

CONNECTICUT SOCIETY OF CERTIFIED PUBLIC ACCOUNTANTS

http://www.cscpa.org/

CSCPA CANDIDATE'S AWARD

Scholarship of $3000 that assists students in complying with the 150-hour requirement of the Connecticut State Board of Accountancy to sit for the Uniform Certified Public Accountant Examination. An overall GPA of 3.0.

Academic Fields/Career Goals: Accounting.

Award: Scholarship for use in senior year; not renewable. *Number:* 8–10. *Amount:* $3000.

Eligibility Requirements: Applicant must be enrolled or expecting to enroll full- or part-time at a four-year institution or university; resident of Connecticut and studying in Connecticut. Applicant must have 3.0 GPA or higher. Available to U.S. citizens.

Application Requirements: Application form, essay, transcript. *Deadline:* August 31.

Contact: Ms. Jill Wise, Program Coordinator
Connecticut Society of Certified Public Accountants
845 Brook Street, Building Two
Rocky Hill, CT 06067

EDUCATIONAL FOUNDATION FOR WOMEN IN ACCOUNTING (EFWA)

http://www.efwa.org/

MICHELE L. MCDONALD SCHOLARSHIP

Individuals eligible for this award will be women who are returning to college from the workforce or after raising children. Scholarship recipients will be awarded $1000 to begin their studies in pursuit of a college degree in accounting.

Academic Fields/Career Goals: Accounting.

Award: Scholarship for use in freshman, sophomore, junior, or senior years; not renewable. *Amount:* $1000.

Eligibility Requirements: Applicant must be enrolled or expecting to enroll full- or part-time at a four-year institution or university and married female. Available to U.S. citizens.

Application Requirements: Application form, financial need analysis, transcript. *Deadline:* April 15.

Contact: Cynthia Hires, Foundation Administrator
Phone: 610-407-9229
Fax: 610-644-3713
E-mail: info@efwa.org

ROWLING, DOLD & ASSOCIATES LLP SCHOLARSHIP

One year $1000 scholarship award for minority women enrolled in an accounting program at an accredited college or university. Women returning to school with undergraduate status; incoming, current, or reentry juniors or seniors; or minority women are all eligible.

Academic Fields/Career Goals: Accounting.

Award: Scholarship for use in junior, senior, or graduate years; not renewable. *Amount:* $1000.

Eligibility Requirements: Applicant must be American Indian/Alaska Native, Asian/Pacific Islander, Black (non-Hispanic), Hispanic; enrolled or expecting to enroll full- or part-time at a four-year institution or university and female. Available to U.S. citizens.

Application Requirements: Application form, financial need analysis, transcript. *Deadline:* April 15.

Contact: Cynthia Hires, Foundation Administrator
Phone: 610-407-9229
Fax: 610-644-3713
E-mail: info@efwa.org

SEATTLE AMERICAN SOCIETY OF WOMEN ACCOUNTANTS CHAPTER SCHOLARSHIP

Scholarship for an amount up to $2000 to be awarded to a women attending an accredited school within the State of Washington. The scholarship will be renewable for one additional year upon satisfactory completion of course requirements. Must pursue a degree in accounting.

Academic Fields/Career Goals: Accounting.

Award: Scholarship for use in freshman, sophomore, junior, or senior years; renewable. *Amount:* up to $2000.

Eligibility Requirements: Applicant must be enrolled or expecting to enroll full- or part-time at a four-year institution or university; female and studying in Washington. Available to U.S. citizens.

Application Requirements: Application form, financial need analysis, transcript. *Deadline:* April 15.

Contact: Cynthia Hires, Foundation Administrator
Phone: 610-407-9229
Fax: 610-644-3713
E-mail: info@efwa.org

WOMEN IN NEED SCHOLARSHIP

Scholarship provides financial assistance to female reentry students who wish to pursue a degree in accounting. Scholarship is available to incoming, current, or reentry juniors.

Academic Fields/Career Goals: Accounting.

Award: Scholarship for use in junior year; renewable. *Number:* 1. *Amount:* $2000.

Eligibility Requirements: Applicant must be enrolled or expecting to enroll full- or part-time at a four-year institution or university and female. Available to U.S. citizens.

Application Requirements: Application form, financial need analysis, transcript. *Deadline:* April 15.

Contact: Cynthia Hires, Foundation Administrator
Phone: 610-407-9229
Fax: 610-644-3713
E-mail: info@efwa.org

WOMEN IN TRANSITION SCHOLARSHIP

Renewable award available to incoming or current freshmen and women returning to school with a freshman status. Scholarship value may be up to $16,000 over four years.

Academic Fields/Career Goals: Accounting.

Award: Scholarship for use in freshman year; renewable. *Number:* 1. *Amount:* up to $4000.

Eligibility Requirements: Applicant must be enrolled or expecting to enroll full- or part-time at a four-year institution or university and female. Available to U.S. citizens.

Application Requirements: Application form, financial need analysis, transcript. *Deadline:* April 15.

Contact: Cynthia Hires, Foundation Administrator
Phone: 610-407-9229
Fax: 610-644-3713
E-mail: info@efwa.org

EDUCATIONAL FOUNDATION OF THE MASSACHUSETTS SOCIETY OF CERTIFIED PUBLIC ACCOUNTANTS

http://www.CPATrack.com/

F. GRANT WAITE, CPA, MEMORIAL SCHOLARSHIP

Scholarship available to undergraduate accounting major who has completed sophomore year. Must demonstrate financial need and superior academic standing. Preference given to married students with children. Information available on website at http://www.cpatrack.com.

Academic Fields/Career Goals: Accounting.

Award: Scholarship for use in junior or senior years; not renewable. *Number:* 1. *Amount:* $1000.

Eligibility Requirements: Applicant must be enrolled or expecting to enroll full-time at a four-year institution or university. Available to U.S. citizens.

Application Requirements: Application form, financial need analysis, recommendations or references, transcript. *Deadline:* March 17.

Contact: Barbara Iannoni, Academic Specialist
Phone: 617-303-2314
Fax: 617-303-2415
E-mail: biannoni@mscpaonline.org

KATHLEEN M. PEABODY, CPA, MEMORIAL SCHOLARSHIP

Scholarship available for Massachusetts resident who has completed sophomore year. Must be accounting major with plans to seek an accounting career in Massachusetts. Must demonstrate academic excellence and financial need. Information on website at http://www.cpatrack.com.

Academic Fields/Career Goals: Accounting.

Award: Scholarship for use in junior or senior years; not renewable. *Number:* 1. *Amount:* $2500.

Eligibility Requirements: Applicant must be enrolled or expecting to enroll full-time at a four-year institution or university and resident of Massachusetts. Available to U.S. citizens.

Application Requirements: Application form, financial need analysis, recommendations or references, transcript. *Deadline:* March 17.

Contact: Barbara Iannoni, Academic Specialist
Phone: 617-303-2314
Fax: 617-303-2415
E-mail: biannoni@mscpaonline.org

MSCPA FIRM SCHOLARSHIP

Scholarship to encourage individuals who have demonstrated academic excellence and financial need to pursue a career in public accounting in Massachusetts.

Academic Fields/Career Goals: Accounting.

Award: Scholarship for use in junior, senior, graduate, or postgraduate years; not renewable. *Number:* 12–16. *Amount:* $2500.

Eligibility Requirements: Applicant must be enrolled or expecting to enroll full-time at a four-year institution or university and resident of Massachusetts. Available to U.S. citizens.

Application Requirements: Application form, essay, financial need analysis, recommendations or references, transcript. *Deadline:* March 17.

Contact: Barbara Iannoni, Academic Coordinator
Educational Foundation of the Massachusetts Society of
Certified Public Accountants
105 Chauncy Street
Boston, MA 02111
Phone: 617-556-4000
Fax: 617-556-4126
E-mail: biannoni@mscpaonline.org

PAYCHEX INC. ENTREPRENEUR SCHOLARSHIP

Scholarships available to students who are residents of Massachusetts and attending a Massachusetts college or university. Must be an accounting major entering their junior year, have a minimum 3.0 GPA, and demonstrate financial need. Application and information on website at http://www.cpatrack.com.

Academic Fields/Career Goals: Accounting.

Award: Scholarship for use in junior year; not renewable. *Number:* 1. *Amount:* $1000.

Eligibility Requirements: Applicant must be enrolled or expecting to enroll full-time at a four-year institution or university; resident of Massachusetts and studying in Massachusetts. Applicant must have 3.0 GPA or higher. Available to U.S. citizens.

Application Requirements: Application form, financial need analysis, transcript. *Deadline:* March 17.

Contact: Barbara Iannoni, Academic Specialist
Phone: 617-303-2314
Fax: 617-303-2415
E-mail: biannoni@mscpaonline.org

FLORIDA INSTITUTE OF CERTIFIED PUBLIC ACCOUNTANTS EDUCATIONAL FOUNDATION, INC.

http://www.ficpa.org/

FICPA EDUCATIONAL FOUNDATION SCHOLARSHIPS

Scholarship for full-time or part-time (minimum of six credit hours), fourth- or fifth-year accounting major at participating Florida colleges or universities. Must be a Florida resident and plan to practice accounting in Florida. See website for list of institutions, http://www1.ficpa.org/ficpa/Visitors/Careers/EdFoundation/Scholarships.

Academic Fields/Career Goals: Accounting.

Award: Scholarship for use in senior or graduate years; not renewable. *Number:* up to 67. *Amount:* $1000–$2000.

Eligibility Requirements: Applicant must be enrolled or expecting to enroll full- or part-time at a four-year institution or university; resident of Florida and studying in Florida. Applicant must have 3.0 GPA or higher. Available to U.S. citizens.

Application Requirements: Application form, must be recommended by faculty committee at school attended, recommendations or references, transcript. *Deadline:* April 15.

Contact: Mrs. Betsy Wilson, Educational Foundation Assistant
Florida Institute of Certified Public Accountants Educational Foundation, Inc.
325 West College Avenue, PO Box 5437
Tallahassee, FL 32314
Phone: 850-224-2727 Ext. 0
Fax: 850-222-8190
E-mail: wilsonb@ficpa.org

MONEY RUN FORMERLY 1040K RUN/WALK SCHOLARSHIPS

Scholarship for African American permanent resident of Miami-Dade, Broward, Monroe or Palm Beach Counties. Applicants must be full-time, 4th- or 5th-year accounting majors at one of the following Florida institutions: Barry University, Florida Atlantic University, Florida International University, Nova Southeastern University, St. Thomas University, or University of Miami. See website for details http://www1.ficpa.org/ficpa/Visitors/Careers/EdFoundation/Scholar.ships/Availa.

Academic Fields/Career Goals: Accounting.

Award: Scholarship for use in senior or graduate years; not renewable. *Number:* up to 3. *Amount:* up to $3000.

Eligibility Requirements: Applicant must be Black (non-Hispanic); enrolled or expecting to enroll full-time at a four-year institution or university; resident of Florida and studying in Florida. Applicant must have 3.0 GPA or higher. Available to U.S. citizens.

Application Requirements: Application form, must be recommended by accounting faculty committee at Florida college or university attended, recommendations or references, transcript. *Deadline:* February 15.

Contact: Mrs. Betsy Wilson, Educational Foundation Assistant
Florida Institute of Certified Public Accountants Educational Foundation, Inc.
325 West College Avenue, PO Box 5437
Tallahassee, FL 32314
Phone: 850-224-2727 Ext. 0
Fax: 850-222-8190
E-mail: wilsonb@ficpa.org

GEORGIA GOVERNMENT FINANCE OFFICERS ASSOCIATION

http://www.ggfoa.org/

GGFOA SCHOLARSHIP

The scholarship recognizes outstanding performance in the study of public finance at the undergraduate and graduate level and encourages careers in state and local government. The GGFOA Scholarship is awarded to undergraduate or graduate students who meet the eligibility requirements and are preparing for a career in public finance. Must have nomination by the head of the applicable program (e.g., public administration, accounting, finance). Preference will be given to GGFOA members and employees of GGFOA governmental entities who are eligible for in-state tuition.

Academic Fields/Career Goals: Accounting; Business/Consumer Services; Finance.

Award: Scholarship for use in freshman, sophomore, junior, senior, or graduate years; not renewable. *Number:* 1–2. *Amount:* $3000.

Eligibility Requirements: Applicant must be enrolled or expecting to enroll full- or part-time at a four-year institution or university and studying in Georgia. Applicant must have 3.0 GPA or higher. Available to U.S. citizens.

Application Requirements: Application form, essay, recommendations or references, resume, test scores, transcript. *Deadline:* September 10.

GOVERNMENT FINANCE OFFICERS ASSOCIATION

http://www.gfoa.org/

MINORITIES IN GOVERNMENT FINANCE SCHOLARSHIP

Awards upper-division undergraduate or graduate students of public administration, governmental accounting, finance, political science, economics, or business administration to recognize outstanding performance by minority students preparing for a career in state and local government finance.

Academic Fields/Career Goals: Accounting; Business/Consumer Services; Economics; Political Science; Public Policy and Administration.

Award: Scholarship for use in freshman, sophomore, junior, senior, or graduate years; not renewable. *Number:* 1. *Amount:* $5000.

Eligibility Requirements: Applicant must be American Indian/Alaska Native, Asian/Pacific Islander, Black (non-Hispanic), Hispanic and enrolled or expecting to enroll full- or part-time at a two-year or four-year institution or university. Available to U.S. and Canadian citizens.

Application Requirements: Application form, essay, recommendations or references, resume, transcript. *Deadline:* February 29.

Contact: Jake Lorentz, Assistant Director
Government Finance Officers Association
203 North LaSalle Street, Suite 2700
Chicago, IL 60601
Phone: 312-977-9700 Ext. 267
Fax: 312-977-4806
E-mail: jlorentz@gfoa.org

GREATER WASHINGTON SOCIETY OF CERTIFIED PUBLIC ACCOUNTANTS

http://www.gwscpa.org/

GREATER WASHINGTON SOCIETY OF CPAS SCHOLARSHIP

Scholarship available to accounting students. School must offer an accounting degree that qualifies graduates to sit for the CPA exam (must meet the 150-hour rule). Minimum 3.0 GPA in major courses required. Application details on our website http://www.gwscpa.org.

Academic Fields/Career Goals: Accounting.

Award: Scholarship for use in junior, senior, or graduate years; not renewable. *Number:* 3–5. *Amount:* $2000–$4500.

Eligibility Requirements: Applicant must be enrolled or expecting to enroll full-time at a four-year institution or university; resident of District of Columbia and studying in District of Columbia. Applicant must have 3.0 GPA or higher. Available to U.S. citizens.

Application Requirements: Application form, essay, financial need analysis, recommendations or references, resume, transcript. *Deadline:* February 15.

Contact: Kari Bedell, Executive Director
Phone: 202-464-6001
E-mail: info@gwscpa.org

HAWAII SOCIETY OF CERTIFIED PUBLIC ACCOUNTANTS

http://www.hscpa.org/

HSCPA SCHOLARSHIP PROGRAM FOR ACCOUNTING STUDENTS

Scholarship for Hawaii resident currently attending an accredited Hawaii college or university. Minimum 3.0 GPA required. Must be majoring, or concentrating, in accounting with the intention to sit for the CPA exam, and have completed an intermediate accounting course. Number of awards vary from year to year.

Academic Fields/Career Goals: Accounting.

Award: Scholarship for use in freshman, sophomore, junior, or senior years; not renewable. *Amount:* $500–$1500.

Eligibility Requirements: Applicant must be enrolled or expecting to enroll full-time at a four-year institution or university; resident of Hawaii and studying in Hawaii. Applicant must have 3.0 GPA or higher. Available to U.S. citizens.

Application Requirements: Application form, community service, recommendations or references, test scores, transcript. *Deadline:* January 31.

Contact: Kathy Castillo, Executive Director
Hawaii Society of Certified Public Accountants
900 Fort Street Mall, Suite 850
Honolulu, HI 96813
Phone: 808-537-9475
Fax: 808-537-3520
E-mail: info@hscpa.org

ILLINOIS CPA SOCIETY/CPA ENDOWMENT FUND OF ILLINOIS

http://www.icpas.org/

ILLINOIS CPA SOCIETY ACCOUNTING SCHOLARSHIP PROGRAM

The Illinois CPA Society has numerous scholarships available to support accounting students who are studying accounting and planning to become a CPA. Candidates must demonstrate a course of study which reflects a goal to sit for the CPA exam in Illinois. The scholarship program supports diversity of students, investing in their success and helping them to realize their dream of becoming CPAs. Scholarship recipients have studied at a variety of schools throughout the state, from large state universities to small private schools to community colleges. Some scholarships have supported students with their graduate studies, while others support a fifth year of undergraduate education.

Academic Fields/Career Goals: Accounting.

Award: Scholarship for use in junior, senior, graduate, or postgraduate years; not renewable. *Number:* 12–20. *Amount:* $500–$4000.

Eligibility Requirements: Applicant must be enrolled or expecting to enroll full- or part-time at a four-year institution or university; resident of Illinois and studying in Illinois. Applicant must have 3.0 GPA or higher. Available to U.S. citizens.

Application Requirements: Application form, essay, recommendations or references, resume, transcript. *Deadline:* April 1.

Contact: Kari Natale, Development Manager
Phone: 312-993-0407 Ext. 290
Fax: 312-993-9954
E-mail: natalek@icpas.org

INSTITUTE OF INTERNAL AUDITORS RESEARCH FOUNDATION

http://www.theiia.org/

ESTHER R. SAWYER RESEARCH AWARD

Awarded to a student entering or currently enrolled in an internal auditing program at an IIA-affiliated school. Awarded based on submission of an original manuscript on a specific topic related to modern internal auditing.

Academic Fields/Career Goals: Accounting.

Award: Prize for use in freshman, sophomore, junior, senior, or graduate years; not renewable. *Number:* 1. *Amount:* $5000.

Eligibility Requirements: Applicant must be enrolled or expecting to enroll full-time at a four-year institution or university. Available to U.S. and non-U.S. citizens.

Application Requirements: Application form, entry in a contest, essay, recommendations or references. *Deadline:* March 1.

Contact: Susan Dworkis, Research Foundation Administrator
Phone: 407-937-1357
E-mail: research@theiia.org

INSTITUTE OF MANAGEMENT ACCOUNTANTS

http://www.imanet.org/

INSTITUTE OF MANAGEMENT ACCOUNTANTS MEMORIAL EDUCATION FUND SCHOLARSHIPS

Scholarships for IMA undergraduate or graduate student members studying at accredited institutions in the U.S. and Puerto Rico. Must be pursuing a career in management accounting, financial management, or information technology, and have a minimum GPA of 3.0. Awards based on academic merit, IMA participation, strength of recommendations, and quality of written statements.

Academic Fields/Career Goals: Accounting; Business/Consumer Services.

Award: Scholarship for use in sophomore, junior, senior, or graduate years; not renewable. *Number:* 6–15. *Amount:* $1000–$2500.

Eligibility Requirements: Applicant must be enrolled or expecting to enroll full- or part-time at a two-year or four-year institution or university. Applicant must have 3.0 GPA or higher. Available to U.S. citizens.

Application Requirements: Application form, essay, recommendations or references, resume, transcript. *Deadline:* February 15.

Contact: Tara Barker, Research and Academic Community Manager
Institute of Management Accountants
IMA
10 Paragon Drive, Suite 1
Montvale, NJ 07628
Phone: 800-638-4427 Ext. 1535
E-mail: tbarker@imanet.org

ROLF S. JAEHNIGEN FAMILY SCHOLARSHIP

A scholarship to recognize a student who is passionate not only about his/her business career, but about the arts as well. You must be a junior or senior accounting, finance or information systems major at an accredited business school.

Academic Fields/Career Goals: Accounting; Computer Science/Data Processing; Finance.

Award: Scholarship for use in junior or senior years; not renewable. *Amount:* $1000.

Eligibility Requirements: Applicant must be enrolled or expecting to enroll at a four-year institution or university. Available to U.S. citizens.

Application Requirements: *Deadline:* October 31.

Contact: Tara Barker, Research and Academic Community Manager
Institute of Management Accountants
IMA
10 Paragon Drive, Suite 1
Montvale, NJ 07628
Phone: 800-638-4427 Ext. 1535
E-mail: tbarker@imanet.org

STUART CAMERON AND MARGARET MCLEOD MEMORIAL SCHOLARSHIP

Scholarships for IMA undergraduate or graduate student members studying at accredited institutions in the U.S. and Puerto Rico and carrying 12 credits per semester. Must be pursuing a career in management accounting, financial management, or information technology, and have a minimum GPA of 3.0. Awards based on academic merit, IMA participation, strength of recommendations, and quality of written statements.

Academic Fields/Career Goals: Accounting; Business/Consumer Services.

Award: Scholarship for use in junior, senior, or graduate years; not renewable. *Number:* 1. *Amount:* $5000.

Eligibility Requirements: Applicant must be enrolled or expecting to enroll full- or part-time at a two-year or four-year institution or university. Applicant must have 3.0 GPA or higher. Available to U.S. citizens.

Application Requirements: Application form, essay, resume, transcript. *Deadline:* February 15.

Contact: Tara Barker, Research and Academic Community Manager
Institute of Management Accountants
IMA
10 Paragon Drive, Suite 1
Montvale, NJ 07628
Phone: 800-638-4427 Ext. 1535
E-mail: tbarker@imanet.org

KENTUCKY SOCIETY OF CERTIFIED PUBLIC ACCOUNTANTS

http://www.kycpa.org/

KENTUCKY SOCIETY OF CERTIFIED PUBLIC ACCOUNTANTS COLLEGE SCHOLARSHIP

Nonrenewable award for accounting majors at a Kentucky college or university. Must rank in upper third of class or have a minimum 3.0 GPA. Must be a Kentucky resident.

Academic Fields/Career Goals: Accounting.

Award: Scholarship for use in sophomore, junior, or senior years; not renewable. *Number:* up to 23. *Amount:* $1000–$2500.

Eligibility Requirements: Applicant must be enrolled or expecting to enroll full-time at a two-year or four-year institution or university; resident of Kentucky and studying in Kentucky. Applicant must have 3.0 GPA or higher. Available to U.S. and non-U.S. citizens.

Application Requirements: Application form, essay, recommendations or references, transcript. *Deadline:* January 31.

Contact: Becky Ackerman, Foundation Administrator
Phone: 502-266-5272
Fax: 502-261-9512
E-mail: backerman@kycpa.org

LAWRENCE P. DOSS SCHOLARSHIP FOUNDATION

http://www.lawrencepdossfnd.org/

LAWRENCE P. DOSS SCHOLARSHIP FOUNDATION

Renewable scholarships are available to residents of Michigan who are seniors graduating from a high school in the greater Detroit area. Must be pursuing a degree in accounting, finance, management or business. Financial need considered.

Academic Fields/Career Goals: Accounting; Business/Consumer Services.

Award: Scholarship for use in freshman year; renewable. *Number:* 5. *Amount:* $20,000.

Eligibility Requirements: Applicant must be high school student; planning to enroll or expecting to enroll full-time at a four-year institution or university; single and resident of Michigan. Applicant must have 2.5 GPA or higher. Available to U.S. citizens.

Application Requirements: Application form, community service, essay, financial need analysis, interview, recommendations or references, test scores, transcript. *Deadline:* March 15.

Contact: Judith Doss, President and Chief Executive Officer
Lawrence P. Doss Scholarship Foundation
PO Box 351037
Detroit, MI 48235-9998
Phone: 313-891-5834
Fax: 313-891-4520
E-mail: lpdsfoundation@aol.com

MARYLAND ASSOCIATION OF CERTIFIED PUBLIC ACCOUNTANTS EDUCATIONAL FOUNDATION

http://www.tomorrowscpa.org/

STUDENT SCHOLARSHIP IN ACCOUNTING MD ASSOCIATION OF CPAS

Award for Maryland residents who will have completed at least 60 credit hours at a Maryland college or university by the time of the award. Must have 3.0 GPA, demonstrate commitment to 150 semester hours of education, and intend to pursue a career as a certified public accountant. Number of awards varies. Must submit accounting department chairman's signature on required statement. Must be a member of the Tomorrow's CPA program. U.S. citizenship required. See website at http://www.tomorrowscpa.org for further details.

Academic Fields/Career Goals: Accounting.

Award: Scholarship for use in junior or senior years; renewable. *Number:* 10–20. *Amount:* $500–$1500.

Eligibility Requirements: Applicant must be enrolled or expecting to enroll full-time at a four-year institution or university; resident of Maryland and studying in Maryland. Applicant must have 3.0 GPA or higher. Available to U.S. citizens.

Application Requirements: Application form, financial need analysis, recommendations or references, transcript. *Deadline:* April 15.

Contact: Margaret DeRoose, Staff Accountant
Maryland Association of Certified Public Accountants
Educational Foundation
901 Dulaney Valley Road
Suite 710
Towson, MD 21204
Phone: 443-632-2327
E-mail: margaret@macpa.org

MICHIGAN ASSOCIATION OF CPAS

http://www.michcpa.org/

FIFTH/GRADUATE YEAR STUDENT SCHOLARSHIP

Scholarship for a full-time student in senior year, or a student with a combination of education and employment (defined as a minimum of two classes per term and 20 hours per week of employment). Must be majoring in accounting, and a U.S. citizen.

Academic Fields/Career Goals: Accounting.

Award: Scholarship for use in senior year; not renewable. *Number:* 16–25. *Amount:* up to $4000.

Eligibility Requirements: Applicant must be enrolled or expecting to enroll full-time at a four-year institution or university and studying in Michigan. Available to U.S. citizens.

Application Requirements: Application form, essay, financial need analysis, recommendations or references, transcript. *Deadline:* January 31.

MINNESOTA SOCIETY OF CERTIFIED PUBLIC ACCOUNTANTS

http://www.mncpa.org/

MNCPA SCHOLARSHIP PROGRAM

Scholarships given for graduate study in accounting to students from a Minnesota college or university who passed the CPA exam during the previous year. Must be a sophomore, junior or senior (going on to graduate school). At least a 3.0 GPA in accounting.

Academic Fields/Career Goals: Accounting.

Award: Scholarship for use in sophomore, junior, or senior years; not renewable. *Number:* up to 25. *Amount:* up to $1000.

Eligibility Requirements: Applicant must be enrolled or expecting to enroll full-time at a four-year institution or university and studying in Minnesota. Applicant must have 3.0 GPA or higher. Available to U.S. citizens.

Application Requirements: Application form. *Deadline:* varies.

MONTANA SOCIETY OF CERTIFIED PUBLIC ACCOUNTANTS

http://www.mscpa.org/

MONTANA SOCIETY OF CERTIFIED PUBLIC ACCOUNTANTS SCHOLARSHIP

Scholarship available to one student in each of the following four schools: Montana State University Billings, MSU Bozeman, Carroll College, and University of Montana. Must be an accounting major, at least a junior standing with at least one semester of coursework remaining, and have a minimum GPA of 3.0. Graduate students eligible. Preference will be given to student members of the MSCPA. Must be a graduate of a Montana high school and currently a Montana resident. Additional scholarships are awarded through our Endowment Fund and may be applied for through the Montana Community Foundation.

Academic Fields/Career Goals: Accounting.

Award: Scholarship for use in junior, senior, or graduate years; not renewable. *Number:* 4–6. *Amount:* $1000.

Eligibility Requirements: Applicant must be enrolled or expecting to enroll full-time at a four-year institution or university; resident of Montana and studying in Montana. Applicant must have 3.0 GPA or higher. Available to U.S. citizens.

Application Requirements: Application form, essay, resume, transcript. *Deadline:* varies.

Contact: Mrs. Margaret Herriges, Communications Director
Montana Society of Certified Public Accountants
PO Box 138
Helena, MT 59624
Phone: 406-442-7301
E-mail: mscpa@mscpa.org

NATIONAL BLACK MBA ASSOCIATION-TWIN CITIES CHAPTER

http://www.nbmbaatc.org/

TWIN CITIES CHAPTER UNDERGRADUATE SCHOLARSHIP

Award for minority students in first, second, third or fourth year full-time in an accredited undergraduate business or management program during the fall semester working towards a bachelor's degree. Get application from website at http://www.nbmbaatc.org.

Academic Fields/Career Goals: Accounting; Business/Consumer Services.

Award: Scholarship for use in freshman, sophomore, junior, or senior years; not renewable. *Number:* 5. *Amount:* up to $3500.

Eligibility Requirements: Applicant must be Black (non-Hispanic); enrolled or expecting to enroll full-time at a four-year institution or university; resident of Minnesota and studying in Minnesota. Available to U.S. citizens.

Application Requirements: Application form, essay, transcript. *Deadline:* April 7.

Contact: Victor Patterson, President
Phone: 651-223-7373

NATIONAL SOCIETY OF ACCOUNTANTS

http://www.nsacct.org/

CHARLES EARP MEMORIAL SCHOLARSHIP

Annual award for the student designated as most outstanding of all National Society of Accountants scholarship recipients receive an additional stipend of approximately $200.

Academic Fields/Career Goals: Accounting.

Award: Scholarship for use in freshman, sophomore, junior, or senior years; not renewable. *Number:* 1. *Amount:* $200.

Eligibility Requirements: Applicant must be enrolled or expecting to enroll full- or part-time at a four-year institution or university. Available to U.S. and Canadian citizens.

Application Requirements: Application form, appraisal form, financial need analysis, transcript. *Deadline:* March 10.

Contact: Sally Brasse, Director of Education Programs
National Society of Accountants
1010 North Fairfax Street
Alexandria, VA 22314-1574
Phone: 703-549-6400 Ext. 1307
E-mail: sbrasse@nsacct.org

NATIONAL SOCIETY OF ACCOUNTANTS SCHOLARSHIP

One-time award of $500 to $1000 available to undergraduate students. Applicants must maintain a 3.0 GPA and have declared a major in accounting. Must submit an appraisal form and transcripts in addition to application. Must be U.S. or Canadian citizen attending an accredited U.S. school.

Academic Fields/Career Goals: Accounting.

Award: Scholarship for use in freshman, sophomore, junior, or senior years; not renewable. *Number:* up to 40. *Amount:* $500–$1000.

Eligibility Requirements: Applicant must be enrolled or expecting to enroll full- or part-time at a two-year or four-year institution or university. Applicant must have 3.0 GPA or higher. Available to U.S. and Canadian citizens.

Application Requirements: Application form, appraisal form, financial need analysis, transcript. *Deadline:* March 10.

Contact: Susan Noell, Director of Education Programs
National Society of Accountants
1010 North Fairfax Street
Alexandria, VA 22314-1574
Phone: 703-549-6400 Ext. 1312
Fax: 703-549-2984 Ext. 1312
E-mail: snoell@nsacct.org

NSA LOUIS AND FANNIE SAGER MEMORIAL SCHOLARSHIP AWARD

Up to $1000 will be awarded annually to a graduate of a Virginia public high school who is enrolled as an undergraduate at a Virginia college or university. Applicant must major in accounting. Must submit proof of graduation from a Virginia public school.

Academic Fields/Career Goals: Accounting.

Award: Scholarship for use in freshman, sophomore, junior, or senior years; not renewable. *Number:* 1. *Amount:* $500–$1000.

Eligibility Requirements: Applicant must be enrolled or expecting to enroll full- or part-time at a two-year or four-year institution or university; resident of Virginia and studying in Virginia. Applicant must have 3.0 GPA or higher. Available to U.S. and Canadian citizens.

Application Requirements: Application form, appraisal form, financial need analysis, transcript. *Deadline:* March 10.

Contact: Sally Brasse, Director
National Society of Accountants
1010 North Fairfax Street
Alexandria, VA 22314-1574
Phone: 703-549-6400 Ext. 1307
E-mail: sbrasse@nsacct.org

STANLEY H. STEARMAN SCHOLARSHIP

One award for accounting major who is a relative of an active, retired, or deceased member of National Society of Accountants. Must be citizen of the United States or Canada and attend school in the United States. Minimum GPA of 3.0 required. Not available for freshman year. Submit application, appraisal form, and letter of intent.

Academic Fields/Career Goals: Accounting.

Award: Scholarship for use in freshman, sophomore, junior, senior, or graduate years; renewable. *Number:* 1. *Amount:* up to $2000.

Eligibility Requirements: Applicant must be enrolled or expecting to enroll full- or part-time at a two-year or four-year institution or university. Applicant or parent of applicant must be member of National Society of Accountants. Applicant must have 3.0 GPA or higher. Available to U.S. and Canadian citizens.

Application Requirements: Application form, appraisal form, essay, financial need analysis, transcript. *Deadline:* March 10.

Contact: Sally Brasse, Director of Education Programs
National Society of Accountants
1010 North Fairfax Street
Alexandria, VA 22314-1574
Phone: 703-549-6400 Ext. 1307
Fax: 703-549-2984
E-mail: sbrasse@nsacct.org

NC CPA FOUNDATION INC.

http://www.ncacpa.org/Member_Connections/
NC_CPA_Foundation_Inc.aspx

NORTH CAROLINA ASSOCIATION OF CPAS FOUNDATION SCHOLARSHIPS

Scholarship available for North Carolina residents enrolled in a program leading to a degree in accounting or its equivalent in a North Carolina college or university. Must have completed at least one college or university level accounting course and have completed at least 36 semester hours (or equivalent) by the start of the spring semester of the year of application. The applicant must be sponsored by one accounting faculty members. Application and information at http://csbapp.csb.uncw.edu/nccpa.

Academic Fields/Career Goals: Accounting.

Award: Scholarship for use in sophomore, junior, senior, or graduate years; not renewable. *Number:* 50–60. *Amount:* $1000–$5000.

Eligibility Requirements: Applicant must be enrolled or expecting to enroll full- or part-time at a two-year or four-year institution or university; resident of North Carolina and studying in North Carolina. Applicant must have 3.0 GPA or higher. Available to U.S. citizens.

Application Requirements: Application form, application form may be submitted online (http://www.ncacpa.org/Member_Connections/Students/
Foundation.aspx), essay, transcript. *Deadline:* February 10.

Contact: Mr. Jim Ahler, Chief Executive Officer
NC CPA Foundation Inc.
PO Box 80188
Raleigh, NC 27623
Phone: 919-469-1040 Ext. 130
E-mail: jtahler@ncacpa.org

NEBRASKA SOCIETY OF CERTIFIED PUBLIC ACCOUNTANTS

http://www.nescpa.com/

FIFTH-YEAR SCHOLARSHIP AWARDS

The scholarship is for accounting majors who have completed their junior year and are enrolled in a fifth-year (150-hour) program at a Nebraska college or university; accounting students who plan to sit for the CPA exam; accounting students who have the interest and capabilities of becoming a successful accountant and who are considering an accounting career in Nebraska. When candidates are reviewed, scholarship, personality, leadership and character should be considered by the accounting instructional staff at each college or university.

Academic Fields/Career Goals: Accounting.

Award: Scholarship for use in senior year; not renewable.

Eligibility Requirements: Applicant must be enrolled or expecting to enroll at a four-year institution or university and studying in Nebraska. Available to U.S. citizens.

Application Requirements: *Deadline:* April 1.

Contact: Sheila Burroughs, Vice President
Phone: 402-476-8482
Fax: 402-476-8731
E-mail: society@nescpa.org

NEBRASKA SOCIETY OF CPAS SCHOLARSHIP

Scholarship awards are presented to accounting students who have completed their junior year; accounting majors who plan to sit for the CPA exam; students who have the interest and capabilities of becoming a successful accountant and who are considering an accounting career in Nebraska are to be considered. Recipients need not necessarily have the highest scholastic average.

Academic Fields/Career Goals: Accounting.

Award: Scholarship for use in senior year; not renewable.

Eligibility Requirements: Applicant must be enrolled or expecting to enroll full-time at a four-year institution or university. Available to U.S. citizens.

Application Requirements: Application form, nomination letter. *Deadline:* August 1.

Contact: Sheila Burroughs, Vice President
Phone: 402-476-8482
Fax: 402-476-8731
E-mail: society@nescpa.org

NEVADA SOCIETY OF CERTIFIED PUBLIC ACCOUNTANTS

http://www.nevadacpa.org/

NEVADA SOCIETY OF CPAS SCHOLARSHIP

Scholarships available for accounting students in one of Nevada's four community colleges, or for juniors or seniors attending either University of Nevada, Las Vegas, or University of Nevada, Reno. Must be planning a career in accounting.

Academic Fields/Career Goals: Accounting.

Award: Scholarship for use in freshman, sophomore, junior, or senior years; not renewable. *Number:* 6. *Amount:* up to $1500.

Eligibility Requirements: Applicant must be enrolled or expecting to enroll full-time at a two-year or four-year institution or university; resident of Nevada and studying in Nevada. Available to U.S. citizens.

Application Requirements: Application form. *Deadline:* varies.

Contact: Sharon Uithoven, Executive Director
Phone: 775-826-6800 Ext. 104
Fax: 775-826-7942
E-mail: uithoven@nevadacpa.org

NEW ENGLAND EMPLOYEE BENEFITS COUNCIL

http://www.neebc.org/

NEW ENGLAND EMPLOYEE BENEFITS COUNCIL SCHOLARSHIP PROGRAM

Renewable award designed to encourage undergraduate or graduate students to pursue a course of study leading to a bachelor's degree or higher in the employee benefits field. Must be a resident of/or studying in Maine, Massachusetts, New Hampshire, Rhode Island, Connecticut or Vermont. Must have demonstrated interest in the fields of employee benefits, human resources, business law.

Academic Fields/Career Goals: Accounting; Business/Consumer Services; Economics; Health Administration; Human Resources; Insurance and Actuarial Science; Law/Legal Services; Public Health; Public Policy and Administration.

Award: Scholarship for use in freshman, sophomore, junior, or senior years; renewable. *Number:* 1–3. *Amount:* $1000–$5000.

Eligibility Requirements: Applicant must be enrolled or expecting to enroll full- or part-time at a four-year institution or university; resident of Connecticut, Maine, Massachusetts, New Hampshire, Rhode Island, Vermont and studying in Connecticut, Maine, Massachusetts, New Hampshire, Rhode Island, Vermont. Available to U.S. citizens.

Application Requirements: Application form, essay, recommendations or references, transcript. *Deadline:* April 1.

Contact: Linda Viens, Manager of Operations and Member Services
Phone: 781-684-8700
E-mail: linda@neebc.org

NEW HAMPSHIRE SOCIETY OF CERTIFIED PUBLIC ACCOUNTANTS

http://www.nhscpa.org/

NEW HAMPSHIRE SOCIETY OF CERTIFIED PUBLIC ACCOUNTANTS SCHOLARSHIP FUND

One-time award for New Hampshire resident majoring full-time in accounting. Must be entering senior year at a four-year college or university or pursuing a master's degree. Maximum of seven awards of up to $1000 are granted.

Academic Fields/Career Goals: Accounting.

Award: Scholarship for use in senior year; not renewable. *Number:* 1–7. *Amount:* $500–$1000.

Eligibility Requirements: Applicant must be enrolled or expecting to enroll full-time at a four-year institution or university and resident of New Hampshire. Available to U.S. citizens.

Application Requirements: Application form, recommendations or references, transcript. *Deadline:* November 1.

NEW JERSEY SOCIETY OF CERTIFIED PUBLIC ACCOUNTANTS

http://www.njscpa.org/

NEW JERSEY SOCIETY OF CERTIFIED PUBLIC ACCOUNTANTS COLLEGE SCHOLARSHIP PROGRAM

Award for college juniors or those entering an accounting-related graduate program. Must be a New Jersey resident attending a four-year New Jersey institution. Must be nominated by accounting department chair or submit application directly. Minimum 3.0 GPA required. Award values from $4000 to $4500.

Academic Fields/Career Goals: Accounting.

Award: Scholarship for use in junior or senior years; not renewable. *Number:* 40–50. *Amount:* $5000.

Eligibility Requirements: Applicant must be enrolled or expecting to enroll full- or part-time at a four-year institution or university; resident of New Jersey and studying in New Jersey. Applicant must have 3.0 GPA or higher. Available to U.S. citizens.

Application Requirements: Application form, application form may be submitted online (http://www.njscpa.org/scholarships), essay, interview, recommendations or references, resume, transcript. *Deadline:* January 12.

Contact: Janice Amatucci, Membership Manager, NextGen Outreach
New Jersey Society of Certified Public Accountants
425 Eagle Rock Avenue, Suite 100
Roseland, NJ 07068-1723
Phone: 973-226-4494
Fax: 973-226-7425
E-mail: jamatucci@njscpa.org

NEW JERSEY SOCIETY OF CERTIFIED PUBLIC ACCOUNTANTS HIGH SCHOOL SCHOLARSHIP PROGRAM

Renewable scholarship for New Jersey high school seniors who wish to pursue a degree in accounting. Must be resident of New Jersey. Scholarship value is from $6500 to $8500. Deadline is in December.

Academic Fields/Career Goals: Accounting.

Award: Scholarship for use in freshman, sophomore, junior, or senior years; renewable. *Number:* 20–25. *Amount:* $7000–$9000.

Eligibility Requirements: Applicant must be high school student; planning to enroll or expecting to enroll full-time at a four-year institution or university and resident of New Jersey. Applicant must have 3.0 GPA or higher. Available to U.S. citizens.

Application Requirements: Application form, application form may be submitted online (http://www.njscpa.org/scholarships), essay, interview, test scores, transcript. *Deadline:* December 27.

Contact: Janice Amatucci, Membership Manager, NextGen Outreach
New Jersey Society of Certified Public Accountants
425 Eagle Rock Avenue, Suite 100
Roseland, NJ 07068-1723
Phone: 973-226-4494 Ext. 209
Fax: 973-226-7425
E-mail: jamatucci@njscpa.org

NEW YORK STATE SOCIETY OF CERTIFIED PUBLIC ACCOUNTANTS

FOUNDATION FOR ACCOUNTING EDUCATION

http://www.nysscpa.org/page/future-cpas/college-students

FOUNDATION FOR ACCOUNTING EDUCATION SCHOLARSHIP

Awards up to $500 to $2500 scholarships to college students to encourage them to pursue a career in accounting. Must be a New York resident studying in New York and maintaining a 3.0 GPA.

Academic Fields/Career Goals: Accounting.

Award: Scholarship for use in junior, senior, or graduate years; not renewable. *Number:* 1–60. *Amount:* $500–$2500.

Eligibility Requirements: Applicant must be enrolled or expecting to enroll full- or part-time at a four-year institution or university; resident of New York and studying in New York. Applicant must have 3.0 GPA or higher. Available to U.S. citizens.

Application Requirements: Application form, application form may be submitted online (http://www.nysscpa.org), essay, financial need analysis, recommendations or references, transcript. *Deadline:* April 1.

Contact: Ms. Lisa Axisa, Associate Director, Recruitment and Retention
New York State Society of Certified Public Accountants
Foundation for Accounting Education
3 Park Avenue, 18th Floor
New York, NY 10016
Phone: 212-719-8362
E-mail: laxisa@nysspca.org

OREGON ASSOCIATION OF PUBLIC ACCOUNTANTS SCHOLARSHIP FOUNDATION

http://www.oaia.net/

OAIA SCHOLARSHIP

Scholarships of $1000 to $2000 are awarded to full-time students. Must be a resident of the state of Oregon and major in accounting studies at an accredited school in the state of Oregon. The scholarship may be used for tuition, fees, books or other academic expenses incurred during the term.

Academic Fields/Career Goals: Accounting.

Award: Scholarship for use in freshman, sophomore, junior, or senior years; not renewable. *Number:* 5. *Amount:* $1000–$2000.

Eligibility Requirements: Applicant must be enrolled or expecting to enroll full-time at a two-year or four-year institution or university; resident of Oregon and studying in Oregon. Available to U.S. citizens.

Application Requirements: Application form, financial need analysis, recommendations or references, transcript. *Deadline:* April 1.

Contact: Susan Robertson, Treasurer
Phone: 503-282-7247
Fax: 503-282-7406
E-mail: srobertson4oaia@aol.com

OREGON STUDENT ASSISTANCE COMMISSION

http://www.GetCollegeFunds.org/

OREGON ASSOCIATION OF CERTIFIED FRAUD EXAMINERS SCHOLARSHIP

One-time award for students who will enroll as college seniors or above for fall term/semester at Oregon four-year public and nonprofit colleges. Must have minimum 3.25 GPA and be majoring in accounting, business, criminal justice, finance, law, law enforcement, or risk management

Academic Fields/Career Goals: Accounting; Business/Consumer Services; Criminal Justice/Criminology; Finance; Law/Legal Services.

Award: Scholarship for use in senior, graduate, or postgraduate years; not renewable.

Eligibility Requirements: Applicant must be enrolled or expecting to enroll full-time at a four-year institution or university and studying in Oregon. Available to U.S. citizens.

Application Requirements: Application form. *Deadline:* March 1.

OSCPA EDUCATIONAL FOUNDATION

http://www.orcpa.org/

OSCPA EDUCATIONAL FOUNDATION SCHOLARSHIP PROGRAM

One-time award for students majoring in accounting. Must attend an accredited Oregon college/university or community college on full-time basis. High school seniors must have a minimum 3.5 GPA. College students must have a minimum 3.2 GPA. Must be a U.S. citizen and Oregon resident.

Academic Fields/Career Goals: Accounting.

Award: Scholarship for use in freshman, sophomore, junior, senior, or graduate years; not renewable. *Number:* 50–100. *Amount:* $500–$3000.

Eligibility Requirements: Applicant must be enrolled or expecting to enroll full-time at a two-year or four-year or technical institution or university; resident of Oregon and studying in Oregon. Available to U.S. citizens.

Application Requirements: Application form, test scores, transcript. *Deadline:* February 17.

Contact: Tonna Hollis, Member Services and Manager
OSCPA Educational Foundation
PO Box 4555
Beaverton, OR 97076-4555
Phone: 503-641-7200 Ext. 29
Fax: 503-626-2942
E-mail: thollis@orcpa.org

PENNSYLVANIA INSTITUTE OF CERTIFIED PUBLIC ACCOUNTANTS

http://www.cpazone.org/

PENNSYLVANIA INSTITUTE OF CERTIFIED PUBLIC ACCOUNTANTS SOPHOMORE SCHOLARSHIP

To promote the accounting profession and CPA credential as an exciting and rewarding career path. Scholarship amounts range from $1000 to $15,000 and can be renewed annually until you graduate. Candidates must have completed a 36 credit hours and have a minimum 3.0 GPA.

Academic Fields/Career Goals: Accounting.

Award: Scholarship for use in sophomore, junior, senior, graduate, or postgraduate years; renewable. *Number:* 60–85. *Amount:* $1000–$15,000.

Eligibility Requirements: Applicant must be enrolled or expecting to enroll full-time at a four-year institution or university; resident of Pennsylvania and studying in Pennsylvania. Applicant must have 3.0 GPA or higher. Available to U.S. and non-U.S. citizens.

Application Requirements: Application form, essay, recommendations or references, resume, transcript. *Deadline:* March 10.

RHODE ISLAND FOUNDATION

http://www.rifoundation.org/

CARL W. CHRISTIANSEN SCHOLARSHIP

$1000 scholarship for Rhode Island residents pursuing full-time study in accounting or related fields. Must maintain a minimum 3.0 GPA.

Academic Fields/Career Goals: Accounting.

Award: Scholarship for use in freshman, sophomore, junior, senior, or graduate years; not renewable. *Amount:* $1000.

Eligibility Requirements: Applicant must be enrolled or expecting to enroll full-time at a two-year or four-year institution or university and resident of Rhode Island. Applicant must have 3.0 GPA or higher. Available to U.S. citizens.

Application Requirements: Application form. *Deadline:* January 11.

CHERYL A. RUGGIERO SCHOLARSHIP

Award for female Rhode Island residents pursuing full-time study in public accounting. Must maintain a minimum 3.0 GPA.

Academic Fields/Career Goals: Accounting.

Award: Scholarship for use in freshman, sophomore, junior, senior, or graduate years; not renewable. *Amount:* $1000.

Eligibility Requirements: Applicant must be enrolled or expecting to enroll full-time at a two-year or four-year institution or university; female and resident of Rhode Island. Applicant must have 3.0 GPA or higher. Available to U.S. citizens.

Application Requirements: Application form, essay, interview, proof of US citizenship, proof of RI residency, recommendations or references, transcript. *Deadline:* January 11.

RHODE ISLAND SOCIETY OF CERTIFIED PUBLIC ACCOUNTANTS

http://www.riscpa.org/

RHODE ISLAND SOCIETY OF CERTIFIED PUBLIC ACCOUNTANTS SCHOLARSHIP

Annual scholarship for graduates and undergraduates majoring in accounting, who are legal residents of Rhode Island and U.S. citizens. Must have interest in a career in public accounting, and submit one-page memo outlining that interest. Minimum GPA of 3.0 required. For more information, see website http://www.riscpa.org.

Academic Fields/Career Goals: Accounting.

Award: Scholarship for use in freshman, sophomore, junior, senior, or graduate years; not renewable.

Eligibility Requirements: Applicant must be enrolled or expecting to enroll full-time at a four-year institution or university and resident of Rhode Island. Applicant must have 3.0 GPA or higher. Available to U.S. citizens.

Application Requirements: Application form, recommendations or references, resume, test scores, transcript. *Deadline:* January 15.

Contact: Robert Mancini, Executive Director
Phone: 401-331-5720
Fax: 401-454-5780
E-mail: rmancini@riscpa.org

SOCIETY OF AUTOMOTIVE ANALYSTS

http://www.cybersaa.org/

SOCIETY OF AUTOMOTIVE ANALYSTS SCHOLARSHIP

A scholarship of $1500 awarded to students in economics, finance, business administration or marketing management. Minimum 3.0 GPA required. Must submit two letters of recommendation.

Academic Fields/Career Goals: Accounting; Business/Consumer Services; Economics.

Award: Scholarship for use in freshman, sophomore, junior, or senior years; not renewable. *Number:* 2. *Amount:* $1500.

Eligibility Requirements: Applicant must be enrolled or expecting to enroll full-time at a two-year or four-year or technical institution or university. Applicant must have 3.0 GPA or higher. Available to U.S. and non-U.S. citizens.

Application Requirements: Application form, recommendations or references, transcript. *Deadline:* June 1.

Contact: Lynne Hall, Awards and Scholarships
Phone: 313-240-4000
Fax: 313-240-8641

SOCIETY OF LOUISIANA CERTIFIED PUBLIC ACCOUNTANTS

http://www.lcpa.org/

SOCIETY OF LOUISIANA CPAS SCHOLARSHIPS

One-time award for accounting majors. Applicant must be a Louisiana resident attending a four-year college or university in Louisiana. For full-time undergraduates entering their junior or senior year, or full-time graduate students. Minimum 2.5 GPA required. Deadline varies. Must be U.S. citizen.

Academic Fields/Career Goals: Accounting.

Award: Scholarship for use in junior, senior, or graduate years; not renewable. *Amount:* $500–$3000.

Eligibility Requirements: Applicant must be enrolled or expecting to enroll full-time at a four-year institution or university; resident of

Louisiana and studying in Louisiana. Applicant must have 2.5 GPA or higher. Available to U.S. citizens.

Application Requirements: Application form, essay, recommendations or references, transcript. *Deadline:* varies.

Contact: Lisa Richardson, Member Services Manager
Society of Louisiana Certified Public Accountants
2400 Veterans Boulevard, Suite 500
Kenner, LA 70062-4739
Phone: 504-904-1139
Fax: 504-469-7930
E-mail: lrichardson@lcpa.org

SOUTH CAROLINA ASSOCIATION OF CERTIFIED PUBLIC ACCOUNTANTS

http://www.scacpa.org

SCACPA EDUCATIONAL FUND SCHOLARSHIPS

These scholarships are awarded to South Carolina residents who are rising juniors or seniors majoring in accounting, or master's degree students at a South Carolina college or university. Applicants must have a GPA of no less than 3.25 overall and a GPA in accounting no less than 3.5 (on a 4.0 scale).

Academic Fields/Career Goals: Accounting.

Award: Scholarship for use in junior, senior, or graduate years; not renewable. *Number:* 19–25. *Amount:* $500–$2500.

Eligibility Requirements: Applicant must be enrolled or expecting to enroll full-time at a four-year institution or university; resident of South Carolina and studying in South Carolina. Applicant must have 3.0 GPA or higher. Available to U.S. citizens.

Application Requirements: Application form, essay, financial need analysis, recommendations or references, resume, transcript. *Deadline:* June 1.

Contact: Mrs. Glenna Osier, Peer Review Manager
South Carolina Association of Certified Public Accountants
570 Chris Drive
Columbia, SC 29169
Phone: 803-791-4181 Ext. 107
Fax: 803-791-4196
E-mail: gosier@scacpa.org

SOUTH DAKOTA CPA SOCIETY

http://www.sdcpa.org/

5TH YEAR FULL TUITION SCHOLARSHIP

Scholarship pays for the full tuition for a South Dakota student to attend an accredited South Dakota college or university. If awarded the scholarship, the student must become a member of the SD CPA Society, work for or be supervised by a member of the SD CPA Society for 2 years, and upon eligibility, must sit for a minimum of 4 parts of the CPA exam per year for two years or until completed.

Academic Fields/Career Goals: Accounting.

Award: Scholarship for use in senior or graduate years; not renewable. *Number:* 1–2. *Amount:* $6800.

Eligibility Requirements: Applicant must be enrolled or expecting to enroll full-time at a four-year institution or university and studying in South Dakota. Applicant must have 3.0 GPA or higher. Available to U.S. citizens.

Application Requirements: Application form, essay, transcript. *Deadline:* March 30.

Contact: Laura Coome, Executive Director
South Dakota CPA Society
PO Box 2080
Sioux Falls, SD 57101-2080
Phone: 605-334-3848
E-mail: lcoome@iw.net

EXCELLENCE IN ACCOUNTING SCHOLARSHIP

Scholarships available for senior undergraduate and graduate students majoring in accounting. Must have completed 90 credit hours, demonstrated excellence in academics and leadership potential. Application available online at http://www.sdcpa.org.

Academic Fields/Career Goals: Accounting.

Award: Scholarship for use in senior or graduate years; renewable. *Number:* 4–10. *Amount:* $500–$1500.

Eligibility Requirements: Applicant must be enrolled or expecting to enroll full-time at a four-year institution or university and studying in South Dakota. Available to U.S. citizens.

Application Requirements: Application form, transcript. *Deadline:* March 30.

Contact: Laura Coome, Executive Director
South Dakota CPA Society
PO Box 2080
Sioux Falls, SD 57101
Phone: 605-334-3848

SOUTH DAKOTA RETAILERS ASSOCIATION

http://www.sdra.org/

SOUTH DAKOTA RETAILERS ASSOCIATION SCHOLARSHIP PROGRAM

One-time award to assist full-time students studying for a career in retailing. Applicants must have graduated from a South Dakota high school or be enrolled in postsecondary school in South Dakota. The award value and the number of awards granted varies annually.

Academic Fields/Career Goals: Accounting; Business/Consumer Services; Computer Science/Data Processing; Cosmetology; Culinary Arts; Electrical Engineering/Electronics; Graphics/Graphic Arts/Printing; Heating, Air-Conditioning, and Refrigeration Mechanics; Hospitality Management; Interior Design; Landscape Architecture; Pharmacy.

Award: Scholarship for use in sophomore, junior, senior, graduate, or postgraduate years; not renewable. *Number:* 10–15. *Amount:* $250–$1000.

Eligibility Requirements: Applicant must be enrolled or expecting to enroll full-time at a two-year or technical institution or university. Available to U.S. and non-U.S. citizens.

Application Requirements: Application form, application form may be submitted online (http://www.sra.org), essay, recommendations or references, resume, transcript. *Deadline:* April 13.

Contact: Donna Leslie, Communications Director
Phone: 800-658-5545
Fax: 605-224-2059
E-mail: donna@sdra.org

SPECIALTY EQUIPMENT MARKET ASSOCIATION

http://www.sema.org/

SPECIALTY EQUIPMENT MARKET ASSOCIATION MEMORIAL SCHOLARSHIP FUND

Scholarships for college students pursuing careers in or related to the automotive industry. All applicants must be U.S. Citizens who are currently attending U.S. institutions. For more information and to apply, please visit http://www.SEMA.org/scholarships.

Academic Fields/Career Goals: Accounting; Advertising/Public Relations; Business/Consumer Services; Communications; Computer Science/Data Processing; Electrical Engineering/Electronics; Engineering/Technology; Finance; Marketing; Mechanical Engineering; Trade/Technical Specialties; Transportation.

Award: Scholarship for use in sophomore, junior, senior, graduate, or postgraduate years; not renewable. *Number:* 60–90. *Amount:* $2000–$5000.

Eligibility Requirements: Applicant must be enrolled or expecting to enroll full-time at a two-year or four-year or technical institution or university and must have an interest in automotive. Applicant must have 2.5 GPA or higher. Available to U.S. citizens.

Application Requirements: Application form, application form may be submitted online (http://www.SEMA.org/scholarships), essay, recommendations or references, transcript. *Deadline:* March 29.

Contact: Ms. Juliet Marshall, Education Administrator
Phone: 909-978-6655
Fax: 909-860-0184
E-mail: julietm@sema.org

TENNESSEE SOCIETY OF CPAS

http://www.tscpa.com/

TENNESSEE SOCIETY OF CPA SCHOLARSHIP

Scholarships are available only to full-time students who have completed introductory courses in accounting and/or students majoring in accounting. Applicants must be legal residents of Tennessee.

Academic Fields/Career Goals: Accounting.

Award: Scholarship for use in freshman, sophomore, junior, senior, or graduate years; not renewable. *Number:* 120–130. *Amount:* $250–$2500.

Eligibility Requirements: Applicant must be enrolled or expecting to enroll full-time at a four-year institution or university and resident of Tennessee. Available to U.S. citizens.

Application Requirements: Application form, financial need analysis, recommendations or references, transcript. *Deadline:* June 1.

Contact: Wendy Garvin, Member Services Manager
> *Phone:* 615-377-3825
> *Fax:* 390-377-3904
> *E-mail:* wgarvin@tscpa.com

TKE EDUCATIONAL FOUNDATION

http://www.tke.org/

HARRY J. DONNELLY MEMORIAL SCHOLARSHIP

One-time award of $900 given to a member of Tau Kappa Epsilon pursuing an undergraduate degree in accounting or a graduate degree in law. Applicant should have demonstrated leadership ability within his chapter, campus, or community.

Academic Fields/Career Goals: Accounting; Law/Legal Services.

Award: Scholarship for use in freshman, sophomore, junior, senior, or graduate years; not renewable. *Number:* 1. *Amount:* $900.

Eligibility Requirements: Applicant must be enrolled or expecting to enroll full-time at a four-year institution or university and must have an interest in leadership. Applicant or parent of applicant must be member of Tau Kappa Epsilon. Applicant must have 3.0 GPA or higher. Available to U.S. and non-U.S. citizens.

Application Requirements: Application form, essay, narrative summary of how TKE membership has benefited applicant, personal photograph, transcript. *Deadline:* February 29.

Contact: Gary Reed, President and Chief Executive Officer
> TKE Educational Foundation
> 8645 Founders Road
> Indianapolis, IN 46268-1393
> *Phone:* 317-872-6533
> *Fax:* 317-875-8353
> *E-mail:* reedga@tke.org

W. ALLAN HERZOG SCHOLARSHIP

One $3000 award for an undergraduate member of TKE who is a full-time student pursuing a finance or accounting degree. Minimum 2.75 GPA required. Preference given to members of Nu Chapter. Applicant should have record of leadership within chapter and campus organizations.

Academic Fields/Career Goals: Accounting; Business/Consumer Services.

Award: Scholarship for use in freshman, sophomore, junior, or senior years; not renewable. *Number:* 1. *Amount:* $3000.

Eligibility Requirements: Applicant must be enrolled or expecting to enroll full-time at a four-year institution or university; male and must have an interest in leadership. Applicant or parent of applicant must be member of Tau Kappa Epsilon. Available to U.S. and non-U.S. citizens.

Application Requirements: Application form, essay, narrative summary of how TKE membership has benefited applicant, personal photograph, transcript. *Deadline:* February 29.

Contact: Gary Reed, President and Chief Executive Officer
> TKE Educational Foundation
> 8645 Founders Road
> Indianapolis, IN 46268-1393
> *Phone:* 317-872-6533
> *Fax:* 317-875-8353
> *E-mail:* reedga@tke.org

UNITED NEGRO COLLEGE FUND

http://www.uncf.org/

ALFRED CHISHOLM/BASF MEMORIAL SCHOLARSHIP FUND

Scholarship for a student who has a relative employed by the BASF Corporation. Must attend an historically black college or university and have minimum GPA of 2.7 to apply. Eligible majors include engineering, accounting, mathematics, chemistry, biology, computer science, law, electrical engineering, chemical engineering, environmental engineering, mechanical engineering, petroleum engineering, pulp and paper engineering, systems engineering, and construction engineering.

Academic Fields/Career Goals: Accounting; Biology; Computer Science/Data Processing; Construction Engineering/Management; Electrical Engineering/Electronics; Engineering/Technology; Law/Legal Services; Mathematics; Mechanical Engineering; Paper and Pulp Engineering.

Award: Scholarship for use in freshman, sophomore, junior, or senior years; not renewable. *Amount:* $5000.

Eligibility Requirements: Applicant must be Black (non-Hispanic) and enrolled or expecting to enroll full- or part-time at a four-year institution or university. Available to U.S. citizens.

Application Requirements: Application form. *Deadline:* May 31.

AVIS BUDGET GROUP SCHOLARSHIP

$5000 scholarship for second-semester sophomore majoring in business, finance, economics, or accounting. Minimum 3.0 GPA required.

Academic Fields/Career Goals: Accounting; Business/Consumer Services; Economics; Finance.

Award: Scholarship for use in sophomore or junior years; not renewable. *Amount:* $5000.

Eligibility Requirements: Applicant must be Black (non-Hispanic) and enrolled or expecting to enroll full- or part-time at a four-year institution. Applicant must have 3.0 GPA or higher. Available to U.S. citizens.

Application Requirements: Application form. *Deadline:* continuous.

AXA ACHIEVEMENT SCHOLARSHIP PROGRAM

Up to $2000 scholarship available for students attending one of the 38 UNCF membership schools. Must be a sophomore or junior, have a minimum 3.0 GPA, and study accounting, business, or marketing. Employees, financial professionals, or immediate family members of employees or financial professionals of the AXA Group or their affiliates, subsidies, and advertising and promotion agencies are ineligible to apply.

Academic Fields/Career Goals: Accounting; Business/Consumer Services; Marketing.

Award: Scholarship for use in sophomore or junior years; not renewable. *Amount:* up to $2000.

Eligibility Requirements: Applicant must be Black (non-Hispanic) and enrolled or expecting to enroll full-time at a four-year institution or university. Applicant must have 3.0 GPA or higher. Available to U.S. citizens.

Application Requirements: Application form. *Deadline:* April 21.

COMERICA CHARITABLE FOUNDATION SCHOLARSHIP

Scholarship available to students attending UNCF member schools who are residents of the following Comerica market areas: Phoenix, Arizona; or Los Angeles, Oakland, San Diego, San Francisco, or San Jose, CA; or Ann Arbor, Battle Creek, Detroit, Grand Rapids, Jackson, Kalamazoo, Lansing, Midland, or Muskegon, MI; or Austin, Dallas/Ft. Worth, Houston, or San Antonio, TX. Minimum 3.0 GPA required. Must be studying accounting, finance, or business.

Academic Fields/Career Goals: Accounting; Business/Consumer Services; Finance.

Award: Scholarship for use in freshman, sophomore, or junior years; not renewable. *Amount:* up to $2275.

Eligibility Requirements: Applicant must be Black (non-Hispanic); enrolled or expecting to enroll full-time at a four-year institution and resident of Arizona, California, Florida, Michigan, Texas. Applicant must have 3.0 GPA or higher. Available to U.S. citizens.

Application Requirements: Application form. *Deadline:* April 26.

EDWARD M. NAGEL FOUNDATION SCHOLARSHIP

Award for African American residents of California within the top 25 percent of their high school graduating class. Must be enrolled in a UNCF member college or university and pursue a degree in business, economics, or accounting. The scholarship value ranges from $2000 to $5000. For additional information and general scholarship application, visit website: http://www.uncf.org.

Academic Fields/Career Goals: Accounting; Business/Consumer Services; Economics.

Award: Scholarship for use in freshman, sophomore, junior, or senior years; not renewable. *Amount:* $2000–$5000.

Eligibility Requirements: Applicant must be Black (non-Hispanic); enrolled or expecting to enroll full-time at a four-year institution or university and resident of California. Applicant must have 3.0 GPA or higher. Available to U.S. citizens.

Application Requirements: Application form, FAFSA, financial need analysis. *Deadline:* continuous.

FORD/UNCF CORPORATE SCHOLARS PROGRAM

Scholarship of up to $5000 for a college junior studying at a UNCF member school. Must have minimum 3.0 GPA and be studying accounting, computer engineering, electrical engineering, finance, information systems, marketing, mechanical engineering, or operations management.

Academic Fields/Career Goals: Accounting; Computer Science/Data Processing; Electrical Engineering/Electronics; Engineering/Technology; Finance; Marketing; Mechanical Engineering.

Award: Scholarship for use in junior year; not renewable. *Amount:* up to $5000.

Eligibility Requirements: Applicant must be Black (non-Hispanic) and enrolled or expecting to enroll full-time at a four-year institution. Applicant must have 3.0 GPA or higher. Available to U.S. citizens.

Application Requirements: Application form, essay, recommendations or references, transcript. *Deadline:* April 25.

LOCKHEED MARTIN/UNCF SCHOLARSHIP

Scholarship available to African American undergraduate freshman and sophomore students at participating colleges and universities. Eligible majors include business, finance, accounting, computer science, supply chain management, electrical engineering, computer engineering, industrial engineering, mechanical engineering, systems engineering, aerospace engineering, and nuclear engineering. Minimum 3.0 GPA required. For a list of eligible institutions and to apply online, visit website http://www.uncf.org.

Academic Fields/Career Goals: Accounting; Business/Consumer Services; Computer Science/Data Processing; Electrical Engineering/Electronics; Engineering/Technology; Finance; Mechanical Engineering.

Award: Scholarship for use in freshman or sophomore years; not renewable. *Amount:* $5000.

Eligibility Requirements: Applicant must be Black (non-Hispanic) and enrolled or expecting to enroll full-time at a four-year institution or university. Applicant must have 3.0 GPA or higher. Available to U.S. citizens.

Application Requirements: Application form, transcript. *Deadline:* April 28.

NASCAR/WENDELL SCOTT, SR. SCHOLARSHIP

Award for African American junior or senior undergraduates or graduate students. Undergraduates must have a 3.0 GPA and graduate students must have a 3.2 GPA. Please visit website for eligible majors and a list of eligible colleges and universities and to apply online http://www.uncf.org.

Academic Fields/Career Goals: Accounting; Business/Consumer Services; Communications; Computer Science/Data Processing; Engineering/Technology; Finance; Marketing; Mechanical Engineering.

Award: Scholarship for use in junior, senior, or graduate years; renewable. *Amount:* $10,000.

Eligibility Requirements: Applicant must be Black (non-Hispanic) and enrolled or expecting to enroll full- or part-time at a four-year institution or university. Available to U.S. citizens.

Application Requirements: Application form, FAFSA, Student Aid Report (SAR), financial need analysis, personal photograph, recommendations or references, resume, transcript. *Deadline:* continuous.

PACIFIC GAS AND ELECTRIC COMPANY SCHOLARSHIP

Scholarships available to undergraduate freshmen and sophomores who are California residents attending UNCF member colleges and universities. Preference will be given to students from Central and Northern California. Must have minimum 2.5 GPA and major in a number of selected fields.

Academic Fields/Career Goals: Accounting; Business/Consumer Services; Civil Engineering; Computer Science/Data Processing; Economics; Electrical Engineering/Electronics; Engineering/Technology; Finance; Marketing; Mathematics; Mechanical Engineering.

Award: Scholarship for use in freshman or sophomore years; not renewable. *Amount:* $5000.

Eligibility Requirements: Applicant must be Black (non-Hispanic); enrolled or expecting to enroll full-time at a four-year institution or university and resident of California. Applicant must have 2.5 GPA or higher. Available to U.S. citizens.

Application Requirements: Application form. *Deadline:* continuous.

PSE&G SCHOLARSHIP

Scholarships available to New Jersey residents who are enrolled at UNCF colleges and universities and majoring in business, information technology, and engineering. Minimum 3.0 GPA required.

Academic Fields/Career Goals: Accounting; Business/Consumer Services; Computer Science/Data Processing; Economics; Engineering/Technology; Finance; Marketing.

Award: Scholarship for use in freshman, sophomore, junior, or senior years; not renewable. *Amount:* $2500–$3000.

Eligibility Requirements: Applicant must be Black (non-Hispanic); enrolled or expecting to enroll full-time at a four-year institution or university and resident of New Jersey. Applicant must have 3.0 GPA or higher. Available to U.S. citizens.

Application Requirements: Application form. *Deadline:* continuous.

ROBERT HALF INTERNATIONAL SCHOLARSHIP

Scholarships ranging from $1000 to $1750 for students attending UNCF member colleges and universities. Minimum 2.5 GPA required. Must be majoring in business or accounting.

Academic Fields/Career Goals: Accounting; Business/Consumer Services.

Award: Scholarship for use in freshman, sophomore, junior, or senior years; not renewable. *Amount:* $1000–$1750.

Eligibility Requirements: Applicant must be Black (non-Hispanic) and enrolled or expecting to enroll full-time at a four-year institution or university. Applicant must have 2.5 GPA or higher. Available to U.S. citizens.

Application Requirements: Application form. *Deadline:* continuous.

UBS/PAINEWEBBER SCHOLARSHIP

$8000 scholarship available to students majoring in business at one of the UNCF member institutions. Must be an undergraduate sophomore or junior with a minimum 3.0 GPA.

Academic Fields/Career Goals: Accounting; Business/Consumer Services; Economics; Finance; Marketing.

Award: Scholarship for use in sophomore or junior years; not renewable. *Amount:* $8000.

Eligibility Requirements: Applicant must be Black (non-Hispanic) and enrolled or expecting to enroll full- or part-time at a four-year institution or university. Applicant must have 3.0 GPA or higher. Available to U.S. citizens.

Application Requirements: Application form, essay, financial need analysis, recommendations or references, resume, transcript. *Deadline:* November 27.

VIRCHOW, KRAUSE & COMPANY, LLP

http://www.virchowkrause.com/

VIRCHOW, KRAUSE AND COMPANY SCHOLARSHIP

One-time scholarship for students enrolled either full-time or part-time in accredited colleges or universities of Wisconsin, majoring in accounting.

Academic Fields/Career Goals: Accounting.

Award: Scholarship for use in freshman, sophomore, junior, or senior years; not renewable. *Number:* up to 3. *Amount:* up to $1000.

Eligibility Requirements: Applicant must be enrolled or expecting to enroll full- or part-time at a two-year or four-year institution or university and studying in Wisconsin. Available to U.S. citizens.

Application Requirements: Application form, transcript. *Deadline:* varies.

Contact: Darbie Miller, Human Resources Coordinator
Virchow, Krause & Company, LLP
4600 American Parkway, PO Box 7398
Madison, WI 53707-7398
Phone: 608-240-2474
Fax: 608-249-1411
E-mail: dmiller@virchowkrause.com

WYOMING TRUCKING ASSOCIATION SCHOLARSHIP FUND TRUST

http://www.wytruck.org/

WYOMING TRUCKING ASSOCIATION SCHOLARSHIP TRUST FUND

To qualify, students must (1) be a graduate of a Wyoming high school; (2) plan to pursue a course of study which will lead to a career in the Highway Transportation Industry with the following approved courses of study: business management, computer skills, accounting, office procedures and management, safety, diesel mechanics and truck driving; (3) attend a Wyoming school (University, Community College or trade school) approved by the WTA Scholarship Committee.

Academic Fields/Career Goals: Accounting; Business/Consumer Services; Communications; Computer Science/Data Processing; Marketing; Trade/Technical Specialties; Transportation.

Award: Scholarship for use in freshman, sophomore, junior, or senior years; not renewable. *Number:* 4–8. *Amount:* $500–$1000.

Eligibility Requirements: Applicant must be enrolled or expecting to enroll full-time at a two-year or four-year or technical institution or university; resident of Wyoming and studying in Wyoming. Available to U.S. citizens.

Application Requirements: Application form, community service, essay, financial need analysis, recommendations or references, test scores, transcript. *Deadline:* March 10.

Contact: Kathy Cundall, Administrative Assistant
Phone: 307-234-1579
E-mail: wytruck@aol.com

ADVERTISING/PUBLIC RELATIONS

GREAT FALLS ADVERTISING FEDERATION

http://www.gfaf.com/

GREAT FALLS ADVERTISING FEDERATION COLLEGE SCHOLARSHIP

Scholarship of $2000 for college juniors who are residents of Montana. Must intend to pursue a career in communications, marketing, advertising, fine arts, or other related field. The number of awards vary. Must maintain a minimum 3.0 GPA.

Academic Fields/Career Goals: Advertising/Public Relations; Arts; Business/Consumer Services; Communications; Marketing.

Award: Scholarship for use in junior year; renewable. *Amount:* $2000.

Eligibility Requirements: Applicant must be enrolled or expecting to enroll full-time at a four-year institution or university and resident of Montana. Applicant must have 3.0 GPA or higher. Available to U.S. citizens.

Application Requirements: Application form, community service, essay, recommendations or references, resume, transcript, work samples. *Deadline:* February 2.

Contact: Christine Depa, Administrative Assistant
Phone: 406-761-6453
Fax: 406-453-1128
E-mail: gfaf@gfaf.com

HIGH SCHOOL MARKETING/COMMUNICATIONS SCHOLARSHIP

Two scholarships of $2000 for high school seniors who are residents of Montana. Must intend to pursue a career in communications, marketing, advertising, or other related field.

Academic Fields/Career Goals: Advertising/Public Relations; Business/Consumer Services; Communications; Marketing.

Award: Scholarship for use in freshman year; not renewable. *Number:* 2. *Amount:* $2000.

Eligibility Requirements: Applicant must be high school student; planning to enroll or expecting to enroll full-time at a four-year institution or university and resident of Montana. Available to U.S. citizens.

Application Requirements: Application form, cover letter describing how the scholarship money will be used, essay, recommendations or references, resume, self-addressed stamped envelope with application. *Deadline:* February 29.

Contact: Christine Depa, Administrative Assistant
Phone: 406-761-6453
Fax: 406-453-1128
E-mail: gfaf@gfaf.com

INTERNATIONAL FOODSERVICE EDITORIAL COUNCIL

http://www.ifeconline.com/

INTERNATIONAL FOODSERVICE EDITORIAL COUNCIL COMMUNICATIONS SCHOLARSHIP

Applicant must be a full-time student enrolled in an accredited postsecondary educational institution working toward an associate, bachelor's, or master's degree. Must demonstrate financial need, academic achievement, service orientation, and writing ability. Must have background, education, and interests indicating preparedness for entering careers in editorial or public relations within the foodservice industry.

Academic Fields/Career Goals: Advertising/Public Relations; Communications; Culinary Arts; Food Science/Nutrition; Food Service/Hospitality; Graphics/Graphic Arts/Printing; Home Economics; Hospitality Management; Journalism; Literature/English/Writing; Marketing; Photojournalism/Photography.

Award: Scholarship for use in freshman, sophomore, junior, senior, or graduate years; not renewable. *Number:* 1–8. *Amount:* $250–$6000.

Eligibility Requirements: Applicant must be enrolled or expecting to enroll full-time at a two-year or four-year institution or university and must have an interest in photography/photogrammetry/filmmaking or writing. Available to U.S. and non-U.S. citizens.

Application Requirements: Application form, essay, recommendations or references, resume, transcript. *Deadline:* March 15.

Contact: Carol Lally, Executive Director
International Foodservice Editorial Council
PO Box 491
Hyde Park, NY 12538-0491
Phone: 845-229-6973
E-mail: ifec@aol.com

PUBLIC RELATIONS STUDENT SOCIETY OF AMERICA

http://www.prssa.org/

PUBLIC RELATIONS SOCIETY OF AMERICA MULTICULTURAL AFFAIRS SCHOLARSHIP

Two, one-time $1500 awards for members of a principal minority group who are in their junior or senior year at an accredited four-year college or university. Must have at least a 3.0 GPA and be preparing for career in public relations or communications. Must be a full-time student and U.S. citizen.

Academic Fields/Career Goals: Advertising/Public Relations; Communications.

Award: Scholarship for use in freshman, sophomore, junior, or senior years; not renewable. *Number:* 2. *Amount:* $1500.

Eligibility Requirements: Applicant must be American Indian/Alaska Native, Asian/Pacific Islander, Black (non-Hispanic), Hispanic and enrolled or expecting to enroll full-time at a four-year institution or university. Applicant must have 3.0 GPA or higher. Available to U.S. citizens.

Application Requirements: Application form, essay, financial need analysis, recommendations or references, transcript. *Deadline:* April 18.

Contact: Dora Tovar, Chair, Multicultural Communications Section
Public Relations Student Society of America
33 Maiden Lane, 11th Floor
New York, NY 10038-5150
Phone: 212-460-1476
Fax: 212-995-0757
E-mail: jeneen.garcia@prsa.org

RHODE ISLAND FOUNDATION

http://www.rifoundation.org/

J. D. EDSAL SCHOLARSHIP

Award to benefit Rhode Island residents studying advertising (public relations, marketing, graphic design, film, video, television, or broadcast production) with the expectation of pursuing a career in one of more of these fields. Applicants must be college undergraduates, sophomore or above.

Academic Fields/Career Goals: Advertising/Public Relations; Communications; Filmmaking/Video; Graphics/Graphic Arts/Printing; Marketing; TV/Radio Broadcasting.

Award: Scholarship for use in sophomore, junior, or senior years; renewable. *Amount:* $500–$1000.

Eligibility Requirements: Applicant must be enrolled or expecting to enroll full-time at a four-year institution or university and resident of Rhode Island. Available to U.S. citizens.

Application Requirements: Application form, essay, financial need analysis, recommendations or references, self-addressed stamped envelope with application, transcript.

Contact: Libby Monahan, Funds Administrator
Phone: 401-274-4564 Ext. 3117
E-mail: libbym@rifoundation.org

SPECIALTY EQUIPMENT MARKET ASSOCIATION

http://www.sema.org/

SPECIALTY EQUIPMENT MARKET ASSOCIATION MEMORIAL SCHOLARSHIP FUND
• *See page 80*

STRAIGHTFORWARD MEDIA

http://www.straightforwardmedia.com/

STRAIGHTFORWARD MEDIA BUSINESS SCHOOL SCHOLARSHIP

Scholarship of $500 for undergraduate and graduate students pursuing a business-related degree, including but not limited to economics, finance, marketing, and management. Students pursuing an online business degree are also eligible. Awarded four times per year. Deadlines: March 31, June 30, September 30, and December 31.

Academic Fields/Career Goals: Advertising/Public Relations; Business/Consumer Services; Economics; Finance; Marketing.

Award: Scholarship for use in freshman, sophomore, junior, senior, or graduate years; not renewable. *Number:* 4. *Amount:* $500.

Eligibility Requirements: Applicant must be enrolled or expecting to enroll full- or part-time at a two-year or four-year or technical institution or university. Available to U.S. and non-U.S. citizens.

Application Requirements: Essay. *Deadline:* varies.

STRAIGHTFORWARD MEDIA MEDIA & COMMUNICATIONS SCHOLARSHIP

Scholarship of $500 available to students of media and communications. Must be majoring in programs such as journalism, broadcasting, advertising, speech, mass communications, or marketing. Awarded four times per year. Deadlines are March 31, June 30, September 30, and December 31. For more information, visit website at http://www.straightforwardmedia.com/media/form.php.

Academic Fields/Career Goals: Advertising/Public Relations; Communications; Journalism; Marketing; Photojournalism/Photography; TV/Radio Broadcasting.

Award: Scholarship for use in freshman, sophomore, junior, or senior years; not renewable. *Number:* 4. *Amount:* $500.

Eligibility Requirements: Applicant must be enrolled or expecting to enroll full- or part-time at a two-year or four-year or technical institution or university. Available to U.S. and non-U.S. citizens.

Application Requirements: Essay. *Deadline:* varies.

AGRIBUSINESS

ABBIE SARGENT MEMORIAL SCHOLARSHIP INC.

http://www.nhfarmbureau.org/

ABBIE SARGENT MEMORIAL SCHOLARSHIP

Up to three awards between $400 and $500 will be provided to deserving New Hampshire residents, planning to attend an institution of higher learning. Must be a U.S. citizen.

Academic Fields/Career Goals: Agribusiness; Agriculture; Animal/Veterinary Sciences; Environmental Science; Home Economics; Horticulture/Floriculture.

Award: Scholarship for use in freshman, sophomore, junior, senior, graduate, or postgraduate years; not renewable. *Number:* 1–3. *Amount:* $400–$500.

Eligibility Requirements: Applicant must be enrolled or expecting to enroll full- or part-time at a two-year or four-year or technical institution or university and resident of New Hampshire. Applicant or parent of applicant must have employment or volunteer experience in agriculture. Available to U.S. citizens.

Application Requirements: Application form, driver's license, financial need analysis, personal photograph, recommendations or references, transcript. *Deadline:* March 15.

Contact: Diane Clary, Office Administrator
Abbie Sargent Memorial Scholarship Inc.
Abbie Sargent Scholarship
295 Sheep Davis Road
Concord, NH 03301
Phone: 603-224-1934
Fax: 603-228-8432
E-mail: dianec@nhfarmbureau.org

CHS FOUNDATION

http://www.chsfoundation.org/

CHS FOUNDATION HIGH SCHOOL SCHOLARSHIPS

Scholarships available to graduating high school seniors who plan to enroll in an agricultural-related program of study in a two-year or four-year college or university. Student must be a U.S. citizen. For additional information and an application, see website http://www.chsfoundation.org.

Academic Fields/Career Goals: Agribusiness; Agriculture; Horticulture/Floriculture.

Award: Scholarship for use in freshman year; not renewable. *Number:* 50. *Amount:* $1000.

Eligibility Requirements: Applicant must be high school student and planning to enroll or expecting to enroll full- or part-time at a two-year or four-year or technical institution or university. Available to U.S. citizens.

Application Requirements: Application form, essay, recommendations or references, transcript. *Deadline:* April 1.

CHS FOUNDATION TWO-YEAR COLLEGE SCHOLARSHIPS

Non-renewable scholarship available to first-year agricultural students at a two-year college. Must be studying an agricultural-related major; scholarship is intended for the second year of study. Must be a U.S. citizen. For additional information and application, see website http://www.chsfoundation.org.

Academic Fields/Career Goals: Agribusiness; Agriculture; Horticulture/Floriculture.

Award: Scholarship for use in sophomore year; not renewable. *Number:* 25. *Amount:* $1000.

Eligibility Requirements: Applicant must be enrolled or expecting to enroll full- or part-time at a two-year or technical institution. Available to U.S. citizens.

Application Requirements: Application form, essay, recommendations or references, transcript. *Deadline:* April 1.

CHS FOUNDATION UNIVERSITY SCHOLARSHIPS

Renewable scholarship available for students in sophomore, junior, or senior year currently studying agriculture at select universities around the nation. Preference given to students interested in a career in or studying agricultural-based cooperatives and working towards a degree in agribusiness or production agriculture. Students apply to the School of Agriculture or Financial Aid Office at one of the participating universities and follow individual procedures and deadlines for that institution. For additional information and a list of participating universities, see website http://www.chsfoundation.org.

Academic Fields/Career Goals: Agribusiness; Agriculture.

Award: Scholarship for use in sophomore, junior, or senior years; not renewable. *Number:* up to 150. *Amount:* $1000.

Eligibility Requirements: Applicant must be enrolled or expecting to enroll full- or part-time at a four-year institution or university. Available to U.S. citizens.

Application Requirements: Application form, essay, recommendations or references, transcript.

GOLF COURSE SUPERINTENDENTS ASSOCIATION OF AMERICA

http://www.eifg.org/

GOLF COURSE SUPERINTENDENTS ASSOCIATION OF AMERICA STUDENT ESSAY CONTEST

Up to three awards for essays focusing on the golf course management profession. Undergraduates and graduate students pursuing turf grass science, agronomy, or any field related to golf course management may apply. Applicant must be a member of GCSAA. In addition to cash prizes, winning entries may be published or excerpted in News-line or Golf Course Management magazine.

Academic Fields/Career Goals: Agribusiness; Horticulture/Floriculture; Recreation, Parks, Leisure Studies.

Award: Prize for use in freshman, sophomore, junior, or senior years; not renewable. *Number:* up to 3. *Amount:* $1000–$2000.

Eligibility Requirements: Applicant must be enrolled or expecting to enroll full-time at a two-year or four-year institution or university. Applicant or parent of applicant must be member of Golf Course Superintendents Association of America. Available to U.S. and non-U.S. citizens.

Application Requirements: Application form, entry in a contest, essay. *Deadline:* March 31.

Contact: Mischia Wright, Senior Manager, Development
    Phone: 800-472-7878 Ext. 4445
    E-mail: mwright@gcsaa.org

HOLSTEIN ASSOCIATION USA INC.

http://www.holsteinusa.com/

ROBERT H. RUMLER SCHOLARSHIP

Awards to encourage deserving and qualified persons with an established interest in the dairy field, who have demonstrated leadership qualities and managerial abilities to pursue a master's degree in business administration.

Academic Fields/Career Goals: Agribusiness; Business/Consumer Services.

Award: Scholarship for use in freshman, sophomore, junior, senior, or graduate years; not renewable. *Number:* 1. *Amount:* $3000.

Eligibility Requirements: Applicant must be enrolled or expecting to enroll full-time at an institution or university and must have an interest in leadership. Applicant must have 3.0 GPA or higher. Available to U.S. and non-U.S. citizens.

Application Requirements: Application form, essay, personal photograph, recommendations or references, transcript. *Deadline:* April 15.

Contact: John Meyer, Chief Executive Officer
    Holstein Association USA Inc.
    One Holstein Place, PO Box 808
    Brattleboro, VT 05302-0808
    Phone: 802-254-4551
    Fax: 802-254-8251
    E-mail: jmeyer@holstein.com

HORTICULTURAL RESEARCH INSTITUTE

http://www.hriresearch.org/

BRYAN A. CHAMPION MEMORIAL SCHOLARSHIP

On November 10, 2011, Bryan A. Champion, president of Herman Losely and Son, Inc. located in Perry, Ohio, passed away at the age of 47. Champion was diagnosed with cancer in 2007, and fought a courageous 4-year battle to try to beat the devastating disease. Champion was a 5th generation nurseryman with a passion for the nursery and landscape industry. During his career he was involved with local, state and national associations that represent the industry. He sought to advance the industry through sound leadership, volunteer participation, and peer-to-peer networking and education events. He was a Buckeye, and graduated from Ohio State University (OSU) in 1987. Champion understood the value of a quality education and the importance of industry research. During his career at Herman Losely and Son, Inc., he worked with OSU and the United States of America- Agricultural Research Service to successfully solve industry issues. In honor of Champion's legacy and dedication to the nursery and landscape industry, donations have been received from his peers to establish The Bryan A. Champion Memorial Scholarship Fund. Each year, Champion's legacy will be remembered when the fund provides a student scholarship to a deserving horticultural student. It is our hope that each recipient will show a similar passion for the industry as Champion exhibited throughout his life. Applicant must be enrolled in an accredited undergraduate or graduate: landscape, horticulture or related discipline at a two or four-year institution. Students in vocational agriculture programs will also be considered. Undergraduate: Applicant must have at least a sophomore standing in a four-year curriculum or senior standing in a two-year curriculum as of the fall semester of scholarship application year. Graduate: All applicants in graduate school regardless of year in school may apply.

Academic Fields/Career Goals: Agribusiness; Entomology; Horticulture/Floriculture; Landscape Architecture.

Award: Scholarship for use in sophomore, junior, senior, or graduate years; not renewable. *Number:* 1–1. *Amount:* $1000–$1000.

Eligibility Requirements: Applicant must be enrolled or expecting to enroll full-time at a two-year or four-year institution or university and studying in Ohio. Available to U.S. citizens.

Application Requirements: Application form, application form may be submitted online (http://hriresearch.org/index.cfm?page=Content&categoryID=168&ID=7), essay, financial need analysis, recommendations or references, resume, transcript. *Deadline:* May 31.

Contact: Teresa Jodon, Executive Director
Horticultural Research Institute
1200 G Street NW
Suite 800
Washington, DC 20005
Phone: 202-695-2474
Fax: 888-761-7883
E-mail: scholarships@hriresearch.org

TIMOTHY AND PALMER W. BIGELOW JR, SCHOLARSHIP

Award for students who are enrolled in accredited undergraduate or graduate landscape/horticulture program. Must be resident of Connecticut, Maine, Massachusetts, New Hampshire, Rhode Island, or Vermont. Undergraduates must have a GPA of 2.25. Financial need, desire to work in nursery industry are factors. For more information, visit website http://www.hriresearch.org. Application must be completed on the HRI website.

Academic Fields/Career Goals: Agribusiness; Entomology; Horticulture/Floriculture; Landscape Architecture.

Award: Scholarship for use in junior or senior years; not renewable. *Number:* 1. *Amount:* $3000–$3000.

Eligibility Requirements: Applicant must be enrolled or expecting to enroll full-time at a four-year institution or university and resident of Connecticut, Maine, Massachusetts, New Hampshire, Rhode Island, Vermont. Available to U.S. citizens.

Application Requirements: Application form, application form may be submitted online (http://www.hriresearch.org/index.cfm?page=Content&categoryID=168&ID=4), essay, financial need analysis, recommendations or references, resume, transcript. *Deadline:* May 31.

Contact: Ms. Teresa Jodon, Executive Director
Horticultural Research Institute
1200 G Street, NW, Suite 800
Washington, DC 20005
Phone: 202-695-2474
Fax: 888-761-7883
E-mail: scholarships@hriresearch.org

INTERTRIBAL TIMBER COUNCIL

http://www.itcnet.org/

TRUMAN D. PICARD SCHOLARSHIP

The program is dedicated to assisting Native American/Native-Alaskan youth seeking careers in natural resources. Graduating senior high school students and those currently attending institutions of higher education are encouraged to apply. A valid tribal/Alaska native corporation's enrollment card is required.

Academic Fields/Career Goals: Agribusiness; Agriculture; Environmental Science; Natural Resources.

Award: Scholarship for use in freshman, sophomore, junior, senior, or graduate years; not renewable. *Number:* 15–30. *Amount:* $1500–$2000.

Eligibility Requirements: Applicant must be American Indian/Alaska Native and enrolled or expecting to enroll full-time at a two-year or four-year institution or university. Available to U.S. citizens.

Application Requirements: Application form, enrollment card, essay, recommendations or references, resume, transcript. *Deadline:* January 27.

Contact: Laura Alvidrez, Education Committee
Intertribal Timber Council
1112 NE 21st Avenue, Suite 4
Portland, OR 97232-2114
Phone: 503-282-4296
Fax: 503-282-1274
E-mail: itc1@teleport.com

MAINE DEPARTMENT OF AGRICULTURE, FOOD AND RURAL RESOURCES

http://www.maine.gov/agriculture

MAINE RURAL REHABILITATION FUND SCHOLARSHIP PROGRAM

One-time scholarship open to Maine residents enrolled in or accepted by any school, college, or university. Must be full time and demonstrate financial need. Those opting for a Maine institution given preference. Major must lead to an agricultural career. Minimum 3.0 GPA required.

Academic Fields/Career Goals: Agribusiness; Agriculture; Animal/Veterinary Sciences.

Award: Scholarship for use in freshman, sophomore, junior, senior, graduate, or postgraduate years; not renewable. *Number:* 10–20. *Amount:* $800–$2000.

Eligibility Requirements: Applicant must be enrolled or expecting to enroll full-time at a two-year or four-year or technical institution or university and resident of Maine. Applicant must have 3.0 GPA or higher. Available to U.S. citizens.

Application Requirements: Application form, driver's license, financial need analysis, transcript. *Deadline:* June 15.

Contact: Jane Aiudi, Director of Marketing
Phone: 207-287-7628
Fax: 207-287-5576
E-mail: jane.aiudi@maine.gov

MINNESOTA SOYBEAN RESEARCH AND PROMOTION COUNCIL

http://www.mnsoybean.org/

MINNESOTA SOYBEAN RESEARCH AND PROMOTION COUNCIL YOUTH SOYBEAN SCHOLARSHIP

Up to six $1000 awards available to high school seniors who are residents of Minnesota. Must demonstrate activity in agriculture with plans to study in an agricultural related program. For more details see website at http://www.mnsoybean.org.

Academic Fields/Career Goals: Agribusiness; Agriculture; Food Science/Nutrition.

Award: Scholarship for use in freshman year; not renewable. *Number:* 10. *Amount:* up to $1000.

Eligibility Requirements: Applicant must be Hispanic; high school student; planning to enroll or expecting to enroll full-time at a two-year or four-year or technical institution or university and resident of Minnesota. Applicant or parent of applicant must have employment or volunteer experience in agriculture, farming. Available to U.S. citizens.

Application Requirements: Application form, community service, recommendations or references, resume, self-addressed stamped envelope with application, transcript. *Deadline:* February 28.

Contact: Vicki Trudeau, Scholarship Coordinator
Phone: 888-896-9678
E-mail: vicki@mnsoybean.com

MONSANTO AGRIBUSINESS SCHOLARSHIP

http://www.monsanto.ca/

MONSANTO CANADA OPPORTUNITY SCHOLARSHIP PROGRAM

Scholarship available to a first year postsecondary student who is a Canadian citizen. Must be majoring in the agriculture, forestry, business, or biotechnology at a Canadian institution.

Academic Fields/Career Goals: Agribusiness; Agriculture; Science, Technology, and Society.

Award: Scholarship for use in freshman year; not renewable. *Number:* 50–60. *Amount:* $1500.

Eligibility Requirements: Applicant must be of Canadian heritage; high school student and planning to enroll or expecting to enroll full-time at a four-year or technical institution or university. Available to Canadian citizens.

Application Requirements: Application form, community service, essay, recommendations or references, transcript, university/college acceptance letter. *Deadline:* May 16.

NATIONAL CATTLEMEN'S FOUNDATION

http://www.nationalcattlemensfoundation.org/

CME BEEF INDUSTRY SCHOLARSHIP

Ten $1500 scholarships will be awarded to students who intend to pursue a career in the beef industry, including areas such as agricultural education, communications, production, or research. Must be enrolled as an undergraduate student in a four-year institution.

Academic Fields/Career Goals: Agribusiness; Agriculture; Communications.

Award: Scholarship for use in freshman, sophomore, junior, or senior years; not renewable. *Number:* 10. *Amount:* $1500.

Eligibility Requirements: Applicant must be enrolled or expecting to enroll full-time at a four-year institution or university. Available to U.S. citizens.

Application Requirements: Application form, essay, recommendations or references, transcript. *Deadline:* varies.

Contact: RoxAnn Johnson, Executive Director
　　　Phone: 303-850-3388
　　　Fax: 303-694-7372
　　　E-mail: mcf@beef.org

NATIONAL DAIRY SHRINE

http://www.dairyshrine.org/

NDS STUDENT RECOGNITION CONTEST

Awards available to college seniors enrolled in dairy science courses. Applicants must be nominated by their college or university professor and must intend to continue in the dairy field. A college or university may nominate up to 2 applicants.

Academic Fields/Career Goals: Agribusiness; Agriculture; Animal/Veterinary Sciences; Food Science/Nutrition.

Award: Prize for use in senior year; not renewable. *Number:* 2–10. *Amount:* $1000–$2000.

Eligibility Requirements: Applicant must be enrolled or expecting to enroll full-time at a four-year institution or university. Applicant must have 2.5 GPA or higher. Available to U.S. and Canadian citizens.

Application Requirements: Application form, nomination, personal photograph, recommendations or references, transcript. *Deadline:* April 15.

NATIONAL POTATO COUNCIL WOMEN'S AUXILIARY

http://www.nationalpotatocouncil.org/

POTATO INDUSTRY SCHOLARSHIP

The auxiliary scholarship is for full-time students studying in a potato-related field, who desire to work in the potato industry after graduation. Minimum 3.0 GPA required.

Academic Fields/Career Goals: Agribusiness; Agriculture; Food Science/Nutrition; Horticulture/Floriculture.

Award: Scholarship for use in senior year; not renewable. *Number:* 1. *Amount:* $5000.

Eligibility Requirements: Applicant must be enrolled or expecting to enroll full-time at a four-year institution or university. Available to U.S. citizens.

Application Requirements: Application form, essay, recommendations or references, resume, transcript. *Deadline:* June 15.

Contact: John Keeling, Executive Vice President and Chief Executive Officer
　　　National Potato Council Women's Auxiliary
　　　1300 L Street, NW, Suite 910
　　　Washington, DC 20005
　　　Phone: 202-682-9456 Ext. 203
　　　Fax: 202-682-0333
　　　E-mail: johnkeeling@nationalpotatocouncil.org

NATIONAL POULTRY AND FOOD DISTRIBUTORS ASSOCIATION

http://www.npfda.org/

NATIONAL POULTRY AND FOOD DISTRIBUTORS ASSOCIATION SCHOLARSHIP FOUNDATION

The scholarships are awarded to full-time students in their junior or senior years at a U.S. college pursuing degrees in poultry science, food science, agricultural business, or other related areas of study pertaining to the poultry and food industries.

Academic Fields/Career Goals: Agribusiness; Agriculture; Animal/Veterinary Sciences; Food Science/Nutrition; Food Service/Hospitality.

Award: Scholarship for use in junior or senior years; not renewable. *Number:* 4. *Amount:* $1500–$2000.

Eligibility Requirements: Applicant must be enrolled or expecting to enroll full-time at a four-year institution or university. Available to U.S. and non-U.S. citizens.

Application Requirements: Application form, essay, recommendations or references, transcript. *Deadline:* May 31.

Contact: Kristin McWhorter, Executive Director
　　　National Poultry and Food Distributors Association
　　　3150 Highway 34 East, Suite 209
　　　Newnan, GA 30265
　　　Phone: 877-845-1545
　　　Fax: 770-535-7385
　　　E-mail: kkm@npfda.org

NEW YORK STATE ASSOCIATION OF AGRICULTURAL FAIRS

http://www.nyfairs.org/

NEW YORK STATE ASSOCIATION OF AGRICULTURAL FAIRS AND NEW YORK STATE SHOWPEOPLE'S ASSOCIATION ANNUAL SCHOLARSHIP

Scholarship of $1000 given to New York high school seniors and students attending college and planning to pursue, or already pursuing a degree in an agricultural field, a fair management related field or an outdoor amusement related field.

Academic Fields/Career Goals: Agribusiness; Agriculture.

Award: Scholarship for use in freshman, sophomore, junior, senior, or graduate years; not renewable. *Number:* 6. *Amount:* $1000.

Eligibility Requirements: Applicant must be enrolled or expecting to enroll full-time at a two-year or four-year institution or university and resident of New York. Available to U.S. citizens.

Application Requirements: Application form, essay, recommendations or references, transcript. *Deadline:* April 9.

Contact: Mark St. Jacques, President
　　　Phone: 518-692-2464
　　　E-mail: markwashfair@aol.com

OHIO FARMERS UNION

http://www.ohfarmersunion.org/

VIRGIL THOMPSON MEMORIAL SCHOLARSHIP CONTEST

Award available to members of Ohio Farmers Union who are enrolled as full-time college sophomores, juniors or seniors. Awards of $1000 to winner and $500 each to two runners-up.

Academic Fields/Career Goals: Agribusiness; Agriculture.

Award: Scholarship for use in sophomore, junior, or senior years; not renewable. *Number:* 1–3. *Amount:* $500–$1000.

Eligibility Requirements: Applicant must be enrolled or expecting to enroll full-time at a four-year institution or university and resident of Ohio. Applicant or parent of applicant must be member of Ohio Farmers Union. Available to U.S. citizens.

Application Requirements: Application form, entry in a contest, essay. *Deadline:* December 31.

Contact: Ms. Linda Borton, Executive Director
Ohio Farmers Union
PO Box 363
Ottawa, OH 45875
Phone: 419-523.5300
E-mail: lborton@ohfarmersunion.org

OREGON STUDENT ASSISTANCE COMMISSION

http://www.GetCollegeFunds.org/

WILLAMETTE VALLEY AGRICULTURAL ASSOCIATION SCHOLARSHIP

Award for students who enroll as college juniors or above for fall term/semester at Oregon four-year public universities. Must major in agriculture, agriculture education, animal science, or agriculture-related industry. Minimum 3.0 GPA preferred.

Academic Fields/Career Goals: Agribusiness; Agriculture; Animal/Veterinary Sciences.

Award: Scholarship for use in junior, senior, or graduate years; not renewable.

Eligibility Requirements: Applicant must be enrolled or expecting to enroll full-time at a four-year institution or university and studying in Oregon. Applicant must have 3.0 GPA or higher. Available to U.S. citizens.

Application Requirements: Application form. *Deadline:* March 1.

SOCIETY FOR RANGE MANAGEMENT

http://www.rangelands.org/

MASONIC RANGE SCIENCE SCHOLARSHIP

Renewable award for undergraduate students pursuing degree in agribusiness, agriculture, animal/veterinary sciences, earth science, natural resources and range science.

Academic Fields/Career Goals: Agribusiness; Agriculture; Animal/Veterinary Sciences; Environmental Science; Natural Resources.

Award: Scholarship for use in freshman or sophomore years; renewable. *Number:* 1. *Amount:* $1000.

Eligibility Requirements: Applicant must be enrolled or expecting to enroll full-time at a four-year institution or university. Available to U.S. citizens.

Application Requirements: Application form, essay, recommendations or references, test scores, transcript. *Deadline:* January 15.

Contact: Vicky Trujillo, Executive Assistant
Society for Range Management
6901 South Pierce Street, Suite 225
Littleton, CO 80128
Phone: 303-986-3309
Fax: 303-986-3892
E-mail: vtrujillo@rangelands.org

SOIL AND WATER CONSERVATION SOCIETY

http://www.swcs.org

DONALD A. WILLIAMS SCHOLARSHIP SOIL CONSERVATION SCHOLARSHIP

Scholarship providing financial assistance to members of the Soil and Water Conservation Society (SWCS) who are currently employed but who wish to improve their technical or administrative competence in a conservation-related field through course work at an accredited college or through a program of special study. This scholarship is restricted to undergraduates. Must (a) be a member of SWCS for at least one year; (b) have demonstrated integrity, ability, and competence in his or her work and possess skills gained through training or experience; (c) have completed at least one year of full-time employment in a natural resource conservation endeavor; (d) be currently employed in a natural resource-related field; and (e) show reasonable financial need.

Academic Fields/Career Goals: Agribusiness; Agriculture; Earth Science; Environmental Health; Environmental Science; Natural Resources; Natural Sciences.

Award: Scholarship for use in freshman, sophomore, junior, or senior years; not renewable. *Number:* up to 3. *Amount:* $1500.

Eligibility Requirements: Applicant must be enrolled or expecting to enroll full- or part-time at a two-year or four-year or technical institution or university. Applicant or parent of applicant must be member of Soil and Water Conservation Society. Applicant or parent of applicant must have employment or volunteer experience in environmental-related field. Available to U.S. and non-U.S. citizens.

Application Requirements: Application form, application form may be submitted online (http://www.swcs.org), essay, recommendations or references. *Deadline:* February 13.

Contact: Meredith Foley, Program Coordinator
Soil and Water Conservation Society
945 SW Ankeny Road
Ankeny, IA 50023
Phone: 515-289-2331 Ext. 112
Fax: 515-289-1227
E-mail: meredith.foley@swcs.org

MELVILLE H. COHEE STUDENT LEADER CONSERVATION SCHOLARSHIP

Scholarship to honor student members of SWCS who succeed as leaders in their studies, volunteerism, and work. Nominations for this scholarship come from all over the world to compete against other student society members who have interest in conservation or other resource-related fields. The Melville H. Cohee Student Leader Conservation Scholarships provides financial assistance to members of SWCS who are in their junior or senior year of full-time undergraduate study or are pursuing graduate level studies with a natural resource conservation orientation at a properly accredited college or university. An applicant must be a member of SWCS for at least 1 year, not be a family member of the Professional Development Committee, and be in junior or senior year of full-time undergraduate study in fall of 2012 or pursuing graduate level studies in a natural resource field. Financial need is not a consideration

Academic Fields/Career Goals: Agribusiness; Agriculture; Earth Science; Environmental Health; Environmental Science; Natural Resources; Natural Sciences.

Award: Scholarship for use in junior, senior, graduate, or postgraduate years; not renewable. *Number:* 1. *Amount:* up to $500.

Eligibility Requirements: Applicant must be enrolled or expecting to enroll full-time at a four-year institution or university. Applicant or parent of applicant must be member of Soil and Water Conservation Society. Applicant or parent of applicant must have employment or volunteer experience in environmental-related field. Available to U.S. and non-U.S. citizens.

Application Requirements: Application form, essay, recommendations or references, transcript. *Deadline:* February 13.

Contact: Meredith Foley, Program Coordinator
Soil and Water Conservation Society
945 SW Ankeny Road
Ankeny, IA 50023
Phone: 515-289-2331 Ext. 112
Fax: 515-289-1227
E-mail: meredith.foley@swcs.org

SOIL AND WATER CONSERVATION SOCIETY-NEW JERSEY CHAPTER

http://home.comcast.net/~njswcs/scholarship.htm

EDWARD R. HALL SCHOLARSHIP

Two $500 scholarships awarded annually to students attending a New Jersey accredited college or New Jersey residents attending any out-of-state college. Undergraduate students, with the exception of freshmen, are eligible. Must be enrolled in a curriculum related to natural resources. Other areas related to conservation may qualify.

Academic Fields/Career Goals: Agribusiness; Agriculture; Animal/Veterinary Sciences; Biology; Earth Science; Environmental Science; Horticulture/Floriculture; Natural Resources; Natural Sciences.

Award: Scholarship for use in sophomore, junior, or senior years; not renewable. *Number:* 2. *Amount:* $500.

Eligibility Requirements: Applicant must be enrolled or expecting to enroll full-time at a two-year or four-year institution or university and resident of New Jersey. Available to U.S. and non-U.S. citizens.

Application Requirements: Application form, essay, financial need analysis, list of clubs and organizations related to natural resources of which applicant is a member, recommendations or references, transcript. *Deadline:* April 15.

SOUTH DAKOTA BOARD OF REGENTS

http://www.sdbor.edu/

SOUTH DAKOTA BOARD OF REGENTS BJUGSTAD SCHOLARSHIP

Scholarship for graduating North or South Dakota high school senior who is a Native American. Must demonstrate academic achievement, character and leadership abilities. Must submit proof of tribal enrollment. One-time award of $500. Must rank in upper half of class or have a minimum 2.5 GPA. Must be pursuing studies in agriculture, agribusiness, or natural resources.

Academic Fields/Career Goals: Agribusiness; Agriculture; Natural Resources.

Award: Scholarship for use in freshman year; not renewable. *Number:* 2. *Amount:* $500.

Eligibility Requirements: Applicant must be American Indian/Alaska Native; high school student; planning to enroll or expecting to enroll full-time at a four-year institution or university; resident of North Dakota, South Dakota and must have an interest in leadership. Applicant must have 2.5 GPA or higher. Available to U.S. citizens.

Application Requirements: Application form, proof of tribal enrollment, recommendations or references, transcript. *Deadline:* February 15.

Contact: Dr. Paul Turman, System Vice President for Research and
　　　　　 Economic Development
　　　　　 South Dakota Board of Regents
　　　　　 301 East Capital Avenue, Suite 200
　　　　　 Pierre, SD 57501
　　　　　 Phone: 605-773-3455
　　　　　 Fax: 605-773-2422
　　　　　 E-mail: paul.turman@sdbor.edu

UNITED NEGRO COLLEGE FUND

http://www.uncf.org/

MONSANTO/UNCF 1890'S SCHOLARSHIP PROGRAM

Up to $10,000 scholarship for college juniors and seniors at select UNCF colleges and universities studying agriculture, biology, biochemistry, bioengineering technology, biotechnical, electrical engineering, chemical engineering, chemistry, computer science, engineering, or agribusiness. Preference will be given to students who are residents of farm communities which is defined as a city or town that has a population of greater than 50,000 inhabitants, and the urbanized areas contiguous and adjacent to such a city or town. Additionally, at least 30% of the economic development of the community must come from farming. Minimum 3.0 GPA required.

Academic Fields/Career Goals: Agribusiness; Agriculture; Biology; Chemical Engineering; Computer Science/Data Processing; Electrical Engineering/Electronics; Engineering/Technology.

Award: Scholarship for use in junior or senior years; not renewable. *Amount:* up to $10,000.

Eligibility Requirements: Applicant must be Black (non-Hispanic) and enrolled or expecting to enroll full-time at a four-year institution or university. Applicant must have 3.0 GPA or higher. Available to U.S. citizens.

Application Requirements: Application form. *Deadline:* May 31.

AGRICULTURE

ABBIE SARGENT MEMORIAL SCHOLARSHIP INC.

http://www.nhfarmbureau.org/

ABBIE SARGENT MEMORIAL SCHOLARSHIP
• *See page 84*

AGRILIANCE, LAND O' LAKES, AND CROPLAN GENETICS

CAREERS IN AGRICULTURE SCHOLARSHIP PROGRAM

Awards $1000 to 20 high school seniors interested in agriculture-related studies. Must be planning to enroll in a two- or four-year agriculture-related curriculum.

Academic Fields/Career Goals: Agriculture.

Award: Scholarship for use in freshman year; not renewable. *Number:* 20. *Amount:* $1000.

Eligibility Requirements: Applicant must be high school student and planning to enroll or expecting to enroll full-time at a two-year or four-year institution or university. Available to U.S. citizens.

Application Requirements: Application form, essay. *Deadline:* March 1.

Contact: Annette Degnan, Director, Advertising and Communications
　　　　　 Agriliance, Land O' Lakes, and Croplan Genetics
　　　　　 PO Box 64089
　　　　　 St. Paul, MN 55164-0089
　　　　　 Phone: 651-355-5126
　　　　　 E-mail: adegnan@mbrservices.com

ALABAMA GOLF COURSE SUPERINTENDENTS ASSOCIATION

http://www.agcsa.org/

ALABAMA GOLF COURSE SUPERINTENDENT'S ASSOCIATION'S DONNIE ARTHUR MEMORIAL SCHOLARSHIP

One-time award for students majoring in agriculture with an emphasis on turf-grass management. Must have a minimum 2.0 GPA. Applicant must be a full-time student. High school students not considered. Award available to U.S. citizens.

Academic Fields/Career Goals: Agriculture; Horticulture/Floriculture.

Award: Scholarship for use in freshman, sophomore, junior, or senior years; not renewable. *Number:* 1. *Amount:* $2000.

Eligibility Requirements: Applicant must be enrolled or expecting to enroll full-time at a two-year or four-year institution or university. Applicant must have 2.5 GPA or higher. Available to U.S. citizens.

Application Requirements: Application form, essay, recommendations or references, transcript. *Deadline:* October 15.

Contact: Melanie Bonds, Secretary
　　　　　 Phone: 205-967-0397
　　　　　 E-mail: agcsa@charter.net

ALBERTA HERITAGE SCHOLARSHIP FUND

http://www.alis.alberta.ca/

ALBERTA BARLEY COMMISSION-EUGENE BOYKO MEMORIAL SCHOLARSHIP

Award of CAN$500 to recognize and encourage students entering the field of crop production and/or crop processing technology studies. Must be a Canadian citizen or landed immigrant attending an Alberta postsecondary institution. Students must be enrolled in the second or subsequent year of postsecondary study and taking courses that have an emphasis on crop production and/or crop processing technology.

Awarded on basis of academic achievement. For additional information, see website http://alis.alberta.ca.

Academic Fields/Career Goals: Agriculture.

Award: Scholarship for use in sophomore, junior, or senior years; not renewable. *Number:* 1.

Eligibility Requirements: Applicant must be enrolled or expecting to enroll full-time at a four-year institution or university and resident of Alberta. Available to Canadian citizens.

Application Requirements: Application form, transcript. *Deadline:* August 1.

AMERICAN LEGION DEPARTMENT OF NORTH DAKOTA

http://www.ndlegion.org/

O. NESHEIM MEMORIAL SCHOLARSHIP

One-time award of $500 for North Dakota residents who are entering their senior year of college and studying agriculture, dentistry, food science, or pharmacy at a North Dakota college or university. Minimum 2.5 GPA required.

Academic Fields/Career Goals: Agriculture; Dental Health/Services; Food Science/Nutrition; Pharmacy.

Award: Scholarship for use in senior year; not renewable. *Amount:* $500–$500.

Eligibility Requirements: Applicant must be high school student; age 17-18; planning to enroll or expecting to enroll full-time at a two-year or four-year or technical institution or university; single; resident of North Dakota and studying in North Dakota. Applicant must have 2.5 GPA or higher. Available to U.S. citizens. Applicant or parent must meet one or more of the following requirements: general military experience; retired from active duty; disabled or killed as a result of military service; prisoner of war; or missing in action.

Application Requirements: Application form, community service, essay, financial need analysis, recommendations or references, transcript. *Deadline:* April 1.

Contact: Teri Bryant, Programs/Membership Coordinator
   Phone: 701-293-3120
   Fax: 701-293-9951
   E-mail: programs@ndlegion.org

AMERICAN OIL CHEMISTS' SOCIETY

http://www.aocs.org/

AOCS BIOTECHNOLOGY STUDENT EXCELLENCE AWARD

Award to recognize an outstanding paper in the field of biotechnology presented by a student at the AOCS Annual Meeting and Expo. Graduate students presenting within the Biotechnology Division technical program are eligible for the award.

Academic Fields/Career Goals: Agriculture; Chemical Engineering; Food Science/Nutrition.

Award: Prize for use in junior, senior, or graduate years; not renewable. *Number:* 1–3. *Amount:* $100–$300.

Eligibility Requirements: Applicant must be enrolled or expecting to enroll full- or part-time at a four-year institution or university. Available to U.S. and non-U.S. citizens.

Application Requirements: Abstract, application form, essay, recommendations or references. *Deadline:* January 7.

Contact: Barbara Semeraro, Area Manager, Membership
   American Oil Chemists' Society
   AOCS
   PO Box 17190
   Urbana, IL 61803
   Phone: 217-693-4804
   Fax: 217-693-4849
   E-mail: awards@aocs.org

AMERICAN SOCIETY FOR ENOLOGY AND VITICULTURE

http://www.asev.org/

AMERICAN SOCIETY FOR ENOLOGY AND VITICULTURE SCHOLARSHIPS

One-time award for college juniors, seniors, and graduate students residing in North America and enrolled in a program studying viticulture, enology, or any field related to the wine and grape industry. Minimum 3.0 GPA for undergraduates; minimum 3.2 GPA for graduate students. Must be a resident of the United States, Canada, or Mexico.

Academic Fields/Career Goals: Agriculture; Chemical Engineering; Food Science/Nutrition; Horticulture/Floriculture.

Award: Scholarship for use in junior, senior, or graduate years; not renewable. *Number:* up to 30. *Amount:* $500–$4000.

Eligibility Requirements: Applicant must be enrolled or expecting to enroll full-time at a four-year institution or university. Applicant must have 3.0 GPA or higher. Available to U.S. and non-U.S. citizens.

Application Requirements: Application form, essay, financial need analysis, recommendations or references, transcript. *Deadline:* March 1.

Contact: Laurie Radcliff, Office Coordinator
   Phone: 530-753-3142
   Fax: 530-753-3318
   E-mail: society@asev.org

AMERICAN SOCIETY OF AGRONOMY, CROP SCIENCE SOCIETY OF AMERICA, SOIL SCIENCE SOCIETY OF AMERICA

http://www.agronomy.org

HANK BEACHELL FUTURE LEADER SCHOLARSHIP

Scholarship for undergraduate students for $3500 and negotiated travel expenses to the scholarship experience site. Must have completed the sophomore year, and must be majoring in agronomy, crop science, soil science, or other related disciplines. For more information on eligibility criteria and nominee qualifications visit website https://www.agronomy.org/awards

Academic Fields/Career Goals: Agriculture; Earth Science; Entomology; Environmental Science; Natural Resources; Natural Sciences.

Award: Scholarship for use in junior or senior years; not renewable. *Number:* up to 2. *Amount:* up to $4000.

Eligibility Requirements: Applicant must be enrolled or expecting to enroll full-time at a two-year or four-year institution or university. Available to U.S. and non-U.S. citizens.

Application Requirements: Application form, application form may be submitted online (http://www.agronomy.org/awards), letter of interest, nomination letter, recommendations or references, resume. *Deadline:* April 16.

Contact: Sara Uttech, Communications Manager
   American Society of Agronomy, Crop Science Society of
      America, Soil Science Society of America
   5585 Guilford Road
   Madison, WI 53711
   Phone: 608-268-4948
   Fax: 608-273-2021
   E-mail: awards@sciencesocieties.org

J. FIELDING REED SCHOLARSHIP

Scholarship of $1000 to honor an outstanding undergraduate senior pursuing a career in soil or plant sciences. Must have GPA of 3.0, or above, and nominations should contain a history of community and campus leadership activities, specifically in agriculture. For more information on nomination and eligibility criteria, visit website https://www.agronomy.org/awards

Academic Fields/Career Goals: Agriculture; Earth Science; Entomology; Environmental Science; Natural Resources; Natural Sciences.

Award: Scholarship for use in senior year; not renewable. *Number:* 1. *Amount:* up to $1000.

Eligibility Requirements: Applicant must be enrolled or expecting to enroll full-time at a four-year institution or university and must have an interest in leadership. Applicant or parent of applicant must have employment or volunteer experience in community service. Applicant must have 3.0 GPA or higher. Available to U.S. and non-U.S. citizens.

Application Requirements: Application form, application form may be submitted online (http://www.agronomy.org/awards), letter of interest, recommendations or references, resume. *Deadline:* February 26.

Contact: Sara Uttech, Communications Manager
American Society of Agronomy, Crop Science Society of America, Soil Science Society of America
5585 Guilford Road
Madison, WI 53711
Phone: 608-268-4948
Fax: 608-273-2021
E-mail: awards@sciencesocieties.org

ARRL FOUNDATION INC.
http://www.arrl.org/

FRANCIS WALTON MEMORIAL SCHOLARSHIP
Award given to individual with any active Amateur Radio license class, with preference to applicants that provide documentation of CW proficiency of more than 5 wpm. Residents of the ARRL Central Division (Illinois, Indiana, Wisconsin) preferred. Must be studying agriculture, electronics, court reporting, history, broadcasting, communication or related field. Must demonstrate financial need, academic merit, and interest in promoting Amateur Radio.

Academic Fields/Career Goals: Agriculture; Communications; Electrical Engineering/Electronics; History; Journalism; Law/Legal Services; TV/Radio Broadcasting.

Award: Scholarship for use in freshman, sophomore, junior, senior, or graduate years; not renewable. *Number:* 1. *Amount:* $500.

Eligibility Requirements: Applicant must be enrolled or expecting to enroll full-time at a four-year institution or university; resident of Illinois, Indiana, Wisconsin and must have an interest in amateur radio. Available to U.S. citizens.

Application Requirements: Application form, financial need analysis, transcript. *Deadline:* February 1.

Contact: Ms. Mary Hobart, Secretary
Phone: 860-594-0397
E-mail: k1mmh@arrl.org

ASSOCIATION ON AMERICAN INDIAN AFFAIRS, INC.
http://www.indian-affairs.org/

ELIZABETH AND SHERMAN ASCHE MEMORIAL SCHOLARSHIP FUND
Scholarship of up to $1500 available for undergraduate and graduate students seeking a bachelor's or master's degree in science or public health. Students must apply each year. Must be a Native American. See website for details, http://www.indian-affairs.org.

Academic Fields/Career Goals: Agriculture; Animal/Veterinary Sciences; Biology; Chemical Engineering; Dental Health/Services; Earth Science; Health and Medical Sciences; Marine Biology; Natural Sciences; Nursing; Physical Sciences; Public Health.

Award: Scholarship for use in freshman, sophomore, junior, senior, or graduate years; not renewable. *Number:* 6–8. *Amount:* up to $1500.

Eligibility Requirements: Applicant must be American Indian/Alaska Native and enrolled or expecting to enroll full-time at a two-year or four-year institution or university. Available to U.S. citizens.

Application Requirements: Application form, essay, Tribal enrollment. *Deadline:* June 3.

Contact: Lisa Wyzlic, Director of Scholarship Programs
Association on American Indian Affairs, Inc.
966 Hungerford Drive, Suite 12-B
Rockville, MD 20850
Phone: 240-314-7155
Fax: 240-314-7159
E-mail: lw.aaia@indian-affairs.org

CALCOT-SEITZ FOUNDATION
http://www.calcot.com/

CALCOT-SEITZ SCHOLARSHIP
Scholarship for young students from Arizona, New Mexico, Texas, and California who plan to attend a college or are attending a college offering at least a four-year degree in agriculture.

Academic Fields/Career Goals: Agriculture.

Award: Scholarship for use in freshman, sophomore, junior, or senior years; not renewable. *Number:* 1–20. *Amount:* up to $3000.

Eligibility Requirements: Applicant must be enrolled or expecting to enroll full-time at a four-year institution and resident of Arizona, California, New Mexico, Texas. Available to U.S. and non-U.S. citizens.

Application Requirements: Application form, community service, personal photograph, recommendations or references, test scores, transcript. *Deadline:* March 31.

Contact: Marci Cunningham, Scholarship Committee
Calcot-Seitz Foundation
PO Box 259
Bakersfield, CA 93302
Phone: 661-327-5961
Fax: 661-861-9870
E-mail: info@calcot.com

CALIFORNIA CATTLEMEN'S ASSOCIATION
http://www.calcattlemen.org/

CALIFORNIA CATTLEMEN'S ASSOCIATION SCHOLARSHIP
Scholarship is available for YCC members pursuing careers within the industry. Applications are available on the website or through the CCA office. Applicant must be an U.S. citizen.

Academic Fields/Career Goals: Agriculture.

Award: Scholarship for use in freshman year; not renewable. *Number:* up to 5.

Eligibility Requirements: Applicant must be high school student and planning to enroll or expecting to enroll full-time at a two-year or four-year or technical institution or university. Available to U.S. citizens.

Application Requirements: Application form, essay, recommendations or references, transcript. *Deadline:* July 20.

Contact: Megan Huber, Director of Finance
Phone: 916-444-0845
Fax: 916-444-2194
E-mail: megan@calcattlemen.org

CHS FOUNDATION
http://www.chsfoundation.org/

CHS FOUNDATION HIGH SCHOOL SCHOLARSHIPS
• *See page 84*

CHS FOUNDATION TWO-YEAR COLLEGE SCHOLARSHIPS
• *See page 85*

CHS FOUNDATION UNIVERSITY SCHOLARSHIPS
• *See page 85*

DAIRY MANAGEMENT
http://www.dairyinfo.com/

NATIONAL DAIRY PROMOTION AND RESEARCH BOARD SCHOLARSHIP
One-time scholarship of $1500 given to sophomores, juniors and seniors in college/university programs that emphasize dairy. Majors include communications/public relations, journalism, marketing, business, economics, nutrition, food science and agricultural education.

Academic Fields/Career Goals: Agriculture; Business/Consumer Services; Communications; Economics; Food Science/Nutrition; Journalism.

Award: Scholarship for use in sophomore, junior, or senior years; not renewable. *Number:* 19. *Amount:* $1500.

Eligibility Requirements: Applicant must be enrolled or expecting to enroll full-time at a two-year or four-year institution or university. Available to U.S. citizens.

Application Requirements: Application form, recommendations or references, transcript. *Deadline:* May 31.

Contact: Jolene Griffin, Manager of Industry Communications
Dairy Management
10255 West Higgins Road
Rosemont, IL 60018
Phone: 847-627-9920
Fax: 847-803-2077
E-mail: jgriffin@rosedmi.com

GARDEN CLUB OF AMERICA

http://www.gcamerica.org/

THE ELIZABETH GARDNER NORWEB SUMMER ENVIRONMENTAL STUDIES SCHOLARSHIP

Award for college students who wish to pursue summer studies doing field work, research, or classroom work in the environmental field following their freshman, sophomore, or junior years. Work may award academic credit but should be in addition to required courses.

Academic Fields/Career Goals: Agriculture; Earth Science; Environmental Science; Natural Resources.

Award: Scholarship for use in freshman, sophomore, or junior years; not renewable. *Amount:* $2000.

Eligibility Requirements: Applicant must be enrolled or expecting to enroll full-time at a four-year institution or university. Available to U.S. and non-U.S. citizens.

Application Requirements: Application form, essay, recommendations or references, self-addressed stamped envelope with application, transcript. *Deadline:* February 10.

Contact: Connie Yates, Scholarship Committee Administrator
Phone: 212-753-8287
E-mail: cyates@gcamerica.org

GEORGE T. WELCH TRUST

http://www.bakerboyer.com/

BERNICE AND PAT MURPHY SCHOLARSHIP FUND

Grants for students majoring in agriculture. Must be enrolled full-time and maintain a minimum GPA of 2.0. Must reapply. The budget form must be completed and cover the entire school year.

Academic Fields/Career Goals: Agriculture.

Award: Scholarship for use in freshman, sophomore, junior, or senior years; not renewable.

Eligibility Requirements: Applicant must be enrolled or expecting to enroll full-time at a four-year institution or university. Available to U.S. citizens.

Application Requirements: Application form. *Deadline:* April 13.

Contact: Ted Cohan, Trust Portfolio Manager
Phone: 509-526-1204
Fax: 509-522-3136
E-mail: cohant@bakerboyer.com

G.B. PESCIALLO MEMORIAL SCHOLARSHIP FUND

Grants for students majoring in agriculture. Must be enrolled full-time and maintain a minimum GPA of 2.0. Must reapply. The budget form must be completed and cover the entire school year.

Academic Fields/Career Goals: Agriculture.

Award: Scholarship for use in freshman, sophomore, junior, or senior years; not renewable.

Eligibility Requirements: Applicant must be enrolled or expecting to enroll full-time at a four-year institution or university. Available to U.S. citizens.

Application Requirements: Application form, responsibility shown in one or more of the following areas: community, school, home, church. *Deadline:* April 13.

Contact: Ted Cohan, Trust Portfolio Manager
Phone: 509-526-1204
Fax: 509-522-3136
E-mail: cohant@bakerboyer.com

INTERTRIBAL TIMBER COUNCIL

http://www.itcnet.org/

TRUMAN D. PICARD SCHOLARSHIP
• *See page 86*

JAPANESE AMERICAN CITIZENS LEAGUE (JACL)

http://www.jacl.org/

NATIONAL JACL HEADQUARTERS SCHOLARSHIP

Scholarship offers over 30 awards to qualified students nationwide. Scholarships are provided to students at the entering freshman, undergraduate, graduate, law, financial need and creative & performing arts. All scholarships are one-time awards. Every applicant must be an active National JACL member at either an Individual or Student/Youth Level.

Academic Fields/Career Goals: Agriculture; Journalism; Law/Legal Services; Literature/English/Writing; Public Policy and Administration.

Award: Scholarship for use in freshman, sophomore, junior, senior, or graduate years; not renewable. *Number:* 30.

Eligibility Requirements: Applicant must be of Japanese heritage; Asian/Pacific Islander and enrolled or expecting to enroll full-time at a two-year or four-year institution or university. Available to U.S. and non-U.S. citizens.

Application Requirements: Application form, financial need analysis, recommendations or references, transcript. *Deadline:* varies.

MAINE DEPARTMENT OF AGRICULTURE, FOOD AND RURAL RESOURCES

http://www.maine.gov/agriculture

MAINE RURAL REHABILITATION FUND SCHOLARSHIP PROGRAM
• *See page 86*

MINNESOTA SOYBEAN RESEARCH AND PROMOTION COUNCIL

http://www.mnsoybean.org/

COLLEGE SOYBEAN SCHOLARSHIP

Scholarship available for undergraduate junior or senior who is a resident of Minnesota and pursuing an education in soybean agronomy, soil science, or soybean genetics. Must be active in ag-related and/or campus/community activities and maintain a minimum GPA of 2.0. Application must include a paragraph to indicate how student's education will relate back to the soybean farmer or soybean industry.

Academic Fields/Career Goals: Agriculture.

Award: Scholarship for use in junior or senior years; not renewable. *Number:* up to 3. *Amount:* $2000.

Eligibility Requirements: Applicant must be enrolled or expecting to enroll full-time at a four-year institution or university and resident of Minnesota. Available to U.S. citizens.

Application Requirements: Application form, community service, recommendations or references, resume, transcript. *Deadline:* February 28.

Contact: Vicki Trudeau, Scholarship Coordinator
Phone: 888-896-9678
E-mail: vicki@mnsoybean.com

MINNESOTA SOYBEAN RESEARCH AND PROMOTION COUNCIL YOUTH SOYBEAN SCHOLARSHIP
• *See page 86*

MONSANTO AGRIBUSINESS SCHOLARSHIP
http://www.monsanto.ca/

MONSANTO CANADA OPPORTUNITY SCHOLARSHIP PROGRAM
• *See page 86*

NATIONAL CATTLEMEN'S FOUNDATION
http://www.nationalcattlemensfoundation.org/

CME BEEF INDUSTRY SCHOLARSHIP
• *See page 87*

NATIONAL COUNCIL OF STATE GARDEN CLUBS INC. SCHOLARSHIP
http://www.gardenclub.org/

NATIONAL COUNCIL OF STATE GARDEN CLUBS INC. SCHOLARSHIP
Scholarship to students for study in agriculture education, horticulture, floriculture, landscape design, botany, biology, plant pathology/science, forestry, agronomy, environmental concerns.
Academic Fields/Career Goals: Agriculture; Biology; Environmental Science; Horticulture/Floriculture.
Award: Scholarship for use in sophomore, junior, senior, or graduate years; not renewable. *Number:* 34. *Amount:* $3500.
Eligibility Requirements: Applicant must be enrolled or expecting to enroll full-time at a two-year or four-year institution or university. Applicant must have 3.0 GPA or higher. Available to U.S. citizens.
Application Requirements: Application form, financial need analysis, recommendations or references, transcript. *Deadline:* March 1.
Contact: Kathy Romine, National Headquarters
Phone: 314-776-7574 Ext. 15
Fax: 314-776-5108
E-mail: headquarters@gardenclub.org

NATIONAL DAIRY SHRINE
http://www.dairyshrine.org/

KILDEE SCHOLARSHIPS
Top 25 contestants in the three most recent national intercollegiate dairy cattle judging contests are eligible to apply for two $3000 one-time scholarships for graduate study in the field related to dairy cattle production or vet school at the university of their choice. Also the top 25 contestants in the most recent National 4-H and National FFA Dairy Judging contests are eligible to apply for one $2000 scholarship for undergraduate study in the field related to dairy cattle production at the university of their choice.
Academic Fields/Career Goals: Agriculture; Animal/Veterinary Sciences.
Award: Scholarship for use in junior, senior, or postgraduate years; not renewable. *Number:* 3. *Amount:* $2000–$3000.
Eligibility Requirements: Applicant must be enrolled or expecting to enroll full-time at a four-year institution or university. Applicant must have 2.5 GPA or higher. Available to U.S. and Canadian citizens.
Application Requirements: Application form, personal photograph, recommendations or references, transcript. *Deadline:* April 15.

MARSHALL E. MCCULLOUGH-NATIONAL DAIRY SHRINE SCHOLARSHIPS
Scholarship for high school seniors planning to enter a four-year college or university with an intent to major in dairy/animal science with a communications emphasis, or agricultural journalism with a dairy/animal science emphasis.

Academic Fields/Career Goals: Agriculture; Journalism; TV/Radio Broadcasting.
Award: Scholarship for use in freshman year; not renewable. *Number:* 2. *Amount:* $1000–$2500.
Eligibility Requirements: Applicant must be high school student and planning to enroll or expecting to enroll full-time at a four-year institution or university. Applicant must have 2.5 GPA or higher. Available to U.S. citizens.
Application Requirements: Application form, application form may be submitted online (http://www.dairyshrine.org), finalist video, personal photograph, recommendations or references, transcript. *Deadline:* April 15.

NATIONAL DAIRY SHRINE/DAIRY MARKETING INC. MILK MARKETING SCHOLARSHIPS
One-time awards for undergraduate students pursuing careers in marketing of dairy products. Major areas can include: dairy science, animal science, agricultural economics, agricultural communications, agricultural education, general education, food and nutrition, home economics and journalism. For more information, visit website http://www.dairyshrine.org.
Academic Fields/Career Goals: Agriculture; Food Science/Nutrition; Marketing.
Award: Scholarship for use in sophomore or junior years; not renewable. *Number:* 5–9. *Amount:* $1000–$1500.
Eligibility Requirements: Applicant must be enrolled or expecting to enroll full-time at a four-year institution or university. Applicant must have 2.5 GPA or higher. Available to U.S. citizens.
Application Requirements: Application form, personal photograph, recommendations or references, transcript. *Deadline:* April 15.

NATIONAL DAIRY SHRINE/IAGER DAIRY SCHOLARSHIP
$1000 annual scholarship to encourage qualified second-year dairy students in a two-year agricultural school to pursue careers in the dairy industry. Scholarships will be awarded based on academic standing, leadership ability, interest in the dairy industry, and plans for the future. Cumulative 2.5 GPA required.
Academic Fields/Career Goals: Agriculture.
Award: Scholarship for use in sophomore year; not renewable. *Number:* 2. *Amount:* $1000–$1000.
Eligibility Requirements: Applicant must be enrolled or expecting to enroll full-time at a two-year or technical institution. Applicant must have 2.5 GPA or higher. Available to U.S. citizens.
Application Requirements: Application form, application form may be submitted online (http://www.dairyshrine.org), personal photograph, recommendations or references, transcript. *Deadline:* April 15.
Contact: Dr. David Selner, Executive Director
Phone: 920-863-6333
E-mail: info@dairyshrine.org

NATIONAL DAIRY SHRINE/KLUSSENDORF SCHOLARSHIP
The scholarship will be granted to a student successfully completing the first, second or third years at a two-year or four-year college or university. To be eligible, students must major in a dairy science (animal science) curriculum with plans to enter the dairy cattle field as a breeder, owner, herdsperson, or fitter.
Academic Fields/Career Goals: Agriculture; Animal/Veterinary Sciences.
Award: Scholarship for use in freshman, sophomore, or junior years; not renewable. *Number:* 1–7. *Amount:* $1500.
Eligibility Requirements: Applicant must be enrolled or expecting to enroll full-time at a two-year or four-year institution or university. Available to U.S. and Canadian citizens.
Application Requirements: Application form, application form may be submitted online (http://www.dairyshrine.org), personal photograph, recommendations or references, transcript. *Deadline:* April 15.

NATIONAL DAIRY SHRINE/MAURICE E. CORE SCHOLARSHIP
Available to college freshman who are majoring in a dairy/animal industry related field with interest in working in the dairy industry in the

future. Scholarship is based on leadership abilities, volunteerism, activities and plans for the future.

Academic Fields/Career Goals: Agriculture.

Award: Scholarship for use in sophomore year; not renewable. *Number:* 1. *Amount:* $1000.

Eligibility Requirements: Applicant must be enrolled or expecting to enroll full-time at a four-year institution or university. Applicant must have 2.5 GPA or higher. Available to U.S. citizens.

Application Requirements: Application form, application form may be submitted online (http://www.dairyshrine.org), personal photograph, recommendations or references, transcript. *Deadline:* April 15.

Contact: Dr. David Selner, Executive Director
Phone: 920-863-6333
E-mail: info@dairyshrine.org

NDS STUDENT RECOGNITION CONTEST
• *See page 87*

NATIONAL GARDEN CLUBS INC.
http://www.gardenclub.org/

NATIONAL GARDEN CLUBS INC. SCHOLARSHIP PROGRAM

One-time award for full-time students in plant sciences, agriculture and related or allied subjects. Applicants must have at least a 3.25 GPA.

Academic Fields/Career Goals: Agriculture; Biology; Earth Science; Environmental Science; Horticulture/Floriculture; Landscape Architecture.

Award: Scholarship for use in junior, senior, or graduate years; not renewable. *Number:* 34. *Amount:* $3500.

Eligibility Requirements: Applicant must be enrolled or expecting to enroll full-time at a four-year institution or university. Available to U.S. citizens.

Application Requirements: Application form, financial need analysis, personal photograph, recommendations or references, resume, transcript. *Deadline:* March 1.

Contact: Sandra Robinson, Vice President for Scholarship
Phone: 606-878-7281
E-mail: sandyr@kayandkay.com

NATIONAL POTATO COUNCIL WOMEN'S AUXILIARY
http://www.nationalpotatocouncil.org/

POTATO INDUSTRY SCHOLARSHIP
• *See page 87*

NATIONAL POULTRY AND FOOD DISTRIBUTORS ASSOCIATION
http://www.npfda.org/

NATIONAL POULTRY AND FOOD DISTRIBUTORS ASSOCIATION SCHOLARSHIP FOUNDATION
• *See page 87*

NEW YORK STATE ASSOCIATION OF AGRICULTURAL FAIRS
http://www.nyfairs.org/

NEW YORK STATE ASSOCIATION OF AGRICULTURAL FAIRS AND NEW YORK STATE SHOWPEOPLE'S ASSOCIATION ANNUAL SCHOLARSHIP
• *See page 87*

NEW YORK STATE GRANGE
http://www.nysgrange.org/

HOWARD F. DENISE SCHOLARSHIP

Awards for undergraduates under 21 years old to pursue studies in agriculture. Must be a New York resident with a minimum 3.0 GPA. One-time award of $1000.

Academic Fields/Career Goals: Agriculture.

Award: Scholarship for use in freshman, sophomore, junior, or senior years; not renewable. *Number:* 1–6. *Amount:* $1000.

Eligibility Requirements: Applicant must be enrolled or expecting to enroll full-time at a two-year or four-year institution and resident of New York. Applicant must have 3.0 GPA or higher. Available to U.S. citizens.

Application Requirements: Application form, financial need analysis, recommendations or references, transcript. *Deadline:* April 15.

OHIO FARMERS UNION
http://www.ohfarmersunion.org/

JOSEPH FITCHER SCHOLARSHIP CONTEST

Scholarship available to member of Ohio Farmers Union who is a high school junior or senior, or enrolled as a college freshman. Participants are to submit an application obtained from OFU and a typed essay. Essay subject matter changes annually. Award of $1000 to winner and $250 to two runners-up.

Academic Fields/Career Goals: Agriculture.

Award: Scholarship for use in freshman year; not renewable. *Number:* 1–3. *Amount:* $250–$1000.

Eligibility Requirements: Applicant must be high school student; planning to enroll or expecting to enroll full-time at a four-year institution or university and resident of Ohio. Applicant or parent of applicant must be member of Ohio Farmers Union. Available to U.S. citizens.

Application Requirements: Application form, entry in a contest, essay. *Deadline:* December 31.

Contact: Ms. Linda Borton, Executive Director
Ohio Farmers Union
PO Box 363
Ottawa, OH 45875
Phone: 419-523.5300
E-mail: lborton@ohfarmersunion.org

VIRGIL THOMPSON MEMORIAL SCHOLARSHIP CONTEST
• *See page 87*

OREGON STUDENT ASSISTANCE COMMISSION
http://www.GetCollegeFunds.org/

OREGON HORTICULTURE SOCIETY SCHOLARSHIP

Award for college sophomore or above for fall term/semester in undergraduate study, with a preference to those students majoring in horticulture. To be used at Oregon public and nonprofit colleges and universities only. 2.5 GPA or above required.

Academic Fields/Career Goals: Agriculture.

Award: Scholarship for use in sophomore, junior, or senior years; not renewable.

Eligibility Requirements: Applicant must be enrolled or expecting to enroll full-time at a four-year institution or university and studying in Oregon. Applicant must have 2.5 GPA or higher. Available to U.S. citizens.

Application Requirements: Application form, FAFSA, transcript. *Deadline:* March 1.

WILLAMETTE VALLEY AGRICULTURAL ASSOCIATION SCHOLARSHIP
• *See page 88*

PENNSYLVANIA ASSOCIATION OF CONSERVATION DISTRICTS AUXILIARY

http://www.pacd.org/

PACD AUXILIARY SCHOLARSHIPS

Award for residents of Pennsylvania who are upperclassmen pursuing a degree program in agricultural and/or environmental science, and/or environmental education. Must be studying at a two- or four-year Pennsylvania institution. Must be U.S. citizens. Submit resume. One-time award of $500.

Academic Fields/Career Goals: Agriculture; Biology; Environmental Science; Horticulture/Floriculture.

Award: Scholarship for use in junior or senior years; not renewable. *Number:* 1. *Amount:* $500.

Eligibility Requirements: Applicant must be enrolled or expecting to enroll full- or part-time at a four-year institution or university; resident of Pennsylvania and studying in Pennsylvania. Available to U.S. citizens.

Application Requirements: Application form, driver's license, essay, financial need analysis, GPA verification, resume, transcript. *Deadline:* June 15.

PROFESSIONAL GROUNDS MANAGEMENT SOCIETY

http://www.pgms.org/

ANNE SEAMAN PROFESSIONAL GROUNDS MANAGEMENT SOCIETY MEMORIAL SCHOLARSHIP

One-time award for citizens of the United States and Canada who are studying to enter the field of grounds management or a closely related field such as agronomy, horticulture, landscape contracting, and irrigation on a full-time basis. Write for further information. Must be sponsored by a PGMS member. The member must write a letter of recommendation for the applicant.

Academic Fields/Career Goals: Agriculture; Civil Engineering; Horticulture/Floriculture; Landscape Architecture.

Award: Scholarship for use in freshman, sophomore, junior, or senior years; not renewable. *Number:* 3. *Amount:* $250–$1500.

Eligibility Requirements: Applicant must be enrolled or expecting to enroll full-time at a two-year or four-year institution or university. Available to U.S. and Canadian citizens.

Application Requirements: Application form, driver's license, financial need analysis, recommendations or references, resume, self-addressed stamped envelope with application, transcript. *Deadline:* September 15.

Contact: Jenny Smith, Association Coordinator
Professional Grounds Management Society
720 Light Street
Baltimore, MD 21230-3816
Phone: 410-223-2861
Fax: 410-752-8295
E-mail: pgms@assnhqtrs.com

SIGMA XI, THE SCIENTIFIC RESEARCH SOCIETY

http://www.sigmaxi.org/

SIGMA XI GRANTS-IN-AID OF RESEARCH

Award to undergraduate and graduate students currently enrolled in degree seeking programs. Applications are accepted through an online form only. Deadlines for all application material are March 15 and October 15 annually and are available online two months prior to the deadline (January 15 and August 14 respectively).

Academic Fields/Career Goals: Agriculture; Animal/Veterinary Sciences; Biology; Chemical Engineering; Earth Science; Engineering/Technology; Health and Medical Sciences; Mechanical Engineering; Meteorology/Atmospheric Science; Physical Sciences; Science, Technology, and Society; Social Sciences.

Award: Grant for use in freshman, sophomore, junior, senior, or graduate years; not renewable. *Number:* 400. *Amount:* $1000–$5000.

Eligibility Requirements: Applicant must be enrolled or expecting to enroll full-time at a four-year institution or university. Available to U.S. and non-U.S. citizens.

Application Requirements: Application form, recommendations or references. *Deadline:* varies.

Contact: Kevin Bowen, Program Manager, Grants and Society Awards
Sigma Xi, The Scientific Research Society
3106 East NC Highway 54
Research Triangle Park, NC 27709
Phone: 800-243-6534 Ext. 206
E-mail: giar@sigmaxi.org

SOCIETY FOR RANGE MANAGEMENT

http://www.rangelands.org/

MASONIC RANGE SCIENCE SCHOLARSHIP
• *See page 88*

SOIL AND WATER CONSERVATION SOCIETY

http://www.swcs.org

DONALD A. WILLIAMS SCHOLARSHIP SOIL CONSERVATION SCHOLARSHIP
• *See page 88*

MELVILLE H. COHEE STUDENT LEADER CONSERVATION SCHOLARSHIP
• *See page 88*

SOIL AND WATER CONSERVATION SOCIETY-NEW JERSEY CHAPTER

http://home.comcast.net/~njswcs/scholarship.htm

EDWARD R. HALL SCHOLARSHIP
• *See page 88*

SOUTH DAKOTA BOARD OF REGENTS

http://www.sdbor.edu/

SOUTH DAKOTA BOARD OF REGENTS BJUGSTAD SCHOLARSHIP
• *See page 89*

SOUTH FLORIDA FAIR AND PALM BEACH COUNTY EXPOSITIONS INC.

http://www.southfloridafair.com/

SOUTH FLORIDA FAIR AGRICULTURAL COLLEGE SCHOLARSHIP

Renewable award of $2000 for students pursuing a degree in agriculture. Must be a permanent resident of Florida.

Academic Fields/Career Goals: Agriculture.

Award: Scholarship for use in freshman, sophomore, junior, or senior years; renewable. *Number:* 2. *Amount:* $2000.

Eligibility Requirements: Applicant must be enrolled or expecting to enroll full- or part-time at a four-year institution or university and resident of Florida. Available to U.S. and non-U.S. citizens.

Application Requirements: Application form, community service, essay, recommendations or references, test scores, transcript. *Deadline:* October 15.

TURF AND ORNAMENTAL COMMUNICATORS ASSOCIATION

http://www.toca.org/

TURF AND ORNAMENTAL COMMUNICATORS ASSOCIATION SCHOLARSHIP PROGRAM

One-time award for undergraduate students majoring or minoring in technical communications or in a green industry field such as horticulture, plant sciences, botany, or agronomy. The applicant must also demonstrate an interest in using this course of study in the field of communications. An overall GPA of 3.0 is required in major area of study.

Academic Fields/Career Goals: Agriculture; Communications; Horticulture/Floriculture.

Award: Scholarship for use in freshman, sophomore, junior, or senior years; not renewable. *Number:* 1. *Amount:* $2500.

Eligibility Requirements: Applicant must be enrolled or expecting to enroll full-time at a two-year or four-year institution or university. Applicant must have 3.0 GPA or higher. Available to U.S. and non-U.S. citizens.

Application Requirements: Application form, essay, portfolio, recommendations or references, resume, transcript. *Deadline:* March 1.

Contact: Den Gardner, Executive Director
Phone: 952-758-6340
E-mail: toca@gardnerandgardnercommunications.com

UNITED NEGRO COLLEGE FUND

http://www.uncf.org/

MONSANTO/UNCF 1890'S SCHOLARSHIP PROGRAM
• *See page 89*

UNITED STATES DEPARTMENT OF AGRICULTURE

http://www.usda.gov/

USDA/1890 NATIONAL SCHOLARS PROGRAM

The program awards scholarships to students attending one of the eighteen 1890 Historically Black Land-Grant Universities, pursuing a bachelor degree in agriculture, food, natural resource sciences, or related academic disciplines, and willing to work full-time with the USDA upon graduation. Each award provides annual tuition, employment, employee benefits, and use of a laptop computer, printer and software while on scholarship, fees, books, room and board for each of the 4 academic years.

Academic Fields/Career Goals: Agriculture; Food Science/Nutrition; Natural Resources.

Award: Scholarship for use in freshman year; renewable.

Eligibility Requirements: Applicant must be high school student and planning to enroll or expecting to enroll at a four-year institution or university. Applicant must have 3.0 GPA or higher. Available to U.S. citizens.

Application Requirements: *Deadline:* February 1.

USDA/1994 TRIBAL SCHOLARS PROGRAM

Scholarships for applicants attending 1994 Land Grant Tribal Colleges and Universities seeking careers in food, agriculture, and natural resource sciences, and/or other related disciplines. The program offers support for an Associate's Degree (up to 2 Years of support) or Bachelor's of Science Degree (up to 4 Years of support).

Academic Fields/Career Goals: Agriculture; Food Science/Nutrition; Natural Resources.

Award: Scholarship for use in freshman, sophomore, junior, or senior years; renewable.

Eligibility Requirements: Applicant must be American Indian/Alaska Native and enrolled or expecting to enroll at an institution or university. Available to U.S. citizens.

Application Requirements: *Deadline:* February 1.

WILLIAM HELMS SCHOLARSHIP PROGRAM (WHSP)

The USDA APHIS is the agency responsible for safeguarding America's agricultural and natural resources from exotic plant and animal pests and diseases. APHIS' PPQ program deals specifically with plant health issues. Scholarship benefits include: financial aid while pursuing a degree; mentoring; paid work experience during school breaks; possible permanent employment upon graduation. Applicants must be enrolled in programs related to agriculture or the biological sciences and must maintain at least a 2.5 GPA.

Academic Fields/Career Goals: Agriculture; Biology.

Award: Scholarship for use in junior or senior years; renewable. *Number:* up to 5000.

Eligibility Requirements: Applicant must be enrolled or expecting to enroll at a four-year institution or university. Available to U.S. citizens.

Application Requirements: *Deadline:* March 1.

WASHINGTON ASSOCIATION OF WINE GRAPE GROWERS

http://www.wawgg.org/

WALTER J. CLORE SCHOLARSHIP

A scholarship of minimum $500 to a maximum $2000 is awarded to undergraduate and graduate students enrolled in areas of study pertaining to the wine industry. Scholarships will be given to students who are residents of the state of Washington. The number of awards vary each year.

Academic Fields/Career Goals: Agriculture; Food Science/Nutrition.

Award: Scholarship for use in freshman, sophomore, junior, senior, or graduate years; not renewable. *Number:* 6. *Amount:* $500–$2000.

Eligibility Requirements: Applicant must be enrolled or expecting to enroll full-time at a two-year or four-year institution or university and resident of Washington. Available to U.S. and non-U.S. citizens.

Application Requirements: Application form, essay, recommendations or references, resume, transcript. *Deadline:* November 30.

Contact: Vicky Scharlau, Executive Director
Phone: 509-782-8234
E-mail: vicky@501consultants.com

WOMEN GROCERS OF AMERICA

http://www.nationalgrocers.org/

MARY MACEY SCHOLARSHIP

Award for students intending to pursue a career in the independent sector of the grocery industry. One-time award for students who have completed freshman year. Submit statement and recommendation from sponsor in the grocery industry. Applicant should have a minimum 2.0 GPA.

Academic Fields/Career Goals: Agriculture; Business/Consumer Services; Food Service/Hospitality.

Award: Scholarship for use in sophomore, junior, senior, graduate, or postgraduate years; not renewable. *Number:* 2–7. *Amount:* $1000.

Eligibility Requirements: Applicant must be enrolled or expecting to enroll full-time at a two-year or four-year institution or university. Available to U.S. citizens.

Application Requirements: Application form, personal statement, recommendations or references, transcript. *Deadline:* May 15.

Contact: Kristen Comley, Director of Administration
Women Grocers of America
1005 North Glebe Road, Suite 250
Arlington, VA 22201-5758
Phone: 703-516-0700
Fax: 703-516-0115
E-mail: kcomley@nationalgrocers.org

AMERICAN STUDIES

AMERICAN FEDERATION OF STATE, COUNTY, AND MUNICIPAL EMPLOYEES

http://www.afscme.org/

AFSCME/UNCF UNION SCHOLARS PROGRAM

One-time award for a sophomore or junior majoring in ethnic studies, women's studies, labor studies, American studies, sociology, anthropology, history, political science, psychology, social work or economics. Must be African-American, Hispanic-American, Asian Pacific Islander, or American-Indian/Alaska Native. Minimum 2.5 GPA.

Academic Fields/Career Goals: American Studies; Anthropology; History; Political Science; Psychology; Social Sciences; Social Services; Women's Studies.

Award: Scholarship for use in sophomore or junior years; not renewable. *Number:* 10. *Amount:* up to $5000.

Eligibility Requirements: Applicant must be American Indian/Alaska Native, Asian/Pacific Islander, Black (non-Hispanic), Hispanic and enrolled or expecting to enroll full-time at a four-year institution or university. Applicant must have 2.5 GPA or higher. Available to U.S. citizens.

Application Requirements: Application form, essay, recommendations or references, transcript. *Deadline:* February 28.

Contact: Philip Allen, Scholarship Coordinator
Phone: 202-429-1250
Fax: 202-429-1293
E-mail: pallen@asscme.org

ASSOCIATION OF FORMER INTELLIGENCE OFFICERS

http://www.afio.com/13_scholarships.htm

CIA UNDERGRADUATE SCHOLARSHIPS

The type of institution attended is less important than the clarity that the course of study being undertaken leads to a career in the U.S. Intelligence Community. So this covers law enforcement, foreign policy, intelligence analysis, counterterrorism, homeland security, foreign language mastery (Farsi, Tagalog, Pashto, Urdu, Mandarin, Arabic, Hindi, etc.—not Spanish or French), and related disciplines. Applicants seeking funding for law or medical school are placed in a third tier as a currently overabundant category inessential to current needs of the I.C. which already suffers from too many lawyers. Applicants must be a U.S. citizen studying at a U.S. Institution. Advanced knowledge and corroboration of claims of near-native performance in one of the mission-critical languages mentioned above puts applicants at top of consideration. Applicants going to online-only schools are acceptable but only institutions that are on a nationally accredited list maintained by the U.S. Dept of Education. Costly, for-profit and non-profit institutions suspected of gaming the college-loan system, and those with no national accreditation or with fake, odd, bogus, or foreign accreditations, are not considered and cause a student application for support to be set aside.

Academic Fields/Career Goals: American Studies; Aviation/Aerospace; Computer Science/Data Processing; Criminal Justice/Criminology; Foreign Language; History; Law Enforcement/Police Administration; Military and Defense Studies; Natural Sciences; Near and Middle East Studies; Peace and Conflict Studies; Political Science.

Award: Scholarship for use in sophomore, junior, senior, graduate, or postgraduate years; not renewable. *Number:* 15–30. *Amount:* $1000–$4000.

Eligibility Requirements: Applicant must be enrolled or expecting to enroll full- or part-time at a two-year or four-year or technical institution or university. Applicant must have 3.0 GPA or higher. Available to U.S. and Canadian citizens.

Application Requirements: Application form, letter explaining intent and goals, personal photograph, recommendations or references, resume, transcript. *Deadline:* July 1.

Contact: Mrs. Priscilla Adams, Director, AFIO Scholarship Programs
Association of Former Intelligence Officers
7700 Leesburg Pike, Suite 324
Falls Church, VA 22043
Phone: 703-790-0320
Fax: 703-991-1278
E-mail: afio@afio.com

CULTURAL SERVICES OF THE FRENCH EMBASSY

http://www.frenchculture.org/

TEACHING ASSISTANT PROGRAM IN FRANCE

Grants support American students as they teach English for 7 months in the French school system. Monthly stipend of about 790 euros (net) supports recipient in the life-style of a typical French student. Must be U.S. citizen or a permanent resident (not a French citizen). Proficiency in French is required. May not have received a similar grant from the French government for the last three years. For additional information and application, visit website http://highereducation.frenchculture.org/teach-in-france.

Academic Fields/Career Goals: American Studies; Art History; Education; European Studies; Foreign Language; History; Humanities; International Studies; Literature/English/Writing; Political Science; Social Sciences.

Award: Grant for use in junior, senior, graduate, or postgraduate years; not renewable. *Number:* 1120. *Amount:* $1040–$7280.

Eligibility Requirements: Applicant must be age 20-30; enrolled or expecting to enroll full- or part-time at a four-year institution or university and must have an interest in English language, foreign language, French language, or international exchange. Available to U.S. citizens.

Application Requirements: Application form, application form may be submitted online (http://www.tapif.org), essay, passport, personal photograph, recommendations or references, transcript. *Fee:* $40. *Deadline:* January 15.

Contact: Ms. Carolyn Collins, Educational Affairs Program Officer
Cultural Services of the French Embassy
Embassy of France
4101 Reservoir Road, NW
Washington, DC 20007
Phone: 202-944-6011
Fax: 202-944-6268
E-mail: assistant.washington-amba@diplomatie.gouv.fr

THE GEORGIA TRUST FOR HISTORIC PRESERVATION

http://www.georgiatrust.org/

B. PHINIZY SPALDING, HUBERT B. OWENS, AND THE NATIONAL SOCIETY OF THE COLONIAL DAMES OF AMERICA IN THE STATE OF GEORGIA ACADEMIC SCHOLARSHIPS

The Georgia Trust annually awards two $1000 and two $1500 scholarships to encourage the study of historic preservation and related fields. Recipients are chosen on the basis of leadership and academic achievement. Applicants must be residents of Georgia enrolled in an accredited Georgia institution.

Academic Fields/Career Goals: American Studies; Historic Preservation and Conservation; History; Landscape Architecture.

Award: Scholarship for use in sophomore, junior, senior, or graduate years; not renewable. *Number:* 4. *Amount:* $1000–$1500.

Eligibility Requirements: Applicant must be enrolled or expecting to enroll full-time at a four-year institution or university; resident of Georgia and studying in Georgia. Applicant must have 3.0 GPA or higher. Available to U.S. citizens.

Application Requirements: Application form, essay, recommendations or references, resume, transcript. *Deadline:* February 9.

Contact: Ms. Kate Ryan, Director of Preservation
The Georgia Trust for Historic Preservation
1516 Peachtree Street, NW
Atlanta, GA 30309
Phone: 404-885-7817
E-mail: kryan@georgiatrust.org

SONS OF THE REPUBLIC OF TEXAS

http://www.srttexas.org/

PRESIDIO LA BAHIA AWARD

Award of $2000 is available annually for winning participants in the competition, with a minimum first place prize of $1200 for the best published book. Competition is open to any person interested in the Spanish Colonial influence on Texas culture. Refer to website http://www.srttexas.org/labahia.html for details.

Academic Fields/Career Goals: American Studies; History.

Award: Prize for use in freshman, sophomore, junior, senior, graduate, or postgraduate years; not renewable. *Number:* 1. *Amount:* $1200–$2000.

Eligibility Requirements: Applicant must be enrolled or expecting to enroll full- or part-time at a four-year institution or university and must have an interest in writing. Available to U.S. and non-U.S. citizens.

Application Requirements: 4 copies of published writings, entry in a contest. *Deadline:* September 30.

Contact: Janet Knox, Administrative Assistant
Sons of the Republic of Texas
1717 8th Street
Bay City, TX 77414
Phone: 979-245-6644
E-mail: srttexas@srttexas.org

TEXAS HISTORY ESSAY CONTEST

Contest for best essay on the history of Texas written by graduating seniors in any high school in the United States. History, government and English students are particularly encouraged to participate. Prizes will be scholarships to the college of each winner's choice or will be given to the student directly if he or she does not intend to attend a college or university. First prize $3000, second prize $2000, third prize $1000.

Academic Fields/Career Goals: American Studies; History.

Award: Prize for use in freshman year; not renewable. *Number:* 3. *Amount:* $1000–$3000.

Eligibility Requirements: Applicant must be high school student; planning to enroll or expecting to enroll full- or part-time at a two-year or four-year or technical institution or university and must have an interest in writing. Available to U.S. citizens.

Application Requirements: Application form, entry in a contest, essay. *Deadline:* January 31.

Contact: Janet Knox, Administrative Assistant
Sons of the Republic of Texas
1717 Eighth Street
Bay City, TX 77414
Phone: 979-245-6644
E-mail: srttexas@srttexas.org

UNITED NEGRO COLLEGE FUND

http://www.uncf.org/

AFSCME/UNCF/HARVARD UNIVERSITY LWP UNION SCHOLARS PROGRAM

Scholarship available to undergraduate sophomores and juniors who become members of AFSCME and get involved in outreach work for the union. Eligible majors include American studies, anthropology, economics, English, ethnic studies, history, labor studies, political science, psychology, social work, sociology, Spanish, and women's studies. Minimum 2.5 GPA required. For additional information visit website http://www.uncf.org.

Academic Fields/Career Goals: American Studies; Anthropology; Area/Ethnic Studies; Economics; History; Literature/English/Writing; Political Science; Public Policy and Administration; Social Sciences; Social Services; Women's Studies.

Award: Scholarship for use in sophomore or junior years; renewable. *Number:* 1. *Amount:* up to $5000.

Eligibility Requirements: Applicant must be Black (non-Hispanic) and enrolled or expecting to enroll full- or part-time at a four-year institution. Applicant or parent of applicant must be member of American Federation of State, County, and Municipal Employees. Applicant must have 2.5 GPA or higher. Available to U.S. citizens.

Application Requirements: Application form. *Deadline:* March 4.

ANIMAL/VETERINARY SCIENCES

ABBIE SARGENT MEMORIAL SCHOLARSHIP INC.

http://www.nhfarmbureau.org/

ABBIE SARGENT MEMORIAL SCHOLARSHIP
• *See page 84*

AMERICAN PHYSIOLOGICAL SOCIETY

http://www.the-aps.org

DAVID S. BRUCE AWARDS FOR EXCELLENCE IN UNDERGRADUATE RESEARCH

Award available for research in physiology. The student must be enrolled as an undergraduate student at the time of the application. The applicant must be the first author on a submitted abstract for the EB meeting and must be working with an APS member who attests that the student is deserving of the first authorship. Bruce Outstanding Undergraduate Abstract Awards ($100) are given to up to 30 students based on abstract, 1-page letter, and letter of recommendation. Those awardees then compete for Bruce Excellence in Undergraduate Research Awards ($400) by giving oral poster presentations.

Academic Fields/Career Goals: Animal/Veterinary Sciences; Biology; Environmental Science; Health and Medical Sciences; Marine Biology; Natural Sciences; Neurobiology; Sports-Related/Exercise Science.

Award: Prize for use in freshman, sophomore, junior, or senior years; not renewable. *Number:* 10–30. *Amount:* $100–$500.

Eligibility Requirements: Applicant must be enrolled or expecting to enroll full-time at a two-year or four-year institution or university. Available to U.S. and non-U.S. citizens.

Application Requirements: Application form, application form may be submitted online (http://www.the-aps.org/awardapps), essay, first author abstract, recommendations or references. *Deadline:* January 12.

Contact: Melinda Lowy, Higher Education Programs Coordinator
American Physiological Society
9650 Rockville Pike
Bethesda, MD 20814
Phone: 301-634-7787
Fax: 301-634-7098
E-mail: mlowy@the-aps.org

AMERICAN QUARTER HORSE FOUNDATION (AQHF)

http://www.aqha.com/foundation

AQHF RACING SCHOLARSHIPS

Scholarships for members of AQHA/AQHYA who have experience within the racing industry or are seeking a career in the industry. Applicants seeking a career in the racing industry may specialize in veterinary medicine, racetrack management or other related fields.

Academic Fields/Career Goals: Animal/Veterinary Sciences.

Award: Scholarship for use in freshman, sophomore, junior, senior, graduate, or postgraduate years; renewable. *Number:* 1–5. *Amount:* $4000–$8000.

Eligibility Requirements: Applicant must be enrolled or expecting to enroll full-time at a two-year or four-year or technical institution or university. Applicant or parent of applicant must be member of American Quarter Horse Association. Applicant must have 2.5 GPA or higher. Available to U.S. and Canadian citizens.

Application Requirements: Application form, recommendations or references, transcript. *Deadline:* December 1.

JAY PUMPHREY ANIMAL SCIENCES SCHOLARSHIP

Ideal candidate is an AQHA or AQHYA member from Texas with a rural farming and or ranching background who wishes to pursue a major in animal science or a large animal related degree from Tarleton State University or Texas A&M University.

Academic Fields/Career Goals: Animal/Veterinary Sciences.

Award: Scholarship for use in freshman, sophomore, junior, or senior years; renewable. *Number:* 1. *Amount:* $2500.

Eligibility Requirements: Applicant must be high school student; planning to enroll or expecting to enroll full-time at a four-year institution or university; resident of Texas and studying in Texas. Applicant or parent of applicant must be member of American Quarter Horse Association. Applicant must have 3.0 GPA or higher. Available to U.S. citizens.

Application Requirements: Application form, recommendations or references, transcript. *Deadline:* December 1.

APPALOOSA HORSE CLUB-APPALOOSA YOUTH PROGRAM

http://www.appaloosayouth.com/

LEW AND JOANN EKLUND EDUCATIONAL SCHOLARSHIP

One-time award for college juniors and seniors and graduate students studying a field related to the equine industry. Must be member or dependent of member of the Appaloosa Horse Club.

Academic Fields/Career Goals: Animal/Veterinary Sciences.

Award: Scholarship for use in junior, senior, or graduate years; not renewable. *Number:* 1. *Amount:* $2000.

Eligibility Requirements: Applicant must be enrolled or expecting to enroll full-time at a four-year institution or university. Applicant or parent of applicant must be member of Appaloosa Horse Club/Appaloosa Youth Association. Applicant must have 2.5 GPA or higher. Available to U.S. and non-U.S. citizens.

Application Requirements: Application form, entry in a contest, essay, personal photograph, recommendations or references, transcript. *Deadline:* June 1.

Contact: Anna Brown, AYF Coordinator
Appaloosa Horse Club-Appaloosa Youth Program
2720 West Pullman Road
Moscow, ID 83843
Phone: 208-882-5578 Ext. 264
Fax: 208-882-8150
E-mail: youth@appaloosa.com

ASSOCIATION ON AMERICAN INDIAN AFFAIRS, INC.

http://www.indian-affairs.org/

ELIZABETH AND SHERMAN ASCHE MEMORIAL SCHOLARSHIP FUND

• *See page 91*

MAINE DEPARTMENT OF AGRICULTURE, FOOD AND RURAL RESOURCES

http://www.maine.gov/agriculture

MAINE RURAL REHABILITATION FUND SCHOLARSHIP PROGRAM

• *See page 86*

NATIONAL DAIRY SHRINE

http://www.dairyshrine.org/

KILDEE SCHOLARSHIPS

• *See page 93*

NATIONAL DAIRY SHRINE/KLUSSENDORF SCHOLARSHIP

• *See page 93*

NDS STUDENT RECOGNITION CONTEST

• *See page 87*

NATIONAL POULTRY AND FOOD DISTRIBUTORS ASSOCIATION

http://www.npfda.org/

NATIONAL POULTRY AND FOOD DISTRIBUTORS ASSOCIATION SCHOLARSHIP FOUNDATION

• *See page 87*

OREGON STUDENT ASSISTANCE COMMISSION

http://www.GetCollegeFunds.org/

WILLAMETTE VALLEY AGRICULTURAL ASSOCIATION SCHOLARSHIP

• *See page 88*

SIGMA XI, THE SCIENTIFIC RESEARCH SOCIETY

http://www.sigmaxi.org/

SIGMA XI GRANTS-IN-AID OF RESEARCH

• *See page 95*

SOCIETY FOR RANGE MANAGEMENT

http://www.rangelands.org/

MASONIC RANGE SCIENCE SCHOLARSHIP

• *See page 88*

SOIL AND WATER CONSERVATION SOCIETY-NEW JERSEY CHAPTER

http://home.comcast.net/~njswcs/scholarship.htm

EDWARD R. HALL SCHOLARSHIP

• *See page 88*

STRAIGHTFORWARD MEDIA

http://www.straightforwardmedia.com/

STRAIGHTFORWARD MEDIA VOCATIONAL-TECHNICAL SCHOOL SCHOLARSHIP

Scholarship of $500 available to students enrolled in vocational and technical education programs. Awarded four times per year. Deadlines: November 30, February 28, May 31, and August 31. To apply, visit http://www.straightforwardmedia.com/votech/form.php.

Academic Fields/Career Goals: Animal/Veterinary Sciences; Cosmetology; Culinary Arts; Dental Health/Services; Fire Sciences; Heating, Air-Conditioning, and Refrigeration Mechanics; Pharmacy; Real Estate; Sports-Related/Exercise Science; Trade/Technical Specialties.

Award: Scholarship for use in freshman, sophomore, junior, or senior years; not renewable. *Number:* 4. *Amount:* $500.

Eligibility Requirements: Applicant must be enrolled or expecting to enroll full- or part-time at a two-year or four-year or technical institution or university. Available to U.S. and non-U.S. citizens.

Application Requirements: Essay. *Deadline:* varies.

UNITED NEGRO COLLEGE FUND

http://www.uncf.org/

SPRINT SCHOLARS PROGRAM FOR SOPHOMORES, JUNIORS, AND SENIORS

Scholarships for sophomores, juniors, and seniors enrolled at UNCF members schools who are U.S. citizens or permanent residents. Must be majoring in animal science, biochemistry, biology, chemical engineering, chemistry, civil engineering, computer engineering, construction engineering, electrical engineering, environmental engineering, environmental science(s), food science, geophysics, industrial engineering, manufacturing engineering, mathematics, software engineering, computer science, physics, or management information systems. Minimum 3.0 GPA required. Kansas City metropolitan area residents (includes Kansas and Missouri) will be given special consideration.

Academic Fields/Career Goals: Animal/Veterinary Sciences; Biology; Chemical Engineering; Civil Engineering; Computer Science/Data Processing; Electrical Engineering/Electronics; Environmental Science; Food Science/Nutrition; Mathematics; Natural Sciences.

Award: Scholarship for use in sophomore, junior, or senior years; not renewable. *Amount:* up to $5000.

Eligibility Requirements: Applicant must be Black (non-Hispanic) and enrolled or expecting to enroll full-time at a four-year institution or university. Applicant must have 3.0 GPA or higher. Available to U.S. citizens.

Application Requirements: Application form. *Deadline:* May 30.

UNITED STATES DEPARTMENT OF AGRICULTURE

http://www.usda.gov/

SAUL T. WILSON, JR, SCHOLARSHIP PROGRAM (STWJS)

Undergraduate student applicants must have completed at least 2 years (60 semester or 90 quarter hours) of a 4-year pre-veterinary medicine or other biomedical science curriculum. Graduate student applicants must have completed not more than 1 year (18 semester or 27 quarter hours) of study in veterinary medicine. Awards up to $1000 per year for undergraduate studies, up to $5000 for graduate studies. Benefits include paid employment during summers and school breaks, full-time agency employment after graduation.

Academic Fields/Career Goals: Animal/Veterinary Sciences; Biology.

Award: Scholarship for use in junior, senior, or graduate years; renewable. *Amount:* up to $5000.

Eligibility Requirements: Applicant must be enrolled or expecting to enroll full-time at a four-year institution or university. Available to U.S. citizens.

Application Requirements: *Deadline:* March 1.

WILSON ORNITHOLOGICAL SOCIETY

http://www.wilsonsociety.org/

GEORGE A. HALL/HAROLD F. MAYFIELD AWARD

One-time award for scientific research on birds. Available to independent researchers without access to funds or facilities at a college or university. Must be a nonprofessional to apply. Submit research proposal.

Academic Fields/Career Goals: Animal/Veterinary Sciences; Biology; Natural Resources.

Award: Grant for use in freshman, sophomore, junior, or senior years; not renewable. *Number:* 1. *Amount:* $1000.

Eligibility Requirements: Applicant must be enrolled or expecting to enroll full- or part-time at a four-year institution or university. Available to U.S. and non-U.S. citizens.

Application Requirements: Application form, proposal, recommendations or references. *Deadline:* February 1.

Contact: Dr. Carla Dove, Research Grants Coordinator
Phone: 202-633-0787
E-mail: dove@si.edu

PAUL A. STEWART AWARDS

One-time award for studies of bird movements based on banding, analysis of recoveries, and returns of banded birds, or research with an emphasis on economic ornithology. Submit research proposal.

Academic Fields/Career Goals: Animal/Veterinary Sciences; Biology; Natural Resources.

Award: Grant for use in freshman, sophomore, junior, or senior years; not renewable. *Number:* 1–4. *Amount:* up to $500.

Eligibility Requirements: Applicant must be enrolled or expecting to enroll full- or part-time at a four-year institution or university. Available to U.S. and non-U.S. citizens.

Application Requirements: Application form, proposal, recommendations or references. *Deadline:* February 1.

Contact: Dr. Carla Dove, Research Grants Coordinator
Phone: 202-633-0787
E-mail: dove@si.edu

ANTHROPOLOGY

AMERICAN FEDERATION OF STATE, COUNTY, AND MUNICIPAL EMPLOYEES

http://www.afscme.org/

AFSCME/UNCF UNION SCHOLARS PROGRAM
• See page 97

AMERICAN SCHOOL OF CLASSICAL STUDIES AT ATHENS

http://www.ascsa.edu.gr/

ASCSA SUMMER SESSIONS SCHOLARSHIPS

Funding for ASCSA Summer Sessions participants only. Awards for graduate students, high school teachers, and college teachers. One award (Charles Edwards for $500) at undergraduate level used only for participation in the ASCSA Summer Sessions. Six-week sessions in Greece are conducted to become acquainted with Greece and its antiquities. Funding cannot be used for home institution in U.S.

Academic Fields/Career Goals: Anthropology; Archaeology; Architecture; Art History; Arts; Classics; Historic Preservation and Conservation; History; Humanities; Museum Studies; Philosophy; Religion/Theology.

Award: Scholarship for use in senior or graduate years; not renewable. *Number:* 10–11. *Amount:* $500–$4250.

Eligibility Requirements: Applicant must be enrolled or expecting to enroll part-time at a four-year institution or university and must have an interest in international exchange. Available to U.S. and non-U.S. citizens.

Application Requirements: Application form, application form may be submitted online (http://www.ascsa.edu.gr), recommendations or references, transcript. *Fee:* $25. *Deadline:* January 15.

SOCIETY FOR APPLIED ANTHROPOLOGY

http://www.sfaa.net/

ANNUAL SFAA STUDENT ENDOWED AWARD

The Student Endowed Award consists of a $175 travel stipend to cover costs of attending the annual meeting, plus a one-year SfAA membership, (which includes a year's subscription to the journals Human Organization and Practicing Anthropology).

Academic Fields/Career Goals: Anthropology; Applied Sciences; Social Sciences.

Award: Prize for use in freshman, sophomore, junior, senior, graduate, or postgraduate years; not renewable. *Number:* 1–1. *Amount:* $175–$175.

Eligibility Requirements: Applicant must be enrolled or expecting to enroll full- or part-time at a two-year or four-year institution or university. Available to U.S. and non-U.S. citizens.

Application Requirements: Application form, curriculum vitae, essay. *Deadline:* January 14.

Contact: Dr. J.T. May, Executive Director
Society for Applied Anthropology
PO Box 2436
Oklahoma City, OK 73101
Phone: 405-843-5113
Fax: 405-843-8553
E-mail: tom@sfaa.net

BEATRICE MEDICINE AWARDS

Two awards ($500 each) will be made to attend the Annual Meeting of the SfAA.

Academic Fields/Career Goals: Anthropology; Applied Sciences; Social Sciences.

Award: Prize for use in freshman, sophomore, junior, senior, graduate, or postgraduate years; not renewable. *Number:* 2–2. *Amount:* $500–$500.

Eligibility Requirements: Applicant must be American Indian/Alaska Native and enrolled or expecting to enroll full- or part-time at a two-year or four-year institution or university. Available to U.S. and non-U.S. citizens.

Application Requirements: Native Tribe/Community affiliation, career goal statement, transcript. *Deadline:* December 19.

Contact: Dr. J.T. May, Executive Director
Society for Applied Anthropology
PO Box 2436
Oklahoma City, OK 73101
Phone: 405-843-5113
Fax: 405-843-8553
E-mail: tom@sfaa.net

DEL JONES MEMORIAL TRAVEL AWARD

Travel grant for a student to attend the annual meeting of the Society. The Award is intended to increase minority participation in SfAA, particularly African American participation, but also to honor the life and work of Del Jones.

Academic Fields/Career Goals: Anthropology; Applied Sciences; Social Sciences.

Award: Prize for use in freshman, sophomore, junior, senior, or postgraduate years; not renewable. *Number:* 2–2. *Amount:* $500–$500.

Eligibility Requirements: Applicant must be enrolled or expecting to enroll full- or part-time at a two-year or four-year or technical institution or university. Available to U.S. and non-U.S. citizens.

Application Requirements: Abstract, essay. *Deadline:* January 17.

Contact: Dr. J.T. May, Executive Director
Society for Applied Anthropology
PO Box 2436
Oklahoma City, OK 73101
Phone: 405-843-5113
Fax: 405-843-8553
E-mail: tom@sfaa.net

EDWARD H. AND ROSAMOND B. SPICER TRAVEL AWARDS

The Awards commemorate the lifelong concern of Edward H. and Rosamond B. Spicer in furthering the maturation of students in the social sciences, both intellectually and practically, and their lifelong interest in the nature of community as both cause of, and solution to, problems in the human condition.

Academic Fields/Career Goals: Anthropology; Applied Sciences; Social Sciences.

Award: Prize for use in freshman, sophomore, junior, senior, graduate, or postgraduate years; not renewable. *Number:* 2–2. *Amount:* $500–$500.

Eligibility Requirements: Applicant must be enrolled or expecting to enroll full- or part-time at a two-year or four-year institution or university. Available to U.S. and non-U.S. citizens.

Application Requirements: Abstract and written statement. *Deadline:* January 17.

Contact: Dr. J.T. May, Executive Director
Society for Applied Anthropology
PO Box 2436
Oklahoma City, OK 73101
Phone: 405-843-5113
Fax: 405-843-8553
E-mail: tom@sfaa.net

GIL KUSHNER MEMORIAL TRAVEL AWARD

Scholarship of $500 to attend the SfAA annual meeting. Abstracts (paper or poster) should be concerned with the persistence of cultural groups.

Academic Fields/Career Goals: Anthropology; Applied Sciences; Social Sciences.

Award: Prize for use in freshman, sophomore, junior, senior, graduate, or postgraduate years; not renewable. *Number:* 2–2. *Amount:* $500–$500.

Eligibility Requirements: Applicant must be enrolled or expecting to enroll full- or part-time at a two-year or four-year institution or university. Available to U.S. and non-U.S. citizens.

Application Requirements: Abstract, essay. *Deadline:* January 31.

Contact: Dr. J.T. May, Executive Director
Society for Applied Anthropology
PO Box 2436
Oklahoma City, OK 73101
Phone: 405-843-5113
Fax: 405-843-8553
E-mail: tom@sfaa.net

HUMAN RIGHTS DEFENDER STUDENT AWARD

This annual award recognizes the recipient's commitment to the resolution of human rights issues.

Academic Fields/Career Goals: Anthropology; Applied Sciences; Social Sciences.

Award: Prize for use in freshman, sophomore, junior, senior, graduate, or postgraduate years; not renewable. *Number:* 1–1. *Amount:* $500–$500.

Eligibility Requirements: Applicant must be enrolled or expecting to enroll full- or part-time at a two-year or four-year institution or university. Available to U.S. and non-U.S. citizens.

Application Requirements: Written statement. *Deadline:* December 31.

Contact: Dr. J.T. May, Executive Director
Society for Applied Anthropology
PO Box 2436
Oklahoma City, OK 73101
Phone: 405-843-5113
Fax: 405-843-8553
E-mail: tom@sfaa.net

VALENE SMITH PRIZE

The posters which are submitted for the Valene Smith Competition will be set up and exhibited with all other posters at the Annual Meeting of the Society for Applied Anthropology and should be concerned in some way with the applied social science of tourism.

Academic Fields/Career Goals: Anthropology; Applied Sciences; Social Sciences; Travel/Tourism.

Award: Prize for use in freshman, sophomore, junior, senior, graduate, or postgraduate years; not renewable. *Number:* 1–3. *Amount:* $250–$500.

Eligibility Requirements: Applicant must be enrolled or expecting to enroll full- or part-time at a two-year or four-year institution or university. Available to U.S. and non-U.S. citizens.

Application Requirements: Exhibit poster at annual meeting. *Deadline:* October 15.

Contact: Dr. J.T. May, Executive Director
Society for Applied Anthropology
PO Box 2436
Oklahoma City, OK 73101
Phone: 405-843-5113
Fax: 405-843-8553
E-mail: tom@sfaa.net

SOCIETY FOR THE SCIENTIFIC STUDY OF SEXUALITY

http://www.sexscience.org/

SOCIETY FOR THE SCIENTIFIC STUDY OF SEXUALITY STUDENT RESEARCH GRANT

Award to support students doing scientific research related to sexuality. Purpose of research can be master's thesis or doctoral dissertation, but this is not a requirement. Must be enrolled in degree-granting program. Deadlines: February 1 and September 1. One-time award of $1000.

Academic Fields/Career Goals: Anthropology; Behavioral Science; Biology; Education; Health and Medical Sciences; Nursing; Psychology; Public Health; Religion/Theology; Social Sciences; Women's Studies.

Award: Grant for use in freshman, sophomore, junior, senior, or graduate years; not renewable. *Number:* 2. *Amount:* $1000.

Eligibility Requirements: Applicant must be enrolled or expecting to enroll full- or part-time at a four-year institution or university. Available to U.S. and non-U.S. citizens.

Application Requirements: Application form, application form may be submitted online (http://www.sexscience.org), essay, resume. *Deadline:* varies.

Contact: Mandy Peters, Association Manager
Society for the Scientific Study of Sexuality
881 Third Street
Suite B-5
Whitehall, PA 18052
Phone: 610-443-3100
Fax: 610-443-3105
E-mail: thesociety@sexscience.org

UNITED NEGRO COLLEGE FUND

http://www.uncf.org/

AFSCME/UNCF/HARVARD UNIVERSITY LWP UNION SCHOLARS PROGRAM

• See page 98

APPLIED SCIENCES

AMERICAN INDIAN SCIENCE AND ENGINEERING SOCIETY

http://www.aises.org/

A.T. ANDERSON MEMORIAL SCHOLARSHIP PROGRAM

Award for full-time students majoring in math, engineering, science, technology, medicine or natural resources. Must be at least one quarter American-Indian/Alaska Native or have tribal recognition, and be member of AISES. Must have minimum 3.0 GPA.

Academic Fields/Career Goals: Applied Sciences; Biology; Business/Consumer Services; Earth Science; Health and Medical Sciences; Materials Science, Engineering, and Metallurgy; Meteorology/Atmospheric Science; Natural Resources; Natural Sciences; Nuclear Science; Physical Sciences.

Award: Scholarship for use in freshman, sophomore, junior, or senior years; not renewable. *Amount:* $1000–$2000.

Eligibility Requirements: Applicant must be American Indian/Alaska Native and enrolled or expecting to enroll full-time at a two-year or four-year institution or university. Applicant must have 3.0 GPA or higher. Available to U.S. citizens.

Application Requirements: Application form, essay, recommendations or references, resume, transcript, tribal enrollment document. *Deadline:* June 15.

BURLINGTON NORTHERN SANTA FE FOUNDATION SCHOLARSHIP

Award for high school senior for study of science, business, education, and health administration. Must reside in Arizona, Colorado, Kansas, Minnesota, Montana, North Dakota, New Mexico, Oklahoma, Oregon,

South Dakota, Washington, or California. Must be at least one quarter American-Indian or Alaska Native and/or member of federally recognized tribe. Minimum 2.0 GPA required.

Academic Fields/Career Goals: Applied Sciences; Biology; Business/Consumer Services; Education; Engineering/Technology; Health Administration; Meteorology/Atmospheric Science; Natural Sciences; Nuclear Science; Physical Sciences.

Award: Scholarship for use in freshman, sophomore, junior, or senior years; renewable. *Number:* up to 5. *Amount:* up to $2500.

Eligibility Requirements: Applicant must be American Indian/Alaska Native; high school student; planning to enroll or expecting to enroll full-time at a two-year or four-year or technical institution or university and resident of Arizona, California, Colorado, Kansas, Minnesota, Montana, New Mexico, North Dakota, Oklahoma, Oregon, South Dakota, Washington. Available to U.S. citizens.

Application Requirements: Application form, essay, recommendations or references, resume, transcript, tribal identification; certificate of Indian blood (CIB). *Deadline:* April 15.

AMERICAN INSTITUTE OF AERONAUTICS AND ASTRONAUTICS

http://www.aiaa.org/

AIAA FOUNDATION UNDERGRADUATE SCHOLARSHIP

Available to college students that will be sophomores, juniors, and seniors enrolled full-time in an accredited college/university. Must be AIAA student member to apply. Course of study must provide entry into some field of science or engineering encompassed by AIAA. Minimum 3.300 GPA required.

Academic Fields/Career Goals: Applied Sciences; Aviation/Aerospace; Electrical Engineering/Electronics; Engineering-Related Technologies; Engineering/Technology; Materials Science, Engineering, and Metallurgy; Mechanical Engineering; Physical Sciences; Science, Technology, and Society.

Award: Scholarship for use in sophomore, junior, or senior years; not renewable. *Number:* 30. *Amount:* $2000–$2500.

Eligibility Requirements: Applicant must be enrolled or expecting to enroll full-time at a two-year or four-year institution or university. Applicant or parent of applicant must be member of American Institute of Aeronautics and Astronautics. Applicant must have 3.5 GPA or higher. Available to U.S. and non-U.S. citizens.

Application Requirements: Application form, essay, recommendations or references, transcript. *Deadline:* January 31.

Contact: Stephen Brock, Student Programs Team Leader
American Institute of Aeronautics and Astronautics
Suite 500, 1801 Alexander Bell Drive
Reston, VA 20191
Phone: 703-264-7500

AMERICAN SOCIETY FOR ENGINEERING EDUCATION

http://www.asee.org/

SCIENCE, MATHEMATICS, AND RESEARCH FOR TRANSFORMATION DEFENSE SCHOLARSHIP FOR SERVICE PROGRAM

Award established by the Department of Defense to support the education, recruitment, and retention of undergraduate and graduate students in the fields of science, technology, engineering, and mathematics. Available only to full-time undergraduate or graduate students with 3.0 GPA or above.

Academic Fields/Career Goals: Applied Sciences; Engineering-Related Technologies; Engineering/Technology; Mathematics; Physical Sciences.

Award: Scholarship for use in sophomore, junior, or senior years; renewable. *Number:* 200. *Amount:* $22,000–$39,000.

Eligibility Requirements: Applicant must be enrolled or expecting to enroll full-time at a two-year or four-year institution or university. Applicant must have 3.0 GPA or higher. Available to U.S. citizens.

Application Requirements: Application form, essay, recommendations or references, transcript. *Deadline:* December 14.

Contact: Evan Gaines, Project Coordinator
American Society for Engineering Education
1818 North Street, NW, Suite 600
Washington, DC 20036
Phone: 202-331-3544
Fax: 202-265-8504
E-mail: smart@asee.org

AMERICAN SOCIETY OF NAVAL ENGINEERS

http://www.navalengineers.org/

AMERICAN SOCIETY OF NAVAL ENGINEERS SCHOLARSHIP

Award for naval engineering students in the final year of an undergraduate program or after one year of graduate study at an accredited institution. Must be full-time student and a U.S. citizen. Minimum 2.5 GPA required. Award of $2500 for undergraduates and $3500 for graduate students. Graduate student applicants are required to be member of the American Society of Naval Engineers.

Academic Fields/Career Goals: Applied Sciences; Aviation/ Aerospace; Civil Engineering; Electrical Engineering/Electronics; Energy and Power Engineering; Engineering/Technology; Marine/Ocean Engineering; Materials Science, Engineering, and Metallurgy; Mechanical Engineering; Physical Sciences.

Award: Scholarship for use in senior or graduate years; renewable. *Number:* 8–14. *Amount:* $2500–$3500.

Eligibility Requirements: Applicant must be enrolled or expecting to enroll full-time at a four-year institution or university. Applicant must have 2.5 GPA or higher. Available to U.S. citizens.

Application Requirements: Application form, personal photograph, recommendations or references, self-addressed stamped envelope with application, test scores, transcript. *Deadline:* February 15.

Contact: Lonni Jackson, Executive Director
Phone: 703-524-5620 Ext. 111
E-mail: ljackson@msfdn.org

ARRL FOUNDATION INC.

http://www.arrl.org/

CHARLES N. FISHER MEMORIAL SCHOLARSHIP

One-time award available to amateur radio operators in any class. Applicant must be majoring in electronics, communications, or a related field. Preference is given to residents of Arizona and Los Angeles, Orange County, San Diego, or Santa Barbara, California. Must attend a regionally accredited institution.

Academic Fields/Career Goals: Applied Sciences; Communications; Electrical Engineering/Electronics; Engineering/Technology.

Award: Scholarship for use in freshman, sophomore, junior, or senior years; not renewable. *Number:* 1. *Amount:* $1000.

Eligibility Requirements: Applicant must be enrolled or expecting to enroll full-time at a four-year institution or university; resident of Arizona, California and must have an interest in amateur radio. Available to U.S. citizens.

Application Requirements: Application form, transcript. *Deadline:* February 1.

Contact: Ms. Mary Hobart, Secretary
Phone: 860-594-0397
E-mail: k1mmh@arrl.org

MISSISSIPPI SCHOLARSHIP

Available to students pursuing a degree in electronics, communications, or related fields. Must be licensed in any class of amateur radio operators. Preference given to residents of Mississippi attending college in Mississippi. Must be under 30 years of age.

Academic Fields/Career Goals: Applied Sciences; Communications; Electrical Engineering/Electronics; Engineering/Technology.

Award: Scholarship for use in freshman, sophomore, junior, or senior years; not renewable. *Number:* 1. *Amount:* $500.

Eligibility Requirements: Applicant must be enrolled or expecting to enroll full-time at a four-year institution or university; resident of Mississippi; studying in Mississippi and must have an interest in amateur

radio. Applicant or parent of applicant must be member of American Radio Relay League. Available to U.S. citizens.

Application Requirements: Application form, transcript. *Deadline:* February 1.

Contact: Ms. Mary Hobart, Secretary
Phone: 860-594-0397
E-mail: k1mmh@arrl.org

PAUL AND HELEN L. GRAUER SCHOLARSHIP

One award available to students licensed as novice amateur radio operators. Applicant must be majoring in electronics, communications, or a related field. Preference given to residents of Iowa, Kansas, Missouri, and Nebraska. Pursuit of a baccalaureate or higher degree preferred at an institution in Iowa, Kansas, Missouri, or Nebraska.

Academic Fields/Career Goals: Applied Sciences; Communications; Electrical Engineering/Electronics; Engineering/Technology.

Award: Scholarship for use in freshman, sophomore, junior, senior, or graduate years; not renewable. *Number:* 1. *Amount:* $1000.

Eligibility Requirements: Applicant must be enrolled or expecting to enroll full-time at a four-year institution or university; resident of Iowa, Kansas, Missouri, Nebraska; studying in Iowa, Kansas, Missouri, Nebraska and must have an interest in amateur radio. Available to U.S. citizens.

Application Requirements: Application form, transcript. *Deadline:* February 1.

Contact: Ms. Mary Hobart, Secretary
Phone: 860-594-0397
E-mail: k1mmh@arrl.org

ASSOCIATION OF CALIFORNIA WATER AGENCIES

http://www.acwa.com/

ASSOCIATION OF CALIFORNIA WATER AGENCIES SCHOLARSHIPS

Three $3000 awards available to juniors and seniors who are California residents attending California universities. Must be in a water-related field of study. Community college transfers are also eligible as long as they will hold junior class standing as of the fall.

Academic Fields/Career Goals: Applied Sciences; Biology; Civil Engineering; Environmental Science; Hydrology; Natural Resources; Natural Sciences; Surveying, Surveying Technology, Cartography, or Geographic Information Science.

Award: Scholarship for use in junior or senior years; not renewable. *Number:* 3. *Amount:* $3000.

Eligibility Requirements: Applicant must be enrolled or expecting to enroll full-time at a four-year institution or university; resident of California and studying in California. Available to U.S. citizens.

Application Requirements: Application form, essay, recommendations or references, transcript. *Deadline:* April 1.

Contact: Ellen Martin, Outreach Specialist
Association of California Water Agencies
901 K Street, Suite 100
Sacramento, CA 95814
Phone: 916-441-4545
Fax: 916-325-2316
E-mail: ellenm@acwa.com

CLAIR A. HILL SCHOLARSHIP

Scholarship is administered by a different member agency each year and guidelines vary based on the administrator. Contact ACWA for current information. Applicants must be in a water-related field of study and must be a resident of California enrolled in a California four-year college or university.

Academic Fields/Career Goals: Applied Sciences; Biology; Civil Engineering; Environmental Science; Hydrology; Natural Resources; Natural Sciences; Surveying, Surveying Technology, Cartography, or Geographic Information Science.

Award: Scholarship for use in junior or senior years; not renewable. *Number:* 1. *Amount:* $5000.

Eligibility Requirements: Applicant must be enrolled or expecting to enroll full-time at a four-year institution or university; resident of California and studying in California. Available to U.S. citizens.

Application Requirements: Application form, essay, recommendations or references, transcript. *Deadline:* February 1.

Contact: Ellen Martin, Communications Coordinator
Association of California Water Agencies
910 K Street, Suite 100
Sacramento, CA 95814
Phone: 916-441-4545
Fax: 916-325-2316
E-mail: ellenm@acwa.com

ASTRONAUT SCHOLARSHIP FOUNDATION

http://www.astronautscholarship.org/

ASTRONAUT SCHOLARSHIP FOUNDATION

Scholarship candidates must be nominated by the faculty members. Students may not apply directly for the scholarship. Must be U.S. citizens. Scholarship nominees must be engineering or natural or applied science students.

Academic Fields/Career Goals: Applied Sciences; Aviation/Aerospace; Biology; Chemical Engineering; Computer Science/Data Processing; Earth Science; Electrical Engineering/Electronics; Engineering-Related Technologies; Materials Science, Engineering, and Metallurgy; Mechanical Engineering; Meteorology/Atmospheric Science.

Award: Scholarship for use in sophomore, junior, senior, or graduate years; renewable. *Number:* 19. *Amount:* $10,000.

Eligibility Requirements: Applicant must be enrolled or expecting to enroll full-time at a four-year institution or university. Available to U.S. citizens.

Application Requirements: Financial need analysis, recommendations or references, transcript. *Deadline:* varies.

Contact: Linn LeBlanc, Executive Director
Astronaut Scholarship Foundation
6225 Vectorspace Boulevard
Titusville, FL 32780
Phone: 321-269-6101 Ext. 6176
Fax: 321-264-9176
E-mail: linnleblanc@astronautscholarship.org

BARRY M. GOLDWATER SCHOLARSHIP AND EXCELLENCE IN EDUCATION FOUNDATION

http://www.act.org/goldwater

BARRY M. GOLDWATER SCHOLARSHIP AND EXCELLENCE IN EDUCATION PROGRAM

One-time award to college juniors and seniors who will pursue advanced degrees in mathematics, natural sciences, or engineering. Students planning to study medicine are eligible if they plan a career in research. Candidates must be nominated by their college or university. Minimum 3.0 GPA required. Nomination deadline: February 1.

Academic Fields/Career Goals: Applied Sciences; Biology; Chemical Engineering; Civil Engineering; Computer Science/Data Processing; Earth Science; Engineering/Technology; Materials Science, Engineering, and Metallurgy; Mechanical Engineering; Natural Sciences; Nuclear Science; Physical Sciences.

Award: Scholarship for use in junior or senior years; renewable. *Number:* up to 300. *Amount:* up to $7500.

Eligibility Requirements: Applicant must be enrolled or expecting to enroll full-time at a two-year or four-year institution or university. Applicant must have 3.0 GPA or higher. Available to U.S. citizens.

Application Requirements: Application form, application form may be submitted online (http://www.act.org/goldwater), essay, institution nomination, recommendations or references, transcript. *Deadline:* February 1.

Contact: Ms. Lucy Decher, Executive Administrator
Phone: 703-756-6012
Fax: 703-756-6015
E-mail: goldh2o@vacoxmail.com

BRITISH COLUMBIA INNOVATION COUNCIL

http://www.bcic.ca/

BCIC YOUNG INNOVATOR SCHOLARSHIP COMPETITION (IDEA MASH UP)

Awards offered by each secondary school in British Columbia to innovative students who enroll full time in a British Columbia post-secondary institution in the year following graduation from grade 12. Must be enrolled in a program in science, technology, engineering, mathematics, digital arts/media design, or business entrepreneurship. Applicants must describe in detail a new technology that is derived from combining two or more current technologies (mechanisms, methods, objects, tools, processes) that can be used to benefit the community or the world. Must not have any negative impact on humans, any other living thing, or the environment, and must have a practical and positive purpose. See website for additional information http://www.bcic.ca.

Academic Fields/Career Goals: Applied Sciences; Biology; Business/Consumer Services; Earth Science; Engineering-Related Technologies; Engineering/Technology; Environmental Science; Graphics/Graphic Arts/Printing; Mathematics; Natural Sciences; Physical Sciences.

Award: Scholarship for use in freshman year; not renewable. *Amount:* $2000–$4000.

Eligibility Requirements: Applicant must be Canadian citizen; high school student and planning to enroll or expecting to enroll full-time at a four-year institution or university.

Application Requirements: Application form, entry in a contest. *Deadline:* June 30.

Contact: Tera Moon, Programs Specialist
British Columbia Innovation Council
1188 West Georgia Street, 9th Floor
Vancouver, BC V6E 4A2
CAN
Phone: 604-602-5253
Fax: 604-683-6567
E-mail: programs@bcic.ca

PAUL AND HELEN TRUSSELL SCIENCE AND TECHNOLOGY SCHOLARSHIP

CAN $5000 to $20,000 award to a new recipient each year over a 4-year period. Student must be enrolled in the sciences and have graduated high school in the Kootenay/Boundary region of British Columbia. Student must be entering 3rd year of studies at a BC or AB post secondary institution. Available to Canadian citizens and landed immigrants.

Academic Fields/Career Goals: Applied Sciences; Biology; Chemical Engineering; Computer Science/Data Processing; Earth Science; Geography; Meteorology/Atmospheric Science; Natural Resources; Natural Sciences; Nuclear Science; Physical Sciences; Science, Technology, and Society.

Award: Scholarship for use in junior or senior years; renewable. *Number:* 1.

Eligibility Requirements: Applicant must be Canadian citizen; enrolled or expecting to enroll full-time at a two-year or four-year institution or university; resident of British Columbia and studying in Alberta, British Columbia. Applicant must have 3.0 GPA or higher.

Application Requirements: Application form, proof of citizenship, recommendations or references, resume, transcript. *Deadline:* May 31.

ELECTROCHEMICAL SOCIETY INC.

http://www.electrochem.org/

H.H. DOW MEMORIAL STUDENT ACHIEVEMENT AWARD OF THE INDUSTRIAL ELECTROLYSIS AND ELECTROCHEMICAL ENGINEERING DIVISION OF THE ELECTROCHEMICAL SOCIETY INC.

Award to recognize promising young engineers and scientists in the field of electrochemical engineering and applied electrochemistry. Applicant must be enrolled or accepted for enrollment in a college or university as a graduate student. Must submit description of proposed research project and how it relates to the field of electrochemistry, a letter of recommendation from research supervisor, and biography or resume.

Academic Fields/Career Goals: Applied Sciences; Chemical Engineering; Electrical Engineering/Electronics; Energy and Power Engineering; Engineering-Related Technologies; Engineering/Technology; Physical Sciences.

Award: Prize for use in freshman, sophomore, junior, senior, or graduate years; not renewable. *Number:* 1. *Amount:* $1000.

Eligibility Requirements: Applicant must be enrolled or expecting to enroll full-time at a four-year institution or university. Available to U.S. and non-U.S. citizens.

Application Requirements: Abstract of research project, statement of relationship of the project to the field of electrochemical engineering or applied electrochemistry, application form, recommendations or references, resume, transcript. *Deadline:* September 15.

Contact: Mrs. Colleen Klepser, Executive Administrator
Phone: 609-737-1902 Ext. 111
Fax: 609-737-2743
E-mail: awards@electrochem.org

STUDENT RESEARCH AWARDS OF THE BATTERY DIVISION OF THE ELECTROCHEMICAL SOCIETY INC.

Award to recognize promising young engineers and scientists in the field of electrochemical power sources. Student must be enrolled or must have been accepted for enrollment at a college or university.

Academic Fields/Career Goals: Applied Sciences; Chemical Engineering; Electrical Engineering/Electronics; Energy and Power Engineering; Engineering-Related Technologies; Engineering/Technology; Materials Science, Engineering, and Metallurgy; Mechanical Engineering; Natural Sciences; Physical Sciences.

Award: Prize for use in freshman, sophomore, junior, senior, or graduate years; not renewable. *Number:* 1. *Amount:* $1000.

Eligibility Requirements: Applicant must be enrolled or expecting to enroll full-time at a four-year institution or university. Available to U.S. and non-U.S. citizens.

Application Requirements: Application form, recommendations or references, resume, transcript, written summary of research accomplished. *Deadline:* March 15.

Contact: Mrs. Colleen Klepser, Executive Administrator
Phone: 609-737-1902 Ext. 111
Fax: 609-737-2743
E-mail: awards@electrochem.org

FOUNDATION FOR SCIENCE AND DISABILITY

http://stemd.org/

GRANTS FOR DISABLED STUDENTS IN THE SCIENCES

Available to graduate students who are disabled. Awards are given for an assistive device or as financial support for scientific research. Undergraduate seniors may apply. One-time award. Electronic application is available.

Academic Fields/Career Goals: Applied Sciences; Biology; Chemical Engineering; Civil Engineering; Computer Science/Data Processing; Electrical Engineering/Electronics; Engineering/Technology; Health and Medical Sciences; Mechanical Engineering; Physical Sciences.

Award: Grant for use in senior or graduate years; not renewable. *Number:* 1–3. *Amount:* $1000.

Eligibility Requirements: Applicant must be hearing impaired, learning disabled, physically disabled, or visually impaired and enrolled or expecting to enroll full-time at an institution or university. Applicant must be hearing impaired, learning disabled, physically disabled, or visually impaired. Available to U.S. citizens.

Application Requirements: Application form, essay, recommendations or references, transcript. *Deadline:* December 1.

Contact: Richard Mankin, Grants Committee Chair
Foundation for Science and Disability
503 89th Street NW
Gainesville, FL 32607
Phone: 352-374-5774
Fax: 352-374-5781
E-mail: rmankin@nersp.nerdc.ufl.edu

INDIAN HEALTH SERVICES, UNITED STATES DEPARTMENT OF HEALTH AND HUMAN SERVICES

http://www.ihs.gov/scholarship

INDIAN HEALTH SERVICE HEALTH PROFESSIONS PRE-GRADUATE SCHOLARSHIPS

Renewable scholarship for American Indian/ Alaska Native students who are enrolled part-time or full-time in courses leading to a bachelor degree in the areas of pre-medicine, pre-dentistry, pre-optometry, or pre-podiatry. Minimum 2.0 GPA, required, to apply. Must intend to serve AI/AN people upon completion of professional healthcare education.

Academic Fields/Career Goals: Applied Sciences; Biology; Health and Medical Sciences.

Award: Scholarship for use in freshman, sophomore, junior, or senior years; renewable. *Number:* 57–107. *Amount:* $28,823–$35,228.

Eligibility Requirements: Applicant must be American Indian/Alaska Native and enrolled or expecting to enroll full- or part-time at a two-year or four-year or technical institution or university. Applicant must have 2.5 GPA or higher. Available to U.S. citizens.

Application Requirements: Application form, application form may be submitted online (http://www.ihs.gov/scholarship), essay, proof of descent, W-4, curriculum for major, course curriculum verification, recommendations or references, transcript. *Deadline:* March 28.

Contact: Capt. Dawn Kelly, Branch Chief
Indian Health Services, United States Department of Health and Human Services
801 Thompson Avenue
Suite 450-A (TMP)
Rockville, MD 20852
Phone: 301-443-6197
Fax: 301-443-6048
E-mail: dawn.kelly@ihs.gov

INTERNATIONAL SOCIETY FOR OPTICAL ENGINEERING-SPIE

http://www.spie.org/scholarships

SPIE EDUCATIONAL SCHOLARSHIPS IN OPTICAL SCIENCE AND ENGINEERING

Scholarships for high school seniors, undergraduate and graduate students who are SPIE student member. High school students will receive a one-year complimentary student membership. Undergraduate and graduate students must be enrolled in an optics, photonics, imaging, optoelectronics program or related discipline for the full year. More details on eligibility and application requirements/forms can be found at http://spie.org/scholarships.

Academic Fields/Career Goals: Applied Sciences; Chemical Engineering; Electrical Engineering/Electronics; Engineering-Related Technologies; Engineering/Technology; Materials Science, Engineering, and Metallurgy; Mechanical Engineering.

Award: Scholarship for use in freshman, sophomore, junior, senior, or graduate years; not renewable. *Number:* 100–150. *Amount:* $2000–$11,000.

Eligibility Requirements: Applicant must be enrolled or expecting to enroll full- or part-time at a two-year or four-year or technical institution or university. Available to U.S. and non-U.S. citizens.

Application Requirements: Application form, essay, recommendations or references. *Deadline:* January 15.

NASA'S VIRGINIA SPACE GRANT CONSORTIUM

http://www.vsgc.odu.edu/

COMMUNITY COLLEGE STEM SCHOLARSHIPS

Scholarship for Virginia community college students studying STEM fields involving science, technology, engineering, and math with aerospace relevance. Must be U.S. citizen with a minimum GPA of 3.0 currently enrolled full-time with at least one semester of coursework (minimum of 12 credit hours) completed.

Academic Fields/Career Goals: Applied Sciences; Biology; Computer Science/Data Processing; Construction Engineering/Management; Drafting; Electrical Engineering/Electronics; Engineering/Technology; Environmental Science; Industrial Design; Materials Science, Engineering, and Metallurgy; Mathematics; Mechanical Engineering.

Award: Scholarship for use in sophomore year; not renewable. *Number:* 1–12. *Amount:* $2000–$2000.

Eligibility Requirements: Applicant must be enrolled or expecting to enroll full-time at a two-year institution and studying in Virginia. Applicant must have 3.0 GPA or higher. Available to U.S. citizens.

Application Requirements: Application form, application form may be submitted online (http://www.vsgc.odu.edu/sf/ccstem/index.shtml), essay, recommendations or references, resume, transcript. *Deadline:* March 16.

Contact: Mr. Chris Carter, Deputy Director
NASA's Virginia Space Grant Consortium
VSGC ODU, PHEC 600 Butler Farm Road
Hampton, VA 23666
Phone: 757-766-5210
Fax: 757-766-5205
E-mail: cxcarter@odu.edu

UNDERGRADUATE STEM RESEARCH SCHOLARSHIPS

Scholarships designated for undergraduate students pursuing any field of study with aerospace relevance. Must attend one of the five Virginia Space Grant colleges and universities. Must have minimum 3.0 GPA. Please refer to website for further details, http://www.vsgc.odu.edu.

Academic Fields/Career Goals: Applied Sciences; Aviation/Aerospace; Biology; Chemical Engineering; Computer Science/Data Processing; Electrical Engineering/Electronics; Engineering-Related Technologies; Materials Science, Engineering, and Metallurgy; Mathematics; Mechanical Engineering; Physical Sciences; Science, Technology, and Society.

Award: Scholarship for use in junior or senior years; not renewable. *Number:* 1–35. *Amount:* $3000–$8500.

Eligibility Requirements: Applicant must be enrolled or expecting to enroll full-time at a four-year institution or university and studying in Virginia. Applicant must have 3.0 GPA or higher. Available to U.S. citizens.

Application Requirements: Application form, application form may be submitted online (http://www.vsgc.odu.edu/sf/undergrad/index.shtml), essay, recommendations or references, resume, transcript. *Deadline:* February 11.

Contact: Mr. Chris Carter, Deputy Director
NASA's Virginia Space Grant Consortium
VSGC, PHEC 600 Butler Farm Road
Hampton, VA 23666
Phone: 757-766-5210
Fax: 757-766-5205

NATIONAL INVENTORS HALL OF FAME

http://www.invent.org/

COLLEGIATE INVENTORS COMPETITION FOR UNDERGRADUATE STUDENTS

National competition to encourage college students to be active in science, engineering, mathematics, technology, and creative invention, while stimulating their problem solving abilities. This prestigious challenge recognizes the working relationship between student and advisor who are involved in projects that can be patented. The prize winning undergraduate student or student-team receives a $10,000 cash prize.

Academic Fields/Career Goals: Applied Sciences; Biology; Chemical Engineering; Computer Science/Data Processing; Engineering-Related Technologies; Engineering/Technology; Environmental Science; Health and Medical Sciences; Materials Science, Engineering, and Metallurgy; Physical Sciences.

Award: Prize for use in freshman, sophomore, junior, or senior years; not renewable. *Number:* up to 1. *Amount:* up to $10,000.

Eligibility Requirements: Applicant must be enrolled or expecting to enroll full-time at a four-year institution or university. Available to U.S. and non-U.S. citizens.

Application Requirements: Application form, entry in a contest. *Deadline:* May 16.

COLLEGIATE INVENTORS COMPETITION-GRAND PRIZE

The competition was designed to encourage college students to be active in science, engineering, mathematics, technology and creative invention, while stimulating their problem-solving abilities. This prestigious challenge recognizes the working relationship between a student and his or her advisor who are involved in projects leading to inventions that can be patented. The winning student or student team receives a $25,000 cash prize. The advisers of the winning entries will receive $3000.

Academic Fields/Career Goals: Applied Sciences; Biology; Chemical Engineering; Computer Science/Data Processing; Engineering-Related Technologies; Engineering/Technology; Environmental Science; Health and Medical Sciences; Materials Science, Engineering, and Metallurgy; Physical Sciences.

Award: Prize for use in freshman, sophomore, junior, senior, graduate, or postgraduate years; not renewable. *Number:* up to 1. *Amount:* up to $25,000.

Eligibility Requirements: Applicant must be enrolled or expecting to enroll full-time at a two-year or four-year institution or university. Available to U.S. and non-U.S. citizens.

Application Requirements: Application form, entry in a contest. *Deadline:* May 16.

NEVADA NASA SPACE GRANT CONSORTIUM

http://www.nvspacegrant.org/

NATIONAL SPACE GRANT COLLEGE AND FELLOWSHIP PROGRAM

The grant provides graduate fellowships and undergraduate scholarship to qualified students majoring in science, technology, engineering, mathematics and science education. Must be a U.S. citizen (permanent residence status, green card or student visa is not accepted)and enrolled full-time in an accredited educational institution in the state of Nevada. Minimum 3.0 GPA required. Awardees cannot receive other federal training grants during the time they are receiving a Nevada NASA Space Grant award.

Academic Fields/Career Goals: Applied Sciences; Aviation/Aerospace; Chemical Engineering; Civil Engineering; Computer Science/Data Processing; Earth Science; Engineering/Technology; Mathematics; Mechanical Engineering; Natural Sciences; Physical Sciences.

Award: Scholarship for use in freshman, sophomore, junior, senior, or graduate years; not renewable. *Number:* 1–50. *Amount:* $1250–$13,333.

Eligibility Requirements: Applicant must be enrolled or expecting to enroll full-time at a two-year or four-year institution or university; resident of Nevada and studying in Nevada. Applicant must have 3.0 GPA or higher. Available to U.S. citizens.

Application Requirements: Application form, application form may be submitted online (http://www.nvspacegrant.org), essay, recommendations or references, research proposal, resume, transcript. *Deadline:* April 28.

Contact: Leone Thierman, Program Coordinator
Nevada NASA Space Grant Consortium
2601 Enterprise Road
Reno, NV 89512
Phone: 775-784-3476
Fax: 775-784-1127
E-mail: nvspacegrant@nshe.nevada.edu

SOCIETY FOR APPLIED ANTHROPOLOGY

http://www.sfaa.net/

ANNUAL SFAA STUDENT ENDOWED AWARD
• See page 100

BEATRICE MEDICINE AWARDS
• See page 101

DEL JONES MEMORIAL TRAVEL AWARD
• See page 101

EDWARD H. AND ROSAMOND B. SPICER TRAVEL AWARDS
• *See page 101*

GIL KUSHNER MEMORIAL TRAVEL AWARD
• *See page 101*

HUMAN RIGHTS DEFENDER STUDENT AWARD
• *See page 101*

VALENE SMITH PRIZE
• *See page 101*

TKE EDUCATIONAL FOUNDATION

http://www.tke.org/

CARROL C. HALL MEMORIAL SCHOLARSHIP

One-time award of $700 given to a full-time undergraduate member of Tau Kappa Epsilon, who is earning a degree in education or science and has plans to become a teacher or pursue a profession in science. Applicant should have a demonstrated record of leadership within his chapter, on campus and the community.

Academic Fields/Career Goals: Applied Sciences; Biology; Earth Science; Education; Meteorology/Atmospheric Science; Physical Sciences.

Award: Scholarship for use in freshman, sophomore, junior, or senior years; not renewable. *Number:* 1. *Amount:* $700.

Eligibility Requirements: Applicant must be enrolled or expecting to enroll full-time at a four-year institution or university and must have an interest in leadership. Applicant or parent of applicant must be member of Tau Kappa Epsilon. Applicant must have 3.0 GPA or higher. Available to U.S. and non-U.S. citizens.

Application Requirements: Application form, essay, personal photograph, transcript. *Deadline:* February 29.

Contact: Gary Reed, President and Chief Executive Officer
TKE Educational Foundation
8645 Founders Road
Indianapolis, IN 46268-1393
Phone: 317-872-6533
Fax: 317-875-8353
E-mail: reedga@tke.org

UNIVERSITIES SPACE RESEARCH ASSOCIATION

http://www.usra.edu/

UNIVERSITIES SPACE RESEARCH ASSOCIATION SCHOLARSHIP PROGRAM

Award for full-time undergraduate students who have completed at least two years of college credit by the time the award is received. Must be majoring in the physical sciences or engineering; which include, but are not limited to, aerospace engineering, astronomy, biophysics, chemistry, chemical engineering, computer science, electrical engineering, geophysics, geology, mathematics, mechanical engineering, physics, and space science education. Must be U.S. citizen. Minimum 3.5 GPA required.

Academic Fields/Career Goals: Applied Sciences; Aviation/ Aerospace; Chemical Engineering; Civil Engineering; Earth Science; Electrical Engineering/Electronics; Engineering/Technology; Materials Science, Engineering, and Metallurgy; Mechanical Engineering; Nuclear Science; Physical Sciences; Science, Technology, and Society.

Award: Scholarship for use in junior or senior years; not renewable. *Number:* 4. *Amount:* $1000.

Eligibility Requirements: Applicant must be enrolled or expecting to enroll full-time at a four-year institution or university. Applicant must have 3.5 GPA or higher. Available to U.S. citizens.

Application Requirements: Application form, essay, recommendations or references, transcript. *Deadline:* May 1.

Contact: Dr. Hussein Jirdeh, Director of University Relations
Universities Space Research Association
10211 Wincopin Circle, Suite 500
Columbia, MD 21044
Phone: 410-730-2656
Fax: 410-730-3496
E-mail: hjirdeh@usra.edu

VERMONT SPACE GRANT CONSORTIUM

http://www.cems.uvm.edu/vsgc

VERMONT SPACE GRANT CONSORTIUM SCHOLARSHIP PROGRAM

Applicant must be a U.S. citizen, Vermont resident, graduating senior in a Vermont high school, or current undergraduate with a minimum 3.0 GPA enrolled full-time for the following academic year in a degree program in a Vermont institution of higher education. Must plan to pursue a professional career which has direct relevance to the U.S. aerospace industry and the goals of NASA. Three awards will be given to Burlington Technical College Aviation Technology Program.

Academic Fields/Career Goals: Applied Sciences; Aviation/ Aerospace; Biology; Computer Science/Data Processing; Earth Science; Engineering-Related Technologies; Engineering/Technology; Materials Science, Engineering, and Metallurgy; Meteorology/Atmospheric Science; Physical Sciences.

Award: Scholarship for use in freshman, sophomore, junior, or senior years; not renewable. *Number:* up to 15. *Amount:* up to $2500.

Eligibility Requirements: Applicant must be enrolled or expecting to enroll full-time at a two-year or four-year or technical institution or university; resident of Vermont and studying in Vermont. Applicant must have 3.0 GPA or higher. Available to U.S. citizens.

Application Requirements: Application form, application form may be submitted online (http://www.cems.uvm.edu/VSGC), essay, recommendations or references, test scores; transcript. *Deadline:* April 13.

Contact: Laurel Zeno, Program Coordinator
Vermont Space Grant Consortium
University of Vermont, College of Engineering and Math, Votey Hall
Burlington, VT 05405-0156
Phone: 802-656-1429
Fax: 802-656-1102
E-mail: lczeno@uvm.edu

WHOMENTORS.COM, INC.

http://www.WHOmentors.com/

1B USD WORLDWIDE VENTURE CAPITAL

This is an open call for new creative ideas. Any unincorporated, workable nonexempt project proposals will be considered. 1. What is the nonexempt project idea? 2. Who conducts the nonexempt project? 3. When is the nonexempt project conducted? 4. Where is the nonexempt project conducted? 5. How does the nonexempt project further the 501(c)(3) exempt purposes of WHOmentors.com, Inc.? 6. What percentage of your total time is allocated to the nonexempt project? 7. How will the activity earn revenue beyond the startup grant?

Academic Fields/Career Goals: Applied Sciences; Aviation/ Aerospace; Business/Consumer Services; Campus Activities; Communications; Computer Science/Data Processing; Fashion Design; Filmmaking/Video; Industrial Design; Marketing; Materials Science, Engineering, and Metallurgy; Science, Technology, and Society.

Award: Grant for use in freshman, sophomore, junior, senior, graduate, or postgraduate years; not renewable. *Number:* 1–20. *Amount:* $2000–$20,000.

Eligibility Requirements: Applicant must be of Chinese, Japanese, Korean heritage and Chinese, Japanese, Korean citizen; age 12-30; enrolled or expecting to enroll full- or part-time at a two-year or four-year or technical institution or university; single female and must have an interest in Asian language, entrepreneurship, foreign language, international exchange, or public speaking. Available to U.S. and non-U.S. citizens.

Application Requirements: Application form, application form may be submitted online (http://WHOmentors.com/startupgrantapplication), autobiography, community service, complete 10 week, 300 hrs internship., driver's license, essay, financial need analysis, interview, personal photograph, portfolio, recommendations or references, resume, self-addressed stamped envelope with application, test scores, transcript. *Deadline:* continuous.

Contact: Rauhmel Fox, CEO
WHOmentors.com, Inc.
110 Pacific Avenue, Suite 250
San Francisco, CA 94111
Phone: 415-373-6767
E-mail: rauhmel@whomentors.com

ARCHAEOLOGY

AMERICAN PHILOLOGICAL ASSOCIATION

http://www.apaclassics.org/

MINORITY STUDENT SUMMER SCHOLARSHIP

Award to minority undergraduate students for a scholarship to further an undergraduate's preparation for graduate work in classics or archaeology. Applicants should be current students of classics. Eligible proposals might include (but are not limited to) participation in summer programs or field schools in Italy, Greece, Egypt, or language training at institutions in the U.S, Canada, or Europe. Amount of the award will range from $1,500 to $4,000. Application must be supported by a member of the APA.

Academic Fields/Career Goals: Archaeology; Arts; Classics; Foreign Language; History.

Award: Scholarship for use in freshman, sophomore, junior, or senior years; not renewable. *Number:* 2. *Amount:* $1500–$4000.

Eligibility Requirements: Applicant must be American Indian/Alaska Native, Asian/Pacific Islander, Black (non-Hispanic), Hispanic and enrolled or expecting to enroll full-time at a four-year institution or university. Available to U.S. and non-U.S. citizens.

Application Requirements: Application form, essay, financial need analysis, recommendations or references, transcript. *Deadline:* December 11.

Contact: Dr. Adam Blistein, Executive Director
Phone: 215-898-4975
Fax: 215-573-7874
E-mail: apaclassics@sas.upenn.edu

AMERICAN SCHOOL OF CLASSICAL STUDIES AT ATHENS

http://www.ascsa.edu.gr/

ASCSA SUMMER SESSIONS SCHOLARSHIPS

• *See page 100*

ARCHAEOLOGICAL INSTITUTE OF AMERICA

http://www.archaeological.org/

JANE C. WALDBAUM ARCHAEOLOGICAL FIELD SCHOOL SCHOLARSHIP

Scholarship available to support participation in an archaeological excavation or survey project. Open to junior and senior undergraduates and first-year graduate students who are currently enrolled in a U.S. or Canadian college or university. Applicants cannot have previously participated in an archaeological excavation, and must be at least a junior at time of application. Applicants must be at least 18 years of age. The annual deadline is the first Sunday in March (the next deadline is March 10, 2013).

Academic Fields/Career Goals: Archaeology.

Award: Scholarship for use in junior, senior, or graduate years; not renewable. *Number:* 7–15. *Amount:* $1000.

Eligibility Requirements: Applicant must be enrolled or expecting to enroll full- or part-time at a four-year institution or university. Available to U.S. and non-U.S. citizens.

Application Requirements: Application form, application form may be submitted online (http://www.archaeological.org/grants/703), recommendations or references, transcript. *Deadline:* March 1.

Contact: Laurel Sparks, Coordinator, Lecture and Fellowship
Phone: 617-358-4184
Fax: 617-353-6550
E-mail: lsparks@aia.bu.edu

HARVARD TRAVELLERS CLUB

http://www.harvardtravellersclub.org/

HARVARD TRAVELLERS CLUB GRANTS

Approximately three grants made each year to persons with projects that involve intelligent travel and exploration. The travel must be intimately involved with research and/or exploration. Prefer applications from persons working on advanced degrees.

Academic Fields/Career Goals: Archaeology; Area/Ethnic Studies; Geography; History; Humanities; Natural Sciences.

Award: Grant for use in freshman, sophomore, junior, senior, graduate, or postgraduate years; not renewable. *Number:* 3–4. *Amount:* $500–$1000.

Eligibility Requirements: Applicant must be enrolled or expecting to enroll full- or part-time at a four-year institution or university. Available to U.S. and non-U.S. citizens.

Application Requirements: Autobiography, financial need analysis, recommendations or references, resume. *Deadline:* February 28.

Contact: Mr. Jesse Page, Trustee
Harvard Travellers Club
PO Box 162
Lincoln, MA 01773
Phone: 781-259-8665
E-mail: jessepage@comcast.net

ARCHITECTURE

AACE INTERNATIONAL

http://www.aacei.org/

AACE INTERNATIONAL COMPETITIVE SCHOLARSHIP

One-time awards to full-time students pursuing a degree in engineering, construction management, quantity surveying, and related fields. Applications accepted between January 1 and February 15. For more information, visit website http://www.aacei.org/awards/scholarships/.

Academic Fields/Career Goals: Architecture; Aviation/Aerospace; Business/Consumer Services; Chemical Engineering; Civil Engineering; Construction Engineering/Management; Electrical Engineering; Electronics; Engineering-Related Technologies; Engineering/Technology; Mechanical Engineering.

Award: Scholarship for use in freshman, sophomore, junior, senior, or graduate years; not renewable. *Number:* 15–25. *Amount:* $2000–$8000.

Eligibility Requirements: Applicant must be enrolled or expecting to enroll full-time at a two-year or four-year institution or university. Available to U.S. and non-U.S. citizens.

Application Requirements: Application form, application form may be submitted online (http://www.aacei.org/awards/scholarships/), entry in a contest, essay, recommendations or references, transcript. *Deadline:* February 15.

Contact: Ms. Ashley Alexander, Administrator-Education
AACE International
209 Prairie Avenue, Suite 100
Morgantown, WV 26501
Phone: 304-296-8444 Ext. 115
Fax: 304-291-5728
E-mail: aalexander@aacei.org

AIA NEW JERSEY SCHOLARSHIP FOUNDATION, INC.

http://www.aia-nj.org/

AIA NEW JERSEY SCHOLARSHIP PROGRAM

Scholarship available to New Jersey residents or residents from other states attending school in New Jersey. Must be full-time student in an accredited architectural program at a School of Architecture and have completed one full year of study toward a first professional degree. Applicant must indicate interest in and commitment to pursuing an architectural career in New Jersey after graduation. See website for more information and application, http://www.aia-nj.org/about/scholarship.shtml.

Academic Fields/Career Goals: Architecture.

Award: Scholarship for use in sophomore, junior, senior, or graduate years; renewable. *Number:* 3–5. *Amount:* $2500–$5000.

Eligibility Requirements: Applicant must be age 19-26; enrolled or expecting to enroll full-time at a four-year institution or university; resident of New Jersey; studying in New Jersey and must have an interest in art. Available to U.S. citizens.

Application Requirements: Application form, essay, financial need analysis, portfolio, recommendations are optional, transcript. *Fee:* $5. *Deadline:* June 9.

Contact: Ms. Cris Miseo, Secretary/Treasurer, AIA NJ Scholarship Foundation
AIA New Jersey Scholarship Foundation, Inc.
Miseo Associates, Architect
205 Mt. Pleasant Avenue
East Hanover, NH 07936
Phone: 973-533-0002
E-mail: miseoarchitect@yahoo.com

AMERICAN INSTITUTE OF ARCHITECTS

http://www.aia.org/

AIA/AAF MINORITY/DISADVANTAGED SCHOLARSHIP

Award to aid high school seniors and college freshmen from minority or disadvantaged backgrounds who are planning to study architecture in an NAAB accredited program. Twenty awards per year, renewable for two additional years. Amounts based on financial need. Must include one letter of recommendation from a high school guidance counselor, AIA component, architect, or other individual who is aware of the student's interest and aptitude. Applications are due in March.

Academic Fields/Career Goals: Architecture.

Award: Scholarship for use in freshman year; renewable. *Number:* 20. *Amount:* $500–$2500.

Eligibility Requirements: Applicant must be American Indian/Alaska Native, Asian/Pacific Islander, Black (non-Hispanic), Hispanic and enrolled or expecting to enroll full-time at a two-year or four-year or technical institution or university. Available to U.S. citizens.

Application Requirements: Application form, essay, recommendations or references, statement of disadvantaged circumstances, drawing, transcript. *Deadline:* varies.

Contact: Jamie Yeung, AIA Scholarships
American Institute of Architects
1735 New York Avenue, NW
Washington, DC 20006-5292
Phone: 202-626-7529
Fax: 202-626-7509
E-mail: scholarships@aia.org

AMERICAN INSTITUTE OF ARCHITECTS WEST VIRGINIA CHAPTER

http://www.aiawv.org/

AIA WEST VIRGINIA SCHOLARSHIP PROGRAM

Applicant must have completed junior year of an accredited undergraduate architectural program or enrolled in an accredited Master of Architecture program. Applicant must present a portfolio of work to judging committee. The number of scholarships awarded varies based on the number of applicants. Award will be sent to recipient's school for disbursement for the following semester fees. For additional information, go to website http://www.aiawv.org.

Academic Fields/Career Goals: Architecture.

Award: Scholarship for use in senior year; not renewable. *Amount:* up to $12,500.

Eligibility Requirements: Applicant must be enrolled or expecting to enroll full-time at a four-year institution or university and resident of West Virginia. Available to U.S. citizens.

Application Requirements: Application form, personal letter, examples of work, recommendations or references, resume, transcript. *Deadline:* May 30.

Contact: Roberta Guffey, Executive Director
American Institute of Architects West Virginia Chapter
223 Hale Street
Charleston, WV 25301
Phone: 304-344-9872
Fax: 304-343-0205
E-mail: roberta.guffey@aiawv.org

AMERICAN SCHOOL OF CLASSICAL STUDIES AT ATHENS

http://www.ascsa.edu.gr/

ASCSA SUMMER SESSIONS SCHOLARSHIPS

• *See page 100*

AMERICAN SOCIETY OF HEATING, REFRIGERATING, AND AIR CONDITIONING ENGINEERS, INC.

http://www.ashrae.org/

ASHRAE REGION IV BENNY BOOTLE SCHOLARSHIP

One-year scholarship available to an undergraduate engineering or architecture student enrolled full-time in a program accredited by ABET or NAAB and attending a school located within the geographic boundaries of ASHRAE Region IV (North Carolina, South Carolina, Georgia). See website for application and additional information, http://www.ashrae.org.

Academic Fields/Career Goals: Architecture; Engineering/Technology.

Award: Scholarship for use in freshman, sophomore, junior, or senior years; not renewable. *Number:* 1. *Amount:* $3000.

Eligibility Requirements: Applicant must be enrolled or expecting to enroll full-time at a four-year institution or university and studying in Georgia, North Carolina, South Carolina. Applicant must have 3.0 GPA or higher. Available to U.S. and non-U.S. citizens.

Application Requirements: Application form, financial need analysis, recommendations or references, transcript. *Deadline:* December 1.

Contact: Lois Benedict, Scholarship Administrator
Phone: 404-636-8400 Ext. 1120
E-mail: lbenedict@ashrae.org

ASSOCIATION FOR WOMEN IN ARCHITECTURE FOUNDATION

http://www.awa-la.org/

ASSOCIATION FOR WOMEN IN ARCHITECTURE FOUNDATION SCHOLARSHIP

Must be a California resident or attend school in California. Open to women only. Must major in architecture or a related design field and have completed 18 units in that major. Recipients may reapply. Applications available for download on website http://www.awa-la.org/scholarships.

Academic Fields/Career Goals: Architecture; Engineering/Technology; Interior Design; Landscape Architecture; Urban and Regional Planning.

Award: Scholarship for use in sophomore, junior, senior, or graduate years; not renewable. *Number:* 2–6. *Amount:* $1000.

Eligibility Requirements: Applicant must be enrolled or expecting to enroll full-time at a two-year or four-year or technical institution or university and female. Available to U.S. and non-U.S. citizens.

Application Requirements: Application form, personal statement, portfolio, recommendations or references, self-addressed stamped envelope with application, transcript. *Deadline:* April 15.

Contact: Stephanie Oestreich, Scholarship Chair
        E-mail: scholarships@awa-la.org

BRASKEM ODEBRECHT

http://www.odebrechtaward.com

ODEBRECHT AWARD FOR SUSTAINABLE DEVELOPMENT

Award for undergraduate students in all engineering fields, architecture, building and construction management, and chemistry. By submitting a paper that outlines contributions to sustainability, students have an opportunity to win $65,000 in cash prizes for themselves, their faculty advisors and their universities. Ideas can be related to efficient, real-world uses of sustainable materials, new chemical and petrochemical processes or new building techniques. Must register at website to enter.

Academic Fields/Career Goals: Architecture; Chemical Engineering; Civil Engineering; Construction Engineering/Management; Electrical Engineering/Electronics; Energy and Power Engineering; Mechanical Engineering.

Award: Prize for use in freshman, sophomore, junior, or senior years; not renewable.

Eligibility Requirements: Applicant must be enrolled or expecting to enroll at a four-year institution or university. Available to U.S. citizens.

Application Requirements: Application form, application form may be submitted online, recommendations or references, university identification. *Deadline:* May 31.

CENTER FOR ARCHITECTURE

http://www.cfafoundation.org/scholarships

CENTER FOR ARCHITECTURE, DOUGLAS HASKELL AWARD FOR STUDENT JOURNALS

Any journal (online or print) published by a school of architecture, landscape architecture or planning in the United States that is edited by students is eligible. The publication must have been produced in the current or previous school year.

Academic Fields/Career Goals: Architecture; Engineering/Technology; Landscape Architecture; Urban and Regional Planning.

Award: Prize for use in freshman, sophomore, junior, senior, or graduate years; not renewable. *Number:* 1–3. *Amount:* $2000–$5000.

Eligibility Requirements: Applicant must be enrolled or expecting to enroll full- or part-time at a two-year or four-year or technical institution or university and must have an interest in writing. Available to U.S. citizens.

Application Requirements: Application form, essay, portfolio. *Deadline:* May 1.

CENTER FOR ARCHITECTURE, WOMEN'S AUXILIARY ELEANOR ALLWORK SCHOLARSHIP

Students seeking their first degree in architecture from an NAAB accredited school within the State of New York are eligible. The Dean or Chair of the architectural school shall nominate up to three students from their respective college or university to apply. Nominated students will have a high level of academic performance and evidence of financial need. The financial need of each student shall be determined by the guidelines of the Financial Aid Officer of the school nominating the candidate. Students need not be U.S. citizens.

Academic Fields/Career Goals: Architecture.

Award: Scholarship for use in freshman, sophomore, junior, senior, or graduate years; not renewable. *Number:* 1–3. *Amount:* $5000–$15,000.

Eligibility Requirements: Applicant must be enrolled or expecting to enroll full-time at a four-year institution or university; resident of New York and studying in New York. Available to U.S. citizens.

Application Requirements: Application form, portfolio, recommendations or references, resume. *Deadline:* March 15.

THE DALLAS FOUNDATION

http://www.dallasfoundation.org/

DALLAS CENTER FOR ARCHITECTURE FOUNDATION—HKS/JOHN HUMPHRIES SCHOLARSHIP

The scholarship must be used in the year it is awarded. If the funds are not used in this time period, they will be forfeited. The funds are intended to be used for college tuition towards a degree in architecture, and as such, will be routed directly to the appropriate college office for credit towards tuition. Must be a Dallas city resident.

Academic Fields/Career Goals: Architecture.

Award: Scholarship for use in freshman year; not renewable. *Amount:* $2000.

Eligibility Requirements: Applicant must be high school student; planning to enroll or expecting to enroll full-time at a four-year institution or university and resident of Texas.

Application Requirements: Application form, essay, portfolio, recommendations or references, transcript. *Deadline:* March 31.

Contact: Rachel Lasseter, Program Associate
        Phone: 214-741-9898
        E-mail: scholarships@dallasfoundation.org

WHITLEY PLACE SCHOLARSHIP

Established in 2009, the Whitley Place Scholarship seeks to provide aid to graduating seniors in Prosper ISD who plan to study civil engineering, construction science, construction management, architecture, landscape architecture, planning, public administration, mechanical engineering or other math/science related fields.

Academic Fields/Career Goals: Architecture; Civil Engineering; Engineering/Technology; Landscape Architecture; Mathematics; Mechanical Engineering; Physical Sciences; Public Policy and Administration.

Award: Scholarship for use in freshman, sophomore, junior, or senior years; renewable. *Amount:* $2500.

Eligibility Requirements: Applicant must be high school student; planning to enroll or expecting to enroll full-time at a two-year or four-year institution or university and resident of Texas. Applicant must have 3.0 GPA or higher.

Application Requirements: Application form, driver's license, financial need analysis, recommendations or references, resume, transcript. *Deadline:* March 31.

Contact: Rachel Lasseter, Program Associate
        Phone: 214-741-9898
        E-mail: scholarships@dallasfoundation.org

FLORIDA EDUCATIONAL FACILITIES PLANNERS' ASSOCIATION

http://www.fefpa.org/

FEFPA ASSISTANTSHIP

Renewable scholarship for full-time sophomores, juniors, seniors and graduate students enrolled in an accredited four-year Florida university or community college, majoring in facilities planning or a field related to facilities planning. Must be a resident of Florida with a 3.0 GPA.

Academic Fields/Career Goals: Architecture; Construction Engineering/Management.

Award: Scholarship for use in sophomore, junior, senior, or graduate years; renewable. *Number:* 2. *Amount:* $3000.

Eligibility Requirements: Applicant must be enrolled or expecting to enroll full-time at a four-year institution or university; resident of Florida and studying in Florida. Applicant must have 3.0 GPA or higher. Available to U.S. and non-U.S. citizens.

Application Requirements: Application form, essay, financial need analysis, recommendations or references, test scores, transcript. *Deadline:* June 1.

Contact: Robert Griffith, Selection Committee Chair
        Phone: 305-348-4070 Ext. 4002
        Fax: 305-341-3377
        E-mail: griffith@fiu.edu

GARDEN CLUB OF AMERICA

http://www.gcamerica.org/

GCA AWARD IN DESERT STUDIES

One or more awards of $4000 to promote the study of horticulture, conservation, botany, environmental science and landscape design relating to the arid landscape. Open to graduate or advanced undergraduate students studying in an accredited US university.

Academic Fields/Career Goals: Architecture; Environmental Science; Horticulture/Floriculture; Landscape Architecture; Natural Sciences.

Award: Prize for use in junior, senior, or graduate years; not renewable. *Number:* 1. *Amount:* $4000.

Eligibility Requirements: Applicant must be enrolled or expecting to enroll full-time at a four-year institution or university. Available to U.S. citizens.

Application Requirements: Application form, recommendations or references, resume, transcript. *Deadline:* January 15.

Contact: Kenny Zelov, Assistant Director of Horticulture, Desert Botanical Garden
Garden Club of America
1201 North Galvin Parkway
Phoenix, AZ 85008
Phone: 408-481-8162
E-mail: kzelov@dbg.org

THE GEORGIA TRUST FOR HISTORIC PRESERVATION

http://www.georgiatrust.org/

J. NEEL REID PRIZE

A $4000 fellowship is given to an architecture student, architecture intern or a recently-registered architect residing, studying or working in Georgia. Proposed projects should involve the study of an aspect of classic architecture.

Academic Fields/Career Goals: Architecture; Historic Preservation and Conservation; Landscape Architecture.

Award: Prize for use in sophomore, junior, senior, graduate, or postgraduate years; not renewable. *Number:* 1. *Amount:* $4000.

Eligibility Requirements: Applicant must be enrolled or expecting to enroll full- or part-time at a four-year institution or university and resident of Georgia. Available to U.S. and non-U.S. citizens.

Application Requirements: Application form, essay, portfolio, proposed itinerary and budget for travel study, recommendations or references, resume. *Deadline:* February 9.

Contact: Ms. Kate Ryan, Director of Preservation
The Georgia Trust for Historic Preservation
1516 Peachtree Street, NW
Atlanta, GA 30309
Phone: 404-885-7817
E-mail: kryan@georgiatrust.org

HELLENIC UNIVERSITY CLUB OF PHILADELPHIA

http://www.hucphila.org/

DIMITRI J. VERVERELLI MEMORIAL SCHOLARSHIP FOR ARCHITECTURE AND/OR ENGINEERING

$2000 award for full-time student enrolled in an architecture or engineering degree program at an accredited four-year college or university. High school seniors accepted for enrollment in such a degree program may also apply. Must be a U.S. citizen of Greek descent and a resident of particular counties in NJ or PA.

Academic Fields/Career Goals: Architecture; Engineering/ Technology.

Award: Scholarship for use in freshman, sophomore, junior, or senior years; not renewable. *Amount:* up to $2000.

Eligibility Requirements: Applicant must be of Greek heritage; enrolled or expecting to enroll full-time at a four-year institution or university and resident of New Jersey, Pennsylvania. Available to U.S. citizens.

Application Requirements: Application form, financial need analysis, transcript. *Deadline:* April 21.

Contact: Anna Hadgis, Scholarship Chairman
Phone: 610-613-4310
E-mail: hucphila@yahoo.com

ILLUMINATING ENGINEERING SOCIETY OF NORTH AMERICA

http://www.iesna.org/

ROBERT W. THUNEN MEMORIAL SCHOLARSHIPS

One-time award for juniors, seniors, or graduate students enrolled at four-year colleges and universities in northern California, Nevada, Oregon, or Washington pursuing lighting career. Must submit statement describing proposed lighting course work or project and three recommendations, at least one from someone involved professionally or academically with lighting. Curriculum must be accredited by ABET, ACSA, or FIDER.

Academic Fields/Career Goals: Architecture; Engineering-Related Technologies; Engineering/Technology; Interior Design; Performing Arts; TV/Radio Broadcasting.

Award: Scholarship for use in junior, senior, or graduate years; not renewable. *Number:* 2. *Amount:* $2500.

Eligibility Requirements: Applicant must be enrolled or expecting to enroll full-time at a four-year institution or university and studying in California, Nevada, Oregon, Washington. Available to U.S. and non-U.S. citizens.

Application Requirements: Application form, recommendations or references, transcript. *Deadline:* April 1.

Contact: Phil Hall, Chairman
Phone: 510-864-0204
Fax: 510-248-5017
E-mail: mrcatisbac@aol.com

ILLUMINATING ENGINEERING SOCIETY OF NORTH AMERICA–GOLDEN GATE SECTION

http://www.iesgg.org/

ALAN LUCAS MEMORIAL EDUCATIONAL SCHOLARSHIP

Scholarship available to full-time student for pursuit of lighting education or research as part of undergraduate, graduate, or doctoral studies. Scholarships may be made by those who will be a junior, senior, or graduate student in an accredited four-year college or university located in Northern California. The scholarships to be awarded will be at least $1500.

Academic Fields/Career Goals: Architecture; Electrical Engineering/ Electronics; Filmmaking/Video; Interior Design.

Award: Scholarship for use in junior, senior, or graduate years; not renewable. *Number:* 1. *Amount:* $1500.

Eligibility Requirements: Applicant must be enrolled or expecting to enroll full-time at a four-year institution or university and studying in California. Available to U.S. citizens.

Application Requirements: Application form, recommendations or references, statement of purpose, description of work in progress, scholar agreement form, transcript. *Deadline:* April 1.

Contact: Phil Hall, Scholarship Committee
Phone: 510-864-0204
Fax: 510-864-8511
E-mail: iesggthunenfund@aol.com

INTERNATIONAL FACILITY MANAGEMENT ASSOCIATION FOUNDATION

http://www.ifmafoundation.org/

IFMA FOUNDATION SCHOLARSHIPS

One-time scholarships of up to $5000 awarded to students currently enrolled in full-time facility management programs or related programs. Minimum 3.2 GPA required for undergraduates and 3.5 for graduate students.

Academic Fields/Career Goals: Architecture; Construction Engineering/Management; Engineering-Related Technologies; Engineering/Technology; Interior Design; Urban and Regional Planning.

Award: Scholarship for use in junior, senior, graduate, or postgraduate years; not renewable. *Number:* 25–35. *Amount:* $1500–$5000.

Eligibility Requirements: Applicant must be enrolled or expecting to enroll full-time at a four-year institution or university. Available to U.S. and non-U.S. citizens.

Application Requirements: Application form, letter of professional intent, recommendations or references, resume, transcript. *Deadline:* May 31.

Contact: William Rub, Executive Director
International Facility Management Association Foundation
One East Greenway Plaza, Suite 1100
Houston, TX 77046
Phone: 713-623-4362 Ext. 158
E-mail: william.rub@ifma.org

MIDWEST ROOFING CONTRACTORS ASSOCIATION

http://www.mrca.org/

MRCA FOUNDATION SCHOLARSHIP PROGRAM

Renewable scholarships for full-time students enrolled or intending to enroll in an accredited university, college, community college, or trade school. Applicant must be pursuing a curriculum leading to a career in the construction industry or related. Award amount ranges from $500 to $3000.

Academic Fields/Career Goals: Architecture; Civil Engineering; Construction Engineering/Management; Drafting; Engineering/Technology; Industrial Design; Materials Science, Engineering, and Metallurgy; Trade/Technical Specialties.

Award: Scholarship for use in freshman, sophomore, junior, or senior years; not renewable. *Number:* up to 40. *Amount:* $500–$3000.

Eligibility Requirements: Applicant must be enrolled or expecting to enroll full-time at a two-year or four-year or technical institution or university. Applicant or parent of applicant must have employment or volunteer experience in construction. Applicant must have 3.0 GPA or higher. Available to U.S. citizens.

Application Requirements: Application form, community service, essay, financial need analysis, recommendations or references, transcript. *Deadline:* June 20.

Contact: Ms. Peggy Doherty, Operations Manager
Midwest Roofing Contractors Association
4700 West Lake Avenue
Glenview, IL 60025
Phone: 847-375-6378
Fax: 847-375-6473

NATIONAL ASSOCIATION OF WOMEN IN CONSTRUCTION

http://www.nawic.org/

NAWIC UNDERGRADUATE SCHOLARSHIPS

One-time award for any student having at least one year of study remaining in a construction-related program leading to an associate or higher degree. Awards range from $500 to $2000. Submit application and transcript of grades.

Academic Fields/Career Goals: Architecture; Civil Engineering; Drafting; Electrical Engineering/Electronics; Engineering-Related Technologies; Engineering/Technology; Interior Design; Landscape Architecture; Mechanical Engineering; Trade/Technical Specialties.

Award: Scholarship for use in sophomore or junior years; not renewable. *Number:* 40–50. *Amount:* $500–$2000.

Eligibility Requirements: Applicant must be enrolled or expecting to enroll full-time at a two-year or four-year or technical institution or university. Applicant must have 3.0 GPA or higher. Available to U.S. and Canadian citizens.

Application Requirements: Application form, essay, financial need analysis, interview, transcript. *Deadline:* March 15.

OREGON STUDENT ASSISTANCE COMMISSION

http://www.GetCollegeFunds.org/

HOME BUILDERS FOUNDATION JIM IRVINE STATEWIDE SCHOLARSHIP

One-time award for first-year freshmen or other undergraduates studying architecture, construction, engineering (civil, electrical, industrial, management), interior design/architecture, or landscape architecture in an Oregon college or university. Must be enrolled at least half time, write an essay, and complete the FAFSA. Minimum 3.0 GPA preferred.

Academic Fields/Career Goals: Architecture; Civil Engineering; Electrical Engineering/Electronics; Engineering/Technology; Interior Design; Landscape Architecture.

Award: Scholarship for use in freshman, sophomore, junior, or senior years; not renewable.

Eligibility Requirements: Applicant must be enrolled or expecting to enroll full- or part-time at a two-year or four-year institution or university and studying in Oregon. Available to U.S. citizens.

Application Requirements: Application form, essay. *Deadline:* March 1.

SOUTHERN OREGON ARCHITECTS SCHOLARSHIP

Award available to graduating high school seniors (including home-schooled students) and graduates of Curry, Harney, Jackson, Josephine, Klamath, Lake, or Malheur County high schools. Must attend a four-year nonprofit college or university in the United States, major in architecture, and be a U.S. citizen. Apply/compete for one additional year.

Academic Fields/Career Goals: Architecture.

Award: Scholarship for use in freshman, sophomore, junior, or senior years; not renewable.

Eligibility Requirements: Applicant must be enrolled or expecting to enroll full-time at a four-year institution or university and resident of Oregon. Available to U.S. citizens.

Application Requirements: Application form, FAFSA, transcript. *Deadline:* March 1.

RHODE ISLAND FOUNDATION

http://www.rifoundation.org/

NORTON E. SALK SCHOLARSHIP

Scholarship for a student enrolled in an accredited school in Rhode Island and pursuing the study of architecture. Must have completed at least one academic year and demonstrate financial need.

Academic Fields/Career Goals: Architecture.

Award: Scholarship for use in sophomore, junior, or senior years; not renewable.

Eligibility Requirements: Applicant must be enrolled or expecting to enroll full-time at a four-year institution or university and studying in Rhode Island. Available to U.S. citizens.

Application Requirements: Application form, essay, financial need analysis, letter of eligibility for financial aid, recommendations or references. *Deadline:* June 15.

TURNER CONSTRUCTION COMPANY

http://www.turnerconstruction.com/

YOUTHFORCE 2020 SCHOLARSHIP PROGRAM

The scholarship will be awarded to five graduating high school seniors from New York City schools and in the amount of $2000 per year; totaling $8000 after the completion of four years in college. As a scholarship recipient, students must maintain a 2.80 GPA and complete a four-year summer internship at Turner Construction that begins immediately following their first full year of college.

Academic Fields/Career Goals: Architecture; Civil Engineering; Construction Engineering/Management; Electrical Engineering/Electronics; Engineering-Related Technologies; Engineering/Technology; Interior Design; Landscape Architecture; Materials Science, Engineering, and Metallurgy; Mechanical Engineering.

Award: Scholarship for use in freshman, sophomore, junior, or senior years; renewable. *Number:* 5. *Amount:* $8000.

Eligibility Requirements: Applicant must be American Indian/Alaska Native, Asian/Pacific Islander, Black (non-Hispanic), Hispanic; high school student; planning to enroll or expecting to enroll full-time at a four-year institution or university; resident of New York and studying in New York. Applicant must have 3.0 GPA or higher. Available to U.S. citizens.

Application Requirements: Application form, community service, essay, financial need analysis, interview, personal photograph, recommendations or references, resume, test scores, transcript. *Deadline:* April 30.

Contact: Stephanie Burns, Community Affairs Director
Turner Construction Company
375 Hudson Street
6th Floor
New York, NY 10014
Phone: 212-229-6000 Ext. 6480
Fax: 212-229-6083
E-mail: yf2020@tcco.com

UNITED NEGRO COLLEGE FUND

http://www.uncf.org/

GILBANE SCHOLARSHIP PROGRAM

Scholarship provides financial assistance for African American undergraduate sophomores or juniors who are residents of New Jersey, Pennsylvania, and Delaware, and have completed a paid summer internship program with Gilbane. Applicants must major in engineering, mathematics, or architecture at a participating UNCF member, HBCU, or majority institution. Minimum 2.5 GPA required. Information and online application at website http://www.uncf.org.

Academic Fields/Career Goals: Architecture; Engineering/Technology; Mathematics.

Award: Scholarship for use in sophomore or junior years; not renewable. *Number:* 1. *Amount:* $5000–$6000.

Eligibility Requirements: Applicant must be Black (non-Hispanic); enrolled or expecting to enroll full-time at a four-year institution or university and resident of Delaware, New Jersey, Pennsylvania. Applicant must have 2.5 GPA or higher. Available to U.S. citizens.

Application Requirements: Application form. *Deadline:* November 20.

WEST VIRGINIA SOCIETY OF ARCHITECTS/AIA

http://www.aiawv.org/

WEST VIRGINIA SOCIETY OF ARCHITECTS/AIA SCHOLARSHIP

Award for a West Virginia resident who has completed at least their sixth semester of an NAAB-accredited architectural program by application deadline. Must submit resume and letter stating need, qualifications, and desire.

Academic Fields/Career Goals: Architecture.

Award: Scholarship for use in junior, senior, graduate, or postgraduate years; not renewable. *Amount:* up to $11,000.

Eligibility Requirements: Applicant must be enrolled or expecting to enroll full-time at an institution or university and resident of West Virginia. Available to U.S. citizens.

Application Requirements: Application form, recommendations or references, resume, transcript. *Deadline:* May 30.

Contact: Ms. Roberta Guffey, Executive Director
West Virginia Society of Architects/AIA
223 Hale Street
Charleston, WV 25323
Phone: 304-344-9872
Fax: 304-343-0205
E-mail: roberta.guffey@aiawv.org

AREA/ETHNIC STUDIES

AMERICAN COUNCIL FOR POLISH CULTURE

http://www.polishcultureacpc.org/

ACPC SUMMER STUDIES IN POLAND SCHOLARSHIP

Scholarship enables American students of Polish descent to participate in summer study offered by many of Poland's universities. Must be entering junior or senior year at a college or university.

Academic Fields/Career Goals: Area/Ethnic Studies; Foreign Language.

Award: Scholarship for use in junior or senior years; not renewable. *Number:* 2. *Amount:* $2000.

Eligibility Requirements: Applicant must be of Polish heritage and enrolled or expecting to enroll full-time at a four-year institution or university. Available to U.S. citizens.

Application Requirements: Application form, community service, recommendations or references, resume, transcript. *Deadline:* April 1.

Contact: Ms. Camille Kopielski, Chair, ACPC Scholarship Committee
American Council for Polish Culture
1015 Cypress Drive
Arlington Heights, IL 60005
Phone: 847-394-2520

SKALNY SCHOLARSHIP FOR POLISH STUDIES

Scholarships are intended for U.S. citizen students pursuing some Polish studies (major may be in other fields) at universities in the United States who have completed at least two years of college or university work at an accredited institution.

Academic Fields/Career Goals: Area/Ethnic Studies; Foreign Language.

Award: Scholarship for use in junior, senior, graduate, or postgraduate years; not renewable. *Number:* 2. *Amount:* $3000.

Eligibility Requirements: Applicant must be of Polish heritage and enrolled or expecting to enroll full-time at a four-year institution or university. Available to U.S. citizens.

Application Requirements: Application form, community service, copy of an academic project on a Polish topic in English, recommendations or references, resume, transcript. *Deadline:* May 3.

Contact: Ms. Ursula Brodowicz, Chair, Scholarships Committee
American Council for Polish Culture
11 Brinley Way
Newington, CT 06111
Phone: 860-521-0201
E-mail: ubrodowicz@earthlink.net

CANADIAN INSTITUTE OF UKRAINIAN STUDIES

http://www.cius.ca/

CANADIAN INSTITUTE OF UKRAINIAN STUDIES RESEARCH GRANTS

Grants for students who pursue Ukrainian and Ukrainian-Canadian studies in history, literature, language, education, social sciences, women's studies, law, and library sciences.

Academic Fields/Career Goals: Area/Ethnic Studies; Canadian Studies; European Studies.

Award: Grant for use in freshman, sophomore, junior, or senior years; renewable. *Number:* 1.

Eligibility Requirements: Applicant must be enrolled or expecting to enroll full-time at a four-year institution or university. Available to U.S. and non-U.S. citizens.

Application Requirements: Application form. *Deadline:* March 1.

Contact: Iryna Fedoriw, Administrative Assistant
    Phone: 780-492-2972
    E-mail: cius@ualberta.ca

LEO J. KRYSA UNDERGRADUATE SCHOLARSHIP

One-time award for a Canadian citizen or a landed immigrant to enter their final year of undergraduate study in pursuit of a degree with emphasis on Ukrainian and/or Ukrainian-Canadian studies in the disciplines of education, history, humanities, or social sciences. To be used at any Canadian university for an eight-month period of study. Dollar amount CAN$3500.

Academic Fields/Career Goals: Area/Ethnic Studies; Education; History; Humanities; Social Sciences.

Award: Scholarship for use in senior year; not renewable. *Number:* 1.

Eligibility Requirements: Applicant must be Canadian citizen; enrolled or expecting to enroll full-time at a four-year institution or university; resident of Alberta, British Columbia, Manitoba, New Brunswick, Newfoundland, Northwest Territories, Nova Scotia, Ontario, Prince Edward Island, Quebec, Saskatchewan, Yukon and studying in Alberta, British Columbia, Manitoba, New Brunswick, Newfoundland, Nova Scotia, Ontario, Prince Edward Island, Quebec, Saskatchewan.

Application Requirements: Application form, recommendations or references, transcript. *Deadline:* March 1.

Contact: Iryna Fedoriw, Administrative Assistant
    Phone: 780-492-2972
    E-mail: cius@ualberta.ca

CLAN MACBEAN FOUNDATION

http://www.clanmacbean.net/

CLAN MACBEAN FOUNDATION GRANT PROGRAM

Award is open to men and women of any race, color, creed or nationality. Grant is for course of study or project which reflects direct involvement in the preservation or enhancement of Scottish culture, or an effort that would contribute directly to the improvement of the human family.

Academic Fields/Career Goals: Area/Ethnic Studies; Child and Family Studies.

Award: Grant for use in freshman, sophomore, junior, senior, graduate, or postgraduate years; not renewable. *Number:* 1. *Amount:* $500–$3000.

Eligibility Requirements: Applicant must be enrolled or expecting to enroll full-time at a two-year or four-year institution or university. Available to U.S. and non-U.S. citizens.

Application Requirements: Application form, recommendations or references, transcript. *Deadline:* May 1.

Contact: Kenneth Bean, Chairman
    Clan MacBean Foundation
    7475 West 5th Avenue, Suite 201A
    Lakewood, CO 80226
    Phone: 303-233-6002
    Fax: 303-233-6002
    E-mail: macbean@ecentral.com

COSTUME SOCIETY OF AMERICA

http://www.costumesocietyamerica.com/

ADELE FILENE TRAVEL AWARD

One-time award available to society members to assist with travel expenses to attend the Costume Society of America national symposium. Must be currently enrolled students. Recipient will present either a juried paper or a poster.

Academic Fields/Career Goals: Area/Ethnic Studies; Art History; Arts; Historic Preservation and Conservation; History; Home Economics; Museum Studies; Performing Arts.

Award: Prize for use in freshman, sophomore, junior, senior, or graduate years; not renewable. *Number:* 1. *Amount:* $150–$500.

Eligibility Requirements: Applicant must be enrolled or expecting to enroll full- or part-time at a two-year or four-year or technical institution or university. Applicant or parent of applicant must be member of Costume Society of America. Available to U.S. and non-U.S. citizens.

Application Requirements: Application form, entry in a contest, recommendations or references. *Deadline:* March 1.

Contact: Noel Liccardi, Program Contact
    Phone: 800-272-9447
    Fax: 908-450-1118
    E-mail: national.office@costumesocietyamerica.com

STELLA BLUM RESEARCH GRANT

One-time award to support a CSA undergraduate or graduate student member in good standing working on a research project in the field of North American costume. Must be enrolled at an accredited institution. Must submit faculty recommendation. Merit-based award of $3000.

Academic Fields/Career Goals: Area/Ethnic Studies; Art History; Arts; Historic Preservation and Conservation; History; Home Economics; Museum Studies; Performing Arts.

Award: Grant for use in freshman, sophomore, junior, senior, or graduate years; not renewable. *Number:* 1. *Amount:* $3000.

Eligibility Requirements: Applicant must be enrolled or expecting to enroll full-time at a two-year or four-year or technical institution or university. Applicant or parent of applicant must be member of Costume Society of America. Available to U.S. and non-U.S. citizens.

Application Requirements: Application form, essay, proposal of the research project (with budget analysis if necessary), recommendations or references, transcript. *Deadline:* May 1.

Contact: Noel Liccardi, Program Contact
    Phone: 800-272-9447
    Fax: 908-450-1118
    E-mail: national.office@costumesocietyamerica.com

HARVARD TRAVELLERS CLUB

http://www.harvardtravellersclub.org/

HARVARD TRAVELLERS CLUB GRANTS
• See page 108

HAWAIIAN LODGE, F&AM

http://www.hawaiianlodgefreemasons.org/

HAWAIIAN LODGE SCHOLARSHIPS

Scholarship dedicated to worthy students in the areas of engineering, sciences, Hawaiian studies, and education, who would otherwise not be able to attend college.

Academic Fields/Career Goals: Area/Ethnic Studies; Biology; Chemical Engineering; Civil Engineering; Computer Science/Data Processing; Education; Electrical Engineering/Electronics; Energy and Power Engineering; Engineering-Related Technologies; Engineering/Technology; Health and Medical Sciences.

Award: Scholarship for use in freshman, sophomore, junior, or senior years; not renewable. *Number:* 4–16. *Amount:* $1000.

Eligibility Requirements: Applicant must be age 18-25; enrolled or expecting to enroll full-time at a four-year institution or university and resident of Hawaii. Applicant must have 3.0 GPA or higher. Available to U.S. citizens.

Application Requirements: Application form, essay, financial need analysis, interview, recommendations or references, test scores, transcript. *Deadline:* June 31.

Contact: Mr. Robert Schultz, Chairman, Scholarship Committee
Hawaiian Lodge, F&AM
94-1002 Lauwi Place
Waipahu, HI 96797
Phone: 808-220-3859
E-mail: schultzr001@hawaii.rr.com

KE ALI'I PAUAHI FOUNDATION

http://www.pauahi.org/

CHARLES COCKETT 'OHANA SCHOLARSHIP

Applicant must be majoring in Hawaiian Studies/Language/Culture and/or Education. Part-time students are acceptable.

Academic Fields/Career Goals: Area/Ethnic Studies; Education.

Award: Scholarship for use in freshman, sophomore, junior, senior, or graduate years; not renewable. *Number:* 2. *Amount:* $500.

Eligibility Requirements: Applicant must be enrolled or expecting to enroll full- or part-time at a four-year institution or university. Available to U.S. citizens.

Application Requirements: Application form, application form may be submitted online (http://www.pauahi.org/scholarships), Student Aid Report (SAR), college acceptance letter, transcript. *Deadline:* April 1.

Contact: Mavis Shiraishi-Nagao, Scholarship Administrator
Phone: 808-534-3966
E-mail: scholarships@pauahi.org

JOHNNY PINEAPPLE SCHOLARSHIP

Scholarship is for full-time students pursuing a degree in Hawaiian language or Hawaiian studies at an accredited institution of higher learning with minimum GPA of 3.5. Submit two letters of recommendation from school, community organization or religious leaders. Submit essay describing involvement in community service including organizations, number of hours/length of volunteer service and how you intend to continue to benefit the Hawaiian community.

Academic Fields/Career Goals: Area/Ethnic Studies; Foreign Language.

Award: Scholarship for use in freshman, sophomore, junior, senior, or graduate years; not renewable. *Number:* up to 1. *Amount:* up to $1100.

Eligibility Requirements: Applicant must be enrolled or expecting to enroll full-time at a two-year or four-year institution or university and must have an interest in Hawaiian language/culture. Applicant must have 3.5 GPA or higher. Available to U.S. citizens.

Application Requirements: Application form, application form may be submitted online (http://www.pauahi.org/scholarships), college acceptance letter, completed SAR, community service, essay, financial need analysis, recommendations or references, transcript. *Deadline:* April 1.

Contact: Mavis Shiraishi-Nagao, Scholarship Administrator
Phone: 808-534-3966
E-mail: scholarships@pauahi.org

KOSCIUSZKO FOUNDATION

http://www.thekf.org

YEAR ABROAD PROGRAM IN POLAND

Grants for upper division and graduate students who wish to study language and culture at the Center for Polish Language and Culture in the World, Jagiellonian University in Cracow, Poland. US citizens who are undergraduate sophomores, juniors, seniors and graduate students may apply. Scholarship is given towards junior, senior or graduate year of studies. Graduate students receive priority. Must have letters of recommendation, personal statement, and transcript. Covers tuition fees and provides stipend for housing. Application fee: $50. Minimum 3.0 GPA required. Restricted to U.S. citizens.

Academic Fields/Career Goals: Area/Ethnic Studies; Foreign Language.

Award: Scholarship for use in junior, senior, or graduate years; not renewable. *Number:* 5–11. *Amount:* $900–$1,800.

Eligibility Requirements: Applicant must be enrolled or expecting to enroll full-time at a four-year institution or university and must have an interest in Polish language. Applicant must have 3.0 GPA or higher. Available to U.S. citizens.

Application Requirements: Application form, essay, interview, personal photograph, personal statement, recommendations or references, transcript. *Fee:* $50. *Deadline:* December 3.

Contact: Ms. Addy Tymczyszyn, Scholarship and Grant Officer for Americans
Kosciuszko Foundation
15 East 65th Street
New York, NY 10065
Phone: 212-734-2130 Ext. 210
E-mail: addy@thekf.org

NATIONAL ITALIAN AMERICAN FOUNDATION

http://www.niaf.org/

NATIONAL ITALIAN AMERICAN FOUNDATION CATEGORY II SCHOLARSHIP

Award available to students majoring or minoring in Italian language, Italian Studies, Italian-American Studies or a related field who have outstanding potential and high academic achievements. Minimum 3.5 GPA required. Must be a U.S. citizen and be enrolled in an accredited institution of higher education. Application can only be submitted online. For further information, deadlines, and online application visit website http://www.niaf.org/scholarships/index.asp.

Academic Fields/Career Goals: Area/Ethnic Studies.

Award: Scholarship for use in freshman, sophomore, junior, senior, or graduate years; not renewable. *Amount:* $2500–$12,000.

Eligibility Requirements: Applicant must be enrolled or expecting to enroll full-time at a two-year or four-year institution or university and must have an interest in Italian language. Applicant must have 3.5 GPA or higher. Available to U.S. citizens.

Application Requirements: Application form, essay, recommendations or references, transcript. *Deadline:* March 6.

Contact: Serena Cantoni, Director, Culture and Education
National Italian American Foundation
The National Italian American Foundation
1860 19th Street, NW
Washington, DC 20009
Phone: 202-939-3107
E-mail: serena@niaf.org

SONS OF NORWAY FOUNDATION

http://www.sonsofnorway.com/

KING OLAV V NORWEGIAN-AMERICAN HERITAGE FUND

Scholarship available to American students interested in studying Norwegian heritage or modern Norway, or Norwegian students 18 or older interested in studying North American culture. Selection of applicants is based on a 500-word essay, educational and career goals, community service, work experience, and GPA. Must have minimum 3.0 GPA.

Academic Fields/Career Goals: Area/Ethnic Studies.

Award: Scholarship for use in freshman, sophomore, junior, or senior years; not renewable. *Number:* 4–8. *Amount:* $1000–$1500.

Eligibility Requirements: Applicant must be of Norwegian heritage and Norwegian citizen; age 18-30 and enrolled or expecting to enroll full-time at a four-year institution or university. Applicant must have 3.0 GPA or higher. Available to U.S. and non-Canadian citizens.

Application Requirements: Application form, community service, essay, recommendations or references, transcript. *Deadline:* March 1.

STRAIGHTFORWARD MEDIA

http://www.straightforwardmedia.com/

STRAIGHTFORWARD MEDIA LIBERAL ARTS SCHOLARSHIP

Scholarship of $500 available exclusively to liberal arts students. Awarded four times per year. For more information, see web http://www.straightforwardmedia.com/liberal-arts/form.php.

Academic Fields/Career Goals: Area/Ethnic Studies; Art History; Classics; Economics; Foreign Language; History; Humanities; Literature/English/Writing; Philosophy; Political Science; Psychology; Social Sciences.

Award: Scholarship for use in freshman, sophomore, junior, or senior years; not renewable. *Number:* 4. *Amount:* $500.

Eligibility Requirements: Applicant must be enrolled or expecting to enroll full- or part-time at a two-year or four-year or technical institution or university. Available to U.S. and non-U.S. citizens.

Application Requirements: Essay. *Deadline:* varies.

UNITED NEGRO COLLEGE FUND

http://www.uncf.org/

AFSCME/UNCF/HARVARD UNIVERSITY LWP UNION SCHOLARS PROGRAM
• *See page 98*

ART HISTORY

AMERICAN SCHOOL OF CLASSICAL STUDIES AT ATHENS

http://www.ascsa.edu.gr/

ASCSA SUMMER SESSIONS SCHOLARSHIPS
• *See page 100*

COSTUME SOCIETY OF AMERICA

http://www.costumesocietyamerica.com/

ADELE FILENE TRAVEL AWARD
• *See page 114*

STELLA BLUM RESEARCH GRANT
• *See page 114*

CULTURAL SERVICES OF THE FRENCH EMBASSY

http://www.frenchculture.org/

TEACHING ASSISTANT PROGRAM IN FRANCE
• *See page 97*

THE GETTY FOUNDATION

http://www.getty.edu/foundation/

LIBRARY RESEARCH GRANTS

Library Research Grants are intended for scholars of all nationalities and at any level who demonstrate a compelling need to use materials housed in the Getty Research Library, and whose place of residence is more than eighty miles from the Getty Center. Projects must relate to specific items in the library collection. Research period may last several days to a maximum of three months.

Academic Fields/Career Goals: Art History; Arts.

Award: Grant for use in freshman, sophomore, junior, senior, graduate, or postgraduate years; renewable. *Amount:* $500–$2500.

Eligibility Requirements: Applicant must be enrolled or expecting to enroll full- or part-time at a four-year institution or university; studying in California and must have an interest in art. Available to U.S. and non-U.S. citizens.

Application Requirements: Application form, financial need analysis, project proposal, recommendations or references, resume. *Deadline:* November 1.

Contact: Nancy Micklewright, Senior Program Officer
    Phone: 310-440-7320
    E-mail: researchgrants@getty.edu

ROBERT H. MOLLOHAN FAMILY CHARITABLE FOUNDATION, INC.

http://www.mollohanfoundation.org/

MARY OLIVE EDDY JONES ART SCHOLARSHIP

Scholarship awarded to a rising sophomore or junior seriously interested in pursuing an art-related degree. Applicant must be a West Virginia resident attending a West Virginia college or university.

Academic Fields/Career Goals: Art History; Arts; Graphics/Graphic Arts/Printing.

Award: Scholarship for use in sophomore or junior years; not renewable. *Number:* 1–3. *Amount:* up to $1000.

Eligibility Requirements: Applicant must be enrolled or expecting to enroll full- or part-time at a four-year institution or university; resident of West Virginia and studying in West Virginia. Available to U.S. citizens.

Application Requirements: Application form, essay, portfolio, recommendations or references, resume, transcript. *Deadline:* February 9.

Contact: Aime Shaffer, Program Manager
    Robert H. Mollohan Family Charitable Foundation, Inc.
    1000 Technology Drive, Suite 2000
    Fairmont, WV 26554
    Phone: 304-333-6783
    Fax: 304-333-3900
    E-mail: ashaffer@wvhtf.org

STRAIGHTFORWARD MEDIA

http://www.straightforwardmedia.com/

STRAIGHTFORWARD MEDIA LIBERAL ARTS SCHOLARSHIP
• *See page 116*

UNITED NEGRO COLLEGE FUND

http://www.uncf.org/

CATHERINE W. PIERCE SCHOLARSHIP

Up to $5000 scholarship for students at UNCF member colleges and universities studying art and history. For more information, please see website at http://www.uncf.org.

Academic Fields/Career Goals: Art History; Arts; History.

Award: Scholarship for use in freshman, sophomore, junior, or senior years; not renewable. *Amount:* up to $5000.

Eligibility Requirements: Applicant must be Black (non-Hispanic) and enrolled or expecting to enroll full-time at a four-year institution or university. Available to U.S. citizens.

Application Requirements: Application form. *Deadline:* continuous.

ARTS

ALLIANCE FOR YOUNG ARTISTS AND WRITERS INC.

http://www.artandwriting.org/

SCHOLASTIC ART AND WRITING AWARDS-ART SECTION

Awards only graduating students currently enrolled in grades 7 to 12 who attend a public, private, parochial, or home school in the United States, U.S. territories, or U.S. sponsored schools abroad. May submit an art and/or a photography portfolio.

Academic Fields/Career Goals: Arts; Literature/English/Writing.

Award: Scholarship for use in freshman year; not renewable.

Eligibility Requirements: Applicant must be high school student; planning to enroll or expecting to enroll full- or part-time at a four-year institution or university and must have an interest in art or photography/photogrammetry/filmmaking. Available to U.S. and non-U.S. citizens.

Application Requirements: Application form, entry in a contest, essay, original works, electronic files for regional judging, portfolio, recommendations or references. *Deadline:* varies.

SCHOLASTIC ART AND WRITING AWARDS-WRITING SECTION SCHOLARSHIP

Students currently enrolled in grades 7 to 12 who attend a public, private, parochial, or home school in the United States, U.S. territories, or U.S. sponsored schools abroad may apply.

Academic Fields/Career Goals: Arts; Literature/English/Writing.

Award: Scholarship for use in freshman year; not renewable.

Eligibility Requirements: Applicant must be high school student; planning to enroll or expecting to enroll full- or part-time at a four-year institution or university and must have an interest in writing. Available to U.S. and non-U.S. citizens.

Application Requirements: Application form, entry in a contest, essay, manuscript, portfolio, recommendations or references. *Deadline:* varies.

AMERICAN INSTITUTE OF POLISH CULTURE INC.

http://www.ampolinstitute.org/

HARRIET IRSAY SCHOLARSHIP GRANT

Merit-based $1000 scholarships for students studying communications, public relations, and/or journalism. All U.S. citizens may apply, but preference will be given to U.S. citizens of Polish heritage. Must submit three letters of recommendation on appropriate letterhead with application mailed directly to AIPC. For study in the United States only. Non-refundable fee of $10 will be collected.

Academic Fields/Career Goals: Arts; Communications; Education; Foreign Language; Journalism; Public Policy and Administration.

Award: Scholarship for use in freshman, sophomore, junior, senior, or graduate years; not renewable. *Number:* 10–15. *Amount:* $1000.

Eligibility Requirements: Applicant must be enrolled or expecting to enroll full-time at a two-year or four-year institution or university. Available to U.S. citizens.

Application Requirements: Application form, recommendations or references, resume, self-addressed stamped envelope with application, transcript. *Fee:* $10. *Deadline:* April 20.

AMERICAN PHILOLOGICAL ASSOCIATION

http://www.apaclassics.org/

MINORITY STUDENT SUMMER SCHOLARSHIP

• See page 108

AMERICAN SCHOOL OF CLASSICAL STUDIES AT ATHENS

http://www.ascsa.edu.gr/

ASCSA SUMMER SESSIONS SCHOLARSHIPS

• See page 100

ART DIRECTORS CLUB

http://www.adcglobal.org/

ART DIRECTORS CLUB NATIONAL SCHOLARSHIPS

Six $2500 scholarships for sophomores and juniors enrolled in accredited art schools and colleges around the country. Must have successfully completed the first year of an accredited undergraduate or portfolio program.

Academic Fields/Career Goals: Arts.

Award: Scholarship for use in sophomore or junior years; not renewable. *Number:* 6. *Amount:* $2500.

Eligibility Requirements: Applicant must be enrolled or expecting to enroll full-time at a four-year institution or university. Available to U.S. and non-U.S. citizens.

Application Requirements: 5 images of recent work on CD, application form, essay, portfolio, recommendations or references, resume, transcript. *Deadline:* April 30.

BMI FOUNDATION INC.

http://www.bmifoundation.org/

BMI STUDENT COMPOSER AWARDS

One-time awards for original compositions in the classical genre for young student composers who are under age 26 and citizens of the Western Hemisphere. Must submit application and original musical score. Application available at website http://www.bmifoundation.org.

Academic Fields/Career Goals: Arts; Music.

Award: Prize for use in freshman, sophomore, junior, senior, graduate, or postgraduate years; not renewable. *Number:* up to 10. *Amount:* $500–$5000.

Eligibility Requirements: Applicant must be enrolled or expecting to enroll full-time at a two-year or four-year institution or university and must have an interest in music/singing. Available to U.S. and non-U.S. citizens.

Application Requirements: Application form, original musical score, self-addressed stamped envelope with application. *Deadline:* February 1.

Contact: Mr. Ralph Jackson, Director
BMI Foundation Inc.
320 West 57th Street
New York, NY 10019
Phone: 212-586-2000
Fax: 212-245-8986
E-mail: classical@bmi.com

COLLEGEBOUND FOUNDATION

http://www.collegeboundfoundation.org/

JANET B. SONDHEIM SCHOLARSHIP

You must: major in: (a) fine arts (dance, music, art, drama, photography), or (b) any field of study, but you must plan to teach; have a cumulative 3.0 GPA or better; and submit a one-page essay describing your accomplishments to date and your personal and professional goals, focusing on why you are interested in a career in the arts or teaching.

Academic Fields/Career Goals: Arts; Education; Music; Special Education.

Award: Scholarship for use in freshman, sophomore, junior, or senior years; renewable. *Number:* 1. *Amount:* $500.

Eligibility Requirements: Applicant must be high school student; planning to enroll or expecting to enroll full-time at a two-year or four-year institution or university and resident of Maryland. Applicant must have 3.0 GPA or higher. Available to U.S. citizens.

Application Requirements: Application form, application form may be submitted online (http://www.scholarships.mycbf.net/STARS), essay, recommendations or references, resume, transcript. *Deadline:* March 1.

Contact: Michael Thornton, Associate Program Director, Scholarship Programs
Phone: 410-783-2905 Ext. 207
Fax: 410-727-5786
E-mail: mthornton@collegeboundfoundation.org

THE COMMUNITY FOUNDATION FOR GREATER ATLANTA, INC.

http://cfgreateratlanta.org/

JAMES M. AND VIRGINIA M. SMYTH SCHOLARSHIP

Scholarship of $2000 annually for up to four years to students enrolled at an accredited college pursuing an undergraduate degree. Applicant should pursue a degree in the arts and sciences, human services, music or ministry.

Academic Fields/Career Goals: Arts; Humanities; Music; Natural Sciences; Physical Sciences; Religion/Theology.

Award: Scholarship for use in freshman, sophomore, junior, or senior years; renewable. *Number:* 1–15. *Amount:* $2000.

Eligibility Requirements: Applicant must be enrolled or expecting to enroll full-time at a four-year institution or university. Applicant must have 3.0 GPA or higher. Available to U.S. citizens.

Application Requirements: Application form, application form may be submitted online (http://www.cfgreateratlanta.org/Grants-Support/Scholarships.aspx), driver's license, essay, financial need analysis, recommendations or references, transcript. *Deadline:* March 1.

Contact: Kristina Morris, Program Associate
The Community Foundation for Greater Atlanta, Inc.
50 Hurt Plaza
Suite 449
Atlanta, GA 30303
Phone: 404-688-5525
E-mail: scholarships@cfgreateratlanta.org

CONGRESSIONAL BLACK CAUCUS FOUNDATION, INC.

http://www.cbcfinc.org/

CBC SPOUSES VISUAL ARTS SCHOLARSHIP

Award providing financial assistance to undergraduate students pursuing a career in the visual arts.

Academic Fields/Career Goals: Arts.

Award: Scholarship for use in freshman, sophomore, junior, or senior years; not renewable. *Number:* 10. *Amount:* $3000.

Eligibility Requirements: Applicant must be enrolled or expecting to enroll full-time at a two-year or four-year institution. Applicant must have 2.5 GPA or higher. Available to U.S. citizens.

Application Requirements: Application form, application form may be submitted online (http://www.cbcfinc.org/scholarships), essay, financial need analysis, personal photograph, photograph of 5 original pieces of artwork, portfolio, resume, transcript. *Deadline:* May 3.

Contact: Ms. Janet Carter, Program Administrator, Scholarships
Congressional Black Caucus Foundation, Inc.
1720 Massachusetts Avenue, NW
Washington, DC 20036
Phone: 202-263-2800
E-mail: scholarships@cbcfinc.org

CONNECTICUT COMMUNITY FOUNDATION

http://www.conncf.org/

LOIS MCMILLEN MEMORIAL SCHOLARSHIP FUND

One-time scholarship to a woman who is actively pursuing or who would like to pursue an artistic career. Must reside in Connecticut. Preference will be given to artists in the visual arts of painting and design.

Academic Fields/Career Goals: Arts.

Award: Scholarship for use in freshman, sophomore, junior, or senior years; not renewable. *Number:* 1–5. *Amount:* $500–$4000.

Eligibility Requirements: Applicant must be enrolled or expecting to enroll full- or part-time at a two-year or four-year institution or university; female; resident of Connecticut and must have an interest in art. Available to U.S. citizens.

Application Requirements: Application form, essay, financial need analysis, portfolio, recommendations or references, transcript. *Deadline:* March 15.

Contact: Josh Carey, Director of Grants Management
Connecticut Community Foundation
43 Field Street
Waterbury, CT 06702
Phone: 203-753-1315
E-mail: jcarey@conncf.org

COSTUME SOCIETY OF AMERICA

http://www.costumesocietyamerica.com/

ADELE FILENE TRAVEL AWARD
• See page 114

STELLA BLUM RESEARCH GRANT
• See page 114

ELIZABETH GREENSHIELDS FOUNDATION

http://www.elizabethgreenshieldsfoundation.org/

ELIZABETH GREENSHIELDS AWARD/GRANT

Award of $12,500 available to candidates working in painting, drawing, printmaking, or sculpture. Work must be representational or figurative. Must submit at least one color slide of each of six works. Must reapply to renew. Applications from self-taught individuals are also accepted.

Academic Fields/Career Goals: Arts.

Award: Grant for use in freshman, sophomore, junior, or senior years; not renewable. *Number:* 40–60. *Amount:* $12,500.

Eligibility Requirements: Applicant must be enrolled or expecting to enroll full- or part-time at a two-year or four-year or technical institution or university and must have an interest in art. Available to U.S. and non-U.S. citizens.

Application Requirements: Application form, entry in a contest. *Deadline:* continuous.

Contact: Diane Pitcher, Applications Coordinator
Elizabeth Greenshields Foundation
1814 Sherbrooke Street, W, Suite 1
Montreal, QC H3H IE4
CAN
Phone: 514-937-9225
E-mail: greenshields@bellnet.ca

FLORIDA PTA/PTSA

http://www.floridapta.org/

FLORIDA PTA/PTSA FINE ARTS SCHOLARSHIP

Renewable award of $1000 to a graduating Florida high school senior who plans to attend a fine arts program within the State of Florida. Must have a least a two-year attendance in a Florida PTA/PTSA high school. Minimum 3.0 GPA.

Academic Fields/Career Goals: Arts.

Award: Scholarship for use in freshman year; renewable. *Number:* 3. *Amount:* $1000.

Eligibility Requirements: Applicant must be high school student; planning to enroll or expecting to enroll full-time at a four-year institution or university; resident of Florida and studying in Florida. Applicant must have 3.0 GPA or higher. Available to U.S. citizens.

Application Requirements: Application form, essay, recommendations or references. *Deadline:* March 1.

Contact: Janice Bailey, Executive Director
Phone: 407-855-7604
Fax: 407-240-9577
E-mail: janice@floridapta.org

GENERAL FEDERATION OF WOMEN'S CLUBS OF MASSACHUSETTS

http://www.gfwcma.org/

GENERAL FEDERATION OF WOMEN'S CLUBS OF MASSACHUSETTS PENNIES FOR ART SCHOLARSHIP

Scholarship in art for graduating high school seniors who are residents of Massachusetts. The award is for tuition only and will be sent directly to the recipient's college. Must submit letter of recommendation from high school art instructor.

Academic Fields/Career Goals: Arts.

Award: Scholarship for use in freshman year; not renewable. *Amount:* up to $800.

Eligibility Requirements: Applicant must be high school student; planning to enroll or expecting to enroll full-time at a four-year institution or university; resident of Massachusetts and must have an interest in art. Available to U.S. citizens.

Application Requirements: Application form, driver's license, essay, portfolio, recommendations or references, self-addressed stamped envelope with application. *Deadline:* March 1.

Contact: Joan Shanahan, Arts Chairman
General Federation of Women's Clubs of Massachusetts
PO Box 703
Upton, MA 01568-0703
E-mail: cmje@aol.com

THE GETTY FOUNDATION

http://www.getty.edu/foundation/

LIBRARY RESEARCH GRANTS
• *See page 116*

GOLDEN KEY INTERNATIONAL HONOUR SOCIETY

http://www.goldenkey.org/

VISUAL AND PERFORMING ARTS ACHIEVEMENT AWARDS

Award of $500 will be given to winners in each of the following nine categories: painting, drawing, photography, sculpture, computer-generated art/graphic design/illustration, mixed media, instrumental performance, vocal performance, and dance.

Academic Fields/Career Goals: Arts; Graphics/Graphic Arts/Printing.

Award: Prize for use in freshman, sophomore, junior, senior, graduate, or postgraduate years; not renewable. *Number:* 9. *Amount:* $500.

Eligibility Requirements: Applicant must be enrolled or expecting to enroll full- or part-time at a four-year institution or university and must have an interest in art. Available to U.S. and non-U.S. citizens.

Application Requirements: Application form, artwork, cover letter, entry in a contest. *Deadline:* April 1.

GREAT FALLS ADVERTISING FEDERATION

http://www.gfaf.com/

GREAT FALLS ADVERTISING FEDERATION COLLEGE SCHOLARSHIP
• *See page 83*

HIGH SCHOOL ART SCHOLARSHIP

Two scholarships of $2000 for high school seniors who are residents of Montana. Must intend to pursue a career in art or other related field.

Academic Fields/Career Goals: Arts.

Award: Scholarship for use in freshman year; not renewable. *Number:* 2. *Amount:* $2000.

Eligibility Requirements: Applicant must be high school student; planning to enroll or expecting to enroll full-time at a two-year or four-year institution or university and resident of Montana. Available to U.S. citizens.

Application Requirements: Application form, cover letter describing how the scholarship money will be used, essay, portfolio, recommendations or references, resume, self-addressed stamped envelope with application. *Deadline:* February 29.

Contact: Christine Depa, Administrative Assistant
Phone: 406-761-6453
Fax: 406-453-1128
E-mail: gfaf@gfaf.com

IFDA EDUCATIONAL FOUNDATION

http://www.ifdaef.org/

RUTH CLARK FURNITURE DESIGN SCHOLARSHIP

Scholarship available to students studying design at an accredited college or design school with a focus on residential furniture design. Applicant must submit five examples of original designs, three of which must be residential furniture examples. May be CD-ROM (pdf format only), slides, photographs, or copies of drawings no larger than 8 1/2" x 11". Include five sets of each design example with a short description of each illustration.

Academic Fields/Career Goals: Arts; Industrial Design.

Award: Scholarship for use in sophomore, junior, senior, or graduate years; not renewable. *Number:* 1. *Amount:* $3000.

Eligibility Requirements: Applicant must be enrolled or expecting to enroll full-time at a four-year institution or university. Available to U.S. and non-U.S. citizens.

Application Requirements: 2 digital copies of the design work done in class, application form, essay, recommendations or references, transcript. *Deadline:* March 31.

Contact: Sue Williams, Director of Scholarships and Grants
IFDA Educational Foundation
Colleagues
2700 East Grace Street
Richmond, VA 23223
Phone: 804-644-3946
Fax: 804-644-3834
E-mail: colleaguesinc@earthlink.net

JACK J. ISGUR FOUNDATION

http://www.isgur.org

JACK J. ISGUR FOUNDATION SCHOLARSHIP

Awards scholarships to juniors, seniors, and graduate students with intentions of teaching the humanities in grades kindergarten through 8th grade, preferably in rural Missouri.

Academic Fields/Career Goals: Arts; Education; Humanities; Literature/English/Writing; Music; Performing Arts.

Award: Scholarship for use in junior, senior, graduate, or postgraduate years; not renewable. *Number:* 5–40. *Amount:* $1000.

Eligibility Requirements: Applicant must be enrolled or expecting to enroll full- or part-time at a four-year institution or university. Available to U.S. and non-U.S. citizens.

Application Requirements: Application form, application form may be submitted online (http://www.isgur.org), interview, recommendations or references, short answers to 4 questions, transcript. *Deadline:* May 15.

Contact: Mr. Charles Jensen, Administrator,
Jack J. Isgur Foundation
Stinson Morrison Hecker Law Firm
1201 Walnut Street, 29th floor
Kansas City, MO 64106
Phone: 816-691-2760
Fax: 816-691-3495
E-mail: cjensen@stinson.com

JEWISH VOCATIONAL SERVICE CHICAGO

http://www.jvschicago.org/

JEWISH FEDERATION ACADEMIC SCHOLARSHIP PROGRAM

Scholarship for Jewish students who are born or raised in Chicago metropolitan area or Northwest Indiana or one continuous year of full-time employment in Chicago metropolitan area prior to starting professional education. Must intend to remain in the Chicago metropolitan area after completing school. For more details visit website http://jvschicago.org/training-education/scholarship-services/.

Academic Fields/Career Goals: Arts; Education; Health and Medical Sciences; Nursing; Pharmacy; Social Services.

Award: Scholarship for use in junior, senior, or graduate years; renewable. *Number:* up to 100.

Eligibility Requirements: Applicant must be of Jewish heritage; enrolled or expecting to enroll full-time at a four-year institution or university and resident of Illinois, Indiana. Available to U.S. citizens.

Application Requirements: Application form, financial need analysis, interview, recommendations or references, transcript. *Deadline:* February 15.

Contact: Sally Yarberry, Scholarship Coordinator
Phone: 312-673-3444
E-mail: jvsscholarship@jvschicago.org

JOHN F. AND ANNA LEE STACEY SCHOLARSHIP FUND

http://www.nationalcowboymuseum.org/

JOHN F. AND ANNA LEE STACEY SCHOLARSHIP FUND

Scholarships for artists who are high school graduates between the ages of 18 and 35, who are U.S. citizens, and whose work is devoted to the classical or conservative tradition of Western culture. Awards are for drawing or painting only. Must submit no more than six color digital images of work.

Academic Fields/Career Goals: Arts.

Award: Scholarship for use in freshman, sophomore, junior, senior, graduate, or postgraduate years; not renewable. *Number:* 3–5. *Amount:* $1000–$4000.

Eligibility Requirements: Applicant must be age 18-35; enrolled or expecting to enroll full- or part-time at a two-year or four-year or technical institution or university and must have an interest in art. Available to U.S. citizens.

Application Requirements: Application form, application form may be submitted online (http://www.nationalcowboymuseum.org/education/staceyfund/default.aspx), recommendations or references, six digital images of recent artwork. *Deadline:* February 1.

Contact: Ms. Anne Morand, Curator of Art
John F. and Anna Lee Stacey Scholarship Fund
National Cowboy and Western Heritage Museum
1700 NE 63rd Street
Oklahoma City, OK 73111
Phone: 405-478-2250 Ext. 236
Fax: 405-478-4714
E-mail: amorand@nationalcowboymuseum.org

KE ALI'I PAUAHI FOUNDATION

http://www.pauahi.org/

BRUCE T. AND JACKIE MAHI ERICKSON GRANT

Grant to support an undergraduate or graduate student pursuing studies in the creation of crafts, art and photography, and/or independent research relating to historical Hawaiian crafts and arts. Must be in good academic standing, demonstrate financial need, and be pursuing a post-secondary degree.

Academic Fields/Career Goals: Arts; Photojournalism/Photography.

Award: Grant for use in freshman, sophomore, junior, senior, or graduate years; not renewable. *Number:* 1. *Amount:* up to $800.

Eligibility Requirements: Applicant must be enrolled or expecting to enroll full-time at a two-year or four-year institution or university and must have an interest in Hawaiian language/culture. Available to U.S. citizens.

Application Requirements: Application form, application form may be submitted online (http://www.pauahi.org), college acceptance letter, copy of SAR, financial need analysis, recommendations or references, transcript. *Deadline:* April 1.

Contact: Mavis Shiraishi-Nagao, Scholarship Administrator
Ke Ali'i Pauahi Foundation
567 South King Street, Suite 160
Honolulu, HI 96813
Phone: 808-534-3966
E-mail: scholarships@pauahi.org

NATIVE HAWAIIAN VISUAL ARTS SCHOLARSHIP

Scholarship open to University of Hawaii undergraduate or graduate student majoring in art, to encourage studies in the area of visual arts. This includes, but is not limited to, drawing, painting, printmaking, graphic design, fiber arts, sculpture, ceramics, digital art (computer), photography, and film-making or video production. Selection based on artistic merit as demonstrated by an artistic portfolio and academic achievements. Minimum GPA of 3.2 required. Submit hard-copy photos of artistic works created (CD's and DVD's will not be accepted).

Academic Fields/Career Goals: Arts.

Award: Scholarship for use in freshman, sophomore, junior, senior, or graduate years; not renewable. *Number:* 1. *Amount:* $1500.

Eligibility Requirements: Applicant must be enrolled or expecting to enroll full-time at an institution or university; resident of Hawaii; studying in Hawaii and must have an interest in art or photography/photogrammetry/filmmaking. Available to U.S. citizens.

Application Requirements: Application form, application form may be submitted online (http://www.pauahi.org/scholarships), financial need analysis, portfolio, Student Aid Report (SAR), Transcripts & Art Portfolio, transcript. *Deadline:* April 1.

Contact: Mavis Shiraishi-Nagao, Scholarship Administrator
Phone: 808-534-3966
E-mail: scholarships@pauahi.org

MEDIA ACTION NETWORK FOR ASIAN AMERICANS

http://www.manaa.org/

MANAA MEDIA SCHOLARSHIPS FOR ASIAN AMERICAN STUDENTS

One-time award to students pursuing careers in film and television production as writers, directors, producers, and studio executives. Students must have a strong desire to advance a positive and enlightened understanding of the Asian-American experience in mainstream media. See website http://www.manaa.org for application deadline and additional information.

Academic Fields/Career Goals: Arts; Filmmaking/Video; TV/Radio Broadcasting.

Award: Scholarship for use in freshman, sophomore, junior, senior, or graduate years; not renewable. *Number:* 1. *Amount:* $1000.

Eligibility Requirements: Applicant must be Asian/Pacific Islander and enrolled or expecting to enroll full-time at a two-year or four-year or technical institution or university. Available to U.S. citizens.

Application Requirements: Essay, financial need analysis, recommendations or references, transcript, work sample. *Deadline:* varies.

MINNESOTA OFFICE OF HIGHER EDUCATION

http://www.getreadyforcollege.org/

MINNESOTA ACADEMIC EXCELLENCE SCHOLARSHIP

Students must demonstrate outstanding ability, achievement, and potential in one of the following subjects: English or creative writing, fine arts, foreign language, math, science, or social science. Implementation depends on the availability of funds, which are to come from the sale of special collegiate license plates. Apply directly to college. Must be a Minnesota resident and study in Minnesota. At public institutions, the scholarship may cover up to the full price of tuition and fees for one academic year. At private institutions, the scholarship may cover either the actual tuition and fees charged by that school, or the tuition and fees in comparable public institutions whichever is less.

Academic Fields/Career Goals: Arts; Foreign Language; Literature/English/Writing; Mathematics; Science, Technology, and Society; Social Sciences.

Award: Scholarship for use in freshman, sophomore, junior, or senior years; renewable.

Eligibility Requirements: Applicant must be enrolled or expecting to enroll full-time at a four-year institution or university; resident of Minnesota; studying in Minnesota and must have an interest in art, English language, foreign language, science, or writing. Available to U.S. citizens.

Application Requirements: Application form, transcript. *Deadline:* continuous.

Contact: Ginny Dodds, Manager
Phone: 651-355-0610
E-mail: ginny.dodds@state.mn.us

NATIONAL OPERA ASSOCIATION

http://www.noa.org/

NOA VOCAL COMPETITION/LEGACY AWARD PROGRAM

Awards granted based on competitive audition to support study and career development. Singers compete in Scholarship and Artist Division. Legacy Awards are granted for study and career development in any opera-related career to those who further NOA's goal of increased minority participation in the profession.

Academic Fields/Career Goals: Arts; Performing Arts.

Award: Prize for use in freshman, sophomore, junior, senior, graduate, or postgraduate years; not renewable. *Number:* 3–8. *Amount:* $500–$2000.

Eligibility Requirements: Applicant must be age 18-24; enrolled or expecting to enroll full- or part-time at a two-year or four-year or technical institution or university and must have an interest in music or music/singing. Available to U.S. and non-U.S. citizens.

Application Requirements: Application form, audition tape/proposal, driver's license, entry in a contest, personal photograph, recommendations or references. *Fee:* $25. *Deadline:* October 15.

Contact: Robert Hansen, Executive Secretary
National Opera Association
2403 Russell Long Boulevard, PO Box 60869
Canyon, TX 79016-0001
Phone: 806-651-2857
Fax: 806-651-2958
E-mail: hansen@mail.wtamu.edu

NATIONAL SCULPTURE SOCIETY

http://www.nationalsculpture.org/

NSS EDUCATIONAL SCHOLARSHIPS

Scholarships of $2000 each are available for students of figurative or representational sculpture. Scholarships are paid directly to the academic institution through which the student applies. The educational institution the student attends must be an accredited U.S. institution. Please note that work that is inspired by nature—or figurative or realist sculpture—is preferred.

Academic Fields/Career Goals: Arts.

Award: Scholarship for use in sophomore, junior, senior, or graduate years; not renewable. *Number:* 5. *Amount:* $2000.

Eligibility Requirements: Applicant must be enrolled or expecting to enroll full- or part-time at a two-year or four-year or technical institution or university and must have an interest in art. Available to U.S. and non-U.S. citizens.

Application Requirements: Application form, financial need analysis, images of sculpture created by applicant, recommendations or references, transcript. *Deadline:* May 30.

Contact: Elizabeth Helm, Administrative Assistant
National Sculpture Society
75 Varick Street, 11th Floor
New York, NY 10013
Phone: 212-764-5645 Ext. 10
Fax: 212-764-5651
E-mail: elizabeth@nationalsculpture.org

OREGON STUDENT ASSISTANCE COMMISSION

http://www.GetCollegeFunds.org/

KERDRAGON SCHOLARSHIP

Scholarships for students who are graduates (including GED recipients) of Oregon high schools who have not yet attended college and are planning to study fine arts, graphic arts, or photography. Minimum GPA of 3.0 recommended. Semifinalists will be required to submit nonreturnable slides of photos of art samples or film/video of other artistic endeavors. Prior recipients may reapply and must have a 2.75 GPA.

Academic Fields/Career Goals: Arts; Graphics/Graphic Arts/Printing; Photojournalism/Photography.

Award: Scholarship for use in freshman, sophomore, junior, or senior years; not renewable.

Eligibility Requirements: Applicant must be enrolled or expecting to enroll full- or part-time at a four-year institution or university. Available to U.S. citizens.

Application Requirements: Application form, FAFSA. *Deadline:* March 1.

KIRCHHOFF FAMILY FINE ARTS SCHOLARSHIP

Award available to students studying fine art or graphic art at an Oregon four-year nonprofit college or university. Preference will be given to upper-level undergraduates and MFA students. Semifinalists may be asked to submit non-returnable slides or photos of art samples. Recipients may apply for one additional year of funding.

Academic Fields/Career Goals: Arts; Graphics/Graphic Arts/Printing.

Award: Scholarship for use in freshman, sophomore, junior, senior, or graduate years; not renewable.

Eligibility Requirements: Applicant must be enrolled or expecting to enroll full-time at a four-year institution or university. Available to U.S. citizens.

Application Requirements: Application form, FAFSA, portfolio. *Deadline:* March 1.

P. BUCKLEY MOSS FOUNDATION

http://www.mossfoundation.org/

P. BUCKLEY MOSS ENDOWED SCHOLARSHIP

Scholarship of up to $1500 to one or more high school seniors with financial need, a certified language-related learning disability, and artistic talent who plan a career in visual arts.

Academic Fields/Career Goals: Arts.

Award: Scholarship for use in freshman, sophomore, junior, or senior years; renewable. *Number:* 1. *Amount:* up to $1500.

Eligibility Requirements: Applicant must be learning disabled; high school student; age 17-18; planning to enroll or expecting to enroll full-time at a two-year or four-year institution or university and must have an interest in art. Applicant must be learning disabled. Applicant must have 2.5 GPA or higher. Available to U.S. citizens.

Application Requirements: Application form, essay, financial need analysis, portfolio, recommendations or references, transcript. *Deadline:* March 31.

POLISH ARTS CLUB OF BUFFALO SCHOLARSHIP FOUNDATION

http://www.polishartsclubofbuffalo.com/

POLISH ARTS CLUB OF BUFFALO SCHOLARSHIP FOUNDATION TRUST

Provides educational scholarships to students of Polish background who are legal residents of New York. Must be enrolled at the junior level or above in an accredited college or university in NY. Must be a U.S. citizen. For application and additional information, visit website http://www.polishartsclubofbuffalo.com/.

Academic Fields/Career Goals: Arts; Filmmaking/Video; Humanities; Music; Performing Arts.

Award: Scholarship for use in junior, senior, graduate, or postgraduate years; not renewable. *Number:* 1–3. *Amount:* $1000.

Eligibility Requirements: Applicant must be of Polish heritage; enrolled or expecting to enroll full- or part-time at a four-year institution or university and resident of New York. Available to U.S. citizens.

Application Requirements: Application form, essay, interview, portfolio, recommendations or references, resume, self-addressed stamped envelope with application. *Deadline:* June 15.

Contact: Anne Flansburg, Selection Chair
Polish Arts Club of Buffalo Scholarship Foundation
24 Amherston Drive
Williamsville, NY 14221-7002
Phone: 716-863-3631
E-mail: anneflanswz@aol.com

RHODE ISLAND FOUNDATION

http://www.rifoundation.org/

MJSA EDUCATION FOUNDATION JEWELRY SCHOLARSHIP

Scholarships ranging from $500 to $2000 are available for students enrolled in tool making, design, metals fabrication or other jewelry-related courses of study at colleges, universities or non-profit technical schools on the post-secondary level in the United States. Renewable up to four years if the student maintains good academic standing.

Academic Fields/Career Goals: Arts.

Award: Scholarship for use in freshman year; renewable. *Amount:* $500–$2000.

Eligibility Requirements: Applicant must be enrolled or expecting to enroll full-time at a two-year or four-year or technical institution or university and must have an interest in art. Available to U.S. citizens.

Application Requirements: Application form, essay, financial need analysis, self-addressed stamped envelope with application, transcript. *Deadline:* June 14.

Contact: Libby Monahan, Funds Administrator
Phone: 401-274-4564 Ext. 3117
E-mail: libbym@rifoundation.org

PATRICIA W. EDWARDS MEMORIAL ART SCHOLARSHIP

Award to further education of young Rhode Island artists (such as art lessons for high school students in two-dimensional art) and/or scholarships for Rhode Island art students (freshmen, sophomores, and juniors) at Rhode Island institutions.

Academic Fields/Career Goals: Arts.

Award: Scholarship for use in freshman year; not renewable. *Amount:* up to $425.

Eligibility Requirements: Applicant must be high school student; planning to enroll or expecting to enroll full- or part-time at a two-year or four-year institution or university; resident of Rhode Island and studying in Rhode Island. Available to U.S. citizens.

Application Requirements: Application form. *Deadline:* March 4.

Contact: Libby Monahan, Funds Administrator
Phone: 401-274-4564 Ext. 3117
E-mail: libbym@rifoundation.org

ROBERT H. MOLLOHAN FAMILY CHARITABLE FOUNDATION, INC.

http://www.mollohanfoundation.org/

MARY OLIVE EDDY JONES ART SCHOLARSHIP
• See page 116

SERVICE EMPLOYEES INTERNATIONAL UNION (SEIU)

http://www.seiu.org/

SEIU MOE FONER SCHOLARSHIP PROGRAM FOR VISUAL AND PERFORMING ARTS

Scholarship for students pursuing a degree or training full time in the visual or performing arts. Scholarship funding must be applied to tuition at a two- or four-year college, university, or an accredited community college, technical or trade school in an arts-related field.

Academic Fields/Career Goals: Arts; Performing Arts.

Award: Scholarship for use in freshman, sophomore, junior, or senior years; not renewable. *Number:* 1. *Amount:* $5000.

Eligibility Requirements: Applicant must be enrolled or expecting to enroll full-time at a two-year or four-year or technical institution or university. Applicant or parent of applicant must be member of Service Employees International Union. Available to U.S. citizens.

Application Requirements: 6 copies of a single original creative work, application form, essay, transcript. *Deadline:* March 1.

STRAIGHTFORWARD MEDIA

http://www.straightforwardmedia.com/

STRAIGHTFORWARD MEDIA ART SCHOOL SCHOLARSHIP

Award of $500 for students pursuing a degree in any art-related field. May be used for full- or part-time study. Scholarship is awarded four times per year. Deadlines: November 30, February 28, May 31, and August 31. For more information, visit website http://www.straightforwardmedia.com/art/form.php.

Academic Fields/Career Goals: Arts.

Award: Scholarship for use in freshman, sophomore, junior, or senior years; not renewable. *Number:* 4. *Amount:* $500.

Eligibility Requirements: Applicant must be enrolled or expecting to enroll full- or part-time at a two-year or four-year or technical institution or university. Available to U.S. and non-U.S. citizens.

Application Requirements: Essay. *Deadline:* varies.

TELETOON

http://www.teletoon.com/

TELETOON ANIMATION SCHOLARSHIP

Scholarship competition created by TELETOON to encourage creative, original, and imaginative animation by supporting Canadians studying in the animation field or intending to pursue studies in animation. One-time award. Must submit portfolio.

Academic Fields/Career Goals: Arts; Filmmaking/Video.

Award: Scholarship for use in freshman, sophomore, junior, senior, graduate, or postgraduate years; not renewable. *Number:* 9. *Amount:* $5000–$10,000.

Eligibility Requirements: Applicant must be enrolled or expecting to enroll full-time at a two-year or four-year or technical institution or university and resident of Alberta, British Columbia, Manitoba, New Brunswick, Newfoundland, Northwest Territories, Nova Scotia, Ontario, Prince Edward Island, Quebec, Saskatchewan. Available to Canadian citizens.

Application Requirements: 5-minute film, application form, driver's license, essay, portfolio, transcript. *Deadline:* June 15.

Contact: Denise Vaughan, Senior Coordinator, Public Relations
Phone: 416-956-2060
Fax: 416-956-2070
E-mail: denisev@teletoon.com

TEXAS ARTS AND CRAFTS EDUCATIONAL FOUNDATION

http://www.tacef.org/

EMERGING TEXAS ARTIST SCHOLARSHIP

Scholarships for art work offered to students attending colleges or universities in Texas either part-time or full-time. Scholarships are awarded as prizes in a juried art exhibit at the Texas State Arts and Crafts Fair. From 8 to 12 awards are granted annually.

Academic Fields/Career Goals: Arts.

Award: Scholarship for use in freshman, sophomore, junior, senior, graduate, or postgraduate years; not renewable. *Number:* 8–12. *Amount:* $500–$5000.

Eligibility Requirements: Applicant must be enrolled or expecting to enroll full- or part-time at a two-year or four-year or technical institution or university; studying in Texas and must have an interest in art. Available to U.S. citizens.

Application Requirements: 4 color slides of work, application form, entry in a contest, recommendations or references. *Deadline:* March 15.

Contact: Debbie Luce, Assistant Director
> *Phone:* 830-896-5711
> *Fax:* 830-896-5569
> *E-mail:* info@tacef.org

UNITARIAN UNIVERSALIST ASSOCIATION

http://www.uua.org/

MARION BARR STANFIELD ART SCHOLARSHIP

Scholarship for graduate or undergraduate Unitarian Universalist students preparing for a career in fine arts. Eligibility is limited to those in the study of painting, drawing, photography, and/or sculpture. Performing arts majors are not eligible.

Academic Fields/Career Goals: Arts; Photojournalism/Photography.

Award: Scholarship for use in freshman, sophomore, junior, senior, or graduate years; not renewable.

Eligibility Requirements: Applicant must be Unitarian Universalist and enrolled or expecting to enroll full-time at a four-year institution or university. Available to U.S. citizens.

Application Requirements: Application form, essay, financial need analysis, list of works, personal tax information, portfolio, recommendations or references. *Deadline:* varies.

Contact: Ms. Hillary Goodridge, Program Director
> *Phone:* 617-971-9600
> *Fax:* 617-971-0029
> *E-mail:* uufp@aol.com

PAULY D'ORLANDO MEMORIAL ART SCHOLARSHIP

Scholarship for graduate or undergraduate students preparing for a career in fine arts. Student must be studying painting, drawing, photography, and/or sculpture. Performing arts majors are not eligible.

Academic Fields/Career Goals: Arts; Photojournalism/Photography.

Award: Scholarship for use in freshman, sophomore, junior, senior, or graduate years; not renewable.

Eligibility Requirements: Applicant must be Unitarian Universalist and enrolled or expecting to enroll full-time at a four-year institution or university. Available to U.S. citizens.

Application Requirements: Application form, essay, financial need analysis, list of works, personal tax information, recommendations or references. *Deadline:* varies.

Contact: Ms. Hillary Goodridge, Program Director
> *Phone:* 617-971-9600
> *Fax:* 617-971-0029
> *E-mail:* uufp@aol.com

STANFIELD AND D'ORLANDO ART SCHOLARSHIP

Scholarships for both master's and undergraduate Unitarian Universalist students studying the fields of art and law.

Academic Fields/Career Goals: Arts; Law/Legal Services.

Award: Scholarship for use in freshman, sophomore, junior, senior, or graduate years; not renewable.

Eligibility Requirements: Applicant must be Unitarian Universalist and enrolled or expecting to enroll full- or part-time at a four-year institution or university. Available to U.S. citizens.

Application Requirements: Application form. *Deadline:* February 15.

Contact: Ms. Hillary Goodridge, Program Director
> *Phone:* 617-971-9600
> *Fax:* 617-971-0029
> *E-mail:* uufp@aol.com

UNITED NEGRO COLLEGE FUND

http://www.uncf.org/

CATHERINE W. PIERCE SCHOLARSHIP

• *See page 116*

JANET JACKSON/RHYTHM NATION SCHOLARSHIP

$2000 award for students attending select UNCF member colleges and universities. Must be studying communications, art, music, English, or performing arts. May be used for tuition costs, room and board, or to repay federal student loans. Minimum 3.0 GPA required.

Academic Fields/Career Goals: Arts; Communications; Literature/ English/Writing; Music; Performing Arts.

Award: Scholarship for use in freshman year; renewable. *Amount:* $2000.

Eligibility Requirements: Applicant must be Black (non-Hispanic) and enrolled or expecting to enroll full- or part-time at a four-year institution or university. Applicant must have 3.0 GPA or higher. Available to U.S. citizens.

Application Requirements: Application form. *Deadline:* continuous.

MAE MAXEY MEMORIAL SCHOLARSHIP

Award for students with an interest in poetry attending a UNCF member college or university. Minimum 2.5 GPA required. The scholarship value ranges from $1000 to $5000.

Academic Fields/Career Goals: Arts; Literature/English/Writing.

Award: Scholarship for use in freshman, sophomore, junior, or senior years; not renewable. *Amount:* $1000–$5000.

Eligibility Requirements: Applicant must be Black (non-Hispanic) and enrolled or expecting to enroll full- or part-time at a four-year institution or university. Applicant must have 2.5 GPA or higher. Available to U.S. and non-U.S. citizens.

Application Requirements: Application form, financial need analysis. *Deadline:* continuous.

U.S. FISH AND WILDLIFE SERVICE

http://www.fws.gov/duckstamps

FEDERAL JUNIOR DUCK STAMP CONSERVATION AND DESIGN COMPETITION

Any student in grades K-12, public, private, or home schooled, may enter this competition in all 50 states, the District of Columbia, and U.S. Territories. Teachers use the curriculum guide which is provided to teach conservation issues to students. Student then does an artistic rendering of one of the North American Migratory Waterfowl and enters it into their state's Junior Duck Stamp Contest. Each state picks one Best of Show to be sent to the National Office in Arlington, VA. Deadlines: South Carolina, January 30; Florida February 21; all other states and territories March 15. Further information is available at http://duckstamps.fws.gov.

Academic Fields/Career Goals: Arts.

Award: Prize for use in freshman year; not renewable. *Number:* 3. *Amount:* $1000–$4000.

Eligibility Requirements: Applicant must be high school student; planning to enroll or expecting to enroll full- or part-time at a two-year or four-year institution and must have an interest in art. Available to U.S. citizens.

Application Requirements: Application form, entry in a contest. *Deadline:* varies.

Contact: Elizabeth Jackson, Program Coordinator
> U.S. Fish and Wildlife Service
> 4401 North Fairfax Drive, Suite 4073
> Arlington, VA 22203-1622
> *Phone:* 703-358-2073
> *E-mail:* elizabeth_jackson@fws.gov

WARNER BROS. ENTERTAINMENT

http://www.warnerbros.com/

WARNER BROS. ANIMATION/HANNA-BARBERA HONORSHIP

The Honorship will be awarded annually to a graduating high school senior enrolling in a college, university, or trade school to study animation. Applicants must have (1) a passion and talent for a career in animation; (2) a minimum GPA of 3.0 upon graduation; and (3) demonstrate financial need. Each cash scholarship will be for $10,000, disbursed annually in equal amounts over the course of enrollment. In addition, the winner will have the opportunity to receive (4) consecutive, paid summer internships at Warner Bros. Studios in Burbank while at university.

Academic Fields/Career Goals: Arts.

Award: Scholarship for use in freshman, sophomore, junior, or senior years; renewable. *Number:* 1. *Amount:* $10,000.

Eligibility Requirements: Applicant must be high school student and planning to enroll or expecting to enroll at a four-year or technical institution or university. Applicant must have 3.0 GPA or higher. Available to U.S. citizens.

Application Requirements: *Deadline:* March 1.

WOMEN'S JEWELRY ASSOCIATION

http://www.womensjewelry.org/

WJA SCHOLARSHIP PROGRAM

Program is designed to encourage talented female students and help support their studies in the jewelry field. Applicants required to submit original drawings of their jewelry designs. Visit http://www.womensjewelry.org for current information.

Academic Fields/Career Goals: Arts; Trade/Technical Specialties.

Award: Scholarship for use in freshman, sophomore, junior, senior, graduate, or postgraduate years; not renewable. *Number:* 1. *Amount:* $500–$5000.

Eligibility Requirements: Applicant must be enrolled or expecting to enroll full- or part-time at a two-year or four-year or technical institution or university; female and must have an interest in art. Available to U.S. and non-U.S. citizens.

Application Requirements: Application form, essay, portfolio. *Deadline:* May 1.

WORLDSTUDIO FOUNDATION

http://www.aiga.org/

WORLDSTUDIO AIGA SCHOLARSHIPS

Scholarships available for minority and economically disadvantaged students who are pursuing degrees in the design/arts disciplines in colleges and universities in the United States.

Academic Fields/Career Goals: Arts; Graphics/Graphic Arts/Printing.

Award: Scholarship for use in freshman, sophomore, junior, senior, or graduate years; not renewable. *Number:* 10–25. *Amount:* $1000–$5000.

Eligibility Requirements: Applicant must be enrolled or expecting to enroll full-time at a two-year or four-year or technical institution or university. Available to U.S. citizens.

Application Requirements: Application form, application form may be submitted online (http://www.aiga.org/content.cfm/worldstudio-scholarship), essay, portfolio, recommendations or references, transcript. *Deadline:* April 1.

Contact: Tiia Schurig, Web Production Manager
Worldstudio Foundation
164 Fifth Avenue
New York, NY 10010
Phone: 212-807-1990
Fax: 212-807-1799
E-mail: scholarship@aiga.org

AUDIOLOGY

NATIONAL AMBUCS INC.

http://www.ambucs.org/

AMBUCS SCHOLARS-SCHOLARSHIPS FOR THERAPISTS

Scholarships are open to students who are U.S. citizens at a junior level or above in college. Must be enrolled in an accredited program by the appropriate health therapy profession authority in physical therapy, occupational therapy, speech-language pathology, or audiology and must demonstrate a financial need. Application available on website at http://www.ambucs.com. Paper applications are not accepted.

Academic Fields/Career Goals: Audiology; Therapy/Rehabilitation.

Award: Scholarship for use in junior, senior, graduate, or postgraduate years; not renewable. *Number:* 275. *Amount:* $500–$3000.

Eligibility Requirements: Applicant must be enrolled or expecting to enroll full-time at a four-year institution or university. Available to U.S. citizens.

Application Requirements: Application form, enrollment certification form, essay, financial need analysis. *Deadline:* April 15.

Contact: Janice Blankenship, Scholarship Coordinator
National AMBUCS Inc.
PO Box 5127
High Point, NC 27262
Phone: 336-852-0052 Ext. 10
Fax: 336-852-6830
E-mail: janiceb@ambucs.org

AVIATION/AEROSPACE

AACE INTERNATIONAL

http://www.aacei.org/

AACE INTERNATIONAL COMPETITIVE SCHOLARSHIP
• See page 108

AHS INTERNATIONAL—THE VERTICAL FLIGHT TECHNICAL SOCIETY

http://www.vtol.org/

VERTICAL FLIGHT FOUNDATION SCHOLARSHIP

This award is available for undergraduate, graduate, or doctoral study in aerospace, electrical, or mechanical engineering. Applicants must have an interest in vertical flight technology.

Academic Fields/Career Goals: Aviation/Aerospace; Electrical Engineering/Electronics; Engineering-Related Technologies; Engineering/Technology; Mechanical Engineering.

Award: Scholarship for use in junior, senior, graduate, or postgraduate years; not renewable. *Number:* 10–19. *Amount:* $1500–$5000.

Eligibility Requirements: Applicant must be enrolled or expecting to enroll full-time at a four-year institution or university and must have an interest in aviation. Applicant must have 3.5 GPA or higher. Available to U.S. and non-U.S. citizens.

Application Requirements: Application form, essay, recommendations or references, resume, transcript. *Deadline:* February 1.

Contact: Ms. Kay Brackins, Deputy Director
AHS International—The Vertical Flight Technical Society
217 North Washington Street
Alexandria, VA 22314
Phone: 703-684-6777 Ext. 103
Fax: 703-739-9279
E-mail: kbrackins@vtol.org

AIRCRAFT ELECTRONICS ASSOCIATION EDUCATIONAL FOUNDATION

http://www.aea.net/

BUD GLOVER MEMORIAL SCHOLARSHIP

Scholarship available to high school seniors and college students who plan to attend or are attending an avionics or aircraft repair program in an accredited school. Minimum 2.5 GPA required.

Academic Fields/Career Goals: Aviation/Aerospace; Trade/Technical Specialties.

Award: Scholarship for use in freshman, sophomore, junior, or senior years; not renewable. *Number:* 1. *Amount:* $1000.

Eligibility Requirements: Applicant must be enrolled or expecting to enroll full- or part-time at a two-year or four-year or technical institution or university. Applicant must have 2.5 GPA or higher. Available to U.S. and Canadian citizens.

Application Requirements: Application form, essay, recommendations or references, test scores, transcript. *Deadline:* February 15.

Contact: Mike Adamson, Executive Director
Phone: 816-373-6565
E-mail: info@aea.net

CHUCK PEACOCK MEMORIAL SCHOLARSHIP

Scholarship of $1000 for high school seniors or college students who plan to attend or are attending an aviation management program in an accredited school. Minimum 2.5 GPA required.

Academic Fields/Career Goals: Aviation/Aerospace.

Award: Scholarship for use in freshman, sophomore, junior, or senior years; not renewable. *Number:* 1. *Amount:* $1000.

Eligibility Requirements: Applicant must be enrolled or expecting to enroll full- or part-time at a two-year or four-year or technical institution or university. Applicant must have 2.5 GPA or higher. Available to U.S. citizens.

Application Requirements: Application form, essay, transcript. *Deadline:* February 15.

Contact: Mike Adamson, Executive Director
Phone: 816-373-6565
E-mail: info@aea.net

DAVID ARVER MEMORIAL SCHOLARSHIP

Scholarship of $1000 available to high school seniors and college students who plan to or are attending an avionics or aircraft repair program in an accredited school. Restricted to use for study in the following states: Iowa, Illinois, Indiana, Kansas, Michigan, Minnesota, Mississippi, North Dakota, Nebraska, South Dakota, and Wisconsin. Minimum 2.5 GPA required.

Academic Fields/Career Goals: Aviation/Aerospace.

Award: Scholarship for use in freshman, sophomore, junior, or senior years; not renewable. *Number:* 1. *Amount:* $1000.

Eligibility Requirements: Applicant must be enrolled or expecting to enroll full- or part-time at a two-year or four-year or technical institution or university. Applicant must have 2.5 GPA or higher. Available to U.S. and non-U.S. citizens.

Application Requirements: Application form, essay, recommendations or references, test scores, transcript. *Deadline:* February 15.

Contact: Mike Adamson, Executive Director
Phone: 816-373-6565
E-mail: info@aea.net

DUTCH AND GINGER ARVER SCHOLARSHIP

Scholarship available to high school seniors or college students who plan to attend or are attending an avionics or aircraft repair program in an accredited school. Minimum 2.5 GPA required.

Academic Fields/Career Goals: Aviation/Aerospace; Trade/Technical Specialties.

Award: Scholarship for use in freshman, sophomore, junior, or senior years; not renewable. *Number:* 1. *Amount:* $1000.

Eligibility Requirements: Applicant must be enrolled or expecting to enroll full- or part-time at a two-year or four-year or technical institution

or university. Applicant must have 2.5 GPA or higher. Available to U.S. citizens.

Application Requirements: Application form, essay, recommendations or references, test scores, transcript. *Deadline:* February 15.

Contact: Mike Adamson, Executive Director
Phone: 816-373-6565
E-mail: info@aea.net

FIELD AVIATION COMPANY INC. SCHOLARSHIP

Scholarship for high school seniors and college students who plan to or are attending an avionics or aircraft repair program in an accredited college/university. The educational institution must be located in Canada.

Academic Fields/Career Goals: Aviation/Aerospace.

Award: Scholarship for use in freshman, sophomore, junior, or senior years; not renewable. *Number:* 1. *Amount:* $1000.

Eligibility Requirements: Applicant must be enrolled or expecting to enroll full-time at a two-year or four-year or technical institution or university. Applicant must have 2.5 GPA or higher. Available to Canadian citizens.

Application Requirements: Application form, essay, recommendations or references, test scores, transcript. *Deadline:* February 15.

Contact: Mike Adamson, Executive Director
Phone: 816-373-6565
E-mail: info@aea.net

GARMIN-JERRY SMITH MEMORIAL SCHOLARSHIP

Scholarship available for high school, college, or vocational or technical school students who plan to attend or are attending an avionics or aircraft repair program in an accredited vocational or technical school. Minimum 2.5 GPA required.

Academic Fields/Career Goals: Aviation/Aerospace; Trade/Technical Specialties.

Award: Scholarship for use in freshman or sophomore years; not renewable. *Number:* 1. *Amount:* $1000.

Eligibility Requirements: Applicant must be enrolled or expecting to enroll full-time at a two-year or technical institution. Applicant must have 2.5 GPA or higher. Available to U.S. and non-U.S. citizens.

Application Requirements: Application form, community service, essay, transcript. *Deadline:* February 15.

Contact: Mike Adamson, Executive Director
Phone: 816-373-6565
E-mail: info@aea.net

GARMIN SCHOLARSHIP

Scholarship available to high school seniors and college students who plan to attend or are attending an avionics or aircraft repair program in an accredited school. Minimum 2.5 GPA required.

Academic Fields/Career Goals: Aviation/Aerospace; Trade/Technical Specialties.

Award: Scholarship for use in freshman, sophomore, junior, or senior years; not renewable. *Number:* 1. *Amount:* $2000.

Eligibility Requirements: Applicant must be enrolled or expecting to enroll full- or part-time at a two-year or four-year or technical institution or university. Applicant must have 2.5 GPA or higher. Available to U.S. citizens.

Application Requirements: Application form, essay, recommendations or references, test scores, transcript. *Deadline:* February 15.

Contact: Mike Adamson, Executive Director
Phone: 816-373-6565
E-mail: info@aea.net

JOHNNY DAVIS MEMORIAL SCHOLARSHIP

Scholarship of $1000 available to high school seniors and college students who plan to or are attending an avionics or aircraft repair program in an accredited school. Minimum 2.5 GPA required.

Academic Fields/Career Goals: Aviation/Aerospace.

Award: Scholarship for use in freshman, sophomore, junior, or senior years; not renewable. *Number:* 1. *Amount:* $1000.

Eligibility Requirements: Applicant must be enrolled or expecting to enroll full- or part-time at a two-year or four-year or technical institution or university. Applicant must have 2.5 GPA or higher. Available to U.S. citizens.

Application Requirements: Application form, essay, transcript. *Deadline:* February 15.

Contact: Mike Adamson, Executive Director
    Phone: 816-373-6565
    E-mail: info@aea.net

L-3 AVIONICS SYSTEMS SCHOLARSHIP

Scholarship of $2500 available to high school seniors and college students who plan to attend or are attending an avionics or aircraft repair program in an accredited school. Minimum 2.5 GPA required.

Academic Fields/Career Goals: Aviation/Aerospace.

Award: Scholarship for use in freshman, sophomore, junior, or senior years; not renewable. *Number:* 1. *Amount:* $2500.

Eligibility Requirements: Applicant must be enrolled or expecting to enroll full- or part-time at a two-year or four-year or technical institution or university. Applicant must have 2.5 GPA or higher. Available to U.S. citizens.

Application Requirements: Application form, essay, transcript. *Deadline:* February 15.

Contact: Mike Adamson, Executive Director
    Phone: 816-373-6565
    E-mail: info@aea.net

LEE TARBOX MEMORIAL SCHOLARSHIP

Scholarship available to high school seniors or college students who plan to attend or are attending an avionics or aircraft repair program in an accredited school.

Academic Fields/Career Goals: Aviation/Aerospace; Trade/Technical Specialties.

Award: Scholarship for use in freshman, sophomore, junior, or senior years; not renewable. *Number:* 1. *Amount:* $2500.

Eligibility Requirements: Applicant must be enrolled or expecting to enroll full- or part-time at a two-year or four-year or technical institution or university. Applicant must have 2.5 GPA or higher. Available to U.S. citizens.

Application Requirements: Application form, essay, recommendations or references, test scores, transcript. *Deadline:* February 15,

Contact: Mike Adamson, Executive Director
    Phone: 816-373-6565
    E-mail: info@aea.net

LOWELL GAYLOR MEMORIAL SCHOLARSHIP

Scholarship for high school seniors and college students who plan to attend or are attending an avionics or aircraft repair program in an accredited school. Minimum 2.5 GPA required.

Academic Fields/Career Goals: Aviation/Aerospace; Trade/Technical Specialties.

Award: Scholarship for use in freshman, sophomore, junior, or senior years; not renewable. *Number:* 1. *Amount:* $1000.

Eligibility Requirements: Applicant must be enrolled or expecting to enroll full- or part-time at a two-year or four-year or technical institution or university. Applicant must have 2.5 GPA or higher. Available to U.S. and non-U.S. citizens.

Application Requirements: Application form, essay, recommendations or references, test scores, transcript. *Deadline:* February 15.

Contact: Mike Adamson, Executive Director
    Phone: 816-373-6565
    E-mail: info@aea.net

MID-CONTINENT INSTRUMENT SCHOLARSHIP

Scholarship available to high school seniors or college students who plan to attend or are attending an avionics or aircraft repair program in an accredited school. Minimum 2.5 GPA required.

Academic Fields/Career Goals: Aviation/Aerospace; Trade/Technical Specialties.

Award: Scholarship for use in freshman, sophomore, junior, or senior years; not renewable. *Number:* 1. *Amount:* $1000.

Eligibility Requirements: Applicant must be enrolled or expecting to enroll full- or part-time at a two-year or four-year or technical institution

or university. Applicant must have 2.5 GPA or higher. Available to U.S. citizens.

Application Requirements: Application form, essay, recommendations or references, test scores, transcript. *Deadline:* February 15.

Contact: Mike Adamson, Executive Director
    Phone: 816-373-6565
    E-mail: info@aea.net

MONTE R. MITCHELL GLOBAL SCHOLARSHIP

Scholarship of $1000 available to European students pursuing a degree in aviation maintenance technology, avionics, or aircraft repair at an accredited school located in Europe or the United States.

Academic Fields/Career Goals: Aviation/Aerospace.

Award: Scholarship for use in freshman, sophomore, junior, or senior years; not renewable. *Number:* 1. *Amount:* $1000.

Eligibility Requirements: Applicant must be enrolled or expecting to enroll full- or part-time at a two-year or four-year or technical institution or university. Applicant must have 2.5 GPA or higher. Available to citizens of countries other than the U.S. or Canada.

Application Requirements: Application form, essay, recommendations or references, transcript. *Deadline:* February 15.

Contact: Mike Adamson, Executive Director
    Phone: 816-373-6565
    E-mail: info@aea.net

AIRPORT MINORITY ADVISORY COUNCIL EDUCATIONAL AND SCHOLARSHIP PROGRAM

http://www.amac-org.com/

AMACESP STUDENT SCHOLARSHIPS

Applicant must be seeking a BS or BA with interest and desire to pursue a career in the aviation/airport industry and seeking a degree in Aviation, Business Administration, Accounting, Architecture, Engineering or Finance and admitted by an accredited school or university for the current school term in which you are applying for a scholarship. Demonstration of a cumulative 3.0 GPA and involvement in community activities and extracurricular activities. Applicants must be a U.S. Citizen. A commitment to involvement in furthering the mission of the Airport Minority Advisory Council (AMAC) by participating in the AMAC Student Program. AMAC Member Scholarship Awards are offered to Airport Minority Advisory Council (AMAC) members, their spouses, and their children. The AMAC Aviation & Professional Development Committee grant four $2,000 scholarships each year to a number of students who are enrolled in an aviation related program and have a grade point average 3.0 or higher.

Academic Fields/Career Goals: Aviation/Aerospace.

Award: Scholarship for use in sophomore, junior, or senior years; not renewable. *Number:* 1–3. *Amount:* $2000.

Eligibility Requirements: Applicant must be enrolled or expecting to enroll full-time at a four-year institution or university. Applicant must have 3.0 GPA or higher. Available to U.S. citizens.

Application Requirements: Application form, autobiography, essay, personal photograph, recommendations or references, transcript. *Deadline:* May 18.

Contact: Miss Jennifer Ibe, AMACESP Intern
    Airport Minority Advisory Council Educational and
        Scholarship Program
    2345 Crystal Drive, Suite 902
    Arlington, VA 22202
    Phone: 703-414-2622 Ext. 1
    Fax: 703-414-2686
    E-mail: gene.roth@amac-org.com

AIR TRAFFIC CONTROL ASSOCIATION INC.

http://www.atca.org/

AIR TRAFFIC CONTROL ASSOCIATION SCHOLARSHIP

Scholarships for students in programs leading to a bachelor's degree or higher in aviation-related courses of study, and for full-time employees engaged in advanced study to improve their skills in air traffic control or aviation. Visit website for additional information http://www.atca.org.

Academic Fields/Career Goals: Aviation/Aerospace; Engineering/Technology.

Award: Scholarship for use in freshman, sophomore, junior, senior, or graduate years; not renewable. *Number:* 7–12. *Amount:* $2000–$6000.

Eligibility Requirements: Applicant must be enrolled or expecting to enroll full- or part-time at a four-year institution or university and must have an interest in aviation. Applicant or parent of applicant must have employment or volunteer experience in air traffic control. Available to U.S. citizens.

Application Requirements: Application form, driver's license, essay, financial need analysis, recommendations or references, resume, transcript. *Deadline:* May 1.

Contact: Sandra Strickland, Meetings and Programs Coordinator
Air Traffic Control Association Inc.
1101 King Street, Suite 300
Alexandria, VA 22201-2302
Phone: 703-299-2430
Fax: 703-299-2430
E-mail: info@atca.org

ALASKAN AVIATION SAFETY FOUNDATION

http://www.aasfonline.org

ALASKAN AVIATION SAFETY FOUNDATION MEMORIAL SCHOLARSHIP FUND

Scholarships for undergraduate or graduate study in aviation. Must be a resident of Alaska and a U.S. citizen. Write for deadlines and details.

Academic Fields/Career Goals: Aviation/Aerospace.

Award: Scholarship for use in freshman, sophomore, junior, senior, or graduate years; not renewable. *Number:* 1–3. *Amount:* $500–$750.

Eligibility Requirements: Applicant must be enrolled or expecting to enroll full- or part-time at a two-year or four-year or technical institution or university; resident of Alaska and must have an interest in aviation. Available to U.S. citizens.

Application Requirements: Application form, driver's license, financial need analysis, recommendations or references, test scores, transcript. *Deadline:* May 30.

AMERICAN ASSOCIATION OF AIRPORT EXECUTIVES-SOUTHWEST CHAPTER

http://www.swaaae.org/

SWAAAE ACADEMIC SCHOLARSHIPS

A scholarship of $1500 for students pursuing an undergraduate or graduate degree in airport management may apply annually for an academic scholarship. Applicant must attend a college in Arizona, California, Nevada, Utah, or Hawaii.

Academic Fields/Career Goals: Aviation/Aerospace.

Award: Scholarship for use in sophomore, junior, senior, or graduate years; not renewable. *Number:* 5. *Amount:* $500–$1500.

Eligibility Requirements: Applicant must be enrolled or expecting to enroll full- or part-time at a four-year institution or university and studying in Arizona, California, Hawaii, Nevada, Utah. Available to U.S. and non-U.S. citizens.

Application Requirements: Application form. *Deadline:* September 29.

Contact: Charles Mangum, Scholarship Committee
American Association of Airport Executives-Southwest Chapter
8565 North Sand Dune Place
Tucson, AZ 85743
Phone: 520-682-9565
E-mail: cman2122@comcast.net

AMERICAN INSTITUTE OF AERONAUTICS AND ASTRONAUTICS

http://www.aiaa.org/

AIAA FOUNDATION UNDERGRADUATE SCHOLARSHIP

• *See page 102*

AMERICAN SOCIETY OF NAVAL ENGINEERS

http://www.navalengineers.org/

AMERICAN SOCIETY OF NAVAL ENGINEERS SCHOLARSHIP

• *See page 103*

ARMED FORCES COMMUNICATIONS AND ELECTRONICS ASSOCIATION, EDUCATIONAL FOUNDATION

http://www.afcea.org/scholarships

ARMED FORCES COMMUNICATIONS AND ELECTRONICS ASSOCIATION GENERAL EMMETT PAIGE SCHOLARSHIP

Scholarships of $2000 each will be awarded to persons on active duty in the uniformed military services, to veterans, and to their spouses or dependents, who are currently enrolled full-time in an eligible degree program at an accredited four-year college or university in the United States. Candidate must be a U.S. citizen, majoring in the C4I-related fields. Veterans attending college as freshmen are eligible to apply; all others must be at least sophomores.

Academic Fields/Career Goals: Aviation/Aerospace; Chemical Engineering; Communications; Computer Science/Data Processing; Electrical Engineering/Electronics; Engineering-Related Technologies; Engineering/Technology; International Studies; Mathematics; Physical Sciences.

Award: Scholarship for use in freshman, sophomore, or junior years; not renewable. *Number:* 8–12. *Amount:* $2000.

Eligibility Requirements: Applicant must be enrolled or expecting to enroll full-time at a four-year institution or university. Applicant must have 3.0 GPA or higher. Available to U.S. citizens. Applicant must have general military experience.

Application Requirements: Application form, application form may be submitted online (http://www.afcea.org/education/scholarships/undergraduate/genemm.asp), recommendations or references, transcript. *Deadline:* March 1.

Contact: Ms. Norma Corrales, Director, Scholarships and Awards Program
Armed Forces Communications and Electronics Association, Educational Foundation
4400 Fair Lakes Court
Fairfax, VA 22015
Phone: 703-631-6149
E-mail: scholarship@afcea.org

ARMED FORCES COMMUNICATIONS AND ELECTRONICS ASSOCIATION ROTC SCHOLARSHIP PROGRAM

Award for ROTC students in their sophomore or junior years enrolled in four-year accredited colleges or universities in the United States. Eligible fields of study are electronics or electrical, communications, or aerospace engineering; physics; mathematics; and computer science. Must exhibit academic excellence and potential to serve as an officer in the armed forces of the United States. Nominations are submitted by professors of military science, naval science, or aerospace studies.

Academic Fields/Career Goals: Aviation/Aerospace; Communications; Computer Science/Data Processing; Electrical Engineering/Electronics; Engineering-Related Technologies; Engineering/Technology; Foreign Language; International Studies; Mathematics; Physical Sciences.

Award: Scholarship for use in sophomore or junior years; not renewable. *Number:* 35–45. *Amount:* $2000–$4000.

Eligibility Requirements: Applicant must be enrolled or expecting to enroll full-time at a four-year institution or university. Available to U.S. citizens. Applicant must have served in the Air Force, Army, Marine Corps, or Navy.

Application Requirements: Application form, recommendations or references, transcript. *Deadline:* February 15.

Contact: Ms. Norma Corrales, Director, Scholarships and Awards Program
Armed Forces Communications and Electronics Association, Educational Foundation
4400 Fair Lakes Court
Fairfax, VA 22015
Phone: 703-631-6149
E-mail: scholarship@afcea.org

DISABLED WAR VETERANS SCHOLARSHIP

Scholarships are offered to active-duty service personnel, honorably discharged U.S. military veterans, reservists, and National Guard personnel who are disabled because of wounds received during active-duty combat service in Enduring Freedom-Afghanistan or Iraqi Freedom Operations. Candidates must be majoring in fields related to C4I, the support of U.S. intelligence, national security enterprises, or with relevance to the mission of AFCEA.

Academic Fields/Career Goals: Aviation/Aerospace; Computer Science/Data Processing; Education; Electrical Engineering/Electronics; Engineering/Technology; Mathematics; Physical Sciences.

Award: Scholarship for use in freshman, sophomore, junior, or senior years; not renewable. *Number:* 2. *Amount:* $2500.

Eligibility Requirements: Applicant must be hearing impaired, physically disabled, or visually impaired and enrolled or expecting to enroll full- or part-time at a two-year or four-year institution or university. Applicant must be hearing impaired, physically disabled, or visually impaired. Available to U.S. citizens. Applicant must have general military experience.

Application Requirements: Application form, application form may be submitted online (http://www.afcea.org/education/scholarships/undergraduate/DisabledVeteranScholarship.asp), recommendations or references, transcript. *Deadline:* April 1.

Contact: Miss. Norma Corrales, Director of AFCEA Educational Foundation Scholarship Program
Armed Forces Communications and Electronics Association, Educational Foundation
4400 Fair Lakes Parkway
Fairfax, VA 22033
Phone: 703-631-6149
E-mail: ncorrales@afcea.org

LTG DOUGLAS D. BUCHHOLZ MEMORIAL SCHOLARSHIP

Candidates must be current active enlisted soldiers assigned to Fort Gordon, Georgia, and be majoring in the following or related fields of electrical, chemical, systems or aerospace engineering, mathematics, physics, science or mathematics education, or computer science. Majors directly related to the support of U.S. Intelligence enterprises or national security with relevance to the mission of AFCEA will also be eligible.

Academic Fields/Career Goals: Aviation/Aerospace; Chemical Engineering; Computer Science/Data Processing; Electrical Engineering/Electronics; Mathematics; Physical Sciences.

Award: Scholarship for use in freshman, sophomore, junior, or senior years; not renewable. *Number:* 1. *Amount:* $2000.

Eligibility Requirements: Applicant must be enrolled or expecting to enroll full- or part-time at a two-year or four-year institution or university and resident of Georgia. Applicant must have 2.5 GPA or higher. Available to U.S. citizens. Applicant must have general military experience.

Application Requirements: Application form, application form may be submitted online (http://www.afcea.org/education/scholarships/undergraduate/ltgdoug.asp), essay. *Deadline:* varies.

Contact: Mr. Joseph Yavorsky, President, AFCEA Augusta-Fort Gordon Chapter
E-mail: president@afcea-augusta.org

ASSOCIATION OF FORMER INTELLIGENCE OFFICERS

http://www.afio.com/13_scholarships.htm

CIA UNDERGRADUATE SCHOLARSHIPS

• See page 97

ASTRONAUT SCHOLARSHIP FOUNDATION

http://www.astronautscholarship.org/

ASTRONAUT SCHOLARSHIP FOUNDATION

• See page 104

AVIATION COUNCIL OF PENNSYLVANIA

http://www.acpfly.com/

AVIATION COUNCIL OF PENNSYLVANIA SCHOLARSHIP PROGRAM

Awards for Pennsylvania residents to pursue studies at Pennsylvania institutions leading to career as professional pilot or in the fields of aviation technology or aviation management. Awards at discretion of Aviation Council of Pennsylvania. Three to four scholarships ranging from $500 to $1000. Applicants for the aviation management scholarship may attend institutions outside of Pennsylvania.

Academic Fields/Career Goals: Aviation/Aerospace.

Award: Scholarship for use in freshman, sophomore, junior, or senior years; not renewable. *Number:* 3–4. *Amount:* $500–$1000.

Eligibility Requirements: Applicant must be enrolled or expecting to enroll full- or part-time at a two-year or four-year or technical institution or university; resident of Pennsylvania; studying in Pennsylvania and must have an interest in aviation. Available to U.S. citizens.

Application Requirements: Application form, financial need analysis, recommendations or references, transcript. *Deadline:* varies.

Contact: Robert Rockmaker, Coordinator
Aviation Council of Pennsylvania
3111 Arcadia Avenue
Allentown, PA 18103-6903
Phone: 610-797-6911
Fax: 610-797-8238
E-mail: info@acpfly.com

AVIATION DISTRIBUTORS AND MANUFACTURERS ASSOCIATION INTERNATIONAL

http://www.adma.org/

ADMA SCHOLARSHIP

Scholarship to provide assistance to students pursuing careers in the aviation field. Those enrolled in an accredited Aviation program may be eligible.

Academic Fields/Career Goals: Aviation/Aerospace.

Award: Scholarship for use in junior or senior years; not renewable. *Number:* 1. *Amount:* up to $2000.

Eligibility Requirements: Applicant must be enrolled or expecting to enroll full-time at a two-year or four-year institution or university and must have an interest in aviation. Applicant must have 3.0 GPA or higher. Available to U.S. citizens.

Application Requirements: Application form, essay, financial need analysis, recommendations or references, transcript. *Deadline:* March 28.

BOY SCOUTS OF AMERICA-MUSKINGUM VALLEY COUNCIL

http://www.learning-for-life.org/

NATIONAL AVIATION EXPLORER SCHOLARSHIPS

$3000-$10,000 scholarships for aviation Explorers pursuing a career in the aviation industry. The intent of these scholarships is to identify and reward those individuals who best exemplify the qualities that lead to success in the aviation industry. Must be participant of the Learning for Life Exploring program.

Academic Fields/Career Goals: Aviation/Aerospace.

Award: Scholarship for use in freshman, sophomore, junior, or senior years; not renewable. *Number:* 5. *Amount:* $3000–$10,000.

Eligibility Requirements: Applicant must be enrolled or expecting to enroll full- or part-time at a technical institution and must have an interest in aviation or leadership. Available to U.S. and non-U.S. citizens.

Application Requirements: Application form, essay, recommendations or references. *Deadline:* March 31.

Contact: Bill Rogers, Associate Director
>   *Phone:* 972-580-2433
>   *Fax:* 972-580-2137
>   *E-mail:* brogers@lflmail.org

CHARLIE WELLS MEMORIAL SCHOLARSHIP FUND

http://www.wellsscholarship.com/

CHARLIE WELLS MEMORIAL AVIATION GRANT

Applicant must be enrolled in and attending school regularly, or already have a high school diploma or GED. Must be a resident of the United States or one of its territories.

Academic Fields/Career Goals: Aviation/Aerospace.

Award: Grant for use in freshman, sophomore, junior, senior, or graduate years; not renewable.

Eligibility Requirements: Applicant must be enrolled or expecting to enroll full- or part-time at a four-year institution or university. Available to U.S. citizens.

Application Requirements: Application form, recommendations or references, transcript. *Deadline:* April 30.

Contact: Roger Thompson, Manager
>   *Phone:* 217-899-3263
>   *E-mail:* rog@wellsscholarship.com

CHARLIE WELLS MEMORIAL AVIATION SCHOLARSHIP

Scholarship(s) of varying amounts will be awarded each year when funds are available. The applicant must be a resident of the United States or one of its territories. Must be a full-time student majoring in an aviation-oriented curriculum.

Academic Fields/Career Goals: Aviation/Aerospace.

Award: Scholarship for use in freshman, sophomore, junior, senior, or graduate years; not renewable.

Eligibility Requirements: Applicant must be enrolled or expecting to enroll full-time at a four-year institution or university. Available to U.S. citizens.

Application Requirements: Application form, recommendations or references, transcript. *Deadline:* April 30.

Contact: Roger Thompson, Manager
>   *Phone:* 217-899-3263
>   *E-mail:* rog@wellsscholarship.com

CIVIL AIR PATROL, USAF AUXILIARY

http://www.gocivilairpatrol.com/

MAJOR GENERAL LUCAS V. BEAU FLIGHT SCHOLARSHIPS SPONSORED BY THE ORDER OF DAEDALIANS

One-time scholarships for active cadets of the Civil Air Patrol who desire a career in military aviation. Award is to be used toward flight training for a private pilot license. Must be 15 1/2 to 18 1/2 years of age on April 1st of the year for which applying. Must be an active CAP cadet officer. Not open to the general public.

Academic Fields/Career Goals: Aviation/Aerospace.

Award: Scholarship for use in freshman year; not renewable. *Number:* 5. *Amount:* $2100.

Eligibility Requirements: Applicant must be high school student; planning to enroll or expecting to enroll full- or part-time at a four-year institution or university; single and must have an interest in aviation. Applicant or parent of applicant must be member of Civil Air Patrol. Available to U.S. citizens.

Application Requirements: Application form, essay, interview, personal photograph, recommendations or references, test scores, transcript. *Deadline:* March 1.

Contact: Kelly Easterly, Assistant Program Manager
>   Civil Air Patrol, USAF Auxiliary
>   105 South Hansell Street, Building 714
>   Maxwell Air Force Base, AL 36112-6332
>   *Phone:* 334-953-8640
>   *Fax:* 334-953-6699
>   *E-mail:* cpr@capnhq.gov

DAEDALIAN FOUNDATION

http://www.daedalians.org/

DAEDALIAN FOUNDATION MATCHING SCHOLARSHIP PROGRAM

Scholarship program, wherein the foundation matches amounts given by flights, or chapters of the Order of Daedalians, to deserving college and university students who are pursuing a career as a military aviator.

Academic Fields/Career Goals: Aviation/Aerospace.

Award: Scholarship for use in freshman, sophomore, junior, senior, or graduate years; not renewable. *Number:* 75–80. *Amount:* up to $2000.

Eligibility Requirements: Applicant must be enrolled or expecting to enroll full-time at a four-year institution or university. Available to U.S. citizens.

Application Requirements: Application form, flight/ROTC/CAP recommendation, personal photograph, test scores. *Deadline:* December 31.

Contact: Carole Thomson, Program Executive Secretary
>   Daedalian Foundation
>   55 Main Circle, Building 676
>   Randolph AFB, TX 78148
>   *Phone:* 210-945-2113
>   *Fax:* 210-945-2112
>   *E-mail:* icarus@texas.net

EAA AVIATION FOUNDATION, INC.

http://www.eaa.org/

HANSEN SCHOLARSHIP

Renewable scholarship of $1000 for a student enrolled in an accredited institution and pursuing a degree in aerospace engineering or aeronautical engineering. Student must be in good standing; financial need not a requirement. Must be an EAA member. Applications may be downloaded from the website http://www.youngeagles.org.

Academic Fields/Career Goals: Aviation/Aerospace.

Award: Scholarship for use in freshman, sophomore, junior, or senior years; not renewable. *Number:* up to 1. *Amount:* up to $1000.

Eligibility Requirements: Applicant must be enrolled or expecting to enroll full-time at a two-year or four-year or technical institution or university. Applicant or parent of applicant must be member of Experimental Aircraft Association. Available to U.S. and non-U.S. citizens.

Application Requirements: Application form. *Deadline:* February 29.

Contact: Jane Smith, Scholarship Coordinator
>   EAA Aviation Foundation, Inc.
>   PO Box 3086
>   Oshkosh, WI 54903-3086
>   *Phone:* 920-426-6823
>   *Fax:* 920-426-4873
>   *E-mail:* jsmith@eaa.org

PAYZER SCHOLARSHIP

Scholarship for a student accepted or enrolled in an accredited college, university, or postsecondary school with an emphasis on technical information. Awarded to an individual who is seeking a major and declares an intention to pursue a professional career in engineering, mathematics, or the physical/biological sciences. Visit http://www.youngeagles.org for criteria and to download official application. Must be an EAA member or recommended by an EAA member.

Academic Fields/Career Goals: Aviation/Aerospace; Biology; Engineering/Technology; Physical Sciences.

Award: Scholarship for use in freshman, sophomore, junior, or senior years; not renewable. *Number:* up to 1. *Amount:* up to $5000.

Eligibility Requirements: Applicant must be enrolled or expecting to enroll full-time at a two-year or four-year or technical institution or university. Applicant or parent of applicant must be member of Experimental Aircraft Association. Available to U.S. and non-U.S. citizens.

Application Requirements: Application form. *Deadline:* February 29.

Contact: Jane Smith, Scholarship Coordinator
EAA Aviation Foundation, Inc.
PO Box 3086
Oshkosh, WI 54903-3086
Phone: 920-426-6823
Fax: 920-426-4873
E-mail: jsmith@eaa.org

GENERAL AVIATION MANUFACTURERS ASSOCIATION

http://www.gama.aero/

EDWARD W. STIMPSON "AVIATION EXCELLENCE" AWARD

One-time scholarship award for students who are graduating from high school and have been accepted to attend aviation college or university in the upcoming year. See website at http://www.gama.aero for more details.

Academic Fields/Career Goals: Aviation/Aerospace.

Award: Scholarship for use in freshman year; not renewable. *Number:* 1. *Amount:* $500.

Eligibility Requirements: Applicant must be high school student; planning to enroll or expecting to enroll full-time at a four-year institution or university and must have an interest in aviation. Applicant must have 3.0 GPA or higher. Available to U.S. citizens.

Application Requirements: Application form, essay, recommendations or references, transcript. *Deadline:* April 28.

Contact: Katie Pribyl, Director, Communications
Phone: 202-393-1500
Fax: 202-842-4063
E-mail: kpribyl@gama.aero

HAROLD S. WOOD AWARD FOR EXCELLENCE

One-time scholarship award for an university student who is attending a National Intercollegiate Flying Association (NIFA) school. Must have completed at least one semester of coursework. See website at http://www.gama.aero for additional details.

Academic Fields/Career Goals: Aviation/Aerospace.

Award: Scholarship for use in freshman, sophomore, junior, or senior years; not renewable. *Number:* 1. *Amount:* $1000.

Eligibility Requirements: Applicant must be enrolled or expecting to enroll full-time at a four-year institution or university. Applicant must have 3.0 GPA or higher. Available to U.S. citizens.

Application Requirements: Application form, nomination, recommendations or references, transcript. *Deadline:* February 24.

Contact: Katie Pribyl, Director, Communications
Phone: 202-393-1500
Fax: 202-842-4063
E-mail: kpribyl@gama.aero

GRAND RAPIDS COMMUNITY FOUNDATION

http://www.grfoundation.org/

JOSHUA ESCH MITCHELL AVIATION SCHOLARSHIP

For students pursuing studies in the field of professional pilot with an emphasis on general aviation, flight engineer, or airway science. Applicant must be a U.S. citizens enrolled in a full- or part-time program at a college or university in the United States providing an accredited flight science curriculum. Applicant should have a minimum GPA of 2.75.

Academic Fields/Career Goals: Aviation/Aerospace.

Award: Scholarship for use in sophomore, junior, or senior years; not renewable. *Number:* 1. *Amount:* $1000.

Eligibility Requirements: Applicant must be enrolled or expecting to enroll full-time at a four-year institution and must have an interest in aviation. Applicant must have 2.5 GPA or higher. Available to U.S. citizens.

Application Requirements: Application form, financial need analysis, recommendations or references, transcript. *Deadline:* April 1.

Contact: Ruth Bishop, Education Program Officer
Phone: 616-454-1751 Ext. 103
Fax: 616-454-6455
E-mail: rbishop@grfoundation.org

GREAT MINDS IN STEM

http://www.greatmindsinstem.org

HISPANIC ENGINEER NATIONAL ACHIEVEMENT AWARDS CORPORATION SCHOLARSHIP PROGRAM

Scholarships available to Hispanic students maintaining a 3.0 GPA. Must be studying an engineering or science-related field.

Academic Fields/Career Goals: Aviation/Aerospace; Biology; Chemical Engineering; Civil Engineering; Computer Science/Data Processing; Electrical Engineering/Electronics; Engineering/Technology; Materials Science, Engineering, and Metallurgy; Mechanical Engineering; Nuclear Science.

Award: Scholarship for use in freshman, sophomore, junior, or senior years; renewable. *Number:* 12–20. *Amount:* $500–$5000.

Eligibility Requirements: Applicant must be Hispanic and enrolled or expecting to enroll full-time at a four-year institution or university. Applicant must have 3.0 GPA or higher. Available to U.S. and non-U.S. citizens.

Application Requirements: Application form, essay, recommendations or references, resume, transcript. *Deadline:* April 30.

Contact: Kathy Barrera, Manager, Recognition Programs
Phone: 323-262-0997 Ext. 300
E-mail: kathy@henaac.org

ILLINOIS PILOTS ASSOCIATION

http://www.illinoispilots.com/

ILLINOIS PILOTS ASSOCIATION MEMORIAL SCHOLARSHIP

Recipient must be a resident of Illinois established in an Illinois postsecondary institution in a full-time aviation-related program. Applicants will be judged by the scholarship committee, and the award (usually $500 annually) will be sent directly to the recipient's school. For further details visit website http://www.illinoispilots.com.

Academic Fields/Career Goals: Aviation/Aerospace.

Award: Scholarship for use in sophomore, junior, or senior years; not renewable. *Number:* 1. *Amount:* $500–$1000.

Eligibility Requirements: Applicant must be enrolled or expecting to enroll full-time at a two-year or four-year or technical institution or university; resident of Illinois; studying in Illinois and must have an interest in aviation. Available to U.S. citizens.

Application Requirements: Application form, application form may be submitted online (http://www.illinoispilots.com), essay, personal photograph, recommendations or references, transcript. *Deadline:* March 1.

Contact: Ruth Frantz, Scholarship Committee Chairman
Illinois Pilots Association
40W297 Apache Lane
Huntley, IL 60142
Phone: 847-669-3821
E-mail: landings8e@aol.com

AVIATION/AEROSPACE

INTERNATIONAL SOCIETY OF AUTOMATION (ISA)

http://www.isa.org/

INTERNATIONAL SOCIETY OF AUTOMATION EDUCATION FOUNDATION SCHOLARSHIPS

One-time scholarship for students enrolled full-time study majoring in one of the following: heating, air-conditioning, refrigeration mechanics, chemical engineering, mechanical engineering, electrical engineering/electronics or automation curriculum. Must have a minimum GPA of 3.0. The scholarship value is $500 to $5000. Deadline is February 15.

Academic Fields/Career Goals: Aviation/Aerospace; Chemical Engineering; Electrical Engineering/Electronics; Energy and Power Engineering; Engineering-Related Technologies; Engineering/Technology; Heating, Air-Conditioning, and Refrigeration Mechanics; Materials Science, Engineering, and Metallurgy; Mechanical Engineering; Paper and Pulp Engineering; Pharmacy.

Award: Scholarship for use in sophomore, junior, or graduate years; not renewable. *Number:* 5–15. *Amount:* $500–$5000.

Eligibility Requirements: Applicant must be enrolled or expecting to enroll full-time at a two-year or four-year or technical institution or university. Applicant must have 3.0 GPA or higher. Available to U.S. and non-U.S. citizens.

Application Requirements: 2 reference letters, 1 of which must be signed by faculty advisor, application form, essay, recommendations or references, self-addressed stamped envelope with application, transcript. *Deadline:* February 15.

Contact: Stacy Peterson, Scholarship Committee
International Society of Automation (ISA)
67 Alexander Drive, PO Box 1277
Research Triangle Park, NC 27709

INTERNATIONAL SOCIETY OF WOMEN AIRLINE PILOTS (ISA+21)

http://www.iswap.org/

INTERNATIONAL SOCIETY OF WOMEN AIRLINE PILOTS AIRLINE SCHOLARSHIPS

Scholarships are available to women who are pursuing careers as airline pilots. Applicants must demonstrate financial need. Must have a U.S. FAA Commercial Pilot Certificate with an Instrument Rating and First Class Medical Certificate. Must have flight time in a fixed wing aircraft commensurate with the rating sought.

Academic Fields/Career Goals: Aviation/Aerospace.

Award: Scholarship for use in freshman, sophomore, junior, or senior years; not renewable. *Number:* up to 5.

Eligibility Requirements: Applicant must be enrolled or expecting to enroll full-time at a four-year institution or university and female. Available to U.S. and non-U.S. citizens.

Application Requirements: Application form, driver's license, financial need analysis, income tax forms, logbook pages, pilot licenses, medical certificates, interview, personal photograph, recommendations or references, resume, transcript. *Deadline:* December 10.

Contact: Ms. Julie Clippard, Scholarship Chairwoman
E-mail: scholarshipsponsor@iswap.org

INTERNATIONAL SOCIETY OF WOMEN AIRLINE PILOTS FINANCIAL SCHOLARSHIP

Scholarships are available to women who are pursuing careers as airline pilots. Must have flight time in a fixed wing aircraft commensurate with the rating sought. Must have flight time in a fixed wing aircraft commensurate with the rating sought.

Academic Fields/Career Goals: Aviation/Aerospace.

Award: Scholarship for use in freshman, sophomore, junior, or senior years; not renewable. *Number:* 1.

Eligibility Requirements: Applicant must be enrolled or expecting to enroll full-time at a four-year institution or university and female. Available to U.S. and non-U.S. citizens.

Application Requirements: Application form, copies of income tax forms, logbook pages, pilot licenses, medical certificates, driver's license, financial need analysis, interview, personal photograph, recommendations or references, resume, transcript. *Deadline:* December 10.

Contact: Ms. Julie Clippard, Scholarship Chairwoman
E-mail: scholarshipsponsor@iswap.org

INTERNATIONAL SOCIETY OF WOMEN AIRLINE PILOTS FIORENZA DE BERNARDI MERIT SCHOLARSHIP

Financial award will aid those pilots endeavoring to fill some of the basic squares, i.e. a CFI, CFII, MEI or any international equivalents. Must have flight time in a fixed wing aircraft commensurate with the rating sought. Must have flight time in a fixed wing aircraft commensurate with the rating sought.

Academic Fields/Career Goals: Aviation/Aerospace.

Award: Scholarship for use in freshman, sophomore, junior, or senior years; not renewable. *Number:* 1.

Eligibility Requirements: Applicant must be enrolled or expecting to enroll full- or part-time at a four-year institution or university and female. Available to U.S. and non-U.S. citizens.

Application Requirements: Application form, copies of income tax forms, logbook pages, pilot licenses, medical certificates, driver's license, financial need analysis, interview, personal photograph, recommendations or references, resume, transcript. *Deadline:* December 10.

Contact: Ms. Julie Clippard, Scholarship Chairwoman
E-mail: scholarshipsponsor@iswap.org

INTERNATIONAL SOCIETY OF WOMEN AIRLINE PILOTS GRACE MCADAMS HARRIS SCHOLARSHIP

Scholarship may fund any ISA scholarship if the applicant has demonstrated an exceptionally spirited and ingenious attitude under difficult circumstances in the field of aviation. Applicants must have an U.S. FAA Commercial Pilot Certificate with an Instrument Rating and First Class Medical Certificate. Visit website http://www.iswap.org for more details.

Academic Fields/Career Goals: Aviation/Aerospace.

Award: Scholarship for use in freshman, sophomore, junior, or senior years; not renewable. *Number:* 1.

Eligibility Requirements: Applicant must be enrolled or expecting to enroll full-time at a four-year institution or university; female and must have an interest in aviation. Available to U.S. and non-U.S. citizens.

Application Requirements: Application form, copies of income tax forms, logbook pages, pilot licenses, medical certificates, driver's license, financial need analysis, interview, personal photograph, recommendations or references, transcript. *Deadline:* December 10.

Contact: Ms. Julie Clippard, Scholarship Chairwoman
E-mail: scholarshipsponsor@iswap.org

INTERNATIONAL SOCIETY OF WOMEN AIRLINE PILOTS HOLLY MULLENS MEMORIAL SCHOLARSHIP

Financial award is reserved for that applicant who is a single mother. Applicants must have an U.S. FAA Commercial Pilot Certificate with an Instrument Rating and First Class Medical Certificate. Visit website, http://www.iswap.org, for more details.

Academic Fields/Career Goals: Aviation/Aerospace.

Award: Scholarship for use in freshman, sophomore, junior, or senior years; not renewable. *Number:* 1.

Eligibility Requirements: Applicant must be enrolled or expecting to enroll full-time at a four-year institution or university and single female. Available to U.S. and non-U.S. citizens.

Application Requirements: Application form, copies of income tax forms, logbook pages, pilot licenses, medical certificates, driver's license, financial need analysis, interview, recommendations or references, transcript. *Deadline:* December 10.

Contact: Ms. Julie Clippard, Scholarship Chairwoman
E-mail: scholarshipsponsor@iswap.org

INTERNATIONAL SOCIETY OF WOMEN AIRLINE PILOTS NORTH CAROLINA FINANCIAL SCHOLARSHIP

Scholarships for a woman pilot from North Carolina interested in a career in the airline world. Must have flight time in a fixed wing aircraft commensurate with the rating sought. Must have flight time in a fixed wing aircraft commensurate with the rating sought.

Academic Fields/Career Goals: Aviation/Aerospace.

Award: Scholarship for use in freshman, sophomore, junior, or senior years; not renewable. *Number:* 1.

Eligibility Requirements: Applicant must be enrolled or expecting to enroll full-time at a four-year institution or university; female and resident of North Carolina. Available to U.S. and non-U.S. citizens.

Application Requirements: Application form, copies of income tax forms, logbook pages, pilot licenses, medical certificates, driver's license, financial need analysis, interview, personal photograph, recommendations or references, resume, transcript. *Deadline:* December 10.

Contact: Ms. Julie Clippard, Scholarship Chairwoman
E-mail: scholarshipsponsor@iswap.org

MANUFACTURERS ASSOCIATION OF MAINE

http://www.mainemfg.com/

MAINE METAL PRODUCTS EDUCATION FUND SCHOLARSHIP PROGRAM

Manufacturers Education Fund offers scholarship awards to individuals seeking education in the metal trades/precision manufacturing field of study. Any Maine student or worker can apply for tuition assistance at any Maine institute of higher learning. All applicants must be full-time students and maintain a minimum of a C average.

Academic Fields/Career Goals: Aviation/Aerospace; Engineering-Related Technologies; Engineering/Technology; Industrial Design; Marine/Ocean Engineering; Materials Science, Engineering, and Metallurgy; Mechanical Engineering; Trade/Technical Specialties.

Award: Scholarship for use in freshman, sophomore, junior, senior, graduate, or postgraduate years; not renewable. *Number:* 5–25. *Amount:* $250–$1000.

Eligibility Requirements: Applicant must be enrolled or expecting to enroll full- or part-time at a two-year or four-year or technical institution or university; resident of Maine and studying in Maine. Available to U.S. citizens.

Application Requirements: Application form, essay, recommendations or references, transcript. *Deadline:* April 31.

Contact: Marion Sprague, Business and Administration Services
Coordinator
Manufacturers Association of Maine
386 Bridgton Road
Westbrook, ME 04092
Phone: 207-854-2153
Fax: 207-854-3865
E-mail: info@mainemfg.com

NASA FLORIDA SPACE GRANT CONSORTIUM

http://www.floridaspacegrant.org/

FLORIDA SPACE RESEARCH PROGRAM

Grants for faculty researchers from Florida public and private universities and community colleges. One-time award for aerospace and technology research. Submit research proposal with budget.

Academic Fields/Career Goals: Aviation/Aerospace; Earth Science; Materials Science, Engineering, and Metallurgy; Mathematics; Mechanical Engineering.

Award: Grant for use in junior, senior, graduate, or postgraduate years; not renewable. *Number:* 13–15. *Amount:* $12,500–$25,000.

Eligibility Requirements: Applicant must be enrolled or expecting to enroll full- or part-time at a two-year or four-year institution or university; resident of Florida and studying in Florida. Available to U.S. citizens.

Application Requirements: Application form, application form may be submitted online (http://www.floridaspacegrant.org/programs/florida-space-research-program-fsrp/), proposal with budget. *Deadline:* May 30.

Contact: Dr. Jaydeep Mukherjee, FSGC Director
NASA Florida Space Grant Consortium
PO Box 160650, 12354 Research Parkway, Room 218
Orlando, FL 32826
Phone: 407-823-6177
E-mail: fsgc@ucf.edu

NASA/MARYLAND SPACE GRANT CONSORTIUM

http://md.spacegrant.org/

NASA MARYLAND SPACE GRANT CONSORTIUM UNDERGRADUATE SCHOLARSHIPS

Scholarship for full-time student majoring in the biological and life sciences, chemistry, geological sciences, physics, astronomy, engineering, computer science, or other related fields. Must be a U.S. citizen and a Maryland resident. Enrollment in an affiliate institution of the Maryland Space Grant Consortium is necessary.

Academic Fields/Career Goals: Aviation/Aerospace; Biology; Chemical Engineering; Computer Science/Data Processing; Earth Science; Engineering/Technology; Environmental Science; Materials Science, Engineering, and Metallurgy; Mathematics; Physical Sciences.

Award: Scholarship for use in freshman, sophomore, junior, or senior years; not renewable. *Amount:* up to $1000.

Eligibility Requirements: Applicant must be enrolled or expecting to enroll full-time at a four-year institution or university; resident of Maryland and studying in Maryland. Applicant must have 3.0 GPA or higher. Available to U.S. citizens.

Application Requirements: Application form, essay, recommendations or references. *Deadline:* May 15.

Contact: Richard Henry, Director
Phone: 410-516-7350
Fax: 410-516-4109
E-mail: henry@jhu.edu

NASA MINNESOTA SPACE GRANT CONSORTIUM

http://www.aem.umn.edu/mnsgc

MINNESOTA SPACE GRANT CONSORTIUM SCHOLARSHIP PROGRAM

Scholarships for full-time undergraduates attending institutions belonging to the Minnesota Space Grant Consortium—institution list on the website. Preference given to students studying aerospace engineering, space science, and NASA-related math, science, or engineering fields. Minimum 3.0 GPA required. Must be U.S. citizen. For more details go to http://www.aem.umn.edu/mnsgc.

Academic Fields/Career Goals: Aviation/Aerospace; Earth Science; Engineering/Technology; Mathematics; Physical Sciences.

Award: Scholarship for use in sophomore, junior, or senior years; not renewable. *Number:* 25–50. *Amount:* $500–$2500.

Eligibility Requirements: Applicant must be enrolled or expecting to enroll full-time at a two-year or four-year institution or university and studying in Minnesota. Applicant must have 3.0 GPA or higher. Available to U.S. citizens.

Application Requirements: Application form, recommendations or references, transcript. *Deadline:* continuous.

NASA MISSISSIPPI SPACE GRANT CONSORTIUM

http://www.olemiss.edu/programs/nasa

MISSISSIPPI SPACE GRANT CONSORTIUM SCHOLARSHIP

Scholarship of $3000 awarded to undergraduate students in the fields of science, technology, engineering, and math. Must be U.S. citizens, community college graduates, and enrolled in a program of full-time study at one of the MSSGC universities. Minimum 3.0 GPA. Underrepresented minorities, females, and students with disabilities are encouraged to apply.

Academic Fields/Career Goals: Aviation/Aerospace; Engineering-Related Technologies; Engineering/Technology; Mathematics; Physical Sciences.

Award: Scholarship for use in freshman, sophomore, junior, or senior years; not renewable. *Number:* 10. *Amount:* $3000.

Eligibility Requirements: Applicant must be enrolled or expecting to enroll full-time at a four-year institution or university. Applicant must have 3.0 GPA or higher. Available to U.S. citizens.

Application Requirements: Application form, recommendations or references, statement of goals and plan of study, transcript. *Deadline:* March 21.

Contact: Margaret Schaff, Project Coordinator
NASA Mississippi Space Grant Consortium
308 Vardaman Hall
University, MS 38677
Phone: 662-915-1187
Fax: 662-915-3927
E-mail: mschaff@olemiss.edu

NASA MONTANA SPACE GRANT CONSORTIUM

http://www.spacegrant.montana.edu/

MONTANA SPACE GRANT SCHOLARSHIP PROGRAM

Awards are made on a competitive basis to students enrolled in fields of study relevant to the aerospace sciences and engineering. Must be U.S. citizen enrolled as full-time student at a Montana Consortium campus.

Academic Fields/Career Goals: Aviation/Aerospace; Biology; Chemical Engineering; Civil Engineering; Computer Science/Data Processing; Electrical Engineering/Electronics; Engineering/Technology; Mathematics; Mechanical Engineering.

Award: Scholarship for use in freshman, sophomore, junior, or senior years; not renewable. *Number:* 15–20. *Amount:* $1500.

Eligibility Requirements: Applicant must be enrolled or expecting to enroll full-time at a four-year institution or university and studying in Montana. Available to U.S. citizens.

Application Requirements: Application form, essay, recommendations or references, transcript. *Deadline:* April 2.

Contact: Glenda Winslow, Program Coordinator
Phone: 406-994-4223
Fax: 406-994-4452
E-mail: winslow@spacegrant.montana.edu

NASA RHODE ISLAND SPACE GRANT CONSORTIUM

http://brown/initiatives/ri-space-grant

NASA RHODE ISLAND SPACE GRANT CONSORTIUM UNDERGRADUATE RESEARCH SCHOLARSHIP

Scholarship for undergraduate students for study and/or outreach related to NASA and space sciences, engineering and/or technology. Must attend a Rhode Island Space Grant Consortium participating school. Recipients are expected to devote a maximum of 4 hours per week in science education for K-12 children and teachers. See website for additional information http://www.spacegrant.brown.edu.

Academic Fields/Career Goals: Aviation/Aerospace; Engineering/Technology; Meteorology/Atmospheric Science.

Award: Scholarship for use in sophomore, junior, or senior years; not renewable. *Number:* up to 2. *Amount:* up to $4000.

Eligibility Requirements: Applicant must be enrolled or expecting to enroll full-time at a four-year institution or university and studying in Rhode Island. Applicant must have 3.0 GPA or higher. Available to U.S. citizens.

Application Requirements: Application form, essay, recommendations or references, resume, transcript. *Deadline:* varies.

Contact: Nancy Ciminelli, Program Manager
NASA Rhode Island Space Grant Consortium
Brown University
Box 1846, Lincoln Field
Providence, RI 02912
Phone: 401-863-1151
Fax: 401-863-3978
E-mail: nancy_ciminelli@brown.edu

NASA RISGC SCIENCE EN ESPANOL SCHOLARSHIP FOR UNDERGRADUATE STUDENTS

Award for undergraduate students attending a Rhode Island Space Grant Consortium participating school and studying in any space-related field of science, math, engineering, or other field with applications in space study. Recipients are expected to devote a maximum of 8 hours per week in outreach activities, supporting ESL teachers with science instruction.

Academic Fields/Career Goals: Aviation/Aerospace; Engineering/Technology; Mathematics.

Award: Scholarship for use in sophomore, junior, or senior years; not renewable. *Number:* 2. *Amount:* up to $4000.

Eligibility Requirements: Applicant must be enrolled or expecting to enroll full-time at a four-year institution or university and studying in Rhode Island. Applicant must have 3.0 GPA or higher. Available to U.S. citizens.

Application Requirements: Application form, essay, resume, transcript. *Deadline:* varies.

Contact: Nancy Ciminelli, Program Manager
NASA Rhode Island Space Grant Consortium
Brown University
Box 1846, Lincoln Field
Providence, RI 02912
Phone: 401-863-1151
Fax: 401-863-3978
E-mail: nancy_ciminelli@brown.edu

NASA RISGC SUMMER SCHOLARSHIP FOR UNDERGRADUATE STUDENTS

Scholarship for full-time summer study. Students are expected to devote 75 percent of their time to a research project with a faculty adviser and 25 percent to outreach activities in science education for K-12 students and teachers. Must attend a Rhode Island Space Grant Consortium participating school. See website for additional information http://www.spacegrant.brown.edu.

Academic Fields/Career Goals: Aviation/Aerospace; Education.

Award: Scholarship for use in sophomore, junior, or senior years; not renewable. *Number:* up to 2. *Amount:* up to $4000.

Eligibility Requirements: Applicant must be enrolled or expecting to enroll full-time at a four-year institution or university and studying in Rhode Island. Applicant must have 3.0 GPA or higher. Available to U.S. citizens.

Application Requirements: Application form, letter of interest, recommendations or references, resume. *Deadline:* varies.

Contact: Nancy Ciminelli, Program Manager
NASA Rhode Island Space Grant Consortium
Brown University
Box 1846, Lincoln Field
Providence, RI 02912
Phone: 401-863-1151
Fax: 401-863-3978
E-mail: nancy_ciminelli@brown.edu

NASA SOUTH CAROLINA SPACE GRANT CONSORTIUM

http://www.cofc.edu/~scsgrant

UNDERGRADUATE RESEARCH AWARD PROGRAM

The undergraduate research program is designed to increase the number of highly trained scientists and engineers and enable undergraduate students to conduct NASA-related research. Awards: Research money awarded by the SC Space Grant Consortium will be administered as a stipend through the Financial Aid office on whose campus the Scholar is working. The full research stipend amount is $5,000. Two types of Undergraduate Research stipends are available, each $5,000. Up to $500 of the $5,000 will be available for research related expenses, not including any application fees. The applicant may select which one they wish to apply for: (a) An academic year award given to students interested in conducting research on an aerospace- or space science-related topic during the academic calendar year or (b) A student may conduct aerospace or space science related research for 10 weeks in the summer. For details refer to website: http://spinner.cofc.edu/~scsgrant/scholar/undergraduate.html

Academic Fields/Career Goals: Aviation/Aerospace; Biology; Earth Science; Engineering-Related Technologies; Engineering/Technology.

Award: Grant for use in freshman, sophomore, junior, or senior years; not renewable. *Number:* 5–10. *Amount:* up to $5000.

Eligibility Requirements: Applicant must be enrolled or expecting to enroll full-time at a four-year institution or university and studying in South Carolina. Available to U.S. citizens.

Application Requirements: Application form, application form may be submitted online (http://spinner.cofc.edu/~scsgrant/scholar/undergraduate.html), entry in a contest, essay, recommendations or references, research proposal, resume, transcript. *Deadline:* February 9.

Contact: Mrs. Tara Scozzaro, Program Manager
NASA South Carolina Space Grant Consortium
College of Charleston, 66 George Street
Charleston, SC 29424
Phone: 843-953-5463
Fax: 843-953-5446
E-mail: scozzarot@cofc.edu

NASA SOUTH DAKOTA SPACE GRANT CONSORTIUM

http://sdspacegrant.sdsmt.edu/

SOUTH DAKOTA SPACE GRANT CONSORTIUM UNDERGRADUATE AND GRADUATE STUDENT SCHOLARSHIPS

Scholarship for undergraduate graduate students pursuing studies in science, technology, engineering, math, aerospace, or related fields at South Dakota institutions. Women and minorities are encouraged to apply. For more information, see website http://sdspacegrant.sdsmt.edu/.

Academic Fields/Career Goals: Aviation/Aerospace; Earth Science; Energy and Power Engineering; Engineering-Related Technologies; Engineering/Technology; Environmental Science; Materials Science, Engineering, and Metallurgy; Mathematics; Natural Sciences; Physical Sciences; Science, Technology, and Society.

Award: Scholarship for use in freshman, sophomore, junior, senior, or graduate years; renewable. *Number:* 45–50. *Amount:* $1000–$14,000.

Eligibility Requirements: Applicant must be enrolled or expecting to enroll full-time at a four-year institution or university and studying in South Dakota. Applicant must have 3.0 GPA or higher. Available to U.S. citizens.

Application Requirements: Application form, recommendations or references, resume, transcript. *Deadline:* varies.

Contact: Mr. Thomas Durkin, Deputy Director
NASA South Dakota Space Grant Consortium
501 East Saint Joseph Street
Rapid City, SD 57701
Phone: 605-394-1975
Fax: 605-394-5360
E-mail: thomas.durkin@sdsmt.edu

NASA'S VIRGINIA SPACE GRANT CONSORTIUM

http://www.vsgc.odu.edu/

UNDERGRADUATE STEM RESEARCH SCHOLARSHIPS
• *See page 106*

NASA WEST VIRGINIA SPACE GRANT CONSORTIUM

http://www.nasa.wvu.edu/

WEST VIRGINIA SPACE GRANT CONSORTIUM UNDERGRADUATE FELLOWSHIP PROGRAM

Scholarships intended to support undergraduate students pursuing a degree in science, technology, engineering, or math. Students are given opportunities to work with faculty members within their major department on research projects, or students may participate in the Consortium Challenge Program. Must be U.S. citizen. Refer to website for further details http://www.nasa.wvu.edu.

Academic Fields/Career Goals: Aviation/Aerospace; Computer Science/Data Processing; Energy and Power Engineering; Engineering-Related Technologies; Engineering/Technology; Environmental Science; Meteorology/Atmospheric Science; Natural Sciences; Nuclear Science; Physical Sciences.

Award: Scholarship for use in freshman, sophomore, junior, or senior years; not renewable. *Amount:* $1000–$2000.

Eligibility Requirements: Applicant must be enrolled or expecting to enroll full-time at a four-year institution or university. Available to U.S. citizens.

Application Requirements: Application form. *Deadline:* March 7.

Contact: Prof. Candy Cordwell, Program Manager
NASA West Virginia Space Grant Consortium
395 Evansdale Drive, G68 ESB
PO Box 6070
Morgantown, WV. 26506
Phone: 304-293-4099 Ext. 3738
Fax: 304-293-4970
E-mail: cordwell@nasa.wvu.edu

NASA WISCONSIN SPACE GRANT CONSORTIUM

http://www.uwgb.edu/WSGC

WISCONSIN SPACE GRANT CONSORTIUM UNDERGRADUATE RESEARCH PROGRAM

One-time award of up to $3500 for a U.S. citizen enrolled full-time, admitted to, or applying to any undergraduate program at a Wisconsin Space Grant Consortium college or university. Award goes to a student to create and implement their own small research study. Minimum 3.0 GPA required. Submit proposal with budget. Refer to website for more information http://www.uwgb.edu/wsgc.

Academic Fields/Career Goals: Aviation/Aerospace.

Award: Grant for use in freshman, sophomore, junior, or senior years; not renewable. *Number:* up to 15. *Amount:* up to $3500.

Eligibility Requirements: Applicant must be enrolled or expecting to enroll full-time at a four-year institution or university; resident of Wisconsin and studying in Wisconsin. Applicant must have 3.0 GPA or higher. Available to U.S. citizens.

Application Requirements: Application form, proposal with budget, recommendations or references, transcript. *Deadline:* February 3.

Contact: Brittany Luedtke, Office Coordinator
Phone: 920-465-2108
Fax: 920-465-2376
E-mail: luedtkeb@uwgb.edu

WISCONSIN SPACE GRANT CONSORTIUM UNDERGRADUATE SCHOLARSHIP PROGRAM

Scholarship of up to $1500 for a U.S. citizen enrolled full-time in, admitted to, or applying to any undergraduate program at a Wisconsin Space Grant Consortium college or university. Awards will be given to students with outstanding potential in programs of aerospace, space science, or other interdisciplinary space-related studies. Minimum 3.0 GPA required. Refer to website for more information http://www.uwgb.edu/wsgc.

Academic Fields/Career Goals: Aviation/Aerospace.

Award: Scholarship for use in freshman, sophomore, junior, or senior years; not renewable. *Number:* 15–20. *Amount:* up to $1500.

Eligibility Requirements: Applicant must be enrolled or expecting to enroll full-time at a four-year institution or university; resident of Wisconsin and studying in Wisconsin. Applicant must have 3.0 GPA or higher. Available to U.S. citizens.

Application Requirements: Application form, essay, recommendations or references, transcript. *Deadline:* February 3.

Contact: Brittany Luedtke, Office Coordinator
Phone: 920-465-2108
Fax: 920-465-2376
E-mail: luedtkeb@uwgb.edu

NATIONAL AIR TRANSPORTATION FOUNDATION

http://www.nata.aero

DAN L. MEISINGER, SR. MEMORIAL LEARN TO FLY SCHOLARSHIP

Scholarship established in the honor and memory of Dan L. Meisinger Sr., whose career in aviation spanned 63 years. He was founder of

Executive Beechcraft and was twice named Beech Aircraft's Man of the Year. The fund provides an annual flight training scholarship to a qualified individual. For more information, visit website http://www.nata.aero/Scholarships/Dan-L.-Meisinger,-Sr.-Memorial-Scholarship.aspx.

Academic Fields/Career Goals: Aviation/Aerospace.

Award: Scholarship for use in freshman, sophomore, junior, or senior years; not renewable. *Number:* 1. *Amount:* $2500.

Eligibility Requirements: Applicant must be enrolled or expecting to enroll full-time at a two-year or four-year institution or university. Applicant must have 3.0 GPA or higher. Available to U.S. citizens.

Application Requirements: Application form, essay, recommendations or references, test scores, transcript. *Deadline:* November 28.

Contact: Ms. Elizabeth Nicholson, Manager, Safety 1st Programs
    Phone: 703-845-9000
    E-mail: safety1st@nata.aero

NATA BUSINESS SCHOLARSHIP

Scholarship available for education or training to establish a career in the business aviation industry. Applicable education includes any aviation-related two-year, four-year or graduate degree program at an accredited college or university. Must be 18 years of age or older, be nominated and endorsed by a representative of a regular or associate member company of the NATA. Applicable training includes any aviation maintenance program under the aegis of Part 147 or 65, any pilot certificate or rating under Part 61 or 141, and any aviation-related two-year, four-year or graduate degree program at an accredited college or university. Visit website for more information http://www.nata.aero/Scholarships/NATA-Business-Scholarship.aspx.

Academic Fields/Career Goals: Aviation/Aerospace.

Award: Scholarship for use in freshman, sophomore, junior, senior, graduate, or postgraduate years; not renewable. *Number:* 1. *Amount:* $2500.

Eligibility Requirements: Applicant must be enrolled or expecting to enroll full- or part-time at a two-year or four-year or technical institution or university. Available to U.S. citizens.

Application Requirements: Application form, essay, recommendations or references, resume, transcript. *Deadline:* December 26.

Contact: Ms. Elizabeth Nicholson, Manager, Safety 1st Programs
    Phone: 703-845-9000
    E-mail: safety1st@nata.aero

NAVIGATE YOUR FUTURE SCHOLARSHIP

$2500 scholarship for a high school senior planning a career in the general aviation field. Must be enrolled or accepted into an aviation-related program at an accredited college or university and be able to demonstrate an interest in pursuing a career in general aviation.

Academic Fields/Career Goals: Aviation/Aerospace.

Award: Scholarship for use in freshman year; not renewable. *Number:* 1. *Amount:* $2500.

Eligibility Requirements: Applicant must be high school student and planning to enroll or expecting to enroll full-time at a four-year institution or university. Applicant must have 3.0 GPA or higher. Available to U.S. citizens.

Application Requirements: Application form, essay, personal statement, recommendations or references, transcript. *Deadline:* June 29.

Contact: Ms. Elizabeth Nicholson, Manager, Safety 1st Programs
    Phone: 703-845-9000
    E-mail: safety1st@nata.aero

PIONEERS OF FLIGHT SCHOLARSHIP

Scholarship recipients will be notified in writing by the end of April. Interested students must complete the attached application and submit it along with a complete transcript of grades, a letter of recommendation, an essay on general aviation and a paper indicating career goals in general aviation postmarked no later than the last Friday in December. For more information, visit website http://www.nata.aero/Scholarships/Pioneers-of-Flight-Scholarship-Program.aspx

Academic Fields/Career Goals: Aviation/Aerospace.

Award: Scholarship for use in sophomore or junior years; not renewable. *Number:* 2. *Amount:* $1000.

Eligibility Requirements: Applicant must be enrolled or expecting to enroll full-time at a four-year institution or university. Applicant must have 3.0 GPA or higher. Available to U.S. citizens.

Application Requirements: Application form, essay, recommendations or references, test scores, transcript. *Deadline:* December 26.

Contact: Ms. Elizabeth Nicholson, Manager, Safety 1st Programs
    Phone: 703-845-9000
    E-mail: safety1st@nata.aero

RICHARD L. TAYLOR FLIGHT TRAINING SCHOLARSHIP

The Richard L. Taylor Flight Training Scholarship applicant must be enrolled in an accredited college/university, be enrolled in a flight program through the college/university with aspirations to become a pilot (general or commercial aviation), have a private pilot's license (a copy must be included in application the packet), have a GPA of 3.0 or greater, show junior and senior grade point averages from high school (if applying as an incoming freshman); and submit an essay about aviation, your goals, and dreams and why you should receive this scholarship.

Academic Fields/Career Goals: Aviation/Aerospace.

Award: Scholarship for use in freshman, sophomore, junior, or senior years; not renewable. *Number:* 1–1. *Amount:* $1500.

Eligibility Requirements: Applicant must be enrolled or expecting to enroll full- or part-time at a two-year or four-year institution or university. Applicant must have 3.0 GPA or higher. Available to U.S. citizens.

Application Requirements: Application form, essay, pilots's license, transcript. *Deadline:* March 29.

Contact: Ms. Elizabeth Nicholson, Manager, Safety 1st Programs
    Phone: 703-845-9000
    E-mail: safety1st@nata.aero

NATIONAL BUSINESS AVIATION ASSOCIATION INC.

http://www.nbaa.org/

ALAN H. CONKLIN BUSINESS AVIATION MANAGEMENT SCHOLARSHIP

$5000 scholarship for students pursuing a career in business aviation management at NBAA and UAA institutions. Minimum 3.0 GPA required. Must be a U.S. citizen.

Academic Fields/Career Goals: Aviation/Aerospace.

Award: Scholarship for use in sophomore, junior, or senior years; not renewable. *Amount:* $5000.

Eligibility Requirements: Applicant must be enrolled or expecting to enroll full-time at a four-year institution or university. Applicant must have 3.0 GPA or higher. Available to U.S. citizens.

Application Requirements: Application form, essay, recommendations or references. *Deadline:* July 31.

Contact: Jay Evans, Director, Operations
    Phone: 202-783-9353
    Fax: 202-331-8364
    E-mail: jevans@nbaa.org

NBAA INTERNATIONAL OPERATORS SCHOLARSHIP

One-time $5000 scholarship offered to one or more recipients. Include with application 500-word essay explaining how this scholarship will help the applicant achieve their international aviation career goals, statement of the funds required to achieve these goals, and at least one professional letter of recommendation, preferably from an NBAA member company employee.

Academic Fields/Career Goals: Aviation/Aerospace.

Award: Scholarship for use in freshman, sophomore, junior, or senior years; not renewable. *Number:* 1. *Amount:* $5000.

Eligibility Requirements: Applicant must be enrolled or expecting to enroll full- or part-time at a two-year or four-year or technical institution or university. Applicant must have 3.0 GPA or higher. Available to U.S. and non-U.S. citizens.

Application Requirements: Application form, essay, recommendations or references. *Deadline:* November 30.

Contact: Jay Evans, Director, Operations
　　　Phone: 202-783-9353
　　　Fax: 202-331-8364
　　　E-mail: jevans@nbaa.org

NBAA JANICE K. BARDEN SCHOLARSHIP

One-time $1000 scholarships for students officially enrolled in NBAA/UAA programs. Must be U.S. citizen, officially enrolled in an aviation-related program with 3.0 minimum GPA. Include with application a 250-word essay describing the applicant's interest and goals for a career in the business aviation industry, and a letter of recommendation from member of aviation department faculty at institution where applicant is enrolled.

Academic Fields/Career Goals: Aviation/Aerospace.

Award: Scholarship for use in sophomore, junior, senior, graduate, or postgraduate years; not renewable. *Number:* 5. *Amount:* $1000.

Eligibility Requirements: Applicant must be enrolled or expecting to enroll full-time at a two-year or four-year institution or university. Applicant must have 3.0 GPA or higher. Available to U.S. citizens.

Application Requirements: Application form, essay, recommendations or references, resume, transcript. *Deadline:* November 1.

Contact: Jay Evans, Director, Operations
　　　Phone: 202-783-9353
　　　Fax: 202-331-8364
　　　E-mail: jevans@nbaa.org

NBAA LAWRENCE GINOCCHIO AVIATION SCHOLARSHIP

One-time $5000 scholarship for students officially enrolled in NBAA/UAA programs. Must be officially enrolled in aviation-related program with 3.0 minimum GPA. Include with application a 500- to 1000-word essay describing interest in and goals for a career in the business aviation industry while demonstrating strength of character. Must also have two letters of recommendation, including one from member of aviation department faculty at institution where applicant is enrolled.

Academic Fields/Career Goals: Aviation/Aerospace.

Award: Scholarship for use in sophomore, junior, senior, or graduate years; not renewable. *Number:* 5. *Amount:* $5000.

Eligibility Requirements: Applicant must be enrolled or expecting to enroll full-time at a four-year institution or university. Applicant must have 3.0 GPA or higher. Available to U.S. and Canadian citizens.

Application Requirements: Application form, essay, proof of enrollment, recommendations or references, resume, transcript. *Deadline:* July 31.

Contact: Jay Evans, Director, Operations
　　　Phone: 202-783-9353
　　　Fax: 202-331-8364
　　　E-mail: jevans@nbaa.org

NBAA WILLIAM M. FANNING MAINTENANCE SCHOLARSHIP

One-time award given to two students pursuing careers as maintenance technicians. One award will benefit a student who is currently enrolled in an accredited Airframe and Power-plant (A&P) program at an approved FAR Part 147 school. The second award will benefit an individual who is not currently enrolled but has been accepted into an A&P program. Include with application a 250-word essay describing applicant's interest in and goals for a career in the aviation maintenance field. A letter of recommendation from an NBAA Member Company representative is encouraged.

Academic Fields/Career Goals: Aviation/Aerospace.

Award: Scholarship for use in freshman, sophomore, junior, senior, or graduate years; not renewable. *Number:* 2. *Amount:* $2500.

Eligibility Requirements: Applicant must be enrolled or expecting to enroll full-time at a two-year or four-year or technical institution or university. Available to U.S. citizens.

Application Requirements: Application form, essay, recommendations or references, resume, transcript. *Deadline:* July 31.

Contact: Jay Evans, Director, Operations
　　　Phone: 202-783-9353
　　　Fax: 202-331-8364
　　　E-mail: jevans@nbaa.org

NATIONAL GAY PILOTS ASSOCIATION

http://www.ngpa.org/

NGPA EDUCATION FUND, INC.

Scholarship for candidates pursuing a career as a professional pilot. Funds cannot be used to pay for the basic private certificate; they must be applied towards advanced fight training at a government certified flight school or to college tuition if enrolled in an accredited aviation degree program. Applicants must provide evidence of their contribution to the gay and lesbian community.

Academic Fields/Career Goals: Aviation/Aerospace.

Award: Scholarship for use in freshman, sophomore, junior, or senior years; not renewable. *Number:* 3–4. *Amount:* $3000–$4000.

Eligibility Requirements: Applicant must be enrolled or expecting to enroll full- or part-time at a two-year or four-year or technical institution or university and must have an interest in aviation or LGBT issues. Applicant or parent of applicant must have employment or volunteer experience in community service. Available to U.S. and non-U.S. citizens.

Application Requirements: Application form, copies of the applicant's pilot certificate, medical certificate, recent logbook page, essay, recommendations or references, transcript. *Deadline:* March 31.

Contact: Capt. Steve Walker, Executive Director
　　　National Gay Pilots Association
　　　PO Box 1652
　　　San Jose, CA 95109
　　　Phone: 214-336-0873
　　　Fax: 214-350-0447
　　　E-mail: ExecDir@ngpa.org

NEVADA NASA SPACE GRANT CONSORTIUM

http://www.nvspacegrant.org/

NATIONAL SPACE GRANT COLLEGE AND FELLOWSHIP PROGRAM

• *See page 106*

PAPA AT CHICAGO EXECUTIVE AIRPORT

http://www.pwkpilots.org

PALWAUKEE AIRPORT PILOTS ASSOCIATION SCHOLARSHIP PROGRAM

Scholarship offered to Illinois residents who are attending accredited programs at Illinois institutions. Must be pursuing a course of study in an aviation-related program. Minimum GPA of 2.0. Applications available on website, http://www.pwkpilots.org.

Academic Fields/Career Goals: Aviation/Aerospace.

Award: Scholarship for use in freshman, sophomore, junior, or senior years; not renewable. *Number:* 2. *Amount:* $500–$1000.

Eligibility Requirements: Applicant must be enrolled or expecting to enroll full-time at a two-year or four-year or technical institution or university; resident of Illinois; studying in Illinois and must have an interest in aviation. Available to U.S. citizens.

Application Requirements: Application form, copy of FAA medical certificate, pilot certificate, driver's license, recommendations or references, transcript. *Deadline:* May 1.

Contact: Raymond Chou, Chairman, Scholarship Committee
　　　PAPA at Chicago Executive Airport
　　　1020 South Plant Road
　　　Wheeling, IL 60090
　　　Phone: 847-537-2580
　　　Fax: 847-537-8183
　　　E-mail: scholarship@pwkpilots.org

PROFESSIONAL AVIATION MAINTENANCE FOUNDATION

http://www.pama.org/

PROFESSIONAL AVIATION MAINTENANCE FOUNDATION STUDENT SCHOLARSHIP PROGRAM

For students enrolled in an airframe and power plant licensing program. Must have a B average and have completed 25 percent of the program. Must reapply each year.

Academic Fields/Career Goals: Aviation/Aerospace; Trade/Technical Specialties.

Award: Scholarship for use in freshman, sophomore, junior, or senior years; not renewable. *Number:* 10–30. *Amount:* $1000.

Eligibility Requirements: Applicant must be enrolled or expecting to enroll full-time at a two-year or four-year or technical institution or university and must have an interest in aviation. Applicant must have 3.0 GPA or higher. Available to U.S. and non-U.S. citizens.

Application Requirements: Application form, financial need analysis, recommendations or references, self-addressed stamped envelope with application, transcript. *Deadline:* October 31.

Contact: Marge Milligan, Marketing Assistant
Professional Aviation Maintenance Foundation
717 Princess Street
Alexandria, VA 22314
Phone: 724-772-4092
Fax: 724-776-3049
E-mail: milligan@sae.org

RHODE ISLAND PILOTS ASSOCIATION

http://www.ripilots.com/

RHODE ISLAND PILOTS ASSOCIATION SCHOLARSHIP

A scholarship open to Rhode Island residents to begin or advance a career in aviation. Must be age 16 or above.

Academic Fields/Career Goals: Aviation/Aerospace.

Award: Scholarship for use in freshman, sophomore, junior, or senior years; not renewable. *Number:* 2–4. *Amount:* $500–$1000.

Eligibility Requirements: Applicant must be enrolled or expecting to enroll full- or part-time at a two-year or four-year or technical institution; resident of Rhode Island and must have an interest in aviation. Available to U.S. citizens.

Application Requirements: Application form, essay, financial need analysis, recommendations or references, test scores, transcript. *Deadline:* February 28.

Contact: Marilyn Biagetti, Scholarship Chair
Phone: 401-568-3497
Fax: 401-568-5392
E-mail: biagettim@cox.net

ROBERT H. MOLLOHAN FAMILY CHARITABLE FOUNDATION, INC.

http://www.mollohanfoundation.org/

MID-ATLANTIC AEROSPACE SCHOLARSHIP

The Mid-Atlantic Aerospace Complex Scholarship provides scholarship opportunities to students who wish to pursue one of the following aerospace programs offered at the Robert C. Byrd National Aerospace Education Center which awards degrees through Fairmont State University and Pierpont Community and Technical College: BS in Aviation Administration Management, BS in Aviation Administration-Professional Flight, BS in Aviation Maintenance Management, AAS in Airframe & Aerospace Electronics Technology, AAS in Aviation Maintenance Technology. The student must have at least a 2.5 GPA, and will be expected to remain actively involved in an aviation program upon receipt of the scholarship.

Academic Fields/Career Goals: Aviation/Aerospace.

Award: Scholarship for use in freshman, sophomore, junior, or senior years. *Amount:* $1000.

Eligibility Requirements: Applicant must be high school student; planning to enroll or expecting to enroll full-time at a four-year institution or university; resident of West Virginia and studying in West Virginia. Applicant must have 2.5 GPA or higher. Available to U.S. citizens.

Application Requirements: Application form, essay, recommendations or references, resume, test scores, transcript.

Contact: Aime Shaffer, Program Manager
Phone: 304-333-6783
E-mail: ashaffer@wvhtf.org

SOCIETY OF AUTOMOTIVE ENGINEERS

http://www.sae.org/

BMW/SAE ENGINEERING SCHOLARSHIP

Scholarship is provided by BMW AG in recognition of its commitment to excellence in engineering. This scholarship is in support of the SAE Foundation to ensure an adequate supply of well-trained engineers for the future. One scholarship will be awarded at $1500 per year, renewable for four years. Must have a 3.75 GPA, rank in the 90th percentile in both math and critical reading on SAT or composite ACT scores. A 3.0 GPA must be maintained to renew the scholarship.

Academic Fields/Career Goals: Aviation/Aerospace; Chemical Engineering; Electrical Engineering/Electronics; Engineering-Related Technologies; Engineering/Technology; Mechanical Engineering.

Award: Scholarship for use in freshman year; renewable. *Number:* 1. *Amount:* $1500.

Eligibility Requirements: Applicant must be high school student and planning to enroll or expecting to enroll full-time at a four-year institution or university. Available to U.S. citizens.

Application Requirements: Application form, essay, test scores, transcript. *Deadline:* December 15.

Contact: Claudia Tremmelling, Scholarship Program Administrator
Phone: 208-388-2200
E-mail: ctremmelling@idahopower.com

EDWARD D. HENDRICKSON/SAE ENGINEERING SCHOLARSHIP

Scholarship of $4000 awarded at $1000 per year for four years. A 3.0 GPA and continued engineering enrollment must be maintained to renew the scholarship. Applicants must have a 3.75 GPA, rank in the 90th percentile in both math and critical reading on SAT or composite ACT scores, and pursue an engineering degree accredited by ABET.

Academic Fields/Career Goals: Aviation/Aerospace; Chemical Engineering; Electrical Engineering/Electronics; Engineering-Related Technologies; Engineering/Technology; Mechanical Engineering.

Award: Scholarship for use in freshman year; renewable. *Number:* 1. *Amount:* $1000.

Eligibility Requirements: Applicant must be high school student and planning to enroll or expecting to enroll full-time at a four-year institution or university. Available to U.S. citizens.

Application Requirements: Application form, essay, test scores, transcript. *Deadline:* December 15.

Contact: Connie Harnish, SAE Educational Relations
Society of Automotive Engineers
400 Commonwealth Drive
Warrendale, PA 15096-0001
Phone: 724-772-4047
Fax: 724-776-0890
E-mail: connie@sae.org

TMC/SAE DONALD D. DAWSON TECHNICAL SCHOLARSHIP

One scholarship of $1500 a year for up to four years as long as a 3.0 GPA and continuing engineering enrollment is maintained. High school seniors must have a 3.25 or higher GPA, SAT math 600 or above and critical reading 550 or above and/or an ACT composite score 27 or above. Transfer students from accredited four-year colleges/universities must have a 3.0 GPA. Students from postsecondary technical/vocational schools must have a 3.5 GPA.

Academic Fields/Career Goals: Aviation/Aerospace; Chemical Engineering; Electrical Engineering/Electronics; Engineering-Related Technologies; Engineering/Technology; Materials Science, Engineering, and Metallurgy; Mechanical Engineering.

Award: Scholarship for use in freshman, sophomore, junior, or senior years; renewable. *Number:* 1. *Amount:* $1500.

Eligibility Requirements: Applicant must be enrolled or expecting to enroll full-time at a two-year or four-year or technical institution or university. Available to U.S. citizens.

Application Requirements: Application form, essay, test scores, transcript. *Deadline:* December 15.

Contact: Connie Harnish, SAE Educational Relations
Society of Automotive Engineers
400 Commonwealth Drive
Warrendale, PA 15096-0001
Phone: 724-772-4047
Fax: 724-776-0890
E-mail: connie@sae.org

SOCIETY OF SATELLITE PROFESSIONALS INTERNATIONAL

http://www.sspi.org/

SSPI INTERNATIONAL SCHOLARSHIPS

Scholarship open to students majoring or planning to major in fields related to satellite communications. Selection is based on academic and leadership achievement, commitment to pursue education and career opportunities in the satellite industry or a field making direct use of satellite technology. Available to members of SSPI.

Academic Fields/Career Goals: Aviation/Aerospace; Communications; Law/Legal Services; Meteorology/Atmospheric Science; Military and Defense Studies.

Award: Scholarship for use in freshman, sophomore, junior, senior, or graduate years; not renewable. *Number:* 1–4. *Amount:* $2500–$4000.

Eligibility Requirements: Applicant must be enrolled or expecting to enroll full-time at a two-year or four-year institution or university. Available to U.S. and non-U.S. citizens.

Application Requirements: Application form may be submitted online (http://www.sspi.org/?Scholarships), essay, financial need analysis, recommendations or references, sample of work, transcript. *Deadline:* May 15.

Contact: Ms. Tamara Bond, Director of Membership
Society of Satellite Professionals International
55 Broad Street, 14th Floor
New York, NY 10004
Phone: 212-809-5199 Ext. 103
Fax: 212-825-0075
E-mail: tbond@sspi.org

STUDENT PILOT NETWORK

STUDENT PILOT NETWORK-FLIGHT DREAM AWARD

Award is for General Aviation Pilot Flight Training. Open to all persons actively engaged in flight training at a registered SPN flight school. Must be a U.S. or Canadian citizen.

Academic Fields/Career Goals: Aviation/Aerospace.

Award: Grant for use in freshman, sophomore, junior, senior, graduate, or postgraduate years; renewable. *Number:* 1–3. *Amount:* $300–$750.

Eligibility Requirements: Applicant must be enrolled or expecting to enroll full- or part-time at a two-year or four-year or technical institution and must have an interest in aviation. Available to U.S. and Canadian citizens.

Application Requirements: Application form, essay. *Deadline:* November 15.

Contact: William Terry, President
Phone: 480-419-7927
E-mail: info@studentpilot.net

UNIVERSITIES SPACE RESEARCH ASSOCIATION

http://www.usra.edu/

UNIVERSITIES SPACE RESEARCH ASSOCIATION SCHOLARSHIP PROGRAM

• See page 107

UNIVERSITY AVIATION ASSOCIATION

http://www.uaa.aero/

CAE SIMUFLITE CITATION TYPE RATING SCHOLARSHIP

Scholarship open to undergraduate seniors and post-baccalaureate graduates of aviation degree programs up to two years after graduation. Must have a minimum 3.25 GPA. Students must attend, or must have graduated from, a University Aviation Association member institution. The application is posted at the University Aviation Association website at www.uaa.aero There are extensive aviation flight certification and flight time requirements for this application, so, please consult the application directly for more details.

Academic Fields/Career Goals: Aviation/Aerospace.

Award: Scholarship for use in senior year; not renewable. *Number:* 4. *Amount:* $10,500.

Eligibility Requirements: Applicant must be enrolled or expecting to enroll full-time at a four-year institution or university and must have an interest in aviation. Available to U.S. citizens.

Application Requirements: Application form, essay, FAA first class medical certificate, recommendations or references, resume, transcript. *Deadline:* March 31.

Contact: Dr. David Newmyer, Professor and Department Chair, Aviation Management and Flight
University Aviation Association
1365 Douglas Drive
Southern Illinois University Carbondale
Carbondale, IL 62901
Phone: 616-453-8898
Fax: 618-453-7286
E-mail: newmyer@siu.edu

CHICAGO AREA BUSINESS AVIATION ASSOCIATION SCHOLARSHIP

One-time awards of $2500 for U.S. citizens who are Illinois residents. Minimum GPA of 2.5. Priority given to Chicagoland residents followed by Illinois residents who are attending, or will attend, a postsecondary aviation degree program in such fields as Aerospace Engineering, Air Traffic Control, Aircraft Charter, Aircraft Maintenance, Aviation Administration/Management, Aviation Flight, Avionics/Aviation Electronics, etc. At least three letters of recommendation required; at least one of these must be from a person currently employed in the field of Business Aviation. The financial statement that is included in the CABAA Scholarship Application must be completed and attached to the application. Application is posted at the website of the University Aviation Association at http://www.uaa.aero.

Academic Fields/Career Goals: Aviation/Aerospace.

Award: Scholarship for use in freshman, sophomore, junior, senior, graduate, or postgraduate years; not renewable. *Number:* 8. *Amount:* $4000.

Eligibility Requirements: Applicant must be enrolled or expecting to enroll full-time at a two-year or four-year or technical institution or university and resident of Illinois. Applicant must have 2.5 GPA or higher. Available to U.S. citizens.

Application Requirements: Application form, essay, recommendations or references. *Deadline:* April 20.

Contact: Dr. David Newmyer, Department Chair, Aviation Management and Flight
University Aviation Association
Southern Illinois University at Carbondale, College of Applied Sciences and Arts
1365 Douglas Drive
Carbondale, IL 62901-6623
Phone: 618-453-8898
Fax: 618-453-7286
E-mail: newmyer@siu.edu

JOSEPH FRASCA EXCELLENCE IN AVIATION SCHOLARSHIP

Established to encourage those who demonstrate the highest level of commitment to and achievement in aviation studies. Applicant must be a junior or senior currently enrolled in a University Aviation Association member institution. Must be FAA certified/qualified in either aviation maintenance or flight, have membership in at least one aviation organization (such as National Intercollegiate Flying Association flying team, Alpha Eta Rho, Warbirds of America, Experimental Aircraft Association, etc), and be involved in aviation activities, projects, and events. Minimum 3.0 GPA required. Application is posted at www.uaa.aero and applications are due on the second Monday of April each year.

Academic Fields/Career Goals: Aviation/Aerospace.

Award: Scholarship for use in junior or senior years; not renewable. *Number:* 2. *Amount:* $2000.

Eligibility Requirements: Applicant must be enrolled or expecting to enroll full- or part-time at a four-year institution or university and must have an interest in aviation. Applicant must have 3.0 GPA or higher. Available to U.S. and non-U.S. citizens.

Application Requirements: Application form, essay, FAA certification as a pilot or mechanic or both, financial need analysis, recommendations or references, transcript. *Deadline:* April 10.

Contact: Dr. David NewMyer, Department Chair, Aviation Management and Flight
University Aviation Association
1365 Douglas Drive
Carbondale, IL 62901-6623
Phone: 618-453-8898
Fax: 618-453-4850
E-mail: newmyer@siu.edu

PAUL A. WHELAN AVIATION SCHOLARSHIP

One-time award of $2000 given to sophomore, junior, senior or graduate. Must be a U.S. citizen. Must be enrolled in University Aviation Association member institution. 2.5 GPA required. Current or past military service (active duty, reserves or national guard, FAA certification, membership in aviation-related association preferred. Application is posted at the University Aviation Association website at www.uaa.aero

Academic Fields/Career Goals: Aviation/Aerospace.

Award: Scholarship for use in sophomore, junior, senior, or graduate years; not renewable. *Number:* 1. *Amount:* $2000.

Eligibility Requirements: Applicant must be enrolled or expecting to enroll full-time at a two-year or four-year institution or university and must have an interest in aviation. Applicant must have 2.5 GPA or higher. Available to U.S. citizens.

Application Requirements: Application form, essay, FAA certification, recommendations or references, transcript. *Deadline:* May 15.

Contact: David Newmyer, Department Chair, Aviation Management and Flight
University Aviation Association
Southern Illinois University at Carbondale, College of Applied Sciences and Arts
1365 Douglas Drive
Carbondale, IL 62901-6623
Phone: 618-453-8898
Fax: 618-453-7268
E-mail: newmyer@siu.edu

VERMONT SPACE GRANT CONSORTIUM

http://www.cems.uvm.edu/vsgc

VERMONT SPACE GRANT CONSORTIUM SCHOLARSHIP PROGRAM

• *See page 107*

VIRGINIA AVIATION AND SPACE EDUCATION FORUM

http://www.doav.virginia.gov/

JOHN R. LILLARD VIRGINIA AIRPORT OPERATORS COUNCIL SCHOLARSHIP PROGRAM

Scholarship of $3000 offered to high school seniors planning a career in the field of aviation. Must be enrolled or accepted into an aviation-related program at an accredited college. Minimum 3.75 unweighted GPA.

Academic Fields/Career Goals: Aviation/Aerospace.

Award: Scholarship for use in freshman year; not renewable. *Number:* 1. *Amount:* $3000.

Eligibility Requirements: Applicant must be high school student; planning to enroll or expecting to enroll full-time at a four-year institution or university and must have an interest in aviation. Available to U.S. and non-U.S. citizens.

Application Requirements: Application form, essay, financial need analysis, recommendations or references, transcript. *Deadline:* February 20.

Contact: Betty Wilson, Program Coordinator
Phone: 804-236-3624
Fax: 804-236-3636
E-mail: betty.wilson@doav.virginia.gov

WILLARD G. PLENTL AVIATION SCHOLARSHIP PROGRAM

Scholarship of $1000 awarded to a high school senior who is planning an aviation career in a non-engineering area.

Academic Fields/Career Goals: Aviation/Aerospace.

Award: Scholarship for use in freshman year; not renewable. *Number:* 1. *Amount:* $1000.

Eligibility Requirements: Applicant must be high school student; planning to enroll or expecting to enroll full-time at a four-year institution or university and must have an interest in aviation. Applicant must have 3.5 GPA or higher. Available to U.S. and non-U.S. citizens.

Application Requirements: Application form, essay, financial need analysis, recommendations or references, transcript. *Deadline:* February 20.

Contact: Betty Wilson, Program Coordinator
Virginia Aviation and Space Education Forum
5702 Gulfstream Road
Richmond, VA 23250-2422
E-mail: betty.wilson@doav.virginia.gov

WHOMENTORS.COM, INC.

http://www.WHOmentors.com/

1B USD WORLDWIDE VENTURE CAPITAL

• *See page 107*

WOMEN IN AVIATION, INTERNATIONAL

http://www.wai.org/

AIRBUS LEADERSHIP GRANT

One scholarship to a college sophomore or higher level student who is pursuing a degree in an aviation-related field. Must have a minimum GPA of 3.0 and must exhibit leadership potential. Must be a WAI member.

Academic Fields/Career Goals: Aviation/Aerospace.

Award: Scholarship for use in sophomore, junior, or senior years; not renewable. *Number:* 1. *Amount:* $5000.

Eligibility Requirements: Applicant must be enrolled or expecting to enroll full- or part-time at a four-year institution or university and must have an interest in leadership. Applicant or parent of applicant must be member of Women in Aviation, International. Applicant must have 3.0 GPA or higher. Available to U.S. and non-U.S. citizens.

Application Requirements: Application form, essay, recommendations or references, resume. *Deadline:* November 12.

Contact: Donna Wallace, Scholarships Committee
Women in Aviation, International
3647 State Rt. 503 South
West Alexandria, OH 45381
Phone: 937-839-4647
Fax: 937-839-4645
E-mail: dwallace@wai.org

BOEING COMPANY CAREER ENHANCEMENT SCHOLARSHIP

Scholarship available for a woman who wishes to advance her career in aerospace technology or a related management field. Open to full-time or part-time employees currently in the aerospace industry or related field. Students pursuing aviation-related degrees that are at the junior level with a minimum GPA of 2.5 are also eligible.

Academic Fields/Career Goals: Aviation/Aerospace.

Award: Scholarship for use in junior or senior years; not renewable. *Number:* 1. *Amount:* $2500.

Eligibility Requirements: Applicant must be enrolled or expecting to enroll full- or part-time at a four-year institution or university and female. Applicant or parent of applicant must be member of Women in Aviation, International. Available to U.S. and non-U.S. citizens.

Application Requirements: Application form, essay, recommendations or references, resume. *Deadline:* November 12.

Contact: Donna Wallace, Scholarships Committee
Women in Aviation, International
3647 State Rt. 503 South
West Alexandria, OH 45381
Phone: 937-839-4647
Fax: 937-839-4645
E-mail: dwallace@wai.org

DASSAULT FALCON JET CORPORATION SCHOLARSHIP

Scholarship of $1000 available for a woman pursuing an undergraduate or graduate degree in an aviation-related field. Applicant must be a U.S. citizen with fluency in English. Must have minimum 3.0 GPA or better (on a 4.0 scale) in her most recent year of schooling. Must be a member of WAI.

Academic Fields/Career Goals: Aviation/Aerospace.

Award: Scholarship for use in freshman, sophomore, junior, or senior years; not renewable. *Number:* 1. *Amount:* $1000.

Eligibility Requirements: Applicant must be enrolled or expecting to enroll full- or part-time at a four-year institution or university and female. Applicant or parent of applicant must be member of Women in Aviation, International. Applicant must have 3.0 GPA or higher. Available to U.S. citizens.

Application Requirements: Application form, essay, recommendations or references, resume. *Deadline:* November 12.

Contact: Donna Wallace, Scholarships Committee
Women in Aviation, International
3647 State Rt. 503 South
West Alexandria, OH 45381
Phone: 937-839-4647
Fax: 937-839-4645
E-mail: dwallace@wai.org

DELTA AIR LINES AIRCRAFT MAINTENANCE TECHNOLOGY SCHOLARSHIP

Scholarship of $5000 available to a student currently enrolled in an aviation maintenance technology program, or pursuing a degree in aviation maintenance technology. Applicant must be a full-time student with a minimum of two semesters left in the program or degree. Must have minimum GPA of 3.0 or better (on a 4.0 scale). Must be a member of WAI. Must be an U.S. citizen or an eligible non-citizen.

Academic Fields/Career Goals: Aviation/Aerospace.

Award: Scholarship for use in freshman, sophomore, or junior years; not renewable. *Number:* 1. *Amount:* $7000.

Eligibility Requirements: Applicant must be enrolled or expecting to enroll full-time at a two-year or four-year or technical institution or university. Applicant or parent of applicant must be member of Women in Aviation, International. Applicant must have 3.0 GPA or higher. Available to U.S. and non-U.S. citizens.

Application Requirements: Application form, essay, recommendations or references, resume. *Deadline:* November 12.

Contact: Donna Wallace, Scholarships Committee
Women in Aviation, International
3647 State Rt. 503 South
West Alexandria, OH 45381
Phone: 937-839-4647
Fax: 937-839-4645
E-mail: dwallace@wai.org

DELTA AIR LINES ENGINEERING SCHOLARSHIP

Scholarship to a student currently enrolled in a baccalaureate degree in aerospace/ aeronautical, electrical, or mechanical engineering. Applicants must be full-time students at the junior or senior level with a minimum of two semesters left. Must have minimum GPA of 3.0. Must be a member of WAI. Must be U.S. citizens or eligible non-citizens.

Academic Fields/Career Goals: Aviation/Aerospace; Electrical Engineering/Electronics; Mechanical Engineering.

Award: Scholarship for use in junior or senior years; not renewable. *Number:* 1. *Amount:* $7000.

Eligibility Requirements: Applicant must be enrolled or expecting to enroll full-time at a four-year institution or university. Applicant or parent of applicant must be member of Women in Aviation, International. Applicant must have 3.0 GPA or higher. Available to U.S. and non-U.S. citizens.

Application Requirements: Application form, essay, recommendations or references, resume. *Deadline:* November 12.

Contact: Donna Wallace, Scholarships Committee
Women in Aviation, International
3647 State Rt. 503 South
West Alexandria, OH 45381
Phone: 937-839-4647
Fax: 937-839-4645
E-mail: dwallace@wai.org

DELTA AIR LINES MAINTENANCE MANAGEMENT/ AVIATION BUSINESS MANAGEMENT SCHOLARSHIP

Scholarship to a student currently enrolled in an associate or baccalaureate degree in aviation maintenance management or aviation business management. Applicant must be a full-time college student, with a minimum of two semesters left. Must have a minimum GPA of 3.0. Must be a member of WAI and be a U.S. citizen or an eligible non-citizen.

Academic Fields/Career Goals: Aviation/Aerospace.

Award: Scholarship for use in freshman, sophomore, or junior years; not renewable. *Number:* 1. *Amount:* $7000.

Eligibility Requirements: Applicant must be enrolled or expecting to enroll full-time at a two-year or four-year institution or university. Applicant or parent of applicant must be member of Women in Aviation, International. Applicant must have 3.0 GPA or higher. Available to U.S. and non-U.S. citizens.

Application Requirements: Application form, essay, recommendations or references, resume. *Deadline:* November 12.

Contact: Donna Wallace, Scholarships Committee
Women in Aviation, International
3647 State Rt. 503 South
West Alexandria, OH 45381
Phone: 937-839-4647
Fax: 937-839-4645
E-mail: dwallace@wai.org

KEEP FLYING SCHOLARSHIP

One scholarship of up to $3000 will be awarded to an individual working on an instrument or multi engine rating, commercial or initial flight instructor certificate. Flight training must be completed within one year. Minimum requirements: private pilot certificate, 100 hours of flight time, and a copy of a current written test (with passing grade) for the certificate/rating sought. Must be a member of WAI. Finalist will only be interviewed at the annual Women in Aviation Conference.

Academic Fields/Career Goals: Aviation/Aerospace.

Award: Scholarship for use in freshman year; not renewable. *Number:* 1. *Amount:* $3000.

Eligibility Requirements: Applicant must be enrolled or expecting to enroll full- or part-time at a technical institution. Applicant or parent of applicant must be member of Women in Aviation, International. Available to U.S. and non-U.S. citizens.

Application Requirements: Application form, essay, recommendations or references, resume. *Deadline:* November 12.

Contact: Donna Wallace, Scholarships Committee
Women in Aviation, International
3647 State Rt. 503 South
West Alexandria, OH 45381
Phone: 937-839-4647
Fax: 937-839-4645
E-mail: dwallace@wai.org

WOMEN IN AVIATION, INTERNATIONAL ACHIEVEMENT AWARDS

Two scholarships will be awarded to a full-time college or university student, and one to an individual, not necessarily a student, pursuing an aviation-related career goal. Must be a member of WAI.

Academic Fields/Career Goals: Aviation/Aerospace.

Award: Scholarship for use in freshman, sophomore, junior, or senior years; not renewable. *Number:* 2. *Amount:* $1000.

Eligibility Requirements: Applicant must be enrolled or expecting to enroll full-time at a two-year or four-year institution or university. Applicant or parent of applicant must be member of Women in Aviation, International. Available to U.S. and non-U.S. citizens.

Application Requirements: Application form. *Deadline:* November 12.

Contact: Donna Wallace, Scholarships Committee
Women in Aviation, International
3647 State Rt. 503 South
West Alexandria, OH 45381
Phone: 937-839-4647
Fax: 937-839-4645
E-mail: dwallace@wai.org

WOMEN IN AVIATION, INTERNATIONAL MANAGEMENT SCHOLARSHIPS

Scholarship available to a female in an aviation management field who has demonstrated traits of leadership, community spirit, and volunteerism. Must be a member of WAI. Scholarship to be used to attend a leadership-related course or seminar or work towards an advanced degree, that raises the individual's level of management.

Academic Fields/Career Goals: Aviation/Aerospace.

Award: Scholarship for use in freshman, sophomore, junior, or senior years; not renewable. *Number:* 1. *Amount:* $1000.

Eligibility Requirements: Applicant must be enrolled or expecting to enroll full- or part-time at a two-year or four-year or technical institution or university; female and must have an interest in leadership. Applicant or parent of applicant must be member of Women in Aviation, International. Available to U.S. and non-U.S. citizens.

Application Requirements: Application form. *Deadline:* November 12.

Contact: Donna Wallace, Scholarships Committee
Women in Aviation, International
3647 State Rt. 503 South
West Alexandria, OH 45381
Phone: 937-839-4647
Fax: 937-839-4645
E-mail: dwallace@wai.org

WOMEN IN CORPORATE AVIATION CAREER SCHOLARSHIPS

Scholarship to a person who is interested in continued pursuit of a career in any job classification in corporate/business aviation. Applicants should be actively working toward their goal and show financial need. Award can be used toward a specific program of education, flight training, dispatcher training, or upgrades in aviation education, and so forth, but cannot include general business course work. Must be a member of WAI.

Academic Fields/Career Goals: Aviation/Aerospace.

Award: Scholarship for use in freshman, sophomore, junior, or senior years; not renewable. *Number:* 1. *Amount:* $2000.

Eligibility Requirements: Applicant must be enrolled or expecting to enroll full- or part-time at a two-year or four-year or technical institution or university and female. Applicant or parent of applicant must be member of Women in Aviation, International. Available to U.S. and non-U.S. citizens.

Application Requirements: Application form, essay, financial need analysis, recommendations or references, resume, transcript. *Deadline:* November 12.

Contact: Donna Wallace, Scholarships Committee
Women in Aviation, International
3647 State Rt. 503 South
West Alexandria, OH 45381
Phone: 937-839-4647
Fax: 937-839-4645
E-mail: dwallace@wai.org

WOMEN MILITARY AVIATORS INC. DREAM OF FLIGHT SCHOLARSHIP

An annual $2500 scholarship for tuition or flight training for a FAA private pilot rating or advanced rating at an accredited institution or school. Applicant must be an academic student or a flight student. Must be able to complete training within one year of the award. Must be a member of WAI.

Academic Fields/Career Goals: Aviation/Aerospace.

Award: Scholarship for use in freshman, sophomore, junior, or senior years; not renewable. *Number:* 1. *Amount:* $2500.

Eligibility Requirements: Applicant must be enrolled or expecting to enroll full- or part-time at a two-year or four-year or technical institution or university. Applicant or parent of applicant must be member of Women in Aviation, International. Available to U.S. and non-U.S. citizens.

Application Requirements: Application form, financial need analysis, recommendations or references, resume. *Deadline:* November 12.

Contact: Donna Wallace, Scholarships Committee
Women in Aviation, International
3647 State Rt. 503 South
West Alexandria, OH 45381
Phone: 937-839-4647
Fax: 937-839-4645
E-mail: dwallace@wai.org

WRIGHT CHAPTER, WOMEN IN AVIATION, INTERNATIONAL, ELISHA HALL MEMORIAL SCHOLARSHIP

Scholarship offered to a woman seeking to further the aviation career in flight training, aircraft scheduling or dispatch, aviation management, aviation maintenance, or avionics. Preference will be given to applicants from Cincinnati Ohio area. Must be a member of WAI, but does not have to be member of Cincinnati Chapter.

Academic Fields/Career Goals: Aviation/Aerospace.

Award: Scholarship for use in freshman, sophomore, junior, or senior years; not renewable. *Number:* 1. *Amount:* $1000.

Eligibility Requirements: Applicant must be enrolled or expecting to enroll full- or part-time at a two-year or four-year or technical institution or university and female. Applicant or parent of applicant must be member of Women in Aviation, International. Available to U.S. and non-U.S. citizens.

Application Requirements: Application form, essay, recommendations or references, resume. *Deadline:* November 12.

Contact: Donna Wallace, Scholarships Committee
Women in Aviation, International
3647 State Rt. 503 South
West Alexandria, OH 45381
Phone: 937-839-4647
Fax: 937-839-4645
E-mail: dwallace@wai.org

BEHAVIORAL SCIENCE

INDIAN HEALTH SERVICES, UNITED STATES DEPARTMENT OF HEALTH AND HUMAN SERVICES

http://www.ihs.gov/scholarship

HEALTH PROFESSIONS PREPARATORY SCHOLARSHIP PROGRAM

Renewable scholarship for undergraduate American Indian/ Alaska Native students enrolled part-time or full-time in programs related to health and allied health professions. Minimum 2.0 GPA required, to apply. Applicant must demonstrate a desire to serve AI/AN people when their health or allied health profession education/ training is complete. The dollar amount and number of awards varies annually.

Academic Fields/Career Goals: Behavioral Science; Health and Medical Sciences; Nursing; Pharmacy; Psychology; Social Sciences.

Award: Scholarship for use in freshman, sophomore, junior, or senior years; renewable. *Number:* 25–50. *Amount:* $26,376–$32,237.

Eligibility Requirements: Applicant must be American Indian/Alaska Native and enrolled or expecting to enroll full- or part-time at a two-year or four-year or technical institution or university. Applicant must have 2.5 GPA or higher. Available to U.S. citizens.

Application Requirements: Application form, application form may be submitted online (http://www.ihs.gov/scholarship), essay, proof of descent, W-4, curriculum for major, course curriculum verification, recommendations or references, transcript. *Deadline:* March 28.

Contact: Capt. Dawn Kelly, Branch Chief
Indian Health Services, United States Department of Health and Human Services
801 Thompson Avenue
Suite 450-A (TMP)
Rockville, MD 20852
Phone: 301-443-6197
Fax: 301-443-6048
E-mail: dawn.kelly@ihs.gov

SOCIETY FOR APPLIED ANTHROPOLOGY

http://www.sfaa.net/

PETER KONG-MING NEW STUDENT PRIZE

Prize awarded for SFAA's annual student research competition in the applied social and behavioral sciences. The issue of research question should be in the domain of health care or human services (broadly construed). The winner of the competition will receive a cash prize of $2000, a crystal trophy, and travel funds to attend the annual meeting of the SFAA. For more details, see website at http://www.sfaa.net.

Academic Fields/Career Goals: Behavioral Science; Health and Medical Sciences; Social Sciences.

Award: Prize for use in freshman, sophomore, junior, or senior years; not renewable. *Number:* 1–2. *Amount:* up to $2000.

Eligibility Requirements: Applicant must be enrolled or expecting to enroll full- or part-time at a two-year or four-year or technical institution or university. Available to U.S. and non-U.S. citizens.

Application Requirements: Application form, entry in a contest, manuscript. *Deadline:* December 31.

Contact: Dr. J.T. May, Executive Director
Society for Applied Anthropology
PO Box 2436
Oklahoma City, OK 73101
Phone: 405-843-5113
Fax: 405-843-8553
E-mail: tom@sfaa.net

SOCIETY FOR THE SCIENTIFIC STUDY OF SEXUALITY

http://www.sexscience.org/

SOCIETY FOR THE SCIENTIFIC STUDY OF SEXUALITY STUDENT RESEARCH GRANT
• See page 102

BIOLOGY

AIST FOUNDATION

http://www.aistfoundation.org/

ASSOCIATION FOR IRON AND STEEL TECHNOLOGY OHIO VALLEY CHAPTER SCHOLARSHIP

Scholarship of $1000 per year for up to four years provided that applicant continues to meet requirements and reapplies for scholarship. Applicant must be a dependent of Ohio Valley Chapter member, or student or Young Professional member. Must attend or plan to attend an accredited school full-time and pursue a degree in any technological field, including engineering, physics, computer sciences, chemistry or other fields approved by the scholarship committee.

Academic Fields/Career Goals: Biology; Computer Science/Data Processing; Electrical Engineering/Electronics; Engineering-Related Technologies; Engineering/Technology; Materials Science, Engineering, and Metallurgy; Physical Sciences.

Award: Scholarship for use in freshman, sophomore, junior, or senior years; not renewable. *Number:* 1–2. *Amount:* $1000.

Eligibility Requirements: Applicant must be enrolled or expecting to enroll full-time at a four-year institution or university. Applicant or parent of applicant must be member of Association for Iron and Steel Technology. Applicant must have 3.0 GPA or higher. Available to U.S. and non-U.S. citizens.

Application Requirements: Application form, essay, recommendations or references, resume, test scores, transcript. *Deadline:* March 31.

Contact: Jeff McKain, Scholarship Chairman
AIST Foundation
11451 Reading Road
Cincinnati, OH 45241
Phone: 724-776-6040
E-mail: jeff.mckain@xtek.com

ALBERTA HERITAGE SCHOLARSHIP FUND

http://www.alis.alberta.ca/

ABORIGINAL HEALTH CAREERS BURSARY

Award for aboriginal students in Alberta, entering their second or subsequent year of postsecondary education in a health field. Must be Indian, Inuit, or Metis students who have been living in Alberta for at least the last three years, and are enrolled full-time at the technical, college, or university level. Students are selected on the basis of financial need, previous academic record, program of study, involvement in the aboriginal community, and experience in the healthcare field. For additional information and an application, visit website http://alis.alberta.ca.

Academic Fields/Career Goals: Biology; Dental Health/Services; Health Administration; Health and Medical Sciences; Nursing; Therapy/Rehabilitation.

Award: Scholarship for use in sophomore, junior, or senior years; not renewable.

Eligibility Requirements: Applicant must be Canadian citizen; American Indian/Alaska Native; enrolled or expecting to enroll full-time at a two-year or four-year or technical institution or university and resident of Alberta.

Application Requirements: Application form, essay, financial need analysis, proof of Aboriginal status, recommendations or references, transcript. *Deadline:* May 1.

AMERICAN ASSOCIATION OF BLOOD BANKS-SBB SCHOLARSHIP AWARDS

http://www.aabb.org/

AABB-FENWAL SCHOLARSHIP AWARD

Scholarship for an individual enrolled, accepted for enrollment in, or having recently completed a program leading to Specialist in Blood Banking certification in an AABB-accredited institution.

Academic Fields/Career Goals: Biology.

Award: Scholarship for use in freshman, sophomore, junior, senior, or graduate years; not renewable. *Number:* 2.

Eligibility Requirements: Applicant must be enrolled or expecting to enroll full- or part-time at an institution or university. Available to U.S. citizens.

Application Requirements: Application form. *Deadline:* June 1.

AMERICAN INDIAN SCIENCE AND ENGINEERING SOCIETY

http://www.aises.org/

A.T. ANDERSON MEMORIAL SCHOLARSHIP PROGRAM
• See page 102

BURLINGTON NORTHERN SANTA FE FOUNDATION SCHOLARSHIP
• See page 102

AMERICAN PHYSIOLOGICAL SOCIETY

http://www.the-aps.org

DAVID S. BRUCE AWARDS FOR EXCELLENCE IN UNDERGRADUATE RESEARCH
• *See page 98*

AMERICAN SOCIETY OF ICHTHYOLOGISTS AND HERPETOLOGISTS

http://www.asih.org/

GAIGE FUND AWARD

Funds are used to provide support to young herpetologists for museum or laboratory study, travel, fieldwork, or any other activity that will effectively enhance their professional careers and their contributions to the science of herpetology. Applicants must be members of ASIH and be enrolled for an advanced degree. Visit website at http://www.asih.org for additional information.

Academic Fields/Career Goals: Biology.

Award: Grant for use in freshman, sophomore, junior, senior, or graduate years; not renewable. *Number:* 5–10. *Amount:* $400–$1000.

Eligibility Requirements: Applicant must be enrolled or expecting to enroll full-time at a four-year institution or university. Applicant or parent of applicant must be member of American Society of Ichthyologists and Herpetologists. Available to U.S. and non-U.S. citizens.

Application Requirements: Application form, financial need analysis, recommendations or references. *Deadline:* March 1.

Contact: Maureen Donnelly, Secretary
Phone: 305-348-1235
Fax: 305-348-1986
E-mail: asih@fiu.edu

RANEY FUND AWARD

Applications are solicited for grants awarded from the Raney Fund for ichthyology. Funds are used to provide support for young ichthyologists for museums or laboratory study, travel, fieldwork, or any activity that will effectively enhance their professional careers and their contributions to the sciences of ichthyology. Must be a member of ASIH and be enrolled for an advanced degree. Visit website at http://www.asih.org for additional information.

Academic Fields/Career Goals: Biology.

Award: Grant for use in freshman, sophomore, junior, senior, or graduate years; not renewable. *Number:* 5–10. *Amount:* $400–$1000.

Eligibility Requirements: Applicant must be enrolled or expecting to enroll full-time at a four-year institution or university. Applicant or parent of applicant must be member of American Society of Ichthyologists and Herpetologists. Available to U.S. and non-U.S. citizens.

Application Requirements: Application form, financial need analysis, recommendations or references. *Deadline:* March 1.

Contact: Maureen Donnelly, Secretary
Phone: 305-348-1235
Fax: 305-348-1986
E-mail: asih@fiu.edu

ARNOLD AND MABEL BECKMAN FOUNDATION

http://www.beckman-foundation.com/

BECKMAN SCHOLARS PROGRAM

Scholarship for four-year college undergraduate students in chemistry, biochemistry, and the biological and medical sciences. Provides undergraduate research experiences and comprehensive faculty mentoring.

Academic Fields/Career Goals: Biology; Health and Medical Sciences; Neurobiology; Physical Sciences.

Award: Scholarship for use in freshman, sophomore, junior, or senior years; not renewable. *Amount:* $19,300.

Eligibility Requirements: Applicant must be enrolled or expecting to enroll full-time at a four-year institution or university. Available to U.S. citizens.

Application Requirements: Application form. *Deadline:* varies.

ARRL FOUNDATION INC.

http://www.arrl.org/

YASME FOUNDATION SCHOLARSHIP

Multiple awards available to students who possess an active amateur radio license. Preference given to high school applicants ranked in top 5-10% of class and college students ranked in top 10% of class who are active in their local Amateur Radio club and community service activities. Must be studying sciences or engineering at an accredited four-year college or university. Previous awardees seeking renewal must submit a new application and transcript each year.

Academic Fields/Career Goals: Biology; Engineering-Related Technologies; Engineering/Technology; Natural Sciences; Science, Technology, and Society.

Award: Scholarship for use in freshman, sophomore, junior, or senior years; not renewable. *Amount:* $2000.

Eligibility Requirements: Applicant must be enrolled or expecting to enroll full- or part-time at a four-year institution or university and must have an interest in amateur radio. Applicant must have 3.5 GPA or higher. Available to U.S. citizens.

Application Requirements: Application form, community service, transcript. *Deadline:* February 1.

Contact: Ms. Mary Hobart, Secretary
Phone: 860-594-0397
E-mail: k1mmh@arrl.org

ASSOCIATION OF CALIFORNIA WATER AGENCIES

http://www.acwa.com/

ASSOCIATION OF CALIFORNIA WATER AGENCIES SCHOLARSHIPS
• *See page 103*

CLAIR A. HILL SCHOLARSHIP
• *See page 103*

ASSOCIATION ON AMERICAN INDIAN AFFAIRS, INC.

http://www.indian-affairs.org/

ELIZABETH AND SHERMAN ASCHE MEMORIAL SCHOLARSHIP FUND
• *See page 91*

ASTRONAUT SCHOLARSHIP FOUNDATION

http://www.astronautscholarship.org/

ASTRONAUT SCHOLARSHIP FOUNDATION
• *See page 104*

BARRY M. GOLDWATER SCHOLARSHIP AND EXCELLENCE IN EDUCATION FOUNDATION

http://www.act.org/goldwater

BARRY M. GOLDWATER SCHOLARSHIP AND EXCELLENCE IN EDUCATION PROGRAM
• *See page 104*

BRITISH COLUMBIA INNOVATION COUNCIL

http://www.bcic.ca/

BCIC YOUNG INNOVATOR SCHOLARSHIP COMPETITION (IDEA MASH UP)
• *See page 104*

PAUL AND HELEN TRUSSELL SCIENCE AND TECHNOLOGY SCHOLARSHIP
• *See page 104*

CONGRESSIONAL BLACK CAUCUS FOUNDATION, INC.

http://www.cbcfinc.org/

CBCF GENERAL MILLS HEALTH SCHOLARSHIP
Scholarship to increase the number of minority students pursuing degrees in the fields of medicine, engineering, technology, nutrition and other health-related professions. Minimum 2.5 GPA required. Preference is given to students who reside or attend school in a congressional district represented by a member of the Congressional Black Caucus.

Academic Fields/Career Goals: Biology; Chemical Engineering; Health Administration; Health and Medical Sciences; Health Information Management/Technology; Science, Technology, and Society.

Award: Scholarship for use in freshman, sophomore, junior, senior, or graduate years; not renewable. *Number:* 70–100. *Amount:* $200–$1800.

Eligibility Requirements: Applicant must be enrolled or expecting to enroll full-time at a two-year or four-year institution or university. Applicant must have 2.5 GPA or higher. Available to U.S. citizens.

Application Requirements: Application form, application form may be submitted online (http://www.cbcfinc.org/scholarships), essay, financial need analysis, personal photograph, recommendations or references, resume, transcript. *Deadline:* May 31.

Contact: Ms. Janet Carter, Program Administrator, Scholarships
Congressional Black Caucus Foundation, Inc.
1720 Massachusetts Avenue, NW
Washington, DC 20036
Phone: 202-263-2800
Fax: 202-263-0845
E-mail: scholarships@cbcfinc.org

THE LOUIS STOKES HEALTH SCHOLARS PROGRAM
Program seeking to increase the number of qualified, yet underrepresented, college students entering the health workforce. Preference will be given to students who demonstrate an interest to work in underserved communities. Students currently attending two-year institutions are strongly encouraged to apply.

Academic Fields/Career Goals: Biology; Health and Medical Sciences; Nursing; Physical Sciences; Public Health; Science, Technology, and Society; Therapy/Rehabilitation.

Award: Scholarship for use in freshman, sophomore, junior, or senior years; not renewable. *Number:* 10–12. *Amount:* $5000–$8000.

Eligibility Requirements: Applicant must be enrolled or expecting to enroll full-time at a two-year or four-year institution or university. Applicant must have 3.0 GPA or higher. Available to U.S. citizens.

Application Requirements: Application form, application form may be submitted online (http://www.cbcfinc.org/scholarships), community service, essay, financial need analysis, personal photograph, recommendations or references, resume, transcript. *Deadline:* March 15.

Contact: Ms. Janet Carter, Program Administrator, Scholarships
Phone: 202-263-2800
E-mail: scholarships@cbcfinc.org

CUSHMAN FOUNDATION FOR FORAMINIFERAL RESEARCH

http://www.cushmanfoundation.org/index.php

LOEBLICH AND TAPPAN STUDENT RESEARCH AWARD
Research award given to both graduate and undergraduates interested in foraminiferal research. The maximum dollar value for the award is $2000.

Academic Fields/Career Goals: Biology; Marine Biology.

Award: Grant for use in freshman, sophomore, junior, senior, or graduate years; not renewable. *Number:* 1–57. *Amount:* $100–$2000.

Eligibility Requirements: Applicant must be enrolled or expecting to enroll full- or part-time at a four-year institution or university. Available to U.S. and non-U.S. citizens.

Application Requirements: Proposal for research, recommendations or references, resume. *Deadline:* September 15.

Contact: Jennifer Jett, Secretary and Treasurer
Cushman Foundation for Foraminiferal Research
MRC 121 Department of Paleobiology, PO Box 37012
Washington, DC 20013-7012
E-mail: jettje@si.edu

EAA AVIATION FOUNDATION, INC.

http://www.eaa.org/

PAYZER SCHOLARSHIP
• *See page 129*

FEDERATED GARDEN CLUBS OF CONNECTICUT

http://www.ctgardenclubs.org/

FEDERATED GARDEN CLUBS OF CONNECTICUT INC. SCHOLARSHIPS
One-time award for Connecticut residents entering his or her junior, senior, or graduate year at a Connecticut college or university and pursuing studies in gardening, landscaping, or biology. Minimum 3.0 GPA. PhD candidates are not eligible.

Academic Fields/Career Goals: Biology; Horticulture/Floriculture; Landscape Architecture.

Award: Scholarship for use in junior, senior, or graduate years; not renewable. *Number:* 2–5. *Amount:* $1000–$5000.

Eligibility Requirements: Applicant must be enrolled or expecting to enroll full-time at a four-year institution or university; resident of Connecticut and studying in Connecticut. Applicant must have 3.0 GPA or higher. Available to U.S. citizens.

Application Requirements: Application form, driver's license, financial need analysis, recommendations or references, self-addressed stamped envelope with application, test scores, transcript. *Deadline:* July 1.

Contact: Barbara Bomblad, Office Manager
Phone: 203-488-5528
Fax: 203-488-5520 Ext. 51
E-mail: fgcctoff@hotmail.com

FOUNDATION FOR SCIENCE AND DISABILITY

http://stemd.org/

GRANTS FOR DISABLED STUDENTS IN THE SCIENCES
• *See page 105*

GREATER KANAWHA VALLEY FOUNDATION

http://www.tgkvf.org/

MATH AND SCIENCE SCHOLARSHIP

Scholarship for students pursuing a degree in math, science, or engineering at any accredited college or university. For purposes of this fund, science shall include chemistry, physics, biology and other scientific fields. Scholarships are awarded for one or more years. Must be a resident of West Virginia.

Academic Fields/Career Goals: Biology; Engineering/Technology; Mathematics; Physical Sciences.

Award: Scholarship for use in freshman, sophomore, junior, or senior years; renewable. *Amount:* $1000.

Eligibility Requirements: Applicant must be enrolled or expecting to enroll full-time at a four-year institution or university and resident of West Virginia. Available to U.S. citizens.

Application Requirements: Application form, essay, recommendations or references, transcript. *Deadline:* January 15.

Contact: Susan Hoover, Scholarship Program Officer
Greater Kanawha Valley Foundation
900 Lee Street East, 16th Floor
Charleston, WV 25301
Phone: 304-346-3620
E-mail: tgkvf@tgkvf.org

GREAT MINDS IN STEM

http://www.greatmindsinstem.org

HISPANIC ENGINEER NATIONAL ACHIEVEMENT AWARDS CORPORATION SCHOLARSHIP PROGRAM

• See page 130

HAWAIIAN LODGE, F&AM

http://www.hawaiianlodgefreemasons.org/

HAWAIIAN LODGE SCHOLARSHIPS

• See page 114

INDEPENDENT LABORATORIES INSTITUTE SCHOLARSHIP ALLIANCE

http://www.acil.org/

INDEPENDENT LABORATORIES INSTITUTE SCHOLARSHIP ALLIANCE

Scholarships are given to full-time undergraduate juniors or seniors, or graduate students majoring in the physical sciences: physics, chemistry, geology, engineering, biology or environmental science.

Academic Fields/Career Goals: Biology; Chemical Engineering; Civil Engineering; Earth Science; Electrical Engineering/Electronics; Engineering-Related Technologies; Engineering/Technology; Environmental Science; Fire Sciences; Materials Science, Engineering, and Metallurgy; Mechanical Engineering; Physical Sciences.

Award: Scholarship for use in freshman, sophomore, junior, senior, or graduate years; not renewable. *Number:* 1–2. *Amount:* $1000–$2000.

Eligibility Requirements: Applicant must be enrolled or expecting to enroll full-time at a four-year institution or university. Available to U.S. citizens.

Application Requirements: Application form, recommendations or references, resume, transcript. *Deadline:* April 7.

Contact: Janet Allen, Senior Administrator
Independent Laboratories Institute Scholarship Alliance
1629 K Street, NW, Suite 400
Washington, DC 20006-1633
Phone: 202-887-5872 Ext. 204
Fax: 202-887-0021
E-mail: jallen@acil.org

INDIAN HEALTH SERVICES, UNITED STATES DEPARTMENT OF HEALTH AND HUMAN SERVICES

http://www.ihs.gov/scholarship

INDIAN HEALTH SERVICE HEALTH PROFESSIONS PRE-GRADUATE SCHOLARSHIPS

• See page 105

INSTITUTE OF INTERNATIONAL EDUCATION (FULBRIGHT PROGRAM)

http://www.us.fulbrightonline.org/

WHITAKER INTERNATIONAL PROGRAM

The program sends emerging leaders in U.S. biomedical engineering (or bioengineering) to undertake a self-designed project that will enhance their own careers within the field. It offers a stipend commensurate with the recipient's experience and expected expenses in the host country.

Academic Fields/Career Goals: Biology; Chemical Engineering; Electrical Engineering/Electronics; Engineering-Related Technologies; Engineering/Technology; Materials Science, Engineering, and Metallurgy; Mechanical Engineering.

Award: Grant for use in sophomore, junior, senior, graduate, or postgraduate years; not renewable. *Number:* 60–100. *Amount:* up to $25,000.

Eligibility Requirements: Applicant must be enrolled or expecting to enroll full- or part-time at a four-year institution or university. Available to U.S. citizens.

Application Requirements: Application form, application form may be submitted online (http://www.whitaker.org), essay, financial need analysis, recommendations or references, transcript. *Deadline:* January 21.

Contact: Ms. Sabeen Altaf, Senior Program Manager, Science and Technology Programs
Institute of International Education (Fulbright Program)
809 United Nations Plaza
New York, NY 10017
Phone: 212-984-5442
Fax: 212-984-5325
E-mail: saltaf@iie.org

KENTUCKY ENERGY AND ENVIRONMENT CABINET

http://www.eec.ky.gov/

ENVIRONMENTAL PROTECTION SCHOLARSHIP

Renewable awards for college juniors, seniors, and graduate students for in-state tuition, fees, room and board, and a book allowance at a Kentucky public university. Minimum 3.0 GPA required. Must work full-time for the Kentucky Department for Environmental Protection upon graduation (six months for each semester of scholarship support received). Interview required. Program not generally appropriate for non-residents.

Academic Fields/Career Goals: Biology; Chemical Engineering; Civil Engineering; Earth Science; Environmental Science; Hydrology; Mechanical Engineering; Natural Sciences.

Award: Scholarship for use in junior, senior, or graduate years; renewable. *Number:* 1–2. *Amount:* $15,000–$30,000.

Eligibility Requirements: Applicant must be enrolled or expecting to enroll full-time at a four-year institution or university and studying in Kentucky. Applicant must have 3.0 GPA or higher. Available to U.S. and non-U.S. citizens.

Application Requirements: Application form, essay, interview, recommendations or references, transcript, valid work permit for non-citizens. *Deadline:* February 15.

Contact: James Kipp, Scholarship Program Coordinator
Kentucky Energy and Environment Cabinet
233 Mining/Mineral Resources Building
Lexington, KY 40506-0107
Phone: 859-257-1299
Fax: 859-323-1049
E-mail: kipp@uky.edu

LOUISIANA OFFICE OF STUDENT FINANCIAL ASSISTANCE

http://www.osfa.la.gov/

ROCKEFELLER STATE WILDLIFE SCHOLARSHIP

For college undergraduates with a minimum of 60 credit hours who are majoring in Forestry, Wildlife, or Marine Science, and for college graduate students who are majoring in Forestry, Wildlife, or Marine Science. College undergraduates must have a grade point average of at least 2.50 to apply. College graduate students must have a grade point average of at least 3.00 in order to apply. Renewable up to three years as an undergraduate and two years as a graduate student.

Academic Fields/Career Goals: Biology; Marine Biology; Marine/Ocean Engineering; Natural Resources; Oceanography.

Award: Scholarship for use in freshman, sophomore, junior, senior, graduate, or postgraduate years; renewable. *Number:* 20–30. *Amount:* $2000–$3000.

Eligibility Requirements: Applicant must be enrolled or expecting to enroll full-time at a four-year institution or university; resident of Louisiana and studying in Louisiana. Applicant must have 2.5 GPA or higher. Available to U.S. citizens.

Application Requirements: Application form, application form may be submitted online (http://www.fafsa.ed.gov), FAFSA, test scores, transcript. *Deadline:* July 1.

Contact: Bonnie Lavergne, Public Information
Louisiana Office of Student Financial Assistance
PO Box 91202
Baton Rouge, LA 70821-9202
Phone: 800-259-5626 Ext. 7714
Fax: 225-612-6508
E-mail: custserv@osfa.la.gov

NASA IDAHO SPACE GRANT CONSORTIUM

http://www.id.spacegrant.org/

NASA IDAHO SPACE GRANT CONSORTIUM SCHOLARSHIP PROGRAM

Applicants must attend an Idaho accredited institution and maintain a 3.0 GPA. Major/career interest in engineering, mathematics, science or secondary education in math or science. Applicants must be a US citizen.

Academic Fields/Career Goals: Biology; Chemical Engineering; Civil Engineering; Computer Science/Data Processing; Earth Science; Electrical Engineering/Electronics; Geography; Materials Science, Engineering, and Metallurgy; Mathematics; Mechanical Engineering; Natural Sciences; Physical Sciences.

Award: Scholarship for use in freshman, sophomore, junior, or senior years; renewable. *Number:* 1–15. *Amount:* $1000–$2500.

Eligibility Requirements: Applicant must be enrolled or expecting to enroll full-time at a two-year or four-year institution or university and studying in Idaho. Applicant must have 3.0 GPA or higher. Available to U.S. citizens.

Application Requirements: Application form, application form may be submitted online (http://www.id.spacegrant.org/index.php?page=scholarships), essay, recommendations or references, resume, test scores, transcript. *Deadline:* March 1.

Contact: Becky Highfill, Program Manager
Phone: 208-885-6438
Fax: 208-885-1339
E-mail: bhighfill@uidaho.edu

NASA/MARYLAND SPACE GRANT CONSORTIUM

http://md.spacegrant.org/

NASA MARYLAND SPACE GRANT CONSORTIUM UNDERGRADUATE SCHOLARSHIPS

• See page 132

NASA MONTANA SPACE GRANT CONSORTIUM

http://www.spacegrant.montana.edu/

MONTANA SPACE GRANT SCHOLARSHIP PROGRAM

• See page 133

NASA SOUTH CAROLINA SPACE GRANT CONSORTIUM

http://www.cofc.edu/~scsgrant

UNDERGRADUATE RESEARCH AWARD PROGRAM

• See page 133

NASA'S VIRGINIA SPACE GRANT CONSORTIUM

http://www.vsgc.odu.edu/

COMMUNITY COLLEGE STEM SCHOLARSHIPS

• See page 105

UNDERGRADUATE STEM RESEARCH SCHOLARSHIPS

• See page 106

NATIONAL ASSOCIATION OF WATER COMPANIES-NEW JERSEY CHAPTER

http://www.nawc.org/

NATIONAL ASSOCIATION OF WATER COMPANIES-NEW JERSEY CHAPTER SCHOLARSHIP

For college students interested in a career in the water utility industry or any related field. Must be U.S. citizen, five-year resident of New Jersey, high school senior attending or enrolled in a New Jersey college or university. Must maintain a 3.0 GPA.

Academic Fields/Career Goals: Biology; Business/Consumer Services; Communications; Computer Science/Data Processing; Earth Science; Economics; Engineering/Technology; Law/Legal Services; Natural Resources; Physical Sciences; Trade/Technical Specialties.

Award: Scholarship for use in freshman, sophomore, junior, senior, or graduate years; not renewable. *Number:* 2. *Amount:* $2500.

Eligibility Requirements: Applicant must be enrolled or expecting to enroll full- or part-time at a two-year or four-year institution or university; resident of New Jersey and studying in New Jersey. Applicant must have 3.0 GPA or higher. Available to U.S. citizens.

Application Requirements: Application form, essay, recommendations or references, transcript. *Deadline:* April 1.

Contact: Gail Brady, Scholarship Committee Chairperson
National Association of Water Companies-New Jersey Chapter
49 Howell Drive
Verona, NJ 07044
Phone: 973-669-5807
E-mail: gbradygbconsult@verizon.net

NATIONAL COUNCIL OF STATE GARDEN CLUBS INC. SCHOLARSHIP

http://www.gardenclub.org/

NATIONAL COUNCIL OF STATE GARDEN CLUBS INC. SCHOLARSHIP
• *See page 93*

NATIONAL GARDEN CLUBS INC.

http://www.gardenclub.org/

NATIONAL GARDEN CLUBS INC. SCHOLARSHIP PROGRAM
• *See page 94*

NATIONAL INSTITUTES OF HEALTH

https://ugsp.nih.gov/

NIH UNDERGRADUATE SCHOLARSHIP PROGRAM FOR STUDENTS FROM DISADVANTAGED BACKGROUNDS

Award to student from a disadvantaged background is one who comes from a family with an annual income below a level based on low-income thresholds according to family size, as published by the U.S. Bureau of the Census. Must be enrolled full-time at a postsecondary institution and have a GPA of 3.5 or higher. Visit website http://www.ugsp.nih.gov for more details.

Academic Fields/Career Goals: Biology; Health and Medical Sciences; Social Sciences.

Award: Scholarship for use in freshman, sophomore, junior, or senior years; renewable. *Number:* 7–10. *Amount:* $20,000.

Eligibility Requirements: Applicant must be enrolled or expecting to enroll full-time at a two-year or four-year institution or university. Applicant must have 3.5 GPA or higher. Available to U.S. citizens.

Application Requirements: Application form, essay, financial need analysis, recommendations or references, transcript. *Deadline:* February 28.

NATIONAL INVENTORS HALL OF FAME

http://www.invent.org/

COLLEGIATE INVENTORS COMPETITION FOR UNDERGRADUATE STUDENTS
• *See page 106*

COLLEGIATE INVENTORS COMPETITION-GRAND PRIZE
• *See page 106*

OREGON STUDENT ASSISTANCE COMMISSION

http://www.GetCollegeFunds.org/

OREGON FOUNDATION FOR BLACKTAIL DEER SCHOLARSHIP

One-time award for Oregon high school graduate enrolled in forestry, biology, wildlife science, or related majors in an Oregon college or university. Must demonstrate a serious commitment to career in wildlife management. Must submit 250-word essay on wildlife management.

Academic Fields/Career Goals: Biology; Environmental Science; Natural Resources.

Award: Scholarship for use in freshman, sophomore, junior, or senior years; not renewable.

Eligibility Requirements: Applicant must be enrolled or expecting to enroll full-time at a four-year institution; resident of Oregon and studying in Oregon. Available to U.S. citizens.

Application Requirements: Activity chart, previous year's hunting license, application form, essay, financial need analysis, recommendations or references, transcript. *Deadline:* March 1.

ROBERTS SCHOLARSHIP

One-time award for graduates of Oregon public high schools attending four-year public and nonprofit colleges at least half time. This award is not open to graduating high school seniors. Preference given to Oregon state residents majoring in the biological and chemical sciences and pursing careers in environmental toxicology and chemistry. Must have completed 1+ year of college-level science by the March scholarship deadline. FAFSA is recommended.

Academic Fields/Career Goals: Biology; Natural Sciences.

Award: Scholarship for use in freshman, sophomore, junior, or senior years; not renewable.

Eligibility Requirements: Applicant must be enrolled or expecting to enroll full- or part-time at a four-year institution. Available to U.S. citizens.

Application Requirements: Application form. *Deadline:* March 1.

PEARSON BENJAMIN CUMMINGS

http://www.pearsonhighered.com/

PEARSON BENJAMIN CUMMINGS ALLIED HEALTH STUDENT SCHOLARSHIP

Two scholarships of $1250 awarded to students currently enrolled in an anatomy, physiology or microbiology course. Students are also eligible if they have successfully completed one of these courses within the past two years.

Academic Fields/Career Goals: Biology; Health and Medical Sciences.

Award: Scholarship for use in freshman, sophomore, junior, or senior years; not renewable. *Number:* 2. *Amount:* $1250.

Eligibility Requirements: Applicant must be enrolled or expecting to enroll full-time at a four-year institution or university. Available to U.S. citizens.

Application Requirements: Application form, essay. *Deadline:* November 1.

PEARSON BENJAMIN CUMMINGS BIOLOGY PRIZE SCHOLARSHIP

Five scholarships of $500 each to biology majors who are currently enrolled in a general biology course or who have successfully completed a general biology course within the past two years.

Academic Fields/Career Goals: Biology.

Award: Scholarship for use in freshman, sophomore, junior, or senior years; not renewable. *Number:* 5. *Amount:* $500.

Eligibility Requirements: Applicant must be enrolled or expecting to enroll full-time at a four-year institution or university. Available to U.S. citizens.

Application Requirements: Application form. *Deadline:* November 6.

PENNSYLVANIA ASSOCIATION OF CONSERVATION DISTRICTS AUXILIARY

http://www.pacd.org/

PACD AUXILIARY SCHOLARSHIPS
• *See page 95*

ROBERT H. MOLLOHAN FAMILY CHARITABLE FOUNDATION, INC.

http://www.mollohanfoundation.org/

HIGH TECHNOLOGY SCHOLARS PROGRAM

Scholarship for West Virginia students pursuing a technology-related career and residing in one of the following counties: Barbour, Brooke, Calhoun, Doddridge, Gilmer, Grant, Hancock, Harrison, Marion, Marshall, Mineral, Monongalia, Ohio, Pleasants, Preston, Ritchie, Taylor, Tucker, Tyler, Wetzel, Wood. Scholarship recipients become eligible for a paid internship with a West Virginia business. Students may also apply for debt-forgiveness loans up to $2000 per year.

Academic Fields/Career Goals: Biology; Chemical Engineering; Computer Science/Data Processing; Electrical Engineering/Electronics; Energy and Power Engineering; Engineering-Related Technologies; Engineering/Technology; Mechanical Engineering; Physical Sciences.

Award: Scholarship for use in freshman year; not renewable. *Number:* 1–60. *Amount:* $500–$2000.

Eligibility Requirements: Applicant must be high school student; planning to enroll or expecting to enroll full-time at a four-year institution or university and resident of West Virginia. Applicant must have 3.0 GPA or higher. Available to U.S. citizens.

Application Requirements: Application form, essay, recommendations or references, resume, test scores, transcript. *Deadline:* February 9.

Contact: Aime Shaffer, Program Manager
Robert H. Mollohan Family Charitable Foundation, Inc.
1000 Technology Drive, Suite 2000
Fairmont, WV 26554
Phone: 304-333-6783
Fax: 304-333-3900
E-mail: ashaffer@wvhtf.org

SIGMA XI, THE SCIENTIFIC RESEARCH SOCIETY

http://www.sigmaxi.org/

SIGMA XI GRANTS-IN-AID OF RESEARCH
• *See page 95*

SOCIETY FOR INTEGRATIVE AND COMPARATIVE BIOLOGY

http://www.sicb.org/

LIBBIE H. HYMAN MEMORIAL SCHOLARSHIP

Scholarship provides assistance to students to take courses or to carry on research on invertebrates at a marine freshwater or terrestrial field station. For more information and/or an application see website, http://www.sicb.org.

Academic Fields/Career Goals: Biology; Marine Biology.

Award: Scholarship for use in senior year; not renewable. *Number:* 1. *Amount:* $750–$1200.

Eligibility Requirements: Applicant must be enrolled or expecting to enroll full- or part-time at a four-year institution or university. Available to U.S. and non-U.S. citizens.

Application Requirements: Application form, essay, financial need analysis, recommendations or references, transcript. *Deadline:* March 6.

Contact: Bruno Pernet, Chair, Scholarship Committee
Society for Integrative and Comparative Biology
California State University
Long Beach, CA 90840
Phone: 562-985-5378
Fax: 562-985-8878
E-mail: bpernet@csulb.edu

SOCIETY FOR THE SCIENTIFIC STUDY OF SEXUALITY

http://www.sexscience.org/

SOCIETY FOR THE SCIENTIFIC STUDY OF SEXUALITY STUDENT RESEARCH GRANT
• *See page 102*

SOIL AND WATER CONSERVATION SOCIETY-NEW JERSEY CHAPTER

http://home.comcast.net/~njswcs/scholarship.htm

EDWARD R. HALL SCHOLARSHIP
• *See page 88*

TKE EDUCATIONAL FOUNDATION

http://www.tke.org/

CARROL C. HALL MEMORIAL SCHOLARSHIP
• *See page 107*

TIMOTHY L. TASCHWER SCHOLARSHIP

Scholarship available to an undergraduate member of Tau Kappa Epsilon. Must be a full-time student with at least sophomore year standing and a minimum GPA of 2.75. Applicant must be pursuing a degree in natural resources, earth sciences or related subjects and have a record of active TKE chapter leadership involvement. Preference shall be given to qualified graduates of the TKE Leadership Academy.

Academic Fields/Career Goals: Biology; Earth Science; Environmental Science; Natural Resources.

Award: Scholarship for use in sophomore, junior, or senior years; not renewable. *Amount:* $500.

Eligibility Requirements: Applicant must be enrolled or expecting to enroll full-time at a four-year institution or university; male and must have an interest in leadership. Applicant or parent of applicant must be member of Tau Kappa Epsilon. Available to U.S. and non-U.S. citizens.

Application Requirements: Application form, narrative summary of how TKE membership has benefited applicant, personal photograph, transcript. *Deadline:* February 29.

UNITED NEGRO COLLEGE FUND

http://www.uncf.org/

ALFRED CHISHOLM/BASF MEMORIAL SCHOLARSHIP FUND
• *See page 81*

CHARLES E. CULPEPPER SCHOLARSHIP

Scholarship of $1000 available for African American students attending UNCF member colleges and universities and completing the Fisk Pre-Medicine program. Should have minimum GPA of 3.0 with majors in science and technology. For additional information and an online general application, visit http://www.uncf.org.

Academic Fields/Career Goals: Biology; Health and Medical Sciences; Natural Sciences.

Award: Scholarship for use in freshman, sophomore, junior, or senior years; not renewable. *Amount:* $1000.

Eligibility Requirements: Applicant must be Black (non-Hispanic) and enrolled or expecting to enroll full- or part-time at a four-year institution or university. Applicant must have 3.0 GPA or higher. Available to U.S. and non-U.S. citizens.

Application Requirements: Application form, FAFSA, Student Aid Report (SAR), financial need analysis. *Deadline:* continuous.

COOPER INDUSTRIES PACESETTER SCHOLARSHIP

$5000 award for students attending UNCF member schools and majoring in engineering, business, mathematics, or science. Minimum 2.75 GPA required.

Academic Fields/Career Goals: Biology; Business/Consumer Services; Engineering/Technology; Mathematics.

Award: Scholarship for use in freshman, sophomore, junior, senior, or graduate years; not renewable. *Amount:* $5000.

Eligibility Requirements: Applicant must be Black (non-Hispanic) and enrolled or expecting to enroll full-time at a four-year institution or university. Available to U.S. citizens.

Application Requirements: Application form. *Deadline:* continuous.

EARL & PATRICIA ARMSTRONG SCHOLARSHIP

Scholarship up to $3000 for students at UNCF member colleges and universities studying pre-medicine, biology, or health. Minimum 3.0 GPA required.

Academic Fields/Career Goals: Biology; Health and Medical Sciences.

Award: Scholarship for use in freshman year; not renewable. *Amount:* up to $3000.

Eligibility Requirements: Applicant must be Black (non-Hispanic) and enrolled or expecting to enroll full- or part-time at a four-year institution or university. Applicant must have 3.0 GPA or higher. Available to U.S. citizens.

Application Requirements: Application form. *Deadline:* continuous.

MONSANTO/UNCF 1890'S SCHOLARSHIP PROGRAM
• *See page 89*

SPRINT SCHOLARS PROGRAM FOR SOPHOMORES, JUNIORS, AND SENIORS
• *See page 100*

UNCF/MERCK SCIENCE INITIATIVE
Award for students who are undergraduate juniors, graduate students, or postdoctoral fellows majoring in the life or physical sciences. Eligible majors include pre-medicine, science, chemistry, biochemistry, biology, microbiology, biotechnical, biomedical research, health, medicine, comp biology, animal science, and chemical engineering. Undergraduate students must have minimum 3.3 GPA; graduate students must have a minimum 3.0 GPA. Application and additional information at http://www.uncf.org.

Academic Fields/Career Goals: Biology; Chemical Engineering; Environmental Science; Health and Medical Sciences; Natural Sciences; Neurobiology; Physical Sciences.

Award: Scholarship for use in junior, senior, graduate, or postgraduate years; not renewable. *Amount:* $25,000–$70,000.

Eligibility Requirements: Applicant must be Black (non-Hispanic) and enrolled or expecting to enroll full-time at an institution or university. Available to U.S. and non-U.S. citizens.

Application Requirements: Application form, recommendations or references, resume, transcript. *Deadline:* December 15.

Contact: Dr. Jerry Bryant, UNCF
United Negro College Fund
8260 Willow Oaks Corporate Drive
Fairfax, VA 22031
E-mail: uncfmerck@uncf.org

UNITED STATES DEPARTMENT OF AGRICULTURE
http://www.usda.gov/

SAUL T. WILSON, JR, SCHOLARSHIP PROGRAM (STWJS)
• *See page 100*

WILLIAM HELMS SCHOLARSHIP PROGRAM (WHSP)
• *See page 96*

VERMONT SPACE GRANT CONSORTIUM
http://www.cems.uvm.edu/vsgc

VERMONT SPACE GRANT CONSORTIUM SCHOLARSHIP PROGRAM
• *See page 107*

WILSON ORNITHOLOGICAL SOCIETY
http://www.wilsonsociety.org/

GEORGE A. HALL/HAROLD F. MAYFIELD AWARD
• *See page 100*

PAUL A. STEWART AWARDS
• *See page 100*

BUSINESS/CONSUMER SERVICES

AACE INTERNATIONAL
http://www.aacei.org/

AACE INTERNATIONAL COMPETITIVE SCHOLARSHIP
• *See page 108*

AMERICAN ASSOCIATION OF HISPANIC CERTIFIED PUBLIC ACCOUNTANTS (AAHCPA)
http://www.alpfa.org/

ALPFA ANNUAL SCHOLARSHIP PROGRAM
• *See page 69*

AMERICAN CONGRESS ON SURVEYING AND MAPPING
http://www.acsm.net/

TRI-STATE SURVEYING AND PHOTOGRAMMETRY KRIS M. KUNZE MEMORIAL SCHOLARSHIP
One-time award of $1000 for students pursuing college-level courses in business administration or business management. Candidates, in order of priority, include professional land surveyors and certified photogrammetrists, land survey interns and students enrolled in a two- or four-year program in surveying and mapping. Must be ACSM member.

Academic Fields/Career Goals: Business/Consumer Services; Surveying, Surveying Technology, Cartography, or Geographic Information Science.

Award: Scholarship for use in freshman, sophomore, junior, or senior years; not renewable. *Number:* 1. *Amount:* $1000.

Eligibility Requirements: Applicant must be enrolled or expecting to enroll full- or part-time at a two-year or four-year institution or university. Applicant or parent of applicant must be member of American Congress on Surveying and Mapping. Available to U.S. citizens.

Application Requirements: Application form, essay, membership proof, recommendations or references, transcript. *Deadline:* October 1.

Contact: Ilse Genovese, Communications Director
American Congress on Surveying and Mapping
6 Montgomery Village Avenue, Suite 403
Gaithersburg, MD 20879
Phone: 240-632-9716 Ext. 113
Fax: 240-632-1321
E-mail: ilse.genovese@acsm.net

AMERICAN INDIAN SCIENCE AND ENGINEERING SOCIETY
http://www.aises.org/

A.T. ANDERSON MEMORIAL SCHOLARSHIP PROGRAM
• *See page 102*

BURLINGTON NORTHERN SANTA FE FOUNDATION SCHOLARSHIP
• *See page 102*

AMERICAN PUBLIC TRANSPORTATION FOUNDATION

http://www.apta.com/

DAN REICHARD JR. SCHOLARSHIP

Scholarship for study towards a career in the business administration/ management area of the transit industry. Must be sponsored by APTA member organization and complete internship with APTA member organization. Minimum GPA of 3.0 required.

Academic Fields/Career Goals: Business/Consumer Services; Transportation.

Award: Scholarship for use in sophomore, junior, senior, or graduate years; renewable. *Number:* 1. *Amount:* $2500.

Eligibility Requirements: Applicant must be enrolled or expecting to enroll full-time at a two-year or four-year institution or university. Applicant must have 3.0 GPA or higher. Available to U.S. and Canadian citizens.

Application Requirements: Application form, essay, financial need analysis, recommendations or references, transcript, verification of enrollment for the current semester, copy of fee schedule from the college/university. *Deadline:* June 16.

Contact: Pamela Boswell, Vice President of Program Management
American Public Transportation Foundation
1666 K Street, NW
Washington, DC 20006-1215
Phone: 202-496-4803
Fax: 202-496-2323
E-mail: pboswell@apta.com

AMERICAN WELDING SOCIETY

http://www.aws.org/

JAMES A. TURNER, JR. MEMORIAL SCHOLARSHIP

Award for a full-time student pursuing minimum four-year bachelor's degree in business that will lead to a management career in welding store operations or a welding distributorship. Applicant must be working in this field at least 10 hours per week. Submit verification of employment, a copy of proposed curriculum, and acceptance letter.

Academic Fields/Career Goals: Business/Consumer Services.

Award: Scholarship for use in freshman, sophomore, junior, or senior years; renewable. *Number:* 1. *Amount:* $3500.

Eligibility Requirements: Applicant must be enrolled or expecting to enroll full-time at a four-year institution or university. Available to U.S. citizens.

Application Requirements: Application form, financial need analysis, recommendations or references, transcript. *Deadline:* February 15.

Contact: Vicki Pinsky, Manager, Foundation
American Welding Society
8669 Doral Boulevard, Suite 130
Doral, FL 33166
Phone: 800-443-9353 Ext. 212
Fax: 305-443-7559
E-mail: vpinsky@aws.org

AMERICAN WHOLESALE MARKETERS ASSOCIATION

http://www.awmanet.org/

RAY FOLEY MEMORIAL YOUTH EDUCATION FOUNDATION SCHOLARSHIP

Scholarship program annually offers two $5000 scholarships to deserving students. Awards are based on academic merit and a career interest in the candy/tobacco/ convenience-products wholesale industry. Must be employed by an AWMA wholesaler distributor member or be an immediate family member. Must be enrolled full-time in an undergraduate or graduate program. For details visit website http://www.awmanet.org/.

Academic Fields/Career Goals: Business/Consumer Services.

Award: Scholarship for use in freshman, sophomore, junior, senior, or graduate years; not renewable. *Number:* 2. *Amount:* $5000.

Eligibility Requirements: Applicant must be enrolled or expecting to enroll full-time at a four-year institution or university. Available to U.S. citizens.

Application Requirements: Application form, essay, recommendations or references. *Deadline:* May 21.

Contact: Kathy Trost, Manager of Education
American Wholesale Marketers Association
2750 Prosperity Avenue, Suite 530
Fairfax, VA 22031
Phone: 800-482-2962 Ext. 648
Fax: 703-573-5738
E-mail: kathyt@awmanet.org

ARRL FOUNDATION INC.

http://www.arrl.org/

ARRL NORTHWESTERN DIVISION SCHOLARSHIP FUND

$1000 scholarship for a student with a General Class radio license or higher who is a resident in the ARRL Northwestern Division (Alaska, Idaho, Montana, Oregon or Washington). Must be studying engineering, medicine, science, or business. Preference given to applicants with 3.0 GPA or higher for the academic year immediately prior to application (high school or college).

Academic Fields/Career Goals: Business/Consumer Services; Engineering-Related Technologies; Engineering/Technology; Science, Technology, and Society.

Award: Scholarship for use in freshman, sophomore, junior, or senior years; not renewable. *Number:* 1. *Amount:* $1000.

Eligibility Requirements: Applicant must be enrolled or expecting to enroll full- or part-time at a two-year or four-year or technical institution or university; resident of Alaska, Idaho, Montana, Oregon, Washington and must have an interest in amateur radio. Applicant must have 3.0 GPA or higher. Available to U.S. citizens.

Application Requirements: Application form, transcript. *Deadline:* February 1.

Contact: Ms. Mary Hobart, Secretary
Phone: 860-594-0397
E-mail: k1mmh@arrl.org

WILLIAM R. GOLDFARB MEMORIAL SCHOLARSHIP

Award for licensed amateur radio operator pursuing baccalaureate study in business, computers, medical sciences, nursing, engineering, or other sciences. Must be a high school senior and demonstrate financial need. Students are expected to maintain a B average and should submit transcripts of academic performance each semester to the ARRL Foundation Office.

Academic Fields/Career Goals: Business/Consumer Services; Computer Science/Data Processing; Engineering/Technology; Health and Medical Sciences; Natural Sciences; Nursing; Physical Sciences.

Award: Scholarship for use in freshman, sophomore, junior, or senior years; not renewable. *Number:* 1. *Amount:* $10,000.

Eligibility Requirements: Applicant must be high school student; planning to enroll or expecting to enroll full-time at a four-year institution or university and must have an interest in amateur radio. Available to U.S. citizens.

Application Requirements: Application form, FAFSA, Student Aid Report (SAR), financial need analysis, transcript. *Deadline:* February 1.

Contact: Ms. Mary Hobart, Secretary
Phone: 860-594-0397
E-mail: k1mmh@arrl.org

ASSOCIATION FOR FOOD AND DRUG OFFICIALS

http://www.afdo.org/

ASSOCIATION FOR FOOD AND DRUG OFFICIALS SCHOLARSHIP FUND

A $1500 scholarship for students in their third or fourth year of college/ university who have demonstrated a desire for a career in research, regulatory work, quality control, or teaching in an area related to some aspect of food, drugs, or consumer products safety. Minimum 3.0 GPA required in first two years of undergraduate study. For further information visit website http://www.afdo.org.

Academic Fields/Career Goals: Business/Consumer Services; Food Science/Nutrition.

Award: Scholarship for use in junior or senior years; not renewable. *Number:* 2. *Amount:* $1500.

Eligibility Requirements: Applicant must be enrolled or expecting to enroll full-time at a four-year institution or university. Applicant must have 3.0 GPA or higher. Available to U.S. and non-U.S. citizens.

Application Requirements: Application form, essay, recommendations or references, transcript. *Deadline:* February 1.

Contact: Leigh Stamdaugh, Administrative/Special Projects Assistant
Association for Food and Drug Officials
2550 Kingston Road, Suite 311
York, PA 17402
Phone: 717-757-2888
Fax: 717-755-8089
E-mail: afdo@afdo.org

BALTIMORE CHAPTER OF THE AMERICAN MARKETING ASSOCIATION

http://www.amabaltimore.org/

UNDERGRADUATE MARKETING EDUCATION MERIT SCHOLARSHIPS

Scholarship of $2500 awarded for first place and two $500 runner-up awards for full-time students in marketing. Must be attending a 4-year college or university in Maryland with credits equivalent to the status of a junior or senior as of September.

Academic Fields/Career Goals: Business/Consumer Services; Marketing.

Award: Scholarship for use in sophomore or junior years; not renewable. *Number:* 3. *Amount:* $500–$2500.

Eligibility Requirements: Applicant must be enrolled or expecting to enroll full-time at a four-year institution or university. Applicant must have 3.0 GPA or higher. Available to U.S. and non-U.S. citizens.

Application Requirements: Application form, test scores. *Deadline:* February 16.

Contact: Marisa O'Brien, Scholarship Committee
Phone: 410-467-2529
E-mail: scholarship@amabaltimore.org

BRITISH COLUMBIA INNOVATION COUNCIL

http://www.bcic.ca/

BCIC YOUNG INNOVATOR SCHOLARSHIP COMPETITION (IDEA MASH UP)

• *See page 104*

CATCHING THE DREAM

http://www.catchingthedream.org/

MATH, ENGINEERING, SCIENCE, BUSINESS, EDUCATION, COMPUTERS SCHOLARSHIPS

Renewable scholarships for Native American students planning to study math, engineering, science, business, education, and computers, or presently studying in these fields. Study of social science, humanities and liberal arts also funded. Scholarships are awarded on merit and on the basis of likelihood of recipient improving the lives of Native American people. Scholarships are available nationwide.

Academic Fields/Career Goals: Business/Consumer Services; Computer Science/Data Processing; Education; Engineering/Technology; Humanities; Physical Sciences; Science, Technology, and Society; Social Sciences.

Award: Scholarship for use in freshman, sophomore, junior, senior, graduate, or postgraduate years; renewable. *Number:* 180. *Amount:* $500–$5000.

Eligibility Requirements: Applicant must be American Indian/Alaska Native and enrolled or expecting to enroll full-time at a two-year or four-year institution or university. Applicant must have 3.0 GPA or higher. Available to U.S. citizens.

Application Requirements: Application form, certificate of Indian blood, essay, financial need analysis, personal photograph, recommendations or references, test scores, transcript. *Deadline:* varies.

Contact: Mary Frost, Recruiter
Catching the Dream
8200 Mountain Road, NE, Suite 203
Albuquerque, NM 87110
Phone: 505-262-2351
Fax: 505-262-0534
E-mail: nscholarsh@aol.com

NATIVE AMERICAN LEADERSHIP IN EDUCATION (NALE)

Renewable scholarships available for Native American and Alaska Native students. Must be at least one-quarter Native American from a federally recognized, state recognized, or terminated tribe. Must be U.S. citizen. Must demonstrate high academic achievement, depth of character, leadership, seriousness of purpose, and service orientation.

Academic Fields/Career Goals: Business/Consumer Services; Education; Humanities; Physical Sciences; Science, Technology, and Society.

Award: Scholarship for use in freshman, sophomore, junior, senior, graduate, or postgraduate years; renewable. *Number:* up to 30. *Amount:* $500–$5000.

Eligibility Requirements: Applicant must be American Indian/Alaska Native and enrolled or expecting to enroll full-time at a four-year institution or university. Applicant must have 3.0 GPA or higher. Available to U.S. citizens.

Application Requirements: Application form, certificate of Indian blood, essay, financial need analysis, personal photograph, recommendations or references, test scores, transcript. *Deadline:* varies.

Contact: Mary Frost, Recruiter
Catching the Dream
8200 Mountain Road, NE, Suite 203
Albuquerque, NM 87110
Phone: 505-262-2351
Fax: 505-262-0534
E-mail: nscholarsh@aol.com

TRIBAL BUSINESS MANAGEMENT PROGRAM (TBM)

• *See page 70*

CENTRAL INTELLIGENCE AGENCY

http://www.cia.gov/

CENTRAL INTELLIGENCE AGENCY UNDERGRADUATE SCHOLARSHIP PROGRAM

• *See page 70*

THE CIRI FOUNDATION (TCF)

http://www.thecirifoundation.org/

CAP LATHROP SCHOLARSHIP PROGRAM

Award for an Alaska Native enrollee or descendant of original enrollee to an ANCSA regional or village corporation. Must be enrolled or accepted into an accredited or authorized college or university as a full-time student and have a minimum 3.0 GPA. An applicant must be a declared major in broadcast, telecommunications, business, engineering, journalism, or other media related degree programs to be considered.

Academic Fields/Career Goals: Business/Consumer Services; Journalism; TV/Radio Broadcasting.

Award: Scholarship for use in freshman, sophomore, junior, senior, or graduate years; not renewable. *Amount:* up to $4000.

Eligibility Requirements: Applicant must be American Indian/Alaska Native and enrolled or expecting to enroll full-time at a two-year or four-year institution or university. Applicant must have 3.0 GPA or higher. Available to U.S. and Canadian citizens.

Application Requirements: Application form, community service, essay, personal photograph, proof of eligibility, statement of purpose, recommendations or references, transcript. *Deadline:* June 1.

Contact: Susan Anderson, President and Chief Executive Officer
   Phone: 907-793-3575
   E-mail: tcf@thecirifoundation.org

COLLEGEBOUND FOUNDATION

http://www.collegeboundfoundation.org/

HILTON BALTIMORE CONVENTION CENTER HOTEL SCHOLARSHIP FUND

This award has been established in order to increase educational opportunities for the young people of Baltimore City. This fund will award those who are enrolled in hotel, hospitality and/or restaurant management programs. You must apply for a CollegeBound Foundation Last Dollar Grant, demonstrate financial need; and major in the field of hotel, hospitality, tourism, restaurant management or business. Preference is given to seniors from National Academy Foundation.

Academic Fields/Career Goals: Business/Consumer Services; Hospitality Management.

Award: Scholarship for use in freshman, sophomore, junior, or senior years; renewable. *Number:* 13–15. *Amount:* $1000–$3000.

Eligibility Requirements: Applicant must be high school student; planning to enroll or expecting to enroll full-time at a four-year institution or university and resident of Maryland. Available to U.S. citizens.

Application Requirements: *Deadline:* March 1.

Contact: Michael Thornton, Associate Program Director, Scholarship
   Programs
   Phone: 410-783-2905 Ext. 207
   Fax: 410-727-5786
   E-mail: mthornton@collegeboundfoundation.org

CONNECTICUT COMMUNITY FOUNDATION

http://www.conncf.org/

MALCOLM BALDRIGE SCHOLARSHIP

One-time award for undergraduates studying in accredited colleges or universities of Connecticut majoring in international business or trade. Must be a Connecticut resident. The award value is in the range of $2000 to $4000 and up to two scholarships are granted annually.

Academic Fields/Career Goals: Business/Consumer Services; International Studies.

Award: Scholarship for use in freshman, sophomore, junior, or senior years; not renewable. *Number:* 1–3. *Amount:* $2000–$4000.

Eligibility Requirements: Applicant must be enrolled or expecting to enroll full- or part-time at a two-year or four-year institution or university; resident of Connecticut and studying in Connecticut. Available to U.S. citizens.

Application Requirements: Application form, essay, financial need analysis, recommendations or references, transcript. *Deadline:* March 15.

Contact: Josh Carey, Director of Grants Management
   Connecticut Community Foundation
   43 Field Street
   Waterbury, CT 06702
   Phone: 203-753-1315
   E-mail: jcarey@conncf.org

CUBAN AMERICAN NATIONAL FOUNDATION

http://www.masscholarships.org/

MAS FAMILY SCHOLARSHIPS

Graduate and undergraduate scholarships in the fields of engineering, business, international relations, economics, communications, and journalism. Applicants must be Cuban-American and have graduated in the top 10 percent of high school class or have minimum 3.5 college GPA. Selection based on need, academic performance, leadership. Those who have already received awards and maintained high level of performance are given preference over new applicants.

Academic Fields/Career Goals: Business/Consumer Services; Chemical Engineering; Communications; Economics; Electrical Engineering/Electronics; Engineering-Related Technologies; Engineering/Technology; Journalism; Mechanical Engineering; Political Science.

Award: Scholarship for use in freshman, sophomore, junior, senior, or graduate years; renewable. *Number:* 10–15. *Amount:* up to $10,000.

Eligibility Requirements: Applicant must be of Latin American/Caribbean heritage; Hispanic; enrolled or expecting to enroll full-time at a two-year or four-year institution or university and must have an interest in leadership. Applicant must have 3.5 GPA or higher. Available to U.S. citizens.

Application Requirements: Application form, driver's license, essay, financial need analysis, proof of Cuban descent, proof of admission, recommendations or references, test scores, transcript. *Deadline:* March 31.

Contact: Melanie Martinez, Director of Community Relations
   Phone: 305-592-0075
   E-mail: mmartinez@jmcffmasscholarships.org

DADE COMMUNITY FOUNDATION

http://www.dadecommunityfoundation.org/

DR. FELIX H. REYLER (FIBA) SCHOLARSHIP

Award for an undergraduate junior or senior enrolled full time in a program of business/finance at a Florida college or university. Must be a resident of Florida. Students graduating from the Academy for International Business and Finance at Miami Jackson Senior High and children of Florida International Bankers Association members may also apply. May reapply for a second year of the award if a 3.0 GPA is maintained. For additional information and application, visit website http://www.dadecommunityfoundation.org.

Academic Fields/Career Goals: Business/Consumer Services; Finance.

Award: Scholarship for use in junior or senior years; not renewable. *Number:* 2. *Amount:* $2500.

Eligibility Requirements: Applicant must be enrolled or expecting to enroll full-time at a four-year institution or university; resident of Florida and studying in Florida. Applicant must have 3.0 GPA or higher. Available to U.S. citizens.

Application Requirements: Application form, financial need analysis, personal statement, resume, transcript. *Deadline:* April 24.

Contact: Ted Seijo, Scholarship Coordinator
   Phone: 305-371-2711
   E-mail: ted.seijo@dadecommunityfoundation.org

SEITLIN FRANKLIN E. WHEELER SCHOLARSHIP

Award available for South Florida high school seniors who are planning to enroll in a two- or four-year college or university studying business or insurance. Applicant must demonstrate the highest ethical standards, commitment to excellence, and involvement in the community. Minimum GPA of 3.0 and a one-page essay on "Ethics" are required. For additional information and application, see website http://www.dadecommunityfoundation.org.

Academic Fields/Career Goals: Business/Consumer Services; Insurance and Actuarial Science.

Award: Scholarship for use in freshman year; not renewable. *Number:* 2. *Amount:* $1500.

Eligibility Requirements: Applicant must be high school student; planning to enroll or expecting to enroll full-time at a two-year or four-year institution or university and resident of Florida. Applicant must have 3.0 GPA or higher. Available to U.S. citizens.

Application Requirements: Application form, community service, essay, recommendations or references, resume, transcript. *Deadline:* May 8.

Contact: Ted Seijo, Scholarship Coordinator
   Phone: 305-371-2711
   E-mail: ted.seijo@dadecommunityfoundation.org

DAIRY MANAGEMENT

http://www.dairyinfo.com/

NATIONAL DAIRY PROMOTION AND RESEARCH BOARD SCHOLARSHIP

• See page 91

DECA (DISTRIBUTIVE EDUCATION CLUBS OF AMERICA)

http://www.deca.org/

HARRY A. APPLEGATE SCHOLARSHIP

Scholarship available to current DECA or Collegiate DECA members for undergraduate study. Must major in marketing education, merchandising, and/or management. Nonrenewable award for high school students based on DECA activities, grades, and need.

Academic Fields/Career Goals: Business/Consumer Services; Education; Fashion Design; Finance; Hospitality Management; Marketing.

Award: Scholarship for use in freshman, sophomore, junior, or senior years; not renewable. *Number:* 20–25. *Amount:* $1000–$5000.

Eligibility Requirements: Applicant must be enrolled or expecting to enroll full-time at a two-year or four-year institution or university. Applicant or parent of applicant must be member of Distribution Ed Club or Future Business Leaders of America. Available to U.S. and non-U.S. citizens.

Application Requirements: Application form, application form may be submitted online (http://www.deca.org/scholarships/), copy of DECA chapter roster, recommendations or references, test scores, transcript. *Deadline:* January 17.

Contact: Kathy Onion, Corporate and External Affairs Assistant
Phone: 703-860-5000 Ext. 248
Fax: 703-860-4013
E-mail: kathy_onion@deca.org

DELTA SIGMA PI LEADERSHIP FOUNDATION

http://www.dspnet.org/

DELTA SIGMA PI UNDERGRADUATE SCHOLARSHIP

Applicant must be a member of Delta Sigma Pi in good standing with at least one full semester or quarter of college remaining in the fall following application.

Academic Fields/Career Goals: Business/Consumer Services.

Award: Scholarship for use in sophomore, junior, or senior years; not renewable. *Number:* 1–40. *Amount:* $250–$3000.

Eligibility Requirements: Applicant must be enrolled or expecting to enroll full-time at a four-year institution or university. Applicant or parent of applicant must be member of Greek Organization. Available to U.S. and non-U.S. citizens.

Application Requirements: Application form, application form may be submitted online (http://www.dspnet.org/scholarship/default.aspx), community service, description of fraternity, campus, community involvement, essay, financial need analysis, recommendations or references, transcript. *Deadline:* June 15.

Contact: Shanda Gray, Executive Vice President
Delta Sigma Pi Leadership Foundation
330 South Campus Avenue
Oxford, OH 45056
Phone: 513-523-1907
Fax: 513-523-7292
E-mail: foundation@dspnet.org

EASTERN STAR-GRAND CHAPTER OF CALIFORNIA

http://www.oescal.org/

SCHOLARSHIPS FOR EDUCATION, BUSINESS AND RELIGION

Scholarship of $500 to $3000 awarded to students residing in California for post-secondary study. These scholarships are awarded for the study of business, education or religion.

Academic Fields/Career Goals: Business/Consumer Services; Education; Religion/Theology.

Award: Scholarship for use in freshman, sophomore, junior, or senior years; renewable. *Amount:* $500–$3000.

Eligibility Requirements: Applicant must be enrolled or expecting to enroll full-time at a two-year or four-year or technical institution or university and resident of California. Applicant must have 3.0 GPA or higher. Available to U.S. citizens.

Application Requirements: Application form, financial need analysis, personal photograph, proof of acceptance to college or university, recommendations or references, self-addressed stamped envelope with application, transcript. *Deadline:* March 8.

Contact: Maryann Barrios, Grand Secretary
Eastern Star-Grand Chapter of California
16960 Bastanchury Road, Suite E
Yorba Linda, CA 92886-1711
Phone: 714-986-2380
Fax: 714-986-2385
E-mail: gsecretary@oescal.org

ELECTRONIC DOCUMENT SYSTEMS FOUNDATION

http://www.edsf.org/

EDSF BOARD OF DIRECTORS SCHOLARSHIPS

Scholarships awarded to full-time students who are committed to pursuing a career in the document management and graphic communications marketplace. The career choices are very broad and include, but are not limited to, computer science and engineering, graphic and media communications, and business. Preference is given to college-level juniors, seniors and advanced degree students. Minimum 3.0 GPA required.

Academic Fields/Career Goals: Business/Consumer Services; Computer Science/Data Processing; Graphics/Graphic Arts/Printing.

Award: Scholarship for use in freshman, sophomore, junior, senior, or graduate years; not renewable. *Amount:* $1000–$5000.

Eligibility Requirements: Applicant must be enrolled or expecting to enroll full-time at a two-year or four-year institution or university. Applicant must have 3.0 GPA or higher. Available to U.S. and non-U.S. citizens.

Application Requirements: Application form, community service, recommendations or references, transcript. *Deadline:* May 1.

Contact: Ms. Brenda Kai, Executive Director
Phone: 817-849-1145
E-mail: brenda.kai@edsf.org

HOODS MEMORIAL SCHOLARSHIP

$2000 award for students whose academic focus includes all document management and graphic communications careers with special consideration given to students interested in marketing and public relations. Minimum 3.0 GPA required.

Academic Fields/Career Goals: Business/Consumer Services; Computer Science/Data Processing; Graphics/Graphic Arts/Printing; Marketing.

Award: Scholarship for use in freshman, sophomore, junior, senior, or graduate years; not renewable. *Amount:* $2000.

Eligibility Requirements: Applicant must be enrolled or expecting to enroll full-time at a two-year or four-year institution or university. Applicant must have 3.0 GPA or higher. Available to U.S. and non-U.S. citizens.

Application Requirements: Application form, community service, essay, recommendations or references, transcript. *Deadline:* May 1.

Contact: Ms. Brenda Kai, Executive Director
Phone: 817-849-1145
E-mail: brenda.kai@edsf.org

LYNDA BABOYIAN MEMORIAL SCHOLARSHIP

$2000 award for full-time students whose academic focus includes all document management and graphic communications careers. Minimum 3.0 GPA required.

Academic Fields/Career Goals: Business/Consumer Services; Computer Science/Data Processing; Graphics/Graphic Arts/Printing.

Award: Scholarship for use in freshman, sophomore, junior, or senior years; not renewable. *Amount:* $2000.

Eligibility Requirements: Applicant must be enrolled or expecting to enroll full-time at a two-year or four-year institution or university.

Applicant must have 3.0 GPA or higher. Available to U.S. and non-U.S. citizens.

Application Requirements: Application form, community service, essay, recommendations or references, transcript. *Deadline:* May 1.

Contact: Ms. Brenda Kai, Executive Director
Phone: 817-849-1145
E-mail: brenda.kai@edsf.org

FAMILY, CAREER AND COMMUNITY LEADERS OF AMERICA-TEXAS ASSOCIATION

http://www.texasfccla.org/

FCCLA HOUSTON LIVESTOCK SHOW AND RODEO SCHOLARSHIP

Renewable scholarship for graduating high school seniors enrolled in full-time program in family and consumer sciences. Must be Texas resident and should study in Texas. Must have minimum GPA of 3.5.

Academic Fields/Career Goals: Business/Consumer Services; Home Economics.

Award: Scholarship for use in freshman year; renewable. *Number:* up to 10. *Amount:* $12,000.

Eligibility Requirements: Applicant must be high school student; planning to enroll or expecting to enroll full-time at a four-year institution or university; single; resident of Texas and studying in Texas. Applicant or parent of applicant must be member of Family, Career and Community Leaders of America. Applicant must have 3.5 GPA or higher. Available to U.S. citizens.

Application Requirements: Application form, essay, personal photograph, recommendations or references, test scores, transcript. *Deadline:* March 1.

FCCLA REGIONAL SCHOLARSHIPS

One-time award for graduating high school seniors enrolled in full-time program in family and consumer sciences. Must be Texas resident and should study in Texas. Must have minimum GPA of 2.5.

Academic Fields/Career Goals: Business/Consumer Services; Home Economics.

Award: Scholarship for use in freshman year; not renewable. *Number:* up to 5. *Amount:* $1000.

Eligibility Requirements: Applicant must be high school student; planning to enroll or expecting to enroll full-time at a four-year institution or university; single; resident of Texas and studying in Texas. Applicant or parent of applicant must be member of Family, Career and Community Leaders of America. Applicant must have 2.5 GPA or higher. Available to U.S. citizens.

Application Requirements: Application form, essay, recommendations or references, test scores, transcript. *Deadline:* March 1.

FCCLA TEXAS FARM BUREAU SCHOLARSHIP

One-time award for a graduating high school senior enrolled in full-time program in family and consumer sciences. Must be a Texas resident and must study in Texas. Must have minimum GPA of 2.5. The award value is $1000.

Academic Fields/Career Goals: Business/Consumer Services; Home Economics.

Award: Scholarship for use in freshman year; not renewable. *Number:* 1. *Amount:* $1000.

Eligibility Requirements: Applicant must be high school student; planning to enroll or expecting to enroll full-time at a four-year institution or university; single; resident of Texas and studying in Texas. Applicant or parent of applicant must be member of Family, Career and Community Leaders of America. Applicant must have 2.5 GPA or higher. Available to U.S. citizens.

Application Requirements: Application form, driver's license, essay, recommendations or references, test scores, transcript. *Deadline:* March 1.

FISHER BROADCASTING COMPANY

http://www.fsci.com/

FISHER BROADCASTING INC. SCHOLARSHIP FOR MINORITIES

Applicant must be of non-white origin, must be at least a sophomore, must be a U.S. citizen and must be in broadcast, marketing or journalism courses. If the applicant is permanent resident of the states of Washington, Oregon, Idaho or Montana, tuition may be applied to an out-of-state school. If the applicant is not a permanent resident of the above-mentioned states, tuition must be applied to a school in Washington, Oregon, Idaho or Montana. Require a minimum of 2.5 GPA.

Academic Fields/Career Goals: Business/Consumer Services; Journalism; TV/Radio Broadcasting.

Award: Scholarship for use in sophomore, junior, or senior years; not renewable. *Number:* up to 5. *Amount:* $1000–$10,000.

Eligibility Requirements: Applicant must be American Indian/Alaska Native, Asian/Pacific Islander, Black (non-Hispanic), Hispanic and enrolled or expecting to enroll full-time at a two-year or four-year or technical institution or university. Applicant must have 2.5 GPA or higher. Available to U.S. citizens.

Application Requirements: Application form, citizenship proof, essay, financial need analysis, interview, recommendations or references, transcript. *Deadline:* April 30.

Contact: Annnarie Hitchcock, Human Resources Administrator
Fisher Broadcasting Company
100 Fourth Avenue North, Suite 510
Seattle, WA 98109
Phone: 206-404-6050
Fax: 206-404-6760
E-mail: ahitchcock@fsci.com

FUKUNAGA SCHOLARSHIP FOUNDATION

http://servco.com/philanthropy/scholarships.php

FUKUNAGA SCHOLARSHIP FOUNDATION

Renewable scholarships available only to Hawaii residents pursuing a business degree at the undergraduate level at an accredited institution. Minimum 3.0 GPA required.

Academic Fields/Career Goals: Business/Consumer Services.

Award: Scholarship for use in freshman, sophomore, junior, or senior years; renewable. *Number:* 10–15. *Amount:* $4000.

Eligibility Requirements: Applicant must be enrolled or expecting to enroll full-time at a four-year institution or university and resident of Hawaii. Applicant must have 3.0 GPA or higher. Available to U.S. citizens.

Application Requirements: Application form, essay, FAFSA, Student Aid Report (SAR), financial need analysis, interview, recommendations or references, test scores, transcript. *Deadline:* March 1.

Contact: Mrs. Sandy Wong, Program Administrator
Fukunaga Scholarship Foundation
PO Box 2788
Honolulu, HI 96803-2788
Phone: 808-564-1386
Fax: 808-523-3937
E-mail: sandyw@servco.com

GEORGIA GOVERNMENT FINANCE OFFICERS ASSOCIATION

http://www.ggfoa.org/

GGFOA SCHOLARSHIP
• *See page 73*

GLOBAL AUTOMOTIVE AFTERMARKET SYMPOSIUM

http://www.automotivescholarships.com/

GAAS SCHOLARSHIP

To receive a scholarship, applicants must be a high school graduate enrolled in a full time college-level program or an ASE/NATEF certified postsecondary automotive technical program, and planning a career in the automotive aftermarket.

Academic Fields/Career Goals: Business/Consumer Services; Engineering-Related Technologies; Marketing; Mechanical Engineering; Trade/Technical Specialties.

Award: Scholarship for use in freshman, sophomore, junior, or senior years; not renewable. *Number:* up to 150. *Amount:* $1000.

Eligibility Requirements: Applicant must be enrolled or expecting to enroll full-time at a four-year or technical institution or university. Available to U.S. and Canadian citizens.

Application Requirements: Application form, application form may be submitted online (http://www.automotivescholarships.com), essay, personal photograph, recommendations or references, transcript. *Deadline:* March 31.

Contact: Emily McConnell, Scholarship Committee
Global Automotive Aftermarket Symposium
PO Box 13966
Research Triangle Park, NC 27709-3966
Phone: 919-406-8802
Fax: 919-549-4824
E-mail: emcconnell@mema.org

GOLDEN KEY INTERNATIONAL HONOUR SOCIETY

http://www.goldenkey.org/

BUSINESS ACHIEVEMENT AWARD

Award to members who excel in the study of business. Applicants will be asked to respond to a problem posed by an honorary member within the discipline. The response will be in the form of a professional business report. One winner will receive a $1000 award. The second place winner will receive $750 and the third place winner will receive $500.

Academic Fields/Career Goals: Business/Consumer Services.

Award: Prize for use in freshman, sophomore, junior, senior, graduate, or postgraduate years; not renewable. *Number:* 3. *Amount:* $500–$1000.

Eligibility Requirements: Applicant must be enrolled or expecting to enroll full- or part-time at a four-year institution or university. Available to U.S. and non-U.S. citizens.

Application Requirements: Application form, business-related report, entry in a contest, essay, recommendations or references, transcript. *Deadline:* March 3.

GOVERNMENT FINANCE OFFICERS ASSOCIATION

http://www.gfoa.org/

FRANK L. GREATHOUSE GOVERNMENT ACCOUNTING SCHOLARSHIP

One to two scholarships awarded to undergraduate or graduate students enrolled full-time, preparing for a career in state or local government finance. Submit resume. One-time award of $3500.

Academic Fields/Career Goals: Business/Consumer Services; Public Policy and Administration.

Award: Scholarship for use in freshman, sophomore, junior, senior, or graduate years; not renewable. *Number:* 1–2. *Amount:* $5000.

Eligibility Requirements: Applicant must be enrolled or expecting to enroll full-time at a two-year or four-year or technical institution or university. Available to U.S. and Canadian citizens.

Application Requirements: Application form, essay, recommendations or references, resume, transcript. *Deadline:* February 29.

Contact: Jake Lorentz, Assistant Director
Government Finance Officers Association
203 North LaSalle Street, Suite 2700
Chicago, IL 60601
Phone: 312-977-9700 Ext. 267
Fax: 312-977-4806
E-mail: jlorentz@gfoa.org

MINORITIES IN GOVERNMENT FINANCE SCHOLARSHIP
• *See page 73*

GREATER KANAWHA VALLEY FOUNDATION

http://www.tgkvf.org/

WILLARD H. ERWIN JR. MEMORIAL SCHOLARSHIP FUND

Award of $600 for West Virginia residents who are starting their junior or senior year of undergraduate or graduate studies in a business or health-care finance degree program. Must be enrolled at a college in West Virginia. Scholarships are awarded on the basis of financial need and scholastic ability.

Academic Fields/Career Goals: Business/Consumer Services; Health Administration.

Award: Scholarship for use in junior, senior, or graduate years; renewable. *Number:* 1. *Amount:* $600.

Eligibility Requirements: Applicant must be enrolled or expecting to enroll full- or part-time at a four-year institution or university; resident of West Virginia and studying in West Virginia. Available to U.S. citizens.

Application Requirements: Application form, essay, financial need analysis, recommendations or references, self-addressed stamped envelope with application, test scores, transcript. *Deadline:* January 15.

Contact: Susan Hoover, Scholarship Program Officer
Greater Kanawha Valley Foundation
900 Lee Street East, 16th Floor
Charleston, WV 25301
Phone: 304-346-3620
E-mail: tgkvf@tgkvf.org

GREAT FALLS ADVERTISING FEDERATION

http://www.gfaf.com/

GREAT FALLS ADVERTISING FEDERATION COLLEGE SCHOLARSHIP
• *See page 83*

HIGH SCHOOL MARKETING/COMMUNICATIONS SCHOLARSHIP
• *See page 83*

HISPANIC HERITAGE FOUNDATION

http://www.hispanicheritage.org/

HISPANIC HERITAGE YOUTH AWARDS

Applicants must be current high school Juniors (not seniors) planning to enroll in college in the following fall, citizens or permanent residents of the US. Award categories include Business & Finance, Community Service, Education (future teachers), Engineering and Mathematics, and Healthcare.

Academic Fields/Career Goals: Business/Consumer Services; Education; Engineering-Related Technologies; Finance; Health and Medical Sciences; Mathematics.

Award: Scholarship for use in freshman year. *Amount:* $1000.

Eligibility Requirements: Applicant must be Hispanic; high school student and planning to enroll or expecting to enroll at an institution or university. Applicant must have 3.0 GPA or higher. Available to U.S. citizens.

Application Requirements: *Deadline:* July 1.

HOLSTEIN ASSOCIATION USA INC.

http://www.holsteinusa.com/

ROBERT H. RUMLER SCHOLARSHIP
• *See page 85*

IDAHO STATE BROADCASTERS ASSOCIATION

http://www.idahobroadcasters.org/

WAYNE C. CORNILS MEMORIAL SCHOLARSHIP

Scholarship for students enrolled in an Idaho school on a full-time basis. Must be majoring in a broadcasting related field. Must have minimum GPA of 2.0 if in the first two years of school or 2.5 in the last two years of school.

Academic Fields/Career Goals: Business/Consumer Services; Engineering/Technology; Journalism; TV/Radio Broadcasting.

Award: Scholarship for use in sophomore, junior, or senior years; not renewable. *Number:* 3. *Amount:* $1000.

Eligibility Requirements: Applicant must be enrolled or expecting to enroll full-time at a four-year institution or university; resident of Idaho and studying in Idaho. Applicant must have 2.5 GPA or higher. Available to U.S. citizens.

Application Requirements: Application form, essay, recommendations or references, transcript. *Deadline:* March 15.

Contact: Connie Searles, President and CEO
Idaho State Broadcasters Association
1674 Hill Road
Suite 3
Boise, ID 83702
Phone: 208-345-3072
Fax: 208-343-8046
E-mail: isba@qwestoffice.net

INSTITUTE FOR OPERATIONS RESEARCH AND THE MANAGEMENT SCIENCES

http://www.informs.org/

GEORGE NICHOLSON STUDENT PAPER COMPETITION

Honors outstanding papers in the field of operations research and the management sciences. Entrant must be student on or after the year of application. Research papers present original results and be written by student. Electronic submission of paper required.

Academic Fields/Career Goals: Business/Consumer Services.

Award: Prize for use in junior, senior, graduate, or postgraduate years; not renewable. *Number:* up to 6. *Amount:* $100–$600.

Eligibility Requirements: Applicant must be enrolled or expecting to enroll full- or part-time at a four-year institution or university. Available to U.S. and non-U.S. citizens.

Application Requirements: Application form, entry in a contest, recommendations or references. *Deadline:* June 30.

Contact: Mark Doherty, Executive Director
Phone: 410-850-0300
Fax: 410-684-2963
E-mail: mark.doherty@informs.org

INSTITUTE OF MANAGEMENT ACCOUNTANTS

http://www.imanet.org/

INSTITUTE OF MANAGEMENT ACCOUNTANTS MEMORIAL EDUCATION FUND SCHOLARSHIPS
• *See page 74*

STUART CAMERON AND MARGARET MCLEOD MEMORIAL SCHOLARSHIP
• *See page 74*

JORGE MAS CANOSA FREEDOM FOUNDATION

http://www.jorgemascanosa.org/

MAS FAMILY SCHOLARSHIP AWARD

Scholarship for Cuban American student who is a direct descendant of those who left Cuba or was born in Cuba. Minimum 3.5 GPA in college. Scholarships available only in the fields of engineering, business, international relations, economics, communications and journalism.

Academic Fields/Career Goals: Business/Consumer Services; Chemical Engineering; Civil Engineering; Communications; Economics; Electrical Engineering/Electronics; Engineering-Related Technologies; International Studies; Journalism; Materials Science, Engineering, and Metallurgy; Mechanical Engineering.

Award: Scholarship for use in freshman, sophomore, junior, senior, or graduate years; renewable. *Number:* 5–10. *Amount:* $8000–$40,000.

Eligibility Requirements: Applicant must be of Latin American/Caribbean heritage; Hispanic and enrolled or expecting to enroll full-time at a two-year or four-year institution or university. Applicant must have 3.5 GPA or higher. Available to U.S. and non-U.S. citizens.

Application Requirements: Application form, essay, financial need analysis, proof of Cuban descent, recommendations or references, test scores, transcript. *Deadline:* April 15.

Contact: Mr. Daniel Lafuente, Mas Scholarship Coordinator
Jorge Mas Canosa Freedom Foundation
1312 SW 27th Avenue
Miami, FL 33145
Phone: 305-592-7768
E-mail: dlafuente@canf.org

KE ALI'I PAUAHI FOUNDATION

http://www.pauahi.org/

NATIVE HAWAIIAN CHAMBER OF COMMERCE SCHOLARSHIP

Scholarship for students enrolled in an undergraduate or graduate degree-seeking program from an accredited post-secondary educational institution majoring in business administration. Minimum 3.0 GPA.

Academic Fields/Career Goals: Business/Consumer Services.

Award: Scholarship for use in freshman, sophomore, junior, senior, or graduate years; not renewable. *Number:* 9. *Amount:* $500–$1000.

Eligibility Requirements: Applicant must be enrolled or expecting to enroll full-time at a four-year institution or university. Applicant must have 3.0 GPA or higher. Available to U.S. citizens.

Application Requirements: Application form, application form may be submitted online (http://www.pauahi.org/scholarships), financial need analysis, recommendations or references, Student Aid Report (SAR), college acceptance letter, transcript. *Deadline:* April 1.

Contact: Mavis Shiraishi-Nagao, Scholarship Administrator
Phone: 808-534-3966
E-mail: scholarships@pauahi.org

LAGRANT FOUNDATION

http://www.lagrantfoundation.org/

LAGRANT FOUNDATION SCHOLARSHIP FOR UNDERGRADUATES

Awards are for undergraduate and graduate minority students who are attending accredited four-year institutions and are pursuing careers in the fields of advertising, marketing, and public relations. Minimum 2.75 GPA required.

Academic Fields/Career Goals: Business/Consumer Services; Communications.

Award: Scholarship for use in freshman, sophomore, junior, senior, or graduate years; renewable. *Number:* 22. *Amount:* up to $5000.

Eligibility Requirements: Applicant must be American Indian/Alaska Native, Asian/Pacific Islander, Black (non-Hispanic), Hispanic and enrolled or expecting to enroll full-time at a four-year institution or university. Available to U.S. citizens.

Application Requirements: Application form, essay, recommendations or references, resume, transcript. *Deadline:* February 28.

LAWRENCE P. DOSS SCHOLARSHIP FOUNDATION

http://www.lawrencepdossfnd.org/

LAWRENCE P. DOSS SCHOLARSHIP FOUNDATION

• *See page 75*

LEAGUE OF UNITED LATIN AMERICAN CITIZENS NATIONAL EDUCATIONAL SERVICE CENTERS INC.

http://www.lnesc.org/

GE/LULAC SCHOLARSHIP

The scholarship for business and engineering students offers outstanding minority or low-income students entering their sophomore year in pursuit of an undergraduate degree a renewable scholarship up to 3 years.

Academic Fields/Career Goals: Business/Consumer Services; Engineering/Technology.

Award: Scholarship for use in sophomore, junior, or senior years; renewable. *Number:* up to 9. *Amount:* up to $5000.

Eligibility Requirements: Applicant must be American Indian/Alaska Native, Asian/Pacific Islander, Black (non-Hispanic), Hispanic and enrolled or expecting to enroll full-time at a four-year institution or university. Applicant must have 3.0 GPA or higher. Available to U.S. citizens.

Application Requirements: Application form, personal statement with career goals, recommendations or references, transcript. *Deadline:* July 15.

MAINE EDUCATION SERVICES

http://www.mesfoundation.com/

MAINE STATE CHAMBER OF COMMERCE SCHOLARSHIP-HIGH SCHOOL SENIOR

Two scholarships available for graduating high school seniors, one who is planning to pursue an associate degree in a technical program, and one who is planning to pursue a bachelor's degree in a business-related area. Preference may be given to students attending Maine colleges. Awards are based on academic excellence, student activities, financial need, letters of recommendation, and a required essay.

Academic Fields/Career Goals: Business/Consumer Services; Engineering/Technology.

Award: Scholarship for use in freshman year; not renewable. *Number:* up to 2. *Amount:* up to $1500.

Eligibility Requirements: Applicant must be high school student; planning to enroll or expecting to enroll full-time at a two-year or four-year or technical institution or university and resident of Maine. Available to U.S. citizens.

Application Requirements: Application form, community service, essay, financial need analysis, recommendations or references, transcript. *Deadline:* April 18.

Contact: Kim Benjamin, Vice President of Operations
Phone: 207-791-3600

MARYLAND ASSOCIATION OF PRIVATE COLLEGES AND CAREER SCHOOLS

http://www.mapccs.org/

MARYLAND ASSOCIATION OF PRIVATE COLLEGES AND CAREER SCHOOLS SCHOLARSHIP

Awards for study at trade schools only. Must enter school same year high school is completed. For use only in Maryland and by Maryland residents.

Academic Fields/Career Goals: Business/Consumer Services; Computer Science/Data Processing; Dental Health/Services; Engineering/Technology; Food Science/Nutrition; Home Economics; Trade/Technical Specialties; TV/Radio Broadcasting.

Award: Scholarship for use in freshman year; not renewable. *Number:* 50. *Amount:* $500–$19,950.

Eligibility Requirements: Applicant must be high school student; planning to enroll or expecting to enroll full-time at a technical institution; resident of Maryland and studying in Maryland. Available to U.S. citizens.

Application Requirements: Application form, letter of eligibility from the MAPCCS career school, recommendations or references, transcript. *Deadline:* April 11.

Contact: Jeannie Schwartz, Director of Placements
Maryland Association of Private Colleges and Career Schools
1539 Merriet Boulevard, PO Box 206
Baltimore, MD 21222
Phone: 410-282-4012
Fax: 410-282-4133
E-mail: jeannie.schwartz@computertraining.com

NATIONAL ASSOCIATION OF WATER COMPANIES-NEW JERSEY CHAPTER

http://www.nawc.org/

NATIONAL ASSOCIATION OF WATER COMPANIES-NEW JERSEY CHAPTER SCHOLARSHIP

• *See page 146*

NATIONAL BLACK MBA ASSOCIATION-TWIN CITIES CHAPTER

http://www.nbmbaatc.org/

TWIN CITIES CHAPTER UNDERGRADUATE SCHOLARSHIP

• *See page 76*

NATIONAL URBAN LEAGUE

http://www.nulbeep.org/

BLACK EXECUTIVE EXCHANGE PROGRAM JERRY BARTOW SCHOLARSHIP FUND

Scholarships for undergraduate students at participating Historically Black Colleges and Universities. Must be sophomore, junior, or senior, majoring in business, management, technology, or education. Must be available to receive award at BEEP's annual conference.

Academic Fields/Career Goals: Business/Consumer Services; Education; Engineering/Technology.

Award: Scholarship for use in sophomore, junior, or senior years; not renewable. *Number:* 2. *Amount:* $5000.

Eligibility Requirements: Applicant must be Black (non-Hispanic) and enrolled or expecting to enroll full-time at a four-year institution or university. Applicant must have 2.5 GPA or higher. Available to U.S. citizens.

Application Requirements: Application form. *Deadline:* February 1.

Contact: William Dawson, Scholarship Committee
National Urban League
120 Wall Street
New York, NY 10005
Phone: 212-558-5300
Fax: 212-344-5332
E-mail: beep2005@nul.org

NEBRASKA DECA

http://www.nedeca.org/

NEBRASKA DECA LEADERSHIP SCHOLARSHIP

Awards applicants who intend to pursue a full-time two- or four-year course of study in a marketing or business-related field. Applicant must be active in DECA and involved in community service activities.

Academic Fields/Career Goals: Business/Consumer Services.

Award: Scholarship for use in freshman year; not renewable. *Number:* 2–9. *Amount:* $250–$1000.

Eligibility Requirements: Applicant must be high school student; planning to enroll or expecting to enroll full-time at a two-year or four-year or technical institution or university and resident of Nebraska. Applicant or parent of applicant must be member of Distribution Ed Club or Future Business Leaders of America. Applicant must have 2.5 GPA or higher. Available to U.S. citizens.

Application Requirements: Application form, DECA participation and accomplishment documents, essay, recommendations or references, resume, test scores, transcript. *Deadline:* February 1.

NEW ENGLAND EMPLOYEE BENEFITS COUNCIL

http://www.neebc.org/

NEW ENGLAND EMPLOYEE BENEFITS COUNCIL SCHOLARSHIP PROGRAM
• See page 77

NEW ENGLAND WATER WORKS ASSOCIATION

http://www.newwa.org/

FRANCIS X. CROWLEY SCHOLARSHIP

Scholarships are awarded to eligible civil engineering, environmental and business management students on the basis of merit, character, and need. Preference given to those students whose programs are considered by a committee as beneficial to water works practice in New England. NEWWA student membership is required to receive a scholarship award. Applicants for scholarships should be residents or attend school in New England. (Maine, New Hampshire, Vermont, Massachusetts, Rhode Island and Connecticut).

Academic Fields/Career Goals: Business/Consumer Services; Civil Engineering; Environmental Science.

Award: Scholarship for use in freshman, sophomore, junior, senior, or graduate years; not renewable. *Number:* 1. *Amount:* up to $3000.

Eligibility Requirements: Applicant must be enrolled or expecting to enroll full-time at a four-year institution or university. Applicant or parent of applicant must be member of New England Water Works Association. Available to U.S. citizens.

Application Requirements: Application form, essay, recommendations or references, transcript. *Fee:* $25. *Deadline:* July 1.

Contact: Thomas MacElhaney, Chair, Scholarship Committee
Phone: 631-231-8100
Fax: 978-418-9156
E-mail: tmacelhaney@preloadinc.com

OREGON STUDENT ASSISTANCE COMMISSION

http://www.GetCollegeFunds.org/

OREGON ASSOCIATION OF CERTIFIED FRAUD EXAMINERS SCHOLARSHIP
• See page 78

OREGON CAREER AND TECHNICAL EDUCATION SCHOLARSHIP

Award for at least part-time study at Oregon public two-year colleges. Major must qualify according to one of these preferences in the following order: (1) industrial mechanics/maintenance, industrial/mechanical engineering, manufacturing technology, or (2) business administration,

commerce, entrepreneurship, and management. FAFSA is required. Automatically renewable if renewal criteria is met.

Academic Fields/Career Goals: Business/Consumer Services; Mechanical Engineering; Trade/Technical Specialties.

Award: Scholarship for use in freshman or sophomore years; renewable.

Eligibility Requirements: Applicant must be enrolled or expecting to enroll full- or part-time at a two-year institution and studying in Oregon. Available to U.S. citizens.

Application Requirements: Application form, FAFSA. *Deadline:* March 1.

PLUMBING-HEATING-COOLING CONTRACTORS EDUCATION FOUNDATION

http://www.phccfoundation.org/

DELTA FAUCET COMPANY SCHOLARSHIP PROGRAM

Applicants must be sponsored by a member of the National Association of Plumbing-Heating-Cooling Contractors. Must pursue studies in a major related to the plumbing-heating-cooling industry. Visit website for additional information.

Academic Fields/Career Goals: Business/Consumer Services; Engineering-Related Technologies; Engineering/Technology; Heating, Air-Conditioning, and Refrigeration Mechanics; Mechanical Engineering; Trade/Technical Specialties.

Award: Scholarship for use in freshman, sophomore, junior, or senior years; renewable. *Number:* 6. *Amount:* $2500.

Eligibility Requirements: Applicant must be enrolled or expecting to enroll full-time at a two-year or four-year or technical institution or university. Applicant must have 2.5 GPA or higher. Available to U.S. and Canadian citizens.

Application Requirements: Application form, community service, essay, interview, recommendations or references, test scores, transcript. *Deadline:* May 1.

Contact: John Zink, Scholarship Coordinator
Phone: 800-533-7694
E-mail: foundation@naphcc.org

PHCC EDUCATIONAL FOUNDATION NEED-BASED SCHOLARSHIP

Need-based scholarship worth $2500 to a student enrolled in an approved four-year PHCC apprenticeship program, or at an accredited two-year technical college, community college, or an accredited four-year college or university.

Academic Fields/Career Goals: Business/Consumer Services; Engineering-Related Technologies; Engineering/Technology; Heating, Air-Conditioning, and Refrigeration Mechanics; Mechanical Engineering; Trade/Technical Specialties.

Award: Scholarship for use in freshman, sophomore, junior, or senior years; not renewable. *Number:* 1. *Amount:* $2500.

Eligibility Requirements: Applicant must be enrolled or expecting to enroll full-time at a two-year or four-year or technical institution or university. Applicant must have 2.5 GPA or higher. Available to U.S. and Canadian citizens.

Application Requirements: Application form, community service, essay, financial need analysis, interview, recommendations or references, test scores, transcript. *Deadline:* May 1.

Contact: John Zink, Scholarship Coordinator
Phone: 800-533-7694
E-mail: foundation@naphcc.org

PHCC EDUCATIONAL FOUNDATION SCHOLARSHIP PROGRAM

Applicants must be sponsored by a member of the National Association of Plumbing-Heating-Cooling Contractors. Must pursue studies in a major related to the plumbing-heating-cooling industry. Visit website for additional information.

Academic Fields/Career Goals: Business/Consumer Services; Engineering-Related Technologies; Engineering/Technology; Heating, Air-Conditioning, and Refrigeration Mechanics; Mechanical Engineering; Trade/Technical Specialties.

Award: Scholarship for use in freshman, sophomore, junior, or senior years; not renewable. *Number:* 1–4. *Amount:* $2500–$5000.

Eligibility Requirements: Applicant must be enrolled or expecting to enroll full-time at a two-year or four-year or technical institution or university. Applicant must have 2.5 GPA or higher. Available to U.S. and Canadian citizens.

Application Requirements: Application form, community service, essay, interview, recommendations or references, test scores, transcript. *Deadline:* May 1.

Contact: John Zink, Scholarship Coordinator
Phone: 800-533-7694
E-mail: foundation@naphcc.org

ROBERT H. MOLLOHAN FAMILY CHARITABLE FOUNDATION, INC.

http://www.mollohanfoundation.org/

TEAMING TO WIN BUSINESS SCHOLARSHIP

Scholarship for a rising college sophomore or junior pursuing a degree in business administration at a West Virginia college or university.

Academic Fields/Career Goals: Business/Consumer Services.

Award: Scholarship for use in sophomore or junior years; not renewable. *Number:* 2. *Amount:* up to $1000.

Eligibility Requirements: Applicant must be enrolled or expecting to enroll full- or part-time at a four-year institution or university; resident of West Virginia; studying in West Virginia and must have an interest in leadership. Applicant must have 3.0 GPA or higher. Available to U.S. citizens.

Application Requirements: Application form, essay, interview, recommendations or references, resume, test scores, transcript. *Deadline:* February 9.

Contact: Aime Shaffer, Program Manager
Robert H. Mollohan Family Charitable Foundation, Inc.
1000 Technology Drive, Suite 2000
Fairmont, WV 26554
Phone: 304-333-6783
Fax: 304-333-3900
E-mail: ashaffer@wvhtf.org

SALES PROFESSIONALS-USA

http://www.salesprofessionals-usa.com/

SALES PROFESSIONALS-USA SCHOLARSHIP

Scholarships are awarded to students furthering their degree or obtaining a degree in business or marketing. The scholarships are initiated and awarded by the individual Sales Pros Clubs (located in Colorado, Kansas and Missouri) and are not nationally awarded. A listing of local clubs can be found at http://www.salesprofessionals-usa.com.

Academic Fields/Career Goals: Business/Consumer Services.

Award: Scholarship for use in freshman, sophomore, junior, or senior years; not renewable. *Number:* 3–5. *Amount:* $600–$1000.

Eligibility Requirements: Applicant must be enrolled or expecting to enroll full- or part-time at a two-year or four-year institution or university; resident of Colorado, Indiana, Kansas and studying in Colorado, Kansas, Missouri. Applicant must have 3.0 GPA or higher. Available to U.S. citizens.

Application Requirements: Application form, essay. *Deadline:* varies.

Contact: Jay Berg, National President
Sales Professionals-USA
2870 North Speer Boulevard
Denver, CO 80001
Phone: 303-433-1051
E-mail: jberg@spacelogic.net

SOCIETY OF AUTOMOTIVE ANALYSTS

http://www.cybersaa.org/

SOCIETY OF AUTOMOTIVE ANALYSTS SCHOLARSHIP

• See page 79

SOUTH DAKOTA RETAILERS ASSOCIATION

http://www.sdra.org/

SOUTH DAKOTA RETAILERS ASSOCIATION SCHOLARSHIP PROGRAM

• See page 80

SPECIALTY EQUIPMENT MARKET ASSOCIATION

http://www.sema.org/

SPECIALTY EQUIPMENT MARKET ASSOCIATION MEMORIAL SCHOLARSHIP FUND

• See page 80

STRAIGHTFORWARD MEDIA

http://www.straightforwardmedia.com/

STRAIGHTFORWARD MEDIA BUSINESS SCHOOL SCHOLARSHIP

• See page 84

TEXAS FAMILY BUSINESS ASSOCIATION AND SCHOLARSHIP FOUNDATION

http://www.texasfamilybusiness.org/

TEXAS FAMILY BUSINESS ASSOCIATION SCHOLARSHIP

Scholarships awarded to eligible Texas family business members to help them obtain an education in business. Applicants must be planning to return to or stay with their family business.

Academic Fields/Career Goals: Business/Consumer Services.

Award: Scholarship for use in freshman, sophomore, junior, or senior years; not renewable. *Number:* 1.

Eligibility Requirements: Applicant must be enrolled or expecting to enroll full- or part-time at a four-year institution or university; resident of Texas; studying in Texas and must have an interest in entrepreneurship. Available to U.S. citizens.

Application Requirements: Application form, essay, transcript. *Deadline:* varies.

Contact: William Kirshner, President
Phone: 361-882-1686
Fax: 361-888-6602
E-mail: info@texasfamilybusiness.org

TKE EDUCATIONAL FOUNDATION

http://www.tke.org/

W. ALLAN HERZOG SCHOLARSHIP

• See page 81

TRUCKLOAD CARRIERS ASSOCIATION

http://www.truckload.org/

TRUCKLOAD CARRIERS ASSOCIATION SCHOLARSHIP FUND

This scholarship fund is for persons affiliated with the trucking industry and their families to pursue higher education. Special consideration will be given to applicants pursuing transportation or business degrees. Minimum 3.3 GPA required. For junior and senior undergraduate students at four-year college or university. Further information and application deadlines available at website http://www.truckload.org.

Academic Fields/Career Goals: Business/Consumer Services; Transportation.

Award: Scholarship for use in junior or senior years; not renewable. *Number:* 18. *Amount:* $1500–$5000.

Eligibility Requirements: Applicant must be enrolled or expecting to enroll full-time at a four-year institution or university. Applicant or parent of applicant must have employment or volunteer experience in transportation industry. Available to U.S. and Canadian citizens.

Application Requirements: Application form, course schedule including tuition and fees, essay, financial need analysis, transcript. *Deadline:* May 23.

Contact: Debbie Sparks, Vice President of Development
　　　　Phone: 703-838-1950
　　　　Fax: 703-836-6610
　　　　E-mail: tca@truckload.org

UNITED DAUGHTERS OF THE CONFEDERACY

http://www.hqudc.org/

WALTER REED SMITH SCHOLARSHIP

Award for full-time female undergraduate students who are descendant of a Confederate soldier, studying nutrition, home economics, nursing, business administration, or computer science in accredited college or university. Minimum 3.0 GPA required. Submit application and letter of endorsement from sponsoring chapter of the United Daughters of the Confederacy.

Academic Fields/Career Goals: Business/Consumer Services; Computer Science/Data Processing; Food Science/Nutrition; Home Economics; Nursing.

Award: Scholarship for use in freshman, sophomore, junior, or senior years; renewable. *Number:* 1–2. *Amount:* $800–$1000.

Eligibility Requirements: Applicant must be enrolled or expecting to enroll full-time at a four-year institution or university and female. Applicant or parent of applicant must be member of United Daughters of the Confederacy. Applicant must have 3.0 GPA or higher. Available to U.S. citizens.

Application Requirements: Application form, copy of applicant's birth certificate, copy of confederate ancestor's proof of service, essay, financial need analysis, personal photograph, recommendations or references, self-addressed stamped envelope with application, test scores, transcript. *Deadline:* March 15.

Contact: Ms. Jamie Davis, Second Vice President General
　　　　Phone: 804-355-1636
　　　　E-mail: hqudc@rcn.com

UNITED NEGRO COLLEGE FUND

http://www.uncf.org/

AVIS BUDGET GROUP SCHOLARSHIP

• *See page 81*

AXA ACHIEVEMENT SCHOLARSHIP PROGRAM

• *See page 81*

BANK OF AMERICA SCHOLARSHIP

Scholarship supports UNCF students attending a UNCF college or university located in any of the Bank of America core states and majoring in business, finance, education, marketing, computer science, or information technology. Minimum 3.0 GPA required. List of eligible institutions and additional information is available at website http://www.uncf.org.

Academic Fields/Career Goals: Business/Consumer Services; Computer Science/Data Processing; Education; Finance; Marketing.

Award: Scholarship for use in freshman, sophomore, junior, or senior years; not renewable. *Number:* 1. *Amount:* $1000.

Eligibility Requirements: Applicant must be Black (non-Hispanic); enrolled or expecting to enroll full-time at a four-year institution or university and studying in Florida, Georgia, North Carolina, South Carolina, Texas. Applicant must have 3.0 GPA or higher. Available to U.S. and non-U.S. citizens.

Application Requirements: Application form, community service, essay, recommendations or references, transcript. *Deadline:* November 25.

COLGATE-PALMOLIVE COMPANY/UNCF SCHOLARSHIP

Scholarship available to UNCF students who have completed their freshman year and are majoring in business, with a concentration in marketing. Must have a minimum 3.0 GPA.

Academic Fields/Career Goals: Business/Consumer Services; Marketing.

Award: Scholarship for use in sophomore, junior, or senior years; not renewable.

Eligibility Requirements: Applicant must be Black (non-Hispanic) and enrolled or expecting to enroll full-time at a four-year institution or university. Applicant must have 3.0 GPA or higher. Available to U.S. citizens.

Application Requirements: Application form. *Deadline:* continuous.

COMERICA CHARITABLE FOUNDATION SCHOLARSHIP

• *See page 81*

COOPER INDUSTRIES PACESETTER SCHOLARSHIP

• *See page 148*

EDWARD M. NAGEL FOUNDATION SCHOLARSHIP

• *See page 82*

JESSE JONES JR. SCHOLARSHIP

Scholarship is funded through the Chrysler Minority Dealership Association for business students attending a UNCF member college or university. Minimum 2.5 GPA required. Scholarship value ranges from $2000 to $5000.

Academic Fields/Career Goals: Business/Consumer Services.

Award: Scholarship for use in freshman, sophomore, junior, or senior years; not renewable. *Amount:* $2000–$5000.

Eligibility Requirements: Applicant must be Black (non-Hispanic) and enrolled or expecting to enroll full- or part-time at a four-year institution or university. Applicant must have 2.5 GPA or higher. Available to U.S. and non-U.S. citizens.

Application Requirements: Application form, financial need analysis. *Deadline:* continuous.

LIBERTY MUTUAL SCHOLARSHIP

$5000 scholarships to provide recognition of and financial assistance to outstanding students from UNCF member institutions who are business or finance majors. Students should live or go to school in California, Pennsylvania, Massachusetts, New York, New Jersey, Illinois, Georgia, Wisconsin, Texas, Florida, or New Hampshire. Minimum 3.4 GPA required. Recipients are encouraged to apply for a summer internship with Liberty Mutual.

Academic Fields/Career Goals: Business/Consumer Services; Finance.

Award: Scholarship for use in freshman, sophomore, junior, or senior years; not renewable. *Amount:* $5000.

Eligibility Requirements: Applicant must be Black (non-Hispanic) and enrolled or expecting to enroll full-time at a four-year institution or university. Available to U.S. citizens.

Application Requirements: Application form. *Deadline:* continuous.

LOCKHEED MARTIN/UNCF SCHOLARSHIP

• *See page 82*

NASCAR/WENDELL SCOTT, SR. SCHOLARSHIP

• *See page 82*

PACIFIC GAS AND ELECTRIC COMPANY SCHOLARSHIP

• *See page 82*

PSE&G SCHOLARSHIP

• *See page 82*

ROBERT HALF INTERNATIONAL SCHOLARSHIP

• *See page 82*

UBS/PAINEWEBBER SCHOLARSHIP
• *See page 82*

WILLIAM WRIGLEY JR. SCHOLARSHIP/INTERNSHIP
Up to $3000 scholarship for sophomore and juniors attending UNCF member colleges and universities. Must be majoring in engineering, business, or chemistry. Minimum 3.0 GPA required. An internship may also be available for the recipient of this scholarship.

Academic Fields/Career Goals: Business/Consumer Services; Engineering/Technology; Physical Sciences.

Award: Scholarship for use in sophomore or junior years; not renewable. *Amount:* up to $3000.

Eligibility Requirements: Applicant must be Black (non-Hispanic) and enrolled or expecting to enroll full-time at a four-year institution or university. Applicant must have 3.0 GPA or higher. Available to U.S. citizens.

Application Requirements: Application form. *Deadline:* continuous.

WHOMENTORS.COM, INC.
http://www.WHOmentors.com/

1B USD WORLDWIDE VENTURE CAPITAL
• *See page 107*

WOMEN GROCERS OF AMERICA
http://www.nationalgrocers.org/

MARY MACEY SCHOLARSHIP
• *See page 96*

WOMEN IN LOGISTICS, NORTHERN CALIFORNIA
http://www.womeninlogistics.org/

WOMEN IN LOGISTICS SCHOLARSHIP
Award for students (undergraduate/graduate, male/female) studying and eventually planning careers in logistics/supply chain management. Applicants must be enrolled in a degree program at an institution within the 9 counties comprising the San Francisco Bay Area and have at least one semester left, as this award goes directly to the institution towards tuition/fees. Deadlines typically fall on November 1st. While student need may considered, awards are based primarily on merit, work experience and demonstrated interest in the field.

Academic Fields/Career Goals: Business/Consumer Services; Trade/Technical Specialties; Transportation.

Award: Scholarship for use in freshman, sophomore, junior, senior, or graduate years; not renewable. *Number:* 1–3. *Amount:* $1000–$2000.

Eligibility Requirements: Applicant must be enrolled or expecting to enroll full- or part-time at a two-year or four-year institution or university; resident of California and studying in California. Applicant or parent of applicant must be member of Women in Logistics. Available to U.S. and non-U.S. citizens.

Application Requirements: Application form, entry in a contest, essay, recommendations or references, resume. *Deadline:* November 1.

Contact: Susan Cholette, Scholarship Director
    Phone: 415-405-2173
    E-mail: cholette@sfsu.edu

WYOMING TRUCKING ASSOCIATION SCHOLARSHIP FUND TRUST
http://www.wytruck.org/

WYOMING TRUCKING ASSOCIATION SCHOLARSHIP TRUST FUND
• *See page 83*

Y'S MEN INTERNATIONAL
http://www.ysmenusa.com/

ALEXANDER SCHOLARSHIP LOAN FUND
The purpose of the fund is to promote the training of staff of the YMCA and/or those seeking to become members or staff of the YMCA. Deadlines are May 30 for fall semester and October 30 for spring semester.

Academic Fields/Career Goals: Business/Consumer Services; Child and Family Studies; Education; Human Resources; Social Sciences; Social Services; Sports-Related/Exercise Science.

Award: Scholarship for use in freshman, sophomore, junior, or senior years; renewable.

Eligibility Requirements: Applicant must be enrolled or expecting to enroll full- or part-time at a two-year or four-year institution or university. Available to U.S. citizens.

Application Requirements: Application form. *Fee:* $1. *Deadline:* varies.

Contact: Dean Currie, Area Service Director
    Phone: 908-753-9493
    Fax: 602-935-6322
    E-mail: kidcurrie@adelphia.net

ZONTA INTERNATIONAL FOUNDATION
http://www.zonta.org/

JANE M. KLAUSMAN WOMEN IN BUSINESS SCHOLARSHIPS
Awards for female students entering their third or fourth year in an undergraduate business degree. Application available at website, http://www.zonta.org.

Academic Fields/Career Goals: Business/Consumer Services.

Award: Scholarship for use in junior or senior years; not renewable. *Number:* up to 12. *Amount:* $4000–$5000.

Eligibility Requirements: Applicant must be enrolled or expecting to enroll full-time at a four-year institution or university and female. Available to U.S. and non-U.S. citizens.

Application Requirements: Application form, essay, recommendations or references. *Deadline:* varies.

Contact: Ana Ubides, Programs Manager
    Fax: 630-928-1559
    E-mail: progrmas@zonta.org

CAMPUS ACTIVITIES

NATIONAL ASSOCIATION FOR CAMPUS ACTIVITIES
http://www.naca.org/

MARKLEY SCHOLARSHIP
Scholarship available to students who are strongly involved in the field of student activities and/or student activities employment, and who have made significant contributions to NACA Central. Must be classified as a junior, senior or graduate student at a four-year school located in the former NACA South Central region, or a sophomore in the former NACA South Central region. Must have minimum 2.5 GPA.

Academic Fields/Career Goals: Campus Activities.

Award: Scholarship for use in junior, senior, or graduate years; not renewable. *Number:* up to 2. *Amount:* $250–$300.

Eligibility Requirements: Applicant must be enrolled or expecting to enroll full- or part-time at a four-year institution and studying in Arkansas, Louisiana, New Mexico, Oklahoma, Texas. Applicant or parent of applicant must have employment or volunteer experience in community service. Applicant must have 2.5 GPA or higher. Available to U.S. citizens.

Application Requirements: Application form, resume. *Deadline:* September 1.

Contact: Dionne Ellison, Administrative Assistant
Phone: 803-732-6222 Ext. 131
Fax: 803-749-1047
E-mail: dionnee@naca.org

WHOMENTORS.COM, INC.

http://www.WHOmentors.com/

1B USD WORLDWIDE VENTURE CAPITAL
• *See page 107*

CANADIAN STUDIES

CANADIAN INSTITUTE OF UKRAINIAN STUDIES

http://www.cius.ca/

CANADIAN INSTITUTE OF UKRAINIAN STUDIES RESEARCH GRANTS
• *See page 114*

CHEMICAL ENGINEERING

AACE INTERNATIONAL

http://www.aacei.org/

AACE INTERNATIONAL COMPETITIVE SCHOLARSHIP
• *See page 108*

AIST FOUNDATION

http://www.aistfoundation.org/

ASSOCIATION FOR IRON AND STEEL TECHNOLOGY BENJAMIN F. FAIRLESS SCHOLARSHIP (AIME)

Scholarship for full-time students of metallurgy, materials science, chemical, mechanical, electrical, environmental, computer science, and industrial engineering. Students must have an interest in a career in the steel industry as demonstrated by an internship or related experience, or who have plans to pursue such experiences during college. Student may apply after first term of freshman year of college. Applications are accepted from 1 Sep through 31 Dec each year. Note: High school students do not qualify but are encouraged to learn about the steel industry and the career opportunities available therein, during their freshman year.

Academic Fields/Career Goals: Chemical Engineering; Electrical Engineering/Electronics; Engineering-Related Technologies; Materials Science, Engineering, and Metallurgy; Mechanical Engineering.

Award: Scholarship for use in sophomore, junior, or senior years; not renewable. *Number:* 2. *Amount:* $3000.

Eligibility Requirements: Applicant must be enrolled or expecting to enroll full-time at a four-year institution or university. Applicant must have 2.5 GPA or higher. Available to U.S. and non-U.S. citizens.

Application Requirements: Application form, essay, recommendations or references, resume, transcript. *Deadline:* December 31.

Contact: Lori Wharrey, AIST Manager, Board Services
AIST Foundation
186 Thorn Hill Road
Warrendale, PA 15086
Phone: 724-814-3044
E-mail: lwharrey@aist.org

ASSOCIATION FOR IRON AND STEEL TECHNOLOGY DAVID H. SAMSON CANADIAN SCHOLARSHIP

Scholarship for full-time students of metallurgy, materials science, chemical, mechanical, electrical, environmental, computer science, and industrial engineering. Students must have an interest in a career in the steel industry as demonstrated by an internship or related experience, or who have plans to pursue such experiences during college. Student may apply after first term of freshman year of college. Applications are accepted from 1 Sep through 31 Dec each year. Note: High school students do not qualify but are encouraged to learn about the steel industry and the career opportunities available therein, during their freshman year.

Academic Fields/Career Goals: Chemical Engineering; Civil Engineering; Electrical Engineering/Electronics; Engineering/Technology; Materials Science, Engineering, and Metallurgy.

Award: Scholarship for use in sophomore, junior, or senior years; not renewable. *Number:* 1. *Amount:* $3000.

Eligibility Requirements: Applicant must be Canadian citizen and enrolled or expecting to enroll full-time at a four-year institution or university. Applicant must have 2.5 GPA or higher.

Application Requirements: Application form, essay, recommendations or references, resume, transcript. *Deadline:* December 31.

Contact: Lori Wharrey, AIST Manager, Board Services
AIST Foundation
186 Thorn HIll Road
Warrendale, PA 15086
Phone: 724-814-3044
E-mail: lwharrey@aist.org

ASSOCIATION FOR IRON AND STEEL TECHNOLOGY WILLY KORF MEMORIAL SCHOLARSHIP

Scholarships are available for full-time students of metallurgy, chemical, materials science, mechanical, electrical, computer science, industrial and environmental engineering who have a genuine demonstrated interest in a career in the steel industry as demonstrated by an internship or related experience, or who have plans to pursue such experiences during college. Student may apply first during the freshman year of college. Applications are accepted 1 Sep through 31 Dec each year. Note: High school seniors are not eligible though are encouraged to learn and investigate the steel industry and the career opportunities available, during their freshman year.

Academic Fields/Career Goals: Chemical Engineering; Computer Science/Data Processing; Electrical Engineering/Electronics; Environmental Science; Industrial Design; Materials Science, Engineering, and Metallurgy; Mechanical Engineering.

Award: Scholarship for use in sophomore, junior, senior, or graduate years; not renewable. *Number:* 2. *Amount:* $3000.

Eligibility Requirements: Applicant must be enrolled or expecting to enroll full-time at a four-year institution or university. Applicant or parent of applicant must have employment or volunteer experience in engineering/technology. Applicant must have 2.5 GPA or higher. Available to U.S. and non-U.S. citizens.

Application Requirements: Application form, essay, recommendations or references, resume, transcript. *Deadline:* December 31.

Contact: Lori Wharrey, AIST Manager, Board Services
AIST Foundation
186 Thorn Hill Road
Warrendale, PA 15086
Phone: 724-814-3044 Ext. 621
E-mail: lwharrey@aist.org

AMERICAN CHEMICAL SOCIETY

http://www.acs.org/

AMERICAN CHEMICAL SOCIETY SCHOLARS PROGRAM

Renewable award for minority students pursuing studies in chemistry, biochemistry, chemical technology, chemical engineering, or any chemical science. Must be U.S. citizen or permanent resident and have minimum 3.0 GPA. Must be Native American, African-American, or Hispanic.

Academic Fields/Career Goals: Chemical Engineering; Environmental Science; Materials Science, Engineering, and Metallurgy; Natural Sciences; Paper and Pulp Engineering.

Award: Scholarship for use in freshman, sophomore, junior, or senior years; renewable. *Number:* 100–200. *Amount:* $1000–$5000.

Eligibility Requirements: Applicant must be American Indian/Alaska Native, Black (non-Hispanic), Hispanic and enrolled or expecting to enroll full-time at a two-year or four-year or technical institution or university. Applicant must have 3.0 GPA or higher. Available to U.S. citizens.

Application Requirements: Application form, application form may be submitted online (http://www.acs.org/scholars), financial need analysis, recommendations or references, test scores, transcript. *Deadline:* March 1.

Contact: Mr. Robert Hughes, Manager, ACS Scholars Program
American Chemical Society
1155 16th Street, NW
Washington, DC 20036
Phone: 202-872-6048
Fax: 202-872-4361
E-mail: scholars@acs.org

AMERICAN CHEMICAL SOCIETY, RUBBER DIVISION

http://www.rubber.org/

AMERICAN CHEMICAL SOCIETY, RUBBER DIVISION UNDERGRADUATE SCHOLARSHIP

Candidate must be majoring in a technical discipline relevant to the rubber industry with a "B" or better overall academic average. Two scholarships are awarded to juniors and seniors enrolled in an accredited college or university in the United States, Canada, Mexico, India or Brazil.

Academic Fields/Career Goals: Chemical Engineering; Engineering/Technology; Materials Science, Engineering, and Metallurgy; Mechanical Engineering; Science, Technology, and Society.

Award: Scholarship for use in junior or senior years; not renewable. *Number:* 3. *Amount:* $5000.

Eligibility Requirements: Applicant must be enrolled or expecting to enroll full-time at a four-year institution or university. Applicant must have 3.0 GPA or higher. Available to U.S. and non-U.S. citizens.

Application Requirements: Application form, essay, interview, recommendations or references, test scores, transcript. *Deadline:* March 1.

Contact: Christie Robinson, Education and Publications Manager
American Chemical Society, Rubber Division
250 South Forge Road, PO Box 499
Akron, OH 44325
Phone: 330-972-7814
Fax: 330-972-5269
E-mail: education@rubber.org

AMERICAN COUNCIL OF ENGINEERING COMPANIES OF PENNSYLVANIA (ACEC/PA)

http://www.acecpa.org/

ENGINEERING SCHOLARSHIP

Scholarship for full-time engineering students enrolled in accredited colleges or universities. Must be U.S. citizen. Up to five awards are granted annually.

Academic Fields/Career Goals: Chemical Engineering; Civil Engineering; Electrical Engineering/Electronics; Engineering-Related Technologies; Engineering/Technology; Materials Science, Engineering, and Metallurgy; Mechanical Engineering.

Award: Scholarship for use in freshman, sophomore, junior, or senior years; not renewable. *Number:* 1–5. *Amount:* $1000–$4000.

Eligibility Requirements: Applicant must be enrolled or expecting to enroll full-time at a four-year institution or university and resident of Pennsylvania. Available to U.S. citizens.

Application Requirements: Application form, essay, recommendations or references, resume, transcript. *Deadline:* December 1.

Contact: Laurie Troutman, Administrative Assistant
American Council of Engineering Companies of Pennsylvania (ACEC/PA)
2040 Linglestown Road, Suite 200
Harrisburg, PA 17110
Phone: 717-540-6811
Fax: 717-540-6815
E-mail: laurie@acecpa.org

AMERICAN INSTITUTE OF CHEMICAL ENGINEERS

http://www.aiche.org/

CHEME-CAR NATIONAL LEVEL COMPETITION

Each student chapter region may send their first and second place winners to the design competition. Multiple entries from a single school may be permitted at the regional competitions, but only one entry per school is allowed at the national competition. Students majoring in chemical engineering can participate.

Academic Fields/Career Goals: Chemical Engineering.

Award: Prize for use in freshman, sophomore, junior, or senior years; not renewable. *Number:* up to 3. *Amount:* $200–$2000.

Eligibility Requirements: Applicant must be enrolled or expecting to enroll full-time at a four-year institution or university. Available to U.S. and non-U.S. citizens.

Application Requirements: Application form, entry in a contest, student chapter name, team contact, list of team members, title of entry, description of chemical reaction/drive system, list of chemicals to be used and estimated quantity needed. *Fee:* $100. *Deadline:* June 30.

Contact: Prof. David Dixon, Department of Chemistry and Chemical Engineering
American Institute of Chemical Engineers
South Dakota School of Mines and Technology
501 East Saint Joseph Street
Rapid City, SD 57701
Phone: 605-394-1235
Fax: 605-394-1232
E-mail: david.dixon@sdsmt.edu

DONALD F. AND MILDRED TOPP OTHMER FOUNDATION-NATIONAL SCHOLARSHIP AWARDS

Awards for 15 national AICHE student members, a scholarship of $1000. Awards are presented on the basis of academic achievement and involvement in student chapter activities. The student chapter advisor must make nominations. Only one nomination will be accepted from each AICHE student chapter or chemical engineering club.

Academic Fields/Career Goals: Chemical Engineering.

Award: Scholarship for use in freshman, sophomore, junior, senior, or graduate years; not renewable. *Number:* 15. *Amount:* $1000.

Eligibility Requirements: Applicant must be enrolled or expecting to enroll full-time at a four-year institution or university. Available to U.S. and non-U.S. citizens.

Application Requirements: Application form, essay, recommendations or references, statement of long-range career plans, transcript. *Deadline:* May 11.

ENVIRONMENTAL DIVISION UNDERGRADUATE STUDENT PAPER AWARD

Cash prizes awarded to full-time undergraduate students who prepare the best original papers based on the results of research or an investigation related to the environment. The work must be performed during the student's undergraduate enrollment, and the paper must be submitted prior to or within six months of graduation. Student must be the sole author of the paper, but faculty guidance is encouraged. Student must be a member of the American Institute of Chemical Engineers Student Chapter.

Academic Fields/Career Goals: Chemical Engineering; Environmental Science.

Award: Prize for use in freshman, sophomore, junior, or senior years; not renewable. *Number:* 3. *Amount:* $100–$300.

Eligibility Requirements: Applicant must be enrolled or expecting to enroll full-time at a four-year institution or university. Available to U.S. and non-U.S. citizens.

Application Requirements: 5 copies of the nomination package, entry in a contest, essay, recommendations or references. *Deadline:* May 15.

Contact: Tapas Das, Environmental Division Awards Committee
American Institute of Chemical Engineers
125 Mandy Place, NE
Olympia, WA 98516
Phone: 360-456-0573
E-mail: shivaniki@comcast.net

JOHN J. MCKETTA UNDERGRADUATE SCHOLARSHIP

A $5000 scholarship will be awarded to a junior or senior student member of AICHE who is planning a career in the chemical engineering process industries. Must maintain a 3.0 GPA. Applicant should show leadership or activity in either the school's AICHE student chapter or other university sponsored campus activities. Must attend ABET-accredited school in the United States, Canada, or Mexico.

Academic Fields/Career Goals: Chemical Engineering.

Award: Scholarship for use in junior or senior years; not renewable. *Number:* 1. *Amount:* $5000.

Eligibility Requirements: Applicant must be enrolled or expecting to enroll full-time at a four-year institution or university and must have an interest in leadership. Applicant must have 3.0 GPA or higher. Available to U.S. and non-U.S. citizens.

Application Requirements: Application form, essay, recommendations or references. *Deadline:* May 25.

MINORITY AFFAIRS COMMITTEE AWARD FOR OUTSTANDING SCHOLASTIC ACHIEVEMENT

Award recognizing the outstanding achievements of a chemical engineering student who serves as a role model for minority students. Offers $1000 award and $500 travel allowance to attend AICHE meeting. Must be nominated.

Academic Fields/Career Goals: Chemical Engineering.

Award: Scholarship for use in freshman, sophomore, junior, senior, or graduate years; not renewable. *Number:* 1. *Amount:* $1500.

Eligibility Requirements: Applicant must be American Indian/Alaska Native, Asian/Pacific Islander, Black (non-Hispanic), Hispanic and enrolled or expecting to enroll full-time at a four-year institution or university. Applicant must have 3.0 GPA or higher. Available to U.S. and non-U.S. citizens.

Application Requirements: Application form. *Deadline:* May 15.

Contact: Dr. Emmanuel Dada, Scholarship Administrator
American Institute of Chemical Engineers
PO Box 8
Princeton, NJ 08543
Phone: 212-591-7107
E-mail: emmanuel_dada@fmc.com

MINORITY SCHOLARSHIP AWARDS FOR COLLEGE STUDENTS

Award for college undergraduates who are studying chemical engineering. Must be a member of a minority group that is underrepresented in chemical engineering. Must be an AICHE national student member at the time of application. Recipients of this scholarship are eligible to reapply.

Academic Fields/Career Goals: Chemical Engineering.

Award: Scholarship for use in freshman, sophomore, junior, or senior years; renewable. *Number:* up to 10. *Amount:* $1000.

Eligibility Requirements: Applicant must be American Indian/Alaska Native, Asian/Pacific Islander, Black (non-Hispanic), Hispanic and enrolled or expecting to enroll full-time at a two-year or four-year institution or university. Applicant must have 3.0 GPA or higher. Available to U.S. and non-U.S. citizens.

Application Requirements: Application form, career objective, essay, financial need analysis, recommendations or references, transcript. *Deadline:* May 15.

Contact: Dr. Emmanuel Dada, FMC Corporation
American Institute of Chemical Engineers
PO Box 8
Princeton, NJ 08543
Phone: 212-591-7107
E-mail: emmanuel_dada@fmc.com

MINORITY SCHOLARSHIP AWARDS FOR INCOMING COLLEGE FRESHMEN

Up to ten awards of $1000 for high school graduates who are members of a minority group that is underrepresented in chemical engineering. Students must be high school seniors planning to enroll during the next academic year in a four-year college or university offering a science/engineering degree.

Academic Fields/Career Goals: Chemical Engineering.

Award: Scholarship for use in freshman year; not renewable. *Number:* up to 10. *Amount:* $1000.

Eligibility Requirements: Applicant must be American Indian/Alaska Native, Asian/Pacific Islander, Black (non-Hispanic), Hispanic; high school student and planning to enroll or expecting to enroll full-time at a four-year institution or university. Applicant must have 3.0 GPA or higher. Available to U.S. and non-U.S. citizens.

Application Requirements: Application form, confirmation of minority status, essay, financial need analysis, recommendations or references, transcript. *Deadline:* May 15.

Contact: Dr. Emmanuel Dada, Minority Affairs Committee
American Institute of Chemical Engineers
PO Box 8
Princeton, NJ 08543
Phone: 212-591-7107
E-mail: emmanuel_dada@fmc.com

NATIONAL STUDENT DESIGN COMPETITION-INDIVIDUAL

Three cash prizes for student contest problem that typifies a real, working, chemical engineering design situation. Competition statements are distributed online to student chapter advisors and department heads.

Academic Fields/Career Goals: Chemical Engineering.

Award: Prize for use in freshman, sophomore, junior, senior, or graduate years; not renewable. *Number:* 3. *Amount:* $200–$500.

Eligibility Requirements: Applicant must be enrolled or expecting to enroll full-time at a four-year institution or university. Available to U.S. and non-U.S. citizens.

Application Requirements: Entry in a contest, essay. *Deadline:* June 6.

NATIONAL STUDENT DESIGN COMPETITION-TEAM (WILLIAM CUNNINGHAM AWARD)

Design contest for chemical engineering students.

Academic Fields/Career Goals: Chemical Engineering.

Award: Prize for use in freshman, sophomore, junior, senior, or graduate years; not renewable. *Number:* 1. *Amount:* up to $600.

Eligibility Requirements: Applicant must be enrolled or expecting to enroll full-time at a four-year institution or university. Available to U.S. and non-U.S. citizens.

Application Requirements: Application form, entry in a contest, essay. *Deadline:* June 6.

NATIONAL STUDENT PAPER COMPETITION

First place winners from each of the nine regional student paper competitions present their prize-winning papers during the American Institute of Chemical Engineers meeting held in the current calendar year. First prize is $500, second prize is $300, and third prize is $200.

Academic Fields/Career Goals: Chemical Engineering.

Award: Prize for use in freshman, sophomore, junior, senior, or graduate years; not renewable. *Number:* 3. *Amount:* $200–$500.

Eligibility Requirements: Applicant must be enrolled or expecting to enroll full-time at a four-year institution or university. Available to U.S. and non-U.S. citizens.

Application Requirements: Entry in a contest, student paper. *Deadline:* varies.

NORTH AMERICAN MIXING FORUM (NAMF) STUDENT AWARD

Award to encourage, recognize, and reward students for quality research in the area of mixing. Any graduate or undergraduate student doing research in the field of fluid mixing at an accredited university in North America is eligible.

Academic Fields/Career Goals: Chemical Engineering.

Award: Prize for use in freshman, sophomore, junior, senior, or graduate years; not renewable. *Number:* 1. *Amount:* up to $500.

Eligibility Requirements: Applicant must be enrolled or expecting to enroll full-time at a four-year institution or university. Available to U.S. and non-U.S. citizens.

Application Requirements: Cover letter including title of work, name and address of author, abstract, theory or model development, experimental setup/procedures, results and discussion, entry in a contest, essay, recommendations or references. *Deadline:* March 15.

Contact: Dr. Ricahrd Grenville, Student Award Committee
American Institute of Chemical Engineers
1007 Market Street, B8214
Wilmington, DE 19898
Phone: 302-774-2256
Fax: 302-774-2457
E-mail: richard.k.grenville@usa.dupont.com

OUTSTANDING STUDENT CHAPTER ADVISOR AWARD

Award for service and leadership in guiding the activities of an AIChE student chapter in accordance with AIChE principles. Must be advisor of a chartered AIChE student chapter for at least the last three years. Award winners cannot be renominated.

Academic Fields/Career Goals: Chemical Engineering.

Award: Prize for use in freshman, sophomore, junior, or senior years; not renewable. *Number:* 1. *Amount:* up to $1000.

Eligibility Requirements: Applicant must be enrolled or expecting to enroll full-time at a four-year institution or university. Available to U.S. and non-U.S. citizens.

Application Requirements: 4 copies of the nomination, application form, recommendations or references. *Deadline:* June 1.

Contact: Marvin Borgmeyer, Scholarship Committee
American Institute of Chemical Engineers
PO Box 1607
Baton Rouge, LA 70821-1607
Phone: 225-977-6206
Fax: 225-977-6396

PROCESS DEVELOPMENT DIVISION STUDENT PAPER AWARD

Award presented to a full-time graduate or undergraduate student who prepares the best technical paper to describe the results of process development related studies within chemical engineering. Must be carried out while the student is enrolled at a university with an accredited chemical engineering program. Student must be the primary author. Paper must be suitable for publication in a refereed journal. Must be a member of AIChE.

Academic Fields/Career Goals: Chemical Engineering.

Award: Prize for use in freshman, sophomore, junior, or graduate years; not renewable. *Number:* 1. *Amount:* $200.

Eligibility Requirements: Applicant must be enrolled or expecting to enroll full-time at a four-year institution or university. Available to U.S. and non-U.S. citizens.

Application Requirements: Original and five copies of the nomination form, recommendations or references. *Deadline:* June 15.

Contact: A.R. Cartolano, Awards Committee Chair
American Institute of Chemical Engineers
7201 Hamilton Boulevard
Allentown, PA 18195-1501
Phone: 610-481-4262
E-mail: cartolar@airproducts.com

REGIONAL STUDENT PAPER COMPETITION

Students present technical papers at the student regional conferences which are held during spring. Deadlines for regional conferences vary. First prize is $200, second prize is $100, and third prize is $50. First place winner from each region present their paper at the regional competition.

Academic Fields/Career Goals: Chemical Engineering.

Award: Prize for use in freshman, sophomore, junior, or senior years; not renewable. *Number:* 3. *Amount:* $50–$200.

Eligibility Requirements: Applicant must be enrolled or expecting to enroll full-time at a four-year institution or university. Available to U.S. and non-U.S. citizens.

Application Requirements: Entry in a contest, student paper. *Deadline:* varies.

SAFETY AND CHEMICAL ENGINEERING EDUCATION (SACHE) STUDENT ESSAY AWARD FOR SAFETY

Awards individuals or a team submitting the best essays on the topic of chemical process safety. Essays may focus on process safety in education, relevance of safety in undergraduate education, or integrating safety principles into the undergraduate chemical engineering curriculum.

Academic Fields/Career Goals: Chemical Engineering.

Award: Prize for use in freshman, sophomore, junior, or senior years; not renewable. *Number:* up to 4. *Amount:* $500.

Eligibility Requirements: Applicant must be enrolled or expecting to enroll full-time at a four-year institution or university. Available to U.S. and non-U.S. citizens.

Application Requirements: Entry in a contest, essay. *Deadline:* June 5.

SAFETY AND HEALTH NATIONAL STUDENT DESIGN COMPETITION AWARD FOR SAFETY

Four $600 awards available for each of the teams or individuals who apply one or more of the following concepts of inherent safety in their designs: design the plant for easier and effective maintainability; design the plant with less waste; design the plant with special features that demonstrate inherent safety; include design concepts regarding the entire life cycle. The school must have a student chapter of AIChE.

Academic Fields/Career Goals: Chemical Engineering; Industrial Design.

Award: Prize for use in freshman, sophomore, junior, senior, or graduate years; not renewable. *Number:* 4. *Amount:* $600.

Eligibility Requirements: Applicant must be enrolled or expecting to enroll full- or part-time at a four-year institution or university. Available to U.S. and non-U.S. citizens.

Application Requirements: Application form, design. *Deadline:* June 6.

AMERICAN OIL CHEMISTS' SOCIETY

http://www.aocs.org/

AOCS ANALYTICAL DIVISION STUDENT AWARD

$250 prize, $500 travel funding and certificate to recognize an outstanding graduate student's presentation in the field of lipid analytical chemistry at the Society's annual meeting.

Academic Fields/Career Goals: Chemical Engineering; Food Science/Nutrition.

Award: Prize for use in junior, senior, or graduate years; not renewable. *Number:* 1–2. *Amount:* $250–$750.

Eligibility Requirements: Applicant must be enrolled or expecting to enroll full- or part-time at a four-year institution or university. Available to U.S. and non-U.S. citizens.

Application Requirements: Abstract, application form, essay, recommendations or references. *Deadline:* October 15.

Contact: Barbara Semeraro, Area Manager, Membership
American Oil Chemists' Society
AOCS
PO Box 17190
Urbana, IL 61803
Phone: 217-693-4804
Fax: 217-693-4849
E-mail: awards@aocs.org

AOCS BIOTECHNOLOGY STUDENT EXCELLENCE AWARD

• *See page 90*

AOCS PROCESSING DIVISION AWARDS

Award and certificate to recognize graduate students presenting an outstanding paper at the Society's annual meeting. All graduate students presenting a paper at any of the AOCS Annual Meeting Processing Division sessions are eligible for the award.

Academic Fields/Career Goals: Chemical Engineering; Food Science/Nutrition.

Award: Prize for use in junior, senior, or graduate years; not renewable. *Number:* 1–1. *Amount:* $1000.

Eligibility Requirements: Applicant must be enrolled or expecting to enroll full-time at a four-year institution or university. Available to U.S. and non-U.S. citizens.

Application Requirements: Abstract, application form, essay, recommendations or references. *Deadline:* January 7.

Contact: Barbara Semeraro, Area Manager, Membership
American Oil Chemists' Society
AOCS
PO Box 17190
Urbana, IL 61803
Phone: 217-693-4804
Fax: 217-693-4849
E-mail: awards@aocs.org

AMERICAN SOCIETY FOR ENOLOGY AND VITICULTURE

http://www.asev.org/

AMERICAN SOCIETY FOR ENOLOGY AND VITICULTURE SCHOLARSHIPS

• *See page 90*

AMERICAN SOCIETY OF HEATING, REFRIGERATING, AND AIR CONDITIONING ENGINEERS, INC.

http://www.ashrae.org/

ASHRAE REGION III BOGGARM SETTY SCHOLARSHIP

One $3000 scholarship for an undergraduate pre-engineering or engineering student enrolled full time in a post-secondary educational institution within the geographic boundaries of ASHRAE Region III (Delaware, Maryland, Pennsylvania, Virginia, Washington, DC). Minimum 3.0 GPA required.

Academic Fields/Career Goals: Chemical Engineering; Construction Engineering/Management; Electrical Engineering/Electronics; Energy and Power Engineering; Engineering-Related Technologies; Engineering/Technology; Mechanical Engineering; Paper and Pulp Engineering.

Award: Scholarship for use in freshman, sophomore, junior, or senior years; not renewable. *Number:* 1. *Amount:* $3000.

Eligibility Requirements: Applicant must be enrolled or expecting to enroll full-time at a four-year institution or university and studying in Delaware, District of Columbia, Maryland, Pennsylvania, Virginia. Applicant must have 3.0 GPA or higher. Available to U.S. citizens.

Application Requirements: Application form, recommendations or references, transcript. *Deadline:* December 1.

Contact: Lois Benedict, Scholarship Administrator
Phone: 404-636-8400 Ext. 1120
E-mail: lbenedict@ashrae.org

ARMED FORCES COMMUNICATIONS AND ELECTRONICS ASSOCIATION, EDUCATIONAL FOUNDATION

http://www.afcea.org/scholarships

ARMED FORCES COMMUNICATIONS AND ELECTRONICS ASSOCIATION GENERAL EMMETT PAIGE SCHOLARSHIP

• *See page 127*

LTG DOUGLAS D. BUCHHOLZ MEMORIAL SCHOLARSHIP

• *See page 128*

ARRL FOUNDATION INC.

http://www.arrl.org/

ALFRED E. FRIEND JR., W4CF, MEMORIAL SCHOLARSHIP

One $5000 scholarship for a student with active Amateur Radio license who is studying engineering.

Academic Fields/Career Goals: Chemical Engineering; Civil Engineering; Construction Engineering/Management; Electrical Engineering/Electronics; Energy and Power Engineering; Engineering/Technology; Marine/Ocean Engineering; Materials Science, Engineering, and Metallurgy; Mechanical Engineering; Paper and Pulp Engineering.

Award: Scholarship for use in freshman, sophomore, junior, or senior years; not renewable. *Number:* 1. *Amount:* $5000.

Eligibility Requirements: Applicant must be enrolled or expecting to enroll full- or part-time at a two-year or four-year or technical institution or university and must have an interest in amateur radio. Available to U.S. citizens.

Application Requirements: Application form, transcript. *Deadline:* February 1.

Contact: Ms. Mary Hobart, Secretary
Phone: 860-594-0397
E-mail: k1mmh@arrl.org

GARY WAGNER, K3OMI, SCHOLARSHIP

One $1000 award available to student who possesses a novice class or higher amateur radio license and who is or will be attending a four-year college or university. Must be a U.S. citizen and resident of North Carolina, Virginia, West Virginia, Maryland, or Tennessee and studying toward a Bachelor of Science degree in any field of engineering. Financial need must be demonstrated.

Academic Fields/Career Goals: Chemical Engineering; Civil Engineering; Construction Engineering/Management; Electrical Engineering/Electronics; Energy and Power Engineering; Engineering-Related Technologies; Engineering/Technology; Materials Science, Engineering, and Metallurgy; Mechanical Engineering.

Award: Scholarship for use in freshman, sophomore, junior, or senior years; not renewable. *Number:* 1. *Amount:* $1000.

Eligibility Requirements: Applicant must be enrolled or expecting to enroll full- or part-time at a four-year institution or university; resident of Maryland, North Carolina, Tennessee, Virginia, West Virginia and must have an interest in amateur radio. Available to U.S. citizens.

Application Requirements: Application form, financial need analysis, transcript. *Deadline:* February 1.

Contact: Ms. Mary Hobart, Secretary
Phone: 860-594-0397
E-mail: k1mmh@arrl.org

ASSOCIATION ON AMERICAN INDIAN AFFAIRS, INC.

http://www.indian-affairs.org/

ELIZABETH AND SHERMAN ASCHE MEMORIAL SCHOLARSHIP FUND

• *See page 91*

ASTRONAUT SCHOLARSHIP FOUNDATION

http://www.astronautscholarship.org/

ASTRONAUT SCHOLARSHIP FOUNDATION

• *See page 104*

BARRY M. GOLDWATER SCHOLARSHIP AND EXCELLENCE IN EDUCATION FOUNDATION

http://www.act.org/goldwater

BARRY M. GOLDWATER SCHOLARSHIP AND EXCELLENCE IN EDUCATION PROGRAM
• See page 104

BRASKEM ODEBRECHT

http://www.odebrechtaward.com

ODEBRECHT AWARD FOR SUSTAINABLE DEVELOPMENT
• See page 110

BRITISH COLUMBIA INNOVATION COUNCIL

http://www.bcic.ca/

PAUL AND HELEN TRUSSELL SCIENCE AND TECHNOLOGY SCHOLARSHIP
• See page 104

CHEMICAL INSTITUTE OF CANADA

http://www.cheminst.ca/

CSCHE CHEMICAL ENGINEERING LOCAL SECTION SCHOLARSHIPS

Scholarships for undergraduate students in chemical engineering who are entering their final year of studies at a Canadian university. Applicants must be paid undergraduate student members of Canadian Society for Chemical Engineering (CSChE). Leadership qualities, demonstrated contributions to the Society such as participation in student chapters, and academic performance will be considered.

Academic Fields/Career Goals: Chemical Engineering.

Award: Scholarship for use in senior year; not renewable. *Number:* 2. *Amount:* $2000.

Eligibility Requirements: Applicant must be enrolled or expecting to enroll full-time at an institution or university and studying in Alberta, British Columbia, Manitoba, New Brunswick, Newfoundland, Northwest Territories, Nova Scotia, Ontario, Prince Edward Island, Quebec, Saskatchewan, Yukon. Applicant or parent of applicant must be member of Canadian Society for Chemical Engineering. Available to U.S. and non-U.S. citizens.

Application Requirements: Application form may be submitted online, recommendations or references, resume, transcript. *Deadline:* April 30.

Contact: Ms. Gale Thirlwall, Awards Manager
Chemical Institute of Canada
130 Slater Street, Suite 550
Ottawa, ON K1P 6E2
CAN
Phone: 613-232-6252 Ext. 223
E-mail: awards@cheminst.ca

CONGRESSIONAL BLACK CAUCUS FOUNDATION, INC.

http://www.cbcfinc.org/

CBCF GENERAL MILLS HEALTH SCHOLARSHIP
• See page 144

CUBAN AMERICAN NATIONAL FOUNDATION

http://www.masscholarships.org/

MAS FAMILY SCHOLARSHIPS
• See page 152

ELECTROCHEMICAL SOCIETY INC.

http://www.electrochem.org/

H.H. DOW MEMORIAL STUDENT ACHIEVEMENT AWARD OF THE INDUSTRIAL ELECTROLYSIS AND ELECTROCHEMICAL ENGINEERING DIVISION OF THE ELECTROCHEMICAL SOCIETY INC.
• See page 104

STUDENT RESEARCH AWARDS OF THE BATTERY DIVISION OF THE ELECTROCHEMICAL SOCIETY INC.
• See page 105

ENGINEERS' SOCIETY OF WESTERN PENNSYLVANIA

http://www.eswp.com/

JOSEPH A. LEVENDUSKY MEMORIAL SCHOLARSHIP

Scholarship of up to $7000 awarded to an undergraduate student in mechanical or chemical engineering. Must be accepted or enrolled in good standing as a student at an accredited institution.

Academic Fields/Career Goals: Chemical Engineering; Mechanical Engineering.

Award: Scholarship for use in sophomore, junior, or senior years; not renewable. *Number:* 1. *Amount:* $7000.

Eligibility Requirements: Applicant must be enrolled or expecting to enroll full-time at a four-year institution or university. Available to U.S. citizens.

Application Requirements: Application form, application form may be submitted online (http://www.eswp.com/water), essay, financial need analysis, recommendations or references, resume, transcript. *Deadline:* September 7.

Contact: Stephanie Mueller, Conference Manager
Engineers' Society of Western Pennsylvania
337 Fourth Avenue
Pittsburgh, PA 15222
Phone: 412-261-0710
Fax: 412-261-1606
E-mail: s.mueller@eswp.com

FOUNDATION FOR SCIENCE AND DISABILITY

http://stemd.org/

GRANTS FOR DISABLED STUDENTS IN THE SCIENCES
• See page 105

GREATER KANAWHA VALLEY FOUNDATION

http://www.tgkvf.org/

STEVEN ENGINEERING SCHOLARSHIP

Renewable award for a West Virginia resident pursuing full-time postsecondary studies in engineering. Preference given to students at West Virginia University Institute of Technology or West Virginia University. Minimum 2.5 GPA required.

Academic Fields/Career Goals: Chemical Engineering; Construction Engineering/Management; Electrical Engineering/Electronics; Energy and Power Engineering; Engineering/Technology; Marine/Ocean

Engineering; Materials Science, Engineering, and Metallurgy; Mechanical Engineering; Paper and Pulp Engineering.

Award: Scholarship for use in freshman, sophomore, junior, or senior years; renewable.

Eligibility Requirements: Applicant must be enrolled or expecting to enroll full-time at a four-year institution or university and resident of West Virginia. Applicant must have 2.5 GPA or higher. Available to U.S. citizens.

Application Requirements: Application form, recommendations or references, transcript. *Deadline:* January 15.

Contact: Susan Hoover, Scholarship Program Officer
Greater Kanawha Valley Foundation
900 Lee Street East, 16th Floor
Charleston, WV 25301
Phone: 304-346-3620
E-mail: tgkvf@tgkvf.org

GREAT MINDS IN STEM

http://www.greatmindsinstem.org

HISPANIC ENGINEER NATIONAL ACHIEVEMENT AWARDS CORPORATION SCHOLARSHIP PROGRAM
• *See page 130*

HAWAIIAN LODGE, F&AM

http://www.hawaiianlodgefreemasons.org/

HAWAIIAN LODGE SCHOLARSHIPS
• *See page 114*

INDEPENDENT LABORATORIES INSTITUTE SCHOLARSHIP ALLIANCE

http://www.acil.org/

INDEPENDENT LABORATORIES INSTITUTE SCHOLARSHIP ALLIANCE
• *See page 145*

INSTITUTE OF INTERNATIONAL EDUCATION (FULBRIGHT PROGRAM)

http://www.us.fulbrightonline.org/

WHITAKER INTERNATIONAL PROGRAM
• *See page 145*

INTERNATIONAL SOCIETY FOR OPTICAL ENGINEERING-SPIE

http://www.spie.org/scholarships

SPIE EDUCATIONAL SCHOLARSHIPS IN OPTICAL SCIENCE AND ENGINEERING
• *See page 105*

INTERNATIONAL SOCIETY OF AUTOMATION (ISA)

http://www.isa.org/

INTERNATIONAL SOCIETY OF AUTOMATION EDUCATION FOUNDATION SCHOLARSHIPS
• *See page 131*

JORGE MAS CANOSA FREEDOM FOUNDATION

http://www.jorgemascanosa.org/

MAS FAMILY SCHOLARSHIP AWARD
• *See page 156*

KENTUCKY ENERGY AND ENVIRONMENT CABINET

http://www.eec.ky.gov/

ENVIRONMENTAL PROTECTION SCHOLARSHIP
• *See page 145*

LOS ANGELES COUNCIL OF BLACK PROFESSIONAL ENGINEERS

http://www.lablackengineers.org/

AL-BEN SCHOLARSHIP FOR ACADEMIC INCENTIVE

One-time scholarship for students enrolled full-time with scholastic achievements in the academic pursuits of engineering, math, computer or scientific studies. Must be from a minority group. Scholarship value is $500 to $1000. Two scholarships are granted annually. Preference given to residents of Southern California.

Academic Fields/Career Goals: Chemical Engineering; Civil Engineering; Computer Science/Data Processing; Electrical Engineering/Electronics; Engineering-Related Technologies; Engineering/Technology; Materials Science, Engineering, and Metallurgy; Mechanical Engineering; Physical Sciences.

Award: Scholarship for use in freshman, sophomore, junior, or senior years; not renewable. *Number:* 2. *Amount:* $500–$1000.

Eligibility Requirements: Applicant must be American Indian/Alaska Native, Asian/Pacific Islander, Black (non-Hispanic), Hispanic and enrolled or expecting to enroll full-time at a four-year institution or university. Available to U.S. citizens.

Application Requirements: Application form, essay, recommendations or references, transcript. *Deadline:* April 2.

Contact: Leroy Freelon, President
Phone: 310-635-7734
E-mail: lfreelonjr@aol.com

AL-BEN SCHOLARSHIP FOR PROFESSIONAL MERIT

One-time scholarship for students enrolled full-time with scholastic achievements in the academic pursuits of engineering, math, computer or scientific studies. Must be from a minority group. Scholarship value is $500 to $1000. Two scholarships are granted annually. Preference given to residents of Southern California.

Academic Fields/Career Goals: Chemical Engineering; Civil Engineering; Computer Science/Data Processing; Electrical Engineering/Electronics; Engineering-Related Technologies; Engineering/Technology; Materials Science, Engineering, and Metallurgy; Mechanical Engineering; Physical Sciences.

Award: Scholarship for use in freshman, sophomore, junior, or senior years; not renewable. *Number:* 2. *Amount:* $500–$1000.

Eligibility Requirements: Applicant must be American Indian/Alaska Native, Asian/Pacific Islander, Black (non-Hispanic), Hispanic and enrolled or expecting to enroll full-time at a four-year institution or university. Available to U.S. citizens.

Application Requirements: Application form, essay, recommendations or references, transcript. *Deadline:* April 2.

Contact: Leroy Freelon, President
Phone: 310-635-7734
E-mail: lfreelonjr@aol.com

AL-BEN SCHOLARSHIP FOR SCHOLASTIC ACHIEVEMENT

Scholarships for students enrolled full-time with scholastic achievements in the academic pursuits of engineering, math, computer or scientific studies. Must be from a minority group.

Academic Fields/Career Goals: Chemical Engineering; Civil Engineering; Computer Science/Data Processing; Electrical Engineering/

Electronics; Engineering-Related Technologies; Engineering/
Technology; Materials Science, Engineering, and Metallurgy;
Mechanical Engineering; Physical Sciences.

Award: Scholarship for use in freshman, sophomore, junior, or senior
years; not renewable. *Number:* 2. *Amount:* $500–$1000.

Eligibility Requirements: Applicant must be American Indian/Alaska
Native, Asian/Pacific Islander, Black (non-Hispanic), Hispanic and
enrolled or expecting to enroll full-time at a four-year institution or
university. Available to U.S. citizens.

Application Requirements: Application form, essay,
recommendations or references, transcript. *Deadline:* April 2.

Contact: Leroy Freelon, President
  Phone: 310-635-7734
  E-mail: lfreelonjr@aol.com

MICHIGAN SOCIETY OF PROFESSIONAL ENGINEERS

http://www.michiganspe.org/

MICHIGAN SOCIETY OF PROFESSIONAL ENGINEERS HARRY R. BALL, P.E. GRANT

One $1000 grant for a Michigan high school student to study engineering
at an ABET-accredited college or university in Michigan. Minimum 3.0
GPA required in grades eleven and twelve.

Academic Fields/Career Goals: Chemical Engineering; Civil
Engineering; Construction Engineering/Management; Electrical
Engineering/Electronics; Engineering/Technology; Mechanical
Engineering.

Award: Grant for use in freshman year; not renewable. *Number:* 1.
Amount: $1000.

Eligibility Requirements: Applicant must be high school student;
planning to enroll or expecting to enroll full-time at a four-year
institution or university; resident of Michigan and studying in Michigan.
Applicant must have 3.0 GPA or higher. Available to U.S. citizens.

Application Requirements: Application form, test scores, transcript.
Deadline: February 15.

Contact: Maura Nessan, Executive Director
  Phone: 517-487-9388
  E-mail: mspe@michiganspe.org

MICHIGAN SOCIETY OF PROFESSIONAL ENGINEERS KENNETH B. FISHBECK, P.E. MEMORIAL GRANT

One $1000 grant for a Michigan high school student to study engineering
at an ABET-accredited college or university in Michigan. Submit
application to local MSPE chapter chair. Applicants should demonstrate
qualifications of high merit and professional ethics.

Academic Fields/Career Goals: Chemical Engineering; Civil
Engineering; Construction Engineering/Management; Electrical
Engineering/Electronics; Engineering/Technology; Mechanical
Engineering.

Award: Grant for use in freshman year; not renewable. *Number:* 1.
Amount: $1000.

Eligibility Requirements: Applicant must be high school student;
planning to enroll or expecting to enroll full-time at a four-year
institution or university; resident of Michigan and studying in Michigan.
Applicant must have 3.0 GPA or higher. Available to U.S. citizens.

Application Requirements: Application form, test scores, transcript.
Deadline: February 15.

Contact: Maura Nessan, Executive Director
  Phone: 517-487-9388
  E-mail: mspe@michiganspe.org

NASA IDAHO SPACE GRANT CONSORTIUM

http://www.id.spacegrant.org/

NASA IDAHO SPACE GRANT CONSORTIUM SCHOLARSHIP PROGRAM
• See page 146

NASA/MARYLAND SPACE GRANT CONSORTIUM

http://md.spacegrant.org/

NASA MARYLAND SPACE GRANT CONSORTIUM UNDERGRADUATE SCHOLARSHIPS
• See page 132

NASA MONTANA SPACE GRANT CONSORTIUM

http://www.spacegrant.montana.edu/

MONTANA SPACE GRANT SCHOLARSHIP PROGRAM
• See page 133

NASA'S VIRGINIA SPACE GRANT CONSORTIUM

http://www.vsgc.odu.edu/

UNDERGRADUATE STEM RESEARCH SCHOLARSHIPS
• See page 106

NATIONAL ASSOCIATION FOR THE ADVANCEMENT OF COLORED PEOPLE

http://www.naacp.org/

HUBERTUS W.V. WELLEMS SCHOLARSHIP FOR MALE STUDENTS

Scholarship for a male, full-time student, majoring in engineering,
chemistry, physics, or mathematical sciences. Graduate student may be
full- or part-time and have 2.5 minimum GPA. Graduating high school
seniors and undergraduates must have 3.0 minimum GPA. Must
demonstrate financial need. Undergraduate scholarship is $2000; and
graduate scholarship is $3000.

Academic Fields/Career Goals: Chemical Engineering; Engineering-
Related Technologies; Engineering/Technology; Physical Sciences.

Award: Scholarship for use in freshman, sophomore, junior, senior, or
graduate years; not renewable. *Number:* 1. *Amount:* $2000–$3000.

Eligibility Requirements: Applicant must be American Indian/Alaska
Native, Asian/Pacific Islander, Black (non-Hispanic), Hispanic; enrolled
or expecting to enroll full- or part-time at a two-year or four-year
institution or university and male. Applicant or parent of applicant must
be member of National Association for the Advancement of Colored
People. Applicant must have 3.0 GPA or higher. Available to U.S.
citizens.

Application Requirements: Application form, financial need
analysis, recommendations or references, transcript. *Deadline:* March 7.

Contact: Victor Goode, Attorney
  Phone: 410-580-5760
  E-mail: info@naacp.org

NATIONAL BOARD OF BOILER AND PRESSURE VESSEL INSPECTORS

http://www.nationalboard.org/

NATIONAL BOARD TECHNICAL SCHOLARSHIP

Two $6000 scholarships to selected students meeting eligibility
standards, who are pursuing a bachelor's degree in certain engineering or
related studies. Must be a child, step-child, grandchild, or great-
grandchild of a past or present National Board member (living or
deceased), or of a past or present Commissioned Inspector (living or
deceased), employed by a member jurisdiction, or of a past or present
National Board employee (living or deceased).

Academic Fields/Career Goals: Chemical Engineering; Electrical
Engineering/Electronics; Mechanical Engineering.

Award: Scholarship for use in freshman, sophomore, junior, or senior
years; not renewable. *Number:* 2. *Amount:* $6000.

Eligibility Requirements: Applicant must be enrolled or expecting to enroll full-time at a four-year or technical institution or university. Applicant or parent of applicant must be member of National Board of Boiler and Pressure Vessel Inspectors. Applicant must have 3.0 GPA or higher. Available to U.S. and Canadian citizens.

Application Requirements: Application form, essay, recommendations or references, transcript. *Deadline:* February 29.

Contact: Donald Tanner, Executive Director
    Phone: 614-888-8320
    Fax: 614-888-0750
    E-mail: dtanner@nationalboard.org

NATIONAL INVENTORS HALL OF FAME

http://www.invent.org/

COLLEGIATE INVENTORS COMPETITION FOR UNDERGRADUATE STUDENTS

• *See page 106*

COLLEGIATE INVENTORS COMPETITION-GRAND PRIZE

• *See page 106*

NATIONAL SOCIETY OF PROFESSIONAL ENGINEERS

http://www.nspe.org/

MAUREEN L. AND HOWARD N. BLITMAN, PE SCHOLARSHIP TO PROMOTE DIVERSITY IN ENGINEERING

Award of $5000 in two disbursements of $2500 to a high school senior from an ethnic minority who has been accepted into an ABET-accredited engineering program at a four-year college or university.

Academic Fields/Career Goals: Chemical Engineering; Civil Engineering; Electrical Engineering/Electronics; Engineering-Related Technologies; Engineering/Technology; Materials Science, Engineering, and Metallurgy; Mechanical Engineering.

Award: Scholarship for use in freshman year; not renewable. *Number:* 1. *Amount:* $5000.

Eligibility Requirements: Applicant must be American Indian/Alaska Native, Black (non-Hispanic), Hispanic; high school student and planning to enroll or expecting to enroll full-time at a four-year institution or university. Applicant must have 2.5 GPA or higher. Available to U.S. citizens.

Application Requirements: Application form, community service, essay, recommendations or references, test scores, transcript. *Deadline:* March 1.

Contact: Cindy Simpson, Director of Education
    Phone: 703-684-2833
    E-mail: csimpson@nspe.org

PAUL H. ROBBINS HONORARY SCHOLARSHIP

Awarded annually to a current engineering undergraduate student entering the junior year in an ABET-accredited engineering program and attending a college/university that participates in the NSPE Professional Engineers in Higher Education (PEHE) Sustaining University Program(SUP).

Academic Fields/Career Goals: Chemical Engineering; Civil Engineering; Electrical Engineering/Electronics; Engineering-Related Technologies; Engineering/Technology; Materials Science, Engineering, and Metallurgy; Mechanical Engineering.

Award: Scholarship for use in junior year; renewable. *Number:* 1. *Amount:* $5000.

Eligibility Requirements: Applicant must be enrolled or expecting to enroll full-time at a four-year institution or university. Applicant or parent of applicant must be member of National Society of Professional Engineers. Available to U.S. citizens.

Application Requirements: Application form, essay, recommendations or references, test scores, transcript. *Deadline:* March 1.

Contact: Cindy Simpson, Director of Education
    Phone: 703-684-2833
    E-mail: csimpson@nspe.org

PROFESSIONAL ENGINEERS IN INDUSTRY SCHOLARSHIP

Applicants must be sponsored by an NSPE/PEI member. Students must have completed a minimum of two semesters or three quarters of undergraduate engineering studies (or be enrolled in graduate study) accredited by ABET.

Academic Fields/Career Goals: Chemical Engineering; Civil Engineering; Electrical Engineering/Electronics; Engineering-Related Technologies; Engineering/Technology; Materials Science, Engineering, and Metallurgy; Mechanical Engineering.

Award: Scholarship for use in sophomore, junior, or senior years; not renewable. *Number:* 1. *Amount:* $2500.

Eligibility Requirements: Applicant must be enrolled or expecting to enroll full-time at a four-year institution or university. Applicant must have 3.5 GPA or higher. Available to U.S. citizens.

Application Requirements: Application form, community service, essay, recommendations or references, resume, transcript, work experience certificates. *Deadline:* April 1.

Contact: Erin Reyes, Practice Division Manager
    National Society of Professional Engineers
    1420 King Street
    Alexandria, VA 22314
    Phone: 703-684-2884
    E-mail: egarcia@nspe.org

NEVADA NASA SPACE GRANT CONSORTIUM

http://www.nvspacegrant.org/

NATIONAL SPACE GRANT COLLEGE AND FELLOWSHIP PROGRAM

• *See page 106*

OREGON STUDENT ASSISTANCE COMMISSION

http://www.GetCollegeFunds.org/

SOCIETY OF AMERICAN MILITARY ENGINEERS PORTLAND POST SCHOLARSHIP

Award for a student who will enroll as college sophomore or above for fall term/semester in undergraduate study. Preference given to ROTC reservist, National Guard reservist, or prior service veteran. Must have a minimum 3.0 GPA and major in aeronautical, biomedical, chemical, civil, electrical, or mechanical engineering. Essay is required.

Academic Fields/Career Goals: Chemical Engineering; Civil Engineering; Electrical Engineering/Electronics; Engineering/Technology; Mechanical Engineering.

Award: Scholarship for use in sophomore, junior, or senior years; not renewable.

Eligibility Requirements: Applicant must be enrolled or expecting to enroll full-time at a four-year institution or university. Applicant must have 3.0 GPA or higher. Available to U.S. citizens.

Application Requirements: Application form, essay, FAFSA. *Deadline:* March 1.

PLASTICS INSTITUTE OF AMERICA

http://www.plasticsinstitute.org/

PLASTICS PIONEERS SCHOLARSHIPS

Financial grants awarded to undergraduate students needing help in their education expenses to enter into a full-time career in any and all segments of the plastics industry, with emphasis on "hands on" participation in the many fields where members of the Plastics Pioneers Association have spent their professional years. Applicants must be U.S. citizens.

Academic Fields/Career Goals: Chemical Engineering; Engineering-Related Technologies; Engineering/Technology; Materials Science, Engineering, and Metallurgy; Trade/Technical Specialties.

Award: Scholarship for use in freshman, sophomore, junior, or senior years; renewable. *Number:* 30–40. *Amount:* $1500–$3000.

Eligibility Requirements: Applicant must be enrolled or expecting to enroll full- or part-time at a two-year or four-year or technical institution. Available to U.S. citizens.

Application Requirements: Application form, essay, recommendations or references, resume, transcript. *Deadline:* April 1.

Contact: Aldo Crugnola, Executive Director
Plastics Institute of America
333 Aiken Street
Lowell, MA 01854
Phone: 978-934-2575
Fax: 978-459-9420
E-mail: pia@uml.edu

ROBERT H. MOLLOHAN FAMILY CHARITABLE FOUNDATION, INC.

http://www.mollohanfoundation.org/

HIGH TECHNOLOGY SCHOLARS PROGRAM
• See page 147

SEMICONDUCTOR RESEARCH CORPORATION (SRC)

http://www.src.org/

MASTER'S SCHOLARSHIP PROGRAM

Scholarship given to women or members of an under represented minority category (African-American, Hispanic, Native American). Scholarships are for study in disciplines related to microelectronics at US-based universities having research funded by the Semiconductor Research Corporation and require US citizenship or permanent resident status.

Academic Fields/Career Goals: Chemical Engineering; Computer Science/Data Processing; Electrical Engineering/Electronics; Engineering/Technology; Materials Science, Engineering, and Metallurgy.

Award: Scholarship for use in senior or graduate years; renewable. *Number:* 1–15. *Amount:* $25,000–$32,000.

Eligibility Requirements: Applicant must be American Indian/Alaska Native, Black (non-Hispanic), Hispanic and enrolled or expecting to enroll full-time at a four-year institution or university. Applicant must have 3.0 GPA or higher. Available to U.S. citizens.

Application Requirements: Application form, recommendations or references, resume, test scores, transcript. *Deadline:* February 15.

Contact: Virginia Wiggins, Student Relations Manager
Phone: 919-941-9453
E-mail: students@src.org

SIGMA XI, THE SCIENTIFIC RESEARCH SOCIETY

http://www.sigmaxi.org/

SIGMA XI GRANTS-IN-AID OF RESEARCH
• See page 95

SOCIETY OF AUTOMOTIVE ENGINEERS

http://www.sae.org/

BMW/SAE ENGINEERING SCHOLARSHIP
• See page 137

EDWARD D. HENDRICKSON/SAE ENGINEERING SCHOLARSHIP
• See page 137

TMC/SAE DONALD D. DAWSON TECHNICAL SCHOLARSHIP
• See page 137

SOCIETY OF PLASTICS ENGINEERS (SPE) FOUNDATION

http://www.4spe.org/

FLEMING/BASZCAK SCHOLARSHIP

Award available for a full-time undergraduate student, with a demonstrated interest in the plastics industry. Must be a U.S. citizen and provide documentation of Mexican heritage.

Academic Fields/Career Goals: Chemical Engineering; Electrical Engineering/Electronics; Engineering/Technology; Industrial Design; Materials Science, Engineering, and Metallurgy; Trade/Technical Specialties.

Award: Scholarship for use in freshman, sophomore, junior, or senior years; not renewable. *Number:* 1. *Amount:* $2000.

Eligibility Requirements: Applicant must be of Mexican heritage; Hispanic and enrolled or expecting to enroll full-time at a two-year or four-year institution or university. Available to U.S. citizens.

Application Requirements: Application form, essay, financial need analysis, recommendations or references, transcript. *Deadline:* February 15.

Contact: Gail Bristol, Managing Director
Society of Plastics Engineers (SPE) Foundation
13 Church Hill Road
Newtown, CT 06470
Phone: 203-740-5447
Fax: 203-775-8490
E-mail: foundation@4spe.org

PLASTICS PIONEERS ASSOCIATION SCHOLARSHIPS

Scholarships available to undergraduate students who are committed to becoming "hands-on" workers in the plastics industry, such as plastics technicians or engineers.

Academic Fields/Career Goals: Chemical Engineering; Engineering/Technology.

Award: Scholarship for use in freshman, sophomore, junior, or senior years; renewable. *Number:* up to 10. *Amount:* $3000.

Eligibility Requirements: Applicant must be enrolled or expecting to enroll full-time at a two-year or four-year or technical institution or university. Available to U.S. and Canadian citizens.

Application Requirements: Application form, essay, financial need analysis, recommendations or references, resume, transcript. *Deadline:* January 15.

Contact: Ms. Gail Bristol, Managing Director
Society of Plastics Engineers (SPE) Foundation
13 Church Hill Road
Newtown, CT 06470
Phone: 203-740-5447
Fax: 203-775-8490
E-mail: foundation@4spe.org

SOCIETY OF PLASTICS ENGINEERS SCHOLARSHIP PROGRAM

Scholarships awarded to full-time students who have demonstrated or expressed an interest in the plastics industry. Major or course of study must be beneficial to a career in the plastics industry.

Academic Fields/Career Goals: Chemical Engineering; Electrical Engineering/Electronics; Engineering/Technology; Industrial Design; Materials Science, Engineering, and Metallurgy; Trade/Technical Specialties.

Award: Scholarship for use in freshman, sophomore, junior, senior, or graduate years; not renewable. *Number:* 25–30. *Amount:* $1000–$5000.

Eligibility Requirements: Applicant must be enrolled or expecting to enroll full-time at a two-year or four-year or technical institution or university. Available to U.S. and non-U.S. citizens.

Application Requirements: Application form, essay, financial need analysis, recommendations or references, transcript. *Deadline:* February 15.

Contact: Gail Bristol, Managing Director
Society of Plastics Engineers (SPE) Foundation
13 Church Hill Road
Newtown, CT 06470
Phone: 203-740-5447
Fax: 203-775-8490
E-mail: foundation@4spe.org

SOCIETY OF WOMEN ENGINEERS
http://www.swe.org/

ACCENTURE SCHOLARSHIP

Five scholarships of $2000 available to two sophomores and three juniors who are women pursuing ABET-accredited baccalaureate or graduate programs in preparation for careers in engineering, engineering technology, and computer science in the United States and Mexico.

Academic Fields/Career Goals: Chemical Engineering; Civil Engineering; Computer Science/Data Processing; Electrical Engineering/Electronics; Mechanical Engineering.

Award: Scholarship for use in sophomore or junior years; not renewable. *Number:* 5. *Amount:* $2000.

Eligibility Requirements: Applicant must be enrolled or expecting to enroll full-time at a four-year institution or university and female. Available to U.S. citizens.

Application Requirements: Application form, recommendations or references. *Deadline:* February 15.

ADA I. PRESSMAN MEMORIAL SCHOLARSHIP

$5000 renewable scholarship for women pursuing ABET-accredited baccalaureate or graduate programs in preparation for careers in engineering, engineering technology, and computer science in the United States and Mexico. Must be a U.S. citizen.

Academic Fields/Career Goals: Chemical Engineering; Construction Engineering/Management; Electrical Engineering/Electronics; Energy and Power Engineering; Engineering/Technology; Marine/Ocean Engineering; Mechanical Engineering; Paper and Pulp Engineering.

Award: Scholarship for use in sophomore, junior, senior, or graduate years; renewable. *Number:* 7. *Amount:* $5000.

Eligibility Requirements: Applicant must be enrolled or expecting to enroll full-time at a four-year institution or university and female. Available to U.S. citizens.

Application Requirements: Application form, recommendations or references. *Deadline:* February 15.

ANNE MAUREEN WHITNEY BARROW MEMORIAL SCHOLARSHIP

$7000 award for women pursuing ABET-accredited baccalaureate programs in preparation for careers in engineering or engineering technology in the United States and Mexico. One award, renewable up to 5 years.

Academic Fields/Career Goals: Chemical Engineering; Construction Engineering/Management; Electrical Engineering/Electronics; Energy and Power Engineering; Engineering/Technology; Marine/Ocean Engineering; Mechanical Engineering; Paper and Pulp Engineering.

Award: Scholarship for use in freshman, sophomore, junior, or senior years; renewable. *Number:* 1. *Amount:* $7000.

Eligibility Requirements: Applicant must be enrolled or expecting to enroll full-time at a four-year institution or university and female. Available to U.S. citizens.

Application Requirements: Application form, recommendations or references. *Deadline:* February 15.

BETTY LOU BAILEY SWE REGION F SCHOLARSHIP

$1500 award for women pursuing ABET-accredited baccalaureate or graduate programs in preparation for careers in engineering, engineering technology and computer science in the United States and Mexico. U.S. citizenship, SWE membership, and financial need required. First choice is for the applicant to attend a college/university within the Region F boundaries of Connecticut, Maine, Massachusetts, New Hampshire, New York (upstate), Rhode Island, and Vermont. Second choice would be for the applicant's home address to be within the Region F boundaries.

Academic Fields/Career Goals: Chemical Engineering; Civil Engineering; Construction Engineering/Management; Electrical Engineering/Electronics; Energy and Power Engineering; Engineering/

Technology; Marine/Ocean Engineering; Materials Science, Engineering, and Metallurgy; Mechanical Engineering; Paper and Pulp Engineering.

Award: Scholarship for use in sophomore, junior, senior, or graduate years; not renewable. *Number:* 1. *Amount:* $1500.

Eligibility Requirements: Applicant must be enrolled or expecting to enroll full-time at a four-year institution or university and female. Applicant or parent of applicant must be member of Society of Women Engineers. Available to U.S. citizens.

Application Requirements: Application form, financial need analysis, recommendations or references. *Deadline:* February 15.

BK KRENZER MEMORIAL REENTRY SCHOLARSHIP

One $2500 award for women pursuing ABET-accredited baccalaureate or graduate programs in preparation for careers in engineering, engineering technology, and computer science in the United States and Mexico. Must have been out of school and the engineering or technology workforce for a minimum of two years prior to beginning the current course of study. The student is not required to have prior engineering experience or education.

Academic Fields/Career Goals: Chemical Engineering; Construction Engineering/Management; Electrical Engineering/Electronics; Energy and Power Engineering; Engineering/Technology; Marine/Ocean Engineering; Materials Science, Engineering, and Metallurgy; Mechanical Engineering; Paper and Pulp Engineering.

Award: Scholarship for use in freshman, sophomore, junior, senior, or graduate years; not renewable. *Number:* 1. *Amount:* $2500.

Eligibility Requirements: Applicant must be enrolled or expecting to enroll full- or part-time at a four-year institution or university and female. Available to U.S. citizens.

Application Requirements: Application form, recommendations or references. *Deadline:* February 15.

BOSTON SCIENTIFIC SCHOLARSHIP

$5000 scholarship for women pursuing ABET-accredited baccalaureate programs in preparation for careers in engineering, engineering technology, or computer science in the United States and Mexico. Minimum 3.5 GPA required. Inquire about preferred schools.

Academic Fields/Career Goals: Chemical Engineering; Computer Science/Data Processing; Electrical Engineering/Electronics; Engineering/Technology; Mechanical Engineering.

Award: Scholarship for use in senior year; not renewable. *Number:* 2. *Amount:* $5000.

Eligibility Requirements: Applicant must be enrolled or expecting to enroll full-time at a four-year institution or university and female. Applicant must have 3.5 GPA or higher. Available to U.S. citizens.

Application Requirements: Application form, recommendations or references. *Deadline:* February 15.

CAROL STEPHENS REGION F SCHOLARSHIP

One $1000 scholarship for women pursuing ABET-accredited baccalaureate or graduate programs in preparation for careers in engineering, engineering technology, and computer science in the United States and Mexico. Must attend a college/university within the Region F boundaries or home address must be within the Region F boundaries.

Academic Fields/Career Goals: Chemical Engineering; Civil Engineering; Construction Engineering/Management; Electrical Engineering/Electronics; Energy and Power Engineering; Engineering/Technology; Marine/Ocean Engineering; Materials Science, Engineering, and Metallurgy; Mechanical Engineering; Paper and Pulp Engineering.

Award: Scholarship for use in sophomore, junior, senior, or graduate years; not renewable. *Number:* 1. *Amount:* $1000.

Eligibility Requirements: Applicant must be enrolled or expecting to enroll full-time at a four-year institution or university and female. Available to U.S. citizens.

Application Requirements: Application form, recommendations or references. *Deadline:* February 15.

CATERPILLAR INC. SCHOLARSHIP

$2400 scholarship for women pursuing ABET-accredited baccalaureate or graduate programs in preparation for careers in engineering, engineering technology, or computer science in the United States and Mexico. Must be part of Regions C, D, H, or I and authorized to work in U.S.

Academic Fields/Career Goals: Chemical Engineering; Electrical Engineering/Electronics; Engineering/Technology; Mechanical Engineering.

Award: Scholarship for use in sophomore, junior, senior, or graduate years; not renewable. *Number:* 3. *Amount:* $2400.

Eligibility Requirements: Applicant must be enrolled or expecting to enroll full-time at a four-year institution or university and female. Available to U.S. citizens.

Application Requirements: Application form, recommendations or references. *Deadline:* February 15.

CUMMINS INC. SCHOLARSHIP

Two $1000 awards for women pursuing ABET-accredited baccalaureate or graduate programs in preparation for careers in engineering, engineering technology, and computer science in the United States and Mexico. Preference given to under-represented groups and those willing to intern.

Academic Fields/Career Goals: Chemical Engineering; Computer Science/Data Processing; Electrical Engineering/Electronics; Engineering/Technology; Materials Science, Engineering, and Metallurgy; Mechanical Engineering.

Award: Scholarship for use in sophomore, junior, senior, or graduate years; not renewable. *Number:* 2. *Amount:* $1000.

Eligibility Requirements: Applicant must be enrolled or expecting to enroll full-time at a four-year institution or university and female. Available to U.S. citizens.

Application Requirements: Application form, recommendations or references. *Deadline:* February 15.

DR. IVY M. PARKER MEMORIAL SCHOLARSHIP

$1500 scholarship for a woman pursuing an ABET-accredited baccalaureate program in preparation for a career in engineering, engineering technology, and computer science in the United States and Mexico. Must demonstrate financial need.

Academic Fields/Career Goals: Chemical Engineering; Civil Engineering; Construction Engineering/Management; Electrical Engineering/Electronics; Energy and Power Engineering; Engineering/Technology; Marine/Ocean Engineering; Materials Science, Engineering, and Metallurgy; Mechanical Engineering; Paper and Pulp Engineering.

Award: Scholarship for use in junior or senior years; not renewable. *Number:* 1. *Amount:* $1500.

Eligibility Requirements: Applicant must be enrolled or expecting to enroll full-time at a four-year institution or university and female. Available to U.S. citizens.

Application Requirements: Application form, financial need analysis, recommendations or references. *Deadline:* February 15.

DOROTHY LEMKE HOWARTH MEMORIAL SCHOLARSHIP

Six scholarships of $3333 awarded to sophomore women pursuing ABET-accredited baccalaureate programs in preparation for careers in engineering, engineering technology, and computer science in the United States and Mexico. Must be a U.S. citizen.

Academic Fields/Career Goals: Chemical Engineering; Civil Engineering; Electrical Engineering/Electronics; Energy and Power Engineering; Engineering/Technology; Marine/Ocean Engineering; Materials Science, Engineering, and Metallurgy; Mechanical Engineering; Paper and Pulp Engineering.

Award: Scholarship for use in sophomore year; not renewable. *Number:* 6. *Amount:* $3333.

Eligibility Requirements: Applicant must be enrolled or expecting to enroll full-time at a four-year institution or university and female. Available to U.S. citizens.

Application Requirements: Application form, recommendations or references. *Deadline:* February 15.

DOROTHY P. MORRIS SCHOLARSHIP

One $1500 scholarship for a woman pursuing an ABET-accredited baccalaureate program in preparation for a career in engineering, engineering technology, or computer science in the United States and Mexico. Must be a U.S. citizen.

Academic Fields/Career Goals: Chemical Engineering; Civil Engineering; Construction Engineering/Management; Electrical Engineering/Electronics; Energy and Power Engineering; Engineering/

Technology; Marine/Ocean Engineering; Materials Science, Engineering, and Metallurgy; Mechanical Engineering; Paper and Pulp Engineering.

Award: Scholarship for use in sophomore, junior, or senior years; not renewable. *Number:* 1. *Amount:* $1500.

Eligibility Requirements: Applicant must be enrolled or expecting to enroll full-time at a four-year institution or university and female. Available to U.S. citizens.

Application Requirements: Application form, recommendations or references. *Deadline:* February 15.

DUPONT COMPANY SCHOLARSHIP

Two $1000 awards for women pursuing ABET-accredited baccalaureate programs in preparation for careers in engineering, engineering technology, and computer science in the United States and Mexico.

Academic Fields/Career Goals: Chemical Engineering; Engineering/Technology; Mechanical Engineering.

Award: Scholarship for use in sophomore, junior, or senior years; not renewable. *Number:* 2. *Amount:* $1000.

Eligibility Requirements: Applicant must be enrolled or expecting to enroll full-time at a four-year institution or university and female. Available to U.S. citizens.

Application Requirements: Application form, recommendations or references. *Deadline:* February 15.

EXELON CORPORATION SCHOLARSHIP

Five awards of $1000 for freshmen women pursuing ABET-accredited baccalaureate programs in preparation for careers in electrical and mechanical engineering in the United States and Mexico. Minimum 3.5 GPA required.

Academic Fields/Career Goals: Chemical Engineering; Mechanical Engineering.

Award: Scholarship for use in freshman year; not renewable. *Number:* 5. *Amount:* $1000.

Eligibility Requirements: Applicant must be enrolled or expecting to enroll full-time at a four-year institution or university and female. Applicant must have 3.5 GPA or higher. Available to U.S. citizens.

Application Requirements: Application form, essay, recommendations or references, self-addressed stamped envelope with application, test scores, transcript. *Deadline:* May 15.

HONEYWELL CORPORATION SCHOLARSHIP

Three $5000 scholarships for women pursuing ABET-accredited baccalaureate or graduate programs in preparation for careers in engineering, engineering technology and computer science in the United States and Mexico. U.S. citizenship required. Financial need and underrepresented students preferred.

Academic Fields/Career Goals: Chemical Engineering; Computer Science/Data Processing; Electrical Engineering/Electronics; Engineering/Technology; Materials Science, Engineering, and Metallurgy; Mechanical Engineering.

Award: Scholarship for use in freshman, sophomore, junior, or senior years; not renewable. *Number:* 3. *Amount:* $5000.

Eligibility Requirements: Applicant must be enrolled or expecting to enroll full-time at a four-year institution or university and female. Available to U.S. citizens.

Application Requirements: Application form, financial need analysis, recommendations or references. *Deadline:* February 15.

JILL S. TIETJEN P.E. SCHOLARSHIP

$1500 award for a woman pursuing an ABET-accredited baccalaureate or graduate program in preparation for a career in engineering, engineering technology, and computer science in the United States and Mexico. Must be a U.S. citizen.

Academic Fields/Career Goals: Chemical Engineering; Civil Engineering; Computer Science/Data Processing; Electrical Engineering/Electronics; Energy and Power Engineering; Engineering/Technology; Marine/Ocean Engineering; Materials Science, Engineering, and Metallurgy; Mechanical Engineering; Paper and Pulp Engineering.

Award: Scholarship for use in sophomore, junior, senior, or graduate years; not renewable. *Number:* 1. *Amount:* $1500.

Eligibility Requirements: Applicant must be enrolled or expecting to enroll full-time at a four-year institution or university and female. Available to U.S. citizens.

Application Requirements: Application form, recommendations or references. *Deadline:* February 15.

KELLOGG SCHOLARSHIP

Three scholarships for women pursuing ABET-accredited baccalaureate programs in preparation for careers in engineering, engineering technology, or computer science in the United States and Mexico. Minimum 3.2 GPA required. SWE membership also required. Two $1,000 scholarships (student at Michigan University and Western Michigan University preferred) and 1 $3,000 scholarship (financial need preferred).

Academic Fields/Career Goals: Chemical Engineering; Mechanical Engineering.

Award: Scholarship for use in sophomore or junior years; not renewable. *Number:* 3. *Amount:* $1000–$3000.

Eligibility Requirements: Applicant must be enrolled or expecting to enroll full-time at a four-year institution or university and female. Applicant or parent of applicant must be member of Society of Women Engineers. Available to U.S. citizens.

Application Requirements: Application form, recommendations or references. *Deadline:* February 15.

LIFE TECHNOLOGIES SCHOLARSHIP

One-time scholarship for women pursuing ABET-accredited baccalaureate programs in preparation for careers in engineering, engineering technology, or computer science in the United States and Mexico. Underrepresented groups preferred.

Academic Fields/Career Goals: Chemical Engineering; Civil Engineering; Computer Science/Data Processing; Electrical Engineering/Electronics; Engineering/Technology; Materials Science, Engineering, and Metallurgy; Mechanical Engineering.

Award: Scholarship for use in sophomore, junior, or senior years; not renewable. *Number:* 3. *Amount:* $2500–$7500.

Eligibility Requirements: Applicant must be enrolled or expecting to enroll full-time at a four-year institution or university and female. Available to U.S. citizens.

Application Requirements: Application form, recommendations or references. *Deadline:* February 15.

LILLIAN MOLLER GILBRETH MEMORIAL SCHOLARSHIP

One award of $12,000 for a woman pursuing an ABET-accredited baccalaureate program in preparation for a career in engineering, engineering technology, and computer science in the United States and Mexico. Renewable for continuing undergraduate study only. Availability dependent upon renewal.

Academic Fields/Career Goals: Chemical Engineering; Civil Engineering; Computer Science/Data Processing; Construction Engineering/Management; Electrical Engineering/Electronics; Energy and Power Engineering; Engineering/Technology; Marine/Ocean Engineering; Materials Science, Engineering, and Metallurgy; Mechanical Engineering; Paper and Pulp Engineering.

Award: Scholarship for use in junior or senior years; not renewable. *Number:* 1. *Amount:* $12,000.

Eligibility Requirements: Applicant must be enrolled or expecting to enroll full-time at a four-year institution or university and female. Available to U.S. citizens.

Application Requirements: Application form, recommendations or references. *Deadline:* February 15.

MARY V. MUNGER SCHOLARSHIP

One $5000 award for a woman pursuing an ABET-accredited baccalaureate or graduate programs in preparation for a career in engineering, engineering technology, or computer science in the United States and Mexico. Must be a U.S. citizen and a member of SWE. For use by college junior or senior or a re-entry/nontraditional student. Re-entry/nontraditional students must have been out of school and the engineering or technology workforce for a minimum of two years prior to beginning the current course of study.

Academic Fields/Career Goals: Chemical Engineering; Civil Engineering; Construction Engineering/Management; Electrical Engineering/Electronics; Energy and Power Engineering; Engineering/Technology; Marine/Ocean Engineering; Materials Science, Engineering, and Metallurgy; Mechanical Engineering; Paper and Pulp Engineering.

Award: Scholarship for use in junior or senior years; not renewable. *Number:* 1. *Amount:* $5000.

Eligibility Requirements: Applicant must be enrolled or expecting to enroll full-time at a four-year institution or university and female. Available to U.S. citizens.

Application Requirements: Application form, recommendations or references. *Deadline:* February 15.

MASWE MEMORIAL SCHOLARSHIP

Four $1500 awards for women pursuing ABET-accredited baccalaureate programs in preparation for careers in engineering, engineering technology, and computer science in the United States and Mexico. Financial need is taken into consideration.

Academic Fields/Career Goals: Chemical Engineering; Civil Engineering; Construction Engineering/Management; Electrical Engineering/Electronics; Energy and Power Engineering; Engineering/Technology; Marine/Ocean Engineering; Materials Science, Engineering, and Metallurgy; Mechanical Engineering; Paper and Pulp Engineering.

Award: Scholarship for use in sophomore, junior, or senior years; not renewable. *Number:* 4. *Amount:* $1500.

Eligibility Requirements: Applicant must be enrolled or expecting to enroll full-time at a four-year institution or university and female. Available to U.S. citizens.

Application Requirements: Application form, recommendations or references. *Deadline:* February 15.

MERIDITH THOMS MEMORIAL SCHOLARSHIPS

Five $2500 scholarships for women pursuing ABET-accredited baccalaureate programs in preparation for careers in engineering, engineering technology, and computer science in the United States and Mexico.

Academic Fields/Career Goals: Chemical Engineering; Civil Engineering; Construction Engineering/Management; Electrical Engineering/Electronics; Energy and Power Engineering; Engineering/Technology; Marine/Ocean Engineering; Materials Science, Engineering, and Metallurgy; Mechanical Engineering; Paper and Pulp Engineering.

Award: Scholarship for use in sophomore, junior, or senior years; not renewable. *Number:* 5. *Amount:* $2500.

Eligibility Requirements: Applicant must be enrolled or expecting to enroll full-time at a four-year institution or university and female. Available to U.S. citizens.

Application Requirements: Application form, recommendations or references. *Deadline:* February 15.

OLIVE LYNN SALEMBIER MEMORIAL REENTRY SCHOLARSHIP

One $1500 scholarship for a women pursuing an ABET-accredited baccalaureate or graduate program in preparation for a career in engineering, engineering technology, and computer science in the United States and Mexico. Must have been out of the engineering work force and out of school for a minimum of two years prior to re-entry. Minimum 3.0 GPA except for first year of reentry.

Academic Fields/Career Goals: Chemical Engineering; Civil Engineering; Construction Engineering/Management; Electrical Engineering/Electronics; Energy and Power Engineering; Engineering/Technology; Marine/Ocean Engineering; Materials Science, Engineering, and Metallurgy; Mechanical Engineering; Paper and Pulp Engineering.

Award: Scholarship for use in freshman, sophomore, junior, senior, or graduate years; not renewable. *Number:* 1. *Amount:* $1500.

Eligibility Requirements: Applicant must be enrolled or expecting to enroll full-time at a four-year institution or university and female. Applicant must have 3.0 GPA or higher. Available to U.S. citizens.

Application Requirements: Application form, recommendations or references. *Deadline:* February 15.

PRAXAIR INC. SCHOLARSHIP

Ten $1000 scholarships for women pursuing ABET-accredited baccalaureate programs in preparation for careers in engineering, engineering technology, and computer science in the United States and Mexico. Students from under-represented populations preferred. Minimum 3.2 GPA required.

Academic Fields/Career Goals: Chemical Engineering; Mechanical Engineering.

Award: Scholarship for use in sophomore, junior, or senior years; not renewable. *Number:* 10. *Amount:* $1000.

Eligibility Requirements: Applicant must be enrolled or expecting to enroll full-time at a four-year institution or university and female. Available to U.S. citizens.

Application Requirements: Application form, recommendations or references. *Deadline:* February 15.

SUSAN MISZKOWICZ MEMORIAL SCHOLARSHIP

$1500 award for a woman pursuing an ABET-accredited baccalaureate program in preparation for a career in engineering, engineering technology, or computer science in the United States and Mexico.

Academic Fields/Career Goals: Chemical Engineering; Civil Engineering; Construction Engineering/Management; Electrical Engineering/Electronics; Energy and Power Engineering; Engineering/Technology; Marine/Ocean Engineering; Materials Science, Engineering, and Metallurgy; Mechanical Engineering; Paper and Pulp Engineering.

Award: Scholarship for use in sophomore, junior, or senior years; not renewable. *Number:* 1. *Amount:* $1500.

Eligibility Requirements: Applicant must be enrolled or expecting to enroll full-time at a four-year institution or university and female. Available to U.S. citizens.

Application Requirements: Application form, recommendations or references. *Deadline:* February 15.

SWE BALTIMORE-WASHINGTON SECTION SCHOLARSHIP

One $1500 award for a woman pursuing an ABET-accredited baccalaureate or graduate program in preparation for a career in engineering, engineering technology, or computer science in the United States and Mexico. For use at a school in DC, MD, or VA. U.S. citizenship and SWE membership required.

Academic Fields/Career Goals: Chemical Engineering; Civil Engineering; Construction Engineering/Management; Electrical Engineering/Electronics; Energy and Power Engineering; Engineering/Technology; Marine/Ocean Engineering; Materials Science, Engineering, and Metallurgy; Mechanical Engineering; Paper and Pulp Engineering.

Award: Scholarship for use in sophomore, junior, senior, or graduate years; not renewable. *Number:* 1. *Amount:* $1500.

Eligibility Requirements: Applicant must be enrolled or expecting to enroll full-time at a four-year institution or university; female and studying in District of Columbia, Maryland, Virginia. Applicant or parent of applicant must be member of Society of Women Engineers. Available to U.S. citizens.

Application Requirements: Application form, recommendations or references. *Deadline:* February 15.

SWE CENTRAL NEW MEXICO PIONEERS SCHOLARSHIP

Renewable $1250 scholarship for a woman pursuing an ABET-accredited baccalaureate program in preparation for a career in engineering, engineering technology, or computer science in the United States and Mexico. Must attend a NM university or 4-year engineering/technology school. US citizenship and SWE membership required. Renewable up to three years.

Academic Fields/Career Goals: Chemical Engineering; Civil Engineering; Construction Engineering/Management; Electrical Engineering/Electronics; Energy and Power Engineering; Engineering/Technology; Marine/Ocean Engineering; Materials Science, Engineering, and Metallurgy; Mechanical Engineering; Paper and Pulp Engineering.

Award: Scholarship for use in sophomore, junior, or senior years; renewable. *Number:* 1. *Amount:* $1250.

Eligibility Requirements: Applicant must be enrolled or expecting to enroll full-time at an institution or university; female and studying in New Mexico. Applicant or parent of applicant must be member of Society of Women Engineers. Available to U.S. citizens.

Application Requirements: Application form, recommendations or references. *Deadline:* February 15.

SWE CENTRAL NEW MEXICO REENTRY SCHOLARSHIP

$1250 scholarship for a woman pursuing an ABET-accredited baccalaureate or graduate program in preparation for a career in engineering, engineering technology, or computer science in the United States and Mexico. Must be a U.S. citizen and have SWE membership. Must attend a university located in NM—New Mexico Institute of

Mining and Technology, New Mexico State University, or University of New Mexico. Reentry for undergraduate sophomore, junior, senior, or graduate student. If there is no qualified candidate, the Scholarship Committee can award a second CNM-Pioneers Scholarship.

Academic Fields/Career Goals: Chemical Engineering; Civil Engineering; Construction Engineering/Management; Electrical Engineering/Electronics; Energy and Power Engineering; Engineering/Technology; Marine/Ocean Engineering; Materials Science, Engineering, and Metallurgy; Mechanical Engineering; Paper and Pulp Engineering.

Award: Scholarship for use in sophomore, junior, senior, or graduate years; renewable. *Number:* 1. *Amount:* $1250.

Eligibility Requirements: Applicant must be enrolled or expecting to enroll full-time at a four-year institution or university; female and studying in New Mexico. Applicant or parent of applicant must be member of Society of Women Engineers. Available to U.S. citizens.

Application Requirements: Application form, recommendations or references. *Deadline:* February 15.

SWE MID-HUDSON SECTION SCHOLARSHIP

$1000 scholarship for a woman pursuing an ABET-accredited baccalaureate or graduate program in preparation for a career in engineering, engineering technology, or computer science in the United States and Mexico. New York is the preferred state for home residence and study.

Academic Fields/Career Goals: Chemical Engineering; Civil Engineering; Construction Engineering/Management; Electrical Engineering/Electronics; Energy and Power Engineering; Engineering/Technology; Marine/Ocean Engineering; Materials Science, Engineering, and Metallurgy; Mechanical Engineering; Paper and Pulp Engineering.

Award: Scholarship for use in sophomore, junior, senior, or graduate years; not renewable. *Number:* 1. *Amount:* $1000.

Eligibility Requirements: Applicant must be enrolled or expecting to enroll full-time at a four-year institution or university; female; resident of New York and studying in New York. Available to U.S. citizens.

Application Requirements: Application form, recommendations or references. *Deadline:* February 15.

SWE PAST PRESIDENTS SCHOLARSHIP

$1500 scholarship for women pursuing ABET-accredited baccalaureate or graduate programs in preparation for careers in engineering, engineering technology, and computer science in the United States and Mexico. Must be a U.S. citizen.

Academic Fields/Career Goals: Chemical Engineering; Civil Engineering; Construction Engineering/Management; Electrical Engineering/Electronics; Energy and Power Engineering; Engineering/Technology; Marine/Ocean Engineering; Materials Science, Engineering, and Metallurgy; Mechanical Engineering; Paper and Pulp Engineering.

Award: Scholarship for use in sophomore, junior, senior, or graduate years; not renewable. *Number:* 2. *Amount:* $1750.

Eligibility Requirements: Applicant must be enrolled or expecting to enroll full-time at a four-year institution or university and female. Available to U.S. citizens.

Application Requirements: Application form, recommendations or references. *Deadline:* February 15.

SWE PHOENIX SECTION SCHOLARSHIP

$2500 scholarship for a woman pursuing an ABET-accredited baccalaureate program in preparation for a career in engineering, engineering technology, or computer science in the United States and Mexico. Must attend a school in Arizona. SWE membership required.

Academic Fields/Career Goals: Chemical Engineering; Civil Engineering; Construction Engineering/Management; Electrical Engineering/Electronics; Energy and Power Engineering; Engineering/Technology; Marine/Ocean Engineering; Materials Science, Engineering, and Metallurgy; Mechanical Engineering; Paper and Pulp Engineering.

Award: Scholarship for use in sophomore, junior, or senior years; not renewable. *Number:* 1. *Amount:* $2500.

Eligibility Requirements: Applicant must be enrolled or expecting to enroll full-time at a four-year institution or university; female and studying in Arizona. Applicant or parent of applicant must be member of Society of Women Engineers. Available to U.S. citizens.

Application Requirements: Application form, recommendations or references. *Deadline:* February 15.

SWE REGION H SCHOLARSHIPS

Two awards ranging from $1000 to $1500 for women pursuing ABET-accredited baccalaureate or graduate programs in preparation for careers in engineering, engineering technology, and computer science in the United States and Mexico. SWE membership required. Must attend a school within Region H boundaries, which includes ND, SD, MN, IA, WI, IL, MI, and IN. Level of involvement in SWE should be high, as well as the amount of time spent volunteering, level of commitment, and years of service.

Academic Fields/Career Goals: Chemical Engineering; Civil Engineering; Construction Engineering/Management; Electrical Engineering/Electronics; Energy and Power Engineering; Engineering/Technology; Marine/Ocean Engineering; Materials Science, Engineering, and Metallurgy; Mechanical Engineering; Paper and Pulp Engineering.

Award: Scholarship for use in sophomore, junior, or graduate years; not renewable. *Number:* 2. *Amount:* $1000–$1500.

Eligibility Requirements: Applicant must be enrolled or expecting to enroll full-time at a four-year institution or university; female and studying in Illinois, Indiana, Iowa, Michigan, Minnesota, North Dakota, South Dakota, Wisconsin. Applicant or parent of applicant must be member of Society of Women Engineers. Available to U.S. citizens.

Application Requirements: Application form, recommendations or references. *Deadline:* February 15.

WANDA MUNN SCHOLARSHIP

One $1500 award for a woman pursuing an ABET-accredited baccalaureate or graduate program in preparation for a career in engineering, engineering technology, or computer science in the United States and Mexico. The student must have been out of school and the engineering or technology workforce for a minimum of two years prior to beginning the current course of study. Home or school must be in Alaska, Idaho, Montana, Oregon, or Washington.

Academic Fields/Career Goals: Chemical Engineering; Civil Engineering; Construction Engineering/Management; Electrical Engineering/Electronics; Energy and Power Engineering; Engineering/Technology; Marine/Ocean Engineering; Materials Science, Engineering, and Metallurgy; Mechanical Engineering; Paper and Pulp Engineering.

Award: Scholarship for use in freshman, sophomore, junior, senior, or graduate years; not renewable. *Number:* 1. *Amount:* $1500.

Eligibility Requirements: Applicant must be enrolled or expecting to enroll full-time at a four-year institution or university and female. Available to U.S. citizens.

Application Requirements: Application form, recommendations or references. *Deadline:* February 15.

SOCIETY OF WOMEN ENGINEERS-ROCKY MOUNTAIN SECTION

http://www.societyofwomenengineers.org/RockyMountain/

SOCIETY OF WOMEN ENGINEERS-ROCKY MOUNTAIN SECTION SCHOLARSHIP PROGRAM

One-time award for graduating female high school seniors and female college students in Colorado and Wyoming (except zip codes 80800 and 81599). Eligibility: 1. Applicant must be a woman enrolled or planning to enroll as an undergraduate or graduate student in an ABET accredited engineering, computing, or engineering technology program (see http://www.abet.org/ for a list of eligible schools and majors). 2. Applicant must meet minimum GPA requirements. 3. Applicant must be able to accept the scholarship for the academic year starting in the Fall and must not already be receiving full funding from another source. For more information visit website http://www.societyofwomenengineers.org/RockyMountain/ and look for local scholarships.

Academic Fields/Career Goals: Chemical Engineering; Civil Engineering; Computer Science/Data Processing; Construction Engineering/Management; Electrical Engineering/Electronics; Energy and Power Engineering; Engineering-Related Technologies; Engineering/Technology; Marine/Ocean Engineering; Materials Science, Engineering, and Metallurgy; Mechanical Engineering.

Award: Scholarship for use in freshman, sophomore, junior, senior, or graduate years; not renewable. *Number:* 3–8. *Amount:* $500–$1500.

Eligibility Requirements: Applicant must be enrolled or expecting to enroll full-time at a four-year institution or university; female and resident of Colorado, Wyoming. Applicant must have 3.5 GPA or higher. Available to U.S. citizens.

Application Requirements: Application form, community service, essay, recommendations or references, resume, test scores, transcript. *Deadline:* February 1.

Contact: Christi Wisleder, Scholarship Chair
Society of Women Engineers-Rocky Mountain Section
PO Box 260692
Lakewood, CO 80226-0692
E-mail: christi.wisleder@gmail.com

SONS OF NORWAY FOUNDATION

http://www.sonsofnorway.com/

NANCY LORRAINE JENSEN MEMORIAL SCHOLARSHIP

Scholarship available for full-time undergraduate study in chemistry, physics or in chemical, electrical, or mechanical engineering by a female student who is a U.S. citizen, and a current member, daughter, or granddaughter of a current member of Sons of Norway. The annual award will be at least 50 percent of the tuition for one semester and no more than 100 percent of the tuition for one year. Must have attained a SAT score of at least 1800, a math score of 600 or better, or an ACT score of at least 26. Applicant must have completed at least one term of studies in the above fields. The award will be made jointly payable to the student and her institution. The award is renewable two times during undergraduate study.

Academic Fields/Career Goals: Chemical Engineering; Electrical Engineering/Electronics; Mechanical Engineering.

Award: Scholarship for use in sophomore, junior, or senior years; not renewable. *Number:* 1–6. *Amount:* $2500–$10,000.

Eligibility Requirements: Applicant must be of Norwegian heritage; age 17-35; enrolled or expecting to enroll full-time at a four-year institution or university; female and must have an interest in science. Applicant must have 3.5 GPA or higher. Available to U.S. citizens.

Application Requirements: Application form, essay, personal photograph, recommendations or references, test scores, transcript. *Deadline:* April 1.

STRAIGHTFORWARD MEDIA

http://www.straightforwardmedia.com/

STRAIGHTFORWARD MEDIA ENGINEERING SCHOLARSHIP

Scholarship of $500 to students attending or planning to enroll in a postsecondary engineering program in the United States or abroad. Scholarship is awarded four times per year. Deadlines: March 31, June 30, September 30, and December 31. For more information, see web http://www.straightforwardmedia.com/engineering/form.php.

Academic Fields/Career Goals: Chemical Engineering; Civil Engineering; Electrical Engineering/Electronics; Energy and Power Engineering; Engineering-Related Technologies; Engineering/Technology; Materials Science, Engineering, and Metallurgy; Mechanical Engineering; Paper and Pulp Engineering.

Award: Scholarship for use in freshman, sophomore, junior, or senior years; not renewable. *Number:* 4. *Amount:* $500.

Eligibility Requirements: Applicant must be enrolled or expecting to enroll full- or part-time at a two-year or four-year or technical institution or university. Available to U.S. and non-U.S. citizens.

Application Requirements: Essay. *Deadline:* varies.

UNITED NEGRO COLLEGE FUND

http://www.uncf.org/

CDM SCHOLARSHIP/INTERNSHIP

$6000 scholarship and summer internship program for up to six students who are majoring in a variety of engineering, science, or construction disciplines. These disciplines include chemical, civil, electrical, environmental, geotechnical, water resources, mechanical and structural engineering, as well as environmental systems, environmental science, geology, hydrogeology, geography and computer science. Must be currently enrolled in an undergraduate academic program or enrolled to pursue a master's degree. Must have a 3.0 GPA or above and be available for a summer internship.

Academic Fields/Career Goals: Chemical Engineering; Civil Engineering; Computer Science/Data Processing; Electrical Engineering/ Electronics; Engineering/Technology; Environmental Science; Geography; Marine/Ocean Engineering; Mechanical Engineering.

Award: Scholarship for use in sophomore, junior, senior, or graduate years; not renewable. *Number:* up to 6. *Amount:* $6000.

Eligibility Requirements: Applicant must be Black (non-Hispanic) and enrolled or expecting to enroll full-time at an institution or university. Applicant must have 3.0 GPA or higher. Available to U.S. citizens.

Application Requirements: Application form. *Deadline:* continuous.

EMERSON PROCESS MANAGEMENT SCHOLARSHIP

Awards of up to $6975 for undergraduate students at UNCF member colleges and universities studying selective engineering fields. Minimum 2.5 GPA required. For additional information, go to website at http://www.uncf.org.

Academic Fields/Career Goals: Chemical Engineering; Civil Engineering; Electrical Engineering/Electronics; Engineering/ Technology; Mechanical Engineering.

Award: Scholarship for use in freshman, sophomore, junior, or senior years; not renewable. *Amount:* up to $6975.

Eligibility Requirements: Applicant must be Black (non-Hispanic) and enrolled or expecting to enroll full- or part-time at a four-year institution. Applicant must have 2.5 GPA or higher. Available to U.S. citizens.

Application Requirements: Application form. *Deadline:* continuous.

INTEL SCHOLARS PROGRAM

Up to $5000 awards to assist sophomores and juniors majoring in various engineering programs attending UNCF institutions and selected universities. The additional participating schools are Florida A & M University, Howard University, North Carolina A&T State University, North Carolina State University, Georgia Institute of Technology and Tennessee State University. Minimum 3.0 GPA required.

Academic Fields/Career Goals: Chemical Engineering; Computer Science/Data Processing; Electrical Engineering/Electronics; Mechanical Engineering.

Award: Scholarship for use in sophomore or junior years; not renewable. *Amount:* up to $5000.

Eligibility Requirements: Applicant must be Black (non-Hispanic) and enrolled or expecting to enroll full-time at a four-year institution or university. Applicant must have 3.0 GPA or higher. Available to U.S. citizens.

Application Requirements: Application form. *Deadline:* continuous.

MONSANTO/UNCF 1890'S SCHOLARSHIP PROGRAM

• See page 89

SPRINT SCHOLARS PROGRAM FOR SOPHOMORES, JUNIORS, AND SENIORS

• See page 100

UNCF/MERCK SCIENCE INITIATIVE

• See page 149

UNIVERSITIES SPACE RESEARCH ASSOCIATION

http://www.usra.edu/

UNIVERSITIES SPACE RESEARCH ASSOCIATION SCHOLARSHIP PROGRAM

• See page 107

UTAH SOCIETY OF PROFESSIONAL ENGINEERS

http://www.uspeonline.com/

UTAH SOCIETY OF PROFESSIONAL ENGINEERS JOE RHOADS SCHOLARSHIP

One-time award for entering freshman pursuing studies in the field of engineering (civil, chemical, electrical, or engineering related

technologies.) Minimum 3.5 GPA required. Must be a U.S. citizen and Utah resident attending school in Utah.

Academic Fields/Career Goals: Chemical Engineering; Civil Engineering; Construction Engineering/Management; Electrical Engineering/Electronics; Energy and Power Engineering; Engineering/ Technology; Marine/Ocean Engineering; Mechanical Engineering.

Award: Scholarship for use in freshman year; not renewable. *Number:* 1. *Amount:* $1000.

Eligibility Requirements: Applicant must be high school student; planning to enroll or expecting to enroll full-time at a four-year institution or university; resident of Utah and studying in Utah. Applicant must have 3.5 GPA or higher. Available to U.S. citizens.

Application Requirements: Application form, essay, recommendations or references, resume, test scores, transcript. *Deadline:* March 23.

Contact: Dan Church, Joe Rhoads Scholarship Chair
Utah Society of Professional Engineers
488 East Winchester Street, Suite 400
Murray, UT 84107
E-mail: churchd@pbworld.com

XEROX

http://www.xerox.com//

TECHNICAL MINORITY SCHOLARSHIP

Scholarships are made available to minority students enrolled in technical degree programs at the bachelor's degree level or above. Eligible students must have a GPA of 3.0 or higher and show financial need. Refer to website, http://www.studentcareers-xerox-com.tmpqa.com/, for details.

Academic Fields/Career Goals: Chemical Engineering; Computer Science/Data Processing; Electrical Engineering/Electronics; Engineering-Related Technologies; Engineering/Technology; Materials Science, Engineering, and Metallurgy; Mechanical Engineering; Physical Sciences.

Award: Scholarship for use in freshman, sophomore, junior, senior, graduate, or postgraduate years; not renewable. *Number:* up to 122. *Amount:* $1000–$10,000.

Eligibility Requirements: Applicant must be American Indian/Alaska Native, Asian/Pacific Islander, Black (non-Hispanic), Hispanic and enrolled or expecting to enroll full-time at a four-year institution or university. Applicant must have 3.0 GPA or higher. Available to U.S. citizens.

Application Requirements: Application form, financial need analysis, resume. *Deadline:* September 30.

CHILD AND FAMILY STUDIES

CALIFORNIA STUDENT AID COMMISSION

http://www.csac.ca.gov/

CHILD DEVELOPMENT TEACHER AND SUPERVISOR GRANT PROGRAM

Award is for those students pursuing an approved course of study leading to a Child Development Permit issued by the California Commission on Teacher Credentialing. In exchange for each year funding is received, recipients agree to provide one year of service in a licensed childcare center.

Academic Fields/Career Goals: Child and Family Studies; Education.

Award: Grant for use in freshman, sophomore, junior, senior, or graduate years; renewable. *Number:* up to 300. *Amount:* $1000–$2000.

Eligibility Requirements: Applicant must be enrolled or expecting to enroll full- or part-time at a two-year or four-year institution or university; resident of California and studying in California. Applicant or parent of applicant must have employment or volunteer experience in teaching/education. Available to U.S. citizens.

Application Requirements: Application form, financial need analysis, GPA verification, recommendations or references. *Deadline:* April 16.

Contact: Catalina Mistler, Chief, Program Administration and Services Division
California Student Aid Commission
PO Box 419026
Rancho Cordova, CA 95741-9026
Phone: 916-526-7268
Fax: 916-526-8002
E-mail: studentsupport@csac.ca.gov

CLAN MACBEAN FOUNDATION

http://www.clanmacbean.net/

CLAN MACBEAN FOUNDATION GRANT PROGRAM
• See page 114

COLLEGEBOUND FOUNDATION

http://www.collegeboundfoundation.org/

JEANETTE R. WOLMAN SCHOLARSHIP

Renewable scholarship of $500 available for students specializing in pre-law, social work, or a field that focuses on child advocacy. Minimum cumulative GPA of 3.0 required.

Academic Fields/Career Goals: Child and Family Studies; Law/Legal Services; Social Services.

Award: Scholarship for use in freshman, sophomore, junior, or senior years; renewable. *Number:* 1. *Amount:* $500.

Eligibility Requirements: Applicant must be high school student; planning to enroll or expecting to enroll full-time at a two-year or four-year institution or university and resident of Maryland. Applicant must have 3.0 GPA or higher. Available to U.S. citizens.

Application Requirements: Application form, application form may be submitted online (http://www.scholarships.mycbf.net/STARS), financial need analysis, recommendations or references, resume, transcript. *Deadline:* March 1.

Contact: Michael Thornton, Associate Program Director, Scholarship Programs
Phone: 410-783-2905 Ext. 207
Fax: 410-727-5786
E-mail: mthornton@collegeboundfoundation.org

KE ALI'I PAUAHI FOUNDATION

http://www.pauahi.org/

MYRON & LAURA THOMPSON SCHOLARSHIP

Scholarships for students pursuing a degree in the field of early childhood education. Preference will be given to students who demonstrate an interest in working with Hawaiian children in Hawaii after completion of their education. Applicants must demonstrate financial need. Submit two letters of recommendation from teachers, counselors or community organization.

Academic Fields/Career Goals: Child and Family Studies; Education.

Award: Scholarship for use in freshman, sophomore, junior, senior, or graduate years; not renewable. *Number:* 2. *Amount:* $1300.

Eligibility Requirements: Applicant must be enrolled or expecting to enroll full-time at a four-year institution or university. Available to U.S. citizens.

Application Requirements: Application form, financial need analysis, recommendations or references, Student Aid Report (SAR), college acceptance letter, transcript. *Deadline:* April 1.

Contact: Mavis Shiraishi-Nagao, Scholarship Administrator
Phone: 808-534-3966
E-mail: scholarships@pauahi.org

KENTUCKY HIGHER EDUCATION ASSISTANCE AUTHORITY (KHEAA)

http://www.kheaa.com/

EARLY CHILDHOOD DEVELOPMENT SCHOLARSHIP

Awards scholarship with conditional service commitment for part-time students currently employed by participating ECD facility or providing training in ECD for an approved organization. For more information, visit website at http://www.kheaa.com.

Academic Fields/Career Goals: Child and Family Studies; Education.

Award: Scholarship for use in freshman, sophomore, junior, or senior years; not renewable. *Number:* 800–1200. *Amount:* up to $1800.

Eligibility Requirements: Applicant must be enrolled or expecting to enroll part-time at a two-year or four-year institution or university; resident of Kentucky and studying in Kentucky. Available to U.S. citizens.

Application Requirements: Application form, application form may be submitted online (http://www.kheaa.com), FAFSA, financial need analysis. *Deadline:* continuous.

Contact: David Lawhorn, Program Coordinator
Kentucky Higher Education Assistance Authority (KHEAA)
PO Box 798
Frankfort, KY 40602-0798
Phone: 800-928-8926 Ext. 67383
Fax: 502-696-7373
E-mail: dlawhorn@kheaa.com

OHIO CHILD CARE RESOURCE & REFERRAL ASSOCIATION

http://www.occrra.org/

T.E.A.C.H. EARLY CHILDHOOD OHIO SCHOLARSHIPS

Award for early childhood professionals working in Ohio. AAS Scholarships available. Must earn under $15/hr and work 30 hours per week with children in licensed child care or preschool.

Academic Fields/Career Goals: Child and Family Studies; Education.

Award: Scholarship for use in freshman, sophomore, junior, or senior years; renewable.

Eligibility Requirements: Applicant must be enrolled or expecting to enroll full- or part-time at a two-year or four-year institution; resident of Ohio and studying in Ohio. Available to U.S. citizens.

Application Requirements: Application form.

Contact: Greg Yorker, Director
E-mail: teach@occrra.org

SOCIETY OF PEDIATRIC NURSES

http://www.pedsnurses.org/

SOCIETY OF PEDIATRIC NURSES EDUCATIONAL SCHOLARSHIP

Award to a member engaged in a BSN completion program or a graduate program that will advance the health of children. Nominee must be a current Society of Pediatric Nurses member.

Academic Fields/Career Goals: Child and Family Studies; Health and Medical Sciences; Nursing.

Award: Scholarship for use in freshman, sophomore, junior, senior, or graduate years; not renewable. *Number:* 1. *Amount:* $500.

Eligibility Requirements: Applicant must be enrolled or expecting to enroll full-time at a four-year institution or university. Applicant or parent of applicant must be member of Society of Pediatric Nurses. Applicant or parent of applicant must have employment or volunteer experience in nursing. Available to U.S. citizens.

Application Requirements: Application form, essay, recommendations or references, resume. *Deadline:* November 14.

Y'S MEN INTERNATIONAL

http://www.ysmenusa.com/

ALEXANDER SCHOLARSHIP LOAN FUND
• See page 161

ZETA PHI BETA SORORITY INC. NATIONAL EDUCATIONAL FOUNDATION

http://www.zpbnef1975.org/

LULLELIA W. HARRISON SCHOLARSHIP IN COUNSELING

Scholarships available for female students enrolled in a graduate or undergraduate degree program in counseling. Awarded for full-time study for one academic year. See website for additional information and application, http://www.zpbnef1975.org/.

Academic Fields/Career Goals: Child and Family Studies; Psychology; Social Sciences; Social Services.

Award: Scholarship for use in freshman, sophomore, junior, senior, or graduate years; not renewable. *Number:* 1. *Amount:* $500–$1000.

Eligibility Requirements: Applicant must be enrolled or expecting to enroll full-time at a four-year institution or university. Applicant or parent of applicant must be member of Zeta Phi Beta. Available to U.S. citizens.

Application Requirements: Application form, essay, proof of enrollment, recommendations or references, transcript. *Deadline:* February 1.

Contact: Cheryl Williams, National Second Vice President
Fax: 318-232-4593
E-mail: 2ndanti@zphib1920.org

CIVIL ENGINEERING

AACE INTERNATIONAL

http://www.aacei.org/

AACE INTERNATIONAL COMPETITIVE SCHOLARSHIP
• See page 108

AIST FOUNDATION

http://www.aistfoundation.org/

ASSOCIATION FOR IRON AND STEEL TECHNOLOGY DAVID H. SAMSON CANADIAN SCHOLARSHIP
• See page 162

AMERICAN COUNCIL OF ENGINEERING COMPANIES OF PENNSYLVANIA (ACEC/PA)

http://www.acecpa.org/

ENGINEERING SCHOLARSHIP
• See page 163

AMERICAN GROUND WATER TRUST

http://www.agwt.org/

AMERICAN GROUND WATER TRUST-THOMAS STETSON SCHOLARSHIP

For students entering their freshman year in a full-time program of study at a four-year accredited university or college located west of the Mississippi River and intending to pursue a career in ground water-related field. Must be U.S. citizen or legal resident with 3.0 GPA or higher. For more information see website http://www.agwt.org.

Academic Fields/Career Goals: Civil Engineering; Hydrology; Natural Resources.

Award: Scholarship for use in freshman year; not renewable. *Number:* 1. *Amount:* up to $1500.

Eligibility Requirements: Applicant must be enrolled or expecting to enroll full-time at a four-year institution or university. Applicant must have 3.0 GPA or higher. Available to U.S. citizens.

Application Requirements: Application form, essay, recommendations or references, transcript. *Deadline:* June 1.

Contact: Garret Graaskamp, Ground Water Specialist
American Ground Water Trust
50 Pleasant Street, Suite 2
Concord, NH 03301-4073
Phone: 603-228-5444
Fax: 603-228-6557
E-mail: trustinfo@agwt.org

AMERICAN PUBLIC TRANSPORTATION FOUNDATION

http://www.apta.com/

TRANSIT HALL OF FAME SCHOLARSHIP AWARD PROGRAM

Renewable award for sophomores, juniors, seniors or graduate students studying transportation or rail transit engineering. Must be sponsored by APTA member organization and complete an internship program with a member organization. Must have a minimum 3.0 GPA and be a U.S. or Canadian citizen.

Academic Fields/Career Goals: Civil Engineering; Electrical Engineering/Electronics; Engineering-Related Technologies; Engineering/Technology; Mechanical Engineering; Transportation.

Award: Scholarship for use in sophomore, junior, senior, or graduate years; renewable. *Number:* 1. *Amount:* $2500.

Eligibility Requirements: Applicant must be enrolled or expecting to enroll full-time at a two-year or four-year institution or university. Applicant must have 3.0 GPA or higher. Available to U.S. and Canadian citizens.

Application Requirements: Application form, essay, financial need analysis, nomination by APTA member, verification of enrollment, copy of fee schedule from the college/university for the academic year, recommendations or references, transcript. *Deadline:* June 16.

Contact: Pamela Boswell, Vice President of Program Management
American Public Transportation Foundation
1666 K Street, NW
Washington, DC 20006-1215
Phone: 202-496-4803
Fax: 202-496-4323

AMERICAN RAILWAY ENGINEERING AND MAINTENANCE OF WAY ASSOCIATION

http://www.aremafoundation.org/

AREMA MICHAEL R. GARCIA SCHOLARSHIP

Award for students enrolled in a four- or five-year program leading to a bachelor's degree in engineering or engineering technology. This scholarship is for students who are married and/or are supporting a family while enrolled as a student.

Academic Fields/Career Goals: Civil Engineering; Construction Engineering/Management; Electrical Engineering/Electronics; Engineering-Related Technologies; Engineering/Technology.

Award: Scholarship for use in freshman, sophomore, junior, or senior years; not renewable. *Number:* 1. *Amount:* $2000.

Eligibility Requirements: Applicant must be enrolled or expecting to enroll full-time at a four-year institution or university and married. Available to U.S. citizens.

Application Requirements: Application form, cover letter, recommendations or references, resume, transcript. *Deadline:* March 8.

Contact: Stacy Spaulding, Director of Committees and Technical Services
Phone: 301-459-3200 Ext. 706
E-mail: sspaulding@arema.org

AREMA PRESIDENTIAL SPOUSE SCHOLARSHIP

Scholarship is awarded to an enrolled female student who has completed at least one quarter or semester in an accredited four- or five-year engineering or engineering technology undergraduate degree program.

Academic Fields/Career Goals: Civil Engineering; Construction Engineering/Management; Electrical Engineering/Electronics; Engineering-Related Technologies; Engineering/Technology.

Award: Scholarship for use in freshman, sophomore, junior, or senior years; not renewable. *Amount:* $1000.

Eligibility Requirements: Applicant must be enrolled or expecting to enroll full-time at a four-year institution or university and female. Available to U.S. citizens.

Application Requirements: Application form, cover letter, recommendations or references, transcript. *Deadline:* March 8.

Contact: Stacy Spaulding, Director of Committees and Technical
Services
Phone: 301-459-3200 Ext. 706
E-mail: sspaulding@arema.org

AREMA UNDERGRADUATE SCHOLARSHIPS

Scholarships are awarded to engineering students who have a potential interest in railway engineering careers. Minimum 2.0 GPA required.

Academic Fields/Career Goals: Civil Engineering; Construction Engineering/Management; Electrical Engineering/Electronics; Engineering-Related Technologies; Engineering/Technology.

Award: Scholarship for use in freshman, sophomore, junior, or senior years; not renewable. *Amount:* $1000.

Eligibility Requirements: Applicant must be enrolled or expecting to enroll full-time at a four-year institution or university. Available to U.S. and Canadian citizens.

Application Requirements: Application form, cover letter, recommendations or references, resume, transcript. *Deadline:* March 8.

Contact: Stacy Spaulding, Director of Committees and Technical
Services
Phone: 301-459-3200 Ext. 706
E-mail: sspaulding@arema.org

AMERICAN SOCIETY OF CIVIL ENGINEERS

http://www.asce.org/

EUGENE C. FIGG JR. CIVIL ENGINEERING SCHOLARSHIP

Applicant must be currently enrolled junior or senior civil engineering student in an ABET-accredited program and an ASCE National Student Member in good standing.

Academic Fields/Career Goals: Civil Engineering.

Award: Scholarship for use in junior or senior years; not renewable. *Number:* 1. *Amount:* $3000.

Eligibility Requirements: Applicant must be enrolled or expecting to enroll full- or part-time at a four-year institution or university. Applicant or parent of applicant must be member of American Society of Civil Engineers. Available to U.S. citizens.

Application Requirements: Application form, financial need analysis, personal statement, recommendations or references, resume, transcript. *Deadline:* February 9.

Contact: Ping Wei, Director, Educational Activities
American Society of Civil Engineers
1801 Alexander Bell Drive
Reston, VA 20191
Phone: 703-295-6300
Fax: 703-295-6132

SAMUEL FLETCHER TAPMAN ASCE STUDENT CHAPTER SCHOLARSHIP

Awards available to currently enrolled undergraduates. Must be a member of local ASCE Student Chapter and an ASCE National Student Member in good standing. Selection is based on the applicant's justification of award, educational plan, academic performance and standing, potential for development, leadership capacity, ASCE activities, and financial need.

Academic Fields/Career Goals: Civil Engineering; Construction Engineering/Management.

Award: Scholarship for use in sophomore, junior, or senior years; not renewable. *Number:* up to 12. *Amount:* up to $2000.

Eligibility Requirements: Applicant must be enrolled or expecting to enroll full- or part-time at a four-year institution or university. Applicant or parent of applicant must be member of American Society of Civil Engineers. Available to U.S. and non-U.S. citizens.

Application Requirements: Annual budget, application form, essay, financial need analysis, recommendations or references, resume, transcript. *Deadline:* February 9.

Contact: Ping Wei, Director, Educational Activities
American Society of Civil Engineers
1801 Alexander Bell Drive
Reston, VA 20191
Phone: 703-295-6300
Fax: 703-295-6132

Y.C. YANG CIVIL ENGINEERING SCHOLARSHIP

Applicants must be student members in good standing of the Society. Currently enrolled junior or senior civil engineering students at an institution with an ABET-accredited program and an interest in structural engineering may apply.

Academic Fields/Career Goals: Civil Engineering.

Award: Scholarship for use in junior or senior years; not renewable. *Number:* up to 2. *Amount:* $2000–$2500.

Eligibility Requirements: Applicant must be enrolled or expecting to enroll full- or part-time at a four-year institution or university. Available to U.S. and non-U.S. citizens.

Application Requirements: Application form, financial need analysis, personal statement, recommendations or references, resume, test scores, transcript. *Deadline:* February 9.

Contact: Ping Wei, Director, Educational Activities
American Society of Civil Engineers
1801 Alexander Bell Drive
Reston, VA 20191
Phone: 703-295-6300
Fax: 703-295-6132

AMERICAN SOCIETY OF CIVIL ENGINEERS-MAINE SECTION

http://www.maineasce.org/

AMERICAN SOCIETY OF CIVIL ENGINEERS-MAINE HIGH SCHOOL SCHOLARSHIP

One-time award available to high school student in senior year, pursuing a course of study in civil engineering. Must be enrolled in a four year ABET accredited Civil Engineering program at the time of award. Must be a resident of Maine. Essay, references and transcript required with application.

Academic Fields/Career Goals: Civil Engineering.

Award: Scholarship for use in freshman year; not renewable. *Number:* 2. *Amount:* $2000.

Eligibility Requirements: Applicant must be high school student; planning to enroll or expecting to enroll full-time at a four-year institution or university and resident of Maine. Available to U.S. citizens.

Application Requirements: Application form, essay, recommendations or references, transcript. *Deadline:* January 31.

Contact: Ms. Leslie Corrow, Senior Engineer P.E.
American Society of Civil Engineers-Maine Section
141 Main Street, PO Box 650
Pittsfield, ME 04967
Phone: 207-487-3328 Ext. 243
Fax: 207-487-3124
E-mail: leslie.corrow@kleinschmidtusa.com

AMERICAN SOCIETY OF NAVAL ENGINEERS

http://www.navalengineers.org/

AMERICAN SOCIETY OF NAVAL ENGINEERS SCHOLARSHIP

• *See page 103*

AMERICAN WELDING SOCIETY

http://www.aws.org/

ARSHAM AMIRIKIAN ENGINEERING SCHOLARSHIP

Awarded to an undergraduate pursuing a minimum four-year degree in civil engineering or welding-related program at an accredited university. Applicant must be a minimum of 18 years of age, have a minimum 3.0 GPA and be a citizen of the United States.

Academic Fields/Career Goals: Civil Engineering; Materials Science, Engineering, and Metallurgy; Trade/Technical Specialties.

Award: Scholarship for use in freshman, sophomore, junior, or senior years; not renewable. *Number:* 1. *Amount:* $2500.

Eligibility Requirements: Applicant must be enrolled or expecting to enroll full- or part-time at a four-year institution or university. Applicant must have 3.0 GPA or higher. Available to U.S. citizens.

Application Requirements: Application form, financial need analysis, recommendations or references, transcript. *Deadline:* February 15.

Contact: Vicki Pinsky, Manager, Foundation
American Welding Society
8669 Doral Boulevard, Suite 130
Doral, FL 33166
Phone: 800-443-9353 Ext. 212
Fax: 305-443-7559
E-mail: vpinsky@aws.org

MATSUO BRIDGE COMPANY LTD. OF JAPAN SCHOLARSHIP

Awarded to a college junior or senior, or graduate student pursuing a minimum four-year degree in civil engineering, welding engineering, welding engineering technology, or related discipline. Applicant must have a minimum 3.0 overall GPA. Financial need is not required to apply. Must be U.S. citizen.

Academic Fields/Career Goals: Civil Engineering; Engineering-Related Technologies; Engineering/Technology; Materials Science, Engineering, and Metallurgy.

Award: Scholarship for use in junior or senior years; not renewable. *Number:* 1. *Amount:* $2500.

Eligibility Requirements: Applicant must be enrolled or expecting to enroll full- or part-time at a two-year or four-year institution or university. Applicant must have 3.0 GPA or higher. Available to U.S. citizens.

Application Requirements: Application form, financial need analysis, recommendations or references, transcript. *Deadline:* January 15.

Contact: Vicki Pinsky, Manager, Foundation
American Welding Society
8669 Doral Boulevard, Suite 130
Doral, FL 33166
Phone: 800-443-9353 Ext. 212
Fax: 305-443-7559
E-mail: vpinsky@aws.org

ARRL FOUNDATION INC.

http://www.arrl.org/

ALFRED E. FRIEND JR., W4CF, MEMORIAL SCHOLARSHIP

• *See page 166*

GARY WAGNER, K3OMI, SCHOLARSHIP

• *See page 166*

ASSOCIATED GENERAL CONTRACTORS EDUCATION AND RESEARCH FOUNDATION

http://www.agcfoundation.org/

AGC EDUCATION AND RESEARCH FOUNDATION UNDERGRADUATE SCHOLARSHIPS

College sophomores and juniors enrolled or planning to enroll in a full-time, four or five-year ABET or ACCE-accredited construction management or construction-related engineering program are eligible to apply. High school seniors and college freshmen are not eligible.

Academic Fields/Career Goals: Civil Engineering; Construction Engineering/Management; Engineering/Technology.

Award: Scholarship for use in sophomore, junior, or senior years; renewable. *Number:* 100. *Amount:* $2500–$7500.

Eligibility Requirements: Applicant must be enrolled or expecting to enroll full-time at a four-year institution or university. Available to U.S. citizens.

Application Requirements: Application form, essay, financial need analysis, recommendations or references, transcript. *Deadline:* November 1.

Contact: Floretta Slade, Director of Programs
Associated General Contractors Education and Research Foundation
2300 Wilson Boulevard, Suite 400
Arlington, VA 22201
Phone: 703-837-5342
Fax: 703-837-5451
E-mail: sladef@agc.org

ASSOCIATED GENERAL CONTRACTORS OF NEW YORK STATE, LLC

http://www.agcnys.org/

ASSOCIATED GENERAL CONTRACTORS NYS SCHOLARSHIP PROGRAM

One-time scholarship for students enrolled full-time study in civil engineering, construction management and construction technology and diesel technology. Must have minimum GPA of 2.5. Scholarship value is from $1500 to $5000. Must be resident of New York.

Academic Fields/Career Goals: Civil Engineering; Construction Engineering/Management; Surveying, Surveying Technology, Cartography, or Geographic Information Science; Trade/Technical Specialties; Transportation.

Award: Scholarship for use in sophomore, junior, senior, or graduate years; not renewable. *Number:* 15–25. *Amount:* $1500–$5000.

Eligibility Requirements: Applicant must be enrolled or expecting to enroll full-time at a two-year or four-year or technical institution or university and resident of New York. Applicant must have 2.5 GPA or higher. Available to U.S. citizens.

Application Requirements: Application form, financial need analysis, recommendations or references, transcript. *Deadline:* May 15.

Contact: Brendan Manning, Education and Environmental Director
Phone: 518-456-1134
E-mail: bmanning@agcnys.org

ASSOCIATION OF CALIFORNIA WATER AGENCIES

http://www.acwa.com/

ASSOCIATION OF CALIFORNIA WATER AGENCIES SCHOLARSHIPS

• *See page 103*

CLAIR A. HILL SCHOLARSHIP

• *See page 103*

BARRY M. GOLDWATER SCHOLARSHIP AND EXCELLENCE IN EDUCATION FOUNDATION

http://www.act.org/goldwater

BARRY M. GOLDWATER SCHOLARSHIP AND EXCELLENCE IN EDUCATION PROGRAM
• See page 104

BRASKEM ODEBRECHT

http://www.odebrechtaward.com

ODEBRECHT AWARD FOR SUSTAINABLE DEVELOPMENT
• See page 110

THE DALLAS FOUNDATION

http://www.dallasfoundation.org/

JERE W. THOMPSON, JR, SCHOLARSHIP FUND
Renewable scholarships awarded to full-time undergraduate juniors or seniors with disadvantaged backgrounds, who are pursuing a degree in civil engineering and closely related disciplines at Texas colleges and universities. Up to $2000 awarded each semester, beginning with junior year. Must maintain 2.5 GPA. Special consideration given to students from Collin, Dallas, Denton, and Tarrant Counties, Texas.

Academic Fields/Career Goals: Civil Engineering.

Award: Scholarship for use in junior or senior years; renewable. *Number:* 1–2. *Amount:* up to $4000.

Eligibility Requirements: Applicant must be enrolled or expecting to enroll full-time at a four-year institution or university; resident of Texas and studying in Texas. Available to U.S. citizens.

Application Requirements: Application form, essay, financial need analysis, recommendations or references, test scores, transcript. *Deadline:* April 1.

Contact: Rachel Lasseter, Program Associate
The Dallas Foundation
900 Jackson Street, Suite 705
Dallas, TX 75202
Phone: 214-741-9898
Fax: 214-741-9848
E-mail: scholarships@dallasfoundation.org

WHITLEY PLACE SCHOLARSHIP
• See page 110

DAVID EVANS AND ASSOCIATES, INC.

http://www.deainc.com/

DAVID EVANS AND ASSOCIATES, INC. SCHOLARSHIP
The goal of the DEA scholarship is to assist the recipients in pursuing a bachelor's degree in Civil Engineering or Geomatics. Two scholarships of $3000 each will be awarded to students attending college in one of the states in which DEA has local offices: AZ, CA, CO, ID, NY, OR, or WA.

Academic Fields/Career Goals: Civil Engineering; Surveying, Surveying Technology, Cartography, or Geographic Information Science.

Award: Scholarship for use in freshman, sophomore, junior, or senior years; not renewable. *Number:* 2. *Amount:* $3000.

Eligibility Requirements: Applicant must be enrolled or expecting to enroll full-time at a four-year institution and studying in Arizona, California, Colorado, Idaho, New York, Oregon, Washington. Applicant must have 3.0 GPA or higher. Available to U.S. and non-U.S. citizens.

Application Requirements: Application form, essay, resume, transcript. *Deadline:* April 30.

Contact: Kim Holcombe, HR Specialist
Phone: 503-499-0414
E-mail: kxho@deainc.com

FLORIDA ENGINEERING SOCIETY

http://www.fleng.org/scholarships.cfm

DAVID F. LUDOVICI SCHOLARSHIP
One-time scholarship of $1000 given to students in their junior or senior year in any Florida university engineering program, with at least 3.0 GPA. Applicants must be interested in civil, structural, or consulting engineering.

Academic Fields/Career Goals: Civil Engineering; Construction Engineering/Management; Engineering/Technology.

Award: Scholarship for use in junior or senior years; not renewable. *Number:* 1. *Amount:* $1000.

Eligibility Requirements: Applicant must be enrolled or expecting to enroll full-time at an institution or university; resident of Florida and studying in Florida. Applicant must have 3.0 GPA or higher. Available to U.S. citizens.

Application Requirements: Application form, recommendations or references, self-addressed stamped envelope with application, transcript. *Deadline:* February 1.

Contact: Abby Andersen, Scholarship Committee Staff Liaison
Phone: 850-224-7121
E-mail: aandersen@fleng.org

FECON SCHOLARSHIP
One-time scholarship of $1000 given to Florida citizens in their junior or senior year, who are enrolled or accepted into a Florida university engineering program. Minimum 3.0 GPA required. Applicant must be interested in pursuing a career in the field of construction.

Academic Fields/Career Goals: Civil Engineering; Construction Engineering/Management.

Award: Scholarship for use in junior or senior years; not renewable. *Number:* 1. *Amount:* $1000.

Eligibility Requirements: Applicant must be enrolled or expecting to enroll full-time at an institution or university; resident of Florida and studying in Florida. Applicant must have 3.0 GPA or higher. Available to U.S. citizens.

Application Requirements: Application form, essay, recommendations or references, self-addressed stamped envelope with application, transcript. *Deadline:* February 15.

Contact: Kelly Harris-Jones, Scholarship Committee Staff Liaison
Florida Engineering Society
125 South Gadsden Street
Tallahassee, FL 32301
Phone: 850-224-7121
Fax: 850-222-4349
E-mail: kelly@fleng.org

FOUNDATION FOR SCIENCE AND DISABILITY

http://stemd.org/

GRANTS FOR DISABLED STUDENTS IN THE SCIENCES
• See page 105

GREAT MINDS IN STEM

http://www.greatmindsinstem.org

HISPANIC ENGINEER NATIONAL ACHIEVEMENT AWARDS CORPORATION SCHOLARSHIP PROGRAM
• See page 130

HAWAIIAN LODGE, F&AM

http://www.hawaiianlodgefreemasons.org/

HAWAIIAN LODGE SCHOLARSHIPS
• See page 114

INDEPENDENT LABORATORIES INSTITUTE SCHOLARSHIP ALLIANCE

http://www.acil.org/

INDEPENDENT LABORATORIES INSTITUTE SCHOLARSHIP ALLIANCE
• *See page 145*

JORGE MAS CANOSA FREEDOM FOUNDATION

http://www.jorgemascanosa.org/

MAS FAMILY SCHOLARSHIP AWARD
• *See page 156*

KENTUCKY ENERGY AND ENVIRONMENT CABINET

http://www.eec.ky.gov/

ENVIRONMENTAL PROTECTION SCHOLARSHIP
• *See page 145*

KENTUCKY TRANSPORTATION CABINET

http://transportation.ky.gov/Education/Pages/
Scholarships.aspx

KENTUCKY TRANSPORTATION CABINET CIVIL ENGINEERING SCHOLARSHIP PROGRAM

Scholarships awarded to qualified Kentucky residents who wish to study civil engineering at University of Kentucky, Western Kentucky University, University of Louisville or Kentucky State University. Applicant should be a graduate of an accredited Kentucky high school or a Kentucky resident. Scholarship recipients are given opportunities to work for the Cabinet during summers and job opportunities upon graduation within the state of KY.

Academic Fields/Career Goals: Civil Engineering.

Award: Scholarship for use in freshman, sophomore, junior, or senior years; renewable. *Number:* 15–25. *Amount:* $10,600–$44,000.

Eligibility Requirements: Applicant must be enrolled or expecting to enroll full-time at a four-year institution or university; resident of Kentucky and studying in Kentucky. Applicant must have 3.0 GPA or higher. Available to U.S. and non-U.S. citizens.

Application Requirements: Application form, essay, interview, recommendations or references, test scores, transcript. *Deadline:* March 1.

Contact: Cherie Mertz, Scholarship Program Coordinator
    Kentucky Transportation Cabinet
    200 Mero Street, 6th Floor West
    Frankfort, KY 40622
    E-mail: Cherie.Mertz@ky.gov

LOS ANGELES COUNCIL OF BLACK PROFESSIONAL ENGINEERS

http://www.lablackengineers.org/

AL-BEN SCHOLARSHIP FOR ACADEMIC INCENTIVE
• *See page 168*

AL-BEN SCHOLARSHIP FOR PROFESSIONAL MERIT
• *See page 168*

AL-BEN SCHOLARSHIP FOR SCHOLASTIC ACHIEVEMENT
• *See page 168*

MICHIGAN SOCIETY OF PROFESSIONAL ENGINEERS

http://www.michiganspe.org/

MICHIGAN SOCIETY OF PROFESSIONAL ENGINEERS HARRY R. BALL, P.E. GRANT
• *See page 169*

MICHIGAN SOCIETY OF PROFESSIONAL ENGINEERS KENNETH B. FISHBECK, P.E. MEMORIAL GRANT
• *See page 169*

MIDWEST ROOFING CONTRACTORS ASSOCIATION

http://www.mrca.org/

MRCA FOUNDATION SCHOLARSHIP PROGRAM
• *See page 112*

NASA IDAHO SPACE GRANT CONSORTIUM

http://www.id.spacegrant.org/

NASA IDAHO SPACE GRANT CONSORTIUM SCHOLARSHIP PROGRAM
• *See page 146*

NASA MONTANA SPACE GRANT CONSORTIUM

http://www.spacegrant.montana.edu/

MONTANA SPACE GRANT SCHOLARSHIP PROGRAM
• *See page 133*

NATIONAL ASPHALT PAVEMENT ASSOCIATION RESEARCH AND EDUCATION FOUNDATION

http://www.asphaltpavement.org

NATIONAL ASPHALT PAVEMENT ASSOCIATION RESEARCH AND EDUCATION FOUNDATION SCHOLARSHIP PROGRAM

Our Scholarship program provides funding for undergraduate and graduate students who are U.S. citizens enrolled in a full time civil engineering, construction management, or construction engineering curriculum at an accredited four year college/university or two-year technical institution. The student must take at least one course on Hot Mix Asphalt (HMA) Technology. Refer to website for more details at http://www.hotmix.org/
index.php?option=com_content&task=view&id=97&Itemid=410.

Academic Fields/Career Goals: Civil Engineering; Construction Engineering/Management.

Award: Scholarship for use in freshman, sophomore, junior, senior, graduate, or postgraduate years; not renewable. *Number:* 50–150. *Amount:* $500–$3000.

Eligibility Requirements: Applicant must be enrolled or expecting to enroll full-time at a two-year or four-year or technical institution or university. Available to U.S. citizens.

Application Requirements: Application form, essay, recommendations or references, transcript. *Deadline:* varies.

Contact: Mrs. Carolyn Wilson, Vice President, Finance and Operations
    National Asphalt Pavement Association Research and
      Education Foundation
    5100 Forbes Boulevard
    Lanham, MD 20706
    Phone: 301-731-4748 Ext. 127
    Fax: 301-731-4621
    E-mail: cwilson@asphaltpavement.org

NATIONAL ASSOCIATION OF WOMEN IN CONSTRUCTION

http://www.nawic.org/

NAWIC UNDERGRADUATE SCHOLARSHIPS
• *See page 112*

NATIONAL SOCIETY OF PROFESSIONAL ENGINEERS

http://www.nspe.org/

MAUREEN L. AND HOWARD N. BLITMAN, PE SCHOLARSHIP TO PROMOTE DIVERSITY IN ENGINEERING
• *See page 170*

PAUL H. ROBBINS HONORARY SCHOLARSHIP
• *See page 170*

PROFESSIONAL ENGINEERS IN INDUSTRY SCHOLARSHIP
• *See page 170*

NEVADA NASA SPACE GRANT CONSORTIUM

http://www.nvspacegrant.org/

NATIONAL SPACE GRANT COLLEGE AND FELLOWSHIP PROGRAM
• *See page 106*

NEW ENGLAND WATER WORKS ASSOCIATION

http://www.newwa.org/

ELSON T. KILLAM MEMORIAL SCHOLARSHIP

Scholarships are awarded to eligible civil and environmental engineering students on the basis of merit, character, and need. Preference given to those students whose programs are considered by a committee as beneficial to water works practice in New England. NEWWA student membership is required to receive a scholarship award. Applicants for scholarships should be residents or attend school in New England. (Maine, New Hampshire, Vermont, Massachusetts, Rhode Island and Connecticut).

Academic Fields/Career Goals: Civil Engineering; Environmental Science.

Award: Scholarship for use in freshman, sophomore, junior, senior, or graduate years; not renewable. *Number:* 1. *Amount:* up to $1500.

Eligibility Requirements: Applicant must be enrolled or expecting to enroll full-time at a four-year institution or university. Applicant or parent of applicant must be member of New England Water Works Association. Available to U.S. citizens.

Application Requirements: Application form, essay, recommendations or references, transcript. *Fee:* $25. *Deadline:* July 1.

Contact: Thomas MacElhaney, Chair, Scholarship Committee
Phone: 631-231-8100
Fax: 978-418-9156
E-mail: tmacelhaney@preloadinc.com

FRANCIS X. CROWLEY SCHOLARSHIP
• *See page 158*

JOSEPH MURPHY SCHOLARSHIP

Scholarships are awarded to eligible civil or environmental engineering students on the basis of merit, character, and need. Preference given to those students whose programs are considered by a committee as beneficial to water works practice in New England. NEWWA student membership is required to receive a scholarship award.

Academic Fields/Career Goals: Civil Engineering; Environmental Science.

Award: Scholarship for use in freshman, sophomore, junior, senior, or graduate years; not renewable. *Number:* 1. *Amount:* up to $1500.

Eligibility Requirements: Applicant must be enrolled or expecting to enroll full-time at a four-year institution or university. Applicant or parent of applicant must be member of New England Water Works Association. Available to U.S. citizens.

Application Requirements: Application form, essay, recommendations or references, transcript. *Fee:* $25. *Deadline:* July 1.

Contact: Thomas MacElhaney, Chair, Scholarship Committee
Phone: 631-231-8100
Fax: 978-418-9156
E-mail: tmacelhaney@preloadinc.com

WORKS GEORGE E. WATTERS MEMORIAL SCHOLARSHIP.

Scholarships are awarded to eligible Civil Engineering students on the basis of merit, character, and need. Preference given to those students whose programs are considered by a committee as beneficial to water works practice in New England. NEWWA student membership is required to receive a scholarship award. Applicants for scholarships should be residents or attend school in New England. (Maine, New Hampshire, Vermont, Massachusetts, Rhode Island and Connecticut).

Academic Fields/Career Goals: Civil Engineering.

Award: Scholarship for use in freshman, sophomore, junior, senior, or graduate years; not renewable. *Number:* 1. *Amount:* up to $5000.

Eligibility Requirements: Applicant must be enrolled or expecting to enroll full-time at a four-year institution or university. Available to U.S. citizens.

Application Requirements: Application form, essay, recommendations or references, transcript. *Fee:* $25. *Deadline:* July 1.

Contact: Thomas MacElhaney, Chair, Scholarship Committee
Phone: 631-231-8100
Fax: 978-418-9156
E-mail: tmacelhaney@preloadinc.com

OREGON STUDENT ASSISTANCE COMMISSION

http://www.GetCollegeFunds.org/

HOME BUILDERS FOUNDATION JIM IRVINE STATEWIDE SCHOLARSHIP
• *See page 112*

SOCIETY OF AMERICAN MILITARY ENGINEERS PORTLAND POST SCHOLARSHIP
• *See page 170*

PROFESSIONAL CONSTRUCTION ESTIMATORS ASSOCIATION

http://www.pcea.org/

TED G. WILSON MEMORIAL SCHOLARSHIP FOUNDATION

Amount up to $1000 to a deserving student (high school senior, college freshman, sophomore, or junior) based on their academic ability, need, and desire to enter the construction industry.

Academic Fields/Career Goals: Civil Engineering; Construction Engineering/Management; Drafting; Electrical Engineering/Electronics; Engineering/Technology; Heating, Air-Conditioning, and Refrigeration Mechanics; Landscape Architecture; Mechanical Engineering; Surveying, Surveying Technology, Cartography, or Geographic Information Science; Trade/Technical Specialties.

Award: Scholarship for use in freshman, sophomore, junior, or senior years; not renewable. *Number:* 5. *Amount:* up to $1000.

Eligibility Requirements: Applicant must be enrolled or expecting to enroll full-time at a two-year or four-year technical institution or university; resident of Florida, Georgia, North Carolina, South Carolina, Virginia and studying in Florida, Georgia, North Carolina, South Carolina, Virginia. Available to U.S. and non-U.S. citizens.

Application Requirements: Application form, financial need analysis, interview, recommendations or references, transcript. *Deadline:* March 15.

Contact: Kim Lybrand, National Office Manager
Professional Construction Estimators Association
PO Box 680336
Charlotte, NC 28216-0336
Phone: 704-987-9978
Fax: 704-987-9979
E-mail: pcea@pcea.org

PROFESSIONAL GROUNDS MANAGEMENT SOCIETY

http://www.pgms.org/

ANNE SEAMAN PROFESSIONAL GROUNDS MANAGEMENT SOCIETY MEMORIAL SCHOLARSHIP
• *See page 95*

ROCKY MOUNTAIN COAL MINING INSTITUTE

http://www.rmcmi.org/

ROCKY MOUNTAIN COAL MINING INSTITUTE SCHOLARSHIP

Must be full-time college sophomore or junior at time of application, pursuing a degree in mining-related fields or engineering disciplines such as mining, geology, mineral processing, or metallurgy. For residents of Arizona, Colorado, Montana, New Mexico, North Dakota, Texas, Utah, and Wyoming. Scholarship value is $2500 per year for two-years sent directly to school for tuition.

Academic Fields/Career Goals: Civil Engineering; Earth Science; Engineering-Related Technologies; Engineering/Technology; Materials Science, Engineering, and Metallurgy.

Award: Scholarship for use in junior or senior years; renewable. *Number:* 8. *Amount:* $2500.

Eligibility Requirements: Applicant must be enrolled or expecting to enroll full-time at a four-year institution or university and resident of Arizona, Colorado, Montana, New Mexico, North Dakota, Texas, Utah, Wyoming. Available to U.S. citizens.

Application Requirements: Application form, interview, recommendations or references. *Deadline:* February 1.

Contact: Karen Inzano, Executive Director
Phone: 303-948-3300
E-mail: mail@rmcmi.org

SOCIETY OF WOMEN ENGINEERS

http://www.swe.org/

ACCENTURE SCHOLARSHIP
• *See page 172*

BETTY LOU BAILEY SWE REGION F SCHOLARSHIP
• *See page 172*

CAROL STEPHENS REGION F SCHOLARSHIP
• *See page 172*

DR. IVY M. PARKER MEMORIAL SCHOLARSHIP
• *See page 173*

DOROTHY LEMKE HOWARTH MEMORIAL SCHOLARSHIP
• *See page 173*

DOROTHY P. MORRIS SCHOLARSHIP
• *See page 173*

GENERAL ELECTRIC WOMEN'S NETWORK SCHOLARSHIP

Scholarships for women pursuing ABET-accredited baccalaureate or graduate programs in preparation for a careers in engineering, engineering technology, or computer science in the United States and Mexico. U.S. citizenship and SWE membership required. Leadership roles outside of academics and involvement in engineering professional organizations, discipline related internships, presentation skills. Recipients should be willing to intern at GE. Inquire for list of preferred schools.

Academic Fields/Career Goals: Civil Engineering; Electrical Engineering/Electronics; Engineering/Technology; Mechanical Engineering.

Award: Scholarship for use in sophomore or junior years; not renewable. *Number:* 15. *Amount:* $5000.

Eligibility Requirements: Applicant must be enrolled or expecting to enroll full-time at a four-year institution or university; female and must have an interest in leadership. Applicant or parent of applicant must be member of Society of Women Engineers. Available to U.S. citizens.

Application Requirements: Application form, recommendations or references. *Deadline:* February 15.

JILL S. TIETJEN P.E. SCHOLARSHIP
• *See page 173*

LIFE TECHNOLOGIES SCHOLARSHIP
• *See page 174*

LILLIAN MOLLER GILBRETH MEMORIAL SCHOLARSHIP
• *See page 174*

MARY V. MUNGER SCHOLARSHIP
• *See page 174*

MASWE MEMORIAL SCHOLARSHIP
• *See page 174*

MERIDITH THOMS MEMORIAL SCHOLARSHIPS
• *See page 174*

OLIVE LYNN SALEMBIER MEMORIAL REENTRY SCHOLARSHIP
• *See page 174*

SUSAN MISZKOWICZ MEMORIAL SCHOLARSHIP
• *See page 175*

SWE BALTIMORE-WASHINGTON SECTION SCHOLARSHIP
• *See page 175*

SWE CENTRAL NEW MEXICO PIONEERS SCHOLARSHIP
• *See page 175*

SWE CENTRAL NEW MEXICO REENTRY SCHOLARSHIP
• *See page 175*

SWE MID-HUDSON SECTION SCHOLARSHIP
• *See page 175*

SWE PAST PRESIDENTS SCHOLARSHIP
• *See page 175*

SWE PHOENIX SECTION SCHOLARSHIP
• *See page 175*

SWE REGION H SCHOLARSHIPS
• *See page 176*

WANDA MUNN SCHOLARSHIP
• *See page 176*

SOCIETY OF WOMEN ENGINEERS-ROCKY MOUNTAIN SECTION

http://www.societyofwomenengineers.org/RockyMountain/

SOCIETY OF WOMEN ENGINEERS-ROCKY MOUNTAIN SECTION SCHOLARSHIP PROGRAM
• See page 176

STRAIGHTFORWARD MEDIA

http://www.straightforwardmedia.com/

STRAIGHTFORWARD MEDIA ENGINEERING SCHOLARSHIP
• See page 176

TEXAS DEPARTMENT OF TRANSPORTATION

http://www.txdot.gov/

CONDITIONAL GRANT PROGRAM
Renewable award to students who are considered economically disadvantaged based on federal guidelines. The maximum amount awarded per semester is $3000 not to exceed $6000 per academic year. Students already enrolled in an undergraduate program should have minimum GPA 2.5 and students newly enrolling should have minimum GPA 3.0.

Academic Fields/Career Goals: Civil Engineering; Computer Science/Data Processing; Occupational Safety and Health.

Award: Grant for use in freshman, sophomore, junior, or senior years; renewable. *Amount:* up to $6000.

Eligibility Requirements: Applicant must be enrolled or expecting to enroll full-time at a four-year institution or university; resident of Texas and studying in Texas. Available to U.S. citizens.

Application Requirements: Application form, essay, interview, recommendations or references, test scores, transcript. *Deadline:* March 1.

Contact: Minnie Brown, Program Coordinator
Texas Department of Transportation
125 East 11th Street
Austin, TX 78701-2483
Phone: 512-416-4979
Fax: 512-416-4980
E-mail: mbrown2@dot.state.tx.us

TURNER CONSTRUCTION COMPANY

http://www.turnerconstruction.com/

YOUTHFORCE 2020 SCHOLARSHIP PROGRAM
• See page 113

UNITED NEGRO COLLEGE FUND

http://www.uncf.org/

CDM SCHOLARSHIP/INTERNSHIP
• See page 176

EMERSON PROCESS MANAGEMENT SCHOLARSHIP
• See page 177

PACIFIC GAS AND ELECTRIC COMPANY SCHOLARSHIP
• See page 82

SPRINT SCHOLARS PROGRAM FOR SOPHOMORES, JUNIORS, AND SENIORS
• See page 100

UNIVERSITIES SPACE RESEARCH ASSOCIATION

http://www.usra.edu/

UNIVERSITIES SPACE RESEARCH ASSOCIATION SCHOLARSHIP PROGRAM
• See page 107

UTAH SOCIETY OF PROFESSIONAL ENGINEERS

http://www.uspeonline.com/

UTAH SOCIETY OF PROFESSIONAL ENGINEERS JOE RHOADS SCHOLARSHIP
• See page 177

WIRE REINFORCEMENT INSTITUTE EDUCATION FOUNDATION

http://www.wirereinforcementinstitute.org/

WRI COLLEGE SCHOLARSHIP PROGRAM
Academic scholarships for qualified high school seniors and current undergraduate and graduate level students intending to or presently pursuing four-year or graduate-level degrees in structural and/or civil engineering at accredited four-year universities or colleges in the U.S. or Canada.

Academic Fields/Career Goals: Civil Engineering; Construction Engineering/Management.

Award: Scholarship for use in freshman, sophomore, junior, senior, or graduate years; not renewable. *Number:* 2–5. *Amount:* $1500–$3000.

Eligibility Requirements: Applicant must be enrolled or expecting to enroll full-time at a four-year institution or university. Available to U.S. and non-U.S. citizens.

Application Requirements: Application form, application form may be submitted online (http://www.wirereinforcementinstitute.org), essay, recommendations or references, resume, test scores, transcript. *Deadline:* April 15.

CLASSICS

ACL/NJCL NATIONAL LATIN EXAM

http://www.nle.org/

NATIONAL LATIN EXAM SCHOLARSHIP
Scholarships to high school seniors who are gold medal winners in Latin III, III-IV Prose, III-IV Poetry, or Latin V-VI. Applicants must agree to take at least one year of Latin or classical Greek in college.

Academic Fields/Career Goals: Classics; Foreign Language.

Award: Scholarship for use in freshman, sophomore, junior, or senior years; renewable. *Number:* 21. *Amount:* $1000.

Eligibility Requirements: Applicant must be high school student; planning to enroll or expecting to enroll full-time at a four-year institution or university and must have an interest in Greek language or Latin language. Available to U.S. and non-U.S. citizens.

Application Requirements: Application form, essay, recommendations or references, test scores, transcript. *Deadline:* May 1.

Contact: Mrs. Ephy Howard, Scholarship Chairperson
Phone: 888-378-7721

AMERICAN CLASSICAL LEAGUE/ NATIONAL JUNIOR CLASSICAL LEAGUE

http://www.aclclassics.org/

NATIONAL JUNIOR CLASSICAL LEAGUE SCHOLARSHIP

A one-time award available to graduating high school seniors, who are members of the Junior Classical League. Preference is given to students who plan to major in the classics.

Academic Fields/Career Goals: Classics; Foreign Language; Humanities.

Award: Scholarship for use in freshman year; not renewable. *Number:* 7. *Amount:* $1000–$2000.

Eligibility Requirements: Applicant must be high school student; planning to enroll or expecting to enroll full-time at a two-year or four-year institution or university and must have an interest in foreign language. Applicant or parent of applicant must be member of Junior Classical League. Available to U.S. and non-U.S. citizens.

Application Requirements: Application form, essay, list of 5 extracurricular activities and 5 community activities, recommendations or references, transcript. *Deadline:* May 1.

Contact: Geri Dutra, Administrator
American Classical League/National Junior Classical League
Miami University, 422 Wells Mill Drive
Oxford, OH 45066
Phone: 513-529-7741
Fax: 513-529-7742
E-mail: info@aclclassics.org

AMERICAN PHILOLOGICAL ASSOCIATION

http://www.apaclassics.org/

MINORITY STUDENT SUMMER SCHOLARSHIP
• See page 108

AMERICAN SCHOOL OF CLASSICAL STUDIES AT ATHENS

http://www.ascsa.edu.gr/

ASCSA SUMMER SESSIONS SCHOLARSHIPS
• See page 100

STRAIGHTFORWARD MEDIA

http://www.straightforwardmedia.com/

STRAIGHTFORWARD MEDIA LIBERAL ARTS SCHOLARSHIP
• See page 116

COMMUNICATIONS

ADC RESEARCH INSTITUTE

http://www.adc.org/

JACK SHAHEEN MASS COMMUNICATIONS SCHOLARSHIP AWARD

Awarded to Arab-American students who excel in the mass communications field (journalism, radio, television or film). Must be a junior or senior undergraduate or graduate student. Must be U.S. citizen. Minimum 3.0 GPA required.

Academic Fields/Career Goals: Communications; Filmmaking/Video; Journalism; TV/Radio Broadcasting.

Award: Scholarship for use in junior, senior, or graduate years; not renewable. *Number:* 1–6. *Amount:* $500–$1000.

Eligibility Requirements: Applicant must be of Arab heritage and enrolled or expecting to enroll full- or part-time at a four-year institution or university. Applicant must have 3.0 GPA or higher. Available to U.S. citizens.

Application Requirements: Application form, copies of original articles, videos, films, essay, recommendations or references, transcript. *Deadline:* April 12.

Contact: Mr. Nawar Shora, Director of Diversity and Law Enforcement Outreach
ADC Research Institute
1732 Wisconsin Avenue, NW
Washington, DC 20007
Phone: 202-244-2990
Fax: 202-244-3196
E-mail: nshora@adc.org

AMERICAN INSTITUTE OF POLISH CULTURE INC.

http://www.ampolinstitute.org/

HARRIET IRSAY SCHOLARSHIP GRANT
• See page 117

AMERICAN LEGION DEPARTMENT OF NEW YORK

http://www.ny.legion.org/

AMERICAN LEGION DEPARTMENT OF NEW YORK PRESS ASSOCIATION SCHOLARSHIP

A $1000 scholarship for children of NY American Legion or American Legion Auxiliary members, members of SAL or ALA Juniors or graduates of NY AL Boys State or Girls State. Must be entering or attending accredited four-year college pursuing communications degree.

Academic Fields/Career Goals: Communications.

Award: Scholarship for use in freshman, sophomore, junior, or senior years; not renewable. *Number:* 1. *Amount:* $1000.

Eligibility Requirements: Applicant must be enrolled or expecting to enroll full-time at a four-year institution or university and resident of New York. Applicant or parent of applicant must be member of American Legion or Auxiliary. Available to U.S. citizens. Applicant or parent must meet one or more of the following requirements: general military experience; retired from active duty; disabled or killed as a result of military service; prisoner of war; or missing in action.

Application Requirements: Application form. *Deadline:* April 15.

AMERICAN LEGION PRESS CLUB OF NEW JERSEY

AMERICAN LEGION PRESS CLUB OF NEW JERSEY AND POST 170 ARTHUR DEHARDT MEMORIAL SCHOLARSHIP

Merit-based scholarship awarded to two students entering their freshman year. Eligible applicants will be the son, daughter, grandson, or granddaughter of a current card-holding member of the American Legion. Any student who has graduated from either American Legion Boys' State or Girls' State program shall be eligible. Must go into communication field.

Academic Fields/Career Goals: Communications; Journalism; Photojournalism/Photography; TV/Radio Broadcasting.

Award: Scholarship for use in freshman year; not renewable. *Number:* 2. *Amount:* $500.

Eligibility Requirements: Applicant must be high school student; planning to enroll or expecting to enroll full-time at a four-year institution or university; single and resident of New Jersey. Applicant or parent of applicant must be member of American Legion or Auxiliary. Available to U.S. citizens. Applicant or parent must meet one or more of the following requirements: general military experience; retired from active duty; disabled or killed as a result of military service; prisoner of war; or missing in action.

Application Requirements: Application form, copy of graduation certificates, DD-214, essay, transcript. *Deadline:* July 1.

Contact: Dorothy Saunders, Scholarship Chairman
American Legion Press Club of New Jersey
Three Lewis Street
Wayne, NJ 07470-4716

AMERICAN QUARTER HORSE FOUNDATION (AQHF)

http://www.aqha.com/foundation

AQHF JOURNALISM OR COMMUNICATIONS SCHOLARSHIP

Ideal candidate is an AQHA or AQHYA member pursuing a college degree in journalism or communications. Recipient must pursue a career in news, editorial or print journalism, photojournalism or a related field.

Academic Fields/Career Goals: Communications; Journalism; Photojournalism/Photography.

Award: Scholarship for use in freshman, sophomore, junior, senior, or graduate years; renewable. *Number:* 1. *Amount:* $8000.

Eligibility Requirements: Applicant must be enrolled or expecting to enroll full-time at a two-year or four-year or technical institution or university and must have an interest in animal/agricultural competition. Applicant or parent of applicant must be member of American Quarter Horse Association. Applicant must have 2.5 GPA or higher. Available to U.S. and non-U.S. citizens.

Application Requirements: Application form, recommendations or references, transcript. *Deadline:* December 1.

ARAB AMERICAN SCHOLARSHIP FOUNDATION

http://www.lahc.org/

LEBANESE AMERICAN HERITAGE CLUB'S SCHOLARSHIP FUND

Scholarship for high school, undergraduate, or graduate students who are of Arab descent. Minimum 3.0 GPA required for high school and undergraduate applicants, 3.5 GPA for graduate student applicants. Must be U.S. citizens.

Academic Fields/Career Goals: Communications; Political Science.

Award: Scholarship for use in freshman, sophomore, junior, senior, or graduate years; not renewable. *Number:* 1. *Amount:* $1000.

Eligibility Requirements: Applicant must be of Arab heritage; enrolled or expecting to enroll full-time at a four-year institution or university and resident of Michigan. Applicant must have 3.0 GPA or higher. Available to U.S. citizens.

Application Requirements: Application form, essay, financial need analysis, recommendations or references, Student Aid Report (SAR), transcript. *Deadline:* April 6.

Contact: Suehalia Amen, Communications Chair
Phone: 313-846-8480
Fax: 313-846-2710
E-mail: sueamen@lahc.org

ARMED FORCES COMMUNICATIONS AND ELECTRONICS ASSOCIATION, EDUCATIONAL FOUNDATION

http://www.afcea.org/scholarships

ARMED FORCES COMMUNICATIONS AND ELECTRONICS ASSOCIATION GENERAL EMMETT PAIGE SCHOLARSHIP
• *See page 127*

ARMED FORCES COMMUNICATIONS AND ELECTRONICS ASSOCIATION ROTC SCHOLARSHIP PROGRAM
• *See page 127*

ARRL FOUNDATION INC.

http://www.arrl.org/

CHARLES CLARKE CORDLE MEMORIAL SCHOLARSHIP

One-time award for licensed amateur radio operators. Must have minimum GPA of 2.5. Preference to students studying electronics, communications, or related fields. Preference given to residents of Georgia or Alabama attending institutions in those states.

Academic Fields/Career Goals: Communications; Electrical Engineering/Electronics.

Award: Scholarship for use in freshman, sophomore, junior, or senior years; not renewable. *Number:* 1. *Amount:* $1000.

Eligibility Requirements: Applicant must be enrolled or expecting to enroll full-time at a four-year institution or university; resident of Alabama, Georgia; studying in Alabama, Georgia and must have an interest in amateur radio. Applicant must have 2.5 GPA or higher. Available to U.S. citizens.

Application Requirements: Application form, transcript. *Deadline:* February 1.

Contact: Ms. Mary Hobart, Secretary
Phone: 860-594-0397
E-mail: k1mmh@arrl.org

CHARLES N. FISHER MEMORIAL SCHOLARSHIP
• *See page 103*

DR. JAMES L. LAWSON MEMORIAL SCHOLARSHIP

One-time award of $500 available to general amateur radio operators. For baccalaureate or higher course of study in electronics, communications, or a related field. Preference given to residents of New England states (ME, NH, VT, CT, RI, MA) and New York State.

Academic Fields/Career Goals: Communications; Electrical Engineering/Electronics.

Award: Scholarship for use in freshman, sophomore, junior, senior, or graduate years; not renewable. *Number:* 1. *Amount:* $500.

Eligibility Requirements: Applicant must be enrolled or expecting to enroll full-time at a four-year institution or university; resident of Connecticut, Maine, Massachusetts, New Hampshire, New York, Rhode Island, Vermont; studying in Connecticut, Maine, Massachusetts, New Hampshire, New York, Rhode Island, Vermont and must have an interest in amateur radio. Available to U.S. citizens.

Application Requirements: Application form, transcript. *Deadline:* February 1.

Contact: Ms. Mary Hobart, Secretary
Phone: 860-594-0397
E-mail: k1mmh@arrl.org

EUGENE "GENE" SALLEE, W4YFR, MEMORIAL SCHOLARSHIP

One $500 award is available to a student who is a Georgia resident and who has a Technician class or higher amateur radio license. Preference given to students studying electronics, communications, or related fields with a GPA of 3.0 or higher. Academic merit, financial need, and interest in promoting Amateur Radio are taken into consideration.

Academic Fields/Career Goals: Communications; Electrical Engineering/Electronics.

Award: Scholarship for use in freshman, sophomore, junior, or senior years; not renewable. *Number:* 1. *Amount:* $500.

Eligibility Requirements: Applicant must be enrolled or expecting to enroll full- or part-time at a two-year or four-year institution or university; resident of Georgia and must have an interest in amateur radio. Applicant must have 3.0 GPA or higher. Available to U.S. citizens.

Application Requirements: Application form, financial need analysis, transcript. *Deadline:* February 1.

Contact: Ms. Mary Hobart, Secretary
Phone: 860-594-0397
E-mail: k1mmh@arrl.org

FRANCIS WALTON MEMORIAL SCHOLARSHIP
• *See page 91*

FRED R. MCDANIEL MEMORIAL SCHOLARSHIP

One $500 award is available to students who possess a general class or higher amateur radio license. Must be studying electronics, communications, or related fields at a four-year college or university. Preference will be given to applicants with a 3.0 GPA or higher who are residents of FCC 5th call district (TX, OK, AR, LA, MS, NM).

Academic Fields/Career Goals: Communications; Electrical Engineering/Electronics.

Award: Scholarship for use in freshman, sophomore, junior, or senior years; not renewable. *Number:* 1. *Amount:* $500.

Eligibility Requirements: Applicant must be enrolled or expecting to enroll full- or part-time at a four-year institution or university; resident of Arkansas, Louisiana, Mississippi, New Mexico, Oklahoma, Texas and must have an interest in amateur radio. Applicant must have 3.0 GPA or higher. Available to U.S. citizens.

Application Requirements: Application form, transcript. *Deadline:* February 1.

Contact: Ms. Mary Hobart, Secretary
Phone: 860-594-0397
E-mail: k1mmh@arrl.org

IRVING W. COOK, WA0CGS, SCHOLARSHIP

One-time award of $1000 to students pursuing a baccalaureate or higher degree in communications, electronics, or related fields. Must be a amateur radio operator. Preference to Kansas resident but may attend school in any state.

Academic Fields/Career Goals: Communications; Electrical Engineering/Electronics.

Award: Scholarship for use in freshman, sophomore, junior, or senior years; not renewable. *Number:* 1. *Amount:* $1000.

Eligibility Requirements: Applicant must be enrolled or expecting to enroll full-time at a four-year institution or university; resident of Kansas and must have an interest in amateur radio. Available to U.S. citizens.

Application Requirements: Application form, transcript. *Deadline:* February 1.

Contact: Ms. Mary Hobart, Secretary
Phone: 860-594-0397
E-mail: k1mmh@arrl.org

L. PHIL AND ALICE J. WICKER SCHOLARSHIP

One-time award available to a licensed general amateur radio operator. Preference given to residents in the ARRL Roanoke Division (North Carolina, South Carolina, Virginia, West Virginia) and attending school in that division. Preference to baccalaureate or higher degree studies in electronics, communications, or related fields.

Academic Fields/Career Goals: Communications; Electrical Engineering/Electronics.

Award: Scholarship for use in freshman, sophomore, junior, senior, or graduate years; not renewable. *Number:* 1. *Amount:* $500.

Eligibility Requirements: Applicant must be enrolled or expecting to enroll full-time at a four-year institution or university; resident of North Carolina, South Dakota, Virginia, West Virginia; studying in North Carolina, South Carolina, Virginia, West Virginia and must have an interest in amateur radio. Available to U.S. citizens.

Application Requirements: Application form, transcript. *Deadline:* February 1.

Contact: Ms. Mary Hobart, Secretary
Phone: 860-594-0397
E-mail: k1mmh@arrl.org

MAGNOLIA DX ASSOCIATION SCHOLARSHIP

One $500 award is available to a student majoring in electronics, communications, computer science, engineering, or a related field. Preference is given to graduating high school seniors who are residents of Mississippi or Delta division planning to study in Mississippi. Must have obtained a technical class or higher amateur radio license.

Academic Fields/Career Goals: Communications; Computer Science/Data Processing; Electrical Engineering/Electronics; Engineering/Technology.

Award: Scholarship for use in freshman, sophomore, junior, or senior years; not renewable. *Number:* 1. *Amount:* $500.

Eligibility Requirements: Applicant must be enrolled or expecting to enroll full- or part-time at a two-year or four-year or technical institution or university; resident of Mississippi; studying in Mississippi and must have an interest in amateur radio. Available to U.S. citizens.

Application Requirements: Application form, transcript. *Deadline:* February 1.

Contact: Ms. Mary Hobart, Secretary
Phone: 860-594-0397
E-mail: k1mmh@arrl.org

MISSISSIPPI SCHOLARSHIP
• See page 103

PAUL AND HELEN L. GRAUER SCHOLARSHIP
• See page 103

ASIAN AMERICAN JOURNALISTS ASSOCIATION

http://www.aaja.org/

ASIAN-AMERICAN JOURNALISTS ASSOCIATION SCHOLARSHIP

Award of $5000 for high school seniors and college students pursuing careers in the news media. Asian heritage is not required. Minimum 2.5 GPA required. Based on scholarship, goals, journalistic ability, financial need, and commitment to the Asian-American community. Visit website http://www.aaja.org for application and details.

Academic Fields/Career Goals: Communications; Journalism; Photojournalism/Photography; TV/Radio Broadcasting.

Award: Scholarship for use in freshman, sophomore, junior, senior, or graduate years; renewable. *Number:* 10. *Amount:* $5000.

Eligibility Requirements: Applicant must be enrolled or expecting to enroll full-time at a two-year or four-year institution or university. Applicant or parent of applicant must have employment or volunteer experience in journalism/broadcasting. Applicant must have 2.5 GPA or higher. Available to U.S. and non-U.S. citizens.

Application Requirements: Application form, essay, financial need analysis, recommendations or references, resume, transcript. *Deadline:* March 28.

Contact: Kim Mizuhara, Programs Coordinator
Asian American Journalists Association
1182 Market Street, Suite 320
San Francisco, CA 94102
Phone: 415-346-2051 Ext. 102
Fax: 415-346-6343
E-mail: programs@aaja.org

CHARLES AND LUCILLE KING FAMILY FOUNDATION, INC.

http://www.kingfoundation.org/

CHARLES AND LUCILLE KING FAMILY FOUNDATION SCHOLARSHIPS

Renewable award for college undergraduates at junior or senior level pursuing television, film, or communication studies to further their education. Must attend a four-year undergraduate institution. Minimum 3.0 GPA required to renew scholarship. Must have completed at least two years of study and be currently enrolled in a U.S. college or university. Application may be downloaded on website.

Academic Fields/Career Goals: Communications; Filmmaking/Video; TV/Radio Broadcasting.

Award: Scholarship for use in junior or senior years; renewable. *Number:* 10–20. *Amount:* $3500–$7000.

Eligibility Requirements: Applicant must be enrolled or expecting to enroll full-time at a four-year institution or university. Applicant must have 3.0 GPA or higher. Available to U.S. and non-U.S. citizens.

Application Requirements: Application form, essay, financial need analysis, recommendations or references, transcript. *Deadline:* March 15.

Contact: Michael Donovan, Educational Director
Charles and Lucille King Family Foundation, Inc.
366 Madison Avenue, Tenth Floor
New York, NY 10017
Phone: 212-682-2913
Fax: 212-949-0728
E-mail: info@kingfoundation.org

CONNECTICUT CHAPTER OF SOCIETY OF PROFESSIONAL JOURNALISTS

http://www.ctspj.org/

CONNECTICUT SPJ BOB EDDY SCHOLARSHIP PROGRAM

One-time awards of $250 to $2000 for college juniors or seniors planning a career in journalism. Must be a Connecticut resident attending a four year college or any student attending a four year college in Connecticut.

Academic Fields/Career Goals: Communications; Journalism; Photojournalism/Photography.

Award: Scholarship for use in junior or senior years; not renewable. *Number:* 5. *Amount:* $250–$2000.

Eligibility Requirements: Applicant must be enrolled or expecting to enroll full-time at a four-year institution or university; resident of Connecticut; studying in Connecticut and must have an interest in writing. Available to U.S. and non-U.S. citizens.

Application Requirements: Application form, entry in a contest, essay, financial need analysis, transcript. *Deadline:* April 4.

Contact: Debra Estock, Scholarship Committee Chairman
Connecticut Chapter of Society of Professional Journalists
71 Kenwood Avenue
Fairfield, CT 06824
Phone: 203-255-2127
E-mail: debae@optonline.net

CUBAN AMERICAN NATIONAL FOUNDATION

http://www.masscholarships.org/

MAS FAMILY SCHOLARSHIPS
• See page 152

DADE COMMUNITY FOUNDATION

http://www.jackituckfield.org/

LEO SUAREZ SCHOLARSHIP

Award available to a public high school senior in the Miami, Dade, and Broward county area who is planning to enroll in a two- or four-year college or university and study journalism, broadcasting, mass communications or related fields. Must be a resident of South Florida, have a 3.0 GPA, and attach writing samples of published work to scholarship application. For additional information, visit website http://www.dadecommunityfoundation.org.

Academic Fields/Career Goals: Communications; Journalism; TV/Radio Broadcasting.

Award: Scholarship for use in freshman year; not renewable. *Number:* 1. *Amount:* $1000.

Eligibility Requirements: Applicant must be high school student; planning to enroll or expecting to enroll full-time at a two-year or four-year institution or university and resident of Florida. Applicant must have 3.0 GPA or higher. Available to U.S. citizens.

Application Requirements: Application form, published examples of writing, recommendations or references, transcript. *Deadline:* March 21.

Contact: Ted Seijo, Scholarship Coordinator
Phone: 305-371-2711
E-mail: ted.seijo@dadecommunityfoundation.org

DAIRY MANAGEMENT

http://www.dairyinfo.com/

NATIONAL DAIRY PROMOTION AND RESEARCH BOARD SCHOLARSHIP
• See page 91

GREAT FALLS ADVERTISING FEDERATION

http://www.gfaf.com/

GREAT FALLS ADVERTISING FEDERATION COLLEGE SCHOLARSHIP
• See page 83

HIGH SCHOOL MARKETING/COMMUNICATIONS SCHOLARSHIP
• See page 83

GREAT LAKES COMMISSION

http://www.glc.org/

CAROL A. RATZA MEMORIAL SCHOLARSHIP

One-time award to full-time students at a college or university in the Great Lake states (IL, IN, MI, MN, NY, OH, PA, WI) or Canadian provinces of Ontario or Quebec. Must have a demonstrated interest in the environmental or economic applications of electronic communications technology, exhibit academic excellence, and have a sincere appreciation for the Great Lakes and their protection.

Academic Fields/Career Goals: Communications; Computer Science/Data Processing; Environmental Science; Graphics/Graphic Arts/Printing; Journalism; Natural Resources; Natural Sciences; Science, Technology, and Society; TV/Radio Broadcasting.

Award: Scholarship for use in freshman, sophomore, junior, or senior years; not renewable. *Number:* 1. *Amount:* $1000.

Eligibility Requirements: Applicant must be enrolled or expecting to enroll full-time at a two-year or four-year or technical institution or university; resident of Illinois, Indiana, Michigan, Minnesota, New York, Ohio, Ontario, Pennsylvania, Quebec, Wisconsin and studying in Illinois, Indiana, Michigan, Minnesota, New York, Ohio, Ontario, Pennsylvania, Quebec, Wisconsin. Available to U.S. and Canadian citizens.

Application Requirements: Application form, essay, letter of intent explaining career goals, recommendations or references, resume, transcript. *Deadline:* March 31.

Contact: Christine Manninen, Program Manager
Great Lakes Commission
Eisenhower Corporate Park, 2805 South Industrial Highway, Suite 100
Ann Arbor, MI 48104-6791
Phone: 734-971-9135
Fax: 734-971-9150
E-mail: manninen@glc.org

INSTITUTE FOR HUMANE STUDIES

http://www.theihs.org/

HUMANE STUDIES FELLOWSHIPS

Renewable award for undergraduate and graduate students in selected disciplines. Applicants should have demonstrated interest in classical liberal or libertarian ideas and must intend to pursue a scholarly career. Minimum 3.5 GPA required. Application fee: $25.

Academic Fields/Career Goals: Communications; Economics; History; Humanities; Law/Legal Services; Literature/English/Writing; Political Science; Social Sciences.

Award: Scholarship for use in junior or senior years; not renewable. *Number:* 140–180. *Amount:* $2000–$12,000.

Eligibility Requirements: Applicant must be enrolled or expecting to enroll full-time at a two-year or four-year institution or university. Applicant must have 3.5 GPA or higher. Available to U.S. and Canadian citizens.

Application Requirements: Application form, essay, recommendations or references, resume, test scores, transcript. *Fee:* $25. *Deadline:* December 31.

INTERNATIONAL COMMUNICATIONS INDUSTRIES FOUNDATION

http://www.infocomm.org/scholarships

ICIF SCHOLARSHIP FOR EMPLOYEES AND DEPENDENTS OF MEMBER ORGANIZATIONS

Scholarship for a spouse, child, stepchild or grandchild of an employee of an InfoComm International member organization or for an employee of an InfoComm International member organization. Must be majoring in audiovisual related fields, such as audio, video, audiovisual, electronics, telecommunications, technical theatre, data networking, software development, and information technology. Minimum of 2.75 GPA required. Must show evidence of AV experience (completed course, job, internship, etc).

Academic Fields/Career Goals: Communications; Computer Science/Data Processing; Electrical Engineering/Electronics; Filmmaking/Video.

Award: Scholarship for use in freshman, sophomore, junior, senior, or graduate years; not renewable. *Number:* 1–50. *Amount:* $1500.

Eligibility Requirements: Applicant must be enrolled or expecting to enroll full-time at a two-year or four-year or technical institution or university. Applicant must have 3.0 GPA or higher. Available to U.S. and non-U.S. citizens.

Application Requirements: Application form, essay, recommendations or references, transcript. *Deadline:* May 10.

Contact: Ms. Shana Rieger, Membership and Social Media Program Manager
International Communications Industries Foundation
11242 Waples Mill Road, Suite 200
Fairfax, VA 22030
Phone: 703-273-7200 Ext. 3690
Fax: 703-278-8082
E-mail: srieger@infocomm.org

INTERNATIONAL COMMUNICATIONS INDUSTRIES FOUNDATION AV SCHOLARSHIP

Scholarship for students majoring in audiovisual related fields such as audio, video, audiovisual, electronics, telecommunications, technical theatre, data networking, software development, information and technology. Minimum 2.75 GPA required. Must provide evidence of audiovisual knowledge (completed course, job, internship, etc.).

Academic Fields/Career Goals: Communications; Computer Science/Data Processing; Electrical Engineering/Electronics; Filmmaking/Video.

Award: Scholarship for use in freshman, sophomore, junior, senior, or graduate years; not renewable. *Number:* 1–50. *Amount:* $1200.

Eligibility Requirements: Applicant must be enrolled or expecting to enroll full-time at a two-year or four-year or technical institution or university. Applicant must have 3.0 GPA or higher. Available to U.S. and Canadian citizens.

Application Requirements: Application form, essay, recommendations or references, transcript. *Deadline:* May 10.

Contact: Ms. Shana Rieger, Membership and Social Media Program Manager
International Communications Industries Foundation
11242 Waples Mill Road, Suite 200
Fairfax, VA 22030
Phone: 703-273-7200 Ext. 3690
Fax: 703-278-8082
E-mail: srieger@infocomm.org

INTERNATIONAL FOODSERVICE EDITORIAL COUNCIL

http://www.ifeconline.com/

INTERNATIONAL FOODSERVICE EDITORIAL COUNCIL COMMUNICATIONS SCHOLARSHIP

• See page 83

JOHN BAYLISS BROADCAST FOUNDATION

http://www.baylissfoundation.org/

JOHN BAYLISS BROADCAST RADIO SCHOLARSHIP

One-time award for college juniors or seniors majoring in broadcast communications with a concentration in radio broadcasting. Must have history of radio-related activities and a GPA of at least 3.0.

Academic Fields/Career Goals: Communications; Journalism; TV/Radio Broadcasting.

Award: Scholarship for use in junior or senior years; not renewable. *Number:* 2–6. *Amount:* $5000.

Eligibility Requirements: Applicant must be enrolled or expecting to enroll full-time at a four-year institution or university. Applicant must have 3.0 GPA or higher. Available to U.S. citizens.

Application Requirements: Application form, essay, recommendations or references, resume, self-addressed stamped envelope with application, transcript. *Deadline:* April 30.

JORGE MAS CANOSA FREEDOM FOUNDATION

http://www.jorgemascanosa.org/

MAS FAMILY SCHOLARSHIP AWARD

• See page 156

KATU THOMAS R. DARGAN MINORITY SCHOLARSHIP

http://www.katu.com/

THOMAS R. DARGAN MINORITY SCHOLARSHIP

Up to four awards for minority students who are citizens of the United States pursuing broadcast or communications studies. Must be a resident of Oregon or Washington attending an out-of-state institution or be enrolled at a four-year college or university in Oregon or Washington. Minimum 3.0 GPA required.

Academic Fields/Career Goals: Communications; Journalism; TV/Radio Broadcasting.

Award: Scholarship for use in freshman, sophomore, junior, or senior years; renewable. *Number:* 1–4. *Amount:* $6000.

Eligibility Requirements: Applicant must be American Indian/Alaska Native, Asian/Pacific Islander, Black (non-Hispanic), Hispanic; enrolled or expecting to enroll full-time at a four-year institution or university and resident of Oregon, Washington. Applicant must have 3.0 GPA or higher. Available to U.S. citizens.

Application Requirements: Application form, essay, financial need analysis, interview, recommendations or references, transcript. *Deadline:* April 30.

KE ALI'I PAUAHI FOUNDATION

http://www.pauahi.org/

JOSEPH A. SOWA SCHOLARSHIP

Award for study in the field of communications. Requires a minimum GPA of 3.0. Must demonstrate financial need. Submit two letters recommendation from a teacher, counselor, employer or community organization. Submit essay demonstrating how to engage young people through communication and describe your leadership potential in the community.

Academic Fields/Career Goals: Communications.

Award: Scholarship for use in freshman, sophomore, junior, senior, or graduate years; not renewable. *Number:* 1. *Amount:* $1500.

Eligibility Requirements: Applicant must be enrolled or expecting to enroll full-time at a four-year institution or university. Applicant must have 3.0 GPA or higher. Available to U.S. citizens.

Application Requirements: Application form, application form may be submitted online (http://www.pauahi.org/scholarships), essay, recommendations or references, Student Aid Report (SAR), college acceptance letter, transcript. *Deadline:* April 1.

Contact: Mavis Shiraishi-Nagao, Scholarship Administrator
Phone: 808-534-3966
E-mail: scholarships@pauahi.org

LAGRANT FOUNDATION

http://www.lagrantfoundation.org/

LAGRANT FOUNDATION SCHOLARSHIP FOR UNDERGRADUATES

• *See page 156*

NATIONAL ACADEMY OF TELEVISION ARTS AND SCIENCES

http://www.emmyonline.tv/

NATIONAL ACADEMY OF TELEVISION ARTS AND SCIENCES JOHN CANNON MEMORIAL SCHOLARSHIP

Scholarships are distributed over a four-year period up to $40,000 awarded prior to the first year of study and three additional awards of $1000 granted in subsequent years if the recipient demonstrates satisfactory progress towards a degree in a communications-oriented program. Must submit SAT or ACT scores. Must be child or grandchild of NATAS member. Application available on the web at http://www.emmyonline.org/emmy/scholr.html.

Academic Fields/Career Goals: Communications; TV/Radio Broadcasting.

Award: Scholarship for use in freshman, sophomore, junior, or senior years; renewable. *Number:* 1–10. *Amount:* $1000–$40,000.

Eligibility Requirements: Applicant must be high school student and planning to enroll or expecting to enroll full-time at a four-year institution or university. Applicant must have 3.0 GPA or higher. Available to U.S. and non-U.S. citizens.

Application Requirements: Application form, essay, recommendations or references, test scores, transcript. *Deadline:* varies.

Contact: Ms. Pamela Kotch, Scholarship Manager
Phone: 212-586-8424
Fax: 212-246-8129
E-mail: pkotch@emmyonline.tv

NATIONAL ASSOCIATION OF BLACK JOURNALISTS

http://www.nabj.org/

NABJ SCHOLARSHIP

Scholarship for a student who is currently attending an accredited four-year college or university. Must be enrolled as an undergraduate or graduate student majoring in journalism (print, radio, online, or television). Minimum 2.5 GPA. Must be a member of NABJ. Scholarship value and the number of awards granted varies annually.

Academic Fields/Career Goals: Communications; Journalism; TV/Radio Broadcasting.

Award: Scholarship for use in freshman, sophomore, junior, senior, or graduate years; not renewable.

Eligibility Requirements: Applicant must be enrolled or expecting to enroll full-time at a four-year institution or university. Applicant must have 2.5 GPA or higher. Available to U.S. and non-U.S. citizens.

Application Requirements: Application form, driver's license, essay, interview, recommendations or references, transcript. *Deadline:* March 17.

Contact: Irving Washington, Manager
Phone: 301-445-7100
Fax: 301-445-7101
E-mail: iwashington@nabj.org

NATIONAL ASSOCIATION OF BROADCASTERS

http://www.nab.org/

NATIONAL ASSOCIATION OF BROADCASTERS GRANTS FOR RESEARCH IN BROADCASTING

Award program is intended to fund research on economic, business, social, and policy issues important to station managers and other decision-makers in the United States commercial broadcast industry. Competition is open to all academic personnel. Graduate students and senior undergraduates are invited to submit proposals. For details refer to website http://www.nab.org.

Academic Fields/Career Goals: Communications; Journalism; TV/Radio Broadcasting.

Award: Grant for use in senior, graduate, or postgraduate years; not renewable. *Number:* 2. *Amount:* $5000.

Eligibility Requirements: Applicant must be enrolled or expecting to enroll full-time at a four-year institution or university. Available to U.S. and non-U.S. citizens.

Application Requirements: Application form, recommendations or references, research proposal, budget. *Deadline:* February 1.

Contact: Debbie Milman, Research Director
National Association of Broadcasters
1771 N Street NW
Washington, DC 20036
Phone: 202-429-5383
Fax: 202-429-4199
E-mail: dmilman@nab.org

NATIONAL ASSOCIATION OF HISPANIC JOURNALISTS (NAHJ)

http://www.nahj.org/

NATIONAL ASSOCIATION OF HISPANIC JOURNALISTS SCHOLARSHIP

One-time award for high school seniors, college undergraduates, and first-year graduate students who are pursuing careers in English- or Spanish-language print, photo, broadcast, or online journalism. Students may major or plan to major in any subject, but must demonstrate a sincere desire to pursue a career in journalism. Must submit resume and work samples. Applications available only on website http://www.nahj.org.

Academic Fields/Career Goals: Communications; Journalism; Photojournalism/Photography; TV/Radio Broadcasting.

Award: Scholarship for use in freshman, sophomore, junior, senior, or graduate years; not renewable. *Amount:* $1000–$2000.

Eligibility Requirements: Applicant must be enrolled or expecting to enroll full-time at a four-year institution or university and must have an interest in photography/photogrammetry/filmmaking or writing. Available to U.S. citizens.

Application Requirements: Application form, essay, financial need analysis, recommendations or references, resume, transcript, work samples. *Deadline:* March 31.

Contact: Virginia Galindo, Program Assistant
Phone: 202-662-7145
E-mail: vgalindo@nahj.org

NATIONAL ASSOCIATION OF WATER COMPANIES-NEW JERSEY CHAPTER

http://www.nawc.org/

NATIONAL ASSOCIATION OF WATER COMPANIES-NEW JERSEY CHAPTER SCHOLARSHIP

• *See page 146*

NATIONAL CATTLEMEN'S FOUNDATION

http://www.nationalcattlemensfoundation.org/

CME BEEF INDUSTRY SCHOLARSHIP

• *See page 87*

NATIONAL INSTITUTE FOR LABOR RELATIONS RESEARCH

http://www.nilrr.org/

NATIONAL INSTITUTE FOR LABOR RELATIONS RESEARCH WILLIAM B. RUGGLES JOURNALISM SCHOLARSHIP

One-time award for undergraduate or graduate study in journalism or mass communications. Submit 500-word essay on the right-to-work principle. High school seniors accepted into certified journalism school may apply. Specify "Journalism" or "Ruggles" scholarship on any correspondence.

Academic Fields/Career Goals: Communications; Journalism.

Award: Scholarship for use in freshman, sophomore, junior, senior, graduate, or postgraduate years; not renewable. *Number:* 1. *Amount:* $2000.

Eligibility Requirements: Applicant must be enrolled or expecting to enroll full-time at a four-year institution or university and must have an interest in writing. Available to U.S. citizens.

Application Requirements: Application form, application form may be submitted online (http://www.nilrr.org), essay, transcript. *Deadline:* December 31.

Contact: Cathy Jones, Scholarship Coordinator
National Institute for Labor Relations Research
5211 Port Royal Road, Suite 510
Springfield, VA 22151
Phone: 703-321-9606 Ext. 2231
Fax: 703-321-7143
E-mail: research@nilrr.org

NEW JERSEY BROADCASTERS ASSOCIATION

http://www.njba.com/

MICHAEL S. LIBRETTI SCHOLARSHIP

Scholarships for undergraduate students in broadcasting, communication and journalism. Must be a New Jersey resident.

Academic Fields/Career Goals: Communications; Journalism; TV/Radio Broadcasting.

Award: Scholarship for use in freshman, sophomore, junior, or senior years; not renewable. *Number:* 1. *Amount:* up to $5000.

Eligibility Requirements: Applicant must be enrolled or expecting to enroll full-time at a four-year institution or university and resident of New Jersey. Available to U.S. citizens.

Application Requirements: Application form. *Deadline:* varies.

Contact: Phil Roberts, Scholarships Coordinator
Phone: 888-652-2366
Fax: 609-860-0110
E-mail: njba@njba.com

OREGON ASSOCIATION OF BROADCASTERS

http://www.theoab.org/

OAB FOUNDATION SCHOLARSHIP

Award for students to begin or continue their education in broadcast and related studies. Must have a minimum GPA of 3.25. Must be a resident of Oregon studying in Oregon. For more details, refer to website at http://www.TheOAB.org.

Academic Fields/Career Goals: Communications; Journalism; TV/Radio Broadcasting.

Award: Scholarship for use in freshman, sophomore, junior, senior, graduate, or postgraduate years; renewable. *Number:* 4. *Amount:* $2500–$3500.

Eligibility Requirements: Applicant must be enrolled or expecting to enroll full-time at a two-year or four-year institution or university and resident of Oregon. Available to U.S. citizens.

Application Requirements: Application form, essay, financial need analysis, recommendations or references, resume, transcript. *Deadline:* May 3.

Contact: Mr. Bill Johnstone, President and Chief Executive Officer
Oregon Association of Broadcasters
9020 SW Washington Square Road
Suite 140
Portland, OR 97223-4433
Phone: 503-443-2299
Fax: 503-443-2488
E-mail: theoab@theoab.org

OUTDOOR WRITERS ASSOCIATION OF AMERICA

http://www.owaa.org/

OUTDOOR WRITERS ASSOCIATION OF AMERICA - BODIE MCDOWELL SCHOLARSHIP AWARD

One-time award for college level candidates who demonstrate outdoor communications talent and intend to make a career in this field. Applicants must include a letter of recommendation from their institution and samples of their outdoor communications work.

Academic Fields/Career Goals: Communications; Filmmaking/Video; Journalism; Literature/English/Writing; Photojournalism/Photography; TV/Radio Broadcasting.

Award: Scholarship for use in junior, senior, graduate, or postgraduate years; not renewable. *Number:* 2–6. *Amount:* $1000–$5000.

Eligibility Requirements: Applicant must be enrolled or expecting to enroll full-time at a four-year institution or university and must have an interest in amateur radio, art, athletics/sports, photography/photogrammetry/filmmaking, or writing. Available to U.S. and non-U.S. citizens.

Application Requirements: Application form, essay, recommendations or references, transcript, work samples. *Deadline:* March 1.

Contact: Ms. Jessica Pollett, Membership and Conference Coordinator
Outdoor Writers Association of America
615 Oak Street, Suite 201
Missoula, MT 59801
Phone: 406-728-7434
Fax: 406-728-7445
E-mail: info@owaa.org

PRINT AND GRAPHIC SCHOLARSHIP FOUNDATION

http://www.printing.org/

PRINT AND GRAPHICS SCHOLARSHIPS FOUNDATION

Applicant must be interested in a career in graphic communications, printing technology or management, or publishing. Selection is based on academic record, class rank, recommendations, biographical information, and extracurricular activities. All applications and letters of recommendation must be submitted online at www.pgsf.org. All applications high school and college applicants must be submitted by April 1. Awards are available to applicants outside United States, as long as they are attending a U.S. institution and meet the basic criteria of the Print and Graphics Scholarship Foundation.

Academic Fields/Career Goals: Communications; Graphics/Graphic Arts/Printing.

Award: Scholarship for use in freshman, sophomore, junior, senior, or graduate years; renewable. *Number:* 150–200. *Amount:* $1500–$5000.

Eligibility Requirements: Applicant must be enrolled or expecting to enroll full-time at a two-year or four-year or technical institution or university. Applicant must have 3.0 GPA or higher. Available to U.S. and non-U.S. citizens.

Application Requirements: Application form, application form may be submitted online (http://www.pgsf.org), essay, recommendations or references, self-addressed stamped envelope with application, test scores, transcript. *Deadline:* April 1.

Contact: Bernie Eckert, Administrator
Print and Graphic Scholarship Foundation
200 Deer Run Road
Sewickley, PA 15143
Phone: 412-259-1740
Fax: 412-741-2311
E-mail: pgsf@printing.org

PRINTING INDUSTRY OF MIDWEST EDUCATION FOUNDATION

http://www.pimn.org/

PRINTING INDUSTRY MIDWEST EDUCATION FOUNDATION SCHOLARSHIP FUND

The fund offers $1000 renewable scholarships to full-time students enrolled in two- or four-year institutions and technical colleges offering degrees in the print communications discipline. Applicant must be a Minnesota resident and be committed to a career in the print communications industry. Minimum 3.0 GPA required. Priority given to children of PIM member company employees.

Academic Fields/Career Goals: Communications; Flexography; Graphics/Graphic Arts/Printing; Journalism.

Award: Scholarship for use in freshman, sophomore, junior, or senior years; renewable. *Number:* 10–15. *Amount:* $1000.

Eligibility Requirements: Applicant must be enrolled or expecting to enroll full-time at a two-year or four-year or technical institution or university and resident of Iowa, Louisiana, Minnesota, North Dakota, South Dakota. Applicant must have 3.0 GPA or higher. Available to U.S. citizens.

Application Requirements: Application form, copy of college admission form, proof of admission, essay, recommendations or references, test scores, transcript. *Deadline:* April 1.

Contact: Kristin Davis, Director of Education Services
Phone: 651-789-5508
Fax: 65-789-5520
E-mail: kristinp@pimn.org

PUBLIC RELATIONS STUDENT SOCIETY OF AMERICA

http://www.prssa.org/

PUBLIC RELATIONS SOCIETY OF AMERICA MULTICULTURAL AFFAIRS SCHOLARSHIP
• *See page 83*

RADIO & TELEVISION NEWS DIRECTORS FOUNDATION

http://www.rtnda.org/

CAROLE SIMPSON SCHOLARSHIP

Award of $2000 for minority sophomore, junior, or senior undergraduate student enrolled in an electronic journalism program. Submit one to three examples of reporting or producing skills on audio cassette tape or videotape, totaling 15 minutes or less, with scripts.

Academic Fields/Career Goals: Communications; Journalism; TV/Radio Broadcasting.

Award: Scholarship for use in sophomore, junior, or senior years; not renewable. *Number:* 1. *Amount:* $2000.

Eligibility Requirements: Applicant must be American Indian/Alaska Native, Asian/Pacific Islander, Black (non-Hispanic), Hispanic; enrolled or expecting to enroll full-time at a four-year institution or university and must have an interest in photography/photogrammetry/filmmaking or writing. Available to U.S. and non-U.S. citizens.

Application Requirements: Application form, essay, recommendations or references, resume, video or audio tape of work. *Deadline:* May 12.

Contact: Melanie Lo, Project Coordinator
Radio & Television News Directors Foundation
1600 K Street, NW, Suite 700
Washington, DC 20006
Phone: 202-467-5218
Fax: 202-223-4007
E-mail: irvingw@rtndf.org

KEN KASHIWAHARA SCHOLARSHIP

One-time award of $2500 for minority sophomore, junior, or senior whose career objective is electronic journalism. Submit examples showing reporting or producing skills on CD or DVD, with scripts.

Academic Fields/Career Goals: Communications; Journalism; TV/Radio Broadcasting.

Award: Scholarship for use in sophomore, junior, or senior years; not renewable. *Number:* 1. *Amount:* $2500.

Eligibility Requirements: Applicant must be American Indian/Alaska Native, Asian/Pacific Islander, Black (non-Hispanic), Hispanic and enrolled or expecting to enroll full-time at a four-year institution or university. Available to U.S. and non-U.S. citizens.

Application Requirements: Application form, essay, recommendations or references, resume, video or audio tape of work, statement explaining career in electronic journalism. *Deadline:* May 12.

Contact: Melanie Lo, Program Coordinator
Radio & Television News Directors Foundation
1600 K Street, NW, Suite 700
Washington, DC 20006
Phone: 202-467-5218
E-mail: melaniel@rtnda.org

LOU AND CAROLE PRATO SPORTS REPORTING SCHOLARSHIP

One-time tuition grant of $1000 is given to a deserving student with strong writing skills and planning a career as a sports reporter in television or radio.

Academic Fields/Career Goals: Communications; Journalism; TV/Radio Broadcasting.

Award: Grant for use in sophomore, junior, or senior years; not renewable. *Number:* 1. *Amount:* $1000.

Eligibility Requirements: Applicant must be enrolled or expecting to enroll full-time at a four-year institution or university and must have an interest in writing. Available to U.S. and non-U.S. citizens.

Application Requirements: Application form, essay, recommendations or references, resume, video or audio tape of work, cover letter with reasons for seeking scholarship. *Deadline:* May 11.

Contact: Stacey Staniak, Project Manager
Phone: 202-467-5214
E-mail: staceys@rtnda.org

PRESIDENTS SCHOLARSHIP

Two Presidents Scholarships available to full-time college sophomore, junior, or senior year whose career objective is electronic journalism. Must have at least one full year of college remaining.

Academic Fields/Career Goals: Communications; Journalism; TV/Radio Broadcasting.

Award: Scholarship for use in sophomore, junior, or senior years; not renewable. *Number:* 2. *Amount:* $2500.

Eligibility Requirements: Applicant must be enrolled or expecting to enroll full-time at a four-year institution or university. Available to U.S. and non-U.S. citizens.

Application Requirements: Application form, CD or DVD of work, essay, recommendations or references, resume. *Deadline:* May 11.

Contact: Stacey Staniak, Project Manager
Phone: 202-467-5214
E-mail: staceys@rtnda.org

RHODE ISLAND FOUNDATION

http://www.rifoundation.org/

J. D. EDSAL SCHOLARSHIP
• *See page 84*

RDW GROUP INC. MINORITY SCHOLARSHIP FOR COMMUNICATIONS

Award to provide support for minority students who wish to pursue a course of study in communications at the undergraduate or graduate level. Must be a Rhode Island resident and must demonstrate financial need.

Academic Fields/Career Goals: Communications.

Award: Scholarship for use in freshman, sophomore, junior, senior, or graduate years; not renewable. *Amount:* $2000.

Eligibility Requirements: Applicant must be American Indian/Alaska Native, Asian/Pacific Islander, Black (non-Hispanic), Hispanic; enrolled or expecting to enroll full-time at a four-year institution or university and resident of Rhode Island. Available to U.S. citizens.

Application Requirements: Application form, essay, self-addressed stamped envelope with application, transcript. *Deadline:* April 26.

Contact: Libby Monahan, Funds Administrator
Phone: 401-274-4564 Ext. 3117
E-mail: libbym@rifoundation.org

ROBERT H. MOLLOHAN FAMILY CHARITABLE FOUNDATION, INC.

http://www.mollohanfoundation.org/

HARRY C. HAMM FAMILY SCHOLARSHIP

The Harry C. Hamm Family Scholarship is awarded to a sophomore, junior, or senior college student who is in serious pursuit of a B.A. in Journalism or Communications at a West Virginia four-year institution. Mr. Hamm was a 50 year veteran reporter/editor with Ogden Newspapers. The applicant must be a graduate of a high school in West Virginia and must have at least a 3.0 GPA.

Academic Fields/Career Goals: Communications; Journalism.

Award: Scholarship for use in sophomore, junior, or senior years; not renewable. *Amount:* $1000.

Eligibility Requirements: Applicant must be high school student; planning to enroll or expecting to enroll full-time at a four-year institution or university; resident of West Virginia and studying in West Virginia. Applicant must have 3.0 GPA or higher. Available to U.S. citizens.

Application Requirements: Application form, essay, recommendations or references, resume, test scores, transcript.

Contact: Aime Shaffer, Program Manager
Phone: 304-333-6783
E-mail: ashaffer@wvhtf.org

SOCIETY FOR TECHNICAL COMMUNICATION

http://www.stc.org/

SOCIETY FOR TECHNICAL COMMUNICATION SCHOLARSHIP PROGRAM

Award for study relating to communication of information about technical subjects. Applicants must be full-time graduate students working toward a master's or doctoral degree, or undergraduate students working toward a bachelor's degree. Must have completed at least one year of postsecondary education and have at least one full year of academic work remaining. Two awards available for undergraduate students, two available for graduate students.

Academic Fields/Career Goals: Communications; Science, Technology, and Society.

Award: Scholarship for use in sophomore, junior, senior, or graduate years; not renewable. *Number:* up to 4. *Amount:* up to $1500.

Eligibility Requirements: Applicant must be enrolled or expecting to enroll full-time at a four-year institution or university. Available to U.S. and non-U.S. citizens.

Application Requirements: Application form, essay, recommendations or references, transcript. *Deadline:* February 15.

Contact: Scott DeLoach, Manager, Scholarship Selection Committee
Society for Technical Communication
834 C Dekalb Avenue, NE
Atlanta, GA 30307

SOCIETY FOR TECHNICAL COMMUNICATION–LONE STAR CHAPTER

http://www.stc-dfw.org/

LONE STAR COMMUNITY SCHOLARSHIPS

Scholarship for graduate or undergraduate student working toward a degree or certificate in the technical communication field. We also provide a scholarship for those returning to school to either further their studies in technical communication through approved training courses or career advancement classes. For further information see website http://www.stc-dfw.org.

Academic Fields/Career Goals: Communications.

Award: Scholarship for use in freshman, sophomore, junior, senior, or graduate years; not renewable. *Number:* 1–4.

Eligibility Requirements: Applicant must be Hispanic; enrolled or expecting to enroll full- or part-time at a four-year institution or university and resident of Oklahoma, Texas. Available to U.S. and non-U.S. citizens.

Application Requirements: Application form, recommendations or references, transcript. *Deadline:* March 28.

Contact: Rob Harris, Scholarship Committee Manager
Phone: 940-391-0167
E-mail: scholarship@stc-dfw.org

SOCIETY OF MOTION PICTURE AND TELEVISION ENGINEERS

http://www.smpte.org/

LOUIS F. WOLF JR. MEMORIAL SCHOLARSHIP

Award for students enrolled in an accredited high school, two-year or four-year college or university. Must be members of Society of Motion Picture and Television Engineers.

Academic Fields/Career Goals: Communications; Electrical Engineering/Electronics; Engineering-Related Technologies; Engineering/Technology; Filmmaking/Video; Science, Technology, and Society; TV/Radio Broadcasting.

Award: Scholarship for use in freshman, sophomore, junior, senior, graduate, or postgraduate years; not renewable. *Number:* 1–3. *Amount:* $1000–$2000.

Eligibility Requirements: Applicant must be enrolled or expecting to enroll full-time at a two-year or four-year or technical institution or university. Applicant or parent of applicant must be member of Society of Motion Picture and Television Engineers. Available to U.S. and non-U.S. citizens.

Application Requirements: Application form, essay, recommendations or references, transcript. *Deadline:* July 1.

Contact: Sally-Ann DAmato, Director of Operations
Society of Motion Picture and Television Engineers (SMPTE)
3 Barker Avenue
White Plains, NY 10601
Phone: 914-761-1100 Ext. 2375
E-mail: sdamato@smpte.org

STUDENT PAPER AWARD

Contest for best paper by a current Student Member of SMPTE. Paper must deal with some technical phase of motion pictures, television, photographic instrumentation, or their closely allied arts and sciences. For more information see website http://www.smpte.org.

Academic Fields/Career Goals: Communications; Electrical Engineering/Electronics; Engineering-Related Technologies; Engineering/Technology; Filmmaking/Video; Science, Technology, and Society; TV/Radio Broadcasting.

Award: Prize for use in freshman, sophomore, junior, senior, graduate, or postgraduate years; not renewable. *Number:* 1–2. *Amount:* up to $1500.

Eligibility Requirements: Applicant must be enrolled or expecting to enroll full- or part-time at a two-year or four-year or technical institution or university. Applicant or parent of applicant must be member of Society of Motion Picture and Television Engineers. Available to U.S. and non-U.S. citizens.

Application Requirements: Application form, entry in a contest, essay, student ID card, transcript. *Deadline:* July 1.

Contact: Sally-Ann D'Amato, Director of Operations
Society of Motion Picture and Television Engineers (SMPTE)
3 Barker Avenue
White Plains, NY 10601
Phone: 914-761-1100 Ext. 2375
E-mail: sdamato@smpte.org

SOCIETY OF SATELLITE PROFESSIONALS INTERNATIONAL
http://www.sspi.org/

SSPI INTERNATIONAL SCHOLARSHIPS
• *See page 138*

SPECIALTY EQUIPMENT MARKET ASSOCIATION
http://www.sema.org/

SPECIALTY EQUIPMENT MARKET ASSOCIATION MEMORIAL SCHOLARSHIP FUND
• *See page 80*

STRAIGHTFORWARD MEDIA
http://www.straightforwardmedia.com/

STRAIGHTFORWARD MEDIA MEDIA & COMMUNICATIONS SCHOLARSHIP
• *See page 84*

TEXAS ASSOCIATION OF BROADCASTERS
http://www.tab.org/

BELO TEXAS BROADCAST EDUCATION FOUNDATION SCHOLARSHIP

Scholarship of $2000 to undergraduate and graduate students enrolled in a fully accredited program of instruction that emphasizes radio or television broadcasting or communications at a four-year college or university in Texas. Student must be a member of the Texas Association of Broadcasters. Must have a GPA of 3.0 minimum.

Academic Fields/Career Goals: Communications; TV/Radio Broadcasting.

Award: Scholarship for use in freshman, sophomore, junior, senior, or graduate years; not renewable. *Number:* 1. *Amount:* $2000.

Eligibility Requirements: Applicant must be enrolled or expecting to enroll full-time at a four-year institution or university and studying in Texas. Applicant or parent of applicant must be member of Texas Association of Broadcasters. Applicant must have 3.0 GPA or higher. Available to U.S. and non-U.S. citizens.

Application Requirements: Application form, essay, financial need analysis, recommendations or references. *Deadline:* May 3.

Contact: Craig Bean, Public Service Manager
Texas Association of Broadcasters
502 East 11th Street, Suite 200
Austin, TX 78701
Phone: 512-322-9944
Fax: 512-322-0522
E-mail: craig@tab.org

BONNER MCLANE TEXAS BROADCAST EDUCATION FOUNDATION SCHOLARSHIP

Scholarship of $2000 to a undergraduate and students enrolled in a fully accredited program of instruction that emphasizes radio or television broadcasting or communications at a four-year college or university in Texas. Student must be a member of the Texas Association of Broadcasters. Must have a GPA of 3.0 minimum.

Academic Fields/Career Goals: Communications; TV/Radio Broadcasting.

Award: Scholarship for use in freshman, sophomore, junior, senior, or graduate years; not renewable. *Number:* 1. *Amount:* $2000.

Eligibility Requirements: Applicant must be enrolled or expecting to enroll full-time at a four-year institution or university and studying in Texas. Applicant or parent of applicant must be member of Texas Association of Broadcasters. Applicant must have 3.0 GPA or higher. Available to U.S. and non-U.S. citizens.

Application Requirements: Application form, essay, financial need analysis, recommendations or references. *Deadline:* May 3.

Contact: Craig Bean, Public Service Manager
Texas Association of Broadcasters
502 East 11th Street, Suite 200
Austin, TX 78701
Phone: 512-322-9944
Fax: 512-322-0522
E-mail: craig@tab.org

STUDENT TEXAS BROADCAST EDUCATION FOUNDATION SCHOLARSHIP

Scholarship of $2000 to a undergraduate or a graduate student enrolled in a program of instruction that emphasizes radio or television broadcasting or communications at a two-year or technical school in Texas. Student must be a member of the Texas Association of Broadcasters. Must have a GPA of 3.0 minimum.

Academic Fields/Career Goals: Communications; TV/Radio Broadcasting.

Award: Scholarship for use in freshman, sophomore, junior, or senior years; not renewable. *Number:* 1. *Amount:* $2000.

Eligibility Requirements: Applicant must be enrolled or expecting to enroll full-time at a two-year or technical institution and studying in Texas. Applicant or parent of applicant must be member of Texas Association of Broadcasters. Applicant must have 3.0 GPA or higher. Available to U.S. and non-U.S. citizens.

Application Requirements: Application form, essay, financial need analysis, recommendations or references. *Deadline:* May 3.

Contact: Craig Bean, Public Service Manager
Texas Association of Broadcasters
502 East 11th Street, Suite 200
Austin, TX 78701
Phone: 512-322-9944
Fax: 512-322-0522
E-mail: craig@tab.org

TOM REIFF TEXAS BROADCAST EDUCATION FOUNDATION SCHOLARSHIP

Scholarship of $2000 to undergraduate and graduate students enrolled in a fully accredited program of instruction that emphasizes radio or television broadcasting or communications at a four-year college or university in Texas. Student must be a member of the Texas Association of Broadcasters. Must have a GPA of 3.0 minimum.

Academic Fields/Career Goals: Communications; TV/Radio Broadcasting.

Award: Scholarship for use in freshman, sophomore, junior, senior, or graduate years; not renewable. *Number:* 1. *Amount:* $2000.

Eligibility Requirements: Applicant must be enrolled or expecting to enroll full-time at a four-year institution or university and studying in Texas. Applicant or parent of applicant must be member of Texas Association of Broadcasters. Applicant must have 3.0 GPA or higher. Available to U.S. and non-U.S. citizens.

Application Requirements: Application form, essay, financial need analysis, recommendations or references. *Deadline:* May 3.

Contact: Craig Bean, Public Service Manager
Texas Association of Broadcasters
502 East 11th Street, Suite 200
Austin, TX 78701
Phone: 512-322-9944
Fax: 512-322-0522
E-mail: craig@tab.org

UNDERGRADUATE TEXAS BROADCAST EDUCATION FOUNDATION SCHOLARSHIP

Scholarship of $2000 to a undergraduate student enrolled in a fully accredited program of instruction that emphasizes radio or television broadcasting or communications at a four-year college or university in Texas. Student must be a member of the Texas Association of Broadcasters. Must have a GPA of 3.0 minimum.

Academic Fields/Career Goals: Communications; TV/Radio Broadcasting.

Award: Scholarship for use in freshman, sophomore, junior, or senior years; not renewable. *Number:* 1. *Amount:* $2000.

Eligibility Requirements: Applicant must be enrolled or expecting to enroll full-time at a four-year institution or university and studying in Texas. Applicant or parent of applicant must be member of Texas Association of Broadcasters. Applicant must have 3.0 GPA or higher. Available to U.S. and non-U.S. citizens.

Application Requirements: Application form, essay, financial need analysis, recommendations or references. *Deadline:* May 3.

Contact: Craig Bean, Public Service Manager
Texas Association of Broadcasters
502 East 11th Street, Suite 200
Austin, TX 78701
Phone: 512-322-9944
Fax: 512-322-0522
E-mail: craig@tab.org

VANN KENNEDY TEXAS BROADCAST EDUCATION FOUNDATION SCHOLARSHIP

Scholarship of $2000 to a undergraduate or graduate student enrolled in a fully accredited program of instruction that emphasizes radio or television broadcasting or communications at college or university in Texas. Student must be a member of the Texas Association of Broadcasters. Must have a GPA of 3.0 minimum.

Academic Fields/Career Goals: Communications; TV/Radio Broadcasting.

Award: Scholarship for use in freshman, sophomore, junior, or senior years; not renewable. *Number:* 1. *Amount:* $2000.

Eligibility Requirements: Applicant must be enrolled or expecting to enroll full-time at a two-year or four-year institution or university and studying in Texas. Applicant or parent of applicant must be member of Texas Association of Broadcasters. Applicant must have 3.0 GPA or higher. Available to U.S. and non-U.S. citizens.

Application Requirements: Application form, essay, financial need analysis, recommendations or references. *Deadline:* May 3.

Contact: Craig Bean, Public Service Manager
Texas Association of Broadcasters
502 East 11th Street, Suite 200
Austin, TX 78701
Phone: 512-322-9944
Fax: 512-322-0522
E-mail: craig@tab.org

TEXAS GRIDIRON CLUB INC.

http://www.spjfw.org/

TEXAS GRIDIRON CLUB SCHOLARSHIPS

$500 to $1000 scholarships for full-time or part-time college juniors, seniors, or graduate students majoring in newspaper, photojournalism, or broadcast fields. Must be Texas resident or going to school in Texas.

Academic Fields/Career Goals: Communications; Journalism; Photojournalism/Photography; TV/Radio Broadcasting.

Award: Scholarship for use in junior, senior, or graduate years; not renewable. *Number:* 10–15. *Amount:* $500–$1000.

Eligibility Requirements: Applicant must be enrolled or expecting to enroll full- or part-time at a four-year institution or university and resident of Texas. Available to U.S. citizens.

Application Requirements: Application form, essay, financial need analysis, recommendations or references, transcript, work samples. *Deadline:* March 3.

Contact: Angie Summers, Scholarships Coordinator
Texas Gridiron Club Inc.
709 Houston Street
Arlington, TX 76012
E-mail: asummers@star-telegram.com

TEXAS OUTDOOR WRITERS ASSOCIATION

http://www.towa.org/

TEXAS OUTDOOR WRITERS ASSOCIATION SCHOLARSHIP

Annual merit award available to students attending an accredited Texas college or university preparing for a career which would incorporate communications skills about the outdoors, environmental conservation, or resource management. Minimum 2.5 GPA required. Submit writing/photo samples.

Academic Fields/Career Goals: Communications; Environmental Science; Natural Resources.

Award: Scholarship for use in freshman, sophomore, junior, senior, graduate, or postgraduate years; not renewable. *Number:* 2. *Amount:* $1000–$1500.

Eligibility Requirements: Applicant must be enrolled or expecting to enroll full- or part-time at a four-year institution or university; resident of Texas; studying in Texas and must have an interest in writing. Applicant must have 2.5 GPA or higher. Available to U.S. citizens.

Application Requirements: Application form, recommendations or references, transcript, writing/photo samples. *Deadline:* February 15.

Contact: Chester Moore, Scholarship Chair
Phone: 409-882-0945
Fax: 409-882-0945
E-mail: saltwater@fishgame.com

TKE EDUCATIONAL FOUNDATION

http://www.tke.org/

GEORGE W. WOOLERY MEMORIAL SCHOLARSHIP

Scholarship available to initiated undergraduate members of Tau Kappa Epsilon who are full-time students in good standing, and pursuing a degree in communications or marketing with a cumulative GPA of 2.5 or higher. Record of leadership within the TKE chapter and on campus should be submitted. Preference will be given to members of Beta-Sigma Chapter, but if no qualified candidate applies, the award will be open to any member of TKE.

Academic Fields/Career Goals: Communications.

Award: Scholarship for use in freshman, sophomore, junior, or senior years; not renewable. *Number:* 1. *Amount:* $600.

Eligibility Requirements: Applicant must be enrolled or expecting to enroll full-time at a four-year institution or university; male and must have an interest in leadership. Applicant or parent of applicant must be member of Tau Kappa Epsilon. Applicant must have 2.5 GPA or higher. Available to U.S. and non-U.S. citizens.

Application Requirements: Application form, essay, narrative summary of how TKE membership has benefited applicant, personal photograph, transcript. *Deadline:* February 29.

TURF AND ORNAMENTAL COMMUNICATORS ASSOCIATION

http://www.toca.org/

TURF AND ORNAMENTAL COMMUNICATORS ASSOCIATION SCHOLARSHIP PROGRAM

• See page 96

UNITED METHODIST COMMUNICATIONS

http://www.umcom.org/

LEONARD M. PERRYMAN COMMUNICATIONS SCHOLARSHIP FOR ETHNIC MINORITY STUDENTS

One-time award to assist United Methodist ethnic minority students who are college students intending to pursue careers in religious communications.

Academic Fields/Career Goals: Communications; Journalism; Photojournalism/Photography; Religion/Theology; TV/Radio Broadcasting.

Award: Scholarship for use in junior or senior years; not renewable. *Number:* 1. *Amount:* $2500.

Eligibility Requirements: Applicant must be Methodist; American Indian/Alaska Native, Asian/Pacific Islander, Black (non-Hispanic), Hispanic and enrolled or expecting to enroll full-time at a two-year or four-year institution or university. Available to U.S. citizens.

Application Requirements: Application form, essay, personal photograph, recommendations or references, transcript. *Deadline:* March 15.

Contact: Michael Neff, Executive Director
  Phone: 703-836-4606 Ext. 325
  Fax: 703-836-2024
  E-mail: mwneff@ashs.org

UNITED NEGRO COLLEGE FUND

http://www.uncf.org/

JANET JACKSON/RHYTHM NATION SCHOLARSHIP
• *See page 123*

JOHN LENNON SCHOLARSHIP

Scholarships for students at UNCF member institutes majoring in performing arts, music, mass communications, and communications. Must have at least 3.0 GPA. Prospective applicants should complete the Student Profile found at website http://www.uncf.org.

Academic Fields/Career Goals: Communications; Music; Performing Arts.

Award: Scholarship for use in freshman, sophomore, junior, or senior years; not renewable. *Number:* 1. *Amount:* $5000.

Eligibility Requirements: Applicant must be Black (non-Hispanic); high school student and planning to enroll or expecting to enroll full- or part-time at a four-year institution or university. Applicant must have 3.0 GPA or higher. Available to U.S. citizens.

Application Requirements: Application form, essay, financial need analysis, personal photograph, recommendations or references, transcript. *Deadline:* April 15.

MICHAEL JACKSON SCHOLARSHIP

Scholarships for students majoring in the performing arts, English, or communications who are attending UNCF member colleges and universities. Funds may be used for tuition, room and board, books, or to repay federal student loans. Minimum 3.0 GPA required.

Academic Fields/Career Goals: Communications; Literature/English/Writing; Performing Arts.

Award: Scholarship for use in freshman year; not renewable. *Amount:* up to $4000.

Eligibility Requirements: Applicant must be Black (non-Hispanic) and enrolled or expecting to enroll full-time at a four-year institution or university. Applicant must have 3.0 GPA or higher. Available to U.S. citizens.

Application Requirements: Application form. *Deadline:* continuous.

NASCAR/WENDELL SCOTT, SR. SCHOLARSHIP
• *See page 82*

READER'S DIGEST FOUNDATION SCHOLARSHIP

$5000 scholarships for students attending UNCF member colleges and universities and majoring in communications, journalism, or English. Students must be in their junior or senior year and have a minimum 3.0 GPA. Must submit a published writing sample with application.

Academic Fields/Career Goals: Communications; Journalism; Literature/English/Writing.

Award: Scholarship for use in junior or senior years; not renewable. *Amount:* $5000.

Eligibility Requirements: Applicant must be Black (non-Hispanic) and enrolled or expecting to enroll full-time at a four-year institution or university. Applicant must have 3.0 GPA or higher. Available to U.S. citizens.

Application Requirements: Application form, published writing sample. *Deadline:* continuous.

VALLEY PRESS CLUB, SPRINGFIELD NEWSPAPERS

http://www.valleypressclub.com/

VALLEY PRESS CLUB SCHOLARSHIPS, THE REPUBLICAN SCHOLARSHIP, CHANNEL 22 SCHOLARSHIP

Nonrenewable award for graduating high school seniors from Connecticut and Massachusetts, who are interested in television journalism, photojournalism, broadcast journalism, or print journalism.

Academic Fields/Career Goals: Communications; Journalism; Photojournalism/Photography; TV/Radio Broadcasting.

Award: Scholarship for use in freshman year; not renewable. *Number:* 5. *Amount:* $1000.

Eligibility Requirements: Applicant must be high school student; planning to enroll or expecting to enroll full-time at a four-year institution or university; resident of Connecticut, Massachusetts and must have an interest in writing. Available to U.S. citizens.

Application Requirements: Application form, financial need analysis, interview, recommendations or references, test scores, transcript. *Deadline:* April 1.

Contact: Robert McClellan, Scholarship Committee Chair
  Valley Press Club, Springfield Newspapers
  PO Box 5475
  Springfield, MA 01101
  Phone: 413-783-3355

VIRGINIA ASSOCIATION OF BROADCASTERS

http://www.vabonline.com/

VIRGINIA ASSOCIATION OF BROADCASTERS SCHOLARSHIP AWARD

Scholarships are available to entering juniors and seniors majoring in mass communications-related courses. Must either be a resident of Virginia or be enrolled at a Virginia college or university. Must be U.S. citizen and enrolled full-time.

Academic Fields/Career Goals: Communications.

Award: Scholarship for use in junior or senior years; renewable. *Number:* 4. *Amount:* $500–$1000.

Eligibility Requirements: Applicant must be enrolled or expecting to enroll full-time at a four-year institution or university; resident of Virginia and studying in Virginia. Available to U.S. and non-U.S. citizens.

Application Requirements: Application form, essay, financial need analysis, transcript. *Deadline:* February 15.

Contact: Ruby Seal, Director of Administration
  Phone: 434-977-3716
  Fax: 434-979-2439
  E-mail: ruby.seal@easterassociates.com

WASHINGTON NEWS COUNCIL

http://www.wanewscouncil.org/

DICK LARSEN SCHOLARSHIP PROGRAM

One-time award for a student at a Washington state four-year public or private college with a serious interest in a career in communications-journalism, public relations, politics, or a related field. Must be resident of Washington state and U.S. citizen. See website for more information.

Academic Fields/Career Goals: Communications; Journalism; Political Science.

Award: Scholarship for use in freshman, sophomore, junior, senior, or graduate years; not renewable. *Number:* 1. *Amount:* $2000.

Eligibility Requirements: Applicant must be enrolled or expecting to enroll full-time at a four-year institution; resident of Washington and studying in Washington. Available to U.S. citizens.

Application Requirements: 3 samples of work, application form, essay, financial need analysis, recommendations or references, transcript. *Deadline:* May 15.

HERB ROBINSON SCHOLARSHIP PROGRAM

One-time award to a graduating Washington state high school senior who is entering a four-year public or private college or university in Washington. Must have a serious interest in a career in communications-journalism, public relations, politics or a related field. Must be resident of Washington state and a U.S. citizen. See website for more information.

Academic Fields/Career Goals: Communications; Journalism; Political Science.

Award: Scholarship for use in freshman year; not renewable. *Number:* 1. *Amount:* $2000.

Eligibility Requirements: Applicant must be high school student; planning to enroll or expecting to enroll full-time at a four-year institution or university; resident of Washington and studying in Washington. Available to U.S. citizens.

Application Requirements: Application form, essay, financial need analysis, recommendations or references, transcript. *Deadline:* May 1.

Contact: John Hamer, Executive Director
Phone: 206-262-9793
E-mail: info@wanewscouncil.org

WHOMENTORS.COM, INC.

http://www.WHOmentors.com/

1B USD WORLDWIDE VENTURE CAPITAL
• *See page 107*

WISCONSIN BROADCASTERS ASSOCIATION FOUNDATION

http://www.wi-broadcasters.org/

WISCONSIN BROADCASTERS ASSOCIATION FOUNDATION SCHOLARSHIP

Four $2000 scholarships offered to assist students enrolled in broadcasting-related educational programs at four-year public or private institutions. Applicants must either have graduated from a Wisconsin high school, or be attending a Wisconsin college or university, must have completed at least 60 credits, and must be planning a career in radio or television broadcasting.

Academic Fields/Career Goals: Communications; TV/Radio Broadcasting.

Award: Scholarship for use in freshman, sophomore, junior, or senior years; not renewable. *Number:* 4. *Amount:* $2000.

Eligibility Requirements: Applicant must be enrolled or expecting to enroll full-time at a four-year institution or university and studying in Wisconsin. Available to U.S. citizens.

Application Requirements: Application form, essay, recommendations or references, transcript. *Deadline:* October 20.

Contact: John Laabs, President
Phone: 608-255-2600
Fax: 608-256-3986
E-mail: jlaabs@aol.com

WOMEN'S BASKETBALL COACHES ASSOCIATION

http://www.wbca.org/

ROBIN ROBERTS/WBCA SPORTS COMMUNICATIONS SCHOLARSHIP AWARD

One-time award for female student athletes who have completed their eligibility and plan to go to graduate school. Must major in communications. Must be nominated by the head coach of women's basketball who is a member of the WBCA.

Academic Fields/Career Goals: Communications; Journalism.

Award: Scholarship for use in senior, graduate, or postgraduate years; not renewable. *Number:* 1. *Amount:* $4000.

Eligibility Requirements: Applicant must be enrolled or expecting to enroll full- or part-time at a four-year institution or university; female and must have an interest in athletics/sports. Available to U.S. and non-U.S. citizens.

Application Requirements: Application form, recommendations or references, statistics. *Deadline:* February 15.

Contact: Betty Jaynes, Consultant
Phone: 770-279-8027 Ext. 102
Fax: 770-279-6290
E-mail: bettyj@wbca.org

WYOMING TRUCKING ASSOCIATION SCHOLARSHIP FUND TRUST

http://www.wytruck.org/

WYOMING TRUCKING ASSOCIATION SCHOLARSHIP TRUST FUND
• *See page 83*

COMPUTER SCIENCE/ DATA PROCESSING

AIST FOUNDATION

http://www.aistfoundation.org/

ASSOCIATION FOR IRON AND STEEL TECHNOLOGY OHIO VALLEY CHAPTER SCHOLARSHIP
• *See page 142*

ASSOCIATION FOR IRON AND STEEL TECHNOLOGY WILLY KORF MEMORIAL SCHOLARSHIP
• *See page 162*

AMERICAN FOUNDATION FOR THE BLIND

http://www.afb.org/

PAUL W. RUCKES SCHOLARSHIP

Scholarship of $1000 to an undergraduate or graduate student studying in the field of engineering or in computer, physical, or life sciences. For more information and application requirements, please visit http://www.afb.org/scholarships.asp.

Academic Fields/Career Goals: Computer Science/Data Processing; Electrical Engineering/Electronics; Engineering/Technology; Natural Sciences; Physical Sciences.

Award: Scholarship for use in freshman, sophomore, junior, or senior years; not renewable. *Number:* 1. *Amount:* $1000.

Eligibility Requirements: Applicant must be visually impaired and enrolled or expecting to enroll full-time at a two-year or four-year institution or university. Applicant must be visually impaired. Available to U.S. citizens.

Application Requirements: Application form, essay, proof of post-secondary acceptance and legal blindness, proof of citizenship, FAFSA, recommendations or references, transcript. *Deadline:* April 30.

Contact: Dawn Bodrogi, Information Center
American Foundation for the Blind
11 Penn Plaza, Suite 300
New York, NY 10001
Phone: 212-502-7661
Fax: 212-502-7771
E-mail: afbinfo@afb.net

AMERICAN SOCIETY FOR INFORMATION SCIENCE AND TECHNOLOGY

http://www.asis.org/

JOHN WILEY & SONS BEST JASIST PAPER AWARD

Award of $1500 to recognize the best refereed paper published in the volume year of the JASIT preceding the ASIST annual meeting. John

Wiley & Sons Inc., shall contribute $500 towards travel expenses to attend the ASIST annual meeting. No nomination procedure is used for this award. All eligible papers are considered.

Academic Fields/Career Goals: Computer Science/Data Processing; Library and Information Sciences.

Award: Prize for use in freshman, sophomore, junior, senior, graduate, or postgraduate years; not renewable. *Number:* 1. *Amount:* $2000.

Eligibility Requirements: Applicant must be enrolled or expecting to enroll full-time at a four-year institution or university. Available to U.S. and non-U.S. citizens.

Application Requirements: Application form, essay. *Deadline:* varies.

ARMED FORCES COMMUNICATIONS AND ELECTRONICS ASSOCIATION, EDUCATIONAL FOUNDATION

http://www.afcea.org/scholarships

ARMED FORCES COMMUNICATIONS AND ELECTRONICS ASSOCIATION GENERAL EMMETT PAIGE SCHOLARSHIP

• *See page 127*

ARMED FORCES COMMUNICATIONS AND ELECTRONICS ASSOCIATION ROTC SCHOLARSHIP PROGRAM

• *See page 127*

DISABLED WAR VETERANS SCHOLARSHIP

• *See page 128*

LTG DOUGLAS D. BUCHHOLZ MEMORIAL SCHOLARSHIP

• *See page 128*

VETERANS OF ENDURING FREEDOM (AFGHANISTAN) AND IRAQI FREEDOM SCHOLARSHIP

Scholarships for active-duty and honorably discharged U.S. military veterans (to include Reservists and National Guard personnel) of the Enduring Freedom (Afghanistan) or Iraqi Freedom operations who are actively pursuing an undergraduate degree in an eligible major at accredited two- or four-year institutions in the United States. Distance-learning or online programs affiliated with a major U.S. institution are eligible. Candidates must be majoring in the following or related fields: electrical, aerospace, systems or computer engineering; computer engineering technology; computer information systems; information systems management; computer science; physics; mathematics; or science or mathematics education. Majors directly related to the support of U.S. intelligence or homeland security enterprises with relevance to the mission of AFCEA will also be eligible.

Academic Fields/Career Goals: Computer Science/Data Processing; Electrical Engineering/Electronics; Mathematics; Physical Sciences.

Award: Scholarship for use in freshman, sophomore, or junior years; not renewable. *Number:* 5–6. *Amount:* $2500.

Eligibility Requirements: Applicant must be enrolled or expecting to enroll full- or part-time at a two-year or four-year institution or university. Available to U.S. citizens. Applicant must have general military experience.

Application Requirements: Application form, Military ID/DD214, recommendations or references, transcript. *Deadline:* May 1.

Contact: Ms. Norma Corrales, Senior Director, Scholarships and Awards
Armed Forces Communications and Electronics Association, Educational Foundation
4400 Fair Lakes Court
Fairfax, VA 22033
Phone: 703-631-6149
E-mail: scholarships@afcea.org

ARRL FOUNDATION INC.

http://www.arrl.org/

ANDROSCOGGIN AMATEUR RADIO CLUB SCHOLARSHIP

Up to 2 awards to students in the ARRL Maine or New England Division (Maine, New Hampshire, Vermont, Rhode Island, Massachusetts or Connecticut) who have an active technician class amateur radio license or higher. Preference given to students studying computer science, TV/radio electronics, or electrical engineering at a two- or four-year college.

Academic Fields/Career Goals: Computer Science/Data Processing; Electrical Engineering/Electronics; TV/Radio Broadcasting.

Award: Scholarship for use in freshman, sophomore, junior, or senior years; not renewable. *Number:* 1–2. *Amount:* $500–$1000.

Eligibility Requirements: Applicant must be enrolled or expecting to enroll full- or part-time at a two-year or four-year or technical institution; resident of Connecticut, Maine, Massachusetts, New Hampshire, Rhode Island, Vermont and must have an interest in amateur radio. Available to U.S. citizens.

Application Requirements: Application form, transcript. *Deadline:* February 1.

Contact: Ms. Mary Hobart, Secretary
Phone: 860-594-0397
E-mail: k1mmh@arrl.org

INDIANAPOLIS AMATEUR RADIO ASSOCIATION SCHOLARSHIP FUND

$1000 award for a student who is a resident of Indiana or the ARRL Central Division (Illinois, Indiana, and Wisconsin). Must be studying electrical or electronics engineering, computer science, or related fields.

Academic Fields/Career Goals: Computer Science/Data Processing; Electrical Engineering/Electronics.

Award: Scholarship for use in freshman, sophomore, junior, or senior years; not renewable. *Number:* 1. *Amount:* $1000.

Eligibility Requirements: Applicant must be enrolled or expecting to enroll full- or part-time at a two-year or four-year or technical institution or university; resident of Illinois, Indiana, Wisconsin and must have an interest in amateur radio. Available to U.S. citizens.

Application Requirements: Application form, transcript. *Deadline:* February 1.

Contact: Ms. Mary Hobart, Secretary
Phone: 860-594-0397
E-mail: k1mmh@arrl.org

JAKE MCCLAIN DRIVER, KC5WXA, SCHOLARSHIP FUND

$1000 scholarship for a resident of Tennessee or the ARRL Delta Division (Arkansas, Louisiana, Mississippi, Tennessee). Must have a Technical Class or higher license and provide at least one QLSL card received within the past 12 months. Must be studying electronics, computers, or journalism.

Academic Fields/Career Goals: Computer Science/Data Processing; Electrical Engineering/Electronics; Journalism.

Award: Scholarship for use in freshman, sophomore, junior, or senior years; not renewable. *Number:* 1. *Amount:* $1000.

Eligibility Requirements: Applicant must be enrolled or expecting to enroll full- or part-time at a two-year or four-year or technical institution or university and resident of Arkansas, Louisiana, Mississippi, Tennessee. Available to U.S. citizens.

Application Requirements: Application form, QLSL card, transcript. *Deadline:* February 1.

Contact: Ms. Mary Hobart, Secretary
Phone: 860-594-0397
E-mail: k1mmh@arrl.org

MAGNOLIA DX ASSOCIATION SCHOLARSHIP

• *See page 189*

NORTH FULTON AMATEUR RADIO LEAGUE SCHOLARSHIP FUND

$900 scholarship for an ARRL member who is studying engineering or computer science. Must be a resident in GA and a member of ARRL. If no qualified applicant, preference will be awarded to an applicant from the ARRL Southeastern Division (Alabama, Florida, Georgia, Puerto Rico and the US Virgin Islands).

Academic Fields/Career Goals: Computer Science/Data Processing; Engineering/Technology.

Award: Scholarship for use in freshman, sophomore, junior, or senior years; not renewable. *Number:* 1. *Amount:* $900.

Eligibility Requirements: Applicant must be enrolled or expecting to enroll full- or part-time at a two-year or four-year or technical institution or university; resident of Alabama, Florida, Georgia, Puerto Rico and must have an interest in amateur radio. Applicant or parent of applicant must be member of American Radio Relay League. Available to U.S. citizens.

Application Requirements: Application form, transcript. *Deadline:* February 1.

Contact: Ms. Mary Hobart, Secretary
    Phone: 860-594-0397
    E-mail: k1mmh@arrl.org

PHD SCHOLARSHIP

One $1000 award for journalism, computer science, or electronic engineering students who are amateur radio operators. Preference given to students who are children of deceased amateur radio operators. Preference given to residents of ARRL Midwest Division (IA, KS, MO, NE).

Academic Fields/Career Goals: Computer Science/Data Processing; Electrical Engineering/Electronics; Journalism.

Award: Scholarship for use in freshman, sophomore, junior, or senior years; not renewable. *Number:* 1. *Amount:* $1000.

Eligibility Requirements: Applicant must be enrolled or expecting to enroll full-time at a four-year institution or university; resident of Iowa, Kansas, Missouri, Nebraska and must have an interest in amateur radio. Applicant or parent of applicant must be member of American Radio Relay League. Available to U.S. citizens.

Application Requirements: Application form, transcript. *Deadline:* February 1.

Contact: Ms. Mary Hobart, Secretary
    Phone: 860-594-0397
    E-mail: k1mmh@arrl.org

RAY, N0RP, & KATIE, W0KTE, PAUTZ SCHOLARSHIP

One award of up to $1000 is available to a resident of the ARRL Midwest Division (IA, KS, NE, MO) studying electronics or computer science at an accredited four-year college or university. Applicant should possess a general class or higher amateur radio license and be a member of the ARRL.

Academic Fields/Career Goals: Computer Science/Data Processing; Electrical Engineering/Electronics.

Award: Scholarship for use in freshman, sophomore, junior, or senior years; not renewable. *Number:* 1. *Amount:* $500–$1000.

Eligibility Requirements: Applicant must be enrolled or expecting to enroll full- or part-time at a four-year institution or university; resident of Iowa, Kansas, Missouri, Nevada and must have an interest in amateur radio. Applicant or parent of applicant must be member of American Radio Relay League. Available to U.S. citizens.

Application Requirements: Application form, transcript. *Deadline:* February 1.

Contact: Ms. Mary Hobart, Secretary
    Phone: 860-594-0397
    E-mail: k1mmh@arrl.org

SOUTHEASTERN DX CLUB SCHOLARSHIP FUND

$500 scholarship for an active member of an amateur radio club affiliated with the ARRL. Preference given to students pursuing engineering or computer science. Must be a resident of Georgia. If no qualified applicant, preference will be awarded to an applicant from the ARRL Southeastern Division (Alabama, Florida, Georgia, Puerto Rico and the US Virgin Islands).

Academic Fields/Career Goals: Computer Science/Data Processing; Engineering/Technology.

Award: Scholarship for use in freshman, sophomore, junior, or senior years; not renewable. *Number:* 1. *Amount:* $500.

Eligibility Requirements: Applicant must be enrolled or expecting to enroll full- or part-time at a two-year or four-year or technical institution

or university; resident of Alabama, Florida, Georgia, Puerto Rico and must have an interest in amateur radio. Available to U.S. citizens.

Application Requirements: Application form, transcript. *Deadline:* February 1.

Contact: Ms. Mary Hobart, Secretary
    Phone: 860-594-0397
    E-mail: k1mmh@arrl.org

WILLIAM R. GOLDFARB MEMORIAL SCHOLARSHIP
• See page 150

ASSOCIATION OF FORMER INTELLIGENCE OFFICERS

http://www.afio.com/13_scholarships.htm

CIA UNDERGRADUATE SCHOLARSHIPS
• See page 97

ASTRONAUT SCHOLARSHIP FOUNDATION

http://www.astronautscholarship.org/

ASTRONAUT SCHOLARSHIP FOUNDATION
• See page 104

BARRY M. GOLDWATER SCHOLARSHIP AND EXCELLENCE IN EDUCATION FOUNDATION

http://www.act.org/goldwater

BARRY M. GOLDWATER SCHOLARSHIP AND EXCELLENCE IN EDUCATION PROGRAM
• See page 104

BRITISH COLUMBIA INNOVATION COUNCIL

http://www.bcic.ca/

PAUL AND HELEN TRUSSELL SCIENCE AND TECHNOLOGY SCHOLARSHIP
• See page 104

CATCHING THE DREAM

http://www.catchingthedream.org/

MATH, ENGINEERING, SCIENCE, BUSINESS, EDUCATION, COMPUTERS SCHOLARSHIPS
• See page 151

TRIBAL BUSINESS MANAGEMENT PROGRAM (TBM)
• See page 70

CENTRAL INTELLIGENCE AGENCY

http://www.cia.gov/

CENTRAL INTELLIGENCE AGENCY UNDERGRADUATE SCHOLARSHIP PROGRAM
• See page 70

ELECTRONIC DOCUMENT SYSTEMS FOUNDATION

http://www.edsf.org/

EDSF BOARD OF DIRECTORS SCHOLARSHIPS
• See page 153

HOODS MEMORIAL SCHOLARSHIP
• *See page 153*

LYNDA BABOYIAN MEMORIAL SCHOLARSHIP
• *See page 153*

FOUNDATION FOR SCIENCE AND DISABILITY

http://stemd.org/

GRANTS FOR DISABLED STUDENTS IN THE SCIENCES
• *See page 105*

GREAT LAKES COMMISSION

http://www.glc.org/

CAROL A. RATZA MEMORIAL SCHOLARSHIP
• *See page 190*

GREAT MINDS IN STEM

http://www.greatmindsinstem.org

HISPANIC ENGINEER NATIONAL ACHIEVEMENT AWARDS CORPORATION SCHOLARSHIP PROGRAM
• *See page 130*

HAWAIIAN LODGE, F&AM

http://www.hawaiianlodgefreemasons.org/

HAWAIIAN LODGE SCHOLARSHIPS
• *See page 114*

HEMOPHILIA HEALTH SERVICES

http://www.hemophiliahealth.com/

SCOTT TARBELL SCHOLARSHIP
Award to U.S. citizens with hemophilia A or B severe and related bleeding disorders. Students must be majoring or seeking a degree or certification in computer science and/or math. Applicants must be high school seniors, high school graduates (or equivalent/GED), college freshmen, sophomores, or juniors.

Academic Fields/Career Goals: Computer Science/Data Processing; Mathematics.

Award: Scholarship for use in freshman, sophomore, junior, or senior years; not renewable. *Number:* 1–2. *Amount:* $1500–$2000.

Eligibility Requirements: Applicant must be physically disabled and enrolled or expecting to enroll full-time at a four-year institution or university. Applicant must be physically disabled. Available to U.S. citizens.

Application Requirements: Application form, doctor-certification form, essay, financial need analysis, recommendations or references, test scores, transcript. *Deadline:* May 1.

Contact: Sally Johnson, Manager, Operations Support
Phone: 615-850-5175
Fax: 615-352-2588
E-mail: scholarship@hemophiliahealth.com

INSTITUTE OF MANAGEMENT ACCOUNTANTS

http://www.imanet.org/

ROLF S. JAEHNIGEN FAMILY SCHOLARSHIP
• *See page 74*

INTERNATIONAL COMMUNICATIONS INDUSTRIES FOUNDATION

http://www.infocomm.org/scholarships

ICIF SCHOLARSHIP FOR EMPLOYEES AND DEPENDENTS OF MEMBER ORGANIZATIONS
• *See page 191*

INTERNATIONAL COMMUNICATIONS INDUSTRIES FOUNDATION AV SCHOLARSHIP
• *See page 191*

LOS ANGELES COUNCIL OF BLACK PROFESSIONAL ENGINEERS

http://www.lablackengineers.org/

AL-BEN SCHOLARSHIP FOR ACADEMIC INCENTIVE
• *See page 168*

AL-BEN SCHOLARSHIP FOR PROFESSIONAL MERIT
• *See page 168*

AL-BEN SCHOLARSHIP FOR SCHOLASTIC ACHIEVEMENT
• *See page 168*

MARYLAND ASSOCIATION OF PRIVATE COLLEGES AND CAREER SCHOOLS

http://www.mapccs.org/

MARYLAND ASSOCIATION OF PRIVATE COLLEGES AND CAREER SCHOOLS SCHOLARSHIP
• *See page 157*

MICROSOFT CORPORATION

http://www.microsoft.com/

YOU CAN MAKE A DIFFERENCE SCHOLARSHIP
Scholarship for high school students who want make an impact with technology. All students who submit proposals will receive a free copy of Microsoft Visual Studio NET Academic Edition.

Academic Fields/Career Goals: Computer Science/Data Processing.

Award: Scholarship for use in freshman year; not renewable. *Number:* 10. *Amount:* $5000.

Eligibility Requirements: Applicant must be high school student and planning to enroll or expecting to enroll full- or part-time at a four-year institution or university. Available to U.S. citizens.

Application Requirements: Application form, transcript. *Deadline:* April 30.

NASA IDAHO SPACE GRANT CONSORTIUM

http://www.id.spacegrant.org/

NASA IDAHO SPACE GRANT CONSORTIUM SCHOLARSHIP PROGRAM
• *See page 146*

NASA/MARYLAND SPACE GRANT CONSORTIUM

http://md.spacegrant.org/

NASA MARYLAND SPACE GRANT CONSORTIUM UNDERGRADUATE SCHOLARSHIPS
• *See page 132*

NASA MONTANA SPACE GRANT CONSORTIUM

http://www.spacegrant.montana.edu/

MONTANA SPACE GRANT SCHOLARSHIP PROGRAM
• See page 133

NASA'S VIRGINIA SPACE GRANT CONSORTIUM

http://www.vsgc.odu.edu/

COMMUNITY COLLEGE STEM SCHOLARSHIPS
• See page 105

UNDERGRADUATE STEM RESEARCH SCHOLARSHIPS
• See page 106

NASA WEST VIRGINIA SPACE GRANT CONSORTIUM

http://www.nasa.wvu.edu/

WEST VIRGINIA SPACE GRANT CONSORTIUM UNDERGRADUATE FELLOWSHIP PROGRAM
• See page 134

NATIONAL ASSOCIATION OF WATER COMPANIES-NEW JERSEY CHAPTER

http://www.nawc.org/

NATIONAL ASSOCIATION OF WATER COMPANIES-NEW JERSEY CHAPTER SCHOLARSHIP
• See page 146

NATIONAL INVENTORS HALL OF FAME

http://www.invent.org/

COLLEGIATE INVENTORS COMPETITION FOR UNDERGRADUATE STUDENTS
• See page 106

COLLEGIATE INVENTORS COMPETITION-GRAND PRIZE
• See page 106

NATIONAL SCIENCE TEACHERS ASSOCIATION

http://www.nsta.org/

TOSHIBA/NSTA EXPLORAVISION AWARDS PROGRAM

A competition for all students in grades K-12 attending a public, private or home school in the United States, Canada, or U.S. Territories. It is designed to encourage students to combine their imagination with their knowledge of science and technology to explore visions of the future.

Academic Fields/Career Goals: Computer Science/Data Processing; Engineering/Technology; Nuclear Science; Physical Sciences.

Award: Prize for use in freshman year; not renewable. *Number:* 16–32. *Amount:* $5000–$10,000.

Eligibility Requirements: Applicant must be high school student and planning to enroll or expecting to enroll full-time at a two-year or four-year or technical institution or university. Available to U.S. and Canadian citizens.

Application Requirements: Application form, entry in a contest, essay, project description, bibliography, 5 web page graphics, abstract. *Deadline:* January 29.

NATIONAL SECURITY AGENCY

http://www.nsa.gov/Careers

NATIONAL SECURITY AGENCY STOKES EDUCATIONAL SCHOLARSHIP PROGRAM

Renewable awards for high school students planning to attend a four-year undergraduate institution to study computer science, electrical engineering, or computer engineering. Must be at least 16 to apply. Must be a U.S. citizen. Minimum 3.0 GPA required, and minimum SAT score of 1600. For application visit website http://www.nsa.gov/careers

Academic Fields/Career Goals: Computer Science/Data Processing; Electrical Engineering/Electronics.

Award: Scholarship for use in freshman, sophomore, junior, or senior years; renewable. *Number:* 15–20. *Amount:* $1000–$30,000.

Eligibility Requirements: Applicant must be high school student and planning to enroll or expecting to enroll full-time at a four-year institution or university. Applicant must have 3.0 GPA or higher. Available to U.S. citizens.

Application Requirements: Application form, application form may be submitted online (http://www.nsa.gov/careers), essay, interview, recommendations or references, resume, test scores, transcript. *Deadline:* November 15.

Contact: Anne Clark, Program Manager
National Security Agency
9800 Savage Road, Suite 6779
Fort Meade, MD 20755-6779
Phone: 866-672-4473
Fax: 410-854-3002
E-mail: amclark@nsa.gov

NEVADA NASA SPACE GRANT CONSORTIUM

http://www.nvspacegrant.org/

NATIONAL SPACE GRANT COLLEGE AND FELLOWSHIP PROGRAM
• See page 106

ROBERT H. MOLLOHAN FAMILY CHARITABLE FOUNDATION, INC.

http://www.mollohanfoundation.org/

HIGH TECHNOLOGY SCHOLARS PROGRAM
• See page 147

RURAL TECHNOLOGY FUND

http://ruraltechfund.org/

SOCIAL ENTREPRENEURSHIP SCHOLARSHIP

This scholarship is open to students from schools in Kentucky who have a passion for using technology skills to make a positive social change in the world or at home in their communities. Applicants must be an active member of the Student Technology Leadership Program at his or her respective high school.

Academic Fields/Career Goals: Computer Science/Data Processing.

Award: Scholarship for use in freshman year; not renewable. *Number:* 1. *Amount:* $500.

Eligibility Requirements: Applicant must be high school student; planning to enroll or expecting to enroll at a four-year institution and studying in Kentucky. Available to U.S. citizens.

Application Requirements: Application form, essay. *Deadline:* April 15.

SEMICONDUCTOR RESEARCH CORPORATION (SRC)

http://www.src.org/

MASTER'S SCHOLARSHIP PROGRAM
• *See page 171*

SOCIETY OF WOMEN ENGINEERS

http://www.swe.org/

ACCENTURE SCHOLARSHIP
• *See page 172*

ADMIRAL GRACE MURRAY HOPPER SCHOLARSHIP

One $1500 scholarship for freshman woman pursuing ABET-accredited baccalaureate program in preparation for a career in engineering, engineering technology, and computer science in the United States and Mexico. Preference is given to student in computer-related engineering majors.

Academic Fields/Career Goals: Computer Science/Data Processing; Engineering-Related Technologies.

Award: Scholarship for use in freshman year; not renewable. *Number:* 3. *Amount:* $1500.

Eligibility Requirements: Applicant must be enrolled or expecting to enroll full-time at a four-year institution or university and female. Applicant must have 3.5 GPA or higher.

Application Requirements: Application form, essay, recommendations or references, self-addressed stamped envelope with application, test scores, transcript. *Deadline:* May 15.

APPLIED COMPUTER SECURITY ASSOCIATION CYBERSECURITY SCHOLARSHIP

$10,000 scholarship for a woman pursuing ABET-accredited baccalaureate or graduate program in preparation for a career in engineering, engineering technology, and computer science in the United States and Mexico. Must have demonstrated interest in security, as evidenced by coursework, outside study, and/or work experience. Must be a U.S. citizen.

Academic Fields/Career Goals: Computer Science/Data Processing; Engineering/Technology.

Award: Scholarship for use in junior, senior, or graduate years; not renewable. *Number:* 1. *Amount:* $10,000.

Eligibility Requirements: Applicant must be enrolled or expecting to enroll full-time at a four-year institution or university and female. Available to U.S. citizens.

Application Requirements: Application form, recommendations or references. *Deadline:* February 15.

BOSTON SCIENTIFIC SCHOLARSHIP
• *See page 172*

CISCO'S FUTURE SCHOLARSHIP

Five $5000 scholarships for women pursuing ABET-accredited baccalaureate or graduate programs in preparation for careers in engineering, engineering technology, or computer science in the United States and Mexico. US citizenship and SWE membership required. Underrepresented groups, disabled candidates, and veteran candidates preferred. Selection also based on financial need.

Academic Fields/Career Goals: Computer Science/Data Processing; Electrical Engineering/Electronics; Engineering/Technology.

Award: Scholarship for use in sophomore or junior years; not renewable. *Number:* 5. *Amount:* $5000.

Eligibility Requirements: Applicant must be enrolled or expecting to enroll full-time at a four-year institution or university and female. Applicant or parent of applicant must be member of Society of Women Engineers. Available to U.S. citizens.

Application Requirements: Application form, financial need analysis, recommendations or references. *Deadline:* February 15.

CUMMINS INC. SCHOLARSHIP
• *See page 173*

DELL SCHOLARSHIP

Two $2250 scholarships for women pursuing ABET-accredited baccalaureate programs in preparation for careers in engineering, engineering technology, and computer science in the United States and Mexico. Financial need also taken into consideration.

Academic Fields/Career Goals: Computer Science/Data Processing; Electrical Engineering/Electronics; Engineering/Technology; Mechanical Engineering.

Award: Scholarship for use in junior or senior years; not renewable. *Number:* 2. *Amount:* $2250.

Eligibility Requirements: Applicant must be enrolled or expecting to enroll full-time at a four-year institution or university and female. Available to U.S. citizens.

Application Requirements: Application form, financial need analysis, recommendations or references. *Deadline:* February 15.

GOLDMAN, SACHS & CO. SCHOLARSHIP

Two $2000 scholarships for junior and senior women pursuing ABET-accredited baccalaureate programs in preparation for careers in engineering, engineering technology, and computer science in the United States and Mexico. Must be a member of SWE and have a minimum 3.2 GPA. Includes travel stipend to Annual Conference.

Academic Fields/Career Goals: Computer Science/Data Processing; Electrical Engineering/Electronics; Engineering/Technology.

Award: Scholarship for use in junior or senior years; not renewable. *Number:* 2. *Amount:* $2000.

Eligibility Requirements: Applicant must be enrolled or expecting to enroll full-time at a four-year institution or university and female. Applicant or parent of applicant must be member of Society of Women Engineers. Available to U.S. citizens.

Application Requirements: Application form, recommendations or references. *Deadline:* February 15.

HONEYWELL CORPORATION SCHOLARSHIP
• *See page 173*

IBM CORPORATION SCHOLARSHIP

Five $1000 scholarships for women pursuing ABET-accredited baccalaureate programs in preparation for careers in engineering, engineering technology, and computer science in the United States and Mexico. Must be a U.S. citizen and have a minimum 3.4 GPA. Preference given to students in underrepresented groups.

Academic Fields/Career Goals: Computer Science/Data Processing; Electrical Engineering/Electronics; Engineering/Technology.

Award: Scholarship for use in sophomore or junior years; not renewable. *Number:* 5. *Amount:* $1000.

Eligibility Requirements: Applicant must be enrolled or expecting to enroll full-time at a four-year institution or university and female. Available to U.S. citizens.

Application Requirements: Application form, recommendations or references. *Deadline:* February 15.

ITW SCHOLARSHIP

Renewable award of $2500 for women pursuing ABET-accredited baccalaureate programs in preparation for careers in engineering, engineering technology, and computer science in the United States and Mexico. Underrepresented groups and UIC preferred. Must be a U.S. citizen and be willing to intern.

Academic Fields/Career Goals: Computer Science/Data Processing; Electrical Engineering/Electronics; Engineering/Technology; Mechanical Engineering.

Award: Scholarship for use in junior year; not renewable. *Number:* 2. *Amount:* $2500.

Eligibility Requirements: Applicant must be enrolled or expecting to enroll full-time at a four-year institution or university and female. Available to U.S. citizens.

Application Requirements: Application form, recommendations or references. *Deadline:* February 15.

JILL S. TIETJEN P.E. SCHOLARSHIP
• *See page 173*

LIFE TECHNOLOGIES SCHOLARSHIP
• *See page 174*

LILLIAN MOLLER GILBRETH MEMORIAL SCHOLARSHIP
• See page 174

LOCKHEED MARTIN AERONAUTICS CORPORATION SCHOLARSHIPS

Four $2000 scholarships for women pursuing ABET-accredited baccalaureate or graduate programs in preparation for careers in engineering, engineering technology, or computer science in the United States and Mexico. Includes travel grant for the SWE Annual Conference. 3.2 minimum GPA for the sophomore-graduate students.

Academic Fields/Career Goals: Computer Science/Data Processing; Electrical Engineering/Electronics; Engineering/Technology.

Award: Scholarship for use in freshman, sophomore, junior, senior, or graduate years; not renewable. *Number:* 4. *Amount:* $2000.

Eligibility Requirements: Applicant must be enrolled or expecting to enroll full-time at a four-year institution or university and female. Available to U.S. citizens.

Application Requirements: Application form, recommendations or references. *Deadline:* February 15.

ROCKWELL COLLINS SCHOLARSHIP

Three $2500 scholarships for women pursuing ABET-accredited baccalaureate programs in preparation for careers in engineering, engineering technology, and computer science in the United States and Mexico. Preference given to under-represented students. SWE membership required. Must be willing to intern.

Academic Fields/Career Goals: Computer Science/Data Processing; Electrical Engineering/Electronics; Engineering/Technology; Mechanical Engineering.

Award: Scholarship for use in sophomore or junior years; not renewable. *Number:* 3. *Amount:* $2500.

Eligibility Requirements: Applicant must be enrolled or expecting to enroll full-time at a four-year institution or university; female and must have an interest in leadership. Applicant or parent of applicant must be member of Society of Women Engineers. Available to U.S. citizens.

Application Requirements: Application form, recommendations or references. *Deadline:* February 15.

VERIZON SCHOLARSHIP

Ten $3000 scholarships for women pursuing ABET-accredited baccalaureate or graduate programs in preparation for careers in engineering, engineering technology and computer science in the United States and Mexico. Must be a U.S. citizen.

Academic Fields/Career Goals: Computer Science/Data Processing; Electrical Engineering/Electronics; Engineering/Technology; Mechanical Engineering.

Award: Scholarship for use in sophomore, junior, senior, or graduate years; not renewable. *Number:* 10. *Amount:* $3000.

Eligibility Requirements: Applicant must be enrolled or expecting to enroll full-time at a four-year institution or university and female. Available to U.S. citizens.

Application Requirements: Application form, recommendations or references. *Deadline:* February 15.

VIASAT SOFTWARE ENGINEERING SCHOLARSHIP

$2200 scholarship for a woman pursuing an ABET-accredited baccalaureate or graduate program in preparation for a career in engineering, engineering technology, or computer science in the United States and Mexico. Home or school must be located in either California, DC, Maryland, or Massachusetts. Minimum 3.2 GPA required.

Academic Fields/Career Goals: Computer Science/Data Processing; Engineering/Technology.

Award: Scholarship for use in junior, senior, or graduate years; not renewable. *Number:* 1. *Amount:* $2200.

Eligibility Requirements: Applicant must be enrolled or expecting to enroll full-time at a four-year institution or university and female. Available to U.S. citizens.

Application Requirements: Application form, recommendations or references. *Deadline:* February 15.

SOCIETY OF WOMEN ENGINEERS-DALLAS SECTION
http://www.dallaswe.org/

NATIONAL SOCIETY OF WOMEN ENGINEERS SCHOLARSHIPS

Provides financial assistance to women admitted to accredited baccalaureate or graduate programs, in preparation for careers in engineering, engineering technology, and computer science. Minimum GPA of 3.5 for freshman applicants and 3.0 for sophomore, junior, senior, and graduate applicants.

Academic Fields/Career Goals: Computer Science/Data Processing; Engineering/Technology.

Award: Scholarship for use in freshman, sophomore, junior, senior, or graduate years; not renewable. *Amount:* $1000–$10,000.

Eligibility Requirements: Applicant must be enrolled or expecting to enroll full-time at a four-year institution or university and female. Applicant must have 3.5 GPA or higher. Available to U.S. and non-U.S. citizens.

Application Requirements: Application form, essay, letter of acceptance from the accredited college or university, recommendations or references, transcript. *Deadline:* May 15.

SOCIETY OF WOMEN ENGINEERS-ROCKY MOUNTAIN SECTION
http://www.societyofwomenengineers.org/RockyMountain/

SOCIETY OF WOMEN ENGINEERS-ROCKY MOUNTAIN SECTION SCHOLARSHIP PROGRAM
• See page 176

SOCIETY OF WOMEN ENGINEERS-TWIN TIERS SECTION
http://www.swetwintiers.org/

SOCIETY OF WOMEN ENGINEERS-TWIN TIERS SECTION SCHOLARSHIP

Scholarship available to female students who reside or attend school in the Twin Tiers SWE section of New York. This is limited to zip codes that begin with 148, 149, 169 and residents of Bradford County, Pennsylvania. Applicant must be accepted or enrolled in an undergraduate degree program in engineering or computer science at an ABET-, CSAB- or SWE-accredited school.

Academic Fields/Career Goals: Computer Science/Data Processing; Engineering/Technology.

Award: Scholarship for use in freshman year; not renewable. *Number:* 4–6. *Amount:* $2000.

Eligibility Requirements: Applicant must be high school student; planning to enroll or expecting to enroll full-time at a four-year institution or university; female and resident of New York, Pennsylvania. Applicant must have 3.0 GPA or higher. Available to U.S. citizens.

Application Requirements: Application form, essay, letter of acceptance, personal information, and achievements, recommendations or references, resume, self-addressed stamped envelope with application, transcript. *Deadline:* March 23.

Contact: Amy Litwiler, Scholarship Chair
  Phone: 607-974-6261
  E-mail: litwilerak@corning.com

SOUTH DAKOTA RETAILERS ASSOCIATION
http://www.sdra.org/

SOUTH DAKOTA RETAILERS ASSOCIATION SCHOLARSHIP PROGRAM
• See page 80

SPECIALTY EQUIPMENT MARKET ASSOCIATION

http://www.sema.org/

SPECIALTY EQUIPMENT MARKET ASSOCIATION MEMORIAL SCHOLARSHIP FUND

• See page 80

TEXAS DEPARTMENT OF TRANSPORTATION

http://www.txdot.gov/

CONDITIONAL GRANT PROGRAM

• See page 186

UNITED DAUGHTERS OF THE CONFEDERACY

http://www.hqudc.org/

WALTER REED SMITH SCHOLARSHIP

• See page 160

UNITED NEGRO COLLEGE FUND

http://www.uncf.org/

ALFRED CHISHOLM/BASF MEMORIAL SCHOLARSHIP FUND

• See page 81

BANK OF AMERICA SCHOLARSHIP

• See page 160

CDM SCHOLARSHIP/INTERNSHIP

• See page 176

CISCO/UNCF SCHOLARS PROGRAM

Scholarship provides financial support for African-American electrical engineering or computer science majors, attending specific UNCF member college or university, with a special focus on women and students who demonstrate community service. Minimum 3.2 GPA required. List of participating institutions and online application are available at website http://www.uncf.org.

Academic Fields/Career Goals: Computer Science/Data Processing; Electrical Engineering/Electronics.

Award: Scholarship for use in sophomore year; not renewable. *Number:* 1. *Amount:* $4000.

Eligibility Requirements: Applicant must be Black (non-Hispanic) and enrolled or expecting to enroll full-time at a four-year institution or university. Available to U.S. and non-U.S. citizens.

Application Requirements: Application form, financial need analysis. *Deadline:* April 15.

COMPUWARE ACADEMIC SCHOLARSHIP

Award available to a resident of Southeast Michigan or student living within a Compuware service area. Must major in the fields of computer science, information technology and software development. Must be African-American student attending a four year institution in Michigan or a Historically Black College or University. Minimum 3.0 GPA required.

Academic Fields/Career Goals: Computer Science/Data Processing.

Award: Scholarship for use in sophomore or junior years; not renewable. *Amount:* $5000.

Eligibility Requirements: Applicant must be Black (non-Hispanic); enrolled or expecting to enroll full- or part-time at a four-year institution and resident of Michigan. Applicant must have 3.0 GPA or higher. Available to U.S. citizens.

Application Requirements: Application form. *Deadline:* continuous.

FORD/UNCF CORPORATE SCHOLARS PROGRAM

• See page 82

GOOGLE SCHOLARSHIP

Scholarships available for African American undergraduate juniors, seniors, graduate students, and postgraduates who are studying computer science, computer engineering, and electrical engineering. Selected students will receive $10,000 for an academic year of study and will be invited to attend the all-expenses-paid Annual Google Scholars' Retreat. Apply online at website http://www.uncf.org.

Academic Fields/Career Goals: Computer Science/Data Processing; Electrical Engineering/Electronics.

Award: Scholarship for use in sophomore, junior, or senior years; not renewable. *Amount:* $10,000.

Eligibility Requirements: Applicant must be Black (non-Hispanic) and enrolled or expecting to enroll full-time at a four-year institution or university. Available to U.S. citizens.

Application Requirements: Application form, transcript. *Deadline:* March 18.

INTEL SCHOLARS PROGRAM

• See page 177

LOCKHEED MARTIN/UNCF SCHOLARSHIP

• See page 82

MONSANTO/UNCF 1890'S SCHOLARSHIP PROGRAM

• See page 89

NASCAR/WENDELL SCOTT, SR. SCHOLARSHIP

• See page 82

PACIFIC GAS AND ELECTRIC COMPANY SCHOLARSHIP

• See page 82

PSE&G SCHOLARSHIP

• See page 82

SANDISK CORPORATION SCHOLARSHIP

$2500 scholarship for an African American student enrolled full-time as a sophomore, junior, or senior at an accredited institution in the U.S., Puerto Rico, Virgin Islands, or Guam. Must also apply for federal student aid. Minimum 3.0 GPA required.

Academic Fields/Career Goals: Computer Science/Data Processing; Engineering/Technology; Mathematics; Natural Sciences; Physical Sciences.

Award: Scholarship for use in sophomore, junior, or senior years; renewable. *Amount:* $2500.

Eligibility Requirements: Applicant must be Black (non-Hispanic) and enrolled or expecting to enroll full-time at a four-year institution or university. Applicant must have 3.0 GPA or higher. Available to U.S. citizens.

Application Requirements: Application form, financial need analysis. *Deadline:* March 15.

SPRINT SCHOLARS PROGRAM FOR SOPHOMORES, JUNIORS, AND SENIORS

• See page 100

VERMONT SPACE GRANT CONSORTIUM

http://www.cems.uvm.edu/vsgc

VERMONT SPACE GRANT CONSORTIUM SCHOLARSHIP PROGRAM

• See page 107

WHOMENTORS.COM, INC.

http://www.WHOmentors.com/

1B USD WORLDWIDE VENTURE CAPITAL

• See page 107

WIFLE FOUNDATION, INC.

http://www.wifle.org/

WIFLE SCHOLARSHIP PROGRAM

Scholarship to encourage women to pursue a career in federal law enforcement. Applicant must be enrolled in, or be transferring to, a four-year program in criminal justice, social sciences, public administration, chemistry, physics, computer science, or related studies and have a minimum GPA of 3.0. May also be in a graduate program. Must demonstrate commitment to the community through volunteer community service or an internship in a law enforcement agency. Must be a United States citizen.

Academic Fields/Career Goals: Computer Science/Data Processing; Law Enforcement/Police Administration; Physical Sciences; Public Policy and Administration; Social Sciences.

Award: Scholarship for use in sophomore, junior, senior, graduate, or postgraduate years; not renewable.

Eligibility Requirements: Applicant must be enrolled or expecting to enroll full-time at a four-year institution or university and female. Applicant or parent of applicant must have employment or volunteer experience in community service. Applicant must have 3.0 GPA or higher. Available to U.S. citizens.

Application Requirements: Application form, community service, essay, recommendations or references, transcript. *Deadline:* May 1.

Contact: Ms. Catherine Sanz, President
      Phone: 301-805-2180
      Fax: 301-560-8836

WYOMING TRUCKING ASSOCIATION SCHOLARSHIP FUND TRUST

http://www.wytruck.org/

WYOMING TRUCKING ASSOCIATION SCHOLARSHIP TRUST FUND
• *See page 83*

XEROX

http://www.xerox.com//

TECHNICAL MINORITY SCHOLARSHIP
• *See page 177*

CONSTRUCTION ENGINEERING/ MANAGEMENT

AACE INTERNATIONAL

http://www.aacei.org/

AACE INTERNATIONAL COMPETITIVE SCHOLARSHIP
• *See page 108*

AMERICAN RAILWAY ENGINEERING AND MAINTENANCE OF WAY ASSOCIATION

http://www.aremafoundation.org/

AREMA MICHAEL R. GARCIA SCHOLARSHIP
• *See page 179*

AREMA PRESIDENTIAL SPOUSE SCHOLARSHIP
• *See page 180*

AREMA UNDERGRADUATE SCHOLARSHIPS
• *See page 180*

AMERICAN SOCIETY OF CIVIL ENGINEERS

http://www.asce.org/

CONSTRUCTION ENGINEERING SCHOLARSHIP

Scholarship for freshman, sophomore, junior, or first-year senior who is a Construction Institute (CI) student member and/or ASCE National Student Member in good standing at the time of application and award.

Academic Fields/Career Goals: Construction Engineering/ Management.

Award: Scholarship for use in freshman, sophomore, junior, or senior years; renewable.

Eligibility Requirements: Applicant must be enrolled or expecting to enroll full- or part-time at a four-year institution or university. Applicant or parent of applicant must be member of American Society of Civil Engineers. Available to U.S. citizens.

Application Requirements: Annual budget, application form, financial need analysis, recommendations or references, resume, transcript. *Deadline:* April 1.

SAMUEL FLETCHER TAPMAN ASCE STUDENT CHAPTER SCHOLARSHIP
• *See page 180*

AMERICAN SOCIETY OF HEATING, REFRIGERATING, AND AIR CONDITIONING ENGINEERS, INC.

http://www.ashrae.org/

ASHRAE REGION III BOGGARM SETTY SCHOLARSHIP
• *See page 166*

ARRL FOUNDATION INC.

http://www.arrl.org/

ALFRED E. FRIEND JR., W4CF, MEMORIAL SCHOLARSHIP
• *See page 166*

GARY WAGNER, K3OMI, SCHOLARSHIP
• *See page 166*

ASSOCIATED GENERAL CONTRACTORS EDUCATION AND RESEARCH FOUNDATION

http://www.agcfoundation.org/

AGC EDUCATION AND RESEARCH FOUNDATION GRADUATE SCHOLARSHIPS

College seniors enrolled in, or others possessing a degree in, an undergraduate construction management or construction-related engineering program, are eligible to apply. Applicant must be enrolled or planning to enroll in a graduate level construction management or construction-related engineering degree program as a full-time student.

Academic Fields/Career Goals: Construction Engineering/ Management.

Award: Scholarship for use in senior or graduate years; not renewable. *Number:* 2. *Amount:* $7500.

Eligibility Requirements: Applicant must be enrolled or expecting to enroll full-time at a four-year institution or university. Available to U.S. citizens.

Application Requirements: Application form, essay, financial need analysis, transcript. *Deadline:* November 1.

Contact: Floretta Slade, Director of Programs
Associated General Contractors Education and Research
Foundation
2300 Wilson Boulevard, Suite 400
Arlington, VA 22201
Phone: 703-837-5342
Fax: 703-837-5451
E-mail: sladef@agc.org

AGC EDUCATION AND RESEARCH FOUNDATION UNDERGRADUATE SCHOLARSHIPS
• See page 181

ASSOCIATED GENERAL CONTRACTORS OF NEW YORK STATE, LLC

http://www.agcnys.org/

ASSOCIATED GENERAL CONTRACTORS NYS SCHOLARSHIP PROGRAM
• See page 181

BRASKEM ODEBRECHT

http://www.odebrechtaward.com

ODEBRECHT AWARD FOR SUSTAINABLE DEVELOPMENT
• See page 110

COLORADO CONTRACTORS ASSOCIATION INC.

http://www.coloradocontractors.org/

COLORADO CONTRACTORS ASSOCIATION SCHOLARSHIP PROGRAM

Scholarships of $2500 for junior and senior students who are interested in pursuing a career in heavy-highway-municipal-utility construction. Scholarships are only awarded to students who attend the following institutions: Colorado School of Mines, Colorado State University-Fort Collins, Colorado State University-Pueblo.

Academic Fields/Career Goals: Construction Engineering/Management.

Award: Scholarship for use in junior or senior years; not renewable. *Amount:* $2500.

Eligibility Requirements: Applicant must be enrolled or expecting to enroll full- or part-time at a four-year institution or university. Available to U.S. citizens.

Application Requirements: Application form. *Deadline:* varies.

FLORIDA EDUCATIONAL FACILITIES PLANNERS' ASSOCIATION

http://www.fefpa.org/

FEFPA ASSISTANTSHIP
• See page 110

FLORIDA ENGINEERING SOCIETY

http://www.fleng.org/scholarships.cfm

DAVID F. LUDOVICI SCHOLARSHIP
• See page 182

FECON SCHOLARSHIP
• See page 182

GREATER KANAWHA VALLEY FOUNDATION

http://www.tgkvf.org/

STEVEN ENGINEERING SCHOLARSHIP
• See page 167

INDIAN HEALTH SERVICES, UNITED STATES DEPARTMENT OF HEALTH AND HUMAN SERVICES

http://www.ihs.gov/scholarship

INDIAN HEALTH SERVICE HEALTH PROFESSIONS SCHOLARSHIP PROGRAM

Renewable scholarship for Native American/Alaska Native students enrolled either part- or full-time in undergraduate or graduate programs leading to health or allied health professions degrees. Scholar must be in good standing with their Program of study to receive continuation funding. Minimum 2.0 GPA, required. Two to four year service obligations are incurred upon acceptance of scholarship funding. Number of awards and dollar values vary.

Academic Fields/Career Goals: Construction Engineering/Management; Dental Health/Services; Engineering-Related Technologies; Environmental Health; Food Science/Nutrition; Health and Medical Sciences; Health Information Management/Technology; Nursing; Optometry; Pharmacy; Psychology; Therapy/Rehabilitation.

Award: Scholarship for use in junior, senior, or graduate years; renewable. *Number:* 257–307. *Amount:* $37,319–$106,110.

Eligibility Requirements: Applicant must be American Indian/Alaska Native and enrolled or expecting to enroll full- or part-time at a two-year or four-year or technical institution or university. Applicant must have 2.5 GPA or higher. Available to U.S. citizens.

Application Requirements: Application form, application form may be submitted online (http://www.ihs.gov/scholarship), essay, proof of descent, W-4, curriculum for major, course curriculum verification, recommendations or references, transcript. *Deadline:* March 28.

Contact: Capt. Dawn Kelly, Branch Chief
Indian Health Services, United States Department of Health
and Human Services
801 Thompson Avenue
Suite 450-A (TMP)
Rockville, MD 20852
Phone: 301-443-6197
Fax: 301-443-6048
E-mail: dawn.kelly@ihs.gov

INTERNATIONAL FACILITY MANAGEMENT ASSOCIATION FOUNDATION

http://www.ifmafoundation.org/

IFMA FOUNDATION SCHOLARSHIPS
• See page 112

MICHIGAN SOCIETY OF PROFESSIONAL ENGINEERS

http://www.michiganspe.org/

MICHIGAN SOCIETY OF PROFESSIONAL ENGINEERS HARRY R. BALL, P.E. GRANT
• See page 169

MICHIGAN SOCIETY OF PROFESSIONAL ENGINEERS KENNETH B. FISHBECK, P.E. MEMORIAL GRANT
• See page 169

MIDWEST ROOFING CONTRACTORS ASSOCIATION

http://www.mrca.org/

MRCA FOUNDATION SCHOLARSHIP PROGRAM
• *See page 112*

NASA'S VIRGINIA SPACE GRANT CONSORTIUM

http://www.vsgc.odu.edu/

COMMUNITY COLLEGE STEM SCHOLARSHIPS
• *See page 105*

NATIONAL ASPHALT PAVEMENT ASSOCIATION RESEARCH AND EDUCATION FOUNDATION

http://www.asphaltpavement.org

NATIONAL ASPHALT PAVEMENT ASSOCIATION RESEARCH AND EDUCATION FOUNDATION SCHOLARSHIP PROGRAM
• *See page 183*

NATIONAL CONSTRUCTION EDUCATION FOUNDATION

http://www.abc.org/

TRIMMER EDUCATION FOUNDATION SCHOLARSHIPS FOR CONSTRUCTION MANAGEMENT
Scholarships are available to students in a major related to the construction industry. Applicants must be enrolled at an educational institution with an ABC student chapter, and be current, active members or employed by an ABC member firm. Architecture and most engineering programs are excluded. Applicants must have a minimum overall GPA of 2.85 and 3.0 in the major. If no courses have been taken in the major, a minimum overall GPA of 3.0 is required. Visit website http://www.abc.org.

Academic Fields/Career Goals: Construction Engineering/Management.

Award: Scholarship for use in sophomore, junior, or senior years; not renewable. *Number:* 10–15. *Amount:* up to $5000.

Eligibility Requirements: Applicant must be enrolled or expecting to enroll full-time at a two-year or four-year institution or university. Available to U.S. citizens.

Application Requirements: Application form, essay, financial need analysis, recommendations or references, Student Aid Report (SAR), transcript. *Deadline:* May 22.

Contact: John Strock, Director, Career and Constructions
  Phone: 703-812-2008
  E-mail: strock@abc.org

PROFESSIONAL CONSTRUCTION ESTIMATORS ASSOCIATION

http://www.pcea.org/

TED G. WILSON MEMORIAL SCHOLARSHIP FOUNDATION
• *See page 184*

SOCIETY OF WOMEN ENGINEERS

http://www.swe.org/

ADA I. PRESSMAN MEMORIAL SCHOLARSHIP
• *See page 172*

ANNE MAUREEN WHITNEY BARROW MEMORIAL SCHOLARSHIP
• *See page 172*

BETTY LOU BAILEY SWE REGION F SCHOLARSHIP
• *See page 172*

BK KRENZER MEMORIAL REENTRY SCHOLARSHIP
• *See page 172*

CAROL STEPHENS REGION F SCHOLARSHIP
• *See page 172*

DR. IVY M. PARKER MEMORIAL SCHOLARSHIP
• *See page 173*

DOROTHY P. MORRIS SCHOLARSHIP
• *See page 173*

LILLIAN MOLLER GILBRETH MEMORIAL SCHOLARSHIP
• *See page 174*

MARY V. MUNGER SCHOLARSHIP
• *See page 174*

MASWE MEMORIAL SCHOLARSHIP
• *See page 174*

MERIDITH THOMS MEMORIAL SCHOLARSHIPS
• *See page 174*

OLIVE LYNN SALEMBIER MEMORIAL REENTRY SCHOLARSHIP
• *See page 174*

SUSAN MISZKOWICZ MEMORIAL SCHOLARSHIP
• *See page 175*

SWE BALTIMORE-WASHINGTON SECTION SCHOLARSHIP
• *See page 175*

SWE CENTRAL NEW MEXICO PIONEERS SCHOLARSHIP
• *See page 175*

SWE CENTRAL NEW MEXICO REENTRY SCHOLARSHIP
• *See page 175*

SWE MID-HUDSON SECTION SCHOLARSHIP
• *See page 175*

SWE PAST PRESIDENTS SCHOLARSHIP
• *See page 175*

SWE PHOENIX SECTION SCHOLARSHIP
• *See page 175*

SWE REGION H SCHOLARSHIPS
• *See page 176*

WANDA MUNN SCHOLARSHIP
• *See page 176*

SOCIETY OF WOMEN ENGINEERS-ROCKY MOUNTAIN SECTION

http://www.societyofwomenengineers.org/RockyMountain/

SOCIETY OF WOMEN ENGINEERS-ROCKY MOUNTAIN SECTION SCHOLARSHIP PROGRAM

• *See page 176*

TURNER CONSTRUCTION COMPANY

http://www.turnerconstruction.com/

YOUTHFORCE 2020 SCHOLARSHIP PROGRAM

• *See page 113*

UNITED NEGRO COLLEGE FUND

http://www.uncf.org/

ALFRED CHISHOLM/BASF MEMORIAL SCHOLARSHIP FUND

• *See page 81*

UTAH SOCIETY OF PROFESSIONAL ENGINEERS

http://www.uspeonline.com/

UTAH SOCIETY OF PROFESSIONAL ENGINEERS JOE RHOADS SCHOLARSHIP

• *See page 177*

WIRE REINFORCEMENT INSTITUTE EDUCATION FOUNDATION

http://www.wirereinforcementinstitute.org/

WRI COLLEGE SCHOLARSHIP PROGRAM

• *See page 186*

COSMETOLOGY

AMERICAN HEALTH AND BEAUTY AIDS INSTITUTE

http://www.ahbai.org/

FRED LUSTER, SR. EDUCATION FOUNDATION SCHOLARSHIP FUND

Scholarship of $250 awarded to cosmetology students currently enrolled in, or accepted by, a state-approved cosmetic art training facility prior to applying for scholarship. Student must have completed initial 300 hours before funds are approved or disbursed to the facility.

Academic Fields/Career Goals: Cosmetology.

Award: Scholarship for use in senior year; not renewable. *Amount:* $250.

Eligibility Requirements: Applicant must be enrolled or expecting to enroll full-time at a four-year institution or university. Available to U.S. and non-U.S. citizens.

Application Requirements: Application form, personal photograph, recommendations or references, transcript. *Deadline:* April 15.

Contact: Geri Jones, Executive Director
Phone: 708-633-6328
Fax: 708-633-6329
E-mail: ahbai1@sbcglobal.net

JOE FRANCIS HAIRCARE SCHOLARSHIP FOUNDATION

http://www.joefrancis.com/

JOE FRANCIS HAIRCARE SCHOLARSHIP PROGRAM

Scholarships are awarded for $1000 each, with 20 scholarships awarded annually. Applicants are evaluated for their potential to successfully complete school, their financial need, and their commitment to a long-term career in cosmetology. Must be enrolled in school by fall of award year.

Academic Fields/Career Goals: Cosmetology.

Award: Scholarship for use in freshman or sophomore years; not renewable. *Number:* 20. *Amount:* $1000.

Eligibility Requirements: Applicant must be enrolled or expecting to enroll full- or part-time at a technical institution. Available to U.S. citizens.

Application Requirements: Application form, essay, financial need analysis, recommendations or references. *Deadline:* June 1.

Contact: Kim Larson, Administrator
Joe Francis Haircare Scholarship Foundation
PO Box 50625
Minneapolis, MN 55405
Phone: 651-769-1757
Fax: 651-459-8371
E-mail: kimlarsonmn@gmail.com

SOUTH DAKOTA RETAILERS ASSOCIATION

http://www.sdra.org/

SOUTH DAKOTA RETAILERS ASSOCIATION SCHOLARSHIP PROGRAM

• *See page 80*

STRAIGHTFORWARD MEDIA

http://www.straightforwardmedia.com/

STRAIGHTFORWARD MEDIA VOCATIONAL-TECHNICAL SCHOOL SCHOLARSHIP

• *See page 99*

CRIMINAL JUSTICE/ CRIMINOLOGY

ALBERTA HERITAGE SCHOLARSHIP FUND

http://www.alis.alberta.ca/

ROBERT C. CARSON MEMORIAL BURSARY

Award of CAN$500 to provide financial assistance to aboriginal students who are Alberta residents and full-time students enrolled in the second year of law enforcement or criminal justice program. Must be attending and nominated by one of the following qualifying Alberta institutions: Lethbridge College, Mount Royal College, Grant MacEwan College, the University of Calgary, or the University of Alberta. For additional information, see website http://alis.alberta.ca.

Academic Fields/Career Goals: Criminal Justice/Criminology; Law Enforcement/Police Administration; Law/Legal Services.

Award: Scholarship for use in sophomore year; not renewable. *Number:* 5.

Eligibility Requirements: Applicant must be Canadian citizen; American Indian/Alaska Native; enrolled or expecting to enroll full-time at a two-year or four-year institution or university; resident of Alberta and studying in Alberta.

Application Requirements: Application form, nomination from educational institution, transcript. *Deadline:* October 1.

AMERICAN CRIMINAL JUSTICE ASSOCIATION-LAMBDA ALPHA EPSILON

http://www.acjalae.org/

AMERICAN CRIMINAL JUSTICE ASSOCIATION-LAMBDA ALPHA EPSILON NATIONAL SCHOLARSHIP

Awarded only to members of the American Criminal Justice Association. One-time award of $100 to $400. Members may reapply each year. Must have minimum 3.0 GPA. Must pursue studies in law/legal services, criminal justice/law, or the social sciences.

Academic Fields/Career Goals: Criminal Justice/Criminology; Law/Legal Services; Social Sciences.

Award: Scholarship for use in freshman, sophomore, junior, senior, or graduate years; not renewable. *Number:* 9. *Amount:* $100–$400.

Eligibility Requirements: Applicant must be enrolled or expecting to enroll full- or part-time at a two-year or four-year institution or university. Applicant or parent of applicant must be member of American Criminal Justice Association. Applicant must have 3.0 GPA or higher. Available to U.S. citizens.

Application Requirements: Application form, entry in a contest, recommendations or references, transcript. *Deadline:* December 31.

Contact: Karen Campbell, Executive Secretary
American Criminal Justice Association-Lambda Alpha
Epsilon
PO Box 601047
Sacramento, CA 95860-1047
Phone: 916-484-6553
Fax: 916-488-2227
E-mail: acjalae@aol.com

AMERICAN SOCIETY OF CRIMINOLOGY

http://www.asc41.com/

AMERICAN SOCIETY OF CRIMINOLOGY GENE CARTE STUDENT PAPER COMPETITION

Award for full-time undergraduate or graduate students. Must submit a conceptual or empirical paper on a subject directly relating to criminology. Papers must be 7500 words or less.

Academic Fields/Career Goals: Criminal Justice/Criminology; Law Enforcement/Police Administration; Law/Legal Services; Social Sciences.

Award: Prize for use in freshman, sophomore, junior, senior, or graduate years; not renewable. *Number:* 3. *Amount:* $200–$500.

Eligibility Requirements: Applicant must be enrolled or expecting to enroll full-time at a four-year institution or university and must have an interest in writing. Available to U.S. and non-U.S. citizens.

Application Requirements: Conceptual or empirical paper on a subject directly relating to criminology, entry in a contest. *Deadline:* April 15.

Contact: Andrew Hochstetlet, Scholarship Committee
American Society of Criminology
Iowa State University, 203D East Hall
Ames, IA 50011-4504
Phone: 515-294-2841
E-mail: hochstet@iastate.edu

ASSOCIATION OF CERTIFIED FRAUD EXAMINERS

http://www.acfe.com/

RITCHIE-JENNINGS MEMORIAL SCHOLARSHIP
• *See page 70*

ASSOCIATION OF FORMER INTELLIGENCE OFFICERS

http://www.afio.com/13_scholarships.htm

CIA UNDERGRADUATE SCHOLARSHIPS
• *See page 97*

CONNECTICUT ASSOCIATION OF WOMEN POLICE

http://www.cawp.net/

CONNECTICUT ASSOCIATION OF WOMEN POLICE SCHOLARSHIP

Available to Connecticut residents graduating from an accredited high school, and entering a college or university in Connecticut as a criminal justice major.

Academic Fields/Career Goals: Criminal Justice/Criminology; Law Enforcement/Police Administration.

Award: Scholarship for use in freshman year; not renewable. *Number:* 1–3. *Amount:* $200–$500.

Eligibility Requirements: Applicant must be high school student; planning to enroll or expecting to enroll full-time at a two-year or four-year institution or university; resident of Connecticut and studying in Connecticut. Available to U.S. citizens.

Application Requirements: Application form, essay, financial need analysis, recommendations or references, transcript. *Deadline:* April 30.

Contact: Gail McDonnell, Scholarship Committee
Connecticut Association of Women Police
PO Box 1653
Hartford, CT 06144
Phone: 860-527-7300

INDIANA SHERIFFS' ASSOCIATION

http://www.indianasheriffs.org/

INDIANA SHERIFFS' ASSOCIATION SCHOLARSHIP PROGRAM

Applicant must be an Indiana resident majoring in a criminal justice/law enforcement field at an Indiana college or university. Must be a member or dependent child or grandchild of a member of the association. Must be a full-time student with at least 12 credit hours.

Academic Fields/Career Goals: Criminal Justice/Criminology; Law Enforcement/Police Administration.

Award: Scholarship for use in freshman, sophomore, junior, or senior years; not renewable. *Number:* up to 40. *Amount:* up to $500.

Eligibility Requirements: Applicant must be enrolled or expecting to enroll full-time at a two-year or four-year institution or university; resident of Indiana and studying in Indiana. Applicant or parent of applicant must be member of Indiana Sheriffs' Association. Available to U.S. citizens.

Application Requirements: Application form, essay, SAT scores, transcript. *Deadline:* April 1.

Contact: Laura Vest, Administrative Director
Indiana Sheriffs' Association
147 East Maryland Street
Indianapolis, IN 46204
Phone: 317-356-3633
Fax: 317-356-3996
E-mail: lvest@indianasheriffs.org

MISSOURI SHERIFFS' ASSOCIATION

http://www.mosheriffs.com/

JOHN DENNIS SCHOLARSHIP

Awards for Missouri high school seniors planning to attend a Missouri college or university and pursuing a career in criminal justice. Award is based on financial need. Students must be in upper one-third of their graduating class and participate in extracurricular activities. Minimum 2.0 GPA required.

Academic Fields/Career Goals: Criminal Justice/Criminology.

Award: Scholarship for use in freshman year; not renewable. *Number:* 16. *Amount:* $1000.

Eligibility Requirements: Applicant must be high school student; planning to enroll or expecting to enroll full-time at a two-year or four-year institution or university; resident of Missouri and studying in Missouri. Available to U.S. citizens.

Application Requirements: Application form, essay, financial need analysis, test scores. *Deadline:* January 31.

Contact: Ms. Karen Logan, Administrative Assistant
Phone: 573-635-5925 Ext. 100
E-mail: karen@mosheriffs.com

NATIONAL BLACK POLICE ASSOCIATION

http://www.blackpolice.org/

ALPHONSO DEAL SCHOLARSHIP AWARD

$500 scholarship for high school senior and U.S. citizen to attend a two-year college or university. Must study law enforcement or other related criminal justice field. Minimum 2.5 GPA required.

Academic Fields/Career Goals: Criminal Justice/Criminology; Law Enforcement/Police Administration; Law/Legal Services; Social Sciences; Social Services.

Award: Scholarship for use in freshman year; not renewable. *Number:* 4. *Amount:* $500.

Eligibility Requirements: Applicant must be high school student and planning to enroll or expecting to enroll full-time at a two-year or four-year institution or university. Available to U.S. citizens.

Application Requirements: Application form, letter of acceptance, personal photograph, recommendations or references, transcript. *Deadline:* June 1.

Contact: Ronald Hampton, Executive Director
National Black Police Association
30 Kennedy Street NW, Suite 101
Washington, DC 20011
Phone: 202-986-2070
Fax: 202-986-0410
E-mail: nbpanatofc@worldnet.att.net

NORTH CAROLINA STATE EDUCATION ASSISTANCE AUTHORITY

http://www.ncseaa.edu/

NORTH CAROLINA SHERIFFS' ASSOCIATION UNDERGRADUATE CRIMINAL JUSTICE SCHOLARSHIPS

One-time award for full-time North Carolina resident undergraduate students majoring in criminal justice at a University of North Carolina school. Priority given to child of any North Carolina law enforcement officer. Letter of recommendation from county sheriff required.

Academic Fields/Career Goals: Criminal Justice/Criminology; Law Enforcement/Police Administration.

Award: Scholarship for use in freshman, sophomore, junior, or senior years; not renewable. *Number:* up to 10. *Amount:* $1000–$2000.

Eligibility Requirements: Applicant must be enrolled or expecting to enroll full-time at a four-year institution or university; resident of North Carolina and studying in North Carolina. Applicant or parent of applicant must have employment or volunteer experience in police/firefighting. Available to U.S. citizens.

Application Requirements: Application form, financial need analysis, recommendations or references, statement of career goals, transcript. *Deadline:* continuous.

Contact: Nolita Goldston, Assistant, Scholarship and Grant Division
North Carolina State Education Assistance Authority
PO Box 13663
Research Triangle Park, NC 27709
Phone: 919-549-8614
Fax: 919-248-4687
E-mail: ngoldston@ncseaa.edu

OREGON STUDENT ASSISTANCE COMMISSION

http://www.GetCollegeFunds.org/

OREGON ASSOCIATION OF CERTIFIED FRAUD EXAMINERS SCHOLARSHIP

• See page 78

CULINARY ARTS

AMERICAN CULINARY FEDERATION

http://www.acfchefs.org/

AMERICAN ACADEMY OF CHEFS COLLEGE SCHOLARSHIP

One-time award to exemplary students currently enrolled in a full-time two- or four-year culinary program. Must have a career goal of becoming a chef or pastry chef.

Academic Fields/Career Goals: Culinary Arts; Food Service/Hospitality.

Award: Scholarship for use in sophomore, junior, or senior years; not renewable. *Number:* 1–10. *Amount:* $1000–$5000.

Eligibility Requirements: Applicant must be enrolled or expecting to enroll full-time at a two-year or four-year or technical institution or university. Available to U.S. and non-U.S. citizens.

Application Requirements: Application form, recommendations or references, transcript. *Deadline:* July 1.

AMERICAN ACADEMY OF CHEFS HIGH SCHOOL SCHOLARSHIP

One-time award to exemplary high schools students accepted in a full-time two-year or four-year culinary program.

Academic Fields/Career Goals: Culinary Arts; Food Service/Hospitality.

Award: Scholarship for use in freshman year; not renewable. *Number:* 1–10. *Amount:* $500–$1000.

Eligibility Requirements: Applicant must be high school student and planning to enroll or expecting to enroll full- or part-time at a two-year or four-year institution. Available to U.S. and non-U.S. citizens.

Application Requirements: Application form, recommendations or references, transcript. *Deadline:* December 1.

Contact: Debra Moore, Academic Administrator
Phone: 800-624-9458
Fax: 904-825-4758
E-mail: academy@acfchefs.net

AMERICAN HOTEL AND LODGING EDUCATIONAL FOUNDATION

http://www.ahlef.org/

AMERICAN HOTEL & LODGING EDUCATIONAL FOUNDATION PEPSI SCHOLARSHIP

Scholarships of $500 to $3000 awarded to graduates of Hospitality High School in Washington, DC. The scholarship recipients are selected by Hospitality High based upon a set of minimum eligibility criteria which includes graduate of Hospitality High, a minimum 2.5 GPA, and at least 250 hours in the hotel/hospitality industry.

Academic Fields/Career Goals: Culinary Arts; Food Service/Hospitality; Hospitality Management; Recreation, Parks, Leisure Studies; Travel/Tourism.

Award: Scholarship for use in freshman, sophomore, junior, or senior years; not renewable. *Amount:* $500–$3000.

Eligibility Requirements: Applicant must be enrolled or expecting to enroll full-time at a two-year or four-year institution or university and resident of District of Columbia. Applicant must have 2.5 GPA or higher. Available to U.S. and non-U.S. citizens.

Application Requirements: Application form, application form may be submitted online (http://www.ahlef.org), essay, financial need analysis, nomination from Hospitality High School, resume, transcript. *Deadline:* May 1.

Contact: Ms. Christa Boatman, Foundation Manager
American Hotel and Lodging Educational Foundation
1201 New York Avenue, NW, Suite 600
Washington, DC 20005
Phone: 202-289-3139
Fax: 202-289-3199
E-mail: cboatman@ahlef.org

ANNUAL SCHOLARSHIP GRANT PROGRAM

Students are selected for this award by their school which must be an AH&LEF affiliated program. Available to full-time students who have completed at least one or two years of a hospitality-related degree, are U.S. citizens or have permanent U.S. resident status. Minimum GPA of 3.0. A list of affiliated schools and designated contacts at the schools is available on http://www.ahlef.org.

Academic Fields/Career Goals: Culinary Arts; Food Service/ Hospitality; Hospitality Management; Recreation, Parks, Leisure Studies; Travel/Tourism.

Award: Scholarship for use in sophomore, junior, or senior years; not renewable. *Amount:* $500–$3000.

Eligibility Requirements: Applicant must be enrolled or expecting to enroll full-time at a two-year or four-year institution or university. Applicant must have 3.0 GPA or higher. Available to U.S. citizens.

Application Requirements: Application form, application form may be submitted online (http://www.ahlef.org), essay, financial need analysis, nomination from school, recommendations or references, transcript. *Deadline:* May 1.

Contact: Ms. Christa Boatman, Foundation Manager
American Hotel and Lodging Educational Foundation
1201 New York Avenue, NW, Suite 600
Washington, DC 20005-3931
Phone: 202-289-3139
Fax: 202-289-3199
E-mail: cboatman@ahlef.org

ARTHUR J. PACKARD MEMORIAL SCHOLARSHIP

Each AH&LEF affiliated university nominates its best qualified student to compete in the national competition. First-place winner receives a $5000 scholarship, second-place receives $3000 and third-place receives $2000. List of affiliated schools and their designated contacts can be found on http://www.ahlef.org.

Academic Fields/Career Goals: Culinary Arts; Food Service/ Hospitality; Hospitality Management; Recreation, Parks, Leisure Studies; Travel/Tourism.

Award: Scholarship for use in junior or senior years; not renewable. *Number:* 3. *Amount:* $2000–$5000.

Eligibility Requirements: Applicant must be enrolled or expecting to enroll full-time at a two-year or four-year institution or university. Applicant must have 3.5 GPA or higher. Available to U.S. citizens.

Application Requirements: Application form, application form may be submitted online (http://www.ahlef.org), essay, financial need analysis, nomination from AH&LEF affiliated school, recommendations or references, resume, transcript. *Deadline:* May 1.

Contact: Ms. Christa Boatman, Foundation Manager
American Hotel and Lodging Educational Foundation
1201 New York Avenue, NW, Suite 600
Washington, DC 20005
Phone: 202-289-3139
Fax: 202-289-3110

ECOLAB SCHOLARSHIP PROGRAM

Award for students enrolled full-time in United States baccalaureate or associate program leading to degree in hospitality management.

Academic Fields/Career Goals: Culinary Arts; Food Service/ Hospitality; Hospitality Management; Recreation, Parks, Leisure Studies; Travel/Tourism.

Award: Scholarship for use in freshman, sophomore, junior, or senior years; not renewable. *Number:* 10–15. *Amount:* $1000–$2000.

Eligibility Requirements: Applicant must be enrolled or expecting to enroll full-time at a two-year or four-year institution or university. Available to U.S. and non-U.S. citizens.

Application Requirements: Application form, application form may be submitted online (http://www.ahlef.org), essay, financial need analysis, resume, transcript. *Deadline:* May 1.

Contact: Ms. Christa Boatman, Foundation Manager
American Hotel and Lodging Educational Foundation
1201 New York Avenue, NW, Suite 600
Washington, DC 20005-3931
Phone: 202-289-3139
Fax: 202-289-3199
E-mail: cboatman@ahlef.org

HYATT HOTELS FUND FOR MINORITY LODGING MANAGEMENT

Scholarship available for African-American, Hispanic, American Indian, Alaskan Native, Asian, or Pacific Islander in a baccalaureate hospitality management program. Must be at least a sophomore in a four-year program.

Academic Fields/Career Goals: Culinary Arts; Food Service/ Hospitality; Hospitality Management; Recreation, Parks, Leisure Studies; Travel/Tourism.

Award: Scholarship for use in sophomore, junior, or senior years; not renewable. *Number:* 10–15. *Amount:* $2000.

Eligibility Requirements: Applicant must be American Indian/Alaska Native, Asian/Pacific Islander, Black (non-Hispanic), Hispanic and enrolled or expecting to enroll full-time at a four-year institution or university. Available to U.S. citizens.

Application Requirements: Application form, application form may be submitted online (http://www.ahlef.org), essay, financial need analysis, recommendations or references, resume, transcript. *Deadline:* May 1.

Contact: Ms. Christa Boatman, Foundation Manager
American Hotel and Lodging Educational Foundation
1201 New York Avenue, NW, Suite 600
Washington, DC 20005
Phone: 202-289-3139
Fax: 202-289-3199
E-mail: cboatman@ahlef.org

INCOMING FRESHMAN SCHOLARSHIPS

This program is exclusively for incoming freshman interested in pursuing hospitality-related undergraduate programs. Preference will be given to any applicant who is a graduate of the Educational Institute's Lodging Management Program (LMP, which is a two-year high school program.) Must have a minimum 2.0 GPA.

Academic Fields/Career Goals: Culinary Arts; Food Service/ Hospitality; Hospitality Management; Recreation, Parks, Leisure Studies; Travel/Tourism.

Award: Scholarship for use in freshman year; not renewable. *Number:* 5–10. *Amount:* $1000–$2000.

Eligibility Requirements: Applicant must be high school student and planning to enroll or expecting to enroll full-time at a two-year or four-year institution or university. Available to U.S. citizens.

Application Requirements: Application form, application form may be submitted online (http://www.ahlef.org), essay, financial need analysis, resume, transcript. *Deadline:* May 1.

Contact: Ms. Christa Boatman, Foundation Manager
American Hotel and Lodging Educational Foundation
1201 New York Avenue, NW, Suite 600
Washington, DC 20005-3197
Phone: 202-289-3139
Fax: 202-289-3199
E-mail: cboatman@ahlef.org

RAMA SCHOLARSHIP FOR THE AMERICAN DREAM

Schools participating in this program include Bethune-Cookman College, California State Polytechnic University, Cornell University, Florida International University, Georgia State university, Greenville Technical College, Howard University, Johnson & Wales University, New York University, University of Central Florida, University of Houston, University of South Carolina, and Virginia Tech. The participating schools select the student nominees based upon a set of minimum eligibility criteria which include: enrolled in at least 9 credit hours for the fall and spring semesters, majoring in an undergraduate or graduate hospitality management program, minimum GPA of 2.5, US citizenship or permanent resident, and schools must give preference to students of Asian-Indian descent or other minority groups, as well as JHM employees and their dependents.

Academic Fields/Career Goals: Culinary Arts; Food Service/ Hospitality; Hospitality Management; Recreation, Parks, Leisure Studies; Travel/Tourism.

Award: Scholarship for use in sophomore, junior, senior, or graduate years; not renewable. *Amount:* $1000–$3000.

Eligibility Requirements: Applicant must be American Indian/Alaska Native, Asian/Pacific Islander, Black (non-Hispanic), Hispanic and enrolled or expecting to enroll full- or part-time at a two-year or four-year institution or university. Applicant must have 2.5 GPA or higher. Available to U.S. citizens.

Application Requirements: Application form, application form may be submitted online (http://www.ahlef.org), essay, financial need analysis, nomination from school, recommendations or references, transcript. *Deadline:* May 1.

Contact: Ms. Christa Boatman, Foundation Manager
American Hotel and Lodging Educational Foundation
1201 New York Avenue, NW, Suite 600
Washington, DC 20005
Phone: 202-289-3139
Fax: 202-289-3199
E-mail: cboatman@ahlef.org

STEVEN HYMANS EXTENDED STAY SCHOLARSHIP

Each year the AH&LA Extended Stay Council selects one AH&LEF affiliated school to receive the fund monies and the selected school designates the winning students. In 2012, Michigan State University has been designated. The minimum eligibility for the student nominees include: full-time enrollment, minimum GPA of 3.0, US citizenship or permanent residency, some experience either working or interning (paid or unpaid) at a lodging property, and preference will be given to those with experience at an extended stay property.

Academic Fields/Career Goals: Culinary Arts; Food Service/ Hospitality; Hospitality Management; Recreation, Parks, Leisure Studies; Travel/Tourism.

Award: Scholarship for use in freshman, sophomore, junior, or senior years; not renewable. *Amount:* $1000–$3000.

Eligibility Requirements: Applicant must be enrolled or expecting to enroll full-time at an institution or university. Applicant must have 3.0 GPA or higher. Available to U.S. citizens.

Application Requirements: Application form, application form may be submitted online (http://www.ahlef.org), essay, financial need analysis, nominees selected by school, resume, transcript. *Deadline:* May 1.

Contact: Ms. Christa Boatman, Foundation Manager
American Hotel and Lodging Educational Foundation
1201 New York Avenue, NW, Suite 600
Washington, DC 20005
Phone: 202-289-3139
Fax: 202-289-3199
E-mail: cboatman@ahlef.org

CANFIT

http://www.canfit.org/

CANFIT NUTRITION, PHYSICAL EDUCATION AND CULINARY ARTS SCHOLARSHIP

Awards undergraduate and graduate African-American, American-Indian/Alaska Native, Asian-American, Pacific Islander or Latino/ Hispanic students who express financial need and are studying nutrition, physical education, or culinary arts in California. GPA of minimum 2.5 for undergraduates and 3.0 for graduates. See website for essay topic http://www.canfit.org.

Academic Fields/Career Goals: Culinary Arts; Food Science/ Nutrition; Food Service/Hospitality; Health and Medical Sciences; Sports-Related/Exercise Science.

Award: Scholarship for use in junior, senior, or graduate years; not renewable. *Number:* 5–10. *Amount:* $500–$1500.

Eligibility Requirements: Applicant must be of African, Chinese, Hispanic, Indian, Japanese heritage; American Indian/Alaska Native, Asian/Pacific Islander, Black (non-Hispanic); enrolled or expecting to enroll full-time at a four-year or technical institution or university; resident of California and studying in California. Applicant must have 2.5 GPA or higher. Available to U.S. citizens.

Application Requirements: Application form, essay, financial need analysis, personal photograph, recommendations or references, transcript. *Deadline:* March 31.

Contact: Ms. Arnell Hinkle, Executive Director
CANFIT
2140 Shattuck Avenue, Suite 610
Berkeley, CA 94704
Phone: 510-644-1533 Ext. 12
Fax: 510-644-1535
E-mail: info@canfit.org

CAREERS THROUGH CULINARY ARTS PROGRAM INC.

http://www.ccapinc.org/

CAREERS THROUGH CULINARY ARTS PROGRAM COOKING COMPETITION FOR SCHOLARSHIPS

Applicants MUST be a senior in a C-CAP designated partner high school in Arizona; Prince George's County, Maryland; Tidewater, Virginia; or the cities of Boston, Chicago, Los Angeles, New York, Philadelphia or Washington, DC. Applicants MUST be accepted into the cooking competition for scholarships.

Academic Fields/Career Goals: Culinary Arts; Hospitality Management.

Award: Scholarship for use in freshman, sophomore, junior, or senior years; not renewable. *Number:* 50–70. *Amount:* $1000–$90,000.

Eligibility Requirements: Applicant must be high school student; planning to enroll or expecting to enroll full- or part-time at a two-year or four-year or technical institution and resident of Arizona, California, Illinois, Maryland, New York, Pennsylvania, Virginia. Available to U.S. and non-U.S. citizens.

Application Requirements: Application form, entry in a contest, essay, financial need analysis, interview, recommendations or references, test scores, transcript. *Deadline:* varies.

THE CULINARY TRUST

http://www.theculinarytrust.org/

CULINARY TRUST SCHOLARSHIP PROGRAM FOR CULINARY STUDY AND RESEARCH

Scholarships provides funds to qualified applicants for beginning, continuing, and specialty education courses at accredited culinary schools worldwide, as well as, independent study for research projects. Applicants must have at least, a minimum 3.0 GPA, must write an essay, submit two letters of recommendation. Application fee: $35.

Academic Fields/Career Goals: Culinary Arts; Food Science/ Nutrition; Food Service/Hospitality.

Award: Scholarship for use in freshman, sophomore, junior, senior, graduate, or postgraduate years; not renewable. *Number:* 21. *Amount:* $1000–$5000.

Eligibility Requirements: Applicant must be enrolled or expecting to enroll full- or part-time at a two-year or four-year or technical institution or university. Applicant must have 3.0 GPA or higher. Available to U.S. and non-U.S. citizens.

Application Requirements: Application form, application form may be submitted online (http://www.theculinarytrust.org), essay, interview, recommendations or references, resume, transcript. *Fee:* $35. *Deadline:* March 1.

Contact: Heather Johnston, Administrator
The Culinary Trust
PO Box 273
New York, NY 10013
Phone: 888-345-4666
Fax: 888-345-4666
E-mail: heather@theculinarytrust.org

GOLDEN GATE RESTAURANT ASSOCIATION

http://www.ggra.org/

GOLDEN GATE RESTAURANT ASSOCIATION SCHOLARSHIP FOUNDATION

One-time award for any student pursuing a food service degree at a 501(c)(3) institution, or institutions approved by the Board of Trustees. California residency and personal interview in San Francisco is required. Minimum GPA of 2.75 required. For further information email donnalyn@ggra.org, or visit ggra.org/scholarships.aspx.

Academic Fields/Career Goals: Culinary Arts; Food Service/ Hospitality; Hospitality Management.

Award: Scholarship for use in freshman, sophomore, junior, or senior years; not renewable. *Number:* 9–15. *Amount:* $1000–$6000.

Eligibility Requirements: Applicant must be enrolled or expecting to enroll full- or part-time at a two-year or four-year or technical institution or university and resident of California. Applicant must have 2.5 GPA or higher. Available to U.S. citizens.

Application Requirements: Application form, application form may be submitted online (https://sams.scholarshipexperts.com/showApp.htx?appId=10687&src=GGRA), essay, financial need analysis, interview, recommendations or references, transcript. *Deadline:* April 30.

Contact: Donnalyn Murphy, Trustee and Secretary
Golden Gate Restaurant Association
100 Montgomery Street, Suite 1280
San Francisco, CA 94104
Phone: 415-781-5348 Ext. 2
Fax: 415-781-3925
E-mail: donnalyn@ggra.org

ILLINOIS RESTAURANT ASSOCIATION EDUCATIONAL FOUNDATION

http://www.illinoisrestaurants.org/

ILLINOIS RESTAURANT ASSOCIATION EDUCATIONAL FOUNDATION SCHOLARSHIPS

Scholarship available to Illinois residents enrolled in a food service management, culinary arts, or hospitality management concentration in an accredited program of a two- or four-year college or university. Must be a U.S. citizen.

Academic Fields/Career Goals: Culinary Arts; Food Science/Nutrition; Food Service/Hospitality; Hospitality Management.

Award: Scholarship for use in freshman, sophomore, junior, senior, graduate, or postgraduate years; not renewable. *Number:* 50–70. *Amount:* $750–$24,000.

Eligibility Requirements: Applicant must be enrolled or expecting to enroll full- or part-time at a two-year or four-year or technical institution or university and resident of Illinois. Applicant or parent of applicant must have employment or volunteer experience in food service, hospitality/hotel administration/operations. Available to U.S. citizens.

Application Requirements: Application form, essay, personal photograph, recommendations or references, transcript. *Deadline:* May 15.

INTERNATIONAL FOODSERVICE EDITORIAL COUNCIL

http://www.ifeconline.com/

INTERNATIONAL FOODSERVICE EDITORIAL COUNCIL COMMUNICATIONS SCHOLARSHIP
• *See page 83*

JAMES BEARD FOUNDATION INC.

http://www.jamesbeard.org/

ALLEN SUSSER SCHOLARSHIP

Up to one scholarship of $5500 for high school seniors or graduates who plan to enroll or students currently enrolled at least part-time in a course of study at a licensed or accredited culinary school. Must reside in the state of Florida or be enrolled in a Florida culinary school.

Academic Fields/Career Goals: Culinary Arts.

Award: Scholarship for use in freshman, sophomore, junior, or senior years; not renewable. *Number:* up to 1. *Amount:* $5500.

Eligibility Requirements: Applicant must be enrolled or expecting to enroll full- or part-time at a two-year or technical institution. Available to U.S. citizens.

Application Requirements: Application form. *Deadline:* May 15.

AMERICAN RESTAURANT SCHOLARSHIP

Up to one award of $5000 available for students who plan to enroll or are already enrolled at a licensed or accredited culinary school.

Academic Fields/Career Goals: Culinary Arts.

Award: Scholarship for use in freshman, sophomore, junior, senior, or graduate years; not renewable. *Number:* up to 1. *Amount:* $5000.

Eligibility Requirements: Applicant must be enrolled or expecting to enroll full-time at a four-year institution or university. Available to U.S. and non-U.S. citizens.

Application Requirements: Application form, essay, financial need analysis, recommendations or references, transcript. *Deadline:* May 15.

AZUREA AT ONE OCEAN RESORT HOTEL & SPA SCHOLARSHIP

Up to one $4000 scholarship for high school seniors or graduates who plan to enroll or students who are currently enrolled at least part-time in a course of study at a licensed or accredited culinary school in the state of Florida.

Academic Fields/Career Goals: Culinary Arts.

Award: Scholarship for use in freshman, sophomore, junior, or senior years; not renewable. *Number:* up to 1. *Amount:* $4000.

Eligibility Requirements: Applicant must be enrolled or expecting to enroll full- or part-time at a two-year or technical institution and studying in Florida. Available to U.S. citizens.

Application Requirements: Application form. *Deadline:* May 15.

BERN LAXER MEMORIAL SCHOLARSHIP

Scholarship for students seeking careers in food service and hospitality management. Up to two scholarships given in one of three programs: culinary, hospitality management, and viticulture/oenology. Program and school must be accredited in accordance with the James Beard Foundation scholarship criteria. Must be resident of Florida and substantiate residency; have a high school diploma or the equivalent; and have a minimum of one-year culinary experience either as a student or employee. Applicants may reapply each year for a maximum of four years.

Academic Fields/Career Goals: Culinary Arts; Food Science/Nutrition; Hospitality Management.

Award: Scholarship for use in freshman, sophomore, junior, or senior years; not renewable. *Number:* up to 2. *Amount:* $4000.

Eligibility Requirements: Applicant must be enrolled or expecting to enroll full- or part-time at a four-year institution or university and resident of Florida. Available to U.S. and non-U.S. citizens.

Application Requirements: Application form, essay, financial need analysis, recommendations or references, transcript. *Deadline:* May 15.

BILL RAMSEY/CRAIG NOONE MEMORIAL SCHOLARSHIP

Up to one scholarship of $5000 for high school seniors or graduates who plan to enroll or students who are already enrolled at least part-time in a course of study at a licensed or accredited culinary school.

Academic Fields/Career Goals: Culinary Arts.

Award: Scholarship for use in freshman, sophomore, junior, or senior years; not renewable. *Number:* up to 1. *Amount:* $5000.

Eligibility Requirements: Applicant must be enrolled or expecting to enroll full- or part-time at a two-year or technical institution. Available to U.S. citizens.

Application Requirements: Application form. *Deadline:* May 15.

BOB ZAPPATELLI MEMORIAL SCHOLARSHIP

Up to one $3000 award is available to applicants who are planning to enroll or currently enrolled in an accredited program of culinary studies or food and beverage studies. Applicant must have work experience in food and beverage and must demonstrate strong leadership skills and passion for the culinary arts. Preference will be given to an employee or relative of a Benchmark employee.

Academic Fields/Career Goals: Culinary Arts.

Award: Scholarship for use in freshman, sophomore, junior, or senior years; not renewable. *Number:* up to 1. *Amount:* $3000.

Eligibility Requirements: Applicant must be enrolled or expecting to enroll full- or part-time at a two-year or four-year institution or university. Available to U.S. citizens.

Application Requirements: Application form, proof of residency. *Deadline:* May 15.

THE CHEFS FOR LOUISIANA COOKERY SCHOLARSHIP

Up to one $5000 awards are available to residents of Louisiana who are pursuing a career in the culinary field at an accredited culinary college/ university located in the state of Louisiana.

Academic Fields/Career Goals: Culinary Arts.

Award: Scholarship for use in freshman, sophomore, junior, or senior years; not renewable. *Number:* up to 1. *Amount:* $5000.

Eligibility Requirements: Applicant must be enrolled or expecting to enroll full- or part-time at a two-year or four-year institution or university; resident of Louisiana and studying in Louisiana.

Application Requirements: Application form, proof of residency. *Deadline:* May 15.

CHRISTIAN WOLFFER SCHOLARSHIP

Up to one $2000 award is available to New York residents planning to enroll or currently enrolled at a licensed or accredited culinary school or wine studies program. Minimum GPA of 3.0 required.

Academic Fields/Career Goals: Culinary Arts.

Award: Scholarship for use in freshman, sophomore, junior, or senior years; not renewable. *Number:* up to 1. *Amount:* $2000.

Eligibility Requirements: Applicant must be enrolled or expecting to enroll full- or part-time at a two-year or four-year institution or university and resident of New York. Applicant must have 3.0 GPA or higher. Available to U.S. citizens.

Application Requirements: Application form, proof of residency. *Deadline:* May 15.

CLAY TRIPLETTE SCHOLARSHIP

$4000 scholarship for deserving students who want to pursue a baking and pastry degree. Applicants must plan to enroll or already be enrolled in an accredited baking or pastry studies program at a licensed or accredited culinary school. Must submit a 250 word essay on the life of James Beard.

Academic Fields/Career Goals: Culinary Arts.

Award: Scholarship for use in freshman, sophomore, junior, or senior years; not renewable. *Number:* up to 1. *Amount:* $4000.

Eligibility Requirements: Applicant must be enrolled or expecting to enroll full-time at a four-year institution or university. Available to U.S. citizens.

Application Requirements: Application form, essay, financial need analysis, recommendations or references, transcript. *Deadline:* May 15.

THE ELKES FAMILY CULINARY SCHOLARSHIP

Up to one $42,500 scholarship for a high school senior or graduate who plans to enroll or is currently enrolled at least part-time in a course of student at a licensed or accredited culinary school. Must demonstrate financial need, submit three letters of recommendation, and write an essay on one of two topics. Finalists must participate in a telephone or in-person interview. Award is intended to cover full tuition and potentially may cover other education-related expenses at the discretion of the Foundation.

Academic Fields/Career Goals: Culinary Arts.

Award: Scholarship for use in freshman, sophomore, junior, or senior years; not renewable. *Number:* up to 1. *Amount:* $42,500.

Eligibility Requirements: Applicant must be enrolled or expecting to enroll full- or part-time at a two-year or technical institution. Available to U.S. citizens.

Application Requirements: Application form, essay, financial need analysis, recommendations or references. *Deadline:* May 15.

FOOD NETWORK SCHOLARSHIP FOR IMMIGRANTS IN THE KITCHEN

Up to two scholarships of $5000 each for a student planning to enroll or currently enrolled in an accredited program of study in the culinary arts or a related field at an accredited culinary school. Must be an immigrant from a country other than the USA and submit proof.

Academic Fields/Career Goals: Culinary Arts.

Award: Scholarship for use in freshman, sophomore, junior, or senior years; not renewable. *Number:* up to 2. *Amount:* $5000.

Eligibility Requirements: Applicant must be enrolled or expecting to enroll full- or part-time at a two-year or technical institution.

Application Requirements: Application form, proof of residency. *Deadline:* May 15.

JOSE AND VICTORIA MARTINEZ MAISON BLANCH SCHOLARSHIP

Up to one award of $2000 for a high school senior or graduate who plans to enroll or a student who is already enrolled at least part-time in a course of study at a licensed or accredited culinary school. Preference will be given to applicants who reside on the Gulf Coast of Florida and must demonstrate financial need. Submit a 250-500-word essay describing a personal path to excellence in the culinary arts.

Academic Fields/Career Goals: Culinary Arts.

Award: Scholarship for use in freshman, sophomore, junior, or senior years; not renewable. *Number:* up to 1. *Amount:* $2000.

Eligibility Requirements: Applicant must be enrolled or expecting to enroll full-time at a two-year or technical institution. Available to U.S. citizens.

Application Requirements: Application form, essay, proof of residency. *Deadline:* May 15.

LACROIX AT THE RITTENHOUSE SCHOLARSHIP

Up to one $2500 scholarship for a high school senior or graduate who is planning to enroll or currently enrolled at least part-time in a course of study at a licensed or accredited culinary school. Must be a resident of Pennsylvania.

Academic Fields/Career Goals: Culinary Arts.

Award: Scholarship for use in freshman, sophomore, junior, or senior years; not renewable. *Number:* up to 1. *Amount:* $2500.

Eligibility Requirements: Applicant must be enrolled or expecting to enroll full- or part-time at a two-year or technical institution and resident of Pennsylvania. Available to U.S. citizens.

Application Requirements: Application form. *Deadline:* May 15.

LA TOQUE SCHOLARSHIP IN WINE STUDIES

Scholarship for $3000 toward tuition in an accredited wine studies program of the student's choice. For both full-time and part-time study.

Academic Fields/Career Goals: Culinary Arts.

Award: Scholarship for use in freshman, sophomore, junior, senior, or graduate years; not renewable. *Number:* 1. *Amount:* $3000.

Eligibility Requirements: Applicant must be enrolled or expecting to enroll full- or part-time at a four-year institution or university. Available to U.S. and non-U.S. citizens.

Application Requirements: Application form, essay, financial need analysis, recommendations or references, transcript. *Deadline:* May 15.

LEMAIRE RESTAURANT AT THE JEFFERSON HOTEL SCHOLARSHIP

Up to one award of $4500 for high school seniors or graduates who plan to enroll or students who are already enrolled at least part-time in a course of study at a licensed or accredited culinary school.

Academic Fields/Career Goals: Culinary Arts.

Award: Scholarship for use in freshman, sophomore, junior, or senior years; not renewable. *Number:* up to 1. *Amount:* $4500.

Eligibility Requirements: Applicant must be enrolled or expecting to enroll full- or part-time at a two-year or technical institution. Available to U.S. citizens.

Application Requirements: Application form, proof of residency. *Deadline:* May 15.

NEW ENGLAND HADASSAH SCHOLARSHIP

Up to one $3000 scholarship for a female high school senior or graduate who plans to enroll or is currently enrolled at least part-time in a course of study at a licensed or accredited culinary school.

Academic Fields/Career Goals: Culinary Arts.

Award: Scholarship for use in freshman, sophomore, junior, or senior years; not renewable. *Number:* up to 1. *Amount:* $3000.

Eligibility Requirements: Applicant must be enrolled or expecting to enroll full- or part-time at a two-year or technical institution and female. Available to U.S. citizens.

Application Requirements: Application form. *Deadline:* May 15.

PETER CAMERON/HOUSEWARES CHARITY FOUNDATION SCHOLARSHIP

Up to one scholarship of $4000 for high school seniors planning to enroll at a licensed or accredited culinary school. Must have a minimum GPA of 3.0.

Academic Fields/Career Goals: Culinary Arts.

Award: Scholarship for use in freshman year; not renewable. *Number:* up to 1. *Amount:* $4000.

Eligibility Requirements: Applicant must be high school student and planning to enroll or expecting to enroll full-time at a four-year institution or university. Applicant must have 3.0 GPA or higher. Available to U.S. and non-U.S. citizens.

Application Requirements: Application form, essay, financial need analysis, recommendations or references, transcript. *Deadline:* May 15.

PETER KUMP MEMORIAL SCHOLARSHIP

One-time award towards tuition at an accredited or licensed culinary school of student's choice. Candidates must have a minimum of one year of experience in the culinary field, demonstrate financial need, and have at least a 3.0 GPA.

Academic Fields/Career Goals: Culinary Arts.

Award: Scholarship for use in freshman year; not renewable. *Number:* up to 5. *Amount:* $5000.

Eligibility Requirements: Applicant must be high school student and planning to enroll or expecting to enroll full- or part-time at a four-year institution or university. Applicant must have 3.0 GPA or higher. Available to U.S. and non-U.S. citizens.

Application Requirements: Application form, essay, financial need analysis, recommendations or references, transcript. *Deadline:* May 15.

THE RANCH HOUSE AT DEVIL'S THUMB RANCH SCHOLARSHIP

Up to one scholarship of $3750 for high school seniors or graduates who plan to enroll or students who are already enrolled at least part-time in a course of study at a licensed or accredited culinary school.

Academic Fields/Career Goals: Culinary Arts.

Award: Scholarship for use in freshman, sophomore, junior, or senior years; not renewable. *Number:* up to 1. *Amount:* $3750.

Eligibility Requirements: Applicant must be enrolled or expecting to enroll full- or part-time at a two-year or technical institution. Available to U.S. citizens.

Application Requirements: Application form. *Deadline:* May 15.

RESTAURANT AT SUNSET MARQUIS SCHOLARSHIP

Up to one scholarship of $3750 for high school seniors or graduates who plan to enroll or students who are already enrolled at least part-time in a course of study at a licensed or accredited culinary school.

Academic Fields/Career Goals: Culinary Arts.

Award: Scholarship for use in freshman, sophomore, junior, or senior years; not renewable. *Number:* up to 1. *Amount:* $3750.

Eligibility Requirements: Applicant must be enrolled or expecting to enroll full- or part-time at a two-year or technical institution. Available to U.S. citizens.

Application Requirements: Application form. *Deadline:* May 15.

SCHNITZER STEEL "RACING TO STOP HUNGER" SCHOLARSHIP

Up to two scholarships of $5000 each for residents of Oregon or those enrolling or planning to attend an Oregon-based culinary school or program. Must submit 500-word essay on "Fighting Hunger in Oregon: What I've Done or Would Like to Do to Make a Difference."

Academic Fields/Career Goals: Culinary Arts.

Award: Scholarship for use in freshman, sophomore, junior, or senior years; not renewable. *Number:* up to 2. *Amount:* $5000.

Eligibility Requirements: Applicant must be enrolled or expecting to enroll full- or part-time at a two-year or technical institution. Available to U.S. citizens.

Application Requirements: Application form, essay, proof of residency. *Deadline:* May 15.

STEVEN SCHER MEMORIAL SCHOLARSHIP FOR ASPIRING RESTAURANTEURS

Awards available to students enrolled or accepted in a culinary or hospitality management program at an accredited institution. Must detail work experience, submit essay, and include a list of top three favorite restaurants and explain why they have earned that ranking. One award is for use at an institution of the recipient's choice and the second is for use

only at the French Culinary Institute in New York City. Special consideration will be given to career changers.

Academic Fields/Career Goals: Culinary Arts.

Award: Scholarship for use in freshman, sophomore, junior, or senior years; not renewable. *Number:* up to 2. *Amount:* $5000.

Eligibility Requirements: Applicant must be enrolled or expecting to enroll full- or part-time at a two-year or four-year institution or university. Available to U.S. citizens.

Application Requirements: Essay, proof of residency. *Deadline:* May 15.

STUDIO AT THE MONTAGE RESORT & SPA SCHOLARSHIP

Up to one $3600 award available to high school senior or graduate who plans to enroll or student who is already enrolled at least part-time in a course of study at a licensed or accredited culinary school.

Academic Fields/Career Goals: Culinary Arts.

Award: Scholarship for use in freshman, sophomore, junior, or senior years; not renewable. *Number:* up to 1. *Amount:* $3600.

Eligibility Requirements: Applicant must be enrolled or expecting to enroll full- or part-time at a two-year or four-year institution or university. Available to U.S. citizens.

Application Requirements: Application form, proof of residency. *Deadline:* May 15.

SUNDAY SUPPER ATLANTA SCHOLARSHIP

Awards for high school seniors or graduates who plan to enroll or students who are already enrolled at least part-time in a course of study at a licensed or accredited culinary school. Two awards for $5000 each, two for $4000 each, and one for $2000 will be distributed.

Academic Fields/Career Goals: Culinary Arts.

Award: Scholarship for use in freshman, sophomore, junior, or senior years; not renewable. *Number:* up to 5. *Amount:* $2000–$5000.

Eligibility Requirements: Applicant must be enrolled or expecting to enroll full- or part-time at a two-year or technical institution. Available to U.S. citizens.

Application Requirements: Application form, proof of residency. *Deadline:* May 15.

ZOV'S BISTRO SCHOLARSHIP

Up to one $3000 award available to high school senior or graduate who plans to enroll or student who is already enrolled at least part-time in a course of study at a licensed or accredited culinary school.

Academic Fields/Career Goals: Culinary Arts.

Award: Scholarship for use in freshman, sophomore, junior, or senior years; not renewable. *Number:* up to 1. *Amount:* $3000.

Eligibility Requirements: Applicant must be enrolled or expecting to enroll full- or part-time at a two-year or four-year institution or university. Available to U.S. citizens.

Application Requirements: Application form, proof of residency. *Deadline:* May 15.

MAINE RESTAURANT ASSOCIATION

http://www.mainerestaurant.com/

MAINE RESTAURANT ASSOCIATION EDUCATION FOUNDATION SCHOLARSHIP FUND

Scholarship available to students (Maine Residents Only) who wish to pursue higher education in culinary arts, restaurant, and hotel or hospitality management. Preference will be given to those in Maine-based institutions and those who intend to pursue a career in food service.

Academic Fields/Career Goals: Culinary Arts; Hospitality Management.

Award: Scholarship for use in freshman, sophomore, junior, or senior years; not renewable. *Number:* 1–8. *Amount:* $500–$2000.

Eligibility Requirements: Applicant must be enrolled or expecting to enroll full- or part-time at a two-year or four-year or technical institution or university and resident of Maine. Available to U.S. citizens.

Application Requirements: Application form, essay, transcript. *Deadline:* April 21.

Contact: Becky Jacobson, Operations Manager
Phone: 207-623-2178
E-mail: info@mainerestaurant.com

MAINE SCHOOL FOOD SERVICE ASSOCIATION (MSFSA) CONTINUING EDUCATION SCHOLARSHIP

http://www.mainesfsa.org/

MAINE SCHOOL FOOD SERVICE ASSOCIATION CONTINUING EDUCATION SCHOLARSHIP

Awarded to students from Maine enrolling in nutrition or culinary arts. It is also available to employees of school nutrition programs wishing to continue their education. Applicant can be a high school senior, college student, or member of MSFSA. Applicant must be attending an institution in Maine.

Academic Fields/Career Goals: Culinary Arts; Food Science/Nutrition; Food Service/Hospitality; Home Economics.

Award: Scholarship for use in freshman, sophomore, junior, senior, graduate, or postgraduate years; not renewable. *Number:* 1–4. *Amount:* $250–$1200.

Eligibility Requirements: Applicant must be enrolled or expecting to enroll full- or part-time at a two-year or four-year or technical institution or university; resident of Maine and studying in Maine. Available to U.S. citizens.

Application Requirements: Acceptance letter, application form, essay, recommendations or references, resume, transcript. *Deadline:* April 1.

Contact: Judith Campbell, Education Committee Chair
Maine School Food Service Association (MSFSA) Continuing Education Scholarship
9 Wentworth Drive
Scarborough, ME 04074
Phone: 207-730-4701
Fax: 207-730-4702

OREGON STUDENT ASSISTANCE COMMISSION

http://www.GetCollegeFunds.org/

OREGON WINE BROTHERHOOD SCHOLARSHIP

Award for residents of Oregon or Washington majoring in enology, viticulture, or culinary arts with an emphasis on wine. Must attend Chemeketa, Central Oregon, Lane, Mt. Hood, Southwestern Oregon, Umpqua, or Walla Walla Community Colleges, Southern Oregon and Oregon State Universities, or University of California at Davis. Must reapply annually for renewal.

Academic Fields/Career Goals: Culinary Arts; Food Science/Nutrition.

Award: Scholarship for use in freshman, sophomore, junior, senior, or graduate years; not renewable.

Eligibility Requirements: Applicant must be enrolled or expecting to enroll full-time at a two-year or four-year institution or university and resident of Oregon, Washington. Available to U.S. citizens.

Application Requirements: Activities chart, FAFSA, application form, essay, financial need analysis, transcript. *Deadline:* March 1.

SOUTH DAKOTA RETAILERS ASSOCIATION

http://www.sdra.org/

SOUTH DAKOTA RETAILERS ASSOCIATION SCHOLARSHIP PROGRAM

• See page 80

STRAIGHTFORWARD MEDIA

http://www.straightforwardmedia.com/

STRAIGHTFORWARD MEDIA VOCATIONAL-TECHNICAL SCHOOL SCHOLARSHIP

• See page 99

WISCONSIN BAKERS ASSOCIATION (WBA)

http://www.umwba.org/

ROBERT W. HILLER SCHOLARSHIP FUND

Scholarship of $1000 awarded for students at all levels in a baking/pastry arts-related program that prepares candidates for a retail baking profession. Minimum 2.85 GPA required.

Academic Fields/Career Goals: Culinary Arts.

Award: Scholarship for use in freshman, sophomore, junior, senior, graduate, or postgraduate years; not renewable. *Amount:* $1000.

Eligibility Requirements: Applicant must be enrolled or expecting to enroll full-time at a four-year institution or university. Available to U.S. citizens.

Application Requirements: Application form, essay, recommendations or references, resume. *Deadline:* June 2.

Contact: Rebeca Borrero-Hoover, Scholarship Committee
Phone: 414-258-5552
Fax: 414-258-5582
E-mail: information@umwba.org

WOMEN CHEFS AND RESTAURATEURS

http://www.womenchefs.org/

FRENCH CULINARY INSTITUTE/ITALIAN CULINARY EXPERIENCE SCHOLARSHIP

Scholarship intended for a culinary student wishing to specialize in Italian cuisine. Recipient must be a new enrollment and satisfy all entrance requirements of the FCI. Scholarship award is applied to total program fee.

Academic Fields/Career Goals: Culinary Arts; Food Service/Hospitality.

Award: Scholarship for use in freshman, sophomore, junior, senior, graduate, or postgraduate years; not renewable. *Number:* 1. *Amount:* $5000.

Eligibility Requirements: Applicant must be enrolled or expecting to enroll full-time at a four-year institution or university. Available to U.S. and non-U.S. citizens.

Application Requirements: Application form, essay. *Fee:* $25. *Deadline:* March 31.

Contact: Dori Sacksteder, Director of Programs
Phone: 502-581-0300 Ext. 219
Fax: 502-589-3602
E-mail: dsacksteder@hqtrs.com

DENTAL HEALTH/ SERVICES

ALBERTA HERITAGE SCHOLARSHIP FUND

http://www.alis.alberta.ca/

ABORIGINAL HEALTH CAREERS BURSARY

• See page 142

JASON LANG SCHOLARSHIP

Award of CAN$1000 to reward the outstanding academic achievement of Alberta postsecondary students who are studying full-time in Alberta. Must be a Canadian citizen or permanent resident and Alberta resident. Must be enrolled full-time in an undergraduate or professional program, such as law, medicine, pharmacy, or dentistry at an eligible Alberta postsecondary institution. Nominated by Awards Office at institution on the basis of achieving a minimum GPA of 3.2 in the previous academic year. May be awarded up to three times to one student. For additional information, see website http://alis.alberta.ca.

Academic Fields/Career Goals: Dental Health/Services; Health and Medical Sciences; Law/Legal Services; Pharmacy.

Award: Scholarship for use in sophomore, junior, or senior years; not renewable.

Eligibility Requirements: Applicant must be Canadian citizen; enrolled or expecting to enroll full-time at a two-year or four-year or technical institution or university; resident of Alberta and studying in Alberta.

Application Requirements: Application form, test scores, transcript. *Deadline:* varies.

NORTHERN ALBERTA DEVELOPMENT COUNCIL BURSARY

Return service bursary awards CAN$6000 per year for up to two years to increase the number of trained professionals in Northern Alberta and to encourage students from Northern Alberta to obtain a postsecondary education. Must be residents of Alberta, and planning to enroll in a full-time postsecondary program in a field in demand in Northern Alberta. Fields in demand include: education, healthcare and medical, engineering and technical fields, social work. Applicants must also be within two years of completion of their postsecondary program. Students must live and work for one year in Northern Alberta for each year of assistance awarded. For additional information, go to website http://alis.alberta.ca.

Academic Fields/Career Goals: Dental Health/Services; Education; Engineering/Technology; Health and Medical Sciences; Social Services.

Award: Scholarship for use in freshman, sophomore, junior, or senior years; not renewable.

Eligibility Requirements: Applicant must be Canadian citizen; enrolled or expecting to enroll full-time at a two-year or four-year or technical institution or university; resident of Alberta and studying in Alberta.

Application Requirements: Application form, essay, financial need analysis, transcript. *Deadline:* April 30.

AMERICAN ACADEMY OF ORAL AND MAXILLOFACIAL RADIOLOGY

http://www.aaomr.org/

CHARLES R. MORRIS STUDENT RESEARCH AWARD

Award to applicants from accredited programs performing research in oral and maxillofacial radiology. Applicant must be a full-time undergraduate or predoctoral student at the time of research, be nominated by the institution where research was carried out, and submit a manuscript detailing the research project.

Academic Fields/Career Goals: Dental Health/Services.

Award: Grant for use in junior, senior, or graduate years; not renewable. *Number:* 1. *Amount:* $1000.

Eligibility Requirements: Applicant must be enrolled or expecting to enroll full-time at a four-year institution or university. Available to U.S. and non-U.S. citizens.

Application Requirements: Application form, manuscript, recommendations or references. *Deadline:* June 16.

Contact: Dr. Michael Shrout, Executive Director
American Academy of Oral and Maxillofacial Radiology
Box 1010
Evans, GA 30809-1010
Phone: 706-271-2881
E-mail: mshrout@mcg.edu

AMERICAN DENTAL ASSISTANTS ASSOCIATION

http://www.dentalassistant.org/

JULIETTE A. SOUTHARD/ORAL B LABORATORIES SCHOLARSHIP

Leadership-based award available to students enrolled in an ADAA dental assistant's program. Proof of acceptance into ADAA program and two letters of reference are required.

Academic Fields/Career Goals: Dental Health/Services.

Award: Scholarship for use in freshman, sophomore, junior, senior, graduate, or postgraduate years; not renewable. *Number:* up to 10.

Eligibility Requirements: Applicant must be enrolled or expecting to enroll full- or part-time at a two-year or four-year institution or university and must have an interest in leadership. Applicant or parent of applicant must be member of American Dental Assistants Association. Available to U.S. citizens.

Application Requirements: Application form, essay, financial need analysis, recommendations or references, transcript. *Deadline:* March 1.

Contact: Erek Armentrout, Membership Development Manager
Phone: 312-541-1550
Fax: 312-541-1496
E-mail: earmentrout@adaa1.com

AMERICAN DENTAL ASSOCIATION (ADA) FOUNDATION

http://www.adafoundation.org/

AMERICAN DENTAL ASSOCIATION FOUNDATION DENTAL ASSISTING SCHOLARSHIP PROGRAM

Applicant must be enrolled as a full-time student with a minimum of 12 credit hours in a dental assistant program accredited by the Commission on Dental Accreditation of the American Dental Association. Must be a U.S. citizen, permanent resident is ineligible to apply. Must have an accumulative 3.5 GPA based on a 4.0 scale. Applicants must be recommended by the dental assisting program director at the school where accepted into the dental assisting program. Applicants must demonstrate a minimum financial need of $1000.

Academic Fields/Career Goals: Dental Health/Services.

Award: Scholarship for use in freshman year; not renewable. *Number:* up to 10. *Amount:* up to $1000.

Eligibility Requirements: Applicant must be enrolled or expecting to enroll full-time at a two-year or four-year institution. Applicant must have 3.5 GPA or higher. Available to U.S. citizens.

Application Requirements: Application form, essay, financial need analysis, recommendations or references. *Deadline:* April 23.

Contact: Rose Famularo, Coordinator
Phone: 312-440-2763
E-mail: famularor@ada.org

AMERICAN DENTAL ASSOCIATION FOUNDATION DENTAL HYGIENE SCHOLARSHIP PROGRAM

Applicant must be enrolled full-time with a minimum of 12 Credit hours as a student in an accredited dental hygiene program accredited by the Commission of Dental Accreditation of the American Dental Association. Must be U.S. citizen, permanent resident is ineligible to apply. Must have a minimum 3.5 GPA on a 4.0 scale. Applicants must be recommended by the dental hygiene program director and may request application materials from that same individual at the school where they are currently enrolled as an entering final year student in a dental hygiene program. Applicants must demonstrate a minimum financial need of $1000.

Academic Fields/Career Goals: Dental Health/Services.

Award: Scholarship for use in senior year; not renewable. *Number:* up to 15. *Amount:* up to $1000.

Eligibility Requirements: Applicant must be enrolled or expecting to enroll full-time at a four-year institution or university. Applicant must have 3.5 GPA or higher. Available to U.S. citizens.

Application Requirements: Application form, essay, financial need analysis, recommendations or references. *Deadline:* April 23.

Contact: Rose Famularo, Coordinator
Phone: 312-440-2763
E-mail: famularor@ada.org

AMERICAN DENTAL ASSOCIATION FOUNDATION DENTAL LAB TECHNOLOGY SCHOLARSHIP

Applicant must be enrolled as a full-time student with a minimum of 12 credit hours as a last-year student in a dental laboratory technology program accredited by the Commission on Dental Accreditation of the American Dental Association. Must be a U.S. citizen, permanent resident is ineligible to apply. Must have an accumulative minimum 3.5 GPA based on a 4.0 scale. Applicants must be recommended by the dental laboratory technology program director at the school where attending. Applicant must demonstrate a $1,000 financial need.

Academic Fields/Career Goals: Dental Health/Services.

Award: Scholarship for use in senior year; not renewable. *Number:* up to 5. *Amount:* up to $1000.

Eligibility Requirements: Applicant must be enrolled or expecting to enroll full-time at a four-year institution or university. Applicant must have 3.5 GPA or higher. Available to U.S. citizens.

Application Requirements: Application form, essay, financial need analysis, recommendations or references. *Deadline:* April 23.

Contact: Rose Famularo, Coordinator
Phone: 312-440-2763
E-mail: famularor@ada.org

AMERICAN DENTAL ASSOCIATION FOUNDATION DENTAL STUDENT SCHOLARSHIP PROGRAM

One-time award for entering second-year students at a dental school accredited by the American Dental Association Commission on Dental Accreditation. Must have 3.0 GPA, and be enrolled full-time (minimum of 12 hours). Must show financial need and be a U.S. citizen, a permanent resident is ineligible to apply. Applicants may request application materials from associate dean for student affairs at the dental school where they are currently enrolled. An applicant must be recommended to the ADA Foundation by the school official.

Academic Fields/Career Goals: Dental Health/Services.

Award: Scholarship for use in sophomore year; not renewable. *Number:* up to 25. *Amount:* up to $2500.

Eligibility Requirements: Applicant must be enrolled or expecting to enroll full-time at a four-year institution or university. Applicant must have 3.0 GPA or higher. Available to U.S. citizens.

Application Requirements: Application form, essay, financial need analysis, recommendations or references. *Deadline:* October 4.

Contact: Rose Famularo, Coordinator
Phone: 312-440-2763
E-mail: famularor@ada.org

AMERICAN DENTAL ASSOCIATION FOUNDATION UNDERREPRESENTED MINORITY DENTAL STUDENT SCHOLARSHIP PROGRAM

One-time scholarship award for entering second-year students at a dental school accredited by the American Dental Association Commission on Dental Accreditation of a minority group that is underrepresented in dental school enrollment. Based on financial need and academic achievement. Must be U.S. citizen, a permanent resident is ineligible to apply. Must be a full-time students (minimum 12 hours). Must have minimum 3.0 GPA. Applicants may request application materials from associate dean for student affairs at the school where they are currently enrolled and must be recommended by the school official. Applicants must demonstrate a minimum financial need of $2500.

Academic Fields/Career Goals: Dental Health/Services.

Award: Scholarship for use in sophomore year; not renewable. *Number:* up to 25. *Amount:* up to $2500.

Eligibility Requirements: Applicant must be American Indian/Alaska Native, Black (non-Hispanic), Hispanic and enrolled or expecting to enroll full-time at a four-year institution or university. Applicant must have 3.0 GPA or higher. Available to U.S. citizens.

Application Requirements: Application form, essay, financial need analysis, recommendations or references. *Deadline:* October 4.

Contact: Rose Famularo, Coordinator
Phone: 312-440-2763
E-mail: famularor@ada.org

AMERICAN DENTAL HYGIENISTS' ASSOCIATION (ADHA) INSTITUTE FOR ORAL HEALTH

http://www.adha.org/institute

CAROL BAUHS BENSON SCHOLARSHIP

Established in the memory of Carol Bauhs Benson, this scholarship is awarded to students at the Certificate/Associate educational level who have completed (or who will complete by the time of the award) a minimum of one year in a dental hygiene curriculum. This scholarship is restricted to students who reside in the following states: Minnesota, North Dakota, South Dakota or Wisconsin.

Academic Fields/Career Goals: Dental Health/Services.

Award: Scholarship for use in sophomore year; not renewable. *Number:* 1. *Amount:* $1000.

Eligibility Requirements: Applicant must be enrolled or expecting to enroll full-time at a two-year institution or university and resident of Minnesota, North Dakota, South Dakota, Wisconsin. Applicant must have 3.5 GPA or higher. Available to U.S. citizens.

Application Requirements: Application form, essay, recommendations or references. *Deadline:* February 1.

Contact: Jessica Mitton, Development Manager
American Dental Hygienists' Association (ADHA) Institute
For Oral Health
444 North Michigan Avenue
Suite 3400
Chicago, IL 60611
Phone: 312-440-8944
Fax: 312-440-6764
E-mail: institute@adha.net

COLGATE "BRIGHT SMILES, BRIGHT FUTURES" MINORITY SCHOLARSHIP

One time award for members of minority groups currently underrepresented in dental hygiene programs at the certificate educational level. Must be an active student member of ADHA. Applicant must have completed one year of dental hygiene curricula at an accredited dental hygiene program in United States. Applicant must demonstrate GPA of at least 3.0, and financial need of $1500 or more.

Academic Fields/Career Goals: Dental Health/Services.

Award: Scholarship for use in sophomore year; not renewable. *Number:* 1–2. *Amount:* $1250.

Eligibility Requirements: Applicant must be American Indian/Alaska Native, Asian/Pacific Islander, Black (non-Hispanic), Hispanic and enrolled or expecting to enroll full-time at a two-year or technical institution. Applicant or parent of applicant must be member of American Dental Hygienist's Association. Applicant must have 3.0 GPA or higher. Available to U.S. citizens.

Application Requirements: Application form, essay, recommendations or references. *Deadline:* February 1.

Contact: Jessica Mitton, Development Manager
American Dental Hygienists' Association (ADHA) Institute
For Oral Health
444 North Michigan Avenue
Suite 3400
Chicago, IL 60611
Phone: 312-440-8944
Fax: 312-440-6764
E-mail: institute@adha.net

CREST ORAL-B LABORATORIES DENTAL HYGIENE SCHOLARSHIP

Scholarships to baccalaureate degree students who demonstrate intent to encourage professional excellence, promote quality research, and support dental hygiene through public and private education. Must be an active SADHA or ADHA member. Must have completed one year of dental hygiene curricula at an accredited dental hygiene program in United States. Must demonstrate GPA of at least 3.5.

Academic Fields/Career Goals: Dental Health/Services.

Award: Scholarship for use in sophomore, junior, or senior years; not renewable. *Number:* 1–2. *Amount:* $1000.

Eligibility Requirements: Applicant must be enrolled or expecting to enroll full-time at a four-year institution or university. Applicant or parent of applicant must be member of American Dental Hygienist's

Association. Applicant must have 3.5 GPA or higher. Available to U.S. citizens.

Application Requirements: Application form, essay, recommendations or references. *Deadline:* May 1.

Contact: Jessica Mitton, Development Manager
American Dental Hygienists' Association (ADHA) Institute
For Oral Health
444 North Michigan Avenue
Suite 3400
Chicago, IL 60611
Phone: 312-440-8944
Fax: 312-440-6764
E-mail: institute@adha.net

HU-FRIEDY/ESTHER WILKINS INSTRUMENT SCHOLARSHIP

These scholarships are awarded to applicants at the certificate/associate or baccalaureate degree level who have completed a minimum of one year in a dental hygiene curriculum. The program awards recipients with the Hu-Friedy dental hygiene instruments of their choice, equivalent to a retail value of $1,000.

Academic Fields/Career Goals: Dental Health/Services.

Award: Scholarship for use in sophomore, junior, or senior years; not renewable. *Amount:* $1000.

Eligibility Requirements: Applicant must be enrolled or expecting to enroll full-time at a two-year or four-year institution or university. Applicant must have 3.0 GPA or higher. Available to U.S. citizens.

Application Requirements: Application form, essay, recommendations or references. *Deadline:* February 1.

Contact: Jessica Mitton, Development Manager
American Dental Hygienists' Association (ADHA) Institute
For Oral Health
444 North Michigan Avenue
Suite 3400
Chicago, IL 60611
Phone: 312-440-8944
Fax: 312-440-6764
E-mail: institute@adha.net

JOHNSON & JOHNSON SCHOLARSHIP

These scholarships are awarded to applicants pursuing a certificate/associate or baccalaureate degree in dental hygiene and have completed a minimum of one year in a dental hygiene curriculum.

Academic Fields/Career Goals: Dental Health/Services.

Award: Scholarship for use in sophomore, junior, or senior years; not renewable. *Number:* 5. *Amount:* $1000.

Eligibility Requirements: Applicant must be enrolled or expecting to enroll full-time at a two-year or four-year institution or university. Applicant must have 3.5 GPA or higher. Available to U.S. citizens.

Application Requirements: Application form, essay, recommendations or references. *Deadline:* February 1.

Contact: Jessica Mitton, Development Manager
American Dental Hygienists' Association (ADHA) Institute
For Oral Health
444 North Michigan Avenue
Suite 3400
Chicago, IL 60611
Phone: 312-440-8944
Fax: 312-440-6764
E-mail: institute@adha.net

KARLA GIRTS MEMORIAL COMMUNITY OUTREACH SCHOLARSHIP

These scholarships are awarded to students enrolled in an associate, baccalaureate or degree completion program and completed a minimum of one year in a dental hygiene curriculum. Applicants will display a commitment to improving oral health within the geriatric population.

Academic Fields/Career Goals: Dental Health/Services.

Award: Scholarship for use in sophomore, junior, or senior years; not renewable. *Number:* 2. *Amount:* $2000.

Eligibility Requirements: Applicant must be enrolled or expecting to enroll full-time at a two-year or four-year institution. Applicant must have 3.0 GPA or higher. Available to U.S. citizens.

Application Requirements: Additional essay as part of the application, application form, essay, recommendations or references. *Deadline:* February 1.

Contact: Jessica Mitton, Development Manager
American Dental Hygienists' Association (ADHA) Institute
For Oral Health
444 North Michigan Avenue
Suite 3400
Chicago, IL 60611
Phone: 312-440-8944
Fax: 312-440-6764
E-mail: institute@adha.net

SIGMA PHI ALPHA UNDERGRADUATE SCHOLARSHIP

Awarded to an outstanding Sigma Phi Alpha member pursuing a certificate/associate or baccalaureate degree at a school with an active chapter of the Sigma Phi Alpha Dental Hygiene Honor Society. Applicant must demonstrate GPA of at least 3.5. Must have completed one year of dental hygiene curricula at an accredited dental hygiene program in United States. Must demonstrate a financial need of $1500 or more. Must be an active SADHA or ADHA member.

Academic Fields/Career Goals: Dental Health/Services.

Award: Scholarship for use in sophomore, junior, or senior years; not renewable. *Number:* 1–1. *Amount:* $1000.

Eligibility Requirements: Applicant must be enrolled or expecting to enroll full-time at a two-year or four-year or technical institution or university. Applicant or parent of applicant must be member of American Dental Hygienist's Association. Applicant must have 3.5 GPA or higher. Available to U.S. citizens.

Application Requirements: Application form, essay, recommendations or references. *Deadline:* February 1.

Contact: Jessica Mitton, Development Manager
American Dental Hygienists' Association (ADHA) Institute
For Oral Health
444 North Michigan Avenue
Suite 3400
Chicago, IL 60611
Phone: 312-440-8944
Fax: 312-440-6764
E-mail: institute@adha.net

WILMA E. MOTLEY SCHOLARSHIP

This scholarship is awarded to applicant(s) pursuing a Baccalaureate degree at an accredited dental hygiene program and will have completed a minimum of one year in a dental hygiene curriculum.

Academic Fields/Career Goals: Dental Health/Services.

Award: Scholarship for use in sophomore, junior, or senior years; not renewable. *Number:* 1. *Amount:* $1000.

Eligibility Requirements: Applicant must be enrolled or expecting to enroll full-time at an institution or university. Applicant must have 3.5 GPA or higher. Available to U.S. citizens.

Application Requirements: Application form, essay, recommendations or references. *Deadline:* February 1.

Contact: Jessica Mitton, Development Manager
American Dental Hygienists' Association (ADHA) Institute
For Oral Health
444 North Michigan Avenue
Suite 3400
Chicago, IL 60611
Phone: 312-440-8944
Fax: 312-440-6764
E-mail: institute@adha.net

WILMA MOTLEY CALIFORNIA MERIT SCHOLARSHIP

Three scholarships available annually to individuals pursuing an certificate/associate, baccalaureate, degree completion in dental hygiene, Registered Dental Hygienist in Alternative Practice (RDHAP) or master's or doctorate degree in dental hygiene or related field. Applicants must either be a resident of California or attending a dental hygiene program in California. Must demonstrate leadership experience and a minim GPA of 3.5. Awarded solely on merit: no financial need requirement.

Academic Fields/Career Goals: Dental Health/Services.

Award: Scholarship for use in sophomore, junior, senior, or graduate years; not renewable. *Number:* 1–3. *Amount:* $2000.

Eligibility Requirements: Applicant must be enrolled or expecting to enroll full-time at a two-year or four-year institution or university; studying in California and must have an interest in leadership. Applicant or parent of applicant must be member of American Dental Hygienist's Association. Applicant must have 3.5 GPA or higher. Available to U.S. citizens.

Application Requirements: Application form, essay, recommendations or references. *Deadline:* February 1.

Contact: Jessica Mitton, Development Manager
American Dental Hygienists' Association (ADHA) Institute
For Oral Health
444 North Michigan Avenue
Suite 3400
Chicago, IL 60611
Phone: 312-440-8944
Fax: 312-440-6764
E-mail: institute@adha.net

AMERICAN LEGION AUXILIARY DEPARTMENT OF WYOMING

AMERICAN LEGION AUXILIARY DEPARTMENT OF WYOMING PAST PRESIDENTS' PARLEY HEALTH CARE SCHOLARSHIP

Scholarship of $300 is available for a student in the human healthcare field. Must be a resident of Wyoming, a U.S. citizen, and attend a school in Wyoming. Minimum 3.5 GPA required.

Academic Fields/Career Goals: Dental Health/Services; Health and Medical Sciences; Nursing; Therapy/Rehabilitation.

Award: Scholarship for use in sophomore year; not renewable. *Number:* up to 2. *Amount:* $300.

Eligibility Requirements: Applicant must be enrolled or expecting to enroll full-time at a two-year or four-year or technical institution or university; resident of Wyoming and studying in Wyoming. Applicant must have 3.5 GPA or higher. Available to U.S. citizens.

Application Requirements: Application form, financial need analysis, transcript. *Deadline:* June 1.

Contact: Sonja Wright, Department Secretary
American Legion Auxiliary Department of Wyoming
PO Box 2198
Gillette, WY 82717
Phone: 307-686-7137
Fax: 307-686-7137
E-mail: deptwy@collinscom.net

AMERICAN LEGION DEPARTMENT OF NORTH DAKOTA

http://www.ndlegion.org/

O. NESHEIM MEMORIAL SCHOLARSHIP

• See page 90

AMERICAN MEDICAL TECHNOLOGISTS

http://www.amt1.com/

AMERICAN MEDICAL TECHNOLOGISTS STUDENT SCHOLARSHIP

One-time award for the undergraduate study of medical technology, medical laboratory technician, office laboratory technician, phlebotomy, or medical, dental assisting. Include SASE.

Academic Fields/Career Goals: Dental Health/Services; Health and Medical Sciences.

Award: Scholarship for use in freshman, sophomore, junior, or senior years; not renewable. *Number:* 5. *Amount:* $500.

Eligibility Requirements: Applicant must be enrolled or expecting to enroll full- or part-time at a two-year or four-year institution or university. Available to U.S. citizens.

Application Requirements: Application form, essay, financial need analysis, recommendations or references, self-addressed stamped envelope with application, transcript. *Deadline:* April 1.

Contact: Carol Lockman, Hagley Center Coordinator
Phone: 302-658-2400 Ext. 243
Fax: 302-655-3188
E-mail: clockman@hagley.org

ARRL FOUNDATION INC.

http://www.arrl.org/

CAROLE J. STREETER, KB9JBR, SCHOLARSHIP

One $750 award is available to a student with a Technician class or higher radio license. Preference for students studying in the health and healing arts fields. Must demonstrate basic Morse Code proficiency, be a U.S. citizen, and attend an accredited college or university.

Academic Fields/Career Goals: Dental Health/Services; Health and Medical Sciences; Nursing; Oncology; Optometry; Osteopathy; Therapy/Rehabilitation.

Award: Scholarship for use in freshman, sophomore, junior, senior, or graduate years; not renewable. *Number:* 1. *Amount:* $750.

Eligibility Requirements: Applicant must be enrolled or expecting to enroll full- or part-time at a two-year or four-year institution or university and must have an interest in amateur radio. Available to U.S. citizens.

Application Requirements: Application form, transcript. *Deadline:* February 1.

Contact: Ms. Mary Hobart, Secretary
Phone: 860-594-0397
E-mail: k1mmh@arrl.org

ASSOCIATION ON AMERICAN INDIAN AFFAIRS, INC.

http://www.indian-affairs.org/

ELIZABETH AND SHERMAN ASCHE MEMORIAL SCHOLARSHIP FUND

• See page 91

BETHESDA LUTHERAN COMMUNITIES

http://www.bethesdalutherancommunities.org/scholarships

DEVELOPMENTAL DISABILITIES SCHOLASTIC ACHIEVEMENT SCHOLARSHIP FOR COLLEGE STUDENTS WHO ARE LUTHERAN

One-time award for Lutheran students who have completed sophomore year in studies related to developmental disabilities. Awards of up to $3000. 3.0 GPA required.

Academic Fields/Career Goals: Dental Health/Services; Education; Health Administration; Health and Medical Sciences; Health Information Management/Technology; Humanities; Religion/Theology; Social Services; Special Education; Therapy/Rehabilitation.

Award: Scholarship for use in junior or senior years; not renewable. *Number:* 1–2. *Amount:* up to $3000.

Eligibility Requirements: Applicant must be Lutheran and enrolled or expecting to enroll full-time at a four-year institution or university. Applicant must have 3.0 GPA or higher. Available to U.S. and Canadian citizens.

Application Requirements: Application form, community service, essay, recommendations or references, resume, transcript. *Deadline:* April 16.

Contact: Pam Bergen, Executive Assistant for Mission Advancement
Bethesda Lutheran Communities
600 Hoffmann Drive
Watertown, WI 53094-6294
Phone: 920-206-4410
Fax: 920-206-7706
E-mail: pam.bergen@mailblc.org

DELAWARE STATE DENTAL SOCIETY

http://www.delawarestatedentalsociety.org/

G. LAYTON GRIER SCHOLARSHIP

One-time award for Delaware residents to study dentistry. Freshmen are not eligible. Must be a U.S. citizen. Student must have financial need and good academic standing.

Academic Fields/Career Goals: Dental Health/Services.

Award: Scholarship for use in sophomore, junior, or senior years; not renewable. *Number:* 3. *Amount:* $1000.

Eligibility Requirements: Applicant must be enrolled or expecting to enroll full-time at a four-year institution or university and resident of Delaware. Available to U.S. citizens.

Application Requirements: Application form, financial need analysis, interview, proof of residency, biographical sketch, recommendations or references, transcript. *Deadline:* March 1.

Contact: Betty Dencler, Executive Director
Phone: 302-368-7634
E-mail: dedentalsociety@gmail.com

HELLENIC UNIVERSITY CLUB OF PHILADELPHIA

http://www.hucphila.org/

NICHOLAS S. HETOS, DDS MEMORIAL GRADUATE SCHOLARSHIP

$2000 scholarships for a senior undergraduate or graduate student with financial need pursuing studies leading to a Doctor of Dental Medicine or Doctor of Dental Surgery degree. Must be a U.S. citizen of Greek descent and a resident of particular counties in NJ or PA.

Academic Fields/Career Goals: Dental Health/Services.

Award: Scholarship for use in senior or graduate years; not renewable. *Number:* up to 1. *Amount:* $2000.

Eligibility Requirements: Applicant must be of Greek heritage; enrolled or expecting to enroll full-time at a four-year institution or university and resident of New Jersey, Pennsylvania. Available to U.S. citizens.

Application Requirements: Application form, financial need analysis, transcript. *Deadline:* April 21.

Contact: Anna Hadgis, Scholarship Chairman
Phone: 610-613-4310
E-mail: hucphila@yahoo.com

HISPANIC DENTAL ASSOCIATION FOUNDATION

http://www.hdassoc.org/

DR. JUAN D. VILLARREAL/HISPANIC DENTAL ASSOCIATION FOUNDATION

Scholarship offered to Hispanic U.S. students who have been accepted into or are currently enrolled in an accredited dental or dental hygiene program in the state of Texas. Scholarship will obligate the grantees to complete the current year of their dental or dental hygiene program. Scholastic achievement, leadership skills, community service and commitment to improving the health of the Hispanic community will all be considered. Must be a current member of the Hispanic Dental Association.

Academic Fields/Career Goals: Dental Health/Services.

Award: Scholarship for use in freshman, sophomore, junior, or senior years; not renewable. *Number:* up to 3. *Amount:* $500–$1000.

Eligibility Requirements: Applicant must be of Hispanic heritage; enrolled or expecting to enroll full-time at a two-year or four-year institution or university; resident of Texas and studying in Texas. Available to U.S. citizens.

Application Requirements: Application form, essay, recommendations or references, transcript. *Deadline:* June 1.

Contact: David Pena, Executive Director
Hispanic Dental Association Foundation
1111 14th Street
Suite 1100
Washington, DC 20005
Phone: 202-629-3726
E-mail: dpena@hdassoc.org

PROCTOR AND GAMBLE ORAL CARE AND HDA FOUNDATION SCHOLARSHIP

Scholarships available to Hispanic students entering into their first year of an accredited dental, dental hygiene, dental assisting, or dental technician program. Scholastic achievement, community service, leadership, and commitment to improving health of the Hispanic community will all be considered. Must be member of the Hispanic Dental Association.

Academic Fields/Career Goals: Dental Health/Services.

Award: Scholarship for use in freshman year; not renewable. *Number:* up to 15. *Amount:* up to $1000.

Eligibility Requirements: Applicant must be high school student and planning to enroll or expecting to enroll full-time at a two-year or four-year or technical institution or university. Available to U.S. citizens.

Application Requirements: Application form, community service, essay, recommendations or references, transcript. *Deadline:* June 1.

Contact: David Pena, Executive Director
Hispanic Dental Association Foundation
1111 14th Street
Suite 1100
Washington, DC 20005
Phone: 202-629-6108
E-mail: dpena@hdassoc.org

INDIAN HEALTH SERVICES, UNITED STATES DEPARTMENT OF HEALTH AND HUMAN SERVICES

http://www.ihs.gov/scholarship

INDIAN HEALTH SERVICE HEALTH PROFESSIONS SCHOLARSHIP PROGRAM

• *See page 208*

INTERNATIONAL ORDER OF THE KING'S DAUGHTERS AND SONS

http://www.iokds.org/

HEALTH CAREERS SCHOLARSHIP

Award for students preparing for careers in medicine, dentistry, pharmacy, physical or occupational therapy, and medical technologies. Must be a U.S. or Canadian citizen, enrolled full-time in a school accredited in the field involved and located in the U.S. or Canada. For all students, except those preparing for an RN degree, application must be for at least the third year of college. RN students must have completed the first year of schooling. Premedicine students are not eligible to apply. For those students seeking degrees of MD or DDS application must be for at least the second year of medical or dental school. Each applicant must supply proof of acceptance in the school involved.

Academic Fields/Career Goals: Dental Health/Services; Health and Medical Sciences; Nursing; Therapy/Rehabilitation.

Award: Scholarship for use in junior, senior, or graduate years; not renewable. *Number:* 20–30. *Amount:* $500–$1000.

Eligibility Requirements: Applicant must be enrolled or expecting to enroll full-time at a four-year institution or university. Available to U.S. and Canadian citizens.

Application Requirements: Application form, essay, itemized budget, recommendations or references, resume, self-addressed stamped envelope with application, transcript. *Deadline:* April 1.

MARYLAND ASSOCIATION OF PRIVATE COLLEGES AND CAREER SCHOOLS

http://www.mapccs.org/

MARYLAND ASSOCIATION OF PRIVATE COLLEGES AND CAREER SCHOOLS SCHOLARSHIP

• See page 157

MARYLAND STATE HIGHER EDUCATION COMMISSION

http://www.mhec.state.md.us/

GRADUATE AND PROFESSIONAL SCHOLARSHIP PROGRAM-MARYLAND

Graduate and professional scholarships provide need-based financial assistance to students attending a Maryland school of medicine, dentistry, law, pharmacy, social work, or nursing. Funds are provided to specific Maryland colleges and universities. Students must demonstrate financial need and be Maryland residents. Contact institution financial aid office for more information.

Academic Fields/Career Goals: Dental Health/Services; Health and Medical Sciences; Law/Legal Services; Nursing; Social Services.

Award: Scholarship for use in freshman, sophomore, junior, or senior years; renewable. *Number:* up to 584. *Amount:* $1000–$5000.

Eligibility Requirements: Applicant must be enrolled or expecting to enroll full- or part-time at a four-year institution or university; resident of Maryland and studying in Maryland. Available to U.S. citizens.

Application Requirements: Application form, contact institution financial aid office, financial need analysis. *Deadline:* March 1.

Contact: Monica Wheatley, Program Manager
Maryland State Higher Education Commission
839 Bestgate Road, Suite 400
Annapolis, MD 21401
Phone: 410-260-4560
Fax: 410-260-3202
E-mail: mwheatle@mhec.state.md.us

NATIONAL ARAB AMERICAN MEDICAL ASSOCIATION

http://www.naama.com/

FOUNDATION SCHOLARSHIP

Scholarship of $1000 each to qualified students of Arabic extraction enrolled in a U.S. or Canadian medical, osteopathic, or dental school.

Academic Fields/Career Goals: Dental Health/Services; Health and Medical Sciences; Osteopathy.

Award: Scholarship for use in freshman, sophomore, junior, senior, or graduate years; not renewable. *Number:* 2. *Amount:* $1000.

Eligibility Requirements: Applicant must be of Arab heritage and enrolled or expecting to enroll full-time at a four-year institution or university. Applicant must have 3.0 GPA or higher. Available to U.S. and Canadian citizens.

Application Requirements: Application form, essay, financial need analysis, transcript. *Deadline:* July 1.

Contact: Mouhanad Hammami, Executive Director
Phone: 248-646-3661
Fax: 248-646-0617
E-mail: naama@naama.com

NATIONAL DENTAL ASSOCIATION FOUNDATION

http://www.ndaonline.org/

NATIONAL DENTAL ASSOCIATION FOUNDATION COLGATE-PALMOLIVE SCHOLARSHIP PROGRAM (UNDERGRADUATES)

A scholarship of up to $1000 is given to sophomores through juniors in a dental school who are under-represented minority students. Applicants should be a member of NDA. Number of scholarships granted varies.

Academic Fields/Career Goals: Dental Health/Services.

Award: Scholarship for use in sophomore, junior, or senior years; not renewable. *Number:* up to 100. *Amount:* $700–$1000.

Eligibility Requirements: Applicant must be American Indian/Alaska Native, Asian/Pacific Islander, Black (non-Hispanic), Hispanic and enrolled or expecting to enroll full-time at a four-year institution or university. Available to U.S. citizens.

Application Requirements: Application form, financial need analysis, letter of request, recommendations or references, resume, transcript. *Deadline:* May 15.

Contact: Roosevelt Brown, President
Phone: 501-681-6110
Fax: 541-376-4008
E-mail: rbndaf1@comcast.net

OREGON STUDENT ASSISTANCE COMMISSION

http://www.GetCollegeFunds.org/

CLARK-PHELPS SCHOLARSHIP

Award for high school graduates who are residents of Oregon or Alaska and are studying nursing (undergraduate or graduate), dentistry, or medicine. Must be enrolled in a public institution in Oregon, with preference for Oregon Health & Science University, and working toward a 4-year degree or graduate degree. Must reapply annually for award renewal.

Academic Fields/Career Goals: Dental Health/Services; Health and Medical Sciences; Nursing.

Award: Scholarship for use in freshman, sophomore, junior, senior, or graduate years; not renewable.

Eligibility Requirements: Applicant must be enrolled or expecting to enroll full-time at a four-year institution or university; resident of Alaska, Oregon and studying in Oregon. Available to U.S. citizens.

Application Requirements: Activities chart, FAFSA, application form, essay, financial need analysis, transcript. *Deadline:* March 1.

STRAIGHTFORWARD MEDIA

http://www.straightforwardmedia.com/

STRAIGHTFORWARD MEDIA MEDICAL PROFESSIONS SCHOLARSHIP

Scholarship of $500 available to full-time students in any health-related field. Awarded four times per year. Deadlines: March 31, June 30, September 30, and December 31.

Academic Fields/Career Goals: Dental Health/Services; Environmental Health; Health Administration; Health and Medical Sciences; Health Information Management/Technology; Nursing; Occupational Safety and Health; Oncology; Optometry; Osteopathy; Pharmacy; Therapy/Rehabilitation.

Award: Scholarship for use in freshman, sophomore, junior, or senior years; not renewable. *Number:* 4. *Amount:* $500.

Eligibility Requirements: Applicant must be enrolled or expecting to enroll full- or part-time at a two-year or four-year or technical institution or university. Available to U.S. and non-U.S. citizens.

Application Requirements: Essay. *Deadline:* varies.

STRAIGHTFORWARD MEDIA VOCATIONAL-TECHNICAL SCHOOL SCHOLARSHIP

• See page 99

SUPREME GUARDIAN COUNCIL, INTERNATIONAL ORDER OF JOB'S DAUGHTERS

http://www.iojd.org/

GROTTO SCHOLARSHIP

Scholarships of $1500 to aid Job's Daughters students of outstanding ability whom have a sincerity of purpose. High school seniors, or graduates, junior college, technical school, or college students who are in early graduation programs, and pursuing an education in dentistry, preferably with some training in the handicapped field are eligible to apply.

Academic Fields/Career Goals: Dental Health/Services.

Award: Scholarship for use in freshman, sophomore, junior, senior, graduate, or postgraduate years; not renewable. *Number:* 1. *Amount:* $1500.

Eligibility Requirements: Applicant must be age 18-30; enrolled or expecting to enroll full- or part-time at a two-year or four-year or technical institution or university and single female. Applicant or parent of applicant must be member of Jobs Daughters. Available to U.S. and non-U.S. citizens.

Application Requirements: Application form, community service, essay, recommendations or references, transcript. *Deadline:* April 30.

Contact: Christal Bindrich, Scholarship Committee Chairman
Supreme Guardian Council, International Order of Job's Daughters
5351 South Butterfield Way
Greenfield, WI 53221
Phone: 414-423-0016
E-mail: christalbindrich@wi.rr.com

U. S. DEPARTMENT OF HEALTH AND HUMAN SERVICES

http://www.hhs.gov/about/whatwedo.html/

U. S. PUBLIC HEALTH SERVICE-HEALTH RESOURCES AND SERVICES ADMINISTRATION, BUREAU OF HEALTH PROFESSIONS SCHOLARSHIPS FOR DISADVANTAGED STUDENTS

One-time award for full-time students from disadvantaged backgrounds enrolled in health professions and nursing programs. Institution must apply for funding and must be eligible to receive SDS funds. Students must contact financial aid office to apply.

Academic Fields/Career Goals: Dental Health/Services; Health and Medical Sciences; Nursing; Therapy/Rehabilitation.

Award: Scholarship for use in freshman, sophomore, junior, senior, or graduate years; not renewable. *Number:* up to 400.

Eligibility Requirements: Applicant must be enrolled or expecting to enroll full-time at a two-year or four-year institution or university. Available to U.S. citizens.

Application Requirements: Application form, financial need analysis. *Deadline:* varies.

Contact: Andrea Stampone, Scholarship Coordinator
U. S. Department of Health and Human Services
Division of Health Careers Diversity Development
5600 Fishers Lane
Rockville, MD 20857
Phone: 301-443-4776
Fax: 301-446-0846
E-mail: callcenter@hrsa.gov

DRAFTING

MIDWEST ROOFING CONTRACTORS ASSOCIATION

http://www.mrca.org/

MRCA FOUNDATION SCHOLARSHIP PROGRAM
• See page 112

NASA'S VIRGINIA SPACE GRANT CONSORTIUM

http://www.vsgc.odu.edu/

COMMUNITY COLLEGE STEM SCHOLARSHIPS
• See page 105

NATIONAL ASSOCIATION OF WOMEN IN CONSTRUCTION

http://www.nawic.org/

NAWIC UNDERGRADUATE SCHOLARSHIPS
• See page 112

PROFESSIONAL CONSTRUCTION ESTIMATORS ASSOCIATION

http://www.pcea.org/

TED G. WILSON MEMORIAL SCHOLARSHIP FOUNDATION
• See page 184

EARTH SCIENCE

AEG FOUNDATION

http://www.aegfoundation.org/

AEG FOUNDATION

One-time award to support undergraduate and graduate students studying engineering geology and geological engineering.

Academic Fields/Career Goals: Earth Science; Engineering/Technology; Science, Technology, and Society.

Award: Scholarship for use in senior or graduate years; not renewable. *Number:* 1. *Amount:* $4000.

Eligibility Requirements: Applicant must be enrolled or expecting to enroll full-time at a four-year institution or university. Available to U.S. and Canadian citizens.

Application Requirements: Application form, application form may be submitted online (http://www.aegfoundation.org), essay, recommendations or references, resume, transcript. *Deadline:* February 1.

Contact: Becky Roland, Executive Director
AEG Foundation
PO Box 460518
Denver, CO 80246
Phone: 303-757-2926
Fax: 720-230-4846
E-mail: staff@aegfoundation.org

TILFORD FIELD STUDIES SCHOLARSHIP

Scholarship of $1000 for student members of AEG. Three to four awards are granted annually. For undergraduate students, the scholarship goes toward the cost of a geology field camp course or senior thesis field research. For graduate students, the scholarship would apply to field research.

Academic Fields/Career Goals: Earth Science.

Award: Scholarship for use in freshman, sophomore, junior, senior, graduate, or postgraduate years; not renewable. *Number:* 4–5. *Amount:* $500–$2500.

Eligibility Requirements: Applicant must be enrolled or expecting to enroll full-time at a four-year institution or university. Applicant or parent of applicant must be member of Association of Engineering Geologists. Available to U.S. and non-U.S. citizens.

Application Requirements: Application form, application form may be submitted online (http://www.aegfoundation.org), essay, recommendations or references, resume, transcript. *Deadline:* February 1.

Contact: Becky Roland, AEG Foundation
AEG Foundation
PO Box 460518
Denver, CO 80246
Phone: 303-757-2926
Fax: 720-230-4846
E-mail: staff@aegfoundation.org

ALASKA GEOLOGICAL SOCIETY INC.

http://www.alaskageology.org/

ALASKA GEOLOGICAL SOCIETY SCHOLARSHIP

Scholarship available for a full-time junior or senior undergraduate or graduate student enrolled at any college or university with academic emphasis in earth sciences. Student must have a project based in Alaska or on a topic directly related to Alaskan geology.

Academic Fields/Career Goals: Earth Science.

Award: Scholarship for use in junior, senior, or graduate years; not renewable. *Number:* 3–6. *Amount:* $500–$2000.

Eligibility Requirements: Applicant must be enrolled or expecting to enroll full-time at a four-year institution or university and studying in Alaska. Available to U.S. and non-U.S. citizens.

Application Requirements: Application form may be submitted online (http://www.alaskageology.org), cover letter, thesis proposal (for graduate students), financial need analysis, recommendations or references, transcript. *Deadline:* February 1.

Contact: Susan Karl, Chair of Scholarship Committee
Alaska Geological Society Inc.
Alaska Geological Society
PO Box 101288
Anchorage, AK 99510
Phone: 907-786-7428
Fax: 907-786-7401
E-mail: skarl@usgs.gov

AMERICAN INDIAN SCIENCE AND ENGINEERING SOCIETY

http://www.aises.org/

A.T. ANDERSON MEMORIAL SCHOLARSHIP PROGRAM

• *See page 102*

AMERICAN SOCIETY OF AGRONOMY, CROP SCIENCE SOCIETY OF AMERICA, SOIL SCIENCE SOCIETY OF AMERICA

http://www.agronomy.org

HANK BEACHELL FUTURE LEADER SCHOLARSHIP

• *See page 90*

J. FIELDING REED SCHOLARSHIP

• *See page 90*

ARIZONA HYDROLOGICAL SOCIETY

http://www.azhydrosoc.org/

ARIZONA HYDROLOGICAL SOCIETY SCHOLARSHIP

One-time award to outstanding undergraduate or graduate students who have demonstrated academic excellence in water resources related fields as a means of encouraging them to continue to develop as water resources professionals. Must be a resident of Arizona and be enrolled in a postsecondary Arizona institution.

Academic Fields/Career Goals: Earth Science; Hydrology; Natural Resources; Nuclear Science; Science, Technology, and Society.

Award: Scholarship for use in sophomore, junior, senior, or graduate years; not renewable. *Number:* 3. *Amount:* $3000.

Eligibility Requirements: Applicant must be enrolled or expecting to enroll full-time at a two-year or four-year or technical institution or university; resident of Arizona and studying in Arizona. Available to U.S. citizens.

Application Requirements: Application form, essay, financial need analysis, recommendations or references, transcript. *Deadline:* April 30.

Contact: Aregai Tecle, Professor
Phone: 928-523-6642
Fax: 928-556-7112
E-mail: aregai.tecle@nau.edu

ASSOCIATION FOR WOMEN GEOSCIENTISTS, PUGET SOUND CHAPTER

http://www.awg.org/

AWG CRAWFORD FIELD CAMP SCHOLARSHIP

Two $500 scholarships will be awarded to promising undergraduate women students who will be attending field camp during the summer.

Academic Fields/Career Goals: Earth Science.

Award: Scholarship for use in freshman, sophomore, junior, or senior years; not renewable. *Number:* 2. *Amount:* $500.

Eligibility Requirements: Applicant must be enrolled or expecting to enroll full-time at a four-year institution or university and female. Applicant must have 3.0 GPA or higher. Available to U.S. citizens.

Application Requirements: Application form, essay, recommendations or references, transcript. *Deadline:* February 16.

Contact: Richard Yuretich, Department of Geosciences, University of Massachusetts-Amherst
Association for Women Geoscientists, Puget Sound Chapter
611 North Pleasant Street, 233 Morrill Science Center
Amherst, MA 01003-9297

AWG MINORITY SCHOLARSHIP

Scholarship available for an African American, Hispanic, or Native American full-time student who is pursuing an undergraduate degree in the geosciences at an accredited college or university.

Academic Fields/Career Goals: Earth Science.

Award: Scholarship for use in freshman, sophomore, junior, or senior years; not renewable. *Number:* 1. *Amount:* up to $5000.

Eligibility Requirements: Applicant must be American Indian/Alaska Native, Black (non-Hispanic), Hispanic; enrolled or expecting to enroll full-time at a four-year institution or university and female. Available to U.S. citizens.

Application Requirements: Application form, recommendations or references, SAT or ACT scores, transcript. *Deadline:* June 30.

Contact: Kim Jackson, Minority Scholarship Coordinator
Association for Women Geoscientists, Puget Sound Chapter
PO Box 30645
Lincoln, NE 68503-0645
E-mail: awgscholarship@yahoo.com

OSAGE CHAPTER SCHOLARSHIP

Scholarship for undergraduate women pursuing independent research in geosciences. Amount varies based on merit up to $500.

Academic Fields/Career Goals: Earth Science.

Award: Scholarship for use in freshman, sophomore, junior, or senior years; not renewable. *Number:* 1. *Amount:* up to $500.

Eligibility Requirements: Applicant must be enrolled or expecting to enroll full-time at a four-year institution or university and female. Available to U.S. citizens.

Application Requirements: Application form, one-page description of research project, budget, letter of support from research supervisor, transcript. *Deadline:* April 1.

Contact: Jessica Finnearty, AWG Osage Chapter President
Association for Women Geoscientists, Puget Sound Chapter
University of Kansas, 1475 Jayhawk Boulevard, Room 120
Lawrence, KS 66045
E-mail: jfinne@ku.edu

PENELOPE HANSHAW SCHOLARSHIP

Scholarship available for women who are currently enrolled as full-time, graduate or undergraduate geoscience majors in an accredited, degree-granting college or university in Delaware, the District of Columbia, Maryland, Virginia, or West Virginia. The candidate must demonstrate academic excellence by a GPA not lower than 3.0 and awareness of the importance of community outreach by participation in geoscience or Earth science education activities.

Academic Fields/Career Goals: Earth Science; Education.

Award: Scholarship for use in freshman, sophomore, junior, senior, or graduate years; not renewable. *Number:* 1. *Amount:* $500.

Eligibility Requirements: Applicant must be enrolled or expecting to enroll full-time at a four-year institution or university; female and studying in Delaware, District of Columbia, Maryland, Virginia, West Virginia. Applicant or parent of applicant must have employment or volunteer experience in teaching/education. Applicant must have 3.0 GPA or higher. Available to U.S. citizens.

Application Requirements: Application form, recommendations or references, transcript. *Deadline:* April 30.

Contact: Laurel Bybell, U.S. Geological Survey
Association for Women Geoscientists, Puget Sound Chapter
926 National Center
Reston, VA 20192

PUGET SOUND CHAPTER SCHOLARSHIP

Scholarship for undergraduate women committed to completing a bachelor's degree and pursuing a career or graduate work in the geosciences, including geology, environmental/engineering geology, geochemistry, geophysics, and hydrology. Must be sophomore, junior, or senior woman enrolled in a university or two-year college in western Washington State, west of the Columbia and Okanogan Rivers. Must have minimum 3.2 GPA. Must be a U.S. citizen or permanent resident.

Academic Fields/Career Goals: Earth Science; Environmental Science; Hydrology; Physical Sciences.

Award: Scholarship for use in freshman, sophomore, junior, or senior years; not renewable. *Number:* 1. *Amount:* $1000.

Eligibility Requirements: Applicant must be enrolled or expecting to enroll full-time at a two-year or four-year institution or university; female and studying in Washington. Available to U.S. citizens.

Application Requirements: Essay, financial need analysis, recommendations or references, transcript. *Deadline:* November 3.

Contact: Anne Udaloy, Scholarship Committee Chair
Association for Women Geoscientists, Puget Sound Chapter
1910 East Fourth Avenue, PO Box 65
Olympia, WA 98506
E-mail: scholarship@awg-ps.org

SUSAN EKDALE MEMORIAL SCHOLARSHIP

A single $1500 scholarship will be awarded to a female student in the geosciences to help defray field camp expenses. Applicant must be attending a Utah institution of higher learning, or be a Utah resident attending college elsewhere.

Academic Fields/Career Goals: Earth Science.

Award: Scholarship for use in freshman, sophomore, junior, senior, or graduate years; not renewable. *Number:* 1. *Amount:* $1500.

Eligibility Requirements: Applicant must be enrolled or expecting to enroll full-time at a four-year institution or university; female and resident of Utah. Available to U.S. citizens.

Application Requirements: Application form, essay, letter of eligibility from the department verifying field of study, recommendations or references, self-addressed stamped envelope with application. *Deadline:* March 28.

Contact: Janae Wallace, Scholarship Committee
Association for Women Geoscientists, Puget Sound Chapter
PO Box 146100
Salt Lake City, UT 84114

WILLIAM RUCKER GREENWOOD SCHOLARSHIP

Scholarship available for minority women who are currently enrolled as full-time, graduate or undergraduate geoscience majors in an accredited, degree-granting college or university in Delaware, the District of Columbia, Maryland, Virginia, or West Virginia. The candidate must demonstrate awareness of the importance of community outreach by participation in geoscience or Earth science education activities that reflect AWG's goals and potential for leadership as a future geoscience professional.

Academic Fields/Career Goals: Earth Science; Education.

Award: Scholarship for use in freshman, sophomore, junior, senior, or graduate years; not renewable. *Number:* 1. *Amount:* $1000.

Eligibility Requirements: Applicant must be American Indian/Alaska Native, Asian/Pacific Islander, Black (non-Hispanic), Hispanic; enrolled or expecting to enroll full-time at a four-year institution or university; female and studying in Delaware, District of Columbia, Maryland, Virginia, West Virginia. Applicant or parent of applicant must have employment or volunteer experience in teaching/education. Available to U.S. citizens.

Application Requirements: Application form, recommendations or references. *Deadline:* April 30.

Contact: Laurel Bybell, U.S. Geological Survey
Association for Women Geoscientists, Puget Sound Chapter
926 National Center
Reston, VA 20192

ASSOCIATION ON AMERICAN INDIAN AFFAIRS, INC.

http://www.indian-affairs.org/

ELIZABETH AND SHERMAN ASCHE MEMORIAL SCHOLARSHIP FUND
• *See page 91*

ASTRONAUT SCHOLARSHIP FOUNDATION

http://www.astronautscholarship.org/

ASTRONAUT SCHOLARSHIP FOUNDATION
• *See page 104*

BARRY M. GOLDWATER SCHOLARSHIP AND EXCELLENCE IN EDUCATION FOUNDATION

http://www.act.org/goldwater

BARRY M. GOLDWATER SCHOLARSHIP AND EXCELLENCE IN EDUCATION PROGRAM
• *See page 104*

BRITISH COLUMBIA INNOVATION COUNCIL

http://www.bcic.ca/

BCIC YOUNG INNOVATOR SCHOLARSHIP COMPETITION (IDEA MASH UP)
• *See page 104*

PAUL AND HELEN TRUSSELL SCIENCE AND TECHNOLOGY SCHOLARSHIP
• *See page 104*

GARDEN CLUB OF AMERICA

http://www.gcamerica.org/

THE ELIZABETH GARDNER NORWEB SUMMER ENVIRONMENTAL STUDIES SCHOLARSHIP
• *See page 92*

INDEPENDENT LABORATORIES INSTITUTE SCHOLARSHIP ALLIANCE

http://www.acil.org/

INDEPENDENT LABORATORIES INSTITUTE SCHOLARSHIP ALLIANCE
• *See page 145*

INTERNATIONAL ASSOCIATION FOR GREAT LAKES RESEARCH

http://www.iaglr.org/

PAUL W. RODGERS SCHOLARSHIP

Award given to any senior undergraduate, master's or doctoral student who wishes to pursue a future in research, conservation, education, communication, management, or other knowledge-based activity pertaining to the Great Lakes.

Academic Fields/Career Goals: Earth Science; Education; Environmental Science; Hydrology; Marine Biology; Natural Resources; Natural Sciences.

Award: Scholarship for use in senior, graduate, or postgraduate years; not renewable. *Number:* 1. *Amount:* $2000.

Eligibility Requirements: Applicant must be enrolled or expecting to enroll full- or part-time at a four-year institution or university. Available to U.S. and non-U.S. citizens.

Application Requirements: Application form, application form may be submitted online, essay, recommendations or references, transcript. *Deadline:* March 1.

Contact: Wendy Foster, Business Manager
    Phone: 734-665-5303
    E-mail: office@iaglr.org

KENTUCKY ENERGY AND ENVIRONMENT CABINET

http://www.eec.ky.gov/

ENVIRONMENTAL PROTECTION SCHOLARSHIP
• *See page 145*

MONTANA FEDERATION OF GARDEN CLUBS

http://www.mtfgc.org/

LIFE MEMBER MONTANA FEDERATION OF GARDEN CLUBS SCHOLARSHIP

Applicant must be at least a sophomore, majoring in conservation, horticulture, park or forestry, floriculture, greenhouse management, land management, or related subjects. Must be in need of assistance. Must have a potential for a successful future. Must be ranked in upper half of class or have a minimum 2.7 GPA. Must be a Montana resident and all study must be done in Montana.

Academic Fields/Career Goals: Earth Science; Horticulture/Floriculture; Landscape Architecture; Natural Resources.

Award: Scholarship for use in sophomore, junior, or senior years; not renewable. *Number:* 1. *Amount:* $1000.

Eligibility Requirements: Applicant must be enrolled or expecting to enroll full-time at a four-year institution or university; resident of Montana and studying in Montana. Applicant must have 2.5 GPA or higher. Available to U.S. citizens.

Application Requirements: Driver's license, recommendations or references, transcript. *Deadline:* May 1.

Contact: Joyce Backa, Life Members Scholarship Chairman
    Montana Federation of Garden Clubs
    513 Skyline Drive
    Craig, MT 59404-8712
    Phone: 406-235-4229
    E-mail: rjback@bresnan.net

NASA FLORIDA SPACE GRANT CONSORTIUM

http://www.floridaspacegrant.org/

FLORIDA SPACE RESEARCH PROGRAM
• *See page 132*

NASA IDAHO SPACE GRANT CONSORTIUM

http://www.id.spacegrant.org/

NASA IDAHO SPACE GRANT CONSORTIUM SCHOLARSHIP PROGRAM
• *See page 146*

NASA/MARYLAND SPACE GRANT CONSORTIUM

http://md.spacegrant.org/

NASA MARYLAND SPACE GRANT CONSORTIUM UNDERGRADUATE SCHOLARSHIPS
• *See page 132*

NASA MINNESOTA SPACE GRANT CONSORTIUM

http://www.aem.umn.edu/mnsgc

MINNESOTA SPACE GRANT CONSORTIUM SCHOLARSHIP PROGRAM
• *See page 132*

NASA SOUTH CAROLINA SPACE GRANT CONSORTIUM

http://www.cofc.edu/~scsgrant

UNDERGRADUATE RESEARCH AWARD PROGRAM
• *See page 133*

NASA SOUTH DAKOTA SPACE GRANT CONSORTIUM

http://sdspacegrant.sdsmt.edu/

SOUTH DAKOTA SPACE GRANT CONSORTIUM UNDERGRADUATE AND GRADUATE STUDENT SCHOLARSHIPS
• *See page 134*

NATIONAL ASSOCIATION OF GEOSCIENCE TEACHERS & FAR WESTERN SECTION

http://www.mlkwolves.org/

NATIONAL ASSOCIATION OF GEOSCIENCE TEACHERS-FAR WESTERN SECTION SCHOLARSHIP

Academically superior students currently enrolled in school in Hawaii, Nevada, or California are eligible to apply for one of three $500 scholarships to the school of their choice. Must be a high school senior or community college student enrolling full time (12 quarter units) in a bachelor's degree program in geology at a four-year institution or an undergraduate geology major enrolling in an upper division field geology course of approximately 30 field mapping days.

Academic Fields/Career Goals: Earth Science.

Award: Scholarship for use in sophomore, junior, or senior years; not renewable. *Number:* 3. *Amount:* $500.

Eligibility Requirements: Applicant must be enrolled or expecting to enroll full- or part-time at a four-year institution or university and studying in California, Hawaii, Nevada. Available to U.S. citizens.

Application Requirements: Application form, endorsement signature of a regular member of NAGT-FWS in the reference letter, recommendations or references, transcript. *Deadline:* April 1.

Contact: Mike Martin, Geology Scholarship Coordinator
    Phone: 951-789-5690
    E-mail: mmartin@rusd.k12.ca.us

NATIONAL ASSOCIATION OF WATER COMPANIES-NEW JERSEY CHAPTER

http://www.nawc.org/

NATIONAL ASSOCIATION OF WATER COMPANIES-NEW JERSEY CHAPTER SCHOLARSHIP
• *See page 146*

NATIONAL GARDEN CLUBS INC.

http://www.gardenclub.org/

NATIONAL GARDEN CLUBS INC. SCHOLARSHIP PROGRAM
• *See page 94*

NATIONAL GROUND WATER RESEARCH AND EDUCATIONAL FOUNDATION

http://www.ngwa.org/Foundation/assante/Pages/default.aspx

NATIONAL GROUND WATER RESEARCH AND EDUCATIONAL FOUNDATION'S LEN ASSANTE SCHOLARSHIP

Scholarships granted to full-time students only, including high school graduates and currently enrolled undergraduates. Previous scholarship recipients are ineligible. Applicant must be entering a field of study that serves, supports, or promotes the ground water industry. Qualifying majors: geology, hydrology, hydrogeology, environmental sciences, microbiology, and well-drilling two-year associate degree programs. Minimum 2.5 GPA required.

Academic Fields/Career Goals: Earth Science; Environmental Science; Hydrology.

Award: Scholarship for use in freshman, sophomore, junior, or senior years; not renewable. *Number:* 5–10. *Amount:* $1000–$5000.

Eligibility Requirements: Applicant must be enrolled or expecting to enroll full-time at a two-year or four-year or technical institution or university. Applicant must have 2.5 GPA or higher. Available to U.S. and non-U.S. citizens.

Application Requirements: Application form, application form may be submitted online (http://www.ngwa.org/Documents/scholarship_application.pdf), essay, transcript. *Deadline:* January 15.

Contact: Ms. Rachel Jones, Scholarship Coordinator
National Ground Water Research and Educational Foundation
601 Dempsey Road
Westerville, OH 43081
Phone: 614-898-7791 Ext. 504
Fax: 614-897-7786
E-mail: rjones@ngwa.org

NEVADA NASA SPACE GRANT CONSORTIUM

http://www.nvspacegrant.org/

NATIONAL SPACE GRANT COLLEGE AND FELLOWSHIP PROGRAM
• *See page 106*

OZARKA NATURAL SPRING WATER

http://www.ozarkawater.com/

EARTH SCIENCE SCHOLARSHIP

Scholarships offered to qualified students who are currently enrolled or planning to enroll in an earth/environmental sciences program at a public or private, not-for-profit, four-year college or university. Must be Texas resident with a minimum 3.0 GPA.

Academic Fields/Career Goals: Earth Science; Environmental Science.

Award: Scholarship for use in freshman, sophomore, junior, or senior years; not renewable. *Number:* 2. *Amount:* $10,000.

Eligibility Requirements: Applicant must be enrolled or expecting to enroll full-time at a four-year institution or university and resident of Texas. Applicant must have 3.0 GPA or higher. Available to U.S. citizens.

Application Requirements: Application form, essay, transcript. *Deadline:* March 31.

Contact: David Feckley, Scholarship Committee
Ozarka Natural Spring Water
3265 FM 2869
Hawkins, TX 75765
Phone: 800-678-4448
E-mail: edcfund@texas.net

ROCKY MOUNTAIN COAL MINING INSTITUTE

http://www.rmcmi.org/

ROCKY MOUNTAIN COAL MINING INSTITUTE SCHOLARSHIP
• *See page 185*

SIGMA XI, THE SCIENTIFIC RESEARCH SOCIETY

http://www.sigmaxi.org/

SIGMA XI GRANTS-IN-AID OF RESEARCH
• *See page 95*

SOIL AND WATER CONSERVATION SOCIETY

http://www.swcs.org

DONALD A. WILLIAMS SCHOLARSHIP SOIL CONSERVATION SCHOLARSHIP
• *See page 88*

MELVILLE H. COHEE STUDENT LEADER CONSERVATION SCHOLARSHIP
• *See page 88*

SOIL AND WATER CONSERVATION SOCIETY-NEW JERSEY CHAPTER

http://home.comcast.net/~njswcs/scholarship.htm

EDWARD R. HALL SCHOLARSHIP
• *See page 88*

TKE EDUCATIONAL FOUNDATION

http://www.tke.org/

CARROL C. HALL MEMORIAL SCHOLARSHIP
• *See page 107*

TIMOTHY L. TASCHWER SCHOLARSHIP
• *See page 148*

UNIVERSITIES SPACE RESEARCH ASSOCIATION

http://www.usra.edu/

UNIVERSITIES SPACE RESEARCH ASSOCIATION SCHOLARSHIP PROGRAM
• *See page 107*

VERMONT SPACE GRANT CONSORTIUM

http://www.cems.uvm.edu/vsgc

VERMONT SPACE GRANT CONSORTIUM SCHOLARSHIP PROGRAM
• *See page 107*

ECONOMICS

CATCHING THE DREAM

http://www.catchingthedream.org/

TRIBAL BUSINESS MANAGEMENT PROGRAM (TBM)
• See page 70

CENTRAL INTELLIGENCE AGENCY

http://www.cia.gov/

CENTRAL INTELLIGENCE AGENCY UNDERGRADUATE SCHOLARSHIP PROGRAM
• See page 70

CUBAN AMERICAN NATIONAL FOUNDATION

http://www.masscholarships.org/

MAS FAMILY SCHOLARSHIPS
• See page 152

DAIRY MANAGEMENT

http://www.dairyinfo.com/

NATIONAL DAIRY PROMOTION AND RESEARCH BOARD SCHOLARSHIP
• See page 91

GOVERNMENT FINANCE OFFICERS ASSOCIATION

http://www.gfoa.org/

MINORITIES IN GOVERNMENT FINANCE SCHOLARSHIP
• See page 73

INSTITUTE FOR HUMANE STUDIES

http://www.theihs.org/

HUMANE STUDIES FELLOWSHIPS
• See page 190

JORGE MAS CANOSA FREEDOM FOUNDATION

http://www.jorgemascanosa.org/

MAS FAMILY SCHOLARSHIP AWARD
• See page 156

NATIONAL ASSOCIATION OF NEGRO BUSINESS AND PROFESSIONAL WOMEN'S CLUBS INC.

http://www.nanbpwc.org/

JULIANNE MALVEAUX SCHOLARSHIP

Scholarship for African-American women who are college sophomores or juniors enrolled in an accredited college or university. Applicants must be majoring in journalism, economics, or a related field. Minimum 3.0 GPA required. Must be a U.S. citizen.

Academic Fields/Career Goals: Economics; Journalism.

Award: Scholarship for use in sophomore or junior years; not renewable. *Number:* 1. *Amount:* $1000.

Eligibility Requirements: Applicant must be Black (non-Hispanic); enrolled or expecting to enroll full-time at a four-year institution or university and female. Applicant must have 3.0 GPA or higher. Available to U.S. citizens.

Application Requirements: Application form, essay, recommendations or references, transcript. *Deadline:* April 30.

NATIONAL ASSOCIATION OF WATER COMPANIES-NEW JERSEY CHAPTER

http://www.nawc.org/

NATIONAL ASSOCIATION OF WATER COMPANIES-NEW JERSEY CHAPTER SCHOLARSHIP
• See page 146

NATIONAL SOCIETY DAUGHTERS OF THE AMERICAN REVOLUTION

http://www.dar.org/

NATIONAL SOCIETY DAUGHTERS OF THE AMERICAN REVOLUTION ENID HALL GRISWOLD MEMORIAL SCHOLARSHIP

Scholarship of $1000 awarded to a deserving junior or senior enrolled in an accredited college or university in the United States who is majoring in political science, history, government, or economics.

Academic Fields/Career Goals: Economics; History; Political Science.

Award: Scholarship for use in junior or senior years; not renewable. *Number:* 1. *Amount:* $1000.

Eligibility Requirements: Applicant must be enrolled or expecting to enroll full-time at a four-year institution or university. Available to U.S. citizens.

Application Requirements: Application form, financial need analysis, letter of sponsorship, recommendations or references, self-addressed stamped envelope with application, transcript. *Deadline:* February 15.

Contact: Tania Tatum, Manager, Office of the Reporter General
  Phone: 202-628-1776
  Fax: 202-879-3348
  E-mail: nsdarscholarships@dar.org

NEW ENGLAND EMPLOYEE BENEFITS COUNCIL

http://www.neebc.org/

NEW ENGLAND EMPLOYEE BENEFITS COUNCIL SCHOLARSHIP PROGRAM
• See page 77

OFFICE AND PROFESSIONAL EMPLOYEES INTERNATIONAL UNION

http://www.opeiu.org/

JOHN KELLY LABOR STUDIES SCHOLARSHIP FUND

Scholarship of up to $3000 given to graduate or undergraduate students who have labor studies, social sciences, industrial relation as their major. Ten scholarships are granted. Applicants should be a member or associate member of the union.

Academic Fields/Career Goals: Economics; Social Sciences.

Award: Scholarship for use in freshman, sophomore, junior, senior, or graduate years; not renewable. *Number:* 10. *Amount:* up to $3000.

Eligibility Requirements: Applicant must be enrolled or expecting to enroll full-time at a four-year institution or university. Available to U.S. citizens.

Application Requirements: Application form, essay, transcript. *Deadline:* March 31.

Contact: Mary Mahoney, Secretary-Treasurer
Phone: 202-393-4464
Fax: 202-887-0910
E-mail: mmahoney@opeiudc.org

SOCIETY OF AUTOMOTIVE ANALYSTS

http://www.cybersaa.org/

SOCIETY OF AUTOMOTIVE ANALYSTS SCHOLARSHIP
• See page 79

STRAIGHTFORWARD MEDIA

http://www.straightforwardmedia.com/

STRAIGHTFORWARD MEDIA BUSINESS SCHOOL SCHOLARSHIP
• See page 84

STRAIGHTFORWARD MEDIA LIBERAL ARTS SCHOLARSHIP
• See page 116

UNITED NEGRO COLLEGE FUND

http://www.uncf.org/

AFSCME/UNCF/HARVARD UNIVERSITY LWP UNION SCHOLARS PROGRAM
• See page 98

AVIS BUDGET GROUP SCHOLARSHIP
• See page 81

EDWARD M. NAGEL FOUNDATION SCHOLARSHIP
• See page 82

PACIFIC GAS AND ELECTRIC COMPANY SCHOLARSHIP
• See page 82

PSE&G SCHOLARSHIP
• See page 82

UBS/PAINEWEBBER SCHOLARSHIP
• See page 82

EDUCATION

ALBERTA HERITAGE SCHOLARSHIP FUND

http://www.alis.alberta.ca/

ANNA AND JOHN KOLESAR MEMORIAL SCHOLARSHIPS

Award of CAN$1500 to recognize and reward the academic excellence of a high school student entering a Faculty of Education. Must be resident of Alberta and plan to enroll full-time in the first year of an education program. Must be from a family where neither parent obtained a university degree. Selection based on the highest average obtained on three grade 12 subjects. Must be a Canadian citizen or permanent resident. For additional information and application, visit website http://alis.alberta.ca.

Academic Fields/Career Goals: Education; Special Education.
Award: Scholarship for use in freshman year; not renewable. *Number:* 1.
Eligibility Requirements: Applicant must be Canadian citizen; high school student; planning to enroll or expecting to enroll full-time at a two-year or four-year institution or university and resident of Alberta. Applicant must have 3.0 GPA or higher.
Application Requirements: Application form, test scores, transcript. *Deadline:* July 1.

LANGUAGES IN TEACHER EDUCATION SCHOLARSHIPS

Awards of CAN$2500 to Alberta students enrolled full-time in the final two years of a recognized teacher preparation program in Alberta, taking courses that will allow them to teach languages other than English in Alberta schools. Must be Canadian citizen or permanent resident and a resident of Alberta. Must intend to teach in Alberta after graduation. Nominations by faculty of education. For additional information, visit website http://alis.alberta.ca.

Academic Fields/Career Goals: Education; Foreign Language.
Award: Scholarship for use in junior or senior years; not renewable. *Number:* 14.
Eligibility Requirements: Applicant must be enrolled or expecting to enroll full-time at a four-year institution or university; resident of Alberta and studying in Alberta. Available to Canadian citizens.
Application Requirements: Nomination by institution. *Deadline:* varies.

NORTHERN ALBERTA DEVELOPMENT COUNCIL BURSARY
• See page 219

AMERICAN ASSOCIATION FOR HEALTH EDUCATION

http://www.aahperd.org/aahe

BILL KANE SCHOLARSHIP

Scholarship available to any undergraduate student officially enrolled as a health education major at an accredited college or university in the United States or a U.S. territory.

Academic Fields/Career Goals: Education.
Award: Scholarship for use in freshman, sophomore, junior, or senior years; not renewable. *Number:* 1. *Amount:* $1000.
Eligibility Requirements: Applicant must be enrolled or expecting to enroll full-time at a four-year institution or university. Applicant must have 3.0 GPA or higher. Available to U.S. citizens.
Application Requirements: Application form, essay, recommendations or references, resume, transcript. *Deadline:* November 15.
Contact: Ms. Linda Moore, Acting Executive Director
American Association for Health Education
1900 Association Drive
Reston, VA 20191-1599
Phone: 703-476-3837
Fax: 703-476-6638
E-mail: aahe@aahperd.org

AMERICAN FEDERATION OF TEACHERS

http://www.aft.org/

ROBERT G. PORTER SCHOLARS PROGRAM-AFT MEMBERS

Nonrenewable grant provides continuing education for school teachers, paraprofessionals and school-related personnel, higher education faculty and professionals, employees of state and local governments, nurses and other health professionals. Must be member of the American Federation of Teachers for at least one year.

Academic Fields/Career Goals: Education.
Award: Grant for use in freshman, sophomore, junior, or senior years; not renewable. *Number:* up to 10. *Amount:* $1000.
Eligibility Requirements: Applicant must be enrolled or expecting to enroll full- or part-time at a four-year institution or university. Applicant or parent of applicant must have employment or volunteer experience in nursing, teaching/education. Available to U.S. citizens.
Application Requirements: Application form, essay, recommendations or references, statement of need. *Deadline:* March 31.

Contact: Bernadette Bailey, Scholarship Coordinator
American Federation of Teachers
555 New Jersey Avenue, NW
Washington, DC 20001
Phone: 202-879-4481
Fax: 202-879-4406
E-mail: bbailey@aft.org

AMERICAN FOUNDATION FOR THE BLIND

http://www.afb.org/

DELTA GAMMA FOUNDATION FLORENCE MARGARET HARVEY MEMORIAL SCHOLARSHIP

The scholarship provides one scholarship of $1000 to an undergraduate or graduate student who has exhibited academic excellence, and is studying in the field of rehabilitation and/or education of persons who are blind or visually impaired. Must submit proof of legal blindness. For additional information and application requirements, refer to website http://www.afb.org/scholarships.asp.

Academic Fields/Career Goals: Education; Therapy/Rehabilitation.

Award: Scholarship for use in freshman, sophomore, junior, or senior years; not renewable. *Number:* 1. *Amount:* $1000.

Eligibility Requirements: Applicant must be visually impaired and enrolled or expecting to enroll full- or part-time at a two-year or four-year institution or university. Applicant must be visually impaired. Available to U.S. citizens.

Application Requirements: Application form, essay, proof of post-secondary acceptance and legal blindness, recommendations or references, transcript. *Deadline:* April 30.

Contact: Dawn Bodrogi, Information Center and Library Coordinator
American Foundation for the Blind
11 Penn Plaza, Suite 300
New York, NY 10001
Phone: 212-502-7661
Fax: 212-502-7771
E-mail: afbinfo@afb.net

RUDOLPH DILLMAN MEMORIAL SCHOLARSHIP

One-time award not open to previous recipients. Four scholarships of $2500 each to undergraduate or graduate students who are studying in the field of rehabilitation and/or education of persons who are blind or visually impaired. One of these grants is specifically for a student who meets all requirements and submits evidence of economic need. Must submit proof of legal blindness. For additional information and application requirements, visit website http://www.afb.org/scholarships.asp.

Academic Fields/Career Goals: Education; Therapy/Rehabilitation.

Award: Scholarship for use in freshman, sophomore, junior, or senior years; not renewable. *Number:* up to 4. *Amount:* $2500.

Eligibility Requirements: Applicant must be visually impaired and enrolled or expecting to enroll full- or part-time at a two-year or four-year institution or university. Applicant must be visually impaired. Available to U.S. citizens.

Application Requirements: Application form, essay, financial need analysis, proof of legal blindness, acceptance letter, recommendations or references, transcript. *Deadline:* April 30.

Contact: Dawn Bodrogi, Information Center and Library Coordinator
American Foundation for the Blind
11 Penn Plaza, Suite 300
New York, NY 10001
Phone: 212-502-7661
Fax: 212-502-7771
E-mail: afbinfo@afb.net

AMERICAN INDIAN SCIENCE AND ENGINEERING SOCIETY

http://www.aises.org/

BURLINGTON NORTHERN SANTA FE FOUNDATION SCHOLARSHIP

• *See page 102*

AMERICAN INSTITUTE OF POLISH CULTURE INC.

http://www.ampolinstitute.org/

HARRIET IRSAY SCHOLARSHIP GRANT

• *See page 117*

AMERICAN LEGION AUXILIARY DEPARTMENT OF IOWA

http://www.ialegion.org/ala

AMERICAN LEGION AUXILIARY DEPARTMENT OF IOWA HARRIET HOFFMAN MEMORIAL MERIT AWARD FOR TEACHER TRAINING

One-time award for Iowa residents attending Iowa institutions who are the children, grandchildren, or great-grandchildren of veterans. Preference given to descendants of deceased veterans.

Academic Fields/Career Goals: Education.

Award: Scholarship for use in freshman, sophomore, junior, or senior years; not renewable. *Number:* 1. *Amount:* $400.

Eligibility Requirements: Applicant must be enrolled or expecting to enroll full-time at a four-year institution or university; resident of Iowa and studying in Iowa. Available to U.S. citizens. Applicant or parent must meet one or more of the following requirements: general military experience; retired from active duty; disabled or killed as a result of military service; prisoner of war; or missing in action.

Application Requirements: Application form, essay, financial need analysis, personal photograph, recommendations or references, self-addressed stamped envelope with application, test scores, transcript. *Deadline:* June 1.

Contact: Marlene Valentine, Secretary and Treasurer
American Legion Auxiliary Department of Iowa
720 Lyon Street
Des Moines, IA 50309
Phone: 515-282-7987
Fax: 515-282-7583
E-mail: alasectreas@ialegion.org

AMERICAN LEGION DEPARTMENT OF MISSOURI

http://www.missourilegion.org/

ERMAN W. TAYLOR MEMORIAL SCHOLARSHIP

Two $500 awards are given annually to a student planning on obtaining a degree in education. Applicants must be unmarried Missouri resident below age 21, and must use the scholarship as a full-time student in an accredited college or university. Must be an unmarried descendant of a veteran having served 90 days on active duty in the Army, Air Force, Navy, Marine Corps, or Coast Guard of the United States, and having an honorable discharge.

Academic Fields/Career Goals: Education.

Award: Scholarship for use in freshman year; not renewable. *Number:* 2. *Amount:* $500.

Eligibility Requirements: Applicant must be high school student; planning to enroll or expecting to enroll full-time at a two-year or four-year institution or university; single and resident of Missouri. Available to U.S. citizens. Applicant or parent must meet one or more of the following requirements: general military experience; retired from active duty; disabled or killed as a result of military service; prisoner of war; or missing in action.

Application Requirements: Application form, discharge certificate, essay, test scores. *Deadline:* April 20.

Contact: John Doane, Chairman
Phone: 417-924-8596
Fax: 573-225-1406
E-mail: info@missourilegion.org

AMERICAN MONTESSORI SOCIETY

http://www.amshq.org/

AMERICAN MONTESSORI SOCIETY TEACHER EDUCATION SCHOLARSHIP FUND

One-time award for aspiring Montessori teacher candidates. Requires verification that applicant has been accepted into the AMS Montessori Teacher Education program.

Academic Fields/Career Goals: Education.

Award: Scholarship for use in freshman, sophomore, junior, senior, or graduate years; not renewable. *Number:* 10–20. *Amount:* $1000–$3000.

Eligibility Requirements: Applicant must be enrolled or expecting to enroll full-time at a two-year or four-year or technical institution or university. Available to U.S. and non-U.S. citizens.

Application Requirements: Application form, essay, financial need analysis, recommendations or references. *Deadline:* May 1.

Contact: Abbie Kelly, Director of Teacher Education Services
American Montessori Society
116 East 16th Street, 6th Floor
New York, NY 10003
Phone: 212-358-1250 Ext. 315
Fax: 212-358-1256
E-mail: abbie@amshq.org

AMERICAN PHYSICAL THERAPY ASSOCIATION

http://www.apta.org/

MARY MCMILLAN SCHOLARSHIP AWARD

Students may be nominated from physical therapist assistant education programs and physical therapist professional education programs accredited by the Commission on Accreditation in Physical Therapy Education (CAPTE) of the association. Student nominees should be in one of the following phases of their educational program: Physical therapist assistant education program students must be enrolled in the final year of study. For physical therapist assistant education programs that have a part-time curriculum, all nominees must be in the final year of the curriculum of that institution. Each institution must determine the minimum number of credit hours required for final year status. Based on this, all nominees must be in the final year of the curriculum to be nominated. [Must be scheduled to graduate between September 1, 2012, and August 31, 2013]. Physical therapist professional education program students must be within 12 months of completing all requirements for graduation from the entry-level program, by the start of the September 1 Honors and Awards nomination process. [Must be scheduled to graduate between September 1, 2012, and August 31, 2013]. Nominations of students from an educational institution will be limited to one (1) physical therapist assistant student, and one (1) physical therapist professional education student. The intent of the award is to recognize those students who exhibit superior scholastic ability and potential for future professional contribution. Awards are made on a competitive basis. Recipients will be selected on the basis of the following criteria: superior scholastic performance, past productivity, evidence of potential contribution to physical therapy, and service to the American Physical Therapy Association.

Academic Fields/Career Goals: Education; Health and Medical Sciences; Therapy/Rehabilitation.

Award: Scholarship for use in senior, graduate, or postgraduate years; not renewable. *Number:* 1–6. *Amount:* $3000–$5000.

Eligibility Requirements: Applicant must be enrolled or expecting to enroll full-time at a two-year or four-year institution or university. Applicant or parent of applicant must have employment or volunteer experience in physical therapy/rehabilitation. Available to U.S. citizens.

Application Requirements: Application form, application form may be submitted online (http://www.apta.org/HonorsAwards/), community service, essay, recommendations or references, resume, transcript. *Deadline:* December 1.

Contact: Stephanie Sadowski, Honors and Awards Program Specialist
American Physical Therapy Association
1111 North Fairfax Street
Alexandria, VA 22314
Phone: 800-999-2782 Ext. 3127
Fax: 703-706-8536
E-mail: stephaniesadowski@apta.org

ARCTIC INSTITUTE OF NORTH AMERICA

http://www.arctic.ucalgary.ca/

JIM BOURQUE SCHOLARSHIP

One-time award of CAN$1000 to Canadian aboriginal student enrolled in postsecondary training in education, environmental studies, traditional knowledge or telecommunications. Must submit, in 500 words or less, a description of their intended program of study and reasons for their choice of program. Must include most recent high school or college/university transcript; a signed letter of recommendation from a community leader, a statement of financial need which indicates funding already received or expected; and proof of enrollment in, or application to, a post secondary institution. Applicants must also provide proof of Canadian Aboriginal descent. Applicants are evaluated based on need, relevance of study, achievements, return of investment and overall presentation of the application.

Academic Fields/Career Goals: Education; Environmental Science; Natural Resources; Natural Sciences.

Award: Scholarship for use in freshman, sophomore, junior, or senior years; not renewable. *Number:* 1. *Amount:* $1000.

Eligibility Requirements: Applicant must be of Canadian heritage and Canadian citizen; American Indian/Alaska Native; enrolled or expecting to enroll full-time at a four-year institution or university and resident of Alberta, British Columbia, Manitoba, New Brunswick, Newfoundland, Northwest Territories, Nova Scotia, Ontario, Prince Edward Island, Quebec, Saskatchewan, Yukon.

Application Requirements: Essay, financial need analysis, proof of enrollment in or application to a post-secondary institution, recommendations or references, transcript. *Deadline:* July 15.

Contact: Melanie Paulson, Administrative Assistant
Arctic Institute of North America
University of Calgary, 2500 University Drive, NW
Calgary, AB T2N 1N4
CAN
Phone: 403-220-7515
Fax: 403-282-4609
E-mail: arctic@ucalgary.ca

ARIZONA BUSINESS EDUCATION ASSOCIATION

http://www.azbea.org/

ABEA STUDENT TEACHER SCHOLARSHIPS

Scholarships awarded to future business education teachers. Must be member of ABEA. Must be a student in last semester or two of an undergraduate Arizona business education teacher program at an accredited university or four-year college or in a post-baccalaureate Arizona business education teacher certification program at an accredited university or four-year college.

Academic Fields/Career Goals: Education.

Award: Scholarship for use in junior or senior years; not renewable. *Number:* up to 3. *Amount:* $500.

Eligibility Requirements: Applicant must be enrolled or expecting to enroll full-time at a four-year institution or university and resident of Arizona. Applicant or parent of applicant must be member of Arizona Business Education Association. Available to U.S. citizens.

Application Requirements: Application form, recommendations or references, resume, transcript. *Deadline:* April 1.

Contact: Shirley Eittreim, Scholarships Committee Chair
Arizona Business Education Association
Northland Pioneer College, PO Box 610
Holbrook, AZ 86025
Phone: 928-532-6151
E-mail: sjeittreim@cybertrails.com

ARMED FORCES COMMUNICATIONS AND ELECTRONICS ASSOCIATION, EDUCATIONAL FOUNDATION

http://www.afcea.org/scholarships

DISABLED WAR VETERANS SCHOLARSHIP
• See page 128

ASRT FOUNDATION

http://www.asrtfoundation.org/

MEDICAL IMAGING EDUCATORS SCHOLARSHIP

Open to ASRT members only who are completing a bachelor's, master's, or doctoral degree to enhance their position as a medical imaging program director, faculty member, clinical coordinator or clinical instructor. One of the following must also be true: applicant holds an unrestricted state license, is registered by the American Registry of Radiologic Technologists, or registered with an equivalent certifying body.

Academic Fields/Career Goals: Education; Health and Medical Sciences; Radiology.

Award: Scholarship for use in freshman, sophomore, junior, senior, or graduate years; not renewable. *Number:* 4. *Amount:* $5000.

Eligibility Requirements: Applicant must be enrolled or expecting to enroll full- or part-time at a four-year institution or university. Applicant or parent of applicant must be member of American Society of Radiologic Technologists. Available to U.S. and Canadian citizens.

Application Requirements: Application form, application form may be submitted online (http://www.asrtfoundation.org), essay, financial need analysis, recommendations or references, resume. *Deadline:* February 1.

Contact: Brooke Palmer, Program Services Specialist
    Phone: 505-298-4500 Ext. 1392
    E-mail: foundation@asrt.org

ASSOCIATION FOR WOMEN GEOSCIENTISTS, PUGET SOUND CHAPTER

http://www.awg.org/

PENELOPE HANSHAW SCHOLARSHIP
• See page 226

WILLIAM RUCKER GREENWOOD SCHOLARSHIP
• See page 227

ASSOCIATION OF RETIRED TEACHERS OF CONNECTICUT

http://www.ctretiredteachers.org/

ARTC GLEN MOON SCHOLARSHIP

Renewable scholarship to Connecticut high school seniors, who intend to pursue a career in teaching. Must demonstrate a positive financial need.

Academic Fields/Career Goals: Education.

Award: Scholarship for use in freshman year; renewable. *Number:* 2–3. *Amount:* $1500–$2000.

Eligibility Requirements: Applicant must be high school student; planning to enroll or expecting to enroll full- or part-time at a four-year institution or university and resident of Connecticut. Available to U.S. citizens.

Application Requirements: Application form, community service, driver's license, financial need analysis, recommendations or references, test scores, transcript. *Deadline:* March 31.

Contact: Teresa Barton, Scholarship Committee
    Phone: 866-343-2782
    E-mail: info@ctretiredteachers.org

BETHESDA LUTHERAN COMMUNITIES

http://www.bethesdalutherancommunities.org/scholarships

DEVELOPMENTAL DISABILITIES SCHOLASTIC ACHIEVEMENT SCHOLARSHIP FOR COLLEGE STUDENTS WHO ARE LUTHERAN
• See page 222

BNY MELLON, N.A.

http://www.bnymellon.com/

JOHN L. BATES SCHOLARSHIP

Scholarship only for students who are pursuing a career in education. Not for graduate study programs. Must be resident of Massachusetts. Eligible applicant must be recommended by educational institution.

Academic Fields/Career Goals: Education.

Award: Scholarship for use in freshman, sophomore, junior, or senior years; not renewable. *Amount:* $300–$2000.

Eligibility Requirements: Applicant must be enrolled or expecting to enroll full-time at a four-year institution or university and resident of Massachusetts. Available to U.S. citizens.

Application Requirements: Application form, essay, transcript. *Deadline:* April 15.

Contact: June Kfoury McNeil, Vice President
    BNY Mellon, N.A.
    201 Washington Street, 024-0092
    Boston, MA 02108
    Phone: 617-722-3891

CALIFORNIA STUDENT AID COMMISSION

http://www.csac.ca.gov/

CHILD DEVELOPMENT TEACHER AND SUPERVISOR GRANT PROGRAM
• See page 177

CALIFORNIA TEACHERS ASSOCIATION (CTA)

http://www.cta.org/

L. GORDON BITTLE MEMORIAL SCHOLARSHIP

Awards scholarships annually to active SCTA members for study in a teacher preparatory program. Students may reapply each year. Not available to those who are currently working in public schools as members of CTA. Minimum 3.5 GPA.

Academic Fields/Career Goals: Education.

Award: Scholarship for use in freshman, sophomore, junior, senior, or graduate years; not renewable. *Number:* up to 3. *Amount:* $2500.

Eligibility Requirements: Applicant must be enrolled or expecting to enroll full-time at a two-year or four-year institution or university and resident of California. Applicant or parent of applicant must be member of California Teachers Association. Applicant must have 3.5 GPA or higher. Available to U.S. citizens.

Application Requirements: Application form, essay, recommendations or references, transcript. *Deadline:* February 8.

Contact: Janeya Collins, Scholarship Coordinator
    California Teachers Association (CTA)
    PO Box 921
    Burlingame, CA 94011-0921
    Phone: 650-552-5468
    Fax: 650-552-5001
    E-mail: scholarships@cta.org

MARTIN LUTHER KING, JR. MEMORIAL SCHOLARSHIP

Awards for ethnic minority members of the California Teachers Association, their dependent children, and ethnic minority members of Student California Teachers Association who want to pursue degrees or credentials in public education. Minimum 3.5 GPA.

Academic Fields/Career Goals: Education.

Award: Scholarship for use in freshman, sophomore, junior, senior, or graduate years; not renewable. *Amount:* $1000–$2000.

Eligibility Requirements: Applicant must be American Indian/Alaska Native, Asian/Pacific Islander, Black (non-Hispanic), Hispanic; enrolled or expecting to enroll full-time at a two-year or four-year institution or university and resident of California. Applicant or parent of applicant must be member of California Teachers Association. Applicant must have 3.5 GPA or higher. Available to U.S. citizens.

Application Requirements: Application form, essay, financial need analysis, recommendations or references. *Deadline:* March 14.

Contact: Janeya Collins, Scholarship Coordinator
California Teachers Association (CTA)
PO Box 921
Burlingame, CA 94011-0921
Phone: 650-552-5468
Fax: 650-552-5001
E-mail: scholarships@cta.org

CANADIAN INSTITUTE OF UKRAINIAN STUDIES

http://www.cius.ca/

LEO J. KRYSA UNDERGRADUATE SCHOLARSHIP
• *See page 114*

PADDLE CANADA (FORMERLY THE CANADIAN RECREATIONAL CANOEING ASSOCIATION

http://www.paddlingcanada.com/

BILL MASON SCHOLARSHIP FUND

The Bill Mason Memorial Scholarship Fund is a tribute to the late Bill Mason, a Canadian recognized both nationally and internationally as an avid canoeist, environmentalist, filmmaker, photographer, artist and public speaker. The scholarship is intended to incorporate some of the characteristics that made Bill Mason unique and to help ensure that the memory, spirit and ideals that he represented are kept fresh in the minds of Canadians. Applicants must demonstrate experience and competency in any or all of the following: canoeing and kayaking skills, wilderness travel experience, wilderness leadership and guiding, environmental issues, communication skills.

Academic Fields/Career Goals: Education; Environmental Science; Natural Resources; Natural Sciences; Recreation, Parks, Leisure Studies; Sports-Related/Exercise Science.

Award: Scholarship for use in sophomore, senior, graduate, or postgraduate years; not renewable. *Number:* 1–1. *Amount:* $943.

Eligibility Requirements: Applicant must be Canadian citizen; enrolled or expecting to enroll full-time at a two-year or four-year or technical institution or university; resident of Alberta, British Columbia, Manitoba, New Brunswick, Newfoundland, Northwest Territories, Nova Scotia, Ontario, Prince Edward Island, Quebec, Saskatchewan, Yukon and studying in Alberta, British Columbia, Manitoba, New Brunswick, Newfoundland, Northwest Territories, Nova Scotia, Ontario, Prince Edward Island, Quebec, Saskatchewan, Yukon. Applicant must have 3.0 GPA or higher.

Application Requirements: Application form, community service, driver's license, entry in a contest, financial need analysis, resume, test scores, transcript. *Deadline:* August 30.

Contact: Mr. Graham Ketcheson, Executive Director
Paddle Canada (formerly the Canadian Recreational Canoeing Association)
PO Box 126 Station Main
Kingston, ON K7L 4V6
CAN
Phone: 888-252 6292
E-mail: info@paddlingcanada.com

CATCHING THE DREAM

http://www.catchingthedream.org/

MATH, ENGINEERING, SCIENCE, BUSINESS, EDUCATION, COMPUTERS SCHOLARSHIPS
• *See page 151*

NATIVE AMERICAN LEADERSHIP IN EDUCATION (NALE)
• *See page 151*

COLLEGEBOUND FOUNDATION

http://www.collegeboundfoundation.org/

ALICE G. PINDERHUGHES SCHOLARSHIP

You must: major in the field of education and plan to teach in grades K-12; have a cumulative 3.0 GPA or better; demonstrate financial need; and submit a one-page typed essay describing a teacher who has made an impact on you and the reasons why you want to become a teacher.

Academic Fields/Career Goals: Education.

Award: Scholarship for use in freshman, sophomore, junior, or senior years; renewable. *Number:* 1. *Amount:* $500.

Eligibility Requirements: Applicant must be high school student; planning to enroll or expecting to enroll full-time at a two-year or four-year institution or university and resident of Maryland. Applicant must have 3.0 GPA or higher. Available to U.S. citizens.

Application Requirements: Application form, application form may be submitted online (http://www.scholarships.mycbf.net/STARS), essay, financial need analysis, recommendations or references, resume, transcript. *Deadline:* March 1.

Contact: Michael Thornton, Associate Program Director, Scholarship Programs
Phone: 410-783-2905 Ext. 207
Fax: 410-727-5786
E-mail: mthornton@collegeboundfoundation.org

JANET B. SONDHEIM SCHOLARSHIP
• *See page 117*

REVEREND NATE BROOKS SCHOLARSHIP

You must be male; major in the field of English, Religion/Biblical Studies or Education; demonstrate financial need; submit an essay (700 words or less) stating the importance of reading, as well as who or what has helped you develop into the person you are today; submit at least one (1) reference from a church pastor or leader and one (1) reference from a teacher or school counselor; and must be accepted to and attend a 4-year college or university.

Academic Fields/Career Goals: Education; Religion/Theology.

Award: Scholarship for use in freshman year; not renewable. *Number:* up to 2. *Amount:* $100.

Eligibility Requirements: Applicant must be high school student; planning to enroll or expecting to enroll full-time at a four-year institution or university and resident of Maryland. Available to U.S. citizens.

Application Requirements: *Deadline:* March 1.

Contact: Michael Thornton, Associate Program Director, Scholarship Programs
Phone: 410-783-2905 Ext. 207
Fax: 410-727-5786
E-mail: mthornton@collegeboundfoundation.org

SHEILA Z. KOLMAN MEMORIAL SCHOLARSHIP

You must: major in the field of education or a related field and aspire to become a teacher; have a cumulative 2.5 GPA or better; demonstrate financial need; and submit an essay (500-1000 words) describing how a teacher affected your life in a positive way.

Academic Fields/Career Goals: Education.

Award: Scholarship for use in freshman, sophomore, junior, or senior years; renewable. *Number:* 1. *Amount:* $1000.

Eligibility Requirements: Applicant must be high school student; planning to enroll or expecting to enroll full-time at a two-year or four-

year institution or university and resident of Maryland. Applicant must have 2.5 GPA or higher. Available to U.S. citizens.

Application Requirements: Application form, application form may be submitted online (http://www.scholarships.mycbf.net/STARS), essay, financial need analysis, recommendations or references, resume, transcript. *Deadline:* March 1.

Contact: Michael Thornton, Associate Program Director, Scholarship Programs
Phone: 410-783-2905 Ext. 207
Fax: 410-727-5786
E-mail: mthornton@collegeboundfoundation.org

CONNECTICUT EDUCATION FOUNDATION INC.

http://www.cea.org/

SCHOLARSHIP FOR MINORITY COLLEGE STUDENTS

An award for qualified minority candidates who have been accepted into a teacher preparation program at an accredited Connecticut college or university. Must have a 2.75 GPA.

Academic Fields/Career Goals: Education.

Award: Scholarship for use in freshman, sophomore, junior, or senior years; not renewable. *Number:* 2. *Amount:* up to $1000.

Eligibility Requirements: Applicant must be American Indian/Alaska Native, Asian/Pacific Islander, Black (non-Hispanic), Hispanic; enrolled or expecting to enroll full-time at a two-year or four-year institution or university and studying in Connecticut. Available to U.S. citizens.

Application Requirements: Application form, essay, income verification, letter of acceptance, copy of SAR, recommendations or references, transcript. *Deadline:* May 1.

Contact: Mr. Jeffrey Leake, President
Connecticut Education Foundation Inc.
Connecticut Education Foundation
21 Oak Street, Suite 500
Hartford, CT 06106
Phone: 860-525-5641 Ext. 6308
E-mail: jeffl@cea.org

SCHOLARSHIP FOR MINORITY HIGH SCHOOL STUDENTS

Award for qualified minority candidates who have been accepted into an accredited two or four-year Connecticut college or university and intend to enter the teaching profession. Must have 2.75 GPA.

Academic Fields/Career Goals: Education.

Award: Scholarship for use in freshman year; not renewable. *Number:* 1. *Amount:* up to $1000.

Eligibility Requirements: Applicant must be American Indian/Alaska Native, Asian/Pacific Islander, Black (non-Hispanic), Hispanic; high school student; planning to enroll or expecting to enroll full-time at a four-year institution or university and studying in Connecticut. Available to U.S. citizens.

Application Requirements: Application form, essay, letter of acceptance, income verification, copy of SAR, recommendations or references, transcript. *Deadline:* May 1.

Contact: Mr. Jeffry Leake, President
Connecticut Education Foundation Inc.
21 Oak Street, Suite 500
Hartford, CT 06106
Phone: 860-525-5641 Ext. 6308
Fax: 860-725-6388
E-mail: jeffl@cea.org

CONNECTICUT OFFICE OF HIGHER EDUCATION

http://www.ctohe.org

MINORITY TEACHER INCENTIVE GRANT PROGRAM

Program provides up to $5000 a year for two years of full-time study in a teacher preparation program for the junior or senior year at a Connecticut college or university. Applicant must be African-American, Hispanic/Latino, Asian American or Native American heritage and be nominated by the Education Dean. Program graduates who teach in Connecticut

public schools may be eligible for loan reimbursement stipends up to $2,500 per year for up to four years.

Academic Fields/Career Goals: Education.

Award: Grant for use in junior or senior years; renewable. *Number:* 71. *Amount:* $2500–$5000.

Eligibility Requirements: Applicant must be American Indian/Alaska Native, Asian/Pacific Islander, Black (non-Hispanic), Hispanic; enrolled or expecting to enroll full-time at a four-year institution or university and studying in Connecticut. Available to U.S. citizens.

Application Requirements: Application form. *Deadline:* October 1.

Contact: Ms. Lynne Little, Executive Assistant
Connecticut Office of Higher Education
61 Woodland Street
Hartford, CT 06105
Phone: 860-947-1855
Fax: 860-947-1838
E-mail: mtip@ctohe.org

CONTINENTAL SOCIETY, DAUGHTERS OF INDIAN WARS

http://www.csdiw.org/

CONTINENTAL SOCIETY, DAUGHTERS OF INDIAN WARS SCHOLARSHIP

Award for a certified Indian tribal member enrolled in an undergraduate degree program in education or social service. Must maintain minimum 3.0 GPA and work with Native Americans in a social service or educational role after graduation. Preference given to those in or entering junior year.

Academic Fields/Career Goals: Education; Social Services.

Award: Scholarship for use in freshman, sophomore, junior, or senior years; not renewable. *Number:* 3. *Amount:* $2500–$5000.

Eligibility Requirements: Applicant must be American Indian/Alaska Native and enrolled or expecting to enroll full-time at a two-year or four-year institution or university. Applicant must have 3.0 GPA or higher. Available to U.S. citizens.

Application Requirements: Application form, essay, financial need analysis, recommendations or references, transcript, tribal membership proof. *Deadline:* June 15.

Contact: Mrs. Leslie Canavan, National Scholarship Chairman
Continental Society, Daughters of Indian Wars
PO Box 6695
Chesterfield, MO 63006-6695
Phone: 314-647-7986
E-mail: Leslie@khs65.com

CULTURAL SERVICES OF THE FRENCH EMBASSY

http://www.frenchculture.org/

TEACHING ASSISTANT PROGRAM IN FRANCE
• See page 97

DECA (DISTRIBUTIVE EDUCATION CLUBS OF AMERICA)

http://www.deca.org/

HARRY A. APPLEGATE SCHOLARSHIP
• See page 153

EASTERN STAR-GRAND CHAPTER OF CALIFORNIA

http://www.oescal.org/

SCHOLARSHIPS FOR EDUCATION, BUSINESS AND RELIGION
• See page 153

GENERAL BOARD OF HIGHER EDUCATION AND MINISTRY

http://www.gbhem.org

EDITH M. ALLEN SCHOLARSHIP

Scholarship for outstanding African-American graduate or undergraduate students pursuing a degree in education, social work, medicine, and/or other health professions. Must be enrolled at a United Methodist college or university and be an active, full member of the United Methodist Church for at least three years.

Academic Fields/Career Goals: Education; Health and Medical Sciences; Social Services.

Award: Scholarship for use in freshman, sophomore, junior, or senior years; not renewable. *Number:* 2. *Amount:* $1200.

Eligibility Requirements: Applicant must be Methodist; Black (non-Hispanic) and enrolled or expecting to enroll full-time at a four-year institution or university. Available to U.S. citizens.

Application Requirements: Application form, essay, recommendations or references, transcript. *Deadline:* March 1.

Contact: Ms. Mary Robinson, Scholarships Coordinator
General Board of Higher Education and Ministry
PO Box 340007
Nashville, TN 37203-0007
Phone: 615-340-7344
Fax: 615-340-7529
E-mail: umscholar@gbhem.org

GENERAL FEDERATION OF WOMEN'S CLUBS OF MASSACHUSETTS

http://www.gfwcma.org/

NEWTONVILLE WOMAN'S CLUB SCHOLARSHIPS

Applicant must be a senior in a Massachusetts high school in who will enroll in a four-year accredited college or university in a teacher-training program that leads to certification to teach.

Academic Fields/Career Goals: Education.

Award: Scholarship for use in freshman year; not renewable. *Number:* 1. *Amount:* $600.

Eligibility Requirements: Applicant must be high school student; planning to enroll or expecting to enroll full-time at a four-year institution or university and resident of Massachusetts. Available to U.S. citizens.

Application Requirements: Application form, driver's license, essay, interview, recommendations or references, self-addressed stamped envelope with application, transcript. *Deadline:* March 1.

Contact: Marta DiBenedetto, Scholarship Chairman
General Federation of Women's Clubs of Massachusetts
245 Dutton Road, PO Box 679
Sudbury, MA 01776-0679
Phone: 978-444-9105
E-mail: marta_dibenedetto@nylim.com

GEORGE T. WELCH TRUST

http://www.bakerboyer.com/

SARA CARLSON MEMORIAL FUND

Grants for students majoring in education. Must be enrolled full-time and maintain a minimum GPA of 2.0. Must reapply. The budget form must be completed and cover the entire school year.

Academic Fields/Career Goals: Education.

Award: Scholarship for use in freshman, sophomore, junior, or senior years; not renewable. *Amount:* up to $300.

Eligibility Requirements: Applicant must be enrolled or expecting to enroll full-time at a four-year institution or university. Available to U.S. citizens.

Application Requirements: Application form. *Deadline:* April 13.

Contact: Ted Cohan, Trust Portfolio Manager
Phone: 509-526-1204
Fax: 509-522-3136
E-mail: cohant@bakerboyer.com

GEORGIA ASSOCIATION OF EDUCATORS

http://www.gae.org/

GAE GFIE SCHOLARSHIP FOR ASPIRING TEACHERS

Scholarships will be awarded to graduating seniors who currently attend a fully accredited public Georgia high school and will attend a fully accredited Georgia college or university within the next twelve months. Must have a 3.0 GPA. Must submit three letters of recommendation. Must have plans to enter the teaching profession.

Academic Fields/Career Goals: Education.

Award: Scholarship for use in freshman year; not renewable. *Number:* up to 20. *Amount:* $1000.

Eligibility Requirements: Applicant must be enrolled or expecting to enroll full-time at a two-year or four-year institution or university; resident of Georgia and studying in Georgia. Applicant must have 3.0 GPA or higher. Available to U.S. citizens.

Application Requirements: Application form, recommendations or references, transcript. *Deadline:* February 1.

Contact: Sharon Henderson, Staff Associate
Phone: 678-837-1114
Fax: 678-837-1150
E-mail: sharon.henderson@gae.org

GOLDEN APPLE FOUNDATION

http://www.goldenapple.org/

GOLDEN APPLE SCHOLARS OF ILLINOIS

Applicants must be between the ages of 16 and 21 and maintain a GPA of 2.5. Eligible applicants must be residents of Illinois studying in Illinois. Recipients must agree to teach in high-need Illinois schools.

Academic Fields/Career Goals: Education.

Award: Scholarship for use in freshman, sophomore, junior, or senior years; renewable. *Number:* 100–150. *Amount:* $23,000.

Eligibility Requirements: Applicant must be age 16-21; enrolled or expecting to enroll full-time at a four-year institution or university; resident of Illinois and studying in Illinois. Available to U.S. citizens.

Application Requirements: Application form, essay, interview, personal photograph, recommendations or references, social security card, test scores, transcript. *Deadline:* November 15.

Contact: Ms. Patricia Kilduff, Director of Recruitment and Placement
Phone: 312-407-0006 Ext. 105
E-mail: kilduff@goldenapple.org

GOLDEN KEY INTERNATIONAL HONOUR SOCIETY

http://www.goldenkey.org/

EDUCATION ACHIEVEMENT AWARDS

Awards members who excel in the study of education. Eligible applicants are undergraduate, graduate and postgraduate members who are currently enrolled in classes at a degree-granting program. One winner will receive a $1000 award. The second place winner will receive $750 and the third place winner will receive $500.

Academic Fields/Career Goals: Education.

Award: Prize for use in freshman, sophomore, junior, senior, graduate, or postgraduate years; not renewable. *Number:* 3. *Amount:* $500–$1000.

Eligibility Requirements: Applicant must be enrolled or expecting to enroll full- or part-time at a four-year institution or university. Available to U.S. and non-U.S. citizens.

Application Requirements: Application form, education related paper or report, entry in a contest, essay, recommendations or references, transcript. *Deadline:* March 3.

GREATER KANAWHA VALLEY FOUNDATION

http://www.tgkvf.org/

JOSEPH C. BASILE, II MEMORIAL SCHOLARSHIP FUND

Award for residents of West Virginia who are majoring in education. Must be an undergraduate at a college or university in West Virginia. Award based on financial need.

Academic Fields/Career Goals: Education.

Award: Scholarship for use in freshman, sophomore, junior, or senior years; not renewable.

Eligibility Requirements: Applicant must be enrolled or expecting to enroll full-time at a four-year institution or university; resident of West Virginia and studying in West Virginia. Available to U.S. citizens.

Application Requirements: Application form, essay, financial need analysis, recommendations or references, self-addressed stamped envelope with application, test scores, transcript. *Deadline:* January 15.

Contact: Susan Hoover, Scholarship Coordinator
Greater Kanawha Valley Foundation
900 Lee Street East, 16th Floor
Charleston, WV 25301
Phone: 304-346-3620
E-mail: tgkvf@tgkvf.org

HAWAIIAN LODGE, F&AM

http://www.hawaiianlodgefreemasons.org/

HAWAIIAN LODGE SCHOLARSHIPS
• *See page 114*

HAWAII EDUCATION ASSOCIATION

http://www.heaed.com/

HAWAII EDUCATION ASSOCIATION STUDENT TEACHER SCHOLARSHIP

Scholarship available to children or grandchildren of HEA members. Intent is to minimize the need for employment during student teaching semester. Must be enrolled full-time in an undergraduate or post-baccalaureate program in accredited institution of higher learning.

Academic Fields/Career Goals: Education.

Award: Scholarship for use in senior, graduate, or postgraduate years; not renewable. *Number:* up to 2. *Amount:* up to $3000.

Eligibility Requirements: Applicant must be enrolled or expecting to enroll full-time at a four-year institution or university. Applicant or parent of applicant must be member of Hawaii Education Association. Available to U.S. citizens.

Application Requirements: Application form, driver's license, financial need analysis, personal photograph, recommendations or references, transcript. *Deadline:* April 1.

HIROSHI BARBARA KIM YAMASHITA HEA SCHOLARSHIP

Two $2000 scholarships awarded to full-time undergraduate education majors currently attending an accredited institution of higher learning and intending to teach in a Hawaii public school. Minimum 3.2 GPA required.

Academic Fields/Career Goals: Education.

Award: Scholarship for use in freshman, sophomore, junior, or senior years; not renewable. *Number:* 2. *Amount:* $2000.

Eligibility Requirements: Applicant must be enrolled or expecting to enroll full-time at a two-year or four-year or technical institution or university. Available to U.S. citizens.

Application Requirements: Application form, financial need analysis, recommendations or references, test scores. *Deadline:* April 1.

Contact: Carol Yoneshige, Executive Director
Phone: 808-949-6657
Fax: 808-944-2032
E-mail: hea.office@heaed.com

HISPANIC HERITAGE FOUNDATION

http://www.hispanicheritage.org/

HISPANIC HERITAGE YOUTH AWARDS
• *See page 155*

ILLINOIS PTA

http://www.illinoispta.org/

ILLINOIS PTA LILLIAN E. GLOVER SCHOLARSHIP

Scholarship has evolved to encourage Illinois college-bound high school seniors entering the field of education or an education-related field at the college/university of their choice.

Academic Fields/Career Goals: Education.

Award: Scholarship for use in freshman year; not renewable. *Number:* up to 2. *Amount:* $500–$1000.

Eligibility Requirements: Applicant must be high school student; planning to enroll or expecting to enroll full-time at a four-year institution or university and resident of Illinois. Applicant must have 3.0 GPA or higher. Available to U.S. citizens.

Application Requirements: Application form, community service, essay, resume, test scores, transcript. *Deadline:* February 15.

Contact: Barb Miller, Scholarship Director
Illinois PTA
PO Box 907
Springfield, IL 62705-0907
Phone: 217-528-9617
Fax: 217-528-9490
E-mail: Bmiller@illinoispta.org

ILLINOIS STUDENT ASSISTANCE COMMISSION (ISAC)

http://www.collegezone.org/

ILLINOIS FUTURE TEACHERS CORPS PROGRAM

Scholarships are available for students planning to become teachers in Illinois. Students must be Illinois residents, enrolled or accepted as a junior or above in a Teacher Education Program at an Illinois college or university. By receiving the award, students agree to teach for five years at either a public, private, or parochial Illinois preschool, or at a public elementary or secondary school.

Academic Fields/Career Goals: Education.

Award: Scholarship for use in junior, senior, or graduate years; renewable. *Amount:* $5000–$10,000.

Eligibility Requirements: Applicant must be enrolled or expecting to enroll full- or part-time at a four-year institution or university; resident of Illinois and studying in Illinois. Available to U.S. citizens.

Application Requirements: Application form, FAFSA, financial need analysis. *Deadline:* March 1.

MINORITY TEACHERS OF ILLINOIS SCHOLARSHIP PROGRAM

Award for minority students intending to become school teachers; teaching commitment attached to receipt. Number of scholarships and the individual dollar amounts vary.

Academic Fields/Career Goals: Education; Special Education.

Award: Scholarship for use in freshman, sophomore, junior, senior, graduate, or postgraduate years; renewable. *Amount:* up to $5000.

Eligibility Requirements: Applicant must be American Indian/Alaska Native, Asian/Pacific Islander, Black (non-Hispanic), Hispanic; enrolled or expecting to enroll full- or part-time at a two-year or four-year institution or university; resident of Illinois and studying in Illinois. Available to U.S. citizens.

Application Requirements: Application form, transcript. *Deadline:* March 1.

INDIANA RETIRED TEACHER'S ASSOCIATION (IRTA)

http://www.retiredteachers.org/

INDIANA RETIRED TEACHERS ASSOCIATION FOUNDATION SCHOLARSHIP

Scholarship available to college sophomores or juniors who are enrolled full-time in an education program at an Indiana college or university for a baccalaureate degree. The applicant must be the child, grandchild, legal dependant or spouse of an active, retired or deceased member of the Indiana State Teachers Retirement Fund.

Academic Fields/Career Goals: Education.

Award: Scholarship for use in sophomore or junior years; not renewable. *Number:* 8. *Amount:* $1500.

Eligibility Requirements: Applicant must be enrolled or expecting to enroll full-time at a four-year institution or university; resident of Indiana and studying in Indiana. Applicant or parent of applicant must have employment or volunteer experience in teaching/education. Available to U.S. and non-U.S. citizens.

Application Requirements: Application form, community service, essay, financial need analysis, recommendations or references, transcript. *Deadline:* February 22.

INTERNATIONAL ASSOCIATION FOR GREAT LAKES RESEARCH

http://www.iaglr.org/

PAUL W. RODGERS SCHOLARSHIP
• See page 227

INTERNATIONAL TECHNOLOGY EDUCATION ASSOCIATION

http://www.iteaconnect.org/

INTERNATIONAL TECHNOLOGY EDUCATION ASSOCIATION UNDERGRADUATE SCHOLARSHIP IN TECHNOLOGY EDUCATION

A scholarship for undergraduate students pursuing a degree in technology education and technological studies. Applicants must be members of the association.

Academic Fields/Career Goals: Education; Engineering/Technology; Science, Technology, and Society.

Award: Scholarship for use in freshman, sophomore, junior, or senior years; not renewable. *Number:* 3. *Amount:* $1000.

Eligibility Requirements: Applicant must be enrolled or expecting to enroll full-time at a four-year institution or university. Applicant or parent of applicant must be member of International Technology Education Association. Applicant must have 2.5 GPA or higher. Available to U.S. and non-U.S. citizens.

Application Requirements: Application form, recommendations or references, resume, transcript. *Deadline:* December 1.

JACK J. ISGUR FOUNDATION

http://www.isgur.org

JACK J. ISGUR FOUNDATION SCHOLARSHIP
• See page 119

JEWISH VOCATIONAL SERVICE CHICAGO

http://www.jvschicago.org/

JEWISH FEDERATION ACADEMIC SCHOLARSHIP PROGRAM
• See page 120

KANSAS BOARD OF REGENTS

http://www.kansasregents.org/

KANSAS TEACHER SERVICE SCHOLARSHIP

Scholarship to encourage talented students to enter the teaching profession and teach in Kansas in specific curriculum areas or in underserved areas of Kansas. Students must be Kansas residents attending a postsecondary institution in Kansas. For more details, refer to website http://www.kansasregents.org.

Academic Fields/Career Goals: Education.

Award: Scholarship for use in junior, senior, or graduate years; renewable. *Amount:* $2206–$5514.

Eligibility Requirements: Applicant must be enrolled or expecting to enroll full- or part-time at a four-year institution or university. Applicant must have 3.0 GPA or higher. Available to U.S. citizens.

Application Requirements: Application form, essay, financial need analysis, recommendations or references, resume, test scores, transcript. *Fee:* $12. *Deadline:* May 1.

Contact: Diane Lindeman, Director of Student Financial Assistance
Kansas Board of Regents
1000 SW Jackson, Suite 520
Topeka, KS 66612
Phone: 785-296-3517
Fax: 785-296-0983
E-mail: dlindeman@ksbor.org

KE ALI'I PAUAHI FOUNDATION

http://www.pauahi.org/

CHARLES COCKETT 'OHANA SCHOLARSHIP
• See page 115

DAN AND RACHEL MAHI EDUCATIONAL SCHOLARSHIP

Scholarship provides support to undergraduate or graduate students. Must demonstrate financial need. Minimum GPA of 2.0 required. Submit two letters of recommendation; one from a teacher or counselor and one from and employer or community or organization.

Academic Fields/Career Goals: Education.

Award: Scholarship for use in freshman, sophomore, junior, senior, or graduate years; not renewable. *Number:* 1–2. *Amount:* $800–$1000.

Eligibility Requirements: Applicant must be enrolled or expecting to enroll full-time at a two-year or four-year institution or university. Available to U.S. citizens.

Application Requirements: Application form, application form may be submitted online (http://www.pauahi.org/scholarships), college acceptance letter, copy of SAR, financial need analysis, recommendations or references, transcript. *Deadline:* April 1.

Contact: Mavis Shiraishi-Nagao, Scholarship Administrator
Ke Ali'i Pauahi Foundation
567 South King Street, Suite 160
Honolulu, HI 96813
Phone: 808-534-3966
E-mail: scholarships@pauahi.org

GLADYS KAMAKAKUOKALANI AINOA BRANDT SCHOLARSHIP

Provides scholarships for full-time junior, senior or graduate students at an accredited university aspiring to enter the educational profession. Applicants must demonstrate financial need, a GPA of 2.5 or higher is required, and priority will be given to current or former residents of Kauai. Submit two letters of recommendation from a teacher, counselor or community organization.

Academic Fields/Career Goals: Education.

Award: Scholarship for use in junior, senior, or graduate years; not renewable. *Number:* up to 4. *Amount:* up to $3000.

Eligibility Requirements: Applicant must be enrolled or expecting to enroll full-time at a four-year institution or university and resident of Hawaii. Applicant must have 2.5 GPA or higher. Available to U.S. citizens.

Application Requirements: Application form, application form may be submitted online (http://www.pauahi.org/scholarships), essay, financial need analysis, recommendations or references, signed application confirmation page, copy of completed Student Aid Report (SAR), transcript. *Deadline:* April 1.

Contact: Mavis Shiraishi-Nagao, Scholarship Administrator
  Phone: 808-534-3966
  E-mail: scholarships@pauahi.org

INSPIRATIONAL EDUCATOR SCHOLARSHIP

In recognition of inspirational educators who have made a difference in the lives of students, this endowment provides educational scholarships for full- or part-time college students pursuing a career in the field of education. Submit two letters or recommendation from teachers, counselors, employers, coaches or other citing examples of how applicant has already worked in and will continue to work with Hawaiian community. Submit essay on applicant's commitment to education and how you would use scholarship funds for educational costs.

Academic Fields/Career Goals: Education.

Award: Scholarship for use in freshman, sophomore, junior, senior, or graduate years; not renewable. *Number:* up to 2. *Amount:* up to $1200.

Eligibility Requirements: Applicant must be enrolled or expecting to enroll full- or part-time at a two-year or four-year institution or university. Available to U.S. citizens.

Application Requirements: Application form, application form may be submitted online (http://www.pauahi.org/scholarships), college acceptance letter, copy of signed online application confirmation page, copy of completed SAR, essay, financial need analysis, recommendations or references, transcript. *Deadline:* April 1.

Contact: Mavis Shiraishi-Nagao, Scholarship Administrator
  Phone: 808-534-3966
  E-mail: scholarships@pauahi.org

MYRON & LAURA THOMPSON SCHOLARSHIP
• *See page 178*

KENTUCKY HIGHER EDUCATION ASSISTANCE AUTHORITY (KHEAA)

http://www.kheaa.com/

EARLY CHILDHOOD DEVELOPMENT SCHOLARSHIP
• *See page 178*

MARION D. AND EVA S. PEEPLES FOUNDATION TRUST SCHOLARSHIP PROGRAM

http://www.jccf.org/

MARION A. AND EVA S. PEEPLES SCHOLARSHIPS

Award for undergraduate study in nursing, dietetics, and teaching in industrial arts. Applicant must reapply each year for renewal. Recipient must maintain 2.5 GPA. Must be Indiana resident and attending an Indiana school.

Academic Fields/Career Goals: Education; Engineering/Technology; Food Science/Nutrition; Nursing; Trade/Technical Specialties.

Award: Scholarship for use in freshman, sophomore, junior, or senior years; not renewable. *Number:* 30–35. *Amount:* $1000–$3000.

Eligibility Requirements: Applicant must be enrolled or expecting to enroll full-time at a two-year or four-year or technical institution or university; resident of Indiana and studying in Indiana. Applicant must have 2.5 GPA or higher. Available to U.S. citizens.

Application Requirements: Application form, driver's license, financial need analysis, interview, recommendations or references, self-addressed stamped envelope with application, test scores, transcript. *Deadline:* March 1.

Contact: Kim Kastings, Scholarship Director
  Phone: 317-738-2213
  Fax: 317-738-9113
  E-mail: kimk@jccf.org

MARYLAND STATE HIGHER EDUCATION COMMISSION

http://www.mhec.state.md.us/

JANET L. HOFFMANN LOAN ASSISTANCE REPAYMENT PROGRAM

Provides assistance for repayment of loan debt to Maryland residents working full-time in nonprofit organizations and state or local governments. Must submit Employment Verification Form and Lender Verification Form.

Academic Fields/Career Goals: Education; Law/Legal Services; Nursing; Social Services; Therapy/Rehabilitation.

Award: Grant for use in freshman, sophomore, junior, or senior years; not renewable. *Number:* up to 700. *Amount:* $1500–$10,000.

Eligibility Requirements: Applicant must be enrolled or expecting to enroll full-time at a four-year institution or university; resident of Maryland and studying in Maryland. Applicant or parent of applicant must have employment or volunteer experience in government/politics. Available to U.S. citizens.

Application Requirements: Application form, IRS 1040 form, transcript. *Deadline:* September 30.

Contact: Tamika McKelvin, Office of Student Financial Assistance
  Maryland State Higher Education Commission
  839 Bestgate Road, Suite 400
  Annapolis, MD 21401
  Phone: 410-260-4546
  Fax: 410-260-3203
  E-mail: tmckelvil@mhec.state.md.us

MASSACHUSETTS OFFICE OF STUDENT FINANCIAL ASSISTANCE

http://www.osfa.mass.edu/

EARLY CHILDHOOD EDUCATORS SCHOLARSHIP PROGRAM

Scholarship to provide financial assistance for currently employed early childhood educators and providers who enroll in an associate or bachelor degree program in Early Childhood Education or related programs. Awards are not based on financial need. Individuals taking their first college-level ECE course are eligible for 100 percent tuition, while subsequent ECE courses are awarded at 50 percent tuition. Can be used for one class each semester.

Academic Fields/Career Goals: Education.

Award: Scholarship for use in freshman, sophomore, junior, or senior years; not renewable. *Amount:* $150–$3600.

Eligibility Requirements: Applicant must be enrolled or expecting to enroll full- or part-time at a four-year institution or university. Available to U.S. citizens.

Application Requirements: Application form. *Deadline:* July 1.

Contact: Robert Brun, Director of Scholarships and Grants
  Phone: 617-727-9420
  Fax: 617-727-0667
  E-mail: osfa@osfa.mass.edu

PARAPROFESSIONAL TEACHER PREPARATION GRANT

Grant providing financial aid assistance to Massachusetts residents, who are currently employed as paraprofessionals in Massachusetts public schools and wish to obtain higher education and become certified as full-time teachers.

Academic Fields/Career Goals: Education.

Award: Grant for use in freshman, sophomore, junior, or senior years; not renewable. *Amount:* $250–$7500.

Eligibility Requirements: Applicant must be enrolled or expecting to enroll full- or part-time at a two-year or four-year institution or university and resident of Massachusetts. Available to U.S. citizens.

Application Requirements: Application form, FAFSA. *Deadline:* August 1.

Contact: Robert Brun, Director of Scholarships and Grants
  Phone: 617-727-9420
  Fax: 617-727-0667
  E-mail: osfa@osfa.mass.edu

MEMORIAL FOUNDATION FOR JEWISH CULTURE

http://www.mfjc.org/

MEMORIAL FOUNDATION FOR JEWISH CULTURE, SCHOLARSHIPS FOR POST-RABBINICAL STUDENTS

Scholarship program is to assist well-qualified individuals to train for careers in the rabbinate, Jewish education, social work, and as religious functionaries in Diaspora Jewish communities in need of such personnel. Open to any individual, regardless of country of origin, who is presently receiving, or plans to undertake, training in a recognized yeshiva, teacher training seminary, school of social work, university or other educational institution.

Academic Fields/Career Goals: Education; Religion/Theology; Social Services.

Award: Scholarship for use in freshman, sophomore, junior, or senior years; renewable.

Eligibility Requirements: Applicant must be Jewish; enrolled or expecting to enroll full- or part-time at a two-year or four-year or technical institution or university and must have an interest in Jewish culture. Available to U.S. and non-U.S. citizens.

Application Requirements: Application form, personal photograph, recommendations or references. *Deadline:* November 30.

Contact: Dr. Jerry Hochbaum, Executive Vice President
Memorial Foundation for Jewish Culture
50 Broadway, 34th Floor
New York, NY 10004
Phone: 212-425-6606
Fax: 212-425-6602
E-mail: office@mfjc.org

NASA RHODE ISLAND SPACE GRANT CONSORTIUM

http://brown/initiatives/ri-space-grant

NASA RISGC SUMMER SCHOLARSHIP FOR UNDERGRADUATE STUDENTS
• *See page 133*

NATIONAL COUNCIL OF TEACHERS OF MATHEMATICS

http://www.nctm.org/

PROSPECTIVE SECONDARY TEACHER COURSE WORK SCHOLARSHIPS

Grant provides financial support to college students preparing for teaching secondary school mathematics. Award of $10,000 will be granted in two phases, with $5000 for the recipient's third year of full-time study, and $5000 for fourth year. Must be student members of NCTM and cannot reapply. Must submit proposal, essay, letters of recommendation, and transcripts.

Academic Fields/Career Goals: Education; Mathematics.

Award: Scholarship for use in junior or senior years; not renewable. *Number:* 2. *Amount:* up to $5000.

Eligibility Requirements: Applicant must be enrolled or expecting to enroll full-time at a four-year institution or university. Available to U.S. and non-U.S. citizens.

Application Requirements: Application form, essay, recommendations or references, transcript, written proposal. *Deadline:* May 9.

NATIONAL INSTITUTE FOR LABOR RELATIONS RESEARCH

http://www.nilrr.org/

APPLEGATE/JACKSON/PARKS FUTURE TEACHER SCHOLARSHIP

Scholarship available to all education majors currently attending school. High school seniors accepted into a teacher education program may also apply. Award is based on an essay demonstrating knowledge of and interest in compulsory unionism in education. Specify "Education" or "Future Teacher Scholarship" on any correspondence.

Academic Fields/Career Goals: Education; Special Education.

Award: Scholarship for use in freshman, sophomore, junior, senior, graduate, or postgraduate years; not renewable. *Number:* 1. *Amount:* $1000.

Eligibility Requirements: Applicant must be enrolled or expecting to enroll full-time at a four-year institution or university. Available to U.S. citizens.

Application Requirements: Application form, application form may be submitted online (http://www.nilrr.org), essay, transcript. *Deadline:* December 31.

Contact: Cathy Jones, Scholarship Coordinator
National Institute for Labor Relations Research
5211 Port Royal Road
Springfield, VA 22151
Phone: 703-321-9606 Ext. 2231
Fax: 703-321-7143
E-mail: research@nilrr.org

NATIONAL URBAN LEAGUE

http://www.nulbeep.org/

BLACK EXECUTIVE EXCHANGE PROGRAM JERRY BARTOW SCHOLARSHIP FUND
• *See page 157*

NORTH CAROLINA ASSOCIATION OF EDUCATORS

http://www.ncae.org/

MARY MORROW-EDNA RICHARDS SCHOLARSHIP

One-time award for junior year of study in four-year education degree program. Preference given to members of the student branch of the North Carolina Association of Educators. Must be North Carolina resident attending a North Carolina institution. Must agree to teach in North Carolina for two years after graduation. Must be a junior in college when application is filed.

Academic Fields/Career Goals: Education.

Award: Scholarship for use in senior year; not renewable. *Number:* 3–8. *Amount:* up to $1000.

Eligibility Requirements: Applicant must be enrolled or expecting to enroll full-time at a four-year institution or university; resident of North Carolina and studying in North Carolina. Applicant or parent of applicant must be member of Other Student Academic Clubs. Available to U.S. citizens.

Application Requirements: Application form, essay, financial need analysis, recommendations or references, transcript. *Deadline:* January 13.

Contact: Annette Montgomery, Communications Secretary
Phone: 800-662-7924
Fax: 919-839-8229
E-mail: annette.montgomery@ncae.org

NORTH CAROLINA STATE EDUCATION ASSISTANCE AUTHORITY

http://www.ncseaa.edu/

TEACHER ASSISTANT SCHOLARSHIP FUND

Funding to attend a public or private four-year college or university in North Carolina with an approved teacher education program. Applicant must be employed full-time as a teacher assistant in an instructional area while pursuing licensure and maintain employment to remain eligible. Must have at least 3.0 cumulative GPA. Refer to website for further details http://www.ncseaa.edu/tas.htm.

Academic Fields/Career Goals: Education.

Award: Scholarship for use in freshman, sophomore, junior, or senior years; renewable. *Amount:* $600–$3600.

Eligibility Requirements: Applicant must be enrolled or expecting to enroll full- or part-time at a four-year institution or university; resident of North Carolina and studying in North Carolina. Applicant or parent of applicant must have employment or volunteer experience in teaching/education. Applicant must have 3.0 GPA or higher. Available to U.S. citizens.

Application Requirements: Application form, FAFSA, financial need analysis, transcript. *Deadline:* March 31.

Contact: Rashonn Albritton, Processing Assistant
North Carolina State Education Assistance Authority
PO Box 13663
Research Triangle Park, NC 27709
Phone: 919-549-8614
Fax: 919-248-4687
E-mail: ralbritton@ncseaa.edu

OHIO CHILD CARE RESOURCE & REFERRAL ASSOCIATION

http://www.occrra.org/

T.E.A.C.H. EARLY CHILDHOOD OHIO SCHOLARSHIPS
• See page 178

OKLAHOMA STATE REGENTS FOR HIGHER EDUCATION

http://www.okhighered.org/

FUTURE TEACHER SCHOLARSHIP-OKLAHOMA

Open to outstanding Oklahoma high school graduates who agree to teach in shortage areas. Must rank in top 15 percent of graduating class or score above 85th percentile on ACT or similar test, or be accepted in an educational program. Students nominated by institution. Reapply to renew. Must attend college/university in Oklahoma.

Academic Fields/Career Goals: Education.

Award: Scholarship for use in freshman, sophomore, junior, senior, or graduate years; not renewable. *Amount:* $500–$1500.

Eligibility Requirements: Applicant must be enrolled or expecting to enroll full- or part-time at a two-year or four-year institution or university; resident of Oklahoma and studying in Oklahoma. Available to U.S. citizens.

Application Requirements: Application form, essay, test scores, transcript. *Deadline:* varies.

OREGON PTA

http://www.oregonpta.org/

TEACHER EDUCATION SCHOLARSHIP

Nonrenewable scholarships to high school seniors or college students who are Oregon residents who want to teach in Oregon at an elementary or secondary school. The scholarship may be used at any Oregon public college or university that trains teachers or that transfers credits in education.

Academic Fields/Career Goals: Education.

Award: Scholarship for use in freshman, sophomore, junior, or senior years; not renewable. *Amount:* $500.

Eligibility Requirements: Applicant must be enrolled or expecting to enroll full-time at a two-year or four-year institution or university; resident of Oregon and studying in Oregon. Available to U.S. citizens.

Application Requirements: Application form, essay, recommendations or references, self-addressed stamped envelope with application, test scores, transcript. *Deadline:* March 21.

OREGON STUDENT ASSISTANCE COMMISSION

http://www.GetCollegeFunds.org/

HARRIET A. SIMMONS SCHOLARSHIP

One-time award available to Oregon residents who are enrolled in an elementary or secondary education program in an Oregon college or university, entering senior or fifth-year, or graduate students in a fifth year for elementary or secondary teaching certificate.

Academic Fields/Career Goals: Education.

Award: Scholarship for use in senior or graduate years; not renewable.

Eligibility Requirements: Applicant must be enrolled or expecting to enroll full-time at a four-year institution or university; resident of Oregon and studying in Oregon. Available to U.S. citizens.

Application Requirements: Application form, essay, FAFSA, financial need analysis, transcript. *Deadline:* March 1.

JAMES CARLSON MEMORIAL SCHOLARSHIP

One-time award for elementary or secondary education majors entering the final year of their program, or graduate students in fifth year for elementary or secondary certificate. Applicants may qualify according to one of the following; (1) Diverse environments essay, (2) dependents of Oregon Education Association members (no essay); or (3) students committed to teaching autistic children.

Academic Fields/Career Goals: Education; Special Education.

Award: Scholarship for use in senior or graduate years; not renewable.

Eligibility Requirements: Applicant must be enrolled or expecting to enroll full-time at a four-year institution or university and resident of Oregon. Applicant or parent of applicant must be member of Oregon Education Association. Available to U.S. citizens.

Application Requirements: Activity chart, application form, essay, financial need analysis, transcript. *Deadline:* March 1.

NETTIE HANSELMAN JAYNES SCHOLARSHIP

One-time award for students majoring in elementary and secondary education entering their senior or fifth year or graduate students in their fifth year for elementary or secondary certificate. To be used at any four-year college in Oregon. May reapply for additional year.

Academic Fields/Career Goals: Education.

Award: Scholarship for use in senior or graduate years; not renewable.

Eligibility Requirements: Applicant must be enrolled or expecting to enroll full-time at a four-year institution; resident of Oregon and studying in Oregon. Available to U.S. citizens.

Application Requirements: Activities chart, FAFSA, application form, essay, financial need analysis, transcript. *Deadline:* March 1.

OREGON ALPHA DELTA KAPPA SCHOLARSHIP

One-time award for elementary or secondary education majors entering senior or fifth-year or graduate students in fifth year for elementary or secondary certificate. For use at Oregon four-year public and nonprofit colleges. FAFSA is required.

Academic Fields/Career Goals: Education.

Award: Scholarship for use in senior or graduate years; not renewable.

Eligibility Requirements: Applicant must be enrolled or expecting to enroll full-time at a four-year institution or university and studying in Oregon. Available to U.S. citizens.

Application Requirements: Application form, FAFSA. *Deadline:* March 1.

OREGON COLLEGE SAVINGS PLAN EDUCATION CELEBRATION SCHOLARSHIP

One-time award for education majors studying at least half-time Oregon public or nonprofit schools. Preference given to college seniors or 5th-year seniors seeking MAT or 2nd-year community college students pursuing AAOT or equivalent. High school seniors must have at least a 3.0 GPA (3.4 preferred) and college students must have a minimum GPA of 3.25. Awardees must be willing to participate in publicity with Oregon 529 College Savings Network. FAFSA is required. Apply/compete annually.

Academic Fields/Career Goals: Education.

Award: Scholarship for use in freshman, sophomore, junior, senior, or graduate years; not renewable.

Eligibility Requirements: Applicant must be enrolled or expecting to enroll full- or part-time at a two-year or four-year institution or university and studying in Oregon. Available to U.S. citizens.

Application Requirements: Application form, FAFSA. *Deadline:* March 1.

PI LAMBDA THETA INC.

http://www.pilambda.org/

DISTINGUISHED STUDENT SCHOLAR AWARD

The award is presented in recognition of an education major who has displayed leadership potential and a strong dedication to education. Award given out in odd years. Minimum 3.5 GPA required.

Academic Fields/Career Goals: Education.

Award: Prize for use in freshman, sophomore, junior, or senior years; not renewable. *Number:* 1. *Amount:* $500.

Eligibility Requirements: Applicant must be enrolled or expecting to enroll full- or part-time at a four-year institution or university and must have an interest in leadership. Applicant or parent of applicant must have employment or volunteer experience in community service. Applicant must have 3.5 GPA or higher. Available to U.S. and non-U.S. citizens.

Application Requirements: 2 letters of support from faculty members other than the nominator, letter of endorsement from the nominee's chapter, application form, recommendations or references, resume, transcript. *Deadline:* April 16.

GRADUATE STUDENT SCHOLAR AWARD

The award is presented in recognition of an outstanding graduate student who is an education major. Award given out in odd years. Minimum 3.5 GPA required.

Academic Fields/Career Goals: Education.

Award: Prize for use in senior or graduate years; not renewable. *Number:* 1. *Amount:* $1000.

Eligibility Requirements: Applicant must be enrolled or expecting to enroll full- or part-time at a four-year institution or university and must have an interest in leadership. Applicant or parent of applicant must have employment or volunteer experience in community service. Applicant must have 3.5 GPA or higher. Available to U.S. and non-U.S. citizens.

Application Requirements: Application form, essay, letter of endorsement from nominee's chapter, recommendations or references, resume, transcript. *Deadline:* April 16.

NADEEN BURKEHOLDER WILLIAMS MUSIC SCHOLARSHIP

The scholarship provides $1000 to an outstanding K-12 teacher who is pursuing a graduate degree at an accredited college or university and who is either a music education teacher or applies music systematically in teaching another subject. Minimum 3.5 GPA required.

Academic Fields/Career Goals: Education; Music.

Award: Scholarship for use in freshman, sophomore, junior, senior, or graduate years; not renewable. *Number:* 1–5. *Amount:* $1000.

Eligibility Requirements: Applicant must be enrolled or expecting to enroll full- or part-time at a four-year institution or university and must have an interest in music. Applicant or parent of applicant must have employment or volunteer experience in teaching/education. Applicant must have 3.5 GPA or higher. Available to U.S. and non-U.S. citizens.

Application Requirements: Application form, essay, portfolio, recommendations or references, resume. *Deadline:* April 16.

STUDENT SUPPORT SCHOLARSHIP

The scholarship is available to current members of Pi Lambda Theta who will be a full-time or part-time student enrolled in a minimum of three semester hours at a regionally accredited institution during the year following the award. Minimum 3.5 GPA required.

Academic Fields/Career Goals: Education.

Award: Scholarship for use in sophomore, junior, senior, graduate, or postgraduate years; not renewable. *Number:* 1–6. *Amount:* $750.

Eligibility Requirements: Applicant must be enrolled or expecting to enroll full- or part-time at a two-year or four-year or technical institution or university. Applicant or parent of applicant must be member of Greek Organization. Applicant must have 3.5 GPA or higher. Available to U.S. and non-U.S. citizens.

Application Requirements: Application form, essay, transcript. *Deadline:* April 16.

TOBIN SORENSON PHYSICAL EDUCATION SCHOLARSHIP

The scholarship provides $1000 for tuition to an outstanding student who intends to pursue a career at the K-12 level as a physical education teacher, adaptive physical education teacher, coach, recreational therapist, dance therapist, or similar professional focusing on teaching the knowledge and use of the human body. Awarded in odd years only. Minimum 3.5 GPA required.

Academic Fields/Career Goals: Education; Sports-Related/Exercise Science; Therapy/Rehabilitation.

Award: Scholarship for use in sophomore, junior, senior, or graduate years; not renewable. *Number:* 1. *Amount:* $1000.

Eligibility Requirements: Applicant must be enrolled or expecting to enroll full- or part-time at a two-year or four-year institution or university. Applicant must have 3.5 GPA or higher. Available to U.S. and non-U.S. citizens.

Application Requirements: Application form, recommendations or references, resume, transcript. *Deadline:* April 16.

PRESBYTERIAN CHURCH (USA)

http://www.pcusa.org/financialaid

STUDENT OPPORTUNITY SCHOLARSHIP

Designed to assist undergraduate students with their junior and senior year of college. Restricted to members of the Presbyterian Church (USA).

Academic Fields/Career Goals: Education; Health and Medical Sciences; Religion/Theology; Social Sciences; Social Services.

Award: Scholarship for use in junior or senior years; renewable. *Number:* 68. *Amount:* up to $3000.

Eligibility Requirements: Applicant must be Presbyterian and enrolled or expecting to enroll full-time at a four-year institution or university. Applicant must have 2.5 GPA or higher. Available to U.S. citizens.

Application Requirements: Application form, essay, financial need analysis, recommendations or references, resume, transcript. *Deadline:* June 1.

Contact: Ms. Laura Bryan, Associate, Financial Aid for Studies
Presbyterian Church (USA)
100 Witherspoon Street
Louisville, KY 40202
Phone: 800-728-7228 Ext. 5735
Fax: 502-569-8766
E-mail: finaid@pcusa.org

SARAH KLENKE MEMORIAL TEACHING SCHOLARSHIP

http://www.sarahklenkescholarship.org/

SARAH ELIZABETH KLENKE MEMORIAL TEACHING SCHOLARSHIP

Scholarship for graduating senior or high school graduate enrolling in secondary schooling. Should have a desire to major in education. Minimum 2.0 GPA required. Participation in JROTC or team sport is required.

Academic Fields/Career Goals: Education.

Award: Scholarship for use in freshman or senior years; not renewable. *Number:* 1. *Amount:* $1000.

Eligibility Requirements: Applicant must be enrolled or expecting to enroll full-time at a two-year or four-year institution or university. Available to U.S. and non-U.S. citizens.

Application Requirements: Application form, essay, letter from coach or teacher confirming participation in ROTC or team sport, recommendations or references. *Deadline:* April 15.

Contact: Aaron Klenke, Scholarship Committee
Sarah Klenke Memorial Teaching Scholarship
3131 Glade Springs
Kingwood, TX 77339
Phone: 281-358-7933
E-mail: aaron.klenke@gmail.com

SOCIETY FOR THE SCIENTIFIC STUDY OF SEXUALITY

http://www.sexscience.org/

SOCIETY FOR THE SCIENTIFIC STUDY OF SEXUALITY STUDENT RESEARCH GRANT

• *See page 102*

SOUTH DAKOTA BOARD OF REGENTS

http://www.sdbor.edu/

HAINES MEMORIAL SCHOLARSHIP

One-time scholarship for South Dakota public university students who are sophomores, juniors, or seniors having at least a 2.5 GPA and majoring in a teacher education program. Must include resume with application. Must be South Dakota resident.

Academic Fields/Career Goals: Education.

Award: Scholarship for use in sophomore, junior, or senior years; not renewable. *Number:* 1. *Amount:* $2150.

Eligibility Requirements: Applicant must be enrolled or expecting to enroll full-time at an institution or university; resident of South Dakota and studying in South Dakota. Applicant must have 3.5 GPA or higher. Available to U.S. citizens.

Application Requirements: Application form, essay, resume, typed statement describing personal philosophy and philosophy of education. *Deadline:* February 8.

Contact: Dr. Paul Turman, System Vice President for Research and
Economic Development
South Dakota Board of Regents
301 East Capital Avenue, Suite 200
Pierre, SD 57501
Phone: 605-773-3455
Fax: 605-773-2422
E-mail: paul.turman@sdbor.edu

SOUTH DAKOTA BOARD OF REGENTS ANNIS I. FOWLER/KADEN SCHOLARSHIP

Scholarship for graduating South Dakota high school seniors to pursue a career in elementary education at a South Dakota public university. Must attend BHSU, BSU, NSU or USD. Applicants must have a cumulative GPA of 3.0 after three years of high school. One-time award.

Academic Fields/Career Goals: Education.

Award: Scholarship for use in freshman year; not renewable. *Number:* 2. *Amount:* $1000.

Eligibility Requirements: Applicant must be high school student; planning to enroll or expecting to enroll full-time at a four-year institution or university; resident of South Dakota and studying in South Dakota. Applicant must have 3.0 GPA or higher. Available to U.S. citizens.

Application Requirements: ACT scores, application form, essay, recommendations or references, test scores, transcript. *Deadline:* February 15.

Contact: Dr. Paul Turman, System Vice President for Research and
Economic Development
South Dakota Board of Regents
301 East Capital Avenue, Suite 200
Pierre, SD 57501
Phone: 605-773-3455
Fax: 605-773-2422
E-mail: paul.turman@sdbor.edu

STATE OF WYOMING, ADMINISTERED BY UNIVERSITY OF WYOMING

http://www.uwyo.edu/scholarships

SUPERIOR STUDENT IN EDUCATION SCHOLARSHIP-WYOMING

Scholarship available each year to sixteen Wyoming high school graduates who plan to teach in Wyoming. The award covers costs of undergraduate tuition at the University of Wyoming or any Wyoming community college.

Academic Fields/Career Goals: Education.

Award: Scholarship for use in freshman, sophomore, junior, or senior years; renewable. *Number:* 16. *Amount:* $1000.

Eligibility Requirements: Applicant must be high school student; planning to enroll or expecting to enroll full-time at a two-year or four-year institution or university; resident of Wyoming and studying in Wyoming. Applicant must have 3.0 GPA or higher. Available to U.S. citizens.

Application Requirements: Application form, recommendations or references, test scores, transcript. *Deadline:* October 31.

Contact: Tammy Mack, Assistant Director, Scholarships
State of Wyoming, Administered by University of Wyoming
Department 3335
1000 East University Avenue
Laramie, WY 82071
Phone: 307-766-2412
Fax: 307-766-3800
E-mail: westmack@uwyo.edu

STRAIGHTFORWARD MEDIA

http://www.straightforwardmedia.com/

STRAIGHTFORWARD MEDIA TEACHER SCHOLARSHIP

Scholarship of $500 for students planning to be teachers of any kind and at any level. Must be U.S. citizen. Awarded four times per year. Deadlines are January 14, April 14, July 14, and October 14. For more information, see website at http://www.straightforwardmedia.com/education/form.php.

Academic Fields/Career Goals: Education; Special Education.

Award: Scholarship for use in freshman, sophomore, junior, or senior years; not renewable. *Number:* 4. *Amount:* $500.

Eligibility Requirements: Applicant must be enrolled or expecting to enroll full- or part-time at a two-year or four-year or technical institution or university. Available to U.S. citizens.

Application Requirements: Essay. *Deadline:* varies.

TENNESSEE EDUCATION ASSOCIATION

http://www.teateachers.org/

TEA DON SAHLI-KATHY WOODALL FUTURE TEACHERS OF AMERICA SCHOLARSHIP

Scholarship is available to a high school senior planning to major in education, attending a high school which has an FTA Chapter affiliated with TEA, and planning to enroll in a Tennessee college.

Academic Fields/Career Goals: Education.

Award: Scholarship for use in freshman year; not renewable. *Number:* 1. *Amount:* $1000.

Eligibility Requirements: Applicant must be high school student; planning to enroll or expecting to enroll full-time at a four-year institution or university; resident of Tennessee and studying in Tennessee. Applicant must have 3.0 GPA or higher. Available to U.S. citizens.

Application Requirements: Application form, entry in a contest, essay, financial need analysis, recommendations or references, statement of income, transcript. *Deadline:* March 1.

Contact: Stephanie Faulkner, Manager of Business Affairs
Phone: 615-242-8392
Fax: 615-259-4581
E-mail: sfaulkner@tea.nea.org

TEA DON SAHLI-KATHY WOODALL MINORITY SCHOLARSHIP

Scholarship is available to a minority high school senior planning to major in education and planning to enroll in a Tennessee college. Application must be made by an FTA Chapter, or by the student with the recommendation of an active TEA member.

Academic Fields/Career Goals: Education.

Award: Scholarship for use in freshman year; not renewable. *Number:* 1. *Amount:* $1000.

Eligibility Requirements: Applicant must be American Indian/Alaska Native, Asian/Pacific Islander, Black (non-Hispanic), Hispanic; high school student; planning to enroll or expecting to enroll full-time at a four-year institution or university; resident of Tennessee and studying in

Tennessee. Applicant must have 3.0 GPA or higher. Available to U.S. citizens.

Application Requirements: Application form, entry in a contest, essay, financial need analysis, recommendations or references, statement of income, transcript. *Deadline:* March 1.

Contact: Stephanie Faulkner, Manager of Business Affairs
　　　　Phone: 615-242-8392
　　　　Fax: 615-259-4581
　　　　E-mail: sfaulkner@tea.nea.org

TEA DON SAHLI-KATHY WOODALL UNDERGRADUATE SCHOLARSHIP

Scholarship is available to undergraduate students who are student TEA members. Application must be made through the local STEA Chapter. Amount varies form $500 to $1000.

Academic Fields/Career Goals: Education.

Award: Scholarship for use in freshman, sophomore, junior, or senior years; not renewable. *Number:* 4. *Amount:* $500–$1000.

Eligibility Requirements: Applicant must be enrolled or expecting to enroll full- or part-time at a four-year institution or university; resident of Tennessee and studying in Tennessee. Applicant or parent of applicant must be member of Tennessee Education Association. Applicant must have 3.0 GPA or higher. Available to U.S. citizens.

Application Requirements: Application form, essay, financial need analysis, recommendations or references, statement of income, transcript. *Deadline:* March 1.

Contact: Stephanie Faulkner, Manager of Business Affairs
　　　　Phone: 615-242-8392
　　　　Fax: 615-259-4581
　　　　E-mail: sfaulkner@tea.nea.org

TENNESSEE STUDENT ASSISTANCE CORPORATION

http://www.tn.gov/collegepays

CHRISTA MCAULIFFE SCHOLARSHIP PROGRAM

Scholarship to assist and support Tennessee students who have demonstrated a commitment to a career in educating the youth of Tennessee. Offered to college seniors for a period of one academic year. Must have a minimum college GPA of 3.5. Must have attained scores on either the ACT or SAT which meet or exceed the national norms. Award is made on a periodic basis as funding becomes available.

Academic Fields/Career Goals: Education.

Award: Scholarship for use in senior year; not renewable. *Number:* up to 1. *Amount:* up to $500.

Eligibility Requirements: Applicant must be enrolled or expecting to enroll full-time at a four-year institution or university; resident of Tennessee and studying in Tennessee. Applicant must have 3.5 GPA or higher. Available to U.S. citizens.

Application Requirements: Application form, application form may be submitted online (http://www.tn.gov/collegepays), essay. *Deadline:* April 1.

Contact: Ms. Kathy Stripling, Scholarship Administrator
　　　　Tennessee Student Assistance Corporation
　　　　Parkway Towers, 404 James Robertson Parkway, Suite 1510
　　　　Nashville, TN 37243-0820
　　　　Phone: 615-253-7480
　　　　Fax: 615-741-6101
　　　　E-mail: kathy.stripling@tn.gov

TKE EDUCATIONAL FOUNDATION

http://www.tke.org/

CARROL C. HALL MEMORIAL SCHOLARSHIP
• *See page 107*

FRANCIS J. FLYNN MEMORIAL SCHOLARSHIP

Award of $1300 for an undergraduate member of TKE who is a full-time student pursuing a degree in mathematics or education. Minimum 2.75 GPA required. Leadership within chapter or campus organizations recognized. Preference will be given to members of Theta-Sigma Chapter.

Academic Fields/Career Goals: Education; Mathematics.

Award: Scholarship for use in freshman, sophomore, junior, or senior years; not renewable. *Number:* 1. *Amount:* $1300.

Eligibility Requirements: Applicant must be enrolled or expecting to enroll full-time at a four-year institution or university; male and must have an interest in leadership. Applicant or parent of applicant must be member of Tau Kappa Epsilon. Available to U.S. and non-U.S. citizens.

Application Requirements: Application form, essay, narrative summary of how TKE membership has benefited applicant, personal photograph, transcript. *Deadline:* February 29.

Contact: Gary Reed, President and Chief Executive Officer
　　　　TKE Educational Foundation
　　　　8645 Founders Road
　　　　Indianapolis, IN 46268-1393
　　　　Phone: 317-872-6533
　　　　Fax: 317-875-8353
　　　　E-mail: reedga@tke.org

UNITED NEGRO COLLEGE FUND

http://www.uncf.org/

BANK OF AMERICA SCHOLARSHIP
• *See page 160*

EARL C. SAMS FOUNDATION SCHOLARSHIP

Award of up to $3000 is available for African American students who are residents of Texas. Must be elementary or secondary education majors attending Jarvis Christian College, Paul Quinn College, or Wiley College. Must have a minimum GPA of 2.5. For additional information and general scholarship application, visit website http://www.uncf.org.

Academic Fields/Career Goals: Education.

Award: Scholarship for use in freshman, sophomore, junior, or senior years; not renewable. *Amount:* up to $3000.

Eligibility Requirements: Applicant must be Black (non-Hispanic); enrolled or expecting to enroll full-time at a two-year or four-year institution or university and resident of Texas. Applicant must have 2.5 GPA or higher. Available to U.S. citizens.

Application Requirements: Application form, FAFSA, Student Aid Report (SAR), financial need analysis. *Deadline:* continuous.

VERMONT-NEA

http://www.vtnea.org/

VERMONT-NEA/MAIDA F. TOWNSEND SCHOLARSHIP

Scholarship of $1000 to sons and daughters of Vermont-NEA members in their last year of high school, undergraduates, and graduate students. Students majoring in any discipline are eligible to apply, but preference may be given to those majoring in education, or having that intention.

Academic Fields/Career Goals: Education.

Award: Scholarship for use in freshman, sophomore, junior, senior, or graduate years; not renewable. *Number:* 5. *Amount:* $1000.

Eligibility Requirements: Applicant must be enrolled or expecting to enroll full- or part-time at a two-year or four-year or technical institution or university. Applicant or parent of applicant must be member of Vermont-NEA. Applicant or parent of applicant must have employment or volunteer experience in teaching/education. Available to U.S. and non-U.S. citizens.

Application Requirements: Application form, community service, cover letter, essay, recommendations or references, test scores, transcript. *Deadline:* February 1.

Contact: Sandy Perkins, Administrative Assistant
　　　　Vermont-NEA
　　　　10 Wheelock Street
　　　　Montpelier, VT 05602-3737
　　　　Phone: 802-223-6375
　　　　E-mail: sperkins@vtnea.org

VIRGINIA CONGRESS OF PARENTS AND TEACHERS

http://www.vapta.org/

FRIEDA L. KOONTZ SCHOLARSHIP

Scholarship of $1200 to graduating high school students planning to enter teaching or other youth-serving professions in Virginia. Must be Virginia residents graduating from a Virginia public high school with a Parent-Teacher-Student Association (PTSA) and attending a Virginia college or university. Minimum 2.5 GPA required.

Academic Fields/Career Goals: Education.

Award: Scholarship for use in freshman year; not renewable. *Number:* 1. *Amount:* $1200.

Eligibility Requirements: Applicant must be high school student; planning to enroll or expecting to enroll full-time at a four-year institution or university; resident of Virginia and studying in Virginia. Applicant or parent of applicant must be member of Parent-Teacher Association/Organization. Applicant must have 2.5 GPA or higher. Available to U.S. citizens.

Application Requirements: Application form, essay, recommendations or references, test scores, transcript. *Deadline:* March 1.

Contact: Daniel Phillips, Scholarship Chair
    Phone: 804-264-1234
    E-mail: info@vapta.org

GENERAL SCHOLARSHIPS

General scholarships in addition to the Freida L. Koontz and John S. Davis Scholarships. Only graduating students enrolled in a Virginia school that is a PTA or PTSA school may apply. See website for application details.

Academic Fields/Career Goals: Education.

Award: Scholarship for use in freshman year; not renewable. *Number:* 10–20. *Amount:* $1000.

Eligibility Requirements: Applicant must be high school student; planning to enroll or expecting to enroll full-time at a four-year institution or university and resident of Virginia. Applicant or parent of applicant must be member of Parent-Teacher Association/Organization. Applicant must have 2.5 GPA or higher. Available to U.S. citizens.

Application Requirements: Application form, essay, recommendations or references, test scores, transcript. *Deadline:* March 1.

Contact: Daniel Phillips, Scholarship Chair
    Phone: 804-264-1234
    E-mail: info@vapta.org

S. JOHN DAVIS SCHOLARSHIP

Scholarship of $1200 to Virginia residents graduating from a Virginia public school that has a Parent-Teacher-Student Association (PTSA) or PTA. Must be planning to attend a Virginia college or university and pursuing a career in teaching or qualifying for service with a youth-serving agency in Virginia. Minimum 2.5 GPA required.

Academic Fields/Career Goals: Education.

Award: Scholarship for use in freshman year; not renewable. *Number:* 1. *Amount:* $1200.

Eligibility Requirements: Applicant must be high school student; planning to enroll or expecting to enroll full-time at a four-year institution or university; resident of Virginia and studying in Virginia. Applicant or parent of applicant must be member of Parent-Teacher Association/Organization. Applicant must have 2.5 GPA or higher. Available to U.S. citizens.

Application Requirements: Application form, essay. *Deadline:* March 1.

Contact: Daniel Phillips, Scholarship Chair
    Phone: 804-264-1234
    E-mail: info@vapta.org

WEST VIRGINIA HIGHER EDUCATION POLICY COMMISSION-STUDENT SERVICES

http://wvhepcnew.wvnet.edu/

UNDERWOOD-SMITH TEACHER SCHOLARSHIP PROGRAM

Award for West Virginia residents at West Virginia institutions pursuing teaching careers. Must have a 3.25 GPA after completion of two years of course work. Must teach two years in West Virginia public schools for each year the award is received. Recipients will be required to sign an agreement acknowledging an understanding of the program's requirements and their willingness to repay the award if appropriate teaching service is not rendered.

Academic Fields/Career Goals: Education.

Award: Scholarship for use in junior, senior, graduate, or postgraduate years; renewable. *Number:* 30–60. *Amount:* $2500–$5000.

Eligibility Requirements: Applicant must be enrolled or expecting to enroll full-time at a four-year institution or university; resident of West Virginia and studying in West Virginia. Applicant must have 3.0 GPA or higher. Available to U.S. citizens.

Application Requirements: Application form, essay, recommendations or references. *Deadline:* March 1.

Contact: Jan Ruge, Scholarship Coordinator
    West Virginia Higher Education Policy Commission-Student Services
    1018 Kanawha Boulevard East, Suite 700
    Charleston, WV 25301
    Phone: 304-558-4618
    Fax: 304-558-4622
    E-mail: jruge@hepc.wvnet.edu

WISCONSIN CONGRESS OF PARENTS AND TEACHERS INC.

http://www.wisconsinpta.org/

BROOKMIRE-HASTINGS SCHOLARSHIPS

One-time award to graduating high school seniors from Wisconsin public schools. Must pursue a degree in education. High school must have an active PTA in good standing of the Wisconsin PTA.

Academic Fields/Career Goals: Education; Special Education.

Award: Scholarship for use in freshman year; not renewable. *Number:* up to 2. *Amount:* $1000.

Eligibility Requirements: Applicant must be high school student; planning to enroll or expecting to enroll full-time at a four-year institution or university and resident of Wisconsin. Available to U.S. citizens.

Application Requirements: Application form, essay, interview, recommendations or references, transcript. *Deadline:* March 1.

Contact: Kim Schwantes, Executive Administrator
    Wisconsin Congress of Parents and Teachers Inc.
    4797 Hayes Road, Suite 2
    Madison, WI 53704-3256
    Phone: 608-244-1455

WISCONSIN MATHEMATICS EDUCATION FOUNDATION

http://wmefonline.org/

ARNE ENGEBRETSEN WISCONSIN MATHEMATICS COUNCIL SCHOLARSHIP

Scholarship for Wisconsin high school senior who is planning to study mathematics education and teach mathematics at K-12 level.

Academic Fields/Career Goals: Education; Mathematics.

Award: Scholarship for use in freshman year; not renewable. *Number:* 1. *Amount:* $2000.

Eligibility Requirements: Applicant must be high school student; planning to enroll or expecting to enroll full-time at a four-year institution or university and resident of Wisconsin. Available to U.S. citizens.

Application Requirements: Application form, essay, recommendations or references, resume, transcript. *Deadline:* March 1.

ETHEL A. NEIJAHR WISCONSIN MATHEMATICS COUNCIL SCHOLARSHIP

Scholarship for a Wisconsin resident who is currently enrolled in teacher education programs in a Wisconsin institution studying mathematics education. Minimum GPA of 3.0 required.

Academic Fields/Career Goals: Education; Mathematics.

Award: Scholarship for use in junior or senior years; not renewable. *Number:* 1. *Amount:* $2000.

Eligibility Requirements: Applicant must be enrolled or expecting to enroll full-time at a four-year institution or university; resident of Wisconsin and studying in Wisconsin. Applicant must have 3.0 GPA or higher. Available to U.S. citizens.

Application Requirements: Application form, essay, recommendations or references, resume, transcript. *Deadline:* March 1.

SISTER MARY PETRONIA VAN STRATEN WISCONSIN MATHEMATICS COUNCIL SCHOLARSHIP

Scholarship for a Wisconsin resident who is currently enrolled in teacher education programs in Wisconsin institution studying mathematics education. Minimum GPA of 3.0 required.

Academic Fields/Career Goals: Education; Mathematics.

Award: Scholarship for use in junior or senior years; not renewable. *Number:* 1. *Amount:* $2000.

Eligibility Requirements: Applicant must be enrolled or expecting to enroll full-time at a four-year institution or university; resident of Wisconsin and studying in Wisconsin. Applicant must have 3.0 GPA or higher. Available to U.S. citizens.

Application Requirements: Application form, essay, recommendations or references, resume, transcript. *Deadline:* March 1.

WOMEN BAND DIRECTORS INTERNATIONAL

http://www.womenbanddirectors.org/

CHARLOTTE PLUMMER OWEN MEMORIAL SCHOLARSHIP

One-time award for women instrumental music majors enrolled in a four-year institution. Applicants must be working toward a degree in music education with the intention of becoming a band director. See website for application http://www.womenbanddirectors.org/.

Academic Fields/Career Goals: Education; Music; Performing Arts.

Award: Scholarship for use in freshman, sophomore, junior, or senior years; not renewable. *Number:* 4. *Amount:* $300.

Eligibility Requirements: Applicant must be enrolled or expecting to enroll full-time at a four-year institution or university; female and must have an interest in music/singing. Available to U.S. and non-U.S. citizens.

Application Requirements: Application form, essay, personal photograph, recommendations or references, transcript. *Deadline:* December 1.

Contact: Nicole Aakre-Rubis, Scholarship Chair
Women Band Directors International
16085 Excel Way
Rosemount, MN 55068

MARTHA ANN STARK MEMORIAL SCHOLARSHIP

One-time award for women instrumental music majors enrolled in a four-year institution. Applicants must be working toward a degree in music education with the intention of becoming a band director. Three of the scholarships are designated for college upperclassmen, and one is open to all levels. See website for application http://www.womenbanddirectors.org/.

Academic Fields/Career Goals: Education; Music; Performing Arts.

Award: Scholarship for use in freshman, sophomore, junior, or senior years; not renewable. *Number:* 1. *Amount:* $300.

Eligibility Requirements: Applicant must be enrolled or expecting to enroll full-time at a four-year institution or university; female and must have an interest in music/singing. Available to U.S. and non-U.S. citizens.

Application Requirements: Application form, essay, personal photograph, recommendations or references, transcript. *Deadline:* December 1.

Contact: Nicole Aakre-Rubis, Scholarship Chair
Women Band Directors International
16085 Excel Way
Rosemount, MN 55068

VOLKWEIN MEMORIAL SCHOLARSHIP

One-time award for female instrumental music majors enrolled in a four-year institution. Applicants must be working toward a degree in music education with the intention of becoming a band director. Three of the scholarships are designated for college upperclassmen, and one is open to all levels. See website for application http://www.womenbanddirectors.org/.

Academic Fields/Career Goals: Education; Music; Performing Arts.

Award: Scholarship for use in freshman, sophomore, junior, senior, or graduate years; not renewable. *Number:* 4. *Amount:* $300–$500.

Eligibility Requirements: Applicant must be enrolled or expecting to enroll full-time at a four-year institution or university; female and must have an interest in music/singing. Available to U.S. and non-U.S. citizens.

Application Requirements: Application form, essay, personal photograph, recommendations or references, self-addressed stamped envelope with application, transcript. *Deadline:* December 1.

Contact: Nicole Aakre-Rubis, Scholarship Chair
Women Band Directors International
16085 Excel Way
Rosemount, MN 55068

Y'S MEN INTERNATIONAL

http://www.ysmenusa.com/

ALEXANDER SCHOLARSHIP LOAN FUND

• *See page 161*

ZETA PHI BETA SORORITY INC. NATIONAL EDUCATIONAL FOUNDATION

http://www.zpbnef1975.org/

ISABEL M. HERSON SCHOLARSHIP IN EDUCATION

Scholarships available for female graduate or undergraduate students enrolled in a degree program in either elementary or secondary education. Award for full-time study for one academic year. See website for additional information and application http://www.zpbnef1975.org/.

Academic Fields/Career Goals: Education.

Award: Scholarship for use in freshman, sophomore, junior, senior, or graduate years; not renewable. *Number:* 1. *Amount:* $500–$1000.

Eligibility Requirements: Applicant must be enrolled or expecting to enroll full-time at a four-year institution or university. Available to U.S. citizens.

Application Requirements: Application form, essay, proof of enrollment, recommendations or references, transcript. *Deadline:* February 1.

Contact: Cheryl Williams, National Second Vice President
Fax: 318-232-4593
E-mail: 2ndanti@zphib1920.org

ELECTRICAL ENGINEERING/ ELECTRONICS

AACE INTERNATIONAL

http://www.aacei.org/

AACE INTERNATIONAL COMPETITIVE SCHOLARSHIP
• *See page 108*

AHS INTERNATIONAL—THE VERTICAL FLIGHT TECHNICAL SOCIETY

http://www.vtol.org/

VERTICAL FLIGHT FOUNDATION SCHOLARSHIP
• *See page 124*

AIST FOUNDATION

http://www.aistfoundation.org/

AISI/AIST FOUNDATION PREMIER SCHOLARSHIP
This award is granted to the highest scoring FeMET at StEEL scholarship applicants. $10,000 scholarships are for full-time students of metallurgy, materials science, chemical, electrical, mechanical, environmental, computer science, and industrial engineering. Students must have an interest in a career in the steel industry as demonstrated by an internship or related experience, or who have plans to pursue such experiences during college. Students must commit to a summer internship at a steel producing company (placement assistance is provided) prior to receiving this scholarship. Student may apply during their sophomore and junior years. Applications are accepted from September 1 through December 31 each year.

Academic Fields/Career Goals: Electrical Engineering/Electronics; Materials Science, Engineering, and Metallurgy; Mechanical Engineering.

Award: Scholarship for use in sophomore or junior years; not renewable. *Number:* 1. *Amount:* $10,000.

Eligibility Requirements: Applicant must be enrolled or expecting to enroll full-time at a four-year institution or university. Applicant must have 2.5 GPA or higher. Available to U.S. and non-U.S. citizens.

Application Requirements: Application form, essay, recommendations or references, resume, transcript. *Deadline:* December 31.

Contact: Lori Wharrey, AIST Manager, Board Services
AIST Foundation
186 Thorn Hill Road
Warrendale, PA 15086
Phone: 724-814-3044
E-mail: lwharrey@aist.org

AIST WILLIAM E. SCHWABE MEMORIAL SCHOLARSHIP
Scholarship for full-time students of metallurgy, materials science, chemical, mechanical, electrical, environmental, computer science, and industrial engineering. Students must have an interest in a career in the steel industry as demonstrated by an internship or related experience, or who have plans to pursue such experiences during college. Student may apply after first term of freshman year of college. Applications are accepted from 1 Sep through 31 Dec each year. Note: High school students do not qualify but are encouraged to learn about the steel industry and the career opportunities available therein, during their freshman year.

Academic Fields/Career Goals: Electrical Engineering/Electronics; Engineering/Technology; Materials Science, Engineering, and Metallurgy; Mechanical Engineering.

Award: Scholarship for use in sophomore, junior, or senior years; not renewable. *Number:* 1. *Amount:* $3000.

Eligibility Requirements: Applicant must be enrolled or expecting to enroll full-time at a four-year institution or university. Applicant must have 2.5 GPA or higher. Available to U.S. and non-U.S. citizens.

Application Requirements: Application form, essay, recommendations or references, resume, transcript. *Deadline:* December 31.

Contact: Lori Wharrey, AIST Manager, Board Services
Warrendale, PA 15086
Phone: 724-814-3044
E-mail: lwharrey@aist.org

ASSOCIATION FOR IRON AND STEEL TECHNOLOGY BENJAMIN F. FAIRLESS SCHOLARSHIP (AIME)
• *See page 162*

ASSOCIATION FOR IRON AND STEEL TECHNOLOGY DAVID H. SAMSON CANADIAN SCHOLARSHIP
• *See page 162*

ASSOCIATION FOR IRON AND STEEL TECHNOLOGY OHIO VALLEY CHAPTER SCHOLARSHIP
• *See page 142*

ASSOCIATION FOR IRON AND STEEL TECHNOLOGY RONALD E. LINCOLN SCHOLARSHIP
Scholarship for full-time students of metallurgy, materials science, chemical, mechanical, electrical, environmental, computer science, and industrial engineering. Students must have an interest in a career in the steel industry as demonstrated by an internship or related experience, or who have plans to pursue such experiences during college. Student may apply after first term of freshman year of college. Applications are accepted from 1 Sep through 31 Dec each year. Note: High school students do not qualify but are encouraged to learn about the steel industry and the career opportunities available therein, during their freshman year.

Academic Fields/Career Goals: Electrical Engineering/Electronics; Materials Science, Engineering, and Metallurgy; Mechanical Engineering.

Award: Scholarship for use in sophomore, junior, or senior years; not renewable. *Number:* 2. *Amount:* $3000.

Eligibility Requirements: Applicant must be enrolled or expecting to enroll full-time at a four-year institution or university. Applicant must have 2.5 GPA or higher. Available to U.S. and non-U.S. citizens.

Application Requirements: Application form, essay, recommendations or references, resume, transcript. *Deadline:* December 31.

Contact: Lori Wharrey, AIST Manager, Board Services
AIST Foundation
186 Thorn Hill Road
Warrendale, PA 15086
Phone: 724-814-3044
E-mail: lwharrey@aist.org

ASSOCIATION FOR IRON AND STEEL TECHNOLOGY WILLY KORF MEMORIAL SCHOLARSHIP
• *See page 162*

STEEL ENGINEERING EDUCATION LINK (STEEL) SCHOLARSHIPS
Scholarships are for full-time students of chemical, electrical, mechanical, computer science, environment, and industrial engineering. Students must have an interest in a career in the steel industry as demonstrated by an internship or related experience, or who have plans to pursue such experiences during college. Students must commit to a paid summer internship at a steel producing company (placement assistance is provided) prior to receiving this scholarship. Student may apply during their sophomore and junior years. Applications are accepted from 1 Sep through 31 Dec each year.

Academic Fields/Career Goals: Electrical Engineering/Electronics; Mechanical Engineering.

Award: Scholarship for use in sophomore or junior years; not renewable. *Number:* 1–10. *Amount:* $5000.

Eligibility Requirements: Applicant must be enrolled or expecting to enroll full-time at a four-year institution or university. Applicant must have 2.5 GPA or higher. Available to U.S. and non-U.S. citizens.

Application Requirements: Application form, essay, recommendations or references, resume, transcript. *Deadline:* December 31.

Contact: Lori Wharrey, AIST Manager, Board Services
AIST Foundation
186 Thorn Hill Road
Warrendale, PA 15086
Phone: 724-814-3044
E-mail: lwharrey@aist.org

AMERICAN COUNCIL OF ENGINEERING COMPANIES OF PENNSYLVANIA (ACEC/PA)

http://www.acecpa.org/

ENGINEERING SCHOLARSHIP
• *See page 163*

AMERICAN FOUNDATION FOR THE BLIND

http://www.afb.org/

PAUL W. RUCKES SCHOLARSHIP
• *See page 199*

AMERICAN INSTITUTE OF AERONAUTICS AND ASTRONAUTICS

http://www.aiaa.org/

AIAA FOUNDATION UNDERGRADUATE SCHOLARSHIP
• *See page 102*

AMERICAN PUBLIC TRANSPORTATION FOUNDATION

http://www.apta.com/

LOUIS T. KLAUDER SCHOLARSHIP

Scholarships for study towards a career in the rail transit industry as an electrical or mechanical engineer. Must be sponsored by APTA member organization and complete internship with APTA member organization. Minimum GPA of 3.0 required.

Academic Fields/Career Goals: Electrical Engineering/Electronics; Mechanical Engineering.

Award: Scholarship for use in sophomore, junior, senior, or graduate years; renewable. *Number:* 1. *Amount:* $2500.

Eligibility Requirements: Applicant must be enrolled or expecting to enroll full-time at a two-year or four-year institution or university. Applicant must have 3.0 GPA or higher. Available to U.S. and Canadian citizens.

Application Requirements: Application form, essay, financial need analysis, recommendations or references, transcript, verification of enrollment for the current semester, copy of fee schedule from the college/university. *Deadline:* June 16.

Contact: Pamela Boswell, Vice President of Program Management
American Public Transportation Foundation
1666 K Street, NW
Washington, DC 20006-1215
Phone: 202-496-4803
Fax: 202-496-2323
E-mail: pboswell@apta.com

TRANSIT HALL OF FAME SCHOLARSHIP AWARD PROGRAM
• *See page 179*

AMERICAN RAILWAY ENGINEERING AND MAINTENANCE OF WAY ASSOCIATION

http://www.aremafoundation.org/

AREMA MICHAEL R. GARCIA SCHOLARSHIP
• *See page 179*

AREMA PRESIDENTIAL SPOUSE SCHOLARSHIP
• *See page 180*

AREMA UNDERGRADUATE SCHOLARSHIPS
• *See page 180*

CHARLES L. STANFORD FAMILY OHIO STATE UNIVERSITY RAILWAY ENGINEERING SCHOLARSHIP

Undergraduate student at Ohio State University enrolled full time in civil, mechanical, electrical or industrial engineering curriculum, having completed at least one full term. All scholarship applicants must having an interest in railway engineering, maintaining a minimum GPA of 2.0, and is available for interview by the AREMA Scholarship Committee.

Academic Fields/Career Goals: Electrical Engineering/Electronics; Entomology; Mechanical Engineering; Transportation.

Award: Scholarship for use in sophomore, junior, or senior years; not renewable. *Number:* 1–1. *Amount:* $1000–$1000.

Eligibility Requirements: Applicant must be enrolled or expecting to enroll full-time at an institution or university. Available to U.S. and non-U.S. citizens.

Application Requirements: Application form, application form may be submitted online (http://www.aremafoundation.org/scholarship_app.cfm), recommendations or references, resume, transcript. *Deadline:* March 8.

Contact: Stacy Spaulding, Director of Committees and Technical Services
American Railway Engineering and Maintenance of Way Association
10003 Derekwood Lane, Suite 210
Lanham, MD 20706
Phone: 301-459-3200 Ext. 706

AMERICAN SOCIETY OF HEATING, REFRIGERATING, AND AIR CONDITIONING ENGINEERS, INC.

http://www.ashrae.org/

ALWIN B. NEWTON SCHOLARSHIP

Scholarship available to undergraduate students pursuing a bachelor of science or engineering degree, who are enrolled full-time in a program accredited by the Accreditation Board for Engineering and Technology. Application and additional information on website http://www.ashrae.org.

Academic Fields/Career Goals: Electrical Engineering/Electronics; Engineering-Related Technologies; Engineering/Technology; Heating, Air-Conditioning, and Refrigeration Mechanics; Mechanical Engineering; Trade/Technical Specialties.

Award: Scholarship for use in sophomore, junior, or senior years; not renewable. *Number:* 1. *Amount:* $3000.

Eligibility Requirements: Applicant must be enrolled or expecting to enroll full-time at a four-year institution or university and must have an interest in leadership. Applicant must have 3.0 GPA or higher. Available to U.S. and non-U.S. citizens.

Application Requirements: Application form, financial need analysis, recommendations or references, transcript. *Deadline:* December 1.

Contact: Lois Benedict, Scholarship Administrator
Phone: 404-636-8400 Ext. 1120
E-mail: lbenedict@ashrae.org

ASHRAE MEMORIAL SCHOLARSHIP

One-time $3000 award for full-time study in heating, ventilating, refrigeration, and air conditioning in an ABET-accredited program at an accredited school. See website for application and additional information, http://www.ashrae.org.

Academic Fields/Career Goals: Electrical Engineering/Electronics; Engineering-Related Technologies; Engineering/Technology; Heating, Air-Conditioning, and Refrigeration Mechanics; Trade/Technical Specialties.

Award: Scholarship for use in freshman, sophomore, junior, or senior years; not renewable. *Number:* 1. *Amount:* $3000.

Eligibility Requirements: Applicant must be enrolled or expecting to enroll full-time at a four-year institution or university. Applicant must have 3.0 GPA or higher. Available to U.S. and non-U.S. citizens.

Application Requirements: Application form, financial need analysis, recommendations or references, transcript. *Deadline:* December 1.

Contact: Lois Benedict, Scholarship Administrator
    Phone: 404-636-8400 Ext. 1120
    E-mail: lbenedict@ashrae.org

ASHRAE REGION III BOGGARM SETTY SCHOLARSHIP
• *See page 166*

DUANE HANSON SCHOLARSHIP
One-time, $3000 scholarship available to undergraduate students pursuing a bachelor of science or engineering degree, who are enrolled full-time in a program. For study in heating, ventilating, refrigeration, and air conditioning in an ABET-accredited program at an accredited school. See website for application and additional information, http://www.ashrae.org.

Academic Fields/Career Goals: Electrical Engineering/Electronics; Engineering-Related Technologies; Engineering/Technology; Heating, Air-Conditioning, and Refrigeration Mechanics; Trade/Technical Specialties.

Award: Scholarship for use in freshman, sophomore, junior, or senior years; not renewable. *Number:* 1. *Amount:* $3000.

Eligibility Requirements: Applicant must be enrolled or expecting to enroll full-time at a four-year institution or university. Applicant must have 3.0 GPA or higher. Available to U.S. and non-U.S. citizens.

Application Requirements: Application form, financial need analysis, recommendations or references, transcript. *Deadline:* December 1.

Contact: Lois Benedict, Scholarship Administrator
    Phone: 404-636-8400 Ext. 1120
    E-mail: lbenedict@ashrae.org

ENGINEERING TECHNOLOGY SCHOLARSHIP
Three one-year $3000 scholarships available annually to full-time engineering technology students enrolled in or accepted to a post-secondary educational institution for a bachelor degree or an associate degree and pursuing a course of study which is a preparatory curriculum for the HVAC&R profession. Minimum 3.0 GPA required.

Academic Fields/Career Goals: Electrical Engineering/Electronics; Energy and Power Engineering; Engineering/Technology; Heating, Air-Conditioning, and Refrigeration Mechanics.

Award: Scholarship for use in freshman year; not renewable. *Number:* 3. *Amount:* $3000.

Eligibility Requirements: Applicant must be enrolled or expecting to enroll full-time at a two-year or four-year institution or university. Applicant must have 3.0 GPA or higher.

Application Requirements: Application form, recommendations or references, transcript. *Deadline:* May 1.

Contact: Lois Benedict, Scholarship Administrator
    Phone: 404-636-8400 Ext. 1120
    E-mail: lbenedict@ashrae.org

FRANK M. CODA SCHOLARSHIP
$5000 award to undergraduate students enrolled full-time in an ABET-accredited program leading to bachelor of science or engineering degree in a course of study that traditionally has been a preparatory curriculum for the HVAC&R profession. Future service to the HVAC&R profession, character and leadership ability are taken into consideration. For application and additional information see website, http://www.ashrae.org.

Academic Fields/Career Goals: Electrical Engineering/Electronics; Engineering-Related Technologies; Engineering/Technology; Heating,

Air-Conditioning, and Refrigeration Mechanics; Mechanical Engineering; Trade/Technical Specialties.

Award: Scholarship for use in sophomore, junior, or senior years; not renewable. *Number:* 1. *Amount:* $5000.

Eligibility Requirements: Applicant must be enrolled or expecting to enroll full-time at a four-year institution or university and must have an interest in leadership. Applicant must have 3.0 GPA or higher. Available to U.S. and non-U.S. citizens.

Application Requirements: Application form, financial need analysis, recommendations or references, transcript. *Deadline:* December 1.

Contact: Lois Benedict, Scholarship Administrator
    Phone: 404-636-8400 Ext. 1120
    E-mail: lbenedict@ashrae.org

HENRY ADAMS SCHOLARSHIP
One-time $3000 award for full-time study in heating, ventilating, refrigeration, and air conditioning in an ABET-accredited program at an accredited school. Must be pursuing a bachelor of science or engineering degree. See website for application and additional information, http://www.ashrae.org.

Academic Fields/Career Goals: Electrical Engineering/Electronics; Engineering-Related Technologies; Engineering/Technology; Heating, Air-Conditioning, and Refrigeration Mechanics; Trade/Technical Specialties.

Award: Scholarship for use in freshman, sophomore, junior, or senior years; not renewable. *Number:* 1. *Amount:* $3000.

Eligibility Requirements: Applicant must be enrolled or expecting to enroll full-time at a four-year institution or university and must have an interest in leadership. Applicant must have 3.0 GPA or higher. Available to U.S. and non-U.S. citizens.

Application Requirements: Application form, financial need analysis, recommendations or references, transcript. *Deadline:* December 1.

Contact: Lois Benedict, Scholarship Administrator
    Phone: 404-636-8400 Ext. 1120
    E-mail: lbenedict@ashrae.org

LYNN G. BELLENGER SCHOLARSHIP
One-year $3000 scholarship available to a female undergraduate engineering technology student enrolled full-time in a post-secondary educational institution and pursuing a bachelor or an associate degree in a course of study which has traditionally been a preparatory curriculum for the HVAC&R profession.

Academic Fields/Career Goals: Electrical Engineering/Electronics; Engineering-Related Technologies; Engineering/Technology; Mechanical Engineering; Trade/Technical Specialties.

Award: Scholarship for use in sophomore, junior, or senior years; not renewable. *Number:* 1. *Amount:* $3000.

Eligibility Requirements: Applicant must be enrolled or expecting to enroll full-time at a two-year or four-year institution or university and female. Applicant must have 3.0 GPA or higher. Available to U.S. citizens.

Application Requirements: Application form, financial need analysis, recommendations or references, transcript. *Deadline:* December 1.

Contact: Lois Benedict, Scholarship Administrator
    Phone: 404-636-8400 Ext. 1120
    E-mail: lbenedict@ashrae.org

REUBEN TRANE SCHOLARSHIP
Undergraduate engineering scholarships awarded in two disbursements of $5000 each at the beginning of the student's junior and senior year. Must be a full-time student enrolled in a bachelor of science or engineering degree accredited by the Accreditation Board for Engineering and Technology. See website for application package and additional information, http://www.ashrae.org.

Academic Fields/Career Goals: Electrical Engineering/Electronics; Energy and Power Engineering; Engineering/Technology; Heating, Air-Conditioning, and Refrigeration Mechanics; Mechanical Engineering; Trade/Technical Specialties.

Award: Scholarship for use in junior or senior years; renewable. *Number:* 2. *Amount:* $10,000.

Eligibility Requirements: Applicant must be enrolled or expecting to enroll full-time at a four-year institution or university. Applicant must have 3.0 GPA or higher. Available to U.S. and non-U.S. citizens.

Application Requirements: Application form, financial need analysis, recommendations or references, transcript. *Deadline:* December 1.

Contact: Lois Benedict, Scholarship Administrator
  Phone: 404-636-8400 Ext. 1120
  E-mail: lbenedict@ashrae.org

WILLIS H. CARRIER SCHOLARSHIPS

Two, one-year scholarships of $10,000 available to undergraduate students enrolled full time in an ABET-accredited program leading to a bachelor of science or engineering degree. Minimum 3.0 GPA required. See website for application and further details, http://www.ashrae.org.

Academic Fields/Career Goals: Electrical Engineering/Electronics; Engineering-Related Technologies; Engineering/Technology; Heating, Air-Conditioning, and Refrigeration Mechanics.

Award: Scholarship for use in sophomore, junior, or senior years; not renewable. *Number:* 2. *Amount:* $10,000.

Eligibility Requirements: Applicant must be enrolled or expecting to enroll full-time at a four-year institution or university. Applicant must have 3.0 GPA or higher. Available to U.S. citizens.

Application Requirements: Application form, financial need analysis, recommendations or references, transcript. *Deadline:* December 1.

Contact: Lois Benedict, Scholarship Administrator
  Phone: 404-636-8400 Ext. 1120
  E-mail: lbenedict@ashrae.org

AMERICAN SOCIETY OF NAVAL ENGINEERS

http://www.navalengineers.org/

AMERICAN SOCIETY OF NAVAL ENGINEERS SCHOLARSHIP
• *See page 103*

ARMED FORCES COMMUNICATIONS AND ELECTRONICS ASSOCIATION, EDUCATIONAL FOUNDATION

http://www.afcea.org/scholarships

ARMED FORCES COMMUNICATIONS AND ELECTRONICS ASSOCIATION GENERAL EMMETT PAIGE SCHOLARSHIP
• *See page 127*

ARMED FORCES COMMUNICATIONS AND ELECTRONICS ASSOCIATION ROTC SCHOLARSHIP PROGRAM
• *See page 127*

DISABLED WAR VETERANS SCHOLARSHIP
• *See page 128*

LTG DOUGLAS D. BUCHHOLZ MEMORIAL SCHOLARSHIP
• *See page 128*

VETERANS OF ENDURING FREEDOM (AFGHANISTAN) AND IRAQI FREEDOM SCHOLARSHIP
• *See page 200*

ARRL FOUNDATION INC.

http://www.arrl.org/

ALFRED E. FRIEND JR., W4CF, MEMORIAL SCHOLARSHIP
• *See page 166*

ANDROSCOGGIN AMATEUR RADIO CLUB SCHOLARSHIP
• *See page 200*

BETTY WEATHERFORD, KQ6RE, MEMORIAL SCHOLARSHIP

$1000 award for a student with an Amateur Radio license in any class. Must be studying electrical or communications engineering.

Academic Fields/Career Goals: Electrical Engineering/Electronics; Engineering/Technology.

Award: Scholarship for use in freshman, sophomore, junior, or senior years; not renewable. *Number:* 1. *Amount:* $1000.

Eligibility Requirements: Applicant must be enrolled or expecting to enroll full- or part-time at a two-year or four-year or technical institution or university and must have an interest in amateur radio.

Application Requirements: Application form, transcript. *Deadline:* February 1.

Contact: Ms. Mary Hobart, Secretary
  Phone: 860-594-0397
  E-mail: k1mmh@arrl.org

CHARLES CLARKE CORDLE MEMORIAL SCHOLARSHIP
• *See page 188*

CHARLES N. FISHER MEMORIAL SCHOLARSHIP
• *See page 103*

DR. JAMES L. LAWSON MEMORIAL SCHOLARSHIP
• *See page 188*

EARL I. ANDERSON SCHOLARSHIP

Award for students in electronic engineering or related technical field. Student must be an amateur radio operator and member of the American Radio Relay League. Preference given to students who are residents of and attend classes in Illinois, Indiana, Michigan, or Florida.

Academic Fields/Career Goals: Electrical Engineering/Electronics.

Award: Scholarship for use in freshman, sophomore, junior, or senior years; not-renewable. *Number:* 3. *Amount:* $1250.

Eligibility Requirements: Applicant must be enrolled or expecting to enroll full-time at a four-year institution or university; resident of Florida, Illinois, Indiana, Michigan; studying in Florida, Illinois, Indiana, Michigan and must have an interest in amateur radio. Applicant or parent of applicant must be member of American Radio Relay League. Available to U.S. citizens.

Application Requirements: Application form, transcript. *Deadline:* February 1.

Contact: Ms. Mary Hobart, Secretary
  Phone: 860-594-0397
  E-mail: k1mmh@arrl.org

EDMOND A. METZGER SCHOLARSHIP

Scholarship for licensed amateur radio operators, at the novice class or above. Applicants must be undergraduate or graduate electrical engineering students and members of the Amateur Radio Relay League.

Academic Fields/Career Goals: Electrical Engineering/Electronics.

Award: Scholarship for use in freshman, sophomore, junior, senior, or graduate years; not renewable. *Number:* 1. *Amount:* $500.

Eligibility Requirements: Applicant must be enrolled or expecting to enroll full-time at a four-year institution or university; resident of Illinois, Indiana, Wisconsin; studying in Illinois, Indiana, Wisconsin and must have an interest in amateur radio. Applicant or parent of applicant must be member of American Radio Relay League. Available to U.S. citizens.

Application Requirements: Application form, transcript. *Deadline:* February 1.

Contact: Ms. Mary Hobart, Secretary
Phone: 860-594-0397
E-mail: k1mmh@arrl.org

EUGENE "GENE" SALLEE, W4YFR, MEMORIAL SCHOLARSHIP
• See page 188

FRANCIS WALTON MEMORIAL SCHOLARSHIP
• See page 91

FRED R. MCDANIEL MEMORIAL SCHOLARSHIP
• See page 188

GARY WAGNER, K3OMI, SCHOLARSHIP
• See page 166

INDIANAPOLIS AMATEUR RADIO ASSOCIATION SCHOLARSHIP FUND
• See page 200

IRARC MEMORIAL, JOSEPH P. RUBINO, WA4MMD, SCHOLARSHIP

Need-based award available to licensed amateur radio operators. Preference is given to Brevard County, FL residents or to all Florida residents. Must maintain 2.5 GPA and pursue an undergraduate degree or electronic technician certification at an accredited institution.

Academic Fields/Career Goals: Electrical Engineering/Electronics.

Award: Scholarship for use in freshman, sophomore, junior, or senior years; not renewable. Amount: $750.

Eligibility Requirements: Applicant must be enrolled or expecting to enroll full-time at a two-year or four-year or technical institution or university; resident of Florida and must have an interest in amateur radio. Applicant or parent of applicant must be member of American Radio Relay League. Applicant must have 2.5 GPA or higher. Available to U.S. citizens.

Application Requirements: Application form, financial need analysis, transcript. Deadline: February 1.

Contact: Ms. Mary Hobart, Secretary
Phone: 860-594-0397
E-mail: k1mmh@arrl.org

IRVING W. COOK, WA0CGS, SCHOLARSHIP
• See page 189

JAKE MCCLAIN DRIVER, KC5WXA, SCHOLARSHIP FUND
• See page 200

L. PHIL AND ALICE J. WICKER SCHOLARSHIP
• See page 189

MAGNOLIA DX ASSOCIATION SCHOLARSHIP
• See page 189

MISSISSIPPI SCHOLARSHIP
• See page 103

PAUL AND HELEN L. GRAUER SCHOLARSHIP
• See page 103

PHD SCHOLARSHIP
• See page 201

RAY, N0RP, & KATIE, W0KTE, PAUTZ SCHOLARSHIP
• See page 201

VICTOR POOR, W5SMM, MEMORIAL SCHOLARSHIP FUND

$2500 scholarship for a student of electrical engineering, with a preference for concentration in digital communications. Must have a Technical Class or higher radio license.

Academic Fields/Career Goals: Electrical Engineering/Electronics.

Award: Scholarship for use in freshman, sophomore, junior, or senior years; not renewable. Number: 1. Amount: $2500.

Eligibility Requirements: Applicant must be enrolled or expecting to enroll full- or part-time at a two-year or four-year or technical institution or university and must have an interest in amateur radio. Available to U.S. citizens.

Application Requirements: Application form, transcript. Deadline: February 1.

Contact: Ms. Mary Hobart, Secretary
Phone: 860-594-0397
E-mail: k1mmh@arrl.org

ASTRONAUT SCHOLARSHIP FOUNDATION
http://www.astronautscholarship.org/

ASTRONAUT SCHOLARSHIP FOUNDATION
• See page 104

BRASKEM ODEBRECHT
http://www.odebrechtaward.com

ODEBRECHT AWARD FOR SUSTAINABLE DEVELOPMENT
• See page 110

CATCHING THE DREAM
http://www.catchingthedream.org/

TRIBAL BUSINESS MANAGEMENT PROGRAM (TBM)
• See page 70

CENTRAL INTELLIGENCE AGENCY
http://www.cia.gov/

CENTRAL INTELLIGENCE AGENCY UNDERGRADUATE SCHOLARSHIP PROGRAM
• See page 70

CUBAN AMERICAN NATIONAL FOUNDATION
http://www.masscholarships.org/

MAS FAMILY SCHOLARSHIPS
• See page 152

ELECTROCHEMICAL SOCIETY INC.
http://www.electrochem.org/

H.H. DOW MEMORIAL STUDENT ACHIEVEMENT AWARD OF THE INDUSTRIAL ELECTROLYSIS AND ELECTROCHEMICAL ENGINEERING DIVISION OF THE ELECTROCHEMICAL SOCIETY INC.
• See page 104

STUDENT RESEARCH AWARDS OF THE BATTERY DIVISION OF THE ELECTROCHEMICAL SOCIETY INC.
• See page 105

FOUNDATION FOR SCIENCE AND DISABILITY
http://stemd.org/

GRANTS FOR DISABLED STUDENTS IN THE SCIENCES
• See page 105

GREATER KANAWHA VALLEY FOUNDATION

http://www.tgkvf.org/

STEVEN ENGINEERING SCHOLARSHIP
• *See page 167*

GREAT MINDS IN STEM

http://www.greatmindsinstem.org

HISPANIC ENGINEER NATIONAL ACHIEVEMENT AWARDS CORPORATION SCHOLARSHIP PROGRAM
• *See page 130*

HAWAIIAN LODGE, F&AM

http://www.hawaiianlodgefreemasons.org/

HAWAIIAN LODGE SCHOLARSHIPS
• *See page 114*

ILLUMINATING ENGINEERING SOCIETY OF NORTH AMERICA–GOLDEN GATE SECTION

http://www.iesgg.org/

ALAN LUCAS MEMORIAL EDUCATIONAL SCHOLARSHIP
• *See page 111*

INDEPENDENT LABORATORIES INSTITUTE SCHOLARSHIP ALLIANCE

http://www.acil.org/

INDEPENDENT LABORATORIES INSTITUTE SCHOLARSHIP ALLIANCE
• *See page 145*

INSTITUTE OF INTERNATIONAL EDUCATION (FULBRIGHT PROGRAM)

http://www.us.fulbrightonline.org/

WHITAKER INTERNATIONAL PROGRAM
• *See page 145*

INTERNATIONAL COMMUNICATIONS INDUSTRIES FOUNDATION

http://www.infocomm.org/scholarships

ICIF SCHOLARSHIP FOR EMPLOYEES AND DEPENDENTS OF MEMBER ORGANIZATIONS
• *See page 191*

INTERNATIONAL COMMUNICATIONS INDUSTRIES FOUNDATION AV SCHOLARSHIP
• *See page 191*

INTERNATIONAL SOCIETY FOR OPTICAL ENGINEERING-SPIE

http://www.spie.org/scholarships

SPIE EDUCATIONAL SCHOLARSHIPS IN OPTICAL SCIENCE AND ENGINEERING
• *See page 105*

INTERNATIONAL SOCIETY OF AUTOMATION (ISA)

http://www.isa.org/

INTERNATIONAL SOCIETY OF AUTOMATION EDUCATION FOUNDATION SCHOLARSHIPS
• *See page 131*

JORGE MAS CANOSA FREEDOM FOUNDATION

http://www.jorgemascanosa.org/

MAS FAMILY SCHOLARSHIP AWARD
• *See page 156*

KOREAN-AMERICAN SCIENTISTS AND ENGINEERS ASSOCIATION

http://www.ksea.org/

KSEA SCHOLARSHIPS
Scholarship for undergraduate or graduate students in the United States with Korean heritage. Applicant should major in science, engineering, or related fields and should be a KSEA member.
Academic Fields/Career Goals: Electrical Engineering/Electronics; Engineering-Related Technologies; Engineering/Technology; Science, Technology, and Society.
Award: Scholarship for use in freshman, sophomore, junior, senior, or graduate years; not renewable. *Number:* 1–35. *Amount:* $1000–$1500.
Eligibility Requirements: Applicant must be of Korean heritage; Asian/Pacific Islander and enrolled or expecting to enroll full-time at a two-year or four-year institution or university. Applicant or parent of applicant must be member of Korean-American Scientists and Engineers Association. Available to U.S. citizens.
Application Requirements: Application form, essay, recommendations or references, resume, transcript. *Deadline:* February 15.

LOS ANGELES COUNCIL OF BLACK PROFESSIONAL ENGINEERS

http://www.lablackengineers.org/

AL-BEN SCHOLARSHIP FOR ACADEMIC INCENTIVE
• *See page 168*

AL-BEN SCHOLARSHIP FOR PROFESSIONAL MERIT
• *See page 168*

AL-BEN SCHOLARSHIP FOR SCHOLASTIC ACHIEVEMENT
• *See page 168*

MICHIGAN SOCIETY OF PROFESSIONAL ENGINEERS

http://www.michiganspe.org/

MICHIGAN SOCIETY OF PROFESSIONAL ENGINEERS HARRY R. BALL, P.E. GRANT
• *See page 169*

MICHIGAN SOCIETY OF PROFESSIONAL ENGINEERS KENNETH B. FISHBECK, P.E. MEMORIAL GRANT
• *See page 169*

NASA IDAHO SPACE GRANT CONSORTIUM

http://www.id.spacegrant.org/

NASA IDAHO SPACE GRANT CONSORTIUM SCHOLARSHIP PROGRAM
• *See page 146*

NASA MONTANA SPACE GRANT CONSORTIUM

http://www.spacegrant.montana.edu/

MONTANA SPACE GRANT SCHOLARSHIP PROGRAM
• *See page 133*

NASA'S VIRGINIA SPACE GRANT CONSORTIUM

http://www.vsgc.odu.edu/

COMMUNITY COLLEGE STEM SCHOLARSHIPS
• *See page 105*

UNDERGRADUATE STEM RESEARCH SCHOLARSHIPS
• *See page 106*

NATIONAL ASSOCIATION OF WOMEN IN CONSTRUCTION

http://www.nawic.org/

NAWIC UNDERGRADUATE SCHOLARSHIPS
• *See page 112*

NATIONAL BOARD OF BOILER AND PRESSURE VESSEL INSPECTORS

http://www.nationalboard.org/

NATIONAL BOARD TECHNICAL SCHOLARSHIP
• *See page 169*

NATIONAL SECURITY AGENCY

http://www.nsa.gov/Careers

NATIONAL SECURITY AGENCY STOKES EDUCATIONAL SCHOLARSHIP PROGRAM
• *See page 203*

NATIONAL SOCIETY OF PROFESSIONAL ENGINEERS

http://www.nspe.org/

MAUREEN L. AND HOWARD N. BLITMAN, PE SCHOLARSHIP TO PROMOTE DIVERSITY IN ENGINEERING
• *See page 170*

PAUL H. ROBBINS HONORARY SCHOLARSHIP
• *See page 170*

PROFESSIONAL ENGINEERS IN INDUSTRY SCHOLARSHIP
• *See page 170*

OREGON STUDENT ASSISTANCE COMMISSION

http://www.GetCollegeFunds.org/

HOME BUILDERS FOUNDATION JIM IRVINE STATEWIDE SCHOLARSHIP
• *See page 112*

SOCIETY OF AMERICAN MILITARY ENGINEERS PORTLAND POST SCHOLARSHIP
• *See page 170*

PROFESSIONAL CONSTRUCTION ESTIMATORS ASSOCIATION

http://www.pcea.org/

TED G. WILSON MEMORIAL SCHOLARSHIP FOUNDATION
• *See page 184*

ROBERT H. MOLLOHAN FAMILY CHARITABLE FOUNDATION, INC.

http://www.mollohanfoundation.org/

HIGH TECHNOLOGY SCHOLARS PROGRAM
• *See page 147*

SEMICONDUCTOR RESEARCH CORPORATION (SRC)

http://www.src.org/

MASTER'S SCHOLARSHIP PROGRAM
• *See page 171*

SOCIETY OF AUTOMOTIVE ENGINEERS

http://www.sae.org/

BMW/SAE ENGINEERING SCHOLARSHIP
• *See page 137*

EDWARD D. HENDRICKSON/SAE ENGINEERING SCHOLARSHIP
• *See page 137*

TMC/SAE DONALD D. DAWSON TECHNICAL SCHOLARSHIP
• *See page 137*

SOCIETY OF BROADCAST ENGINEERS INC.

http://www.sbe.org/

ROBERT GREENBERG/HAROLD E. ENNES SCHOLARSHIP FUND AND ENNES EDUCATIONAL FOUNDATION BROADCAST TECHNOLOGY SCHOLARSHIP

Merit-based awards for undergraduate students to study the technical aspects of broadcast engineering. Students should apply as high school senior or college freshman and may use the award for a two- or four-year college or university program. One-time award of $1000¿$1500.

Academic Fields/Career Goals: Electrical Engineering/Electronics; Engineering-Related Technologies; TV/Radio Broadcasting.

Award: Scholarship for use in freshman, sophomore, junior, or senior years; renewable. *Number:* 3. *Amount:* $1000–$1500.

Eligibility Requirements: Applicant must be enrolled or expecting to enroll full-time at a two-year or four-year institution or university. Applicant must have 3.0 GPA or higher. Available to U.S. citizens.
Application Requirements: Application form, essay, recommendations or references, self-addressed stamped envelope with application, transcript. *Deadline:* July 1.

SOCIETY OF MANUFACTURING ENGINEERS EDUCATION FOUNDATION
http://www.smeef.org/

WILLIAM E. WEISEL SCHOLARSHIP FUND
Scholarship will be given to a full-time undergraduate student enrolled in an engineering or technology degree program in the U.S. or Canada, seeking a career in manufacturing. Consideration will be given to students who intend to apply their knowledge in the sub-specialty of medical robotics. Minimum of 3.0 GPA is required. Scholarships will be limited to United States and Canadian citizens.
Academic Fields/Career Goals: Electrical Engineering/Electronics; Engineering/Technology; Mechanical Engineering; Trade/Technical Specialties.
Award: Scholarship for use in sophomore, junior, or senior years; not renewable. *Number:* 1–10. *Amount:* $1000–$5000.
Eligibility Requirements: Applicant must be enrolled or expecting to enroll full-time at a four-year institution or university. Applicant must have 3.0 GPA or higher. Available to U.S. and Canadian citizens.
Application Requirements: Application form, essay, recommendations or references, resume, transcript. *Deadline:* February 1.

SOCIETY OF MOTION PICTURE AND TELEVISION ENGINEERS
http://www.smpte.org/

LOUIS F. WOLF JR. MEMORIAL SCHOLARSHIP
• *See page 195*

STUDENT PAPER AWARD
• *See page 195*

SOCIETY OF PLASTICS ENGINEERS (SPE) FOUNDATION
http://www.4spe.org/

FLEMING/BASZCAK SCHOLARSHIP
• *See page 171*

SOCIETY OF PLASTICS ENGINEERS SCHOLARSHIP PROGRAM
• *See page 171*

SOCIETY OF WOMEN ENGINEERS
http://www.swe.org/

ACCENTURE SCHOLARSHIP
• *See page 172*

ADA I. PRESSMAN MEMORIAL SCHOLARSHIP
• *See page 172*

ANNE MAUREEN WHITNEY BARROW MEMORIAL SCHOLARSHIP
• *See page 172*

BERTHA LAMME MEMORIAL SCHOLARSHIP
One $1200 award for women pursuing ABET-accredited baccalaureate programs in preparation for careers in electric engineering in the United States and Mexico. Must be a U.S. citizen. Minimum 3.5 GPA required.

Academic Fields/Career Goals: Electrical Engineering/Electronics.
Award: Scholarship for use in freshman year; not renewable. *Number:* 1. *Amount:* $1200.
Eligibility Requirements: Applicant must be enrolled or expecting to enroll full-time at a four-year institution or university and female. Applicant must have 3.5 GPA or higher. Available to U.S. citizens.
Application Requirements: Application form, recommendations or references. *Deadline:* May 15.

BETTY LOU BAILEY SWE REGION F SCHOLARSHIP
• *See page 172*

BK KRENZER MEMORIAL REENTRY SCHOLARSHIP
• *See page 172*

BOSTON SCIENTIFIC SCHOLARSHIP
• *See page 172*

CAROL STEPHENS REGION F SCHOLARSHIP
• *See page 172*

CATERPILLAR INC. SCHOLARSHIP
• *See page 172*

CISCO'S FUTURE SCHOLARSHIP
• *See page 204*

CUMMINS INC. SCHOLARSHIP
• *See page 173*

DELL SCHOLARSHIP
• *See page 204*

DR. IVY M. PARKER MEMORIAL SCHOLARSHIP
• *See page 173*

DOROTHY LEMKE HOWARTH MEMORIAL SCHOLARSHIP
• *See page 173*

DOROTHY P. MORRIS SCHOLARSHIP
• *See page 173*

FORD MOTOR COMPANY SCHOLARSHIP
$1000 scholarship for women pursuing ABET-accredited baccalaureate programs in preparation for careers in engineering and engineering technology in the United States and Mexico. Must have leadership potential.
Academic Fields/Career Goals: Electrical Engineering/Electronics; Engineering/Technology; Mechanical Engineering.
Award: Scholarship for use in sophomore or junior years; not renewable. *Number:* 3. *Amount:* $1000.
Eligibility Requirements: Applicant must be enrolled or expecting to enroll full-time at a four-year institution or university; female and must have an interest in leadership. Available to U.S. citizens.
Application Requirements: Application form, recommendations or references. *Deadline:* February 15.

GENERAL ELECTRIC WOMEN'S NETWORK SCHOLARSHIP
• *See page 185*

GOLDMAN, SACHS & CO. SCHOLARSHIP
• *See page 204*

HONEYWELL CORPORATION SCHOLARSHIP
• *See page 173*

IBM CORPORATION SCHOLARSHIP
• *See page 204*

ITW SCHOLARSHIP
• *See page 204*

JILL S. TIETJEN P.E. SCHOLARSHIP

LIFE TECHNOLOGIES SCHOLARSHIP

LILLIAN MOLLER GILBRETH MEMORIAL SCHOLARSHIP

LOCKHEED MARTIN AERONAUTICS CORPORATION SCHOLARSHIPS

MARY V. MUNGER SCHOLARSHIP

MASWE MEMORIAL SCHOLARSHIP

MERIDITH THOMS MEMORIAL SCHOLARSHIPS

OLIVE LYNN SALEMBIER MEMORIAL REENTRY SCHOLARSHIP

ROCKWELL COLLINS SCHOLARSHIP

SUSAN MISZKOWICZ MEMORIAL SCHOLARSHIP

SWE BALTIMORE-WASHINGTON SECTION SCHOLARSHIP

SWE CENTRAL NEW MEXICO PIONEERS SCHOLARSHIP

SWE CENTRAL NEW MEXICO REENTRY SCHOLARSHIP

SWE MID-HUDSON SECTION SCHOLARSHIP

SWE PAST PRESIDENTS SCHOLARSHIP

SWE PHOENIX SECTION SCHOLARSHIP

SWE REGION H SCHOLARSHIPS

VERIZON SCHOLARSHIP

WANDA MUNN SCHOLARSHIP

SOCIETY OF WOMEN ENGINEERS-ROCKY MOUNTAIN SECTION

http://www.societyofwomenengineers.org/RockyMountain/

SOCIETY OF WOMEN ENGINEERS-ROCKY MOUNTAIN SECTION SCHOLARSHIP PROGRAM

SONS OF NORWAY FOUNDATION

http://www.sonsofnorway.com/

NANCY LORRAINE JENSEN MEMORIAL SCHOLARSHIP

SOUTH DAKOTA RETAILERS ASSOCIATION

http://www.sdra.org/

SOUTH DAKOTA RETAILERS ASSOCIATION SCHOLARSHIP PROGRAM

SPECIALTY EQUIPMENT MARKET ASSOCIATION

http://www.sema.org/

SPECIALTY EQUIPMENT MARKET ASSOCIATION MEMORIAL SCHOLARSHIP FUND

STRAIGHTFORWARD MEDIA

http://www.straightforwardmedia.com/

STRAIGHTFORWARD MEDIA ENGINEERING SCHOLARSHIP

TURNER CONSTRUCTION COMPANY

http://www.turnerconstruction.com/

YOUTHFORCE 2020 SCHOLARSHIP PROGRAM

UNITED NEGRO COLLEGE FUND

http://www.uncf.org/

ALFRED CHISHOLM/BASF MEMORIAL SCHOLARSHIP FUND

CDM SCHOLARSHIP/INTERNSHIP

CISCO/UNCF SCHOLARS PROGRAM

EMERSON PROCESS MANAGEMENT SCHOLARSHIP

FORD/UNCF CORPORATE SCHOLARS PROGRAM

GOOGLE SCHOLARSHIP

INTEL SCHOLARS PROGRAM

LOCKHEED MARTIN/UNCF SCHOLARSHIP

MONSANTO/UNCF 1890'S SCHOLARSHIP PROGRAM

PACIFIC GAS AND ELECTRIC COMPANY SCHOLARSHIP
• *See page 82*

SPRINT SCHOLARS PROGRAM FOR SOPHOMORES, JUNIORS, AND SENIORS
• *See page 100*

UNIVERSITIES SPACE RESEARCH ASSOCIATION

http://www.usra.edu/

UNIVERSITIES SPACE RESEARCH ASSOCIATION SCHOLARSHIP PROGRAM
• *See page 107*

UTAH SOCIETY OF PROFESSIONAL ENGINEERS

http://www.uspeonline.com/

UTAH SOCIETY OF PROFESSIONAL ENGINEERS JOE RHOADS SCHOLARSHIP
• *See page 177*

WEST VIRGINIA HIGHER EDUCATION POLICY COMMISSION-STUDENT SERVICES

http://wvhepcnew.wvnet.edu/

WEST VIRGINIA ENGINEERING, SCIENCE AND TECHNOLOGY SCHOLARSHIP PROGRAM
Award for full-time students attending West Virginia institutions, pursuing a degree in engineering, science, or technology. Must be a resident of West Virginia. Must have a 3.0 GPA, and after graduation, must work in the fields of engineering, science, or technology in West Virginia one year for each year the award was received.
Academic Fields/Career Goals: Electrical Engineering/Electronics; Engineering-Related Technologies; Engineering/Technology; Science, Technology, and Society.
Award: Scholarship for use in freshman, sophomore, junior, or senior years; renewable. *Number:* 200–300. *Amount:* $1500–$3000.
Eligibility Requirements: Applicant must be enrolled or expecting to enroll full-time at a two-year or four-year or technical institution or university; resident of West Virginia and studying in West Virginia. Applicant must have 3.0 GPA or higher. Available to U.S. citizens.
Application Requirements: Application form, essay, test scores, transcript. *Deadline:* March 1.
Contact: Jan Ruge, Scholarship Coordinator
Phone: 304-558-4618
Fax: 304-558-4266
E-mail: jruge@hepc.wvnet.edu

WOMEN IN AVIATION, INTERNATIONAL

http://www.wai.org/

DELTA AIR LINES ENGINEERING SCHOLARSHIP
• *See page 140*

XEROX

http://www.xerox.com//

TECHNICAL MINORITY SCHOLARSHIP
• See page 177

ENERGY AND POWER ENGINEERING

AMERICAN NUCLEAR SOCIETY

http://www.ans.org/

DECOMMISSIONING, DECONTAMINATION, AND REUTILIZATION UNDERGRADUATE SCHOLARSHIP
Undergraduate scholarship for students who have completed two or more years in a course of study leading to a degree in nuclear science, nuclear engineering, or a nuclear-related field.
Academic Fields/Career Goals: Energy and Power Engineering; Nuclear Science.
Award: Scholarship for use in junior or senior years; not renewable. *Number:* 1. *Amount:* $2000.
Eligibility Requirements: Applicant must be enrolled or expecting to enroll full-time at a four-year institution or university. Available to U.S. citizens.
Application Requirements: Application form, essay, recommendations or references, transcript. *Deadline:* February 1.

AMERICAN SOCIETY OF HEATING, REFRIGERATING, AND AIR CONDITIONING ENGINEERS, INC.

http://www.ashrae.org/

ASHRAE REGION III BOGGARM SETTY SCHOLARSHIP
• *See page 166*

ENGINEERING TECHNOLOGY SCHOLARSHIP
• *See page 250*

REUBEN TRANE SCHOLARSHIP
• *See page 250*

AMERICAN SOCIETY OF NAVAL ENGINEERS

http://www.navalengineers.org/

AMERICAN SOCIETY OF NAVAL ENGINEERS SCHOLARSHIP
• *See page 103*

ARRL FOUNDATION INC.

http://www.arrl.org/

ALFRED E. FRIEND JR., W4CF, MEMORIAL SCHOLARSHIP
• *See page 166*

GARY WAGNER, K3OMI, SCHOLARSHIP
• *See page 166*

BRASKEM ODEBRECHT

http://www.odebrechtaward.com

ODEBRECHT AWARD FOR SUSTAINABLE DEVELOPMENT
• *See page 110*

ELECTROCHEMICAL SOCIETY INC.

http://www.electrochem.org/

H.H. DOW MEMORIAL STUDENT ACHIEVEMENT AWARD OF THE INDUSTRIAL ELECTROLYSIS AND ELECTROCHEMICAL ENGINEERING DIVISION OF THE ELECTROCHEMICAL SOCIETY INC.
• *See page 104*

STUDENT RESEARCH AWARDS OF THE BATTERY DIVISION OF THE ELECTROCHEMICAL SOCIETY INC.
• *See page 105*

GREATER KANAWHA VALLEY FOUNDATION

http://www.tgkvf.org/

LEOPOLD & ELIZABETH MARMET SCHOLARSHIP
Renewable award to West Virginia residents pursuing full-time postsecondary studies in science, production or conservation of energy, or natural resources. Award may not be used for medical studies. Minimum 2.5 GPA required. Preference given to graduate students.
Academic Fields/Career Goals: Energy and Power Engineering; Natural Resources.
Award: Scholarship for use in freshman, sophomore, junior, senior, or graduate years; renewable. *Amount:* $3000.
Eligibility Requirements: Applicant must be enrolled or expecting to enroll full-time at a four-year institution or university and resident of West Virginia. Applicant must have 2.5 GPA or higher. Available to U.S. citizens.
Application Requirements: Application form, financial need analysis, recommendations or references, test scores, transcript. *Deadline:* January 15.
Contact: Susan Hoover, Scholarship Program Officer
        Charleston, WV 25301
        Phone: 304-346-3620
        E-mail: tgkvf@tgkvf.org

STEVEN ENGINEERING SCHOLARSHIP
• *See page 167*

HAWAIIAN LODGE, F&AM

http://www.hawaiianlodgefreemasons.org/

HAWAIIAN LODGE SCHOLARSHIPS
• *See page 114*

INTERNATIONAL SOCIETY OF AUTOMATION (ISA)

http://www.isa.org/

INTERNATIONAL SOCIETY OF AUTOMATION EDUCATION FOUNDATION SCHOLARSHIPS
• *See page 131*

NASA SOUTH DAKOTA SPACE GRANT CONSORTIUM

http://sdspacegrant.sdsmt.edu/

SOUTH DAKOTA SPACE GRANT CONSORTIUM UNDERGRADUATE AND GRADUATE STUDENT SCHOLARSHIPS
• *See page 134*

NASA WEST VIRGINIA SPACE GRANT CONSORTIUM

http://www.nasa.wvu.edu/

WEST VIRGINIA SPACE GRANT CONSORTIUM UNDERGRADUATE FELLOWSHIP PROGRAM
• *See page 134*

ROBERT H. MOLLOHAN FAMILY CHARITABLE FOUNDATION, INC.

http://www.mollohanfoundation.org/

HIGH TECHNOLOGY SCHOLARS PROGRAM
• *See page 147*

SOCIETY OF WOMEN ENGINEERS

http://www.swe.org/

ADA I. PRESSMAN MEMORIAL SCHOLARSHIP
• *See page 172*

ANNE MAUREEN WHITNEY BARROW MEMORIAL SCHOLARSHIP
• *See page 172*

BETTY LOU BAILEY SWE REGION F SCHOLARSHIP
• *See page 172*

BK KRENZER MEMORIAL REENTRY SCHOLARSHIP
• *See page 172*

CAROL STEPHENS REGION F SCHOLARSHIP
• *See page 172*

DR. IVY M. PARKER MEMORIAL SCHOLARSHIP
• *See page 173*

DOROTHY LEMKE HOWARTH MEMORIAL SCHOLARSHIP
• *See page 173*

DOROTHY P. MORRIS SCHOLARSHIP
• *See page 173*

JILL S. TIETJEN P.E. SCHOLARSHIP
• *See page 173*

LILLIAN MOLLER GILBRETH MEMORIAL SCHOLARSHIP
• *See page 174*

MARY V. MUNGER SCHOLARSHIP
• *See page 174*

MASWE MEMORIAL SCHOLARSHIP
• *See page 174*

MERIDITH THOMS MEMORIAL SCHOLARSHIPS
• *See page 174*

OLIVE LYNN SALEMBIER MEMORIAL REENTRY SCHOLARSHIP
• *See page 174*

SUSAN MISZKOWICZ MEMORIAL SCHOLARSHIP
• *See page 175*

SWE BALTIMORE-WASHINGTON SECTION SCHOLARSHIP
• *See page 175*

SWE CENTRAL NEW MEXICO PIONEERS SCHOLARSHIP

SWE CENTRAL NEW MEXICO REENTRY SCHOLARSHIP

SWE MID-HUDSON SECTION SCHOLARSHIP

SWE PAST PRESIDENTS SCHOLARSHIP

SWE PHOENIX SECTION SCHOLARSHIP

SWE REGION H SCHOLARSHIPS

WANDA MUNN SCHOLARSHIP

SOCIETY OF WOMEN ENGINEERS-ROCKY MOUNTAIN SECTION
http://www.societyofwomenengineers.org/RockyMountain/

SOCIETY OF WOMEN ENGINEERS-ROCKY MOUNTAIN SECTION SCHOLARSHIP PROGRAM

STRAIGHTFORWARD MEDIA
http://www.straightforwardmedia.com/

STRAIGHTFORWARD MEDIA ENGINEERING SCHOLARSHIP

UTAH SOCIETY OF PROFESSIONAL ENGINEERS
http://www.uspeonline.com/

UTAH SOCIETY OF PROFESSIONAL ENGINEERS JOE RHOADS SCHOLARSHIP

ENGINEERING-RELATED TECHNOLOGIES

AACE INTERNATIONAL
http://www.aacei.org/

AACE INTERNATIONAL COMPETITIVE SCHOLARSHIP

AHS INTERNATIONAL—THE VERTICAL FLIGHT TECHNICAL SOCIETY
http://www.vtol.org/

VERTICAL FLIGHT FOUNDATION SCHOLARSHIP

AIST FOUNDATION
http://www.aistfoundation.org/

ASSOCIATION FOR IRON AND STEEL TECHNOLOGY BALTIMORE CHAPTER SCHOLARSHIP
Scholarship for child, grandchild, or spouse of a member of the Baltimore Chapter of AIST. Must be high school seniors who are currently enrolled undergraduate students pursuing a career in engineering or metallurgy. Student may reapply each year for the term of their college education.

Academic Fields/Career Goals: Engineering-Related Technologies; Engineering/Technology; Materials Science, Engineering, and Metallurgy.

Award: Scholarship for use in freshman, sophomore, junior, or senior years; not renewable. *Number:* 1. *Amount:* $1500.

Eligibility Requirements: Applicant must be enrolled or expecting to enroll full-time at a four-year institution or university. Applicant or parent of applicant must be member of Association for Iron and Steel Technology. Available to U.S. citizens.

Application Requirements: Application form, essay, test scores, transcript. *Deadline:* April 30.

Contact: Thomas Russo, Program Coordinator
AIST Foundation
1430 Sparrows Point Boulevard
Sparrows Point, MD 21219-1014

ASSOCIATION FOR IRON AND STEEL TECHNOLOGY BENJAMIN F. FAIRLESS SCHOLARSHIP (AIME)

ASSOCIATION FOR IRON AND STEEL TECHNOLOGY OHIO VALLEY CHAPTER SCHOLARSHIP

AMERICAN COUNCIL OF ENGINEERING COMPANIES OF PENNSYLVANIA (ACEC/PA)
http://www.acecpa.org/

ENGINEERING SCHOLARSHIP

AMERICAN INSTITUTE OF AERONAUTICS AND ASTRONAUTICS
http://www.aiaa.org/

AIAA FOUNDATION UNDERGRADUATE SCHOLARSHIP

AMERICAN PUBLIC TRANSPORTATION FOUNDATION
http://www.apta.com/

TRANSIT HALL OF FAME SCHOLARSHIP AWARD PROGRAM

AMERICAN RAILWAY ENGINEERING AND MAINTENANCE OF WAY ASSOCIATION
http://www.aremafoundation.org/

AREMA MICHAEL R. GARCIA SCHOLARSHIP

AREMA PRESIDENTIAL SPOUSE SCHOLARSHIP

AREMA UNDERGRADUATE SCHOLARSHIPS
• *See page 180*

COMMITTEE 12-RAIL TRANSIT UNDERGRADUATE SCHOLARSHIP

Applicants must be enrolled as full-time students, or as part-time students working full time in the railway industry, in an accredited four- or five-year program leading to a bachelor's degree in engineering or engineering technology. Must have completed at least one quarter or semester in college prior to submitting an application and have a minimum 2.00 GPA.

Academic Fields/Career Goals: Engineering-Related Technologies; Engineering/Technology.

Award: Scholarship for use in freshman, sophomore, junior, or senior years; not renewable. *Amount:* $1000.

Eligibility Requirements: Applicant must be enrolled or expecting to enroll full- or part-time at a four-year institution or university. Available to U.S. citizens.

Application Requirements: Application form, cover letter, recommendations or references, resume, transcript. *Deadline:* March 8.

Contact: Stacy Spaulding, Director of Committees and Technical Services
    Phone: 301-459-3200 Ext. 706
    E-mail: sspaulding@arema.org

CSX SCHOLARSHIP

Applicants must be enrolled as full-time students in a four- or five-year program leading to a bachelor's degree in engineering or engineering technology in a curriculum which has been accredited by the Accreditation Board of Engineering and Technology (or comparable accreditation in Canada and Mexico). Must have completed at least one quarter or semester in college prior to submitting an application and have a minimum 2.00 GPA.

Academic Fields/Career Goals: Engineering-Related Technologies; Engineering/Technology.

Award: Scholarship for use in freshman, sophomore, junior, or senior years; not renewable. *Amount:* $1000.

Eligibility Requirements: Applicant must be enrolled or expecting to enroll full-time at a four-year institution or university. Available to U.S. citizens.

Application Requirements: Application form, cover letter, recommendations or references, resume, self-addressed stamped envelope with application, transcript. *Deadline:* March 8.

Contact: Stacy Spaulding, Director of Committees and Technical Services
    Phone: 301-459-3200 Ext. 706
    E-mail: sspaulding@arema.org

NORFOLK SOUTHERN FOUNDATION SCHOLARSHIP

Applicants must be enrolled as full-time students in a four- or five-year undergraduate program in engineering or engineering technology. Institution must be located in Norfolk Southern's service area (22 states, the District of Columbia, and Ontario, Canada). Must have completed at least one quarter or semester in college prior to submitting an application and have a minimum 2.00 GPA.

Academic Fields/Career Goals: Engineering-Related Technologies; Engineering/Technology.

Award: Scholarship for use in freshman, sophomore, junior, or senior years; not renewable. *Amount:* $1000.

Eligibility Requirements: Applicant must be enrolled or expecting to enroll full-time at a four-year institution or university and resident of Alabama, Delaware, Florida, Georgia, Illinois, Indiana, Iowa, Kentucky, Louisiana, Maryland, Minnesota, Missouri, Montana, New Jersey, North Carolina. Available to U.S. citizens.

Application Requirements: Application form, cover letter, recommendations or references, resume, transcript. *Deadline:* March 8.

Contact: Stacy Spaulding, Director of Committees and Technical Services
    Phone: 301-459-3200 Ext. 706
    E-mail: sspaulding@arema.org

PB RAIL ENGINEERING SCHOLARSHIP

Applicants must be enrolled as full-time students in a four- or five-year program leading to a bachelor's degree in engineering or engineering technology in a curriculum which has been accredited by the Accreditation Board of Engineering and Technology (or comparable accreditation in Canada and Mexico). Must have completed at least one quarter or semester in college prior to submitting an application and have a minimum 2.00 GPA.

Academic Fields/Career Goals: Engineering-Related Technologies; Engineering/Technology.

Award: Scholarship for use in freshman, sophomore, junior, or senior years; not renewable. *Amount:* $2000.

Eligibility Requirements: Applicant must be enrolled or expecting to enroll full-time at a four-year institution or university. Available to U.S. citizens.

Application Requirements: Application form, cover letter, recommendations or references, resume, self-addressed stamped envelope with application, transcript. *Deadline:* March 8.

Contact: Stacy Spaulding, Director of Committees and Technical Services
    Phone: 301-459-3200 Ext. 706
    E-mail: sspaulding@arema.org

REMSA SCHOLARSHIP

Applicants must be enrolled as full-time students in a four- or five-year program leading to a bachelor's degree in engineering or engineering technology in a curriculum which has been accredited by the Accreditation Board of Engineering and Technology (or comparable accreditation in Canada and Mexico). Must have completed at least one quarter or semester in college prior to submitting an application and have a minimum 2.0 GPA.

Academic Fields/Career Goals: Engineering-Related Technologies; Engineering/Technology.

Award: Scholarship for use in freshman, sophomore, junior, or senior years; not renewable. *Amount:* $1000.

Eligibility Requirements: Applicant must be enrolled or expecting to enroll full-time at a four-year institution or university. Available to U.S. citizens.

Application Requirements: Application form, cover letter, recommendations or references, resume, self-addressed stamped envelope with application, transcript. *Deadline:* March 8.

Contact: Stacy Spaulding, Director of Committees and Technical Services
    Phone: 301-459-3200 Ext. 706
    E-mail: sspaulding@arema.org

AMERICAN SOCIETY FOR ENGINEERING EDUCATION
http://www.asee.org/

SCIENCE, MATHEMATICS, AND RESEARCH FOR TRANSFORMATION DEFENSE SCHOLARSHIP FOR SERVICE PROGRAM
• *See page 102*

AMERICAN SOCIETY OF HEATING, REFRIGERATING, AND AIR CONDITIONING ENGINEERS, INC.
http://www.ashrae.org/

ALWIN B. NEWTON SCHOLARSHIP
• *See page 249*

ASHRAE GENERAL SCHOLARSHIPS

One-time award of $3000 for full-time study in heating, ventilating, refrigeration, and air conditioning in an ABET-accredited program at an accredited school. Must be pursuing a bachelor of science or engineering degree and have a minimum GPA of 3.0. See website for application and additional information, http://www.ashrae.org.

Academic Fields/Career Goals: Engineering-Related Technologies; Engineering/Technology; Heating, Air-Conditioning, and Refrigeration Mechanics; Trade/Technical Specialties.

Award: Scholarship for use in freshman, sophomore, junior, or senior years; not renewable. *Number:* 2. *Amount:* $3000.

Eligibility Requirements: Applicant must be enrolled or expecting to enroll full-time at a four-year institution or university and must have an interest in leadership. Applicant must have 3.0 GPA or higher. Available to U.S. and non-U.S. citizens.

Application Requirements: Application form, financial need analysis, recommendations or references, transcript. *Deadline:* December 1.

Contact: Lois Benedict, Scholarship Administrator
Phone: 404-636-8400 Ext. 1120
E-mail: lbenedict@ashrae.org

ASHRAE MEMORIAL SCHOLARSHIP
• *See page 249*

ASHRAE REGION III BOGGARM SETTY SCHOLARSHIP
• *See page 166*

ASHRAE REGION VIII SCHOLARSHIP

One-year scholarship available to undergraduate engineering student enrolled full time in an ABET-accredited program at a school located within the geographic boundaries of ASHRAE'S Region VIII or accredited by the Consejo de Acreditacion de la Ensenanza de la Ingenieria in Mexico. This region includes Arkansas, Louisiana, Texas, and Oklahoma as well as Mexico. See website for application and additional information, http://www.ashrae.org.

Academic Fields/Career Goals: Engineering-Related Technologies; Engineering/Technology.

Award: Scholarship for use in freshman, sophomore, junior, or senior years; not renewable. *Number:* 1. *Amount:* $3000.

Eligibility Requirements: Applicant must be enrolled or expecting to enroll full-time at a four-year institution or university and studying in Arkansas, Louisiana, Oklahoma, Texas. Applicant must have 3.0 GPA or higher. Available to U.S. and non-U.S. citizens.

Application Requirements: Application form, financial need analysis, recommendations or references, transcript. *Deadline:* December 1.

Contact: Lois Benedict, Scholarship Administrator
Phone: 404-636-8400 Ext. 1120
E-mail: lbenedict@ashrae.org

DUANE HANSON SCHOLARSHIP
• *See page 250*

FRANK M. CODA SCHOLARSHIP
• *See page 250*

HENRY ADAMS SCHOLARSHIP
• *See page 250*

HIGH SCHOOL SENIOR SCHOLARSHIPS

Two $3000 scholarships for college freshmen enrolled full-time in an undergraduate pre-engineering, engineering, or engineering technology program leading to a bachelor degree in a course of study that traditionally has been a preparatory curriculum for the HVAC&R profession. Must be high school senior who has been accepted into a pre-engineering, engineering, or engineering technology program at a post-secondary educational institution. Minimum 3.0 GPA required.

Academic Fields/Career Goals: Engineering-Related Technologies; Engineering/Technology.

Award: Scholarship for use in freshman year; not renewable. *Number:* 2. *Amount:* $3000.

Eligibility Requirements: Applicant must be high school student and planning to enroll or expecting to enroll full-time at a four-year institution or university. Applicant must have 3.0 GPA or higher.

Application Requirements: Application form, letter of college acceptance, recommendations or references. *Deadline:* May 1.

Contact: Lois Benedict, Scholarship Administrator
Phone: 404-636-8400 Ext. 1120
E-mail: lbenedict@ashrae.org

LYNN G. BELLENGER SCHOLARSHIP
• *See page 250*

WILLIS H. CARRIER SCHOLARSHIPS
• *See page 251*

AMERICAN WELDING SOCIETY

http://www.aws.org/

AIRGAS-JERRY BAKER SCHOLARSHIP

Awarded to full-time undergraduate pursuing a minimum four-year degree in welding engineering or welding engineering technology. Applicant must be a minimum of 18 years of age and have a 3.0 GPA. Priority will be given to those individuals residing or attending school in the states of Alabama, Georgia or Florida.

Academic Fields/Career Goals: Engineering-Related Technologies; Materials Science, Engineering, and Metallurgy.

Award: Scholarship for use in freshman, sophomore, junior, or senior years; not renewable. *Number:* 1. *Amount:* $2500.

Eligibility Requirements: Applicant must be enrolled or expecting to enroll full-time at a four-year institution or university. Applicant must have 3.0 GPA or higher. Available to U.S. and Canadian citizens.

Application Requirements: Application form, essay, financial need analysis, recommendations or references, transcript. *Deadline:* January 15.

Contact: Vicki Pinsky, Manager, Foundation
American Welding Society
8669 Doral Boulevard, Suite 130
Doral, FL 33166
Phone: 800-443-9353 Ext. 212
Fax: 305-443-7559
E-mail: vpinsky@aws.org

AIRGAS-TERRY JARVIS MEMORIAL SCHOLARSHIP

Award for a full-time undergraduate pursuing a minimum four-year degree in welding engineering or welding engineering technology. Must have a minimum 2.8 overall GPA with a 3.0 GPA in engineering courses. Priority given to applicants residing or attending school in Florida, Georgia, or Alabama.

Academic Fields/Career Goals: Engineering-Related Technologies; Engineering/Technology; Materials Science, Engineering, and Metallurgy.

Award: Scholarship for use in freshman, sophomore, junior, or senior years; not renewable. *Number:* 1. *Amount:* $2500.

Eligibility Requirements: Applicant must be enrolled or expecting to enroll full-time at a four-year institution or university. Applicant must have 3.0 GPA or higher. Available to U.S. and Canadian citizens.

Application Requirements: Application form, essay, financial need analysis, recommendations or references, transcript. *Deadline:* February 15.

Contact: Vicki Pinsky, Manager, Foundation
American Welding Society
8669 Doral Boulevard, Suite 130
Doral, FL 33166
Phone: 800-443-9353 Ext. 212
Fax: 305-443-7559
E-mail: vpinsky@aws.org

AMERICAN WELDING SOCIETY DISTRICT SCHOLARSHIP PROGRAM

Award for students in vocational training, community college, or a degree program in welding or a related field of study. Applicants must be high school graduates or equivalent. Must reside in the United States and attend a U.S. institution. Recipients may reapply. Must include personal statement of career goals.

Academic Fields/Career Goals: Engineering-Related Technologies; Trade/Technical Specialties.

Award: Scholarship for use in freshman, sophomore, junior, or senior years; not renewable. *Number:* 150–200. *Amount:* $100–$2500.

Eligibility Requirements: Applicant must be enrolled or expecting to enroll full- or part-time at a two-year or four-year or technical institution or university. Available to U.S. citizens.

Application Requirements: Application form, financial need analysis, transcript. *Deadline:* March 1.

Contact: Nazdhia Prado-Pulido, Assistant, Foundation
American Welding Society
8669 Doral Boulevard, Suite 130
Doral, FL 33166
Phone: 800-443-9353 Ext. 250
Fax: 305-443-7559
E-mail: nprado-pulido@aws.org

AMERICAN WELDING SOCIETY INTERNATIONAL SCHOLARSHIP

Award for full-time international students pursuing a bachelor's or graduate degree in joining technologies. Scholarship not available to students residing in North America. Applicants must have completed at least one year of welding or related field of study at a baccalaureate degree-granting institution and be in the top 20 percent of that institution's grading system. For more information see website http://www.aws.org/foundation/intl_scholarships.html.

Academic Fields/Career Goals: Engineering-Related Technologies; Engineering/Technology; Materials Science, Engineering, and Metallurgy; Trade/Technical Specialties.

Award: Scholarship for use in freshman, sophomore, junior, senior, or graduate years; not renewable. *Number:* 1. *Amount:* up to $2500.

Eligibility Requirements: Applicant must be enrolled or expecting to enroll full-time at a four-year institution or university. Available to citizens of countries other than the U.S. or Canada.

Application Requirements: Application form, essay, financial need analysis, proof of citizenship, proof of acceptance, recommendations or references, resume, transcript. *Deadline:* April 1.

Contact: Vicki Pinsky, Manager, Foundation
American Welding Society
8669 Doral Boulevard, Suite 130
Doral, FL 33166
Phone: 800-443-9353 Ext. 212
Fax: 305-443-7559
E-mail: vpinsky@aws.org

DONALD F. HASTINGS SCHOLARSHIP

Award for undergraduate pursuing a four-year degree either full-time or part-time in welding engineering or welding engineering technology. Preference given to students residing or attending school in California or Ohio. Submit copy of proposed curriculum. Must rank in upper half of class or have a minimum GPA of 2.5. Must also include acceptance letter.

Academic Fields/Career Goals: Engineering-Related Technologies; Engineering/Technology; Trade/Technical Specialties.

Award: Scholarship for use in freshman, sophomore, junior, or senior years; renewable. *Number:* 1. *Amount:* $2500.

Eligibility Requirements: Applicant must be enrolled or expecting to enroll full- or part-time at a four-year institution or university. Applicant must have 2.5 GPA or higher. Available to U.S. citizens.

Application Requirements: Application form, financial need analysis, recommendations or references, transcript. *Deadline:* February 15.

Contact: Vicki Pinsky, Manager, Foundation
American Welding Society
8669 Doral Boulevard, Suite 130
Doral, FL 33166
Phone: 800-443-9353 Ext. 212
Fax: 305-443-7559
E-mail: vpinsky@aws.org

EDWARD J. BRADY MEMORIAL SCHOLARSHIP

Award for an undergraduate student pursuing a four-year degree either full- or part-time in welding engineering or welding engineering technology.

Academic Fields/Career Goals: Engineering-Related Technologies; Engineering/Technology; Trade/Technical Specialties.

Award: Scholarship for use in freshman, sophomore, junior, or senior years; not renewable. *Number:* 1. *Amount:* $2500.

Eligibility Requirements: Applicant must be enrolled or expecting to enroll full- or part-time at a four-year institution or university. Available to U.S. citizens.

Application Requirements: Application form, copy of proposed curriculum, acceptance letter, essay, financial need analysis, recommendations or references, transcript. *Deadline:* February 15.

Contact: Ms. Vicki Pinsky, Manager, AWS Foundation
American Welding Society
8669 Doral Boulevard, Suite 130
Doral, FL 33166
Phone: 305-443-9353 Ext. 212

HOWARD E. AND WILMA J. ADKINS MEMORIAL SCHOLARSHIP

Award for a full-time junior or senior in welding engineering or welding engineering technology. Preference to welding engineering students and those residing or attending school in Wisconsin or Kentucky. Must have at least 3.2 GPA in engineering, scientific, and technical subjects and a 2.8 GPA overall. No financial need is required to apply. Award may be granted a maximum of two years. Reapply each year. Submit copy of proposed curriculum and an acceptance letter.

Academic Fields/Career Goals: Engineering-Related Technologies; Engineering/Technology; Trade/Technical Specialties.

Award: Scholarship for use in junior or senior years; not renewable. *Number:* 1. *Amount:* $2500.

Eligibility Requirements: Applicant must be enrolled or expecting to enroll full-time at a four-year institution. Available to U.S. citizens.

Application Requirements: Application form, essay, recommendations or references, transcript. *Deadline:* February 15.

Contact: Vicki Pinsky, Manager, Foundation
American Welding Society
8669 Doral Boulevard, Suite 130
Doral, FL 33166
Phone: 800-443-9353 Ext. 212
Fax: 305-443-7559
E-mail: vpinsky@aws.org

JOHN C. LINCOLN MEMORIAL SCHOLARSHIP

Award for an undergraduate pursuing a four-year degree either full time or part time in engineering or welding engineering technology. Priority given to welding engineering students residing or attending school in the states of Ohio or Arizona. Applicant must have a minimum 2.5 overall GPA. Proof of financial need is required to qualify.

Academic Fields/Career Goals: Engineering-Related Technologies; Engineering/Technology; Materials Science, Engineering, and Metallurgy.

Award: Scholarship for use in freshman, sophomore, junior, or senior years; not renewable. *Number:* 1. *Amount:* $3500.

Eligibility Requirements: Applicant must be enrolled or expecting to enroll full- or part-time at a four-year institution. Applicant must have 2.5 GPA or higher. Available to U.S. citizens.

Application Requirements: Application form, financial need analysis, recommendations or references, transcript. *Deadline:* February 15.

Contact: Vicki Pinsky, Manager, Foundation
American Welding Society
8669 Doral Boulevard, Suite 130
Doral, FL 33166
Phone: 800-443-9353 Ext. 212
Fax: 305-443-7559
E-mail: vpinsky@aws.org

MATSUO BRIDGE COMPANY LTD. OF JAPAN SCHOLARSHIP

• See page 181

MILLER ELECTRIC INTERNATIONAL WORLD SKILLS COMPETITION SCHOLARSHIP

Applicant must compete in the National Skills USA-VICA Competition for Welding, and advance to the AWS Weld Trials at the AWS International Welding and Fabricating Exposition and Convention, which is held on a bi-annual basis. The winner of the U.S. Weld Trial Competition will receive the scholarship for $10,000 and runner up will receive $1000. For additional information, see website http://www.aws.org/foundation/national_scholarships.html.

Academic Fields/Career Goals: Engineering-Related Technologies; Engineering/Technology; Materials Science, Engineering, and Metallurgy; Trade/Technical Specialties.

Award: Scholarship for use in freshman, sophomore, junior, or senior years; renewable. *Number:* 1. *Amount:* $1000–$10,000.

Eligibility Requirements: Applicant must be enrolled or expecting to enroll full- or part-time at a four-year institution or university. Available to U.S. citizens.

Application Requirements: Entry in a contest.

Contact: Vicki Pinsky, Manager, Foundation
American Welding Society
8669 Doral Boulevard, Suite 130
Doral, FL 33166
Phone: 800-443-9353 Ext. 212
Fax: 305-443-7559
E-mail: vpinsky@aws.org

MILLER ELECTRIC MFG. CO. SCHOLARSHIP

Two awards of $3000 each are available for undergraduate students who will be seniors in a four-year bachelor's degree in welding engineering technology or welding engineering. Applicant must be U.S. citizen planning to attend a U.S. institution and have a minimum 3.0 GPA. Priority given to students attending Ferris State University. Must exhibit a strong interest in welding equipment and have prior work experience in the welding equipment field.

Academic Fields/Career Goals: Engineering-Related Technologies; Engineering/Technology; Materials Science, Engineering, and Metallurgy; Trade/Technical Specialties.

Award: Scholarship for use in senior year; not renewable. *Number:* 2. *Amount:* $3000.

Eligibility Requirements: Applicant must be enrolled or expecting to enroll full- or part-time at a four-year institution or university. Applicant must have 3.0 GPA or higher. Available to U.S. citizens.

Application Requirements: Application form, transcript. *Deadline:* February 15.

Contact: Vicki Pinsky, Manager, Foundation
American Welding Society
8669 Doral Boulevard, Suite 130
Doral, FL 33166
Phone: 800-443-9353 Ext. 212
Fax: 305-443-7559
E-mail: vpinsky@aws.org

PRAXAIR INTERNATIONAL SCHOLARSHIP

Award for a full-time student demonstrating leadership and pursuing a four-year degree in welding engineering or welding engineering technology. Priority given to welding engineering students. Must be a U.S. or Canadian citizen. Financial need is not required. Must have minimum 2.5 GPA.

Academic Fields/Career Goals: Engineering-Related Technologies; Engineering/Technology; Materials Science, Engineering, and Metallurgy.

Award: Scholarship for use in freshman, sophomore, junior, or senior years; not renewable. *Number:* 1. *Amount:* $2500.

Eligibility Requirements: Applicant must be enrolled or expecting to enroll full-time at a four-year institution or university. Applicant must have 2.5 GPA or higher. Available to U.S. and Canadian citizens.

Application Requirements: Application form, financial need analysis, recommendations or references, transcript. *Deadline:* February 15.

Contact: Vicki Pinsky, Manager, Foundation
American Welding Society
8669 Doral Boulevard, Suite 130
Doral, FL 33166
Phone: 800-443-9353 Ext. 212
Fax: 305-443-7559
E-mail: vpinsky@aws.org

WILLIAM A. AND ANN M. BROTHERS SCHOLARSHIP

Awarded to a full-time undergraduate pursuing a bachelor's degree in welding or welding-related program at an accredited university. Applicant must have a minimum 2.5 overall GPA. Proof of financial need is required.

Academic Fields/Career Goals: Engineering-Related Technologies; Materials Science, Engineering, and Metallurgy.

Award: Scholarship for use in freshman, sophomore, junior, or senior years; not renewable. *Number:* 1. *Amount:* $3500.

Eligibility Requirements: Applicant must be enrolled or expecting to enroll full-time at a four-year institution or university. Applicant must have 2.5 GPA or higher. Available to U.S. citizens.

Application Requirements: Application form, financial need analysis, recommendations or references, transcript. *Deadline:* February 15.

Contact: Vicki Pinsky, Manager, Foundation
American Welding Society
8669 Doral Boulevard, Suite 130
Doral, FL 33166
Phone: 800-443-9353 Ext. 212
Fax: 305-443-7559
E-mail: vpinsky@aws.org

WILLIAM B. HOWELL MEMORIAL SCHOLARSHIP

Awarded to a full-time undergraduate student pursuing a minimum four-year degree in a welding program at an accredited university. Priority will be given to those individuals residing or attending schools in the state of Florida, Michigan, and Ohio. Minimum 2.5 GPA required.

Academic Fields/Career Goals: Engineering-Related Technologies; Engineering/Technology; Materials Science, Engineering, and Metallurgy.

Award: Scholarship for use in freshman, sophomore, junior, or senior years; not renewable. *Number:* 1. *Amount:* $2500.

Eligibility Requirements: Applicant must be enrolled or expecting to enroll full-time at a four-year institution; resident of Florida, Michigan, Ohio and studying in Florida, Michigan, Ohio. Applicant must have 2.5 GPA or higher. Available to U.S. citizens.

Application Requirements: Application form, essay, financial need analysis, recommendations or references, transcript. *Deadline:* February 15.

Contact: Vicki Pinsky, Manager, Foundation
American Welding Society
8669 Doral Boulevard, Suite 130
Doral, FL 33166
Phone: 305-443-9353 Ext. 212
Fax: 305-443-7559
E-mail: vpinsky@aws.org

ARMED FORCES COMMUNICATIONS AND ELECTRONICS ASSOCIATION, EDUCATIONAL FOUNDATION

http://www.afcea.org/scholarships

ARMED FORCES COMMUNICATIONS AND ELECTRONICS ASSOCIATION GENERAL EMMETT PAIGE SCHOLARSHIP

• *See page 127*

ARMED FORCES COMMUNICATIONS AND ELECTRONICS ASSOCIATION ROTC SCHOLARSHIP PROGRAM

• *See page 127*

ARRL FOUNDATION INC.

http://www.arrl.org/

ARRL NORTHWESTERN DIVISION SCHOLARSHIP FUND

• *See page 150*

GARY WAGNER, K3OMI, SCHOLARSHIP

• *See page 166*

HENRY BROUGHTON, K2AE, MEMORIAL SCHOLARSHIP

At least one $1000 award is available to students located within 70 miles of Schenectady, NY. Must possess a general class amateur radio license and pursue a Baccalaureate or higher course of study in engineering, sciences, or similar field at an accredited four-year college or university.

Academic Fields/Career Goals: Engineering-Related Technologies; Engineering/Technology.

Award: Scholarship for use in freshman, sophomore, junior, senior, or graduate years; not renewable. *Number:* 1. *Amount:* $1000.

Eligibility Requirements: Applicant must be enrolled or expecting to enroll full- or part-time at a four-year institution or university; resident of New York and must have an interest in amateur radio. Available to U.S. citizens.

Application Requirements: Application form, transcript. *Deadline:* February 1.

Contact: Ms. Mary Hobart, Secretary
Phone: 860-594-0397
E-mail: k1mmh@arrl.org

YASME FOUNDATION SCHOLARSHIP
• *See page 143*

ASTRONAUT SCHOLARSHIP FOUNDATION
http://www.astronautscholarship.org/

ASTRONAUT SCHOLARSHIP FOUNDATION
• *See page 104*

BRITISH COLUMBIA INNOVATION COUNCIL
http://www.bcic.ca/

BCIC YOUNG INNOVATOR SCHOLARSHIP COMPETITION (IDEA MASH UP)
• *See page 104*

CATCHING THE DREAM
http://www.catchingthedream.org/

TRIBAL BUSINESS MANAGEMENT PROGRAM (TBM)
• *See page 70*

CUBAN AMERICAN NATIONAL FOUNDATION
http://www.masscholarships.org/

MAS FAMILY SCHOLARSHIPS
• *See page 152*

DELAWARE HIGHER EDUCATION OFFICE
http://www.doe.k12.de.us

DELAWARE SOLID WASTE AUTHORITY JOHN P. "PAT" HEALY SCHOLARSHIP

Award for legal residents of Delaware who are U.S. citizens or eligible non-citizens. Must be high school seniors or full-time college students in their freshman or sophomore years. Must major in either environmental engineering or environmental sciences at a Delaware college. Selection based on financial need, academic performance, community and school involvement, and leadership ability.

Academic Fields/Career Goals: Engineering-Related Technologies; Environmental Science.

Award: Scholarship for use in freshman or sophomore years; renewable. *Number:* 1. *Amount:* $2000.

Eligibility Requirements: Applicant must be enrolled or expecting to enroll full-time at a two-year or four-year institution or university; resident of Delaware; studying in Delaware and must have an interest in leadership. Applicant or parent of applicant must have employment or volunteer experience in community service. Applicant must have 3.0 GPA or higher. Available to U.S. citizens.

Application Requirements: Application form, FAFSA, Student Aid Report (SAR), financial need analysis. *Deadline:* March 14.

Contact: Carylin Brinkley, Program Administrator
Phone: 302-735-4120
Fax: 302-739-5894
E-mail: cbrinkley@doe.k12.de.us

ELECTROCHEMICAL SOCIETY INC.
http://www.electrochem.org/

H.H. DOW MEMORIAL STUDENT ACHIEVEMENT AWARD OF THE INDUSTRIAL ELECTROLYSIS AND ELECTROCHEMICAL ENGINEERING DIVISION OF THE ELECTROCHEMICAL SOCIETY INC.
• *See page 104*

STUDENT RESEARCH AWARDS OF THE BATTERY DIVISION OF THE ELECTROCHEMICAL SOCIETY INC.
• *See page 105*

ENGINEERS FOUNDATION OF OHIO
http://www.ohioengineer.com/

ENGINEERS FOUNDATION OF OHIO GENERAL FUND SCHOLARSHIP

Applicant must be a college junior or senior at the end of the academic year in which the application is submitted. Must be enrolled full-time at an Ohio college or university in a curriculum leading to a BS degree in engineering or its equivalent. Minimum GPA of 3.0 required. Must be a U.S. citizen and permanent resident of Ohio.

Academic Fields/Career Goals: Engineering-Related Technologies.

Award: Scholarship for use in junior or senior years; not renewable. *Number:* 1. *Amount:* $1000.

Eligibility Requirements: Applicant must be enrolled or expecting to enroll full-time at a four-year institution or university; resident of Ohio and studying in Ohio. Applicant must have 3.0 GPA or higher. Available to U.S. citizens.

Application Requirements: Application form, essay, financial need analysis, recommendations or references, test scores, transcript. *Deadline:* December 15.

Contact: Pam McClure, Manager of Administration
Phone: 614-223-1177
E-mail: efo@ohioengineer.com

LLOYD A. CHACEY, PE-OHIO SOCIETY OF PROFESSIONAL ENGINEERS MEMORIAL SCHOLARSHIP

Scholarship available for a son, daughter, brother, sister, niece, nephew, spouse or grandchild of a current member of the Ohio Society of Professional Engineers, or of a deceased member who was in good standing at the time of his or her death. Must be enrolled full-time at an Ohio college or university in a curriculum leading to a degree in engineering or its equivalent. Must have a minimum of 3.0 GPA. Must be a U.S. citizen and permanent resident of Ohio.

Academic Fields/Career Goals: Engineering-Related Technologies.

Award: Scholarship for use in junior or senior years; renewable. *Number:* up to 2. *Amount:* $2000.

Eligibility Requirements: Applicant must be enrolled or expecting to enroll full-time at a four-year institution or university; resident of Ohio and studying in Ohio. Applicant must have 3.0 GPA or higher. Available to U.S. citizens.

Application Requirements: Application form, essay, financial need analysis, recommendations or references, test scores, transcript. *Deadline:* December 15.

Contact: Pam McClure, Manager of Administration
Phone: 614-223-1177
E-mail: efo@ohioengineer.com

RAYMOND H. FULLER, PE MEMORIAL SCHOLARSHIP

Scholarship of $1000 to graduating high school seniors who will enter their freshman year in college the next fall. Recipients must be accepted for enrollment in an engineering program at an Ohio college or university. Must have a minimum of 3.0 GPA. Must be a U.S. citizen and permanent resident of Ohio. Consideration will be given to the prospective recipient's academic achievement, interest in a career in engineering and financial need as determined by interviews and from references.

Academic Fields/Career Goals: Engineering-Related Technologies.

Award: Scholarship for use in freshman year; not renewable. *Number:* 1. *Amount:* $1000.

Eligibility Requirements: Applicant must be high school student; planning to enroll or expecting to enroll full-time at a four-year institution or university; resident of Ohio and studying in Ohio. Applicant must have 3.0 GPA or higher. Available to U.S. citizens.

Application Requirements: Application form, essay, financial need analysis, interview, recommendations or references, test scores, transcript. *Deadline:* December 15.

Contact: Pam McClure, Manager of Administration
   Phone: 614-223-1177
   E-mail: efo@ohioengineer.com

GLOBAL AUTOMOTIVE AFTERMARKET SYMPOSIUM

http://www.automotivescholarships.com/

GAAS SCHOLARSHIP
• *See page 155*

HAWAIIAN LODGE, F&AM

http://www.hawaiianlodgefreemasons.org/

HAWAIIAN LODGE SCHOLARSHIPS
• *See page 114*

HISPANIC HERITAGE FOUNDATION

http://www.hispanicheritage.org/

HISPANIC HERITAGE YOUTH AWARDS
• *See page 155*

ILLUMINATING ENGINEERING SOCIETY OF NORTH AMERICA

http://www.iesna.org/

ROBERT W. THUNEN MEMORIAL SCHOLARSHIPS
• *See page 111*

INDEPENDENT LABORATORIES INSTITUTE SCHOLARSHIP ALLIANCE

http://www.acil.org/

INDEPENDENT LABORATORIES INSTITUTE SCHOLARSHIP ALLIANCE
• *See page 145*

INDIAN HEALTH SERVICES, UNITED STATES DEPARTMENT OF HEALTH AND HUMAN SERVICES

http://www.ihs.gov/scholarship

INDIAN HEALTH SERVICE HEALTH PROFESSIONS SCHOLARSHIP PROGRAM
• *See page 208*

INSTITUTE OF INTERNATIONAL EDUCATION (FULBRIGHT PROGRAM)

http://www.us.fulbrightonline.org/

WHITAKER INTERNATIONAL PROGRAM
• *See page 145*

INTERNATIONAL FACILITY MANAGEMENT ASSOCIATION FOUNDATION

http://www.ifmafoundation.org/

IFMA FOUNDATION SCHOLARSHIPS
• *See page 112*

INTERNATIONAL SOCIETY FOR OPTICAL ENGINEERING-SPIE

http://www.spie.org/scholarships

SPIE EDUCATIONAL SCHOLARSHIPS IN OPTICAL SCIENCE AND ENGINEERING
• *See page 105*

INTERNATIONAL SOCIETY OF AUTOMATION

http://www.isa.org/

ISA EDUCATIONAL FOUNDATION SCHOLARSHIPS

Scholarships to graduate and undergraduate students who demonstrate outstanding potential for long-range contribution to the fields of automation, systems, and control.

Academic Fields/Career Goals: Engineering-Related Technologies.

Award: Scholarship for use in sophomore, junior, or graduate years; not renewable. *Number:* up to 15. *Amount:* $500–$5000.

Eligibility Requirements: Applicant must be enrolled or expecting to enroll full-time at a two-year or four-year institution or university. Applicant must have 2.5 GPA or higher. Available to U.S. and non-U.S. citizens.

Application Requirements: Application form, essay, recommendations or references, transcript. *Deadline:* February 15.

INTERNATIONAL SOCIETY OF AUTOMATION (ISA)

http://www.isa.org/

INTERNATIONAL SOCIETY OF AUTOMATION EDUCATION FOUNDATION SCHOLARSHIPS
• *See page 131*

INTERNATIONAL SOCIETY OF EXPLOSIVES ENGINEERS

http://www.isee.org/

JERRY MCDOWELL FUND

Scholarship of $1000 to $5000 to students whose field of education is related to the commercial explosives industry.

Academic Fields/Career Goals: Engineering-Related Technologies; Engineering/Technology.

Award: Scholarship for use in freshman, sophomore, junior, or senior years; not renewable. *Number:* 1–3. *Amount:* $1000–$5000.

Eligibility Requirements: Applicant must be enrolled or expecting to enroll full-time at a two-year or four-year institution or university. Available to U.S. and non-U.S. citizens.

Application Requirements: Application form, financial need analysis, recommendations or references, statement of goal, transcript. *Deadline:* May 1.

Contact: Arlene Chafe, Assistant to the Executive Director
   Phone: 440-349-4400
   Fax: 440-349-3788
   E-mail: foundation@isee.org

JORGE MAS CANOSA FREEDOM FOUNDATION

http://www.jorgemascanosa.org/

MAS FAMILY SCHOLARSHIP AWARD
• See page 156

KOREAN-AMERICAN SCIENTISTS AND ENGINEERS ASSOCIATION

http://www.ksea.org/

KSEA SCHOLARSHIPS
• See page 253

LOS ANGELES COUNCIL OF BLACK PROFESSIONAL ENGINEERS

http://www.lablackengineers.org/

AL-BEN SCHOLARSHIP FOR ACADEMIC INCENTIVE
• See page 168

AL-BEN SCHOLARSHIP FOR PROFESSIONAL MERIT
• See page 168

AL-BEN SCHOLARSHIP FOR SCHOLASTIC ACHIEVEMENT
• See page 168

MAINE SOCIETY OF PROFESSIONAL ENGINEERS

http://www.mespe.org/

MAINE SOCIETY OF PROFESSIONAL ENGINEERS VERNON T. SWAINE-ROBERT E. CHUTE SCHOLARSHIP

Nonrenewable scholarship for full-time study for freshmen only. Must be a Maine resident. Application can also be obtained by sending e-mail to rgmglads@twi.net.

Academic Fields/Career Goals: Engineering-Related Technologies; Engineering/Technology.

Award: Scholarship for use in freshman year; not renewable. *Number:* 1–2. *Amount:* $1500.

Eligibility Requirements: Applicant must be high school student; planning to enroll or expecting to enroll full-time at a four-year institution or university; resident of Maine and studying in Maine. Applicant must have 2.5 GPA or higher. Available to U.S. citizens.

Application Requirements: Application form, essay, interview, recommendations or references, self-addressed stamped envelope with application, test scores, transcript. *Deadline:* March 1.

Contact: Robert Martin, Scholarship Committee Chairman
Maine Society of Professional Engineers
1387 Augusta Road
Belgrade, ME 04917
Phone: 207-495-2244
E-mail: rgmglads@twi.net

MANUFACTURERS ASSOCIATION OF MAINE

http://www.mainemfg.com/

MAINE METAL PRODUCTS EDUCATION FUND SCHOLARSHIP PROGRAM
• See page 132

MINERALS, METALS, AND MATERIALS SOCIETY (TMS)

http://www.tms.org/

TMS/EMPMD GILBERT CHIN SCHOLARSHIP

One $2000 scholarship is available to an undergraduate students in their sophomore and junior years, who are studying subjects in relation to synthesis and processing, structure, properties, and performance of electronic, photonic, magnetic, and superconducting materials as well as materials used in packaging, and interconnecting such materials in device structures. An additional $500 for travel expenses is available to the recipient in order to personally accept the award at the TMS Annual Meeting and Exhibition. The scholarship recipient is known as the EMPMD Gilbert Chin Scholar.

Academic Fields/Career Goals: Engineering-Related Technologies; Engineering/Technology; Materials Science, Engineering, and Metallurgy.

Award: Scholarship for use in sophomore or junior years; not renewable. *Number:* 1. *Amount:* $2000.

Eligibility Requirements: Applicant must be enrolled or expecting to enroll full-time at a four-year institution or university. Available to U.S. and non-U.S. citizens.

Application Requirements: Application form, essay, recommendations or references, resume, transcript. *Deadline:* March 15.

TMS/EPD SCHOLARSHIP

Four $2000 scholarships are available to full-time undergraduate applicants in their sophomore or junior years, who are majoring in the extraction and processing of minerals, metals and materials. Each scholarship recipient is also given the opportunity to select up to five Extraction & Processing Division-sponsored conference proceedings or textbooks to be donated in the recipient's name to his/her college or university library. Awards are presented during the Extraction & Processing Division luncheon at the TMS Annual Meeting and Exhibition. Up to $500 for travel expenses is available to each recipient in order to accept the award at the luncheon. Scholarship recipients are known as EPD Scholars.

Academic Fields/Career Goals: Engineering-Related Technologies; Engineering/Technology; Materials Science, Engineering, and Metallurgy.

Award: Scholarship for use in sophomore or junior years; not renewable. *Number:* 4. *Amount:* $2000.

Eligibility Requirements: Applicant must be enrolled or expecting to enroll full-time at a four-year institution or university. Available to U.S. and non-U.S. citizens.

Application Requirements: Application form, essay, recommendations or references, resume, transcript. *Deadline:* March 15.

TMS/INTERNATIONAL SYMPOSIUM ON SUPERALLOYS SCHOLARSHIP PROGRAM

Scholarships with up to $500 in travel reimbursements are available to undergraduate and graduate students majoring in metallurgical and/or materials science and engineering with an emphasis on all aspects of the high-temperature, high-performance materials used in the gas turbine industry and all other applications. Awards are presented in conjunction with the Materials Science and Technology Conference.

Academic Fields/Career Goals: Engineering-Related Technologies; Engineering/Technology; Materials Science, Engineering, and Metallurgy.

Award: Scholarship for use in sophomore, junior, senior, or graduate years; not renewable. *Number:* 2. *Amount:* $2500.

Eligibility Requirements: Applicant must be enrolled or expecting to enroll full-time at a four-year institution or university. Available to U.S. and non-U.S. citizens.

Application Requirements: Application form, essay, recommendations or references, resume, transcript. *Deadline:* March 15.

TMS J. KEITH BRIMACOMBE PRESIDENTIAL SCHOLARSHIP

One $5000 cash award scholarship is made to an undergraduate student majoring in metallurgical engineering, materials science and engineering, or minerals processing/extraction programs. In addition, a travel stipend of $1000 is available for the recipient to attend the TMS Annual Meeting, to formally receive the scholarship.

Academic Fields/Career Goals: Engineering-Related Technologies; Engineering/Technology; Materials Science, Engineering, and Metallurgy.

Award: Scholarship for use in sophomore or junior years; not renewable. *Number:* 1. *Amount:* $5000.

Eligibility Requirements: Applicant must be enrolled or expecting to enroll full-time at a four-year institution or university. Available to U.S. and non-U.S. citizens.

Application Requirements: Application form, essay, recommendations or references, resume, transcript. *Deadline:* March 15.

TMS/LMD SCHOLARSHIP PROGRAM

Scholarships are available to full-time undergraduate applicants who are majoring in metallurgical and/or materials science and engineering with an emphasis on both traditional (aluminum, magnesium, beryllium, titanium, lithium and other reactive metals) and emerging (composites, laminates, etc.) light metals. Additionally, recipients may select up to $300 worth of Light Metals Division-sponsored conference proceedings or textbooks to be donated in the recipient's name to his/her college or university library. Each recipient may also choose up to $400 worth of books for his/her personal use. As the awards are presented during the Light Metals Division luncheon at the TMS Annual Meeting and Exhibition, up to $600 for travel expenses is available to each recipient.

Academic Fields/Career Goals: Engineering-Related Technologies; Engineering/Technology; Materials Science, Engineering, and Metallurgy.

Award: Scholarship for use in sophomore or junior years; not renewable. *Number:* 3. *Amount:* $4000.

Eligibility Requirements: Applicant must be enrolled or expecting to enroll full-time at a four-year institution or university. Available to U.S. and non-U.S. citizens.

Application Requirements: Application form, essay, recommendations or references, resume, transcript. *Deadline:* March 15.

TMS OUTSTANDING STUDENT PAPER CONTEST-UNDERGRADUATE

This contest is open all student members of TMS and offers an undergraduate and graduate division. Students are encouraged to submit essays on global or national issues as well as technical research papers, relating to any field of metallurgy or materials science. Students should display original thought and creativity in the development of the essays, which should include a comprehensive bibliography on which the paper is based.

Academic Fields/Career Goals: Engineering-Related Technologies; Engineering/Technology; Materials Science, Engineering, and Metallurgy.

Award: Prize for use in freshman, sophomore, junior, or senior years; not renewable. *Number:* 2. *Amount:* $500–$1000.

Eligibility Requirements: Applicant must be enrolled or expecting to enroll full-time at a four-year institution or university. Available to U.S. and non-U.S. citizens.

Application Requirements: Application form, entry in a contest, essay. *Deadline:* May 1.

TMS/STRUCTURAL MATERIALS DIVISION SCHOLARSHIP

Scholarships are available to full-time undergraduate applicants who are majoring in metallurgical and/or materials science and engineering with an emphasis on the science and engineering of load-bearing materials, including studies into the nature of a material's physical properties based upon its microstructure and operating environment. Awards are presented at the TMS Annual Meeting and Exhibition, and up to $500 is available for each recipient's travel expenses.

Academic Fields/Career Goals: Engineering-Related Technologies; Engineering/Technology; Materials Science, Engineering, and Metallurgy.

Award: Scholarship for use in sophomore or junior years; not renewable. *Number:* 2. *Amount:* $2500.

Eligibility Requirements: Applicant must be enrolled or expecting to enroll full-time at a four-year institution or university. Available to U.S. and non-U.S. citizens.

Application Requirements: Application form, essay, recommendations or references, resume, transcript. *Deadline:* March 15.

NASA MISSISSIPPI SPACE GRANT CONSORTIUM

http://www.olemiss.edu/programs/nasa

MISSISSIPPI SPACE GRANT CONSORTIUM SCHOLARSHIP
• See page 132

NASA RHODE ISLAND SPACE GRANT CONSORTIUM

http://brown/initiatives/ri-space-grant

NASA RHODE ISLAND SPACE GRANT CONSORTIUM OUTREACH SCHOLARSHIP FOR UNDERGRADUATE STUDENTS

Scholarship for undergraduate students attending a Rhode Island Space Grant Consortium participating institution and studying in any space-related field of science, math, engineering, or other field with applications in space study. Recipients are expected to devote a maximum of 8 hours per week to outreach activities in science education for K-12 children and teachers.

Academic Fields/Career Goals: Engineering-Related Technologies; Mathematics; Science, Technology, and Society.

Award: Scholarship for use in sophomore, junior, or senior years; not renewable. *Number:* up to 2. *Amount:* up to $4000.

Eligibility Requirements: Applicant must be enrolled or expecting to enroll full-time at a four-year institution or university and studying in Rhode Island. Applicant must have 3.0 GPA or higher. Available to U.S. citizens.

Application Requirements: Application form, essay, letter of interest, recommendations or references, resume, transcript. *Deadline:* varies.

Contact: Nancy Ciminelli, Program Manager
NASA Rhode Island Space Grant Consortium
Brown University
Box 1846, Lincoln Field
Providence, RI 02912
Phone: 401-863-1151
Fax: 401-863-3978
E-mail: nancy_ciminelli@brown.edu

NASA SOUTH CAROLINA SPACE GRANT CONSORTIUM

http://www.cofc.edu/~scsgrant

UNDERGRADUATE RESEARCH AWARD PROGRAM
• See page 133

NASA SOUTH DAKOTA SPACE GRANT CONSORTIUM

http://sdspacegrant.sdsmt.edu/

SOUTH DAKOTA SPACE GRANT CONSORTIUM UNDERGRADUATE AND GRADUATE STUDENT SCHOLARSHIPS
• See page 134

NASA'S VIRGINIA SPACE GRANT CONSORTIUM

http://www.vsgc.odu.edu/

UNDERGRADUATE STEM RESEARCH SCHOLARSHIPS
• See page 106

NASA WEST VIRGINIA SPACE GRANT CONSORTIUM

http://www.nasa.wvu.edu/

WEST VIRGINIA SPACE GRANT CONSORTIUM UNDERGRADUATE FELLOWSHIP PROGRAM
• See page 134

NATIONAL ASSOCIATION FOR THE ADVANCEMENT OF COLORED PEOPLE

http://www.naacp.org/

HUBERTUS W.V. WELLEMS SCHOLARSHIP FOR MALE STUDENTS
• See page 169

NATIONAL ASSOCIATION OF WOMEN IN CONSTRUCTION

http://www.nawic.org/

NAWIC UNDERGRADUATE SCHOLARSHIPS
• See page 112

NATIONAL INVENTORS HALL OF FAME

http://www.invent.org/

COLLEGIATE INVENTORS COMPETITION FOR UNDERGRADUATE STUDENTS
• See page 106

COLLEGIATE INVENTORS COMPETITION-GRAND PRIZE
• See page 106

NATIONAL SOCIETY OF BLACK ENGINEERS

http://www.nsbe.org/

NSBE O-I CORPORATE SCHOLARSHIP PROGRAM

The goals of this scholarship are to encourage and reward academic excellence for African-American students and to promote O-I's Wellness Culture that values each person, encourages him/her to be great and appreciates individual unique talents and strengths. Applicants should major in: chemical, mechanical, material science, ceramic, glass, manufacturing, or industrial Engineering; and have demonstrated leadership and community service.

Academic Fields/Career Goals: Engineering-Related Technologies; Engineering/Technology.

Award: Scholarship for use in junior or senior years. *Number:* 2. *Amount:* $2500.

Eligibility Requirements: Applicant must be Black (non-Hispanic) and enrolled or expecting to enroll at a four-year institution or university. Applicant must have 3.0 GPA or higher. Available to U.S. citizens.

Application Requirements: *Deadline:* June 30.

NATIONAL SOCIETY OF PROFESSIONAL ENGINEERS

http://www.nspe.org/

MAUREEN L. AND HOWARD N. BLITMAN, PE SCHOLARSHIP TO PROMOTE DIVERSITY IN ENGINEERING
• See page 170

PAUL H. ROBBINS HONORARY SCHOLARSHIP
• See page 170

PROFESSIONAL ENGINEERS IN INDUSTRY SCHOLARSHIP
• See page 170

NATIONAL STONE, SAND AND GRAVEL ASSOCIATION (NSSGA)

http://www.nssga.org/

BARRY K. WENDT MEMORIAL SCHOLARSHIP

Scholarship is restricted to a student in an engineering school who plans to pursue a career in the aggregates industry. One-time award for full-time students attending a four-year college or university.

Academic Fields/Career Goals: Engineering-Related Technologies; Materials Science, Engineering, and Metallurgy.

Award: Scholarship for use in freshman, sophomore, junior, or senior years; not renewable. *Number:* 1. *Amount:* up to $2500.

Eligibility Requirements: Applicant must be enrolled or expecting to enroll full-time at a four-year institution or university. Available to U.S. and non-U.S. citizens.

Application Requirements: 300- to 500-word statement of plans for career in the aggregates industry, application form, essay, recommendations or references, transcript. *Deadline:* June 2.

PLASTICS INSTITUTE OF AMERICA

http://www.plasticsinstitute.org/

PLASTICS PIONEERS SCHOLARSHIPS
• See page 170

PLUMBING-HEATING-COOLING CONTRACTORS EDUCATION FOUNDATION

http://www.phccfoundation.org/

DELTA FAUCET COMPANY SCHOLARSHIP PROGRAM
• See page 158

PHCC EDUCATIONAL FOUNDATION NEED-BASED SCHOLARSHIP
• See page 158

PHCC EDUCATIONAL FOUNDATION SCHOLARSHIP PROGRAM
• See page 158

ROBERT H. MOLLOHAN FAMILY CHARITABLE FOUNDATION, INC.

http://www.mollohanfoundation.org/

HIGH TECHNOLOGY SCHOLARS PROGRAM
• See page 147

ROCKY MOUNTAIN COAL MINING INSTITUTE

http://www.rmcmi.org/

ROCKY MOUNTAIN COAL MINING INSTITUTE SCHOLARSHIP
• See page 185

SIMPLEHUMAN

http://www.simplehuman.com/

SIMPLE SOLUTIONS DESIGN COMPETITION

IDSA-endorsed competition to promote creative problem-solving through product design and increase public awareness of industrial design. Applicants must be enrolled in an Industrial Design program or a closely related program at a design school or university and must design a new, innovative product/technology/concept for making household chores easier. Entries evaluated on utility, efficiency, innovation, research, and aesthetics. See website for details http://www.simplehuman.com/design.

Academic Fields/Career Goals: Engineering-Related Technologies; Engineering/Technology; Industrial Design.

Award: Prize for use in freshman, sophomore, junior, or senior years; not renewable. *Number:* 1. *Amount:* $5000.

Eligibility Requirements: Applicant must be enrolled or expecting to enroll full- or part-time at a two-year or four-year or technical institution or university. Available to U.S. and non-U.S. citizens.

Application Requirements: Application form, entry in a contest, one PDF or JPEG of design, specs, materials, explanation. *Deadline:* February 27.

Contact: Sarah Beachler, Marketing and Communications Associate
Phone: 310-436-2278
Fax: 310-538-9196
E-mail: sbeachler@simplehuman.com

SOCIETY OF AUTOMOTIVE ENGINEERS

http://www.sae.org/

BMW/SAE ENGINEERING SCHOLARSHIP

• *See page 137*

DETROIT SECTION SAE TECHNICAL SCHOLARSHIP

Two $3500 renewable freshman scholarships will be awarded. Applicants must be a child or grandchild of a current SAE Detroit Section member. Student must maintain a 2.5 GPA and remain in good standing at the college or university in order to qualify for scholarship renewal. A student having completed a two-year program may continue for an additional consecutive two years at a second school offering a complete engineering or science baccalaureate degree program.

Academic Fields/Career Goals: Engineering-Related Technologies; Engineering/Technology; Mechanical Engineering.

Award: Scholarship for use in freshman or junior years; renewable. *Number:* 2. *Amount:* $3500.

Eligibility Requirements: Applicant must be enrolled or expecting to enroll full-time at a two-year or four-year institution or university. Applicant or parent of applicant must be member of Society of Automotive Engineers. Applicant must have 2.5 GPA or higher. Available to U.S. citizens.

Application Requirements: Application form, FAFSA, financial need analysis, test scores, transcript. *Deadline:* December 1.

Contact: Connie Harnish, SAE Educational Relations
Society of Automotive Engineers
400 Commonwealth Drive
Warrendale, PA 15096-0001
Phone: 724-772-4047
E-mail: connie@sae.org

EDWARD D. HENDRICKSON/SAE ENGINEERING SCHOLARSHIP

• *See page 137*

RALPH K. HILLQUIST HONORARY SAE SCHOLARSHIP

A $1000 nonrenewable scholarship awarded every other year at the SAE Noise and Vibration Conference. Applicants must be U.S. citizens enrolled full-time as a junior in a U.S. university. A minimum 3.0 GPA with significant academic and leadership achievements is required. The student must also have a declared major in mechanical engineering or an automotive-related engineering discipline, with preference given to those with studies in the areas of expertise related to noise and vibration.

Academic Fields/Career Goals: Engineering-Related Technologies; Engineering/Technology; Mechanical Engineering.

Award: Scholarship for use in junior year; not renewable. *Number:* 1. *Amount:* $1000.

Eligibility Requirements: Applicant must be enrolled or expecting to enroll full-time at a four-year institution or university. Applicant or parent

of applicant must be member of Society of Automotive Engineers. Applicant must have 3.0 GPA or higher. Available to U.S. citizens.

Application Requirements: Application form, essay, transcript. *Deadline:* February 1.

Contact: Connie Harnish, SAE Educational Relations
Society of Automotive Engineers
400 Commonwealth Drive
Warrendale, PA 15096-0001
Phone: 724-772-4047
E-mail: connie@sae.org

SAE WILLIAM G. BELFREY MEMORIAL GRANT

Two $1000 grants awarded annually. One grant will be awarded to a Canadian citizen enrolled at any Canadian university, and one grant will be specific to the University of Toronto. Applicants must be citizens of Canada.

Academic Fields/Career Goals: Engineering-Related Technologies; Engineering/Technology.

Award: Grant for use in junior year; not renewable. *Number:* 2. *Amount:* $1000.

Eligibility Requirements: Applicant must be Canadian citizen and enrolled or expecting to enroll full-time at a four-year institution or university.

Application Requirements: Application form, essay, recommendations or references, resume, transcript. *Deadline:* April 1.

Contact: Connie Harnish, SAE Educational Relations
Society of Automotive Engineers
400 Commonwealth Drive
Warrendale, PA 15096-0001
Phone: 724-772-4047
E-mail: connie@sae.org

TMC/SAE DONALD D. DAWSON TECHNICAL SCHOLARSHIP

• *See page 137*

YANMAR/SAE SCHOLARSHIP

Eligible applicants will be citizens of North America (U.S., Canada, Mexico) and will be entering their junior year of undergraduate engineering or enrolled in a postgraduate engineering or related science program. Applicants must be pursuing a course of study or research related to the conservation of energy in transportation, agriculture, construction, and power generation. Emphasis will be placed on research or study related to the internal combustion engine.

Academic Fields/Career Goals: Engineering-Related Technologies; Engineering/Technology; Materials Science, Engineering, and Metallurgy; Mechanical Engineering.

Award: Scholarship for use in junior, senior, or graduate years; renewable. *Number:* 1. *Amount:* $1000.

Eligibility Requirements: Applicant must be enrolled or expecting to enroll full-time at a four-year institution or university. Available to U.S. and non-U.S. citizens.

Application Requirements: Application form, essay, self-addressed stamped envelope with application, test scores, transcript. *Deadline:* April 1.

Contact: Connie Harnish, SAE Educational Relations
Society of Automotive Engineers
400 Commonwealth Drive
Warrendale, PA 15096
Phone: 724-772-4047
E-mail: connie@sae.org

SOCIETY OF BROADCAST ENGINEERS INC.

http://www.sbe.org/

ROBERT GREENBERG/HAROLD E. ENNES SCHOLARSHIP FUND AND ENNES EDUCATIONAL FOUNDATION BROADCAST TECHNOLOGY SCHOLARSHIP

• *See page 254*

SOCIETY OF MANUFACTURING ENGINEERS EDUCATION FOUNDATION

http://www.smeef.org/

MYRTLE AND EARL WALKER SCHOLARSHIP FUND

Scholarship available to full-time undergraduate students enrolled in a degree program in manufacturing engineering or technology in the United States or Canada. Minimum GPA of 3.0. Scholarship value and number of awards granted varies.

Academic Fields/Career Goals: Engineering-Related Technologies; Engineering/Technology; Mechanical Engineering.

Award: Scholarship for use in freshman, sophomore, junior, or senior years; not renewable. *Number:* 1–25. *Amount:* $1000–$7000.

Eligibility Requirements: Applicant must be enrolled or expecting to enroll full-time at a two-year or four-year or technical institution or university. Applicant must have 3.0 GPA or higher. Available to U.S. and Canadian citizens.

Application Requirements: Application form, essay, recommendations or references, resume, test scores, transcript. *Deadline:* February 1.

SOCIETY OF MOTION PICTURE AND TELEVISION ENGINEERS

http://www.smpte.org/

LOUIS F. WOLF JR. MEMORIAL SCHOLARSHIP

• *See page 195*

STUDENT PAPER AWARD

• *See page 195*

SOCIETY OF WOMEN ENGINEERS

http://www.swe.org/

ADMIRAL GRACE MURRAY HOPPER SCHOLARSHIP

• *See page 204*

SOCIETY OF WOMEN ENGINEERS-ROCKY MOUNTAIN SECTION

http://www.societyofwomenengineers.org/RockyMountain/

SOCIETY OF WOMEN ENGINEERS-ROCKY MOUNTAIN SECTION SCHOLARSHIP PROGRAM

• *See page 176*

STRAIGHTFORWARD MEDIA

http://www.straightforwardmedia.com/

STRAIGHTFORWARD MEDIA ENGINEERING SCHOLARSHIP

• *See page 176*

TAG AND LABEL MANUFACTURERS INSTITUTE, INC.

http://www.tlmi.com/

TLMI 4 YEAR COLLEGE DEGREE SCHOLARSHIP PROGRAM

A $5000 scholarship awarded to a sophomore or junior attending a four-year accredited college or university on a full-time basis for their junior or senior year studies. Applicants must demonstrate interest in pursuing a career in the tag and label industry.

Academic Fields/Career Goals: Engineering-Related Technologies; Flexography; Graphics/Graphic Arts/Printing.

Award: Scholarship for use in junior or senior years; renewable. *Number:* up to 6. *Amount:* $5000.

Eligibility Requirements: Applicant must be enrolled or expecting to enroll full-time at a four-year institution or university and must have an interest in designated field specified by sponsor. Applicant must have 3.0 GPA or higher. Available to U.S. and Canadian citizens.

Application Requirements: Application form, interview, portfolio, recommendations or references, resume, transcript. *Deadline:* March 31.

TECHNICAL ASSOCIATION OF THE PULP & PAPER INDUSTRY (TAPPI)

http://www.tappi.org/

CORRUGATED PACKAGING DIVISION SCHOLARSHIPS

Award to applicants working full time or part time in the box business and attending day/night school for a graduate or undergraduate degree or to a full-time student in a two- or four-year college, university or technical school. Information can be found at http://www.tappi.org/ s_tappi/sec.asp?CID=6101&DID=546695.

Academic Fields/Career Goals: Engineering-Related Technologies; Paper and Pulp Engineering.

Award: Scholarship for use in freshman, sophomore, junior, senior, or graduate years; not renewable. *Number:* 1–4. *Amount:* $1000–$2000.

Eligibility Requirements: Applicant must be enrolled or expecting to enroll full- or part-time at a four-year or technical institution or university. Applicant must have 3.0 GPA or higher. Available to U.S. and non-U.S. citizens.

Application Requirements: Application form, recommendations or references, transcript.

Contact: Mr. Charles Bohanan, Director of Standards and Awards
Technical Association of the Pulp & Paper Industry (TAPPI)
15 Technology Parkway South
Peachtree Corners, GA 30092
Phone: 770-209-7276
Fax: 770-446-6947
E-mail: standards@tappi.org

TRANSPORTATION CLUBS INTERNATIONAL

http://www.transportationclubsinternational.com/

TRANSPORTATION CLUBS INTERNATIONAL FRED A. HOOPER MEMORIAL SCHOLARSHIP

Merit-based award available to currently enrolled college students majoring in traffic management, transportation, physical distribution, logistics, or a related field. Must have completed at least one year of post-high school education. One-time award of $1500. Must submit three references. Available to citizens of the United States, Canada, and Mexico.

Academic Fields/Career Goals: Engineering-Related Technologies; Transportation.

Award: Scholarship for use in freshman, sophomore, junior, or senior years; not renewable. *Number:* 1. *Amount:* $1500.

Eligibility Requirements: Applicant must be enrolled or expecting to enroll full- or part-time at a two-year or four-year or technical institution or university. Available to U.S. and non-U.S. citizens.

Application Requirements: Application form, essay, personal photograph, recommendations or references, transcript. *Deadline:* April 30.

Contact: Bill Blair, Scholarships Trustee
Phone: 832-300-5905
E-mail: bblair@zimmerworldwide.com

TURNER CONSTRUCTION COMPANY

http://www.turnerconstruction.com/

YOUTHFORCE 2020 SCHOLARSHIP PROGRAM

• *See page 113*

UNITED NEGRO COLLEGE FUND

http://www.uncf.org/

NAACP/HUBERTUS W.V. WILLEMS SCHOLARSHIP FOR MALE SCHOLARS

Scholarship awarded to male students who are U.S. citizens and plan to study engineering, chemistry, physics, or mathematical sciences in undergraduate or graduate school. Must be a full-time undergraduate or full- or part-time graduate student at an accredited college or university. Undergraduates receive $2000 and graduate students receive $3000. Minimum 3.0 GPA required. Members of the National NAACP Board of Directors, SCF Trustees, National Youth Work Committee, the NAACP Scholarship Selection Committee, employees and their spouses or families to the first degree of consanguinity, are not eligible to apply for or receive this scholarship.

Academic Fields/Career Goals: Engineering-Related Technologies; Mathematics; Natural Sciences.

Award: Scholarship for use in freshman, sophomore, junior, senior, or graduate years; not renewable. *Amount:* $2000–$3000.

Eligibility Requirements: Applicant must be Black (non-Hispanic); enrolled or expecting to enroll full- or part-time at a four-year institution or university and male. Applicant must have 3.0 GPA or higher. Available to U.S. citizens.

Application Requirements: Application form, financial need analysis. *Deadline:* continuous.

VERMONT SPACE GRANT CONSORTIUM

http://www.cems.uvm.edu/vsgc

VERMONT SPACE GRANT CONSORTIUM SCHOLARSHIP PROGRAM

• See page 107

WEST VIRGINIA HIGHER EDUCATION POLICY COMMISSION-STUDENT SERVICES

http://wvhepcnew.wvnet.edu/

WEST VIRGINIA ENGINEERING, SCIENCE AND TECHNOLOGY SCHOLARSHIP PROGRAM

• See page 257

XEROX

http://www.xerox.com//

TECHNICAL MINORITY SCHOLARSHIP

• See page 177

ENGINEERING/ TECHNOLOGY

AACE INTERNATIONAL

http://www.aacei.org/

AACE INTERNATIONAL COMPETITIVE SCHOLARSHIP

• See page 108

AEG FOUNDATION

http://www.aegfoundation.org/

AEG FOUNDATION

• See page 225

AHS INTERNATIONAL—THE VERTICAL FLIGHT TECHNICAL SOCIETY

http://www.vtol.org/

VERTICAL FLIGHT FOUNDATION SCHOLARSHIP

• See page 124

AIR TRAFFIC CONTROL ASSOCIATION INC.

http://www.atca.org/

AIR TRAFFIC CONTROL ASSOCIATION SCHOLARSHIP

• See page 126

AIST FOUNDATION

http://www.aistfoundation.org/

AIST ALFRED B. GLOSSBRENNER AND JOHN KLUSCH SCHOLARSHIPS

Scholarship intended to award high school senior who plans on pursuing a degree in metallurgy or engineering. Student must have previous academic excellence in science courses. Applicant must be a dependent of a AIST Northeastern Ohio chapter member.

Academic Fields/Career Goals: Engineering/Technology; Materials Science, Engineering, and Metallurgy.

Award: Scholarship for use in freshman year; not renewable. *Number:* 2. *Amount:* $1000.

Eligibility Requirements: Applicant must be high school student and planning to enroll or expecting to enroll full-time at a four-year institution or university. Applicant or parent of applicant must be member of Association for Iron and Steel Technology. Available to U.S. and non-U.S. citizens.

Application Requirements: Application form, essay, recommendations or references, resume, test scores, transcript. *Deadline:* April 30.

Contact: Richard Kurz, Chapter Secretary
AIST Foundation
22831 East State Street, Route 62
Alliance, OH 44601

AIST WILLIAM E. SCHWABE MEMORIAL SCHOLARSHIP

• See page 248

ASSOCIATION FOR IRON AND STEEL TECHNOLOGY BALTIMORE CHAPTER SCHOLARSHIP

• See page 259

ASSOCIATION FOR IRON AND STEEL TECHNOLOGY DAVID H. SAMSON CANADIAN SCHOLARSHIP

• See page 162

ASSOCIATION FOR IRON AND STEEL TECHNOLOGY MIDWEST CHAPTER BETTY MCKERN SCHOLARSHIP

Scholarship awarded to a graduating female high school senior, or to an undergraduate freshman, sophomore, or junior enrolled in a fully AIST-accredited college or university. Applicant must be in good academic standing. Must be a dependant of an AIST Midwest chapter member.

Academic Fields/Career Goals: Engineering/Technology.

Award: Scholarship for use in freshman, sophomore, junior, or senior years; not renewable. *Number:* 1. *Amount:* $3000.

Eligibility Requirements: Applicant must be enrolled or expecting to enroll full-time at a four-year institution or university and female. Applicant or parent of applicant must be member of Association for Iron and Steel Technology. Available to U.S. and non-U.S. citizens.

Application Requirements: Application form, essay, recommendations or references, resume, test scores, transcript. *Deadline:* March 15.

ASSOCIATION FOR IRON AND STEEL TECHNOLOGY MIDWEST CHAPTER DON NELSON SCHOLARSHIP

One scholarship for a graduating high school senior, or undergraduate freshman, sophomore or junior enrolled in a fully AIST-accredited college or university. Applicant must be in good academic standing. Must be a dependent of an AIST Midwest chapter member. May reapply each year for the duration of college education.

Academic Fields/Career Goals: Engineering/Technology.

Award: Scholarship for use in freshman, sophomore, junior, or senior years; not renewable. *Number:* 1. *Amount:* up to $1000.

Eligibility Requirements: Applicant must be enrolled or expecting to enroll full-time at a four-year institution or university. Applicant or parent of applicant must be member of Association for Iron and Steel Technology. Available to U.S. and non-U.S. citizens.

Application Requirements: Application form, essay, recommendations or references, resume, test scores, transcript. *Deadline:* March 15.

ASSOCIATION FOR IRON AND STEEL TECHNOLOGY MIDWEST CHAPTER ENGINEERING SCHOLARSHIP

Two four-year scholarships awarded to graduating high school senior or undergraduate freshman, sophomore or junior enrolled in a fully AIST-accredited college or university majoring engineering. Applicant must be in good academic standing. Must be a dependent of an AIST Midwest chapter member. May reapply each year for the duration of college education.

Academic Fields/Career Goals: Engineering/Technology.

Award: Scholarship for use in freshman, sophomore, or junior years; renewable. *Number:* 2. *Amount:* $1500.

Eligibility Requirements: Applicant must be enrolled or expecting to enroll full-time at a four-year institution or university. Applicant or parent of applicant must be member of Association for Iron and Steel Technology. Available to U.S. and non-U.S. citizens.

Application Requirements: Application form, essay, recommendations or references, resume, test scores, transcript. *Deadline:* March 15.

ASSOCIATION FOR IRON AND STEEL TECHNOLOGY MIDWEST CHAPTER JACK GILL SCHOLARSHIP

Scholarship for a graduating high school senior, or undergraduate freshman, sophomore, or junior enrolled in a fully AIST-accredited college or university majoring engineering. Applicant must be in good academic standing. Must be a dependent of an AIST Midwest chapter member. May reapply each year for the duration of college education.

Academic Fields/Career Goals: Engineering/Technology.

Award: Scholarship for use in freshman, sophomore, junior, or senior years; not renewable. *Number:* 1. *Amount:* $3000.

Eligibility Requirements: Applicant must be enrolled or expecting to enroll full-time at a four-year institution or university. Applicant or parent of applicant must be member of Association for Iron and Steel Technology. Available to U.S. and non-U.S. citizens.

Application Requirements: Application form, essay, recommendations or references, resume, test scores, transcript. *Deadline:* March 15.

ASSOCIATION FOR IRON AND STEEL TECHNOLOGY MIDWEST CHAPTER MEL NICKEL SCHOLARSHIP

Scholarship awarded to a graduating high school senior, or undergraduate freshman, sophomore or junior enrolled in a fully AIST-accredited college or university majoring engineering. Applicant must be in good academic standing. Must be a dependent of an AIST Midwest chapter member. May reapply each year for the term of their college education.

Academic Fields/Career Goals: Engineering/Technology.

Award: Scholarship for use in freshman, sophomore, junior, or senior years; not renewable. *Number:* 1. *Amount:* $3000.

Eligibility Requirements: Applicant must be enrolled or expecting to enroll full-time at a four-year institution or university. Applicant or parent of applicant must be member of Association for Iron and Steel Technology. Available to U.S. and non-U.S. citizens.

Application Requirements: Application form, essay, recommendations or references, resume, test scores, transcript. *Deadline:* March 15.

ASSOCIATION FOR IRON AND STEEL TECHNOLOGY MIDWEST CHAPTER NON-ENGINEERING SCHOLARSHIP

Scholarship for graduating high school senior, or undergraduate freshman, sophomore, or junior enrolled in a fully AIST-accredited college or university. Applicant must be in good academic standing and dependent of an AIST Midwest chapter member. Recipients may reapply each year for the term of their college education.

Academic Fields/Career Goals: Engineering/Technology.

Award: Scholarship for use in freshman, sophomore, junior, or senior years; not renewable. *Number:* 3. *Amount:* $1500.

Eligibility Requirements: Applicant must be enrolled or expecting to enroll full-time at a four-year institution or university. Applicant or parent of applicant must be member of Association for Iron and Steel Technology. Available to U.S. and non-U.S. citizens.

Application Requirements: Application form, essay, recommendations or references, resume, test scores, transcript. *Deadline:* March 15.

ASSOCIATION FOR IRON AND STEEL TECHNOLOGY MIDWEST CHAPTER WESTERN STATES SCHOLARSHIP

Scholarship of $3000 awarded to a graduating high school senior, or undergraduate freshman, sophomore, junior, or senior enrolled in a fully AIST-accredited college or university. Applicant must be in good academic standing and a dependant of an AIST Midwest chapter member. Recipients may reapply each year for the term of their college education.

Academic Fields/Career Goals: Engineering/Technology.

Award: Scholarship for use in freshman, sophomore, junior, or senior years; not renewable. *Number:* 1. *Amount:* $3000.

Eligibility Requirements: Applicant must be enrolled or expecting to enroll full-time at a four-year institution or university. Applicant or parent of applicant must be member of Association for Iron and Steel Technology. Available to U.S. and non-U.S. citizens.

Application Requirements: Application form, essay, recommendations or references, resume, test scores, transcript. *Deadline:* March 15.

ASSOCIATION FOR IRON AND STEEL TECHNOLOGY NORTHWEST MEMBER CHAPTER SCHOLARSHIP

Scholarships of $1000 available to encourage a Pacific Northwest area student to prepare for a career in engineering. Must be the child, grandchild, spouse, or niece/nephew of a member in good standing of the AIST Northwest Chapter. Award based on academic achievements in chemistry, mathematics, and physics.

Academic Fields/Career Goals: Engineering/Technology; Materials Science, Engineering, and Metallurgy.

Award: Scholarship for use in freshman, sophomore, junior, or senior years; not renewable. *Number:* 2. *Amount:* $1000.

Eligibility Requirements: Applicant must be enrolled or expecting to enroll full- or part-time at a four-year institution or university. Applicant or parent of applicant must be member of Association for Iron and Steel Technology. Available to U.S. citizens.

Application Requirements: Application form, essay, recommendations or references, resume, test scores, transcript. *Deadline:* April 30.

Contact: Gerardo Giraldo, AIST Northwest Chapter Secretary
AIST Foundation
2434 Eyres Place West
Seattle, WA 98199
Phone: 206-285-7897
E-mail: acero9938@comcast.net

ASSOCIATION FOR IRON AND STEEL TECHNOLOGY OHIO VALLEY CHAPTER SCHOLARSHIP

• *See page 142*

ASSOCIATION FOR IRON AND STEEL TECHNOLOGY PITTSBURGH CHAPTER SCHOLARSHIP

Scholarships of $2500 for children, stepchildren, grandchildren, or spouse of a member in good standing of the Pittsburgh Chapter. Applicant must be a high school senior or currently enrolled undergraduate preparing for a career in engineering or metallurgy.

Academic Fields/Career Goals: Engineering/Technology; Materials Science, Engineering, and Metallurgy.

Award: Scholarship for use in freshman, sophomore, junior, or senior years; not renewable. *Number:* 2–3. *Amount:* $2500.

Eligibility Requirements: Applicant must be enrolled or expecting to enroll full-time at a four-year institution or university. Applicant or parent of applicant must be member of Association for Iron and Steel Technology. Available to U.S. citizens.

Application Requirements: Application form, essay, recommendations or references, resume, test scores, transcript. *Deadline:* April 30.

Contact: Daniel Kos, Program Coordinator
AIST Foundation
375 Saxonburg Boulevard
Saxonburg, PA 16056
E-mail: dkos@ii-vi.com

ASSOCIATION FOR IRON AND STEEL TECHNOLOGY SOUTHEAST MEMBER CHAPTER SCHOLARSHIP

Scholarship of $3000 for children, stepchildren, grandchildren, or spouse of active Southeast Chapter members who are pursuing a career in engineering, the sciences, or other majors relating to iron and steel production. Students may reapply for the scholarship each year for their term of college.

Academic Fields/Career Goals: Engineering/Technology; Materials Science, Engineering, and Metallurgy.

Award: Scholarship for use in freshman, sophomore, junior, or senior years; renewable. *Number:* 1. *Amount:* $3000.

Eligibility Requirements: Applicant must be enrolled or expecting to enroll full- or part-time at a four-year institution or university. Applicant or parent of applicant must be member of Association for Iron and Steel Technology. Available to U.S. citizens.

Application Requirements: Application form, essay, recommendations or references, resume, test scores, transcript. *Deadline:* April 30.

Contact: Mike Hutson, AIST Southeast Chapter Secretary
AIST Foundation
803 Floyd Street
Kings Mountain, NC 29086
Phone: 704-730-8320
Fax: 704-730-8321
E-mail: mike@johnhutsoncompany.com

ALBERTA HERITAGE SCHOLARSHIP FUND

http://www.alis.alberta.ca/

NORTHERN ALBERTA DEVELOPMENT COUNCIL BURSARY
• See page 219

AMERICAN CHEMICAL SOCIETY, RUBBER DIVISION

http://www.rubber.org/

AMERICAN CHEMICAL SOCIETY, RUBBER DIVISION UNDERGRADUATE SCHOLARSHIP
• See page 163

AMERICAN COUNCIL OF ENGINEERING COMPANIES OF PENNSYLVANIA (ACEC/PA)

http://www.acecpa.org/

ENGINEERING SCHOLARSHIP
• See page 163

AMERICAN FOUNDATION FOR THE BLIND

http://www.afb.org/

PAUL W. RUCKES SCHOLARSHIP
• See page 199

AMERICAN INDIAN SCIENCE AND ENGINEERING SOCIETY

http://www.aises.org/

BURLINGTON NORTHERN SANTA FE FOUNDATION SCHOLARSHIP
• See page 102

AMERICAN INSTITUTE OF AERONAUTICS AND ASTRONAUTICS

http://www.aiaa.org/

AIAA FOUNDATION UNDERGRADUATE SCHOLARSHIP
• See page 102

AMERICAN NUCLEAR SOCIETY

http://www.ans.org/

AMERICAN NUCLEAR SOCIETY VOGT RADIOCHEMISTRY SCHOLARSHIP

One-time award for juniors, seniors, and first-year graduate students enrolled or proposing research in radio-analytical or analytical application of nuclear science. Must be U.S. citizen or permanent resident.

Academic Fields/Career Goals: Engineering/Technology; Nuclear Science.

Award: Scholarship for use in junior, senior, or graduate years; not renewable. *Number:* 1. *Amount:* $3000.

Eligibility Requirements: Applicant must be enrolled or expecting to enroll full-time at a four-year institution or university. Available to U.S. citizens.

Application Requirements: Application form, recommendations or references, sponsorship letter from ANS organization, transcript. *Deadline:* February 1.

AMERICAN PUBLIC TRANSPORTATION FOUNDATION

http://www.apta.com/

JACK GILSTRAP SCHOLARSHIP

Awarded the APTF scholarship to the applicant with the highest score. Must be in public transportation industry-related fields of study. Must be sponsored by AFTA member organization and complete an internship program with a member organization. Minimum 3.0 GPA required.

Academic Fields/Career Goals: Engineering/Technology; Transportation.

Award: Scholarship for use in sophomore, junior, senior, or graduate years; renewable. *Number:* 1. *Amount:* $2500.

Eligibility Requirements: Applicant must be enrolled or expecting to enroll full-time at a two-year or four-year institution or university. Applicant must have 3.0 GPA or higher. Available to U.S. and Canadian citizens.

Application Requirements: Application form, essay, financial need analysis, recommendations or references, transcript, verification of enrollment for the current semester and copy of fee schedule from the college/university. *Deadline:* June 16.

Contact: Pamela Boswell, Vice President of Program Management
American Public Transportation Foundation
1666 K Street, NW
Washington, DC 20006-1215
Phone: 202-496-4803
Fax: 202-496-2323
E-mail: pboswell@apta.com

TRANSIT HALL OF FAME SCHOLARSHIP AWARD PROGRAM
• See page 179

AMERICAN RAILWAY ENGINEERING AND MAINTENANCE OF WAY ASSOCIATION

http://www.aremafoundation.org/

AREMA MICHAEL R. GARCIA SCHOLARSHIP
• *See page 179*

AREMA PRESIDENTIAL SPOUSE SCHOLARSHIP
• *See page 180*

AREMA UNDERGRADUATE SCHOLARSHIPS
• *See page 180*

COMMITTEE 12-RAIL TRANSIT UNDERGRADUATE SCHOLARSHIP
• *See page 260*

CSX SCHOLARSHIP
• *See page 260*

JOHN J. CUNNINGHAM MEMORIAL SCHOLARSHIP (SPONSORED JOINTLY BY COMMITTEES 11 AND 17)
Scholarship awarded to a junior or senior college student pursuing an undergraduate degree in a professional field that has direct applications in the passenger rail sector. Minimum 2.00 GPA required.

Academic Fields/Career Goals: Engineering/Technology; Transportation.

Award: Scholarship for use in junior or senior years; not renewable. *Amount:* $1000.

Eligibility Requirements: Applicant must be enrolled or expecting to enroll full-time at a four-year institution or university. Available to U.S. citizens.

Application Requirements: Application form, cover letter, recommendations or references, resume, transcript. *Deadline:* March 8.

Contact: Stacy Spaulding, Director of Committees and Technical
      Services
      Phone: 301-459-3200 Ext. 706
      E-mail: sspaulding@arema.org

NORFOLK SOUTHERN FOUNDATION SCHOLARSHIP
• *See page 260*

PB RAIL ENGINEERING SCHOLARSHIP
• *See page 260*

REMSA SCHOLARSHIP
• *See page 260*

AMERICAN SOCIETY FOR ENGINEERING EDUCATION

http://www.asee.org/

SCIENCE, MATHEMATICS, AND RESEARCH FOR TRANSFORMATION DEFENSE SCHOLARSHIP FOR SERVICE PROGRAM
• *See page 102*

AMERICAN SOCIETY OF CERTIFIED ENGINEERING TECHNICIANS

http://www.ascet.org/

JOSEPH C. JOHNSON MEMORIAL GRANT
Grant for $750 given to qualified applicants in order to offset the cost of tuition, books and lab fees. Applicant must be a U.S. citizen or a legal resident of the country in which the applicant is currently living, as well as be either a student, certified, regular, registered or associate member of ASCET. Student must be enrolled in an engineering technology program. For further information, visit http://www.ascet.org.

Academic Fields/Career Goals: Engineering/Technology.

Award: Grant for use in freshman, sophomore, junior, or senior years; not renewable. *Number:* 1. *Amount:* $750.

Eligibility Requirements: Applicant must be enrolled or expecting to enroll full- or part-time at a two-year or four-year or technical institution or university. Applicant must have 3.0 GPA or higher. Available to U.S. citizens.

Application Requirements: Application form, financial need analysis, personal photograph, recommendations or references, transcript. *Deadline:* April 1.

Contact: Mr. Tim Latham, General Manager
      American Society of Certified Engineering Technicians
      PO Box 1536
      Brandon, MS 39043
      Phone: 601-824-8991
      E-mail: tim-latham@ascet.org

JOSEPH M. PARISH MEMORIAL GRANT
Grant of $500 will be awarded to a student to be used to offset the cost of tuition, books and lab fees. Applicant must be a student member of ASCET and be a U.S. citizen or a legal resident of the country in which the applicant is currently living. The award will be given to full time students enrolled in an engineering technology program; students pursuing a BS degree in engineering are not eligible for this grant. For more information, visit http://www.ascet.org.

Academic Fields/Career Goals: Engineering/Technology.

Award: Grant for use in freshman, sophomore, junior, or senior years; not renewable. *Number:* 1. *Amount:* $500.

Eligibility Requirements: Applicant must be enrolled or expecting to enroll full- or part-time at a two-year or four-year or technical institution or university. Applicant must have 3.0 GPA or higher. Available to U.S. citizens.

Application Requirements: Application form, financial need analysis, personal photograph, recommendations or references, transcript. *Deadline:* April 1.

Contact: Mr. Tim Latham, General Manager
      American Society of Certified Engineering Technicians
      PO Box 1536
      Brandon, MS 39043
      Phone: 601-824-8991
      E-mail: tim-latham@ascet.org

AMERICAN SOCIETY OF HEATING, REFRIGERATING, AND AIR CONDITIONING ENGINEERS, INC.

http://www.ashrae.org/

ALWIN B. NEWTON SCHOLARSHIP
• *See page 249*

ASHRAE GENERAL SCHOLARSHIPS
• *See page 260*

ASHRAE MEMORIAL SCHOLARSHIP
• *See page 249*

ASHRAE REGION III BOGGARM SETTY SCHOLARSHIP
• *See page 166*

ASHRAE REGION IV BENNY BOOTLE SCHOLARSHIP
• *See page 109*

ASHRAE REGION VIII SCHOLARSHIP
• *See page 261*

DUANE HANSON SCHOLARSHIP
• *See page 250*

ENGINEERING TECHNOLOGY SCHOLARSHIP
• *See page 250*

FRANK M. CODA SCHOLARSHIP
• *See page 250*

HENRY ADAMS SCHOLARSHIP
• *See page 250*

HIGH SCHOOL SENIOR SCHOLARSHIPS
• *See page 261*

LYNN G. BELLENGER SCHOLARSHIP
• *See page 250*

REUBEN TRANE SCHOLARSHIP
• *See page 250*

WILLIS H. CARRIER SCHOLARSHIPS
• *See page 251*

AMERICAN SOCIETY OF NAVAL ENGINEERS
http://www.navalengineers.org/

AMERICAN SOCIETY OF NAVAL ENGINEERS SCHOLARSHIP
• *See page 103*

AMERICAN SOCIETY OF PLUMBING ENGINEERS
http://www.aspe.org/

ALFRED STEELE ENGINEERING SCHOLARSHIP
Scholarships of $1000 are awarded for the members of American society of plumbing engineers towards education and professional development on plumbing engineering and designing.

Academic Fields/Career Goals: Engineering/Technology; Industrial Design.

Award: Scholarship for use in freshman, sophomore, junior, or senior years; not renewable. *Number:* 5. *Amount:* $1000.

Eligibility Requirements: Applicant must be enrolled or expecting to enroll full-time at a two-year or four-year or technical institution or university. Applicant must have 3.0 GPA or higher. Available to U.S. and non-U.S. citizens.

Application Requirements: Application form, community service, essay, recommendations or references, statement of personal achievement, transcript. *Deadline:* September 1.

Contact: Stacey Kidd, Membership Director
    Phone: 773-693-2773
    Fax: 773-695-9007
    E-mail: skidd@aspe.org

AMERICAN WELDING SOCIETY
http://www.aws.org/

AIRGAS-TERRY JARVIS MEMORIAL SCHOLARSHIP
• *See page 261*

AMERICAN WELDING SOCIETY INTERNATIONAL SCHOLARSHIP
• *See page 262*

D. FRED AND MARIAN L. BOVIE NATIONAL SCHOLARSHIP
Scholarship for welding engineering at The Ohio State University.

Academic Fields/Career Goals: Engineering/Technology.

Award: Scholarship for use in freshman, sophomore, junior, or senior years; not renewable. *Number:* 1–1. *Amount:* up to $3000.

Eligibility Requirements: Applicant must be enrolled or expecting to enroll full-time at an institution or university and studying in Ohio. Applicant must have 3.0 GPA or higher. Available to U.S. citizens.

Application Requirements: Application form, financial need analysis, recommendations or references, transcript. *Deadline:* February 15.

Contact: Vicki Pinsky, Manager, AWS Foundation
    American Welding Society
    8669 Doral Boulevard, Suite 130
    Doral, FL 33166
    Phone: 305-443-9353 Ext. 212
    Fax: 305-443-7559
    E-mail: vpinsky@aws.org

DONALD AND SHIRLEY HASTINGS SCHOLARSHIP
Award for U.S. citizen at least 18 years of age pursuing a four-year undergraduate degree in welding engineering or welding engineering technology. Priority given to welding engineering students. Preference is given to students residing or attending school in California or Ohio. Submit copy of proposed curriculum. Minimum GPA of 2.5 required.

Academic Fields/Career Goals: Engineering/Technology; Materials Science, Engineering, and Metallurgy.

Award: Scholarship for use in freshman, sophomore, junior, or senior years; not renewable. *Number:* 1. *Amount:* $2500.

Eligibility Requirements: Applicant must be enrolled or expecting to enroll full- or part-time at a four-year institution or university. Available to U.S. citizens.

Application Requirements: Application form, FAFSA, financial need analysis, recommendations or references, transcript. *Deadline:* February 15.

Contact: Vicki Pinsky, Manager, Foundation
    American Welding Society
    8669 Doral Boulevard, Suite 130
    Doral, FL 33166
    Phone: 800-443-9353 Ext. 212
    Fax: 305-443-7559
    E-mail: vpinsky@aws.org

DONALD F. HASTINGS SCHOLARSHIP
• *See page 262*

EDWARD J. BRADY MEMORIAL SCHOLARSHIP
• *See page 262*

HOWARD E. AND WILMA J. ADKINS MEMORIAL SCHOLARSHIP
• *See page 262*

JACK R. BARCKHOFF WELDING MANAGEMENT SCHOLARSHIP
Scholarship for a college junior at The Ohio State University. Must complete course in Total Welding Management. Essay required on improving the world of welding and the welding industry in the US.

Academic Fields/Career Goals: Engineering/Technology.

Award: Scholarship for use in junior year; not renewable. *Number:* 2. *Amount:* up to $2500.

Eligibility Requirements: Applicant must be enrolled or expecting to enroll full- or part-time at an institution or university and studying in Ohio. Available to U.S. citizens.

Application Requirements: Application form, essay, financial need analysis, recommendations or references, transcript. *Deadline:* February 15.

Contact: Vicki Pinsky, Manager, AWS Foundation
    American Welding Society
    8669 Doral Boulevard, Suite 130
    Doral, FL 33166
    Phone: 305-443-9353 Ext. 212
    Fax: 305-443-7559
    E-mail: vpinsky@aws.org

JOHN C. LINCOLN MEMORIAL SCHOLARSHIP
• *See page 262*

MATSUO BRIDGE COMPANY LTD. OF JAPAN SCHOLARSHIP
• *See page 181*

MILLER ELECTRIC INTERNATIONAL WORLD SKILLS COMPETITION SCHOLARSHIP
• *See page 262*

MILLER ELECTRIC MFG. CO. SCHOLARSHIP
• *See page 263*

PAST PRESIDENTS' SCHOLARSHIP

Scholarship available to students pursuing a bachelor's degree in welding engineering, welding engineering technology, or an engineering program with emphasis on welding. Also open to graduate students pursuing a master's or doctorate in engineering or management.

Academic Fields/Career Goals: Engineering/Technology; Mechanical Engineering.

Award: Scholarship for use in junior or senior years; not renewable. *Number:* 1. *Amount:* $2500.

Eligibility Requirements: Applicant must be enrolled or expecting to enroll full- or part-time at a four-year institution. Available to U.S. citizens.

Application Requirements: Application form, financial need analysis, recommendations or references, transcript. *Deadline:* February 15.

Contact: Ms. Vicki Pinsky, Manager
American Welding Society
8669 Doral Boulevard, Suite 130
Doral, FL 33166

PRAXAIR INTERNATIONAL SCHOLARSHIP
• *See page 263*

RESISTANCE WELDER MANUFACTURERS' ASSOCIATION SCHOLARSHIP

$2500 award to students who express an interest in the resistance welding process while pursuing a career in welding engineering. Available to U.S. and Canadian citizens. Must be a junior in a four-year program only and maintain a minimum 3.0 GPA.

Academic Fields/Career Goals: Engineering/Technology; Materials Science, Engineering, and Metallurgy.

Award: Scholarship for use in junior year; not renewable. *Number:* 1. *Amount:* $2500.

Eligibility Requirements: Applicant must be enrolled or expecting to enroll full- or part-time at a four-year institution or university. Applicant must have 3.0 GPA or higher. Available to U.S. and Canadian citizens.

Application Requirements: Application form, essay, resume, transcript. *Deadline:* February 15.

Contact: Vicki Pinsky, Manager, Foundation
American Welding Society
8669 Doral Boulevard, Suite 130
Doral, FL 33166
Phone: 800-443-9353 Ext. 212
Fax: 305-443-7559
E-mail: vpinsky@aws.org

ROBERT L. PEASLEE BRAZING SCHOLARSHIP

$2500 award for students pursuing a minimum four-year bachelor's degree in welding engineering or welding engineering technology with an emphasis on brazing and soldering applications. Must be minimum 18 years of age and at least a college junior. 3.0 GPA required.

Academic Fields/Career Goals: Engineering/Technology; Materials Science, Engineering, and Metallurgy.

Award: Scholarship for use in junior or senior years; not renewable. *Number:* 1. *Amount:* $2500.

Eligibility Requirements: Applicant must be enrolled or expecting to enroll full- or part-time at a four-year institution or university. Applicant must have 3.0 GPA or higher. Available to U.S. and Canadian citizens.

Application Requirements: Application form, financial need analysis, recommendations or references, resume, statement of unmet financial need, transcript. *Deadline:* February 15.

Contact: Vicki Pinsky, Manager, Foundation
American Welding Society
8669 Doral Boulevard, Suite 130
Doral, FL 33166
Phone: 800-443-9353 Ext. 212
Fax: 305-443-7559
E-mail: vpinsky@aws.org

WILLIAM B. HOWELL MEMORIAL SCHOLARSHIP
• *See page 263*

ARIZONA PROFESSIONAL CHAPTER OF AISES

ARIZONA PROFESSIONAL CHAPTER OF AISES SCHOLARSHIP

Scholarship awarded to American Indian/Alaska Natives attending Arizona schools of higher education pursuing degrees in the sciences, engineering, medicine, natural resources, math, and technology. Student must be a full-time undergraduate student (at least 12 hours per semester) at an accredited two-year or four-year college or university.

Academic Fields/Career Goals: Engineering/Technology; Health and Medical Sciences; Natural Resources; Physical Sciences.

Award: Scholarship for use in freshman, sophomore, junior, or senior years; not renewable.

Eligibility Requirements: Applicant must be American Indian/Alaska Native; enrolled or expecting to enroll full-time at a two-year or four-year institution or university and studying in Arizona. Applicant must have 2.5 GPA or higher. Available to U.S. citizens.

Application Requirements: Application form, essay, portfolio, proof of tribal enrollment, copy of AISES membership card, recommendations or references, resume, transcript. *Deadline:* August 17.

Contact: Jaime Ashike, Scholarship Committee
Arizona Professional Chapter of AISES
PO Box 2528
Phoenix, AZ 85002
Phone: 480-326-0958
E-mail: amazing_butterfly@hotmail.com

ARMED FORCES COMMUNICATIONS AND ELECTRONICS ASSOCIATION, EDUCATIONAL FOUNDATION

http://www.afcea.org/scholarships

ARMED FORCES COMMUNICATIONS AND ELECTRONICS ASSOCIATION GENERAL EMMETT PAIGE SCHOLARSHIP
• *See page 127*

ARMED FORCES COMMUNICATIONS AND ELECTRONICS ASSOCIATION ROTC SCHOLARSHIP PROGRAM
• *See page 127*

DISABLED WAR VETERANS SCHOLARSHIP
• *See page 128*

ARRL FOUNDATION INC.

http://www.arrl.org/

ALFRED E. FRIEND JR., W4CF, MEMORIAL SCHOLARSHIP
• *See page 166*

ALLEN AND BERTHA WATSON MEMORIAL SCHOLARSHIP

$500 award for the study of science, technology, or engineering. Must be a resident of Oklahoma or attend a 4-year university or college in Oklahoma. If no qualified applicant is identified, an applicant from the ARRL West Gulf Division (Texas and Oklahoma) will be chosen.

Academic Fields/Career Goals: Engineering/Technology; Science, Technology, and Society.

Award: Scholarship for use in freshman, sophomore, junior, or senior years; not renewable. *Number:* 1. *Amount:* $500.

Eligibility Requirements: Applicant must be enrolled or expecting to enroll full- or part-time at a four-year institution or university and must have an interest in amateur radio. Available to U.S. citizens.

Application Requirements: Application form, transcript. *Deadline:* February 1.

Contact: Ms. Mary Hobart, Secretary
Phone: 860-594-0397
E-mail: k1mmh@arrl.org

ARRL NORTHWESTERN DIVISION SCHOLARSHIP FUND
• See page 150

BETTY WEATHERFORD, KQ6RE, MEMORIAL SCHOLARSHIP
• See page 251

CHARLES N. FISHER MEMORIAL SCHOLARSHIP
• See page 103

GARY WAGNER, K3OMI, SCHOLARSHIP
• See page 166

HENRY BROUGHTON, K2AE, MEMORIAL SCHOLARSHIP
• See page 263

MAGNOLIA DX ASSOCIATION SCHOLARSHIP
• See page 189

MISSISSIPPI SCHOLARSHIP
• See page 103

NORTH FULTON AMATEUR RADIO LEAGUE SCHOLARSHIP FUND
• See page 200

PAUL AND HELEN L. GRAUER SCHOLARSHIP
• See page 103

SOUTHEASTERN DX CLUB SCHOLARSHIP FUND
• See page 201

WILLIAM R. GOLDFARB MEMORIAL SCHOLARSHIP
• See page 150

YASME FOUNDATION SCHOLARSHIP
• See page 143

ASM MATERIALS EDUCATION FOUNDATION

http://www.asmfoundation.org/

ASM OUTSTANDING SCHOLARS AWARDS

Awards for student members of ASM International studying metallurgy or materials science and engineering. Must have completed at least one year of college to apply. Awards are merit-based; financial need is not considered.

Academic Fields/Career Goals: Engineering/Technology; Materials Science, Engineering, and Metallurgy.

Award: Scholarship for use in sophomore, junior, or senior years; not renewable. *Number:* 3. *Amount:* $2000.

Eligibility Requirements: Applicant must be enrolled or expecting to enroll full-time at a four-year institution or university. Applicant or parent of applicant must be member of ASM International. Available to U.S. and non-U.S. citizens.

Application Requirements: Application form, essay, personal photograph, recommendations or references, transcript. *Deadline:* May 1.

Contact: Pergentina Deatherage, Administrator, Foundation Programs
ASM Materials Education Foundation
9639 Kinsman Road
Materials Park, OH 44073-0002
Phone: 440-338-5151
Fax: 440-338-4634

EDWARD J. DULIS SCHOLARSHIP

Award of $1500 for student members of ASM International studying metallurgy or materials science and engineering. Award is merit based; financial need is not considered.

Academic Fields/Career Goals: Engineering/Technology; Materials Science, Engineering, and Metallurgy.

Award: Scholarship for use in freshman, sophomore, junior, or senior years; not renewable. *Number:* 1. *Amount:* $1500.

Eligibility Requirements: Applicant must be enrolled or expecting to enroll full-time at a four-year institution or university. Applicant or parent of applicant must be member of ASM International. Available to U.S. and Canadian citizens.

Application Requirements: Application form, personal photograph, recommendations or references, transcript. *Deadline:* May 1.

Contact: Pergentina Deatherage, Administrator, Foundation Programs
ASM Materials Education Foundation
9639 Kinsman Road
Materials Park, OH 44073-0002
Phone: 440-338-5151
Fax: 440-338-4634

GEORGE A. ROBERTS SCHOLARSHIP

Awards for college juniors or seniors studying metallurgy or materials engineering in North America. Applicants must be student members of ASM International. Awards based on need, interest in field, academics, and character.

Academic Fields/Career Goals: Engineering/Technology; Materials Science, Engineering, and Metallurgy.

Award: Scholarship for use in junior or senior years; not renewable. *Number:* 7. *Amount:* $6000.

Eligibility Requirements: Applicant must be enrolled or expecting to enroll full-time at an institution or university. Applicant or parent of applicant must be member of ASM International. Available to U.S. and Canadian citizens.

Application Requirements: Application form, essay, financial need analysis, personal photograph, recommendations or references, transcript. *Deadline:* May 1.

Contact: Pergentina Deatherage, Administrator, Foundation Programs
ASM Materials Education Foundation
9639 Kinsman Road
Materials Park, OH 44073-0002
Phone: 440-338-5151
Fax: 440-338-4634

JOHN M. HANIAK SCHOLARSHIP

Award for student members of ASM International studying metallurgy or materials science and engineering. Must have completed at least one year of college to apply. Award is merit based; financial need is not considered.

Academic Fields/Career Goals: Engineering/Technology; Materials Science, Engineering, and Metallurgy.

Award: Scholarship for use in freshman, sophomore, junior, or senior years; not renewable. *Number:* 1. *Amount:* $1500.

Eligibility Requirements: Applicant must be enrolled or expecting to enroll full-time at a four-year institution or university. Applicant or parent of applicant must be member of ASM International. Available to U.S. and Canadian citizens.

Application Requirements: Application form, essay, recommendations or references, self-addressed stamped envelope with application, transcript. *Deadline:* May 1.

Contact: Pergentina Deatherage, Administrator, Foundation Programs
ASM Materials Education Foundation
9639 Kinsman Road
Materials Park, OH 44073-0002
Phone: 440-338-5151
Fax: 440-338-4634

WILLIAM P. WOODSIDE FOUNDER'S SCHOLARSHIP

$10,000 scholarship for college junior or senior studying metallurgy or materials engineering in North America. Must be a student member of ASM International. Award based on need, interest in field, academics, and character.

Academic Fields/Career Goals: Engineering/Technology; Materials Science, Engineering, and Metallurgy.

Award: Scholarship for use in junior or senior years; not renewable. *Number:* 1. *Amount:* up to $10,000.

Eligibility Requirements: Applicant must be enrolled or expecting to enroll full-time at an institution or university. Applicant or parent of applicant must be member of ASM International. Available to U.S. and Canadian citizens.

Application Requirements: Application form, essay, financial need analysis, personal photograph, recommendations or references, transcript. *Deadline:* May 1.

Contact: Pergentina Deatherage, Administrator, Foundation Programs
ASM Materials Education Foundation
9639 Kinsman Road
Materials Park, OH 44073-0002
Phone: 440-338-5151
Fax: 440-338-4634

ASPRS, THE IMAGING AND GEOSPATIAL INFORMATION SOCIETY

http://www.asprs.org/

ABRAHAM ANSON MEMORIAL SCHOLARSHIP

Award to encourage students to pursue education in geospatial science or technology related to photogrammetry, remote sensing, surveying and mapping. Must be enrolled or intending to enroll in a U.S. college or university in geospatial science, surveying and mapping and related fields. Must submit with application a list of all applicable courses taken, a statement of work experience including internships, special projects, technical papers, and courses taught that may support the student's capabilities in this field. For additional information and online application, see website http://www.asprs.org/membership/scholar.html.

Academic Fields/Career Goals: Engineering/Technology; Surveying, Surveying Technology, Cartography, or Geographic Information Science.

Award: Scholarship for use in freshman, sophomore, junior, or senior years; not renewable. *Number:* 1. *Amount:* $2000.

Eligibility Requirements: Applicant must be enrolled or expecting to enroll full-time at a four-year institution or university. Available to U.S. citizens.

Application Requirements: Application form, essay, recommendations or references, resume, transcript. *Deadline:* October 17.

FRANCIS H. MOFFITT MEMORIAL SCHOLARSHIP

Award to encourage upper-division undergraduate and graduate-level students to pursue a course of study in surveying and photogrammetry leading to a career in the mapping profession. Must be enrolled or intending to enroll in a college or university in the U.S. in the field of surveying or photogrammetry. Application must include listing of all courses taken in the field, internships, special projects, courses taught, technical papers that demonstrate applicant's capabilities in the field, two letters of recommendation, and a short statement detailing contributions to the field and future career plans. For additional information, see website http://www.asprs.org.

Academic Fields/Career Goals: Engineering/Technology; Surveying, Surveying Technology, Cartography, or Geographic Information Science.

Award: Scholarship for use in junior or senior years; not renewable. *Number:* 1. *Amount:* $3000.

Eligibility Requirements: Applicant must be enrolled or expecting to enroll full-time at a four-year institution or university. Available to U.S. citizens.

Application Requirements: Application form, essay, recommendations or references, transcript. *Deadline:* October 17.

JOHN O. BEHRENS INSTITUTE FOR LAND INFORMATION MEMORIAL SCHOLARSHIP

Award to encourage study in geospatial science or technology or land information systems/records. Must be an undergraduate student enrolled or intending to enroll in a U.S. college or university in the designated field. Application must be submitted electronically and must include a list of completed courses in the field, papers, research reports, or other items produced by the applicant that demonstrate capability in the field, and internships, work experience, special projects or courses taught that support potential excellence in the field. Additional information and application on website http://www.asprs.org/membership/scholar.html.

Academic Fields/Career Goals: Engineering/Technology; Surveying, Surveying Technology, Cartography, or Geographic Information Science.

Award: Scholarship for use in freshman, sophomore, junior, or senior years; not renewable. *Number:* 1. *Amount:* $2000.

Eligibility Requirements: Applicant must be enrolled or expecting to enroll full-time at a four-year institution or university. Available to U.S. citizens.

Application Requirements: Application form, essay, recommendations or references, resume, transcript. *Deadline:* October 17.

KENNETH J. OSBORN MEMORIAL SCHOLARSHIP

Award to encourage students who display the interest and aptitude to enter the profession of surveying, mapping, geospatial information and technology, and photogrammetry. Student must be enrolled or intending to enroll in a college or university in the U.S. in a program of study to prepare for the profession. Application must be submitted electronically. For additional requirements that must accompany electronic application, visit website http://www.asprs.org/membership/scholar.html.

Academic Fields/Career Goals: Engineering/Technology; Surveying, Surveying Technology, Cartography, or Geographic Information Science.

Award: Scholarship for use in freshman, sophomore, junior, or senior years; not renewable. *Number:* 1. *Amount:* $2000.

Eligibility Requirements: Applicant must be enrolled or expecting to enroll full-time at a four-year institution or university. Available to U.S. citizens.

Application Requirements: Application form, essay, recommendations or references, resume, transcript. *Deadline:* October 17.

ROBERT E. ALTENHOFEN MEMORIAL SCHOLARSHIP

One-time award of $2000 available for undergraduate or graduate study in theoretical photogrammetry. Applicant must supply a sample of work in photogrammetry and a statement of plans for future study in the field. Must be a member of ASPRS.

Academic Fields/Career Goals: Engineering/Technology; Surveying, Surveying Technology, Cartography, or Geographic Information Science.

Award: Scholarship for use in junior, senior, or graduate years; not renewable. *Number:* 1. *Amount:* $2000.

Eligibility Requirements: Applicant must be enrolled or expecting to enroll full-time at a four-year institution or university and must have an interest in photography/photogrammetry/filmmaking. Applicant or parent of applicant must be member of American Society for Photogrammetry and Remote Sensing. Available to U.S. and non-U.S. citizens.

Application Requirements: Application form, essay, recommendations or references, transcript, work sample. *Deadline:* October 17.

ASSOCIATED GENERAL CONTRACTORS EDUCATION AND RESEARCH FOUNDATION

http://www.agcfoundation.org/

AGC EDUCATION AND RESEARCH FOUNDATION UNDERGRADUATE SCHOLARSHIPS
• *See page 181*

ASSOCIATION FOR WOMEN IN ARCHITECTURE FOUNDATION

http://www.awa-la.org/

ASSOCIATION FOR WOMEN IN ARCHITECTURE FOUNDATION SCHOLARSHIP
• *See page 109*

BARRY M. GOLDWATER SCHOLARSHIP AND EXCELLENCE IN EDUCATION FOUNDATION

http://www.act.org/goldwater

BARRY M. GOLDWATER SCHOLARSHIP AND EXCELLENCE IN EDUCATION PROGRAM
• *See page 104*

BOYS AND GIRLS CLUBS OF SAN DIEGO

http://www.sdyouth.org/

SPENCE REESE SCHOLARSHIP

Renewable scholarship for graduating male high school seniors in the United States for study of law, medicine, engineering, and political science. Awarded based on academic standing, academic ability, financial need, and character.

Academic Fields/Career Goals: Engineering/Technology; Health and Medical Sciences; Law/Legal Services; Political Science.

Award: Scholarship for use in freshman, sophomore, junior, or senior years; renewable. *Number:* up to 8. *Amount:* $2000.

Eligibility Requirements: Applicant must be high school student; planning to enroll or expecting to enroll full-time at a four-year institution or university and male. Applicant must have 3.5 GPA or higher. Available to U.S. citizens.

Application Requirements: Application form, application form may be submitted online (http://www.sdyouth.org/about/college-scholarships), essay, financial need analysis, interview, recommendations or references, self-addressed stamped envelope with application, test scores, transcript. *Deadline:* April 1.

BRITISH COLUMBIA INNOVATION COUNCIL

http://www.bcic.ca/

BCIC YOUNG INNOVATOR SCHOLARSHIP COMPETITION (IDEA MASH UP)
• *See page 104*

CATCHING THE DREAM

http://www.catchingthedream.org/

MATH, ENGINEERING, SCIENCE, BUSINESS, EDUCATION, COMPUTERS SCHOLARSHIPS
• *See page 151*

CENTER FOR ARCHITECTURE

http://www.cfafoundation.org/scholarships

CENTER FOR ARCHITECTURE, DOUGLAS HASKELL AWARD FOR STUDENT JOURNALS
• *See page 110*

COLLEGEBOUND FOUNDATION

http://www.collegeboundfoundation.org/

DR. FREEMAN A. HRABOWSKI, III SCHOLARSHIP

You must: be accepted to and attend UMBC; major in the field of engineering or science or technology; have a cumulative 3.0 GPA or better; and an SAT (CR+M) score of at least 1000.

Academic Fields/Career Goals: Engineering/Technology; Mathematics; Science, Technology, and Society.

Award: Scholarship for use in freshman, sophomore, junior, or senior years; renewable. *Number:* 1. *Amount:* $1500.

Eligibility Requirements: Applicant must be high school student; planning to enroll or expecting to enroll full-time at a four-year institution or university; resident of Maryland and studying in Maryland. Applicant must have 3.0 GPA or higher. Available to U.S. citizens.

Application Requirements: Application form, application form may be submitted online (http://www.scholarships.mycbf.net/STARS), financial need analysis, recommendations or references, resume, test scores, transcript. *Deadline:* March 1.

Contact: Michael Thornton, Associate Program Director, Scholarship Programs
Phone: 410-783-2905 Ext. 207
Fax: 410-727-5786
E-mail: mthornton@collegeboundfoundation.org

GEORGE V. MCGOWAN SCHOLARSHIP

You must: major in the field of engineering; have a cumulative 3.0 GPA or better and an SAT (CR+M) score of at least 1000.

Academic Fields/Career Goals: Engineering/Technology.

Award: Scholarship for use in freshman year; renewable. *Number:* 1. *Amount:* $1500.

Eligibility Requirements: Applicant must be high school student; planning to enroll or expecting to enroll full-time at a four-year institution or university; resident of Maryland and studying in Maryland. Applicant must have 3.0 GPA or higher. Available to U.S. citizens.

Application Requirements: Application form, application form may be submitted online (http://www.scholarships.mycbf.net/STARS), financial need analysis, recommendations or references, resume, test scores, transcript. *Deadline:* March 1.

Contact: Michael Thornton, Associate Program Director, Scholarship Programs
Phone: 410-783-2905 Ext. 207
Fax: 410-727-5786
E-mail: mthornton@collegeboundfoundation.org

THE COMMUNITY FOUNDATION FOR GREATER ATLANTA, INC.

http://cfgreateratlanta.org/

TECH HIGH SCHOOL ALUMNI ASSOCIATION/W.O. CHENEY MERIT SCHOLARSHIP FUND

Scholarship for students pursuing degrees in mathematics, engineering, or one of the physical sciences. Cumulative high school GPA of 3.7 or higher or in upper 10 percent of graduating class. SAT (math and critical reading) of at least 1300. For complete eligibility requirements and application, visit http://www.cfgreateratlanta.org.

Academic Fields/Career Goals: Engineering/Technology; Mathematics; Physical Sciences.

Award: Scholarship for use in freshman, sophomore, junior, or senior years; renewable. *Number:* 1–4. *Amount:* up to $5000.

Eligibility Requirements: Applicant must be high school student; planning to enroll or expecting to enroll full-time at a four-year institution or university and resident of Georgia. Applicant must have 3.5 GPA or higher. Available to U.S. citizens.

Application Requirements: Application form, application form may be submitted online (http://www.cfgreateratlanta.org/Grants-Support/Scholarships.aspx), community service, driver's license, essay, financial need analysis, recommendations or references, test scores, transcript. *Deadline:* March 1.

Contact: Kristina Morris, Program Associate
The Community Foundation for Greater Atlanta, Inc.
50 Hurt Plaza
Suite 449
Atlanta, GA 30303
Phone: 404-688-5525
E-mail: scholarships@cfgreateratlanta.org

CUBAN AMERICAN NATIONAL FOUNDATION

http://www.masscholarships.org/

MAS FAMILY SCHOLARSHIPS
• *See page 152*

THE DALLAS FOUNDATION

http://www.dallasfoundation.org/

WHITLEY PLACE SCHOLARSHIP
• *See page 110*

DENVER FOUNDATION

http://www.denverfoundation.org/

RBC DAIN RAUSCHER COLORADO SCHOLARSHIP FUND

Scholarships for undergraduate education to outstanding Colorado high school seniors. Five $5000 scholarships will be awarded to students intending to pursue a degree in science or engineering. Must have at least a 3.75 cumulative GPA. Students who have a parent, step-parent, grandparent, aunt, or uncle who is employed by RBC Dain Rauscher are not eligible to apply.

Academic Fields/Career Goals: Engineering/Technology; Science, Technology, and Society.

Award: Scholarship for use in freshman year; not renewable. *Number:* 5. *Amount:* $5000.

Eligibility Requirements: Applicant must be high school student; planning to enroll or expecting to enroll full-time at a four-year institution or university and studying in Colorado. Available to U.S. citizens.

Application Requirements: Application form, test scores, transcript. *Deadline:* April 4.

Contact: Karla Bieniulis, Scholarship Committee
　　　Phone: 303-300-1790 Ext. 103
　　　Fax: 303-300-6547
　　　E-mail: info@denverfoundation.org

EAA AVIATION FOUNDATION, INC.

http://www.eaa.org/

PAYZER SCHOLARSHIP
• *See page 129*

ELECTROCHEMICAL SOCIETY INC.

http://www.electrochem.org/

H.H. DOW MEMORIAL STUDENT ACHIEVEMENT AWARD OF THE INDUSTRIAL ELECTROLYSIS AND ELECTROCHEMICAL ENGINEERING DIVISION OF THE ELECTROCHEMICAL SOCIETY INC.
• *See page 104*

STUDENT RESEARCH AWARDS OF THE BATTERY DIVISION OF THE ELECTROCHEMICAL SOCIETY INC.
• *See page 105*

FLORIDA ENGINEERING SOCIETY

http://www.fleng.org/scholarships.cfm

ACEC/FLORIDA SCHOLARSHIP

One-time scholarship of $5000 given to Florida citizen pursuing a bachelor's, master's or doctoral degree in an ABET-approved engineering program or in an accredited land surveying program. Students must be entering their junior, senior, or fifth year of college.

Academic Fields/Career Goals: Engineering/Technology; Surveying, Surveying Technology, Cartography, or Geographic Information Science.

Award: Scholarship for use in junior or senior years; not renewable. *Number:* 1. *Amount:* $5000.

Eligibility Requirements: Applicant must be enrolled or expecting to enroll full-time at a four-year institution or university and resident of Florida. Available to U.S. citizens.

Application Requirements: Application form, essay, recommendations or references, test scores, transcript. *Deadline:* February 15.

Contact: Debbie Hall, Scholarship Committee Staff Liaison
　　　Florida Engineering Society
　　　125 South Gadsden Street
　　　Tallahassee, FL 32301
　　　Phone: 850-224-7121
　　　Fax: 850-222-4349
　　　E-mail: dhall@fleng.org

DAVID F. LUDOVICI SCHOLARSHIP
• *See page 182*

ERIC PRIMAVERA MEMORIAL SCHOLARSHIP

One-time scholarship of $1000 given to students in their junior or senior year in a Florida university engineering program. Minimum 3.0 GPA required.

Academic Fields/Career Goals: Engineering/Technology.

Award: Scholarship for use in junior or senior years; not renewable. *Number:* 1. *Amount:* $1000.

Eligibility Requirements: Applicant must be enrolled or expecting to enroll full-time at an institution or university; resident of Florida and studying in Florida. Applicant must have 3.0 GPA or higher. Available to U.S. citizens.

Application Requirements: Application form, recommendations or references, self-addressed stamped envelope with application, transcript. *Deadline:* February 1.

Contact: Abby Andersen, Scholarship Committee Staff Liaison
　　　Phone: 850-224-7121
　　　E-mail: aandersen@fleng.org

HIGH SCHOOL SCHOLARSHIP

One-time scholarship given to high school seniors who are residents of Florida. Minimum 3.5 GPA required. Applicant must have genuine interest in engineering.

Academic Fields/Career Goals: Engineering/Technology.

Award: Scholarship for use in freshman year; not renewable. *Number:* 6. *Amount:* $1500–$2500.

Eligibility Requirements: Applicant must be high school student; planning to enroll or expecting to enroll full-time at a four-year institution or university and resident of Florida. Applicant must have 3.5 GPA or higher. Available to U.S. citizens.

Application Requirements: Application form, IB and AP exam results, interview, test scores, transcript. *Deadline:* February 1.

Contact: Abby Andersen, Scholarship Committee Staff Liaison
　　　Phone: 850-224-7121
　　　E-mail: aandersen@fleng.org

RAYMOND W. MILLER, PE SCHOLARSHIP

One-time scholarship given to students in their junior or senior year in a Florida university engineering program. Minimum 3.0 GPA required.

Academic Fields/Career Goals: Engineering/Technology.

Award: Scholarship for use in junior or senior years; not renewable. *Number:* 1. *Amount:* $1500–$2500.

Eligibility Requirements: Applicant must be enrolled or expecting to enroll full-time at an institution or university; resident of Florida and studying in Florida. Applicant must have 3.0 GPA or higher. Available to U.S. citizens.

Application Requirements: Application form, recommendations or references, self-addressed stamped envelope with application, transcript. *Deadline:* February 1.

Contact: Abby Andersen, Scholarship Committee Staff Liaison
　　　Phone: 850-224-7121
　　　E-mail: aandersen@fleng.org

RICHARD B. GASSETT, PE SCHOLARSHIP

One-time scholarship given to students in their junior or senior year in a Florida university engineering program. Minimum 3.0 GPA required.

Academic Fields/Career Goals: Engineering/Technology.

Award: Scholarship for use in junior or senior years; not renewable. *Number:* 1. *Amount:* $1500–$2500.

Eligibility Requirements: Applicant must be enrolled or expecting to enroll full-time at an institution or university; resident of Florida and studying in Florida. Applicant must have 3.0 GPA or higher. Available to U.S. citizens.

Application Requirements: Application form, recommendations or references, self-addressed stamped envelope with application, transcript. *Deadline:* February 1.

Contact: Abby Andersen, Scholarship Committee Staff Liaison
　　　Phone: 850-224-7121
　　　E-mail: aandersen@fleng.org

FOUNDATION FOR SCIENCE AND DISABILITY

http://stemd.org/

GRANTS FOR DISABLED STUDENTS IN THE SCIENCES
• *See page 105*

GEORGIA SOCIETY OF PROFESSIONAL ENGINEERS/GEORGIA ENGINEERING FOUNDATION

http://www.gefinc.org/

GEORGIA ENGINEERING FOUNDATION SCHOLARSHIP PROGRAM

Awards scholarships to students who are preparing for a career in engineering or engineering technology. Must be U.S. citizens and legal residents of Georgia. Must be attending or accepted in an ABET-accredited program. Separate applications are available: one for use by high school seniors and new college freshmen and one for use by college upperclassmen.

Academic Fields/Career Goals: Engineering/Technology.

Award: Scholarship for use in freshman, sophomore, junior, or senior years; not renewable. *Number:* 45. *Amount:* $1000–$5000.

Eligibility Requirements: Applicant must be enrolled or expecting to enroll full-time at a four-year institution or university and resident of Georgia. Applicant or parent of applicant must have employment or volunteer experience in community service. Available to U.S. citizens.

Application Requirements: Application form, personal photograph, recommendations or references, test scores, transcript. *Deadline:* August 31.

Contact: Roseana Richards, Scholarship Committee Chairman
Georgia Society of Professional Engineers/Georgia
Engineering Foundation
233 Peachtree Street, Suite 700, Harris Tower
Atlanta, GA 30303
Phone: 404-521-2324
E-mail: richardsr@pondco.com

GOLDEN KEY INTERNATIONAL HONOUR SOCIETY

http://www.goldenkey.org/

ENGINEERING/TECHNOLOGY ACHIEVEMENT AWARD

Award to members who excel in the study of engineering or technology. Applicants will be asked to respond to a problem posed by an honorary member within the discipline. One winner will receive a $1000 award. The second place winner will receive $750 and the third place winner will receive $500.

Academic Fields/Career Goals: Engineering/Technology.

Award: Prize for use in freshman, sophomore, junior, senior, graduate, or postgraduate years; not renewable. *Number:* 3. *Amount:* $500–$1000.

Eligibility Requirements: Applicant must be enrolled or expecting to enroll full- or part-time at a four-year institution or university. Available to U.S. and non-U.S. citizens.

Application Requirements: Application form, engineering-related report, cover page from the online registration, entry in a contest, essay, recommendations or references, transcript. *Deadline:* March 3.

GREATER KANAWHA VALLEY FOUNDATION

http://www.tgkvf.org/

MATH AND SCIENCE SCHOLARSHIP
• *See page 145*

STEVEN ENGINEERING SCHOLARSHIP
• *See page 167*

GREAT MINDS IN STEM

http://www.greatmindsinstem.org

HISPANIC ENGINEER NATIONAL ACHIEVEMENT AWARDS CORPORATION SCHOLARSHIP PROGRAM
• *See page 130*

HAWAIIAN LODGE, F&AM

http://www.hawaiianlodgefreemasons.org/

HAWAIIAN LODGE SCHOLARSHIPS
• *See page 114*

HELLENIC UNIVERSITY CLUB OF PHILADELPHIA

http://www.hucphila.org/

DIMITRI J. VERVERELLI MEMORIAL SCHOLARSHIP FOR ARCHITECTURE AND/OR ENGINEERING
• *See page 111*

IDAHO STATE BROADCASTERS ASSOCIATION

http://www.idahobroadcasters.org/

WAYNE C. CORNILS MEMORIAL SCHOLARSHIP
• *See page 156*

ILLINOIS SOCIETY OF PROFESSIONAL ENGINEERS

http://www.illinoisengineer.com/

ILLINOIS SOCIETY OF PROFESSIONAL ENGINEERS/ MELVIN E. AMSTUTZ MEMORIAL AWARD

Applicant must attend an Illinois university approved by the Accreditation Board of Engineering. Applicant must be at least a junior in university he or she attends, and must prove financial need. Essay must address why applicant wishes to become a professional engineer. Must have a B average.

Academic Fields/Career Goals: Engineering/Technology.

Award: Scholarship for use in junior or senior years; not renewable. *Number:* 1. *Amount:* $1500.

Eligibility Requirements: Applicant must be enrolled or expecting to enroll full-time at a four-year institution and studying in Illinois. Applicant must have 3.0 GPA or higher. Available to U.S. and non-U.S. citizens.

Application Requirements: Application form, application form may be submitted online (http://illinoisengineer.com/scholarships.shtml), essay, financial need analysis, recommendations or references, resume, transcript. *Deadline:* March 31.

Contact: Mrs. Nicole Palmisano, Scholarship Coordinator
Springfield, IL 62701
Phone: 217-544-7424 Ext. 238
Fax: 217-528-6545
E-mail: NicolePalmisano@illinoisengineer.com

ILLUMINATING ENGINEERING SOCIETY OF NORTH AMERICA

http://www.iesna.org/

ROBERT W. THUNEN MEMORIAL SCHOLARSHIPS
• *See page 111*

INDEPENDENT LABORATORIES INSTITUTE SCHOLARSHIP ALLIANCE

http://www.acil.org/

INDEPENDENT LABORATORIES INSTITUTE SCHOLARSHIP ALLIANCE

• *See page 145*

INDIANA SOCIETY OF PROFESSIONAL ENGINEERS

http://www.indspe.org/

INDIANA ENGINEERING SCHOLARSHIP

Award for Indiana resident who attends an Indiana educational institution, or commutes daily to a school outside Indiana. Applicant must have accrued the minimum of one-half the credits required for an undergraduate ABET-accredited engineering degree. For details and an application visit website http://indspe.org.

Academic Fields/Career Goals: Engineering/Technology.

Award: Scholarship for use in junior or senior years; not renewable. *Number:* 3. *Amount:* $750.

Eligibility Requirements: Applicant must be enrolled or expecting to enroll full- or part-time at a four-year institution or university and resident of Indiana. Available to U.S. citizens.

Application Requirements: Application form, community service, recommendations or references, resume, transcript. *Deadline:* May 1.

Contact: Mr. Harold Dungan, Scholarship Coordinator
Indiana Society of Professional Engineers
HNTB, 111 Monument Circle, Suite 1200
Indianapolis, IN 46204
Phone: 317-636-4682 Ext. 75245
Fax: 317-917-5211
E-mail: hdungan@hntb.com

INSTITUTE OF INDUSTRIAL ENGINEERS

http://www.iienet.org/

A.O. PUTNAM MEMORIAL SCHOLARSHIP

$700 award for undergraduate students enrolled in any school in the United States and its territories, Canada, and Mexico pursuing a course of study in industrial engineering. The school's industrial engineering program or equivalent must be accredited by an agency or organization recognized by IIE. Priority is given to students who have demonstrated an interest in management consulting. Minimum 3.4 GPA required.

Academic Fields/Career Goals: Engineering/Technology.

Award: Scholarship for use in freshman, sophomore, junior, or senior years; not renewable. *Number:* 1. *Amount:* up to $4000.

Eligibility Requirements: Applicant must be enrolled or expecting to enroll full-time at a four-year institution or university. Applicant or parent of applicant must be member of Institute of Industrial Engineers. Available to U.S. and non-U.S. citizens.

Application Requirements: Application form, nomination, recommendations or references, transcript. *Deadline:* November 15.

Contact: Bonnie Cameron, Operations Administrator
Phone: 770-449-0461 Ext. 105
E-mail: bcameron@iienet.org

C.B. GAMBRELL UNDERGRADUATE SCHOLARSHIP

One-time award for undergraduate industrial engineering students who are U.S. citizens, have graduated from a U.S. high school, and have a class standing above freshman level in an ABET-accredited IE program. Must be a member of Industrial Engineers, have a minimum GPA of 3.4, and be nominated by a department head.

Academic Fields/Career Goals: Engineering/Technology.

Award: Scholarship for use in sophomore, junior, or senior years; not renewable. *Number:* 1. *Amount:* up to $4000.

Eligibility Requirements: Applicant must be enrolled or expecting to enroll full-time at a four-year institution or university. Applicant or parent of applicant must be member of Institute of Industrial Engineers. Available to U.S. citizens.

Application Requirements: Application form, nomination, recommendations or references, transcript. *Deadline:* November 15.

Contact: Bonnie Cameron, Operations Administrator
Phone: 770-449-0461 Ext. 105
E-mail: bcameron@iienet.org

CIE UNDERGRADUATE SCHOLARSHIP

$2000 scholarship will be awarded to an undergraduate industrial engineering student for the best application of corporate social responsibility, resilience, or sustainability principals aligned with classic industrial engineering techniques to a project for an enterprise. Interested candidates must complete an application form, as well as submit a complete description of the project, including provision of a financial analysis using the triple-bottom line definitions of sustainability, showing a positive cash flow or return on investment to the enterprise over the project life. Applicants should have at least a 3.4 GPA.

Academic Fields/Career Goals: Engineering/Technology.

Award: Scholarship for use in freshman, sophomore, junior, or senior years; not renewable. *Number:* 1. *Amount:* $2000.

Eligibility Requirements: Applicant must be enrolled or expecting to enroll full-time at a four-year institution or university. Available to U.S. citizens.

Application Requirements: Application form, project description, recommendations or references, transcript. *Deadline:* February 1.

Contact: Bonnie Cameron, Operations Administrator
Phone: 770-449-0461 Ext. 105
E-mail: bcameron@iienet.org

DWIGHT D. GARDNER SCHOLARSHIP

$3000 scholarship available to undergraduate students enrolled in an industrial engineering program in any school in the United States and its territories, Canada, and Mexico, provided the school's engineering program or equivalent is accredited by an agency recognized by IIE. Must be an IIE member. Minimum 3.4 GPA required. Must be nominated by department head.

Academic Fields/Career Goals: Engineering/Technology.

Award: Scholarship for use in freshman, sophomore, junior, or senior years; not renewable. *Number:* 3. *Amount:* up to $4000.

Eligibility Requirements: Applicant must be enrolled or expecting to enroll full-time at a four-year institution or university. Applicant or parent of applicant must be member of Institute of Industrial Engineers. Available to U.S. and non-U.S. citizens.

Application Requirements: Application form, essay, financial need analysis, nomination, recommendations or references, transcript. *Deadline:* November 15.

Contact: Bonnie Cameron, Operations Administrator
Phone: 770-449-0461 Ext. 105
E-mail: bcameron@iienet.org

HAROLD AND INGE MARCUS SCHOLARSHIP

Available to undergraduate students enrolled in any school in the United States provided the school's engineering program is accredited by an agency recognized by IIE and the student is pursuing a course of study in industrial engineering. This award is intended to recognize academic excellence and noteworthy contribution to the development of the industrial engineering profession. Must have at least a 3.4 GPA.

Academic Fields/Career Goals: Engineering/Technology.

Award: Scholarship for use in freshman, sophomore, junior, or senior years; not renewable. *Amount:* up to $4000.

Eligibility Requirements: Applicant must be enrolled or expecting to enroll full-time at a two-year or four-year institution or university. Available to U.S. citizens.

Application Requirements: Application form, nominations, recommendations or references, transcript. *Deadline:* November 15.

Contact: Bonnie Cameron, Operations Administrator
Phone: 770-449-0461 Ext. 105
E-mail: bcameron@iienet.org

IIE COUNCIL OF FELLOWS UNDERGRADUATE SCHOLARSHIP

Awards to undergraduate students enrolled in any school in the United States and its territories, Canada and Mexico, provided the school's engineering program or equivalent is accredited by an agency recognized by IIE and the student is pursuing a course of study in industrial engineering. Must be IIE member and have minimum 3.4 GPA.

Academic Fields/Career Goals: Engineering/Technology.

Award: Scholarship for use in freshman, sophomore, junior, or senior years; not renewable. *Amount:* up to $4000.

Eligibility Requirements: Applicant must be enrolled or expecting to enroll full-time at a four-year institution or university. Applicant or parent of applicant must be member of Institute of Industrial Engineers. Available to U.S. and non-U.S. citizens.

Application Requirements: Application form, nomination form, recommendations or references, transcript. *Deadline:* November 15.

Contact: Bonnie Cameron, Operations Administrator
  Phone: 770-449-0461 Ext. 105
  E-mail: bcameron@iienet.org

JOHN L. IMHOFF SCHOLARSHIP

At least one award for a student pursuing an industrial engineering degree who, by academic, employment and/or professional achievements, has made noteworthy contributions to the development of the industrial engineering profession through international understanding. IIE membership is not required. Must have at least a 3.4 GPA.

Academic Fields/Career Goals: Engineering/Technology.

Award: Scholarship for use in freshman, sophomore, junior, or senior years; not renewable. *Number:* 1. *Amount:* $1000.

Eligibility Requirements: Applicant must be enrolled or expecting to enroll full-time at a four-year institution or university. Available to U.S. citizens.

Application Requirements: Application form, essay, nomination, recommendations or references, transcript. *Deadline:* November 15.

Contact: Bonnie Cameron, Operations Administrator
  Phone: 770-449-0461 Ext. 105
  E-mail: bcameron@iienet.org

LISA ZAKEN AWARD FOR EXCELLENCE

Award for undergraduate and graduate students enrolled in any school, and pursuing a course of study in industrial engineering. Award is intended to recognize excellence in scholarly activities and leadership related to the industrial engineering profession on campus. Must maintain at least a 3.0 GPA.

Academic Fields/Career Goals: Engineering/Technology.

Award: Prize for use in freshman, sophomore, junior, senior, or graduate years; not renewable. *Number:* up to 1. *Amount:* up to $4000.

Eligibility Requirements: Applicant must be enrolled or expecting to enroll full-time at a four-year institution or university. Applicant or parent of applicant must be member of Institute of Industrial Engineers. Applicant must have 3.0 GPA or higher. Available to U.S. and non-U.S. citizens.

Application Requirements: Application form, essay, nomination form, recommendations or references, transcript. *Deadline:* November 15.

Contact: Bonnie Cameron, Operations Administrator
  Phone: 770-449-0461 Ext. 105
  E-mail: bcameron@iienet.org

MARVIN MUNDEL MEMORIAL SCHOLARSHIP

Scholarship awarded to undergraduate students enrolled in any school in the United States, Canada, or Mexico with an accredited industrial engineering program. Priority given to students who have demonstrated an interest in work measurement and methods engineering. Must be active Institute members with 3.4 GPA or above. Must be nominated by department head or faculty adviser.

Academic Fields/Career Goals: Engineering/Technology.

Award: Scholarship for use in freshman, sophomore, junior, or senior years; not renewable. *Amount:* up to $4000.

Eligibility Requirements: Applicant must be enrolled or expecting to enroll full-time at a four-year institution or university. Applicant or parent of applicant must be member of Institute of Industrial Engineers. Available to U.S. and non-U.S. citizens.

Application Requirements: Application form, nomination, recommendations or references, transcript. *Deadline:* November 15.

Contact: Bonnie Cameron, Operations Administrator
  Phone: 770-449-0461 Ext. 105
  E-mail: bcameron@iienet.org

PRESIDENTS SCHOLARSHIP

$1000 scholarship available to undergraduate student pursuing a course of study in industrial engineering. This award is intended to recognize excellence in scholarly activities and leadership of the industrial engineering profession. Must be active in a student chapter and must have demonstrated leadership and promoted IIE involvement on campus. Must have at least a 3.4 GPA.

Academic Fields/Career Goals: Engineering/Technology.

Award: Scholarship for use in freshman, sophomore, junior, or senior years; not renewable. *Number:* 1. *Amount:* $1000.

Eligibility Requirements: Applicant must be enrolled or expecting to enroll full-time at a four-year institution or university. Applicant or parent of applicant must be member of Institute of Industrial Engineers. Available to U.S. citizens.

Application Requirements: Application form, nomination, recommendations or references, transcript. *Deadline:* November 15.

Contact: Bonnie Cameron, Operations Administrator
  Phone: 770-449-0461 Ext. 105
  E-mail: bcameron@iienet.org

SOCIETY FOR HEALTH SYSTEMS SCHOLARSHIP

$1000 award for undergraduate students enrolled full-time in an industrial engineering program in any accredited school in the United States and its territories, Canada and Mexico. Must be pursuing a course of study in industrial engineering and operations research with a definite interest in the area of health care. Must be an active Society for Health Systems student member with a minimum 3.4 GPA. Nomination required.

Academic Fields/Career Goals: Engineering/Technology.

Award: Scholarship for use in freshman, sophomore, junior, or senior years; not renewable. *Amount:* $1000.

Eligibility Requirements: Applicant must be enrolled or expecting to enroll full-time at a four-year institution or university. Available to U.S. citizens.

Application Requirements: Application form, essay, nomination, recommendations or references, resume, transcript. *Deadline:* December 1.

Contact: Bonnie Cameron, Operations Administrator
  Phone: 770-449-0461 Ext. 105
  E-mail: bcameron@iienet.org

UPS SCHOLARSHIP FOR FEMALE STUDENTS

One-time award for female undergraduate students enrolled at any school in the United States, Canada, or Mexico in an industrial engineering program. Must be a member of Institute of Industrial Engineers, have a minimum GPA of 3.4, and be nominated by a department head.

Academic Fields/Career Goals: Engineering/Technology.

Award: Scholarship for use in freshman, sophomore, junior, or senior years; not renewable. *Number:* 1. *Amount:* up to $4000.

Eligibility Requirements: Applicant must be enrolled or expecting to enroll full-time at a four-year or technical institution or university and female. Applicant or parent of applicant must be member of Institute of Industrial Engineers. Available to U.S. and non-U.S. citizens.

Application Requirements: Application form, nomination, recommendations or references, transcript. *Deadline:* November 15.

Contact: Bonnie Cameron, Operations Administrator
  Phone: 770-449-0461 Ext. 105
  E-mail: bcameron@iienet.org

UPS SCHOLARSHIP FOR MINORITY STUDENTS

One-time award for minority undergraduate students enrolled at any school in the United States, Canada, or Mexico in an industrial engineering program. Must be a member of Institute of Industrial Engineers. Nominated students by IE department heads will be sent an application package to complete and return before November 15. Minimum GPA of 3.4 required.

Academic Fields/Career Goals: Engineering/Technology.

Award: Scholarship for use in freshman, sophomore, junior, or senior years; not renewable. *Number:* 1. *Amount:* up to $4000.

Eligibility Requirements: Applicant must be American Indian/Alaska Native, Asian/Pacific Islander, Black (non-Hispanic), Hispanic and enrolled or expecting to enroll full-time at a four-year institution or university. Applicant or parent of applicant must be member of Institute of Industrial Engineers. Available to U.S. and non-U.S. citizens.

Application Requirements: Application form, nomination, recommendations or references, transcript. *Deadline:* November 15.

Contact: Bonnie Cameron, Operations Administrator
 Phone: 770-449-0461 Ext. 105
 E-mail: bcameron@iienet.org

INSTITUTE OF INTERNATIONAL EDUCATION (FULBRIGHT PROGRAM)

http://www.us.fulbrightonline.org/

WHITAKER INTERNATIONAL PROGRAM
• *See page 145*

INTERNATIONAL FACILITY MANAGEMENT ASSOCIATION FOUNDATION

http://www.ifmafoundation.org/

IFMA FOUNDATION SCHOLARSHIPS
• *See page 112*

INTERNATIONAL SOCIETY FOR OPTICAL ENGINEERING-SPIE

http://www.spie.org/scholarships

SPIE EDUCATIONAL SCHOLARSHIPS IN OPTICAL SCIENCE AND ENGINEERING
• *See page 105*

INTERNATIONAL SOCIETY OF AUTOMATION (ISA)

http://www.isa.org/

INTERNATIONAL SOCIETY OF AUTOMATION EDUCATION FOUNDATION SCHOLARSHIPS
• *See page 131*

INTERNATIONAL SOCIETY OF EXPLOSIVES ENGINEERS

http://www.isee.org/

JERRY MCDOWELL FUND
• *See page 265*

INTERNATIONAL TECHNOLOGY EDUCATION ASSOCIATION

http://www.iteaconnect.org/

INTERNATIONAL TECHNOLOGY EDUCATION ASSOCIATION UNDERGRADUATE SCHOLARSHIP IN TECHNOLOGY EDUCATION
• *See page 239*

KOREAN-AMERICAN SCIENTISTS AND ENGINEERS ASSOCIATION

http://www.ksea.org/

INYONG HAM SCHOLARSHIP

Scholarship of $1000 awarded to undergraduate and graduate students of Korean heritage majoring in science, engineering or related fields. Must be KSEA members or apply for membership at the time of scholarship application.

Academic Fields/Career Goals: Engineering/Technology.

Award: Scholarship for use in freshman, sophomore, junior, senior, or graduate years; not renewable. *Number:* 1. *Amount:* $1000.

Eligibility Requirements: Applicant must be of Korean heritage; Asian/Pacific Islander and enrolled or expecting to enroll full-time at a two-year or four-year institution or university. Applicant or parent of applicant must be member of Korean-American Scientists and Engineers Association. Available to U.S. citizens.

Application Requirements: Application form, essay, recommendations or references, resume, test scores, transcript. *Deadline:* February 15.

KSEA SCHOLARSHIPS
• *See page 253*

LEAGUE OF UNITED LATIN AMERICAN CITIZENS NATIONAL EDUCATIONAL SERVICE CENTERS INC.

http://www.lnesc.org/

GE/LULAC SCHOLARSHIP
• *See page 157*

GM/LULAC SCHOLARSHIP

Renewable award for minority students who are pursuing an undergraduate degree in engineering at an accredited college or university. Must maintain a minimum 3.0 GPA. Selection is based in part on the likelihood of pursuing a successful career in engineering.

Academic Fields/Career Goals: Engineering/Technology.

Award: Scholarship for use in freshman, sophomore, junior, or senior years; renewable. *Number:* up to 20. *Amount:* up to $2000.

Eligibility Requirements: Applicant must be American Indian/Alaska Native, Asian/Pacific Islander, Black (non-Hispanic), Hispanic and enrolled or expecting to enroll full-time at a four-year institution or university. Applicant must have 3.0 GPA or higher. Available to U.S. citizens.

Application Requirements: Application form, essay, recommendations or references, transcript. *Deadline:* July 15.

LOS ANGELES COUNCIL OF BLACK PROFESSIONAL ENGINEERS

http://www.lablackengineers.org/

AL-BEN SCHOLARSHIP FOR ACADEMIC INCENTIVE
• *See page 168*

AL-BEN SCHOLARSHIP FOR PROFESSIONAL MERIT
• *See page 168*

AL-BEN SCHOLARSHIP FOR SCHOLASTIC ACHIEVEMENT
• *See page 168*

MAINE EDUCATION SERVICES

http://www.mesfoundation.com/

MAINE STATE CHAMBER OF COMMERCE SCHOLARSHIP-HIGH SCHOOL SENIOR
• *See page 157*

MAINE SOCIETY OF PROFESSIONAL ENGINEERS

http://www.mespe.org/

MAINE SOCIETY OF PROFESSIONAL ENGINEERS VERNON T. SWAINE-ROBERT E. CHUTE SCHOLARSHIP
• *See page 266*

MANUFACTURERS ASSOCIATION OF MAINE

http://www.mainemfg.com/

MAINE METAL PRODUCTS EDUCATION FUND SCHOLARSHIP PROGRAM
• *See page 132*

MARINE TECHNOLOGY SOCIETY

http://www.mtsociety.org/

MTS STUDENT SCHOLARSHIP FOR GRADUATING HIGH SCHOOL SENIORS
Scholarship of $2000 available to high school seniors who have been accepted into a full-time undergraduate program and have an interest in marine technology.
Academic Fields/Career Goals: Engineering/Technology; Marine/Ocean Engineering.
Award: Scholarship for use in freshman year; not renewable. *Amount:* $2000.
Eligibility Requirements: Applicant must be high school student and planning to enroll or expecting to enroll full-time at a four-year institution or university. Available to U.S. and non-U.S. citizens.
Application Requirements: Application form, college acceptance letter, essay, recommendations or references, transcript. *Deadline:* April 15.
Contact: Suzanne Voelker, Operations Administrator
Marine Technology Society
5565 Sterrett Place, Suite 108
Columbia, MD 21044
Phone: 410-884-5330
E-mail: suzanne.voelker@mtsociety.org

MARION D. AND EVA S. PEEPLES FOUNDATION TRUST SCHOLARSHIP PROGRAM

http://www.jccf.org/

MARION A. AND EVA S. PEEPLES SCHOLARSHIPS
• *See page 240*

MARYLAND ASSOCIATION OF PRIVATE COLLEGES AND CAREER SCHOOLS

http://www.mapccs.org/

MARYLAND ASSOCIATION OF PRIVATE COLLEGES AND CAREER SCHOOLS SCHOLARSHIP
• *See page 157*

MICHIGAN SOCIETY OF PROFESSIONAL ENGINEERS

http://www.michiganspe.org/

MICHIGAN SOCIETY OF PROFESSIONAL ENGINEERS HARRY R. BALL, P.E. GRANT
• *See page 169*

MICHIGAN SOCIETY OF PROFESSIONAL ENGINEERS KENNETH B. FISHBECK, P.E. MEMORIAL GRANT
• *See page 169*

MIDWEST ROOFING CONTRACTORS ASSOCIATION

http://www.mrca.org/

MRCA FOUNDATION SCHOLARSHIP PROGRAM
• *See page 112*

MINERALS, METALS, AND MATERIALS SOCIETY (TMS)

http://www.tms.org/

TMS/EMPMD GILBERT CHIN SCHOLARSHIP
• *See page 266*

TMS/EPD SCHOLARSHIP
• *See page 266*

TMS/INTERNATIONAL SYMPOSIUM ON SUPERALLOYS SCHOLARSHIP PROGRAM
• *See page 266*

TMS J. KEITH BRIMACOMBE PRESIDENTIAL SCHOLARSHIP
• *See page 266*

TMS/LMD SCHOLARSHIP PROGRAM
• *See page 267*

TMS OUTSTANDING STUDENT PAPER CONTEST-UNDERGRADUATE
• *See page 267*

TMS/STRUCTURAL MATERIALS DIVISION SCHOLARSHIP
• *See page 267*

NASA/MARYLAND SPACE GRANT CONSORTIUM

http://md.spacegrant.org/

NASA MARYLAND SPACE GRANT CONSORTIUM UNDERGRADUATE SCHOLARSHIPS
• *See page 132*

NASA MINNESOTA SPACE GRANT CONSORTIUM

http://www.aem.umn.edu/mnsgc

MINNESOTA SPACE GRANT CONSORTIUM SCHOLARSHIP PROGRAM
• *See page 132*

NASA MISSISSIPPI SPACE GRANT CONSORTIUM

http://www.olemiss.edu/programs/nasa

MISSISSIPPI SPACE GRANT CONSORTIUM SCHOLARSHIP
• *See page 132*

NASA MONTANA SPACE GRANT CONSORTIUM

http://www.spacegrant.montana.edu/

MONTANA SPACE GRANT SCHOLARSHIP PROGRAM
• *See page 133*

NASA RHODE ISLAND SPACE GRANT CONSORTIUM

http://brown/initiatives/ri-space-grant

NASA RHODE ISLAND SPACE GRANT CONSORTIUM UNDERGRADUATE RESEARCH SCHOLARSHIP
• *See page 133*

NASA RISGC SCIENCE EN ESPANOL SCHOLARSHIP FOR UNDERGRADUATE STUDENTS
• *See page 133*

NASA SOUTH CAROLINA SPACE GRANT CONSORTIUM

http://www.cofc.edu/~scsgrant

UNDERGRADUATE RESEARCH AWARD PROGRAM
• *See page 133*

NASA SOUTH DAKOTA SPACE GRANT CONSORTIUM

http://sdspacegrant.sdsmt.edu/

SOUTH DAKOTA SPACE GRANT CONSORTIUM UNDERGRADUATE AND GRADUATE STUDENT SCHOLARSHIPS
• *See page 134*

NASA'S VIRGINIA SPACE GRANT CONSORTIUM

http://www.vsgc.odu.edu/

COMMUNITY COLLEGE STEM SCHOLARSHIPS
• *See page 105*

NASA WEST VIRGINIA SPACE GRANT CONSORTIUM

http://www.nasa.wvu.edu/

WEST VIRGINIA SPACE GRANT CONSORTIUM UNDERGRADUATE FELLOWSHIP PROGRAM
• *See page 134*

NATIONAL ACTION COUNCIL FOR MINORITIES IN ENGINEERING-NACME INC.

http://www.nacme.org/

NACME SCHOLARS PROGRAM
Renewable award for African-American, American-Indian, or Latino student enrolled in a baccalaureate engineering program. Must attend an ABET-accredited institution full-time and complete one semester with a minimum 2.7 GPA. Must be a U.S. citizen. Award money is given to participating institutions who select applicants and disperse funds. Check website for details http://www.nacme.org.

Academic Fields/Career Goals: Engineering/Technology.
Award: Scholarship for use in freshman, sophomore, junior, or senior years; renewable. *Amount:* up to $5000.
Eligibility Requirements: Applicant must be American Indian/Alaska Native, Black (non-Hispanic), Hispanic and enrolled or expecting to enroll full-time at a four-year institution or university. Available to U.S. citizens.
Application Requirements: Application form, financial need analysis, recommendations or references. *Deadline:* continuous.
Contact: Aileen Walter, Director, Scholar Management
National Action Council for Minorities in Engineering-
NACME Inc.
440 Hamilton Avenue, Suite 302
White Plains, NY 10601
Phone: 914-539-4010

NATIONAL ASSOCIATION FOR THE ADVANCEMENT OF COLORED PEOPLE

http://www.naacp.org/

HUBERTUS W.V. WELLEMS SCHOLARSHIP FOR MALE STUDENTS
• *See page 169*

NATIONAL ASSOCIATION OF WATER COMPANIES-NEW JERSEY CHAPTER

http://www.nawc.org/

NATIONAL ASSOCIATION OF WATER COMPANIES-NEW JERSEY CHAPTER SCHOLARSHIP
• *See page 146*

NATIONAL ASSOCIATION OF WOMEN IN CONSTRUCTION

http://www.nawic.org/

NAWIC UNDERGRADUATE SCHOLARSHIPS
• *See page 112*

NATIONAL INVENTORS HALL OF FAME

http://www.invent.org/

COLLEGIATE INVENTORS COMPETITION FOR UNDERGRADUATE STUDENTS
• *See page 106*

COLLEGIATE INVENTORS COMPETITION-GRAND PRIZE
• *See page 106*

NATIONAL SCIENCE TEACHERS ASSOCIATION

http://www.nsta.org/

TOSHIBA/NSTA EXPLORAVISION AWARDS PROGRAM
• *See page 203*

NATIONAL SOCIETY OF BLACK ENGINEERS

http://www.nsbe.org/

NSBE O-I CORPORATE SCHOLARSHIP PROGRAM
• *See page 268*

S. D. BECHTEL JR. FOUNDATION ENGINEERING SCHOLARSHIP

The purpose of this scholarship is to provide financial scholarships for students pursuing undergraduate degrees in Engineering and collegiate members of the National Society of Black Engineers (NSBE). Applicants must be NSBE members, majoring in civil engineering or mechanical engineering.

Academic Fields/Career Goals: Engineering/Technology.
Award: Scholarship for use in freshman, sophomore, junior, or senior years; renewable. *Number:* 3. *Amount:* $15,000.
Eligibility Requirements: Applicant must be Black (non-Hispanic) and enrolled or expecting to enroll at a four-year institution or university. Applicant must have 3.0 GPA or higher. Available to U.S. citizens.
Application Requirements: *Deadline:* June 30.

NATIONAL SOCIETY OF PROFESSIONAL ENGINEERS

http://www.nspe.org/

MAUREEN L. AND HOWARD N. BLITMAN, PE SCHOLARSHIP TO PROMOTE DIVERSITY IN ENGINEERING
• *See page 170*

PAUL H. ROBBINS HONORARY SCHOLARSHIP
• *See page 170*

PROFESSIONAL ENGINEERS IN INDUSTRY SCHOLARSHIP
• *See page 170*

NATIONAL URBAN LEAGUE

http://www.nulbeep.org/

BLACK EXECUTIVE EXCHANGE PROGRAM JERRY BARTOW SCHOLARSHIP FUND
• *See page 157*

NEVADA NASA SPACE GRANT CONSORTIUM

http://www.nvspacegrant.org/

NATIONAL SPACE GRANT COLLEGE AND FELLOWSHIP PROGRAM
• *See page 106*

OREGON STUDENT ASSISTANCE COMMISSION

http://www.GetCollegeFunds.org/

HOME BUILDERS FOUNDATION JIM IRVINE STATEWIDE SCHOLARSHIP
• *See page 112*

JEFFREY ALAN SCOGGINS MEMORIAL SCHOLARSHIP

Award for college junior or above for fall term/semester in undergraduate study in engineering at an Oregon four-year nonprofit college or university. Membership in the Sigma Chi fraternity is preferred. May reapply for additional year of funding, which may be used towards graduate study. Minimum 3.0 GPA is preferred.
Academic Fields/Career Goals: Engineering/Technology.
Award: Scholarship for use in junior, senior, or graduate years; not renewable.

Eligibility Requirements: Applicant must be enrolled or expecting to enroll full-time at a four-year institution or university and studying in Oregon. Applicant must have 3.0 GPA or higher. Available to U.S. citizens.
Application Requirements: Application form, FAFSA, transcript. *Deadline:* March 1.

SOCIETY OF AMERICAN MILITARY ENGINEERS PORTLAND POST SCHOLARSHIP
• *See page 170*

WILLIAM D. AND RUTH D. ROY SCHOLARSHIP

Scholarships available for Oregon high school graduates, home scholars, and GED recipients. Preference given to older, nontraditional students or students who are the first generation in their family to attend college. Must major in engineering and attend Portland State University or Oregon State University. Minimum 2.75 GPA required. Must enroll at least half-time. Must compete annually for renewal.
Academic Fields/Career Goals: Engineering/Technology.
Award: Scholarship for use in freshman, sophomore, junior, or senior years; not renewable.
Eligibility Requirements: Applicant must be enrolled or expecting to enroll full- or part-time at a four-year institution or university; resident of Oregon and studying in Oregon. Available to U.S. citizens.
Application Requirements: Activities chart, FAFSA, application form, essay, financial need analysis, transcript. *Deadline:* March 1.

PLASTICS INSTITUTE OF AMERICA

http://www.plasticsinstitute.org/

PLASTICS PIONEERS SCHOLARSHIPS
• *See page 170*

PLUMBING-HEATING-COOLING CONTRACTORS EDUCATION FOUNDATION

http://www.phccfoundation.org/

DELTA FAUCET COMPANY SCHOLARSHIP PROGRAM
• *See page 158*

PHCC EDUCATIONAL FOUNDATION NEED-BASED SCHOLARSHIP
• *See page 158*

PHCC EDUCATIONAL FOUNDATION SCHOLARSHIP PROGRAM
• *See page 158*

PROFESSIONAL CONSTRUCTION ESTIMATORS ASSOCIATION

http://www.pcea.org/

TED G. WILSON MEMORIAL SCHOLARSHIP FOUNDATION
• *See page 184*

ROBERT H. MOLLOHAN FAMILY CHARITABLE FOUNDATION, INC.

http://www.mollohanfoundation.org/

HIGH TECHNOLOGY SCHOLARS PROGRAM
• *See page 147*

ROCKY MOUNTAIN COAL MINING INSTITUTE

http://www.rmcmi.org/

ROCKY MOUNTAIN COAL MINING INSTITUTE SCHOLARSHIP

• See page 185

SALT RIVER PROJECT (SRP)

http://www.srpnet.com/

NAVAJO GENERATING STATION NAVAJO SCHOLARSHIP

Applicants must be enrolled members of the Navajo Nation who will be full-time students at an accredited college or university. Priority will be given to the math, engineering and environmental studies. Awards are made based on the field of study, and academic excellence and achievement. Award amounts are determined by the NGS Scholarship Committee following an evaluation of the Financial Needs Analysis of each applicant.

Academic Fields/Career Goals: Engineering/Technology; Environmental Science; Mathematics.

Award: Scholarship for use in junior year; renewable.

Eligibility Requirements: Applicant must be American Indian/Alaska Native and enrolled or expecting to enroll full-time at a four-year institution or university. Applicant must have 3.0 GPA or higher.

Application Requirements: *Deadline:* April 25.

SEMICONDUCTOR RESEARCH CORPORATION (SRC)

http://www.src.org/

MASTER'S SCHOLARSHIP PROGRAM

• See page 171

SIGMA XI, THE SCIENTIFIC RESEARCH SOCIETY

http://www.sigmaxi.org/

SIGMA XI GRANTS-IN-AID OF RESEARCH

• See page 95

SIMPLEHUMAN

http://www.simplehuman.com/

SIMPLE SOLUTIONS DESIGN COMPETITION

• See page 268

SOCIETY FOR IMAGING SCIENCE AND TECHNOLOGY

http://www.imaging.org/

RAYMOND DAVIS SCHOLARSHIP

Award available to an undergraduate junior or senior or graduate student enrolled full-time in an accredited program of photographic, imaging science or engineering. Minimum award is $1000. Applications processed between October 1 and December 15 only.

Academic Fields/Career Goals: Engineering/Technology; Physical Sciences.

Award: Scholarship for use in junior, senior, or graduate years; renewable. *Number:* 1–2. *Amount:* $1000.

Eligibility Requirements: Applicant must be enrolled or expecting to enroll full-time at a four-year institution or university. Available to U.S. and non-U.S. citizens.

Application Requirements: Application form, application form may be submitted online (http://imaging.org), recommendations or references, transcript. *Deadline:* October 1.

Contact: Donna Smith, Executive Assistant
Society for Imaging Science and Technology
7003 Kilworth Lane
Springfield, VA 22151
Phone: 703-642-9090 Ext. 107
Fax: 703-642-9094
E-mail: info@imaging.org

SOCIETY OF AUTOMOTIVE ENGINEERS

http://www.sae.org/

BMW/SAE ENGINEERING SCHOLARSHIP

• See page 137

DETROIT SECTION SAE TECHNICAL SCHOLARSHIP

• See page 269

EDWARD D. HENDRICKSON/SAE ENGINEERING SCHOLARSHIP

• See page 137

FRED M. YOUNG SR./SAE ENGINEERING SCHOLARSHIP

Scholarship of $4000 awarded at $1000 per year for four years. Applicants must have a 3.75 GPA, rank in the 90th percentile in both math and critical reading on SAT or composite ACT scores, and pursue an engineering degree accredited by ABET. A 3.0 GPA and continued engineering enrollment must be maintained to renew the scholarship.

Academic Fields/Career Goals: Engineering/Technology.

Award: Scholarship for use in freshman year; renewable. *Number:* 1. *Amount:* $1000.

Eligibility Requirements: Applicant must be high school student and planning to enroll or expecting to enroll full-time at a four-year institution or university. Available to U.S. citizens.

Application Requirements: Application form, essay, test scores, transcript. *Deadline:* December 15.

Contact: Connie Harnish, SAE Educational Relations
Society of Automotive Engineers
400 Commonwealth Drive
Warrendale, PA 15096
Phone: 724-772-4047
E-mail: connie@sae.org

RALPH K. HILLQUIST HONORARY SAE SCHOLARSHIP

• See page 269

SAE BALTIMORE SECTION BILL BRUBAKER SCHOLARSHIP

Nonrenewable scholarship for any family member of a Baltimore SAE member, or any high school senior accepted to an engineering program at a Maryland university.

Academic Fields/Career Goals: Engineering/Technology.

Award: Scholarship for use in freshman year; not renewable. *Number:* 1. *Amount:* up to $1000.

Eligibility Requirements: Applicant must be high school student; planning to enroll or expecting to enroll full-time at an institution or university and studying in Maryland. Applicant or parent of applicant must be member of Society of Automotive Engineers. Available to U.S. citizens.

Application Requirements: Application form, essay, resume, transcript. *Deadline:* May 10.

Contact: Marguerite Milligan, Marketing Assistant
Phone: 724-772-7158
Fax: 724-776-3049
E-mail: customerservice@sae.org

SAE LONG TERM MEMBER SPONSORED SCHOLARSHIP

The scholarship recognizes outstanding SAE student members who actively support SAE and its activities. Applications may be submitted by the student or by the SAE faculty advisor, an SAE Section officer or a community leader. The student must be a junior who will be entering the senior year of undergraduate engineering studies. Number of award varies.

Academic Fields/Career Goals: Engineering/Technology.

Award: Scholarship for use in senior year; not renewable. *Amount:* $1000.

Eligibility Requirements: Applicant must be enrolled or expecting to enroll full-time at a four-year institution or university. Applicant or parent of applicant must be member of Society of Automotive Engineers. Available to U.S. citizens.

Application Requirements: Application form, recommendations or references. *Deadline:* April 1.

Contact: Connie Harnish, SAE Educational Relations
Society of Automotive Engineers
400 Commonwealth Drive
Warrendale, PA 15096
Phone: 724-772-4047
E-mail: connie@sae.org

SAE WILLIAM G. BELFREY MEMORIAL GRANT

• *See page 269*

TAU BETA PI/SAE ENGINEERING SCHOLARSHIP

Six scholarships valued at $1000 each will be awarded for the freshman year only. Applicants must have a 3.75 GPA, rank in the 90th percentile in both math and critical reading for SAT scores or for composite ACT scores, and pursue an engineering program accredited by the engineering accreditation commission of the Accreditation Board for Engineering and Technology.

Academic Fields/Career Goals: Engineering/Technology.

Award: Scholarship for use in freshman year; not renewable. *Number:* 6. *Amount:* $1000.

Eligibility Requirements: Applicant must be high school student and planning to enroll or expecting to enroll full- or part-time at a four-year institution or university. Available to U.S. citizens.

Application Requirements: Application form, essay, test scores, transcript. *Deadline:* December 15.

Contact: Connie Harnish, SAE Educational Relations
Society of Automotive Engineers
400 Commonwealth Drive
Warrendale, PA 15096
Phone: 724-772-4047
E-mail: connie@sae.org

TMC/SAE DONALD D. DAWSON TECHNICAL SCHOLARSHIP

• *See page 137*

YANMAR/SAE SCHOLARSHIP

• *See page 269*

SOCIETY OF HISPANIC PROFESSIONAL ENGINEERS

http://www.shpe.org/

AHETEMS SCHOLARSHIPS

Merit-based and need-based scholarships are awarded, in the amount of $1000 to $5000 to high school graduating seniors, undergraduate students, and graduate students who demonstrate both significant motivation and aptitude for a career in science, technology, engineering or mathematics. Must have a minimum GPA of 3.0 (for high school seniors and undergraduates) and 3.25 for graduate students.

Academic Fields/Career Goals: Engineering/Technology; Mathematics; Science, Technology, and Society.

Award: Scholarship for use in freshman, sophomore, junior, senior, or graduate years; not renewable. *Number:* up to 100. *Amount:* $1000–$5000.

Eligibility Requirements: Applicant must be enrolled or expecting to enroll full-time at a two-year or four-year or technical institution or university. Applicant must have 3.0 GPA or higher. Available to U.S. and non-U.S. citizens.

Application Requirements: Application form, personal statement, recommendations or references, transcript. *Deadline:* April 1.

Contact: Rafaela Schwan, AHETEMS Office
Society of Hispanic Professional Engineers
The University of Texas at Arlington, College of Engineering, PO Box 19019
Arlington, TX 76019-0019
Phone: 817-272-0776
Fax: 817-272-2548
E-mail: rschwan@shpe.org

SOCIETY OF MANUFACTURING ENGINEERS EDUCATION FOUNDATION

http://www.smeef.org/

ALBERT E. WISCHMEYER MEMORIAL SCHOLARSHIP AWARD

Applicants must be residents of Western New York State, graduating high school seniors or current undergraduate students enrolled in an accredited degree program in manufacturing engineering, manufacturing engineering technology or mechanical technology in New York. Must have an GPA of 3.0.

Academic Fields/Career Goals: Engineering/Technology.

Award: Scholarship for use in freshman, sophomore, junior, or senior years; not renewable. *Number:* 1–10. *Amount:* $1000–$5000.

Eligibility Requirements: Applicant must be enrolled or expecting to enroll full-time at a four-year institution or university; resident of New York and studying in New York. Applicant must have 3.0 GPA or higher. Available to U.S. citizens.

Application Requirements: Application form, essay, recommendations or references, resume, transcript. *Deadline:* February 1.

ARTHUR AND GLADYS CERVENKA SCHOLARSHIP AWARD

One-time award to full-time students enrolled in a degree program in manufacturing engineering or technology. Preference given to students attending a Florida institution. Minimum 3.0 GPA required.

Academic Fields/Career Goals: Engineering/Technology.

Award: Scholarship for use in freshman, sophomore, junior, or senior years; not renewable. *Number:* 1–10. *Amount:* $1000–$5000.

Eligibility Requirements: Applicant must be enrolled or expecting to enroll full-time at a four-year institution or university. Applicant must have 3.0 GPA or higher. Available to U.S. citizens.

Application Requirements: Application form, essay, recommendations or references, resume, transcript. *Deadline:* February 1.

CATERPILLAR SCHOLARS AWARD FUND

Supports five one-time scholarships for full-time students enrolled in a manufacturing engineering program. Minority applicants may apply as incoming freshmen. Applicants must have an overall minimum GPA of 3.0.

Academic Fields/Career Goals: Engineering/Technology.

Award: Scholarship for use in freshman, sophomore, junior, or senior years; not renewable. *Number:* 1–15. *Amount:* $1000–$5000.

Eligibility Requirements: Applicant must be enrolled or expecting to enroll full-time at a four-year institution or university. Applicant must have 3.0 GPA or higher. Available to U.S. and Canadian citizens.

Application Requirements: Application form, essay, recommendations or references, resume, transcript. *Deadline:* February 1.

CHAPTER 17-ST. LOUIS SCHOLARSHIP

Scholarship will be given to full-time or part-time students enrolled in a manufacturing engineering, industrial technology, or other related program. Must study in Missouri or Illinois. Minimum of 2.5 GPA is required.

Academic Fields/Career Goals: Engineering/Technology.

Award: Scholarship for use in freshman, sophomore, junior, or senior years; not renewable.

Eligibility Requirements: Applicant must be enrolled or expecting to enroll full-time at a four-year institution or university and studying in

Illinois, Missouri. Applicant must have 2.5 GPA or higher. Available to U.S. and Canadian citizens.

Application Requirements: Application form, essay, recommendations or references, resume, transcript. *Deadline:* February 1.

CHAPTER 198-DOWNRIVER DETROIT SCHOLARSHIP

One-time award for an individual seeking an associates degree, bachelor's degree, or graduate degree in manufacturing, mechanical or industrial engineering, engineering technology, or industrial technology at an accredited public or private college or university in Michigan. Must have a minimum GPA of 2.5. Preference is given to applicants who are a child or grandchild of a current SME Downriver Chapter No. 198 member, a member of its student chapter, or a Michigan resident.

Academic Fields/Career Goals: Engineering/Technology; Industrial Design; Mechanical Engineering; Trade/Technical Specialties.

Award: Scholarship for use in freshman, sophomore, junior, senior, or graduate years; not renewable. *Number:* 1–5. *Amount:* $1000–$5000.

Eligibility Requirements: Applicant must be enrolled or expecting to enroll full-time at a two-year or four-year institution or university and studying in Michigan. Applicant must have 2.5 GPA or higher. Available to U.S. citizens.

Application Requirements: Application form, essay, recommendations or references, resume, student statement letter, test scores, transcript. *Deadline:* February 1.

CHAPTER 23-QUAD CITIES IOWA/ILLINOIS SCHOLARSHIP

Scholarship applicant must be entering freshman or current undergraduate student pursuing a bachelor's degree in manufacturing engineering or a related field at an accredited college or university in Iowa or Illinois.

Academic Fields/Career Goals: Engineering/Technology.

Award: Scholarship for use in freshman, sophomore, or junior years; not renewable. *Number:* up to 5. *Amount:* $1000–$5000.

Eligibility Requirements: Applicant must be enrolled or expecting to enroll full-time at a four-year institution or university and studying in Illinois, Iowa. Available to U.S. and Canadian citizens.

Application Requirements: Application form, essay, recommendations or references, resume, test scores, transcript. *Deadline:* February 1.

CHAPTER 31-TRI CITY SCHOLARSHIP

Applicants must be seeking a bachelor's degree in manufacturing, mechanical, or industrial engineering, engineering technology, industrial technology or closely related field of study. Must be enrolled in or plan to attend an accredited college or university in the state of Michigan.

Academic Fields/Career Goals: Engineering/Technology.

Award: Scholarship for use in freshman, sophomore, junior, or senior years; not renewable. *Number:* up to 5. *Amount:* $1000–$5000.

Eligibility Requirements: Applicant must be enrolled or expecting to enroll full-time at a two-year or four-year or technical institution or university and studying in Michigan. Applicant must have 3.0 GPA or higher. Available to U.S. and Canadian citizens.

Application Requirements: Application form, essay, resume, test scores, transcript. *Deadline:* February 1.

CHAPTER 3-PEORIA ENDOWED SCHOLARSHIP

Applicants must be seeking a bachelor's degree in manufacturing engineering, industrial engineering, manufacturing technology, or a manufacturing-related degree program at either Bradley University (Peoria, Illinois) or Illinois State University (Normal, Illinois).

Academic Fields/Career Goals: Engineering/Technology.

Award: Scholarship for use in freshman, sophomore, or junior years; not renewable. *Number:* up to 5. *Amount:* $1000–$5000.

Eligibility Requirements: Applicant must be enrolled or expecting to enroll full-time at a two-year or four-year or technical institution or university; resident of Illinois and studying in Illinois. Applicant must have 3.0 GPA or higher. Available to U.S. and Canadian citizens.

Application Requirements: Application form, essay, recommendations or references, resume, test scores, transcript. *Deadline:* February 1.

CHAPTER 4-LAWRENCE A. WACKER MEMORIAL SCHOLARSHIP

Awards available to full-time students enrolled in or accepted to a degree program in manufacturing, mechanical or industrial engineering at a college or university in the state of Wisconsin. One scholarship will be granted to a graduating high school senior and the other will be granted to a current undergraduate student. Minimum GPA of 3.0 required.

Academic Fields/Career Goals: Engineering/Technology; Mechanical Engineering.

Award: Scholarship for use in freshman, sophomore, junior, or senior years; not renewable. *Number:* 1–10. *Amount:* $1000–$5000.

Eligibility Requirements: Applicant must be enrolled or expecting to enroll full-time at a four-year institution or university and studying in Wisconsin. Applicant must have 3.0 GPA or higher. Available to U.S. citizens.

Application Requirements: Application form, essay, recommendations or references, resume, transcript. *Deadline:* February 1.

CHAPTER 63-PORTLAND JAMES E. MORROW SCHOLARSHIP

Applicants must be pursuing a career in manufacturing or a related field. Preference will be given to students planning to attend Oregon or southwest Washington schools. Preference will also be given to applicants who reside within the states of Oregon or southwest Washington.

Academic Fields/Career Goals: Engineering/Technology.

Award: Scholarship for use in freshman, sophomore, or junior years; not renewable. *Number:* up to 5. *Amount:* $1000–$5000.

Eligibility Requirements: Applicant must be enrolled or expecting to enroll full-time at a two-year or four-year or technical institution or university; resident of Oregon, Washington and studying in Oregon, Washington. Available to U.S. and Canadian citizens.

Application Requirements: Application form, essay, recommendations or references, resume, test scores, transcript. *Deadline:* February 1.

CHAPTER 63-PORTLAND UNCLE BUD SMITH SCHOLARSHIP

Applicants must be pursuing a career in manufacturing or a related field. Preference will be given to students planning to attend Oregon or southwest Washington schools. Preference will also be given to applicants who reside within the states of Oregon or southwest Washington.

Academic Fields/Career Goals: Engineering/Technology.

Award: Scholarship for use in freshman, sophomore, or junior years; not renewable. *Number:* up to 5. *Amount:* $1000–$5000.

Eligibility Requirements: Applicant must be enrolled or expecting to enroll full-time at a two-year or four-year or technical institution or university; resident of Oregon, Washington and studying in Oregon, Washington. Available to U.S. and Canadian citizens.

Application Requirements: Application form, essay, recommendations or references, resume, test scores, transcript. *Deadline:* February 1.

CHAPTER 67-PHOENIX SCHOLARSHIP

Award for a high school senior who plans on enrolling in a manufacturing program technology or manufacturing technology program or an undergraduate student enrolled in a manufacturing engineering technology, manufacturing technology, industrial technology, or closely related program at an accredited college or university in Arizona. Applicants must have an overall GPA of 2.5. Scholarship ranges from $1000 to $5000.

Academic Fields/Career Goals: Engineering/Technology; Industrial Design; Mechanical Engineering; Trade/Technical Specialties.

Award: Scholarship for use in freshman, sophomore, junior, or senior years; not renewable. *Number:* 1–5. *Amount:* $1000–$5000.

Eligibility Requirements: Applicant must be enrolled or expecting to enroll full-time at a two-year or four-year institution or university and studying in Arizona. Applicant must have 2.5 GPA or higher. Available to U.S. citizens.

Application Requirements: Application form, essay, recommendations or references, resume, test scores, transcript. *Deadline:* February 1.

CHAPTER 6-FAIRFIELD COUNTY SCHOLARSHIP

Scholarship applicants must be full-time undergraduate students enrolled in a degree program in manufacturing engineering, technology, or a closely related field in the United States or Canada. Preference is given to residents of, or students studying in, the eastern part of the United States.

Academic Fields/Career Goals: Engineering/Technology.

Award: Scholarship for use in freshman, sophomore, or junior years; not renewable. *Number:* up to 4. *Amount:* $1000–$5000.

Eligibility Requirements: Applicant must be enrolled or expecting to enroll full-time at a two-year or four-year or technical institution. Applicant must have 3.0 GPA or higher. Available to U.S. and Canadian citizens.

Application Requirements: Application form, essay, recommendations or references, resume, test scores, transcript. *Deadline:* February 1.

CHAPTER 93-ALBUQUERQUE SCHOLARSHIP

Scholarship to students entering freshmen or current undergraduate students pursuing a bachelor's degree in manufacturing engineering or a related field who plan to or are attending an accredited college or university in New Mexico.

Academic Fields/Career Goals: Engineering/Technology.

Award: Scholarship for use in freshman, sophomore, junior, or senior years; not renewable. *Number:* 1–5. *Amount:* $1000–$5000.

Eligibility Requirements: Applicant must be enrolled or expecting to enroll full-time at a four-year institution or university and studying in New Mexico. Available to U.S. citizens.

Application Requirements: Application form, essay, recommendations or references, resume, test scores, transcript. *Deadline:* February 1.

CLARENCE AND JOSEPHINE MYERS SCHOLARSHIP

Applicants must be an undergraduate or graduate student pursuing a degree in engineering or a manufacturing-related field at a college within the state of Indiana.

Academic Fields/Career Goals: Engineering/Technology.

Award: Scholarship for use in freshman, sophomore, junior, or senior years; not renewable. *Number:* up to 5. *Amount:* $1000–$5000.

Eligibility Requirements: Applicant must be enrolled or expecting to enroll full-time at a two-year or four-year or technical institution or university and studying in Indiana. Available to U.S. and Canadian citizens.

Application Requirements: Application form, essay, recommendations or references, test scores, transcript. *Deadline:* February 1.

CLINTON J. HELTON MANUFACTURING SCHOLARSHIP AWARD FUND

One-time award to full-time students enrolled in a degree program in manufacturing engineering or technology at Colorado State University or University of Colorado. Applicants must possess an overall minimum GPA of 3.3.

Academic Fields/Career Goals: Engineering/Technology; Trade/Technical Specialties.

Award: Scholarship for use in freshman, sophomore, junior, or senior years; not renewable. *Number:* 1–5. *Amount:* $1000–$5000.

Eligibility Requirements: Applicant must be enrolled or expecting to enroll full-time at a four-year institution or university and studying in Colorado. Available to U.S. citizens.

Application Requirements: Application form, essay, recommendations or references, test scores, transcript. *Deadline:* February 1.

CONNIE AND ROBERT T. GUNTER SCHOLARSHIP

One-time award will be given for full-time undergraduate students enrolled in a degree program in manufacturing engineering or technology. Minimum 3.5 GPA is required. Must study in Georgia.

Academic Fields/Career Goals: Engineering/Technology.

Award: Scholarship for use in freshman, sophomore, junior, or senior years; not renewable. *Number:* 1–5. *Amount:* $1000–$5000.

Eligibility Requirements: Applicant must be enrolled or expecting to enroll full-time at a four-year institution or university and studying in

Georgia. Applicant must have 3.5 GPA or higher. Available to U.S. citizens.

Application Requirements: Application form, essay, recommendations or references, resume, transcript. *Deadline:* February 1.

DETROIT CHAPTER ONE-FOUNDING CHAPTER SCHOLARSHIP

Several awards will be available in each of the following: associate degree and equivalent, baccalaureate degree and graduate degree programs. Minimum GPA of 3.5 is required. Preference given to undergraduate or graduate student enrolled in a manufacturing engineering or technology program at one of the sponsored institutions.

Academic Fields/Career Goals: Engineering/Technology.

Award: Scholarship for use in freshman, sophomore, junior, senior, or graduate years; not renewable. *Number:* 3. *Amount:* $1000.

Eligibility Requirements: Applicant must be enrolled or expecting to enroll full- or part-time at a two-year or four-year institution or university and studying in Michigan. Applicant must have 3.5 GPA or higher. Available to U.S. citizens.

Application Requirements: Application form, recommendations or references. *Deadline:* February 1.

DIRECTOR'S SCHOLARSHIP AWARD

Scholarship award for full-time undergraduate students enrolled in a manufacturing or related degree program in the United States or Canada. Preference will be given to students who demonstrate leadership skills in a community, academic, or professional environment. Average GPA of 3.5 required.

Academic Fields/Career Goals: Engineering/Technology.

Award: Scholarship for use in freshman, sophomore, junior, or senior years; not renewable. *Number:* 1–5. *Amount:* $1000–$10,000.

Eligibility Requirements: Applicant must be enrolled or expecting to enroll full-time at a four-year institution or university and must have an interest in leadership. Applicant must have 3.5 GPA or higher. Available to U.S. and Canadian citizens.

Application Requirements: Application form, essay, recommendations or references, resume, transcript. *Deadline:* February 1.

EDWARD S. ROTH MANUFACTURING ENGINEERING SCHOLARSHIP

Award to a graduating high school senior, a current full-time undergraduate or graduate student enrolled in an accredited four-year degree program in manufacturing engineering at a sponsored ABET-accredited school. Minimum GPA of 3.0 and be a U.S. citizen.

Academic Fields/Career Goals: Engineering/Technology.

Award: Scholarship for use in freshman, sophomore, junior, senior, or graduate years; not renewable. *Number:* 1–10. *Amount:* $1000–$5000.

Eligibility Requirements: Applicant must be enrolled or expecting to enroll full-time at a four-year institution or university and studying in California, Florida, Illinois, Massachusetts, Minnesota, Ohio, Texas, Utah. Applicant must have 3.0 GPA or higher. Available to U.S. citizens.

Application Requirements: Application form, interview, recommendations or references, resume, transcript. *Deadline:* February 1.

E. WAYNE KAY COMMUNITY COLLEGE SCHOLARSHIP AWARD

One-time award to full-time students enrolled at an accredited community college or trade school which offers programs in manufacturing or closely related field in the United States or Canada. Minimum GPA of 3.0 required. Scholarship applicants may be entering freshmen or sophomore students with less than 60 college credit hours completed and be seeking a career in manufacturing engineering or technology.

Academic Fields/Career Goals: Engineering/Technology; Trade/Technical Specialties.

Award: Scholarship for use in freshman or sophomore years; not renewable. *Number:* 1–20. *Amount:* $1000–$10,000.

Eligibility Requirements: Applicant must be enrolled or expecting to enroll full-time at a two-year or four-year or technical institution or university. Applicant must have 3.0 GPA or higher. Available to U.S. and Canadian citizens.

Application Requirements: Application form, essay, recommendations or references, resume, transcript. *Deadline:* February 1.

E. WAYNE KAY CO-OP SCHOLARSHIP

Scholarship will be awarded for graduating high school senior or full-time undergraduate student enrolled in a degree program in manufacturing or a closely related field at a two year Community College or trade school in the United States or Canada. Average of 3.0 GPA is required.

Academic Fields/Career Goals: Engineering/Technology.

Award: Scholarship for use in freshman, sophomore, junior, or senior years; not renewable. *Number:* 1–10. *Amount:* $1000–$5000.

Eligibility Requirements: Applicant must be enrolled or expecting to enroll full-time at a two-year or four-year or technical institution or university. Applicant must have 3.0 GPA or higher. Available to U.S. and non-U.S. citizens.

Application Requirements: Application form, essay, recommendations or references, resume, transcript. *Deadline:* February 1.

E. WAYNE KAY HIGH SCHOOL SCHOLARSHIP

Scholarship available for student enrolled full-time in manufacturing engineering or technology program at an accredited college or university. Minimum 3.0 GPA required.

Academic Fields/Career Goals: Engineering/Technology.

Award: Scholarship for use in freshman, sophomore, junior, or senior years; renewable. *Number:* 1–20. *Amount:* $1000–$2500.

Eligibility Requirements: Applicant must be enrolled or expecting to enroll full-time at a four-year institution or university. Applicant must have 3.0 GPA or higher. Available to U.S. and Canadian citizens.

Application Requirements: Application form, essay, recommendations or references, test scores, transcript. *Deadline:* February 1.

E. WAYNE KAY SCHOLARSHIP

Scholarship for full-time undergraduate students enrolled in a degree program in manufacturing engineering, technology, or a closely related field in the United States or Canada. Minimum of 3.0 GPA is required.

Academic Fields/Career Goals: Engineering/Technology; Trade/Technical Specialties.

Award: Scholarship for use in freshman, sophomore, junior, or senior years; not renewable. *Number:* 10–30. *Amount:* $2500–$7500.

Eligibility Requirements: Applicant must be enrolled or expecting to enroll full-time at a four-year institution or university. Applicant must have 3.0 GPA or higher. Available to U.S. and Canadian citizens.

Application Requirements: Application form, essay, recommendations or references, resume, test scores, transcript. *Deadline:* February 1.

FORT WAYNE CHAPTER 56 SCHOLARSHIP

One-time award for an individual seeking an associates degree, bachelor's degree, or graduate degree in manufacturing, mechanical or industrial engineering, engineering technology, or industrial technology at an accredited public or private college or university in Indiana. Must have a minimum GPA of 2.5. Preference given to applicants who are a child or grandchild of a current SME Fort Wayne Chapter No. 56 member, a member of its student chapter, or an Indiana resident.

Academic Fields/Career Goals: Engineering/Technology; Industrial Design; Mechanical Engineering; Trade/Technical Specialties.

Award: Scholarship for use in freshman, sophomore, junior, senior, or graduate years; not renewable. *Number:* 1–10. *Amount:* $1000–$5000.

Eligibility Requirements: Applicant must be enrolled or expecting to enroll full-time at a two-year or four-year institution or university and studying in Indiana. Applicant must have 2.5 GPA or higher. Available to U.S. citizens.

Application Requirements: Application form, essay, recommendations or references, resume, transcript. *Deadline:* February 1.

GUILIANO MAZZETTI SCHOLARSHIP AWARD

One-time award available to full-time students enrolled in a degree program in manufacturing engineering or technology in the United States or Canada. Minimum GPA of 3.0 required.

Academic Fields/Career Goals: Engineering/Technology.

Award: Scholarship for use in freshman, sophomore, junior, or senior years; not renewable. *Number:* 1–10. *Amount:* $1000–$5000.

Eligibility Requirements: Applicant must be enrolled or expecting to enroll full-time at a four-year institution or university. Applicant must have 3.0 GPA or higher. Available to U.S. and Canadian citizens.

Application Requirements: Application form, essay, recommendations or references, resume, transcript. *Deadline:* February 1.

LUCILE B. KAUFMAN WOMEN'S SCHOLARSHIP

Scholarships available for female full-time undergraduate students enrolled in a degree program in manufacturing engineering, technology or a closely related field in the United States or Canada. Minimum of 3.0 GPA is required. Scholarship value and the number of awards granted varies.

Academic Fields/Career Goals: Engineering/Technology.

Award: Scholarship for use in freshman, sophomore, junior, or senior years; not renewable. *Number:* 1–5. *Amount:* $1000–$5000.

Eligibility Requirements: Applicant must be enrolled or expecting to enroll full-time at a four-year institution or university and female. Applicant must have 3.0 GPA or higher. Available to U.S. and Canadian citizens.

Application Requirements: Application form, essay, recommendations or references, resume, transcript. *Deadline:* February 1.

MYRTLE AND EARL WALKER SCHOLARSHIP FUND

• *See page 270*

NORTH CENTRAL REGION 9 SCHOLARSHIP

Award to a full-time student enrolled in a manufacturing, mechanical, or industrial engineering degree program in North Central Region 9 (Iowa, Minnesota, Nebraska, North Dakota, South Dakota, Wisconsin, and the upper peninsula of Michigan). Applicants must have a 3.0 GPA.

Academic Fields/Career Goals: Engineering/Technology; Industrial Design; Mechanical Engineering; Trade/Technical Specialties.

Award: Scholarship for use in freshman, sophomore, junior, or senior years; not renewable. *Number:* 1–10. *Amount:* $1000–$5000.

Eligibility Requirements: Applicant must be enrolled or expecting to enroll full-time at a four-year institution or university and studying in Iowa, Michigan, Minnesota, Nebraska, North Dakota, South Dakota, Wisconsin. Applicant must have 3.0 GPA or higher. Available to U.S. citizens.

Application Requirements: Application form, essay, recommendations or references, resume, transcript. *Deadline:* February 1.

SME FAMILY SCHOLARSHIP

Scholarships awarded to children or grandchildren of Society of Manufacturing Engineers members. Must be graduating high school senior planning to pursue full-time studies for an undergraduate degree in manufacturing engineering, manufacturing engineering technology, or a closely related engineering study at an accredited college or university. Minimum GPA of 3.0 required. Scholarship value and the number of awards granted varies annually.

Academic Fields/Career Goals: Engineering/Technology.

Award: Scholarship for use in freshman, sophomore, junior, or senior years; renewable. *Number:* 1–10. *Amount:* $5000–$80,000.

Eligibility Requirements: Applicant must be enrolled or expecting to enroll full-time at a four-year institution or university. Applicant must have 3.0 GPA or higher. Available to U.S. and non-U.S. citizens.

Application Requirements: Application form, essay, interview, personal photograph, recommendations or references, resume, test scores, transcript. *Deadline:* February 1.

WALT BARTRAM MEMORIAL EDUCATION AWARD

Scholarship available for graduating high school seniors who commit to enroll in, or full-time college or university students pursuing a degree in, manufacturing engineering or a closely related field within the areas of New Mexico, Arizona or Southern California.

Academic Fields/Career Goals: Engineering/Technology.

Award: Scholarship for use in freshman, sophomore, junior, or senior years; not renewable. *Number:* 1. *Amount:* $1500.

Eligibility Requirements: Applicant must be enrolled or expecting to enroll full-time at a four-year institution or university; resident of Arizona, California, New Mexico and studying in Arizona, California, New Mexico. Applicant or parent of applicant must be member of Soil and Water Conservation Society. Available to U.S. and Canadian citizens.

Application Requirements: 2 copies of student statement letter, application form, recommendations or references, resume, transcript. *Deadline:* February 1.

WICHITA CHAPTER 52 SCHOLARSHIP

Award for an individual seeking an associates degree, bachelor's degree, or graduate degree in manufacturing, mechanical or industrial engineering, engineering technology, or industrial technology at an accredited public or private college or university in Kansas, Oklahoma or Missouri. Applicants must have a minimum GPA of 2.5. Preference given to applicants who are a relative of a current SME Wichita Chapter No. 52 member or a Kansas resident.

Academic Fields/Career Goals: Engineering/Technology; Industrial Design; Mechanical Engineering; Trade/Technical Specialties.

Award: Scholarship for use in freshman, sophomore, junior, senior, or graduate years; not renewable. *Number:* 1. *Amount:* up to $1500.

Eligibility Requirements: Applicant must be enrolled or expecting to enroll full-time at a two-year or four-year institution or university and studying in Kansas, Missouri, Oklahoma. Applicant must have 2.5 GPA or higher. Available to U.S. citizens.

Application Requirements: Application form, recommendations or references, resume, student statement letter, transcript. *Deadline:* February 1.

WILLIAM E. WEISEL SCHOLARSHIP FUND
• *See page 255*

SOCIETY OF MOTION PICTURE AND TELEVISION ENGINEERS
http://www.smpte.org/

LOUIS F. WOLF JR. MEMORIAL SCHOLARSHIP
• *See page 195*

STUDENT PAPER AWARD
• *See page 195*

SOCIETY OF PETROLEUM ENGINEERS
http://www.spe.org/

GUS ARCHIE MEMORIAL SCHOLARSHIPS

Renewable award for students who have not attended college or university before and are planning to enroll in a petroleum engineering degree program at a four-year institution. Must have minimum 3.0 GPA.

Academic Fields/Career Goals: Engineering/Technology.

Award: Scholarship for use in freshman, sophomore, junior, or senior years; renewable. *Number:* 1–2. *Amount:* $6000.

Eligibility Requirements: Applicant must be enrolled or expecting to enroll full-time at a four-year institution or university. Applicant must have 3.0 GPA or higher. Available to U.S. and non-U.S. citizens.

Application Requirements: Application form, financial need analysis, personal photograph, recommendations or references, test scores, transcript. *Deadline:* April 30.

SOCIETY OF PLASTICS ENGINEERS (SPE) FOUNDATION
http://www.4spe.org/

FLEMING/BASZCAK SCHOLARSHIP
• *See page 171*

PLASTICS PIONEERS ASSOCIATION SCHOLARSHIPS
• *See page 171*

SOCIETY OF PLASTICS ENGINEERS SCHOLARSHIP PROGRAM
• *See page 171*

SOCIETY OF WOMEN ENGINEERS
http://www.swe.org/

ADA I. PRESSMAN MEMORIAL SCHOLARSHIP
• *See page 172*

ANNE MAUREEN WHITNEY BARROW MEMORIAL SCHOLARSHIP
• *See page 172*

APPLIED COMPUTER SECURITY ASSOCIATION CYBERSECURITY SCHOLARSHIP
• *See page 204*

BECHTEL CORPORATION SCHOLARSHIP

Two $1400 scholarships for women pursuing ABET-accredited baccalaureate or graduate programs in preparation for careers in engineering, engineering technology and computer science in the United States and Mexico. SWE membership required.

Academic Fields/Career Goals: Engineering/Technology.

Award: Scholarship for use in sophomore, junior, senior, or graduate years; not renewable. *Number:* 2. *Amount:* $1400.

Eligibility Requirements: Applicant must be enrolled or expecting to enroll full-time at a four-year institution or university and female. Applicant or parent of applicant must be member of Society of Women Engineers. Available to U.S. citizens.

Application Requirements: Application form, recommendations or references. *Deadline:* February 15.

BETTY LOU BAILEY SWE REGION F SCHOLARSHIP
• *See page 172*

B.J. HARROD SCHOLARSHIP

Two $1500 scholarships for women pursuing ABET-accredited baccalaureate or graduate programs in preparation for careers in engineering, engineering technology, and computer science in the United States and Mexico.

Academic Fields/Career Goals: Engineering/Technology.

Award: Scholarship for use in freshman year; not renewable. *Number:* 2. *Amount:* $1500.

Eligibility Requirements: Applicant must be enrolled or expecting to enroll full-time at a four-year institution or university and female. Applicant must have 3.5 GPA or higher. Available to U.S. citizens.

Application Requirements: Application form, essay, recommendations or references, self-addressed stamped envelope with application, test scores, transcript. *Deadline:* May 15.

BK KRENZER MEMORIAL REENTRY SCHOLARSHIP
• *See page 172*

BOSTON SCIENTIFIC SCHOLARSHIP
• *See page 172*

BRILL FAMILY SCHOLARSHIP

$1500 award for a woman pursuing an ABET-accredited baccalaureate or graduate program in preparation for a career in engineering, engineering technology, and computer science in the United States and Mexico. Preference given to a student pursuing study in aeronautical/aerospace engineering or biomedical engineering.

Academic Fields/Career Goals: Engineering/Technology.

Award: Scholarship for use in sophomore, junior, or senior years; not renewable. *Number:* 1. *Amount:* $1500.

Eligibility Requirements: Applicant must be enrolled or expecting to enroll full-time at a four-year institution or university and female. Available to U.S. citizens.

Application Requirements: Application form, recommendations or references. *Deadline:* February 15.

CAROL STEPHENS REGION F SCHOLARSHIP
• *See page 172*

CATERPILLAR INC. SCHOLARSHIP
• *See page 172*

CISCO'S FUTURE SCHOLARSHIP
• *See page 204*

CUMMINS INC. SCHOLARSHIP
• *See page 173*

DELL SCHOLARSHIP
• *See page 204*

DR. IVY M. PARKER MEMORIAL SCHOLARSHIP
• *See page 173*

DOROTHY LEMKE HOWARTH MEMORIAL SCHOLARSHIP
• *See page 173*

DOROTHY P. MORRIS SCHOLARSHIP
• *See page 173*

DUPONT COMPANY SCHOLARSHIP
• *See page 173*

ELIZABETH MCLEAN MEMORIAL SCHOLARSHIP
$1500 scholarship for a woman pursuing an ABET-accredited baccalaureate program in preparation for a career in civil engineering in the United States and Mexico.

Academic Fields/Career Goals: Engineering/Technology.

Award: Scholarship for use in sophomore, junior, or senior years; not renewable. *Number:* 1. *Amount:* $1500.

Eligibility Requirements: Applicant must be enrolled or expecting to enroll full-time at a four-year institution or university and female. Available to U.S. citizens.

Application Requirements: Application form, recommendations or references. *Deadline:* February 15.

FORD MOTOR COMPANY SCHOLARSHIP
• *See page 255*

GENERAL ELECTRIC WOMEN'S NETWORK SCHOLARSHIP
• *See page 185*

GOLDMAN, SACHS & CO. SCHOLARSHIP
• *See page 204*

HONEYWELL CORPORATION SCHOLARSHIP
• *See page 173*

IBM CORPORATION SCHOLARSHIP
• *See page 204*

ITW SCHOLARSHIP
• *See page 204*

JILL S. TIETJEN P.E. SCHOLARSHIP
• *See page 173*

JUDITH RESNICK MEMORIAL SCHOLARSHIP
$3000 scholarship for a women pursuing an ABET-accredited baccalaureate program in preparation for a career in engineering, engineering technology, and computer science in the United States and Mexico. Must be a member of SWE and pursuing a space-related engineering major.

Academic Fields/Career Goals: Engineering/Technology.

Award: Scholarship for use in sophomore, junior, or senior years; not renewable. *Number:* 1. *Amount:* $3000.

Eligibility Requirements: Applicant must be enrolled or expecting to enroll full-time at a four-year institution or university and female. Applicant or parent of applicant must be member of Society of Women Engineers. Available to U.S. citizens.

Application Requirements: Application form, recommendations or references. *Deadline:* February 15.

LIFE TECHNOLOGIES SCHOLARSHIP
• *See page 174*

LILLIAN MOLLER GILBRETH MEMORIAL SCHOLARSHIP
• *See page 174*

LOCKHEED MARTIN AERONAUTICS CORPORATION SCHOLARSHIPS
• *See page 205*

MARY GUNTHER MEMORIAL SCHOLARSHIP
Four $3000 scholarships for women pursuing ABET-accredited baccalaureate programs in preparation for careers in engineering, engineering technology, and computer science in the United States and Mexico. Preference given to students pursuing studies in architectural and environmental engineering.

Academic Fields/Career Goals: Engineering/Technology.

Award: Scholarship for use in freshman, sophomore, junior, or senior years; not renewable. *Number:* 4. *Amount:* $3000.

Eligibility Requirements: Applicant must be enrolled or expecting to enroll full-time at a four-year institution or university and female. Available to U.S. citizens.

Application Requirements: Application form, recommendations or references. *Deadline:* February 15.

MARY V. MUNGER SCHOLARSHIP
• *See page 174*

MASWE MEMORIAL SCHOLARSHIP
• *See page 174*

MERIDITH THOMS MEMORIAL SCHOLARSHIPS
• *See page 174*

OLIVE LYNN SALEMBIER MEMORIAL REENTRY SCHOLARSHIP
• *See page 174*

ROCKWELL COLLINS SCHOLARSHIP
• *See page 205*

SUSAN MISZKOWICZ MEMORIAL SCHOLARSHIP
• *See page 175*

SWE BALTIMORE-WASHINGTON SECTION SCHOLARSHIP
• *See page 175*

SWE CENTRAL NEW MEXICO PIONEERS SCHOLARSHIP
• *See page 175*

SWE CENTRAL NEW MEXICO REENTRY SCHOLARSHIP
• *See page 175*

SWE MID-HUDSON SECTION SCHOLARSHIP
• *See page 175*

SWE NEW JERSEY SECTION SCHOLARSHIP
Scholarship available for a female New Jersey resident majoring in engineering. Available to incoming freshman. Minimum 3.5 GPA required. Must have attended high school in New Jersey.

Academic Fields/Career Goals: Engineering/Technology.

Award: Scholarship for use in freshman year; not renewable. *Number:* 1. *Amount:* $2000.

Eligibility Requirements: Applicant must be enrolled or expecting to enroll full-time at a four-year institution or university; female and resident of New Jersey. Applicant must have 3.5 GPA or higher. Available to U.S. citizens.

Application Requirements: Application form, essay, recommendations or references, self-addressed stamped envelope with application, test scores, transcript. *Deadline:* May 15.

SWE PAST PRESIDENTS SCHOLARSHIP
• *See page 175*

SWE PHOENIX SECTION SCHOLARSHIP
• *See page 175*

SWE REGION H SCHOLARSHIPS
• *See page 176*

VERIZON SCHOLARSHIP
• *See page 205*

VIASAT SOFTWARE ENGINEERING SCHOLARSHIP
• *See page 205*

WANDA MUNN SCHOLARSHIP
• *See page 176*

SOCIETY OF WOMEN ENGINEERS-DALLAS SECTION
http://www.dallaswe.org/

GRADUATING HIGH SCHOOL SENIORSENGINEERING SCHOLARSHIP FOR DALLAS WOMEN
Scholarship for graduating high school senior women who wish to pursue a degree in engineering. Applicant must be a Texas resident. Please refer to website for further details, http://www.dallaswe.org.

Academic Fields/Career Goals: Engineering/Technology.

Award: Scholarship for use in freshman, sophomore, junior, or senior years; renewable. *Number:* 2–4. *Amount:* $500–$1000.

Eligibility Requirements: Applicant must be high school student; planning to enroll or expecting to enroll full-time at a four-year institution or university; female and resident of Texas. Available to U.S. citizens.

Application Requirements: Application form, confirmation of enrollment, essay, personal photograph, recommendations or references, resume, transcript. *Deadline:* May 15.

Contact: Barbara Vilbig, Scholarship Coordinator
Society of Women Engineers-Dallas Section
PO Box 852022
Richardson, TX 75085-2022
Phone: 214-352-7333

NATIONAL SOCIETY OF WOMEN ENGINEERS SCHOLARSHIPS
• *See page 205*

SOCIETY OF WOMEN ENGINEERS-ROCKY MOUNTAIN SECTION
http://www.societyofwomenengineers.org/RockyMountain/

SOCIETY OF WOMEN ENGINEERS-ROCKY MOUNTAIN SECTION SCHOLARSHIP PROGRAM
• *See page 176*

SOCIETY OF WOMEN ENGINEERS-TWIN TIERS SECTION
http://www.swetwintiers.org/

SOCIETY OF WOMEN ENGINEERS-TWIN TIERS SECTION SCHOLARSHIP
• *See page 205*

SPECIALTY EQUIPMENT MARKET ASSOCIATION
http://www.sema.org/

SPECIALTY EQUIPMENT MARKET ASSOCIATION MEMORIAL SCHOLARSHIP FUND
• *See page 80*

STRAIGHTFORWARD MEDIA
http://www.straightforwardmedia.com/

STRAIGHTFORWARD MEDIA ENGINEERING SCHOLARSHIP
• *See page 176*

TAU BETA PI ASSOCIATION
http://www.tbp.org/

TAU BETA PI SCHOLARSHIP PROGRAM
One-time award for initiated members of Tau Beta Pi in their senior year of full-time undergraduate engineering study.

Academic Fields/Career Goals: Engineering/Technology.

Award: Scholarship for use in senior year; not renewable. *Number:* 150–200. *Amount:* $2000.

Eligibility Requirements: Applicant must be enrolled or expecting to enroll full-time at a four-year institution or university. Applicant or parent of applicant must be member of Tau Beta Pi Association. Available to U.S. and non-U.S. citizens.

Application Requirements: Application form, essay, recommendations or references. *Deadline:* April 1.

Contact: Dylan Lane, Communications Specialist
Phone: 865-546-4578
E-mail: dylan@tbp.org

TECHNICAL ASSOCIATION OF THE PULP & PAPER INDUSTRY (TAPPI)
http://www.tappi.org/

NONWOVENS DIVISION SCHOLARSHIP
Award to applicants enrolled as full-time students in a state accredited undergraduate program. Must be in a program preparatory to a career in the nonwovens industry or demonstrate an interest in the areas, be recommended and endorsed by an instructor or faculty member and maintain a 3.0 GPA. Information can be found at http://www.tappi.org/s_tappi/sec.asp?CID=6101&DID=546695.

Academic Fields/Career Goals: Engineering/Technology; Paper and Pulp Engineering.

Award: Scholarship for use in freshman, sophomore, junior, or senior years; not renewable. *Number:* 1. *Amount:* $1000.

Eligibility Requirements: Applicant must be enrolled or expecting to enroll full-time at a four-year institution or university. Applicant must have 3.0 GPA or higher. Available to U.S. and non-U.S. citizens.

Application Requirements: Application form, recommendations or references, transcript. *Deadline:* February 15.

Contact: Mr. Charles Bohanan, Director of Standards and Awards
Technical Association of the Pulp & Paper Industry (TAPPI)
15 Technology Parkway South
Peachtree Corners, GA 30092
Phone: 770-209-7276
Fax: 770-446-6947
E-mail: standards@tappi.org

PAPER AND BOARD DIVISION SCHOLARSHIPS

Award to TAPPI student member or an undergraduate member of a TAPPI Student Chapter enrolled as a college or university undergraduate in an engineering or science program. Must be sophomore, junior, or senior and able to show a significant interest in the paper industry. Information can be found at http://www.tappi.org/s_tappi/sec.asp?CID=6101&DID=546695.

Academic Fields/Career Goals: Engineering/Technology; Paper and Pulp Engineering.

Award: Scholarship for use in sophomore, junior, or senior years; not renewable. *Number:* 1–4. *Amount:* $1000.

Eligibility Requirements: Applicant must be enrolled or expecting to enroll full-time at a four-year institution or university. Available to U.S. and non-U.S. citizens.

Application Requirements: Application form, recommendations or references, transcript. *Deadline:* February 15.

Contact: Mr. Charles Bohanan, Director of Standards and Awards
Technical Association of the Pulp & Paper Industry (TAPPI)
15 Technology Parkway South
Peachtree Corners, GA 30092
Phone: 770-209-7276
Fax: 770-446-6947
E-mail: standards@tappi.org

TAPPI PROCESS AND PRODUCT QUALITY DIVISION SCHOLARSHIP

The TAPPI Process and Product Quality Scholarship is awarded to TAPPI student members or student chapter members to encourage them to pursue careers in the pulp and paper industry and to develop awareness of quality management.

Academic Fields/Career Goals: Engineering/Technology.

Award: Scholarship for use in sophomore, junior, or senior years; not renewable. *Number:* 1. *Amount:* $500.

Eligibility Requirements: Applicant must be enrolled or expecting to enroll full-time at a four-year institution or university. Available to U.S. and non-U.S. citizens.

Application Requirements: Application form, recommendations or references, transcript. *Deadline:* February 15.

Contact: Mr. Charles Bohanan, Director of Standards and Awards
Technical Association of the Pulp & Paper Industry (TAPPI)
15 Technology Parkway South
Peachtree Corners, GA 30092
Phone: 770-209-7276
Fax: 770-446-6947
E-mail: standards@tappi.org

TRIANGLE EDUCATION FOUNDATION

http://www.triangle.org/

KAPADIA SCHOLARSHIPS

Award ranges from $1500 to $8000 to an undergraduate or graduate Triangle members in good standing, with preference to engineering majors, non-US citizens, members of the Zoroastrian religion and Michigan State student.

Academic Fields/Career Goals: Engineering/Technology.

Award: Scholarship for use in freshman, sophomore, junior, senior, or graduate years; not renewable. *Amount:* $1500–$8000.

Eligibility Requirements: Applicant must be enrolled or expecting to enroll full-time at a four-year institution or university and male. Applicant must have 3.0 GPA or higher. Available to U.S. and non-U.S. citizens.

Application Requirements: Application form, essay, financial need analysis, recommendations or references, self-addressed stamped envelope with application, transcript. *Deadline:* February 15.

Contact: Scott Bova, President
Phone: 317-705-9803
Fax: 317-837-9642
E-mail: sbova@triangle.org

RUST SCHOLARSHIP

Awards $5500 annually based on a combination of need, grades and participation in campus and Triangle Activities. All other things being equal, preference is given to applicants in the core engineering disciplines or hard sciences.

Academic Fields/Career Goals: Engineering/Technology.

Award: Scholarship for use in freshman, sophomore, junior, or senior years; not renewable. *Number:* 1. *Amount:* up to $5500.

Eligibility Requirements: Applicant must be enrolled or expecting to enroll full-time at a four-year institution or university and male. Applicant must have 3.0 GPA or higher. Available to U.S. and non-U.S. citizens.

Application Requirements: Application form, essay, financial need analysis, recommendations or references, self-addressed stamped envelope with application, transcript. *Deadline:* February 15.

Contact: Scott Bova, President
Phone: 317-705-9803
Fax: 317-837-9642
E-mail: sbova@triangle.org

SEVCIK SCHOLARSHIP

One-time award up to $1000 annually for active member of the Triangle Fraternity based on need, preference to an Ohio State student, preference to an Engineering student. Refer to website, http://www.triangle.org/programs/scholarshipsloans/, for details.

Academic Fields/Career Goals: Engineering/Technology.

Award: Scholarship for use in freshman, sophomore, junior, or senior years; not renewable. *Number:* 1. *Amount:* up to $1000.

Eligibility Requirements: Applicant must be American Indian/Alaska Native, Asian/Pacific Islander, Black (non-Hispanic), Hispanic; enrolled or expecting to enroll full-time at a four-year institution or university and male. Applicant must have 3.0 GPA or higher. Available to U.S. and non-U.S. citizens.

Application Requirements: Application form, essay, financial need analysis, recommendations or references, self-addressed stamped envelope with application, transcript. *Deadline:* February 15.

Contact: Scott Bova, President
Phone: 317-705-9803
Fax: 317-837-9642
E-mail: sbova@triangle.org

TURNER CONSTRUCTION COMPANY

http://www.turnerconstruction.com/

YOUTHFORCE 2020 SCHOLARSHIP PROGRAM
• See page 113

UNITED NEGRO COLLEGE FUND

http://www.uncf.org/

ALFRED CHISHOLM/BASF MEMORIAL SCHOLARSHIP FUND
• See page 81

CARTER AND BURGESS SCHOLARSHIP

Need-based scholarship for students from Ft. Worth, Texas. If there aren't enough engineering students in Ft. Worth, the scholarship pool may extend to the entire state of Texas and HBCUs. Students studying engineering with minimum GPA of 2.5 are eligible. The scholarship value varies, based on need.

Academic Fields/Career Goals: Engineering/Technology.

Award: Scholarship for use in freshman, sophomore, junior, or senior years; renewable. *Number:* 1.

Eligibility Requirements: Applicant must be Black (non-Hispanic); enrolled or expecting to enroll full-time at a four-year institution or university and resident of Texas. Applicant must have 2.5 GPA or higher. Available to U.S. citizens.

Application Requirements: Application form, FAFSA, Student Aid Report (SAR), financial need analysis. *Deadline:* continuous.

CDM SCHOLARSHIP/INTERNSHIP
• *See page 176*

COOPER INDUSTRIES PACESETTER SCHOLARSHIP
• *See page 148*

EMERSON PROCESS MANAGEMENT SCHOLARSHIP
• *See page 177*

FORD/UNCF CORPORATE SCHOLARS PROGRAM
• *See page 82*

GILBANE SCHOLARSHIP PROGRAM
• *See page 113*

LOCKHEED MARTIN/UNCF SCHOLARSHIP
• *See page 82*

MONSANTO/UNCF 1890'S SCHOLARSHIP PROGRAM
• *See page 89*

NASCAR/WENDELL SCOTT, SR. SCHOLARSHIP
• *See page 82*

PACIFIC GAS AND ELECTRIC COMPANY SCHOLARSHIP
• *See page 82*

PSE&G SCHOLARSHIP
• *See page 82*

SANDISK CORPORATION SCHOLARSHIP
• *See page 206*

WILLIAM WRIGLEY JR. SCHOLARSHIP/INTERNSHIP
• *See page 161*

UNIVERSITIES SPACE RESEARCH ASSOCIATION

http://www.usra.edu/

UNIVERSITIES SPACE RESEARCH ASSOCIATION SCHOLARSHIP PROGRAM
• *See page 107*

UTAH SOCIETY OF PROFESSIONAL ENGINEERS

http://www.uspeonline.com/

UTAH SOCIETY OF PROFESSIONAL ENGINEERS JOE RHOADS SCHOLARSHIP
• *See page 177*

VERMONT SPACE GRANT CONSORTIUM

http://www.cems.uvm.edu/vsgc

VERMONT SPACE GRANT CONSORTIUM SCHOLARSHIP PROGRAM
• *See page 107*

WEST VIRGINIA HIGHER EDUCATION POLICY COMMISSION-STUDENT SERVICES

http://wvhepcnew.wvnet.edu/

WEST VIRGINIA ENGINEERING, SCIENCE AND TECHNOLOGY SCHOLARSHIP PROGRAM
• *See page 257*

WISCONSIN SOCIETY OF PROFESSIONAL ENGINEERS

http://www.wspe.org/

WISCONSIN SOCIETY OF PROFESSIONAL ENGINEERS SCHOLARSHIPS

Scholarships are awarded each year to high school seniors having qualifications for success in engineering education. Must be a U.S. citizen and Wisconsin resident and have a minimum GPA of 3.0.

Academic Fields/Career Goals: Engineering/Technology.

Award: Scholarship for use in freshman year; not renewable. *Number:* 3. *Amount:* $1000.

Eligibility Requirements: Applicant must be high school student; planning to enroll or expecting to enroll full-time at a four-year institution or university and resident of Wisconsin. Applicant must have 3.0 GPA or higher. Available to U.S. citizens.

Application Requirements: Application form, essay, interview, recommendations or references, self-addressed stamped envelope with application, test scores, transcript. *Deadline:* December 28.

Contact: Mr. Christopher Roper, Executive Director
  Phone: 414-908-4950 Ext. 107
  E-mail: c.roper@wspe.org

XEROX

http://www.xerox.com//

TECHNICAL MINORITY SCHOLARSHIP
• *See page 177*

ENTOMOLOGY

AMERICAN RAILWAY ENGINEERING AND MAINTENANCE OF WAY ASSOCIATION

http://www.aremafoundation.org/

CHARLES L. STANFORD FAMILY OHIO STATE UNIVERSITY RAILWAY ENGINEERING SCHOLARSHIP
• *See page 249*

AMERICAN SOCIETY OF AGRONOMY, CROP SCIENCE SOCIETY OF AMERICA, SOIL SCIENCE SOCIETY OF AMERICA

http://www.agronomy.org

HANK BEACHELL FUTURE LEADER SCHOLARSHIP
• *See page 90*

J. FIELDING REED SCHOLARSHIP
• *See page 90*

ENTOMOLOGICAL FOUNDATION

http://www.entfdn.org/

BIOQUIP UNDERGRADUATE SCHOLARSHIP

Award to assist students in obtaining a degree in entomology or pursuing a career as an entomologist. Must have minimum of 90 college credit hours by September 1 following the application deadline, and either completed two junior-level entomology courses or a research project in entomology. Preference will be given to students with demonstrated financial need.

Academic Fields/Career Goals: Entomology.

Award: Scholarship for use in sophomore, junior, or senior years; not renewable. *Number:* up to 1. *Amount:* $2000.

Eligibility Requirements: Applicant must be enrolled or expecting to enroll full- or part-time at a four-year institution or university. Available to U.S. and non-U.S. citizens.

Application Requirements: Application form, application form may be submitted online (http://www.entfdn.org), recommendations or references, resume, transcript. *Deadline:* July 1.

Contact: Melodie Dziduch, Awards Coordinator
  E-mail: melodie@entfdn.org

HORTICULTURAL RESEARCH INSTITUTE

http://www.hriresearch.org/

BRYAN A. CHAMPION MEMORIAL SCHOLARSHIP

• *See page 85*

CARVILLE M. AKEHURST MEMORIAL SCHOLARSHIP

Scholarship is available to resident of Maryland, Virginia, or West Virginia. Applicant must be enrolled in an accredited undergraduate or graduate landscape/ horticulture program or related discipline at a two- or four-year institution and must have minimum 3.0 GPA. Online application only. http://www.HRIResearch.org for complete information.

Academic Fields/Career Goals: Entomology; Horticulture/Floriculture; Landscape Architecture.

Award: Scholarship for use in junior or senior years; not renewable. *Number:* 2–2. *Amount:* $2000–$2000.

Eligibility Requirements: Applicant must be enrolled or expecting to enroll full-time at a two-year or four-year or technical institution or university and resident of Maryland, Virginia, West Virginia. Applicant must have 3.0 GPA or higher. Available to U.S. citizens.

Application Requirements: Application form, essay, financial need analysis, recommendations or references, resume, transcript. *Deadline:* May 31.

Contact: Ms. Teresa Jodon, Executive Director
  Horticultural Research Institute
  1200 G Street, NW, Suite 800
  Washington, DC 20005
  Phone: 202-695-2474
  Fax: 888-761-7883
  E-mail: scholarships@hriresearch.org

TIMOTHY AND PALMER W. BIGELOW JR, SCHOLARSHIP

• *See page 86*

USREY FAMILY SCHOLARSHIP

Award for students accredited in undergraduate or graduate landscape horticulture program or related discipline at a two- or four-year institution. Preference given to applicants who plan to work within the industry. Must have a minimum 2.5 GPA. For more information, visit website http://www.hriresearch.org.

Academic Fields/Career Goals: Entomology; Horticulture/Floriculture; Landscape Architecture.

Award: Scholarship for use in sophomore, junior, senior, or graduate years; not renewable. *Amount:* $500–$500.

Eligibility Requirements: Applicant must be enrolled or expecting to enroll full-time at a two-year or four-year or technical institution or university and studying in California. Applicant must have 2.5 GPA or higher. Available to U.S. and non-U.S. citizens.

Application Requirements: Application form, application form may be submitted online (http://www.hriresearch.org/)

index.cfm?page=Content&categoryID=168&ID=5), essay, financial need analysis, recommendations or references, resume, transcript. *Deadline:* May 31.

ENVIRONMENTAL HEALTH

ASSOCIATION OF ENVIRONMENTAL HEALTH ACADEMIC PROGRAMS (AEHAP)

http://www.aehap.org/

NSF INTERNATIONAL SCHOLAR PROGRAM

Award available for college junior or senior in an AEHAP Environmental Health Academic Program. Student will spend summer on an independent research project in conjunction with their home university and NSF International and the AEHAP Office. Must have consent and commitment from advisor to help develop and oversee research project. Stipend will be paid in two sums, and advisor will receive $500 stipend.

Academic Fields/Career Goals: Environmental Health.

Award: Scholarship for use in junior or senior years; not renewable. *Number:* 1. *Amount:* $3500.

Eligibility Requirements: Applicant must be enrolled or expecting to enroll full-time at a four-year institution or university and must have an interest in writing. Available to U.S. citizens.

Application Requirements: Application form, cover letter, letter of adviser support, essay, recommendations or references, resume. *Deadline:* April 16.

Contact: Yalonda Sinde, AEHAP Scholarship Committee
  Association of Environmental Health Academic Programs
    (AEHAP)
  8620 Roosevelt Way, NE, Suite A
  Seattle, WA 98115
  Phone: 206-522-5272
  E-mail: info@aehap.org

CYNTHIA E. MORGAN SCHOLARSHIP FUND (CEMS)

http://www.cemsfund.com/

CYNTHIA E. MORGAN MEMORIAL SCHOLARSHIP FUND, INC.

Award for a high school junior or senior, or a current college student, who is a Maryland resident and first generation college student. No previous generation (parents or grandparents) may have attended any college/university. Scholarship for use only at a Maryland post-secondary school or medical school. Must be majoring in, or plan to enter, a medical-related field (for example: doctor, nurse, radiologist).

Academic Fields/Career Goals: Environmental Health; Health and Medical Sciences; Health Information Management/Technology; Neurobiology; Nursing; Occupational Safety and Health; Oncology; Osteopathy; Pharmacy; Psychology; Radiology; Therapy/Rehabilitation.

Award: Scholarship for use in freshman, sophomore, junior, senior, graduate, or postgraduate years; not renewable. *Number:* 1. *Amount:* $1000.

Eligibility Requirements: Applicant must be enrolled or expecting to enroll full- or part-time at a two-year or four-year or technical institution or university; resident of Maryland and studying in Maryland. Available to U.S. citizens.

Application Requirements: Application form, application form may be submitted online (http://www.cemsfund.com), essay. *Deadline:* February 25.

Contact: Mr. John Kantorski, Founder and President
  Cynthia E. Morgan Scholarship Fund (CEMS)
  5516 Maudes Way
  White Marsh, MD 21162-3417
  Phone: 410-458-6312
  Fax: 443-927-7321
  E-mail: administrator@cemsfund.com

FLORIDA ENVIRONMENTAL HEALTH ASSOCIATION

http://www.feha.org/

FLORIDA ENVIRONMENTAL HEALTH ASSOCIATION EDUCATIONAL SCHOLARSHIP AWARDS

Scholarships offered to students interested in pursuing a career in the field of environmental health, or to enhance an existing career in environmental health. Applicant must be a member of FEHA in good standing.

Academic Fields/Career Goals: Environmental Health; Public Health.

Award: Scholarship for use in junior, senior, graduate, or postgraduate years; not renewable. *Number:* 1–4. *Amount:* $500–$1000.

Eligibility Requirements: Applicant must be enrolled or expecting to enroll full- or part-time at a four-year institution or university. Applicant or parent of applicant must be member of Florida Environmental Health Association. Applicant must have 2.5 GPA or higher. Available to U.S. and non-U.S. citizens.

Application Requirements: Application form, recommendations or references, transcript. *Deadline:* varies.

Contact: Kim Duffek, Scholarship Committee Chair
Phone: 407-317-7325
E-mail: duffekkj@gmail.com

INDIAN HEALTH SERVICES, UNITED STATES DEPARTMENT OF HEALTH AND HUMAN SERVICES

http://www.ihs.gov/scholarship

INDIAN HEALTH SERVICE HEALTH PROFESSIONS SCHOLARSHIP PROGRAM

• *See page 208*

NATIONAL ENVIRONMENTAL HEALTH ASSOCIATION/AMERICAN ACADEMY OF SANITARIANS

http://www.neha.org/

NATIONAL ENVIRONMENTAL HEALTH ASSOCIATION/AMERICAN ACADEMY OF SANITARIANS SCHOLARSHIP

One-time award for college juniors, seniors, and graduate students pursuing studies in environmental health sciences or public health. Undergraduates must be enrolled full-time in an approved program that is accredited by the Environmental Health Accreditation Council (EHAC) or a NEHA institutional/educational or sustaining member school.

Academic Fields/Career Goals: Environmental Health; Public Health.

Award: Scholarship for use in junior or senior years; renewable. *Number:* 3–4. *Amount:* $1000–$2000.

Eligibility Requirements: Applicant must be enrolled or expecting to enroll full-time at a two-year or four-year institution or university. Available to U.S. citizens.

Application Requirements: Application form, recommendations or references, transcript. *Deadline:* February 1.

Contact: Cindy Dimmitt, Scholarship Coordinator
National Environmental Health Association/American
Academy of Sanitarians
720 South Colorado Boulevard, Suite 1000-N
Denver, CO 80246-1926
Phone: 303-756-9090
Fax: 303-691-9490
E-mail: cdimmitt@neha.org

SAEMS-SOUTHERN ARIZONA ENVIRONMENTAL MANAGEMENT SOCIETY

http://www.saems.org/

ENVIRONMENTAL SCHOLARSHIPS

Applicant must be a student in any accredited Southern Arizona college or university. Student must have a minimum GPA of 2.5 or be a full- or part-time student and plan on pursuing a career in the environmental arena.

Academic Fields/Career Goals: Environmental Health; Environmental Science; Natural Resources.

Award: Scholarship for use in freshman, sophomore, junior, senior, or graduate years; not renewable. *Number:* 2. *Amount:* $3000.

Eligibility Requirements: Applicant must be enrolled or expecting to enroll full- or part-time at a two-year or four-year institution or university and studying in Arizona. Applicant must have 2.5 GPA or higher. Available to U.S. and non-U.S. citizens.

Application Requirements: Application form, essay, interview. *Deadline:* March 15.

Contact: Dan Uthe, Scholarship Committee Chair
SAEMS-Southern Arizona Environmental Management
Society
PO Box 41433
Tucson, AZ 85717
Phone: 520-791-5630
Fax: 520-791-5346
E-mail: dan.uthe@tucsonaz.com

SOIL AND WATER CONSERVATION SOCIETY

http://www.swcs.org

DONALD A. WILLIAMS SCHOLARSHIP SOIL CONSERVATION SCHOLARSHIP

• *See page 88*

MELVILLE H. COHEE STUDENT LEADER CONSERVATION SCHOLARSHIP

• *See page 88*

STRAIGHTFORWARD MEDIA

http://www.straightforwardmedia.com/

STRAIGHTFORWARD MEDIA MEDICAL PROFESSIONS SCHOLARSHIP

• *See page 224*

WASHINGTON STATE ENVIRONMENTAL HEALTH ASSOCIATION

http://www.wseha.org/

CIND M. TRESER MEMORIAL SCHOLARSHIP PROGRAM

Scholarships are available for undergraduate students pursuing a major in environmental health or related science and intending to practice environmental health. Must be a resident of Washington. For more details see website at http://www.wseha.org.

Academic Fields/Career Goals: Environmental Health.

Award: Scholarship for use in freshman, sophomore, junior, or senior years; not renewable. *Number:* 1–2. *Amount:* $500–$1000.

Eligibility Requirements: Applicant must be enrolled or expecting to enroll full-time at a four-year institution or university and resident of Washington. Applicant must have 3.0 GPA or higher. Available to U.S. citizens.

Application Requirements: Application form, recommendations or references, transcript. *Deadline:* March 15.

Contact: Mr. Charles Treser, Scholarship Committee Chair
Phone: 206-616-2097
E-mail: ctreser@u.washington.edu

WINDSTAR FOUNDATION

WINDSTAR ENVIRONMENTAL STUDIES SCHOLARSHIPS

Two $500 scholarships for qualified undergraduates entering their junior or senior year of college, and one $1000 scholarship for graduate students entering their second year of graduate school.

Academic Fields/Career Goals: Environmental Health; Environmental Science.

Award: Scholarship for use in junior, senior, or graduate years; renewable. *Number:* up to 3. *Amount:* $500–$1000.

Eligibility Requirements: Applicant must be enrolled or expecting to enroll full-time at a four-year institution or university. Applicant must have 3.0 GPA or higher. Available to U.S. citizens.

Application Requirements: Application form, essay, transcript. *Deadline:* June 1.

WISCONSIN ASSOCIATION FOR FOOD PROTECTION

http://www.wafp-wi.org/

E.H. MARTH FOOD PROTECTION AND FOOD SCIENCES SCHOLARSHIP

Scholarship awarded to promote and sustain interest in the fields of study that may lead to a career in dairy, food, or environmental sanitation. One scholarship is awarded per year and previous applicants and recipients may reapply.

Academic Fields/Career Goals: Environmental Health; Food Science/Nutrition.

Award: Scholarship for use in sophomore, junior, senior, or graduate years; not renewable. *Number:* 1. *Amount:* $1500.

Eligibility Requirements: Applicant must be enrolled or expecting to enroll full-time at a four-year institution or university; resident of Wisconsin and studying in Wisconsin. Available to U.S. citizens.

Application Requirements: Application form, recommendations or references, transcript. *Deadline:* July 1.

Contact: Mr. Jim Wickert, Chairman, Scholarship Committee
Wisconsin Association for Food Protection
3834 Ridgeway Avenue
Madison, WI 53704
Phone: 608-241-2438
E-mail: jwick16060@tds.net

ENVIRONMENTAL SCIENCE

ABBIE SARGENT MEMORIAL SCHOLARSHIP INC.

http://www.nhfarmbureau.org/

ABBIE SARGENT MEMORIAL SCHOLARSHIP
• *See page 84*

AIR & WASTE MANAGEMENT ASSOCIATION–ALLEGHENY MOUNTAIN SECTION

http://www.ams-awma.org/

ALLEGHENY MOUNTAIN SECTION AIR & WASTE MANAGEMENT ASSOCIATION SCHOLARSHIP

Scholarships for qualified students enrolled in an undergraduate program leading to a career in a field related directly to the environment. Open to current undergraduate students or high school students accepted full-time in a four-year college or university program in Western Pennsylvania or West Virginia. Applicants must have a minimum B average or a 3.0 GPA.

Academic Fields/Career Goals: Environmental Science.

Award: Scholarship for use in freshman, sophomore, junior, or senior years; not renewable. *Number:* up to 2. *Amount:* up to $1500.

Eligibility Requirements: Applicant must be enrolled or expecting to enroll full-time at a four-year institution or university; resident of Pennsylvania, West Virginia and studying in Pennsylvania, West Virginia. Applicant must have 3.0 GPA or higher. Available to U.S. citizens.

Application Requirements: Application form, essay, plan of study, recommendations or references, resume, transcript. *Deadline:* March 31.

Contact: David Testa, Scholarship Chair
Air & Waste Management Association–Allegheny Mountain Section
c/o Equitable Resources Inc., 225 North Shore Drive
Pittsburgh, PA 15212
Phone: 412-787-6803
Fax: 412-787-6717
E-mail: dtesta@calgoncarbon-us.com

AIR & WASTE MANAGEMENT ASSOCIATION–COASTAL PLAINS CHAPTER

http://www.awmacoastalplains.org/

COASTAL PLAINS CHAPTER OF THE AIR AND WASTE MANAGEMENT ASSOCIATION ENVIRONMENTAL STEWARD SCHOLARSHIP

Scholarships awarded to first- or second-year students pursuing a career in environmental science or physical science. Minimum high school and college GPA of 2.5 required. A 500-word paper on personal and professional goals must be submitted.

Academic Fields/Career Goals: Environmental Science; Physical Sciences.

Award: Scholarship for use in freshman or sophomore years; not renewable. *Number:* 5. *Amount:* $800.

Eligibility Requirements: Applicant must be enrolled or expecting to enroll full-time at a two-year or four-year institution or university. Applicant must have 2.5 GPA or higher. Available to U.S. citizens.

Application Requirements: 500-word paper on personal and professional goals, application form, recommendations or references, test scores. *Deadline:* varies.

Contact: Dwain Waters, Treasurer
Air & Waste Management Association–Coastal Plains Chapter
One Energy Place
Pensacola, FL 32520-0328
Phone: 850-444-6527
Fax: 850-444-6217
E-mail: gdwaters@southernco.com

AIST FOUNDATION

http://www.aistfoundation.org/

ASSOCIATION FOR IRON AND STEEL TECHNOLOGY WILLY KORF MEMORIAL SCHOLARSHIP
• *See page 162*

AMERICAN CHEMICAL SOCIETY

http://www.acs.org/

AMERICAN CHEMICAL SOCIETY SCHOLARS PROGRAM
• See page 162

AMERICAN INSTITUTE OF CHEMICAL ENGINEERS

http://www.aiche.org/

ENVIRONMENTAL DIVISION UNDERGRADUATE STUDENT PAPER AWARD
• See page 163

AMERICAN METEOROLOGICAL SOCIETY

http://www.ametsoc.org/

AMS FRESHMAN UNDERGRADUATE SCHOLARSHIP

Scholarships will be awarded, based on academic excellence, to high school seniors entering their freshman year of study in the atmospheric, oceanic, or hydrologic sciences. For use in freshman and sophomore years, with second-year funding dependent on successful completion of first year.

Academic Fields/Career Goals: Environmental Science; Hydrology; Marine/Ocean Engineering; Meteorology/Atmospheric Science.

Award: Scholarship for use in freshman year; not renewable. *Number:* 14. *Amount:* $5000.

Eligibility Requirements: Applicant must be high school student and planning to enroll or expecting to enroll full-time at a two-year or four-year or technical institution or university. Applicant must have 3.0 GPA or higher. Available to U.S. and non-U.S. citizens.

Application Requirements: Application form, essay, recommendations or references, test scores, transcript. *Deadline:* February 22.

Contact: Mrs. Donna Sampson, Development and Student Program
      Manager
      American Meteorological Society
      45 Beacon Street
      Boston, MA 02108
      Phone: 617-227-2426 Ext. 246
      Fax: 617-742-8718
      E-mail: dfernand@ametsoc.org

AMERICAN PHYSIOLOGICAL SOCIETY

http://www.the-aps.org

DAVID S. BRUCE AWARDS FOR EXCELLENCE IN UNDERGRADUATE RESEARCH
• See page 98

AMERICAN SOCIETY OF AGRONOMY, CROP SCIENCE SOCIETY OF AMERICA, SOIL SCIENCE SOCIETY OF AMERICA

http://www.agronomy.org

HANK BEACHELL FUTURE LEADER SCHOLARSHIP
• See page 90

J. FIELDING REED SCHOLARSHIP
• See page 90

ARCTIC INSTITUTE OF NORTH AMERICA

http://www.arctic.ucalgary.ca/

JIM BOURQUE SCHOLARSHIP
• See page 233

ASSOCIATION FOR WOMEN GEOSCIENTISTS, PUGET SOUND CHAPTER

http://www.awg.org/

PUGET SOUND CHAPTER SCHOLARSHIP
• See page 227

ASSOCIATION OF CALIFORNIA WATER AGENCIES

http://www.acwa.com/

ASSOCIATION OF CALIFORNIA WATER AGENCIES SCHOLARSHIPS
• See page 103

CLAIR A. HILL SCHOLARSHIP
• See page 103

ASSOCIATION OF NEW JERSEY ENVIRONMENTAL COMMISSIONS

http://www.anjec.org/

LECHNER SCHOLARSHIP

Award of $1000 scholarship for a student entering his/her junior or senior year at an accredited New Jersey college or university. Must be a New Jersey resident and have a minimum GPA of 3.0.

Academic Fields/Career Goals: Environmental Science.

Award: Scholarship for use in junior or senior years; not renewable. *Number:* 1. *Amount:* $1000.

Eligibility Requirements: Applicant must be enrolled or expecting to enroll full-time at a four-year institution or university; resident of New Jersey and studying in New Jersey. Applicant must have 3.0 GPA or higher. Available to U.S. citizens.

Application Requirements: Application form, essay, recommendations or references, transcript.

Contact: Sandy Batty, Executive Director
      Phone: 973-539-7547
      Fax: 973-539-7713
      E-mail: sbatty@anjec.org

AUDUBON SOCIETY OF WESTERN PENNSYLVANIA

http://www.aswp.org/

BEULAH FREY ENVIRONMENTAL SCHOLARSHIP

Scholarship available to high school seniors pursuing studies in the environmental and natural sciences. Students who are applying to a two- or four-year college to further their studies in an environmentally-related field are eligible to apply. Scholarship is restricted to the residents of the seven counties around Pittsburgh.

Academic Fields/Career Goals: Environmental Science; Natural Sciences.

Award: Scholarship for use in freshman year; not renewable. *Number:* 1–2. *Amount:* $1000.

Eligibility Requirements: Applicant must be high school student; planning to enroll or expecting to enroll full-time at a two-year or four-year institution or university and resident of Pennsylvania. Available to U.S. citizens.

Application Requirements: Application form, essay, recommendations or references, test scores, transcript. *Deadline:* March 31.

Contact: Patricia O'Neill, Director of Education
Audubon Society of Western Pennsylvania
614 Dorseyville Road
Pittsburgh, PA 15238
Phone: 412-963-6100
Fax: 412-963-6761
E-mail: toneill@aswp.org

BRITISH COLUMBIA INNOVATION COUNCIL

http://www.bcic.ca/

BCIC YOUNG INNOVATOR SCHOLARSHIP COMPETITION (IDEA MASH UP)

• See page 104

PADDLE CANADA (FORMERLY THE CANADIAN RECREATIONAL CANOEING ASSOCIATION

http://www.paddlingcanada.com/

BILL MASON SCHOLARSHIP FUND

• See page 235

CONSERVATION FEDERATION OF MISSOURI

http://www.confedmo.org/

CHARLES P. BELL CONSERVATION SCHOLARSHIP

Eight scholarships of $250 to $600 for Missouri students and/or teachers whose studies or projects are related to natural science, resource conservation, earth resources, or environmental protection. Must be used for study in Missouri. See application for eligibility details.

Academic Fields/Career Goals: Environmental Science; Natural Resources; Natural Sciences.

Award: Scholarship for use in freshman, sophomore, junior, senior, or graduate years; not renewable. *Number:* 8. *Amount:* $250–$600.

Eligibility Requirements: Applicant must be enrolled or expecting to enroll full- or part-time at a four-year institution or university; resident of Missouri and studying in Missouri. Available to U.S. citizens.

Application Requirements: Application form, community service, financial need analysis, recommendations or references, transcript, work experience certificate. *Deadline:* January 15.

DELAWARE HIGHER EDUCATION OFFICE

http://www.doe.k12.de.us

DELAWARE SOLID WASTE AUTHORITY JOHN P. "PAT" HEALY SCHOLARSHIP

• See page 264

EARTH ISLAND INSTITUTE

http://www.earthisland.org/

BROWER YOUTH AWARDS

Annual national award that recognizes six young people for outstanding activism and achievements in the fields of environmental and social justice advocacy. The winners of the award receive $3000 in cash, a trip to California for the award ceremony and Yosemite camping trip, and ongoing access to resources and opportunities to further their work at Earth Island Institute. Applicant's age must be between 13 and 22.

Academic Fields/Career Goals: Environmental Science; Peace and Conflict Studies.

Award: Prize for use in freshman, sophomore, junior, or senior years; not renewable. *Number:* 6. *Amount:* $3000.

Eligibility Requirements: Applicant must be age 13-22 and enrolled or expecting to enroll full- or part-time at a two-year or four-year or technical institution or university. Available to U.S. and non-U.S. citizens.

Application Requirements: Application form, essay, personal photograph, recommendations or references. *Deadline:* May 15.

Contact: Ms. Anisha Desai, Program Director
Earth Island Institute
300 Broadway, Suite 28
San Francisco, CA 94133
Phone: 510-859-9144 Ext. 144
E-mail: bya@earthisland.org

ENVIRONMENTAL PROFESSIONALS' ORGANIZATION OF CONNECTICUT

http://www.epoc.org/

EPOC ENVIRONMENTAL SCHOLARSHIP FUND

Scholarships awarded annually to junior, senior, and graduate level students (full- or part-time) enrolled in accepted programs of study leading the student to become an environmental professional in Connecticut.

Academic Fields/Career Goals: Environmental Science.

Award: Scholarship for use in junior, senior, or graduate years; not renewable. *Number:* 2–3.

Eligibility Requirements: Applicant must be enrolled or expecting to enroll full- or part-time at a four-year institution or university. Available to U.S. citizens.

Application Requirements: Application form, essay, financial need analysis, recommendations or references, transcript. *Deadline:* May 7.

Contact: John Figurelli, Scholarship Fund Coordinator
Environmental Professionals' Organization of Connecticut
PO Box 176
Amston, CT 06231-0176
Phone: 860-513-1473
Fax: 860-228-4902
E-mail: figurelj@wseinc.com

FRIENDS OF THE FRELINGHUYSEN ARBORETUM

http://www.arboretumfriends.org/

BENJAMIN C. BLACKBURN SCHOLARSHIP

One-time award for undergraduate and graduate students who are pursuing degrees in horticulture, landscape architecture, or environmental studies. Must be a New Jersey resident. Minimum 3.0 GPA required.

Academic Fields/Career Goals: Environmental Science; Horticulture/Floriculture; Landscape Architecture; Natural Resources.

Award: Scholarship for use in sophomore, junior, senior, or graduate years; not renewable. *Number:* 1. *Amount:* $5000.

Eligibility Requirements: Applicant must be enrolled or expecting to enroll full- or part-time at a four-year institution or university and resident of New Jersey. Applicant must have 3.0 GPA or higher. Available to U.S. citizens.

Application Requirements: Application form, community service, essay, recommendations or references, transcript. *Deadline:* April 14.

Contact: Ann Abrams, Scholarship Committee
Friends of the Frelinghuysen Arboretum
53 East Hanover Avenue, PO Box 1295
Morristown, NJ 07962-1295
Phone: 973-326-7603
E-mail: aabrams@morrisparks.net

GARDEN CLUB OF AMERICA

http://www.gcamerica.org/

CAROLINE THORN KISSEL SUMMER ENVIRONMENTAL STUDIES SCHOLARSHIP

Scholarship for students to promote environmental studies by students who are either residents of the state of New Jersey or non-residents pursuing study in New Jersey or its surrounding waters. Open to college students, graduate students, Ph.D. candidates, or non-degree-seeking applicants above the high school level. Must be a U.S. citizen.

Academic Fields/Career Goals: Environmental Science.

Award: Scholarship for use in freshman, sophomore, junior, or senior years; not renewable. *Number:* 1. *Amount:* $2000.

Eligibility Requirements: Applicant must be enrolled or expecting to enroll full- or part-time at a two-year or four-year or technical institution or university; resident of New Jersey and studying in New Jersey. Available to U.S. citizens.

Application Requirements: Application form, essay, recommendations or references. *Deadline:* February 10.

Contact: Connie Yates, Garden Club of America
Garden Club of America
14 East 60th Street
New York, NY 10022-1006
Phone: 212-753-8287
Fax: 212-753-0134
E-mail: cyates@gcamerica.org

CLARA CARTER HIGGINS SCHOLARSHIP/GCA AWARDS FOR SUMMER ENVIRONMENTAL SCHOLARSHIP

Scholarship to encourage studies and careers in the environmental field, with the opportunity to gain knowledge and experience beyond the regular course of study. Annually funds one Clara Carter Higgins scholar and one or more GCA Summer Environmental Studies scholars at $2000 per recipient in financial assistance for summer coursework in environmental studies.

Academic Fields/Career Goals: Environmental Science.

Award: Scholarship for use in sophomore, junior, or senior years; not renewable. *Amount:* $2000.

Eligibility Requirements: Applicant must be enrolled or expecting to enroll full- or part-time at a four-year institution or university. Available to U.S. citizens.

Application Requirements: Application form, essay, recommendations or references, transcript. *Deadline:* February 10.

THE ELIZABETH GARDNER NORWEB SUMMER ENVIRONMENTAL STUDIES SCHOLARSHIP
• See page 92

GCA AWARD IN DESERT STUDIES
• See page 111

MARY T. CAROTHERS SUMMER ENVIRONMENTAL STUDIES SCHOLARSHIP

Scholarship to encourage studies and careers in the environmental field, with the opportunity to gain knowledge and experience beyond the regular course of study. Provides financial assistance of $2000 to one student annually for field work, research, or classroom work. Open to college undergraduates for summer study following the freshman, sophomore, or junior year.

Academic Fields/Career Goals: Environmental Science.

Award: Scholarship for use in sophomore, junior, or senior years; not renewable. *Number:* 1. *Amount:* $2000.

Eligibility Requirements: Applicant must be enrolled or expecting to enroll full-time at a four-year institution or university. Available to U.S. citizens.

Application Requirements: Application form, essay, recommendations or references, transcript. *Deadline:* February 10.

GREAT LAKES COMMISSION
http://www.glc.org/

CAROL A. RATZA MEMORIAL SCHOLARSHIP
• See page 190

GREEN CHEMISTRY INSTITUTE-AMERICAN CHEMICAL SOCIETY
http://www.acs.org/greenchemistry

CIBA TRAVEL AWARDS IN GREEN CHEMISTRY

The award sponsors the participation of students (high school, undergraduate, and graduate students) in an American Chemical Society (ACS) technical meeting, conference or training program, having a significant green chemistry or sustainability component, to expand the students' education in green chemistry. The applicant must demonstrate research or educational interest in green chemistry. The award amount is based on estimated travel expenses.

Academic Fields/Career Goals: Environmental Science.

Award: Grant for use in freshman, sophomore, junior, senior, graduate, or postgraduate years; not renewable. *Number:* 3–4. *Amount:* up to $2000.

Eligibility Requirements: Applicant must be enrolled or expecting to enroll full-time at a four-year institution or university. Available to U.S. citizens.

Application Requirements: Application form, application form may be submitted online, essay, recommendations or references, resume, transcript. *Deadline:* October 12.

Contact: Ms. Joyce Kilgore, Program Manager
Green Chemistry Institute-American Chemical Society
1155 16th Street, NW
Washington, DC 20036
Phone: 202-872-6109
E-mail: gci@acs.org

JOSEPH BREEN MEMORIAL FELLOWSHIP IN GREEN CHEMISTRY

The award sponsors the participation of a young international Green Chemistry scholar in a Green Chemistry technical meeting, conference, or training program of their choice. International scholar is defined as undergraduate students and above, but below the level of assistant professor and within the first seven years of a professional career.

Academic Fields/Career Goals: Environmental Science.

Award: Prize for use in freshman, sophomore, junior, senior, graduate, or postgraduate years; not renewable. *Number:* 1–2. *Amount:* $1–$2000.

Eligibility Requirements: Applicant must be enrolled or expecting to enroll full-time at a four-year institution or university. Available to U.S. and non-U.S. citizens.

Application Requirements: Application form, application form may be submitted online, essay, recommendations or references, resume. *Deadline:* March 1.

Contact: Mrs. Jennifer MacKellar, Program Manager
Green Chemistry Institute-American Chemical Society
1155 16th Street, NW
Washington, DC 20036
Phone: 202-872-6173
E-mail: gci@acs.org

KENNETH G. HANCOCK MEMORIAL AWARD IN GREEN CHEMISTRY

Award of $1000 for the students who have completed their education or research in green chemistry. The scholarship provides national recognition for outstanding student contributions to furthering the goals of green chemistry through research or education.

Academic Fields/Career Goals: Environmental Science.

Award: Prize for use in freshman, sophomore, junior, senior, or graduate years; not renewable. *Number:* 1–2. *Amount:* $1000.

Eligibility Requirements: Applicant must be enrolled or expecting to enroll full-time at a four-year institution or university. Available to U.S. and non-U.S. citizens.

Application Requirements: Application form, application form may be submitted online, essay. *Deadline:* March 1.

Contact: Mrs. Jennifer MacKellar, Program Manager
Green Chemistry Institute-American Chemical Society
1155 16th Street, NW
Washington, DC 20036
Phone: 202-872-6173
E-mail: gci@acs.org

INDEPENDENT LABORATORIES INSTITUTE SCHOLARSHIP ALLIANCE

http://www.acil.org/

INDEPENDENT LABORATORIES INSTITUTE SCHOLARSHIP ALLIANCE

• See page 145

INDIANA WILDLIFE FEDERATION ENDOWMENT

http://www.indianawildlife.org/

CHARLES A. HOLT INDIANA WILDLIFE FEDERATION ENDOWMENT SCHOLARSHIP

A $1000 scholarship will be awarded to an Indiana resident enrolled in or planning to enroll in a course of study related to resource conservation or environmental education at the undergraduate level. A 6-12 month internship with the Indiana Wildlife Federation is offered in conjunction with the scholarship.

Academic Fields/Career Goals: Environmental Science; Natural Resources.

Award: Scholarship for use in sophomore, junior, or senior years; not renewable. *Number:* 1. *Amount:* $1000.

Eligibility Requirements: Applicant must be enrolled or expecting to enroll full-time at a four-year institution or university; resident of Indiana and studying in Indiana. Available to U.S. citizens.

Application Requirements: Application form, essay, recommendations or references. *Deadline:* June 15.

Contact: Barbara Simpson, Executive Director
Indiana Wildlife Federation Endowment
4715 W. 106th Street
Zionsville, IN 46077
Phone: 317-875-9453
E-mail: info@indianawildlife.org

INTERNATIONAL ASSOCIATION FOR GREAT LAKES RESEARCH

http://www.iaglr.org/

PAUL W. RODGERS SCHOLARSHIP

• See page 227

INTERTRIBAL TIMBER COUNCIL

http://www.itcnet.org/

TRUMAN D. PICARD SCHOLARSHIP

• See page 86

KENTUCKY ENERGY AND ENVIRONMENT CABINET

http://www.eec.ky.gov/

ENVIRONMENTAL PROTECTION SCHOLARSHIP

• See page 145

LAND CONSERVANCY OF NEW JERSEY

http://www.tlc-nj.org/

ROGERS FAMILY SCHOLARSHIP

Scholarship to deserving individuals who plan careers in environmental science, natural resource management, conservation, horticulture, park administration, or a related field. Must be a resident of New Jersey and considering a career in New Jersey. Payment is made directly to the institution that the successful candidate attends.

Academic Fields/Career Goals: Environmental Science; Horticulture/Floriculture; Natural Resources; Recreation, Parks, Leisure Studies.

Award: Scholarship for use in freshman, sophomore, junior, or senior years; not renewable. *Amount:* up to $7000.

Eligibility Requirements: Applicant must be enrolled or expecting to enroll full- or part-time at a four-year institution or university and resident of New Jersey. Applicant must have 3.0 GPA or higher. Available to U.S. citizens.

Application Requirements: Application form, essay, recommendations or references, resume, transcript. *Deadline:* April 1.

RUSSELL W. MYERS SCHOLARSHIP

Scholarship to deserving individuals who plan careers in environmental science, natural resource management, conservation, horticulture, park administration, or a related field. Must be a resident of New Jersey and considering a career in New Jersey. Payment is made directly to the institution that the successful candidate attends.

Academic Fields/Career Goals: Environmental Science; Horticulture/Floriculture; Landscape Architecture; Natural Resources; Recreation, Parks, Leisure Studies.

Award: Scholarship for use in freshman, sophomore, junior, or senior years; not renewable. *Amount:* up to $7000.

Eligibility Requirements: Applicant must be enrolled or expecting to enroll full-time at a four-year institution or university and resident of New Jersey. Applicant must have 3.0 GPA or higher. Available to U.S. citizens.

Application Requirements: Application form, essay, recommendations or references, resume, transcript. *Deadline:* April 1.

MANITOBA FORESTRY ASSOCIATION

http://www.thinktrees.org/

DR. ALAN BEAVEN FORESTRY SCHOLARSHIP

Awarded annually to a Manitoba resident selected by a committee of association members. Must be a recent high school graduate entering first year forestry program at a Canadian university or technical school. Scholarship of $500 (Canadian Dollars) will be paid in the student's name to the university or school as part of the tuition.

Academic Fields/Career Goals: Environmental Science; Natural Resources.

Award: Scholarship for use in freshman year; not renewable. *Number:* 1. *Amount:* $300–$475.

Eligibility Requirements: Applicant must be Canadian citizen; high school student; planning to enroll or expecting to enroll full-time at a two-year or four-year or technical institution or university and resident of Manitoba.

Application Requirements: Application form, recommendations or references, transcript. *Deadline:* July 31.

MISSOURI DEPARTMENT OF NATURAL RESOURCES

http://www.dnr.mo.gov/

ENVIRONMENTAL EDUCATION SCHOLARSHIP PROGRAM (EESP)

Scholarship to minority and other underrepresented students pursuing a bachelor's or master's degree in an environmental course of study. Must be a Missouri resident having a cumulative high school GPA of 3.0 or if enrolled in college, must have cumulative GPA of 2.5.

Academic Fields/Career Goals: Environmental Science.

Award: Scholarship for use in freshman, sophomore, junior, senior, or graduate years; renewable. *Number:* 16. *Amount:* $2000.

Eligibility Requirements: Applicant must be American Indian/Alaska Native, Asian/Pacific Islander, Black (non-Hispanic), Hispanic; enrolled or expecting to enroll full-time at a four-year institution or university and resident of Missouri. Applicant must have 3.0 GPA or higher. Available to U.S. citizens.

Application Requirements: Application form, community service, essay, recommendations or references, transcript. *Deadline:* June 1.

Contact: Dana Muessig, Executive
Phone: 800-361-4827
Fax: 573-526-3878
E-mail: danamuessig@dnr.mo.gov

NASA/MARYLAND SPACE GRANT CONSORTIUM

http://md.spacegrant.org/

NASA MARYLAND SPACE GRANT CONSORTIUM UNDERGRADUATE SCHOLARSHIPS
• See page 132

NASA SOUTH DAKOTA SPACE GRANT CONSORTIUM

http://sdspacegrant.sdsmt.edu/

SOUTH DAKOTA SPACE GRANT CONSORTIUM UNDERGRADUATE AND GRADUATE STUDENT SCHOLARSHIPS
• See page 134

NASA'S VIRGINIA SPACE GRANT CONSORTIUM

http://www.vsgc.odu.edu/

COMMUNITY COLLEGE STEM SCHOLARSHIPS
• See page 105

NASA WEST VIRGINIA SPACE GRANT CONSORTIUM

http://www.nasa.wvu.edu/

WEST VIRGINIA SPACE GRANT CONSORTIUM UNDERGRADUATE FELLOWSHIP PROGRAM
• See page 134

NATIONAL COUNCIL OF STATE GARDEN CLUBS INC. SCHOLARSHIP

http://www.gardenclub.org/

NATIONAL COUNCIL OF STATE GARDEN CLUBS INC. SCHOLARSHIP
• See page 93

NATIONAL GARDEN CLUBS INC.

http://www.gardenclub.org/

NATIONAL GARDEN CLUBS INC. SCHOLARSHIP PROGRAM
• See page 94

NATIONAL GROUND WATER RESEARCH AND EDUCATIONAL FOUNDATION

http://www.ngwa.org/Foundation/assante/Pages/default.aspx

NATIONAL GROUND WATER RESEARCH AND EDUCATIONAL FOUNDATION'S LEN ASSANTE SCHOLARSHIP
• See page 229

NATIONAL INVENTORS HALL OF FAME

http://www.invent.org/

COLLEGIATE INVENTORS COMPETITION FOR UNDERGRADUATE STUDENTS
• See page 106

COLLEGIATE INVENTORS COMPETITION-GRAND PRIZE
• See page 106

NATIONAL SAFETY COUNCIL

http://www.cshema.org/

CAMPUS SAFETY, HEALTH AND ENVIRONMENTAL MANAGEMENT ASSOCIATION SCHOLARSHIP AWARD PROGRAM

One $2000 scholarship available to full-time undergraduate or graduate students in all majors to encourage the study of safety and environmental management. The program is open to all college undergraduate and graduate students in all majors/disciplines enrolled in 12 credit hours per semester, trimester, or quarter.

Academic Fields/Career Goals: Environmental Science; Occupational Safety and Health.

Award: Scholarship for use in freshman, sophomore, junior, senior, or graduate years; not renewable. *Number:* 1. *Amount:* $2000.

Eligibility Requirements: Applicant must be enrolled or expecting to enroll full-time at a four-year institution or university. Available to U.S. and Canadian citizens.

Application Requirements: Application form, essay, transcript. *Deadline:* March 1.

NEW ENGLAND WATER WORKS ASSOCIATION

http://www.newwa.org/

ELSON T. KILLAM MEMORIAL SCHOLARSHIP
• See page 184

FRANCIS X. CROWLEY SCHOLARSHIP
• See page 158

JOSEPH MURPHY SCHOLARSHIP
• See page 184

OHIO ACADEMY OF SCIENCE/OHIO ENVIRONMENTAL EDUCATION FUND

http://www.ohiosci.org/

OHIO ENVIRONMENTAL SCIENCE & ENGINEERING SCHOLARSHIPS

Merit-based, non-renewable, tuition-only scholarships awarded to undergraduate students admitted to Ohio state or private colleges and universities. Must be able to demonstrate knowledge of, and commitment to, careers in environmental sciences or environmental engineering.

Academic Fields/Career Goals: Environmental Science.

Award: Scholarship for use in senior year; not renewable. *Number:* 18. *Amount:* $1250–$2500.

Eligibility Requirements: Applicant must be enrolled or expecting to enroll full- or part-time at a two-year or four-year institution or university and studying in Ohio. Applicant must have 3.0 GPA or higher. Available to U.S. citizens.

Application Requirements: Application form, community service, essay, recommendations or references, resume, self-addressed stamped envelope with application, transcript. *Deadline:* June 1.

Contact: Dr. Lynn Elfner, Chief Executive Officer
Ohio Academy of Science/Ohio Environmental Education Fund
1500 West Third Avenue, Suite 228
Columbus, OH 43212-2817
Phone: 614-488-2228
Fax: 614-488-7629
E-mail: oas@iwaynet.net

OREGON STUDENT ASSISTANCE COMMISSION

http://www.GetCollegeFunds.org/

OREGON FOUNDATION FOR BLACKTAIL DEER SCHOLARSHIP
• *See page 147*

ROYDEN M. BODLEY SCHOLARSHIP

One-time award open to Oregon high school graduates who earned their Eagle rank in Boy Scouts of America Cascade Pacific Council. Must be enrolled, or planning to enroll, in an Oregon college or university in an undergraduate program in forestry, wildlife conservation, environmental studies, or related fields that continue interest in the outdoors. Must reapply annually to renew award.

Academic Fields/Career Goals: Environmental Science; Natural Resources; Natural Sciences.

Award: Scholarship for use in freshman year; not renewable.

Eligibility Requirements: Applicant must be enrolled or expecting to enroll full-time at a four-year institution or university; male; resident of Oregon and studying in Oregon. Applicant or parent of applicant must be member of Boy Scouts. Available to U.S. citizens.

Application Requirements: Activity chart, FAFSA, application form, essay, financial need analysis, transcript. *Deadline:* March 1.

OZARKA NATURAL SPRING WATER

http://www.ozarkawater.com/

EARTH SCIENCE SCHOLARSHIP
• *See page 229*

PENNSYLVANIA ASSOCIATION OF CONSERVATION DISTRICTS AUXILIARY

http://www.pacd.org/

PACD AUXILIARY SCHOLARSHIPS
• *See page 95*

SAEMS-SOUTHERN ARIZONA ENVIRONMENTAL MANAGEMENT SOCIETY

http://www.saems.org/

ENVIRONMENTAL SCHOLARSHIPS
• *See page 299*

SALT RIVER PROJECT (SRP)

http://www.srpnet.com/

NAVAJO GENERATING STATION NAVAJO SCHOLARSHIP
• *See page 288*

SOCIETY FOR RANGE MANAGEMENT

http://www.rangelands.org/

MASONIC RANGE SCIENCE SCHOLARSHIP
• *See page 88*

SOIL AND WATER CONSERVATION SOCIETY

http://www.swcs.org

DONALD A. WILLIAMS SCHOLARSHIP SOIL CONSERVATION SCHOLARSHIP
• *See page 88*

MELVILLE H. COHEE STUDENT LEADER CONSERVATION SCHOLARSHIP
• *See page 88*

SOIL AND WATER CONSERVATION SOCIETY-NEW JERSEY CHAPTER

http://home.comcast.net/~njswcs/scholarship.htm

EDWARD R. HALL SCHOLARSHIP
• *See page 88*

TECHNICAL ASSOCIATION OF THE PULP & PAPER INDUSTRY (TAPPI)

http://www.tappi.org/

ENVIRONMENTAL WORKING GROUP SCHOLARSHIP

Annual awards for SME student members who are undergraduate students at or above the level of a sophomore and enrolled at an ABET-accredited or equivalent college. Minimum of one $2500 scholarship. Information can be found at http://www.tappi.org/s_tappi/sec.asp?CID=6101&DID=546695.

Academic Fields/Career Goals: Environmental Science; Paper and Pulp Engineering.

Award: Scholarship for use in sophomore, junior, or senior years; not renewable. *Number:* 1. *Amount:* $2500.

Eligibility Requirements: Applicant must be enrolled or expecting to enroll full-time at a four-year institution or university. Applicant must have 3.0 GPA or higher. Available to U.S. and non-U.S. citizens.

Application Requirements: Application form, interview, recommendations or references, transcript. *Deadline:* February 15.

Contact: Mr. Charles Bohanan, Director of Standards and Awards
Technical Association of the Pulp & Paper Industry (TAPPI)
15 Technology Parkway South
Peachtree Corners, GA 30033
Phone: 770-209-7276
Fax: 770-446-6947
E-mail: standards@tappi.org

TEXAS OUTDOOR WRITERS ASSOCIATION

http://www.towa.org/

TEXAS OUTDOOR WRITERS ASSOCIATION SCHOLARSHIP
• *See page 197*

TKE EDUCATIONAL FOUNDATION

http://www.tke.org/

TIMOTHY L. TASCHWER SCHOLARSHIP
• *See page 148*

UNITED NEGRO COLLEGE FUND

http://www.uncf.org/

CDM SCHOLARSHIP/INTERNSHIP
• *See page 176*

SPRINT SCHOLARS PROGRAM FOR SOPHOMORES, JUNIORS, AND SENIORS
• See page 100

UNCF/MERCK SCIENCE INITIATIVE
• See page 149

UNITED STATES ENVIRONMENTAL PROTECTION AGENCY

http://www.epa.gov/enviroed

NATIONAL NETWORK FOR ENVIRONMENTAL MANAGEMENT STUDIES FELLOWSHIP

Fellowship program designed to provide undergraduate and graduate students with research opportunities at one of EPA's facilities nationwide. EPA awards approximately 40 NNEMS fellowships per year. Selected students receive a stipend for performing their research project. EPA develops an annual catalog of research projects available for student application. Submit a complete application package as described in the annual catalog. Minimum 3.0 GPA required.

Academic Fields/Career Goals: Environmental Science; Natural Resources.

Award: Grant for use in freshman, sophomore, junior, senior, graduate, or postgraduate years; not renewable. *Number:* 20–25.

Eligibility Requirements: Applicant must be enrolled or expecting to enroll full- or part-time at a two-year or four-year institution or university. Applicant must have 3.0 GPA or higher. Available to U.S. citizens.

Application Requirements: Application form, recommendations or references, resume, transcript. *Deadline:* January 22.

Contact: Michael Baker, Acting Director
United States Environmental Protection Agency
Environmental Education Division, 1200 Pennsylvania
    Avenue, NW, MC 1704A
Washington, DC 20460
Phone: 202-564-0446
Fax: 202-564-2754
E-mail: baker.michael@epa.gov

VIRGINIA ASSOCIATION OF SOIL AND WATER CONSERVATION DISTRICTS EDUCATIONAL FOUNDATION INC.

http://www.vaswcd.org/

VASWCD EDUCATIONAL FOUNDATION INC. SCHOLARSHIP AWARDS PROGRAM

Scholarship to provide financial support to Virginia residents majoring in, or showing a strong desire to major in, a course curriculum related to natural resource conservation and/or environmental studies. Applicants must be full-time students who have applied to an undergraduate freshman-level curriculum. Must rank in the top 20 percent of graduating class or have a 3.0 or greater GPA, and demonstrate an active interest in conservation. Recipients may reapply to their individual SWCD for scholarship consideration in ensuing years.

Academic Fields/Career Goals: Environmental Science; Natural Resources.

Award: Scholarship for use in freshman year; not renewable. *Number:* 4. *Amount:* $1000.

Eligibility Requirements: Applicant must be high school student; planning to enroll or expecting to enroll full-time at a four-year institution or university and resident of Virginia. Applicant must have 3.0 GPA or higher. Available to U.S. citizens.

Application Requirements: Application form, essay, financial need analysis, recommendations or references, transcript. *Deadline:* March 1.

Contact: Jennifer Krick, District Manager
Phone: 540-347-3120 Ext. 116
Fax: 540-349-0878
E-mail: jennifer.krick@va.nacdnet.net

WINDSTAR FOUNDATION

WINDSTAR ENVIRONMENTAL STUDIES SCHOLARSHIPS
• See page 300

EUROPEAN STUDIES

CANADIAN INSTITUTE OF UKRAINIAN STUDIES

http://www.cius.ca/

CANADIAN INSTITUTE OF UKRAINIAN STUDIES RESEARCH GRANTS
• See page 114

CULTURAL SERVICES OF THE FRENCH EMBASSY

http://www.frenchculture.org/

TEACHING ASSISTANT PROGRAM IN FRANCE
• See page 97

FASHION DESIGN

DECA (DISTRIBUTIVE EDUCATION CLUBS OF AMERICA)

http://www.deca.org/

HARRY A. APPLEGATE SCHOLARSHIP
• See page 153

NATIONAL ASSOCIATION TO ADVANCE FAT ACCEPTANCE

http://www.naafa.org/

NAAFA PLUS-SIZE FASHION DESIGN SCHOLARSHIP

The purpose of this scholarship is to encourage student fashion designers to specialize in the design of fashions for the plus-size body.

Academic Fields/Career Goals: Fashion Design.

Award: Scholarship for use in freshman, sophomore, junior, senior, or graduate years; not renewable. *Amount:* $1000.

Eligibility Requirements: Applicant must be enrolled or expecting to enroll full-time at a two-year or four-year or technical institution. Available to U.S. and Canadian citizens.

Application Requirements: Application form, essay, interview, portfolio, recommendations or references. *Deadline:* July 1.

Contact: Ms. Peggy Howell, Public Relations Director
National Association to Advance Fat Acceptance
PO Box 4662
Foster City, CA 94404
Phone: 916-558-6880
E-mail: pr@naafa.org

WHOMENTORS.COM, INC.
http://www.WHOmentors.com/

1B USD WORLDWIDE VENTURE CAPITAL
- *See page 107*

FILMMAKING/VIDEO

ACADEMY FOUNDATION OF THE ACADEMY OF MOTION PICTURE ARTS AND SCIENCES
http://www.oscars.org/saa

ACADEMY OF MOTION PICTURE ARTS AND SCIENCES STUDENT ACADEMY AWARDS

Award available to students who have made a narrative, documentary, alternative, foreign or animated film of up to 60 minutes within the curricular structure of an accredited college or university. Initial entry must be on DVD-R. 16mm or larger format print, digital beta-cam tape, HD-Cam or DCP required for further rounds. Prizes awarded in four categories. Each category awards gold ($5000), silver ($3000), and bronze ($2000). Visit website for details and application http://www.oscars.org/saa.

Academic Fields/Career Goals: Filmmaking/Video.

Award: Prize for use in freshman, sophomore, junior, senior, or graduate years; not renewable. *Number:* 3–15. *Amount:* $2000–$5000.

Eligibility Requirements: Applicant must be enrolled or expecting to enroll full-time at a two-year or four-year institution or university. Available to U.S. and non-U.S. citizens.

Application Requirements: 16mm or larger format film print or NTSC digital betacam version of the entry (BetaSP format is not acceptable), DVD, application form, application form may be submitted online (http://www.oscars.org/saa), entry in a contest. *Deadline:* April 1.

Contact: Richard Miller, Awards Administration Director
Academy Foundation of the Academy of Motion Picture Arts and Sciences
8949 Wilshire Boulevard
Beverly Hills, CA 90211-1972
Phone: 310-247-3000 Ext. 1129
Fax: 310-859-9619
E-mail: rmiller@oscars.org

ADC RESEARCH INSTITUTE
http://www.adc.org/

JACK SHAHEEN MASS COMMUNICATIONS SCHOLARSHIP AWARD
- *See page 187*

CHARLES AND LUCILLE KING FAMILY FOUNDATION, INC.
http://www.kingfoundation.org/

CHARLES AND LUCILLE KING FAMILY FOUNDATION SCHOLARSHIPS
- *See page 189*

ILLUMINATING ENGINEERING SOCIETY OF NORTH AMERICA–GOLDEN GATE SECTION
http://www.iesgg.org/

ALAN LUCAS MEMORIAL EDUCATIONAL SCHOLARSHIP
- *See page 111*

INTERNATIONAL COMMUNICATIONS INDUSTRIES FOUNDATION
http://www.infocomm.org/scholarships

ICIF SCHOLARSHIP FOR EMPLOYEES AND DEPENDENTS OF MEMBER ORGANIZATIONS
- *See page 191*

INTERNATIONAL COMMUNICATIONS INDUSTRIES FOUNDATION AV SCHOLARSHIP
- *See page 191*

MEDIA ACTION NETWORK FOR ASIAN AMERICANS
http://www.manaa.org/

MANAA MEDIA SCHOLARSHIPS FOR ASIAN AMERICAN STUDENTS
- *See page 120*

OUTDOOR WRITERS ASSOCIATION OF AMERICA
http://www.owaa.org/

OUTDOOR WRITERS ASSOCIATION OF AMERICA - BODIE MCDOWELL SCHOLARSHIP AWARD
- *See page 193*

PHI DELTA THETA FOUNDATION
http://www.phideltathetafoundation.org/

FRANCIS D. LYON SCHOLARSHIP FOR FILM STUDENT

One scholarship for up to $3000 for an undergraduate or graduate student of filmmaking. Must have completed two full years of college and be enrolled in an institution in the U.S. or Canada. Award based on talent, academic excellence, and financial need. Application deadline is March 18.

Academic Fields/Career Goals: Filmmaking/Video.

Award: Scholarship for use in junior or senior years; not renewable. *Number:* 1. *Amount:* $2000–$3000.

Eligibility Requirements: Applicant must be enrolled or expecting to enroll full-time at a four-year institution or university. Available to U.S. and non-U.S. citizens.

Application Requirements: Application form, essay, personal photograph, recommendations or references, sample of work, transcript. *Deadline:* March 18.

Contact: Linda Brattain, Director of Stewardship
Phi Delta Theta Foundation
2 South Campus Avenue
Oxford, OH 45056
Phone: 513-523-6345
Fax: 513-523-9200
E-mail: linda@phideltatheta.org

POLISH ARTS CLUB OF BUFFALO SCHOLARSHIP FOUNDATION

http://www.pacb.bfn.org/

POLISH ARTS CLUB OF BUFFALO SCHOLARSHIP FOUNDATION TRUST
• *See page 121*

PRINCESS GRACE FOUNDATION-USA

http://www.pgfusa.org/

PRINCESS GRACE AWARDS IN DANCE, THEATER, AND FILM

One-time scholarship for students enrolled full-time in film or video, dance, or theater program. For dance, applicant must have completed at least one year of undergraduate study; for theater, final year of study in either undergraduate or graduate level; and for film, must be in thesis program. The number of scholarships varies from ten to twelve annually.

Academic Fields/Career Goals: Filmmaking/Video; Performing Arts.

Award: Grant for use in sophomore, junior, senior, or graduate years; not renewable. *Number:* 15–25. *Amount:* $5000–$25,000.

Eligibility Requirements: Applicant must be enrolled or expecting to enroll full-time at a four-year institution or university. Available to U.S. citizens.

Application Requirements: Application form, entry in a contest, essay, nomination, personal photograph, portfolio, recommendations or references, resume, self-addressed stamped envelope with application.

Contact: Ms. Jelena Tadic, Program Manager
   Phone: 212-317-1470
   E-mail: grants@pgfusa.org

RHODE ISLAND FOUNDATION

http://www.rifoundation.org/

J. D. EDSAL SCHOLARSHIP
• *See page 84*

SAN FRANCISCO FOUNDATION

http://www.sff.org/

PHELAN ART AWARD IN FILMMAKING

Award presented in every even-numbered year to recognize achievement in film making. Must have been born in California, but need not be a current resident. Applicants must provide a copy of their birth certificate with their application. Scholarship values from $5000 to $10,000. Deadline varies.

Academic Fields/Career Goals: Filmmaking/Video.

Award: Prize for use in freshman, sophomore, junior, senior, graduate, or postgraduate years; not renewable. *Number:* 3. *Amount:* $5000–$10,000.

Eligibility Requirements: Applicant must be enrolled or expecting to enroll full- or part-time at a two-year or four-year institution or university. Available to U.S. citizens.

Application Requirements: Application form, entry in a contest, self-addressed stamped envelope with application. *Deadline:* varies.

PHELAN ART AWARD IN VIDEO

Award presented in every even-numbered year to recognize achievement in video. Must have been born in California, but need not be a current resident. Applicants must provide a copy of their birth certificates with their application. Scholarship value is $5000 to $10,000. Deadline varies.

Academic Fields/Career Goals: Filmmaking/Video.

Award: Prize for use in freshman, sophomore, junior, senior, graduate, or postgraduate years; not renewable. *Number:* 3. *Amount:* $5000–$10,000.

Eligibility Requirements: Applicant must be enrolled or expecting to enroll full- or part-time at a two-year or four-year institution or university. Available to U.S. citizens.

Application Requirements: Application form, entry in a contest, self-addressed stamped envelope with application. *Deadline:* varies.

SOCIETY OF MOTION PICTURE AND TELEVISION ENGINEERS

http://www.smpte.org/

LOUIS F. WOLF JR. MEMORIAL SCHOLARSHIP
• *See page 195*

STUDENT PAPER AWARD
• *See page 195*

TELETOON

http://www.teletoon.com/

TELETOON ANIMATION SCHOLARSHIP
• *See page 122*

UNIVERSITY FILM AND VIDEO ASSOCIATION

http://www.ufva.org/

UNIVERSITY FILM AND VIDEO ASSOCIATION CAROLE FIELDING STUDENT GRANTS

Up to $4000 is available for production grants in narrative, documentary, experimental, new-media/installation, or animation. Up to $1000 is available for grants in research. Applicant must be sponsored by a faculty person who is an active member of the University Film and Video Association. Fifty percent of award distributed upon completion of project.

Academic Fields/Career Goals: Filmmaking/Video.

Award: Grant for use in freshman, sophomore, junior, senior, or graduate years; not renewable. *Number:* up to 5. *Amount:* $1000–$4000.

Eligibility Requirements: Applicant must be enrolled or expecting to enroll full- or part-time at a two-year or four-year institution or university. Available to U.S. and non-U.S. citizens.

Application Requirements: Application form, essay, project description, budget, recommendations or references, resume. *Deadline:* December 15.

Contact: Prof. Robert Johnson, Chair
   University Film and Video Association
   Framingham State College, 100 State Street
   Framingham, MA 01701-9101
   Phone: 508-626-4684
   Fax: 508-626-4847
   E-mail: rjohnso@frc.mass.edu

WHOMENTORS.COM, INC.

http://www.WHOmentors.com/

I B USD WORLDWIDE VENTURE CAPITAL
• *See page 107*

WOMEN IN FILM AND TELEVISION (WIFT)

http://www.wif.org/

WIF FOUNDATION SCHOLARSHIP

Scholarships for female students based on their academic standing, artistic talents and commitment to a film-based curriculum with special consideration for financial need, regardless of age, ethnicity or religious affiliation. Scholarships to such schools as University of California, Los Angeles, University of Southern California, Chapman University and AFI are available to female students who are already enrolled and have been nominated by instructors and faculty at respective schools.

Academic Fields/Career Goals: Filmmaking/Video.

Award: Scholarship for use in freshman, sophomore, junior, or senior years; not renewable. *Number:* up to 3. *Amount:* up to $1000.

Eligibility Requirements: Applicant must be enrolled or expecting to enroll part-time at a two-year or four-year or technical institution or university and female. Available to U.S. citizens.

Application Requirements: Application form, essay, financial need analysis, recommendations or references, transcript. *Deadline:* varies.

Contact: Gayle Nachlis, Executive Director
　　　Phone: 310-657-5144 Ext. 28
　　　Fax: 310-657-5154
　　　E-mail: gnachlis@wif.org

WORLDFEST INTERNATIONAL FILM AND VIDEO FESTIVAL

http://www.worldfest.org/

WORLDFEST STUDENT FILM AWARD

Award for students enrolled full-time or part-time in accredited colleges or universities majoring filmmaking.

Academic Fields/Career Goals: Filmmaking/Video.

Award: Prize for use in freshman, sophomore, junior, senior, or graduate years; not renewable. *Number:* 10. *Amount:* $1000–$10,000.

Eligibility Requirements: Applicant must be enrolled or expecting to enroll full- or part-time at a two-year or four-year or technical institution or university. Available to U.S. and non-U.S. citizens.

Application Requirements: Application form, entry in a contest, film/tape entry, student ID, recommendations or references. *Fee:* $45. *Deadline:* December 15.

Contact: Hunter Todd, Executive Director
　　　Phone: 713-965-9955
　　　Fax: 713-965-9960
　　　E-mail: hunter@worldfest.org

FINANCE

COMMUNITY FOUNDATION OF WESTERN MASSACHUSETTS

http://www.communityfoundation.org/

GREATER SPRINGFIELD ACCOUNTANTS SCHOLARSHIP
• *See page 71*

DADE COMMUNITY FOUNDATION

http://www.jackituckfield.org/

DR. FELIX H. REYLER (FIBA) SCHOLARSHIP
• *See page 152*

DECA (DISTRIBUTIVE EDUCATION CLUBS OF AMERICA)

http://www.deca.org/

HARRY A. APPLEGATE SCHOLARSHIP
• *See page 153*

GEORGIA GOVERNMENT FINANCE OFFICERS ASSOCIATION

http://www.ggfoa.org/

GGFOA SCHOLARSHIP
• *See page 73*

HISPANIC HERITAGE FOUNDATION

http://www.hispanicheritage.org/

HISPANIC HERITAGE YOUTH AWARDS
• *See page 155*

INSTITUTE OF MANAGEMENT ACCOUNTANTS

http://www.imanet.org/

ROLF S. JAEHNIGEN FAMILY SCHOLARSHIP
• *See page 74*

OREGON STUDENT ASSISTANCE COMMISSION

http://www.GetCollegeFunds.org/

OREGON ASSOCIATION OF CERTIFIED FRAUD EXAMINERS SCHOLARSHIP
• *See page 78*

SPECIALTY EQUIPMENT MARKET ASSOCIATION

http://www.sema.org/

SPECIALTY EQUIPMENT MARKET ASSOCIATION MEMORIAL SCHOLARSHIP FUND
• *See page 80*

STRAIGHTFORWARD MEDIA

http://www.straightforwardmedia.com/

STRAIGHTFORWARD MEDIA BUSINESS SCHOOL SCHOLARSHIP
• *See page 84*

UNITED NEGRO COLLEGE FUND

http://www.uncf.org/

AVIS BUDGET GROUP SCHOLARSHIP
• *See page 81*

BANK OF AMERICA SCHOLARSHIP
• *See page 160*

COMERICA CHARITABLE FOUNDATION SCHOLARSHIP
• *See page 81*

FORD/UNCF CORPORATE SCHOLARS PROGRAM
• *See page 82*

LIBERTY MUTUAL SCHOLARSHIP
• *See page 160*

LOCKHEED MARTIN/UNCF SCHOLARSHIP
• *See page 82*

NASCAR/WENDELL SCOTT, SR. SCHOLARSHIP
• *See page 82*

PACIFIC GAS AND ELECTRIC COMPANY SCHOLARSHIP
• *See page 82*

PSE&G SCHOLARSHIP
• *See page 82*

UBS/PAINEWEBBER SCHOLARSHIP
• *See page 82*

FIRE SCIENCES

BOY SCOUTS OF AMERICA-MUSKINGUM VALLEY COUNCIL
http://www.learning-for-life.org/

INTERNATIONAL ASSOCIATION OF FIRE CHIEFS FOUNDATION SCHOLARSHIP
Two $500 scholarships for Explorers who are pursuing a full-time career in the fire sciences. Must be high school senior and participant of the Learning for Life Exploring program.
Academic Fields/Career Goals: Fire Sciences.
Award: Scholarship for use in freshman year; not renewable. *Number:* 2. *Amount:* $500.
Eligibility Requirements: Applicant must be high school student and planning to enroll or expecting to enroll full-time at a four-year institution or university. Available to U.S. and non-U.S. citizens.
Application Requirements: Application form, essay, personal photograph, recommendations or references, test scores, transcript. *Deadline:* July 1.

INDEPENDENT LABORATORIES INSTITUTE SCHOLARSHIP ALLIANCE
http://www.acil.org/

INDEPENDENT LABORATORIES INSTITUTE SCHOLARSHIP ALLIANCE
• *See page 145*

IAAI FOUNDATION, INC.
http://www.firearson.com/

JOHN CHARLES WILSON SCHOLARSHIP & ROBERT DORAN SCHOLARSHIP
One-time award to members in good standing of IAAI or the immediate family of a member or must be sponsored by an IAAI member. Must enroll or plan to enroll full-time in an accredited college or university that offers courses in police, fire sciences, or any arson investigation-related field. Application available at website.
Academic Fields/Career Goals: Fire Sciences; Law Enforcement/Police Administration.
Award: Scholarship for use in freshman, sophomore, junior, senior, or graduate years; not renewable. *Number:* up to 4. *Amount:* $500–$1000.
Eligibility Requirements: Applicant must be enrolled or expecting to enroll full-time at a two-year or four-year institution or university. Available to U.S. and non-U.S. citizens.
Application Requirements: Application form, application form may be submitted online (http://www.firearson.com/iaai-foundation/scholarships), driver's license, essay, recommendations or references, resume, test scores, transcript. *Deadline:* February 15.
Contact: Gloria Guernsey Ryan, Office Manager
IAAI Foundation, Inc.
2111 Baldwin Avenue Suite 203
Crofton, MD 21114
Phone: 410-451-FIRE Ext. 3473
Fax: 410-451-9049
E-mail: iaai@firearson.com

INTERNATIONAL ASSOCIATION OF FIRE CHIEFS FOUNDATION
http://www.iafcf.org/

INTERNATIONAL ASSOCIATION OF FIRE CHIEFS FOUNDATION SCHOLARSHIP AWARD
One-time award, open to any person who is an active member (volunteer or paid) of an emergency or fire department. Must use the scholarship funds for an accredited, recognized institution of higher education.
Academic Fields/Career Goals: Fire Sciences.
Award: Scholarship for use in senior, graduate, or postgraduate years; not renewable. *Number:* 10–25. *Amount:* $500–$2500.
Eligibility Requirements: Applicant must be enrolled or expecting to enroll full- or part-time at a four-year institution or university. Available to U.S. citizens.
Application Requirements: Application form, essay, letters of endorsement, recommendations or references, resume, transcript. *Deadline:* June 1.
Contact: Sharon Baroncelli, Association and Services Manager
Phone: 703-896-4822
Fax: 703-273-9363
E-mail: sbaroncelli@iafc.org

LEARNING FOR LIFE
http://www.learning-for-life.org/

INTERNATIONAL ASSOCIATIONS OF FIRE CHIEFS FOUNDATION SCHOLARSHIP
Applicant must be a graduating high school senior in May or June of the year the application is issued and a Fire Service Explorer. The school selected by the applicant must be an accredited public or proprietary institution.
Academic Fields/Career Goals: Fire Sciences.
Award: Scholarship for use in freshman year; not renewable. *Number:* 2. *Amount:* $500.
Eligibility Requirements: Applicant must be high school student and planning to enroll or expecting to enroll full- or part-time at a two-year or four-year institution or university. Applicant or parent of applicant must be member of Explorer Program/Learning for Life. Available to U.S. citizens.
Application Requirements: Application form, essay, personal photograph, recommendations or references, transcript. *Deadline:* July 1.
Contact: William Taylor, Scholarships and Awards Coordinator
E-mail: btaylor@lflmail.org

MARYLAND STATE HIGHER EDUCATION COMMISSION
http://www.mhec.state.md.us/

CHARLES W. RILEY FIRE AND EMERGENCY MEDICAL SERVICES TUITION REIMBURSEMENT PROGRAM
Award intended to reimburse members of rescue organizations serving Maryland communities for tuition costs of course work towards a degree or certificate in fire service or medical technology. Must attend a two- or four-year school in Maryland. Minimum 2.0 GPA. The scholarship is worth up to $6500.
Academic Fields/Career Goals: Fire Sciences; Health and Medical Sciences; Trade/Technical Specialties.
Award: Scholarship for use in freshman, sophomore, junior, or senior years; not renewable. *Number:* up to 150. *Amount:* up to $6500.
Eligibility Requirements: Applicant must be enrolled or expecting to enroll full- or part-time at a two-year or four-year institution or university; resident of Maryland and studying in Maryland. Applicant or parent of applicant must have employment or volunteer experience in police/firefighting. Available to U.S. citizens.
Application Requirements: Application form, transcript, tuition receipt, proof of enrollment. *Deadline:* July 1.

Contact: Maura Sappington, Office of Student Financial Assistance
Maryland State Higher Education Commission
839 Bestgate Road, Suite 400
Annapolis, MD 21401-3013
Phone: 410-260-4569
Fax: 410-260-3203
E-mail: msapping@mhec.state.md.us

STRAIGHTFORWARD MEDIA

http://www.straightforwardmedia.com/

STRAIGHTFORWARD MEDIA VOCATIONAL-TECHNICAL SCHOOL SCHOLARSHIP

• *See page 99*

FLEXOGRAPHY

FOUNDATION OF FLEXOGRAPHIC TECHNICAL ASSOCIATION

http://www.flexography.org/

FOUNDATION OF FLEXOGRAPHIC TECHNICAL ASSOCIATION SCHOLARSHIP COMPETITION

Awards students enrolled in a FFTA Flexo in Education Program with plans to attend a postsecondary institution, or be currently enrolled in a postsecondary institution offering a course of study in flexography. Must demonstrate an interest in a career in flexography, and maintain an overall GPA of at least 3.0. Must reapply.

Academic Fields/Career Goals: Flexography.

Award: Scholarship for use in freshman, sophomore, junior, or senior years; not renewable. *Number:* 6–8. *Amount:* up to $3000.

Eligibility Requirements: Applicant must be enrolled or expecting to enroll full-time at a two-year or four-year or technical institution or university. Applicant must have 3.0 GPA or higher. Available to U.S. and Canadian citizens.

Application Requirements: Application form, application form may be submitted online (http://www.flexography.org), essay, recommendations or references, transcript. *Deadline:* March 15.

Contact: Shelley Rubin, Manager of Educational Programs
Foundation of Flexographic Technical Association
3920 Veterans Memorial Highway, Suite 9
Bohemia, NY 11716
Phone: 631-737-6020 Ext. 36
Fax: 631-737-6813

PRINTING INDUSTRY OF MIDWEST EDUCATION FOUNDATION

http://www.pimn.org/

PRINTING INDUSTRY MIDWEST EDUCATION FOUNDATION SCHOLARSHIP FUND

• *See page 194*

TAG AND LABEL MANUFACTURERS INSTITUTE, INC.

http://www.tlmi.com/

TLMI 4 YEAR COLLEGE DEGREE SCHOLARSHIP PROGRAM

• *See page 270*

FOOD SCIENCE/ NUTRITION

AMERICAN DIETETIC ASSOCIATION

http://www.eatright.org/

AMERICAN DIETETIC ASSOCIATION FOUNDATION SCHOLARSHIP PROGRAM

ADAF scholarships are available for undergraduate and graduate students enrolled in programs, including dietetic internships, preparing for entry to dietetics practice as well as dietetics professionals engaged in continuing education at the graduate level. Scholarship funds are provided by many state dietetic associations, dietetic practice groups, past ADA leaders and corporate donors. Scholarships require ADA membership. Details available on website http://www.eatright.org/CADE/content.aspx?id=7934.

Academic Fields/Career Goals: Food Science/Nutrition.

Award: Scholarship for use in sophomore, junior, or senior years; not renewable. *Number:* 200–225. *Amount:* $500–$3000.

Eligibility Requirements: Applicant must be enrolled or expecting to enroll full- or part-time at a two-year or four-year institution or university. Applicant or parent of applicant must be member of American Dietetic Association. Available to U.S. citizens.

Application Requirements: Application form, essay, financial need analysis, recommendations or references, transcript. *Deadline:* February 15.

Contact: Eva Donovan, Education Coordinator
Phone: 312-899-0040 Ext. 4876
E-mail: education@eatright.org

AMERICAN INSTITUTE OF WINE AND FOOD-PACIFIC NORTHWEST CHAPTER

http://www.aiwf.org/

CULINARY, VINIFERA, AND HOSPITALITY SCHOLARSHIP

One-time award available to residents of Washington State. Must be enrolled full-time in an accredited culinary, vinifera, or hospitality program in Washington State. Must have completed two years. Minimum 3.0 GPA required.

Academic Fields/Career Goals: Food Science/Nutrition; Food Service/Hospitality; Hospitality Management.

Award: Scholarship for use in junior or senior years; not renewable. *Number:* 4. *Amount:* $1500.

Eligibility Requirements: Applicant must be enrolled or expecting to enroll full-time at a two-year or four-year or technical institution or university; resident of Washington and studying in Washington. Applicant must have 3.0 GPA or higher. Available to U.S. and non-U.S. citizens.

Application Requirements: Application form, recommendations or references, resume. *Deadline:* continuous.

Contact: Brad Sturman, Scholarship Coordinator
American Institute of Wine and Food-Pacific Northwest Chapter
224 18th Avenue
Kirkland, WA 98033
Phone: 206-679-6228

AMERICAN LEGION DEPARTMENT OF NORTH DAKOTA

http://www.ndlegion.org/

O. NESHEIM MEMORIAL SCHOLARSHIP

• *See page 90*

AMERICAN OIL CHEMISTS' SOCIETY

http://www.aocs.org/

AOCS ANALYTICAL DIVISION STUDENT AWARD
• *See page 165*

AOCS BIOTECHNOLOGY STUDENT EXCELLENCE AWARD
• *See page 90*

AOCS HEALTH AND NUTRITION DIVISION STUDENT EXCELLENCE AWARD

$500 award and certificate to recognize the outstanding merit and performance of a student in the health and nutrition field. Student will present a paper at the Annual Meeting of the Society.

Academic Fields/Career Goals: Food Science/Nutrition.

Award: Prize for use in senior or graduate years; not renewable. *Number:* 1–1. *Amount:* $500.

Eligibility Requirements: Applicant must be enrolled or expecting to enroll full-time at a four-year institution or university. Available to U.S. and non-U.S. citizens.

Application Requirements: Abstract, application form, essay, recommendations or references. *Deadline:* October 15.

Contact: Barbara Semeraro, Area Manager, Membership
American Oil Chemists' Society
AOCS
PO Box 17190
Urbana, IL 61803
Phone: 217-693-4804
Fax: 217-693-4849
E-mail: awards@aocs.org

AOCS PROCESSING DIVISION AWARDS
• *See page 166*

AMERICAN SOCIETY FOR ENOLOGY AND VITICULTURE

http://www.asev.org/

AMERICAN SOCIETY FOR ENOLOGY AND VITICULTURE SCHOLARSHIPS
• *See page 90*

ASSOCIATION FOR FOOD AND DRUG OFFICIALS

http://www.afdo.org/

ASSOCIATION FOR FOOD AND DRUG OFFICIALS SCHOLARSHIP FUND
• *See page 150*

CANFIT

http://www.canfit.org/

CANFIT NUTRITION, PHYSICAL EDUCATION AND CULINARY ARTS SCHOLARSHIP
• *See page 214*

CHILD NUTRITION FOUNDATION

http://www.schoolnutrition.org/

NANCY CURRY SCHOLARSHIP

Scholarship assists members of the American School Food Service Association and their dependents to pursue educational and career advancement in school food-service or child nutrition.

Academic Fields/Career Goals: Food Science/Nutrition; Food Service/Hospitality.

Award: Scholarship for use in freshman, sophomore, junior, senior, graduate, or postgraduate years; not renewable.

Eligibility Requirements: Applicant must be enrolled or expecting to enroll full- or part-time at a two-year or four-year or technical institution or university. Applicant or parent of applicant must have employment or volunteer experience in food service. Applicant must have 3.0 GPA or higher. Available to U.S. citizens.

Application Requirements: Application form, essay, proof of enrollment, recommendations or references, resume, test scores, transcript. *Deadline:* April 15.

Contact: Ruth O'Brien, Scholarship Manager
Child Nutrition Foundation
700 South Washington Street, Suite 300
Alexandria, VA 22314
Phone: 703-739-3900 Ext. 150
E-mail: robrien@asfsa.org

PROFESSIONAL GROWTH SCHOLARSHIP

Scholarships for child nutrition professionals who are pursuing graduate education in a food science management or nutrition-related field of study.

Academic Fields/Career Goals: Food Science/Nutrition; Food Service/Hospitality.

Award: Scholarship for use in freshman, sophomore, junior, senior, graduate, or postgraduate years; not renewable.

Eligibility Requirements: Applicant must be enrolled or expecting to enroll full- or part-time at a two-year or four-year or technical institution or university. Applicant or parent of applicant must have employment or volunteer experience in food service. Applicant must have 3.5 GPA or higher. Available to U.S. citizens.

Application Requirements: Application form, essay, proof of enrollment, official program requirement, recommendations or references, resume, transcript. *Deadline:* April 15.

SCHWAN'S FOOD SERVICE SCHOLARSHIP

Program is designed to assist members of the American School Food Service Association and their dependents as they pursue educational advancement in the field of child nutrition.

Academic Fields/Career Goals: Food Science/Nutrition; Food Service/Hospitality.

Award: Scholarship for use in freshman, sophomore, junior, senior, graduate, or postgraduate years; not renewable.

Eligibility Requirements: Applicant must be enrolled or expecting to enroll full- or part-time at a two-year or four-year or technical institution or university. Applicant or parent of applicant must have employment or volunteer experience in food service. Applicant must have 2.5 GPA or higher. Available to U.S. citizens.

Application Requirements: Application form, essay, proof of enrollment, official program requirements, recommendations or references, resume, transcript. *Deadline:* April 15.

Contact: Ruth O'Brien, Scholarship Manager
Child Nutrition Foundation
700 South Washington Street, Suite 300
Alexandria, VA 22314
Phone: 703-739-3900 Ext. 150
E-mail: robrien@asfsa.org

THE CULINARY TRUST

http://www.theculinarytrust.org/

CULINARY TRUST SCHOLARSHIP PROGRAM FOR CULINARY STUDY AND RESEARCH
• *See page 214*

DAIRY MANAGEMENT

http://www.dairyinfo.com/

NATIONAL DAIRY PROMOTION AND RESEARCH BOARD SCHOLARSHIP
• *See page 91*

ILLINOIS RESTAURANT ASSOCIATION EDUCATIONAL FOUNDATION

http://www.illinoisrestaurants.org/

ILLINOIS RESTAURANT ASSOCIATION EDUCATIONAL FOUNDATION SCHOLARSHIPS
• See page 215

INDIAN HEALTH SERVICES, UNITED STATES DEPARTMENT OF HEALTH AND HUMAN SERVICES

http://www.ihs.gov/scholarship

INDIAN HEALTH SERVICE HEALTH PROFESSIONS SCHOLARSHIP PROGRAM
• See page 208

INSTITUTE OF FOOD TECHNOLOGISTS

http://www.ift.org/

DR. C. ANN HOLLINGSWORTH STUDENT LEADERSHIP SCHOLARSHIP

One $1000 award to recognize student leaders that have demonstrated outstanding leadership at their university and the IFT Student Association, along with a passion for student advocacy, IFT, and the food science profession. Must be a college junior or senior and have a minimum 3.0 GPA.

Academic Fields/Career Goals: Food Science/Nutrition.

Award: Scholarship for use in junior or senior years; not renewable. *Number:* 1. *Amount:* $1000.

Eligibility Requirements: Applicant must be enrolled or expecting to enroll full-time at an institution or university and must have an interest in leadership. Applicant must have 3.0 GPA or higher. Available to U.S. and non-U.S. citizens.

Application Requirements: Application form, recommendations or references, resume, test scores, transcript. *Deadline:* April 2.

DR. JOHN J. & IRENE POWERS SCHOLARSHIP

One $1500 scholarship for an upper-division undergraduate student pursuing a curriculum in food science or food technology at an educational institution having an IFT approved degree program. Minimum 3.0 GPA required.

Academic Fields/Career Goals: Food Science/Nutrition.

Award: Scholarship for use in junior or senior years; not renewable. *Number:* 1. *Amount:* $1500.

Eligibility Requirements: Applicant must be enrolled or expecting to enroll full-time at an institution or university. Applicant must have 3.0 GPA or higher. Available to U.S. and non-U.S. citizens.

Application Requirements: Application form, recommendations or references, resume, test scores, transcript. *Deadline:* April 2.

FEEDING TOMORROW FRESHMAN SCHOLARSHIP

$1000 scholarship for high school seniors who demonstrate exceptional scholastic achievements, leadership experience, and a keen interest in the food science and technology profession. Must be pursuing an undergraduate degree in food science within an IFT-approved food science program. Minimum 3.0 GPA required.

Academic Fields/Career Goals: Food Science/Nutrition.

Award: Scholarship for use in freshman year; not renewable. *Amount:* $1000.

Eligibility Requirements: Applicant must be high school student and planning to enroll or expecting to enroll full-time at a four-year institution or university. Applicant must have 3.0 GPA or higher. Available to U.S. citizens.

Application Requirements: Application form, recommendations or references, test scores, transcript. *Deadline:* May 13.

FEEDING TOMORROW UNDERGRADUATE SCHOLARSHIPS

Multiple scholarships for college freshmen, sophomores, juniors, and seniors demonstrating exceptional scholastic achievements, leadership experience and a devotion to the food science and technology profession. Minimum 3.0 GPA required.

Academic Fields/Career Goals: Food Science/Nutrition.

Award: Scholarship for use in freshman, sophomore, junior, or senior years; not renewable. *Amount:* $1000–$2000.

Eligibility Requirements: Applicant must be enrolled or expecting to enroll full-time at a four-year institution or university. Applicant must have 3.0 GPA or higher. Available to U.S. and non-U.S. citizens.

Application Requirements: Application form, recommendations or references, resume, test scores, transcript. *Deadline:* April 2.

IFT FOOD ENGINEERING DIVISION SCHOLARSHIP

$1000 award available to an undergraduate student who will pursue a research project focusing on some aspect of food engineering. The research will occur during the academic year or summer. The student will work with a faculty member who is part of the Food Engineering Division. Minimum 3.0 GPA required. Must submit project outline and a 2-page research statement on the relevance, approach, and expected outcome of their research project.

Academic Fields/Career Goals: Food Science/Nutrition.

Award: Scholarship for use in junior or senior years; not renewable. *Number:* 1. *Amount:* $1000.

Eligibility Requirements: Applicant must be enrolled or expecting to enroll full-time at an institution or university. Applicant must have 3.0 GPA or higher. Available to U.S. and non-U.S. citizens.

Application Requirements: Application form, project outline, research statement, recommendations or references, resume, test scores, transcript. *Deadline:* April 2.

IFT FOOD MICROBIOLOGY DIVISION UNDERGRADUATE SCHOLARSHIP

$500 scholarship available to an undergraduate student studying food microbiology. Minimum 3.0 GPA required.

Academic Fields/Career Goals: Food Science/Nutrition.

Award: Scholarship for use in freshman, sophomore, junior, or senior years; not renewable. *Number:* 1. *Amount:* $500.

Eligibility Requirements: Applicant must be enrolled or expecting to enroll full-time at a four-year institution or university. Applicant must have 3.0 GPA or higher. Available to U.S. and non-U.S. citizens.

Application Requirements: Application form, recommendations or references, test scores, transcript. *Deadline:* April 2.

IFT PAST PRESIDENTS SCHOLARSHIP

$1000 scholarship for college juniors and seniors that honors past IFT presidents. Minimum 3.0 GPA required. Must be pursuing a curriculum in food science or food technology in an educational institution having an IFT approved degree program.

Academic Fields/Career Goals: Food Science/Nutrition.

Award: Scholarship for use in junior or senior years; not renewable. *Number:* 1. *Amount:* $1000.

Eligibility Requirements: Applicant must be enrolled or expecting to enroll full-time at an institution or university. Applicant must have 3.0 GPA or higher. Available to U.S. and non-U.S. citizens.

Application Requirements: Application form, recommendations or references, resume, test scores, transcript. *Deadline:* April 2.

INAUGURAL EDLONG DAIRY FLAVORS SCHOLARSHIP

One $3000 scholarship to a graduate student and one to a junior/senior undergraduate student. The student must be enrolled in a Masters or Ph.D food science program with a focus in dairy science and/or dairy flavors or pursuing an undergraduate degree in food science with a focus in dairy flavors at an IFT approved university.

Academic Fields/Career Goals: Food Science/Nutrition.

Award: Scholarship for use in junior, senior, or graduate years; not renewable. *Number:* 2. *Amount:* $3000.

Eligibility Requirements: Applicant must be enrolled or expecting to enroll full-time at an institution or university. Applicant must have 3.0 GPA or higher. Available to U.S. and non-U.S. citizens.

Application Requirements: Application form, recommendations or references, resume, test scores, transcript. *Deadline:* April 2.

INSTITUTE FOR THERMAL PROCESSING SPECIALISTS IRVING PFLUG SCHOLARSHIP

One $1500 scholarship for an upper-level undergraduate student studying food science, food engineering, or applied microbiology as it relates to food preservation. Minimum 3.0 GPA required. Must reapply each year.

Academic Fields/Career Goals: Food Science/Nutrition.

Award: Scholarship for use in junior or senior years; not renewable. *Number:* 1. *Amount:* $1500.

Eligibility Requirements: Applicant must be enrolled or expecting to enroll full-time at an institution or university. Applicant must have 3.0 GPA or higher. Available to U.S. and non-U.S. citizens.

Application Requirements: Application form, recommendations or references, resume, test scores, transcript. *Deadline:* April 2.

JULIE VANDE VELDE LEADERSHIP SCHOLARSHIP

One $1500 scholarship in memory of a former IFT Development Director. Must be an upper-division undergraduate student pursuing a curriculum in food science or food technology in an educational institution having an IFT approved degree program. Minimum 3.0 GPA required.

Academic Fields/Career Goals: Food Science/Nutrition.

Award: Scholarship for use in junior or senior years; not renewable. *Number:* 1. *Amount:* $1000.

Eligibility Requirements: Applicant must be enrolled or expecting to enroll full-time at an institution or university and must have an interest in leadership. Applicant must have 3.0 GPA or higher. Available to U.S. and non-U.S. citizens.

Application Requirements: Application form, recommendations or references, resume, test scores, transcript. *Deadline:* April 2.

MCCORMICK & COMPANY ENDOWMENT SCHOLARSHIP

One $2500 scholarship for an upper-division undergraduate student pursuing a curriculum in food science or food technology in an educational institution having an IFT approved degree program. Minimum 3.0 GPA required.

Academic Fields/Career Goals: Food Science/Nutrition.

Award: Scholarship for use in junior or senior years; not renewable. *Number:* 1. *Amount:* $2500.

Eligibility Requirements: Applicant must be enrolled or expecting to enroll full-time at an institution or university. Applicant must have 3.0 GPA or higher. Available to U.S. and non-U.S. citizens.

Application Requirements: Application form, recommendations or references, resume, test scores, transcript. *Deadline:* April 2.

INTERNATIONAL FOODSERVICE EDITORIAL COUNCIL

http://www.ifeconline.com/

INTERNATIONAL FOODSERVICE EDITORIAL COUNCIL COMMUNICATIONS SCHOLARSHIP
• See page 83

JAMES BEARD FOUNDATION INC.

http://www.jamesbeard.org/

BERN LAXER MEMORIAL SCHOLARSHIP
• See page 215

MAINE SCHOOL FOOD SERVICE ASSOCIATION (MSFSA) CONTINUING EDUCATION SCHOLARSHIP

http://www.mainesfsa.org/

MAINE SCHOOL FOOD SERVICE ASSOCIATION CONTINUING EDUCATION SCHOLARSHIP
• See page 218

MARION D. AND EVA S. PEEPLES FOUNDATION TRUST SCHOLARSHIP PROGRAM

http://www.jccf.org/

MARION A. AND EVA S. PEEPLES SCHOLARSHIPS
• See page 240

MARYLAND ASSOCIATION OF PRIVATE COLLEGES AND CAREER SCHOOLS

http://www.mapccs.org/

MARYLAND ASSOCIATION OF PRIVATE COLLEGES AND CAREER SCHOOLS SCHOLARSHIP
• See page 157

MINNESOTA SOYBEAN RESEARCH AND PROMOTION COUNCIL

http://www.mnsoybean.org/

MINNESOTA SOYBEAN RESEARCH AND PROMOTION COUNCIL YOUTH SOYBEAN SCHOLARSHIP
• See page 86

NATIONAL DAIRY SHRINE

http://www.dairyshrine.org/

NATIONAL DAIRY SHRINE/DAIRY MARKETING INC. MILK MARKETING SCHOLARSHIPS
• See page 93

NDS STUDENT RECOGNITION CONTEST
• See page 87

NATIONAL POTATO COUNCIL WOMEN'S AUXILIARY

http://www.nationalpotatocouncil.org/

POTATO INDUSTRY SCHOLARSHIP
• See page 87

NATIONAL POULTRY AND FOOD DISTRIBUTORS ASSOCIATION

http://www.npfda.org/

NATIONAL POULTRY AND FOOD DISTRIBUTORS ASSOCIATION SCHOLARSHIP FOUNDATION
• See page 87

OREGON STUDENT ASSISTANCE COMMISSION

http://www.GetCollegeFunds.org/

OREGON WINE BROTHERHOOD SCHOLARSHIP
• See page 218

UNITED DAUGHTERS OF THE CONFEDERACY

http://www.hqudc.org/

WALTER REED SMITH SCHOLARSHIP
• See page 160

UNITED NEGRO COLLEGE FUND

http://www.uncf.org/

SPRINT SCHOLARS PROGRAM FOR SOPHOMORES, JUNIORS, AND SENIORS
• *See page 100*

UNITED STATES DEPARTMENT OF AGRICULTURE

http://www.usda.gov/

USDA/1890 NATIONAL SCHOLARS PROGRAM
• *See page 96*

USDA/1994 TRIBAL SCHOLARS PROGRAM
• *See page 96*

WASHINGTON ASSOCIATION OF WINE GRAPE GROWERS

http://www.wawgg.org/

WALTER J. CLORE SCHOLARSHIP
• *See page 96*

WISCONSIN ASSOCIATION FOR FOOD PROTECTION

http://www.wafp-wi.org/

E.H. MARTH FOOD PROTECTION AND FOOD SCIENCES SCHOLARSHIP
• *See page 300*

FOOD SERVICE/ HOSPITALITY

AMERICAN CULINARY FEDERATION

http://www.acfchefs.org/

AMERICAN ACADEMY OF CHEFS COLLEGE SCHOLARSHIP
• *See page 212*

AMERICAN ACADEMY OF CHEFS HIGH SCHOOL SCHOLARSHIP
• *See page 212*

AMERICAN HOTEL AND LODGING EDUCATIONAL FOUNDATION

http://www.ahlef.org/

AMERICAN HOTEL & LODGING EDUCATIONAL FOUNDATION PEPSI SCHOLARSHIP
• *See page 212*

ANNUAL SCHOLARSHIP GRANT PROGRAM
• *See page 213*

ARTHUR J. PACKARD MEMORIAL SCHOLARSHIP
• *See page 213*

ECOLAB SCHOLARSHIP PROGRAM
• *See page 213*

HYATT HOTELS FUND FOR MINORITY LODGING MANAGEMENT
• *See page 213*

INCOMING FRESHMAN SCHOLARSHIPS
• *See page 213*

RAMA SCHOLARSHIP FOR THE AMERICAN DREAM
• *See page 213*

STEVEN HYMANS EXTENDED STAY SCHOLARSHIP
• *See page 214*

AMERICAN INSTITUTE OF WINE AND FOOD-PACIFIC NORTHWEST CHAPTER

http://www.aiwf.org/

CULINARY, VINIFERA, AND HOSPITALITY SCHOLARSHIP
• *See page 312*

CALIFORNIA RESTAURANT ASSOCIATION EDUCATIONAL FOUNDATION

http://www.calrest.org/

ACADEMIC SCHOLARSHIP FOR HIGH SCHOOL SENIORS

One-time scholarship awarded to high school seniors to support their education in the restaurant and/or food service industry. Applicants must be citizens of the United States or its territories (American Samoa, Guam, Puerto Rico, and U.S. Virgin Islands).

Academic Fields/Career Goals: Food Service/Hospitality.

Award: Scholarship for use in freshman year; not renewable. *Amount:* up to $2000.

Eligibility Requirements: Applicant must be high school student; planning to enroll or expecting to enroll full-time at a two-year or four-year or technical institution or university and resident of California. Applicant must have 2.5 GPA or higher. Available to U.S. and non-U.S. citizens.

Application Requirements: Application form, essay, interview, recommendations or references, resume, transcript. *Deadline:* April 15.

Contact: Mrs. Kathie Griley, Director, Industry Education
Phone: 800-765-4842 Ext. 2756
E-mail: kgriley@calrest.org

ACADEMIC SCHOLARSHIP FOR UNDERGRADUATE STUDENTS

Scholarships awarded to college students to support their education in the restaurant and food service industry. Minimum 2.75 GPA required. Individuals must be citizens of the United States or its territories (American Samoa, Guam, Puerto Rico, and U.S. Virgin Islands).

Academic Fields/Career Goals: Food Service/Hospitality.

Award: Scholarship for use in freshman, sophomore, junior, or senior years; not renewable.

Eligibility Requirements: Applicant must be enrolled or expecting to enroll full-time at a four-year institution or university and resident of California. Applicant must have 2.5 GPA or higher. Available to U.S. and non-U.S. citizens.

Application Requirements: Application form, essay, interview, recommendations or references, transcript. *Deadline:* March 31.

Contact: Mrs. Kathie Griley, Director, Industry Education
Phone: 800-765-4842 Ext. 2756
E-mail: kgriley@calrest.org

CANFIT

http://www.canfit.org/

CANFIT NUTRITION, PHYSICAL EDUCATION AND CULINARY ARTS SCHOLARSHIP
• *See page 214*

CHILD NUTRITION FOUNDATION

http://www.schoolnutrition.org/

NANCY CURRY SCHOLARSHIP
• See page 313

PROFESSIONAL GROWTH SCHOLARSHIP
• See page 313

SCHWAN'S FOOD SERVICE SCHOLARSHIP
• See page 313

COLORADO RESTAURANT ASSOCIATION

http://www.coloradorestaurant.com/

CRA UNDERGRADUATE SCHOLARSHIPS

Scholarship of $1000 to $2000 for applicants intending to pursue education in the undergraduate level in the field of food service or hospitality and have a GPA of at least 2.75.

Academic Fields/Career Goals: Food Service/Hospitality.

Award: Scholarship for use in freshman, sophomore, junior, or senior years; not renewable. *Number:* 15. *Amount:* $1000–$2000.

Eligibility Requirements: Applicant must be enrolled or expecting to enroll full- or part-time at a four-year institution or university. Available to U.S. and non-U.S. citizens.

Application Requirements: Application form, recommendations or references, resume, transcript. *Deadline:* April 6.

Contact: Mary Mino, President
Phone: 800-522-2972
Fax: 303-830-2973
E-mail: info@coloradorestaurant.com

PROSTART SCHOLARSHIPS

Scholarship of $500 to $1000 for applicants currently in high school and intending to pursue education in the field of food service or hospitality and have a GPA of at least 3.0.

Academic Fields/Career Goals: Food Service/Hospitality.

Award: Scholarship for use in freshman year; not renewable. *Number:* 15. *Amount:* $500–$1000.

Eligibility Requirements: Applicant must be high school student and planning to enroll or expecting to enroll full- or part-time at a four-year institution or university. Applicant must have 3.0 GPA or higher. Available to U.S. and non-U.S. citizens.

Application Requirements: Application form, recommendations or references, resume, transcript. *Deadline:* April 6.

Contact: Mary Mino, President
Phone: 800-522-2972
Fax: 303-830-2973
E-mail: info@coloradorestaurant.com

THE CULINARY TRUST

http://www.theculinarytrust.org/

CULINARY TRUST SCHOLARSHIP PROGRAM FOR CULINARY STUDY AND RESEARCH
• See page 214

GOLDEN GATE RESTAURANT ASSOCIATION

http://www.ggra.org/

GOLDEN GATE RESTAURANT ASSOCIATION SCHOLARSHIP FOUNDATION
• See page 214

ILLINOIS RESTAURANT ASSOCIATION EDUCATIONAL FOUNDATION

http://www.illinoisrestaurants.org/

ILLINOIS RESTAURANT ASSOCIATION EDUCATIONAL FOUNDATION SCHOLARSHIPS
• See page 215

INTERNATIONAL EXECUTIVE HOUSEKEEPERS ASSOCIATION

http://www.ieha.org/

INTERNATIONAL EXECUTIVE HOUSEKEEPERS EDUCATIONAL FOUNDATION

One-time award of up to $800 for students planning careers in the area of facilities management. Must be enrolled in IEHA-approved courses at a participating college or university. Must be a member of IEHA.

Academic Fields/Career Goals: Food Service/Hospitality; Home Economics; Trade/Technical Specialties.

Award: Scholarship for use in freshman, sophomore, junior, or senior years; not renewable. *Number:* 10. *Amount:* $800.

Eligibility Requirements: Applicant must be enrolled or expecting to enroll full- or part-time at a two-year or four-year or technical institution or university. Applicant or parent of applicant must be member of International Executive Housekeepers Association. Available to U.S. and non-U.S. citizens.

Application Requirements: Application form, essay, transcript. *Deadline:* January 10.

Contact: Beth Risinger, Chief Executive Officer and Executive Director
International Executive Housekeepers Association
Education Department, 1001 Eastwind Drive, Suite 301
Westerville, OH 43081-3361
Phone: 800-200-6342
Fax: 614-895-7166
E-mail: excel@ieha.org

INTERNATIONAL FOODSERVICE EDITORIAL COUNCIL

http://www.ifeconline.com/

INTERNATIONAL FOODSERVICE EDITORIAL COUNCIL COMMUNICATIONS SCHOLARSHIP
• See page 83

INTERNATIONAL FOOD SERVICE EXECUTIVES ASSOCIATION

http://www.ifsea.com/

WORTHY GOAL SCHOLARSHIP FUND

Scholarships to assist individuals in receiving food service management or vocational training beyond high school. Applicant must be enrolled or accepted as full-time student in a food service related major for the fall term following the award.

Academic Fields/Career Goals: Food Service/Hospitality.

Award: Scholarship for use in freshman, sophomore, junior, or senior years; not renewable. *Number:* 15. *Amount:* $1000–$1500.

Eligibility Requirements: Applicant must be enrolled or expecting to enroll full-time at a two-year or four-year or technical institution or university. Available to U.S. citizens.

Application Requirements: Essay, financial need analysis, financial statement summary, work experience documentation, recommendations or references, transcript. *Deadline:* March 1.

Contact: Steve Schroeder, IFSEA President
International Food Service Executives Association
500 Ryland Street Suite 200
Reno, NV 89502
Phone: 775-825-2665
Fax: 775-825-6411
E-mail: steve@IFSEA.com

KENTUCKY RESTAURANT ASSOCIATION EDUCATIONAL FOUNDATION

http://www.kyra.org/

KENTUCKY RESTAURANT ASSOCIATION EDUCATIONAL FOUNDATION SCHOLARSHIP

Scholarship available for high school graduate or equivalent accepted to an associate or bachelor's degree program in food service, or student already enrolled in an associate, bachelor's, or master's degree food service program. Applicant must be a resident of Kentucky or within 25 miles of Kentucky's borders for previous 18 months.

Academic Fields/Career Goals: Food Service/Hospitality.

Award: Scholarship for use in freshman, sophomore, junior, or senior years; renewable.

Eligibility Requirements: Applicant must be enrolled or expecting to enroll full-time at a four-year institution or university and resident of Kentucky. Available to U.S. citizens.

Application Requirements: Application form, proof of acceptance, recommendations or references, transcript. *Deadline:* varies.

MAINE SCHOOL FOOD SERVICE ASSOCIATION (MSFSA) CONTINUING EDUCATION SCHOLARSHIP

http://www.mainesfsa.org/

MAINE SCHOOL FOOD SERVICE ASSOCIATION CONTINUING EDUCATION SCHOLARSHIP

• *See page 218*

MISSOURI TRAVEL COUNCIL

http://www.missouritravel.com/

MISSOURI TRAVEL COUNCIL TOURISM SCHOLARSHIP

One-time award for Missouri resident pursuing hospitality-related major such as hotel/restaurant management or parks and recreation. Applicant must be currently enrolled in an accredited college or university in the state of Missouri. Selection is based on essay, GPA, community involvement, academic activities, and hospitality-related experience.

Academic Fields/Career Goals: Food Service/Hospitality; Hospitality Management; Travel/Tourism.

Award: Scholarship for use in sophomore, junior, or senior years; not renewable. *Number:* 2. *Amount:* $1000.

Eligibility Requirements: Applicant must be enrolled or expecting to enroll full-time at a four-year institution or university; resident of Missouri and studying in Missouri. Applicant must have 3.0 GPA or higher. Available to U.S. citizens.

Application Requirements: Application form, essay, recommendations or references, transcript. *Deadline:* March 1.

Contact: Pat Amick, Executive Director
Phone: 573-636-2814
Fax: 573-636-5783
E-mail: pamick@sockets.net

NATIONAL POULTRY AND FOOD DISTRIBUTORS ASSOCIATION

http://www.npfda.org/

NATIONAL POULTRY AND FOOD DISTRIBUTORS ASSOCIATION SCHOLARSHIP FOUNDATION

• *See page 87*

NATIONAL RESTAURANT ASSOCIATION EDUCATIONAL FOUNDATION

http://www.nraef.org/

COCA-COLA SALUTE TO EXCELLENCE SCHOLARSHIP AWARD

Scholarship for a student currently enrolled in college who has completed at least one semester in a restaurant and/or foodservice-related program.

Academic Fields/Career Goals: Food Service/Hospitality.

Award: Scholarship for use in sophomore, junior, senior, graduate, or postgraduate years; not renewable. *Number:* 2. *Amount:* $5000.

Eligibility Requirements: Applicant must be enrolled or expecting to enroll full-time at a two-year or four-year or technical institution or university. Applicant or parent of applicant must have employment or volunteer experience in food service. Available to U.S. citizens.

Application Requirements: Application form, essay, proof of total hours worked, transcript. *Deadline:* March 21.

Contact: Shanna Young, Manager
Phone: 800-765-2122 Ext. 744
Fax: 312-566-9733
E-mail: syoung@nraef.org

NATIONAL RESTAURANT ASSOCIATION EDUCATIONAL FOUNDATION UNDERGRADUATE SCHOLARSHIPS FOR COLLEGE STUDENTS

Awarded to college students who have demonstrated a commitment to both postsecondary hospitality education and to a career in the industry with 750 hours of industry work experience. Minimum 2.75 GPA required. Application deadlines: March 31, July 31 and October 31.

Academic Fields/Career Goals: Food Service/Hospitality; Hospitality Management.

Award: Scholarship for use in sophomore, junior, or senior years; not renewable. *Amount:* $2000.

Eligibility Requirements: Applicant must be enrolled or expecting to enroll full- or part-time at a four-year institution or university. Applicant or parent of applicant must have employment or volunteer experience in food service. Available to U.S. citizens.

Application Requirements: Application form, copies of paycheck stubs or a letter from employers verifying total work hours, essay, recommendations or references, resume, transcript. *Deadline:* varies.

Contact: Shanna Young, Manager
Phone: 800-765-2122 Ext. 744
Fax: 312-566-9733
E-mail: syoung@nraef.org

NATIONAL RESTAURANT ASSOCIATION EDUCATIONAL FOUNDATION UNDERGRADUATE SCHOLARSHIPS FOR HIGH SCHOOL SENIORS AND GENERAL EDUCATION DIPLOMA (GED) GRADUATE S

Scholarship awarded to high school students who have demonstrated a commitment to both postsecondary hospitality education and to a career in the industry. Must have 250 hours of industry experience, be between ages of 17 and 19, and have minimum 2.75 GPA.

Academic Fields/Career Goals: Food Service/Hospitality; Hospitality Management.

Award: Scholarship for use in freshman year; not renewable. *Amount:* $2000.

Eligibility Requirements: Applicant must be age 17-19 and enrolled or expecting to enroll full-time at a four-year institution or university. Applicant or parent of applicant must have employment or volunteer experience in food service. Available to U.S. citizens.

Application Requirements: Application form, essay, letter of acceptance, industrial experience letter, recommendations or references, transcript. *Deadline:* May 16.

Contact: Shanna Young, Manager
Phone: 800-765-2122 Ext. 744
Fax: 312-566-9733
E-mail: syoung@nraef.org

PROSTART® NATIONAL CERTIFICATE OF ACHIEVEMENT SCHOLARSHIP

For high school junior and senior students who have earned Pro Start National Certificate of Achievement and are continuing their education in a restaurant or foodservice program. For application and details visit website http://nraef.org.

Academic Fields/Career Goals: Food Service/Hospitality.

Award: Scholarship for use in freshman year; not renewable. *Amount:* $2000.

Eligibility Requirements: Applicant must be high school student and planning to enroll or expecting to enroll full- or part-time at a four-year institution or university. Available to U.S. citizens.

Application Requirements: Application form. *Deadline:* August 15.

Contact: Shanna Young, Manager
Phone: 800-765-2122 Ext. 744
Fax: 312-566-9733
E-mail: syoung@nraef.org

TOURISM CARES

http://www.tourismcares.org

NEW HORIZONS KATHY LETARTE SCHOLARSHIP

One $1000 scholarship awarded to an undergraduate student entering his or her junior year of study. Applicant must be enrolled in a tourism-related program at an accredited four-year college or university. Must have minimum 3.0 GPA. Applicant must be Michigan resident. Refer to website for further details http://www.ntfonline.com/scholarships/index.php.

Academic Fields/Career Goals: Food Service/Hospitality; Hospitality Management; Travel/Tourism.

Award: Scholarship for use in freshman, sophomore, junior, or senior years; not renewable. *Number:* 1. *Amount:* $1000.

Eligibility Requirements: Applicant must be enrolled or expecting to enroll full-time at a two-year or four-year institution or university and resident of Michigan. Applicant must have 3.0 GPA or higher. Available to U.S. citizens.

Application Requirements: Application form, essay, recommendations or references, resume, transcript. *Deadline:* May 10.

Contact: Amanda D'Aiuto, Student Programs Manager
Phone: 781-821-5990
Fax: 781-821-8949
E-mail: info@tourismcares.org

SOCIETIE DES CASINOS DU QUEBEC SCHOLARSHIP

Award for resident of Quebec who is pursuing travel and tourism studies. May attend a four-year college or university. Minimum 3.0 GPA required.

Academic Fields/Career Goals: Food Service/Hospitality; Hospitality Management; Travel/Tourism.

Award: Scholarship for use in freshman, sophomore, junior, or senior years; not renewable. *Number:* 1. *Amount:* $1000.

Eligibility Requirements: Applicant must be enrolled or expecting to enroll full-time at a two-year or four-year institution and resident of Quebec. Applicant must have 3.0 GPA or higher. Available to Canadian citizens.

Application Requirements: Application form, essay, recommendations or references, resume, transcript. *Deadline:* May 10.

Contact: Amanda D'Aiuto, Student Programs Manager
Phone: 781-821-5990
Fax: 781-821-8949
E-mail: info@tourismcares.org

WOMEN CHEFS AND RESTAURATEURS

http://www.womenchefs.org/

FRENCH CULINARY INSTITUTE/ITALIAN CULINARY EXPERIENCE SCHOLARSHIP

• *See page 218*

WOMEN GROCERS OF AMERICA

http://www.nationalgrocers.org/

MARY MACEY SCHOLARSHIP

• *See page 96*

FOREIGN LANGUAGE

ACL/NJCL NATIONAL LATIN EXAM

http://www.nle.org/

NATIONAL LATIN EXAM SCHOLARSHIP

• *See page 186*

ALBERTA HERITAGE SCHOLARSHIP FUND

http://www.alis.alberta.ca/

FELLOWSHIPS FOR FULL-TIME STUDIES IN FRENCH

Awards of between CAN$500 and CAN$1000 to assist Albertans in pursuing postsecondary studies taught in French. Must be Alberta resident, Canadian citizen, or landed immigrant, and plan to register full-time in a postsecondary program in Alberta of at least one semester in length. Must be enrolled in a minimum of three courses per semester which have French as the language of instruction. For additional information and application, see website http://alis.alberta.ca.

Academic Fields/Career Goals: Foreign Language.

Award: Scholarship for use in freshman, sophomore, junior, or senior years; not renewable.

Eligibility Requirements: Applicant must be Canadian citizen; enrolled or expecting to enroll full-time at a two-year or four-year or technical institution or university; resident of Alberta and must have an interest in French language.

Application Requirements: Application form, transcript. *Deadline:* November 15.

LANGUAGE BURSARY PROGRAM FOR TEACHING FNMI LANGUAGES

Award of CAN$2500 to assist Alberta teachers, Elders, or instructors who currently provide instruction of an FNMI language and intend to take a summer post-secondary program in an indigenous language teaching methodology. Applicants must hold a valid Alberta professional teaching certificate or be working towards Alberta certification, have been teaching in Alberta for a minimum of one year by the end of the current school year, demonstrate a background in FNMI language learning and culture, or have recently initiated the study of an FNMI language. For additional information, see website http://alis.alberta.ca.

Academic Fields/Career Goals: Foreign Language.

Award: Scholarship for use in freshman, sophomore, junior, senior, or graduate years; not renewable. *Number:* 2.

Eligibility Requirements: Applicant must be Canadian citizen; enrolled or expecting to enroll at a two-year or four-year institution or university and resident of Alberta. Applicant or parent of applicant must have employment or volunteer experience in teaching/education.

Application Requirements: Application form, recommendations or references. *Deadline:* February 10.

LANGUAGES IN TEACHER EDUCATION SCHOLARSHIPS

• *See page 231*

ALPHA MU GAMMA, THE NATIONAL COLLEGIATE FOREIGN LANGUAGE SOCIETY

http://www.lacitycollege.edu/

NATIONAL ALPHA MU GAMMA SCHOLARSHIPS

One-time award to student members of Alpha Mu Gamma with a minimum 3.5 GPA, who plan to continue study of a foreign language. Must participate in a national scholarship competition. Apply through local chapter advisers. Freshmen are not eligible. Must submit a copy of Alpha Mu Gamma membership certificate. Can study overseas if part of his/her school program.

Academic Fields/Career Goals: Foreign Language.

Award: Scholarship for use in sophomore, junior, senior, graduate, or postgraduate years; not renewable. *Number:* 3. *Amount:* up to $750.

Eligibility Requirements: Applicant must be enrolled or expecting to enroll full- or part-time at a two-year or four-year institution or university. Applicant or parent of applicant must be member of Alpha Mu Gamma. Applicant must have 3.5 GPA or higher. Available to U.S. and non-U.S. citizens.

Application Requirements: Application form, entry in a contest, essay, photocopy of Alpha Mud Gamma membership, recommendations or references, transcript. *Deadline:* February 1.

Contact: Hisham Malek, Scholarship Coordinator
 Phone: 323-644-9752
 Fax: 323-644-9752
 E-mail: amgnat@lacitycollege.edu

AMERICAN CLASSICAL LEAGUE/ NATIONAL JUNIOR CLASSICAL LEAGUE

http://www.aclclassics.org/

NATIONAL JUNIOR CLASSICAL LEAGUE SCHOLARSHIP
• *See page 187*

AMERICAN COUNCIL FOR POLISH CULTURE

http://www.polishcultureacpc.org/

ACPC SUMMER STUDIES IN POLAND SCHOLARSHIP
• *See page 113*

SKALNY SCHOLARSHIP FOR POLISH STUDIES
• *See page 113*

AMERICAN FOUNDATION FOR TRANSLATION AND INTERPRETATION

http://www.afti.org/

AFTI SCHOLARSHIPS IN SCIENTIFIC AND TECHNICAL TRANSLATION, LITERARY TRANSLATION, AND INTERPRETATION

Scholarships for full-time students enrolled or planning to enroll in a degree program in scientific and technical translation, literary translation, or interpreter training. Must have a 3.0 GPA.

Academic Fields/Career Goals: Foreign Language.

Award: Scholarship for use in sophomore, junior, or senior years; not renewable. *Number:* 1–3. *Amount:* $2500.

Eligibility Requirements: Applicant must be enrolled or expecting to enroll full-time at a four-year institution or university. Applicant must have 3.0 GPA or higher. Available to U.S. citizens.

Application Requirements: Application form, essay, proof of admission to T/I program, recommendations or references, transcript. *Deadline:* June 1.

Contact: Walter Bacak, Secretary
 American Foundation for Translation and Interpretation
 225 Reinekers Lane, Suite 590
 Alexandria, VA 22314
 Phone: 703-683-6100
 E-mail: walter@atanet.org

AMERICAN INSTITUTE OF POLISH CULTURE INC.

http://www.ampolinstitute.org/

HARRIET IRSAY SCHOLARSHIP GRANT
• *See page 117*

AMERICAN PHILOLOGICAL ASSOCIATION

http://www.apaclassics.org/

MINORITY STUDENT SUMMER SCHOLARSHIP
• *See page 108*

AMERICAN RESEARCH INSTITUTE IN TURKEY (ARIT)

http://ccat.sas.upenn.edu/ARIT/FellowshipPrograms.html

CRITICAL LANGUAGES SCHOLARSHIPS FOR INTENSIVE SUMMER INSTITUTE IN TURKISH LANGUAGE

Scholarships available for Intensive Summer Institute in Turkish Language. The program places students in intensive, eight-week summer courses in Turkish at all levels held at institutions in five locations in Turkey. See website for additional information and application http://www.caorc.org/centers/arit.htm.

Academic Fields/Career Goals: Foreign Language.

Award: Scholarship for use in freshman, sophomore, junior, or senior years; not renewable. *Number:* 50–60. *Amount:* $8000–$8500.

Eligibility Requirements: Applicant must be enrolled or expecting to enroll full-time at a four-year institution or university and must have an interest in Turkish language. Applicant must have 3.0 GPA or higher. Available to U.S. citizens.

Application Requirements: Application form, essay, language test, recommendations or references, test scores, transcript. *Deadline:* November 1.

ARMED FORCES COMMUNICATIONS AND ELECTRONICS ASSOCIATION, EDUCATIONAL FOUNDATION

http://www.afcea.org/scholarships

ARMED FORCES COMMUNICATIONS AND ELECTRONICS ASSOCIATION ROTC SCHOLARSHIP PROGRAM
• *See page 127*

ASSOCIATION OF FORMER INTELLIGENCE OFFICERS

http://www.afio.com/13_scholarships.htm

CIA UNDERGRADUATE SCHOLARSHIPS
• *See page 97*

CENTRAL INTELLIGENCE AGENCY

http://www.cia.gov/

CENTRAL INTELLIGENCE AGENCY UNDERGRADUATE SCHOLARSHIP PROGRAM
• *See page 70*

CULTURAL SERVICES OF THE FRENCH EMBASSY

http://www.frenchculture.org/

TEACHING ASSISTANT PROGRAM IN FRANCE
• *See page 97*

DONALD KEENE CENTER OF JAPANESE CULTURE

http://www.donaldkeenecenter.org/

JAPAN-U.S. FRIENDSHIP COMMISSION PRIZE FOR THE TRANSLATION OF JAPANESE LITERATURE

Annual prize for the best translation into English of a modern work of literature or for the best classical literary translation, or the prize is divided between a classical and a modern work. To qualify, works must be book-length translations of Japanese literary works: novels, collections of short stories, literary essays, memoirs, drama or poetry.

Academic Fields/Career Goals: Foreign Language.

Award: Prize for use in freshman, sophomore, junior, or senior years; not renewable. *Number:* 2. *Amount:* $3000.

Eligibility Requirements: Applicant must be enrolled or expecting to enroll full- or part-time at a two-year or four-year or technical institution or university. Available to U.S. citizens.

Application Requirements: Application form, entry in a contest, resume, unpublished manuscripts. *Deadline:* February 29.

Contact: Kia Cheleen, Assistant Director
Phone: 212-854-5036
E-mail: donald-keene-center@columbia.edu

GERMAN ACADEMIC EXCHANGE SERVICE (DAAD)

http://www.daad.org/

DAAD UNIVERSITY SUMMER COURSE GRANT

Scholarships are awarded to full-time degree students of Canadian or US colleges, sophomore/2nd year and higher, for the pursuit of summer courses at universities in Germany. It is open to applicants of any major but there is a prerequisite of at least two years of college level German or the equivalent German language fluency. Courses are three to four weeks in duration, take place at many locations in Germany (universities), are taught in German, and topics include German language, literature, current affairs, political science, history, culture, arts, film and media, economics, linguistics, law, translation and interpretation, and test prep for German language proficiency examinations. The scholarship is approximately €850 to cover course fees, and room and board in whole or in part, with an additional international travel reimbursement ranging from €300 to €450. Accommodations are arranged by the host institution.

Academic Fields/Career Goals: Foreign Language.

Award: Grant for use in sophomore, junior, senior, or graduate years; not renewable.

Eligibility Requirements: Applicant must be enrolled or expecting to enroll full-time at a four-year institution or university and must have an interest in German language/culture. Available to U.S. and non-U.S. citizens.

Application Requirements: Application form, application form may be submitted online (http://www.daad.org/?p=summercourse), essay, recommendations or references, resume, transcript. *Deadline:* December 15.

Contact: Jane Fu, Information Officer
Phone: 212-758-3223
E-mail: daadny@daad.org

KE ALI'I PAUAHI FOUNDATION

http://www.pauahi.org/

JOHNNY PINEAPPLE SCHOLARSHIP
• *See page 115*

SARAH KELI'ILOLENA LUM KONIA NAKOA SCHOLARSHIP

Award to recognize the academic achievements of students pursuing the study and perpetuation of the Hawaiian language, including Hawaiian culture and history. Must be a Hawaii resident, and demonstrate a financial need. Submit essay demonstrating applicant's achievements in studying Hawaiian Language, culture and history; propose a realistic plan to complete college level Hawaiian language studies; and plan to share this knowledge with others in the Hawaiian community.

Academic Fields/Career Goals: Foreign Language; History.

Award: Scholarship for use in freshman, sophomore, junior, senior, or graduate years; not renewable. *Number:* 1. *Amount:* $600.

Eligibility Requirements: Applicant must be enrolled or expecting to enroll full-time at a four-year institution or university; resident of Hawaii; studying in Hawaii and must have an interest in Hawaiian language/culture. Available to U.S. citizens.

Application Requirements: Application form, essay, financial need analysis, Student Aid Report (SAR), college acceptance letter, transcript. *Deadline:* April 1.

Contact: Mavis Shiraishi-Nagao, Scholarship Administrator
Phone: 808-534-3966
E-mail: scholarships@pauahi.org

KLINGON LANGUAGE INSTITUTE

http://www.kli.org/

KOR MEMORIAL SCHOLARSHIP

Scholarship for undergraduate or graduate student in a program leading to a degree in a field related to language studies. Must send application materials by mail.

Academic Fields/Career Goals: Foreign Language.

Award: Scholarship for use in freshman, sophomore, junior, senior, or graduate years; not renewable. *Number:* 1. *Amount:* $500.

Eligibility Requirements: Applicant must be enrolled or expecting to enroll full-time at a four-year institution or university and must have an interest in foreign language. Available to U.S. citizens.

Application Requirements: Application form, nominating letter from chair, head, or dean, a brief statement of goals, recommendations or references, resume. *Deadline:* June 1.

Contact: Dr. Lawrence Schoen, Director
Klingon Language Institute
PO Box 634
Flourtown, PA 19031
E-mail: lawrence@kli.org

KOSCIUSZKO FOUNDATION

http://www.thekf.org

YEAR ABROAD PROGRAM IN POLAND
• *See page 115*

MINNESOTA OFFICE OF HIGHER EDUCATION

http://www.getreadyforcollege.org/

MINNESOTA ACADEMIC EXCELLENCE SCHOLARSHIP
• *See page 120*

NATIONAL ASSOCIATION OF HISPANIC JOURNALISTS (NAHJ)

http://www.nahj.org/

MARIA ELENA SALINAS SCHOLARSHIP

One-time scholarship for high school seniors, college undergraduates, and first-year graduate students who are pursuing careers in Spanish-language broadcast (radio or TV) journalism. Students may major or plan to major in any subject, but must demonstrate a sincere desire to pursue a career in this field. Must submit essays and demo tapes (audio or video) in Spanish. Scholarship includes the opportunity to serve an internship with Univision Spanish-language television news network.

Academic Fields/Career Goals: Foreign Language; Journalism; TV/Radio Broadcasting.

Award: Scholarship for use in freshman, sophomore, junior, senior, or graduate years; not renewable. *Number:* 2. *Amount:* $5000.

Eligibility Requirements: Applicant must be enrolled or expecting to enroll full-time at a four-year institution or university and must have an interest in Spanish language. Available to U.S. citizens.

Application Requirements: Application form, driver's license, essay, financial need analysis, recommendations or references, resume, transcript. *Deadline:* March 31.

Contact: Virginia Galindo, Program Assistant
>   *Phone:* 202-662-7145
>   *E-mail:* vgalindo@nahj.org

NORWICH JUBILEE ESPERANTO FOUNDATION

http://www.esperanto-gb.org/

NOJEF TRAVEL GRANTS

Grants to help young Esperanto-speakers to use and improve their knowledge of the language, by traveling to congresses, and summer courses. Applicant must already speak Esperanto sufficiently well enough to take part in planned activity, and should be under 26 years old. For more information, refer to website http://www.esperanto-gb.org/nojef/nojef-en.htm.

Academic Fields/Career Goals: Foreign Language.

Award: Grant for use in freshman, sophomore, junior, senior, or graduate years; not renewable. *Number:* 1–20. *Amount:* $64–$1600.

Eligibility Requirements: Applicant must be enrolled or expecting to enroll full- or part-time at a two-year or four-year or technical institution or university and must have an interest in Spanish language. Available to U.S. and non-U.S. citizens.

Application Requirements: Application form, essay, recommendations or references. *Deadline:* continuous.

Contact: Dr. Kathleen Hall, Scholarship Committee
>   Norwich Jubilee Esperanto Foundation
>   37 Granville Court, Cheney Lane
>   Oxford OX3 0HS
>   GBR
>   *Phone:* 44-1865-245-509

SONS OF ITALY FOUNDATION

http://www.osia.org/

SONS OF ITALY NATIONAL LEADERSHIP GRANTS COMPETITION LANGUAGE SCHOLARSHIP

Scholarships for undergraduate students in their junior or senior year of study who are majoring in Italian language studies. Must be a U.S. citizen of Italian descent. For more details see website, http://www.osia.org.

Academic Fields/Career Goals: Foreign Language.

Award: Scholarship for use in junior or senior years; not renewable. *Number:* up to 1. *Amount:* $4000–$10,000.

Eligibility Requirements: Applicant must be of Italian heritage and enrolled or expecting to enroll full-time at a four-year institution or university. Available to U.S. citizens.

Application Requirements: Application form, community service, driver's license, essay, recommendations or references, resume, self-addressed stamped envelope with application, test scores, transcript. *Fee:* $30. *Deadline:* February 28.

Contact: Ms. Laura Kelly, Scholarship Coordinator
>   *Phone:* 202-547-2900
>   *E-mail:* scholarships@osia.org

STRAIGHTFORWARD MEDIA

http://www.straightforwardmedia.com/

STRAIGHTFORWARD MEDIA LIBERAL ARTS SCHOLARSHIP
• *See page 116*

FUNERAL SERVICES/ MORTUARY SCIENCE

ALABAMA FUNERAL DIRECTORS ASSOCIATION INC.

http://www.alabamafda.org/

ALABAMA FUNERAL DIRECTORS ASSOCIATION SCHOLARSHIP

Two $1000 scholarships available to Alabama residents. Applicant must have been accepted by an accredited mortuary science school and be sponsored by a member of the AFDA. Must maintain a minimum 2.5 GPA. Deadline: no later than 30 days prior to the AFDA mid winter meeting and annual convention.

Academic Fields/Career Goals: Funeral Services/Mortuary Science.

Award: Scholarship for use in freshman, sophomore, junior, or senior years; not renewable. *Number:* 2. *Amount:* $1000.

Eligibility Requirements: Applicant must be enrolled or expecting to enroll full- or part-time at a four-year institution or university and resident of Alabama. Applicant must have 2.5 GPA or higher. Available to U.S. citizens.

Application Requirements: Application form, essay, personal photograph, recommendations or references, transcript, two proofs of residency (such as voter registration, drivers license, or tax returns). *Deadline:* varies.

Contact: Denise Edmisten, Executive Director
>   Alabama Funeral Directors Association Inc.
>   7956 Vaughn Road, PO Box 380
>   Montgomery, AL 36116
>   *Phone:* 334-956-8000
>   *Fax:* 334-956-8001

AMERICAN BOARD OF FUNERAL SERVICE EDUCATION

http://www.abfse.org/

AMERICAN BOARD OF FUNERAL SERVICE EDUCATION SCHOLARSHIPS

One-time award for students who are enrolled in an accredited funeral science education program and have completed at least one term/semester. Deadlines: March 1 and September 1. For more details see website, http://www.abfse.org.

Academic Fields/Career Goals: Funeral Services/Mortuary Science.

Award: Scholarship for use in freshman, sophomore, junior, or senior years; not renewable. *Number:* 5–15. *Amount:* $500–$2500.

Eligibility Requirements: Applicant must be enrolled or expecting to enroll full-time at a two-year or four-year institution or university. Available to U.S. and non-U.S. citizens.

Application Requirements: Application form, essay, financial need analysis, recommendations or references, transcript. *Deadline:* varies.

Contact: Dr. Michael Smith, Executive Director
>   American Board of Funeral Service Education
>   3414 Ashland Avenue Suite G
>   St. Joseph, MO 64506
>   *Phone:* 816-233-3747
>   *Fax:* 816-233-3793
>   *E-mail:* exdir@abfse.org

INTERNATIONAL ORDER OF THE GOLDEN RULE

http://www.ogr.org/

INTERNATIONAL ORDER OF THE GOLDEN RULE AWARDS OF EXCELLENCE SCHOLARSHIP

One-time scholarship for mortuary science students to prepare for a career in funeral service. Must: be enrolled in a mortuary science degree program at an accredited mortuary school, have a minimum 3.0 GPA, commit to working at an independently owned funeral home, and be scheduled to graduate within this calendar year.

Academic Fields/Career Goals: Funeral Services/Mortuary Science.

Award: Scholarship for use in freshman, sophomore, junior, or senior years; not renewable. *Number:* 2. *Amount:* $2000–$3500.

Eligibility Requirements: Applicant must be enrolled or expecting to enroll full- or part-time at a two-year or four-year or technical institution or university. Applicant must have 3.0 GPA or higher. Available to U.S. and non-U.S. citizens.

Application Requirements: Application form, essay, transcript. *Deadline:* January 31.

Contact: Lisa Krabbenhoft, Director of Education
Phone: 800-637-8030
Fax: 512-334-5514
E-mail: lkrabbenhoft@ogr.org

MISSOURI FUNERAL DIRECTORS & EMBALMERS ASSOCIATION

http://www.mofuneral.org/

MISSOURI FUNERAL DIRECTORS ASSOCIATION SCHOLARSHIPS

Scholarship to Missouri residents pursuing a career in funeral services or mortuary science.

Academic Fields/Career Goals: Funeral Services/Mortuary Science.

Award: Scholarship for use in freshman, sophomore, junior, or senior years; not renewable. *Number:* up to 5. *Amount:* $300–$600.

Eligibility Requirements: Applicant must be enrolled or expecting to enroll full- or part-time at a technical institution and resident of Missouri. Available to U.S. citizens.

Application Requirements: Application form, recommendations or references, resume. *Deadline:* April 15.

Contact: Don Otto, Executive Director
Missouri Funeral Directors & Embalmers Association
1105 Southwest Boulevard, Suite A
Jefferson City, MO 65109
Phone: 573-635-1661
Fax: 573-635-9494
E-mail: info@mofuneral.org

NATIONAL FUNERAL DIRECTORS AND MORTICIANS ASSOCIATION

http://www.nfdma.com/

NATIONAL FUNERAL DIRECTORS AND MORTICIANS ASSOCIATION SCHOLARSHIP

Awards for high school graduates who have preferably worked in or had one year of apprenticeship in the funeral home business.

Academic Fields/Career Goals: Funeral Services/Mortuary Science.

Award: Scholarship for use in freshman year; not renewable. *Number:* 1. *Amount:* $1500.

Eligibility Requirements: Applicant must be high school student and planning to enroll or expecting to enroll full- or part-time at a four-year institution or university. Available to U.S. citizens.

Application Requirements: Application form, recommendations or references, resume, test scores. *Deadline:* April 15.

Contact: Eva Cranford, Scholarship Coordinator
Phone: 718-625-4656
E-mail: lladyc23@aol.com

GEOGRAPHY

ASSOCIATION OF AMERICAN GEOGRAPHERS

http://www.aag.org/

DARREL HESS COMMUNITY COLLEGE GEOGRAPHY SCHOLARSHIPS

Two $1000 scholarships will be awarded to students from community colleges, junior colleges, city colleges, or similar two-year educational institutions who will be transferring as geography majors to four year colleges and universities.

Academic Fields/Career Goals: Geography.

Award: Grant for use in junior year; not renewable. *Number:* 2–4. *Amount:* $1000.

Eligibility Requirements: Applicant must be enrolled or expecting to enroll at a two-year institution.

Application Requirements: Applications consist of a form, unofficial transcripts and two letters of reference to be submitted online.

Contact: Dr. Patricia Solis, Director of Outreach and Strategic Initiatives
Association of American Geographers
1710 16th Street, NW
Washington, DC 20009
Phone: 202-234-1450
E-mail: grantsawards@aag.org

BRITISH COLUMBIA INNOVATION COUNCIL

http://www.bcic.ca/

PAUL AND HELEN TRUSSELL SCIENCE AND TECHNOLOGY SCHOLARSHIP
• *See page 104*

CENTRAL INTELLIGENCE AGENCY

http://www.cia.gov/

CENTRAL INTELLIGENCE AGENCY UNDERGRADUATE SCHOLARSHIP PROGRAM
• *See page 70*

GAMMA THETA UPSILON-INTERNATIONAL GEOGRAPHIC HONOR SOCIETY

http://www.gtuhonors.org/

BUZZARD-MAXFIELD-RICHASON AND RECHLIN SCHOLARSHIP

Award is granted to a student who is a Gamma Theta Upsilon member, majoring in geography, will be a senior undergraduate and who has been accepted into a graduate program in geography.

Academic Fields/Career Goals: Geography.

Award: Scholarship for use in senior or graduate years; not renewable. *Number:* 5. *Amount:* $1000.

Eligibility Requirements: Applicant must be enrolled or expecting to enroll full-time at a four-year institution or university. Applicant or parent of applicant must be member of Gamma Theta Upsilon. Applicant must have 3.0 GPA or higher. Available to U.S. and non-U.S. citizens.

Application Requirements: Application form, recommendations or references, transcript. *Deadline:* May 31.

Contact: Dr. Donald Zeigler, Scholarship Committee
Gamma Theta Upsilon-International Geographic Honor Society
Old Dominion University, 1881 University Drive
Virginia Beach, VA 23453
E-mail: dzeigler@odu.edu

HARVARD TRAVELLERS CLUB

http://www.harvardtravellersclub.org/

HARVARD TRAVELLERS CLUB GRANTS
• *See page 108*

NASA IDAHO SPACE GRANT CONSORTIUM

http://www.id.spacegrant.org/

NASA IDAHO SPACE GRANT CONSORTIUM SCHOLARSHIP PROGRAM
• *See page 146*

UNITED NEGRO COLLEGE FUND

http://www.uncf.org/

CDM SCHOLARSHIP/INTERNSHIP
• *See page 176*

GRAPHICS/GRAPHIC ARTS/ PRINTING

BRITISH COLUMBIA INNOVATION COUNCIL

http://www.bcic.ca/

BCIC YOUNG INNOVATOR SCHOLARSHIP COMPETITION (IDEA MASH UP)
• *See page 104*

CENTRAL INTELLIGENCE AGENCY

http://www.cia.gov/

CENTRAL INTELLIGENCE AGENCY UNDERGRADUATE SCHOLARSHIP PROGRAM
• *See page 70*

ELECTRONIC DOCUMENT SYSTEMS FOUNDATION

http://www.edsf.org/

EDSF BOARD OF DIRECTORS SCHOLARSHIPS
• *See page 153*

HOODS MEMORIAL SCHOLARSHIP
• *See page 153*

LYNDA BABOYIAN MEMORIAL SCHOLARSHIP
• *See page 153*

GOLDEN KEY INTERNATIONAL HONOUR SOCIETY

http://www.goldenkey.org/

VISUAL AND PERFORMING ARTS ACHIEVEMENT AWARDS
• *See page 119*

GRAVURE EDUCATION FOUNDATION

http://www.gaa.org/

GEF RESOURCE CENTER SCHOLARSHIPS

Scholarships are awarded annually to students enrolled full-time at one of the designated GEF gravure printing resource centers: Arizona State University, California Polytechnic State University, Clemson University, Murray State University, Rochester Institute of Technology, University of Wisconsin-Stout, and Western Michigan University.

Academic Fields/Career Goals: Graphics/Graphic Arts/Printing.

Award: Scholarship for use in sophomore, junior, senior, or graduate years; not renewable.

Eligibility Requirements: Applicant must be enrolled or expecting to enroll full-time at a four-year institution or university. Applicant must have 3.0 GPA or higher. Available to U.S. citizens.

Application Requirements: Application form. *Deadline:* May 31.

Contact: Bernadette Carlson, Director of Development
    Phone: 201-523-6042
    E-mail: bcarlson@gaa.org

GRAVURE CATALOG AND INSERT COUNCIL SCHOLARSHIP

Scholarship of up to $1000 for a student enrolled full-time at a college or university designated by GEF as a gravure printing resource center. Must be at least a junior and have a minimum GPA of 3.0.

Academic Fields/Career Goals: Graphics/Graphic Arts/Printing.

Award: Scholarship for use in junior or senior years; not renewable. *Number:* 1. *Amount:* up to $1000.

Eligibility Requirements: Applicant must be enrolled or expecting to enroll full-time at a four-year institution or university. Applicant must have 3.0 GPA or higher. Available to U.S. and non-U.S. citizens.

Application Requirements: Application form, essay, transcript. *Deadline:* May 31.

Contact: Bernadette Carlson, Director of Development
    Phone: 201-523-6042
    E-mail: bcarlson@gaa.org

GRAVURE EDUCATION FOUNDATION CORPORATE LEADERSHIP SCHOLARSHIPS

Scholarships for full-time sophomore, junior, senior, or graduate students enrolled at any of the GEF-funded colleges or universities. Must demonstrate a declared major in printing, graphic arts, or graphic communications. Minimum 3.0 GPA required.

Academic Fields/Career Goals: Graphics/Graphic Arts/Printing.

Award: Scholarship for use in sophomore, junior, senior, or graduate years; not renewable. *Number:* 3–6. *Amount:* $1000–$1500.

Eligibility Requirements: Applicant must be enrolled or expecting to enroll full-time at a four-year institution or university. Applicant must have 3.0 GPA or higher. Available to U.S. and non-U.S. citizens.

Application Requirements: Application form, essay, transcript. *Deadline:* April 20.

Contact: Bernadette Carlson, Director of Development
    Gravure Education Foundation
    GEF, PO Box 14625
    Rochester, NY 14625
    Phone: 201-523-6042
    E-mail: bcarlson@gaa.org

WERNER B. THIELE MEMORIAL SCHOLARSHIP

Two scholarships of up to $1250 each are awarded to students enrolled full-time at a college or university designated by GEF as a gravure printing resource center: Arizona State University, California Polytechnic State University, Clemson University, Murray State University, Rochester Institute of Technology, University of Wisconsin-Stout, and Western Michigan University. Minimum GPA of 3.0 required.

Academic Fields/Career Goals: Graphics/Graphic Arts/Printing.

Award: Scholarship for use in junior or senior years; not renewable. *Number:* up to 2. *Amount:* up to $1250.

Eligibility Requirements: Applicant must be enrolled or expecting to enroll full-time at a four-year institution or university. Applicant must have 3.0 GPA or higher. Available to U.S. citizens.

Application Requirements: Application form, essay, transcript. *Deadline:* May 31.

Contact: Bernadette Carlson, Director of Development
Phone: 201-523-6042
E-mail: bcarlson@gaa.org

GREAT LAKES COMMISSION

http://www.glc.org/

CAROL A. RATZA MEMORIAL SCHOLARSHIP
• *See page 190*

INTERNATIONAL FOODSERVICE EDITORIAL COUNCIL

http://www.ifeconline.com/

INTERNATIONAL FOODSERVICE EDITORIAL COUNCIL COMMUNICATIONS SCHOLARSHIP
• *See page 83*

MAINE GRAPHICS ARTS ASSOCIATION

http://www.megaa.org/

MAINE GRAPHICS ART ASSOCIATION

One-time award for Maine high school students majoring in graphic arts at any university. Must submit transcript and references with application.

Academic Fields/Career Goals: Graphics/Graphic Arts/Printing.

Award: Scholarship for use in freshman year; not renewable. *Number:* up to 20. *Amount:* $100–$500.

Eligibility Requirements: Applicant must be high school student; planning to enroll or expecting to enroll full- or part-time at a four-year institution or university and resident of Maine. Available to U.S. citizens.

Application Requirements: Application form, recommendations or references, transcript. *Deadline:* May 15.

Contact: Angie Dougherty, Director
Maine Graphics Arts Association
PO Box 874
Auburn, ME 04212-0874
Phone: 207-883-9525
Fax: 207-883-3158
E-mail: edpougher@maine.rr.com

NATIONAL ASSOCIATION OF HISPANIC JOURNALISTS (NAHJ)

http://www.nahj.org/

NEWHOUSE SCHOLARSHIP PROGRAM

Two-year $5000 annually award for students who are pursuing careers in the newspaper industry as reporters, editors, graphic artists, or photojournalists. Recipient is expected to participate in summer internship at a Newhouse newspaper following their junior year. Students must submit resume and writing samples.

Academic Fields/Career Goals: Graphics/Graphic Arts/Printing; Journalism; Photojournalism/Photography.

Award: Scholarship for use in junior or senior years; not renewable. *Amount:* $5000.

Eligibility Requirements: Applicant must be enrolled or expecting to enroll full-time at a four-year institution or university. Available to U.S. citizens.

Application Requirements: Application form, essay, financial need analysis, recommendations or references, resume, transcript, work samples. *Deadline:* March 31.

Contact: Virginia Galindo, Program Assistant
Phone: 202-662-7145
E-mail: vgalindo@nahj.org

NEW ENGLAND PRINTING AND PUBLISHING COUNCIL

http://www.ppcne.org/

NEW ENGLAND GRAPHIC ARTS SCHOLARSHIP

Applicants must be residents of New England who have admission to an accredited two-year vocational or technical college or a four-year college or university that offers a degree program related to printing or graphic arts. Renewable for up to four years if student maintains 2.5 GPA.

Academic Fields/Career Goals: Graphics/Graphic Arts/Printing.

Award: Scholarship for use in freshman, sophomore, junior, or senior years; renewable. *Amount:* up to $2500.

Eligibility Requirements: Applicant must be enrolled or expecting to enroll full-time at a two-year or four-year or technical institution or university and resident of Connecticut, Maine, Massachusetts, New Hampshire, Rhode Island, Vermont. Applicant must have 2.5 GPA or higher. Available to U.S. citizens.

Application Requirements: Application form, financial need analysis, test scores, transcript. *Deadline:* May 15.

Contact: Jay Smith, Scholarship Chair
New England Printing and Publishing Council
166 New Boston Street
Woburn, MA 01801
Phone: 781-944-1116
Fax: 781-944-3905
E-mail: jay@mhcp.com

OREGON STUDENT ASSISTANCE COMMISSION

http://www.GetCollegeFunds.org/

HB DESIGN SCHOLARSHIP

Award for college junior or above studying graphic design or interactive/web design at any U.S. college or university. Minimum 3.0 GPA required. Semifinalists will be required to e-mail a design sample along with a 200-word description about the concept. Apply/compete annually.

Academic Fields/Career Goals: Graphics/Graphic Arts/Printing.

Award: Scholarship for use in junior, senior, or graduate years; not renewable.

Eligibility Requirements: Applicant must be enrolled or expecting to enroll full-time at a four-year institution or university. Applicant must have 3.0 GPA or higher. Available to U.S. citizens.

Application Requirements: Application form, FAFSA. *Deadline:* March 1.

KERDRAGON SCHOLARSHIP
• *See page 121*

KIRCHHOFF FAMILY FINE ARTS SCHOLARSHIP
• *See page 121*

PRINT AND GRAPHIC SCHOLARSHIP FOUNDATION

http://www.printing.org/

PRINT AND GRAPHICS SCHOLARSHIPS FOUNDATION
• *See page 193*

PRINTING INDUSTRY OF MIDWEST EDUCATION FOUNDATION

http://www.pimn.org/

PRINTING INDUSTRY MIDWEST EDUCATION FOUNDATION SCHOLARSHIP FUND
• *See page 194*

RHODE ISLAND FOUNDATION

http://www.rifoundation.org/

J. D. EDSAL SCHOLARSHIP
• *See page 84*

ROBERT H. MOLLOHAN FAMILY CHARITABLE FOUNDATION, INC.

http://www.mollohanfoundation.org/

MARY OLIVE EDDY JONES ART SCHOLARSHIP
• *See page 116*

SAN FRANCISCO FOUNDATION

http://www.sff.org/

PHELAN AWARD IN PRINTMAKING
Award presented in every odd-numbered year to recognize achievement in printmaking for students. Must have been born in California, but need not be a current resident. Applicants must provide a copy of their birth certificate with their application. This award is not a scholarship.
Academic Fields/Career Goals: Graphics/Graphic Arts/Printing.
Award: Prize for use in freshman, sophomore, junior, senior, graduate, or postgraduate years; not renewable. *Number:* 2. *Amount:* up to $4000.
Eligibility Requirements: Applicant must be enrolled or expecting to enroll full- or part-time at a two-year or four-year institution or university. Available to U.S. citizens.
Application Requirements: Application form, entry in a contest, self-addressed stamped envelope with application. *Deadline:* May 4.

SOUTH DAKOTA RETAILERS ASSOCIATION

http://www.sdra.org/

SOUTH DAKOTA RETAILERS ASSOCIATION SCHOLARSHIP PROGRAM
• *See page 80*

TAG AND LABEL MANUFACTURERS INSTITUTE, INC.

http://www.tlmi.com/

TLMI 4 YEAR COLLEGE DEGREE SCHOLARSHIP PROGRAM
• *See page 270*

TECHNICAL ASSOCIATION OF THE PULP & PAPER INDUSTRY (TAPPI)

http://www.tappi.org/

COATING AND GRAPHIC ARTS DIVISION SCHOLARSHIP
Scholarship to encourage talented science and engineering students to pursue careers in the paper industry and to utilize their capabilities in advancing the science and technology of coated paper and paperboard manufacturing and the graphic arts industry. The division may award up to four $1000 awards annually. Information can be found at http://www.tappi.org/s_tappi/sec.asp?CID=6101&DID=546695.
Academic Fields/Career Goals: Graphics/Graphic Arts/Printing; Paper and Pulp Engineering.
Award: Scholarship for use in freshman, sophomore, junior, or senior years; not renewable. *Number:* 1–4. *Amount:* $1000.
Eligibility Requirements: Applicant must be enrolled or expecting to enroll full-time at a four-year institution or university. Applicant must have 3.0 GPA or higher. Available to U.S. and non-U.S. citizens.

Application Requirements: Application form, recommendations or references, transcript. *Deadline:* February 15.
Contact: Mr. Charles Bohanan, Director of Standards and Awards
Technical Association of the Pulp & Paper Industry (TAPPI)
15 Technology Parkway South
Peachtree Corners, GA 30092
Phone: 770-209-7276
Fax: 770-446-6947
E-mail: standards@tappi.org

WORLDSTUDIO FOUNDATION

http://www.aiga.org/

WORLDSTUDIO AIGA SCHOLARSHIPS
• *See page 124*

HEALTH ADMINISTRATION

ALBERTA HERITAGE SCHOLARSHIP FUND

http://www.alis.alberta.ca/

ABORIGINAL HEALTH CAREERS BURSARY
• *See page 142*

AMERICAN INDIAN SCIENCE AND ENGINEERING SOCIETY

http://www.aises.org/

BURLINGTON NORTHERN SANTA FE FOUNDATION SCHOLARSHIP
• *See page 102*

BETHESDA LUTHERAN COMMUNITIES

http://www.bethesdalutherancommunities.org/scholarships

DEVELOPMENTAL DISABILITIES SCHOLASTIC ACHIEVEMENT SCHOLARSHIP FOR COLLEGE STUDENTS WHO ARE LUTHERAN
• *See page 222*

CANADIAN SOCIETY FOR MEDICAL LABORATORY SCIENCE

http://www.csmls.org/

E.V. BOOTH SCHOLARSHIP AWARD
The fund was established to assist CSMLS members in fulfilling their vision of achieving university level education in the medical laboratory sciences. One-time award of CAN$500. Must be a Canadian citizen.
Academic Fields/Career Goals: Health Administration; Health and Medical Sciences; Health Information Management/Technology.
Award: Scholarship for use in freshman, sophomore, junior, or senior years; not renewable. *Number:* 2.
Eligibility Requirements: Applicant must be Canadian citizen and enrolled or expecting to enroll full- or part-time at a four-year institution or university. Applicant or parent of applicant must be member of Canadian Society for Medical Laboratory Science.
Application Requirements: Application form, community service, financial need analysis, self-addressed stamped envelope with application, transcript. *Deadline:* April 1.

Contact: Norah Langham, Marketing Assistant
Canadian Society for Medical Laboratory Science
33 Wellington Street North
Hamilton, ON L8R 1M7
CAN
Phone: 905-528-8642 Ext. 8688
Fax: 905-528-4968
E-mail: norahl@csmls.org

CONGRESSIONAL BLACK CAUCUS FOUNDATION, INC.

http://www.cbcfinc.org/

CBCF GENERAL MILLS HEALTH SCHOLARSHIP
• See page 144

GREATER KANAWHA VALLEY FOUNDATION

http://www.tgkvf.org/

WILLARD H. ERWIN JR. MEMORIAL SCHOLARSHIP FUND
• See page 155

HEALTHCARE INFORMATION AND MANAGEMENT SYSTEMS SOCIETY FOUNDATION

http://www.himss.org/

HIMSS FOUNDATION SCHOLARSHIP PROGRAM
The Foundation Scholarships can be awarded to undergraduate, Masters or PhD students enrolled in a program related to the healthcare information and management systems field. In addition to the $5000 scholarship award, the winner also receives an all-expense paid trip to the Annual HIMSS Conference and Exhibition. Applicants must be member in good standing of HIMS. Primary occupation must be that of student in an accredited program related to the healthcare information or management systems field. The specific degree program is not a critical factor, although it is expected that programs similar to those in industrial engineering, operations research, healthcare informatics, computer science and information systems, mathematics, and quantitative programs in business administration and hospital administration will predominate. Undergraduate applicants must be at least a first-term junior when the scholarship is awarded. Previous Foundation Scholarship winners are ineligible.

Academic Fields/Career Goals: Health Administration; Health and Medical Sciences; Health Information Management/Technology; Science, Technology, and Society.

Award: Scholarship for use in junior, senior, graduate, or postgraduate years; not renewable. *Number:* 4–12. *Amount:* $5000.

Eligibility Requirements: Applicant must be enrolled or expecting to enroll full-time at a four-year institution or university. Applicant or parent of applicant must be member of Healthcare Information and Management Systems Society. Available to U.S. and non-U.S. citizens.

Application Requirements: Application form, community service, essay, recommendations or references, resume, transcript. *Deadline:* October 15.

Contact: Helen Figge, Senior Director, Professional Development, Career Services
Healthcare Information and Management Systems Society Foundation
33 West Monroe Street, Suite 1700
Chicago, IL 60603
Phone: 312-915-9548
E-mail: hfigge@himss.org

HEALTH RESEARCH COUNCIL OF NEW ZEALAND

http://www.hrc.govt.nz/

PACIFIC HEALTH WORKFORCE AWARD
Intended to support students studying towards a health or health-related qualification. The eligible courses of study are: health, health administration, or a recognized qualification aligned with the Pacific Island. Priority given to management training, medical, and nursing students. Applicants should be New Zealand citizens or hold residency in New Zealand at the time of application and be of Pacific Island descent. The value of the awards and dollar value will vary and for one year of study.

Academic Fields/Career Goals: Health Administration; Health and Medical Sciences; Health Information Management/Technology; Nursing.

Award: Scholarship for use in freshman, sophomore, junior, senior, graduate, or postgraduate years; not renewable.

Eligibility Requirements: Applicant must be New Zealander citizen; Asian/Pacific Islander and enrolled or expecting to enroll full-time at a two-year or four-year institution or university. Available to citizens of countries other than the U.S. or Canada.

Application Requirements: Application form, driver's license, essay, financial need analysis, recommendations or references, transcript. *Deadline:* October 10.

Contact: Ngamau Tou, Manager, Pacific Health Research
Phone: 64 9 3035255
Fax: 64 9 377 9988
E-mail: nwichmantou@hrc.govt.nz

PACIFIC MENTAL HEALTH WORK FORCE AWARD
Intended to provide one year of support for students studying towards a mental health or mental health-related qualification. Eligible courses of study include: nursing, psychology, health, health administration or a recognized qualification aligned with the Pacific Island mental health priority areas. Applicants should be New Zealand citizens or hold residency in New Zealand at the time of application and be of Pacific Island descent.

Academic Fields/Career Goals: Health Administration; Health and Medical Sciences; Health Information Management/Technology; Nursing; Psychology.

Award: Scholarship for use in freshman, sophomore, junior, senior, graduate, or postgraduate years; not renewable.

Eligibility Requirements: Applicant must be New Zealander citizen; Asian/Pacific Islander and enrolled or expecting to enroll full-time at a two-year or four-year institution or university. Available to citizens of countries other than the U.S. or Canada.

Application Requirements: Application form, essay, financial need analysis, recommendations or references, resume, transcript. *Deadline:* October 10.

Contact: Ngamau Tou, Manager, Pacific Health Research
Phone: 64 9 3035255
Fax: 64 9 377 9988
E-mail: nwichmantou@hrc.govt.nz

NATIONAL SOCIETY OF THE COLONIAL DAMES OF AMERICA

http://www.nscda.org/

AMERICAN INDIAN NURSE SCHOLARSHIP AWARDS
Renewable award of $500 to $1000. Currently able to fund between 10 and 15 students. Intended originally to benefit females only, the program has expanded to include males and the career goals now include not only nursing careers, but jobs in health care and health education, as well.

Academic Fields/Career Goals: Health Administration; Nursing.

Award: Scholarship for use in freshman, sophomore, junior, senior, graduate, or postgraduate years; renewable. *Number:* 10–15. *Amount:* $500–$1000.

Eligibility Requirements: Applicant must be American Indian/Alaska Native and enrolled or expecting to enroll full-time at a two-year or four-year or technical institution or university. Applicant must have 2.5 GPA or higher. Available to U.S. citizens.

Application Requirements: Application form, driver's license, financial need analysis, personal photograph, recommendations or references, transcript. *Deadline:* continuous.

Contact: Mrs. Joe Calvin, Scholarship Awards Consultant
National Society of The Colonial Dames of America
Nine Cross Creek Drive
Birmingham, AL 35213
Phone: 205-871-4072
E-mail: info@nscda.org

NEW ENGLAND EMPLOYEE BENEFITS COUNCIL

http://www.neebc.org/

NEW ENGLAND EMPLOYEE BENEFITS COUNCIL SCHOLARSHIP PROGRAM

• *See page 77*

STRAIGHTFORWARD MEDIA

http://www.straightforwardmedia.com/

STRAIGHTFORWARD MEDIA MEDICAL PROFESSIONS SCHOLARSHIP

• *See page 224*

HEALTH AND MEDICAL SCIENCES

101ST AIRBORNE DIVISION ASSOCIATION

http://www.screamingeagle.org/

AL & WILLIAMARY VISTE SCHOLARSHIP

Scholarship to provide financial assistance to students who have the potential to become assets to our nation. The major factors to be considered in the evaluation and rating of applicants are eligibility, career objectives, academic record, and insight gained from the letter requesting consideration and letters of recommendation. Preference will be given, but is not limited, to obtaining a degree in one of the physical sciences, medical, or scientific research fields. Must be an upperclassman and have a minimum 3.75 GPA. Applicant's parents, grandparent, husband or wife is (or if deceased was) a regular or life (not Associate) member of the 101st Airborne Division Association.

Academic Fields/Career Goals: Health and Medical Sciences; Physical Sciences.

Award: Scholarship for use in junior, senior, or graduate years; not renewable.

Eligibility Requirements: Applicant must be enrolled or expecting to enroll full-time at a four-year institution or university. Available to U.S. citizens.

Application Requirements: Application form, essay, personal photograph, proof of membership, recommendations or references, transcript. *Deadline:* May 10.

Contact: Mr. Sam Bass, Executive Secretary-Treasurer
Phone: 931-431-0199 Ext. 35
E-mail: 101exec@comcast.net

ALBERTA HERITAGE SCHOLARSHIP FUND

http://www.alis.alberta.ca/

ABORIGINAL HEALTH CAREERS BURSARY

• *See page 142*

JASON LANG SCHOLARSHIP

• *See page 218*

NORTHERN ALBERTA DEVELOPMENT COUNCIL BURSARY

• *See page 219*

ALPENA REGIONAL MEDICAL CENTER

http://www.alpenaregionalmedicalcenter.org/

THELMA ORR MEMORIAL SCHOLARSHIP

Two $1500 scholarships for students pursuing a course of study related to human medicine at any state accredited Michigan college or university.

Academic Fields/Career Goals: Health and Medical Sciences.

Award: Scholarship for use in freshman, sophomore, junior, or senior years; not renewable. *Number:* 2. *Amount:* $1500.

Eligibility Requirements: Applicant must be enrolled or expecting to enroll full-time at a four-year institution or university; resident of Michigan and studying in Michigan. Available to U.S. citizens.

Application Requirements: Application form. *Deadline:* April 15.

Contact: Marlene Pear, Director, Voluntary Services
Phone: 989-356-7351
E-mail: info@agh.org

ALPHA OMEGA ALPHA

http://www.alphaomegaalpha.org/

HELEN H. GLASER STUDENT ESSAY AWARDS

Award of $2000 first, $750 second, $500 third, and honorable mention awards of $250 each. Authors must be enrolled at medical schools with active Alpha Omega Alpha chapters. The essay may be on any nontechnical subject related to medicine, including ethics, history, education, philosophy, and policy. Well-referenced, scholarly fiction is an acceptable genre, as is creative narrative from personal experience.

Academic Fields/Career Goals: Health and Medical Sciences.

Award: Prize for use in freshman, sophomore, junior, or senior years; not renewable. *Amount:* $250–$2000.

Eligibility Requirements: Applicant must be enrolled or expecting to enroll full-time at a two-year or four-year or technical institution or university. Available to U.S. and non-U.S. citizens.

Application Requirements: Application form, application form may be submitted online (http://www.alphaomegaalpha.org/submit_essay.php), essay. *Deadline:* January 31.

Contact: Debbie Lancaster, Managing Editor
Alpha Omega Alpha
525 Middlefield Road, Suite 130
Menlo Park, CA 94025
Phone: 650-329-0291
Fax: 650-329-1618
E-mail: d.lancaster@alphaomegaalpha.org

PHAROS POETRY COMPETITION

Awards of $500, $250, $100 and $75; to encourage medical students to write poetry on medical subjects and to recognize and reward excellent and thoughtful compositions. Students must be enrolled at medical schools with active Alpha Omega Alpha chapters, but need not be members.

Academic Fields/Career Goals: Health and Medical Sciences.

Award: Prize for use in freshman, sophomore, junior, or senior years; not renewable. *Number:* 4. *Amount:* $75–$500.

Eligibility Requirements: Applicant must be enrolled or expecting to enroll full- or part-time at a two-year or four-year or technical institution or university and must have an interest in writing. Available to U.S. and non-U.S. citizens.

Application Requirements: Application form, application form may be submitted online (http://www.alphaomegaalpha.org/submit_poetry.php), essay. *Deadline:* January 31.

Contact: Debbie Lancaster, Managing Editor
Alpha Omega Alpha
525 Middlefield Road, Suite 130
Menlo Park, CA 94025
Phone: 650-329-0291
E-mail: d.lancaster@alphaomegaalpha.org

AMERICAN INDIAN SCIENCE AND ENGINEERING SOCIETY

http://www.aises.org/

A.T. ANDERSON MEMORIAL SCHOLARSHIP PROGRAM
• *See page 102*

AMERICAN LEGION AUXILIARY DEPARTMENT OF ARIZONA

http://wwwaladeptaz.org

AMERICAN LEGION AUXILIARY DEPARTMENT OF ARIZONA HEALTH CARE OCCUPATION SCHOLARSHIPS

Award for Arizona residents enrolled at an institution in Arizona that awards degrees or certificates in health occupations. Preference given to an immediate family member of a veteran. Must be a U.S. citizen and Arizona resident for at least one year.

Academic Fields/Career Goals: Health and Medical Sciences.

Award: Scholarship for use in freshman, sophomore, junior, or senior years; not renewable. *Amount:* $500.

Eligibility Requirements: Applicant must be enrolled or expecting to enroll full- or part-time at a two-year or four-year or technical institution or university; resident of Arizona and studying in Arizona. Available to U.S. citizens.

Application Requirements: Application form, essay, financial need analysis, personal photograph, recommendations or references, test scores, transcript. *Deadline:* May 15.

Contact: Mrs. Barbara Matteson, Department Secretary and Treasurer
American Legion Auxiliary Department of Arizona
4701 North 19th Avenue, Suite 100
Phoenix, AZ 85015-3727
Phone: 602-241-1080
Fax: 602-604-9640
E-mail: secretary@aladeptaz.org

AMERICAN LEGION AUXILIARY DEPARTMENT OF MAINE

http://www.mainelegion.org/

AMERICAN LEGION AUXILIARY DEPARTMENT OF MAINE PAST PRESIDENTS' PARLEY NURSES SCHOLARSHIP

One-time award for child, grandchild, sister, or brother of veteran. Must be resident of Maine and wishing to continue education at accredited school in medical field. Must submit photo, doctor's statement, and evidence of civic activity. Minimum 3.5 GPA required.

Academic Fields/Career Goals: Health and Medical Sciences; Nursing.

Award: Scholarship for use in freshman, sophomore, junior, or senior years; not renewable. *Number:* 1. *Amount:* $300.

Eligibility Requirements: Applicant must be enrolled or expecting to enroll full-time at a two-year or four-year or technical institution or university and resident of Maine. Applicant or parent of applicant must have employment or volunteer experience in community service. Applicant must have 2.5 GPA or higher. Available to U.S. citizens. Applicant or parent must meet one or more of the following requirements: general military experience; retired from active duty; disabled or killed as a result of military service; prisoner of war; or missing in action.

Application Requirements: Application form, doctor's statement, personal photograph, recommendations or references, transcript. *Deadline:* March 31.

Contact: Mary Wells, Education Chairman
Phone: 207-532-6007
E-mail: aladeptsecme@verizon.net

AMERICAN LEGION AUXILIARY DEPARTMENT OF MICHIGAN

http://www.michalaux.org/

AMERICAN LEGION AUXILIARY DEPARTMENT OF MICHIGAN MEDICAL CAREER SCHOLARSHIP

Award for training in Michigan as registered nurse, licensed practical nurse, physical therapist, respiratory therapist, or in any medical career. Must be child, grandchild, great-grandchild, wife, or widow of honorably discharged or deceased veteran who has served during the eligibility dates for American Legion membership. Must be Michigan resident attending a Michigan school.

Academic Fields/Career Goals: Health and Medical Sciences; Nursing; Therapy/Rehabilitation.

Award: Scholarship for use in freshman year; not renewable. *Number:* 10–20. *Amount:* $500.

Eligibility Requirements: Applicant must be high school student; planning to enroll or expecting to enroll full-time at a two-year or four-year or technical institution or university; resident of Michigan and studying in Michigan. Available to U.S. citizens. Applicant must have general military experience.

Application Requirements: Application form, financial need analysis, recommendations or references, transcript, veteran's discharge papers, copy of pages 1 and 2 of federal income tax return. *Deadline:* March 15.

AMERICAN LEGION AUXILIARY DEPARTMENT OF MINNESOTA

http://www.mnlegion.org/

AMERICAN LEGION AUXILIARY DEPARTMENT OF MINNESOTA PAST PRESIDENTS' PARLEY HEALTH CARE SCHOLARSHIP

One-time $1000 award for American Legion Auxiliary Department of Minnesota member for at least three years who is needy and deserving, to begin or continue education in any phase of the health care field. Must be a Minnesota resident, attend a vocational or postsecondary institution and maintain at least a C average in school.

Academic Fields/Career Goals: Health and Medical Sciences.

Award: Scholarship for use in freshman, sophomore, junior, or senior years; not renewable. *Number:* 1–10. *Amount:* $1000.

Eligibility Requirements: Applicant must be enrolled or expecting to enroll full-time at a two-year or four-year or technical institution or university; resident of Minnesota and studying in Minnesota. Applicant or parent of applicant must be member of American Legion or Auxiliary. Available to U.S. citizens.

Application Requirements: Application form, financial need analysis. *Deadline:* March 15.

Contact: Eleanor Johnson, Executive Secretary
American Legion Auxiliary Department of Minnesota
State Veterans Service Building
20 West 12th Street, Room 314
St. Paul, MN 55155
Phone: 651-224-7634
Fax: 651-224-5243

AMERICAN LEGION AUXILIARY DEPARTMENT OF TEXAS

http://www.alatexas.org/

AMERICAN LEGION AUXILIARY DEPARTMENT OF TEXAS PAST PRESIDENTS' PARLEY MEDICAL SCHOLARSHIP

Scholarships available for full-time students pursuing studies in human health care. Must be a resident of Texas. Must be a veteran or child, grandchild, great grandchild of a veteran who served in the Armed Forces during period of eligibility.

Academic Fields/Career Goals: Health and Medical Sciences.

Award: Scholarship for use in freshman, sophomore, junior, or senior years; not renewable. *Number:* 1–10. *Amount:* $1000.

Eligibility Requirements: Applicant must be enrolled or expecting to enroll full-time at a two-year or four-year or technical institution or university and resident of Texas. Available to U.S. citizens. Applicant must have general military experience.

Application Requirements: Application form, community service, financial need analysis, letter stating qualifications and intentions, recommendations or references, transcript. *Deadline:* June 1.

Contact: Paula Raney, State Secretary
Phone: 512-476-7278
Fax: 512-482-8391
E-mail: alatexas@txlegion.org

AMERICAN LEGION AUXILIARY DEPARTMENT OF WYOMING

AMERICAN LEGION AUXILIARY DEPARTMENT OF WYOMING PAST PRESIDENTS' PARLEY HEALTH CARE SCHOLARSHIP
• *See page 222*

AMERICAN MEDICAL ASSOCIATION FOUNDATION

http://www.amafoundation.org/

AMA FOUNDATION MINORITY SCHOLARS AWARD

Awards $10,000 scholarships annually. Applicant must be a current first- or second-year medical student and a permanent resident or citizen of the United States. Eligible students of minority background include African American/Black, American Indian, Native Hawaiian, Alaska Native and Hispanic/Latino. Each medical school dean or dean's designate is invited to submit up to 2 nominees.

Academic Fields/Career Goals: Health and Medical Sciences.

Award: Scholarship for use in sophomore, junior, or senior years; not renewable. *Number:* 10. *Amount:* $10,000.

Eligibility Requirements: Applicant must be American Indian/Alaska Native, Black (non-Hispanic), Hispanic and enrolled or expecting to enroll full-time at an institution or university. Available to U.S. citizens.

Application Requirements: Application form, community service, essay, financial need analysis, nomination from dean, recommendations or references, transcript. *Deadline:* April 15.

Contact: Dina Lindenberg, Minority Scholars Award
American Medical Association Foundation
515 North State Street
Chicago, IL 60654
Phone: 312-464-4193
Fax: 312-464-4142
E-mail: scholarships@ama-assn.org

AMA FOUNDATION PHYSICIANS OF TOMORROW SCHOLARSHIP

Scholarship of $10,000 will be awarded to current third-year medical students, who are entering their fourth-year of study. Based on academic excellence and/or financial need. Awards four scholarships. Applicant must be nominated by medical school dean or dean's designate.

Academic Fields/Career Goals: Health and Medical Sciences.

Award: Scholarship for use in senior year; not renewable. *Number:* 1–12. *Amount:* $10,000.

Eligibility Requirements: Applicant must be enrolled or expecting to enroll full-time at an institution or university. Available to U.S. citizens.

Application Requirements: Application form, essay, financial need analysis, nomination from dean, recommendations or references. *Deadline:* May 31.

Contact: Dina Lindenberg, Program Officer
American Medical Association Foundation
515 North State Street
Chicago, IL 60654
Phone: 312-464-4193
Fax: 312-464-4142
E-mail: scholarships@ama-assn.org

AMERICAN MEDICAL TECHNOLOGISTS

http://www.amt1.com/

AMERICAN MEDICAL TECHNOLOGISTS STUDENT SCHOLARSHIP
• *See page 222*

AMERICAN OCCUPATIONAL THERAPY FOUNDATION INC.

http://www.aotf.org/

AMERICAN OCCUPATIONAL THERAPY FOUNDATION STATE ASSOCIATION SCHOLARSHIPS

Awards offered at the state association level by the Foundation, for study leading to associate and graduate degrees in occupational therapy. Must be a member of the American Occupational Therapy Association. Requirements vary by state. See website at http://www.aotf.org for further details.

Academic Fields/Career Goals: Health and Medical Sciences; Therapy/Rehabilitation.

Award: Scholarship for use in sophomore, junior, senior, or graduate years; not renewable. *Amount:* $150–$5000.

Eligibility Requirements: Applicant must be enrolled or expecting to enroll full-time at a two-year or four-year institution or university. Available to U.S. citizens.

Application Requirements: Application form, Curriculum Director's statement, essay, recommendations or references. *Deadline:* March 1.

Contact: Jeanne Cooper, Scholarship Coordinator
Phone: 301-652-6611 Ext. 2550
Fax: 301-656-3620
E-mail: jcooper@aotf.org

CARLOTTA WELLES SCHOLARSHIP

Award for study leading to an occupational therapy associate degree at an accredited institution. Must be a member of the American Occupational Therapy Association.

Academic Fields/Career Goals: Health and Medical Sciences; Therapy/Rehabilitation.

Award: Scholarship for use in sophomore year; not renewable. *Amount:* $500.

Eligibility Requirements: Applicant must be enrolled or expecting to enroll full-time at a two-year institution. Applicant or parent of applicant must be member of American Occupational Therapy Association. Available to U.S. citizens.

Application Requirements: Application form, application form may be submitted online (http://www.aotf.org), Curriculum Director's statement, essay, recommendations or references. *Deadline:* varies.

Contact: Ms. Jeanne Cooper, Scholarship Coordinator
Phone: 301-652-6611 Ext. 2550
Fax: 301-656-3620
E-mail: jcooper@aotf.org

AMERICAN PHYSICAL THERAPY ASSOCIATION

http://www.apta.org/

MARY MCMILLAN SCHOLARSHIP AWARD
• *See page 233*

MINORITY SCHOLARSHIP AWARD

Three scholarship awards are supported by the Minority Scholarship Fund. These scholarships are awarded annually to physical therapy students in their final year of physical therapy education and faculty members pursuing their post-professional doctoral degree.

Academic Fields/Career Goals: Health and Medical Sciences.

Award: Scholarship for use in senior, graduate, or postgraduate years; not renewable. *Number:* 5–10. *Amount:* $2000–$6000.

Eligibility Requirements: Applicant must be American Indian/Alaska Native, Asian/Pacific Islander, Black (non-Hispanic), Hispanic and enrolled or expecting to enroll full- or part-time at a two-year or four-year institution or university. Applicant or parent of applicant must have employment or volunteer experience in physical therapy/rehabilitation. Available to U.S. citizens.

Application Requirements: Application form, application form may be submitted online (http://www.apta.org/HonorsAwards/), community service, essay, recommendations or references, resume, transcript. *Deadline:* December 1.

Contact: Stephanie Sadowski, Honors and Awards Program Specialist
American Physical Therapy Association
1111 North Fairfax Street
Alexandria, VA 22314
Phone: 800-999-2783 Ext. 3127
Fax: 703-706-8536
E-mail: stephaniesadowski@apta.org

AMERICAN PHYSIOLOGICAL SOCIETY

http://www.the-aps.org

DAVID S. BRUCE AWARDS FOR EXCELLENCE IN UNDERGRADUATE RESEARCH
• *See page 98*

AMERICAN RESPIRATORY CARE FOUNDATION

http://www.arcfoundation.org/

JIMMY A. YOUNG MEMORIAL EDUCATION RECOGNITION AWARD

Award available to students studying respiratory care at an American Medical Association-approved institution. Preference given to minority students. Must submit letters of recommendation and a paper on a respiratory care topic. Must have a minimum 3.0 GPA.

Academic Fields/Career Goals: Health and Medical Sciences; Therapy/Rehabilitation.

Award: Prize for use in freshman, sophomore, junior, or senior years; not renewable. *Number:* 1. *Amount:* up to $1000.

Eligibility Requirements: Applicant must be enrolled or expecting to enroll full- or part-time at a two-year or four-year institution or university. Applicant must have 3.0 GPA or higher. Available to U.S. citizens.

Application Requirements: Application form, paper on respiratory care topic, recommendations or references, transcript. *Deadline:* June 16.

Contact: Jill Nelson, Administrative Coordinator
American Respiratory Care Foundation
9425 North MacArthur Boulevard, Suite 100
Irving, TX 75063-4706
Phone: 972-243-2272
Fax: 972-484-2720
E-mail: info@arcfoundation.org

MORTON B. DUGGAN, JR. MEMORIAL EDUCATION RECOGNITION AWARD

Awards students with a minimum 3.0 GPA, enrolled in an American Medical Association-approved respiratory care program. Must be U.S. citizen or permanent resident. Need proof of college enrollment. Must submit an original referenced paper on respiratory care. Preference given to Georgia and South Carolina residents. One-time merit-based award of up to $1000, and includes airfare, registration to AARC Congress, and one night's lodging.

Academic Fields/Career Goals: Health and Medical Sciences; Therapy/Rehabilitation.

Award: Scholarship for use in freshman, sophomore, junior, or senior years; not renewable. *Number:* 1. *Amount:* up to $1000.

Eligibility Requirements: Applicant must be enrolled or expecting to enroll full- or part-time at a two-year or four-year institution or university. Applicant must have 3.0 GPA or higher. Available to U.S. citizens.

Application Requirements: Application form, paper on respiratory care, recommendations or references, transcript. *Deadline:* June 16.

Contact: Jill Nelson, Administrative Coordinator
American Respiratory Care Foundation
9425 North MacArthur Boulevard, Suite 100
Irving, TX 75063-4706
Phone: 972-243-2272
Fax: 972-484-2720
E-mail: info@arcfoundation.org

NBRC/AMP ROBERT M. LAWRENCE, MD EDUCATION RECOGNITION AWARD

Merit-based award to a third- or fourth-year student with a minimum 3.0 GPA, enrolled in an accredited undergraduate respiratory therapy program leading to a baccalaureate degree.

Academic Fields/Career Goals: Health and Medical Sciences; Therapy/Rehabilitation.

Award: Scholarship for use in junior or senior years; not renewable. *Number:* 1. *Amount:* up to $2500.

Eligibility Requirements: Applicant must be enrolled or expecting to enroll full- or part-time at a four-year institution or university. Applicant must have 3.0 GPA or higher. Available to U.S. and non-U.S. citizens.

Application Requirements: Application form, paper on respiratory care, recommendations or references, transcript. *Deadline:* June 16.

Contact: Jill Nelson, Administrative Coordinator
American Respiratory Care Foundation
9425 North MacArthur Boulevard, Suite 100
Irving, TX 75063-4706
Phone: 972-243-2272
Fax: 972-484-2720
E-mail: info@arcfoundation.org

NBRC/AMP WILLIAM W. BURGIN, MD EDUCATION RECOGNITION AWARD

Merit-based award for second-year students enrolled in an accredited respiratory therapy program leading to an associate degree. Minimum GPA of 3.0 required. For more information visit website, http://www.arcfoundation.org/awards/undergraduate/burgin.cfm.

Academic Fields/Career Goals: Health and Medical Sciences; Therapy/Rehabilitation.

Award: Prize for use in sophomore year; not renewable. *Number:* 1. *Amount:* up to $2500.

Eligibility Requirements: Applicant must be enrolled or expecting to enroll full- or part-time at a two-year institution. Applicant must have 3.0 GPA or higher. Available to U.S. and non-U.S. citizens.

Application Requirements: Application form, paper on respiratory care, recommendations or references, transcript. *Deadline:* June 16.

Contact: Jill Nelson, Administrative Coordinator
American Respiratory Care Foundation
9425 North MacArthur Boulevard, Suite 100
Irving, TX 75063-4706
Phone: 972-243-2272
Fax: 972-484-2720
E-mail: info@arcfoundation.org

SEPRACOR ACHIEVEMENT AWARD FOR EXCELLENCE IN PULMONARY DISEASE STATE MANAGEMENT

Nominations may be made by anyone by submitting a paper of not more than 1000 words describing why a nominee should be considered for the award. Must be a member of the American Association for Respiratory Care. Must be a respiratory therapist or other healthcare professional, including physician. Nominees must have demonstrated the attainment of positive healthcare outcomes as a direct result of their disease-oriented practice of respiratory care, regardless of care setting.

Academic Fields/Career Goals: Health and Medical Sciences; Therapy/Rehabilitation.

Award: Prize for use in freshman, sophomore, junior, senior, graduate, or postgraduate years; not renewable. *Number:* 1. *Amount:* up to $2500.

Eligibility Requirements: Applicant must be enrolled or expecting to enroll full- or part-time at a four-year institution or university. Applicant or parent of applicant must have employment or volunteer experience in physical therapy/rehabilitation. Available to U.S. and non-U.S. citizens.

Application Requirements: Paper describing why a nominee should be considered for the award, recommendations or references, resume. *Deadline:* June 1.

Contact: Jill Nelson, Administrative Coordinator
American Respiratory Care Foundation
9425 North MacArthur Boulevard, Suite 100
Irving, TX 75063-4706
Phone: 972-243-2272
Fax: 972-484-2720
E-mail: info@arcfoundation.org

ARIZONA PROFESSIONAL CHAPTER OF AISES

ARIZONA PROFESSIONAL CHAPTER OF AISES SCHOLARSHIP
• See page 276

ARNOLD AND MABEL BECKMAN FOUNDATION
http://www.beckman-foundation.com/

BECKMAN SCHOLARS PROGRAM
• See page 143

ARRL FOUNDATION INC.
http://www.arrl.org/

CAROLE J. STREETER, KB9JBR, SCHOLARSHIP
• See page 222

WILLIAM R. GOLDFARB MEMORIAL SCHOLARSHIP
• See page 150

ASRT FOUNDATION
http://www.asrtfoundation.org/

ELEKTA RADIATION THERAPY SCHOLARSHIP

Open to students in an entry-level radiation therapy program. Is a merit-based scholarship awarded on financial need, academic performance, recommendation, and essays.

Academic Fields/Career Goals: Health and Medical Sciences; Oncology.

Award: Scholarship for use in freshman, sophomore, junior, or senior years; not renewable. *Number:* 4. *Amount:* $5000.

Eligibility Requirements: Applicant must be enrolled or expecting to enroll full- or part-time at a two-year or four-year or technical institution or university. Applicant or parent of applicant must be member of American Society of Radiologic Technologists. Applicant must have 3.0 GPA or higher. Available to U.S. and Canadian citizens.

Application Requirements: Application form, application form may be submitted online (http://www.asrtfoundation.org), essay, financial need analysis, recommendations or references, resume. *Deadline:* February 1.

Contact: Brooke Palmer, Program Services Specialist
Phone: 505-298-4500 Ext. 1392
E-mail: foundation@asrt.org

JERMAN-CAHOON STUDENT SCHOLARSHIP

Merit scholarship for certificate or undergraduate students. Must have completed at least one semester in the radiological sciences to apply. Financial need is a factor. Requirements include 3.0 GPA, recommendation and several short answer essays.

Academic Fields/Career Goals: Health and Medical Sciences; Oncology; Radiology.

Award: Scholarship for use in freshman, sophomore, or junior years; not renewable. *Number:* 4–7. *Amount:* up to $2500.

Eligibility Requirements: Applicant must be enrolled or expecting to enroll full- or part-time at a two-year or four-year or technical institution or university. Applicant must have 3.0 GPA or higher. Available to U.S. citizens.

Application Requirements: Application form, application form may be submitted online (http://www.asrtfoundation.org), essay, financial

need analysis, recommendations or references, transcript. *Deadline:* February 1.

Contact: Brooke Palmer, Program Services Specialist
Phone: 505-298-4500 Ext. 1392
E-mail: foundation@asrt.org

MEDICAL IMAGING EDUCATORS SCHOLARSHIP
• See page 234

PROFESSIONAL ADVANCEMENT SCHOLARSHIP

Open to ASRT members only who are certificate, undergraduate or graduate students pursuing any degree or certificate intended to further a career in the radiologic sciences profession. One of the following must also be true: applicant holds an unrestricted state license, is registered by the American Registry of Radiologic Technologists, or registered with an equivalent certifying body.

Academic Fields/Career Goals: Health and Medical Sciences; Oncology; Radiology.

Award: Scholarship for use in freshman, sophomore, junior, senior, graduate, or postgraduate years; not renewable. *Number:* 5–15. *Amount:* up to $1500.

Eligibility Requirements: Applicant must be enrolled or expecting to enroll full- or part-time at a two-year or four-year or technical institution or university. Applicant or parent of applicant must be member of American Society of Radiologic Technologists. Available to U.S. and Canadian citizens.

Application Requirements: Application form, application form may be submitted online (http://www.asrtfoundation.org), essay, financial need analysis, recommendations or references, resume. *Deadline:* February 1.

Contact: Brooke Palmer, Program Services Specialist
Phone: 505-298-4500 Ext. 1392
E-mail: foundation@asrt.org

ROYCE OSBORN MINORITY STUDENT SCHOLARSHIP

Minority scholarship for certificate or undergraduate students. Must have completed at least one semester in the radiological sciences to apply. Financial need is a factor. Requirements include 3.0 GPA, recommendation and several short answer essays.

Academic Fields/Career Goals: Health and Medical Sciences; Radiology.

Award: Scholarship for use in freshman, sophomore, or junior years; not renewable. *Number:* 5–7. *Amount:* up to $4000.

Eligibility Requirements: Applicant must be American Indian/Alaska Native, Asian/Pacific Islander, Black (non-Hispanic), Hispanic and enrolled or expecting to enroll full- or part-time at a two-year or four-year or technical institution or university. Applicant must have 3.0 GPA or higher. Available to U.S. citizens.

Application Requirements: Application form, application form may be submitted online (http://www.asrtfoundation.org), essay, financial need analysis, recommendations or references, transcript. *Deadline:* February 1.

Contact: Brooke Palmer, Program Services Specialist
Phone: 505-298-4500 Ext. 1392
E-mail: foundation@asrt.org

SIEMENS CLINICAL ADVANCEMENT SCHOLARSHIP

Open to ASRT members only who are pursuing a bachelor's or master's degree in the radiologic sciences to advance patient care skills or pursuing a certificate in a specialty discipline. One of the following must also be true: applicant holds an unrestricted state license, is registered by the American Registry of Radiologic Technologists, or registered with an equivalent certifying body.

Academic Fields/Career Goals: Health and Medical Sciences; Oncology; Radiology.

Award: Scholarship for use in freshman, sophomore, junior, senior, graduate, or postgraduate years; not renewable. *Number:* 4. *Amount:* $5000.

Eligibility Requirements: Applicant must be enrolled or expecting to enroll full- or part-time at a two-year or four-year or technical institution or university. Applicant or parent of applicant must be member of American Society of Radiologic Technologists. Available to U.S. and Canadian citizens.

Application Requirements: Application form, application form may be submitted online (http://www.asrtfoundation.org), essay, financial need analysis, recommendations or references, resume. *Deadline:* February 1.

Contact: Brooke Palmer, Program Services Specialist
Phone: 505-298-4500 Ext. 1392
E-mail: foundation@asrt.org

VARIAN RADIATION THERAPY ADVANCEMENT SCHOLARSHIP

Merit scholarship for radiation therapists and medical dosimetrists or for current radiologic technologists in an entry-level radiation therapy program. Financial need is a factor. Requirements include recommendation and several short answer essays.

Academic Fields/Career Goals: Health and Medical Sciences; Oncology.

Award: Scholarship for use in freshman, sophomore, junior, senior, graduate, or postgraduate years; not renewable. *Number:* 19. *Amount:* $5000.

Eligibility Requirements: Applicant must be enrolled or expecting to enroll full- or part-time at a two-year or four-year or technical institution or university. Available to U.S. and Canadian citizens.

Application Requirements: Application form, application form may be submitted online (http://www.asrtfoundation.org), essay, financial need analysis, recommendations or references, transcript. *Deadline:* February 1.

Contact: Brooke Palmer, Program Services Specialist
Phone: 505-298-4500 Ext. 1392
E-mail: foundation@asrt.org

ASSOCIATION OF SURGICAL TECHNOLOGISTS

http://www.ast.org/

DELMAR CENGAGE LEARNING SURGICAL TECHNOLOGY SCHOLARSHIP

Scholarship offers students in CAAHEP-accredited surgical technology programs the opportunity to apply for financial assistance. Must have a 2.5 GPA.

Academic Fields/Career Goals: Health and Medical Sciences.

Award: Scholarship for use in freshman, sophomore, junior, or senior years; not renewable. *Number:* 1. *Amount:* $1000.

Eligibility Requirements: Applicant must be enrolled or expecting to enroll full-time at a two-year or four-year institution or university. Applicant must have 2.5 GPA or higher. Available to U.S. citizens.

Application Requirements: Application form, course fee schedule, essay, recommendations or references, self-addressed stamped envelope with application, transcript. *Deadline:* April 1.

Contact: Karen Ludwig, Director of Publishing
Phone: 800-637-7433
Fax: 303-694-9169
E-mail: kludwig@ast.org

FOUNDATION STUDENT SCHOLARSHIP

Scholarship to encourage and reward educational excellence as well as to respond to the financial need demonstrated by the surgical technology student and offer assistance to those who seek a career in surgical technology. High school students also eligible to apply. Minimum GPA 3.2 is required.

Academic Fields/Career Goals: Health and Medical Sciences.

Award: Scholarship for use in freshman, sophomore, junior, or senior years; not renewable. *Number:* up to 12. *Amount:* $500–$2000.

Eligibility Requirements: Applicant must be enrolled or expecting to enroll full-time at a two-year or four-year institution or university. Available to U.S. citizens.

Application Requirements: Application form, essay, financial need analysis, recommendations or references, self-addressed stamped envelope with application, transcript. *Deadline:* April 1.

Contact: Karen Ludwig, Director of Publishing
Phone: 800-637-7433
Fax: 303-694-9169
E-mail: kludwig@ast.org

ASSOCIATION ON AMERICAN INDIAN AFFAIRS, INC.

http://www.indian-affairs.org/

ELIZABETH AND SHERMAN ASCHE MEMORIAL SCHOLARSHIP FUND

• *See page 91*

ATLANTIC HEALTH SYSTEM OVERLOOK HOSPITAL FOUNDATION

http://www.overlookfoundation.org

OVERLOOK HOSPITAL FOUNDATION PROFESSIONAL DEVELOPMENT PROGRAM

Nursing and other allied health students who live in New Jersey are eligible to apply. Pays for one to two years of tuition in exchange for a commitment to work at Overlook Hospital upon graduation.

Academic Fields/Career Goals: Health and Medical Sciences; Nursing.

Award: Scholarship for use in freshman, sophomore, junior, or senior years; not renewable.

Eligibility Requirements: Applicant must be enrolled or expecting to enroll full- or part-time at a two-year or four-year institution and resident of New Jersey. Available to U.S. citizens.

Application Requirements: Application form. *Deadline:* varies.

Contact: Betsy Koehler, Scholarship Coordinator
Atlantic Health System Overlook Hospital Foundation
99 Beauvoir Avenue
Summit, NJ 07902
Phone: 908-522-2835
E-mail: betsy.koehler@ahsys.org

BETHESDA LUTHERAN COMMUNITIES

http://www.bethesdalutherancommunities.org/scholarships

DEVELOPMENTAL DISABILITIES AWARENESS AWARDS FOR HIGH SCHOOL STUDENTS WHO ARE LUTHERAN

Award available to high school seniors interested in the developmental disabilities field. Students must complete two activities from a suggested list, which, together with the application process, are designed to promote the student's knowledge of careers in the field of developmental disabilities services. Two $500 awards are given. For more information, visit website at http://www.blhs.org.

Academic Fields/Career Goals: Health and Medical Sciences; Nursing; Social Services; Special Education; Therapy/Rehabilitation.

Award: Scholarship for use in freshman year; not renewable. *Number:* 2. *Amount:* up to $500.

Eligibility Requirements: Applicant must be Lutheran; high school student and planning to enroll or expecting to enroll full-time at a two-year or four-year or technical institution or university. Applicant must have 3.0 GPA or higher. Available to U.S. and Canadian citizens.

Application Requirements: Application form, community service, essay, recommendations or references, resume, transcript. *Deadline:* April 16.

Contact: Pam Bergen, Executive Assistant for Mission Advancement
Bethesda Lutheran Communities
600 Hoffmann Drive
Watertown, WI 53094
Phone: 920-206-4410
Fax: 920-206-7706
E-mail: pam.bergen@mailblc.org

DEVELOPMENTAL DISABILITIES SCHOLASTIC ACHIEVEMENT SCHOLARSHIP FOR COLLEGE STUDENTS WHO ARE LUTHERAN

• *See page 222*

BOYS AND GIRLS CLUBS OF SAN DIEGO

http://www.sdyouth.org/

SPENCE REESE SCHOLARSHIP
• *See page 279*

CANADIAN SOCIETY FOR MEDICAL LABORATORY SCIENCE

http://www.csmls.org/

CANADIAN SOCIETY OF LABORATORY TECHNOLOGISTS STUDENT SCHOLARSHIP PROGRAM

Four one-time awards of CAN$500 available to students enrolled in their final year of general medical laboratory technology, cytotechnology, or clinical genetic studies. Must be student member of Canadian Society for Medical Laboratory Science, and Canadian citizen or permanent resident of Canada.

Academic Fields/Career Goals: Health and Medical Sciences.

Award: Scholarship for use in senior year; not renewable. *Number:* 4.

Eligibility Requirements: Applicant must be Canadian citizen and enrolled or expecting to enroll full-time at an institution or university. Applicant or parent of applicant must be member of Canadian Society for Medical Laboratory Science.

Application Requirements: Application form, financial need analysis, recommendations or references, self-addressed stamped envelope with application, transcript. *Deadline:* October 1.

Contact: Norah Langham, Marketing Assistant
Canadian Society for Medical Laboratory Science
33 Wellington Street North
Hamilton, ON L8R 1M7
CAN
Phone: 905-528-8642 Ext. 8688
Fax: 905-528-4968
E-mail: norahl@csmls.org

E.V. BOOTH SCHOLARSHIP AWARD
• *See page 326*

CANFIT

http://www.canfit.org/

CANFIT NUTRITION, PHYSICAL EDUCATION AND CULINARY ARTS SCHOLARSHIP
• *See page 214*

CENTRAL SCHOLARSHIP

http://www.central-scholarship.org

CHESAPEAKE UROLOGY ASSOCIATES SCHOLARSHIP

Scholarship provides assistance to Maryland residents who are full-time undergraduate students pursuing a degree in pre-medicine, pre-nursing, and ancillary health fields. Recipients will be selected based on demonstrated commitment to the medical field, financial need, and academic achievement.

Academic Fields/Career Goals: Health and Medical Sciences; Nursing.

Award: Scholarship for use in sophomore, junior, or senior years; renewable. *Number:* 3. *Amount:* $1500–$5000.

Eligibility Requirements: Applicant must be enrolled or expecting to enroll full-time at a two-year or four-year institution or university and resident of Maryland. Applicant must have 3.0 GPA or higher. Available to U.S. citizens.

Application Requirements: Application form, essay, financial need analysis, interview, resume, transcript. *Deadline:* May 1.

Contact: Roberta Goldman, Program Director
Phone: 410-415-5558
Fax: 410-415-5501
E-mail: rgoldman@centralsb.org

CHRISTIANA CARE HEALTH SYSTEMS

http://www.christianacare.org/

RUTH SHAW JUNIOR BOARD SCHOLARSHIP

Offers financial assistance to students currently enrolled in nursing and selected allied health programs. Applicants are selected based on academic achievement and a proven commitment to quality patient care. Students receiving assistance are required to commit to a minimum of one year of employment with Christiana Care.

Academic Fields/Career Goals: Health and Medical Sciences; Nursing.

Award: Scholarship for use in freshman, sophomore, junior, or senior years; not renewable.

Eligibility Requirements: Applicant must be enrolled or expecting to enroll full- or part-time at a four-year institution or university. Applicant or parent of applicant must have employment or volunteer experience in nursing. Available to U.S. citizens.

Application Requirements: Application form, driver's license, recommendations or references, resume, transcript. *Deadline:* April 30.

Contact: Wendy Gable, Scholarship Committee
Christiana Care Health Systems
200 Hygeia Drive, PO Box 6001
Newark, DE 19713
Phone: 302-428-5710
E-mail: wgable@christianacare.org

THE COMMUNITY FOUNDATION FOR GREATER ATLANTA, INC.

http://cfgreateratlanta.org/

STEVE DEARDUFF SCHOLARSHIP

Scholarship for undergraduate and graduate students pursuing degrees in medicine or social work. Legal resident of Georgia. Minimum 2.0 GPA. Previous recipients are encouraged to reapply, but are not guaranteed additional awards. For complete eligibility requirements or to submit an application, visit http://www.cfgreateratlanta.org.

Academic Fields/Career Goals: Health and Medical Sciences; Social Services.

Award: Scholarship for use in freshman, sophomore, junior, senior, or graduate years; not renewable. *Number:* 1–3. *Amount:* $1000–$2500.

Eligibility Requirements: Applicant must be enrolled or expecting to enroll full- or part-time at a four-year institution or university and resident of Georgia. Available to U.S. citizens.

Application Requirements: Application form, application form may be submitted online (http://www.cfgreateratlanta.org/Grants-Support/Scholarships.aspx), driver's license, essay, financial need analysis, recommendations or references, test scores, transcript. *Deadline:* March 1.

Contact: Kristina Morris, Program Associate
The Community Foundation for Greater Atlanta, Inc.
50 Hurt Plaza
Suite 449
Atlanta, GA 30303
Phone: 404-688-5525
E-mail: scholarships@cfgreateratlanta.org

CONGRESSIONAL BLACK CAUCUS FOUNDATION, INC.

http://www.cbcfinc.org/

CBCF GENERAL MILLS HEALTH SCHOLARSHIP
• *See page 144*

THE LOUIS STOKES HEALTH SCHOLARS PROGRAM
• *See page 144*

CROHN'S & COLITIS FOUNDATION OF AMERICA INC.

http://www.ccfa.org/

CROHN'S & COLITIS FOUNDATION OF AMERICA STUDENT RESEARCH FELLOWSHIP AWARDS

Student Research Fellowship Awards will be available for full time research with a mentor investigating a subject relevant to IBD. Mentors may not be a relative of the applicant and may not work in their lab. The mentor must be a faculty member who directs a research project highly relevant to the study of IBD at an accredited institution. Awards will be payable to the institution, not the individual. A complete financial statement and scientific report are due September 1 of the year of the award. All publications arising from work funded by this project must acknowledge support of CCFA. Candidates may be undergraduate, medical or graduate students (not yet engaged in thesis research) in accredited United States institutions. Candidates may not hold similar salary support from other agencies.

Academic Fields/Career Goals: Health and Medical Sciences.

Award: Scholarship for use in freshman, sophomore, junior, senior, or graduate years; not renewable. *Amount:* $2500–$2500.

Eligibility Requirements: Applicant must be enrolled or expecting to enroll full-time at a four-year institution or university. Available to U.S. and non-U.S. citizens.

Application Requirements: Abstract, research plan description, application form, application form may be submitted online (https://proposalcentral.altum.com/default.asp?GMID=96), resume. *Deadline:* March 15.

Contact: Joseph O'Keefe, Director, Grants Administration
Crohn's & Colitis Foundation of America Inc.
386 Park Avenue South
17th Floor
New York, NY 10016-8804
Phone: 646-943-7505
Fax: 212-779-4098
E-mail: grants@ccfa.org

CYNTHIA E. MORGAN SCHOLARSHIP FUND (CEMS)

http://www.cemsfund.com/

CYNTHIA E. MORGAN MEMORIAL SCHOLARSHIP FUND, INC.

• See page 298

FOUNDATION FOR SCIENCE AND DISABILITY

http://stemd.org/

GRANTS FOR DISABLED STUDENTS IN THE SCIENCES

• See page 105

FOUNDATION FOR SURGICAL TECHNOLOGY

http://www.ffst.org/

FOUNDATION FOR SURGICAL TECHNOLOGY SCHOLARSHIP FUND

Scholarships available for students who are currently enrolled in an accredited surgical technology program whose graduates are eligible to sit for the NBSTSA surgical technologist certifying examination. Must be preparing for a career as a surgical technologist. Minimum 3.0 GPA is required. One-time award. Amount varies from year to year. Applicant must be selected by sponsoring institution. Visit website for more information.

Academic Fields/Career Goals: Health and Medical Sciences.

Award: Scholarship for use in freshman, sophomore, junior, or senior years; not renewable. *Number:* 10–20. *Amount:* $500–$2500.

Eligibility Requirements: Applicant must be enrolled or expecting to enroll full-time at a two-year or four-year or technical institution or university. Applicant must have 3.0 GPA or higher. Available to U.S. citizens.

Application Requirements: Application form, financial need analysis, recommendations or references, transcript. *Deadline:* March 1.

Contact: Karen Ludwig, Director of Publishing
Foundation for Surgical Technology
6 West Dry Creek Circle
Littleton, CO 80120
Phone: 303-694-9130
Fax: 303-694-9169

GARDEN CLUB OF AMERICA

http://www.gcamerica.org/

ZELLER SUMMER SCHOLARSHIP IN MEDICINAL BOTANY

One $2000 award open to undergraduate students enrolled in an accredited US college or university for study or work during the summer following the freshman, sophomore, junior, or senior year.

Academic Fields/Career Goals: Health and Medical Sciences; Horticulture/Floriculture; Natural Sciences.

Award: Scholarship for use in freshman, sophomore, junior, or senior years; not renewable. *Number:* 1. *Amount:* $2000.

Eligibility Requirements: Applicant must be enrolled or expecting to enroll full-time at a four-year institution or university. Available to U.S. citizens.

Application Requirements: Application form, essay, recommendations or references, resume, transcript. *Deadline:* February 1.

Contact: Connie Yates, Garden Club of America
Garden Club of America
14 East 60th Street
New York, NY 10022-1006
Phone: 212-753-8287
Fax: 212-753-0134
E-mail: cyates@gcamerica.org

GENERAL BOARD OF HIGHER EDUCATION AND MINISTRY

http://www.gbhem.org

EDITH M. ALLEN SCHOLARSHIP

• See page 237

GREATER KANAWHA VALLEY FOUNDATION

http://www.tgkvf.org/

NICHOLAS AND MARY AGNES TRIVILLIAN MEMORIAL SCHOLARSHIP FUND

Renewable award for West Virginia residents pursuing medical or pharmacy programs. Must show financial need and academic merit.

Academic Fields/Career Goals: Health and Medical Sciences; Pharmacy.

Award: Scholarship for use in freshman, sophomore, junior, or senior years; renewable. *Amount:* $1000.

Eligibility Requirements: Applicant must be enrolled or expecting to enroll full-time at a four-year institution or university and resident of West Virginia. Available to U.S. citizens.

Application Requirements: Application form, essay, financial need analysis, recommendations or references, self-addressed stamped envelope with application, test scores, transcript. *Deadline:* January 15.

Contact: Susan Hoover, Scholarship Program Officer
Greater Kanawha Valley Foundation
900 Lee Street East, 16th Floor
Charleston, WV 25301
Phone: 304-346-3620
E-mail: tgkvf@tgkvf.org

HAWAIIAN LODGE, F&AM

http://www.hawaiianlodgefreemasons.org/

HAWAIIAN LODGE SCHOLARSHIPS
• *See page 114*

HEALTHCARE INFORMATION AND MANAGEMENT SYSTEMS SOCIETY FOUNDATION

http://www.himss.org/

HIMSS FOUNDATION SCHOLARSHIP PROGRAM
• *See page 327*

HEALTH PROFESSIONS EDUCATION FOUNDATION

http://www.healthprofessions.ca.gov/

KAISER PERMANENTE ALLIED HEALTHCARE SCHOLARSHIP

One-time award available to students enrolled in, or accepted to California accredited allied health education programs. Scholarship worth up to $4500. Deadlines are March 24 and September 11.

Academic Fields/Career Goals: Health and Medical Sciences; Social Services; Therapy/Rehabilitation.

Award: Scholarship for use in freshman, sophomore, junior, senior, graduate, or postgraduate years; not renewable. *Number:* up to 40. *Amount:* $3000–$4000.

Eligibility Requirements: Applicant must be enrolled or expecting to enroll full- or part-time at a two-year or four-year or technical institution or university; resident of California and studying in California. Available to U.S. citizens.

Application Requirements: Application form, driver's license, financial need analysis, recommendations or references, resume, Student Aid Report (SAR) or tax return with W2, transcript. *Deadline:* varies.

Contact: Margarita Miranda, Program Administrator
Health Professions Education Foundation
818 K Street, Suite 210
Sacramento, CA 95814
Phone: 916-326-3640
Fax: 916-324-6585

HEALTH RESEARCH COUNCIL OF NEW ZEALAND

http://www.hrc.govt.nz/

PACIFIC HEALTH WORKFORCE AWARD
• *See page 327*

PACIFIC MENTAL HEALTH WORK FORCE AWARD
• *See page 327*

HELLENIC UNIVERSITY CLUB OF PHILADELPHIA

http://www.hucphila.org/

DR. PETER A. THEODOS MEMORIAL GRADUATE SCHOLARSHIP

$2500 scholarship awarded to a senior undergraduate or graduate student with financial need pursuing studies leading to a Doctor of Medicine degree. Must be a U.S. citizen of Greek descent and a resident of particular counties in NJ or PA.

Academic Fields/Career Goals: Health and Medical Sciences.

Award: Scholarship for use in senior or graduate years; not renewable. *Number:* up to 1. *Amount:* up to $2500.

Eligibility Requirements: Applicant must be of Greek heritage; enrolled or expecting to enroll full-time at a four-year institution or

university and resident of New Jersey, Pennsylvania. Available to U.S. citizens.

Application Requirements: Application form, financial need analysis, transcript. *Deadline:* April 21.

Contact: Anna Hadgis, Scholarship Chairman
Phone: 610-613-4310
E-mail: hucphila@yahoo.com

HISPANIC HERITAGE FOUNDATION

http://www.hispanicheritage.org/

HISPANIC HERITAGE YOUTH AWARDS
• *See page 155*

INDIAN HEALTH SERVICES, UNITED STATES DEPARTMENT OF HEALTH AND HUMAN SERVICES

http://www.ihs.gov/scholarship

HEALTH PROFESSIONS PREPARATORY SCHOLARSHIP PROGRAM
• *See page 141*

INDIAN HEALTH SERVICE HEALTH PROFESSIONS PRE-GRADUATE SCHOLARSHIPS
• *See page 105*

INDIAN HEALTH SERVICE HEALTH PROFESSIONS SCHOLARSHIP PROGRAM
• *See page 208*

INTERNATIONAL ORDER OF THE KING'S DAUGHTERS AND SONS

http://www.iokds.org/

HEALTH CAREERS SCHOLARSHIP
• *See page 223*

JEWISH VOCATIONAL SERVICE CHICAGO

http://www.jvschicago.org/

JEWISH FEDERATION ACADEMIC SCHOLARSHIP PROGRAM
• *See page 120*

LADIES AUXILIARY TO THE VETERANS OF FOREIGN WARS, DEPARTMENT OF MAINE

http://mainevfw.org/

FRANCES L. BOOTH MEDICAL SCHOLARSHIP SPONSORED BY LAVFW DEPARTMENT OF MAINE

Award for an undergraduate student majoring in the field of medicine who has a parent or grandparent who is a member of the Maine VFW or VFW auxiliary.

Academic Fields/Career Goals: Health and Medical Sciences; Humanities; Nursing; Therapy/Rehabilitation.

Award: Scholarship for use in freshman, sophomore, junior, or senior years; renewable. *Number:* 2. *Amount:* $500–$1000.

Eligibility Requirements: Applicant must be enrolled or expecting to enroll full-time at a two-year or four-year institution or university and resident of Maine. Applicant or parent of applicant must be member of Veterans of Foreign Wars or Auxiliary. Applicant must have 3.0 GPA or higher. Available to U.S. citizens. Applicant or parent must meet one or more of the following requirements: general military experience; retired from active duty; disabled or killed as a result of military service; prisoner of war; or missing in action.

Application Requirements: Application form, community service, essay, financial need analysis, personal letter, recommendations or references, resume, transcript. *Deadline:* March 31.

Contact: Sheila Webber, Chairman, FBMS
Ladies Auxiliary to the Veterans of Foreign Wars, Department of Maine
PO Box 493
Old Orchard Beach, ME 04064
Phone: 207-934-2405
E-mail: swebber2@maine.rr.com

MAINE OSTEOPATHIC ASSOCIATION MEMORIAL SCHOLARSHIP/MAINE OSTEOPATHIC ASSOCIATION

http://www.mainedo.org/

BEALE FAMILY MEMORIAL SCHOLARSHIP

One award of $1000 is made to a well qualified student in their second, third or fourth year of study at an osteopathic college, who has evidence of interest in returning to Maine to practice or in teaching in an osteopathic college in New England.

Academic Fields/Career Goals: Health and Medical Sciences; Osteopathy.

Award: Scholarship for use in sophomore, junior, or senior years; not renewable. *Number:* 1. *Amount:* $1000.

Eligibility Requirements: Applicant must be enrolled or expecting to enroll full- or part-time at a four-year institution or university. Available to U.S. citizens.

Application Requirements: Application form, proof of residence. *Deadline:* May 1.

Contact: Dianne Jackson, Office Manager and Convention Coordinator
Phone: 207-623-1101
Fax: 207-623-4228
E-mail: djackson@mainedo.org

MAINE OSTEOPATHIC ASSOCIATION MEMORIAL SCHOLARSHIP

One award of $1000 to a second, third, or fourth year student who is a resident of Maine. Must present proof of enrollment at an approved osteopathic college.

Academic Fields/Career Goals: Health and Medical Sciences; Osteopathy.

Award: Scholarship for use in sophomore, junior, or senior years; not renewable. *Number:* 1. *Amount:* $1000.

Eligibility Requirements: Applicant must be enrolled or expecting to enroll full- or part-time at a four-year institution or university and resident of Maine. Available to U.S. citizens.

Application Requirements: Application form, proof of residence, proof of enrollment at an approved osteopathic college. *Deadline:* May 1.

Contact: Dianne Jackson, Office Manager and Convention Coordinator
Phone: 207-623-1101
Fax: 207-623-4228
E-mail: djackson@mainedo.org

MAINE OSTEOPATHIC ASSOCIATION SCHOLARSHIP

One award of $1000 to a student who is a resident of Maine and able to present proof of enrollment at an approved osteopathic college.

Academic Fields/Career Goals: Health and Medical Sciences; Osteopathy.

Award: Scholarship for use in freshman year; not renewable. *Number:* 1. *Amount:* $1000.

Eligibility Requirements: Applicant must be high school student; planning to enroll or expecting to enroll full- or part-time at a two-year or four-year or technical institution or university and resident of Maine. Available to U.S. citizens.

Application Requirements: Application form, proof of Maine residence, transcript. *Deadline:* May 1.

Contact: Dianne Jackson, Office Manager and Convention Coordinator
Phone: 207-623-1101
Fax: 207-623-4228
E-mail: djackson@mainedo.org

MARYLAND STATE HIGHER EDUCATION COMMISSION

http://www.mhec.state.md.us/

CHARLES W. RILEY FIRE AND EMERGENCY MEDICAL SERVICES TUITION REIMBURSEMENT PROGRAM
• *See page 311*

GRADUATE AND PROFESSIONAL SCHOLARSHIP PROGRAM-MARYLAND
• *See page 224*

NATIONAL ARAB AMERICAN MEDICAL ASSOCIATION

http://www.naama.com/

FOUNDATION SCHOLARSHIP
• *See page 224*

NATIONAL ATHLETIC TRAINERS' ASSOCIATION RESEARCH AND EDUCATION FOUNDATION

http://www.natafoundation.org/

NATIONAL ATHLETIC TRAINERS' ASSOCIATION RESEARCH AND EDUCATION FOUNDATION SCHOLARSHIP PROGRAM

One-time award available to full-time students who are members of NATA. Minimum 3.2 GPA required. Open to undergraduate upperclassmen and graduate/postgraduate students.

Academic Fields/Career Goals: Health and Medical Sciences; Health Information Management/Technology; Sports-Related/Exercise Science; Therapy/Rehabilitation.

Award: Scholarship for use in junior, senior, graduate, or postgraduate years; not renewable. *Number:* 70. *Amount:* $2000.

Eligibility Requirements: Applicant must be enrolled or expecting to enroll full-time at a four-year institution or university. Applicant or parent of applicant must be member of National Athletic Trainers Association. Available to U.S. and non-U.S. citizens.

Application Requirements: Application form, essay, recommendations or references, transcript. *Deadline:* February 10.

Contact: Patsy Brown, Scholarship Coordinator
National Athletic Trainers' Association Research and Education Foundation
2952 Stemmons Freeway, Suite 200
Dallas, TX 75247
Phone: 214-637-6282 Ext. 151
Fax: 214-637-2206
E-mail: patsyb@nata.org

NATIONAL INSTITUTES OF HEALTH

https://ugsp.nih.gov/

NIH UNDERGRADUATE SCHOLARSHIP PROGRAM FOR STUDENTS FROM DISADVANTAGED BACKGROUNDS
• *See page 147*

NATIONAL INVENTORS HALL OF FAME

http://www.invent.org/

COLLEGIATE INVENTORS COMPETITION FOR UNDERGRADUATE STUDENTS
• *See page 106*

COLLEGIATE INVENTORS COMPETITION-GRAND PRIZE
• *See page 106*

OREGON COMMUNITY FOUNDATION

http://www.oregoncf.org/

FRANZ STENZEL M.D. AND KATHRYN STENZEL SCHOLARSHIP FUND

Scholarships for Oregon residents, with a focus on three types of students: (a) those pursuing any type of undergraduate degree, (b) those pursuing a nursing education through a two-year, four-year, or graduate program, and (c) medical students.

Academic Fields/Career Goals: Health and Medical Sciences; Nursing.

Award: Scholarship for use in freshman, sophomore, junior, or senior years; renewable. *Number:* up to 70. *Amount:* $2000–$5000.

Eligibility Requirements: Applicant must be enrolled or expecting to enroll full-time at a two-year or four-year institution or university and resident of Oregon. Available to U.S. citizens.

Application Requirements: Application form, recommendations or references. *Deadline:* March 1.

Contact: Dianne Causey, Program Associate for Scholarships and Grants
    Phone: 503-227-6846 Ext. 1418
    E-mail: dcausey@oregoncf.org

OREGON STUDENT ASSISTANCE COMMISSION

http://www.GetCollegeFunds.org/

CHESTER AND HELEN LUTHER SCHOLARSHIP

Award available to graduates of any high school in Oregon or Clark County, Washington. Applicants must also be residents of either Oregon or Clark County, Washington. Preference is given to first-generation college attendees. Must attend a college or university in Oregon or Clark County, Washington, enroll at least half-time, and be at least 25 years old as of the March scholarship deadline. Minimum 3.0 GPA required.

Academic Fields/Career Goals: Health and Medical Sciences; Nursing.

Award: Scholarship for use in freshman, sophomore, junior, senior, or graduate years; not renewable.

Eligibility Requirements: Applicant must be enrolled or expecting to enroll full- or part-time at a two-year or four-year institution or university; resident of Oregon, Washington and studying in Oregon, Washington. Applicant must have 3.0 GPA or higher. Available to U.S. citizens.

Application Requirements: Application form, FAFSA, transcript. *Deadline:* March 1.

CLARK-PHELPS SCHOLARSHIP

• *See page 224*

HELEN HALL AND JOHN SEELY MEMORIAL SCHOLARSHIP

Award is open to graduates of Douglas County high schools. Minimum GPA of 3.0 is required. Preference for majors in medical, nursing, or other health-related fields. Evidence of healthcare, community-related activities, and financial need will be taken into consideration. Must reapply annually for renewal.

Academic Fields/Career Goals: Health and Medical Sciences; Nursing.

Award: Scholarship for use in freshman, sophomore, junior, senior, or graduate years; not renewable.

Eligibility Requirements: Applicant must be enrolled or expecting to enroll full- or part-time at a four-year institution or university and resident of Oregon. Applicant must have 3.0 GPA or higher. Available to U.S. citizens.

Application Requirements: Application form, community service, FAFSA, financial need analysis, test scores, transcript. *Deadline:* March 1.

MARION A. LINDEMAN SCHOLARSHIP

Award for Willamette View Health Center or Willamette View Terrace employees who have completed one or more years of service. Must be pursuing a degree or certificate in nursing, speech, physical or occupational therapy, or other health-related fields. Must enroll at least half time in a U.S. college or university and reapply annually for award renewal. Oregon residency is not required.

Academic Fields/Career Goals: Health and Medical Sciences; Nursing; Therapy/Rehabilitation.

Award: Scholarship for use in freshman, sophomore, junior, or senior years; not renewable.

Eligibility Requirements: Applicant must be enrolled or expecting to enroll full- or part-time at a two-year or four-year institution. Applicant or parent of applicant must be affiliated with Willamette View. Available to U.S. citizens.

Application Requirements: Activity chart, application form, essay, financial need analysis, recommendations or references, transcript. *Deadline:* March 1.

PACERS FOUNDATION INC.

http://www.pacersfoundation.org/

LINDA CRAIG MEMORIAL SCHOLARSHIP PRESENTED BY ST. VINCENT SPORTS MEDICINE

Scholarship presented by St. Vincent Sports Medicine is for currently-enrolled juniors and seniors with declared majors of medicine, sports medicine, and/or physical therapy. Students must have completed at least 4 semesters and attend a school in Indiana. Minimum 3.0 GPA required.

Academic Fields/Career Goals: Health and Medical Sciences; Sports-Related/Exercise Science; Therapy/Rehabilitation.

Award: Scholarship for use in junior, senior, graduate, or postgraduate years; renewable. *Number:* 1–2. *Amount:* $2000.

Eligibility Requirements: Applicant must be enrolled or expecting to enroll full-time at a two-year or four-year institution or university and studying in Indiana. Applicant must have 3.0 GPA or higher. Available to U.S. citizens.

Application Requirements: Application form, essay, recommendations or references, transcript. *Deadline:* March 1.

Contact: Jami Marsh, Executive Director
    Pacers Foundation Inc.
    125 South Pennsylvania Street
    Indianapolis, IN 46204
    Phone: 317-917-2856
    E-mail: foundation@pacers.com

PEARSON BENJAMIN CUMMINGS

http://www.pearsonhighered.com/

PEARSON BENJAMIN CUMMINGS ALLIED HEALTH STUDENT SCHOLARSHIP

• *See page 147*

PHYSICIAN ASSISTANT FOUNDATION

http://www.aapa.org/paf

PHYSICIAN ASSISTANT FOUNDATION ANNUAL SCHOLARSHIP

One-time award for student members of the American Academy of Physician Assistants enrolled in an ARC PA-accredited physician assistant program. Award based on financial need, academic achievement, and goals.

Academic Fields/Career Goals: Health and Medical Sciences.

Award: Scholarship for use in junior or senior years; not renewable. *Number:* up to 75. *Amount:* $2000.

Eligibility Requirements: Applicant must be enrolled or expecting to enroll full- or part-time at a four-year institution or university. Applicant or parent of applicant must be member of American Academy of Physicians Assistants. Available to U.S. and non-U.S. citizens.

Application Requirements: Application form, essay, financial need analysis, personal photograph, test scores, transcript. *Deadline:* January 15.

Contact: Tara Burnett, Scholarship Committee
Physician Assistant Foundation
950 North Washington Street
Alexandria, VA 22314-1552
Phone: 703-519-5686
Fax: 703-684-1924
E-mail: tburnett@aapa.org

PILOT INTERNATIONAL FOUNDATION

http://www.pilotinternational.org/

PILOT INTERNATIONAL FOUNDATION RUBY NEWHALL MEMORIAL SCHOLARSHIP

Scholarship available to international students for full-time study in the United States or Canada. Applicants must have visa or green card and must be majoring in a field related to human health and welfare. Minimum of one full academic semester in an accredited college in the United States or Canada must be completed before applying for the scholarship. Applicants must be sponsored by Pilot Club in their home town, or in the city in which their college or university is located.

Academic Fields/Career Goals: Health and Medical Sciences; Nursing; Psychology; Public Health; Social Services; Special Education; Therapy/Rehabilitation.

Award: Scholarship for use in freshman, sophomore, junior, or senior years; not renewable. *Number:* 8–10. *Amount:* up to $1500.

Eligibility Requirements: Applicant must be enrolled or expecting to enroll full- or part-time at a two-year or four-year or technical institution. Applicant must have 3.0 GPA or higher. Available to Canadian and non-U.S. citizens.

Application Requirements: Application form, essay, financial need analysis, recommendations or references, self-addressed stamped envelope with application, transcript, visa or F1 status. *Deadline:* March 1.

Contact: Jennifer Overbay, Foundation Services Director
Phone: 478-743-7403
Fax: 478-474-7229
E-mail: pifinfo@pilothq.org

PILOT INTERNATIONAL FOUNDATION SCHOLARSHIP PROGRAM

Scholarship program for undergraduate students preparing for a career helping those with brain related disorders or disabilities. Applicant must have visa or green card. Minimum GPA Score to be 3.25.

Academic Fields/Career Goals: Health and Medical Sciences; Nursing; Psychology; Special Education; Therapy/Rehabilitation.

Award: Scholarship for use in freshman, sophomore, or junior years; not renewable. *Number:* 8–10. *Amount:* up to $2000.

Eligibility Requirements: Applicant must be enrolled or expecting to enroll full- or part-time at a two-year or four-year or technical institution. Available to U.S. and non-U.S. citizens.

Application Requirements: Application form, essay, financial need analysis, recommendations or references, self-addressed stamped envelope with application, transcript, visa or F1 status. *Deadline:* March 1.

Contact: Jennifer Overbay, Foundation Services Director
Phone: 478-743-7403
Fax: 478-474-7229
E-mail: pifinfo@pilothq.org

PRESBYTERIAN CHURCH (USA)

http://www.pcusa.org/financialaid

STUDENT OPPORTUNITY SCHOLARSHIP
• See page 243

SIGMA XI, THE SCIENTIFIC RESEARCH SOCIETY

http://www.sigmaxi.org/

SIGMA XI GRANTS-IN-AID OF RESEARCH
• See page 95

SOCIETY FOR APPLIED ANTHROPOLOGY

http://www.sfaa.net/

PETER KONG-MING NEW STUDENT PRIZE
• See page 142

SOCIETY FOR THE SCIENTIFIC STUDY OF SEXUALITY

http://www.sexscience.org/

SOCIETY FOR THE SCIENTIFIC STUDY OF SEXUALITY STUDENT RESEARCH GRANT
• See page 102

SOCIETY OF NUCLEAR MEDICINE AND MOLECULAR IMAGING

http://www.snmmi.org/

PAUL COLE TECHNOLOGIST SCHOLARSHIP

Scholarship for students who are enrolled in or accepted for enrollment in associate, baccalaureate or certificate programs in nuclear medicine technology. Academic merit considered. Minimum 2.5 GPA required.

Academic Fields/Career Goals: Health and Medical Sciences; Nuclear Science; Radiology.

Award: Scholarship for use in freshman, sophomore, junior, or senior years; not renewable. *Number:* 15–25. *Amount:* $1000.

Eligibility Requirements: Applicant must be enrolled or expecting to enroll full- or part-time at a two-year or four-year or technical institution or university. Applicant must have 2.5 GPA or higher. Available to U.S. and non-U.S. citizens.

Application Requirements: Acceptance letter, application form, application form may be submitted online (http://www.snmmi.org/grants), essay, financial need analysis, recommendations or references, resume, transcript. *Deadline:* March 31.

Contact: Kristi Padley, SNMMI Development Office
Phone: 703-652-6780
Fax: 703-708-9013
E-mail: kpadley@snmmi.org

SOCIETY OF PEDIATRIC NURSES

http://www.pedsnurses.org/

SOCIETY OF PEDIATRIC NURSES EDUCATIONAL SCHOLARSHIP
• See page 178

STRAIGHTFORWARD MEDIA

http://www.straightforwardmedia.com/

STRAIGHTFORWARD MEDIA MEDICAL PROFESSIONS SCHOLARSHIP
• See page 224

UNITED NEGRO COLLEGE FUND

http://www.uncf.org/

CHARLES E. CULPEPPER SCHOLARSHIP
• See page 148

EARL & PATRICIA ARMSTRONG SCHOLARSHIP
• See page 148

HARRY C. JAECKER SCHOLARSHIP

Award for pre-medical students attending a UNCF member college or university. Minimum 2.5 GPA required. For additional information, go to website http://www.uncf.org.

Academic Fields/Career Goals: Health and Medical Sciences.

Award: Scholarship for use in freshman, sophomore, junior, or senior years; not renewable. *Amount:* $2000–$5000.

Eligibility Requirements: Applicant must be Black (non-Hispanic) and enrolled or expecting to enroll full- or part-time at a four-year institution or university. Applicant must have 2.5 GPA or higher. Available to U.S. and non-U.S. citizens.

Application Requirements: Application form, financial need analysis. *Deadline:* continuous.

HARRY C. JAECKER SCHOLARSHIP

Scholarship for premedical students who attend a UNCF member college or university. Minimum 2.5 GPA required.

Academic Fields/Career Goals: Health and Medical Sciences.

Award: Scholarship for use in freshman, sophomore, junior, or senior years; not renewable. *Amount:* $2000–$5000.

Eligibility Requirements: Applicant must be Black (non-Hispanic) and enrolled or expecting to enroll full-time at a four-year institution or university. Applicant must have 2.5 GPA or higher. Available to U.S. citizens.

Application Requirements: Application form. *Deadline:* continuous.

UNCF/MERCK SCIENCE INITIATIVE
• *See page 149*

WILMA WARBURG SCHOLARSHIP

Scholarships for students attending Clark Atlanta University, Morehouse College, Morris Brown College, Spelman College, or ITC. Minimum 2.5 GPA required. Must be majoring in science or health.

Academic Fields/Career Goals: Health and Medical Sciences; Natural Sciences; Physical Sciences.

Award: Scholarship for use in freshman, sophomore, junior, or senior years; not renewable.

Eligibility Requirements: Applicant must be Black (non-Hispanic) and enrolled or expecting to enroll full-time at a four-year institution. Applicant must have 2.5 GPA or higher. Available to U.S. citizens.

Application Requirements: Application form. *Deadline:* continuous.

U. S. DEPARTMENT OF HEALTH AND HUMAN SERVICES

http://www.hhs.gov/about/whatwedo.html/

U. S. PUBLIC HEALTH SERVICE-HEALTH RESOURCES AND SERVICES ADMINISTRATION, BUREAU OF HEALTH PROFESSIONS SCHOLARSHIPS FOR DISADVANTAGED STUDENTS
• *See page 225*

VESALIUS TRUST FOR VISUAL COMMUNICATION IN THE HEALTH SCIENCES

http://www.vesaliustrust.org/

STUDENT RESEARCH SCHOLARSHIP

Scholarships available to students currently enrolled in an undergraduate or graduate school program of bio-communications (medical illustration) who have completed one full year of the curriculum.

Academic Fields/Career Goals: Health and Medical Sciences.

Award: Scholarship for use in junior, senior, or graduate years; not renewable. *Number:* 10–15. *Amount:* $500.

Eligibility Requirements: Applicant must be enrolled or expecting to enroll full- or part-time at a four-year institution or university and must have an interest in art. Available to U.S. and non-U.S. citizens.

Application Requirements: Application form, portfolio, recommendations or references, resume, transcript. *Deadline:* November 7.

Contact: Wendy Gee, Student Grants and Scholarships
Vesalius Trust for Visual Communication in the Health Sciences
1100 Grundy Lane
San Bruno, CA 94066
Phone: 650-244-4320
E-mail: wendy.hillergee@krames.com

ZETA PHI BETA SORORITY INC. NATIONAL EDUCATIONAL FOUNDATION

http://www.zpbnef1975.org/

S. EVELYN LEWIS MEMORIAL SCHOLARSHIP IN MEDICAL HEALTH SCIENCES

Scholarships available for graduate or undergraduate women enrolled in a program leading to a degree in medicine or health sciences. Must be a full-time student. See website for information and application, http://www.zpbnef1975.org/.

Academic Fields/Career Goals: Health and Medical Sciences.

Award: Scholarship for use in freshman, sophomore, junior, senior, or graduate years; not renewable. *Number:* 1. *Amount:* $500–$1000.

Eligibility Requirements: Applicant must be enrolled or expecting to enroll full-time at a four-year institution or university and female. Available to U.S. citizens.

Application Requirements: Application form, essay, proof of enrollment, recommendations or references, transcript. *Deadline:* February 1.

Contact: Cheryl Williams, National Second Vice President
Fax: 318-232-4593
E-mail: 2ndanti@zphib1920.org

HEALTH INFORMATION MANAGEMENT/ TECHNOLOGY

AHIMA FOUNDATION

http://ahimafoundation.org/

AHIMA FOUNDATION STUDENT MERIT SCHOLARSHIP

Merit scholarships for undergraduate, Masters, and Doctoral health information management students. Must be a member of AHIMA. One standard application for all available scholarships. Applicant must have a minimum cumulative GPA of 3.5 (out of 4.0) or 4.5 (out of 5.0). Applications can be downloaded at http://ahimafoundation.org/Scholarships/meritscholarships.aspx

Academic Fields/Career Goals: Health Information Management/Technology.

Award: Scholarship for use in sophomore, junior, senior, graduate, or postgraduate years; not renewable. *Number:* 1. *Amount:* $1000–$2500.

Eligibility Requirements: Applicant must be enrolled or expecting to enroll full- or part-time at a two-year or four-year institution or university. Applicant or parent of applicant must be member of American Health Information Management Association. Applicant must have 3.5 GPA or higher. Available to U.S. and non-U.S. citizens.

Application Requirements: Application form, application form may be submitted online (http://ahimafoundation.org/Scholarships/meritscholarships.aspx), community service, essay, program director verification, recommendations or references, transcript. *Deadline:* September 30.

ALICE L. HALTOM EDUCATIONAL FUND

http://www.alhef.org/

ALICE L. HALTOM EDUCATIONAL FUND

Award for students pursuing a career in information and records management. Up to $1000 for those in an associate degree program, and up to $2000 for students in a baccalaureate or advanced degree program. Students must be citizens of the United States, Canada or Mexico.

Academic Fields/Career Goals: Health Information Management/Technology; Library and Information Sciences.

Award: Scholarship for use in freshman, sophomore, junior, senior, or graduate years; not renewable. *Number:* 5–25. *Amount:* $1000–$2000.

Eligibility Requirements: Applicant must be enrolled or expecting to enroll full- or part-time at a two-year or four-year institution or university. Available to U.S. and non-U.S. citizens.

Application Requirements: Application form, essay, recommendations or references, transcript. *Deadline:* May 1.

BETHESDA LUTHERAN COMMUNITIES

http://www.bethesdalutherancommunities.org/scholarships

DEVELOPMENTAL DISABILITIES SCHOLASTIC ACHIEVEMENT SCHOLARSHIP FOR COLLEGE STUDENTS WHO ARE LUTHERAN
• See page 222

CANADIAN SOCIETY FOR MEDICAL LABORATORY SCIENCE

http://www.csmls.org/

E.V. BOOTH SCHOLARSHIP AWARD
• See page 326

CONGRESSIONAL BLACK CAUCUS FOUNDATION, INC.

http://www.cbcfinc.org/

CBCF GENERAL MILLS HEALTH SCHOLARSHIP
• See page 144

CYNTHIA E. MORGAN SCHOLARSHIP FUND (CEMS)

http://www.cemsfund.com/

CYNTHIA E. MORGAN MEMORIAL SCHOLARSHIP FUND, INC.
• See page 298

HEALTHCARE INFORMATION AND MANAGEMENT SYSTEMS SOCIETY FOUNDATION

http://www.himss.org/

HIMSS FOUNDATION SCHOLARSHIP PROGRAM
• See page 327

HEALTH RESEARCH COUNCIL OF NEW ZEALAND

http://www.hrc.govt.nz/

PACIFIC HEALTH WORKFORCE AWARD
• See page 327

PACIFIC MENTAL HEALTH WORK FORCE AWARD
• See page 327

INDIAN HEALTH SERVICES, UNITED STATES DEPARTMENT OF HEALTH AND HUMAN SERVICES

http://www.ihs.gov/scholarship

INDIAN HEALTH SERVICE HEALTH PROFESSIONS SCHOLARSHIP PROGRAM
• See page 208

NATIONAL ATHLETIC TRAINERS' ASSOCIATION RESEARCH AND EDUCATION FOUNDATION

http://www.natafoundation.org/

NATIONAL ATHLETIC TRAINERS' ASSOCIATION RESEARCH AND EDUCATION FOUNDATION SCHOLARSHIP PROGRAM
• See page 337

STRAIGHTFORWARD MEDIA

http://www.straightforwardmedia.com/

STRAIGHTFORWARD MEDIA MEDICAL PROFESSIONS SCHOLARSHIP
• See page 224

HEATING, AIR-CONDITIONING, AND REFRIGERATION MECHANICS

AMERICAN SOCIETY OF HEATING, REFRIGERATING, AND AIR CONDITIONING ENGINEERS, INC.

http://www.ashrae.org/

ALWIN B. NEWTON SCHOLARSHIP
• See page 249

ASHRAE GENERAL SCHOLARSHIPS
• See page 260

ASHRAE MEMORIAL SCHOLARSHIP
• See page 249

DUANE HANSON SCHOLARSHIP
• See page 250

ENGINEERING TECHNOLOGY SCHOLARSHIP
• See page 250

FRANK M. CODA SCHOLARSHIP
• See page 250

HENRY ADAMS SCHOLARSHIP
• See page 250

REUBEN TRANE SCHOLARSHIP
• *See page 250*

WILLIS H. CARRIER SCHOLARSHIPS
• *See page 251*

INTERNATIONAL SOCIETY OF AUTOMATION (ISA)

http://www.isa.org/

INTERNATIONAL SOCIETY OF AUTOMATION EDUCATION FOUNDATION SCHOLARSHIPS
• *See page 131*

PLUMBING-HEATING-COOLING CONTRACTORS EDUCATION FOUNDATION

http://www.phccfoundation.org/

BRADFORD WHITE CORPORATION SCHOLARSHIP

Scholarship for students enrolled in either an approved four-year PHCC apprenticeship program or at an accredited two-year community college, technical college, or trade school.

Academic Fields/Career Goals: Heating, Air-Conditioning, and Refrigeration Mechanics; Trade/Technical Specialties.

Award: Scholarship for use in freshman, sophomore, junior, or senior years; not renewable. *Number:* 3. *Amount:* $2500.

Eligibility Requirements: Applicant must be enrolled or expecting to enroll full-time at a two-year or technical institution. Applicant must have 2.5 GPA or higher. Available to U.S. and Canadian citizens.

Application Requirements: Application form, recommendations or references, test scores, transcript. *Deadline:* May 1.

Contact: John Zink, Scholarship Coordinator
  Phone: 800-533-7694
  E-mail: foundation@naphcc.org

DELTA FAUCET COMPANY SCHOLARSHIP PROGRAM
• *See page 158*

PHCC EDUCATIONAL FOUNDATION NEED-BASED SCHOLARSHIP
• *See page 158*

PHCC EDUCATIONAL FOUNDATION SCHOLARSHIP PROGRAM
• *See page 158*

PROFESSIONAL CONSTRUCTION ESTIMATORS ASSOCIATION

http://www.pcea.org/

TED G. WILSON MEMORIAL SCHOLARSHIP FOUNDATION
• *See page 184*

SOUTH CAROLINA ASSOCIATION OF HEATING AND AIR CONDITIONING CONTRACTORS

http://www.schvac.org/

SOUTH CAROLINA ASSOCIATION OF HEATING AND AIR CONDITIONING CONTRACTORS SCHOLARSHIP

Scholarship of $500 to pursue a career in the heating and air conditioning industry. Participating students must maintain an overall GPA of 2.5 and a GPA of 3.0 in all major topics. Deadline varies.

Academic Fields/Career Goals: Heating, Air-Conditioning, and Refrigeration Mechanics.

Award: Scholarship for use in freshman year; renewable. *Amount:* $500.

Eligibility Requirements: Applicant must be high school student and planning to enroll or expecting to enroll full- or part-time at a technical institution. Applicant must have 2.5 GPA or higher. Available to U.S. and non-U.S. citizens.

Application Requirements: Application form, recommendations or references. *Deadline:* varies.

Contact: Leigh Faircloth, Scholarship Committee
  Phone: 800-395-9276
  Fax: 803-252-7799
  E-mail: staff@schvac.org

SOUTH DAKOTA RETAILERS ASSOCIATION

http://www.sdra.org/

SOUTH DAKOTA RETAILERS ASSOCIATION SCHOLARSHIP PROGRAM
• *See page 80*

STRAIGHTFORWARD MEDIA

http://www.straightforwardmedia.com/

STRAIGHTFORWARD MEDIA VOCATIONAL-TECHNICAL SCHOOL SCHOLARSHIP
• *See page 99*

HISTORIC PRESERVATION AND CONSERVATION

AMERICAN SCHOOL OF CLASSICAL STUDIES AT ATHENS

http://www.ascsa.edu.gr/

ASCSA SUMMER SESSIONS SCHOLARSHIPS
• *See page 100*

COSTUME SOCIETY OF AMERICA

http://www.costumesocietyamerica.com/

ADELE FILENE TRAVEL AWARD
• *See page 114*

STELLA BLUM RESEARCH GRANT
• *See page 114*

THE GEORGIA TRUST FOR HISTORIC PRESERVATION

http://www.georgiatrust.org/

B. PHINIZY SPALDING, HUBERT B. OWENS, AND THE NATIONAL SOCIETY OF THE COLONIAL DAMES OF AMERICA IN THE STATE OF GEORGIA ACADEMIC SCHOLARSHIPS
• *See page 97*

J. NEEL REID PRIZE
• *See page 111*

HISTORY

AMERICAN FEDERATION OF STATE, COUNTY, AND MUNICIPAL EMPLOYEES

http://www.afscme.org/

AFSCME/UNCF UNION SCHOLARS PROGRAM
• *See page 97*

AMERICAN PHILOLOGICAL ASSOCIATION

http://www.apaclassics.org/

MINORITY STUDENT SUMMER SCHOLARSHIP
• *See page 108*

AMERICAN SCHOOL OF CLASSICAL STUDIES AT ATHENS

http://www.ascsa.edu.gr/

ASCSA SUMMER SESSIONS SCHOLARSHIPS
• *See page 100*

ARRL FOUNDATION INC.

http://www.arrl.org/

FRANCIS WALTON MEMORIAL SCHOLARSHIP
• *See page 91*

ASSOCIATION OF FORMER INTELLIGENCE OFFICERS

http://www.afio.com/13_scholarships.htm

CIA UNDERGRADUATE SCHOLARSHIPS
• *See page 97*

CANADIAN INSTITUTE OF UKRAINIAN STUDIES

http://www.cius.ca/

LEO J. KRYSA UNDERGRADUATE SCHOLARSHIP
• *See page 114*

COLLEGEBOUND FOUNDATION

http://www.collegeboundfoundation.org/

DECATUR H. MILLER SCHOLARSHIP
You must: major in the field of political science, history, or pre-law; have a cumulative 3.0 GPA or better; and an SAT (CR+M) score of at least 1100.
Academic Fields/Career Goals: History; Law/Legal Services; Political Science.
Award: Scholarship for use in freshman, sophomore, junior, or senior years; renewable. *Number:* 1. *Amount:* $1500.
Eligibility Requirements: Applicant must be high school student; planning to enroll or expecting to enroll full-time at a four-year institution or university; resident of Maryland and studying in Maryland. Applicant must have 3.0 GPA or higher. Available to U.S. citizens.
Application Requirements: Application form, application form may be submitted online (http://www.scholarships.mycbf.net/STARS), financial need analysis, recommendations or references, resume, test scores, transcript. *Deadline:* March 1.

Contact: Michael Thornton, Associate Program Director, Scholarship Programs
Phone: 410-783-2905 Ext. 207
Fax: 410-727-5786
E-mail: mthornton@collegeboundfoundation.org

THE ROBERT SPAR MEMORIAL SCHOLARSHIP
You must major in the field of political science, history, or pre-law; have a cumulative 3.0 GPA or better; and be accepted to and attend Bowie State University, Coppin State University, Frostburg State University, Morgan State University, St. Mary's College of Maryland, Stevenson University, Towson University, University of Maryland College Park, or University of Maryland Eastern Shore.
Academic Fields/Career Goals: History; Law/Legal Services; Political Science.
Award: Scholarship for use in freshman, sophomore, junior, or senior years; renewable. *Number:* up to 1. *Amount:* $1500.
Eligibility Requirements: Applicant must be high school student; planning to enroll or expecting to enroll full-time at a two-year or four-year institution or university; resident of Maryland and studying in Maryland. Applicant must have 3.0 GPA or higher. Available to U.S. citizens.
Application Requirements: *Deadline:* March 1.
Contact: Michael Thornton, Associate Program Director, Scholarship Programs
Phone: 410-783-2905 Ext. 207
Fax: 410-727-5786
E-mail: mthornton@collegeboundfoundation.org

COSTUME SOCIETY OF AMERICA

http://www.costumesocietyamerica.com/

ADELE FILENE TRAVEL AWARD
• *See page 114*

STELLA BLUM RESEARCH GRANT
• *See page 114*

CULTURAL SERVICES OF THE FRENCH EMBASSY

http://www.frenchculture.org/

TEACHING ASSISTANT PROGRAM IN FRANCE
• *See page 97*

THE GEORGIA TRUST FOR HISTORIC PRESERVATION

http://www.georgiatrust.org/

B. PHINIZY SPALDING, HUBERT B. OWENS, AND THE NATIONAL SOCIETY OF THE COLONIAL DAMES OF AMERICA IN THE STATE OF GEORGIA ACADEMIC SCHOLARSHIPS
• *See page 97*

GREATER SALINA COMMUNITY FOUNDATION

http://www.gscf.org/

KANSAS FEDERATION OF REPUBLICAN WOMEN SCHOLARSHIP
Awards female students currently attending a Kansas college or university with declared major of political science, history, or public administration. Must be entering junior or senior year of undergraduate study, or attending graduate school. Must be Kansas residents and maintain cumulative GPA of 3.0 or better. Applicants must be registered members of the Republican Party. Must be involved in extracurricular activities.

Academic Fields/Career Goals: History; Political Science; Public Policy and Administration.

Award: Scholarship for use in junior, senior, or graduate years; renewable. *Number:* 1. *Amount:* up to $1000.

Eligibility Requirements: Applicant must be enrolled or expecting to enroll full-time at a two-year or four-year institution or university; female; resident of Kansas and studying in Kansas. Applicant must have 3.0 GPA or higher. Available to U.S. citizens.

Application Requirements: Application form, essay. *Deadline:* March 31.

Contact: Michelle Griffin, Scholarship and Affiliate Coordinator
Greater Salina Community Foundation
PO Box 2876
Salina, KS 67402-2876
Phone: 785-823-1800
E-mail: michellegriffin@gscf.org

HARVARD TRAVELLERS CLUB

http://www.harvardtravellersclub.org/

HARVARD TRAVELLERS CLUB GRANTS
• *See page 108*

INSTITUTE FOR HUMANE STUDIES

http://www.theihs.org/

HUMANE STUDIES FELLOWSHIPS
• *See page 190*

KE ALI'I PAUAHI FOUNDATION

http://www.pauahi.org/

SARAH KELI'ILOLENA LUM KONIA NAKOA SCHOLARSHIP
• *See page 321*

THE LYNDON BAINES JOHNSON FOUNDATION

http://www.lbjfoundation.org/

MOODY RESEARCH GRANTS

Grants to defray travel and other expenses incurred while conducting research at LBJ Library. September 15 deadline for spring term (January 1 to August 31). March 15 deadline for fall term (June 1 to December 31). Must contact Archives regarding availability of material. Should state clearly how Library's holdings will contribute to completion of project.

Academic Fields/Career Goals: History; Political Science.

Award: Grant for use in senior, graduate, or postgraduate years; not renewable. *Number:* 10–15. *Amount:* $500–$2500.

Eligibility Requirements: Applicant must be enrolled or expecting to enroll full- or part-time at an institution or university and studying in Texas. Available to U.S. and non-U.S. citizens.

Application Requirements: Application form, application form may be submitted online (http://www.lbjfoundation.org), recommendations or references, research proposal. *Deadline:* varies.

Contact: Mrs. Stephanie Savage, Director of Grants and Programs
Phone: 512-232-2280
Fax: 512-232-2285
E-mail: ssavage@lbjfoundation.org

NATIONAL SOCIETY DAUGHTERS OF THE AMERICAN REVOLUTION

http://www.dar.org/

NATIONAL SOCIETY DAUGHTERS OF THE AMERICAN REVOLUTION DR. AURA-LEE A. PITTENGER AND JAMES HOBBS PITTENGER AMERICAN HISTORY SCHOLARSHIP

Scholarship of $2000 each year for up to four consecutive years to a graduating high school senior who will have a concentrated study of a minimum of 24 credit hours in American history or American government while in college. United States citizens residing abroad may apply through a Units Overseas chapter.

Academic Fields/Career Goals: History; Political Science.

Award: Scholarship for use in freshman year; renewable. *Number:* 1. *Amount:* $2000.

Eligibility Requirements: Applicant must be high school student and planning to enroll or expecting to enroll full-time at a four-year institution or university. Available to U.S. citizens.

Application Requirements: Application form, letter of sponsorship, recommendations or references, self-addressed stamped envelope with application, transcript. *Deadline:* February 15.

Contact: Tania Tatum, Manager, Office of the Reporter General
Phone: 202-628-1776
Fax: 202-879-3348
E-mail: nsdarscholarships@dar.org

NATIONAL SOCIETY DAUGHTERS OF THE AMERICAN REVOLUTION ENID HALL GRISWOLD MEMORIAL SCHOLARSHIP
• *See page 230*

PHI ALPHA THETA HISTORY HONOR SOCIETY, INC.

http://www.phialphatheta.org/

PHI ALPHA THETA PAPER PRIZES

Award for best graduate and undergraduate student papers. Grants $500 prize for best graduate student paper, $500 prize for best undergraduate paper, and four $350 prizes for either graduate or undergraduate papers. All applicants must be members of the association.

Academic Fields/Career Goals: History.

Award: Prize for use in freshman, sophomore, junior, senior, or graduate years; not renewable. *Number:* 6. *Amount:* $350–$500.

Eligibility Requirements: Applicant must be enrolled or expecting to enroll full-time at a four-year institution or university. Applicant or parent of applicant must be member of Phi Alpha Theta. Applicant must have 3.0 GPA or higher. Available to U.S. and non-U.S. citizens.

Application Requirements: Essay, recommendations or references. *Deadline:* June 30.

Contact: Dr. Clayton Drees, Department of History
Phi Alpha Theta History Honor Society, Inc.
Virginia Wesleyan College, 1584 Wesleyan Drive
Norfolk, VA 23502-5599
E-mail: cdrees@vwc.edu

PHI ALPHA THETA UNDERGRADUATE STUDENT SCHOLARSHIP

Awards of $1000 available to exceptional juniors entering the senior year and majoring in modern European history (1815 to present). Must be Phi Alpha Theta members. Based on both financial need and merit.

Academic Fields/Career Goals: History.

Award: Scholarship for use in senior year; not renewable. *Number:* 1. *Amount:* $1000.

Eligibility Requirements: Applicant must be enrolled or expecting to enroll full-time at a four-year institution or university. Applicant or parent of applicant must be member of Phi Alpha Theta. Available to U.S. and non-U.S. citizens.

Application Requirements: Application form, recommendations or references, resume, transcript. *Deadline:* March 1.

Contact: Dr. Graydon Tunstall, Executive Director
Phi Alpha Theta History Honor Society, Inc.
University of South Florida
4202 East Fowler Avenue, SOC 107
Tampa, FL 33620-8100
Phone: 800-394-8195
Fax: 813-974-8215
E-mail: info@phialphatheta.org

PHI ALPHA THETA/WESTERN FRONT ASSOCIATION PAPER PRIZE

Essay competition open to full-time undergraduate members of the association. The paper must be from 12 to 15 typed pages and must address the American experience in World War I, must be dealing with virtually any aspect of American involvement during the period from 1912 (second Moroccan crisis) to 1924 (Dawes plan). Primary source material must be used. For further details visit http://www.phialphatheta.org.

Academic Fields/Career Goals: History.

Award: Prize for use in freshman, sophomore, junior, or senior years; not renewable. *Number:* 1. *Amount:* $1000.

Eligibility Requirements: Applicant must be enrolled or expecting to enroll full-time at a four-year institution or university and must have an interest in writing. Applicant or parent of applicant must be member of Phi Alpha Theta. Applicant must have 3.0 GPA or higher. Available to U.S. and non-U.S. citizens.

Application Requirements: 5 copies of the paper, CD-ROM containing a file of the paper and cover letter, application form, essay. *Deadline:* December 1.

Contact: Dr. Graydon Tunstall, Executive Director
Phi Alpha Theta History Honor Society, Inc.
University of South Florida
4202 East Fowler Avenue, SOC 107
Tampa, FL 33620-8100
Phone: 800-394-8195
Fax: 813-974-8215
E-mail: info@phialphatheta.org

PHI ALPHA THETA WORLD HISTORY ASSOCIATION PAPER PRIZE

Awards one undergraduate and one graduate-level prize for papers examining any historical issue with global implications such as: exchange or interchange of cultures, comparison of civilizations or cultures. This is a joint award with the World History Association. Must be a member of the World History Association or Phi Alpha Theta. Paper must have been composed while enrolled at an accredited college or university. Must send in four copies of paper along with professor's letter.

Academic Fields/Career Goals: History; Humanities; International Studies; Social Sciences.

Award: Prize for use in freshman, sophomore, junior, senior, or graduate years; not renewable. *Number:* 2. *Amount:* $500.

Eligibility Requirements: Applicant must be enrolled or expecting to enroll full-time at a four-year institution or university. Applicant or parent of applicant must be member of Other Student Academic Clubs, Phi Alpha Theta. Applicant must have 3.0 GPA or higher. Available to U.S. and non-U.S. citizens.

Application Requirements: 4 copies of paper, abstract, letter from faculty member or professor, recommendations or references. *Deadline:* June 30.

SONS OF THE REPUBLIC OF TEXAS

http://www.srttexas.org/

PRESIDIO LA BAHIA AWARD
• *See page 98*

TEXAS HISTORY ESSAY CONTEST
• *See page 98*

STRAIGHTFORWARD MEDIA

http://www.straightforwardmedia.com/

STRAIGHTFORWARD MEDIA LIBERAL ARTS SCHOLARSHIP
• *See page 116*

TOPSFIELD HISTORICAL SOCIETY

http://www.topsfieldhistory.org/

JOHN KIMBALL MEMORIAL TRUST SCHOLARSHIP PROGRAM FOR THE STUDY OF HISTORY

Scholarship grants funds for tuition, books, and other educational and research expenses to undergraduate and graduate students; as well as college, university, and graduate school instructors and professors who have excelled in, and/or have a passion for the study of history and related disciplines; and who reside in, or have a substantial connection to Topsfield, Massachusetts.

Academic Fields/Career Goals: History.

Award: Grant for use in freshman, sophomore, junior, senior, graduate, or postgraduate years; not renewable. *Number:* 3–10. *Amount:* $300–$5000.

Eligibility Requirements: Applicant must be enrolled or expecting to enroll full- or part-time at a two-year or four-year or technical institution or university and resident of Massachusetts. Available to U.S. citizens.

Application Requirements: Application form. *Deadline:* April 15.

Contact: Mr. Norman Isler, Trustee, John Kimball Scholarship Program
Topsfield Historical Society
PO Box 323
Topsfield, MA 01983
Phone: 978-887-9724
Fax: 978-887-0185
E-mail: normisler@comcast.net

UNITED DAUGHTERS OF THE CONFEDERACY

http://www.hqudc.org/

HELEN JAMES BREWER SCHOLARSHIP

Award for full-time undergraduate student who is a descendant of a Confederate soldier, sailor or marine. Must be from Alabama, Florida, Georgia, South Carolina, Tennessee or Virginia. Recipient must be enrolled in an accredited college or university and studying history and literature. Must be a member or former member of the Children of the Confederacy. Minimum 3.0 GPA required.

Academic Fields/Career Goals: History; Literature/English/Writing.

Award: Scholarship for use in freshman, sophomore, junior, or senior years; renewable. *Number:* 1–2. *Amount:* $800–$1000.

Eligibility Requirements: Applicant must be enrolled or expecting to enroll full-time at a four-year institution or university and resident of Alabama, Florida, Georgia, South Carolina, Tennessee, Virginia. Applicant or parent of applicant must be member of Children of the Confederacy, United Daughters of the Confederacy. Applicant must have 3.0 GPA or higher. Available to U.S. citizens.

Application Requirements: Application form, copy of applicant's birth certificate, copy of confederate ancestor's proof of service, essay, financial need analysis, personal photograph, recommendations or references, self-addressed stamped envelope with application, test scores, transcript. *Deadline:* March 15.

Contact: Ms. Jamie Davis, Second Vice President General
Phone: 804-355-1636
E-mail: hqudc@rcn.com

UNITED NEGRO COLLEGE FUND

http://www.uncf.org/

AFSCME/UNCF/HARVARD UNIVERSITY LWP UNION SCHOLARS PROGRAM
• *See page 98*

CATHERINE W. PIERCE SCHOLARSHIP
• *See page 116*

HOME ECONOMICS

ABBIE SARGENT MEMORIAL SCHOLARSHIP INC.

http://www.nhfarmbureau.org/

ABBIE SARGENT MEMORIAL SCHOLARSHIP
• See page 84

AMERICAN ASSOCIATION OF FAMILY & CONSUMER SERVICES

http://www.aafcs.org/

AMERICAN ASSOCIATION OF FAMILY & CONSUMER SCIENCES NATIONAL UNDERGRADUATE SCHOLARSHIP

The association awards scholarships to individuals who have exhibited the potential to make contributions to the family and consumer sciences profession.

Academic Fields/Career Goals: Home Economics.

Award: Scholarship for use in sophomore, junior, or senior years; not renewable. *Number:* up to 1. *Amount:* up to $5000.

Eligibility Requirements: Applicant must be enrolled or expecting to enroll full-time at a four-year institution or university. Available to U.S. citizens.

Application Requirements: Application form, application form may be submitted online (http://www.aafcs.org), recommendations or references, resume, transcript. *Deadline:* January 15.

COSTUME SOCIETY OF AMERICA

http://www.costumesocietyamerica.com/

ADELE FILENE TRAVEL AWARD
• See page 114

STELLA BLUM RESEARCH GRANT
• See page 114

FAMILY, CAREER AND COMMUNITY LEADERS OF AMERICA-TEXAS ASSOCIATION

http://www.texasfccla.org/

C.J. DAVIDSON SCHOLARSHIP FOR FCCLA

Renewable award for graduating high school seniors enrolled in full-time program in family and consumer sciences. Must be Texas resident and should study in Texas. Must have minimum GPA of 2.5.

Academic Fields/Career Goals: Home Economics.

Award: Scholarship for use in freshman year; renewable. *Number:* up to 10. *Amount:* up to $18,000.

Eligibility Requirements: Applicant must be high school student; planning to enroll or expecting to enroll full-time at a four-year institution or university; single; resident of Texas and studying in Texas. Applicant or parent of applicant must be member of Family, Career and Community Leaders of America. Applicant must have 2.5 GPA or higher. Available to U.S. citizens.

Application Requirements: Application form, essay, recommendations or references, test scores, transcript. *Deadline:* March 1.

FCCLA HOUSTON LIVESTOCK SHOW AND RODEO SCHOLARSHIP
• See page 154

FCCLA REGIONAL SCHOLARSHIPS
• See page 154

FCCLA TEXAS FARM BUREAU SCHOLARSHIP
• See page 154

INTERNATIONAL EXECUTIVE HOUSEKEEPERS ASSOCIATION

http://www.ieha.org/

INTERNATIONAL EXECUTIVE HOUSEKEEPERS EDUCATIONAL FOUNDATION
• See page 317

INTERNATIONAL FOODSERVICE EDITORIAL COUNCIL

http://www.ifeconline.com/

INTERNATIONAL FOODSERVICE EDITORIAL COUNCIL COMMUNICATIONS SCHOLARSHIP
• See page 83

MAINE SCHOOL FOOD SERVICE ASSOCIATION (MSFSA) CONTINUING EDUCATION SCHOLARSHIP

http://www.mainesfsa.org/

MAINE SCHOOL FOOD SERVICE ASSOCIATION CONTINUING EDUCATION SCHOLARSHIP
• See page 218

MARYLAND ASSOCIATION OF PRIVATE COLLEGES AND CAREER SCHOOLS

http://www.mapccs.org/

MARYLAND ASSOCIATION OF PRIVATE COLLEGES AND CAREER SCHOOLS SCHOLARSHIP
• See page 157

UNITED DAUGHTERS OF THE CONFEDERACY

http://www.hqudc.org/

WALTER REED SMITH SCHOLARSHIP
• See page 160

HORTICULTURE/ FLORICULTURE

ABBIE SARGENT MEMORIAL SCHOLARSHIP INC.

http://www.nhfarmbureau.org/

ABBIE SARGENT MEMORIAL SCHOLARSHIP
• See page 84

ALABAMA GOLF COURSE SUPERINTENDENTS ASSOCIATION

http://www.agcsa.org/

ALABAMA GOLF COURSE SUPERINTENDENT'S ASSOCIATION'S DONNIE ARTHUR MEMORIAL SCHOLARSHIP
• See page 89

AMERICAN SOCIETY FOR ENOLOGY AND VITICULTURE

http://www.asev.org/

AMERICAN SOCIETY FOR ENOLOGY AND VITICULTURE SCHOLARSHIPS
• See page 90

AMERICAN SOCIETY FOR HORTICULTURAL SCIENCE

http://www.ashs.org/

ASHS SCHOLARS AWARD

Two annual scholarships of $1500 given to undergraduate students majoring in horticulture at a four-year institution. Applicants must be nominated by the chair/head of the department in which they are majoring, but only one applicant per department may be nominated.

Academic Fields/Career Goals: Horticulture/Floriculture.

Award: Scholarship for use in freshman, sophomore, junior, or senior years; not renewable. *Number:* 2. *Amount:* $1500.

Eligibility Requirements: Applicant must be enrolled or expecting to enroll full-time at a four-year institution or university and must have an interest in leadership. Applicant or parent of applicant must have employment or volunteer experience in community service. Available to U.S. and non-U.S. citizens.

Application Requirements: Application form, essay, recommendations or references, resume, transcript. *Deadline:* February 4.

Contact: Michael Neff, Executive Director
  Phone: 703-836-4606 Ext. 106
  Fax: 703-836-2024
  E-mail: mwneff@ashs.org

ARIZONA NURSERY ASSOCIATION

http://www.azna.org/

ARIZONA NURSERY ASSOCIATION FOUNDATION SCHOLARSHIP

Provides research grants and scholarships for the Green Industry. Applicant must be an Arizona resident currently or planning to be enrolled in a horticultural related curriculum at an Arizona university, community college, or continuing education program. See website for further details http://www.azna.org.

Academic Fields/Career Goals: Horticulture/Floriculture.

Award: Scholarship for use in freshman, sophomore, junior, or senior years; renewable. *Number:* 12–16. *Amount:* $500–$3000.

Eligibility Requirements: Applicant must be enrolled or expecting to enroll full- or part-time at a two-year or four-year or technical institution or university. Available to U.S. citizens.

Application Requirements: Application form, recommendations or references, transcript. *Deadline:* April 15.

Contact: Cheryl Goar, Executive Director
  Phone: 480-966-1610
  E-mail: cgoar@azna.org

CALIFORNIA ASSOCIATION OF NURSERYMEN ENDOWMENT FOR RESEARCH AND SCHOLARSHIPS

http://www.cangc.org/

CANERS FOUNDATION ENDOWMENT SCHOLARSHIP

Applicants must be college students who are currently enrolled in no fewer than six units within a program related to the nursery industry and who are entering or returning to college in a horticulture-related field in the fall.

Academic Fields/Career Goals: Horticulture/Floriculture.

Award: Scholarship for use in freshman, sophomore, junior, or senior years; not renewable.

Eligibility Requirements: Applicant must be enrolled or expecting to enroll full-time at a four-year institution or university. Available to U.S. citizens.

Application Requirements: Application form, transcript. *Deadline:* varies.

Contact: Darrelyn Adams, Membership Director
  Phone: 916-928-3900 Ext. 13
  Fax: 916-567-0505
  E-mail: dadams@cangc.org

CHS FOUNDATION

http://www.chsfoundation.org/

CHS FOUNDATION HIGH SCHOOL SCHOLARSHIPS
• See page 84

CHS FOUNDATION TWO-YEAR COLLEGE SCHOLARSHIPS
• See page 85

FEDERATED GARDEN CLUBS OF CONNECTICUT

http://www.ctgardenclubs.org/

FEDERATED GARDEN CLUBS OF CONNECTICUT INC. SCHOLARSHIPS
• See page 144

FEDERATED GARDEN CLUBS OF MARYLAND

http://www.fgcofmd.org/

ROBERT LEWIS BAKER SCHOLARSHIP

Scholarship awards of up to $5000 to encourage the study of ornamental horticulture, and landscape design. Applicants must be high school graduates, current college and/or graduate students, and Maryland residents. Can attend any accredited college/university in the United States.

Academic Fields/Career Goals: Horticulture/Floriculture; Landscape Architecture.

Award: Scholarship for use in freshman, sophomore, junior, senior, or graduate years; not renewable. *Number:* 1. *Amount:* $5000.

Eligibility Requirements: Applicant must be enrolled or expecting to enroll full-time at a four-year institution or university and resident of Maryland. Available to U.S. citizens.

Application Requirements: Application form. *Deadline:* June 30.

Contact: Marjorie Schiebel, Scholarship Chairman
  Phone: 410-296-6961
  E-mail: fgcofmd@aol.com

VIRGINIA P. HENRY SCHOLARSHIP

Scholarship of up to $1000 available to qualified undergraduate students enrolled in horticultural studies. For full-time study. Must be legal residents of Maryland.

Academic Fields/Career Goals: Horticulture/Floriculture.

Award: Scholarship for use in freshman, sophomore, junior, or senior years; not renewable. *Number:* 1. *Amount:* $1000.

Eligibility Requirements: Applicant must be enrolled or expecting to enroll full-time at a four-year institution or university and resident of Maryland. Available to U.S. citizens.

Application Requirements: Application form. *Deadline:* May 1.

Contact: Marjorie Schiebel, Scholarship Chairman
Phone: 410-296-6961
E-mail: fgcofmd@aol.com

FRIENDS OF THE FRELINGHUYSEN ARBORETUM

http://www.arboretumfriends.org/

BENJAMIN C. BLACKBURN SCHOLARSHIP
• See page 302

GARDEN CLUB OF AMERICA

http://www.gcamerica.org/

CORLISS KNAPP ENGLE SCHOLARSHIP IN HORTICULTURE

$2500 award to support horticultural study at an accredited college, university, or major botanic garden or arboretum. Open to college undergraduates and graduate students, advanced degree candidates, or non-degree-seeking applicants above the high school level.

Academic Fields/Career Goals: Horticulture/Floriculture.

Award: Scholarship for use in freshman, sophomore, junior, senior, or graduate years; not renewable. *Number:* 1. *Amount:* $2500.

Eligibility Requirements: Applicant must be enrolled or expecting to enroll at an institution or university. Available to U.S. citizens.

Application Requirements: Application form, essay, recommendations or references. *Deadline:* February 10.

Contact: Connie Yates, Garden Club of America
Garden Club of America
14 East 60th Street
New York, NY 10022
Phone: 212-753-8287
Fax: 212-753-0134
E-mail: cyates@gcamerica.org

GCA AWARD IN DESERT STUDIES
• See page 111

GCA SUMMER SCHOLARSHIP IN FIELD BOTANY

Scholarship of $2000 to undergraduate or graduate students up to master's level wishing to pursue summer field work in botany. All candidates must be enrolled in a U.S. college or university.

Academic Fields/Career Goals: Horticulture/Floriculture; Natural Sciences.

Award: Scholarship for use in freshman, sophomore, junior, senior, or graduate years; not renewable. *Number:* 1. *Amount:* $2000.

Eligibility Requirements: Applicant must be enrolled or expecting to enroll full-time at a four-year institution or university. Available to U.S. citizens.

Application Requirements: Application form, essay, recommendations or references, resume, transcript. *Deadline:* February 1.

Contact: Connie Yates, Garden Club of America
Garden Club of America
14 East 60th Street
New York, NY 10022-1006
Phone: 212-753-8287
Fax: 212-753-0134
E-mail: cyates@gcamerica.org

JOAN K. HUNT AND RACHEL M. HUNT SUMMER SCHOLARSHIP IN FIELD BOTANY

One or more scholarships of $2000 towards summer study in field botany to promote the awareness of the importance of botany to horticulture. Open to undergraduates and graduate students up to the masters degree level with preference given to undergraduate students. Must be enrolled in an accredited United States institution.

Academic Fields/Career Goals: Horticulture/Floriculture; Natural Sciences.

Award: Scholarship for use in freshman, sophomore, junior, senior, or graduate years; not renewable. *Number:* 1. *Amount:* $2000.

Eligibility Requirements: Applicant must be enrolled or expecting to enroll full-time at a four-year institution or university. Available to U.S. citizens.

Application Requirements: Application form, essay, recommendations or references, resume, transcript. *Deadline:* February 1.

Contact: Connie Yates, Garden Club of America
Garden Club of America
14 East 60th Street
New York, NY 10022-1006
Phone: 212-753-8287
Fax: 212-753-0134
E-mail: cyates@gcamerica.org

KATHARINE M. GROSSCUP SCHOLARSHIPS IN HORTICULTURE

Scholarships to encourage the study of horticulture and related fields by providing financial assistance to college juniors, seniors, or graduate students who wish to pursue these academic endeavors. Preference is given to students from Ohio, Pennsylvania, West Virginia, Michigan, Indiana, and Kentucky.

Academic Fields/Career Goals: Horticulture/Floriculture; Landscape Architecture.

Award: Scholarship for use in junior, senior, or graduate years; not renewable. *Amount:* up to $3500.

Eligibility Requirements: Applicant must be enrolled or expecting to enroll full-time at a four-year institution or university and resident of Indiana, Kentucky, Michigan, Ohio, Pennsylvania, West Virginia. Available to U.S. citizens.

Application Requirements: Application form, interview, recommendations or references, self-addressed stamped envelope with application, transcript. *Deadline:* January 11.

LOY MCCANDLESS MARKS SCHOLARSHIP IN TROPICAL HORTICULTURE

Award of $5000 to graduate or advanced undergraduate student specializing in tropical horticulture, botany, or landscape architecture. Provides an opportunity to study at a leading foreign institution that specializes in the field of tropical plants. Travel must commence within 12 months of the award. Awarded only in even numbered years.

Academic Fields/Career Goals: Horticulture/Floriculture.

Award: Scholarship for use in sophomore, junior, or senior years; not renewable. *Number:* 1. *Amount:* $5000.

Eligibility Requirements: Applicant must be enrolled or expecting to enroll full-time at a four-year institution or university. Available to U.S. citizens.

Application Requirements: Application form, budget, interview, recommendations or references, self-addressed stamped envelope with application, transcript. *Deadline:* January 15.

Contact: Connie Yates, Garden Club of America
Garden Club of America
14 East 60th Street
New York, NY 10022-1006
Phone: 212-753-8287
Fax: 212-753-0134
E-mail: cyates@gcamerica.org

SARA SHALLENBERGER BROWN GCA NATIONAL PARKS CONSERVATION SCHOLARSHIP

Scholarship to encourage students to pursue careers in conservation by providing hands-on field training experience protecting the treasured resources of America's national parks. Open to college undergraduates aged 19 to 20, with preference given to those with prior SCA experience.

Academic Fields/Career Goals: Horticulture/Floriculture; Natural Resources.

Award: Scholarship for use in freshman or sophomore years; not renewable.

Eligibility Requirements: Applicant must be age 19-20 and enrolled or expecting to enroll full-time at a four-year institution or university. Available to U.S. citizens.

Application Requirements: Application form, transcript. *Deadline:* February 15.

ZELLER SUMMER SCHOLARSHIP IN MEDICINAL BOTANY
• *See page 335*

GOLDEN STATE BONSAI FEDERATION
http://www.gsbf-bonsai.org/

HORTICULTURE SCHOLARSHIPS
Scholarship for study towards a certificate in ornamental horticulture from an accredited school. Applicant must be a current member of a GSBF member club and have a letter of recommendation from club president, or a responsible spokesperson from GSBF. Deadline varies.

Academic Fields/Career Goals: Horticulture/Floriculture.

Award: Scholarship for use in freshman, sophomore, junior, senior, graduate, or postgraduate years; not renewable. *Number:* 1–5. *Amount:* up to $400.

Eligibility Requirements: Applicant must be enrolled or expecting to enroll full-time at a two-year or four-year or technical institution or university. Applicant or parent of applicant must be member of Golden State Bonsai Federation. Available to U.S. citizens.

Application Requirements: Application form, recommendations or references. *Deadline:* varies.

Contact: Abe Far, Grants and Scholarship Committee
Golden State Bonsai Federation
2451 Galahad Road
San Diego, CA 92123
Phone: 619-234-3434
E-mail: abefar@cox.net

GOLF COURSE SUPERINTENDENTS ASSOCIATION OF AMERICA
http://www.eifg.org/

GCSAA SCHOLARS COMPETITION
Competition for outstanding students planning careers in golf course management. Must be full-time college undergraduates currently enrolled in a two-year or more accredited program related to golf course management and have completed one year of program. Must be member of GCSAA.

Academic Fields/Career Goals: Horticulture/Floriculture.

Award: Scholarship for use in sophomore, junior, or senior years; not renewable. *Amount:* $500–$6000.

Eligibility Requirements: Applicant must be enrolled or expecting to enroll full-time at a two-year or four-year institution or university. Applicant or parent of applicant must be member of Golf Course Superintendents Association of America. Available to U.S. and non-U.S. citizens.

Application Requirements: Adviser's report, superintendent's report, application form, entry in a contest, essay, recommendations or references, transcript. *Deadline:* June 1.

Contact: Mischia Wright, Senior Manager, Development
Phone: 800-472-7878 Ext. 4445
E-mail: mwright@gcsaa.org

GOLF COURSE SUPERINTENDENTS ASSOCIATION OF AMERICA STUDENT ESSAY CONTEST
• *See page 85*

SCOTTS COMPANY SCHOLARS PROGRAM
Applicant must be a graduating high school senior or freshman, sophomore, or junior in college. Applicants must be pursuing a career in the green industry.

Academic Fields/Career Goals: Horticulture/Floriculture.

Award: Scholarship for use in freshman, sophomore, or junior years; not renewable. *Number:* up to 5. *Amount:* $500–$2500.

Eligibility Requirements: Applicant must be enrolled or expecting to enroll full-time at a two-year or four-year institution or university. Available to U.S. and non-U.S. citizens.

Application Requirements: Application form, essay, recommendations or references, transcript. *Deadline:* March 1.

Contact: Mischia Wright, Senior Manager, Development
Phone: 800-472-7878 Ext. 4445
E-mail: mwright@gcsaa.org

HERB SOCIETY OF AMERICA, WESTERN RESERVE UNIT
http://www.herbsociety.org/units/western-reserve.html

FRANCIS SYLVIA ZVERINA SCHOLARSHIP
Awards are given to needy students who plan a career in horticulture or related field. Preference will be given to applicants whose horticultural career goals involve teaching, research, or work in the public or nonprofit sector, such as public gardens, botanical gardens, parks, arboreta, city planning, public education, and awareness.

Academic Fields/Career Goals: Horticulture/Floriculture; Landscape Architecture.

Award: Scholarship for use in sophomore, junior, or senior years; not renewable. *Number:* 1. *Amount:* $5000.

Eligibility Requirements: Applicant must be enrolled or expecting to enroll full-time at a four-year institution or university. Available to U.S. citizens.

Application Requirements: Application form, essay, recommendations or references, transcript. *Deadline:* April 1.

Contact: Jewelann Stefanar, Committee Chair
Herb Society of America, Western Reserve Unit
4706 Bentwood Drive
Brooklyn, OH 44144
Phone: 216-741-0985
E-mail: jewelann1@roadrunner.com

WESTERN RESERVE HERB SOCIETY SCHOLARSHIP
Awards are given to needy students who plan a career in horticulture or related field. Preference will be given to applicants whose horticultural career goals involve teaching, research, or work in the public or nonprofit sector, such as public gardens, botanical gardens, parks, arboreta, city planning, public education and awareness.

Academic Fields/Career Goals: Horticulture/Floriculture; Landscape Architecture.

Award: Scholarship for use in sophomore, junior, senior, or graduate years; not renewable. *Number:* 1. *Amount:* $4000.

Eligibility Requirements: Applicant must be enrolled or expecting to enroll full-time at a four-year institution or university and resident of Ohio. Available to U.S. citizens.

Application Requirements: Application form, essay, recommendations or references, transcript. *Deadline:* April 1.

Contact: Jewelann Stefanar, Committee Chair
Herb Society of America, Western Reserve Unit
4706 Bentwood Drive
Brooklyn, OH 44144
Phone: 216-741-0985
E-mail: jewelann1@roadrunner.com

HORTICULTURAL RESEARCH INSTITUTE
http://www.hriresearch.org/

BRYAN A. CHAMPION MEMORIAL SCHOLARSHIP
• *See page 85*

CARVILLE M. AKEHURST MEMORIAL SCHOLARSHIP
• *See page 298*

MUGGETS SCHOLARSHIP
Annual scholarship available to students enrolled in an accredited undergraduate or graduate horticulture, landscape, or related discipline at a two- or four-year institution. Students in vocational agriculture programs will also be considered. High school seniors may apply for this

scholarship. Minimum 2.5 GPA required. Online application submission. Visit http://www.HRIresearch.org for details.

Academic Fields/Career Goals: Horticulture/Floriculture; Landscape Architecture.

Award: Scholarship for use in sophomore, junior, senior, or graduate years; not renewable. *Number:* 1–1. *Amount:* $1500–$1500.

Eligibility Requirements: Applicant must be enrolled or expecting to enroll full-time at a two-year or four-year or technical institution or university. Applicant must have 2.5 GPA or higher. Available to U.S. and non-U.S. citizens.

Application Requirements: Application form, essay, financial need analysis, recommendations or references, resume, transcript. *Deadline:* May 31.

Contact: Ms. Teresa Jodon, Executive Director
Horticultural Research Institute
1200 G Street, NW, Suite 800
Washington, DC 20005
Phone: 202-695-2474
Fax: 888-761-7883
E-mail: scholarships@hriresearch.org

SPRING MEADOW NURSERY SCHOLARSHIP

Scholarship for the full-time study of horticulture or landscape architecture students in undergraduate or graduate horticulture program or related discipline at a two- or four-year institution. Applicant must have minimum 2.5 GPA. Spring Meadow Nursery's goal is to grant scholarships to students with an interest in woody plant production, woody plant propagation, woody plant breeding, horticultural sales and marketing. Undergraduate: Applicant must have at least a Sophomore standing in a four-year curriculum or Senior standing in a two-year curriculum as of the Fall semester of scholarship application year. Graduate: All applicants in graduate school regardless of year in school may apply. Online application only.

Academic Fields/Career Goals: Horticulture/Floriculture; Landscape Architecture.

Award: Scholarship for use in junior, senior, or graduate years; not renewable. *Number:* 3–3. *Amount:* $3000–$3000.

Eligibility Requirements: Applicant must be enrolled or expecting to enroll full-time at a two-year or four-year or technical institution or university. Applicant must have 2.5 GPA or higher. Available to U.S. and Canadian citizens.

Application Requirements: Application form, essay, financial need analysis, recommendations or references, resume, transcript. *Deadline:* May 31.

Contact: Ms. Teresa Jodon, Executive Director
Horticultural Research Institute
1200 G Street, NW, Suite 800
Washington, DC 20005
Phone: 202-695-2474
Fax: 888-761-7883
E-mail: scholarships@hriresearch.org

TIMOTHY AND PALMER W. BIGELOW JR. SCHOLARSHIP
• *See page 86*

USREY FAMILY SCHOLARSHIP
• *See page 298*

IDAHO NURSERY AND LANDSCAPE ASSOCIATION

http://www.inlagrow.org/

IDAHO NURSERY AND LANDSCAPE ASSOCIATION SCHOLARSHIPS

To encourage study of Horticulture, Floriculture, Plant Pathology, Landscape Design, Turfgrass Management, Botany and other allied subjects that pertain to the green industry. Applicant must be an Idaho resident.

Academic Fields/Career Goals: Horticulture/Floriculture.

Award: Scholarship for use in freshman, sophomore, junior, or senior years; not renewable. *Number:* 1–5. *Amount:* $750.

Eligibility Requirements: Applicant must be enrolled or expecting to enroll full- or part-time at a two-year or four-year or technical institution or university; resident of Idaho and studying in Idaho. Available to U.S. citizens.

Application Requirements: Application form, application form may be submitted online (http://www.inlagrow.org), community service, essay, recommendations or references, transcript. *Deadline:* November 1.

Contact: Ann Bates, Executive Director
Phone: 208-522-7307
Fax: 208-529-0832
E-mail: abates@inlagrow.org

JOSEPH SHINODA MEMORIAL SCHOLARSHIP FOUNDATION

http://www.shinodascholarship.org/

JOSEPH SHINODA MEMORIAL SCHOLARSHIP

One-time award for undergraduates in accredited colleges and universities. Must be furthering their education in the field of floriculture (production, distribution, research, or retail).

Academic Fields/Career Goals: Horticulture/Floriculture.

Award: Scholarship for use in sophomore, junior, or senior years; not renewable. *Number:* 8–15. *Amount:* $1000–$5000.

Eligibility Requirements: Applicant must be enrolled or expecting to enroll full-time at a four-year institution or university. Available to U.S. citizens.

Application Requirements: Application form, essay, financial need analysis, recommendations or references, transcript. *Deadline:* March 30.

Contact: Barbara McCaleb, Executive Secretary
Joseph Shinoda Memorial Scholarship Foundation
234 Via La Paz
San Luis Obispo, CA 93401
Phone: 805-544-0717

LAND CONSERVANCY OF NEW JERSEY

http://www.tlc-nj.org/

ROGERS FAMILY SCHOLARSHIP
• *See page 304*

RUSSELL W. MYERS SCHOLARSHIP
• *See page 304*

MONTANA FEDERATION OF GARDEN CLUBS

http://www.mtfgc.org/

LIFE MEMBER MONTANA FEDERATION OF GARDEN CLUBS SCHOLARSHIP
• *See page 228*

NATIONAL GARDEN CLUBS SCHOLARSHIP

Scholarship for a college student majoring in some branch of horticulture. Applicants must have sophomore or higher standing and be a legal resident of Montana.

Academic Fields/Career Goals: Horticulture/Floriculture.

Award: Scholarship for use in sophomore, junior, or senior years; not renewable. *Number:* 1. *Amount:* up to $3500.

Eligibility Requirements: Applicant must be enrolled or expecting to enroll full-time at a four-year institution or university and resident of Montana. Available to U.S. citizens.

Application Requirements: Application form, financial need analysis. *Deadline:* February 28.

Contact: Margaret Yaw, Scholarship Committee, State Chairman
Montana Federation of Garden Clubs
2603 Spring Creek Drive
Bozeman, MT 59715-3621
Phone: 406-587-3621

NATIONAL COUNCIL OF STATE GARDEN CLUBS INC. SCHOLARSHIP

http://www.gardenclub.org/

NATIONAL COUNCIL OF STATE GARDEN CLUBS INC. SCHOLARSHIP
• *See page 93*

NATIONAL GARDEN CLUBS INC.

http://www.gardenclub.org/

NATIONAL GARDEN CLUBS INC. SCHOLARSHIP PROGRAM
• *See page 94*

NATIONAL POTATO COUNCIL WOMEN'S AUXILIARY

http://www.nationalpotatocouncil.org/

POTATO INDUSTRY SCHOLARSHIP
• *See page 87*

PENNSYLVANIA ASSOCIATION OF CONSERVATION DISTRICTS AUXILIARY

http://www.pacd.org/

PACD AUXILIARY SCHOLARSHIPS
• *See page 95*

PROFESSIONAL GROUNDS MANAGEMENT SOCIETY

http://www.pgms.org/

ANNE SEAMAN PROFESSIONAL GROUNDS MANAGEMENT SOCIETY MEMORIAL SCHOLARSHIP
• *See page 95*

SOIL AND WATER CONSERVATION SOCIETY-NEW JERSEY CHAPTER

http://home.comcast.net/~njswcs/scholarship.htm

EDWARD R. HALL SCHOLARSHIP
• *See page 88*

SOUTHERN NURSERY ASSOCIATION

http://www.sna.org/

SIDNEY B. MEADOWS SCHOLARSHIP
Scholarship up to $2500 to students enrolled in an accredited undergraduate or graduate ornamental horticulture program or related discipline at a four-year institution. Student must be in a junior or senior standing at time of application. For undergraduate students minimum grade point average of 2.25 or 3.0 on a scale of 4.0 for graduate students.
Academic Fields/Career Goals: Horticulture/Floriculture.
Award: Scholarship for use in junior, senior, or graduate years; not renewable. *Number:* 10–15. *Amount:* $1500–$2500.
Eligibility Requirements: Applicant must be enrolled or expecting to enroll full-time at a four-year institution or university and resident of Arkansas, Florida, Georgia, Kentucky, Louisiana, Maryland, Mississippi, Missouri, North Carolina, Oklahoma, South Carolina, Tennessee, Texas, Virginia. Available to U.S. and non-U.S. citizens.
Application Requirements: Application form, recommendations or references, resume, self-addressed stamped envelope with application, transcript. *Deadline:* May 31.

TURF AND ORNAMENTAL COMMUNICATORS ASSOCIATION

http://www.toca.org/

TURF AND ORNAMENTAL COMMUNICATORS ASSOCIATION SCHOLARSHIP PROGRAM
• *See page 96*

WOMAN'S NATIONAL FARM AND GARDEN ASSOCIATION

http://www.wnfga.org/

WOMAN'S NATIONAL FARM AND GARDEN ASSOCIATION, INC. BURLINGAME/GERRITY HORTICULTURAL THERAPY SCHOLARSHIP
$500 scholarship for a student enrolled in a bachelor's degree program in horticultural therapy. The recipient is chosen by their college.
Academic Fields/Career Goals: Horticulture/Floriculture.
Award: Scholarship for use in freshman, sophomore, junior, or senior years; not renewable. *Number:* 1. *Amount:* $500.
Eligibility Requirements: Applicant must be enrolled or expecting to enroll full- or part-time at a four-year institution or university and female. Available to U.S. citizens.
Application Requirements: Application form. *Deadline:* varies.
Contact: Mrs. EmmaJane Brice, Scholarship Coordinator
Woman's National Farm and Garden Association
PO Box 1175
Midland, MI 48641-1175
Phone: 248-620-9281
E-mail: mgbertolini@aol.com

HOSPITALITY MANAGEMENT

AMERICAN HOTEL AND LODGING EDUCATIONAL FOUNDATION

http://www.ahlef.org/

AMERICAN EXPRESS SCHOLARSHIP PROGRAM
Award for full- and part-time students in undergraduate program leading to degree in hospitality management. Must be employed at hotel which is a member of AH&LA, and must work a minimum of 20 hours per week. Dependents of hotel employees may also apply.
Academic Fields/Career Goals: Hospitality Management.
Award: Scholarship for use in freshman, sophomore, junior, or senior years; not renewable. *Number:* 5–8. *Amount:* $500–$2000.
Eligibility Requirements: Applicant must be enrolled or expecting to enroll full- or part-time at a two-year or four-year institution or university. Applicant or parent of applicant must have employment or volunteer experience in hospitality/hotel administration/operations. Available to U.S. and non-U.S. citizens.
Application Requirements: Application form, application form may be submitted online (http://www.ahlef.org), essay, financial need analysis, resume, transcript. *Deadline:* May 1.
Contact: Christa Boatman, Foundation Manager
American Hotel and Lodging Educational Foundation
1201 New York Avenue, NW, Suite 600
Washington, DC 20005-3931
Phone: 202-289-3139
Fax: 202-289-3199
E-mail: cboatman@ahlef.org

AMERICAN HOTEL & LODGING EDUCATIONAL FOUNDATION PEPSI SCHOLARSHIP
• *See page 212*

ANNUAL SCHOLARSHIP GRANT PROGRAM
• *See page 213*

ARTHUR J. PACKARD MEMORIAL SCHOLARSHIP
• *See page 213*

ECOLAB SCHOLARSHIP PROGRAM
• *See page 213*

HYATT HOTELS FUND FOR MINORITY LODGING MANAGEMENT
• *See page 213*

INCOMING FRESHMAN SCHOLARSHIPS
• *See page 213*

RAMA SCHOLARSHIP FOR THE AMERICAN DREAM
• *See page 213*

STEVEN HYMANS EXTENDED STAY SCHOLARSHIP
• *See page 214*

AMERICAN INSTITUTE OF WINE AND FOOD-PACIFIC NORTHWEST CHAPTER

http://www.aiwf.org/

CULINARY, VINIFERA, AND HOSPITALITY SCHOLARSHIP
• *See page 312*

CAREERS THROUGH CULINARY ARTS PROGRAM INC.

http://www.ccapinc.org/

CAREERS THROUGH CULINARY ARTS PROGRAM COOKING COMPETITION FOR SCHOLARSHIPS
• *See page 214*

CLUB FOUNDATION

http://www.clubfoundation.org/

JOE PERDUE SCHOLARSHIP PROGRAM
Awards for candidates seeking a managerial career in the private club industry and currently attending an accredited four year college or university. Must have completed freshman year and be enrolled full-time. Must have achieved and continue to maintain a GPA of at least 2.5. Minimum two awards of $2500 granted annually.
Academic Fields/Career Goals: Hospitality Management.
Award: Scholarship for use in sophomore, junior, or senior years; not renewable. *Number:* 2. *Amount:* $2500.
Eligibility Requirements: Applicant must be enrolled or expecting to enroll full-time at a four-year institution or university. Applicant must have 2.5 GPA or higher. Available to U.S. citizens.
Application Requirements: Application form, essay, recommendations or references, resume, self-addressed stamped envelope with application, transcript. *Deadline:* May 1.
Contact: Ashleigh Hill, Program Specialist
    Phone: 703-299-4268 Ext. 268
    Fax: 703-739-0124
    E-mail: ashleigh.hill@cmaa.org

COLLEGEBOUND FOUNDATION

http://www.collegeboundfoundation.org/

HILTON BALTIMORE CONVENTION CENTER HOTEL SCHOLARSHIP FUND
• *See page 152*

DECA (DISTRIBUTIVE EDUCATION CLUBS OF AMERICA)

http://www.deca.org/

HARRY A. APPLEGATE SCHOLARSHIP
• *See page 153*

GOLDEN GATE RESTAURANT ASSOCIATION

http://www.ggra.org/

GOLDEN GATE RESTAURANT ASSOCIATION SCHOLARSHIP FOUNDATION
• *See page 214*

HAWAII LODGING & TOURISM ASSOCIATION

http://www.hawaiilodging.org

CLEM JUDD, JR. MEMORIAL SCHOLARSHIP
Scholarship for a Hawaii resident who must be able to prove Hawaiian ancestry. Applicant must be enrolled full-time at a U.S. accredited university/college majoring in hotel management. Must have a minimum 3.0 GPA.
Academic Fields/Career Goals: Hospitality Management.
Award: Scholarship for use in junior or senior years; not renewable. *Number:* 2. *Amount:* $1000–$2500.
Eligibility Requirements: Applicant must be Asian/Pacific Islander; enrolled or expecting to enroll full-time at a four-year institution and resident of Hawaii. Applicant must have 3.0 GPA or higher. Available to U.S. citizens.
Application Requirements: Application form, essay, personal photograph, recommendations or references, resume. *Deadline:* July 1.

R.W. "BOB" HOLDEN SCHOLARSHIP
One $1000 award for a student attending an accredited university or college in Hawaii, majoring in hotel management. Must be a Hawaii resident and a U.S. citizen. Must have a minimum 3.0 GPA.
Academic Fields/Career Goals: Hospitality Management; Travel/ Tourism.
Award: Scholarship for use in junior or senior years; not renewable. *Number:* 1–5. *Amount:* $1000.
Eligibility Requirements: Applicant must be enrolled or expecting to enroll full-time at a four-year institution or university. Applicant must have 3.0 GPA or higher. Available to U.S. citizens.
Application Requirements: Application form, essay, personal photograph, recommendations or references, resume, self-addressed stamped envelope with application, transcript. *Deadline:* July 1.
Contact: Karen Nakaoka, Director of Member Relations and Operations
    Hawaii Lodging & Tourism Association
    2270 Kalakaua Avenue, Suite 1506
    Honolulu, HI 96815
    Phone: 808-923-0407
    E-mail: info@hawaiilodging.org

ILLINOIS RESTAURANT ASSOCIATION EDUCATIONAL FOUNDATION

http://www.illinoisrestaurants.org/

ILLINOIS RESTAURANT ASSOCIATION EDUCATIONAL FOUNDATION SCHOLARSHIPS
• *See page 215*

INTERNATIONAL AIRLINES TRAVEL AGENT NETWORK

http://www.iatan.org/

INTERNATIONAL AIRLINES TRAVEL AGENT NETWORK FOUNDATION SCHOLARSHIP

Scholarships available annually to individuals who are interested in pursuing or enhancing their careers in travel. Must be U.S. citizens or permanent legal residents of the United States and not less than 17 years of age. Must have been employed for at least six months by an IATAN accredited travel agency or who are registered students at a recognized postsecondary educational/vocational institution having direct links with the travel industry.

Academic Fields/Career Goals: Hospitality Management; Travel/Tourism.

Award: Scholarship for use in freshman, sophomore, junior, senior, graduate, or postgraduate years; not renewable. *Number:* 10–15. *Amount:* $500–$3000.

Eligibility Requirements: Applicant must be enrolled or expecting to enroll full- or part-time at a two-year or four-year or technical institution or university. Applicant or parent of applicant must have employment or volunteer experience in travel and tourism industry. Available to U.S. citizens.

Application Requirements: Application form, essay, recommendations or references, resume, transcript. *Deadline:* April 25.

Contact: Neil Scotten, Customer Service Representative
International Airlines Travel Agent Network
800 Place Victoria, Suite 800, PO Box 113
Montreal, QC H4Z 1M1
CAN
Phone: 514-868-8800 Ext. 4407
Fax: 514-868-8850
E-mail: scottenn@iata.org

INTERNATIONAL FLIGHT SERVICES ASSOCIATION

http://www.ifsanet.com

THE HOFFMAN GROUP SCHOLARSHIP AWARD

Individuals are selected to receive the award based on scholastic merit and dedication to an advanced education. Must be an employee of a current IFSA member company in good standing, or a relative of an employee of a current IFSA member company.

Academic Fields/Career Goals: Hospitality Management.

Award: Scholarship for use in freshman, sophomore, junior, or senior years; not renewable. *Number:* 1. *Amount:* $2000.

Eligibility Requirements: Applicant must be enrolled or expecting to enroll full- or part-time at an institution or university. Applicant or parent of applicant must have employment or volunteer experience in hospitality/hotel administration/operations. Applicant must have 3.0 GPA or higher. Available to U.S. and non-U.S. citizens.

Application Requirements: Application form, essay, recommendations or references, transcript. *Deadline:* May 14.

Contact: Jacqueline Petty, Communications Manager
International Flight Services Association
1100 Johnson Ferry Road NE
Suite 300
Atlanta, GA 30342
Phone: 404-252-3663 Ext. 2969
Fax: 404-252-0774
E-mail: jpetty@kellencompany.com

INTERNATIONAL FOODSERVICE EDITORIAL COUNCIL

http://www.ifeconline.com/

INTERNATIONAL FOODSERVICE EDITORIAL COUNCIL COMMUNICATIONS SCHOLARSHIP

• See page 83

JAMES BEARD FOUNDATION INC.

http://www.jamesbeard.org/

BERN LAXER MEMORIAL SCHOLARSHIP

• See page 215

MAINE RESTAURANT ASSOCIATION

http://www.mainerestaurant.com/

MAINE RESTAURANT ASSOCIATION EDUCATION FOUNDATION SCHOLARSHIP FUND

• See page 217

MISSOURI TRAVEL COUNCIL

http://www.missouritravel.com/

MISSOURI TRAVEL COUNCIL TOURISM SCHOLARSHIP

• See page 318

NATIONAL RESTAURANT ASSOCIATION EDUCATIONAL FOUNDATION

http://www.nraef.org/

NATIONAL RESTAURANT ASSOCIATION EDUCATIONAL FOUNDATION UNDERGRADUATE SCHOLARSHIPS FOR COLLEGE STUDENTS

• See page 318

NATIONAL RESTAURANT ASSOCIATION EDUCATIONAL FOUNDATION UNDERGRADUATE SCHOLARSHIPS FOR HIGH SCHOOL SENIORS AND GENERAL EDUCATION DIPLOMA (GED) GRADUATE S

• See page 318

TOURISM CARES

http://www.tourismcares.org

NEW HORIZONS KATHY LETARTE SCHOLARSHIP

• See page 319

PAT AND JIM HOST SCHOLARSHIP

Award for students who have a degree emphasis in a travel and tourism related field. Must maintain a 3.0 GPA for renewal.

Academic Fields/Career Goals: Hospitality Management; Travel/Tourism.

Award: Scholarship for use in freshman, sophomore, junior, or senior years; renewable. *Number:* 1. *Amount:* $2000–$8000.

Eligibility Requirements: Applicant must be enrolled or expecting to enroll full-time at a four-year institution or university. Applicant must have 3.0 GPA or higher. Available to U.S. citizens.

Application Requirements: Application form, essay, recommendations or references, resume, transcript. *Deadline:* May 10.

Contact: Amanda D'Aiuto, Student Programs Manager
Phone: 781-821-5990
Fax: 781-821-8949
E-mail: info@tourismcares.org

SOCIETIE DES CASINOS DU QUEBEC SCHOLARSHIP

• See page 319

OHIO TRAVEL ASSOCIATION

http://www.ohiotravel.org/

BILL SCHWARTZ MEMORIAL SCHOLARSHIP

Scholarship will be granted to a qualified full-time, Ohio student after the completion of their freshman year. Must be studying hospitality management or travel/tourism with a minimum 2.5 GPA. As part of the scholarship program, the recipient will be invited to various OTA events throughout the year.

Academic Fields/Career Goals: Hospitality Management; Travel/Tourism.

Award: Scholarship for use in sophomore, junior, or senior years; not renewable. *Number:* 1. *Amount:* $1000.

Eligibility Requirements: Applicant must be enrolled or expecting to enroll full-time at a two-year or four-year or technical institution or university; resident of Ohio and studying in Ohio. Applicant or parent of applicant must have employment or volunteer experience in travel and tourism industry. Applicant must have 2.5 GPA or higher. Available to U.S. citizens.

Application Requirements: Application form, financial need analysis, recommendations or references, transcript. *Deadline:* June 15.

Contact: Ms. Betsy Decillis, Membership and Community Manager
Phone: 800-896-4682 Ext. 0#
E-mail: betsy@ohiotravel.org

SOUTH DAKOTA RETAILERS ASSOCIATION

http://www.sdra.org/

SOUTH DAKOTA RETAILERS ASSOCIATION SCHOLARSHIP PROGRAM
• *See page 80*

UNITED NEGRO COLLEGE FUND

http://www.uncf.org/

AMERICAN HOTEL FOUNDATION SCHOLARSHIP

Scholarship available to hotel management majors attending UNCF member colleges and universities. Minimum 2.5 GPA required. Prospective applicants should complete the Student Profile found at website, http://www.uncf.org.

Academic Fields/Career Goals: Hospitality Management.

Award: Scholarship for use in freshman, sophomore, junior, or senior years; not renewable. *Amount:* $1500.

Eligibility Requirements: Applicant must be Black (non-Hispanic) and enrolled or expecting to enroll full-time at a four-year institution or university. Applicant must have 2.5 GPA or higher. Available to U.S. and non-U.S. citizens.

Application Requirements: Application form. *Deadline:* May 1.

MARRIOTT SCHOLARS PROGRAM

Up to $9000 scholarship per year for four years coupled with opportunities for ongoing career guidance and mentoring by Marriott hotel managers and corporate executives. Must be a student attending a UNCF member college or university, major in hotel or restaurant management, and have a minimum 3.0 GPA.

Academic Fields/Career Goals: Hospitality Management.

Award: Scholarship for use in freshman, sophomore, junior, or senior years; renewable. *Amount:* up to $9000.

Eligibility Requirements: Applicant must be Black (non-Hispanic) and enrolled or expecting to enroll full-time at a four-year institution or university. Applicant must have 3.0 GPA or higher. Available to U.S. citizens.

Application Requirements: Application form. *Deadline:* continuous.

HUMANITIES

ALBERTA HERITAGE SCHOLARSHIP FUND

http://www.alis.alberta.ca/

LOIS HOLE HUMANITIES AND SOCIAL SCIENCES SCHOLARSHIP

Award of CAN$5000 available to Alberta residents who are students enrolled full time in the second or subsequent year of postsecondary study in the Faculty of Humanities or the Faculty of Social Sciences at University of Alberta, University of Calgary, University of Lethbridge, or Athabasca University. Awarded on the basis of academic merit, demonstrated leadership, and community service. For further information, see website http://alis.alberta.ca.

Academic Fields/Career Goals: Humanities; Social Sciences.

Award: Scholarship for use in sophomore, junior, or senior years; not renewable. *Number:* 4.

Eligibility Requirements: Applicant must be Canadian citizen; enrolled or expecting to enroll full-time at a four-year institution or university; resident of Alberta; studying in Alberta and must have an interest in leadership.

Application Requirements: Application form, community service, transcript. *Deadline:* varies.

AMERICAN CLASSICAL LEAGUE/ NATIONAL JUNIOR CLASSICAL LEAGUE

http://www.aclclassics.org/

NATIONAL JUNIOR CLASSICAL LEAGUE SCHOLARSHIP
• *See page 187*

AMERICAN SCHOOL OF CLASSICAL STUDIES AT ATHENS

http://www.ascsa.edu.gr/

ASCSA SUMMER SESSIONS SCHOLARSHIPS
• *See page 100*

BETHESDA LUTHERAN COMMUNITIES

http://www.bethesdalutherancommunities.org/scholarships

DEVELOPMENTAL DISABILITIES SCHOLASTIC ACHIEVEMENT SCHOLARSHIP FOR COLLEGE STUDENTS WHO ARE LUTHERAN
• *See page 222*

CANADIAN INSTITUTE OF UKRAINIAN STUDIES

http://www.cius.ca/

LEO J. KRYSA UNDERGRADUATE SCHOLARSHIP
• *See page 114*

CATCHING THE DREAM

http://www.catchingthedream.org/

MATH, ENGINEERING, SCIENCE, BUSINESS, EDUCATION, COMPUTERS SCHOLARSHIPS
• *See page 151*

NATIVE AMERICAN LEADERSHIP IN EDUCATION (NALE)
• *See page 151*

THE COMMUNITY FOUNDATION FOR GREATER ATLANTA, INC.

http://cfgreateratlanta.org/

JAMES M. AND VIRGINIA M. SMYTH SCHOLARSHIP
• *See page 118*

CULTURAL SERVICES OF THE FRENCH EMBASSY

http://www.frenchculture.org/

TEACHING ASSISTANT PROGRAM IN FRANCE
• *See page 97*

HARVARD TRAVELLERS CLUB

http://www.harvardtravellersclub.org/

HARVARD TRAVELLERS CLUB GRANTS
• *See page 108*

INSTITUTE FOR HUMANE STUDIES

http://www.theihs.org/

HUMANE STUDIES FELLOWSHIPS
• *See page 190*

JACK J. ISGUR FOUNDATION

http://www.isgur.org

JACK J. ISGUR FOUNDATION SCHOLARSHIP
• *See page 119*

LADIES AUXILIARY TO THE VETERANS OF FOREIGN WARS, DEPARTMENT OF MAINE

http://mainevfw.org/

FRANCES L. BOOTH MEDICAL SCHOLARSHIP SPONSORED BY LAVFW DEPARTMENT OF MAINE
• *See page 336*

PHI ALPHA THETA HISTORY HONOR SOCIETY, INC.

http://www.phialphatheta.org/

PHI ALPHA THETA WORLD HISTORY ASSOCIATION PAPER PRIZE
• *See page 345*

POLISH ARTS CLUB OF BUFFALO SCHOLARSHIP FOUNDATION

http://www.pacb.bfn.org/

POLISH ARTS CLUB OF BUFFALO SCHOLARSHIP FOUNDATION TRUST
• *See page 121*

STRAIGHTFORWARD MEDIA

http://www.straightforwardmedia.com/

STRAIGHTFORWARD MEDIA LIBERAL ARTS SCHOLARSHIP
• *See page 116*

HUMAN RESOURCES

NEW ENGLAND EMPLOYEE BENEFITS COUNCIL

http://www.neebc.org/

NEW ENGLAND EMPLOYEE BENEFITS COUNCIL SCHOLARSHIP PROGRAM
• *See page 77*

SHRM FOUNDATION-SOCIETY FOR HUMAN RESOURCE MANAGEMENT

http://www.shrmfoundation.org

SHRM FOUNDATION STUDENT SCHOLARSHIPS
Applicants must be SHRM student members and must be pursuing a college degree in HR or a related field. Undergraduates must have a cumulative GPA of at least 3.0 on a 4.0 point scale, and graduate applicants must have at least a 3.5 GPA on a 4.0 scale. Course work in HR management is required. Awards are primarily merit-based. Scholarships are also available for students sitting for the Assurance of Learning Assessment.
Academic Fields/Career Goals: Human Resources.
Award: Scholarship for use in junior, senior, or graduate years; not renewable. *Number:* 40. *Amount:* $200–$5000.
Eligibility Requirements: Applicant must be enrolled or expecting to enroll full- or part-time at a four-year institution or university. Applicant or parent of applicant must be member of Society for Human Resource Management. Applicant must have 3.0 GPA or higher. Available to U.S. and non-U.S. citizens.
Application Requirements: Application form, application form may be submitted online (http://www.shrm.org/ABOUT/FOUNDATION/SCHOLARSHIPS/Pages/default.aspx), community service, essay, recommendations or references, resume. *Deadline:* November 1.
Contact: Beth McFarland, Manager, Special Projects
   Phone: 703-535-6371
   E-mail: beth.mcfarland@shrm.org

Y'S MEN INTERNATIONAL

http://www.ysmenusa.com/

ALEXANDER SCHOLARSHIP LOAN FUND
• *See page 161*

HYDROLOGY

AMERICAN GROUND WATER TRUST

http://www.agwt.org/

AMERICAN GROUND WATER TRUST-AMTROL INC. SCHOLARSHIP
Award for college/university entry-level students intending to pursue a career in ground water-related field. Must either have completed a science/environmental project involving ground water resources or have had vacation work experience related to the environment and natural resources. Must be U.S. citizen or legal resident with minimum 3.0 GPA. Submit two letters of recommendation and transcript.
Academic Fields/Career Goals: Hydrology; Natural Resources.
Award: Scholarship for use in freshman year; not renewable. *Number:* 2. *Amount:* up to $1500.
Eligibility Requirements: Applicant must be enrolled or expecting to enroll full-time at a four-year institution or university. Applicant must have 3.0 GPA or higher. Available to U.S. citizens.

Application Requirements: Application form, essay, recommendations or references, transcript. *Deadline:* June 1.

Contact: Garret Grasskamp, Ground Water Specialist
American Ground Water Trust
50 Pleasant Street, Suite 2
Concord, NH 03301-4073
Phone: 603-228-5444
Fax: 603-228-6557
E-mail: trustinfo@agwt.org

AMERICAN GROUND WATER TRUST-THOMAS STETSON SCHOLARSHIP

• *See page 179*

AMERICAN METEOROLOGICAL SOCIETY

http://www.ametsoc.org/

AMERICAN METEOROLOGICAL SOCIETY DR. PEDRO GRAU UNDERGRADUATE SCHOLARSHIP

Award for full-time undergraduate students majoring in atmospheric or related oceanic and hydrologic sciences. Must be enrolled at a U.S. institution. Minimum GPA of 3.25 required. Must be U.S. citizen or permanent resident to apply. Award of $2500 annually for four years.

Academic Fields/Career Goals: Hydrology; Meteorology/Atmospheric Science; Oceanography.

Award: Scholarship for use in freshman, sophomore, junior, or senior years; not renewable. *Number:* 1. *Amount:* $2500.

Eligibility Requirements: Applicant must be enrolled or expecting to enroll full-time at a four-year institution or university. Available to U.S. citizens.

Application Requirements: Application form, essay, recommendations or references, transcript. *Deadline:* February 20.

Contact: Donna Fernandez, Development Program Coordinator
American Meteorological Society
45 Beacon Street
Boston, MA 02108-3693
Phone: 617-227-2426 Ext. 246
Fax: 617-742-8718
E-mail: dfernand@ametsoc.org

AMERICAN METEOROLOGICAL SOCIETY/INDUSTRY MINORITY SCHOLARSHIPS

Two-year scholarship of $3000 per year for minority students entering their freshman year of college. Must plan to pursue careers in the atmospheric and related oceanic and hydrologic sciences. Must be U.S. citizen or permanent resident to apply.

Academic Fields/Career Goals: Hydrology; Meteorology/Atmospheric Science; Oceanography.

Award: Scholarship for use in freshman year; not renewable. *Number:* 6–13. *Amount:* $3000.

Eligibility Requirements: Applicant must be American Indian/Alaska Native, Asian/Pacific Islander, Black (non-Hispanic), Hispanic; high school student and planning to enroll or expecting to enroll full-time at a four-year institution or university. Applicant must have 3.0 GPA or higher. Available to U.S. citizens.

Application Requirements: Application form, recommendations or references, test scores, transcript. *Deadline:* February 22.

Contact: Donna Sampson, Development and Student Program Manager
American Meteorological Society
45 Beacon Street
Boston, MA 02108-3693
Phone: 617-227-2426 Ext. 246
Fax: 617-742-8718
E-mail: dfernand@ametsoc.org

AMERICAN METEOROLOGICAL SOCIETY MARK J. SCHROEDER SCHOLARSHIP IN METEOROLOGY

Award for full-time students entering their final year of undergraduate study majoring in atmospheric or related oceanic and hydrologic sciences. Must be enrolled at a U.S. institution. Minimum GPA of 3.25 is required. Must be U.S. citizen or permanent resident to apply.

Academic Fields/Career Goals: Hydrology; Meteorology/Atmospheric Science; Oceanography.

Award: Scholarship for use in senior year; not renewable.

Eligibility Requirements: Applicant must be enrolled or expecting to enroll full-time at a four-year institution or university. Available to U.S. citizens.

Application Requirements: Application form, essay, financial need analysis, recommendations or references, transcript. *Deadline:* February 20.

Contact: Donna Fernandez, Development Program Coordinator
American Meteorological Society
45 Beacon Street
Boston, MA 02108-3693
Phone: 617-227-2426 Ext. 246
Fax: 617-742-8718
E-mail: dfernand@ametsoc.org

AMERICAN METEOROLOGICAL SOCIETY RICHARD AND HELEN HAGEMEYER SCHOLARSHIP

Award for full-time students entering their final year of undergraduate study majoring in atmospheric or related oceanic and hydrologic sciences. Must be enrolled at a U.S. institution. Minimum GPA of 3.25 is required. One-time award of $3000. Must be U.S. citizen or permanent resident to apply.

Academic Fields/Career Goals: Hydrology; Meteorology/Atmospheric Science; Oceanography.

Award: Scholarship for use in junior or senior years; not renewable. *Amount:* $3000.

Eligibility Requirements: Applicant must be enrolled or expecting to enroll full-time at a two-year or four-year institution or university. Available to U.S. citizens.

Application Requirements: Application form, essay, recommendations or references, transcript. *Deadline:* February 20.

Contact: Donna Fernandez, Development Program Coordinator
American Meteorological Society
45 Beacon Street
Boston, MA 02108-3693
Phone: 617-227-2426 Ext. 246
Fax: 617-742-8718
E-mail: dfernand@ametsoc.org

AMERICAN METEOROLOGICAL SOCIETY WERNER A. BAUM UNDERGRADUATE SCHOLARSHIP

Award for full-time students entering final year of undergraduate study majoring in atmospheric or related oceanic or hydrologic science, and/or must show clear intent to make the atmospheric or related sciences their career. Must be enrolled at a U.S. institution. Minimum GPA of 3.25 is required. Must be U.S. citizen or permanent resident.

Academic Fields/Career Goals: Hydrology; Meteorology/Atmospheric Science; Oceanography.

Award: Scholarship for use in senior year; not renewable. *Amount:* $5000.

Eligibility Requirements: Applicant must be enrolled or expecting to enroll full-time at a four-year institution or university. Applicant must have 3.5 GPA or higher. Available to U.S. citizens.

Application Requirements: Application form, essay, financial need analysis, recommendations or references, transcript. *Deadline:* February 20.

Contact: Donna Fernandez, Development Program Coordinator
American Meteorological Society
45 Beacon Street
Boston, MA 02108-3693
Phone: 617-227-2426 Ext. 246
Fax: 617-742-8718
E-mail: dfernand@ametsoc.org

AMS FRESHMAN UNDERGRADUATE SCHOLARSHIP

• *See page 301*

CARL W. KREITZBERG ENDOWED SCHOLARSHIP

Scholarships of $2000 for full-time students entering their final year of undergraduate study, majoring in atmospheric or related oceanic/hydrologic science programs at accredited U.S. institutions. Minimum 3.25 GPA required. Must be U.S. citizen.

Academic Fields/Career Goals: Hydrology; Meteorology/Atmospheric Science; Oceanography.

Award: Scholarship for use in senior year; not renewable. *Number:* 1. *Amount:* up to $2000.

Eligibility Requirements: Applicant must be enrolled or expecting to enroll full-time at a four-year institution or university. Available to U.S. citizens.

Application Requirements: Application form, essay, recommendations or references, transcript. *Deadline:* February 20.

Contact: Donna Fernandez, Development Program Coordinator
American Meteorological Society
45 Beacon Street
Boston, MA 02108-3693
Phone: 617-227-2426 Ext. 246
Fax: 617-742-8718
E-mail: dfernand@ametsoc.org

ETHAN AND ALLAN MURPHY MEMORIAL SCHOLARSHIP

Award for entering their final year of undergraduate study majoring in atmospheric or related oceanic and hydrologic science. Must show clear intent to make the atmospheric or related sciences a career. Must be enrolled in an accredited U.S. institution. Minimum 3.25 GPA required. Must be a U.S. citizen.

Academic Fields/Career Goals: Hydrology; Meteorology/Atmospheric Science; Oceanography.

Award: Scholarship for use in senior year; not renewable. *Amount:* $2000.

Eligibility Requirements: Applicant must be enrolled or expecting to enroll full-time at a four-year institution or university. Available to U.S. citizens.

Application Requirements: Application form, essay, recommendations or references, transcript. *Deadline:* February 20.

Contact: Donna Fernandez, Development Program Coordinator
American Meteorological Society
45 Beacon Street
Boston, MA 02108-3693
Phone: 617-227-2426 Ext. 246
Fax: 617-742-8718
E-mail: dfernand@ametsoc.org

GEORGE S. BENTON SCHOLARSHIP

Scholarships are awarded to full-time students entering their final year of undergraduate study at accredited U.S. institutions for study in atmospheric sciences or related oceanic or hydrologic science. Minimum 3.25 GPA required. Must be U.S. citizen or permanent resident.

Academic Fields/Career Goals: Hydrology; Meteorology/Atmospheric Science; Oceanography.

Award: Scholarship for use in senior year; not renewable. *Number:* 1. *Amount:* up to $3500.

Eligibility Requirements: Applicant must be enrolled or expecting to enroll full-time at a four-year institution or university. Available to U.S. citizens.

Application Requirements: Application form, financial need analysis, resume, transcript. *Deadline:* February 20.

Contact: Donna Fernandez, Development Program Coordinator
American Meteorological Society
45 Beacon Street
Boston, MA 02108-3693
Phone: 617-227-2426 Ext. 246
Fax: 617-742-8718
E-mail: dfernand@ametsoc.org

GUILLERMO SALAZAR RODRIGUES SCHOLARSHIP

Award for full-time undergraduate students majoring in atmospheric or related oceanic and hydrologic science. Must show clear intent to make the atmospheric or related sciences a career. Must be enrolled in an accredited U.S. institution. Minimum 3.25 GPA required. Must be a U.S. citizen. Award of $2,500 annually for four years.

Academic Fields/Career Goals: Hydrology; Meteorology/Atmospheric Science; Oceanography.

Award: Scholarship for use in freshman, sophomore, junior, or senior years; not renewable. *Amount:* $2500.

Eligibility Requirements: Applicant must be enrolled or expecting to enroll full-time at a four-year institution or university. Available to U.S. citizens.

Application Requirements: Application form, essay, recommendations or references, transcript. *Deadline:* February 20.

Contact: Donna Fernandez, Development Program Coordinator
American Meteorological Society
45 Beacon Street
Boston, MA 02108-3693
Phone: 617-227-2426 Ext. 246
Fax: 617-742-8718
E-mail: dfernand@ametsoc.org

JOHN R. HOPE SCHOLARSHIP

Award for students entering their final year of undergraduate study majoring in atmospheric or related oceanic and hydrological science. Must show clear intent to make the atmospheric or related science a career. Minimum 3.25 GPA required. Must be enrolled in an accredited U.S. institution. Must be a U.S. citizen to apply.

Academic Fields/Career Goals: Hydrology; Meteorology/Atmospheric Science; Oceanography.

Award: Scholarship for use in senior year; not renewable. *Number:* 1. *Amount:* up to $2500.

Eligibility Requirements: Applicant must be enrolled or expecting to enroll full-time at a four-year institution or university. Available to U.S. citizens.

Application Requirements: Application form, essay, recommendations or references, transcript. *Deadline:* February 20.

Contact: Donna Fernandez, Development Program Coordinator
American Meteorological Society
45 Beacon Street
Boston, MA 02108-3693
Phone: 617-227-2426 Ext. 246
Fax: 617-742-8718
E-mail: dfernand@ametsoc.org

LOREN W. CROW SCHOLARSHIP

One-time award for full-time students entering their final year of undergraduate study majoring in atmospheric or related oceanic and hydrologic sciences. Must be enrolled full-time at a U.S. institution with a 3.25 GPA. Must be U.S. citizen or permanent resident to apply.

Academic Fields/Career Goals: Hydrology; Meteorology/Atmospheric Science; Oceanography.

Award: Scholarship for use in senior year; not renewable. *Amount:* up to $2000.

Eligibility Requirements: Applicant must be enrolled or expecting to enroll full-time at a four-year institution or university. Available to U.S. citizens.

Application Requirements: Application form, essay, recommendations or references, transcript. *Deadline:* February 20.

Contact: Donna Fernandez, Development Program Coordinator
American Meteorological Society
45 Beacon Street
Boston, MA 02108-3693
Phone: 617-227-2426 Ext. 246
Fax: 617-742-8718
E-mail: dfernand@ametsoc.org

ARIZONA HYDROLOGICAL SOCIETY

http://www.azhydrosoc.org/

ARIZONA HYDROLOGICAL SOCIETY SCHOLARSHIP
• See page 226

ASSOCIATION FOR WOMEN GEOSCIENTISTS, PUGET SOUND CHAPTER

http://www.awg.org/

PUGET SOUND CHAPTER SCHOLARSHIP
• See page 227

ASSOCIATION OF CALIFORNIA WATER AGENCIES

http://www.acwa.com/

ASSOCIATION OF CALIFORNIA WATER AGENCIES SCHOLARSHIPS
• *See page 103*

CLAIR A. HILL SCHOLARSHIP
• *See page 103*

CALIFORNIA GROUNDWATER ASSOCIATION

http://www.groundh2o.org/

CALIFORNIA GROUNDWATER ASSOCIATION SCHOLARSHIP

Award for California residents who demonstrate an interest in some facet of groundwater technology. One to two $1000 awards. Must use for study in California. Submit letter of recommendation.

Academic Fields/Career Goals: Hydrology; Natural Resources.

Award: Scholarship for use in freshman, sophomore, junior, or senior years; not renewable. *Number:* 1–2. *Amount:* $1000.

Eligibility Requirements: Applicant must be enrolled or expecting to enroll full-time at a two-year or four-year or technical institution or university; resident of California and studying in California. Available to U.S. citizens.

Application Requirements: Application form, essay, recommendations or references, transcript. *Deadline:* April 1.

Contact: Mike Mortensson, Executive Director
California Groundwater Association
PO Box 14369
Santa Rosa, CA 95402
Phone: 707-578-4408
Fax: 707-546-4906
E-mail: wellguy@groundh2o.org

INTERNATIONAL ASSOCIATION FOR GREAT LAKES RESEARCH

http://www.iaglr.org/

PAUL W. RODGERS SCHOLARSHIP
• *See page 227*

KENTUCKY ENERGY AND ENVIRONMENT CABINET

http://www.eec.ky.gov/

ENVIRONMENTAL PROTECTION SCHOLARSHIP
• *See page 145*

NATIONAL GROUND WATER RESEARCH AND EDUCATIONAL FOUNDATION

http://www.ngwa.org/Foundation/assante/Pages/default.aspx

NATIONAL GROUND WATER RESEARCH AND EDUCATIONAL FOUNDATION'S LEN ASSANTE SCHOLARSHIP
• *See page 229*

INDUSTRIAL DESIGN

AIST FOUNDATION

http://www.aistfoundation.org/

ASSOCIATION FOR IRON AND STEEL TECHNOLOGY WILLY KORF MEMORIAL SCHOLARSHIP
• *See page 162*

AMERICAN INSTITUTE OF CHEMICAL ENGINEERS

http://www.aiche.org/

SAFETY AND HEALTH NATIONAL STUDENT DESIGN COMPETITION AWARD FOR SAFETY
• *See page 165*

AMERICAN SOCIETY OF PLUMBING ENGINEERS

http://www.aspe.org/

ALFRED STEELE ENGINEERING SCHOLARSHIP
• *See page 275*

IFDA EDUCATIONAL FOUNDATION

http://www.ifdaef.org/

RUTH CLARK FURNITURE DESIGN SCHOLARSHIP
• *See page 119*

INDUSTRIAL DESIGNERS SOCIETY OF AMERICA

http://www.idsa.org/

INDUSTRIAL DESIGNERS SOCIETY OF AMERICA UNDERGRADUATE SCHOLARSHIP

One-time award to a U.S. citizen or permanent U.S. resident currently enrolled in an industrial design program. Must submit twenty visual examples of work and study full-time.

Academic Fields/Career Goals: Industrial Design.

Award: Scholarship for use in junior year; not renewable. *Number:* 2. *Amount:* $2500.

Eligibility Requirements: Applicant must be enrolled or expecting to enroll full-time at an institution or university. Applicant must have 3.0 GPA or higher. Available to U.S. citizens.

Application Requirements: Application form, recommendations or references, transcript, twenty visual examples of work. *Deadline:* May 18.

Contact: Max Taylor, Executive Assistant
Industrial Designers Society of America
45195 Business Court, Suite 250
Dulles, VA 20166
Phone: 703-707-6000
Fax: 703-787-8501
E-mail: maxt@idsa.org

MANUFACTURERS ASSOCIATION OF MAINE

http://www.mainemfg.com/

MAINE METAL PRODUCTS EDUCATION FUND SCHOLARSHIP PROGRAM
• *See page 132*

MIDWEST ROOFING CONTRACTORS ASSOCIATION

http://www.mrca.org/

MRCA FOUNDATION SCHOLARSHIP PROGRAM
• See page 112

NASA'S VIRGINIA SPACE GRANT CONSORTIUM

http://www.vsgc.odu.edu/

COMMUNITY COLLEGE STEM SCHOLARSHIPS
• See page 105

RHODE ISLAND FOUNDATION

http://www.rifoundation.org/

JAMES J. BURNS AND C. A. HAYNES SCHOLARSHIP
Award of $1000 for students enrolled in a textile program at an educational institution offering this type of program. Preference given to children of members of National Association of Textile Supervisors. Must demonstrate financial need.

Academic Fields/Career Goals: Industrial Design.

Award: Scholarship for use in freshman, sophomore, junior, or senior years; not renewable. *Amount:* $1000.

Eligibility Requirements: Applicant must be enrolled or expecting to enroll full-time at a two-year or four-year institution or university. Available to U.S. citizens.

Application Requirements: Application form, essay, financial need analysis, recommendations or references, transcript. *Deadline:* June 3.

Contact: Libby Monahan, Funds Administrator
    Phone: 401-274-4564 Ext. 3117
    E-mail: libbym@rifoundation.org

SIMPLEHUMAN

http://www.simplehuman.com/

SIMPLE SOLUTIONS DESIGN COMPETITION
• See page 268

SOCIETY OF MANUFACTURING ENGINEERS EDUCATION FOUNDATION

http://www.smeef.org/

CHAPTER 198-DOWNRIVER DETROIT SCHOLARSHIP
• See page 290

CHAPTER 67-PHOENIX SCHOLARSHIP
• See page 290

FORT WAYNE CHAPTER 56 SCHOLARSHIP
• See page 292

NORTH CENTRAL REGION 9 SCHOLARSHIP
• See page 292

WICHITA CHAPTER 52 SCHOLARSHIP
• See page 293

SOCIETY OF PLASTICS ENGINEERS (SPE) FOUNDATION

http://www.4spe.org/

FLEMING/BASZCAK SCHOLARSHIP
• See page 171

SOCIETY OF PLASTICS ENGINEERS SCHOLARSHIP PROGRAM
• See page 171

WHOMENTORS.COM, INC.

http://www.WHOmentors.com/

IB USD WORLDWIDE VENTURE CAPITAL
• See page 107

INSURANCE AND ACTUARIAL SCIENCE

THE ACTUARIAL FOUNDATION

http://www.actuarialfoundation.org/programs/actuarial/scholarships.shtml

ACTUARIAL DIVERSITY SCHOLARSHIP
The Actuarial Diversity Scholarship promotes diversity through an annual scholarship program for Black/African American, Hispanic, Native North American and Pacific Islander students. The scholarship award recognizes and encourages the academic achievements of full-time undergraduate students pursuing a degree that may lead to a career in the actuarial profession.

Academic Fields/Career Goals: Insurance and Actuarial Science; Mathematics.

Award: Scholarship for use in freshman, sophomore, junior, or senior years; not renewable. *Amount:* $1000–$3000.

Eligibility Requirements: Applicant must be American Indian/Alaska Native, Asian/Pacific Islander, Black (non-Hispanic), Hispanic and enrolled or expecting to enroll full-time at a two-year or four-year institution or university. Applicant must have 3.0 GPA or higher. Available to U.S. and non-U.S. citizens.

Application Requirements: Application form, application form may be submitted online (http://www.actuarialfoundation.org/programs/actuarial/act-diversity.shtml), essay, recommendations or references, test scores, transcript. *Deadline:* May 3.

ACTUARY OF TOMORROW—STUART A. ROBERTSON MEMORIAL SCHOLARSHIP
The Actuary of Tomorrow—Stuart A. Robertson Memorial Scholarship recognizes and encourages the academic achievements of undergraduate students pursuing a career in actuarial science. Applicants must be full-time students entering as a sophomore, junior or senior, must have a minimum cumulative GPA of 3.0 (on 4.0 scale) and must have successfully completed two actuarial exams. The Actuarial Foundation will provide an award of $7,500 for education expenses at any accredited U.S. educational institution.

Academic Fields/Career Goals: Insurance and Actuarial Science.

Award: Scholarship for use in sophomore, junior, or senior years; not renewable. *Amount:* $7500.

Eligibility Requirements: Applicant must be enrolled or expecting to enroll full-time at a four-year institution. Applicant must have 3.0 GPA or higher. Available to U.S. and non-U.S. citizens.

Application Requirements: Application form, application form may be submitted online (http://www.actuarialfoundation.org/programs/actuarial/robertson.shtml), essay, must have successfully completed two actuarial exams, recommendations or references, transcript. *Deadline:* June 1.

JOHN CULVER WOODDY SCHOLARSHIP
The John Culver Wooddy Scholarship is awarded annually to college seniors who have successfully completed at least one actuarial examination, rank in the top quartile of their class and are nominated by a professor at their school.

Academic Fields/Career Goals: Insurance and Actuarial Science; Mathematics.

Award: Scholarship for use in senior year; not renewable. *Amount:* $2000.

Eligibility Requirements: Applicant must be enrolled or expecting to enroll full-time at a four-year institution or university. Applicant must have 3.5 GPA or higher. Available to U.S. and non-U.S. citizens.

Application Requirements: Application form, essay, recommendations or references. *Deadline:* June 21.

DADE COMMUNITY FOUNDATION

http://www.jackituckfield.org/

SEITLIN FRANKLIN E. WHEELER SCHOLARSHIP
• *See page 152*

D.W. SIMPSON & COMPANY

http://www.dwsimpson.com/

D.W. SIMPSON ACTUARIAL SCIENCE SCHOLARSHIP

One-time award for full-time actuarial science students. Must be entering senior year of undergraduate study in actuarial science. GPA of 3.2 or better in actuarial science and an overall GPA of 3.0 or better required. Must have passed at least one actuarial exam and be eligible to work in the U.S. Deadlines: April 30 for fall and October 31 for spring.

Academic Fields/Career Goals: Insurance and Actuarial Science.

Award: Scholarship for use in senior year; not renewable. *Number:* up to 2. *Amount:* up to $1000.

Eligibility Requirements: Applicant must be enrolled or expecting to enroll full-time at a four-year institution or university. Applicant must have 3.0 GPA or higher. Available to U.S. citizens.

Application Requirements: Application form, essay, resume, test scores. *Deadline:* varies.

Contact: Bethany Rave, Partner-Operations
Phone: 312-867-2300
Fax: 312-951-8386
E-mail: scholarship@dwsimpson.com

MISSOURI INSURANCE EDUCATION FOUNDATION

http://www.mief.org/

MISSOURI INSURANCE EDUCATION FOUNDATION SCHOLARSHIP

One $2500 scholarship and five $2000 scholarships available to college and university students in their junior or senior year. Must be Missouri resident.

Academic Fields/Career Goals: Insurance and Actuarial Science.

Award: Scholarship for use in junior or senior years; renewable. *Number:* 6. *Amount:* $2000–$2500.

Eligibility Requirements: Applicant must be enrolled or expecting to enroll full-time at a four-year institution or university; resident of Missouri and studying in Missouri. Applicant must have 2.5 GPA or higher. Available to U.S. citizens.

Application Requirements: Application form, financial need analysis, recommendations or references, transcript. *Deadline:* March 31.

Contact: Amy Hamacher, Scholarship Chairman
Phone: 573-893-4234
Fax: 573-893-4996
E-mail: miis@midamerica.net

NEW ENGLAND EMPLOYEE BENEFITS COUNCIL

http://www.neebc.org/

NEW ENGLAND EMPLOYEE BENEFITS COUNCIL SCHOLARSHIP PROGRAM
• *See page 77*

SPENCER EDUCATIONAL FOUNDATION INC.

http://www.spencered.org/

SPENCER EDUCATIONAL FOUNDATION SCHOLARSHIP

Scholarship is available to outstanding applicants who are focused on a career in risk management, insurance, and related disciplines. If student is attending a two year college, he/she must have intentions of transferring to a four year college.

Academic Fields/Career Goals: Insurance and Actuarial Science.

Award: Scholarship for use in junior, senior, graduate, or postgraduate years; renewable. *Number:* 30–40. *Amount:* $5000–$10,000.

Eligibility Requirements: Applicant must be enrolled or expecting to enroll full- or part-time at a two-year or four-year institution or university. Applicant must have 3.0 GPA or higher. Available to U.S. and non-U.S. citizens.

Application Requirements: Application form, application form may be submitted online (http://www.spencered.org), essay, resume, transcript. *Deadline:* January 31.

Contact: Ms. Angela Sabatino, Programs Director
Spencer Educational Foundation Inc.
1065 Avenue of the Americas, 13th Floor
New York, NY 10018
Phone: 212-655-6223
E-mail: asabatino@spencered.org

INTERIOR DESIGN

AMERICAN SOCIETY OF INTERIOR DESIGNERS (ASID) EDUCATION FOUNDATION INC.

http://www.asidfoundation.org

ASID FOUNDATION LEGACY SCHOLARSHIP FOR UNDERGRADUATES

Open to all students in their junior or senior year of undergraduate study enrolled in at least a three-year program of interior design. The award will be given to a creatively outstanding student as demonstrated through their portfolio.

Academic Fields/Career Goals: Interior Design.

Award: Scholarship for use in junior or senior years; not renewable. *Number:* 1. *Amount:* $4000.

Eligibility Requirements: Applicant must be enrolled or expecting to enroll full- or part-time at a four-year institution or university. Available to U.S. citizens.

Application Requirements: Application form, application form may be submitted online (http://www.asidfoundation.org), portfolio, recommendations or references, transcript. *Deadline:* March 12.

Contact: Valerie O'Keefe, Executive Assistant and Foundation Manager
Phone: 202-546-3480
Fax: 202-546-3240
E-mail: foundation@asid.org

ASSOCIATION FOR WOMEN IN ARCHITECTURE FOUNDATION

http://www.awa-la.org/

ASSOCIATION FOR WOMEN IN ARCHITECTURE FOUNDATION SCHOLARSHIP
• *See page 109*

IFDA EDUCATIONAL FOUNDATION

http://www.ifdaef.org/

IFDA LEADERS COMMEMORATIVE SCHOLARSHIP

Scholarship available to students who have completed four courses related to the field of interior design. Award is made to a to full-time student. Applicant does not have to be IFDA student member. Applicant must submit 300 to 500 word essay explaining future plans and goals, indicating why they believe that they are deserving of this award. Decision based upon student's academic achievement, awards and accomplishments, future plans and goals, and letter of recommendation. Documents sent along with the application should be sent individually to the four judges (4 copies).

Academic Fields/Career Goals: Interior Design; Trade/Technical Specialties.

Award: Scholarship for use in sophomore or junior years; not renewable. *Number:* 1. *Amount:* $1500.

Eligibility Requirements: Applicant must be enrolled or expecting to enroll full-time at a four-year institution or university. Available to U.S. and Canadian citizens.

Application Requirements: 2 digital pictures of design work done in class, application form, essay, recommendations or references, transcript. *Deadline:* March 31.

Contact: Sue Williams, Director of Scholarships and Grants
IFDA Educational Foundation
Colleagues
2700 East Grace Street
Richmond, VA 23223
Phone: 804-644-3946
Fax: 804-644-3834
E-mail: colleaguesinc@earthlink.net

IFDA STUDENT MEMBER SCHOLARSHIP

Scholarship available to students who have completed four courses related to the field of interior design. Award of $2000 to full-time student. Applicant must be IFDA student member. Applicant must submit 300 to 500 word essay explaining why they joined IFDA, discuss future plans and goals, and indicate why they are deserving of this award. Decision based upon student's academic achievement, awards and accomplishments, future plans and goals, and letter of recommendation. Documents sent along with the application should be sent individually to the four judges (4 copies).

Academic Fields/Career Goals: Interior Design; Trade/Technical Specialties.

Award: Scholarship for use in sophomore or junior years; not renewable. *Number:* 1. *Amount:* $2000.

Eligibility Requirements: Applicant must be enrolled or expecting to enroll full-time at a four-year institution or university. Available to U.S. and non-U.S. citizens.

Application Requirements: 2 digital copies of the design work done in class, application form, essay, recommendations or references, transcript. *Deadline:* March 31.

Contact: Sue Williams, Director of Scholarships and Grants
IFDA Educational Foundation
Colleagues
2700 East Grace Street
Richmond, VA 23233
Phone: 804-664-3946
Fax: 804-644-3834
E-mail: colleaguesinc@earthlink.net

ILLUMINATING ENGINEERING SOCIETY OF NORTH AMERICA

http://www.iesna.org/

ROBERT W. THUNEN MEMORIAL SCHOLARSHIPS

• *See page 111*

ILLUMINATING ENGINEERING SOCIETY OF NORTH AMERICA–GOLDEN GATE SECTION

http://www.iesgg.org/

ALAN LUCAS MEMORIAL EDUCATIONAL SCHOLARSHIP

• *See page 111*

INTERNATIONAL FACILITY MANAGEMENT ASSOCIATION FOUNDATION

http://www.ifmafoundation.org/

IFMA FOUNDATION SCHOLARSHIPS

• *See page 112*

INTERNATIONAL INTERIOR DESIGN ASSOCIATION (IIDA) FOUNDATION

http://www.iida.org/

KIMBALL OFFICE SCHOLARSHIP FUND

Three-year program that will award $5000 to a senior year student pursuing a degree in interior design. Deadline varies.

Academic Fields/Career Goals: Interior Design.

Award: Scholarship for use in senior year; not renewable. *Number:* 1. *Amount:* $5000.

Eligibility Requirements: Applicant must be enrolled or expecting to enroll full- or part-time at a four-year institution or university. Available to U.S. citizens.

Application Requirements: Application form, resume. *Deadline:* varies.

Contact: Jocelyn Pysarchuk, Senior Director, Communications and Marketing
Phone: 312-467-1950
Fax: 312-467-0779
E-mail: jpysarchuk@iida.org

NATIONAL ASSOCIATION OF WOMEN IN CONSTRUCTION

http://www.nawic.org/

NAWIC UNDERGRADUATE SCHOLARSHIPS

• *See page 112*

OREGON STUDENT ASSISTANCE COMMISSION

http://www.GetCollegeFunds.org/

HOME BUILDERS FOUNDATION JIM IRVINE STATEWIDE SCHOLARSHIP

• *See page 112*

SOUTH DAKOTA RETAILERS ASSOCIATION

http://www.sdra.org/

SOUTH DAKOTA RETAILERS ASSOCIATION SCHOLARSHIP PROGRAM

• *See page 80*

TURNER CONSTRUCTION COMPANY

http://www.turnerconstruction.com/

YOUTHFORCE 2020 SCHOLARSHIP PROGRAM
• *See page 113*

INTERNATIONAL STUDIES

ARMED FORCES COMMUNICATIONS AND ELECTRONICS ASSOCIATION, EDUCATIONAL FOUNDATION

http://www.afcea.org/scholarships

ARMED FORCES COMMUNICATIONS AND ELECTRONICS ASSOCIATION GENERAL EMMETT PAIGE SCHOLARSHIP
• *See page 127*

ARMED FORCES COMMUNICATIONS AND ELECTRONICS ASSOCIATION ROTC SCHOLARSHIP PROGRAM
• *See page 127*

ARRL FOUNDATION INC.

http://www.arrl.org/

DON RIEBHOFF MEMORIAL SCHOLARSHIP

One $1000 award available to students with a technician or higher class license for radio operation. Must be pursuing a baccalaureate or higher degree in international studies at any accredited institution above the high school level. Preference given to ARRL members.

Academic Fields/Career Goals: International Studies.

Award: Scholarship for use in freshman, sophomore, junior, senior, or graduate years; not renewable. *Number:* 1. *Amount:* $1000.

Eligibility Requirements: Applicant must be enrolled or expecting to enroll full-time at a four-year institution or university and must have an interest in amateur radio. Applicant or parent of applicant must be member of American Radio Relay League. Available to U.S. citizens.

Application Requirements: Application form, transcript. *Deadline:* February 1.

Contact: Ms. Mary Hobart, Secretary
Phone: 860-594-0397
E-mail: k1mmh@arrl.org

CENTRAL INTELLIGENCE AGENCY

http://www.cia.gov/

CENTRAL INTELLIGENCE AGENCY UNDERGRADUATE SCHOLARSHIP PROGRAM
• *See page 70*

CONNECTICUT COMMUNITY FOUNDATION

http://www.conncf.org/

MALCOLM BALDRIGE SCHOLARSHIP
• *See page 152*

CULTURAL SERVICES OF THE FRENCH EMBASSY

http://www.frenchculture.org/

TEACHING ASSISTANT PROGRAM IN FRANCE
• *See page 97*

JORGE MAS CANOSA FREEDOM FOUNDATION

http://www.jorgemascanosa.org/

MAS FAMILY SCHOLARSHIP AWARD
• *See page 156*

PHI ALPHA THETA HISTORY HONOR SOCIETY, INC.

http://www.phialphatheta.org/

PHI ALPHA THETA WORLD HISTORY ASSOCIATION PAPER PRIZE
• *See page 345*

UNITED STATES INSTITUTE OF PEACE

http://www.usip.org/

NATIONAL PEACE ESSAY CONTEST

Essay contest designed to have high school students research and write about international peace and conflict resolution. Topic changes yearly. State winners are awarded $10,000 and invited to Washington, D.C. for an awards program. Must be enrolled in a U.S. high school, home school, or be a U.S. citizen enrolled in a high school abroad.

Academic Fields/Career Goals: International Studies; Peace and Conflict Studies.

Award: Scholarship for use in freshman, sophomore, junior, senior, or graduate years; not renewable. *Number:* 50–53. *Amount:* $1000–$10,000.

Eligibility Requirements: Applicant must be high school student; planning to enroll or expecting to enroll full-time at a two-year or four-year institution or university and must have an interest in writing. Available to U.S. citizens.

Application Requirements: Application form, application form may be submitted online (http://www.usip.org/npec), bibliography, essay. *Deadline:* February 1.

WOMEN IN INTERNATIONAL TRADE (WIIT)

http://www.wiit.org/

WIIT SCHOLARSHIP PROGRAM

This award is given to women students who are currently studying or want to study international trade.

Academic Fields/Career Goals: International Studies.

Award: Scholarship for use in freshman, sophomore, junior, senior, graduate, or postgraduate years; not renewable. *Number:* 1–2. *Amount:* $1500.

Eligibility Requirements: Applicant must be enrolled or expecting to enroll full-time at a two-year or four-year institution or university and female. Available to U.S. and non-U.S. citizens.

Application Requirements: Application form, application form may be submitted online, entry in a contest, essay, proof of admittance to U.S. institution. *Deadline:* April 15.

JOURNALISM

ADC RESEARCH INSTITUTE
http://www.adc.org/

JACK SHAHEEN MASS COMMUNICATIONS SCHOLARSHIP AWARD
• *See page 187*

AMERICAN COPY EDITORS SOCIETY
http://www.copydesk.org/

ACES COPY EDITING SCHOLARSHIP
Several $2500 scholarships awarded each year. Students not chosen as an Aubespin scholar are automatically eligible for ACES' other awards of $1000 each. Open to undergraduate students entering their junior or senior year, graduate students, and graduating students who will take full-time copy editing jobs or internships.

Academic Fields/Career Goals: Journalism.

Award: Scholarship for use in junior, senior, or graduate years; not renewable. *Amount:* $1000–$2500.

Eligibility Requirements: Applicant must be enrolled or expecting to enroll full-time at a four-year institution or university and must have an interest in writing. Applicant must have 2.5 GPA or higher. Available to U.S. citizens.

Application Requirements: Application form, entry in a contest, essay, list of course work relevant to copy editing, copy of a story edited by the applicant, copies of five to ten headlines, recommendations or references. *Deadline:* November 15.

Contact: Kathy Schenck, Assistant Managing Editor
American Copy Editors Society
Milwaukee Journal Sentinel, 333 West State Street
Milwaukee, WI 53203
Phone: 414-224-2237

AMERICAN INSTITUTE OF POLISH CULTURE INC.
http://www.ampolinstitute.org/

HARRIET IRSAY SCHOLARSHIP GRANT
• *See page 117*

AMERICAN LEGION PRESS CLUB OF NEW JERSEY

AMERICAN LEGION PRESS CLUB OF NEW JERSEY AND POST 170 ARTHUR DEHARDT MEMORIAL SCHOLARSHIP
• *See page 187*

AMERICAN QUARTER HORSE FOUNDATION (AQHF)
http://www.aqha.com/foundation

AQHF JOURNALISM OR COMMUNICATIONS SCHOLARSHIP
• *See page 188*

ARRL FOUNDATION INC.
http://www.arrl.org/

FRANCIS WALTON MEMORIAL SCHOLARSHIP
• *See page 91*

JAKE MCCLAIN DRIVER, KC5WXA, SCHOLARSHIP FUND
• *See page 200*

PHD SCHOLARSHIP
• *See page 201*

ASIAN AMERICAN JOURNALISTS ASSOCIATION
http://www.aaja.org/

AAJA/COX FOUNDATION SCHOLARSHIP
Award of up to $1250 to full-time students pursuing careers in print, broadcast, or photo journalism. Must maintain an minimum GPA of 2.5.

Academic Fields/Career Goals: Journalism; TV/Radio Broadcasting.

Award: Scholarship for use in freshman, sophomore, junior, senior, or graduate years; not renewable. *Amount:* $1250.

Eligibility Requirements: Applicant must be Asian/Pacific Islander and enrolled or expecting to enroll full-time at a two-year or four-year or technical institution or university. Applicant must have 2.5 GPA or higher. Available to U.S. and non-U.S. citizens.

Application Requirements: Application form, essay, financial need analysis, recommendations or references, resume, transcript. *Deadline:* March 28.

Contact: Kim Mizuhara, Program Coordinator
Asian American Journalists Association
1182 Market Street, Suite 320
San Francisco, CA 94102
Phone: 415-346-2051 Ext. 102
Fax: 415-346-6343
E-mail: programs@aaja.org

ASIAN-AMERICAN JOURNALISTS ASSOCIATION SCHOLARSHIP
• *See page 189*

MARY MOY QUAN ING MEMORIAL SCHOLARSHIP AWARD
One-time award of up to $2000 for a deserving high school senior for undergraduate study. Must intend to pursue a journalism career and must show a commitment to the Asian-American community. Visit website http://www.aaja.org for application and details.

Academic Fields/Career Goals: Journalism.

Award: Scholarship for use in freshman year; not renewable. *Number:* 1. *Amount:* up to $2000.

Eligibility Requirements: Applicant must be Asian/Pacific Islander; high school student and planning to enroll or expecting to enroll full-time at a two-year or four-year institution. Available to U.S. and non-U.S. citizens.

Application Requirements: Application form, essay, financial need analysis, recommendations or references, resume, transcript. *Deadline:* March 28.

Contact: Kim Mizuhara, Programs Coordinator
Asian American Journalists Association
1182 Market Street, Suite 320
San Francisco, CA 94102
Phone: 415-346-2051 Ext. 102
Fax: 415-346-6343
E-mail: programs@aaja.org

MINORU YASUI MEMORIAL SCHOLARSHIP AWARD
One-time award of $2000 for a promising Asian undergraduate male who will pursue a broadcasting career. For use at an accredited two- or four-year institution. Visit website http://www.aaja.org for application and details.

Academic Fields/Career Goals: Journalism; TV/Radio Broadcasting.

Award: Scholarship for use in freshman, sophomore, junior, or senior years; not renewable. *Number:* 1. *Amount:* $2000.

Eligibility Requirements: Applicant must be Asian/Pacific Islander; enrolled or expecting to enroll full-time at a two-year or four-year institution or university and male. Available to U.S. and non-U.S. citizens.

Application Requirements: Application form, essay, financial need analysis, recommendations or references, resume, transcript. *Deadline:* March 28.

Contact: Kim Mizuhara, Programs Coordinator
Asian American Journalists Association
1182 Market Street, Suite 320
San Francisco, CA 94102
Phone: 415-346-2051 Ext. 102
Fax: 415-346-6343
E-mail: programs@aaja.org

NATIONAL ASIAN-AMERICAN JOURNALISTS ASSOCIATION NEWHOUSE SCHOLARSHIP

Awards up to $5000 for high school seniors and college students who plan to or are currently enrolled in a journalism program at any two- or four-year postsecondary institution. Scholarship awardees will be eligible for summer internships with a Newhouse publication. Applicants from underrepresented Asian Pacific American groups including Vietnamese, Hmong, Cambodians, and other Southeast Asians, South Asians, and Pacific Islanders are especially encouraged. Visit website http://www.aaja.org for application and details.

Academic Fields/Career Goals: Journalism.

Award: Scholarship for use in freshman, sophomore, junior, or senior years; not renewable. *Number:* 5. *Amount:* $1000–$5000.

Eligibility Requirements: Applicant must be enrolled or expecting to enroll full-time at a two-year or four-year institution or university. Applicant must have 2.5 GPA or higher. Available to U.S. and non-U.S. citizens.

Application Requirements: Application form, essay, financial need analysis, recommendations or references, resume, transcript. *Deadline:* March 28.

Contact: Kim Mizuhara, Programs Coordinator
Asian American Journalists Association
1182 Market Street, Suite 320
San Francisco, CA 94102
Phone: 415-346-2051 Ext. 102
Fax: 415-346-6343
E-mail: programs@aaja.org

VINCENT CHIN MEMORIAL SCHOLARSHIP

$5000 award to a journalism student committed to keeping Vincent Chin's memory alive. Minimum GPA of 2.5.

Academic Fields/Career Goals: Journalism.

Award: Scholarship for use in freshman, sophomore, junior, senior, or graduate years; not renewable. *Number:* 1. *Amount:* up to $5000.

Eligibility Requirements: Applicant must be Asian/Pacific Islander and enrolled or expecting to enroll full-time at a two-year or four-year or technical institution or university. Applicant must have 2.5 GPA or higher. Available to U.S. and non-U.S. citizens.

Application Requirements: Application form, essay, financial need analysis, recommendations or references, resume, transcript, work samples. *Deadline:* March 28.

Contact: Kim Mizuhara, Program Coordinator
Asian American Journalists Association
1182 Market Street, Suite 320
San Francisco, CA 94102
Phone: 415-346-2051 Ext. 102
Fax: 415-346-6343
E-mail: programs@aaja.org

ASIAN AMERICAN JOURNALISTS ASSOCIATION (SEATTLE CHAPTER)

http://www.aajaseattle.org/

NORTHWEST JOURNALISTS OF COLOR SCHOLARSHIP

One-time award for Washington state high school and college students seeking careers in journalism. Must be an undergraduate enrolled in an accredited college or university or a senior in high school. Must be Asian-American, African-American, Native-American, or Latino.

Academic Fields/Career Goals: Journalism.

Award: Scholarship for use in freshman, sophomore, junior, or senior years; not renewable. *Number:* 1–4. *Amount:* $500–$2500.

Eligibility Requirements: Applicant must be American Indian/Alaska Native, Asian/Pacific Islander, Black (non-Hispanic), Hispanic; enrolled or expecting to enroll full-time at a two-year or four-year or technical institution or university and resident of Washington. Available to U.S. citizens.

Application Requirements: Application form, community service, essay, financial need analysis, recommendations or references, transcript, work samples. *Deadline:* May 1.

Contact: Ms. Mai Hoang, AAJA Chapter Treasurer
Asian American Journalists Association (Seattle chapter)
Yakima Herald--Republic
114 North Fourth Street
Yakima, WA 98909
Phone: 509-577-7724
E-mail: mhoang@yakimaherald.com

ASSOCIATED PRESS

http://www.aptra.org/

ASSOCIATED PRESS TELEVISION/RADIO ASSOCIATION-CLETE ROBERTS JOURNALISM SCHOLARSHIP AWARDS

Award for college undergraduates and graduate students studying in California, Nevada or Hawaii and pursuing careers in broadcast journalism. Submit application, references, and examples of broadcast-related work.

Academic Fields/Career Goals: Journalism; TV/Radio Broadcasting.

Award: Scholarship for use in freshman, sophomore, junior, or senior years; not renewable. *Number:* 3. *Amount:* $1500.

Eligibility Requirements: Applicant must be enrolled or expecting to enroll full-time at a two-year or four-year institution or university and studying in California, Hawaii, Nevada. Available to U.S. citizens.

Application Requirements: Application form, recommendations or references. *Deadline:* December 14.

Contact: Roberta Gonzales, Scholarship Committee
Associated Press
CBS 5 TV, 855 Battery Street
San Francisco, CA 94111

KATHRYN DETTMAN MEMORIAL JOURNALISM SCHOLARSHIP

One-time award of $1500 for broadcast journalism students, enrolled at a California, Hawaii or Nevada college or university. Must submit entry form and examples of broadcast-related work.

Academic Fields/Career Goals: Journalism; TV/Radio Broadcasting.

Award: Scholarship for use in freshman, sophomore, junior, or senior years; renewable. *Number:* 1–4. *Amount:* $1500.

Eligibility Requirements: Applicant must be enrolled or expecting to enroll full-time at a two-year or four-year institution or university and studying in California, Hawaii, Nevada. Available to U.S. citizens.

Application Requirements: Application form, examples of broadcast-related work. *Deadline:* December 14.

Contact: Roberta Gonzales, Scholarship Committee
Associated Press
CBS 5 TV, 855 Battery Street
San Francisco, CA 94111

ASSOCIATION FOR WOMEN IN COMMUNICATIONS-SEATTLE PROFESSIONAL CHAPTER

http://www.seattleawc.org/

SEATTLE PROFESSIONAL CHAPTER OF THE ASSOCIATION FOR WOMEN IN COMMUNICATIONS

Scholarship of $3000 for women pursuing journalism in the state of Washington. For more details on eligibility criteria or selection procedure, refer to website at http://www.seattleawc.org/scholarships.html.

Academic Fields/Career Goals: Journalism.

Award: Scholarship for use in sophomore, junior, or senior years; not renewable. *Number:* 2. *Amount:* $3000.

Eligibility Requirements: Applicant must be enrolled or expecting to enroll full-time at a two-year or four-year or technical institution or university; female; resident of Washington and studying in Washington. Available to U.S. citizens.

Application Requirements: Application form, resume, sample of work, cover letter, transcript. *Deadline:* March 16.

Contact: Jaron Snow, Office Administrator
Phone: 425-771-4189
E-mail: awcseattle@verizon.net

ATLANTA PRESS CLUB INC.

http://www.atlantapressclub.org/

ATLANTA PRESS CLUB JOURNALISM SCHOLARSHIP PROGRAM

Awards outstanding Georgia college or university sophomores, juniors, and seniors who are pursuing careers in journalism. Must attend an interview with the selection committee. Must be a U.S. citizen.

Academic Fields/Career Goals: Journalism; TV/Radio Broadcasting.

Award: Scholarship for use in sophomore, junior, or senior years; not renewable. *Number:* 4. *Amount:* $1500.

Eligibility Requirements: Applicant must be enrolled or expecting to enroll full- or part-time at a four-year institution or university; resident of Georgia; studying in Georgia and must have an interest in writing. Available to U.S. citizens.

Application Requirements: Application form, clips/tapes/CD, essay, interview, portfolio, transcript. *Deadline:* February 15.

Contact: Elaine Hudson, Assistant Director, Scholarship Committee
Atlanta Press Club Inc.
34 Broad Street, 18th Floor
Atlanta, GA 30303
Phone: 404-577-7377
Fax: 404-223-3706
E-mail: ehudson@atlpressclub.org

BAY AREA BLACK JOURNALISTS ASSOCIATION SCHOLARSHIP CONTEST

http://www.babja.org/

YOUNG JOURNALISTS SCHOLARSHIP

Nonrenewable scholarship of $2500 open to photojournalism students. Applicant must be enrolled in any college or university nationwide. Must be studying journalism (television, radio, print, online).

Academic Fields/Career Goals: Journalism; Photojournalism/Photography.

Award: Scholarship for use in freshman, sophomore, junior, senior, or graduate years; not renewable. *Amount:* $2500.

Eligibility Requirements: Applicant must be enrolled or expecting to enroll full- or part-time at a four-year institution or university. Available to U.S. citizens.

Application Requirements: Application form, essay, recommendations or references, resume, transcript, work samples. *Deadline:* October 2.

CANADIAN PRESS

http://www.thecanadianpress.com/

GIL PURCELL MEMORIAL JOURNALISM SCHOLARSHIP FOR NATIVE CANADIANS

Scholarship is designed to encourage native Canadian students to enter the field of journalism in Canada. Awards aboriginal Canadians (status or non-status Indian, Metis, or Inuit) who are pursuing postsecondary studies and intend to work in the field of journalism.

Academic Fields/Career Goals: Journalism.

Award: Scholarship for use in freshman, sophomore, junior, or senior years; not renewable. *Number:* 1. *Amount:* $4000.

Eligibility Requirements: Applicant must be of Canadian heritage and Canadian citizen; American Indian/Alaska Native and enrolled or

expecting to enroll full- or part-time at a four-year institution or university.

Application Requirements: Application form, resume. *Deadline:* November 15.

Contact: Marissa D'Mello, Human Resources Coordinator
Canadian Press
36 King Street East
Toronto, ON M5C 2L9
CAN

CCNMA: LATINO JOURNALISTS OF CALIFORNIA

http://www.ccnma.org/

CCNMA SCHOLARSHIPS

Scholarships for Latinos interested in pursuing a career in journalism. Awards based on scholastic achievement, financial need, and community awareness. Submit sample of work. Award limited to California residents or those attending school in California.

Academic Fields/Career Goals: Journalism; Photojournalism/Photography; TV/Radio Broadcasting.

Award: Scholarship for use in freshman, sophomore, junior, senior, or graduate years; not renewable. *Number:* 5–10. *Amount:* $500–$1000.

Eligibility Requirements: Applicant must be of Latin American/Caribbean heritage; Hispanic; enrolled or expecting to enroll full-time at a two-year or four-year institution or university and resident of California. Available to U.S. and non-U.S. citizens.

Application Requirements: Application form, entry in a contest, essay, financial need analysis, interview, portfolio, recommendations or references, resume, transcript. *Deadline:* April 1.

Contact: Julio Moran, Executive Director
CCNMA: Latino Journalists of California
ASU Walter Cronkite School of Journalism and Mass Communication
725 Arizona Avenue, Suite 206
Santa Monica, CA 90401-1734
Phone: 310-458-8040
Fax: 310-576-0502
E-mail: ccnmainfo@ccnma.org

THE CIRI FOUNDATION (TCF)

http://www.thecirifoundation.org/

CAP LATHROP SCHOLARSHIP PROGRAM
• See page 151

CONNECTICUT CHAPTER OF SOCIETY OF PROFESSIONAL JOURNALISTS

http://www.ctspj.org/

CONNECTICUT SPJ BOB EDDY SCHOLARSHIP PROGRAM
• See page 190

CUBAN AMERICAN NATIONAL FOUNDATION

http://www.masscholarships.org/

MAS FAMILY SCHOLARSHIPS
• See page 152

DADE COMMUNITY FOUNDATION

http://www.jackituckfield.org/

LEO SUAREZ SCHOLARSHIP
• See page 190

DAIRY MANAGEMENT

http://www.dairyinfo.com/

NATIONAL DAIRY PROMOTION AND RESEARCH BOARD SCHOLARSHIP

• *See page 91*

DOW JONES NEWS FUND, INC.

https://www.newsfund.org/

DOW JONES NEWS FUND HIGH SCHOOL JOURNALISM WORKSHOPS WRITING, PHOTOGRAPHY AND MULTIMEDIA COMPETITION

Participants in DJNF summer workshops are nominated for writing, multimedia and photography awards based on their published work. Scholarships are presented to the best writers, digital producers and photographers to pursue media careers.

Academic Fields/Career Goals: Journalism.

Award: Scholarship for use in freshman year; not renewable. *Number:* 8. *Amount:* up to $1000.

Eligibility Requirements: Applicant must be high school student and planning to enroll or expecting to enroll full-time at a four-year institution or university. Available to U.S. and non-U.S. citizens.

Application Requirements: Application form, entry in a contest, essay, portfolio, recommendations or references. *Deadline:* October 1.

Contact: Mrs. Linda Shockley, Deputy Director
Dow Jones News Fund, Inc.
PO Box 300
Princeton, NJ 08543-0300
Phone: 609-452-2820
Fax: 609-520-5804
E-mail: djnf@dowjones.com

FISHER BROADCASTING COMPANY

http://www.fsci.com/

FISHER BROADCASTING INC. SCHOLARSHIP FOR MINORITIES

• *See page 154*

FREEDOM FORUM

http://www.freedomforum.org/

AL NEUHARTH FREE SPIRIT AND JOURNALISM CONFERENCE PROGRAM

One-time award for high school juniors interested in pursuing a career in journalism. Must be actively involved in high school journalism and demonstrate qualities such as being a visionary, an innovative leader, an entrepreneur or a courageous achiever. Scholars come to Washington D.C. to receive their awards and participate in an all-expense paid journalism conference. See website at http://www.freespirit.org for further information.

Academic Fields/Career Goals: Journalism.

Award: Scholarship for use in freshman year; not renewable. *Number:* 51. *Amount:* $1000.

Eligibility Requirements: Applicant must be high school student; planning to enroll or expecting to enroll full-time at a two-year or four-year institution or university and must have an interest in entrepreneurship, leadership, photography/photogrammetry/filmmaking, or writing. Available to U.S. citizens.

Application Requirements: Application form, essay, personal photograph, recommendations or references, sample of journalistic work, transcript. *Deadline:* February 15.

Contact: Karen Catone, Director/Al Neuharth Free Spirit Program
Freedom Forum
555 Pennsylvania Avenue, NW
Washington, DC 20001
Phone: 202-292-6271
Fax: 202-292-6275
E-mail: freespirit@freedomforum.org

GEORGIA PRESS EDUCATIONAL FOUNDATION INC.

http://www.gapress.org/

DURWOOD MCALISTER SCHOLARSHIP

Scholarship awarded annually to an outstanding student majoring in print journalism at a Georgia college or university.

Academic Fields/Career Goals: Journalism.

Award: Scholarship for use in freshman, sophomore, junior, senior, graduate, or postgraduate years; not renewable. *Number:* 1. *Amount:* $500–$1500.

Eligibility Requirements: Applicant must be enrolled or expecting to enroll full-time at a two-year or four-year or technical institution or university; resident of Georgia and must have an interest in writing. Available to U.S. citizens.

Application Requirements: Application form, essay, personal photograph, recommendations or references, transcript. *Deadline:* March 1.

Contact: Jenifer Farmer, Manager
Phone: 770-454-6776
Fax: 770-454-6778

GEORGIA PRESS EDUCATIONAL FOUNDATION SCHOLARSHIPS

One-time awards to Georgia high school seniors and college undergraduates. Based on prior interest in newspaper journalism. Must be recommended by high school counselor, professor, and/or Georgia Press Educational Foundation member. Must reside and attend school in Georgia.

Academic Fields/Career Goals: Journalism.

Award: Scholarship for use in freshman, sophomore, junior, or senior years; not renewable. *Number:* 16. *Amount:* $500–$1500.

Eligibility Requirements: Applicant must be enrolled or expecting to enroll full-time at a two-year or four-year institution or university; resident of Georgia; studying in Georgia and must have an interest in writing. Available to U.S. citizens.

Application Requirements: Application form, financial need analysis, personal photograph, recommendations or references, test scores, transcript. *Deadline:* March 1.

Contact: Jenifer Farmer, Manager
Georgia Press Educational Foundation Inc.
3066 Mercer University Drive, Suite 200
Atlanta, GA 30341-4137
Phone: 770-454-6776
Fax: 770-454-6778

KIRK SUTLIVE SCHOLARSHIP

Scholarship awarded annually to a junior or senior majoring in either the news-editorial or public relations sequence.

Academic Fields/Career Goals: Journalism.

Award: Scholarship for use in junior or senior years; not renewable. *Number:* 1. *Amount:* $500–$1500.

Eligibility Requirements: Applicant must be enrolled or expecting to enroll full-time at a four-year institution or university. Available to U.S. citizens.

Application Requirements: Application form, essay, financial need analysis, personal photograph, transcript. *Deadline:* March 1.

Contact: Jenifer Farmer, Manager
Phone: 770-454-6776
Fax: 770-454-6778

MORRIS NEWSPAPER CORPORATION SCHOLARSHIP

Scholarship awarded annually to an outstanding print journalism student. Applications are submitted through newspapers in the Morris Newspaper Corporation chain and recipients are named by the Foundation.

Academic Fields/Career Goals: Journalism.

Award: Scholarship for use in freshman, sophomore, junior, or senior years; not renewable. *Number:* 1. *Amount:* $500–$1500.

Eligibility Requirements: Applicant must be enrolled or expecting to enroll full-time at a four-year or technical institution or university; resident of Georgia and must have an interest in writing. Available to U.S. citizens.

Application Requirements: Application form, essay, personal photograph, recommendations or references, transcript. *Deadline:* March 1.

Contact: Jenifer Farmer, Manager
Phone: 770-454-6776
Fax: 770-454-6778

WILLIAM C. ROGERS SCHOLARSHIP

Scholarship awarded to a junior or senior majoring in the news-editorial sequence. For full-time study only. Must be a resident of Georgia.

Academic Fields/Career Goals: Journalism.

Award: Scholarship for use in junior or senior years; not renewable. *Number:* 1. *Amount:* $500–$1500.

Eligibility Requirements: Applicant must be enrolled or expecting to enroll full-time at a four-year institution or university; resident of Georgia and must have an interest in writing. Available to U.S. citizens.

Application Requirements: Application form, essay, personal photograph, recommendations or references, transcript. *Deadline:* March 1.

Contact: Jenifer Farmer, Manager
Phone: 770-454-6776
Fax: 770-454-6778

GREAT LAKES COMMISSION

http://www.glc.org/

CAROL A. RATZA MEMORIAL SCHOLARSHIP
• *See page 190*

IDAHO STATE BROADCASTERS ASSOCIATION

http://www.idahobroadcasters.org/

WAYNE C. CORNILS MEMORIAL SCHOLARSHIP
• *See page 156*

INDIANA BROADCASTERS ASSOCIATION

http://www.indianabroadcasters.org/

INDIANA BROADCASTERS FOUNDATION SCHOLARSHIP

Awards a student majoring in broadcasting, electronic media, or journalism. Must maintain a 3.0 GPA and be a resident of Indiana. One-time award for full-time undergraduate study in Indiana.

Academic Fields/Career Goals: Journalism; TV/Radio Broadcasting.

Award: Scholarship for use in freshman, sophomore, junior, or senior years; not renewable. *Number:* up to 10. *Amount:* $500–$2000.

Eligibility Requirements: Applicant must be enrolled or expecting to enroll full-time at a two-year or four-year or technical institution or university; resident of Indiana and studying in Indiana. Applicant must have 3.0 GPA or higher. Available to U.S. citizens.

Application Requirements: Application form, application form may be submitted online (http://www.indianabroadcasters.org), essay, recommendations or references, transcript. *Deadline:* March 4.

Contact: Gwen Piening, Scholarship Administrator
Indiana Broadcasters Association
3003 East 98th Street, Suite 161
Indianapolis, IN 46280
Phone: 317-573-0119
Fax: 317-573-0895
E-mail: indba@aol.com

INTERNATIONAL FOODSERVICE EDITORIAL COUNCIL

http://www.ifeconline.com/

INTERNATIONAL FOODSERVICE EDITORIAL COUNCIL COMMUNICATIONS SCHOLARSHIP
• *See page 83*

JAMES BEARD FOUNDATION INC.

http://www.jamesbeard.org/

DANA CAMPBELL MEMORIAL SCHOLARSHIP

Up to one $2000 award for a student in their second or third year of study in an accredited bachelor degree program in journalism or a food-related curriculum at any U.S. college or university. Must be a resident of Alabama, Florida, Georgia, North Carolina, South Carolina, Louisiana, Virginia, Arkansas, Texas, Mississippi, Kentucky, Maryland, Missouri, Oklahoma, West Virginia, or Delaware and substantiate residency. Must have a career interest in food journalism.

Academic Fields/Career Goals: Journalism.

Award: Scholarship for use in sophomore or junior years; not renewable. *Number:* up to 1. *Amount:* $2000.

Eligibility Requirements: Applicant must be enrolled or expecting to enroll full- or part-time at a four-year institution or university. Available to U.S. citizens.

Application Requirements: Application form, proof of residency. *Deadline:* May 15.

JAPANESE AMERICAN CITIZENS LEAGUE (JACL)

http://www.jacl.org/

NATIONAL JACL HEADQUARTERS SCHOLARSHIP
• *See page 92*

JOHN BAYLISS BROADCAST FOUNDATION

http://www.baylissfoundation.org/

JOHN BAYLISS BROADCAST RADIO SCHOLARSHIP
• *See page 191*

JORGE MAS CANOSA FREEDOM FOUNDATION

http://www.jorgemascanosa.org/

MAS FAMILY SCHOLARSHIP AWARD
• *See page 156*

KATU THOMAS R. DARGAN MINORITY SCHOLARSHIP

http://www.katu.com/

THOMAS R. DARGAN MINORITY SCHOLARSHIP
• *See page 191*

LIN TELEVISION CORPORATION

http://www.lintv.com/

LINTV MINORITY SCHOLARSHIP

Scholarship to help educate and train outstanding minority candidates who seek to enter the television broadcast field. Minimum 3.0 cumulative GPA required. Must have declared major in journalism or related broadcast field at an accredited university or college. Must be a sophomore or have completed sufficient semester hours or similar educational units to be within two years of receiving a bachelor's degree.

Academic Fields/Career Goals: Journalism; TV/Radio Broadcasting.

Award: Scholarship for use in sophomore year; not renewable. *Number:* 1.

Eligibility Requirements: Applicant must be American Indian/Alaska Native, Asian/Pacific Islander, Black (non-Hispanic), Hispanic and enrolled or expecting to enroll full-time at a two-year or four-year institution or university. Applicant must have 3.0 GPA or higher. Available to U.S. citizens.

Application Requirements: Application form, transcript. *Deadline:* March 15.

Contact: Don Donohue, Director, Human Resources
Lin Television Corporation
One Richmond Square, Suite 230E
Providence, RI 02906
Phone: 401-457-9402
E-mail: dan.donohue@lintv.com

MARYLAND/DELAWARE/DISTRICT OF COLUMBIA PRESS FOUNDATION

http://www.mddcpress.com/

MICHAEL J. POWELL HIGH SCHOOL JOURNALIST OF THE YEAR

Scholarship of $1500 to an outstanding high school student. Applicant must submit five samples of work, mounted on unlined paper, a letter of recommendation from the nominee's advisor, an autobiography geared to the publication activities in which the nominee participated, and the nominee should write a paragraph or two on the most important aspect of scholastic journalism.

Academic Fields/Career Goals: Journalism.

Award: Scholarship for use in freshman year; not renewable. *Number:* 1. *Amount:* $1500.

Eligibility Requirements: Applicant must be high school student; planning to enroll or expecting to enroll full- or part-time at a four-year institution or university and must have an interest in writing. Available to U.S. citizens.

Application Requirements: Application form, driver's license, entry in a contest, five sample articles, recommendations or references. *Deadline:* January 31.

Contact: Jennifer Thornberry, Administration Associate Coordinator
Phone: 410-721-4000 Ext. 20
Fax: 410-721-4557
E-mail: info@mddcpress.com

MISSISSIPPI ASSOCIATION OF BROADCASTERS

http://www.msbroadcasters.org/

MISSISSIPPI ASSOCIATION OF BROADCASTERS SCHOLARSHIP

Scholarship available to a student enrolled in a fully accredited broadcast curriculum at a Mississippi two- or four-year college.

Academic Fields/Career Goals: Journalism; TV/Radio Broadcasting.

Award: Scholarship for use in freshman, sophomore, junior, or senior years; not renewable. *Number:* up to 8. *Amount:* $2000.

Eligibility Requirements: Applicant must be enrolled or expecting to enroll full-time at a two-year or four-year institution or university; resident of Mississippi and studying in Mississippi. Available to U.S. citizens.

Application Requirements: Application form, extracurricular activities and community involvement also considered, financial need analysis, recommendations or references. *Deadline:* May 1.

Contact: Jackie Lett, Scholarship Coordinator
Phone: 601-957-9121
Fax: 601-957-9175
E-mail: jackie@msbroadcasters.org

MISSISSIPPI PRESS ASSOCIATION EDUCATION FOUNDATION

http://mspa.affiniscape.com

MISSISSIPPI PRESS ASSOCIATION EDUCATION FOUNDATION SCHOLARSHIP

The foundation annually offers $1000 ($500 per semester) scholarships to qualified students enrolled in print journalism, and who are residents of Mississippi. The recipient who maintains a 3.0 GPA. Total value of the scholarship can be as much as $4000 when awarded to an incoming freshman who remains qualified throughout their four years of print journalism education.

Academic Fields/Career Goals: Journalism.

Award: Scholarship for use in freshman, sophomore, junior, or senior years; renewable. *Number:* 1. *Amount:* $1000–$4000.

Eligibility Requirements: Applicant must be enrolled or expecting to enroll full-time at a two-year or four-year institution or university and resident of Mississippi. Applicant must have 3.0 GPA or higher. Available to U.S. citizens.

Application Requirements: Application form, recommendations or references, resume, sample of work. *Deadline:* April 1.

Contact: Beth Boone, Scholarship Coordinator
Phone: 601-981-3060
Fax: 601-981-3676
E-mail: bboone@mspress.org

NATIONAL ACADEMY OF TELEVISION ARTS AND SCIENCES-NATIONAL CAPITAL/CHESAPEAKE BAY CHAPTER

http://www.natasdc.org/

BETTY ENDICOTT/NTA-NCCB STUDENT SCHOLARSHIP

Scholarship for a full-time sophomore, junior or non-graduating senior student pursuing a career in communication, television or broadcast journalism. Must be enrolled in an accredited four-year college or university in Maryland, Virginia or Washington, D.C. Minimum GPA of 3.0 required. Must demonstrate an aptitude or interest in communication, television or broadcast journalism. Application URL http://capitalemmys.tv/betty_endicott.htm.

Academic Fields/Career Goals: Journalism; TV/Radio Broadcasting.

Award: Scholarship for use in sophomore, junior, or senior years; not renewable. *Number:* 1. *Amount:* $5000.

Eligibility Requirements: Applicant must be enrolled or expecting to enroll full-time at a four-year institution or university and studying in District of Columbia, Maryland, Virginia. Applicant must have 3.0 GPA or higher. Available to U.S. citizens.

Application Requirements: Application form, essay, recommendations or references, resume, transcript, work samples (resume tape in VHS format and radio or television broadcast scripts). *Deadline:* April 22.

Contact: Diane Bruno, Student Affairs Committee
National Academy of Television Arts and Sciences-National Capital/Chesapeake Bay Chapter
9405 Russell Road
Silver Spring, MD 20910
Phone: 301-587-3993
E-mail: capitalemmys@aol.com

NATIONAL ASSOCIATION OF BLACK JOURNALISTS

http://www.nabj.org/

ALLISON FISHER SCHOLARSHIP

Scholarship for students currently attending an accredited college or university. Must be majoring in print journalism and maintain a 3.0 GPA. Recipient will attend NABJ convention and participate in the mentor program. Scholarship value and the number of awards granted varies.

Academic Fields/Career Goals: Journalism.

Award: Scholarship for use in freshman, sophomore, junior, senior, or graduate years; not renewable.

Eligibility Requirements: Applicant must be enrolled or expecting to enroll full-time at a four-year institution or university. Applicant must have 3.0 GPA or higher. Available to U.S. and non-U.S. citizens.

Application Requirements: Driver's license, proof of enrollment, recommendations or references. *Deadline:* March 17.

Contact: Irving Washington, Manager
Phone: 301-445-7100
Fax: 301-445-7101
E-mail: iwashington@nabj.org

GERALD BOYD/ROBIN STONE NON-SUSTAINING SCHOLARSHIP

One-time scholarship for students enrolled in an accredited four-year institution. Must be enrolled as an undergraduate or graduate student and maintain a 3.0 GPA. Must major in print journalism. Must be a member of NABJ. Scholarship value and the number of awards granted annually varies.

Academic Fields/Career Goals: Journalism.

Award: Scholarship for use in freshman, sophomore, junior, senior, or graduate years; not renewable.

Eligibility Requirements: Applicant must be enrolled or expecting to enroll full-time at a four-year institution or university. Applicant must have 3.0 GPA or higher. Available to U.S. and non-U.S. citizens.

Application Requirements: 6 samples of work, application form, essay, personal photograph, recommendations or references, transcript. *Deadline:* March 17.

Contact: Irving Washington, Manager
Phone: 301-445-7100
Fax: 301-445-7101
E-mail: iwashington@nabj.org

NABJ SCHOLARSHIP
• *See page 192*

NATIONAL ASSOCIATION OF BLACK JOURNALISTS AND NEWHOUSE FOUNDATION SCHOLARSHIP

Award for high school seniors planning to attend an accredited four-year college or university and major in journalism. Minimum 3.0 GPA required. Must be a member of NABJ. The scholarship value and the number of awards granted varies.

Academic Fields/Career Goals: Journalism.

Award: Scholarship for use in freshman, sophomore, junior, or senior years; not renewable.

Eligibility Requirements: Applicant must be enrolled or expecting to enroll full-time at a four-year institution or university and must have an interest in writing. Applicant must have 3.0 GPA or higher. Available to U.S. and non-U.S. citizens.

Application Requirements: Application form, driver's license, essay, interview, recommendations or references, transcript. *Deadline:* March 17.

Contact: Irving Washington, Manager
Phone: 301-445-7100
Fax: 301-445-7101
E-mail: iwashington@nabj.org

NATIONAL ASSOCIATION OF BLACK JOURNALISTS NON-SUSTAINING SCHOLARSHIP AWARDS

One-time award for college students attending a four-year institution and majoring in journalism. Minimum 2.5 GPA required. Must be a member of NABJ. Scholarship value and the number of awards varies annually.

Academic Fields/Career Goals: Journalism; Photojournalism/Photography; TV/Radio Broadcasting.

Award: Scholarship for use in freshman, sophomore, junior, or senior years; not renewable.

Eligibility Requirements: Applicant must be enrolled or expecting to enroll full-time at a four-year institution or university and must have an interest in writing. Applicant must have 2.5 GPA or higher. Available to U.S. and non-U.S. citizens.

Application Requirements: Application form, driver's license, personal photograph, proof of enrollment, recommendations or references, transcript. *Deadline:* March 17.

Contact: Irving Washington, Manager
Phone: 301-445-7100
Fax: 301-445-7101
E-mail: iwashington@nabj.org

NATIONAL ASSOCIATION OF BROADCASTERS

http://www.nab.org/

NATIONAL ASSOCIATION OF BROADCASTERS GRANTS FOR RESEARCH IN BROADCASTING
• *See page 192*

NATIONAL ASSOCIATION OF HISPANIC JOURNALISTS (NAHJ)

http://www.nahj.org/

GERALDO RIVERA SCHOLARSHIP

Awards available to college undergraduates and graduate students pursuing careers in English- or Spanish-language TV broadcast journalism. Applications available on website, http://www.nahj.org.

Academic Fields/Career Goals: Journalism; TV/Radio Broadcasting.

Award: Scholarship for use in senior or graduate years; not renewable. *Amount:* $1000–$5000.

Eligibility Requirements: Applicant must be enrolled or expecting to enroll full-time at a four-year institution or university. Available to U.S. citizens.

Application Requirements: Application form, financial need analysis, recommendations or references, resume, transcript. *Deadline:* March 31.

Contact: Virginia Galindo, Program Assistant
Phone: 202-662-7145
E-mail: vgalindo@nahj.org

MARIA ELENA SALINAS SCHOLARSHIP
• *See page 321*

NATIONAL ASSOCIATION OF HISPANIC JOURNALISTS SCHOLARSHIP
• *See page 192*

NEWHOUSE SCHOLARSHIP PROGRAM
• *See page 325*

WASHINGTON POST YOUNG JOURNALISTS SCHOLARSHIP

Four-year award of $10,000 for high school seniors in D.C. metropolitan area. Contact educational programs manager for application and information.

Academic Fields/Career Goals: Journalism.

Award: Scholarship for use in freshman year; not renewable. *Amount:* $10,000.

Eligibility Requirements: Applicant must be high school student; planning to enroll or expecting to enroll full-time at a four-year institution or university and resident of District of Columbia, Maryland, Virginia. Available to U.S. citizens.

Application Requirements: Application form, recommendations or references, transcript. *Deadline:* March 31.

Contact: Virginia Galindo, Program Assistant
Phone: 202-662-7145
E-mail: vgalindo@nahj.org

NATIONAL ASSOCIATION OF NEGRO BUSINESS AND PROFESSIONAL WOMEN'S CLUBS INC.

http://www.nanbpwc.org/

JULIANNE MALVEAUX SCHOLARSHIP
• *See page 230*

NATIONAL DAIRY SHRINE

http://www.dairyshrine.org/

MARSHALL E. MCCULLOUGH-NATIONAL DAIRY SHRINE SCHOLARSHIPS

• See page 93

NATIONAL INSTITUTE FOR LABOR RELATIONS RESEARCH

http://www.nilrr.org/

NATIONAL INSTITUTE FOR LABOR RELATIONS RESEARCH WILLIAM B. RUGGLES JOURNALISM SCHOLARSHIP

• See page 193

NATIONAL PRESS CLUB

http://www.npc.press.org/

NATIONAL PRESS CLUB SCHOLARSHIP FOR JOURNALISM DIVERSITY

Scholarship of $2500 per year awarded to a talented minority student planning to pursue a career in journalism. Applicant must be a high school senior. Must have applied to or been accepted by a college or university for the upcoming year.

Academic Fields/Career Goals: Journalism.

Award: Scholarship for use in freshman year; not renewable. *Number:* 1. *Amount:* $2500.

Eligibility Requirements: Applicant must be high school student and planning to enroll or expecting to enroll full-time at a four-year institution or university. Available to U.S. and non-U.S. citizens.

Application Requirements: Application form, essay, financial need analysis, recommendations or references, self-addressed stamped envelope with application, transcript, work samples demonstrating an ongoing interest in journalism. *Deadline:* March 1.

Contact: Joann Booze, Scholarship Coordinator
 Phone: 202-662-7532
 E-mail: jbooze@press.org

NATIONAL PRESS FOUNDATION

http://www.nationalpress.org/

EVERT CLARK/SETH PAYNE AWARD

Award to recognize outstanding reporting and writing in any field of science. Limited to non-technical, print journalism only. Articles published in newspapers (including college newspapers), magazines, and newsletters are eligible. Both freelancers and staff writers are eligible.

Academic Fields/Career Goals: Journalism; Literature/English/ Writing.

Award: Prize for use in freshman, sophomore, junior, senior, graduate, or postgraduate years; not renewable. *Number:* 1000.

Eligibility Requirements: Applicant must be enrolled or expecting to enroll full- or part-time at a two-year or four-year or technical institution or university and must have an interest in writing. Available to U.S. citizens.

Application Requirements: Application form, entry in a contest, five photocopies of each article. *Deadline:* June 30.

Contact: John Carey, Scholarship Committee
 National Press Foundation
 1211 Connecticut Avenue, Suite 310
 Washington, DC 20036
 Phone: 202-383-2100

NATIONAL SCHOLASTIC PRESS ASSOCIATION

http://www.studentpress.org/

NSPA JOURNALISM HONOR ROLL SCHOLARSHIP

Scholarship to student journalists who have achieved a 3.75 or higher GPA and have worked in student media for two or more years.

Academic Fields/Career Goals: Journalism.

Award: Scholarship for use in freshman year; not renewable. *Number:* 1–3. *Amount:* $1000.

Eligibility Requirements: Applicant must be high school student and planning to enroll or expecting to enroll full-time at a four-year institution or university. Applicant or parent of applicant must have employment or volunteer experience in journalism/broadcasting. Available to U.S. and non-U.S. citizens.

Application Requirements: Application form, essay, proof of NSPA membership required, recommendations or references, resume, transcript. *Deadline:* February 15.

Contact: Marisa Dobson, Sponsorship Contest Coordinator
 Phone: 612-625-6519
 Fax: 612-626-0720
 E-mail: marisa@studentpress.org

NATIONAL WRITERS ASSOCIATION FOUNDATION

http://www.nationalwriters.com/

NATIONAL WRITERS ASSOCIATION FOUNDATION SCHOLARSHIPS

Scholarships available to talented young writers with serious interest in any writing field.

Academic Fields/Career Goals: Journalism; Literature/English/ Writing.

Award: Scholarship for use in freshman, sophomore, junior, senior, graduate, or postgraduate years; not renewable. *Number:* 1–4. *Amount:* $1000.

Eligibility Requirements: Applicant must be enrolled or expecting to enroll full- or part-time at a two-year or four-year or technical institution or university and must have an interest in writing. Available to U.S. and non-U.S. citizens.

Application Requirements: Application form, transcript, writing samples. *Deadline:* January 15.

Contact: Sandy Welchel, Executive Director
 National Writers Association Foundation
 10940 South Parker Road, Suite 508
 Parker, CO 80134
 Phone: 303-841-0246
 Fax: 303-841-2607
 E-mail: natlwritersassn@hotmail.com

NATIVE AMERICAN JOURNALISTS ASSOCIATION

http://www.naja.com/

NATIVE AMERICAN JOURNALISTS ASSOCIATION SCHOLARSHIPS

One-time award for undergraduate study leading to journalism career at accredited colleges and universities. Applicants must be current members of Native-American Journalists Association or may join at time of application. Applicants must have proof of tribal association. Send cover letter, letters of reference, and work samples with application. Financial need considered.

Academic Fields/Career Goals: Journalism.

Award: Scholarship for use in freshman, sophomore, junior, or senior years; not renewable. *Number:* 10. *Amount:* $500–$5000.

Eligibility Requirements: Applicant must be American Indian/Alaska Native; enrolled or expecting to enroll full-time at a two-year or four-year institution or university and must have an interest in writing. Applicant or parent of applicant must be member of Native American Journalists Association. Applicant must have 2.5 GPA or higher. Available to U.S. and Canadian citizens.

Application Requirements: Application form, community service, essay, financial need analysis, interview, personal photograph, portfolio, recommendations or references, resume, test scores, transcript. *Deadline:* April 1.

Contact: Jeffrey Palmer, Education Director
    Phone: 405-325-9008
    Fax: 866-325-7565
    E-mail: jeffrey.p.palmer@ou.edu

NEBRASKA PRESS ASSOCIATION

http://www.nebpress.com/

NEBRASKA PRESS ASSOCIATION FOUNDATION INC. SCHOLARSHIP

Award for graduates of Nebraska high schools who have a minimum GPA of 2.5 and are enrolled or planning to enroll in programs in Nebraska colleges or universities leading to careers in print journalism.

Academic Fields/Career Goals: Journalism; Photojournalism/Photography.

Award: Scholarship for use in freshman, sophomore, or junior years; not renewable. *Number:* 2–4. *Amount:* $2000.

Eligibility Requirements: Applicant must be enrolled or expecting to enroll full-time at a four-year institution or university; resident of Nebraska and studying in Nebraska. Applicant must have 2.5 GPA or higher. Available to U.S. citizens.

Application Requirements: Application form, essay, recommendations or references, up to 3 work samples, if available. *Deadline:* February 22.

Contact: Allen Beermann, Executive Director
    Nebraska Press Association
    845 S Street
    Lincoln, NE 68508-1226
    Phone: 402-476-2851
    Fax: 402-476-2942
    E-mail: abeermann@nebpress.com

NEW JERSEY BROADCASTERS ASSOCIATION

http://www.njba.com/

MICHAEL S. LIBRETTI SCHOLARSHIP
• *See page 193*

NEW JERSEY PRESS FOUNDATION

http://www.njpressfoundation.org/

BERNARD KILGORE MEMORIAL SCHOLARSHIP FOR THE NJ HIGH SCHOOL JOURNALIST OF THE YEAR

Program co-sponsored with the Garden State Scholastic Press Association. Winning student is nominated to the Journalism Education Association for the National High School Journalist of the Year Competition. Must be in high school with plans of entering a four-year college or university on a full-time basis. Minimum 3.0 GPA required.

Academic Fields/Career Goals: Journalism.

Award: Scholarship for use in freshman year; not renewable. *Number:* 1. *Amount:* $5000.

Eligibility Requirements: Applicant must be high school student; planning to enroll or expecting to enroll full-time at a four-year institution or university; resident of New Jersey and must have an interest in writing. Applicant must have 3.0 GPA or higher. Available to U.S. citizens.

Application Requirements: Application form, entry in a contest, essay, portfolio, recommendations or references, resume, transcript. *Deadline:* February 15.

Contact: Thomas Engleman, Program Director
    Phone: 609-406-0600 Ext. 19
    E-mail: programs@njpressfoundation.org

OHIO NEWSPAPERS FOUNDATION

http://www.ohionews.org/foundation.html

OHIO NEWSPAPERS FOUNDATION MINORITY SCHOLARSHIP

One scholarship for minority high school seniors who plan to pursue a newspaper journalism career. Applicants must be enrolled in an accredited Ohio college or university. Must be African-American, Hispanic, Asian-American or American-Indian. A minimum high school GPA of 2.5 required.

Academic Fields/Career Goals: Journalism.

Award: Scholarship for use in freshman year; not renewable. *Number:* 1. *Amount:* $1500.

Eligibility Requirements: Applicant must be American Indian/Alaska Native, Asian/Pacific Islander, Black (non-Hispanic), Hispanic; high school student; planning to enroll or expecting to enroll full-time at a four-year institution or university; resident of Ohio and studying in Ohio. Applicant must have 2.5 GPA or higher. Available to U.S. citizens.

Application Requirements: Application form, application form may be submitted online (http://www.ohionews.org), driver's license, essay, recommendations or references, transcript. *Deadline:* March 31.

OHIO NEWSPAPERS FOUNDATION UNIVERSITY JOURNALISM SCHOLARSHIP

One-time $1500 scholarship for a student who is enrolled in an Ohio college or university, majoring in journalism or equivalent degree program. Preference will be given to students demonstrating a career commitment to newspaper journalism. A minimum GPA of 2.5 required.

Academic Fields/Career Goals: Journalism.

Award: Scholarship for use in freshman, sophomore, junior, or senior years; not renewable. *Number:* 3. *Amount:* $1500.

Eligibility Requirements: Applicant must be enrolled or expecting to enroll full-time at a four-year institution or university; resident of Ohio and studying in Ohio. Applicant must have 2.5 GPA or higher. Available to U.S. citizens.

Application Requirements: Application form, application form may be submitted online (http://www.ohionews.org), driver's license, essay, recommendations or references, transcript. *Deadline:* March 31.

OHIO NEWSPAPER WOMEN'S SCHOLARSHIP

One-time scholarship for female student who is enrolled as a junior or senior in an Ohio college or university, majoring in journalism or an equivalent degree program. Must be U.S. citizen.

Academic Fields/Career Goals: Journalism.

Award: Scholarship for use in junior or senior years; not renewable. *Number:* 1. *Amount:* $1500.

Eligibility Requirements: Applicant must be enrolled or expecting to enroll full-time at a four-year institution or university; female and studying in Ohio. Applicant must have 2.5 GPA or higher. Available to U.S. citizens.

Application Requirements: Application form, application form may be submitted online (http://www.ohionews.org), driver's license, recommendations or references, test scores, transcript. *Deadline:* March 31.

OREGON ASSOCIATION OF BROADCASTERS

http://www.theoab.org/

OAB FOUNDATION SCHOLARSHIP
• *See page 193*

OREGON COMMUNITY FOUNDATION

http://www.oregoncf.org/

JACKSON FOUNDATION JOURNALISM SCHOLARSHIP FUND

Scholarship for students attending an Oregon college or university and majoring in, or with emphasis on, journalism. For both full time and part time. Must be a resident of Oregon.

Academic Fields/Career Goals: Journalism.

Award: Scholarship for use in freshman, sophomore, junior, or senior years; renewable. *Number:* 5. *Amount:* $1500–$2000.

Eligibility Requirements: Applicant must be enrolled or expecting to enroll full-time at a four-year institution or university; resident of Oregon and studying in Oregon. Available to U.S. citizens.

Application Requirements: Application form. *Deadline:* March 1.

Contact: Dianne Causey, Program Associate for Scholarships and
      Grants
      Phone: 503-227-6846 Ext. 1418
      E-mail: dcausey@oregoncf.org

OREGON STUDENT ASSISTANCE COMMISSION

http://www.GetCollegeFunds.org/

BUERKLE SCHOLARSHIP

Award available to graduates of Clackamas, Linn, and Washington County high schools (including GED recipients and home-schooled graduates). Preference for older, nontraditional students or students who are returning to college after a long absence. Must be intending to major in English, journalism, math, music or physical education and have at least a 3.6 GPA. Prior recipients may reapply regardless of high school counties where school was attended.

Academic Fields/Career Goals: Journalism; Literature/English/ Writing; Mathematics; Music.

Award: Scholarship for use in freshman, sophomore, junior, or senior years; not renewable.

Eligibility Requirements: Applicant must be enrolled or expecting to enroll full-time at a two-year or four-year institution or university. Available to U.S. citizens.

Application Requirements: Application form, FAFSA, transcript. *Deadline:* March 1.

JACKSON FOUNDATION JOURNALISM SCHOLARSHIP

Renewable award for students at Oregon public and nonprofit colleges who are journalism majors or whose course of study emphasizes journalism. Preference given to students who have taken the SAT and have received good essay scores. FAFSA is required.

Academic Fields/Career Goals: Journalism.

Award: Scholarship for use in freshman, sophomore, junior, or senior years; not renewable.

Eligibility Requirements: Applicant must be enrolled or expecting to enroll full-time at a two-year or four-year institution; resident of Oregon and studying in Oregon. Available to U.S. citizens.

Application Requirements: Activity chart, SAT scores, FAFSA, application form, essay, financial need analysis, recommendations or references, test scores, transcript. *Deadline:* March 1.

OUTDOOR WRITERS ASSOCIATION OF AMERICA

http://www.owaa.org/

OUTDOOR WRITERS ASSOCIATION OF AMERICA - BODIE MCDOWELL SCHOLARSHIP AWARD

• See page 193

OVERSEAS PRESS CLUB FOUNDATION

http://www.overseaspressclubfoundation.org/

OVERSEAS PRESS CLUB FOUNDATION SCHOLARSHIPS

Students aspiring to become foreign correspondents can apply. Must write an essay of no more than 500 words concentrating on an area of the world or an international issue that is in keeping with the applicant's interest. Must be studying at an American college or university or be an American student studying abroad. Winners receive either a $2,000 scholarship or a $3,000 to be used to fund an internship at an overseas media organization.

Academic Fields/Career Goals: Journalism.

Award: Scholarship for use in freshman, sophomore, junior, or senior years; not renewable. *Number:* 14. *Amount:* $2000–$3000.

Eligibility Requirements: Applicant must be enrolled or expecting to enroll full- or part-time at a two-year or four-year institution or university and must have an interest in writing. Available to Canadian and non-U.S. citizens.

Application Requirements: Application form may be submitted online (http://overseaspressclubfoundation.org), cover letter, entry in a contest, essay, resume. *Deadline:* December 1.

Contact: Jane Reilly, Executive Director
      Overseas Press Club Foundation
      40 West 45th Street
      New York, NY 10036
      Phone: 201-493-9087
      Fax: 201-612-9915
      E-mail: foundation@opcofamerica.org

PALM BEACH ASSOCIATION OF BLACK JOURNALISTS

PALM BEACH ASSOCIATION OF BLACK JOURNALISTS SCHOLARSHIP

Scholarship of $1000 are awarded to African-American graduating high school seniors plan to pursue a degree in journalism-print, television, radio broadcasting or photography industries. Have a GPA of 2.7 or better.

Academic Fields/Career Goals: Journalism; Photojournalism/ Photography; TV/Radio Broadcasting.

Award: Scholarship for use in freshman year; not renewable. *Number:* 1. *Amount:* $1000.

Eligibility Requirements: Applicant must be Black (non-Hispanic); high school student and planning to enroll or expecting to enroll full- or part-time at a four-year institution or university. Available to U.S. and non-U.S. citizens.

Application Requirements: Application form, college acceptance proof, driver's license, transcript. *Deadline:* March 30.

Contact: Christopher Smith, Scholarship Chair
      Palm Beach Association of Black Journalists
      PO Box 19533
      West Palm Beach, FL 33416

PHILADELPHIA ASSOCIATION OF BLACK JOURNALISTS

http://www.pabj.org/

PHILADELPHIA ASSOCIATION OF BLACK JOURNALISTS SCHOLARSHIP

One-time award available to deserving high school students in the Delaware Valley who are interested in becoming journalists. Must have a 2.5 GPA. All applicants must state their intention to pursue journalism careers.

Academic Fields/Career Goals: Journalism.

Award: Scholarship for use in freshman, sophomore, junior, or senior years; not renewable. *Number:* 2. *Amount:* up to $1000.

Eligibility Requirements: Applicant must be Black (non-Hispanic); enrolled or expecting to enroll full-time at a four-year institution or university; resident of Pennsylvania and must have an interest in writing. Applicant must have 2.5 GPA or higher. Available to U.S. citizens.

Application Requirements: Application form, driver's license, essay, recommendations or references, transcript. *Deadline:* May 1.

Contact: Manny Smith, Scholarship Committee
      Philadelphia Association of Black Journalists
      PO Box 8232
      Philadelphia, PA 19101
      E-mail: manuelsmith@gmail.com

PRINTING INDUSTRY OF MIDWEST EDUCATION FOUNDATION

http://www.pimn.org/

PRINTING INDUSTRY MIDWEST EDUCATION FOUNDATION SCHOLARSHIP FUND
• See page 194

QUILL AND SCROLL FOUNDATION

http://www.uiowa.edu/~quill-sc

EDWARD J. NELL MEMORIAL SCHOLARSHIP IN JOURNALISM

Merit-based award for high school seniors planning to major in journalism. Must have won a National Quill and Scroll Writing Award or a Photography or Yearbook Excellence contest. Entry forms available from journalism adviser or Quill and Scroll. Must rank in upper third of class or have a minimum 3.0 GPA.

Academic Fields/Career Goals: Journalism.

Award: Scholarship for use in freshman year; not renewable. *Number:* 1–6. *Amount:* $500–$1500.

Eligibility Requirements: Applicant must be high school student; planning to enroll or expecting to enroll full-time at a four-year institution or university and must have an interest in photography/ photogrammetry/filmmaking or writing. Applicant must have 3.0 GPA or higher. Available to U.S. citizens.

Application Requirements: Application form, entry in a contest, essay, personal photograph, recommendations or references, test scores, transcript. *Deadline:* May 10.

Contact: Vanessa Shelton, Executive Director
Quill and Scroll Foundation
School of Journalism, E346AJB
Iowa City, IA 52242-1528
Phone: 319-335-3457
Fax: 319-335-3989
E-mail: quill-scroll@uiowa.edu

RADIO & TELEVISION NEWS DIRECTORS FOUNDATION

http://www.rtnda.org/

CAROLE SIMPSON SCHOLARSHIP
• See page 194

ED BRADLEY SCHOLARSHIP

One-time, $10,000 award for minority sophomore, junior, or senior undergraduate student enrolled in an electronic journalism program. Submit examples of reporting or producing skills on CD or DVD, totaling 15 minutes or less, with scripts, resume and application form available at RTNDA.org.

Academic Fields/Career Goals: Journalism; TV/Radio Broadcasting.

Award: Scholarship for use in sophomore, junior, or senior years; not renewable. *Number:* 1. *Amount:* $10,000.

Eligibility Requirements: Applicant must be American Indian/Alaska Native, Asian/Pacific Islander, Black (non-Hispanic), Hispanic and enrolled or expecting to enroll full-time at a four-year institution or university. Available to U.S. and non-U.S. citizens.

Application Requirements: Application form, DVD or CD with work samples, essay, recommendations or references, resume. *Deadline:* May 11.

Contact: Stacey Staniak, Project Manager
Phone: 202-467-5214
E-mail: staceys@rtnda.org

KEN KASHIWAHARA SCHOLARSHIP
• See page 194

LOU AND CAROLE PRATO SPORTS REPORTING SCHOLARSHIP
• See page 194

PRESIDENTS SCHOLARSHIP
• See page 194

ROBERT H. MOLLOHAN FAMILY CHARITABLE FOUNDATION, INC.

http://www.mollohanfoundation.org/

HARRY C. HAMM FAMILY SCHOLARSHIP
• See page 195

ST. PETERSBURG TIMES FUND INC.

http://www.sptimes.com/

ST. PETERSBURG TIMES JOURNALISM SCHOLARSHIPS

Scholarship to high school seniors in the Times' circulation area who have a demonstrated interest in pursuing journalism major in college and career after graduation.

Academic Fields/Career Goals: Journalism.

Award: Scholarship for use in freshman year; renewable. *Number:* 1. *Amount:* $2500.

Eligibility Requirements: Applicant must be high school student; planning to enroll or expecting to enroll full-time at a four-year institution or university and resident of Florida. Available to U.S. citizens.

Application Requirements: Application form, essay, portfolio, recommendations or references, resume. *Deadline:* January 5.

Contact: Nancy Waclawek, Director
Phone: 727-893-8780
Fax: 727-892-2257
E-mail: waclawek@sptimes.com

SEATTLE POST-INTELLIGENCER

http://www.seattlepi.com/

BOBBI MCCALLUM MEMORIAL SCHOLARSHIP

Scholarship for female college juniors and seniors who are Washington residents studying in Washington and have an interest in print journalism. Minimum 3.0 GPA required. Must submit clips of published stories with transcripts, financial need analysis, application, and two letters of recommendation.

Academic Fields/Career Goals: Journalism.

Award: Scholarship for use in junior or senior years; not renewable. *Number:* 1. *Amount:* $1000.

Eligibility Requirements: Applicant must be enrolled or expecting to enroll full- or part-time at a four-year institution or university; female; resident of Washington and studying in Washington. Applicant must have 3.0 GPA or higher. Available to U.S. citizens.

Application Requirements: Application form, financial need analysis, portfolio, recommendations or references, resume, transcript. *Deadline:* April 1.

Contact: Janet Grimley, Assistant Managing Editor
Seattle Post-Intelligencer
101 Elliot Avenue West
Seattle, WA 98119
Phone: 206-448-8316
Fax: 206-448-8305
E-mail: janetgrimley@seattlep-i.com

SIGMA DELTA CHI FOUNDATION OF WASHINGTON D.C.

http://www.spj.org/washdcpro

SIGMA DELTA CHI SCHOLARSHIPS

One-time award to help pay tuition for full-time students in their junior or senior year demonstrating a clear intention to become journalists. Must demonstrate financial need. Grades and skills are also considered. Must be enrolled in a college or university in the Washington, D.C., metropolitan area. Sponsored by the Society of Professional Journalists.

Academic Fields/Career Goals: Journalism.

Award: Scholarship for use in sophomore or junior years; not renewable. *Number:* 5. *Amount:* $4000.

Eligibility Requirements: Applicant must be enrolled or expecting to enroll full-time at a four-year institution or university and studying in District of Columbia, Maryland, Virginia. Applicant must have 3.0 GPA or higher. Available to U.S. and non-U.S. citizens.

Application Requirements: Application form, essay, financial need analysis, interview, portfolio, recommendations or references, transcript. *Deadline:* March 1.

SOCIETY OF PROFESSIONAL JOURNALISTS, LOS ANGELES CHAPTER

http://www.spj.org/losangeles

BILL FARR SCHOLARSHIP

Award available to a student who is either a resident of Los Angeles, Ventura or Orange counties or is enrolled at a university in one of those counties. Must have completed sophomore year and be enrolled in or accepted to a journalism program.

Academic Fields/Career Goals: Journalism.

Award: Scholarship for use in junior, senior, or graduate years; not renewable. *Number:* 1. *Amount:* $500–$1000.

Eligibility Requirements: Applicant must be enrolled or expecting to enroll full-time at a four-year institution or university; resident of California and studying in California. Available to U.S. citizens.

Application Requirements: Application form, essay, financial need analysis, recommendations or references, resume, work samples. *Deadline:* April 15.

Contact: Daniel Garvey, Scholarship Chairman
Society of Professional Journalists, Los Angeles Chapter
1250 Bellflower
Long Beach, CA 90840
Phone: 562-985-5779

CARL GREENBERG SCHOLARSHIP

Award for a student who is either a resident of Los Angeles, Ventura or Orange counties or is enrolled at a university in one of those three California counties. Must have completed sophomore year and be enrolled in or accepted to an investigative or political journalism program.

Academic Fields/Career Goals: Journalism.

Award: Scholarship for use in junior, senior, or graduate years; not renewable. *Number:* 1. *Amount:* $1000.

Eligibility Requirements: Applicant must be enrolled or expecting to enroll full-time at a four-year institution or university; resident of California and studying in California. Available to U.S. citizens.

Application Requirements: Application form, essay, financial need analysis, recommendations or references, resume, work samples. *Deadline:* April 15.

Contact: Daniel Garvey, Scholarship Chairman
Society of Professional Journalists, Los Angeles Chapter
1250 Bellflower
Long Beach, CA 90840
Phone: 562-985-5779

HELEN JOHNSON SCHOLARSHIP

Awards are available to a student who is a resident of Los Angeles, Ventura or Orange counties or is enrolled at a university in one of those three California counties. Must have completed sophomore year and be enrolled in or accepted to a broadcast journalism program.

Academic Fields/Career Goals: Journalism; TV/Radio Broadcasting.

Award: Scholarship for use in junior, senior, or graduate years; not renewable. *Number:* 1. *Amount:* $500–$1000.

Eligibility Requirements: Applicant must be enrolled or expecting to enroll full-time at a four-year institution or university; resident of California and studying in California. Available to U.S. citizens.

Application Requirements: Application form, essay, financial need analysis, recommendations or references, resume, work samples. *Deadline:* April 15.

Contact: Daniel Garvey, Scholarship Chairman
Society of Professional Journalists, Los Angeles Chapter
1250 Bellflower
Long Beach, CA 90840
Phone: 562-985-5779

KEN INOUYE SCHOLARSHIP

Awards are available to a minority student who is either a resident of Los Angeles, Ventura, or Orange counties or is enrolled at a university in one of those three California counties. Must have completed sophomore year and be enrolled in or accepted to a journalism program.

Academic Fields/Career Goals: Journalism.

Award: Scholarship for use in junior, senior, or graduate years; renewable. *Number:* 1. *Amount:* $500–$1000.

Eligibility Requirements: Applicant must be American Indian/Alaska Native, Asian/Pacific Islander, Black (non-Hispanic), Hispanic; enrolled or expecting to enroll full-time at a four-year institution or university; resident of California and studying in California. Available to U.S. citizens.

Application Requirements: Application form, essay, financial need analysis, recommendations or references, resume, work samples. *Deadline:* April 15.

Contact: Daniel Garvey, Scholarship Chairman
Society of Professional Journalists, Los Angeles Chapter
1250 Bellflower
Long Beach, CA 90840
Phone: 562-985-5779

SOCIETY OF PROFESSIONAL JOURNALISTS MARYLAND PRO CHAPTER

http://www.spj.org/mdpro

MARYLAND SPJ PRO CHAPTER COLLEGE SCHOLARSHIP

Scholarships for journalism students whose regular home residence is in Maryland. May attend colleges or universities in Virginia, Washington D.C., or Pennsylvania.

Academic Fields/Career Goals: Journalism.

Award: Scholarship for use in freshman, sophomore, junior, or senior years; not renewable.

Eligibility Requirements: Applicant must be enrolled or expecting to enroll full- or part-time at a four-year institution or university; resident of Maryland and studying in District of Columbia, Maryland, Pennsylvania, Virginia. Available to U.S. citizens.

Application Requirements: Application form, awards or honors received, essay, financial need analysis, recommendations or references, transcript. *Deadline:* May 9.

Contact: Sue Katcef, Scholarship Chair
Society of Professional Journalists Maryland Pro Chapter
402 Fox Hollow Lane
Annapolis, MD 21403
Phone: 301-405-7526
E-mail: susiekk@aol.com

SOUTH ASIAN JOURNALISTS ASSOCIATION (SAJA)

http://www.saja.org/

SAJA JOURNALISM SCHOLARSHIP

Scholarships for students in North America who are of South Asian descent (includes Bangladesh, Bhutan, India, Maldives, Nepal, Pakistan and Sri Lanka, Indo-Caribbean) or those with a demonstrated interest in South Asia or South Asian issues. Must be interested in pursuing journalism. Applicant must be a high school senior, undergraduate student or graduate-level student.

Academic Fields/Career Goals: Journalism.

Award: Scholarship for use in freshman, sophomore, junior, senior, graduate, or postgraduate years; not renewable. *Number:* 1–4. *Amount:* $1000–$2000.

Eligibility Requirements: Applicant must be Asian/Pacific Islander and enrolled or expecting to enroll full-time at a two-year or four-year institution or university. Available to U.S. and non-U.S. citizens.

Application Requirements: Application form, essay, financial need analysis, journalism clips or work samples, portfolio, recommendations or references, resume. *Deadline:* February 15.

Contact: Amita Parashar, Student Committee and Scholarships
  Phone: 202-513-2845
  E-mail: students@saja.org

SOUTH CAROLINA PRESS ASSOCIATION FOUNDATION

http://www.scpress.org/

SOUTH CAROLINA PRESS ASSOCIATION FOUNDATION NEWSPAPER SCHOLARSHIPS

Renewable award for students entering junior year at a South Carolina institution. Based on grades, journalistic activities in college, and recommendations. Must agree to work in the newspaper field for two years after graduation or repay as loan.

Academic Fields/Career Goals: Journalism.

Award: Scholarship for use in junior year; renewable. *Number:* up to 3. *Amount:* $500–$1375.

Eligibility Requirements: Applicant must be enrolled or expecting to enroll full-time at a four-year institution or university and studying in South Carolina. Available to U.S. and non-U.S. citizens.

Application Requirements: Application form, essay, financial need analysis, portfolio, recommendations or references, resume, transcript. *Deadline:* January 20.

Contact: William Rogers, Secretary
  South Carolina Press Association Foundation
  PO Box 11429
  Columbia, SC 29211-1429
  Phone: 803-750-9561
  Fax: 803-551-0903
  E-mail: brogers@scpress.org

STRAIGHTFORWARD MEDIA

http://www.straightforwardmedia.com/

STRAIGHTFORWARD MEDIA MEDIA & COMMUNICATIONS SCHOLARSHIP

• *See page 84*

TEXAS GRIDIRON CLUB INC.

http://www.spjfw.org/

TEXAS GRIDIRON CLUB SCHOLARSHIPS

• *See page 197*

UNITED METHODIST COMMUNICATIONS

http://www.umcom.org/

LEONARD M. PERRYMAN COMMUNICATIONS SCHOLARSHIP FOR ETHNIC MINORITY STUDENTS

• *See page 197*

UNITED NEGRO COLLEGE FUND

http://www.uncf.org/

READER'S DIGEST FOUNDATION SCHOLARSHIP

• *See page 198*

VALLEY PRESS CLUB, SPRINGFIELD NEWSPAPERS

http://www.valleypressclub.com/

VALLEY PRESS CLUB SCHOLARSHIPS, THE REPUBLICAN SCHOLARSHIP, CHANNEL 22 SCHOLARSHIP

• *See page 198*

WASHINGTON NEWS COUNCIL

http://www.wanewscouncil.org/

DICK LARSEN SCHOLARSHIP PROGRAM

• *See page 198*

HERB ROBINSON SCHOLARSHIP PROGRAM

• *See page 199*

WOMEN'S BASKETBALL COACHES ASSOCIATION

http://www.wbca.org/

ROBIN ROBERTS/WBCA SPORTS COMMUNICATIONS SCHOLARSHIP AWARD

• *See page 199*

LANDSCAPE ARCHITECTURE

ASSOCIATION FOR WOMEN IN ARCHITECTURE FOUNDATION

http://www.awa-la.org/

ASSOCIATION FOR WOMEN IN ARCHITECTURE FOUNDATION SCHOLARSHIP

• *See page 109*

CENTER FOR ARCHITECTURE

http://www.cfafoundation.org/scholarships

CENTER FOR ARCHITECTURE, DOUGLAS HASKELL AWARD FOR STUDENT JOURNALS

• *See page 110*

THE DALLAS FOUNDATION

http://www.dallasfoundation.org/

WHITLEY PLACE SCHOLARSHIP

• *See page 110*

FEDERATED GARDEN CLUBS OF CONNECTICUT

http://www.ctgardenclubs.org/

FEDERATED GARDEN CLUBS OF CONNECTICUT INC. SCHOLARSHIPS

• *See page 144*

FEDERATED GARDEN CLUBS OF MARYLAND

http://www.fgcofmd.org/

ROBERT LEWIS BAKER SCHOLARSHIP
• See page 347

FRIENDS OF THE FRELINGHUYSEN ARBORETUM

http://www.arboretumfriends.org/

BENJAMIN C. BLACKBURN SCHOLARSHIP
• See page 302

GARDEN CLUB OF AMERICA

http://www.gcamerica.org/

GCA AWARD IN DESERT STUDIES
• See page 111

KATHARINE M. GROSSCUP SCHOLARSHIPS IN HORTICULTURE
• See page 348

THE GEORGIA TRUST FOR HISTORIC PRESERVATION

http://www.georgiatrust.org/

B. PHINIZY SPALDING, HUBERT B. OWENS, AND THE NATIONAL SOCIETY OF THE COLONIAL DAMES OF AMERICA IN THE STATE OF GEORGIA ACADEMIC SCHOLARSHIPS
• See page 97

J. NEEL REID PRIZE
• See page 111

HERB SOCIETY OF AMERICA, WESTERN RESERVE UNIT

http://www.herbsociety.org/units/western-reserve.html

FRANCIS SYLVIA ZVERINA SCHOLARSHIP
• See page 349

WESTERN RESERVE HERB SOCIETY SCHOLARSHIP
• See page 349

HORTICULTURAL RESEARCH INSTITUTE

http://www.hriresearch.org/

BRYAN A. CHAMPION MEMORIAL SCHOLARSHIP
• See page 85

CARVILLE M. AKEHURST MEMORIAL SCHOLARSHIP
• See page 298

MUGGETS SCHOLARSHIP
• See page 349

SPRING MEADOW NURSERY SCHOLARSHIP
• See page 350

TIMOTHY AND PALMER W. BIGELOW JR., SCHOLARSHIP
• See page 86

USREY FAMILY SCHOLARSHIP
• See page 298

LAND CONSERVANCY OF NEW JERSEY

http://www.tlc-nj.org/

RUSSELL W. MYERS SCHOLARSHIP
• See page 304

LANDSCAPE ARCHITECTURE FOUNDATION

http://www.lafoundation.org

ASLA COUNCIL OF FELLOWS SCHOLARSHIP

This scholarship was established to: 1) aid outstanding students with unmet financial need; 2) increase participation of economically disadvantaged and under-represented populations; and 3) enrich the profession of landscape architecture through a more diverse population. Eligible applicants must be Student ASLA members and third, fourth, or fifth-year undergraduates in Landscape Architecture Accreditation Board (LAAB) accredited programs.

Academic Fields/Career Goals: Landscape Architecture.

Award: Scholarship for use in junior or senior years; not renewable. *Number:* 1–2. *Amount:* up to $4000.

Eligibility Requirements: Applicant must be enrolled or expecting to enroll full- or part-time at a four-year institution or university. Available to U.S. citizens.

Application Requirements: Application form, application form may be submitted online (http://www.lafoundation.org/scholarship/leadership-in-landscape/awards-available/asla-council-of-fellows-scholarships/), essay, financial need analysis, recommendations or references. *Deadline:* February 15.

Contact: Heather Whitlow, Director of Programs and Communications
Phone: 202-331-7070 Ext. 14
E-mail: hwhitlow@lafoundation.org

COURTLAND PAUL SCHOLARSHIP

Scholarship for undergraduate students in the final two years of study in landscape architecture accreditation board accredited schools. Applicants must demonstrate financial need, must be U.S. citizens, and have a minimum C average.

Academic Fields/Career Goals: Landscape Architecture.

Award: Scholarship for use in junior or senior years; not renewable. *Number:* 1. *Amount:* up to $5000.

Eligibility Requirements: Applicant must be enrolled or expecting to enroll full- or part-time at a four-year institution or university. Applicant must have 2.5 GPA or higher. Available to U.S. citizens.

Application Requirements: Application form, application form may be submitted online (http://www.lafoundation.org/scholarship/leadership-in-landscape/awards-available/courtland-paul-scholarship/), essay, financial need analysis, recommendations or references. *Deadline:* February 15.

Contact: Heather Whitlow, Director of Programs and Communications
Phone: 202-331-7070 Ext. 14
E-mail: hwhitlow@lafoundation.org

EDSA MINORITY SCHOLARSHIP

Scholarship established to help African American, Hispanic, Native American and minority students of other cultural and ethnic backgrounds to continue their landscape architecture education as they pursue a graduate degree or enter into their final two years of undergraduate study.

Academic Fields/Career Goals: Landscape Architecture.

Award: Scholarship for use in junior, senior, or graduate years; not renewable. *Number:* up to 1. *Amount:* up to $5000.

Eligibility Requirements: Applicant must be American Indian/Alaska Native, Asian/Pacific Islander, Black (non-Hispanic), Hispanic and enrolled or expecting to enroll full- or part-time at a four-year institution or university. Available to U.S. and non-U.S. citizens.

Application Requirements: 3 work samples, application form, application form may be submitted online (http://www.lafoundation.org/scholarship/leadership-in-landscape/awards-available/edsa-scholarship/), essay, recommendations or references. *Deadline:* February 15.

Contact: Heather Whitlow, Director of Programs and Communications
Phone: 202-331-7070 Ext. 14
E-mail: hwhitlow@lafoundation.org

HAWAII CHAPTER/DAVID T. WOOLSEY SCHOLARSHIP

The award provides funds for educational or professional development purposes for a third-, fourth-, or fifth-year undergraduate or graduate student of landscape architecture in a Landscape Architecture Accreditation Board (LAAB) accredited program. Student must be a permanent resident of Hawaii.

Academic Fields/Career Goals: Landscape Architecture.

Award: Scholarship for use in junior, senior, or graduate years; not renewable. *Number:* 1. *Amount:* $2000.

Eligibility Requirements: Applicant must be enrolled or expecting to enroll full- or part-time at a four-year institution or university and resident of Hawaii. Available to U.S. and non-U.S. citizens.

Application Requirements: 3 work samples, proof of Hawaii residency, application form, application form may be submitted online (http://www.lafoundation.org/scholarship/leadership-in-landscape/awards-available/hawaii-woolsey-scholarship/), essay, recommendations or references. *Deadline:* February 15.

Contact: Heather Whitlow, Director of Programs and Communications
Phone: 202-331-7070 Ext. 14
E-mail: hwhitlow@lafoundation.org

LANDSCAPE FORMS DESIGN FOR PEOPLE SCHOLARSHIP

This $3000 scholarship honors landscape architecture students with a proven contribution to the design of public spaces that integrate landscape design and the use of amenities to promote social interaction.

Academic Fields/Career Goals: Landscape Architecture.

Award: Scholarship for use in senior year; not renewable. *Number:* 1. *Amount:* $3000.

Eligibility Requirements: Applicant must be enrolled or expecting to enroll full-time at a four-year institution or university. Available to U.S. and non-U.S. citizens.

Application Requirements: 3 work samples, application form, application form may be submitted online (http://www.lafoundation.org/scholarship/leadership-in-landscape/awards-available/landscape-forms-scholarship/), essay, recommendations or references. *Deadline:* February 15.

Contact: Heather Whitlow, Director of Programs and Communications
Phone: 202-331-7070 Ext. 14
E-mail: hwhitlow@lafoundation.org

PERIDIAN INTERNATIONAL, INC./RAE L. PRICE, FASLA SCHOLARSHIP

This $5000 scholarship helps landscape architecture students in the UCLA Extension Program or Cal Poly Pomona who may not otherwise have the financial ability to cover all the costs of their educational program. The award must be used only for tuition and/or books within the school year of the award.

Academic Fields/Career Goals: Landscape Architecture.

Award: Scholarship for use in junior or senior years; not renewable. *Number:* 1. *Amount:* $5000.

Eligibility Requirements: Applicant must be enrolled or expecting to enroll full- or part-time at a four-year institution or university and studying in California. Applicant must have 3.0 GPA or higher. Available to U.S. citizens.

Application Requirements: Application form, application form may be submitted online (http://www.lafoundation.org/scholarship/leadership-in-landscape/awards-available/peridian-rae-price-scholarship/), essay, financial need analysis, personal photograph, recommendations or references. *Deadline:* February 15.

Contact: Heather Whitlow, Director of Programs and Communications
Phone: 202-331-7070 Ext. 14
E-mail: hwhitlow@lafoundation.org

RAIN BIRD INTELLIGENT USE OF WATER SCHOLARSHIP

This award recognizes an outstanding landscape architecture, horticulture or irrigation science student. Eligible applicants are in the final two years of undergraduate study with demonstrated commitment to these professions through participation in extracurricular activities and exemplary scholastic achievements.

Academic Fields/Career Goals: Landscape Architecture.

Award: Scholarship for use in junior or senior years; not renewable. *Number:* 1. *Amount:* $2500.

Eligibility Requirements: Applicant must be enrolled or expecting to enroll full- or part-time at a four-year institution or university. Available to U.S. and non-U.S. citizens.

Application Requirements: Application form, application form may be submitted online (http://www.lafoundation.org/scholarship/leadership-in-landscape/awards-available/rain-bird-scholarship/), cover letter, essay, recommendations or references. *Deadline:* February 15.

Contact: Heather Whitlow, Director of Programs and Communications
Phone: 202-331-7070 Ext. 14
E-mail: hwhitlow@lafoundation.org

STEVEN G. KING PLAY ENVIRONMENTS SCHOLARSHIP

This $5000 scholarship recognizes landscape architecture students with a demonstrated interest and aptitude in the design of play environments.

Academic Fields/Career Goals: Landscape Architecture.

Award: Scholarship for use in junior, senior, or graduate years; not renewable. *Number:* 1. *Amount:* $5000.

Eligibility Requirements: Applicant must be enrolled or expecting to enroll full- or part-time at a four-year institution or university. Available to U.S. and non-U.S. citizens.

Application Requirements: Application form, application form may be submitted online (http://www.lafoundation.org/scholarship/leadership-in-landscape/awards-available/steven-king-scholarship/), essay, personal photograph, plan and details of play environment design, recommendations or references. *Deadline:* February 15.

Contact: Heather Whitlow, Director of Programs and Communications
Phone: 202-331-7070 Ext. 14
E-mail: hwhitlow@lafoundation.org

MONTANA FEDERATION OF GARDEN CLUBS

http://www.mtfgc.org/

LIFE MEMBER MONTANA FEDERATION OF GARDEN CLUBS SCHOLARSHIP

• *See page 228*

NATIONAL ASSOCIATION OF WOMEN IN CONSTRUCTION

http://www.nawic.org/

NAWIC UNDERGRADUATE SCHOLARSHIPS

• *See page 112*

NATIONAL GARDEN CLUBS INC.

http://www.gardenclub.org/

NATIONAL GARDEN CLUBS INC. SCHOLARSHIP PROGRAM

• *See page 94*

OREGON STUDENT ASSISTANCE COMMISSION

http://www.GetCollegeFunds.org/

HOME BUILDERS FOUNDATION JIM IRVINE STATEWIDE SCHOLARSHIP

• *See page 112*

PROFESSIONAL CONSTRUCTION ESTIMATORS ASSOCIATION

http://www.pcea.org/

TED G. WILSON MEMORIAL SCHOLARSHIP FOUNDATION
• *See page 184*

PROFESSIONAL GROUNDS MANAGEMENT SOCIETY

http://www.pgms.org/

ANNE SEAMAN PROFESSIONAL GROUNDS MANAGEMENT SOCIETY MEMORIAL SCHOLARSHIP
• *See page 95*

SOUTH DAKOTA RETAILERS ASSOCIATION

http://www.sdra.org/

SOUTH DAKOTA RETAILERS ASSOCIATION SCHOLARSHIP PROGRAM
• *See page 80*

TURNER CONSTRUCTION COMPANY

http://www.turnerconstruction.com/

YOUTHFORCE 2020 SCHOLARSHIP PROGRAM
• *See page 113*

LAW ENFORCEMENT/ POLICE ADMINISTRATION

ALBERTA HERITAGE SCHOLARSHIP FUND
http://www.alis.alberta.ca/

ROBERT C. CARSON MEMORIAL BURSARY
• *See page 210*

AMERICAN SOCIETY OF CRIMINOLOGY
http://www.asc41.com/

AMERICAN SOCIETY OF CRIMINOLOGY GENE CARTE STUDENT PAPER COMPETITION
• *See page 211*

ASSOCIATION OF FORMER INTELLIGENCE OFFICERS

http://www.afio.com/13_scholarships.htm

CIA UNDERGRADUATE SCHOLARSHIPS
• *See page 97*

BOY SCOUTS OF AMERICA-MUSKINGUM VALLEY COUNCIL

http://www.learning-for-life.org/

SHERYL A. HORAK MEMORIAL SCHOLARSHIP
$1000 one-time scholarship for students enrolled either for full- or part-time study in a law enforcement field. Must be participant of the Learning for Life Exploring program.

Academic Fields/Career Goals: Law Enforcement/Police Administration.

Award: Scholarship for use in freshman, sophomore, junior, or senior years; not renewable. *Number:* 1. *Amount:* $1000.

Eligibility Requirements: Applicant must be enrolled or expecting to enroll full- or part-time at a two-year or four-year or technical institution or university. Available to U.S. and non-U.S. citizens.

Application Requirements: Application form, essay, personal photograph, recommendations or references, transcript. *Deadline:* March 31.

CONNECTICUT ASSOCIATION OF WOMEN POLICE

http://www.cawp.net/

CONNECTICUT ASSOCIATION OF WOMEN POLICE SCHOLARSHIP
• *See page 211*

INDIANA SHERIFFS' ASSOCIATION
http://www.indianasheriffs.org/

INDIANA SHERIFFS' ASSOCIATION SCHOLARSHIP PROGRAM
• *See page 211*

IAAI FOUNDATION, INC.
http://www.firearson.com/

JOHN CHARLES WILSON SCHOLARSHIP & ROBERT DORAN SCHOLARSHIP
• *See page 311*

LEARNING FOR LIFE
http://www.learning-for-life.org/

CAPTAIN JAMES J. REGAN SCHOLARSHIP
Two one-time $500 scholarships are presented annually to Law Enforcement Explorers graduating from high school or from an accredited college program. Evaluation will be based on academic record.

Academic Fields/Career Goals: Law Enforcement/Police Administration.

Award: Scholarship for use in freshman, sophomore, junior, or senior years; not renewable. *Number:* 2. *Amount:* $500.

Eligibility Requirements: Applicant must be enrolled or expecting to enroll full-time at a two-year or four-year or technical institution or university. Applicant or parent of applicant must be member of Explorer Program/Learning for Life. Available to U.S. citizens.

Application Requirements: Application form, essay, personal photograph, recommendations or references, transcript. *Deadline:* March 31.

Contact: William Taylor, Scholarships and Awards Coordinator
Learning for Life
1329 West Walnut Hill Lane, PO Box 152225
Irving, TX 75015-2225
Phone: 972-580-2241
E-mail: btaylor@lflmail.org

DEA DRUG ABUSE PREVENTION SERVICE AWARDS

The award recognizes a Law Enforcement Explorer for outstanding service in drug abuse prevention.

Academic Fields/Career Goals: Law Enforcement/Police Administration.

Award: Prize for use in freshman, sophomore, junior, or senior years; not renewable. *Number:* 1. *Amount:* $1000.

Eligibility Requirements: Applicant must be enrolled or expecting to enroll full-time at a two-year or four-year institution or university. Applicant or parent of applicant must be member of Explorer Program/Learning for Life. Applicant or parent of applicant must have employment or volunteer experience in alcohol or drug abuse counseling/treatment/prevention. Available to U.S. citizens.

Application Requirements: Application form, personal photograph. *Deadline:* March 31.

Contact: William Taylor, Scholarships and Awards Coordinator
    E-mail: btaylor@lflmail.org

FEDERAL CRIMINAL INVESTIGATORS SERVICE AWARD

The award recognizes Law Enforcement Explorers who render outstanding service to law enforcement agencies.

Academic Fields/Career Goals: Law Enforcement/Police Administration.

Award: Prize for use in freshman, sophomore, junior, or senior years; not renewable. *Number:* 1. *Amount:* $500.

Eligibility Requirements: Applicant must be enrolled or expecting to enroll full- or part-time at a two-year or four-year institution or university. Applicant or parent of applicant must be member of Explorer Program/Learning for Life. Available to U.S. citizens.

Application Requirements: Application form, essay, personal photograph, recommendations or references. *Deadline:* March 31.

Contact: William Taylor, Scholarships and Awards Coordinator
    E-mail: btaylor@lflmail.org

SHERYL A. HORAK MEMORIAL SCHOLARSHIP

Award for graduating high school students who are Law Enforcement Explorers joining a program in law enforcement in accredited college or university. Provides a one-time scholarship of $1000.

Academic Fields/Career Goals: Law Enforcement/Police Administration.

Award: Scholarship for use in freshman year; not renewable. *Number:* 1. *Amount:* $1000.

Eligibility Requirements: Applicant must be enrolled or expecting to enroll full-time at a two-year or four-year institution or university. Applicant or parent of applicant must be member of Explorer Program/Learning for Life. Available to U.S. citizens.

Application Requirements: Application form, essay, personal photograph, recommendations or references, transcript. *Deadline:* March 31.

Contact: William Taylor, Scholarships and Awards Coordinator
    E-mail: btaylor@lflmail.org

NATIONAL BLACK POLICE ASSOCIATION

http://www.blackpolice.org/

ALPHONSO DEAL SCHOLARSHIP AWARD
• *See page 212*

NORTH CAROLINA STATE EDUCATION ASSISTANCE AUTHORITY

http://www.ncseaa.edu/

NORTH CAROLINA SHERIFFS' ASSOCIATION UNDERGRADUATE CRIMINAL JUSTICE SCHOLARSHIPS
• *See page 212*

SOUTH CAROLINA POLICE CORPS

http://www.citadel.edu/

SOUTH CAROLINA POLICE CORPS SCHOLARSHIP

Tuition reimbursement scholarship available to a full-time student of an U.S. accredited college. Must agree to serve for four years on community patrol with a participating South Carolina police or sheriff's department. Up to $7500 per academic year with a limit of $30,000 per student.

Academic Fields/Career Goals: Law Enforcement/Police Administration.

Award: Scholarship for use in freshman, sophomore, junior, senior, or graduate years; renewable. *Number:* 20. *Amount:* $7500–$30,000.

Eligibility Requirements: Applicant must be enrolled or expecting to enroll full-time at a four-year institution or university. Available to U.S. citizens.

Application Requirements: Application form, driver's license, essay, interview, recommendations or references, test scores, transcript. *Deadline:* varies.

Contact: Bryan Jones, Community Action Team
    South Carolina Police Corps
    5623 Two Notch Road
    Columbia, SC 29223
    Phone: 803-865-4486
    E-mail: bryan.jones@hcahealthcare.com

WIFLE FOUNDATION, INC.

http://www.wifle.org/

WIFLE SCHOLARSHIP PROGRAM
• *See page 207*

LAW/LEGAL SERVICES

ALBERTA HERITAGE SCHOLARSHIP FUND

http://www.alis.alberta.ca/

JASON LANG SCHOLARSHIP
• *See page 218*

ROBERT C. CARSON MEMORIAL BURSARY
• *See page 210*

AMERICAN CRIMINAL JUSTICE ASSOCIATION-LAMBDA ALPHA EPSILON

http://www.acjalae.org/

AMERICAN CRIMINAL JUSTICE ASSOCIATION-LAMBDA ALPHA EPSILON NATIONAL SCHOLARSHIP
• *See page 211*

AMERICAN SOCIETY OF CRIMINOLOGY

http://www.asc41.com/

AMERICAN SOCIETY OF CRIMINOLOGY GENE CARTE STUDENT PAPER COMPETITION
• *See page 211*

ARRL FOUNDATION INC.

http://www.arrl.org/

FRANCIS WALTON MEMORIAL SCHOLARSHIP
• *See page 91*

BLACK ENTERTAINMENT AND SPORTS LAWYERS ASSOCIATION INC.

http://www.besla.org/

BESLA SCHOLARSHIP LEGAL WRITING COMPETITION

$1500 award for the best 1000-word, or two-page essay on a compelling legal issue facing the entertainment or sports industry. Essay must be written by law school student who has completed at least one full year at an accredited law school. Minimum GPA of 2.8 required.

Academic Fields/Career Goals: Law/Legal Services.

Award: Scholarship for use in freshman, sophomore, junior, senior, or graduate years; not renewable. *Number:* 2. *Amount:* $1500.

Eligibility Requirements: Applicant must be enrolled or expecting to enroll full-time at a four-year institution or university. Available to U.S. and non-U.S. citizens.

Application Requirements: Application form, essay, resume, transcript. *Deadline:* varies.

Contact: Rev. Phyllicia Hatton, Executive Administrator
　　　　　Phone: 301-248-1818
　　　　　Fax: 301-248-0700
　　　　　E-mail: beslamailbox@aol.com

BOYS AND GIRLS CLUBS OF SAN DIEGO

http://www.sdyouth.org/

SPENCE REESE SCHOLARSHIP

• *See page 279*

COLLEGEBOUND FOUNDATION

http://www.collegeboundfoundation.org/

DECATUR H. MILLER SCHOLARSHIP

• *See page 343*

JEANETTE R. WOLMAN SCHOLARSHIP

• *See page 178*

THE ROBERT SPAR MEMORIAL SCHOLARSHIP

• *See page 343*

GRAND RAPIDS COMMUNITY FOUNDATION

http://www.grfoundation.org/

WARNER NORCROSS AND JUDD LLP SCHOLARSHIP FOR MINORITY STUDENTS

Financial assistance to students who are residents of Michigan, or attend a college/university/vocational school in Michigan, and are of racial and ethnic minority heritage pursuing a career in law, paralegal, or a legal secretarial program. Law school scholarship ($5000), paralegal scholarship ($2000), legal secretary scholarship ($1000).

Academic Fields/Career Goals: Law/Legal Services.

Award: Scholarship for use in freshman, sophomore, junior, senior, or graduate years; not renewable. *Number:* up to 3. *Amount:* $1000–$5000.

Eligibility Requirements: Applicant must be American Indian/Alaska Native, Asian/Pacific Islander, Black (non-Hispanic), Hispanic; enrolled or expecting to enroll full-time at a two-year or four-year institution or university; resident of Michigan and studying in Michigan. Applicant must have 2.5 GPA or higher. Available to U.S. citizens.

Application Requirements: Application form, essay, financial need analysis, recommendations or references, transcript. *Deadline:* April 15.

Contact: Ruth Bishop, Education Program Officer
　　　　　Phone: 616-454-1751 Ext. 103
　　　　　Fax: 616-454-6455
　　　　　E-mail: rbishop@grfoundation.org

GREATER KANAWHA VALLEY FOUNDATION

http://www.tgkvf.org/

BERNICE PICKINS PARSONS FUND

Renewable award of $1000 open to students pursuing education or training in the fields of library science, nursing, and paraprofessional training in the legal field. Grant based on financial need. Must be a resident of West Virginia; preference given to Jackson county residents.

Academic Fields/Career Goals: Law/Legal Services; Library and Information Sciences; Nursing.

Award: Grant for use in freshman, sophomore, junior, or senior years; renewable. *Amount:* $1000.

Eligibility Requirements: Applicant must be enrolled or expecting to enroll full-time at a two-year or four-year institution or university and resident of West Virginia. Available to U.S. citizens.

Application Requirements: Application form, essay, financial need analysis, recommendations or references, self-addressed stamped envelope with application, test scores, transcript. *Deadline:* January 15.

Contact: Susan Hoover, Scholarship Program Officer
　　　　　Greater Kanawha Valley Foundation
　　　　　900 Lee Street East, 16th Floor
　　　　　Charleston, WV 25301
　　　　　Phone: 304-346-3620
　　　　　E-mail: tgkvf@tgkvf.org

INSTITUTE FOR HUMANE STUDIES

http://www.theihs.org/

HUMANE STUDIES FELLOWSHIPS

• *See page 190*

JAPANESE AMERICAN CITIZENS LEAGUE (JACL)

http://www.jacl.org/

NATIONAL JACL HEADQUARTERS SCHOLARSHIP

• *See page 92*

KE ALI'I PAUAHI FOUNDATION

http://www.pauahi.org/

WILLIAM S. RICHARDSON COMMEMORATIVE SCHOLARSHIP

This scholarship was established to honor William S. Richardson, retired Trustee of the Kamehameha Schools Bishop Estate and provides support for students of character and exceptional ability pursuing law degrees from the University of Hawai'i-Manoa William S. Richardson School of Law. Applicants must be a resident of the State of Hawai'i and preference will be given to applicants demonstrating financial need and commitment to contributing to the greater community.

Academic Fields/Career Goals: Law/Legal Services.

Award: Scholarship for use in freshman, sophomore, junior, senior, or graduate years; not renewable. *Number:* 5. *Amount:* up to $1000.

Eligibility Requirements: Applicant must be enrolled or expecting to enroll full-time at a four-year institution or university and resident of Hawaii. Available to U.S. citizens.

Application Requirements: Application form, application form may be submitted online (http://www.pauahi.org/scholarships), college acceptance letter for first-year students, financial need analysis, recommendations or references, transcript. *Deadline:* April 1.

Contact: Mavis Shiraishi-Nagao, Scholarship Coordinator
　　　　　Phone: 808-534-3966
　　　　　E-mail: scholarships@pauahi.org

LAW/LEGAL SERVICES

MARYLAND STATE HIGHER EDUCATION COMMISSION

http://www.mhec.state.md.us/

GRADUATE AND PROFESSIONAL SCHOLARSHIP PROGRAM-MARYLAND
• See page 224

JANET L. HOFFMANN LOAN ASSISTANCE REPAYMENT PROGRAM
• See page 240

NATIONAL ASSOCIATION OF WATER COMPANIES-NEW JERSEY CHAPTER

http://www.nawc.org/

NATIONAL ASSOCIATION OF WATER COMPANIES-NEW JERSEY CHAPTER SCHOLARSHIP
• See page 146

NATIONAL BLACK POLICE ASSOCIATION

http://www.blackpolice.org/

ALPHONSO DEAL SCHOLARSHIP AWARD
• See page 212

NATIONAL COURT REPORTERS ASSOCIATION

http://www.ncraonline.org/

COUNCIL ON APPROVED STUDENT EDUCATION'S SCHOLARSHIP FUND

Applicant must have a writing speed of 140 to 180 words/min, and must be in an NCRA-approved court reporting program. Must write a two-page essay on topic chosen for the year and is also required to enter the competition.

Academic Fields/Career Goals: Law/Legal Services.

Award: Scholarship for use in sophomore year; not renewable. *Number:* 3. *Amount:* $500–$1500.

Eligibility Requirements: Applicant must be enrolled or expecting to enroll full- or part-time at a two-year or four-year or technical institution. Applicant must have 3.0 GPA or higher. Available to U.S. and Canadian citizens.

Application Requirements: Application form, entry in a contest, essay, recommendations or references, transcript. *Deadline:* April 1.

Contact: Donna Gaede, Approval Program Manager
National Court Reporters Association
8224 Old Courthouse Road
Vienna, VA 22182
Phone: 703-556-6272 Ext. 171
Fax: 703-556-6291
E-mail: dgaede@ncrahq.org

FRANK SARLI MEMORIAL SCHOLARSHIP

One-time award to a student who is nearing graduation from a trade/technical school or four-year college. Must be enrolled in a court reporting program. Minimum 3.5 GPA required.

Academic Fields/Career Goals: Law/Legal Services.

Award: Scholarship for use in senior year; not renewable. *Number:* 1. *Amount:* $2000.

Eligibility Requirements: Applicant must be enrolled or expecting to enroll full- or part-time at a four-year or technical institution or university. Applicant or parent of applicant must be member of National Federation of Press Women. Applicant must have 3.5 GPA or higher. Available to U.S. and non-U.S. citizens.

Application Requirements: Application form. *Deadline:* February 28.

Contact: B. Shorak, Deputy Executive Director
National Court Reporters Association
8224 Old Courthouse Road
Vienna, VA 22182-3808
Phone: 703-556-6272 Ext. 126
Fax: 703-556-6291
E-mail: bjshorak@ncrahq.org

STUDENT MEMBER TUITION GRANT

Four $500 awards for students in good academic standing in a court reporting program. Students are required to write 120 to 200 words/min.

Academic Fields/Career Goals: Law/Legal Services.

Award: Grant for use in freshman, sophomore, junior, or senior years; not renewable. *Number:* 4. *Amount:* $500.

Eligibility Requirements: Applicant must be enrolled or expecting to enroll full- or part-time at a four-year or technical institution or university. Available to U.S. and non-U.S. citizens.

Application Requirements: Application form. *Deadline:* May 31.

Contact: Amy Davidson, Assistant Director of Membership
National Court Reporters Association
8224 Old Courthouse Road
Vienna, VA 22182
Phone: 703-556-6272 Ext. 123
E-mail: adavidson@ncrahq.org

NATIONAL FEDERATION OF PARALEGAL ASSOCIATIONS INC. (NFPA)

http://www.paralegals.org/

NATIONAL FEDERATION OF PARALEGAL ASSOCIATES INC. THOMSON REUTERS SCHOLARSHIP

Applicants must be full- or part-time students enrolled in an accredited paralegal education program or college-level program with emphasis in paralegal studies. Minimum GPA of 3.0 required. NFPA membership is not required. Travel stipend to annual convention, where recipients will receive awards, also provided.

Academic Fields/Career Goals: Law/Legal Services.

Award: Scholarship for use in freshman, sophomore, junior, senior, graduate, or postgraduate years; not renewable. *Number:* 2. *Amount:* $2000–$3000.

Eligibility Requirements: Applicant must be enrolled or expecting to enroll full- or part-time at a two-year or four-year or technical institution or university. Applicant must have 3.0 GPA or higher. Available to U.S. and non-U.S. citizens.

Application Requirements: Application form, essay, recommendations or references, transcript. *Deadline:* July 31.

Contact: Cindy Byfield, Managing Director
Phone: 425-967-0045
E-mail: info@paralegals.org

NEW ENGLAND EMPLOYEE BENEFITS COUNCIL

http://www.neebc.org/

NEW ENGLAND EMPLOYEE BENEFITS COUNCIL SCHOLARSHIP PROGRAM
• See page 77

OKLAHOMA PARALEGAL ASSOCIATION

http://www.okparalegal.org/

JAMIE BOWIE MEMORIAL SCHOLARSHIP

Applicant must be currently enrolled in a legal assistant program at an ABA-approved institution and have successfully completed at least six credit hours. The director of the legal assistant program must provide verification of current enrollment. Recipient must be present at the presentation of the scholarship on the date to be announced.

Academic Fields/Career Goals: Law/Legal Services.

Award: Scholarship for use in freshman, sophomore, junior, or senior years; not renewable. *Number:* 1. *Amount:* $250.

Eligibility Requirements: Applicant must be enrolled or expecting to enroll full- or part-time at a four-year institution or university. Available to U.S. citizens.

Application Requirements: Application form, financial need analysis, transcript. *Deadline:* April 15.

Contact: Emily Buckmaster, Student Director
 Phone: 405-235-7000
 E-mail: ebuckmaster@hartzoglaw.com

OREGON STUDENT ASSISTANCE COMMISSION

http://www.GetCollegeFunds.org/

OREGON ASSOCIATION OF CERTIFIED FRAUD EXAMINERS SCHOLARSHIP
• *See page 78*

RICHARD V. CRUZ MEMORIAL FOUNDATION

http://www.rvcruzfoundation.2givenow.org/

RICHARD V. CRUZ MEMORIAL FOUNDATION SCHOLARSHIP

$2000 scholarships to students from underserved populations enrolled in a California ABA-accredited law school. Applicants must have begun or completed their first year of law school and must be in good academic standing.

Academic Fields/Career Goals: Law/Legal Services.

Award: Scholarship for use in sophomore, junior, senior, or graduate years; not renewable. *Amount:* $2000.

Eligibility Requirements: Applicant must be Hispanic; enrolled or expecting to enroll full-time at a four-year institution or university and studying in California. Available to U.S. citizens.

Application Requirements: Application form, community service, financial need analysis, interview, personal statement, recommendations or references, resume. *Deadline:* April 17.

SOCIETY OF SATELLITE PROFESSIONALS INTERNATIONAL

http://www.sspi.org/

SSPI INTERNATIONAL SCHOLARSHIPS
• *See page 138*

TKE EDUCATIONAL FOUNDATION

http://www.tke.org/

HARRY J. DONNELLY MEMORIAL SCHOLARSHIP
• *See page 81*

UNITARIAN UNIVERSALIST ASSOCIATION

http://www.uua.org/

STANFIELD AND D'ORLANDO ART SCHOLARSHIP
• *See page 123*

UNITED NEGRO COLLEGE FUND

http://www.uncf.org/

ALFRED CHISHOLM/BASF MEMORIAL SCHOLARSHIP FUND
• *See page 81*

MCCA LLOYD M. JOHNSON JR. SCHOLARSHIP

Scholarship support for newly entering first year law students pursuing a Juris Doctor (non-LL.M.) degree. Must be a U.S. citizen and have a minimum undergraduate 3.2 GPA. Should an interest in corporate law, including working in a corporate law department and/or law firm. Must be financially disadvantaged and have completed the FAFSA and provide additional documents as requested, and demonstrate community service and leadership qualities.

Academic Fields/Career Goals: Law/Legal Services.

Award: Scholarship for use in senior or graduate years; not renewable. *Amount:* up to $10,000.

Eligibility Requirements: Applicant must be Black (non-Hispanic); enrolled or expecting to enroll full-time at a four-year institution or university and must have an interest in leadership. Available to U.S. citizens.

Application Requirements: Application form, community service, essay, FAFSA, financial need analysis, resume, transcript. *Deadline:* May 30.

MCCA LLOYD M. JOHNSON JR. SCHOLARSHIP PROGRAM

Scholarship available to student interested in corporate law, including working in a corporate law department and/or law firm. Must have an interest in diversity, be financially disadvantaged, have completed the FAFSA, and provide additional documents as requested. Must also demonstrate community service, leadership qualities, and have an undergraduate or graduate cumulative GPA of 3.2 or higher.

Academic Fields/Career Goals: Law/Legal Services.

Award: Scholarship for use in senior or graduate years; renewable. *Number:* 10. *Amount:* $10,000.

Eligibility Requirements: Applicant must be Black (non-Hispanic) and enrolled or expecting to enroll full-time at a four-year institution or university. Available to U.S. citizens.

Application Requirements: Application form. *Deadline:* May 31.

RAYMOND W. CANNON MEMORIAL SCHOLARSHIP

Annual scholarship awarded to undergraduate juniors majoring in pharmacy or pre-law, who have demonstrated leadership in high school and college. Minimum 2.5 GPA required. Must be enrolled in a UNCF member institution or a HBCU.

Academic Fields/Career Goals: Law/Legal Services; Pharmacy.

Award: Scholarship for use in junior year; not renewable. *Amount:* $2000–$5000.

Eligibility Requirements: Applicant must be Black (non-Hispanic) and enrolled or expecting to enroll full- or part-time at a four-year institution or university. Applicant must have 2.5 GPA or higher. Available to U.S. and non-U.S. citizens.

Application Requirements: Application form, financial need analysis. *Deadline:* continuous.

VIRGINIA STATE BAR

http://www.vsb.org/

LAW IN SOCIETY AWARD COMPETITION

Participants write an essay in response to a hypothetical situation dealing with legal issues. Awards are based on superior understanding of the value of law in everyday life. The top thirty essays are awarded prizes of a plaque and dictionary/thesaurus set. First place receives $2000 U.S. Savings Bond or $1000 cash; second place, $1,500 bond or $750 cash; third place, $1,000 bond or $500 cash; honorable mentions, $200 bond or $100 cash.

Academic Fields/Career Goals: Law/Legal Services.

Award: Prize for use in freshman year; not renewable. *Number:* up to 10. *Amount:* $100–$1000.

Eligibility Requirements: Applicant must be high school student; planning to enroll or expecting to enroll full- or part-time at a four-year institution or university; resident of Virginia and must have an interest in writing. Available to U.S. citizens.

Application Requirements: Application form, entry in a contest, essay. *Deadline:* February 1.

Contact: Sandy Adkins, Public Relations Assistant
 Virginia State Bar
 707 East Main Street, Suite 1500
 Richmond, VA 23219-2800
 Phone: 804-775-0594
 Fax: 804-775-0582
 E-mail: adkins@vsb.org

WASHINGTON STATE TRIAL LAWYERS ASSOCIATION

http://www.wstla.org/

WSTLA AMERICAN JUSTICE ESSAY SCHOLARSHIP CONTEST

The purpose of the scholarship is to foster an awareness and understanding of the American justice system. The essay contest deals with advocacy in the American justice system and related topics. Three scholarships are available to students who are attending high school in Washington state.

Academic Fields/Career Goals: Law/Legal Services.

Award: Scholarship for use in freshman year; not renewable. *Number:* 3. *Amount:* $2000–$3000.

Eligibility Requirements: Applicant must be high school student; planning to enroll or expecting to enroll full- or part-time at a two-year or four-year institution or university and studying in Washington. Available to U.S. and non-U.S. citizens.

Application Requirements: Application form, entry in a contest, essay. *Deadline:* March 21.

Contact: Adrianne Williams, Scholarship Coordinator
Washington State Trial Lawyers Association
1511 State Avenue, NW
Olympia, WA 98506

LIBRARY AND INFORMATION SCIENCES

ALICE L. HALTOM EDUCATIONAL FUND

http://www.alhef.org/

ALICE L. HALTOM EDUCATIONAL FUND
• *See page 341*

AMERICAN SOCIETY FOR INFORMATION SCIENCE AND TECHNOLOGY

http://www.asis.org/

JOHN WILEY & SONS BEST JASIST PAPER AWARD
• *See page 199*

BIBLIOGRAPHICAL SOCIETY OF AMERICA

http://www.bibsocamer.org/

JUSTIN G. SCHILLER PRIZE FOR BIBLIOGRAPHICAL WORK IN PRE-20TH-CENTURY CHILDREN'S BOOKS

Award for bibliographic work in the field of pre-20th century children's books. Winner will receive a cash award of $2000 and a year's membership in the Society.

Academic Fields/Career Goals: Library and Information Sciences; Literature/English/Writing.

Award: Prize for use in freshman, sophomore, junior, or senior years; not renewable. *Number:* 1. *Amount:* $2000.

Eligibility Requirements: Applicant must be enrolled or expecting to enroll full- or part-time at a four-year institution or university. Available to U.S. and non-U.S. citizens.

Application Requirements: Application form, documentation regarding the approval of a thesis or dissertation or confirming the date of publication, entry in a contest, resume. *Deadline:* September 1.

Contact: Michele Randall, Executive Secretary
Bibliographical Society of America
PO Box 1537, Lenox Hill Station
New York, NY 10021
Phone: 212-452-2710
Fax: 212-452-2710
E-mail: bsa@bibsocamer.org

CALIFORNIA SCHOOL LIBRARY ASSOCIATION

http://www.csla.net/

JOHN BLANCHARD MEMORIAL FUND SCHOLARSHIP

Provides assistance to school library paraprofessional in obtaining preparation needed to qualify and serve as a school library media teacher in California. Applicant must be a member of the California School Library Association.

Academic Fields/Career Goals: Library and Information Sciences.

Award: Scholarship for use in freshman, sophomore, junior, or senior years; not renewable. *Number:* 1. *Amount:* $1000.

Eligibility Requirements: Applicant must be enrolled or expecting to enroll full- or part-time at an institution or university; resident of California and studying in California. Applicant or parent of applicant must have employment or volunteer experience in library work. Available to U.S. citizens.

Application Requirements: Application form, recommendations or references. *Deadline:* April 30.

Contact: Deidre Bryant, Executive Director
Phone: 916-447-2684
E-mail: info@csla.net

FLORIDA ASSOCIATION FOR MEDIA IN EDUCATION

http://www.floridamedia.org/

FAME/SANDY ULM SCHOLARSHIP

Scholarship for students studying to be school library media specialists. The scholarship awards at least $1000 to one or more students each year. Deadlines are September 15 and February 15.

Academic Fields/Career Goals: Library and Information Sciences.

Award: Scholarship for use in freshman year; not renewable. *Amount:* $1000.

Eligibility Requirements: Applicant must be high school student; planning to enroll or expecting to enroll full-time at a two-year or four-year or technical institution or university and studying in Florida. Available to U.S. citizens.

Application Requirements: Application form. *Deadline:* varies.

Contact: Larry Bodkin, Executive Director
Phone: 850-531-8350
Fax: 850-531-8344
E-mail: lbodkin@floridamedia.org

FLORIDA LIBRARY ASSOCIATION

http://www.flalib.org/

FLORIDA LIBRARY ASSOCIATION-ASSOCIATE'S DEGREE SCHOLARSHIP

Scholarship will be awarded to a Florida resident with library experience who is pursuing an associate degree. Applicants must be members of the Florida Library Association. For further details, visit website at http://www.flalib.org.

Academic Fields/Career Goals: Library and Information Sciences.

Award: Scholarship for use in freshman or sophomore years; not renewable. *Number:* 1. *Amount:* up to $350.

Eligibility Requirements: Applicant must be enrolled or expecting to enroll full- or part-time at a two-year or four-year institution or university; resident of Florida and studying in Florida. Applicant or parent of applicant must have employment or volunteer experience in library work. Available to U.S. and non-U.S. citizens.

Application Requirements: Application form, essay, recommendations or references, resume. *Deadline:* February 1.

Contact: Faye Roberts, Executive Director
Florida Library Association
PO Box 1571
Lake City, FL 32056
Phone: 386-438-5795
E-mail: faye.roberts@comcast.net

FLORIDA LIBRARY ASSOCIATION-BACHELOR'S DEGREE SCHOLARSHIP

Scholarship will be awarded to a Florida resident with library experience who is pursuing a bachelor's degree. Applicants must be members of Florida Library Association. For further details, visit website at http://www.flalib.org.

Academic Fields/Career Goals: Library and Information Sciences.

Award: Scholarship for use in freshman, sophomore, junior, or senior years; not renewable. *Number:* 1. *Amount:* up to $750.

Eligibility Requirements: Applicant must be enrolled or expecting to enroll full- or part-time at a two-year or four-year institution or university; resident of Florida and studying in Florida. Applicant or parent of applicant must have employment or volunteer experience in library work. Available to U.S. and non-U.S. citizens.

Application Requirements: Application form, essay, recommendations or references, resume. *Deadline:* February 1.

Contact: Faye Roberts, Executive Director
Florida Library Association
PO Box 1571
Lake City, FL 32056
Phone: 386-438-5795
E-mail: faye.roberts@comcast.net

GREATER KANAWHA VALLEY FOUNDATION

http://www.tgkvf.org/

BERNICE PICKINS PARSONS FUND
• *See page 380*

IDAHO LIBRARY ASSOCIATION

http://www.idaholibraries.org/

IDAHO LIBRARY ASSOCIATION GARDNER HANKS SCHOLARSHIP

Scholarship for students who are beginning or continuing formal library education, pursuing a Master's of Library Science degree or Media Generalist certification. Must be an ILA member.

Academic Fields/Career Goals: Library and Information Sciences.

Award: Scholarship for use in freshman, sophomore, junior, or senior years; not renewable. *Number:* 1. *Amount:* $500.

Eligibility Requirements: Applicant must be enrolled or expecting to enroll full-time at a four-year institution or university. Applicant or parent of applicant must be member of Idaho Library Association. Available to U.S. citizens.

Application Requirements: Application form, community service, financial need analysis, recommendations or references. *Deadline:* May 1.

Contact: Amy Vecchione, Scholarships and Awards Committee Chair
Phone: 208-426-1625
E-mail: amyvecchione@boisestate.edu

INDIANA LIBRARY FEDERATION

http://www.ilfonline.org/

AISLE SCHOLARSHIP FUND

Scholarships are provided for undergraduate or graduate students entering or currently enrolled in a program to receive educational certification in the field of school library media services. For more details, visit http://www.ilfonline.org.

Academic Fields/Career Goals: Library and Information Sciences.

Award: Scholarship for use in freshman, sophomore, junior, senior, or graduate years; not renewable.

Eligibility Requirements: Applicant must be enrolled or expecting to enroll full-time at a four-year institution or university and resident of Indiana. Available to U.S. citizens.

Application Requirements: Application form, recommendations or references, transcript. *Deadline:* June 30.

Contact: Amanda Turney, Communications
Phone: 317-257-2040
Fax: 317-257-1389
E-mail: aturney@ilfonline.org

NEBRASKA LIBRARY ASSOCIATION

http://www.nebraskalibraries.org/

NEBRASKA LIBRARY ASSOCIATION DUANE MUNSON SCHOLARSHIP

Award for practicing librarians and paraprofessionals to gain additional professional training on a part- or full-time basis. Must be employee of Nebraska library or educational unit and member of NLA, both for at least one year. Submit employment record, two letters of recommendation, proof of acceptance, and estimate of expenses.

Academic Fields/Career Goals: Library and Information Sciences.

Award: Scholarship for use in freshman, sophomore, junior, senior, graduate, or postgraduate years; not renewable. *Number:* 1. *Amount:* $250.

Eligibility Requirements: Applicant must be enrolled or expecting to enroll full- or part-time at a two-year or four-year institution or university and resident of Nebraska. Applicant or parent of applicant must be member of Nebraska Library Association. Applicant or parent of applicant must have employment or volunteer experience in library work. Available to U.S. and non-U.S. citizens.

Application Requirements: Application form, application form may be submitted online (https://nlia.memberclicks.net/index.php?option=com_mc&view=mc&mcid=form_107921), essay, financial need analysis, personal statement, proof of acceptance, recommendations or references. *Deadline:* April 15.

Contact: Michael Straatmann, Executive Director
Nebraska Library Association
PO Box 21756
Lincoln, NE 68542
Phone: 402-216-0727
E-mail: NLAExecutivedirector@gmail.com

WISCONSIN LIBRARY ASSOCIATION

http://wla.wisconsinlibraries.org/

SCHOLARSHIP FOR THE EDUCATION OF RURAL LIBRARIANS GLORIA HOEGH MEMORIAL FUND

Scholarship awarded to librarians planning to attend a workshop, conference, and/or a continuing education program within or outside Wisconsin. Applicant must be a library employee working in a Wisconsin community with a current population of 5000 or less or who works with library employees in those communities.

Academic Fields/Career Goals: Library and Information Sciences.

Award: Scholarship for use in freshman, sophomore, junior, senior, or graduate years; not renewable. *Number:* 1. *Amount:* $1000.

Eligibility Requirements: Applicant must be enrolled or expecting to enroll full- or part-time at a four-year institution or university and resident of Wisconsin. Available to U.S. citizens.

Application Requirements: Application form, essay, financial need analysis. *Deadline:* August 1.

Contact: Brigitte Rupp Vacha, Member Services Coordinator
Phone: 608-245-3640
E-mail: ruppvacha@scls.lib.wi.us

WLA CONTINUING EDUCATION SCHOLARSHIP

Scholarship awarded to employee who is planning to attend a continuing education program within or outside of Wisconsin. Applicant must be able to communicate the knowledge gained from the continuing education program to fellow librarians and information professionals in Wisconsin, employed in a library and information agency in Wisconsin.

Academic Fields/Career Goals: Library and Information Sciences.

Award: Scholarship for use in freshman, sophomore, junior, senior, graduate, or postgraduate years; not renewable. *Number:* 1.

Eligibility Requirements: Applicant must be enrolled or expecting to enroll full- or part-time at a four-year institution or university and resident of Wisconsin. Available to U.S. citizens.

Application Requirements: Application form, copy of the continuing education program. *Deadline:* June 1.

Contact: Brigitte Rupp Vacha, Member Services Coordinator
Phone: 608-245-3640
E-mail: ruppvacha@scls.lib.wi.us

LITERATURE/ENGLISH/ WRITING

AIM MAGAZINE SHORT STORY CONTEST

http://www.aimmagazine.org/

AMERICA'S INTERCULTURAL MAGAZINE (AIM) SHORT STORY CONTEST

Short fiction award for a previously unpublished story that embodies the magazine's goal of furthering the brotherhood of man through the written word. Must provide proof that people from different racial/ethnic backgrounds are more alike than they are different. Maximum length 4000 words. Story should not moralize.

Academic Fields/Career Goals: Literature/English/Writing.

Award: Prize for use in freshman, sophomore, junior, senior, or graduate years; not renewable. *Number:* 1–2. *Amount:* $75–$100.

Eligibility Requirements: Applicant must be enrolled or expecting to enroll full- or part-time at a two-year or four-year or technical institution or university and must have an interest in writing. Available to U.S. and Canadian citizens.

Application Requirements: Application form, entry in a contest, essay. *Deadline:* August 15.

Contact: Mark Boone, Fiction Editor
Aim Magazine Short Story Contest
PO Box 1174
Maywood, IL 60153
Phone: 708-344-4414
E-mail: apiladoone@aol.com

ALLIANCE FOR YOUNG ARTISTS AND WRITERS INC.

http://www.artandwriting.org/

SCHOLASTIC ART AND WRITING AWARDS-ART SECTION
• *See page 117*

SCHOLASTIC ART AND WRITING AWARDS-WRITING SECTION SCHOLARSHIP
• *See page 117*

AMERICAN FOUNDATION FOR THE BLIND

http://www.afb.org/

R.L. GILLETTE SCHOLARSHIP

Two scholarships of $1000 each to women who are enrolled in a four-year undergraduate degree program in literature or music. In addition to the general requirements, applicants must submit a performance tape not to exceed 30 minutes, or a creative writing sample. Must submit proof of legal blindness. For additional information and application requirements, refer to website http://www.afb.org/scholarships.asp.

Academic Fields/Career Goals: Literature/English/Writing; Music.

Award: Scholarship for use in freshman, sophomore, junior, or senior years; not renewable. *Number:* up to 2. *Amount:* $1000.

Eligibility Requirements: Applicant must be visually impaired; enrolled or expecting to enroll full-time at a four-year institution or university and female. Applicant must be visually impaired. Available to U.S. citizens.

Application Requirements: Application form, essay, financial need analysis, performance tape (not to exceed 30 minutes) or creative writing sample, proof of legal blindness, acceptance letter, recommendations or references, transcript. *Deadline:* April 30.

Contact: Dawn Bodrogi, Information Center and Library Coordinator
American Foundation for the Blind
11 Penn Plaza, Suite 300
New York, NY 10001
Phone: 212-502-7661
Fax: 212-502-7771
E-mail: afbinfo@afb.net

AMERICAN-SCANDINAVIAN FOUNDATION

http://www.amscan.org/

AMERICAN-SCANDINAVIAN FOUNDATION TRANSLATION PRIZE

Two prizes are awarded for outstanding English translations of poetry, fiction, drama, or literary prose originally written in Danish, Finnish, Icelandic, Norwegian, or Swedish. One-time award of $2000.

Academic Fields/Career Goals: Literature/English/Writing.

Award: Prize for use in freshman, sophomore, junior, or senior years; not renewable. *Number:* 2. *Amount:* $1000–$2000.

Eligibility Requirements: Applicant must be enrolled or expecting to enroll full- or part-time at a two-year or four-year or technical institution or university and must have an interest in Scandinavian language. Available to U.S. and non-U.S. citizens.

Application Requirements: Application form, entry in a contest, resume, translation sample. *Deadline:* June 1.

AMY LOWELL POETRY TRAVELLING SCHOLARSHIP TRUST

http://www.amylowell.org/

AMY LOWELL POETRY TRAVELING SCHOLARSHIP

Scholarship to a poet of American birth. Upon acceptance, the recipient agrees to spend one year outside the continent of North America in a place deemed by the recipient suitable to advance the art of poetry. At the end of the year, the recipient shall submit at least three poems for consideration by the trust's committee. For additional information visit website http://www.amylowell.org.

Academic Fields/Career Goals: Literature/English/Writing.

Award: Scholarship for use in freshman, sophomore, junior, or senior years; not renewable. *Number:* 1. *Amount:* up to $52,000.

Eligibility Requirements: Applicant must be enrolled or expecting to enroll full- or part-time at a two-year or four-year or technical institution or university and must have an interest in writing. Available to U.S. citizens.

Application Requirements: Application form, entry in a contest, poetry sample. *Deadline:* October 15.

Contact: Laura Reidy, Administrator
Phone: 617-248-5000
E-mail: amylowell@choate.com

BIBLIOGRAPHICAL SOCIETY OF AMERICA

http://www.bibsocamer.org/

JUSTIN G. SCHILLER PRIZE FOR BIBLIOGRAPHICAL WORK IN PRE-20TH-CENTURY CHILDREN'S BOOKS
• *See page 383*

CULTURAL SERVICES OF THE FRENCH EMBASSY

http://www.frenchculture.org/

TEACHING ASSISTANT PROGRAM IN FRANCE
• *See page 97*

DAVIDSON INSTITUTE FOR TALENT DEVELOPMENT

http://www.davidsongifted.org/

DAVIDSON FELLOWS SCHOLARSHIP PROGRAM

One-time award to recognize outstanding achievements of young people. Must be 18 or younger as of October 10, 2012. Must have completed a significant piece of work in one of the following areas: science, technology, mathematics, humanities (music, literature or philosophy) or outside the box. Must be a U.S. citizen or a permanent resident.

Academic Fields/Career Goals: Literature/English/Writing; Mathematics; Music; Philosophy; Science, Technology, and Society.

Award: Scholarship for use in freshman, sophomore, junior, senior, or graduate years; not renewable. *Number:* 15–20. *Amount:* $10,000–$50,000.

Eligibility Requirements: Applicant must be enrolled or expecting to enroll full- or part-time at a two-year or four-year or technical institution or university. Available to U.S. citizens.

Application Requirements: Application form, application form may be submitted online (http://www.DavidsonGifted.org/Fellows), essay, portfolio, recommendations or references. *Deadline:* February 1.

Contact: Tacie Moessner, Davidson Fellows Program Manager
Davidson Institute for Talent Development
9665 Gateway Drive, Suite B
Reno, NV 89521
Phone: 775-852-3483 Ext. 423
Fax: 775-852-2184
E-mail: davidsonfellows@davidsongifted.org

GOLDEN KEY INTERNATIONAL HONOUR SOCIETY

http://www.goldenkey.org/

LITERARY ACHIEVEMENT AWARDS

Award of $1000 will be given to winners in each of the following four categories: fiction, non-fiction, poetry, and feature writing. Eligible applicants are undergraduate, graduate and postgraduate members who are currently enrolled in classes at a degree-granting program.

Academic Fields/Career Goals: Literature/English/Writing.

Award: Prize for use in freshman, sophomore, junior, senior, graduate, or postgraduate years; not renewable. *Number:* 4. *Amount:* $1000.

Eligibility Requirements: Applicant must be enrolled or expecting to enroll full- or part-time at a four-year institution or university and must have an interest in writing. Available to U.S. and non-U.S. citizens.

Application Requirements: Application form, entry in a contest, essay, original composition. *Deadline:* April 1.

INSTITUTE FOR HUMANE STUDIES

http://www.theihs.org/

HUMANE STUDIES FELLOWSHIPS
• *See page 190*

INTERNATIONAL FOODSERVICE EDITORIAL COUNCIL

http://www.ifeconline.com/

INTERNATIONAL FOODSERVICE EDITORIAL COUNCIL COMMUNICATIONS SCHOLARSHIP
• *See page 83*

JACK J. ISGUR FOUNDATION

http://www.isgur.org

JACK J. ISGUR FOUNDATION SCHOLARSHIP
• *See page 119*

JAPANESE AMERICAN CITIZENS LEAGUE (JACL)

http://www.jacl.org/

NATIONAL JACL HEADQUARTERS SCHOLARSHIP
• *See page 92*

JOHN F. KENNEDY LIBRARY FOUNDATION

http://www.jfklibrary.org/

PROFILE IN COURAGE ESSAY CONTEST

Essay contest open to all high school students, grades nine to twelve. Students in U.S. territories and U.S. citizens attending schools overseas may also apply. All essays will be judged on the overall originality of topic and the clear communication of ideas through language. Winner and their nominating teacher are invited to Kennedy Library to accept award. Winner receives $3000, nomination teacher receives grant of $500; second place receives $1000 and five finalists receive $500.

Academic Fields/Career Goals: Literature/English/Writing.

Award: Prize for use in freshman year; not renewable. *Number:* 7. *Amount:* $500–$3000.

Eligibility Requirements: Applicant must be high school student; planning to enroll or expecting to enroll full-time at a four-year institution and must have an interest in writing. Available to U.S. citizens.

Application Requirements: Application form, bibliography, entry in a contest, essay. *Deadline:* January 7.

Contact: Esther Kohn, Essay Contest Coordinator
John F. Kennedy Library Foundation
Columbia Point
Boston, MA 02125
Phone: 617-514-1649
Fax: 617-514-1641
E-mail: profiles@nara.gov

LAMBDA IOTA TAU, COLLEGE LITERATURE HONOR SOCIETY

http://www.bsu.edu/english/undergraduate/lit

LAMBDA IOTA TAU LITERATURE SCHOLARSHIP

Scholarships for members of Lambda Iota Tau who are pursuing the study of literature. Must be nominated by chapter sponsor and have 3.5 GPA.

Academic Fields/Career Goals: Literature/English/Writing.

Award: Scholarship for use in sophomore, junior, senior, or graduate years; not renewable. *Number:* 2–4. *Amount:* $1000.

Eligibility Requirements: Applicant must be enrolled or expecting to enroll full-time at a two-year or four-year institution or university. Applicant or parent of applicant must be member of Lambda Iota Tau Literature Honor Society. Applicant must have 3.5 GPA or higher. Available to U.S. citizens.

Application Requirements: Application form, essay, nomination letter from chapter sponsor, recommendations or references, transcript. *Deadline:* May 31.

Contact: Mrs. Mary Clark-Upchurch, Executive Secretary and Treasurer
Phone: 765-285-8382
E-mail: mcupchurchi@bsu.edu

MINNESOTA OFFICE OF HIGHER EDUCATION

http://www.getreadyforcollege.org/

MINNESOTA ACADEMIC EXCELLENCE SCHOLARSHIP
• *See page 120*

NATIONAL PRESS FOUNDATION

http://www.nationalpress.org/

EVERT CLARK/SETH PAYNE AWARD
• *See page 370*

NATIONAL WRITERS ASSOCIATION FOUNDATION

http://www.nationalwriters.com/

NATIONAL WRITERS ASSOCIATION FOUNDATION SCHOLARSHIPS
• *See page 370*

OREGON STUDENT ASSISTANCE COMMISSION

http://www.GetCollegeFunds.org/

BUERKLE SCHOLARSHIP
• *See page 372*

SEHAR SALEHA AHMAD AND ABRAHIM EKRAMULLAH ZAFAR FOUNDATION SCHOLARSHIP
Scholarship available to female Oregon residents who are graduating seniors from Oregon high schools (including GED recipients and home schooled students). Minimum 3.8 GPA required. Must be an English major at a 4-year public or nonprofit college or university in Oregon.
Academic Fields/Career Goals: Literature/English/Writing.
Award: Scholarship for use in freshman year; renewable.
Eligibility Requirements: Applicant must be high school student; planning to enroll or expecting to enroll full-time at a four-year institution or university; female; resident of Oregon and studying in Oregon. Available to U.S. citizens.
Application Requirements: Activity chart, application form, essay, financial need analysis, recommendations or references, transcript. *Deadline:* March 1.

OUTDOOR WRITERS ASSOCIATION OF AMERICA

http://www.owaa.org/

OUTDOOR WRITERS ASSOCIATION OF AMERICA - BODIE MCDOWELL SCHOLARSHIP AWARD
• *See page 193*

STRAIGHTFORWARD MEDIA

http://www.straightforwardmedia.com/

STRAIGHTFORWARD MEDIA LIBERAL ARTS SCHOLARSHIP
• *See page 116*

UNITED DAUGHTERS OF THE CONFEDERACY

http://www.hqudc.org/

HELEN JAMES BREWER SCHOLARSHIP
• *See page 345*

UNITED NEGRO COLLEGE FUND

http://www.uncf.org/

AFSCME/UNCF/HARVARD UNIVERSITY LWP UNION SCHOLARS PROGRAM
• *See page 98*

JANET JACKSON/RHYTHM NATION SCHOLARSHIP
• *See page 123*

MAE MAXEY MEMORIAL SCHOLARSHIP
• *See page 123*

MICHAEL JACKSON SCHOLARSHIP
• *See page 198*

READER'S DIGEST FOUNDATION SCHOLARSHIP
• *See page 198*

WILLA CATHER FOUNDATION

http://www.willacather.org/

NORMA ROSS WALTER SCHOLARSHIP
The award is to provide scholarship support to female Nebraska high school graduates who continue their higher education as English majors in accredited colleges or universities.
Academic Fields/Career Goals: Literature/English/Writing.
Award: Scholarship for use in freshman year; not renewable. *Number:* 1. *Amount:* $1000.
Eligibility Requirements: Applicant must be high school student; planning to enroll or expecting to enroll full-time at a four-year institution or university; female and resident of Nebraska. Applicant must have 3.0 GPA or higher. Available to U.S. citizens.
Application Requirements: Application form, essay, recommendations or references, test scores, transcript. *Deadline:* January 31.
Contact: Ashley Olson, Associate Executive Director
Willa Cather Foundation
413 North Webster Street
Red Cloud, NE 68970
Phone: 402-746-2653
Fax: 402-746-2652
E-mail: info@willacather.org

MARINE BIOLOGY

AMERICAN PHYSIOLOGICAL SOCIETY

http://www.the-aps.org

DAVID S. BRUCE AWARDS FOR EXCELLENCE IN UNDERGRADUATE RESEARCH
• *See page 98*

ASSOCIATION ON AMERICAN INDIAN AFFAIRS, INC.

http://www.indian-affairs.org/

ELIZABETH AND SHERMAN ASCHE MEMORIAL SCHOLARSHIP FUND
• *See page 91*

CUSHMAN FOUNDATION FOR FORAMINIFERAL RESEARCH

http://www.cushmanfoundation.org/index.php

LOEBLICH AND TAPPAN STUDENT RESEARCH AWARD
• *See page 144*

INTERNATIONAL ASSOCIATION FOR GREAT LAKES RESEARCH

http://www.iaglr.org/

PAUL W. RODGERS SCHOLARSHIP
• *See page 227*

LOUISIANA OFFICE OF STUDENT FINANCIAL ASSISTANCE

http://www.osfa.la.gov/

ROCKEFELLER STATE WILDLIFE SCHOLARSHIP
• *See page 146*

MARINE TECHNOLOGY SOCIETY

http://www.mtsociety.org/

CHARLES H. BUSSMAN UNDERGRADUATE SCHOLARSHIP

Scholarship for undergraduate students enrolled full-time in a marine-related field. Must be a member of Marine Technology Society.

Academic Fields/Career Goals: Marine Biology; Marine/Ocean Engineering; Oceanography.

Award: Scholarship for use in freshman, sophomore, junior, or senior years; not renewable. *Amount:* up to $2500.

Eligibility Requirements: Applicant must be enrolled or expecting to enroll full-time at a four-year institution or university. Applicant or parent of applicant must be member of Marine Technology Society. Available to U.S. and non-U.S. citizens.

Application Requirements: Application form, driver's license, proof of acceptance for an undergraduate course, recommendations or references, transcript. *Deadline:* April 15.

Contact: Suzanne Voelker, Operations Administrator
Phone: 410-884-5330
Fax: 410-884-9060
E-mail: suzanne.voelker@mtsociety.org

JOHN C. BAJUS SCHOLARSHIP

Scholarship available to undergraduate and graduate students enrolled full-time in a marine-related field. Must be a MTS student member with demonstrated commitment to community service/volunteer activities.

Academic Fields/Career Goals: Marine Biology; Marine/Ocean Engineering; Oceanography.

Award: Scholarship for use in freshman, sophomore, junior, senior, or graduate years; not renewable. *Amount:* up to $1000.

Eligibility Requirements: Applicant must be enrolled or expecting to enroll full-time at a four-year institution or university. Applicant or parent of applicant must be member of Marine Technology Society. Available to U.S. and non-U.S. citizens.

Application Requirements: Application form, driver's license, recommendations or references, transcript. *Deadline:* April 15.

Contact: Suzanne Voelker, Operations Administrator
Phone: 410-884-5330
Fax: 410-884-9060
E-mail: suzanne.voelker@mtsociety.org

MTS STUDENT SCHOLARSHIP

Scholarships available to both Marine Technology Society members and non-members, undergraduates and graduate students, enrolled full-time in a marine-related field.

Academic Fields/Career Goals: Marine Biology; Marine/Ocean Engineering; Oceanography.

Award: Scholarship for use in freshman, sophomore, junior, senior, or graduate years; not renewable. *Amount:* up to $2000.

Eligibility Requirements: Applicant must be enrolled or expecting to enroll full-time at a four-year institution or university. Available to U.S. and non-U.S. citizens.

Application Requirements: Application form, driver's license, recommendations or references, transcript. *Deadline:* April 15.

Contact: Suzanne Voelker, Operations Administrator
Phone: 410-884-5330
Fax: 410-884-9060
E-mail: suzanne.voelker@mtsociety.org

MTS STUDENT SCHOLARSHIP FOR GRADUATE AND UNDERGRADUATE STUDENTS

Scholarship of $2000 available to undergraduate students who are enrolled full-time in a marine-related field.

Academic Fields/Career Goals: Marine Biology; Marine/Ocean Engineering.

Award: Scholarship for use in freshman, sophomore, junior, senior, or graduate years; not renewable. *Amount:* $2000.

Eligibility Requirements: Applicant must be enrolled or expecting to enroll full-time at a four-year institution or university. Available to U.S. and non-U.S. citizens.

Application Requirements: Application form, essay, recommendations or references, transcript. *Deadline:* April 15.

Contact: Suzanne Voelker, Operations Administrator
Marine Technology Society
5565 Sterrett Place, Suite 108
Columbia, MD 21044
Phone: 410-884-5330
E-mail: suzanne.voelker@mtsociety.org

MTS STUDENT SCHOLARSHIP FOR TWO-YEAR TECHNICAL, ENGINEERING AND COMMUNITY COLLEGE STUDENTS

Scholarship of $2000 available to students enrolled in a two-year technical, engineering, or community college in a marine-related field.

Academic Fields/Career Goals: Marine Biology; Marine/Ocean Engineering.

Award: Scholarship for use in freshman or sophomore years; not renewable. *Amount:* $2000.

Eligibility Requirements: Applicant must be enrolled or expecting to enroll full-time at a two-year institution. Available to U.S. and non-U.S. citizens.

Application Requirements: Application form, essay, recommendations or references, transcript. *Deadline:* April 15.

Contact: Suzanne Voelker, Operations Administrator
Marine Technology Society
5565 Sterrett Place, Suite 108
Columbia, MD 21044
Phone: 410-884-5330
E-mail: suzanne.voelker@mtsociety.org

PAROS-DIGIQUARTZ SCHOLARSHIP

Scholarships available to both MTS members and non-members, undergraduates and graduate students, enrolled full-time in a marine-related field with an interest in marine instrumentation. High school seniors who have been accepted into a full-time undergraduate program in a marine-related field are also eligible to apply.

Academic Fields/Career Goals: Marine Biology; Marine/Ocean Engineering; Oceanography.

Award: Scholarship for use in freshman, sophomore, junior, senior, or graduate years; not renewable. *Amount:* up to $2000.

Eligibility Requirements: Applicant must be enrolled or expecting to enroll full-time at a four-year institution or university. Available to U.S. and non-U.S. citizens.

Application Requirements: Application form, driver's license, recommendations or references, transcript. *Deadline:* April 15.

Contact: Suzanne Voelker, Operations Administrator
    Phone: 410-884-5330
    Fax: 410-884-9060
    E-mail: suzanne.voelker@mtsociety.org

ROV SCHOLARSHIP

Scholarships for undergraduate and graduate students interested in remotely operated vehicles or underwater work that furthers the use of ROVs. Open to MTS student members and non-MTS members.

Academic Fields/Career Goals: Marine Biology; Marine/Ocean Engineering; Oceanography.

Award: Scholarship for use in freshman, sophomore, junior, senior, or graduate years; not renewable. *Amount:* up to $10,000.

Eligibility Requirements: Applicant must be enrolled or expecting to enroll full-time at a four-year institution or university. Available to U.S. and non-U.S. citizens.

Application Requirements: Application form, driver's license, essay, recommendations or references, transcript. *Deadline:* April 15.

Contact: Chuck Richards, Chair, Scholarship Committee
    Marine Technology Society
    c/o C.A. Richards and Associates Inc.
    777 North Eldridge Parkway, Suite 280
    Houston, TX 77079

SOCIETY FOR INTEGRATIVE AND COMPARATIVE BIOLOGY

http://www.sicb.org/

LIBBIE H. HYMAN MEMORIAL SCHOLARSHIP

• *See page 148*

WOMAN'S SEAMEN'S FRIEND SOCIETY OF CONNECTICUT INC.

FINANCIAL SUPPORT FOR MARINE OR MARITIME STUDIES

Applicant must be full-time student. High school students not considered. Award available to U.S. citizens. Must be majoring in marine sciences at any college or university.

Academic Fields/Career Goals: Marine Biology; Oceanography.

Award: Scholarship for use in freshman, sophomore, junior, or senior years; not renewable.

Eligibility Requirements: Applicant must be enrolled or expecting to enroll full-time at a four-year institution or university. Available to U.S. citizens.

Application Requirements: Application form, financial need analysis, recommendations or references, resume, test scores, transcript. *Deadline:* varies.

Contact: Marshall Davidson, Executive Director
    Phone: 203-777-2165
    Fax: 203-777-5774
    E-mail: wsfsofct@earthlink.net

YOUTH MARITIME TRAINING ASSOCIATION

http://ymta.net/

NORM MANLY—YMTA MARITIME EDUCATIONAL SCHOLARSHIPS

The scholarships may be used by students pursuing marine-related and maritime training and education in community colleges, technical and vocational programs, colleges, universities, maritime academies or other educational institutions. Scholarships will be awarded in the amounts of one $5,000, one $3,000, one $2,000 two $1,000 and one $500. In addition, Pacific Maritime Magazine will award a $500 scholarship to one of the finalists planning to pursue a seagoing maritime career. Requires 2.5 GPA or submit an additional letter of recommendation from a second teacher.

Academic Fields/Career Goals: Marine Biology; Marine/Ocean Engineering; Oceanography; Trade/Technical Specialties.

Award: Scholarship for use in freshman year; not renewable. *Number:* 6–7. *Amount:* $500–$5000.

Eligibility Requirements: Applicant must be high school student; planning to enroll or expecting to enroll full- or part-time at a two-year or four-year or technical institution or university and resident of Washington. Available to U.S. citizens.

Application Requirements: Application form, essay, recommendations or references, transcript. *Deadline:* February 22.

Contact: Carleen See, Chairperson, YMTA Scholarship Committee
    Youth Maritime Training Association
    PO Box 70425
    Seattle, WA 98127
    E-mail: carleeninballard@yahoo.com

MARINE/OCEAN ENGINEERING

AMERICAN METEOROLOGICAL SOCIETY

http://www.ametsoc.org/

AMS FRESHMAN UNDERGRADUATE SCHOLARSHIP

• *See page 301*

AMERICAN SOCIETY OF NAVAL ENGINEERS

http://www.navalengineers.org/

AMERICAN SOCIETY OF NAVAL ENGINEERS SCHOLARSHIP

• *See page 103*

ARRL FOUNDATION INC.

http://www.arrl.org/

ALFRED E. FRIEND JR., W4CF, MEMORIAL SCHOLARSHIP

• *See page 166*

GREATER KANAWHA VALLEY FOUNDATION

http://www.tgkvf.org/

STEVEN ENGINEERING SCHOLARSHIP

• *See page 167*

LOUISIANA OFFICE OF STUDENT FINANCIAL ASSISTANCE

http://www.osfa.la.gov/

ROCKEFELLER STATE WILDLIFE SCHOLARSHIP

• *See page 146*

MANUFACTURERS ASSOCIATION OF MAINE

http://www.mainemfg.com/

MAINE METAL PRODUCTS EDUCATION FUND SCHOLARSHIP PROGRAM
• *See page 132*

MARINE TECHNOLOGY SOCIETY

http://www.mtsociety.org/

CHARLES H. BUSSMAN UNDERGRADUATE SCHOLARSHIP
• *See page 388*

JOHN C. BAJUS SCHOLARSHIP
• *See page 388*

MTS STUDENT SCHOLARSHIP
• *See page 388*

MTS STUDENT SCHOLARSHIP FOR GRADUATE AND UNDERGRADUATE STUDENTS
• *See page 388*

MTS STUDENT SCHOLARSHIP FOR GRADUATING HIGH SCHOOL SENIORS
• *See page 285*

MTS STUDENT SCHOLARSHIP FOR TWO-YEAR TECHNICAL, ENGINEERING AND COMMUNITY COLLEGE STUDENTS
• *See page 388*

PAROS-DIGIQUARTZ SCHOLARSHIP
• *See page 388*

ROV SCHOLARSHIP
• *See page 389*

SOCIETY OF WOMEN ENGINEERS

http://www.swe.org/

ADA I. PRESSMAN MEMORIAL SCHOLARSHIP
• *See page 172*

ANNE MAUREEN WHITNEY BARROW MEMORIAL SCHOLARSHIP
• *See page 172*

BETTY LOU BAILEY SWE REGION F SCHOLARSHIP
• *See page 172*

BK KRENZER MEMORIAL REENTRY SCHOLARSHIP
• *See page 172*

CAROL STEPHENS REGION F SCHOLARSHIP
• *See page 172*

DR. IVY M. PARKER MEMORIAL SCHOLARSHIP
• *See page 173*

DOROTHY LEMKE HOWARTH MEMORIAL SCHOLARSHIP
• *See page 173*

DOROTHY P. MORRIS SCHOLARSHIP
• *See page 173*

JILL S. TIETJEN P.E. SCHOLARSHIP
• *See page 173*

LILLIAN MOLLER GILBRETH MEMORIAL SCHOLARSHIP
• *See page 174*

MARY V. MUNGER SCHOLARSHIP
• *See page 174*

MASWE MEMORIAL SCHOLARSHIP
• *See page 174*

MERIDITH THOMS MEMORIAL SCHOLARSHIPS
• *See page 174*

OLIVE LYNN SALEMBIER MEMORIAL REENTRY SCHOLARSHIP
• *See page 174*

SUSAN MISZKOWICZ MEMORIAL SCHOLARSHIP
• *See page 175*

SWE BALTIMORE-WASHINGTON SECTION SCHOLARSHIP
• *See page 175*

SWE CENTRAL NEW MEXICO PIONEERS SCHOLARSHIP
• *See page 175*

SWE CENTRAL NEW MEXICO REENTRY SCHOLARSHIP
• *See page 175*

SWE MID-HUDSON SECTION SCHOLARSHIP
• *See page 175*

SWE PAST PRESIDENTS SCHOLARSHIP
• *See page 175*

SWE PHOENIX SECTION SCHOLARSHIP
• *See page 175*

SWE REGION H SCHOLARSHIPS
• *See page 176*

WANDA MUNN SCHOLARSHIP
• *See page 176*

SOCIETY OF WOMEN ENGINEERS-ROCKY MOUNTAIN SECTION

http://www.societyofwomenengineers.org/RockyMountain/

SOCIETY OF WOMEN ENGINEERS-ROCKY MOUNTAIN SECTION SCHOLARSHIP PROGRAM
• *See page 176*

UNITED NEGRO COLLEGE FUND

http://www.uncf.org/

CDM SCHOLARSHIP/INTERNSHIP
• *See page 176*

UTAH SOCIETY OF PROFESSIONAL ENGINEERS

http://www.uspeonline.com/

UTAH SOCIETY OF PROFESSIONAL ENGINEERS JOE RHOADS SCHOLARSHIP
• *See page 177*

YOUTH MARITIME TRAINING ASSOCIATION

http://ymta.net/

NORM MANLY—YMTA MARITIME EDUCATIONAL SCHOLARSHIPS
• *See page 389*

MARKETING

BALTIMORE CHAPTER OF THE AMERICAN MARKETING ASSOCIATION

http://www.amabaltimore.org/

UNDERGRADUATE MARKETING EDUCATION MERIT SCHOLARSHIPS
• *See page 151*

DECA (DISTRIBUTIVE EDUCATION CLUBS OF AMERICA)

http://www.deca.org/

HARRY A. APPLEGATE SCHOLARSHIP
• *See page 153*

ELECTRONIC DOCUMENT SYSTEMS FOUNDATION

http://www.edsf.org/

HOODS MEMORIAL SCHOLARSHIP
• *See page 153*

GLOBAL AUTOMOTIVE AFTERMARKET SYMPOSIUM

http://www.automotivescholarships.com/

GAAS SCHOLARSHIP
• *See page 155*

GREAT FALLS ADVERTISING FEDERATION

http://www.gfaf.com/

GREAT FALLS ADVERTISING FEDERATION COLLEGE SCHOLARSHIP
• *See page 83*

HIGH SCHOOL MARKETING/COMMUNICATIONS SCHOLARSHIP
• *See page 83*

INTERNATIONAL FOODSERVICE EDITORIAL COUNCIL

http://www.ifeconline.com/

INTERNATIONAL FOODSERVICE EDITORIAL COUNCIL COMMUNICATIONS SCHOLARSHIP
• *See page 83*

NATIONAL DAIRY SHRINE

http://www.dairyshrine.org/

NATIONAL DAIRY SHRINE/DAIRY MARKETING INC. MILK MARKETING SCHOLARSHIPS
• *See page 93*

RHODE ISLAND FOUNDATION

http://www.rifoundation.org/

J. D. EDSAL SCHOLARSHIP
• *See page 84*

SPECIALTY EQUIPMENT MARKET ASSOCIATION

http://www.sema.org/

SPECIALTY EQUIPMENT MARKET ASSOCIATION MEMORIAL SCHOLARSHIP FUND
• *See page 80*

STRAIGHTFORWARD MEDIA

http://www.straightforwardmedia.com/

STRAIGHTFORWARD MEDIA BUSINESS SCHOOL SCHOLARSHIP
• *See page 84*

STRAIGHTFORWARD MEDIA MEDIA & COMMUNICATIONS SCHOLARSHIP
• *See page 84*

UNITED NEGRO COLLEGE FUND

http://www.uncf.org/

AXA ACHIEVEMENT SCHOLARSHIP PROGRAM
• *See page 81*

BANK OF AMERICA SCHOLARSHIP
• *See page 160*

COLGATE-PALMOLIVE COMPANY/UNCF SCHOLARSHIP
• *See page 160*

FORD/UNCF CORPORATE SCHOLARS PROGRAM
• *See page 82*

NASCAR/WENDELL SCOTT, SR. SCHOLARSHIP
• *See page 82*

PACIFIC GAS AND ELECTRIC COMPANY SCHOLARSHIP
• *See page 82*

PSE&G SCHOLARSHIP
• *See page 82*

UBS/PAINEWEBBER SCHOLARSHIP
• *See page 82*

WHOMENTORS.COM, INC.

http://www.WHOmentors.com/

I B USD WORLDWIDE VENTURE CAPITAL
• *See page 107*

WYOMING TRUCKING ASSOCIATION SCHOLARSHIP FUND TRUST

http://www.wytruck.org/

WYOMING TRUCKING ASSOCIATION SCHOLARSHIP TRUST FUND
• *See page 83*

MATERIALS SCIENCE, ENGINEERING, AND METALLURGY

AIST FOUNDATION

http://www.aistfoundation.org/

AISI/AIST FOUNDATION PREMIER SCHOLARSHIP
• *See page 248*

AIST ALFRED B. GLOSSBRENNER AND JOHN KLUSCH SCHOLARSHIPS
• *See page 271*

AIST WILLIAM E. SCHWABE MEMORIAL SCHOLARSHIP
• *See page 248*

ASSOCIATION FOR IRON AND STEEL TECHNOLOGY BALTIMORE CHAPTER SCHOLARSHIP
• *See page 259*

ASSOCIATION FOR IRON AND STEEL TECHNOLOGY BENJAMIN F. FAIRLESS SCHOLARSHIP (AIME)
• *See page 162*

ASSOCIATION FOR IRON AND STEEL TECHNOLOGY DAVID H. SAMSON CANADIAN SCHOLARSHIP
• *See page 162*

ASSOCIATION FOR IRON AND STEEL TECHNOLOGY NORTHWEST MEMBER CHAPTER SCHOLARSHIP
• *See page 272*

ASSOCIATION FOR IRON AND STEEL TECHNOLOGY OHIO VALLEY CHAPTER SCHOLARSHIP
• *See page 142*

ASSOCIATION FOR IRON AND STEEL TECHNOLOGY PITTSBURGH CHAPTER SCHOLARSHIP
• *See page 272*

ASSOCIATION FOR IRON AND STEEL TECHNOLOGY RONALD E. LINCOLN SCHOLARSHIP
• *See page 248*

ASSOCIATION FOR IRON AND STEEL TECHNOLOGY SOUTHEAST MEMBER CHAPTER SCHOLARSHIP
• *See page 273*

ASSOCIATION FOR IRON AND STEEL TECHNOLOGY WILLY KORF MEMORIAL SCHOLARSHIP
• *See page 162*

FERROUS METALLURGY EDUCATION TODAY (FEMET)
Scholarships are for full-time students of metallurgy or materials science engineering. Students must have an interest in a career in the steel industry as demonstrated by an internship or related experience, or who have plans to pursue such experiences during college. Students must commit to a summer internship at a steel producing company (placement assistance is provided) prior to receiving this scholarship. Student may apply during their sophomore and junior years. Applications are accepted from 1 Sep through 31 Dec each year.

Academic Fields/Career Goals: Materials Science, Engineering, and Metallurgy.

Award: Scholarship for use in sophomore or junior years; not renewable. *Number:* 1–10. *Amount:* $5000.

Eligibility Requirements: Applicant must be enrolled or expecting to enroll full-time at a four-year institution or university. Applicant must have 2.5 GPA or higher. Available to U.S. and non-U.S. citizens.

Application Requirements: Application form, essay, recommendations or references, resume, transcript. *Deadline:* December 31.

Contact: Lori Wharrey, AIST Manager, Board Services
AIST Foundation
186 Thorn HIll Road
Warrendale, PA 15086
Phone: 724-814-3044
E-mail: lwharrey@aist.org

AMERICAN CHEMICAL SOCIETY

http://www.acs.org/

AMERICAN CHEMICAL SOCIETY SCHOLARS PROGRAM
• *See page 162*

AMERICAN CHEMICAL SOCIETY, RUBBER DIVISION

http://www.rubber.org/

AMERICAN CHEMICAL SOCIETY, RUBBER DIVISION UNDERGRADUATE SCHOLARSHIP
• *See page 163*

AMERICAN COUNCIL OF ENGINEERING COMPANIES OF PENNSYLVANIA (ACEC/PA)

http://www.acecpa.org/

ENGINEERING SCHOLARSHIP
• *See page 163*

AMERICAN INDIAN SCIENCE AND ENGINEERING SOCIETY

http://www.aises.org/

A.T. ANDERSON MEMORIAL SCHOLARSHIP PROGRAM
• *See page 102*

AMERICAN INSTITUTE OF AERONAUTICS AND ASTRONAUTICS

http://www.aiaa.org/

AIAA FOUNDATION UNDERGRADUATE SCHOLARSHIP
• *See page 102*

AMERICAN SOCIETY OF NAVAL ENGINEERS

http://www.navalengineers.org/

AMERICAN SOCIETY OF NAVAL ENGINEERS SCHOLARSHIP
• *See page 103*

AMERICAN WELDING SOCIETY

http://www.aws.org/

AIRGAS-JERRY BAKER SCHOLARSHIP
• *See page 261*

AIRGAS-TERRY JARVIS MEMORIAL SCHOLARSHIP
• *See page 261*

AMERICAN WELDING SOCIETY INTERNATIONAL SCHOLARSHIP
• *See page 262*

ARSHAM AMIRIKIAN ENGINEERING SCHOLARSHIP
• *See page 181*

DONALD AND SHIRLEY HASTINGS SCHOLARSHIP
• *See page 275*

JOHN C. LINCOLN MEMORIAL SCHOLARSHIP
• *See page 262*

MATSUO BRIDGE COMPANY LTD. OF JAPAN SCHOLARSHIP
• *See page 181*

MILLER ELECTRIC INTERNATIONAL WORLD SKILLS COMPETITION SCHOLARSHIP
• *See page 262*

MILLER ELECTRIC MFG. CO. SCHOLARSHIP
• *See page 263*

PRAXAIR INTERNATIONAL SCHOLARSHIP
• *See page 263*

RESISTANCE WELDER MANUFACTURERS' ASSOCIATION SCHOLARSHIP
• *See page 276*

ROBERT L. PEASLEE BRAZING SCHOLARSHIP
• *See page 276*

WILLIAM A. AND ANN M. BROTHERS SCHOLARSHIP
• *See page 263*

WILLIAM B. HOWELL MEMORIAL SCHOLARSHIP
• *See page 263*

ARRL FOUNDATION INC.

http://www.arrl.org/

ALFRED E. FRIEND JR., W4CF, MEMORIAL SCHOLARSHIP
• *See page 166*

GARY WAGNER, K3OMI, SCHOLARSHIP
• *See page 166*

ASM MATERIALS EDUCATION FOUNDATION

http://www.asmfoundation.org/

ASM OUTSTANDING SCHOLARS AWARDS
• *See page 277*

EDWARD J. DULIS SCHOLARSHIP
• *See page 277*

GEORGE A. ROBERTS SCHOLARSHIP
• *See page 277*

JOHN M. HANIAK SCHOLARSHIP
• *See page 277*

WILLIAM P. WOODSIDE FOUNDER'S SCHOLARSHIP
• *See page 277*

ASTRONAUT SCHOLARSHIP FOUNDATION

http://www.astronautscholarship.org/

ASTRONAUT SCHOLARSHIP FOUNDATION
• *See page 104*

BARRY M. GOLDWATER SCHOLARSHIP AND EXCELLENCE IN EDUCATION FOUNDATION

http://www.act.org/goldwater

BARRY M. GOLDWATER SCHOLARSHIP AND EXCELLENCE IN EDUCATION PROGRAM
• *See page 104*

ELECTROCHEMICAL SOCIETY INC.

http://www.electrochem.org/

STUDENT RESEARCH AWARDS OF THE BATTERY DIVISION OF THE ELECTROCHEMICAL SOCIETY INC.
• *See page 105*

GREATER KANAWHA VALLEY FOUNDATION

http://www.tgkvf.org/

STEVEN ENGINEERING SCHOLARSHIP
• *See page 167*

GREAT MINDS IN STEM

http://www.greatmindsinstem.org

HISPANIC ENGINEER NATIONAL ACHIEVEMENT AWARDS CORPORATION SCHOLARSHIP PROGRAM
• *See page 130*

INDEPENDENT LABORATORIES INSTITUTE SCHOLARSHIP ALLIANCE

http://www.acil.org/

INDEPENDENT LABORATORIES INSTITUTE SCHOLARSHIP ALLIANCE
• *See page 145*

INSTITUTE OF INTERNATIONAL EDUCATION (FULBRIGHT PROGRAM)

http://www.us.fulbrightonline.org/

WHITAKER INTERNATIONAL PROGRAM
• *See page 145*

INTERNATIONAL SOCIETY FOR OPTICAL ENGINEERING-SPIE

http://www.spie.org/scholarships

SPIE EDUCATIONAL SCHOLARSHIPS IN OPTICAL SCIENCE AND ENGINEERING
• *See page 105*

INTERNATIONAL SOCIETY OF AUTOMATION (ISA)

http://www.isa.org/

INTERNATIONAL SOCIETY OF AUTOMATION EDUCATION FOUNDATION SCHOLARSHIPS
• *See page 131*

JORGE MAS CANOSA FREEDOM FOUNDATION

http://www.jorgemascanosa.org/

MAS FAMILY SCHOLARSHIP AWARD
• *See page 156*

LOS ANGELES COUNCIL OF BLACK PROFESSIONAL ENGINEERS

http://www.lablackengineers.org/

AL-BEN SCHOLARSHIP FOR ACADEMIC INCENTIVE
• *See page 168*

AL-BEN SCHOLARSHIP FOR PROFESSIONAL MERIT
• *See page 168*

AL-BEN SCHOLARSHIP FOR SCHOLASTIC ACHIEVEMENT
• *See page 168*

MANUFACTURERS ASSOCIATION OF MAINE

http://www.mainemfg.com/

MAINE METAL PRODUCTS EDUCATION FUND SCHOLARSHIP PROGRAM
• *See page 132*

MIDWEST ROOFING CONTRACTORS ASSOCIATION

http://www.mrca.org/

MRCA FOUNDATION SCHOLARSHIP PROGRAM
• *See page 112*

MINERALS, METALS, AND MATERIALS SOCIETY (TMS)

http://www.tms.org/

TMS/EMPMD GILBERT CHIN SCHOLARSHIP
• *See page 266*

TMS/EPD SCHOLARSHIP
• *See page 266*

TMS/INTERNATIONAL SYMPOSIUM ON SUPERALLOYS SCHOLARSHIP PROGRAM
• *See page 266*

TMS J. KEITH BRIMACOMBE PRESIDENTIAL SCHOLARSHIP
• *See page 266*

TMS/LMD SCHOLARSHIP PROGRAM
• *See page 267*

TMS OUTSTANDING STUDENT PAPER CONTEST-UNDERGRADUATE
• *See page 267*

TMS/STRUCTURAL MATERIALS DIVISION SCHOLARSHIP
• *See page 267*

NASA FLORIDA SPACE GRANT CONSORTIUM

http://www.floridaspacegrant.org/

FLORIDA SPACE RESEARCH PROGRAM
• *See page 132*

NASA IDAHO SPACE GRANT CONSORTIUM

http://www.id.spacegrant.org/

NASA IDAHO SPACE GRANT CONSORTIUM SCHOLARSHIP PROGRAM
• *See page 146*

NASA/MARYLAND SPACE GRANT CONSORTIUM

http://md.spacegrant.org/

NASA MARYLAND SPACE GRANT CONSORTIUM UNDERGRADUATE SCHOLARSHIPS
• *See page 132*

NASA SOUTH DAKOTA SPACE GRANT CONSORTIUM

http://sdspacegrant.sdsmt.edu/

SOUTH DAKOTA SPACE GRANT CONSORTIUM UNDERGRADUATE AND GRADUATE STUDENT SCHOLARSHIPS
• *See page 134*

NASA'S VIRGINIA SPACE GRANT CONSORTIUM

http://www.vsgc.odu.edu/

COMMUNITY COLLEGE STEM SCHOLARSHIPS
• *See page 105*

UNDERGRADUATE STEM RESEARCH SCHOLARSHIPS
• See page 106

NATIONAL INVENTORS HALL OF FAME

http://www.invent.org/

COLLEGIATE INVENTORS COMPETITION FOR UNDERGRADUATE STUDENTS
• See page 106

COLLEGIATE INVENTORS COMPETITION-GRAND PRIZE
• See page 106

NATIONAL SOCIETY OF PROFESSIONAL ENGINEERS

http://www.nspe.org/

MAUREEN L. AND HOWARD N. BLITMAN, PE SCHOLARSHIP TO PROMOTE DIVERSITY IN ENGINEERING
• See page 170

PAUL H. ROBBINS HONORARY SCHOLARSHIP
• See page 170

PROFESSIONAL ENGINEERS IN INDUSTRY SCHOLARSHIP
• See page 170

NATIONAL STONE, SAND AND GRAVEL ASSOCIATION (NSSGA)

http://www.nssga.org/

BARRY K. WENDT MEMORIAL SCHOLARSHIP
• See page 268

PLASTICS INSTITUTE OF AMERICA

http://www.plasticsinstitute.org/

PLASTICS PIONEERS SCHOLARSHIPS
• See page 170

ROCKY MOUNTAIN COAL MINING INSTITUTE

http://www.rmcmi.org/

ROCKY MOUNTAIN COAL MINING INSTITUTE SCHOLARSHIP
• See page 185

SEMICONDUCTOR RESEARCH CORPORATION (SRC)

http://www.src.org/

MASTER'S SCHOLARSHIP PROGRAM
• See page 171

SOCIETY OF AUTOMOTIVE ENGINEERS

http://www.sae.org/

TMC/SAE DONALD D. DAWSON TECHNICAL SCHOLARSHIP
• See page 137

YANMAR/SAE SCHOLARSHIP
• See page 269

SOCIETY OF PLASTICS ENGINEERS (SPE) FOUNDATION

http://www.4spe.org/

FLEMING/BASZCAK SCHOLARSHIP
• See page 171

SOCIETY OF PLASTICS ENGINEERS SCHOLARSHIP PROGRAM
• See page 171

SOCIETY OF WOMEN ENGINEERS

http://www.swe.org/

BETTY LOU BAILEY SWE REGION F SCHOLARSHIP
• See page 172

BK KRENZER MEMORIAL REENTRY SCHOLARSHIP
• See page 172

CAROL STEPHENS REGION F SCHOLARSHIP
• See page 172

CUMMINS INC. SCHOLARSHIP
• See page 173

DR. IVY M. PARKER MEMORIAL SCHOLARSHIP
• See page 173

DOROTHY LEMKE HOWARTH MEMORIAL SCHOLARSHIP
• See page 173

DOROTHY P. MORRIS SCHOLARSHIP
• See page 173

HONEYWELL CORPORATION SCHOLARSHIP
• See page 173

JILL S. TIETJEN P.E. SCHOLARSHIP
• See page 173

LIFE TECHNOLOGIES SCHOLARSHIP
• See page 174

LILLIAN MOLLER GILBRETH MEMORIAL SCHOLARSHIP
• See page 174

MARY V. MUNGER SCHOLARSHIP
• See page 174

MASWE MEMORIAL SCHOLARSHIP
• See page 174

MERIDITH THOMS MEMORIAL SCHOLARSHIPS
• See page 174

OLIVE LYNN SALEMBIER MEMORIAL REENTRY SCHOLARSHIP
• See page 174

SUSAN MISZKOWICZ MEMORIAL SCHOLARSHIP
• See page 175

SWE BALTIMORE-WASHINGTON SECTION SCHOLARSHIP
• See page 175

SOCIETY OF WOMEN ENGINEERS-ROCKY MOUNTAIN SECTION

http://www.societyofwomenengineers.org/RockyMountain/

STRAIGHTFORWARD MEDIA

http://www.straightforwardmedia.com/

TURNER CONSTRUCTION COMPANY

http://www.turnerconstruction.com/

UNIVERSITIES SPACE RESEARCH ASSOCIATION

http://www.usra.edu/

VERMONT SPACE GRANT CONSORTIUM

http://www.cems.uvm.edu/vsgc

WHOMENTORS.COM, INC.

http://www.WHOmentors.com/

XEROX

http://www.xerox.com//

MATHEMATICS

THE ACTUARIAL FOUNDATION

http://www.actuarialfoundation.org/programs/actuarial/scholarships.shtml

AMERICAN LEGION DEPARTMENT OF MARYLAND

http://www.mdlegion.org/

AMERICAN LEGION DEPARTMENT OF MARYLAND MATH-SCIENCE SCHOLARSHIP

Scholarship for study in math or the sciences. Must be a Maryland resident and the dependent child of a veteran. Must submit essay, financial need analysis, and transcript with application. Nonrenewable award for freshman. Application available on website http://mdlegion.org.

Academic Fields/Career Goals: Mathematics; Physical Sciences.

Award: Scholarship for use in freshman year; not renewable. *Number:* 1–3. *Amount:* $500–$1500.

Eligibility Requirements: Applicant must be high school student; planning to enroll or expecting to enroll full-time at a two-year or four-year institution or university and resident of Maryland. Available to U.S. citizens. Applicant or parent must meet one or more of the following requirements: general military experience; retired from active duty; disabled or killed as a result of military service; prisoner of war; or missing in action.

Application Requirements: Application form, essay, financial need analysis, transcript. *Deadline:* April 1.

Contact: Russell Myers, Department Adjutant
American Legion Department of Maryland
101 North Gay, Room E
Baltimore, MD 21202
Phone: 410-752-1405
Fax: 410-752-3822
E-mail: russell@mdlegion.org

AMERICAN MATHEMATICAL ASSOCIATION OF TWO YEAR COLLEGES

http://www.amatyc.org/

CHARLES MILLER SCHOLARSHIP

A grand prize of $3000 for the qualified individual with the highest total score of the student mathematics league exam. Funds to continue education at an accredited four-year institution. In the case of a tie for the grand prize, the scholarship will be evenly divided.

Academic Fields/Career Goals: Mathematics.

Award: Scholarship for use in freshman or sophomore years; not renewable. *Number:* 1. *Amount:* $3000.

Eligibility Requirements: Applicant must be enrolled or expecting to enroll full-time at a two-year institution. Available to U.S. citizens.

Application Requirements: Entry in a contest, test scores. *Deadline:* September 30.

Contact: Cheryl Cleaves, Executive Director of Office Operations
Phone: 901-333-4643
Fax: 901-333-4651
E-mail: amatyc@amatyc.org

AMERICAN SOCIETY FOR ENGINEERING EDUCATION

http://www.asee.org/

SCIENCE, MATHEMATICS, AND RESEARCH FOR TRANSFORMATION DEFENSE SCHOLARSHIP FOR SERVICE PROGRAM

• See page 102

ARMED FORCES COMMUNICATIONS AND ELECTRONICS ASSOCIATION, EDUCATIONAL FOUNDATION

http://www.afcea.org/scholarships

ARMED FORCES COMMUNICATIONS AND ELECTRONICS ASSOCIATION GENERAL EMMETT PAIGE SCHOLARSHIP

• See page 127

ARMED FORCES COMMUNICATIONS AND ELECTRONICS ASSOCIATION ROTC SCHOLARSHIP PROGRAM

• See page 127

DISABLED WAR VETERANS SCHOLARSHIP

• See page 128

LTG DOUGLAS D. BUCHHOLZ MEMORIAL SCHOLARSHIP

• See page 128

VETERANS OF ENDURING FREEDOM (AFGHANISTAN) AND IRAQI FREEDOM SCHOLARSHIP

• See page 200

ASSOCIATION FOR WOMEN IN MATHEMATICS

http://www.awm-math.org/

ALICE T. SCHAFER MATHEMATICS PRIZE FOR EXCELLENCE IN MATHEMATICS BY AN UNDERGRADUATE WOMAN

One-time merit award for women undergraduates in the math field. Based on quality of performance in math courses and special programs, ability to work independently, interest in math, and performance in competitions. Must be nominated by a professor or an adviser.

Academic Fields/Career Goals: Mathematics.

Award: Prize for use in freshman, sophomore, junior, or senior years; not renewable. *Number:* 1. *Amount:* $250–$1000.

Eligibility Requirements: Applicant must be enrolled or expecting to enroll full-time at a four-year institution or university and female. Available to U.S. citizens.

Application Requirements: Application form, application form may be submitted online (http://awm-math.org), recommendations or references, transcript. *Deadline:* October 1.

Contact: Jennifer Lewis, Managing Director
Phone: 703-934-0163 Ext. 213
Fax: 703-359-7562
E-mail: jennifer@awm-math.org

BRITISH COLUMBIA INNOVATION COUNCIL

http://www.bcic.ca/

BCIC YOUNG INNOVATOR SCHOLARSHIP COMPETITION (IDEA MASH UP)

• See page 104

CALIFORNIA MATHEMATICS COUNCIL-SOUTH

http://www.cmc-math.org/

CALIFORNIA MATHEMATICS COUNCIL-SOUTH SECONDARY EDUCATION SCHOLARSHIPS

Scholarships for students enrolled in accredited Southern California secondary education credential programs with math as a major. Applicants must be members of the California Math Council-South.

Academic Fields/Career Goals: Mathematics.

Award: Scholarship for use in freshman, sophomore, junior, or senior years; renewable. *Number:* 2–5. *Amount:* $100–$2000.

Eligibility Requirements: Applicant must be enrolled or expecting to enroll full- or part-time at a four-year institution or university; resident of California and studying in California. Available to U.S. and non-U.S. citizens.

Application Requirements: Application form, essay, recommendations or references, transcript. *Deadline:* January 31.

Contact: Dr. Sid Kolpas, Professor of Mathematics
Phone: 818-240-1000 Ext. 5378
E-mail: sjkolpas@sprintmail.com

COLLEGEBOUND FOUNDATION

http://www.collegeboundfoundation.org/

DR. FREEMAN A. HRABOWSKI, III SCHOLARSHIP

• See page 279

THE COMMUNITY FOUNDATION FOR GREATER ATLANTA, INC.

http://cfgreateratlanta.org/

TECH HIGH SCHOOL ALUMNI ASSOCIATION/W.O. CHENEY MERIT SCHOLARSHIP FUND

• See page 279

THE DALLAS FOUNDATION

http://www.dallasfoundation.org/

WHITLEY PLACE SCHOLARSHIP

• See page 110

DAVIDSON INSTITUTE FOR TALENT DEVELOPMENT

http://www.davidsongifted.org/

DAVIDSON FELLOWS SCHOLARSHIP PROGRAM

• See page 386

DAYTON FOUNDATION

http://www.daytonfoundation.org/

THRYSA FRAZIER SVAGER SCHOLARSHIP

Scholarship for African-American female students majoring in mathematics and attending Central State University, Wilberforce University, Wright State University, University of Dayton, Howard

University or Spelman College. Must maintain average grade of 3.0 or better.

Academic Fields/Career Goals: Mathematics.

Award: Scholarship for use in sophomore, junior, or senior years; renewable. *Number:* 1–2. *Amount:* $2000.

Eligibility Requirements: Applicant must be Black (non-Hispanic); enrolled or expecting to enroll full-time at a four-year institution or university; female and studying in District of Columbia, Georgia, Ohio. Applicant must have 3.0 GPA or higher. Available to U.S. citizens.

Application Requirements: Application form, essay, recommendations or references, transcript. *Deadline:* March 25.

Contact: Elizabeth Horner, Scholarship Program Officer
Dayton Foundation
500 Kettering Tower
Dayton, OH 45423
Phone: 937-222-9955
Fax: 937-222-0636
E-mail: ehorner@daytonfoundation.org

GREATER KANAWHA VALLEY FOUNDATION

http://www.tgkvf.org/

MATH AND SCIENCE SCHOLARSHIP
• *See page 145*

HEMOPHILIA HEALTH SERVICES

http://www.hemophiliahealth.com/

SCOTT TARBELL SCHOLARSHIP
• *See page 202*

HISPANIC HERITAGE FOUNDATION

http://www.hispanicheritage.org/

HISPANIC HERITAGE YOUTH AWARDS
• *See page 155*

MICHIGAN COUNCIL OF TEACHERS OF MATHEMATICS

http://www.mictm.org/

MIRIAM SCHAEFER SCHOLARSHIP

A scholarship of $1500 is given to a senior or a junior enrolled full-time in undergraduate degree with mathematics specialty. Applicants should be a resident of Michigan but citizenship does not matter.

Academic Fields/Career Goals: Mathematics.

Award: Scholarship for use in junior or senior years; not renewable. *Number:* 3–5. *Amount:* $1500.

Eligibility Requirements: Applicant must be enrolled or expecting to enroll full-time at a four-year institution or university and resident of Michigan. Applicant must have 3.0 GPA or higher. Available to U.S. and non-U.S. citizens.

Application Requirements: Application form, essay, recommendations or references, transcript. *Deadline:* April 1.

Contact: Mr. Chris Berry, Executive Director
Michigan Council of Teachers of Mathematics
4767 Stadler Road
Monroe, MI 48162
Phone: 734-477-0421
Fax: 734-241-4128
E-mail: info@mictm.org

MINNESOTA OFFICE OF HIGHER EDUCATION

http://www.getreadyforcollege.org/

MINNESOTA ACADEMIC EXCELLENCE SCHOLARSHIP
• *See page 120*

NASA FLORIDA SPACE GRANT CONSORTIUM

http://www.floridaspacegrant.org/

FLORIDA SPACE RESEARCH PROGRAM
• *See page 132*

NASA IDAHO SPACE GRANT CONSORTIUM

http://www.id.spacegrant.org/

NASA IDAHO SPACE GRANT CONSORTIUM SCHOLARSHIP PROGRAM
• *See page 146*

NASA/MARYLAND SPACE GRANT CONSORTIUM

http://md.spacegrant.org/

NASA MARYLAND SPACE GRANT CONSORTIUM UNDERGRADUATE SCHOLARSHIPS
• *See page 132*

NASA MINNESOTA SPACE GRANT CONSORTIUM

http://www.aem.umn.edu/mnsgc

MINNESOTA SPACE GRANT CONSORTIUM SCHOLARSHIP PROGRAM
• *See page 132*

NASA MISSISSIPPI SPACE GRANT CONSORTIUM

http://www.olemiss.edu/programs/nasa

MISSISSIPPI SPACE GRANT CONSORTIUM SCHOLARSHIP
• *See page 132*

NASA MONTANA SPACE GRANT CONSORTIUM

http://www.spacegrant.montana.edu/

MONTANA SPACE GRANT SCHOLARSHIP PROGRAM
• *See page 133*

NASA RHODE ISLAND SPACE GRANT CONSORTIUM

http://brown/initiatives/ri-space-grant

NASA RHODE ISLAND SPACE GRANT CONSORTIUM OUTREACH SCHOLARSHIP FOR UNDERGRADUATE STUDENTS
• *See page 267*

NASA RISGC SCIENCE EN ESPANOL SCHOLARSHIP FOR UNDERGRADUATE STUDENTS
• See page 133

NASA SOUTH DAKOTA SPACE GRANT CONSORTIUM
http://sdspacegrant.sdsmt.edu/

SOUTH DAKOTA SPACE GRANT CONSORTIUM UNDERGRADUATE AND GRADUATE STUDENT SCHOLARSHIPS
• See page 134

NASA'S VIRGINIA SPACE GRANT CONSORTIUM
http://www.vsgc.odu.edu/

COMMUNITY COLLEGE STEM SCHOLARSHIPS
• See page 105

UNDERGRADUATE STEM RESEARCH SCHOLARSHIPS
• See page 106

NATIONAL COUNCIL OF TEACHERS OF MATHEMATICS
http://www.nctm.org/

PROSPECTIVE SECONDARY TEACHER COURSE WORK SCHOLARSHIPS
• See page 241

NEVADA NASA SPACE GRANT CONSORTIUM
http://www.nvspacegrant.org/

NATIONAL SPACE GRANT COLLEGE AND FELLOWSHIP PROGRAM
• See page 106

OREGON STUDENT ASSISTANCE COMMISSION
http://www.GetCollegeFunds.org/

BUERKLE SCHOLARSHIP
• See page 372

SALT RIVER PROJECT (SRP)
http://www.srpnet.com/

NAVAJO GENERATING STATION NAVAJO SCHOLARSHIP
• See page 288

SOCIETY OF HISPANIC PROFESSIONAL ENGINEERS
http://www.shpe.org/

AHETEMS SCHOLARSHIPS
• See page 289

TKE EDUCATIONAL FOUNDATION
http://www.tke.org/

FRANCIS J. FLYNN MEMORIAL SCHOLARSHIP
• See page 245

UNITED NEGRO COLLEGE FUND
http://www.uncf.org/

ALFRED CHISHOLM/BASF MEMORIAL SCHOLARSHIP FUND
• See page 81

COOPER INDUSTRIES PACESETTER SCHOLARSHIP
• See page 148

GATES MILLENNIUM SCHOLARSHIP
Award is aimed at increasing minority enrollment in undergraduate and graduate degree programs. This program is available to entering freshman with at least a 3.3 GPA attending any college or university. Award is for students intending to study mathematics or science. Community service and leadership potential are taken into consideration.

Academic Fields/Career Goals: Mathematics; Science, Technology, and Society.

Award: Scholarship for use in freshman year; renewable.

Eligibility Requirements: Applicant must be Black (non-Hispanic); enrolled or expecting to enroll full-time at a four-year institution or university and must have an interest in leadership. Available to U.S. citizens.

Application Requirements: Application form, financial need analysis, nomination packet. *Deadline:* January 17.

GILBANE SCHOLARSHIP PROGRAM
• See page 113

NAACP/HUBERTUS W.V. WILLEMS SCHOLARSHIP FOR MALE SCHOLARS
• See page 271

PACIFIC GAS AND ELECTRIC COMPANY SCHOLARSHIP
• See page 82

SANDISK CORPORATION SCHOLARSHIP
• See page 206

SPRINT SCHOLARS PROGRAM FOR SOPHOMORES, JUNIORS, AND SENIORS
• See page 100

WISCONSIN MATHEMATICS EDUCATION FOUNDATION
http://wmefonline.org/

ARNE ENGEBRETSEN WISCONSIN MATHEMATICS COUNCIL SCHOLARSHIP
• See page 246

ETHEL A. NEIJAHR WISCONSIN MATHEMATICS COUNCIL SCHOLARSHIP
• See page 247

SISTER MARY PETRONIA VAN STRATEN WISCONSIN MATHEMATICS COUNCIL SCHOLARSHIP
• See page 247

MECHANICAL ENGINEERING

AACE INTERNATIONAL
http://www.aacei.org/

AACE INTERNATIONAL COMPETITIVE SCHOLARSHIP

AHS INTERNATIONAL—THE VERTICAL FLIGHT TECHNICAL SOCIETY
http://www.vtol.org/

VERTICAL FLIGHT FOUNDATION SCHOLARSHIP

AIST FOUNDATION
http://www.aistfoundation.org/

AISI/AIST FOUNDATION PREMIER SCHOLARSHIP

AIST WILLIAM E. SCHWABE MEMORIAL SCHOLARSHIP

ASSOCIATION FOR IRON AND STEEL TECHNOLOGY BENJAMIN F. FAIRLESS SCHOLARSHIP (AIME)

ASSOCIATION FOR IRON AND STEEL TECHNOLOGY RONALD E. LINCOLN SCHOLARSHIP

ASSOCIATION FOR IRON AND STEEL TECHNOLOGY WILLY KORF MEMORIAL SCHOLARSHIP

STEEL ENGINEERING EDUCATION LINK (STEEL) SCHOLARSHIPS

AMERICAN CHEMICAL SOCIETY, RUBBER DIVISION
http://www.rubber.org/

AMERICAN CHEMICAL SOCIETY, RUBBER DIVISION UNDERGRADUATE SCHOLARSHIP

AMERICAN COUNCIL OF ENGINEERING COMPANIES OF PENNSYLVANIA (ACEC/PA)
http://www.acecpa.org/

ENGINEERING SCHOLARSHIP

AMERICAN INSTITUTE OF AERONAUTICS AND ASTRONAUTICS
http://www.aiaa.org/

AIAA FOUNDATION UNDERGRADUATE SCHOLARSHIP

AMERICAN PUBLIC TRANSPORTATION FOUNDATION
http://www.apta.com/

LOUIS T. KLAUDER SCHOLARSHIP

TRANSIT HALL OF FAME SCHOLARSHIP AWARD PROGRAM

AMERICAN RAILWAY ENGINEERING AND MAINTENANCE OF WAY ASSOCIATION
http://www.aremafoundation.org/

CHARLES L. STANFORD FAMILY OHIO STATE UNIVERSITY RAILWAY ENGINEERING SCHOLARSHIP

AMERICAN SOCIETY OF HEATING, REFRIGERATING, AND AIR CONDITIONING ENGINEERS, INC.
http://www.ashrae.org/

ALWIN B. NEWTON SCHOLARSHIP

ASHRAE REGION III BOGGARM SETTY SCHOLARSHIP

FRANK M. CODA SCHOLARSHIP

LYNN G. BELLENGER SCHOLARSHIP

REUBEN TRANE SCHOLARSHIP

AMERICAN SOCIETY OF MECHANICAL ENGINEERS (ASME)
http://www.asme.org/

KENNETH ANDREW ROE SCHOLARSHIP
Award of $10,000 for college juniors and seniors who are student members of ASME. Must be U.S. citizens and North American residents. Must be enrolled in an ABET-accredited, or substantially equivalent, mechanical engineering baccalaureate program in the United States.

Academic Fields/Career Goals: Mechanical Engineering.

Award: Scholarship for use in junior or senior years; not renewable. *Number:* 1. *Amount:* $10,000.

Eligibility Requirements: Applicant must be enrolled or expecting to enroll full-time at a four-year institution or university. Applicant must have 3.0 GPA or higher. Available to U.S. citizens.

Application Requirements: Application form, essay, financial need analysis, recommendations or references, transcript. *Deadline:* March 15.

Contact: Ms. Beth Lefever, Administrator, Centers Programs
American Society of Mechanical Engineers (ASME)
Three Park Avenue, 22nd Floor
New York, NY 10016-5990
Phone: 212-591-7790
Fax: 212-591-7856
E-mail: lefeverb@asme.org

AMERICAN SOCIETY OF MECHANICAL ENGINEERS AUXILIARY INC.

http://www.asme.org/

AGNES MALAKATE KEZIOS SCHOLARSHIP

Scholarship to college juniors for use in final year at a four year college. Must be majoring in mechanical engineering, be member of ASME (if available), and exhibit leadership values. Must be U.S. citizen enrolled in a college/university in the United States that has ABET accreditation. Scholarship value is $2000 and the number of awards granted varies.

Academic Fields/Career Goals: Mechanical Engineering.

Award: Scholarship for use in junior or senior years; not renewable. *Number:* 1–2. *Amount:* $2000.

Eligibility Requirements: Applicant must be enrolled or expecting to enroll full-time at a four-year institution or university. Available to U.S. citizens.

Application Requirements: Application form, driver's license, recommendations or references, self-addressed stamped envelope with application, transcript. *Deadline:* March 15.

Contact: Saraswati Sahay, Undergraduate Scholarships
American Society of Mechanical Engineers Auxiliary Inc.
170 East Opal Drive
Glastonbury, CT 06033
Phone: 860-659-3828
E-mail: uma.sahay@gmail.com

ALLEN J. BALDWIN SCHOLARSHIP

Scholarship available to college juniors for use in final year at a four year college. Must be majoring in mechanical engineering, be member of ASME (if available), and exhibit leadership values. Must be U.S. citizen enrolled in a college/university in the United States that has ABET accreditation. Scholarship value is $2000 and the number of awards granted varies.

Academic Fields/Career Goals: Mechanical Engineering.

Award: Scholarship for use in junior year; not renewable. *Number:* 1–2. *Amount:* $2000.

Eligibility Requirements: Applicant must be enrolled or expecting to enroll full-time at a four-year institution or university. Available to U.S. citizens.

Application Requirements: Application form, driver's license, financial need analysis, recommendations or references, self-addressed stamped envelope with application, transcript. *Deadline:* March 15.

Contact: Saraswati Sahay, Undergraduate Scholarships
American Society of Mechanical Engineers Auxiliary Inc.
170 East Opal Drive
Glastonbury, CT 06033
Phone: 860-659-3828
E-mail: uma.sahay@gmail.com

ASME AUXILIARY UNDERGRADUATE SCHOLARSHIP CHARLES B. SHARP

Award of $2000 available only to ASME student members to be used in final year of undergraduate study in mechanical engineering. Must be a U.S. citizen.

Academic Fields/Career Goals: Mechanical Engineering.

Award: Scholarship for use in junior year; not renewable. *Number:* 1–2. *Amount:* $2000.

Eligibility Requirements: Applicant must be enrolled or expecting to enroll full-time at a four-year institution or university. Applicant or parent of applicant must be member of American Society of Mechanical Engineers. Available to U.S. citizens.

Application Requirements: Application form, financial need analysis, recommendations or references, transcript. *Deadline:* March 15.

Contact: Mrs. Saraswati Sahay, Undergraduate Scholarships Chair
American Society of Mechanical Engineers Auxiliary Inc.
170 East Opal Drive
Glastonbury, CT 06033
Phone: 860-659-3828
E-mail: uma.sahay@gmail.com

BERNA LOU CARTWRIGHT SCHOLARSHIP

Scholarship for college juniors for use in final year at a four year college. Must be majoring in mechanical engineering. Must be a U.S. citizen, enrolled in a college/university in the United States that has ABET accreditation. Number of awards varies.

Academic Fields/Career Goals: Mechanical Engineering.

Award: Scholarship for use in junior year; not renewable. *Number:* 1–2. *Amount:* $2000.

Eligibility Requirements: Applicant must be enrolled or expecting to enroll full-time at a four-year institution or university and must have an interest in leadership. Applicant or parent of applicant must be member of Other Student Academic Clubs. Available to U.S. citizens.

Application Requirements: Application form, financial need analysis, recommendations or references, resume, transcript. *Deadline:* March 15.

Contact: Saraswati Sahay, Undergraduate Scholarships
American Society of Mechanical Engineers Auxiliary Inc.
170 East Opal Drive
Glastonbury, CT 06033
Phone: 860-659-3828
E-mail: uma.sahay@gmail.com

SYLVIA W. FARNY SCHOLARSHIP

One-time awards of $2000 to ASME student members for the final year of undergraduate study in mechanical engineering. Must be a U.S. citizen, enrolled in a college/university in the United States that has ABET accreditation. Number of scholarships granted varies.

Academic Fields/Career Goals: Mechanical Engineering.

Award: Scholarship for use in junior year; not renewable. *Number:* 1–2. *Amount:* $2000.

Eligibility Requirements: Applicant must be enrolled or expecting to enroll full-time at a four-year institution or university. Applicant or parent of applicant must be member of Other Student Academic Clubs. Available to U.S. citizens.

Application Requirements: Application form, recommendations or references, transcript. *Deadline:* March 15.

Contact: Saraswati Sahay, Undergraduate Scholarships
American Society of Mechanical Engineers Auxiliary Inc.
170 East Opal Drive
Glastonbury, CT 06033
Phone: 860-659-3828
E-mail: uma.sahay@gmail.com

AMERICAN SOCIETY OF NAVAL ENGINEERS

http://www.navalengineers.org/

AMERICAN SOCIETY OF NAVAL ENGINEERS SCHOLARSHIP

• See page 103

AMERICAN WELDING SOCIETY

http://www.aws.org/

PAST PRESIDENTS' SCHOLARSHIP

• See page 276

ARRL FOUNDATION INC.

http://www.arrl.org/

ALFRED E. FRIEND JR, W4CF, MEMORIAL SCHOLARSHIP

• See page 166

GARY WAGNER, K3OMI, SCHOLARSHIP
• See page 166

ASTRONAUT SCHOLARSHIP FOUNDATION

http://www.astronautscholarship.org/

ASTRONAUT SCHOLARSHIP FOUNDATION
• See page 104

BARRY M. GOLDWATER SCHOLARSHIP AND EXCELLENCE IN EDUCATION FOUNDATION

http://www.act.org/goldwater

BARRY M. GOLDWATER SCHOLARSHIP AND EXCELLENCE IN EDUCATION PROGRAM
• See page 104

BRASKEM·ODEBRECHT

http://www.odebrechtaward.com

ODEBRECHT AWARD FOR SUSTAINABLE DEVELOPMENT
• See page 110

CUBAN AMERICAN NATIONAL FOUNDATION

http://www.masscholarships.org/

MAS FAMILY SCHOLARSHIPS
• See page 152

THE DALLAS FOUNDATION

http://www.dallasfoundation.org/

WHITLEY PLACE SCHOLARSHIP
• See page 110

ELECTROCHEMICAL SOCIETY INC.

http://www.electrochem.org/

STUDENT RESEARCH AWARDS OF THE BATTERY DIVISION OF THE ELECTROCHEMICAL SOCIETY INC.
• See page 105

ENGINEERS' SOCIETY OF WESTERN PENNSYLVANIA

http://www.eswp.com/

JOSEPH A. LEVENDUSKY MEMORIAL SCHOLARSHIP
• See page 167

FOUNDATION FOR SCIENCE AND DISABILITY

http://stemd.org/

GRANTS FOR DISABLED STUDENTS IN THE SCIENCES
• See page 105

GLOBAL AUTOMOTIVE AFTERMARKET SYMPOSIUM

http://www.automotivescholarships.com/

GAAS SCHOLARSHIP
• See page 155

GREATER KANAWHA VALLEY FOUNDATION

http://www.tgkvf.org/

STEVEN ENGINEERING SCHOLARSHIP
• See page 167

GREAT MINDS IN STEM

http://www.greatmindsinstem.org

HISPANIC ENGINEER NATIONAL ACHIEVEMENT AWARDS CORPORATION SCHOLARSHIP PROGRAM
• See page 130

INDEPENDENT LABORATORIES INSTITUTE SCHOLARSHIP ALLIANCE

http://www.acil.org/

INDEPENDENT LABORATORIES INSTITUTE SCHOLARSHIP ALLIANCE
• See page 145

INSTITUTE OF INTERNATIONAL EDUCATION (FULBRIGHT PROGRAM)

http://www.us.fulbrightonline.org/

WHITAKER INTERNATIONAL PROGRAM
• See page 145

INTERNATIONAL SOCIETY FOR OPTICAL ENGINEERING-SPIE

http://www.spie.org/scholarships

SPIE EDUCATIONAL SCHOLARSHIPS IN OPTICAL SCIENCE AND ENGINEERING
• See page 105

INTERNATIONAL SOCIETY OF AUTOMATION (ISA)

http://www.isa.org/

INTERNATIONAL SOCIETY OF AUTOMATION EDUCATION FOUNDATION SCHOLARSHIPS
• See page 131

JORGE MAS CANOSA FREEDOM FOUNDATION

http://www.jorgemascanosa.org/

MAS FAMILY SCHOLARSHIP AWARD
• See page 156

KENTUCKY ENERGY AND ENVIRONMENT CABINET

http://www.eec.ky.gov/

ENVIRONMENTAL PROTECTION SCHOLARSHIP
• *See page 145*

LOS ANGELES COUNCIL OF BLACK PROFESSIONAL ENGINEERS

http://www.lablackengineers.org/

AL-BEN SCHOLARSHIP FOR ACADEMIC INCENTIVE
• *See page 168*

AL-BEN SCHOLARSHIP FOR PROFESSIONAL MERIT
• *See page 168*

AL-BEN SCHOLARSHIP FOR SCHOLASTIC ACHIEVEMENT
• *See page 168*

MAINE EDUCATION SERVICES

http://www.mesfoundation.com/

MAINE METAL PRODUCTS ASSOCIATION SCHOLARSHIP

Awards available for individuals demonstrating an outstanding record and overall potential to attend an institution of higher learning majoring in: mechanical engineering, machine tool technician, sheet metal fabrication, welding, CAD/CAM for metals industry. Restricted to the study of metal working trades. The award value and the number of awards granted varies annually.

Academic Fields/Career Goals: Mechanical Engineering; Trade/Technical Specialties.

Award: Scholarship for use in freshman, sophomore, junior, or senior years; not renewable.

Eligibility Requirements: Applicant must be enrolled or expecting to enroll full- or part-time at a two-year or four-year or technical institution or university; resident of Maine and studying in Maine. Available to U.S. citizens.

Application Requirements: Application form, community service, recommendations or references, transcript. *Deadline:* April 18.

Contact: Kim Benjamin, Vice President of Operations
   Phone: 207-791-3600

MANUFACTURERS ASSOCIATION OF MAINE

http://www.mainemfg.com/

MAINE METAL PRODUCTS EDUCATION FUND SCHOLARSHIP PROGRAM
• *See page 132*

MICHIGAN SOCIETY OF PROFESSIONAL ENGINEERS

http://www.michiganspe.org/

MICHIGAN SOCIETY OF PROFESSIONAL ENGINEERS HARRY R. BALL, P.E. GRANT
• *See page 169*

MICHIGAN SOCIETY OF PROFESSIONAL ENGINEERS KENNETH B. FISHBECK, P.E. MEMORIAL GRANT
• *See page 169*

NASA FLORIDA SPACE GRANT CONSORTIUM

http://www.floridaspacegrant.org/

FLORIDA SPACE RESEARCH PROGRAM
• *See page 132*

NASA IDAHO SPACE GRANT CONSORTIUM

http://www.id.spacegrant.org/

NASA IDAHO SPACE GRANT CONSORTIUM SCHOLARSHIP PROGRAM
• *See page 146*

NASA MONTANA SPACE GRANT CONSORTIUM

http://www.spacegrant.montana.edu/

MONTANA SPACE GRANT SCHOLARSHIP PROGRAM
• *See page 133*

NASA'S VIRGINIA SPACE GRANT CONSORTIUM

http://www.vsgc.odu.edu/

COMMUNITY COLLEGE STEM SCHOLARSHIPS
• *See page 105*

UNDERGRADUATE STEM RESEARCH SCHOLARSHIPS
• *See page 106*

NATIONAL ASSOCIATION OF WOMEN IN CONSTRUCTION

http://www.nawic.org/

NAWIC UNDERGRADUATE SCHOLARSHIPS
• *See page 112*

NATIONAL BOARD OF BOILER AND PRESSURE VESSEL INSPECTORS

http://www.nationalboard.org/

NATIONAL BOARD TECHNICAL SCHOLARSHIP
• *See page 169*

NATIONAL SOCIETY OF PROFESSIONAL ENGINEERS

http://www.nspe.org/

MAUREEN L. AND HOWARD N. BLITMAN, PE SCHOLARSHIP TO PROMOTE DIVERSITY IN ENGINEERING
• *See page 170*

PAUL H. ROBBINS HONORARY SCHOLARSHIP
• *See page 170*

PROFESSIONAL ENGINEERS IN INDUSTRY SCHOLARSHIP
• *See page 170*

NEVADA NASA SPACE GRANT CONSORTIUM

http://www.nvspacegrant.org/

NATIONAL SPACE GRANT COLLEGE AND FELLOWSHIP PROGRAM

OREGON STUDENT ASSISTANCE COMMISSION

http://www.GetCollegeFunds.org/

OREGON CAREER AND TECHNICAL EDUCATION SCHOLARSHIP

SOCIETY OF AMERICAN MILITARY ENGINEERS PORTLAND POST SCHOLARSHIP

PLUMBING-HEATING-COOLING CONTRACTORS EDUCATION FOUNDATION

http://www.phccfoundation.org/

DELTA FAUCET COMPANY SCHOLARSHIP PROGRAM

PHCC EDUCATIONAL FOUNDATION NEED-BASED SCHOLARSHIP

PHCC EDUCATIONAL FOUNDATION SCHOLARSHIP PROGRAM

PROFESSIONAL CONSTRUCTION ESTIMATORS ASSOCIATION

http://www.pcea.org/

TED G. WILSON MEMORIAL SCHOLARSHIP FOUNDATION

ROBERT H. MOLLOHAN FAMILY CHARITABLE FOUNDATION, INC.

http://www.mollohanfoundation.org/

HIGH TECHNOLOGY SCHOLARS PROGRAM

SIGMA XI, THE SCIENTIFIC RESEARCH SOCIETY

http://www.sigmaxi.org/

SIGMA XI GRANTS-IN-AID OF RESEARCH

SOCIETY OF AUTOMOTIVE ENGINEERS

http://www.sae.org/

BMW/SAE ENGINEERING SCHOLARSHIP

DETROIT SECTION SAE TECHNICAL SCHOLARSHIP

EDWARD D. HENDRICKSON/SAE ENGINEERING SCHOLARSHIP

RALPH K. HILLQUIST HONORARY SAE SCHOLARSHIP

TMC/SAE DONALD D. DAWSON TECHNICAL SCHOLARSHIP

YANMAR/SAE SCHOLARSHIP

SOCIETY OF MANUFACTURING ENGINEERS EDUCATION FOUNDATION

http://www.smeef.org/

CHAPTER 198-DOWNRIVER DETROIT SCHOLARSHIP

CHAPTER 4-LAWRENCE A. WACKER MEMORIAL SCHOLARSHIP

CHAPTER 67-PHOENIX SCHOLARSHIP

FORT WAYNE CHAPTER 56 SCHOLARSHIP

MYRTLE AND EARL WALKER SCHOLARSHIP FUND

NORTH CENTRAL REGION 9 SCHOLARSHIP

WICHITA CHAPTER 52 SCHOLARSHIP

WILLIAM E. WEISEL SCHOLARSHIP FUND

SOCIETY OF WOMEN ENGINEERS

http://www.swe.org/

ACCENTURE SCHOLARSHIP

ADA I. PRESSMAN MEMORIAL SCHOLARSHIP

ANNE MAUREEN WHITNEY BARROW MEMORIAL SCHOLARSHIP

BETTY LOU BAILEY SWE REGION F SCHOLARSHIP

BK KRENZER MEMORIAL REENTRY SCHOLARSHIP

BOSTON SCIENTIFIC SCHOLARSHIP

CAROL STEPHENS REGION F SCHOLARSHIP

CATERPILLAR INC. SCHOLARSHIP

CUMMINS INC. SCHOLARSHIP

DELL SCHOLARSHIP

DR. IVY M. PARKER MEMORIAL SCHOLARSHIP

DOROTHY LEMKE HOWARTH MEMORIAL SCHOLARSHIP

DOROTHY P. MORRIS SCHOLARSHIP

DUPONT COMPANY SCHOLARSHIP

EXELON CORPORATION SCHOLARSHIP

FORD MOTOR COMPANY SCHOLARSHIP

GENERAL ELECTRIC WOMEN'S NETWORK SCHOLARSHIP

HONEYWELL CORPORATION SCHOLARSHIP

ITW SCHOLARSHIP

JILL S. TIETJEN P.E. SCHOLARSHIP

KELLOGG SCHOLARSHIP

LIFE TECHNOLOGIES SCHOLARSHIP

LILLIAN MOLLER GILBRETH MEMORIAL SCHOLARSHIP

MARY V. MUNGER SCHOLARSHIP

MASWE MEMORIAL SCHOLARSHIP

MERIDITH THOMS MEMORIAL SCHOLARSHIPS

OLIVE LYNN SALEMBIER MEMORIAL REENTRY SCHOLARSHIP

PRAXAIR INC. SCHOLARSHIP

ROCKWELL COLLINS SCHOLARSHIP

SUSAN MISZKOWICZ MEMORIAL SCHOLARSHIP

SWE BALTIMORE-WASHINGTON SECTION SCHOLARSHIP

SWE CENTRAL NEW MEXICO PIONEERS SCHOLARSHIP

SWE CENTRAL NEW MEXICO REENTRY SCHOLARSHIP

SWE MID-HUDSON SECTION SCHOLARSHIP

SWE PAST PRESIDENTS SCHOLARSHIP

SWE PHOENIX SECTION SCHOLARSHIP

SWE REGION H SCHOLARSHIPS

VERIZON SCHOLARSHIP

WANDA MUNN SCHOLARSHIP

SOCIETY OF WOMEN ENGINEERS-ROCKY MOUNTAIN SECTION

http://www.societyofwomenengineers.org/RockyMountain/

SOCIETY OF WOMEN ENGINEERS-ROCKY MOUNTAIN SECTION SCHOLARSHIP PROGRAM

SONS OF NORWAY FOUNDATION

http://www.sonsofnorway.com/

NANCY LORRAINE JENSEN MEMORIAL SCHOLARSHIP

SPECIALTY EQUIPMENT MARKET ASSOCIATION

http://www.sema.org/

SPECIALTY EQUIPMENT MARKET ASSOCIATION MEMORIAL SCHOLARSHIP FUND

STRAIGHTFORWARD MEDIA

http://www.straightforwardmedia.com/

STRAIGHTFORWARD MEDIA ENGINEERING SCHOLARSHIP

TURNER CONSTRUCTION COMPANY

http://www.turnerconstruction.com/

YOUTHFORCE 2020 SCHOLARSHIP PROGRAM

UNITED NEGRO COLLEGE FUND

http://www.uncf.org/

ALFRED CHISHOLM/BASF MEMORIAL SCHOLARSHIP FUND
• *See page 81*

CDM SCHOLARSHIP/INTERNSHIP
• *See page 176*

EMERSON PROCESS MANAGEMENT SCHOLARSHIP
• *See page 177*

FORD/UNCF CORPORATE SCHOLARS PROGRAM
• *See page 82*

INTEL SCHOLARS PROGRAM
• *See page 177*

LOCKHEED MARTIN/UNCF SCHOLARSHIP
• *See page 82*

NASCAR/WENDELL SCOTT, SR. SCHOLARSHIP
• *See page 82*

PACIFIC GAS AND ELECTRIC COMPANY SCHOLARSHIP
• *See page 82*

UNIVERSITIES SPACE RESEARCH ASSOCIATION

http://www.usra.edu/

UNIVERSITIES SPACE RESEARCH ASSOCIATION SCHOLARSHIP PROGRAM
• *See page 107*

UTAH SOCIETY OF PROFESSIONAL ENGINEERS

http://www.uspeonline.com/

UTAH SOCIETY OF PROFESSIONAL ENGINEERS JOE RHOADS SCHOLARSHIP
• *See page 177*

WOMEN IN AVIATION, INTERNATIONAL

http://www.wai.org/

DELTA AIR LINES ENGINEERING SCHOLARSHIP
• *See page 140*

XEROX

http://www.xerox.com//

TECHNICAL MINORITY SCHOLARSHIP
• *See page 177*

METEOROLOGY/ ATMOSPHERIC SCIENCE

AMERICAN INDIAN SCIENCE AND ENGINEERING SOCIETY

http://www.aises.org/

A.T. ANDERSON MEMORIAL SCHOLARSHIP PROGRAM
• *See page 102*

BURLINGTON NORTHERN SANTA FE FOUNDATION SCHOLARSHIP
• *See page 102*

AMERICAN METEOROLOGICAL SOCIETY

http://www.ametsoc.org/

AMERICAN METEOROLOGICAL SOCIETY DR. PEDRO GRAU UNDERGRADUATE SCHOLARSHIP
• *See page 356*

AMERICAN METEOROLOGICAL SOCIETY HOWARD H. HANKS, JR. METEOROLOGICAL SCHOLARSHIP

Scholarship of $700 available for college or university student entering final year in undergraduate study. Applicant must be a major in a meteorology department or other department actively engaged in work on some aspect of the atmospheric sciences, and must intend to make atmospheric science his or her career. Must be enrolled full-time at a U.S. institution with a 3.25 minimum GPA. U.S. citizenship required.

Academic Fields/Career Goals: Meteorology/Atmospheric Science.

Award: Scholarship for use in senior year; not renewable. *Number:* 1. *Amount:* $700.

Eligibility Requirements: Applicant must be enrolled or expecting to enroll full-time at a four-year institution or university. Available to U.S. citizens.

Application Requirements: Application form, essay, recommendations or references, transcript. *Deadline:* varies.

Contact: Donna Fernandez, Development Program Coordinator
American Meteorological Society
45 Beacon Street
Boston, MA 02108-3693
Phone: 617-227-2426 Ext. 246
Fax: 617-742-8718
E-mail: dfernand@ametsoc.org

AMERICAN METEOROLOGICAL SOCIETY HOWARD T. ORVILLE METEOROLOGY SCHOLARSHIP

One-time award for full-time students entering their final year of undergraduate study. Must major in a meteorology department or other department actively engaged in work on some aspect of the atmospheric sciences, and must intend to make atmospheric science his or her career. Must be enrolled full-time at a U.S. institution with a minimum of 3.25 GPA. Must be U.S. citizen or permanent resident to apply.

Academic Fields/Career Goals: Meteorology/Atmospheric Science.

Award: Scholarship for use in senior year; not renewable. *Amount:* up to $5000.

Eligibility Requirements: Applicant must be enrolled or expecting to enroll full-time at a four-year institution or university. Applicant must have 3.5 GPA or higher. Available to U.S. citizens.

Application Requirements: Application form, essay, recommendations or references, transcript. *Deadline:* February 20.

Contact: Donna Fernandez, Development Program Coordinator
American Meteorological Society
45 Beacon Street
Boston, MA 02108-3693
Phone: 617-227-2426 Ext. 246
Fax: 617-742-8718
E-mail: dfernand@ametsoc.org

AMERICAN METEOROLOGICAL SOCIETY/INDUSTRY MINORITY SCHOLARSHIPS
• See page 356

AMERICAN METEOROLOGICAL SOCIETY MARK J. SCHROEDER SCHOLARSHIP IN METEOROLOGY
• See page 356

AMERICAN METEOROLOGICAL SOCIETY RICHARD AND HELEN HAGEMEYER SCHOLARSHIP
• See page 356

AMERICAN METEOROLOGICAL SOCIETY WERNER A. BAUM UNDERGRADUATE SCHOLARSHIP
• See page 356

AMS FRESHMAN UNDERGRADUATE SCHOLARSHIP
• See page 301

CARL W. KREITZBERG ENDOWED SCHOLARSHIP
• See page 356

ETHAN AND ALLAN MURPHY MEMORIAL SCHOLARSHIP
• See page 357

FATHER JAMES B. MACELWANE ANNUAL AWARDS
Available to enrolled undergraduates who submit a paper on a phase of atmospheric sciences with a statement from a supervisor on the student's original contribution to the work. Minimum 3.0 GPA required. No more than two students from any one institution may enter papers in one contest. Must submit letter from department head or faculty member confirming applicant's undergraduate status and paper's originality. Must be a U.S. citizen.

Academic Fields/Career Goals: Meteorology/Atmospheric Science.

Award: Prize for use in sophomore, junior, or senior years; not renewable. *Number:* 1. *Amount:* $1000.

Eligibility Requirements: Applicant must be enrolled or expecting to enroll full-time at a four-year institution or university. Applicant must have 3.0 GPA or higher. Available to U.S. citizens.

Application Requirements: Entry in a contest, original copy of paper, letter of application from the author, letter from the department head, abstract of no more than 250 words, recommendations or references. *Deadline:* June 14.

GEORGE S. BENTON SCHOLARSHIP
• See page 357

GUILLERMO SALAZAR RODRIGUES SCHOLARSHIP
• See page 357

JOHN R. HOPE SCHOLARSHIP
• See page 357

LOREN W. CROW SCHOLARSHIP
• See page 357

OM AND SARASWATI BAHETHI SCHOLARSHIP
Assists full-time students pursuing degrees in the atmospheric and related sciences. Minimum GPA of 3.25 required.

Academic Fields/Career Goals: Meteorology/Atmospheric Science.

Award: Scholarship for use in junior or senior years; not renewable. *Number:* 1. *Amount:* up to $2000.

Eligibility Requirements: Applicant must be enrolled or expecting to enroll full-time at a two-year or four-year institution or university. Available to U.S. citizens.

Application Requirements: Application form, essay, recommendations or references, transcript. *Deadline:* February 10.

Contact: Donna Fernandez, Development Program Coordinator
American Meteorological Society
45 Beacon Street
Boston, MA 02108-3693
Phone: 617-227-2426 Ext. 246
Fax: 617-742-8718
E-mail: dfernand@ametsoc.org

ASTRONAUT SCHOLARSHIP FOUNDATION
http://www.astronautscholarship.org/

ASTRONAUT SCHOLARSHIP FOUNDATION
• See page 104

BRITISH COLUMBIA INNOVATION COUNCIL
http://www.bcic.ca/

PAUL AND HELEN TRUSSELL SCIENCE AND TECHNOLOGY SCHOLARSHIP
• See page 104

NASA RHODE ISLAND SPACE GRANT CONSORTIUM
http://brown/initiatives/ri-space-grant

NASA RHODE ISLAND SPACE GRANT CONSORTIUM UNDERGRADUATE RESEARCH SCHOLARSHIP
• See page 133

NASA WEST VIRGINIA SPACE GRANT CONSORTIUM
http://www.nasa.wvu.edu/

WEST VIRGINIA SPACE GRANT CONSORTIUM UNDERGRADUATE FELLOWSHIP PROGRAM
• See page 134

SIGMA XI, THE SCIENTIFIC RESEARCH SOCIETY
http://www.sigmaxi.org/

SIGMA XI GRANTS-IN-AID OF RESEARCH
• See page 95

SOCIETY OF SATELLITE PROFESSIONALS INTERNATIONAL
http://www.sspi.org/

SSPI INTERNATIONAL SCHOLARSHIPS
• See page 138

TKE EDUCATIONAL FOUNDATION
http://www.tke.org/

CARROL C. HALL MEMORIAL SCHOLARSHIP
• See page 107

VERMONT SPACE GRANT CONSORTIUM

http://www.cems.uvm.edu/vsgc

VERMONT SPACE GRANT CONSORTIUM SCHOLARSHIP PROGRAM
• *See page 107*

MILITARY AND DEFENSE STUDIES

ASSOCIATION OF FORMER INTELLIGENCE OFFICERS

http://www.afio.com/13_scholarships.htm

CIA UNDERGRADUATE SCHOLARSHIPS
• *See page 97*

NATIONAL MILITARY INTELLIGENCE FOUNDATION

http://www.nmia.org/

NATIONAL MILITARY INTELLIGENCE ASSOCIATION SCHOLARSHIP
Scholarships to support the growth of professional studies in the field of military intelligence and to recognize and reward excellence in the development and transfer of knowledge about military and associated intelligence disciplines.

Academic Fields/Career Goals: Military and Defense Studies.

Award: Scholarship for use in freshman, sophomore, junior, or senior years; not renewable. *Number:* 3. *Amount:* $1000.

Eligibility Requirements: Applicant must be enrolled or expecting to enroll full-time at a four-year institution or university. Applicant or parent of applicant must be member of National Military Intelligence Association. Applicant must have 3.0 GPA or higher. Available to U.S. citizens.

Application Requirements: Application form, test scores. *Deadline:* August 1.

Contact: Dr. Forrest Frank, Secretary-Treasurer
National Military Intelligence Foundation
PO Box 6844
Arlington, VA 22311
Phone: 703-578-2841
E-mail: ffrank54@comcast.net

SOCIETY OF SATELLITE PROFESSIONALS INTERNATIONAL

http://www.sspi.org/

SSPI INTERNATIONAL SCHOLARSHIPS
• *See page 138*

WOMEN IN DEFENSE (WID), A NATIONAL SECURITY ORGANIZATION

http://wid.ndia.org

HORIZONS SCHOLARSHIP
Scholarships awarded to provide financial assistance to further educational objectives of women either currently employed in, or planning careers in, defense or national security arenas (not law enforcement or criminal justice). Must be U.S. citizen. Minimum 3.5 GPA required.

Academic Fields/Career Goals: Military and Defense Studies.

Award: Scholarship for use in junior, senior, graduate, or postgraduate years; renewable. *Number:* 5–6. *Amount:* $500–$10,000.

Eligibility Requirements: Applicant must be enrolled or expecting to enroll full- or part-time at a four-year institution or university and female. Applicant must have 3.5 GPA or higher. Available to U.S. citizens.

Application Requirements: Application form, essay, financial need analysis, proof of citizenship, recommendations or references, transcript. *Deadline:* July 1.

MUSEUM STUDIES

AMERICAN SCHOOL OF CLASSICAL STUDIES AT ATHENS

http://www.ascsa.edu.gr/

ASCSA SUMMER SESSIONS SCHOLARSHIPS
• *See page 100*

COSTUME SOCIETY OF AMERICA

http://www.costumesocietyamerica.com/

ADELE FILENE TRAVEL AWARD
• *See page 114*

STELLA BLUM RESEARCH GRANT
• *See page 114*

MUSIC

AMERICAN COLLEGE OF MUSICIANS/ NATIONAL GUILD OF PIANO TEACHERS

http://www.pianoguild.com/

AMERICAN COLLEGE OF MUSICIANS/NATIONAL GUILD OF PIANO TEACHERS $200 SCHOLARSHIPS
Award available only to student affiliate members who have participated in National Guild of Piano Teachers auditions over a ten-year period. Must be Paderewski Medal winner and be sponsored by Guild member. Contact American College of Musicians for more information.

Academic Fields/Career Goals: Music.

Award: Scholarship for use in freshman, sophomore, junior, or senior years; not renewable. *Number:* up to 150. *Amount:* $200.

Eligibility Requirements: Applicant must be enrolled or expecting to enroll full-time at a two-year or four-year or technical institution or university and must have an interest in music. Applicant or parent of applicant must be member of American College of Musicians. Available to U.S. and non-U.S. citizens.

Application Requirements: Application form, test scores. *Deadline:* September 15.

AMERICAN COUNCIL FOR POLISH CULTURE

http://www.polishcultureacpc.org/

MARCELLA KOCHANSKA SEMBRICH VOCAL COMPETITION
Prize of $1500 given to high school graduates, male or female up to the age of 35 years who have pursued or are currently pursuing higher education study in voice or in the early stage of their vocal career. Contestant must be a U.S. citizen of Polish descent.

Academic Fields/Career Goals: Music.

Award: Prize for use in freshman, sophomore, junior, senior, graduate, or postgraduate years; not renewable. *Number:* 1. *Amount:* $1500.

Eligibility Requirements: Applicant must be of Polish heritage; enrolled or expecting to enroll full- or part-time at a two-year or four-year institution or university and must have an interest in music/singing. Available to U.S. citizens.

Application Requirements: 3 copies of a cassette or CD containing applicant's operatic vocal performance, application form, entry in a contest, recommendations or references. *Deadline:* April 1.

Contact: Mrs. Alicia Dutka, ACPC Music Committee Chair
American Council for Polish Culture
1991 Selkirk Court
Inverness, IL 60010
Phone: 847-382-6339
Fax: 847-382-6338
E-mail: aldutka@comcast.net

AMERICAN FOUNDATION FOR THE BLIND

http://www.afb.org/

GLADYS C. ANDERSON MEMORIAL SCHOLARSHIP

Non-renewable award available to a legally-blind female undergraduate or graduate student studying religious or classical music. Must submit a letter from a post-secondary institution as proof of enrollment in a program in music. For online application and more information, visit website http://www.afb.org.

Academic Fields/Career Goals: Music.

Award: Scholarship for use in freshman, sophomore, junior, or senior years; not renewable. *Number:* 1. *Amount:* $1000.

Eligibility Requirements: Applicant must be visually impaired; enrolled or expecting to enroll full-time at a four-year institution or university and female. Applicant must be visually impaired. Available to U.S. citizens.

Application Requirements: Application form, essay, proof of enrollment letter from post secondary institution, proof of blindness letter from agency or medical doctor, recommendations or references, transcript. *Deadline:* April 30.

Contact: Dawn Bodrogi, Information Center and Library Coordinator
Phone: 212-502-7661
E-mail: dbodrogi@afb.net

R.L. GILLETTE SCHOLARSHIP
• See page 385

AMERICAN LEGION DEPARTMENT OF KANSAS

http://www.ksamlegion.org/

MUSIC COMMITTEE SCHOLARSHIP

One-time award open to a high school senior or college freshman or sophomore. Must be a Kansas resident. Must have distinguished background in the field of music at an approved Kansas junior college, college or university. Award of $1000, with the disbursement as $500 award for each of the two semesters.

Academic Fields/Career Goals: Music; Performing Arts.

Award: Scholarship for use in freshman or sophomore years; not renewable. *Number:* 1. *Amount:* $1000.

Eligibility Requirements: Applicant must be enrolled or expecting to enroll full-time at a two-year or four-year or technical institution or university; resident of Kansas; studying in Kansas and must have an interest in music/singing. Available to U.S. citizens.

Application Requirements: Application form, financial need analysis, latest 1040 income statement of supporting parents, personal photograph, recommendations or references, transcript. *Deadline:* February 15.

Contact: Jim Gravenstein, Chairman, Scholarship Committee
American Legion Department of Kansas
1314 Topeka Boulevard, SW
Topeka, KS 66612
Phone: 785-232-9315
Fax: 782-232-1399

BMI FOUNDATION INC.

http://www.bmifoundation.org/

BMI STUDENT COMPOSER AWARDS
• See page 117

JOHN LENNON SCHOLARSHIP PROGRAM

Scholarships available to songwriters and composers from music schools, universities, and youth orchestras. Also submissions from the Music Educators National Conference are solicited. The submitted work must be an original song with lyrics accompanied by whatever instrumentation is chosen by the applicant.

Academic Fields/Career Goals: Music.

Award: Scholarship for use in freshman, sophomore, junior, senior, graduate, or postgraduate years; not renewable. *Number:* up to 3. *Amount:* $5000–$10,000.

Eligibility Requirements: Applicant must be age 15-24; enrolled or expecting to enroll full- or part-time at a two-year or four-year or technical institution or university and must have an interest in music. Available to U.S. citizens.

Application Requirements: Application form, CD or audio tape of a song written by the applicant with original words and music, three typed copies of the lyric, entry in a contest. *Deadline:* January 26.

Contact: Mr. Ralph Jackson, President
BMI Foundation Inc.
320 West 57th Street
New York, NY 10019
Phone: 212-586-2000
Fax: 212-245-8986
E-mail: info@bmifoundation.org

PEERMUSIC LATIN SCHOLARSHIP

Award for the best song or instrumental work in any Latin genre. The competition is open to songwriters and composers between the ages of 16 and 24 who are current students at colleges and universities. Must submit an original work. Applicants must not have had any musical work commercially recorded or distributed.

Academic Fields/Career Goals: Music.

Award: Scholarship for use in freshman, sophomore, junior, senior, graduate, or postgraduate years; not renewable. *Number:* 1. *Amount:* up to $5000.

Eligibility Requirements: Applicant must be age 16-24; enrolled or expecting to enroll full-time at a two-year or four-year or technical institution or university and must have an interest in music. Available to U.S. citizens.

Application Requirements: Application form, CD of original song or instrumental work, three typed lyric sheets, entry in a contest. *Deadline:* varies.

Contact: Mr. Ralph Jackson, President
BMI Foundation Inc.
320 West 57th Street
New York, NY 10019
Phone: 212-586-2000
Fax: 212-245-8986
E-mail: rjackson@bmi.com

BNY MELLON, N.A.

http://www.bnymellon.com/

SUSAN GLOVER HITCHCOCK SCHOLARSHIP

Award for women who are majoring in music. Must be a Massachusetts resident. Eligible applicant must be recommended by educational institution. Not for graduate study programs.

Academic Fields/Career Goals: Music.

Award: Scholarship for use in freshman, sophomore, junior, or senior years; not renewable. *Amount:* up to $2000.

Eligibility Requirements: Applicant must be enrolled or expecting to enroll full-time at a two-year or four-year or technical institution or university; female and resident of Massachusetts. Available to U.S. citizens.

Application Requirements: Application form, essay, transcript. *Deadline:* April 15.

Contact: June Kfoury McNeil, Vice President
BNY Mellon, N.A.
201 Washington Street, 024-0092
Boston, MA 02108
Phone: 617-722-3891

THE CHOPIN FOUNDATION OF THE UNITED STATES

http://www.chopin.org/

SCHOLARSHIP PROGRAM FOR YOUNG AMERICAN PIANISTS

Program aimed to help young American pianists to continue their piano education. Award(s) are available to students between ages 14 and 17 whose field of study is music and whose major is piano. Renewable for up to four years. Students will be assisted in preparing to qualify for the National Chopin Piano Competition. Must be U.S. citizen or legal resident. For more information, see website http://www.chopin.org.

Academic Fields/Career Goals: Music; Performing Arts.

Award: Scholarship for use in freshman, sophomore, junior, or senior years; renewable. *Number:* 1–10. *Amount:* $1000.

Eligibility Requirements: Applicant must be age 14-17; enrolled or expecting to enroll full- or part-time at a four-year institution or university and must have an interest in music. Available to U.S. citizens.

Application Requirements: Application form, entry in a contest, recommendations or references, unedited video recording of applicant playing specific required pieces. *Fee:* $25. *Deadline:* April 15.

Contact: Jadwiga Gewert, Executive Director
The Chopin Foundation of the United States
1440 79th Street Causeway, Suite 117
Miami, FL 33141
Phone: 305-868-0624
Fax: 305-865-5150
E-mail: info@chopin.org

COLLEGEBOUND FOUNDATION

http://www.collegeboundfoundation.org/

JANET B. SONDHEIM SCHOLARSHIP
• *See page 117*

THE COMMUNITY FOUNDATION FOR GREATER ATLANTA, INC.

http://cfgreateratlanta.org/

JAMES M. AND VIRGINIA M. SMYTH SCHOLARSHIP
• *See page 118*

DAVIDSON INSTITUTE FOR TALENT DEVELOPMENT

http://www.davidsongifted.org/

DAVIDSON FELLOWS SCHOLARSHIP PROGRAM
• *See page 386*

DELTA OMICRON FOUNDATION

http://www.delta-omicron.org/

DELTA OMICRON FOUNDATION EDUCATIONAL GRANTS IN MUSIC

Grants available to those studying music at a four-year college or university. Must have a minimum 2.5 GPA. Must be a member of Delta Omicron International Music Fraternity. For more information, visit website http://www.dofoundation.org.

Academic Fields/Career Goals: Music.

Award: Grant for use in freshman, sophomore, junior, or senior years; not renewable. *Number:* 10–20. *Amount:* $500.

Eligibility Requirements: Applicant must be enrolled or expecting to enroll full- or part-time at a four-year institution or university and must have an interest in music. Applicant must have 3.5 GPA or higher. Available to U.S. and non-U.S. citizens.

Application Requirements: Application form, recommendations or references, resume. *Deadline:* April 30.

Contact: Kay Wideman, President
Delta Omicron Foundation
503 Greystone Lane
Douglasville, GA 30134
Phone: 770-920-2417
Fax: 770-577-5863
E-mail: widemans@bellsouth.net

DELTA OMICRON SUMMER SCHOLARSHIPS

Scholarships awarded to assist with summer study in the area of music for summer workshops, seminars and study abroad. Award cannot be used for college tuition. Recipients must be members of Delta Omicron International Music Fraternity.

Academic Fields/Career Goals: Music.

Award: Scholarship for use in freshman, sophomore, junior, or senior years; not renewable. *Number:* 8. *Amount:* $400–$500.

Eligibility Requirements: Applicant must be enrolled or expecting to enroll part-time at a four-year institution or university and must have an interest in music. Available to U.S. and non-U.S. citizens.

Application Requirements: Application form. *Deadline:* April 2.

Contact: Ms. Michelle May, Chair, Summer Scholarships
Delta Omicron Foundation
1635 West Boston Boulevard
Detroit, MI 48206
Phone: 313-865-1149
E-mail: maybiz@aol.com

DOMENIC TROIANO GUITAR SCHOLARSHIP

http://www.domenictroiano.com/

DOMENIC TROIANO GUITAR SCHOLARSHIP

Scholarship of $3000 is presented annually to a Canadian guitarist who will be pursuing postsecondary guitar education in Canada or elsewhere. Any university, college or private institution guitar program will be funded. Funds will be forwarded directly to the chosen institution of the winner. Must submit a one-page letter outlining background and reasons why applicant should be considered for the scholarship.

Academic Fields/Career Goals: Music.

Award: Scholarship for use in freshman, sophomore, junior, or senior years; not renewable. *Number:* up to 2. *Amount:* $3000.

Eligibility Requirements: Applicant must be Canadian citizen; enrolled or expecting to enroll full-time at a four-year institution or university and must have an interest in music.

Application Requirements: Recommendations or references, two-song demo of the applicant playing guitar. *Deadline:* October 31.

Contact: Clinton Somerton, Administrator
Domenic Troiano Guitar Scholarship
18 Sherbourne Street
Toronto, ON M5A 2R2
CAN
Phone: 416-367-0178
Fax: 416-367-0178
E-mail: clinton@domenictroiano.com

GENERAL FEDERATION OF WOMEN'S CLUBS OF MASSACHUSETTS

http://www.gfwcma.org/

DORCHESTER WOMEN'S CLUB MUSIC SCHOLARSHIP

Scholarship for undergraduate major in voice. Applicant must be a Massachusetts resident and an undergraduate currently enrolled in a four-year accredited college, university or school of music, majoring in voice.

Academic Fields/Career Goals: Music; Performing Arts.

Award: Scholarship for use in freshman, sophomore, junior, or senior years; not renewable. *Number:* 1. *Amount:* $500.

Eligibility Requirements: Applicant must be enrolled or expecting to enroll full-time at a four-year institution or university; resident of Massachusetts and must have an interest in music/singing. Available to U.S. and Canadian citizens.

Application Requirements: Application form, driver's license, entry in a contest, interview, recommendations or references, self-addressed stamped envelope with application, transcript. *Deadline:* March 1.

Contact: Joan Korslund, Music Chairman
General Federation of Women's Clubs of Massachusetts
25 Apple Lane
Wrentham, MA 02093
E-mail: nonnalda@aol.com

GENERAL FEDERATION OF WOMEN'S CLUBS OF MASSACHUSETTS NICKEL FOR NOTES MUSIC SCHOLARSHIP

Scholarship for high school seniors majoring in piano, instrument, music education, music therapy or voice. Applicant must be a senior in a Massachusetts high school.

Academic Fields/Career Goals: Music; Performing Arts.

Award: Scholarship for use in freshman year; not renewable. *Amount:* up to $800.

Eligibility Requirements: Applicant must be high school student; planning to enroll or expecting to enroll full-time at a four-year institution or university; resident of Massachusetts and must have an interest in music/singing. Available to U.S. citizens.

Application Requirements: Application form, essay, interview, recommendations or references, self-addressed stamped envelope with application, transcript. *Deadline:* March 1.

Contact: Joan Korslund, Music Chairman
General Federation of Women's Clubs of Massachusetts
25 Apple Lane
Wrentham, MA 02093
E-mail: nonnalda@aol.com

GLENN MILLER BIRTHPLACE SOCIETY

http://www.glennmiller.org/

GMBS-3RD PLACE INSTRUMENTAL SCHOLARSHIP

One scholarship for a male or female instrumentalist will be awarded as a competition prize to be used for any education-related expenses. Must submit 10-minute, high-quality audio tape of pieces selected for competition or those of similar style. Applicant is responsible for travel to and lodging during the competition. One-time award for high school seniors and college freshmen.

Academic Fields/Career Goals: Music.

Award: Scholarship for use in freshman year; not renewable. *Number:* 1. *Amount:* up to $1000.

Eligibility Requirements: Applicant must be enrolled or expecting to enroll full-time at a four-year institution or university. Available to U.S. and non-U.S. citizens.

Application Requirements: Application form, essay, performance tape or CD. *Deadline:* March 10.

Contact: Arlene Leonard, Secretary
Glenn Miller Birthplace Society
PO Box 61
Clarinda, IA 51632
Phone: 712-542-2461
Fax: 712-542-2461
E-mail: gmbs@heartland.net

GMBS-BILL BAKER/HANS STARREVELD SCHOLARSHIP

One scholarship for a male or female instrumentalist will be awarded as a competition prize to be used for any education-related expenses. Must submit 10-minute, high-quality audio tape of pieces selected for competition or those of similar style. Applicant is responsible for travel to and lodging during the competition. One-time award for high school seniors and college freshmen.

Academic Fields/Career Goals: Music.

Award: Scholarship for use in freshman year; not renewable. *Number:* 1. *Amount:* up to $2000.

Eligibility Requirements: Applicant must be enrolled or expecting to enroll full-time at a four-year institution or university. Available to U.S. and non-U.S. citizens.

Application Requirements: Application form, essay, performance tape or CD. *Deadline:* March 10.

Contact: Arlene Leonard, Secretary
Glenn Miller Birthplace Society
PO Box 61
Clarinda, IA 51632
Phone: 712-542-2461
Fax: 712-542-2461
E-mail: gmbs@heartland.net

GMBS-RAY EBERLE VOCAL SCHOLARSHIP

One scholarship for a male or female vocalist will be awarded as a competition prize to be used for any education-related expenses. Must submit 10-minute, high-quality audio tape of pieces selected for competition or those of similar style. Applicant is responsible for travel to and lodging during the competition. One-time award for high school seniors and college freshmen.

Academic Fields/Career Goals: Music.

Award: Scholarship for use in freshman year; not renewable. *Number:* 1. *Amount:* up to $4000.

Eligibility Requirements: Applicant must be enrolled or expecting to enroll full-time at a four-year institution. Available to U.S. and non-U.S. citizens.

Application Requirements: Application form, essay, performance tape or CD. *Deadline:* March 10.

Contact: Arlene Leonard, Secretary
Glenn Miller Birthplace Society
PO Box 61
Clarinda, IA 51632
Phone: 712-542-2461
Fax: 712-542-2461
E-mail: gmbs@heartland.net

GRAND RAPIDS COMMUNITY FOUNDATION

http://www.grfoundation.org/

LLEWELLYN L. CAYVAN STRING INSTRUMENT SCHOLARSHIP

Scholarship for undergraduate students studying the violin, the viola, the violoncello, and/or the bass viol. High school students not considered. To apply, submit required application form, transcript, essay, reference.

Academic Fields/Career Goals: Music.

Award: Scholarship for use in freshman, sophomore, junior, or senior years; not renewable. *Number:* 6. *Amount:* $1000.

Eligibility Requirements: Applicant must be enrolled or expecting to enroll full-time at a four-year institution or university and must have an interest in music. Available to U.S. citizens.

Application Requirements: Application form, recommendations or references, transcript. *Deadline:* April 1.

Contact: Ruth Bishop, Education Program Officer
Phone: 616-454-1751 Ext. 103
Fax: 616-454-6455
E-mail: rbishop@grfoundation.org

GREATER KANAWHA VALLEY FOUNDATION

http://www.tgkvf.org/

HERB SMITH/EUNICE FLEMING SCHOLARSHIP

Renewable award for a West Virginia resident pursuing full-time postsecondary studies in music, theater, musical theatre, and/or dance. Preference given to Fayette, Kanawha or Wood County residents. Minimum 3.5 GPA required.

Academic Fields/Career Goals: Music; Performing Arts.

Award: Scholarship for use in freshman, sophomore, junior, or senior years; renewable. *Amount:* $1000.

Eligibility Requirements: Applicant must be enrolled or expecting to enroll full-time at a four-year institution or university and resident of West Virginia. Applicant must have 3.5 GPA or higher. Available to U.S. citizens.

Application Requirements: Application form, financial need analysis, recommendations or references, test scores, transcript. *Deadline:* January 15.

Contact: Susan Hoover, Scholarship Program Officer
Greater Kanawha Valley Foundation
900 Lee Street East, 16th Floor
Charleston, WV 25301
Phone: 304-346-3620
E-mail: tgkvf@tgkvf.org

HAPCO MUSIC FOUNDATION INC.

http://www.hapcopromo.org/

TRADITIONAL MARCHING BAND EXTRAVAGANZA SCHOLARSHIP AWARD

Scholarship is offered to deserving students who will continue their participation in any college music program. Minimum 3.0 GPA required. Applicant should have best composite score of 970 SAT or 20 ACT.

Academic Fields/Career Goals: Music.

Award: Scholarship for use in freshman year; not renewable. *Amount:* $250–$1000.

Eligibility Requirements: Applicant must be enrolled or expecting to enroll full-time at a two-year or four-year institution or university and must have an interest in music. Applicant must have 3.0 GPA or higher. Available to U.S. citizens.

Application Requirements: Application form, essay, personal photograph, recommendations or references, test scores, transcript. *Deadline:* varies.

Contact: Joseph McMullen, President
Phone: 407-877-2262
Fax: 407-654-0308
E-mail: hapcopromo@aol.com

HARTFORD JAZZ SOCIETY INC.

http://www.hartfordjazzsociety.com/

HARTFORD JAZZ SOCIETY SCHOLARSHIPS

Scholarship of up to $3000 is awarded to graduating high school senior attending a four-year college or university. Must be a Connecticut resident. Music major with interest in jazz required.

Academic Fields/Career Goals: Music.

Award: Scholarship for use in freshman year; not renewable. *Number:* 2–3. *Amount:* up to $3000.

Eligibility Requirements: Applicant must be high school student; planning to enroll or expecting to enroll full- or part-time at a four-year institution or university; resident of Connecticut and must have an interest in music. Available to U.S. and Canadian citizens.

Application Requirements: Application form, cassette tape or CD, recommendations or references. *Deadline:* May 1.

HOUSTON SYMPHONY

http://www.houstonsymphony.org/

HOUSTON SYMPHONY IMA HOGG COMPETITION

Competition for musicians ages 16 to 29 who play standard instruments of the symphony orchestra. Goal is to offer a review by panel of music professionals and further career of an advanced student or a professional musician. Participants must be U.S. citizens or studying in the United States. Application fee is $30.

Academic Fields/Career Goals: Music.

Award: Prize for use in freshman, sophomore, junior, senior, graduate, or postgraduate years; not renewable. *Number:* 5. *Amount:* $300–$5000.

Eligibility Requirements: Applicant must be age 16-29; enrolled or expecting to enroll full- or part-time at a two-year or four-year or

technical institution or university and must have an interest in music. Available to U.S. and non-U.S. citizens.

Application Requirements: Application form, CD with required repertoire, entry in a contest. *Fee:* $30. *Deadline:* February 13.

Contact: Carol Wilson, Manager, Music Matters!
Houston Symphony
615 Louisiana Street, Suite 102
Houston, TX 77002
Phone: 713-238-1447
Fax: 713-224-0453
E-mail: e&o@houstonsymphony.org

HOUSTON SYMPHONY LEAGUE CONCERTO COMPETITION

Competition is open to student musicians 18 years of age or younger who have not yet graduated from high school and who play any standard orchestral instrument or piano. Must live within a 200-mile radius of Houston and submit a screening CD of one movement of their concerto.

Academic Fields/Career Goals: Music.

Award: Prize for use in freshman year; not renewable. *Number:* up to 3. *Amount:* $250–$1000.

Eligibility Requirements: Applicant must be high school student; planning to enroll or expecting to enroll full-time at a two-year or four-year institution; resident of Texas and must have an interest in music. Available to U.S. citizens.

Application Requirements: Application form, CD, entry in a contest. *Fee:* $25. *Deadline:* November 18.

Contact: Carol Wilson, Manager, Music Matters!
Houston Symphony
615 Louisiana Street, Suite 102
Houston, TX 77002
Phone: 713-238-1449
Fax: 713-224-0453
E-mail: e&o@houstonsymphony.org

JACK J. ISGUR FOUNDATION

http://www.isgur.org

JACK J. ISGUR FOUNDATION SCHOLARSHIP
• See page 119

KE ALI'I PAUAHI FOUNDATION

http://www.pauahi.org/

EDWIN MAHIAI COPP BEAMER SCHOLARSHIP

Award supports a post-secondary student pursuing a career in music, specifically piano and/or voice, with emphasis on Hawaiian music, opera or musical theatre. Must demonstrate a serious commitment to music training, a career in music and dedication to artistic excellence, and demonstrate financial need. Submit two letter of recommendations from teachers (piano, voice), counselor or music professionals. One-page essay describing the applicant's music background/education to-date, including any awards or special recognitions. Finalist may be asked to conduct an informal musical performance or provide a video of their performance.

Academic Fields/Career Goals: Music; Performing Arts.

Award: Scholarship for use in freshman, sophomore, junior, senior, graduate, or postgraduate years; not renewable. *Number:* up to 1. *Amount:* up to $1000.

Eligibility Requirements: Applicant must be enrolled or expecting to enroll full-time at a two-year or four-year or technical institution or university and must have an interest in Hawaiian language/culture, music, or music/singing. Available to U.S. citizens.

Application Requirements: Application form, application form may be submitted online (http://www.pauahi.org/scholarships), college acceptance letter, copy of completed SAR, essay, financial need analysis, recommendations or references, transcript. *Deadline:* April 1.

Contact: Mavis Shiraishi-Nagao, Scholarship Administrator
Phone: 808-534-3966
E-mail: scholarships@pauahi.org

KOSCIUSZKO FOUNDATION

http://www.thekf.org

KOSCIUSZKO FOUNDATION CHOPIN PIANO COMPETITION

Three awards for students majoring or planning to major in piano studies, who are between the ages of 16 and 22. Application fee: $50. Must be U.S. citizen or full-time international student in the United States with valid visa.

Academic Fields/Career Goals: Music; Performing Arts.

Award: Prize for use in freshman, sophomore, junior, or senior years; not renewable. *Number:* 3. *Amount:* $1500–$5000.

Eligibility Requirements: Applicant must be age 16-22; enrolled or expecting to enroll full- or part-time at a four-year institution or university and must have an interest in music/singing. Available to U.S. and non-U.S. citizens.

Application Requirements: Application form, entry in a contest, personal photograph, proof of age, recommendations or references, resume. *Fee:* $50. *Deadline:* March 7.

Contact: Tom Pniewski, Director of Cultural Programs
Kosciuszko Foundation
15 East 65th Street
New York, NY 10021-6595
Phone: 212-734-2130
Fax: 212-628-4552
E-mail: tompkf@aol.com

NATIONAL ASSOCIATION OF PASTORAL MUSICIANS

http://www.npm.org/

DAN SCHUTTE SCHOLARSHIP

Scholarship for NPM members enrolled full-or part-time in an undergraduate or graduate pastoral music program. Applicant must intend to work at least two years in the field of pastoral music following graduation/program completion.

Academic Fields/Career Goals: Music.

Award: Scholarship for use in freshman, sophomore, junior, senior, or graduate years; not renewable. *Number:* 1. *Amount:* $1000.

Eligibility Requirements: Applicant must be enrolled or expecting to enroll full- or part-time at a two-year or four-year institution or university and must have an interest in music/singing. Applicant or parent of applicant must be member of National Association of Pastoral Musicians. Available to U.S. and non-U.S. citizens.

Application Requirements: Application form, CD of performance, essay, financial need analysis, recommendations or references, resume. *Deadline:* March 5.

Contact: Kathleen Haley, Director of Membership Services
Phone: 240-247-3000
E-mail: haley@npm.org

ELAINE RENDLER-RENE DOSOGNE-GEORGETOWN CHORALE SCHOLARSHIP

Awards NPM members enrolled full-time or part-time in a graduate or undergraduate degree program of studies related to the field of pastoral music. Applicant must intend to work at least two years in the field of pastoral music following graduation or program completion.

Academic Fields/Career Goals: Music; Religion/Theology.

Award: Scholarship for use in freshman, sophomore, junior, senior, or graduate years; not renewable. *Number:* 1. *Amount:* $1000.

Eligibility Requirements: Applicant must be enrolled or expecting to enroll full- or part-time at a two-year or four-year institution or university and must have an interest in music/singing. Applicant or parent of applicant must be member of National Association of Pastoral Musicians. Available to U.S. and non-U.S. citizens.

Application Requirements: Application form, CD of performance, essay, financial need analysis, recommendations or references, resume. *Deadline:* March 5.

Contact: Kathleen Haley, Director of Membership Services
Phone: 240-247-3000
E-mail: haley@npm.org

FUNK FAMILY MEMORIAL SCHOLARSHIP

Awards NPM members enrolled full-time or part-time in a graduate or undergraduate degree program of studies related to the field of pastoral music. Applicant must intend to work at least two years in the field of pastoral music following graduation or program completion.

Academic Fields/Career Goals: Music; Religion/Theology.

Award: Scholarship for use in freshman, sophomore, junior, senior, or graduate years; not renewable. *Number:* 1. *Amount:* $1000.

Eligibility Requirements: Applicant must be enrolled or expecting to enroll full- or part-time at a two-year or four-year or technical institution or university and must have an interest in music/singing. Applicant or parent of applicant must be member of National Association of Pastoral Musicians. Available to U.S. and non-U.S. citizens.

Application Requirements: Application form, CD of performance, essay, financial need analysis, recommendations or references, resume. *Deadline:* March 5.

Contact: Kathleen Haley, Director of Membership Services
Phone: 240-247-3000
E-mail: haley@npm.org

GIA PUBLICATION PASTORAL MUSICIAN SCHOLARSHIP

Awards NPM members enrolled full-time or part-time in a graduate or undergraduate degree program of studies related to the field of pastoral music. Applicant must intend to work at least two years in the field of pastoral music following graduation or program completion.

Academic Fields/Career Goals: Music; Religion/Theology.

Award: Scholarship for use in freshman, sophomore, junior, senior, or graduate years; not renewable. *Number:* 1. *Amount:* $2000.

Eligibility Requirements: Applicant must be enrolled or expecting to enroll full- or part-time at a two-year or four-year institution or university and must have an interest in music/singing. Applicant or parent of applicant must be member of National Association of Pastoral Musicians. Available to U.S. and non-U.S. citizens.

Application Requirements: Application form, CD of performance, essay, financial need analysis, recommendations or references, resume. *Deadline:* March 5.

Contact: Kathleen Haley, Director of Membership Services
Phone: 240-247-3000
E-mail: haley@npm.org

MUSONICS SCHOLARSHIP

Awards NPM members enrolled full-time or part-time in a graduate or undergraduate degree program of studies related to the field of pastoral music. Applicant must intend to work at least two years in the field of pastoral music following graduation or program completion. One award available for graduate study and one award available for undergraduate study.

Academic Fields/Career Goals: Music; Religion/Theology.

Award: Scholarship for use in freshman, sophomore, junior, senior, or graduate years; not renewable. *Number:* 2. *Amount:* $2000.

Eligibility Requirements: Applicant must be enrolled or expecting to enroll full- or part-time at a two-year or four-year institution or university and must have an interest in music/singing. Applicant or parent of applicant must be member of National Association of Pastoral Musicians. Available to U.S. and non-U.S. citizens.

Application Requirements: Application form, CD of performance, essay, financial need analysis, recommendations or references, resume. *Deadline:* March 5.

Contact: Kathleen Haley, Director of Membership Services
Phone: 240-247-3000
E-mail: haley@npm.org

NATIONAL ASSOCIATION OF PASTORAL MUSICIANS MEMBERS' SCHOLARSHIP

Awards NPM members enrolled full-time or part-time in a graduate or undergraduate degree program of studies related to the field of pastoral music. Applicant must intend to work at least two years in the field of pastoral music following graduation or program completion.

Academic Fields/Career Goals: Music; Religion/Theology.

Award: Scholarship for use in freshman, sophomore, junior, senior, or graduate years; not renewable. *Number:* 1. *Amount:* $3000.

Eligibility Requirements: Applicant must be enrolled or expecting to enroll full- or part-time at a two-year or four-year or technical institution or university and must have an interest in music/singing. Applicant or parent of applicant must be member of National Association of Pastoral Musicians. Available to U.S. and non-U.S. citizens.

Application Requirements: Application form, CD of performance, essay, financial need analysis, recommendations or references, resume. *Deadline:* March 5.

Contact: Kathleen Haley, Director of Membership Services
> *Phone:* 240-247-3000
> *E-mail:* haley@npm.org

NPM BOARD OF DIRECTORS SCHOLARSHIP

Scholarship for NPM members enrolled full- or part-time in an undergraduate or graduate pastoral music program. Must intend to work at least two years in the field of pastoral music following graduation/program completion.

Academic Fields/Career Goals: Music.

Award: Scholarship for use in freshman, sophomore, junior, senior, or graduate years; not renewable. *Number:* 1. *Amount:* $2000.

Eligibility Requirements: Applicant must be enrolled or expecting to enroll full- or part-time at a two-year or four-year institution or university and must have an interest in music/singing. Applicant or parent of applicant must be member of National Association of Pastoral Musicians. Available to U.S. and non-U.S. citizens.

Application Requirements: Application form, CD of performance, essay, financial need analysis, recommendations or references, resume. *Deadline:* March 5.

Contact: Kathleen Haley, Director of Membership Services
> *Phone:* 240-247-3000
> *E-mail:* haley@npm.org

NPM KOINONIA/BOARD OF DIRECTORS SCHOLARSHIP

Awards NPM members enrolled full-time or part-time in a graduate or undergraduate degree program of studies related to the field of pastoral music. Applicant must intend to work at least two years in the field of pastoral music following graduation or program completion.

Academic Fields/Career Goals: Music; Religion/Theology.

Award: Scholarship for use in freshman, sophomore, junior, senior, or graduate years; not renewable. *Number:* 1. *Amount:* $2000.

Eligibility Requirements: Applicant must be enrolled or expecting to enroll full- or part-time at a two-year or four-year institution or university and must have an interest in music/singing. Applicant or parent of applicant must be member of National Association of Pastoral Musicians. Available to U.S. and non-U.S. citizens.

Application Requirements: Application form, CD of performance, essay, financial need analysis, recommendations or references, resume. *Deadline:* March 5.

Contact: Kathleen Haley, Director of Membership Services
> *Phone:* 240-247-3000
> *E-mail:* haley@npm.org

NPM PERROT SCHOLARSHIP

Awards NPM members enrolled full-time or part-time in a graduate or undergraduate degree program of studies related to the field of pastoral music. Applicant must intend to work at least two years in the field of pastoral music following graduation or program completion.

Academic Fields/Career Goals: Music.

Award: Scholarship for use in freshman, sophomore, junior, senior, or graduate years; not renewable. *Number:* 1. *Amount:* $3000.

Eligibility Requirements: Applicant must be enrolled or expecting to enroll full- or part-time at a two-year or four-year institution or university. Applicant or parent of applicant must be member of National Association of Pastoral Musicians. Available to U.S. and non-U.S. citizens.

Application Requirements: Application form, CD of performance, essay, financial need analysis, recommendations or references, resume. *Deadline:* March 5.

Contact: Kathleen Haley, Director of Membership Services
> *Phone:* 240-247-3000
> *E-mail:* haley@npm.org

OREGON CATHOLIC PRESS SCHOLARSHIP

Awards NPM members enrolled full-time or part-time in a graduate or undergraduate degree program of studies related to the field of pastoral music. Applicant must intend to work at least two years in the field of pastoral music following graduation or program completion.

Academic Fields/Career Goals: Music; Religion/Theology.

Award: Scholarship for use in freshman, sophomore, junior, senior, or graduate years; not renewable. *Number:* 1. *Amount:* up to $2500.

Eligibility Requirements: Applicant must be enrolled or expecting to enroll full- or part-time at a two-year or four-year institution or university and must have an interest in music/singing. Available to U.S. and non-U.S. citizens.

Application Requirements: Application form, CD of performance, essay, financial need analysis, recommendations or references, resume. *Deadline:* March 5.

Contact: Kathleen Haley, Director of Membership Services
> *Phone:* 240-247-3000
> *E-mail:* haley@npm.org

PALUCH FAMILY FOUNDATION/WORLD LIBRARY PUBLICATIONS SCHOLARSHIP

Awards NPM members enrolled full-time or part-time in a graduate or undergraduate degree program of studies related to the field of pastoral music. Applicant must intend to work at least two years in the field of pastoral music following graduation or program completion.

Academic Fields/Career Goals: Music; Religion/Theology.

Award: Scholarship for use in freshman, sophomore, junior, senior, or graduate years; not renewable. *Number:* 1. *Amount:* up to $2500.

Eligibility Requirements: Applicant must be enrolled or expecting to enroll full- or part-time at a two-year or four-year institution or university and must have an interest in music/singing. Available to U.S. and non-U.S. citizens.

Application Requirements: Application form, CD of performance, essay, financial need analysis, recommendations or references, resume. *Deadline:* March 5.

Contact: Kathleen Haley, Director of Membership Services
> *Phone:* 240-247-3000
> *E-mail:* haley@npm.org

STEVEN C. WARNER SCHOLARSHIP

Scholarship for NPM members enrolled full-or part-time in an undergraduate or graduate pastoral music program. Applicant must intend to work at least two years in the field of pastoral music following graduation/program completion.

Academic Fields/Career Goals: Music.

Award: Scholarship for use in freshman, sophomore, junior, senior, or graduate years; not renewable. *Number:* 1. *Amount:* $1000.

Eligibility Requirements: Applicant must be enrolled or expecting to enroll full- or part-time at a two-year or four-year institution or university and must have an interest in music/singing. Applicant or parent of applicant must be member of National Association of Pastoral Musicians. Available to U.S. and non-U.S. citizens.

Application Requirements: Application form, CD of performance, essay, financial need analysis, recommendations or references, resume. *Deadline:* March 5.

Contact: Kathleen Haley, Director of Membership Services
> *Phone:* 240-247-3000
> *E-mail:* haley@npm.org

OREGON STUDENT ASSISTANCE COMMISSION

http://www.GetCollegeFunds.org/

BUERKLE SCHOLARSHIP
• *See page 372*

FARROLD STEPHENS SCHOLARSHIP

Awards for students that have experience in vocal performance or music education. Must enroll at least half time as college junior or above for fall term working towards a degree as a vocal performer or music educator. Oregon residency is not required. Semifinalists will be invited to submit a non-returnable CD of a musical performance.

Academic Fields/Career Goals: Music.

Award: Scholarship for use in junior, senior, or graduate years; not renewable.

Eligibility Requirements: Applicant must be enrolled or expecting to enroll full- or part-time at a four-year institution or university. Available to U.S. citizens.

Application Requirements: Application form, FAFSA. *Deadline:* March 1.

PI LAMBDA THETA INC.

http://www.pilambda.org/

NADEEN BURKEHOLDER WILLIAMS MUSIC SCHOLARSHIP

• *See page 243*

POLISH ARTS CLUB OF BUFFALO SCHOLARSHIP FOUNDATION

http://www.pacb.bfn.org/

POLISH ARTS CLUB OF BUFFALO SCHOLARSHIP FOUNDATION TRUST

• *See page 121*

QUEEN ELISABETH INTERNATIONAL MUSIC COMPETITION OF BELGIUM

http://www.qeimc.be

QUEEN ELISABETH COMPETITION

Competition is open to musicians who have already completed their training and who are ready to launch their international careers. The competition covers the following musical disciplines: piano, voice and violin.

Academic Fields/Career Goals: Music.

Award: Prize for use in freshman, sophomore, junior, senior, or graduate years; not renewable. *Amount:* $1–$33.

Eligibility Requirements: Applicant must be age 18-30; enrolled or expecting to enroll full- or part-time at a two-year or four-year or technical institution or university and must have an interest in music or music/singing. Available to U.S. and non-U.S. citizens.

Application Requirements: Application form, application form may be submitted online (http://www.qeimc.be), CD/DVD recording, personal photograph. *Fee:* $130. *Deadline:* January 15.

Contact: Michel-Etienne Van Neste, Secretary General
    Phone: 32 2 213 40 50
    Fax: 32 2 514 32 97
    E-mail: info@qeimc.be

RHODE ISLAND FOUNDATION

http://www.rifoundation.org/

BACH ORGAN AND KEYBOARD MUSIC SCHOLARSHIP

Scholarship for college music majors who are Rhode Island residents or attending college in Rhode Island. Must demonstrate good grades, financial need, and be an ABO member. Must include music sample.

Academic Fields/Career Goals: Music.

Award: Scholarship for use in freshman, sophomore, junior, or senior years; not renewable. *Amount:* $800–$1000.

Eligibility Requirements: Applicant must be enrolled or expecting to enroll full-time at a two-year or four-year institution or university; resident of Rhode Island and must have an interest in music/singing. Available to U.S. citizens.

Application Requirements: Application form, financial need analysis, recommendations or references, self-addressed stamped envelope with application, transcript. *Deadline:* June 14.

Contact: Libby Monahan, Funds Administrator
    Phone: 401-274-4564 Ext. 3117
    E-mail: libbym@rifoundation.org

SAN ANGELO SYMPHONY SOCIETY

http://www.sanangelosymphony.org/

SORANTIN YOUNG ARTIST AWARD

Prizes awarded to full-time or part-time students in the field of music (pianists and string instrumentalists), who are under 28 years of age. Award amount ranges from $1000 to $3000. Overall winner will appear in concert with the San Angelo Symphony Orchestra. Application fee of $75 is required. An eligible applicant must submit all required materials which must be received by the San Angelo Symphony on or before October 9, 2012.

Academic Fields/Career Goals: Music; Performing Arts.

Award: Prize for use in freshman, sophomore, junior, senior, graduate, or postgraduate years; not renewable. *Number:* 5–12. *Amount:* $1000–$3000.

Eligibility Requirements: Applicant must be enrolled or expecting to enroll full- or part-time at a two-year or four-year or technical institution or university and must have an interest in music. Available to U.S. and non-U.S. citizens.

Application Requirements: 3 video DVD copies of a recorded performance by the applicant., application form, application form may be submitted online (http://www.sanangelosymphony.org/storage/afm_uploads/Sorantin%202012%20Application.pdf), driver's license, entry in a contest, personal photograph. *Fee:* $75. *Deadline:* October 9.

UNITED NEGRO COLLEGE FUND

http://www.uncf.org/

ELLA FITZGERALD CHARITABLE FOUNDATION SCHOLARSHIP

Scholarship available to students at UNCF member colleges and universities who are studying music. Minimum 2.5 GPA required. For more information please see website, http://www.uncf.org.

Academic Fields/Career Goals: Music.

Award: Scholarship for use in freshman year; not renewable.

Eligibility Requirements: Applicant must be Black (non-Hispanic) and enrolled or expecting to enroll full- or part-time at a four-year institution or university. Applicant must have 2.5 GPA or higher. Available to U.S. citizens.

Application Requirements: Application form. *Deadline:* continuous.

JANET JACKSON/RHYTHM NATION SCHOLARSHIP

• *See page 123*

JIMI HENDRIX ENDOWMENT FUND SCHOLARSHIP

Scholarship supports undergraduate students majoring in music and attending a UNCF member college or university. Minimum 2.5 GPA required. The scholarship value ranges from $2000 to $5000.

Academic Fields/Career Goals: Music.

Award: Scholarship for use in sophomore, junior, or senior years; not renewable. *Amount:* $2000–$5000.

Eligibility Requirements: Applicant must be Black (non-Hispanic) and enrolled or expecting to enroll full- or part-time at a four-year institution or university. Applicant must have 2.5 GPA or higher. Available to U.S. and non-U.S. citizens.

Application Requirements: Application form, financial need analysis. *Deadline:* continuous.

JOHN LENNON SCHOLARSHIP

• *See page 198*

WOMEN BAND DIRECTORS INTERNATIONAL

http://www.womenbanddirectors.org/

CHARLOTTE PLUMMER OWEN MEMORIAL SCHOLARSHIP

• *See page 247*

MARTHA ANN STARK MEMORIAL SCHOLARSHIP
• *See page 247*

VOLKWEIN MEMORIAL SCHOLARSHIP
• *See page 247*

NATURAL RESOURCES

AMERICAN GROUND WATER TRUST

http://www.agwt.org/

AMERICAN GROUND WATER TRUST-AMTROL INC. SCHOLARSHIP
• *See page 355*

AMERICAN GROUND WATER TRUST-BAROID SCHOLARSHIP

Award for entry-level students intending to pursue a career in ground water-related field. Must either have completed a science/environmental project involving ground water resources or have had vacation work experience related to the environment and natural resources. Must be a U.S. citizen or legal resident with minimum 3.0 GPA. Submit two letters of recommendation and transcript.

Academic Fields/Career Goals: Natural Resources.

Award: Scholarship for use in freshman year; not renewable. *Number:* 1. *Amount:* up to $2000.

Eligibility Requirements: Applicant must be enrolled or expecting to enroll full-time at a four-year institution or university. Applicant must have 3.0 GPA or higher. Available to U.S. citizens.

Application Requirements: Application form, essay, recommendations or references, transcript. *Deadline:* June 1.

Contact: Garret Grasskamp, Ground Water Specialist
American Ground Water Trust
50 Pleasant Street, Suite 2
Concord, NH 03301-4073
Phone: 603-228-5444
Fax: 603-228-6557
E-mail: ggraaskamp@agwt.org

AMERICAN GROUND WATER TRUST-THOMAS STETSON SCHOLARSHIP
• *See page 179*

AMERICAN INDIAN SCIENCE AND ENGINEERING SOCIETY

http://www.aises.org/

A.T. ANDERSON MEMORIAL SCHOLARSHIP PROGRAM
• *See page 102*

AMERICAN SOCIETY OF AGRONOMY, CROP SCIENCE SOCIETY OF AMERICA, SOIL SCIENCE SOCIETY OF AMERICA

http://www.agronomy.org

HANK BEACHELL FUTURE LEADER SCHOLARSHIP
• *See page 90*

J. FIELDING REED SCHOLARSHIP
• *See page 90*

AMERICAN WATER RESOURCES ASSOCIATION

http://www.awra.org/

AWRA RICHARD A. HERBERT MEMORIAL SCHOLARSHIP

At least two scholarships are available: one for full-time undergraduate student and one for a full-time graduate student, each working toward a degree in water resources. All applicants must be national AWRA members.

Academic Fields/Career Goals: Natural Resources.

Award: Scholarship for use in freshman, sophomore, junior, senior, or graduate years; not renewable. *Number:* 2–4. *Amount:* $1000–$2000.

Eligibility Requirements: Applicant must be enrolled or expecting to enroll full-time at a four-year institution or university. Available to U.S. and non-U.S. citizens.

Application Requirements: Application form, application form may be submitted online (http://www.awra.org), essay, recommendations or references, resume, transcript. *Deadline:* April 22.

Contact: Jacque Towner, Office Manager
American Water Resources Association
4 West Federal Street, PO Box 1626
Middleburg, VA 20118-1626
Phone: 540-687-8390
Fax: 540-687-8395
E-mail: info@awra.org

ARCTIC INSTITUTE OF NORTH AMERICA

http://www.arctic.ucalgary.ca/

JIM BOURQUE SCHOLARSHIP
• *See page 233*

ARIZONA HYDROLOGICAL SOCIETY

http://www.azhydrosoc.org/

ARIZONA HYDROLOGICAL SOCIETY SCHOLARSHIP
• *See page 226*

ARIZONA PROFESSIONAL CHAPTER OF AISES

ARIZONA PROFESSIONAL CHAPTER OF AISES SCHOLARSHIP
• *See page 276*

ASSOCIATION OF CALIFORNIA WATER AGENCIES

http://www.acwa.com/

ASSOCIATION OF CALIFORNIA WATER AGENCIES SCHOLARSHIPS
• *See page 103*

CLAIR A. HILL SCHOLARSHIP
• *See page 103*

BRITISH COLUMBIA INNOVATION COUNCIL

http://www.bcic.ca/

PAUL AND HELEN TRUSSELL SCIENCE AND TECHNOLOGY SCHOLARSHIP
• *See page 104*

CALIFORNIA GROUNDWATER ASSOCIATION

http://www.groundh2o.org/

CALIFORNIA GROUNDWATER ASSOCIATION SCHOLARSHIP
• *See page 358*

PADDLE CANADA (FORMERLY THE CANADIAN RECREATIONAL CANOEING ASSOCIATION

http://www.paddlingcanada.com/

BILL MASON SCHOLARSHIP FUND
• *See page 235*

CONNECTICUT FOREST AND PARK ASSOCIATION

http://www.ctwoodlands.org/

JAMES L. AND GENEVIEVE H. GOODWIN MEMORIAL SCHOLARSHIP
Scholarship to support Connecticut residents enrolled in a curriculum of silviculture or forest resource management.
Academic Fields/Career Goals: Natural Resources.
Award: Scholarship for use in freshman, sophomore, junior, or senior years; not renewable. *Number:* up to 10. *Amount:* $1000–$5000.
Eligibility Requirements: Applicant must be enrolled or expecting to enroll full-time at a two-year or four-year institution or university and resident of Connecticut. Available to U.S. citizens.
Application Requirements: Application form, essay, financial need analysis, transcript. *Deadline:* March 15.
Contact: Eric Hammerling, Executive Director
Connecticut Forest and Park Association
16 Meriden Road
Rockfall, CT 06481-2961
Phone: 860-346-2372
Fax: 860-347-7463
E-mail: info@ctwoodlands.org

CONSERVATION FEDERATION OF MISSOURI

http://www.confedmo.org/

CHARLES P. BELL CONSERVATION SCHOLARSHIP
• *See page 302*

FRIENDS OF THE FRELINGHUYSEN ARBORETUM

http://www.arboretumfriends.org/

BENJAMIN C. BLACKBURN SCHOLARSHIP
• *See page 302*

GARDEN CLUB OF AMERICA

http://www.gcamerica.org/

THE ELIZABETH GARDNER NORWEB SUMMER ENVIRONMENTAL STUDIES SCHOLARSHIP
• *See page 92*

SARA SHALLENBERGER BROWN GCA NATIONAL PARKS CONSERVATION SCHOLARSHIP
• *See page 348*

GREATER KANAWHA VALLEY FOUNDATION

http://www.tgkvf.org/

LEOPOLD & ELIZABETH MARMET SCHOLARSHIP
• *See page 258*

GREAT LAKES COMMISSION

http://www.glc.org/

CAROL A. RATZA MEMORIAL SCHOLARSHIP
• *See page 190*

INDIANA WILDLIFE FEDERATION ENDOWMENT

http://www.indianawildlife.org/

CHARLES A. HOLT INDIANA WILDLIFE FEDERATION ENDOWMENT SCHOLARSHIP
• *See page 304*

INTERNATIONAL ASSOCIATION FOR GREAT LAKES RESEARCH

http://www.iaglr.org/

PAUL W. RODGERS SCHOLARSHIP
• *See page 227*

INTERTRIBAL TIMBER COUNCIL

http://www.itcnet.org/

TRUMAN D. PICARD SCHOLARSHIP
• *See page 86*

LAND CONSERVANCY OF NEW JERSEY

http://www.tlc-nj.org/

ROGERS FAMILY SCHOLARSHIP
• *See page 304*

RUSSELL W. MYERS SCHOLARSHIP
• *See page 304*

LOUISIANA OFFICE OF STUDENT FINANCIAL ASSISTANCE

http://www.osfa.la.gov/

ROCKEFELLER STATE WILDLIFE SCHOLARSHIP
• *See page 146*

MANITOBA FORESTRY ASSOCIATION

http://www.thinktrees.org/

DR. ALAN BEAVEN FORESTRY SCHOLARSHIP
• *See page 304*

MONTANA FEDERATION OF GARDEN CLUBS

http://www.mtfgc.org/

LIFE MEMBER MONTANA FEDERATION OF GARDEN CLUBS SCHOLARSHIP
• See page 228

NATIONAL ASSOCIATION OF WATER COMPANIES-NEW JERSEY CHAPTER

http://www.nawc.org/

NATIONAL ASSOCIATION OF WATER COMPANIES-NEW JERSEY CHAPTER SCHOLARSHIP
• See page 146

OHIO FORESTRY ASSOCIATION

http://www.ohioforest.org/

OHIO FORESTRY ASSOCIATION MEMORIAL SCHOLARSHIP

Minimum of one scholarship will be awarded to provide assistance toward forest resource education to quality college students. Preference given to students attending Ohio colleges and universities.

Academic Fields/Career Goals: Natural Resources.

Award: Scholarship for use in freshman, sophomore, junior, or senior years; not renewable. *Number:* 1. *Amount:* $1000.

Eligibility Requirements: Applicant must be enrolled or expecting to enroll full-time at a two-year or four-year or technical institution or university and resident of Ohio. Available to U.S. citizens.

Application Requirements: Application form, essay, test scores. *Deadline:* April 15.

Contact: John Dorka, Executive Director
Ohio Forestry Association
1100-H Brandywine Boulevard
Zanesville, OH 43701
Phone: 614-497-9580
Fax: 614-497-9581
E-mail: johnd@ohioforest.org

OREGON STUDENT ASSISTANCE COMMISSION

http://www.GetCollegeFunds.org/

OREGON FOUNDATION FOR BLACKTAIL DEER SCHOLARSHIP
• See page 147

ROYDEN M. BODLEY SCHOLARSHIP
• See page 306

RAILWAY TIE ASSOCIATION

http://www.rta.org/

JOHN MABRY FORESTRY SCHOLARSHIP

One-time award to potential forestry industry leaders. Open to junior and senior undergraduates who will be enrolled in accredited forestry schools. One scholarship is also available to second-year students in a two-year college. Applications reviewed with emphasis on leadership qualities, career objectives, scholastic achievement, and financial need.

Academic Fields/Career Goals: Natural Resources.

Award: Scholarship for use in sophomore, junior, or senior years; not renewable. *Number:* 2. *Amount:* $2000.

Eligibility Requirements: Applicant must be enrolled or expecting to enroll full-time at a two-year or four-year institution or university. Available to U.S. and Canadian citizens.

Application Requirements: Application form, application form may be submitted online (http://www.rta.org/scholarships), essay, financial need analysis, personal photograph, recommendations or references, transcript. *Deadline:* June 30.

Contact: Mrs. Barbara Stacey, Committee Director
Railway Tie Association
115 Commerce Drive, Suite C
Fayetteville, GA 30214
Phone: 770-460-5553
Fax: 770-460-5573
E-mail: ties@rta.org

ROCKY MOUNTAIN ELK FOUNDATION

http://www.elkfoundation.org/

WILDLIFE LEADERSHIP AWARDS

Program established to recognize, encourage and promote leadership among future wildlife management professionals. Candidates must be an undergraduate in a recognized wildlife program, have at least a junior standing (completed a minimum of 56 semester hours or 108 quarter hours), and have at least one semester or two quarters remaining in their degree program.

Academic Fields/Career Goals: Natural Resources; Natural Sciences.

Award: Scholarship for use in junior or senior years; not renewable. *Number:* 1–10. *Amount:* $2000.

Eligibility Requirements: Applicant must be enrolled or expecting to enroll full- or part-time at a four-year institution or university and must have an interest in wildlife conservation/animal rescue. Available to U.S. and Canadian citizens.

Application Requirements: Application form, letters of recommendation from faculty. *Deadline:* March 1.

Contact: Floretta Slade, Director of Programs
Phone: 703-837-5342
Fax: 703-837-5451
E-mail: sladef@agc.org

SAEMS-SOUTHERN ARIZONA ENVIRONMENTAL MANAGEMENT SOCIETY

http://www.saems.org/

ENVIRONMENTAL SCHOLARSHIPS
• See page 299

SOCIETY FOR RANGE MANAGEMENT

http://www.rangelands.org/

MASONIC RANGE SCIENCE SCHOLARSHIP
• See page 88

SOIL AND WATER CONSERVATION SOCIETY

http://www.swcs.org

DONALD A. WILLIAMS SCHOLARSHIP SOIL CONSERVATION SCHOLARSHIP
• See page 88

MELVILLE H. COHEE STUDENT LEADER CONSERVATION SCHOLARSHIP
• See page 88

SOIL AND WATER CONSERVATION SOCIETY-NEW JERSEY CHAPTER

http://home.comcast.net/~njswcs/scholarship.htm

EDWARD R. HALL SCHOLARSHIP
• See page 88

SOUTH DAKOTA BOARD OF REGENTS

http://www.sdbor.edu/

SOUTH DAKOTA BOARD OF REGENTS BJUGSTAD SCHOLARSHIP
• *See page 89*

TECHNICAL ASSOCIATION OF THE PULP & PAPER INDUSTRY (TAPPI)

http://www.tappi.org/

WILLIAM L. CULLISON SCHOLARSHIP
Scholarship provides incentive for students to pursue an academic path related to the pulp and paper industry. Eligible students must meet all criteria and will have completed two years of undergraduate school with two years (or three years in a five-year program) remaining. For details, refer to website http://www.tappi.org/s_tappi/doc.asp?CID=6101&DID=561682.
Academic Fields/Career Goals: Natural Resources; Paper and Pulp Engineering.
Award: Scholarship for use in junior or senior years; renewable. *Number:* 1–2. *Amount:* $2000–$4000.
Eligibility Requirements: Applicant must be enrolled or expecting to enroll full-time at a four-year institution or university. Available to U.S. and non-U.S. citizens.
Application Requirements: Application form, recommendations or references, transcript. *Deadline:* May 1.
Contact: Mr. Charles Bohanan, Director of Standards and Awards
Technical Association of the Pulp & Paper Industry (TAPPI)
15 Technology Parkway South
Peachtree Corners, GA 30092
Phone: 770-209-7276
Fax: 770-446-6947
E-mail: standards@tappi.org

TEXAS OUTDOOR WRITERS ASSOCIATION

http://www.towa.org/

TEXAS OUTDOOR WRITERS ASSOCIATION SCHOLARSHIP
• *See page 197*

TKE EDUCATIONAL FOUNDATION

http://www.tke.org/

TIMOTHY L. TASCHWER SCHOLARSHIP
• *See page 148*

UNITED STATES DEPARTMENT OF AGRICULTURE

http://www.usda.gov/

USDA/1890 NATIONAL SCHOLARS PROGRAM
• *See page 96*

USDA/1994 TRIBAL SCHOLARS PROGRAM
• *See page 96*

UNITED STATES ENVIRONMENTAL PROTECTION AGENCY

http://www.epa.gov/enviroed

NATIONAL NETWORK FOR ENVIRONMENTAL MANAGEMENT STUDIES FELLOWSHIP
• *See page 307*

VIRGINIA ASSOCIATION OF SOIL AND WATER CONSERVATION DISTRICTS EDUCATIONAL FOUNDATION INC.

http://www.vaswcd.org/

VASWCD EDUCATIONAL FOUNDATION INC. SCHOLARSHIP AWARDS PROGRAM
• *See page 307*

WILSON ORNITHOLOGICAL SOCIETY

http://www.wilsonsociety.org/

GEORGE A. HALL/HAROLD F. MAYFIELD AWARD
• *See page 100*

PAUL A. STEWART AWARDS
• *See page 100*

NATURAL SCIENCES

AMERICAN CHEMICAL SOCIETY

http://www.acs.org/

AMERICAN CHEMICAL SOCIETY SCHOLARS PROGRAM
• *See page 162*

AMERICAN FOUNDATION FOR THE BLIND

http://www.afb.org/

PAUL W. RUCKES SCHOLARSHIP
• *See page 199*

AMERICAN INDIAN SCIENCE AND ENGINEERING SOCIETY

http://www.aises.org/

A.T. ANDERSON MEMORIAL SCHOLARSHIP PROGRAM
• *See page 102*

BURLINGTON NORTHERN SANTA FE FOUNDATION SCHOLARSHIP
• *See page 102*

AMERICAN PHYSIOLOGICAL SOCIETY

http://www.the-aps.org

DAVID S. BRUCE AWARDS FOR EXCELLENCE IN UNDERGRADUATE RESEARCH
• *See page 98*

AMERICAN SOCIETY OF AGRONOMY, CROP SCIENCE SOCIETY OF AMERICA, SOIL SCIENCE SOCIETY OF AMERICA

http://www.agronomy.org

HANK BEACHELL FUTURE LEADER SCHOLARSHIP
• *See page 90*

J. FIELDING REED SCHOLARSHIP
• *See page 90*

ARCTIC INSTITUTE OF NORTH AMERICA
http://www.arctic.ucalgary.ca/

JIM BOURQUE SCHOLARSHIP
• *See page 233*

ARRL FOUNDATION INC.
http://www.arrl.org/

WILLIAM R. GOLDFARB MEMORIAL SCHOLARSHIP
• *See page 150*

YASME FOUNDATION SCHOLARSHIP
• *See page 143*

ASSOCIATION OF CALIFORNIA WATER AGENCIES
http://www.acwa.com/

ASSOCIATION OF CALIFORNIA WATER AGENCIES SCHOLARSHIPS
• *See page 103*

CLAIR A. HILL SCHOLARSHIP
• *See page 103*

ASSOCIATION OF FORMER INTELLIGENCE OFFICERS
http://www.afio.com/13_scholarships.htm

CIA UNDERGRADUATE SCHOLARSHIPS
• *See page 97*

ASSOCIATION ON AMERICAN INDIAN AFFAIRS, INC.
http://www.indian-affairs.org/

ELIZABETH AND SHERMAN ASCHE MEMORIAL SCHOLARSHIP FUND
• *See page 91*

AUDUBON SOCIETY OF WESTERN PENNSYLVANIA
http://www.aswp.org/

BEULAH FREY ENVIRONMENTAL SCHOLARSHIP
• *See page 301*

BARRY M. GOLDWATER SCHOLARSHIP AND EXCELLENCE IN EDUCATION FOUNDATION
http://www.act.org/goldwater

BARRY M. GOLDWATER SCHOLARSHIP AND EXCELLENCE IN EDUCATION PROGRAM
• *See page 104*

BRITISH COLUMBIA INNOVATION COUNCIL
http://www.bcic.ca/

BCIC YOUNG INNOVATOR SCHOLARSHIP COMPETITION (IDEA MASH UP)
• *See page 104*

PAUL AND HELEN TRUSSELL SCIENCE AND TECHNOLOGY SCHOLARSHIP
• *See page 104*

PADDLE CANADA (FORMERLY THE CANADIAN RECREATIONAL CANOEING ASSOCIATION
http://www.paddlingcanada.com/

BILL MASON SCHOLARSHIP FUND
• *See page 235*

THE COMMUNITY FOUNDATION FOR GREATER ATLANTA, INC.
http://cfgreateratlanta.org/

JAMES M. AND VIRGINIA M. SMYTH SCHOLARSHIP
• *See page 118*

CONSERVATION FEDERATION OF MISSOURI
http://www.confedmo.org/

CHARLES P. BELL CONSERVATION SCHOLARSHIP
• *See page 302*

ELECTROCHEMICAL SOCIETY INC.
http://www.electrochem.org/

STUDENT RESEARCH AWARDS OF THE BATTERY DIVISION OF THE ELECTROCHEMICAL SOCIETY INC.
• *See page 105*

EXPLORERS CLUB
http://www.explorers.org/

YOUTH ACTIVITY FUND
Award given to college students or high school students pursuing a research project in the field of science. Applicants must have two letter of recommendation, one-page description of project, a budget or plan, and proof of student enrollment with dates.

Academic Fields/Career Goals: Natural Sciences; Science, Technology, and Society.

Award: Grant for use in freshman, sophomore, junior, or senior years; not renewable. *Number:* 10–30. *Amount:* $500–$5000.

Eligibility Requirements: Applicant must be enrolled or expecting to enroll full-time at a four-year institution or university. Available to U.S. and non-U.S. citizens.

Application Requirements: Application form, essay, financial need analysis, recommendations or references. *Deadline:* varies.

Contact: Annie Lee, Member Services
Explorers Club
46 East 70th Street
New York, NY 10021
Fax: 212-288-4449
E-mail: alee@explorers.org

GARDEN CLUB OF AMERICA

http://www.gcamerica.org/

FRANCES M. PEACOCK SCHOLARSHIP FOR NATIVE BIRD HABITAT

Up to $4500 award provides financial aid to study areas in the United States that provide seasonal habitat for threatened or endangered native birds and to tend useful information for land-management decisions. Open to college seniors and graduate students only (second-semester juniors may apply for their senior year).

Academic Fields/Career Goals: Natural Sciences.

Award: Scholarship for use in senior or graduate years; not renewable. *Number:* 1. *Amount:* $4500.

Eligibility Requirements: Applicant must be enrolled or expecting to enroll full- or part-time at a four-year institution or university. Available to U.S. citizens.

Application Requirements: Application form, budget, essay, recommendations or references, resume, self-addressed stamped envelope with application, transcript. *Deadline:* January 15.

Contact: Scott Sutcliffe, Scholarship Committee
Garden Club of America
Cornell Lab of Ornithology
159 Sapsucker Woods Road
Ithaca, NY 14850-1999
E-mail: sas10@cornell.edu

GCA AWARD IN DESERT STUDIES
• *See page 111*

GCA SUMMER SCHOLARSHIP IN FIELD BOTANY
• *See page 348*

JOAN K. HUNT AND RACHEL M. HUNT SUMMER SCHOLARSHIP IN FIELD BOTANY
• *See page 348*

ZELLER SUMMER SCHOLARSHIP IN MEDICINAL BOTANY
• *See page 335*

GREAT LAKES COMMISSION

http://www.glc.org/

CAROL A. RATZA MEMORIAL SCHOLARSHIP
• *See page 190*

HARVARD TRAVELLERS CLUB

http://www.harvardtravellersclub.org/

HARVARD TRAVELLERS CLUB GRANTS
• *See page 108*

INTERNATIONAL ASSOCIATION FOR GREAT LAKES RESEARCH

http://www.iaglr.org/

PAUL W. RODGERS SCHOLARSHIP
• *See page 227*

KENTUCKY ENERGY AND ENVIRONMENT CABINET

http://www.eec.ky.gov/

ENVIRONMENTAL PROTECTION SCHOLARSHIP
• *See page 145*

NASA IDAHO SPACE GRANT CONSORTIUM

http://www.id.spacegrant.org/

NASA IDAHO SPACE GRANT CONSORTIUM SCHOLARSHIP PROGRAM
• *See page 146*

NASA SOUTH DAKOTA SPACE GRANT CONSORTIUM

http://sdspacegrant.sdsmt.edu/

SOUTH DAKOTA SPACE GRANT CONSORTIUM UNDERGRADUATE AND GRADUATE STUDENT SCHOLARSHIPS
• *See page 134*

NASA WEST VIRGINIA SPACE GRANT CONSORTIUM

http://www.nasa.wvu.edu/

WEST VIRGINIA SPACE GRANT CONSORTIUM UNDERGRADUATE FELLOWSHIP PROGRAM
• *See page 134*

NEVADA NASA SPACE GRANT CONSORTIUM

http://www.nvspacegrant.org/

NATIONAL SPACE GRANT COLLEGE AND FELLOWSHIP PROGRAM
• *See page 106*

OREGON STUDENT ASSISTANCE COMMISSION

http://www.GetCollegeFunds.org/

ROBERTS SCHOLARSHIP
• *See page 147*

ROYDEN M. BODLEY SCHOLARSHIP
• *See page 306*

ROBERT H. MOLLOHAN FAMILY CHARITABLE FOUNDATION, INC.

http://www.mollohanfoundation.org/

JOHN M. MURPHY SCHOLARSHIP

The John M. Murphy Scholarship is a $500 scholarship that will be awarded to a Pendleton County High School senior who is planning to major in any natural science related field at a West Virginia college or university. Furthermore, the recipient will be eligible for summer internship opportunities within his or her field of study.

Academic Fields/Career Goals: Natural Sciences.

Award: Scholarship for use in senior year; not renewable. *Amount:* $500.

Eligibility Requirements: Applicant must be high school student; planning to enroll or expecting to enroll at a four-year institution or university; resident of West Virginia and studying in West Virginia. Available to U.S. citizens.

Application Requirements: Application form, essay, recommendations or references, resume, test scores, transcript.

Contact: Aime Shaffer, Program Manager
Phone: 304-333-6783
E-mail: ashaffer@wvhtf.org

ROCKY MOUNTAIN ELK FOUNDATION

http://www.elkfoundation.org/

WILDLIFE LEADERSHIP AWARDS
• *See page 418*

SOIL AND WATER CONSERVATION SOCIETY

http://www.swcs.org

DONALD A. WILLIAMS SCHOLARSHIP SOIL CONSERVATION SCHOLARSHIP
• *See page 88*

MELVILLE H. COHEE STUDENT LEADER CONSERVATION SCHOLARSHIP
• *See page 88*

SOIL AND WATER CONSERVATION SOCIETY-NEW JERSEY CHAPTER

http://home.comcast.net/~njswcs/scholarship.htm

EDWARD R. HALL SCHOLARSHIP
• *See page 88*

UNITED NEGRO COLLEGE FUND

http://www.uncf.org/

CHARLES E. CULPEPPER SCHOLARSHIP
• *See page 148*

NAACP/HUBERTUS W.V. WILLEMS SCHOLARSHIP FOR MALE SCHOLARS
• *See page 271*

SANDISK CORPORATION SCHOLARSHIP
• *See page 206*

SPRINT SCHOLARS PROGRAM FOR SOPHOMORES, JUNIORS, AND SENIORS
• *See page 100*

UNCF/MERCK SCIENCE INITIATIVE
• *See page 149*

WILMA WARBURG SCHOLARSHIP
• *See page 340*

NEAR AND MIDDLE EAST STUDIES

ASSOCIATION OF FORMER INTELLIGENCE OFFICERS

http://www.afio.com/13_scholarships.htm

CIA UNDERGRADUATE SCHOLARSHIPS
• *See page 97*

NEUROBIOLOGY

AMERICAN PHYSIOLOGICAL SOCIETY

http://www.the-aps.org

DAVID S. BRUCE AWARDS FOR EXCELLENCE IN UNDERGRADUATE RESEARCH
• *See page 98*

ARNOLD AND MABEL BECKMAN FOUNDATION

http://www.beckman-foundation.com/

BECKMAN SCHOLARS PROGRAM
• *See page 143*

CYNTHIA E. MORGAN SCHOLARSHIP FUND (CEMS)

http://www.cemsfund.com/

CYNTHIA E. MORGAN MEMORIAL SCHOLARSHIP FUND, INC.
• *See page 298*

UNITED NEGRO COLLEGE FUND

http://www.uncf.org/

UNCF/MERCK SCIENCE INITIATIVE
• *See page 149*

NUCLEAR SCIENCE

AMERICAN INDIAN SCIENCE AND ENGINEERING SOCIETY

http://www.aises.org/

A.T. ANDERSON MEMORIAL SCHOLARSHIP PROGRAM
• *See page 102*

BURLINGTON NORTHERN SANTA FE FOUNDATION SCHOLARSHIP
• *See page 102*

AMERICAN NUCLEAR SOCIETY

http://www.ans.org/

AMERICAN NUCLEAR SOCIETY OPERATIONS AND POWER SCHOLARSHIP
Undergraduate scholarship for students who have completed two or more years in a course of study leading to a degree in nuclear science, nuclear engineering, or a nuclear-related field.

Academic Fields/Career Goals: Nuclear Science.

Award: Scholarship for use in junior or senior years; not renewable. *Number:* 1. *Amount:* $2500.

Eligibility Requirements: Applicant must be enrolled or expecting to enroll full- or part-time at a four-year institution or university. Available to U.S. citizens.

Application Requirements: Application form, recommendations or references, transcript. *Deadline:* February 1.

AMERICAN NUCLEAR SOCIETY UNDERGRADUATE SCHOLARSHIPS

Maximum of four scholarships for students who have completed one year in a course of study leading to a degree in nuclear science, nuclear engineering, or a nuclear-related field and who will be sophomores in the upcoming academic year; and a maximum of twenty one scholarships for students who have completed two or more years and will be entering as juniors or seniors. Must be sponsored by ANS member or branch. Must be U.S. citizen or permanent resident.

Academic Fields/Career Goals: Nuclear Science.

Award: Scholarship for use in junior or senior years; not renewable. *Number:* 4–21. *Amount:* $2000.

Eligibility Requirements: Applicant must be enrolled or expecting to enroll full-time at a four-year institution or university. Available to U.S. citizens.

Application Requirements: Application form, recommendations or references, transcript. *Deadline:* February 1.

AMERICAN NUCLEAR SOCIETY VOGT RADIOCHEMISTRY SCHOLARSHIP

• See page 273

ANS INCOMING FRESHMAN SCHOLARSHIP

Scholarship for graduating high school seniors who have enrolled or plan to enroll full-time in a nuclear engineering degree program. Scholarships will be awarded based on an applicant's high school academic achievement and course of undergraduate study.

Academic Fields/Career Goals: Nuclear Science.

Award: Scholarship for use in freshman year; not renewable. *Number:* 1–4. *Amount:* $1000.

Eligibility Requirements: Applicant must be high school student and planning to enroll or expecting to enroll full-time at a four-year institution or university. Available to U.S. and non-U.S. citizens.

Application Requirements: Application form, essay, recommendations or references, transcript. *Deadline:* April 1.

CHARLES (TOMMY) THOMAS MEMORIAL SCHOLARSHIP DIVISION SCHOLARSHIP

Undergraduate scholarship for students who have completed two or more years in a course of study leading to a degree in nuclear science, nuclear engineering, or a nuclear-related field.

Academic Fields/Career Goals: Nuclear Science.

Award: Scholarship for use in junior or senior years; not renewable. *Number:* 1. *Amount:* $3000.

Eligibility Requirements: Applicant must be enrolled or expecting to enroll full-time at a four-year institution or university. Available to U.S. citizens.

Application Requirements: Application form, recommendations or references, transcript. *Deadline:* February 1.

DECOMMISSIONING, DECONTAMINATION, AND REUTILIZATION UNDERGRADUATE SCHOLARSHIP

• See page 257

DELAYED EDUCATION FOR WOMEN SCHOLARSHIPS

One-time award given to enable mature women whose formal studies in nuclear science, nuclear engineering, or related fields have been delayed or interrupted at least one year. Must be U.S. citizen or permanent resident. Minimum GPA of 2.5 required.

Academic Fields/Career Goals: Nuclear Science.

Award: Scholarship for use in freshman, sophomore, junior, or senior years; not renewable. *Number:* 1. *Amount:* $5000.

Eligibility Requirements: Applicant must be enrolled or expecting to enroll full-time at a four-year institution or university and female. Applicant must have 2.5 GPA or higher. Available to U.S. citizens.

Application Requirements: Application form, financial need analysis, recommendations or references, transcript. *Deadline:* February 1.

JOHN AND MURIEL LANDIS SCHOLARSHIP AWARDS

Maximum of eight scholarships are awarded to undergraduate and graduate students who have greater than average financial need. Applicants should be planning a career in nuclear science, nuclear engineering, or a nuclear related field and be enrolled or planning to enroll in a college or university located in the United States, but need not be U.S. citizens.

Academic Fields/Career Goals: Nuclear Science.

Award: Scholarship for use in freshman, sophomore, junior, senior, or graduate years; not renewable. *Number:* 1–8. *Amount:* $5000.

Eligibility Requirements: Applicant must be enrolled or expecting to enroll full-time at a four-year institution or university. Available to U.S. and non-U.S. citizens.

Application Requirements: Application form, financial need analysis, recommendations or references, transcript. *Deadline:* February 1.

JOHN R. LAMARSH SCHOLARSHIP

Undergraduate scholarship for students who have completed two or more years in a course of study leading to a degree in nuclear science, nuclear engineering, or a nuclear-related field.

Academic Fields/Career Goals: Nuclear Science.

Award: Scholarship for use in junior or senior years; not renewable. *Number:* 1. *Amount:* $2000.

Eligibility Requirements: Applicant must be enrolled or expecting to enroll full- or part-time at a four-year institution or university. Available to U.S. citizens.

Application Requirements: Application form, recommendations or references, transcript. *Deadline:* February 1.

JOSEPH R. DIETRICH SCHOLARSHIP

Undergraduate scholarship for students who have completed two or more years in a course of study leading to a degree in nuclear science, nuclear engineering, or a nuclear-related field.

Academic Fields/Career Goals: Nuclear Science.

Award: Scholarship for use in junior or senior years; not renewable. *Number:* 1. *Amount:* $2000.

Eligibility Requirements: Applicant must be enrolled or expecting to enroll full- or part-time at a four-year institution or university. Available to U.S. citizens.

Application Requirements: Application form, recommendations or references, transcript. *Deadline:* February 1.

RAYMOND DISALVO SCHOLARSHIP

Undergraduate scholarship for students who have completed two or more years in a course of study leading to a degree in nuclear science, nuclear engineering, or a nuclear-related field.

Academic Fields/Career Goals: Nuclear Science.

Award: Scholarship for use in junior or senior years; not renewable. *Number:* 1–21. *Amount:* $2000.

Eligibility Requirements: Applicant must be enrolled or expecting to enroll full-time at a four-year institution or university. Available to U.S. and non-U.S. citizens.

Application Requirements: Application form, recommendations or references, sponsorship letter from ANS organization, transcript. *Deadline:* February 1.

ROBERT G. LACY SCHOLARSHIP

Undergraduate scholarship for students who have completed two or more years in a course of study leading to a degree in nuclear science, nuclear engineering, or a nuclear-related field.

Academic Fields/Career Goals: Nuclear Science.

Award: Scholarship for use in junior or senior years; not renewable. *Number:* 1. *Amount:* $2000.

Eligibility Requirements: Applicant must be enrolled or expecting to enroll full-time at a four-year institution or university. Available to U.S. and non-U.S. citizens.

Application Requirements: Application form, recommendations or references, sponsorship letter from ANS organization, transcript. *Deadline:* February 1.

ROBERT T. "BOB" LINER SCHOLARSHIP

Undergraduate scholarship for students who have completed two or more years in a course of study leading to a degree in nuclear science, nuclear engineering, or a nuclear-related field.

Academic Fields/Career Goals: Nuclear Science.

Award: Scholarship for use in junior or senior years; not renewable. *Number:* 1. *Amount:* $2000.

Eligibility Requirements: Applicant must be enrolled or expecting to enroll full-time at a four-year institution or university. Available to U.S. and non-U.S. citizens.

Application Requirements: Application form, recommendations or references, sponsorship letter from ANS organization, transcript. *Deadline:* February 1.

ARIZONA HYDROLOGICAL SOCIETY

http://www.azhydrosoc.org/

ARIZONA HYDROLOGICAL SOCIETY SCHOLARSHIP
• *See page 226*

BARRY M. GOLDWATER SCHOLARSHIP AND EXCELLENCE IN EDUCATION FOUNDATION

http://www.act.org/goldwater

BARRY M. GOLDWATER SCHOLARSHIP AND EXCELLENCE IN EDUCATION PROGRAM
• *See page 104*

BRITISH COLUMBIA INNOVATION COUNCIL

http://www.bcic.ca/

PAUL AND HELEN TRUSSELL SCIENCE AND TECHNOLOGY SCHOLARSHIP
• *See page 104*

GREAT MINDS IN STEM

http://www.greatmindsinstem.org

HISPANIC ENGINEER NATIONAL ACHIEVEMENT AWARDS CORPORATION SCHOLARSHIP PROGRAM
• *See page 130*

NASA WEST VIRGINIA SPACE GRANT CONSORTIUM

http://www.nasa.wvu.edu/

WEST VIRGINIA SPACE GRANT CONSORTIUM UNDERGRADUATE FELLOWSHIP PROGRAM
• *See page 134*

NATIONAL SCIENCE TEACHERS ASSOCIATION

http://www.nsta.org/

TOSHIBA/NSTA EXPLORAVISION AWARDS PROGRAM
• *See page 203*

SOCIETY OF NUCLEAR MEDICINE AND MOLECULAR IMAGING

http://www.snmmi.org/

PAUL COLE TECHNOLOGIST SCHOLARSHIP
• *See page 339*

UNIVERSITIES SPACE RESEARCH ASSOCIATION

http://www.usra.edu/

UNIVERSITIES SPACE RESEARCH ASSOCIATION SCHOLARSHIP PROGRAM
• *See page 107*

NURSING

AIR FORCE RESERVE OFFICER TRAINING CORPS

http://www.afrotc.com/

AIR FORCE ROTC FOUR-YEAR NURSING SCHOLARSHIP

Scholarship offers qualified individuals the chance to compete for scholarships of up to $15,000 per academic year. Nursing students can compete for scholarships through the In-College Scholarship Program, or may qualify for a nursing scholarship.

Academic Fields/Career Goals: Nursing.

Award: Scholarship for use in sophomore, junior, or senior years; not renewable. *Amount:* up to $15,000.

Eligibility Requirements: Applicant must be enrolled or expecting to enroll full-time at a four-year institution or university. Available to U.S. citizens.

Application Requirements: Application form. *Deadline:* varies.

Contact: Capt. Elmarko Magee, Chief of Advertising
Air Force Reserve Officer Training Corps
551 East Maxwell Boulevard
Maxwell AFB, AL 36112-6106
Phone: 866-423-7682

ALBERTA HERITAGE SCHOLARSHIP FUND

http://www.alis.alberta.ca/

ABORIGINAL HEALTH CAREERS BURSARY
• *See page 142*

AMARILLO AREA FOUNDATION

http://www.amarilloareafoundation.org/

E. EUGENE WAIDE, MD MEMORIAL SCHOLARSHIP

Scholarship for graduating senior from Ochiltree, Hansford, Lipscomb, Hutchinson, Roberts or Hemphill counties. Applicant must pursue a career as LVN, BSN (junior or senior), or MSN.

Academic Fields/Career Goals: Nursing.

Award: Scholarship for use in freshman, sophomore, junior, senior, or graduate years; not renewable.

Eligibility Requirements: Applicant must be enrolled or expecting to enroll full- or part-time at a two-year or four-year or technical institution or university and resident of Texas. Available to U.S. citizens.

Application Requirements: Application form, personal photograph. *Deadline:* February 1.

NANCY GERALD MEMORIAL NURSING SCHOLARSHIP

Scholarship of $500 for graduating senior from one of the 26 counties in Texas. Applicant must be majoring in the field of nursing at Amarillo College or West Texas A & M University pursuing AAS, BSN, or MSN degree.

Academic Fields/Career Goals: Nursing.

Award: Scholarship for use in freshman, sophomore, junior, senior, or graduate years; not renewable. *Amount:* $500.

Eligibility Requirements: Applicant must be enrolled or expecting to enroll full- or part-time at a two-year or four-year institution or university; resident of Texas and studying in Texas. Applicant must have 2.5 GPA or higher. Available to U.S. citizens.

Application Requirements: Application form, personal photograph. *Deadline:* February 1.

AMERICAN ASSOCIATION OF NEUROSCIENCE NURSES

http://www.aann.org/

NEUROSCIENCE NURSING FOUNDATION SCHOLARSHIP

Scholarship available for registered nurse to attend an NLN accredited school. Submit letter of school acceptance along with application, transcript, and copy of current RN license. Applicants should have diploma or AD.

Academic Fields/Career Goals: Nursing.

Award: Scholarship for use in freshman, sophomore, junior, senior, or graduate years; not renewable. *Amount:* $1500.

Eligibility Requirements: Applicant must be enrolled or expecting to enroll full- or part-time at a two-year or four-year institution or university. Applicant must have 3.0 GPA or higher. Available to U.S. citizens.

Application Requirements: Application form, letter of acceptance, transcript. *Deadline:* January 15.

AMERICAN LEGION AUXILIARY DEPARTMENT OF ARIZONA

http://wwwaladeptaz.org

AMERICAN LEGION AUXILIARY DEPARTMENT OF ARIZONA NURSES' SCHOLARSHIPS

Award for Arizona residents enrolled in their second year at an institution in Arizona awarding degrees as a registered nurse. Preference given to immediate family member of a veteran. Must be a U.S. citizen and resident of Arizona for one year.

Academic Fields/Career Goals: Nursing.

Award: Scholarship for use in sophomore, junior, or senior years; not renewable. *Number:* 4. *Amount:* $600.

Eligibility Requirements: Applicant must be enrolled or expecting to enroll full-time at a two-year or four-year institution or university; resident of Arizona and studying in Arizona. Available to U.S. citizens.

Application Requirements: Application form, essay, financial need analysis, personal photograph, recommendations or references, test scores, transcript. *Deadline:* May 15.

Contact: Mrs. Barbara Matteson, Department Secretary and Treasurer
American Legion Auxiliary Department of Arizona
4701 North 19th Avenue, Suite 100
Phoenix, AZ 85015-3727
Phone: 602-241-1080
Fax: 602-604-9640
E-mail: secretary@aladeptaz.org

AMERICAN LEGION AUXILIARY DEPARTMENT OF CALIFORNIA

http://www.calegionaux.org/

AMERICAN LEGION AUXILIARY DEPARTMENT OF CALIFORNIA PAST PRESIDENTS' PARLEY NURSING SCHOLARSHIPS

Award for student entering into or continuing studies in a nursing program.

Academic Fields/Career Goals: Nursing.

Award: Scholarship for use in freshman, sophomore, junior, or senior years; not renewable. *Amount:* $500–$1000.

Eligibility Requirements: Applicant must be enrolled or expecting to enroll full- or part-time at a four-year institution or university. Available to U.S. citizens. Applicant or parent must meet one or more of the following requirements: Army experience; retired from active duty; disabled or killed as a result of military service; prisoner of war; or missing in action.

Application Requirements: Application form, recommendations or references, transcript. *Deadline:* April 4.

Contact: Theresa Jacob, Secretary/Treasurer
Phone: 415-862-5092
Fax: 415-861-8365
E-mail: calegionaux@calegionaux.org

AMERICAN LEGION AUXILIARY DEPARTMENT OF COLORADO

http://www.alacolorado.com

AMERICAN LEGION AUXILIARY DEPARTMENT OF COLORADO PAST PRESIDENTS' PARLEY NURSES SCHOLARSHIP

Open to children, spouses, grandchildren, and great-grandchildren of American Legion veterans, and veterans who served in the armed forces during eligibility dates for membership in the American Legion. Must be Colorado residents who have been accepted by an accredited school of nursing in Colorado.

Academic Fields/Career Goals: Nursing.

Award: Scholarship for use in freshman, sophomore, junior, senior, or graduate years; not renewable. *Number:* 3–5. *Amount:* up to $500.

Eligibility Requirements: Applicant must be enrolled or expecting to enroll full- or part-time at a four-year institution or university; resident of Colorado and studying in Colorado. Applicant or parent of applicant must be member of American Legion or Auxiliary. Available to U.S. citizens. Applicant or parent must meet one or more of the following requirements: general military experience; retired from active duty; disabled or killed as a result of military service; prisoner of war; or missing in action.

Application Requirements: Application form, essay, financial need analysis, recommendations or references. *Deadline:* April 1.

Contact: Lynn Cody, Department Secretary-Treasurer
American Legion Auxiliary Department of Colorado
7465 East First Avenue, Suite D
Denver, CO 80230
Phone: 303-367-5388
Fax: 303-367-5388
E-mail: www.dept-sec@alacolorado.com

AMERICAN LEGION AUXILIARY DEPARTMENT OF IDAHO

http://www.idahoala.org/

AMERICAN LEGION AUXILIARY DEPARTMENT OF IDAHO NURSING SCHOLARSHIP

Scholarship available to veterans or the children of veterans who are majoring in nursing. Applicants must be 17 to 35 years of age and residents of Idaho for five years prior to applying. One-time award of $1000.

Academic Fields/Career Goals: Nursing.

Award: Scholarship for use in freshman, sophomore, junior, or senior years; not renewable. *Number:* 1. *Amount:* $1000.

Eligibility Requirements: Applicant must be age 17-35; enrolled or expecting to enroll full- or part-time at a four-year institution or university and resident of Idaho. Available to U.S. citizens. Applicant or parent must meet one or more of the following requirements: general military experience; retired from active duty; disabled or killed as a result of military service; prisoner of war; or missing in action.

Application Requirements: Application form, financial need analysis, personal photograph, recommendations or references, self-addressed stamped envelope with application, transcript. *Deadline:* May 15.

Contact: Mary Sue Chase, Secretary
American Legion Auxiliary Department of Idaho
905 Warren Street
Boise, ID 83706-3825
Phone: 208-342-7066
Fax: 208-342-7066
E-mail: idalegionaux@msn.com

AMERICAN LEGION AUXILIARY DEPARTMENT OF IOWA

http://www.ialegion.org/ala

AMERICAN LEGION AUXILIARY DEPARTMENT OF IOWA M.V. MCCRAE MEMORIAL NURSES MERIT AWARD

One-time award available to the child of an Iowa American Legion Post member or Iowa American Legion Auxiliary Unit member. Award is for full-time study in an accredited nursing program. Must be U.S. citizen and Iowa resident. Must attend an Iowa institution.

Academic Fields/Career Goals: Nursing.

Award: Scholarship for use in freshman, sophomore, junior, or senior years; not renewable. *Number:* 1. *Amount:* $400.

Eligibility Requirements: Applicant must be enrolled or expecting to enroll full-time at a two-year or four-year or technical institution or university; resident of Iowa and studying in Iowa. Applicant or parent of applicant must be member of American Legion or Auxiliary. Available to U.S. citizens. Applicant or parent must meet one or more of the following requirements; general military experience; retired from active duty; disabled or killed as a result of military service; prisoner of war; or missing in action.

Application Requirements: Application form, essay, financial need analysis, personal photograph, recommendations or references, self-addressed stamped envelope with application, test scores, transcript. *Deadline:* June 1.

Contact: Marlene Valentine, Secretary and Treasurer
American Legion Auxiliary Department of Iowa
720 Lyon Street
Des Moines, IA 50309
Phone: 515-282-7987
Fax: 515-282-7583
E-mail: alasectreas@ialegion.org

AMERICAN LEGION AUXILIARY DEPARTMENT OF MAINE

http://www.mainelegion.org/

AMERICAN LEGION AUXILIARY DEPARTMENT OF MAINE PAST PRESIDENTS' PARLEY NURSES SCHOLARSHIP

• *See page 329*

AMERICAN LEGION AUXILIARY DEPARTMENT OF MARYLAND

http://www.alamd.org/

AMERICAN LEGION AUXILIARY DEPARTMENT OF MARYLAND PAST PRESIDENTS' PARLEY NURSES SCHOLARSHIP

One scholarship of $2000 for undergraduate students enrolled full-time in nursing study at accredited colleges or universities. Must be U.S. citizen and a descendant of an ex-service veteran.

Academic Fields/Career Goals: Nursing.

Award: Scholarship for use in freshman, sophomore, junior, or senior years; renewable. *Number:* 1. *Amount:* $2000.

Eligibility Requirements: Applicant must be enrolled or expecting to enroll full-time at a four-year institution or university and female. Available to U.S. citizens. Applicant or parent must meet one or more of the following requirements: general military experience; retired from active duty; disabled or killed as a result of military service; prisoner of war; or missing in action.

Application Requirements: Application form, community service, financial need analysis, recommendations or references, transcript. *Deadline:* May 1.

Contact: Pamela Miller, Secretary
Phone: 410-242-9519
E-mail: hq@alamd.org

AMERICAN LEGION AUXILIARY DEPARTMENT OF MICHIGAN

http://www.michalaux.org/

AMERICAN LEGION AUXILIARY DEPARTMENT OF MICHIGAN MEDICAL CAREER SCHOLARSHIP

• *See page 329*

AMERICAN LEGION AUXILIARY DEPARTMENT OF MISSOURI

http://www.missourilegion.org/

AMERICAN LEGION AUXILIARY DEPARTMENT OF MISSOURI PAST PRESIDENTS' PARLEY SCHOLARSHIP

Scholarship of $500 is awarded to high school graduate who has chosen to study nursing. $500 will be awarded upon receipt of verification from the college that student is enrolled. The applicant must be a resident of Missouri and a member of a veteran's family. The applicant must be validated by the sponsoring unit. Check with sponsoring unit for details on required recommendation letters.

Academic Fields/Career Goals: Nursing.

Award: Scholarship for use in freshman year; not renewable. *Number:* 2. *Amount:* $500.

Eligibility Requirements: Applicant must be high school student; planning to enroll or expecting to enroll full-time at a two-year or four-year or technical institution or university and resident of Missouri. Applicant or parent of applicant must be member of American Legion or Auxiliary. Available to U.S. citizens. Applicant or parent must meet one or more of the following requirements: general military experience; retired from active duty; disabled or killed as a result of military service; prisoner of war; or missing in action.

Application Requirements: Application form, personal photograph, resume. *Deadline:* March 1.

Contact: Karen Larson, Department Secretary/Treasurer
Phone: 573-636-9133
E-mail: dptmoala@embarqmail.com

AMERICAN LEGION AUXILIARY DEPARTMENT OF NORTH DAKOTA

http://www.ndlegion.org/

AMERICAN LEGION AUXILIARY DEPARTMENT OF NORTH DAKOTA PAST PRESIDENTS' PARLEY NURSES SCHOLARSHIP

One-time award for North Dakota resident who is the child, grandchild, or great-grandchild of a member of the American Legion or Auxiliary. Must be a graduate of a North Dakota high school and attending a nursing program in North Dakota. A minimum 2.5 GPA is required.

Academic Fields/Career Goals: Nursing.

Award: Scholarship for use in freshman year; not renewable. *Number:* 5. *Amount:* $500.

Eligibility Requirements: Applicant must be enrolled or expecting to enroll full- or part-time at a four-year institution or university; resident of North Dakota and studying in North Dakota. Applicant or parent of applicant must be member of American Legion or Auxiliary. Applicant must have 2.5 GPA or higher. Available to U.S. citizens. Applicant or parent must meet one or more of the following requirements: general military experience; retired from active duty; disabled or killed as a result of military service; prisoner of war; or missing in action.

Application Requirements: Application form, driver's license, essay, financial need analysis, self-addressed stamped envelope with application, test scores, transcript. *Deadline:* May 15.

Contact: Myrna Ronholm, Department Secretary
American Legion Auxiliary Department of North Dakota
PO Box 1060
Jamestown, ND 58402-1060
Phone: 701-253-5992
E-mail: ala-hq@ndlegion.org

AMERICAN LEGION AUXILIARY DEPARTMENT OF OHIO

http://www.alaohio.org/

AMERICAN LEGION AUXILIARY DEPARTMENT OF OHIO PAST PRESIDENTS' PARLEY NURSES SCHOLARSHIP

One-time award worth $300 to $500 for Ohio residents who are the children or grandchildren of a veteran, living or deceased. Must enroll or be enrolled in a nursing program. Application requests must be received by May 1.

Academic Fields/Career Goals: Nursing.

Award: Scholarship for use in freshman, sophomore, junior, or senior years; not renewable. *Number:* 15–20. *Amount:* $300–$500.

Eligibility Requirements: Applicant must be enrolled or expecting to enroll full-time at a two-year or four-year institution or university and resident of Ohio. Available to U.S. citizens. Applicant or parent must meet one or more of the following requirements: general military experience; retired from active duty; disabled or killed as a result of military service; prisoner of war; or missing in action.

Application Requirements: Application form, recommendations or references. *Deadline:* May 1.

Contact: Katie Tucker, Scholarship Coordinator
Phone: 740-452-8245
Fax: 740-452-2620
E-mail: ala_katie@rrohio.com

AMERICAN LEGION AUXILIARY DEPARTMENT OF OREGON

http://www.alaoregon.org/

AMERICAN LEGION AUXILIARY DEPARTMENT OF OREGON NURSES SCHOLARSHIP

One-time award for Oregon residents who are in their senior year of High School, who are the children of veterans who served during eligibility dates for American Legion membership. Must enroll in a nursing program. Contact local units for application.

Academic Fields/Career Goals: Nursing.

Award: Scholarship for use in freshman year; not renewable. *Number:* 1. *Amount:* $1500.

Eligibility Requirements: Applicant must be high school student; planning to enroll or expecting to enroll full- or part-time at a four-year institution or university and resident of Oregon. Available to U.S. citizens. Applicant or parent must meet one or more of the following requirements: general military experience; retired from active duty; disabled or killed as a result of military service; prisoner of war; or missing in action.

Application Requirements: Application form, essay, financial need analysis, interview, transcript. *Deadline:* May 15.

Contact: Virginia Biddle, Secretary/Treasurer
American Legion Auxiliary Department of Oregon
PO Box 1730
Wilsonville, OR 97070
Phone: 503-682-3162
Fax: 503-685-5008
E-mail: alaor@pcez.com

AMERICAN LEGION AUXILIARY DEPARTMENT OF WISCONSIN

http://www.amlegionauxwi.org/

AMERICAN LEGION AUXILIARY DEPARTMENT OF WISCONSIN PAST PRESIDENTS' PARLEY REGISTERED NURSE SCHOLARSHIP

One-time award of $1000. Applicant must be in nursing school or have positive acceptance to an accredited hospital or university registered nursing program. Applicant must be a daughter, son, wife, or widow of a veteran. Granddaughters and great-granddaughters of veterans who are auxiliary members may also apply. Must submit certification of an American Legion Auxiliary unit president, copy of proof that veteran was in service (i.e. discharge papers), letters of recommendation, transcripts, and essay. Must have minimum 3.5 GPA, show financial need, and be a resident of Wisconsin. Applications available on website http://www.legion-aux.org.

Academic Fields/Career Goals: Nursing.

Award: Scholarship for use in freshman, sophomore, junior, or senior years; not renewable. *Number:* 1–2. *Amount:* $750–$1000.

Eligibility Requirements: Applicant must be enrolled or expecting to enroll full- or part-time at an institution or university and resident of Wisconsin. Applicant or parent of applicant must be member of American Legion or Auxiliary. Applicant must have 3.5 GPA or higher. Available to U.S. citizens. Applicant or parent must meet one or more of the following requirements: general military experience; retired from active duty; disabled or killed as a result of military service; prisoner of war; or missing in action.

Application Requirements: Application form, essay, financial need analysis, recommendations or references, transcript. *Deadline:* March 15.

Contact: Bonnie Dorniak, Department Secretary
Phone: 608-745-0124
Fax: 608-745-1947
E-mail: deptsec@amlegionauxwi.org

AMERICAN LEGION AUXILIARY DEPARTMENT OF WYOMING

AMERICAN LEGION AUXILIARY DEPARTMENT OF WYOMING PAST PRESIDENTS' PARLEY HEALTH CARE SCHOLARSHIP

• See page 222

AMERICAN LEGION DEPARTMENT OF KANSAS

http://www.ksamlegion.org/

HOBBLE (LPN) NURSING SCHOLARSHIP

Award of $300, payable one-time at the start of the first semester. Awarded only upon acceptance and verification of enrollment by the scholarship winner in an accredited Kansas school which awards a diploma for Licensed Practical Nursing (LPN). Must pursue this profession in a health related institution such as a nursing home or hospital in Kansas. Must have attained the age of 18 prior to taking the Kansas state board examination. Must be a Kansas resident.

Academic Fields/Career Goals: Nursing.

Award: Scholarship for use in freshman year; not renewable. *Number:* 1. *Amount:* $300.

Eligibility Requirements: Applicant must be enrolled or expecting to enroll full-time at a two-year institution; resident of Kansas and studying in Kansas. Available to U.S. citizens.

Application Requirements: Application form, financial need analysis. *Deadline:* February 15.

Contact: Jim Gravenstein, Chairman, Scholarship Committee
American Legion Department of Kansas
1314 Topeka Boulevard, SW
Topeka, MD 66612
Phone: 785-232-9513
Fax: 785-232-1399

AMERICAN LEGION DEPARTMENT OF MISSOURI

http://www.missourilegion.org/

M.D. "JACK" MURPHY MEMORIAL SCHOLARSHIP

One $750 award for two successive semesters will be given to a Missouri resident who is a RN and under the age of 21. Applicant must be unmarried and a descendant of a veteran with at least ninety days active service in the U.S. Army, Navy, Air Force, Marines, or Coast Guard receiving a Honorable Discharge for service. Applicant must have graduated in the top orty percent of their high school class or have a "C" average or equivalent.

Academic Fields/Career Goals: Nursing.

Award: Scholarship for use in freshman year; not renewable. *Number:* 1. *Amount:* $750.

Eligibility Requirements: Applicant must be high school student; planning to enroll or expecting to enroll full-time at a two-year or four-year institution or university; single female and resident of Missouri. Available to U.S. citizens. Applicant or parent must meet one or more of the following requirements: general military experience; retired from active duty; disabled or killed as a result of military service; prisoner of war; or missing in action.

Application Requirements: Application form, copy of the veteran's discharge or separation notice, financial need analysis, test scores. *Deadline:* April 20.

Contact: John Doane, Chairman
American Legion Department of Missouri
PO Box 179
Jefferson City, MO 65102-0179
Phone: 417-924-8186
Fax: 573-893-2980

AMERICAN LEGION NATIONAL HEADQUARTERS

http://www.legion.org/

EIGHT AND FORTY LUNG AND RESPIRATORY NURSING SCHOLARSHIP FUND

The fund was established to assist registered nurses with advanced preparation for positions in supervision, administration, or teaching. Students are to have prospects of being employed in specific positions in hospitals, clinics, or health departments on completion of their education and the position must have a full-time and direct relationship to lung and respiratory control. Scholarship value is $3000.

Academic Fields/Career Goals: Nursing.

Award: Scholarship for use in junior or senior years; not renewable. *Number:* 1–22. *Amount:* up to $3000.

Eligibility Requirements: Applicant must be enrolled or expecting to enroll full-time at an institution or university. Available to U.S. citizens.

Application Requirements: Application form. *Deadline:* May 15.

Contact: Jason Kees, Program Coordinator
American Legion National Headquarters
The American Legion, PO Box 1055
Indianapolis, IN 46206
Phone: 317-630-1323
Fax: 317-630-1369
E-mail: jkees@legion.org

AMERICAN MOBILE HEALTHCARE

http://www.americanmobile.com/

AMERICAN MOBILE HEALTHCARE ANNUAL SCHOLARSHIP

Scholarship of $2000 awarded to students enrolled in a bachelor's degree in nursing or master's degree in nursing program. Applicant must be enrolled in full time study.

Academic Fields/Career Goals: Nursing.

Award: Scholarship for use in freshman, sophomore, junior, senior, or graduate years; not renewable. *Number:* 1. *Amount:* up to $2000.

Eligibility Requirements: Applicant must be enrolled or expecting to enroll full-time at a four-year institution or university. Available to U.S. citizens.

Application Requirements: Application form. *Deadline:* June 1.

AMERICAN NEPHROLOGY NURSES' ASSOCIATION

http://www.annanurse.org/

ABBOTT/PAMELA BALZER CAREER MOBILITY SCHOLARSHIP

Scholarships available to support qualified ANNA members, who have been members for a minimum of two years, in the pursuit of either a BSN or advanced degree in nursing that will enhance their nephrology nursing practice. Details on website, http://www.annanurse.org.

Academic Fields/Career Goals: Nursing.

Award: Scholarship for use in freshman, sophomore, junior, senior, graduate, or postgraduate years; not renewable. *Number:* 1. *Amount:* $2500.

Eligibility Requirements: Applicant must be enrolled or expecting to enroll full- or part-time at a four-year institution or university. Applicant or parent of applicant must be member of American Nephrology Nurses' Association. Applicant or parent of applicant must have employment or volunteer experience in nursing. Available to U.S. citizens.

Application Requirements: Application form, essay, recommendations or references, transcript. *Deadline:* October 15.

Contact: Sharon Longton, Awards, Scholarships, and Grants
Chairperson
American Nephrology Nurses' Association
200 East Holly Avenue, PO Box 56
Pitman, NJ 08071-0056
Phone: 313-966-2674
E-mail: slongton@dmc.org

AMERICAN NEPHROLOGY NURSES' ASSOCIATION CAREER MOBILITY SCHOLARSHIP

Scholarships available to support qualified ANNA members, who have been a member for a minimum two years, in the pursuit of either BSN or advanced degrees in nursing that will enhance their nephrology nursing practice. Must be accepted or enrolled in baccalaureate or higher degree program in nursing. Must be actively involved in nephrology nursing related health care services. Details on website http://www.annanurse.org.

Academic Fields/Career Goals: Nursing.

Award: Scholarship for use in freshman, sophomore, junior, senior, graduate, or postgraduate years; not renewable. *Number:* 5. *Amount:* $2000.

Eligibility Requirements: Applicant must be enrolled or expecting to enroll full- or part-time at a four-year institution or university. Applicant or parent of applicant must be member of American Nephrology Nurses' Association. Applicant or parent of applicant must have employment or volunteer experience in nursing. Available to U.S. citizens.

Application Requirements: Acceptance letter, application form, essay, recommendations or references, transcript. *Deadline:* October 15.

Contact: Sharon Longton, Awards, Scholarships, and Grants
Chairperson
American Nephrology Nurses' Association
200 East Holly Avenue, PO Box 56
Pitman, NJ 08071-0056
Phone: 313-966-2674
E-mail: slongton@dmc.org

AMERICAN NEPHROLOGY NURSES' ASSOCIATION NNCC CAREER MOBILITY SCHOLARSHIP

Applicants must be current full member of ANNA, having been a member for a minimum of two years. Must have been accepted or enrolled in a baccalaureate or higher degree program in nursing. Must be actively involved in nephrology nursing related health care services. The applicant must hold a current credential as a certified nephrology nurse (CNN) or certified dialysis nurse (CDN) administered by the Nephrology Nursing Certification Commission (NNCC).

Academic Fields/Career Goals: Nursing.

Award: Scholarship for use in freshman, sophomore, junior, senior, graduate, or postgraduate years; not renewable. *Number:* 3. *Amount:* $2000.

Eligibility Requirements: Applicant must be enrolled or expecting to enroll full- or part-time at a four-year institution or university. Applicant or parent of applicant must be member of American Nephrology Nurses' Association. Applicant or parent of applicant must have employment or volunteer experience in nursing. Available to U.S. citizens.

Application Requirements: Application form, essay, recommendations or references, transcript. *Deadline:* October 15.

Contact: Sharon Longton, Awards, Scholarships, and Grants
Chairperson
American Nephrology Nurses' Association
200 East Holly Avenue, PO Box 56
Pitman, NJ 08071-0056
Phone: 313-966-2674
E-mail: slongton@dmc.org

AMERICAN NEPHROLOGY NURSES' ASSOCIATION WATSON PHARMA INC. CAREER MOBILITY SCHOLARSHIP

Applicants must be current full member of ANNA, having been a member for a minimum of two years. Must have been accepted or enrolled in a baccalaureate or higher degree program in nursing. Must be actively involved in nephrology nursing related health care services. For details visit the website http://www.annanurse.org.

Academic Fields/Career Goals: Nursing.

Award: Scholarship for use in freshman, sophomore, junior, senior, graduate, or postgraduate years; not renewable. *Number:* 1. *Amount:* $2500.

Eligibility Requirements: Applicant must be enrolled or expecting to enroll full- or part-time at a four-year institution or university. Applicant or parent of applicant must be member of American Nephrology Nurses' Association. Applicant or parent of applicant must have employment or volunteer experience in nursing. Available to U.S. citizens.

Application Requirements: Application form, essay, recommendations or references, transcript. *Deadline:* October 15.

Contact: Sharon Longton, Awards, Scholarships, and Grants
Chairperson
American Nephrology Nurses' Association
200 East Holly Avenue, PO Box 56
Pitman, NJ 08071-0056
Phone: 313-966-2674
E-mail: slongton@dmc.org

JANEL PARKER CAREER MOBILITY SCHOLARSHIP

Applicants must be current full member of ANNA, having been a member for a minimum of two years. Must have been accepted or enrolled in a baccalaureate or higher degree program in nursing. Must be actively involved in nephrology nursing related health care services. For details visit the website http://www.annanurse.org.

Academic Fields/Career Goals: Nursing.

Award: Scholarship for use in freshman, sophomore, junior, senior, graduate, or postgraduate years; not renewable. *Number:* 1. *Amount:* up to $2500.

Eligibility Requirements: Applicant must be enrolled or expecting to enroll full- or part-time at a two-year or four-year institution or university. Applicant or parent of applicant must be member of American Nephrology Nurses' Association. Applicant or parent of applicant must have employment or volunteer experience in nursing. Available to U.S. citizens.

Application Requirements: Application form, essay, recommendations or references, transcript. *Deadline:* October 15.

Contact: Sharon Longton, Awards, Scholarships, and Grants
Chairperson
American Nephrology Nurses' Association
200 East Holly Avenue, PO Box 56
Pitman, NJ 08071-0056
Phone: 313-966-2674
E-mail: slongton@dmc.org

ARRL FOUNDATION INC.

http://www.arrl.org/

CAROLE J. STREETER, KB9JBR, SCHOLARSHIP
• See page 222

WILLIAM R. GOLDFARB MEMORIAL SCHOLARSHIP
• See page 150

ASSOCIATION ON AMERICAN INDIAN AFFAIRS, INC.

http://www.indian-affairs.org/

ELIZABETH AND SHERMAN ASCHE MEMORIAL SCHOLARSHIP FUND
• See page 91

ATLANTIC HEALTH SYSTEM OVERLOOK HOSPITAL FOUNDATION

http://www.overlookfoundation.org

OVERLOOK HOSPITAL FOUNDATION PROFESSIONAL DEVELOPMENT PROGRAM
• See page 333

BETHESDA LUTHERAN COMMUNITIES

http://www.bethesdalutherancommunities.org/scholarships

DEVELOPMENTAL DISABILITIES AWARENESS AWARDS FOR HIGH SCHOOL STUDENTS WHO ARE LUTHERAN
• See page 333

CAMBRIDGE HOME HEALTH CARE

http://www.cambridgehomehealth.com/

CAMBRIDGE HOME HEALTH CARE NURSING EXCELLENCE SCHOLARSHIPS

Scholarships available for study towards LPN or RN degree. Must be a home health aide/nurse's aide or LPN who has worked for two of the past three years in that position. Two scholarships awarded to Cambridge employees, and two scholarships awarded to residents of the counties where Cambridge Home Health Care offices are located.

Academic Fields/Career Goals: Nursing.

Award: Scholarship for use in freshman, sophomore, junior, or senior years; not renewable. *Number:* up to 4. *Amount:* up to $1000.

Eligibility Requirements: Applicant must be enrolled or expecting to enroll full-time at a four-year institution or university. Applicant or parent of applicant must have employment or volunteer experience in nursing. Available to U.S. citizens.

Application Requirements: Application form, essay, recommendations or references. *Deadline:* May 15.

Contact: Elizabeth Bever, Director of Community Relations
Phone: 330-668-1922 Ext. 105
Fax: 330-668-1311
E-mail: lbever@cambridgehomehealth.com

CANADIAN NURSES FOUNDATION

http://www.cnf-fiic.ca/

CANADIAN NURSES FOUNDATION SCHOLARSHIPS

Study awards are granted annually to Canadian nurses wishing to pursue education and research. Must be a Canadian citizen or permanent resident and provide proof of citizenship. Must be studying in Canada at a Canadian institution. Baccalaureate students must be full-time, masters and doctoral students may be full- or part-time. Additional restrictions vary by specific scholarship.

Academic Fields/Career Goals: Nursing.

Award: Scholarship for use in sophomore, junior, senior, graduate, or postgraduate years; not renewable. *Number:* 50–60. *Amount:* $1500–$10,000.

Eligibility Requirements: Applicant must be Canadian citizen and enrolled or expecting to enroll full- or part-time at a four-year institution or university. Applicant or parent of applicant must have employment or volunteer experience in nursing.

Application Requirements: Application form, application form may be submitted online (http://www.cnf-fiic.ca), community service, recommendations or references, transcript. *Fee:* $35. *Deadline:* March 31.

CENTRAL SCHOLARSHIP

http://www.central-scholarship.org

CHESAPEAKE UROLOGY ASSOCIATES SCHOLARSHIP
• See page 334

CHRISTIANA CARE HEALTH SYSTEMS

http://www.christianacare.org/

RUTH SHAW JUNIOR BOARD SCHOLARSHIP
• *See page 334*

CONGRESSIONAL BLACK CAUCUS FOUNDATION, INC.

http://www.cbcfinc.org/

THE LOUIS STOKES HEALTH SCHOLARS PROGRAM
• *See page 144*

CYNTHIA E. MORGAN SCHOLARSHIP FUND (CEMS)

http://www.cemsfund.com/

CYNTHIA E. MORGAN MEMORIAL SCHOLARSHIP FUND, INC.
• *See page 298*

DADE COMMUNITY FOUNDATION

http://www.jackituckfield.org/

JENNET COLLIFLOWER SCHOLARSHIP

Award for Florida residents enrolled full-time in the junior or senior year of an undergraduate nursing program at a public or private Florida college or university. For additional information and application, go to website at http://www.dadecommunityfoundation.org.

Academic Fields/Career Goals: Nursing.

Award: Scholarship for use in junior or senior years; not renewable. *Number:* 2. *Amount:* $1000.

Eligibility Requirements: Applicant must be enrolled or expecting to enroll full-time at a four-year institution or university; resident of Florida and studying in Florida. Available to U.S. citizens.

Application Requirements: Application form, financial need analysis, personal statement, recommendations or references, transcript. *Deadline:* May 1.

Contact: Ted Seijo, Scholarship Coordinator
    Phone: 305-371-2711
    E-mail: ted.seijo@dadecommunityfoundation.org

DEPARTMENT OF THE ARMY

http://www.goarmy.com/rotc

U.S. ARMY ROTC FOUR-YEAR NURSING SCHOLARSHIP

One-time award for freshman interested in nursing and accepted into an accredited nursing program. Must join ROTC program at the institution, pass physical evaluation, and have minimum GPA of 2.5. Applicant must be a U.S. citizen, have a qualifying SAT or ACT score, and be at least 17 years of age by college enrollment and under 31 years of age at time of graduation. Online application available.

Academic Fields/Career Goals: Nursing.

Award: Scholarship for use in freshman, sophomore, junior, or senior years; not renewable. *Number:* 175. *Amount:* $5000–$50,000.

Eligibility Requirements: Applicant must be physically disabled; age 17-26 and enrolled or expecting to enroll full-time at a four-year institution or university. Applicant must be physically disabled. Applicant must have 2.5 GPA or higher. Available to U.S. citizens. Applicant must have national guard experience.

Application Requirements: Application form, application form may be submitted online (http://www.goarmy.com/rotc/high-school-students/four-year-scholarship.html), essay, interview, test scores, transcript. *Deadline:* January 10.

Contact: Mr. Rodney Roederer, Chief of Scholarship management
    Branch
    Department of the Army
    U.S. Army Cadet Command, Bldg 1002, 204 1st Cavalry
    Regiment Road
    Fort Knox, KY 40121-5123
    Phone: 502-624-7023
    Fax: 502-624-1120
    E-mail: rodney.l.roederer.civ@mail.mil

DERMATOLOGY NURSES' ASSOCIATION

http://www.dnanurse.org/

CAREER MOBILITY SCHOLARSHIP

Provides financial assistance to members of the Dermatology Nurses' Association (DNA) who are pursuing an undergraduate or graduate degree. The candidate must be a DNA member for two years, and be employed in the specialty of dermatology.

Academic Fields/Career Goals: Nursing.

Award: Scholarship for use in freshman, sophomore, junior, senior, or graduate years; not renewable. *Number:* 2. *Amount:* $2500.

Eligibility Requirements: Applicant must be enrolled or expecting to enroll full- or part-time at a four-year or technical institution or university. Applicant or parent of applicant must be member of Dermatology Nurses' Association. Applicant or parent of applicant must have employment or volunteer experience in nursing. Available to U.S. and non-U.S. citizens.

Application Requirements: Application form, essay, financial need analysis, recommendations or references, transcript. *Deadline:* August 31.

EQUALITY SCHOLARSHIP COLLABORATIVE

http://www.equalityscholarship.org

NURSING SCHOLARSHIP

Applicants must be enrolled or accepted for enrollment by the interview date in an accredited ADN or BSN RN program in California. Master's prepared programs with a BA/BS in a field other than nursing will be considered eligible. Current Kaiser Permanente employees or their dependents, RN reentry programs, or current RN to BSN or MSN programs are not eligible for these scholarships. Diploma programs are not eligible.

Academic Fields/Career Goals: Nursing.

Award: Scholarship for use in freshman, sophomore, junior, or graduate years; not renewable. *Number:* 1–2. *Amount:* $6000.

Eligibility Requirements: Applicant must be enrolled or expecting to enroll full- or part-time at a two-year or four-year institution or university; studying in California and must have an interest in LGBT issues. Applicant or parent of applicant must have employment or volunteer experience in community service. Applicant must have 3.0 GPA or higher. Available to U.S. and non-U.S. citizens.

Application Requirements: Application form, application form may be submitted online (http://www.scholarselect.com/scholarships/4662-2013-equality-scholarships), essay, interview, recommendations or references, transcript. *Deadline:* February 1.

EXCEPTIONALNURSE.COM

http://www.exceptionalnurse.com/

ANNA May ROLANDO SCHOLARSHIP AWARD

Scholarship of $500 awarded to a nursing student with a disability. Preference will be given to a graduate student who has demonstrated a commitment to working with people with disabilities.

Academic Fields/Career Goals: Nursing.

Award: Scholarship for use in freshman, sophomore, junior, senior, graduate, or postgraduate years; not renewable. *Number:* 1. *Amount:* $500.

Eligibility Requirements: Applicant must be hearing impaired, learning disabled, physically disabled, or visually impaired and enrolled or expecting to enroll full-time at a four-year institution or university.

Applicant must be hearing impaired, learning disabled, physically disabled, or visually impaired. Available to U.S. citizens.

Application Requirements: Application form, essay, medical verification of disability form, recommendations or references, transcript. *Deadline:* June 1.

Contact: Donna Maheady, Founder
> *Phone:* 561-627-9872
> *Fax:* 561-776-9254
> *E-mail:* exceptionalnurse@aol.com

BRUNO ROLANDO SCHOLARSHIP AWARD

Scholarship of $250 awarded to a nursing student with a disability. Preference will be given to a nursing student who is employed at a Veteran's Hospital.

Academic Fields/Career Goals: Nursing.

Award: Scholarship for use in freshman, sophomore, junior, senior, graduate, or postgraduate years; not renewable. *Number:* 1. *Amount:* $250.

Eligibility Requirements: Applicant must be hearing impaired, learning disabled, physically disabled, or visually impaired and enrolled or expecting to enroll full-time at a four-year institution or university. Applicant or parent of applicant must have employment or volunteer experience in nursing. Applicant must be hearing impaired, learning disabled, physically disabled, or visually impaired. Available to U.S. citizens.

Application Requirements: Application form, essay, medical verification of disability form, recommendations or references, transcript. *Deadline:* June 1.

Contact: Donna Maheady, Founder
> *Phone:* 561-627-9872
> *Fax:* 561-776-9254
> *E-mail:* exceptionalnurse@aol.com

CAROLINE SIMPSON MAHEADY SCHOLARSHIP AWARD

Scholarship of $250 awarded to a nursing student with a disability. Preference will be given to an undergraduate student, of Scottish descent, who has demonstrated a commitment to working with people with disabilities.

Academic Fields/Career Goals: Nursing.

Award: Scholarship for use in freshman, sophomore, junior, senior, graduate, or postgraduate years; not renewable. *Number:* 1. *Amount:* $250.

Eligibility Requirements: Applicant must be hearing impaired, learning disabled, physically disabled, or visually impaired and enrolled or expecting to enroll full-time at a four-year institution or university. Applicant must be hearing impaired, learning disabled, physically disabled, or visually impaired. Available to U.S. citizens.

Application Requirements: Application form, essay, medical verification of disability form, recommendations or references, transcript. *Deadline:* June 1.

Contact: Donna Maheady, Founder
> *Phone:* 561-627-9872
> *Fax:* 561-776-9254
> *E-mail:* exceptionalnurse@aol.com

GENEVIEVE SARAN RICHMOND AWARD

Scholarship of $500 awarded to a nursing student with a disability.

Academic Fields/Career Goals: Nursing.

Award: Scholarship for use in freshman, sophomore, junior, senior, graduate, or postgraduate years; not renewable. *Number:* 1. *Amount:* $500.

Eligibility Requirements: Applicant must be hearing impaired, learning disabled, physically disabled, or visually impaired and enrolled or expecting to enroll full-time at a four-year institution or university. Applicant must be hearing impaired, learning disabled, physically disabled, or visually impaired. Available to U.S. citizens.

Application Requirements: Application form, essay, medical verification of disability form, recommendations or references, transcript. *Deadline:* June 1.

Contact: Donna Maheady, Founder
> *Phone:* 561-627-9872
> *Fax:* 561-776-9254
> *E-mail:* exceptionalnurse@aol.com

JILL LAURA CREEDON SCHOLARSHIP AWARD

Scholarship of $500 awarded to a nursing student with a disability or medical challenge.

Academic Fields/Career Goals: Nursing.

Award: Scholarship for use in freshman, sophomore, junior, senior, graduate, or postgraduate years; not renewable. *Number:* 1. *Amount:* $500.

Eligibility Requirements: Applicant must be hearing impaired, learning disabled, physically disabled, or visually impaired and enrolled or expecting to enroll full-time at a four-year institution or university. Applicant must be hearing impaired, learning disabled, physically disabled, or visually impaired. Available to U.S. citizens.

Application Requirements: Application form, essay, medical verification of disability form, recommendations or references, transcript. *Deadline:* June 1.

Contact: Donna Maheady, Founder
> *Phone:* 561-627-9872
> *Fax:* 561-776-9254
> *E-mail:* exceptionalnurse@aol.com

MARY SERRA GILI SCHOLARSHIP AWARD

Scholarship of $250 awarded to a nursing student with a disability.

Academic Fields/Career Goals: Nursing.

Award: Scholarship for use in freshman, sophomore, junior, senior, graduate, or postgraduate years; not renewable. *Number:* 1. *Amount:* $250.

Eligibility Requirements: Applicant must be hearing impaired, learning disabled, physically disabled, or visually impaired and enrolled or expecting to enroll full-time at a four-year institution or university. Applicant must be hearing impaired, learning disabled, physically disabled, or visually impaired. Available to U.S. citizens.

Application Requirements: Application form, essay, medical verification of disability form, recommendations or references, transcript. *Deadline:* June 1.

Contact: Donna Maheady, Founder
> *Phone:* 561-627-9872
> *Fax:* 561-776-9254
> *E-mail:* exceptionalnurse@aol.com

PETER GILI SCHOLARSHIP AWARD

Scholarship of $500 awarded to a nursing student with a disability.

Academic Fields/Career Goals: Nursing.

Award: Scholarship for use in freshman, sophomore, junior, senior, graduate, or postgraduate years; not renewable. *Number:* 1. *Amount:* $500.

Eligibility Requirements: Applicant must be hearing impaired, learning disabled, physically disabled, or visually impaired and enrolled or expecting to enroll full-time at a four-year institution or university. Applicant must be hearing impaired, learning disabled, physically disabled, or visually impaired. Available to U.S. citizens.

Application Requirements: Application form, essay, medical verification of disability form, recommendations or references, transcript. *Deadline:* June 1.

Contact: Donna Maheady, Founder
> *Phone:* 561-627-9872
> *Fax:* 561-776-9254
> *E-mail:* exceptionalnurse@aol.com

FLORIDA NURSES FOUNDATION

http://www.floridanurse.org/

AGNES NAUGHTON RN-BSN FUND

This fund is established to honor Agnes Naughton who was a lifelong FNA member and the mother of FNA Executive Director Paula Massey. She valued education and this scholarship will assist a RN who is continuing his or her education.

Academic Fields/Career Goals: Nursing.

Award: Scholarship for use in freshman, sophomore, junior, or senior years; not renewable. *Number:* 1. *Amount:* $500.

Eligibility Requirements: Applicant must be enrolled or expecting to enroll full- or part-time at a four-year institution or university; resident of

Florida and studying in Florida. Applicant must have 2.5 GPA or higher. Available to U.S. citizens.

Application Requirements: Application form, application form may be submitted online (http://www.floridanurse.org), essay, recommendations or references, transcript, validation of Florida residency.

Contact: Willa Fuller, Executive Director
E-mail: foundation@floridanurse.org

EDNA HICKS FUND SCHOLARSHIP

Applicant should be enrolled in a nationally accredited nursing program. Must be in associate, baccalaureate, or master's degree nursing programs or doctoral programs. Preference given to nurse researchers from South Florida.

Academic Fields/Career Goals: Nursing.

Award: Scholarship for use in freshman, sophomore, junior, senior, graduate, or postgraduate years; not renewable. *Number:* 1–1. *Amount:* $500–$500.

Eligibility Requirements: Applicant must be enrolled or expecting to enroll full- or part-time at a two-year or four-year institution or university; resident of Florida and studying in Florida. Applicant must have 2.5 GPA or higher. Available to U.S. citizens.

Application Requirements: Application form, driver's license, recommendations or references, transcript. *Deadline:* June 1.

Contact: Willa Fuller, Executive Director
Florida Nurses Foundation
PO Box 536985
Orlando, FL 32803
E-mail: foundation@floridanurse.org

MARY YORK SCHOLARSHIP FUND

Need criteria for the Mary York Scholarship Fund is not restricted at this time.

Academic Fields/Career Goals: Nursing.

Award: Scholarship for use in freshman, sophomore, junior, senior, graduate, or postgraduate years; not renewable. *Number:* 1–1. *Amount:* $500–$500.

Eligibility Requirements: Applicant must be enrolled or expecting to enroll full- or part-time at a two-year or four-year or technical institution or university; resident of Florida and studying in Florida. Applicant must have 2.5 GPA or higher. Available to U.S. citizens.

Application Requirements: Application form, essay, financial need analysis, proof of Florida residency, recommendations or references, transcript. *Deadline:* June 1.

Contact: Willa Fuller, Executive Director
Florida Nurses Foundation
PO Box 536985
Orlando, FL 32803
Phone: 407-896-3261
E-mail: foundation@floridanurse.org

RUTH FINAMORE SCHOLARSHIP FUND

The Ruth Finamore Scholarship Fund is available to all levels of Florida nursing students.

Academic Fields/Career Goals: Nursing.

Award: Scholarship for use in freshman, sophomore, junior, senior, graduate, or postgraduate years; not renewable. *Number:* 1. *Amount:* $500.

Eligibility Requirements: Applicant must be enrolled or expecting to enroll full- or part-time at a two-year or four-year or technical institution or university; resident of Florida and studying in Florida. Applicant must have 2.5 GPA or higher. Available to U.S. citizens.

Application Requirements: Application form, driver's license, essay, financial need analysis, recommendations or references, transcript, validation of Florida residency. *Deadline:* June 1.

Contact: Willa Fuller, Executive Director
Florida Nurses Foundation
PO Box 536985
Orlando, FL 32803
E-mail: foundation@floridanurse.org

UNDINE SAMS AND FRIENDS SCHOLARSHIP FUND

The Undine Sams and Friends Scholarship Fund is available statewide to all levels of Nursing students.

Academic Fields/Career Goals: Nursing.

Award: Scholarship for use in freshman, sophomore, junior, senior, or graduate years; not renewable. *Number:* 1. *Amount:* $500.

Eligibility Requirements: Applicant must be enrolled or expecting to enroll full- or part-time at a two-year or four-year or technical institution or university; resident of Florida and studying in Florida. Applicant must have 2.5 GPA or higher. Available to U.S. citizens.

Application Requirements: Application form, application form may be submitted online (http://www.floridanurse.org), financial need analysis, proof of Florida residency, recommendations or references, transcript. *Deadline:* June 1.

Contact: Willa Fuller, Executive Director
Florida Nurses Foundation
PO Box 536985
Orlando, FL 32803
Phone: 407-896-3261
E-mail: foundation@floridanurse.org

FOUNDATION OF THE NATIONAL STUDENT NURSES' ASSOCIATION

http://www.nsna.org/

BREAKTHROUGH TO NURSING SCHOLARSHIPS FOR RACIAL/ETHNIC MINORITIES

Available to minority students enrolled in nursing or pre-nursing programs. Awards based on need, scholarship, and health-related activities. Application fee of $10. Send self-addressed stamped envelope with two stamps along with application request. Number of awards varies based on donors.

Academic Fields/Career Goals: Nursing.

Award: Scholarship for use in freshman, sophomore, junior, or senior years; not renewable. *Amount:* $1000–$2500.

Eligibility Requirements: Applicant must be American Indian/Alaska Native, Asian/Pacific Islander, Black (non-Hispanic), Hispanic and enrolled or expecting to enroll full- or part-time at a two-year or four-year institution or university. Available to U.S. citizens.

Application Requirements: Application form, financial need analysis, self-addressed stamped envelope with application, transcript. *Fee:* $10. *Deadline:* January 11.

Contact: Lauren Sperle, Scholarship Chairperson
Phone: 718-210-0705
Fax: 718-210-0710
E-mail: lauren@nsna.org

FOUNDATION OF THE NATIONAL STUDENT NURSES' ASSOCIATION CAREER MOBILITY SCHOLARSHIP

One-time award open to registered nurses enrolled in nursing or licensed practical or vocational nurses enrolled in a program leading to licensure as a registered nurse. The award value is $1000 to $2500 and the number of awards varies. Submit copy of license. Application fee: $10. Send self-addressed stamped envelope.

Academic Fields/Career Goals: Nursing.

Award: Scholarship for use in freshman, sophomore, junior, or senior years; not renewable. *Amount:* $1000–$2500.

Eligibility Requirements: Applicant must be enrolled or expecting to enroll full- or part-time at a two-year or four-year institution or university. Available to U.S. citizens.

Application Requirements: Application form, financial need analysis, self-addressed stamped envelope with application, transcript. *Fee:* $10. *Deadline:* January 11.

Contact: Lauren Sperle, Scholarship Chairperson
Phone: 718-210-0705
Fax: 718-210-0710
E-mail: lauren@nsna.org

FOUNDATION OF THE NATIONAL STUDENT NURSES' ASSOCIATION GENERAL SCHOLARSHIPS

One-time award for National Student Nurses' Association members and nonmembers enrolled in nursing programs. Graduating high school seniors are not eligible. Send self-addressed stamped envelope with two stamps for application.

Academic Fields/Career Goals: Nursing.

Award: Scholarship for use in freshman, sophomore, junior, or senior years; not renewable. *Amount:* $1000–$2500.

Eligibility Requirements: Applicant must be enrolled or expecting to enroll full- or part-time at a two-year or four-year institution or university. Available to U.S. citizens.

Application Requirements: Application form, financial need analysis, self-addressed stamped envelope with application, transcript. *Fee:* $10. *Deadline:* January 11.

Contact: Lauren Sperle, Scholarship Chairperson
Phone: 718-210-0705
Fax: 718-210-0710
E-mail: lauren@nsna.org

FOUNDATION OF THE NATIONAL STUDENT NURSES' ASSOCIATION SPECIALTY SCHOLARSHIP

One-time award available to students currently enrolled in a state-approved school of nursing or prenursing. Must have interest in a specialty area of nursing. The award value is $1000 to $2500 and the number of awards granted varies.

Academic Fields/Career Goals: Nursing.

Award: Scholarship for use in freshman, sophomore, junior, or senior years; not renewable. *Amount:* $1000–$2500.

Eligibility Requirements: Applicant must be enrolled or expecting to enroll full- or part-time at a two-year or four-year institution or university. Available to U.S. citizens.

Application Requirements: Application form, financial need analysis, self-addressed stamped envelope with application, transcript. *Fee:* $10. *Deadline:* January 11.

Contact: Lauren Sperle, Scholarship Chairperson
Phone: 718-210-0705
Fax: 718-210-0710
E-mail: lauren@nsna.org

PROMISE OF NURSING SCHOLARSHIP

Applicants attending nursing school in California, South Florida, Georgia, Illinois, Massachusetts, Michigan, New Jersey, Tennessee, or Dallas/Fort Worth, Texas are eligible. Number of awards granted varies.

Academic Fields/Career Goals: Nursing.

Award: Scholarship for use in freshman, sophomore, junior, or senior years; renewable. *Amount:* $1000–$5000.

Eligibility Requirements: Applicant must be enrolled or expecting to enroll full- or part-time at a two-year or four-year institution or university and studying in California, Florida, Georgia, Illinois, Massachusetts, Michigan, New Jersey, Tennessee, Texas. Available to U.S. citizens.

Application Requirements: Application form, financial need analysis, self-addressed stamped envelope with application, transcript. *Fee:* $10. *Deadline:* January 11.

Contact: Lauren Sperle, Scholarship Chairperson
Phone: 718-210-0705
Fax: 718-210-0710
E-mail: lauren@nsna.org

GENESIS HEALTH SERVICES FOUNDATION

http://www.genesishealth.com/

GALA NURSING SCHOLARSHIPS

Scholarships of $6000 for up to five recipients who are seeking admission to, or have been accepted into, an undergraduate baccalaureate program in nursing.

Academic Fields/Career Goals: Nursing.

Award: Scholarship for use in freshman, sophomore, junior, or senior years; not renewable. *Number:* up to 5. *Amount:* $6000.

Eligibility Requirements: Applicant must be enrolled or expecting to enroll full-time at a four-year institution or university; resident of Illinois, Iowa and studying in Illinois, Iowa. Available to U.S. citizens.

Application Requirements: Application form, transcript. *Deadline:* March 8.

Contact: Melinda Gowey, Executive Director
Phone: 563-421-6865
Fax: 563-421-6869
E-mail: goweym@genesishealth.com

GOOD SAMARITAN FOUNDATION

http://www.gsftx.org/

GOOD SAMARITAN FOUNDATION SCHOLARSHIP

Scholarship for nursing students in their clinical level of education. Must be a resident of Texas and plan to work in a U.S. health-care system.

Academic Fields/Career Goals: Nursing.

Award: Scholarship for use in freshman, sophomore, junior, senior, graduate, or postgraduate years; renewable. *Amount:* $1000.

Eligibility Requirements: Applicant must be enrolled or expecting to enroll full-time at a four-year institution or university and resident of Texas. Available to U.S. and non-U.S. citizens.

Application Requirements: Application form. *Deadline:* varies.

Contact: Kay Crawford, Scholarship Director
Phone: 713-529-4646
Fax: 713-521-1169
E-mail: kcrawford@gsftx.org

GREATER KANAWHA VALLEY FOUNDATION

http://www.tgkvf.org/

BERNICE PICKINS PARSONS FUND
• See page 380

ELEANORA G. WYLIE SCHOLARSHIP

Renewable award for West Virginia residents pursuing postsecondary studies in nursing or gerontology. Minimum 2.5 GPA required.

Academic Fields/Career Goals: Nursing.

Award: Scholarship for use in freshman, sophomore, junior, senior, or graduate years; renewable. *Amount:* $350.

Eligibility Requirements: Applicant must be enrolled or expecting to enroll full-time at a four-year institution or university and resident of West Virginia. Applicant must have 2.5 GPA or higher. Available to U.S. citizens.

Application Requirements: Application form, financial need analysis, recommendations or references, test scores, transcript. *Deadline:* January 15.

Contact: Susan Hoover, Scholarship Program Officer
Greater Kanawha Valley Foundation
900 Lee Street East, 16th Floor
Charleston, WV 25301
Phone: 304-346-3620
E-mail: tgkvf@tgkvf.org

GUSTAVUS B. CAPITO FUND

Scholarships awarded to students who show financial need and are seeking education in nursing at any accredited college or university with a nursing program in West Virginia. Scholarships are awarded for one or more years. Must be a resident of West Virginia.

Academic Fields/Career Goals: Nursing.

Award: Scholarship for use in freshman, sophomore, junior, or senior years; renewable. *Amount:* $1000.

Eligibility Requirements: Applicant must be enrolled or expecting to enroll full-time at a four-year institution or university; resident of West Virginia and studying in West Virginia. Available to U.S. citizens.

Application Requirements: Application form, essay, financial need analysis, recommendations or references, transcript. *Deadline:* January 15.

Contact: Susan Hoover, Scholarship Program Officer
Greater Kanawha Valley Foundation
900 Lee Street East, 16th Floor
Charleston, WV 25301
Phone: 304-346-3620
E-mail: tgkvf@tgkvf.org

HEALTH PROFESSIONS EDUCATION FOUNDATION

http://www.healthprofessions.ca.gov/

ASSOCIATE DEGREE NURSING SCHOLARSHIP PROGRAM

One-time award to nursing students accepted to or enrolled in associate degree nursing programs. Eligible applicants may receive up to $8000 per year in financial assistance. Deadlines: March 24 and September 11. Must be a resident of California. Minimum 2.0 GPA.

Academic Fields/Career Goals: Nursing.

Award: Scholarship for use in freshman, sophomore, junior, senior, graduate, or postgraduate years; not renewable. *Number:* up to 30. *Amount:* up to $8000.

Eligibility Requirements: Applicant must be enrolled or expecting to enroll full- or part-time at a two-year or four-year institution or university; resident of California and studying in California. Available to U.S. citizens.

Application Requirements: Application form, essay, financial need analysis, graduation date verification form, verification of language fluency, recommendations or references, transcript. *Deadline:* varies.

Contact: James Hall, Program Administrator
Health Professions Education Foundation
400 R Street
Sacramento, CA 95811
Phone: 916-326-3640
Fax: 916-324-6585

HEALTH PROFESSIONS EDUCATION FOUNDATION BACHELOR OF SCIENCE NURSING SCHOLARSHIP PROGRAM

Scholarship of up to $10,000 for students pursuing bachelor's degree in nursing. Available for both full- and part-time students. Must be U.S. citizen.

Academic Fields/Career Goals: Nursing.

Award: Scholarship for use in freshman, sophomore, junior, senior, graduate, or postgraduate years; not renewable. *Number:* up to 40. *Amount:* up to $10,000.

Eligibility Requirements: Applicant must be enrolled or expecting to enroll full- or part-time at a two-year or four-year institution or university. Available to U.S. citizens.

Application Requirements: Application form, personal statement, Student Aid Report (SAR) or tax return with W2, certification of enrollment, recommendations or references, transcript. *Deadline:* varies.

Contact: Margarita Miranda, Program Administrator
Health Professions Education Foundation
400 R Street
Sacramento, CA 95811
Phone: 916-326-3640

REGISTERED NURSE EDUCATION LOAN REPAYMENT PROGRAM

Repays governmental and commercial loans that were obtained for tuition expenses, books, equipment, and reasonable living expenses associated with attending college. In return for the repayment of educational debt, loan repayment recipients are required to practice full-time in direct patient care in a medically underserved area or county health facility. Deadlines: March 24 and September 11. Must be resident of California.

Academic Fields/Career Goals: Nursing.

Award: Grant for use in senior, graduate, or postgraduate years; not renewable. *Number:* 50–70. *Amount:* up to $10,000.

Eligibility Requirements: Applicant must be enrolled or expecting to enroll full- or part-time at a four-year institution or university; resident of California and studying in California. Available to U.S. citizens.

Application Requirements: Application form, financial need analysis, recommendations or references, transcript. *Deadline:* varies.

Contact: Monique Scott, Program Director
Health Professions Education Foundation
818 K Street, Suite 210
Sacramento, CA 95814
Phone: 916-324-6500
Fax: 916-324-6585
E-mail: mvoss@oshpd.state.ca.us

RN EDUCATION SCHOLARSHIP PROGRAM

One-time award to nursing students accepted to or enrolled in baccalaureate degree nursing programs in California. Eligible applicants may receive up to $10,000 per year in financial assistance. Deadlines: March 24 and September 11. Must be resident of California and a U.S. citizen. Minimum 2.0 GPA.

Academic Fields/Career Goals: Nursing.

Award: Scholarship for use in freshman, sophomore, junior, or senior years; not renewable. *Number:* 50–70. *Amount:* up to $10,000.

Eligibility Requirements: Applicant must be enrolled or expecting to enroll full- or part-time at a two-year or four-year institution or university; resident of California and studying in California. Available to U.S. citizens.

Application Requirements: Application form, employment verification form, proof of RN license, verification of language fluency, essay, financial need analysis, recommendations or references, transcript. *Deadline:* varies.

Contact: Monique Scott, Program Director
Health Professions Education Foundation
818 K Street, Suite 210
Sacramento, CA 95814
Phone: 916-324-6500
Fax: 916-324-6585
E-mail: mvoss@oshpd.state.ca.us

VOCATIONAL NURSE SCHOLARSHIP PROGRAM

Scholarships are available to students who are enrolled or accepted in an accredited Vocational Nurse program. Awardees must sign a contract with the Office of Statewide Health Planning and Development. Minimum 2.0 GPA required. Deadlines: March 24 and September 11.

Academic Fields/Career Goals: Nursing.

Award: Scholarship for use in freshman or sophomore years; not renewable. *Amount:* $4000–$8000.

Eligibility Requirements: Applicant must be enrolled or expecting to enroll full- or part-time at a two-year or technical institution and resident of California. Available to U.S. citizens.

Application Requirements: Application form, recommendations or references, Student Aid Report (SAR), personal statement, educational debt reporting form, transcript. *Deadline:* varies.

HEALTH RESEARCH COUNCIL OF NEW ZEALAND

http://www.hrc.govt.nz/

PACIFIC HEALTH WORKFORCE AWARD
• See page 327

PACIFIC MENTAL HEALTH WORK FORCE AWARD
• See page 327

ILLINOIS NURSES ASSOCIATION

http://www.illinoisnurses.com/

SONNE SCHOLARSHIP

One-time award of up to $3000 available to nursing students. Funds may be used to cover tuition, fees, or any other cost encountered by students enrolled in Illinois state-approved nursing program. Award limited to U.S. citizens who are residents of Illinois. Recipients will receive a year's free membership in INA upon graduation.

Academic Fields/Career Goals: Nursing.

Award: Scholarship for use in freshman, sophomore, junior, or senior years; not renewable. *Number:* 2–4. *Amount:* $1000–$3000.

Eligibility Requirements: Applicant must be enrolled or expecting to enroll full-time at a four-year institution or university; resident of Illinois and studying in Illinois. Applicant must have 3.5 GPA or higher. Available to U.S. citizens.

Application Requirements: Application form, essay, financial need analysis, recommendations or references, transcript. *Deadline:* March 15.

Contact: Melinda Sweeney, Sonne Scholarship Committee
Illinois Nurses Association
105 West Adams Street, Suite 2101
Chicago, IL 60603
Phone: 312-419-2900 Ext. 222
Fax: 312-419-2920
E-mail: msweeney@illinoisnurses.com

INDEPENDENT COLLEGE FUND OF NEW JERSEY

http://www.njcolleges.org/

C.R. BARD FOUNDATION, INC. NURSING SCHOLARSHIP

Applicant must be entering at least the second semester of their sophomore year or the second semester of the second year of their nursing program and be enrolled full time at an ICFNJ member college or university. Must maintain a minimum GPA of 3.0.

Academic Fields/Career Goals: Nursing.

Award: Scholarship for use in junior or senior years; not renewable. *Number:* 10. *Amount:* $2500.

Eligibility Requirements: Applicant must be enrolled or expecting to enroll full-time at a four-year institution or university and studying in New Jersey. Applicant must have 3.0 GPA or higher. Available to U.S. citizens.

Application Requirements: Application form, community service, essay, financial need analysis, recommendations or references, resume, transcript. *Deadline:* April 30.

Contact: Ms. Yvette Panella, Scholarship Coordinator
Independent College Fund of New Jersey
797 Springfield Avenue
Summit, NJ 07901
Phone: 908-277-3424
Fax: 908-277-0851
E-mail: scholarships@njcolleges.org

INDIANA HEALTH CARE POLICY INSTITUTE

http://www.ihca.org/

INDIANA HEALTH CARE POLICY INSTITUTE NURSING SCHOLARSHIP

Scholarship is for students pursuing a career in long-term care. One-time award of up to $5000 for Indiana residents studying nursing at an institution in Indiana, Ohio, Kentucky, Illinois or Michigan. Minimum 2.5 GPA required. Total number of awards varies.

Academic Fields/Career Goals: Nursing.

Award: Scholarship for use in freshman, sophomore, junior, or senior years; not renewable. *Number:* 1–5. *Amount:* $750–$5000.

Eligibility Requirements: Applicant must be enrolled or expecting to enroll full- or part-time at a two-year or four-year or technical institution or university; resident of Indiana and studying in Illinois, Indiana, Kentucky, Michigan, Ohio. Applicant must have 2.5 GPA or higher. Available to U.S. citizens.

Application Requirements: Application form, essay, interview, recommendations or references, transcript. *Deadline:* May 13.

Contact: Dorothy Henry, Executive Director
Indiana Health Care Policy Institute
One North Capitol Avenue, Suite 100
Indianapolis, IN 46204
Phone: 317-616-9028
Fax: 877-298-3749
E-mail: dhenry@ihca.org

INDIAN HEALTH SERVICES, UNITED STATES DEPARTMENT OF HEALTH AND HUMAN SERVICES

http://www.ihs.gov/scholarship

HEALTH PROFESSIONS PREPARATORY SCHOLARSHIP PROGRAM
• *See page 141*

INDIAN HEALTH SERVICE HEALTH PROFESSIONS SCHOLARSHIP PROGRAM
• *See page 208*

INTERNATIONAL ORDER OF THE KING'S DAUGHTERS AND SONS

http://www.iokds.org/

HEALTH CAREERS SCHOLARSHIP
• *See page 223*

JEWISH VOCATIONAL SERVICE CHICAGO

http://www.jvschicago.org/

JEWISH FEDERATION ACADEMIC SCHOLARSHIP PROGRAM
• *See page 120*

KAISER PERMANENTE

http://kpapan.org/

DELORAS JONES RN EXCELLENCE IN BACHELOR'S DEGREE NURSING SCHOLARSHIP

Merit-based scholarships of $5000 are awarded to Kaiser Permanente employees who are pursuing a bachelor's degree in nursing. Minimum 3.0 GPA required.

Academic Fields/Career Goals: Nursing.

Award: Scholarship for use in freshman, sophomore, junior, or senior years; not renewable. *Amount:* $5000.

Eligibility Requirements: Applicant must be enrolled or expecting to enroll full-time at a four-year institution or university and resident of California. Applicant or parent of applicant must be affiliated with Kaiser Permanente. Applicant must have 3.0 GPA or higher. Available to U.S. citizens.

Application Requirements: Application form, transcript. *Deadline:* varies.

Contact: Dr. Michael Tran, KPAPAN Scholarship Committee Chairman
E-mail: michael.j.tran@kp.org

DELORAS JONES RN NURSING AS A SECOND CAREER SCHOLARSHIP

Need-based scholarships of $1000 to $2500 are offered to students enrolled in approved nursing degree programs in California. Applicants must be pursuing nursing as a second career. Minimum 2.5 GPA required.

Academic Fields/Career Goals: Nursing.

Award: Scholarship for use in freshman, sophomore, junior, senior, or graduate years; not renewable. *Amount:* $1000–$2500.

Eligibility Requirements: Applicant must be enrolled or expecting to enroll full-time at a four-year institution or university; resident of California and studying in California. Applicant must have 2.5 GPA or higher. Available to U.S. citizens.

Application Requirements: Application form, transcript. *Deadline:* varies.

Contact: Dr. Michael Tran, KPAPAN Scholarship Committee Chairman
E-mail: michael.j.tran@kp.org

DELORAS JONES RN SCHOLARSHIP PROGRAM

Scholarship of up to $2500 awarded to nursing students in California having completed at least one academic term with minimum GPA of 2.5.

Academic Fields/Career Goals: Nursing.

Award: Scholarship for use in sophomore, junior, or senior years; not renewable. *Amount:* $1000–$2500.

Eligibility Requirements: Applicant must be enrolled or expecting to enroll full-time at a four-year institution or university; resident of California and studying in California. Applicant must have 2.5 GPA or higher. Available to U.S. citizens.

Application Requirements: Application form, copy of federal income tax return, financial need analysis, recommendations or references, transcript. *Deadline:* March 15.

Contact: Dr. Michael Tran, KPAPAN Scholarship Committee Chairman
E-mail: michael.j.tran@kp.org

DELORAS JONES RN UNDERREPRESENTED GROUPS IN NURSING SCHOLARSHIP

Need-based scholarships of $1000 to $2500 are offered to minority and male students enrolled in approved nursing degree programs in California.

Academic Fields/Career Goals: Nursing.

Award: Scholarship for use in freshman, sophomore, junior, senior, or graduate years; not renewable. *Amount:* $1000–$2500.

Eligibility Requirements: Applicant must be American Indian/Alaska Native, Asian/Pacific Islander, Black (non-Hispanic), Hispanic; enrolled or expecting to enroll full- or part-time at a four-year institution or university; resident of California and studying in California. Available to U.S. citizens.

Application Requirements: Application form. *Deadline:* varies.

Contact: Dr. Michael Tran, KPAPAN Scholarship Committee Chairman
E-mail: michael.j.tran@kp.org

KANSAS BOARD OF REGENTS

http://www.kansasregents.org/

KANSAS NURSING SERVICE SCHOLARSHIP PROGRAM

This is a service scholarship loan program available to students attending two-year or four-year public and private postsecondary institutions as well as vocational technical schools with nursing education programs. Students can be pursuing either LPN or RN licensure. This is a service obligation scholarship, therefore students must agree to work in the field of nursing one year for each year they have received the scholarship or must repay the amount of the scholarship award that they received plus interest. Students must be Kansas residents attending a postsecondary institution in Kansas.

Academic Fields/Career Goals: Nursing.

Award: Scholarship for use in freshman, sophomore, junior, or senior years; renewable. *Amount:* $2500–$3500.

Eligibility Requirements: Applicant must be enrolled or expecting to enroll full-time at a two-year or four-year or technical institution or university. Available to U.S. citizens.

Application Requirements: Application form, financial need analysis. *Fee:* $12. *Deadline:* May 1.

Contact: Diane Lindeman, Director of Student Financial Assistance
Kansas Board of Regents
1000 SW Jackson, Suite 520
Topeka, KS 66612
Phone: 785-296-3517
Fax: 785-296-0983
E-mail: dlindeman@ksbor.org

LADIES AUXILIARY TO THE VETERANS OF FOREIGN WARS, DEPARTMENT OF MAINE

http://mainevfw.org/

FRANCES L. BOOTH MEDICAL SCHOLARSHIP SPONSORED BY LAVFW DEPARTMENT OF MAINE

• See page 336

MARION D. AND EVA S. PEEPLES FOUNDATION TRUST SCHOLARSHIP PROGRAM

http://www.jccf.org/

MARION A. AND EVA S. PEEPLES SCHOLARSHIPS

• See page 240

MARSHA'S ANGELS SCHOLARSHIP FUND

http://www.marshasangels.org/

MARSHA'S ANGELS SCHOLARSHIP FUND

Scholarship for students who have completed all prerequisites to enter their first year of an accredited nursing program. Applicants who are residents of Sedgwick County, Kansas or one of the surrounding counties may attend an accredited nursing program anywhere in the U.S.; applicants from any other state in the U.S. may use the scholarship to attend a qualified program in Sedgwick County, Kansas, one of the surrounding counties, or St. Luke's College in Kansas City, Missouri.

Academic Fields/Career Goals: Nursing.

Award: Scholarship for use in freshman year; renewable. *Number:* 1. *Amount:* $2000.

Eligibility Requirements: Applicant must be enrolled or expecting to enroll full-time at a two-year or four-year institution or university. Available to U.S. citizens.

Application Requirements: Application form, application form may be submitted online (http://www.marshasangels.org), community service, essay, recommendations or references. *Deadline:* June 30.

MARYLAND STATE HIGHER EDUCATION COMMISSION

http://www.mhec.state.md.us/

GRADUATE AND PROFESSIONAL SCHOLARSHIP PROGRAM-MARYLAND

• See page 224

JANET L. HOFFMANN LOAN ASSISTANCE REPAYMENT PROGRAM

• See page 240

TUITION REDUCTION FOR NON-RESIDENT NURSING STUDENTS

Available to nonresidents of Maryland who attend a two-year or four-year public institution in Maryland. It is renewable provided student maintains academic requirements designated by institution attended. Recipient must agree to serve as a full-time nurse in a hospital or related institution for two to four years.

Academic Fields/Career Goals: Nursing.

Award: Scholarship for use in freshman, sophomore, junior, or senior years; renewable.

Eligibility Requirements: Applicant must be enrolled or expecting to enroll full- or part-time at a two-year or four-year institution and studying in Maryland. Available to U.S. citizens.

Application Requirements: Application form. *Deadline:* varies.

Contact: Robert Parker, Director
Phone: 410-260-4558
E-mail: rparker@mhec.state.md.us

MICHIGAN LEAGUE FOR NURSING

http://www.michleaguenursing.org/

NURSING STUDENT SCHOLARSHIP

Four $500 scholarships will be awarded to students currently enrolled in a licensed practical nurse, associate degree, or bachelors degree nursing education program. Must have successfully completed at least one nursing course with a clinical component. For Michigan residents to use at colleges and universities within the state of Michigan.

Academic Fields/Career Goals: Nursing.

Award: Scholarship for use in sophomore, junior, or senior years; not renewable. *Number:* 4. *Amount:* $500.

Eligibility Requirements: Applicant must be enrolled or expecting to enroll full-time at a two-year or four-year institution; resident of Michigan and studying in Michigan. Available to U.S. and non-U.S. citizens.

Application Requirements: Application form, community service, essay, letters of endorsement, recommendations or references, transcript. *Deadline:* January 1.

Contact: Carole Stacy, Director
Michigan League for Nursing
2410 Woodlake Drive
Okemos, MI 48864
Phone: 517-347-8091
Fax: 517-347-4096
E-mail: cstacy@mhc.org

MINORITY NURSE MAGAZINE

http://www.minoritynurse.com/

MINORITY NURSE MAGAZINE SCHOLARSHIP PROGRAM

Scholarships to help academically excellent, financially needy racial and ethnic minority nursing students complete a BSN degree.

Academic Fields/Career Goals: Nursing.

Award: Scholarship for use in junior or senior years; not renewable. *Number:* 3. *Amount:* $1000–$3000.

Eligibility Requirements: Applicant must be American Indian/Alaska Native, Asian/Pacific Islander, Black (non-Hispanic), Hispanic and enrolled or expecting to enroll full- or part-time at a four-year institution or university. Applicant must have 3.0 GPA or higher. Available to U.S. citizens.

Application Requirements: Application form, community service, essay, recommendations or references, transcript. *Deadline:* February 1.

Contact: Ms. Pam Chwedyk, Senior Editor and Editorial Manager
Phone: 312-525-3095
E-mail: pchwedyk@alloyeducation.com

MISSISSIPPI NURSES' ASSOCIATION (MNA)

http://www.msnurses.org/

MISSISSIPPI NURSES' ASSOCIATION FOUNDATION SCHOLARSHIP

Scholarship of $1000 to a Mississippi resident. Applicant should major in nursing and be a member of MASN.

Academic Fields/Career Goals: Nursing.

Award: Scholarship for use in freshman, sophomore, junior, or senior years; not renewable. *Number:* 1. *Amount:* $1000.

Eligibility Requirements: Applicant must be enrolled or expecting to enroll full- or part-time at a four-year institution or university and resident of Mississippi. Available to U.S. citizens.

Application Requirements: Application form, essay, recommendations or references, transcript. *Deadline:* October 1.

MOUNT SINAI HOSPITAL DEPARTMENT OF NURSING

http://www.mountsinai.org/

BSN STUDENT SCHOLARSHIP/WORK REPAYMENT PROGRAM

$3000 award for senior nursing student or in the last semester/year of the program. Minimum GPA is 3.25.

Academic Fields/Career Goals: Nursing.

Award: Scholarship for use in senior year; not renewable. *Amount:* $3000.

Eligibility Requirements: Applicant must be enrolled or expecting to enroll full-time at a four-year institution or university. Available to U.S. citizens.

Application Requirements: Application form, recommendations or references, resume, transcript. *Deadline:* October 1.

Contact: Maria Vezina, Director, Nursing Education and Recruitment
Mount Sinai Hospital Department of Nursing
One Gustave Levy Place, PO Box 1144
New York, NY 10029

NATIONAL ASSOCIATION DIRECTORS OF NURSING ADMINISTRATION

http://www.nadona.org/

NADONA/LTC STEPHANIE CARROLL MEMORIAL SCHOLARSHIP

Scholarship is for nursing student enrolled in an accredited nursing program or nursing students in an undergraduate or graduate program. Also for employees in the long term care continuum achieving an LPN/LVN.

Academic Fields/Career Goals: Nursing.

Award: Scholarship for use in freshman, sophomore, junior, senior, or graduate years; not renewable. *Number:* 1–20. *Amount:* $1000–$5000.

Eligibility Requirements: Applicant must be enrolled or expecting to enroll full- or part-time at a two-year or four-year or technical institution or university. Available to U.S. citizens.

Application Requirements: Application form, essay, financial need analysis, personal photograph, transcript. *Deadline:* May 15.

Contact: Sherrie Dornberger, Executive Director
National Association Directors of Nursing Administration
11353 Reed Hartman Highway, Suite 210, Reed Hartman Tower
Cincinnati, OH 45241
Phone: 800-222-0539
Fax: 513-791-3699
E-mail: sherrie@nadona.org

NATIONAL ASSOCIATION OF HISPANIC NURSES

http://www.nahnnet.org

NAHN SCHOLARSHIPS

Awards are presented to NAHN members only (must be a member for at least 6 months) enrolled in associate, diploma, baccalaureate, graduate or practical/vocational nursing programs. Selection based on current academic standing. Scholarship award recipients are a select group of Hispanic students who demonstrate promise of future professional contributions to the nursing profession and who have the potential to act as role models for other aspiring nursing students.

Academic Fields/Career Goals: Nursing.

Award: Scholarship for use in freshman, sophomore, junior, senior, or graduate years; not renewable.

Eligibility Requirements: Applicant must be of Hispanic heritage and enrolled or expecting to enroll full-time at a four-year or technical institution or university. Available to U.S. citizens.

Application Requirements: Application form, essay, recommendations or references, transcript. *Deadline:* varies.

Contact: Celia Besore, Executive Director and CEO
Phone: 202-387-2477
Fax: 202-483-7183
E-mail: info@thehispanicnurses.org

NATIONAL BLACK NURSES ASSOCIATION INC.

http://www.nbna.org/

DR. HILDA RICHARDS SCHOLARSHIP

Scholarship for nurses currently enrolled in a nursing program who are members of NBNA. Applicant must have at least one full year of school remaining.

Academic Fields/Career Goals: Nursing.

Award: Scholarship for use in freshman, sophomore, junior, senior, graduate, or postgraduate years; not renewable. *Number:* 1. *Amount:* $1000–$2000.

Eligibility Requirements: Applicant must be enrolled or expecting to enroll full-time at a two-year or four-year institution or university. Applicant or parent of applicant must be member of National Black Nurses' Association. Applicant or parent of applicant must have employment or volunteer experience in community service. Available to U.S. and non-U.S. citizens.

Application Requirements: Application form, essay, personal photograph, recommendations or references, self-addressed stamped envelope with application, transcript. *Deadline:* April 15.

DR. LAURANNE SAMS SCHOLARSHIP

Award available for NBNA member who is currently enrolled full-time in a nursing program. Applicant must have at least one full year of school remaining. Scholarships will range from $1000 to $2000.

Academic Fields/Career Goals: Nursing.

Award: Scholarship for use in freshman, sophomore, junior, senior, graduate, or postgraduate years; not renewable. *Number:* up to 5. *Amount:* $1000–$2000.

Eligibility Requirements: Applicant must be enrolled or expecting to enroll full-time at a two-year or four-year institution or university. Applicant or parent of applicant must be member of National Black Nurses' Association. Available to U.S. and non-U.S. citizens.

Application Requirements: Application form, essay, recommendations or references, self-addressed stamped envelope with application, transcript. *Deadline:* April 15.

KAISER PERMANENTE SCHOOL OF ANESTHESIA SCHOLARSHIP

Scholarship for nurses currently enrolled in a nursing program who are active members of NBNA. Must have at least one full year of school remaining.

Academic Fields/Career Goals: Nursing.

Award: Scholarship for use in freshman, sophomore, junior, senior, graduate, or postgraduate years; not renewable. *Number:* 1. *Amount:* $1000–$2000.

Eligibility Requirements: Applicant must be enrolled or expecting to enroll full-time at a two-year or four-year institution or university. Applicant or parent of applicant must be member of National Black Nurses' Association. Available to U.S. and non-U.S. citizens.

Application Requirements: Application form, essay, recommendations or references, self-addressed stamped envelope with application, transcript. *Deadline:* April 15.

MARTHA R. DUDLEY LVN/LPN SCHOLARSHIP

Scholarship available for nurses currently enrolled full-time in a nursing program and must be a member of NBNA. Applicant must have at least one full year of school remaining. Scholarships will range from $1000 to $2000.

Academic Fields/Career Goals: Nursing.

Award: Scholarship for use in freshman, sophomore, junior, senior, graduate, or postgraduate years; not renewable. *Number:* 1. *Amount:* $1000–$2000.

Eligibility Requirements: Applicant must be Black (non-Hispanic) and enrolled or expecting to enroll full-time at a two-year or four-year institution or university. Applicant or parent of applicant must be member of National Black Nurses' Association. Applicant or parent of applicant must have employment or volunteer experience in community service. Available to U.S. and non-U.S. citizens.

Application Requirements: Application form, essay, personal photograph, recommendations or references, self-addressed stamped envelope with application, transcript. *Deadline:* April 15.

MAYO FOUNDATIONS SCHOLARSHIP

Scholarship for nurses currently enrolled full-time in a nursing program who are members of NBNA. Applicant must have at least one full year of school remaining.

Academic Fields/Career Goals: Nursing.

Award: Scholarship for use in freshman, sophomore, junior, senior, graduate, or postgraduate years; not renewable. *Number:* 1. *Amount:* $1000–$2000.

Eligibility Requirements: Applicant must be enrolled or expecting to enroll full-time at a two-year or four-year institution or university. Applicant or parent of applicant must be member of National Black Nurses' Association. Available to U.S. and non-U.S. citizens.

Application Requirements: Application form, essay, personal photograph, recommendations or references, self-addressed stamped envelope with application, transcript. *Deadline:* April 15.

NBNA BOARD OF DIRECTORS SCHOLARSHIP

The scholarship enables nurses to grow and better contribute their talents to the health and healthcare of communities. Candidate must be currently enrolled in a nursing program with at least one full year of school remaining and must be a member of NBNA.

Academic Fields/Career Goals: Nursing.

Award: Scholarship for use in freshman, sophomore, junior, senior, graduate, or postgraduate years; not renewable. *Number:* up to 2. *Amount:* $1000–$2000.

Eligibility Requirements: Applicant must be enrolled or expecting to enroll full-time at a two-year or four-year institution or university. Applicant or parent of applicant must be member of National Black Nurses' Association. Applicant or parent of applicant must have employment or volunteer experience in community service. Available to U.S. and non-U.S. citizens.

Application Requirements: Application form, essay, personal photograph, recommendations or references, self-addressed stamped envelope with application, transcript. *Deadline:* April 15.

NURSING SPECTRUM SCHOLARSHIP

Scholarship enables nurses to grow and better contribute their talents to the health and healthcare of communities. Candidate must be currently enrolled in a nursing program and be a member of NBNA. Applicant must have at least one full year of school remaining.

Academic Fields/Career Goals: Nursing.

Award: Scholarship for use in freshman, sophomore, junior, senior, graduate, or postgraduate years; not renewable. *Number:* 1. *Amount:* $1000–$2000.

Eligibility Requirements: Applicant must be enrolled or expecting to enroll full-time at a two-year or four-year institution or university. Applicant or parent of applicant must be member of National Black Nurses' Association. Available to U.S. and non-U.S. citizens.

Application Requirements: Application form, essay, recommendations or references, self-addressed stamped envelope with application, transcript. *Deadline:* April 15.

NATIONAL SOCIETY DAUGHTERS OF THE AMERICAN REVOLUTION

http://www.dar.org/

NATIONAL SOCIETY DAUGHTERS OF THE AMERICAN REVOLUTION CAROLINE E. HOLT NURSING SCHOLARSHIPS

One-time award of $1000 for students who are in financial need and have been accepted or are enrolled in an accredited school of nursing. A letter of acceptance into the nursing program or the transcript stating that the applicant is enrolled in the nursing program must be included with the application.

Academic Fields/Career Goals: Nursing.

Award: Scholarship for use in freshman, sophomore, junior, or senior years; not renewable. *Amount:* $1000.

Eligibility Requirements: Applicant must be enrolled or expecting to enroll full-time at a two-year or four-year institution or university. Available to U.S. citizens.

Application Requirements: Application form, financial need analysis, letter of sponsorship, self-addressed stamped envelope with application, transcript. *Deadline:* February 15.

Contact: Tania Tatum, Manager, Office of the Reporter General
   Phone: 202-628-1776
   Fax: 202-879-3348
   E-mail: nsdarscholarships@dar.org

NATIONAL SOCIETY DAUGHTERS OF THE AMERICAN REVOLUTION MADELINE PICKETT (HALBERT) COGSWELL NURSING SCHOLARSHIP

Scholarship available to students who have been accepted or are currently enrolled in an accredited school of nursing, who are members of NSDAR, descendants of members of NSDAR, or are eligible to be members of NSDAR. A letter of acceptance into the nursing program or transcript showing enrollment in nursing program must be included with the application. DAR member number must be on the application.

Academic Fields/Career Goals: Nursing.

Award: Scholarship for use in freshman, sophomore, junior, or senior years; not renewable. *Amount:* $1000.

Eligibility Requirements: Applicant must be enrolled or expecting to enroll full-time at a two-year or four-year institution or university. Applicant or parent of applicant must be member of Daughters of the American Revolution. Available to U.S. and non-U.S. citizens.

Application Requirements: Application form, letter of sponsorship, recommendations or references, self-addressed stamped envelope with application. *Deadline:* February 15.

Contact: Tania Tatum, Manager, Office of the Reporter General
 Phone: 202-628-1776
 Fax: 202-879-3348
 E-mail: nsdarscholarships@dar.org

NATIONAL SOCIETY DAUGHTERS OF THE AMERICAN REVOLUTION MILDRED NUTTING NURSING SCHOLARSHIP

A one-time $1000 scholarship for students who are in financial need and who have been accepted or are currently enrolled in an accredited school of nursing. A letter of acceptance into the nursing program or the transcript stating that the applicant is in the nursing program must be enclosed with the application. Preference will be given to candidates from the Lowell, Massachusetts area.

Academic Fields/Career Goals: Nursing.

Award: Scholarship for use in freshman, sophomore, junior, or senior years; not renewable. *Amount:* $1000.

Eligibility Requirements: Applicant must be enrolled or expecting to enroll full-time at a two-year or four-year institution or university. Available to U.S. citizens.

Application Requirements: Application form, essay, financial need analysis, letter of sponsorship, recommendations or references, self-addressed stamped envelope with application, test scores, transcript. *Deadline:* February 15.

Contact: Tania Tatum, Manager, Office of the Reporter General
 Phone: 202-628-1776
 Fax: 202-879-3348
 E-mail: nsdarscholarships@dar.org

NATIONAL SOCIETY OF THE COLONIAL DAMES OF AMERICA

http://www.nscda.org/

AMERICAN INDIAN NURSE SCHOLARSHIP AWARDS
• See page 327

NEW JERSEY STATE NURSES ASSOCIATION

http://www.njsna.org/

INSTITUTE FOR NURSING SCHOLARSHIP

Applicants must be New Jersey residents currently enrolled in a diploma, associate, baccalaureate, master's, or doctoral program in nursing or a related field. The amount awarded in each scholarship will be $1000 per recipient.

Academic Fields/Career Goals: Nursing.

Award: Scholarship for use in freshman, sophomore, junior, senior, or graduate years; not renewable. *Number:* 14. *Amount:* $1000.

Eligibility Requirements: Applicant must be enrolled or expecting to enroll full-time at a two-year or four-year institution or university and resident of New Jersey. Available to U.S. citizens.

Application Requirements: Application form, recommendations or references, tax form, transcript. *Deadline:* varies.

Contact: Sandy Kerr, Executive Assistant
 Phone: 609-883-5335
 Fax: 609-883-5343
 E-mail: sandy@njsna.org

NEW YORK STATE EMERGENCY NURSES ASSOCIATION (ENA)

http://www.ena.org/

NEW YORK STATE ENA September 11 SCHOLARSHIP FUND

Scholarships to rescue workers who are going to school to obtain their undergraduate nursing degree. Eligible rescue workers include prehospital care providers, fire fighters, and police officers. The scholarship is not limited geographically. The scholarship winner will also be awarded a complimentary one year ENA membership.

Academic Fields/Career Goals: Nursing.

Award: Scholarship for use in freshman, sophomore, junior, senior, graduate, or postgraduate years; not renewable. *Number:* 1. *Amount:* $2000.

Eligibility Requirements: Applicant must be enrolled or expecting to enroll full- or part-time at a four-year institution or university. Available to U.S. citizens.

Application Requirements: Application form. *Deadline:* varies.

NEW YORK STATE GRANGE

http://www.nysgrange.org/

June GILL NURSING SCHOLARSHIP

One annual scholarship award to verified NYS Grange member pursuing a career in nursing. Selection based on verification of NYS Grange membership and enrollment in a nursing program, as well as applicant's career statement, academic records, and financial need. Payment made after successful completion of one term.

Academic Fields/Career Goals: Nursing.

Award: Scholarship for use in freshman, sophomore, junior, or senior years; not renewable. *Number:* 2. *Amount:* $1000.

Eligibility Requirements: Applicant must be enrolled or expecting to enroll full-time at a two-year or four-year institution and resident of New York. Applicant or parent of applicant must be member of Grange Association. Available to U.S. citizens.

Application Requirements: Application form, financial need analysis, nursing program enrollment letter, career statement, transcript. *Deadline:* April 15.

NIGHTINGALE AWARDS OF PENNSYLVANIA

http://www.nightingaleawards.org/

NIGHTINGALE AWARDS OF PENNSYLVANIA NURSING SCHOLARSHIP

Scholarships for students who are studying nursing at the basic or advanced level and intend to practice in Pennsylvania. Regardless of the type of nursing program, all candidates accepted into or presently enrolled in accredited nursing programs in Pennsylvania may apply. Scholarships are awarded to students who enter professional nursing programs, practical nursing programs, and advanced degree programs.

Academic Fields/Career Goals: Nursing.

Award: Scholarship for use in freshman, sophomore, junior, senior, or graduate years; not renewable. *Number:* up to 6. *Amount:* $6000–$10,000.

Eligibility Requirements: Applicant must be enrolled or expecting to enroll full-time at a four-year institution or university and studying in Pennsylvania. Available to U.S. citizens.

Application Requirements: Application form, recommendations or references, test scores, transcript. *Deadline:* January 31.

Contact: Christine Filipovich, President
 Phone: 717-909-0350
 Fax: 717-234-6798
 E-mail: nightingale@pronursingresources.com

ODD FELLOWS AND REBEKAHS

http://www.ioofme.org/

ODD FELLOWS AND REBEKAHS ELLEN F. WASHBURN NURSES TRAINING AWARD

Award for high school seniors and college undergraduates to attend an accredited Maine institution and pursue a registered nursing degree. Must have a minimum 2.5 GPA. Can reapply for award for up to four years.

Academic Fields/Career Goals: Nursing.

Award: Scholarship for use in freshman, sophomore, junior, or senior years; renewable. *Number:* up to 30. *Amount:* $150–$400.

Eligibility Requirements: Applicant must be enrolled or expecting to enroll full- or part-time at a two-year or four-year institution or university and studying in Maine. Applicant must have 2.5 GPA or higher. Available to U.S. citizens.

Application Requirements: Application form, financial need analysis, personal photograph, recommendations or references. *Deadline:* April 15.

Contact: Joyce Young, Chairman
　　Phone: 207-839-4723

ONS FOUNDATION

http://www.onsfoundation.org

ONS FOUNDATION JOSH GOTTHEIL MEMORIAL BONE MARROW TRANSPLANT CAREER DEVELOPMENT AWARDS

Awards available to any professional registered nurse in field of bone marrow transplant nursing for further study in a bachelor's or master's program. Submit examples of contributions to BMT nursing.

Academic Fields/Career Goals: Nursing.

Award: Scholarship for use in junior, senior, or graduate years; not renewable. *Number:* 4. *Amount:* $2000.

Eligibility Requirements: Applicant must be enrolled or expecting to enroll full- or part-time at a four-year institution or university. Available to U.S. and non-U.S. citizens.

Application Requirements: Application form, essay, recommendations or references, resume. *Deadline:* December 1.

Contact: Bonny Revo, Executive Assistant
　　Phone: 412-859-6278
　　E-mail: brevo@onsfoundation.org

ONS FOUNDATION/ONCOLOGY NURSING CERTIFICATION CORPORATION BACHELOR'S SCHOLARSHIPS

One-time awards to improve oncology nursing by assisting registered nurses in furthering their education. Applicants must hold a current license to practice and be enrolled in an undergraduate nursing degree program at an NLN-accredited school.

Academic Fields/Career Goals: Nursing; Oncology.

Award: Scholarship for use in freshman, sophomore, junior, or senior years; not renewable. *Amount:* $2000.

Eligibility Requirements: Applicant must be enrolled or expecting to enroll full- or part-time at a four-year institution or university. Available to U.S. and non-U.S. citizens.

Application Requirements: Application form, transcript. *Fee:* $5. *Deadline:* February 1.

Contact: Bonny Revo, Executive Assistant
　　Phone: 412-859-6278
　　E-mail: brevo@onsfoundation.org

ONS FOUNDATION/PEARL MOORE CAREER DEVELOPMENT AWARDS

Awards to practicing staff nurses who possess or are pursuing a BSN and have two years oncology practice experience.

Academic Fields/Career Goals: Nursing; Oncology.

Award: Prize for use in junior, senior, or graduate years; not renewable. *Number:* 3. *Amount:* $3000.

Eligibility Requirements: Applicant must be enrolled or expecting to enroll full- or part-time at a four-year institution or university. Available to U.S. citizens.

Application Requirements: Application form, recommendations or references. *Deadline:* December 1.

Contact: Bonny Revo, Executive Assistant
　　Phone: 412-859-6278
　　E-mail: brevo@onsfoundation.org

OREGON COMMUNITY FOUNDATION

http://www.oregoncf.org/

FRANZ STENZEL M.D. AND KATHRYN STENZEL SCHOLARSHIP FUND

• See page 338

NLN ELLA MCKINNEY SCHOLARSHIP FUND

Award for Oregon high school graduates (or the equivalent) for use in the pursuit of an undergraduate or graduate nursing education. Must attend a nonprofit college or university in Oregon accredited by the NLN Accrediting Commission. For more information, see web http://www.getcollegefunds.org.

Academic Fields/Career Goals: Nursing.

Award: Scholarship for use in freshman, sophomore, junior, or senior years; renewable. *Number:* up to 2. *Amount:* $1000–$2000.

Eligibility Requirements: Applicant must be enrolled or expecting to enroll full-time at a two-year or four-year institution or university; resident of Oregon and studying in Oregon. Available to U.S. citizens.

Application Requirements: Application form, recommendations or references. *Deadline:* March 1.

Contact: Dianne Causey, Program Associate for Scholarships and Grants
　　Phone: 503-227-6846 Ext. 1418
　　E-mail: dcausey@oregoncf.org

OREGON STUDENT ASSISTANCE COMMISSION

http://www.GetCollegeFunds.org/

BERTHA P. SINGER NURSES SCHOLARSHIP

Renewable award for Oregon residents pursuing a nursing career. Must attend a college or university in Oregon. Minimum GPA of 3.0 required. Proof of enrollment in second year of four-year nursing degree program is required. Transcripts alone are not sufficient proof, must obtain a form or letter from department. U.S. Bank employees, their children, or close relatives are not eligible.

Academic Fields/Career Goals: Nursing.

Award: Scholarship for use in sophomore, junior, or senior years; renewable.

Eligibility Requirements: Applicant must be enrolled or expecting to enroll full-time at a four-year institution or university; resident of Oregon and studying in Oregon. Applicant must have 3.0 GPA or higher. Available to U.S. citizens.

Application Requirements: Application form, essay, form or letter from department, transcript. *Deadline:* March 1.

CHESTER AND HELEN LUTHER SCHOLARSHIP

• See page 338

CLARK-PHELPS SCHOLARSHIP

• See page 224

FRANKS FOUNDATION SCHOLARSHIP

Awards to students who are nursing or theology majors and residents of Crook, Deschutes, or Jefferson County (first preference) or residents of Grant, Harney, Klamath, or Lake County (second preference). High school seniors must have a minimum GPA of 2.5, college students must have a minimum GPA of 2.0. Must reapply annually for renewal. U.S. Bank employees, their children, and near relatives are not eligible.

Academic Fields/Career Goals: Nursing; Religion/Theology.

Award: Scholarship for use in freshman, sophomore, junior, senior, or graduate years; not renewable.

Eligibility Requirements: Applicant must be enrolled or expecting to enroll full- or part-time at a four-year institution or university and resident of Oregon. Available to U.S. citizens.

Application Requirements: Application form, FAFSA, test scores, transcript. *Deadline:* March 1.

HELEN HALL AND JOHN SEELY MEMORIAL SCHOLARSHIP
• *See page 338*

MARION A. LINDEMAN SCHOLARSHIP
• *See page 338*

WALTER C. AND MARIE C. SCHMIDT SCHOLARSHIP

Scholarship available to Oregon students enrolling in programs to become registered nurses and intending to pursue careers in geriatric health care. Must submit an additional essay describing their desire to pursue a nursing career in geriatrics. Preference to students attending Lane County Community College, but students may attend any other two-year college nursing program. Essay required describing desire to pursue nursing career in geriatric health care. U.S. Bank employees, their children, or near relatives are not eligible.

Academic Fields/Career Goals: Nursing.

Award: Scholarship for use in freshman or sophomore years; renewable.

Eligibility Requirements: Applicant must be enrolled or expecting to enroll full- or part-time at a two-year institution and resident of Oregon. Available to U.S. citizens.

Application Requirements: Activity chart, application form, essay, financial need analysis, recommendations or references, transcript. *Deadline:* March 1.

PILOT INTERNATIONAL FOUNDATION

http://www.pilotinternational.org/

PILOT INTERNATIONAL FOUNDATION RUBY NEWHALL MEMORIAL SCHOLARSHIP
• *See page 339*

PILOT INTERNATIONAL FOUNDATION SCHOLARSHIP PROGRAM
• *See page 339*

RHODE ISLAND FOUNDATION

http://www.rifoundation.org/

ALBERT E. AND FLORENCE W. NEWTON NURSE SCHOLARSHIP

Scholarship for student studying nursing on a full- or part-time basis. Preference will be given to Rhode Island residents committed to practicing in Rhode Island. Must be able to demonstrate financial need. Must be either a licensed RN enrolled in a nursing baccalaureate degree program; a student enrolled in a baccalaureate nursing program; a student in a diploma nursing program; or a student in a two-year associate degree nursing program.

Academic Fields/Career Goals: Nursing.

Award: Scholarship for use in freshman, sophomore, junior, or senior years; renewable. *Amount:* $500–$2000.

Eligibility Requirements: Applicant must be enrolled or expecting to enroll full- or part-time at a two-year or four-year institution or university. Available to U.S. citizens.

Application Requirements: Application form, copy of college acceptance letter, copy of most recent income tax return, essay, financial need analysis, self-addressed stamped envelope with application, transcript. *Deadline:* April 19.

Contact: Libby Monahan, Funds Administrator
   Phone: 401-274-4564 Ext. 3117
   E-mail: libbym@rifoundation.org

EDWARD J. AND VIRGINIA M. ROUTHIER NURSING SCHOLARSHIP

Renewable scholarship for licensed RNs seeking baccalaureate or graduate nursing degrees in Rhode Island. Must demonstrate financial need.

Academic Fields/Career Goals: Nursing.

Award: Scholarship for use in freshman, sophomore, junior, senior, or graduate years; renewable. *Amount:* $500–$3000.

Eligibility Requirements: Applicant must be enrolled or expecting to enroll full- or part-time at a four-year institution or university and studying in Rhode Island. Available to U.S. citizens.

Application Requirements: Application form. *Deadline:* April 19.

Contact: Libby Monahan, Funds Administrator
   Phone: 401-274-4564 Ext. 3117
   E-mail: libbym@rifoundation.org

WILLARD & MARJORIE SCHEIBE NURSING SCHOLARSHIP

Renewable scholarship for Rhode Island residents pursuing LPN, RN, or advanced nursing degrees. Must demonstrate financial need.

Academic Fields/Career Goals: Nursing.

Award: Scholarship for use in freshman, sophomore, junior, senior, or graduate years; renewable.

Eligibility Requirements: Applicant must be enrolled or expecting to enroll full-time at a four-year institution or university and resident of Rhode Island. Available to U.S. citizens.

Application Requirements: Application form, financial need analysis. *Deadline:* April 19.

Contact: Libby Monahan, Funds Administrator
   Phone: 401-274-4564 Ext. 3117
   E-mail: libbym@rifoundation.org

SOCIETY FOR THE SCIENTIFIC STUDY OF SEXUALITY

http://www.sexscience.org/

SOCIETY FOR THE SCIENTIFIC STUDY OF SEXUALITY STUDENT RESEARCH GRANT
• *See page 102*

SOCIETY OF PEDIATRIC NURSES

http://www.pedsnurses.org/

SOCIETY OF PEDIATRIC NURSES EDUCATIONAL SCHOLARSHIP
• *See page 178*

STATE STUDENT ASSISTANCE COMMISSION OF INDIANA (SSACI)

http://www.in.gov/ssaci

INDIANA NURSING SCHOLARSHIP FUND

Need-based tuition funding for nursing students enrolled full- or part-time at an eligible Indiana institution. Must be a U.S. citizen and an Indiana resident and have a minimum 2.0 GPA or meet the minimum requirements for the nursing program. Upon graduation, recipients must practice as a nurse in an Indiana health care setting for two years.

Academic Fields/Career Goals: Nursing.

Award: Scholarship for use in freshman, sophomore, junior, or senior years; not renewable. *Number:* 490–690. *Amount:* $200–$5000.

Eligibility Requirements: Applicant must be enrolled or expecting to enroll full- or part-time at a two-year or four-year institution or university; resident of Indiana and studying in Indiana. Available to U.S. citizens.

Application Requirements: Application form, FAFSA, financial need analysis. *Deadline:* continuous.

Contact: Yvonne Heflin, Director, Special Programs
   State Student Assistance Commission of Indiana (SSACI)
   150 West Market Street, Suite 500
   Indianapolis, IN 46204-2805
   Phone: 317-232-2350
   Fax: 317-232-3260

STRAIGHTFORWARD MEDIA

http://www.straightforwardmedia.com/

STRAIGHTFORWARD MEDIA MEDICAL PROFESSIONS SCHOLARSHIP

• *See page 224*

STRAIGHTFORWARD MEDIA NURSING SCHOOL SCHOLARSHIP

Scholarship of $500 available to students majoring in nursing. Awarded four times per year. Deadlines are April 14, July 14, October 14, and January 14. To apply, go to http://www.straightforwardmedia.com/nursing/form.php.

Academic Fields/Career Goals: Nursing.

Award: Scholarship for use in freshman, sophomore, junior, or senior years; not renewable. *Number:* 4. *Amount:* $500.

Eligibility Requirements: Applicant must be enrolled or expecting to enroll full- or part-time at a two-year or four-year or technical institution or university. Available to U.S. and non-U.S. citizens.

Application Requirements: Essay. *Deadline:* varies.

TAFFORD UNIFORMS

http://www.tafford.com/

TAFFORD UNIFORMS NURSING SCHOLARSHIP PROGRAM

Two scholarships of $1000 each awarded to nursing students enrolled in undergraduate and graduate study. Minimum 2.5 GPA required.

Academic Fields/Career Goals: Nursing.

Award: Scholarship for use in freshman, sophomore, junior, or senior years; not renewable. *Number:* 2. *Amount:* $1000.

Eligibility Requirements: Applicant must be enrolled or expecting to enroll full-time at a two-year or four-year institution or university. Applicant must have 2.5 GPA or higher. Available to U.S. citizens.

Application Requirements: Application form. *Deadline:* continuous.

TEXAS HIGHER EDUCATION COORDINATING BOARD

http://www.collegefortexans.com/

TEXAS PROFESSIONAL NURSING SCHOLARSHIPS

Award to provide financial assistance to encourage students to become Professional Nurses. Only in-state (Texas) colleges or universities may participate in the program. Both public and private, non-profit colleges or universities with professional nursing programs may participate in the programs.

Academic Fields/Career Goals: Nursing.

Award: Scholarship for use in freshman, sophomore, junior, or senior years; not renewable. *Amount:* $2500.

Eligibility Requirements: Applicant must be enrolled or expecting to enroll at a two-year or four-year or technical institution; resident of Texas and studying in Texas.

Application Requirements: Application form, financial need analysis.

TEXAS VOCATIONAL NURSING SCHOLARSHIPS

Awards to encourage individuals to pursue vocational nursing. Both public and private, non-profit colleges or universities with vocational nursing programs may participate in the programs. No individual award may be more than the student's financial need. The maximum award is $1500.

Academic Fields/Career Goals: Nursing.

Award: Scholarship for use in freshman or sophomore years; not renewable. *Amount:* $1500.

Eligibility Requirements: Applicant must be enrolled or expecting to enroll at a two-year or technical institution; resident of Texas and studying in Texas.

Application Requirements: Application form, financial need analysis.

TOUCHMARK FOUNDATION

http://www.touchmarkfoundation.org/

TOUCHMARK FOUNDATION NURSING SCHOLARSHIP

Students pursuing nursing degrees at any level are encouraged to apply, including nurses interested pursuing advanced degrees in order to teach. Scholarship application deadlines are June 30 and December 30 of each year.

Academic Fields/Career Goals: Nursing.

Award: Scholarship for use in freshman, sophomore, junior, senior, graduate, or postgraduate years; not renewable. *Amount:* $500–$1000.

Eligibility Requirements: Applicant must be enrolled or expecting to enroll full-time at a four-year institution or university and studying in Alberta, Idaho, Minnesota, Montana, North Dakota, Oklahoma, Oregon, South Dakota, Washington, Wisconsin. Available to U.S. citizens.

Application Requirements: Application form, essay, FAFSA, copy of acceptance letter, recommendations or references, transcript. *Deadline:* continuous.

Contact: Bret Cope, Chairman
    Phone: 800-796-8744
    E-mail: bjc@touchmark.com

UNICO FOUNDATION INC.

http://www.unico.org/

BERNARD AND CAROLYN TORRACO MEMORIAL NURSING SCHOLARSHIP PROGRAM

$2500 award for students currently enrolled in an accredited nursing degree program in the United States, completing core nursing courses at either an associate degree School of Nursing, a collegiate School of Nursing, or a diploma School of Nursing. Proof of enrollment must be provided. Preference will be given to applicants demonstrating financial need. A current FAFSA Student Aid Report (SAR) is required. Must hold U.S. citizenship. Applications must be acquired from and submitted through a participating, local UNICO chapter. To locate contact information for the nearest chapter, access the UNICO National website, http://www.unico.org, and click on Find a Chapter.

Academic Fields/Career Goals: Nursing.

Award: Scholarship for use in sophomore, junior, or senior years. *Number:* 2. *Amount:* $2500.

Eligibility Requirements: Applicant must be enrolled or expecting to enroll at a two-year or four-year institution or university. Available to U.S. citizens.

Application Requirements: Application form, financial need analysis, proof of college enrollment. *Deadline:* April 15.

Contact: Joan Tidona, Scholarship Director
    Phone: 973-808-0035
    Fax: 973-808-0043
    E-mail: uniconational@unico.org

UNITED DAUGHTERS OF THE CONFEDERACY

http://www.hqudc.org/

PHOEBE PEMBER MEMORIAL SCHOLARSHIP

Award for full-time undergraduate students who are descendants of a Confederate soldier, enrolled in a school of nursing. Must be enrolled in an accredited college or university and have a minimum 3.0 GPA. Submit letter of endorsement from sponsoring Chapter of the United Daughters of the Confederacy.

Academic Fields/Career Goals: Nursing.

Award: Scholarship for use in freshman, sophomore, junior, or senior years; renewable. *Number:* 1–2. *Amount:* $800–$1000.

Eligibility Requirements: Applicant must be enrolled or expecting to enroll full-time at a four-year institution or university. Applicant or parent of applicant must be member of United Daughters of the Confederacy. Applicant must have 3.0 GPA or higher. Available to U.S. citizens.

Application Requirements: Application form, copy of applicant's birth certificate, copy of confederate ancestor's proof of service, essay, financial need analysis, personal photograph, recommendations or references, self-addressed stamped envelope with application, test scores, transcript. *Deadline:* March 15.

Contact: Ms. Jamie Davis, Second Vice President General
Phone: 804-355-1636
E-mail: hqudc@rcn.com

WALTER REED SMITH SCHOLARSHIP
• *See page 160*

U. S. DEPARTMENT OF HEALTH AND HUMAN SERVICES
http://www.hhs.gov/about/whatwedo.html/

U. S. PUBLIC HEALTH SERVICE-HEALTH RESOURCES AND SERVICES ADMINISTRATION, BUREAU OF HEALTH PROFESSIONS SCHOLARSHIPS FOR DISADVANTAGED STUDENTS
• *See page 225*

VIRGINIA DEPARTMENT OF HEALTH, OFFICE OF MINORITY HEALTH AND HEALTH EQUITY
http://www.vdh.virginia.gov/

MARY MARSHALL PRACTICAL NURSING SCHOLARSHIP (LPN)

Scholarship provides annual nursing scholarships for part-time and full-time students that are residents of Virginia and enrolled in a Licensed Practical Nursing (LPN) program. This fund also includes any funds appropriated by the General Assembly for the purposes of the fund; and any gifts, grants, or bequests received from any private person or organization. All scholarship awards vary from year to year and are made by an Advisory Committee appointed by the Virginia State Board of Health. The Virginia Department of Health (VDH)-Office of Minority Health and Health Equity (OMHHE)-Health Workforce serves as the staff element to the Advisory Committee and plays no role in the determination of scholarship recipients. The Advisory Committee recommends to the State Commissioner of Health the award selection with due regard given to scholastic attainment, financial need, character, and adaptability to the nursing profession. Recipient must agree to work in Virginia after graduation as a LPN within a certain amount of time until their service obligation is fulfilled. The recipient service obligation is one month for every $100 received.

Academic Fields/Career Goals: Nursing.

Award: Scholarship for use in freshman, sophomore, junior, or senior years; not renewable. *Number:* 50–150. *Amount:* $150–$500.

Eligibility Requirements: Applicant must be enrolled or expecting to enroll full- or part-time at a two-year or four-year or technical institution or university; resident of Virginia and studying in Virginia. Applicant must have 2.5 GPA or higher. Available to U.S. citizens.

Application Requirements: Application form, driver's license, essay, financial need analysis, recommendations or references, transcript. *Deadline:* June 30.

Contact: Mrs. Dena Schall, Healthcare Workforce Manager/Program Specialist
Virginia Department of Health, Office of Minority Health and Health Equity
PO Box 2448, 109 Governor Street, Suite 1016-E
Richmond, VA 23218-2448
Phone: 804-864-7435
Fax: 804-864-7440
E-mail: IncentivePrograms@vdh.virginia.gov

MARY MARSHALL REGISTERED NURSING SCHOLARSHIPS

Scholarship provides annual nursing scholarships for part-time and full-time students that are residents of Virginia and enrolled in a Licensed Practical Nursing (LPN) program. This fund also includes any funds appropriated by the General Assembly for the purposes of the fund; and any gifts, grants, or bequests received from any private person or organization. All scholarship awards are made by an Advisory Committee appointed by the Virginia State Board of Health. The Virginia Department of Health (VDH)-Office of Minority Health and Health Equity (OMHHE)-Health Workforce serves as the staff element to the Advisory Committee and plays no role in the determination of scholarship recipients. The Advisory Committee recommends to the State Commissioner of Health the award selection with due regard given to scholastic attainment, financial need, character, and adaptability to the nursing profession. Recipients are required to start employment as a RN in Virginia within a certain amount of time as a service obligation. The service obligation is one month for every $100 received.

Academic Fields/Career Goals: Nursing.

Award: Scholarship for use in freshman, sophomore, junior, or senior years; not renewable. *Number:* up to 150. *Amount:* $150–$2000.

Eligibility Requirements: Applicant must be enrolled or expecting to enroll full- or part-time at a two-year or four-year institution or university; resident of Virginia and studying in Virginia. Applicant must have 2.5 GPA or higher. Available to U.S. citizens.

Application Requirements: Application form, driver's license, essay, financial need analysis, recommendations or references, transcript. *Deadline:* June 30.

Contact: Mrs. Dena Schall, Healthcare Workforce Manager/Program Specialist
Virginia Department of Health, Office of Minority Health and Health Equity
PO Box 2448, 109 Governor Street, Suite 1016-E
Richmond, VA 23218-2448
Phone: 804-864-7435
Fax: 804-864-7440
E-mail: IncentivePrograms@vdh.virginia.gov

WISCONSIN LEAGUE FOR NURSING, INC.
http://www.wisconsinwln.org/

NURSING SCHOLARSHIP FOR HIGH SCHOOL SENIORS

One scholarship for a Wisconsin high school senior who will be pursuing a professional nursing career. The senior must have been accepted by a Wisconsin NLN accredited school of nursing, have financial need, demonstrate scholastic excellence and leadership potential. Contact the WLN office by mail to request an application.

Academic Fields/Career Goals: Nursing.

Award: Scholarship for use in freshman year; not renewable. *Number:* 1. *Amount:* $500.

Eligibility Requirements: Applicant must be high school student; planning to enroll or expecting to enroll full-time at a two-year or four-year institution or university; resident of Wisconsin and studying in Wisconsin. Available to U.S. citizens.

Application Requirements: Application form, financial need analysis. *Deadline:* March 1.

Contact: Mary Ann Tanner, Administrative Secretary
Phone: 888-755-3329
E-mail: wln@wisconsinwln.org

WISCONSIN LEAGUE FOR NURSING, INC. SCHOLARSHIP

One-time award for Wisconsin residents who have completed half of an accredited Wisconsin school of nursing program. Financial need of student must be demonstrated. Scholarship applications are mailed by WLN office ONLY to Wisconsin nursing schools in January for distribution to students. Students interested in obtaining an application must contact their nursing school and submit completed applications to their school. Applications sent directly to WLN office will be returned to applicant. For further information visit website http://www.wisconsinwln.org/Scholarships.htm.

Academic Fields/Career Goals: Nursing.

Award: Scholarship for use in junior or senior years; not renewable. *Number:* 11–35. *Amount:* $500–$1000.

Eligibility Requirements: Applicant must be enrolled or expecting to enroll full-time at a two-year or four-year or technical institution or university; resident of Wisconsin and studying in Wisconsin. Available to U.S. citizens.

Application Requirements: Application form, essay, financial need analysis. *Deadline:* March 1.

Contact: Mary Ann Tanner, Administrative Secretary
Phone: 888-755-3329
E-mail: wln@wisconsinwln.org

WOUND, OSTOMY AND CONTINENCE NURSES SOCIETY

http://www.wocn.org/

WOCN ACCREDITED NURSING EDUCATION PROGRAM SCHOLARSHIP

Scholarships are awarded to deserving individuals committed to working within the wound, ostomy and continence nursing specialty. Applicants must agree to support the WOCN Society philosophy and scope of practice. Number of scholarships and the dollar value varies annually. Deadlines: May 1 or November 1.

Academic Fields/Career Goals: Nursing.

Award: Scholarship for use in freshman, sophomore, junior, or senior years; not renewable.

Eligibility Requirements: Applicant must be enrolled or expecting to enroll full-time at a two-year or four-year or technical institution or university. Available to U.S. and non-U.S. citizens.

Application Requirements: Acceptance letter, proof of current enrollment or certificate of completion from a WOCN accredited education program, application form, recommendations or references. *Deadline:* varies.

OCCUPATIONAL SAFETY AND HEALTH

AMERICAN SOCIETY OF SAFETY ENGINEERS (ASSE) FOUNDATION

http://www.asse.org/

AMERICA RESPONDS MEMORIAL SCHOLARSHIP

Scholarship of $1000 will be awarded to a student pursuing an undergraduate degree in occupational safety and health or a closely related field. Must have completed 60 semester hours and maintain at least a 3.0 GPA. Must be a member of ASSE and be a U.S. citizen. Students who have experience working as an emergency responder will have priority on this award.

Academic Fields/Career Goals: Occupational Safety and Health.

Award: Scholarship for use in sophomore, junior, or senior years; not renewable. *Number:* 1. *Amount:* $1000.

Eligibility Requirements: Applicant must be enrolled or expecting to enroll full-time at a four-year institution or university. Applicant or parent of applicant must be member of American Society of Safety Engineers. Applicant must have 3.0 GPA or higher. Available to U.S. citizens.

Application Requirements: Application form, essay, financial need analysis, recommendations or references, transcript. *Deadline:* December 1.

Contact: Brenda Zylstra, Scholarship Coordinator
American Society of Safety Engineers (ASSE) Foundation
1800 East Oakton Street
Des Plaines, IL 60018
E-mail: bzylstra@asse.org

APPLICATIONS INTERNATIONAL CORPORATION SCHOLARSHIP

$2500 scholarship awarded to a student pursuing an undergraduate or graduate degree in occupational safety and health or a closely related field. Priority will be given to students that have served in the military. GPA of 3.0 required for undergraduates, 3.5 for graduate students. ASSE membership is preferred but not required.

Academic Fields/Career Goals: Occupational Safety and Health.

Award: Scholarship for use in sophomore, junior, senior, or graduate years; not renewable. *Number:* 9. *Amount:* $2500.

Eligibility Requirements: Applicant must be enrolled or expecting to enroll full-time at a four-year institution or university. Available to U.S. citizens.

Application Requirements: Application form, essay, financial need analysis, recommendations or references, transcript. *Deadline:* December 1.

Contact: Brenda Zylstra, Scholarship Coordinator
American Society of Safety Engineers (ASSE) Foundation
1800 East Oakton Street
Des Plaines, IL 60018
E-mail: bzylstra@asse.org

ASSE CONSTRUCTION SAFETY SCHOLARSHIP

One $1500 scholarship for a student pursuing an undergraduate degree in occupational safety and health or a closely related field. Must have completed 60 semester hours and maintain at least a 3.0 GPA. Priority will be given to students with an emphasis in construction safety, and enrolled in an ABET accredited OSH program.

Academic Fields/Career Goals: Occupational Safety and Health.

Award: Scholarship for use in sophomore, junior, or senior years; not renewable. *Number:* 1. *Amount:* $1500.

Eligibility Requirements: Applicant must be enrolled or expecting to enroll full-time at a four-year institution or university. Applicant must have 3.0 GPA or higher. Available to U.S. citizens.

Application Requirements: Application form, essay, financial need analysis, recommendations or references, transcript. *Deadline:* December 1.

Contact: Brenda Zylstra, Scholarship Coordinator
American Society of Safety Engineers (ASSE) Foundation
1800 East Oakton Street
Des Plaines, IL 60018
E-mail: bzylstra@asse.org

ASSED FOUNDATION MILITARY SERVICE SCHOLARSHIP

Scholarship of $1000 will be awarded to a student pursuing an undergraduate or graduate degree in occupational safety and health or a closely related field. Students that have served in the military will have priority on this award. Minimum 3.0 GPA for undergraduates, 3.5 for graduate students.

Academic Fields/Career Goals: Occupational Safety and Health.

Award: Scholarship for use in sophomore, junior, senior, or graduate years; not renewable. *Number:* 1. *Amount:* $1000.

Eligibility Requirements: Applicant must be enrolled or expecting to enroll full-time at a four-year institution or university. Available to U.S. citizens.

Application Requirements: Application form, essay, financial need analysis, recommendations or references, transcript. *Deadline:* December 1.

Contact: Brenda Zylstra, Scholarship Coordinator
American Society of Safety Engineers (ASSE) Foundation
1800 East Oakton Street
Des Plaines, IL 60018
E-mail: bzylstra@asse.org

ASSE DIVERSITY COMMITTEE SCHOLARSHIP

Scholarship of $1000 will be awarded to a student pursuing an undergraduate or graduate degree in occupational safety and health or a closely related field. Award is open to any individual regardless of race, ethnicity, gender, religion, personal beliefs, age, sexual orientation, physical challenges, geographic location, university or specific area of study. Minimum 3.0 GPA required for undergraduates, 3.5 for graduates.

Academic Fields/Career Goals: Occupational Safety and Health.

Award: Scholarship for use in sophomore, junior, senior, or graduate years; not renewable. *Number:* 1. *Amount:* $1000.

Eligibility Requirements: Applicant must be enrolled or expecting to enroll full-time at a four-year institution or university. Available to U.S. citizens.

Application Requirements: Application form, essay, financial need analysis, recommendations or references, transcript. *Deadline:* December 1.

Contact: Brenda Zylstra, Scholarship Coordinator
American Society of Safety Engineers (ASSE) Foundation
1800 East Oakton Street
Des Plaines, IL 60018
E-mail: bzylstra@asse.org

ASSE-GULF COAST PAST PRESIDENTS SCHOLARSHIP

Scholarship of $1500 will be awarded to a part- or full-time student pursuing an undergraduate degree in occupational safety and health or a closely related field. Must have completed 60 semester hours and maintain at least a 3.0 GPA. ASSE general or professional membership preferred if applicant is a part-time student.

Academic Fields/Career Goals: Occupational Safety and Health.

Award: Scholarship for use in sophomore, junior, or senior years; not renewable. *Number:* 2. *Amount:* $1500.

Eligibility Requirements: Applicant must be enrolled or expecting to enroll full- or part-time at a four-year institution or university. Applicant or parent of applicant must be member of American Society of Safety Engineers. Applicant must have 3.0 GPA or higher. Available to U.S. citizens.

Application Requirements: Application form, essay, financial need analysis, recommendations or references, transcript. *Deadline:* December 1.

Contact: Brenda Zylstra, Scholarship Coordinator
American Society of Safety Engineers (ASSE) Foundation
1800 East Oakton Street
Des Plaines, IL 60018
E-mail: bzylstra@asse.org

ASSE-MARSH RISK CONSULTING SCHOLARSHIP

Scholarship for students pursuing an undergraduate degree in occupational safety. Completion of at least 60 credit hours and minimum GPA of 3.0 required. Must be a student member of ASSE.

Academic Fields/Career Goals: Occupational Safety and Health.

Award: Scholarship for use in sophomore, junior, or senior years; not renewable. *Number:* 1. *Amount:* $1000.

Eligibility Requirements: Applicant must be enrolled or expecting to enroll full-time at a four-year institution or university. Applicant or parent of applicant must be member of American Society of Safety Engineers. Applicant must have 3.0 GPA or higher. Available to U.S. and non-U.S. citizens.

Application Requirements: Application form, essay, recommendations or references, transcript. *Deadline:* December 1.

Contact: Brenda Zylstra, Scholarship Coordinator
American Society of Safety Engineers (ASSE) Foundation
1800 East Oakton Street
Des Plaines, IL 60018
E-mail: bzylstra@asse.org

ASSE-UNITED PARCEL SERVICE SCHOLARSHIP

Scholarships for students pursuing a four-year BS or BA degree in occupational safety and health or related area. Completion of at least 60 current semester hours and a minimum 3.0 GPA is required. Must be a student member of ASSE.

Academic Fields/Career Goals: Occupational Safety and Health.

Award: Scholarship for use in sophomore, junior, or senior years; not renewable. *Number:* 4. *Amount:* $5250.

Eligibility Requirements: Applicant must be enrolled or expecting to enroll full-time at a four-year institution or university. Applicant or parent of applicant must be member of American Society of Safety Engineers. Applicant must have 3.0 GPA or higher. Available to U.S. and non-U.S. citizens.

Application Requirements: Application form, essay, recommendations or references, transcript. *Deadline:* December 1.

Contact: Brenda Zylstra, Scholarship Coordinator
American Society of Safety Engineers (ASSE) Foundation
1800 East Oakton Street
Des Plaines, IL 60018
E-mail: bzylstra@asse.org

BCSP FRED A. MANUELE PROFESSIONAL SCHOLARSHIP

$1000 scholarship for students pursuing an undergraduate degree in occupational safety and health or a closely related field. Minimum 3.0 GPA required. Priority will be given to students attending a school with an ASAC/ABET accredited safety program.

Academic Fields/Career Goals: Occupational Safety and Health.

Award: Scholarship for use in sophomore, junior, or senior years; not renewable. *Number:* 1. *Amount:* $1000.

Eligibility Requirements: Applicant must be enrolled or expecting to enroll full-time at a four-year institution or university. Applicant must have 3.0 GPA or higher. Available to U.S. citizens.

Application Requirements: Application form, essay, financial need analysis, recommendations or references, transcript. *Deadline:* December 1.

Contact: Brenda Zylstra, Scholarship Coordinator
American Society of Safety Engineers (ASSE) Foundation
1800 East Oakton Street
Des Plaines, IL 60018
E-mail: bzylstra@asse.org

BCSP KEVIN MOORHEAD TECHNICIAN/TECHNOLOGIST, SUPERVISORY SCHOLARSHIP

$1000 scholarship for students pursuing an undergraduate degree in occupational safety and health or a closely related field. Minimum 3.0 GPA required. Priority will be given to students attending a school with an ASAC/ABET accredited safety program.

Academic Fields/Career Goals: Occupational Safety and Health.

Award: Scholarship for use in sophomore, junior, or senior years; not renewable. *Number:* 1. *Amount:* $1000.

Eligibility Requirements: Applicant must be enrolled or expecting to enroll full-time at a four-year institution or university. Applicant must have 3.0 GPA or higher. Available to U.S. citizens.

Application Requirements: Application form, essay, financial need analysis, recommendations or references, transcript. *Deadline:* December 1.

Contact: Brenda Zylstra, Scholarship Coordinator
American Society of Safety Engineers (ASSE) Foundation
1800 East Oakton Street
Des Plaines, IL 30018
E-mail: bzylstra@asse.org

BERVIN HALL MEMORIAL SCHOLARSHIP

Scholarship of $1000 will be awarded to a student pursuing an undergraduate degree in occupational safety and health or a closely related field. Must have completed 60 semester hours and maintain at least a 3.0 GPA. Priority will be given to Colorado Chapter members or to students attending school within Region II.

Academic Fields/Career Goals: Occupational Safety and Health.

Award: Scholarship for use in sophomore, junior, or senior years; not renewable. *Number:* 1. *Amount:* $1000.

Eligibility Requirements: Applicant must be enrolled or expecting to enroll full-time at a four-year institution or university. Applicant must have 3.0 GPA or higher. Available to U.S. citizens.

Application Requirements: Application form, essay, financial need analysis, recommendations or references, transcript. *Deadline:* December 1.

Contact: Brenda Zylstra, Scholarship Coordinator
American Society of Safety Engineers (ASSE) Foundation
1800 East Oakton Street
Des Plaines, IL 60018
E-mail: bzylstra@asse.org

BLACKS IN SAFETY ENGINEERING SCHOLARSHIP

Scholarship of $1000 will be awarded to a black student pursuing an undergraduate degree in occupational safety and health or a closely related field. Must have completed 60 semester hours and maintain at least a 3.0 GPA.

Academic Fields/Career Goals: Occupational Safety and Health.

Award: Scholarship for use in sophomore, junior, or senior years; not renewable. *Number:* 1. *Amount:* $1000.

Eligibility Requirements: Applicant must be Black (non-Hispanic) and enrolled or expecting to enroll full-time at a four-year institution or university. Applicant must have 3.0 GPA or higher. Available to U.S. citizens.

Application Requirements: Application form, essay, financial need analysis, recommendations or references, transcript. *Deadline:* December 1.

Contact: Brenda Zylstra, Scholarship Coordinator
American Society of Safety Engineers (ASSE) Foundation
1800 East Oakton Street
Des Plaines, IL 60018
E-mail: bzylstra@asse.org

CENTRAL INDIANA ASSE JIM KRINER MEMORIAL SCHOLARSHIP

Scholarships will be awarded to students pursuing an undergraduate or graduate degree in occupational safety and health or a closely related field. Priority will be given to Indiana residents attending school in Indiana or anywhere in the U.S. or to non-residents attending an Indiana university. Minimum 3.0 GPA for undergraduate students, 3.5 GPA for graduate students.

Academic Fields/Career Goals: Occupational Safety and Health.

Award: Scholarship for use in sophomore, junior, senior, or graduate years; not renewable. *Number:* 3. *Amount:* $1000–$3000.

Eligibility Requirements: Applicant must be enrolled or expecting to enroll full-time at a four-year institution or university. Available to U.S. citizens.

Application Requirements: Application form, essay, financial need analysis, recommendations or references, transcript. *Deadline:* December 1.

Contact: Brenda Zylstra, Scholarship Coordinator
American Society of Safety Engineers (ASSE) Foundation
1800 East Oakton Street
Des Plaines, IL 60018
E-mail: bzylstra@asse.org

COLUMBIA-WILLAMETTE CHAPTER PRESIDENT SCHOLARSHIP

One $1000 scholarship will be awarded to a student pursuing an undergraduate degree in occupational safety and health or a closely related field. Minimum 3.0 GPA for undergraduate students, 3.5 for graduate students. Priority will be given to Columbia-Willamette chapter members, students attending school in Oregon or Washington state or to residents of Oregon or Washington state attending school elsewhere.

Academic Fields/Career Goals: Occupational Safety and Health.

Award: Scholarship for use in sophomore, junior, senior, or graduate years; not renewable. *Number:* 1. *Amount:* $1000.

Eligibility Requirements: Applicant must be enrolled or expecting to enroll full-time at a four-year institution or university. Available to U.S. citizens.

Application Requirements: Application form, essay, financial need analysis, recommendations or references, transcript. *Deadline:* December 1.

Contact: Brenda Zylstra, Scholarship Coordinator
American Society of Safety Engineers (ASSE) Foundation
1800 East Oakton Street
Des Plaines, IL 60018
E-mail: bzylstra@asse.org

EDWIN P. LOCKE HSE SCHOLARSHIP

$2000 scholarship for students pursuing an undergraduate degree in occupational safety and health or a closely related field. Minimum 3.0 GPA required. Priority will be given to students residing in Texas or students attending a Texas university.

Academic Fields/Career Goals: Occupational Safety and Health.

Award: Scholarship for use in sophomore, junior, or senior years; not renewable. *Number:* 1. *Amount:* $2000.

Eligibility Requirements: Applicant must be enrolled or expecting to enroll full-time at a four-year institution or university. Applicant must have 3.0 GPA or higher. Available to U.S. citizens.

Application Requirements: Application form, essay, financial need analysis, recommendations or references, transcript. *Deadline:* December 1.

Contact: Brenda Zylstra, Scholarship Coordinator
American Society of Safety Engineers (ASSE) Foundation
1800 East Oakton Street
Des Plaines, IL 60018
E-mail: bzylstra@asse.org

FLATIRON CONSTRUCTION CHRISTOPHER GONZALEZ MEMORIAL SCHOLARSHIP

One scholarship of $4700 will be awarded to a student pursuing an undergraduate degree in occupational safety and health or a closely related field. Must have completed 60 semester hours and maintain at least a 3.0 GPA. Priority will be given to students with an emphasis in construction safety.

Academic Fields/Career Goals: Occupational Safety and Health.

Award: Scholarship for use in sophomore, junior, or senior years; not renewable. *Number:* 1. *Amount:* $4700.

Eligibility Requirements: Applicant must be enrolled or expecting to enroll full-time at a four-year institution or university. Applicant must have 3.0 GPA or higher. Available to U.S. citizens.

Application Requirements: Application form, essay, financial need analysis, recommendations or references, transcript. *Deadline:* December 1.

Contact: Brenda Zylstra, Scholarship Coordinator
American Society of Safety Engineers (ASSE) Foundation
1800 East Oakton Street
Des Plaines, IL 60018
E-mail: bzylstra@asse.org

FOUR CORNERS CHAPTER SCHOLARSHIP

Scholarship of $1000 will be awarded to a student pursuing an undergraduate degree in occupational safety and health or a closely related field. Must have completed 60 semester hours and maintain at least a 3.0 GPA. Priority will be given to students from the Four Corner's Chapter, a New Mexico or Colorado Chapter member, or from a student that resides in R2 (in that order).

Academic Fields/Career Goals: Occupational Safety and Health.

Award: Scholarship for use in sophomore, junior, or senior years; not renewable. *Number:* 1. *Amount:* $1000.

Eligibility Requirements: Applicant must be enrolled or expecting to enroll full-time at a four-year institution or university. Applicant must have 3.0 GPA or higher. Available to U.S. citizens.

Application Requirements: Application form, essay, financial need analysis, recommendations or references, transcript. *Deadline:* December 1.

Contact: Brenda Zylstra, Scholarship Coordinator
American Society of Safety Engineers (ASSE) Foundation
1800 East Oakton Street
Des Plaines, IL 60018
E-mail: bzylstra@asse.org

GEORGE GUSTAFSON HSE MEMORIAL SCHOLARSHIP

Scholarship of $2000 will be awarded to a student pursuing an undergraduate or a graduate degree in occupational safety and health or a closely related field. Minimum GPA of 3.0 for undergraduates, 3.5 for graduate students. Priority will be given to students residing in Texas or attending a Texas university.

Academic Fields/Career Goals: Occupational Safety and Health.

Award: Scholarship for use in sophomore, junior, senior, or graduate years; not renewable. *Number:* 1. *Amount:* $2000.

Eligibility Requirements: Applicant must be enrolled or expecting to enroll full-time at a four-year institution or university. Available to U.S. citizens.

Application Requirements: Application form, essay, financial need analysis, recommendations or references, transcript. *Deadline:* December 1.

Contact: Brenda Zylstra, Scholarship Coordinator
American Society of Safety Engineers (ASSE) Foundation
1800 East Oakton Street
Des Plaines, IL 60018
E-mail: bzylstra@asse.org

GRANBERRY, FLEMING & ROSS SCHOLARSHIP

Scholarship of $1500 will be awarded to a student pursuing an undergraduate degree in occupational safety and health or a closely related field. Must have completed 60 semester hours and maintain at least a 3.0 GPA. Priority will be given to students that attend school within the Region IV area.

Academic Fields/Career Goals: Occupational Safety and Health.

Award: Scholarship for use in sophomore, junior, or senior years; not renewable. *Number:* 1. *Amount:* $1500.

Eligibility Requirements: Applicant must be enrolled or expecting to enroll full-time at a four-year institution or university. Applicant must have 3.0 GPA or higher. Available to U.S. citizens.

Application Requirements: Application form, essay, financial need analysis, recommendations or references, transcript. *Deadline:* December 1.

Contact: Brenda Zylstra, Scholarship Coordinator
American Society of Safety Engineers (ASSE) Foundation
1800 Oakton Street
Des Plaines, IL 60018
E-mail: bzylstra@asse.org

HAROLD F. POLSTON SCHOLARSHIP

Scholarship of $1500 for students pursuing undergraduate or graduate degree in occupational safety and health or a closely related field. Priority will be given to students that belong to the Middle Tennessee Chapter, attending Middle Tennessee State University in Murfreesboro, TN, Murray State University in Murray, KY and those that live in the Region VII. Must have a minimum GPA of 3.0 for undergraduate study and 3.5 for graduate study. Must be a student member of ASSE.

Academic Fields/Career Goals: Occupational Safety and Health.

Award: Scholarship for use in sophomore, junior, senior, or graduate years; not renewable. *Number:* 1. *Amount:* $1500.

Eligibility Requirements: Applicant must be enrolled or expecting to enroll full-time at a four-year institution or university. Applicant or parent of applicant must be member of American Society of Safety Engineers. Available to U.S. and non-U.S. citizens.

Application Requirements: Application form, essay, financial need analysis, recommendations or references, transcript. *Deadline:* December 1.

Contact: Brenda Zylstra, Scholarship Coordinator
American Society of Safety Engineers (ASSE) Foundation
1800 East Oakton Street
Des Plaines, IL 60018
E-mail: bzylstra@asse.org

HARRY TABACK 9/11 MEMORIAL SCHOLARSHIP

Scholarship for students pursuing an undergraduate or graduate degree in occupational safety and health or a closely related field. Preference given to student who is a natural born United States citizen. Minimum GPA is 3.0 for undergraduates and 3.5 for graduates. Must be a student member of ASSE.

Academic Fields/Career Goals: Occupational Safety and Health.

Award: Scholarship for use in sophomore, junior, senior, or graduate years; not renewable. *Number:* 1. *Amount:* $1000.

Eligibility Requirements: Applicant must be enrolled or expecting to enroll full-time at a four-year institution or university. Applicant or parent of applicant must be member of American Society of Safety Engineers. Available to U.S. citizens.

Application Requirements: Application form, financial need analysis, recommendations or references, transcript. *Deadline:* December 1.

Contact: Brenda Zylstra, Scholarship Coordinator
American Society of Safety Engineers (ASSE) Foundation
1800 East Oakton Street
Des Plaines, IL 60018
E-mail: bzylstra@asse.org

HEART OF AMERICA SCHOLARSHIP

Scholarship of $1000 will be awarded to a student pursuing an undergraduate or graduate degree in occupational safety and health or a closely related field. Minimum GPA of 3.0 for undergraduate students, 3.5 for graduate students. Priority will be given to students attending University of Central Missouri in Warrensburg, MO or Pittsburg State University in Pittsburgh, KS or to those attending a university in KS or MO, or to those attending a university within Region V (in that order).

Academic Fields/Career Goals: Occupational Safety and Health.

Award: Scholarship for use in sophomore, junior, senior, or graduate years; not renewable. *Number:* 1. *Amount:* $1000.

Eligibility Requirements: Applicant must be enrolled or expecting to enroll full-time at a four-year institution or university. Available to U.S. citizens.

Application Requirements: Application form, essay, financial need analysis, recommendations or references, transcript. *Deadline:* December 1.

Contact: Brenda Zylstra, Scholarship Coordinator
American Society of Safety Engineers (ASSE) Foundation
1800 East Oakton Street
Des Plaines, IL 60018
E-mail: bzylstra@asse.org

ISNETWORLD SCHOLARSHIP

Scholarship of $1000 will be awarded to a student pursuing an undergraduate degree in occupational safety and health or a closely related field. Must have completed 60 semester hours and maintain at least a 3.0 GPA. Priority will be given to students living in OK, TX, NM, LA or AK.

Academic Fields/Career Goals: Occupational Safety and Health.

Award: Scholarship for use in sophomore, junior, or senior years; not renewable. *Number:* 1. *Amount:* $1000.

Eligibility Requirements: Applicant must be enrolled or expecting to enroll full-time at a four-year institution or university and resident of Alaska, Louisiana, New Mexico, Oklahoma, Texas. Applicant must have 3.0 GPA or higher. Available to U.S. citizens.

Application Requirements: Application form, essay, financial need analysis, recommendations or references, transcript. *Deadline:* December 1.

Contact: Brenda Zylstra, Scholarship Coordinator
American Society of Safety Engineers (ASSE) Foundation
1800 East Oakton Street
Des Plaines, IL 60018
E-mail: bzylstra@asse.org

JANET SPRICKMAN AWARD

$1000 scholarship awarded to a student pursuing an undergraduate or graduate degree in occupational safety and health or a closely related field. Minimum GPA of 3.0 for undergraduates, 3.5 for graduate students. Students from Region VI, IV, VII and VIII will have priority (in that order).

Academic Fields/Career Goals: Occupational Safety and Health.

Award: Scholarship for use in sophomore, junior, senior, or graduate years; not renewable. *Number:* 1. *Amount:* $1000.

Eligibility Requirements: Applicant must be enrolled or expecting to enroll full-time at a four-year institution or university. Available to U.S. citizens.

Application Requirements: Application form, essay, financial need analysis, recommendations or references, transcript. *Deadline:* December 1.

Contact: Brenda Zylstra, Scholarship Coordinator
American Society of Safety Engineers (ASSE) Foundation
1800 East Oakton Street
Des Plaines, IL 60018
E-mail: bzylstra@asse.org

JIM & TIFFANY KREINBRINK SCHOLARSHIP

Scholarship of $1500 will be awarded to a student pursuing an undergraduate degree in occupational safety and health or a closely related field. Must have completed 60 semester hours and maintain at least a 3.0 GPA. Priority will be given to students that belong to the Middle Tennessee Chapter, attending Middle Tennessee State University in Murfreesboro, TN, Murray State University in Murray, KY and those that live in the Region VII area (in that order).

Academic Fields/Career Goals: Occupational Safety and Health.

Award: Scholarship for use in sophomore, junior, or senior years; not renewable. *Number:* 1. *Amount:* $1500.

Eligibility Requirements: Applicant must be enrolled or expecting to enroll full-time at a four-year institution or university. Applicant must have 3.0 GPA or higher. Available to U.S. citizens.

Application Requirements: Application form, essay, financial need analysis, recommendations or references, transcript. *Deadline:* December 1.

Contact: Brenda Zylstra, Scholarship Coordinator
American Society of Safety Engineers (ASSE) Foundation
1800 East Oakton Street
Des Plaines, IL 60018
E-mail: bzylstra@asse.org

KEITH BAIN SCHOLARSHIP

$1500 scholarship for students pursuing an undergraduate degree in occupational safety and health or a closely related field. Minimum 3.0 GPA required. Priority will be given to students that belong to the Middle Tennessee Chapter, attending Middle Tennessee State University in Murfreesboro, TN, Murray State University in Murray, KY and those that live in the Region VII area (in that order).

Academic Fields/Career Goals: Occupational Safety and Health.

Award: Scholarship for use in sophomore, junior, or senior years; not renewable. *Number:* 1. *Amount:* $1500.

Eligibility Requirements: Applicant must be enrolled or expecting to enroll full-time at a four-year institution or university. Applicant must have 3.0 GPA or higher. Available to U.S. citizens.

Application Requirements: Application form, essay, financial need analysis, recommendations or references, transcript. *Deadline:* December 1.

Contact: Brenda Zylstra, Scholarship Coordinator
American Society of Safety Engineers (ASSE) Foundation
1800 East Oakton Street
Des Plaines, IL 60018
E-mail: bzylstra@asse.org

LIBERTY MUTUAL SCHOLARSHIP

Scholarship of $4000 for students pursuing an undergraduate degree in occupational safety and health or a closely related field. ASSE student membership required. Minimum 3.0 GPA required. Must have completed 60 semester hours in the study program. Students may also be provided with the opportunity to attend a professional development conference related to safety.

Academic Fields/Career Goals: Occupational Safety and Health.

Award: Scholarship for use in sophomore, junior, or senior years; not renewable. *Number:* 2. *Amount:* $4000.

Eligibility Requirements: Applicant must be enrolled or expecting to enroll full-time at a four-year institution or university. Applicant or parent of applicant must be member of American Society of Safety Engineers. Applicant must have 3.0 GPA or higher. Available to U.S. and non-U.S. citizens.

Application Requirements: Application form, financial need analysis, transcript. *Deadline:* December 1.

Contact: Brenda Zylstra, Scholarship Coordinator
American Society of Safety Engineers (ASSE) Foundation
1800 East Oakton Street
Des Plaines, IL 60018
E-mail: bzylstra@asse.org

LINDA & BRAD GILES SCHOLARSHIP

One $2500 scholarship will be awarded to a student pursuing an undergraduate degree in occupational safety and health or a closely related field. Must have completed 60 semester hours and maintain at least a 3.0 GPA. Priority will be given to students attending a school with an ASAC/ABET accredited safety program. Students with a military background attending Murray State University, Oakland or Central Missouri University will also have priority.

Academic Fields/Career Goals: Occupational Safety and Health.

Award: Scholarship for use in sophomore, junior, or senior years; not renewable. *Number:* 1. *Amount:* $2500.

Eligibility Requirements: Applicant must be enrolled or expecting to enroll full-time at a four-year institution or university. Applicant must have 3.0 GPA or higher. Available to U.S. citizens.

Application Requirements: Application form, essay, financial need analysis, recommendations or references, transcript. *Deadline:* December 1.

Contact: Brenda Zylstra, Scholarship Coordinator
American Society of Safety Engineers (ASSE) Foundation
1800 East Oakton Street
Des Plaines, IL 60018
E-mail: bzylstra@asse.org

NEW ENGLAND AREA FUTURE LEADERSHIP AWARD

One $1500 award will be given to a student pursuing an undergraduate degree or graduate degree in occupational safety and health or a closely related field. Minimum GPA of 3.0 for undergraduates, 3.5 for graduate students. Priority will be given to students residing in the New England area, or the Region VIII area (in that order).

Academic Fields/Career Goals: Occupational Safety and Health.

Award: Scholarship for use in sophomore, junior, senior, or graduate years; not renewable. *Number:* 1. *Amount:* $1500.

Eligibility Requirements: Applicant must be enrolled or expecting to enroll full-time at a four-year institution or university. Available to U.S. citizens.

Application Requirements: Application form, essay, financial need analysis, recommendations or references, transcript. *Deadline:* December 1.

Contact: Brenda Zylstra, Scholarship Coordinator
American Society of Safety Engineers (ASSE) Foundation
1800 East Oakton Street
Des Plaines, IL 60018
E-mail: bzylstra@asse.org

NORTHEASTERN ILLINOIS CHAPTER SCHOLARSHIP

Scholarship of $2000 for students pursuing an undergraduate or graduate degree in occupational safety and health or a closely related field. Priority will be given to students that attend Northern Illinois University in DeKalb, IL; members of the NE IL chapter, regardless of school location; offspring of NE IL chapter members, regardless of school location; or to students attending school in the northeastern Illinois region. ASSE student membership required. Undergraduate students must have completed at least 60 semester hours. Minimum GPA is 3.0 for undergraduates and 3.5 for graduates.

Academic Fields/Career Goals: Occupational Safety and Health.

Award: Scholarship for use in sophomore, junior, senior, graduate, or postgraduate years; not renewable. *Number:* 1. *Amount:* $2000.

Eligibility Requirements: Applicant must be enrolled or expecting to enroll full-time at a four-year institution or university and resident of Illinois, Wisconsin. Applicant or parent of applicant must be member of American Society of Safety Engineers. Available to U.S. citizens.

Application Requirements: Application form, financial need analysis, transcript. *Deadline:* December 1.

Contact: Brenda Zylstra, Scholarship Coordinator
American Society of Safety Engineers (ASSE) Foundation
1800 East Oakton Street
Des Plaines, IL 60018
E-mail: bzylstra@asse.org

NORTH FLORIDA CHAPTER SAFETY EDUCATION SCHOLARSHIP

One $1000 scholarship for to a student pursuing an undergraduate or graduate degree in occupational safety and health or a closely related field. Minimum GPA of 3.0 for undergraduates, 3.5 for graduate students. Priority will be given to part-time or full-time students that belong to the North Florida Chapter, full-time students that attend any Florida college or university or to full-time students that attend an ASAC/ABET accredited program nationwide (in that order). ASSE general or professional membership is preferred if applicant is a part-time student.

Academic Fields/Career Goals: Occupational Safety and Health.

Award: Scholarship for use in sophomore, junior, senior, or graduate years; not renewable. *Number:* 1. *Amount:* $1000.

Eligibility Requirements: Applicant must be enrolled or expecting to enroll full- or part-time at a four-year institution or university. Available to U.S. citizens.

Application Requirements: Application form, essay, financial need analysis, recommendations or references, transcript. *Deadline:* December 1.

Contact: Brenda Zylstra, Scholarship Coordinator
American Society of Safety Engineers (ASSE) Foundation
1800 East Oakton Street
Des Plaines, IL 60018
E-mail: bzylstra@asse.org

PERMIAN BASIN CHAPTER ENDOWMENT SCHOLARSHIP

Scholarship of $1000 will be awarded to a student pursuing an undergraduate or graduate degree in occupational safety and health or a closely related field. Minimum GPA of 3.0 for undergraduates, 3.5 for graduate students. Priority will be given to students that attend a school within the Region III area.

Academic Fields/Career Goals: Occupational Safety and Health.

Award: Scholarship for use in sophomore, junior, senior, or graduate years; not renewable. *Number:* 1. *Amount:* $1000.

Eligibility Requirements: Applicant must be enrolled or expecting to enroll full-time at a four-year institution or university. Available to U.S. citizens.

Application Requirements: Application form, essay, financial need analysis, recommendations or references, transcript. *Deadline:* December 1.

Contact: Brenda Zylstra, Scholarship Coordinator
American Society of Safety Engineers (ASSE) Foundation
1800 East Oakton Street
Des Plaines, IL 60018
E-mail: bzylstra@asse.org

RAYMOND P. BOYLSTON MEMORIAL SCHOLARSHIP

$1000 scholarship for students pursuing an undergraduate degree in occupational safety and health or a closely related field. Minimum 3.0 GPA required.

Academic Fields/Career Goals: Occupational Safety and Health.

Award: Scholarship for use in sophomore, junior, or senior years; not renewable. *Number:* 1. *Amount:* $1000.

Eligibility Requirements: Applicant must be enrolled or expecting to enroll full-time at a four-year institution or university. Applicant must have 3.0 GPA or higher. Available to U.S. citizens.

Application Requirements: Application form, essay, financial need analysis, recommendations or references, transcript. *Deadline:* December 1.

Contact: Brenda Zylstra, Scholarship Coordinator
American Society of Safety Engineers (ASSE) Foundation
1800 East Oakton Street
Des Plaines, IL 60018
E-mail: bzylstra@asse.org

RIXIO MEDINA & ASSOCIATES HISPANICS IN SAFETY SCHOLARSHIP

$4000 award for a student pursuing an undergraduate or graduate degree in occupational safety and health or a closely related field. Minimum GPA of 3.0 for undergraduates, 3.5 for graduate students. Must be bilingual (Spanish-English); Hispanic ethnicity preferred. Student attending an ASAC/ABET accredited safety program is also preferred.

Academic Fields/Career Goals: Occupational Safety and Health.

Award: Scholarship for use in sophomore, junior, senior, or graduate years; not renewable. *Number:* 1. *Amount:* $4000.

Eligibility Requirements: Applicant must be enrolled or expecting to enroll full-time at a four-year institution or university. Available to U.S. citizens.

Application Requirements: Application form, essay, financial need analysis, recommendations or references, transcript. *Deadline:* December 1.

Contact: Brenda Zylstra, Scholarship Coordinator
American Society of Safety Engineers (ASSE) Foundation
1800 East Oakton Street
Des Plaines, IL 60018
E-mail: bzylstra@asse.org

SCOTT DOMINGUEZ-CRATERS OF THE MOON CHAPTER SCHOLARSHIP

Scholarship for part-or full-time students pursuing an undergraduate or graduate degree in occupational safety and health or a closely related field. Students residing within the Craters of the Moon Chapter, Idaho, and Region II (MT, ID, WY, CO, UT, NV, AZ, NM) will have priority. Students that are employees or dependents of a sponsoring organization, serve the country through active duty in the armed forces or honorably discharged, members of the Boy Scouts, Girl Scouts, FFA, 4H, etc. in previous years, recipients of awards from service organizations, or have provided volunteer service to an ASSE chapter in a leadership role will also receive priority on this award. ASSE student membership required for full-time student. ASSE general or professional membership required for part-time students. Minimum GPA is 3.0 for undergraduates and 3.5 for graduates.

Academic Fields/Career Goals: Occupational Safety and Health.

Award: Scholarship for use in sophomore, junior, senior, or graduate years; not renewable. *Number:* 1. *Amount:* $1000.

Eligibility Requirements: Applicant must be enrolled or expecting to enroll full- or part-time at a four-year institution or university and resident of Arizona, Colorado, Idaho, Montana, Nevada, New Mexico,

Utah, Wyoming. Applicant or parent of applicant must be member of American Society of Safety Engineers. Available to U.S. citizens.

Application Requirements: Application form, financial need analysis, transcript. *Deadline:* December 1.

Contact: Brenda Zylstra, Scholarship Coordinator
American Society of Safety Engineers (ASSE) Foundation
1800 East Oakton Street
Des Plaines, IL 60018
E-mail: bzylstra@asse.org

SITEHAWK SAFETY SCHOLARSHIP

Scholarship of $1000 will be awarded to a student pursuing an undergraduate degree in occupational safety and health or a closely related field. Must have completed 60 semester hours and maintain at least a 3.0 GPA.

Academic Fields/Career Goals: Occupational Safety and Health.

Award: Scholarship for use in sophomore, junior, or senior years; not renewable. *Number:* 1. *Amount:* $1000.

Eligibility Requirements: Applicant must be enrolled or expecting to enroll full-time at a four-year institution or university. Applicant must have 3.0 GPA or higher. Available to U.S. citizens.

Application Requirements: Application form, essay, financial need analysis, recommendations or references, transcript. *Deadline:* December 1.

Contact: Brenda Zylstra, Scholarship Coordinator
American Society of Safety Engineers (ASSE) Foundation
1800 East Oakton Street
Des Plaines, IL 60018
E-mail: bzylstra@asse.org

STEVEN F. KANE MEMORIAL SCHOLARSHIP

$1000 scholarship for students pursuing an undergraduate degree in occupational safety and health or a closely related field. Minimum 3.0 GPA required.

Academic Fields/Career Goals: Occupational Safety and Health.

Award: Scholarship for use in sophomore, junior, or senior years; not renewable. *Number:* 1. *Amount:* $1000.

Eligibility Requirements: Applicant must be enrolled or expecting to enroll full-time at a four-year institution or university. Applicant must have 3.0 GPA or higher. Available to U.S. citizens.

Application Requirements: Application form, essay, financial need analysis, recommendations or references, transcript. *Deadline:* December 1.

Contact: Brenda Zylstra, Scholarship Coordinator
American Society of Safety Engineers (ASSE) Foundation
1800 East Oakton Street
Des Plaines, IL 60018
E-mail: bzylstra@asse.org

UNITED PARCEL SERVICE DIVERSITY SCHOLARSHIP PROGRAM

Scholarship for students pursuing an undergraduate degree in occupational safety and health or a closely related field. Must be of a minority ethnic or racial group. U.S. citizenship preferred but not required. Must be an ASSE member and have a minimum 3.0 GPA. Students may also be provided with the opportunity to attend a professional development conference related to safety.

Academic Fields/Career Goals: Occupational Safety and Health.

Award: Scholarship for use in sophomore, junior, or senior years; not renewable. *Amount:* $5250.

Eligibility Requirements: Applicant must be American Indian/Alaska Native, Asian/Pacific Islander, Black (non-Hispanic), Hispanic and enrolled or expecting to enroll full-time at a four-year institution or university. Applicant or parent of applicant must be member of American Society of Safety Engineers. Applicant must have 3.0 GPA or higher. Available to U.S. citizens.

Application Requirements: Application form, essay, financial need analysis, recommendations or references, transcript. *Deadline:* December 1.

Contact: Brenda Zylstra, Scholarship Coordinator
American Society of Safety Engineers (ASSE) Foundation
1800 East Oakton Street
Des Plaines, IL 60018
E-mail: bzylstra@asse.org

URS SAFETY SCHOLARSHIP

$6000 scholarship awarded to a student pursuing an undergraduate degree in occupational safety and health or a closely related field. Must have completed 60 semester hours and maintain at least a 3.0 GPA. Student attending school with an ASAC/ABET-accredited safety program is required. Student may also be provided with the opportunity to attend a professional development conference as it relates to safety and an internship that includes salary and living expenses.

Academic Fields/Career Goals: Occupational Safety and Health.

Award: Scholarship for use in sophomore, junior, or senior years; not renewable. *Number:* 1. *Amount:* $6000.

Eligibility Requirements: Applicant must be enrolled or expecting to enroll full-time at a four-year institution or university. Applicant must have 3.0 GPA or higher. Available to U.S. citizens.

Application Requirements: Application form, essay, financial need analysis, recommendations or references, transcript. *Deadline:* December 1.

Contact: Brenda Zylstra, Scholarship Coordinator
American Society of Safety Engineers (ASSE) Foundation
1800 East Oakton Street
Des Plaines, IL 60018
E-mail: bzylstra@asse.org

UTAH CHAPTER ASSE SCHOLARSHIP

Two awards of of $1000 will be awarded to students pursuing an undergraduate or graduate degree in occupational safety and health or a closely related field. Minimum GPA of 3.0 for undergraduates, 3.5 for graduate students. Priority will be given to students residing in Utah or Wyoming.

Academic Fields/Career Goals: Occupational Safety and Health.

Award: Scholarship for use in sophomore, junior, senior, or graduate years; not renewable. *Number:* 2. *Amount:* $1000.

Eligibility Requirements: Applicant must be enrolled or expecting to enroll full-time at a four-year institution or university and resident of Utah, Washington. Available to U.S. citizens.

Application Requirements: Application form, essay, financial need analysis, recommendations or references, transcript. *Deadline:* December 1.

Contact: Brenda Zylstra, Scholarship Coordinator
American Society of Safety Engineers (ASSE) Foundation
1800 East Oakton Street
Des Plaines, IL 60018
E-mail: bzylstra@asse.org

WILLIAM C. RAY, CIH, CSP ARIZONA SCHOLARSHIP

Scholarship of $2500 will be awarded to a student pursuing an undergraduate or graduate degree in occupational safety and health or a closely related field. Minimum GPA of 3.0 for undergraduates, 3.5 for graduate students. Priority will be given to students residing in Arizona or within the Region II area.

Academic Fields/Career Goals: Occupational Safety and Health.

Award: Scholarship for use in sophomore, junior, senior, or graduate years; not renewable. *Number:* 1. *Amount:* $2500.

Eligibility Requirements: Applicant must be enrolled or expecting to enroll full-time at a four-year institution or university. Available to U.S. citizens.

Application Requirements: Application form, essay, financial need analysis, recommendations or references, transcript. *Deadline:* December 1.

Contact: Brenda Zylstra, Scholarship Coordinator
American Society of Safety Engineers (ASSE) Foundation
1800 East Oakton Street
Des Plaines, IL 60018
E-mail: bzylstra@asse.org

CYNTHIA E. MORGAN SCHOLARSHIP FUND (CEMS)

http://www.cemsfund.com/

CYNTHIA E. MORGAN MEMORIAL SCHOLARSHIP FUND, INC.
• *See page 298*

NATIONAL SAFETY COUNCIL

http://www.cshema.org/

CAMPUS SAFETY, HEALTH AND ENVIRONMENTAL MANAGEMENT ASSOCIATION SCHOLARSHIP AWARD PROGRAM
• *See page 305*

STRAIGHTFORWARD MEDIA

http://www.straightforwardmedia.com/

STRAIGHTFORWARD MEDIA MEDICAL PROFESSIONS SCHOLARSHIP
• *See page 224*

TEXAS DEPARTMENT OF TRANSPORTATION

http://www.txdot.gov/

CONDITIONAL GRANT PROGRAM
• *See page 186*

OCEANOGRAPHY

AMERICAN METEOROLOGICAL SOCIETY

http://www.ametsoc.org/

AMERICAN METEOROLOGICAL SOCIETY DR. PEDRO GRAU UNDERGRADUATE SCHOLARSHIP
• *See page 356*

AMERICAN METEOROLOGICAL SOCIETY/INDUSTRY MINORITY SCHOLARSHIPS
• *See page 356*

AMERICAN METEOROLOGICAL SOCIETY MARK J. SCHROEDER SCHOLARSHIP IN METEOROLOGY
• *See page 356*

AMERICAN METEOROLOGICAL SOCIETY RICHARD AND HELEN HAGEMEYER SCHOLARSHIP
• *See page 356*

AMERICAN METEOROLOGICAL SOCIETY WERNER A. BAUM UNDERGRADUATE SCHOLARSHIP
• *See page 356*

CARL W. KREITZBERG ENDOWED SCHOLARSHIP
• *See page 356*

ETHAN AND ALLAN MURPHY MEMORIAL SCHOLARSHIP
• *See page 357*

GEORGE S. BENTON SCHOLARSHIP
• *See page 357*

GUILLERMO SALAZAR RODRIGUES SCHOLARSHIP
• *See page 357*

JOHN R. HOPE SCHOLARSHIP
• *See page 357*

LOREN W. CROW SCHOLARSHIP
• *See page 357*

LOUISIANA OFFICE OF STUDENT FINANCIAL ASSISTANCE

http://www.osfa.la.gov/

ROCKEFELLER STATE WILDLIFE SCHOLARSHIP
• *See page 146*

MARINE TECHNOLOGY SOCIETY

http://www.mtsociety.org/

CHARLES H. BUSSMAN UNDERGRADUATE SCHOLARSHIP
• *See page 388*

JOHN C. BAJUS SCHOLARSHIP
• *See page 388*

MTS STUDENT SCHOLARSHIP
• *See page 388*

PAROS-DIGIQUARTZ SCHOLARSHIP
• *See page 388*

ROV SCHOLARSHIP
• *See page 389*

WOMAN'S NATIONAL FARM AND GARDEN ASSOCIATION

http://www.wnfga.org/

WARREN, SANDERS, MCNAUGHTON OCEANOGRAPHIC SCHOLARSHIP

Upon receiving this award the student agrees to follow and complete the program of study or research as outlined in the application, and to communicate with the Scholarship Chair any changes in the program, as well as periodic progress reports. For further information visit website http://www.wnfga.org/code/scholarships.htm.

Academic Fields/Career Goals: Oceanography.

Award: Scholarship for use in freshman, sophomore, junior, senior, graduate, or postgraduate years; not renewable. *Number:* 1. *Amount:* $1500.

Eligibility Requirements: Applicant must be enrolled or expecting to enroll full- or part-time at a four-year institution or university. Available to U.S. citizens.

Application Requirements: Recommendations or references, resume, transcript. *Deadline:* May 25.

Contact: Mrs. EmmaJane Brice, Scholarship Coordinator
Woman's National Farm and Garden Association
PO Box 1175
Midland, MI 48641-1175
Phone: 248-620-9281
E-mail: mgbertolini@aol.com

WOMAN'S SEAMEN'S FRIEND SOCIETY OF CONNECTICUT INC.

FINANCIAL SUPPORT FOR MARINE OR MARITIME STUDIES
• *See page 389*

YOUTH MARITIME TRAINING ASSOCIATION

http://ymta.net/

NORM MANLY—YMTA MARITIME EDUCATIONAL SCHOLARSHIPS
• *See page 389*

ONCOLOGY

ARRL FOUNDATION INC.

http://www.arrl.org/

CAROLE J. STREETER, KB9JBR, SCHOLARSHIP
• *See page 222*

ASRT FOUNDATION

http://www.asrtfoundation.org/

ELEKTA RADIATION THERAPY SCHOLARSHIP
• *See page 332*

JERMAN-CAHOON STUDENT SCHOLARSHIP
• *See page 332*

PROFESSIONAL ADVANCEMENT SCHOLARSHIP
• *See page 332*

SIEMENS CLINICAL ADVANCEMENT SCHOLARSHIP
• *See page 332*

VARIAN RADIATION THERAPY ADVANCEMENT SCHOLARSHIP
• *See page 333*

CYNTHIA E. MORGAN SCHOLARSHIP FUND (CEMS)

http://www.cemsfund.com/

CYNTHIA E. MORGAN MEMORIAL SCHOLARSHIP FUND, INC.
• *See page 298*

ONS FOUNDATION

http://www.onsfoundation.org

ONS FOUNDATION/ONCOLOGY NURSING CERTIFICATION CORPORATION BACHELOR'S SCHOLARSHIPS
• *See page 440*

ONS FOUNDATION/PEARL MOORE CAREER DEVELOPMENT AWARDS
• *See page 440*

STRAIGHTFORWARD MEDIA

http://www.straightforwardmedia.com/

STRAIGHTFORWARD MEDIA MEDICAL PROFESSIONS SCHOLARSHIP
• *See page 224*

OPTOMETRY

AMERICAN OPTOMETRIC FOUNDATION

http://www.aaopt.org/

VISTAKON AWARD OF EXCELLENCE IN CONTACT LENS PATIENT CARE

Open to any fourth-year student attending any school or college of optometry. Must have 3.0 GPA. Student's knowledge of subject matter and skillful, professional clinical contact lens patient care are considered. School makes selection and sends application to AOF.

Academic Fields/Career Goals: Optometry.

Award: Scholarship for use in senior or graduate years; not renewable. *Number:* 19. *Amount:* $1000.

Eligibility Requirements: Applicant must be enrolled or expecting to enroll full-time at a four-year institution or university. Applicant must have 3.0 GPA or higher. Available to U.S. and non-U.S. citizens.

Application Requirements: Application form, recommendations or references. *Deadline:* September 1.

Contact: Alisa Moore, Program Administrator
Phone: 240-880-3084
Fax: 301-984-4737
E-mail: alisam@aaopt.org

ARRL FOUNDATION INC.

http://www.arrl.org/

CAROLE J. STREETER, KB9JBR, SCHOLARSHIP
• *See page 222*

INDIAN HEALTH SERVICES, UNITED STATES DEPARTMENT OF HEALTH AND HUMAN SERVICES

http://www.ihs.gov/scholarship

INDIAN HEALTH SERVICE HEALTH PROFESSIONS SCHOLARSHIP PROGRAM
• *See page 208*

STRAIGHTFORWARD MEDIA

http://www.straightforwardmedia.com/

STRAIGHTFORWARD MEDIA MEDICAL PROFESSIONS SCHOLARSHIP
• *See page 224*

OSTEOPATHY

ARRL FOUNDATION INC.

http://www.arrl.org/

CAROLE J. STREETER, KB9JBR, SCHOLARSHIP
• *See page 222*

CYNTHIA E. MORGAN SCHOLARSHIP FUND (CEMS)

http://www.cemsfund.com/

CYNTHIA E. MORGAN MEMORIAL SCHOLARSHIP FUND, INC.
• *See page 298*

MAINE OSTEOPATHIC ASSOCIATION MEMORIAL SCHOLARSHIP/MAINE OSTEOPATHIC ASSOCIATION

http://www.mainedo.org/

BEALE FAMILY MEMORIAL SCHOLARSHIP
• *See page 337*

MAINE OSTEOPATHIC ASSOCIATION MEMORIAL SCHOLARSHIP
• *See page 337*

MAINE OSTEOPATHIC ASSOCIATION SCHOLARSHIP
• *See page 337*

NATIONAL ARAB AMERICAN MEDICAL ASSOCIATION

http://www.naama.com/

FOUNDATION SCHOLARSHIP
• *See page 224*

STRAIGHTFORWARD MEDIA

http://www.straightforwardmedia.com/

STRAIGHTFORWARD MEDIA MEDICAL PROFESSIONS SCHOLARSHIP
• *See page 224*

PAPER AND PULP ENGINEERING

AMERICAN CHEMICAL SOCIETY

http://www.acs.org/

AMERICAN CHEMICAL SOCIETY SCHOLARS PROGRAM
• *See page 162*

AMERICAN SOCIETY OF HEATING, REFRIGERATING, AND AIR CONDITIONING ENGINEERS, INC.

http://www.ashrae.org/

ASHRAE REGION III BOGGARM SETTY SCHOLARSHIP
• *See page 166*

ARRL FOUNDATION INC.

http://www.arrl.org/

ALFRED E. FRIEND JR., W4CF, MEMORIAL SCHOLARSHIP
• *See page 166*

GREATER KANAWHA VALLEY FOUNDATION

http://www.tgkvf.org/

STEVEN ENGINEERING SCHOLARSHIP
• *See page 167*

INTERNATIONAL SOCIETY OF AUTOMATION (ISA)

http://www.isa.org/

INTERNATIONAL SOCIETY OF AUTOMATION EDUCATION FOUNDATION SCHOLARSHIPS
• *See page 131*

SOCIETY OF WOMEN ENGINEERS

http://www.swe.org/

ADA I. PRESSMAN MEMORIAL SCHOLARSHIP
• *See page 172*

ANNE MAUREEN WHITNEY BARROW MEMORIAL SCHOLARSHIP
• *See page 172*

BETTY LOU BAILEY SWE REGION F SCHOLARSHIP
• *See page 172*

BK KRENZER MEMORIAL REENTRY SCHOLARSHIP
• *See page 172*

CAROL STEPHENS REGION F SCHOLARSHIP
• *See page 172*

DR. IVY M. PARKER MEMORIAL SCHOLARSHIP
• *See page 173*

DOROTHY LEMKE HOWARTH MEMORIAL SCHOLARSHIP
• *See page 173*

DOROTHY P. MORRIS SCHOLARSHIP
• *See page 173*

JILL S. TIETJEN P.E. SCHOLARSHIP
• *See page 173*

LILLIAN MOLLER GILBRETH MEMORIAL SCHOLARSHIP
• *See page 174*

MARY V. MUNGER SCHOLARSHIP
• *See page 174*

MASWE MEMORIAL SCHOLARSHIP
• *See page 174*

MERIDITH THOMS MEMORIAL SCHOLARSHIPS
• *See page 174*

OLIVE LYNN SALEMBIER MEMORIAL REENTRY SCHOLARSHIP
• *See page 174*

SUSAN MISZKOWICZ MEMORIAL SCHOLARSHIP
• *See page 175*

SWE BALTIMORE-WASHINGTON SECTION SCHOLARSHIP
• *See page 175*

SWE CENTRAL NEW MEXICO PIONEERS SCHOLARSHIP
• *See page 175*

SWE CENTRAL NEW MEXICO REENTRY SCHOLARSHIP
• *See page 175*

SWE MID-HUDSON SECTION SCHOLARSHIP
• *See page 175*

SWE PAST PRESIDENTS SCHOLARSHIP
• *See page 175*

SWE PHOENIX SECTION SCHOLARSHIP
• *See page 175*

SWE REGION H SCHOLARSHIPS
• *See page 176*

WANDA MUNN SCHOLARSHIP
• *See page 176*

STRAIGHTFORWARD MEDIA

http://www.straightforwardmedia.com/

STRAIGHTFORWARD MEDIA ENGINEERING SCHOLARSHIP
• *See page 176*

TECHNICAL ASSOCIATION OF THE PULP & PAPER INDUSTRY (TAPPI)

http://www.tappi.org/

COATING AND GRAPHIC ARTS DIVISION SCHOLARSHIP
• *See page 326*

CORRUGATED PACKAGING DIVISION SCHOLARSHIPS
• *See page 270*

ENGINEERING DIVISION SCHOLARSHIP

Up to two $1500 scholarships offered. One may be awarded to a student who will be in his or her junior year, and the other will be offered to a student who will be in his or her senior year at the beginning of the next academic year. Information can be found at http://www.tappi.org/s_tappi/sec.asp?CID=6101&DID=546695.

Academic Fields/Career Goals: Paper and Pulp Engineering.

Award: Scholarship for use in junior or senior years; not renewable. *Number:* 1–2. *Amount:* up to $1500.

Eligibility Requirements: Applicant must be enrolled or expecting to enroll full-time at a four-year institution or university. Applicant must have 3.0 GPA or higher. Available to U.S. and non-U.S. citizens.

Application Requirements: Application form, recommendations or references, transcript. *Deadline:* February 15.

Contact: Mr. Charles Bohanan, Director of Standards and Awards
Technical Association of the Pulp & Paper Industry (TAPPI)
15 Technology Parkway South
Peachtree Corners, GA 30092
Phone: 770-209-7276
Fax: 770-446-6947
E-mail: standards@tappi.org

ENVIRONMENTAL WORKING GROUP SCHOLARSHIP
• *See page 306*

NONWOVENS DIVISION SCHOLARSHIP
• *See page 295*

PAPER AND BOARD DIVISION SCHOLARSHIPS
• *See page 296*

WILLIAM L. CULLISON SCHOLARSHIP
• *See page 419*

UNITED NEGRO COLLEGE FUND

http://www.uncf.org/

ALFRED CHISHOLM/BASF MEMORIAL SCHOLARSHIP FUND
• *See page 81*

PEACE AND CONFLICT STUDIES

ASSOCIATION OF FORMER INTELLIGENCE OFFICERS

http://www.afio.com/13_scholarships.htm

CIA UNDERGRADUATE SCHOLARSHIPS
• *See page 97*

EARTH ISLAND INSTITUTE

http://www.earthisland.org/

BROWER YOUTH AWARDS
• *See page 302*

UNITED STATES INSTITUTE OF PEACE

http://www.usip.org/

NATIONAL PEACE ESSAY CONTEST
• *See page 362*

PERFORMING ARTS

AMERICAN LEGION DEPARTMENT OF KANSAS

http://www.ksamlegion.org/

MUSIC COMMITTEE SCHOLARSHIP
• *See page 409*

THE CHOPIN FOUNDATION OF THE UNITED STATES

http://www.chopin.org/

SCHOLARSHIP PROGRAM FOR YOUNG AMERICAN PIANISTS
• *See page 410*

CONGRESSIONAL BLACK CAUCUS FOUNDATION, INC.

http://www.cbcfinc.org/

CONGRESSIONAL BLACK CAUCUS SPOUSES HEINEKEN USA PERFORMING ARTS SCHOLARSHIP
Award for minority students pursuing a career in the performing arts. Must be a full-time undergraduate student enrolled in a performing arts program. Minimum 2.5 GPA required. Applicants must submit a video performance.

Academic Fields/Career Goals: Performing Arts.
Award: Scholarship for use in freshman, sophomore, junior, or senior years; not renewable. *Number:* 10–20. *Amount:* $3000.
Eligibility Requirements: Applicant must be enrolled or expecting to enroll full-time at a two-year or four-year or technical institution or university. Applicant must have 2.5 GPA or higher. Available to U.S. citizens.
Application Requirements: Application form, application form may be submitted online (http://www.cbcfinc.org/scholarships), essay, financial need analysis, personal photograph, recommendations or references, transcript, visual recording of performance. *Deadline:* May 3.
Contact: Ms. Janet Carter, Program Administrator, Scholarships
  Congressional Black Caucus Foundation, Inc.
  1720 Massachusetts Avenue, NW
  Washington, DC 20036
  Phone: 202-263-2800
  Fax: 202-263-0845
  E-mail: scholarships@cbcfinc.org

COSTUME SOCIETY OF AMERICA

http://www.costumesocietyamerica.com/

ADELE FILENE TRAVEL AWARD
• *See page 114*

STELLA BLUM RESEARCH GRANT
• *See page 114*

GENERAL FEDERATION OF WOMEN'S CLUBS OF MASSACHUSETTS

http://www.gfwcma.org/

DORCHESTER WOMEN'S CLUB MUSIC SCHOLARSHIP
• *See page 410*

GENERAL FEDERATION OF WOMEN'S CLUBS OF MASSACHUSETTS NICKEL FOR NOTES MUSIC SCHOLARSHIP
• *See page 411*

GREATER KANAWHA VALLEY FOUNDATION

http://www.tgkvf.org/

HERB SMITH/EUNICE FLEMING SCHOLARSHIP
• *See page 411*

HOSTESS COMMITTEE SCHOLARSHIPS/ MISS AMERICA PAGEANT

http://www.missamerica.org/

EUGENIA VELLNER FISCHER AWARD FOR PERFORMING ARTS
Scholarship for Miss America contestants pursuing degree in performing arts. Award available to women who have competed within the Miss America system on the local, state, or national level from 1998 to the present, regardless of whether title was won. One or more scholarships are awarded annually, depending on qualifications of applicants. Late or incomplete applications are not accepted.
Academic Fields/Career Goals: Performing Arts.
Award: Scholarship for use in freshman, sophomore, junior, senior, or graduate years; not renewable.
Eligibility Requirements: Applicant must be enrolled or expecting to enroll full- or part-time at a four-year institution or university; female and must have an interest in beauty pageant. Available to U.S. citizens.
Application Requirements: Application form, essay, financial need analysis, recommendations or references, transcript. *Deadline:* June 30.

Contact: Doreen Lindell Gordon, Controller and Scholarship
Administrator
Phone: 609-345-7571 Ext. 27
Fax: 609-347-6079
E-mail: doreen@missamerica.org

ILLUMINATING ENGINEERING SOCIETY OF NORTH AMERICA

http://www.iesna.org/

ROBERT W. THUNEN MEMORIAL SCHOLARSHIPS
• *See page 111*

JACK J. ISGUR FOUNDATION

http://www.isgur.org

JACK J. ISGUR FOUNDATION SCHOLARSHIP
• *See page 119*

KE ALI'I PAUAHI FOUNDATION

http://www.pauahi.org/

EDWIN MAHIAI COPP BEAMER SCHOLARSHIP
• *See page 412*

KOSCIUSZKO FOUNDATION

http://www.thekf.org

KOSCIUSZKO FOUNDATION CHOPIN PIANO COMPETITION
• *See page 413*

NATIONAL OPERA ASSOCIATION

http://www.noa.org/

NOA VOCAL COMPETITION/LEGACY AWARD PROGRAM
• *See page 121*

POLISH ARTS CLUB OF BUFFALO SCHOLARSHIP FOUNDATION

http://www.pacb.bfn.org/

POLISH ARTS CLUB OF BUFFALO SCHOLARSHIP FOUNDATION TRUST
• *See page 121*

PRINCESS GRACE FOUNDATION-USA

http://www.pgfusa.org/

PRINCESS GRACE AWARDS IN DANCE, THEATER, AND FILM
• *See page 309*

SAN ANGELO SYMPHONY SOCIETY

http://www.sanangelosymphony.org/

SORANTIN YOUNG ARTIST AWARD
• *See page 415*

SERVICE EMPLOYEES INTERNATIONAL UNION (SEIU)

http://www.seiu.org/

SEIU MOE FONER SCHOLARSHIP PROGRAM FOR VISUAL AND PERFORMING ARTS
• *See page 122*

UNITED NEGRO COLLEGE FUND

http://www.uncf.org/

JANET JACKSON/RHYTHM NATION SCHOLARSHIP
• *See page 123*

JOHN LENNON SCHOLARSHIP
• *See page 198*

MICHAEL JACKSON SCHOLARSHIP
• *See page 198*

VSA

http://www.kennedy-center.org/education/vsa/

VSA INTERNATIONAL YOUNG SOLOISTS AWARD
Musical performance competition for persons with disabilities. Age limit for U.S residents is 25 or below and for international applicants is 30 or below. One-time award of $5000. Submit audio or video recording of performance. Contact VSA for information and application materials.
Academic Fields/Career Goals: Performing Arts.
Award: Prize for use in freshman, sophomore, junior, or senior years; not renewable. *Number:* 4. *Amount:* $5000.
Eligibility Requirements: Applicant must be hearing impaired, learning disabled, physically disabled, or visually impaired; enrolled or expecting to enroll full- or part-time at a four-year institution or university and must have an interest in music/singing. Applicant must be hearing impaired, learning disabled, physically disabled, or visually impaired. Available to U.S. and non-U.S. citizens.
Application Requirements: Application form, audition recording, driver's license, entry in a contest. *Deadline:* November 15.
Contact: Sonja Cendak, VSA Programs Manager
Phone: 800-416-8898
Fax: 202-429-0868
E-mail: scendak@kennedy-center.org

WAMSO-MINNESOTA ORCHESTRA VOLUNTEER ASSOCIATION

http://www.wamso.org/

YOUNG ARTIST COMPETITION
Scholarship of $500 to $5000 for graduates and undergraduates. Applicant should be Canadian/ U.S citizens.
Academic Fields/Career Goals: Performing Arts.
Award: Prize for use in freshman, sophomore, junior, senior, graduate, or postgraduate years; not renewable. *Number:* 8. *Amount:* $500–$5000.
Eligibility Requirements: Applicant must be age 15-26; enrolled or expecting to enroll full- or part-time at a two-year or four-year or technical institution or university; resident of Illinois, Indiana, Iowa, Kansas, Manitoba, Michigan, Minnesota, Missouri, Nebraska, North Dakota, Ontario, South Dakota, Wisconsin and must have an interest in music. Available to U.S. and Canadian citizens.
Application Requirements: Application form, entry in a contest, taped performance of specific repertoire. *Fee:* $75. *Deadline:* varies.
Contact: Eloise Breikjern, Executive Director
Phone: 612-371-5654
E-mail: wamso@mnorch.org

WOMEN BAND DIRECTORS INTERNATIONAL

http://www.womenbanddirectors.org/

CHARLOTTE PLUMMER OWEN MEMORIAL SCHOLARSHIP
• *See page 247*

MARTHA ANN STARK MEMORIAL SCHOLARSHIP
• *See page 247*

VOLKWEIN MEMORIAL SCHOLARSHIP
• *See page 247*

PHARMACY

ALBERTA HERITAGE SCHOLARSHIP FUND

http://www.alis.alberta.ca/

JASON LANG SCHOLARSHIP
• *See page 218*

AMERICAN FOUNDATION FOR PHARMACEUTICAL EDUCATION

http://www.afpenet.org/

KAPPA EPSILON-NELLIE WAKEMAN-AFPE FIRST YEAR GRADUATE SCHOOL SCHOLARSHIP

Applicant must be in final year of a pharmacy college BS or PharmD program or have completed a pharmacy degree. At time of application, the Kappa Epsilon member must be in good financial standing with the Fraternity and planning to pursue a PhD, master's degree, or combined Residency/master's degree program at an accredited U.S. College or School of Pharmacy.

Academic Fields/Career Goals: Pharmacy.

Award: Scholarship for use in senior year; not renewable. *Number:* 1. *Amount:* $7500.

Eligibility Requirements: Applicant must be enrolled or expecting to enroll full-time at a four-year institution or university. Available to U.S. citizens.

Application Requirements: Application form, recommendations or references, resume, student statement of interest in graduate school, transcript. *Deadline:* February 1.

Contact: Ms. Nancy Stankiewicz, Executive Director, Kappa Epsilon
American Foundation for Pharmaceutical Education
7700 Shawnee Mission Parkway
Overland Park, KS 66202
Phone: 913-262-2749
Fax: 913-432-9040
E-mail: kefrat@aol.com

PHI LAMBDA SIGMA-GLAXOSMITHKLINE-AFPE FIRST YEAR GRADUATE SCHOOL SCHOLARSHIP

Applicant must be in final year of pharmacy college BS or PharmD program and be a member of Phi Lambda Sigma.

Academic Fields/Career Goals: Pharmacy.

Award: Scholarship for use in senior year; not renewable. *Number:* 1. *Amount:* $7500.

Eligibility Requirements: Applicant must be enrolled or expecting to enroll full-time at an institution or university. Available to U.S. citizens.

Application Requirements: Application form, essay, recommendations or references, resume, statement of interest in graduate school, test scores, transcript. *Deadline:* February 1.

Contact: Mary Euler, Executive Director, Phi Lambda Sigma
American Foundation for Pharmaceutical Education
5005 Rockhill Road
Kansas City, MO 64110
Phone: 816-235-1738
Fax: 816-235-5190
E-mail: eulerm@umkc.edu

AMERICAN LEGION DEPARTMENT OF NORTH DAKOTA

http://www.ndlegion.org/

O. NESHEIM MEMORIAL SCHOLARSHIP
• *See page 90*

CYNTHIA E. MORGAN SCHOLARSHIP FUND (CEMS)

http://www.cemsfund.com/

CYNTHIA E. MORGAN MEMORIAL SCHOLARSHIP FUND, INC.
• *See page 298*

GREATER KANAWHA VALLEY FOUNDATION

http://www.tgkvf.org/

NICHOLAS AND MARY AGNES TRIVILLIAN MEMORIAL SCHOLARSHIP FUND
• *See page 335*

INDIAN HEALTH SERVICES, UNITED STATES DEPARTMENT OF HEALTH AND HUMAN SERVICES

http://www.ihs.gov/scholarship

HEALTH PROFESSIONS PREPARATORY SCHOLARSHIP PROGRAM
• *See page 141*

INDIAN HEALTH SERVICE HEALTH PROFESSIONS SCHOLARSHIP PROGRAM
• *See page 208*

INTERNATIONAL SOCIETY OF AUTOMATION (ISA)

http://www.isa.org/

INTERNATIONAL SOCIETY OF AUTOMATION EDUCATION FOUNDATION SCHOLARSHIPS
• *See page 131*

JEWISH VOCATIONAL SERVICE CHICAGO

http://www.jvschicago.org/

JEWISH FEDERATION ACADEMIC SCHOLARSHIP PROGRAM
• *See page 120*

NATIONAL COMMUNITY PHARMACIST ASSOCIATION (NCPA) FOUNDATION

http://www.ncpanet.org/

NATIONAL COMMUNITY PHARMACIST ASSOCIATION FOUNDATION PRESIDENTIAL SCHOLARSHIP

One-time award to student members of NCPA. Must be enrolled in an accredited U.S. school or college of pharmacy on a full-time basis. Award based on leadership qualities and accomplishments with a demonstrated interest in independent pharmacy, as well as involvement in extracurricular activities.

Academic Fields/Career Goals: Pharmacy.

Award: Scholarship for use in freshman, sophomore, junior, or senior years; not renewable. *Number:* up to 15. *Amount:* up to $2000.

Eligibility Requirements: Applicant must be enrolled or expecting to enroll full-time at a four-year institution or university and must have an interest in leadership. Applicant must have 2.5 GPA or higher. Available to U.S. citizens.

Application Requirements: Application form, essay, recommendations or references, resume, transcript. *Deadline:* March 15.

Contact: Jackie Lopez, Administrative Assistant
National Community Pharmacist Association (NCPA)
Foundation
100 Daingerfield Road
Alexandria, VA 22314
Phone: 703-683-8200
Fax: 703-683-3619
E-mail: jackie.lopez@ncpanet.org

SOUTH DAKOTA RETAILERS ASSOCIATION

http://www.sdra.org/

SOUTH DAKOTA RETAILERS ASSOCIATION SCHOLARSHIP PROGRAM
• See page 80

STRAIGHTFORWARD MEDIA

http://www.straightforwardmedia.com/

STRAIGHTFORWARD MEDIA MEDICAL PROFESSIONS SCHOLARSHIP
• See page 224

STRAIGHTFORWARD MEDIA VOCATIONAL-TECHNICAL SCHOOL SCHOLARSHIP
• See page 99

UNITED NEGRO COLLEGE FUND

http://www.uncf.org/

CVS/PHARMACY SCHOLARSHIP

$2000 scholarship awarded to African American third and fourth year pharmacy majors from the Washington, D.C. area or Detroit, Michigan. Must have minimum 2.8 GPA.

Academic Fields/Career Goals: Pharmacy.

Award: Scholarship for use in junior or senior years; not renewable. *Amount:* $2000.

Eligibility Requirements: Applicant must be Black (non-Hispanic); enrolled or expecting to enroll full-time at a four-year institution or university and resident of District of Columbia, Michigan. Available to U.S. citizens.

Application Requirements: Application form, FAFSA, Student Aid Report (SAR), financial need analysis. *Deadline:* continuous.

RAYMOND W. CANNON MEMORIAL SCHOLARSHIP
• See page 382

PHILOSOPHY

AMERICAN SCHOOL OF CLASSICAL STUDIES AT ATHENS

http://www.ascsa.edu.gr/

ASCSA SUMMER SESSIONS SCHOLARSHIPS
• See page 100

DAVIDSON INSTITUTE FOR TALENT DEVELOPMENT

http://www.davidsongifted.org/

DAVIDSON FELLOWS SCHOLARSHIP PROGRAM
• See page 386

STRAIGHTFORWARD MEDIA

http://www.straightforwardmedia.com/

STRAIGHTFORWARD MEDIA LIBERAL ARTS SCHOLARSHIP
• See page 116

PHOTOJOURNALISM/ PHOTOGRAPHY

AMERICAN LEGION PRESS CLUB OF NEW JERSEY

AMERICAN LEGION PRESS CLUB OF NEW JERSEY AND POST 170 ARTHUR DEHARDT MEMORIAL SCHOLARSHIP
• See page 187

AMERICAN QUARTER HORSE FOUNDATION (AQHF)

http://www.aqha.com/foundation

AQHF JOURNALISM OR COMMUNICATIONS SCHOLARSHIP
• See page 188

ASIAN AMERICAN JOURNALISTS ASSOCIATION

http://www.aaja.org/

ASIAN-AMERICAN JOURNALISTS ASSOCIATION SCHOLARSHIP
• See page 189

BAY AREA BLACK JOURNALISTS ASSOCIATION SCHOLARSHIP CONTEST

http://www.babja.org/

LUCI S. WILLIAMS HOUSTON MEMORIAL SCHOLARSHIP

Nonrenewable scholarship of $2500 to photojournalism students. Applicant must be enrolled in any college or university nationwide. Must be studying photojournalism (including print, television, and online).

Academic Fields/Career Goals: Photojournalism/Photography.

Award: Scholarship for use in freshman, sophomore, junior, senior, or graduate years; not renewable. *Amount:* $2500.

Eligibility Requirements: Applicant must be enrolled or expecting to enroll full- or part-time at a four-year institution or university. Available to U.S. citizens.

Application Requirements: Application form, essay, recommendations or references, resume, transcript, work samples. *Deadline:* October 2.

YOUNG JOURNALISTS SCHOLARSHIP

• *See page 365*

CCNMA: LATINO JOURNALISTS OF CALIFORNIA

http://www.ccnma.org/

CCNMA SCHOLARSHIPS

• *See page 365*

COLLEGE PHOTOGRAPHER OF THE YEAR

http://www.cpoy.org/

COLLEGE PHOTOGRAPHER OF THE YEAR COMPETITION

Awards undergraduate and graduate students for juried contest of individual photographs, picture stories and photographic essay and multimedia presentations. Two awards in the dollar value of $500 and $1000 are granted. Deadline varies.

Academic Fields/Career Goals: Photojournalism/Photography.

Award: Prize for use in freshman, sophomore, junior, senior, or graduate years; not renewable. *Number:* up to 2. *Amount:* $500–$1000.

Eligibility Requirements: Applicant must be enrolled or expecting to enroll full- or part-time at a four-year institution or university. Available to U.S. and non-U.S. citizens.

Application Requirements: Application form, entry in a contest, essay, personal photograph, portfolio. *Deadline:* varies.

Contact: Rita Ann Reed, Program Director
College Photographer of the Year
University of Missouri, School of Journalism, 107 Lee Hills Hall
Columbia, MO 65211
Phone: 573-882-2198
Fax: 573-884-4999
E-mail: info@cpoy.org

CONNECTICUT CHAPTER OF SOCIETY OF PROFESSIONAL JOURNALISTS

http://www.ctspj.org/

CONNECTICUT SPJ BOB EDDY SCHOLARSHIP PROGRAM

• *See page 190*

DAYTON FOUNDATION

http://www.daytonfoundation.org/

LARRY FULLERTON PHOTOJOURNALISM SCHOLARSHIP

One-time scholarship for Ohio residents pursuing careers in photojournalism. Must have experience and submit examples of work. Award for use in sophomore, junior or senior year at an Ohio two- or four-year college or university. High school students are ineligible. Minimum 2.5 GPA required. Must be U.S. citizen.

Academic Fields/Career Goals: Photojournalism/Photography.

Award: Scholarship for use in sophomore, junior, or senior years; not renewable. *Number:* 1–2. *Amount:* $500–$2500.

Eligibility Requirements: Applicant must be enrolled or expecting to enroll full-time at a two-year or four-year institution or university; resident of Ohio; studying in Ohio and must have an interest in photography/photogrammetry/filmmaking. Applicant must have 2.5 GPA or higher. Available to U.S. citizens.

Application Requirements: Application form, financial need analysis, portfolio, slide portfolio, transcript. *Deadline:* January 31.

Contact: Elizabeth Horner, Scholarship Program Officer
Dayton Foundation
500 Kettering Tower
Dayton, OH 45423
Phone: 937-222-9955
Fax: 937-222-0636
E-mail: ehorner@daytonfoundation.org

INTERNATIONAL FOODSERVICE EDITORIAL COUNCIL

http://www.ifeconline.com/

INTERNATIONAL FOODSERVICE EDITORIAL COUNCIL COMMUNICATIONS SCHOLARSHIP

• *See page 83*

KE ALI'I PAUAHI FOUNDATION

http://www.pauahi.org/

BRUCE T. AND JACKIE MAHI ERICKSON GRANT

• *See page 120*

NATIONAL ASSOCIATION OF BLACK JOURNALISTS

http://www.nabj.org/

NATIONAL ASSOCIATION OF BLACK JOURNALISTS NON-SUSTAINING SCHOLARSHIP AWARDS

• *See page 369*

VISUAL TASK FORCE SCHOLARSHIP

Scholarship for students attending an accredited four-year college or university and majoring in visual journalism. Minimum 3.0 GPA required. Must be a member of NABJ. Scholarship value and the number of scholarships granted varies annually.

Academic Fields/Career Goals: Photojournalism/Photography.

Award: Scholarship for use in freshman, sophomore, junior, senior, or graduate years; not renewable.

Eligibility Requirements: Applicant must be enrolled or expecting to enroll full-time at a four-year institution or university. Applicant must have 3.0 GPA or higher. Available to U.S. and non-U.S. citizens.

Application Requirements: Application form, driver's license, essay, interview, recommendations or references, transcript. *Deadline:* March 17.

Contact: Irving Washington, Manager
Phone: 301-445-7100
Fax: 301-445-7101
E-mail: iwashington@nabj.org

NATIONAL ASSOCIATION OF HISPANIC JOURNALISTS (NAHJ)

http://www.nahj.org/

NATIONAL ASSOCIATION OF HISPANIC JOURNALISTS SCHOLARSHIP
• *See page 192*

NEWHOUSE SCHOLARSHIP PROGRAM
• *See page 325*

NEBRASKA PRESS ASSOCIATION

http://www.nebpress.com/

NEBRASKA PRESS ASSOCIATION FOUNDATION INC. SCHOLARSHIP
• *See page 371*

OREGON STUDENT ASSISTANCE COMMISSION

http://www.GetCollegeFunds.org/

KERDRAGON SCHOLARSHIP
• *See page 121*

OUTDOOR WRITERS ASSOCIATION OF AMERICA

http://www.owaa.org/

OUTDOOR WRITERS ASSOCIATION OF AMERICA - BODIE MCDOWELL SCHOLARSHIP AWARD
• *See page 193*

PALM BEACH ASSOCIATION OF BLACK JOURNALISTS

PALM BEACH ASSOCIATION OF BLACK JOURNALISTS SCHOLARSHIP
• *See page 372*

SAN FRANCISCO FOUNDATION

http://www.sff.org/

PHELAN AWARD IN PHOTOGRAPHY
Award presented in every odd-numbered year to recognize achievement in photography. Applicants must provide a copy of their birth certificate with their application.
Academic Fields/Career Goals: Photojournalism/Photography.
Award: Prize for use in freshman, sophomore, junior, senior, graduate, or postgraduate years; not renewable. *Number:* 3. *Amount:* $2500.
Eligibility Requirements: Applicant must be enrolled or expecting to enroll full- or part-time at a two-year or four-year institution or university. Available to U.S. citizens.
Application Requirements: Application form, entry in a contest, self-addressed stamped envelope with application. *Deadline:* May 4.

STRAIGHTFORWARD MEDIA

http://www.straightforwardmedia.com/

STRAIGHTFORWARD MEDIA MEDIA & COMMUNICATIONS SCHOLARSHIP
• *See page 84*

TEXAS GRIDIRON CLUB INC.

http://www.spjfw.org/

TEXAS GRIDIRON CLUB SCHOLARSHIPS
• *See page 197*

UNITARIAN UNIVERSALIST ASSOCIATION

http://www.uua.org/

MARION BARR STANFIELD ART SCHOLARSHIP
• *See page 123*

PAULY D'ORLANDO MEMORIAL ART SCHOLARSHIP
• *See page 123*

UNITED METHODIST COMMUNICATIONS

http://www.umcom.org/

LEONARD M. PERRYMAN COMMUNICATIONS SCHOLARSHIP FOR ETHNIC MINORITY STUDENTS
• *See page 197*

VALLEY PRESS CLUB, SPRINGFIELD NEWSPAPERS

http://www.valleypressclub.com/

VALLEY PRESS CLUB SCHOLARSHIPS, THE REPUBLICAN SCHOLARSHIP, CHANNEL 22 SCHOLARSHIP
• *See page 198*

PHYSICAL SCIENCES

101ST AIRBORNE DIVISION ASSOCIATION

http://www.screamingeagle.org/

AL & WILLIAMARY VISTE SCHOLARSHIP
• *See page 328*

AIR & WASTE MANAGEMENT ASSOCIATION–COASTAL PLAINS CHAPTER

http://www.awmacoastalplains.org/

COASTAL PLAINS CHAPTER OF THE AIR AND WASTE MANAGEMENT ASSOCIATION ENVIRONMENTAL STEWARD SCHOLARSHIP
• *See page 300*

AIST FOUNDATION

http://www.aistfoundation.org/

ASSOCIATION FOR IRON AND STEEL TECHNOLOGY OHIO VALLEY CHAPTER SCHOLARSHIP
• *See page 142*

AMERICAN FOUNDATION FOR THE BLIND

http://www.afb.org/

PAUL W. RUCKES SCHOLARSHIP
• See page 199

AMERICAN INDIAN SCIENCE AND ENGINEERING SOCIETY

http://www.aises.org/

A.T. ANDERSON MEMORIAL SCHOLARSHIP PROGRAM
• See page 102

BURLINGTON NORTHERN SANTA FE FOUNDATION SCHOLARSHIP
• See page 102

AMERICAN INSTITUTE OF AERONAUTICS AND ASTRONAUTICS

http://www.aiaa.org/

AIAA FOUNDATION UNDERGRADUATE SCHOLARSHIP
• See page 102

AMERICAN LEGION DEPARTMENT OF MARYLAND

http://www.mdlegion.org/

AMERICAN LEGION DEPARTMENT OF MARYLAND MATH-SCIENCE SCHOLARSHIP
• See page 396

AMERICAN PHYSICAL SOCIETY

http://www.aps.org/

AMERICAN PHYSICAL SOCIETY SCHOLARSHIP FOR MINORITY UNDERGRADUATE PHYSICS MAJORS

One-time renewable award for high school seniors, college freshmen and sophomores planning to major in physics. Must be African-American, Hispanic, or Native American. Must be a U.S. citizen or a legal resident. For legal residents, a copy of alien registration card is required.

Academic Fields/Career Goals: Physical Sciences.

Award: Scholarship for use in freshman or sophomore years; not renewable. *Number:* 30–40. *Amount:* $2000–$3000.

Eligibility Requirements: Applicant must be American Indian/Alaska Native, Black (non-Hispanic), Hispanic and enrolled or expecting to enroll full-time at a four-year institution or university. Available to U.S. citizens.

Application Requirements: Application form, copy of alien registration card, if applicable, essay, recommendations or references, test scores, transcript. *Deadline:* February 3.

Contact: Ms. Arlene Modeste Knowles, Scholarship Administrator
American Physical Society
One Physics Ellipse
College Park, MD 20740
Phone: 847-209-3232
Fax: 301-209-0865
E-mail: knowles@aps.org

AMERICAN SOCIETY FOR ENGINEERING EDUCATION

http://www.asee.org/

SCIENCE, MATHEMATICS, AND RESEARCH FOR TRANSFORMATION DEFENSE SCHOLARSHIP FOR SERVICE PROGRAM
• See page 102

AMERICAN SOCIETY OF NAVAL ENGINEERS

http://www.navalengineers.org/

AMERICAN SOCIETY OF NAVAL ENGINEERS SCHOLARSHIP
• See page 103

ARIZONA PROFESSIONAL CHAPTER OF AISES

ARIZONA PROFESSIONAL CHAPTER OF AISES SCHOLARSHIP
• See page 276

ARMED FORCES COMMUNICATIONS AND ELECTRONICS ASSOCIATION, EDUCATIONAL FOUNDATION

http://www.afcea.org/scholarships

ARMED FORCES COMMUNICATIONS AND ELECTRONICS ASSOCIATION GENERAL EMMETT PAIGE SCHOLARSHIP
• See page 127

ARMED FORCES COMMUNICATIONS AND ELECTRONICS ASSOCIATION ROTC SCHOLARSHIP PROGRAM
• See page 127

DISABLED WAR VETERANS SCHOLARSHIP
• See page 128

LTG DOUGLAS D. BUCHHOLZ MEMORIAL SCHOLARSHIP
• See page 128

VETERANS OF ENDURING FREEDOM (AFGHANISTAN) AND IRAQI FREEDOM SCHOLARSHIP
• See page 200

ARNOLD AND MABEL BECKMAN FOUNDATION

http://www.beckman-foundation.com/

BECKMAN SCHOLARS PROGRAM
• See page 143

ARRL FOUNDATION INC.

http://www.arrl.org/

WILLIAM R. GOLDFARB MEMORIAL SCHOLARSHIP
• See page 150

ASSOCIATION FOR WOMEN GEOSCIENTISTS, PUGET SOUND CHAPTER

http://www.awg.org/

PUGET SOUND CHÁPTER SCHOLARSHIP

ASSOCIATION ON AMERICAN INDIAN AFFAIRS, INC.

http://www.indian-affairs.org/

ELIZABETH AND SHERMAN ASCHE MEMORIAL SCHOLARSHIP FUND

BARRY M. GOLDWATER SCHOLARSHIP AND EXCELLENCE IN EDUCATION FOUNDATION

http://www.act.org/goldwater

BARRY M. GOLDWATER SCHOLARSHIP AND EXCELLENCE IN EDUCATION PROGRAM

BRITISH COLUMBIA INNOVATION COUNCIL

http://www.bcic.ca/

BCIC YOUNG INNOVATOR SCHOLARSHIP COMPETITION (IDEA MASH UP)

PAUL AND HELEN TRUSSELL SCIENCE AND TECHNOLOGY SCHOLARSHIP

CATCHING THE DREAM

http://www.catchingthedream.org/

MATH, ENGINEERING, SCIENCE, BUSINESS, EDUCATION, COMPUTERS SCHOLARSHIPS

NATIVE AMERICAN LEADERSHIP IN EDUCATION (NALE)

THE COMMUNITY FOUNDATION FOR GREATER ATLANTA, INC.

http://cfgreateratlanta.org/

JAMES M. AND VIRGINIA M. SMYTH SCHOLARSHIP

TECH HIGH SCHOOL ALUMNI ASSOCIATION/W.O. CHENEY MERIT SCHOLARSHIP FUND

CONGRESSIONAL BLACK CAUCUS FOUNDATION, INC.

http://www.cbcfinc.org/

THE LOUIS STOKES HEALTH SCHOLARS PROGRAM

THE DALLAS FOUNDATION

http://www.dallasfoundation.org/

WHITLEY PLACE SCHOLARSHIP

EAA AVIATION FOUNDATION, INC.

http://www.eaa.org/

PAYZER SCHOLARSHIP

ELECTROCHEMICAL SOCIETY INC.

http://www.electrochem.org/

H.H. DOW MEMORIAL STUDENT ACHIEVEMENT AWARD OF THE INDUSTRIAL ELECTROLYSIS AND ELECTROCHEMICAL ENGINEERING DIVISION OF THE ELECTROCHEMICAL SOCIETY INC.

STUDENT RESEARCH AWARDS OF THE BATTERY DIVISION OF THE ELECTROCHEMICAL SOCIETY INC.

FOUNDATION FOR SCIENCE AND DISABILITY

http://stemd.org/

GRANTS FOR DISABLED STUDENTS IN THE SCIENCES

GREATER KANAWHA VALLEY FOUNDATION

http://www.tgkvf.org/

MATH AND SCIENCE SCHOLARSHIP

INDEPENDENT LABORATORIES INSTITUTE SCHOLARSHIP ALLIANCE

http://www.acil.org/

INDEPENDENT LABORATORIES INSTITUTE SCHOLARSHIP ALLIANCE

LOS ANGELES COUNCIL OF BLACK PROFESSIONAL ENGINEERS

http://www.lablackengineers.org/

AL-BEN SCHOLARSHIP FOR ACADEMIC INCENTIVE

AL-BEN SCHOLARSHIP FOR PROFESSIONAL MERIT

AL-BEN SCHOLARSHIP FOR SCHOLASTIC ACHIEVEMENT

NASA IDAHO SPACE GRANT CONSORTIUM

http://www.id.spacegrant.org/

NASA IDAHO SPACE GRANT CONSORTIUM SCHOLARSHIP PROGRAM
• *See page 146*

NASA/MARYLAND SPACE GRANT CONSORTIUM

http://md.spacegrant.org/

NASA MARYLAND SPACE GRANT CONSORTIUM UNDERGRADUATE SCHOLARSHIPS
• *See page 132*

NASA MINNESOTA SPACE GRANT CONSORTIUM

http://www.aem.umn.edu/mnsgc

MINNESOTA SPACE GRANT CONSORTIUM SCHOLARSHIP PROGRAM
• *See page 132*

NASA MISSISSIPPI SPACE GRANT CONSORTIUM

http://www.olemiss.edu/programs/nasa

MISSISSIPPI SPACE GRANT CONSORTIUM SCHOLARSHIP
• *See page 132*

NASA SOUTH DAKOTA SPACE GRANT CONSORTIUM

http://sdspacegrant.sdsmt.edu/

SOUTH DAKOTA SPACE GRANT CONSORTIUM UNDERGRADUATE AND GRADUATE STUDENT SCHOLARSHIPS
• *See page 134*

NASA'S VIRGINIA SPACE GRANT CONSORTIUM

http://www.vsgc.odu.edu/

UNDERGRADUATE STEM RESEARCH SCHOLARSHIPS
• *See page 106*

NASA WEST VIRGINIA SPACE GRANT CONSORTIUM

http://www.nasa.wvu.edu/

WEST VIRGINIA SPACE GRANT CONSORTIUM UNDERGRADUATE FELLOWSHIP PROGRAM
• *See page 134*

NATIONAL ASSOCIATION FOR THE ADVANCEMENT OF COLORED PEOPLE

http://www.naacp.org/

HUBERTUS W.V. WELLEMS SCHOLARSHIP FOR MALE STUDENTS
• *See page 169*

NATIONAL ASSOCIATION OF WATER COMPANIES-NEW JERSEY CHAPTER

http://www.nawc.org/

NATIONAL ASSOCIATION OF WATER COMPANIES-NEW JERSEY CHAPTER SCHOLARSHIP
• *See page 146*

NATIONAL INVENTORS HALL OF FAME

http://www.invent.org/

COLLEGIATE INVENTORS COMPETITION FOR UNDERGRADUATE STUDENTS
• *See page 106*

COLLEGIATE INVENTORS COMPETITION-GRAND PRIZE
• *See page 106*

NATIONAL SCIENCE TEACHERS ASSOCIATION

http://www.nsta.org/

TOSHIBA/NSTA EXPLORAVISION AWARDS PROGRAM
• *See page 203*

NATIONAL SOCIETY OF BLACK PHYSICISTS

http://www.nsbp.org/

AMERICAN PHYSICAL SOCIETY CORPORATE-SPONSORED SCHOLARSHIP FOR MINORITY UNDERGRADUATE STUDENTS WHO MAJOR IN PHYSICS

Scholarship available for minority undergraduate students majoring in physics. Award of $2000 per year for new corporate scholars, and $3000 per year for renewal students. In addition, each physics department that hosts one or more APS minority undergraduate scholars and assigns a mentor for their students will receive a $500 award for programs to encourage minority students.

Academic Fields/Career Goals: Physical Sciences.

Award: Scholarship for use in freshman, sophomore, junior, or senior years; not renewable. *Amount:* $2000–$3000.

Eligibility Requirements: Applicant must be American Indian/Alaska Native, Asian/Pacific Islander, Black (non-Hispanic), Hispanic and enrolled or expecting to enroll full- or part-time at a two-year or four-year institution or university. Available to U.S. citizens.

Application Requirements: Application form, recommendations or references, transcript. *Deadline:* December 1.

Contact: Dr. Kennedy Reed, Scholarship Chairman
    Phone: 703-536-4207
    Fax: 703-536-4203
    E-mail: scholarships@nsbp.org

CHARLES S. BROWN SCHOLARSHIP IN PHYSICS

Scholarship providing and African-American student with financial assistance while enrolled in a physics degree program. Number of awards and dollar value varies.

Academic Fields/Career Goals: Physical Sciences.

Award: Scholarship for use in freshman, sophomore, junior, senior, or graduate years; not renewable.

Eligibility Requirements: Applicant must be Black (non-Hispanic) and enrolled or expecting to enroll full- or part-time at a four-year institution or university. Available to U.S. and non-U.S. citizens.

Application Requirements: Application form, financial need analysis, self-addressed stamped envelope with application. *Deadline:* January 12.

ELMER S. IMES SCHOLARSHIP IN PHYSICS

Graduating high school seniors and undergraduate students already enrolled in college as physics majors may apply for the scholarship. U.S citizenship is required.

Academic Fields/Career Goals: Physical Sciences.

Award: Scholarship for use in freshman, sophomore, junior, or senior years; not renewable. *Number:* 1. *Amount:* $1000.

Eligibility Requirements: Applicant must be enrolled or expecting to enroll full-time at a two-year or four-year institution or university. Available to U.S. citizens.

Application Requirements: Application form, driver's license, essay, recommendations or references, resume, transcript. *Deadline:* January 12.

HARVEY WASHINGTON BANKS SCHOLARSHIP IN ASTRONOMY

One-time award for an African American student pursuing an undergraduate degree in astronomy/physics.

Academic Fields/Career Goals: Physical Sciences.

Award: Scholarship for use in freshman, sophomore, junior, or senior years; not renewable. *Number:* 1. *Amount:* $1000.

Eligibility Requirements: Applicant must be Black (non-Hispanic) and enrolled or expecting to enroll full-time at a two-year or four-year institution or university. Available to U.S. citizens.

Application Requirements: Application form, essay, recommendations or references, transcript. *Deadline:* January 12.

Contact: Dr. Kennedy Reed, Scholarship Chairman
>   *Phone:* 703-536-4207
>   *Fax:* 703-536-4203
>   *E-mail:* scholarships@nsbp.org

MICHAEL P. ANDERSON SCHOLARSHIP IN SPACE SCIENCE

One-time award for an African American undergraduate student majoring in space science/physics.

Academic Fields/Career Goals: Physical Sciences.

Award: Scholarship for use in freshman, sophomore, junior, or senior years; not renewable. *Number:* 1. *Amount:* $1000.

Eligibility Requirements: Applicant must be Black (non-Hispanic) and enrolled or expecting to enroll full-time at a two-year or four-year institution or university. Available to U.S. citizens.

Application Requirements: Application form, essay, recommendations or references, transcript. *Deadline:* January 12.

Contact: Dr. Kennedy Reed, Scholarship Chairman
>   *Phone:* 703-536-4207
>   *Fax:* 703-536-4203
>   *E-mail:* scholarships@nsbp.org

NATIONAL SOCIETY OF BLACK PHYSICISTS AND LAWRENCE LIVERMORE NATIONAL LIBRARY UNDERGRADUATE SCHOLARSHIP

Scholarship for a graduating high school senior or undergraduate student enrolled in a physics major. Scholarship renewable up to four years if student maintains a 3.0 GPA and remains a physics major.

Academic Fields/Career Goals: Physical Sciences.

Award: Scholarship for use in freshman, sophomore, junior, or senior years; renewable. *Number:* 1. *Amount:* $5000.

Eligibility Requirements: Applicant must be Black (non-Hispanic) and enrolled or expecting to enroll full-time at a two-year or four-year institution or university. Applicant must have 3.0 GPA or higher. Available to U.S. citizens.

Application Requirements: Application form, essay, recommendations or references, transcript. *Deadline:* December 1.

Contact: Dr. Kennedy Reed, Scholarship Chairman
>   *Phone:* 703-536-4207
>   *Fax:* 703-536-4203
>   *E-mail:* scholarships@nsbp.org

RONALD E. MCNAIR SCHOLARSHIP IN SPACE AND OPTICAL PHYSICS

One-time award for African American undergraduate student majoring in physics. Must be U.S. citizen.

Academic Fields/Career Goals: Physical Sciences.

Award: Scholarship for use in freshman, sophomore, junior, or senior years; not renewable. *Number:* 1. *Amount:* $1000.

Eligibility Requirements: Applicant must be Black (non-Hispanic) and enrolled or expecting to enroll full-time at a two-year or four-year institution or university. Available to U.S. citizens.

Application Requirements: Application form, essay, recommendations or references, transcript. *Deadline:* January 12.

Contact: Dr. Kennedy Reed, Scholarship Chairman
>   *Phone:* 703-536-4207
>   *Fax:* 703-536-4203
>   *E-mail:* scholarships@nsbp.org

WALTER SAMUEL MCAFEE SCHOLARSHIP IN SPACE PHYSICS

One-time scholarship for African American full-time undergraduate student majoring in physics. Must be U.S. citizen.

Academic Fields/Career Goals: Physical Sciences.

Award: Scholarship for use in freshman, sophomore, junior, or senior years; not renewable. *Number:* 1. *Amount:* $1000.

Eligibility Requirements: Applicant must be Black (non-Hispanic) and enrolled or expecting to enroll full-time at a two-year or four-year institution or university. Available to U.S. citizens.

Application Requirements: Application form, essay, recommendations or references, transcript. *Deadline:* January 12.

Contact: Dr. Kennedy Reed, Scholarship Chairman
>   *Phone:* 703-536-4207
>   *Fax:* 703-536-4203
>   *E-mail:* scholarships@nsbp.org

WILLIE HOBBS MOORE, HARRY L. MORRISON, AND ARTHUR B.C. WALKER PHYSICS SCHOLARSHIPS

Scholarships are intended for African American undergraduate physics majors. Applicants should be either sophomores or juniors. Award for use in junior or senior year of study.

Academic Fields/Career Goals: Physical Sciences.

Award: Scholarship for use in sophomore, junior, or senior years; not renewable. *Number:* 3. *Amount:* $1000.

Eligibility Requirements: Applicant must be Black (non-Hispanic) and enrolled or expecting to enroll full-time at a two-year or four-year institution or university. Available to U.S. citizens.

Application Requirements: Application form, essay, recommendations or references, transcript. *Deadline:* January 12.

Contact: Dr. Kennedy Reed, Scholarship Chairman
>   *Phone:* 703-536-4207
>   *Fax:* 703-536-4203
>   *E-mail:* scholarships@nsbp.org

NEVADA NASA SPACE GRANT CONSORTIUM

http://www.nvspacegrant.org/

NATIONAL SPACE GRANT COLLEGE AND FELLOWSHIP PROGRAM
• *See page 106*

ROBERT H. MOLLOHAN FAMILY CHARITABLE FOUNDATION, INC.

http://www.mollohanfoundation.org/

HIGH TECHNOLOGY SCHOLARS PROGRAM
• *See page 147*

SIGMA XI, THE SCIENTIFIC RESEARCH SOCIETY

http://www.sigmaxi.org/

SIGMA XI GRANTS-IN-AID OF RESEARCH
• *See page 95*

SOCIETY FOR IMAGING SCIENCE AND TECHNOLOGY

http://www.imaging.org/

RAYMOND DAVIS SCHOLARSHIP

• *See page 288*

SOCIETY OF PHYSICS STUDENTS

http://www.spsnational.org/

SOCIETY OF PHYSICS STUDENTS LEADERSHIP SCHOLARSHIPS

Scholarships of $2000 to $5000 are awarded to members of Society of Physics Students (SPS) for undergraduate study. The number of awards granted ranges from 17 to 22.

Academic Fields/Career Goals: Physical Sciences.

Award: Scholarship for use in sophomore, junior, or senior years; not renewable. *Number:* 17–22. *Amount:* $2000–$5000.

Eligibility Requirements: Applicant must be enrolled or expecting to enroll full-time at a two-year or four-year institution or university. Applicant or parent of applicant must be member of Society of Physics Students. Available to U.S. and non-U.S. citizens.

Application Requirements: Application form, recommendations or references, transcript. *Deadline:* February 15.

SOCIETY OF PHYSICS STUDENTS OUTSTANDING STUDENT IN RESEARCH

Available to members of the Society of Physics Students. Winners will receive a $500 honorarium and a $500 award for their SPS Chapter. In addition, expenses for transportation, room, board, and registration for the ICPS will by paid by SPS.

Academic Fields/Career Goals: Physical Sciences.

Award: Prize for use in freshman, sophomore, junior, or senior years; not renewable. *Number:* 1–2. *Amount:* $500–$2500.

Eligibility Requirements: Applicant must be enrolled or expecting to enroll full-time at a two-year or four-year institution or university. Applicant or parent of applicant must be member of Society of Physics Students. Available to U.S. and non-U.S. citizens.

Application Requirements: Abstract, application form, recommendations or references. *Deadline:* April 15.

SOCIETY OF PHYSICS STUDENTS PEGGY DIXON TWO-YEAR COLLEGE SCHOLARSHIP

Scholarship available to Society of Physics Students (SPS) members. Award based on performance both in physics and overall studies, and SPS participation. Must have completed at least one semester or quarter of the introductory physics sequence, and be currently registered in the appropriate subsequent physics courses.

Academic Fields/Career Goals: Physical Sciences.

Award: Scholarship for use in freshman or sophomore years; not renewable. *Number:* 1. *Amount:* $2000.

Eligibility Requirements: Applicant must be enrolled or expecting to enroll full-time at a two-year or four-year institution or university. Applicant or parent of applicant must be member of Society of Physics Students. Available to U.S. and non-U.S. citizens.

Application Requirements: Application form, financial need analysis, letters from at least two faculty members, transcript. *Deadline:* February 15.

Contact: Sacha Purnell, Administrative Assistant
Phone: 301-209-3007
E-mail: sps@aip.org

TKE EDUCATIONAL FOUNDATION

http://www.tke.org/

CARROL C. HALL MEMORIAL SCHOLARSHIP

• *See page 107*

UNITED NEGRO COLLEGE FUND

http://www.uncf.org/

SANDISK CORPORATION SCHOLARSHIP

• *See page 206*

UNCF/MERCK SCIENCE INITIATIVE

• *See page 149*

WILLIAM WRIGLEY JR. SCHOLARSHIP/INTERNSHIP

• *See page 161*

WILMA WARBURG SCHOLARSHIP

• *See page 340*

UNIVERSITIES SPACE RESEARCH ASSOCIATION

http://www.usra.edu/

UNIVERSITIES SPACE RESEARCH ASSOCIATION SCHOLARSHIP PROGRAM

• *See page 107*

VERMONT SPACE GRANT CONSORTIUM

http://www.cems.uvm.edu/vsgc

VERMONT SPACE GRANT CONSORTIUM SCHOLARSHIP PROGRAM

• *See page 107*

WIFLE FOUNDATION, INC.

http://www.wifle.org/

WIFLE SCHOLARSHIP PROGRAM

• *See page 207*

XEROX

http://www.xerox.com//

TECHNICAL MINORITY SCHOLARSHIP

• *See page 177*

POLITICAL SCIENCE

AMERICAN FEDERATION OF STATE, COUNTY, AND MUNICIPAL EMPLOYEES

http://www.afscme.org/

AFSCME/UNCF UNION SCHOLARS PROGRAM

• *See page 97*

JERRY CLARK MEMORIAL SCHOLARSHIP

Renewable award for a student majoring in political science for his or her junior and senior years of study. Must be a child of an AFSCME member. Minimum 2.5 GPA required. Once awarded, the scholarship will be renewed for the senior year provided the student remains enrolled full-time as a political science major.

Academic Fields/Career Goals: Political Science.

Award: Scholarship for use in junior or senior years; renewable. *Number:* 2. *Amount:* $5000.

Eligibility Requirements: Applicant must be enrolled or expecting to enroll full-time at a four-year institution or university. Applicant or parent of applicant must be member of American Federation of State, County, and Municipal Employees. Applicant must have 2.5 GPA or higher. Available to U.S. citizens.

Application Requirements: Application form, proof of parent, transcript. *Deadline:* July 1.

Contact: Philip Allen, Scholarship Coordinator
Phone: 202-429-1250
Fax: 202-429-1293
E-mail: pallen@asscme.org

AMERICAN LEGION AUXILIARY DEPARTMENT OF ARIZONA

http://wwwaladeptaz.org

AMERICAN LEGION AUXILIARY DEPARTMENT OF ARIZONA WILMA HOYAL-MAXINE CHILTON MEMORIAL SCHOLARSHIP

Annual scholarship to a student in second year or higher in one of the three state universities in Arizona. Must be enrolled in a program of study in political science, public programs, or special education. Must be a citizen of United States and of Arizona for at least one year. Honorably discharged veterans or immediate family members are given preference.

Academic Fields/Career Goals: Political Science; Public Policy and Administration; Social Services; Special Education.

Award: Scholarship for use in sophomore, junior, or senior years; not renewable. *Number:* 3. *Amount:* $1000.

Eligibility Requirements: Applicant must be enrolled or expecting to enroll full- or part-time at a two-year or four-year institution or university; resident of Arizona and studying in Arizona. Available to U.S. citizens.

Application Requirements: Application form, essay, financial need analysis, personal photograph, recommendations or references, test scores, transcript. *Deadline:* May 15.

Contact: Mr. Barbara Matteson, Department Secretary/Treasurer
American Legion Auxiliary Department of Arizona
4701 North 19th Avenue, Suite 100
Phoenix, AZ 85015
Phone: 602-241-1080
Fax: 602-602-9640
E-mail: secretary@aladeptaz.org

ARAB AMERICAN SCHOLARSHIP FOUNDATION

http://www.lahc.org/

LEBANESE AMERICAN HERITAGE CLUB'S SCHOLARSHIP FUND
• See page 188

ASSOCIATION OF FORMER INTELLIGENCE OFFICERS

http://www.afio.com/13_scholarships.htm

CIA UNDERGRADUATE SCHOLARSHIPS
• See page 97

BOYS AND GIRLS CLUBS OF SAN DIEGO

http://www.sdyouth.org/

SPENCE REESE SCHOLARSHIP
• See page 279

CENTRAL INTELLIGENCE AGENCY

http://www.cia.gov/

CENTRAL INTELLIGENCE AGENCY UNDERGRADUATE SCHOLARSHIP PROGRAM
• See page 70

COLLEGEBOUND FOUNDATION

http://www.collegeboundfoundation.org/

DECATUR H. MILLER SCHOLARSHIP
• See page 343

THE ROBERT SPAR MEMORIAL SCHOLARSHIP
• See page 343

CUBAN AMERICAN NATIONAL FOUNDATION

http://www.masscholarships.org/

MAS FAMILY SCHOLARSHIPS
• See page 152

CULTURAL SERVICES OF THE FRENCH EMBASSY

http://www.frenchculture.org/

TEACHING ASSISTANT PROGRAM IN FRANCE
• See page 97

GOVERNMENT FINANCE OFFICERS ASSOCIATION

http://www.gfoa.org/

MINORITIES IN GOVERNMENT FINANCE SCHOLARSHIP
• See page 73

GREATER SALINA COMMUNITY FOUNDATION

http://www.gscf.org/

KANSAS FEDERATION OF REPUBLICAN WOMEN SCHOLARSHIP
• See page 343

HARRY S. TRUMAN SCHOLARSHIP FOUNDATION

http://www.truman.gov/

HARRY S. TRUMAN SCHOLARSHIP

Scholarships for U.S. citizens or U.S. nationals who are college or university students with junior-level academic standing and who wish to attend professional or graduate school to prepare for careers in government or the nonprofit and advocacy sectors. Candidates must be nominated by their institution. Public service and leadership record considered. Visit website http://www.truman.gov for further information and application.

Academic Fields/Career Goals: Political Science; Public Policy and Administration.

Award: Scholarship for use in junior year; renewable. *Number:* 65. *Amount:* $30,000.

Eligibility Requirements: Applicant must be enrolled or expecting to enroll full-time at a four-year institution or university and must have an interest in leadership. Available to U.S. citizens.

Application Requirements: Application form, interview, policy proposal, recommendations or references. *Deadline:* February 5.

Contact: Tonji Wade, Program Officer
Harry S. Truman Scholarship Foundation
712 Jackson Place, NW
Washington, DC 20006
Phone: 202-395-4831
Fax: 202-395-6995
E-mail: office@truman.gov

INSTITUTE FOR HUMANE STUDIES

http://www.theihs.org/

HUMANE STUDIES FELLOWSHIPS
• *See page 190*

THE LYNDON BAINES JOHNSON FOUNDATION

http://www.lbjfoundation.org/

MOODY RESEARCH GRANTS
• *See page 344*

NATIONAL SOCIETY DAUGHTERS OF THE AMERICAN REVOLUTION

http://www.dar.org/

NATIONAL SOCIETY DAUGHTERS OF THE AMERICAN REVOLUTION DR. AURA-LEE A. PITTENGER AND JAMES HOBBS PITTENGER AMERICAN HISTORY SCHOLARSHIP
• *See page 344*

NATIONAL SOCIETY DAUGHTERS OF THE AMERICAN REVOLUTION ENID HALL GRISWOLD MEMORIAL SCHOLARSHIP
• *See page 230*

STRAIGHTFORWARD MEDIA

http://www.straightforwardmedia.com/

STRAIGHTFORWARD MEDIA LIBERAL ARTS SCHOLARSHIP
• *See page 116*

TKE EDUCATIONAL FOUNDATION

http://www.tke.org/

BRUCE B. MELCHERT SCHOLARSHIP
One-time award of $500 given to an undergraduate member of Tau Kappa Epsilon with sophomore, junior, or senior standing. Must be pursuing a degree in political science or government and have a record of leadership within his fraternity and other campus organizations. Should have as a goal to serve in a political or government position. Recent head and shoulders photograph must be submitted with application. Minimum 3.0 GPA required.

Academic Fields/Career Goals: Political Science.

Award: Scholarship for use in sophomore, junior, or senior years; not renewable. *Number:* 1. *Amount:* $500.

Eligibility Requirements: Applicant must be enrolled or expecting to enroll full-time at a four-year institution or university and must have an interest in leadership. Applicant or parent of applicant must be member of Tau Kappa Epsilon. Applicant must have 3.0 GPA or higher. Available to U.S. and non-U.S. citizens.

Application Requirements: Application form, essay, narrative summary of how TKE membership has benefited applicant, personal photograph, transcript. *Deadline:* February 29.

Contact: Gary Reed, President and Chief Executive Officer
TKE Educational Foundation
8645 Founders Road
Indianapolis, IN 46268-1393
Phone: 317-872-6533
Fax: 317-875-8353
E-mail: reedga@tke.org

UNITED NEGRO COLLEGE FUND

http://www.uncf.org/

AFSCME/UNCF/HARVARD UNIVERSITY LWP UNION SCHOLARS PROGRAM
• *See page 98*

WASHINGTON CROSSING FOUNDATION

http://www.gwcf.org/

WASHINGTON CROSSING FOUNDATION SCHOLARSHIP
Renewable, merit-based awards available to high school seniors who are planning a career in government service. Must write an essay stating reason for deciding on a career in public service. Minimum 3.0 GPA required.

Academic Fields/Career Goals: Political Science; Public Policy and Administration.

Award: Scholarship for use in freshman year; renewable. *Number:* 5–10. *Amount:* $1000–$20,000.

Eligibility Requirements: Applicant must be high school student and planning to enroll or expecting to enroll full-time at a four-year institution or university. Applicant must have 3.0 GPA or higher. Available to U.S. citizens.

Application Requirements: Application form, essay, interview, personal photograph, recommendations or references, test scores, transcript. *Deadline:* January 15.

Contact: Eugene Fish, Vice Chairman
Washington Crossing Foundation
PO Box 503
Levittown, PA 19058-0503
Phone: 215-949-8841
Fax: 215-949-8843
E-mail: info@gwcf.org

WASHINGTON NEWS COUNCIL

http://www.wanewscouncil.org/

DICK LARSEN SCHOLARSHIP PROGRAM
• *See page 198*

HERB ROBINSON SCHOLARSHIP PROGRAM
• *See page 199*

PSYCHOLOGY

AMERICAN FEDERATION OF STATE, COUNTY, AND MUNICIPAL EMPLOYEES

http://www.afscme.org/

AFSCME/UNCF UNION SCHOLARS PROGRAM
• *See page 97*

CYNTHIA E. MORGAN SCHOLARSHIP FUND (CEMS)

http://www.cemsfund.com/

CYNTHIA E. MORGAN MEMORIAL SCHOLARSHIP FUND, INC.
• See page 298

HEALTH RESEARCH COUNCIL OF NEW ZEALAND

http://www.hrc.govt.nz/

PACIFIC MENTAL HEALTH WORK FORCE AWARD
• See page 327

INDIAN HEALTH SERVICES, UNITED STATES DEPARTMENT OF HEALTH AND HUMAN SERVICES

http://www.ihs.gov/scholarship

HEALTH PROFESSIONS PREPARATORY SCHOLARSHIP PROGRAM
• See page 141

INDIAN HEALTH SERVICE HEALTH PROFESSIONS SCHOLARSHIP PROGRAM
• See page 208

PILOT INTERNATIONAL FOUNDATION

http://www.pilotinternational.org/

PILOT INTERNATIONAL FOUNDATION RUBY NEWHALL MEMORIAL SCHOLARSHIP
• See page 339

PILOT INTERNATIONAL FOUNDATION SCHOLARSHIP PROGRAM
• See page 339

SOCIETY FOR THE SCIENTIFIC STUDY OF SEXUALITY

http://www.sexscience.org/

SOCIETY FOR THE SCIENTIFIC STUDY OF SEXUALITY STUDENT RESEARCH GRANT
• See page 102

STRAIGHTFORWARD MEDIA

http://www.straightforwardmedia.com/

STRAIGHTFORWARD MEDIA LIBERAL ARTS SCHOLARSHIP
• See page 116

ZETA PHI BETA SORORITY INC. NATIONAL EDUCATIONAL FOUNDATION

http://www.zpbnef1975.org/

LULLELIA W. HARRISON SCHOLARSHIP IN COUNSELING
• See page 179

PUBLIC HEALTH

ASSOCIATION ON AMERICAN INDIAN AFFAIRS, INC.

http://www.indian-affairs.org/

ELIZABETH AND SHERMAN ASCHE MEMORIAL SCHOLARSHIP FUND
• See page 91

CONGRESSIONAL BLACK CAUCUS FOUNDATION, INC.

http://www.cbcfinc.org/

THE LOUIS STOKES HEALTH SCHOLARS PROGRAM
• See page 144

FLORIDA ENVIRONMENTAL HEALTH ASSOCIATION

http://www.feha.org/

FLORIDA ENVIRONMENTAL HEALTH ASSOCIATION EDUCATIONAL SCHOLARSHIP AWARDS
• See page 299

GENERAL FEDERATION OF WOMEN'S CLUBS OF MASSACHUSETTS

http://www.gfwcma.org/

CATHERINE E. PHILBIN SCHOLARSHIP
One scholarship of $500 will be awarded to a graduate or undergraduate student studying public health. Eligible applicants will be residents of Massachusetts. Along with the application, students must send a personal statement of no more than 500 words addressing professional goals and financial need.

Academic Fields/Career Goals: Public Health.

Award: Scholarship for use in freshman, sophomore, junior, senior, or graduate years; not renewable. *Number:* 1. *Amount:* $500.

Eligibility Requirements: Applicant must be enrolled or expecting to enroll full-time at a four-year institution or university and resident of Massachusetts. Available to U.S. citizens.

Application Requirements: Application form, essay, recommendations or references, transcript. *Deadline:* March 1.

Contact: Jane Howard, Scholarship Chairman
General Federation of Women's Clubs of Massachusetts
PO Box 679
Sudbury, MA 01776-0679
E-mail: jhoward@mountida.edu

NATIONAL ENVIRONMENTAL HEALTH ASSOCIATION/AMERICAN ACADEMY OF SANITARIANS

http://www.neha.org/

NATIONAL ENVIRONMENTAL HEALTH ASSOCIATION/AMERICAN ACADEMY OF SANITARIANS SCHOLARSHIP
• See page 299

NEW ENGLAND EMPLOYEE BENEFITS COUNCIL

http://www.neebc.org/

NEW ENGLAND EMPLOYEE BENEFITS COUNCIL SCHOLARSHIP PROGRAM
• *See page 77*

OREGON STUDENT ASSISTANCE COMMISSION

http://www.GetCollegeFunds.org/

LAURENCE R. FOSTER MEMORIAL SCHOLARSHIP
One-time award to students enrolled or planning to enroll in a public health degree program. First preference given to those working in the public health field and those pursuing a graduate degree in public health. Undergraduates entering junior or senior year health programs may apply if seeking a public health career, and not private practice. Applicants from diverse cultures preferred. Additional essays required.

Academic Fields/Career Goals: Public Health.

Award: Scholarship for use in freshman, sophomore, junior, or senior years; renewable.

Eligibility Requirements: Applicant must be enrolled or expecting to enroll full- or part-time at a four-year institution. Available to U.S. citizens.

Application Requirements: Activity chart, application form, essay, financial need analysis, recommendations or references, transcript. *Deadline:* March 1.

PILOT INTERNATIONAL FOUNDATION

http://www.pilotinternational.org/

PILOT INTERNATIONAL FOUNDATION RUBY NEWHALL MEMORIAL SCHOLARSHIP
• *See page 339*

SOCIETY FOR THE SCIENTIFIC STUDY OF SEXUALITY

http://www.sexscience.org/

SOCIETY FOR THE SCIENTIFIC STUDY OF SEXUALITY STUDENT RESEARCH GRANT
• *See page 102*

SOUTH CAROLINA PUBLIC HEALTH ASSOCIATION

http://www.scpha.com/

SOUTH CAROLINA PUBLIC HEALTH ASSOCIATION PUBLIC HEALTH SCHOLARSHIPS
Current member of the SCPHA with more than 6 hours remaining and enrolled in a accredited higher education program for public health or related field. Dantzler- exhibit significant commitment to the public health profession through volunteer and/or professional activity as indicated on the application. Public Health Scholarship- exhibit significant commitment to the public health profession through volunteer and/or professional activity as indicated on the application.

Academic Fields/Career Goals: Public Health.

Award: Scholarship for use in freshman, sophomore, junior, senior, graduate, or postgraduate years; not renewable. *Number:* 2. *Amount:* $500–$750.

Eligibility Requirements: Applicant must be enrolled or expecting to enroll full- or part-time at a four-year institution or university. Applicant must have 3.5 GPA or higher. Available to U.S. citizens.

Application Requirements: Application form, proof of number of hours remaining., transcript. *Deadline:* March 31.

Contact: Mr. Larry White, Scholarship Committee Chair
South Carolina Public Health Association
PO Box 3051
Conway, SC 29528
Phone: 843-488-1329 Ext. 225
Fax: 843-488-1330
E-mail: larry@smokefreehorry.org

PUBLIC POLICY AND ADMINISTRATION

AMERICAN INSTITUTE OF POLISH CULTURE INC.

http://www.ampolinstitute.org/

HARRIET IRSAY SCHOLARSHIP GRANT
• *See page 117*

AMERICAN LEGION AUXILIARY DEPARTMENT OF ARIZONA

http://wwwaladeptaz.org

AMERICAN LEGION AUXILIARY DEPARTMENT OF ARIZONA WILMA HOYAL-MAXINE CHILTON MEMORIAL SCHOLARSHIP
• *See page 465*

THE DALLAS FOUNDATION

http://www.dallasfoundation.org/

WHITLEY PLACE SCHOLARSHIP
• *See page 110*

GOVERNMENT FINANCE OFFICERS ASSOCIATION

http://www.gfoa.org/

FRANK L. GREATHOUSE GOVERNMENT ACCOUNTING SCHOLARSHIP
• *See page 155*

MINORITIES IN GOVERNMENT FINANCE SCHOLARSHIP
• *See page 73*

GREATER SALINA COMMUNITY FOUNDATION

http://www.gscf.org/

KANSAS FEDERATION OF REPUBLICAN WOMEN SCHOLARSHIP
• *See page 343*

HARRY S. TRUMAN SCHOLARSHIP FOUNDATION

http://www.truman.gov/

HARRY S. TRUMAN SCHOLARSHIP
• *See page 465*

JAPANESE AMERICAN CITIZENS LEAGUE (JACL)

http://www.jacl.org/

NATIONAL JACL HEADQUARTERS SCHOLARSHIP
• *See page 92*

NEW ENGLAND EMPLOYEE BENEFITS COUNCIL

http://www.neebc.org/

NEW ENGLAND EMPLOYEE BENEFITS COUNCIL SCHOLARSHIP PROGRAM
• *See page 77*

UNITED NEGRO COLLEGE FUND

http://www.uncf.org/

AFSCME/UNCF/HARVARD UNIVERSITY LWP UNION SCHOLARS PROGRAM
• *See page 98*

WASHINGTON CROSSING FOUNDATION

http://www.gwcf.org/

WASHINGTON CROSSING FOUNDATION SCHOLARSHIP
• *See page 466*

WIFLE FOUNDATION, INC.

http://www.wifle.org/

WIFLE SCHOLARSHIP PROGRAM
• *See page 207*

RADIOLOGY

ASRT FOUNDATION

http://www.asrtfoundation.org/

JERMAN-CAHOON STUDENT SCHOLARSHIP
• *See page 332*

MEDICAL IMAGING EDUCATORS SCHOLARSHIP
• *See page 234*

PROFESSIONAL ADVANCEMENT SCHOLARSHIP
• *See page 332*

ROYCE OSBORN MINORITY STUDENT SCHOLARSHIP
• *See page 332*

SIEMENS CLINICAL ADVANCEMENT SCHOLARSHIP
• *See page 332*

CYNTHIA E. MORGAN SCHOLARSHIP FUND (CEMS)

http://www.cemsfund.com/

CYNTHIA E. MORGAN MEMORIAL SCHOLARSHIP FUND, INC.
• *See page 298*

SOCIETY OF NUCLEAR MEDICINE AND MOLECULAR IMAGING

http://www.snmmi.org/

PAUL COLE TECHNOLOGIST SCHOLARSHIP
• *See page 339*

REAL ESTATE

APPRAISAL INSTITUTE EDUCATION TRUST

http://www.aiedtrust.org/

AIET MINORITIES AND WOMEN EDUCATIONAL SCHOLARSHIP

Awarded to minorities and women undergraduate students pursuing academic degrees in real estate appraisal or related fields.

Academic Fields/Career Goals: Real Estate.

Award: Scholarship for use in freshman, sophomore, junior, senior, graduate, or postgraduate years; not renewable. *Amount:* $1000.

Eligibility Requirements: Applicant must be American Indian/Alaska Native, Asian/Pacific Islander, Black (non-Hispanic), Hispanic; enrolled or expecting to enroll full- or part-time at a four-year institution or university and female. Applicant must have 2.5 GPA or higher. Available to U.S. citizens.

Application Requirements: Application form, essay, financial need analysis, personal photograph, recommendations or references, resume, transcript. *Deadline:* April 15.

APPRAISAL INSTITUTE EDUCATION TRUST EDUCATION SCHOLARSHIPS

Awarded on the basis of academic excellence, this scholarship helps finance the educational endeavors of undergraduate and graduate students concentrating in real estate appraisal, land economics, real estate or allied fields.

Academic Fields/Career Goals: Real Estate.

Award: Scholarship for use in sophomore, junior, senior, or graduate years; not renewable. *Amount:* $1000–$2000.

Eligibility Requirements: Applicant must be enrolled or expecting to enroll full-time at a four-year institution or university. Available to U.S. citizens.

Application Requirements: Application form, essay, recommendations or references, resume, transcript. *Deadline:* March 15.

C.A.R. SCHOLARSHIP FOUNDATION

http://www.car.org/

C.A.R. SCHOLARSHIP FOUNDATION AWARD

Scholarships to students enrolled at a California college or niversity for professions which are centered on, or support a career in real estate transactional activity. Must have maintained a cumulative GPA of 2.6 or higher.

Academic Fields/Career Goals: Real Estate.

Award: Scholarship for use in sophomore, junior, senior, or graduate years; not renewable. *Number:* 20–30. *Amount:* $2000–$4000.

Eligibility Requirements: Applicant must be enrolled or expecting to enroll full-time at a two-year or four-year institution or university; resident of California and studying in California. Available to U.S. citizens.

Application Requirements: Application form, driver's license, essay, interview, recommendations or references, transcript.

Contact: Lynette Flores, Scholarship Coordinator
C.A.R. Scholarship Foundation
525 South Virgil Avenue
Los Angeles, CA 90020
Phone: 213-739-8200
Fax: 213-480-7724
E-mail: lynettef@car.org

ILLINOIS REAL ESTATE EDUCATIONAL FOUNDATION

http://www.ilreef.org/

ILLINOIS REAL ESTATE EDUCATIONAL FOUNDATION ACADEMIC SCHOLARSHIPS

Awards for Illinois residents attending an accredited two-or four-year junior college, college or university in Illinois. Must have completed 30 college credit hours and be pursuing a degree with an emphasis in real estate. Must be a U.S. citizen.

Academic Fields/Career Goals: Real Estate.

Award: Scholarship for use in freshman, sophomore, junior, or senior years; not renewable. *Amount:* $1000.

Eligibility Requirements: Applicant must be enrolled or expecting to enroll full-time at a two-year or four-year institution or university; resident of Illinois and studying in Illinois. Available to U.S. citizens.

Application Requirements: Application form, essay, recommendations or references, resume, transcript. *Deadline:* April 1.

Contact: Laurie Clayton, Foundation Manager
Illinois Real Estate Educational Foundation
522 South 5th Street, PO Box 2607
Springfield, IL 62708
Phone: 866-854-7333
Fax: 217-529-5893
E-mail: lclayton@iar.org

THOMAS F. SEAY SCHOLARSHIP

Award of $2000 to students pursuing a degree with an emphasis in real estate. Must be a U.S. citizen and attending any accredited U.S. college or university full-time. Must have completed at least 30 college credit hours. Minimum 3.5 GPA required.

Academic Fields/Career Goals: Real Estate.

Award: Scholarship for use in junior or senior years; not renewable. *Amount:* $2000.

Eligibility Requirements: Applicant must be enrolled or expecting to enroll full-time at a four-year institution or university; resident of Illinois and studying in Illinois. Applicant must have 3.5 GPA or higher. Available to U.S. citizens.

Application Requirements: Application form, community service, essay, recommendations or references, resume, transcript. *Deadline:* April 1.

Contact: Laurie Clayton, Foundation Manager
Illinois Real Estate Educational Foundation
522 South 5th Street, PO Box 2607
Springfield, IL 62708
Phone: 866-854-7333
Fax: 217-529-5893
E-mail: lclayton@iar.org

INTERNATIONAL COUNCIL OF SHOPPING CENTERS FOUNDATION

http://www.icscfoundation.org/

JOHN T. RIORDAN SCHOOL FOR PROFESSIONAL DEVELOPMENT

Award for higher education for shopping center professionals. Must be a official ICSC member in good standing, actively employed in the shopping center industry for a minimum of one year, or recent graduate of college/university with coursework emphasis in real estate; or a graduate of REAP or Inroads programs within the past eighteen months prior to year end when the application is submitted.

Academic Fields/Career Goals: Real Estate.

Award: Scholarship for use in freshman, sophomore, junior, senior, graduate, or postgraduate years; not renewable. *Number:* 10–15. *Amount:* up to $3000.

Eligibility Requirements: Applicant must be enrolled or expecting to enroll full- or part-time at a technical institution. Available to U.S. and non-U.S. citizens.

Application Requirements: Application form, essay, recommendations or references, resume. *Deadline:* March 14.

Contact: Valerie Cammiso, Executive Director
Phone: 646-728-3559
E-mail: vcammiso@icsc.org

NEW JERSEY ASSOCIATION OF REALTORS

http://www.njar.com/

NEW JERSEY ASSOCIATION OF REALTORS EDUCATIONAL FOUNDATION SCHOLARSHIP PROGRAM

One-time awards for New Jersey residents who are high school seniors pursuing studies in real estate or allied fields. Preference to students considering a career in real estate. Must be member of NJAR or relative of a member. Selected candidates are interviewed in June. Must be a U.S. citizen.

Academic Fields/Career Goals: Real Estate.

Award: Scholarship for use in freshman year; not renewable. *Number:* 20–32. *Amount:* $1000–$2500.

Eligibility Requirements: Applicant must be high school student; planning to enroll or expecting to enroll full-time at a four-year institution or university and resident of New Jersey. Applicant or parent of applicant must be member of New Jersey Association of Realtors. Available to U.S. citizens.

Application Requirements: Application form, essay, financial need analysis, interview, letter of verification of realtor/realtor associate/ association staff, transcript. *Deadline:* April 9.

Contact: Diane Hatley, Educational Foundation
New Jersey Association of Realtors
PO Box 2098
Edison, NJ 08818
Phone: 732-494-5616
Fax: 732-494-4723

STRAIGHTFORWARD MEDIA

http://www.straightforwardmedia.com/

STRAIGHTFORWARD MEDIA VOCATIONAL-TECHNICAL SCHOOL SCHOLARSHIP
• *See page 99*

RECREATION, PARKS, LEISURE STUDIES

AMERICAN ALLIANCE FOR HEALTH, PHYSICAL EDUCATION, RECREATION AND DANCE

http://www.aahperd.org/

ROBERT W. CRAWFORD STUDENT LITERARY AWARD

Annual award recognizing writing excellence among graduate and undergraduate students. Any student enrolled in an HPERD professional track (health, physical education, recreation or dance) is eligible to submit. Applicants must submit manuscripts with a focus on leisure and recreation. Students must have a faculty sponsor to submit a paper for this award.

Academic Fields/Career Goals: Recreation, Parks, Leisure Studies.

Award: Scholarship for use in freshman, sophomore, junior, senior, or graduate years; not renewable. *Number:* 2. *Amount:* $500.

Eligibility Requirements: Applicant must be enrolled or expecting to enroll full- or part-time at a four-year institution or university. Available to U.S. and non-U.S. citizens.

Application Requirements: Application form, entry in a contest, essay, faculty sponsor, sample evaluation sheets, resume. *Deadline:* January 1.

Contact: Chris Neumann, Senior Program Manager
American Alliance for Health, Physical Education, Recreation and Dance
1900 Association Drive
Reston, VA 20191
Phone: 703-476-3432
Fax: 703-476-9527
E-mail: aapar@aahperd.org

RUTH ABERNATHY PRESIDENTIAL SCHOLARSHIP

Three award for undergraduate students and two for graduate students in January of each year. Must be majoring in the field of health, physical education, recreation or dance. Undergraduate awards are in the amount of $1,250 each and graduate awards are in the amount of $1,750 each. Recipients also receive a complimentary three-year AAHPERD membership. Applicant must be current member of AAHPERD.

Academic Fields/Career Goals: Recreation, Parks, Leisure Studies; Sports-Related/Exercise Science.

Award: Scholarship for use in junior, senior, or graduate years; not renewable. *Number:* 5. *Amount:* $1250–$1750.

Eligibility Requirements: Applicant must be enrolled or expecting to enroll full-time at a four-year institution or university and must have an interest in leadership. Applicant must have 3.5 GPA or higher. Available to U.S. and non-U.S. citizens.

Application Requirements: Application form, letter from the school's dean/registrar indicating full-time status, recommendations or references, transcript. *Deadline:* October 15.

Contact: Deb Callis, Secretary to Chief Executive Officer
American Alliance for Health, Physical Education, Recreation and Dance
1900 Association Drive
Reston, VA 20191
Phone: 703-476-3405
Fax: 703-476-9537
E-mail: dcallis@aahperd.org

AMERICAN HOTEL AND LODGING EDUCATIONAL FOUNDATION

http://www.ahlef.org/

AMERICAN HOTEL & LODGING EDUCATIONAL FOUNDATION PEPSI SCHOLARSHIP
• *See page 212*

ANNUAL SCHOLARSHIP GRANT PROGRAM
• *See page 213*

ARTHUR J. PACKARD MEMORIAL SCHOLARSHIP
• *See page 213*

ECOLAB SCHOLARSHIP PROGRAM
• *See page 213*

HYATT HOTELS FUND FOR MINORITY LODGING MANAGEMENT
• *See page 213*

INCOMING FRESHMAN SCHOLARSHIPS
• *See page 213*

RAMA SCHOLARSHIP FOR THE AMERICAN DREAM
• *See page 213*

STEVEN HYMANS EXTENDED STAY SCHOLARSHIP
• *See page 214*

PADDLE CANADA (FORMERLY THE CANADIAN RECREATIONAL CANOEING ASSOCIATION

http://www.paddlingcanada.com/

BILL MASON SCHOLARSHIP FUND
• *See page 235*

GOLF COURSE SUPERINTENDENTS ASSOCIATION OF AMERICA

http://www.eifg.org/

GOLF COURSE SUPERINTENDENTS ASSOCIATION OF AMERICA STUDENT ESSAY CONTEST
• *See page 85*

LAND CONSERVANCY OF NEW JERSEY

http://www.tlc-nj.org/

ROGERS FAMILY SCHOLARSHIP
• *See page 304*

RUSSELL W. MYERS SCHOLARSHIP
• *See page 304*

MAINE CAMPGROUND OWNERS ASSOCIATION

http://www.campmaine.com/home.php

MAINE CAMPGROUND OWNERS ASSOCIATION SCHOLARSHIP

One-time award of $500 to a Maine resident pursuing a career in outdoor recreation. Must have completed one year of study and have a minimum GPA of 2.5.

Academic Fields/Career Goals: Recreation, Parks, Leisure Studies.

Award: Scholarship for use in sophomore, junior, senior, graduate, or postgraduate years; not renewable. *Number:* 1. *Amount:* $500.

Eligibility Requirements: Applicant must be enrolled or expecting to enroll full-time at a two-year or four-year or technical institution or university and resident of Maine. Applicant must have 2.5 GPA or higher. Available to U.S. and non-U.S. citizens.

Application Requirements: Application form, essay, financial need analysis, transcript. *Deadline:* March 31.

Contact: Richard Abare, Executive Director
Maine Campground Owners Association
10 Falcon Road, Suite 1
Lewiston, ME 04240
Phone: 207-782-5874
Fax: 207-782-4497
E-mail: info@campmaine.com

NATIONAL RECREATION AND PARK ASSOCIATION

http://www.nrpa.org/

AFRS STUDENT SCHOLARSHIP

Applicant must be currently enrolled in a NRPA accredited recreation/parks curriculum or related field. Number of awards varies.

Academic Fields/Career Goals: Recreation, Parks, Leisure Studies.

Award: Scholarship for use in freshman or sophomore years; not renewable. *Amount:* $500.

Eligibility Requirements: Applicant must be enrolled or expecting to enroll full- or part-time at a four-year institution or university. Applicant must have 3.0 GPA or higher. Available to U.S. citizens.

Application Requirements: Application form, essay, recommendations or references, test scores, transcript. *Deadline:* June 1.

Contact: Jessica Lytle, Senior Manager
Phone: 703-858-2150
Fax: 703-858-0974
E-mail: jlytle@nrpa.org

RELIGION/THEOLOGY

AMERICAN ACADEMY OF RELIGION

http://www.aarweb.org/

AWARDS FOR EXCELLENCE IN THE STUDY OF RELIGION

Awards recognizing new scholarly publications that make significant contributions to the study of religion. The Awards honor works of distinctive originality, intelligence, creativity and importance, books that affect decisively how religion is examined, understood, and interpreted. Awards for Excellence are given in four categories: 1) Analytical-Descriptive; 2) Constructive-Reflective; 3) Historical; and 4) Textual. For more information about our Awards, visit http://www.aarweb.org/Programs/Awards/Book_Awards/rules-excellence.asp. The deadline for submissions is March 20.

Academic Fields/Career Goals: Religion/Theology.

Award: Prize for use in freshman, sophomore, junior, senior, graduate, or postgraduate years; not renewable. *Number:* 4. *Amount:* $1000.

Eligibility Requirements: Applicant must be enrolled or expecting to enroll at a two-year or four-year institution or university. Available to U.S. and non-U.S. citizens.

Application Requirements: Copy of book, rationale letter, entry in a contest. *Deadline:* March 20.

RELIGION AND THE ARTS AWARD

The award in Religion and the Arts is presented annually to an artist, performer, critic, curator, or scholar who has made a recent significant contribution to the understanding of the relations among the arts and religions, both for the Academy and for a broader public.Nominations are accepted from AAR members, though nominees need not be AAR members. Nominations must include a supporting letter (no more than 1,000 words), and any relevant supporting materials (images, DVDs, books, catalogs, etc.). Please, no self-nominations. To be considered for the 2013 award, nominations must be made by February 1, 2013 (the 2012 award deadline has already passed).Send nominations to Brent Plate, Department of Religious Studies, 198 College Hill Road, Clinton, NY 13323, USA. Electronic submissions can be sent to splate@hamilton.edu.

Academic Fields/Career Goals: Religion/Theology.

Award: Prize for use in freshman, sophomore, junior, senior, graduate, or postgraduate years; not renewable. *Number:* 1. *Amount:* $1000.

Eligibility Requirements: Applicant must be enrolled or expecting to enroll at a two-year or four-year institution or university. Available to U.S. and non-U.S. citizens.

Application Requirements: Application form may be submitted online (http://www.aarweb.org/Programs/Awards/Arts_Award), letter of support, supporting materials (optional). *Deadline:* February 1.

AMERICAN SCHOOL OF CLASSICAL STUDIES AT ATHENS

http://www.ascsa.edu.gr/

ASCSA SUMMER SESSIONS SCHOLARSHIPS
• *See page 100*

BETHESDA LUTHERAN COMMUNITIES

http://www.bethesdalutherancommunities.org/scholarships

DEVELOPMENTAL DISABILITIES SCHOLASTIC ACHIEVEMENT SCHOLARSHIP FOR COLLEGE STUDENTS WHO ARE LUTHERAN
• *See page 222*

COLLEGEBOUND FOUNDATION

http://www.collegeboundfoundation.org/

REVEREND NATE BROOKS SCHOLARSHIP
• *See page 235*

THE COMMUNITY FOUNDATION FOR GREATER ATLANTA, INC.

http://cfgreateratlanta.org/

JAMES M. AND VIRGINIA M. SMYTH SCHOLARSHIP
• *See page 118*

DISCIPLES OF CHRIST HOMELAND MINISTRIES

http://www.discipleshomemissions.org/

DAVID TAMOTSU KAGIWADA MEMORIAL SCHOLARSHIP

Scholarship of $2000 is available to Asian-American ministerial students. Must be a member of the Christian Church (Disciples of Christ), demonstrate financial need, have a C+ average, be a full-time student, and be under care of a regional Commission on the Ministry. Application may be submitted electronically.

Academic Fields/Career Goals: Religion/Theology.

Award: Scholarship for use in freshman, sophomore, junior, or senior years; not renewable. *Amount:* $2000.

Eligibility Requirements: Applicant must be Disciple of Christ; Asian/Pacific Islander and enrolled or expecting to enroll full-time at a two-year or four-year institution or university. Applicant must have 2.5 GPA or higher. Available to U.S. and Canadian citizens.

Application Requirements: Application form, financial need analysis, recommendations or references, transcript. *Deadline:* March 15.

Contact: Lorna Hernandez, Administrative Assistant
Phone: 317-713-2666
E-mail: amoyars@dhm.disciples.org

DISCIPLE CHAPLAINS SCHOLARSHIP

Scholarship of $2000 is available to first year seminarians. Must be a member of the Christian Church (Disciples of Christ), demonstrate financial need, have a C+ average, be a full-time student, and be under the care of a regional Commission on the Ministry. Application may be submitted electronically.

Academic Fields/Career Goals: Religion/Theology.

Award: Scholarship for use in freshman year; not renewable. *Amount:* $2000.

Eligibility Requirements: Applicant must be Disciple of Christ; high school student and planning to enroll or expecting to enroll full-time at a four-year institution or university. Applicant must have 2.5 GPA or higher. Available to U.S. citizens.

Application Requirements: Application form, financial need analysis, recommendations or references, transcript. *Deadline:* March 15.

Contact: Lorna Hernandez, Administrative Assistant
Phone: 317-713-2666
E-mail: amoyars@dhm.disciples.org

EDWIN G. AND LAURETTA M. MICHAEL SCHOLARSHIP

Scholarship of $2000 available to ministers wives. Must be a member of the Christian Church (Disciples of Christ), demonstrate financial need, have a C+ average, be a full-time student, and be under the care of a regional Commission on the Ministry. Application may be submitted electronically.

Academic Fields/Career Goals: Religion/Theology.

Award: Scholarship for use in freshman, sophomore, junior, or senior years; not renewable. *Amount:* $2000.

Eligibility Requirements: Applicant must be Disciple of Christ; enrolled or expecting to enroll full-time at a two-year or four-year institution or university and married female. Applicant must have 2.5 GPA or higher. Available to U.S. and non-U.S. citizens.

Application Requirements: Application form, financial need analysis, recommendations or references, transcript. *Deadline:* March 15.

Contact: Lorna Hernandez, Administrative Assistant
Phone: 317-713-2666
E-mail: amoyars@dhm.disciples.org

KATHERINE J. SHUTZE MEMORIAL SCHOLARSHIP

Scholarship of $2000 is available to female seminary students. Must be a member of the Christian Church (Disciples of Christ), demonstrate financial need, have a C+ average, be a full-time student, and be under the care of a regional Commission on the Ministry. Application may be submitted electronically.

Academic Fields/Career Goals: Religion/Theology.

Award: Scholarship for use in freshman, sophomore, junior, or graduate years; not renewable. *Amount:* $2000.

Eligibility Requirements: Applicant must be Disciple of Christ; enrolled or expecting to enroll full-time at a four-year institution or university and female. Applicant must have 2.5 GPA or higher. Available to U.S. and non-U.S. citizens.

Application Requirements: Application form, financial need analysis, recommendations or references, transcript. *Deadline:* March 15.

Contact: Lorna Hernandez, Administrative Assistant
Phone: 317-713-2666
E-mail: amoyars@dhm.disciples.org

ROWLEY/MINISTERIAL EDUCATION SCHOLARSHIP

Scholarship of $2000 is available to seminary students preparing for the ministry. Must be a member of the Christian Church (Disciples of Christ), demonstrate financial need, have a C+ average, be a full-time student and be under the care of a regional Commission on the Ministry. Application may be submitted electronically.

Academic Fields/Career Goals: Religion/Theology.

Award: Scholarship for use in freshman, sophomore, junior, senior, or graduate years; not renewable. *Amount:* $2000.

Eligibility Requirements: Applicant must be Disciple of Christ and enrolled or expecting to enroll full-time at a two-year or four-year institution or university. Applicant must have 2.5 GPA or higher. Available to U.S. and non-U.S. citizens.

Application Requirements: Application form, financial need analysis, recommendations or references, transcript. *Deadline:* March 15.

Contact: Lorna Hernandez, Administrative Assistant
Phone: 317-713-2666
E-mail: amoyars@dhm.disciples.org

EASTERN STAR-GRAND CHAPTER OF CALIFORNIA

http://www.oescal.org/

SCHOLARSHIPS FOR EDUCATION, BUSINESS AND RELIGION

• See page 153

ED E. AND GLADYS HURLEY FOUNDATION

ED E. AND GLADYS HURLEY FOUNDATION SCHOLARSHIP

Provides scholarships up to $1000 per year per student. Applicant must be Protestant enrolled or expecting to enroll full or part-time at a two-year or four-year institution or university and studying in Texas. Available to U.S. citizens.

Academic Fields/Career Goals: Religion/Theology.

Award: Scholarship for use in freshman, sophomore, junior, senior, graduate, or postgraduate years; not renewable. *Number:* 100–150. *Amount:* up to $1000.

Eligibility Requirements: Applicant must be Protestant; enrolled or expecting to enroll full- or part-time at a two-year or four-year institution or university; resident of Arkansas, Louisiana, Texas and studying in Texas. Available to U.S. citizens.

Application Requirements: Application form, financial need analysis, recommendations or references. *Deadline:* April 30.

Contact: Rose Davis, Financial Aid Coordinator
Ed E. and Gladys Hurley Foundation
Houston Graduate School-Theology
2501 Central Parkway, Suite A19
Houston, TX 77092
Phone: 713-942-9505
E-mail: rdavis@hgst.edu

FIRST PRESBYTERIAN CHURCH

http://www.firstchurchtulsa.org/

ULLERY CHARITABLE TRUST FUND

This fund was formed in 1972 from the estate of Miss Jimmie Ullery, a member of First Presbyterian Church in Tulsa, Oklahoma. Interest from the original corpus of the trust is used to assist students pursuing full-time Christian work with the Presbyterian Church (U.S.A.).

Academic Fields/Career Goals: Religion/Theology.

Award: Scholarship for use in freshman, sophomore, junior, or senior years; not renewable. *Number:* 5–7. *Amount:* $500–$2000.

Eligibility Requirements: Applicant must be Presbyterian and enrolled or expecting to enroll at a four-year institution or university. Available to U.S. and non-U.S. citizens.

Application Requirements: Application form, financial need analysis, interview, recommendations or references, transcript. *Deadline:* April 1.

Contact: Tonye Briscoe, Facilities and Benefits Coordinator
First Presbyterian Church
709 South Boston Avenue
Tulsa, OK 74119
Phone: 918-301-1035
Fax: 918-584-5233
E-mail: tbriscoe@firstchurchtulsa.org

MEMORIAL FOUNDATION FOR JEWISH CULTURE

http://www.mfjc.org/

MEMORIAL FOUNDATION FOR JEWISH CULTURE, SCHOLARSHIPS FOR POST-RABBINICAL STUDENTS

• See page 241

NATIONAL ASSOCIATION OF PASTORAL MUSICIANS

http://www.npm.org/

ELAINE RENDLER-RENE DOSOGNE-GEORGETOWN CHORALE SCHOLARSHIP

• See page 413

FUNK FAMILY MEMORIAL SCHOLARSHIP

• See page 413

GIA PUBLICATION PASTORAL MUSICIAN SCHOLARSHIP

• See page 413

MUSONICS SCHOLARSHIP

• See page 413

NATIONAL ASSOCIATION OF PASTORAL MUSICIANS MEMBERS' SCHOLARSHIP

NPM KOINONIA/BOARD OF DIRECTORS SCHOLARSHIP

OREGON CATHOLIC PRESS SCHOLARSHIP

PALUCH FAMILY FOUNDATION/WORLD LIBRARY PUBLICATIONS SCHOLARSHIP

OREGON STUDENT ASSISTANCE COMMISSION
http://www.GetCollegeFunds.org/

FRANKS FOUNDATION SCHOLARSHIP

PRESBYTERIAN CHURCH (USA)
http://www.pcusa.org/financialaid

STUDENT OPPORTUNITY SCHOLARSHIP

SOCIETY FOR THE SCIENTIFIC STUDY OF SEXUALITY
http://www.sexscience.org/

SOCIETY FOR THE SCIENTIFIC STUDY OF SEXUALITY STUDENT RESEARCH GRANT

UNITARIAN UNIVERSALIST ASSOCIATION
http://www.uua.org/

ROY H. POLLACK SCHOLARSHIP
Scholarship given to a junior or senior student with academic excellence and good character, studying for ordained ministry who actively participates in extracurricular activities at their theological school. Applicant must be pursuing in Divinity degree.
Academic Fields/Career Goals: Religion/Theology.
Award: Scholarship for use in junior or senior years; not renewable.
Eligibility Requirements: Applicant must be Unitarian Universalist and enrolled or expecting to enroll full- or part-time at a four-year institution or university. Available to U.S. citizens.
Application Requirements: Application form, financial need analysis. *Deadline:* April 15.
Contact: Ms. Hillary Goodridge, Program Director
Phone: 617-971-9600
Fax: 617-971-0029
E-mail: uufp@aol.com

UNITED METHODIST COMMUNICATIONS
http://www.umcom.org/

LEONARD M. PERRYMAN COMMUNICATIONS SCHOLARSHIP FOR ETHNIC MINORITY STUDENTS

UNITED NEGRO COLLEGE FUND
http://www.uncf.org/

DR. JOE RATLIFF CHALLENGE SCHOLARSHIP
Award for students at UNCF member colleges and universities pursing majors in religious study. Minimum 2.5 GPA required.
Academic Fields/Career Goals: Religion/Theology.
Award: Scholarship for use in freshman year; not renewable.
Eligibility Requirements: Applicant must be Black (non-Hispanic) and enrolled or expecting to enroll full- or part-time at a four-year institution or university. Applicant must have 2.5 GPA or higher. Available to U.S. citizens.
Application Requirements: Application form. *Deadline:* continuous.

SCIENCE, TECHNOLOGY, AND SOCIETY

AEG FOUNDATION
http://www.aegfoundation.org/

AEG FOUNDATION

AMERICAN CHEMICAL SOCIETY, RUBBER DIVISION
http://www.rubber.org/

AMERICAN CHEMICAL SOCIETY, RUBBER DIVISION UNDERGRADUATE SCHOLARSHIP

AMERICAN INSTITUTE OF AERONAUTICS AND ASTRONAUTICS
http://www.aiaa.org/

AIAA FOUNDATION UNDERGRADUATE SCHOLARSHIP

ARIZONA HYDROLOGICAL SOCIETY
http://www.azhydrosoc.org/

ARIZONA HYDROLOGICAL SOCIETY SCHOLARSHIP

ARRL FOUNDATION INC.
http://www.arrl.org/

ALLEN AND BERTHA WATSON MEMORIAL SCHOLARSHIP

ARRL NORTHWESTERN DIVISION SCHOLARSHIP FUND

YASME FOUNDATION SCHOLARSHIP

BRITISH COLUMBIA INNOVATION COUNCIL

http://www.bcic.ca/

PAUL AND HELEN TRUSSELL SCIENCE AND TECHNOLOGY SCHOLARSHIP
• *See page 104*

CATCHING THE DREAM

http://www.catchingthedream.org/

MATH, ENGINEERING, SCIENCE, BUSINESS, EDUCATION, COMPUTERS SCHOLARSHIPS
• *See page 151*

NATIVE AMERICAN LEADERSHIP IN EDUCATION (NALE)
• *See page 151*

COLLEGEBOUND FOUNDATION

http://www.collegeboundfoundation.org/

DR. FREEMAN A. HRABOWSKI, III SCHOLARSHIP
• *See page 279*

CONGRESSIONAL BLACK CAUCUS FOUNDATION, INC.

http://www.cbcfinc.org/

CBCF GENERAL MILLS HEALTH SCHOLARSHIP
• *See page 144*

THE LOUIS STOKES HEALTH SCHOLARS PROGRAM
• *See page 144*

DAVIDSON INSTITUTE FOR TALENT DEVELOPMENT

http://www.davidsongifted.org/

DAVIDSON FELLOWS SCHOLARSHIP PROGRAM
• *See page 386*

DENVER FOUNDATION

http://www.denverfoundation.org/

RBC DAIN RAUSCHER COLORADO SCHOLARSHIP FUND
• *See page 280*

EXPLORERS CLUB

http://www.explorers.org/

YOUTH ACTIVITY FUND
• *See page 420*

GREAT LAKES COMMISSION

http://www.glc.org/

CAROL A. RATZA MEMORIAL SCHOLARSHIP
• *See page 190*

HEALTHCARE INFORMATION AND MANAGEMENT SYSTEMS SOCIETY FOUNDATION

http://www.himss.org/

HIMSS FOUNDATION SCHOLARSHIP PROGRAM
• *See page 327*

INTERNATIONAL TECHNOLOGY EDUCATION ASSOCIATION

http://www.iteaconnect.org/

INTERNATIONAL TECHNOLOGY EDUCATION ASSOCIATION UNDERGRADUATE SCHOLARSHIP IN TECHNOLOGY EDUCATION
• *See page 239*

KOREAN-AMERICAN SCIENTISTS AND ENGINEERS ASSOCIATION

http://www.ksea.org/

KSEA SCHOLARSHIPS
• *See page 253*

MINNESOTA OFFICE OF HIGHER EDUCATION

http://www.getreadyforcollege.org/

MINNESOTA ACADEMIC EXCELLENCE SCHOLARSHIP
• *See page 120*

MONSANTO AGRIBUSINESS SCHOLARSHIP

http://www.monsanto.ca/

MONSANTO CANADA OPPORTUNITY SCHOLARSHIP PROGRAM
• *See page 86*

NASA RHODE ISLAND SPACE GRANT CONSORTIUM

http://brown/initiatives/ri-space-grant

NASA RHODE ISLAND SPACE GRANT CONSORTIUM OUTREACH SCHOLARSHIP FOR UNDERGRADUATE STUDENTS
• *See page 267*

NASA SOUTH DAKOTA SPACE GRANT CONSORTIUM

http://sdspacegrant.sdsmt.edu/

SOUTH DAKOTA SPACE GRANT CONSORTIUM UNDERGRADUATE AND GRADUATE STUDENT SCHOLARSHIPS
• *See page 134*

NASA'S VIRGINIA SPACE GRANT CONSORTIUM

http://www.vsgc.odu.edu/

UNDERGRADUATE STEM RESEARCH SCHOLARSHIPS
• *See page 106*

SIGMA XI, THE SCIENTIFIC RESEARCH SOCIETY

http://www.sigmaxi.org/

SIGMA XI GRANTS-IN-AID OF RESEARCH
• *See page 95*

SOCIETY FOR TECHNICAL COMMUNICATION

http://www.stc.org/

SOCIETY FOR TECHNICAL COMMUNICATION SCHOLARSHIP PROGRAM
• *See page 195*

SOCIETY OF HISPANIC PROFESSIONAL ENGINEERS

http://www.shpe.org/

AHETEMS SCHOLARSHIPS
• *See page 289*

SOCIETY OF MOTION PICTURE AND TELEVISION ENGINEERS

http://www.smpte.org/

LOUIS F. WOLF JR. MEMORIAL SCHOLARSHIP
• *See page 195*

STUDENT PAPER AWARD
• *See page 195*

UNITED NEGRO COLLEGE FUND

http://www.uncf.org/

GATES MILLENNIUM SCHOLARSHIP
• *See page 399*

UNIVERSITIES SPACE RESEARCH ASSOCIATION

http://www.usra.edu/

UNIVERSITIES SPACE RESEARCH ASSOCIATION SCHOLARSHIP PROGRAM
• *See page 107*

WEST VIRGINIA HIGHER EDUCATION POLICY COMMISSION-STUDENT SERVICES

http://wvhepcnew.wvnet.edu/

WEST VIRGINIA ENGINEERING, SCIENCE AND TECHNOLOGY SCHOLARSHIP PROGRAM
• *See page 257*

WHOMENTORS.COM, INC.

http://www.WHOmentors.com/

IB USD WORLDWIDE VENTURE CAPITAL
• *See page 107*

SOCIAL SCIENCES

ALBERTA HERITAGE SCHOLARSHIP FUND

http://www.alis.alberta.ca/

LOIS HOLE HUMANITIES AND SOCIAL SCIENCES SCHOLARSHIP
• *See page 354*

AMERICAN CRIMINAL JUSTICE ASSOCIATION-LAMBDA ALPHA EPSILON

http://www.acjalae.org/

AMERICAN CRIMINAL JUSTICE ASSOCIATION-LAMBDA ALPHA EPSILON NATIONAL SCHOLARSHIP
• *See page 211*

AMERICAN FEDERATION OF STATE, COUNTY, AND MUNICIPAL EMPLOYEES

http://www.afscme.org/

AFSCME/UNCF UNION SCHOLARS PROGRAM
• *See page 97*

AMERICAN SOCIETY OF CRIMINOLOGY

http://www.asc41.com/

AMERICAN SOCIETY OF CRIMINOLOGY GENE CARTE STUDENT PAPER COMPETITION
• *See page 211*

CANADIAN INSTITUTE OF UKRAINIAN STUDIES

http://www.cius.ca/

LEO J. KRYSA UNDERGRADUATE SCHOLARSHIP
• *See page 114*

CATCHING THE DREAM

http://www.catchingthedream.org/

MATH, ENGINEERING, SCIENCE, BUSINESS, EDUCATION, COMPUTERS SCHOLARSHIPS
• *See page 151*

CULTURAL SERVICES OF THE FRENCH EMBASSY

http://www.frenchculture.org/

TEACHING ASSISTANT PROGRAM IN FRANCE
• *See page 97*

INDIAN HEALTH SERVICES, UNITED STATES DEPARTMENT OF HEALTH AND HUMAN SERVICES

http://www.ihs.gov/scholarship

HEALTH PROFESSIONS PREPARATORY SCHOLARSHIP PROGRAM
• See page 141

INSTITUTE FOR HUMANE STUDIES

http://www.theihs.org/

HUMANE STUDIES FELLOWSHIPS
• See page 190

MINNESOTA OFFICE OF HIGHER EDUCATION

http://www.getreadyforcollege.org/

MINNESOTA ACADEMIC EXCELLENCE SCHOLARSHIP
• See page 120

NATIONAL BLACK POLICE ASSOCIATION

http://www.blackpolice.org/

ALPHONSO DEAL SCHOLARSHIP AWARD
• See page 212

NATIONAL INSTITUTES OF HEALTH

https://ugsp.nih.gov/

NIH UNDERGRADUATE SCHOLARSHIP PROGRAM FOR STUDENTS FROM DISADVANTAGED BACKGROUNDS
• See page 147

OFFICE AND PROFESSIONAL EMPLOYEES INTERNATIONAL UNION

http://www.opeiu.org/

JOHN KELLY LABOR STUDIES SCHOLARSHIP FUND
• See page 230

ORGONE BIOPHYSICAL RESEARCH LABORATORY

http://www.orgonelab.org/

LOU HOCHBERG-HIGH SCHOOL ESSAY AWARDS
One-time award of up to $500 will be given for the best high school student essay paper addressing Wilhlem Reich's sociological discoveries. Maximum length of 25 pages.

Academic Fields/Career Goals: Social Sciences.

Award: Prize for use in freshman year; not renewable. *Number:* 1. *Amount:* up to $500.

Eligibility Requirements: Applicant must be high school student and planning to enroll or expecting to enroll full- or part-time at a four-year institution or university. Available to U.S. and non-U.S. citizens.

Application Requirements: Entry in a contest, essay, photocopy of student ID, transcript. *Deadline:* continuous.

PARAPSYCHOLOGY FOUNDATION

http://www.parapsychology.org/

CHARLES T. AND JUDITH A. TART STUDENT INCENTIVE
An annual incentive is awarded to promote the research of an undergraduate or graduate student, who shows dedication to work within parapsychology. For more details see website http://www.parapsychology.org.

Academic Fields/Career Goals: Social Sciences.

Award: Scholarship for use in freshman, sophomore, junior, senior, graduate, or postgraduate years; not renewable. *Number:* 1. *Amount:* $500.

Eligibility Requirements: Applicant must be enrolled or expecting to enroll full-time at a two-year or four-year institution or university. Available to U.S. citizens.

Application Requirements: Application form, essay, recommendations or references, transcript. *Deadline:* October 15.

Contact: Lisette Coly, Vice President
Phone: 212-628-1550
Fax: 212-628-1559
E-mail: office@parapsychology.org

EILEEN J. GARRETT SCHOLARSHIP FOR PARAPSYCHOLOGICAL RESEARCH
Scholarship requires applicants to demonstrate academic interest in the science of parapsychology through completed research, term papers, and courses for which credit was received. Those with only a general interest will not be considered. Visit website for additional information.

Academic Fields/Career Goals: Social Sciences.

Award: Scholarship for use in freshman, sophomore, junior, senior, graduate, or postgraduate years; not renewable. *Number:* 1. *Amount:* $3000.

Eligibility Requirements: Applicant must be enrolled or expecting to enroll full-time at a two-year or four-year institution or university. Available to U.S. citizens.

Application Requirements: Application form, essay, recommendations or references, transcript. *Deadline:* July 15.

Contact: Lisette Coly, Vice President
Parapsychology Foundation
PO Box 1562
New York, NY 10021-0043
Phone: 212-628-1550
Fax: 212-628-1559
E-mail: office@parapsychology.org

PHI ALPHA THETA HISTORY HONOR SOCIETY, INC.

http://www.phialphatheta.org/

PHI ALPHA THETA WORLD HISTORY ASSOCIATION PAPER PRIZE
• See page 345

PRESBYTERIAN CHURCH (USA)

http://www.pcusa.org/financialaid

STUDENT OPPORTUNITY SCHOLARSHIP
• See page 243

SIGMA XI, THE SCIENTIFIC RESEARCH SOCIETY

http://www.sigmaxi.org/

SIGMA XI GRANTS-IN-AID OF RESEARCH
• See page 95

SOCIETY FOR APPLIED ANTHROPOLOGY

http://www.sfaa.net/

ANNUAL SFAA STUDENT ENDOWED AWARD
• *See page 100*

BEATRICE MEDICINE AWARDS
• *See page 101*

DEL JONES MEMORIAL TRAVEL AWARD
• *See page 101*

EDWARD H. AND ROSAMOND B. SPICER TRAVEL AWARDS
• *See page 101*

GIL KUSHNER MEMORIAL TRAVEL AWARD
• *See page 101*

HUMAN RIGHTS DEFENDER STUDENT AWARD
• *See page 101*

PETER KONG-MING NEW STUDENT PRIZE
• *See page 142*

VALENE SMITH PRIZE
• *See page 101*

SOCIETY FOR THE SCIENTIFIC STUDY OF SEXUALITY

http://www.sexscience.org/

SOCIETY FOR THE SCIENTIFIC STUDY OF SEXUALITY STUDENT RESEARCH GRANT
• *See page 102*

STRAIGHTFORWARD MEDIA

http://www.straightforwardmedia.com/

STRAIGHTFORWARD MEDIA LIBERAL ARTS SCHOLARSHIP
• *See page 116*

UNITED NEGRO COLLEGE FUND

http://www.uncf.org/

AFSCME/UNCF/HARVARD UNIVERSITY LWP UNION SCHOLARS PROGRAM
• *See page 98*

WIFLE FOUNDATION, INC.

http://www.wifle.org/

WIFLE SCHOLARSHIP PROGRAM
• *See page 207*

Y'S MEN INTERNATIONAL

http://www.ysmenusa.com/

ALEXANDER SCHOLARSHIP LOAN FUND
• *See page 161*

ZETA PHI BETA SORORITY INC. NATIONAL EDUCATIONAL FOUNDATION

http://www.zpbnef1975.org/

LULLELIA W. HARRISON SCHOLARSHIP IN COUNSELING
• *See page 179*

SOCIAL SERVICES

ALBERTA HERITAGE SCHOLARSHIP FUND

http://www.alis.alberta.ca/

NORTHERN ALBERTA DEVELOPMENT COUNCIL BURSARY
• *See page 219*

AMERICAN FEDERATION OF STATE, COUNTY, AND MUNICIPAL EMPLOYEES

http://www.afscme.org/

AFSCME/UNCF UNION SCHOLARS PROGRAM
• *See page 97*

AMERICAN LEGION AUXILIARY DEPARTMENT OF ARIZONA

http://wwwaladeptaz.org

AMERICAN LEGION AUXILIARY DEPARTMENT OF ARIZONA WILMA HOYAL-MAXINE CHILTON MEMORIAL SCHOLARSHIP
• *See page 465*

BETHESDA LUTHERAN COMMUNITIES

http://www.bethesdalutherancommunities.org/scholarships

DEVELOPMENTAL DISABILITIES AWARENESS AWARDS FOR HIGH SCHOOL STUDENTS WHO ARE LUTHERAN
• *See page 333*

DEVELOPMENTAL DISABILITIES SCHOLASTIC ACHIEVEMENT SCHOLARSHIP FOR COLLEGE STUDENTS WHO ARE LUTHERAN
• *See page 222*

COLLEGEBOUND FOUNDATION

http://www.collegeboundfoundation.org/

JEANETTE R. WOLMAN SCHOLARSHIP
• *See page 178*

THE COMMUNITY FOUNDATION FOR GREATER ATLANTA, INC.

http://cfgreateratlanta.org/

STEVE DEARDUFF SCHOLARSHIP
• *See page 334*

CONTINENTAL SOCIETY, DAUGHTERS OF INDIAN WARS

http://www.csdiw.org/

CONTINENTAL SOCIETY, DAUGHTERS OF INDIAN WARS SCHOLARSHIP
• *See page 236*

GENERAL BOARD OF HIGHER EDUCATION AND MINISTRY

http://www.gbhem.org

EDITH M. ALLEN SCHOLARSHIP
• *See page 237*

HEALTH PROFESSIONS EDUCATION FOUNDATION

http://www.healthprofessions.ca.gov/

KAISER PERMANENTE ALLIED HEALTHCARE SCHOLARSHIP
• *See page 336*

JEWISH VOCATIONAL SERVICE CHICAGO

http://www.jvschicago.org/

JEWISH FEDERATION ACADEMIC SCHOLARSHIP PROGRAM
• *See page 120*

MARYLAND STATE HIGHER EDUCATION COMMISSION

http://www.mhec.state.md.us/

GRADUATE AND PROFESSIONAL SCHOLARSHIP PROGRAM-MARYLAND
• *See page 224*

JANET L. HOFFMANN LOAN ASSISTANCE REPAYMENT PROGRAM
• *See page 240*

MEMORIAL FOUNDATION FOR JEWISH CULTURE

http://www.mfjc.org/

MEMORIAL FOUNDATION FOR JEWISH CULTURE, SCHOLARSHIPS FOR POST-RABBINICAL STUDENTS
• *See page 241*

NATIONAL BLACK POLICE ASSOCIATION

http://www.blackpolice.org/

ALPHONSO DEAL SCHOLARSHIP AWARD
• *See page 212*

PILOT INTERNATIONAL FOUNDATION

http://www.pilotinternational.org/

PILOT INTERNATIONAL FOUNDATION RUBY NEWHALL MEMORIAL SCHOLARSHIP
• *See page 339*

PRESBYTERIAN CHURCH (USA)

http://www.pcusa.org/financialaid

STUDENT OPPORTUNITY SCHOLARSHIP
• *See page 243*

UNITED COMMUNITY SERVICES FOR WORKING FAMILIES

http://www.ucswf.org

TED BRICKER SCHOLARSHIP
One-time award available to child of a union member who is a parent or guardian. Must be a member of a union affiliated with the Berks County United Labor Council, AFL-CIO. Must submit essay that is clear, concise, persuasive, and shows a commitment to the community.
Academic Fields/Career Goals: Social Services.
Award: Scholarship for use in freshman year; not renewable. *Number:* 1. *Amount:* up to $500.
Eligibility Requirements: Applicant must be high school student; planning to enroll or expecting to enroll full-time at a four-year institution or university and resident of Pennsylvania. Applicant or parent of applicant must be member of AFL-CIO. Available to U.S. citizens.
Application Requirements: Application form, essay, financial need analysis, transcript. *Deadline:* July 27.
Contact: Ruth Mathews, Executive Director
   Phone: 610-374-3319 Ext. 101
   E-mail: ruth.mathews@comcast.net

UNITED NEGRO COLLEGE FUND

http://www.uncf.org/

AFSCME/UNCF/HARVARD UNIVERSITY LWP UNION SCHOLARS PROGRAM
• *See page 98*

Y'S MEN INTERNATIONAL

http://www.ysmenusa.com/

ALEXANDER SCHOLARSHIP LOAN FUND
• *See page 161*

ZETA PHI BETA SORORITY INC. NATIONAL EDUCATIONAL FOUNDATION

http://www.zpbnef1975.org/

LULLELIA W. HARRISON SCHOLARSHIP IN COUNSELING
• *See page 179*

SPECIAL EDUCATION

ALBERTA HERITAGE SCHOLARSHIP FUND

http://www.alis.alberta.ca/

ANNA AND JOHN KOLESAR MEMORIAL SCHOLARSHIPS
• *See page 231*

AMERICAN LEGION AUXILIARY DEPARTMENT OF ARIZONA

http://wwwaladeptaz.org

AMERICAN LEGION AUXILIARY DEPARTMENT OF ARIZONA WILMA HOYAL-MAXINE CHILTON MEMORIAL SCHOLARSHIP
• *See page 465*

ARC OF WASHINGTON TRUST FUND

http://www.arcwa.org/

ARC OF WASHINGTON TRUST FUND STIPEND PROGRAM

Stipends of up to $5000 will be awarded to upper division or graduate students in schools in the states of Washington, Alaska, Oregon or Idaho. Applicants must have a demonstrated interest in the field of mental retardation. The application can be downloaded from the website http://www.arcwa.org.

Academic Fields/Career Goals: Special Education.

Award: Scholarship for use in junior, senior, graduate, or postgraduate years; not renewable. *Number:* 1–8. *Amount:* up to $5000.

Eligibility Requirements: Applicant must be enrolled or expecting to enroll full- or part-time at a four-year institution or university and studying in Alaska, Idaho, Oregon, Washington. Available to U.S. citizens.

Application Requirements: Application form, driver's license, essay, recommendations or references, transcript. *Deadline:* February 29.

Contact: Neal Lessenger, Secretary
Phone: 206-363-2206
E-mail: arcwatrust@charter.net

BETHESDA LUTHERAN COMMUNITIES

http://www.bethesdalutherancommunities.org/scholarships

DEVELOPMENTAL DISABILITIES AWARENESS AWARDS FOR HIGH SCHOOL STUDENTS WHO ARE LUTHERAN
• *See page 333*

DEVELOPMENTAL DISABILITIES SCHOLASTIC ACHIEVEMENT SCHOLARSHIP FOR COLLEGE STUDENTS WHO ARE LUTHERAN
• *See page 222*

COLLEGEBOUND FOUNDATION

http://www.collegeboundfoundation.org/

JANET B. SONDHEIM SCHOLARSHIP
• *See page 117*

ILLINOIS STUDENT ASSISTANCE COMMISSION (ISAC)

http://www.collegezone.org/

ILLINOIS SPECIAL EDUCATION TEACHER TUITION WAIVER

Teachers or students who are pursuing a career in special education as public, private or parochial preschool, elementary or secondary school teachers in Illinois may be eligible for this program. This program will exempt such individuals from paying tuition and mandatory fees at an eligible institution, for up to four years. The individual dollar amount awarded are subject to sufficient annual appropriations by the Illinois General Assembly.

Academic Fields/Career Goals: Special Education.

Award: Scholarship for use in freshman, sophomore, junior, senior, or graduate years; renewable.

Eligibility Requirements: Applicant must be enrolled or expecting to enroll full- or part-time at a four-year institution or university; resident of Illinois and studying in Illinois. Available to U.S. citizens.

Application Requirements: Application form. *Deadline:* March 1.

MINORITY TEACHERS OF ILLINOIS SCHOLARSHIP PROGRAM
• *See page 238*

NATIONAL INSTITUTE FOR LABOR RELATIONS RESEARCH

http://www.nilrr.org/

APPLEGATE/JACKSON/PARKS FUTURE TEACHER SCHOLARSHIP
• *See page 241*

OREGON STUDENT ASSISTANCE COMMISSION

http://www.GetCollegeFunds.org/

JAMES CARLSON MEMORIAL SCHOLARSHIP
• *See page 242*

PILOT INTERNATIONAL FOUNDATION

http://www.pilotinternational.org/

PILOT INTERNATIONAL FOUNDATION RUBY NEWHALL MEMORIAL SCHOLARSHIP
• *See page 339*

PILOT INTERNATIONAL FOUNDATION SCHOLARSHIP PROGRAM
• *See page 339*

STRAIGHTFORWARD MEDIA

http://www.straightforwardmedia.com/

STRAIGHTFORWARD MEDIA TEACHER SCHOLARSHIP
• *See page 244*

WISCONSIN CONGRESS OF PARENTS AND TEACHERS INC.

http://www.wisconsinpta.org/

BROOKMIRE-HASTINGS SCHOLARSHIPS
• *See page 246*

SPORTS-RELATED/ EXERCISE SCIENCE

AMERICAN ALLIANCE FOR HEALTH, PHYSICAL EDUCATION, RECREATION AND DANCE

http://www.aahperd.org/

RUTH ABERNATHY PRESIDENTIAL SCHOLARSHIP
• *See page 471*

AMERICAN PHYSIOLOGICAL SOCIETY

http://www.the-aps.org

DAVID S. BRUCE AWARDS FOR EXCELLENCE IN UNDERGRADUATE RESEARCH
• *See page 98*

PADDLE CANADA (FORMERLY THE CANADIAN RECREATIONAL CANOEING ASSOCIATION

http://www.paddlingcanada.com/

BILL MASON SCHOLARSHIP FUND
• *See page 235*

CANFIT

http://www.canfit.org/

CANFIT NUTRITION, PHYSICAL EDUCATION AND CULINARY ARTS SCHOLARSHIP
• *See page 214*

NATIONAL ATHLETIC TRAINERS' ASSOCIATION RESEARCH AND EDUCATION FOUNDATION

http://www.natafoundation.org/

NATIONAL ATHLETIC TRAINERS' ASSOCIATION RESEARCH AND EDUCATION FOUNDATION SCHOLARSHIP PROGRAM
• *See page 337*

PACERS FOUNDATION INC.

http://www.pacersfoundation.org/

LINDA CRAIG MEMORIAL SCHOLARSHIP PRESENTED BY ST. VINCENT SPORTS MEDICINE
• *See page 338*

PI LAMBDA THETA INC.

http://www.pilambda.org/

TOBIN SORENSON PHYSICAL EDUCATION SCHOLARSHIP
• *See page 243*

STRAIGHTFORWARD MEDIA

http://www.straightforwardmedia.com/

STRAIGHTFORWARD MEDIA VOCATIONAL-TECHNICAL SCHOOL SCHOLARSHIP
• *See page 99*

Y'S MEN INTERNATIONAL

http://www.ysmenusa.com/

ALEXANDER SCHOLARSHIP LOAN FUND
• *See page 161*

SURVEYING, SURVEYING TECHNOLOGY, CARTOGRAPHY, OR GEOGRAPHIC INFORMATION SCIENCE

AMERICAN CONGRESS ON SURVEYING AND MAPPING

http://www.acsm.net/

ACSM FELLOWS SCHOLARSHIP
One-time award available to a student with a junior or higher standing in any ACSM discipline (surveying, mapping, geographic information systems, and geodetic science). Must be ACSM member.
Academic Fields/Career Goals: Surveying, Surveying Technology, Cartography, or Geographic Information Science.
Award: Scholarship for use in freshman, sophomore, junior, or senior years; not renewable. *Number:* 1. *Amount:* $2000.
Eligibility Requirements: Applicant must be enrolled or expecting to enroll full- or part-time at a four-year institution or university. Applicant or parent of applicant must be member of American Congress on Surveying and Mapping. Available to U.S. citizens.
Application Requirements: Application form, essay, membership proof, recommendations or references, transcript. *Deadline:* October 1.
Contact: Ilse Genovese, Communications Director
American Congress on Surveying and Mapping
6 Montgomery Village Avenue, Suite 403
Gaithersburg, MD 20879
Phone: 240-632-9716 Ext. 113
Fax: 240-632-1321
E-mail: ilse.genovese@acsm.net

ACSM LOWELL H. AND DOROTHY LOVING UNDERGRADUATE SCHOLARSHIP
Scholarship available for a junior or senior in a college or university in the U.S. studying surveying. Program of study must include courses in two of the following areas: land surveying, geometric geodesy, photogrammetry/remote sensing, or analysis and design of spatial measurement systems.
Academic Fields/Career Goals: Surveying, Surveying Technology, Cartography, or Geographic Information Science.
Award: Scholarship for use in freshman, sophomore, junior, or senior years; not renewable. *Number:* 1. *Amount:* $2500.
Eligibility Requirements: Applicant must be enrolled or expecting to enroll full- or part-time at a four-year institution or university. Applicant or parent of applicant must be member of American Congress on Surveying and Mapping. Available to U.S. citizens.
Application Requirements: Application form, essay, membership proof, recommendations or references, transcript. *Deadline:* October 1.
Contact: Ilse Genovese, Communications Director
American Congress on Surveying and Mapping
6 Montgomery Village Avenue, Suite 403
Gaithersbutg, MD 20879
Phone: 240-632-9716
Fax: 240-632-1321
E-mail: ilse.genovese@acsm.net

AMERICAN ASSOCIATION FOR GEODETIC SURVEYING JOSEPH F. DRACUP SCHOLARSHIP AWARD
Award for students enrolled in a four-year degree program in surveying (or in closely-related degree programs such as geomatics or surveying engineering). Preference given to applicants from programs with significant focus on geodetic surveying. Must be ACSM member.
Academic Fields/Career Goals: Surveying, Surveying Technology, Cartography, or Geographic Information Science.

Award: Scholarship for use in freshman, sophomore, junior, or senior years; not renewable. *Number:* 1. *Amount:* $2000.

Eligibility Requirements: Applicant must be enrolled or expecting to enroll full- or part-time at a four-year institution or university. Applicant or parent of applicant must be member of American Congress on Surveying and Mapping. Available to U.S. and non-Canadian citizens.

Application Requirements: Application form, essay, recommendations or references, transcript. *Deadline:* October 1.

Contact: Ilse Genovese, ACSM Communications Director
American Congress on Surveying and Mapping
6 Montgomery Village Avenue, Suite 403
Gaithersburg, MD 20879
Phone: 240-632-9716 Ext. 113
Fax: 240-632-1321
E-mail: ilse.genovese@acsm.net

BERNTSEN INTERNATIONAL SCHOLARSHIP IN SURVEYING

Award of $1500 for full-time students enrolled in a four-year degree program in surveying or in a closely-related degree program, such as geomatics or surveying engineering. Must be ACSM member.

Academic Fields/Career Goals: Surveying, Surveying Technology, Cartography, or Geographic Information Science.

Award: Scholarship for use in freshman, sophomore, junior, or senior years; not renewable. *Number:* 1. *Amount:* $1500.

Eligibility Requirements: Applicant must be enrolled or expecting to enroll full-time at a four-year institution or university. Applicant or parent of applicant must be member of American Congress on Surveying and Mapping. Available to U.S. citizens.

Application Requirements: Application form, essay, recommendations or references, transcript. *Deadline:* October 1.

Contact: Ilse Genovese, ACSM Communications Director
American Congress on Surveying and Mapping
6 Montgomery Village Avenue, Suite 403
Gaithersburg, MD 20879
Phone: 240-632-9716 Ext. 113
Fax: 240-632-1321
E-mail: ilse.genovese@acsm.net

BERNTSEN INTERNATIONAL SCHOLARSHIP IN SURVEYING TECHNOLOGY

Award for full-time undergraduate students enrolled in a two-year degree program in surveying technology. For U.S. study only. Must be a member of the American Congress on Surveying and Mapping. See website for application and more details http://www.acsm.net/scholar.html.

Academic Fields/Career Goals: Surveying, Surveying Technology, Cartography, or Geographic Information Science.

Award: Scholarship for use in freshman or sophomore years; not renewable. *Number:* 1. *Amount:* $500.

Eligibility Requirements: Applicant must be enrolled or expecting to enroll full-time at a two-year or four-year institution. Applicant or parent of applicant must be member of American Congress on Surveying and Mapping. Available to U.S. and non-Canadian citizens.

Application Requirements: Application form, essay, proof of membership in ACSM, recommendations or references, transcript. *Deadline:* varies.

Contact: Ilse Genovese, ACSM Communications Director
American Congress on Surveying and Mapping
6 Montgomery Village Avenue, Suite 403
Gaithersburg, MD 20879
Phone: 240-632-9716 Ext. 113
Fax: 240-632-1321
E-mail: ilse.genovese@acsm.net

CADY MCDONNELL MEMORIAL SCHOLARSHIP

Award of $1000 for female surveying student. Must be a resident of one of the following western states: Alaska, Arizona, California, Colorado, Hawaii, Idaho, Montana, Nevada, New Mexico, Oregon, Utah, Washington, and Wyoming. Must provide proof of legal home residence and be a member of the American Congress on Surveying and Mapping.

Academic Fields/Career Goals: Surveying, Surveying Technology, Cartography, or Geographic Information Science.

Award: Scholarship for use in freshman, sophomore, junior, or senior years; not renewable. *Number:* 1. *Amount:* $1000.

Eligibility Requirements: Applicant must be enrolled or expecting to enroll full- or part-time at a two-year or four-year institution or university; female and resident of Alaska, Arizona, California, Colorado, Hawaii, Idaho, Montana, Nevada, New Mexico, Oregon, Utah, Washington, Wyoming. Applicant or parent of applicant must be member of American Congress on Surveying and Mapping. Available to U.S. citizens.

Application Requirements: Application form, essay, financial need analysis, proof of residence, membership proof, personal statement, recommendations or references, transcript. *Deadline:* October 1.

Contact: Ilse Genovese, ACSM Communications Director
American Congress on Surveying and Mapping
6 Montgomery Village Avenue, Suite 403
Gaithersburg, MD 20879
Phone: 240-632-9716 Ext. 113
Fax: 240-632-1321
E-mail: ilse.genovese@acsm.net

NATIONAL SOCIETY OF PROFESSIONAL SURVEYORS BOARD OF GOVERNORS SCHOLARSHIP

Award available to students enrolled in surveying program entering junior year of study at four-year institution. Minimum 3.0 GPA required. Must be ACSM member.

Academic Fields/Career Goals: Surveying, Surveying Technology, Cartography, or Geographic Information Science.

Award: Scholarship for use in junior year; not renewable. *Number:* 1. *Amount:* up to $1000.

Eligibility Requirements: Applicant must be enrolled or expecting to enroll full- or part-time at a four-year institution or university. Applicant or parent of applicant must be member of American Congress on Surveying and Mapping. Applicant must have 3.0 GPA or higher. Available to U.S. citizens.

Application Requirements: Application form, essay, financial need analysis, membership proof, recommendations or references, transcript. *Deadline:* October 1.

Contact: Ilse Genovese, Communications Director
American Congress on Surveying and Mapping
6 Montgomery Village Avenue, Suite 403
Gaithersburg, MD 20879
Phone: 240-632-9716 Ext. 113
Fax: 240-632-1321
E-mail: ilse.genovese@acsm.net

NATIONAL SOCIETY OF PROFESSIONAL SURVEYORS SCHOLARSHIPS

Two awards of $1000 each to students enrolled full-time in a four-year undergraduate surveying program. Must be ACSM member.

Academic Fields/Career Goals: Surveying, Surveying Technology, Cartography, or Geographic Information Science.

Award: Scholarship for use in freshman, sophomore, junior, or senior years; not renewable. *Number:* 2. *Amount:* $1000.

Eligibility Requirements: Applicant must be enrolled or expecting to enroll full-time at a four-year institution or university. Applicant or parent of applicant must be member of American Congress on Surveying and Mapping. Available to U.S. and non-Canadian citizens.

Application Requirements: ACSM membership proof, application form, essay, recommendations or references, transcript. *Deadline:* October 1.

Contact: Ilse Genovese, ACSM Communications Director
American Congress on Surveying and Mapping
6 Montgomery Village Avenue, Suite 403
Gaithersburg, MD 20879
Phone: 240-632-9716 Ext. 113
Fax: 240-632-1321
E-mail: ilse.genovese@acsm.net

NETTIE DRACUP MEMORIAL SCHOLARSHIP

Award for undergraduate student enrolled in a four-year geodetic surveying program at an accredited college or university. Must be U.S. citizen. Must be ACSM member.

Academic Fields/Career Goals: Surveying, Surveying Technology, Cartography, or Geographic Information Science.

Award: Scholarship for use in freshman, sophomore, junior, or senior years; not renewable. *Number:* 2. *Amount:* $2000.

Eligibility Requirements: Applicant must be enrolled or expecting to enroll full-time at a four-year institution or university. Applicant or parent of applicant must be member of American Congress on Surveying and Mapping. Available to U.S. citizens.

Application Requirements: ACSM membership proof, application form, essay, financial need analysis, recommendations or references, transcript. *Deadline:* October 1.

Contact: Ilse Genovese, Communications Director
American Congress on Surveying and Mapping
6 Montgomery Village Avenue, Suite 403
Gaithersburg, MD 20879
Phone: 240-632-9716 Ext. 113
Fax: 240-632-1321
E-mail: ilse.genovese@acsm.net

SCHONSTEDT SCHOLARSHIP IN SURVEYING

Award preference given to applicants with junior or senior standing in a four-year program in surveying. Schonstedt donates magnetic locator to surveying program at each recipient's school. Must be ACSM member.

Academic Fields/Career Goals: Surveying, Surveying Technology, Cartography, or Geographic Information Science.

Award: Scholarship for use in junior or senior years; not renewable. *Number:* 2. *Amount:* $1500.

Eligibility Requirements: Applicant must be enrolled or expecting to enroll full-time at a four-year institution or university. Applicant or parent of applicant must be member of American Congress on Surveying and Mapping. Available to U.S. citizens.

Application Requirements: ACSM membership proof, application form, essay, recommendations or references, transcript. *Deadline:* October 1.

Contact: Ilse Genovese, Communications Director
American Congress on Surveying and Mapping
6 Montgomery Village Avenue, Suite 403
Gaithersburg, MD 20879
Phone: 240-632-9716 Ext. 113
Fax: 240-632-1321
E-mail: ilse.genovese@acsm.net

TRI-STATE SURVEYING AND PHOTOGRAMMETRY KRIS M. KUNZE MEMORIAL SCHOLARSHIP

• *See page 149*

ASPRS, THE IMAGING AND GEOSPATIAL INFORMATION SOCIETY

http://www.asprs.org/

ABRAHAM ANSON MEMORIAL SCHOLARSHIP

• *See page 278*

FRANCIS H. MOFFITT MEMORIAL SCHOLARSHIP

• *See page 278*

JOHN O. BEHRENS INSTITUTE FOR LAND INFORMATION MEMORIAL SCHOLARSHIP

• *See page 278*

KENNETH J. OSBORN MEMORIAL SCHOLARSHIP

• *See page 278*

ROBERT E. ALTENHOFEN MEMORIAL SCHOLARSHIP

• *See page 278*

ASSOCIATED GENERAL CONTRACTORS OF NEW YORK STATE, LLC

http://www.agcnys.org/

ASSOCIATED GENERAL CONTRACTORS NYS SCHOLARSHIP PROGRAM

• *See page 181*

ASSOCIATION OF CALIFORNIA WATER AGENCIES

http://www.acwa.com/

ASSOCIATION OF CALIFORNIA WATER AGENCIES SCHOLARSHIPS

• *See page 103*

CLAIR A. HILL SCHOLARSHIP

• *See page 103*

CENTRAL INTELLIGENCE AGENCY

http://www.cia.gov/

CENTRAL INTELLIGENCE AGENCY UNDERGRADUATE SCHOLARSHIP PROGRAM

• *See page 70*

DAVID EVANS AND ASSOCIATES, INC.

http://www.deainc.com/

DAVID EVANS AND ASSOCIATES, INC. SCHOLARSHIP

• *See page 182*

FLORIDA ENGINEERING SOCIETY

http://www.fleng.org/scholarships.cfm

ACEC/FLORIDA SCHOLARSHIP

• *See page 280*

OREGON STUDENT ASSISTANCE COMMISSION

http://www.GetCollegeFunds.org/

PROFESSIONAL LAND SURVEYORS OF OREGON SCHOLARSHIP

Award for first-time freshmen enrolled in Oregon public and nonprofit colleges and engaged in a course of study leading to land-surveying career. Community college applicants must intend to transfer to four-year college. Oregon residency not required. Must intend to take Fundamentals of Land Surveying exam. Additional essay stating education/career goals and their relation to land surveying is required. FAFSA and two references also required.

Academic Fields/Career Goals: Surveying, Surveying Technology, Cartography, or Geographic Information Science.

Award: Scholarship for use in freshman year; renewable.

Eligibility Requirements: Applicant must be enrolled or expecting to enroll full-time at a four-year institution or university and studying in Oregon. Available to U.S. citizens.

Application Requirements: Activity chart, application form, essay, financial need analysis, recommendations or references, transcript. *Deadline:* March 1.

PROFESSIONAL CONSTRUCTION ESTIMATORS ASSOCIATION

http://www.pcea.org/

TED G. WILSON MEMORIAL SCHOLARSHIP FOUNDATION

• *See page 184*

RHODE ISLAND SOCIETY OF PROFESSIONAL LAND SURVEYORS

http://www.rispls.org/

PIERRE H. GUILLEMETTE SCHOLARSHIP

Scholarship available to any Rhode Island resident enrolled in a certificate or degree program in land surveying at a qualified institution of higher learning.

Academic Fields/Career Goals: Surveying, Surveying Technology, Cartography, or Geographic Information Science.

Award: Scholarship for use in freshman, sophomore, junior, or senior years; not renewable.

Eligibility Requirements: Applicant must be enrolled or expecting to enroll full- or part-time at a four-year institution or university and resident of Rhode Island. Available to U.S. citizens.

Application Requirements: Application form, resume, transcript. *Deadline:* October 30.

THERAPY/ REHABILITATION

ALBERTA HERITAGE SCHOLARSHIP FUND

http://www.alis.alberta.ca/

ABORIGINAL HEALTH CAREERS BURSARY
• *See page 142*

AMERICAN FOUNDATION FOR THE BLIND

http://www.afb.org/

DELTA GAMMA FOUNDATION FLORENCE MARGARET HARVEY MEMORIAL SCHOLARSHIP
• *See page 232*

RUDOLPH DILLMAN MEMORIAL SCHOLARSHIP
• *See page 232*

AMERICAN LEGION AUXILIARY DEPARTMENT OF MICHIGAN

http://www.michalaux.org/

AMERICAN LEGION AUXILIARY DEPARTMENT OF MICHIGAN MEDICAL CAREER SCHOLARSHIP
• *See page 329*

AMERICAN LEGION AUXILIARY DEPARTMENT OF WYOMING

AMERICAN LEGION AUXILIARY DEPARTMENT OF WYOMING PAST PRESIDENTS' PARLEY HEALTH CARE SCHOLARSHIP
• *See page 222*

AMERICAN OCCUPATIONAL THERAPY FOUNDATION INC.

http://www.aotf.org/

AMERICAN OCCUPATIONAL THERAPY FOUNDATION STATE ASSOCIATION SCHOLARSHIPS
• *See page 330*

CARLOTTA WELLES SCHOLARSHIP
• *See page 330*

AMERICAN PHYSICAL THERAPY ASSOCIATION

http://www.apta.org/

MARY MCMILLAN SCHOLARSHIP AWARD
• *See page 233*

AMERICAN QUARTER HORSE FOUNDATION (AQHF)

http://www.aqha.com/foundation

EAAT HIPPOTHERAPY SCHOLARSHIP

Ideal candidate is an AQHA member pursuing a career in the field of hippotherapy through physical therapy, occupational therapy and or speech language pathology. Related majors may include, but are not limited to, communication disorders, sports and exercise science or kinesiology.

Academic Fields/Career Goals: Therapy/Rehabilitation.

Award: Scholarship for use in freshman, sophomore, junior, senior, or graduate years; renewable. *Number:* 1. *Amount:* $10,000.

Eligibility Requirements: Applicant must be enrolled or expecting to enroll full-time at a two-year or four-year institution or university. Applicant or parent of applicant must be member of American Quarter Horse Association. Applicant must have 2.5 GPA or higher. Available to U.S. and non-U.S. citizens.

Application Requirements: Application form, recommendations or references, transcript. *Deadline:* December 1.

AMERICAN RESPIRATORY CARE FOUNDATION

http://www.arcfoundation.org/

JIMMY A. YOUNG MEMORIAL EDUCATION RECOGNITION AWARD
• *See page 331*

MORTON B. DUGGAN, JR. MEMORIAL EDUCATION RECOGNITION AWARD
• *See page 331*

NBRC/AMP ROBERT M. LAWRENCE, MD EDUCATION RECOGNITION AWARD
• *See page 331*

NBRC/AMP WILLIAM W. BURGIN, MD EDUCATION RECOGNITION AWARD
• *See page 331*

SEPRACOR ACHIEVEMENT AWARD FOR EXCELLENCE IN PULMONARY DISEASE STATE MANAGEMENT
• *See page 331*

ARRL FOUNDATION INC.

http://www.arrl.org/

CAROLE J. STREETER, KB9JBR, SCHOLARSHIP
• *See page 222*

BETHESDA LUTHERAN COMMUNITIES

http://www.bethesdalutherancommunities.org/scholarships

DEVELOPMENTAL DISABILITIES AWARENESS AWARDS FOR HIGH SCHOOL STUDENTS WHO ARE LUTHERAN
• *See page 333*

DEVELOPMENTAL DISABILITIES SCHOLASTIC ACHIEVEMENT SCHOLARSHIP FOR COLLEGE STUDENTS WHO ARE LUTHERAN
• *See page 222*

CONGRESSIONAL BLACK CAUCUS FOUNDATION, INC.

http://www.cbcfinc.org/

THE LOUIS STOKES HEALTH SCHOLARS PROGRAM
• *See page 144*

CYNTHIA E. MORGAN SCHOLARSHIP FUND (CEMS)

http://www.cemsfund.com/

CYNTHIA E. MORGAN MEMORIAL SCHOLARSHIP FUND, INC.
• *See page 298*

HEALTH PROFESSIONS EDUCATION FOUNDATION

http://www.healthprofessions.ca.gov/

KAISER PERMANENTE ALLIED HEALTHCARE SCHOLARSHIP
• *See page 336*

INDIAN HEALTH SERVICES, UNITED STATES DEPARTMENT OF HEALTH AND HUMAN SERVICES

http://www.ihs.gov/scholarship

INDIAN HEALTH SERVICE HEALTH PROFESSIONS SCHOLARSHIP PROGRAM
• *See page 208*

INTERNATIONAL ORDER OF THE KING'S DAUGHTERS AND SONS

http://www.iokds.org/

HEALTH CAREERS SCHOLARSHIP
• *See page 223*

LADIES AUXILIARY TO THE VETERANS OF FOREIGN WARS, DEPARTMENT OF MAINE

http://mainevfw.org/

FRANCES L. BOOTH MEDICAL SCHOLARSHIP SPONSORED BY LAVFW DEPARTMENT OF MAINE
• *See page 336*

MARYLAND STATE HIGHER EDUCATION COMMISSION

http://www.mhec.state.md.us/

JANET L. HOFFMANN LOAN ASSISTANCE REPAYMENT PROGRAM
• *See page 240*

NATIONAL AMBUCS INC.

http://www.ambucs.org/

AMBUCS SCHOLARS-SCHOLARSHIPS FOR THERAPISTS
• *See page 124*

NATIONAL ATHLETIC TRAINERS' ASSOCIATION RESEARCH AND EDUCATION FOUNDATION

http://www.natafoundation.org/

NATIONAL ATHLETIC TRAINERS' ASSOCIATION RESEARCH AND EDUCATION FOUNDATION SCHOLARSHIP PROGRAM
• *See page 337*

NATIONAL SOCIETY DAUGHTERS OF THE AMERICAN REVOLUTION

http://www.dar.org/

NATIONAL SOCIETY DAUGHTERS OF THE AMERICAN REVOLUTION OCCUPATIONAL THERAPY SCHOLARSHIP
Scholarship of $1000 for students who are in financial need and have been accepted or are attending an accredited school of occupational therapy including art, music or physical therapy. A letter of acceptance into the occupational therapy program or the transcript stating the applicant is in the occupational therapy program must be included with the application.

Academic Fields/Career Goals: Therapy/Rehabilitation.

Award: Scholarship for use in freshman, sophomore, junior, senior, or graduate years; not renewable. *Amount:* $1000.

Eligibility Requirements: Applicant must be enrolled or expecting to enroll full- or part-time at a two-year or four-year institution or university. Available to U.S. citizens.

Application Requirements: Application form, essay, financial need analysis, letter of sponsorship, recommendations or references, self-addressed stamped envelope with application, transcript. *Deadline:* February 15.

Contact: Tania Tatum, Manager, Office of the Reporter General
    Phone: 202-628-1776
    Fax: 202-879-3348
    E-mail: nsdarscholarships@dar.org

OREGON STUDENT ASSISTANCE COMMISSION

http://www.GetCollegeFunds.org/

MARION A. LINDEMAN SCHOLARSHIP
• *See page 338*

PACERS FOUNDATION INC.

http://www.pacersfoundation.org/

LINDA CRAIG MEMORIAL SCHOLARSHIP PRESENTED BY ST. VINCENT SPORTS MEDICINE
• *See page 338*

PI LAMBDA THETA INC.

http://www.pilambda.org/

TOBIN SORENSON PHYSICAL EDUCATION SCHOLARSHIP
• *See page 243*

PILOT INTERNATIONAL FOUNDATION

http://www.pilotinternational.org/

PILOT INTERNATIONAL FOUNDATION RUBY NEWHALL MEMORIAL SCHOLARSHIP
• *See page 339*

PILOT INTERNATIONAL FOUNDATION SCHOLARSHIP PROGRAM
• *See page 339*

STRAIGHTFORWARD MEDIA

http://www.straightforwardmedia.com/

STRAIGHTFORWARD MEDIA MEDICAL PROFESSIONS SCHOLARSHIP
• *See page 224*

U. S. DEPARTMENT OF HEALTH AND HUMAN SERVICES

http://www.hhs.gov/about/whatwedo.html/

U. S. PUBLIC HEALTH SERVICE-HEALTH RESOURCES AND SERVICES ADMINISTRATION, BUREAU OF HEALTH PROFESSIONS SCHOLARSHIPS FOR DISADVANTAGED STUDENTS
• *See page 225*

TRADE/TECHNICAL SPECIALTIES

AIRCRAFT ELECTRONICS ASSOCIATION EDUCATIONAL FOUNDATION

http://www.aea.net/

BUD GLOVER MEMORIAL SCHOLARSHIP
• *See page 125*

DUTCH AND GINGER ARVER SCHOLARSHIP
• *See page 125*

GARMIN-JERRY SMITH MEMORIAL SCHOLARSHIP
• *See page 125*

GARMIN SCHOLARSHIP
• *See page 125*

LEE TARBOX MEMORIAL SCHOLARSHIP
• *See page 126*

LOWELL GAYLOR MEMORIAL SCHOLARSHIP
• *See page 126*

MID-CONTINENT INSTRUMENT SCHOLARSHIP
• *See page 126*

ALBERTA HERITAGE SCHOLARSHIP FUND

http://www.alis.alberta.ca/

REGISTERED APPRENTICESHIP PROGRAM/CAREER AND TECHNOLOGIES STUDIES (RAPS/CTS) SCHOLARSHIPS

Scholarships of CAN$1000 available for high school graduates who are registered as apprentices in a trade while in high school to encourage recipients to continue their apprenticeship or occupational training programs after graduation. Must be a Canadian citizen or landed immigrant and Alberta resident. For more details see website http://alis.alberta.ca.

Academic Fields/Career Goals: Trade/Technical Specialties.

Award: Scholarship for use in freshman year; not renewable. *Number:* 500.

Eligibility Requirements: Applicant must be enrolled or expecting to enroll full-time at a technical institution and resident of Alberta. Available to Canadian citizens.

Application Requirements: Application form, essay, recommendations or references. *Deadline:* June 29.

AMERICAN LEGION DEPARTMENT OF PENNSYLVANIA

http://www.pa-legion.com/

ROBERT W. VALIMONT ENDOWMENT FUND SCHOLARSHIP (PART II)

Scholarships for any Pennsylvania high school senior seeking admission to a two-year college, post-high school trade/technical school, or training program. Must attend school in Pennsylvania. Continuation of award is based on grades. Renewable award of $600. Number of awards varies from year to year. Membership in an American Legion post in Pennsylvania is not required, but it must be documented if it does apply.

Academic Fields/Career Goals: Trade/Technical Specialties.

Award: Scholarship for use in freshman year; renewable. *Amount:* $600.

Eligibility Requirements: Applicant must be high school student; planning to enroll or expecting to enroll full-time at a two-year or technical institution; resident of Pennsylvania and studying in Pennsylvania. Applicant must have 2.5 GPA or higher. Available to U.S. citizens.

Application Requirements: Application form, financial need analysis, test scores, transcript. *Deadline:* May 30.

Contact: Debbie Watson, Emblem Sales Supervisor
American Legion Department of Pennsylvania
PO Box 2324
Harrisburg, PA 17105-2324
Phone: 717-730-9100
Fax: 717-975-2836
E-mail: hq@pa-legion.com

AMERICAN SOCIETY OF HEATING, REFRIGERATING, AND AIR CONDITIONING ENGINEERS, INC.

http://www.ashrae.org/

ALWIN B. NEWTON SCHOLARSHIP
• *See page 249*

ASHRAE GENERAL SCHOLARSHIPS
• *See page 260*

ASHRAE MEMORIAL SCHOLARSHIP
• *See page 249*

DUANE HANSON SCHOLARSHIP
• *See page 250*

FRANK M. CODA SCHOLARSHIP
• *See page 250*

HENRY ADAMS SCHOLARSHIP
• *See page 250*

LYNN G. BELLENGER SCHOLARSHIP
• *See page 250*

REUBEN TRANE SCHOLARSHIP
• *See page 250*

AMERICAN WELDING SOCIETY

http://www.aws.org/

AMERICAN WELDING SOCIETY DISTRICT SCHOLARSHIP PROGRAM
• *See page 261*

AMERICAN WELDING SOCIETY INTERNATIONAL SCHOLARSHIP
• *See page 262*

ARSHAM AMIRIKIAN ENGINEERING SCHOLARSHIP
• *See page 181*

DONALD F. HASTINGS SCHOLARSHIP
• *See page 262*

EDWARD J. BRADY MEMORIAL SCHOLARSHIP
• *See page 262*

HOWARD E. AND WILMA J. ADKINS MEMORIAL SCHOLARSHIP
• *See page 262*

MILLER ELECTRIC INTERNATIONAL WORLD SKILLS COMPETITION SCHOLARSHIP
• *See page 262*

MILLER ELECTRIC MFG. CO. SCHOLARSHIP
• *See page 263*

ASSOCIATED GENERAL CONTRACTORS OF NEW YORK STATE, LLC

http://www.agcnys.org/

ASSOCIATED GENERAL CONTRACTORS NYS SCHOLARSHIP PROGRAM
• *See page 181*

BOY SCOUTS OF AMERICA-MUSKINGUM VALLEY COUNCIL

http://www.learning-for-life.org/

AFL-CIO SKILL TRADES SCHOLARSHIP

Two $1000 scholarships awarded annually to skilled trade explorers to help them support their education. Must be a graduating high school senior in May or June of the year the application is made. School selected by the applicant must be an accredited public or proprietary institution or union apprentice program.
Academic Fields/Career Goals: Trade/Technical Specialties.
Award: Scholarship for use in freshman year; not renewable. *Number:* 2. *Amount:* $1000.
Eligibility Requirements: Applicant must be high school student and planning to enroll or expecting to enroll full- or part-time at a technical institution. Available to U.S. and non-U.S. citizens.
Application Requirements: Application form, essay, personal photograph, recommendations or references, transcript. *Deadline:* April 30.

Contact: Bill Rogers, Associate Director
Phone: 972-580-2433
Fax: 972-580-2137
E-mail: brogers@lflmail.org

GLOBAL AUTOMOTIVE AFTERMARKET SYMPOSIUM

http://www.automotivescholarships.com/

GAAS SCHOLARSHIP
• *See page 155*

IFDA EDUCATIONAL FOUNDATION

http://www.ifdaef.org/

IFDA LEADERS COMMEMORATIVE SCHOLARSHIP
• *See page 361*

IFDA STUDENT MEMBER SCHOLARSHIP
• *See page 361*

INTERNATIONAL EXECUTIVE HOUSEKEEPERS ASSOCIATION

http://www.ieha.org/

INTERNATIONAL EXECUTIVE HOUSEKEEPERS EDUCATIONAL FOUNDATION
• *See page 317*

LEARNING FOR LIFE

http://www.learning-for-life.org/

AFL-CIO SKILLED TRADES EXPLORING SCHOLARSHIPS

Two $1000 scholarships awarded annually to Explorers to help them support their education toward a career in skilled trades. Applicant must be a graduating high school senior in May or June of the year the application is issued. The school selected by the applicant must be an accredited public or proprietary institution or a union apprentice program.
Academic Fields/Career Goals: Trade/Technical Specialties.
Award: Scholarship for use in freshman year; not renewable. *Number:* up to 2. *Amount:* $1000.
Eligibility Requirements: Applicant must be high school student and planning to enroll or expecting to enroll full- or part-time at a technical institution. Applicant or parent of applicant must be member of Explorer Program/Learning for Life. Available to U.S. citizens.
Application Requirements: Application form, essay, personal photograph, recommendations or references, transcript. *Deadline:* April 30.

MAINE EDUCATION SERVICES

http://www.mesfoundation.com/

MAINE METAL PRODUCTS ASSOCIATION SCHOLARSHIP
• *See page 403*

MANUFACTURERS ASSOCIATION OF MAINE

http://www.mainemfg.com/

MAINE METAL PRODUCTS EDUCATION FUND SCHOLARSHIP PROGRAM
• *See page 132*

MARION D. AND EVA S. PEEPLES FOUNDATION TRUST SCHOLARSHIP PROGRAM

http://www.jccf.org/

MARION A. AND EVA S. PEEPLES SCHOLARSHIPS
• *See page 240*

MARYLAND ASSOCIATION OF PRIVATE COLLEGES AND CAREER SCHOOLS

http://www.mapccs.org/

MARYLAND ASSOCIATION OF PRIVATE COLLEGES AND CAREER SCHOOLS SCHOLARSHIP
• *See page 157*

MARYLAND STATE HIGHER EDUCATION COMMISSION

http://www.mhec.state.md.us/

CHARLES W. RILEY FIRE AND EMERGENCY MEDICAL SERVICES TUITION REIMBURSEMENT PROGRAM
• *See page 311*

MIDWEST ROOFING CONTRACTORS ASSOCIATION

http://www.mrca.org/

MRCA FOUNDATION SCHOLARSHIP PROGRAM
• *See page 112*

NATIONAL ASSOCIATION OF WATER COMPANIES-NEW JERSEY CHAPTER

http://www.nawc.org/

NATIONAL ASSOCIATION OF WATER COMPANIES-NEW JERSEY CHAPTER SCHOLARSHIP
• *See page 146*

NATIONAL ASSOCIATION OF WOMEN IN CONSTRUCTION

http://www.nawic.org/

NAWIC CONSTRUCTION TRADES SCHOLARSHIP
Scholarship for women pursuing a trade apprenticeship program. Only for students attending school in the United States or Canada.

Academic Fields/Career Goals: Trade/Technical Specialties.

Award: Scholarship for use in sophomore or junior years; not renewable. *Number:* 1. *Amount:* $1000–$2000.

Eligibility Requirements: Applicant must be enrolled or expecting to enroll full-time at a technical institution. Available to U.S. and Canadian citizens.

Application Requirements: Application form, essay, transcript. *Deadline:* March 15.

NAWIC UNDERGRADUATE SCHOLARSHIPS
• *See page 112*

NORTH CAROLINA COMMUNITY COLLEGE SYSTEM-STUDENT DEVELOPMENT SERVICES

WACHOVIA TECHNICAL SCHOLARSHIP PROGRAM
One scholarship per college valued at $500 each. These scholarships are distributed among the 58 colleges in the community college system, which may be distributed in two payments: fall semester, $250; and spring semester, $250. To qualify as a candidate for these scholarships, a person must meet the following criteria: 1. Is a full-time student enrolled in the second year of a two-year educational/technical program. 2. Demonstrate financial need. 3. Demonstrate scholastic promise. 4. Use the scholarship to pay for tuition, books, and transportation. The recipients of the scholarships will be selected each year from applicants meeting the above criteria at local colleges.

Academic Fields/Career Goals: Trade/Technical Specialties.

Award: Scholarship for use in freshman or sophomore years; not renewable. *Amount:* $500.

Eligibility Requirements: Applicant must be enrolled or expecting to enroll full-time at a two-year or technical institution; resident of North Carolina and studying in North Carolina. Available to U.S. citizens.

Application Requirements: Application form, essay. *Deadline:* continuous.

Contact: Charletta Sims Evans, Associate Director of Student Development Services
Phone: 919-807-7106
E-mail: simsc@nccommunitycolleges.edu

OREGON STUDENT ASSISTANCE COMMISSION

http://www.GetCollegeFunds.org/

DAVID L. MASSEE EDUCATION SCHOLARSHIP
Award for first-time freshmen and undergraduate students who are enrolled at least half time in trade or vocational programs in private or two-year public colleges in the U.S. Apply/compete annually.

Academic Fields/Career Goals: Trade/Technical Specialties.

Award: Scholarship for use in freshman, sophomore, junior, or senior years; not renewable.

Eligibility Requirements: Applicant must be enrolled or expecting to enroll full- or part-time at a two-year or four-year institution. Available to U.S. citizens.

Application Requirements: Application form. *Deadline:* March 1.

JIM AND DIANNA MURPHY SCHOLARSHIP
Scholarship for graduates of Oregon high schools who are majoring in programs to become diesel mechanic/technician, driver/operator of commercial vehicle/bus/truck, and related areas leading to a career in the commercial trucking industry or in diesel technologies. Must enroll at least half time at a Oregon two-year community college or for-profit school. FAFSA is recommended.

Academic Fields/Career Goals: Trade/Technical Specialties.

Award: Scholarship for use in freshman, sophomore, junior, or senior years; not renewable.

Eligibility Requirements: Applicant must be enrolled or expecting to enroll full- or part-time at a two-year or technical institution and studying in Oregon. Available to U.S. citizens.

Application Requirements: Application form. *Deadline:* March 1.

OREGON CAREER AND TECHNICAL EDUCATION SCHOLARSHIP
• *See page 158*

PLASTICS INSTITUTE OF AMERICA

http://www.plasticsinstitute.org/

PLASTICS PIONEERS SCHOLARSHIPS
• *See page 170*

PLUMBING-HEATING-COOLING CONTRACTORS EDUCATION FOUNDATION

http://www.phccfoundation.org/

BRADFORD WHITE CORPORATION SCHOLARSHIP
• See page 342

DELTA FAUCET COMPANY SCHOLARSHIP PROGRAM
• See page 158

PHCC EDUCATIONAL FOUNDATION NEED-BASED SCHOLARSHIP
• See page 158

PHCC EDUCATIONAL FOUNDATION SCHOLARSHIP PROGRAM
• See page 158

PROFESSIONAL AVIATION MAINTENANCE FOUNDATION

http://www.pama.org/

PROFESSIONAL AVIATION MAINTENANCE FOUNDATION STUDENT SCHOLARSHIP PROGRAM
• See page 137

PROFESSIONAL CONSTRUCTION ESTIMATORS ASSOCIATION

http://www.pcea.org/

TED G. WILSON MEMORIAL SCHOLARSHIP FOUNDATION
• See page 184

ROCKY MOUNTAIN COAL MINING INSTITUTE

http://www.rmcmi.org/

ROCKY MOUNTAIN COAL MINING INSTITUTE TECHNICAL SCHOLARSHIP

Scholarship for a first or second year student at a two-year technical/trade school in good standing at the time of selection. The student must be in a discipline related to potential use in the coal mining industry. Must be U.S. citizen and a legal resident of one of the Rocky Mountain Coal Mining Institute member states.

Academic Fields/Career Goals: Trade/Technical Specialties.

Award: Scholarship for use in freshman or sophomore years; not renewable. *Number:* 8. *Amount:* $1000.

Eligibility Requirements: Applicant must be enrolled or expecting to enroll full-time at a technical institution and resident of Arizona, Colorado, Montana, New Mexico, North Dakota, Texas, Utah, Wyoming. Available to U.S. citizens.

Application Requirements: Application form, essay, interview. *Deadline:* February 1.

Contact: Shahreen Salam, Executive Assistant
Rocky Mountain Coal Mining Institute
8057 South Yukon Way
Littleton, CO 80128-5510
Phone: 303-948-3300
Fax: 303-948-1132
E-mail: mail@rmcmi.org

SOCIETY OF MANUFACTURING ENGINEERS EDUCATION FOUNDATION

http://www.smeef.org/

CHAPTER 198-DOWNRIVER DETROIT SCHOLARSHIP
• See page 290

CHAPTER 67-PHOENIX SCHOLARSHIP
• See page 290

CLINTON J. HELTON MANUFACTURING SCHOLARSHIP AWARD FUND
• See page 291

E. WAYNE KAY COMMUNITY COLLEGE SCHOLARSHIP AWARD
• See page 291

E. WAYNE KAY SCHOLARSHIP
• See page 292

FORT WAYNE CHAPTER 56 SCHOLARSHIP
• See page 292

NORTH CENTRAL REGION 9 SCHOLARSHIP
• See page 292

WICHITA CHAPTER 52 SCHOLARSHIP
• See page 293

WILLIAM E. WEISEL SCHOLARSHIP FUND
• See page 255

SOCIETY OF PLASTICS ENGINEERS (SPE) FOUNDATION

http://www.4spe.org/

FLEMING/BASZCAK SCHOLARSHIP
• See page 171

SOCIETY OF PLASTICS ENGINEERS SCHOLARSHIP PROGRAM
• See page 171

SPECIALTY EQUIPMENT MARKET ASSOCIATION

http://www.sema.org/

SPECIALTY EQUIPMENT MARKET ASSOCIATION MEMORIAL SCHOLARSHIP FUND
• See page 80

STRAIGHTFORWARD MEDIA

http://www.straightforwardmedia.com/

STRAIGHTFORWARD MEDIA VOCATIONAL-TECHNICAL SCHOOL SCHOLARSHIP
• See page 99

UNITED COMMUNITY SERVICES FOR WORKING FAMILIES

http://www.ucswf.org

RONALD LORAH MEMORIAL SCHOLARSHIP

One-time award available to a union member, spouse of a union member, or child of a union member who is a resident of Pennsylvania. Must submit essay that is clear, concise, persuasive and show an understanding of unions.

Academic Fields/Career Goals: Trade/Technical Specialties.

Award: Scholarship for use in freshman, sophomore, junior, or senior years; not renewable. *Number:* 2. *Amount:* $750–$1000.

Eligibility Requirements: Applicant must be enrolled or expecting to enroll full-time at a two-year or four-year or technical institution or university and resident of Pennsylvania. Applicant or parent of applicant must be member of AFL-CIO. Available to U.S. citizens.

Application Requirements: Application form, essay, financial need analysis. *Deadline:* July 27.

Contact: Ruth Mathews, Executive Director
Phone: 610-374-3319 Ext. 101
E-mail: ruth.mathews@comcast.net

WOMEN IN LOGISTICS, NORTHERN CALIFORNIA

http://www.womeninlogistics.org/

WOMEN IN LOGISTICS SCHOLARSHIP
• *See page 161*

WOMEN'S JEWELRY ASSOCIATION

http://www.womensjewelry.org/

WJA SCHOLARSHIP PROGRAM
• *See page 124*

WYOMING TRUCKING ASSOCIATION SCHOLARSHIP FUND TRUST

http://www.wytruck.org/

WYOMING TRUCKING ASSOCIATION SCHOLARSHIP TRUST FUND
• *See page 83*

YOUTH MARITIME TRAINING ASSOCIATION

http://ymta.net/

NORM MANLY—YMTA MARITIME EDUCATIONAL SCHOLARSHIPS
• *See page 389*

TRANSPORTATION

AMERICAN PUBLIC TRANSPORTATION FOUNDATION

http://www.apta.com/

DAN REICHARD JR. SCHOLARSHIP
• *See page 150*

DR. GEORGE M. SMERK SCHOLARSHIP
Scholarship for study towards a career in career in public transit management. Must be sponsored by APTA member organization. Minimum GPA of 3.0 required. College sophomores (30 hours or more satisfactorily completed), juniors, seniors, or those seeking advanced degrees may apply.

Academic Fields/Career Goals: Transportation.

Award: Scholarship for use in sophomore, junior, senior, or graduate years; not renewable. *Number:* 1. *Amount:* $2500.

Eligibility Requirements: Applicant must be enrolled or expecting to enroll full-time at a two-year or four-year institution or university. Applicant must have 3.0 GPA or higher. Available to U.S. citizens.

Application Requirements: Application form, essay, financial need analysis, recommendations or references, test scores, transcript, verification of enrollment for the fall semester, copy of fee schedule from the college/university. *Deadline:* June 16.

Contact: Pamela Boswell, Vice President of Program Management
American Public Transportation Foundation
1666 K Street, NW
Washington, DC 20006-1215
Phone: 202-496-4803
Fax: 202-496-2323
E-mail: pboswell@apta.com

DONALD C. HYDE ESSAY PROGRAM
Award of $500 for the best response to the required essay component of the program.

Academic Fields/Career Goals: Transportation.

Award: Prize for use in sophomore, junior, senior, or graduate years; not renewable. *Number:* 1. *Amount:* $500.

Eligibility Requirements: Applicant must be enrolled or expecting to enroll full-time at a two-year or four-year institution or university. Applicant must have 3.0 GPA or higher. Available to U.S. and Canadian citizens.

Application Requirements: Application form, entry in a contest, essay, financial need analysis, recommendations or references, transcript. *Deadline:* June 16.

Contact: Pamela Boswell, Vice President of Program Management
American Public Transportation Foundation
1666 K Street, NW
Washington, DC 20006-1215
Phone: 202-496-4803
Fax: 202-496-2323
E-mail: pboswell@apta.com

JACK GILSTRAP SCHOLARSHIP
• *See page 273*

PARSONS BRINCKERHOFF-JIM LAMMIE SCHOLARSHIP
Scholarship for study in public transportation engineering field. Must be sponsored by APTA member organization and complete internship with APTA member organization. Minimum GPA of 3.0 required.

Academic Fields/Career Goals: Transportation.

Award: Scholarship for use in sophomore, junior, senior, or graduate years; renewable. *Number:* 1. *Amount:* $2500.

Eligibility Requirements: Applicant must be enrolled or expecting to enroll full-time at a two-year or four-year institution or university. Applicant must have 3.0 GPA or higher. Available to U.S. and Canadian citizens.

Application Requirements: Application form, essay, financial need analysis, recommendations or references, transcript, verification of enrollment for the current year and copy of fee schedule from the college/university. *Deadline:* June 16.

Contact: Pamela Boswell, Vice President of Program Management
American Public Transportation Foundation
1666 K Street, NW
Washington, DC 20006-1215
Phone: 202-496-4803
Fax: 202-496-2323
E-mail: pboswell@apta.com

TRANSIT HALL OF FAME SCHOLARSHIP AWARD PROGRAM
• *See page 179*

AMERICAN RAILWAY ENGINEERING AND MAINTENANCE OF WAY ASSOCIATION

http://www.aremafoundation.org/

CHARLES L. STANFORD FAMILY OHIO STATE UNIVERSITY RAILWAY ENGINEERING SCHOLARSHIP
• *See page 249*

JOHN J. CUNNINGHAM MEMORIAL SCHOLARSHIP (SPONSORED JOINTLY BY COMMITTEES 11 AND 17)
• See page 274

ASSOCIATED GENERAL CONTRACTORS OF NEW YORK STATE, LLC

http://www.agcnys.org/

ASSOCIATED GENERAL CONTRACTORS NYS SCHOLARSHIP PROGRAM
• See page 181

NATIONAL CUSTOMS BROKERS AND FORWARDERS ASSOCIATION OF AMERICA

http://www.ncbfaa.org/

NATIONAL CUSTOMS BROKERS AND FORWARDERS ASSOCIATION OF AMERICA SCHOLARSHIP AWARD

One-time award for employees of National Customs Broker & Forwarders Association of America, Inc. (NCBFAA) regular member organizations and their children. Must be studying transportation logistics or international trade full time. Require minimum 2.0 GPA.

Academic Fields/Career Goals: Transportation.

Award: Scholarship for use in freshman, sophomore, junior, or senior years; not renewable. *Number:* 1. *Amount:* $5000.

Eligibility Requirements: Applicant must be enrolled or expecting to enroll full-time at a four-year institution or university. Available to U.S. citizens.

Application Requirements: Employment verification letter from NCBFAA regular member firm, proof of acceptance to or current enrollment in an accredited college or university, essay. *Deadline:* February 1.

Contact: Mr. Tom Mathers, Director, Communications
National Customs Brokers and Forwarders Association of America
1200 18th Street, NW, Suite 901
Washington, DC 20036
Phone: 202-466-0222
Fax: 202-466-0226
E-mail: tom@ncbfaa.org

SPECIALTY EQUIPMENT MARKET ASSOCIATION

http://www.sema.org/

SPECIALTY EQUIPMENT MARKET ASSOCIATION MEMORIAL SCHOLARSHIP FUND
• See page 80

TRANSPORTATION CLUBS INTERNATIONAL

http://www.transportationclubinternational.com/

ALICE GLAISYER WARFIELD MEMORIAL SCHOLARSHIP

Award is available to currently enrolled students majoring in transportation, logistics, traffic management, or related fields. Available to citizens of the United States, Canada, and Mexico. See website for application, http://www.transportationclubinternational.com/.

Academic Fields/Career Goals: Transportation.

Award: Scholarship for use in freshman, sophomore, junior, or senior years; not renewable. *Number:* 1. *Amount:* $1500.

Eligibility Requirements: Applicant must be enrolled or expecting to enroll full- or part-time at a two-year or four-year or technical institution or university. Applicant or parent of applicant must be member of Transportation Club International. Available to U.S. and non-U.S. citizens.

Application Requirements: Application form, essay, personal photograph, recommendations or references, transcript. *Deadline:* April 30.

Contact: Bill Blair, Scholarships Trustee
Phone: 832-300-5905
E-mail: bblair@zimmerworldwide.com

DENNY LYDIC SCHOLARSHIP

Award is available to currently enrolled college students majoring in transportation, logistics, traffic management, or related fields. Available to citizens of the United States, Canada, and Mexico. See website for application, http://www.transportationclubinternational.com/.

Academic Fields/Career Goals: Transportation.

Award: Scholarship for use in freshman, sophomore, junior, or senior years; not renewable. *Number:* 1. *Amount:* $1000.

Eligibility Requirements: Applicant must be enrolled or expecting to enroll full- or part-time at a two-year or four-year or technical institution or university. Applicant or parent of applicant must be member of Transportation Club International. Available to U.S. and non-U.S. citizens.

Application Requirements: Application form, essay, personal photograph, recommendations or references, transcript. *Deadline:* April 30.

Contact: Bill Blair, Scholarships Trustee
Phone: 832-300-5905
E-mail: bblair@zimmerworldwide.com

TEXAS TRANSPORTATION SCHOLARSHIP

Merit-based award for a student who is at least a sophomore studying transportation, traffic management, and related fields. Must have been enrolled in a school in Texas during some phase of education (elementary, secondary, high school). Must include photo and submit three references. One-time scholarship of $1000. See website for application http://www.transportationclubinternational.com/.

Academic Fields/Career Goals: Transportation.

Award: Scholarship for use in sophomore, junior, or senior years; not renewable. *Number:* 1. *Amount:* $1000.

Eligibility Requirements: Applicant must be enrolled or expecting to enroll full- or part-time at a two-year or four-year or technical institution or university. Applicant or parent of applicant must be member of Transportation Club International. Available to U.S. citizens.

Application Requirements: Application form, essay, personal photograph, recommendations or references, transcript. *Deadline:* April 30.

Contact: Bill Blair, Scholarships Trustee
Phone: 832-300-5905
E-mail: bblair@zimmerworldwide.com

TRANSPORTATION CLUBS INTERNATIONAL CHARLOTTE WOODS SCHOLARSHIP

Award available to an enrolled college student majoring in transportation or traffic management. Must be a member or a dependant of a member of Transportation Clubs International. Must have completed at least one year of post-high school education. One-time award of $1000. See website for application http://www.transportationclubinternational.com/

Academic Fields/Career Goals: Transportation.

Award: Scholarship for use in freshman, sophomore, junior, or senior years; not renewable. *Number:* 1. *Amount:* $1000.

Eligibility Requirements: Applicant must be enrolled or expecting to enroll full- or part-time at a two-year or four-year or technical institution or university. Applicant or parent of applicant must be member of Transportation Club International. Available to U.S. and non-U.S. citizens.

Application Requirements: Application form, essay, personal photograph, recommendations or references, transcript. *Deadline:* April 30.

Contact: Crystal Hunter, Program Manager
Phone: 800-377-2401
E-mail: awards@goldenkey.org

TRANSPORTATION CLUBS INTERNATIONAL FRED A. HOOPER MEMORIAL SCHOLARSHIP
• See page 270

TRANSPORTATION CLUBS INTERNATIONAL GINGER AND FRED DEINES CANADA SCHOLARSHIP

One-time award for a student of Canadian heritage, who is attending college or university in Canada or the United States and majoring in transportation, traffic management, logistics, or a related field. Academic merit is considered. See website for application http://www.transportationclubsinternational.com/.

Academic Fields/Career Goals: Transportation.

Award: Scholarship for use in freshman, sophomore, junior, or senior years; not renewable. *Number:* 1. *Amount:* $1500.

Eligibility Requirements: Applicant must be of Canadian heritage and Canadian citizen and enrolled or expecting to enroll full- or part-time at a two-year or four-year or technical institution or university. Applicant or parent of applicant must be member of Transportation Club International.

Application Requirements: Application form, essay, personal photograph, recommendations or references, transcript. *Deadline:* April 30.

Contact: Bill Blair, Scholarships Trustee
   Phone: 832-300-5905
   E-mail: bblair@zimmerworldwide.com

TRANSPORTATION CLUBS INTERNATIONAL GINGER AND FRED DEINES MEXICO SCHOLARSHIP

Scholarship of $2000 for a Mexican student who is enrolled in an accredited institution of higher learning in a vocational or degree program in the fields of transportation, logistics or traffic management, or related fields. May be enrolled in a U.S. or Canadian institution. See website for application http://www.transportationclubinternational.com/

Academic Fields/Career Goals: Transportation.

Award: Scholarship for use in freshman, sophomore, junior, or senior years; not renewable. *Number:* 1. *Amount:* $2000.

Eligibility Requirements: Applicant must be Mexican citizen and enrolled or expecting to enroll full- or part-time at a two-year or four-year or technical institution or university. Applicant or parent of applicant must be member of Transportation Club International. Available to Canadian and non-U.S. citizens.

Application Requirements: Application form, essay, personal photograph, recommendations or references, transcript. *Deadline:* April 30.

Contact: Bill Blair, Scholarships Trustee
   Phone: 832-300-5905
   E-mail: bblair@zimmerworldwide.com

TRUCKLOAD CARRIERS ASSOCIATION

http://www.truckload.org/

TRUCKLOAD CARRIERS ASSOCIATION SCHOLARSHIP FUND

• See page 159

WOMEN IN LOGISTICS, NORTHERN CALIFORNIA

http://www.womeninlogistics.org/

WOMEN IN LOGISTICS SCHOLARSHIP

• See page 161

WYOMING TRUCKING ASSOCIATION SCHOLARSHIP FUND TRUST

http://www.wytruck.org/

WYOMING TRUCKING ASSOCIATION SCHOLARSHIP TRUST FUND

• See page 83

TRAVEL/TOURISM

AMERICAN HOTEL AND LODGING EDUCATIONAL FOUNDATION

http://www.ahlef.org/

AMERICAN HOTEL & LODGING EDUCATIONAL FOUNDATION PEPSI SCHOLARSHIP

• See page 212

ANNUAL SCHOLARSHIP GRANT PROGRAM

• See page 213

ARTHUR J. PACKARD MEMORIAL SCHOLARSHIP

• See page 213

ECOLAB SCHOLARSHIP PROGRAM

• See page 213

HYATT HOTELS FUND FOR MINORITY LODGING MANAGEMENT

• See page 213

INCOMING FRESHMAN SCHOLARSHIPS

• See page 213

RAMA SCHOLARSHIP FOR THE AMERICAN DREAM

• See page 213

STEVEN HYMANS EXTENDED STAY SCHOLARSHIP

• See page 214

AMERICAN SOCIETY OF TRAVEL AGENTS (ASTA) FOUNDATION

http://www.asta.org/

AMERICAN EXPRESS TRAVEL SCHOLARSHIP

Candidate must be enrolled in a travel or tourism program in either a two- or four-year college or university or proprietary travel school. Must write 500-word essay on student's view of travel industry's future. Minimum 2.5 GPA required.

Academic Fields/Career Goals: Travel/Tourism.

Award: Scholarship for use in freshman, sophomore, junior, or senior years; not renewable.

Eligibility Requirements: Applicant must be enrolled or expecting to enroll full- or part-time at a two-year or four-year institution or university. Applicant must have 2.5 GPA or higher. Available to U.S. and Canadian citizens.

Application Requirements: 500-word paper detailing the student's plans in travel, application form, recommendations or references, resume, transcript. *Deadline:* July 31.

Contact: Verlette Mitchell, Manager
   American Society of Travel Agents (ASTA) Foundation
   1101 King Street
   Alexandria, VA 22314-2187
   Phone: 703-739-8721
   Fax: 703-684-8319
   E-mail: scholarship@astahq.com

ARIZONA CHAPTER DEPENDENT/EMPLOYEE MEMBERSHIP SCHOLARSHIP

Candidate must be a dependent of an ASTA Arizona Chapter Active, Active Associate or Travel Professional member, or an employee of an Arizona ASTA member agency for a minimum of six months whose ASTA membership dues are current. One award of $1500 will be given. Must attend Arizona institution. Must be enrolled in their final year in a two year college, or as a junior or senior in a four-year college/university. Minimum 2.5 GPA required.

Academic Fields/Career Goals: Travel/Tourism.

Award: Scholarship for use in sophomore, junior, or senior years; not renewable. *Number:* 1. *Amount:* $1500.

Eligibility Requirements: Applicant must be enrolled or expecting to enroll full- or part-time at a two-year or four-year institution or university; resident of Arizona and studying in Arizona. Applicant or parent of applicant must be member of American Society of Travel Agents. Applicant must have 2.5 GPA or higher. Available to U.S. and Canadian citizens.

Application Requirements: 500-word paper entitled "My Career Goals," application form, recommendations or references, transcript. *Deadline:* July 31.

Contact: Verlette Mitchell, Manager
American Society of Travel Agents (ASTA) Foundation
1101 King Street
Alexandria, VA 22314-2187
Phone: 703-739-8721
Fax: 703-684-8319
E-mail: scholarship@astahq.com

ARIZONA CHAPTER GOLD SCHOLARSHIP

One-time award for college undergraduates who are Arizona residents pursuing a travel or tourism degree at a four-year Arizona institution. Freshmen are not eligible. Must submit essay on career plans and interests. Minimum 2.5 GPA required. Must be a U.S. citizen or Canadian citizen.

Academic Fields/Career Goals: Travel/Tourism.

Award: Scholarship for use in sophomore, junior, or senior years; not renewable. *Number:* 1. *Amount:* $3000.

Eligibility Requirements: Applicant must be enrolled or expecting to enroll full- or part-time at a four-year institution or university; resident of Arizona and studying in Arizona. Applicant must have 2.5 GPA or higher. Available to U.S. and Canadian citizens.

Application Requirements: Application form, recommendations or references, transcript. *Deadline:* July 31.

Contact: Verlette Mitchell, Manager
American Society of Travel Agents (ASTA) Foundation
1101 King Street
Alexandria, VA 22314-2187
Phone: 703-739-8721
Fax: 703-684-8319
E-mail: scholarship@astahq.com

AVIS SCHOLARSHIP

Scholarship of $2000 for individuals who have already gained experience and/or training in the travel industry. Candidate must have a minimum of two years of full-time travel industry experience or an undergraduate degree in travel/tourism and must currently be employed in the travel industry. Must be enrolled in a minimum of two courses per semester in an accredited undergraduate or graduate level degree program in business, or equivalent degree program. Minimum GPA of 3.0 required.

Academic Fields/Career Goals: Travel/Tourism.

Award: Scholarship for use in freshman, sophomore, junior, senior, or graduate years; renewable. *Number:* 1. *Amount:* $2000.

Eligibility Requirements: Applicant must be enrolled or expecting to enroll full- or part-time at a four-year institution or university. Applicant must have 3.0 GPA or higher. Available to U.S. and Canadian citizens.

Application Requirements: Application form, proof of current employment in the travel industry, recommendations or references, transcript. *Deadline:* July 31.

Contact: Verlette Mitchell, Manager
American Society of Travel Agents (ASTA) Foundation
1101 King Street
Alexandria, VA 22314-2187
Phone: 703-739-8721
Fax: 703-684-8319
E-mail: scholarship@astahq.com

DONALD ESTEY SCHOLARSHIP FUND-ROCKY MOUNTAIN CHAPTER

Applicants must be enrolled in a licensed preparatory travel program or must be participating in either an ASTA sponsored training program, The Travel Institute Destination Specialist, or other industry training programs. Must have letter of recommendation from ASTA Rocky Mountain Chapter. Must be Colorado, Utah, or Wyoming resident. Must have a minimum of 2.5 GPA. Must be a U.S. citizen or Canadian citizen.

Academic Fields/Career Goals: Travel/Tourism.

Award: Scholarship for use in freshman or sophomore years; not renewable. *Number:* 3. *Amount:* $1000.

Eligibility Requirements: Applicant must be enrolled or expecting to enroll full- or part-time at a two-year or technical institution; resident of Colorado, Utah, Wyoming and studying in Colorado, Utah, Wyoming. Applicant or parent of applicant must be member of American Society of Travel Agents. Applicant or parent of applicant must have employment or volunteer experience in travel and tourism industry. Applicant must have 2.5 GPA or higher. Available to U.S. and Canadian citizens.

Application Requirements: Application form, financial need analysis, recommendations or references, statement indicating the program's expected benefit, test scores, transcript. *Deadline:* varies.

Contact: Verlette Mitchell, Manager
American Society of Travel Agents (ASTA) Foundation
1101 King Street
Alexandria, VA 22314-2187
Phone: 703-739-8721
Fax: 703-684-8319
E-mail: scholarship@astahq.com

GEORGE REINKE SCHOLARSHIPS

Applicant must write a 500-word essay on career goals in the travel or tourism industry. Must be a U.S. citizen living and studying in the United States and enrolled in a travel agent studies program in a junior college or travel school. Must have a minimum GPA of 2.5.

Academic Fields/Career Goals: Travel/Tourism.

Award: Scholarship for use in freshman or sophomore years; not renewable. *Number:* up to 6. *Amount:* $2000.

Eligibility Requirements: Applicant must be enrolled or expecting to enroll full- or part-time at a two-year institution. Applicant must have 2.5 GPA or higher. Available to U.S. citizens.

Application Requirements: 500-word paper entitled "My Objectives in the Travel Agency Industry," application form, recommendations or references, transcript. *Deadline:* July 31.

Contact: Verlette Mitchell, Manager
American Society of Travel Agents (ASTA) Foundation
1101 King Street
Alexandria, VA 22314-2187
Phone: 703-739-8721
Fax: 703-684-8319
E-mail: scholarship@astahq.com

HEALY SCHOLARSHIP

One-time award of $2000 for a college undergraduate pursuing a travel or tourism degree. Must submit essay suggesting improvements for the travel industry. Must be a citizen of United States or Canada. Minimum 2.5 GPA required.

Academic Fields/Career Goals: Travel/Tourism.

Award: Scholarship for use in freshman, sophomore, junior, or senior years; not renewable. *Number:* 1. *Amount:* $2000.

Eligibility Requirements: Applicant must be enrolled or expecting to enroll full- or part-time at a four-year institution or university. Applicant must have 2.5 GPA or higher. Available to U.S. and Canadian citizens.

Application Requirements: 500-word paper suggesting improvements in the travel industry, application form, recommendations or references, self-addressed stamped envelope with application, transcript. *Deadline:* July 31.

Contact: Carmen Gordon, Program Officer
Phone: 202-502-7542
E-mail: ope_javits_program@ed.gov

HOLLAND-AMERICA LINE WESTOURS SCHOLARSHIPS

Students must write 500-word essay on the future of the cruise industry and must be enrolled in travel or tourism program at a two- or four-year college or proprietary travel school. Minimum 2.5 GPA required. Must be a U.S. or Canadian citizen.

Academic Fields/Career Goals: Travel/Tourism.

Award: Scholarship for use in freshman, sophomore, junior, or senior years; not renewable. *Number:* 2. *Amount:* $3000.

Eligibility Requirements: Applicant must be enrolled or expecting to enroll full- or part-time at a two-year or four-year institution or university. Applicant must have 2.5 GPA or higher. Available to U.S. and Canadian citizens.

Application Requirements: 500-word paper on the future of the cruise industry, application form, financial need analysis, recommendations or references, resume, transcript. *Deadline:* July 31.

Contact: Verlette Mitchell, Manager
American Society of Travel Agents (ASTA) Foundation
1101 King Street
Alexandria, VA 22314-2187
Phone: 703-739-8721
Fax: 703-684-8319
E-mail: scholarship@astahq.com

JOHN HJORTH SCHOLARSHIP FUND-SAN DIEGO CHAPTER

Any employee of a San Diego ASTA Chapter member pursuing one of the Travel Institute certification programs, The Travel Institute Destination Specialists programs, or any ASTA Educational program is eligible to apply. Must have a minimum of two years travel industry experience. Must be a U.S. citizen or Canadian citizen.

Academic Fields/Career Goals: Travel/Tourism.

Award: Scholarship for use in freshman or sophomore years; not renewable. *Number:* 3. *Amount:* up to $250.

Eligibility Requirements: Applicant must be enrolled or expecting to enroll full- or part-time at a technical institution and resident of California. Applicant or parent of applicant must be member of American Society of Travel Agents. Applicant or parent of applicant must have employment or volunteer experience in travel and tourism industry. Applicant must have 2.5 GPA or higher. Available to U.S. and Canadian citizens.

Application Requirements: Application form, essay, letter of interest and/or need, recommendations or references. *Deadline:* July 31.

Contact: Verlette Mitchell, Manager
American Society of Travel Agents (ASTA) Foundation
1101 King Street
Alexandria, VA 22314-2187
Phone: 703-739-8721
Fax: 703-684-8319
E-mail: scholarship@astahq.com

JOSEPH R. STONE SCHOLARSHIPS

One-time award for high school senior or college undergraduate pursuing a travel or tourism degree. Must have a parent in the industry and proof of employment. Must submit a 500-word essay explaining career goals. Minimum 2.5 GPA required. Must be a citizen of United States or Canada.

Academic Fields/Career Goals: Travel/Tourism.

Award: Scholarship for use in freshman, sophomore, junior, or senior years; not renewable. *Number:* 3. *Amount:* $2400.

Eligibility Requirements: Applicant must be enrolled or expecting to enroll full- or part-time at a four-year institution or university. Applicant must have 2.5 GPA or higher. Available to U.S. and Canadian citizens.

Application Requirements: 500-word paper on applicant's goals, application form, recommendations or references, transcript. *Deadline:* July 31.

Contact: Verlette Mitchell, Manager
American Society of Travel Agents (ASTA) Foundation
1101 King Street
Alexandria, VA 22314-2187
Phone: 703-739-8721
Fax: 703-684-8319
E-mail: scholarship@astahq.com

NANCY STEWART SCHOLARSHIP FUND-ALLEGHENY CHAPTER

One-time award for travel professionals working for an agency that is a member of American Society of Travel Agents' Allegheny Chapter. Must be pursuing one of The Travel Institute's four certification programs: CTC accreditation, Destination Specialist, Travel Career Development, Professional Management; or an ASTA educational program. Must be Pennsylvania resident. Must also have at least three years of travel industry experience. Must have a minimum of 2.5 GPA.

Academic Fields/Career Goals: Travel/Tourism.

Award: Scholarship for use in freshman or sophomore years; not renewable. *Number:* 3. *Amount:* $400.

Eligibility Requirements: Applicant must be enrolled or expecting to enroll part-time at a technical institution and resident of Pennsylvania.

Applicant or parent of applicant must be member of American Society of Travel Agents. Applicant or parent of applicant must have employment or volunteer experience in travel and tourism industry. Applicant must have 2.5 GPA or higher. Available to U.S. and Canadian citizens.

Application Requirements: Application form, essay, letter of intent, recommendations or references. *Deadline:* July 31.

Contact: Verlette Mitchell, Manager
American Society of Travel Agents (ASTA) Foundation
1101 King Street
Alexandria, VA 22314-2187
Phone: 703-739-8721
Fax: 703-684-8319
E-mail: scholarship@astahq.com

NORTHERN CALIFORNIA CHAPTER RICHARD EPPING SCHOLARSHIP

Scholarship of $2000. Applicant must be currently enrolled in a travel and tourism curriculum at a college, university, or proprietary travel and tourism school in Northern California or Northern Nevada. Minimum 2.5 GPA required. Must be a U.S. or Canadian citizen.

Academic Fields/Career Goals: Travel/Tourism.

Award: Scholarship for use in freshman, sophomore, junior, or senior years; not renewable. *Number:* 1. *Amount:* $2000.

Eligibility Requirements: Applicant must be enrolled or expecting to enroll full- or part-time at a two-year or four-year institution or university and studying in California, Nevada. Applicant must have 2.5 GPA or higher. Available to U.S. and Canadian citizens.

Application Requirements: Application form, essay, recommendations or references, transcript. *Deadline:* July 31.

Contact: Verlette Mitchell, Manager
American Society of Travel Agents (ASTA) Foundation
1101 King Street
Alexandria, VA 22314-2187
Phone: 703-739-8721
Fax: 703-684-8319
E-mail: scholarship@astahq.com

ORANGE COUNTY CHAPTER/HARRY JACKSON SCHOLARSHIP FUND

Awards are available to any Active or Associate member of the Orange County ASTA office pursuing one of the following programs: ASTA Educational Programs, The Travel Institute certification programs, CTC, Destination Specialist, The Travel Institute Educational Programs, and The Travel Institute forums. The applicant must also have at least two years of travel industry experience. Must have a minimum of 2.5 GPA.

Academic Fields/Career Goals: Travel/Tourism.

Award: Scholarship for use in freshman or sophomore years; not renewable. *Amount:* $250.

Eligibility Requirements: Applicant must be enrolled or expecting to enroll full- or part-time at a technical institution and resident of California. Applicant or parent of applicant must be member of American Society of Travel Agents. Applicant must have 2.5 GPA or higher. Available to U.S. and Canadian citizens.

Application Requirements: Application form, financial need analysis, letter of interest, recommendations or references, resume, transcript. *Deadline:* July 31.

Contact: Verlette Mitchell, Manager
American Society of Travel Agents (ASTA) Foundation
1101 King Street
Alexandria, VA 22314-2187
Phone: 703-739-8721
Fax: 703-684-8319
E-mail: scholarship@astahq.com

PACIFIC NORTHWEST CHAPTER-WILLIAM HUNT SCHOLARSHIP FUND

One-time award for travel professionals. Applicant must be employed in the travel industry in an ASTA office or enrolled in a travel and tourism program in either a two- or four-year college, university or proprietary travel school. Must be a resident of and studying in one of the following states: Alaska, Idaho, Montana, Oregon, or Washington. Must be a U.S. or Canadian citizen. Must have a minimum of 2.5 GPA.

Academic Fields/Career Goals: Travel/Tourism.

Award: Scholarship for use in freshman, sophomore, junior, or senior years; not renewable. *Number:* up to 3. *Amount:* up to $1000.

Eligibility Requirements: Applicant must be enrolled or expecting to enroll full- or part-time at a two-year or four-year or technical institution or university; resident of Alaska, Idaho, Montana, Oregon, Washington and studying in Alaska, Idaho, Montana, Oregon, Washington. Applicant or parent of applicant must be member of American Society of Travel Agents. Applicant must have 2.5 GPA or higher. Available to U.S. and Canadian citizens.

Application Requirements: 300-word letter explaining reasons for interest in further training in travel, application form, essay, recommendations or references, transcript. *Deadline:* July 31.

Contact: Verlette Mitchell, Manager
American Society of Travel Agents (ASTA) Foundation
1101 King Street
Alexandria, VA 22314-2187
Phone: 703-739-8721
Fax: 703-684-8319
E-mail: scholarship@astahq.com

PRINCESS CRUISES AND PRINCESS TOURS SCHOLARSHIP

Merit-based award for student accepted or enrolled as an undergraduate in a travel or tourism program. Submit 300-word essay on two features cruise ships will need to offer passengers in the next ten years. Minimum 2.5 GPA required. Must be a U.S. citizen or Canadian citizen.

Academic Fields/Career Goals: Travel/Tourism.

Award: Scholarship for use in freshman, sophomore, junior, or senior years; not renewable. *Number:* 2. *Amount:* $2000.

Eligibility Requirements: Applicant must be enrolled or expecting to enroll full- or part-time at a two-year or four-year institution or university. Applicant must have 2.5 GPA or higher. Available to U.S. and Canadian citizens.

Application Requirements: 300-word paper on the two features cruise ships will need to offer passengers in the next ten years, application form, recommendations or references, transcript. *Deadline:* July 31.

Contact: Verlette Mitchell, Manager
American Society of Travel Agents (ASTA) Foundation
1101 King Street
Alexandria, VA 22314-2187
Phone: 703-739-8721
Fax: 703-684-8319
E-mail: scholarship@astahq.com

SOUTHEAST AMERICAN SOCIETY OF TRAVEL AGENTS CHAPTER SCHOLARSHIP

Applicants must be Active Associate members in good standing of the SEASTA chapter, and have at least two years of travel industry experience. Applicants must be pursuing any of the ASTA Specialist certification programs, ASTA educational conferences, The Travel Institute CTA, The Travel Institute CTC, or The Travel Institute Destination certification programs. Applicant must apply for scholarship within one year of receiving certification.

Academic Fields/Career Goals: Travel/Tourism.

Award: Scholarship for use in freshman year; not renewable. *Number:* up to 6. *Amount:* $350.

Eligibility Requirements: Applicant must be enrolled or expecting to enroll part-time at a technical institution; resident of Alabama, Georgia, Kentucky, Louisiana, Mississippi, North Carolina, South Carolina, Tennessee and studying in Alabama, Georgia, Kentucky, Louisiana, Mississippi, North Carolina, South Carolina, Tennessee. Applicant or parent of applicant must be member of American Society of Travel Agents. Applicant or parent of applicant must have employment or volunteer experience in travel and tourism industry. Applicant must have 2.5 GPA or higher. Available to U.S. and Canadian citizens.

Application Requirements: Application form, letter of interest or need, proof of course certification, recommendations or references. *Deadline:* July 31.

Contact: Verlette Mitchell, Manager
American Society of Travel Agents (ASTA) Foundation
1101 King Street
Alexandria, VA 22314-2187
Phone: 703-739-8721
Fax: 703-684-8319
E-mail: scholarship@astahq.com

SOUTHERN CALIFORNIA CHAPTER/PLEASANT HAWAIIAN HOLIDAYS SCHOLARSHIP

Two awards for students pursuing travel or tourism degrees. One award given to student attending college in southern California, and one award given to a student attending school anywhere in the United States. Applicant must be U.S. citizens. Minimum 2.5 GPA required.

Academic Fields/Career Goals: Travel/Tourism.

Award: Scholarship for use in freshman, sophomore, junior, or senior years; not renewable. *Number:* 2. *Amount:* $2500.

Eligibility Requirements: Applicant must be enrolled or expecting to enroll full- or part-time at a four-year institution or university. Applicant must have 2.5 GPA or higher. Available to U.S. citizens.

Application Requirements: 500-word paper entitled "My Goals in the Travel Industry," application form, recommendations or references, transcript. *Deadline:* July 31.

Contact: Verlette Mitchell, Manager
American Society of Travel Agents (ASTA) Foundation
1101 King Street
Alexandria, VA 22314-2187
Phone: 703-739-8721
Fax: 703-684-8319
E-mail: scholarship@astahq.com

STAN AND LEONE POLLARD SCHOLARSHIPS

Candidate must be re-entering the job market by being enrolled in a travel and tourism curriculum in either a recognized proprietary travel school or a two-year junior college. Two awards of $2000 each will be given. Must have a minimum GPA of 2.5 and be a U.S. or Canadian citizen.

Academic Fields/Career Goals: Travel/Tourism.

Award: Scholarship for use in freshman or sophomore years; not renewable. *Number:* 2. *Amount:* $2000.

Eligibility Requirements: Applicant must be enrolled or expecting to enroll full- or part-time at a two-year or technical institution. Applicant must have 2.5 GPA or higher. Available to U.S. and Canadian citizens.

Application Requirements: 500-word paper on the student's objectives in the travel and tourism industry, application form, recommendations or references, transcript. *Deadline:* July 31.

Contact: Verlette Mitchell, Manager
American Society of Travel Agents (ASTA) Foundation
1101 King Street
Alexandria, VA 22314-2187
Phone: 703-739-8721
Fax: 703-684-8319
E-mail: scholarship@astahq.com

HAWAII LODGING & TOURISM ASSOCIATION

http://www.hawaiilodging.org

R.W. "BOB" HOLDEN SCHOLARSHIP
• See page 352

INTERNATIONAL AIRLINES TRAVEL AGENT NETWORK

http://www.iatan.org/

INTERNATIONAL AIRLINES TRAVEL AGENT NETWORK FOUNDATION SCHOLARSHIP
• See page 353

MISSOURI TRAVEL COUNCIL

http://www.missouritravel.com/

MISSOURI TRAVEL COUNCIL TOURISM SCHOLARSHIP
• See page 318

TOURISM CARES

http://www.tourismcares.org

NEW HORIZONS KATHY LETARTE SCHOLARSHIP
• *See page 319*

PAT AND JIM HOST SCHOLARSHIP
• *See page 353*

SOCIETIE DES CASINOS DU QUEBEC SCHOLARSHIP
• *See page 319*

OHIO TRAVEL ASSOCIATION

http://www.ohiotravel.org/

BILL SCHWARTZ MEMORIAL SCHOLARSHIP
• *See page 353*

SOCIETY FOR APPLIED ANTHROPOLOGY

http://www.sfaa.net/

VALENE SMITH PRIZE
• *See page 101*

TV/RADIO BROADCASTING

ADC RESEARCH INSTITUTE

http://www.adc.org/

JACK SHAHEEN MASS COMMUNICATIONS SCHOLARSHIP AWARD
• *See page 187*

ALABAMA BROADCASTERS ASSOCIATION

http://www.al-ba.com/

ALABAMA BROADCASTERS ASSOCIATION SCHOLARSHIP

Scholarship available to Alabama residents studying broadcasting at any accredited Alabama technical school, 2- or 4-year college, or university.

Academic Fields/Career Goals: TV/Radio Broadcasting.

Award: Scholarship for use in junior or senior years; not renewable. *Number:* up to 4. *Amount:* up to $2500.

Eligibility Requirements: Applicant must be enrolled or expecting to enroll full-time at a two-year or four-year or technical institution or university; resident of Alabama and studying in Alabama. Available to U.S. citizens.

Application Requirements: Application form, recommendations or references. *Deadline:* April 30.

Contact: Sharon Tinsley, President
Phone: 205-982-5001
Fax: 205-982-0015
E-mail: stinsley@al-ba.com

ALBERTA HERITAGE SCHOLARSHIP FUND

http://www.alis.alberta.ca/

TIESSEN FOUNDATION BROADCAST SCHOLARSHIP

CAN$750 to recognize an outstanding Alberta high school student and to encourage and assist them with their post-secondary studies at any recognized post-secondary institution in Canada that offers degree or diploma, programs in broadcasting. For additional information, see website http://alis.alberta.ca.

Academic Fields/Career Goals: TV/Radio Broadcasting.

Award: Scholarship for use in freshman year; not renewable.

Eligibility Requirements: Applicant must be Canadian citizen; high school student; planning to enroll or expecting to enroll full-time at a two-year or four-year or technical institution or university and resident of Alberta.

Application Requirements: Application form, essay, recommendations or references. *Deadline:* June 1.

AMERICAN LEGION PRESS CLUB OF NEW JERSEY

AMERICAN LEGION PRESS CLUB OF NEW JERSEY AND POST 170 ARTHUR DEHARDT MEMORIAL SCHOLARSHIP
• *See page 187*

ARRL FOUNDATION INC.

http://www.arrl.org/

ANDROSCOGGIN AMATEUR RADIO CLUB SCHOLARSHIP
• *See page 200*

FRANCIS WALTON MEMORIAL SCHOLARSHIP
• *See page 91*

ASIAN AMERICAN JOURNALISTS ASSOCIATION

http://www.aaja.org/

AAJA/COX FOUNDATION SCHOLARSHIP
• *See page 363*

ASIAN-AMERICAN JOURNALISTS ASSOCIATION SCHOLARSHIP
• *See page 189*

MINORU YASUI MEMORIAL SCHOLARSHIP AWARD
• *See page 363*

ASSOCIATED PRESS

http://www.aptra.org/

ASSOCIATED PRESS TELEVISION/RADIO ASSOCIATION-CLETE ROBERTS JOURNALISM SCHOLARSHIP AWARDS
• *See page 364*

KATHRYN DETTMAN MEMORIAL JOURNALISM SCHOLARSHIP
• *See page 364*

ATLANTA PRESS CLUB INC.

http://www.atlantapressclub.org/

ATLANTA PRESS CLUB JOURNALISM SCHOLARSHIP PROGRAM
• *See page 365*

CALIFORNIA BROADCASTERS FOUNDATION

http://www.yourcba.com/scholarships/

CALIFORNIA BROADCASTERS FOUNDATION INTERN SCHOLARSHIP

Two $500 scholarships awarded to radio interns and two $500 scholarships awarded to television interns each semester. Any enrolled college student working as an intern at any California Broadcasters Foundation or Association member radio or television station is eligible. No minimum number of hours per week required. Immediate family of current Foundation Board Members are not eligible. Deadlines: June 18 for fall and December 10 for spring.

Academic Fields/Career Goals: TV/Radio Broadcasting.

Award: Scholarship for use in freshman, sophomore, junior, senior, graduate, or postgraduate years; not renewable. *Number:* up to 4. *Amount:* $500.

Eligibility Requirements: Applicant must be enrolled or expecting to enroll full- or part-time at a two-year or four-year or technical institution or university and resident of California. Available to U.S. citizens.

Application Requirements: Application form, essay, recommendations or references. *Deadline:* varies.

Contact: Mark Powers, Government Affairs
California Broadcasters Foundation
915 L Street, Suite 1150
Sacramento, CA 95814
Phone: 916-444-2237
E-mail: cbapowers@cabroadcasters.org

CCNMA: LATINO JOURNALISTS OF CALIFORNIA

http://www.ccnma.org/

CCNMA SCHOLARSHIPS
• *See page 365*

CHARLES AND LUCILLE KING FAMILY FOUNDATION, INC.

http://www.kingfoundation.org/

CHARLES AND LUCILLE KING FAMILY FOUNDATION SCHOLARSHIPS
• *See page 189*

THE CIRI FOUNDATION (TCF)

http://www.thecirifoundation.org/

CAP LATHROP SCHOLARSHIP PROGRAM
• *See page 151*

DADE COMMUNITY FOUNDATION

http://www.jackituckfield.org/

LEO SUAREZ SCHOLARSHIP
• *See page 190*

FISHER BROADCASTING COMPANY

http://www.fsci.com/

FISHER BROADCASTING INC. SCHOLARSHIP FOR MINORITIES
• *See page 154*

GREAT LAKES COMMISSION

http://www.glc.org/

CAROL A. RATZA MEMORIAL SCHOLARSHIP
• *See page 190*

HAWAII ASSOCIATION OF BROADCASTERS INC.

http://www.hawaiibroadcasters.com/

HAWAII ASSOCIATION OF BROADCASTERS SCHOLARSHIP

Renewable scholarship for full-time college students with the career goal of working in the broadcast industry in Hawaii upon graduation. Minimum GPA of 2.75 required. Number of awards granted ranges between twenty and thirty. For more information, visit website http://www.hawaiibroadcasters.com.

Academic Fields/Career Goals: TV/Radio Broadcasting.

Award: Scholarship for use in freshman, sophomore, junior, or senior years; renewable. *Number:* 20–30. *Amount:* $500–$4500.

Eligibility Requirements: Applicant must be enrolled or expecting to enroll full-time at a two-year or four-year institution or university. Applicant must have 2.5 GPA or higher. Available to U.S. and non-U.S. citizens.

Application Requirements: Application form, recommendations or references, transcript. *Deadline:* April 30.

IDAHO STATE BROADCASTERS ASSOCIATION

http://www.idahobroadcasters.org/

WAYNE C. CORNILS MEMORIAL SCHOLARSHIP
• *See page 156*

ILLUMINATING ENGINEERING SOCIETY OF NORTH AMERICA

http://www.iesna.org/

ROBERT W. THUNEN MEMORIAL SCHOLARSHIPS
• *See page 111*

INDIANA BROADCASTERS ASSOCIATION

http://www.indianabroadcasters.org/

INDIANA BROADCASTERS FOUNDATION SCHOLARSHIP
• *See page 367*

JOHN BAYLISS BROADCAST FOUNDATION

http://www.baylissfoundation.org/

JOHN BAYLISS BROADCAST RADIO SCHOLARSHIP
• *See page 191*

KATU THOMAS R. DARGAN MINORITY SCHOLARSHIP

http://www.katu.com/

THOMAS R. DARGAN MINORITY SCHOLARSHIP
• *See page 191*

LIN TELEVISION CORPORATION

http://www.lintv.com/

LINTV MINORITY SCHOLARSHIP

• See page 367

LOUISIANA ASSOCIATION OF BROADCASTERS

http://www.broadcasters.org/

BROADCAST SCHOLARSHIP PROGRAM

Scholarship to students enrolled and attending classes, full-time, in a fully accredited broadcast curriculum at a Louisiana four-year college. Must be a Louisiana resident and maintain a minimum 2.5 GPA. Previous LAB Scholarship Award winners are eligible.

Academic Fields/Career Goals: TV/Radio Broadcasting.

Award: Scholarship for use in junior or senior years; not renewable. *Number:* 2. *Amount:* $2000.

Eligibility Requirements: Applicant must be enrolled or expecting to enroll full-time at a four-year institution or university; resident of Louisiana and studying in Louisiana. Applicant must have 2.5 GPA or higher. Available to U.S. citizens.

Application Requirements: Application form, essay, recommendations or references, transcript. *Deadline:* February 1.

Contact: Louise Munson, Scholarship Coordinator
Louisiana Association of Broadcasters
660 Florida Boulevard
Baton Rouge, LA 70801
Phone: 225-267-4522
Fax: 225-267-4329
E-mail: lmunson@broadcasters.org

MARYLAND ASSOCIATION OF PRIVATE COLLEGES AND CAREER SCHOOLS

http://www.mapccs.org/

MARYLAND ASSOCIATION OF PRIVATE COLLEGES AND CAREER SCHOOLS SCHOLARSHIP

• See page 157

MASSACHUSETTS BROADCASTERS ASSOCIATION

http://www.massbroadcasters.org/

MBA STUDENT BROADCASTER SCHOLARSHIP

Scholarship available to permanent residents of Massachusetts who will be enrolling or are currently enrolled at an accredited vocational school, two- or four-year college or university in the United States. Must be full-time students pursuing studies in radio and television broadcasting.

Academic Fields/Career Goals: TV/Radio Broadcasting.

Award: Scholarship for use in freshman, sophomore, junior, or senior years; not renewable. *Amount:* $2000.

Eligibility Requirements: Applicant must be enrolled or expecting to enroll full-time at a two-year or four-year or technical institution or university and resident of Massachusetts. Available to U.S. citizens.

Application Requirements: Application form, financial need analysis, recommendations or references, transcript. *Deadline:* April 4.

Contact: B. Sprague, President
Phone: 800-471-1875
Fax: 800-471-1876
E-mail: als@massbroadcasters.org

MEDIA ACTION NETWORK FOR ASIAN AMERICANS

http://www.manaa.org/

MANAA MEDIA SCHOLARSHIPS FOR ASIAN AMERICAN STUDENTS

• See page 120

MICHIGAN ASSOCIATION OF BROADCASTERS FOUNDATION

http://www.michmab.com/

WXYZ-TV BROADCASTING SCHOLARSHIP

One-time $1000 scholarship to assist students who are actively pursuing a career in a broadcast-related field. No limit on the number of awards within the program. Interested applicants should send a cover letter, resume, letters of recommendation, and an essay (200 to 300 words). The scholarship is open to Michigan residents currently attending college in Michigan.

Academic Fields/Career Goals: TV/Radio Broadcasting.

Award: Scholarship for use in freshman year; not renewable. *Number:* 1. *Amount:* $1000.

Eligibility Requirements: Applicant must be high school student; planning to enroll or expecting to enroll full-time at a two-year or four-year institution or university; resident of Michigan and studying in Michigan. Available to U.S. citizens.

Application Requirements: Application form, driver's license, essay, recommendations or references. *Deadline:* January 15.

Contact: Julie Sochay, Executive Vice President
Michigan Association of Broadcasters Foundation
819 North Washington Avenue
Lansing, MI 48906
Phone: 517-484-7444
Fax: 517-484-5810
E-mail: mabf@michmab.com

MINNESOTA BROADCASTERS ASSOCIATION

http://www.minnesotabroadcasters.com/

JAMES J. WYCHOR SCHOLARSHIP

One-time scholarships to Minnesota residents interested in broadcasting who are planning to enter the broadcasting field or other electronic media. Minimum 3.0 GPA is required. Submit proof of enrollment at an accredited postsecondary institution.

Academic Fields/Career Goals: TV/Radio Broadcasting.

Award: Scholarship for use in freshman, sophomore, junior, senior, or graduate years; not renewable. *Number:* 10. *Amount:* $1500.

Eligibility Requirements: Applicant must be enrolled or expecting to enroll full-time at a two-year or four-year or technical institution or university and resident of Minnesota. Applicant must have 2.5 GPA or higher. Available to U.S. citizens.

Application Requirements: Application form, essay, recommendations or references, transcript. *Deadline:* May 31.

Contact: Linda Lasere, Administrative Assistant
Phone: 612-926-8123
Fax: 612-926-9761
E-mail: llasere@minnesotabroadcasters.com

MISSISSIPPI ASSOCIATION OF BROADCASTERS

http://www.msbroadcasters.org/

MISSISSIPPI ASSOCIATION OF BROADCASTERS SCHOLARSHIP

• See page 368

MISSOURI BROADCASTERS ASSOCIATION SCHOLARSHIP PROGRAM

http://www.mbaweb.org/

MISSOURI BROADCASTERS ASSOCIATION SCHOLARSHIP

Scholarship for a Missouri resident enrolled or planning to enroll in a broadcast or related curriculum which provides training and expertise applicable to a broadcast operation. Must maintain a GPA of at least 3.0 or equivalent. Multiple awards may be assigned each year and the amount of the scholarship will vary.

Academic Fields/Career Goals: TV/Radio Broadcasting.

Award: Scholarship for use in freshman, sophomore, junior, or senior years; not renewable. *Number:* 3. *Amount:* $1000–$2500.

Eligibility Requirements: Applicant must be enrolled or expecting to enroll full-time at a two-year or four-year institution or university; resident of Missouri and studying in Missouri. Applicant must have 3.0 GPA or higher. Available to U.S. citizens.

Application Requirements: Application form, financial need analysis, recommendations or references. *Deadline:* March 31.

Contact: Conny Heiland, Executive Assistant
Phone: 573-636-6692
Fax: 573-634-8258
E-mail: cheiland@mbaweb.org

MONTANA BROADCASTERS ASSOCIATION

http://www.mtbroadcasters.org/

GREAT FALLS BROADCASTERS ASSOCIATION SCHOLARSHIP

Scholarship available to a student who has graduated from a north-central Montana high school (Cascade, Meagher, Judith Basin, Fergus, Choteau, Teton, Pondera, Glacier, Toole, Liberty, Hill, Blaine, Phillips, and Valley counties) and is enrolled as at least a second year student in radio-TV at any public or private Montana college or university.

Academic Fields/Career Goals: TV/Radio Broadcasting.

Award: Scholarship for use in sophomore year; not renewable. *Number:* 1. *Amount:* $2000–$5000.

Eligibility Requirements: Applicant must be enrolled or expecting to enroll full-time at a two-year or four-year institution or university; resident of Montana and studying in Montana. Available to U.S. citizens.

Application Requirements: Application form, essay, recommendations or references, transcript. *Deadline:* March 15.

Contact: Gregory McDonald, Scholarship Coordinator
Montana Broadcasters Association
HC 70 PO Box 98
Bonner, MT 59823
Phone: 406-244-4622
Fax: 406-244-5518
E-mail: mba@mtbroadcasters.org

NATIONAL ACADEMY OF TELEVISION ARTS AND SCIENCES

http://www.emmyonline.tv/

NATIONAL ACADEMY OF TELEVISION ARTS AND SCIENCES JOHN CANNON MEMORIAL SCHOLARSHIP
• *See page 192*

NATIONAL ACADEMY OF TELEVISION ARTS AND SCIENCES-NATIONAL CAPITAL/CHESAPEAKE BAY CHAPTER

http://www.natasdc.org/

BETTY ENDICOTT/NTA-NCCB STUDENT SCHOLARSHIP
• *See page 368*

NATIONAL ASSOCIATION OF BLACK JOURNALISTS

http://www.nabj.org/

NABJ SCHOLARSHIP
• *See page 192*

NATIONAL ASSOCIATION OF BLACK JOURNALISTS NON-SUSTAINING SCHOLARSHIP AWARDS
• *See page 369*

NATIONAL ASSOCIATION OF BROADCASTERS

http://www.nab.org/

NATIONAL ASSOCIATION OF BROADCASTERS GRANTS FOR RESEARCH IN BROADCASTING
• *See page 192*

NATIONAL ASSOCIATION OF HISPANIC JOURNALISTS (NAHJ)

http://www.nahj.org/

GERALDO RIVERA SCHOLARSHIP
• *See page 369*

MARIA ELENA SALINAS SCHOLARSHIP
• *See page 321*

NATIONAL ASSOCIATION OF HISPANIC JOURNALISTS SCHOLARSHIP
• *See page 192*

NATIONAL DAIRY SHRINE

http://www.dairyshrine.org/

MARSHALL E. MCCULLOUGH-NATIONAL DAIRY SHRINE SCHOLARSHIPS
• *See page 93*

NEW JERSEY BROADCASTERS ASSOCIATION

http://www.njba.com/

MICHAEL S. LIBRETTI SCHOLARSHIP
• *See page 193*

NORTH CAROLINA ASSOCIATION OF BROADCASTERS

http://www.ncbroadcast.com/

NCAB SCHOLARSHIP

One-time scholarship for high school seniors enrolled as full-time students in a North Carolina college or university with an interest in broadcasting. Must be between ages 17 and 20.

Academic Fields/Career Goals: TV/Radio Broadcasting.

Award: Scholarship for use in freshman year; not renewable. *Number:* 2. *Amount:* $10,000.

Eligibility Requirements: Applicant must be high school student; age 17-20; planning to enroll or expecting to enroll full-time at a two-year or four-year institution or university and studying in North Carolina. Available to U.S. citizens.

Application Requirements: Application form, essay, recommendations or references, transcript. *Deadline:* April 15.

Contact: Lisa Reynolds, Executive Manager
North Carolina Association of Broadcasters
PO Box 627
Raleigh, NC 27602
Phone: 919-821-7300
Fax: 919-839-0304

OREGON ASSOCIATION OF BROADCASTERS

http://www.theoab.org/

OAB FOUNDATION SCHOLARSHIP
• *See page 193*

OUTDOOR WRITERS ASSOCIATION OF AMERICA

http://www.owaa.org/

OUTDOOR WRITERS ASSOCIATION OF AMERICA - BODIE MCDOWELL SCHOLARSHIP AWARD
• *See page 193*

PALM BEACH ASSOCIATION OF BLACK JOURNALISTS

PALM BEACH ASSOCIATION OF BLACK JOURNALISTS SCHOLARSHIP
• *See page 372*

RADIO & TELEVISION NEWS DIRECTORS FOUNDATION

http://www.rtnda.org/

CAROLE SIMPSON SCHOLARSHIP
• *See page 194*

ED BRADLEY SCHOLARSHIP
• *See page 373*

KEN KASHIWAHARA SCHOLARSHIP
• *See page 194*

LOU AND CAROLE PRATO SPORTS REPORTING SCHOLARSHIP
• *See page 194*

PRESIDENTS SCHOLARSHIP
• *See page 194*

RHODE ISLAND FOUNDATION

http://www.rifoundation.org/

J. D. EDSAL SCHOLARSHIP
• *See page 84*

SOCIETY OF BROADCAST ENGINEERS INC.

http://www.sbe.org/

ROBERT GREENBERG/HAROLD E. ENNES SCHOLARSHIP FUND AND ENNES EDUCATIONAL FOUNDATION BROADCAST TECHNOLOGY SCHOLARSHIP
• *See page 254*

YOUTH SCHOLARSHIP
Award available to senior in high school with a serious interest in pursuing studies leading to a career in broadcast engineering or closely related field.

Academic Fields/Career Goals: TV/Radio Broadcasting.

Award: Scholarship for use in freshman year; renewable. *Number:* 1. *Amount:* $1000–$1500.

Eligibility Requirements: Applicant must be high school student and planning to enroll or expecting to enroll full-time at a four-year institution. Applicant must have 3.0 GPA or higher. Available to U.S. citizens.

Application Requirements: Application form, transcript, written statement of education plans after high school. *Deadline:* July 1.

Contact: Debbie Hennessey, Executive Secretary
Society of Broadcast Engineers Inc.
9102 North Meridian Street, Suite 150
Indianapolis, IN 46260
Phone: 317-846-9000
Fax: 317-846-9120
E-mail: dhennessey@sbe.org

SOCIETY OF MOTION PICTURE AND TELEVISION ENGINEERS

http://www.smpte.org/

LOUIS F. WOLF JR. MEMORIAL SCHOLARSHIP
• *See page 195*

STUDENT PAPER AWARD
• *See page 195*

SOCIETY OF PROFESSIONAL JOURNALISTS, LOS ANGELES CHAPTER

http://www.spj.org/losangeles

HELEN JOHNSON SCHOLARSHIP
• *See page 374*

STRAIGHTFORWARD MEDIA

http://www.straightforwardmedia.com/

STRAIGHTFORWARD MEDIA MEDIA & COMMUNICATIONS SCHOLARSHIP
• *See page 84*

TEXAS ASSOCIATION OF BROADCASTERS

http://www.tab.org/

BELO TEXAS BROADCAST EDUCATION FOUNDATION SCHOLARSHIP
• *See page 196*

BONNER MCLANE TEXAS BROADCAST EDUCATION FOUNDATION SCHOLARSHIP
• *See page 196*

STUDENT TEXAS BROADCAST EDUCATION FOUNDATION SCHOLARSHIP
• *See page 196*

TOM REIFF TEXAS BROADCAST EDUCATION FOUNDATION SCHOLARSHIP
• *See page 196*

UNDERGRADUATE TEXAS BROADCAST EDUCATION FOUNDATION SCHOLARSHIP
• *See page 196*

VANN KENNEDY TEXAS BROADCAST EDUCATION FOUNDATION SCHOLARSHIP
• *See page 197*

TEXAS GRIDIRON CLUB INC.
http://www.spjfw.org/

TEXAS GRIDIRON CLUB SCHOLARSHIPS
• *See page 197*

UNITED METHODIST COMMUNICATIONS
http://www.umcom.org/

LEONARD M. PERRYMAN COMMUNICATIONS SCHOLARSHIP FOR ETHNIC MINORITY STUDENTS
• *See page 197*

VALLEY PRESS CLUB, SPRINGFIELD NEWSPAPERS
http://www.valleypressclub.com/

VALLEY PRESS CLUB SCHOLARSHIPS, THE REPUBLICAN SCHOLARSHIP, CHANNEL 22 SCHOLARSHIP
• *See page 198*

WISCONSIN BROADCASTERS ASSOCIATION FOUNDATION
http://www.wi-broadcasters.org/

WISCONSIN BROADCASTERS ASSOCIATION FOUNDATION SCHOLARSHIP
• *See page 199*

WOWT-TV–OMAHA, NEBRASKA
http://www.wowt.com/

WOWT-TV BROADCASTING SCHOLARSHIP PROGRAM
Two annual scholarships of $1000 for high school graduates in the Channel 6 viewing area of Nebraska. Must be pursuing a full-time career in broadcasting and have a minimum GPA of 3.0.

Academic Fields/Career Goals: TV/Radio Broadcasting.

Award: Scholarship for use in freshman year; not renewable. *Number:* up to 2. *Amount:* up to $1000.

Eligibility Requirements: Applicant must be high school student; planning to enroll or expecting to enroll full-time at a two-year or four-year institution or university and resident of Nebraska. Applicant must have 3.0 GPA or higher. Available to U.S. citizens.

Application Requirements: Application form, community service, essay, interview, recommendations or references, test scores, transcript. *Deadline:* March 15.

Contact: Gail Backer, Scholarship Committee
WOWT-TV–Omaha, Nebraska
3501 Farnam Street
Omaha, NE 68131
Phone: 402-346-6666
Fax: 402-233-7880

YOUNG AMERICAN BROADCASTERS SCHOLARSHIP
http://www.youngamericanbroadcasters.org/

YOUNG AMERICAN BROADCASTERS SCHOLARSHIP
Scholarship for ethnically diverse college population to encourage pursuit of studies in radio and Internet broadcasting. One-time scholarship for part-time students who have completed at least one year of study.

Academic Fields/Career Goals: TV/Radio Broadcasting.

Award: Scholarship for use in sophomore, junior, or senior years; not renewable. *Amount:* up to $5000.

Eligibility Requirements: Applicant must be enrolled or expecting to enroll part-time at a four-year institution or university. Available to U.S. and non-U.S. citizens.

Application Requirements: Application form, entry in a contest, transcript. *Deadline:* varies.

URBAN AND REGIONAL PLANNING

AMERICAN PLANNING ASSOCIATION
http://www.planning.org/

JUDITH MCMANUS PRICE SCHOLARSHIP
Scholarship available to women and underrepresented minority students enrolled in an approved Planning Accreditation Board (PAB) planning program who are U.S. citizens and intend to pursue careers as practicing planners in the public sector. Must demonstrate financial need. For further information visit http://www.planning.org/institutions/scholarship.htm.

Academic Fields/Career Goals: Urban and Regional Planning.

Award: Scholarship for use in freshman, sophomore, junior, or senior years; not renewable. *Amount:* $2000–$5000.

Eligibility Requirements: Applicant must be American Indian/Alaska Native, Black (non-Hispanic), Hispanic and enrolled or expecting to enroll full-time at a four-year institution or university. Available to U.S. citizens.

Application Requirements: 2- to 5-page personal and background statement written by the school, 2 letters of recommendation, acceptance letter, application form, financial need analysis, resume, transcript. *Deadline:* April 30.

Contact: Kriss Blank, Leadership Affairs Associate
American Planning Association
122 South Michigan Avenue, Suite 1600
Chicago, IL 60603
Phone: 312-786-6722
Fax: 312-786-6727
E-mail: kblank@planning.org

ASSOCIATION FOR WOMEN IN ARCHITECTURE FOUNDATION
http://www.awa-la.org/

ASSOCIATION FOR WOMEN IN ARCHITECTURE FOUNDATION SCHOLARSHIP
• *See page 109*

CENTER FOR ARCHITECTURE
http://www.cfafoundation.org/scholarships

CENTER FOR ARCHITECTURE, DOUGLAS HASKELL AWARD FOR STUDENT JOURNALS
• *See page 110*

CONNECTICUT CHAPTER OF THE AMERICAN PLANNING ASSOCIATION

http://www.ccapa.org/

DIANA DONALD SCHOLARSHIP

One-time award of $2500 for full-time students enrolled in a graduate or undergraduate program in city planning or a closely related field. Must be resident of Connecticut and study in Connecticut. Deadline varies.

Academic Fields/Career Goals: Urban and Regional Planning.

Award: Scholarship for use in freshman, sophomore, junior, senior, or graduate years; not renewable. *Number:* up to 1. *Amount:* up to $2500.

Eligibility Requirements: Applicant must be enrolled or expecting to enroll full-time at a four-year institution or university; resident of Connecticut and studying in Connecticut. Available to U.S. and non-U.S. citizens.

Application Requirements: Application form, essay, financial need analysis, recommendations or references, transcript. *Deadline:* varies.

Contact: Mary Savage-Dunham, Town Planner
Connecticut Chapter of the American Planning Association
75 Main Street
Southington, CT 06489
Phone: 860-276-6248
E-mail: savagem@southington.org

INTERNATIONAL FACILITY MANAGEMENT ASSOCIATION FOUNDATION

http://www.ifmafoundation.org/

IFMA FOUNDATION SCHOLARSHIPS
• See page 112

WOMEN'S STUDIES

AMERICAN FEDERATION OF STATE, COUNTY, AND MUNICIPAL EMPLOYEES

http://www.afscme.org/

AFSCME/UNCF UNION SCHOLARS PROGRAM
• See page 97

SOCIETY FOR THE SCIENTIFIC STUDY OF SEXUALITY

http://www.sexscience.org/

SOCIETY FOR THE SCIENTIFIC STUDY OF SEXUALITY STUDENT RESEARCH GRANT
• See page 102

UNITED NEGRO COLLEGE FUND

http://www.uncf.org/

AFSCME/UNCF/HARVARD UNIVERSITY LWP UNION SCHOLARS PROGRAM
• See page 98

Nonacademic/Noncareer Criteria

CIVIC, PROFESSIONAL, SOCIAL, OR UNION AFFILIATION

AIR LINE PILOTS ASSOCIATION, INTERNATIONAL

http://www.alpa.org/

AIRLINE PILOTS ASSOCIATION SCHOLARSHIP PROGRAM

Scholarship for children of medically retired, long-term disabled, or deceased pilot members of the Air Line Pilots Association. The total monetary value is $12,000 with $3000 disbursed annually to the recipient for four consecutive years, provided that a GPA of 3.0 is maintained. An additional $2000 per year is available which may be awarded to one or two additional applicants as a one-year special award, which is not renewable.

Award: Scholarship for use in freshman, sophomore, junior, or senior years; renewable. *Number:* 1–3. *Amount:* $1000–$12,000.

Eligibility Requirements: Applicant must be enrolled or expecting to enroll full-time at a four-year institution or university. Applicant or parent of applicant must be member of Airline Pilots Association. Applicant must have 3.0 GPA or higher. Available to U.S. and Canadian citizens.

Application Requirements: Application form, financial need analysis, recommendations or references, test scores, transcript. *Deadline:* April 1.

Contact: Maggie Erzen, Coordinator
Phone: 202-797-4059
Fax: 202-797-4014
E-mail: maggie.erzen@alpa.org

ALBERTA AGRICULTURE FOOD AND RURAL DEVELOPMENT 4-H BRANCH

http://www.4h.ab.ca/

ALBERTA AGRICULTURE FOOD AND RURAL DEVELOPMENT 4-H SCHOLARSHIP PROGRAM

Awards will be given to current and incoming students attending any institute of higher learning. Must have been a member of the Alberta 4-H Program and be a Canadian citizen. Must be a resident of Alberta.

Award: Scholarship for use in freshman, sophomore, junior, senior, or graduate years; not renewable. *Number:* 115–120. *Amount:* $200–$1500.

Eligibility Requirements: Applicant must be enrolled or expecting to enroll full-time at a two-year or four-year or technical institution or university and resident of Alberta. Applicant or parent of applicant must be member of National 4-H. Available to Canadian citizens.

Application Requirements: Application form, essay, recommendations or references, transcript. *Deadline:* May 5.

Contact: Susann Stone, Scholarship Coordinator
Phone: 780-682-2153
Fax: 780-682-3784
E-mail: foundation@4hab.com

AMERICAN BOWLING CONGRESS

http://www.bowl.com/

CHUCK HALL STAR OF TOMORROW SCHOLARSHIP

$1500 scholarship, renewable for up to three years, available to male high school seniors or college students who hold an average bowling score of 175 or greater. Minimum 2.5 GPA required. Must be a current USBC Youth or USBC member in good standing and currently compete in certified events.

Award: Scholarship for use in freshman, sophomore, junior, or senior years; renewable. *Number:* 1. *Amount:* $1500.

Eligibility Requirements: Applicant must be enrolled or expecting to enroll full- or part-time at a two-year or four-year or technical institution or university; male and must have an interest in bowling. Applicant or parent of applicant must be member of Young American Bowling Alliance. Applicant must have 2.5 GPA or higher. Available to U.S. and Canadian citizens.

Application Requirements: Application form, essay, recommendations or references, self-addressed stamped envelope with application, transcript. *Deadline:* October 1.

Contact: Ed Gocha, Scholarship Administrator
Phone: 800-514-2695 Ext. 3343
Fax: 414-423-3014
E-mail: smart@bowl.com

AMERICAN FEDERATION OF STATE, COUNTY, AND MUNICIPAL EMPLOYEES

http://www.afscme.org/

AMERICAN FEDERATION OF STATE, COUNTY, AND MUNICIPAL EMPLOYEES SCHOLARSHIP PROGRAM

Scholarship for family dependents of American Federation of State, County, and Municipal Employees members. Must be a graduating high school senior planning to pursue postsecondary education at a four-year institution. Submit proof of parent's membership. Renewable award of $2000.

Award: Scholarship for use in freshman, sophomore, junior, or senior years; renewable. *Number:* 13. *Amount:* $2000.

Eligibility Requirements: Applicant must be high school student and planning to enroll or expecting to enroll full-time at a four-year institution or university. Applicant or parent of applicant must be member of American Federation of State, County, and Municipal Employees. Available to U.S. citizens.

Application Requirements: Application form, essay, recommendations or references, test scores, transcript. *Deadline:* December 31.

Contact: Philip Allen, Scholarship Coordinator
Phone: 202-429-1250
Fax: 202-429-1293
E-mail: pallen@asscme.org

UNION PLUS CREDIT CARD SCHOLARSHIP PROGRAM

One-time award for AFSCME members, their spouses and dependent children. Graduate students and grandchildren are not eligible.

Award: Scholarship for use in freshman, sophomore, junior, or senior years; not renewable. *Amount:* $500–$4000.

Eligibility Requirements: Applicant must be enrolled or expecting to enroll full-time at a two-year or four-year or technical institution or university. Applicant or parent of applicant must be member of American Federation of State, County, and Municipal Employees. Available to U.S. citizens.

Application Requirements: Application form, driver's license, essay, recommendations or references, transcript. *Deadline:* January 31.

Contact: Philip Allen, Scholarship Coordinator
Phone: 202-429-1250
Fax: 202-429-1293
E-mail: pallen@asscme.org

AMERICAN FEDERATION OF TEACHERS

http://www.aft.org/

ROBERT G. PORTER SCHOLARS PROGRAM-AMERICAN FEDERATION OF TEACHERS DEPENDENTS

Scholarship of up to $8000 for high school seniors who are dependents of AFT members. Must submit transcript, test scores, essay, and recommendations with application. Must be U.S. citizen.

Award: Scholarship for use in freshman year; renewable. *Number:* 4. *Amount:* $8000.

Eligibility Requirements: Applicant must be high school student and planning to enroll or expecting to enroll full-time at a four-year institution or university. Applicant or parent of applicant must be member of American Federation of Teachers. Applicant or parent of applicant must have employment or volunteer experience in nursing, teaching/education. Available to U.S. citizens.

Application Requirements: Application form, community service, essay, recommendations or references, test scores, transcript. *Deadline:* March 31.

Contact: Ms. Bernadette Bailey, Scholarship Coordinator
Phone: 202-879-4481
E-mail: bbailey@aft.org

AMERICAN FOREIGN SERVICE ASSOCIATION

http://www.afsa.org/

AMERICAN FOREIGN SERVICE ASSOCIATION (AFSA) FINANCIAL AID AWARD PROGRAM

Need-based financial aid scholarship program is open only to students whose parents are members of The American Foreign Service Association (AFSA). A parent who is in the Civil Service or in the Military, will not qualify the student. The student must attend school full-time as an undergraduate at a two- or four-year accredited college, university, community college, art school, or conservatory. Must maintain a 2.0 GPA and have demonstrated financial need by completing the CSS PROFILE and submitting transcripts.

Award: Scholarship for use in freshman, sophomore, junior, or senior years; not renewable. *Number:* 50–60. *Amount:* $1000–$3500.

Eligibility Requirements: Applicant must be Asian/Pacific Islander; age 18-23; enrolled or expecting to enroll full-time at a two-year or four-year institution or university and single. Applicant or parent of applicant must be member of American Foreign Service Association. Applicant must have 2.5 GPA or higher. Available to U.S. citizens.

Application Requirements: Application form, application form may be submitted online (http://www.afsa.org/scholar), CSS profile, financial need analysis, transcript. *Deadline:* February 6.

Contact: Lori Dec, Scholarship Director
American Foreign Service Association
2101 E Street, NW
Washington, DC 20037
Phone: 202-944-5504
Fax: 202-338-8244
E-mail: scholar@afsa.org

AMERICAN LEGION AUXILIARY DEPARTMENT OF CALIFORNIA

http://www.calegionaux.org/

AMERICAN LEGION AUXILIARY DEPARTMENT OF CALIFORNIA JUNIOR SCHOLARSHIP

Award for undergraduate students. Must be a California resident. Must have consecutive membership as a Junior for three years and be current with membership in the American Legion Auxiliary.

Award: Scholarship for use in freshman year; not renewable. *Number:* 1. *Amount:* $300–$1000.

Eligibility Requirements: Applicant must be high school student; planning to enroll or expecting to enroll full- or part-time at a four-year institution or university and resident of California. Applicant or parent of applicant must be member of American Legion or Auxiliary. Available to U.S. citizens. Applicant or parent must meet one or more of the following requirements: Army experience; retired from active duty; disabled or killed as a result of military service; prisoner of war; or missing in action.

Application Requirements: Application form. *Deadline:* April 13.

Contact: Theresa Jacob, Secretary/Treasurer
> *Phone:* 415-862-5092
> *Fax:* 415-861-8365
> *E-mail:* calegionaux@calegionaux.org

AMERICAN LEGION AUXILIARY DEPARTMENT OF CONNECTICUT

http://www.ct.legion.org/

AMERICAN LEGION AUXILIARY DEPARTMENT OF CONNECTICUT MEMORIAL EDUCATIONAL GRANT

Half the number of available grants are awarded to children of veterans who are also residents of CT. Remaining grants awarded to child or grandchild of a member (or member at time of death) of the CT Departments of the American Legion/American Legion Auxiliary, regardless of residency; or are members of the CT Departments of the American Legion Auxiliary/Sons of the American Legion, regardless of residency. Contact local unit President. Must include list of community service activities.

Award: Grant for use in freshman, sophomore, junior, or senior years; not renewable. *Number:* 4. *Amount:* $500.

Eligibility Requirements: Applicant must be age 16-23 and enrolled or expecting to enroll full-time at a two-year or four-year or technical institution or university. Applicant or parent of applicant must be member of American Legion or Auxiliary. Available to U.S. citizens. Applicant must have general military experience.

Application Requirements: Application form, community service, essay, financial need analysis, recommendations or references, self-addressed stamped envelope with application, transcript. *Deadline:* March 10.

Contact: Rita Barylski, State Secretary
> *Phone:* 860-721-5945
> *E-mail:* ctalahq@juno.com

AMERICAN LEGION AUXILIARY DEPARTMENT OF CONNECTICUT PAST PRESIDENTS' PARLEY MEMORIAL EDUCATION GRANT

The program gives preference a child or grandchild of an ex-service woman, who was or is a member of the CT departments of the American Legion/American Legion Auxiliary. In the event of a deficiency of preferred applicants, award may be granted to child or grandchild of a member of the CT Departments of the American Legion/American Legion Auxiliary or Sons of the American Legion. Minimum three-year membership required, or three years prior to death. Contact local unit President. Must include list of community service activities.

Award: Grant for use in freshman, sophomore, junior, or senior years; not renewable. *Number:* 4. *Amount:* up to $500.

Eligibility Requirements: Applicant must be age 16-23; enrolled or expecting to enroll full-time at a two-year or four-year or technical institution or university and resident of Connecticut. Applicant or parent of applicant must be member of American Legion or Auxiliary. Available to U.S. citizens. Applicant must have general military experience.

Application Requirements: Application form, community service, financial need analysis, list of school and community activities, recommendations or references, test scores, transcript. *Deadline:* March 10.

Contact: Rita Barylski, State Secretary
> *Phone:* 860-721-5945
> *E-mail:* ctalahq@juno.com

AMERICAN LEGION AUXILIARY DEPARTMENT OF FLORIDA

http://www.alafl.org/

AMERICAN LEGION AUXILIARY DEPARTMENT OF FLORIDA MEMORIAL SCHOLARSHIP

Scholarship for a member, daughter, or granddaughter of a member of Florida American Legion Auxiliary with a minimum three-year membership. Award for Florida resident for undergraduate study in Florida school. Minimum 2.5 GPA required.

Award: Scholarship for use in freshman, sophomore, junior, or senior years; renewable. *Number:* 1–6. *Amount:* $500–$1000.

Eligibility Requirements: Applicant must be enrolled or expecting to enroll full-time at a two-year or four-year or technical institution or university; female; resident of Florida and studying in Florida. Applicant or parent of applicant must be member of American Legion or Auxiliary. Applicant must have 2.5 GPA or higher. Available to U.S. citizens. Applicant or parent must meet one or more of the following requirements: general military experience; retired from active duty; disabled or killed as a result of military service; prisoner of war; or missing in action.

Application Requirements: Application form, financial need analysis, recommendations or references, transcript. *Deadline:* March 1.

Contact: Robin Briere, Department Secretary and Treasurer
> *Phone:* 407-293-7411
> *Fax:* 407-299-6522
> *E-mail:* contact@alafl.org

AMERICAN LEGION AUXILIARY DEPARTMENT OF MARYLAND

http://www.alamd.org/

AMERICAN LEGION AUXILIARY DEPARTMENT OF MARYLAND GIRL SCOUT ACHIEVEMENT AWARD

Scholarship available to a Girl Scout who has received the Girl Scout Gold Award. Must be a senior in high school, an active member of her religious institution, and must have received the appropriate religious emblem, Cadette or Senior Scout level.

Award: Scholarship for use in freshman year; not renewable. *Number:* 1. *Amount:* $500.

Eligibility Requirements: Applicant must be high school student; planning to enroll or expecting to enroll full-time at a four-year institution or university and female. Applicant or parent of applicant must be member of Girl Scouts. Available to U.S. citizens.

Application Requirements: Application form, essay, recommendations or references, transcript. *Deadline:* April 1.

Contact: Pamela Miller, Secretary
> *Phone:* 410-242-9519
> *E-mail:* hq@alamd.org

AMERICAN LEGION AUXILIARY DEPARTMENT OF MISSOURI

http://www.missourilegion.org/

AMERICAN LEGION AUXILIARY DEPARTMENT OF MISSOURI LELA MURPHY SCHOLARSHIP

Scholarship of $500 for high school graduate. $250 will be awarded each semester. Applicant must be Missouri resident and the granddaughter or great-granddaughter of a living or deceased Auxiliary member. Sponsoring unit and department must validate application.

Award: Scholarship for use in freshman year; not renewable. *Number:* 1. *Amount:* $500.

Eligibility Requirements: Applicant must be high school student; planning to enroll or expecting to enroll full-time at a two-year or four-year or technical institution or university; female and resident of Missouri. Applicant or parent of applicant must be member of American Legion or Auxiliary. Available to U.S. citizens. Applicant or parent must meet one or more of the following requirements: general military experience; retired from active duty; disabled or killed as a result of military service; prisoner of war; or missing in action.

Application Requirements: Application form. *Deadline:* March 1.

Contact: Karen Larson, Department Secretary/Treasurer
Phone: 573-636-9133
E-mail: dptmoala@embarqmail.com

AMERICAN LEGION AUXILIARY DEPARTMENT OF MISSOURI NATIONAL PRESIDENT'S SCHOLARSHIP

State-level award. Offers one $500 scholarship. Applicant must complete 50 hours of community service during their high school years. Sponsoring unit and department must validate application. Applicant must be a Missouri resident.

Award: Scholarship for use in freshman year; not renewable. *Number:* 1. *Amount:* $500.

Eligibility Requirements: Applicant must be high school student; planning to enroll or expecting to enroll full-time at a two-year or four-year or technical institution or university and resident of Missouri. Applicant or parent of applicant must be member of American Legion or Auxiliary. Available to U.S. citizens. Applicant or parent must meet one or more of the following requirements: general military experience; retired from active duty; disabled or killed as a result of military service; prisoner of war; or missing in action.

Application Requirements: Application form, community service, resume. *Deadline:* March 1.

Contact: Karen Larson, Department Secretary/Treasurer
Phone: 573-636-9133
E-mail: dptmoala@embarqmail.com

AMERICAN LEGION AUXILIARY DEPARTMENT OF NEBRASKA

http://www.nebraskalegionaux.net/

AMERICAN LEGION AUXILIARY DEPARTMENT OF NEBRASKA RUBY PAUL CAMPAIGN FUND SCHOLARSHIP

One-time award for Nebraska residents who are children, grandchildren, or great-grandchildren of an American Legion Auxiliary member, or who have been members of the American Legion, American Legion Auxiliary, or Sons of the American Legion or Auxiliary for two years prior to issuing the application. Must rank in upper third of class or have minimum 3.0 GPA.

Award: Scholarship for use in freshman year; not renewable. *Number:* 1–3. *Amount:* $100–$300.

Eligibility Requirements: Applicant must be high school student; planning to enroll or expecting to enroll full-time at a four-year institution or university and resident of Nebraska. Applicant or parent of applicant must be member of American Legion or Auxiliary. Applicant must have 3.0 GPA or higher. Available to U.S. citizens. Applicant or parent must meet one or more of the following requirements: general military experience; retired from active duty; disabled or killed as a result of military service; prisoner of war; or missing in action.

Application Requirements: Application form, essay, financial need analysis, letter of acceptance, proof of enrollment, recommendations or references, test scores, transcript. *Deadline:* March 15.

Contact: Jacki O'Neill, Department Secretary
Phone: 402-466-1808
E-mail: neaux@alltel.net

AMERICAN LEGION AUXILIARY DEPARTMENT OF OREGON

http://www.alaoregon.org/

AMERICAN LEGION AUXILIARY DEPARTMENT OF OREGON SPIRIT OF YOUTH SCHOLARSHIP

One-time award available to Oregon high school seniors. Must be a current female junior member of the American Legion Auxiliary with a three-year membership history. Apply through local units.

Award: Scholarship for use in freshman year; not renewable. *Number:* 1. *Amount:* $1000.

Eligibility Requirements: Applicant must be high school student; planning to enroll or expecting to enroll full- or part-time at a four-year institution or university; female and resident of Oregon. Applicant or parent of applicant must be member of American Legion or Auxiliary. Available to U.S. citizens. Applicant or parent must meet one or more of

the following requirements: general military experience; retired from active duty; disabled or killed as a result of military service; prisoner of war; or missing in action.

Application Requirements: Application form, essay, financial need analysis, interview, recommendations or references, transcript. *Deadline:* March 1.

Contact: Virginia Biddle, Secretary/Treasurer
American Legion Auxiliary Department of Oregon
PO Box 1730
Wilsonville, OR 97070
Phone: 503-682-3162
Fax: 503-685-5008
E-mail: alaor@pcez.com

AMERICAN LEGION AUXILIARY DEPARTMENT OF SOUTH DAKOTA

http://www.sdlegion-aux.org/

AMERICAN LEGION AUXILIARY DEPARTMENT OF SOUTH DAKOTA COLLEGE SCHOLARSHIPS

One-time award of $500 to assist veterans children or auxiliary members' children from South Dakota ages 16 to 22 to secure an education at a four-year school. Write for more information.

Award: Scholarship for use in freshman, sophomore, junior, or senior years; not renewable. *Number:* 2. *Amount:* $500.

Eligibility Requirements: Applicant must be age 16-22; enrolled or expecting to enroll full-time at a four-year institution or university and resident of South Dakota. Applicant or parent of applicant must be member of American Legion or Auxiliary. Available to U.S. and non-U.S. citizens. Applicant or parent must meet one or more of the following requirements: general military experience; retired from active duty; disabled or killed as a result of military service; prisoner of war; or missing in action.

Application Requirements: Application form, entry in a contest, essay, financial need analysis, recommendations or references. *Deadline:* March 1.

Contact: Dianne Hudson, Executive Secretary
American Legion Auxiliary Department of South Dakota
PO Box 1819
Sioux Falls, SD 57101
Phone: 605-338-9774
Fax: 605-332-3032
E-mail: legionauxiliary.sd@gmail.com

AMERICAN LEGION AUXILIARY DEPARTMENT OF SOUTH DAKOTA SENIOR SCHOLARSHIP

Award of $400 for current senior member of South Dakota American Legion Auxiliary who has been a member for three years. Based on financial need.

Award: Scholarship for use in freshman year; not renewable. *Number:* 1. *Amount:* $400.

Eligibility Requirements: Applicant must be high school student; planning to enroll or expecting to enroll full-time at a two-year or four-year or technical institution; female and resident of South Dakota. Applicant or parent of applicant must be member of American Legion or Auxiliary. Available to U.S. and non-U.S. citizens. Applicant or parent must meet one or more of the following requirements: general military experience; retired from active duty; disabled or killed as a result of military service; prisoner of war; or missing in action.

Application Requirements: Application form, essay, financial need analysis, recommendations or references, transcript. *Deadline:* March 1.

Contact: Dianne Hudson, Executive Secretary
American Legion Auxiliary Department of South Dakota
PO Box 1819
Sioux Falls, SD 57101
Phone: 605-338-9774
Fax: 605-332-3032
E-mail: legionauxiliary.sd@gmail.com

AMERICAN LEGION AUXILIARY DEPARTMENT OF SOUTH DAKOTA THELMA FOSTER SCHOLARSHIP FOR SENIOR AUXILIARY MEMBERS

One-time award of $300 must be used within twelve months for a current senior member of the South Dakota American Legion Auxiliary who has been a member for three years. Applicant may be a high school senior or older and must be female.

Award: Scholarship for use in freshman year; not renewable. *Number:* 1. *Amount:* $300.

Eligibility Requirements: Applicant must be enrolled or expecting to enroll full-time at a four-year institution or university and female. Applicant or parent of applicant must be member of American Legion or Auxiliary. Available to U.S. and non-U.S. citizens. Applicant or parent must meet one or more of the following requirements: general military experience; retired from active duty; disabled or killed as a result of military service; prisoner of war; or missing in action.

Application Requirements: Application form, essay, financial need analysis, recommendations or references. *Deadline:* March 1.

Contact: Dianne Hudson, Executive Secretary
American Legion Auxiliary Department of South Dakota
PO Box 1819
Sioux Falls, SD 57101
Phone: 605-338-9774
Fax: 605-332-3032
E-mail: legionauxiliary.sd@gmail.com

AMERICAN LEGION AUXILIARY DEPARTMENT OF SOUTH DAKOTA THELMA FOSTER SCHOLARSHIPS FOR JUNIOR AUXILIARY MEMBERS

One-time award of $300 for junior member of the South Dakota American Legion Auxiliary who has held membership for the past three years and holds a membership card for the current year. Must be a senior in high school.

Award: Scholarship for use in freshman year; not renewable. *Number:* 1. *Amount:* $300.

Eligibility Requirements: Applicant must be high school student; planning to enroll or expecting to enroll full-time at a four-year institution or university and female. Applicant or parent of applicant must be member of American Legion or Auxiliary. Available to U.S. and non-U.S. citizens. Applicant or parent must meet one or more of the following requirements: general military experience; retired from active duty; disabled or killed as a result of military service; prisoner of war; or missing in action.

Application Requirements: Application form, essay, financial need analysis, recommendations or references, transcript. *Deadline:* March 1.

Contact: Dianne Hudson, Executive Secretary
American Legion Auxiliary Department of South Dakota
PO Box 1819
Sioux Falls, SD 57101
Phone: 605-338-9774
Fax: 605-332-3032
E-mail: legionauxiliary.sd@gmail.com

AMERICAN LEGION AUXILIARY DEPARTMENT OF SOUTH DAKOTA VOCATIONAL SCHOLARSHIP

One-time award of $500 to assist veterans children or auxiliary members children from South Dakota ages 16 to 22, secure a vocational education beyond the high school level. Write for more information.

Award: Scholarship for use in freshman or sophomore years; not renewable. *Number:* 2. *Amount:* $500.

Eligibility Requirements: Applicant must be age 16-22; enrolled or expecting to enroll full-time at a technical institution; resident of South Dakota and studying in South Dakota. Applicant or parent of applicant must be member of American Legion or Auxiliary. Available to U.S. and non-U.S. citizens. Applicant or parent must meet one or more of the following requirements: general military experience; retired from active duty; disabled or killed as a result of military service; prisoner of war; or missing in action.

Application Requirements: Application form, essay, financial need analysis, recommendations or references. *Deadline:* March 1.

Contact: Dianne Hudson, Executive Secretary
American Legion Auxiliary Department of South Dakota
PO Box 1819
Sioux Falls, SD 57101
Phone: 605-338-9774
Fax: 605-332-3032
E-mail: legionauxiliary.sd@gmail.com

AMERICAN LEGION AUXILIARY DEPARTMENT OF UTAH

http://www.legion-aux.org/

AMERICAN LEGION AUXILIARY DEPARTMENT OF UTAH NATIONAL PRESIDENT'S SCHOLARSHIP

Scholarships available for graduating high school seniors. Must be a resident of Utah, a U.S. citizen, and the direct descendant of a veteran.

Award: Scholarship for use in freshman year; not renewable. *Number:* 15. *Amount:* $1000–$2500.

Eligibility Requirements: Applicant must be high school student; planning to enroll or expecting to enroll full-time at a two-year or four-year or technical institution or university; single and resident of Utah. Applicant or parent of applicant must be member of American Legion or Auxiliary. Available to U.S. citizens. Applicant or parent must meet one or more of the following requirements: general military experience; retired from active duty; disabled or killed as a result of military service; prisoner of war; or missing in action.

Application Requirements: Application form, essay, recommendations or references, statement of parent's military service, test scores, transcript. *Deadline:* March 1.

Contact: Lucia Anderson, Public Relations Manager and Associate Editor
Phone: 801-539-1015
Fax: 801-521-9191
E-mail: landerson@legion-aux.org

AMERICAN LEGION AUXILIARY DEPARTMENT OF WISCONSIN

http://www.amlegionauxwi.org/

AMERICAN LEGION AUXILIARY DEPARTMENT OF WISCONSIN DELLA VAN DEUREN MEMORIAL SCHOLARSHIP

One-time award of $1000 for Wisconsin residents. Applicant or mother of applicant must be a member of an American Legion Auxiliary unit. Must submit certification of an American Legion Auxiliary unit president, copy of proof that veteran was in service (i.e. discharge papers), letters of recommendation, transcripts, and essay. Minimum 3.5 GPA required. Must demonstrate financial need. Applications available on website http://www.amlegionauxwi.org.

Award: Scholarship for use in freshman, sophomore, junior, or senior years; not renewable. *Number:* 2. *Amount:* $1000.

Eligibility Requirements: Applicant must be enrolled or expecting to enroll full- or part-time at a four-year institution or university and resident of Wisconsin. Applicant or parent of applicant must be member of American Legion or Auxiliary. Applicant must have 3.5 GPA or higher. Available to U.S. citizens. Applicant or parent must meet one or more of the following requirements: general military experience; retired from active duty; disabled or killed as a result of military service; prisoner of war; or missing in action.

Application Requirements: Application form, essay, financial need analysis, recommendations or references, transcript. *Deadline:* March 15.

Contact: Bonnie Dorniak, Department Secretary
Phone: 608-745-0124
Fax: 608-745-1947
E-mail: deptsec@amlegionauxwi.org

AMERICAN LEGION AUXILIARY DEPARTMENT OF WISCONSIN H.S. AND ANGELINE LEWIS SCHOLARSHIPS

One-time award of $1000. Applicant must be a daughter, son, wife, or widow of a veteran. Granddaughters and great-granddaughters of veterans who are auxiliary members may also apply. Must submit certification of an American Legion Auxiliary unit president, copy of proof that veteran was in service (i.e. discharge papers), letters of recommendation, transcripts and essay. Must have minimum 3.5 GPA, show financial need, and be a resident of Wisconsin. Applications available on website http://www.amlegionauxwi.org.

Award: Scholarship for use in freshman, sophomore, junior, senior, or graduate years; not renewable. *Number:* 4–6. *Amount:* $1000.

Eligibility Requirements: Applicant must be enrolled or expecting to enroll full- or part-time at a two-year or four-year institution or university and resident of Wisconsin. Applicant or parent of applicant must be member of American Legion or Auxiliary. Applicant must have 3.5 GPA or higher. Available to U.S. citizens. Applicant or parent must meet one or more of the following requirements: general military experience; retired from active duty; disabled or killed as a result of military service; prisoner of war; or missing in action.

Application Requirements: Application form, essay, financial need analysis, recommendations or references, transcript. *Deadline:* March 15.

Contact: Bonnie Dorniak, Department Secretary
    Phone: 608-745-0124
    Fax: 608-745-1947
    E-mail: deptsec@amlegionauxwi.org

AMERICAN LEGION AUXILIARY DEPARTMENT OF WISCONSIN MERIT AND MEMORIAL SCHOLARSHIPS

One-time award of $1000. Applicant must be a daughter, son, wife, or widow of a veteran. Granddaughters and great-granddaughters of veterans who are auxiliary members may also apply. Must submit certification of an American Legion Auxiliary unit president, copy of proof that veteran was in service (i.e. discharge papers), letters of recommendation, transcripts, and essay. Must have minimum 3.5 GPA, show financial need, and be a resident of Wisconsin. Applications available on website http://www.legion-aux.org.

Award: Scholarship for use in freshman, sophomore, junior, or senior years; not renewable. *Number:* 6. *Amount:* $1000.

Eligibility Requirements: Applicant must be enrolled or expecting to enroll full- or part-time at a four-year institution or university and resident of Wisconsin. Applicant or parent of applicant must be member of American Legion or Auxiliary. Applicant must have 3.5 GPA or higher. Available to U.S. citizens. Applicant or parent must meet one or more of the following requirements: general military experience; retired from active duty; disabled or killed as a result of military service; prisoner of war; or missing in action.

Application Requirements: Application form, essay, financial need analysis, recommendations or references, transcript. *Deadline:* March 15.

Contact: Bonnie Dorniak, Department Secretary
    Phone: 608-745-0124
    Fax: 608-745-1947
    E-mail: deptsec@amlegionauxwi.org

AMERICAN LEGION AUXILIARY DEPARTMENT OF WISCONSIN PAST PRESIDENTS' PARLEY HEALTH CAREER SCHOLARSHIPS

One-time award of $1000. Course of study need not be a four-year program. A hospital, university, or technical school program is also acceptable. Applicant must be a daughter, son, wife, or widow of a veteran. Granddaughters and great-granddaughters of veterans who are auxiliary members may also apply. Must submit certification of an American Legion Auxiliary unit president, copy of proof that veteran was in service (i.e. discharge papers), letters of recommendation, transcripts, and essay. Must have minimum 3.5 GPA, show financial need, and be a resident of Wisconsin. Applications available on website http://www.amlegionauxwi.org.

Award: Scholarship for use in freshman, sophomore, junior, or senior years; not renewable. *Number:* 1–2. *Amount:* $750–$1000.

Eligibility Requirements: Applicant must be enrolled or expecting to enroll full- or part-time at a two-year or four-year or technical institution or university and resident of Wisconsin. Applicant or parent of applicant must be member of American Legion or Auxiliary. Applicant must have 3.5 GPA or higher. Available to U.S. citizens. Applicant or parent must meet one or more of the following requirements: general military experience; retired from active duty; disabled or killed as a result of military service; prisoner of war; or missing in action.

Application Requirements: Application form, essay, financial need analysis, recommendations or references, transcript. *Deadline:* March 15.

Contact: Bonnie Dorniak, Department Secretary
    Phone: 608-745-0124
    Fax: 608-745-1947
    E-mail: deptsec@amlegionauxwi.org

AMERICAN LEGION AUXILIARY DEPARTMENT OF WISCONSIN PRESIDENT'S SCHOLARSHIPS

One-time award of $1000. The mother of the applicant or the applicant must be a member of an Auxiliary unit. Must submit certification of an American Legion Auxiliary unit president, copy of proof that veteran was in service (i.e. discharge papers), letters of recommendation, transcripts, and essay. Must have minimum 3.5 GPA, show financial need, and be a resident of Wisconsin. Applications available on website http://www.legion-aux.org.

Award: Scholarship for use in freshman, sophomore, junior, or senior years; not renewable. *Number:* 3. *Amount:* $1000.

Eligibility Requirements: Applicant must be enrolled or expecting to enroll full- or part-time at a four-year institution or university and resident of Wisconsin. Applicant or parent of applicant must be member of American Legion or Auxiliary. Applicant must have 3.5 GPA or higher. Available to U.S. citizens. Applicant or parent must meet one or more of the following requirements: general military experience; retired from active duty; disabled or killed as a result of military service; prisoner of war; or missing in action.

Application Requirements: Application form, essay, financial need analysis, recommendations or references, transcript. *Deadline:* March 15.

Contact: Bonnie Dorniak, Department Secretary
    Phone: 608-745-0124
    Fax: 608-745-1947
    E-mail: deptsec@amlegionauxwi.org

AMERICAN LEGION AUXILIARY NATIONAL HEADQUARTERS

http://www.ALAforVeterans.org

AMERICAN LEGION AUXILIARY NON-TRADITIONAL STUDENTS SCHOLARSHIPS

One-time award for students returning to the classroom after some period of time in which his/her formal schooling was interrupted or a student who has had at least one year of college and is in need of financial assistance to pursue an undergraduate degree. Must be a member of the American Legion, American Legion Auxiliary or Sons of the American Legion.

Award: Scholarship for use in freshman, sophomore, junior, or senior years; not renewable. *Number:* 5. *Amount:* $1000.

Eligibility Requirements: Applicant must be enrolled or expecting to enroll full-time at a two-year or four-year or technical institution or university. Applicant or parent of applicant must be member of American Legion or Auxiliary. Available to U.S. citizens.

Application Requirements: Application form, essay, financial need analysis, recommendations or references, test scores, transcript. *Deadline:* March 1.

Contact: Maria Potts, Program Coordinator
    Phone: 317-569-4555
    E-mail: mpotts@ALAforVeterans.org

AMERICAN LEGION AUXILIARY SPIRIT OF YOUTH SCHOLARSHIPS FOR JUNIOR MEMBERS

Renewable scholarship for graduating high school seniors. Must be a woman and a current junior member of the American Legion Auxiliary, with a three-year membership history. Scholarship is awarded in $1000 increments over four years if applicant meets criteria.

Award: Scholarship for use in freshman, sophomore, junior, or senior years; renewable. *Number:* 5. *Amount:* $1000.

Eligibility Requirements: Applicant must be high school student; planning to enroll or expecting to enroll full-time at a four-year institution or university and female. Applicant or parent of applicant must be member of American Legion or Auxiliary. Applicant must have 3.0 GPA or higher. Available to U.S. citizens.

Application Requirements: Application form, essay, recommendations or references, self-addressed stamped envelope with application, test scores, transcript. *Deadline:* March 1.

Contact: Maria Potts, Program Coordinator
    Phone: 317-569-4555
    E-mail: mpotts@ALAforVeterans.org

AMERICAN LEGION DEPARTMENT OF ARKANSAS

http://www.arklegion.homestead.com/

AMERICAN LEGION DEPARTMENT OF ARKANSAS COUDRET SCHOLARSHIP AWARD

Awards child, grandchild, or great-grandchild of American Legionnaire in good standing for two years. Two-year requirement is waived for Desert Storm and deceased veterans. One-time award for graduating Arkansas high school seniors.

Award: Scholarship for use in freshman year; not renewable. *Number:* 4. *Amount:* $1000.

Eligibility Requirements: Applicant must be high school student; age 16–24; planning to enroll or expecting to enroll full-time at a two-year or four-year or technical institution or university and resident of Arkansas. Applicant or parent of applicant must be member of American Legion or Auxiliary. Applicant must have 2.5 GPA or higher. Available to U.S. citizens. Applicant or parent must meet one or more of the following requirements: general military experience; retired from active duty; disabled or killed as a result of military service; prisoner of war; or missing in action.

Application Requirements: Application form, driver's license, essay, financial need analysis, personal photograph, recommendations or references, transcript. *Deadline:* April 15.

Contact: William Winchell, Department Adjutant
American Legion Department of Arkansas
PO Box 3280
Little Rock, AR 72203-3280
Phone: 501-375-1104
Fax: 501-375-4236
E-mail: alegion@swbell.net

AMERICAN LEGION DEPARTMENT OF IDAHO

http://www.idlegion.home.mindspring.com/

AMERICAN LEGION DEPARTMENT OF IDAHO SCHOLARSHIP

One-time award of $500 to $750 for residents of Idaho studying at an Idaho institution. Must be related to a Idaho American Member.

Award: Scholarship for use in freshman year; not renewable. *Number:* 1–3. *Amount:* $500–$750.

Eligibility Requirements: Applicant must be high school student; planning to enroll or expecting to enroll full-time at a four-year institution or university; resident of Idaho and studying in Idaho. Applicant or parent of applicant must be member of American Legion or Auxiliary. Available to U.S. citizens. Applicant or parent must meet one or more of the following requirements: general military experience; retired from active duty; disabled or killed as a result of military service; prisoner of war; or missing in action.

Application Requirements: Application form, financial need analysis, recommendations or references, resume, self-addressed stamped envelope with application, test scores, transcript. *Deadline:* June 1.

Contact: Jimmie Foster, Adjutant
American Legion Department of Idaho
901 West Warren Street
Boise, ID 83706-3825
Phone: 208-342-7061
Fax: 208-342-1964
E-mail: idlegion@mindspring.com

AMERICAN LEGION DEPARTMENT OF ILLINOIS

http://www.illegion.org/

AMERICAN ESSAY CONTEST SCHOLARSHIP

Scholarship for students in 7th to 12th grades of any accredited Illinois high school. Must write a 500-word essay on selected topic.

Award: Prize for use in freshman year; not renewable. *Number:* up to 60. *Amount:* $100–$1200.

Eligibility Requirements: Applicant must be high school student; planning to enroll or expecting to enroll full- or part-time at a two-year or four-year institution or university; resident of Illinois and must have an interest in writing. Applicant or parent of applicant must be member of American Legion or Auxiliary. Available to U.S. citizens.

Application Requirements: Application form, entry in a contest, essay. *Deadline:* February 1.

Contact: Mr. Gary Jenson, American Legion Department Assistant
Adjutant
American Legion Department of Illinois
2720 East Lincoln Street
Bloomington, IL 61704
Phone: 309-663-0361
Fax: 309-663-5783
E-mail: gjenson@illegion.org

AMERICAN LEGION DEPARTMENT OF ILLINOIS BOY SCOUT/EXPLORER SCHOLARSHIP

Scholarship for a graduating high school senior who is a qualified Boy Scout or Explorer and a resident of Illinois. Must write a 500-word essay on Legion's Americanism and Boy Scout programs.

Award: Scholarship for use in freshman year; not renewable. *Number:* up to 5. *Amount:* $200–$1000.

Eligibility Requirements: Applicant must be high school student; planning to enroll or expecting to enroll full- or part-time at a four-year institution or university; male and resident of Illinois. Applicant or parent of applicant must be member of Boy Scouts. Available to U.S. citizens.

Application Requirements: Application form, entry in a contest, essay. *Deadline:* April 30.

Contact: Mr. Gary Jenson, American Legion Assistant Adjutant
American Legion Department of Illinois
2720 East Lincoln Street
Bloomington, IL 61704
Phone: 309-663-0361
Fax: 309-663-5783
E-mail: gjenson@illegion.org

AMERICAN LEGION DEPARTMENT OF ILLINOIS SCHOLARSHIPS

Awards twenty $1000 scholarships for graduating students of Illinois high schools. May be used at any accredited college, university, trade or technical school. Applicant must be a child or grandchild of members of the American Legion-Illinois. Awards will be based on academic merit and financial need.

Award: Scholarship for use in freshman year; not renewable. *Number:* up to 20. *Amount:* $1000–$1000.

Eligibility Requirements: Applicant must be high school student; planning to enroll or expecting to enroll full- or part-time at a two-year or four-year or technical institution or university and resident of Illinois. Applicant or parent of applicant must be member of American Legion or Auxiliary. Available to U.S. citizens. Applicant or parent must meet one or more of the following requirements: general military experience; retired from active duty; disabled or killed as a result of military service; prisoner of war; or missing in action.

Application Requirements: Application form, financial need analysis, test scores, transcript. *Deadline:* March 15.

Contact: Mr. Gary Jenson, American Legion Assistant Adjutant
American Legion Department of Illinois
2720 East Lincoln Street
Bloomington, IL 61704
Phone: 309-663-0361
Fax: 309-663-5783
E-mail: gjenson@illegion.org

AMERICAN LEGION DEPARTMENT OF INDIANA

http://www.hoosierlegionnaire.org

AMERICAN LEGION FAMILY SCHOLARSHIP

Scholarship open to children and grandchildren of current members of The American Legion, American Legion Auxiliary, and The Sons of the American Legion. Also open to the children and grandchildren of deceased members who were current paid members of the above organizations at the time of their death. Applicants must be attending or planning to attend an Indiana institution of higher education.

Award: Scholarship for use in freshman, sophomore, junior, or senior years; not renewable. *Number:* 5. *Amount:* $1000–$1500.

Eligibility Requirements: Applicant must be enrolled or expecting to enroll full- or part-time at a two-year or four-year or technical institution or university; resident of Indiana and studying in Indiana. Applicant or parent of applicant must be member of American Legion or Auxiliary. Applicant must have 3.5 GPA or higher. Available to U.S. citizens.

Application Requirements: Application form, essay, transcript. *Deadline:* April 1.

Contact: Susan Long, Program Coordinator
Phone: 317-630-1264
Fax: 317-237-9891
E-mail: slong@indlegion.org

AMERICAN LEGION DEPARTMENT OF IOWA

http://www.ialegion.org/

AMERICAN LEGION DEPARTMENT OF IOWA EAGLE SCOUT OF THE YEAR SCHOLARSHIP

Three one-time award for Eagle Scouts who are residents of Iowa. For full-time study only.

Award: Scholarship for use in freshman year; not renewable. *Number:* up to 3. *Amount:* $250–$1000.

Eligibility Requirements: Applicant must be high school student; planning to enroll or expecting to enroll full-time at a two-year or four-year institution or university; male and resident of Iowa. Applicant or parent of applicant must be member of Boy Scouts. Available to U.S. citizens.

Application Requirements: Application form, entry in a contest, recommendations or references. *Deadline:* March 1.

AMERICAN LEGION DEPARTMENT OF KANSAS

http://www.ksamlegion.org/

ALBERT M. LAPPIN SCHOLARSHIP

Scholarship for children of the members of Kansas American Legion or its auxiliary. Membership must have been active for the past three years. The children of deceased members are also eligible if parents' dues were paid at the time of death. Applicant must be a son/daughter of a veteran. Must be high school senior or college freshman or sophomore. Must use award at a Kansas college, university, or trade school.

Award: Scholarship for use in freshman or sophomore years; not renewable. *Number:* 1. *Amount:* $1000.

Eligibility Requirements: Applicant must be enrolled or expecting to enroll full-time at a two-year or four-year or technical institution or university and studying in Kansas. Applicant or parent of applicant must be member of American Legion or Auxiliary. Available to U.S. citizens. Applicant or parent must meet one or more of the following requirements: general military experience; retired from active duty; disabled or killed as a result of military service; prisoner of war; or missing in action.

Application Requirements: Application form, essay, financial need analysis, personal photograph, transcript. *Deadline:* February 15.

Contact: Jim Gravenstein, Chairman, Scholarship Committee
American Legion Department of Kansas
1314 Topeka Boulevard, SW
Topeka, KS 66612
Phone: 785-232-9513
Fax: 785-232-1399

CHARLES W. AND ANNETTE HILL SCHOLARSHIP

Scholarship of $1000 to the descendants of veterans who are American Legion members or American Legion Auxiliary members holding membership for the past three consecutive years. Descendants of deceased members can also apply. Must be high school seniors or college freshmen or sophomores in a Kansas institution. Scholarship for use at an approved college, university, or trade school in Kansas. Must maintain a 3.0 GPA. Disbursement: $500 at beginning each semester for one year.

Award: Scholarship for use in freshman or sophomore years; not renewable. *Number:* 1. *Amount:* $1000.

Eligibility Requirements: Applicant must be enrolled or expecting to enroll full-time at a two-year or four-year or technical institution or university; resident of Kansas and studying in Kansas. Applicant or parent of applicant must be member of American Legion or Auxiliary. Applicant must have 3.0 GPA or higher. Available to U.S. citizens. Applicant or parent must meet one or more of the following requirements: general military experience; retired from active duty; disabled or killed as a result of military service; prisoner of war; or missing in action.

Application Requirements: Application form, essay, latest 1040 income statement of supporting parents, recommendations or references, transcript. *Deadline:* February 15.

Contact: Jim Gravenstein, Chairman, Scholarship Committee
American Legion Department of Kansas
1314 Topeka Boulevard, SW
Topeka, KS 66612
Phone: 785-232-9513
Fax: 785-232-1399

HUGH A. SMITH SCHOLARSHIP FUND

One-year scholarship of $500 to the children of American Legion/Auxiliary members holding membership for the past three consecutive years. Children of a deceased member can also apply. Parent of the applicant must be a veteran. Must be high school seniors or college freshmen or sophomores in a Kansas institution. Scholarship for use at an approved college, university, or trade school in Kansas. Must maintain a C average in college.

Award: Scholarship for use in freshman or sophomore years; not renewable. *Number:* 1. *Amount:* $500.

Eligibility Requirements: Applicant must be enrolled or expecting to enroll full-time at a two-year or four-year or technical institution or university; resident of Kansas and studying in Kansas. Applicant or parent of applicant must be member of American Legion or Auxiliary. Available to U.S. citizens. Applicant or parent must meet one or more of the following requirements: general military experience; retired from active duty; disabled or killed as a result of military service; prisoner of war; or missing in action.

Application Requirements: Application form, financial need analysis, latest 1040 income statement of supporting parents, personal photograph, recommendations or references, transcript. *Deadline:* February 15.

Contact: Jim Gravenstein, Chairman, Scholarship Committee
American Legion Department of Kansas
1314 Topeka Boulevard, SW
Topeka, KS 66612
Phone: 785-232-9513
Fax: 785-232-1399

ROSEDALE POST 346 SCHOLARSHIP

Two scholarships of $1500 each awarded to the children of American Legion members or of American Legion Auxiliary members holding membership for the past three consecutive years. Children of a deceased member can also apply. Parent of the applicant must be a veteran. Must be high school seniors or college freshmen or sophomores in a Kansas institution. Scholarship for use at an approved college, university, or trade school in Kansas. Must maintain a C average in college.

Award: Scholarship for use in freshman or sophomore years; not renewable. *Number:* 2. *Amount:* $1500.

Eligibility Requirements: Applicant must be enrolled or expecting to enroll full-time at a two-year or four-year or technical institution or university; resident of Kansas and studying in Kansas. Applicant or parent of applicant must be member of American Legion or Auxiliary. Available to U.S. citizens. Applicant or parent must meet one or more of the following requirements: general military experience; retired from active duty; disabled or killed as a result of military service; prisoner of war; or missing in action.

Application Requirements: Application form, essay, financial need analysis, latest 1040 income statement of supporting parents), personal photograph, recommendations or references, transcript. *Deadline:* February 15.

Contact: Jim Gravenstein, Chairman, Scholarship Committee
American Legion Department of Kansas
1314 Topeka Boulevard, SW
Topeka, KS 66612
Phone: 785-232-9513
Fax: 785-232-1399

TED AND NORA ANDERSON SCHOLARSHIPS

Scholarship of $250 for each semester (one year only) given to the children of American Legion members or Auxiliary members who are holding membership for the past three consecutive years. Children of a deceased member can also apply. Parent of the applicant must be a veteran. Must be high school seniors or college freshmen or sophomores in a Kansas institution. Scholarship for use at an approved college, university, or trade school in Kansas. Must maintain a C average in college.

Award: Scholarship for use in freshman or sophomore years; not renewable. *Number:* 4. *Amount:* $250–$500.

Eligibility Requirements: Applicant must be enrolled or expecting to enroll full-time at a two-year or four-year or technical institution or university; resident of Kansas and studying in Kansas. Applicant or parent of applicant must be member of American Legion or Auxiliary. Available to U.S. citizens. Applicant or parent must meet one or more of the following requirements: general military experience; retired from active duty; disabled or killed as a result of military service; prisoner of war; or missing in action.

Application Requirements: Application form, essay, financial need analysis, personal photograph, recommendations or references, transcript. *Deadline:* February 15.

Contact: Jim Gravenstein, Chairman, Scholarship Committee
American Legion Department of Kansas
1314 Topeka Boulevard, SW
Topeka, KS 66612
Phone: 785-232-9315
Fax: 785-232-1399

AMERICAN LEGION DEPARTMENT OF MAINE

http://www.mainelegion.org/

JAMES V. DAY SCHOLARSHIP

One-time $500 award for a Maine resident whose parent is a member of the American Legion or Auxiliary in Maine, or is a member of Sons of the American Legion in Maine. Must be a U.S. citizen. Based on character and financial need.

Award: Scholarship for use in freshman, sophomore, junior, or senior years; not renewable. *Number:* 1–2. *Amount:* up to $500.

Eligibility Requirements: Applicant must be enrolled or expecting to enroll full-time at a two-year or four-year or technical institution or university and resident of Maine. Applicant or parent of applicant must be member of American Legion or Auxiliary. Available to U.S. citizens. Applicant or parent must meet one or more of the following requirements: general military experience; retired from active duty; disabled or killed as a result of military service; prisoner of war; or missing in action.

Application Requirements: Application form, recommendations or references, transcript. *Deadline:* May 1.

Contact: Mr. Lloyd Woods, Department Adjutant
American Legion Department of Maine
PO Box 900
Waterville, ME 04903
Phone: 207-873-3229
Fax: 207-872-0501
E-mail: legionme@mainelegion.org

AMERICAN LEGION DEPARTMENT OF MINNESOTA

http://www.mnlegion.org/

AMERICAN LEGION DEPARTMENT OF MINNESOTA MEMORIAL SCHOLARSHIP

Scholarship available to Minnesota residents who are dependents of members of the Minnesota American Legion or auxiliary. One-time award of $500 for study at a Minnesota institution or neighboring state with reciprocating agreement. See website for application information http://www.mnlegion.org.

Award: Scholarship for use in freshman, sophomore, junior, or senior years; not renewable. *Number:* 6. *Amount:* $500.

Eligibility Requirements: Applicant must be enrolled or expecting to enroll full- or part-time at a two-year or four-year or technical institution or university; resident of Minnesota and studying in Iowa, Minnesota, North Dakota, South Dakota, Wisconsin. Applicant or parent of applicant must be member of American Legion or Auxiliary. Available to U.S. citizens. Applicant or parent must meet one or more of the following requirements: general military experience; retired from active duty; disabled or killed as a result of military service; prisoner of war; or missing in action.

Application Requirements: Application form, essay, financial need analysis, recommendations or references, transcript. *Deadline:* April 1.

Contact: Jennifer Kelley, Program Coordinator
American Legion Department of Minnesota
20 West 12th Street, Room 300-A
St. Paul, MN 55155
Phone: 651-291-1800
Fax: 651-291-1057
E-mail: department@mnlegion.org

MINNESOTA LEGIONNAIRES INSURANCE TRUST SCHOLARSHIP

Scholarship for Minnesota residents who are veterans or dependents of veterans. One-time award of $500 for study at a Minnesota institution or neighboring state with reciprocating agreement. All applications must be approved and recommended by a post of the American Legion. See website for application information http://www.mnlegion.org.

Award: Scholarship for use in freshman, sophomore, junior, or senior years; not renewable. *Number:* 3. *Amount:* $500.

Eligibility Requirements: Applicant must be enrolled or expecting to enroll full- or part-time at a two-year or four-year or technical institution or university; resident of Minnesota and studying in Iowa, Minnesota, North Dakota, South Dakota, Wisconsin. Applicant or parent of applicant must be member of American Legion or Auxiliary. Available to U.S. citizens. Applicant or parent must meet one or more of the following requirements: general military experience; retired from active duty; disabled or killed as a result of military service; prisoner of war; or missing in action.

Application Requirements: Application form, essay, financial need analysis, recommendations or references, transcript. *Deadline:* April 1.

Contact: Jennifer Kelley, Program Coordinator
American Legion Department of Minnesota
20 West 12th Street, Room 300-A
St. Paul, MN 55155
Phone: 651-291-1800
Fax: 651-291-1057
E-mail: department@mnlegion.org

AMERICAN LEGION DEPARTMENT OF MISSOURI

http://www.missourilegion.org/

CHARLES L. BACON MEMORIAL SCHOLARSHIP

Two awards of $500 are given to members of The American Legion, the American Legion Auxiliary, or the Sons of The American Legion, or a descendant of a member of any thereof. Applicants must be unmarried Missouri resident below age 21, and must use the scholarship as a full-time student in an accredited college or university in Missouri. Must submit proof of American Legion membership.

Award: Scholarship for use in freshman year; not renewable. *Number:* 2. *Amount:* $500.

Eligibility Requirements: Applicant must be high school student; planning to enroll or expecting to enroll full-time at a two-year or four-year institution or university; single and resident of Missouri. Applicant or parent of applicant must be member of American Legion or Auxiliary. Available to U.S. citizens. Applicant or parent must meet one or more of the following requirements: general military experience; retired from active duty; disabled or killed as a result of military service; prisoner of war; or missing in action.

Application Requirements: Application form, discharge certificate, financial need analysis, test scores. *Deadline:* April 20.

Contact: John Doane, Chairman
Phone: 417-924-8596
Fax: 573-225-1406
E-mail: info@missourilegion.org

AMERICAN LEGION DEPARTMENT OF NEBRASKA

http://www.nebraskalegion.net/

EAGLE SCOUT OF THE YEAR SCHOLARSHIP

Scholarship of $1000 is awarded to one recipient each year by The American Legion, Department of Nebraska. The Department recipient is then entered into The American Legion National Eagle Scout of the Year and is eligible to receive a $10,000 scholarship, or one of three second place scholarships of $2500.

Award: Scholarship for use in freshman, sophomore, junior, or senior years; not renewable. *Number:* 1. *Amount:* $1000–$10,000.

Eligibility Requirements: Applicant must be enrolled or expecting to enroll full- or part-time at a two-year or four-year or technical institution or university; male and resident of Nebraska. Applicant or parent of applicant must be member of Boy Scouts. Available to U.S. citizens.

Application Requirements: Application form, community service, personal photograph, recommendations or references, transcript. *Deadline:* March 1.

Contact: Brent Hagel-Pitt, Activities Director
American Legion Department of Nebraska
PO Box 5205
Lincoln, NE 68505-0205
Phone: 402-464-6338
Fax: 402-464-6330
E-mail: actdirlegion@windstream.net

MAYNARD JENSEN AMERICAN LEGION MEMORIAL SCHOLARSHIP

Scholarship for dependents or grandchildren of members, prisoner-of-war, missing-in-action veterans, killed-in-action veterans, or any deceased veterans of the American Legion. One-time award is based on academic achievement and financial need for Nebraska residents attending Nebraska institutions. Several scholarships of $500 each. Must have minimum 2.5 GPA and must submit school certification of GPA.

Award: Scholarship for use in freshman, sophomore, junior, or senior years; not renewable. *Number:* 1–10. *Amount:* $500.

Eligibility Requirements: Applicant must be enrolled or expecting to enroll full-time at a two-year or four-year or technical institution or university; resident of Nebraska and studying in Nebraska. Applicant or parent of applicant must be member of American Legion or Auxiliary. Applicant must have 2.5 GPA or higher. Available to U.S. citizens. Applicant or parent must meet one or more of the following requirements: general military experience; retired from active duty; disabled or killed as a result of military service; prisoner of war; or missing in action.

Application Requirements: Application form, financial need analysis, test scores. *Deadline:* March 1.

Contact: David Salak, Adjutant
American Legion Department of Nebraska
PO Box 5205
Lincoln, NE 68505-0205
Phone: 402-464-6338
Fax: 402-464-6330
E-mail: nebraska@legion.org

AMERICAN LEGION DEPARTMENT OF NEW JERSEY

http://www.njamericanlegion.org/

AMERICAN LEGION DEPARTMENT OF NEW JERSEY SCHOLARSHIP

Applicant must be a natural or adopted descendant of a member of The American Legion, Department of New Jersey. Applicant must be a member of the graduating class of high school including Vo-tech.

Award: Scholarship for use in freshman, sophomore, junior, or senior years; not renewable. *Number:* 8. *Amount:* $1000–$4000.

Eligibility Requirements: Applicant must be high school student and planning to enroll or expecting to enroll full-time at a two-year or four-year or technical institution or university. Applicant or parent of applicant must be member of American Legion or Auxiliary. Available to U.S.

citizens. Applicant or parent must meet one or more of the following requirements: Army experience; retired from active duty; disabled or killed as a result of military service; prisoner of war; or missing in action.

Application Requirements: Application form, community service, essay, recommendations or references, transcript. *Deadline:* February 15.

Contact: John Baker, Department Adjutant
Phone: 609-695-5418
Fax: 609-394-1532
E-mail: adjutant@njamericanlegion.org

AMERICAN LEGION DEPARTMENT OF OHIO

http://www.ohiolegion.com/

OHIO AMERICAN LEGION SCHOLARSHIPS

One-time award for full-time students attending an accredited institution. Open to students of any postsecondary academic year. Must have minimum 3.0 GPA. Must be a member of the American Legion, a direct descendent of a Legionnaire (living or deceased), or surviving spouse or child of a deceased U.S. military person who died on active duty or of injuries received on active duty.

Award: Scholarship for use in freshman, sophomore, junior, or senior years; not renewable. *Number:* 15–18. *Amount:* $2000–$3000.

Eligibility Requirements: Applicant must be enrolled or expecting to enroll full-time at a two-year or four-year or technical institution or university. Applicant or parent of applicant must be member of American Legion or Auxiliary. Applicant must have 3.0 GPA or higher. Available to U.S. and non-U.S. citizens. Applicant or parent must meet one or more of the following requirements: general military experience; retired from active duty; disabled or killed as a result of military service; prisoner of war; or missing in action.

Application Requirements: Application form, resume, transcript. *Deadline:* April 15.

Contact: Donald Lanthorn, Service Director
American Legion Department of Ohio
60 Big Run Road, PO Box 8007
Delaware, OH 43015
Phone: 740-362-7478
Fax: 740-362-1429
E-mail: dlanthorn@iwaynet.net

AMERICAN LEGION DEPARTMENT OF PENNSYLVANIA

http://www.pa-legion.com/

JOSEPH P. GAVENONIS COLLEGE SCHOLARSHIP (PLAN I)

Scholarships for Pennsylvania residents seeking a four-year degree from a Pennsylvania college or university. Must be the child of a member of a Pennsylvania American Legion post. Must be a graduating high school senior. Award amount and number of awards determined annually. Renewable award. Must maintain 2.5 GPA in college. Total number of awards varies.

Award: Scholarship for use in freshman year; renewable. *Amount:* $500–$1000.

Eligibility Requirements: Applicant must be high school student; planning to enroll or expecting to enroll full-time at a four-year institution or university; resident of Pennsylvania and studying in Pennsylvania. Applicant or parent of applicant must be member of American Legion or Auxiliary. Applicant must have 2.5 GPA or higher. Available to U.S. citizens.

Application Requirements: Application form, financial need analysis, test scores, transcript. *Deadline:* May 30.

Contact: Debbie Watson, Emblem Sales Supervisor
American Legion Department of Pennsylvania
PO Box 2324
Harrisburg, PA 17105-2324
Phone: 717-730-9100
Fax: 717-975-2836
E-mail: hq@pa-legion.com

AMERICAN LEGION DEPARTMENT OF TENNESSEE

http://www.tennesseelegion.org/

AMERICAN LEGION DEPARTMENT OF TENNESSEE EAGLE SCOUT OF THE YEAR

$1500 scholarship for graduating high school seniors who are Eagle Scouts, enrolled either part-time or full-time for study in accredited colleges or universities. Deadline varies.

Award: Scholarship for use in freshman, sophomore, junior, or senior years; renewable. *Number:* 1. *Amount:* $1500.

Eligibility Requirements: Applicant must be high school student; age 15-18; planning to enroll or expecting to enroll full- or part-time at a four-year institution or university; male and resident of Tennessee. Applicant or parent of applicant must be member of Boy Scouts. Available to U.S. citizens.

Application Requirements: Application form, community service, personal photograph, portfolio, resume, transcript. *Deadline:* varies.

Contact: Darlene Burgess, Executive Secretary
Phone: 615-391-5088
E-mail: taltnadj@bellsouth.net

AMERICAN LEGION DEPARTMENT OF VERMONT

http://www.vtlegion.org

AMERICAN LEGION EAGLE SCOUT OF THE YEAR

Awarded to the Boy Scout chosen for outstanding service to his religious institution, school, and community. Must receive the award and reside in Vermont.

Award: Scholarship for use in freshman year; not renewable. *Number:* 1. *Amount:* $1000.

Eligibility Requirements: Applicant must be high school student; planning to enroll or expecting to enroll full-time at a two-year or four-year or technical institution or university and resident of Vermont. Applicant or parent of applicant must be member of Boy Scouts. Applicant or parent of applicant must have employment or volunteer experience in community service. Available to U.S. citizens.

Application Requirements: Application form, community service, essay, personal photograph. *Deadline:* March 1.

Contact: Francis Killay, Chairman
American Legion Department of Vermont
PO Box 396
Montpelier, VT 05601-0396
Phone: 802-223-7131
Fax: 802-223-0318
E-mail: alvthq@myfairpoint.net

AMERICAN LEGION DEPARTMENT OF WASHINGTON

http://www.walegion.org/

AMERICAN LEGION DEPARTMENT OF WASHINGTON CHILDREN AND YOUTH SCHOLARSHIPS

One-time award for the son or daughter of a Washington American Legion or Auxiliary member, living or deceased. Must be high school senior and Washington resident planning to attend an accredited institution of higher education in Washington. Award based on need.

Award: Scholarship for use in freshman year; not renewable. *Number:* 2. *Amount:* $1500–$2500.

Eligibility Requirements: Applicant must be high school student; planning to enroll or expecting to enroll full- or part-time at a four-year institution or university; resident of Washington and studying in Washington. Applicant or parent of applicant must be member of American Legion or Auxiliary. Available to U.S. citizens. Applicant or parent must meet one or more of the following requirements: general military experience; retired from active duty; disabled or killed as a result of military service; prisoner of war; or missing in action.

Application Requirements: Application form, financial need analysis, transcript. *Deadline:* April 1.

Contact: Marc O'Connor, Chairman, Children and Youth Commission
Phone: 360-423-9542
E-mail: oconnorred@comcast.net

AMERICAN LEGION DEPARTMENT OF WEST VIRGINIA

http://www.wvlegion.org/

SONS OF THE AMERICAN LEGION WILLIAM F. "BILL" JOHNSON MEMORIAL SCHOLARSHIP

Applicant is required to write an essay based on a different question each year. Award is given during the second semester of college provided the winner has passing grades in the first semester. Must submit a copy of passing GPA of their first semester of college. Must be a resident of West Virginia and the child or grandchild of a member of The American Legion.

Award: Scholarship for use in freshman year; not renewable. *Number:* up to 2. *Amount:* up to $1500.

Eligibility Requirements: Applicant must be high school student; planning to enroll or expecting to enroll full-time at a two-year or four-year institution or university and resident of West Virginia. Applicant or parent of applicant must be member of American Legion or Auxiliary. Available to U.S. citizens. Applicant or parent must meet one or more of the following requirements: general military experience; retired from active duty; disabled or killed as a result of military service; prisoner of war; or missing in action.

Application Requirements: Application form, essay, transcript. *Deadline:* May 15.

Contact: Ms. Lois Moles, Executive Secretary
American Legion Department of West Virginia
2016 Kanawha Boulevard East, PO Box 3191
Charleston, WV 25332-3191
Phone: 304-343-7591
Fax: 304-343-7592
E-mail: wvlegion@suddenlinkmail.com

AMERICAN POSTAL WORKERS UNION

http://www.apwu.org/

E.C. HALLBECK SCHOLARSHIP FUND

Scholarship for children of American Postal Workers Union members. Applicant must be a child, grandchild, stepchild, or legally adopted child of an active member, Retirees Department member, or deceased member of American Postal Workers Union. Must be a senior attending high school or other corresponding secondary school. Must be 18 years or older. Recipient must attend accredited community college or university as a full-time student. Scholarship will be $1000 for each year of four consecutive years of college. Scholarship will provide five area winners. For additional information and to download applications go to website http://www.apwu.org.

Award: Scholarship for use in freshman year; renewable. *Number:* 5. *Amount:* $1000.

Eligibility Requirements: Applicant must be high school student and planning to enroll or expecting to enroll full-time at a two-year or four-year or technical institution or university. Applicant or parent of applicant must be member of American Postal Workers Union. Applicant or parent of applicant must have employment or volunteer experience in federal/postal service. Available to U.S. citizens.

Application Requirements: Application form, essay, recommendations or references, test scores, transcript. *Deadline:* March 15.

Contact: Terry Stapleton, Secretary and Treasurer
American Postal Workers Union
1300 L Street, NW
Washington, DC 20005
Phone: 202-842-4215
Fax: 202-842-8530

VOCATIONAL SCHOLARSHIP PROGRAM

A scholarship for a child, grandchild, stepchild, or legally adopted child of an active member, Retiree's Department member, or deceased member of the American Postal Workers Union. Applicant must be a senior attending high school who plans on attending an accredited vocational school or community college vocational program as a full-time student.

The award is $1000 per year consecutively or until completion of the course. For additional information see website http://www.apwu.org.

Award: Scholarship for use in freshman year; renewable. *Number:* 5. *Amount:* $1000.

Eligibility Requirements: Applicant must be high school student and planning to enroll or expecting to enroll full-time at a four-year institution or university. Applicant or parent of applicant must be member of American Postal Workers Union. Applicant or parent of applicant must have employment or volunteer experience in federal/postal service. Available to U.S. citizens.

Application Requirements: Application form, essay, recommendations or references, test scores, transcript. *Deadline:* March 15.

Contact: Terry Stapleton, Secretary and Treasurer
American Postal Workers Union
1300 L Street, NW
Washington, DC 20005
Phone: 202-842-4215
Fax: 202-842-8530

AMERICAN QUARTER HORSE FOUNDATION (AQHF)

http://www.aqha.com/foundation

AQHF GENERAL SCHOLARSHIP

Ideal candidates are current AQHA or AQHYA members.

Award: Scholarship for use in freshman, sophomore, junior, senior, graduate, or postgraduate years; renewable. *Number:* 1–15. *Amount:* $4000.

Eligibility Requirements: Applicant must be enrolled or expecting to enroll full-time at a two-year or four-year or technical institution or university. Applicant or parent of applicant must be member of American Quarter Horse Association. Applicant must have 2.5 GPA or higher. Available to U.S. and non-U.S. citizens.

Application Requirements: Application form, recommendations or references, transcript. *Deadline:* December 1.

AQHF YOUTH SCHOLARSHIPS

Ideal candidates are members of AQHA or AQHYA who have completed a minimum of three years cumulative membership; exhibit an affinity for the American Quarter Horse, and demonstrate leadership potential.

Award: Scholarship for use in freshman, sophomore, junior, senior, or graduate years; renewable. *Number:* 1–15. *Amount:* $8000.

Eligibility Requirements: Applicant must be high school student and planning to enroll or expecting to enroll full-time at a two-year or four-year or technical institution or university. Applicant or parent of applicant must be member of American Quarter Horse Association. Applicant must have 3.5 GPA or higher. Available to U.S. and non-U.S. citizens.

Application Requirements: Application form, recommendations or references, transcript. *Deadline:* December 1.

ARIZONA QUARTER HORSE YOUTH SCHOLARSHIP

Ideal candidate is an AQHA or AQHYA member from Arizona who is a current or previous member of the Arizona Quarter Horse Youth Association, and must be actively involved with AzQHA.

Award: Scholarship for use in freshman, sophomore, junior, senior, or graduate years; renewable. *Number:* 1. *Amount:* $5000.

Eligibility Requirements: Applicant must be enrolled or expecting to enroll full-time at a two-year or four-year or technical institution or university and resident of Arizona. Applicant or parent of applicant must be member of American Quarter Horse Association. Applicant must have 2.5 GPA or higher. Available to U.S. citizens.

Application Requirements: Application form, recommendations or references, transcript. *Deadline:* December 1.

ARIZONA QUARTER RACING SCHOLARSHIP

Ideal candidate is an AQHA or AQHYA member from Arizona who has experience within, or is seeking a career in the racing industry. Recipient may specialize in veterinary medicine, racetrack management or other related field.

Award: Scholarship for use in freshman, sophomore, junior, senior, graduate, or postgraduate years; not renewable. *Number:* 1. *Amount:* $500.

Eligibility Requirements: Applicant must be enrolled or expecting to enroll full-time at a two-year or four-year or technical institution or university and resident of Arizona. Applicant or parent of applicant must be member of American Quarter Horse Association. Applicant must have 2.5 GPA or higher. Available to U.S. citizens.

Application Requirements: Application form, proof of residency, recommendations or references, transcript. *Deadline:* December 1.

BOON SAN KITTY SCHOLARSHIP

Ideal candidate is a current AQHA or AQHYA member.

Award: Scholarship for use in freshman, sophomore, junior, or senior years; renewable. *Number:* 1. *Amount:* $7500.

Eligibility Requirements: Applicant must be high school student and planning to enroll or expecting to enroll full-time at a two-year or four-year or technical institution or university. Applicant or parent of applicant must be member of American Quarter Horse Association. Applicant must have 3.0 GPA or higher. Available to U.S. and non-U.S. citizens.

Application Requirements: Application form, recommendations or references, transcript. *Deadline:* December 1.

CHRISTOPHER LAWRENCE JUNKER NEBRASKA SCHOLARSHIP

Ideal candidate is an AQHA or AQHYA member from Nebraska.

Award: Scholarship for use in freshman, sophomore, junior, or senior years; not renewable. *Number:* 1. *Amount:* $500.

Eligibility Requirements: Applicant must be enrolled or expecting to enroll full-time at a two-year or four-year or technical institution or university and resident of Nebraska. Applicant or parent of applicant must be member of American Quarter Horse Association. Applicant must have 2.5 GPA or higher. Available to U.S. citizens.

Application Requirements: Application form, recommendations or references, transcript. *Deadline:* December 1.

DR. GERALD O'CONNOR MICHIGAN QHY SCHOLARSHIP

Ideal candidate is an AQHA or AQHYA member from Michigan. Scholarship is available once every four years.

Award: Scholarship for use in freshman, sophomore, junior, senior, or graduate years; renewable. *Number:* 1. *Amount:* $2000.

Eligibility Requirements: Applicant must be enrolled or expecting to enroll full-time at a two-year or four-year or technical institution or university; resident of Michigan and must have an interest in animal/agricultural competition. Applicant or parent of applicant must be member of American Quarter Horse Association. Applicant must have 2.5 GPA or higher. Available to U.S. and Canadian citizens.

Application Requirements: Application form, recommendations or references, transcript. *Deadline:* December 1.

DOGWOOD SCHOLARSHIP

Ideal candidate is a current AQHA or AQHYA member.

Award: Scholarship for use in freshman, sophomore, junior, or senior years; renewable. *Number:* 1. *Amount:* $4000.

Eligibility Requirements: Applicant must be enrolled or expecting to enroll full-time at a two-year or four-year or technical institution or university. Applicant or parent of applicant must be member of American Quarter Horse Association. Applicant must have 3.0 GPA or higher. Available to U.S. and non-U.S. citizens.

Application Requirements: Application form, recommendations or references, transcript. *Deadline:* December 1.

EXCELLENCE IN EQUINE/AGRICULTURAL INVOLVEMENT SCHOLARSHIP

Ideal candidate is an AQHA or AQHYA member who exemplifies the characteristics of leadership and excellence acquired through participation in equine and or agriculture activities. Applicant should not compete in AQHA-approved shows.

Award: Scholarship for use in freshman, sophomore, junior, senior, or graduate years; renewable. *Number:* 1. *Amount:* $25,000.

Eligibility Requirements: Applicant must be enrolled or expecting to enroll full-time at a two-year or four-year or technical institution or university. Applicant or parent of applicant must be member of American Quarter Horse Association. Applicant or parent of applicant must have employment or volunteer experience in agriculture. Applicant must have 3.5 GPA or higher. Available to U.S. and non-U.S. citizens.

Application Requirements: Application form, recommendations or references, transcript. *Deadline:* December 1.

FARM AND RANCH HERITAGE SCHOLARSHIP

Ideal candidates are AQHA or AQHYA members from farming and or ranching backgrounds who represent the outstanding education, expertise and life skills gained through participation in agricultural activities. Applicants may not compete in AQHA-approved shows.

Award: Scholarship for use in freshman, sophomore, junior, senior, or graduate years; renewable. *Number:* 1–3. *Amount:* $12,500.

Eligibility Requirements: Applicant must be enrolled or expecting to enroll full-time at a two-year or four-year or technical institution or university. Applicant or parent of applicant must be member of American Quarter Horse Association. Applicant or parent of applicant must have employment or volunteer experience in agriculture, farming. Applicant must have 3.0 GPA or higher. Available to U.S. and non-U.S. citizens.

Application Requirements: Application form, recommendations or references, transcript. *Deadline:* December 1.

GUY STOOPS PROFESSIONAL HORSEMEN'S FAMILY SCHOLARSHIP

Ideal candidates are AQHA or AQHYA members whose parent(s) are a current member of the AQHA Professional Horseman's Association, with membership in good standing for three or more years.

Award: Scholarship for use in freshman, sophomore, junior, senior, graduate, or postgraduate years; not renewable. *Number:* 1–2. *Amount:* $500.

Eligibility Requirements: Applicant must be enrolled or expecting to enroll full-time at a two-year or four-year or technical institution or university. Applicant or parent of applicant must be member of American Quarter Horse Association, Professional Horsemen Association. Applicant must have 2.5 GPA or higher. Available to U.S. and non-U.S. citizens.

Application Requirements: Application form, recommendations or references, transcript. *Deadline:* December 1.

INDIANA QUARTER HORSE YOUTH SCHOLARSHIP

Ideal candidate an AQHA or AQHYA member from Indiana who is a current member of the Indiana Quarter Horse Association, and has maintained two or more years membership with that association.

Award: Scholarship for use in freshman, sophomore, junior, or senior years; not renewable. *Number:* 1. *Amount:* $1000.

Eligibility Requirements: Applicant must be enrolled or expecting to enroll full-time at a two-year or four-year or technical institution or university and resident of Indiana. Applicant or parent of applicant must be member of American Quarter Horse Association. Applicant must have 2.5 GPA or higher. Available to U.S. citizens.

Application Requirements: Application form, recommendations or references, transcript. *Deadline:* December 1.

JAMES F. AND DORIS M. BARTON SCHOLARSHIP

Ideal candidate is an AQHA or AQHYA member from New York who is a current member of the Empire State Youth Quarter Horse Association.

Award: Scholarship for use in freshman, sophomore, junior, senior, graduate, or postgraduate years; renewable. *Number:* 1. *Amount:* $5000.

Eligibility Requirements: Applicant must be enrolled or expecting to enroll full-time at a two-year or four-year or technical institution or university and resident of New York. Applicant or parent of applicant must be member of American Quarter Horse Association. Applicant must have 3.0 GPA or higher. Available to U.S. citizens.

Application Requirements: Application form, recommendations or references, transcript. *Deadline:* December 1.

JOAN CAIN FLORIDA QUARTER HORSE YOUTH SCHOLARSHIP

Ideal candidate is an AQHA or AQHYA member from Florida who is a current member of the Florida Quarter Horse Youth Association, and has maintained two or more years of membership.

Award: Scholarship for use in freshman, sophomore, junior, senior, graduate, or postgraduate years; not renewable. *Number:* 1. *Amount:* $1000.

Eligibility Requirements: Applicant must be enrolled or expecting to enroll full-time at a two-year or four-year or technical institution or university and resident of Florida. Applicant or parent of applicant must

be member of American Quarter Horse Association. Applicant must have 2.5 GPA or higher. Available to U.S. citizens.

Application Requirements: Application form, recommendations or references, transcript. *Deadline:* December 1.

JOYCE WYATT PENNSYLVANIA QUARTER HORSE YOUTH SCHOLARSHIP

Ideal candidate is an AQHA or AQHYA member from Pennsylvania. Scholarship is available once every four years.

Award: Scholarship for use in freshman, sophomore, junior, senior, or graduate years; renewable. *Number:* 1. *Amount:* $2000.

Eligibility Requirements: Applicant must be enrolled or expecting to enroll full-time at a two-year or four-year or technical institution or university and resident of Pennsylvania. Applicant or parent of applicant must be member of American Quarter Horse Association. Applicant must have 3.0 GPA or higher. Available to U.S. citizens.

Application Requirements: Application form, recommendations or references, transcript. *Deadline:* December 1.

NEBRASKA QUARTER HORSE YOUTH SCHOLARSHIP

Ideal candidate is an AQHA or AQHYA member from Nebraska.

Award: Scholarship for use in freshman, sophomore, junior, senior, or graduate years; renewable. *Number:* 1. *Amount:* $2000.

Eligibility Requirements: Applicant must be enrolled or expecting to enroll full-time at a two-year or four-year or technical institution or university and resident of Nebraska. Applicant or parent of applicant must be member of American Quarter Horse Association. Applicant must have 2.5 GPA or higher. Available to U.S. citizens.

Application Requirements: Application form, recommendations or references, transcript. *Deadline:* December 1.

OKLAHOMA QUARTER HORSE YOUTH SCHOLARSHIP

Ideal candidates are AQHA or AQHYA members from Oklahoma who are current members of the Oklahoma Quarter Horse Association, and have maintained two or more years of membership. Applicants should be actively involved with OkQHA.

Award: Scholarship for use in freshman, sophomore, junior, or senior years; renewable. *Number:* 1–2. *Amount:* $2000.

Eligibility Requirements: Applicant must be enrolled or expecting to enroll full-time at a two-year or four-year or technical institution or university and resident of Oklahoma. Applicant or parent of applicant must be member of American Quarter Horse Association. Applicant must have 2.5 GPA or higher. Available to U.S. citizens.

Application Requirements: Application form, recommendations or references, transcript. *Deadline:* December 1.

SCOOP VESSELS SCHOLARSHIP

Ideal candidate is a member of AQHA who demonstrates a strong work ethic and financial need.

Award: Scholarship for use in junior, senior, graduate, or postgraduate years; renewable. *Number:* 1. *Amount:* $5000.

Eligibility Requirements: Applicant must be enrolled or expecting to enroll full-time at a four-year institution or university. Applicant or parent of applicant must be member of American Quarter Horse Association. Applicant must have 2.5 GPA or higher. Available to U.S. and non-U.S. citizens.

Application Requirements: Application form, recommendations or references, transcript. *Deadline:* December 1.

SWAYZE WOODRUFF MEMORIAL MID-SOUTH SCHOLARSHIP

Ideal candidate is an AQHA or AQHYA member from Alabama, Arkansas, Louisiana, Mississippi or Tennessee who competes in AQHA-approved shows.

Award: Scholarship for use in freshman, sophomore, junior, senior, or graduate years; renewable. *Number:* 1. *Amount:* $8000.

Eligibility Requirements: Applicant must be enrolled or expecting to enroll full-time at a two-year or four-year or technical institution or university; resident of Alabama, Arkansas, Louisiana, Mississippi, Tennessee and must have an interest in animal/agricultural competition. Applicant or parent of applicant must be member of American Quarter Horse Association. Applicant must have 2.5 GPA or higher. Available to U.S. and Canadian citizens.

Application Requirements: Application form, recommendations or references, transcript. *Deadline:* December 1.

AMERICAN WATER SKI EDUCATIONAL FOUNDATION

http://www.waterskihalloffame.com/

AMERICAN WATER SKI EDUCATIONAL FOUNDATION SCHOLARSHIP

Awards for incoming college sophomores through incoming seniors who are members of USA Water Ski. Awards are based upon academics, leadership, extracurricular activities, recommendations, essay and financial need.

Award: Scholarship for use in sophomore, junior, or senior years; renewable. *Number:* 5. *Amount:* $1500–$3000.

Eligibility Requirements: Applicant must be enrolled or expecting to enroll full-time at a two-year or four-year institution or university. Applicant or parent of applicant must be member of USA Water Ski. Available to U.S. citizens.

Application Requirements: Application form, essay, financial need analysis, recommendations or references, self-addressed stamped envelope with application, transcript. *Deadline:* March 1.

Contact: Carole Lowe, Scholarship Director
Phone: 863-324-2472 Ext. 127
Fax: 863-324-3996
E-mail: awsefhalloffame@cs.com

AMVETS AUXILIARY

http://amvetsaux.org/

AMVETS NATIONAL LADIES AUXILIARY SCHOLARSHIP

One-time award of up to $1000 for a member of AMVETS or the Auxiliary. Applicant may also be the family member of a member. Award for full-time study at any accredited U.S. institution. Minimum 2.5 GPA required.

Award: Scholarship for use in sophomore, junior, or senior years; not renewable. *Number:* up to 7. *Amount:* $750–$1000.

Eligibility Requirements: Applicant must be enrolled or expecting to enroll full-time at a two-year or four-year or technical institution. Applicant or parent of applicant must be member of AMVETS Auxiliary. Applicant must have 2.5 GPA or higher. Available to U.S. citizens. Applicant or parent must meet one or more of the following requirements: general military experience; retired from active duty; disabled or killed as a result of military service; prisoner of war; or missing in action.

Application Requirements: Application form, essay, recommendations or references, transcript. *Deadline:* June 1.

Contact: Kellie Haggerty, Executive Administrator
AMVETS Auxiliary
4647 Forbes Boulevard
Lanham, MD 20706-4380
Phone: 301-459-6255
Fax: 301-459-5403
E-mail: auxhdqs@amvets.org

APPALOOSA HORSE CLUB-APPALOOSA YOUTH PROGRAM

http://www.appaloosayouth.com/

APPALOOSA YOUTH EDUCATIONAL SCHOLARSHIPS

Scholarship of up to $1000 available for members or dependents of members of the Appaloosa Youth Association or Appaloosa Horse Club. Based on academics, leadership, sportsmanship, and horsemanship. Printable application is available http://www.appaloosayouth.com.

Award: Scholarship for use in freshman, sophomore, junior, or senior years; not renewable. *Number:* 6–8. *Amount:* $100–$1000.

Eligibility Requirements: Applicant must be enrolled or expecting to enroll full-time at a two-year or four-year institution or university and must have an interest in animal/agricultural competition or leadership. Applicant or parent of applicant must be member of Appaloosa Horse Club/Appaloosa Youth Association. Applicant must have 3.5 GPA or higher. Available to U.S. citizens.

Application Requirements: Application form, entry in a contest, essay, personal photograph, recommendations or references, test scores, transcript. *Deadline:* June 1.

Contact: Anna Brown, AYF Coordinator
Appaloosa Horse Club-Appaloosa Youth Program
2720 West Pullman Road
Moscow, ID 83843
Phone: 208-882-5578 Ext. 264
Fax: 208-882-8150
E-mail: youth@appaloosa.com

ARRL FOUNDATION INC.

http://www.arrl.org/

YOU'VE GOT A FRIEND IN PENNSYLVANIA SCHOLARSHIP

One-time award available to licensed general amateur radio operators. Must be a member of American Radio Relay League and have an A or equivalent grade point average including graded courses in mathematics, science and languages and excluding grades in sports or physical education. Preference given to residents of the Commonwealth of Pennsylvania.

Award: Scholarship for use in freshman, sophomore, junior, senior, graduate, or postgraduate years; not renewable. *Number:* 2. *Amount:* $2000.

Eligibility Requirements: Applicant must be enrolled or expecting to enroll full-time at a two-year or four-year or technical institution or university; resident of Pennsylvania and must have an interest in amateur radio. Applicant or parent of applicant must be member of American Radio Relay League. Applicant must have 3.5 GPA or higher. Available to U.S. citizens.

Application Requirements: Application form, transcript. *Deadline:* February 1.

Contact: Ms. Mary Hobart, Secretary
Phone: 860-594-0397
E-mail: k1mmh@arrl.org

AUTOMOTIVE RECYCLERS ASSOCIATION SCHOLARSHIP FOUNDATION

http://www.a-r-a.org/

AUTOMOTIVE RECYCLERS ASSOCIATION SCHOLARSHIP FOUNDATION SCHOLARSHIP

Scholarships are available for the post-high school educational pursuits of the children of employees of direct ARA member companies.

Award: Scholarship for use in freshman, sophomore, junior, or senior years; not renewable.

Eligibility Requirements: Applicant must be enrolled or expecting to enroll full-time at a two-year or four-year institution or university. Applicant or parent of applicant must be member of Automotive Recyclers Association. Applicant must have 3.0 GPA or higher. Available to U.S. and non-U.S. citizens.

Application Requirements: Application form, letter verifying parents' employment, personal photograph, transcript. *Deadline:* March 15.

Contact: Kelly Badillo, Director, Member Services
Automotive Recyclers Association Scholarship Foundation
3975 Fair Ridge Drive, Suite 20-North
Fairfax, VA 22033
Phone: 703-385-1001 Ext. 26
Fax: 703-385-1494
E-mail: kelly@a-r-a.org

BOYS AND GIRLS CLUBS OF CHICAGO

http://www.bgcc.org/

BOYS AND GIRLS CLUBS OF CHICAGO SCHOLARSHIPS

Scholarships are awarded to graduating high school seniors who are local Club members. Scholarships are based upon academic achievement, club involvement, financial need, and personal interviews. Students are asked to maintain their grades, seek internships and job opportunities, and lend guidance to younger children.

Award: Scholarship for use in freshman year; renewable. *Amount:* $3000–$5000.

Eligibility Requirements: Applicant must be high school student; planning to enroll or expecting to enroll full- or part-time at a two-year or four-year or technical institution or university and resident of Illinois. Applicant or parent of applicant must be member of Boys or Girls Club. Applicant must have 3.5 GPA or higher. Available to U.S. citizens.

Application Requirements: Application form, essay, financial need analysis, interview, recommendations or references, test scores, transcript. *Deadline:* varies.

Contact: Katie Huckaby, Project Director
    Phone: 312-235-8000 Ext. 8008
    E-mail: khuckaby@bgcc.org

BUFFALO AFL-CIO COUNCIL

http://www.wnyalf.org/

AFL-CIO COUNCIL OF BUFFALO SCHOLARSHIP WNY ALF SCHOLARSHIP

One-time award of up to $1000 for a high school senior who is a son or daughter of a member of a local union affiliated with the Buffalo AFL-CIO Council. Must be a New York resident and use the award for study in New York.

Award: Scholarship for use in freshman year; not renewable. *Number:* up to 3. *Amount:* up to $1000.

Eligibility Requirements: Applicant must be high school student; planning to enroll or expecting to enroll full-time at a two-year or four-year institution or university; resident of New York and studying in New York. Applicant or parent of applicant must be member of AFL-CIO. Available to U.S. and Canadian citizens.

Application Requirements: Application form, essay, recommendations or references, transcript. *Deadline:* March 31.

Contact: Mike Hoffert, President
    Phone: 716-852-0375
    Fax: 716-855-1802
    E-mail: mhoffert@wnyalf.org

CALIFORNIA GRANGE FOUNDATION

http://www.californiagrange.org/

CALIFORNIA GRANGE FOUNDATION SCHOLARSHIP

Scholarship program available for Grange members residing in California who wish to attend a higher institution of learning of their choice.

Award: Scholarship for use in freshman, sophomore, junior, or senior years; renewable. *Number:* 5–8. *Amount:* $250–$1000.

Eligibility Requirements: Applicant must be enrolled or expecting to enroll full- or part-time at a two-year or four-year or technical institution or university and resident of California. Applicant or parent of applicant must be member of Grange Association. Available to U.S. citizens.

Application Requirements: Application form, community service, essay, financial need analysis, recommendations or references, transcript. *Deadline:* April 1.

Contact: Mrs. Leslie Parker, Executive Assistant
    California Grange Foundation
    3830 U Street
    Sacramento, CA 95817
    Phone: 916-454-5805 Ext. 21
    Fax: 916-739-8189
    E-mail: info@californiagrange.org

CALIFORNIA STATE PARENT-TEACHER ASSOCIATION

http://www.capta.org/

CONTINUING EDUCATION-PTA VOLUNTEERS SCHOLARSHIP

Scholarships are available annually from the California State PTA to be used for continuing education at accredited colleges, universities, trade or technical schools. These scholarships recognize volunteer service in PTA and enable PTA volunteers to continue their education.

Award: Scholarship for use in freshman, sophomore, junior, senior, or graduate years; not renewable. *Amount:* $500.

Eligibility Requirements: Applicant must be enrolled or expecting to enroll full- or part-time at a two-year or four-year or technical institution or university and resident of California. Applicant or parent of applicant must be member of Parent-Teacher Association/Organization. Applicant or parent of applicant must have employment or volunteer experience in community service. Available to U.S. citizens.

Application Requirements: Application form, copy of membership card, essay, recommendations or references, transcript. *Deadline:* November 15.

Contact: Becky Reece, Scholarship and Award Chairman
    California State Parent-Teacher Association
    930 Georgia Street
    Los Angeles, CA 90015-1322
    Phone: 213-620-1100
    Fax: 213-620-1141

CALIFORNIA TEACHERS ASSOCIATION (CTA)

http://www.cta.org/

CALIFORNIA TEACHERS ASSOCIATION SCHOLARSHIP FOR DEPENDENT CHILDREN

Awards scholarships annually for dependant children of active, retired, or deceased members of California Teachers Association. Minimum 3.5 GPA required.

Award: Scholarship for use in freshman, sophomore, junior, senior, or graduate years; not renewable. *Number:* up to 25. *Amount:* $2500.

Eligibility Requirements: Applicant must be enrolled or expecting to enroll full-time at a two-year or four-year or technical institution or university. Applicant or parent of applicant must be member of California Teachers Association. Applicant must have 3.5 GPA or higher. Available to U.S. citizens.

Application Requirements: Application form, essay, recommendations or references, transcript. *Deadline:* February 8.

Contact: Janeya Collins, Scholarship Coordinator
    California Teachers Association (CTA)
    PO Box 921
    Burlingame, CA 94011-0921
    Phone: 650-552-5468
    Fax: 650-552-5001
    E-mail: scholarships@cta.org

CALIFORNIA TEACHERS ASSOCIATION SCHOLARSHIP FOR MEMBERS

Must be an active member of California Teachers Association (including members working on an emergency credential). Available for study in a degree, credential, or graduate program.

Award: Scholarship for use in freshman, sophomore, junior, senior, or graduate years; not renewable. *Number:* 5. *Amount:* $2500.

Eligibility Requirements: Applicant must be enrolled or expecting to enroll full-time at a two-year or four-year institution or university and resident of California. Applicant or parent of applicant must be member of California Teachers Association. Applicant or parent of applicant must have employment or volunteer experience in teaching/education. Applicant must have 3.0 GPA or higher. Available to U.S. citizens.

Application Requirements: Application form, essay, recommendations or references, transcript. *Deadline:* February 8.

Contact: Janeya Collins, Scholarship Coordinator
    California Teachers Association (CTA)
    PO Box 921
    Burlingame, CA 94011-0921
    Phone: 650-552-5468
    E-mail: scholarships@cta.org

CIVIL AIR PATROL, USAF AUXILIARY

http://www.gocivilairpatrol.com/

CIVIL AIR PATROL ACADEMIC SCHOLARSHIPS

One-time award for active members of the Civil Air Patrol to pursue undergraduate, graduate, or trade or technical education. Must be a current CAP member. Significant restrictions apply. Not open to the general public.

Award: Scholarship for use in freshman, sophomore, junior, senior, or graduate years; not renewable. *Number:* up to 40. *Amount:* $1000–$7500.

Eligibility Requirements: Applicant must be enrolled or expecting to enroll full-time at a two-year or four-year or technical institution or university. Applicant or parent of applicant must be member of Civil Air Patrol. Available to U.S. citizens.

Application Requirements: Application form, essay, personal photograph, recommendations or references, resume, test scores, transcript. *Deadline:* January 31.

Contact: Kelly Easterly, Assistant Program Manager
Civil Air Patrol, USAF Auxiliary
105 South Hansell Street, Building 714
Maxwell Air Force Base, AL 36112-6332
Phone: 334-953-8640
Fax: 334-953-6699
E-mail: cpr@capnhq.gov

COMMUNITY BANKERS ASSOCIATION OF ILLINOIS

http://www.cbai.com/

COMMUNITY BANKERS ASSOC OF IL CHILD OF A BANKER SCHOLARSHIP

Eligible Illinois community banks can submit one or more names for based on a sliding scale relative to their donations made to the CBAI Foundation. Children of eligible community bankers and part-time bank employees entering freshman year of higher education are eligible. Winner determined by drawing. Must be Illinois resident. For more details see website http://www.cbai.com.

Award: Scholarship for use in freshman year; renewable. *Number:* 2. *Amount:* $1000–$4000.

Eligibility Requirements: Applicant must be high school student; planning to enroll or expecting to enroll full-time at a two-year or four-year or technical institution or university and resident of Illinois. Applicant or parent of applicant must be member of Community Banker Association of Illinois. Applicant or parent of applicant must have employment or volunteer experience in banking. Available to U.S. citizens.

Application Requirements: Application form. *Deadline:* August 15.

Contact: Ms. Andrea Cusick, Senior Vice President of Communications
Community Bankers Association of Illinois
901 Community Drive
Springfield, IL 62703
Phone: 217-529-2265
Fax: 217-585-8738
E-mail: cbaicom@cbai.com

COMMUNITY FOUNDATION OF WESTERN MASSACHUSETTS

http://www.communityfoundation.org/

HORACE HILL SCHOLARSHIP

Scholarships are given to children or grandchildren of a member of the Springfield Newspapers 25-Year Club. For more information or application visit http://www.communityfoundation.org.

Award: Scholarship for use in freshman, sophomore, junior, senior, or graduate years; not renewable. *Number:* 2. *Amount:* up to $1000.

Eligibility Requirements: Applicant must be enrolled or expecting to enroll full- or part-time at a two-year or four-year institution or university. Applicant or parent of applicant must be member of Springfield Newspaper 25-Year Club. Available to U.S. citizens.

Application Requirements: Application form, application form may be submitted online (http://www.communityfoundation.org), financial need analysis, Student Aid Report (SAR), transcript. *Deadline:* March 29.

Contact: Dorothy Theriaque, Education Associate
Community Foundation of Western Massachusetts
1500 Main Street, PO Box 15769
Springfield, MA 01115
Phone: 413-732-2858
Fax: 413-733-8565
E-mail: scholar@communityfoundation.org

DAUGHTERS OF PENELOPE FOUNDATION

http://daughtersofpenelope.org/

ALEXANDRA APOSTOLIDES SONENFELD SCHOLARSHIP

Annual award for female graduating high school seniors or undergraduate students who are members of the Daughters of Penelope or the Maids of Athena, or have a member of the immediate family in the Daughters of Penelope, or the Order of AHEPA. Membership must be for a minimum of two years in good standing.

Award: Scholarship for use in freshman, sophomore, junior, or senior years; not renewable. *Number:* 1. *Amount:* up to $1500.

Eligibility Requirements: Applicant must be of Greek heritage; enrolled or expecting to enroll full-time at a two-year or four-year or technical institution or university and female. Applicant or parent of applicant must be member of Daughters of Penelope/Maids of Athena/Order of Ahepa. Available to U.S. citizens.

Application Requirements: Application form, essay, IRS forms, recommendations or references, test scores, transcript. *Deadline:* June 1.

Contact: Helen Santire, National Scholarship Chairman
Phone: 713-468-6531
E-mail: helen.santire@duchesne.org

JOANNE V. HOLOGGITAS, PHD SCHOLARSHIP

Annual award for female graduating high school seniors or undergraduate students who are related to an AHEPAN or a Daughter of Penelope, or must be members of the Maids of Athens. Membership must be for a minimum of two years in good standing.

Award: Scholarship for use in freshman, sophomore, junior, or senior years; not renewable. *Number:* 1. *Amount:* up to $1500.

Eligibility Requirements: Applicant must be of Greek heritage; enrolled or expecting to enroll full-time at a two-year or four-year or technical institution or university and female. Applicant or parent of applicant must be member of Daughters of Penelope/Maids of Athena/Order of Ahepa. Available to U.S. and Canadian citizens.

Application Requirements: Application form, essay, IRS forms, recommendations or references, test scores, transcript. *Deadline:* June 1.

Contact: Helen Santire, National Scholarship Chairman
Phone: 713-468-6531
E-mail: helen.santire@duchesne.org

KOTTIS FAMILY SCHOLARSHIP

Annual award for female graduating high school seniors or undergraduate students who are related to an AHEPAN or a Daughter of Penelope, or a member of the Maids of Athens. Membership must be for a minimum of two years in good standing.

Award: Scholarship for use in freshman, sophomore, junior, or senior years; not renewable. *Number:* 1. *Amount:* up to $1500.

Eligibility Requirements: Applicant must be of Greek heritage; enrolled or expecting to enroll full-time at a two-year or four-year or technical institution or university and female. Applicant or parent of applicant must be member of Daughters of Penelope/Maids of Athena/Order of Ahepa. Available to U.S. and Canadian citizens.

Application Requirements: Application form, essay, IRS forms, recommendations or references, test scores, transcript. *Deadline:* June 1.

Contact: Helen Santire, National Scholarship Chairman
Phone: 713-468-6531
E-mail: helen.santire@duchesne.org

MARY M. VERGES SCHOLARSHIP

Annual award for female graduating high school seniors or undergraduate students who are members of the Daughters of Penelope or the Maids of Athena, or have a member of the immediate family in the

Daughters of Penelope, or the Order of AHEPA. Membership must be for a minimum of two years in good standing.

Award: Scholarship for use in freshman, sophomore, junior, or senior years; not renewable. *Number:* 1. *Amount:* up to $1500.

Eligibility Requirements: Applicant must be of Greek heritage; enrolled or expecting to enroll full-time at a two-year or four-year or technical institution or university and female. Applicant or parent of applicant must be member of Daughters of Penelope/Maids of Athena/Order of Ahepa. Available to U.S. and Canadian citizens.

Application Requirements: Application form, essay, IRS forms, recommendations or references, test scores, transcript. *Deadline:* June 1.

Contact: Helen Santire, National Scholarship Chairman
   Phone: 713-468-6531
   E-mail: helen.santire@duchesne.org

PAST GRAND PRESIDENTS SCHOLARSHIP

Scholarship for female students of Greek descent. Must be a graduating high school senior or an undergraduate student who is related to an AHEPAN or a Daughter of Penelope, or must be a member of the Maids of Athens. Must be a citizen of the United States, Canada, Greece, or any country in which there is an established Daughters of Penelope chapter.

Award: Scholarship for use in freshman, sophomore, junior, or senior years; not renewable. *Number:* 1. *Amount:* up to $1500.

Eligibility Requirements: Applicant must be of Greek heritage; enrolled or expecting to enroll full-time at a two-year or four-year or technical institution or university and female. Applicant or parent of applicant must be member of Daughters of Penelope/Maids of Athena/Order of Ahepa. Available to U.S. and Canadian citizens.

Application Requirements: Application form, essay, IRS forms, recommendations or references, test scores, transcript. *Deadline:* June 1.

Contact: Helen Santire, National Scholarship Chairman
   Phone: 713-468-6531
   E-mail: helen.santire@duchesne.org

DELTA DELTA DELTA FOUNDATION

http://www.tridelta.org/

DELTA DELTA DELTA UNDERGRADUATE SCHOLARSHIP

One-time award to any initiated sophomore or junior member in good-standing of Delta Delta Delta based on academic achievement, campus, chapter, and community involvement. Application and information available at website http://www.tridelta.org.

Award: Scholarship for use in sophomore or junior years; not renewable. *Number:* 48–50. *Amount:* $500–$1500.

Eligibility Requirements: Applicant must be enrolled or expecting to enroll full-time at a four-year institution or university and single female. Applicant or parent of applicant must be member of Greek Organization. Applicant or parent of applicant must have employment or volunteer experience in community service. Available to U.S. and Canadian citizens.

Application Requirements: Alumna adviser check-off, personal statement, application form, recommendations or references, transcript. *Deadline:* March 15.

Contact: Laura Allen, Foundation Manager of Scholarships and
      Financial Services
   Delta Delta Delta Foundation
   PO Box 5987
   Arlington, TX 76005
   Phone: 817-633-8001
   Fax: 817-652-0212
   E-mail: lallen@trideltaeo.org

DELTA PHI EPSILON EDUCATIONAL FOUNDATION

http://www.dphie.org/

DELTA PHI EPSILON EDUCATIONAL FOUNDATION GRANT

Scholarships are awarded based on three criteria: service and involvement, academics, and need. Applications may be submitted for undergraduate only. Applicants must be members of Delta Phi Epsilon or the sons/daughters of members. Refer to website http://www.dphie.org/foundation/apply.shtml for details.

Award: Grant for use in freshman, sophomore, junior, or senior years; not renewable. *Number:* 6–8. *Amount:* $1000.

Eligibility Requirements: Applicant must be enrolled or expecting to enroll full-time at a four-year institution or university. Applicant or parent of applicant must be member of Greek Organization. Available to U.S. and non-U.S. citizens.

Application Requirements: Application form, community service, driver's license, essay, financial need analysis, personal photograph, recommendations or references, transcript. *Deadline:* April 15.

Contact: Nicole DeFeo, Executive Director
   Phone: 215-732-5901
   Fax: 215-275-2655
   E-mail: info@dphie.org

EASTERN ORTHODOX COMMITTEE ON SCOUTING

http://www.eocs.org/

EASTERN ORTHODOX COMMITTEE ON SCOUTING SCHOLARSHIPS

One-time award for high school seniors planning to attend a four-year institution. Must be a registered member of a Boy or Girl Scout unit, an Eagle Scout or Gold Award recipient, active member of an Eastern Orthodox Church, and recipient of the Alpha Omega religious award.

Award: Scholarship for use in freshman year; not renewable. *Number:* 2. *Amount:* $500–$1000.

Eligibility Requirements: Applicant must be Eastern Orthodox; high school student; planning to enroll or expecting to enroll full-time at a four-year institution or university and single. Applicant or parent of applicant must be member of Boy Scouts, Girl Scouts. Available to U.S. citizens.

Application Requirements: Application form, community service, recommendations or references, self-addressed stamped envelope with application, test scores, transcript. *Deadline:* May 1.

Contact: George Boulukos, Scholarship Chairman
   Eastern Orthodox Committee on Scouting
   862 Guy Lombardo Avenue
   Freeport, NY 11520
   Phone: 516-868-4050
   E-mail: geobou03@aol.com

EASTERN SURFING ASSOCIATION (ESA)

http://www.surfesa.org/

ESA MARSH SCHOLARSHIP PROGRAM

Grants are awarded to ESA current members in good standing on the basis of academics and U.S. citizenship rather than athletic ability.

Award: Scholarship for use in freshman, sophomore, junior, or senior years; not renewable. *Number:* 2. *Amount:* up to $8000.

Eligibility Requirements: Applicant must be enrolled or expecting to enroll full-time at a four-year institution or university. Applicant or parent of applicant must be member of Eastern Surfing Association. Available to U.S. citizens.

Application Requirements: Application form, essay, recommendations or references, transcript. *Deadline:* May 15.

Contact: Debbie Hodges, Scholarship Committee
   Phone: 757-233-1790
   E-mail: centralhq@surfesa.org

ELKS NATIONAL FOUNDATION

http://www.elks.org/enf

ELKS EMERGENCY EDUCATIONAL GRANTS

Grant available to children of Elks who are deceased or totally incapacitated. Applicants for the one-year renewable awards must be unmarried, under the age of 23, be a full-time undergraduate student, and demonstrate financial need.

Award: Scholarship for use in freshman, sophomore, junior, or senior years; not renewable. *Amount:* $1000–$4000.

Eligibility Requirements: Applicant must be enrolled or expecting to enroll full-time at a two-year or four-year institution or university and single. Applicant or parent of applicant must be member of Elks Club. Available to U.S. citizens.

Application Requirements: Application form, community service, entry in a contest, essay, financial need analysis, recommendations or references, self-addressed stamped envelope with application, test scores, transcript. *Deadline:* December 31.

ELKS NATIONAL FOUNDATION LEGACY AWARDS

$4000 four-year scholarships available for children and grandchildren of Elks in good standing. Parent or grandparent must have been an Elk for two years. Must be high school senior and apply through the related member's Elks Lodge. Applications available after September 1 online only, http://www.elks.org/enf/scholars/legacy.cfm.

Award: Scholarship for use in freshman, sophomore, junior, or senior years; renewable. *Number:* 250. *Amount:* $4000.

Eligibility Requirements: Applicant must be high school student and planning to enroll or expecting to enroll full-time at a two-year or four-year institution or university. Applicant or parent of applicant must be member of Elks Club. Available to U.S. citizens.

Application Requirements: Application form, application form may be submitted online (http://www.elks.org/legacyawards), community service, essay, test scores, transcript. *Deadline:* February 1.

FEDERATION OF AMERICAN CONSUMERS AND TRAVELERS

http://www.usafact.org/

FEDERATION OF AMERICAN CONSUMERS AND TRAVELERS GRADUATING HIGH SCHOOL SENIOR SCHOLARSHIP

One $10,000 scholarship and one $2500 scholarship are given to graduating high school seniors per year. Eligible applicants must be a member or the child or grandchild of a member of FACT. Awards are designed for the average student: the young man or woman who may never have made the honor roll or who did not excel on the athletic field and wants to obtain a higher education, but is all too often overlooked by other scholarship sources.

Award: Scholarship for use in freshman year; not renewable. *Number:* 2. *Amount:* $2500–$10,000.

Eligibility Requirements: Applicant must be high school student and planning to enroll or expecting to enroll full-time at a two-year or four-year institution or university. Applicant or parent of applicant must be member of Federation of American Consumers and Travelers. Available to U.S. citizens.

Application Requirements: Application form, essay, recommendations or references, test scores, transcript. *Deadline:* January 15.

Contact: Vicki Rolens, Managing Director
Federation of American Consumers and Travelers
PO Box 104
Edwardsville, IL 62025
Phone: 800-872-3228
Fax: 618-656-5369
E-mail: vrolens@usafact.org

FEDERATION OF AMERICAN CONSUMERS AND TRAVELERS TRADE/TECHNICAL SCHOOL SCHOLARSHIP

Scholarships offered in four categories: current high school seniors, persons who graduated from high school four or more years ago and now plan to go to a university or college, students currently enrolled in a college or university, and trade or technical school aspirants. Members of FACT, their children and grandchildren are eligible to apply.

Award: Scholarship for use in freshman, sophomore, junior, or senior years; not renewable. *Number:* 1–3. *Amount:* $1000–$5000.

Eligibility Requirements: Applicant must be enrolled or expecting to enroll full- or part-time at a technical institution. Applicant or parent of applicant must be member of Federation of American Consumers and Travelers. Available to U.S. citizens.

Application Requirements: Application form, essay, recommendations or references, resume, test scores, transcript. *Deadline:* January 15.

Contact: Vicki Rolens, Managing Director
Federation of American Consumers and Travelers
PO Box 104
Edwardsville, IL 62025
Phone: 800-872-3228
Fax: 618-656-5369
E-mail: vrolens@usafact.org

FIRST CATHOLIC SLOVAK LADIES ASSOCIATION

http://www.fcsla.org/

FIRST CATHOLIC SLOVAK LADIES ASSOCIATION HIGH SCHOOL SCHOLARSHIPS

Scholarship for high school students, A written report of approximately 250 words on "What This High School Scholarship Will Do for Me" must be submitted with application. Candidate must have been a beneficial member of the Association for at least three years prior to date of application.

Award: Scholarship for use in freshman year; renewable. *Number:* up to 32. *Amount:* $1000.

Eligibility Requirements: Applicant must be high school student and planning to enroll or expecting to enroll full-time at a four-year institution or university. Applicant or parent of applicant must be member of First Catholic Slovak Ladies Association. Available to U.S. and Canadian citizens.

Application Requirements: Application form, community service, essay, personal photograph, transcript. *Deadline:* March 1.

FRA EDUCATION FOUNDATION

http://www.fra.org/foundation

COLONEL HAZEL ELIZABETH BENN U.S.M.C. SCHOLARSHIP

You may apply only if: (1) you are a U.S. citizen; (2) you are an unmarried dependent child of a member in good standing of the FRA, currently or at time of death, who has US Navy service and served or is now serving in the U.S. Navy as an enlisted medical rating assigned to and serving with the U.S. Marine Corps; and (3) you will attend post-high school freshman or sophomore undergraduate education at a state or regionally accredited institution of post- secondary education situated in the United States.

Award: Scholarship for use in freshman or sophomore years; not renewable. *Number:* 1–10. *Amount:* $1000–$5000.

Eligibility Requirements: Applicant must be enrolled or expecting to enroll full-time at a two-year or four-year institution and single. Applicant or parent of applicant must be member of Fleet Reserve Association/Auxiliary. Available to U.S. citizens. Applicant must have served in the Navy.

Application Requirements: Application form, community service, essay, recommendations or references, transcript. *Deadline:* April 15.

Contact: Mrs. Marilyn Smith, Scholarship Administrator
FRA Education Foundation
125 North West Street
Alexandria, VA 22314-2754
Phone: 703-683-1400 Ext. 107
E-mail: scholars@fra.org

STANLEY A. DORAN MEMORIAL SCHOLARSHIP

Only dependent children of members in good standing of the FRA, currently or at time of death, are eligible for this award. Applicant must be a U.S. citizen, registered as a full time student in an accredited college located in the United States of America.

Award: Scholarship for use in freshman, sophomore, junior, or senior years; not renewable. *Number:* 1. *Amount:* $1000–$5000.

Eligibility Requirements: Applicant must be enrolled or expecting to enroll full-time at a two-year or four-year institution or university. Applicant or parent of applicant must be member of Fleet Reserve

Association/Auxiliary. Available to U.S. citizens. Applicant must have served in the Coast Guard, Marine Corps, or Navy.

Application Requirements: Application form, community service, essay, recommendations or references, transcript. *Deadline:* April 15.

Contact: Mrs. Marilyn Smith, Scholarship Administrator
FRA Education Foundation
125 North West Street
Alexandria, VA 22314-2754
Phone: 703-683-1400 Ext. 107
E-mail: scholars@fra.org

GEOLOGICAL SOCIETY OF AMERICA

http://www.geosociety.org/

NORTHEASTERN SECTION UNDERGRADUATE STUDENT RESEARCH GRANTS

Grants to support individual research by sophomore or junior undergraduates attending universities within geographic boundaries of the Northeastern Section. Must be a student associate or a member of GSA.

Award: Grant for use in sophomore or junior years; not renewable.

Eligibility Requirements: Applicant must be enrolled or expecting to enroll full- or part-time at a four-year institution or university. Applicant or parent of applicant must be member of Geological Society of America. Available to U.S. citizens.

Application Requirements: Application form, financial need analysis, proposal text, endorsement form. *Deadline:* February 28.

Contact: Stephen Pollock, Secretary
Geological Society of America
37 College Avenue
Gorham, ME 04038
Phone: 207-780-5353
Fax: 207-228-8361
E-mail: pollock@usm.maine.edu

GIRL SCOUTS OF CONNECTICUT

http://www.gsofct.org/

EMILY CHAISON GOLD AWARD SCHOLARSHIP

An annual scholarship of $750 is awarded each year to one Gold Award recipient from the state of Connecticut during her senior year.

Award: Scholarship for use in freshman year; not renewable. *Number:* 1. *Amount:* $750.

Eligibility Requirements: Applicant must be high school student; planning to enroll or expecting to enroll full-time at a four-year institution or university; female and resident of Connecticut. Applicant or parent of applicant must be member of Girl Scouts. Available to U.S. citizens.

Application Requirements: Application form, community service, essay, recommendations or references. *Deadline:* April 1.

Contact: Nancy Bussman, Scholarship Committee
Girl Scouts of Connecticut
340 Washington Street
Hartford, CT 06106
Phone: 203-239-2922
E-mail: nbussman@gsofct.org

GLASS, MOLDERS, POTTERY, PLASTICS AND ALLIED WORKERS INTERNATIONAL UNION

http://www.gmpiu.org/

GMP MEMORIAL SCHOLARSHIP PROGRAM

Six college scholarships of $4000 per year available to the sons and daughters of members of the union. Renewable each year for a full four-year college program if adequate academic standards are maintained. Four vocational/technical/two-year associate degree scholarships of $2000 also available (not to exceed the cost of the program).

Award: Scholarship for use in freshman year; renewable. *Number:* 10. *Amount:* $2000–$4000.

Eligibility Requirements: Applicant must be high school student and planning to enroll or expecting to enroll full-time at a two-year or four-year or technical institution or university. Applicant or parent of applicant must be member of Glass, Molders, Pottery, Plastics and Allied Workers International Union. Available to U.S. and Canadian citizens.

Application Requirements: Application form, test scores. *Deadline:* November 1.

Contact: Bruce Smith, International Secretary and Treasurer
Glass, Molders, Pottery, Plastics and Allied Workers
International Union
608 East Baltimore Pike, PO Box 607
Media, PA 19063
Phone: 610-565-5051 Ext. 220
Fax: 610-565-0983

GOLDEN KEY INTERNATIONAL HONOUR SOCIETY

http://www.goldenkey.org/

GEICO LIFE SCHOLARSHIP

Ten $1000 awards will be given to outstanding students while balancing additional responsibilities. Must have completed at least 12 undergraduate credit hours in the previous year. Must be enrolled at the time of application and must be working toward a baccalaureate degree.

Award: Scholarship for use in freshman, sophomore, junior, or senior years; not renewable. *Number:* 10. *Amount:* $1000.

Eligibility Requirements: Applicant must be enrolled or expecting to enroll full- or part-time at a four-year institution or university. Applicant or parent of applicant must be member of Golden Key National Honor Society. Available to U.S. and non-U.S. citizens.

Application Requirements: Application form, essay, recommendations or references, transcript. *Deadline:* April 1.

GOLDEN KEY STUDY ABROAD SCHOLARSHIPS

Ten $1000 scholarships will be awarded each year to assist students in the pursuit of a study abroad program. Eligible members are undergraduate members who are currently enrolled in a study abroad program or will be enrolled in the academic year immediately following the granting of the award. Deadlines: April 15 and October 20.

Award: Scholarship for use in freshman, sophomore, junior, or senior years; not renewable. *Number:* 10. *Amount:* $1000.

Eligibility Requirements: Applicant must be enrolled or expecting to enroll full-time at a four-year institution or university. Applicant or parent of applicant must be member of Golden Key National Honor Society. Available to U.S. and non-U.S. citizens.

Application Requirements: Application form, description of the planned academic program, essay, transcript. *Deadline:* varies.

GOLF COURSE SUPERINTENDENTS ASSOCIATION OF AMERICA

http://www.eifg.org/

GOLF COURSE SUPERINTENDENTS ASSOCIATION OF AMERICA LEGACY AWARD

Awards of $1500 for the children or grandchildren of Golf Course Superintendents Association of America members. Applicants must be enrolled full-time at an accredited institution of higher learning, or for high school seniors, they must have been accepted at such an institution for the next academic year.

Award: Scholarship for use in freshman, sophomore, junior, or senior years; not renewable. *Number:* 20. *Amount:* $1500.

Eligibility Requirements: Applicant must be enrolled or expecting to enroll full-time at a two-year or four-year or technical institution or university. Applicant or parent of applicant must be member of Golf Course Superintendents Association of America. Available to U.S. and non-U.S. citizens.

Application Requirements: Application form, essay, recommendations or references, transcript. *Deadline:* April 15.

Contact: Mischia Wright, Senior Manager, Development
Phone: 800-472-7878 Ext. 4445
E-mail: mwright@gcsaa.org

JOSEPH S. GARSKE COLLEGIATE GRANT PROGRAM

Renewable award available to children/step children of GCSAA members who have been active members for five or more consecutive years for use at an accredited college or trade school. Applicant must be a graduating high school senior and be accepted at an institution of higher learning for the upcoming year.

Award: Scholarship for use in freshman year; not renewable. *Number:* 1–4. *Amount:* $1500–$2500.

Eligibility Requirements: Applicant must be high school student and planning to enroll or expecting to enroll full-time at a two-year or four-year or technical institution or university. Applicant or parent of applicant must be member of Golf Course Superintendents Association of America. Available to U.S. and non-U.S. citizens.

Application Requirements: Application form, essay, letter of acceptance, transcript. *Deadline:* March 15.

Contact: Mischia Wright, Senior Manager, Development
Phone: 800-472-7878 Ext. 4445
E-mail: mwright@gcsaa.org

HAWAII EDUCATION ASSOCIATION

http://www.heaed.com/

HAWAII EDUCATION ASSOCIATION HIGH SCHOOL STUDENT SCHOLARSHIP

Scholarship available to high school seniors planning on attending four-year college/university. Must be children or grandchildren of HEA members. Membership must be for at least one year.

Award: Scholarship for use in freshman year; not renewable. *Number:* up to 5. *Amount:* up to $1000.

Eligibility Requirements: Applicant must be high school student; planning to enroll or expecting to enroll full-time at a four-year institution or university and resident of Hawaii. Applicant or parent of applicant must be member of Hawaii Education Association. Available to U.S. citizens.

Application Requirements: Application form, driver's license, financial need analysis, personal photograph, recommendations or references, transcript. *Deadline:* April 1.

HAWAII EDUCATION ASSOCIATION UNDERGRADUATE COLLEGE STUDENT SCHOLARSHIP

Scholarships to children and grandchildren of HEA members. To qualify, the HEA member should have at least one year membership in HEA. Four scholarships of $1000 each are offered to deserving continuing, full-time undergraduate college students in any two- or four-year accredited institution of higher learning.

Award: Scholarship for use in freshman, sophomore, junior, or senior years; not renewable. *Number:* up to 4. *Amount:* up to $1000.

Eligibility Requirements: Applicant must be enrolled or expecting to enroll full-time at a two-year or four-year institution or university. Applicant or parent of applicant must be member of Hawaii Education Association. Available to U.S. citizens.

Application Requirements: Application form, financial need analysis, personal statement, recommendations or references, transcript. *Deadline:* April 1.

Contact: Carol Yoneshige, Executive Director
Hawaii Education Association
1953 South Beretania Street, Suite 3C
Honolulu, HI 96826-1304
Phone: 808-949-6657
Fax: 808-944-2032

HEBREW IMMIGRANT AID SOCIETY

http://www.hias.org/

HEBREW IMMIGRANT AID SOCIETY SCHOLARSHIP AWARDS COMPETITION

Contestants must be Hebrew Immigrant Aid Society-assisted refugee who came to the United States after January 1, 1992. Must have completed two semesters at a U.S. high school, college, or graduate school. Application and information are available at website http://www.hias.org. Applications will be accepted only if submitted online.

Award: Scholarship for use in freshman, sophomore, junior, senior, or graduate years; not renewable. *Number:* 75–150. *Amount:* $2000.

Eligibility Requirements: Applicant must be of Jewish heritage and enrolled or expecting to enroll full-time at a two-year or four-year or technical institution or university. Applicant or parent of applicant must be member of Hebrew Immigrant Aid Society. Available to U.S. citizens.

Application Requirements: Application form, community service, essay, financial need analysis, test scores, transcript. *Deadline:* March 1.

Contact: Miriam Ignatoff, Scholarship Committee
Phone: 212-613-1358
E-mail: scholarship@hias.org

HELLENIC UNIVERSITY CLUB OF PHILADELPHIA

http://www.hucphila.org/

PAIDEIA SCHOLARSHIP

$3000 merit scholarship awarded to the child of a Hellenic University Club of Philadelphia member. Must be a U.S. citizen of Greek descent and a resident of particular counties in NJ or PA.

Award: Scholarship for use in freshman, sophomore, junior, or senior years; not renewable. *Number:* 1. *Amount:* up to $3000.

Eligibility Requirements: Applicant must be of Greek heritage; enrolled or expecting to enroll full-time at a four-year institution or university and resident of New Jersey, Pennsylvania. Applicant or parent of applicant must be member of Hellenic University Club of Pennsylvania. Available to U.S. citizens.

Application Requirements: Application form, financial need analysis, transcript. *Deadline:* April 21.

Contact: Anna Hadgis, Scholarship Chairman
Phone: 610-613-4310
E-mail: hucphila@yahoo.com

HONOR SOCIETY OF PHI KAPPA PHI

http://www.PhiKappaPhi.org/

LITERACY GRANT COMPETITION

Grants up to $2500 are awarded to Phi Kappa Phi members for projects relating to a broad definition of literacy (math, science, music, art, reading, health, etc.). These projects should fulfill the spirit of volunteerism and community. Eligible applicants must be Active members of Phi Kappa Phi.

Award: Grant for use in freshman, sophomore, junior, senior, graduate, or postgraduate years; not renewable. *Number:* up to 18. *Amount:* $300–$2500.

Eligibility Requirements: Applicant must be enrolled or expecting to enroll full- or part-time at a two-year or four-year or technical institution or university. Applicant or parent of applicant must be member of Phi Kappa Phi. Available to U.S. and non-U.S. citizens.

Application Requirements: Application form, application form may be submitted online (http://apply.phikappaphi.org/Awards/SignIn.aspx?ReturnUrl=/Awards/Programs/Literacy/ApplicantInformation.aspx), itemized budget. *Deadline:* April 1.

Contact: Mrs. Maria Davis, Awards and Benefits Manager
Honor Society of Phi Kappa Phi
7576 Goodwood Boulevard
Baton Rouge, LA 70806
Phone: 225-388-4917 Ext. 35
Fax: 225-388-4900
E-mail: mdavis@phikappaphi.org

INDEPENDENT OFFICE PRODUCTS AND FURNITURE DEALERS ASSOCIATION

http://www.iopfda.org/

NOPA AND OFDA SCHOLARSHIP AWARD

Candidates must have graduated from high school or its equivalent before July 1 of the year in which they would use the scholarship. Must have an academic record sufficient to be accepted by an accredited college, junior college, or technical institute. Must be a relative of a member of NOPA or OFDA.

Award: Scholarship for use in freshman, sophomore, junior, or senior years; not renewable. *Number:* up to 25. *Amount:* $2000.

Eligibility Requirements: Applicant must be enrolled or expecting to enroll full- or part-time at a two-year or four-year or technical institution or university. Applicant or parent of applicant must be member of Independent Office Products and Furniture Dealers Association. Available to U.S. and non-U.S. citizens.

Application Requirements: Application form, recommendations or references, transcript. *Deadline:* March 16.

Contact: Billie Zidek, Scholarship Administrator
Phone: 703-549-9040 Ext. 121
E-mail: bzidek@iopfda.org

INTERNATIONAL BROTHERHOOD OF TEAMSTERS SCHOLARSHIP FUND

http://www.teamster.org/

JAMES R. HOFFA MEMORIAL SCHOLARSHIP FUND

Scholarships available to children and grandchildren of members of the International Brotherhood of Teamsters (in good standing). Thirty-one of the awards are renewed on an annual basis. Sixty-nine of the awards are a one-time award (non-renewable). The recipient plan to attend a four-year institution and must maintain 3.0 GPA.

Award: Scholarship for use in freshman, sophomore, junior, or senior years; renewable. *Number:* 1–100. *Amount:* $1000–$10,000.

Eligibility Requirements: Applicant must be high school student and planning to enroll or expecting to enroll full-time at a four-year institution or university. Applicant or parent of applicant must be member of International Brotherhood of Teamsters. Applicant must have 3.0 GPA or higher. Available to U.S. and Canadian citizens.

Application Requirements: Application form, entry in a contest, list of activities, recommendations or references, test scores, transcript. *Deadline:* March 31.

Contact: Mrs. Traci Jacobs, Administrative Manager
International Brotherhood of Teamsters Scholarship Fund
25 Louisiana Avenue, NW
Washington, DC 20001
Phone: 202-624-8735
Fax: 202-624-7457
E-mail: scholarship@teamster.org

INTERNATIONAL CHEMICAL WORKERS UNION

http://www.icwuc.org/

WALTER L. MITCHELL MEMORIAL AWARDS

Award available to children of International Chemical Workers Union members. Applicants must be starting their freshman year of college.

Award: Scholarship for use in freshman year; not renewable. *Number:* 12. *Amount:* $1500.

Eligibility Requirements: Applicant must be high school student and planning to enroll or expecting to enroll full-time at a two-year or four-year or technical institution or university. Applicant or parent of applicant must be member of International Chemical Workers Union. Available to U.S. citizens.

Application Requirements: Application form, biographical questionnaire, test scores, transcript. *Deadline:* April 23.

Contact: Sue Everhart, Secretary for Research and Education
International Chemical Workers Union
1799 Akron-Peninsula Road
Akron, OH 44313
Phone: 330-926-1444 Ext. 134
Fax: 330-926-0816
E-mail: severhart@icwuc.org

INTERNATIONAL EXECUTIVE HOUSEKEEPERS ASSOCIATION

http://www.ieha.org/

INTERNATIONAL EXECUTIVE HOUSEKEEPERS ASSOCIATION EDUCATIONAL FOUNDATION SPARTAN SCHOLARSHIP

Award available to IEHA members and their immediate families. Scholarship will be awarded to the best qualified candidate as determined by IEHA's education committee.

Award: Scholarship for use in freshman, sophomore, junior, or senior years; not renewable. *Number:* 1. *Amount:* $1500.

Eligibility Requirements: Applicant must be enrolled or expecting to enroll full- or part-time at a four-year institution or university. Applicant or parent of applicant must be member of International Executive Housekeepers Association. Available to U.S. and non-U.S. citizens.

Application Requirements: Application form, financial need analysis. *Deadline:* September 10.

INTERNATIONAL FEDERATION OF PROFESSIONAL AND TECHNICAL ENGINEERS

http://www.ifpte.org/

INTERNATIONAL FEDERATION OF PROFESSIONAL AND TECHNICAL ENGINEERS ANNUAL SCHOLARSHIP

Scholarship for high school seniors who have demonstrated academic achievement and service to their school and community. Only children or grandchildren of IFPTE members are eligible. Must be a U.S. or Canadian citizen. Three scholarships of $1500 are granted.

Award: Scholarship for use in freshman year; not renewable. *Number:* 3. *Amount:* $1500.

Eligibility Requirements: Applicant must be high school student and planning to enroll or expecting to enroll full-time at a four-year institution or university. Applicant or parent of applicant must be member of International Federation of Professional and Technical Engineers. Applicant or parent of applicant must have employment or volunteer experience in community service. Available to U.S. and Canadian citizens.

Application Requirements: Application form, essay, recommendations or references, transcript. *Deadline:* March 15.

Contact: Candace Rhett, Communications Representative
International Federation of Professional and Technical Engineers
8630 Fenton Street, Suite 400
Silver Spring, MD 20910
Phone: 301-565-9016
Fax: 301-565-0018
E-mail: crhett@ifpte.org

INTERNATIONAL UNION OF BRICKLAYERS AND ALLIED CRAFTSMEN

http://www.bacweb.org/

CANADIAN BATES SCHOLARSHIP PROGRAM

Renewable scholarship for high school seniors for their undergraduate study. Two scholarships are granted annually and the award value is CAN$1200 or CAN$1500. Must be the son or daughter of a Canadian BAC member in good standing of a Canadian BAC local, and a high school senior planning to attend college in the fall.

Award: Scholarship for use in freshman year; renewable. *Number:* 2.

Eligibility Requirements: Applicant must be Canadian citizen; high school student and planning to enroll or expecting to enroll full- or part-time at a four-year institution or university. Applicant or parent of applicant must be member of International Union of Bricklayers and Allied Craftworkers.

Application Requirements: Application form. *Deadline:* March 1.

Contact: Mrs. Constance Lambert, Director of Education
International Union of Bricklayers and Allied Craftsmen
620 F Street, NW
Washington, DC 20004
Phone: 202-383-3110
E-mail: mmccarthy@bacweb.org

U.S. BATES SCHOLARSHIP PROGRAM

Scholarship awards a stipend of $2500 per year for up to four years to two students annually. The program is open to sons and daughters of U.S. BAC members in good standing of U.S. BAC locals who are in their junior year of high school, and who either have taken or plan to take the standardized PSAT exam.

Award: Scholarship for use in freshman year; renewable. *Number:* 3. *Amount:* $2500.

Eligibility Requirements: Applicant must be high school student and planning to enroll or expecting to enroll full- or part-time at a four-year institution or university. Applicant or parent of applicant must be member of International Union of Bricklayers and Allied Craftworkers. Available to U.S. citizens.

Application Requirements: Application form. *Deadline:* March 1.

Contact: Mrs. Constance Lambert, Director of Education
International Union of Bricklayers and Allied Craftsmen
620 F Street, NW
Washington, DC 20004
Phone: 202-383-3110
E-mail: mmccarthy@bacweb.org

ITALIAN CATHOLIC FEDERATION INC.

http://www.icf.org/

ITALIAN CATHOLIC FEDERATION FIRST YEAR SCHOLARSHIP

Scholarship for undergraduate students of the Catholic faith and of Italian heritage (or children or grand children of non-Italian ICF members). Must have minimum 3.2 GPA.

Award: Scholarship for use in freshman year; not renewable. *Number:* 180–200.

Eligibility Requirements: Applicant must be Roman Catholic; high school student; planning to enroll or expecting to enroll full-time at a four-year institution or university and resident of Arizona, California, Illinois, Nevada. Applicant or parent of applicant must be member of Italian Catholic Federation. Available to U.S. citizens.

Application Requirements: Application form, essay, financial need analysis, recommendations or references, test scores, transcript. *Deadline:* March 15.

JUNIOR ACHIEVEMENT

http://www.ja.org/

JOE FRANCOMANO SCHOLARSHIP

Renewable award to high school seniors who have demonstrated academic achievement, leadership skills, and financial need. May be used at any accredited post secondary educational institution for any field of study resulting in a baccalaureate degree. Must have completed JA Company Program or JA Economics.

Award: Scholarship for use in freshman year; renewable. *Number:* 1. *Amount:* $5000.

Eligibility Requirements: Applicant must be high school student; planning to enroll or expecting to enroll full-time at a four-year institution or university and must have an interest in leadership. Applicant or parent of applicant must be member of Junior Achievement. Applicant must have 3.0 GPA or higher. Available to U.S. citizens.

Application Requirements: Application form, essay, financial need analysis, recommendations or references, transcript. *Deadline:* February 1.

Contact: Gwen Rose, Scholarship Coordinator
Phone: 719-540-6134
E-mail: dterry@ja.org

KAPPA ALPHA THETA FOUNDATION

http://www.kappaalphathetafoundation.org/

KAPPA ALPHA THETA FOUNDATION NON-DEGREE EDUCATIONAL GRANT PROGRAM

Kappa Alpha Theta Foundation grants provide funds for collegian and alumnae members of Kappa Alpha Theta Fraternity for leadership training and non-degree educational opportunities. Individual Thetas, collegian or alumna, and college and alumnae chapters are eligible to apply.

Award: Grant for use in freshman, sophomore, junior, senior, graduate, or postgraduate years; not renewable. *Number:* 1–50. *Amount:* $100–$5000.

Eligibility Requirements: Applicant must be enrolled or expecting to enroll full- or part-time at an institution or university and female. Applicant or parent of applicant must be member of Greek Organization. Available to U.S. and non-U.S. citizens.

Application Requirements: Application form, application form may be submitted online, recommendations or references. *Deadline:* continuous.

Contact: Ms. Gaylena Merritt, Manager of Programs
Phone: 317-876-1870 Ext. 148
E-mail: gmerritt@kappaalphatheta.org

KAPPA ALPHA THETA FOUNDATION SCHOLARSHIP PROGRAM

Kappa Alpha Theta Foundation awards scholarships to graduate and undergraduate members of Kappa Alpha Theta Fraternity. Scholarships are awarded based upon academic performance, fraternity activities, campus and/or community activities, financial need (for need-based awards), and references.

Award: Scholarship for use in sophomore, junior, senior, graduate, or postgraduate years; not renewable. *Number:* 200–230. *Amount:* $1000–$12,000.

Eligibility Requirements: Applicant must be enrolled or expecting to enroll full- or part-time at a two-year or four-year institution or university and female. Applicant or parent of applicant must be member of Greek Organization. Available to U.S. and non-U.S. citizens.

Application Requirements: Application form, application form may be submitted online, community service, essay, financial need analysis, recommendations or references, transcript. *Deadline:* March 1.

Contact: Ms. Gaylena Merritt, Manager of Programs
Phone: 317-876-1870 Ext. 148
E-mail: gmerritt@kappaalphatheta.org

KNIGHTS OF COLUMBUS

http://www.kofc.org/

FOURTH DEGREE PRO DEO AND PRO PATRIA (CANADA)

Renewable scholarships for members of Canadian Knights of Columbus councils and their children who are entering first year of study for baccalaureate degree. Based on academic excellence. Award not limited to Fourth Degree members.

Award: Scholarship for use in freshman year; renewable. *Amount:* $1500.

Eligibility Requirements: Applicant must be Roman Catholic; Canadian citizen and enrolled or expecting to enroll full-time at a four-year institution or university. Applicant or parent of applicant must be member of Knights of Columbus. Applicant must have 3.0 GPA or higher.

Application Requirements: Application form, recommendations or references, test scores, transcript. *Deadline:* May 1.

FOURTH DEGREE PRO DEO AND PRO PATRIA SCHOLARSHIPS

Award available to students entering freshman year at a Catholic university or college in United States. Applicant must be a member or child of a member of Knights of Columbus or Columbian Squires. Scholarships are awarded on the basis of academic excellence. Minimum 3.0 GPA required. See website for additional information http://www.kofc.org.

Award: Scholarship for use in freshman, sophomore, junior, or senior years; renewable. *Amount:* $1500.

Eligibility Requirements: Applicant must be Roman Catholic and enrolled or expecting to enroll full-time at a four-year institution or university. Applicant or parent of applicant must be member of Columbian Squires, Knights of Columbus. Applicant must have 3.0 GPA or higher. Available to U.S. citizens.

Application Requirements: Application form, essay, recommendations or references, test scores, transcript. *Deadline:* March 1.

Contact: Rev. Donald Barry, Scholarship Coordinator
Knights of Columbus
Department of Scholarships, PO Box 1670
New Haven, CT 06507-0901
Phone: 202-336-6800
Fax: 202-408-8102
E-mail: info@kofc.org

FRANCIS P. MATTHEWS AND JOHN E. SWIFT EDUCATIONAL TRUST SCHOLARSHIPS

Available to dependent children of Knights of Columbus who died or became permanently disabled while in military service during a time of conflict, from a cause connected with military service, or who died as the result of criminal violence while in the performance of their duties as full-time law enforcement officers or firemen. The scholarship is awarded at a Catholic college in the amount not covered by other financial aid for tuition up to $25,000 annually.

Award: Scholarship for use in freshman, sophomore, junior, or senior years; renewable. *Amount:* up to $25,000.

Eligibility Requirements: Applicant must be Roman Catholic and enrolled or expecting to enroll full-time at a four-year institution or university. Applicant or parent of applicant must be member of Knights of Columbus. Available to U.S. citizens. Applicant or parent must meet one or more of the following requirements: general military experience; retired from active duty; disabled or killed as a result of military service; prisoner of war; or missing in action.

Application Requirements: Application form, proof of parent's military service or employment in law enforcement services. *Deadline:* March 1.

JOHN W. MCDEVITT (FOURTH DEGREE) SCHOLARSHIPS

Scholarship for students entering freshman year at a Catholic college or university in United States. Applicant must submit Pro Deo and Pro Patria Scholarship application. Must be a member or wife, son, or daughter of a member of the Knights of Columbus. Minimum 3.0 GPA required. See website for additional information http://www.fofc.org.

Award: Scholarship for use in freshman year; renewable. *Amount:* $1500.

Eligibility Requirements: Applicant must be Roman Catholic and enrolled or expecting to enroll full-time at a four-year institution or university. Applicant or parent of applicant must be member of Knights of Columbus. Applicant must have 3.0 GPA or higher. Available to U.S. citizens.

Application Requirements: Application form, recommendations or references, test scores, transcript. *Deadline:* March 1.

PERCY J. JOHNSON ENDOWED SCHOLARSHIPS

Renewable scholarship for young men entering freshman year at a Catholic college or university. Applicants must submit Pro Deo and Pro Patria Scholarship application and a copy of Student Aid Report (SAR). Must be a member or a son of a member of the Knights of Columbus. Must also rank in upper third of class or have 3.0 GPA. See website for additional information http://www.kofc.org.

Award: Scholarship for use in freshman year; renewable. *Amount:* $1500.

Eligibility Requirements: Applicant must be Roman Catholic; enrolled or expecting to enroll full-time at a four-year institution or university and male. Applicant or parent of applicant must be member of Knights of Columbus. Applicant must have 3.0 GPA or higher. Available to U.S. citizens.

Application Requirements: Application form, financial need analysis, recommendations or references, test scores, transcript. *Deadline:* March 1.

LADIES AUXILIARY OF THE FLEET RESERVE ASSOCIATION

http://www.fra.org/

ALLIE MAE ODEN MEMORIAL SCHOLARSHIP

Scholarships are given to the children/grandchildren of members of the FRA or LA FRA. Selections are based on financial need, academic standing, character, and leadership qualities. Must be sponsored by a FRA member in good standing.

Award: Scholarship for use in freshman, sophomore, junior, senior, graduate, or postgraduate years; not renewable. *Amount:* $1500.

Eligibility Requirements: Applicant must be enrolled or expecting to enroll full-time at a two-year or four-year institution or university. Applicant or parent of applicant must be member of Fleet Reserve Association/Auxiliary. Available to U.S. citizens. Applicant or parent must meet one or more of the following requirements: Coast Guard, Marine Corps, or Navy experience; retired from active duty; disabled or killed as a result of military service; prisoner of war; or missing in action.

Application Requirements: Application form, essay, recommendations or references, transcript. *Deadline:* April 15.

Contact: Ruth Boggs, Scholarship Chairman
Phone: 209-295-4567

LADIES AUXILIARY OF THE FLEET RESERVE ASSOCIATION-NATIONAL PRESIDENT'S SCHOLARSHIP

Scholarships are given to children/grandchildren of U.S. Navy, Marine Corps and Coast Guard personnel active Fleet Reserve, Fleet Marine Corps Reserve and Coast Guard Reserve, retired with pay or deceased. Selections are based on financial need, academic standing, character, and leadership qualities. Must be sponsored by a FRA member in good standing.

Award: Scholarship for use in freshman, sophomore, junior, or senior years; not renewable. *Number:* 1. *Amount:* $1500.

Eligibility Requirements: Applicant must be enrolled or expecting to enroll full-time at a four-year institution or university. Applicant or parent of applicant must be member of Fleet Reserve Association/Auxiliary. Available to U.S. citizens. Applicant or parent must meet one or more of the following requirements: Coast Guard, Marine Corps, or Navy experience; retired from active duty; disabled or killed as a result of military service; prisoner of war; or missing in action.

Application Requirements: Application form, essay, recommendations or references, transcript. *Deadline:* April 15.

Contact: Ruth Boggs, National Scholarship Chair
Ladies Auxiliary of the Fleet Reserve Association
PO Box 3459
Pahrump, NV 89041-3459
Phone: 775-751-3309

LADIES AUXILIARY OF THE FLEET RESERVE ASSOCIATION SCHOLARSHIP

Scholarships are given to the daughters/granddaughters of U.S. Navy, Marine Corps, and Coast Guard personnel, active Fleet Reserve, Fleet Marine Corps Reserve, and Coast Guard Reserve, retired with pay or deceased. Selections are based on financial need, academic standing, character, and leadership qualities. Must be sponsored by a FRA member in good standing.

Award: Scholarship for use in freshman, sophomore, junior, or senior years; not renewable. *Amount:* $1500.

Eligibility Requirements: Applicant must be enrolled or expecting to enroll full-time at a four-year institution or university and female. Applicant or parent of applicant must be member of Fleet Reserve Association/Auxiliary. Available to U.S. citizens. Applicant or parent must meet one or more of the following requirements: Coast Guard, Marine Corps, or Navy experience; retired from active duty; disabled or killed as a result of military service; prisoner of war; or missing in action.

Application Requirements: Application form, essay, recommendations or references, transcript. *Deadline:* April 15.

Contact: Ruth Boggs, National Scholarship Chair
Ladies Auxiliary of the Fleet Reserve Association
PO Box 3459
Pahrump, NV 89041-3459
Phone: 775-751-3309

SAM ROSE MEMORIAL SCHOLARSHIP

Scholarships are given to the child/grandchild of a deceased FRA member or persons who were eligible to be FRA members at the time of death. Selections are based on financial need, academic standing, character, and leadership qualities. Must be sponsored by a FRA member in good standing.

Award: Scholarship for use in freshman, sophomore, junior, or senior years; not renewable. *Amount:* $1500.

Eligibility Requirements: Applicant must be enrolled or expecting to enroll full-time at a four-year institution or university. Applicant or parent of applicant must be member of Fleet Reserve Association/Auxiliary. Available to U.S. citizens. Applicant or parent must meet one or more of the following requirements: Coast Guard, Marine Corps, or Navy experience; retired from active duty; disabled or killed as a result of military service; prisoner of war; or missing in action.

Application Requirements: Application form, essay, recommendations or references, transcript. *Deadline:* April 15.

Contact: Ruth Boggs, National Scholarship Chair
Ladies Auxiliary of the Fleet Reserve Association
PO Box 3459
Pahrump, NV 89041-3459
Phone: 775-751-3309

LADIES AUXILIARY TO THE VETERANS OF FOREIGN WARS

http://www.ladiesauxvfw.org/

JUNIOR GIRLS SCHOLARSHIP PROGRAM

One-time awards available to female high school students under age 17 who have been members of Junior Girls Unit of Ladies Auxiliary for one year. Awards based on scholastic aptitude, participation in Junior Girls Unit, and school activities.

Award: Scholarship for use in freshman year; not renewable. *Number:* 1. *Amount:* $7500.

Eligibility Requirements: Applicant must be high school student; age 13-16; planning to enroll or expecting to enroll full-time at a two-year or four-year or technical institution; single female and must have an interest in leadership. Applicant or parent of applicant must be member of Veterans of Foreign Wars or Auxiliary. Available to U.S. citizens.

Application Requirements: Application form, entry in a contest, recommendations or references, transcript. *Deadline:* March 12.

Contact: Judith Millick, Administrator of Programs
Ladies Auxiliary to the Veterans of Foreign Wars
406 West 34th Street, 10th Floor
Kansas City, MO 64111
Phone: 816-561-8655 Ext. 19
Fax: 816-931-4753
E-mail: jmillick@ladiesauxvfw.org

LEARNING ALLY

http://www.learningally.org/

MARION HUBER LEARNING THROUGH LISTENING AWARDS

Awards presented to Learning Ally members who are high school seniors with learning disabilities, in recognition of extraordinary leadership, scholarship, enterprise and service to others. Must have minimum 3.0 GPA.

Award: Prize for use in freshman year; not renewable. *Number:* 6. *Amount:* $2000–$6000.

Eligibility Requirements: Applicant must be learning disabled; high school student; planning to enroll or expecting to enroll full-time at a two-year or four-year institution and must have an interest in leadership. Applicant or parent of applicant must be member of Learning Ally. Applicant or parent of applicant must have employment or volunteer experience in community service. Applicant must be learning disabled. Applicant must have 3.0 GPA or higher. Available to U.S. citizens.

Application Requirements: Application form, community service, essay, recommendations or references, transcript. *Deadline:* March 3.

Contact: Julie Haggith, Strategic Communications Department
Learning Ally
20 Roszel Road
Princeton, NJ 08540
Phone: 609-520-8044
Fax: 609-520-7990
E-mail: jhaggith@learningally.org

MARY P. OENSLAGER SCHOLASTIC ACHIEVEMENT AWARDS

Award presented to Learning Ally members who are college seniors and blind or visually impaired, in recognition of extraordinary leadership, scholarship, enterprise, and service to others.

Award: Prize for use in senior or graduate years; not renewable. *Number:* up to 9. *Amount:* $1000–$6000.

Eligibility Requirements: Applicant must be visually impaired; enrolled or expecting to enroll full-time at a four-year institution or university and must have an interest in leadership. Applicant or parent of applicant must be member of Learning Ally. Applicant or parent of applicant must have employment or volunteer experience in community service. Applicant must be visually impaired. Applicant must have 3.0 GPA or higher. Available to U.S. citizens.

Application Requirements: Application form, community service, essay, recommendations or references, transcript. *Deadline:* April 14.

Contact: Julie Haggith, Strategic Communications Department
Learning Ally
20 Roszel Road
Princeton, NJ 08540
Phone: 609-520-8044
Fax: 609-520-7990
E-mail: jhaggith@learningally.org

MINNESOTA AFL-CIO

http://www.mnaflcio.org/

BILL PETERSON SCHOLARSHIP

Scholarship available to an union member, spouse, or dependent to attend a postsecondary institution. Must have participated in, or made a donation to the Bill Peterson Golf Tournament. See website for additional information, http://www.mnaflcio.org.

Award: Scholarship for use in freshman, sophomore, junior, or senior years; not renewable. *Number:* 20. *Amount:* $1000.

Eligibility Requirements: Applicant must be enrolled or expecting to enroll full-time at a four-year institution or university; resident of Minnesota; studying in Minnesota and must have an interest in golf. Applicant or parent of applicant must be member of AFL-CIO. Available to U.S. citizens.

Application Requirements: Application form, essay. *Deadline:* April 30.

MARTIN DUFFY ADULT LEARNER SCHOLARSHIP AWARD

Scholarship available for union members affiliated with the Minnesota AFL-CIO or the Minnesota Joint Council 32. May be used at any postsecondary institution in Minnesota. Information available on website at http://www.mnaflcio.org.

Award: Scholarship for use in freshman, sophomore, junior, or senior years; not renewable. *Number:* 4. *Amount:* $500.

Eligibility Requirements: Applicant must be enrolled or expecting to enroll full-time at a four-year institution or university; resident of Minnesota and studying in Minnesota. Applicant or parent of applicant must be member of AFL-CIO. Available to U.S. citizens.

Application Requirements: Application form. *Deadline:* April 30.

MINNESOTA AFL-CIO SCHOLARSHIPS

Applicant must be attending a college or university located in Minnesota. Must have a parent or legal guardian, who has held a one year membership in a local union which is an affiliate of the Minnesota AFL-CIO. Winners are selected by lot. Academic eligibility based on a straight "B" average or better. See website http://www.mnaflcio.org for information and application.

Award: Scholarship for use in freshman year; not renewable. *Number:* up to 5. *Amount:* $1000.

Eligibility Requirements: Applicant must be high school student; planning to enroll or expecting to enroll full-time at a two-year or four-year or technical institution or university and studying in Minnesota. Applicant or parent of applicant must be member of AFL-CIO. Applicant must have 3.0 GPA or higher. Available to U.S. citizens.

Application Requirements: Application form, transcript. *Deadline:* April 30.

NAAS-USA FUND, INC.

http://www.naas.org/

NAAS AWARDS

Merit-based scholarships available for tuition, room, board, books, and academically-related supplies. Applicants must be high school seniors or equivalent home-school seniors. Application periods are September 15 to May 1. Required 2.0 GPA. Electronic applications available to NAAS Subscribers; no fees for NAAS Subscribers.

Award: Scholarship for use in freshman year; renewable. *Number:* 10–14. *Amount:* $200–$10,000.

Eligibility Requirements: Applicant must be high school student and planning to enroll or expecting to enroll full-time at a four-year institution or university. Applicant or parent of applicant must be member of National Academy of American Scholars. Available to U.S. and non-U.S. citizens.

Application Requirements: Application form, application form may be submitted online (http://naas.org/). *Deadline:* May 1.

Contact: Mr. R. Thomas, c/o Scholarship Committee
NAAS-USA FUND, INC.
601 South Figueroa Street, Suite #4050
Los Angeles, CA 90017
E-mail: staff@naas.org

NATIONAL AGRICULTURAL AVIATION ASSOCIATION

http://www.agaviation.org/

WNAAA ANNUAL SCHOLARSHIP ESSAY CONTEST

Awards two prizes of $1000 and $2000 to entrants who are members of NAAA or to children, grandchildren, sons-in-law, daughters-in-law, or spouse of any NAAA operator. Must be high school graduate and enrolled in continuing education during the year of entry. Essays judged on content, theme development, clarity, originality, and proper grammar.

Award: Prize for use in freshman, sophomore, junior, senior, graduate, or postgraduate years; not renewable. *Number:* 2. *Amount:* $1000–$2000.

Eligibility Requirements: Applicant must be enrolled or expecting to enroll full- or part-time at a two-year or four-year or technical institution or university. Applicant or parent of applicant must be member of National Agricultural Aviation Association. Available to U.S. citizens.

Application Requirements: Application form, driver's license, entry in a contest, essay, one copy of the manuscript, personal photograph. *Deadline:* August 15.

NATIONAL ALLIANCE OF POSTAL AND FEDERAL EMPLOYEES (NAPFE)

http://www.napfe.com/

ASHBY B. CARTER MEMORIAL SCHOLARSHIP FUND FOUNDERS AWARD

Scholarships available to high school seniors. Must be a U.S. citizen. Applicant must be a dependent of NAPFE Labor Union member with a minimum three year membership. Applicant must take the SAT on or before March 1 of the year they apply for award.

Award: Scholarship for use in freshman year; not renewable. *Number:* 3. *Amount:* $2000–$5000.

Eligibility Requirements: Applicant must be high school student and planning to enroll or expecting to enroll full-time at a four-year institution or university. Applicant or parent of applicant must be member of National Alliance of Postal and Federal Employees. Available to U.S. citizens.

Application Requirements: Application form, community service, personal photograph, recommendations or references, self-addressed

stamped envelope with application, test scores, transcript. *Deadline:* April 1.

Contact: Melissa Jeffries-Stewart, Director
Phone: 202-939-6325 Ext. 239
Fax: 202-939-6389
E-mail: headquarters@napfe.org

NATIONAL ASSOCIATION FOR THE ADVANCEMENT OF COLORED PEOPLE

http://www.naacp.org/

AGNES JONES JACKSON SCHOLARSHIP

Scholarship for undergraduate and graduate students who have been members of the NAACP for at least one year, or fully paid life members. Undergraduates must have 2.5 GPA and graduate students must have 3.0 GPA.

Award: Scholarship for use in freshman, sophomore, junior, senior, or graduate years; not renewable. *Number:* 1. *Amount:* $1500–$2500.

Eligibility Requirements: Applicant must be American Indian/Alaska Native, Asian/Pacific Islander, Black (non-Hispanic), Hispanic and enrolled or expecting to enroll full- or part-time at a two-year or four-year institution or university. Applicant or parent of applicant must be member of National Association for the Advancement of Colored People. Available to U.S. citizens.

Application Requirements: Application form, evidence of NAACP membership, financial need analysis, recommendations or references, transcript. *Deadline:* March 7.

Contact: Victor Goode, Attorney
Phone: 410-580-5760
E-mail: info@naacp.org

NATIONAL ASSOCIATION FOR THE SELF-EMPLOYED

http://www.NASE.org/

NASE FUTURE ENTREPRENEUR SCHOLARSHIP

Scholarship of $12,000 given to undergraduate and young micro-business owner in any field of study. May renew for a $4000 scholarship each additional year for up to three consecutive years of undergraduate work for a maximum award of $24,000. Applicant must be child or dependent of an NASE Member.

Award: Scholarship for use in freshman, sophomore, junior, or senior years; not renewable. *Number:* 1. *Amount:* up to $12,000.

Eligibility Requirements: Applicant must be enrolled or expecting to enroll full-time at a four-year institution or university and must have an interest in entrepreneurship. Applicant or parent of applicant must be member of National Association for the Self-Employed. Available to U.S. citizens.

Application Requirements: Application form, application form may be submitted online (http://www.nase.org/Membership/MembersBenefits/BenefitDetails.aspx?BenefitId=71), essay, financial need analysis, interview, recommendations or references, transcript. *Deadline:* April 1.

Contact: Molly Nelson, Member Communications Manager
Phone: 202-466-2100
Fax: 202-466-2123
E-mail: mnelson@NASEadmin.org

NASE SCHOLARSHIPS

Scholarship of $4000 for high school students or college undergraduates enrolled in full-time program of study. Total number of available awards varies. Applicants must be children or dependents of NASE Members and between the ages of 16 and 24.

Award: Scholarship for use in freshman, sophomore, junior, or senior years; not renewable. *Amount:* $4000.

Eligibility Requirements: Applicant must be age 16-24; enrolled or expecting to enroll full-time at a four-year institution or university and must have an interest in leadership. Applicant or parent of applicant must be member of National Association for the Self-Employed. Available to U.S. citizens.

Application Requirements: Application form, application form may be submitted online (http://www.nase.org/Membership/

MembersBenefits/BenefitDetails.aspx?BenefitId=71), essay, financial need analysis, recommendations or references, resume, transcript. *Deadline:* April 1.

Contact: Molly Nelson, Member Communications Manager
Phone: 202-466-2100
Fax: 202-466-2123
E-mail: mnelson@NASEadmin.org

NATIONAL ASSOCIATION OF ENERGY SERVICE COMPANIES

http://www.aesc.net/

ASSOCIATION OF ENERGY SERVICE COMPANIES SCHOLARSHIP PROGRAM

Applicant must be the legal dependent of an employee of an AESC member company, or an employee. Dependents of company officers are not eligible. Must submit application to local AESC chapter chairman. Application must include ACT or SAT test scores.

Award: Scholarship for use in freshman, sophomore, junior, senior, or graduate years; renewable. *Number:* 150–200. *Amount:* $1000.

Eligibility Requirements: Applicant must be enrolled or expecting to enroll full-time at a two-year or four-year or technical institution or university. Applicant or parent of applicant must be member of Association of Energy Service Companies. Available to U.S. and non-U.S. citizens.

Application Requirements: Application form, essay, test scores, transcript. *Deadline:* March 14.

Contact: Nikki James, Administrative Assistant
Phone: 800-692-0771
Fax: 713-781-7542
E-mail: njames@aesc.net

NATIONAL ASSOCIATION OF LETTER CARRIERS

http://www.nalc.org/

COSTAS G. LEMONOPOULOS SCHOLARSHIP

Scholarships to children of NALC members attending public, four-year colleges or universities supported by the state of Florida or St. Petersburg Junior College. Scholarships are renewable one time.

Award: Scholarship for use in freshman, sophomore, junior, or senior years; renewable. *Number:* 1–20.

Eligibility Requirements: Applicant must be enrolled or expecting to enroll full-time at a two-year or four-year institution or university and studying in Florida. Applicant or parent of applicant must be member of National Association of Letter Carriers. Available to U.S. citizens.

Application Requirements: Application form, recommendations or references, transcript. *Deadline:* June 1.

Contact: Ann Porch, Membership Committee
Phone: 202-393-4695
E-mail: nalcinf@nalc.org

JOHN T. DONELON SCHOLARSHIP

Scholarship for sons and daughters of NALC members who are high school seniors when making application. The $1000 scholarship will be renewable for four years.

Award: Scholarship for use in freshman year; renewable. *Number:* 5. *Amount:* $1000.

Eligibility Requirements: Applicant must be high school student and planning to enroll or expecting to enroll full-time at a four-year institution or university. Applicant or parent of applicant must be member of National Association of Letter Carriers. Available to U.S. citizens.

Application Requirements: Application form, recommendations or references, transcript. *Deadline:* December 31.

Contact: Ann Porch, Membership Committee
Phone: 202-393-4695
E-mail: nalcinf@nalc.org

UNION PLUS SCHOLARSHIP PROGRAM

One-time cash award available for undergraduate and graduate study programs. Scholarship ranges from $500 to $4000. Three awards are granted. Must be children of members of NALC.

Award: Scholarship for use in freshman year; not renewable. *Number:* 3. *Amount:* $500–$4000.

Eligibility Requirements: Applicant must be high school student and planning to enroll or expecting to enroll full-time at a four-year institution or university. Applicant or parent of applicant must be member of National Association of Letter Carriers. Available to U.S. citizens.

Application Requirements: Application form, recommendations or references, transcript. *Deadline:* January 31.

Contact: Ann Porch, Membership Committee
Phone: 202-393-4695
E-mail: nalcinf@nalc.org

WILLIAM C. DOHERTY SCHOLARSHIP FUND

Five scholarships of $4000 each are awarded to children of members in NALC. Renewable for three consecutive years thereafter providing the winner maintains satisfactory grades. Applicant must be a high school senior when making application.

Award: Scholarship for use in freshman year; renewable. *Number:* 5. *Amount:* $4000.

Eligibility Requirements: Applicant must be high school student and planning to enroll or expecting to enroll full-time at a four-year institution or university. Applicant or parent of applicant must be member of National Association of Letter Carriers. Available to U.S. citizens.

Application Requirements: Application form, test scores, transcript. *Deadline:* December 31.

Contact: Ann Porch, Membership Committee
Phone: 202-393-4695
E-mail: nalcinf@nalc.org

NATIONAL ASSOCIATION OF SECONDARY SCHOOL PRINCIPALS

http://www.nhs.us/

NATIONAL HONOR SOCIETY SCHOLARSHIPS

One-time award to high school seniors who are National Honor Society members for use at an accredited two- or four-year college or university in the U.S. Application fee $6. Contact school counselor or NHS chapter adviser as they must nominate seniors in good standing for the award. Minimum 3.0 GPA.

Award: Scholarship for use in freshman year; not renewable. *Number:* 200. *Amount:* $1000–$13,000.

Eligibility Requirements: Applicant must be high school student and planning to enroll or expecting to enroll full-time at a two-year or four-year institution or university. Applicant or parent of applicant must be member of National Honor Society. Applicant must have 3.0 GPA or higher. Available to U.S. and non-U.S. citizens.

Application Requirements: Application form, essay, nomination by NHS adviser, recommendations or references, test scores, transcript. *Fee:* $6. *Deadline:* January 23.

Contact: Wanda Carroll, Program Manager
Phone: 703-860-0200
E-mail: carrollw@principals.org

NATIONAL BETA CLUB

http://www.betaclub.org/

NATIONAL BETA CLUB SCHOLARSHIP

Applicant must be in twelfth grade and a member of the National Beta Club. Must be nominated by school chapter of the National Beta Club, therefore, applications will not be sent to the individual students. Renewable and nonrenewable awards available. Contact school Beta Club sponsor for more information.

Award: Scholarship for use in freshman year; renewable. *Number:* 221. *Amount:* $1000–$15,000.

Eligibility Requirements: Applicant must be high school student and planning to enroll or expecting to enroll full-time at a two-year or four-year institution or university. Applicant or parent of applicant must be member of National Beta Club. Available to U.S. citizens.

Application Requirements: Application form, application form may be submitted online, essay, recommendations or references, test scores, transcript. *Fee:* $10. *Deadline:* December 10.

Contact: Mrs. Joan Burnett, Scholarship Coordinator
  Phone: 864-583-4553
  Fax: 864-542-9300
  E-mail: jburnett@betaclub.org

NATIONAL BICYCLE LEAGUE (NBL)

http://www.nbl.org/

BOB WARNICKE MEMORIAL SCHOLARSHIP PROGRAM

Scholarship assists students and their families in meeting the costs of undergraduate or trade school education. Applicant must be a high school senior, graduate or attending a postsecondary school at the time of application, or accepted and plan to attend an accredited postsecondary school as a full-time or part-time student for the complete award year. Must be an active member or official of the National Bicycle League.

Award: Scholarship for use in freshman year; not renewable.

Eligibility Requirements: Applicant must be enrolled or expecting to enroll full- or part-time at a two-year or four-year or technical institution or university. Applicant or parent of applicant must be member of National Bicycle League. Available to U.S. citizens.

Application Requirements: Acceptance letter from the school, application form, personal photograph, recommendations or references, transcript. *Deadline:* December 15.

Contact: Alyson Willett, Scholarship Committee
  Phone: 800-886-2691
  Fax: 614-777-1680
  E-mail: awillett@nbl.org

NATIONAL FFA ORGANIZATION

http://www.ffa.org/

NATIONAL FFA COLLEGIATE SCHOLARSHIP PROGRAM

Scholarships to high school seniors planning to enroll in a full-time course of study at an accredited vocational/technical school, college or university. A smaller number of awards are available to currently enrolled undergraduates. Most awards require the applicant be an FFA member. Some awards are available to non-members.

Award: Scholarship for use in freshman, sophomore, junior, or senior years; not renewable. *Number:* 1500–1600. *Amount:* $300–$26,000.

Eligibility Requirements: Applicant must be age 17-23 and enrolled or expecting to enroll full-time at a two-year or four-year or technical institution or university. Applicant or parent of applicant must be member of Future Farmers of America. Available to U.S. citizens.

Application Requirements: Application form, application form may be submitted online (http://www.ffa.org), signature page mailed by deadline. *Deadline:* February 15.

NATIONAL FOSTER PARENT ASSOCIATION

http://www.nfpaonline.org/

NATIONAL FOSTER PARENT ASSOCIATION YOUTH SCHOLARSHIP

Award for high school senior who will be entering first year of college, comparable education, or training program. Six $1000 awards, three for foster children currently in foster care with an NFPA member family, and one each for birth and adopted children of foster parents. NFPA family membership required ($35 membership fee).

Award: Scholarship for use in freshman year; not renewable. *Number:* 6. *Amount:* $1000.

Eligibility Requirements: Applicant must be high school student and planning to enroll or expecting to enroll full- or part-time at a two-year or four-year or technical institution or university. Applicant or parent of applicant must be member of National Foster Parent Association. Available to U.S. citizens.

Application Requirements: Application form, driver's license, essay, recommendations or references, test scores, transcript. *Deadline:* March 31.

Contact: Karen Jorgenson, Executive Director
  National Foster Parent Association
  7512 Stanich Avenue, Suite 6
  Gig Harbor, WA 98335
  Phone: 253-853-4000
  Fax: 253-853-4001
  E-mail: info@nfpaonline.org

NATIONAL JUNIOR ANGUS ASSOCIATION

http://www.angus.org/njaa/

ANGUS FOUNDATION SCHOLARSHIPS

Applicants must have at one time been a National Junior Angus Association member and currently be a junior, regular or life member of the association. Must have applied to undergraduate studies in any field. Applicants must have a minimum 2.0 GPA. See website for further information and to download application.

Award: Scholarship for use in freshman, sophomore, junior, senior, or graduate years; not renewable. *Number:* 75–90. *Amount:* $250–$5000.

Eligibility Requirements: Applicant must be enrolled or expecting to enroll full-time at a two-year or four-year or technical institution or university. Applicant or parent of applicant must be member of American Angus Association. Available to U.S. and Canadian citizens.

Application Requirements: Application form, recommendations or references, transcript. *Deadline:* May 1.

Contact: Mr. Milford Jenkins, Angus Foundation President
  National Junior Angus Association
  3201 Frederick Avenue
  St. Joseph, MO 64506
  Phone: 816-383-5100 Ext. 163
  Fax: 816-383-5146
  E-mail: mjenkins@angusfoundation.org

NATIONAL ORDER OF OMEGA

http://www.orderofomega.org/

FOUNDERS SCHOLARSHIP

Scholarship of $1000 available to juniors or seniors displaying leadership and service to their Order of Omega chapter.

Award: Scholarship for use in junior or senior years; not renewable. *Number:* 1. *Amount:* $1000.

Eligibility Requirements: Applicant must be enrolled or expecting to enroll full-time at a four-year institution or university and must have an interest in leadership. Applicant or parent of applicant must be member of Order of Omega. Available to U.S. and Canadian citizens.

Application Requirements: Application form, essay, personal photograph, recommendations or references, transcript. *Deadline:* November 16.

NATIONAL RIFLE ASSOCIATION

http://www.friendsofnra.org/yes

JEANNE E. BRAY MEMORIAL SCHOLARSHIP PROGRAM

Renewable scholarship of $2000 for a maximum of four years for undergraduate students enrolled full-time in accredited colleges or universities. Must have a minimum GPA of 2.5.

Award: Scholarship for use in freshman, sophomore, junior, or senior years; renewable. *Number:* 1. *Amount:* $2000.

Eligibility Requirements: Applicant must be enrolled or expecting to enroll full-time at a two-year or four-year institution or university. Applicant or parent of applicant must be member of National Rifle Association. Applicant must have 2.5 GPA or higher. Available to U.S. citizens.

Application Requirements: Application form, essay, proof of acceptance to college or university, referral on letterhead signed by agency official documenting qualifying parent, recommendations or references, test scores, transcript. *Deadline:* November 15.

Contact: Sandy Elkin, Grants Manager
 Phone: 703-267-1131
 Fax: 703-267-1083
 E-mail: selkin@nrahqn.org

NATIONAL SOCIETY DAUGHTERS OF THE AMERICAN REVOLUTION

http://www.dar.org/

NATIONAL SOCIETY DAUGHTERS OF THE AMERICAN REVOLUTION LILLIAN AND ARTHUR DUNN SCHOLARSHIP

A $2000 scholarship awarded for up to four years to well-qualified, deserving sons and daughters of members of the NSDAR. Outstanding recipients will be considered for an additional period of up to four years of study. Must include DAR member number.

Award: Scholarship for use in freshman, sophomore, junior, or senior years; renewable. *Amount:* $2000.

Eligibility Requirements: Applicant must be enrolled or expecting to enroll full-time at a four-year institution or university. Applicant or parent of applicant must be member of Daughters of the American Revolution. Available to U.S. citizens.

Application Requirements: Application form, financial need analysis, letter of sponsorship, recommendations or references, self-addressed stamped envelope with application, transcript. *Deadline:* February 15.

Contact: Tania Tatum, Manager, Office of the Reporter General
 Phone: 202-628-1776
 Fax: 202-879-3348
 E-mail: nsdarscholarships@dar.org

NATIONAL SOCIETY OF COLLEGIATE SCHOLARS (NSCS)

http://www.nscs.org/

NSCS EXEMPLARY SCHOLAR AWARD

Scholarship of $1000 available to outstanding undergraduates among the NSCS members for their high academic achievement as well as additional scholarly pursuits outside of the classroom. They should exemplify the NSCS mission: "Honoring and inspiring academic excellence and engaged citizenship for a lifetime" and show integrity in everything they do. Must have a completed profile and resume in NSCS database. Apply on website http://www.nscs.org/exemplary_scholar_award.

Award: Scholarship for use in freshman, sophomore, junior, or senior years; not renewable. *Number:* 3. *Amount:* $1000.

Eligibility Requirements: Applicant must be enrolled or expecting to enroll full- or part-time at a four-year institution or university and must have an interest in leadership. Applicant or parent of applicant must be member of National Society of Collegiate Scholars. Available to U.S. and non-U.S. citizens.

Application Requirements: Application form. *Deadline:* April 30.

Contact: Stephen Loflin, Executive Director
 Phone: 202-965-9000
 E-mail: nscs@nscs.org

NSCS INTEGRITY SCHOLARSHIP

Award of $1000 to ten NSCS members who demonstrate a true commitment to integrity through a series of short answer questions describing a time when their integrity has been challenged. Must be working towards an undergraduate or graduate degree at an accredited university. Must have minimum GPA of 3.4 and have their resume in the NSCS database. Apply on website http://www.nscs.org/integrity-scholarship.

Award: Scholarship for use in freshman, sophomore, junior, senior, or graduate years; not renewable. *Number:* 10. *Amount:* $1000.

Eligibility Requirements: Applicant must be enrolled or expecting to enroll full- or part-time at a four-year institution or university. Applicant or parent of applicant must be member of National Society of Collegiate Scholars. Available to U.S. and non-U.S. citizens.

Application Requirements: Application form, resume. *Deadline:* January 13.

Contact: Stephen Loflin, Executive Director
 Phone: 202-965-9000
 E-mail: nscs@nscs.org

NSCS MERIT AWARD

Fifty merit awards to outstanding new NSCS members around the country. Student is chosen based upon how they exemplify the mission of NSCS. Must have a resume in the NSCS database and be a member who has joined between August of the previous year and July of the present year. Must have a minimum GPA of 3.4 and be enrolled in an accredited institution. For additional information, see website http://www.nscs.org.

Award: Scholarship for use in freshman, sophomore, junior, or senior years; not renewable. *Number:* 50. *Amount:* $1000.

Eligibility Requirements: Applicant must be enrolled or expecting to enroll full- or part-time at a two-year or four-year or technical institution or university. Applicant or parent of applicant must be member of National Society of Collegiate Scholars. Available to U.S. and non-U.S. citizens.

Application Requirements: Application form, recommendations or references, resume, transcript. *Deadline:* July 31.

Contact: Stephen Loflin, Executive Director
 Phone: 202-965-9000
 E-mail: nscs@nscs.org

NSCS SCHOLAR ABROAD SCHOLARSHIP

Scholarship for an active NSCS member who has been accepted to and enrolled in an accredited study abroad program. One $5000 scholarship is awarded each fall and spring semester and one $2500 scholarship is awarded for the summer term. Must have profile and resume in NSCS database and have a minimum 3.4 GPA. Apply at website http://www.nscs.org/scholar-abroad-scholarship.

Award: Scholarship for use in freshman, sophomore, junior, or senior years; not renewable. *Number:* 3. *Amount:* $2500–$5000.

Eligibility Requirements: Applicant must be enrolled or expecting to enroll full-time at a two-year or four-year institution or university. Applicant or parent of applicant must be member of National Society of Collegiate Scholars. Available to U.S. and non-U.S. citizens.

Application Requirements: Application form, resume. *Deadline:* April 15.

Contact: Stephen Loflin, Executive Director
 Phone: 202-965-9000
 E-mail: nscs@nscs.org

NATIONAL SOCIETY OF HIGH SCHOOL SCHOLARS

http://www.nshss.org/

ABERCROMBIE & FITCH GLOBAL DIVERSITY & LEADERSHIP SCHOLAR AWARDS

Ten scholarships of $1000 to high school seniors who are members of NSHSS. Must submit written response to the question posed by A&F regarding diversity and inclusion.

Award: Scholarship for use in freshman year; not renewable. *Number:* 10. *Amount:* $1000.

Eligibility Requirements: Applicant must be high school student and planning to enroll or expecting to enroll full-time at a four-year institution or university. Applicant or parent of applicant must be member of National Society of High School Scholars. Applicant must have 3.5 GPA or higher. Available to U.S. and non-U.S. citizens.

Application Requirements: Application form, essay, personal photograph, recommendations or references, transcript. *Deadline:* April 1.

Contact: Dr. Susan Thurman, Scholarship Director
 National Society of High School Scholars
 1936 North Druid Hills Road
 Atlanta, GA 30319
 Phone: 866-343-1800
 Fax: 404-235-5510
 E-mail: susan.thurman@nshss.org

CLAES NOBEL ACADEMIC SCHOLARSHIPS FOR NSHSS MEMBERS

Scholarship of $5000 to current high school seniors who are members of NSHSS. Award is based upon community service, leadership, academic performance, and school and extracurricular activities. Must complete an online application form. Deadline varies.

Award: Scholarship for use in freshman year; not renewable. *Number:* 5–10. *Amount:* $5000.

Eligibility Requirements: Applicant must be high school student; planning to enroll or expecting to enroll full- or part-time at a four-year institution or university and must have an interest in leadership. Applicant or parent of applicant must be member of National Society of High School Scholars. Applicant must have 3.5 GPA or higher. Available to U.S. and non-U.S. citizens.

Application Requirements: Application form, essay, personal photograph, recommendations or references, transcript. *Deadline:* November 30.

Contact: Dr. Susan Thurman, Scholarship Director
National Society of High School Scholars
1936 North Druid Hills Road
Atlanta, GA 30319
Phone: 404-235-5500
Fax: 404-235-5510

GRIFFITH COLLEGE SCHOLARS SCHOLARSHIPS FOR NSHSS MEMBERS

Five $1000 scholarships awarded to NSHSS members who are part- and full-time students. May be used at any college or university.

Award: Scholarship for use in freshman year; not renewable. *Number:* 5. *Amount:* $1000.

Eligibility Requirements: Applicant must be high school student and planning to enroll or expecting to enroll full- or part-time at a four-year institution or university. Applicant or parent of applicant must be member of National Society of High School Scholars. Applicant must have 3.5 GPA or higher. Available to U.S. and non-U.S. citizens.

Application Requirements: Application form, essay, personal photograph, recommendations or references, resume, transcript. *Deadline:* May 15.

Contact: Dr. Susan Thurman, Scholarship Director
National Society of High School Scholars
1936 North Druid Hills Road
Atlanta, GA 30319
Phone: 404-235-5500
Fax: 404-235-5510
E-mail: information@nshss.org

NATIONAL SCHOLAR AWARDS FOR NSHSS MEMBERS

Scholarship of $1000 for undergraduate study. Applicant must be a member of NSHSS.

Award: Scholarship for use in freshman year; not renewable. *Number:* 10–30. *Amount:* $1000.

Eligibility Requirements: Applicant must be high school student and planning to enroll or expecting to enroll full- or part-time at a two-year or four-year or technical institution or university. Applicant or parent of applicant must be member of National Society of High School Scholars. Available to U.S. and non-U.S. citizens.

Application Requirements: Application form, personal photograph, recommendations or references, resume, transcript. *Deadline:* November 30.

Contact: Dr. Susan Thurman, Scholarship Director
Phone: 866-343-1800
E-mail: information@nshss.org

NEW YORK STATE GRANGE

http://www.nysgrange.org/

CAROLINE KARK AWARD

Award available to a Grange member who is preparing for a career working with the deaf, or a deaf individual who is furthering his or her education beyond high school. The recipient must be a New York State resident. The award is based on funds available.

Award: Scholarship for use in freshman year; not renewable. *Number:* 1.

Eligibility Requirements: Applicant must be hearing impaired; high school student; planning to enroll or expecting to enroll full- or part-time at a four-year institution or university and resident of New York. Applicant or parent of applicant must be member of Grange Association. Applicant must be hearing impaired. Available to U.S. citizens.

Application Requirements: Application form. *Deadline:* April 15.

SUSAN W. FREESTONE EDUCATION AWARD

Grants for members of Junior Grange and Subordinate Grange in New York State. Students must enroll in an approved two or four-year college in New York State. Second grants available with reapplication.

Award: Scholarship for use in freshman or sophomore years; renewable. *Number:* 1–4. *Amount:* $1000.

Eligibility Requirements: Applicant must be high school student; planning to enroll or expecting to enroll full-time at a two-year or four-year institution; resident of New York and studying in New York. Applicant or parent of applicant must be member of Grange Association. Applicant must have 2.5 GPA or higher. Available to U.S. citizens.

Application Requirements: Application form, financial need analysis, recommendations or references, self-addressed stamped envelope with application, transcript. *Deadline:* April 15.

NORTHEASTERN LOGGERS' ASSOCIATION INC.

http://www.northernlogger.com/

NORTHEASTERN LOGGERS' ASSOCIATION SCHOLARSHIPS

Scholarships available to those whose family belongs to the Northeastern Loggers' Association or whose family member is an employee of the Industrial and Associate Members of the Northeastern Loggers' Association. Must submit paper on topic of "What it means to grow up in the forest industry."

Award: Scholarship for use in freshman, sophomore, junior, or senior years; not renewable. *Number:* 8. *Amount:* $500–$1000.

Eligibility Requirements: Applicant must be enrolled or expecting to enroll full-time at a two-year or four-year or technical institution or university. Applicant or parent of applicant must be member of Northeastern Loggers Association. Available to U.S. and non-U.S. citizens.

Application Requirements: Application form, entry in a contest, essay, transcript. *Deadline:* March 31.

Contact: Mona Lincoln, Director, Training and Safety
Northeastern Loggers' Association Inc.
PO Box 69
Old Forge, NY 13420-0069
Phone: 315-369-3078
Fax: 315-369-3736
E-mail: mona@northernlogger.com

NORTH EAST ROOFING EDUCATIONAL FOUNDATION

http://www.nerca.org/

NORTH EAST ROOFING EDUCATIONAL FOUNDATION SCHOLARSHIP

Applicants must be a member of NERCA, their employees, or their respective immediate family. Immediate family is defined as self, spouse, or child. The child may be natural, legally adopted, or a stepchild. Also must be a high school senior or graduate who plans to enroll in a full-time undergraduate course of study at an accredited two-year or four-year college, university, or vocational-technical school.

Award: Scholarship for use in freshman, sophomore, junior, or senior years; not renewable. *Number:* 11. *Amount:* up to $2000.

Eligibility Requirements: Applicant must be enrolled or expecting to enroll full-time at a two-year or four-year or technical institution or university. Applicant or parent of applicant must be member of North East Roofing Contractors Association. Available to U.S. and Canadian citizens.

Application Requirements: Application form, recommendations or references, self-addressed stamped envelope with application, transcript. *Deadline:* May 1.

Contact: Patsy Sweeney, Clerk
North East Roofing Educational Foundation
150 Grossman Drive Street, Suite 313
Braintree, MA 02184
Phone: 781-849-0555
Fax: 781-849-3223
E-mail: info@nerca.org

OFFICE AND PROFESSIONAL EMPLOYEES INTERNATIONAL UNION

http://www.opeiu.org/

OFFICE AND PROFESSIONAL EMPLOYEES INTERNATIONAL UNION HOWARD COUGHLIN MEMORIAL SCHOLARSHIP FUND

Scholarship of twelve full-time awards of $6000 and six part-time awards of $2400 is given to undergraduate students. Applicants should be a member or associate member of the Union.

Award: Scholarship for use in freshman, sophomore, junior, or senior years; not renewable. *Number:* 18. *Amount:* $2400–$6000.

Eligibility Requirements: Applicant must be enrolled or expecting to enroll full- or part-time at a two-year or four-year or technical institution or university. Applicant or parent of applicant must be member of Office and Professional Employees International Union. Available to U.S. citizens.

Application Requirements: Application form, SAT/CAT scores, transcript. *Deadline:* March 31.

Contact: Mary Mahoney, Secretary-Treasurer
Phone: 202-393-4464
Fax: 202-887-0910
E-mail: mmahoney@opeiudc.org

OHIO CIVIL SERVICE EMPLOYEES ASSOCIATION

http://www.ocsea.org/

LES BEST SCHOLARSHIP

Scholarships will be awarded to eligible union members, spouses and their dependent children. For more details see website http://www.ocsea.org.

Award: Scholarship for use in freshman, sophomore, junior, or senior years; not renewable. *Number:* 8–10. *Amount:* $500–$2000.

Eligibility Requirements: Applicant must be enrolled or expecting to enroll full- or part-time at a two-year or four-year or technical institution or university and resident of Ohio. Applicant or parent of applicant must be member of Ohio Civil Service Employee Association. Available to U.S. citizens.

Application Requirements: Application form, essay, proof of enrollment, recommendations or references, transcript. *Deadline:* April 30.

OKLAHOMA ALUMNI & ASSOCIATES OF FHA, HERO AND FCCLA INC.

http://www.okfccla.net/

OKLAHOMA ALUMNI & ASSOCIATES OF FHA, HERO, AND FCCLA INC. SCHOLARSHIP

One-time award for FCCLA members who will be pursuing a postsecondary education. Must be a resident of Oklahoma. Scholarship value is $1000. Two scholarships are granted.

Award: Scholarship for use in freshman year; not renewable. *Number:* 2. *Amount:* $1000.

Eligibility Requirements: Applicant must be high school student; planning to enroll or expecting to enroll full-time at a two-year or four-year or technical institution or university and resident of Oklahoma. Applicant or parent of applicant must be member of Family, Career and Community Leaders of America. Applicant must have 3.0 GPA or higher. Available to U.S. citizens.

Application Requirements: Application form, essay, recommendations or references, transcript. *Deadline:* March 1.

Contact: Denise Morris, State FCCLA Adviser
Oklahoma Alumni & Associates of FHA, HERO and FCCLA Inc.
1500 West Seventh Avenue
Stillwater, OK 74074
Phone: 405-743-5467
Fax: 405-743-6809
E-mail: dmorr@okcareertech.org

OREGON STUDENT ASSISTANCE COMMISSION

http://www.GetCollegeFunds.org/

AFSCME: AMERICAN FEDERATION OF STATE, COUNTY, AND MUNICIPAL EMPLOYEES COUNCIL # 75 SCHOLARSHIP

Renewable award for active, laid-off, retired, or disabled members in good standing or spouses (including life partners and their children), natural children, or grandchildren of active, laid-off, retired, disabled, or deceased members of AFSCME Council #75 in good standing. Qualifying members must have been active in AFSCME Council # 75 one year or more as of the March 1 scholarship deadline or have been a member one year or more preceding the date of layoff, death, disability, or retirement. Enrollment of at least half-time is required. FAFSA and essay required. Financial need may or may not be considered.

Award: Scholarship for use in freshman, sophomore, junior, senior, or graduate years; renewable.

Eligibility Requirements: Applicant must be enrolled or expecting to enroll full- or part-time at a two-year or four-year institution or university. Applicant or parent of applicant must be member of American Federation of State, County, and Municipal Employees. Available to U.S. citizens.

Application Requirements: Activity chart, FAFSA, application form, essay, financial need analysis, transcript. *Deadline:* March 1.

AFSCME: AMERICAN FEDERATION OF STATE, COUNTY, AND MUNICIPAL EMPLOYEES LOCAL 2067 SCHOLARSHIP

Award for active members in good standing or spouses, children, or grandchildren of active members in good standing of Oregon AFSCME Local 2067. Qualifying members must have been active in AFSCME Local 2067 one+ year as of the March scholarship deadline. Oregon residency is not required. FAFSA and essay required. Financial need is not a requirement, and may or may not be considered.

Award: Scholarship for use in freshman, sophomore, junior, or senior years; not renewable.

Eligibility Requirements: Applicant must be enrolled or expecting to enroll full- or part-time at a four-year institution or university and resident of Oregon. Applicant or parent of applicant must be member of American Federation of State, County, and Municipal Employees. Applicant must have 2.5 GPA or higher. Available to U.S. citizens.

Application Requirements: Activity chart, application form, essay, financial need analysis, recommendations or references, transcript. *Deadline:* March 1.

INTERNATIONAL BROTHERHOOD OF ELECTRICAL WORKERS LOCAL 280 SCHOLARSHIP

One-time award available for children or grandchildren of active or retired members of IBEW Local 280. Must be graduating high school seniors enrolling as first-time freshman in any college or university in the U.S. Oregon residency not required. Not based on financial need.

Award: Scholarship for use in freshman year; not renewable.

Eligibility Requirements: Applicant must be enrolled or expecting to enroll full-time at a four-year institution or university. Applicant or parent of applicant must be member of International Brotherhood of Electrical Workers. Available to U.S. citizens.

Application Requirements: Application form, essay, transcript. *Deadline:* March 1.

INTERNATIONAL UNION OF OPERATING ENGINEERS LOCAL 701 SCHOLARSHIP

One-time award available for graduating high school seniors who are children of International Union of Operating Engineers Local 701 members. Not based on financial need. Oregon residency is not required.

Award: Scholarship for use in freshman year; not renewable.

Eligibility Requirements: Applicant must be high school student and planning to enroll or expecting to enroll full-time at a four-year institution or university. Applicant or parent of applicant must be member of International Union of Operating Engineers. Available to U.S. citizens.

Application Requirements: Activities chart, application form, essay, transcript. *Deadline:* March 1.

JOSH HIETER MEMORIAL/TEAMSTERS LOCAL 223 SCHOLARSHIP

One-time award for active members or dependent children or stepchildren of active, retired, disabled, or deceased members of Local 223 of the Joint Council of Teamsters #37. Member must have been active 1+ year as of the March scholarship deadline or have been a member 1+ year preceding the date of retirement, disability, or death. For use at Oregon public or nonprofit colleges and universities. Essay is required, minimum 3.0 GPA is preferred.

Award: Scholarship for use in freshman, sophomore, junior, or senior years; not renewable.

Eligibility Requirements: Applicant must be enrolled or expecting to enroll full-time at a two-year or four-year or technical institution or university and studying in Oregon. Applicant or parent of applicant must be member of Teamsters. Available to U.S. citizens.

Application Requirements: Application form, essay, FAFSA, transcript. *Deadline:* March 1.

NORTHWEST AUTOMATIC VENDING ASSOCIATION SCHOLARSHIP

One-time award to recent high school graduates who are first-time freshmen and either children (natural, adopted, or stepchildren) or grandchildren of members or associate members of Northwest Automatic Vending Association. Oregon residency not required. For use at public or nonprofit universities only.

Award: Scholarship for use in freshman year; not renewable.

Eligibility Requirements: Applicant must be high school student and planning to enroll or expecting to enroll full-time at a four-year institution or university. Applicant or parent of applicant must be member of Northwest Automatic Vending Association. Available to U.S. citizens.

Application Requirements: Activities chart, application form, essay, financial need analysis, transcript. *Deadline:* March 1.

OREGON STATE FISCAL ASSOCIATION SCHOLARSHIP

One-time award for OSFA members or their children. Members must enroll in an Oregon public or nonprofit institution at least half-time and must study public administration, finance, economics, or related fields. Children of members must enroll full-time in an Oregon institution and may enter any program of study. Must reapply annually.

Award: Scholarship for use in freshman, sophomore, junior, or senior years; not renewable.

Eligibility Requirements: Applicant must be enrolled or expecting to enroll full- or part-time at a two-year or four-year institution; resident of Oregon and studying in Oregon. Applicant or parent of applicant must be member of Oregon State Fiscal Association. Available to U.S. citizens.

Application Requirements: Activity chart, application form, essay, financial need analysis, recommendations or references, transcript. *Deadline:* March 1.

TEAMSTERS CLYDE C. CROSBY/JOSEPH M. EDGAR MEMORIAL SCHOLARSHIP

Renewable scholarship available for Oregon resident who is a graduating high school senior with a minimum 3.0 cumulative GPA and is a child, or dependent stepchild of an active, retired, disabled, or deceased member of local union affiliated with Teamsters 37. Member must have been active for at least one year.

Award: Scholarship for use in freshman, sophomore, junior, or senior years; renewable.

Eligibility Requirements: Applicant must be high school student; planning to enroll or expecting to enroll full-time at a four-year institution and resident of Oregon. Applicant or parent of applicant must be member of Teamsters. Applicant must have 3.0 GPA or higher. Available to U.S. citizens.

Application Requirements: Activity chart, application form, essay, financial need analysis, transcript. *Deadline:* March 1.

TEAMSTERS COUNCIL 37 FEDERAL CREDIT UNION SCHOLARSHIP

One-time award for members (or dependents of members) of Council 37 Federal Credit Union who are active for one year as of the March 1 deadline, in a local that is affiliated with the Joint Council of Teamsters 37. Applicant must have a minimum GPA between 2.0 and 3.0, and be enrolled at least half-time in a two- or four-year college or university in the U.S.

Award: Scholarship for use in freshman, sophomore, junior, or senior years; not renewable.

Eligibility Requirements: Applicant must be enrolled or expecting to enroll full- or part-time at a two-year or four-year institution or university. Applicant or parent of applicant must be member of Teamsters. Available to U.S. citizens.

Application Requirements: Application form, financial need analysis, recommendations or references, transcript. *Deadline:* March 1.

TEAMSTERS LOCAL 305 SCHOLARSHIP

Renewable award for graduating Oregon high school seniors who are children or dependent stepchildren of active, retired, disabled, or deceased members of Local 305 of the Joint Council of Teamsters #37. Members must have been active at least one year. Not based on financial need. Oregon state residency is not required.

Award: Scholarship for use in freshman, sophomore, junior, or senior years; renewable.

Eligibility Requirements: Applicant must be enrolled or expecting to enroll full-time at a four-year institution or university. Applicant or parent of applicant must be member of Teamsters. Available to U.S. citizens.

Application Requirements: Application form, essay, transcript. *Deadline:* March 1.

PENNSYLVANIA AFL-CIO

http://www.paaflcio.org/

PA AFL-CIO UNIONISM IN AMERICA ESSAY CONTEST

Contest consists of three categories: high school seniors, students currently attending an accredited postsecondary institution, and affiliated members attending an accredited postsecondary institution. Must be a U.S. citizen.

Award: Prize for use in freshman, sophomore, junior, or senior years; not renewable. *Number:* 9. *Amount:* $500–$2000.

Eligibility Requirements: Applicant must be enrolled or expecting to enroll full-time at a two-year or four-year or technical institution or university. Applicant or parent of applicant must be member of AFL-CIO. Available to U.S. citizens.

Application Requirements: Application form, entry in a contest, hard copy, CD copy of essay, recommendations or references. *Deadline:* January 31.

Contact: Carl Dillinger, Education Director
     Pennsylvania AFL-CIO
     231 State Street
     Harrisburg, PA 17101-1110
     Phone: 717-231-2843
     Fax: 717-238-8541
     E-mail: cdillinger@paaflcio.org

PENNSYLVANIA FEDERATION OF DEMOCRATIC WOMEN INC.

http://www.pfdw.org/

PENNSYLVANIA FEDERATION OF DEMOCRATIC WOMEN INC. ANNUAL SCHOLARSHIP AWARDS

Award of up to $1000 for any female resident of Pennsylvania who is a junior at an accredited college or university and is a registered Democrat. Award if for their senior year. Applicants must possess a Democratic Party family background and be an active participant in activities of the Democratic Party.

Award: Scholarship for use in senior year; not renewable. *Number:* 1–4. *Amount:* $250–$1000.

Eligibility Requirements: Applicant must be enrolled or expecting to enroll full-time at a four-year institution or university; female and resident of Pennsylvania. Applicant or parent of applicant must be member of Democratic Party. Available to U.S. citizens.

Application Requirements: Application form, essay, recommendations or references, transcript. *Deadline:* May 1.

Contact: Bonita Hannis, Scholarship Chair
Pennsylvania Federation of Democratic Women Inc.
36 Betts Lane
Lock Haven, PA 17745
Phone: 570-769-7175
E-mail: behannis@kcnet.org

PENNSYLVANIA YOUTH FOUNDATION

http://www.pmyf.org/

PENNSYLVANIA MASONIC YOUTH FOUNDATION EDUCATIONAL ENDOWMENT FUND SCHOLARSHIPS

Grants for children, stepchildren, grandchildren, siblings, or dependents of members in good standing of a Pennsylvania Masonic Lodge, or members in good standing of a PA Masonic-sponsored youth group. Applicants must be high school graduates or high school seniors pursuing a college education. Minimum GPA 3.0.

Award: Grant for use in freshman, sophomore, junior, or senior years; not renewable. *Amount:* $1000–$3000.

Eligibility Requirements: Applicant must be enrolled or expecting to enroll full-time at a two-year or four-year or technical institution or university. Applicant or parent of applicant must be member of Freemasons. Applicant must have 3.0 GPA or higher. Available to U.S. and non-U.S. citizens.

Application Requirements: Application form, essay, financial need analysis, proof of relationship to a Pennsylvania Masonic or membership in a Pennsylvania Masonic-sponsored youth group, test scores, transcript. *Deadline:* March 15.

Contact: Amy Nace, Executive Assistant
Phone: 717-367-1536 Ext. 2
E-mail: pmyf@pagrandlodge.org

PHILIPINO-AMERICAN ASSOCIATION OF NEW ENGLAND

http://www.pamas.org/

PAMAS RESTRICTED SCHOLARSHIP AWARD

Award of $500 for any sons or daughters of PAMAS members who are currently active in PAMAS projects and activities. Must be of Filipino descent, a resident of New England, a high school senior at the time of award, and have college acceptance letter from accredited institution. Minimum of 3.3 GPA required. For application details visit http://www.pamas.org.

Award: Scholarship for use in freshman year; not renewable. *Number:* 1. *Amount:* $500.

Eligibility Requirements: Applicant must be Asian/Pacific Islander; high school student; planning to enroll or expecting to enroll full-time at a four-year institution or university and resident of Connecticut, Maine, Massachusetts, New Hampshire, Rhode Island, Vermont. Applicant or parent of applicant must be member of Philipino-American Association. Available to U.S. citizens.

Application Requirements: Application form, college acceptance letter, essay, recommendations or references, transcript. *Deadline:* May 31.

Contact: Amanda Kalb, First Vice President
Phone: 617-471-3513
E-mail: balic2ss@comcast.net

PHI SIGMA KAPPA INTERNATIONAL HEADQUARTERS

http://www.phisigmakappa.org/

WENDEROTH UNDERGRADUATE SCHOLARSHIP

Available to sophomores and juniors on the basis of academic criteria. Must submit an essay and letter of recommendation along with the application.

Award: Scholarship for use in sophomore or junior years; not renewable. *Number:* 1–4. *Amount:* $1750–$4000.

Eligibility Requirements: Applicant must be enrolled or expecting to enroll full-time at a four-year institution or university. Applicant or parent of applicant must be member of Phi Sigma Kappa. Available to U.S. and non-U.S. citizens.

Application Requirements: Application form, essay, personal photograph, recommendations or references, resume, transcript. *Deadline:* January 31.

Contact: Michael Carey, Executive Director
Phone: 317-573-5420
Fax: 317-573-5430
E-mail: michael@phisigmakappa.org

ZETA SCHOLARSHIP

Scholarships are available following a generous gift to the Phi Sigma Kappa Foundation from the Zeta Alumni Association. Phi Sig or a child of a Phi Sig having minimum 3.0 GPA are eligible to apply.

Award: Scholarship for use in freshman, sophomore, junior, senior, or graduate years; not renewable. *Number:* 2. *Amount:* $2500.

Eligibility Requirements: Applicant must be enrolled or expecting to enroll full-time at a four-year institution or university. Applicant or parent of applicant must be member of Phi Sigma Kappa. Applicant must have 3.0 GPA or higher. Available to U.S. citizens.

Application Requirements: Application form, community service, personal photograph, recommendations or references, resume, test scores, transcript. *Deadline:* January 31.

PHI SIGMA PI NATIONAL HONOR FRATERNITY

http://www.phisigmapi.org/

RICHARD CECIL TODD AND CLAUDA PENNOCK TODD TRIPOD SCHOLARSHIP

Scholarship to promote the future academic opportunity of brothers (members) of the fraternity, who have excelled in embodying the ideals of scholarship, leadership, and fellowship. One-time award for full-time student, sophomore level or higher, with minimum 3.0 GPA.

Award: Scholarship for use in sophomore, junior, or senior years; not renewable. *Number:* 1. *Amount:* up to $1500.

Eligibility Requirements: Applicant must be enrolled or expecting to enroll full-time at a two-year or four-year or technical institution or university and must have an interest in leadership. Applicant or parent of applicant must be member of Greek Organization. Applicant must have 3.0 GPA or higher. Available to U.S. and non-U.S. citizens.

Application Requirements: Application form, driver's license, essay, recommendations or references, transcript. *Deadline:* April 15.

Contact: Suzanne Schaffer, Executive Director
Phone: 717-299-4710
Fax: 717-390-3054
E-mail: schaffer@phisigmapi.org

PONY OF THE AMERICAS CLUB

http://www.poac.org/

PONY OF THE AMERICAS SCHOLARSHIP

Two to four renewable awards that may be used for any year or any institution but must be for full-time undergraduate study. Application and transcript required. Award restricted to those who have interest in animal or agricultural competition and active involvement in Pony of the Americas.

Award: Scholarship for use in freshman, sophomore, junior, or senior years; not renewable. *Number:* 2–4. *Amount:* $500–$1000.

Eligibility Requirements: Applicant must be enrolled or expecting to enroll full- or part-time at a two-year or four-year or technical institution or university and must have an interest in animal/agricultural competition. Applicant or parent of applicant must be member of Pony of the Americas Club. Available to U.S. and non-U.S. citizens.

Application Requirements: Application form, driver's license, entry in a contest, essay, recommendations or references, transcript. *Deadline:* March 1.

Contact: Lynda Corn, Scholarship Administrator
Pony of the Americas Club
3828 South Emerson Avenue
Indianapolis, IN 46203
Phone: 317-788-0107 Ext. 2
Fax: 317-788-8974
E-mail: poac@poac.org

PROFESSIONAL HORSEMEN'S SCHOLARSHIP FUND INC.

http://www.nationalpha.com/

PROFESSIONAL HORSEMEN'S SCHOLARSHIP FUND

Scholarship provides financial assistance from a fund established for children of professional members or professional members of more than two years who are enrolled in an approved school for the advancement of their education beyond the secondary level.

Award: Scholarship for use in freshman, sophomore, junior, senior, graduate, or postgraduate years; not renewable. *Number:* 10–20. *Amount:* $500–$1000.

Eligibility Requirements: Applicant must be enrolled or expecting to enroll full-time at a two-year or four-year or technical institution or university. Applicant or parent of applicant must be member of Professional Horsemen Association. Available to U.S. citizens.

Application Requirements: Application form, application form may be submitted online, essay, financial need analysis, recommendations or references, transcript. *Deadline:* May 1.

Contact: Mrs. Ann Grenci, Chairman, Scholarship Committee
Phone: 561-707-9094
Fax: 914-206-4574
E-mail: foxhill33@aol.com

PROJECT BEST SCHOLARSHIP FUND

http://www.projectbest.com/

PROJECT BEST SCHOLARSHIP

One-time award of $1000 to $2000 for employees or children or spouses of employees working for a company or labor union in the construction industry that is affiliated with Project BEST. Must be residents of West Virginia, Pennsylvania, or Ohio and attend a West Virginia or Ohio postsecondary institution. Must be U.S. citizens.

Award: Scholarship for use in freshman, sophomore, junior, senior, or graduate years; renewable. *Number:* 11–22. *Amount:* $1000–$2000.

Eligibility Requirements: Applicant must be enrolled or expecting to enroll full-time at a two-year or four-year institution or university; resident of Ohio, Pennsylvania, West Virginia and studying in Ohio, West Virginia. Applicant or parent of applicant must be member of AFL-CIO. Applicant or parent of applicant must have employment or volunteer experience in construction. Available to U.S. citizens.

Application Requirements: Application form. *Deadline:* continuous.

Contact: Mary Jo Klempa, Director
Project BEST Scholarship Fund
21 Armory Drive
Wheeling, WV 26003
Phone: 304-242-0520
Fax: 304-242-7261
E-mail: best2003@swave.net

PUEBLO OF ISLETA, DEPARTMENT OF EDUCATION

http://www.isletapueblo.com/

HIGHER EDUCATION SUPPLEMENTAL SCHOLARSHIP
ISLETA PUEBLO HIGHER EDUCATION DEPARTMENT

Applicants must be students seeking a postsecondary degree. The degree granting institution must be a nationally accredited vocational or postsecondary institution offering a certificate, associate, bachelors, master's or doctorate degree. Enrolled tribal members of the Isleta Pueblo may apply for this scholarship if they also apply for additional

scholarships from different sources. Deadlines: April 1 for summer, November 1 for spring and July 1 for fall.

Award: Scholarship for use in freshman, sophomore, junior, senior, graduate, or postgraduate years; renewable.

Eligibility Requirements: Applicant must be American Indian/Alaska Native and enrolled or expecting to enroll full- or part-time at a two-year or four-year or technical institution or university. Applicant or parent of applicant must be member of Ice Skating Institute. Available to U.S. citizens.

Application Requirements: Application form, certificate of Indian blood, class schedule, financial need analysis, transcript. *Deadline:* varies.

RAILWAY SUPPLY INSTITUTE

http://www.rsiweb.org/

RSI UNDERGRADUATE SCHOLARSHIP PROGRAM

Scholarship available to a full-time student enrolled in a four- or five-year program leading to a bachelor's degree. Applicants must be 22 years old or under and be the dependant son, daughter, grandson or granddaughter of a railroad employee, who is a member of one of the mechanical associations listed in the website. For application and association list go to http://www.rsiweb.org/scholarship.

Award: Scholarship for use in sophomore, junior, or senior years; not renewable. *Number:* 4. *Amount:* $3000.

Eligibility Requirements: Applicant must be enrolled or expecting to enroll full-time at a four-year institution or university. Applicant or parent of applicant must be member of Mutual Benefit Society. Available to U.S. and Canadian citizens.

Application Requirements: Application form, essay, recommendations or references, resume, transcript. *Deadline:* April 2.

Contact: Thomas Simpson, Executive Director
Phone: 202-347-4664
E-mail: rsi@railwaysupply.org

RED ANGUS ASSOCIATION OF AMERICA

http://www.redangus.org/

4 RAAA/JUNIOR RED ANGUS SCHOLARSHIP

Scholarship of $500 given to active members of the National Junior Red Angus Association. Must be high school seniors or college underclassmen.

Award: Scholarship for use in freshman or sophomore years; not renewable. *Number:* 2. *Amount:* $500.

Eligibility Requirements: Applicant must be enrolled or expecting to enroll full-time at a two-year or four-year institution or university. Applicant or parent of applicant must be member of National Junior Red Angus Association. Available to U.S. citizens.

Application Requirements: Application form, personal photograph, recommendations or references, transcript. *Deadline:* March 31.

Contact: Betty Grimshaw, Association Administrative Director
Phone: 940-387-3502
Fax: 940-383-4036
E-mail: betty@redangus.org

DEE SONSTEGARD MEMORIAL SCHOLARSHIP

Scholarship of $500 given to active members of the National Junior Red Angus Association. Must be high school seniors or college underclassmen.

Award: Scholarship for use in freshman or sophomore years; not renewable. *Number:* 2. *Amount:* $500.

Eligibility Requirements: Applicant must be enrolled or expecting to enroll full-time at a two-year or four-year institution or university. Applicant or parent of applicant must be member of National Junior Red Angus Association. Available to U.S. citizens.

Application Requirements: Application form, personal photograph, recommendations or references, transcript. *Deadline:* March 31.

Contact: Betty Grimshaw, Association Administrative Director
Phone: 940-387-3502
Fax: 940-383-4036
E-mail: betty@redangus.org

FARM AND RANCH CONNECTION SCHOLARSHIP

Scholarship of $500 given to active members of the National Junior Red Angus Association. Must be high school seniors or college underclassmen.

Award: Scholarship for use in freshman or sophomore years; not renewable. *Number:* 1. *Amount:* $500.

Eligibility Requirements: Applicant must be enrolled or expecting to enroll full-time at a two-year or four-year institution or university. Applicant or parent of applicant must be member of National Junior Red Angus Association. Available to U.S. citizens.

Application Requirements: Application form, personal photograph, recommendations or references, transcript. *Deadline:* March 31.

Contact: Betty Grimshaw, Association Administrative Director
Phone: 940-387-3502
Fax: 940-383-4036
E-mail: betty@redangus.org

LEONARD A. LORENZEN MEMORIAL SCHOLARSHIP

Scholarship of $500 given to active members of the National Junior Red Angus Association. Must be high school seniors or college underclassmen.

Award: Scholarship for use in freshman or sophomore years; not renewable. *Number:* 2. *Amount:* $500.

Eligibility Requirements: Applicant must be enrolled or expecting to enroll full-time at a two-year or four-year institution or university. Applicant or parent of applicant must be member of National Junior Red Angus Association. Available to U.S. citizens.

Application Requirements: Application form, personal photograph, recommendations or references, transcript. *Deadline:* March 31.

Contact: Betty Grimshaw, Association Administrative Director
Phone: 940-387-3502
Fax: 940-383-4036
E-mail: betty@redangus.org

THE RESERVE OFFICERS ASSOCIATION

http://www.roa.org/

HENRY J. REILLY MEMORIAL SCHOLARSHIP-HIGH SCHOOL SENIORS AND FIRST YEAR FRESHMEN

One-time award for high school seniors or college freshmen who are U.S. citizens and children or grandchildren of active members of the Reserve Officers Association. Must demonstrate leadership, have minimum 3.0 GPA and 1250 on the SAT. Must submit sponsor verification. College freshmen must submit college transcript.

Award: Scholarship for use in freshman year; not renewable. *Number:* 25–30. *Amount:* $1000.

Eligibility Requirements: Applicant must be enrolled or expecting to enroll full-time at a four-year institution or university and must have an interest in leadership. Applicant or parent of applicant must be member of Reserve Officers Association. Applicant must have 3.0 GPA or higher. Available to U.S. citizens. Applicant or parent must meet one or more of the following requirements: general military experience; retired from active duty; disabled or killed as a result of military service; prisoner of war; or missing in action.

Application Requirements: Application form, essay, test scores, transcript. *Deadline:* May 15.

Contact: Rebecca Riedler, Executive Administrator
Phone: 202-646-7706
E-mail: scholarship@roa.org

HENRY J. REILLY MEMORIAL UNDERGRADUATE SCHOLARSHIP PROGRAM FOR COLLEGE ATTENDEES

One-time award of $1000 for members and children or grandchildren of members of the Reserve Officers Association or its Auxiliary. Must be a U.S. citizen, 26 years old or younger, and enrolled at an accredited four-year institution. Must submit sponsor verification. Minimum 3.0 GPA required. Submit SAT or ACT scores; contact for score requirements.

Award: Scholarship for use in freshman, sophomore, junior, or senior years; not renewable. *Number:* 25–30. *Amount:* $1000.

Eligibility Requirements: Applicant must be enrolled or expecting to enroll full-time at a two-year or four-year institution or university. Applicant or parent of applicant must be member of Reserve Officers Association. Applicant must have 3.0 GPA or higher. Available to U.S.

citizens. Applicant or parent must meet one or more of the following requirements: general military experience; retired from active duty; disabled or killed as a result of military service; prisoner of war; or missing in action.

Application Requirements: Application form, essay, sponsor verification, test scores, transcript. *Deadline:* May 15.

Contact: Rebecca Riedler, Executive Administrator
Phone: 202-646-7706
E-mail: scholarship@roa.org

RETAIL, WHOLESALE AND DEPARTMENT STORE UNION

http://www.rwdsu.org/

ALVIN E. HEAPS MEMORIAL SCHOLARSHIP

Scholarship for RWDSU members or members of an RWDSU family. Applicant must submit 500-word essay on the benefits of union membership. See website for application, http://www.rwdsu.info/heapsscholar.htm.

Award: Scholarship for use in freshman, sophomore, junior, or senior years; not renewable.

Eligibility Requirements: Applicant must be enrolled or expecting to enroll full- or part-time at a two-year or four-year institution or university. Applicant or parent of applicant must be member of Retail, Wholesale and Department Store Union. Available to U.S. citizens.

Application Requirements: Application form, essay, transcript. *Deadline:* varies.

RHODE ISLAND FOUNDATION

http://www.rifoundation.org/

EDWARD LEON DUHAMEL FREEMASONS SCHOLARSHIP

Renewable scholarship for descendants of members of Franklin Lodge in Westerly Rhode Island. Must be accepted into an accredited postsecondary institution. Must demonstrate scholastic achievement, financial need, and good citizenship.

Award: Scholarship for use in freshman, sophomore, junior, or senior years; renewable. *Amount:* $500–$1000.

Eligibility Requirements: Applicant must be enrolled or expecting to enroll full-time at a four-year institution or university. Applicant or parent of applicant must be member of Freemasons. Available to U.S. citizens.

Application Requirements: Application form, essay, financial need analysis, self-addressed stamped envelope with application, transcript. *Deadline:* varies.

Contact: Libby Monahan, Funds Administrator
Phone: 401-274-4564 Ext. 3117
E-mail: libbym@rifoundation.org

SERVICE EMPLOYEES INTERNATIONAL UNION (SEIU)

http://www.seiu.org/

SEIU JESSE JACKSON SCHOLARSHIP PROGRAM

Renewable scholarship of $5000 given to a student whose work and aspirations for economic and social justice reflect the values and accomplishments of the Rev. Jackson.

Award: Scholarship for use in freshman, sophomore, junior, or senior years; renewable. *Number:* 1. *Amount:* $5000.

Eligibility Requirements: Applicant must be enrolled or expecting to enroll full-time at a four-year institution or university. Applicant or parent of applicant must be member of Service Employees International Union. Available to U.S. citizens.

Application Requirements: Application form, essay. *Deadline:* March 1.

SEIU JOHN GEAGAN SCHOLARSHIP

Scholarship to SEIU members or their children or SEIU local union staff. Priority will be given to those applicants who are not served by traditional education institutions-typically adults who have been in the workforce and have decided to go, or return to, college.

Award: Scholarship for use in freshman, sophomore, junior, or senior years; not renewable. *Number:* 1. *Amount:* $2500.

Eligibility Requirements: Applicant must be enrolled or expecting to enroll full-time at a two-year or four-year or technical institution or university. Applicant or parent of applicant must be member of Service Employees International Union. Available to U.S. citizens.

Application Requirements: Application form, essay. *Deadline:* March 1.

SEIU NORA PIORE SCHOLARSHIP PROGRAM

Renewable award of $4375 to SEIU members enrolled full-time in an undergraduate study. Applicant's financial need will be considered during the selection process.

Award: Scholarship for use in freshman, sophomore, junior, or senior years; renewable. *Number:* 1. *Amount:* $4375.

Eligibility Requirements: Applicant must be enrolled or expecting to enroll full-time at a four-year institution or university. Applicant or parent of applicant must be member of Service Employees International Union. Available to U.S. citizens.

Application Requirements: Application form. *Deadline:* March 1.

SEIU SCHOLARSHIP PROGRAM

Fifteen $1000 scholarships available in annual installments for up to four years. Applicants must graduate from a high school or GED program by August. Must be enrolled as a full-time college freshman by the fall semester at an accredited, four-year college or university.

Award: Scholarship for use in freshman year; renewable. *Number:* 15. *Amount:* $1000.

Eligibility Requirements: Applicant must be high school student and planning to enroll or expecting to enroll full-time at a four-year institution or university. Applicant or parent of applicant must be member of Service Employees International Union. Available to U.S. citizens.

Application Requirements: Application form. *Deadline:* March 1.

SIGMA ALPHA MU

http://www.sam-fdn.org

UNDERGRADUATE ACHIEVEMENT AWARDS

Scholarship for seniors or juniors of undergraduate students enrolled full-time study. Must be member of Sigma Alpha Mu Foundation. Scholarship value varies.

Award: Scholarship for use in junior or senior years; not renewable. *Number:* 2.

Eligibility Requirements: Applicant must be enrolled or expecting to enroll full-time at a four-year institution or university. Applicant or parent of applicant must be member of Sigma Alpha Mu Foundation. Available to U.S. citizens.

Application Requirements: Application form, transcript. *Deadline:* March 1.

Contact: Maria Mandel, Scholarship and Foundation Coordinator
Phone: 317-789-8339
Fax: 317-824-1505
E-mail: mariam@sam-fdn.org

YOUNG SCHOLARS PROGRAM

Scholarship for candidates achieving a 3.75 GPA (or equivalent) for courses taken in the academic term of the undergraduate study. Must be member of Sigma Alpha Mu Foundation. Deadline varies.

Award: Scholarship for use in freshman, sophomore, junior, or senior years; not renewable. *Amount:* $200.

Eligibility Requirements: Applicant must be enrolled or expecting to enroll full-time at a four-year institution or university. Applicant or parent of applicant must be member of Sigma Alpha Mu Foundation. Applicant must have 3.5 GPA or higher. Available to U.S. citizens.

Application Requirements: Application form, transcript. *Deadline:* varies.

Contact: Maria Mandel, Scholarship and Foundation Coordinator
Phone: 317-789-8339
Fax: 317-824-1505
E-mail: mariam@sam-fdn.org

SIGMA CHI FOUNDATION

http://foundation.sigmachi.org

GENERAL SCHOLARSHIP GRANTS

Applicants must have completed three semesters (or four quarters) of undergraduate study to be considered for current year awards. Funds are available for tuition/fees payments only.

Award: Scholarship for use in sophomore, junior, or senior years; not renewable.

Eligibility Requirements: Applicant must be enrolled or expecting to enroll full-time at a four-year institution or university and male. Applicant or parent of applicant must be member of Sigma Chi Fraternity. Available to U.S. and non-U.S. citizens.

Application Requirements: Application form, financial need analysis, recommendations or references, transcript. *Deadline:* April 13.

Contact: Heidi Holley, Scholarship Administrator
Phone: 847-869-3655 Ext. 270
Fax: 847-869-4906
E-mail: heidi.holley@sigmachi.org

SLOVAK GYMNASTIC UNION SOKOL, USA

http://www.sokolusa.org/

SLOVAK GYMNASTIC UNION SOKOL, USA/MILAN GETTING SCHOLARSHIP

Available to members of SOKOL, U.S.A who have been in good standing for at least three years. Must have plans to attend college. Renewable for a maximum of four years, based upon academic achievement. Minimum GPA 2.5 required.

Award: Scholarship for use in freshman, sophomore, junior, or senior years; renewable. *Number:* 4–8. *Amount:* $500.

Eligibility Requirements: Applicant must be enrolled or expecting to enroll full-time at a four-year institution or university. Applicant or parent of applicant must be member of SOKOL, USA. Applicant must have 2.5 GPA or higher. Available to U.S. citizens.

Application Requirements: Application form, member of the Slovak Gymnastic Union Sokol of the U.S.A. for at least 3 years, recommendations or references, transcript. *Deadline:* April 15.

Contact: Milan Kovac, Supreme Secretary
Slovak Gymnastic Union SOKOL, USA
276 Prospect Street, PO Box 189
East Orange, NJ 07019
Phone: 973-676-0280
Fax: 973-676-3348
E-mail: sokolusahqs@aol.com

SLOVENIAN WOMEN'S UNION SCHOLARSHIP FOUNDATION

http://www.swua.org/

SLOVENIAN WOMEN'S UNION OF AMERICA SCHOLARSHIP FOUNDATION

One-time award for full-time study only. Applicant must have been an active participant or member of Slovenian Women's Union for the past three years. Essay, transcripts, letters of recommendation from principal/teacher and SWU branch officer, financial need form, photo, civic and church activities information required. Open to high school seniors.One graduate school scholarship of $2,000 available to student majoring in education. Membership in Slovenian Women's Unon not required. Applicant must be of Slovenian ancestry.One Graudate school scholarship of $2,000 available to student majoring in science, mathematics, or engineering. Membership in Slovenian Women' s Union not required. Applicant must be of Slovenian ancestry.

Award: Scholarship for use in freshman, sophomore, junior, senior, or graduate years; not renewable. *Number:* 5–6. *Amount:* $1000–$2000.

Eligibility Requirements: Applicant must be enrolled or expecting to enroll full-time at a two-year or four-year or technical institution or university. Applicant or parent of applicant must be member of Slovenian Women's Union of America. Available to U.S. citizens.

Application Requirements: Application form, community service, essay, financial need analysis, personal photograph, recommendations or references, resume, self-addressed stamped envelope with application, test scores, transcript. *Deadline:* March 1.

Contact: Mary Turvey, Director
Slovenian Women's Union Scholarship Foundation
4 Lawrence Drive
Marquette, MI 49855
Phone: 906-249-4288
E-mail: mturvey@aol.com

SONS OF NORWAY FOUNDATION

http://www.sonsofnorway.com/

ASTRID G. CATES AND MYRTLE BEINHAUER SCHOLARSHIP FUNDS

Merit and need-based award available to students ages 17 to 22 who are members, children, or grandchildren of members of the Sons of Norway. School transcript required. Academic potential and clarity of study plan is key criterion for award. Minimum 3.0 GPA required.

Award: Scholarship for use in freshman, sophomore, junior, or senior years; not renewable. *Number:* 2–7. *Amount:* $1000–$3000.

Eligibility Requirements: Applicant must be age 17-22; enrolled or expecting to enroll full-time at a two-year or four-year institution or university and resident of Yukon. Applicant or parent of applicant must be member of Mutual Benefit Society. Applicant must have 3.0 GPA or higher. Available to U.S. citizens.

Application Requirements: Application form, community service, essay, financial need analysis, personal photograph, recommendations or references, test scores, transcript. *Deadline:* March 1.

SOUTH CAROLINA STATE EMPLOYEES ASSOCIATION

http://www.scsea.com/

ANNE A. AGNEW SCHOLARSHIP

Nonrenewable scholarship for full-time study only. Must be a sophomore, junior, senior, graduate or postgraduate student. Application forms are available after January 1 of each year.

Award: Scholarship for use in sophomore, junior, senior, graduate, or postgraduate years; not renewable. *Number:* 3. *Amount:* $1000.

Eligibility Requirements: Applicant must be enrolled or expecting to enroll full-time at a four-year institution or university and resident of South Carolina. Applicant or parent of applicant must be member of South Carolina State Employees Association. Available to U.S. and non-U.S. citizens.

Application Requirements: Application form, essay, financial need analysis, transcript. *Deadline:* March 12.

Contact: Broadus Jamerson, Executive Director
South Carolina State Employees Association
PO Box 8447
Columbia, SC 29202
Phone: 803-765-0680
Fax: 803-779-6558
E-mail: scsea@scsea.com

RICHLAND/LEXINGTON SCSEA SCHOLARSHIP

Scholarships available to SCSEA members or their relatives, with priority given to Richland-Lexington Chapter members, spouses and/or children of Chapter members. The awardees must be currently enrolled at a recognized and accredited college, university, trade school or other institution of higher learning and must have completed at least one academic semester/quarter.

Award: Scholarship for use in sophomore, junior, senior, graduate, or postgraduate years; not renewable. *Number:* 3. *Amount:* $750.

Eligibility Requirements: Applicant must be enrolled or expecting to enroll full-time at a two-year or four-year institution or university and resident of South Carolina. Applicant or parent of applicant must be member of Society of Architectural Historians. Available to U.S. citizens.

Application Requirements: Application form, essay, transcript. *Deadline:* March 12.

Contact: Broadus Jamerson, Executive Director
Phone: 803-765-0680
Fax: 803-779-6558
E-mail: scsea@scsea.com

SUPREME GUARDIAN COUNCIL, INTERNATIONAL ORDER OF JOB'S DAUGHTERS

http://www.iojd.org/

SUPREME GUARDIAN COUNCIL SCHOLARSHIP

Scholarships of $750 to aid Job's Daughters students of outstanding ability whom have a sincerity of purpose. High school seniors, or graduates, junior college, technical school, or college students who are in early graduation programs, are eligible to apply.

Award: Scholarship for use in freshman, sophomore, junior, senior, graduate, or postgraduate years; not renewable. *Number:* 5–10. *Amount:* $750.

Eligibility Requirements: Applicant must be age 18-30; enrolled or expecting to enroll full- or part-time at a two-year or four-year or technical institution or university and single female. Applicant or parent of applicant must be member of Jobs Daughters. Available to U.S. and non-U.S. citizens.

Application Requirements: Application form, community service, essay, financial need analysis, recommendation from Executive Bethel Guardian Council, achievements outside of Job's Daughters, recommendations or references. *Deadline:* April 30.

Contact: Christal Bindrich, Scholarship Committee Chairman
Supreme Guardian Council, International Order of Job's Daughters
5351 South Butterfield Way
Greenfield, WI 53221
Phone: 414-423-0016
E-mail: christalbindrich@wi.rr.com

SUSIE HOLMES MEMORIAL SCHOLARSHIP

Scholarships of $1000 awarded to Job's Daughters high school students with a minimum of 2.5 GPA.

Award: Scholarship for use in freshman, sophomore, junior, senior, graduate, or postgraduate years; not renewable. *Number:* 1. *Amount:* $1000.

Eligibility Requirements: Applicant must be age 18-30; enrolled or expecting to enroll full-time at a two-year or four-year or technical institution or university and single female. Applicant or parent of applicant must be member of Jobs Daughters. Applicant must have 2.5 GPA or higher. Available to U.S. and non-U.S. citizens.

Application Requirements: Application form, community service, essay, recommendations or references, test scores, transcript. *Deadline:* April 30.

Contact: Christal Bindrich, Scholarship Committee Chairman
Supreme Guardian Council, International Order of Job's Daughters
5351 South Butterfield Way
Greenfield, WI 53221
Phone: 414-423-0016
E-mail: christalbindrich@wi.rr.com

TENNESSEE EDUCATION ASSOCIATION

http://www.teateachers.org/

TEA DON SAHLI-KATHY WOODALL SONS AND DAUGHTERS SCHOLARSHIP

Scholarship is available to a TEA member's child who is a high school senior, undergraduate or graduate student, and is planning to enroll, or is already enrolled, in a Tennessee college.

Award: Scholarship for use in freshman, sophomore, junior, senior, or graduate years; not renewable. *Number:* 1. *Amount:* $1000.

Eligibility Requirements: Applicant must be enrolled or expecting to enroll full-time at a four-year institution or university; resident of Tennessee and studying in Tennessee. Applicant or parent of applicant must be member of Tennessee Education Association. Applicant must have 3.0 GPA or higher. Available to U.S. citizens.

Application Requirements: Application form, entry in a contest, essay, financial need analysis, recommendations or references, statement of income, transcript. *Deadline:* March 1.

Contact: Stephanie Faulkner, Manager of Business Affairs
    Phone: 615-242-8392
    Fax: 615-259-4581
    E-mail: sfaulkner@tea.nea.org

TEXAS AFL-CIO

http://www.texasaflcio.org/

TEXAS AFL-CIO SCHOLARSHIP PROGRAM

Award for sons or daughters of members of unions affiliated with the Texas AFL-CIO and the appropriate Central Labor Council. Selection by interview/testing process. One-time awards of $1000. Applicant must be a graduating high school senior and Texas resident. Previous winners may apply for a limited number of continuing scholarships.

Award: Scholarship for use in freshman, sophomore, junior, or senior years; not renewable. *Number:* 20–35. *Amount:* $1000.

Eligibility Requirements: Applicant must be high school student; planning to enroll or expecting to enroll full-time at a two-year or four-year institution or university and resident of Texas. Applicant or parent of applicant must be member of AFL-CIO. Available to U.S. citizens.

Application Requirements: Application form, essay, financial need analysis, interview, personal photograph, test scores, transcript. *Deadline:* January 31.

Contact: Mr. Edward Sills, Director of Communications
    Texas AFL-CIO
    1106 Lavaca Street, Suite 200
    Austin, TX 78701
    Phone: 512-477-6195
    E-mail: ed@texasaflcio.org

TEXAS WOMEN IN LAW ENFORCEMENT

VANESSA RUDLOFF SCHOLARSHIP PROGRAM

Scholarships of $1000 awarded to qualified TWLE members and their dependents who are entering or continuing students at an accredited college or university. For details refer to website, http://www.twle.net/.

Award: Scholarship for use in freshman, sophomore, junior, senior, graduate, or postgraduate years; not renewable. *Number:* 4. *Amount:* $1000.

Eligibility Requirements: Applicant must be enrolled or expecting to enroll full- or part-time at a two-year or four-year or technical institution or university. Applicant or parent of applicant must be member of Texas Women in Law Enforcement. Applicant must have 3.0 GPA or higher. Available to U.S. and non-U.S. citizens.

Application Requirements: Application form, essay, recommendations or references. *Deadline:* April 15.

Contact: Glenda Baker, Scholarship Awards Chairperson
    Texas Women in Law Enforcement
    12605 Rhea Court
    Austin, TX 78727
    E-mail: gbakerab@aol.com

TKE EDUCATIONAL FOUNDATION

http://www.tke.org/

ALL-TKE ACADEMIC TEAM RECOGNITION AND JOHN A. COURSON TOP SCHOLAR AWARD

One-time award given to full-time students who are active members of Tau Kappa Epsilon with junior or senior standing. Candidates should be able to maintain excellent academic standing while making positive contributions to chapter, campus, and community. Must have a minimum of 3.0 GPA.

Award: Scholarship for use in junior or senior years; not renewable. *Number:* 10. *Amount:* up to $3250.

Eligibility Requirements: Applicant must be enrolled or expecting to enroll full-time at a four-year institution or university and must have an interest in leadership. Applicant or parent of applicant must be member of Tau Kappa Epsilon. Applicant must have 3.0 GPA or higher. Available to U.S. and Canadian citizens.

Application Requirements: Application form, personal photograph, transcript. *Deadline:* February 29.

Contact: Gary Reed, President and Chief Executive Officer
    TKE Educational Foundation
    8645 Founders Road
    Indianapolis, IN 46268-1393
    Phone: 317-872-6533
    Fax: 317-875-8353
    E-mail: reedga@tke.org

CANADIAN TKE SCHOLARSHIP

Scholarship available to an undergraduate who has been initiated into a Canadian TKE chapter and has demonstrated leadership qualities within the fraternity and the campus community, while maintaining a good academic record.

Award: Scholarship for use in freshman, sophomore, junior, or senior years; not renewable. *Number:* 1. *Amount:* $250.

Eligibility Requirements: Applicant must be enrolled or expecting to enroll full-time at a four-year institution or university; male and must have an interest in leadership. Applicant or parent of applicant must be member of Tau Kappa Epsilon. Applicant must have 2.5 GPA or higher. Available to U.S. and non-U.S. citizens.

Application Requirements: Application form, essay, personal photograph, transcript. *Deadline:* February 28.

Contact: Gary Reed, President and Chief Executive Officer
    Phone: 317-872-6533
    Fax: 317-875-8353
    E-mail: reedga@tke.org

CHARLES WALGREEN JR. SCHOLARSHIP

Award given in recognition of outstanding leadership, as demonstrated by the activities and accomplishments of an individual within the chapter, on campus and in the community, while maintaining a good academic record. All initiated undergraduate members of TKE, in good standing with a cumulative GPA of 3.0 or higher, are eligible to apply.

Award: Scholarship for use in freshman, sophomore, junior, or senior years; not renewable. *Number:* 1. *Amount:* $2500.

Eligibility Requirements: Applicant must be enrolled or expecting to enroll full-time at a four-year institution or university; male and must have an interest in leadership. Applicant or parent of applicant must be member of Tau Kappa Epsilon. Applicant must have 3.0 GPA or higher. Available to U.S. and non-U.S. citizens.

Application Requirements: Application form, essay, narrative summary of how TKE membership has benefited applicant, personal photograph, transcript. *Deadline:* February 29.

DONALD A. AND JOHN R. FISHER MEMORIAL SCHOLARSHIP

One-time award of $1400 given to an undergraduate member of Tau Kappa Epsilon, who has demonstrated leadership ability within his chapter, campus, or community. Must be a full-time student in good standing with a GPA of 3.0 or higher.

Award: Scholarship for use in freshman, sophomore, junior, or senior years; not renewable. *Number:* 1. *Amount:* $1400.

Eligibility Requirements: Applicant must be enrolled or expecting to enroll full-time at a four-year institution or university and must have an interest in leadership. Applicant or parent of applicant must be member of Tau Kappa Epsilon. Applicant must have 3.0 GPA or higher. Available to U.S. and non-U.S. citizens.

Application Requirements: Application form, essay, personal photograph, transcript. *Deadline:* February 29.

Contact: Gary Reed, President and Chief Executive Officer
    TKE Educational Foundation
    8645 Founders Road
    Indianapolis, IN 46268-1393
    Phone: 317-872-6533
    Fax: 317-875-8353
    E-mail: reedga@tke.org

DWAYNE R. WOERPEL MEMORIAL LEADERSHIP AWARD

Award available to an undergraduate Tau Kappa Epsilon member who is a full-time student and graduate of the TKE Leadership Academy. Applicants should have demonstrated leadership qualities in service to the Fraternity and to the civic and religious community while maintaining a 3.0 GPA or higher.

Award: Scholarship for use in freshman, sophomore, junior, or senior years; not renewable. *Number:* 1. *Amount:* $700.

Eligibility Requirements: Applicant must be enrolled or expecting to enroll full-time at a four-year institution or university; male and must have an interest in leadership. Applicant or parent of applicant must be member of Tau Kappa Epsilon. Applicant must have 3.0 GPA or higher. Available to U.S. and non-U.S. citizens.

Application Requirements: Application form, essay, personal photograph, transcript. *Deadline:* February 29.

ELMER AND DORIS SCHMITZ SR. MEMORIAL SCHOLARSHIP

One-time award of $500 given to an undergraduate member of Tau Kappa Epsilon from Wisconsin who has demonstrated leadership ability within his chapter, campus, or community. Must be a full-time student in good standing with a GPA of 2.5 or higher.

Award: Scholarship for use in freshman, sophomore, junior, or senior years; not renewable. *Number:* 1. *Amount:* $500.

Eligibility Requirements: Applicant must be enrolled or expecting to enroll full-time at a four-year institution or university; resident of Wisconsin and must have an interest in leadership. Applicant or parent of applicant must be member of Tau Kappa Epsilon. Applicant must have 2.5 GPA or higher. Available to U.S. and non-U.S. citizens.

Application Requirements: Application form, essay, narrative summary of how TKE membership has benefited applicant, personal photograph, transcript. *Deadline:* February 29.

Contact: Gary Reed, President and Chief Executive Officer
TKE Educational Foundation
8645 Founders Road
Indianapolis, IN 46268-1393
Phone: 317-872-6533
Fax: 317-875-8353
E-mail: reedga@tke.org

EUGENE C. BEACH MEMORIAL SCHOLARSHIP

One-time award of $400 given to an undergraduate member of Tau Kappa Epsilon who has demonstrated leadership ability within chapter, campus, or community. Must be a full-time student in good standing with a GPA of 3.0 or higher.

Award: Scholarship for use in freshman, sophomore, junior, or senior years; not renewable. *Number:* 1. *Amount:* $400.

Eligibility Requirements: Applicant must be enrolled or expecting to enroll full-time at a four-year institution or university and must have an interest in leadership. Applicant or parent of applicant must be member of Tau Kappa Epsilon. Applicant must have 3.0 GPA or higher. Available to U.S. and non-U.S. citizens.

Application Requirements: Application form, essay, narrative summary of how TKE membership has benefited applicant, personal photograph, transcript. *Deadline:* February 29.

Contact: Gary Reed, President and Chief Executive Officer
TKE Educational Foundation
8645 Founders Road
Indianapolis, IN 46268-1393
Phone: 317-872-6533
Fax: 317-875-8353
E-mail: reedga@tke.org

J. RUSSEL SALSBURY MEMORIAL SCHOLARSHIP

One-time award of $300 given to an undergraduate member of Tau Kappa Epsilon who has demonstrated leadership ability within his chapter, campus, or community. Must be a full-time student in good standing with a GPA of 3.0 or higher.

Award: Scholarship for use in freshman, sophomore, junior, or senior years; not renewable. *Number:* 1. *Amount:* $300.

Eligibility Requirements: Applicant must be enrolled or expecting to enroll full-time at a four-year institution or university and must have an interest in leadership. Applicant or parent of applicant must be member of Tau Kappa Epsilon. Applicant must have 3.0 GPA or higher. Available to U.S. and non-U.S. citizens.

Application Requirements: Application form, essay, personal photograph, transcript. *Deadline:* February 29.

Contact: Gary Reed, President and Chief Executive Officer
TKE Educational Foundation
8645 Founders Road
Indianapolis, IN 46268-1393
Phone: 317-872-6533
Fax: 317-875-8353
E-mail: reedga@tke.org

MICHAEL J. MORIN MEMORIAL SCHOLARSHIP

One-time award for any undergraduate member of Tau Kappa Epsilon who has demonstrated leadership capacity within his chapter, on campus or the community. Must have a cumulative GPA of 3.0 or higher and be a full-time student in good standing.

Award: Scholarship for use in freshman, sophomore, junior, or senior years; not renewable. *Number:* 1. *Amount:* $400.

Eligibility Requirements: Applicant must be enrolled or expecting to enroll full-time at a four-year institution or university and must have an interest in leadership. Applicant or parent of applicant must be member of Tau Kappa Epsilon. Applicant must have 3.0 GPA or higher. Available to U.S. and non-U.S. citizens.

Application Requirements: Application form, essay, narrative summary of how TKE membership has benefited applicant, personal photograph, transcript. *Deadline:* February 29.

MILES GRAY MEMORIAL SCHOLARSHIP

One-time award of $400 given to an undergraduate member of Tau Kappa Epsilon who has demonstrated leadership ability within his chapter, campus, or community. Must be a full-time student in good standing with a GPA of 3.0 or higher.

Award: Scholarship for use in freshman, sophomore, junior, or senior years; not renewable. *Number:* 1. *Amount:* $400.

Eligibility Requirements: Applicant must be enrolled or expecting to enroll full-time at a four-year institution or university and must have an interest in leadership. Applicant or parent of applicant must be member of Tau Kappa Epsilon. Applicant must have 3.0 GPA or higher. Available to U.S. and non-U.S. citizens.

Application Requirements: Application form, essay, personal photograph, transcript. *Deadline:* February 29.

Contact: Gary Reed, President and Chief Executive Officer
TKE Educational Foundation
8645 Founders Road
Indianapolis, IN 46268-1393
Phone: 317-872-6533
Fax: 317-875-8353
E-mail: reedga@tke.org

RONALD REAGAN LEADERSHIP AWARD

One-time award of $2000 for initiated undergraduate member of Tau Kappa Epsilon, given in recognition of outstanding leadership, as demonstrated by activities and accomplishments within chapter, on campus, and in community. Recipient should attend official fraternity function to accept award.

Award: Scholarship for use in freshman, sophomore, junior, or senior years; not renewable. *Number:* 1. *Amount:* $2000.

Eligibility Requirements: Applicant must be enrolled or expecting to enroll full-time at a four-year institution or university and must have an interest in leadership. Applicant or parent of applicant must be member of Tau Kappa Epsilon. Applicant must have 3.0 GPA or higher. Available to U.S. and non-U.S. citizens.

Application Requirements: Application form, essay, narrative summary of how TKE membership has benefited applicant, personal photograph, transcript. *Deadline:* February 29.

Contact: Gary Reed, President and Chief Executive Officer
TKE Educational Foundation
8645 Founders Road
Indianapolis, IN 46268-1393
Phone: 317-872-6533
Fax: 317-875-8353
E-mail: reedga@tke.org

T.J. SCHMITZ SCHOLARSHIP

Award for an initiated undergraduate member of TKE. Must be a full-time student in good standing with a minimum cumulative GPA of 3.0. Must have demonstrated leadership capability within chapter, campus, or community.

Award: Scholarship for use in freshman, sophomore, junior, or senior years; not renewable. *Number:* 1. *Amount:* $800.

Eligibility Requirements: Applicant must be enrolled or expecting to enroll full-time at a four-year institution or university; male and must have an interest in leadership. Applicant or parent of applicant must be member of Tau Kappa Epsilon. Applicant must have 3.0 GPA or higher. Available to U.S. and non-U.S. citizens.

Application Requirements: Application form, essay, narrative summary of how TKE membership has benefited applicant, personal photograph, transcript. *Deadline:* February 29.

Contact: Gary Reed, President and Chief Executive Officer
TKE Educational Foundation
8645 Founders Road
Indianapolis, IN 46268-1393
Phone: 317-872-6533
Fax: 317-875-8353
E-mail: reedga@tke.org

WALLACE MCCAULEY MEMORIAL SCHOLARSHIP

One-time award to undergraduate member of Tau Kappa Epsilon with junior or senior standing. Must have demonstrated understanding of the importance of good alumni relations. Must have excelled in the development, promotion, and execution of programs which increase alumni contact, awareness, and participation in fraternity activities.

Award: Scholarship for use in junior or senior years; not renewable. *Number:* 1. *Amount:* $500.

Eligibility Requirements: Applicant must be enrolled or expecting to enroll full-time at a four-year institution or university and must have an interest in leadership. Applicant or parent of applicant must be member of Tau Kappa Epsilon. Applicant must have 3.0 GPA or higher. Available to U.S. and non-U.S. citizens.

Application Requirements: Application form, essay, narrative summary of how TKE membership has benefited applicant, personal photograph, transcript. *Deadline:* February 29.

Contact: Gary Reed, President and Chief Executive Officer
TKE Educational Foundation
8645 Founders Road
Indianapolis, IN 46268-1393
Phone: 317-872-6533
Fax: 317-875-8353
E-mail: reedga@tke.org

WILLIAM V. MUSE SCHOLARSHIP

Award of $700 given to an undergraduate member of Tau Kappa Epsilon who has completed at least 30 semester hours of course work. Applicant should demonstrate leadership within chapter and maintain 3.0 GPA. Preference given to members of Epsilon-Upsilon Chapter.

Award: Scholarship for use in freshman, sophomore, junior, or senior years; not renewable. *Number:* 1. *Amount:* $700.

Eligibility Requirements: Applicant must be enrolled or expecting to enroll full-time at a four-year institution or university and must have an interest in leadership. Applicant or parent of applicant must be member of Tau Kappa Epsilon. Applicant must have 3.0 GPA or higher. Available to U.S. and non-U.S. citizens.

Application Requirements: Application form, essay, narrative summary of how TKE membership has benefited applicant, personal photograph, transcript. *Deadline:* February 29.

Contact: Gary Reed, President and Chief Executive Officer
TKE Educational Foundation
8645 Founders Road
Indianapolis, IN 46268-1393
Phone: 317-872-6533
Fax: 317-875-8353
E-mail: reedga@tke.org

WILLIAM WILSON MEMORIAL SCHOLARSHIP

One-time award given to undergraduate member of Tau Kappa Epsilon with junior or senior standing. Must have demonstrated understanding of the importance of good alumni relations. Must have excelled in the development, promotion, and execution of programs which increase alumni contact, awareness, and participation in fraternity activities.

Award: Scholarship for use in junior or senior years; not renewable. *Number:* 1. *Amount:* $500.

Eligibility Requirements: Applicant must be enrolled or expecting to enroll full-time at a four-year institution or university and must have an interest in leadership. Applicant or parent of applicant must be member

of Tau Kappa Epsilon. Applicant must have 3.0 GPA or higher. Available to U.S. and non-U.S. citizens.

Application Requirements: Application form, essay, narrative summary of how TKE membership has benefited applicant, personal photograph, transcript. *Deadline:* February 29.

Contact: Gary Reed, President and Chief Executive Officer
TKE Educational Foundation
8645 Founders Road
Indianapolis, IN 46268-1393
Phone: 317-872-6533
Fax: 317-875-8353
E-mail: reedga@tke.org

UNION PLUS SCHOLARSHIP PROGRAM

http://www.unionplus.org/

UNION PLUS EDUCATION FOUNDATION SCHOLARSHIP PROGRAM

One-time cash award for current or retired union members affiliated with the AFL-CIO, their spouses, and dependent children. Based upon academic achievement, character, leadership, career goals, social awareness and financial need. Must be from Canada or U.S., including Puerto Rico and the Virgin Islands. Members must download application from website: http://www.unionplus.org/scholarships.

Award: Scholarship for use in freshman, sophomore, junior, senior, or graduate years; not renewable. *Number:* 100–120. *Amount:* $500–$4000.

Eligibility Requirements: Applicant must be enrolled or expecting to enroll full- or part-time at a two-year or four-year or technical institution or university. Applicant or parent of applicant must be member of AFL-CIO. Available to U.S. and non-U.S. citizens.

Application Requirements: Application form, application form may be submitted online (http://www.unionplus.org/college-education-financing/union-plus-scholarship), essay, financial need analysis, recommendations or references, test scores. *Deadline:* January 31.

Contact: Mrs. Shana Higgins, Union Plus Education Foundation
Union Plus Scholarship Program
Union Privilege, 1125 15th Street, NW, Suite 300
Washington, DC 20005
E-mail: shiggins@unionprivilege.org

UNITED DAUGHTERS OF THE CONFEDERACY

http://www.hqudc.org/

BARBARA JACKSON SICHEL MEMORIAL SCHOLARSHIP

Renewable award for undergraduate students who are descendant of a Confederate soldier, sailor or marine. Must be enrolled in an accredited college or university. Minimum of 3.0 GPA required. Submit a letter of endorsement from sponsoring Chapter of the United Daughters of the Confederacy.

Award: Scholarship for use in freshman, sophomore, junior, or senior years; renewable. *Number:* 1–2. *Amount:* $800–$1000.

Eligibility Requirements: Applicant must be enrolled or expecting to enroll full-time at a four-year institution or university. Applicant or parent of applicant must be member of United Daughters of the Confederacy. Applicant must have 3.0 GPA or higher. Available to U.S. citizens.

Application Requirements: Application form, essay, financial need analysis, personal photograph, proof of confederate ancestor's service, copy of applicant's birth certificate, recommendations or references, self-addressed stamped envelope with application, test scores, transcript. *Deadline:* March 15.

Contact: Ms. Jamie Davis, Second Vice President General
Phone: 804-355-1636
E-mail: hqudc@rcn.com

CHARLOTTE M. F. BENTLEY/NEW YORK CHAPTER 103 SCHOLARSHIP

Renewable award for undergraduate students who are descendant of a Confederate soldier, sailor or marine. Must be enrolled in an accredited college or university. Minimum of 3.0 GPA required. Must be members of United Daughters of the Confederacy and Children of the Confederacy from New York.

Award: Scholarship for use in freshman, sophomore, junior, or senior years; renewable. *Number:* 1–2. *Amount:* $800–$1000.

Eligibility Requirements: Applicant must be enrolled or expecting to enroll full-time at a four-year institution or university and resident of New York. Applicant or parent of applicant must be member of Children of the Confederacy, United Daughters of the Confederacy. Applicant must have 3.0 GPA or higher. Available to U.S. citizens.

Application Requirements: Application form, essay, financial need analysis, personal photograph, proof of confederate ancestor's service, copy of applicant's birth certificate, recommendations or references, self-addressed stamped envelope with application, test scores, transcript. *Deadline:* March 15.

Contact: Ms. Jamie Davis, Second Vice President General
Phone: 804-355-1636
E-mail: hqudc@rcn.com

ELIZABETH AND WALLACE KINGSBURY SCHOLARSHIP

Award for full-time undergraduate students who are descendants of a Confederate soldier, studying at an accredited college or university. Must have been a member of the Children of the Confederacy for a minimum of three years. Minimum 3.0 GPA required.

Award: Scholarship for use in freshman, sophomore, junior, or senior years; renewable. *Number:* 1–2. *Amount:* $800–$1000.

Eligibility Requirements: Applicant must be enrolled or expecting to enroll full-time at a four-year institution or university. Applicant or parent of applicant must be member of Children of the Confederacy. Applicant must have 3.0 GPA or higher. Available to U.S. citizens.

Application Requirements: Application form, copy of applicant's birth certificate, copy of confederate ancestor's proof of service, essay, financial need analysis, personal photograph, recommendations or references, self-addressed stamped envelope with application, test scores, transcript. *Deadline:* March 15.

Contact: Ms. Jamie Davis, Second Vice President General
Phone: 804-355-1636
E-mail: hqudc@rcn.com

GERTRUDE BOTTS-SAUCIER SCHOLARSHIP

Award for full-time undergraduate students who are descendants of a Confederate soldier, sailor or marine. Must be from Texas, Mississippi or Louisiana. Must be enrolled in an accredited college or university and have a minimum 3.0 GPA. Submit application and letter of endorsement from sponsoring chapter of the United Daughters of the Confederacy.

Award: Scholarship for use in freshman, sophomore, junior, or senior years; renewable. *Number:* 1–2. *Amount:* $800–$1000.

Eligibility Requirements: Applicant must be enrolled or expecting to enroll full-time at a four-year institution or university and resident of Louisiana, Mississippi, Texas. Applicant or parent of applicant must be member of United Daughters of the Confederacy. Applicant must have 3.0 GPA or higher. Available to U.S. citizens.

Application Requirements: Application form, copy of applicant's birth certificate, copy of confederate ancestor's proof of service, essay, financial need analysis, personal photograph, recommendations or references, self-addressed stamped envelope with application, test scores, transcript. *Deadline:* March 15.

Contact: Ms. Jamie Davis, Second Vice President General
Phone: 804-355-1636
E-mail: hqudc@rcn.com

LOLA B. CURRY SCHOLARSHIP

Award for full-time undergraduate students from Alabama who are descendants of a Confederate soldier. Must be enrolled in an accredited college or university in Alabama. Minimum 3.0 GPA required. Submit letter of endorsement from sponsoring chapter of the United Daughters of the Confederacy.

Award: Scholarship for use in freshman, sophomore, junior, or senior years; renewable. *Number:* 1–2. *Amount:* $800–$1000.

Eligibility Requirements: Applicant must be enrolled or expecting to enroll full-time at a four-year institution or university; resident of Alabama and studying in Alabama. Applicant or parent of applicant must be member of United Daughters of the Confederacy. Applicant must have 3.0 GPA or higher. Available to U.S. citizens.

Application Requirements: Application form, copy of applicant's birth certificate, copy of confederate ancestor's proof of service, essay,

financial need analysis, personal photograph, recommendations or references, self-addressed stamped envelope with application, test scores, transcript. *Deadline:* March 15.

Contact: Ms. Jamie Davis, Second Vice President General
Phone: 804-355-1636
E-mail: hqudc@rcn.com

UNITED DAUGHTERS OF THE CONFEDERACY UNDERGRADUATE SCHOLARSHIPS

Renewable award for undergraduate students who are descendants of an eligible Confederate soldier. Must be enrolled in an accredited college or university. Minimum 3.0 GPA required. Applicants must be endorsed by the President and the Second Vice President/Education Chairman of Chapter and Division, and by the Second Vice President General. Applications are submitted through local chapters.

Award: Scholarship for use in freshman, sophomore, junior, or senior years; renewable. *Number:* 18–30. *Amount:* $800–$1000.

Eligibility Requirements: Applicant must be enrolled or expecting to enroll full-time at a two-year or four-year institution or university. Applicant or parent of applicant must be member of United Daughters of the Confederacy. Applicant must have 3.0 GPA or higher. Available to U.S. citizens.

Application Requirements: Application form, copy of applicant's birth certificate, copy of confederate ancestor's proof of service, essay, financial need analysis, personal photograph, recommendations or references, self-addressed stamped envelope with application, test scores, transcript. *Deadline:* March 15.

Contact: Ms. Jamie Davis, Second Vice President General
Phone: 804-355-1636
E-mail: hqudc@rcn.com

WINNIE DAVIS-CHILDREN OF THE CONFEDERACY SCHOLARSHIP

Award for full-time undergraduate students who are descendants of a Confederate soldier, enrolled in an accredited college or university. Recipient must be, or have been until age of 18, a participating member of the Children of the Confederacy and approved by the Third Vice President General. Minimum 3.0 GPA required.

Award: Scholarship for use in freshman, sophomore, junior, or senior years; renewable. *Number:* 1–2. *Amount:* $800–$1000.

Eligibility Requirements: Applicant must be enrolled or expecting to enroll full-time at a four-year institution or university. Applicant or parent of applicant must be member of Children of the Confederacy. Applicant must have 3.0 GPA or higher. Available to U.S. citizens.

Application Requirements: Application form, copy of applicant's birth certificate, copy of confederate ancestor's proof of service, essay, financial need analysis, personal photograph, recommendations or references, self-addressed stamped envelope with application, test scores, transcript. *Deadline:* March 15.

Contact: Ms. Jamie Davis, Second Vice President General
Phone: 804-355-1636
E-mail: hqudc@rcn.com

UNITED FOOD AND COMMERCIAL WORKERS INTERNATIONAL UNION

http://www.ufcw.org/

JAMES A. SUFFRIDGE UNITED FOOD AND COMMERCIAL WORKERS SCHOLARSHIP PROGRAM

Scholarships available to graduating high school seniors and college students during the specific program year. Must be an active member of UFCW or unmarried dependent under age 20 of a UFCW member. Scholarship is disbursed over a four-year period.

Award: Scholarship for use in freshman, sophomore, junior, or senior years; renewable. *Number:* 14–20. *Amount:* up to $8000.

Eligibility Requirements: Applicant must be enrolled or expecting to enroll full- or part-time at a two-year or four-year or technical institution or university. Applicant or parent of applicant must be member of United Food and Commercial Workers. Available to U.S. and Canadian citizens.

Application Requirements: Application form, community service, essay, transcript. *Deadline:* April 15.

UNITED STATES JUNIOR CHAMBER OF COMMERCE

http://www.usjaycees.org/

CHARLES R. FORD SCHOLARSHIP

One-time award of $3000 available to active members of Jaycee wishing to return to college to complete his/her formal education. Must be U.S. citizen, possess academic potential and leadership qualities and show financial need. To receive an application, send $10 application fee and self-addressed stamped envelope by February 1.

Award: Scholarship for use in freshman, sophomore, junior, senior, graduate, or postgraduate years; not renewable. *Number:* 1. *Amount:* $3000.

Eligibility Requirements: Applicant must be age 18-40 and enrolled or expecting to enroll full- or part-time at a two-year or four-year institution or university. Applicant or parent of applicant must be member of Jaycees. Available to U.S. citizens.

Application Requirements: Application form, financial need analysis, self-addressed stamped envelope with application, transcript. *Fee:* $10. *Deadline:* February 1.

Contact: Karen Fitzgerald, Customer Service and Data Processing
Phone: 918-584-2481
E-mail: customerservice@usjaycees.org

THOMAS WOOD BALDRIDGE SCHOLARSHIP

One-time award of $3000 available to a Jaycee immediate family member or a descendant of a Jaycee member. Must be U.S. citizen, possess academic potential and leadership qualities and show financial need. To receive an application, send $10 application fee and self-addressed stamped envelope by February 1.

Award: Scholarship for use in freshman, sophomore, junior, senior, graduate, or postgraduate years; not renewable. *Number:* 1. *Amount:* $3000.

Eligibility Requirements: Applicant must be age 18-40 and enrolled or expecting to enroll full- or part-time at a two-year or four-year or technical institution or university. Applicant or parent of applicant must be member of Jaycees. Available to U.S. citizens.

Application Requirements: Application form, financial need analysis, self-addressed stamped envelope with application, transcript. *Fee:* $10. *Deadline:* February 1.

Contact: Karen Fitzgerald, Customer Service and Data Processing
Phone: 918-584-2481
E-mail: customerservice@usjaycees.org

UNITED STATES MARINE CORPS SCHOLARSHIP FOUNDATION, INC.

http://www.mcsf.org/

MARINE CORPS SCHOLARSHIP FOUNDATION

Available to the sons and daughters of active duty Marines and to the children of former and deceased Marines whose family income does not exceed $82,000. Must submit proof of parent's service. Apply online at mcsf.org and call for further information 1-800-292-7777.

Award: Scholarship for use in freshman, sophomore, junior, or senior years; not renewable. *Number:* 1000–1500. *Amount:* $500–$10,000.

Eligibility Requirements: Applicant must be enrolled or expecting to enroll full- or part-time at a two-year or four-year or technical institution or university. Applicant or parent of applicant must be member of American Legion or Auxiliary, Boy Scouts. Available to U.S. citizens. Applicant must have served in the Marine Corps.

Application Requirements: Application form, essay, financial need analysis, Marine parent DD-214 or active duty statement of service, pages 1 and 2 of Federal Income Tax Return, transcript. *Deadline:* April 1.

Contact: June Hering, Scholarship Program Director
United States Marine Corps Scholarship Foundation, Inc.
PO Box 3008
Princeton, NJ 08543-3008
Phone: 800-292-7777
Fax: 609-452-2259
E-mail: mcsf@marine-scholars.org

UNITED STATES NAVAL SEA CADET CORPS

http://www.seacadets.org/

HARRY AND ROSE HOWELL SCHOLARSHIP

Renewable award for Sea Cadets only. Two Howell Scholarships of $2500 each and one scholarship of $2000. Applicants must be U.S. citizens with a minimum 3.0 GPA.

Award: Scholarship for use in freshman, sophomore, junior, or senior years; renewable. *Number:* 3. *Amount:* $2000–$2500.

Eligibility Requirements: Applicant must be enrolled or expecting to enroll full-time at a two-year or four-year institution or university. Applicant or parent of applicant must be member of Naval Sea Cadet Corps. Applicant must have 3.0 GPA or higher. Available to U.S. citizens.

Application Requirements: Application form, financial need analysis, recommendations or references, test scores, transcript. *Deadline:* May 1.

Contact: M.J. Ford, Executive Director
Phone: 703-243-6910
Fax: 703-243-3985
E-mail: mford@navyleague.org

KINGSLEY FOUNDATION AWARDS

One-time award to assist Cadets in continuing their education at an accredited four-year college or university. Must be a member of NSCC for at least two years. Minimum 3.0 GPA required.

Award: Scholarship for use in freshman, sophomore, junior, or senior years; not renewable. *Number:* 5. *Amount:* $1000.

Eligibility Requirements: Applicant must be enrolled or expecting to enroll full-time at a four-year institution or university. Applicant or parent of applicant must be member of Naval Sea Cadet Corps. Applicant must have 3.0 GPA or higher. Available to U.S. citizens.

Application Requirements: Application form, financial need analysis, recommendations or references, test scores, transcript. *Deadline:* May 1.

Contact: M.J. Ford, Executive Director
Phone: 703-243-6910
Fax: 703-243-3985
E-mail: mford@navyleague.org

NAVAL SEA CADET CORPS BOARD OF DIRECTORS SCHOLARSHIP

Renewable award up to $1400 is available for Sea Cadets. Award available to U.S. citizens and minimum GPA of 3.0 is required.

Award: Scholarship for use in freshman, sophomore, junior, or senior years; renewable. *Number:* 1. *Amount:* $1200–$1400.

Eligibility Requirements: Applicant must be enrolled or expecting to enroll full-time at a two-year or four-year institution. Applicant or parent of applicant must be member of Naval Sea Cadet Corps. Applicant must have 3.0 GPA or higher. Available to U.S. citizens.

Application Requirements: Application form, financial need analysis, recommendations or references, test scores, transcript. *Deadline:* May 1.

Contact: M.J. Ford, Executive Director
Phone: 703-243-6910
Fax: 703-243-3985
E-mail: mford@navyleague.org

NAVAL SEA CADET CORPS SCHOLARSHIP PROGRAM

One-time award to assist Cadets in continuing their education at an accredited four-year college or university. Must be a member of NSCC for at least two years. Minimum 3.0 GPA required.

Award: Scholarship for use in freshman, sophomore, junior, or senior years; not renewable. *Number:* up to 5. *Amount:* $1000.

Eligibility Requirements: Applicant must be enrolled or expecting to enroll full-time at a four-year institution or university. Applicant or parent of applicant must be member of Naval Sea Cadet Corps. Applicant must have 3.0 GPA or higher. Available to U.S. citizens.

Application Requirements: Application form, financial need analysis, recommendations or references, test scores, transcript. *Deadline:* May 1.

Contact: M.J. Ford, Executive Director
Phone: 703-243-6910
Fax: 703-243-3985
E-mail: mford@navyleague.org

ROBERT AND HELEN HUTTON SCHOLARSHIP

One renewable award of $1000 is available for Sea Cadets to assist them in continuing their education at an accredited four-year college or university. Minimum 3.0 GPA required.

Award: Scholarship for use in freshman, sophomore, junior, or senior years; renewable. *Number:* 1. *Amount:* $1000.

Eligibility Requirements: Applicant must be enrolled or expecting to enroll full-time at a two-year or four-year institution or university. Applicant or parent of applicant must be member of Naval Sea Cadet Corps. Applicant must have 3.0 GPA or higher. Available to U.S. citizens.

Application Requirements: Application form, financial need analysis, recommendations or references, test scores, transcript. *Deadline:* May 1.

Contact: M.J. Ford, Executive Director
Phone: 703-243-6910
Fax: 703-243-3985
E-mail: mford@navyleague.org

STOCKHOLM SCHOLARSHIP PROGRAM

Renewable award for a selected Cadet, to be designated a Stockholm Scholar. Must be a member of NSCC for at least two years. Assistance provided for no more than four consecutive years at an accredited college or university. Minimum 3.0 GPA required.

Award: Scholarship for use in freshman, sophomore, junior, or senior years; renewable. *Number:* 1. *Amount:* $2000–$2500.

Eligibility Requirements: Applicant must be enrolled or expecting to enroll full-time at a four-year institution or university. Applicant or parent of applicant must be member of Naval Sea Cadet Corps. Applicant must have 3.0 GPA or higher. Available to U.S. citizens.

Application Requirements: Application form, financial need analysis, recommendations or references, test scores, transcript. *Deadline:* May 1.

Contact: M.J. Ford, Executive Director
Phone: 703-243-6910
Fax: 703-243-3985
E-mail: mford@navyleague.org

UNITED STATES SUBMARINE VETERANS

http://www.ussvcf.org/

UNITED STATES SUBMARINE VETERANS INC. NATIONAL SCHOLARSHIP PROGRAM

Program requires the sponsor to be a qualified Base Member or Member-at-Large in good standing. Must demonstrate financial need, have a minimum 2.5 GPA, and submit an essay. Open to children, stepchildren, and grandchildren of qualified members. Applicants must be between the ages of 17 to 23 and must be unmarried.

Award: Scholarship for use in freshman, sophomore, junior, or senior years; not renewable. *Number:* 2–18. *Amount:* $950–$1500.

Eligibility Requirements: Applicant must be age 17-23; enrolled or expecting to enroll full-time at a two-year or four-year or technical institution or university and single. Applicant or parent of applicant must be member of Veterans of Foreign Wars or Auxiliary. Applicant or parent of applicant must have employment or volunteer experience in seafaring/fishing industry. Applicant must have 3.5 GPA or higher. Available to U.S. citizens. Applicant or parent must meet one or more of the following requirements: Navy experience; retired from active duty; disabled or killed as a result of military service; prisoner of war; or missing in action.

Application Requirements: Application form, essay, financial need analysis, recommendations or references, test scores, transcript. *Deadline:* April 15.

Contact: Paul Orstad, National Scholarship Chairman
United States Submarine Veterans
30 Surrey Lane
Norwich, CT 06369-6541
Phone: 860-889-4750
Fax: 860-334-6457
E-mail: hogan343@aol.com

UTILITY WORKERS UNION OF AMERICA

http://www.uwua.net/

UTILITY WORKERS UNION OF AMERICA SCHOLARSHIP AWARDS PROGRAM

Renewable award for high school juniors who are children of active members of the Utility Workers Union of America. Must take the PSAT National Merit Scholarship Qualifying Test in junior year and plan to enter college in the fall after high school graduation.

Award: Scholarship for use in freshman, sophomore, junior, or senior years; renewable. *Number:* 2. *Amount:* $500–$2000.

Eligibility Requirements: Applicant must be high school student and planning to enroll or expecting to enroll full-time at a four-year institution or university. Applicant or parent of applicant must be member of Utility Workers Union of America. Available to U.S. citizens.

Application Requirements: Application form, application form may be submitted online (http://uwua.net), test scores. *Deadline:* December 31.

Contact: Rosanna Farley, Office Manager
Phone: 202-974-8200
E-mail: rfarley@aflcio.org

VIETNOW NATIONAL HEADQUARTERS

http://www.vietnow.com/

VIETNOW NATIONAL SCHOLARSHIP

One-time award available to dependants of members of VietNow only. Applicants' academic achievements, abilities and extracurricular activities will be reviewed. Must be U.S. citizen and under the age of 35.

Award: Scholarship for use in freshman, sophomore, junior, senior, or graduate years; not renewable. *Amount:* $500–$1000.

Eligibility Requirements: Applicant must be enrolled or expecting to enroll full-time at a four-year institution or university. Applicant or parent of applicant must be member of VietNow. Available to U.S. citizens.

Application Requirements: Application form, driver's license, essay, test scores, transcript. *Deadline:* April 1.

Contact: Eileen Shoemaker, Executive Assistant
VietNow National Headquarters
1835 Broadway
Rockford, IL 61104
Phone: 815-227-5100
Fax: 815-227-5127
E-mail: vnnatl@inwave.com

WESTERN FRATERNAL LIFE ASSOCIATION

http://www.wflains.org/

WESTERN FRATERNAL LIFE ASSOCIATION NATIONAL SCHOLARSHIP

Ten national scholarships will be awarded annually for up to $1000 to qualified members attending college or vocational programs. Traditional and non-traditional students are eligible. Must be a WFLA member in good standing for two years prior to the application deadline. A member is an individual who has life insurance or an annuity with WFLA. High school seniors may apply. Members who are qualified for the National Scholarship may also qualify for 3 state scholarships.

Award: Scholarship for use in freshman, sophomore, junior, senior, or graduate years; renewable. *Number:* 10. *Amount:* $1000.

Eligibility Requirements: Applicant must be enrolled or expecting to enroll full-time at a two-year or four-year or technical institution or university. Applicant or parent of applicant must be member of Western Fraternal Life Association. Available to U.S. citizens.

Application Requirements: Application form, essay, recommendations or references, test scores, transcript. *Deadline:* March 1.

Contact: Linda Grove, Publication Coordinator
Phone: 877-935-2467
Fax: 319-363-8806
E-mail: wflains@wflains.org

WISCONSIN ASSOCIATION FOR FOOD PROTECTION

http://www.wafp-wi.org/

WAFP MEMORIAL SCHOLARSHIP

Scholarship for a child or dependent of a current or deceased WAFP member, or the applicant may be a WAFP student member. Must have been accepted into an accredited degree program in a university, college, or technical institute.

Award: Scholarship for use in sophomore, junior, senior, or graduate years; not renewable. *Number:* 1. *Amount:* $1000.

Eligibility Requirements: Applicant must be enrolled or expecting to enroll full-time at a two-year or four-year or technical institution or university. Applicant or parent of applicant must be member of Wisconsin Association for Food Protection. Available to U.S. and non-U.S. citizens.

Application Requirements: Application form. *Deadline:* July 1.

Contact: Mr. Jim Wickert, Scholarship Committee Chairman
Wisconsin Association for Food Protection
3834 Ridgeway Avenue
Madison, WI 53704
Phone: 608-241-2438
E-mail: jwick16060@tds.net

WOODMEN OF THE WORLD AND/OR ASSURED LIFE ASSOCIATION

http://www.denverwoodmen.com/

WOODMEN OF THE WORLD AND/OR ASSURED LIFE ASSOCIATION ENDOWMENT SCHOLARSHIP PROGRAM

Award for full-time study at a trade/technical school, two-year college, four-year college or university. Applicant must be a benefit member, or a child or grandchild of a benefit member of Woodmen the World and/or Assured Life Association of Colorado. Applicant may reapply each year he/she is a full-time student.

Award: Scholarship for use in freshman, sophomore, junior, senior, or graduate years; not renewable. *Number:* 70–75. *Amount:* $500–$1500.

Eligibility Requirements: Applicant must be enrolled or expecting to enroll full-time at a two-year or four-year or technical institution or university. Applicant or parent of applicant must be member of Woodmen of the World. Available to U.S. and Canadian citizens.

Application Requirements: Application form, community service, essay, personal photograph, transcript. *Deadline:* March 15.

Contact: Mr. Jerome Christensen, Vice President of Fraternal Affairs
Woodmen of the World and/or Assured Life Association
6030 Greenwood Plaza Boulevard, Suite 100
Greenwood Village, CO 80111
Phone: 303-468-3773
Fax: 303-792-9793
E-mail: jlc@denverwoodmen.com

WYOMING FARM BUREAU FEDERATION

http://www.wyfb.org/

KING-LIVINGSTON SCHOLARSHIP

One-time award given to graduates of Wyoming high schools. Must attend a Wyoming junior college or the University of Wyoming. Minimum 2.5 GPA required. Applicant's family must be a current member of the Wyoming Farm Bureau.

Award: Scholarship for use in freshman, sophomore, junior, senior, or graduate years; not renewable. *Number:* 1. *Amount:* $1000.

Eligibility Requirements: Applicant must be enrolled or expecting to enroll full-time at a two-year or four-year institution or university; resident of Wyoming and studying in Wyoming. Applicant or parent of applicant must be member of Wyoming Farm Bureau. Applicant must have 2.5 GPA or higher. Available to U.S. and non-U.S. citizens.

Application Requirements: Application form, financial need analysis, personal photograph, recommendations or references, resume, transcript. *Deadline:* March 1.

Contact: Ellen Westbrook, Executive Secretary
Phone: 307-721-7719
E-mail: ewestbrook@wyfb.org

WYOMING FARM BUREAU CONTINUING EDUCATION SCHOLARSHIPS

Award to students attending a two-year college in Wyoming or the University of Wyoming. Must be a resident of Wyoming and applicant's family must be a current member of the Wyoming Farm Bureau. Must submit at least two semesters of college grade transcripts. Freshmen must submit first semester grades and proof of enrollment in second semester. Minimum 2.5 GPA.

Award: Scholarship for use in freshman, sophomore, junior, senior, or graduate years; not renewable. *Number:* 3. *Amount:* $500.

Eligibility Requirements: Applicant must be enrolled or expecting to enroll full-time at a two-year or four-year institution or university; resident of Wyoming and studying in Wyoming. Applicant or parent of applicant must be member of Wyoming Farm Bureau. Applicant must have 2.5 GPA or higher. Available to U.S. and non-U.S. citizens.

Application Requirements: Application form, financial need analysis, personal photograph, recommendations or references, resume, test scores, transcript. *Deadline:* March 1.

Contact: Ellen Westbrook, Executive Secretary
Phone: 307-721-7719
E-mail: ewestbrook@wyfb.org

WYOMING FARM BUREAU FEDERATION SCHOLARSHIPS

Five $500 scholarships will be given to graduates of Wyoming high schools. Eligible candidates must be enrolled in a two-year college in Wyoming or the University of Wyoming and must have a minimum 2.5 GPA. Applicant's family should be current member of the Wyoming Farm Bureau Federation.

Award: Scholarship for use in freshman, sophomore, junior, senior, or graduate years; not renewable. *Number:* 5. *Amount:* $500.

Eligibility Requirements: Applicant must be enrolled or expecting to enroll full-time at a two-year or four-year institution or university; resident of Wyoming and studying in Wyoming. Applicant or parent of applicant must be member of Wyoming Farm Bureau. Applicant must have 2.5 GPA or higher. Available to U.S. and non-U.S. citizens.

Application Requirements: Application form, financial need analysis, personal photograph, recommendations or references, resume, transcript. *Deadline:* March 1.

Contact: Ellen Westbrook, Executive Secretary
Phone: 307-721-7719
E-mail: ewestbrook@wyfb.org

UNITED STATES BOWLING CONGRESS (USBC)

http://www.bowl.com/

GIFT FOR LIFE SCHOLARSHIP

The Gift for Life Scholarships are available to any USBC Youth member currently in high school and holding a GPA of 2.0 or better who can demonstrate financial need.

Award: Scholarship for use in freshman year; not renewable. *Number:* 12. *Amount:* $1000.

Eligibility Requirements: Applicant must be high school student; planning to enroll or expecting to enroll full- or part-time at a four-year institution or university and must have an interest in bowling. Applicant or parent of applicant must be member of Young American Bowling Alliance. Available to U.S. citizens.

Application Requirements: Application form, recommendations or references, transcript. *Deadline:* April 1.

USBC EARL ANTHONY MEMORIAL SCHOLARSHIP

Annually recognizes five USBC Youth bowlers for their community involvement and academic achievements.

Award: Scholarship for use in freshman, sophomore, junior, or senior years; not renewable. *Number:* 5. *Amount:* $5000.

Eligibility Requirements: Applicant must be high school student; planning to enroll or expecting to enroll full- or part-time at a two-year or four-year institution or university and must have an interest in bowling. Applicant or parent of applicant must be member of Young American

Bowling Alliance. Applicant must have 3.0 GPA or higher. Available to U.S. citizens.

Application Requirements: Application form, community service, entry in a contest, essay, recommendations or references, transcript. *Deadline:* December 1.

Contact: Denise Lish, SMART Program Administrator
　　　　 Phone: 800-514-2695
　　　　 E-mail: smart@bowl.com

CORPORATE AFFILIATION

BUTLER MANUFACTURING COMPANY

http://www.butlermfg.com/

BUTLER MANUFACTURING COMPANY FOUNDATION SCHOLARSHIP PROGRAM

Award for high school seniors who are the children of full-time employees of Butler Manufacturing Company and its subsidiaries. Award is renewable for up to four years. Must enroll full-time and stay in upper half of class.

Award: Scholarship for use in freshman year; renewable. *Number:* 8. *Amount:* $3000.

Eligibility Requirements: Applicant must be high school student and planning to enroll or expecting to enroll full-time at a four-year institution or university. Applicant or parent of applicant must be affiliated with Butler Manufacturing Company. Available to U.S. and Canadian citizens.

Application Requirements: Application form, essay, financial need analysis, recommendations or references, test scores, transcript. *Deadline:* February 15.

Contact: Jill Harmon, Foundation Administrator
　　　　 Phone: 816-968-3208
　　　　 Fax: 816-968-6501
　　　　 E-mail: jcharmon@butlermfg.org

CHICK-FIL-A INC.

http://www.chick-fil-a.com/

CHICK-FIL-A LEADERSHIP SCHOLARSHIP

Scholarships available to current employees of Chick-fil-A restaurants. Must show proof of enrollment in technical school, two- or four-year college or university. Must demonstrate solid work ethic, be actively involved in school or community activities, and possess strong leadership abilities. Must apply with approval of a Unit Operator accompanied by their letter of recommendation. Letter of recommendation from non-work-related individual also required.

Award: Scholarship for use in freshman, sophomore, junior, or senior years; not renewable. *Number:* up to 1400. *Amount:* $1000.

Eligibility Requirements: Applicant must be enrolled or expecting to enroll full- or part-time at a two-year or four-year or technical institution or university. Applicant or parent of applicant must be affiliated with Chick-Fil-A, Inc.. Applicant or parent of applicant must have employment or volunteer experience in food service. Available to U.S. citizens.

Application Requirements: Application form, letter of acceptance, recommendations or references, transcript. *Deadline:* continuous.

S. TRUETT CATHY SCHOLAR AWARDS

This award is given to the top twenty-five Chick-fil-A Leadership Scholarship recipients each year. Scholarship amount is $1000.

Award: Scholarship for use in freshman, sophomore, junior, or senior years; not renewable. *Number:* up to 25. *Amount:* up to $1000.

Eligibility Requirements: Applicant must be enrolled or expecting to enroll full- or part-time at a two-year or four-year or technical institution or university. Applicant or parent of applicant must be affiliated with Chick-Fil-A, Inc.. Available to U.S. citizens.

Application Requirements: Application form, recommendations or references, transcript, unit operator approval, proof of enrollment. *Deadline:* continuous.

COMMUNITY FOUNDATION OF WESTERN MASSACHUSETTS

http://www.communityfoundation.org/

DEERFIELD PLASTICS/BARKER FAMILY SCHOLARSHIP

Children, step-children, and grandchildren of employees of the former Deerfield Plastics Company, Inc. as of October 1996. Fifteen awards totaling $40,000 were made in 2012. The 2013-2014 will be the last year this scholarship will be awarded.

Award: Scholarship for use in freshman, sophomore, junior, senior, or graduate years; not renewable. *Number:* 1. *Amount:* $1500–$3000.

Eligibility Requirements: Applicant must be enrolled or expecting to enroll full-time at a two-year or four-year institution or university and resident of Kentucky, Massachusetts. Applicant or parent of applicant must be affiliated with Deerfield Plastics. Available to U.S. citizens.

Application Requirements: Application form, application form may be submitted online (http://www.communityfoundation.org), financial need analysis, Student Aid Report (SAR), transcript. *Deadline:* March 29.

Contact: Dorothy Theriaque, Education Associate
　　　　 Community Foundation of Western Massachusetts
　　　　 1500 Main Street, PO Box 15769
　　　　 Springfield, MA 01115
　　　　 Phone: 413-732-2858
　　　　 Fax: 413-733-8565
　　　　 E-mail: scholar@communityfoundation.org

DEMOLAY FOUNDATION INCORPORATED

http://www.demolay.org/

FRANK S. LAND SCHOLARSHIP

Scholarship awarded to members of DeMolay International only, who have not yet reached the age of 21, to assist in financing their education. Must be U.S. resident.

Award: Scholarship for use in freshman, sophomore, junior, or senior years; not renewable. *Number:* 10–15. *Amount:* $1000.

Eligibility Requirements: Applicant must be enrolled or expecting to enroll full-time at a two-year or four-year institution or university and male. Applicant or parent of applicant must be affiliated with DeMolay. Available to U.S. citizens.

Application Requirements: Application form, recommendations or references, self-addressed stamped envelope with application, transcript. *Deadline:* April 1.

Contact: Jeffrey Kitsmiller, Executive Director
　　　　 DeMolay Foundation Incorporated
　　　　 10200 Northwest Ambassador Drive
　　　　 Kansas City, MO 64153
　　　　 Phone: 800-336-6529
　　　　 Fax: 816-891-9062
　　　　 E-mail: admin@demolay.org

DONALDSON COMPANY

http://www.donaldson.com/

THE DONALDSON COMPANY, INC. SCHOLARSHIP PROGRAM

Scholarships for children of U.S. employees of Donaldson Company Inc. Any form of accredited postsecondary education is eligible. The amount of the award can range from $1000 to $3000 for each year of full-time study and may be renewed for up to a total of four years. The number of scholarships awarded is limited to a maximum of 25 percent of the number of applicants.

Award: Scholarship for use in freshman, sophomore, junior, or senior years; renewable. *Amount:* $1000–$3000.

Eligibility Requirements: Applicant must be enrolled or expecting to enroll full-time at a two-year or four-year institution or university.

Applicant or parent of applicant must be affiliated with Donaldson Company. Available to U.S. citizens.

Application Requirements: Application form, essay, financial need analysis, recommendations or references, transcript. *Deadline:* March 15.

Contact: Norm Linnell, Vice President, General Counsel and Secretary
Phone: 952-887-3631
Fax: 952-887-3005
E-mail: norm.linnell@donaldson.com

DUKE ENERGY CORPORATION
http://www.duke-energy.com/

DUKE ENERGY SCHOLARS PROGRAM
The scholarship is for undergraduate study at accredited, two-year technical schools and/or four-year colleges or universities in the United States and Canada who are children of eligible employees and retirees of Duke Energy and its subsidiaries. Recipients selected by five-member outside committee.

Award: Scholarship for use in freshman, sophomore, junior, or senior years; renewable. *Number:* 15. *Amount:* $1000–$5000.

Eligibility Requirements: Applicant must be enrolled or expecting to enroll full-time at a two-year or four-year or technical institution or university. Applicant or parent of applicant must be affiliated with Duke Energy Corporation. Available to U.S. and Canadian citizens.

Application Requirements: Application form, driver's license, essay, financial need analysis, recommendations or references, test scores, transcript. *Deadline:* December 1.

Contact: Celia Beam, Scholarship Administrator
Phone: 704-382-5544
Fax: 704-382-3553
E-mail: chbeam@duke-energy.com

GANNETT FOUNDATION
http://www.gannettfoundation.org/

GANNETT FOUNDATION/MADELYN P. JENNINGS SCHOLARSHIP AWARD
One-time awards for high school students whose parents are current full-time Gannett Company employees. Must be planning to attend a 4-year college or university for full-time study in the fall after graduation. Students must meet all requirements for participation in the National Merit Scholarship Program and take the PSAT/NMSQT in their junior year of high school. For more information, call Collette Horton at Gannett Co., Inc., (703) 854-6254.

Award: Scholarship for use in freshman year; not renewable. *Number:* 12. *Amount:* $3000.

Eligibility Requirements: Applicant must be high school student and planning to enroll or expecting to enroll full-time at a four-year institution or university. Applicant or parent of applicant must be affiliated with Gannett Company, Inc.. Available to U.S. citizens.

Application Requirements: Application form, application form may be submitted online (https://programentry.nationalmerit.org/DHNNGDCT). *Deadline:* March 1.

Contact: Collette Horton, Benefits Representative
Gannett Foundation
7950 Jones Branch Drive
McLean, VA 22107
Phone: 703-854-6254
E-mail: cnhorton@gannett.com

GATEWAY PRESS INC. OF LOUISVILLE
http://www.gatewaypressinc.com/

GATEWAY PRESS SCHOLARSHIP
Scholarship for graduating high school seniors whose parents have been employees of Gateway Press Inc. for a minimum of 5 years. Applicant must be accepted at a college or university and maintain a minimum GPA of 2.25.

Award: Scholarship for use in freshman year; renewable. *Amount:* up to $3000.

Eligibility Requirements: Applicant must be high school student and planning to enroll or expecting to enroll full-time at a four-year

institution or university. Applicant or parent of applicant must be affiliated with Gateway Press Inc.. Available to U.S. citizens.

Application Requirements: Application form, recommendations or references, transcript. *Deadline:* January 1.

Contact: Chris Georgehead, Human Resources Manager
Phone: 502-454-0431
Fax: 502-459-7930
E-mail: kit@gatewaypressinc.com

GRACO INC.
http://www.graco.com/

GRACO EXCELLENCE SCHOLARSHIP
Three awards of $7500 (one for athletic achievement) for children of Graco employees with at least one year of company service. Award based on academics, financial need, and tuition costs. Must be under 25 years of age.

Award: Scholarship for use in freshman, sophomore, junior, senior, or graduate years; renewable. *Number:* 3. *Amount:* $7500.

Eligibility Requirements: Applicant must be enrolled or expecting to enroll full-time at a two-year or four-year or technical institution or university and must have an interest in athletics/sports. Applicant or parent of applicant must be affiliated with Graco, Inc.. Available to U.S. and non-U.S. citizens.

Application Requirements: Application form, financial need analysis, test scores, transcript. *Deadline:* March 15.

Contact: Kristin Ridley, Grants Administration Manager
Graco Inc.
PO Box 1441
Minneapolis, MN 55440-1441
Phone: 612-623-6684
Fax: 612-623-6944

GRACO INC. SCHOLARSHIP PROGRAM
Renewable award for children of Graco employees under 26 years of age pursuing undergraduate or graduate education. Awards are based upon academics, financial need, and tuition costs. Submit transcripts, test scores, and financial need analysis with application.

Award: Scholarship for use in freshman, sophomore, junior, senior, or graduate years; renewable. *Amount:* $3500–$5000.

Eligibility Requirements: Applicant must be enrolled or expecting to enroll full-time at a two-year or four-year or technical institution or university. Applicant or parent of applicant must be affiliated with Graco, Inc.. Available to U.S. and non-U.S. citizens.

Application Requirements: Application form, financial need analysis, test scores, transcript. *Deadline:* March 15.

Contact: Kristin Ridley, Grants Administration Manager
Graco Inc.
PO Box 1441
Minneapolis, MN 55440-1441
Phone: 612-623-6684
Fax: 612-623-6944

HERMAN O. WEST FOUNDATION
http://www.westpharma.com/

HERMAN O. WEST FOUNDATION SCHOLARSHIP PROGRAM
Awards up to seven scholarships per year to high school seniors who will be attending college in the fall after graduation. The scholarship may only be applied toward tuition cost up to $2500 per year for up to four years. Available only to children of active employees of West Pharmaceutical Services, Inc.

Award: Scholarship for use in freshman, sophomore, junior, or senior years; renewable. *Number:* 1–7. *Amount:* $2500–$10,000.

Eligibility Requirements: Applicant must be high school student and planning to enroll or expecting to enroll full-time at a two-year or four-year institution or university. Applicant or parent of applicant must be affiliated with West Pharmaceuticals. Available to U.S. citizens.

Application Requirements: Application form, essay, recommendations or references, test scores, transcript. *Deadline:* February 28.

Contact: Maureen Goebel, Administrator
Herman O. West Foundation
101 Gordon Drive
Lionville, PA 19341
Phone: 610-594-2945
Fax: 610-594-3011
E-mail: maureen.goebel@westpharma.com

JOHNSON CONTROLS INC.

http://www.johnsoncontrols.com/

JOHNSON CONTROLS FOUNDATION SCHOLARSHIP PROGRAM

Available to high school seniors who are children of Johnson Controls, Inc. U.S. employees only. Twenty one-time awards of $2000 and 25 renewable scholarships of $2000 a year for up to four years.

Award: Scholarship for use in freshman year; renewable. *Number:* up to 45. *Amount:* $2000.

Eligibility Requirements: Applicant must be high school student and planning to enroll or expecting to enroll full-time at a four-year institution or university. Applicant or parent of applicant must be affiliated with Johnson Controls, Inc.. Applicant must have 3.0 GPA or higher. Available to U.S. citizens.

Application Requirements: Application form, application form may be submitted online, community service, essay, test scores, transcript. *Deadline:* March 15.

Contact: Marlene Griffith, Human Resources Administration Coordinator
Phone: 414-524-2425
Fax: 414-524-2299
E-mail: marlene.f.griffith@jci.com

NEW HAMPSHIRE FOOD INDUSTRIES EDUCATION FOUNDATION

http://www.grocers.org/

NEW HAMPSHIRE FOOD INDUSTRY SCHOLARSHIPS

Awards are $1000 each. The purpose is to assist students who are employees or children of employees working for New Hampshire Grocers Association member firms (either retailer or supplier).

Award: Scholarship for use in freshman, sophomore, junior, or senior years; renewable. *Number:* up to 35. *Amount:* $1000.

Eligibility Requirements: Applicant must be enrolled or expecting to enroll full- or part-time at a two-year or four-year or technical institution or university and resident of New Hampshire. Applicant or parent of applicant must be affiliated with New Hampshire Grocers Association member companies. Available to U.S. citizens.

Application Requirements: Application form, essay, recommendations or references, test scores, transcript. *Deadline:* April 1.

Contact: Mr. John Dumais, Secretary and Treasurer
New Hampshire Food Industries Education Foundation
110 Stark Street
Manchester, NH 03101-1977
Phone: 603-669-9333 Ext. 110
Fax: 603-623-1137
E-mail: scholarships@grocers.org

OREGON STUDENT ASSISTANCE COMMISSION

http://www.GetCollegeFunds.org/

ALBINA FUEL COMPANY SCHOLARSHIP

Scholarship available to a dependent child of a current Albina Fuel Company employee. The employee must have been employed for at least one full year as of October 1 prior to the scholarship deadline. Must reapply annually. Oregon residency not required.

Award: Scholarship for use in freshman, sophomore, junior, or senior years; not renewable.

Eligibility Requirements: Applicant must be enrolled or expecting to enroll full-time at a four-year institution. Applicant or parent of applicant must be affiliated with Albina Fuel Company. Available to U.S. citizens.

Application Requirements: Activity chart, application form, essay, transcript. *Deadline:* March 1.

A. VICTOR ROSENFELD SCHOLARSHIP

Award for dependents of employees of Calbag Metals of Portland, Oregon who have worked for that company for three or more years prior to the March 1 scholarship deadline. Applicants must be enrolled at any public or nonprofit U.S. college or university. Must reapply annually for award renewal. FAFSA required.

Award: Scholarship for use in freshman, sophomore, junior, or senior years; not renewable.

Eligibility Requirements: Applicant must be enrolled or expecting to enroll full-time at a four-year institution or university and resident of Oregon. Applicant or parent of applicant must be affiliated with Calbag Metals. Available to U.S. citizens.

Application Requirements: Application form, essay, FAFSA, financial need analysis, recommendations or references, transcript. *Deadline:* March 1.

ESSEX GENERAL CONSTRUCTION SCHOLARSHIP

Award for an employee, or dependent of a current employee of Essex General Construction. Employee must have been continuously employed at Essex for one year or more at no fewer than 20 hours per week as of the March 1 application deadline. Applicant must be a high school graduate. Oregon residency is not required. Must be enrolling as an undergraduate in a college or university in the U.S. Must reapply each year to renew award for up to four years.

Award: Scholarship for use in freshman, sophomore, junior, or senior years; not renewable.

Eligibility Requirements: Applicant must be enrolled or expecting to enroll full- or part-time at a four-year institution and resident of Oregon. Applicant or parent of applicant must be affiliated with Essex General Construction. Available to U.S. citizens.

Application Requirements: Activities chart, application form, essay, financial need analysis, transcript. *Deadline:* March 1.

GLENN JACKSON SCHOLARS SCHOLARSHIPS

Renewable award for Oregon graduating high school seniors who are dependents of employees or retirees of Oregon Department of Transportation or Parks and Recreation Department. Employees must have worked in their department at least three years as of the March 1 scholarship deadline.

Award: Scholarship for use in freshman, sophomore, junior, or senior years; renewable.

Eligibility Requirements: Applicant must be high school student; planning to enroll or expecting to enroll full- or part-time at a two-year or four-year institution or university and resident of Oregon. Applicant or parent of applicant must be affiliated with Oregon Department of Transportation Parks and Recreation. Available to U.S. citizens.

Application Requirements: Activity chart, application form, essay, financial need analysis, recommendations or references, transcript. *Deadline:* March 1.

KONNIE MEMORIAL DEPENDENTS SCHOLARSHIP

Renewable award for graduating high school seniors who are children of Swanson Brothers Lumber Co. employees. Must be an Oregon resident and enrolled in an Oregon public college.

Award: Scholarship for use in freshman year; renewable.

Eligibility Requirements: Applicant must be high school student; planning to enroll or expecting to enroll full-time at a two-year or four-year or technical institution or university; resident of Oregon and studying in Oregon. Applicant or parent of applicant must be affiliated with Swanson Brothers Lumber Company. Available to U.S. citizens.

Application Requirements: Activity chart, application form, essay, recommendations or references, transcript. *Deadline:* March 1.

OREGON TRUCKING ASSOCIATION SAFETY MANAGEMENT COUNCIL SCHOLARSHIP

One-time award available to a child of an Oregon Trucking Association member, or child of an employee of OTA member. Applicants must be graduating high school seniors from an Oregon high school planning to attend a public or nonprofit college or university. Oregon residency is not required.

Award: Scholarship for use in freshman year; not renewable.

Eligibility Requirements: Applicant must be high school student and planning to enroll or expecting to enroll full-time at a four-year institution. Applicant or parent of applicant must be affiliated with Oregon Trucking Association. Available to U.S. citizens.

Application Requirements: Activity chart, application form, essay, financial need analysis, recommendations or references, transcript. *Deadline:* March 1.

PACIFICSOURCE HEALTH PLANS SCHOLARSHIP

Award for high school graduates or GED recipients who are the dependents of PacificSource Health Plans employees. Employee must have been continuously employed at PacificSource for at least two years at no fewer than 20 hours per week as of the March 1 application deadline. Dependents of company officers are not eligible. Award is to be used for undergraduate study at a U.S. college or university. Minimum 3.0 GPA required. Oregon residency is not required.

Award: Scholarship for use in freshman, sophomore, junior, or senior years; not renewable.

Eligibility Requirements: Applicant must be enrolled or expecting to enroll full-time at a four-year institution or university. Applicant or parent of applicant must be affiliated with PacificSource. Applicant must have 3.0 GPA or higher. Available to U.S. citizens.

Application Requirements: Activities chart, application form, essay, transcript. *Deadline:* March 1.

RICHARD F. BRENTANO MEMORIAL SCHOLARSHIP

One-time award for legal dependents of eligible employees of Waste Control Systems Inc., and subsidiaries. Employees must be employed at least one year as of the March 1 scholarship deadline. Oregon residency is not required. Must reapply annually to renew award.

Award: Scholarship for use in freshman, sophomore, junior, or senior years; not renewable.

Eligibility Requirements: Applicant must be enrolled or expecting to enroll full-time at a four-year institution. Applicant or parent of applicant must be affiliated with Waste Control Systems, Inc.. Available to U.S. citizens.

Application Requirements: Activity chart, application form, essay, recommendations or references, transcript. *Deadline:* March 1.

ROBERT D. FORSTER SCHOLARSHIP

One scholarship available to an employee of Walsh Construction Co. or a dependent child of an employee. Oregon residency not required. Award may be renewed for a maximum of twelve quarters of undergraduate study if renewal criteria are met, and may be used at any four-year college or university in the U.S.

Award: Scholarship for use in freshman, sophomore, junior, or senior years; renewable.

Eligibility Requirements: Applicant must be enrolled or expecting to enroll full-time at a four-year institution or university. Applicant or parent of applicant must be affiliated with Walsh Construction Company. Available to U.S. citizens.

Application Requirements: Activity chart, application form, essay, financial need analysis, recommendations or references, transcript. *Deadline:* March 1.

ROGER W. EMMONS MEMORIAL SCHOLARSHIP

Scholarship available to a graduating Oregon high school senior who is a child or grandchild of an employee (for at least three years) of member of the Oregon Refuse and Recycling Association. Oregon residency is not required; award may be used at any accredited U.S. public or nonprofit college or university.

Award: Scholarship for use in freshman year; renewable.

Eligibility Requirements: Applicant must be high school student and planning to enroll or expecting to enroll full-time at a four-year institution. Applicant or parent of applicant must be affiliated with Oregon Refuse and Recycling Association. Available to U.S. citizens.

Application Requirements: Activity chart, application form, essay, recommendations or references, transcript. *Deadline:* March 1.

STIMSON LUMBER COMPANY SCHOLARSHIP

Award for dependents of Stimson Lumber Company employees who are graduating seniors that have a minimum 3.0 GPA. Oregon residency is not required. One-year-only scholarships available for students attending two- or four-year public or nonprofit colleges. Renewable scholarships are for students enrolled in four-year public or nonprofit colleges who meet renewal criteria and maintain 2.7 GPA.

Award: Scholarship for use in freshman year; not renewable.

Eligibility Requirements: Applicant must be enrolled or expecting to enroll full-time at a two-year or four-year institution. Applicant or parent of applicant must be affiliated with Stimson Lumber Company. Applicant must have 3.0 GPA or higher. Available to U.S. citizens.

Application Requirements: Activity chart, application form, essay, financial need analysis, recommendations or references, transcript. *Deadline:* March 1.

TAYLOR MADE LABELS SCHOLARSHIP

Award available to dependents of active employees of Taylor Made Label Company. Employee must have been employed by Taylor Made for a minimum of one year as of the March 1 scholarship deadline. Oregon residency is not required. Applicant must be enrolled as an undergraduate in a U.S. college or university and must reapply annually for award renewal.

Award: Scholarship for use in freshman, sophomore, junior, or senior years; not renewable.

Eligibility Requirements: Applicant must be enrolled or expecting to enroll full- or part-time at a four-year institution or university. Applicant or parent of applicant must be affiliated with Taylor Made Label Company. Available to U.S. citizens.

Application Requirements: Activity chart, FAFSA, application form, essay, financial need analysis, recommendations or references, transcript. *Deadline:* March 1.

WALTER DAVIES SCHOLARSHIP

Award for current U.S. Bank employees or employees' natural or adopted children. Must be Oregon high school graduate. Oregon residency is not required; must re-apply annually. Financial need will be considered.

Award: Scholarship for use in freshman, sophomore, junior, or senior years; not renewable.

Eligibility Requirements: Applicant must be enrolled or expecting to enroll full-time at a four-year institution. Applicant or parent of applicant must be affiliated with U.S. Bancorp. Available to U.S. citizens.

Application Requirements: Activity chart, FAFSA, application form, essay, financial need analysis, recommendations or references, transcript. *Deadline:* March 1.

WILLETT AND MARGUERITE LAKE SCHOLARSHIP

Scholarship awards for children, stepchildren, and grandchildren of current employees of Bonita Pioneer Packaging Company who have been employed by the company for two years. Open to high school seniors and undergraduates who are Oregon residents. Reapply annually.

Award: Scholarship for use in freshman, sophomore, junior, or senior years; not renewable.

Eligibility Requirements: Applicant must be enrolled or expecting to enroll full-time at a four-year institution or university and resident of Oregon. Applicant or parent of applicant must be affiliated with Bonita Pioneer Packaging Company. Available to U.S. citizens.

Application Requirements: Activity chart, application form, essay, financial need analysis, transcript. *Deadline:* March 1.

WOODARD FAMILY SCHOLARSHIP

Scholarships are available to employees and dependents of eligible employees of Kimwood Corporation. Awards may be used at Oregon public and nonprofit colleges only. FAFSA required. May reapply annually for award.

Award: Scholarship for use in freshman, sophomore, junior, or senior years; renewable.

Eligibility Requirements: Applicant must be enrolled or expecting to enroll full-time at a two-year or four-year institution; resident of Oregon and studying in Oregon. Applicant or parent of applicant must be affiliated with Kimwood Corporation or Middlefield Village. Available to U.S. citizens.

Application Requirements: Application form, essay, financial need analysis, recommendations or references, transcript. *Deadline:* March 1.

RHODE ISLAND FOUNDATION

http://www.rifoundation.org/

A.T. CROSS SCHOLARSHIP

Renewable scholarships ranging from $1000 to $3000 for new applicants and from $300 to $2000 for renewals are available to children of full-time employees of A.T. Cross Company. Must be Rhode Island residents.

Award: Scholarship for use in freshman, sophomore, junior, or senior years; renewable. *Amount:* $1000–$3000.

Eligibility Requirements: Applicant must be enrolled or expecting to enroll full-time at a four-year institution or university and resident of Rhode Island. Applicant or parent of applicant must be affiliated with A.T. Cross. Available to U.S. citizens.

Application Requirements: Application form, essay, financial need analysis, recommendations or references, self-addressed stamped envelope with application, transcript. *Deadline:* May 15.

Contact: Libby Monahan, Funds Administrator
Phone: 401-274-4564 Ext. 3117
E-mail: libbym@rifoundation.org

THEODORE R. AND VIVIAN M. JOHNSON SCHOLARSHIP FOUNDATION INC.

http://www.jsf.bz/

THEODORE R. AND VIVIAN M. JOHNSON SCHOLARSHIP PROGRAM FOR CHILDREN OF UPS EMPLOYEES OR UPS RETIREES

The children of United Parcel Service employees or retirees who live in Florida are eligible for scholarship funds to attend college or vocational school in Florida. Awards are for undergraduate study only and ranges from $1000 to $10,000. Community college students and vocational school students may receive a maximum of $10,000 per year.

Award: Scholarship for use in freshman, sophomore, junior, or senior years; renewable. *Number:* 1–250. *Amount:* $1000–$10,000.

Eligibility Requirements: Applicant must be enrolled or expecting to enroll full-time at a two-year or four-year or technical institution or university; resident of Florida and studying in Florida. Applicant or parent of applicant must be affiliated with UPS-United Parcel Service. Available to U.S. citizens.

Application Requirements: Application form, financial need analysis, transcript. *Deadline:* April 15.

Contact: Mrs. Sharon Wood, Office Manager/Program Officer
Theodore R. and Vivian M. Johnson Scholarship Foundation Inc.
505 South Flagler Drive
Suite 1460
West Palm Beach, FL 33401
Phone: 561-659-2005 Ext. 3
Fax: 561-659-1054
E-mail: wood@jsf.bz

VERIZON FOUNDATION

http://www.verizonfoundation.org/grants/

VERIZON FOUNDATION SCHOLARSHIP

Award up to 250 four-year scholarships to high school seniors who are children of Verizon employees in the United States, and are planning to attend a four-year college or university. Deadline varies.

Award: Scholarship for use in freshman year; renewable. *Number:* up to 250. *Amount:* $5000–$20,000.

Eligibility Requirements: Applicant must be high school student and planning to enroll or expecting to enroll full- or part-time at a four-year institution or university. Applicant or parent of applicant must be affiliated with Verizon. Available to U.S. citizens.

Application Requirements: Application form. *Deadline:* varies.

WAL-MART FOUNDATION

http://www.walmartfoundation.org/

WAL-MART ASSOCIATE SCHOLARSHIPS

Awards for college-bound graduating high school seniors, those receiving a home-school diploma, or receiving a GED equivalency who work for Wal-Mart at least six months. Based on minimum 2.5 cumulative high school GPA and can prove financial need by required documents. One-time award of up to $3000. For use at an accredited two- or four-year U.S. institution. Apply online at https//www.applyists.net, Access Key: WMAS.

Award: Scholarship for use in freshman year; not renewable. *Amount:* up to $3000.

Eligibility Requirements: Applicant must be high school student and planning to enroll or expecting to enroll full-time at a two-year or four-year institution or university. Applicant or parent of applicant must be affiliated with Wal-Mart Foundation. Applicant must have 2.5 GPA or higher. Available to U.S. citizens.

Application Requirements: Application form, federal income tax return, test scores, transcript. *Deadline:* January 31.

WAL-MART HIGHER REACH SCHOLARSHIP

Applicant must be full-time or part-time Wal-Mart Associate. Must have been employed by Wal-Mart Stores for at least six months. Must have been out of high school for at least one year or have equivalent home school or GED. Award is based on financial need and community involvement. Applications available online https://www.applyists.net. Access key: WALMT.

Award: Scholarship for use in freshman, sophomore, junior, or senior years; not renewable. *Amount:* $250–$3000.

Eligibility Requirements: Applicant must be enrolled or expecting to enroll full- or part-time at a two-year or four-year institution or university. Applicant or parent of applicant must be affiliated with Wal-Mart Foundation. Available to U.S. citizens.

Application Requirements: Application form, federal tax form, test scores. *Deadline:* January 31.

WALTON FAMILY FOUNDATION SCHOLARSHIP

Award for high-school seniors, or those receiving a home-school diploma, or receiving a GED-equivalency who are children of a Wal-Mart associate who has been employed as a full-time associate for at least one year. A $13,000 undergraduate scholarship is payable over four years. Minimum of 22 (ACT) or 1030 (SAT) score and can prove financial need by required documents. Application available online at https://www.applyists.net. Access key: WFFS.

Award: Scholarship for use in freshman year; renewable. *Number:* 175. *Amount:* $13,000.

Eligibility Requirements: Applicant must be high school student and planning to enroll or expecting to enroll full-time at a two-year or four-year institution or university. Applicant or parent of applicant must be affiliated with Wal-Mart Foundation. Available to U.S. citizens.

Application Requirements: Application form, federal income tax return, test scores, transcript. *Deadline:* January 31.

WEYERHAEUSER COMPANY FOUNDATION

http://www.weyerhaeuser.com/

WEYERHAEUSER COMPANY FOUNDATION SCHOLARSHIPS

Renewable awards for children of Weyerhaeuser Company employees. Must be in senior year in high school. Thirty scholarships to four-year institutions and 20 scholarships to community colleges or vocational/technical schools are awarded each year.

Award: Scholarship for use in freshman year; renewable. *Number:* 50. *Amount:* $1000–$4000.

Eligibility Requirements: Applicant must be high school student and planning to enroll or expecting to enroll full-time at a two-year or four-year or technical institution. Applicant or parent of applicant must be affiliated with Weyerhauser Company. Available to U.S. and Canadian citizens.

Application Requirements: Application form. *Deadline:* January 15.

WILLITS FOUNDATION

WILLITS FOUNDATION SCHOLARSHIP PROGRAM

Renewable awards for children of full-time employees of C. R. Bard Inc. Children of Bard officers are not eligible. Must be pursuing, or planning to pursue, full-time postsecondary studies in the year in which the application is made.

Award: Scholarship for use in freshman, sophomore, junior, or senior years; renewable. *Number:* 10–15. *Amount:* $5000.

Eligibility Requirements: Applicant must be enrolled or expecting to enroll full-time at a four-year institution or university. Applicant or parent of applicant must be affiliated with C.R. Bard, Inc.. Available to U.S. and Canadian citizens.

Application Requirements: Application form, essay, personal photograph, recommendations or references, test scores, transcript. *Deadline:* March 1.

Contact: Linda Hrevnack, Program Manager
Willits Foundation
730 Central Avenue
Murray Hill, NJ 07974
Phone: 908-277-8182
Fax: 908-277-8098

EMPLOYMENT/ VOLUNTEER EXPERIENCE

AIR TRAFFIC CONTROL ASSOCIATION INC.

http://www.atca.org/

BUCKINGHAM MEMORIAL SCHOLARSHIP

Scholarships granted to children of air traffic control specialists pursuing a bachelor's degree or higher in any course of study. Must be the child, natural or by adoption, of a person serving, or having served as an air traffic control specialist, be it with the U.S. government, U.S. military, or in a private facility in the United States.

Award: Scholarship for use in freshman, sophomore, junior, senior, or graduate years; not renewable. *Number:* 15–20. *Amount:* $2000–$6000.

Eligibility Requirements: Applicant must be enrolled or expecting to enroll full-time at a four-year institution or university. Applicant or parent of applicant must have employment or volunteer experience in air traffic control. Available to U.S. citizens.

Application Requirements: Application form, driver's license, essay, financial need analysis, recommendations or references, transcript. *Deadline:* May 1.

Contact: Sandra Strickland, Meetings and Programs Coordinator
Air Traffic Control Association Inc.
1101 King Street, Suite 300
Alexandria, VA 22201
Phone: 703-299-2430
Fax: 703-299-2430
E-mail: info@atca.org

AMERICAN FEDERATION OF TEACHERS

http://www.aft.org/

ROBERT G. PORTER SCHOLARS PROGRAM-AMERICAN FEDERATION OF TEACHERS DEPENDENTS
• *See page 503*

AMERICAN LEGION AUXILIARY DEPARTMENT OF MAINE

http://www.mainelegion.org/

AMERICAN LEGION AUXILIARY DEPARTMENT OF MAINE NATIONAL PRESIDENT'S SCHOLARSHIP

Scholarships to children of veterans who served in the Armed Forces during the eligibility dates for The American Legion. One $2500, one $2000, and one $1000 scholarship will be awarded. Applicant must complete 50 hours of community service during his/her high school years.

Award: Scholarship for use in freshman year; not renewable. *Number:* 3. *Amount:* $1000–$2500.

Eligibility Requirements: Applicant must be high school student; planning to enroll or expecting to enroll full-time at a four-year institution or university and resident of Maine. Applicant or parent of applicant must have employment or volunteer experience in community service. Available to U.S. citizens. Applicant or parent must meet one or more of the following requirements: general military experience; retired from active duty; disabled or killed as a result of military service; prisoner of war; or missing in action.

Application Requirements: Application form, essay, recommendations or references, test scores, transcript. *Deadline:* March 1.

Contact: Mary Wells, Education Chairman
Phone: 207-532-6007
E-mail: aladeptsecme@verizon.net

AMERICAN LEGION AUXILIARY DEPARTMENT OF MASSACHUSETTS

http://www.masslegion-aux.org/

AMERICAN LEGION AUXILIARY DEPARTMENT OF MASSACHUSETTS DEPARTMENT PRESIDENT'S SCHOLARSHIP

Awarded to children of veterans who served in the armed forces during the eligibility dates specified by the legion. The applicant must complete 50 hours of community service during high school years to be eligible for this scholarship.

Award: Scholarship for use in freshman, sophomore, junior, or senior years; not renewable. *Number:* 12. *Amount:* $200–$750.

Eligibility Requirements: Applicant must be age 16-22; enrolled or expecting to enroll full-time at a two-year or four-year institution or university; resident of Massachusetts and studying in Massachusetts. Applicant or parent of applicant must have employment or volunteer experience in community service. Available to U.S. citizens. Applicant or parent must meet one or more of the following requirements; general military experience; retired from active duty; disabled or killed as a result of military service; prisoner of war; or missing in action.

Application Requirements: Application form. *Deadline:* March 1.

Contact: Beverly Monaco, Secretary and Treasurer
Phone: 617-727-2958
Fax: 617-727-0741

AMERICAN LEGION AUXILIARY DEPARTMENT OF NORTH DAKOTA

http://www.ndlegion.org/

AMERICAN LEGION AUXILIARY DEPARTMENT OF NORTH DAKOTA NATIONAL PRESIDENT'S SCHOLARSHIP

Three division scholarships for children of veterans who served in the Armed Forces during eligible dates for American Legion membership. Must be U.S. citizen and a high school senior with a minimum 2.5 GPA. Must be entered by local American Legion Auxiliary Unit.

Award: Scholarship for use in freshman year; not renewable. *Number:* 3. *Amount:* $1000–$2500.

Eligibility Requirements: Applicant must be high school student; planning to enroll or expecting to enroll full-time at a four-year institution or university; resident of North Dakota and studying in North Dakota. Applicant or parent of applicant must have employment or volunteer experience in community service. Applicant must have 2.5 GPA or higher. Available to U.S. citizens. Applicant or parent must meet one or more of the following requirements: general military experience; retired from active duty; disabled or killed as a result of military service; prisoner of war; or missing in action.

Application Requirements: Application form, essay, financial need analysis, proof of 50 hours voluntary service, recommendations or references, test scores, transcript. *Deadline:* March 1.

Contact: Myrna Runholm, Department Secretary
　　　　　　Phone: 701-253-5992
　　　　　　Fax: 701-952-5993
　　　　　　E-mail: ala-hq@ndlegion.org

AMERICAN LEGION DEPARTMENT OF VERMONT

http://www.vtlegion.org

AMERICAN LEGION EAGLE SCOUT OF THE YEAR

• See page 512

AMERICAN LEGION NATIONAL HEADQUARTERS

http://www.legion.org/

AMERICAN LEGION NATIONAL HEADQUARTERS EAGLE SCOUT OF THE YEAR

The winner of the competition receives a $10,000 scholarship and 3 runners-up are each awarded $2500 scholarships. May be used to attend any state accredited postsecondary institution in the U.S.

Award: Scholarship for use in freshman, sophomore, junior, or senior years; not renewable. *Number:* 4. *Amount:* $2500–$10,000.

Eligibility Requirements: Applicant must be high school student; age 15-18; planning to enroll or expecting to enroll full-time at a two-year or four-year institution or university and male. Applicant or parent of applicant must have employment or volunteer experience in community service. Available to U.S. citizens.

Application Requirements: Application form, essay, recommendations or references, transcript. *Deadline:* March 1.

Contact: Michael Buss, Assistant Director
　　　　　　American Legion National Headquarters
　　　　　　The American Legion, PO Box 1055
　　　　　　Indianapolis, IN 46206
　　　　　　Phone: 317-630-1249
　　　　　　Fax: 317-630-1369
　　　　　　E-mail: mbuss@legion.org

AMERICAN POSTAL WORKERS UNION

http://www.apwu.org/

E.C. HALLBECK SCHOLARSHIP FUND

• See page 512

VOCATIONAL SCHOLARSHIP PROGRAM

• See page 512

AMERICAN QUARTER HORSE FOUNDATION (AQHF)

http://www.aqha.com/foundation

EXCELLENCE IN EQUINE/AGRICULTURAL INVOLVEMENT SCHOLARSHIP

• See page 513

FARM AND RANCH HERITAGE SCHOLARSHIP

• See page 514

AMERICAN ROAD & TRANSPORTATION BUILDERS ASSOCIATION-

TRANSPORTATION DEVELOPMENT FOUNDATION (ARTBA-TDF)

http://www.artba.org/

ARTBA-TDF LANFORD FAMILY HIGHWAY WORKERS MEMORIAL SCHOLARSHIP PROGRAM

The ARTBA-TDF Highway Worker Memorial Scholarship Program provides financial assistance to help the sons, daughters or legally adopted children of highway workers killed or permanently disabled in the line of duty pursue post-high school education. Minimum 2.5 GPA required.

Award: Scholarship for use in freshman, sophomore, junior, or senior years; not renewable. *Amount:* $1000–$5000.

Eligibility Requirements: Applicant must be enrolled or expecting to enroll full-time at a two-year or four-year or technical institution or university. Applicant or parent of applicant must have employment or volunteer experience in construction, roadway work. Applicant must have 2.5 GPA or higher. Available to U.S. citizens.

Application Requirements: Application form, copy of current year's federal tax return, copy of parent's current year federal tax return, essay, financial need analysis, personal photograph, recommendations or references, transcript. *Deadline:* April 5.

Contact: Holly Bolton, Scholarship and Awards Manager
　　　　　　American Road & Transportation Builders Association-
　　　　　　　　Transportation Development Foundation (ARTBA-TDF)
　　　　　　1219 28th Street, NW
　　　　　　Washington, DC 20007
　　　　　　Phone: 202-289-4434 Ext. 411
　　　　　　E-mail: hbolton@artba.org

A.W. BODINE-SUNKIST GROWERS INC.

http://www.sunkist.com/

A.W. BODINE-SUNKIST MEMORIAL SCHOLARSHIP

Renewable award for undergraduate study for applicants whose family derives most of its income from the agriculture industry in Arizona or California. Award is based on minimum 2.7 GPA and financial need.

Award: Scholarship for use in freshman, sophomore, junior, or senior years; renewable. *Number:* 20. *Amount:* $2000.

Eligibility Requirements: Applicant must be enrolled or expecting to enroll full-time at a two-year or four-year institution or university and resident of Arizona, California. Applicant or parent of applicant must have employment or volunteer experience in agriculture. Available to U.S. citizens.

Application Requirements: Application form, essay, financial need analysis, recommendations or references, resume, test scores, transcript. *Deadline:* April 30.

Contact: Claire Smith, Scholarship Administrator
　　　　　　Phone: 818-986-4800
　　　　　　Fax: 818-986-7511

BOY SCOUTS OF AMERICA-MUSKINGUM VALLEY COUNCIL

http://www.learning-for-life.org/

YOUNG AMERICAN AWARD

Award for young adults between the ages of 15 and 25, who have achieved excellence in the fields of art, athletics, business, education, government, humanities, literature, music, religion, science, or service. Applicant must have been involved in service to their community, state, or country that adds to the quality of life. Must be participant of the Learning for Life Exploring program.

Award: Prize for use in freshman year; not renewable. *Number:* 5. *Amount:* $7500.

Eligibility Requirements: Applicant must be high school student; age 15-25 and planning to enroll or expecting to enroll full-time at a four-year institution or university. Applicant or parent of applicant must have employment or volunteer experience in community service. Available to U.S. and non-U.S. citizens.

Application Requirements: Application form, entry in a contest, recommendations or references, transcript. *Deadline:* December 1.

Contact: Bill Rogers, Associate Director
Phone: 972-580-2433
Fax: 972-580-2137
E-mail: brogers@lflmail.org

CALIFORNIA CORRECTIONAL PEACE OFFICERS ASSOCIATION

http://www.ccpoa.org/

CALIFORNIA CORRECTIONAL PEACE OFFICERS ASSOCIATION JOE HARPER SCHOLARSHIP

Scholarship program for immediate relatives of current, retired, or deceased correctional peace officers working the toughest beat in the state. Must be or must have been members in good standing of CCPOA. Applicant must be a high school senior with minimum 3.0 GPA or currently enrolled college student.

Award: Scholarship for use in freshman, sophomore, junior, senior, or graduate years; not renewable. *Number:* 100–200. *Amount:* $500–$1000.

Eligibility Requirements: Applicant must be enrolled or expecting to enroll full- or part-time at a two-year or four-year or technical institution or university and resident of California. Applicant or parent of applicant must have employment or volunteer experience in police/firefighting. Applicant must have 3.0 GPA or higher. Available to U.S. citizens.

Application Requirements: Application form, copies of federal income tax return from the previous year, essay, financial need analysis, personal photograph, recommendations or references, test scores, transcript. *Deadline:* April 30.

Contact: Marcia Bartlett, CCPOA Membership Committee
California Correctional Peace Officers Association
755 Riverpoint Drive, Suite 200
West Sacramento, CA 95605-1634
Phone: 916-372-6060
Fax: 916-372-6623
E-mail: marcia.bartlett@ccpoa.org

CALIFORNIA STATE PARENT-TEACHER ASSOCIATION

http://www.capta.org/

CONTINUING EDUCATION-PTA VOLUNTEERS SCHOLARSHIP

• *See page 516*

GRADUATING HIGH SCHOOL SENIOR SCHOLARSHIP

Available to high school seniors graduating between January 1 and June 30 of the current academic year from high schools in California with a PTA/PTSA unit in good standing. Must be a California resident. Must have volunteered in the school and community volunteer service.

Award: Scholarship for use in freshman year; renewable. *Amount:* $500.

Eligibility Requirements: Applicant must be high school student; planning to enroll or expecting to enroll full-time at a two-year or four-year or technical institution or university and resident of California. Applicant or parent of applicant must have employment or volunteer experience in community service. Available to U.S. citizens.

Application Requirements: Application form, community service, copy of current PTA/PTSA membership card, essay, recommendations or references, transcript. *Deadline:* February 1.

Contact: Becky Reece, Scholarship and Award Chairman
California State Parent-Teacher Association
930 Georgia Street
Los Angeles, CA 90015-1322
Phone: 213-620-1100
Fax: 213-620-1411
E-mail: info@capta.org

CALIFORNIA STUDENT AID COMMISSION

http://www.csac.ca.gov/

LAW ENFORCEMENT PERSONNEL DEPENDENTS SCHOLARSHIP

Provides college grants to needy dependents of California law enforcement officers, officers and employees of the Department of Corrections and Department of Youth Authority, and firefighters killed or disabled in the line of duty.

Award: Grant for use in freshman, sophomore, junior, or senior years; renewable. *Amount:* $100–$13,665.

Eligibility Requirements: Applicant must be enrolled or expecting to enroll full- or part-time at a two-year or four-year institution or university; resident of California and studying in California. Applicant or parent of applicant must have employment or volunteer experience in police/firefighting. Available to U.S. citizens.

Application Requirements: Application form, birth certificate, death certificate of parents or spouse, police report, financial need analysis, transcript. *Deadline:* continuous.

Contact: Catalina Mistler, Chief, Program Administration and Services Division
California Student Aid Commission
PO Box 419026
Rancho Cordova, CA 95741-9026
Phone: 916-526-7268
Fax: 916-526-8002
E-mail: studentsupport@csac.ca.gov

CALIFORNIA TABLE GRAPE COMMISSION

http://www.freshcaliforniagrapes.com/

CALIFORNIA TABLE GRAPE FARM WORKERS SCHOLARSHIP PROGRAM

Applicants must be high school graduates who plan to attend any college or university in California. The applicant, a parent, or a legal guardian must have worked in the California table grape harvest during the last season. School activities, personal references, and financial need are considered. Must be a U.S. citizen.

Award: Scholarship for use in freshman year; not renewable. *Number:* 3. *Amount:* $16,000.

Eligibility Requirements: Applicant must be enrolled or expecting to enroll full-time at a four-year institution or university and studying in California. Applicant or parent of applicant must have employment or volunteer experience in agriculture. Available to U.S. citizens.

Application Requirements: Application form, essay, recommendations or references, test scores, transcript. *Deadline:* March 19.

CALIFORNIA TEACHERS ASSOCIATION (CTA)

http://www.cta.org/

CALIFORNIA TEACHERS ASSOCIATION SCHOLARSHIP FOR MEMBERS

• *See page 516*

CHICK-FIL-A INC.

http://www.chick-fil-a.com/

CHICK-FIL-A LEADERSHIP SCHOLARSHIP

• *See page 545*

COCA-COLA SCHOLARS FOUNDATION INC.

http://www.coca-colascholars.org/

COCA-COLA TWO-YEAR COLLEGES SCHOLARSHIP

Nonrenewable awards based on community involvement, leadership, and academic performance. Must pursue a two-year degree. Each institution may nominate up to two applicants. Minimum 2.5 GPA is required.

Award: Scholarship for use in freshman or sophomore years; not renewable. *Number:* 350–400. *Amount:* $1000.

Eligibility Requirements: Applicant must be enrolled or expecting to enroll full- or part-time at a two-year institution and must have an interest in leadership. Applicant or parent of applicant must have employment or volunteer experience in community service. Applicant must have 2.5 GPA or higher. Available to U.S. citizens.

Application Requirements: Application form, essay, nomination from institution. *Deadline:* May 31.

Contact: Ryan Rodriguez, Program Facilitator
Coca-Cola Scholars Foundation Inc.
PO Box 442
Atlanta, GA 30301-0442
Phone: 800-306-2653
Fax: 404-733-5439
E-mail: scholars@na.ko.com

COLLEGEBOUND FOUNDATION

http://www.collegeboundfoundation.org/

BALTIMORE ROTARY SERVICE ABOVE SELF AWARD PROGRAM

One time scholarship awards ranging from $1000 to $1500 for high school graduates who possess a minimum GPA of 2.5. Must have verifiable community service. For more information visit website, http://www.collegeboundfoundation.org.

Award: Scholarship for use in freshman year; not renewable. *Number:* 1–4. *Amount:* $1000–$1500.

Eligibility Requirements: Applicant must be high school student and planning to enroll or expecting to enroll full-time at a two-year or four-year institution or university. Applicant or parent of applicant must have employment or volunteer experience in community service. Applicant must have 2.5 GPA or higher. Available to U.S. citizens.

Application Requirements: Application form, application form may be submitted online (http://www.scholarships.mycbf.net/STARS), community service, essay, financial aid award letters, Student Aid Report (SAR), financial need analysis, recommendations or references, transcript. *Deadline:* March 1.

Contact: Michael Thornton, Associate Program Director, Scholarship Programs
Phone: 410-783-2905 Ext. 207
Fax: 410-727-5786
E-mail: mthornton@collegeboundfoundation.org

COMCAST LEADERS AND ACHIEVERS SCHOLARSHIP PROGRAM

http://www.com/cast.com/

COMCAST LEADERS AND ACHIEVERS SCHOLARSHIP

Nominees must be full-time high school seniors, must demonstrate a strong commitment to community service and display leadership abilities. Minimum 2.8 GPA required. Must be nominated by their high school principal. Employees of Comcast, its subsidiaries and affiliates, and their families, are not eligible. E-mail for nomination form: comcast@spaprog.com.

Award: Scholarship for use in freshman year; not renewable. *Amount:* $1000.

Eligibility Requirements: Applicant must be high school student and planning to enroll or expecting to enroll full-time at a two-year or four-year institution or university. Applicant or parent of applicant must have employment or volunteer experience in community service. Applicant must have 3.0 GPA or higher. Available to U.S. and non-U.S. citizens.

Application Requirements: Community service. *Deadline:* January 29.

COMMUNITY BANKERS ASSOCIATION OF ILLINOIS

http://www.cbai.com/

COMMUNITY BANKERS ASSOC OF IL CHILD OF A BANKER SCHOLARSHIP

• See page 517

DELAWARE HIGHER EDUCATION OFFICE

http://www.doe.k12.de.us

AGENDA FOR DELAWARE WOMEN TRAILBLAZER SCHOLARSHIP

Award for women legal residents of Delaware who are U.S. citizens or eligible non-citizens. Must enroll in a public or private nonprofit college in Delaware as an undergraduate student. Must have a cumulative GPA of 2.5 or higher. Award based 50 percent on financial need, 50 percent on community and school activities, vision, participation, and leadership.

Award: Scholarship for use in freshman, sophomore, junior, or senior years; renewable. *Number:* 2. *Amount:* $2500.

Eligibility Requirements: Applicant must be enrolled or expecting to enroll full-time at a four-year institution or university; female; resident of Delaware; studying in Delaware and must have an interest in leadership. Applicant or parent of applicant must have employment or volunteer experience in community service. Applicant must have 2.5 GPA or higher. Available to U.S. citizens.

Application Requirements: Application form, FAFSA, Student Aid Report (SAR), financial need analysis. *Deadline:* April 11.

Contact: Carylin Brinkley, Program Administrator
Phone: 302-735-4120
Fax: 302-739-5894
E-mail: cbrinkley@doe.k12.de.us

EDUCATIONAL BENEFITS FOR CHILDREN OF DECEASED VETERANS

Award for children between the ages of 16 and 24 of deceased/MIA/POW veterans or state police officers. Must have been a resident of Delaware for 3 or more years prior to the date of application. If the applicant's parent is a member of the armed forces, the parent must have been a resident of Delaware at the time of death or declaration of missing in action or prisoner of war status. Award will not exceed tuition and fees at a Delaware public college.

Award: Grant for use in freshman, sophomore, junior, or senior years; renewable.

Eligibility Requirements: Applicant must be age 16-24; enrolled or expecting to enroll full-time at a two-year or four-year institution or university and resident of Delaware. Applicant or parent of applicant must have employment or volunteer experience in police/firefighting. Available to U.S. citizens. Applicant or parent must meet one or more of the following requirements: general military experience; retired from active duty; disabled or killed as a result of military service; prisoner of war; or missing in action.

Application Requirements: Application form, verification of service-related death. *Deadline:* continuous.

Contact: Carylin Brinkley, Program Administrator
Phone: 302-735-4120
Fax: 302-739-5894
E-mail: cbrinkley@doe.k12.de.us

DELTA DELTA DELTA FOUNDATION

http://www.tridelta.org/

DELTA DELTA DELTA UNDERGRADUATE SCHOLARSHIP

• See page 518

DIAMANTE, INC.

http://www.diamanteinc.org/

LATINO DIAMANTE SCHOLARSHIP FUND

Awards for Hispanic high school seniors recognizing their contributions to the community and their leadership qualities. Graduating high school seniors in North Carolina who plan to enroll at North Carolina institutions of higher education, and first-year undergraduates can apply for this scholarship. Must maintain a GPA of at least 2.5.

Award: Scholarship for use in freshman year; not renewable. *Number:* 2. *Amount:* $500.

Eligibility Requirements: Applicant must be Hispanic; enrolled or expecting to enroll full- or part-time at a two-year or four-year institution or university; resident of North Carolina; studying in North Carolina and must have an interest in leadership. Applicant or parent of applicant must have employment or volunteer experience in community service. Applicant must have 2.5 GPA or higher. Available to U.S. citizens.

Application Requirements: Application form, community service, essay, recommendations or references, transcript.

DISABLED AMERICAN VETERANS

http://www.dav.org/

JESSE BROWN MEMORIAL YOUTH SCHOLARSHIP PROGRAM

Scholarship awarded annually to outstanding youth volunteers who are active in Department of Veterans Affairs Voluntary Services (VAVS) programs and activities.

Award: Scholarship for use in freshman, sophomore, junior, senior, graduate, or postgraduate years; renewable. *Number:* 12. *Amount:* $5000–$15,000.

Eligibility Requirements: Applicant must be enrolled or expecting to enroll full-time at a two-year or four-year or technical institution or university. Applicant or parent of applicant must have employment or volunteer experience in community service, helping handicapped. Available to U.S. citizens.

Application Requirements: Application form, community service, essay. *Deadline:* varies.

Contact: Edward Hartman, National Director of Voluntary Services
    Phone: 202-554-3501
    Fax: 202-354-3581
    E-mail: ehartman@davmail.org

EQUALITY SCHOLARSHIP COLLABORATIVE

http://www.equalityscholarship.org

SCHOLARSHIPS FOR HIGH SCHOOL GRADUATES

eQuality scholarships for high school graduates recognize graduating high school seniors and recent graduates in northern and central California students for their service to the lesbian/gay/bisexual/transgender community. Applicants must plan to attend or have begun attending an accredited post-secondary institution for the first time in the award year.

Award: Scholarship for use in freshman, sophomore, or junior years; not renewable. *Number:* 9–12. *Amount:* $6000.

Eligibility Requirements: Applicant must be enrolled or expecting to enroll full- or part-time at a two-year or four-year or technical institution or university; resident of California and must have an interest in LGBT issues. Applicant or parent of applicant must have employment or volunteer experience in community service. Available to U.S. and non-U.S. citizens.

Application Requirements: Application form, application form may be submitted online (http://www.scholarselect.com/scholarships/4662-2013-equality-scholarships), essay, interview, recommendations or references, transcript. *Deadline:* February 1.

EOD WARRIOR FOUNDATION

http://www.eodwarriorfoundation.org

EXPLOSIVE ORDNANCE DISPOSAL MEMORIAL SCHOLARSHIP

Award based on academic merit, community involvement, and financial need for the children, grandchildren, and spouses of military Explosive Ordnance Disposal technicians. This scholarship is for students enrolled or planning to enroll full-time as an undergraduate in a U.S. accredited two year, four year college. Applications are only available on the website at http://www.eodwarriorfoundation.org.

Award: Scholarship for use in freshman, sophomore, junior, or senior years; not renewable. *Number:* 25–75. *Amount:* $1000–$5000.

Eligibility Requirements: Applicant must be enrolled or expecting to enroll full-time at a two-year or four-year institution or university. Applicant or parent of applicant must have employment or volunteer experience in explosive ordnance disposal. Available to U.S. citizens.

Applicant or parent must meet one or more of the following requirements: general military experience; retired from active duty; disabled or killed as a result of military service; prisoner of war; or missing in action.

Application Requirements: Application form, application form may be submitted online (http://www.eodmemorial.org/scholarship), community service, essay, recommendations or references, transcript. *Deadline:* March 15.

Contact: Nicole Motsek, Executive Director
    EOD Warrior Foundation
    33735 Snickersville Turnpike
    PO Box 309
    Bluemont, VA 20135
    Phone: 540-554-4550
    E-mail: nicole.motsek@eodmemorial.org

FINANCE AUTHORITY OF MAINE

http://www.famemaine.com/

TUITION WAIVER PROGRAMS

Provides tuition waivers for children and spouses of EMS personnel, firefighters, and law enforcement officers who have been killed in the line of duty and for students who were foster children under the custody of the Department of Human Services when they graduated from high school. Waivers valid at the University of Maine System, the Maine Technical College System, and Maine Maritime Academy. Applicant must reside and study in Maine.

Award: Grant for use in freshman, sophomore, junior, or senior years; renewable. *Number:* up to 30.

Eligibility Requirements: Applicant must be enrolled or expecting to enroll full- or part-time at a four-year institution or university; resident of Maine and studying in Maine. Applicant or parent of applicant must have employment or volunteer experience in police/firefighting. Available to U.S. citizens.

Application Requirements: Application form, letter from the Department of Human Services documenting that applicant is in their custody and residing in foster care at the time of graduation from high school or its equivalent. *Deadline:* continuous.

Contact: Claude Roy, Education Services Officer
    Phone: 207-620-3507
    E-mail: education@famemaine.com

FRATERNAL ORDER OF POLICE ASSOCIATES OF OHIO INC.

http://www.fopaohio.org/

FRATERNAL ORDER OF POLICE ASSOCIATES, STATE LODGE OF OHIO INC., SCHOLARSHIP FUND

Scholarship available to a graduating high school senior whose parent or guardian is a member in good standing of the Fraternal Order of Police, State Lodge of Ohio Inc. The amount of each scholarship will be up to $4000 payable over a four-year period. A one-time award of $500 will be given to the first runner-up. Scholarships will be awarded on the basis of scholastic merit, economic need and goals in life.

Award: Scholarship for use in freshman year; renewable. *Number:* 1–4. *Amount:* $500–$1000.

Eligibility Requirements: Applicant must be high school student; planning to enroll or expecting to enroll full-time at a four-year institution or university and resident of Ohio. Applicant or parent of applicant must have employment or volunteer experience in police/firefighting. Available to U.S. citizens.

Application Requirements: Application form, community service, essay, financial need analysis, personal photograph, proof of guardianship, recommendations or references, test scores, transcript. *Deadline:* May 1.

Contact: Mr. Michael Esposito, FOPA Scholarship Assistance Program
    Fraternal Order of Police Associates of Ohio Inc.
    PO Box 14564
    Cincinnati, OH 45250-0564
    Phone: 513-684-4755
    E-mail: mje@fopaohio.org

GREATER WASHINGTON URBAN LEAGUE

http://www.gwul.org/

SAFEWAY/GREATER WASHINGTON URBAN LEAGUE SCHOLARSHIP

Award to graduating high school students who reside in the service area of the League. Applicants must complete an essay on a subject selected by the sponsors and must have completed 90 percent of their school district's community service requirement. Minimum GPA of 2.7 required.

Award: Scholarship for use in freshman year; not renewable. *Number:* 6. *Amount:* $3000.

Eligibility Requirements: Applicant must be high school student; planning to enroll or expecting to enroll full-time at a four-year institution or university and resident of District of Columbia. Applicant or parent of applicant must have employment or volunteer experience in community service. Available to U.S. citizens.

Application Requirements: Application form, community service, entry in a contest, essay, test scores. *Deadline:* February 12.

Contact: Audrey Epperson, Director of Education
    Phone: 202-265-8200
    Fax: 202-387-7019
    E-mail: epperson@gwulparentcenter.org

GREENHOUSE SCHOLARS

http://www.greenhousescholars.org/

GREENHOUSE SCHOLARS

Greenhouse Scholars provides comprehensive personal and financial support to high-performing, under-resourced college students. Using our unique Whole Person approach, which offers intellectual, academic, professional, and financial support, we are cultivating the next generation of community leaders. The day our Scholars leave college they'll be prepared to succeed in their professional endeavors and make significant contributions in their communities. Applicants should be able to demonstrate a strong interest and commitment to the community; demonstrate an ability to persevere through difficult circumstances; possess excellent leadership skills; and demonstrate financial need [annual household income no greater than $70,000].

Award: Scholarship for use in freshman, sophomore, junior, or senior years; renewable. *Number:* 20–35. *Amount:* $500–$5000.

Eligibility Requirements: Applicant must be high school student; planning to enroll or expecting to enroll full-time at a four-year institution or university; resident of Colorado, Illinois and must have an interest in leadership. Applicant or parent of applicant must have employment or volunteer experience in community service. Applicant must have 3.5 GPA or higher. Available to U.S. citizens.

Application Requirements: Application form, application form may be submitted online (http://www.greenhousescholars.org), community service, essay, financial need analysis, interview, recommendations or references, test scores, transcript. *Deadline:* January 20.

Contact: Bess Moodie, Associate
    Greenhouse Scholars
    1881 9th Street, Suite 200
    Boulder, CO 80121
    Phone: 303-460-1735
    E-mail: scholars@greenhousescholars.org

HARNESS HORSE YOUTH FOUNDATION

http://www.hhyf.org/

CURT GREENE MEMORIAL SCHOLARSHIP

One-time award with preference given to those under age 24 who have a passion for harness racing. Based on need, merit, need, and passion for harness racing. Available for study in any field. May reapply.

Award: Scholarship for use in freshman, sophomore, junior, or senior years; not renewable. *Number:* 1–2. *Amount:* $2500.

Eligibility Requirements: Applicant must be age 18-24; enrolled or expecting to enroll full-time at a two-year or four-year or technical institution or university and must have an interest in animal/agricultural competition. Applicant or parent of applicant must have employment or volunteer experience in harness racing. Available to U.S. and Canadian citizens.

Application Requirements: Application form, community service, essay, financial need analysis, page 1 of parent's IRS form, test scores, transcript. *Deadline:* April 30.

Contact: Ellen Taylor, Executive Director
    Harness Horse Youth Foundation
    16575 Carey Road
    Westfield, IN 46074
    Phone: 317-867-5877
    Fax: 317-867-5896
    E-mail: ellen@hhyf.org

HARNESS TRACKS OF AMERICA

http://www.harnesstracks.com/

HARNESS TRACKS OF AMERICA SCHOLARSHIP

One-time, merit-based award of $5000 for students actively involved in harness racing or the children of licensed drivers, trainers, breeders, or caretakers, living or deceased. Based on financial need, academic merit, and active harness racing involvement by applicant or family member. High school seniors may apply for the following school year award.

Award: Scholarship for use in freshman, sophomore, junior, senior, or graduate years; not renewable. *Number:* 3. *Amount:* $5000.

Eligibility Requirements: Applicant must be enrolled or expecting to enroll full-time at a two-year or four-year or technical institution or university. Applicant or parent of applicant must have employment or volunteer experience in harness racing. Available to U.S. and Canadian citizens.

Application Requirements: Application form, essay, financial need analysis, IRS 1040 of parents and/or applicant, transcript. *Deadline:* May 15.

Contact: Mrs. Delight Craddock, Executive Assistant
    Harness Tracks of America
    12025 East Dry Gulch Place
    Tucson, AZ 85749
    Phone: 520-529-2525
    Fax: 520-529-3235
    E-mail: delight@harnesstracks.com

HEART OF A MARINE FOUNDATION

http://www.heartofamarine.org/

LANCE CORPORAL PHILLIP E. FRANK - FIFTH THIRD BANK MEMORIAL SCHOLARSHIP

Scholarships available nationally to graduating high school seniors who will be enrolling at an accredited college or trade school within one year of receiving the award. Applicants should exemplify the spirit of "The Heart of a Marine" ideal, which is honor, patriotism, loyalty, respect and concern for others and are required to submit an essay on how they demonstrate these qualities, as well as documentation of community service. There is no GPA requirement; character is what counts the most. Discharged military personnel continuing their education are also encouraged to apply.

Award: Scholarship for use in freshman year; not renewable. *Number:* 6. *Amount:* $2000.

Eligibility Requirements: Applicant must be enrolled or expecting to enroll full-time at a two-year or four-year or technical institution or university. Applicant or parent of applicant must have employment or volunteer experience in community service. Available to U.S. citizens.

Application Requirements: Application form, community service, driver's license, essay, letter of recommendation from a school official (guidance counselor, teacher, or administrator), personal photograph. *Deadline:* March 31.

Contact: Georgette Frank, Executive Director
    Heart of a Marine Foundation
    PO Box 1732
    Elk Grove Village, IL 60007
    E-mail: theheartofamarine@comcast.net

HERB KOHL EDUCATIONAL FOUNDATION INC.

http://www.kohleducation.org/

HERB KOHL EXCELLENCE SCHOLARSHIP PROGRAM

Scholarships of $1000 to Wisconsin high school graduates awarded annually. Applicants must be Wisconsin residents. Recipients are chosen for their demonstrated academic potential, outstanding leadership, citizenship, community service, integrity and other special talents.

Award: Scholarship for use in freshman year; not renewable. *Number:* 100. *Amount:* $1000.

Eligibility Requirements: Applicant must be high school student; planning to enroll or expecting to enroll full-time at a two-year or four-year or technical institution or university; resident of Wisconsin and must have an interest in leadership. Applicant or parent of applicant must have employment or volunteer experience in community service. Available to U.S. citizens.

Application Requirements: Application form, essay, recommendations or references, transcript. *Deadline:* November 16.

HISPANIC ANNUAL SALUTE

http://www.hispanicannualsalute.org/

HISPANIC ANNUAL SALUTE SCHOLARSHIP

Scholarships of $2000 are awarded to graduating high school seniors. Program is intended to help foster a strong Hispanic presence within colleges and universities that will ultimately lead to active community leadership and volunteerism. Applicant must maintain a minimum GPA of 2.5.

Award: Scholarship for use in freshman year; not renewable. *Number:* 10. *Amount:* $2000.

Eligibility Requirements: Applicant must be Hispanic; high school student and planning to enroll or expecting to enroll full-time at a four-year institution or university. Applicant or parent of applicant must have employment or volunteer experience in community service. Applicant must have 2.5 GPA or higher. Available to U.S. citizens.

Application Requirements: Application form, essay, recommendations or references, test scores. *Deadline:* December 4.

Contact: Dan Sandos, President
Phone: 303-699-0715
Fax: 303-627-4205
E-mail: dcsandos@aol.com

HOSPITAL CENTRAL SERVICES INC.

http://www.giveapint.org/

HOSPITAL CENTRAL SERVICES STUDENT VOLUNTEER SCHOLARSHIP

Award to a graduating high school senior. Must have completed a minimum of 135 hours of volunteer service to the Blood Center in no less than a two calendar year period. Minimum 2.5 GPA required. Children of employees of Hospital Central Services or its affiliates are not eligible.

Award: Scholarship for use in freshman year; not renewable. *Number:* up to 2. *Amount:* $1000.

Eligibility Requirements: Applicant must be high school student and planning to enroll or expecting to enroll full- or part-time at a two-year or four-year institution or university. Applicant or parent of applicant must have employment or volunteer experience in community service. Applicant must have 2.5 GPA or higher. Available to U.S. citizens.

Application Requirements: Application form, recommendations or references, test scores, transcript. *Deadline:* March 31.

Contact: Sandra Thomas, Director of Development and Customer Service
Hospital Central Services Inc.
1465 Valley Center Parkway
Bethlehem, PA 18017
Phone: 610-691-5850 Ext. 292

HOSTESS COMMITTEE SCHOLARSHIPS/ MISS AMERICA PAGEANT

http://www.missamerica.org/

MISS AMERICA COMMUNITY SERVICE SCHOLARSHIPS

Award to assist in the expansion of scholarship provision throughout the state and local programs. Each eligible state will receive a $1000 scholarship for a contestant demonstrating exemplary community service initiatives. Only opened to those contestants competing at the state level.

Award: Scholarship for use in freshman, sophomore, junior, senior, or graduate years; not renewable. *Amount:* $1000.

Eligibility Requirements: Applicant must be enrolled or expecting to enroll full- or part-time at a four-year institution or university; female and must have an interest in beauty pageant. Applicant or parent of applicant must have employment or volunteer experience in community service. Available to U.S. citizens.

Application Requirements: Application form. *Deadline:* varies.

Contact: Doreen Lindell Gordon, Controller and Scholarship Administrator
Phone: 609-345-7571 Ext. 27
Fax: 609-347-6079
E-mail: doreen@missamerica.org

IDAHO STATE BOARD OF EDUCATION

http://www.boardofed.idaho.gov/

IDAHO GOVERNOR'S CUP SCHOLARSHIP

Renewable scholarship available to Idaho residents enrolled full-time in an undergraduate academic or vocational-technical program at an eligible Idaho public or private college or university. Minimum GPA of 2.8 required. Must demonstrate commitment to public service and submit forms documenting service. Must be a high school senior and U.S. citizen to apply. For additional information and application, see website http://www.boardofed.idaho.gov/scholarship/gov_cup.asp.

Award: Scholarship for use in freshman year; renewable. *Number:* up to 25. *Amount:* $3000.

Eligibility Requirements: Applicant must be high school student; planning to enroll or expecting to enroll full-time at a two-year or four-year or technical institution or university; resident of Idaho and studying in Idaho. Applicant or parent of applicant must have employment or volunteer experience in community service. Available to U.S. citizens.

Application Requirements: Application form, community service, essay, portfolio, recommendations or references, test scores, transcript. *Deadline:* February 15.

PUBLIC SAFETY OFFICER DEPENDENT SCHOLARSHIP

Scholarship for dependents of full-time Idaho public safety officers who were killed or disabled in the line of duty. Recipients will attend an Idaho postsecondary institution with a full waiver of fees, on-campus housing and campus meal plan, and up to $500 per semester for books and supplies. For complete information, see website http://www.boardofed.idaho.gov/scholarship/pub_safety.asp.

Award: Scholarship for use in freshman year; renewable.

Eligibility Requirements: Applicant must be enrolled or expecting to enroll full- or part-time at a two-year or four-year institution or university; resident of Idaho and studying in Idaho. Applicant or parent of applicant must have employment or volunteer experience in police/firefighting. Available to U.S. citizens.

Application Requirements: Application form. *Deadline:* February 15.

INTERNATIONAL ASSOCIATION OF FIRE FIGHTERS

http://www.iaff.org/

W. H. "HOWIE" MCCLENNAN SCHOLARSHIP

Sons, daughters, or legally adopted children of IAFF members killed in the line of duty who are planning to attend an institution of higher learning can apply. Award of $2500 for each year. Renewable up to four years. Applicant must have a GPA of 2.0.

Award: Scholarship for use in freshman year; renewable. *Number:* 20–25. *Amount:* $2500.

Eligibility Requirements: Applicant must be enrolled or expecting to enroll full- or part-time at a two-year or four-year or technical institution. Applicant or parent of applicant must have employment or volunteer experience in police/firefighting. Available to U.S. citizens.

Application Requirements: Application form, essay, financial need analysis, recommendations or references, transcript. *Deadline:* February 1.

Contact: L. Harrington, International Association of Fire Fighters
International Association of Fire Fighters
1750 New York Avenue, NW
Education Department, 3rd Floor
Washington, DC 20006-5395
Phone: 202-737-8484
Fax: 202-737-8418

INTERNATIONAL FEDERATION OF PROFESSIONAL AND TECHNICAL ENGINEERS

http://www.ifpte.org/

INTERNATIONAL FEDERATION OF PROFESSIONAL AND TECHNICAL ENGINEERS ANNUAL SCHOLARSHIP
• *See page 522*

INTERNATIONAL FLIGHT SERVICES ASSOCIATION

http://www.ifsanet.com

AMI GROUP SCHOLARSHIP AWARD

Individuals are selected based on scholastic merit and dedication to an advanced education. Must be an employee of a current IFSA member company in good standing and able to pursue the course of study within the full calendar year following acceptance of the award. Please address financial need within essay.

Award: Scholarship for use in freshman, sophomore, junior, senior, graduate, or postgraduate years; not renewable. *Number:* 1. *Amount:* $4500.

Eligibility Requirements: Applicant must be enrolled or expecting to enroll full- or part-time at an institution or university. Applicant or parent of applicant must have employment or volunteer experience in hospitality/hotel administration/operations. Applicant must have 3.0 GPA or higher. Available to U.S. and non-U.S. citizens.

Application Requirements: Application form, essay, recommendations or references, resume, transcript. *Deadline:* May 14.

Contact: Jacqueline Petty, Communications Manager
International Flight Services Association
1100 Johnson Ferry Road NE
Suite 300
Atlanta, GA 30342
Phone: 404-252-3663 Ext. 2969
Fax: 404-252-0774
E-mail: jpetty@kellencompany.com

DHL AIRLINE BUSINESS SOLUTIONS SCHOLARSHIP AWARD

Individuals are selected to receive the award based on scholastic merit and dedication to an advanced education. Must be an employee of a current IFSA member company in good standing, or a relative of an employee of a current IFSA member company. Please address financial need within essay.

Award: Scholarship for use in freshman, sophomore, junior, or senior years; not renewable. *Number:* 1. *Amount:* $2250.

Eligibility Requirements: Applicant must be enrolled or expecting to enroll full- or part-time at an institution or university. Applicant or parent of applicant must have employment or volunteer experience in hospitality/hotel administration/operations. Applicant must have 3.0 GPA or higher. Available to U.S. and non-U.S. citizens.

Application Requirements: Application form, essay, recommendations or references, transcript. *Deadline:* May 14.

Contact: Jacqueline Petty, Communications Manager
International Flight Services Association
1100 Johnson Ferry Road NE
Suite 300
Atlanta, GA 30342
Phone: 404-252-3663 Ext. 2969
Fax: 404-252-0774
E-mail: jpetty@kellencompany.com

FLYING FOOD GROUP SCHOLARSHIP AWARD

Individuals are selected to receive the award based on scholastic merit and dedication to an advanced education. Must be an employee of a current IFSA member company in good standing, or a relative of an employee of a current IFSA member company.

Award: Scholarship for use in freshman, sophomore, junior, or senior years; not renewable. *Number:* 1. *Amount:* $2250.

Eligibility Requirements: Applicant must be enrolled or expecting to enroll full- or part-time at an institution or university. Applicant or parent of applicant must have employment or volunteer experience in hospitality/hotel administration/operations. Applicant must have 3.0 GPA or higher. Available to U.S. and non-U.S. citizens.

Application Requirements: Application form, essay, recommendations or references, transcript. *Deadline:* May 14.

Contact: Jacqueline Petty, Communications Manager
International Flight Services Association
1100 Johnson Ferry Road NE
Suite 300
Atlanta, GA 30342
Phone: 404-252-3663 Ext. 2969
Fax: 404-252-0774
E-mail: jpetty@kellencompany.com

IFSA MEMBER FAMILY SCHOLARSHIP AWARD

Individuals are selected based upon scholastic merit and dedication to pursuing an advanced degree. Must be an employee of a current IFSA member company in good standing, or a relative of an employee of a current IFSA member company.

Award: Scholarship for use in freshman, sophomore, junior, or senior years; not renewable. *Number:* 2. *Amount:* $2250.

Eligibility Requirements: Applicant must be enrolled or expecting to enroll full- or part-time at an institution or university. Applicant or parent of applicant must have employment or volunteer experience in hospitality/hotel administration/operations. Applicant must have 3.0 GPA or higher. Available to U.S. and non-U.S. citizens.

Application Requirements: Application form, essay, recommendations or references, transcript. *Deadline:* May 14.

Contact: Jacqueline Petty, Communications Manager
International Flight Services Association
1100 Johnson Ferry Road NE
Suite 300
Atlanta, GA 30342
Phone: 404-252-3663 Ext. 2969
Fax: 404-252-0774
E-mail: jpetty@kellencompany.com

JOHN & GINNIE LONG SCHOLARSHIP AWARD

Individuals are selected to receive the award based on scholastic merit and dedication to an advanced education. Must be an employee of a current IFSA member company in good standing, or a relative of an employee of a current IFSA member company.

Award: Scholarship for use in freshman, sophomore, junior, or senior years; not renewable. *Number:* 1. *Amount:* $2250.

Eligibility Requirements: Applicant must be enrolled or expecting to enroll full- or part-time at an institution or university. Applicant or parent of applicant must have employment or volunteer experience in hospitality/hotel administration/operations. Applicant must have 3.0 GPA or higher. Available to U.S. and non-U.S. citizens.

Application Requirements: Application form, essay, recommendations or references, transcript. *Deadline:* May 14.

Contact: Jacqueline Petty, Communications Manager
International Flight Services Association
1100 Johnson Ferry Road NE
Suite 300
Atlanta, GA 30342
Phone: 404-252-3663 Ext. 2969
Fax: 404-252-0774
E-mail: jpetty@kellencompany.com

JOHN LOUIS FOUNDATION SCHOLARSHIP AWARD

Individuals are selected to receive the award based on scholastic merit and dedication to an advanced education. Must be an employee of a current IFSA member company in good standing, or a relative of an employee of a current IFSA member company. Please address financial need within essay.

Award: Scholarship for use in freshman, sophomore, junior, or senior years; not renewable. *Number:* 1. *Amount:* $5000.

Eligibility Requirements: Applicant must be enrolled or expecting to enroll full- or part-time at an institution or university. Applicant or parent of applicant must have employment or volunteer experience in hospitality/hotel administration/operations. Applicant must have 3.0 GPA or higher. Available to U.S. and non-U.S. citizens.

Application Requirements: Application form, essay, recommendations or references, transcript. *Deadline:* May 14.

Contact: Jacqueline Petty, Communications Manager
International Flight Services Association
1100 Johnson Ferry Road NE
Suite 300
Atlanta, GA 30342
Phone: 404-252-3663 Ext. 2969
Fax: 404-252-0774
E-mail: jpetty@kellencompany.com

KING NUT COMPANIES SCHOLARSHIP AWARD

Individuals are selected to receive the award based on scholastic merit and dedication to an advanced education. Must be an employee of a current IFSA member company in good standing, or a relative of an employee of a current IFSA member company. Please address financial need within essay.

Award: Scholarship for use in freshman, sophomore, junior, or senior years; not renewable. *Number:* 1. *Amount:* $2250.

Eligibility Requirements: Applicant must be enrolled or expecting to enroll full- or part-time at an institution or university. Applicant or parent of applicant must have employment or volunteer experience in hospitality/hotel administration/operations. Applicant must have 3.0 GPA or higher. Available to U.S. and non-U.S. citizens.

Application Requirements: Application form, essay, recommendations or references, transcript. *Deadline:* May 14.

Contact: Jacqueline Petty, Communications Manager
International Flight Services Association
1100 Johnson Ferry Road NE
Suite 300
Atlanta, GA 30342
Phone: 404-252-3663 Ext. 2969
Fax: 404-252-0774
E-mail: jpetty@kellencompany.com

OAKFIELD FARMS SOLUTIONS SCHOLARSHIP AWARD

Individuals are selected to receive the award based on scholastic merit and dedication to pursuing a career in onboard services operations. Must be an employee of a current IFSA member company in good standing, or a relative of an employee of a current IFSA member company.

Award: Scholarship for use in freshman, sophomore, junior, or senior years; not renewable. *Number:* 1. *Amount:* $5000.

Eligibility Requirements: Applicant must be enrolled or expecting to enroll full- or part-time at an institution or university. Applicant or parent of applicant must have employment or volunteer experience in hospitality/hotel administration/operations. Applicant must have 3.0 GPA or higher. Available to U.S. and non-U.S. citizens.

Application Requirements: Application form, essay, recommendations or references, transcript. *Deadline:* May 14.

Contact: Jacqueline Petty, Communications Manager
International Flight Services Association
1100 Johnson Ferry Road NE
Suite 300
Atlanta, GA 30342
Phone: 404-252-3663 Ext. 2969
Fax: 404-252-0774
E-mail: jpetty@kellencompany.com

WESSCO INTERNATIONAL SCHOLARSHIP AWARD

Individuals are selected to receive the award based on scholastic merit and dedication to an advanced education. Must be an employee of a current IFSA member company in good standing, or a relative of an employee of a current IFSA member company. Please address financial need within essay.

Award: Scholarship for use in freshman, sophomore, junior, or senior years; not renewable. *Number:* 1. *Amount:* $5000.

Eligibility Requirements: Applicant must be enrolled or expecting to enroll full- or part-time at an institution or university. Applicant or parent of applicant must have employment or volunteer experience in hospitality/hotel administration/operations. Applicant must have 3.0 GPA or higher. Available to U.S. and non-U.S. citizens.

Application Requirements: Application form, essay, recommendations or references, transcript. *Deadline:* May 14.

Contact: Jacqueline Petty, Communications Manager
International Flight Services Association
1100 Johnson Ferry Road NE
Suite 300
Atlanta, GA 30342
Phone: 404-252-3663 Ext. 2969
Fax: 404-252-0774
E-mail: jpetty@kellencompany.com

INTERNATIONAL ORGANIZATION OF MASTERS, MATES AND PILOTS HEALTH AND BENEFIT PLAN

http://www.bridgedeck.org/

M.M. & P. HEALTH AND BENEFIT PLAN SCHOLARSHIP PROGRAM

Scholarships available to dependent children (under 23 years of age) of parents who meet the eligibility requirements set forth by the MM&P Health and Benefit Plan. Selection of winners will be based on test scores, high school record, extracurricular activities, leadership qualities, recommendations, and students' own statements.

Award: Scholarship for use in freshman, sophomore, junior, or senior years; renewable. *Number:* 6. *Amount:* up to $5000.

Eligibility Requirements: Applicant must be enrolled or expecting to enroll full-time at a four-year institution or university and single. Applicant or parent of applicant must have employment or volunteer experience in seafaring/fishing industry. Available to U.S. citizens.

Application Requirements: Application form, test scores. *Deadline:* November 30.

Contact: Mary Ellen Beach, Scholarship Committee
Phone: 410-850-8624
Fax: 410-871-8747
E-mail: communications@bridgedeck.org

JACKIE ROBINSON FOUNDATION

http://www.jackierobinson.org/

JACKIE ROBINSON SCHOLARSHIP

Scholarship for graduating high school seniors accepted to accredited four-year colleges or universities. Must be a minority student, United States citizen, and demonstrate leadership potential and financial need. See website for additional details.

Award: Scholarship for use in freshman, sophomore, junior, senior, or graduate years; renewable. *Number:* 200–250. *Amount:* up to $7500.

Eligibility Requirements: Applicant must be American Indian/Alaska Native, Asian/Pacific Islander, Black (non-Hispanic), Hispanic; high school student; planning to enroll or expecting to enroll full-time at a four-year institution or university and must have an interest in leadership.

Applicant or parent of applicant must have employment or volunteer experience in community service. Available to U.S. citizens.

Application Requirements: Application form, application form may be submitted online (http://www.jackierobinson.org), essay, financial need analysis, recommendations or references, test scores, transcript. *Deadline:* March 31.

KE ALI'I PAUAHI FOUNDATION

http://www.pauahi.org/

DANIEL KAHIKINA AND MILLIE AKAKA SCHOLARSHIP

Educational scholarships for undergraduate or graduate students demonstrating financial need. Minimum GPA of 3.2 required. Recipients are strongly encouraged to provide a minimum of 10 hours of community service to the Council for Native Hawaiian Advancement. Submit two letters of recommendation.

Award: Scholarship for use in freshman, sophomore, junior, senior, or graduate years; not renewable. *Number:* up to 2. *Amount:* up to $900.

Eligibility Requirements: Applicant must be enrolled or expecting to enroll full-time at a two-year or four-year institution or university and resident of Hawaii. Applicant or parent of applicant must have employment or volunteer experience in community service. Available to U.S. citizens.

Application Requirements: Application form, college acceptance letter, copy of SAR, community service, essay, financial need analysis, recommendations or references, transcript. *Deadline:* April 1.

KAMEHAMEHA SCHOOLS ALUMNI ASSOCIATION-MAUI REGION SCHOLARSHIP

Scholarship available to assist students who are residents of the island of Maui and did not graduate from Kamehameha Schools in pursuing a postsecondary education. Applicants must demonstrate academic achievement or excellence, service to the community, financial need. Submit two letters of recommendation from school, employer or community organization.

Award: Scholarship for use in freshman, sophomore, junior, senior, or graduate years; not renewable. *Number:* 1. *Amount:* $500.

Eligibility Requirements: Applicant must be enrolled or expecting to enroll full-time at a four-year institution or university and resident of Hawaii. Applicant or parent of applicant must have employment or volunteer experience in community service. Available to U.S. citizens.

Application Requirements: Application form, application form may be submitted online (http://www.pauahi.org/scholarships), financial need analysis, recommendations or references, Student Aid Report (SAR), college acceptance letter, transcript. *Deadline:* April 1.

Contact: Mavis Shiraishi-Nagao, Scholarship Administrator
  Phone: 808-534-3966
  E-mail: scholarships@pauahi.org

KAMEHAMEHA SCHOOLS CLASS OF 1960 GRANT

Grant recognizes a Hawaii resident who has demonstrated scholastic excellence, provided service to the community, demonstrated good character, and demonstrated an intent to utilize special skills in order to benefit the Hawaiian community.

Award: Grant for use in freshman, sophomore, junior, senior, or graduate years; not renewable. *Number:* 1. *Amount:* $1200.

Eligibility Requirements: Applicant must be enrolled or expecting to enroll full-time at a four-year institution or university. Applicant or parent of applicant must have employment or volunteer experience in community service. Available to U.S. citizens.

Application Requirements: Application form, financial need analysis, Student Aid Report (SAR), college acceptance letter, transcript. *Deadline:* April 1.

Contact: Mavis Shiraishi-Nagao, Scholarship Administrator
  Phone: 808-534-3966
  E-mail: scholarships@pauahi.org

KAMEHAMEHA SCHOOLS CLASS OF 1970 SCHOLARSHIP

Scholarship recognizes a student who has a minimum GPA of 2.0. Submit essay describing involvement in community service (beyond what required through their school)including organizations, numbers or hours/length of volunteer service and how applicant intends to continue to serve the Hawaiian community.

Award: Scholarship for use in freshman, sophomore, junior, senior, or graduate years; not renewable. *Number:* 2. *Amount:* $1300.

Eligibility Requirements: Applicant must be enrolled or expecting to enroll full-time at a four-year institution or university. Applicant or parent of applicant must have employment or volunteer experience in community service. Available to U.S. citizens.

Application Requirements: Application form, application form may be submitted online (http://www.pauahi.org/scholarships), essay, financial need analysis, Student Aid Report (SAR), college acceptance letter, transcript. *Deadline:* April 1.

Contact: Mavis Shiraishi-Nagao, Scholarship Administrator
  Phone: 808-534-3966
  E-mail: scholarships@pauahi.org

LEARNING ALLY

http://www.learningally.org/

MARION HUBER LEARNING THROUGH LISTENING AWARDS

• *See page 525*

MARY P. OENSLAGER SCHOLASTIC ACHIEVEMENT AWARDS

• *See page 525*

LOWE'S COMPANIES INC.

http://www.lowes.com/

LOWE'S EDUCATIONAL SCHOLARSHIP

$1000-$15,000 scholarships available to all high school seniors who plan to attend any accredited 2-year or 4-year college or university within the United States. Selection based upon leadership skills, community service, and academic achievement.

Award: Scholarship for use in freshman year; not renewable. *Number:* up to 375. *Amount:* $1000–$15,000.

Eligibility Requirements: Applicant must be high school student; planning to enroll or expecting to enroll full- or part-time at a two-year or four-year or technical institution or university and must have an interest in leadership. Applicant or parent of applicant must have employment or volunteer experience in community service. Available to U.S. citizens.

Application Requirements: Application form, resume. *Deadline:* March 15.

MAGIC JOHNSON FOUNDATION INC.

http://www.magicjohnson.org/

TAYLOR MICHAELS SCHOLARSHIP FUND

Scholarship to provide support for deserving minority high school students who exemplify a strong potential for academic achievement but face social-economic conditions that hinder them from reaching their full potential. Must have strong community service involvement.

Award: Scholarship for use in freshman year; renewable. *Amount:* $1000–$5000.

Eligibility Requirements: Applicant must be American Indian/Alaska Native, Asian/Pacific Islander, Black (non-Hispanic), Hispanic; high school student and planning to enroll or expecting to enroll full-time at a four-year institution or university. Applicant or parent of applicant must have employment or volunteer experience in community service. Applicant must have 2.5 GPA or higher. Available to U.S. and non-U.S. citizens.

Application Requirements: Application form, community service, essay, recommendations or references, transcript. *Deadline:* February 5.

MANA DE SAN DIEGO

http://www.manasd.org/

MANA DE SAN DIEGO SYLVIA CHAVEZ MEMORIAL SCHOLARSHIP

Scholarship for Latinas with permanent residence in San Diego County who are enrolled or about to enroll in a two-year, four-year, or graduate program. Must have a minimum 2.75 GPA and demonstrate financial need. For an application and additional information visit http://www.sdmana.org.

Award: Scholarship for use in freshman, sophomore, junior, or senior years; not renewable. *Amount:* $500–$2000.

Eligibility Requirements: Applicant must be Hispanic; enrolled or expecting to enroll full- or part-time at a two-year or four-year institution or university; female; resident of California and must have an interest in leadership. Applicant or parent of applicant must have employment or volunteer experience in community service. Available to U.S. citizens.

Application Requirements: Application form, essay, recommendations or references, transcript. *Deadline:* February 13.

Contact: Lucy Hernandez, Scholarship Director
MANA de San Diego
PO Box 81364
San Diego, CA 92138-1364
Phone: 619-225-9594
Fax: 619-225-0500
E-mail: scholarships@sdmana.org

MARYLAND STATE HIGHER EDUCATION COMMISSION

http://www.mhec.state.md.us/

EDWARD T. CONROY MEMORIAL SCHOLARSHIP PROGRAM

Scholarship for dependents of deceased or 100 percent disabled U.S. Armed Forces personnel; the son, daughter, or surviving spouse of a victim of the September 11, 2001 terrorist attacks who died as a result of the attacks on the World Trade Center in New York City, the attack on the Pentagon in Virginia, or the crash of United Airlines Flight 93 in Pennsylvania; a POW/MIA of the Vietnam Conflict or his/her son or daughter; the son, daughter or surviving spouse (who has not remarried) of a state or local public safety employee or volunteer who died in the line of duty; or a state or local public safety employee or volunteer who was 100 percent disabled in the line of duty. Must be Maryland resident at time of disability. Submit applicable VA certification. Must be at least 16 years of age and attend Maryland institution.

Award: Scholarship for use in freshman, sophomore, junior, or senior years; renewable. *Number:* up to 121. *Amount:* $7200–$9000.

Eligibility Requirements: Applicant must be age 16-24; enrolled or expecting to enroll full- or part-time at a two-year or four-year institution or university; resident of Maryland and studying in Maryland. Applicant or parent of applicant must have employment or volunteer experience in police/firefighting. Available to U.S. citizens. Applicant or parent must meet one or more of the following requirements: general military experience; retired from active duty; disabled or killed as a result of military service; prisoner of war; or missing in action.

Application Requirements: Application form, birth and death certificate, disability papers. *Deadline:* July 15.

Contact: Linda Asplin, Office of Student Financial Assistance
Maryland State Higher Education Commission
839 Bestgate Road, Suite 400
Annapolis, MD 21401-3013
Phone: 410-260-4563
Fax: 410-260-3203
E-mail: lasplin@mhec.state.md.us

MASSACHUSETTS OFFICE OF STUDENT FINANCIAL ASSISTANCE

http://www.osfa.mass.edu/

MASSACHUSETTS PUBLIC SERVICE GRANT PROGRAM

Scholarships for children and/or spouses of deceased members of fire, police, and corrections departments, who were killed in the line of duty. Awards Massachusetts residents attending Massachusetts institutions. Applicant should have not received a prior bachelor's degree or its equivalent.

Award: Grant for use in freshman, sophomore, junior, or senior years; not renewable. *Amount:* $910–$1714.

Eligibility Requirements: Applicant must be enrolled or expecting to enroll full-time at a four-year institution or university; resident of Massachusetts and studying in Massachusetts. Applicant or parent of

applicant must have employment or volunteer experience in police/firefighting. Available to U.S. citizens. Applicant must have general military experience.

Application Requirements: Application form, copy of birth certificate, copy of veteran's death certificate, financial need analysis. *Deadline:* May 1.

MINNESOTA DEPARTMENT OF MILITARY AFFAIRS

http://www.minnesotanationalguard.org/

LEADERSHIP, EXCELLENCE, AND DEDICATED SERVICE SCHOLARSHIP

Scholarship provides a maximum of thirty $1000 to selected high school seniors who become a member of the Minnesota National Guard and complete the application process. The award recognizes demonstrated leadership, community services and potential for success in the Minnesota National Guard.

Award: Scholarship for use in freshman year; not renewable. *Number:* up to 30. *Amount:* $1000.

Eligibility Requirements: Applicant must be high school student; planning to enroll or expecting to enroll full- or part-time at a two-year or four-year or technical institution or university; resident of Minnesota and must have an interest in leadership. Applicant or parent of applicant must have employment or volunteer experience in community service. Available to U.S. citizens. Applicant or parent must meet one or more of the following requirements: national guard experience; retired from active duty; disabled or killed as a result of military service; prisoner of war; or missing in action.

Application Requirements: Essay, recommendations or references, resume, transcript. *Deadline:* March 15.

Contact: Barbara O'Reilly, Education Services Officer
Phone: 651-282-4508
E-mail: barbara.oreilly@mn.ngb.army.mil

MINNESOTA OFFICE OF HIGHER EDUCATION

http://www.getreadyforcollege.org/

SAFETY OFFICERS' SURVIVOR GRANT PROGRAM

Grant for eligible survivors of Minnesota public safety officers killed in the line of duty. Safety officers who have been permanently or totally disabled in the line of duty are also eligible. Must be used at a Minnesota institution participating in State Grant Program. Write for details. Must submit proof of death or disability and Public Safety Officers Benefit Fund Certificate. Must apply for renewal each year. Five-year limit on awards.

Award: Grant for use in freshman, sophomore, junior, senior, or graduate years; not renewable. *Number:* 1. *Amount:* up to $10,488.

Eligibility Requirements: Applicant must be enrolled or expecting to enroll full- or part-time at a two-year or four-year or technical institution or university; resident of Minnesota and studying in Minnesota. Applicant or parent of applicant must have employment or volunteer experience in police/firefighting. Available to U.S. citizens.

Application Requirements: Application form, proof of death or disability. *Deadline:* continuous.

Contact: Brenda Larter, Program Administrator
Phone: 651-355-0612
Fax: 651-642-0675
E-mail: brenda.larter@state.mn.us

MISSISSIPPI OFFICE OF STUDENT FINANCIAL AID

http://www.mississippi.edu/financialaid

LAW ENFORCEMENT OFFICERS/FIREMEN SCHOLARSHIP

Financial assistance to dependent children and spouses of any Mississippi law enforcement officer, full-time fire fighter or volunteer fire fighter who has suffered fatal injuries or wounds or become permanently and totally disabled as a result of injuries or wounds which occurred in the performance of the official and appointed duties of his or her office. This financial assistance is offered as an eight semester tuition and room scholarship at any state-supported college or university in Mississippi.

Award: Scholarship for use in freshman, sophomore, junior, or senior years; not renewable. *Amount:* $1705–$12,707.

Eligibility Requirements: Applicant must be enrolled or expecting to enroll full-time at a four-year institution or university; resident of Mississippi and studying in Mississippi. Applicant or parent of applicant must have employment or volunteer experience in police/firefighting. Available to U.S. citizens.

Application Requirements: Application form, application form may be submitted online (http://www.mississippi.edu/financialaid), residency documentation, documentation of parent's death/disability in line of duty. *Deadline:* continuous.

Contact: Mrs. Jennifer Rogers, Director of Student Financial Aid
Phone: 601-432-6997
E-mail: sfa@mississippi.edu

NATIONAL ASSOCIATION FOR CAMPUS ACTIVITIES

http://www.naca.org/

LORI RHETT MEMORIAL SCHOLARSHIP

Scholarships will be given to undergraduate or graduate students with a cumulative GPA of 2.5 or better at the time of the application and during the academic term in which the scholarship is awarded. Must demonstrate significant leadership skill and ability while holding a significant leadership position on campus. Applicants must have made contributions via volunteer involvement, either on or off campus.

Award: Scholarship for use in freshman, sophomore, junior, senior, or graduate years; not renewable. *Number:* 1. *Amount:* $250–$300.

Eligibility Requirements: Applicant must be enrolled or expecting to enroll full- or part-time at a two-year or four-year institution or university; studying in Alaska, Idaho, Montana, Oregon, Washington and must have an interest in leadership. Applicant or parent of applicant must have employment or volunteer experience in community service. Applicant must have 2.5 GPA or higher. Available to U.S. citizens.

Application Requirements: Application form, recommendations or references, resume, transcript. *Deadline:* June 30.

Contact: Dionne Ellison, Administrative Assistant
Phone: 803-732-6222 Ext. 131
Fax: 803-749-1047
E-mail: dionnee@naca.org

NATIONAL ASSOCIATION FOR CAMPUS ACTIVITIES EAST COAST UNDERGRADUATE SCHOLARSHIP FOR STUDENT LEADERS

Scholarship for undergraduate students who are in good standing at the time of the application and during the academic term in which the scholarship is awarded. Applicants must maintain a 2.5 GPA, demonstrate leadership skills and abilities while holding a significant leadership position on campus or in community, and have made significant contributions via volunteer involvement. Eligible students must be attending a college or university within the NACA East Coast Region.

Award: Scholarship for use in freshman, sophomore, junior, or senior years; not renewable. *Number:* up to 2. *Amount:* $250–$300.

Eligibility Requirements: Applicant must be enrolled or expecting to enroll full- or part-time at a two-year or four-year institution or university; studying in Delaware, District of Columbia, Maryland, New Jersey, New York, Pennsylvania and must have an interest in leadership. Applicant or parent of applicant must have employment or volunteer experience in community service. Applicant must have 2.5 GPA or higher. Available to U.S. citizens.

Application Requirements: Application form, current enrollment form, essay, recommendations or references, resume, transcript. *Deadline:* March 31.

Contact: Dionne Ellison, Administrative Assistant
Phone: 803-732-6222 Ext. 131
Fax: 803-749-1047
E-mail: dionnee@naca.org

NATIONAL ASSOCIATION FOR CAMPUS ACTIVITIES SOUTHEAST REGION STUDENT LEADERSHIP SCHOLARSHIP

Scholarships will be given to full-time undergraduate students in good standing at the time of the application and during the academic term in which the scholarship is awarded. Must demonstrate significant leadership skill and ability while holding a significant leadership position on campus. Applicants must have made contributions via volunteer involvement, either on or off campus. Must be enrolled in a college/university in the NACA Southeast Region.

Award: Scholarship for use in freshman, sophomore, junior, or senior years; not renewable. *Number:* up to 4. *Amount:* $250–$300.

Eligibility Requirements: Applicant must be enrolled or expecting to enroll full-time at a two-year or four-year institution or university; studying in Alabama, Florida, Georgia, Mississippi, North Carolina, Puerto Rico, South Carolina, Tennessee, Virginia and must have an interest in leadership. Applicant or parent of applicant must have employment or volunteer experience in community service. Available to U.S. citizens.

Application Requirements: Application form, enrollment form, essay, recommendations or references, resume, transcript. *Deadline:* March 31.

Contact: Dionne Ellison, Administrative Assistant
Phone: 803-732-6222 Ext. 131
Fax: 803-749-1047
E-mail: dionnee@naca.org

NATIONAL ASSOCIATION FOR CAMPUS ACTIVITIES WISCONSIN REGION STUDENT LEADERSHIP SCHOLARSHIP

Scholarships will be awarded to undergraduate or graduate students in good standing and enrolled in the equivalent of at least six academic credits at the time of the application and during the academic term in which the scholarship is awarded. Must be currently enrolled in or received a degree from a college or university within the NACA Wisconsin Region or Michigan (area code 906) and demonstrated leadership skill and significant service to their campus community.

Award: Scholarship for use in freshman, sophomore, junior, senior, or graduate years; not renewable. *Number:* 1. *Amount:* $250–$300.

Eligibility Requirements: Applicant must be enrolled or expecting to enroll full- or part-time at a two-year or four-year institution or university; studying in Michigan, Wisconsin and must have an interest in leadership. Applicant or parent of applicant must have employment or volunteer experience in community service. Available to U.S. citizens.

Application Requirements: Application form, essay, recommendations or references, resume, transcript. *Deadline:* January 15.

Contact: Dionne Ellison, Administrative Assistant
Phone: 803-732-6222 Ext. 131
Fax: 803-749-1047
E-mail: dionnee@naca.org

SCHOLARSHIPS FOR STUDENT LEADERS

Scholarships will be awarded to undergraduate students in good standing at the time of the application and who, during the academic term in which the scholarship is awarded, hold a significant leadership position on their campus. Must make significant contributions to their campus communities and demonstrate leadership skills and abilities.

Award: Scholarship for use in freshman, sophomore, junior, or senior years; not renewable. *Number:* up to 6. *Amount:* $250–$300.

Eligibility Requirements: Applicant must be enrolled or expecting to enroll full- or part-time at a two-year or four-year institution or university and must have an interest in leadership. Applicant or parent of applicant must have employment or volunteer experience in community service. Available to U.S. and non-U.S. citizens.

Application Requirements: Application form, current enrollment form, recommendations or references, resume, transcript. *Deadline:* November 1.

Contact: Dionne Ellison, Administrative Assistant
Phone: 803-732-6222 Ext. 131
Fax: 803-749-1047
E-mail: dionnee@naca.org

NATIONAL BURGLAR AND FIRE ALARM ASSOCIATION

http://www.alarm.org/

NBFAA YOUTH SCHOLARSHIP PROGRAM

One-time award for high school seniors entering postsecondary education, who are deserving sons or daughters of police and fire officials. The number of awards granted varies annually.

Award: Scholarship for use in freshman year; not renewable. *Amount:* $500–$10,000.

Eligibility Requirements: Applicant must be high school student; age 15–20; planning to enroll or expecting to enroll full-time at a four-year institution or university and resident of California, Connecticut, Georgia, Indiana, Kentucky, Louisiana, Maryland, Minnesota, New Jersey, New York, North Carolina, Pennsylvania, Tennessee, Virginia, Washington. Applicant or parent of applicant must have employment or volunteer experience in police/firefighting. Available to U.S. citizens.

Application Requirements: Application form, essay, test scores, transcript. *Deadline:* March 30.

Contact: Georjia Calaway, Marketing Coordinator
National Burglar and Fire Alarm Association
8380 Colesville Road, Suite 750
Silver Spring, MD 20910
Phone: 301-585-1855 Ext. 133
Fax: 301-585-1866
E-mail: georjiac@alarm.org

NATSO FOUNDATION

http://www.natso.com/

BILL MOON SCHOLARSHIP

Available to employees or dependents of NATSO-affiliated truck stops/travel plazas. Visit website at http://www.natsofoundation.org for additional information.

Award: Scholarship for use in freshman, sophomore, junior, senior, or graduate years; not renewable. *Number:* 13. *Amount:* $2500.

Eligibility Requirements: Applicant must be enrolled or expecting to enroll full- or part-time at a two-year or four-year institution or university. Applicant or parent of applicant must have employment or volunteer experience in transportation industry. Available to U.S. and non-U.S. citizens.

Application Requirements: Application form, essay, financial need analysis, recommendations or references, signature from employer, transcript. *Deadline:* April 14.

Contact: Sharon Corigliano, Executive Director
Phone: 703-549-2100 Ext. 8561
Fax: 703-684-9667
E-mail: scorigliano@natso.com

NETAID FOUNDATION/MERCY CORPS

GLOBAL ACTION AWARDS

Awards honor high school students who have taken outstanding actions to fight global poverty. Honorees receive $5000 for their education or a charity of their choice. College freshman who completed their project while in a U.S. high school may apply.

Award: Scholarship for use in freshman year; not renewable. *Number:* 5. *Amount:* $5000.

Eligibility Requirements: Applicant must be high school student; planning to enroll or expecting to enroll full-time at a four-year institution and must have an interest in leadership. Applicant or parent of applicant must have employment or volunteer experience in community service. Available to U.S. citizens.

Application Requirements: Application form, projects, recommendations or references. *Deadline:* varies.

Contact: Suzanne Guthrie, Manager, Education and Youth Programs
NetAid Foundation/Mercy Corps
75 Broad Street, Suite 2410
New York, NY 10004
Phone: 212-537-0518
Fax: 212-537-0501
E-mail: gaa@nyc.mercycorps.org

NEW JERSEY HIGHER EDUCATION STUDENT ASSISTANCE AUTHORITY

http://www.hesaa.org/

LAW ENFORCEMENT OFFICER MEMORIAL SCHOLARSHIP

Scholarships for full-time undergraduate study at approved New Jersey institutions for the dependent children of New Jersey law enforcement officers killed in the line of duty. Value of scholarship will be established annually. Deadline varies.

Award: Scholarship for use in freshman, sophomore, junior, or senior years; renewable.

Eligibility Requirements: Applicant must be enrolled or expecting to enroll full-time at a four-year institution or university; resident of New Jersey and studying in New Jersey. Applicant or parent of applicant must have employment or volunteer experience in police/firefighting. Available to U.S. citizens.

Application Requirements: Application form. *Deadline:* varies.

Contact: Carol Muka, Assistant Director of Grants and Scholarships
New Jersey Higher Education Student Assistance Authority
PO Box 540
Trenton, NJ 08625
Phone: 800-792-8670 Ext. 3266
Fax: 609-588-2228
E-mail: cmuka@hesaa.org

SURVIVOR TUITION BENEFITS PROGRAM

The scholarship provides tuition fees for spouses and dependents of law enforcement officers, fire, or emergency services personnel killed in the line of duty. Eligible recipients may attend any independent institution in the state; however, the annual value of the grant cannot exceed the highest tuition charged at a New Jersey public institution.

Award: Scholarship for use in freshman, sophomore, junior, or senior years; renewable. *Number:* up to 99,999. *Amount:* up to $99,999.

Eligibility Requirements: Applicant must be enrolled or expecting to enroll full- or part-time at a two-year or four-year institution or university; resident of New Jersey and studying in New Jersey. Applicant or parent of applicant must have employment or volunteer experience in police/firefighting. Available to U.S. citizens.

Application Requirements: Application form. *Deadline:* varies.

Contact: Carol Muka, Scholarship Coordinator
New Jersey Higher Education Student Assistance Authority
PO Box 540
Trenton, NJ 08625
Phone: 800-792-8670 Ext. 3266
Fax: 609-588-2228
E-mail: cmuka@hesaa.org

OREGON STUDENT ASSISTANCE COMMISSION

http://www.GetCollegeFunds.org/

MANUP SCHOLARSHIP

Scholarship for current or previous Oregon DOC prisoners within DOC or OYA custody who have been incarcerated for three years minimum. Must have participated in and completed required treatment and have pursued other education and job opportunities while in prison, within 2 years before release or within one year after release. Should be pursuing programs that provide certification for job preparation instead of general studies. Participation in community service opportunities is required.

Award: Scholarship for use in freshman, sophomore, junior, senior, or graduate years.

Eligibility Requirements: Applicant must be enrolled or expecting to enroll full- or part-time at a two-year or technical institution. Applicant or parent of applicant must have employment or volunteer experience in community service. Available to U.S. citizens.

Application Requirements: Application form. *Deadline:* March 1.

PACERS FOUNDATION INC.

http://www.pacersfoundation.org/

PACERS TEAMUP SCHOLARSHIP

Scholarship is awarded to Indiana high school seniors for their first year of undergraduate study at any accredited four-year college or university or two-year college or junior college. Primary selection criteria is student involvement in community service.

Award: Scholarship for use in freshman year; not renewable. *Number:* 5. *Amount:* $2000.

Eligibility Requirements: Applicant must be enrolled or expecting to enroll full-time at a two-year or four-year institution or university and resident of Indiana. Applicant or parent of applicant must have employment or volunteer experience in community service. Available to U.S. citizens.

Application Requirements: Application form, community service, essay, recommendations or references, transcript. *Deadline:* March 1.

Contact: Jami Marsh, Executive Director
Pacers Foundation Inc.
125 South Pennsylvania Street
Indianapolis, IN 46204
Phone: 317-917-2856
E-mail: foundation@pacers.com

PENNSYLVANIA BURGLAR AND FIRE ALARM ASSOCIATION

http://www.pbfaa.com/

PENNSYLVANIA BURGLAR AND FIRE ALARM ASSOCIATION YOUTH SCHOLARSHIP PROGRAM

Non-renewable scholarships available to sons and daughters of active Pennsylvania police and fire personnel, and volunteer fire department personnel for full-time study at a two- or four-year college, or university. Must be a senior attending a Pennsylvania high school. Scholarship amount in the range of $500 to $6500.

Award: Scholarship for use in freshman year; not renewable. *Number:* 6–8. *Amount:* $500–$6500.

Eligibility Requirements: Applicant must be high school student; planning to enroll or expecting to enroll full-time at a two-year or four-year institution or university and resident of Pennsylvania. Applicant or parent of applicant must have employment or volunteer experience in police/firefighting. Available to U.S. citizens.

Application Requirements: Application form, essay, resume, test scores, transcript. *Deadline:* March 1.

Contact: Dale Eller, Executive Director
Phone: 814-838-3093
Fax: 814-838-5127
E-mail: info@pbfaa.com

PHOENIX SUNS CHARITIES/SUN STUDENTS SCHOLARSHIP

http://www.suns.com/

SUN STUDENT COLLEGE SCHOLARSHIP PROGRAM

Applicants must be seniors preparing to graduate from a high school in Arizona. Eligible applicants must have a minimum 2.5 GPA. Must provide evidence of regular involvement in charitable activities or volunteer service in school, church, or community organizations. Fifteen $2000 scholarships and one $5000 scholarship will be awarded.

Award: Scholarship for use in freshman year; not renewable. *Number:* 1–16. *Amount:* $2000–$5000.

Eligibility Requirements: Applicant must be high school student; planning to enroll or expecting to enroll full- or part-time at a two-year or four-year institution or university and resident of Arizona. Applicant or parent of applicant must have employment or volunteer experience in community service. Applicant must have 2.5 GPA or higher. Available to U.S. citizens.

Application Requirements: Application form, community service, essay, recommendations or references, transcript. *Deadline:* February 15.

Contact: Janell Jakubowski, Administrative Assistant
Phone: 602-379-7767
Fax: 602-379-7922
E-mail: jornelas@suns.com

PROJECT BEST SCHOLARSHIP FUND

http://www.projectbest.com/

PROJECT BEST SCHOLARSHIP
• *See page 534*

PUEBLO OF SAN JUAN, DEPARTMENT OF EDUCATION

http://www.sanjuaned.org/

OHKAY OWINGEH TRIBAL SCHOLARSHIP OF THE PUEBLO OF SAN JUAN

Scholarship for residents of New Mexico enrolled either full-time or part-time in accredited colleges or universities. Minimum GPA of 2.0 required. Must complete required number of hours of community service in the San Juan Pueblo. Up to thirty scholarships are granted and the value of the award ranges from $300 to $600. Deadline varies.

Award: Scholarship for use in freshman, sophomore, junior, or senior years; renewable. *Number:* 1–30. *Amount:* $300–$600.

Eligibility Requirements: Applicant must be American Indian/Alaska Native; enrolled or expecting to enroll full- or part-time at a two-year or four-year or technical institution or university and resident of New Mexico. Applicant or parent of applicant must have employment or volunteer experience in community service. Available to U.S. citizens.

Application Requirements: Application form, letter of acceptance, transcript. *Deadline:* varies.

Contact: Adam Garcia, Education Coordinator
Phone: 505-852-3477
Fax: 505-852-3030
E-mail: wevog68@valornet.com

POP'AY SCHOLARSHIP

Scholarship for members of Pueblo of San Juan tribe pursuing their first associate or baccalaureate degree. Must complete a minimum of 20 hours of community service within the San Juan Pueblo. Scholarship value is $2500. Seventeen awards are granted. Deadlines: December 30 for spring, April 30 for summer, and June 30 for fall.

Award: Scholarship for use in freshman, sophomore, junior, or senior years; renewable. *Number:* up to 17. *Amount:* $2500.

Eligibility Requirements: Applicant must be American Indian/Alaska Native; enrolled or expecting to enroll full-time at a two-year or four-year institution or university and resident of New Mexico. Applicant or parent of applicant must have employment or volunteer experience in community service. Available to U.S. citizens.

Application Requirements: Application form, letter of acceptance, transcript. *Deadline:* varies.

Contact: Adam Garcia, Education Coordinator
Phone: 505-852-3477
Fax: 505-852-3030
E-mail: wevog68@valornet.com

ST. CLAIRE REGIONAL MEDICAL CENTER

http://www.st-claire.org/

SR. MARY JEANNETTE WESS, S.N.D. SCHOLARSHIP

Scholarships available for undergraduates in their junior or senior year of study, or graduate students. Must have graduated from an eastern Kentucky high school in one of the following counties: Bath, Carter, Elliott, Fleming, Lewis, Magoffin, Menifee, Montgomery, Morgan, Rowan, or Wolfe. Must demonstrate academic achievement, leadership, service, and financial need.

Award: Scholarship for use in junior, senior, or graduate years; renewable. *Number:* 2. *Amount:* $750.

Eligibility Requirements: Applicant must be enrolled or expecting to enroll full-time at a four-year institution or university; resident of Kentucky and must have an interest in leadership. Applicant or parent of applicant must have employment or volunteer experience in community service. Available to U.S. and non-U.S. citizens.

Application Requirements: Application form, financial need analysis, recommendations or references, self-addressed stamped envelope with application, transcript. *Deadline:* varies.

Contact: Tom Lewis, Director of Development
    Phone: 606-783-6511
    Fax: 606-783-6795
    E-mail: telewis@st-claire.org

SKILLSUSA

http://www.skillsusa.org/

SKILLSUSA ALUMNI AND FRIENDS MERIT SCHOLARSHIP

Scholarship of up to $1000 recognizes qualities of leadership, commitment to community service, improving the image of career and technical education, and improving the image of his/her chosen occupation.

Award: Scholarship for use in freshman, sophomore, junior, senior, graduate, or postgraduate years; not renewable. *Number:* 1. *Amount:* $500–$1000.

Eligibility Requirements: Applicant must be enrolled or expecting to enroll full-time at a two-year or four-year or technical institution or university and must have an interest in leadership. Applicant or parent of applicant must have employment or volunteer experience in community service. Available to U.S. citizens.

Application Requirements: Application form, community service, recommendations or references. *Deadline:* May 15.

Contact: Karen Perrino, Associate Director
    Phone: 703-737-0610
    Fax: 703-777-8999
    E-mail: kperrino@skillsusa.org

STATE FARM COMPANIES/YOUTH SERVICE AMERICA

http://www.ysa.org/

HARRIS WOFFORD AWARDS

Awards recognize extraordinary achievements in three categories: youth (ages 12 to 25), organization (nonprofit, corporate, foundation), and media (organization or individual) for actively contributing towards, "Making service and service-learning the common expectation and common experience of every young person."

Award: Grant for use in freshman, sophomore, junior, senior, graduate, or postgraduate years; not renewable. *Number:* up to 3. *Amount:* $500–$1000.

Eligibility Requirements: Applicant must be age 12-25 and enrolled or expecting to enroll full- or part-time at a two-year or four-year or technical institution or university. Applicant or parent of applicant must have employment or volunteer experience in community service. Available to U.S. citizens.

Application Requirements: Application form. *Deadline:* October 19.

Contact: Julie Mancuso, Grant Manager
    Phone: 202-296-2992 Ext. 111
    Fax: 202-296-4030
    E-mail: jmancuso@ysa.org

STONEWALL COMMUNITY FOUNDATION

http://www.stonewallfoundation.org/

HARRY BARTEL MEMORIAL SCHOLARSHIP

Scholarship for gay male students in New York City who are 23 years or younger with a record of community service. Deadline varies. Applications available through YES Program at LGBT Center.

Award: Scholarship for use in freshman, sophomore, junior, senior, graduate, or postgraduate years; not renewable. *Number:* 1–2. *Amount:* $500.

Eligibility Requirements: Applicant must be enrolled or expecting to enroll full-time at a two-year or four-year or technical institution or university; male and must have an interest in LGBT issues. Applicant or

parent of applicant must have employment or volunteer experience in community service. Available to U.S. citizens.

Application Requirements: Application form. *Deadline:* varies.

Contact: Nicole Avallone, Director of Youth Services
    Stonewall Community Foundation
    c/o The Lesbian, Gay, Bisexual, and Transgender Community
      Center
    208 West 13th Street
    New York, NY 10011
    Phone: 212-620-7310
    Fax: 646-486-9381
    E-mail: YES@gaycenter.org

SYNOD OF THE COVENANT

http://www.synodofthecovenant.org/

RACIAL ETHNIC SCHOLARSHIP

Scholarship will be awarded for full- or part-time study toward baccalaureate degree or certification at colleges, universities, and vocational schools. Award also available for full-time students enrolled in master's degree programs for church vocations at approved Presbyterian theological institutions. Priority will be given to Presbyterian applicants from the states of Michigan and Ohio. Applicants must maintain a minimum 2.0 GPA. Deadline: September 1.

Award: Scholarship for use in freshman, sophomore, junior, senior, or graduate years; not renewable. *Number:* 30. *Amount:* $400–$800.

Eligibility Requirements: Applicant must be Presbyterian; American Indian/Alaska Native, Asian/Pacific Islander, Black (non-Hispanic), Hispanic; enrolled or expecting to enroll full- or part-time at a four-year institution or university and resident of Michigan, Ohio. Applicant or parent of applicant must have employment or volunteer experience in engineering/technology. Available to U.S. and non-U.S. citizens.

Application Requirements: Application form, application form may be submitted online (http://www.synodofthecovenant.org), community service, financial need analysis, test scores, transcript, verification enrollment letter. *Deadline:* September 1.

Contact: Ms. Janet Fehlen, Executive Assistant
    Phone: 419-754-4050
    Fax: 419-754-4051
    E-mail: j.fehlen@synodofthecovenant.org

TERRY FOX HUMANITARIAN AWARD PROGRAM

http://www.terryfox.org/

TERRY FOX HUMANITARIAN AWARD

Award granted to Canadian students entering postsecondary education. Criteria includes commitment to voluntary humanitarian work, courage in overcoming obstacles, excellence in academics, fitness and amateur sports. Value of award is CAN$7000 awarded annually for maximum of four years. Must be no older than age 25.

Award: Scholarship for use in freshman, sophomore, junior, or senior years; renewable. *Number:* up to 20.

Eligibility Requirements: Applicant must be Canadian citizen; enrolled or expecting to enroll full-time at a two-year or four-year institution or university and must have an interest in athletics/sports. Applicant or parent of applicant must have employment or volunteer experience in community service.

Application Requirements: Application form, recommendations or references, self-addressed stamped envelope with application, transcript. *Deadline:* February 1.

Contact: W.L. Davis, Executive Director
    Phone: 604-291-3057
    Fax: 604-291-3311
    E-mail: terryfox@sfu.ca

TEXAS RESTAURANT ASSOCIATION

http://www.restaurantville.com/

W. PRICE JR. MEMORIAL SCHOLARSHIP

Scholarships of $5000 for recipients attending a four-year university, culinary academy, or graduate program, and $2000 for recipients attending a two-year college. Applicant must be employed by an ARA member in good standing, must have an overall B grade average, and must submit an essay summarizing how their experience in the food service industry has affected their career goals.

Award: Scholarship for use in freshman, sophomore, junior, or senior years; not renewable. *Number:* 4. *Amount:* $2000–$5000.

Eligibility Requirements: Applicant must be enrolled or expecting to enroll full-time at a two-year or four-year institution or university. Applicant or parent of applicant must have employment or volunteer experience in food service. Available to U.S. citizens.

Application Requirements: Application form, recommendations or references, transcript. *Deadline:* February 1.

Contact: Susan Petty, Scholarship Coordinator
Phone: 512-457-4100
Fax: 512-472-2777
E-mail: spetty@tramail.org

TUITION EXCHANGE INC.

http://www.tuitionexchange.org/

TUITION EXCHANGE SCHOLARSHIPS

The Tuition Exchange is an association of over 600 colleges and universities awarding over 6000 full or substantial scholarships each year for children and other family members of faculty and staff employed at participating institutions. Students must maintain satisfactory academic progress and a cumulative GPA as established by each institution. Application procedures and deadlines vary by school. Contact Tuition Exchange Liaison Officer at home institution for details.

Award: Scholarship for use in freshman, sophomore, junior, senior, graduate, or postgraduate years; renewable. *Number:* 5000–7000. *Amount:* $4000–$47,000.

Eligibility Requirements: Applicant must be enrolled or expecting to enroll full- or part-time at a two-year or four-year institution or university. Applicant or parent of applicant must have employment or volunteer experience in teaching/education. Available to U.S. and non-U.S. citizens.

Application Requirements: Application form. *Deadline:* continuous.

Contact: Mr. Robert Shorb, Executive Director/CEO
Tuition Exchange Inc.
3 Bethesda Metro Center
Suite 700
Bethesda, MD 20814
Phone: 301-941-1827
Fax: 301-657-9776
E-mail: rshorb@tuitionexchange.org

TWO TEN FOOTWEAR FOUNDATION

http://www.twoten.org/

TWO TEN FOOTWEAR FOUNDATION SCHOLARSHIP

Renewable, merit and need-based award available to students who have 500 hours work experience in footwear, leather, or allied industries during year of application, or have a parent employed in one of these fields for at least two years. Must have proof of employment and maintain 2.5 GPA.

Award: Scholarship for use in freshman, sophomore, junior, or senior years; renewable. *Number:* 200–300. *Amount:* $500–$3000.

Eligibility Requirements: Applicant must be enrolled or expecting to enroll full- or part-time at a two-year or four-year institution or university. Applicant or parent of applicant must have employment or volunteer experience in leather/footwear industry. Available to U.S. citizens.

Application Requirements: Application form, application form may be submitted online (http://www.twoten.org), essay, financial need analysis, recommendations or references, transcript. *Deadline:* February 16.

Contact: Phyllis Molta, Director of Scholarship
Phone: 781-736-1510
E-mail: scholarship@twoten.org

UNITED NEGRO COLLEGE FUND

http://www.uncf.org/

MAYA ANGELOU/VIVIAN BAXTER SCHOLARSHIP

Scholarships for North Carolina students who will enroll at North Carolina UNCF member institutions, have an unmet financial need, and are involved in school/community services. Minimum 2.5 GPA required. For more information, see website http://www.uncf.org.

Award: Scholarship for use in freshman year; not renewable. *Amount:* $2500.

Eligibility Requirements: Applicant must be Black (non-Hispanic); enrolled or expecting to enroll full-time at a four-year institution or university; resident of North Carolina and studying in North Carolina. Applicant or parent of applicant must have employment or volunteer experience in community service. Applicant must have 2.5 GPA or higher. Available to U.S. citizens.

Application Requirements: Application form. *Deadline:* continuous.

RYAN HOWARD FAMILY FOUNDATION SCHOLARSHIP-ST. LOUIS/PHILADELPHIA

Scholarship for graduating high school students who are residents of Philadelphia, PA or St. Louis, MO. Students should have a minimum GPA 2.5, possess leadership qualities, have performed no less than 20 hours of community service, have the potential for success in college, and be involved in school and the community. To be used at four-colleges or universities only.

Award: Scholarship for use in freshman year; not renewable. *Amount:* $1000.

Eligibility Requirements: Applicant must be Black (non-Hispanic); high school student; planning to enroll or expecting to enroll full-time at a four-year institution or university and resident of Missouri, Pennsylvania. Applicant or parent of applicant must have employment or volunteer experience in community service. Applicant must have 2.5 GPA or higher. Available to U.S. citizens.

Application Requirements: Application form. *Deadline:* continuous.

UNITED STATES SUBMARINE VETERANS

http://www.ussvcf.org/

UNITED STATES SUBMARINE VETERANS INC. NATIONAL SCHOLARSHIP PROGRAM

• See page 543

WESTERN GOLF ASSOCIATION-EVANS SCHOLARS FOUNDATION

http://www.wgaesf.org

CHICK EVANS CADDIE SCHOLARSHIP

Full tuition and housing awards renewable up to four years available to high school seniors who have worked at least two years as a caddie at a Western Golf Association member club. Must demonstrate need, outstanding character and at least a B average in college preparatory courses. Limited to use at universities where Evans Foundation maintains a Scholarship House, where recipients are required to reside. See www.wgaesf.org for complete list.

Award: Scholarship for use in freshman, sophomore, junior, or senior years; renewable. *Number:* up to 240.

Eligibility Requirements: Applicant must be high school student; planning to enroll or expecting to enroll full-time at a four-year institution or university and studying in Colorado, Illinois, Indiana, Michigan, Minnesota, Missouri, Ohio, Oregon, Washington, Wisconsin. Applicant or parent of applicant must have employment or volunteer experience in private club/caddying. Available to U.S. and non-U.S. citizens.

Application Requirements: Application form, application form may be submitted online (http://www.wgaesf.org/apply), essay, financial need analysis, interview, personal photograph, recommendations or references, test scores, transcript. *Deadline:* September 30.

UNITED STATES BOWLING CONGRESS (USBC)

http://www.bowl.com/

USBC ANNUAL ZEB SCHOLARSHIP

Scholarship is awarded to a USBC Youth member who achieves academic success and gives back to his/her community through service. Candidates must have a current GPA of 3.0 or better.

Award: Scholarship for use in junior or senior years; not renewable. *Number:* 1. *Amount:* $2500.

Eligibility Requirements: Applicant must be high school student; planning to enroll or expecting to enroll full- or part-time at a four-year institution or university and must have an interest in bowling. Applicant or parent of applicant must have employment or volunteer experience in community service. Applicant must have 3.0 GPA or higher. Available to U.S. citizens.

Application Requirements: Application form, recommendations or references, transcript. *Deadline:* December 1.

Contact: Denise Lish, SMART Program Administrator
  Phone: 800-514-2695
  E-mail: smart@bowl.com

YOUTH FOUNDATION INC.

http://www.foundationcenter.org/grantmaker/youthfdn/index.html

ALEXANDER AND MAUDE HADDEN SCHOLARSHIP

Youth Foundation offers exceptional students with financial need an award of $2500 to $4000 per year which is renewable for four years at the foundation's discretion. Minimum GPA of 3.5 required, community service and extra curricular activities expected. Must write Foundation for information and application request form.

Award: Scholarship for use in freshman, sophomore, junior, or senior years; renewable. *Amount:* $2500–$4000.

Eligibility Requirements: Applicant must be enrolled or expecting to enroll full- or part-time at a four-year institution or university. Applicant or parent of applicant must have employment or volunteer experience in community service. Applicant must have 3.5 GPA or higher. Available to U.S. citizens.

Application Requirements: Application form, essay, test scores, transcript. *Deadline:* February 29.

IMPAIRMENT

ALEXANDER GRAHAM BELL ASSOCIATION FOR THE DEAF AND HARD OF HEARING

http://www.ListeningAndSpokenLanguage.org/

AG BELL COLLEGE SCHOLARSHIP PROGRAM

Available to students with pre-lingual bilateral hearing loss in the moderate-severe to profound range who attend a mainstream and accredited college or university on a full-time basis. Specific eligibility criteria, submission guidelines, deadline and application available on AG Bell website at http://www.ListeningAndSpokenLanguage.org.

Award: Scholarship for use in freshman, sophomore, junior, senior, graduate, or postgraduate years; not renewable. *Number:* 15–25. *Amount:* $1000–$10,000.

Eligibility Requirements: Applicant must be hearing impaired and enrolled or expecting to enroll full-time at a four-year institution or university. Applicant must be hearing impaired. Applicant must have 3.5 GPA or higher. Available to U.S. and non-U.S. citizens.

Application Requirements: Application form, essay, recommendations or references, transcript, unaided audiogram or CI programming report. *Deadline:* varies.

Contact: Wendy Will, Youth and Family Programs Manager
  Phone: 202-337-5220
  E-mail: financialaid@agbell.org

AMERICAN CANCER SOCIETY

http://www.cancer.org/

AMERICAN CANCER SOCIETY, FLORIDA DIVISION R.O.C.K. COLLEGE SCHOLARSHIP PROGRAM

Applicants must have had a personal diagnosis of cancer, be a Florida resident between the ages of 18 and 21, and plan to attend college in Florida. Minimum 2.5 GPA required. Awards will be based on financial need, scholarship, community service, cancer diagnosis, type and length of treatment.

Award: Scholarship for use in freshman, sophomore, junior, or senior years; renewable. *Number:* 200–225. *Amount:* $300–$3300.

Eligibility Requirements: Applicant must be physically disabled; age 18-21; enrolled or expecting to enroll full- or part-time at a two-year or four-year or technical institution or university; resident of Florida; studying in Florida and must have an interest in leadership. Applicant must be physically disabled. Applicant must have 2.5 GPA or higher. Available to U.S. citizens.

Application Requirements: Application form, essay, financial need analysis, interview, letter from physician, personal photograph, recommendations or references, resume, test scores, transcript. *Deadline:* April 10.

Contact: Susan Lee, Director of Childhood Cancer Programs
  American Cancer Society
  3709 West Jetton Avenue
  Tampa, FL 33629
  Phone: 800-444-1410 Ext. 4405
  Fax: 813-254-5857
  E-mail: susan.bellomy@cancer.org

AMERICAN COUNCIL OF THE BLIND

http://www.acb.org/

AMERICAN COUNCIL OF THE BLIND SCHOLARSHIPS

Merit-based award available to undergraduate students who are legally blind in both eyes. Submit certificate of legal blindness and proof of acceptance at an accredited postsecondary institution.

Award: Scholarship for use in freshman, sophomore, junior, or senior years; renewable. *Number:* 16–20. *Amount:* $1000–$2500.

Eligibility Requirements: Applicant must be visually impaired and enrolled or expecting to enroll full- or part-time at a four-year institution or university. Applicant must be visually impaired. Applicant must have 3.5 GPA or higher. Available to U.S. citizens.

Application Requirements: Application form, driver's license, essay, evidence of legal blindness, proof of post-secondary school acceptance, recommendations or references, transcript. *Deadline:* March 1.

Contact: Tatricia Castillo, Scholarship Coordinator
  American Council of the Blind
  1155 15th Street, NW, Suite 1004
  Washington, DC 20005
  Phone: 202-467-5081
  Fax: 202-467-5085
  E-mail: tcastillo@acp.org

AMERICAN FOUNDATION FOR THE BLIND

http://www.afb.org/

FERDINAND TORRES SCHOLARSHIP

Awards one scholarship of $2500 to a full-time undergraduate or graduate student who presents evidence of economic need. To be eligible the applicant must reside in the U.S., but need not be a citizen of the U.S. Preference will be given to applicants residing in the New York City metropolitan area and new immigrants to the U.S. Must submit proof of legal blindness. For additional information and application requirements, visit http://www.afb.org/scholarships.asp.

Award: Scholarship for use in freshman, sophomore, junior, senior, or graduate years; not renewable. *Number:* 1. *Amount:* $2500.

Eligibility Requirements: Applicant must be visually impaired and enrolled or expecting to enroll full-time at a two-year or four-year institution or university. Applicant must be visually impaired. Available to U.S. and non-U.S. citizens.

Application Requirements: Application form, essay, financial need analysis, proof of acceptance in an accredited full-time undergraduate or graduate program, proof of legal blindness, recommendations or references, transcript. *Deadline:* April 30.

Contact: Dawn Bodrogi, Information Center and Library Coordinator
American Foundation for the Blind
11 Penn Plaza, Suite 300
New York, NY 10001
Phone: 212-502-7661
Fax: 212-502-7771
E-mail: dbodrogi@afb.net

ARRL FOUNDATION INC.

http://www.arrl.org/

CHALLENGE MET SCHOLARSHIP

Multiple $500 awards are available to students with any active amateur radio license who are studying at an accredited two- or four-year college, university, or technical school. Preference to applicants with documented learning disabilities (by physician or school) and indications that applicant is putting forth substantial effort regardless of resulting academic grades.

Award: Scholarship for use in freshman, sophomore, junior, or senior years; not renewable. *Amount:* $500.

Eligibility Requirements: Applicant must be hearing impaired, learning disabled, physically disabled, or visually impaired; enrolled or expecting to enroll full- or part-time at a two-year or four-year or technical institution or university and must have an interest in amateur radio. Applicant must be hearing impaired, learning disabled, physically disabled, or visually impaired. Available to U.S. citizens.

Application Requirements: Application form, documentation of learning disability. *Deadline:* February 1.

Contact: Ms. Mary Hobart, Secretary
Phone: 860-594-0397
E-mail: k1mmh@arrl.org

ASSOCIATION FOR EDUCATION AND REHABILITATION OF THE BLIND AND VISUALLY IMPAIRED

http://www.aerbvi.org/

WILLIAM AND DOROTHY FERREL SCHOLARSHIP

Nonrenewable scholarship given in even years for postsecondary education leading to career in services for blind or visually impaired. Applicant must submit proof of legal blindness or visual field impairment of 20 percent or less.

Award: Scholarship for use in freshman, sophomore, junior, or senior years; not renewable. *Number:* 2. *Amount:* $1000.

Eligibility Requirements: Applicant must be visually impaired and enrolled or expecting to enroll full- or part-time at a two-year or four-year or technical institution or university. Applicant must be visually impaired. Available to U.S. and non-U.S. citizens.

Application Requirements: Application form, proof of legal blindness. *Deadline:* February 15.

ASSOCIATION OF BLIND CITIZENS

http://www.blindcitizens.org/

REGGIE JOHNSON MEMORIAL SCHOLARSHIP

Award for high school or college student who is legally blind. High school or college transcript, certificate of legal blindness, or a letter from ophthalmologist required. Must submit two letters of reference and a CD copy of your biographical sketch.

Award: Scholarship for use in freshman, sophomore, junior, senior, graduate, or postgraduate years; not renewable. *Number:* 1–4. *Amount:* $1000–$2000.

Eligibility Requirements: Applicant must be visually impaired; enrolled or expecting to enroll full-time at a two-year or four-year institution or university and resident of California, Connecticut, Florida, Maine, Massachusetts, New Hampshire, Rhode Island, Vermont. Applicant must be visually impaired. Available to U.S. citizens.

Application Requirements: Application form, application form may be submitted online (http://www.blindcitizens.org), certificate of legal blindness or a letter from an ophthalmologist, essay, recommendations or references, transcript. *Deadline:* April 15.

Contact: John Oliveira, President
Association of Blind Citizens
PO Box 246
Holbrook, MA 02343
Phone: 781-961-1023
Fax: 781-961-0004
E-mail: president@blindcitizens.org

CALIFORNIA COUNCIL OF THE BLIND

http://www.ccbnet.org/

CALIFORNIA COUNCIL OF THE BLIND SCHOLARSHIPS

Scholarships available to blind student applicants who are California residents entering or continuing studies at an accredited California college, university, or vocational training school. Must be a full-time student registered for at least twelve units for the entire academic year. Applications must be typed and all blanks must be filled to be considered for scholarship. Applications available at website http://www.ccbnet.org.

Award: Scholarship for use in freshman, sophomore, junior, or senior years; renewable. *Number:* up to 20. *Amount:* $375–$2500.

Eligibility Requirements: Applicant must be visually impaired; enrolled or expecting to enroll full-time at a two-year or four-year or technical institution or university; resident of California and studying in California. Applicant must be visually impaired. Available to U.S. and non-U.S. citizens.

Application Requirements: Application form, interview, proof of blindness, recommendations or references, transcript. *Deadline:* June 15.

CHAIRSCHOLARS FOUNDATION INC.

http://www.chairscholars.org/

NATIONAL SCHOLARSHIP PROGRAM

Award for students who are severely physically challenged. Applicants may be high school seniors or college undergraduate. Must be outstanding citizen with history of public service. Minimum 3.5 GPA required. Ten to twelve renewable awards of up to $6000 per year are granted.

Award: Scholarship for use in freshman, sophomore, junior, or senior years; renewable. *Number:* 10–40. *Amount:* $1000–$6000.

Eligibility Requirements: Applicant must be hearing impaired, physically disabled, or visually impaired and enrolled or expecting to enroll full- or part-time at a two-year or four-year institution or university. Applicant must be hearing impaired, physically disabled, or visually impaired. Applicant must have 3.5 GPA or higher. Available to U.S. citizens.

Application Requirements: Application form, community service, essay, parent's tax return from previous year, personal photograph, recommendations or references, resume, test scores, transcript. *Deadline:* April 15.

Contact: Alicia Keim, Founder
Chairscholars Foundation Inc.
16101 Carencia Lane
Odessa, FL 33556
Phone: 866-926-0544
Fax: 813-920-7661
E-mail: programs@chairscholars.org

CHRISTIAN RECORD SERVICES INC.

http://www.christianrecord.org/

CHRISTIAN RECORD SERVICES INC. SCHOLARSHIPS

One-time award for legally blind or blind college undergraduates. Submit application, essay-autobiography, photo, references, and financial information by April 1.

Award: Scholarship for use in freshman, sophomore, junior, or senior years; renewable. *Number:* 7–10. *Amount:* $250–$500.

Eligibility Requirements: Applicant must be visually impaired and enrolled or expecting to enroll full-time at a four-year institution or university. Applicant must be visually impaired. Available to U.S. citizens.

Application Requirements: Application form, driver's license, essay, financial need analysis, personal photograph, recommendations or references. *Deadline:* April 1.

Contact: Shelly Kittleson, Assistant to Treasurer
Phone: 402-488-0981 Ext. 216
Fax: 402-488-7582
E-mail: info@christianrecord.org

CIEE: COUNCIL ON INTERNATIONAL EDUCATIONAL EXCHANGE

http://www.ciee.org/

ROBERT B. BAILEY SCHOLARSHIP

One-time award for students from underrepresented groups in study abroad participating in CIEE-administered study abroad programs only. Deadlines are April 1 and November 1. Must be self-identified as belonging to an underrepresented group in study abroad. Students may only apply for this award as part of their CIEE Study Abroad online program application. Written/mailed applications are not accepted.

Award: Scholarship for use in freshman, sophomore, junior, or senior years; not renewable. *Number:* 20–30. *Amount:* $1000–$1500.

Eligibility Requirements: Applicant must be hearing impaired, learning disabled, physically disabled, or visually impaired; American Indian/Alaska Native, Asian/Pacific Islander, Black (non-Hispanic), Hispanic and enrolled or expecting to enroll full-time at a two-year or four-year institution or university. Applicant must be hearing impaired, learning disabled, physically disabled, or visually impaired. Available to U.S. and non-U.S. citizens.

Application Requirements: Application form, application form may be submitted online (http://www.ciee.org), CIEE Study Abroad Program Application, essay, financial need analysis, personal photograph, recommendations or references, transcript. *Deadline:* varies.

COALITION OF TEXANS WITH DISABILITIES

http://www.cotwd.org/

KENNY MURGIA MEMORIAL SCHOLARSHIP

Awarded annually to a high school senior who has demonstrated activism on disability issues. This program also provides for a part-time paid internship for a college student with disabilities at CTD's Austin office.

Award: Scholarship for use in freshman year; not renewable. *Number:* 1. *Amount:* $1000.

Eligibility Requirements: Applicant must be hearing impaired, learning disabled, physically disabled, or visually impaired; high school student; planning to enroll or expecting to enroll full-time at a four-year institution or university and resident of Texas. Applicant must be hearing impaired, learning disabled, physically disabled, or visually impaired. Available to U.S. citizens.

Application Requirements: Application form, recommendations or references, transcript. *Deadline:* May 31.

Contact: Jodi Park, Director of Projects and Communications
Phone: 512-478-3366
Fax: 512-478-3370
E-mail: cotwd@cotwd.org

COLLEGE WOMEN'S ASSOCIATION OF JAPAN

http://www.cwaj.org/

SCHOLARSHIP FOR THE VISUALLY IMPAIRED TO STUDY ABROAD

Scholarship for visually impaired Japanese nationals or permanent residents of Japan who have been accepted into an undergraduate or graduate degree program at an accredited English-speaking university or research institution. Former recipients of CWAJ awards and members of CWAJ are ineligible. Award value is JPY3 million. Deadline on or between November 1 and November 30.

Award: Scholarship for use in junior or senior years; not renewable. *Number:* 1.

Eligibility Requirements: Applicant must be visually impaired; of Japanese heritage and Japanese citizen and enrolled or expecting to enroll full-time at a four-year institution or university. Applicant must be visually impaired. Available to citizens of countries other than the U.S. or Canada.

Application Requirements: Application form, certificate of disability, essay, recommendations or references, test scores, transcript. *Fee:* $10. *Deadline:* varies.

SCHOLARSHIP FOR THE VISUALLY IMPAIRED TO STUDY IN JAPAN

Scholarship for visually impaired Japanese or permanent resident students for graduate or undergraduate study in Japan. Former recipients of CWAJ awards and members of CWAJ are ineligible. Award Value is JPY2.0 million. Deadline on or between November 1 and November 30.

Award: Scholarship for use in junior or senior years; not renewable. *Number:* 1–2.

Eligibility Requirements: Applicant must be visually impaired; of Japanese heritage and Japanese citizen and enrolled or expecting to enroll full-time at a four-year institution or university. Applicant must be visually impaired. Available to citizens of countries other than the U.S. or Canada.

Application Requirements: Application form, certificate of disability, essay, recommendations or references, self-addressed stamped envelope with application, transcript. *Fee:* $10. *Deadline:* varies.

COMMITTEE OF TEN THOUSAND

http://www.cott1.org/

RACHEL WARNER SCHOLARSHIP

Scholarship for persons with any bleeding disorder. For educational use, both undergraduate and graduate studies. Scholarship amount and the number of available awards varies.

Award: Scholarship for use in freshman, sophomore, junior, senior, or graduate years; not renewable. *Amount:* up to $1000.

Eligibility Requirements: Applicant must be physically disabled and enrolled or expecting to enroll full- or part-time at a two-year or four-year or technical institution or university. Applicant must be physically disabled. Available to U.S. citizens.

Application Requirements: Application form, essay, recommendations or references. *Deadline:* May 1.

CYSTIC FIBROSIS SCHOLARSHIP FOUNDATION

http://www.cfscholarship.org/

CYSTIC FIBROSIS SCHOLARSHIP

One-time $1000 to $10,000 scholarships for young adults with cystic fibrosis to be used to further their education after high school. Awards may be used for tuition, books, and fees. Students may reapply in subsequent years.

Award: Scholarship for use in freshman, sophomore, junior, or senior years; not renewable. *Number:* 40–50. *Amount:* $1000–$10,000.

Eligibility Requirements: Applicant must be physically disabled and enrolled or expecting to enroll full-time at a two-year or four-year or technical institution or university. Applicant must be physically disabled. Available to U.S. citizens.

Application Requirements: Application form, essay, financial need analysis, recommendations or references, test scores, transcript. *Deadline:* March 21.

Contact: Mary Bottorff, President
Cystic Fibrosis Scholarship Foundation
2814 Grant Street
Evanston, IL 60201
Phone: 847-328-0127
Fax: 847-328-0127
E-mail: mkbcfsf@aol.com

DEPARTMENT OF THE ARMY

http://www.goarmy.com/rotc

ARMY (ROTC) RESERVE OFFICERS TRAINING CORPS TWO-, THREE-, FOUR-YEAR CAMPUS-BASED SCHOLARSHIPS

One-time award for college freshmen, sophomores, or juniors or students with BA who need two years to obtain graduate degree. Must be a member of school's ROTC program. Must pass physical. Minimum 2.5 GPA required. Professor of military science must submit application. Applicant must be at least 17 when enrolled in college and under thirty-one years of age in the year of graduation. Must be U.S. citizen/national at time of award. Open year-round.

Award: Scholarship for use in freshman, sophomore, junior, senior, or graduate years; not renewable. *Number:* 1200–2500. *Amount:* $10,000–$40,000.

Eligibility Requirements: Applicant must be physically disabled; age 17-30 and enrolled or expecting to enroll full-time at a four-year institution or university. Applicant must be physically disabled. Applicant must have 2.5 GPA or higher. Available to U.S. citizens. Applicant or parent must meet one or more of the following requirements: national guard experience; retired from active duty; disabled or killed as a result of military service; prisoner of war; or missing in action.

Application Requirements: Application form, interview, test scores, transcript. *Deadline:* continuous.

Contact: Mr. Joseph O'Donnell, Incentives Division Chief
Department of the Army
U.S. Army Cadet Command, Bldg 1002, 204 1st Cavalry
Regiment Road
Fort Knox, KY 40121-5123
Phone: 502-624-7046
Fax: 502-624-1120
E-mail: joseph.f.odonnell3.civ@mail.mil

U.S. ARMY ROTC FOUR-YEAR HISTORICALLY BLACK COLLEGE/UNIVERSITY SCHOLARSHIP

One-time award for students attending college for the first time Must attend a historically black college or university and must join school's ROTC program. Must pass physical. Must have a qualifying SAT or ACT score and minimum GPA of 2.5. Applicant must be at least 17 by college enrollment and under thirty-one years of age in the year of graduation. Must be a U.S. citizen/national at time of award. Application available online.

Award: Scholarship for use in freshman, sophomore, junior, senior, or graduate years; not renewable. *Number:* 20–200. *Amount:* $9000–$40,000.

Eligibility Requirements: Applicant must be physically disabled; age 17-26 and enrolled or expecting to enroll full-time at a four-year institution or university. Applicant must be physically disabled. Applicant must have 2.5 GPA or higher. Available to U.S. citizens. Applicant must have national guard experience.

Application Requirements: Application form, application form may be submitted online (http://www.goarmy.com/rotc/high-school-students/four-year-scholarship.html), essay, interview, test scores, transcript. *Deadline:* January 10.

Contact: Ms. Kathleen Barnes, Supervisor, Human Resources Specialist
Department of the Army
U.S. Army Cadet Command, Bldg 1002, 204 1st Cavalry
Regiment Road
Fort Knox, KY 40121-5123
Phone: 502-624-7371
Fax: 502-624-1120
E-mail: kathleen.m.barnes19.civ@mail.mil

U.S. ARMY ROTC GUARANTEED RESERVE FORCES DUTY (GRFD), (ARNG/USAR) AND DEDICATED ARNG SCHOLARSHIPS

One-time award for college sophomores and juniors, or two-year graduate degree students. Must be a member of school's ROTC program. Must pass physical. Minimum 2.5 GPA required. Applicant must be at least seventeen years of age when enrolled in college and under thirty-one years of age in the year of graduation. Must be a U.S. citizen/national at the time of award.

Award: Scholarship for use in sophomore, junior, senior, or graduate years; renewable. *Number:* 800–1000. *Amount:* $10,000–$12,000.

Eligibility Requirements: Applicant must be physically disabled; age 17-30 and enrolled or expecting to enroll full-time at a two-year or four-year institution or university. Applicant must be physically disabled. Applicant must have 2.5 GPA or higher. Available to U.S. citizens. Applicant must have national guard experience.

Application Requirements: Application form, interview, test scores, transcript. *Deadline:* June 15.

Contact: Capt. Melvin Kindle, Program Manager
Department of the Army
U.S. Army Cadet Command, Bldg 1002, 204 1st Cavalry
Regiment Road
Fort Knox, KY 40121-5123
Phone: 502-624-6928
Fax: 502-624-1120
E-mail: melvin.e.kindle.mil@mail.mil

U.S. ARMY ROTC MILITARY JUNIOR COLLEGE (MJC) SCHOLARSHIP

One-time award for high school graduates who wish to attend a two-year military junior college. Must serve simultaneously in the Army National Guard or Reserve and qualify for the ROTC Advanced Course. Must have a minimum GPA of 2.5. Must be a U.S. citizen/national at time of award. Must also be eighteen years of age by October 1 and under twenty-seven years of age on June 30 in the year of graduation. On-line application available. Must be used at one of five military junior colleges. See Professor of Military Science at college for application.

Award: Scholarship for use in freshman or sophomore years; renewable. *Number:* 110–150. *Amount:* $2705–$25,000.

Eligibility Requirements: Applicant must be physically disabled; age 18-26 and enrolled or expecting to enroll full-time at a two-year institution. Applicant must be physically disabled. Applicant must have 2.5 GPA or higher. Available to U.S. citizens. Applicant must have national guard experience.

Application Requirements: Application form, essay, interview, physical, physical fitness test, height/weight, test scores, transcript. *Deadline:* August 25.

Contact: Mr. Larry Waller, Program Manager
Department of the Army
U.S. Army Cadet Command, Bldg 1002, 204 1st Cavalry
Regiment Road
Fort Knox, KY 40121-5123
Phone: 502-624-7023
Fax: 502-624-1120
E-mail: larry.j.waller.civ@mail.mil

DISABLEDPERSON INC. COLLEGE SCHOLARSHIP

http://www.disabledperson.com/

DISABLEDPERSON INC. NATIONAL COLLEGE SCHOLARSHIP AWARD FOR COLLEGE STUDENTS WITH DISABILITIES

Essay contest for college students with disabilities who are enrolled as full-time students in a two- or four-year accredited college or university. Length of the essay must not exceed 1000 words. We offer two scholarships per school year.

Award: Scholarship for use in freshman, sophomore, junior, senior, graduate, or postgraduate years; not renewable. *Number:* up to 1. *Amount:* up to $1000.

Eligibility Requirements: Applicant must be hearing impaired, learning disabled, physically disabled, or visually impaired and enrolled or expecting to enroll full-time at a two-year or four-year or technical institution or university. Applicant must be hearing impaired, learning disabled, physically disabled, or visually impaired. Available to U.S. citizens.

Application Requirements: Application form, application form may be submitted online (http://www.disABLEDperson.com), entry in a contest, essay, proof of disability, transcript.

Contact: Diana Corso, Executive Director
disABLEDperson Inc. College Scholarship
PO Box 230636
Encinitas, CA 92023
E-mail: scholarships@disabledperson.com

EASTERN AMPUTEE GOLF ASSOCIATION

http://www.eaga.org/

EASTERN AMPUTEE GOLF ASSOCIATION SCHOLARSHIP FUND

Six $1000 college scholarships are available to any EAGA amputee member and/or a member of his or her family. Amputee is define as one who has had the loss of a limb at a major joint (ie Ankle , Wrist etc) due to trauma or congenital birth defect. Award recipients do not need to be in attendance. Award covers each of the four school years depending on when applications are accepted. Award recipient must maintain a 2.0 GPA.

Award: Scholarship for use in freshman, sophomore, junior, or senior years; renewable. *Number:* 6. *Amount:* $1000.

Eligibility Requirements: Applicant must be physically disabled and enrolled or expecting to enroll full-time at a four-year institution or university. Applicant must be physically disabled. Available to U.S. and Canadian citizens.

Application Requirements: Application form, application form may be submitted online, community service, essay, financial need analysis, resume, Student Aid Report (SAR), transcript. *Deadline:* June 25.

Contact: Bob Buck, Secretary
Phone: 888-868-0992
E-mail: info@eaga.org

ELAINE CHAPIN MEMORIAL SCHOLARSHIP FUND

http://www.elainememorial.com/

ELAINE CHAPIN MEMORIAL SCHOLARSHIP FUND

Scholarship program that benefits students whose lives are impacted by multiple sclerosis.

Award: Scholarship for use in freshman, sophomore, junior, or senior years; not renewable. *Number:* 8. *Amount:* $1000.

Eligibility Requirements: Applicant must be physically disabled; age 17-99 and enrolled or expecting to enroll full-time at a two-year or four-year or technical institution or university. Applicant must be physically disabled. Available to U.S. citizens.

Application Requirements: Application form, essay, recommendations or references, transcript. *Deadline:* April 30.

Contact: Joseph Chapin, Chairman
Elaine Chapin Memorial Scholarship Fund
4367 Humber Circle
St. Louis, MO 63129
Phone: 314-225-7007
E-mail: elainememorial@sbcglobal.net

EPILEPSY FOUNDATION OF IDAHO

http://www.epilepsyidaho.org/

MARK MUSIC MEMORIAL SCHOLARSHIP

One-time award of $500 to promote educational opportunities for Idaho residents with epilepsy. Applicant must be a high school graduate or hold an equivalent certificate, and be either entering or continuing school and pursuing an academic or vocational undergraduate degree or certificate.

Award: Scholarship for use in freshman, sophomore, junior, or senior years; not renewable. *Number:* 1. *Amount:* $500.

Eligibility Requirements: Applicant must be physically disabled; enrolled or expecting to enroll full-time at a two-year or four-year or technical institution or university and resident of Idaho. Applicant must be physically disabled. Available to U.S. citizens.

Application Requirements: Application form, doctor's statement, essay, recommendations or references. *Deadline:* March 15.

Contact: Diane Foote, Client Services and Program Director
Epilepsy Foundation of Idaho
310 West Idaho Street
Boise, ID 83702
E-mail: dfoote@epilepsyidaho.org

FACTOR SUPPORT NETWORK

http://www.factorsupport.com/

MIKE HYLTON AND RON NIEDERMAN MEMORIAL SCHOLARSHIPS

One-time scholarship for men with hemophilia or von Willebrand Disease and their immediate family members. Must be attending or entering a college, university, trade or technical school, either full-time or part-time. Only U.S. residents are eligible.

Award: Scholarship for use in freshman, sophomore, junior, or senior years; not renewable. *Number:* 5. *Amount:* $1000.

Eligibility Requirements: Applicant must be physically disabled; enrolled or expecting to enroll full- or part-time at a two-year or four-year or technical institution or university and male. Applicant must be physically disabled. Available to U.S. citizens.

Application Requirements: Application form, essay, proof of diagnosis from physician, recommendations or references. *Deadline:* April 30.

MILLIE GONZALEZ MEMORIAL SCHOLARSHIP

Scholarship for women with hemophilia or von Willebrand Disease who are attending or entering a college, university, trade or technical school, either full-time or part-time. Must be U.S. resident.

Award: Scholarship for use in freshman, sophomore, junior, senior, or graduate years; not renewable. *Number:* 2. *Amount:* $1000.

Eligibility Requirements: Applicant must be physically disabled; enrolled or expecting to enroll full- or part-time at a two-year or four-year or technical institution or university and female. Applicant must be physically disabled. Available to U.S. citizens.

Application Requirements: Application form, essay, proof of diagnosis from physician, recommendations or references. *Deadline:* April 30.

GEORGIA STUDENT FINANCE COMMISSION

http://www.GAcollege411.org/

GEORGIA TUITION EQUALIZATION GRANT (GTEG)

Award for Georgia residents pursuing undergraduate study at an accredited two- or four-year Georgia private postsecondary institution.

Award: Grant for use in freshman, sophomore, junior, or senior years; not renewable. *Number:* 1–35,000.

Eligibility Requirements: Applicant must be learning disabled; Hispanic; enrolled or expecting to enroll full-time at a two-year or four-year institution or university; resident of Georgia and studying in Georgia. Applicant must be learning disabled. Available to U.S. citizens.

Application Requirements: Application form, application form may be submitted online (http://www.gacollege411.org), social security number.

Contact: Ms. Caylee French, Director, Student Aid Services
Georgia Student Finance Commission
2082 East Exchange Place, Suite 100
Tucker, GA 30084
Phone: 770-724-9244
Fax: 770-724-9249
E-mail: cayleef@gsfc.org

GREAT LAKES HEMOPHILIA FOUNDATION

http://www.glhf.org/

GLHF INDIVIDUAL CLASS SCHOLARSHIP

Scholarship available to members of the Wisconsin bleeding disorder community, individuals with a bleeding disorder and their immediate families. Provides funding assistance for tuition and enrollment fees relevant to continuing education in a non-traditional or non-degree format.

Award: Scholarship for use in freshman, sophomore, junior, or senior years; not renewable. *Number:* 1. *Amount:* up to $500.

Eligibility Requirements: Applicant must be physically disabled; enrolled or expecting to enroll full- or part-time at a two-year or four-year or technical institution or university and resident of Wisconsin. Applicant must be physically disabled. Available to U.S. citizens.

Application Requirements: Application form, essay, recommendations or references, transcript. *Deadline:* varies.

Contact: Karin Koppen, Program Services Coordinator
Great Lakes Hemophilia Foundation
638 North 18 Street, Suite 108
Milwaukee, WI 53233
Phone: 414-257-0200
Fax: 414-257-1225
E-mail: kkoppen@glhf.org

GREAT LAKES HEMOPHILIA FOUNDATION EDUCATION SCHOLARSHIP

This scholarship not only targets the traditional college and vocational students, but also looks at retraining adults with bleeding disorders who are finding it difficult to function in their chosen field because of health complications. It also targets parents of children with bleeding disorders who through career advancement can better meet the financial needs of caring for their child.

Award: Scholarship for use in freshman, sophomore, junior, senior, graduate, or postgraduate years; not renewable. *Number:* 5–6. *Amount:* $500–$2000.

Eligibility Requirements: Applicant must be physically disabled; enrolled or expecting to enroll full- or part-time at a two-year or four-year or technical institution or university and resident of Wisconsin. Applicant must be physically disabled. Available to U.S. citizens.

Application Requirements: Application form, essay, recommendations or references, transcript. *Deadline:* May 1.

Contact: Karin Koppen, Program Services Coordinator
Great Lakes Hemophilia Foundation
638 North 18 Street, Suite 108
Milwaukee, WI 53233
Phone: 414-257-0200
Fax: 414-257-1225
E-mail: kkoppen@glhf.org

HEARING BRIDGES (FORMERLY LEAGUE FOR THE DEAF AND HARD OF HEARING AND EAR FOUNDATION)

http://www.hearingbridges.org/

LINDA COWDEN MEMORIAL SCHOLARSHIP

Non-renewable award offered to deaf and hard of hearing individuals who are attending or planning to attend a trade school, junior college, college, or university and individuals in a program leading to a profession serving the deaf or hard of hearing community. Applicants must live in one of 16 Tennessee counties served by Hearing Bridges (formerly the League for the Deaf and Hard of Hearing and EAR Foundation).

Award: Scholarship for use in freshman, sophomore, junior, or senior years; not renewable. *Number:* 1. *Amount:* $1000.

Eligibility Requirements: Applicant must be hearing impaired; enrolled or expecting to enroll full- or part-time at a two-year or four-year or technical institution or university and resident of Tennessee. Applicant must be hearing impaired. Available to U.S. citizens.

Application Requirements: Application form, audiology repor, essay, interview, personal photograph, recommendations or references, transcript. *Deadline:* March 12.

Contact: Nikki Ringenberg, Director, Marketing and Special Projects
Phone: 615-248-8828
E-mail: nr@hearingbridges.org

MINNIE PEARL SCHOLARSHIP

Renewable scholarship for full-time college students with a severe to profound bilateral hearing loss. Initially, recipients must be mainstreamed high school seniors with at least a 3.0 GPA. Renewals based upon maintenance of 3.0 GPA, with a $500 bonus per year for a cumulative GPA of at least 3.5. The scholarship is available for up to four years of undergraduate study at schools in the United States.

Award: Scholarship for use in freshman, sophomore, junior, or senior years; renewable. *Number:* 1. *Amount:* up to $10,000.

Eligibility Requirements: Applicant must be hearing impaired; high school student and planning to enroll or expecting to enroll full-time at a two-year or four-year or technical institution or university. Applicant must be hearing impaired. Applicant must have 3.0 GPA or higher. Available to U.S. citizens.

Application Requirements: Application form, audiology report, essay, personal photograph, recommendations or references, transcript. *Deadline:* March 12.

Contact: Nikki Ringenberg, Director, Marketing and Special Projects
Phone: 615-248-8828
E-mail: nr@hearingbridges.org

HEMOPHILIA FEDERATION OF AMERICA

ARTISTIC ENCOURAGEMENT GRANT

Grant available for an individual with hemophilia or von Willebrand (VWD). Award may be used for mounting an exhibition of applicant's artistic work, publishing a story/ book or animation, writing a play, holding a recital, or any kind of creative endeavor.

Award: Grant for use in freshman, sophomore, junior, senior, graduate, or postgraduate years; not renewable. *Number:* 1. *Amount:* $1500.

Eligibility Requirements: Applicant must be physically disabled; enrolled or expecting to enroll full- or part-time at a two-year or four-year or technical institution or university and must have an interest in art, theater, or writing. Applicant must be physically disabled. Available to U.S. citizens.

Application Requirements: Application form, brief summary of project, timeline, essay, financial need analysis, portfolio, recommendations or references. *Deadline:* April 30.

HEMOPHILIA FEDERATION OF AMERICA EDUCATIONAL SCHOLARSHIP

One-time scholarship for persons with hemophilia, attending either full-time or part-time in any accredited two- or four-year college, university, or vocation/technical school in the United States.

Award: Scholarship for use in freshman, sophomore, junior, or senior years; not renewable. *Number:* 1–3. *Amount:* $1500.

Eligibility Requirements: Applicant must be physically disabled and enrolled or expecting to enroll full- or part-time at a two-year or four-year or technical institution or university. Applicant must be physically disabled. Available to U.S. citizens.

Application Requirements: Application form, essay, financial need analysis, recommendations or references. *Deadline:* April 30.

HEMOPHILIA FOUNDATION OF MICHIGAN

http://www.hfmich.org/

BILL MCADAM SCHOLARSHIP FUND

Scholarship for a person with hemophilia, including their spouse, partner, child or sibling, planning to attend an accredited college, university, trade, or technical school.

Award: Scholarship for use in freshman, sophomore, junior, senior, graduate, or postgraduate years; not renewable. *Number:* 1. *Amount:* $2000.

Eligibility Requirements: Applicant must be physically disabled and enrolled or expecting to enroll full- or part-time at a two-year or four-year or technical institution or university. Applicant must be physically disabled. Available to U.S. citizens.

Application Requirements: Application form. *Deadline:* May 15.

HEMOPHILIA FOUNDATION OF MICHIGAN ACADEMIC SCHOLARSHIP

Scholarship for individuals or immediate family members, with hemophilia or other inherited bleeding disorder and residing in Michigan. Must be pursuing education in accredited colleges or universities in the United States.

Award: Scholarship for use in freshman, sophomore, junior, or senior years; not renewable. *Number:* 3. *Amount:* $1500–$2000.

Eligibility Requirements: Applicant must be physically disabled and enrolled or expecting to enroll full- or part-time at a two-year or four-year or technical institution or university. Applicant must be physically disabled. Available to U.S. citizens.

Application Requirements: Application form. *Deadline:* March 14.

HEMOPHILIA FOUNDATION OF SOUTHERN CALIFORNIA

http://www.hemosocal.org/

CHRISTOPHER MARK PITKIN MEMORIAL SCHOLARSHIP

Scholarship open to all members of the hemophilia community, including spouses and siblings. Applicants must be pursuing a college or technical/ trade school education.

Award: Scholarship for use in freshman, sophomore, junior, or senior years; not renewable. *Number:* 2. *Amount:* $500–$1000.

Eligibility Requirements: Applicant must be physically disabled and enrolled or expecting to enroll full- or part-time at a two-year or four-year or technical institution or university. Applicant must be physically disabled. Available to U.S. citizens.

Application Requirements: Application form, recommendations or references. *Deadline:* July 25.

HEMOPHILIA HEALTH SERVICES

http://www.hemophiliahealth.com/

HEMOPHILIA HEALTH SERVICES MEMORIAL SCHOLARSHIP

Award to U.S. citizens with hemophilia and related bleeding disorders. Applicants must be high school seniors, college freshmen, sophomores, or juniors. Also eligible to apply are college seniors who are planning to attend graduate school, or students who are already enrolled in graduate school.

Award: Scholarship for use in freshman, sophomore, junior, senior, graduate, or postgraduate years; not renewable. *Number:* 7–10. *Amount:* $1500–$2000.

Eligibility Requirements: Applicant must be physically disabled and enrolled or expecting to enroll full-time at a four-year institution or university. Applicant must be physically disabled. Available to U.S. citizens.

Application Requirements: Application form, essay, financial need analysis, physician certification form, recommendations or references, test scores, transcript. *Deadline:* May 1.

Contact: Sally Johnson, Manager, Operations Support
Phone: 615-850-5175
Fax: 615-352-2588
E-mail: scholarship@hemophiliahealth.com

ILLINOIS COUNCIL OF THE BLIND

http://www.icbonline.org/

FLOYD R. CARGILL SCHOLARSHIP

Award for a visually impaired Illinois resident attending or planning to attend an Illinois college. One-time award of $1000.

Award: Scholarship for use in freshman, sophomore, junior, or senior years; not renewable. *Number:* 1. *Amount:* $1000.

Eligibility Requirements: Applicant must be visually impaired; enrolled or expecting to enroll full-time at a two-year or four-year or

technical institution or university; resident of Illinois and studying in Illinois. Applicant must be visually impaired. Applicant must have 3.5 GPA or higher. Available to U.S. citizens.

Application Requirements: Application form, recommendations or references, test scores, transcript. *Deadline:* July 15.

Contact: Maggie Ulrich, Office Manager
Phone: 217-523-4967
E-mail: icb@icbonline.org

IMMUNE DEFICIENCY FOUNDATION

http://www.primaryimmune.org/

IMMUNE DEFICIENCY FOUNDATION SCHOLARSHIP

One-time award available to individuals diagnosed with a primary immune deficiency disease. Must submit medical verification of diagnosis. Available for study at the undergraduate level at any postsecondary institution. Must be U.S. citizen.

Award: Scholarship for use in freshman, sophomore, junior, or senior years; not renewable. *Number:* 30–40. *Amount:* $750–$2000.

Eligibility Requirements: Applicant must be physically disabled and enrolled or expecting to enroll full- or part-time at a two-year or four-year or technical institution or university. Applicant must be physically disabled. Available to U.S. citizens.

Application Requirements: Application form, driver's license, essay, financial need analysis, medical verification of diagnosis, recommendations or references. *Deadline:* March 31.

Contact: Diana Gill, Director of Patient Programs
Phone: 800-296-4433 Ext. 2545
Fax: 410-321-9165
E-mail: dgill@primaryimmune.org

JEWISH GUILD HEALTHCARE

http://www.guildhealth.org

GUILDSCHOLAR AWARD

Annual scholarship program for college-bound high school students who are legally blind. Applications will be accepted from students at the beginning of the senior year (September. 15th). For more information, visit website at http://www.guildhealth.org/guildscholar

Award: Scholarship for use in freshman year; not renewable. *Number:* up to 16. *Amount:* $10,000–$15,000.

Eligibility Requirements: Applicant must be visually impaired; high school student and planning to enroll or expecting to enroll full-time at a four-year institution or university. Applicant must be visually impaired. Applicant must have 3.0 GPA or higher. Available to U.S. citizens.

Application Requirements: Application form, application form may be submitted online (http://www.guildhealth.org/guildscholar), autobiography, community service, essay, leadership, extracurricular activities, recommendations or references, test scores, transcript. *Deadline:* September 15.

Contact: Mr. Gordon Rovins, Director of Special Programs
Jewish Guild HealthCare
15 West 65th Street
New York, NY 10023
Phone: 212-769-7801
Fax: 212-579-3251
E-mail: guildscholar@guildhealth.org

LAWRENCE MADEIROS MEMORIAL SCHOLARSHIP

http://www.adirondackspintacular.com/

LAWRENCE MADEIROS MEMORIAL SCHOLARSHIP

Award to a high school student with bleeding disorder or other chronic disorder. Applicant must have applied to and been accepted at an accredited college or university and must be graduating high school in the year of the scholarship award.

Award: Scholarship for use in freshman year; not renewable. *Number:* 1. *Amount:* $1000.

Eligibility Requirements: Applicant must be physically disabled; high school student and planning to enroll or expecting to enroll full- or part-time at a two-year or four-year institution or university. Applicant must be physically disabled. Available to U.S. citizens.

Application Requirements: Application form, interview. *Deadline:* June 1.

Contact: Carol Madeiros, Scholarship Committee
Lawrence Madeiros Memorial Scholarship
PO Box 11
Mayfield, NY 12117
Phone: 518-661-6005
Fax: 518-863-6126
E-mail: carol@adirondackspintacular.com

LEARNING ALLY

http://www.learningally.org/

MARION HUBER LEARNING THROUGH LISTENING AWARDS

• *See page 525*

MARY P. OENSLAGER SCHOLASTIC ACHIEVEMENT AWARDS

• *See page 525*

LILLY REINTEGRATION PROGRAMS

http://www.reintegration.com/

LILLY REINTEGRATION SCHOLARSHIP

Scholarships available to students diagnosed with schizophrenia, bipolar, schizophreniform, or a schizoaffective disorder. Must be currently receiving medical treatment for the disease, including medications and psychiatric follow-up. Must also be U.S. citizen and actively involved in rehabilitative or reintegration efforts. Applicants must be at least 18 years of age.

Award: Scholarship for use in freshman, sophomore, junior, senior, graduate, or postgraduate years; not renewable. *Number:* 70–100. *Amount:* $2500–$5000.

Eligibility Requirements: Applicant must be physically disabled and enrolled or expecting to enroll full- or part-time at a two-year or four-year or technical institution or university. Applicant must be physically disabled. Available to U.S. citizens.

Application Requirements: Application form, essay, recommendations or references, transcript. *Deadline:* January 25.

NATIONAL CENTER FOR LEARNING DISABILITIES, INC.

http://www.ld.org/

ANNE FORD & ALLEGRA FORD SCHOLARSHIP

Award of $10,000 given to two high school seniors of high merit with an identified learning disability who is pursuing a college degree. The ideal candidate is a person who has faced the challenges of having a learning disability and who, through perseverance and academic endeavor, has created a life of purpose and achievement.

Award: Scholarship for use in freshman, sophomore, junior, or senior years; not renewable. *Number:* 2. *Amount:* $10,000.

Eligibility Requirements: Applicant must be learning disabled; high school student and planning to enroll or expecting to enroll full-time at a four-year institution or university. Applicant must be learning disabled. Applicant must have 3.0 GPA or higher. Available to U.S. citizens.

Application Requirements: Application form, essay, financial need analysis, recommendations or references, test scores, transcript. *Deadline:* December 31.

Contact: Catherine Boswell, Coordinator
National Center for Learning Disabilities, Inc.
381 Park Avenue South, Suite 1401
New York, NY 10016-8806
Phone: 646-616-1233
Fax: 212-545-9665
E-mail: afscholarship@ncld.org

NATIONAL COUNCIL OF JEWISH WOMEN NEW YORK SECTION

http://www.ncjwny.org/

JACKSON-STRICKS SCHOLARSHIP

Scholarship provides financial aid to a physically challenged person for academic study or vocational training that leads to independent living.

Award: Scholarship for use in sophomore, junior, senior, graduate, or postgraduate years; not renewable. *Number:* 1–7. *Amount:* $1500–$2500.

Eligibility Requirements: Applicant must be physically disabled; enrolled or expecting to enroll full- or part-time at a two-year or four-year institution or university; resident of New York and studying in New York. Applicant must be physically disabled. Available to U.S. citizens.

Application Requirements: Application form, essay, recommendations or references, transcript. *Deadline:* April 15.

NATIONAL FEDERATION OF BLIND OF MISSOURI

http://www.nfbmo.org/

NATIONAL FEDERATION OF THE BLIND OF MISSOURI SCHOLARSHIPS TO LEGALLY BLIND STUDENTS

Awards are based on achievement, commitment to community, and financial need. Recipients must be legally blind. Amount of money each year available for program will vary.

Award: Scholarship for use in freshman, sophomore, junior, senior, or graduate years; not renewable. *Number:* up to 3. *Amount:* $500–$1500.

Eligibility Requirements: Applicant must be visually impaired; enrolled or expecting to enroll full- or part-time at a two-year or four-year or technical institution or university; resident of Missouri and studying in Missouri. Applicant must be visually impaired. Available to U.S. citizens.

Application Requirements: Application form, essay, financial need analysis, interview, recommendations or references, transcript. *Deadline:* February 1.

Contact: Ms. Shelia Wright, Chair, NFB of Missouri Scholarship Program
National Federation of Blind of Missouri
7928 NW Milrey Drive
Kansas City, MO 64152-2143
Phone: 816-741-6402
Fax: 816-746-1748
E-mail: firstvice.president@nfbmo.org

NATIONAL FEDERATION OF THE BLIND (NFB)

http://www.nfb.org/scholarships

CHARLES AND MELVA T. OWEN MEMORIAL SCHOLARSHIP FOR $3,000

Merit-based scholarship requires academic excellence and leadership, permanent residency in United States/Puerto Rico, and accredited institution's degree program (in US/PR) directed toward financial independence (excludes degrees in religious studies or solely for cultural education). Winner assisted to attend NFB annual convention to receive this award. Membership not required.

Award: Scholarship for use in freshman, sophomore, junior, senior, graduate, or postgraduate years; not renewable. *Number:* 1. *Amount:* $3000.

Eligibility Requirements: Applicant must be visually impaired and enrolled or expecting to enroll full- or part-time at a two-year or four-year institution or university. Applicant must be visually impaired. Available to U.S. and non-U.S. citizens.

Application Requirements: Application form, essay, interview, proof of legal blindness in both eyes, recommendations or references, test scores, transcript. *Deadline:* March 31.

Contact: Ms. Patti Chang, Chairperson, NFB Scholarship Committee
National Federation of the Blind (NFB)
200 East Wells Street
Baltimore, MD 21230
Phone: 410-659-9314 Ext. 2415
E-mail: scholarships@nfb.org

CHARLES AND MELVA T. OWEN SCHOLARSHIP FOR $10,000

Merit-based scholarship requires academic excellence and leadership, permanent residency in United States/Puerto Rico, and accredited institution's degree program (in US/PR) directed toward financial independence (excludes degrees in religious studies or solely for cultural education). Winner assisted to attend NFB annual convention to receive this award. Membership not required.

Award: Scholarship for use in freshman, sophomore, junior, senior, graduate, or postgraduate years; not renewable. *Number:* 1. *Amount:* $10,000.

Eligibility Requirements: Applicant must be visually impaired and enrolled or expecting to enroll full- or part-time at a two-year or four-year institution or university. Applicant must be visually impaired. Available to U.S. and non-U.S. citizens.

Application Requirements: Application form, essay, interview, proof of legal blindness in both eyes, recommendations or references, test scores, transcript. *Deadline:* March 31.

Contact: Ms. Patti Chang, Chairperson, NFB Scholarship Committee
National Federation of the Blind (NFB)
200 East Wells Street
Baltimore, MD 21230
Phone: 410-659-9314 Ext. 2415
E-mail: scholarships@nfb.org

KENNETH JERNIGAN SCHOLARSHIP FOR $12,000

$12,000 award to honor the top blind college student residing in and attending an accredited institution in the US or Puerto Rico. Winner receives financial assistance to attend NFB convention to receive scholarship.

Award: Scholarship for use in freshman, sophomore, junior, senior, graduate, or postgraduate years; not renewable. *Number:* 1. *Amount:* $12,000.

Eligibility Requirements: Applicant must be visually impaired and enrolled or expecting to enroll full- or part-time at a two-year or four-year institution or university. Applicant must be visually impaired. Available to U.S. and non-U.S. citizens.

Application Requirements: Application form, essay, interview, proof of legal blindness, recommendations or references, test scores, transcript. *Deadline:* March 31.

Contact: Ms. Patti Chang, Chairperson
National Federation of the Blind (NFB)
NFB Scholarship Committee
200 East Wells Street
Baltimore, MD 21230
Phone: 410-659-9314 Ext. 2415
E-mail: scholarships@nfb.org

LARRY STREETER MEMORIAL SCHOLARSHIP FOR $3,000

$3000 scholarship for legally blind, permanent residents of the U.S. or Puerto Rico, pursuing a postsecondary degree at an accredited institution in U.S. or PR. Created to assist blind students to elevate their quality of life, equipping them to be active, productive participants in their family, community, and the workplace.

Award: Scholarship for use in freshman, sophomore, junior, or senior years; not renewable. *Number:* 1. *Amount:* $3000.

Eligibility Requirements: Applicant must be visually impaired and enrolled or expecting to enroll full- or part-time at a four-year institution or university. Applicant must be visually impaired. Available to U.S. citizens.

Application Requirements: Application form, essay, financial need analysis, proof of blindness in both eyes, transcript. *Deadline:* March 31.

Contact: Ms. Patti Chang, Chairperson, NFB Scholarship Program
National Federation of the Blind (NFB)
200 East Wells Street
Baltimore, MD 21230
Phone: 410-659-9314 Ext. 2415
E-mail: scholarships@nfb.org

NATIONAL FEDERATION OF THE BLIND SCHOLARSHIP FOR $3,000

$3000 scholarship for legally blind, permanent residents of the U.S. or Puerto Rico, pursuing a postsecondary degree at an accredited institution in U.S. or PR. Selection is merit-based on academic excellence and leadership. With NFB assistance, winner attends NFB annual convention to receive award. Membership in NFB is not required.

Award: Scholarship for use in freshman, sophomore, junior, senior, graduate, or postgraduate years; not renewable. *Number:* 20. *Amount:* $3000.

Eligibility Requirements: Applicant must be visually impaired and enrolled or expecting to enroll full- or part-time at a two-year or four-year institution or university. Applicant must be visually impaired. Available to U.S. and non-U.S. citizens.

Application Requirements: Application form, essay, interview, proof of legal blindness in both eyes, recommendations or references, test scores, transcript. *Deadline:* March 31.

Contact: Ms. Patti Chang, Chairperson, Scholarship Committee
National Federation of the Blind (NFB)
200 East Wells Street
Baltimore, MD 21230
Phone: 410-659-9314 Ext. 2415
E-mail: scholarships@nfb.org

NATIONAL FEDERATION OF THE BLIND SCHOLARSHIP FOR $7,000

$7000 scholarship for legally blind, permanent residents of the U.S. or Puerto Rico, pursuing a postsecondary degree at an accredited institution in U.S. or PR. Selection is merit-based on academic excellence and leadership. With NFB assistance, winner attends NFB annual convention to receive award. Membership in NFB is not required.

Award: Scholarship for use in freshman, sophomore, junior, senior, graduate, or postgraduate years; not renewable. *Number:* 2. *Amount:* $7000.

Eligibility Requirements: Applicant must be visually impaired and enrolled or expecting to enroll full- or part-time at a two-year or four-year institution or university. Applicant must be visually impaired. Available to U.S. and non-U.S. citizens.

Application Requirements: Application form, essay, interview, proof of legal blindness in both eyes, recommendations or references, test scores, transcript. *Deadline:* March 31.

Contact: Ms. Patti Chang, Chairperson, NFB Scholarship Committee
National Federation of the Blind (NFB)
200 East Wells Street
Baltimore, MD 21230
Phone: 410-659-9314 Ext. 2415
E-mail: scholarships@nfb.org

NFB SCHOLARSHIP FOR $5,000

$5000 scholarship for legally blind, permanent residents of the U.S. or Puerto Rico, pursuing a postsecondary degree at an accredited institution in U.S. or PR. Selection is merit-based on academic excellence and leadership. With NFB assistance, winner attends NFB annual convention to receive award. Membership in NFB is not required.

Award: Scholarship for use in freshman, sophomore, junior, senior, graduate, or postgraduate years; not renewable. *Number:* 4. *Amount:* $5000.

Eligibility Requirements: Applicant must be visually impaired and enrolled or expecting to enroll full- or part-time at a two-year or four-year institution or university. Applicant must be visually impaired. Available to U.S. and non-U.S. citizens.

Application Requirements: Application form, essay, interview, proof of legal blindness in both eyes, recommendations or references, test scores, transcript. *Deadline:* March 31.

Contact: Ms. Patti Chang, Chairperson, NFB Scholarship Program
National Federation of the Blind (NFB)
200 East Wells Street
Baltimore, MD 21230
Phone: 410-659-9314 Ext. 2415
E-mail: scholarships@nfb.org

NATIONAL FEDERATION OF THE BLIND OF CALIFORNIA

http://www.nfbcal.org/

GERALD DRAKE MEMORIAL SCHOLARSHIP

One-time award for legally blind students pursuing an undergraduate or graduate degree. Must be a California resident and full-time student.

Award: Scholarship for use in freshman, sophomore, junior, senior, or graduate years; not renewable. *Number:* up to 5. *Amount:* $1500.

Eligibility Requirements: Applicant must be visually impaired; enrolled or expecting to enroll full-time at a four-year institution or university and resident of California. Applicant must be visually impaired. Available to U.S. and non-U.S. citizens.

Application Requirements: Application form. *Deadline:* March 31.

Contact: Robert Stigile, President
Phone: 818-342-6524
Fax: 818-344-7930
E-mail: nfbcal@yahoo.com

JULIE LANDUCCI SCHOLARSHIP

Award for legally blind students pursuing an undergraduate or graduate degree. Must be a California resident and full-time student. Award available to U.S. citizens.

Award: Scholarship for use in freshman, sophomore, junior, senior, or graduate years; renewable. *Number:* 1. *Amount:* up to $2000.

Eligibility Requirements: Applicant must be visually impaired; enrolled or expecting to enroll full-time at a four-year institution or university and resident of California. Applicant must be visually impaired. Available to U.S. citizens.

Application Requirements: Application form. *Deadline:* March 31.

Contact: Robert Stigile, President
Phone: 818-342-6524
Fax: 818-344-7930
E-mail: nfbcal@yahoo.com

LA VYRL "PINKY" JOHNSON MEMORIAL SCHOLARSHIP

One-time award up to $2000 for legally blind students pursuing an undergraduate or graduate degree. Must be a California resident and full-time student.

Award: Scholarship for use in freshman, sophomore, junior, senior, or graduate years; renewable. *Number:* 1. *Amount:* $2000.

Eligibility Requirements: Applicant must be visually impaired; enrolled or expecting to enroll full-time at a four-year institution or university and resident of California. Applicant must be visually impaired. Available to U.S. citizens.

Application Requirements: Application form. *Deadline:* March 31.

Contact: Robert Stigile, President
Phone: 818-342-6524
Fax: 818-344-7930
E-mail: nfbcal@yahoo.com

LAWRENCE "MUZZY" MARCELINO MEMORIAL SCHOLARSHIP

Scholarship provides financial assistance for graduate or undergraduate education to blind students in California. Any legally blind student may apply for a scholarship but must attend the convention of the National Federation of the Blind of California. Selection is based first on academic merit and second on financial need.

Award: Scholarship for use in freshman, sophomore, junior, senior, or graduate years; renewable. *Number:* up to 4. *Amount:* $1500.

Eligibility Requirements: Applicant must be visually impaired; enrolled or expecting to enroll full-time at a four-year institution or university and resident of California. Applicant must be visually impaired. Available to U.S. citizens.

Application Requirements: Application form. *Deadline:* March 15.

Contact: Robert Stigile, President
Phone: 818-342-6524
Fax: 818-344-7930
E-mail: nfbcal@yahoo.com

NATIONAL FEDERATION OF THE BLIND OF CALIFORNIA MERIT SCHOLARSHIPS

Scholarships to qualified blind students pursuing undergraduate or graduate studies in order to achieve an academic degree. This opportunity is also available to high school seniors preparing to enter undergraduate programs.

Award: Scholarship for use in freshman, sophomore, junior, senior, or graduate years; renewable. *Number:* up to 5. *Amount:* $1000.

Eligibility Requirements: Applicant must be visually impaired; enrolled or expecting to enroll full-time at a four-year institution or university and resident of California. Applicant must be visually impaired. Available to U.S. citizens.

Application Requirements: Application form. *Deadline:* March 15.

Contact: Robert Stigile, President
Phone: 818-342-6524
Fax: 818-344-7930
E-mail: nfbcal@yahoo.com

NATIONAL KIDNEY FOUNDATION OF INDIANA INC.

http://www.kidneyindiana.org/

LARRY SMOCK SCHOLARSHIP

Scholarship provides financial assistance for kidney dialysis and transplant patients to pursue post-secondary education. Applicant must be resident of Indiana over the age of 18. Must have a high school diploma or its equivalent.

Award: Scholarship for use in freshman, sophomore, junior, or senior years; renewable. *Number:* 2–6. *Amount:* $500–$1000.

Eligibility Requirements: Applicant must be physically disabled; enrolled or expecting to enroll full- or part-time at a two-year or four-year or technical institution or university and resident of Indiana. Applicant must be physically disabled. Available to U.S. citizens.

Application Requirements: Application form, recommendations or references, transcript.

Contact: Nicki Howard, Public Health Coordinator
National Kidney Foundation of Indiana Inc.
911 East 86th Street, Suite 100
Indianapolis, IN 46240-1840
Phone: 317-722-5640
Fax: 317-722-5650
E-mail: nhoward@kidneyindiana.org

NATIONAL MULTIPLE SCLEROSIS SOCIETY–MID AMERICA CHAPTER

http://www.msmidamerica.org/

NATIONAL MULTIPLE SCLEROSIS SOCIETY MID AMERICA CHAPTER SCHOLARSHIP

Scholarships available from $1000 to $3000 to high school seniors and graduates (or GED) with MS, or who are children of people with MS. Must be attending a postsecondary school for the first time.

Award: Scholarship for use in freshman, sophomore, junior, or senior years; not renewable. *Number:* 100. *Amount:* $1000–$3000.

Eligibility Requirements: Applicant must be physically disabled and enrolled or expecting to enroll full- or part-time at a two-year or four-year or technical institution or university. Applicant must be physically disabled. Available to U.S. citizens.

Application Requirements: Application form, driver's license, essay, financial need analysis, recommendations or references, test scores, transcript. *Deadline:* January 15.

NATIONAL PKU NEWS

http://www.pkunews.org/

ROBERT GUTHRIE PKU SCHOLARSHIP AND AWARDS

Scholarship for persons with phenylketonuria (PKU) who are on a special diet for PKU treatment. Award is for full-time or part-time study at any accredited U.S. institution. Up to 8 scholarships of between $500 and $3500 are granted.

Award: Scholarship for use in freshman, sophomore, junior, or senior years; not renewable. *Number:* 4–8. *Amount:* $500–$3500.

Eligibility Requirements: Applicant must be physically disabled and enrolled or expecting to enroll full- or part-time at a two-year or four-year or technical institution or university. Applicant must be physically disabled. Available to U.S. and non-U.S. citizens.

Application Requirements: Application form, essay, personal photograph, recommendations or references, resume, test scores, transcript. *Deadline:* October 15.

Contact: Virginia Schuett, Director
 Phone: 206-525-8140
 E-mail: schuett@pkunews.org

NEW YORK STATE GRANGE

http://www.nysgrange.org/

CAROLINE KARK AWARD
• *See page 530*

NORTH CAROLINA DIVISION OF SERVICES FOR THE BLIND

http://www.ncdhhs.gov/

NORTH CAROLINA DIVISION OF SERVICES FOR THE BLIND REHABILITATION SERVICES

Financial assistance is available for North Carolina residents who are blind or visually impaired and who require vocational rehabilitation to help find employment. Tuition and other assistance provided based on need. Open to U.S. citizens and legal residents of United States. Applicants goal must be to work after receiving vocational services. To apply, contact the local DSB office and apply for vocational rehabilitation services.

Award: Scholarship for use in freshman, sophomore, junior, or senior years; renewable.

Eligibility Requirements: Applicant must be visually impaired; enrolled or expecting to enroll full-time at a two-year or four-year or technical institution or university and resident of North Carolina. Applicant must be visually impaired. Available to U.S. citizens.

Application Requirements: Application form, financial need analysis, interview, proof of eligibility. *Deadline:* continuous.

Contact: JoAnn Strader, Chief of Rehabilitation Field Services
 North Carolina Division of Services for the Blind
 2601 Mail Service Center
 Raleigh, NC 27699-2601
 Phone: 919-733-9700
 Fax: 919-715-8771
 E-mail: joann.strader@ncmail.net

NORTH CAROLINA DIVISION OF VOCATIONAL REHABILITATION SERVICES

http://www.dhhs.state.nc.us/

TRAINING SUPPORT FOR YOUTH WITH DISABILITIES

Public service program that helps persons with disabilities obtain competitive employment. To qualify, student must have a mental, physical, or learning disability that is an impediment to employment. A Rehabilitation Counselor along with the eligible student individually develops a rehabilitation program to achieve an employment outcome which requires post secondary training. Financial assistance is based on NC Division of Vocational Rehabilitation demonstrated financial need and type of program in which the student enrolls.

Award: Grant for use in freshman, sophomore, junior, or senior years; renewable.

Eligibility Requirements: Applicant must be hearing impaired, learning disabled, physically disabled, or visually impaired; enrolled or expecting to enroll full- or part-time at a two-year or four-year or technical institution or university and resident of North Carolina. Applicant must be hearing impaired, learning disabled, physically disabled, or visually impaired. Available to U.S. citizens.

Application Requirements: Application form, financial need analysis, interview, medical and psychological records, must be under an Individualized Plan for Employment, test scores, transcript. *Deadline:* continuous.

Contact: Alice Farrar, Program Specialist for Transition
 Phone: 919-855-3572
 E-mail: alice.farrar@dhhs.nc.gov

NUFACTOR

http://www.nufactor.com/

ERIC DOSTIE MEMORIAL COLLEGE SCHOLARSHIP

Scholarship for persons or family members with hemophilia or other bleeding disorder, enrolled full-time in an accredited college. Must be a U.S. citizen.

Award: Scholarship for use in freshman, sophomore, junior, senior, or graduate years; not renewable. *Number:* 10. *Amount:* $1000.

Eligibility Requirements: Applicant must be physically disabled and enrolled or expecting to enroll full-time at a two-year or four-year institution or university. Applicant must be physically disabled. Applicant must have 2.5 GPA or higher. Available to U.S. citizens.

Application Requirements: Application form, essay, personal photograph, recommendations or references, request application after November 1, test scores, transcript. *Deadline:* March 1.

OPTIMIST INTERNATIONAL FOUNDATION

http://www.optimist.org/

COMMUNICATION CONTEST FOR THE DEAF AND HARD OF HEARING

College scholarship (district level) for young people through grade twelve in the U.S. and Canada, to CEGEP in Quebec and grade thirteen in the Caribbean. Students interested in participating must submit the results of an audiogram conducted no longer than twenty-four months prior to the date of the contest from a qualified audiologist. Students must be certified to have a hearing loss of forty decibels or more and supported by the audiogram to be eligible to compete. Students attending either public school or schools providing special services are eligible to enter if criteria are met.

Award: Scholarship for use in freshman, sophomore, junior, or senior years; not renewable. *Number:* 1–30. *Amount:* up to $2500.

Eligibility Requirements: Applicant must be hearing impaired and enrolled or expecting to enroll full- or part-time at a two-year or four-year or technical institution or university. Applicant must be hearing impaired. Available to U.S. and Canadian citizens.

Application Requirements: Application form, entry in a contest, self-addressed stamped envelope with application, speech/presentation, audiogram. *Deadline:* varies.

Contact: Danielle Baugher, Director of International Programs
 Optimist International Foundation
 4494 Lindell Boulevard
 St. Louis, MO 63108
 Phone: 800-500-8130
 Fax: 314-371-6006
 E-mail: programs@optimist.org

OREGON COMMUNITY FOUNDATION

http://www.oregoncf.org/

HARRY LUDWIG SCHOLARSHIP FUND

Scholarship for visually impaired students for use in the pursuit of a postsecondary education at a college or university. For full-time students only.

Award: Scholarship for use in freshman, sophomore, junior, or senior years; renewable. *Number:* 1–3. *Amount:* $500–$5000.

Eligibility Requirements: Applicant must be visually impaired and enrolled or expecting to enroll full-time at a four-year institution or university. Applicant must be visually impaired. Available to U.S. citizens.

Application Requirements: Application form, recommendations or references. *Deadline:* March 1.

Contact: Dianne Causey, Program Associate for Scholarships and
Grants
Phone: 503-227-6846 Ext. 1418
E-mail: dcausey@oregoncf.org

OREGON STUDENT ASSISTANCE COMMISSION

http://www.GetCollegeFunds.org/

HARRY LUDWIG MEMORIAL SCHOLARSHIP

Award for visually-impaired Oregon residents planning to enroll full-time
in undergraduate or graduate studies at an Oregon college or university.
Must document visual impairment with a letter from a physician. Must
reapply for award annually. FAFSA is required.

Award: Scholarship for use in freshman, sophomore, junior, senior, or
graduate years; not renewable.

Eligibility Requirements: Applicant must be visually impaired;
enrolled or expecting to enroll full-time at a two-year or four-year
institution or university; resident of Oregon and studying in Oregon.
Applicant must be visually impaired. Available to U.S. citizens.

Application Requirements: Application form, documentation of
visual impairment, FAFSA, essay, financial need analysis,
recommendations or references, transcript. *Deadline:* March 1.

SALEM FOUNDATION ANSEL & MARIE SOLIE SCHOLARSHIP

Award is available to visually impaired Oregon residents planning to
enroll in full-time undergraduate studies. Must be a U.S. citizen. Award
may be used only at a four-year, nonprofit Oregon college or university.
Must submit proof of visual impairment.

Award: Scholarship for use in freshman, sophomore, junior, or senior
years; not renewable.

Eligibility Requirements: Applicant must be visually impaired;
enrolled or expecting to enroll full-time at a four-year institution or
university; resident of Oregon and studying in Oregon. Applicant must be
visually impaired. Available to U.S. citizens.

Application Requirements: Application form, proof of visual
impairment, FAFSA. *Deadline:* March 1.

P. BUCKLEY MOSS FOUNDATION

http://www.mossfoundation.org/

ANNE AND MATT HARBISON SCHOLARSHIP

Scholarship of up to $1500 to one high school senior with a certified
language-related learning difference who is pursuing postsecondary
education.

Award: Scholarship for use in freshman, sophomore, junior, or senior
years; renewable. *Number:* 1. *Amount:* $1500.

Eligibility Requirements: Applicant must be learning disabled; high
school student; age 17-18 and planning to enroll or expecting to enroll
full- or part-time at a four-year institution or university. Applicant must
be learning disabled. Applicant must have 2.5 GPA or higher. Available
to U.S. citizens.

Application Requirements: Application form, essay, transcript.
Deadline: March 31.

PFIZER

http://www.epilepsy-scholarship.com/

PFIZER EPILEPSY SCHOLARSHIP AWARD

Award for students with epilepsy who excel academically and in
extracurricular activities. Must be pursuing an undergraduate degree or
be a college senior entering first year of graduate school. Must be under
the care of a physician for epilepsy to qualify.

Award: Scholarship for use in freshman, sophomore, junior, senior, or
graduate years; not renewable. *Number:* 40. *Amount:* up to $2000.

Eligibility Requirements: Applicant must be physically disabled and
enrolled or expecting to enroll full- or part-time at a two-year or four-year
or technical institution or university. Applicant must be physically
disabled. Available to U.S. citizens.

Application Requirements: Application form, essay,
recommendations or references, test scores, transcript. *Deadline:*
June 15.

Contact: Love Vieira, Coordinator
Pfizer
Pfizer Epilepsy Scholarship Award, c/o AdelphiEden Health
Communications
New York, NY 10003
Phone: 800-292-7373

RYU FAMILY FOUNDATION, INC.

http://www.seolbong.org/

SEOL BONG SCHOLARSHIP

One-time award to support and advance education and research. Must be
Korean residing in DE, PA, NJ, NY, CT, VT, RI, NH, MA, or ME.
Minimum 3.5 GPA required.

Award: Scholarship for use in freshman, sophomore, junior, senior, or
graduate years; not renewable. *Number:* 21. *Amount:* $2000–$3000.

Eligibility Requirements: Applicant must be learning disabled; of
Korean heritage; Asian/Pacific Islander; enrolled or expecting to enroll
full-time at a four-year institution or university; resident of Connecticut,
Delaware, Maine, Massachusetts, New Hampshire, New Jersey, New
York, Pennsylvania, Rhode Island, Vermont and studying in Connecticut,
Delaware, Maine, Massachusetts, New Hampshire, New Jersey, New
York, Pennsylvania, Rhode Island, Vermont. Applicant must be learning
disabled. Applicant must have 3.5 GPA or higher. Available to U.S. and
non-Canadian citizens.

Application Requirements: Application form, essay, financial need
analysis, personal photograph, portfolio, recommendations or references,
resume, test scores, transcript. *Deadline:* November 15.

Contact: Jenny Kang, Scholarship Secretary
Phone: 973-692-9696 Ext. 20
E-mail: jennyk@toplineus.com

SERTOMA, INC.

http://www.sertoma.org/

SERTOMA SCHOLARSHIP FOR STUDENTS WHO ARE HARD OF HEARING OR DEAF

Applicants must have a minimum of 40dB bilateral hearing loss, as
evidenced on audiogram by an SRT of 40dB or greater in both ears. Must
have a minimum cumulative 3.2 GPA on a 4.0 un-weighted scale.

Award: Scholarship for use in freshman, sophomore, junior, or senior
years; not renewable. *Number:* 45. *Amount:* $1000.

Eligibility Requirements: Applicant must be hearing impaired and
enrolled or expecting to enroll full-time at a four-year institution or
university. Applicant must be hearing impaired. Applicant must have 3.0
GPA or higher. Available to U.S. citizens.

Application Requirements: Application form, audiogram (proof of
hearing loss), recommendations or references, transcript. *Deadline:*
May 1.

Contact: Mrs. Laura Hanavan, Development and Mission Activities
Manager
Phone: 816-333-8300
E-mail: LHanavan@sertomahq.org

SISTER KENNY REHABILITATION INSTITUTE

http://www.allina.com/ahs/ski.nsf

INTERNATIONAL ART SHOW FOR ARTISTS WITH DISABILITIES

One-time award for artwork submitted by artists of any age with visual,
hearing, physical, or learning impairment. Contact Sister Kenny
Rehabilitation Institute for show information. This is a one-time prize,
not an academic scholarship.

Award: Prize for use in freshman, sophomore, junior, senior, or graduate
years; not renewable. *Number:* 25–70. *Amount:* $25–$500.

Eligibility Requirements: Applicant must be hearing impaired,
learning disabled, physically disabled, or visually impaired; enrolled or

expecting to enroll full- or part-time at a four-year institution or university and must have an interest in art. Applicant must be hearing impaired, learning disabled, physically disabled, or visually impaired. Available to U.S. and non-U.S. citizens.

Application Requirements: Application form, entry in a contest. *Deadline:* March 17.

Contact: Laura Swift, Administrative Assistant
  Sister Kenny Rehabilitation Institute
  800 East 28th Street
  Minneapolis, MN 55407-3799
  Phone: 612-863-4466
  Fax: 612-863-8942
  E-mail: laura.swift@allina.com

SPINA BIFIDA ASSOCIATION OF AMERICA

http://www.sbaa.org/

SBAA ONE-YEAR SCHOLARSHIP

Scholarship available for a student with spina bifida who has applied for, enrolled in, or accepted by a junior college, approved trade, vocational or business school. Applicant must be high school graduate or possess a GED.

Award: Scholarship for use in freshman year; not renewable. *Number:* up to 5. *Amount:* $2000.

Eligibility Requirements: Applicant must be physically disabled and enrolled or expecting to enroll full-time at a four-year or technical institution or university. Applicant must be physically disabled. Available to U.S. citizens.

Application Requirements: Application form, physician's statement of disability, transcript. *Deadline:* March 2.

Contact: Caroline Alston, Director of Programs
  Phone: 202-944-3285
  Fax: 202-944-3295
  E-mail: sbaa@sbaa.org

SPINA BIFIDA ASSOCIATION OF AMERICA EDUCATIONAL SCHOLARSHIP

One-time award to enhance opportunities for persons born with spina bifida to achieve their full potential through higher education. Minimum 2.5 GPA required. Must submit doctor's statement of disability and acceptance letter from college/university/school.

Award: Scholarship for use in freshman, sophomore, junior, or senior years; not renewable. *Amount:* $1000.

Eligibility Requirements: Applicant must be physically disabled and enrolled or expecting to enroll full-time at a four-year or technical institution or university. Applicant must be physically disabled. Applicant must have 2.5 GPA or higher. Available to U.S. citizens.

Application Requirements: Application form, essay, financial need analysis, recommendations or references, statement of disability, test scores, transcript. *Deadline:* March 2.

Contact: Caroline Alston, Director of Programs
  Phone: 202-944-3285
  Fax: 202-944-3295
  E-mail: sbaa@sbaa.org

SPINA BIFIDA ASSOCIATION OF AMERICA FOUR-YEAR SCHOLARSHIP FUND

Renewable award for a young person born with spina bifida to achieve full potential through higher education, and attend a four-year college otherwise outside of their family's financial reach. Open to U.S. citizens.

Award: Scholarship for use in freshman, sophomore, junior, or senior years; renewable. *Number:* 1. *Amount:* $5000.

Eligibility Requirements: Applicant must be physically disabled and enrolled or expecting to enroll full-time at a four-year institution or university. Applicant must be physically disabled. Available to U.S. citizens.

Application Requirements: Application form, essay, financial need analysis, physician's statement of disability, recommendations or references, test scores, transcript. *Deadline:* March 2.

Contact: Caroline Alston, Director of Programs
  Phone: 202-944-3285
  Fax: 202-944-3295
  E-mail: sbaa@sbaa.org

TPA SCHOLARSHIP TRUST FOR THE DEAF AND NEAR DEAF

http://www.tpahq.org/

TRAVELERS PROTECTIVE ASSOCIATION SCHOLARSHIP TRUST FOR THE HEARING IMPAIRED

Scholarships are awarded to deaf or hearing-impaired persons of any age, race, or religion for specialized education, mechanical devices, or medical or specialized treatment. Based on financial need.

Award: Scholarship for use in freshman, sophomore, junior, or senior years; not renewable. *Amount:* $200–$600.

Eligibility Requirements: Applicant must be hearing impaired and enrolled or expecting to enroll full- or part-time at a two-year or four-year or technical institution or university. Applicant must be hearing impaired. Available to U.S. citizens.

Application Requirements: Application form, financial need analysis, personal photograph. *Deadline:* March 1.

Contact: Brian Schulte, Chief Administrative Officer
  TPA Scholarship Trust for the Deaf and Near Deaf
  3755 Lindell Boulevard
  St. Louis, MO 63108
  Phone: 314-371-0533
  Fax: 314-371-0537

UCB, INC.

http://www.ucb.com/

UCB CROHN'S SCHOLARSHIP PROGRAM

Awards twenty one-time scholarships of up to $5000 each to people diagnosed with Crohn's disease who are entering college or are currently enrolled in college or to adults of any age returning to school. Students of all ages are welcome to apply, and the scholarship can be used for a two-year, four-year, trade or specialty school.

Award: Scholarship for use in freshman, sophomore, junior, senior, or graduate years; not renewable. *Number:* up to 20. *Amount:* up to $5000.

Eligibility Requirements: Applicant must be physically disabled and enrolled or expecting to enroll full- or part-time at a two-year or four-year or technical institution or university. Applicant must be physically disabled. Available to U.S. citizens.

Application Requirements: Application form, application form may be submitted online (http://www.crohnsandme.com), essay, medical certificate, personal photograph, recommendations or references, self-addressed stamped envelope with application, test scores, transcript. *Deadline:* July 27.

UCB FAMILY EPILEPSY SCHOLARSHIP

Awards twenty-five one-time scholarships of up to $5000 each to people diagnosed with epilepsy and their immediate family members (parents, spouses, children or siblings) and caregivers who are entering college or are currently enrolled in college or to adults of any age returning to school. Students of all ages are welcome to apply and the scholarship can be used for a two-year, four-year, trade or specialty school.

Award: Scholarship for use in freshman, sophomore, junior, senior, or graduate years; not renewable. *Number:* up to 25. *Amount:* up to $5000.

Eligibility Requirements: Applicant must be physically disabled and enrolled or expecting to enroll full- or part-time at a two-year or four-year or technical institution or university. Applicant must be physically disabled. Available to U.S. citizens.

Application Requirements: Application form, essay, personal photograph, Physician's letter and medical history form, recommendations or references, test scores, transcript. *Deadline:* May 15.

UCB RA SCHOLARSHIP

Awards fifteen one-time scholarships of up to $5000 each to people diagnosed with rheumatoid arthritis who are entering college or are currently enrolled in college or to adults of any age returning to school. Students of all ages are welcome to apply and the scholarship can be used for a two-year, four-year, trade or specialty school.

Award: Scholarship for use in freshman, sophomore, junior, senior, or graduate years; not renewable. *Number:* up to 15. *Amount:* up to $5000.

Eligibility Requirements: Applicant must be physically disabled and enrolled or expecting to enroll full- or part-time at a two-year or four-year or technical institution or university. Applicant must be physically disabled. Available to U.S. citizens.

Application Requirements: Application form, application form may be submitted online (http://www.reachbeyondra.com), essay, personal photograph, Physician's letter and medical history form, recommendations or references, test scores, transcript. *Deadline:* June 26.

ULMAN CANCER FUND FOR YOUNG ADULTS

http://www.ulmanfund.org/

SEAN SILVER MEMORIAL SCHOLARSHIP AWARD

The Sean Silver Memorial Award is available to young adults, aged 30 or younger, currently undergoing treatment for cancer and seeking a 4-year degree.

Award: Scholarship for use in freshman, sophomore, junior, or senior years; not renewable. *Number:* 1. *Amount:* $2500.

Eligibility Requirements: Applicant must be physically disabled; age 17-30 and enrolled or expecting to enroll full- or part-time at a four-year institution. Applicant must be physically disabled. Available to U.S. citizens.

Application Requirements: Application form, community service, essay, financial need analysis, recommendations or references. *Deadline:* May 1.

VERA YIP MEMORIAL SCHOLARSHIP

Scholarships for college students who were diagnosed with cancer between the ages of 15 and 35, or who have lost a parent to cancer, or whose parent is currently fighting cancer. Applicants must be age 35 or younger at the time of application and be currently attending or accepted into a 4-year college/university, seeking a bachelor's degree or higher. Must have commitment to community service and using their cancer experience to influence the lives of other young adults confronted by cancer. Must be a resident of Maryland, Virginia, or Washington, D.C., or enrolled in a college/university in Maryland, Virginia, or Washington, D.C. Visit http://www.ulmancancerfund for more information and application.

Award: Scholarship for use in freshman, sophomore, junior, or senior years; not renewable. *Number:* 1. *Amount:* $2500.

Eligibility Requirements: Applicant must be physically disabled; enrolled or expecting to enroll full- or part-time at a four-year institution or university; resident of District of Columbia, Maryland, Virginia and studying in District of Columbia, Maryland, Virginia. Applicant must be physically disabled. Available to U.S. and non-U.S. citizens.

Application Requirements: Application form, community service, essay, pertinent medical history, recommendations or references. *Deadline:* May 1.

Contact: Fay Baker, Scholarship Coordinator
Phone: 410-964-0202
E-mail: scholarship@ulmanfund.org

UNITED NEGRO COLLEGE FUND

http://www.uncf.org/

ROBERT DOLE SCHOLARSHIP FOR DISABLED STUDENTS

Scholarship for students with a physical or mental disability who are attending UNCF member colleges and universities and demonstrate financial need. Minimum GPA 2.5 required. For more information, see website at http://www.uncf.org.

Award: Scholarship for use in freshman year; not renewable. *Amount:* up to $3500.

Eligibility Requirements: Applicant must be hearing impaired, learning disabled, physically disabled, or visually impaired; Black (non-Hispanic) and enrolled or expecting to enroll full-time at a four-year institution or university. Applicant must be hearing impaired, learning disabled, physically disabled, or visually impaired. Applicant must have 2.5 GPA or higher. Available to U.S. citizens.

Application Requirements: Application form, financial need analysis. *Deadline:* continuous.

UNITED STATES ASSOCIATION FOR BLIND ATHLETES

http://www.usaba.org/

ARTHUR E. AND HELEN COPELAND SCHOLARSHIPS

Scholarship for a full-time college student who is blind or visually impaired. All applicants must be current members of USABA.

Award: Scholarship for use in freshman, sophomore, junior, or senior years; not renewable. *Number:* 1–2. *Amount:* $500.

Eligibility Requirements: Applicant must be visually impaired and enrolled or expecting to enroll full-time at a four-year institution or university. Applicant must be visually impaired. Available to U.S. citizens.

Application Requirements: Application form, driver's license, proof of acceptance, recommendations or references, transcript. *Deadline:* October 1.

Contact: Mark Lucas, Executive Director
United States Association for Blind Athletes
33 North Institute Street
Colorado Springs, CO 80903
Phone: 719-630-0422 Ext. 13
Fax: 719-630-0616
E-mail: mlucas@usaba.org

WISCONSIN HIGHER EDUCATIONAL AID BOARD

http://www.heab.wi.gov/

HANDICAPPED STUDENT GRANT-WISCONSIN

One-time award available to residents of Wisconsin who have severe or profound hearing or visual impairment. Must be enrolled at least half-time at a nonprofit institution. If the handicap prevents the student from attending a Wisconsin school, the award may be used out-of-state in a specialized college. Refer to website for further details http://www.heab.state.wi.us.

Award: Grant for use in freshman, sophomore, junior, or senior years; not renewable. *Amount:* $250–$1800.

Eligibility Requirements: Applicant must be hearing impaired or visually impaired; enrolled or expecting to enroll full- or part-time at a four-year institution or university and resident of Wisconsin. Applicant must be hearing impaired or visually impaired. Available to U.S. citizens.

Application Requirements: Application form, financial need analysis. *Deadline:* continuous.

Contact: Sandy Thomas, Program Coordinator
Wisconsin Higher Educational Aid Board
PO Box 7885
Madison, WI 53707-7885
Phone: 608-266-0888
Fax: 608-267-2808
E-mail: sandy.thomas@wi.gov

MILITARY SERVICE: AIR FORCE

AIR FORCE AID SOCIETY

http://www.afas.org/

GENERAL HENRY H. ARNOLD EDUCATION GRANT PROGRAM

Need-based grants awarded to dependent sons and daughters of active duty, Title 10 AGR/Reserve, Title 32 AGR performing full-time active duty, retired, retired reserve and deceased Air Force members; spouses of active members and Title 10 AGR/Reservist; and surviving spouses of deceased personnel for their undergraduate studies. Dependent children must be unmarried and under the age of 23. High school seniors may apply. Minimum 2.0 GPA is required. Students must reapply and compete each year. Full-time enrollment status required.

Award: Grant for use in freshman, sophomore, junior, or senior years; not renewable. *Number:* 3000. *Amount:* $2000.

Eligibility Requirements: Applicant must be enrolled or expecting to enroll full-time at a two-year or four-year or technical institution or university. Available to U.S. citizens. Applicant or parent must meet one or more of the following requirements: national guard experience; retired from active duty; disabled or killed as a result of military service; prisoner of war; or missing in action.

Application Requirements: Application form, application form may be submitted online (http://www.afas.org/education-grants), financial need analysis, program's own financial forms, USAF military orders (member/parent), student's military ID card, transcript. *Deadline:* March 8.

AIR FORCE RESERVE OFFICER TRAINING CORPS

http://www.afrotc.com/

AFROTC HBCU SCHOLARSHIP PROGRAM

Up to $15,000 awarded to student studying at a historically black college or university (HBCU). Please refer to website for more information http://www.afrotc.com/scholarships/incolschol/minority/hbcu.php.

Award: Scholarship for use in freshman, sophomore, junior, or senior years; not renewable. *Number:* up to 15. *Amount:* up to $15,000.

Eligibility Requirements: Applicant must be enrolled or expecting to enroll full-time at a four-year institution or university. Available to U.S. citizens. Applicant must have national guard experience.

Application Requirements: Application form. *Deadline:* varies.

Contact: Elmarko Magee, Chief of Advertising
Air Force Reserve Officer Training Corps
551 East Maxwell Boulevard
Maxwell AFB, AL 36112
Phone: 866-423-7682

AFROTC HSI SCHOLARSHIP PROGRAM

$15,000 scholarships to students at colleges and universities defined as Hispanic Serving Institutions by the United States Department of Education. Student must already be enrolled in school to receive award.

Award: Scholarship for use in freshman, sophomore, junior, or senior years; not renewable. *Number:* up to 15. *Amount:* $15,000.

Eligibility Requirements: Applicant must be enrolled or expecting to enroll full-time at a four-year institution or university. Available to U.S. citizens. Applicant must have national guard experience.

Application Requirements: Application form. *Deadline:* varies.

Contact: Capt. Elmarko Magee, Chief of Advertising
Phone: 334-953-2278
E-mail: elmarko.magee@maxwell.af.mil

AIR FORCE ROTC COLLEGE SCHOLARSHIP

Scholarship program provides three- and four-year scholarships in three different types to high school seniors. All scholarship cadets receive a nontaxable monthly allowance (stipend) during the academic year. For more details refer to website http://www.afrotc.com/scholarships/hsschol/types.php.

Award: Scholarship for use in freshman, sophomore, junior, or senior years; renewable. *Number:* 2000–4000. *Amount:* $9000–$15,000.

Eligibility Requirements: Applicant must be age 17-30 and enrolled or expecting to enroll full-time at a two-year or four-year institution or university. Applicant must have 3.0 GPA or higher. Available to U.S. citizens. Applicant or parent must meet one or more of the following requirements: Air Force experience; retired from active duty; disabled or killed as a result of military service; prisoner of war; or missing in action.

Application Requirements: Application form, interview, test scores, transcript. *Deadline:* December 1.

Contact: Ty Christian, Chief Air Force ROTC Advertising Manager
Air Force Reserve Officer Training Corps
551 East Maxwell Boulevard
Maxwell Air Force Base, AL 36112-6106
Phone: 334-953-2278
Fax: 334-953-4384
E-mail: ty.christian@maxwell.af.mil

AIRMEN MEMORIAL FOUNDATION/AIR FORCE SERGEANTS ASSOCIATION

http://www.hqafsa.org/

AIR FORCE SERGEANTS ASSOCIATION SCHOLARSHIP

Scholarships awarded to dependent youth of Air Force Sergeants Association/Auxiliary members. Must be under the age of 23, be enrolled or accepted as an undergraduate in an accredited college or university, have minimum combined score of 1650 on SAT or 24 on ACT, and a minimum GPA of 3.5.

Award: Scholarship for use in freshman, sophomore, junior, or senior years; not renewable. *Number:* up to 30. *Amount:* $500–$3000.

Eligibility Requirements: Applicant must be enrolled or expecting to enroll full-time at a four-year institution or university. Applicant must have 3.5 GPA or higher. Available to U.S. and non-U.S. citizens. Applicant or parent must meet one or more of the following requirements: national guard experience; retired from active duty; disabled or killed as a result of military service; prisoner of war; or missing in action.

Application Requirements: Application form, essay, recommendations or references, transcript. *Deadline:* March 31.

Contact: Melanie Shirley, Scholarship Coordinator
Phone: 301-899-3500
Fax: 301-899-8136
E-mail: staff@afsahq.org

AIRMEN MEMORIAL FOUNDATION SCHOLARSHIP

Scholarship for full-time undergraduate studies of dependent children of Air Force, Air Force Reserve Command and Air National Guard members in active duty, retired or veteran status. Must be under age of 23, have minimum combined score of 1650 on SAT or 24 on ACT, and a minimum GPA of 3.5.

Award: Scholarship for use in freshman, sophomore, junior, or senior years; not renewable. *Number:* 20. *Amount:* $500–$2000.

Eligibility Requirements: Applicant must be enrolled or expecting to enroll full-time at a four-year institution or university. Applicant must have 3.5 GPA or higher. Available to U.S. and non-U.S. citizens. Applicant or parent must meet one or more of the following requirements: national guard experience; retired from active duty; disabled or killed as a result of military service; prisoner of war; or missing in action.

Application Requirements: Application form, essay, recommendations or references, transcript. *Deadline:* March 31.

Contact: Melanie Shirley, Scholarship Coordinator
Phone: 301-899-3500
Fax: 301-899-8136
E-mail: staff@afsahq.org

CHIEF MASTER SERGEANTS OF THE AIR FORCE SCHOLARSHIP PROGRAM

Scholarship to financially assist the full-time undergraduate studies of dependent children of Air Force, Air Force Reserve Command and Air National Guard enlisted members in active duty, retired or veteran status. Must be under age twenty-three and participate in the Airmen Memorial Foundation Scholarship Program. Must have minimum combined score of 1650 on SAT or 24 on ACT, and a minimum GPA of 3.5.

Award: Scholarship for use in freshman, sophomore, junior, or senior years; not renewable. *Number:* up to 30. *Amount:* $500–$3000.

Eligibility Requirements: Applicant must be enrolled or expecting to enroll full-time at a four-year institution or university. Applicant must have 3.5 GPA or higher. Available to U.S. and non-U.S. citizens. Applicant or parent must meet one or more of the following requirements: national guard experience; retired from active duty; disabled or killed as a result of military service; prisoner of war; or missing in action.

Application Requirements: Application form, essay, recommendations or references, transcript. *Deadline:* March 31.

Contact: Melanie Shirley, Scholarship Coordinator
Phone: 301-899-3500
Fax: 301-899-8136
E-mail: staff@afsahq.org

DAUGHTERS OF THE CINCINNATI

http://www.daughters1894.org/

DAUGHTERS OF THE CINCINNATI SCHOLARSHIP

Need and merit-based award available to graduating high school seniors. Minimum GPA of 3.0 required. Must be daughter of commissioned officer in regular Army, Navy, Coast Guard, Air Force, Marines (active, retired, or deceased). Must submit parent's rank and branch of service. Application can be completed and downloaded from website http://www.daughters1894.org.

Award: Scholarship for use in freshman year; renewable. *Number:* 4–5. *Amount:* $3000–$5000.

Eligibility Requirements: Applicant must be high school student; planning to enroll or expecting to enroll full-time at a four-year institution or university and female. Applicant must have 3.0 GPA or higher. Available to U.S. citizens. Applicant or parent must meet one or more of the following requirements: Air Force, Army, Coast Guard, Marine Corps, or Navy experience; retired from active duty; disabled or killed as a result of military service; prisoner of war; or missing in action.

Application Requirements: Application form, essay, financial need analysis, recommendations or references, test scores, transcript. *Deadline:* March 15.

Contact: Mrs. Jane Gonzalez, Scholarship Administrator
  Phone: 212-991-9945
  E-mail: scholarships@daughters1894.org

DEPARTMENT OF VETERANS AFFAIRS (VA)

http://www.gibill.va.gov/

MONTGOMERY GI BILL (SELECTED RESERVE)

Educational assistance program for members of the selected reserve of the Army, Navy, Air Force, Marine Corps and Coast Guard, as well as the Army and Air National Guard. Available to all reservists and National Guard personnel who commit to a six-year obligation, and remain in the Reserve or Guard during the six years. Award is renewable. Monthly benefit is $309 for up to thirty-six months for full-time.

Award: Scholarship for use in freshman, sophomore, junior, senior, or postgraduate years; renewable.

Eligibility Requirements: Applicant must be enrolled or expecting to enroll full- or part-time at a two-year or four-year or technical institution or university. Available to U.S. citizens. Applicant or parent must meet one or more of the following requirements: general military experience; retired from active duty; disabled or killed as a result of military service; prisoner of war; or missing in action.

Application Requirements: Application form, proof of military service of six years in the reserve or guard. *Deadline:* continuous.

Contact: Keith Wilson, Director, Education Service
  Phone: 888-442-4551

FOUNDATION OF THE 1ST CAVALRY DIVISION ASSOCIATION

http://www.1cda.org/

FOUNDATION OF THE 1ST CAVALRY DIVISION ASSOCIATION (IA DRANG) SCHOLARSHIP

Award for children and grandchildren of soldiers of 1st Cavalry Division, U.S. Air Force Forward Air Controllers and A1E pilots, and war correspondents who served in designated qualifying units which were involved in battles of the Ia Drang Valley during the period of November 3–19, 1965. Include self-addressed stamped envelope. More information on http://www.1cda.org.

Award: Scholarship for use in freshman, sophomore, junior, or senior years; not renewable. *Amount:* up to $1200.

Eligibility Requirements: Applicant must be enrolled or expecting to enroll full-time at a two-year or four-year institution or university.

Available to U.S. citizens. Applicant or parent must meet one or more of the following requirements: Air Force or Army experience; retired from active duty; disabled or killed as a result of military service; prisoner of war; or missing in action.

Application Requirements: Application form, birth certificate, proof of father or grandfather's participation in specified units and battles, proof of registration for Selective Service for males, self-addressed stamped envelope with application. *Deadline:* continuous.

Contact: Dennis Webster, Executive Director
  Foundation of the 1st Cavalry Division Association
  302 North Main Street
  Copperas Cove, TX 76522-1703
  Phone: 254-547-6537
  Fax: 254-547-8853
  E-mail: firstcav@1cda.org

IMAGINE AMERICA FOUNDATION

http://www.imagine-america.org

MILITARY AWARD PROGRAM (MAP)

The Military Award Program offers scholarships for veterans and other military students who decide to pursue career college training. This $1000 career education award is available to any qualified active duty, reservist, honorably discharged or retired veteran of a U.S. military service branch for attendance at a participating career college.

Award: Grant for use in freshman, sophomore, junior, or senior years; not renewable. *Number:* up to 1500. *Amount:* $1000.

Eligibility Requirements: Applicant must be enrolled or expecting to enroll full- or part-time at a two-year or four-year or technical institution. Available to U.S. citizens. Applicant must have general military experience.

Application Requirements: Application form, application form may be submitted online (http://www.imagine-america.org/grantsformilitary). *Deadline:* continuous.

Contact: Lee Doubleday, Student Services Representative
  Imagine America Foundation
  12001 Sunrise Valley Drive, Suite 203
  Reston, VA 20191
  Phone: 571-267-3015
  Fax: 866-734-5812
  E-mail: leed@imagine-america.org

INDIANA DEPARTMENT OF VETERANS AFFAIRS

http://www.in.gov/dva

RESIDENT TUITION FOR ACTIVE DUTY MILITARY PERSONNEL

Applicant must be a nonresident of Indiana serving on active duty and stationed in Indiana and attending any state-supported college or university. Dependents remain eligible for the duration of their enrollment, even if the active duty person is no longer in Indiana. Entitlement is to the resident tuition rate.

Award: Grant for use in freshman, sophomore, junior, senior, graduate, or postgraduate years; renewable.

Eligibility Requirements: Applicant must be enrolled or expecting to enroll full- or part-time at a two-year or four-year or technical institution or university and studying in Indiana. Available to U.S. citizens. Applicant or parent must meet one or more of the following requirements: Air Force, Army, Marine Corps, or Navy experience; retired from active duty; disabled or killed as a result of military service; prisoner of war; or missing in action.

Application Requirements: Application form. *Deadline:* continuous.

Contact: Jon Brinkley, State Service Officer
  Phone: 317-232-3910
  Fax: 317-232-7721
  E-mail: jbrinkley@dva.in.gov

WISCONSIN DEPARTMENT OF VETERANS AFFAIRS (WDVA)

http://www.dva.state.wi.us/

VETERANS EDUCATION (VETED) REIMBURSEMENT GRANT

The grant is for eligible Wisconsin veterans enrolled at approved schools who have not yet earned a BS/BA. Reimburses up to 120 credits or eight semesters at the UW Madison rate for the same number of credits taken in one semester or term. The number of credits or semesters is based on length of time serving on active duty in the armed forces (active duty for training does not apply). Application is due no later than 60 days after the course start date. The student must earn a 2.0 or better for the semester. An eligible veteran will have entered active duty as a Wisconsin resident or lived in state for twelve consecutive months since entering active duty.

Award: Grant for use in freshman, sophomore, junior, or senior years; renewable. *Number:* up to 350. *Amount:* up to $4000.

Eligibility Requirements: Applicant must be enrolled or expecting to enroll full- or part-time at a two-year or four-year or technical institution or university; resident of Wisconsin and studying in Minnesota, Wisconsin. Available to U.S. citizens. Applicant must have served in the Air Force, Army, Coast Guard, Marine Corps, or Navy.

Application Requirements: Application form, certified Wisconsin veteran. *Deadline:* continuous.

Contact: Mrs. Leslie Busby-Amegashie, Analyst
Wisconsin Department of Veterans Affairs (WDVA)
PO Box 7843
Madison, WI 53707-7843
Phone: 800-947-8387
Fax: 608-267-0403
E-mail: leslie.busby-amegashie@dva.wisconsin.gov

MILITARY SERVICE: AIR FORCE NATIONAL GUARD

AIR FORCE AID SOCIETY

http://www.afas.org/

GENERAL HENRY H. ARNOLD EDUCATION GRANT PROGRAM
• See page 579

AIR FORCE RESERVE OFFICER TRAINING CORPS

http://www.afrotc.com/

AFROTC HBCU SCHOLARSHIP PROGRAM
• See page 580

AFROTC HSI SCHOLARSHIP PROGRAM
• See page 580

AIRMEN MEMORIAL FOUNDATION/AIR FORCE SERGEANTS ASSOCIATION

http://www.hqafsa.org/

AIR FORCE SERGEANTS ASSOCIATION SCHOLARSHIP
• See page 580

AIRMEN MEMORIAL FOUNDATION SCHOLARSHIP
• See page 580

CHIEF MASTER SERGEANTS OF THE AIR FORCE SCHOLARSHIP PROGRAM
• See page 580

ALABAMA COMMISSION ON HIGHER EDUCATION

http://www.ache.alabama.gov/

ALABAMA NATIONAL GUARD EDUCATIONAL ASSISTANCE PROGRAM

Renewable award aids Alabama residents who are members of the Alabama National Guard and are enrolled in a nationally recognized accredited college in Alabama. Forms must be signed by a representative of the Alabama Military Department and financial aid officer. Recipient must be in a degree-seeking program.

Award: Scholarship for use in freshman, sophomore, junior, senior, or graduate years; renewable. *Number:* up to 800. *Amount:* $25–$1000.

Eligibility Requirements: Applicant must be enrolled or expecting to enroll full- or part-time at a two-year or four-year or technical institution or university; resident of Alabama and studying in Alabama. Available to U.S. citizens. Applicant must have national guard experience.

Application Requirements: Application form. *Deadline:* continuous.

Contact: Cheryl Newton, Grants Coordinator
Phone: 334-242-2273
Fax: 334-242-2269
E-mail: cheryl.newton@ache.alabama.gov

AMERICAN LEGION DEPARTMENT OF TENNESSEE

http://www.tennesseelegion.org/

JROTC SCHOLARSHIP

One scholarship of $2000 available to a Tennessee JROTC cadet who has been awarded either The American Legion General Military Excellence, or The American Legion Scholastic Award Medal. JROTC Senior Instructor must provide the recommendation for the award. Information and recommendation forms are provided each JROTC Unit in Tennessee. Must be U.S. citizen.

Award: Scholarship for use in freshman, sophomore, junior, or senior years; not renewable. *Number:* 1. *Amount:* $3000.

Eligibility Requirements: Applicant must be high school student; planning to enroll or expecting to enroll full- or part-time at a four-year institution or university; resident of Tennessee and studying in Tennessee. Available to U.S. citizens. Applicant must have national guard experience.

Application Requirements: Application form, JROTC Scholastic or Military Excellence Award, recommendations or references. *Deadline:* May 15.

Contact: Darlene Burgess, Executive Secretary
Phone: 615-391-5088
E-mail: taltnadj@bellsouth.net

DELAWARE NATIONAL GUARD

http://www.delawarenationalguard.com/

STATE TUITION ASSISTANCE

You must enlist in the Delaware National Guard to be eligible for this scholarship award. Award providing tuition assistance for any member of the Air or Army National Guard attending a Delaware two-year or four-year college. Awards are renewable. Applicant's minimum GPA must be 2.0.

Award: Scholarship for use in freshman, sophomore, junior, or senior years; renewable. *Number:* 1–200. *Amount:* up to $10,000.

Eligibility Requirements: Applicant must be enrolled or expecting to enroll full- or part-time at a two-year or four-year institution or university and studying in Delaware. Available to U.S. citizens. Applicant or parent must meet one or more of the following requirements: national guard experience; retired from active duty; disabled or killed as a result of military service; prisoner of war; or missing in action.

Application Requirements: Application form, transcript.

Contact: Robert Csizmadia, State Tuition Assistance Manager
Delaware National Guard
1st Regiment Road
Wilmington, DE 19808-2191
Phone: 302-326-7012
Fax: 302-326-7029
E-mail: robert.csizmadia@us.army.mil

DEPARTMENT OF VETERANS AFFAIRS (VA)

http://www.gibill.va.gov/

MONTGOMERY GI BILL (SELECTED RESERVE)

• *See page 581*

RESERVE EDUCATION ASSISTANCE PROGRAM

The program provides educational assistance to members of National Guard and reserve components. Selected Reserve and Individual Ready Reserve (IRR) who are called or ordered to active duty service in response to a war or national emergency as declared by the president or Congress are eligible. For further information see website http://www.GIBILL.va.gov.

Award: Scholarship for use in freshman, sophomore, junior, senior, graduate, or postgraduate years; renewable.

Eligibility Requirements: Applicant must be enrolled or expecting to enroll full- or part-time at a two-year or four-year or technical institution or university. Available to U.S. citizens. Applicant or parent must meet one or more of the following requirements: general military experience; retired from active duty; disabled or killed as a result of military service; prisoner of war; or missing in action.

Application Requirements: Application form. *Deadline:* continuous.

Contact: Keith Wilson, Director, Education Service
Phone: 888-442-4551

EDUCATION FOUNDATION. INC. NATIONAL GUARD ASSOCIATION OF COLORADO

http://www.ngaco.org/

EDUCATION FOUNDATION, INC. NATIONAL GUARD ASSOCIATION OF COLORADO SCHOLARSHIPS

Scholarships for current members of the Colorado National Guard. Applicants must be enrolled as full or part-time at a college, university, trade or business school. Deadlines: August 1st for the fall semester and December 1st for the spring semester.

Award: Scholarship for use in freshman, sophomore, junior, senior, graduate, or postgraduate years; not renewable. *Number:* 20–30. *Amount:* $500–$2500.

Eligibility Requirements: Applicant must be enrolled or expecting to enroll full- or part-time at a two-year or four-year or technical institution or university and resident of Colorado. Available to U.S. citizens. Applicant must have national guard experience.

Application Requirements: Application form, community service, essay, financial need analysis, recommendations or references, transcript. *Deadline:* varies.

Contact: Mr. Bernie Rogoff, Executive Director
Education Foundation. Inc. National Guard Association of Colorado
PO Box 440889
Aurora, CO 80044-8889
Phone: 303-909-6369
Fax: 720-535-5925
E-mail: BernieRogoff@Comcast.net

ENLISTED ASSOCIATION OF THE NATIONAL GUARD OF NEW JERSEY

http://www.eang-nj.org/

CSM VINCENT BALDASSARI MEMORIAL SCHOLARSHIP PROGRAM

Scholarships open to the legal children of New Jersey National Guard Members who are also members of the Enlisted Association. Also open to any drilling guardsperson who is a member of the Enlisted Association. Along with application, submit proof of parent's membership and a letter stating the reason for applying and future intents.

Award: Scholarship for use in freshman, sophomore, junior, senior, graduate, or postgraduate years; not renewable. *Number:* 5. *Amount:* $1000.

Eligibility Requirements: Applicant must be enrolled or expecting to enroll full- or part-time at a two-year or four-year or technical institution or university and resident of New Jersey. Available to U.S. and non-U.S. citizens. Applicant or parent must meet one or more of the following requirements: national guard experience; retired from active duty; disabled or killed as a result of military service; prisoner of war; or missing in action.

Application Requirements: Application form, essay, personal photograph, recommendations or references, transcript. *Deadline:* May 15.

Contact: Michael Amoroso, Scholarship Committee Chairman
Phone: 609-562-0754
Fax: 609-562-0731
E-mail: michael.c@us.army.mil

USAA SCHOLARSHIP

Scholarship of $1000 open to any drilling guardsperson (need not be a member of the EANGNJ).

Award: Scholarship for use in freshman, sophomore, junior, senior, graduate, or postgraduate years; not renewable. *Number:* 1. *Amount:* $1000.

Eligibility Requirements: Applicant must be enrolled or expecting to enroll full- or part-time at a two-year or four-year or technical institution or university. Available to U.S. and non-U.S. citizens. Applicant or parent must meet one or more of the following requirements: national guard experience; retired from active duty; disabled or killed as a result of military service; prisoner of war; or missing in action.

Application Requirements: Application form, essay, personal photograph, transcript. *Deadline:* May 15.

Contact: Michael Amoroso, Scholarship Committee Chairman
Phone: 609-562-0754
Fax: 609-562-0731
E-mail: michael.c@us.army.mil

ILLINOIS STUDENT ASSISTANCE COMMISSION (ISAC)

http://www.collegezone.org/

ILLINOIS NATIONAL GUARD GRANT PROGRAM

Active duty members of the Illinois National Guard, or who are within 12 months of discharge, and who have completed one full year of service are eligible. May be used for study at Illinois two- or four-year public colleges for a maximum of the equivalent of four academic years of full-time enrollment. Deadlines: October 1 of the academic year for full year, March 1 for second/third term, or June 15 for the summer term.

Award: Grant for use in freshman, sophomore, junior, senior, or graduate years; renewable.

Eligibility Requirements: Applicant must be enrolled or expecting to enroll full- or part-time at a two-year or four-year institution or university; resident of Illinois and studying in Illinois. Available to U.S. citizens. Applicant or parent must meet one or more of the following requirements: national guard experience; retired from active duty; disabled or killed as a result of military service; prisoner of war; or missing in action.

Application Requirements: Application form, documentation of service. *Deadline:* varies.

IMAGINE AMERICA FOUNDATION

http://www.imagine-america.org

MILITARY AWARD PROGRAM (MAP)
• *See page 581*

INDIANA DEPARTMENT OF VETERANS AFFAIRS

http://www.in.gov/dva

NATIONAL GUARD SCHOLARSHIP EXTENSION PROGRAM

A scholarship extension applicant is eligible for a tuition scholarship under Indiana Code 21-13-5-4 for a period not to exceed the period of scholarship extension the applicant served on active duty as a member of the National Guard (mobilized and deployed). Must apply not later than one (1) year after the applicant ceases to be a member of the Indiana National Guard. Applicant should apply through the education officer of their last unit of assignment.

Award: Grant for use in freshman, sophomore, junior, or senior years; renewable.

Eligibility Requirements: Applicant must be enrolled or expecting to enroll full- or part-time at a two-year or four-year or technical institution or university and studying in Indiana. Available to U.S. citizens. Applicant must have national guard experience.

Application Requirements: Application form. *Deadline:* continuous.

Contact: Pamela Moody, National Guard Education Officer
Indiana Department of Veterans Affairs
302 West Washington Street, Suite E120
Indianapolis, IN 46204
Phone: 317-964-7017
Fax: 317-232-7721
E-mail: pamela.moody@in.ngb.army.mil

NATIONAL GUARD TUITION SUPPLEMENT PROGRAM

Applicant must be a member of the Indiana National Guard, in active drilling status, who has not been AWOL during the last 12 months, does not possess a bachelor's degree, possesses the requisite academic qualifications, meets the requirements of the state-supported college or university, and meets all National Guard requirements.

Award: Grant for use in freshman, sophomore, junior, or senior years; renewable.

Eligibility Requirements: Applicant must be enrolled or expecting to enroll full- or part-time at a two-year or four-year or technical institution or university and studying in Indiana. Available to U.S. citizens. Applicant must have national guard experience.

Application Requirements: Application form, FAFSA. *Deadline:* continuous.

Contact: Jon Brinkley, State Service Officer
Phone: 317-232-3910
Fax: 317-232-7721
E-mail: jbrinkley@dva.in.gov

TUITION AND FEE REMISSION FOR CHILDREN AND SPOUSES OF NATIONAL GUARD MEMBERS

Award to an individual whose father, mother or spouse was a member of the Indiana National Guard and suffered a service-connected death while serving on state active duty (which includes mobilized and deployed for federal active duty). The student must be eligible to pay the resident tuition rate at the state-supported college or university and must possess the requisite academic qualifications.

Award: Grant for use in freshman, sophomore, junior, or senior years; renewable.

Eligibility Requirements: Applicant must be enrolled or expecting to enroll full- or part-time at a two-year or four-year or technical institution or university and studying in Indiana. Available to U.S. citizens. Applicant or parent must meet one or more of the following requirements: national guard experience; retired from active duty; disabled or killed as a result of military service; prisoner of war; or missing in action.

Application Requirements: Application form, FAFSA. *Deadline:* continuous.

Contact: R. Martin Umbarger, Adjutant General
Indiana Department of Veterans Affairs
2002 South Holt Road
Indianapolis, IN 46241
Phone: 317-247-3559
Fax: 317-247-3540
E-mail: r.martin.umbarger@in.ngb.army.mil

IOWA COLLEGE STUDENT AID COMMISSION

http://www.iowacollegeaid.gov/

IOWA NATIONAL GUARD EDUCATION ASSISTANCE PROGRAM

Program provides postsecondary tuition assistance to members of Iowa National Guard Units. Must study at a postsecondary institution in Iowa. Contact the office for additional information.

Award: Grant for use in freshman, sophomore, junior, or senior years; not renewable. *Number:* 700–1500.

Eligibility Requirements: Applicant must be enrolled or expecting to enroll full- or part-time at a two-year or four-year or technical institution or university; resident of Iowa and studying in Iowa. Available to U.S. citizens. Applicant must have national guard experience.

Application Requirements: Application form, application form may be submitted online (http://www.iowacollegeaid.gov). *Deadline:* continuous.

Contact: Todd Brown, Director, Scholarships, Grants, and Loan Forgiveness
Iowa College Student Aid Commission
603 East 12th Street, 5th Floor
Des Moines, IA 50319
Phone: 877-272-4456
Fax: 515-725-3401
E-mail: todd.brown@iowa.gov

LOUISIANA NATIONAL GUARD, JOINT TASK FORCE LA

http://geauxguard.com/

LOUISIANA NATIONAL GUARD STATE TUITION EXEMPTION PROGRAM

Renewable award for college undergraduates to receive tuition exemption upon satisfactory performance in the Louisiana National Guard. Applicant must attend a state-funded institution in Louisiana, be a resident and registered voter in Louisiana, meet the academic and residency requirements of the university attended, and provide documentation of Louisiana National Guard enlistment. The exemption can be used for up to 15 semesters. Minimum 2.5 GPA required.

Award: Scholarship for use in freshman, sophomore, junior, or senior years; renewable.

Eligibility Requirements: Applicant must be enrolled or expecting to enroll full- or part-time at a two-year or four-year or technical institution or university; resident of Louisiana and studying in Louisiana. Applicant must have 2.5 GPA or higher. Available to U.S. citizens. Applicant or parent must meet one or more of the following requirements: national guard experience; retired from active duty; disabled or killed as a result of military service; prisoner of war; or missing in action.

Application Requirements: Application form, test scores, transcript. *Deadline:* continuous.

Contact: Jona Hughes, Education Services Officer
Louisiana National Guard, Joint Task Force LA
Building 35, Jackson Barracks, JI-PD
New Orleans, LA 70146-0330
Phone: 504-278-8531 Ext. 8304
Fax: 504-278-8025
E-mail: hughesj@la-arng.ngb.army.mil

MINNESOTA DEPARTMENT OF MILITARY AFFAIRS

http://www.minnesotanationalguard.org/

LEADERSHIP, EXCELLENCE, AND DEDICATED SERVICE SCHOLARSHIP

• *See page 560*

NORTH CAROLINA NATIONAL GUARD

http://www.nc.ngb.army.mil/

NORTH CAROLINA NATIONAL GUARD TUITION ASSISTANCE PROGRAM

Scholarship for members of the North Carolina Air and Army National Guard who will remain in the service for two years following the period for which assistance is provided. Must reapply for each academic period. For use at approved North Carolina institutions.

Award: Grant for use in freshman, sophomore, junior, senior, or graduate years; not renewable. *Amount:* up to $2000.

Eligibility Requirements: Applicant must be enrolled or expecting to enroll full- or part-time at a two-year or four-year or technical institution or university; resident of North Carolina and studying in North Carolina. Available to U.S. citizens. Applicant or parent must meet one or more of the following requirements: national guard experience; retired from active duty; disabled or killed as a result of military service; prisoner of war; or missing in action.

Application Requirements: Application form. *Deadline:* varies.

Contact: Anne Gildhouse, Education Services Officer
Phone: 919-664-6000
Fax: 919-664-6520
E-mail: anne.gildhouse@nc.ngb.army.mil

OHIO NATIONAL GUARD

http://www.ongsp.org/

OHIO NATIONAL GUARD SCHOLARSHIP PROGRAM

Scholarships are for undergraduate studies at an approved Ohio post-secondary institution. Applicants must enlist for six or three years of Selective Service Reserve Duty in the Ohio National Guard. Scholarship pays 100% instructional and general fees for public institutions and an average of cost of public universities is available for private schools. May reapply up to four years of studies (12 quarters or 8 semesters) for six year enlistment and two years of studies (6 quarters or 4 semesters) for three year enlistment. Deadlines: July 1 (fall), November 1 (winter quarter/spring semester), February 1 (spring quarter), April 1 (summer).

Award: Scholarship for use in freshman, sophomore, junior, or senior years; not renewable. *Number:* up to 3500. *Amount:* up to $4006.

Eligibility Requirements: Applicant must be enrolled or expecting to enroll full- or part-time at a two-year or four-year or technical institution or university; resident of Ohio and studying in Ohio. Available to U.S. citizens. Applicant must have national guard experience.

Application Requirements: Application form. *Deadline:* varies.

Contact: Mrs. Toni Davis, Grants Administrator
Ohio National Guard
2825 West Dublin Granville Road, ONGSP
Columbus, OH 43235-2789
Phone: 614-336-7143
Fax: 614-336-7318
E-mail: toni.davis7@us.army.mil

PENNSYLVANIA HIGHER EDUCATION ASSISTANCE AGENCY

http://www.pheaa.org/

POSTSECONDARY EDUCATION GRATUITY PROGRAM

The program offers waiver of tuition and fees for children of Pennsylvania police officers, firefighters, rescue or ambulance squad members, corrections facility employees, or National Guard members who died in line of duty after January 1, 1976.

Award: Grant for use in freshman, sophomore, junior, or senior years; renewable.

Eligibility Requirements: Applicant must be enrolled or expecting to enroll full-time at a two-year or four-year institution or university; resident of Pennsylvania and studying in Pennsylvania. Available to U.S. citizens. Applicant or parent must meet one or more of the following requirements: national guard experience; retired from active duty; disabled or killed as a result of military service; prisoner of war; or missing in action.

Application Requirements: Application form. *Deadline:* August 1.

Contact: Keith New, Director of Public Relations
Phone: 717-720-2509
E-mail: knew@pheaa.org

STATE STUDENT ASSISTANCE COMMISSION OF INDIANA (SSACI)

http://www.in.gov/ssaci

INDIANA NATIONAL GUARD SUPPLEMENTAL GRANT

The award is a supplement to the Indiana Higher Education Grant program. Applicants must be members of the Indiana National Guard. All Guard paperwork must be completed prior to the start of each semester. The FAFSA must be received by March 10. Award covers certain tuition and fees at select public colleges.

Award: Grant for use in freshman, sophomore, junior, or senior years; not renewable. *Number:* 503–925. *Amount:* $20–$7110.

Eligibility Requirements: Applicant must be enrolled or expecting to enroll full- or part-time at a two-year or four-year institution or university; resident of Indiana and studying in Indiana. Available to U.S. citizens. Applicant or parent must meet one or more of the following requirements: national guard experience; retired from active duty; disabled or killed as a result of military service; prisoner of war; or missing in action.

Application Requirements: Application form. *Deadline:* March 10.

Contact: Kathryn Moore, Grants Counselor
State Student Assistance Commission of Indiana (SSACI)
150 West Market Street, Suite 500
Indianapolis, IN 46204-2805
Phone: 317-232-2350
Fax: 317-232-2360
E-mail: kmoore@ssaci.in.gov

TEXAS HIGHER EDUCATION COORDINATING BOARD

http://www.collegefortexans.com/

TEXAS NATIONAL GUARD TUITION ASSISTANCE PROGRAM

Provides exemption from the payment of tuition to certain members of the Texas National Guard, Texas Air Guard or the State Guard. Must be Texas resident and attend school in Texas. Deadline varies.

Award: Scholarship for use in freshman, sophomore, junior, or senior years; renewable.

Eligibility Requirements: Applicant must be enrolled or expecting to enroll full- or part-time at a four-year institution or university; resident of Texas and studying in Texas. Available to U.S. citizens. Applicant or parent must meet one or more of the following requirements: national guard experience; retired from active duty; disabled or killed as a result of military service; prisoner of war; or missing in action.

Application Requirements: Application form. *Deadline:* varies.

MILITARY SERVICE: ARMY

1ST INFANTRY DIVISION FOUNDATION
http://www.bigredone.org/

LIEUTENANT GENERAL CLARENCE R. HUEBNER SCHOLARSHIP PROGRAM

Award for undergraduate study for children and grandchildren of veterans of the 1st Infantry Division, U.S. Army (Big Red One). Essay, letter of acceptance, high school transcript, test scores, letters of recommendation, proof of registration with selective service (if male), and proof of parent's or grandparent's service required. Must be high school senior to apply. Send self-addressed stamped envelope for essay topic and details or send request for application to Fdn1ID@aol.com.

Award: Scholarship for use in freshman, sophomore, junior, or senior years; renewable. *Number:* 5. *Amount:* $10,000.

Eligibility Requirements: Applicant must be high school student and planning to enroll or expecting to enroll full-time at a four-year institution or university. Available to U.S. citizens. Applicant or parent must meet one or more of the following requirements: Army experience; retired from active duty; disabled or killed as a result of military service; prisoner of war; or missing in action.

Application Requirements: Application form, essay, letter of acceptance, proof of parent's or grandparent's service with the First Infantry Division, recommendations or references, test scores, transcript. *Deadline:* June 1.

Contact: Rosemary Wirs, Secretary-Treasurer
1st Infantry Division Foundation
PO Box 607
Ambler, PA 19002
E-mail: Fdn1ID@aol.com

AMERICAN LEGION AUXILIARY DEPARTMENT OF CALIFORNIA
http://www.calegionaux.org/

AMERICAN LEGION AUXILIARY DEPARTMENT OF CALIFORNIA JUNIOR SCHOLARSHIP
• *See page 503*

AMERICAN LEGION AUXILIARY DEPARTMENT OF KENTUCKY
http://www.kylegion.org/

AMERICAN LEGION AUXILIARY DEPARTMENT OF KENTUCKY LAURA BLACKBURN MEMORIAL SCHOLARSHIP

Scholarship to the child, grandchild, or great grandchild of a veteran who served in the Armed Forces. Applicant must be a Kentucky resident.

Award: Scholarship for use in freshman year; not renewable. *Number:* 1. *Amount:* $1000.

Eligibility Requirements: Applicant must be high school student; planning to enroll or expecting to enroll full-time at a four-year institution or university and resident of Kentucky. Available to U.S. citizens. Applicant or parent must meet one or more of the following requirements: Army experience; retired from active duty; disabled or killed as a result of military service; prisoner of war; or missing in action.

Application Requirements: Application form, financial need analysis, transcript. *Deadline:* March 31.

Contact: Betty Cook, Secretary and Treasurer
Phone: 270-932-7533
Fax: 270-932-7672
E-mail: secretarykyala@aol.com

AMERICAN LEGION DEPARTMENT OF NEW JERSEY
http://www.njamericanlegion.org/

AMERICAN LEGION DEPARTMENT OF NEW JERSEY SCHOLARSHIP
• *See page 511*

ARMY OFFICERS' WIVES CLUB OF GREATER WASHINGTON AREA
http://www.aowcgwa.org/

ARMY OFFICERS WIVES CLUB OF THE GREATER WASHINGTON AREA SCHOLARSHIP

Scholarship for high school seniors, college students or children or spouses of U.S. Army personnel. Scholarship awards are based on scholastic merit and community involvement.

Award: Scholarship for use in freshman, sophomore, junior, or senior years; not renewable. *Number:* 1–3. *Amount:* $100–$500.

Eligibility Requirements: Applicant must be enrolled or expecting to enroll full-time at a four-year institution or university. Available to U.S. citizens. Applicant or parent must meet one or more of the following requirements: Army experience; retired from active duty; disabled or killed as a result of military service; prisoner of war; or missing in action.

Application Requirements: Application form, essay, military dependent ID card, recommendations or references, self-addressed stamped envelope with application, transcript. *Deadline:* March 31.

Contact: Janis Waller, Scholarship Committee Chair
Army Officers' Wives Club of Greater Washington Area
12025 William and Mary Circle
Woodbridge, VA 22192-1634

DAUGHTERS OF THE CINCINNATI
http://www.daughters1894.org/

DAUGHTERS OF THE CINCINNATI SCHOLARSHIP
• *See page 581*

DEPARTMENT OF THE ARMY
http://www.goarmy.com/rotc

ARMY ROTC GREEN TO GOLD SCHOLARSHIP PROGRAM FOR TWO-YEAR, THREE-YEAR AND FOUR-YEAR SCHOLARSHIPS, ACTIVE DUTY ENLISTED PERSONNEL

Award for freshman, sophomore, and junior year for use at a four-year institution for Army enlisted personnel. Merit considered. Must also be member of the school's ROTC program. Must pass physical and have completed two years of active duty. Applicant must be at least seventeen years of age by college enrollment and under thirty-one years of age in the year of graduation. Submit recommendations from Commanding Officer and Field Grade Commander. Include DODMERB Physical Forms and DA Form 2A.

Award: Scholarship for use in freshman, sophomore, junior, senior, or graduate years; not renewable. *Number:* 200–400. *Amount:* $10,000–$130,000.

Eligibility Requirements: Applicant must be age 17-30 and enrolled or expecting to enroll full-time at a four-year institution or university. Applicant must have 2.5 GPA or higher. Available to U.S. citizens. Applicant must have served in the Army.

Application Requirements: Application form, application form may be submitted online (http://www.goarmy.com/rotc/enlisted-soldiers/green-to-gold-scholarship.html), Enlisted Record Brief, DODMERB physical, APFT, GT, essay, personal photograph, recommendations or references, test scores, transcript. *Deadline:* February 1.

Contact: Mr. Joseph O'Donnell, Scholarship Management Branch
Department of the Army
Building 1002, 204 1st Cavalry Regiment Road
Fort Knox, KY 40121-5123
Phone: 502-624-7046
Fax: 502-624-1120
E-mail: joseph.f.odonnell3.civ@mail.mil

ARMY (ROTC) RESERVE OFFICERS TRAINING CORPS TWO-, THREE-, FOUR-YEAR CAMPUS-BASED SCHOLARSHIPS
• *See page 569*

U.S. ARMY ROTC FOUR-YEAR COLLEGE SCHOLARSHIP
One-time award for students entering college for the first time, or freshmen in a documented five-year degree program. Must join school's ROTC program, pass physical, and submit teacher evaluations. Must be a U.S. citizen and have a qualifying SAT or ACT score. Applicant must be at least seventeen years of age by college enrollment and under thirty-one years of age in the year of graduation. Online application available.

Award: Scholarship for use in freshman, sophomore, junior, or senior years; renewable. *Number:* 1000–2000. *Amount:* $9000–$40,000.

Eligibility Requirements: Applicant must be age 17-26 and enrolled or expecting to enroll full-time at a four-year institution or university. Applicant must have 2.5 GPA or higher. Available to U.S. citizens. Applicant must have national guard experience.

Application Requirements: Application form, application form may be submitted online (http://www.goarmy.com/rotc/high-school-students/four-year-scholarship.html), essay, interview, test scores, transcript. *Deadline:* January 10.

Contact: Ms. Kathleen Barnes, Supervisor, Human Resources Specialist
Department of the Army
U.S. Army Cadet Command, Bldg 1002, 204 1st Cavalry
Regiment Road
Fort Knox, KY 40121-5123
Phone: 502-624-7371
Fax: 502-624-1120
E-mail: kathleen.m.barnes19.civ@mail.mil

U.S. ARMY ROTC FOUR-YEAR HISTORICALLY BLACK COLLEGE/UNIVERSITY SCHOLARSHIP
• *See page 569*

U.S. ARMY ROTC MILITARY JUNIOR COLLEGE (MJC) SCHOLARSHIP
• *See page 569*

DEPARTMENT OF VETERANS AFFAIRS (VA)
http://www.gibill.va.gov/

MONTGOMERY GI BILL (SELECTED RESERVE)
• *See page 581*

FOUNDATION OF THE 1ST CAVALRY DIVISION ASSOCIATION
http://www.1cda.org/

FOUNDATION OF THE 1ST CAVALRY DIVISION ASSOCIATION (IA DRANG) SCHOLARSHIP
• *See page 581*

IMAGINE AMERICA FOUNDATION
http://www.imagine-america.org

MILITARY AWARD PROGRAM (MAP)
• *See page 581*

INDIANA DEPARTMENT OF VETERANS AFFAIRS
http://www.in.gov/dva

RESIDENT TUITION FOR ACTIVE DUTY MILITARY PERSONNEL
• *See page 581*

SOCIETY OF DAUGHTERS OF THE UNITED STATES ARMY

SOCIETY OF DAUGHTERS OF THE UNITED STATES ARMY SCHOLARSHIPS
Scholarship for daughters or granddaughters of career warrant or commissioned officer in the U.S. Army who is: on active duty; retired from active duty after 20 years of service; medically retired before 20 years of active service; died while on active duty or died after retiring from active duty. Send the following information to request an application: applicant's name, name of officer, rank, component (Active, Reserve, Retired), dates of active duty service, and relationship to the applicant. Send information only, no documentation at this time. Send to: Mary P. Maroney, DUSA Scholarship Chairman, 11804 Grey Birch Pl., Reston, VA 20191.

Award: Scholarship for use in freshman, sophomore, junior, or senior years; renewable. *Number:* 8–12. *Amount:* $1000.

Eligibility Requirements: Applicant must be enrolled or expecting to enroll full-time at a two-year or four-year or technical institution or university; female and must have an interest in leadership. Applicant must have 3.0 GPA or higher. Available to U.S. citizens. Applicant or parent must meet one or more of the following requirements: national guard experience; retired from active duty; disabled or killed as a result of military service; prisoner of war; or missing in action.

Application Requirements: Application form, entry in a contest, essay, proof of service of qualifying service member (state relationship to member), recommendations or references, resume, self-addressed stamped envelope with application, test scores, transcript. *Deadline:* March 1.

Contact: Mary Maroney, Chairperson, Memorial and Scholarship Funds
Society of Daughters of the United States Army
11804 Grey Birch Place
Reston, VA 20191

WISCONSIN DEPARTMENT OF VETERANS AFFAIRS (WDVA)
http://www.dva.state.wi.us/

VETERANS EDUCATION (VETED) REIMBURSEMENT GRANT
• *See page 582*

WOMEN'S ARMY CORPS VETERANS' ASSOCIATION
http://www.armywomen.org/

WOMEN'S ARMY CORPS VETERANS' ASSOCIATION SCHOLARSHIP
Scholarship to graduating high school senior showing academic promise. Must be a child, grandchild, niece or nephew of an Army servicewoman. Minimum cumulative GPA of 3.5 required. Applicants must plan to enroll in a degree program as a full-time student at an accredited college or university in the United States.

Award: Scholarship for use in freshman year; not renewable. *Number:* 1. *Amount:* $1500.

Eligibility Requirements: Applicant must be high school student and planning to enroll or expecting to enroll full-time at a four-year institution or university. Applicant must have 3.5 GPA or higher. Available to U.S. citizens. Applicant or parent must meet one or more of the following requirements: Army experience; retired from active duty; disabled or killed as a result of military service; prisoner of war; or missing in action.

Application Requirements: Application form, documentation of sponsor's military service, recommendations or references, transcript. *Deadline:* May 1.

Contact: Eldora Engebretson, Scholarship Committee
　　　Phone: 623-566-9299
　　　E-mail: info@armywomen.org

MILITARY SERVICE: ARMY NATIONAL GUARD

ALABAMA COMMISSION ON HIGHER EDUCATION

http://www.ache.alabama.gov/

ALABAMA NATIONAL GUARD EDUCATIONAL ASSISTANCE PROGRAM
• *See page 582*

AMERICAN LEGION DEPARTMENT OF TENNESSEE

http://www.tennesseelegion.org/

JROTC SCHOLARSHIP
• *See page 582*

CONNECTICUT ARMY NATIONAL GUARD

http://www.ct.ngb.army.mil/

CONNECTICUT ARMY NATIONAL GUARD 100% TUITION WAIVER

Program is for any active member of the Connecticut Army National Guard in good standing. Must be a resident of Connecticut attending any Connecticut state (public) university, community-technical college or regional vocational-technical school. The total number of available awards is unlimited.

Award: Scholarship for use in freshman, sophomore, junior, or senior years; not renewable. *Amount:* $16,000.

Eligibility Requirements: Applicant must be age 17-65; enrolled or expecting to enroll full- or part-time at a two-year or four-year or technical institution or university; resident of Connecticut and studying in Connecticut. Available to U.S. and non-U.S. citizens. Applicant or parent must meet one or more of the following requirements: national guard experience; retired from active duty; disabled or killed as a result of military service; prisoner of war; or missing in action.

Application Requirements: Application form. *Deadline:* July 1.

Contact: Capt. Jeremy Lingenfelser, Education Services Officer
　　　Connecticut Army National Guard
　　　360 Broad Street
　　　Hartford, CT 06105-3795
　　　Phone: 860-524-4816
　　　Fax: 860-524-4904
　　　E-mail: education@ct.ngb.army.mil

DELAWARE NATIONAL GUARD

http://www.delawarenationalguard.com/

STATE TUITION ASSISTANCE
• *See page 582*

DEPARTMENT OF THE ARMY

http://www.goarmy.com/rotc

ARMY (ROTC) RESERVE OFFICERS TRAINING CORPS TWO-, THREE-, FOUR-YEAR CAMPUS-BASED SCHOLARSHIPS
• *See page 569*

U.S. ARMY ROTC FOUR-YEAR COLLEGE SCHOLARSHIP
• *See page 587*

U.S. ARMY ROTC FOUR-YEAR HISTORICALLY BLACK COLLEGE/UNIVERSITY SCHOLARSHIP
• *See page 569*

U.S. ARMY ROTC GUARANTEED RESERVE FORCES DUTY (GRFD), (ARNG/USAR) AND DEDICATED ARNG SCHOLARSHIPS
• *See page 569*

U.S. ARMY ROTC MILITARY JUNIOR COLLEGE (MJC) SCHOLARSHIP
• *See page 569*

DEPARTMENT OF VETERANS AFFAIRS (VA)

http://www.gibill.va.gov/

MONTGOMERY GI BILL (SELECTED RESERVE)
• *See page 581*

RESERVE EDUCATION ASSISTANCE PROGRAM
• *See page 583*

EDUCATION FOUNDATION. INC. NATIONAL GUARD ASSOCIATION OF COLORADO

http://www.ngaco.org/

EDUCATION FOUNDATION, INC. NATIONAL GUARD ASSOCIATION OF COLORADO SCHOLARSHIPS
• *See page 583*

ENLISTED ASSOCIATION OF THE NATIONAL GUARD OF NEW JERSEY

http://www.eang-nj.org/

CSM VINCENT BALDASSARI MEMORIAL SCHOLARSHIP PROGRAM
• *See page 583*

USAA SCHOLARSHIP
• *See page 583*

ILLINOIS STUDENT ASSISTANCE COMMISSION (ISAC)

http://www.collegezone.org/

ILLINOIS NATIONAL GUARD GRANT PROGRAM
• *See page 583*

IMAGINE AMERICA FOUNDATION

http://www.imagine-america.org

MILITARY AWARD PROGRAM (MAP)
• *See page 581*

INDIANA DEPARTMENT OF VETERANS AFFAIRS

http://www.in.gov/dva

NATIONAL GUARD SCHOLARSHIP EXTENSION PROGRAM
• *See page 584*

NATIONAL GUARD TUITION SUPPLEMENT PROGRAM
• *See page 584*

TUITION AND FEE REMISSION FOR CHILDREN AND SPOUSES OF NATIONAL GUARD MEMBERS
• *See page 584*

IOWA COLLEGE STUDENT AID COMMISSION

http://www.iowacollegeaid.gov/

IOWA NATIONAL GUARD EDUCATION ASSISTANCE PROGRAM
• *See page 584*

LOUISIANA NATIONAL GUARD, JOINT TASK FORCE LA

http://geauxguard.com/

LOUISIANA NATIONAL GUARD STATE TUITION EXEMPTION PROGRAM
• *See page 584*

MINNESOTA DEPARTMENT OF MILITARY AFFAIRS

http://www.minnesotanationalguard.org/

LEADERSHIP, EXCELLENCE, AND DEDICATED SERVICE SCHOLARSHIP
• *See page 560*

NORTH CAROLINA NATIONAL GUARD

http://www.nc.ngb.army.mil/

NORTH CAROLINA NATIONAL GUARD TUITION ASSISTANCE PROGRAM
• *See page 585*

OHIO NATIONAL GUARD

http://www.ongsp.org/

OHIO NATIONAL GUARD SCHOLARSHIP PROGRAM
• *See page 585*

PENNSYLVANIA HIGHER EDUCATION ASSISTANCE AGENCY

http://www.pheaa.org/

POSTSECONDARY EDUCATION GRATUITY PROGRAM
• *See page 585*

SOCIETY OF DAUGHTERS OF THE UNITED STATES ARMY

SOCIETY OF DAUGHTERS OF THE UNITED STATES ARMY SCHOLARSHIPS
• *See page 587*

STATE STUDENT ASSISTANCE COMMISSION OF INDIANA (SSACI)

http://www.in.gov/ssaci

INDIANA NATIONAL GUARD SUPPLEMENTAL GRANT
• *See page 585*

TEXAS HIGHER EDUCATION COORDINATING BOARD

http://www.collegefortexans.com/

TEXAS NATIONAL GUARD TUITION ASSISTANCE PROGRAM
• *See page 585*

MILITARY SERVICE: COAST GUARD

DAUGHTERS OF THE CINCINNATI

http://www.daughters1894.org/

DAUGHTERS OF THE CINCINNATI SCHOLARSHIP
• *See page 581*

DEPARTMENT OF VETERANS AFFAIRS (VA)

http://www.gibill.va.gov/

MONTGOMERY GI BILL (SELECTED RESERVE)
• *See page 581*

FRA EDUCATION FOUNDATION

http://www.fra.org/foundation

FLEET RESERVE ASSOCIATION EDUCATION FOUNDATION SCHOLARSHIPS

Only members, spouses, dependent biological, step or adoptive children; or biological, step, or adoptive grandchildren of members in good standing of the FRA currently or at time of death, are eligible for this award. Applicant must be a U.S. citizen, registered as a full time student in an accredited college located in the United States of America.

Award: Scholarship for use in freshman, sophomore, junior, senior, graduate, or postgraduate years; not renewable. *Number:* 1–15. *Amount:* $1000–$5000.

Eligibility Requirements: Applicant must be enrolled or expecting to enroll full-time at a two-year or four-year institution or university. Available to U.S. citizens. Applicant must have served in the Coast Guard, Marine Corps, or Navy.

Application Requirements: Application form, community service, essay, recommendations or references, transcript. *Deadline:* April 15.

Contact: Mrs. Marilyn Smith, Scholarship Administrator
FRA Education Foundation
125 North West Street
Alexandria, VA 22314-2754
Phone: 703-683-1400 Ext. 107
E-mail: scholars@fra.org

STANLEY A. DORAN MEMORIAL SCHOLARSHIP
• *See page 519*

IMAGINE AMERICA FOUNDATION

http://www.imagine-america.org

MILITARY AWARD PROGRAM (MAP)
• *See page 581*

LADIES AUXILIARY OF THE FLEET RESERVE ASSOCIATION

http://www.fra.org/

ALLIE MAE ODEN MEMORIAL SCHOLARSHIP
• *See page 524*

LADIES AUXILIARY OF THE FLEET RESERVE ASSOCIATION-NATIONAL PRESIDENT'S SCHOLARSHIP
• *See page 524*

LADIES AUXILIARY OF THE FLEET RESERVE ASSOCIATION SCHOLARSHIP
• *See page 524*

SAM ROSE MEMORIAL SCHOLARSHIP
• *See page 525*

TAILHOOK EDUCATIONAL FOUNDATION

http://www.tailhook.org/

TAILHOOK EDUCATIONAL FOUNDATION SCHOLARSHIP

Applicant must be a high school graduate and the natural, step or adopted son or daughter of a current or former Naval Aviator, Naval Flight Officer or Naval Air-crewman. Individuals or children of individuals serving or having served on board a U.S. Navy Aircraft Carrier in ship's company or the Air Wing also eligible.

Award: Scholarship for use in freshman, sophomore, junior, or senior years; not renewable. *Number:* 70. *Amount:* $2000–$10,000.

Eligibility Requirements: Applicant must be enrolled or expecting to enroll full-time at a two-year or four-year institution or university. Applicant must have 3.0 GPA or higher. Available to U.S. citizens. Applicant or parent must meet one or more of the following requirements: Coast Guard, Marine Corps, or Navy experience; retired from active duty; disabled or killed as a result of military service; prisoner of war; or missing in action.

Application Requirements: Application form, essay, proof of eligibility, recommendations or references, test scores, transcript. *Deadline:* March 15.

Contact: Marc Ostertag, Executive Director of Education
Tailhook Educational Foundation
9696 Businesspark Avenue
San Diego, CA 92196
Phone: 800-269-8267
Fax: 858-578-8839
E-mail: tag@tailhook.net

WISCONSIN DEPARTMENT OF VETERANS AFFAIRS (WDVA)

http://www.dva.state.wi.us/

VETERANS EDUCATION (VETED) REIMBURSEMENT GRANT
• *See page 582*

MILITARY SERVICE: GENERAL

37TH DIVISION VETERANS ASSOCIATION

http://www.37thdva.org/

37TH DIVISION VETERANS ASSOCIATION SCHOLARSHIP

Scholarships are awarded annually to a son or a daughter of a 37th Division veteran who served in World War I, World War II, or the Korean War. Applicants must display financial need and academic excellence.

Award: Scholarship for use in freshman, sophomore, junior, senior, or graduate years; not renewable.

Eligibility Requirements: Applicant must be enrolled or expecting to enroll full- or part-time at a two-year or four-year institution or university. Available to U.S. citizens. Applicant or parent must meet one or more of the following requirements: general military experience; retired from active duty; disabled or killed as a result of military service; prisoner of war; or missing in action.

Application Requirements: Application form, financial need analysis, recommendations or references. *Deadline:* April 1.

Contact: Cyril Sedlacko, Secretary and Treasurer
Phone: 614-228-3788
Fax: 614-228-3793
E-mail: ops@37thdva.org

ALABAMA DEPARTMENT OF VETERANS AFFAIRS

http://www.va.alabama.gov/

ALABAMA G.I. DEPENDENTS SCHOLARSHIP PROGRAM

Full scholarship for dependents of Alabama disabled, prisoner-of-war, or missing-in-action veterans. Child or stepchild must initiate training before 26th birthday; age 30 deadline may apply in certain situations. No age deadline for spouses or widows.

Award: Scholarship for use in freshman, sophomore, junior, or senior years; renewable.

Eligibility Requirements: Applicant must be enrolled or expecting to enroll full- or part-time at a four-year institution or university; resident of Alabama and studying in Alabama. Available to U.S. and non-U.S. citizens. Applicant or parent must meet one or more of the following requirements: general military experience; retired from active duty; disabled or killed as a result of military service; prisoner of war; or missing in action.

Application Requirements: Application form. *Deadline:* varies.

Contact: Willie Moore, Scholarship Administrator
Alabama Department of Veterans Affairs
PO Box 1509
Montgomery, AL 36102-1509
Phone: 334-242-5077
Fax: 334-242-5102
E-mail: wmoore@va.state.al.us

AMERICAN LEGION AUXILIARY DEPARTMENT OF ALABAMA

http://americanlegionalabama.org/

AMERICAN LEGION AUXILIARY DEPARTMENT OF ALABAMA SCHOLARSHIP PROGRAM

Merit-based scholarships for Alabama residents, preferably ages 17 to 25, who are children or grandchildren of veterans of World War I, World War II, Korea, Vietnam, Operation Desert Storm, Beirut, Grenada, or Panama. Submit proof of relationship and service record. Renewable awards of $850 each. Must send self-addressed stamped envelope for application.

Award: Scholarship for use in freshman, sophomore, junior, or senior years; renewable. *Number:* up to 40. *Amount:* $850.

Eligibility Requirements: Applicant must be age 17-25; enrolled or expecting to enroll full-time at a four-year institution or university and resident of Alabama. Applicant must have 3.5 GPA or higher. Available to U.S. citizens. Applicant or parent must meet one or more of the following requirements: general military experience; retired from active duty; disabled or killed as a result of military service; prisoner of war; or missing in action.

Application Requirements: Application form, birth certificate, service record, financial need analysis, personal photograph, recommendations or references, self-addressed stamped envelope with application, test scores, transcript. *Deadline:* April 1.

AMERICAN LEGION AUXILIARY DEPARTMENT OF COLORADO

http://www.alacolorado.com

AMERICAN LEGION AUXILIARY DEPARTMENT OF COLORADO DEPARTMENT PRESIDENT'S SCHOLARSHIP FOR JUNIOR MEMBER

Open to children, spouses, grandchildren, and great-grandchildren of veterans, and veterans who served in the Armed Forces during eligibility dates for membership in the American Legion. Applicants must be Colorado residents who have been accepted by an accredited school in Colorado.

Award: Scholarship for use in freshman year; not renewable. *Number:* 1–2. *Amount:* up to $500.

Eligibility Requirements: Applicant must be high school student; planning to enroll or expecting to enroll full- or part-time at a four-year institution or university; resident of Colorado and studying in Colorado. Available to U.S. citizens. Applicant or parent must meet one or more of the following requirements: general military experience; retired from active duty; disabled or killed as a result of military service; prisoner of war; or missing in action.

Application Requirements: Application form, essay, recommendations or references, transcript. *Deadline:* April 15.

Contact: Lynn Cody, Department Secretary and Treasurer
American Legion Auxiliary Department of Colorado
7465 East First Avenue, Suite D
Denver, CO 80230
Phone: 303-367-5388
Fax: 303-367-5388
E-mail: www.dept-sec@alacolorado.com

AMERICAN LEGION AUXILIARY DEPARTMENT OF CONNECTICUT

http://www.ct.legion.org/

AMERICAN LEGION AUXILIARY DEPARTMENT OF CONNECTICUT MEMORIAL EDUCATIONAL GRANT

• See page 504

AMERICAN LEGION AUXILIARY DEPARTMENT OF CONNECTICUT PAST PRESIDENTS' PARLEY MEMORIAL EDUCATION GRANT

• See page 504

AMERICAN LEGION AUXILIARY DEPARTMENT OF FLORIDA

http://www.alafl.org/

AMERICAN LEGION AUXILIARY DEPARTMENT OF FLORIDA DEPARTMENT SCHOLARSHIPS

Scholarship for children of veterans who were honorably discharged. Must be Florida resident attending an institution within Florida for full-time undergraduate study. Minimum 2.5 GPA. Must submit copy of parent's military discharge.

Award: Scholarship for use in freshman, sophomore, junior, or senior years; renewable. *Number:* 16–22. *Amount:* $500–$1000.

Eligibility Requirements: Applicant must be enrolled or expecting to enroll full-time at a two-year or four-year or technical institution or university; resident of Florida and studying in Florida. Applicant must have 2.5 GPA or higher. Available to U.S. citizens. Applicant or parent must meet one or more of the following requirements: general military experience; retired from active duty; disabled or killed as a result of military service; prisoner of war; or missing in action.

Application Requirements: Application form, financial need analysis, proof of discharge from armed services, recommendations or references, transcript. *Deadline:* March 1.

Contact: Robin Briere, Department Secretary and Treasurer
Phone: 407-293-7411
Fax: 407-299-6522
E-mail: contact@alafl.org

AMERICAN LEGION AUXILIARY DEPARTMENT OF FLORIDA MEMORIAL SCHOLARSHIP

• See page 504

AMERICAN LEGION AUXILIARY DEPARTMENT OF INDIANA

http://www.amlegauxin.org/

AMERICAN LEGION AUXILIARY DEPARTMENT OF INDIANA EDNA M. BURCUS/HOOSIER SCHOOLHOUSE MEMORIAL SCHOLARSHIP

One-time award for child, grandchild, or great-grandchild of veteran who served during American Legion eligibility dates. Must be Indiana resident and graduating high school senior enrolled as full-time undergraduate at an accredited Indiana institution.

Award: Scholarship for use in freshman year; not renewable. *Number:* 3. *Amount:* $500.

Eligibility Requirements: Applicant must be high school student; planning to enroll or expecting to enroll full-time at a two-year or four-year institution or university; resident of Indiana and studying in Indiana. Available to U.S. citizens. Applicant or parent must meet one or more of the following requirements: general military experience; retired from active duty; disabled or killed as a result of military service; prisoner of war; or missing in action.

Application Requirements: Application form, essay, financial need analysis, self-addressed stamped envelope with application. *Deadline:* April 1.

Contact: Judy Otey, Department Secretary and Treasurer
Phone: 317-630-1390
Fax: 317-630-1277
E-mail: ala777@sbcglobal.net

AMERICAN LEGION AUXILIARY DEPARTMENT OF IOWA

http://www.ialegion.org/ala

AMERICAN LEGION AUXILIARY DEPARTMENT OF IOWA CHILDREN OF VETERANS MERIT AWARD

One-time award available to a high school senior, child of a veteran who served in the armed forces during eligibility dates for American Legion membership. Must be U.S. citizen and Iowa resident enrolled at an Iowa institution.

Award: Scholarship for use in freshman year; not renewable. *Number:* 10. *Amount:* $300.

Eligibility Requirements: Applicant must be high school student; planning to enroll or expecting to enroll full- or part-time at a two-year or four-year or technical institution or university; resident of Iowa and studying in Iowa. Available to U.S. citizens. Applicant or parent must meet one or more of the following requirements: general military experience; retired from active duty; disabled or killed as a result of military service; prisoner of war; or missing in action.

Application Requirements: Application form, essay, financial need analysis, personal photograph, recommendations or references, self-addressed stamped envelope with application, test scores, transcript. *Deadline:* June 1.

Contact: Marlene Valentine, Executive Secretary and Treasurer
American Legion Auxiliary Department of Iowa
720 Lyon Street
Des Moines, IA 50309
Phone: 515-282-7987
Fax: 515-282-7583
E-mail: alasectreas@ialegion.org

AMERICAN LEGION AUXILIARY DEPARTMENT OF KENTUCKY

http://www.kylegion.org/

AMERICAN LEGION AUXILIARY DEPARTMENT OF KENTUCKY MARY BARRETT MARSHALL SCHOLARSHIP

Scholarship to the daughter or grand daughter of a veteran in The American Legion. Applicant must attend a Kentucky college, and demonstrate financial need.

Award: Scholarship for use in freshman year; not renewable. *Number:* 1. *Amount:* $1000.

Eligibility Requirements: Applicant must be high school student; planning to enroll or expecting to enroll full-time at a four-year institution or university; female and studying in Kentucky. Available to U.S. citizens. Applicant or parent must meet one or more of the following requirements: general military experience; retired from active duty; disabled or killed as a result of military service; prisoner of war; or missing in action.

Application Requirements: Application form, financial need analysis, transcript. *Deadline:* April 1.

Contact: Betty Cook, Secretary and Treasurer
Phone: 270-932-7533
Fax: 270-932-7672
E-mail: secretarykyala@aol.com

AMERICAN LEGION AUXILIARY DEPARTMENT OF MAINE

http://www.mainelegion.org/

AMERICAN LEGION AUXILIARY DEPARTMENT OF MAINE DANIEL E. LAMBERT MEMORIAL SCHOLARSHIP

Scholarships to assist young men and women in continuing their education beyond high school. Must demonstrate financial need, must be a resident of the State of Maine, U.S. citizen, and parent must be a veteran.

Award: Scholarship for use in freshman year; not renewable. *Number:* up to 2. *Amount:* $1000.

Eligibility Requirements: Applicant must be high school student; planning to enroll or expecting to enroll full-time at a four-year institution or university and resident of Maine. Available to U.S. citizens. Applicant or parent must meet one or more of the following requirements: general military experience; retired from active duty; disabled or killed as a result of military service; prisoner of war; or missing in action.

Application Requirements: Application form, financial need analysis. *Deadline:* May 1.

Contact: Mary Wells, Education Chairman
Phone: 207-532-6007
E-mail: aladeptsecme@verizon.net

AMERICAN LEGION AUXILIARY DEPARTMENT OF MAINE NATIONAL PRESIDENT'S SCHOLARSHIP
• *See page 550*

AMERICAN LEGION AUXILIARY DEPARTMENT OF MARYLAND

http://www.alamd.org/

AMERICAN LEGION AUXILIARY DEPARTMENT OF MARYLAND CHILDREN AND YOUTH SCHOLARSHIPS

One scholarship of $2000 for undergraduate student enrolled in full-time study at an accredited college or university. Must be U.S. citizen, Maryland resident, and child of a military veteran.

Award: Scholarship for use in freshman, sophomore, junior, or senior years; renewable. *Number:* 1. *Amount:* $2000.

Eligibility Requirements: Applicant must be enrolled or expecting to enroll full-time at a four-year institution or university; female and resident of Maryland. Available to U.S. citizens. Applicant or parent must meet one or more of the following requirements: general military experience; retired from active duty; disabled or killed as a result of military service; prisoner of war; or missing in action.

Application Requirements: Application form, community service, financial need analysis, recommendations or references, transcript. *Deadline:* May 1.

Contact: Pamela Miller, Secretary
Phone: 410-242-9519
E-mail: hq@alamd.org

AMERICAN LEGION AUXILIARY DEPARTMENT OF MASSACHUSETTS

http://www.masslegion-aux.org/

AMERICAN LEGION AUXILIARY DEPARTMENT OF MASSACHUSETTS DEPARTMENT PRESIDENT'S SCHOLARSHIP
• *See page 550*

AMERICAN LEGION AUXILIARY DEPARTMENT OF MASSACHUSETTS PAST PRESIDENTS' PARLEY SCHOLARSHIP

One-time awards of $200 to $750 for residents of Massachusetts who are children of living or deceased veterans. Must be between the ages of 16 to 22 years and enrolled full-time at a Massachusetts institution.

Award: Scholarship for use in freshman, sophomore, junior, or senior years; not renewable. *Number:* 1. *Amount:* $200–$750.

Eligibility Requirements: Applicant must be age 16-22; enrolled or expecting to enroll full-time at a two-year or four-year institution or university; resident of Massachusetts and studying in Massachusetts. Available to U.S. citizens. Applicant or parent must meet one or more of the following requirements: general military experience; retired from active duty; disabled or killed as a result of military service; prisoner of war; or missing in action.

Application Requirements: Application form. *Deadline:* March 1.

Contact: Beverly Monaco, Secretary and Treasurer
Phone: 617-727-2958
Fax: 617-727-0741

AMERICAN LEGION AUXILIARY DEPARTMENT OF MICHIGAN

http://www.michalaux.org/

AMERICAN LEGION AUXILIARY DEPARTMENT OF MICHIGAN MEMORIAL SCHOLARSHIP

Scholarship for daughter, granddaughter, and great-granddaughter of any honorably discharged or deceased veteran of U.S. wars or conflicts. Must be Michigan resident for minimum of one year, female between 16 and 21 years, and attend college in Michigan. Must include copy of military discharge and copy of parent or guardian's IRS 1040 form.

Award: Scholarship for use in freshman or sophomore years; not renewable. *Number:* 10–20. *Amount:* $500.

Eligibility Requirements: Applicant must be age 16-21; enrolled or expecting to enroll full-time at a two-year or four-year or technical institution or university; female; resident of Michigan and studying in Michigan. Available to U.S. citizens. Applicant must have general military experience.

Application Requirements: Application form, discharge papers, financial need analysis, recommendations or references, transcript. *Deadline:* March 15.

AMERICAN LEGION AUXILIARY DEPARTMENT OF MICHIGAN SCHOLARSHIP FOR NON-TRADITIONAL STUDENT

Applicant must be a dependent of a veteran. Must be one of the following: nontraditional student returning to classroom after some period of time in which their education was interrupted, student over the age of 22 attending college for the first time to pursue a degree, or student over the age of 22 attending a trade or vocational school. Applicants must be Michigan residents only and attend Michigan institution. Judging based on need, character/leadership, scholastic standing, and initiative/goal.

Award: Scholarship for use in freshman, sophomore, junior, or senior years; renewable. *Number:* 1. *Amount:* $500.

Eligibility Requirements: Applicant must be age 23-99; enrolled or expecting to enroll full- or part-time at a two-year or four-year or technical institution or university; resident of Michigan and studying in Michigan. Available to U.S. citizens. Applicant must have general military experience.

Application Requirements: Application form, copy of veteran's discharge papers, financial need analysis, transcript. *Deadline:* March 15.

AMERICAN LEGION AUXILIARY NATIONAL PRESIDENT'S SCHOLARSHIP

One-time scholarship for son or daughter of veterans, who were in armed forces during the eligibility dates for American Legion membership. Must be high school senior. Only one candidate per Auxiliary Unit. Applicant must complete 50 hours of volunteer service in the community. Must submit essay of no more than 1000 words on a specified topic.

Award: Scholarship for use in freshman year; not renewable. *Number:* 15. *Amount:* $2500–$3500.

Eligibility Requirements: Applicant must be high school student and planning to enroll or expecting to enroll full-time at a two-year or four-year institution or university. Available to U.S. citizens. Applicant must have general military experience.

Application Requirements: Application form, community service, entry in a contest, essay, financial need analysis, original article (1000-word maximum), recommendations or references, test scores, transcript. *Deadline:* March 1.

AMERICAN LEGION AUXILIARY SPIRIT OF YOUTH SCHOLARSHIP

Scholarship valued at $5000 is available to one Junior American Legion Auxiliary member in each division. The applicant must have held membership in the American Legion Auxiliary for the past three years, must hold a current membership card, and must continue to maintain their membership throughout the four-year scholarship period.

Award: Scholarship for use in freshman, sophomore, junior, or senior years; renewable. *Number:* 5. *Amount:* $5000.

Eligibility Requirements: Applicant must be high school student; planning to enroll or expecting to enroll full-time at a two-year or four-year or technical institution or university and female. Applicant must have 3.0 GPA or higher. Available to U.S. citizens. Applicant must have general military experience.

Application Requirements: Application form, entry in a contest, essay, financial need analysis, original article (1000-word maximum, typed and double-spaced), recommendations or references, transcript. *Deadline:* March 1.

AMERICAN LEGION AUXILIARY DEPARTMENT OF MINNESOTA

http://www.mnlegion.org/

AMERICAN LEGION AUXILIARY DEPARTMENT OF MINNESOTA SCHOLARSHIPS

Seven $1000 awards for the sons, daughters, grandsons, or granddaughters of veterans who served in the Armed Forces during specific eligibility dates. Must be a Minnesota resident, a high school senior or graduate, in need of financial assistance, of good character, having a good scholastic record and at least a C average. Must be planning to attend a Minnesota post secondary institution.

Award: Scholarship for use in freshman, sophomore, junior, or senior years; not renewable. *Number:* up to 7. *Amount:* $1000.

Eligibility Requirements: Applicant must be enrolled or expecting to enroll full-time at a two-year or four-year or technical institution or university; resident of Minnesota and studying in Minnesota. Available to U.S. citizens. Applicant or parent must meet one or more of the following requirements: general military experience; retired from active duty; disabled or killed as a result of military service; prisoner of war; or missing in action.

Application Requirements: Application form, essay, financial need analysis, recommendations or references, transcript. *Deadline:* March 15.

Contact: Eleanor Johnson, Executive Secretary
American Legion Auxiliary Department of Minnesota
State Veterans Service Building, 20 West 12th Street, Room 314
St. Paul, MN 55155
Phone: 651-224-7634
Fax: 651-224-5243

AMERICAN LEGION AUXILIARY DEPARTMENT OF MISSOURI

http://www.missourilegion.org/

AMERICAN LEGION AUXILIARY DEPARTMENT OF MISSOURI LELA MURPHY SCHOLARSHIP
• *See page 504*

AMERICAN LEGION AUXILIARY DEPARTMENT OF MISSOURI NATIONAL PRESIDENT'S SCHOLARSHIP
• *See page 505*

AMERICAN LEGION AUXILIARY DEPARTMENT OF NEBRASKA

http://www.nebraskalegionaux.net/

AMERICAN LEGION AUXILIARY DEPARTMENT OF NEBRASKA RUBY PAUL CAMPAIGN FUND SCHOLARSHIP
• *See page 505*

AMERICAN LEGION AUXILIARY DEPARTMENT OF NORTH DAKOTA

http://www.ndlegion.org/

AMERICAN LEGION AUXILIARY DEPARTMENT OF NORTH DAKOTA NATIONAL PRESIDENT'S SCHOLARSHIP
• *See page 550*

AMERICAN LEGION AUXILIARY DEPARTMENT OF OHIO

http://www.alaohio.org/

AMERICAN LEGION AUXILIARY DEPARTMENT OF OHIO CONTINUING EDUCATION FUND

One-time award for Ohio residents who are the children or grandchildren of veterans, living or deceased, honorably discharged during eligibility dates for American Legion membership. Awards are for undergraduate use, based on need. Freshmen not eligible. Application must be signed by a unit representative.

Award: Scholarship for use in sophomore, junior, or senior years; not renewable. *Number:* 15. *Amount:* $200.

Eligibility Requirements: Applicant must be enrolled or expecting to enroll full-time at a two-year or four-year institution or university and resident of Ohio. Available to U.S. citizens. Applicant or parent must meet one or more of the following requirements: general military experience; retired from active duty; disabled or killed as a result of military service; prisoner of war; or missing in action.

Application Requirements: Application form, financial need analysis, transcript. *Deadline:* November 1.

Contact: Katie Tucker, Scholarship Coordinator
Phone: 740-452-8245
Fax: 740-452-2620
E-mail: ala_katie@rrohio.com

AMERICAN LEGION AUXILIARY DEPARTMENT OF OHIO DEPARTMENT PRESIDENT'S SCHOLARSHIP

Scholarship for children or grandchildren of veterans who served in Armed Forces during eligibility dates for American Legion membership. Must be high school senior, ages 16 to 18, Ohio resident, and U.S. citizen. Award for full-time undergraduate study. One-time award of $1000 to $1500.

Award: Scholarship for use in freshman year; not renewable. *Number:* 2. *Amount:* $1000–$1500.

Eligibility Requirements: Applicant must be high school student; age 16-18; planning to enroll or expecting to enroll full-time at a two-year or four-year institution or university and resident of Ohio. Available to U.S. citizens. Applicant or parent must meet one or more of the following requirements: general military experience; retired from active duty; disabled or killed as a result of military service; prisoner of war; or missing in action.

Application Requirements: Application form, essay, financial need analysis, recommendations or references, transcript. *Deadline:* March 1.

AMERICAN LEGION AUXILIARY DEPARTMENT OF OREGON

http://www.alaoregon.org/

AMERICAN LEGION AUXILIARY DEPARTMENT OF OREGON DEPARTMENT GRANTS

One-time award for educational use in the state of Oregon. Must be a resident of Oregon who is the child or widow of a veteran or the wife of a disabled veteran.

Award: Grant for use in freshman, sophomore, junior, or senior years; not renewable. *Number:* 2. *Amount:* $1000.

Eligibility Requirements: Applicant must be enrolled or expecting to enroll full- or part-time at a two-year or four-year or technical institution or university and resident of Oregon. Available to U.S. citizens. Applicant or parent must meet one or more of the following requirements: general military experience; retired from active duty; disabled or killed as a result of military service; prisoner of war; or missing in action.

Application Requirements: Application form, essay, financial need analysis, interview, recommendations or references, test scores, transcript. *Deadline:* March 10.

Contact: Virginia Biddle, Secretary/Treasurer
American Legion Auxiliary Department of Oregon
PO Box 1730
Wilsonville, OR 97070
Phone: 503-682-3162
Fax: 503-685-5008
E-mail: alaor@pcez.com

AMERICAN LEGION AUXILIARY DEPARTMENT OF OREGON NATIONAL PRESIDENT'S SCHOLARSHIP

One-time award for children of veterans who served in the Armed Forces during eligibility dates for American Legion membership. Must be high school senior and Oregon resident. Must be entered by a local American Legion auxiliary unit. Three scholarships of varying amounts.

Award: Scholarship for use in freshman year; not renewable. *Number:* 3. *Amount:* $1000–$2500.

Eligibility Requirements: Applicant must be high school student; planning to enroll or expecting to enroll full-time at a four-year institution or university and resident of Oregon. Available to U.S. citizens. Applicant or parent must meet one or more of the following requirements: general military experience; retired from active duty; disabled or killed as a result of military service; prisoner of war; or missing in action.

Application Requirements: Application form, essay, financial need analysis, interview, recommendations or references, transcript. *Deadline:* March 1.

Contact: Virginia Biddle, Secretary/Treasurer
American Legion Auxiliary Department of Oregon
PO Box 1730
Wilsonville, OR 97070
Phone: 503-682-3162
Fax: 503-685-5008
E-mail: alaor@pcez.com

AMERICAN LEGION AUXILIARY DEPARTMENT OF OREGON SPIRIT OF YOUTH SCHOLARSHIP
• See page 505

AMERICAN LEGION AUXILIARY DEPARTMENT OF SOUTH DAKOTA

http://www.sdlegion-aux.org/

AMERICAN LEGION AUXILIARY DEPARTMENT OF SOUTH DAKOTA COLLEGE SCHOLARSHIPS
• See page 505

AMERICAN LEGION AUXILIARY DEPARTMENT OF SOUTH DAKOTA SENIOR SCHOLARSHIP
• See page 505

AMERICAN LEGION AUXILIARY DEPARTMENT OF SOUTH DAKOTA THELMA FOSTER SCHOLARSHIP FOR SENIOR AUXILIARY MEMBERS
• See page 505

AMERICAN LEGION AUXILIARY DEPARTMENT OF SOUTH DAKOTA THELMA FOSTER SCHOLARSHIPS FOR JUNIOR AUXILIARY MEMBERS
• See page 506

AMERICAN LEGION AUXILIARY DEPARTMENT OF SOUTH DAKOTA VOCATIONAL SCHOLARSHIP
• See page 506

AMERICAN LEGION AUXILIARY DEPARTMENT OF TENNESSEE

http://www.legion-aux.org/

AMERICAN LEGION AUXILIARY DEPARTMENT OF TENNESSEE VARA GRAY SCHOLARSHIP-GENERAL

One-time award for high school senior who is the child of a veteran (Verification of veteran eligibility is required.) Must be Tennessee resident and single. Must have completed 50 hours of voluntary community service. Award must be used within one year. A written essay is required covering a topic determined by the Auxiliary yearly.

Award: Scholarship for use in freshman year; not renewable. *Number:* 3. *Amount:* $500.

Eligibility Requirements: Applicant must be high school student; planning to enroll or expecting to enroll full-time at a two-year or four-year institution or university; single and resident of Tennessee. Available to U.S. citizens. Applicant or parent must meet one or more of the following requirements: general military experience; retired from active duty; disabled or killed as a result of military service; prisoner of war; or missing in action.

Application Requirements: Application form, community service, essay, financial need analysis, recommendations or references, test scores, transcript. *Deadline:* March 15.

Contact: Mrs. Sue Milliken, Department Secretary and Treasurer
American Legion Auxiliary Department of Tennessee
104 Point East Drive
Nashville, TN 37216
Phone: 615-226-8648
Fax: 615-226-8649
E-mail: alatn@bellsouth.net

AMERICAN LEGION AUXILIARY DEPARTMENT OF TEXAS

http://www.alatexas.org/

AMERICAN LEGION AUXILIARY DEPARTMENT OF TEXAS GENERAL EDUCATION SCHOLARSHIP

Scholarships available for Texas residents. Must be a child of a veteran who served in the Armed Forces during eligibility dates. Some additional criteria used for selection are recommendations, academics, and finances.

Award: Scholarship for use in freshman, sophomore, junior, or senior years; not renewable. *Number:* 1–10. *Amount:* $500.

Eligibility Requirements: Applicant must be enrolled or expecting to enroll full-time at a two-year or four-year or technical institution or university and resident of Texas. Available to U.S. citizens. Applicant must have general military experience.

Application Requirements: Application form, community service, financial need analysis, letter stating qualifications and intentions, recommendations or references, resume, transcript. *Deadline:* June 1.

Contact: Paula Raney, State Secretary
American Legion Auxiliary Department of Texas
PO Box 140407
Austin, TX 78714
Phone: 512-476-7278
Fax: 512-482-8391
E-mail: alatexas@txlegion.org

AMERICAN LEGION AUXILIARY DEPARTMENT OF UTAH

http://www.legion-aux.org/

AMERICAN LEGION AUXILIARY DEPARTMENT OF UTAH NATIONAL PRESIDENT'S SCHOLARSHIP
• *See page 506*

AMERICAN LEGION AUXILIARY DEPARTMENT OF WISCONSIN

http://www.amlegionauxwi.org/

AMERICAN LEGION AUXILIARY DEPARTMENT OF WISCONSIN DELLA VAN DEUREN MEMORIAL SCHOLARSHIP
• *See page 506*

AMERICAN LEGION AUXILIARY DEPARTMENT OF WISCONSIN H.S. AND ANGELINE LEWIS SCHOLARSHIPS
• *See page 506*

AMERICAN LEGION AUXILIARY DEPARTMENT OF WISCONSIN MERIT AND MEMORIAL SCHOLARSHIPS
• *See page 507*

AMERICAN LEGION AUXILIARY DEPARTMENT OF WISCONSIN PAST PRESIDENTS' PARLEY HEALTH CAREER SCHOLARSHIPS
• *See page 507*

AMERICAN LEGION AUXILIARY DEPARTMENT OF WISCONSIN PRESIDENT'S SCHOLARSHIPS
• *See page 507*

AMERICAN LEGION AUXILIARY NATIONAL HEADQUARTERS

http://www.ALAforVeterans.org

AMERICAN LEGION AUXILIARY NATIONAL PRESIDENT'S SCHOLARSHIPS

One-time scholarship for high school children of veterans who served in the Armed Forces during the eligibility dates for The American Legion. The applicant must complete 50 hours of community service during his/her high school years to be eligible for one of these scholarships.

Award: Scholarship for use in freshman year; not renewable. *Number:* 15. *Amount:* $1000–$2500.

Eligibility Requirements: Applicant must be high school student and planning to enroll or expecting to enroll full-time at a four-year institution or university. Available to U.S. citizens. Applicant or parent must meet one or more of the following requirements: general military experience; retired from active duty; disabled or killed as a result of military service; prisoner of war; or missing in action.

Application Requirements: Application form, community service, essay, recommendations or references, self-addressed stamped envelope with application, test scores, transcript. *Deadline:* March 1.

Contact: Maria Potts, Program Coordinator
Phone: 317-569-4555
E-mail: mpotts@ALAforVeterans.org

AMERICAN LEGION DEPARTMENT OF ARKANSAS

http://www.arklegion.homestead.com/

AMERICAN LEGION DEPARTMENT OF ARKANSAS COUDRET SCHOLARSHIP AWARD
• *See page 508*

AMERICAN LEGION DEPARTMENT OF IDAHO

http://www.idlegion.home.mindspring.com/

AMERICAN LEGION DEPARTMENT OF IDAHO SCHOLARSHIP
• *See page 508*

AMERICAN LEGION DEPARTMENT OF ILLINOIS

http://www.illegion.org/

AMERICAN LEGION DEPARTMENT OF ILLINOIS SCHOLARSHIPS
• *See page 508*

AMERICAN LEGION DEPARTMENT OF KANSAS

http://www.ksamlegion.org/

ALBERT M. LAPPIN SCHOLARSHIP
• *See page 509*

CHARLES W. AND ANNETTE HILL SCHOLARSHIP
• *See page 509*

HUGH A. SMITH SCHOLARSHIP FUND
• *See page 509*

ROSEDALE POST 346 SCHOLARSHIP
• *See page 509*

TED AND NORA ANDERSON SCHOLARSHIPS
• *See page 510*

AMERICAN LEGION DEPARTMENT OF MAINE

http://www.mainelegion.org/

AMERICAN LEGION DEPARTMENT OF MAINE CHILDREN AND YOUTH SCHOLARSHIP

Scholarships available to high school seniors, college students, and veterans who are residents of Maine. Must be in upper half of high school class. One-time award of $500.

Award: Scholarship for use in freshman, sophomore, junior, or senior years; not renewable. *Number:* 7. *Amount:* $500.

Eligibility Requirements: Applicant must be enrolled or expecting to enroll full-time at a two-year or four-year or technical institution or university and resident of Maine. Available to U.S. citizens. Applicant or parent must meet one or more of the following requirements: general military experience; retired from active duty; disabled or killed as a result of military service; prisoner of war; or missing in action.

Application Requirements: Application form, essay, financial need analysis, recommendations or references, transcript. *Deadline:* May 1.

Contact: Mr. Lloyd Woods, Department Adjutant
American Legion Department of Maine
PO Box 900
Waterville, ME 04903
Phone: 207-873-3229
Fax: 207-872-0501
E-mail: legionme@mainelegion.org

DANIEL E. LAMBERT MEMORIAL SCHOLARSHIP

One-time award for undergraduate and graduate student whose parents are veterans. Award is based on financial need and good character. Must be U.S. citizen. Applicant must show evidence of being enrolled, or attending accredited college or vocational technical school. Scholarship value is from $500 to $1000.

Award: Scholarship for use in freshman, sophomore, junior, or senior years; not renewable. *Number:* 1–2. *Amount:* $500–$1000.

Eligibility Requirements: Applicant must be enrolled or expecting to enroll full-time at a two-year or four-year or technical institution or university and resident of Maine. Available to U.S. citizens. Applicant or parent must meet one or more of the following requirements: general military experience; retired from active duty; disabled or killed as a result of military service; prisoner of war; or missing in action.

Application Requirements: Application form, recommendations or references. *Deadline:* May 1.

Contact: Mr. Lloyd Woods, Department Adjutant
American Legion Department of Maine
PO Box 900
Waterville, ME 04903
Phone: 207-873-3229
Fax: 207-872-0501
E-mail: legionme@mainelegion.org

JAMES V. DAY SCHOLARSHIP
• *See page 510*

AMERICAN LEGION DEPARTMENT OF MARYLAND

http://www.mdlegion.org/

AMERICAN LEGION DEPARTMENT OF MARYLAND GENERAL SCHOLARSHIP FUND

Nonrenewable scholarship for veterans or children of veterans who served in the Armed Forces during dates of eligibility for American Legion membership. Merit-based award. Application available on website, http://mdlegion.org.

Award: Scholarship for use in freshman, sophomore, junior, or senior years; not renewable. *Number:* 1–10. *Amount:* up to $500.

Eligibility Requirements: Applicant must be enrolled or expecting to enroll full-time at a four-year institution or university and resident of Maryland. Available to U.S. citizens. Applicant or parent must meet one or more of the following requirements: general military experience; retired from active duty; disabled or killed as a result of military service; prisoner of war; or missing in action.

Application Requirements: Application form, essay, financial need analysis, transcript. *Deadline:* April 1.

Contact: Russell Myers, Department Adjutant
American Legion Department of Maryland
101 North Gay, Room E
Baltimore, MD 21202
Phone: 410-752-1405
Fax: 410-752-3822
E-mail: russell@mdlegion.org

AMERICAN LEGION DEPARTMENT OF MICHIGAN

http://www.michiganlegion.org/

GUY M. WILSON SCHOLARSHIPS

Scholarship for undergraduate use at a Michigan college. Must be resident of Michigan and the son, daughter, grandchild, or great grandchild of a veteran, living or deceased. Must submit copy of veteran's honorable discharge. Must have minimum 2.5 GPA. Total number of awards given vary each year depending upon the number of applications received. Applicants have to refer the website for the deadline.

Award: Scholarship for use in freshman year; not renewable. *Number:* 11. *Amount:* $500.

Eligibility Requirements: Applicant must be high school student; planning to enroll or expecting to enroll full- or part-time at a two-year or four-year institution or university; resident of Michigan and studying in Michigan. Applicant must have 2.5 GPA or higher. Available to U.S. citizens. Applicant or parent must meet one or more of the following requirements: general military experience; retired from active duty; disabled or killed as a result of military service; prisoner of war; or missing in action.

Application Requirements: Application form, essay, financial need analysis, test scores, transcript.

Contact: Deanna Clark, Department Administrative Assistant for Programs
American Legion Department of Michigan
212 North Verlinden Avenue, Suite A
Lansing, MI 48915
Phone: 517-371-4720 Ext. 11
Fax: 517-371-2401
E-mail: programs@michiganlegion.org

WILLIAM D. AND JEWELL W. BREWER SCHOLARSHIP TRUSTS

One-time award for residents of Michigan who are the son, daughter, grandchild, or great grandchild of veterans, living or deceased. Must submit copy of veteran's honorable discharge. Several scholarships of $500 each. Must have minimum 2.5 GPA. Scholarship can be applied to any college or university within the United States.

Award: Scholarship for use in freshman, sophomore, junior, or senior years; not renewable. *Number:* 4. *Amount:* $500.

Eligibility Requirements: Applicant must be enrolled or expecting to enroll full- or part-time at a two-year or four-year institution or university and resident of Michigan. Applicant must have 2.5 GPA or higher.

Available to U.S. citizens. Applicant or parent must meet one or more of the following requirements: general military experience; retired from active duty; disabled or killed as a result of military service; prisoner of war; or missing in action.

Application Requirements: Application form, essay, financial need analysis, test scores, transcript.

Contact: Deanna Clark, Department Administrative Assistant for Programs
American Legion Department of Michigan
212 North Verlinden Avenue, Suite A
Lansing, MI 48915
Phone: 517-371-4720 Ext. 11
Fax: 517-371-2401
E-mail: programs@michiganlegion.org

AMERICAN LEGION DEPARTMENT OF MINNESOTA

http://www.mnlegion.org/

AMERICAN LEGION DEPARTMENT OF MINNESOTA MEMORIAL SCHOLARSHIP
• *See page 510*

MINNESOTA LEGIONNAIRES INSURANCE TRUST SCHOLARSHIP
• *See page 510*

AMERICAN LEGION DEPARTMENT OF MISSOURI

http://www.missourilegion.org/

CHARLES L. BACON MEMORIAL SCHOLARSHIP
• *See page 510*

LILLIE LOIS FORD SCHOLARSHIP FUND

Two awards of $1000 each are given each year to one boy and one girl. Applicant must have attended a full session of Missouri Boys/Girls State or Missouri Cadet Patrol Academy. Must be a Missouri resident below age 21, attending an accredited college/university as a full-time student. Must be an unmarried descendant of a veteran having served at least 90 days on active duty in the Army, Air Force, Navy, Marine Corps, or Coast Guard of the United States.

Award: Scholarship for use in freshman year; not renewable. *Number:* 2. *Amount:* $1000.

Eligibility Requirements: Applicant must be high school student; planning to enroll or expecting to enroll full-time at a two-year or four-year institution or university; single and resident of Missouri. Available to U.S. citizens. Applicant or parent must meet one or more of the following requirements: general military experience; retired from active duty; disabled or killed as a result of military service; prisoner of war; or missing in action.

Application Requirements: Application form, copy of the veteran's discharge certificate, financial need analysis, test scores. *Deadline:* April 20.

Contact: John Doane, Chairman, Education and Scholarship Committee
American Legion Department of Missouri
PO Box 179
Jefferson City, MO 65102-0179
Phone: 417-924-8186

AMERICAN LEGION DEPARTMENT OF NEBRASKA

http://www.nebraskalegion.net/

MAYNARD JENSEN AMERICAN LEGION MEMORIAL SCHOLARSHIP
• *See page 511*

AMERICAN LEGION DEPARTMENT OF NORTH DAKOTA

http://www.ndlegion.org/

HATTIE TEDROW MEMORIAL FUND SCHOLARSHIP

Applicants must be legal residents of North Dakota, high school seniors, and direct descendents of a veteran with honorable service in the U.S. military. The student will have two years from the date of graduation from high school to use his/her award.

Award: Scholarship for use in freshman, sophomore, junior, or senior years; not renewable. *Amount:* $200–$500.

Eligibility Requirements: Applicant must be American Indian/Alaska Native, Asian/Pacific Islander, Black (non-Hispanic), Hispanic; high school student; age 17–18; planning to enroll or expecting to enroll full-time at a two-year or four-year or technical institution or university and resident of North Dakota. Available to U.S. citizens. Applicant or parent must meet one or more of the following requirements: general military experience; retired from active duty; disabled or killed as a result of military service; prisoner of war; or missing in action.

Application Requirements: Application form, self-addressed stamped envelope with application, test scores. *Deadline:* April 15.

Contact: Teri Bryant, Programs/Membership Coordinator
Phone: 701-293-3120
Fax: 701-293-9951
E-mail: programs@ndlegion.org

AMERICAN LEGION DEPARTMENT OF OHIO

http://www.ohiolegion.com/

OHIO AMERICAN LEGION SCHOLARSHIPS
• *See page 511*

AMERICAN LEGION DEPARTMENT OF WASHINGTON

http://www.walegion.org/

AMERICAN LEGION DEPARTMENT OF WASHINGTON CHILDREN AND YOUTH SCHOLARSHIPS
• *See page 512*

AMERICAN LEGION DEPARTMENT OF WEST VIRGINIA

http://www.wvlegion.org/

SONS OF THE AMERICAN LEGION WILLIAM F. "BILL" JOHNSON MEMORIAL SCHOLARSHIP
• *See page 512*

AMERICAN LEGION NATIONAL HEADQUARTERS

http://www.legion.org/

AMERICAN LEGION LEGACY SCHOLARSHIP

Scholarship for child/children or legally adopted child/children of active duty U.S. military, National Guard, and Reserve personnel who were federalized and died on active duty on or after September 11, 2001. Must be a high school senior or high school graduate. For undergraduate study at a U.S. school of higher education.

Award: Scholarship for use in freshman, sophomore, junior, or senior years; not renewable. *Amount:* $2000–$5000.

Eligibility Requirements: Applicant must be enrolled or expecting to enroll full-time at a two-year or four-year or technical institution or university. Available to U.S. citizens. Applicant or parent must meet one or more of the following requirements: general military experience; retired from active duty; disabled or killed as a result of military service; prisoner of war; or missing in action.

Application Requirements: Application form, financial need analysis, photocopy of veteran's certificate of death, test scores, transcript. *Deadline:* April 15.

Contact: Charles Graybiel, Assistant Director
American Legion National Headquarters
The American Legion, PO Box 1055
Indianapolis, IN 46206
Phone: 317-630-1212
Fax: 317-630-1369
E-mail: mnovak@legion.org

SAMSUNG AMERICAN LEGION SCHOLARSHIP

Scholarship for high school juniors who participate in and complete either an American Legion Boys State or American Legion Auxiliary Girls State program and are a direct descendant or a legally adopted child of a U.S. wartime veteran. For undergraduate study only and may be used for tuition, books, fees, and room and board.

Award: Scholarship for use in freshman, sophomore, junior, or senior years; not renewable. *Number:* 98. *Amount:* $1000–$20,000.

Eligibility Requirements: Applicant must be high school student and planning to enroll or expecting to enroll full-time at a four-year institution or university. Available to U.S. citizens. Applicant or parent must meet one or more of the following requirements: general military experience; retired from active duty; disabled or killed as a result of military service; prisoner of war; or missing in action.

Application Requirements: Application form, financial need analysis, grandparent's Military discharge papers, test scores, transcript. *Deadline:* May 1.

Contact: Charles Graybiel, Assistant Director
American Legion National Headquarters
The American Legion, PO Box 1055
Indianapolis, IN 46206
Phone: 317-630-1212
Fax: 317-630-1369
E-mail: mnovak@legion.org

AMERICAN MILITARY RETIREES ASSOCIATION

http://www.amra1973.org/

SERGEANT MAJOR DOUGLAS R. DRUM MEMORIAL SCHOLARSHIP

Applicant's sponsor must be a current member of our association.

Award: Scholarship for use in freshman, sophomore, junior, or senior years; not renewable. *Number:* 1–24. *Amount:* $1000–$5000.

Eligibility Requirements: Applicant must be enrolled or expecting to enroll full-time at a two-year or four-year institution or university. Available to U.S. citizens. Applicant must have general military experience.

Application Requirements: Application form, application form may be submitted online(amra1973.org/scholarship), community service, essay, recommendations or references, test scores, transcript. *Deadline:* March 1.

Contact: Ms. Crystal Mang, Office Manager
Phone: 800-424-2969
Fax: 518-324-5204
E-mail: info@amra1973.org

AMVETS AUXILIARY

http://amvetsaux.org/

AMVETS NATIONAL LADIES AUXILIARY SCHOLARSHIP

• See page 515

ARKANSAS DEPARTMENT OF HIGHER EDUCATION

http://www.adhe.edu/

MILITARY DEPENDENT'S SCHOLARSHIP PROGRAM

Renewable waiver of tuition, fees, room and board undergraduate students seeking a bachelor's degree or certificate of completion at any public college, university or technical school in Arkansas who qualify as a spouse or dependent child of an Arkansas resident who has been declared to be missing in action, killed in action, a POW, or killed on ordnance delivery, or a veteran who has been declared to be 100 percent totally and permanently disabled during, or as a result of, active military service.

Award: Scholarship for use in freshman, sophomore, junior, or senior years; renewable. *Number:* 1–60.

Eligibility Requirements: Applicant must be enrolled or expecting to enroll full-time at a two-year or four-year or technical institution or university; resident of Arkansas and studying in Arkansas. Available to U.S. citizens. Applicant or parent must meet one or more of the following requirements: general military experience; retired from active duty; disabled or killed as a result of military service; prisoner of war; or missing in action.

Application Requirements: Application form, recommendations or references, report of casualty. *Deadline:* June 1.

Contact: Tara Smith, Director of Financial Aid
Arkansas Department of Higher Education
114 East Capitol Avenue
Little Rock, AR 72201-3818
Phone: 501-371-2000
Fax: 501-371-2001
E-mail: taras@adhe.edu

ARMED FORCES COMMUNICATIONS AND ELECTRONICS ASSOCIATION, EDUCATIONAL FOUNDATION

http://www.afcea.org/scholarships

AFGHANISTAN AND IRAQ WAR VETERANS SCHOLARSHIP

Applications are requested from U.S. Armed Forces and National Guard personnel either currently on active-duty or honorably discharged veterans or reservists who have served in either Enduring Freedom-Afghanistan or Iraqi Freedom. Candidates must be majoring in the following or related fields: electrical, aerospace, systems or computer engineering; computer engineering technology; computer information systems; information systems management; computer science; physics; mathematics; or science or mathematics education. Majors directly related to the support of U.S. intelligence or homeland security enterprises with relevance to the mission of AFCEA will also be eligible.

Award: Scholarship for use in freshman, sophomore, or junior years; not renewable. *Number:* 1–2. *Amount:* $2500.

Eligibility Requirements: Applicant must be enrolled or expecting to enroll full- or part-time at a two-year or four-year institution or university. Available to U.S. citizens. Applicant must have general military experience.

Application Requirements: Application form, application form may be submitted online, Military ID/DD214, recommendations or references. *Deadline:* May 1.

Contact: Ms. Norma Corrales, Senior Director, Scholarships and Awards
Armed Forces Communications and Electronics Association, Educational Foundation
4400 Fair Lakes Court
Fairfax, VA 22033
Phone: 703-631-6141
E-mail: scholarships@afcea.org

DISABLED WAR VETERANS SCHOLARSHIP (AFGHANISTAN & IRAQ)

Applications are requested from U.S. Armed Forces and National Guard personnel either currently on active-duty or honorably discharged veterans or reservists who have served in either Enduring Freedom-Afghanistan or Iraqi Freedom. Applicants must be currently enrolled and attending either a two-year or four-year accredited college or university in the United States. Students may also be enrolled in an accredited distance-learning or online degree program affiliated with a major, accredited two-year or four-year college or university in the United States. Applications will be accepted from qualified freshmen, sophomore, junior, and senior undergraduate students enrolled either part-time or full-time in an eligible degree program. Candidates must be majoring in the following or related fields: electrical, aerospace, systems or computer engineering; computer engineering technology; computer information systems; information systems management; computer science; physics; mathematics; or science or mathematics education. Majors directly related to the support of U.S. intelligence or homeland security enterprises with relevance to the mission of AFCEA will also be eligible.

Award: Scholarship for use in freshman, sophomore, or junior years; not renewable. *Number:* 1–2. *Amount:* $2500.

Eligibility Requirements: Applicant must be enrolled or expecting to enroll full- or part-time at a two-year or four-year institution or university. Available to U.S. citizens. Applicant must have general military experience.

Application Requirements: Application form, Military ID or DD214, recommendations or references, transcript. *Deadline:* May 1.

Contact: Ms. Norma Corrales, Senior Director, Scholarships and Awards
Armed Forces Communications and Electronics Association, Educational Foundation
4400 Fair Lakes Court
Fairfax, VA 22033
Phone: 703-631-6141
E-mail: scholarships@afcea.org

BLINDED VETERANS ASSOCIATION

http://www.bva.org/

KATHERN F. GRUBER SCHOLARSHIP

Award for undergraduate or graduate study is available to dependent children and spouses of legally blind veterans to include Active Duty Armed Forces members. The veteran's blindness may be either service or non-service connected. High school seniors may apply. Applicant must be enrolled or accepted for admission as a full-time student in an accredited institution of higher learning, business, secretarial, or vocational school. Six awards of $2000 each are given.

Award: Scholarship for use in freshman, sophomore, junior, senior, or graduate years; not renewable. *Number:* 6. *Amount:* $2000.

Eligibility Requirements: Applicant must be enrolled or expecting to enroll full-time at a two-year or four-year or technical institution or university. Available to U.S. citizens. Applicant or parent must meet one or more of the following requirements: general military experience; retired from active duty; disabled or killed as a result of military service; prisoner of war; or missing in action.

Application Requirements: Application form, essay, recommendations or references, transcript. *Deadline:* April 16.

Contact: Kathy Cundall, Administrative Assistant
Phone: 307-234-1579
E-mail: wytruck@aol.com

DEFENSE COMMISSARY AGENCY

http://www.militaryscholar.org/

SCHOLARSHIPS FOR MILITARY CHILDREN

One-time award to unmarried dependants of military personnel for full-time undergraduate study at a four-year institution. Must be 23 years of age. Minimum 3.0 GPA required. Further information and applications available at website at http://www.militaryscholar.org.

Award: Scholarship for use in freshman, sophomore, or junior years; not renewable. *Number:* 500. *Amount:* $1500.

Eligibility Requirements: Applicant must be enrolled or expecting to enroll full-time at a four-year institution or university and single. Applicant must have 3.0 GPA or higher. Available to U.S. citizens. Applicant or parent must meet one or more of the following requirements: general military experience; retired from active duty; disabled or killed as a result of military service; prisoner of war; or missing in action.

Application Requirements: Application form, essay, transcript. *Deadline:* February 20.

Contact: Mr. Bernard Cote, Scholarship Coordinator
Defense Commissary Agency
307 Provincetown Road
Cherry Hill, NJ 08134
Phone: 856-573-9400
E-mail: militaryscholar@scholarshipmanagers.com

DELAWARE HIGHER EDUCATION OFFICE

http://www.doe.k12.de.us

EDUCATIONAL BENEFITS FOR CHILDREN OF DECEASED VETERANS

• See page 553

DEPARTMENT OF EDUCATION, DIVISION OF HIGHER LEARNING, HIGHER EDUCATION COMMISSION

http://www.nh.gov/postsecondary

SCHOLARSHIPS FOR ORPHANS OF VETERANS-NEW HAMPSHIRE

Scholarship to provide financial assistance (room, board, books and supplies) to children of parents) who served in World War II, Korean Conflict, Vietnam (Southeast Asian Conflict) or the Gulf Wars, or any other operation for which the armed forces expeditionary medal or theater of operations service medal was awarded to the veteran.

Award: Scholarship for use in freshman, sophomore, junior, or senior years; renewable. *Number:* 1–10. *Amount:* up to $2500.

Eligibility Requirements: Applicant must be age 16-25; enrolled or expecting to enroll full-time at a two-year or four-year institution or university; resident of New Hampshire and studying in New Hampshire. Available to U.S. citizens. Applicant or parent must meet one or more of the following requirements: general military experience; retired from active duty; disabled or killed as a result of military service; prisoner of war; or missing in action.

Application Requirements: Application form. *Deadline:* varies.

Contact: Ms. Cynthia Capodestria, Student Financial Aid Administrator
Phone: 603-271-2555 Ext. 360
E-mail: cynthia.capodestria@pec.state.nh.us

DEPARTMENT OF VETERANS AFFAIRS (VA)

http://www.gibill.va.gov/

MONTGOMERY GI BILL (ACTIVE DUTY) CHAPTER 30

Award provides up to thirty-six months of education benefits to eligible veterans for college, business school, technical courses, vocational courses, correspondence courses, apprenticeships/job training, or flight training. Must be an eligible veteran with an Honorable Discharge and have high school diploma or GED before applying for benefits.

Award: Scholarship for use in freshman, sophomore, junior, senior, or graduate years; renewable.

Eligibility Requirements: Applicant must be enrolled or expecting to enroll full- or part-time at a two-year or four-year or technical institution or university. Available to U.S. citizens. Applicant or parent must meet one or more of the following requirements: general military experience; retired from active duty; disabled or killed as a result of military service; prisoner of war; or missing in action.

Application Requirements: Application form, proof of active military service of at least 2 years. *Deadline:* continuous.

Contact: Keith Wilson, Director, Education Service
Phone: 888-442-4551

MONTGOMERY GI BILL (SELECTED RESERVE)

• See page 581

RESERVE EDUCATION ASSISTANCE PROGRAM

• See page 583

SURVIVORS AND DEPENDENTS EDUCATIONAL ASSISTANCE (CHAPTER 35)-VA

Monthly $860 benefits for up to 45 months. Must be spouses or children under age 26 of current veterans missing in action or of deceased or totally and permanently disabled (service-related) service persons. For more information visit the following website http://www.gibill.va.gov.

Award: Scholarship for use in freshman, sophomore, junior, or senior years; renewable.

Eligibility Requirements: Applicant must be enrolled or expecting to enroll full- or part-time at a two-year or four-year or technical institution or university. Available to U.S. and non-U.S. citizens. Applicant or parent must meet one or more of the following requirements: general military experience; retired from active duty; disabled or killed as a result of military service; prisoner of war; or missing in action.

Application Requirements: Application form, proof of parent or spouse's qualifying service. *Deadline:* continuous.

Contact: Keith Wilson, Director, Education Service
　　　　Phone: 888-442-4551

DEVRY, INC.

http://www.devry.edu/

DEVRY/KELLER MILITARY SERVICE GRANT

Grant is available to students called to active duty at a time which necessitates the interruption of studies during a term. The grant is available only to those students who resume their studies following their active duty service. Upon resuming their studies, students must provide written documentation of active duty service. The grant is to be used during the first term the student resumes. For details visit http://finance.devry.edu/devrygrants_scholarships.html#military.

Award: Grant for use in freshman, sophomore, junior, senior, or graduate years; not renewable. *Amount:* $1000–$4500.

Eligibility Requirements: Applicant must be enrolled or expecting to enroll full- or part-time at an institution or university. Available to U.S. citizens. Applicant or parent must meet one or more of the following requirements: general military experience; retired from active duty; disabled or killed as a result of military service; prisoner of war; or missing in action.

Application Requirements: Documentation of active duty service. *Deadline:* varies.

Contact: Thonie Simpson, National High School Program Manager
　　　　Phone: 630-706-3122
　　　　E-mail: scholarships@devry.edu

EOD WARRIOR FOUNDATION

http://www.eodwarriorfoundation.org

EXPLOSIVE ORDNANCE DISPOSAL MEMORIAL SCHOLARSHIP

• *See page 554*

FLORIDA STATE DEPARTMENT OF EDUCATION

http://www.floridastudentfinancialaid.org/

SCHOLARSHIPS FOR CHILDREN & SPOUSES OF DECEASED OR DISABLED VETERANS

Renewable scholarships for children and spouses of deceased or disabled veterans. Children must be between the ages of 16 and 22, and attend an eligible Florida postsecondary institution and enrolled at least part-time. Must ensure that the Florida Department of Veterans Affairs certifies the applicant's eligibility. Must maintain GPA of 2.0. For more details, visit the website at http://www.FloridaStudentFinancialAid.org/SSFAD/home/uamain.htm.

Award: Scholarship for use in freshman, sophomore, junior, or senior years; renewable.

Eligibility Requirements: Applicant must be age 16-22; enrolled or expecting to enroll full- or part-time at a two-year or four-year or technical institution or university; resident of Florida and studying in Florida. Available to U.S. citizens. Applicant or parent must meet one or more of the following requirements: general military experience; retired

from active duty; disabled or killed as a result of military service; prisoner of war; or missing in action.

Application Requirements: Application form. *Deadline:* April 1.

FOUNDATION OF THE 1ST CAVALRY DIVISION ASSOCIATION

http://www.1cda.org/

FOUNDATION OF THE 1ST CAVALRY DIVISION ASSOCIATION SCHOLARSHIP

Scholarships for children of soldiers of the 1st Cavalry Division who died or have been declared permanently and totally (100%) disabled from combat with the 1st Cavalry Division. Show proof of service with the division, relationship to parent, death or disability of parent, and acceptance at higher education institution. Include self-addressed stamped envelope.

Award: Scholarship for use in freshman, sophomore, junior, senior, graduate, or postgraduate years; not renewable. *Amount:* up to $1200.

Eligibility Requirements: Applicant must be enrolled or expecting to enroll full- or part-time at a two-year or four-year or technical institution or university. Available to U.S. citizens. Applicant or parent must meet one or more of the following requirements: general military experience; retired from active duty; disabled or killed as a result of military service; prisoner of war; or missing in action.

Application Requirements: Application form, birth certificate, proof of service with the division, proof of disability or death of parent due to service with the 1st Cavalry Division in combat, self-addressed stamped envelope with application. *Deadline:* continuous.

Contact: Dennis Webster, Executive Director
　　　　Foundation of the 1st Cavalry Division Association
　　　　302 North Main Street
　　　　Copperas Cove, TX 76522-1703
　　　　Phone: 254-547-6537
　　　　Fax: 254-547-8853
　　　　E-mail: firstcav@1cda.org

IDAHO STATE BOARD OF EDUCATION

http://www.boardofed.idaho.gov/

FREEDOM SCHOLARSHIP

Waiver of scholastic fees up to $500 per semester for books in addition to on-campus housing and subsistence for children of Idaho citizens determined by the federal government to have been prisoners of war, missing in action, or killed in action or died of injuries or wounds sustained in action in southeast Asia, including Korea, or who shall become so hereafter, in any area of armed conflicts in which the United States is a party. For additional information, see website http://www.boardofed.idaho.gov/scholarship/freedom.asp.

Award: Scholarship for use in freshman, sophomore, junior, or senior years; not renewable. *Amount:* up to $500.

Eligibility Requirements: Applicant must be enrolled or expecting to enroll full- or part-time at a two-year or four-year or technical institution or university; resident of Idaho and studying in Idaho. Available to U.S. citizens. Applicant or parent must meet one or more of the following requirements: general military experience; retired from active duty; disabled or killed as a result of military service; prisoner of war; or missing in action.

Application Requirements: Application form. *Deadline:* February 15.

ILLINOIS AMVETS

http://www.ilamvets.org/

ILLINOIS AMVETS LADIES AUXILIARY MEMORIAL SCHOLARSHIP

Applicant must be an Illinois student and a child of an honorably discharged veteran who served after September 15, 1940. Must submit ACT scores, IRS 1040 form, high school rank and grades.

Award: Scholarship for use in freshman year; not renewable. *Number:* 1–3. *Amount:* $500.

Eligibility Requirements: Applicant must be high school student; planning to enroll or expecting to enroll full-time at a two-year or four-

year or technical institution or university and resident of Illinois. Available to U.S. citizens. Applicant or parent must meet one or more of the following requirements: general military experience; retired from active duty; disabled or killed as a result of military service; prisoner of war; or missing in action.

Application Requirements: Application form, financial need analysis, IRS 1040 form, test scores, transcript. *Deadline:* March 1.

ILLINOIS AMVETS LADIES AUXILIARY WORCHID SCHOLARSHIPS

Applicant must be an Illinois student and the child of an honorably discharged, deceased veteran who served after September 15, 1940. Must submit ACT score and IRS 1040 form.

Award: Scholarship for use in freshman year; not renewable. *Number:* 1–3. *Amount:* $500.

Eligibility Requirements: Applicant must be high school student; age 17-18; planning to enroll or expecting to enroll full-time at a two-year or four-year or technical institution or university and resident of Illinois. Available to U.S. citizens. Applicant or parent must meet one or more of the following requirements: general military experience; retired from active duty; disabled or killed as a result of military service; prisoner of war; or missing in action.

Application Requirements: Application form, financial need analysis, IRS 1040 form, test scores, transcript. *Deadline:* March 1.

ILLINOIS AMVETS SERVICE FOUNDATION

Applicant must be a resident of Illinois and accepted for training at an approved school. Preference given to child of deceased veteran and/or student nurse in training in the order: third, second, first-year student. Must submit IRS 1040 form.

Award: Scholarship for use in freshman year; not renewable. *Number:* 10–30. *Amount:* $1000.

Eligibility Requirements: Applicant must be high school student; age 17-19; planning to enroll or expecting to enroll full-time at a two-year or four-year institution or university; resident of Illinois and studying in Illinois. Applicant must have 2.5 GPA or higher. Available to U.S. citizens. Applicant must have general military experience.

Application Requirements: Application form, community service, financial need analysis, IRS 1040 form, acceptance letter, recommendations or references, test scores, transcript. *Deadline:* March 1.

ILLINOIS AMVETS TRADE SCHOOL SCHOLARSHIP

Applicant must be an Illinois student who has been accepted in a pre-approved trade school program. Must be a child or grandchild of a veteran who served after September 15th, 1940 and was honorably discharged or is presently serving in the military.

Award: Scholarship for use in freshman year; not renewable. *Number:* 1–2. *Amount:* $1000.

Eligibility Requirements: Applicant must be age 17-18; enrolled or expecting to enroll full-time at a technical institution and resident of Illinois. Available to U.S. citizens. Applicant or parent must meet one or more of the following requirements: general military experience; retired from active duty; disabled or killed as a result of military service; prisoner of war; or missing in action.

Application Requirements: Acceptance letter, application form. *Deadline:* March 1.

ILLINOIS DEPARTMENT OF VETERANS' AFFAIRS

http://www.state.il.us/agency/dva

MIA/POW SCHOLARSHIPS

One-time award for spouse, child, or step-child of veterans who are missing in action or were a prisoner of war. Must be enrolled at a state-supported school in Illinois. Candidate must be U.S. citizen. Must apply and be accepted before beginning of school. Also for children and spouses of veterans who are determined to be 100 percent disabled as established by the Veterans Administration. Scholarship value and the number of awards granted varies.

Award: Scholarship for use in freshman, sophomore, junior, or senior years; renewable.

Eligibility Requirements: Applicant must be enrolled or expecting to enroll full- or part-time at a two-year or four-year institution or university; resident of Illinois and studying in Illinois. Available to U.S. citizens. Applicant or parent must meet one or more of the following requirements: general military experience; retired from active duty; disabled or killed as a result of military service; prisoner of war; or missing in action.

Application Requirements: Application form. *Deadline:* continuous.

Contact: Ms. Tracy Smith, Grants Section
Illinois Department of Veterans' Affairs
833 South Spring Street
Springfield, IL 62794-9432
Phone: 217-782-3564
Fax: 217-782-4161

VETERANS' CHILDREN EDUCATIONAL OPPORTUNITIES

$250 award for each child aged 10 to 18 of a veteran who died or became totally disabled as a result of service during World War I, World War II, Korean, or Vietnam War. Must be Illinois resident studying in Illinois. Death must be service-connected. Disability must be rated 100 percent for two or more years.

Award: Grant for use in freshman year; not renewable. *Amount:* $250.

Eligibility Requirements: Applicant must be age 10-18; enrolled or expecting to enroll full- or part-time at a two-year or four-year institution or university; resident of Illinois and studying in Illinois. Available to U.S. citizens. Applicant or parent must meet one or more of the following requirements: general military experience; retired from active duty; disabled or killed as a result of military service; prisoner of war; or missing in action.

Application Requirements: Application form. *Deadline:* June 30.

Contact: Tracy Smith, Grants Section
Illinois Department of Veterans' Affairs
833 South Spring Street
Springfield, IL 62794-9432
Phone: 217-782-3564
Fax: 217-782-4161

ILLINOIS STUDENT ASSISTANCE COMMISSION (ISAC)

http://www.collegezone.org/

ILLINOIS VETERAN GRANT PROGRAM-IVG

Awards qualified veterans and pays eligible tuition and fees for study in Illinois public universities or community colleges. Program eligibility units are based on the enrolled hours for a particular term, not the dollar amount of the benefits paid. Applications are available at college financial aid office and can be submitted any time during the academic year for which assistance is being requested.

Award: Grant for use in freshman, sophomore, junior, senior, or graduate years; renewable.

Eligibility Requirements: Applicant must be enrolled or expecting to enroll full- or part-time at a two-year or four-year institution or university; resident of Illinois and studying in Illinois. Available to U.S. citizens. Applicant or parent must meet one or more of the following requirements: general military experience; retired from active duty; disabled or killed as a result of military service; prisoner of war; or missing in action.

Application Requirements: Application form. *Deadline:* continuous.

IMAGINE AMERICA FOUNDATION

http://www.imagine-america.org

MILITARY AWARD PROGRAM (MAP)

• *See page 581*

INDIANA DEPARTMENT OF VETERANS AFFAIRS

http://www.in.gov/dva

CHILD OF DISABLED VETERAN GRANT OR PURPLE HEART RECIPIENT GRANT

Free tuition at Indiana state-supported colleges or universities for children of disabled veterans or Purple Heart recipients. Must submit form DD214 or service record. Covers tuition and mandatory fees.

Award: Grant for use in freshman, sophomore, junior, senior, graduate, or postgraduate years; renewable.

Eligibility Requirements: Applicant must be enrolled or expecting to enroll full- or part-time at a two-year or four-year institution or university; resident of Indiana and studying in Indiana. Available to U.S. citizens. Applicant or parent must meet one or more of the following requirements: general military experience; retired from active duty; disabled or killed as a result of military service; prisoner of war; or missing in action.

Application Requirements: Application form, FAFSA. *Deadline:* continuous.

Contact: Jon Brinkley, State Service Officer
Indiana Department of Veterans Affairs
302 West Washington Street, Room E-120
Indianapolis, IN 46204-2738
Phone: 317-232-3910
Fax: 317-232-7721
E-mail: jbrinkley@dva.in.gov

DEPARTMENT OF VETERANS AFFAIRS FREE TUITION FOR CHILDREN OF POW/MIA'S IN VIETNAM

Renewable award for residents of Indiana who are the children of veterans declared missing in action or prisoner-of-war after January 1, 1960. Provides tuition at Indiana state-supported institutions for undergraduate study.

Award: Grant for use in freshman, sophomore, junior, senior, graduate, or postgraduate years; renewable.

Eligibility Requirements: Applicant must be enrolled or expecting to enroll full- or part-time at a two-year or four-year institution or university; resident of Indiana and studying in Indiana. Available to U.S. citizens. Applicant or parent must meet one or more of the following requirements: general military experience; retired from active duty; disabled or killed as a result of military service; prisoner of war; or missing in action.

Application Requirements: Application form. *Deadline:* continuous.

Contact: Jon Brinkley, State Service Officer
Indiana Department of Veterans Affairs
302 West Washington Street, Room E-120
Indianapolis, IN 46204-2738
Phone: 317-232-3910
Fax: 317-232-7721
E-mail: jbrinkley@dva.in.gov

KANSAS COMMISSION ON VETERANS AFFAIRS

http://www.kcva.org/

KANSAS EDUCATIONAL BENEFITS FOR CHILDREN OF MIA, POW, AND DECEASED VETERANS OF THE VIETNAM WAR

Scholarship awarded to students who are children of veterans. Must show proof of parent's status as missing in action, prisoner-of-war, or killed in action in the Vietnam War. Kansas residence required of veteran at time of entry to service. Must attend a state-supported postsecondary school.

Award: Scholarship for use in freshman, sophomore, junior, or senior years; not renewable. *Number:* 1.

Eligibility Requirements: Applicant must be enrolled or expecting to enroll full-time at a two-year or four-year or technical institution or university and studying in Kansas. Available to U.S. citizens. Applicant or parent must meet one or more of the following requirements: general military experience; retired from active duty; disabled or killed as a result of military service; prisoner of war; or missing in action.

Application Requirements: Application form, birth certificate, school acceptance letter, military discharge of veteran. *Deadline:* varies.

Contact: Wayne Bollig, Program Director
Phone: 785-296-3976
Fax: 785-296-1462
E-mail: wbollig@kcva.org

KNIGHTS OF COLUMBUS

http://www.kofc.org/

FRANCIS P. MATTHEWS AND JOHN E. SWIFT EDUCATIONAL TRUST SCHOLARSHIPS
• *See page 524*

LOUISIANA DEPARTMENT OF VETERAN AFFAIRS

http://www.vetaffairs.la.gov

LOUISIANA DEPARTMENT OF VETERANS AFFAIRS STATE EDUCATIONAL AID PROGRAM

Waiver of tuition and school-imposed fees at any state supported college, university, or technical institute in Louisiana for dependent children, aged 16-25, of service connected disabled veterans, service connected deceased veterans, or veterans rated 100% service connected due to individual unemployability. Tuition waiver also available for an unremarried surviving spouse of a service connected deceased veteran. Residency restricted to Louisiana.

Award: Scholarship for use in freshman, sophomore, junior, or senior years; not renewable.

Eligibility Requirements: Applicant must be age 16-25; enrolled or expecting to enroll full-time at a two-year or four-year or technical institution or university; resident of Louisiana and studying in Louisiana. Available to U.S. citizens. Applicant or parent must meet one or more of the following requirements: general military experience; retired from active duty; disabled or killed as a result of military service; prisoner of war; or missing in action.

Application Requirements: Application form. *Deadline:* continuous.

Contact: Mrs. Charmagne Scott, Administrative Assistant 6
Louisiana Department of Veteran Affairs
PO Box 94095 Capitol Station
Baton Rouge, LA 70804-9095
Phone: 225-219-5031
Fax: 225-219-5590
E-mail: charmagne.scott@vetaffairs.la.gov

MAINE DIVISION OF VETERANS SERVICES

http://www.maine.gov/dvem/bvs

VETERANS DEPENDENTS EDUCATIONAL BENEFITS-MAINE

Tuition waiver award for dependent children who have not reached their 22nd birthday or spouses of veterans permanently and totally disabled resulting from service-connected disability; died from a service-connected disability; at time of death was totally and permanently disabled due to service-connected disability, but whose death was not related to the service-connected disability; or member of the Armed Forces on active duty who has been listed for more than 90 days as missing in action, captured or forcibly detained or interned in the line of duty. Benefits apply only to the University of Maine System, Maine community colleges and Maine Maritime Academy. Must be high school graduate. Must submit with application proof of veteran's VA disability along with dependent verification paperwork such as birth, marriage, or adoption certificate and proof of enrollment in degree program.

Award: Scholarship for use in freshman, sophomore, junior, or senior years; not renewable.

Eligibility Requirements: Applicant must be enrolled or expecting to enroll full- or part-time at a two-year or four-year institution or university; resident of Maine and studying in Maine. Available to U.S. citizens. Applicant or parent must meet one or more of the following requirements: general military experience; retired from active duty; disabled or killed as a result of military service; prisoner of war; or missing in action.

Application Requirements: Application form,.

Contact: Mrs. Paula Gagnon, Office Associate II
Maine Division of Veterans Services
State House Station 117
Augusta, ME 04333-0117
Phone: 207-430-6035
Fax: 207-626-4471
E-mail: mainebvs@maine.gov

MARYLAND STATE HIGHER EDUCATION COMMISSION

http://www.mhec.state.md.us/

EDWARD T. CONROY MEMORIAL SCHOLARSHIP PROGRAM

• *See page 560*

VETERANS OF THE AFGHANISTAN AND IRAQ CONFLICTS SCHOLARSHIP PROGRAM

Provides financial assistance to Maryland resident U.S. Armed Forces personnel who served in Afghanistan or Iraq Conflicts and their children or spouses who are attending Maryland institutions.

Award: Scholarship for use in freshman, sophomore, junior, or senior years; renewable. *Number:* 123. *Amount:* $8850.

Eligibility Requirements: Applicant must be enrolled or expecting to enroll full- or part-time at a two-year or four-year institution or university; resident of Maryland and studying in Maryland. Available to U.S. citizens. Applicant or parent must meet one or more of the following requirements: general military experience; retired from active duty; disabled or killed as a result of military service; prisoner of war; or missing in action.

Application Requirements: Application form, birth certificate/marriage certificate, documentation of military order, financial need analysis. *Deadline:* March 1.

Contact: Linda Asplin, Program Administrator
Maryland State Higher Education Commission
839 Bestgate Road, Suite 400
Annapolis, MD 21401-3013
Phone: 410-260-4563
Fax: 410-260-3203
E-mail: lasplin@mhec.state.md.us

MASSACHUSETTS OFFICE OF STUDENT FINANCIAL ASSISTANCE

http://www.osfa.mass.edu/

MASSACHUSETTS PUBLIC SERVICE GRANT PROGRAM

• *See page 560*

MILITARY OFFICERS ASSOCIATION OF AMERICA (MOAA) SCHOLARSHIP FUND

http://www.moaa.org/scholarshipfund

GENERAL JOHN RATAY EDUCATIONAL FUND GRANTS

Grants available to the children of the surviving spouse of retired officers. Must be under 24 years old and the child of a deceased retired officer who was a member of MOAA. For more details and an application go to website http://www.moaa.org/education.

Award: Grant for use in freshman, sophomore, junior, or senior years; renewable. *Number:* 1–5. *Amount:* $4000–$5000.

Eligibility Requirements: Applicant must be enrolled or expecting to enroll full-time at a two-year or four-year institution or university. Applicant must have 3.0 GPA or higher. Available to U.S. citizens. Applicant or parent must meet one or more of the following requirements: general military experience; retired from active duty; disabled or killed as a result of military service; prisoner of war; or missing in action.

Application Requirements: Application form, extracurricular activities, financial need analysis, test scores, transcript. *Deadline:* March 1.

Contact: Laurie Wavering, Program Director
Military Officers Association of America (MOAA)
Scholarship Fund
201 North Washington Street
Alexandria, VA 22314
Phone: 800-234-6622 Ext. 163
Fax: 703-838-5819

MOAA AMERICAN PATRIOT SCHOLARSHIP

Scholarships are available to a student under the age of 24 and who are children of MOAA members and children of active-duty, reserve, National Guard, or enlisted personnel whose military parent has died on active service are eligible to apply. For more information and to access the online application go to website http://www.moaa.org/education.

Award: Grant for use in freshman, sophomore, junior, or senior years; renewable. *Number:* up to 65. *Amount:* $2500–$5000.

Eligibility Requirements: Applicant must be enrolled or expecting to enroll full-time at a two-year or four-year institution or university. Applicant must have 3.0 GPA or higher. Available to U.S. citizens. Applicant or parent must meet one or more of the following requirements: general military experience; retired from active duty; disabled or killed as a result of military service; prisoner of war; or missing in action.

Application Requirements: Application form, extracurricular activities, death certificate, test scores, transcript. *Deadline:* March 1.

Contact: Laurie Wavering, Program Director
Military Officers Association of America (MOAA)
Scholarship Fund
201 North Washington Street
Alexandria, VA 22314
Phone: 800-234-6622 Ext. 163
Fax: 703-838-5819
E-mail: edassist@moaa.org

MILITARY ORDER OF THE PURPLE HEART

http://www.purpleheart.org/

MILITARY ORDER OF THE PURPLE HEART SCHOLARSHIP

Scholarship for Military Order of the Purple Heart (MOPH) Members/spouses or children, stepchildren, adopted children or grandchildren, veterans killed-in-action or veterans who died of wounds and did not have the opportunity to join the MOPH. Must submit $10 application fee, essay, high school/college transcript, and letters of recommendation. Must be U.S. citizen and high school graduate with minimum GPA of 2.75 and accepted or enrolled as a full-time student at a U.S. college, university of trade school at the time the scholarship is awarded.

Award: Scholarship for use in freshman, sophomore, junior, or senior years; not renewable. *Number:* up to 83. *Amount:* $3000.

Eligibility Requirements: Applicant must be enrolled or expecting to enroll full-time at a two-year or four-year or technical institution or university. Applicant must have 3.0 GPA or higher. Available to U.S. citizens. Applicant or parent must meet one or more of the following requirements: general military experience; retired from active duty; disabled or killed as a result of military service; prisoner of war; or missing in action.

Application Requirements: Application form, essay, MOPH membership proof, recommendations or references, transcript. *Fee:* $10. *Deadline:* February 17.

Contact: Mr. Stewart Mckeown, Scholarship Coordinator
Military Order of the Purple Heart
5413-B Backlick Road
Springfield, VA 22151-3960
Phone: 703-642-5360
Fax: 703-642-2054
E-mail: info@purpleheart.org

MINNESOTA OFFICE OF HIGHER EDUCATION

http://www.getreadyforcollege.org/

MINNESOTA GI BILL PROGRAM

Provides financial assistance to eligible Minnesota veterans and non-veterans who have served 5 or more years cumulatively as a member of the National Guard or Reserves, and served on or after September 11, 2001. Surviving spouses and children of service members who have died or have a total and permanent disability and who served on or after September 11, 2001, may also be eligible. Full-time students may receive up to $1000 per term, and part-time students up to $500 per term up to $3,000 per year. Maximum lifetime benefit is $10,000.

Award: Scholarship for use in freshman, sophomore, junior, senior, graduate, or postgraduate years; not renewable. *Amount:* up to $3000.

Eligibility Requirements: Applicant must be enrolled or expecting to enroll full- or part-time at a two-year or four-year or technical institution or university; resident of Minnesota and studying in Minnesota. Available to U.S. citizens. Applicant or parent must meet one or more of the following requirements: general military experience; retired from active duty; disabled or killed as a result of military service; prisoner of war; or missing in action.

Application Requirements: Application form, application form may be submitted online (http://www.getreadyforcollege.org), financial need analysis, military records. *Deadline:* continuous.

MINNESOTA STATE VETERANS' DEPENDENTS ASSISTANCE PROGRAM

Tuition assistance to dependents of persons considered to be prisoner-of-war or missing in action after August 1, 1958. Must be Minnesota resident attending Minnesota two- or four-year school.

Award: Scholarship for use in freshman, sophomore, junior, or senior years; renewable. *Amount:* up to $250.

Eligibility Requirements: Applicant must be enrolled or expecting to enroll full- or part-time at a two-year or four-year institution; resident of Minnesota and studying in Minnesota. Available to U.S. citizens. Applicant or parent must meet one or more of the following requirements: general military experience; retired from active duty; disabled or killed as a result of military service; prisoner of war; or missing in action.

Application Requirements: Application form. *Deadline:* continuous.

Contact: Ginny Dodds, Manager
  Phone: 651-355-0610
  E-mail: ginny.dodds@state.mn.us

NATIONAL MILITARY FAMILY ASSOCIATION

http://www.MilitaryFamily.org

NATIONAL MILITARY FAMILY ASSOCATION'S JOANNE HOLBROOK PATTON MILITARY SPOUSE SCHOLARSHIPS

Scholarships ranging from $500 to $1500 are awarded to spouses of Uniformed Services members (active duty, National Guard and Reserve, retirees, and survivors) for professional certification, licensing fees, postsecondary school, graduate school and Mental Health Career fields. Award number and amount varies. You must be a military spouse to apply.

Award: Scholarship for use in freshman, sophomore, junior, senior, graduate, or postgraduate years; not renewable. *Amount:* $500–$1500.

Eligibility Requirements: Applicant must be enrolled or expecting to enroll full- or part-time at a two-year or four-year or technical institution or university and married. Available to U.S. citizens. Applicant or parent must meet one or more of the following requirements: general military experience; retired from active duty; disabled or killed as a result of military service; prisoner of war; or missing in action.

Application Requirements: Application form, application form may be submitted online (https:// militaryfamily.scholarships.ngwebsolutions.com/CMXAdmin/ Cmx_Content.aspx?cpId=561), essay, marriage license and verifying military documentation. *Deadline:* January 31.

Contact: Mrs. Allison Jones, Military Spouse Scholarship Program
  Coordinator
  National Military Family Association
  2500 North Van Dorn Street, Suite 102
  Alexandria, VA 22302
  Phone: 703-931-6632
  Fax: 703-931-4600
  E-mail: scholarships@militaryfamily.org

NEW JERSEY DEPARTMENT OF MILITARY AND VETERANS AFFAIRS

http://www.state.nj.us/military

NEW JERSEY WAR ORPHANS TUITION ASSISTANCE

$500 scholarship to children of those service personnel who died while in the military or due to service-connected disabilities, or who are officially listed as missing in action by the U.S. Department of Defense. Must be a resident of New Jersey for at least one year immediately preceding the filing of the application and be between the ages of 16 and 21 at the time of application.

Award: Scholarship for use in freshman, sophomore, junior, or senior years; renewable. *Amount:* $500.

Eligibility Requirements: Applicant must be age 16-21; enrolled or expecting to enroll full-time at a four-year institution or university and resident of New Jersey. Available to U.S. citizens. Applicant or parent must meet one or more of the following requirements: general military experience; retired from active duty; disabled or killed as a result of military service; prisoner of war; or missing in action.

Application Requirements: Application form, transcript. *Deadline:* varies.

Contact: Patricia Richter, Grants Manager
  New Jersey Department of Military and Veterans Affairs
  PO Box 340
  Trenton, NJ 08625-0340
  Phone: 609-530-6854
  Fax: 609-530-6970
  E-mail: patricia.richter@njdmava.state.nj.us

POW-MIA TUITION BENEFIT PROGRAM

Free undergraduate college tuition provided to any child born or adopted before or during the period of time his or her parent was officially declared a prisoner of war or person missing in action after January 1, 1960. The POW-MIA must have been a New Jersey resident at the time he or she entered the service. Child of veteran must attend either a public or private institution in New Jersey. A copy of DD 1300 must be furnished with the application. Minimum 2.5 GPA required.

Award: Scholarship for use in freshman, sophomore, junior, or senior years; renewable.

Eligibility Requirements: Applicant must be enrolled or expecting to enroll full-time at a two-year or four-year or technical institution or university; resident of New Jersey and studying in New Jersey. Applicant must have 2.5 GPA or higher. Available to U.S. citizens. Applicant or parent must meet one or more of the following requirements: general military experience; retired from active duty; disabled or killed as a result of military service; prisoner of war; or missing in action.

Application Requirements: Application form, copy of DD 1300, transcript. *Deadline:* varies.

Contact: Patricia Richter, Grants Manager
  New Jersey Department of Military and Veterans Affairs
  PO Box 340
  Trenton, NJ 08625-0340
  Phone: 609-530-6854
  Fax: 609-530-6970
  E-mail: patricia.richter@njdmava.state.nj.us

VETERANS TUITION CREDIT PROGRAM-NEW JERSEY

Award for New Jersey resident veterans who served in the armed forces between December 31, 1960, and May 7, 1975. Must have been a New Jersey resident at time of induction or discharge or for two years immediately prior to application.

Award: Scholarship for use in freshman, sophomore, junior, or senior years; renewable. *Amount:* $200–$400.

Eligibility Requirements: Applicant must be enrolled or expecting to enroll full- or part-time at a two-year or four-year or technical institution or university and resident of New Jersey. Available to U.S. citizens.

Applicant or parent must meet one or more of the following requirements: general military experience; retired from active duty; disabled or killed as a result of military service; prisoner of war; or missing in action.

Application Requirements: Application form. *Deadline:* varies.

Contact: Patricia Richter, Grants Manager
New Jersey Department of Military and Veterans Affairs
PO Box 340
Trenton, NJ 08625-0340
Phone: 609-530-6854
Fax: 609-530-6970
E-mail: patricia.richter@njdmava.state.nj.us

NEW MEXICO COMMISSION ON HIGHER EDUCATION

http://www.hed.state.nm.us/

VIETNAM VETERANS' SCHOLARSHIP PROGRAM

Renewable scholarship program created to provide aid for Vietnam veterans who are undergraduate and graduate students attending public postsecondary institutions or select private colleges in New Mexico. Private colleges include: College of Santa Fe, St. John's College and College of the Southwest.

Award: Scholarship for use in freshman, sophomore, junior, or senior years; renewable. *Number:* 1.

Eligibility Requirements: Applicant must be enrolled or expecting to enroll full-time at a two-year or four-year institution; resident of New Mexico and studying in New Mexico. Available to U.S. citizens. Applicant or parent must meet one or more of the following requirements: general military experience; retired from active duty; disabled or killed as a result of military service; prisoner of war; or missing in action.

Application Requirements: Application form, certification by the NM Veteran's commission. *Deadline:* varies.

Contact: Tashina Moore, Director of Financial Aid
New Mexico Commission on Higher Education
1068 Cerrillos Road
Santa Fe, NM 87505-1650
Phone: 505-476-6549
Fax: 505-476-6511
E-mail: tashina.banks-moore@state.nm.us

NEW MEXICO DEPARTMENT OF VETERANS' SERVICES

http://www.dvs.state.nm.us/

CHILDREN OF DECEASED VETERANS SCHOLARSHIP-NEW MEXICO

Award for New Mexico residents who are children of veterans killed or disabled as a result of service, prisoner of war, or veterans missing in action. Must be between ages 16 and 26. For use at New Mexico schools for undergraduate study. Must submit parent's death certificate and DD form 214.

Award: Scholarship for use in freshman, sophomore, junior, or senior years; renewable. *Amount:* $300.

Eligibility Requirements: Applicant must be age 16-26; enrolled or expecting to enroll full- or part-time at a two-year or four-year institution or university; resident of New Mexico and studying in New Mexico. Available to U.S. citizens. Applicant or parent must meet one or more of the following requirements: general military experience; retired from active duty; disabled or killed as a result of military service; prisoner of war; or missing in action.

Application Requirements: Application form, death certificate or notice of casualty, DD form 214, transcript. *Deadline:* continuous.

Contact: Alan Martinez, Deputy Secretary
Phone: 505-827-6300
E-mail: alan.martinez@state.nm.us

NEW MEXICO VIETNAM VETERAN SCHOLARSHIP

Award for Vietnam veterans who have been New Mexico residents for a minimum of ten years and are attending state-funded postsecondary schools. Must have been awarded the Vietnam Campaign medal. Must submit DD 214 and discharge papers.

Award: Scholarship for use in freshman, sophomore, junior, or senior years; renewable. *Number:* 100. *Amount:* $3500–$4000.

Eligibility Requirements: Applicant must be enrolled or expecting to enroll full- or part-time at a two-year or four-year or technical institution or university; resident of New Mexico and studying in New Mexico. Available to U.S. citizens. Applicant or parent must meet one or more of the following requirements: general military experience; retired from active duty; disabled or killed as a result of military service; prisoner of war; or missing in action.

Application Requirements: Application form, copy of DD Form 214. *Deadline:* continuous.

Contact: Alan Martinez, Deputy Secretary
Phone: 505-827-6300
E-mail: alan.martinez@state.nm.us

NEW YORK STATE HIGHER EDUCATION SERVICES CORPORATION

http://www.hesc.com/

NEW YORK VIETNAM/PERSIAN GULF/AFGHANISTAN VETERANS TUITION AWARDS

Scholarship for veterans who served in Vietnam, the Persian Gulf, or Afghanistan. Must be a New York resident attending a New York institution. Must establish eligibility by September 1.

Award: Scholarship for use in freshman, sophomore, junior, or senior years; renewable.

Eligibility Requirements: Applicant must be enrolled or expecting to enroll full- or part-time at a two-year or four-year or technical institution or university; resident of New York and studying in New York. Available to U.S. citizens. Applicant or parent must meet one or more of the following requirements: general military experience; retired from active duty; disabled or killed as a result of military service; prisoner of war; or missing in action.

Application Requirements: Application form, financial need analysis. *Deadline:* May 1.

REGENTS AWARD FOR CHILD OF VETERAN

Award for students whose parent, as a result of service in U.S. Armed Forces during war or national emergency, died; suffered a 40 percent or more disability; or is classified as missing in action or a prisoner of war. Veteran must be current New York State resident or have been so at time of death. Student must be a New York resident, attending, or planning to attend, college in New York State. Must establish eligibility before applying for payment.

Award: Scholarship for use in freshman, sophomore, junior, or senior years; not renewable. *Amount:* up to $450.

Eligibility Requirements: Applicant must be enrolled or expecting to enroll full-time at a two-year or four-year institution or university; resident of New York and studying in New York. Available to U.S. citizens. Applicant or parent must meet one or more of the following requirements: general military experience; retired from active duty; disabled or killed as a result of military service; prisoner of war; or missing in action.

Application Requirements: Application form, proof of eligibility. *Deadline:* May 1.

Contact: Rita McGivern, Student Information
New York State Higher Education Services Corporation
99 Washington Avenue, Room 1320
Albany, NY 12255
E-mail: rmcgivern@hesc.com

NORTH CAROLINA DIVISION OF VETERANS AFFAIRS

http://www.doa.state.nc.us/vets/va.htm

NORTH CAROLINA VETERANS SCHOLARSHIPS CLASS I-A

Scholarships for children of certain deceased, disabled or POW/MIA veterans. Award value is $4500 per nine-month academic year in private colleges and junior colleges. No limit on number awarded each year.

Award: Scholarship for use in freshman, sophomore, junior, or senior years; renewable. *Amount:* $4500.

Eligibility Requirements: Applicant must be enrolled or expecting to enroll full-time at a two-year or four-year or technical institution or university; resident of North Carolina and studying in North Carolina. Available to U.S. citizens. Applicant or parent must meet one or more of the following requirements: general military experience; retired from active duty; disabled or killed as a result of military service; prisoner of war; or missing in action.

Application Requirements: Application form, financial need analysis, interview, transcript. *Deadline:* continuous.

Contact: Charles Smith, Assistant Secretary
  Phone: 919-733-3851
  Fax: 919-733-2834
  E-mail: charlie.smith@ncmail.net

NORTH CAROLINA VETERANS SCHOLARSHIPS CLASS I-B

Awards for children of veterans rated by USDVA as 100 percent disabled due to wartime service as defined in the law, and currently or at time of death drawing compensation for such disability. Parent must have been a North Carolina resident at time of entry into service. Duration of the scholarship is four academic years (8 semesters) if used within 8 years. No limit on number awarded each year.

Award: Scholarship for use in freshman, sophomore, junior, or senior years; renewable. *Amount:* $1500.

Eligibility Requirements: Applicant must be enrolled or expecting to enroll full- or part-time at a two-year or four-year or technical institution or university; resident of North Carolina and studying in North Carolina. Available to U.S. citizens. Applicant or parent must meet one or more of the following requirements: general military experience; retired from active duty; disabled or killed as a result of military service; prisoner of war; or missing in action.

Application Requirements: Application form, financial need analysis, interview, transcript. *Deadline:* continuous.

Contact: Charles Smith, Assistant Secretary
  Phone: 919-733-3851
  Fax: 919-733-2834
  E-mail: charlie.smith@ncmail.net

NORTH CAROLINA VETERANS SCHOLARSHIPS CLASS II

Awards for children of veterans rated by USDVA as much as 20 percent but less than 100 percent disabled due to wartime service as defined in the law, or awarded Purple Heart Medal for wounds received. Parent must have been a North Carolina resident at time of entry into service. Duration of the scholarship is four academic years (8 semesters) if used within 8 years. Free tuition and exemption from certain mandatory fees as set forth in the law in Public, Community and Technical Colleges.

Award: Scholarship for use in freshman, sophomore, junior, or senior years; renewable. *Number:* up to 100. *Amount:* $4500.

Eligibility Requirements: Applicant must be enrolled or expecting to enroll full- or part-time at a two-year or four-year or technical institution or university; resident of North Carolina and studying in North Carolina. Available to U.S. citizens. Applicant or parent must meet one or more of the following requirements: general military experience; retired from active duty; disabled or killed as a result of military service; prisoner of war; or missing in action.

Application Requirements: Application form, financial need analysis, interview, transcript. *Deadline:* March 1.

Contact: Charles Smith, Assistant Secretary
  Phone: 919-733-3851
  Fax: 919-733-2834
  E-mail: charlie.smith@ncmail.net

NORTH CAROLINA VETERANS SCHOLARSHIPS CLASS III

Awards for children of a deceased war veteran, who was honorably discharged and who does not qualify under any other provision within this synopsis or veteran who served in a combat zone or waters adjacent to a combat zone and received a campaign badge or medal and who does not qualify under any other provision within this synopsis. Duration of the scholarship is four academic years (8 semesters) if used within 8 years.

Award: Scholarship for use in freshman, sophomore, junior, or senior years; renewable. *Number:* up to 100. *Amount:* $4500.

Eligibility Requirements: Applicant must be enrolled or expecting to enroll full- or part-time at a two-year or four-year or technical institution or university; resident of North Carolina and studying in North Carolina. Available to U.S. citizens. Applicant or parent must meet one or more of the following requirements: general military experience; retired from active duty; disabled or killed as a result of military service; prisoner of war; or missing in action.

Application Requirements: Application form, financial need analysis, interview, transcript. *Deadline:* March 1.

Contact: Charles Smith, Assistant Secretary
  Phone: 919-733-3851
  Fax: 919-733-2834
  E-mail: charlie.smith@ncmail.net

NORTH CAROLINA VETERANS SCHOLARSHIPS CLASS IV

Awards for children of veterans, who were prisoner of war or missing in action. Duration of the scholarship is four academic years (8 semesters) if used within 8 years. No limit on number awarded each year. Award value is $4500 per nine-month academic year in private colleges and junior colleges.

Award: Scholarship for use in freshman, sophomore, junior, or senior years; renewable. *Amount:* $4500.

Eligibility Requirements: Applicant must be enrolled or expecting to enroll full- or part-time at a two-year or four-year or technical institution or university; resident of North Carolina and studying in North Carolina. Available to U.S. citizens. Applicant or parent must meet one or more of the following requirements: general military experience; retired from active duty; disabled or killed as a result of military service; prisoner of war; or missing in action.

Application Requirements: Application form, financial need analysis, interview, transcript. *Deadline:* continuous.

Contact: Charles Smith, Assistant Secretary
  Phone: 919-733-3851
  Fax: 919-733-2834
  E-mail: charlie.smith@ncmail.net

OHIO BOARD OF REGENTS

http://www.ohiohighered.org

OHIO WAR ORPHANS SCHOLARSHIP

Aids Ohio residents attending an eligible college in Ohio. Must be between the ages of 16 and 25, the child of a disabled or deceased veteran, and enrolled full-time. Renewable up to five years. Amount of award varies. Must include Form DD214.

Award: Scholarship for use in freshman, sophomore, junior, or senior years; renewable.

Eligibility Requirements: Applicant must be age 16-25; enrolled or expecting to enroll full-time at a two-year or four-year institution or university; resident of Ohio and studying in Ohio. Available to U.S. citizens. Applicant or parent must meet one or more of the following requirements: general military experience; retired from active duty; disabled or killed as a result of military service; prisoner of war; or missing in action.

Application Requirements: Application form, Form DD214. *Deadline:* July 1.

Contact: Amber Brady, Program Manager
  Ohio Board of Regents
  Ohio Board of Regents
  25 South Front Street
  Columbus, OH 43215
  Phone: 614-752-9528
  Fax: 614-752-5903
  E-mail: wo_admin@regents.state.oh.us

OREGON DEPARTMENT OF VETERANS' AFFAIRS

http://www.oregon.gov/odva

OREGON VETERANS' EDUCATION AID

To be eligible, veteran must have actively served in U.S. armed forces 90 days and been discharged under honorable conditions. Must be U.S. citizen and Oregon resident. Korean War veteran or received campaign or expeditionary medal or ribbon awarded by U.S. armed forces for services after June 30, 1958. Full-time students receive up to $150 per month, and part-time students receive up to $100 per month for a maximum of 36 months. Length of benefits depend on length of service. Payments contingent upon available funding.

Award: Grant for use in freshman, sophomore, junior, senior, graduate, or postgraduate years; not renewable. *Number:* 1–200. *Amount:* $3600–$5400.

Eligibility Requirements: Applicant must be enrolled or expecting to enroll full- or part-time at a two-year or four-year or technical institution or university; resident of Oregon and studying in Oregon. Available to U.S. citizens. Applicant must have general military experience.

Application Requirements: Application form, certified copy of DD Form 214. *Deadline:* continuous.

Contact: Loriann Sheridan, Veterans Programs Consultant
Oregon Department of Veterans' Affairs
700 Summer Street, NE
Salem, OR 97301-1289
Phone: 503-373-2264
Fax: 503-373-2393
E-mail: sheridl@odva.state.or.us

OREGON STUDENT ASSISTANCE COMMISSION

http://www.GetCollegeFunds.org/

DARLENE HOOLEY FOR OREGON VETERANS SCHOLARSHIP

Award for first-time freshmen, undergraduate, and graduate students who have actively served in the military post-09/11/2001; no minimum length of service required. Must enroll at least half-time in an Oregon college or university. If you are selected as a semifinalist, you will be required to submit a copy of your DD214 showing service during the correct time frame.

Award: Scholarship for use in freshman, sophomore, junior, senior, or graduate years; not renewable.

Eligibility Requirements: Applicant must be enrolled or expecting to enroll full- or part-time at a two-year or four-year institution or university and studying in Oregon. Available to U.S. citizens. Applicant must have general military experience.

Application Requirements: Application form, proof of military service, FAFSA. *Deadline:* March 1.

MARIA C. JACKSON/GENERAL GEORGE A. WHITE SCHOLARSHIP

Available to Oregon residents who served or whose parents serve or have served in the U.S. Armed Forces and resided in Oregon at time of enlistment. Must have at least 3.75 GPA and submit documentation of service. (No GPA requirement for graduate-level students and students attending a technical school). For use at Oregon colleges only. U.S. Bank employees, their children, and near relatives are not eligible.

Award: Scholarship for use in freshman, sophomore, junior, senior, or graduate years; not renewable.

Eligibility Requirements: Applicant must be enrolled or expecting to enroll full-time at a two-year or four-year or technical institution or university; resident of Oregon and studying in Oregon. Available to U.S. citizens. Applicant or parent must meet one or more of the following requirements: general military experience; retired from active duty; disabled or killed as a result of military service; prisoner of war; or missing in action.

Application Requirements: Application form, essay, proof of service (DD93, DD214, or discharge papers), transcript. *Deadline:* March 1.

PETER CONNACHER MEMORIAL SCHOLARSHIP

Renewable award for American prisoners-of-war and their descendants. Written proof of prisoner-of-war status and discharge papers from the U.S. Armed Forces must accompany application. Statement of relationship between applicant and former prisoner-of-war is required. Oregon residency preferred but not required.

Award: Scholarship for use in freshman, sophomore, junior, senior, or graduate years; renewable.

Eligibility Requirements: Applicant must be enrolled or expecting to enroll full-time at a two-year or four-year institution. Available to U.S.

citizens. Applicant or parent must meet one or more of the following requirements: general military experience; retired from active duty; disabled or killed as a result of military service; prisoner of war; or missing in action.

Application Requirements: Application form, essay, financial need analysis, military discharge papers, documentation of POW status , transcript. *Deadline:* March 1.

PARALYZED VETERANS OF AMERICA-SPINAL CORD RESEARCH FOUNDATION

http://www.pva.org/

PARALYZED VETERANS OF AMERICA EDUCATIONAL SCHOLARSHIP PROGRAM

Open to PVA members, their spouses and unmarried children, under 24 years of age, to obtain a postsecondary education. Applicants must be U.S. citizens accepted or enrolled as full-time students in a degree program. For details and application visit website http://www.pva.org.

Award: Scholarship for use in freshman, sophomore, junior, or senior years; renewable. *Number:* 10–20. *Amount:* $500–$1000.

Eligibility Requirements: Applicant must be enrolled or expecting to enroll full- or part-time at a four-year institution or university. Available to U.S. citizens. Applicant or parent must meet one or more of the following requirements: general military experience; retired from active duty; disabled or killed as a result of military service; prisoner of war; or missing in action.

Application Requirements: Application form, personal statement, verification of enrollment, recommendations or references, transcript. *Deadline:* June 30.

Contact: Patricia Rollins, Member Services Coordinator
Paralyzed Veterans of America-Spinal Cord Research Foundation
801 Eighteenth Street, NW
Washington, DC 20006-3517
Phone: 800-424-8200 Ext. 619
E-mail: trishr@pva.org

THE RESERVE OFFICERS ASSOCIATION

http://www.roa.org/

HENRY J. REILLY MEMORIAL SCHOLARSHIP-HIGH SCHOOL SENIORS AND FIRST YEAR FRESHMEN
• See page 535

HENRY J. REILLY MEMORIAL UNDERGRADUATE SCHOLARSHIP PROGRAM FOR COLLEGE ATTENDEES
• See page 535

RETIRED ENLISTED ASSOCIATION

http://www.trea.org/

RETIRED ENLISTED ASSOCIATION SCHOLARSHIP

One-time award for dependent children or grandchildren of a TREA member or TREA auxiliary member in good standing.

Award: Scholarship for use in freshman, sophomore, junior, senior, graduate, or postgraduate years; not renewable. *Amount:* $1000–$1500.

Eligibility Requirements: Applicant must be enrolled or expecting to enroll full-time at a two-year or four-year or technical institution or university. Available to U.S. citizens. Applicant or parent must meet one or more of the following requirements: general military experience; retired from active duty; disabled or killed as a result of military service; prisoner of war; or missing in action.

Application Requirements: Application form, copy of IRS tax forms, essay, financial need analysis, personal photograph, recommendations or references, test scores, transcript. *Deadline:* April 30.

Contact: Donnell Minnis, Executive Assistant
Phone: 303-752-0660
Fax: 303-752-0835
E-mail: execasst@trea.org

SOUTH CAROLINA DIVISION OF VETERANS AFFAIRS

http://www.govoepp.state.sc.us/vetaff.htm

EDUCATIONAL ASSISTANCE FOR CERTAIN WAR VETERANS DEPENDENTS SCHOLARSHIP-SOUTH CAROLINA

Free tuition for South Carolina residents whose parent is a resident, wartime veteran, and meets one of these criteria; awarded Purple Heart or Congressional Medal of Honor; permanently and totally disabled or killed as a result of military service; prisoner of war; or missing in action. Must be age 18–26 and enrolled or expecting to enroll full or part-time at a two-year or four-year technical institution or university in South Carolina. Complete information and qualifications for this award are on website http://www.govoepp.state.sc.us.

Award: Scholarship for use in freshman, sophomore, junior, or senior years; not renewable.

Eligibility Requirements: Applicant must be age 18-26; enrolled or expecting to enroll full- or part-time at a two-year or four-year or technical institution or university; resident of South Carolina and studying in South Carolina. Available to U.S. citizens. Applicant or parent must meet one or more of the following requirements: general military experience; retired from active duty; disabled or killed as a result of military service; prisoner of war; or missing in action.

Application Requirements: Application form, proof of qualification of veteran, transcript. *Deadline:* continuous.

Contact: Dianne Coley, Free Tuition Program Assistant
Phone: 803-647-2434
E-mail: va@oepp.sc.gov

STATE OF WYOMING, ADMINISTERED BY UNIVERSITY OF WYOMING

http://www.uwyo.edu/scholarships

VIETNAM VETERANS AWARD-WYOMING

Scholarship available to Wyoming residents who served in the armed forces between August 5, 1964 and May 7, 1975, and received a Vietnam service medal.

Award: Scholarship for use in freshman, sophomore, junior, or senior years; renewable.

Eligibility Requirements: Applicant must be enrolled or expecting to enroll full- or part-time at a two-year or four-year institution or university and resident of Wyoming. Available to U.S. citizens. Applicant or parent must meet one or more of the following requirements: general military experience; retired from active duty; disabled or killed as a result of military service; prisoner of war; or missing in action.

Application Requirements: Application form. *Deadline:* continuous.

Contact: Tammy Mack, Assistant Director, Scholarships
State of Wyoming, Administered by University of Wyoming
Department 3335
1000 East University Avenue
Laramie, WY 82071
Phone: 307-766-2412
Fax: 307-766-3800
E-mail: westmack@uwyo.edu

TENNESSEE STUDENT ASSISTANCE CORPORATION

http://www.tn.gov/collegepays

HELPING HEROES GRANT

Provides assistance to Tennessee veterans who have been awarded the Iraq Campaign Medal, Afghanistan Campaign Medal, or Global War on Terrorism Expeditionary Medal (on or after 9/11/01) and who meet eligibility requirements for the program. Award is up to $2,000 per year. For more information, visit http://www.TN.gov/collegepays.

Award: Grant for use in freshman, sophomore, junior, or senior years; not renewable. *Amount:* up to $2000.

Eligibility Requirements: Applicant must be enrolled or expecting to enroll full- or part-time at a two-year or four-year institution or university. Available to U.S. citizens. Applicant must have general military experience.

Application Requirements: Application form, application form may be submitted online (http://www.tn.gov/collegepays), DD-214. *Deadline:* September 1.

Contact: Mr. Robert Biggers, Director of Lottery Programs
Tennessee Student Assistance Corporation
Parkway Towers, Suite 1510, 404 James Robertson Parkway
Nashville, TN 37243
Phone: 615-253-7453
Fax: 615-741-6101
E-mail: robert.biggers@tn.gov

VETERANS UNITED HOME LOANS

http://www.veteransunited.com

MILITARY EDUCATION SCHOLARSHIP

This scholarship is for active military members, veterans, spouses of military members, and children of military members. Applicants must submit a 750 word (or less) essay on a topic chosen by our Scholarship Committee. For more information visit http://www.veteransunited.com/about/scholarships/

Award: Scholarship for use in freshman, sophomore, junior, senior, graduate, or postgraduate years; not renewable. *Number:* 10. *Amount:* $2000.

Eligibility Requirements: Applicant must be enrolled or expecting to enroll full- or part-time at a two-year or four-year or technical institution or university. Applicant must have 2.5 GPA or higher. Available to U.S. citizens. Applicant or parent must meet one or more of the following requirements: general military experience; retired from active duty; disabled or killed as a result of military service; prisoner of war; or missing in action.

Application Requirements: Application form, application form may be submitted online (http://www.veteransunited.com/about/scholarships/), essay, transcript. *Deadline:* continuous.

Contact: Ms. Miranda Chapin, Scholarship Committee
Veterans United Home Loans
2101 Chapel Plaza Court, Suite 107
Columbia, MO 65203
Phone: 800-814-1103 Ext. 3867
Fax: 573-445-8073
E-mail: mchapin@veteransunited.com

VIRGINIA DEPARTMENT OF VETERANS SERVICES

http://www.dvs.virginia.gov/

VIRGINIA MILITARY SURVIVORS AND DEPENDENTS EDUCATION PROGRAM

Scholarships for post-secondary students between ages 16 and 29 to attend Virginia state-supported institutions. Must be child or surviving spouse of veteran who has either been permanently or totally disabled due to war or other armed conflict; died as a result of war or other armed conflict; or been listed as a POW or MIA. Parent must also meet Virginia residency requirements.

Award: Scholarship for use in freshman, sophomore, junior, senior, or graduate years; renewable.

Eligibility Requirements: Applicant must be age 16-29; enrolled or expecting to enroll full-time at a two-year or four-year or technical institution or university; resident of Virginia and studying in Virginia. Available to U.S. citizens. Applicant or parent must meet one or more of the following requirements: general military experience; retired from active duty; disabled or killed as a result of military service; prisoner of war; or missing in action.

Application Requirements: Application form, DD214 of service member, birth certificate of applicant, marriage certificate, acceptance letter from institution. *Deadline:* varies.

Contact: Mrs. Doris Sullivan, Coordinator
Virginia Department of Veterans Services
1351 Hershberger Road, Suite 220
Roanoke, VA 24012
Phone: 540-561-6625
Fax: 540-857-7573

MILITARY SERVICE: MARINES

DAUGHTERS OF THE CINCINNATI
http://www.daughters1894.org/

DAUGHTERS OF THE CINCINNATI SCHOLARSHIP
• *See page 581*

DEPARTMENT OF VETERANS AFFAIRS (VA)
http://www.gibill.va.gov/

MONTGOMERY GI BILL (SELECTED RESERVE)
• *See page 581*

FIRST MARINE DIVISION ASSOCIATION
http://www.1stmarinedivisionassociation.org/

FIRST MARINE DIVISION ASSOCIATION SCHOLARSHIP FUND
Scholarship to assist dependents of deceased or 100 percent permanently disabled veterans of service with the 1st Marine Division in furthering their education towards a bachelor's degree. Awarded to full-time, undergraduate students who are attending an accredited college, university, or higher technical trade school, up to a maximum of four years.

Award: Scholarship for use in freshman, sophomore, junior, or senior years; not renewable. *Amount:* up to $1750.

Eligibility Requirements: Applicant must be enrolled or expecting to enroll full-time at a four-year or technical institution or university and single. Available to U.S. citizens. Applicant or parent must meet one or more of the following requirements: Marine Corps experience; retired from active duty; disabled or killed as a result of military service; prisoner of war; or missing in action.

Application Requirements: Application form, essay, personal photograph, social security number, birth certificate, proof of parent's death, transcript. *Deadline:* continuous.

Contact: Col. Len Hayes, Executive Director
Phone: 760-967-8561
Fax: 760-967-8567
E-mail: oldbreed@sbcglobal.net

FRA EDUCATION FOUNDATION
http://www.fra.org/foundation

FLEET RESERVE ASSOCIATION EDUCATION FOUNDATION SCHOLARSHIPS
• *See page 589*

STANLEY A. DORAN MEMORIAL SCHOLARSHIP
• *See page 519*

IMAGINE AMERICA FOUNDATION
http://www.imagine-america.org

MILITARY AWARD PROGRAM (MAP)
• *See page 581*

INDIANA DEPARTMENT OF VETERANS AFFAIRS
http://www.in.gov/dva

RESIDENT TUITION FOR ACTIVE DUTY MILITARY PERSONNEL
• *See page 581*

LADIES AUXILIARY OF THE FLEET RESERVE ASSOCIATION
http://www.fra.org/

ALLIE MAE ODEN MEMORIAL SCHOLARSHIP
• *See page 524*

LADIES AUXILIARY OF THE FLEET RESERVE ASSOCIATION-NATIONAL PRESIDENT'S SCHOLARSHIP
• *See page 524*

LADIES AUXILIARY OF THE FLEET RESERVE ASSOCIATION SCHOLARSHIP
• *See page 524*

SAM ROSE MEMORIAL SCHOLARSHIP
• *See page 525*

MARINE CORPS TANKERS ASSOCIATION INC.
http://www.USMarinetankers.org/

MARINE CORPS TANKERS ASSOCIATION, JOHN CORNELIUS/MAX ENGLISH SCHOLARSHIP
Award for Marine tankers or former Marine tankers, or dependents of Marines who served in a tank unit and are on active duty, retired, reserve or have been honorably discharged. Applicant must be a high school graduate or planning to graduate in June. May be enrolled in college, undergraduate or graduate or have previously attended college. Must be a member of MCTA or intends to join in the future.

Award: Scholarship for use in freshman, sophomore, junior, senior, or graduate years; not renewable. *Number:* 10. *Amount:* up to $2000.

Eligibility Requirements: Applicant must be enrolled or expecting to enroll full-time at a two-year or four-year or technical institution or university. Available to U.S. citizens. Applicant or parent must meet one or more of the following requirements: Marine Corps experience; retired from active duty; disabled or killed as a result of military service; prisoner of war; or missing in action.

Application Requirements: Application form, essay, personal photograph, recommendations or references, test scores, transcript. *Deadline:* March 15.

Contact: Phil Morell, Scholarship Chair
Marine Corps Tankers Association Inc.
1112 Alpine Heights Road
Alpine, CA 91901-2814
Phone: 619-445-8423
Fax: 619-445-8423
E-mail: mpmorell@cox.net

NAVY-MARINE CORPS RELIEF SOCIETY
http://www.nmcrs.org/education

JOSEPH A. MCALINDEN DIVERS SCHOLARSHIP
Navy-Marine Corps Divers: active duty/retired and dependents pursuing study in the area of ocean agriculture, Oceanography, Aquaculture. Or advanced diver training, certifications and recertifications.

Award: Scholarship for use in freshman, sophomore, junior, or senior years; not renewable. *Amount:* $500–$3000.

Eligibility Requirements: Applicant must be enrolled or expecting to enroll full- or part-time at a two-year or four-year or technical institution or university. Available to U.S. citizens. Applicant must have served in the Marine Corps or Navy.

Application Requirements: Application form.

Contact: Mrs. Beverly Langdon, Education, Program Manager

NMCRS GOLD STAR SCHOLARSHIPS FOR CHILDREN OF DECEASED SERVICE MEMBERS

Scholarship for full-time undergraduate students enrolled in accredited colleges or universities. Must be 22 years of age or younger. Must have minimum 2.0 GPA.

Award: Scholarship for use in freshman, sophomore, junior, or senior years; not renewable. *Number:* 1–100. *Amount:* $500–$2500.

Eligibility Requirements: Applicant must be enrolled or expecting to enroll full-time at a two-year or four-year or technical institution or university and single. Available to U.S. citizens. Applicant or parent must meet one or more of the following requirements: Marine Corps or Navy experience; retired from active duty; disabled or killed as a result of military service; prisoner of war; or missing in action.

Application Requirements: Application form, financial need analysis. *Deadline:* April 1.

Contact: Mrs. Beverly Langdon, Education, Program Manager
Navy-Marine Corps Relief Society
875 North Randolph Street, Suite 225
Arlington, VA 22203
Phone: 703-696-4960
E-mail: education@nmcrs.org

SECOND MARINE DIVISION ASSOCIATION

http://www.2dmardiv.com/

SECOND MARINE DIVISION ASSOCIATION MEMORIAL SCHOLARSHIP FUND

Renewable award for students who are unmarried, dependent sons, daughters or grandchildren of former or current members of Second Marine Division or attached units. Must submit proof of parent's or grandparent's service. Family adjusted gross income must not exceed $70,000. Award is merit-based. Minimum 2.5 GPA required.

Award: Scholarship for use in freshman, sophomore, junior, or senior years; not renewable. *Number:* 35–42. *Amount:* $1200.

Eligibility Requirements: Applicant must be enrolled or expecting to enroll full-time at a two-year or four-year or technical institution or university and single. Applicant must have 2.5 GPA or higher. Available to U.S. and non-U.S. citizens. Applicant must have served in the Marine Corps or Navy.

Application Requirements: Application form, essay, financial need analysis, personal photograph, recommendations or references, self-addressed stamped envelope with application, transcript. *Deadline:* April 1.

Contact: Mr. Martin McNulty, Chairman, Board of Trustees, SMDA
Memorial Scholarship Fund
Second Marine Division Association
280 Briarwood Road
Tyrone, GA 30290
Phone: 678-364-1328

TAILHOOK EDUCATIONAL FOUNDATION

http://www.tailhook.org/

TAILHOOK EDUCATIONAL FOUNDATION SCHOLARSHIP

• *See page 590*

THIRD MARINE DIVISION ASSOCIATION, INC.

http://www.caltrap.com/

THIRD MARINE DIVISION ASSOCIATION MEMORIAL SCHOLARSHIP FUND

Scholarship assistance for dependents of qualified Third Marine Division Association members (Marine or Navy), or qualified service-connected deceased 3d Marine Division veterans. For further details visit website, http://www.caltrap.com. Total number of awards varies.

Award: Scholarship for use in freshman, sophomore, junior, or senior years; renewable. *Number:* 5–25. *Amount:* $500–$1500.

Eligibility Requirements: Applicant must be age 16-23; enrolled or expecting to enroll full-time at a two-year or four-year or technical institution or university and single. Available to U.S. citizens. Applicant must have served in the Marine Corps or Navy.

Application Requirements: Application form, birth certificate/adoption order (if applicable), financial need analysis, personal photograph, transcript. *Deadline:* April 15.

Contact: James Kyser, Secretary, Memorial Scholarship Fund
Third Marine Division Association, Inc.
15727 Vista Drive
Dumfries, VA 22025-1810
E-mail: supertop@aol.com

UNITED STATES MARINE CORPS SCHOLARSHIP FOUNDATION, INC.

http://www.mcsf.org/

MARINE CORPS SCHOLARSHIP FOUNDATION

• *See page 542*

WISCONSIN DEPARTMENT OF VETERANS AFFAIRS (WDVA)

http://www.dva.state.wi.us/

VETERANS EDUCATION (VETED) REIMBURSEMENT GRANT

• *See page 582*

MILITARY SERVICE: NAVY

ANCHOR SCHOLARSHIP FOUNDATION

http://www.anchorscholarship.com/

ANCHOR SCHOLARSHIP FOUNDATION PROGRAM

Must be dependent child or spouse of US Navy service member (active or retired) having served at least six years under administrative control of US Naval Surface Forces, Atlantic or Pacific Fleets. Eligibility must first be determined by submitting an eligibility application. This application is available online in the fall. Be prepared to submit sponsor's full name, rank/rate, list of duty stations, home-ports, ship hull numbers, dates served aboard and supporting documentation. Once eligibility is confirmed, the scholarship application will be sent via email. Selection basis: academics, extracurricular activities, character, and financial need.

Award: Scholarship for use in freshman, sophomore, junior, or senior years; not renewable. *Number:* 35–43. *Amount:* $2000–$5000.

Eligibility Requirements: Applicant must be enrolled or expecting to enroll full-time at a four-year institution or university. Available to U.S. citizens. Applicant or parent must meet one or more of the following requirements: Navy experience; retired from active duty; disabled or killed as a result of military service; prisoner of war; or missing in action.

Application Requirements: Application form, eligibility application (online), essay, financial need analysis, recommendations or references, self-addressed stamped envelope with application, test scores, transcript. *Deadline:* March 1.

Contact: Mrs. Danielle Dawley, Executive Director
Anchor Scholarship Foundation
4966 Euclid Road
Suite 109
Virginia Beach, VA 23462
Phone: 757-671-3200 Ext. 116
E-mail: admin@anchorscholarship.com

DAUGHTERS OF THE CINCINNATI

http://www.daughters1894.org/

DAUGHTERS OF THE CINCINNATI SCHOLARSHIP
• *See page 581*

DEPARTMENT OF VETERANS AFFAIRS (VA)

http://www.gibill.va.gov/

MONTGOMERY GI BILL (SELECTED RESERVE)
• *See page 581*

DOLPHIN SCHOLARSHIP FOUNDATION

http://www.dolphinscholarship.org/

DOLPHIN SCHOLARSHIPS
Renewable award for undergraduate students. Applicant's parent/stepparent must meet one of the following requirements: be current/former member of the U.S. Navy who qualified in submarines and served in the Submarine Force for at least eight years; current or former member of the Navy who served in submarine support activities for at least ten years; or Navy member who died while on active duty in the Submarine Force. Must be single, under age 24.

Award: Scholarship for use in freshman, sophomore, junior, or senior years; renewable. *Number:* 25–30. *Amount:* up to $3400.

Eligibility Requirements: Applicant must be enrolled or expecting to enroll full-time at a four-year institution or university and single. Available to U.S. citizens. Applicant or parent must meet one or more of the following requirements: Navy experience; retired from active duty; disabled or killed as a result of military service; prisoner of war; or missing in action.

Application Requirements: Application form, application form may be submitted online (http://www.dolphinscholarship.org), essay, financial need analysis, recommendations or references, self-addressed stamped envelope with application, test scores, transcript. *Deadline:* March 15.

Contact: Mr. Andrew Clark, Executive Director
Dolphin Scholarship Foundation
4966 Euclid Road
Suite 109
Virginia Beach, VA 23462
Phone: 757-671-3200 Ext. 114
Fax: 757-671-3330
E-mail: scholars@dolphinscholarship.org

FRA EDUCATION FOUNDATION

http://www.fra.org/foundation

COLONEL HAZEL ELIZABETH BENN U.S.M.C. SCHOLARSHIP
• *See page 519*

FLEET RESERVE ASSOCIATION EDUCATION FOUNDATION SCHOLARSHIPS
• *See page 589*

STANLEY A. DORAN MEMORIAL SCHOLARSHIP
• *See page 519*

GAMEWARDENS OF VIETNAM ASSOCIATION INC.

http://www.tf116.org/

GAMEWARDENS OF VIETNAM SCHOLARSHIP
Scholarship for entering freshman who is a descendant of a U.S. Navy man or woman who worked with TF-116 in Vietnam. One-time award, but applicant may reapply.

Award: Scholarship for use in freshman year; not renewable. *Number:* 1–3. *Amount:* $500.

Eligibility Requirements: Applicant must be high school student; age 16-21 and planning to enroll or expecting to enroll full-time at a two-year or four-year or technical institution or university. Applicant must have 2.5 GPA or higher. Available to U.S. and non-U.S. citizens. Applicant or parent must meet one or more of the following requirements: Navy experience; retired from active duty; disabled or killed as a result of military service; prisoner of war; or missing in action.

Application Requirements: Application form, recommendations or references, resume, test scores, transcript. *Deadline:* April 1.

Contact: David Ajax, Scholarship Coordinator
Gamewardens of Vietnam Association Inc.
6630 Perry Court
Arvada, CO 80003
Phone: 303-426-6385
Fax: 303-426-6186
E-mail: dpajax@comcast.net

IMAGINE AMERICA FOUNDATION

http://www.imagine-america.org

MILITARY AWARD PROGRAM (MAP)
• *See page 581*

INDIANA DEPARTMENT OF VETERANS AFFAIRS

http://www.in.gov/dva

RESIDENT TUITION FOR ACTIVE DUTY MILITARY PERSONNEL
• *See page 581*

LADIES AUXILIARY OF THE FLEET RESERVE ASSOCIATION

http://www.fra.org/

ALLIE MAE ODEN MEMORIAL SCHOLARSHIP
• *See page 524*

LADIES AUXILIARY OF THE FLEET RESERVE ASSOCIATION-NATIONAL PRESIDENT'S SCHOLARSHIP
• *See page 524*

LADIES AUXILIARY OF THE FLEET RESERVE ASSOCIATION SCHOLARSHIP
• *See page 524*

SAM ROSE MEMORIAL SCHOLARSHIP
• *See page 525*

NAVAL RESERVE ASSOCIATION

http://www.navyreserve.com

NAVAL RESERVE ASSOCIATION SCHOLARSHIP PROGRAM
Award is given to children of active members of the association. Must be U.S. citizens and under the age of 24. Must be enrolled in or accepted for full-time enrollment at an accredited college, university or a fully-accredited technical school.

Award: Scholarship for use in freshman, sophomore, junior, or senior years; not renewable. *Amount:* $1000–$5000.

Eligibility Requirements: Applicant must be enrolled or expecting to enroll full-time at a two-year or four-year or technical institution or university. Available to U.S. citizens. Applicant or parent must meet one or more of the following requirements: Navy experience; retired from active duty; disabled or killed as a result of military service; prisoner of war; or missing in action.

Application Requirements: Application form, community service, driver's license, essay, financial need analysis, recommendations or references, test scores, transcript. *Deadline:* May 1.

Contact: Mr. Bob Lyman, Chief Financial Officer
Naval Reserve Association
1619 King Street
Alexandria, VA 22314
Phone: 703-548-5800
Fax: 703-683-3647
E-mail: cfo@navy-reserve.org

NAVY-MARINE CORPS RELIEF SOCIETY

http://www.nmcrs.org/education

JOSEPH A. MCALINDEN DIVERS SCHOLARSHIP

• *See page 609*

NMCRS GOLD STAR SCHOLARSHIPS FOR CHILDREN OF DECEASED SERVICE MEMBERS

• *See page 610*

SEABEE MEMORIAL SCHOLARSHIP ASSOCIATION, INC.

http://www.seabee.org/

SEABEE MEMORIAL ASSOCIATION SCHOLARSHIP

Award available to children or grandchildren of current or former members of the Naval Construction Force (Seabees) or Naval Civil Engineer Corps. Not available for graduate study or to great-grandchildren of Seabees.

Award: Scholarship for use in freshman, sophomore, junior, or senior years; renewable. *Number:* 99. *Amount:* $1800.

Eligibility Requirements: Applicant must be enrolled or expecting to enroll full-time at a four-year institution or university. Available to U.S. citizens. Applicant or parent must meet one or more of the following requirements: Navy experience; retired from active duty; disabled or killed as a result of military service; prisoner of war; or missing in action.

Application Requirements: Application form, essay, financial need analysis, IRS Form 1040, test scores, transcript. *Deadline:* April 15.

Contact: Sheryl Chiogioji, Administrative Assistant
Seabee Memorial Scholarship Association, Inc.
PO Box 6574
Silver Spring, MD 20916
Phone: 301-570-2850
Fax: 301-570-2873
E-mail: smsa@erols.com

SECOND MARINE DIVISION ASSOCIATION

http://www.2dmardiv.com/

SECOND MARINE DIVISION ASSOCIATION MEMORIAL SCHOLARSHIP FUND

• *See page 610*

TAILHOOK EDUCATIONAL FOUNDATION

http://www.tailhook.org/

TAILHOOK EDUCATIONAL FOUNDATION SCHOLARSHIP

• *See page 590*

THIRD MARINE DIVISION ASSOCIATION, INC.

http://www.caltrap.com/

THIRD MARINE DIVISION ASSOCIATION MEMORIAL SCHOLARSHIP FUND

• *See page 610*

UDT-SEAL ASSOCIATION

http://www.nswfoundation.org/

HAD RICHARDS UDT-SEAL MEMORIAL SCHOLARSHIP

One-time award for dependent children of UDT-SEAL association members. Freshmen given priority. Applicant may not be older than 22 and not married. Must be U.S. citizen.

Award: Scholarship for use in freshman, sophomore, junior, or senior years; not renewable. *Number:* 1–2.

Eligibility Requirements: Applicant must be enrolled or expecting to enroll full-time at a two-year or four-year institution or university and single. Available to U.S. citizens. Applicant or parent must meet one or more of the following requirements: Navy experience; retired from active duty; disabled or killed as a result of military service; prisoner of war; or missing in action.

Application Requirements: Application form, essay, personal photograph, proof of active duty or parent/spouse's active duty, test scores, transcript. *Deadline:* varies.

Contact: Robert Rieve, President and CEO
Phone: 757-363-7490
E-mail: info@nswfoundation.org

NAVAL SPECIAL WARFARE SCHOLARSHIP

Awards given to active duty SEAL's, SWCC's, and other active duty military serving in a Naval Special Warfare command or their spouses and dependents.

Award: Scholarship for use in freshman, sophomore, junior, or senior years; not renewable. *Number:* 80–100.

Eligibility Requirements: Applicant must be enrolled or expecting to enroll full- or part-time at a two-year or four-year institution or university. Available to U.S. citizens. Applicant or parent must meet one or more of the following requirements: Navy experience; retired from active duty; disabled or killed as a result of military service; prisoner of war; or missing in action.

Application Requirements: Application form, essay, personal photograph, proof of active duty or parent/spouse's active duty, transcript.

Contact: Robert Rieve, President and CEO
Phone: 757-363-7490
E-mail: info@nswfoundation.org

UDT-SEAL SCHOLARSHIP

Award for dependent children of UDT-SEAL association members. Freshmen given priority. Applicant may not be older than 22 and not married. Must be U.S. citizen.

Award: Scholarship for use in freshman, sophomore, junior, or senior years; not renewable. *Number:* 10–20.

Eligibility Requirements: Applicant must be enrolled or expecting to enroll full-time at a two-year or four-year or technical institution or university and single. Available to U.S. citizens. Applicant or parent must meet one or more of the following requirements: Navy experience; retired from active duty; disabled or killed as a result of military service; prisoner of war; or missing in action.

Application Requirements: Application form, essay, personal photograph, proof of active duty or parent/spouse's active duty, test scores, transcript. *Deadline:* varies.

Contact: Robert Rieve, President and CEO
Phone: 757-363-7490
E-mail: info@nswfoundation.org

UNITED STATES SUBMARINE VETERANS

http://www.ussvcf.org/

UNITED STATES SUBMARINE VETERANS INC. NATIONAL SCHOLARSHIP PROGRAM

• *See page 543*

WINGS OVER AMERICA SCHOLARSHIP FOUNDATION

http://www.wingsoveramerica.us/

WINGS OVER AMERICA SCHOLARSHIP

Applicant must be graduates of an accredited high school or the equivalent home school or institution and must plan to attend an accredited academic institution.

Award: Scholarship for use in freshman, sophomore, or junior years; not renewable. *Number:* 40. *Amount:* $1000–$3000.

Eligibility Requirements: Applicant must be enrolled or expecting to enroll full- or part-time at a two-year or four-year institution or university. Available to U.S. citizens. Applicant must have served in the Navy.

Application Requirements: Application form, essay, pre-qualification form based on military service of sponsor, recommendations or references, transcript. *Deadline:* March 1.

Contact: Susan Hunter, Scholarship Administrator
    Phone: 757-671-3200
    E-mail: info@wingsoveramerica.us

WISCONSIN DEPARTMENT OF VETERANS AFFAIRS (WDVA)

http://www.dva.state.wi.us/

VETERANS EDUCATION (VETED) REIMBURSEMENT GRANT

• *See page 582*

NATIONALITY OR ETHNIC HERITAGE

ADELANTE! U.S. EDUCATION LEADERSHIP FUND

http://www.adelantefund.org/

ADELANTE FUND SCHOLARSHIPS

Awards are primarily created to enhance the leadership qualities of the recipients for transition into postgraduate education, business, and/or corporate America. Financial need is a factor for these awards. Minimum 3.0 GPA is required for all scholarships. Awards are available for colleges located in the states of California, New Mexico, Arizona, Texas, Florida, Illinois, and New York. Applicants should view website for all award criteria and for scholarship application forms.

Award: Scholarship for use in sophomore, junior, or senior years; renewable. *Number:* 30–45. *Amount:* $1000–$3000.

Eligibility Requirements: Applicant must be of Hispanic heritage; enrolled or expecting to enroll full-time at a two-year or four-year institution or university; studying in Arizona, California, Florida, Illinois, New Mexico, New York, Texas and must have an interest in leadership. Applicant must have 3.0 GPA or higher. Available to U.S. citizens.

Application Requirements: Application form, essay, financial need analysis, recommendations or references, resume, transcript. *Deadline:* April 30.

Contact: Miss. Sarah Ramos, Assistant Director of Student Services
    Adelante! U.S. Education Leadership Fund
    8415 Datapoint Drive, Suite 400
    San Antonio, TX 78229
    Phone: 210-692-1971
    Fax: 210-692-1951
    E-mail: sramos@adelantefund.org

ALABAMA INDIAN AFFAIRS COMMISSION

http://www.aiac.alabama.gov/

AIAC SCHOLARSHIP

Must be a member of a state or federally recognized Indian tribe. Must have a tribal roll card. Must be a resident of the state of Alabama. Must attend a school in the state of Alabama, unless program is not offered in an Alabama school.

Award: Scholarship for use in freshman, sophomore, junior, senior, or graduate years; not renewable. *Number:* 25–55. *Amount:* $500.

Eligibility Requirements: Applicant must be American Indian/Alaska Native; enrolled or expecting to enroll full-time at a two-year or four-year or technical institution or university; resident of Alabama and studying in Alabama. Applicant must have 2.5 GPA or higher. Available to U.S. citizens.

Application Requirements: Application form, community service, essay, financial need analysis, recommendations or references, test scores, transcript, tribal certification, letter of acceptance from school of choice. *Deadline:* March 7.

Contact: Mrs. Eloise Josey, Executive Director
    Alabama Indian Affairs Commission
    771 South Lawrence Street
    Suite 106
    Montgomery, AL 36104
    Phone: 334-242-2831
    Fax: 334-240-3408
    E-mail: aiac@att.net

ALBERTA HERITAGE SCHOLARSHIP FUND

http://www.alis.alberta.ca/

ADULT HIGH SCHOOL EQUIVALENCY SCHOLARSHIPS

Awards of CAN$500 to recognize and reward the academic achievement of mature students in the attainment of high school equivalency and provide an incentive for students to continue their education at the postsecondary level. Applicants must be residents of Alberta, have been out of high school for a minimum of three years prior to commencing a high school equivalency program, and be enrolled full-time in a high school equivalency program. Must be nominated by high school. See website for additional information and application http://alis.alberta.ca.

Award: Scholarship for use in freshman year; not renewable. *Number:* up to 200.

Eligibility Requirements: Applicant must be Canadian citizen; enrolled or expecting to enroll full-time at a two-year or four-year or technical institution or university; resident of Alberta and studying in Alberta. Applicant must have 3.0 GPA or higher.

Application Requirements: Application form, nomination. *Deadline:* September 1.

ALBERTA CENTENNIAL SCHOLARSHIPS-ALBERTA

Awards of CAN$2005 to commemorate the province of Alberta's centennial. Twenty-five awards have been established. Must be Canadian citizens or permanent residents of Canada and Alberta residents. Awards students entering any level of postsecondary study at any university, college, technical institute, or apprenticeship program in Canada. Each high school in Alberta nominates a recipient and all are considered for the 25 awards. For additional information and application form, visit website http://alis.alberta.ca.

Award: Scholarship for use in freshman, sophomore, junior, or senior years; not renewable. *Number:* 25.

Eligibility Requirements: Applicant must be Canadian citizen; high school student; planning to enroll or expecting to enroll full-time at a two-year or four-year or technical institution or university and resident of Alberta.

Application Requirements: Nomination from high school counselors. *Deadline:* June 1.

ALEXANDER RUTHERFORD SCHOLARSHIPS FOR HIGH SCHOOL ACHIEVEMENT

Award of up to CAN$2500 available to high school students who are residents of Alberta and plan to enroll or are enrolled in a full-time postsecondary program of at least one semester. Awarded on the basis of achieving an 75 percent average on seven designated subjects in grades 10, 11 and 12. For additional information, see website http://alis.alberta.ca.

Award: Scholarship for use in freshman year; not renewable.

Eligibility Requirements: Applicant must be Canadian citizen; high school student; planning to enroll or expecting to enroll full-time at a two-year or four-year or technical institution or university and resident of Alberta.

Application Requirements: Application form, transcript. *Deadline:* May 1.

CHARLES S. NOBLE JUNIOR A HOCKEY SCHOLARSHIPS

Awards of CAN$2000 to reward the athletic and academic excellence of Junior A Hockey league players and to provide an incentive and means for these players to continue their postsecondary education. Must be Alberta residents and enrolled full-time at a postsecondary institution in Alberta. Interested applicants should contact their team coach or manager, as nominations must come from the participant's hockey team. For additional information, see website http://alis.alberta.ca.

Award: Scholarship for use in freshman, sophomore, junior, or senior years; not renewable. *Number:* 10.

Eligibility Requirements: Applicant must be Canadian citizen; enrolled or expecting to enroll full-time at a two-year or four-year or technical institution or university; resident of Alberta; studying in Alberta and must have an interest in athletics/sports.

Application Requirements: Application form, essay, transcript. *Deadline:* December 1.

CHARLES S. NOBLE JUNIOR FOOTBALL SCHOLARSHIPS

Scholarships of up to CAN$1000 available to reward the athletic and academic excellence of junior football players at universities, colleges, and technical institutes in Alberta. Must be Alberta residents and enrolled full-time in an undergraduate, professional, or graduate program at a university, college, or technical institute in Alberta. Must be a playing member on an Alberta junior football team and maintain 2.0 average in the previous semester. Interested applicants should contact their team coach or manager as nominations must come from the football team. For additional information, visit website http://alis.alberta.ca.

Award: Scholarship for use in freshman, sophomore, junior, senior, or graduate years; not renewable. *Number:* 30.

Eligibility Requirements: Applicant must be Canadian citizen; enrolled or expecting to enroll full-time at a two-year or four-year or technical institution or university; resident of Alberta; studying in Alberta and must have an interest in athletics/sports.

Application Requirements: Nomination from junior football team. *Deadline:* October 1.

DR. ERNEST AND MINNIE MEHL SCHOLARSHIP

Award of CAN$3500 to encourage students to pursue a postsecondary education and to recognize and reward exceptional academic achievement at the senior high school level. Applicants must be Canadian citizens or landed immigrants who have completed their grade twelve in Alberta at a school that follows the Alberta Education Curriculum. Applicants must be continuing their studies at a degree granting postsecondary institution in Canada. University transfer programs are acceptable. For additional information and application, see website http://alis.alberta.ca.

Award: Scholarship for use in freshman, sophomore, junior, or senior years; not renewable. *Number:* 1.

Eligibility Requirements: Applicant must be Canadian citizen; high school student; planning to enroll or expecting to enroll full-time at a two-year or four-year or technical institution or university; resident of Alberta and studying in Alberta, British Columbia, Manitoba, New Brunswick, Newfoundland, Northwest Territories, Nova Scotia, Ontario, Prince Edward Island, Quebec, Saskatchewan.

Application Requirements: Application form, financial need analysis, transcript. *Deadline:* June 1.

EARL AND COUNTESS OF WESSEX-WORLD CHAMPIONSHIPS IN ATHLETICS SCHOLARSHIPS

Award of CAN$3000 to recognize the top male and female Alberta students who have excelled in track and field, have a strong academic record, and plan to continue their studies at the postsecondary level in Alberta. Must be Canadian citizens or landed immigrants and residents of

Alberta. Must have completed grade twelve in Alberta in the same year they apply for the scholarship. Must be planning on attending University of Alberta, University of Calgary or University of Lethbridge. For additional information and application, go to website http://alis.alberta.ca.

Award: Scholarship for use in freshman year; not renewable. *Number:* 2.

Eligibility Requirements: Applicant must be Canadian citizen; high school student; planning to enroll or expecting to enroll full-time at a two-year or four-year or technical institution or university; resident of Alberta; studying in Alberta and must have an interest in athletics/sports.

Application Requirements: Application form, recommendations or references, transcript. *Deadline:* October 1.

GRANT MACEWAN UNITED WORLD COLLEGE SCHOLARSHIPS

Award to reward Alberta's best grade eleven students with a chance to complete their high school at one of the twelve United World Colleges located throughout the world. Applicants must be Alberta residents and be between the ages of 16 and 17 and a half. Applicants are normally in the process of completing their grade eleven. Scholarship is based on a student's academic record, breadth of study, personal accomplishments, community involvement, and interest in the goals of the United World Colleges. For additional information and application, see website http://alis.alberta.ca.

Award: Scholarship for use in freshman year; renewable.

Eligibility Requirements: Applicant must be Canadian citizen; high school student; age 16-17; planning to enroll or expecting to enroll full-time at a four-year institution or university and resident of Alberta.

Application Requirements: Application form, essay, interview, recommendations or references, transcript. *Deadline:* February 15.

INTERNATIONAL EDUCATION AWARDS-UKRAINE

Awards of CAN$5000 to recognize the accomplishments of intern, co-op, practicum, apprenticeship, and research students. Must be a postsecondary student or an apprenticeship student taking a practicum, internship, co-op, apprenticeship program, or a student conducting research (one-term). Recipient will be selected based on demonstrated past accomplishments and potential for improving relations between Ukraine and Alberta. For additional information and application, see website http://alis.alberta.ca.

Award: Scholarship for use in freshman, sophomore, junior, or senior years; not renewable. *Number:* 5.

Eligibility Requirements: Applicant must be Canadian, Ukrainian citizen; enrolled or expecting to enroll full-time at a two-year or four-year or technical institution or university and studying in Alberta. Available to Canadian and non-U.S. citizens.

Application Requirements: Application form, recommendations or references. *Deadline:* February 1.

JIMMIE CONDON ATHLETIC SCHOLARSHIPS

Award of CAN$1800 available to Alberta residents enrolled full-time in an undergraduate, professional, or graduate program at a university, college, or technical institute in Alberta. Must be a member of a designated sports team or a Provincial Disabled Athletic Team recognized by the Alberta Athlete Development Program, and must be nominated by coach. For additional information, go to website http://alis.alberta.ca.

Award: Scholarship for use in freshman, sophomore, junior, or senior years; not renewable.

Eligibility Requirements: Applicant must be Canadian citizen; enrolled or expecting to enroll full-time at a two-year or four-year or technical institution or university; resident of Alberta; studying in Alberta and must have an interest in athletics/sports.

Application Requirements: Application form, nomination by athletic coach. *Deadline:* November 1.

JO-ANNE KOCH-ABC SOCIETY SCHOLARSHIP

Up to two scholarships of CAN$500 supports gifted learners in their post-secondary studies. Applicants must have completed Grade 12 requirements at a publicly funded high school in Alberta and plan to pursue post-secondary studies. Applicants must meet the criteria for Giftedness as determined by their school jurisdiction. Preference will be given to applicants who have received extra support for their learning needs. For additional information, see website http://alis.alberta.ca.

Award: Scholarship for use in freshman year; not renewable. *Number:* 2.

Eligibility Requirements: Applicant must be Canadian citizen; high school student; planning to enroll or expecting to enroll full-time at a two-year or four-year institution or university and resident of Alberta.

Application Requirements: Application form, essay, recommendations or references. *Deadline:* April 1.

KEYERA ENERGY-PETER J. RENTON MEMORIAL SCHOLARSHIP

The scholarship is intended to assist and encourage Alberta students to pursue full-time studies in a post-secondary program in a field related to the oil and gas industry. CAN$3000 for first year of study and CAN$3000 renewable in second year providing recipient maintains GPA of 3.0 on a 4.0 scale. For additional information, see website http://alis.alberta.ca.

Award: Scholarship for use in freshman or sophomore years; renewable.

Eligibility Requirements: Applicant must be Canadian citizen; high school student; planning to enroll or expecting to enroll full-time at a two-year or four-year or technical institution or university; resident of Alberta and studying in Alberta.

Application Requirements: Application form, essay, recommendations or references.

LAURENCE DECORE AWARDS FOR STUDENT LEADERSHIP

Awards of CAN$500 for postsecondary students who have demonstrated outstanding dedication and leadership to fellow students and to their community. Must be Alberta residents who are currently enrolled in a minimum of three full courses at a designated Alberta postsecondary institution. Selected on the basis of involvement in either student government or student societies, clubs, or organizations. For additional information, visit website http://alis.alberta.ca.

Award: Scholarship for use in freshman, sophomore, junior, or senior years; not renewable. *Number:* 100.

Eligibility Requirements: Applicant must be Canadian citizen; enrolled or expecting to enroll full- or part-time at a two-year or four-year or technical institution or university; resident of Alberta; studying in Alberta and must have an interest in leadership.

Application Requirements: Application form, nomination from school. *Deadline:* March 1.

LOUISE MCKINNEY POSTSECONDARY SCHOLARSHIPS

Student awards of up to CAN$2500 to residents of Alberta who are enrolled at a university, college, or technical institute in the second or subsequent year of full-time study. Alberta students studying out-of-province because their program of study is not offered in Alberta will be considered for a scholarship if their class standing is in the top two percent of their program. For additional information, go to website http://alis.alberta.ca.

Award: Scholarship for use in sophomore, junior, or senior years; not renewable.

Eligibility Requirements: Applicant must be Canadian citizen; enrolled or expecting to enroll full-time at a two-year or four-year institution or university and resident of Alberta.

Application Requirements: Application form, test scores, transcript. *Deadline:* varies.

PERSONS CASE SCHOLARSHIPS

Awards of up to CAN$5000 to assist female students whose studies will ultimately contribute to the advancement of women, or who are studying in a field that is non-traditional for women. Applicants must be residents of Alberta and enrolled full-time at a postsecondary institution in Alberta. Students studying out-of-province may be considered for this award if their program of study is not available in Alberta. Selection is based on chosen program of study, financial need, and academic achievement. For additional information and application, visit website http://alis.alberta.ca.

Award: Scholarship for use in freshman, sophomore, junior, or senior years; not renewable. *Number:* 5–10.

Eligibility Requirements: Applicant must be Canadian citizen; enrolled or expecting to enroll full-time at a two-year or four-year or technical institution or university; female; resident of Alberta and studying in Alberta. Applicant must have 3.0 GPA or higher.

Application Requirements: Application form, essay, financial need analysis, resume, transcript. *Deadline:* September 30.

QUEEN ELIZABETH II GOLDEN JUBILEE CITIZENSHIP MEDAL

Award of CAN$5000, a medal, and letter of commendation from the Lieutenant Governor to recognize the eight most outstanding high school students among those who received a Premier's Citizenship award in recognition of the Queen's Golden Jubilee. Premier's Citizenship Award is for each high school in Alberta to nominate one student for superior public service. For additional information, see website http://alis.alberta.ca.

Award: Prize for use in freshman year; not renewable. *Number:* 8.

Eligibility Requirements: Applicant must be Canadian citizen; high school student; planning to enroll or expecting to enroll full-time at a four-year institution or university and resident of Alberta.

Application Requirements: Community service, proof of winning the Premier's Citizenship Award. *Deadline:* June 1.

RUTHERFORD SCHOLARS

Recipients are selected on the basis of results obtained on Diploma Examinations in English 30, or Francais 30, Social Studies 30 and three other subjects. Averages normally are in the 98.0 to 98.8 percent range. Only the first writing of the diploma exam will be considered. No application is required. Recipients are selected from all Alexander Rutherford Scholarship applications received before August 1. Amount of award is CAN$2500.

Award: Scholarship for use in freshman year; not renewable. *Number:* 10.

Eligibility Requirements: Applicant must be Canadian citizen; high school student; planning to enroll or expecting to enroll full-time at a four-year institution or university and resident of Alberta.

Application Requirements: Test scores, transcript. *Deadline:* August 1.

AMERICAN BAPTIST FINANCIAL AID PROGRAM

http://www.abc-usa.org/

AMERICAN BAPTIST FINANCIAL AID PROGRAM NATIVE AMERICAN GRANTS

Renewable award of $1000 to $2000 for Native Americans who are members of an American Baptist Church/USA congregation. Must be a U.S. citizen. Must be attending an accredited educational institution in the United States.

Award: Grant for use in freshman, sophomore, junior, senior, or graduate years; renewable. *Number:* 1–5. *Amount:* $1000–$2000.

Eligibility Requirements: Applicant must be Baptist; American Indian/Alaska Native and enrolled or expecting to enroll full-time at a four-year institution or university. Available to U.S. citizens.

Application Requirements: Application form, financial need analysis, recommendations or references. *Deadline:* May 31.

Contact: Lynne Eckman, Director of Financial Aid
Phone: 610-768-2067
Fax: 610-768-2470
E-mail: lynne.eckman@abc-usa.org

AMERICAN FOREIGN SERVICE ASSOCIATION

http://www.afsa.org/

AMERICAN FOREIGN SERVICE ASSOCIATION (AFSA) FINANCIAL AID AWARD PROGRAM

• *See page 503*

AMERICAN INDIAN EDUCATION FOUNDATION

http://www.aiefprograms.org/

AMERICAN INDIAN EDUCATION FOUNDATION SCHOLARSHIP

AIEF provides tuition and books for American Indian students. 200 undergraduate, 25 graduate scholarships.

Award: Scholarship for use in freshman, sophomore, junior, senior, or graduate years; not renewable. *Number:* 200. *Amount:* $2000.

Eligibility Requirements: Applicant must be of Indian heritage; American Indian/Alaska Native and enrolled or expecting to enroll full- or part-time at a two-year or four-year or technical institution or university. Available to U.S. citizens.

Application Requirements: Application form, certificate of Tribal enrollment, community service, essay, personal photograph, transcript. *Deadline:* April 4.

Contact: Murray Lee, Scholarship Specialist
American Indian Education Foundation
2401 Eglin Street
Rapid City, SD 57703
Phone: 605-342-9968
E-mail: mlee@nrc1.org

AMERICAN INDIAN GRADUATE CENTER

http://www.aigcs.org/

ACCENTURE AMERICAN INDIAN SCHOLARSHIP

Scholarships awarded to American Indian and Alaska Natives from U.S. federally recognized tribes. This program is for first year college freshmen (undergraduate) students. Must have a cumulative GPA of a 3.25 on a 4.0 scale and demonstrate financial need. Areas of study: engineering, computer science, operations management, finance, marketing and business.

Award: Scholarship for use in freshman year; renewable. *Number:* up to 10. *Amount:* $2000–$20,000.

Eligibility Requirements: Applicant must be American Indian/Alaska Native; high school student and planning to enroll or expecting to enroll full-time at a four-year institution or university. Available to U.S. citizens.

Application Requirements: Application form, application form may be submitted online (http://aigcs.org), community service, essay, financial need analysis, personal photograph, recommendations or references, transcript, tribal eligibility certificate. *Deadline:* April 27.

Contact: Marveline Vallo Gabbard, Program Associate
American Indian Graduate Center
3701 San Mateo Boulevard, NE, Suite 200
Albuquerque, NM 87110
Phone: 505-881-4584
Fax: 505-884-0427
E-mail: fellowships@aigcs.org

GATES MILLENNIUM SCHOLARS PROGRAM

Award enables American-Indian/Alaska native students to complete an undergraduate and graduate education. Must be entering a U.S. accredited college or university as a full-time student. Minimum 3.3 GPA required. Must demonstrate leadership abilities. Must meet federal Pell Grant eligibility criteria. Visit website at http://www.gmsp.org.

Award: Scholarship for use in freshman, sophomore, junior, senior, or graduate years; renewable. *Number:* 150. *Amount:* $500–$20,000.

Eligibility Requirements: Applicant must be American Indian/Alaska Native; enrolled or expecting to enroll full-time at a two-year or four-year institution or university and must have an interest in leadership. Available to U.S. citizens.

Application Requirements: Application form, financial need analysis, nomination packet, recommendations or references. *Deadline:* January 16.

Contact: Christa Moya, GMS Representative
American Indian Graduate Center
4520 Montgomery Boulevard, NE
Suite 1-B
Albuquerque, NM 87109
Phone: 866-884-7007
Fax: 505-884-8683
E-mail: christa@aigcs.org

WELLS FARGO SCHOLARSHIP AMERICAN INDIAN SCHOLARSHIP

Must be an enrolled member of a U.S. federally recognized American Indian or Alaska Native tribe. Be pursuing a degree in the banking, resort management, gaming operations, management and administration,

including accounting, finance, information technology and human resources. Must have a cumulative GPA of a 3.0 on a 4.0 scale and demonstrate financial need.

Award: Scholarship for use in junior, senior, or graduate years; renewable. *Number:* up to 10.

Eligibility Requirements: Applicant must be American Indian/Alaska Native and enrolled or expecting to enroll full-time at a four-year institution or university. Applicant must have 3.0 GPA or higher. Available to U.S. citizens.

Application Requirements: Application form, application form may be submitted online (http://aigcs.org), community service, essay, financial need analysis, personal photograph, transcript, tribal eligibility certificate. *Deadline:* May 4.

Contact: Marveline Vallo Gabbard, Program Associate
American Indian Graduate Center
3701 San Mateo Boulevard, NE, Suite 200
Albuquerque, NM 87110
Phone: 505-881-4584
Fax: 505-884-0427
E-mail: fellowships@aigcs.org

AMERICAN INSTITUTE FOR FOREIGN STUDY

http://www.aifsabroad.com/

AIFS DIVERSITYABROAD.COM SCHOLARSHIP

Scholarships are available for students studying abroad on any program offered by a DiversityAbroad.com member organization. African-American, Asian-American, Hispanic/Latino and Native-American students are strongly encouraged to apply. Visit http://www.aifsabroad.com/scholarships.asp for more information.

Award: Scholarship for use in freshman, sophomore, junior, or senior years; not renewable. *Number:* up to 20. *Amount:* up to $1000.

Eligibility Requirements: Applicant must be American Indian/Alaska Native, Asian/Pacific Islander, Black (non-Hispanic), Hispanic; enrolled or expecting to enroll full-time at a two-year or four-year institution or university and must have an interest in international exchange. Applicant must have 3.5 GPA or higher. Available to U.S. citizens.

Application Requirements: Application form, essay, personal photograph, recommendations or references, resume, transcript. *Fee:* $95. *Deadline:* varies.

Contact: David Mauro, Admissions Counselor
American Institute for Foreign Study
River Plaza, 9 West Broad Street
Stamford, CT 06902-3788
Phone: 800-727-2437 Ext. 5163
Fax: 203-399-5463
E-mail: dmauro@aifs.com

AIFS-HACU SCHOLARSHIPS

Scholarships to outstanding Hispanic students to study abroad with AIFS. Available to students attending HACU member schools. Students will receive scholarships of up to 50 percent of the full program fee. Students must meet all standard AIFS eligibility requirements. Deadlines: April 15 for fall, October 1 for spring, and March 15 for summer.

Award: Scholarship for use in freshman, sophomore, junior, or senior years; not renewable. *Amount:* $6000–$8000.

Eligibility Requirements: Applicant must be Hispanic; enrolled or expecting to enroll full-time at a two-year or four-year institution or university and must have an interest in international exchange. Applicant must have 3.0 GPA or higher. Available to U.S. and non-U.S. citizens.

Application Requirements: Application form, essay, personal photograph, recommendations or references, transcript. *Fee:* $95. *Deadline:* varies.

Contact: David Mauro, Admissions Counselor
American Institute for Foreign Study
River Plaza, 9 West Broad Street
Stamford, CT 06902-3788
Phone: 800-727-2437 Ext. 5163
Fax: 203-399-5463
E-mail: dmauro@aifs.com

AMERICAN LEGION DEPARTMENT OF NORTH DAKOTA

http://www.ndlegion.org/

HATTIE TEDROW MEMORIAL FUND SCHOLARSHIP
• *See page 597*

ARMENIAN RELIEF SOCIETY OF EASTERN USA INC.-REGIONAL OFFICE

http://www.arseastusa.org/

ARMENIAN RELIEF SOCIETY UNDERGRADUATE SCHOLARSHIP

Applicant must be an undergraduate student of Armenian heritage attending an accredited four-year college or university in the United States. Award for full-time students only. Must be U.S. or Canadian citizen. High school students may not apply.

Award: Scholarship for use in freshman, sophomore, junior, or senior years; not renewable. *Amount:* $13,000–$15,000.

Eligibility Requirements: Applicant must be of Armenian heritage and enrolled or expecting to enroll full-time at a four-year institution or university. Available to U.S. and Canadian citizens.

Application Requirements: Application form, financial need analysis, recommendations or references, self-addressed stamped envelope with application, transcript. *Deadline:* April 1.

ARMENIAN STUDENTS ASSOCIATION OF AMERICA INC.

http://www.asainc.org/

ARMENIAN STUDENTS ASSOCIATION OF AMERICA INC. SCHOLARSHIPS

One-time award for students of Armenian descent. Must be an undergraduate in sophomore, junior, or senior years, or graduate student, attending an accredited U.S. institution. Award based on need, merit, and character. Application fee: $15.

Award: Scholarship for use in sophomore, junior, senior, or graduate years; not renewable. *Number:* 30. *Amount:* $1000–$3500.

Eligibility Requirements: Applicant must be of Armenian heritage and enrolled or expecting to enroll full-time at a four-year institution or university. Available to U.S. citizens.

Application Requirements: Application form, essay, financial need analysis, proof of tuition costs and enrollment, recommendations or references, transcript. *Fee:* $15. *Deadline:* March 15.

Contact: Anne Gildhouse, Education Services Officer
Phone: 919-664-6000
Fax: 919-664-6520
E-mail: anne.gildhouse@nc.ngb.army.mil

ASIAN PROFESSIONAL EXTENSION INC.

http://www.apex-ny.org/

APEX SCHOLARSHIP

Scholarship to students based on academic excellence, personal essays, letters of recommendation, extracurricular activities/volunteer service, and financial need. Two winners will receive scholarships of $500 and $1000. Deadline varies.

Award: Scholarship for use in freshman, sophomore, junior, senior, or graduate years; not renewable. *Number:* 2. *Amount:* $500–$1000.

Eligibility Requirements: Applicant must be American Indian/Alaska Native or Asian/Pacific Islander and enrolled or expecting to enroll full- or part-time at a four-year institution or university. Available to U.S. citizens.

Application Requirements: Application form, entry in a contest, essay, financial need analysis, recommendations or references, transcript. *Deadline:* varies.

Contact: Trang Le-Chan, Deputy Director of Programs
Phone: 212-748-1225 Ext. 101
Fax: 212-748-1250
E-mail: trang.le-chan@apex-ny.org

ASIAN REPORTER

http://www.arfoundation.net/

ASIAN REPORTER SCHOLARSHIP

Scholarship available to graduating high school student or currently enrolled college student of Asian descent. Must be a resident of Washington or Oregon and attend school full-time in either state. Minimum 3.5 GPA required. Must demonstrate financial need, and involvement in community or school-related activities.

Award: Scholarship for use in freshman, sophomore, junior, or senior years; renewable. *Number:* 4. *Amount:* $500–$2000.

Eligibility Requirements: Applicant must be Asian/Pacific Islander; enrolled or expecting to enroll full-time at a four-year institution or university; resident of Oregon, Washington and studying in Oregon, Washington. Applicant must have 3.5 GPA or higher. Available to U.S. citizens.

Application Requirements: Application form, community service, essay, financial need analysis, personal photograph, recommendations or references, transcript. *Deadline:* February 28.

Contact: Jason Lim, Program Director
Phone: 503-283-0595
Fax: 503-283-4445
E-mail: arfoundation@asianreporter.com

ASSOCIATION ON AMERICAN INDIAN AFFAIRS, INC.

http://www.indian-affairs.org/

ADOLPH VAN PELT SPECIAL FUND FOR INDIAN SCHOLARSHIPS

Scholarship is open to undergraduate students pursuing a bachelor's degree in any curriculum. Must be an American Indian/Alaska Native. See website, http://www.indian-affairs.org, for specific details.

Award: Scholarship for use in freshman, sophomore, junior, or senior years; not renewable. *Number:* 5–15. *Amount:* up to $1500.

Eligibility Requirements: Applicant must be American Indian/Alaska Native and enrolled or expecting to enroll full-time at a two-year or four-year institution or university. Available to U.S. citizens.

Application Requirements: Application form, essay, Tribal enrollment. *Deadline:* June 3.

Contact: Lisa Wyzlic, Director of Scholarship Programs
Association on American Indian Affairs, Inc.
966 Hungerford Drive, Suite 12-B
Rockville, MD 20850
Phone: 240-314-7155
Fax: 240-314-7155
E-mail: lw.aaia@indian-affairs.org

ALLOGAN SLAGLE MEMORIAL SCHOLARSHIP

Scholarship available for American Indian undergraduate and graduate students who are members of tribes that are not federally recognized. Students must apply each year. See website, http://www.indian-affairs.org, for specific details.

Award: Scholarship for use in freshman, sophomore, junior, senior, or graduate years; not renewable. *Number:* 4–8. *Amount:* $1500.

Eligibility Requirements: Applicant must be American Indian/Alaska Native and enrolled or expecting to enroll full-time at a two-year or four-year institution or university. Available to U.S. citizens.

Application Requirements: Application form, essay, Tribal enrollment. *Deadline:* June 3.

Contact: Lisa Wyzlic, Director of Scholarship Programs
Association on American Indian Affairs, Inc.
966 Hungerford Drive, Suite 12-B
Rockville, MD 20850
Phone: 240-314-7155
Fax: 240-314-7159
E-mail: lw.aaia@indian-affairs.org

DAVID RISLING EMERGENCY AID SCHOLARSHIP

Scholarship is for acute, temporary, unexpected emergencies that would keep students from attending school. Tuition, books, computers and other expected expenses are NOT considered emergencies. Must be Native American/Alaska Native. See our website at http://www.indian-affairs.org for details AND call the Rockville office prior to submission to see if funding is available and if your situation qualifies as an emergency. We do not fund summer session or expenses incurred over the summer.

Award: Scholarship for use in freshman, sophomore, junior, senior, or graduate years; not renewable. *Amount:* $100–$400.

Eligibility Requirements: Applicant must be American Indian/Alaska Native and enrolled or expecting to enroll full-time at a two-year or four-year institution or university. Available to U.S. citizens.

Application Requirements: Application form, essay, financial need analysis, recommendations or references, transcript, Tribal enrollment, financial aid award letter, full time class schedule, explanation of need, proof of need. *Deadline:* continuous.

Contact: Lisa Wyzlic, Director of Scholarship Programs
Association on American Indian Affairs, Inc.
966 Hungerford Drive, Suite 12-B
Rockville, MD 20850
Phone: 240-314-7155
Fax: 240-314-7159
E-mail: lw.aaia@indian-affairs.org

DISPLACED HOMEMAKER SCHOLARSHIP

This undergraduate scholarship is for men and women 30+ who would not otherwise be able to complete their educational goals due to family responsibilities. Must be an American Indian/Alaska Native. See website, http://www.indian-affairs.org, for complete details.

Award: Scholarship for use in freshman, sophomore, junior, or senior years; not renewable. *Number:* 2–10. *Amount:* $1500.

Eligibility Requirements: Applicant must be American Indian/Alaska Native and enrolled or expecting to enroll full-time at a two-year or four-year institution or university. Available to U.S. citizens.

Application Requirements: Application form, essay, Tribal enrollment. *Deadline:* June 3.

Contact: Lisa Wyzlic, Director of Scholarship Programs
Association on American Indian Affairs, Inc.
966 Hungerford Drive, Suite 12-B
Rockville, MD 20850
Phone: 240-314-7155
Fax: 240-314-7159
E-mail: lw.aaia@indian-affairs.org

BLACKFEET NATION HIGHER EDUCATION PROGRAM

http://www.blackfeetnation.com/

BLACKFEET NATION HIGHER EDUCATION GRANT

Grants of $2800-$3000 will be awarded to students who are enrolled members of the Blackfeet Tribe and actively pursuing an undergraduate degree. Must submit a certification of Blackfeet blood.

Award: Grant for use in freshman, sophomore, junior, or senior years; not renewable. *Number:* 180. *Amount:* $2800–$3000.

Eligibility Requirements: Applicant must be American Indian/Alaska Native and enrolled or expecting to enroll full-time at a two-year or four-year or technical institution or university. Available to U.S. citizens.

Application Requirements: Application form, certification of Blackfeet blood, essay, financial need analysis, transcript. *Deadline:* March 1.

Contact: Conrad LaFromboise, Director
Blackfeet Nation Higher Education Program
PO Box 850
Browning, MT 59417
Phone: 406-338-7539
Fax: 406-338-7529
E-mail: bhep@3rivers.net

BUREAU OF INDIAN AFFAIRS OFFICE OF INDIAN EDUCATION PROGRAMS

http://www.bie.edu/

BUREAU OF INDIAN EDUCATION GRANT PROGRAM

Grants are provided to supplement financial assistance to eligible American Indian/Alaska Native students entering college seeking a baccalaureate degree. A student must be a member of, or at least one-quarter degree Indian blood descendent of a member of an American Indian tribe who are eligible for the special programs and services provided by the United States through the Bureau of Indian Affairs to Indians because of their status as Indians.

Award: Grant for use in freshman year; not renewable.

Eligibility Requirements: Applicant must be American Indian/Alaska Native; high school student and planning to enroll or expecting to enroll full-time at a two-year or four-year institution or university. Available to U.S. citizens.

Application Requirements: Application form, recommendations or references, test scores, transcript. *Deadline:* varies.

Contact: Paulina Bell, Office Automation Assistant
Phone: 202-208-6123
Fax: 202-208-3312

CABRILLO CIVIC CLUBS OF CALIFORNIA INC.

http://www.cabrillocivicclubs.org/

CABRILLO CIVIC CLUBS OF CALIFORNIA SCHOLARSHIP

Applicants must be graduating California high school seniors of Portuguese heritage and American citizenship, with an overall 3.5 GPA.

Award: Scholarship for use in freshman year; not renewable. *Number:* 75–100. *Amount:* $500.

Eligibility Requirements: Applicant must be of Portuguese heritage; high school student; planning to enroll or expecting to enroll full-time at a technical institution and resident of California. Applicant must have 3.5 GPA or higher. Available to U.S. citizens.

Application Requirements: Application form, driver's license, personal photograph, recommendations or references, resume, self-addressed stamped envelope with application, transcript. *Deadline:* March 15.

Contact: Breck Austin, Scholarship Chairperson
Cabrillo Civic Clubs of California Inc.
2174 South Coast Highway
Oceanside, CA 92054
E-mail: shampoobla@sbcglobal.net

CENTRAL COUNCIL, TLINGIT AND HAIDA INDIAN TRIBES OF ALASKA

http://www.hied.org/

ALUMNI STUDENT ASSISTANCE PROGRAM

The program provides annual scholarship awards to all enrolled Tlingit or Haida tribal members regardless of service area, community affiliation, origination, residence, tribal compact, or signatory status.

Award: Scholarship for use in freshman, sophomore, junior, senior, graduate, or postgraduate years; not renewable. *Number:* 1–100. *Amount:* $300–$500.

Eligibility Requirements: Applicant must be American Indian/Alaska Native and enrolled or expecting to enroll full-time at a two-year or four-year institution or university. Applicant must have 2.5 GPA or higher. Available to U.S. citizens.

Application Requirements: Application form, community service, essay, financial need analysis, recommendations or references, transcript, tribal enrollment certification form, letter of admission. *Deadline:* September 15.

Contact: Miss. Leslie Rae Isturis, Education Specialist
Central Council, Tlingit and Haida Indian Tribes of Alaska
3239 Hospital Drive
Juneau, AK 99801
Phone: 907-463-7375
Fax: 907-463-7173
E-mail: listuris@ccthita.org

COLLEGE STUDENT ASSISTANCE PROGRAM

A federally funded program which authorizes a program of assistance, by educational grants, to Indians seeking higher education. Awards available only to enrolled T&H members. Minimum 2.0 GPA required.

Award: Scholarship for use in freshman, sophomore, junior, senior, graduate, or postgraduate years; renewable. *Number:* 1–200. *Amount:* up to $2000.

Eligibility Requirements: Applicant must be American Indian/Alaska Native and enrolled or expecting to enroll full-time at a two-year or four-year institution or university. Available to U.S. citizens.

Application Requirements: Application form, letter of admission, test scores, transcript. *Deadline:* May 15.

Contact: Miss. Leslie Rae Isturis, Education Specialist
Central Council, Tlingit and Haida Indian Tribes of Alaska
3239 Hospital Drive
Juneau, AK 99801
Phone: 907-463-7375
Fax: 907-463-7173
E-mail: listuris@ccthita.org

CENTRAL SCHOLARSHIP

http://www.central-scholarship.org

LESSANS FAMILY SCHOLARSHIP

Scholarship available for Jewish students from Maryland who attend undergraduate colleges, universities or vocational schools full-time. Students can attend any accredited U.S. college or university. Awards are based on need and merit. The scholarship committee determines award amounts. For more information, visit website http://www.centralsb.org.

Award: Scholarship for use in freshman, sophomore, junior, or senior years; renewable. *Number:* 12–20. *Amount:* $1000–$2500.

Eligibility Requirements: Applicant must be Jewish; of Jewish heritage; enrolled or expecting to enroll full-time at a two-year or four-year institution or university and resident of Maryland. Applicant must have 3.0 GPA or higher. Available to U.S. citizens.

Application Requirements: Application form, essay, financial need analysis, interview, resume, transcript. *Deadline:* May 1.

Contact: Roberta Goldman, Program Director
Phone: 410-415-5558
Fax: 410-415-5501
E-mail: rgoldman@centralsb.org

CHEROKEE NATION OF OKLAHOMA

http://www.cherokee.org/

CHEROKEE NATION HIGHER EDUCATION SCHOLARSHIP

A supplementary program that provides financial assistance to Cherokee Nation Members only. It is a need-based program which provides assistance in seeking a bachelor's degree.

Award: Scholarship for use in freshman, sophomore, junior, or senior years; renewable. *Number:* up to 2800. *Amount:* $100–$1000.

Eligibility Requirements: Applicant must be American Indian/Alaska Native and enrolled or expecting to enroll full-time at a four-year institution or university. Applicant must have 2.5 GPA or higher. Available to U.S. citizens.

Application Requirements: Test scores, transcript, written request for application. *Deadline:* June 13.

Contact: Nita Wilson, Higher Education Specialist
Cherokee Nation of Oklahoma
PO Box 948
Tahlequah, OK 74465
Phone: 918-458-6195
E-mail: nwilson@cherokee.org

CHICANA/LATINA FOUNDATION

http://www.chicanalatina.org/

SCHOLARSHIPS FOR LATINA STUDENTS ENROLLED IN COLLEGES/UNIVERSITIES IN NORTHERN CALIFORNIA

Scholarships are awarded to female Latina students enrolled in two-year, four-year or graduate levels. Applicants must be from and/or attending colleges in the nine counties of Northern California listed on the application.

Award: Scholarship for use in freshman, sophomore, junior, or senior years; not renewable. *Number:* 25–30. *Amount:* $1500.

Eligibility Requirements: Applicant must be of Hispanic heritage; enrolled or expecting to enroll full-time at a two-year or four-year institution or university; female and resident of California. Available to U.S. citizens.

Application Requirements: Application form, essay, interview, leadership qualities, recommendations or references, transcript.

Contact: Claudia Leon, Program Coordinator
Chicana/Latina Foundation
1419 Burlingame Avenue, Suite N
Burlingame, CA 94010
Phone: 650-373-1085
Fax: 650-373-1090
E-mail: claudia@chicanalatina.org

CHINESE AMERICAN ASSOCIATION OF MINNESOTA

http://www.caam.org/

CHINESE AMERICAN ASSOCIATION OF MINNESOTA (CAAM) SCHOLARSHIPS

Merit and need scholarships of $1000 each are available for college and graduate students of Chinese descent and a resident of Minnesota. Applicants will be evaluated on their academic records, leadership qualities, and community service.

Award: Scholarship for use in freshman, sophomore, junior, senior, or graduate years; not renewable. *Amount:* $1000.

Eligibility Requirements: Applicant must be of Chinese heritage; Asian/Pacific Islander; enrolled or expecting to enroll full-time at a two-year or four-year or technical institution or university and resident of Minnesota. Available to U.S. citizens.

Application Requirements: Application form, financial need analysis, recommendations or references, SAT score. *Deadline:* November 15.

CIEE: COUNCIL ON INTERNATIONAL EDUCATIONAL EXCHANGE

http://www.ciee.org/

ROBERT B. BAILEY SCHOLARSHIP
• *See page 568*

THE CIRI FOUNDATION (TCF)

http://www.thecirifoundation.org/

CAREER UPGRADE GRANTS

Original enrollees of CIRI and their direct lineal descendants. Should have a high school diploma or GED; should maintain at least a 2.5 grade point average (2.0 GPA for TNC applicants); must be prepared to demonstrate the availability of employment upon completion of the training.

Award: Grant for use in freshman, sophomore, junior, senior, graduate, or postgraduate years; not renewable. *Amount:* up to $4500.

Eligibility Requirements: Applicant must be American Indian/Alaska Native and enrolled or expecting to enroll part-time at a two-year or four-year institution or university. Applicant must have 2.5 GPA or higher. Available to U.S. and non-U.S. citizens.

Application Requirements: Application form, essay, proof of eligibility, birth certificate or adoption decree, recommendations or references, transcript. *Deadline:* varies.

Contact: Susan Anderson, President and Chief Executive Officer
  Phone: 907-793-3575
  E-mail: tcf@thecirifoundation.org

CIRI FOUNDATION GENERAL SCHOLARSHIP

For original enrollees or CIRI and their direct lineal descendants. For full-time and part-time, degree-seeking students at an accredited or recognized institution. Provides funding for the academic year, deadline is June 1. Must have a cumulative GPA of 2.5 or above. Must apply online. Full-time students up to $5,000 per academic year, part-time students up to $4,500 per academic year. Mid-year awards are offered at December 1 deadline for eligible applicants beginnings winter/spring term. Provides funding to support one (1) semester or term. Must have a cumulative GPA of 2.5 or above. Must apply online. Full-time students up to $2,500 per term, part-time students up to $2,250 per term.

Award: Scholarship for use in freshman, sophomore, junior, senior, graduate, or postgraduate years; not renewable. *Amount:* up to $5000.

Eligibility Requirements: Applicant must be American Indian/Alaska Native and enrolled or expecting to enroll full- or part-time at a two-year or four-year institution or university. Applicant must have 2.5 GPA or higher. Available to U.S. and non-U.S. citizens.

Application Requirements: Application form, essay, proof of eligibility, birth certificate or adoption decree, recommendations or references, transcript. *Deadline:* June 1.

Contact: Susan Anderson, President and Chief Executive Officer
  Phone: 907-793-3575
  E-mail: tcf@thecirifoundation.org

HOWARD ROCK FOUNDATION SCHOLARSHIP PROGRAM

Scholarships are available to undergraduate and graduate students, who are Alaska Native original enrollees of an ANCSA regional and/or village corporation, a direct lineal descendant, or a member of a tribal or other organization. Preference is given to junior and senior standing students. Affiliated regional and/or village corporations must be current members of Alaska Village Initiatives. Must have a minimum GPA of 2.5 for undergraduates and 3.0 for graduates.

Award: Scholarship for use in freshman, sophomore, junior, senior, or graduate years; not renewable. *Number:* 3. *Amount:* $2500–$5000.

Eligibility Requirements: Applicant must be American Indian/Alaska Native and enrolled or expecting to enroll full-time at a four-year institution or university. Available to U.S. and Canadian citizens.

Application Requirements: Application form, essay, financial need analysis, personal photograph, proof of eligibility, statement of purpose, recommendations or references, transcript. *Deadline:* March 31.

Contact: Susan Anderson, President and Chief Executive Officer
  Phone: 907-793-3575
  E-mail: tcf@thecirifoundation.org

NINILCHIK NATIVE ASSOCIATION INC. SCHOLARSHIP AND GRANT PROGRAM

Original enrollees of NNAI and their direct lineal descendants. Must be accepted or enrolled full-time in an undergraduate or graduate degree program or technical skills training program. For tuition, required fees, books, on-campus-related room, and meal plan and for other direct school related costs. Should have a cumulative 2.5 grade point average or better. Deadline: June 1 and December 1 for scholarship, June 30 for grant Duration of award is one semester.

Award: Scholarship for use in freshman, sophomore, junior, senior, or graduate years; not renewable. *Amount:* $1000–$2000.

Eligibility Requirements: Applicant must be American Indian/Alaska Native and enrolled or expecting to enroll full-time at a two-year or four-year or technical institution or university. Applicant must have 2.5 GPA or higher. Available to U.S. citizens.

Application Requirements: Application form, essay, personal photograph, recommendations or references, test scores, transcript. *Deadline:* varies.

Contact: Susan Anderson, President and Chief Executive Officer
  Phone: 907-793-3575
  E-mail: tcf@thecirifoundation.org

SALAMATOF NATIVE ASSOCIATION INC. SCHOLARSHIP PROGRAM

Two annual scholarships or education grants are awarded to qualified applicants. Alaska Native original enrollees of SNAI and their lineal descendants and spouses may apply. Must be accepted or enrolled full-time in an undergraduate or graduate degree program or technical skills training program. For tuition, required fees, books, on-campus-related room, and meal plan and for other direct school related costs. Should have a cumulative 2.5 grade point average or better. Deadline is June 1.

Award: Scholarship for use in freshman, sophomore, junior, senior, or graduate years; not renewable.

Eligibility Requirements: Applicant must be American Indian/Alaska Native and enrolled or expecting to enroll full-time at a two-year or four-year or technical institution or university. Applicant must have 2.5 GPA or higher. Available to U.S. and non-U.S. citizens.

Application Requirements: Application form, essay, proof of eligibility, birth certificate or adoption degree, recommendations or references, transcript. *Deadline:* June 1.

Contact: Susan Anderson, President and Chief Executive Officer
  Phone: 907-793-3575
  E-mail: tcf@thecirifoundation.org

VOCATIONAL TRAINING GRANTS

Original enrollees of CIRI and their direct lineal descendants. Should have a high school diploma or GED; should maintain at least a 2.5 grade point average. For students enrolled in a technical skills training program at an accredited or recognized institution and earning a certificate/certification or a professional license.

Award: Grant for use in freshman, sophomore, junior, senior, graduate, or postgraduate years; not renewable. *Amount:* up to $4500.

Eligibility Requirements: Applicant must be American Indian/Alaska Native and enrolled or expecting to enroll full- or part-time at a two-year or four-year or technical institution or university. Applicant must have 2.5 GPA or higher. Available to U.S. and non-U.S. citizens.

Application Requirements: Application form, essay, proof of eligibility, birth certificate or adoption decree, recommendations or references, transcript. *Deadline:* varies.

Contact: Susan Anderson, President and Chief Executive Officer
  Phone: 907-793-3575
  E-mail: tcf@thecirifoundation.org

CITIZEN POTAWATOMI NATION

http://www.potawatomi.org/

CITIZEN POTAWATOMI NATION TRIBAL SCHOLARSHIP

Provides financial assistance for payment of tuition for members of the Citizen Potawatomi Nation. Minimum 2.0 GPA required. Deadlines are December 1 for spring, August 1 for fall, and June 1 for summer. Award amount varies from $750 to $1500.

Award: Scholarship for use in freshman, sophomore, junior, senior, or graduate years; renewable. *Amount:* $750–$1500.

Eligibility Requirements: Applicant must be American Indian/Alaska Native and enrolled or expecting to enroll full- or part-time at a two-year or four-year or technical institution or university. Available to U.S. citizens.

Application Requirements: Application form, financial need analysis, test scores, transcript. *Deadline:* varies.

Contact: Charles Clark, Director, Tribal Rolls
  Phone: 800-880-9880
  Fax: 405-275-0198
  E-mail: cclark@potawatomi.org

COLLEGEBOUND FOUNDATION

http://www.collegeboundfoundation.org/

LORENZO FELDER SCHOLARSHIP

You must be an African-American male, be a graduate from a Baltimore City public school, have a cumulative GPA of 3.0 or better, have demonstrated financial need, have verifiable community service or extracurricular activity; and write an essay of 500 words or less, describing how you have been helped by those around you and, in turn, how you have used your talents and skills to help others.

Award: Scholarship for use in freshman year; not renewable. *Number:* 1–3. *Amount:* $1000–$1500.

Eligibility Requirements: Applicant must be Black (non-Hispanic); high school student; planning to enroll or expecting to enroll full-time at a two-year or four-year institution; male and resident of Maryland. Applicant must have 3.0 GPA or higher. Available to U.S. citizens.

Application Requirements: Application form, application form may be submitted online (http://www.scholarships.mycbf.net/STARS), community service, essay, recommendations or references, resume, transcript. *Deadline:* March 1.

Contact: Deana Carr-Davis, Associate Program Director, Scholarship Programs
CollegeBound Foundation
300 Water Street, Suite 300
Baltimore, MD 21202
Phone: 410-783-2905 Ext. 207

COLLEGE WOMEN'S ASSOCIATION OF JAPAN
http://www.cwaj.org/

SCHOLARSHIP FOR THE VISUALLY IMPAIRED TO STUDY ABROAD
• *See page 568*

SCHOLARSHIP FOR THE VISUALLY IMPAIRED TO STUDY IN JAPAN
• *See page 568*

CONGRESSIONAL HISPANIC CAUCUS INSTITUTE
http://www.chci.org/

CONGRESSIONAL HISPANIC CAUCUS INSTITUTE SCHOLARSHIP AWARDS
Needs Based Scholarship award for Latino students who have a history of public service-oriented activities. Provides scholarships to students enrolled full time in school. Scholarship levels are: $1000 for community college, $2500 for four year academic institution, $5000 for graduate level institution. See website at http://www.chci.org for further information.

Award: Scholarship for use in freshman, sophomore, junior, senior, or graduate years; renewable. *Number:* 100–150. *Amount:* $1000–$5000.

Eligibility Requirements: Applicant must be Hispanic and enrolled or expecting to enroll full-time at a two-year or four-year institution or university. Available to U.S. citizens.

Application Requirements: Application form, application form may be submitted online (http://www.chci.org), community service, essay, financial need analysis, recommendations or references, resume, transcript. *Deadline:* April 16.

Contact: Anissa Perez, Scholarship Specialist
Congressional Hispanic Caucus Institute
911 2nd Street, NE
Washington, DC 20002
Phone: 202-543-1771
Fax: 202-546-2143
E-mail: aperez@chci.org

CONNECTICUT ASSOCIATION OF LATINOS IN HIGHER EDUCATION (CALAHE)
http://www.calahe.org/

CONNECTICUT ASSOCIATION OF LATINOS IN HIGHER EDUCATION SCHOLARSHIPS
Must demonstrate involvement with, and commitment to, activities that promote Latinos in pursuit of education. Must have a 3.0 GPA, be a U.S. citizen or permanent resident, and be a resident of Connecticut.

Award: Scholarship for use in freshman, sophomore, junior, or senior years; not renewable. *Number:* 17–17. *Amount:* $1000.

Eligibility Requirements: Applicant must be of Hispanic heritage; enrolled or expecting to enroll full-time at a two-year or four-year institution or university; resident of Connecticut and studying in Connecticut. Applicant must have 3.0 GPA or higher. Available to U.S. citizens.

Application Requirements: Application form, essay, financial need analysis, Student Aid Report (SAR), transcript. *Deadline:* April 15.

Contact: Dr. Wilson Luna, Gateway Community-Technical College
Connecticut Association of Latinos in Higher Education (CALAHE)
20 Church Street
New Haven, CT 06510
Phone: 203-285-2210
Fax: 203-285-2211
E-mail: wluna@gatewayct.edu

CROATIAN SCHOLARSHIP FUND
http://www.croatianscholarship.org/

CROATIAN SCHOLARSHIP FUND
Scholarship for students of Croatian heritage. Award based on academic achievement and financial need. Must demonstrate appropriate degree selection. Scholarships are awarded depending on availability of funds and number of applicants.

Award: Scholarship for use in freshman, sophomore, junior, or senior years; renewable. *Amount:* $1500–$1500.

Eligibility Requirements: Applicant must be of Croatian/Serbian heritage; age 18-25 and enrolled or expecting to enroll full-time at a four-year institution or university. Applicant must have 2.5 GPA or higher. Available to U.S. and non-U.S. citizens.

Application Requirements: Application form, application form may be submitted online, autobiography, financial need analysis, personal photograph, recommendations or references, test scores, transcript. *Deadline:* May 15.

Contact: Vesna Brekalo, Scholarship Liaison
Croatian Scholarship Fund
31 Mesa Vista Court
P O box 290
San Ramon, CA 94583
Phone: 925-556-6263
Fax: 925-556-6263
E-mail: vbrekalo@msn.com

DADE COMMUNITY FOUNDATION
http://www.jackituckfield.org/

RODNEY THAXTON/MARTIN E. SEGAL SCHOLARSHIP
Award available to a graduating high school senior who is African American and a Miami-Dade county area resident. Must demonstrate a commitment to social justice and have financial need. For additional information and application, visit website at http://www.dadecommunityfoundation.org.

Award: Scholarship for use in freshman year; not renewable. *Number:* 11. *Amount:* $1000.

Eligibility Requirements: Applicant must be Black (non-Hispanic); high school student; planning to enroll or expecting to enroll full-time at a four-year institution or university and resident of Florida. Available to U.S. citizens.

Application Requirements: Application form, resume, transcript. *Deadline:* April 17.

Contact: Ted Seijo, Scholarship Coordinator
Phone: 305-371-2711
E-mail: ted.seijo@dadecommunityfoundation.org

SIDNEY M. ARONOVITZ SCHOLARSHIP
Award available for minority students who are seniors at a Miami-Dade county public school or GED recipient from Miami-Dade area. Must be enrolled or planning to enroll in a college or university and plan to live and work in South Florida. Must have a minimum of 3.0 GPA. Additional information and application on website http://www.dadecommunityfoundation.org.

Award: Scholarship for use in freshman year; not renewable. *Number:* 1. *Amount:* $500.

Eligibility Requirements: Applicant must be American Indian/Alaska Native, Black (non-Hispanic), Hispanic; high school student; planning to enroll or expecting to enroll full-time at a four-year institution or university and resident of Florida. Applicant must have 3.0 GPA or higher. Available to U.S. citizens.

Application Requirements: Application form, financial need analysis, transcript. *Deadline:* March 20.

Contact: Ted Seijo, Scholarship Coordinator
Phone: 305-371-2711
E-mail: ted.seijo@dadecommunityfoundation.org

THE DALLAS FOUNDATION
http://www.dallasfoundation.org/

DR. DAN J. AND PATRICIA S. PICKARD SCHOLARSHIP
The Dr. Dan J. and Patricia S. Pickard Scholarship Fund was established at the Dallas Foundation in 2004 to assist African-American male students in Dallas County. Dr. Pickard was an optometrist and founder of the Pickard eye clinic. He believed that if you did something nice for someone and they do something nice for someone else, you can affect the lives of many people. The Scholarship Fund is his way of "passing it on."

Award: Scholarship for use in freshman year; renewable. *Number:* 1–2. *Amount:* $1000–$2000.

Eligibility Requirements: Applicant must be Black (non-Hispanic); high school student; planning to enroll or expecting to enroll full-time at a two-year or four-year institution; male; resident of Texas and studying in Texas. Applicant must have 2.5 GPA or higher. Available to U.S. citizens.

Application Requirements: Application form, community service, essay, financial need analysis, recommendations or references, transcript. *Deadline:* April 1.

Contact: Ms. Rachel Lasseter, Program Associate
The Dallas Foundation
900 Jackson Street, Suite 705
Dallas, TX 75202
Phone: 214-741-9898
Fax: 214-741-9848
E-mail: scholarships@dallasfoundation.org

DAUGHTERS OF PENELOPE FOUNDATION
http://daughtersofpenelope.org/

ALEXANDRA APOSTOLIDES SONENFELD SCHOLARSHIP
• *See page 517*

JOANNE V. HOLOGGITAS, PHD SCHOLARSHIP
• *See page 517*

KOTTIS FAMILY SCHOLARSHIP
• *See page 517*

MARY M. VERGES SCHOLARSHIP
• *See page 517*

PAST GRAND PRESIDENTS SCHOLARSHIP
• *See page 518*

DIAMANTE, INC.
http://www.diamanteinc.org/

LATINO DIAMANTE SCHOLARSHIP FUND
• *See page 553*

DIVERSITY CITY MEDIA
http://www.blacknews.com/

BLACKNEWS.COM SCHOLARSHIP ESSAY CONTEST
Scholarship of $500 awarded to an African-American student for the best essay submitted. Must be a U.S. citizen.

Award: Scholarship for use in freshman, sophomore, junior, or senior years; not renewable. *Number:* up to 4. *Amount:* $500.

Eligibility Requirements: Applicant must be Black (non-Hispanic); enrolled or expecting to enroll full- or part-time at a two-year or four-year or technical institution or university and must have an interest in writing. Available to U.S. citizens.

Application Requirements: Application form, entry in a contest, essay. *Deadline:* April 31.

Contact: Dante Lee, President and Chief Executive Officer
Phone: 866-910-6277
E-mail: scholarship@blacknews.com

EDGAR ALLEN POE LITERARY SOCIETY
http://www.ravens.org/

DISTINGUISHED RAVEN FAC MEMORIAL SCHOLARSHIP
Scholarship provides educational assistance to the descendants of those Lao/Hmong who served alongside the Ravens in defense of their country.

Award: Scholarship for use in freshman, sophomore, junior, or senior years; not renewable. *Number:* 5–10. *Amount:* $500–$3000.

Eligibility Requirements: Applicant must be of Lao/Hmong heritage; Asian/Pacific Islander and enrolled or expecting to enroll full-time at a two-year or four-year or technical institution or university. Available to U.S. and non-U.S. citizens.

Application Requirements: Application form, essay, recommendations or references, transcript. *Deadline:* March 1.

Contact: Col. Jerry Milam, Scholarship Administrator
Edgar Allen Poe Literary Society
4320 Saddle Ridge Trail
Flower Mound, TX 75028
Phone: 972-691-2569
E-mail: spikemilam@verizon.net

EDMONTON COMMUNITY FOUNDATION
http://www.DollarsForLearners.com/

YOUTH FORMERLY IN CARE BURSARY
Scholarship funds awarded to disadvantaged young people to support their postsecondary education and training. Supports students who are residents of Alberta and who have spent a minimum of two years in the care and/or guardianship of Alberta Children's Services. Students considering part-time studies may be considered for an award.

Award: Grant for use in freshman, sophomore, junior, or senior years; renewable. *Number:* 1. *Amount:* $1000.

Eligibility Requirements: Applicant must be Canadian citizen; enrolled or expecting to enroll full- or part-time at a four-year institution or university and resident of Alberta.

Application Requirements: Application form, financial need analysis, personal letter, recommendations or references, transcript. *Deadline:* May 15.

Contact: Craig Stumpf-Allen, Associate Director, Scholarships
Phone: 780-426-0015
Fax: 780-425-0121
E-mail: info@dollarsforlearners.com

EDSOUTH
http://www.edsouth.org/

ECAMPUSTOURS SCHOLARSHIP DRAWING
Two $1000 awards are available.

Award: Scholarship for use in freshman, sophomore, junior, senior, or graduate years; not renewable. *Number:* 2. *Amount:* $1000.

Eligibility Requirements: Applicant must be Hispanic and enrolled or expecting to enroll full- or part-time at a two-year or four-year or technical institution or university. Available to U.S. citizens.

Application Requirements: Entry in a contest, online registration form. *Deadline:* March 31.

EPSILON SIGMA ALPHA

http://www.epsilonsigmaalpha.org/Homepage

EPSILON SIGMA ALPHA FOUNDATION SCHOLARSHIPS

Awards for various fields of study. Required GPA vary with scholarship. Applications must be sent to the Epsilon Sigma Alpha designated state counselor. See website at http://www.esaintl.com/esaf for further information, application forms, and a list of state counselors.

Award: Scholarship for use in freshman, sophomore, junior, senior, graduate, or postgraduate years; not renewable. *Number:* 125–175. *Amount:* $350–$7500.

Eligibility Requirements: Applicant must be American Indian/Alaska Native, Asian/Pacific Islander, Black (non-Hispanic), Hispanic and enrolled or expecting to enroll full- or part-time at a two-year or four-year or technical institution or university. Applicant must have 3.0 GPA or higher. Available to U.S. and non-U.S. citizens.

Application Requirements: Application form, essay, recommendations or references, test scores, transcript. *Fee:* $5. *Deadline:* February 1.

Contact: Kathy Loyd, Scholarship Chairman
Epsilon Sigma Alpha
1222 NW 651
Blairstown, MO 64726
Phone: 660-678-2611
Fax: 660-747-0807
E-mail: kloyd@knoxy.net

FIRST CATHOLIC SLOVAK LADIES ASSOCIATION

http://www.fcsla.org/

FIRST CATHOLIC SLOVAK LADIES ASSOCIATION FRATERNAL SCHOLARSHIP AWARD

Must be FCSLA member in good standing for at least three years. Must attend accredited college in the United States or Canada in undergraduate or graduate degree program. Must submit certified copy of college acceptance. Award value is $1250 for undergraduate and $1750 for graduate students.

Award: Scholarship for use in freshman, sophomore, junior, senior, or graduate years; not renewable. *Number:* 133. *Amount:* $1250–$1750.

Eligibility Requirements: Applicant must be of Slavic/Czech heritage and enrolled or expecting to enroll full-time at a two-year or four-year institution or university. Available to U.S. and Canadian citizens.

Application Requirements: Application form, driver's license, essay, personal photograph, recommendations or references, test scores, transcript. *Deadline:* March 1.

Contact: Dorothy Szumski, Director of Fraternal Scholarships
First Catholic Slovak Ladies Association
24950 Chagrin Boulevard
Beachwood, OH 44122
Phone: 216-464-8015 Ext. 134
Fax: 216-464-9260
E-mail: info@fcsla.com

FLORIDA STATE DEPARTMENT OF EDUCATION

http://www.floridastudentfinancialaid.org/

JOSE MARTI SCHOLARSHIP CHALLENGE GRANT FUND

Award available to Hispanic-American students who were born in, or whose parent was born in a Hispanic country. Must be a Florida resident, be enrolled full-time in Florida at an eligible school, and have a GPA of 3.0 or above. Must be U.S. citizen or eligible non-citizen. FAFSA must be processed by May 15. For more details, visit the website at http://www.FloridaStudentFinancialAid.org/SSFAD/home/uamain.htm.

Award: Scholarship for use in freshman, sophomore, junior, or senior years; renewable. *Amount:* $2000.

Eligibility Requirements: Applicant must be of Hispanic heritage; high school student; planning to enroll or expecting to enroll full-time at a two-year or four-year institution or university; resident of Florida and studying in Florida. Applicant must have 3.0 GPA or higher. Available to U.S. citizens.

Application Requirements: Application form, financial need analysis. *Deadline:* April 1.

GENERAL BOARD OF HIGHER EDUCATION AND MINISTRY

http://www.gbhem.org

BISHOP JOSEPH B. BETHEA SCHOLARSHIP

Undergraduate scholarship for full-time African American students. Must be a member of the Southeastern Jurisdiction Black Methodists for Church Renewal (SEJBMCR) and an active, full member of a United Methodist Church for at least one year prior to applying. Must be U.S. citizen or permanent resident, maintain a GPA of 2.8, and demonstrate financial need.

Award: Scholarship for use in freshman, sophomore, junior, or senior years; not renewable.

Eligibility Requirements: Applicant must be Methodist; Black (non-Hispanic) and enrolled or expecting to enroll full-time at a four-year institution or university. Available to U.S. citizens.

Application Requirements: Application form, application form may be submitted online (http://www.gbhem.org/loans-scholarships), essay, recommendations or references, transcript. *Deadline:* March 1.

Contact: Ms. Mary Robinson, Scholarships Coordinator
General Board of Higher Education and Ministry
PO Box 340007
Nashville, TN 37203-0007
Phone: 615-340-7344
Fax: 615-340-7529
E-mail: umscholar@gbhem.org

ETHNIC MINORITY SCHOLARSHIP

Undergraduate award for U.S. citizens who are Native American, Asian, African American, Hispanic or Pacific Islanders. Must maintain a GPA of 2.5 or higher, and be a full and active member of a United Methodist Church for at least one year.

Award: Scholarship for use in freshman, sophomore, junior, or senior years; not renewable. *Number:* 500–1000.

Eligibility Requirements: Applicant must be Methodist; American Indian/Alaska Native, Asian/Pacific Islander, Black (non-Hispanic), Hispanic and enrolled or expecting to enroll full-time at a two-year or four-year institution or university. Applicant must have 2.5 GPA or higher. Available to U.S. and non-Canadian citizens.

Application Requirements: Application form, application form may be submitted online (http://www.gbhem.org), essay, recommendations or references, transcript. *Deadline:* March 1.

Contact: Ms. Mary Robinson, Scholarships Coordinator
General Board of Higher Education and Ministry
PO Box 340007
Nashville, TN 37203-0007
Phone: 615-340-7344
Fax: 615-340-7529
E-mail: umscholar@gbhem.org

HANA SCHOLARSHIP

Award for a full-time college junior, senior, or graduate student of Hispanic, Asian, Native American/Alaskan Indian, or Pacific Islander parentage. Must be an active, full member of the United Methodist Church for at least three years prior to application. Undergraduates must have GPA of 2.85, graduate students must have 3.0 GPA. Must demonstrate leadership ability within UMC.

Award: Scholarship for use in junior, senior, graduate, or postgraduate years; not renewable. *Amount:* $1000–$2500.

Eligibility Requirements: Applicant must be Methodist; American Indian/Alaska Native, Asian/Pacific Islander, or Hispanic; enrolled or expecting to enroll full-time at a four-year institution or university and must have an interest in leadership. Applicant must have 3.0 GPA or higher. Available to U.S. and non-Canadian citizens.

Application Requirements: Application form, application form may be submitted online (http://www.gbhem.org/loans-scholarships), leadership development plan, recommendations or references, transcript. *Deadline:* March 1.

Contact: Ms. Mary Robinson, Scholarships Coordinator
General Board of Higher Education and Ministry
PO Box 340007
Nashville, TN 37203-0007
Phone: 615-340-7344
Fax: 615-340-7529
E-mail: umscholar@gbhem.org

GEORGIA STUDENT FINANCE COMMISSION

http://www.GAcollege411.org/

GEORGIA TUITION EQUALIZATION GRANT (GTEG)
• *See page 570*

HBCUCONNECT.COM

http://www.hbcuconnect.com/

HBCUCONNECT.COM MINORITY SCHOLARSHIP PROGRAM

Scholarship to minorities attending a historically Black college or university. Must attend or be enrolled into an HBCU. Selection based on quality of content in the online registration, and financial need.

Award: Scholarship for use in freshman, sophomore, junior, senior, graduate, or postgraduate years; not renewable. *Number:* 1–12. *Amount:* $1000–$2500.

Eligibility Requirements: Applicant must be American Indian/Alaska Native, Asian/Pacific Islander, Black (non-Hispanic), Hispanic and enrolled or expecting to enroll full- or part-time at a two-year or four-year institution or university. Available to U.S. citizens.

Application Requirements: Application form, application form may be submitted online (http://www.hbcuconnect.com/scholarships.shtml), essay, resume. *Deadline:* continuous.

Contact: Mr. William Moss, CEO
Phone: 614-416-5515
Fax: 614-864-8901
E-mail: wrmoss@hbcuconnect.com

HEBREW IMMIGRANT AID SOCIETY

http://www.hias.org/

HEBREW IMMIGRANT AID SOCIETY SCHOLARSHIP AWARDS COMPETITION
• *See page 521*

HELLENIC TIMES SCHOLARSHIP FUND

http://www.htsf.org/

HELLENIC TIMES SCHOLARSHIP FUND

One-time award to students of Greek/Hellenic descent. Must be between the ages of 17 and 25. For use in any year of undergraduate education. Employees of the Hellenic Times and their families are not eligible.

Award: Scholarship for use in freshman, sophomore, junior, or senior years; not renewable. *Number:* 30–40. *Amount:* $500–$10,000.

Eligibility Requirements: Applicant must be of Greek heritage; age 17-25 and enrolled or expecting to enroll full-time at a two-year or four-year or technical institution or university. Available to U.S. and non-U.S. citizens.

Application Requirements: Application form, financial need analysis, recommendations or references, resume, transcript. *Deadline:* February 19.

Contact: Nick Katsoris, President of Scholarship Fund
Hellenic Times Scholarship Fund
823 11th Avenue, Fifth Floor
New York, NY 10019-3535
Phone: 212-986-6881
Fax: 212-977-3662
E-mail: htsfund@aol.com

HELLENIC UNIVERSITY CLUB OF PHILADELPHIA

http://www.hucphila.org/

CHRISTOPHER DEMETRIS SCHOLARSHIP

$1200 scholarship for a full-time student enrolled in a degree program at an accredited four-year college or university. High school seniors accepted for enrollment in such a degree program may also apply. Must be a U.S. citizen of Greek descent and a resident of particular counties in NJ or PA.

Award: Scholarship for use in freshman, sophomore, junior, or senior years; not renewable. *Amount:* up to $1200.

Eligibility Requirements: Applicant must be of Greek heritage; enrolled or expecting to enroll full-time at a four-year institution or university and resident of New Jersey, Pennsylvania. Available to U.S. citizens.

Application Requirements: Application form, financial need analysis, transcript. *Deadline:* April 21.

Contact: Anna Hadgis, Scholarship Chairman
Phone: 610-613-4310
E-mail: hucphila@yahoo.com

DR. NICHOLAS PADIS MEMORIAL GRADUATE SCHOLARSHIP

$5000 scholarship for a qualifying senior undergraduate or graduate student pursuing a full-time degree at an accredited university or professional school. Must be a U.S. citizen of Greek descent and a resident of particular counties in NJ or PA. Academic excellence is the primary consideration for this scholarship.

Award: Scholarship for use in senior or graduate years; not renewable. *Number:* up to 1. *Amount:* up to $5000.

Eligibility Requirements: Applicant must be of Greek heritage; enrolled or expecting to enroll full-time at a four-year institution or university and resident of New Jersey, Pennsylvania. Available to U.S. citizens.

Application Requirements: Application form, financial need analysis, transcript. *Deadline:* April 21.

Contact: Anna Hadgis, Scholarship Chairman
Phone: 610-613-4310
E-mail: hucphila@yahoo.com

DORIZAS MEMORIAL SCHOLARSHIP

$3000 award for a full-time student enrolled in a degree program at an accredited four-year college or university. Must be a U.S. citizen of Greek descent and a resident of particular counties in NJ or PA.

Award: Scholarship for use in freshman, sophomore, junior, or senior years; not renewable. *Amount:* up to $3000.

Eligibility Requirements: Applicant must be of Greek heritage; enrolled or expecting to enroll full-time at a four-year institution or university and resident of New Jersey, Pennsylvania. Available to U.S. citizens.

Application Requirements: Application form, financial need analysis, transcript. *Deadline:* April 21.

Contact: Anna Hadgis, Scholarship Chairman
Phone: 610-613-4310
E-mail: hucphila@yahoo.com

FOUNDERS SCHOLARSHIP

$3000 award for a full-time student enrolled in a degree program at an accredited four-year college or university. Must be a U.S. citizen of Greek descent and a resident of particular counties in NJ or PA.

Award: Scholarship for use in freshman, sophomore, junior, or senior years; not renewable. *Amount:* up to $3000.

Eligibility Requirements: Applicant must be of Greek heritage; enrolled or expecting to enroll full-time at a four-year institution or university and resident of New Jersey, Pennsylvania. Available to U.S. citizens.

Application Requirements: Application form, financial need analysis, transcript. *Deadline:* April 21.

Contact: Anna Hadgis, Scholarship Chairman
Phone: 610-613-4310
E-mail: hucphila@yahoo.com

JAMES COSMOS MEMORIAL SCHOLARSHIP

Scholarship of up to $1000 for students enrolled full-time in a degree program at an accredited four-year college or university. High school seniors accepted for enrollment in such a degree program may also apply. Must be a U.S. citizen of Greek descent and a resident of particular counties in NJ or PA.

Award: Scholarship for use in freshman, sophomore, junior, or senior years; not renewable. *Amount:* $1000.

Eligibility Requirements: Applicant must be of Greek heritage; enrolled or expecting to enroll full-time at a four-year institution or university and resident of New Jersey, Pennsylvania. Available to U.S. citizens.

Application Requirements: Application form, financial need analysis. *Deadline:* April 20.

Contact: Anna Hadgis, Scholarship Chairman
Phone: 610-613-4310
E-mail: hucphila@yahoo.com

PAIDEIA SCHOLARSHIP
• *See page 521*

HENRY SACHS FOUNDATION
http://www.sachsfoundation.org/

SACHS FOUNDATION SCHOLARSHIPS

Award to undergraduate students based on performance, financial need, and applicant's area of study and life goals. Must be African-American and a resident of Colorado. Minimum 3.5 GPA required.

Award: Scholarship for use in freshman year; renewable. *Number:* up to 50. *Amount:* up to $4000.

Eligibility Requirements: Applicant must be Black (non-Hispanic); high school student; planning to enroll or expecting to enroll full-time at a four-year institution or university and resident of Colorado. Applicant must have 3.5 GPA or higher. Available to U.S. citizens.

Application Requirements: Application form, financial need analysis, personal photograph. *Deadline:* March 1.

Contact: Lisa Harris, Secretary and Treasurer
Phone: 719-633-2353
E-mail: Lisa@sachsfoundation.org

HISPANIC ANNUAL SALUTE
http://www.hispanicannualsalute.org/

HISPANIC ANNUAL SALUTE SCHOLARSHIP
• *See page 556*

HISPANIC COLLEGE FUND
http://www.hispanicfund.org/

HISPANIC COLLEGE FUND SCHOLARSHIP PROGRAM

Scholarships to U.S. citizens or permanent residents who are Hispanic or of Hispanic descent. Must be studying at an accredited university in the United States or Puerto Rico and enrolled full-time as an undergraduate for the upcoming academic year. Must maintain GPA of 3.0.

Award: Scholarship for use in freshman, sophomore, junior, or senior years; renewable. *Number:* 500–600. *Amount:* $500–$10,000.

Eligibility Requirements: Applicant must be Hispanic and enrolled or expecting to enroll full-time at a two-year or four-year institution or university. Applicant must have 3.0 GPA or higher. Available to U.S. citizens.

Application Requirements: Application form, copy of tax return, Student Aid Report (SAR), proof of citizenship status, essay, financial need analysis, recommendations or references, resume, transcript. *Deadline:* March 15.

Contact: Tatiana Santiago, Scholarship Program Assistant
Phone: 202-296-5400 Ext. 117
E-mail: tsantiago@hispanicfund.org

HISPANIC METROPOLITAN CHAMBER SCHOLARSHIPS
http://www.hmccoregon.com/

HISPANIC METROPOLITAN CHAMBER SCHOLARSHIPS

Scholarships to encourage Hispanics to pursue higher education. Applicant must have a minimum 3.00 GPA. For full-time study only. The award is available only to Hispanic students from Oregon and Southwest Washington.

Award: Scholarship for use in freshman, sophomore, junior, senior, graduate, or postgraduate years; renewable. *Number:* up to 40. *Amount:* $1000–$5000.

Eligibility Requirements: Applicant must be of Hispanic heritage; enrolled or expecting to enroll full- or part-time at a four-year institution or university and resident of Oregon, Washington. Applicant must have 3.0 GPA or higher. Available to U.S. citizens.

Application Requirements: Application form, community service, essay, extracurricular activities, recommendations or references, transcript. *Deadline:* January 29.

Contact: Nicole Ferr, Scholarship Coordinator
E-mail: scholarship@hmccoregon.com

HISPANIC SCHOLARSHIP FUND
http://www.hsf.net/

GATES MILLENNIUM SCHOLARS PROGRAM

Award enables Hispanic-American students to complete an undergraduate or graduate education. Applicant may be pursuing undergraduate studies in any discipline; graduate studies limited to fields of mathematics, science, engineering, education, public health, or library science. Must be entering a U.S. accredited college or university as a full-time degree-seeking student. Minimum 3.3 GPA required. Must demonstrate leadership abilities and significant financial need. Information and application can be found at http://www.gmsp.org.

Award: Scholarship for use in freshman, sophomore, junior, senior, or graduate years; renewable. *Number:* 350.

Eligibility Requirements: Applicant must be Hispanic and enrolled or expecting to enroll full-time at a four-year institution or university. Applicant must have 3.5 GPA or higher. Available to U.S. and non-Canadian citizens.

Application Requirements: Application form, financial need analysis. *Deadline:* January 10.

HSF/GENERAL COLLEGE SCHOLARSHIP PROGRAM

Merit-based award for U.S. citizens or permanent residents of Hispanic heritage with plans to enroll full time in a degree-seeking program at a U.S. accredited institution in the upcoming academic year. Applicants must have a minimum 3.0 GPA. Must complete FAFSA. Must include official transcript and SAR. For additional information please go to http://www.hsf.net/innercontent.aspx?id=34.

Award: Scholarship for use in freshman, sophomore, junior, or senior years; not renewable. *Number:* 2900–3500. *Amount:* $1000–$10,000.

Eligibility Requirements: Applicant must be of Hispanic, Latin American/Caribbean, Mexican, Spanish heritage and enrolled or expecting to enroll full-time at a two-year or four-year institution or university. Applicant must have 3.0 GPA or higher. Available to U.S. citizens.

Application Requirements: Application form, essay, financial need analysis, recommendations or references, Student Aid Report (SAR), transcript. *Deadline:* varies.

HOPI TRIBE
http://www.hopi-nsn.gov/

BIA HIGHER EDUCATION GRANT

Grant provides financial support for eligible Hopi individuals pursuing postsecondary education. Minimum 2.5 CGPA required. Deadlines are July 1 for fall, and December 1 for spring.

Award: Grant for use in freshman, sophomore, junior, or senior years; not renewable. *Number:* 1–150. *Amount:* $50–$2500.

Eligibility Requirements: Applicant must be American Indian/Alaska Native and enrolled or expecting to enroll full-time at a two-year or four-year institution or university. Applicant must have 2.5 GPA or higher. Available to U.S. citizens.

Application Requirements: Application form, financial need analysis, test scores, transcript, verification of Hopi Indian blood. *Deadline:* varies.

Contact: Theresa Lomakema, Financial Aid Processor/Monitor
Phone: 928-734-3533
E-mail: info@hopi.nsn.us

HOPI EDUCATION AWARD

Grant provides financial support for eligible Hopi individuals pursuing postsecondary education. Minimum 2.5 CGPA required. Deadlines are April 1 for summer, July 1 for fall, and December 1 for spring.

Award: Scholarship for use in freshman, sophomore, junior, or senior years; not renewable. *Number:* 1–400. *Amount:* $50–$2500.

Eligibility Requirements: Applicant must be American Indian/Alaska Native and enrolled or expecting to enroll full- or part-time at a two-year or four-year institution or university. Applicant must have 2.5 GPA or higher. Available to U.S. citizens.

Application Requirements: Application form, financial need analysis, test scores, transcript, verification of Hopi Indian blood. *Deadline:* varies.

Contact: Theresa Lomakema, Financial Aid Processor/Monitor
Phone: 928-734-3533
E-mail: info@hopi.nsn.us

TRIBAL PRIORITY AWARD

Scholarship provides financial support for eligible Hopi individuals pursuing postsecondary education. Minimum 3.0 GPA required.

Award: Scholarship for use in junior or senior years; not renewable. *Number:* 1–5. *Amount:* $2500–$15,000.

Eligibility Requirements: Applicant must be American Indian/Alaska Native and enrolled or expecting to enroll full-time at a two-year or four-year institution or university. Applicant must have 3.0 GPA or higher. Available to U.S. citizens.

Application Requirements: Application form, financial need analysis, interview, recommendations or references, test scores, transcript, verification of Hopi Indian blood. *Deadline:* July 1.

Contact: Theresa Lomakema, Financial Aid Processor/Monitor
Phone: 928-734-3533
E-mail: info@hopi.nsn.us

HOUSTON COMMUNITY SERVICES

AZTECA SCHOLARSHIP

Scholarships are awarded annually to a male and a female high school senior planning to attend a university or a college as first-time, first-year students. Must be Texas resident.

Award: Scholarship for use in freshman year; not renewable. *Number:* 2. *Amount:* $500.

Eligibility Requirements: Applicant must be of Mexican heritage; Hispanic; high school student; planning to enroll or expecting to enroll full-time at a two-year or four-year institution or university and resident of Texas. Available to U.S. citizens.

Application Requirements: Application form, essay, income tax report, letter of acceptance, personal photograph, transcript. *Deadline:* March 28.

Contact: Edward Castillo, Coordinator
Phone: 713-926-8771
E-mail: hcsaztlan@sbcglobal.net

INDIAN AMERICAN CULTURAL ASSOCIATION

http://www.iasf.org/

INDIAN AMERICAN SCHOLARSHIP FUND

Scholarships for descendents of families who are from modern-day India and are graduating from public or private high schools in Georgia. They must be enrolled in four-year colleges or universities. There are both academic and need-based awards available through this program.

Award: Scholarship for use in freshman year; renewable. *Number:* 3. *Amount:* $500–$5000.

Eligibility Requirements: Applicant must be of Indian heritage; Asian/Pacific Islander; high school student; planning to enroll or expecting to enroll full-time at a four-year institution or university and resident of Georgia. Applicant must have 3.0 GPA or higher. Available to U.S. citizens.

Application Requirements: Application form, essay, financial need analysis, IRS 1040 form, resume, test scores, transcript. *Deadline:* varies.

Contact: Rajesh Kurup, Scholarship Coordinator
E-mail: rajnina@mindspring.com

INTERNATIONAL ORDER OF THE KING'S DAUGHTERS AND SONS

http://www.iokds.org/

INTERNATIONAL ORDER OF THE KING'S DAUGHTERS AND SONS NORTH AMERICAN INDIAN SCHOLARSHIP

Scholarships available for Native American students. Proof of reservation registration, college acceptance letter, and financial aid office address required. Merit-based award. Send self-addressed stamped envelope. Must maintain minimum 2.5 GPA.

Award: Scholarship for use in freshman, sophomore, junior, or senior years; renewable. *Number:* 45–60. *Amount:* $500–$650.

Eligibility Requirements: Applicant must be American Indian/Alaska Native and enrolled or expecting to enroll full-time at a two-year or four-year or technical institution or university. Applicant must have 2.5 GPA or higher. Available to U.S. and Canadian citizens.

Application Requirements: Application form, essay, financial need analysis, recommendations or references, self-addressed stamped envelope with application, transcript, written documentation of reservation registration. *Deadline:* varies.

INTERNATIONAL UNION OF BRICKLAYERS AND ALLIED CRAFTSMEN

http://www.bacweb.org/

CANADIAN BATES SCHOLARSHIP PROGRAM
• *See page 522*

ITALIAN-AMERICAN CHAMBER OF COMMERCE OF CHICAGO

http://www.iacc-chicago.com/

ITALIAN-AMERICAN CHAMBER OF COMMERCE OF CHICAGO SCHOLARSHIP

One-time awards for Illinois residents of Italian descent. Available to high school seniors and college students for use at a four-year institution. Applicants must have a 3.5 GPA. Must reside in Cook, Du Page, Kane, Lake, McHenry, or Will counties of Illinois. Must submit a letter including a biographical account of themselves and two letters of recommendation, one from a teacher and one from their counselor.

Award: Scholarship for use in freshman, sophomore, junior, or senior years; not renewable. *Number:* 1. *Amount:* up to $1000.

Eligibility Requirements: Applicant must be of Italian heritage; enrolled or expecting to enroll full-time at a four-year institution and resident of Illinois. Applicant must have 2.5 GPA or higher. Available to U.S. and non-U.S. citizens.

Application Requirements: Application form, essay, personal photograph, recommendations or references, self-addressed stamped envelope with application, transcript. *Deadline:* May 31.

Contact: Frank Pugno, Scholarship Chairman
Italian-American Chamber of Commerce of Chicago
30 South Michigan Avenue, Suite 504
Chicago, IL 60603
Phone: 312-553-9137 Ext. 13
Fax: 312-553-9142
E-mail: info.chicago@italchambers.net

JACKIE ROBINSON FOUNDATION

http://www.jackierobinson.org/

JACKIE ROBINSON SCHOLARSHIP

• See page 558

JA LIVING LEGACY

http://www.jalivinglegacy.org/

TERI AND ART IWASAKI SCHOLARSHIP

The scholarship is to support the rising costs of education. Applicant must be a descendent of a Japanese-American World War II veteran that served in the United States military units. Descendents include grandchild, great grandchild, grand niece/nephew as well as extended family.

Award: Scholarship for use in freshman year; not renewable. *Number:* 1. *Amount:* $2000.

Eligibility Requirements: Applicant must be of Japanese heritage; Asian/Pacific Islander; high school student and planning to enroll or expecting to enroll at an institution or university. Available to U.S. citizens.

Application Requirements: *Deadline:* continuous.

JEWISH VOCATIONAL SERVICE LOS ANGELES

http://www.jvsla.org/

JEWISH VOCATIONAL SERVICE SCHOLARSHIP FUND

Need-based scholarships to support Jewish students from Los Angeles County in their pursuit of college, graduate, and vocational education. Applicants must be Jewish, permanent residents of Los Angeles, maintain a minimum 2.7 GPA, and demonstrate verifiable financial need.

Award: Scholarship for use in freshman, sophomore, junior, senior, or graduate years; not renewable. *Number:* 125–200. *Amount:* $1000–$5000.

Eligibility Requirements: Applicant must be Jewish; of Jewish heritage; enrolled or expecting to enroll full-time at a two-year or four-year or technical institution or university and resident of California. Applicant must have 3.0 GPA or higher. Available to U.S. citizens.

Application Requirements: Application form, essay, FAFSA, Student Aid Report (SAR), financial need analysis, interview, recommendations or references, resume, transcript. *Deadline:* March 12.

Contact: Cathy Kersh, Scholarship Program Manager
Jewish Vocational Service Los Angeles
6505 Wilshire Boulevard, Suite 200
Los Angeles, CA 90048
Phone: 323-761-8888 Ext. 8868
Fax: 323-761-8575
E-mail: scholarship@jvsla.org

JOHN M. AZARIAN MEMORIAL ARMENIAN YOUTH SCHOLARSHIP FUND

http://azariangroup.com/scholarship.html

JOHN M. AZARIAN MEMORIAL ARMENIAN YOUTH SCHOLARSHIP FUND

Grants awarded to undergraduate students of Armenian descent, attending a full-time four-year college or university within the United States. Compelling financial need is the main criteria. Minimum 2.5 GPA required. Activity/involvement in the Armenian church / community a plus.

Award: Grant for use in freshman, sophomore, junior, or senior years; not renewable. *Number:* 1–5. *Amount:* $500–$5000.

Eligibility Requirements: Applicant must be of Armenian heritage and enrolled or expecting to enroll full-time at a four-year institution or university. Applicant must have 2.5 GPA or higher. Available to U.S. citizens.

Application Requirements: Application form, autobiography, essay, financial need analysis, personal photograph, recommendations or references, resume, test scores, transcript. *Deadline:* June 30.

Contact: Mr. John Azarian, CEO
John M. Azarian Memorial Armenian Youth Scholarship Fund
The Azarian Group, LLC, The Azarian Building
6 Prospect Street, Suite 1B
Midland Park, NJ 07432
Phone: 201-444-7111 Ext. 27
Fax: 201-444-6655
E-mail: jazarian@azariangroup.com

KANSAS BOARD OF REGENTS

http://www.kansasregents.org/

KANSAS ETHNIC MINORITY SCHOLARSHIP

Scholarship program designed to assist financially needy, academically competitive students who are identified as members of any of the following ethnic/racial groups: African-American, American Indian or Alaskan Native, Asian or Pacific Islander, or Hispanic. Priority is given to applicants who are freshmen. Students must be Kansas residents attending postsecondary institutions in Kansas. For more details refer to website http://www.kansasregents.org/financial_aid/minority.html.

Award: Scholarship for use in freshman, sophomore, junior, or senior years; renewable. *Amount:* up to $1850.

Eligibility Requirements: Applicant must be American Indian/Alaska Native, Asian/Pacific Islander, Black (non-Hispanic), Hispanic; enrolled or expecting to enroll full-time at a two-year or four-year institution or university; resident of Kansas and studying in Kansas. Applicant must have 3.0 GPA or higher. Available to U.S. citizens.

Application Requirements: Application form, financial need analysis, test scores. *Fee:* $12. *Deadline:* May 1.

Contact: Diane Lindeman, Director of Student Financial Assistance
Kansas Board of Regents
1000 SW Jackson, Suite 520
Topeka, KS 66612
Phone: 785-296-3517
Fax: 785-296-0983
E-mail: dlindeman@ksbor.org

KIMBO FOUNDATION

http://www.kimbofoundation.org/

KIMBO FOUNDATION SCHOLARSHIP

Scholarship available to Korean-American students only. Full time study only. Application deadline varies every year.

Award: Scholarship for use in freshman, sophomore, junior, senior, graduate, or postgraduate years; not renewable. *Number:* 30–50. *Amount:* $1500.

Eligibility Requirements: Applicant must be of Korean heritage; Asian/Pacific Islander and enrolled or expecting to enroll full-time at a two-year or four-year or technical institution or university. Available to citizens of countries other than the U.S. or Canada.

Application Requirements: Application form, copy of household income tax return, essay, recommendations or references, transcript. *Deadline:* varies.

Contact: Jennifer Chung, Program Coordinator
Kimbo Foundation
430 Shotwell Street
San Francisco, CA 94110
Phone: 415-285-4100
Fax: 415-285-4103
E-mail: info@kimbofoundation.org

KNIGHTS OF COLUMBUS

http://www.kofc.org/

FOURTH DEGREE PRO DEO AND PRO PATRIA (CANADA)

• See page 523

KONIAG EDUCATION FOUNDATION

http://www.koniageducation.org/

GLENN GODFREY MEMORIAL SCHOLARSHIP

Scholarship for sophomore, junior, or seniors in their undergraduate study. Applicants must be Alaska Native shareholders or descendants (may be adopted) of the Koniag Region. Must have and maintain a minimum cumulative GPA of 2.5.

Award: Scholarship for use in sophomore, junior, or senior years; not renewable. *Number:* 1. *Amount:* up to $5000.

Eligibility Requirements: Applicant must be American Indian/Alaska Native and enrolled or expecting to enroll full-time at a four-year institution or university. Applicant must have 2.5 GPA or higher. Available to U.S. citizens.

Application Requirements: Application form, birth certificate (for descendants only), essay, interview, personal photograph, recommendations or references, resume, transcript. *Deadline:* varies.

Contact: Tyan Hayes, Executive Director
 Phone: 907-562-9093
 Fax: 907-562-9023

KONIAG EDUCATION CAREER DEVELOPMENT GRANT

Applicants must be Alaska Native shareholders or descendents (may be adopted) of the Koniag Region. Applicants must be accepted or enrolled in a career development course and able to demonstrate how the training will assist the student in gaining employment or job security and/or advancement. Awards up to $1000.

Award: Grant for use in freshman year; not renewable. *Number:* 1. *Amount:* $1000.

Eligibility Requirements: Applicant must be American Indian/Alaska Native and enrolled or expecting to enroll part-time at a technical institution. Available to U.S. and non-Canadian citizens.

Application Requirements: Application form, driver's license, resume. *Deadline:* varies.

Contact: Tyan Hayes, Executive Director
 Phone: 907-562-9093
 Fax: 907-562-9023

KONIAG EDUCATION FOUNDATION ACADEMIC/ GRADUATE SCHOLARSHIP

Scholarships to honor students who excel academically, and who show the potential to succeed in college studies. Applicants must be Alaska Native shareholders or descendents (may be adopted) of the Koniag Region. Deadlines are March 15 for summer term and June 1 for fall/ spring terms.

Award: Scholarship for use in freshman, sophomore, junior, senior, graduate, or postgraduate years; not renewable. *Number:* 130–170. *Amount:* $500–$2500.

Eligibility Requirements: Applicant must be American Indian/Alaska Native and enrolled or expecting to enroll full- or part-time at a two-year or four-year or technical institution or university. Applicant must have 3.0 GPA or higher. Available to U.S. citizens.

Application Requirements: Application form, driver's license, essay, financial need analysis, personal photograph, proof of eligibility from Koniag Inc, recommendations or references, transcript. *Deadline:* varies.

Contact: Tyan Hayes, Executive Director
 Phone: 907-562-9093
 Fax: 907-562-9023

KONIAG EDUCATION FOUNDATION COLLEGE/ UNIVERSITY BASIC SCHOLARSHIP

Scholarship to honor students who show the potential to succeed in college studies. Applicants must be Alaska Native shareholders or descendants (may be adopted) of the Koniag Region. Must maintain a minimum cumulative GPA of 2.0 or equivalent scores. Awarded up to $1000 a year. Deadlines: March 15 for summer term, June 1 for fall/ spring terms.

Award: Scholarship for use in freshman, sophomore, junior, senior, graduate, or postgraduate years; not renewable. *Amount:* up to $1000.

Eligibility Requirements: Applicant must be American Indian/Alaska Native and enrolled or expecting to enroll full- or part-time at a two-year or four-year or technical institution or university. Available to U.S. citizens.

Application Requirements: Application form, essay, recommendations or references, transcript. *Deadline:* varies.

Contact: Tyan Hayes, Executive Director
 Phone: 907-562-9093
 Fax: 907-562-9023

KOREAN AMERICAN SCHOLARSHIP FOUNDATION

http://www.kasf.org/

KOREAN-AMERICAN SCHOLARSHIP FOUNDATION EASTERN REGION SCHOLARSHIPS

Scholarships available to Korean-American and Korean students enrolled in a full-time undergraduate or graduate program in the United States. Selection based on financial need, academic achievement, school activities, and community services. Each applicant must submit an application to the respective KASF region. For more details and an application see website http://www.kasf.org.

Award: Scholarship for use in freshman, sophomore, junior, senior, or graduate years; not renewable. *Amount:* $1000.

Eligibility Requirements: Applicant must be of Korean heritage; Asian/Pacific Islander; enrolled or expecting to enroll full-time at a four-year institution or university and studying in Delaware, District of Columbia, Kentucky, Maryland, North Carolina, Pennsylvania, Virginia, West Virginia. Available to U.S. and non-U.S. citizens.

Application Requirements: Application form, essay, financial need analysis, personal photograph, recommendations or references, self-addressed stamped envelope with application, transcript. *Deadline:* May 31.

Contact: Dr. Brandon Yi, Scholarship Committee
 Korean American Scholarship Foundation
 803 Russell Avenue, Suite 2C
 Reston, VA 20879
 E-mail: eastern@kasf.org

KOREAN-AMERICAN SCHOLARSHIP FOUNDATION NORTHEASTERN REGION SCHOLARSHIPS

Scholarships available to Korean-American and Korean students enrolled in a full-time undergraduate or graduate program in the United States. Selection based on financial need, academic achievement, school activities, and community services. Each applicant must submit an application to the respective KASF region. For more details and an application see website http://www.kasf.org.

Award: Scholarship for use in freshman, sophomore, junior, senior, graduate, or postgraduate years; not renewable. *Number:* 60. *Amount:* $1000–$2500.

Eligibility Requirements: Applicant must be of Korean heritage; Asian/Pacific Islander; enrolled or expecting to enroll full-time at a four-year institution or university and studying in Connecticut, Maine, Massachusetts, New Hampshire, New Jersey, New York, Rhode Island, Vermont. Available to U.S. citizens.

Application Requirements: Application form, essay, financial need analysis, personal photograph, recommendations or references, transcript. *Deadline:* June 23.

Contact: Mr. William Kim, Scholarship Committee Chairman
 Korean American Scholarship Foundation
 51 West Overlook
 Port Washington, NY 11050
 Phone: 516-883-1142
 Fax: 516-883-1964
 E-mail: kim.william@gmail.com

KOREAN-AMERICAN SCHOLARSHIP FOUNDATION SOUTHERN REGION SCHOLARSHIPS

Scholarships available to Korean-American and Korean students enrolled in a full-time undergraduate or graduate program in the United States. Selection based on financial need, academic achievement, school activities, and community services. Each applicant must submit an application to the respective KASF region. For more details and an application see website http://www.kasf.org.

Award: Scholarship for use in freshman, sophomore, junior, senior, or graduate years; not renewable. *Number:* up to 45. *Amount:* $1000.

Eligibility Requirements: Applicant must be of Korean heritage; Asian/Pacific Islander; enrolled or expecting to enroll full-time at a four-year institution or university and studying in Alabama, Arkansas, Florida, Georgia, Louisiana, Mississippi, North Carolina, Oklahoma, South Carolina, Tennessee, Texas. Available to U.S. citizens.

Application Requirements: Application form, essay, financial need analysis, personal photograph, recommendations or references, transcript. *Deadline:* June 10.

Contact: Dr. Sam Sook Chung, Scholarship Committee
Korean American Scholarship Foundation
2989 Preston Drive
Rex, GA 30273
Phone: 770-968-6768
E-mail: samsookchung@hotmail.com

KOREAN-AMERICAN SCHOLARSHIP FOUNDATION WESTERN REGION SCHOLARSHIPS

Scholarships available to Korean-American and Korean students enrolled in a full-time undergraduate or graduate program in the United States. Selection based on financial need, academic achievement, school activities, and community services. Each applicant must submit an application to the respective KASF region. For more details and an application see website http://www.kasf.org.

Award: Scholarship for use in freshman, sophomore, junior, senior, or graduate years; not renewable. *Amount:* $2000.

Eligibility Requirements: Applicant must be of Korean heritage; Asian/Pacific Islander; enrolled or expecting to enroll full-time at a four-year institution or university and studying in Alaska, Arizona, California, Colorado, Hawaii, Idaho, Montana, Nevada, New Mexico, Oregon, Utah, Washington, Wyoming. Applicant must have 3.0 GPA or higher. Available to U.S. citizens.

Application Requirements: Application form, essay, financial need analysis, personal photograph, recommendations or references, transcript. *Deadline:* May 31.

KOSCIUSZKO FOUNDATION

http://www.thekf.org

MASSACHUSETTS FEDERATION OF POLISH WOMEN'S CLUBS SCHOLARSHIPS

Nonrenewable award to American students of Polish descent for sophomore, junior, and senior year who are attending an accredited four-year college or university. The scholarship is awarded to residents of Massachusetts. If no residents of Massachusetts apply, the award(s) may be offered to residents of New England. Applicants must submit proof of Polish ancestry. Minimum 3.0 GPA required.

Award: Scholarship for use in sophomore, junior, or senior years; not renewable. *Number:* 1–3. *Amount:* $1250.

Eligibility Requirements: Applicant must be of Polish heritage; enrolled or expecting to enroll full-time at a four-year institution or university and resident of Connecticut, Maine, Massachusetts, New Hampshire, Rhode Island, Vermont. Applicant must have 3.0 GPA or higher. Available to U.S. citizens.

Application Requirements: Application form, essay, financial need analysis, personal photograph, proof of Polish ancestry, recommendations or references, transcript. *Fee:* $35. *Deadline:* January 5.

Contact: Ms. Addy Tymczyszyn, Scholarship and Grant Officer for Americans
Kosciuszko Foundation
15 East 65th Street
New York, NY 10065
Phone: 212-734-2130 Ext. 210
E-mail: Addy@thekf.org

POLISH AMERICAN CLUB OF NORTH JERSEY SCHOLARSHIPS

Scholarships of $1000 to $1700 awarded to qualified students for full-time undergraduate and graduate studies at accredited colleges and universities in the United States. The scholarship is renewable. U.S. citizens of Polish descent and Polish citizens with permanent residency status in the United States with minimum GPA of 3.0 are eligible.

Applicants must be members of the Polish American Club of North Jersey.

Award: Scholarship for use in freshman, sophomore, junior, senior, or graduate years; not renewable. *Number:* 1–5. *Amount:* $1000–$1700.

Eligibility Requirements: Applicant must be of Polish heritage; enrolled or expecting to enroll full-time at a four-year institution or university and resident of New Jersey. Applicant must have 3.0 GPA or higher. Available to U.S. citizens.

Application Requirements: Application form, essay, personal photograph, proof of Polish ancestry, recommendations or references, transcript. *Fee:* $35. *Deadline:* January 15.

Contact: Ms. Addy Tymczyszyn, Scholarship and Grant Officer for Americans
Kosciuszko Foundation
15 East 65th Street
New York, NY 10065
Phone: 212-734 2130 Ext. 210
E-mail: addy@thekf.org

POLISH NATIONAL ALLIANCE OF BROOKLYN USA INC. SCHOLARSHIPS

Scholarships of $2000 available to qualified undergraduate students for full-time studies at accredited colleges and universities in the United States. U.S. citizens of Polish descent and Polish citizens with permanent residency status in the United States with minimum GPA of 3.0 are eligible. Applicants must be members in good standing of the Polish National Alliance of Brooklyn Lodge#1903.

Award: Scholarship for use in freshman, sophomore, junior, or senior years; not renewable. *Number:* 1–2. *Amount:* $2000.

Eligibility Requirements: Applicant must be of Polish heritage; enrolled or expecting to enroll full-time at a four-year institution or university and resident of New York. Applicant must have 3.0 GPA or higher. Available to U.S. and non-Canadian citizens.

Application Requirements: Application form, essay, personal photograph, proof of Polish ancestry, recommendations or references, transcript. *Fee:* $35. *Deadline:* January 5.

Contact: Ms. Addy Tymczyszyn, Scholarship and Grant Officer for Americans
Kosciuszko Foundation
15 East 65th Street
New York, NY 10065
Phone: 212-734-2130 Ext. 210
E-mail: Addy@thekf.org

TOMASZKIEWICZ-FLORIO SCHOLARSHIP

The Tomaszkiewicz-Florio Scholarship supports Kosciuszko Foundation's Summer language and culture program at the Jagiellonian University in Krakow, Poland. The scholarship covers program fees (tuition, 3 meals a day, sightseeing on weekends and a shared room) for a 3 week intensive language program. Some funding may be awarded towards airfare. High school seniors who expect to be 18 and have a high school diploma by the first day of the program may apply. Credit is available. Students who receive scholarship funding are responsible for $95 non-refundable registration fees, airfare and spending money. Group flights are available.

Award: Scholarship for use in freshman, sophomore, junior, or senior years; not renewable. *Number:* up to 13. *Amount:* $1985.

Eligibility Requirements: Applicant must be of Polish heritage and enrolled or expecting to enroll full-time at a four-year institution or university. Applicant must have 3.0 GPA or higher. Available to U.S. citizens.

Application Requirements: Application fee, application form, essay, financial need analysis, personal photograph, recommendations or references, transcript. *Fee:* $35. *Deadline:* April 15.

Contact: Addy Tymczyszyn, Summer Study Abroad Coordinator
Kosciuszko Foundation
15 East 65th Street
New York, NY 10065
Phone: 212-734 2130 Ext. 210

LATIN AMERICAN EDUCATIONAL FOUNDATION

http://www.laef.org/

LATIN AMERICAN EDUCATIONAL FOUNDATION SCHOLARSHIPS

Scholarship for Colorado residents of Hispanic heritage. Applicant should be accepted in an accredited college, university or vocational school. Must maintain a minimum GPA of 3.0.

Award: Scholarship for use in freshman, sophomore, junior, senior, or graduate years; not renewable.

Eligibility Requirements: Applicant must be Hispanic and enrolled or expecting to enroll full-time at a four-year institution or university. Applicant must have 3.0 GPA or higher. Available to U.S. citizens.

Application Requirements: Application form, community service, essay, financial need analysis, interview, recommendations or references, transcript. *Deadline:* March 1.

LEAGUE OF UNITED LATIN AMERICAN CITIZENS NATIONAL EDUCATIONAL SERVICE CENTERS INC.

http://www.lnesc.org/

LULAC NATIONAL SCHOLARSHIP FUND

Awards scholarships to Hispanic students who are enrolled or planning to enroll in accredited colleges or universities in the United States. Applicants must be U.S. citizens or legal residents. Scholarships may be used for the payment of tuition, academic fees, room, board and the purchase of required educational materials. For additional information visit website http://www.lnesc.org to see a list of participating councils or send a self-addressed stamped envelope.

Award: Scholarship for use in freshman, sophomore, junior, or senior years; not renewable. *Number:* 1000. *Amount:* $250–$2000.

Eligibility Requirements: Applicant must be Hispanic and enrolled or expecting to enroll full-time at a two-year or four-year institution or university. Available to U.S. citizens.

Application Requirements: Application form, driver's license, essay, financial need analysis, interview, recommendations or references, self-addressed stamped envelope with application, test scores, transcript. *Deadline:* March 31.

LOS PADRES FOUNDATION

http://www.lospadresfoundation.com/

COLLEGE TUITION ASSISTANCE PROGRAM

Program for eligible students who are the first family member to attend college. Must be a legal resident or citizen of the U.S. and a resident of New York or New Jersey. Must have a 3.0 GPA. For further information, refer to website at http://www.lospadresfoundation.com.

Award: Scholarship for use in freshman, sophomore, junior, or senior years; not renewable. *Number:* 25–30. *Amount:* $2000–$3000.

Eligibility Requirements: Applicant must be of Hispanic heritage; high school student; planning to enroll or expecting to enroll full-time at a two-year or four-year institution or university and resident of New Jersey, New York. Applicant must have 3.0 GPA or higher. Available to U.S. citizens.

Application Requirements: Application form, application form may be submitted online (http://www.lospadresfoundation.com), essay, financial need analysis, interview, personal photograph, recommendations or references, test scores, transcript. *Deadline:* January 16.

Contact: Mrs. Andrea Betancourt, Office Manager
Phone: 800-528-4105
Fax: 866-810-1361
E-mail: lpfadmin@lospadresfoundation.com

SECOND CHANCE SCHOLARSHIPS

Scholarships granted to Puerto Rican/Latinos students who wish to return to college, trade school or apprenticeship program. Must be a resident of New York or New Jersey. Must demonstrate financial need. For further information, refer to website at http://www.lospadresfoundation.com.

Award: Scholarship for use in freshman year; renewable. *Number:* 1–5. *Amount:* $2000–$2000.

Eligibility Requirements: Applicant must be of Hispanic, Latin American/Caribbean heritage; enrolled or expecting to enroll full-time at a two-year or four-year or technical institution or university and resident of New Jersey, New York. Applicant must have 3.0 GPA or higher. Available to U.S. citizens.

Application Requirements: Application form, application form may be submitted online (http://www.lospadresfoundation.com), essay, financial need analysis, interview, personal photograph, recommendations or references, transcript. *Deadline:* June 1.

Contact: Mrs. Andrea Betancourt, Office Manager
Phone: 800-528-4105
Fax: 866-810-1361
E-mail: lpfadmin@lospadresfoundation.com

MAGIC JOHNSON FOUNDATION INC.

http://www.magicjohnson.org/

TAYLOR MICHAELS SCHOLARSHIP FUND
• *See page 559*

MANA DE SAN DIEGO

http://www.manasd.org/

MANA DE SAN DIEGO SYLVIA CHAVEZ MEMORIAL SCHOLARSHIP
• *See page 559*

MENOMINEE INDIAN TRIBE OF WISCONSIN

http://www.menominee-nsn.gov/

MENOMINEE INDIAN TRIBE ADULT VOCATIONAL TRAINING PROGRAM

Renewable award for enrolled Menominee tribal members to use at vocational or technical schools. Must be at least 1/4 Menominee and show proof of Indian blood. Must complete financial aid form.

Award: Grant for use in freshman or sophomore years; renewable. *Number:* 50–70. *Amount:* $100–$2200.

Eligibility Requirements: Applicant must be American Indian/Alaska Native and enrolled or expecting to enroll full- or part-time at a technical institution. Available to U.S. citizens.

Application Requirements: Application form, financial need analysis, proof of Indian blood. *Deadline:* varies.

Contact: Virginia Nuske, Education Director
Menominee Indian Tribe of Wisconsin
PO Box 910
Keshena, WI 54135
Phone: 715-799-5110
Fax: 715-799-5102
E-mail: vnuske@mitw.org

MENOMINEE INDIAN TRIBE OF WISCONSIN HIGHER EDUCATION GRANTS

Renewable award for only enrolled Menominee tribal members to use at a two- or four-year college or university. Must be at least 1/4 Menominee and show proof of Indian blood. Must complete the Free Application for Federal Student Aid (FAFSA)financial aid form and demonstrate financial need.

Award: Grant for use in freshman, sophomore, junior, or senior years; renewable. *Number:* 136. *Amount:* $100–$2200.

Eligibility Requirements: Applicant must be American Indian/Alaska Native and enrolled or expecting to enroll full- or part-time at a two-year or four-year institution or university. Available to U.S. citizens.

Application Requirements: Application form, financial need analysis, proof of Indian blood. *Deadline:* continuous.

Contact: Virginia Nuske, Education Director
Menominee Indian Tribe of Wisconsin
PO Box 910
Keshena, WI 54135
Phone: 715-799-5110
Fax: 715-799-5102
E-mail: vnuske@mitw.org

MINNESOTA OFFICE OF HIGHER EDUCATION

http://www.getreadyforcollege.org/

MINNESOTA INDIAN SCHOLARSHIP

Scholarship for Minnesota residents who are one-fourth or more American Indian ancestry and attending an eligible Minnesota postsecondary institution. Maximum award is $4000 for undergraduate students and $6000 for graduate students. Scholarships are limited to 3 years for certificate or AA/AS programs, 5 years for bachelor's degree programs, and 5 years for graduate programs. Applicants must maintain satisfactory academic progress, not be in default on student loans, and be eligible to receive Pell or State Grant and have remaining need. Undergraduates must be enrolled on a least a 3/4-time basis.

Award: Scholarship for use in freshman, sophomore, junior, senior, graduate, or postgraduate years; not renewable. *Number:* 500–600. *Amount:* up to $6000.

Eligibility Requirements: Applicant must be American Indian/Alaska Native; enrolled or expecting to enroll full- or part-time at a two-year or four-year or technical institution or university; resident of Minnesota and studying in Minnesota. Available to U.S. citizens.

Application Requirements: American Indian ancestry documentation, application form, financial need analysis. *Deadline:* continuous.

MONGOLIA SOCIETY, INC.

http://www.mongoliasociety.org/

DR. GOMBOJAB HANGIN MEMORIAL SCHOLARSHIP

One-time award for students of Mongolian heritage only. Must have permanent residency in Mongolia, the People's Republic of China, or the former Soviet Union. Award is for tuition at U.S. institutions. Must state they are Mongolian on their passport or ID papers. Upon conclusion of award year, recipient must write a report of his or her activities. Application requests must be in English and the application must be filled out in English. Write for application.

Award: Scholarship for use in freshman, sophomore, junior, senior, graduate, or postgraduate years; not renewable. *Number:* 1. *Amount:* up to $1000.

Eligibility Requirements: Applicant must be of Mongolian heritage; Asian/Pacific Islander and enrolled or expecting to enroll full-time at a two-year or four-year or technical institution or university. Available to citizens of countries other than the U.S. or Canada.

Application Requirements: Application form, curriculum vitae, copy of ID card, and passport, essay, personal photograph, recommendations or references. *Deadline:* January 1.

Contact: Mrs. Susie Drost, Executive Director
Phone: 812-855-4078
E-mail: monsoc@indiana.edu

NAACP LEGAL DEFENSE AND EDUCATIONAL FUND INC.

http://www.naacpldf.org/

HERBERT LEHMAN SCHOLARSHIP PROGRAM

Renewable award for successful African-American high school seniors and freshmen to attend a four-year college on a full-time basis. Candidates are required to be U.S. citizens and must have outstanding potential as evidenced by their high school academic records, test scores, and personal essays.

Award: Scholarship for use in freshman, sophomore, junior, or senior years; renewable. *Number:* 25–30. *Amount:* $2000.

Eligibility Requirements: Applicant must be Black (non-Hispanic) and enrolled or expecting to enroll full-time at a four-year institution or university. Applicant must have 2.5 GPA or higher. Available to U.S. citizens.

Application Requirements: Application form, community service, essay, personal photograph, recommendations or references, resume, test scores, transcript. *Deadline:* March 31.

NANA (NORTHWEST ALASKA NATIVE ASSOCIATION) REGIONAL CORPORATION

http://www.nana.com/

ROBERT AQQALUK NEWLIN SR. MEMORIAL TRUST SCHOLARSHIP

Scholarship for NANA shareholders, descendants of NANA shareholders, or dependents of NANA shareholders or their descendants. Applicant must be enrolled or accepted for admittance at a postsecondary educational institution or vocational school.

Award: Scholarship for use in freshman, sophomore, junior, or senior years; not renewable. *Number:* 250–400. *Amount:* $1000–$2000.

Eligibility Requirements: Applicant must be American Indian/Alaska Native and enrolled or expecting to enroll full- or part-time at a two-year or four-year or technical institution or university. Available to U.S. citizens.

Application Requirements: Application form, college acceptance letter, enrollment proof, financial need analysis, recommendations or references, transcript. *Deadline:* varies.

Contact: Erica Nelson, Education Director
NANA (Northwest Alaska Native Association) Regional Corporation
PO Box 509
Kotzebue, AK 99752
Phone: 907-442-1607
Fax: 907-442-2289
E-mail: erica.nelson@nana.org

NATIONAL ASSOCIATION FOR CAMPUS ACTIVITIES

http://www.naca.org/

MULTICULTURAL SCHOLARSHIP PROGRAM

Scholarships will be given to applicants identified as African-American, Latina/Latino, Native-American, Asian-American or Pacific Islander ethnic minorities. A letter of recommendation affirming his/her ethnic minority status, his/her financial need, and that he/she will be in the campus activity field at least one year following the program for which a scholarship is being sought, should accompany applications.

Award: Scholarship for use in freshman, sophomore, junior, senior, or graduate years; not renewable. *Number:* up to 4. *Amount:* $250–$300.

Eligibility Requirements: Applicant must be American Indian/Alaska Native, Asian/Pacific Islander, Black (non-Hispanic), Hispanic; enrolled or expecting to enroll full- or part-time at a two-year or four-year institution or university and must have an interest in leadership. Available to U.S. and non-U.S. citizens.

Application Requirements: Application form, essay, financial need analysis, recommendations or references. *Deadline:* May 1.

Contact: Dionne Ellison, Administrative Assistant
Phone: 803-732-6222 Ext. 131
Fax: 803-749-1047
E-mail: dionnee@naca.org

NATIONAL ASSOCIATION FOR THE ADVANCEMENT OF COLORED PEOPLE

http://www.naacp.org/

AGNES JONES JACKSON SCHOLARSHIP

• See page 526

NATIONAL ASSOCIATION OF COLORED WOMEN'S CLUBS

http://www.nacwc.org/

HALLIE Q. BROWN SCHOLARSHIP

One-time $1000-$2000 scholarship for high school graduates who have completed at least one semester in a postsecondary accredited institution with a minimum "C" average.

Award: Scholarship for use in freshman year; not renewable. *Number:* 4–6. *Amount:* $1000–$2000.

Eligibility Requirements: Applicant must be Black (non-Hispanic); high school student and planning to enroll or expecting to enroll full-time at a two-year or four-year institution or university. Available to U.S. citizens.

Application Requirements: Application form, recommendations or references, transcript. *Deadline:* March 30.

Contact: Dr. Gerldine Jenkins, Program Coordinator
National Association of Colored Women's Clubs
Program Coordinator
Washington, DC 20009
Phone: 202-667-4080
Fax: 202-667-2574

NATIONAL ASSOCIATION OF NEGRO BUSINESS AND PROFESSIONAL WOMEN'S CLUBS INC.

http://www.nanbpwc.org/

NATIONAL SCHOLARSHIP

Scholarship for African-American graduating high school seniors with a minimum 3.0 GPA. Must submit 300-word essay on the topic "Why Education is Important to Me."

Award: Scholarship for use in freshman year; not renewable. *Number:* 6–8. *Amount:* $500–$1000.

Eligibility Requirements: Applicant must be Black (non-Hispanic); high school student and planning to enroll or expecting to enroll full-time at a four-year institution or university. Applicant must have 3.0 GPA or higher. Available to U.S. citizens.

Application Requirements: Application form, community service, essay, recommendations or references, test scores, transcript. *Deadline:* March 1.

Contact: Twyla Whitby, National Director of Education Scholarship Program
National Association of Negro Business and Professional Women's Clubs Inc.
1806 New Hampshire Avenue, NW
Washington, DC 20009-3298
Phone: 202-483-4206
E-mail: info@nanbpwc.org

NATIONAL ITALIAN AMERICAN FOUNDATION

http://www.niaf.org/

NATIONAL ITALIAN AMERICAN FOUNDATION CATEGORY I SCHOLARSHIP

Award available to Italian-American students who have outstanding potential and high academic achievements. Minimum 3.5 GPA required. Must be a U.S. citizen and be enrolled in an accredited institution of higher education. Application can only be submitted online. For further information, deadlines, and online application visit website http://www.niaf.org/scholarships/index.asp.

Award: Scholarship for use in freshman, sophomore, junior, senior, graduate, or postgraduate years; not renewable. *Number:* 40–45. *Amount:* $2500–$10,000.

Eligibility Requirements: Applicant must be of Italian heritage and enrolled or expecting to enroll full-time at a two-year or four-year institution or university. Applicant must have 3.5 GPA or higher. Available to U.S. citizens.

Application Requirements: Application form, application form may be submitted online (http://www.niaf.org/scholarships), essay, recommendations or references, transcript. *Deadline:* March 2.

NATIONAL SOCIETY DAUGHTERS OF THE AMERICAN REVOLUTION

http://www.dar.org/

NATIONAL SOCIETY DAUGHTERS OF THE AMERICAN REVOLUTION AMERICAN INDIAN SCHOLARSHIP

One-time scholarship available to Native Americans. All awards are judged based on financial need and academic achievement. Undergraduate students are given preference. GPA of 2.75 or higher is required. Deadlines are April 1 for fall term and October 1 for spring term.

Award: Scholarship for use in freshman, sophomore, junior, senior, or graduate years; not renewable. *Amount:* $500.

Eligibility Requirements: Applicant must be American Indian/Alaska Native and enrolled or expecting to enroll full-time at a two-year or four-year or technical institution or university. Available to U.S. citizens.

Application Requirements: Application form, proof of American Indian blood, self-addressed stamped envelope with application. *Deadline:* varies.

Contact: Tania Tatum, Manager, Office of the Reporter General
Phone: 202-628-1776
Fax: 202-879-3348
E-mail: nsdarscholarships@dar.org

NATIONAL SOCIETY DAUGHTERS OF THE AMERICAN REVOLUTION FRANCES CRAWFORD MARVIN AMERICAN INDIAN SCHOLARSHIP

Nonrenewable award available for a Native American to attend any two- or four-year college or university. Must demonstrate financial need, academic achievement, and have a 3.0 GPA or higher. Must submit a self-addressed stamped envelope to be considered.

Award: Scholarship for use in freshman, sophomore, junior, or senior years; not renewable. *Number:* 1.

Eligibility Requirements: Applicant must be American Indian/Alaska Native and enrolled or expecting to enroll full-time at a two-year or four-year institution or university. Applicant must have 3.0 GPA or higher. Available to U.S. citizens.

Application Requirements: Application form, financial need analysis, letter or proof papers, self-addressed stamped envelope with application, transcript. *Deadline:* February 1.

Contact: Tania Tatum, Manager, Office of the Reporter General
Phone: 202-628-1776
Fax: 202-879-3348
E-mail: nsdarscholarships@dar.org

NATIONAL WELSH-AMERICAN FOUNDATION

http://www.wales-usa.org/

EXCHANGE SCHOLARSHIP

Limited to colleges/universities in Wales only. Applicant must have a Welsh background through birth and be willing to promote Welsh-American relations both here and abroad. Requested to consider becoming a member of NWAF upon completion of study. Required to complete four-year college study in United States. Applicant must be 21 years of age or older.

Award: Scholarship for use in freshman, sophomore, junior, senior, graduate, or postgraduate years; not renewable. *Number:* 1. *Amount:* $5000.

Eligibility Requirements: Applicant must be of Welsh heritage and enrolled or expecting to enroll full-time at a four-year institution or university. Available to U.S. and Canadian citizens.

Application Requirements: Application form, essay, recommendations or references, test scores. *Deadline:* March 1.

Contact: Donna Lloyd-Kolkin, Scholarship Committee
Phone: 570-925-6923
E-mail: nwaf@epix.net

NATIVEVISION SCHOLARSHIP

http://www.nativevision.org/

NATIVEVISION

Scholarship available to any American Indian high school senior who has been accepted to college.

Award: Scholarship for use in freshman year; not renewable. *Number:* 2. *Amount:* $5000.

Eligibility Requirements: Applicant must be American Indian/Alaska Native; high school student and planning to enroll or expecting to enroll full-time at a four-year institution or university. Applicant must have 3.0 GPA or higher. Available to U.S. and non-U.S. citizens.

Application Requirements: Application form, essay, proof of membership in a federally recognized tribe., recommendations or references, transcript. *Deadline:* May 3.

Contact: Marlena Hammen, Scholarship Coordinator
NativeVision Scholarship
621 North Washington Street
Baltimore, MD 21205
Phone: 410-955-6931
Fax: 410-955-2010
E-mail: mhammen@jhsph.edu

NEED

http://www.needld.org/

UNMET NEED GRANT PROGRAM

The program provides "last dollar" funding to lower-income students that still have a need for aid after all federal, state, local and private scholarships and grants have been secured. Must be a U.S. citizen, high school graduate, resident of one of nine participating counties in Southwestern Pennsylvania (Allegheny, Armstrong, Beaver, Butler, Fayette, Greene, Lawrence, Washington or Westmoreland county), and have a minimum 2.0 GPA.

Award: Grant for use in freshman, sophomore, junior, or senior years; not renewable. *Number:* 10–500. *Amount:* $1000–$3500.

Eligibility Requirements: Applicant must be Black (non-Hispanic); enrolled or expecting to enroll full- or part-time at a two-year or four-year or technical institution or university and resident of Pennsylvania. Available to U.S. citizens.

Application Requirements: Application form, essay, financial need analysis, personal photograph, transcript. *Deadline:* May 31.

Contact: Arlene Holland, Student Services Manager
Phone: 412-566-2760
E-mail: atyler@needld.org

NEW YORK STATE HIGHER EDUCATION SERVICES CORPORATION

http://www.hesc.com/

NEW YORK STATE AID TO NATIVE AMERICANS

Award for enrolled members of a New York State tribe and their children who are attending or planning to attend a New York State college and who are New York State residents. Deadlines: July 15 for the fall semester, December 31 for the spring semester, and May 20 for summer session.

Award: Scholarship for use in freshman, sophomore, junior, or senior years; renewable. *Amount:* $85–$2000.

Eligibility Requirements: Applicant must be American Indian/Alaska Native; enrolled or expecting to enroll full- or part-time at a two-year or four-year or technical institution or university; resident of New York and studying in New York. Available to U.S. citizens.

Application Requirements: Application form, financial need analysis, recommendations or references, transcript. *Deadline:* varies.

NEXTGEN NETWORK INC.

http://www.nextgennetwork.com/

DONNA JAMISON LAGO MEMORIAL SCHOLARSHIP

Awards to assist with future educational expenses of African-American, U.S. citizens. The essay competition is open to those who would complete their studies in that current year. Applicants must be seeking acceptance to an accredited U.S. college or university. The essay competition encourages high school seniors to think critically about important issues that affect their lives.

Award: Scholarship for use in freshman year; not renewable. *Number:* 9. *Amount:* $500–$2500.

Eligibility Requirements: Applicant must be Black (non-Hispanic); high school student; planning to enroll or expecting to enroll full-time at a two-year or four-year institution or university and must have an interest in writing. Available to U.S. citizens.

Application Requirements: Application form, driver's license, entry in a contest, essay, personal photograph, recommendations or references. *Deadline:* May 30.

Contact: Mr. K.J. Mburu, Scholarship Committee
Phone: 202-686-9260 Ext. 101
Fax: 202-944-3322
E-mail: info@nextgennetwork.com

NISEI STUDENT RELOCATION COMMEMORATIVE FUND

http://www.nsrcfund.org/

NISEI STUDENT RELOCATION COMMEMORATIVE FUND

Eligibility: only high school seniors of Southeast Asian (from Vietnam, Cambodia, Laos) ancestry living in the U.S. Deadline to apply varies. Scholarships awarded in a different city/region each year. Check the website (www.nsrcfund.org) for current information or email: jeanhibino@aol.com.

Award: Scholarship for use in freshman year; not renewable. *Number:* 30–50. *Amount:* $250–$2000.

Eligibility Requirements: Applicant must be of Lao/Hmong, Vietnamese heritage; Asian/Pacific Islander; high school student and planning to enroll or expecting to enroll full- or part-time at a two-year or four-year or technical institution or university. Available to U.S. citizens.

Application Requirements: Application form, community service, essay, financial need analysis, personal photograph, recommendations or references, transcript.

Contact: Ms. Jean Hibino, Executive Secretary
Nisei Student Relocation Commemorative Fund
19 Scenic Drive
Portland, CT 06480
E-mail: jeanhibino@aol.com

NORTH CAROLINA SOCIETY OF HISPANIC PROFESSIONALS

http://www.thencshp.org/

NORTH CAROLINA HISPANIC COLLEGE FUND SCHOLARSHIP

Four-year renewable scholarship for Hispanic students. Must have graduated from a North Carolina high school within the past 2 years, have a four-year cumulative GPA of 2.5, and be accepted into a two- or four-year college or university. Preference is given to full-time students but part-time students may apply. Preference will be given to foreign-born applicants or native-born children of foreign-born parents. Applications are available online at http://www.thencshp.org/.

Award: Scholarship for use in freshman, sophomore, junior, or senior years; renewable. *Amount:* $500–$2500.

Eligibility Requirements: Applicant must be Hispanic; enrolled or expecting to enroll full- or part-time at a two-year or four-year institution or university and resident of North Carolina. Applicant must have 2.5 GPA or higher. Available to U.S. and non-U.S. citizens.

Application Requirements: Application form, application form may be submitted online (http://www.thencshp.org), transcript. *Deadline:* continuous.

Contact: Marco Zarate, President
North Carolina Society of Hispanic Professionals
8450 Chapel Hill Road, Suite 209
Cary, NC 27513
Phone: 919-467-8424
Fax: 919-469-1785
E-mail: mailbox@thencshp.org

NORTH DAKOTA UNIVERSITY SYSTEM
http://www.ndus.edu/

NORTH DAKOTA INDIAN SCHOLARSHIP PROGRAM

Award of $800 to $2000 per year to assist American Indian students who are North Dakota residents in obtaining a college education. Must have been accepted for admission at an institution of higher learning or state vocational education program within North Dakota. Based upon scholastic ability and unmet financial need. Minimum 2.0 GPA required.

Award: Scholarship for use in freshman, sophomore, junior, senior, graduate, or postgraduate years; renewable. *Number:* 175–230. *Amount:* $800–$2000.

Eligibility Requirements: Applicant must be American Indian/Alaska Native; enrolled or expecting to enroll full- or part-time at a two-year or four-year or technical institution or university; resident of North Dakota and studying in North Dakota. Available to U.S. citizens.

Application Requirements: Application form, financial need analysis, proof of tribal enrollment, budget, transcript. *Deadline:* July 15.

NORTHERN CHEYENNE TRIBAL EDUCATION DEPARTMENT
http://www.cheyennenation.com/education.html

HIGHER EDUCATION SCHOLARSHIP PROGRAM

Scholarships will be provided for enrolled Northern Cheyenne Tribal members who meet the requirements listed in the higher education guidelines. Must be U.S. citizen enrolled in a postsecondary institution. Minimum 2.0 GPA required.

Award: Scholarship for use in freshman, sophomore, junior, or senior years; renewable. *Number:* 72. *Amount:* $50–$6000.

Eligibility Requirements: Applicant must be American Indian/Alaska Native and enrolled or expecting to enroll full- or part-time at a two-year or four-year institution or university. Available to U.S. citizens.

Application Requirements: Application form, essay, financial need analysis, recommendations or references, test scores, transcript. *Deadline:* March 1.

Contact: Norma Bixby, Director
Phone: 406-477-6602
Fax: 406-477-8150
E-mail: norma@rangeweb.net

OCA
http://www.ocanational.org/

OCA-AXA ACHIEVEMENT SCHOLARSHIP

College achievement scholarship for Asian Pacific Americans entering their first year of college. For full-time study only. Must have an minimum GPA of 3.0.

Award: Scholarship for use in freshman year; not renewable. *Number:* 10. *Amount:* $2000.

Eligibility Requirements: Applicant must be Asian/Pacific Islander; high school student and planning to enroll or expecting to enroll full-time at a two-year or four-year institution or university. Applicant must have 3.0 GPA or higher. Available to U.S. citizens.

Application Requirements: Application form, application form may be submitted online (http://www.ocanational.org), essay, financial need analysis, self-addressed stamped envelope with application, transcript. *Deadline:* April 18.

Contact: Jeffrey Moy, Scholarship Coordinator
OCA
1322 18th Street, NW
Washington, DC 20036
Phone: 202-223-5500 Ext. 116
Fax: 202-296-0540
E-mail: jmoy@ocanational.org

OCA/UPS FOUNDATION GOLD MOUNTAIN SCHOLARSHIP

Scholarships for Asian Pacific Americans who are the first person in their immediate family to attend college. Must be entering first year of college in the upcoming fall. Please see website, http://www.ocanational.org for more information.

Award: Scholarship for use in freshman year; not renewable. *Number:* 10–15. *Amount:* $2000–$2000.

Eligibility Requirements: Applicant must be Asian/Pacific Islander; high school student and planning to enroll or expecting to enroll full-time at a two-year or four-year institution or university. Applicant must have 3.0 GPA or higher. Available to U.S. citizens.

Application Requirements: Application form, application form may be submitted online (http://www.ocanational.org), essay, financial need analysis, resume, self-addressed stamped envelope with application, transcript. *Deadline:* April 18.

Contact: Jeffrey Moy, Scholarship Coordinator
OCA
1322 18th Street, NW
Washington, DC 20036
Phone: 202-223-5500
Fax: 202-296-0540
E-mail: oca@ocanational.org

OCA-VERIZON COLLEGE SCHOLARSHIP

Up to $3000 award for students who are Asian/Pacific Islanders having a minimum 3.0 GPA. For more information, see the OCA website at http://www.ocanational.org.

Award: Scholarship for use in sophomore, junior, or senior years; not renewable. *Number:* 15. *Amount:* up to $2000.

Eligibility Requirements: Applicant must be Asian/Pacific Islander and enrolled or expecting to enroll full-time at a two-year or four-year institution or university. Applicant must have 3.0 GPA or higher. Available to U.S. citizens.

Application Requirements: Application form, essay, financial need analysis, self-addressed stamped envelope with application, transcript. *Deadline:* April 18.

Contact: Jeffrey Moy, Scholarship Coordinator
OCA
1322 18th Street, NW
Washington, DC 20036
Phone: 202-223-5500 Ext. 116
E-mail: jmoy@ocanational.org

OFFICE OF NAVAJO NATION SCHOLARSHIP AND FINANCIAL ASSISTANCE
http://www.onnsfa.org/

CHIEF MANUELITO SCHOLARSHIP PROGRAM

Award programs established to recognize and award undergraduate students with high test scores and GPA of 3.0. Priorities to Navajo Nation applicants. Must be enrolled as a full-time undergraduate and pursue a degree program leading to a baccalaureate. For further details visit website http://www.onnsfa.org/docs/polproc.pdf.

Award: Scholarship for use in freshman, sophomore, junior, or senior years; not renewable. *Number:* 1. *Amount:* $7000.

Eligibility Requirements: Applicant must be American Indian/Alaska Native and enrolled or expecting to enroll full-time at a two-year or four-year institution or university. Applicant must have 3.0 GPA or higher. Available to U.S. citizens.

Application Requirements: Application form, financial need analysis, test scores, transcript. *Deadline:* April 1.

Contact: Maxine Damon, Financial Aid Counselor
Phone: 800-243-2956
Fax: 928-871-6561
E-mail: maxinedamon@navajo.org

ONEIDA TRIBE OF INDIANS OF WISCONSIN

http://www.oneidanation.org/highered

ONEIDA HIGHER EDUCATION GRANT PROGRAM

Renewable award available to enrolled members of the Oneida Tribe of Indians of Wisconsin, who are accepted into an accredited postsecondary institution within the United States. Must have a high school diploma, HSED or GED.

Award: Grant for use in freshman, sophomore, junior, senior, graduate, or postgraduate years; renewable. *Number:* up to 1300. *Amount:* up to $20,000.

Eligibility Requirements: Applicant must be American Indian/Alaska Native and enrolled or expecting to enroll full- or part-time at a two-year or four-year or technical institution or university. Available to U.S. citizens.

Application Requirements: Application form, financial need analysis, Oneida tribal enrollment. *Deadline:* April 15.

OREGON NATIVE AMERICAN CHAMBER OF COMMERCE SCHOLARSHIP

http://www.onacc.org/

OREGON NATIVE AMERICAN CHAMBER OF COMMERCE SCHOLARSHIP

Scholarships available to Native American students studying in Oregon. Must verify Native American status and be actively involved in the Native American community.

Award: Scholarship for use in freshman, sophomore, junior, or senior years; not renewable. *Number:* 1. *Amount:* $1000.

Eligibility Requirements: Applicant must be American Indian/Alaska Native; enrolled or expecting to enroll full- or part-time at a four-year institution or university and studying in Oregon. Available to U.S. and Canadian citizens.

Application Requirements: Application form, proof of Native American descent, transcript. *Deadline:* varies.

Contact: Kelly Anne Ilagan, Secretary
Phone: 503-654-2138
E-mail: kellyanne@onacc.org

OSAGE TRIBAL EDUCATION COMMITTEE

http://www.osagetribe.com/education/

OSAGE TRIBAL EDUCATION COMMITTEE SCHOLARSHIP

Available for Osage Tribal members only. 150 to 250 renewable scholarship awards. Spring deadline is December 31; fall deadline is July 1; summer deadline is May 1.

Award: Scholarship for use in freshman, sophomore, junior, or senior years; renewable. *Number:* 150–250. *Amount:* $200.

Eligibility Requirements: Applicant must be American Indian/Alaska Native and enrolled or expecting to enroll full- or part-time at a two-year or four-year or technical institution or university. Applicant must have 2.5 GPA or higher. Available to U.S. and non-U.S. citizens.

Application Requirements: Application form, essay, personal photograph, recommendations or references, transcript. *Deadline:* varies.

Contact: Cheryl Lewis, Business Manager
Osage Tribal Education Committee
4149 Highline Boulevard, Suite 380
Oklahoma City, OK 73108
Phone: 405-605-6051 Ext. 304
Fax: 405-605-6057

OSAGE TRIBAL EDUCATION DEPARTMENT

http://www.osagetribe.com/education

OSAGE HIGHER EDUCATION SCHOLARSHIP

Award available only to those who have proof of Osage Indian descent. Must submit proof of financial need. Deadlines: July 1 for fall, December 31 for spring, May 1 for summer.

Award: Scholarship for use in freshman, sophomore, junior, senior, graduate, or postgraduate years; renewable. *Number:* up to 1000. *Amount:* $1200–$2100.

Eligibility Requirements: Applicant must be American Indian/Alaska Native and enrolled or expecting to enroll full- or part-time at a two-year or four-year institution or university. Available to U.S. citizens.

Application Requirements: Application form, financial need analysis, transcript, verification of enrollment, Osage Indian descent proof, copy of CDIB card, copy of membership card. *Deadline:* varies.

Contact: Jennifer Holding, Scholarship Coordinator
Phone: 800-390-6724
Fax: 918-287-5567
E-mail: jholding@osagetribe.org

PETER AND ALICE KOOMRUIAN FUND

PETER AND ALICE KOOMRUIAN ARMENIAN EDUCATION FUND

Award for students of Armenian descent to pursue postsecondary studies in any field at any accredited college or university in the U.S. Submit student identification and letter of enrollment. Must rank in upper third of class or have minimum GPA of 3.0.

Award: Scholarship for use in freshman, sophomore, junior, senior, or graduate years; not renewable. *Number:* 4–20. *Amount:* $1000–$2300.

Eligibility Requirements: Applicant must be of Armenian heritage and enrolled or expecting to enroll full-time at a two-year or four-year institution or university. Applicant must have 3.0 GPA or higher. Available to U.S. and non-U.S. citizens.

Application Requirements: Application form, personal photograph, recommendations or references, school ID, current enrollment letter, self-addressed stamped envelope with application, transcript. *Deadline:* April 15.

Contact: Mr. Terenik Koujakian, Awards Committee Member
Peter and Alice Koomruian Fund
15915 Ventura Boulevard, Suite 201
Encino, CA 91436
Phone: 818-990-7454
Fax: 818-990-7466
E-mail: terenikkoujakian@hotmail.com

PETER DOCTOR MEMORIAL INDIAN SCHOLARSHIP FOUNDATION INC.

PETER DOCTOR MEMORIAL IROQUOIS SCHOLARSHIP

One-time award available to enrolled New York state Iroquois Indian students. Must be a full-time student at the sophomore level or above.

Award: Scholarship for use in sophomore, junior, senior, or graduate years; not renewable. *Number:* 1–2. *Amount:* $700–$1500.

Eligibility Requirements: Applicant must be American Indian/Alaska Native; enrolled or expecting to enroll full-time at a two-year or four-year or technical institution or university and resident of New York. Available to U.S. citizens.

Application Requirements: Application form, driver's license, financial need analysis, recommendations or references, tribal certification. *Deadline:* May 31.

Contact: Clara Hill, Treasurer
Peter Doctor Memorial Indian Scholarship Foundation Inc.
PO Box 431
Basom, NY 14013
Phone: 716-542-2025
E-mail: ceh3936@hughes.net

PHILIPINO-AMERICAN ASSOCIATION OF NEW ENGLAND

http://www.pamas.org/

BLESSED LEON OF OUR LADY OF THE ROSARY AWARD

Award for any Filipino-American high school student. Must be of Filipino descent, and have a minimum GPA of 3.3. Application details are available at http://www.pamas.org.

Award: Scholarship for use in freshman year; not renewable. *Number:* 1. *Amount:* $250.

Eligibility Requirements: Applicant must be Asian/Pacific Islander; high school student; planning to enroll or expecting to enroll full-time at a two-year or four-year or technical institution or university and resident of Connecticut, Maine, Massachusetts, New Hampshire, Rhode Island, Vermont. Available to U.S. citizens.

Application Requirements: Application form, college acceptance letter, essay, recommendations or references, transcript. *Deadline:* May 31.

Contact: Amanda Kalb, First Vice President
    Phone: 617-471-3513
    E-mail: balic2ss@comcast.net

PAMAS RESTRICTED SCHOLARSHIP AWARD

• *See page 533*

RAVENSCROFT FAMILY AWARD

Award for any Filipino-American high school student, who is active in the Filipino community. Must be of Filipino descent, a resident of New England, and have a minimum GPA of 3.3. Application details are available at http://www.pamas.org.

Award: Scholarship for use in freshman year; not renewable. *Number:* 1. *Amount:* $250.

Eligibility Requirements: Applicant must be Asian/Pacific Islander; high school student; planning to enroll or expecting to enroll full-time at a four-year institution or university and resident of Connecticut, Maine, Massachusetts, New Hampshire, Rhode Island, Vermont. Available to U.S. citizens.

Application Requirements: Application form, college acceptance letter, essay, recommendations or references, transcript. *Deadline:* May 31.

Contact: Amanda Kalb, First Vice President
    Phone: 617-471-3513
    E-mail: balic2ss@comcast.net

POLISH HERITAGE ASSOCIATION OF MARYLAND

http://www.pha-md.org/

POLISH HERITAGE SCHOLARSHIP

$2500 scholarships given to individuals of Polish descent (at least two Polish grandparents) who demonstrates academic excellence, financial need, and promotes their Polish Heritage. Must be a legal Maryland resident.

Award: Scholarship for use in freshman, sophomore, junior, or senior years; not renewable. *Number:* 1–9. *Amount:* $1500–$2500.

Eligibility Requirements: Applicant must be of Polish heritage; enrolled or expecting to enroll full-time at a two-year or four-year institution or university and resident of Maryland. Available to U.S. citizens.

Application Requirements: Application form, essay, financial need analysis, interview, recommendations or references, transcript. *Deadline:* March 15.

Contact: Thomas Hollowak, Scholarship Chair
    Phone: 410-837-4268
    E-mail: thollowalk@ubmail.ubalt.edu

POLISH WOMEN'S ALLIANCE

http://www.pwaa.org/

POLISH WOMEN'S ALLIANCE SCHOLARSHIP

Scholarships are given to members of the Polish Women's Alliance of America who have been in good standing for five years. Awards are given for the sophomore, junior, and senior year level of undergraduate study. For details visit website, http://www.pwaa.org.

Award: Scholarship for use in sophomore, junior, or senior years; renewable. *Number:* 5. *Amount:* $1000.

Eligibility Requirements: Applicant must be of Polish heritage and enrolled or expecting to enroll full-time at a four-year institution or university. Available to U.S. citizens.

Application Requirements: Application form, essay, personal photograph, transcript. *Deadline:* May 15.

Contact: Sharon Zago, Vice President and Scholarship Chairman
    Phone: 847-384-1208
    E-mail: vpres@pwaa.org

PORTUGUESE FOUNDATION INC.

http://www.pfict.org/

PORTUGUESE FOUNDATION SCHOLARSHIP PROGRAM

Scholarships of $4000 to four deserving students. Student must be of Portuguese ancestry, resident of Connecticut, U.S. citizen or a permanent resident, applying for, or currently in college, full-time student in an undergraduate degree conferring program or a part-time student in a master's or doctorate program.

Award: Scholarship for use in freshman, sophomore, junior, senior, or graduate years; not renewable. *Number:* 4. *Amount:* $4000.

Eligibility Requirements: Applicant must be of Portuguese heritage; enrolled or expecting to enroll full- or part-time at a four-year institution or university and resident of Connecticut. Applicant must have 2.5 GPA or higher. Available to U.S. citizens.

Application Requirements: Application form, essay, FAFSA, copy of recent federal income tax return, financial need analysis, recommendations or references, test scores, transcript. *Deadline:* March 15.

Contact: John Bairos, President
    Phone: 860-614-8614
    E-mail: info@pfict.org

PRESBYTERIAN CHURCH (USA)

http://www.pcusa.org/financialaid

NATIVE AMERICAN EDUCATION GRANTS

Award to assist members of any tribe with their education. First degree students only. Preference for Presbyterian Church (U.S.A.) members who are also awarded a supplemental grant and invited to participate in discernment of vocation dialog through a series of essay prompts and online events to promote a deeper understanding Christian vocation.

Award: Grant for use in freshman, sophomore, junior, or senior years; not renewable. *Number:* 10–30. *Amount:* $500–$1500.

Eligibility Requirements: Applicant must be American Indian/Alaska Native and enrolled or expecting to enroll full-time at a two-year or four-year or technical institution or university. Applicant must have 2.5 GPA or higher. Available to U.S. citizens.

Application Requirements: Application form, essay, financial need analysis, transcript, tribal membership. *Deadline:* June 15.

Contact: Ms. Laura Bryan, Associate
    Presbyterian Church (USA)
    100 Witherspoon Street
    Louisville, KY 40202-1396
    Phone: 502-569-5224
    Fax: 502-569-8766
    E-mail: finaid@pcusa.org

PUEBLO OF ISLETA, DEPARTMENT OF EDUCATION

http://www.isletapueblo.com/

HIGHER EDUCATION SUPPLEMENTAL SCHOLARSHIP ISLETA PUEBLO HIGHER EDUCATION DEPARTMENT
• See page 534

PUEBLO OF SAN JUAN, DEPARTMENT OF EDUCATION

http://www.sanjuaned.org/

OHKAY OWINGEH TRIBAL SCHOLARSHIP OF THE PUEBLO OF SAN JUAN
• See page 563

POP'AY SCHOLARSHIP
• See page 563

ROMAN CATHOLIC DIOCESE OF TULSA

http://www.dioceseoftulsa.org/

MAE LASSLEY OSAGE SCHOLARSHIP
This scholarship fund gives the Catholic Church an opportunity to continue it's educational work with the Osage Tribe.
Award: Scholarship for use in freshman, sophomore, junior, or senior years; renewable. *Amount:* $500–$1000.
Eligibility Requirements: Applicant must be Roman Catholic; American Indian/Alaska Native and enrolled or expecting to enroll full-time at a two-year or four-year institution or university. Applicant must have 2.5 GPA or higher. Available to U.S. citizens.
Application Requirements: Application form, copy of CDIB card or Osage Tribal Membership card, financial need analysis, recommendations or references, transcript. *Deadline:* April 15.
Contact: Mrs. Sarah Jameson, Assistant Director, Youth, Young Adult
and Campus Ministry
Roman Catholic Diocese of Tulsa
Roman Catholic Diocese of Tulsa, PO Box 690240
Tulsa, OK 74169-0240
Phone: 918-307-4939
Fax: 918-294-0920
E-mail: sarah.jameson@dioceseoftulsa.org

RON BROWN SCHOLAR FUND

http://www.ronbrown.org/

RON BROWN SCHOLAR PROGRAM
The program seeks to identify African-American high school seniors who will make significant contributions to the society. Applicants must excel academically, show exceptional leadership potential, participate in community service activities, and demonstrate financial need. Must be a U.S. citizen or hold permanent resident visa. Must plan to attend a four-year college or university. Deadlines: November 1 and January 9.
Award: Scholarship for use in freshman, sophomore, junior, or senior years; renewable. *Number:* 10–20. *Amount:* $10,000–$40,000.
Eligibility Requirements: Applicant must be Black (non-Hispanic); high school student; planning to enroll or expecting to enroll full-time at a four-year institution or university and must have an interest in leadership. Available to U.S. citizens.
Application Requirements: Application form, community service, essay, financial need analysis, interview, personal photograph, recommendations or references, test scores, transcript.
Contact: Ms. Vanessa Evans, Associate Director
Ron Brown Scholar Fund
1160 Pepsi Place, Suite 206
Charlottesville, VA 22901
Phone: 434-964-1588
Fax: 434-964-1589
E-mail: info@ronbrown.org

RYU FAMILY FOUNDATION, INC.

http://www.seolbong.org/

SEOL BONG SCHOLARSHIP
• See page 577

SAINT ANDREW'S SOCIETY OF THE STATE OF NEW YORK

http://www.standrewsny.org/

ST. ANDREWS SCHOLARSHIP
Scholarship for senior undergraduate students who will obtain a bachelor's degree from an accredited college or university in the spring and can demonstrate the significance of studying in Scotland. Proof of application to their selected school will be required for finalists. Applicant must be of Scottish descent.
Award: Scholarship for use in senior year; not renewable. *Number:* 2. *Amount:* $20,000–$30,000.
Eligibility Requirements: Applicant must be of Scottish heritage and enrolled or expecting to enroll full-time at a four-year institution or university. Applicant must have 2.5 GPA or higher. Available to U.S. citizens.
Application Requirements: Application form. *Deadline:* December 15.
Contact: Samuel Abernethy, President
Phone: 212-223-4248
Fax: 212-223-0748
E-mail: office@standrewsny.org

ST. ANDREW'S SOCIETY OF WASHINGTON, DC

http://www.saintandrewsociety.org/

DONALD MALCOLM MACARTHUR SCHOLARSHIP
One-time award is available for U.S. students to study in Scotland or students from Scotland to study in the United States. Special attention will be given to applicants whose work would demonstrably contribute to enhanced knowledge of Scottish history or culture. Must be a college junior, senior, or graduate student to apply. Need for financial assistance and academic record considered. Visit website for details and application http://www.thecapitalscot.com/standrew/scholarships.html.
Award: Scholarship for use in junior, senior, or graduate years; not renewable. *Number:* 1. *Amount:* up to $2500.
Eligibility Requirements: Applicant must be of Scottish heritage; enrolled or expecting to enroll full-time at a four-year institution or university and resident of Delaware, District of Columbia, Maryland, New Jersey, North Carolina, Pennsylvania, Virginia, Wisconsin. Available to U.S. and non-U.S. citizens.
Application Requirements: Application form, essay, financial need analysis, interview, recommendations or references, self-addressed stamped envelope with application. *Deadline:* April 30.
Contact: T.J. Holland, Chairman, Scholarship Committee
St. Andrew's Society of Washington, DC
1443 Laurel Hill Road
Vienna, VA 22182-1711
E-mail: tjholland@wmalumni.com

SALVADORAN AMERICAN LEADERSHIP AND EDUCATIONAL FUND

http://www.salef.org/

FULFILLING OUR DREAMS SCHOLARSHIP FUND
Up to 60 scholarships ranging from $500 to $2500 will be awarded to students who come from a Latino heritage. Must have a 2.5 GPA. See website for more details http://www.salef.org.
Award: Scholarship for use in freshman, sophomore, junior, senior, graduate, or postgraduate years; not renewable. *Number:* 50–60. *Amount:* $500–$2500.

Eligibility Requirements: Applicant must be of Hispanic, Latin American/Caribbean heritage; enrolled or expecting to enroll full- or part-time at a two-year or four-year institution or university; resident of California and studying in California. Applicant must have 2.5 GPA or higher. Available to U.S. and non-U.S. citizens.

Application Requirements: Application form, community service, essay, financial need analysis, interview, personal photograph, recommendations or references, resume, self-addressed stamped envelope with application, test scores, transcript. *Deadline:* June 30.

Contact: Mayra Soriano, Educational and Youth Programs Manager
Salvadoran American Leadership and Educational Fund
1625 West Olympic Boulevard, Suite 718
Los Angeles, CA 90015
Phone: 213-480-1052
Fax: 213-487-2530
E-mail: msoriano@salef.org

SANTO DOMINGO SCHOLARSHIP PROGRAM

SANTO DOMINGO SCHOLARSHIP

An organization instituted for the welfare of the Santo Domingo Pueblo enrolled members. Santo Domingo Tribe—Education Office offers scholarships in Higher Education and Adult Education. To be considered an applicant, you must fill out an application. Deadlines: Fall semester—March 1 and Spring semester—October 1.

Award: Scholarship for use in freshman, sophomore, junior, or senior years; renewable. *Amount:* $200–$1000.

Eligibility Requirements: Applicant must be American Indian/Alaska Native and enrolled or expecting to enroll full- or part-time at a two-year or four-year or technical institution or university. Applicant must have 2.5 GPA or higher. Available to U.S. citizens.

Application Requirements: Application form, certificate of Indian blood, financial need analysis, recommendations or references, transcript. *Deadline:* varies.

Contact: Rita Lujan, Education Director
Santo Domingo Scholarship Program
PO Box 160
Santo Domingo Pueblo, NM 87052
Phone: 505-465-2214 Ext. 2211
Fax: 505-465-2542
E-mail: rlujan@kewa-nsn.us

SENECA NATION OF INDIANS
http://www.sni.org/

SENECA NATION HIGHER EDUCATION PROGRAM

Renewable award for enrolled Senecas of the Cattaraugus and Allegheny Indian reservations who are in need of financial assistance. Application deadlines: July 1 for fall; December 1 for spring; May 1 for summer. Must be degree seeking and enrolled in a two-year college, four-year college or university. Must have GPA of 2.0.

Award: Scholarship for use in freshman, sophomore, junior, senior, graduate, or postgraduate years; renewable. *Amount:* $6000–$11,000.

Eligibility Requirements: Applicant must be American Indian/Alaska Native and enrolled or expecting to enroll full- or part-time at a two-year or four-year institution or university. Available to U.S. citizens.

Application Requirements: Application form, essay, financial need analysis, recommendations or references, transcript, tribal certification. *Deadline:* varies.

Contact: Debra Hoag, Higher Education Coordinator
Phone: 716-945-1790 Ext. 3103
E-mail: dhoag@sni.org

SONS OF ITALY FOUNDATION
http://www.osia.org/

SONS OF ITALY FOUNDATION'S NATIONAL LEADERSHIP GRANT COMPETITION

Scholarships for undergraduate or graduate students who are U.S. citizens of Italian descent. Must demonstrate academic excellence. For more details see website, http://www.osia.org.

Award: Scholarship for use in freshman, sophomore, junior, senior, or graduate years; not renewable. *Number:* 8–14. *Amount:* $4000–$25,000.

Eligibility Requirements: Applicant must be of Italian heritage and enrolled or expecting to enroll full-time at a four-year institution or university. Available to U.S. citizens.

Application Requirements: Application form, community service, essay, recommendations or references, resume, self-addressed stamped envelope with application, test scores, transcript. *Fee:* $30. *Deadline:* February 27.

SONS OF ITALY NATIONAL LEADERSHIP GRANTS COMPETITION HENRY SALVATORI SCHOLARSHIPS

Scholarships for college-bound high school seniors who demonstrate exceptional leadership, distinguished scholarship, and a deep understanding and respect for the principles upon which our nation was founded: liberty, freedom, and equality. Must be a U.S. citizen of Italian descent. For more details see website http://www.osia.org.

Award: Scholarship for use in freshman year; not renewable. *Number:* up to 1. *Amount:* up to $5000.

Eligibility Requirements: Applicant must be of Italian heritage; high school student and planning to enroll or expecting to enroll full-time at a four-year institution or university. Available to U.S. citizens.

Application Requirements: Application form, community service, essay, recommendations or references, resume, self-addressed stamped envelope with application, test scores, transcript. *Fee:* $30. *Deadline:* February 27.

STEVEN KNEZEVICH TRUST

STEVEN KNEZEVICH GRANT

One-time grant for students of Serbian descent. Award not restricted to citizens of the United States. Amount of award varies. Applicants must be attending an accredited institution of higher learning. Grant will be applied toward student's spring semester. To receive additional information and the application itself, applicant must send SASE, along with proof of Serbian descent.

Award: Grant for use in freshman, sophomore, junior, senior, or graduate years; not renewable.

Eligibility Requirements: Applicant must be of Croatian/Serbian heritage and enrolled or expecting to enroll full- or part-time at a two-year or four-year or technical institution or university. Available to U.S. and non-U.S. citizens.

Application Requirements: Application form, proof of Serbian heritage, self-addressed stamped envelope with application, transcript. *Deadline:* November 30.

STRAIGHTFORWARD MEDIA
http://www.straightforwardmedia.com/

STRAIGHTFORWARD MEDIA MINORITY SCHOLARSHIP

Four scholarships a year offered to students who are members of racial or ethnic minority groups and who are currently enrolled in or planning to enroll in postsecondary education. For more information, see website at http://www.straightforwardmedia.com/minority/form.php.

Award: Scholarship for use in freshman, sophomore, junior, or senior years; not renewable. *Number:* 4. *Amount:* $500.

Eligibility Requirements: Applicant must be American Indian/Alaska Native, Asian/Pacific Islander, Black (non-Hispanic), Hispanic and enrolled or expecting to enroll full- or part-time at a two-year or four-year or technical institution or university. Available to U.S. and non-U.S. citizens.

Application Requirements: Essay. *Deadline:* varies.

SWISS BENEVOLENT SOCIETY OF CHICAGO

http://www.sbschicago.org/

SWISS BENEVOLENT SOCIETY OF CHICAGO SCHOLARSHIPS

Scholarship for undergraduate college students of Swiss descent, having permanent residence in Illinois or Southern Wisconsin. Must have 3.3 GPA. High school students need a 26 on ACT or 1050 on SAT.

Award: Scholarship for use in freshman, sophomore, junior, or senior years; renewable. *Number:* 30. *Amount:* $750–$2500.

Eligibility Requirements: Applicant must be of Swiss heritage; enrolled or expecting to enroll full-time at a four-year institution or university and resident of Illinois, Wisconsin. Available to U.S. citizens.

Application Requirements: Application form, essay, self-addressed stamped envelope with application, test scores, transcript. *Deadline:* April 1.

Contact: Franziska Lys, Chair
　　　　Swiss Benevolent Society of Chicago
　　　　PO Box 2137
　　　　Chicago, IL 60690-2137
　　　　Phone: 847-491-8298
　　　　E-mail: education@sbschicago.org

SWISS BENEVOLENT SOCIETY OF NEW YORK

http://www.sbsny.org/

MEDICUS STUDENT EXCHANGE

One-time award to students of Swiss nationality or parentage. Open to U.S. residents for study in Switzerland and to Swiss residents for study in the U.S. Must be proficient in foreign language of instruction.

Award: Grant for use in junior, senior, or graduate years; not renewable. *Number:* 1–10. *Amount:* $2000–$10,000.

Eligibility Requirements: Applicant must be of Swiss heritage; enrolled or expecting to enroll full-time at a four-year institution or university and must have an interest in foreign language. Applicant must have 3.5 GPA or higher. Available to U.S. and non-Canadian citizens.

Application Requirements: Application form, recommendations or references, test scores, transcript. *Deadline:* March 31.

PELLEGRINI SCHOLARSHIP GRANTS

Award to students who have a minimum 3.0 GPA and show financial need. Must submit proof of Swiss nationality or descent. Must be a permanent resident of Connecticut, Delaware, New Jersey, New York, or Pennsylvania.

Award: Scholarship for use in freshman, sophomore, junior, senior, or graduate years; renewable. *Number:* 50. *Amount:* $500–$5000.

Eligibility Requirements: Applicant must be of Swiss heritage; enrolled or expecting to enroll full-time at a two-year or four-year or technical institution or university and resident of Connecticut, Delaware, New Jersey, New York, Pennsylvania. Applicant must have 3.0 GPA or higher. Available to U.S. citizens.

Application Requirements: Application form, copies of tax return, financial need analysis, recommendations or references, test scores, transcript. *Deadline:* March 31.

SYNOD OF THE COVENANT

http://www.synodofthecovenant.org/

RACIAL ETHNIC SCHOLARSHIP

• *See page 564*

TERRY FOX HUMANITARIAN AWARD PROGRAM

http://www.terryfox.org/

TERRY FOX HUMANITARIAN AWARD

• *See page 564*

TEXAS BLACK BAPTIST SCHOLARSHIP COMMITTEE

TEXAS BLACK BAPTIST SCHOLARSHIP

Renewable award for Texas residents attending a Baptist educational institution in Texas. Must be of African-American descent with a minimum 2.0 GPA. Must be a member in good standing of a Baptist church.

Award: Scholarship for use in freshman, sophomore, junior, or senior years; renewable. *Amount:* $1600.

Eligibility Requirements: Applicant must be Baptist; Black (non-Hispanic); enrolled or expecting to enroll full- or part-time at a two-year or four-year institution or university; resident of Texas and studying in Texas. Available to U.S. citizens.

Application Requirements: Application form, driver's license, financial need analysis, interview, personal photograph, portfolio, recommendations or references, resume, test scores, transcript. *Deadline:* continuous.

Contact: Charlie Singleton, Director
　　　　Phone: 214-828-5130
　　　　Fax: 214-828-5284
　　　　E-mail: charlie.singleton@bgct.org

TLICHO GOVERNMENT

http://www.tlicho.ca/

BHP BILLITON UNIVERSITY SCHOLARSHIPS

Award for undergraduate, master's or PhD degree students of Tlicho ancestry. Applicants should be a member of Tlicho Citizens. Must be enrolled full-time in a Canadian university degree program and be interested and active in community affairs. Scholarship value is $5000.

Award: Scholarship for use in junior, senior, graduate, or postgraduate years; not renewable. *Number:* 4. *Amount:* $5000.

Eligibility Requirements: Applicant must be Canadian citizen; American Indian/Alaska Native and enrolled or expecting to enroll full-time at an institution or university. Applicant must have 2.5 GPA or higher.

Application Requirements: Application form, Indian Status Card, acceptance letter, recommendations or references, transcript. *Deadline:* July 15.

Contact: Bertha Black, Career Development Coordinator
　　　　Tlicho Government
　　　　PO Box 412
　　　　Behchoko, NT X0E 0Y0
　　　　CAN
　　　　Phone: 867-392-6381 Ext. 211
　　　　E-mail: berthablack@tlicho.com

DIAVIK DIAMONDS INC. SCHOLARSHIPS FOR COLLEGE STUDENTS

Scholarship for students enrolled full-time in a Canadian college diploma program. Must be of Tlicho ancestry. Must be interested and active in community affairs. Applicants should be a member of Tilcho Citizens. Scholarship value is $3000.

Award: Scholarship for use in freshman, sophomore, junior, or senior years; not renewable. *Number:* 10. *Amount:* $3000.

Eligibility Requirements: Applicant must be Canadian citizen; American Indian/Alaska Native and enrolled or expecting to enroll full-time at a two-year or four-year or technical institution. Applicant must have 2.5 GPA or higher.

Application Requirements: Application form, essay, personal letter, acceptance letter, and Indian Status Card, recommendations or references, transcript. *Deadline:* July 15.

Contact: Bertha Black, Career Development Coordinator
　　　　Tlicho Government
　　　　PO Box 412
　　　　Behchoko, NT X0E 0Y0
　　　　CAN
　　　　Phone: 867-392-6381 Ext. 211
　　　　E-mail: berthablack@tlicho.com

TUSKEGEE AIRMEN SCHOLARSHIP FOUNDATION

http://www.taisf.org/

TUSKEGEE AIRMEN SCHOLARSHIP

Each year the Foundation grants scholarship awards to deserving young men and women. The number of available scholarship awards is directly related to income received from investments. The selection committee uses academic achievement, extra curricular and community activities, relative financial need, recommendations, and both essays to competitively rank applicants.

Award: Scholarship for use in freshman year; not renewable. *Number:* 40. *Amount:* $1500.

Eligibility Requirements: Applicant must be Black (non-Hispanic); high school student and planning to enroll or expecting to enroll at an institution or university. Applicant must have 3.0 GPA or higher. Available to U.S. citizens.

Application Requirements: *Deadline:* January 15.

UNICO FOUNDATION INC.

http://www.unico.org/

ALPHONSE A. MIELE SCHOLARSHIP

Scholarship available to a graduating high school senior of Italian heritage. Must reside and attend high school within the corporate limits or adjoining suburbs of a city wherein an active chapter of UNICO National is located. Application must be signed by student's guidance counselor and properly certified by sponsoring chapter president or scholarship chair. Must have letter of endorsement from the sponsoring chapter. This scholarship is valued at $6,000; paid out at $1,500 per year, over four years.

Award: Scholarship for use in freshman, sophomore, junior, or senior years; renewable. *Number:* 1. *Amount:* $1500.

Eligibility Requirements: Applicant must be of Italian heritage; high school student and planning to enroll or expecting to enroll full-time at a four-year institution or university. Applicant must have 3.0 GPA or higher. Available to U.S. citizens.

Application Requirements: Application form, essay, financial need analysis, recommendations or references, test scores, transcript. *Deadline:* April 15.

Contact: Joan Tidona, Scholarship Director
Phone: 973-808-0035
Fax: 973-808-0043
E-mail: uniconational@unico.org

MAJOR DON S. GENTILE SCHOLARSHIP

Scholarship available to a graduating high school senior of Italian heritage. Must reside and attend high school within the corporate limits or adjoining suburbs of a city wherein an active chapter of UNICO National is located. Application must be signed by student's guidance counselor and properly certified by sponsoring chapter president or scholarship chair. Must have letter of endorsement from the sponsoring chapter. This scholarship is valued at $6,000; paid out at $1,500 per year, over four years.

Award: Scholarship for use in freshman, sophomore, junior, or senior years; renewable. *Number:* 1. *Amount:* $1500.

Eligibility Requirements: Applicant must be of Italian heritage; high school student and planning to enroll or expecting to enroll full-time at a four-year institution or university. Applicant must have 3.0 GPA or higher. Available to U.S. citizens.

Application Requirements: Application form, essay, financial need analysis, recommendations or references, test scores, transcript. *Deadline:* April 15.

Contact: Joan Tidona, Scholarship Director
Phone: 973-808-0035
Fax: 973-808-0043
E-mail: uniconational@unico.org

THEODORE MAZZA SCHOLARSHIP

Scholarship available to a graduating high school senior of Italian heritage. Must reside and attend high school within the corporate limits or adjoining suburbs of a city wherein an active chapter of UNICO National is located. Application must be signed by student's guidance counselor and properly certified by sponsoring chapter president or scholarship chair. Must have letter of endorsement from the sponsoring chapter. This scholarship is valued at $6,000; paid out at $1,500 per year, over four years.

Award: Scholarship for use in freshman, sophomore, junior, or senior years; renewable. *Number:* 1. *Amount:* $1500.

Eligibility Requirements: Applicant must be of Italian heritage; high school student and planning to enroll or expecting to enroll full-time at a four-year institution or university. Applicant must have 3.0 GPA or higher. Available to U.S. citizens.

Application Requirements: Application form, essay, financial need analysis, recommendations or references, test scores, transcript. *Deadline:* April 15.

Contact: Joan Tidona, Scholarship Director
Phone: 973-808-0035
Fax: 973-808-0043
E-mail: uniconational@unico.org

WILLIAM C. DAVINI SCHOLARSHIP

Scholarship available to a graduating high school senior of Italian heritage. Must reside and attend high school within the corporate limits or adjoining suburbs of a city wherein an active chapter of UNICO National is located. Application must be signed by student's guidance counselor and properly certified by sponsoring chapter president or scholarship chair. Must have letter of endorsement from the sponsoring chapter. This scholarship is valued at $6,000; paid out at $1,500 per year, over four years.

Award: Scholarship for use in freshman, sophomore, junior, or senior years; renewable. *Number:* 1. *Amount:* $1500.

Eligibility Requirements: Applicant must be of Italian heritage; high school student and planning to enroll or expecting to enroll full-time at a four-year institution or university. Applicant must have 3.0 GPA or higher. Available to U.S. citizens.

Application Requirements: Application form, essay, financial need analysis, recommendations or references, test scores, transcript. *Deadline:* April 15.

Contact: Joan Tidona, Scholarship Director
Phone: 973-808-0035
Fax: 973-808-0043
E-mail: uniconational@unico.org

UNITED METHODIST CHURCH

http://www.gbhem.org/

UNITED METHODIST CHURCH ETHNIC SCHOLARSHIP

Awards for minority students pursuing undergraduate degree. Must have been certified members of the United Methodist Church for one year. Proof of membership and pastor's statement required. One-time award but applicant may re-apply each year. Minimum 2.5 GPA required.

Award: Scholarship for use in freshman, sophomore, junior, or senior years; not renewable.

Eligibility Requirements: Applicant must be Methodist; American Indian/Alaska Native, Asian/Pacific Islander, Black (non-Hispanic), Hispanic and enrolled or expecting to enroll full-time at a two-year or four-year institution or university. Applicant must have 2.5 GPA or higher. Available to U.S. citizens.

Application Requirements: Application form, essay, membership proof, pastor's statement, recommendations or references, transcript. *Deadline:* May 1.

Contact: Patti Zimmerman, Scholarships Administrator
United Methodist Church
PO Box 340007
Nashville, TN 37203-0007
Phone: 615-340-7344
E-mail: pzimmer@gbhem.org

UNITED METHODIST CHURCH HISPANIC, ASIAN, AND NATIVE AMERICAN SCHOLARSHIP

Award for members of United Methodist Church who are Hispanic, Asian, Native-American, or Pacific Islander college juniors, seniors, or graduate students. Proof of membership and pastor's letter required. Minimum 2.85 GPA.

Award: Scholarship for use in freshman, sophomore, junior, senior, or graduate years; not renewable.

Eligibility Requirements: Applicant must be Methodist; American Indian/Alaska Native, Asian/Pacific Islander, or Hispanic and enrolled or expecting to enroll full-time at a four-year institution or university. Available to U.S. citizens.

Application Requirements: Application form, essay, membership proof, pastor's letter, recommendations or references, transcript. *Deadline:* April 1.

Contact: Patti Zimmerman, Scholarships Administrator
United Methodist Church
PO Box 340007
Nashville, TN 37203-0007
Phone: 615-340-7344
E-mail: pzimmer@gbhem.org

UNITED METHODIST YOUTH ORGANIZATION

http://globalyoungpeople.org

RICHARD S. SMITH SCHOLARSHIP

Open to racial/ethnic minority youth only. Must be a United Methodist Youth who has been active in local church for at least one year prior to application. Must be a graduating senior in high school (who maintained at least a C average) entering the first year of undergraduate study and be pursuing a "church-related" career.

Award: Scholarship for use in freshman year; not renewable. *Number:* 1–5. *Amount:* $100–$2200.

Eligibility Requirements: Applicant must be Methodist; American Indian/Alaska Native, Asian/Pacific Islander, Black (non-Hispanic), Hispanic; high school student and planning to enroll or expecting to enroll full-time at a two-year or four-year or technical institution or university. Available to U.S. citizens.

Application Requirements: Application form, certification of church membership by pastor, essay, financial need analysis, recommendations or references, transcript. *Deadline:* March 4.

Contact: Kelsey Tinker, Grant and Scholarships Administrator
Phone: 615-340-7184
E-mail: youngpeople@gbod.org

UNITED NEGRO COLLEGE FUND

http://www.uncf.org/

ALASKA SCHOLARSHIP PROGRAM

5 renewable scholarships of up to $1000 for Alaska residents planning to enroll at UNCF schools. Minimum 2.5 GPA required.

Award: Scholarship for use in freshman, sophomore, junior, or senior years; renewable. *Number:* 5. *Amount:* up to $1000.

Eligibility Requirements: Applicant must be Black (non-Hispanic); high school student; planning to enroll or expecting to enroll full-time at a two-year or four-year or technical institution or university and resident of Alaska. Applicant must have 2.5 GPA or higher. Available to U.S. citizens.

Application Requirements: Application form. *Deadline:* April 12.

ALLEN AND JOAN BILDNER SCHOLARSHIP

Scholarship open to New Jersey residents attending a UNCF member college or university. Must have minimum 2.5 GPA. Prospective applicants should complete the Student Profile found at website, http://www.uncf.org.

Award: Scholarship for use in freshman, sophomore, junior, or senior years; not renewable. *Amount:* $2000–$2500.

Eligibility Requirements: Applicant must be Black (non-Hispanic); enrolled or expecting to enroll full- or part-time at a four-year institution or university and resident of New Jersey. Applicant must have 2.5 GPA or higher. Available to U.S. citizens.

Application Requirements: Application form. *Deadline:* continuous.

ANHEUSER-BUSCH LEGENDS OF THE CROWN SCHOLARSHIP PROGRAM

$5000 scholarship award to each select student leader entering their sophomore, junior, or senior year of study at a four year accredited Historically Black College or University. Minimum 3.0 GPA required. Finalists must be available to attend a one-of-a-kind leadership seminar and community service project with Anheuser-Busch senior leaders in St. Louis, MO.

Award: Scholarship for use in sophomore, junior, or senior years; not renewable. *Amount:* up to $5000.

Eligibility Requirements: Applicant must be Black (non-Hispanic); enrolled or expecting to enroll full-time at a four-year institution or university and must have an interest in leadership. Applicant must have 3.0 GPA or higher. Available to U.S. citizens.

Application Requirements: Application form, essay, recommendations or references, transcript. *Deadline:* May 31.

ARTHUR ROSS FOUNDATION SCHOLARSHIP

Up to $3000 scholarship for students attending UNCF member schools and residing in the 5 boroughs of New York City or Kentucky, Georgia, Florida, Alabama, South Carolina, Tennessee, Louisiana, Mississippi, or North Carolina. Minimum 2.5 GPA required.

Award: Scholarship for use in freshman year; not renewable. *Amount:* $1000–$3000.

Eligibility Requirements: Applicant must be Black (non-Hispanic) and enrolled or expecting to enroll full- or part-time at a four-year institution or university. Applicant must have 2.5 GPA or higher. Available to U.S. citizens.

Application Requirements: Application form. *Deadline:* continuous.

BRISTOL-MYERS SQUIBB SCHOLARSHIP

This scholarship is a last dollar award directed to New Jersey residents. Must attend college or university within New Jersey or at one of the UNCF member institutions. Minimum 2.5 GPA required.

Award: Scholarship for use in freshman year; not renewable. *Amount:* $500–$650.

Eligibility Requirements: Applicant must be Black (non-Hispanic); enrolled or expecting to enroll full- or part-time at a four-year institution or university and resident of New Jersey. Applicant must have 2.5 GPA or higher. Available to U.S. citizens.

Application Requirements: Application form. *Deadline:* continuous.

CAREER AGENCY COMPANIES SCHOLARSHIP

$5000 scholarship offered only to existing policyholders of one of the Career Agency Companies (The Reliable Life Insurance Company, Old Reliable Casualty Company, Capitol County Mutual, United Insurance Company of America, United Casualty, Union National Life Insurance Company and Union National Fire Insurance Company). Students must attend UNCF member colleges and universities or HBCU schools. Must have minimum 2.5 GPA and reside in one of 27 states.

Award: Scholarship for use in freshman year; not renewable. *Amount:* $5000.

Eligibility Requirements: Applicant must be Black (non-Hispanic) and enrolled or expecting to enroll full- or part-time at a four-year institution or university. Applicant must have 2.5 GPA or higher. Available to U.S. citizens.

Application Requirements: Application form. *Deadline:* continuous.

CARNIVAL & MIAMI HEAT SCHOLARSHIP PROGRAM

Scholarship for full-time undergraduate students attending UNCF colleges who have completed the Carnival or Miami HEAT School to Work Mentoring Program. Must have unmet financial need, a minimum 2.8 GPA, and be a U.S. citizen or permanent resident.

Award: Scholarship for use in freshman, sophomore, junior, or senior years; not renewable. *Amount:* up to $5000.

Eligibility Requirements: Applicant must be Black (non-Hispanic) and enrolled or expecting to enroll full-time at a two-year or four-year institution. Available to U.S. citizens.

Application Requirements: Application form, financial need analysis. *Deadline:* April 30.

CHARLES & ELLORA ALLIS FOUNDATION SCHOLARSHIP

Award of up to $3000 for Minnesota residents attending a UNCF college or university. May be used for any year of undergraduate study. Must have minimum 2.5 GPA.

Award: Scholarship for use in freshman, sophomore, junior, or senior years; not renewable. *Amount:* up to $3000.

Eligibility Requirements: Applicant must be Black (non-Hispanic); enrolled or expecting to enroll at a four-year institution and resident of

Minnesota. Applicant must have 2.5 GPA or higher. Available to U.S. citizens.

Application Requirements: Application form. *Deadline:* continuous.

CHICAGO PUBLIC SCHOOLS UNCF CAMPAIGN

Scholarship open to African American students who have attended Chicago public schools. Minimum 2.5 GPA required and must be accepted to a UNCF member college or university. The scholarship pays tuition and fees for four years; amount varies according to need. General scholarship application and additional information are at website http://www.uncf.org.

Award: Scholarship for use in freshman, sophomore, junior, or senior years; renewable. *Amount:* up to $10,000.

Eligibility Requirements: Applicant must be Black (non-Hispanic); enrolled or expecting to enroll full-time at a four-year institution or university and resident of Illinois. Applicant must have 2.5 GPA or higher. Available to U.S. citizens.

Application Requirements: Application form, FAFSA, Student Aid Report (SAR), financial need analysis. *Deadline:* continuous.

CITY OF CLEVELAND: MAYOR JACKSON SCHOLARSHIP FOR CLEVELAND METROPOLITAN SCHOOL DISTRICT

Scholarships awarded to African American residents of Cleveland, who are graduating seniors from a Cleveland Metropolitan School District high school with minimum GPA of 2.5. Must be accepted at any two- or four-year college or university. Apply online at website http://www.uncf.org.

Award: Scholarship for use in freshman year; not renewable. *Number:* 16. *Amount:* $2500.

Eligibility Requirements: Applicant must be Black (non-Hispanic); high school student; planning to enroll or expecting to enroll full-time at a four-year institution or university and resident of Ohio. Applicant must have 2.5 GPA or higher. Available to U.S. citizens.

Application Requirements: Application form, FAFSA, Student Aid Report (SAR), financial need analysis. *Deadline:* April 30.

CITY OF CLEVELAND: MAYOR JACKSON SCHOLARSHIP FOR HISTORICALLY BLACK COLLEGES AND UNIVERSITIES

Award available to graduating African American high school seniors in Ohio who have been accepted for enrollment at a four-year historically black college or university and have a minimum GPA of 2.5. Emphasis is placed on students with a high level of commitment to community service. For complete list of HBCU schools and to apply online, go to website http://www.uncf.org.

Award: Scholarship for use in freshman year; not renewable. *Amount:* up to $2500.

Eligibility Requirements: Applicant must be Black (non-Hispanic); high school student; planning to enroll or expecting to enroll full-time at a four-year institution or university and resident of Ohio. Applicant must have 2.5 GPA or higher. Available to U.S. citizens.

Application Requirements: Application form, community service. *Deadline:* April 29.

CLARENCE S. WRIGHT AND FLORENCE F. WRIGHT ENDOWED SCHOLARSHIP

Scholarships available to students attending historically black colleges and universities. Minimum 2.5 GPA required. Amount of scholarship varies based on need.

Award: Scholarship for use in freshman, sophomore, junior, or senior years; not renewable.

Eligibility Requirements: Applicant must be Black (non-Hispanic) and enrolled or expecting to enroll full-time at a four-year institution or university. Applicant must have 2.5 GPA or higher. Available to U.S. citizens.

Application Requirements: Application form, financial need analysis. *Deadline:* continuous.

DALLAS INDEPENDENT SCHOOL DISTRICT SCHOLARSHIP

Applicant must be a African American high school senior from the Dallas Independent School District with minimum GPA of 2.5. Must attend a UNCF member college/university or any other Historically Black College or University. Award based on financial need and academic potential. Apply online at http://www.uncf.org.

Award: Scholarship for use in freshman year; not renewable. *Amount:* up to $2500.

Eligibility Requirements: Applicant must be Black (non-Hispanic); high school student; planning to enroll or expecting to enroll full-time at a four-year institution or university and resident of Texas. Applicant must have 2.5 GPA or higher. Available to U.S. citizens.

Application Requirements: Application form, essay, FAFSA, financial need analysis. *Deadline:* April 25.

Contact: Dr. Kendall Beck, Scholarship Coordinator
United Negro College Fund
2538 South Ervay
Dallas, TX 75215
Phone: 972-925-4893

DAVENPORT FORTE PEDESTAL FUND

Scholarship of $10,000 available for African American students who graduated from the Detroit Public School system. Applicant must be a first semester freshman attending a UNCF member college or university. Must have a minimum of 2.7 GPA. For additional information and to complete general scholarship application, visit website: http://www.uncf.org.

Award: Scholarship for use in freshman or sophomore years; not renewable. *Number:* 1. *Amount:* $10,000.

Eligibility Requirements: Applicant must be Black (non-Hispanic); enrolled or expecting to enroll full-time at a four-year institution or university and resident of Michigan. Available to U.S. citizens.

Application Requirements: Application form, FAFSA, Student Aid Report (SAR), financial need analysis. *Deadline:* continuous.

DAVID GEFFEN FOUNDATION SCHOLARSHIP

$5000 scholarship for Los Angeles, CA residents attending UNCF member colleges and universities. Minimum 3.0 GPA required.

Award: Scholarship for use in freshman, sophomore, junior, or senior years; not renewable. *Amount:* $5000.

Eligibility Requirements: Applicant must be Black (non-Hispanic); enrolled or expecting to enroll full-time at a four-year institution or university and resident of California. Applicant must have 3.0 GPA or higher. Available to U.S. citizens.

Application Requirements: Application form. *Deadline:* continuous.

DEBORAH L. VINCENT FAHRO EDUCATION SCHOLARSHIP AWARD

Award for residents of federally assisted housing or a recipient of assistance through the Community Development Block Grant program in Florida. Must be a high school senior and meet income requirements as defined by HUD for public/assisted housing and Community Development Block Grant targeted area recipients. Must have a sponsor that is an active member of FAHRO as a housing authority/agency or community development agency that is willing to support travel expenses to attend Annual Convention awards banquet to receive scholarship if selected. Minimum 2.5 GPA required.

Award: Scholarship for use in freshman year; not renewable. *Amount:* $2500.

Eligibility Requirements: Applicant must be Black (non-Hispanic); high school student; planning to enroll or expecting to enroll full-time at a two-year or four-year institution and resident of Florida. Applicant must have 2.5 GPA or higher. Available to U.S. citizens.

Application Requirements: Application form. *Deadline:* May 31.

DOMINIQUE AND JACQUES CASIMIR SCHOLARSHIP

Scholarship is available for two male and two female African American undergraduate sophomores or juniors from the state of Texas. Minimum GPA of 2.5 is required. For additional information and a general scholarship application online, visit http://www.uncf.org.

Award: Scholarship for use in sophomore or junior years; renewable. *Number:* 4. *Amount:* $1500.

Eligibility Requirements: Applicant must be Black (non-Hispanic); enrolled or expecting to enroll full-time at a four-year institution or university and resident of Texas. Applicant must have 2.5 GPA or higher. Available to U.S. citizens.

Application Requirements: Application form, FAFSA, Student Aid Report (SAR), financial need analysis. *Deadline:* continuous.

DORIS AND JOHN CARPENTER SCHOLARSHIP

Award for undergraduate freshmen showing great financial need and attending UNCF member colleges and universities. Minimum 2.5 GPA required.

Award: Scholarship for use in freshman year; not renewable. *Amount:* $2000–$5000.

Eligibility Requirements: Applicant must be Black (non-Hispanic) and enrolled or expecting to enroll at a four-year institution. Applicant must have 2.5 GPA or higher. Available to U.S. citizens.

Application Requirements: Financial need analysis. *Deadline:* continuous.

DOROTHY N. MCNEAL SCHOLARSHIP

Award for students at UNCF member colleges and universities pursuing careers in community service. Minimum 2.5 GPA required. Scholarship value varies based on need.

Award: Scholarship for use in freshman, sophomore, junior, or senior years; not renewable.

Eligibility Requirements: Applicant must be Black (non-Hispanic) and enrolled or expecting to enroll full- or part-time at a four-year institution or university. Applicant must have 2.5 GPA or higher. Available to U.S. citizens.

Application Requirements: Application form. *Deadline:* continuous.

EDNA F. BLUM FOUNDATION SCHOLARSHIP

Scholarship available to students at UNCF member colleges and universities who are residents of New York. Minimum 2.5 GPA required.

Award: Scholarship for use in freshman year; not renewable. *Amount:* $1000–$3000.

Eligibility Requirements: Applicant must be Black (non-Hispanic); enrolled or expecting to enroll full- or part-time at a four-year institution or university and resident of New York. Applicant must have 2.5 GPA or higher. Available to U.S. citizens.

Application Requirements: Application form. *Deadline:* continuous.

EDWARD FITTERMAN FOUNDATION SCHOLARSHIP

Awards for Minnesota students attending UNCF member colleges and universities. Minimum 2.5 GPA required. For more information, please go to website at http://www.uncf.org/forstudents/scholarship.asp.

Award: Scholarship for use in freshman year; not renewable. *Amount:* up to $3000.

Eligibility Requirements: Applicant must be Black (non-Hispanic); enrolled or expecting to enroll full- or part-time at a four-year institution or university and resident of Minnesota. Applicant must have 2.5 GPA or higher. Available to U.S. citizens.

Application Requirements: Application form. *Deadline:* continuous.

ELAINE B. HANCOCK ENDOWED SCHOLARSHIP

Scholarship of up to $5000 for students at UNCF member institutions and Howard University. Must be juniors or seniors who have a minimum 3.0 GPA. Scholars will be selected based on the quality and responsiveness of their essay.

Award: Scholarship for use in junior or senior years; renewable. *Amount:* up to $5000.

Eligibility Requirements: Applicant must be Black (non-Hispanic) and enrolled or expecting to enroll full-time at an institution or university. Applicant must have 3.0 GPA or higher. Available to U.S. citizens.

Application Requirements: Application form, essay. *Deadline:* May 31.

ELMER ROE DEAVER FOUNDATION SCHOLARSHIP

$4000 scholarships available to students attending UNCF member colleges and universities who are residents of Pennsylvania, New Jersey, or Delaware. Minimum 2.5 GPA required.

Award: Scholarship for use in freshman year; not renewable. *Amount:* $4000.

Eligibility Requirements: Applicant must be Black (non-Hispanic); enrolled or expecting to enroll full- or part-time at a four-year institution or university and resident of Delaware, New Jersey, Pennsylvania. Applicant must have 2.5 GPA or higher. Available to U.S. citizens.

Application Requirements: Application form. *Deadline:* continuous.

ESSENCE SCHOLARS PROGRAM

$10,000 scholarship for African American women attending one of the UNCF member institutions, Hampton University, or Howard University. Must be undergraduate sophomore or junior. Minimum 3.0 GPA required.

Award: Scholarship for use in sophomore or junior years; not renewable. *Amount:* $10,000.

Eligibility Requirements: Applicant must be Black (non-Hispanic); enrolled or expecting to enroll full- or part-time at a four-year institution and female. Applicant must have 3.0 GPA or higher. Available to U.S. citizens.

Application Requirements: Application form. *Deadline:* continuous.

EVELYN LEVINA WRIGHT SCHOLARSHIP

Scholarship of $3500 is available to an African American resident of the Philadelphia, Pennsylvania; Wilmington, Delaware; or Camden, New Jersey, area who is enrolled at a UNCF member college or university. Must have a minimum GPA of 2.5. For information and general scholarship application, visit website http://www.uncf.org.

Award: Scholarship for use in freshman, sophomore, junior, or senior years; renewable. *Number:* 1. *Amount:* $3500.

Eligibility Requirements: Applicant must be Black (non-Hispanic); enrolled or expecting to enroll full- or part-time at a four-year institution or university and resident of Delaware, New Jersey, Pennsylvania. Applicant must have 2.5 GPA or higher. Available to U.S. citizens.

Application Requirements: Application form, FAFSA, financial need analysis. *Deadline:* continuous.

FEDERAL EXPRESS/UNCF SCHOLARSHIP INITIATIVE

Scholarship provides up to $4000 annually ($2000 per semester) to graduating high school seniors planning to enroll at an historically black college or university. Must be Pell Grant eligible and have a demonstrated financial need. Minimum 3.0 GPA required.

Award: Scholarship for use in freshman year; not renewable. *Amount:* up to $4000.

Eligibility Requirements: Applicant must be Black (non-Hispanic); high school student; planning to enroll or expecting to enroll full-time at a four-year institution or university and resident of Indiana. Applicant must have 3.0 GPA or higher. Available to U.S. citizens.

Application Requirements: Application form, essay, financial need analysis, proof of college enrollment, recommendations or references, transcript. *Deadline:* May 18.

FOOT LOCKER FOUNDATION, INC./UNCF SCHOLARSHIP

Scholarship for African American high school seniors or students attending or planning to attend a UNCF member college or university. Minimum GPA of 2.5 required. Officers and directors of the Foundation and of Foot Locker, Inc. and its affiliates and family members of these officers and directors are not eligible to apply.

Award: Scholarship for use in freshman, sophomore, junior, or senior years; not renewable. *Amount:* up to $5000.

Eligibility Requirements: Applicant must be Black (non-Hispanic) and enrolled or expecting to enroll full-time at a four-year institution or university. Applicant must have 2.5 GPA or higher. Available to U.S. citizens.

Application Requirements: Application form, financial need analysis, transcript. *Deadline:* April 24.

FORT WORTH INDEPENDENT SCHOOL DISTRICT SCHOLARSHIP

Scholarship awarded to graduating African American high school senior from the Fort Worth Independent School District. Applicants must be enrolled full-time at a UNCF member institution or Historically Black College or University (HBCU). Special consideration given to students who will be attending or attend a UNCF school in the state of Texas which include Paul Quinn College, Texas College, Jarvis Christian College, Wiley College, or Huston-Tillotson University. Scholarship award amount is up to $5000 and will be awarded to students who demonstrate financial need and academic potential.

Award: Scholarship for use in freshman, sophomore, junior, or senior years; not renewable. *Amount:* up to $5000.

Eligibility Requirements: Applicant must be Black (non-Hispanic); high school student; planning to enroll or expecting to enroll full- or part-time at a four-year institution or university and resident of Texas. Applicant must have 3.0 GPA or higher. Available to U.S. citizens.

Application Requirements: Application form, FAFSA, Student Aid Report (SAR), financial need analysis. *Deadline:* April 15.

GERALD W. & JEAN PURMAL ENDOWED SCHOLARSHIP

Awards of $1000-$4000 available to students attending UNCF member colleges and universities. Minimum 2.5 GPA required. For additional information, see website at http://www.uncf.org.

Award: Scholarship for use in freshman year; not renewable. *Amount:* $1000–$4000.

Eligibility Requirements: Applicant must be Black (non-Hispanic) and enrolled or expecting to enroll full- or part-time at a four-year institution or university. Applicant must have 2.5 GPA or higher. Available to U.S. citizens.

Application Requirements: Application form. *Deadline:* continuous.

HARRY PINKERTON SCHOLARSHIP

Award for students attending UNCF member colleges and universities who are residents of New York. Minimum 2.5 GPA required. For more information, see website at http://www.uncf.org.

Award: Scholarship for use in freshman year; not renewable.

Eligibility Requirements: Applicant must be Black (non-Hispanic); enrolled or expecting to enroll full- or part-time at a four-year institution or university and resident of New York. Applicant must have 2.5 GPA or higher. Available to U.S. citizens.

Application Requirements: Application form. *Deadline:* continuous.

IOWA STUDENT AID SCHOLARSHIP

Award for students attending UNCF member colleges and universities who are residents of Iowa. Minimum 2.5 GPA required. For more information, see website at http://www.uncf.org.

Award: Scholarship for use in freshman year; not renewable.

Eligibility Requirements: Applicant must be Black (non-Hispanic); enrolled or expecting to enroll full- or part-time at an institution or university and resident of Iowa. Applicant must have 2.5 GPA or higher. Available to U.S. citizens.

Application Requirements: Application form. *Deadline:* continuous.

JACK AND JILL OF AMERICA FOUNDATION SCHOLARSHIP

Scholarship available to any African-American high school senior. The applicant must become and maintain full-time status at an accredited, post secondary institution. Minimum 3.0 GPA required.

Award: Scholarship for use in freshman year; not renewable. *Amount:* $1500–$2500.

Eligibility Requirements: Applicant must be Black (non-Hispanic); high school student and planning to enroll or expecting to enroll full-time at a four-year institution or university. Applicant must have 3.0 GPA or higher. Available to U.S. citizens.

Application Requirements: Application form. *Deadline:* continuous.

JAY CHARLES LEVINE SCHOLARSHIP

$3,000 tuition scholarship and a $200 book scholarship for graduates of the 3 target high schools in the Detroit Public Schools System. Must be a resident of Detroit, Michigan with at least a 3.0 GPA on a 4.0 scale, a minimum SAT score of 800 out of 1600 (Critical Reading and Mathmatics) and must be admitted to a UNCF member school as a full-time student.

Award: Scholarship for use in freshman year; not renewable. *Amount:* up to $3200.

Eligibility Requirements: Applicant must be Black (non-Hispanic); high school student; planning to enroll or expecting to enroll full-time at a four-year institution or university and resident of Michigan. Applicant must have 3.0 GPA or higher. Available to U.S. citizens.

Application Requirements: Application form, recommendations or references. *Deadline:* May 31.

JOHN W. ANDERSON FOUNDATION SCHOLARSHIP

Need-based scholarship of up to $3000 for students from Indiana attending UNCF member colleges and universities. Minimum 2.5 GPA required. Prospective applicants should complete the Student Profile found at website. http://www.uncf.org.

Award: Scholarship for use in freshman, sophomore, junior, or senior years; not renewable. *Number:* 1. *Amount:* up to $3000.

Eligibility Requirements: Applicant must be Black (non-Hispanic); enrolled or expecting to enroll full- or part-time at a four-year institution or university and resident of Indiana. Applicant must have 2.5 GPA or higher. Available to U.S. citizens.

Application Requirements: Application form, financial need analysis. *Deadline:* continuous.

JOSEPH AND SYLVIA SLIFKA FOUNDATION SCHOLARSHIP

Four-year scholarship offering full tuition, room and board, fees, and books to entering freshman at a UNCF member institution. Must be US citizen, have a minimum 2.5 grade point average, and a demonstrated need. Scholarship amounts will vary depending on tuition.

Award: Scholarship for use in freshman, sophomore, junior, or senior years; renewable. *Amount:* up to $20,000.

Eligibility Requirements: Applicant must be Black (non-Hispanic); high school student and planning to enroll or expecting to enroll full-time at a four-year institution or university. Applicant must have 2.5 GPA or higher. Available to U.S. citizens.

Application Requirements: Application form, financial need analysis. *Deadline:* continuous.

JOSEPH A. TOWLES AFRICAN STUDY ABROAD SCHOLARSHIP

Scholarship enabling black Americans, conscious of their African descent, to have an opportunity to experience the richness of African cultures. Available to UNCF students who have been accepted into a study abroad program in Africa and have a minimum 3.0 GPA.

Award: Scholarship for use in sophomore or junior years; not renewable. *Amount:* up to $15,000.

Eligibility Requirements: Applicant must be Black (non-Hispanic) and enrolled or expecting to enroll full-time at a four-year institution or university. Applicant must have 3.0 GPA or higher. Available to U.S. citizens.

Application Requirements: Application form. *Deadline:* April 15.

JP MORGAN CHASE/JOHN F. MCGUILLICUDDY SCHOLARSHIP

Full tuition scholarship for graduating high school seniors entering a UNCF college/university as a full-time college freshman. Student must be resident of Missouri, California, Indiana, Arizona, New York, New Jersey, Connecticut, Illinois, Ohio, Kentucky, Wisconsin, Delaware, Michigan, Texas, Florida, Oklahoma, Colorado, Louisiana, Utah, or West Virginia. Minimum 3.0 GPA required.

Award: Scholarship for use in freshman year; not renewable.

Eligibility Requirements: Applicant must be Black (non-Hispanic); high school student and planning to enroll or expecting to enroll full-time at a four-year institution or university. Applicant must have 3.0 GPA or higher. Available to U.S. citizens.

Application Requirements: Application form. *Deadline:* continuous.

KECK FOUNDATION SCHOLARSHIP

Scholarship is available to African American students attending UNCF colleges and universities whose families have suffered a financial hardship as a result of the September 11 tragedy. Minimum 2.5 GPA required. For additional information and general scholarship application, visit website http://www.uncf.org.

Award: Scholarship for use in freshman, sophomore, junior, or senior years; renewable. *Amount:* $2000–$5000.

Eligibility Requirements: Applicant must be Black (non-Hispanic) and enrolled or expecting to enroll full- or part-time at a four-year institution or university. Applicant must have 2.5 GPA or higher. Available to U.S. citizens.

Application Requirements: Application form. *Deadline:* continuous.

LEON JACKSON JR. SCHOLARSHIP

$2500 scholarship established for current UNCF employees who desire to return to school to complete their associate, undergraduate, or graduate education. Minimum 2.5 GPA required.

Award: Scholarship for use in freshman, sophomore, junior, senior, or graduate years; not renewable. *Amount:* $2500.

Eligibility Requirements: Applicant must be Black (non-Hispanic) and enrolled or expecting to enroll full-time at a four-year institution or university. Applicant must have 2.5 GPA or higher. Available to U.S. citizens.

Application Requirements: Application form. *Deadline:* continuous.

LETTY GAROFALO SCHOLARSHIP

Awards for students attending UNCF colleges and universities. Minimum 2.5 GPA required. From more information, see website at http://www.uncf.org.

Award: Scholarship for use in freshman year; not renewable.

Eligibility Requirements: Applicant must be Black (non-Hispanic) and enrolled or expecting to enroll full- or part-time at a four-year institution or university. Applicant must have 2.5 GPA or higher. Available to U.S. citizens.

Application Requirements: Application form. *Deadline:* continuous.

LETTY GAROFALO SCHOLARSHIP

Scholarships available for students enrolled at UNCF member schools. Minimum 2.5 GPA required.

Award: Scholarship for use in freshman, sophomore, junior, or senior years; not renewable.

Eligibility Requirements: Applicant must be Black (non-Hispanic) and enrolled or expecting to enroll full-time at a four-year institution or university. Applicant must have 2.5 GPA or higher. Available to U.S. citizens.

Application Requirements: Application form. *Deadline:* continuous.

LOUISVILLE GALA SCHOLARSHIP

Awards for students planning to attend UNCF member colleges and universities who are residents of Kentucky. Must be a high school graduate and have minimum 2.5 GPA. For more information, see website at http://www.uncf.org.

Award: Scholarship for use in freshman year; not renewable.

Eligibility Requirements: Applicant must be Black (non-Hispanic); high school student; planning to enroll or expecting to enroll full- or part-time at an institution or university and resident of Kentucky. Applicant must have 2.5 GPA or higher. Available to U.S. citizens.

Application Requirements: Application form. *Deadline:* continuous.

MALCOLM X SCHOLARSHIP FOR EXCEPTIONAL COURAGE

Scholarship for students attending UNCF member colleges and universities who have overcome tremendous hardships and special circumstances. Students must also demonstrate academic excellence, as well as campus and community leadership. Minimum 2.5 GPA required.

Award: Scholarship for use in freshman year; not renewable. *Amount:* $4000.

Eligibility Requirements: Applicant must be Black (non-Hispanic); enrolled or expecting to enroll full-time at a four-year institution or university and must have an interest in leadership. Applicant must have 2.5 GPA or higher. Available to U.S. citizens.

Application Requirements: Application form. *Deadline:* continuous.

MARY OENSLAGER SCHOLARSHIP

Scholarships for students attending UNCF member colleges and universities. Must have minimum 2.5 GPA. For more information, see website at http://www.uncf.org.

Award: Scholarship for use in freshman year; not renewable. *Amount:* $2000–$5000.

Eligibility Requirements: Applicant must be Black (non-Hispanic) and enrolled or expecting to enroll full- or part-time at a four-year institution or university. Applicant must have 2.5 GPA or higher. Available to U.S. citizens.

Application Requirements: Application form. *Deadline:* continuous.

MASSMUTUAL SCHOLARS PROGRAM

Scholarships for African American/Black, Asian/Pacific Islander American and Hispanic American students attending or planning to attend a UNCF college or university. Must reside or plan to attend an institution in one of the following metropolitan areas: Atlanta, GA; Chicago, IL; New Jersey; Denver, CO; Houston, TX; Miami, FL; Los Angeles, CA; San Antonio, TX; or San Francisco, CA. Must demonstrate leadership and extra curricular activities and an interest in insurance and financial services careers. Must be U.S. citizen and have minimum 3.0 GPA.

Award: Scholarship for use in freshman, sophomore, junior, or senior years; not renewable. *Amount:* $5000.

Eligibility Requirements: Applicant must be Asian/Pacific Islander, Black (non-Hispanic), Hispanic; enrolled or expecting to enroll full-time at a four-year institution or university and must have an interest in leadership. Applicant must have 3.0 GPA or higher. Available to U.S. citizens.

Application Requirements: Application form. *Deadline:* May 2.

MASTERCARD WORLDWIDE SPECIAL SUPPORT PROGRAM

Scholarship designed to award students attending an UNCF member institution with a last dollar scholarship ranging between $2000-$3000. Minimum GPA of 2.5 required. Apply online at website, http://www.uncf.org.

Award: Scholarship for use in freshman, sophomore, junior, or senior years; not renewable. *Number:* 1. *Amount:* $2000–$3000.

Eligibility Requirements: Applicant must be Black (non-Hispanic) and enrolled or expecting to enroll full-time at a four-year institution or university. Applicant must have 2.5 GPA or higher. Available to U.S. and Canadian citizens.

Application Requirements: Application form, financial need analysis. *Deadline:* continuous.

MAYA ANGELOU/VIVIAN BAXTER SCHOLARSHIP

• *See page 565*

MAYOR DOUGLAS PALMER TRENTON/UNCF SCHOLARSHIP

$3000 scholarship for New Jersey residents who are from the city of Trenton and attending a UNCF member college or other HBCU. Minimum 2.5 GPA required.

Award: Scholarship for use in freshman, sophomore, junior, or senior years; not renewable. *Amount:* $3000.

Eligibility Requirements: Applicant must be Black (non-Hispanic); enrolled or expecting to enroll full-time at a four-year institution or university and resident of New Jersey. Applicant must have 2.5 GPA or higher. Available to U.S. citizens.

Application Requirements: Application form. *Deadline:* continuous.

MICHAEL & DONNA GRIFFITH SCHOLARSHIP

Scholarships for students attending UNCF member colleges and universities. Awards range from $2500 to $5000. Minimum 2.5 GPA required.

Award: Scholarship for use in freshman, sophomore, junior, or senior years; not renewable. *Amount:* $2500–$5000.

Eligibility Requirements: Applicant must be Black (non-Hispanic) and enrolled or expecting to enroll full-time at a four-year institution or university. Applicant must have 2.5 GPA or higher. Available to U.S. citizens.

Application Requirements: Application form. *Deadline:* continuous.

MINNESOTA STUDENT AID SCHOLARSHIP

Scholarship awarded to students from Minnesota who are attending a UNCF member college or university and have an unmet financial need. Minimum 2.5 GPA required.

Award: Scholarship for use in freshman, sophomore, junior, or senior years; not renewable.

Eligibility Requirements: Applicant must be Black (non-Hispanic); enrolled or expecting to enroll full-time at a four-year institution or university and resident of Minnesota. Applicant must have 2.5 GPA or higher. Available to U.S. citizens.

Application Requirements: Application form, financial need analysis. *Deadline:* June 30.

NAACP/AGNES JONES JACKSON SCHOLARSHIP

Scholarships for students attending UNCF member colleges and universities. Must be U.S. resident and demonstrate financial need. Undergraduates must be studying full-time; graduate students may be full or part-time students. Graduate students must possess a 3.0 GPA; all others, 2.5. Graduate students can receive up to $2,500; undergraduate students may receive $1,500. All students must be under the age of 25.

Award: Scholarship for use in freshman, sophomore, junior, senior, or graduate years; not renewable. *Amount:* $1500–$2500.

Eligibility Requirements: Applicant must be Black (non-Hispanic) and enrolled or expecting to enroll full- or part-time at an institution or university. Applicant must have 2.5 GPA or higher. Available to U.S. citizens.

Application Requirements: Application form, financial need analysis. *Deadline:* continuous.

NEBRASKA STUDENT AID SCHOLARSHIP

Funded by corporations, foundations, and individuals from Nebraska, this program provides scholarships to students from the state attending a UNCF member college or university. Must have a minimum GPA of 2.5.

Award: Scholarship for use in freshman year; not renewable.

Eligibility Requirements: Applicant must be Black (non-Hispanic); enrolled or expecting to enroll full- or part-time at a four-year institution or university and resident of Nebraska. Applicant must have 2.5 GPA or higher. Available to U.S. citizens.

Application Requirements: Application form. *Deadline:* continuous.

OKLAHOMA GOVERNOR'S LUNCHEON SCHOLARSHIP

$1000 scholarship for financially challenged, Oklahoma-based college students. Students must be enrolled at Langston University or any UNCF member institution or U.S 4-year fully-accredited college or university. In addition, eligible applicants must have a minimum GPA of 2.5 on a 4.0 scale and submit a 300-500 word essay describing what this scholarship means to them.

Award: Scholarship for use in freshman, sophomore, junior, or senior years; not renewable. *Amount:* up to $1000.

Eligibility Requirements: Applicant must be Black (non-Hispanic); enrolled or expecting to enroll full-time at a two-year or four-year institution and resident of Oklahoma. Applicant must have 2.5 GPA or higher. Available to U.S. citizens.

Application Requirements: Application form, essay, financial need analysis. *Deadline:* May 31.

ORACLE COMMUNITY IMPACT SCHOLARSHIP

Award for deserving but financially challenged African American students from East Palo Alto, Bay View, Hunter's Point, Richmond, Marin City, and Oakland, California, who are attending UNCF colleges and universities. Minimum GPA of 2.5 required. Apply online at website http://www.uncf.org.

Award: Grant for use in freshman, sophomore, junior, or senior years; not renewable. *Amount:* $5000–$10,000.

Eligibility Requirements: Applicant must be Black (non-Hispanic); enrolled or expecting to enroll full-time at a four-year institution or university and resident of California. Applicant must have 2.5 GPA or higher. Available to U.S. citizens.

Application Requirements: Application form, transcript. *Deadline:* April 5.

PENNSYLVANIA STATE EMPLOYEES SCHOLARSHIP (SECA)

Scholarships for UNCF students from Pennsylvania. Funds may be used for tuition, room and board, books, or to repay federal student loans. Minimum 2.5 GPA required. Prospective applicants should complete the Student Profile found at website http://www.uncf.org.

Award: Scholarship for use in freshman, sophomore, junior, or senior years; not renewable. *Amount:* up to $4000.

Eligibility Requirements: Applicant must be Black (non-Hispanic); enrolled or expecting to enroll full-time at a four-year institution or university and resident of Pennsylvania. Applicant must have 2.5 GPA or higher. Available to U.S. citizens.

Application Requirements: Application form, financial need analysis, student profile. *Deadline:* July 14.

ROBERT DOLE SCHOLARSHIP FOR DISABLED STUDENTS

• See page 579

RONALD MCDONALD'S CHICAGOLAND AND NORTHWEST INDIANA SCHOLARSHIP

$3000 scholarships awarded to students attending a UNCF member college or university who are residents of the following counties in Illinois and Indiana: Cook, Lake, Will, DuPage, Kankakee, Kendall, Jasper, Kane, La Salle, Livingston, McHenry, Iroquois, Boone, Bureau, Decal, Ford, and Grundy in IL; Lake, La Porte, and Porter in Indiana.

Must maintain minimum GPA of 2.5 and is applicable for four years of study.

Award: Scholarship for use in freshman, sophomore, junior, or senior years; renewable. *Amount:* $3000.

Eligibility Requirements: Applicant must be Black (non-Hispanic); enrolled or expecting to enroll full-time at a four-year institution or university and resident of Illinois, Indiana. Applicant must have 2.5 GPA or higher. Available to U.S. citizens.

Application Requirements: Application form, financial need analysis. *Deadline:* continuous.

RYAN HOWARD FAMILY FOUNDATION SCHOLARSHIP-ST. LOUIS/PHILADELPHIA

• See page 565

SAFE PASSAGE FOUNDATION EDUCATIONAL AND SCHOLARSHIP FUND

$4000 scholarship for tennis athletes at selected UNCF institutions. Minimum 2.5 GPA required. For more information, see website at http://www.uncf.org.

Award: Scholarship for use in freshman, sophomore, or junior years; not renewable. *Amount:* $4000.

Eligibility Requirements: Applicant must be Black (non-Hispanic); enrolled or expecting to enroll full-time at a four-year institution or university and must have an interest in athletics/sports. Applicant must have 2.5 GPA or higher. Available to U.S. citizens.

Application Requirements: Application form. *Deadline:* continuous.

ST. PETERSBURG GOLF CLASSIC SCHOLARSHIP

Scholarship available for African American undergraduate students from Florida who are enrolled at a UNCF member colleges or universities, and have a minimum 2.5 GPA. Visit website for more information, http://www.uncf.org.

Award: Scholarship for use in freshman, sophomore, junior, or senior years; renewable. *Amount:* up to $6000.

Eligibility Requirements: Applicant must be Black (non-Hispanic); enrolled or expecting to enroll full- or part-time at a four-year institution or university and resident of Florida. Applicant must have 2.5 GPA or higher. Available to U.S. citizens.

Application Requirements: Application form, FAFSA, Student Aid Report (SAR), financial need analysis. *Deadline:* May 31.

SIRAGUSA FOUNDATION SCHOLARSHIP

Scholarships available to students attending a UNCF member college or university. Minimum 2.5 GPA required. Apply online at website http://www.uncf.org.

Award: Scholarship for use in freshman, sophomore, junior, or senior years; not renewable. *Number:* 1. *Amount:* $2000.

Eligibility Requirements: Applicant must be Black (non-Hispanic) and enrolled or expecting to enroll full-time at a four-year institution or university. Applicant must have 2.5 GPA or higher. Available to U.S. and non-U.S. citizens.

Application Requirements: Application form, financial need analysis. *Deadline:* continuous.

SPRINT SCHOLARS PROGRAM FOR FRESHMEN

Need-based scholarships, to a maximum of $5000, for current high school seniors entering UNCF member colleges. Qualified applicants must be U.S. citizens or permanent residents. Minimum 3.0 GPA required. Students with the highest numerical scores will be considered for the scholarships; Kansas City metropolitan area residents (includes Kansas and Missouri) will be given special consideration.

Award: Scholarship for use in freshman year; not renewable. *Amount:* up to $5000.

Eligibility Requirements: Applicant must be Black (non-Hispanic); high school student and planning to enroll or expecting to enroll full-time at a four-year institution or university. Applicant must have 3.0 GPA or higher. Available to U.S. citizens.

Application Requirements: Application form, financial need analysis. *Deadline:* May 30.

SYLVIA SHAPIRO SCHOLARSHIP

Scholarship available for students at UNCF member colleges and universities. Minimum 2.5 GPA required. For more information, see website at http://www.uncf.org.

Award: Scholarship for use in freshman, sophomore, junior, or senior years; not renewable.

Eligibility Requirements: Applicant must be Black (non-Hispanic) and enrolled or expecting to enroll full-time at a four-year institution or university. Applicant must have 2.5 GPA or higher. Available to U.S. citizens.

Application Requirements: Application form. *Deadline:* continuous.

TARGET COMMUNITY LEADERS SCHOLARSHIP PROGRAM

$5000 award providing financial assistance to deserving students that are enrolled at UNCF colleges and universities, have an unmet financial need, and have demonstrated a commitment to giving back to their communities. Minimum 3.0 GPA required.

Award: Scholarship for use in junior year; not renewable. *Amount:* $5000.

Eligibility Requirements: Applicant must be Black (non-Hispanic) and enrolled or expecting to enroll full-time at a four-year institution or university. Applicant must have 3.0 GPA or higher. Available to U.S. citizens.

Application Requirements: Application form. *Deadline:* continuous.

UNCF GENERAL SCHOLARSHIP

Scholarships for students enrolled full-time and attending UNCF Institutes. Minimum 2.5 GPA required. This application information will be used to match students to specific programs administered by UNCF. For more information see website, http://www.uncf.org.

Award: Scholarship for use in freshman, sophomore, junior, senior, or graduate years; not renewable. *Amount:* up to $5000.

Eligibility Requirements: Applicant must be Black (non-Hispanic) and enrolled or expecting to enroll full-time at a four-year institution or university. Applicant must have 2.5 GPA or higher. Available to U.S. citizens.

Application Requirements: Application form, FAFSA. *Deadline:* May 15.

UNITED PARCEL SERVICE FOUNDATION SCHOLARSHIP

Award available to provide African American undergraduate students with financial support for tuition and other education costs. Applicants must be enrolled at UNCF member colleges and universities and have a minimum 2.5 GPA. Amount of scholarship varies based on need. Please visit website for more information and general scholarship application http://www.uncf.org.

Award: Scholarship for use in freshman, sophomore, junior, or senior years; renewable.

Eligibility Requirements: Applicant must be Black (non-Hispanic) and enrolled or expecting to enroll full-time at a four-year institution or university. Applicant must have 2.5 GPA or higher. Available to U.S. citizens.

Application Requirements: Application form, FAFSA, Student Aid Report (SAR), financial need analysis. *Deadline:* continuous.

USA FUNDS

Scholarships to assist students and their families in gaining access to postsecondary education at UNCF colleges/universities. For more information, see website at http://www.uncf.org.

Award: Scholarship for use in freshman, sophomore, junior, or senior years; not renewable.

Eligibility Requirements: Applicant must be Black (non-Hispanic) and enrolled or expecting to enroll full-time at a four-year institution or university. Available to U.S. citizens.

Application Requirements: Application form. *Deadline:* continuous.

VALLANTEEN ABBINGTON SCHOLARSHIP

Scholarship of $5000 to high school students who plan to attend a UNCF member college or university. Applicant must be a resident of the Greater St. Louis, Missouri, metropolitan area. Scholarship is renewed annually. Minimum 3.0 GPA in high school. GPA requirement increases to 3.3 after the sophomore year and 3.5 after the junior year. Visit website for more information http://www.uncf.org.

Award: Scholarship for use in freshman year; renewable. *Amount:* $5000.

Eligibility Requirements: Applicant must be Black (non-Hispanic); high school student; planning to enroll or expecting to enroll full- or part-time at a four-year institution or university and resident of Missouri. Applicant must have 3.0 GPA or higher. Available to U.S. citizens.

Application Requirements: Application form, FAFSA, Student Aid Report (SAR), financial need analysis. *Deadline:* continuous.

WHIRLPOOL FOUNDATION SCHOLARSHIP

Renewable award for African American students participating in Whirlpool's INROADS program in LaPorte, IN; Benton Harbor, MI; and LaVerne, TN. Must have 3.0 GPA and be enrolled in a UNCF member college or university. For additional information see website http://www.uncf.org.

Award: Scholarship for use in freshman, sophomore, junior, or senior years; renewable. *Amount:* $2500.

Eligibility Requirements: Applicant must be Black (non-Hispanic); enrolled or expecting to enroll full-time at a four-year institution or university and resident of Indiana, Michigan, Tennessee. Applicant must have 3.0 GPA or higher. Available to U.S. citizens.

Application Requirements: Application form, FAFSA, Student Aid Report (SAR), financial need analysis. *Deadline:* continuous.

YOUTH EMPOWERMENT SCHOLARSHIP

This scholarship is open to freshmen attending UNCF schools, Lincoln, Cheyney, or Temple Universities, and residing in Bucks, Montgomery, Chester, Philadelphia or Delaware County in Pennsylvania; Gloucester, Camden, Burlington or Mercer County in New Jersey; or New Castle County in Delaware. Student must come from a single-parent household and have a minimum 3.0 GPA. For application and information, visit http://www.uncf.org.

Award: Scholarship for use in freshman year; not renewable. *Number:* 1. *Amount:* up to $4000.

Eligibility Requirements: Applicant must be Black (non-Hispanic); enrolled or expecting to enroll full- or part-time at a four-year institution or university and resident of Delaware, New Jersey, Pennsylvania. Applicant must have 3.0 GPA or higher. Available to U.S. citizens.

Application Requirements: Application form, financial need analysis. *Deadline:* October 30.

UNITED SOUTH AND EASTERN TRIBES INC.

http://www.usetinc.org/

UNITED SOUTH AND EASTERN TRIBES SCHOLARSHIP FUND

One-time scholarship for Native American students who are members of United South and Eastern Tribes, enrolled or accepted in a postsecondary educational institution.

Award: Scholarship for use in freshman, sophomore, junior, or senior years; not renewable. *Number:* 4–8. *Amount:* $500.

Eligibility Requirements: Applicant must be Indian citizen; American Indian/Alaska Native and enrolled or expecting to enroll full- or part-time at a four-year institution or university.

Application Requirements: Application form, essay, financial need analysis, proof of tribal enrollment, transcript. *Deadline:* April 30.

Contact: Theresa Embry, Executive Assistant to Director
United South and Eastern Tribes Inc.
711 Stewarts Ferry Pike, Suite 100
Nashville, TN 37214-2634
Phone: 615-872-7900
Fax: 615-872-7417

UNITED STATES DEPARTMENT OF AGRICULTURE

http://www.usda.gov/

USDA/PUBLIC SERVICE LEADER SCHOLARS (PSLS)

The Public Service Leaders Scholarship Program provides combined scholarship and internship opportunities to undergraduate and graduate students leading to permanent employment upon completion of their degree. Benefits include: Full-tuition scholarships; paid internship (minimum 640 hours) prior to graduation, leading to permanent employment; employee benefits such as mentoring, career development, leadership training, use of a personal computer.

Award: Scholarship for use in sophomore, junior, senior, or graduate years.

Eligibility Requirements: Applicant must be Hispanic and enrolled or expecting to enroll at a four-year institution or university. Available to U.S. citizens.

Application Requirements: *Deadline:* May 20.

Contact: Sandra Cortez, HSI National Student Program Manager
   Phone: 202-720-6506
   E-mail: Sandra.Cortez@ars.usda.gov

UNITED STATES HISPANIC LEADERSHIP INSTITUTE

http://www.ushli.org/

DR. JUAN ANDRADE, JR. SCHOLARSHIP

Scholarship for young Hispanic leaders. Applicants must be enrolled or accepted for enrollment as a full-time student in a four-year institution in the United States or U.S. territories, and demonstrate a verifiable need for financial support. At least one parent must be of Hispanic ancestry.

Award: Scholarship for use in freshman, sophomore, junior, or senior years; not renewable. *Number:* 30. *Amount:* $500–$1000.

Eligibility Requirements: Applicant must be Hispanic and enrolled or expecting to enroll full-time at a two-year or four-year institution or university. Available to U.S. citizens.

Application Requirements: Application form, driver's license, essay, personal photograph, recommendations or references, resume, transcript. *Deadline:* January 11.

Contact: Isabel Reyes, Scholarship Coordinator
   Phone: 312-427-8683
   Fax: 312-427-5183
   E-mail: ireyes@ushli.org

URBAN LEAGUE OF RHODE ISLAND INC.

http://www.ulri.org/

URBAN LEAGUE OF RHODE ISLAND SCHOLARSHIP

Scholarship offered to minority students who are Rhode Island residents seeking postsecondary education. Priority is given to recent high school graduates.

Award: Scholarship for use in freshman, sophomore, junior, or senior years; not renewable.

Eligibility Requirements: Applicant must be American Indian/Alaska Native, Asian/Pacific Islander, Black (non-Hispanic), Hispanic; enrolled or expecting to enroll full-time at a two-year or four-year or technical institution or university and resident of Rhode Island. Available to U.S. citizens.

Application Requirements: Application form, financial need analysis, interview, recommendations or references, transcript. *Deadline:* April 30.

Contact: Marcia Ranglin-Vassell, Associate Director
   Phone: 401-351-5000
   Fax: 401-454-1946
   E-mail: education@ulri.org

US PAN ASIAN AMERICAN CHAMBER OF COMMERCE EDUCATION FOUNDATION

http://www.uspaacc.com/

DRS. POH SHIEN & JUDY YOUNG SCHOLARSHIP

The applicant should demonstrate: academic achievement of 3.3 GPA or higher; leadership in extracurricular activities; involvement in community service; financial need. The amount of the scholarship depends on the sponsors' contributions and varies between $2,000 and $5,000.

Award: Scholarship for use in freshman year; not renewable. *Amount:* $2000–$5000.

Eligibility Requirements: Applicant must be Asian/Pacific Islander; high school student and planning to enroll or expecting to enroll full-time at an institution or university. Available to U.S. citizens.

Application Requirements: *Deadline:* March 18.

MACY'S HALLMARK SCHOLARSHIP

The applicant should demonstrate: academic achievement of 3.3 GPA or higher; leadership in extracurricular activities; involvement in community service; financial need. The amount of the scholarship depends on the sponsors' contributions and varies between $2,000 and $5,000.

Award: Scholarship for use in freshman year. *Number:* 1. *Amount:* $2000–$5000.

Eligibility Requirements: Applicant must be Asian/Pacific Islander; high school student and planning to enroll or expecting to enroll full-time at an institution or university. Available to U.S. citizens.

Application Requirements: *Deadline:* March 18.

PAUL SHEARMAN ALLEN & ASSOCIATES SCHOLARSHIP

The applicant should demonstrate: academic achievement of 3.3 GPA or higher; leadership in extracurricular activities; involvement in community service; financial need. The amount of the scholarship depends on the sponsors' contributions and varies between $2,000 and $5,000.

Award: Scholarship for use in freshman year. *Number:* 1. *Amount:* $2000–$5000.

Eligibility Requirements: Applicant must be Asian/Pacific Islander; high school student and planning to enroll or expecting to enroll full-time at an institution or university. Available to U.S. citizens.

Application Requirements: *Deadline:* March 18.

PEPSICO HALLMARK SCHOLARSHIPS

The applicant should demonstrate: academic achievement of 3.3 GPA or higher; leadership in extracurricular activities; involvement in community service; financial need. The amount of the scholarship depends on the sponsors' contributions and varies between $2,000 and $5,000.

Award: Scholarship for use in freshman year; not renewable. *Number:* 1. *Amount:* $2000–$5000.

Eligibility Requirements: Applicant must be Asian/Pacific Islander; high school student and planning to enroll or expecting to enroll full-time at an institution or university. Available to U.S. citizens.

Application Requirements: *Deadline:* March 18.

PLANNED SYSTEMS INTERNATIONAL SCHOLARSHIP

The applicant should demonstrate: academic achievement of 3.3 GPA or higher; leadership in extracurricular activities; involvement in community service; financial need. The amount of the scholarship depends on the sponsors' contributions and varies between $2,000 and $5,000.

Award: Scholarship for use in freshman year; not renewable. *Amount:* $2000–$5000.

Eligibility Requirements: Applicant must be Asian/Pacific Islander; high school student and planning to enroll or expecting to enroll full-time at an institution or university. Available to U.S. citizens.

Application Requirements: *Deadline:* March 18.

UPS HALLMARK SCHOLARSHIPS

The applicant should demonstrate: academic achievement of 3.3 GPA or higher; leadership in extracurricular activities; involvement in community service; financial need. The amount of the scholarship depends on the sponsors' contributions and varies between $2,000 and $5,000.

Award: Scholarship for use in freshman year; not renewable. *Amount:* $2000–$5000.

Eligibility Requirements: Applicant must be Asian/Pacific Islander; high school student and planning to enroll or expecting to enroll full-time at an institution or university. Available to U.S. citizens.

Application Requirements: *Deadline:* March 18.

VIKKI CARR SCHOLARSHIP FOUNDATION

http://vikkicarr.com

VIKKI CARR SCHOLARSHIPS

Scholarship awarded for high school senior entering the first year of college. Applicant must be of Mexican-American descent and Texas resident.

Award: Scholarship for use in freshman year; not renewable.

Eligibility Requirements: Applicant must be Hispanic; high school student; planning to enroll or expecting to enroll full- or part-time at a two-year or four-year institution and resident of Texas. Available to U.S. citizens.

Application Requirements: Application form, essay, financial need analysis, personal photograph, test scores, transcript. *Deadline:* March 1.

WASHINGTON STATE HIGHER EDUCATION COORDINATING BOARD

http://www.hecb.wa.gov/

AMERICAN INDIAN ENDOWED SCHOLARSHIP

Awarded to financially needy undergraduate and graduate students with close social and cultural ties with a Native-American community. Must be Washington resident and enrolled full-time at Washington public or private school. Must be committed to use education to return service to the state's American Indian community.

Award: Scholarship for use in freshman, sophomore, junior, senior, graduate, or postgraduate years; not renewable. *Number:* 11–20. *Amount:* $500–$2000.

Eligibility Requirements: Applicant must be American Indian/Alaska Native; enrolled or expecting to enroll full-time at a two-year or four-year or technical institution or university; resident of Washington and studying in Washington. Available to U.S. citizens.

Application Requirements: 2 written personal statements, one describing one's social and cultural ties to the American Indian community in WA state; and the other describing how one will use one's education to serve the American Indian community within the state of Washington, application form, recommendations or references, transcript. *Deadline:* February 1.

Contact: Ann Voyles, Program Manager
Washington State Higher Education Coordinating Board
917 Lakeridge Way, PO Box 43430
Olympia, WA 98504-3430
Phone: 360-753-7843
Fax: 360-704-6243
E-mail: annv@wsac.wa.gov

WHITE EARTH TRIBAL COUNCIL

http://www.whiteearth.com/

WHITE EARTH SCHOLARSHIP PROGRAM

Renewable scholarship for students who are enrolled in postsecondary institutions. Must have a GPA of 2.5. Must be U.S. citizen.

Award: Scholarship for use in freshman, sophomore, junior, senior, graduate, or postgraduate years; renewable. *Number:* 200. *Amount:* $3000.

Eligibility Requirements: Applicant must be American Indian/Alaska Native and enrolled or expecting to enroll full- or part-time at a two-year or four-year or technical institution or university. Applicant must have 2.5 GPA or higher. Available to U.S. citizens.

Application Requirements: Application form, financial need analysis, transcript. *Deadline:* May 31.

Contact: Leslie Nessman, Scholarship Manager
Phone: 218-983-3285
Fax: 218-983-4299

WILLIAM E. DOCTER EDUCATIONAL FUND/ST. MARY ARMENIAN CHURCH

http://www.wedfund.org/

WILLIAM ERVANT DOCTER EDUCATIONAL FUND

Grant up to $2000 available to worthy students regardless of age, gender, or level of education or training. Funds given to American citizens of Armenian ancestry to pursue studies and training in the United States or Canada.

Award: Grant for use in freshman, sophomore, junior, senior, graduate, or postgraduate years; not renewable. *Number:* 20. *Amount:* $1000–$2000.

Eligibility Requirements: Applicant must be of Armenian heritage and enrolled or expecting to enroll full- or part-time at a two-year or four-year or technical institution or university. Available to U.S. citizens.

Application Requirements: Application form, essay, financial need analysis, proof of U.S. citizenship, test scores, transcript. *Deadline:* June 30.

Contact: Edward Alexander, Scholarship Committee Chairman
Fax: 202-364-1441
E-mail: wedfund@aol.com

WISCONSIN HIGHER EDUCATIONAL AID BOARD

http://www.heab.wi.gov/

MINORITY UNDERGRADUATE RETENTION GRANT-WISCONSIN

The grant provides financial assistance to African-American, Native-American, Hispanic, and former citizens of Laos, Vietnam, and Cambodia, for study in Wisconsin. Must be Wisconsin resident, enrolled at least half-time in Wisconsin Technical College System schools, non-profit independent colleges and universities, and tribal colleges. Refer to website for further details http://www.heab.state.wi.us.

Award: Grant for use in sophomore, junior, or senior years; not renewable. *Amount:* $250–$2500.

Eligibility Requirements: Applicant must be American Indian/Alaska Native, Asian/Pacific Islander, Black (non-Hispanic), Hispanic; enrolled or expecting to enroll full- or part-time at a two-year or four-year or technical institution or university; resident of Wisconsin and studying in Wisconsin. Available to U.S. and non-U.S. citizens.

Application Requirements: Application form, financial need analysis. *Deadline:* continuous.

Contact: Mary Lou Kuzdas, Program Coordinator
Wisconsin Higher Educational Aid Board
PO Box 7885
Madison, WI 53707-7885
Phone: 608-267-2212
Fax: 608-267-2808
E-mail: mary.kuzdas@wi.gov

WISCONSIN NATIVE AMERICAN/INDIAN STUDENT ASSISTANCE GRANT

Grants for Wisconsin residents who are at least one-quarter American Indian. Must be attending a college or university within the state. Refer to website for further details, http://www.heab.state.wi.us.

Award: Grant for use in freshman, sophomore, junior, or senior years; not renewable. *Amount:* $250–$1100.

Eligibility Requirements: Applicant must be American Indian/Alaska Native; enrolled or expecting to enroll full- or part-time at a two-year or four-year or technical institution or university; resident of Wisconsin and studying in Wisconsin. Available to U.S. citizens.

Application Requirements: Application form, financial need analysis. *Deadline:* continuous.

Contact: Sandra Thomas, Program Coordinator
Wisconsin Higher Educational Aid Board
PO Box 7885
Madison, WI 53707-7885
Phone: 608-266-0888
Fax: 608-267-2808
E-mail: sandy.thomas@wi.gov

WOMEN OF THE EVANGELICAL LUTHERAN CHURCH IN AMERICA

http://www.womenoftheelca.org/

AMELIA KEMP SCHOLARSHIP

Scholarship for ELCA women who are of an ethnic minority in undergraduate, graduate, professional, or vocational courses of study. Must be at least 21 years old and hold membership in the ELCA. Must have experienced an interruption of two or more years in education since the completion of high school.

Award: Scholarship for use in freshman, sophomore, junior, senior, or graduate years; not renewable. *Number:* 1. *Amount:* up to $1000.

Eligibility Requirements: Applicant must be Lutheran; American Indian/Alaska Native, Asian/Pacific Islander, Black (non-Hispanic), Hispanic; enrolled or expecting to enroll full- or part-time at a two-year or four-year or technical institution or university and female. Available to U.S. citizens.

Application Requirements: Application form, recommendations or references, resume, transcript. *Deadline:* February 15.

Contact: Emily Hansen, Scholarship Committee
　　　　Phone: 800-638-3522 Ext. 2736
　　　　Fax: 773-380-2419
　　　　E-mail: womenelca@elca.org

RELIGIOUS AFFILIATION

AMERICAN BAPTIST FINANCIAL AID PROGRAM

http://www.abc-usa.org/

AMERICAN BAPTIST FINANCIAL AID PROGRAM NATIVE AMERICAN GRANTS

• See page 615

AMERICAN BAPTIST SCHOLARSHIPS

One-time award for undergraduates who are members of an American Baptist Church. Must be attending an accredited college or university in the United States or Puerto Rico. If attending an ABC-related school, the scholarship amount is $2000 for the year. If not ABC-related, the amount is $1000. Minimum GPA of 2.75 required.

Award: Scholarship for use in freshman, sophomore, junior, or senior years; not renewable. *Number:* 1–5. *Amount:* $1000–$2000.

Eligibility Requirements: Applicant must be Baptist and enrolled or expecting to enroll full-time at a four-year institution or university. Available to U.S. citizens.

Application Requirements: Application form, financial need analysis, recommendations or references. *Deadline:* May 31.

Contact: Lynne Eckman, Director of Financial Aid
　　　　Phone: 610-768-2067
　　　　Fax: 610-768-2470
　　　　E-mail: lynne.eckman@abc-usa.org

AMERICAN SEPHARDI FOUNDATION

http://www.americansephardifederation.org/

BROOME AND ALLEN BOYS CAMP AND SCHOLARSHIP FUND

The Broome and Allen Scholarship is awarded to students of Sephardic origin or those working in Sephardic studies. Both graduate and undergraduate degree candidates as well as those doing research projects will be considered. It is awarded for one year and must be renewed for successive years. Enclose copy of tax returns with application.

Award: Scholarship for use in freshman, sophomore, junior, senior, graduate, or postgraduate years; not renewable. *Number:* 20–60. *Amount:* $500–$2000.

Eligibility Requirements: Applicant must be Jewish and enrolled or expecting to enroll full- or part-time at a two-year or four-year or technical institution or university. Available to U.S. and non-U.S. citizens.

Application Requirements: Application form, copy of tax returns, essay, financial need analysis, recommendations or references, transcript. *Deadline:* May 15.

Contact: Ms. Ellen Cohen, Membership and Outreach Coordinator
　　　　American Sephardi Foundation
　　　　15 West 16th Street
　　　　New York, NY 10011
　　　　Phone: 212-294-8350 Ext. 4
　　　　Fax: 212-294-8348
　　　　E-mail: ecohen@asf.cjh.org

BNY MELLON, N.A.

http://www.bnymellon.com/

HENRY FRANCIS BARROWS SCHOLARSHIP

Award for Protestant males only. Must be a resident of Massachusetts and applying to a non-Catholic U.S. institution of higher learning. Eligible applicant must be recommended by educational institution. Not for graduate study programs.

Award: Scholarship for use in freshman, sophomore, junior, or senior years; not renewable. *Amount:* up to $2000.

Eligibility Requirements: Applicant must be Protestant; enrolled or expecting to enroll full-time at a two-year or four-year or technical institution or university; male and resident of Massachusetts. Available to U.S. citizens.

Application Requirements: Application form, essay, transcript. *Deadline:* April 15.

Contact: June Kfoury McNeil, Vice President
　　　　BNY Mellon, N.A.
　　　　201 Washington Street, 024-0092
　　　　Boston, MA 02108
　　　　Phone: 617-722-3891

CENTRAL SCHOLARSHIP

http://www.central-scholarship.org

LESSANS FAMILY SCHOLARSHIP

• See page 619

EASTERN ORTHODOX COMMITTEE ON SCOUTING

http://www.eocs.org/

EASTERN ORTHODOX COMMITTEE ON SCOUTING SCHOLARSHIPS

• See page 518

FADEL EDUCATIONAL FOUNDATION, INC.

http://www.fadelfoundation.org/

ANNUAL AWARD PROGRAM

Grants of $800 to $3500 awarded on the basis of merit and financial need.

Award: Grant for use in freshman, sophomore, junior, senior, or graduate years; renewable. *Number:* 20–45. *Amount:* $800–$3500.

Eligibility Requirements: Applicant must be Muslim faith and enrolled or expecting to enroll full- or part-time at a two-year or four-year or technical institution or university. Available to U.S. citizens.

Application Requirements: Application form, essay, financial need analysis, recommendations or references, test scores, transcript. *Deadline:* May 28.

Contact: Mr. Ayman Fadel, Secretary
　　　　Phone: 484-694-1783
　　　　E-mail: secretary@fadelfoundation.org

FOUNDATION FOR CHRISTIAN COLLEGE LEADERS

http://www.collegechristianleader.com/

FOUNDATION FOR COLLEGE CHRISTIAN LEADERS SCHOLARSHIP

Applicant must be accepted to or currently enrolled in an undergraduate degree program. Candidate must demonstrate Christian leadership. Combined income of parents and student must be less than $60,000. Minimum 3.0 GPA required.

Award: Scholarship for use in freshman, sophomore, junior, senior, or graduate years; not renewable.

Eligibility Requirements: Applicant must be Christian; enrolled or expecting to enroll full- or part-time at a four-year institution or university and must have an interest in leadership. Applicant must have 3.0 GPA or higher. Available to U.S. citizens.

Application Requirements: Application form, financial need analysis, interview, leadership assessment form, cover sheet, recommendations or references. *Deadline:* May 7.

GENERAL BOARD OF HIGHER EDUCATION AND MINISTRY

http://www.gbhem.org

BISHOP JOSEPH B. BETHEA SCHOLARSHIP
• *See page 623*

E. CRAIG BRANDENBURG GRADUATE AWARD

Scholarship for students 35 years of age or older, desiring to continue their education or to go into a second career. Must be enrolled full time at an accredited institution, and be active, full-time members of the United Methodist Church for at least one year.

Award: Scholarship for use in freshman, sophomore, junior, senior, or graduate years; not renewable.

Eligibility Requirements: Applicant must be Methodist and enrolled or expecting to enroll full-time at a four-year institution or university. Available to U.S. citizens.

Application Requirements: Application form, application form may be submitted online (http://www.gbhem.org), essay, recommendations or references, resume, transcript. *Deadline:* March 1.

Contact: Ms. Mary Robinson, Scholarships Coordinator
General Board of Higher Education and Ministry
PO Box 340007
Nashville, TN 37203-0007
Phone: 615-340-7344
Fax: 615-340-7529
E-mail: umscholar@gbhem.org

ETHNIC MINORITY SCHOLARSHIP
• *See page 623*

HANA SCHOLARSHIP
• *See page 623*

HELEN AND ALLEN BROWN SCHOLARSHIP

Scholarship for outstanding high school graduates and undergraduate college students who are members of the Nashville District of the Tennessee Annual Conference of UMC or members of the New Orleans District of the Louisiana Annual Conference of UMC. Must have been full and active members of The United Methodist Church for at least three years and maintain a GPA of 3.0.

Award: Scholarship for use in freshman, sophomore, junior, or senior years; not renewable.

Eligibility Requirements: Applicant must be Methodist and enrolled or expecting to enroll full-time at a four-year institution or university. Applicant must have 3.0 GPA or higher. Available to U.S. citizens.

Application Requirements: Application form, application form may be submitted online (http://www.gbhem.org/loans-scholarships), essay, recommendations or references, transcript. *Deadline:* March 1.

Contact: Ms. Mary Robinson, Scholarships Coordinator
General Board of Higher Education and Ministry
PO Box 340007
Nashville, TN 37203-0007
Phone: 615-340-7344
Fax: 615-340-7529
E-mail: umscholar@gbhem.org

THE REV. DR. KAREN LAYMAN GIFT OF HOPE: 21ST CENTURY SCHOLARS PROGRAM

$1000 scholarship to United Methodist undergraduate students who are full-time, active members of UMC for at least three years prior to applying. Must demonstrate leadership in the United Methodist Church and be enrolled in a full-time degree program at a regionally accredited U.S. institution. Cumulative GPA of 3.0 or higher required.

Award: Scholarship for use in freshman, sophomore, junior, or senior years; not renewable. *Amount:* $1000.

Eligibility Requirements: Applicant must be Methodist; enrolled or expecting to enroll full-time at a two-year or four-year institution or university and must have an interest in leadership. Applicant must have 3.0 GPA or higher. Available to U.S. and non-Canadian citizens.

Application Requirements: Application form, application form may be submitted online (http://www.gbhem.org), essay, recommendations or references, transcript. *Deadline:* March 1.

Contact: Ms. Mary Robinson, Scholarships Coordinator
General Board of Higher Education and Ministry
PO Box 340007
Nashville, TN 37203-0007
Phone: 615-340-7344
Fax: 615-340-7529
E-mail: umscholar@gbhem.org

GREATER KANAWHA VALLEY FOUNDATION

http://www.tgkvf.org/

STUART & LUCILLE ARMSTRONG SCHOLARSHIP

Renewable scholarship for an Episcopalian in the Diocese of West Virginia. Must maintain a 3.0 GPA and continue to pursue the same major or degree program. Seminarians are not eligible. Preference given to applicants from St. Christopher in Charleston.

Award: Scholarship for use in freshman, sophomore, junior, or senior years; renewable. *Amount:* $1500.

Eligibility Requirements: Applicant must be Episcopalian; enrolled or expecting to enroll full-time at a four-year institution or university and resident of West Virginia. Applicant must have 3.0 GPA or higher. Available to U.S. citizens.

Application Requirements: Application form, essay, financial need analysis, name and location of home parish along with Rectors name and contact information, recommendations or references, test scores, transcript. *Deadline:* January 15.

Contact: Susan Hoover, Scholarship Program Officer
Greater Kanawha Valley Foundation
900 Lee Street East, 16th Floor
Charleston, WV 25301
Phone: 304-346-3620
E-mail: tgkvf@tgkvf.org

ITALIAN CATHOLIC FEDERATION INC.

http://www.icf.org/

ITALIAN CATHOLIC FEDERATION FIRST YEAR SCHOLARSHIP
• *See page 523*

JEWISH VOCATIONAL SERVICE LOS ANGELES

http://www.jvsla.org/

JEWISH VOCATIONAL SERVICE SCHOLARSHIP FUND
• *See page 627*

KNIGHTS OF COLUMBUS

http://www.kofc.org/

FOURTH DEGREE PRO DEO AND PRO PATRIA (CANADA)
• *See page 523*

FOURTH DEGREE PRO DEO AND PRO PATRIA SCHOLARSHIPS
• *See page 523*

FRANCIS P. MATTHEWS AND JOHN E. SWIFT EDUCATIONAL TRUST SCHOLARSHIPS
• *See page 524*

JOHN W. MCDEVITT (FOURTH DEGREE) SCHOLARSHIPS
• *See page 524*

PERCY J. JOHNSON ENDOWED SCHOLARSHIPS
• *See page 524*

PRESBYTERIAN CHURCH (USA)

http://www.pcusa.org/financialaid

NATIONAL PRESBYTERIAN COLLEGE SCHOLARSHIP

Scholarships between $1000 and $1500 available to incoming undergraduate enrolled in full-time programs in colleges associated with the Presbyterian Church (U.S.A.). Applicants must have a minimum GPA of 2.5 and demonstrate financial need. Students are required to participate in campus ministry or a worshiping community proximate to the college they attend and respond to an annual essay question exploring aspects of vocation.

Award: Scholarship for use in freshman, sophomore, junior, or senior years; not renewable. *Number:* 25–100. *Amount:* $1000–$1500.

Eligibility Requirements: Applicant must be Presbyterian and enrolled or expecting to enroll full-time at a four-year institution or university. Applicant must have 2.5 GPA or higher. Available to U.S. and non-U.S. citizens.

Application Requirements: Application form, essay, financial need analysis, recommendations or references, resume, transcript. *Deadline:* March 1.

Contact: Ms. Laura Bryan, Associate, Financial Aid for Studies
Presbyterian Church (USA)
100 Witherspoon Street
Louisville, KY 40202-1396
Phone: 800-728-7228 Ext. 5735
Fax: 502-569-8776
E-mail: finaid@pcusa.org

SAMUEL ROBINSON AWARD

Prize granted to full-time junior and senior students attending a Presbyterian related college or university who successfully recite answers to the Westminster Shorter Catechism and write an essay on an assigned topic.

Award: Prize for use in junior or senior years; not renewable. *Number:* 16. *Amount:* $250–$5000.

Eligibility Requirements: Applicant must be Presbyterian and enrolled or expecting to enroll full-time at a four-year institution or university. Available to U.S. citizens.

Application Requirements: Application form, entry in a contest, essay. *Deadline:* April 1.

Contact: Ms. Laura Bryan, Associate, Financial Aid for Studies
Presbyterian Church (USA)
100 Witherspoon Street
Louisville, KY 40202
Phone: 800-728-7228 Ext. 5735
Fax: 502-569-8766
E-mail: finaid@pcusa.org

ROMAN CATHOLIC DIOCESE OF TULSA

http://www.dioceseoftulsa.org/

MAE LASSLEY OSAGE SCHOLARSHIP
• *See page 637*

SYNOD OF THE COVENANT

http://www.synodofthecovenant.org/

RACIAL ETHNIC SCHOLARSHIP
• *See page 564*

TEXAS BLACK BAPTIST SCHOLARSHIP COMMITTEE

TEXAS BLACK BAPTIST SCHOLARSHIP
• *See page 639*

UNITARIAN UNIVERSALIST ASSOCIATION

http://www.uua.org/

CHILDREN OF UNITARIAN UNIVERSALIST MINISTERS

Non-renewable scholarship available to children of Unitarian Universalist Ministers to defray undergraduate college expenses. Dollar value and number of awards varies. Priority is given to applicants whose family income does not exceed $50,000.

Award: Scholarship for use in freshman, sophomore, junior, or senior years; not renewable.

Eligibility Requirements: Applicant must be Unitarian Universalist and enrolled or expecting to enroll full- or part-time at a four-year institution or university. Available to U.S. citizens.

Application Requirements: Application form. *Deadline:* July 31.

Contact: Ms. Hillary Goodridge, Program Director
Phone: 617-971-9600
Fax: 617-971-0029
E-mail: uufp@aol.com

JOSEPH SUMNER SMITH SCHOLARSHIP

Funds are available for Unitarian Universalist (UU) students attending Antioch (including satellite and nonresidential campuses) and Harvard. While there is no restriction on the course of studies the student may elect to pursue, nor any restrictions on choice of career, student interested in pursuing the ministry after graduation are especially urged to apply.

Award: Scholarship for use in freshman, sophomore, junior, senior, or graduate years; not renewable. *Amount:* $500–$1000.

Eligibility Requirements: Applicant must be Unitarian Universalist and enrolled or expecting to enroll full- or part-time at a two-year or four-year or technical institution or university. Available to U.S. citizens.

Application Requirements: Application form. *Deadline:* April 30.

Contact: Ms. Hillary Goodridge, Program Director
Phone: 617-971-9600
Fax: 617-971-0029
E-mail: uufp@aol.com

UNITED METHODIST CHURCH

http://www.gbhem.org/

J. A. KNOWLES MEMORIAL SCHOLARSHIP

One-time award for Texas residents attending a United Methodist institution in Texas. Must have been United Methodist Church member for at least one year. Must be U.S. citizens or permanent residents. Minimum 2.5 GPA required.

Award: Scholarship for use in freshman, sophomore, junior, senior, or graduate years; not renewable.

Eligibility Requirements: Applicant must be Methodist; enrolled or expecting to enroll full-time at a two-year or four-year institution or university; resident of Texas and studying in Texas. Applicant must have 2.5 GPA or higher. Available to U.S. citizens.

Application Requirements: Application form, essay, recommendations or references, transcript. *Deadline:* May 15.

UNITED METHODIST CHURCH ETHNIC SCHOLARSHIP
• *See page 640*

UNITED METHODIST CHURCH HISPANIC, ASIAN, AND NATIVE AMERICAN SCHOLARSHIP
• *See page 640*

UNITED METHODIST YOUTH ORGANIZATION
http://globalyoungpeople.org

DAVID W. SELF SCHOLARSHIP
Must be a United Methodist Youth who has been active in local church for at least one year prior to application. Must be a graduating senior in high school (who maintained at least a C average) entering the first year of undergraduate study. Must be pursuing a "church-related" career and should have maintained at least a "C" average throughout high school.

Award: Scholarship for use in freshman year; not renewable. *Number:* 1–5. *Amount:* $100–$2200.

Eligibility Requirements: Applicant must be Methodist; high school student and planning to enroll or expecting to enroll full-time at a two-year or four-year institution or university. Available to U.S. citizens.

Application Requirements: Application form, certification of church membership, essay, financial need analysis, transcript. *Deadline:* March 4.

Contact: Kelsey Tinker, Grant and Scholarships Administrator
Phone: 615-340-7184
E-mail: youngpeople@gbod.org

RICHARD S. SMITH SCHOLARSHIP
• *See page 641*

WOMAN'S MISSIONARY UNION FOUNDATION
http://www.wmufoundation.com/

WOMAN'S MISSIONARY UNION SCHOLARSHIP PROGRAM
The program is primarily for Baptist young women with high scholastic accomplishments and service through Baptist organizations. Must have an interest in Christian women's leadership development or missionary service. Preference is given for WMU/Acteen membership in a Baptist church. The total number of available awards and dollar amount varies. For more information, see website http://www.wmufoundation.com.

Award: Scholarship for use in freshman, sophomore, junior, or senior years; renewable. *Number:* 5–10. *Amount:* $500–$1500.

Eligibility Requirements: Applicant must be Baptist; enrolled or expecting to enroll full-time at a two-year or four-year institution or university and female. Available to U.S. and non-U.S. citizens.

Application Requirements: Application form, recommendations or references, transcript. *Deadline:* March 1.

Contact: Mrs. Linda Lucas, Administrative Assistant
Phone: 205-408-5525
E-mail: llucas@wmu.org

WOMEN OF THE EVANGELICAL LUTHERAN CHURCH IN AMERICA
http://www.womenoftheelca.org/

AMELIA KEMP SCHOLARSHIP
• *See page 650*

BELMER/FLORA PRINCE SCHOLARSHIP
Scholarship for women who have experienced an interruption of two or more years in education since the completion of high school. Must be member of ELCA and be at least 21 years old.

Award: Scholarship for use in freshman, sophomore, junior, senior, or graduate years; not renewable. *Number:* 2. *Amount:* up to $1000.

Eligibility Requirements: Applicant must be Lutheran; enrolled or expecting to enroll full- or part-time at a two-year or four-year or technical institution or university and female. Available to U.S. citizens.

Application Requirements: Application form, recommendations or references, resume, transcript. *Deadline:* February 15.

Contact: Emily Hansen, Scholarship Committee
Phone: 800-638-3522 Ext. 2736
Fax: 773-380-2419
E-mail: womenelca@elca.org

RESIDENCE

AIKEN ELECTRIC COOPERATIVE INC.
http://www.aikenco-op.org/

TRUSTEE SCHOLARSHIP
Scholarship awarded to high school graduating senior in the cooperative service area. Award based on need and academic performance. The primary residence of the applicant must have an account with either Aiken Electric Cooperative Inc. or Aikenelectric.net.

Award: Scholarship for use in freshman year; not renewable. *Number:* 1. *Amount:* up to $1000.

Eligibility Requirements: Applicant must be high school student; planning to enroll or expecting to enroll full-time at a two-year or four-year institution or university and resident of South Carolina. Available to U.S. citizens.

Application Requirements: Application form, essay, financial need analysis. *Deadline:* January 12.

Contact: Marilyn Gerrity, Manager, Marketing and Strategic Services
Phone: 803-649-6245
Fax: 803-641-8310
E-mail: aec@aikenco-op.org

ALABAMA COMMISSION ON HIGHER EDUCATION
http://www.ache.alabama.gov/

ALABAMA NATIONAL GUARD EDUCATIONAL ASSISTANCE PROGRAM
• *See page 582*

ALABAMA STUDENT ASSISTANCE PROGRAM
Scholarship award of $300 to $5000 per academic year given to undergraduate students residing in the state of Alabama and attending a college or university in Alabama.

Award: Grant for use in freshman, sophomore, junior, or senior years; not renewable. *Amount:* $300–$5000.

Eligibility Requirements: Applicant must be enrolled or expecting to enroll full- or part-time at a two-year or four-year or technical institution or university; resident of Alabama and studying in Alabama. Available to U.S. citizens.

Application Requirements: Application form. *Deadline:* continuous.

Contact: Cheryl Newton, Grants Coordinator
Phone: 334-242-2273
Fax: 334-242-2269
E-mail: cheryl.newton@ache.alabama.gov

ALABAMA STUDENT GRANT PROGRAM
Nonrenewable awards available to Alabama residents for undergraduate study at certain independent colleges within the state. Both full and half-time students are eligible. Deadlines: September 15, January 15, and February 15.

Award: Grant for use in freshman, sophomore, junior, or senior years; not renewable. *Number:* up to 1200. *Amount:* up to $1200.

Eligibility Requirements: Applicant must be enrolled or expecting to enroll full- or part-time at a four-year institution or university; resident of Alabama and studying in Alabama. Available to U.S. citizens.

Application Requirements: 5 proofs of Alabama residency, application form.

Contact: Cheryl Newton, Grants Coordinator
　　　Phone: 334-242-2273
　　　Fax: 334-242-2269
　　　E-mail: cheryl.newton@ache.alabama.gov

POLICE OFFICERS AND FIREFIGHTERS SURVIVORS EDUCATION ASSISTANCE PROGRAM-ALABAMA

Provides tuition, fees, books, and supplies to dependents of full-time police officers and firefighters killed or totally disabled in the line of duty. Must attend an Alabama public college as an undergraduate. Must be Alabama resident.

Award: Scholarship for use in freshman, sophomore, junior, or senior years; renewable. *Number:* 15–30. *Amount:* $1600–$12,000.

Eligibility Requirements: Applicant must be enrolled or expecting to enroll full- or part-time at a two-year or four-year or technical institution or university; single; resident of Alabama and studying in Alabama. Available to U.S. citizens.

Application Requirements: Application form, birth certificate, marriage license, death certificate, letter from medical doctor, transcript. *Deadline:* continuous.

Contact: Cheryl Newton, Grants Coordinator
　　　Phone: 334-242-2273
　　　Fax: 334-242-2269
　　　E-mail: cheryl.newton@ache.alabama.gov

ALABAMA DEPARTMENT OF VETERANS AFFAIRS

http://www.va.alabama.gov/

ALABAMA G.I. DEPENDENTS SCHOLARSHIP PROGRAM
• See page 590

ALABAMA INDIAN AFFAIRS COMMISSION

http://www.aiac.alabama.gov/

AIAC SCHOLARSHIP
• See page 613

ALASKA COMMISSION ON POSTSECONDARY EDUCATION

http://www.acpe.alaska.gov

ALASKADVANTAGE EDUCATION GRANT

The Alaska legislature created the AlaskAdvantage Education Grant Program (AEG) to provide need-based financial assistance to eligible Alaska students attending qualifying postsecondary educational institutions in Alaska. Students apply by completing the FAFSA annually.

Award: Grant for use in freshman, sophomore, junior, or senior years; not renewable. *Amount:* $500–$3000.

Eligibility Requirements: Applicant must be enrolled or expecting to enroll full- or part-time at a two-year or four-year institution or university; resident of Alaska and studying in Alaska. Available to U.S. citizens.

Application Requirements: Completed FAFSA.

Contact: Adam Weed, Special Programs Coordinator
　　　Phone: 907-465-6685
　　　E-mail: customer_service@acpe.state.ak.us

ALASKA PERFORMANCE SCHOLARSHIP

To qualify, students must take a specific, rigorous high school curriculum; earn a minimum 2.5 GPA; and do well on college or career readiness exam. Students apply by completing the FAFSA by the annual deadline. Awards can be used at any regionally accredited college or university in Alaska, or for approved career and technical education programs in the state. Students must use scholarship within 6 years of high school graduation. Students cannot receive award for more than 8 semesters.

Award: Scholarship for use in freshman, sophomore, junior, senior, graduate, or postgraduate years; not renewable. *Amount:* $500–$4755.

Eligibility Requirements: Applicant must be enrolled or expecting to enroll full- or part-time at a two-year or four-year or technical institution or university; resident of Alaska and studying in Alaska. Applicant must have 2.5 GPA or higher. Available to U.S. citizens.

Application Requirements: FAFSA.

Contact: Adam Weed, Special Programs Coordinator
　　　Phone: 907-465-6685
　　　E-mail: customer_service@acpe.state.ak.us

ALBERTA AGRICULTURE FOOD AND RURAL DEVELOPMENT 4-H BRANCH

http://www.4h.ab.ca/

ALBERTA AGRICULTURE FOOD AND RURAL DEVELOPMENT 4-H SCHOLARSHIP PROGRAM
• See page 502

ALBERTA HERITAGE SCHOLARSHIP FUND

http://www.alis.alberta.ca/

ADULT HIGH SCHOOL EQUIVALENCY SCHOLARSHIPS
• See page 613

ALBERTA APPRENTICESHIP AND INDUSTRY TRAINING SCHOLARSHIPS

Awards of CAN$1000 to recognize the accomplishments of Alberta high school students taking the registered apprenticeship program and to encourage recipients to continue their apprenticeship training after completing high school. Must be a Canadian citizen or landed immigrant and a resident of Alberta, must have completed the requirements for high school graduation between August 1 and July 31 of the current year and must be registered as an Alberta apprentice in a trade while still attending high school. For additional information, please visit website http://alis.alberta.ca.

Award: Scholarship for use in freshman year; not renewable.

Eligibility Requirements: Applicant must be enrolled or expecting to enroll full-time at a two-year or four-year or technical institution or university and resident of Alberta. Available to Canadian citizens.

Application Requirements: Application form, essay, recommendations or references. *Deadline:* June 29.

ALBERTA CENTENNIAL SCHOLARSHIPS-ALBERTA
• See page 613

ALEXANDER RUTHERFORD SCHOLARSHIPS FOR HIGH SCHOOL ACHIEVEMENT
• See page 613

CHARLES S. NOBLE JUNIOR A HOCKEY SCHOLARSHIPS
• See page 614

CHARLES S. NOBLE JUNIOR FOOTBALL SCHOLARSHIPS
• See page 614

DR. ERNEST AND MINNIE MEHL SCHOLARSHIP
• See page 614

EARL AND COUNTESS OF WESSEX-WORLD CHAMPIONSHIPS IN ATHLETICS SCHOLARSHIPS
• See page 614

GRANT MACEWAN UNITED WORLD COLLEGE SCHOLARSHIPS
• See page 614

JIMMIE CONDON ATHLETIC SCHOLARSHIPS

• See page 614

JO-ANNE KOCH-ABC SOCIETY SCHOLARSHIP

• See page 614

KEYERA ENERGY-PETER J. RENTON MEMORIAL SCHOLARSHIP

• See page 615

LAURENCE DECORE AWARDS FOR STUDENT LEADERSHIP

• See page 615

LOUISE MCKINNEY POSTSECONDARY SCHOLARSHIPS

• See page 615

PERSONS CASE SCHOLARSHIPS

• See page 615

PRAIRIE BASEBALL ACADEMY SCHOLARSHIPS

Scholarships of between CAN$500 and CAN$2500 reward athletic and academic excellence of Alberta baseball players, and provides an incentive and means for these players to continue with their postsecondary education. Must be Alberta residents and enrolled full-time at a postsecondary institution in Alberta. Applicants must be a participant in the Prairie Baseball Academy and must have achieved a minimum GPA of 2.0 in their previous semester. For additional information, visit website http://alis.alberta.ca.

Award: Scholarship for use in freshman, sophomore, junior, or senior years; not renewable.

Eligibility Requirements: Applicant must be enrolled or expecting to enroll full-time at a two-year or four-year or technical institution or university; resident of Alberta; studying in Alberta and must have an interest in athletics/sports. Available to Canadian citizens.

Application Requirements: Application form, community service, recommendations or references. *Deadline:* October 15.

QUEEN ELIZABETH II GOLDEN JUBILEE CITIZENSHIP MEDAL

• See page 615

RUTHERFORD SCHOLARS

• See page 615

ALBUQUERQUE COMMUNITY FOUNDATION

http://www.albuquerquefoundation.org/

NEW MEXICO MANUFACTURED HOUSING SCHOLARSHIP PROGRAM

The scholarship is to be used for study in a four-year college or university. The total number of available awards and the dollar value of each award varies. Deadline varies. Refer to website for details and application, http://www.albuquerquefoundation.org.

Award: Scholarship for use in freshman year; not renewable. *Number:* 1–2. *Amount:* $740–$1000.

Eligibility Requirements: Applicant must be high school student; planning to enroll or expecting to enroll full-time at a four-year institution or university; resident of New Mexico and studying in New Mexico. Applicant must have 3.0 GPA or higher. Available to U.S. citizens.

Application Requirements: Application form, financial need analysis, recommendations or references, resume, test scores, transcript.

Contact: Ms. Nancy Johnson, Program Director
Albuquerque Community Foundation
PO Box 25266
Albuquerque, NM 87125
Phone: 505-883-6240
E-mail: njohnson@albuquerquefoundation.org

SUSSMAN-MILLER EDUCATIONAL ASSISTANCE FUND

The program provides financial aid to enable students to continue with an undergraduate program. This is a gap program based on financial need. Must be resident of New Mexico. Minimum 3.0 GPA required. Deadline varies. The fund requests not to write or call for information. Please visit website http://www.albuquerquefoundation.org for complete information.

Award: Scholarship for use in freshman, sophomore, junior, or senior years; renewable. *Number:* 25–30. *Amount:* $500–$2500.

Eligibility Requirements: Applicant must be enrolled or expecting to enroll full-time at a four-year institution or university and resident of New Mexico. Applicant must have 3.0 GPA or higher. Available to U.S. citizens.

Application Requirements: Application form, essay, financial need analysis, recommendations or references, resume, test scores, transcript.

Contact: Ms. Nancy Johnson, Program Director
Albuquerque Community Foundation
PO Box 25266
Albuquerque, NM 87125
Phone: 505-883-6240
E-mail: njohnson@albuquerquefoundation.org

YOUTH IN FOSTER CARE SCHOLARSHIP PROGRAM

This award is designed to support youth who have been in the New Mexico foster care system.

Award: Scholarship for use in freshman, sophomore, junior, or senior years; not renewable. *Number:* 1–4. *Amount:* $500–$1000.

Eligibility Requirements: Applicant must be age 17-21; enrolled or expecting to enroll full- or part-time at a two-year or four-year or technical institution or university and resident of New Mexico. Available to U.S. citizens.

Application Requirements: Application form, essay, recommendations or references, resume, transcript. *Deadline:* June 2.

Contact: Nancy Johnson, Program Director
Albuquerque Community Foundation
PO Box 25266
Albuquerque, NM 87125
Phone: 505-883-6240
E-mail: njohnson@albuquerquefoundation.org

ALERT SCHOLARSHIP

http://www.alertmagazine.org/

ALERT SCHOLARSHIP

$500 scholarship for the best essay on drug / alcohol abuse from each state. Applicant must be current high school senior in Alaska, Nebraska, Oregon, Washington, Idaho, Montana, Minnesota, Wyoming, Colorado, North Dakota, or South Dakota. Minimum 2.5 GPA required. For more information visit: http://www.alertmagazine.org/scholarship.php.

Award: Scholarship for use in freshman year; not renewable. *Amount:* $500.

Eligibility Requirements: Applicant must be high school student; planning to enroll or expecting to enroll full- or part-time at a four-year institution or university; resident of Alaska, Colorado, Idaho, Minnesota, Montana, Nebraska, North Dakota, Oregon, South Dakota, Washington, Wyoming and must have an interest in writing. Applicant must have 2.5 GPA or higher. Available to U.S. citizens.

Application Requirements: Entry in a contest, essay, personal photograph, transcript. *Deadline:* continuous.

THE ALEXANDER FOUNDATION

http://www.thealexanderfoundation.org/

THE ALEXANDER FOUNDATION SCHOLARSHIP PROGRAM

Alexander scholarships provide financial assistance to undergraduate or graduate students accepted or enrolled in Colorado institutions of higher education. Applicants must be gay, lesbian, bisexual, or transgendered and reside in Colorado, must demonstrate financial need, and should be active/supporting/contributing members of the community.

Award: Scholarship for use in freshman, sophomore, junior, senior, graduate, or postgraduate years; not renewable. *Number:* 6–35. *Amount:* $300–$3000.

Eligibility Requirements: Applicant must be enrolled or expecting to enroll full- or part-time at a two-year or four-year or technical institution or university; resident of Colorado; studying in Colorado and must have an interest in LGBT issues. Available to U.S. citizens.

Application Requirements: Application form, essay, financial need analysis, recommendations or references, transcript. *Deadline:* April 15.

AMERICAN CANCER SOCIETY

http://www.cancer.org/

AMERICAN CANCER SOCIETY, FLORIDA DIVISION R.O.C.K. COLLEGE SCHOLARSHIP PROGRAM
• *See page 566*

AMERICAN LEGION AUXILIARY DEPARTMENT OF ALABAMA

http://americanlegionalabama.org/

AMERICAN LEGION AUXILIARY DEPARTMENT OF ALABAMA SCHOLARSHIP PROGRAM
• *See page 591*

AMERICAN LEGION AUXILIARY DEPARTMENT OF CALIFORNIA

http://www.calegionaux.org/

AMERICAN LEGION AUXILIARY DEPARTMENT OF CALIFORNIA CONTINUING/RE-ENTRY STUDENT SCHOLARSHIP

Awarded to undergraduate students. Must be a continuing or re-entry college student and attend a California college or university.

Award: Scholarship for use in freshman, sophomore, junior, or senior years; not renewable. *Number:* 2–3. *Amount:* $500–$1000.

Eligibility Requirements: Applicant must be enrolled or expecting to enroll full- or part-time at a two-year or four-year institution or university; resident of California and studying in California. Available to U.S. citizens.

Application Requirements: Application form. *Deadline:* March 16.

Contact: Theresa Jacob, Secretary/Treasurer
　　　Phone: 415-862-5092
　　　Fax: 415-861-8365
　　　E-mail: calegionaux@calegionaux.org

AMERICAN LEGION AUXILIARY DEPARTMENT OF CALIFORNIA GENERAL SCHOLARSHIP

Award ranges from $500 to $1000 for high school senior or graduate of an accredited high school who has not been able to begin college due to circumstances of illness or finance. Student must attend a California college or university. Deadline is March 16.

Award: Scholarship for use in freshman, sophomore, junior, or senior years; not renewable. *Amount:* $500–$1000.

Eligibility Requirements: Applicant must be enrolled or expecting to enroll full- or part-time at a two-year or four-year institution or university; resident of California and studying in California. Available to U.S. citizens.

Application Requirements: Application form. *Deadline:* March 16.

Contact: Theresa Jacob, Secretary/Treasurer
　　　Phone: 415-862-5092
　　　Fax: 415-861-8365
　　　E-mail: calegionaux@calegionaux.org

AMERICAN LEGION AUXILIARY DEPARTMENT OF CALIFORNIA JUNIOR SCHOLARSHIP
• *See page 503*

AMERICAN LEGION AUXILIARY DEPARTMENT OF COLORADO

http://www.alacolorado.com

AMERICAN LEGION AUXILIARY DEPARTMENT OF COLORADO DEPARTMENT PRESIDENT'S SCHOLARSHIP FOR JUNIOR MEMBER
• *See page 591*

AMERICAN LEGION AUXILIARY DEPARTMENT OF CONNECTICUT

http://www.ct.legion.org/

AMERICAN LEGION AUXILIARY DEPARTMENT OF CONNECTICUT PAST PRESIDENTS' PARLEY MEMORIAL EDUCATION GRANT
• *See page 504*

AMERICAN LEGION AUXILIARY DEPARTMENT OF FLORIDA

http://www.alafl.org/

AMERICAN LEGION AUXILIARY DEPARTMENT OF FLORIDA DEPARTMENT SCHOLARSHIPS
• *See page 591*

AMERICAN LEGION AUXILIARY DEPARTMENT OF FLORIDA MEMORIAL SCHOLARSHIP
• *See page 504*

AMERICAN LEGION AUXILIARY DEPARTMENT OF INDIANA

http://www.amlegauxin.org/

AMERICAN LEGION AUXILIARY DEPARTMENT OF INDIANA EDNA M. BURCUS/HOOSIER SCHOOLHOUSE MEMORIAL SCHOLARSHIP
• *See page 591*

AMERICAN LEGION AUXILIARY DEPARTMENT OF IOWA

http://www.ialegion.org/ala

AMERICAN LEGION AUXILIARY DEPARTMENT OF IOWA CHILDREN OF VETERANS MERIT AWARD
• *See page 591*

AMERICAN LEGION AUXILIARY DEPARTMENT OF KENTUCKY

http://www.kylegion.org/

AMERICAN LEGION AUXILIARY DEPARTMENT OF KENTUCKY LAURA BLACKBURN MEMORIAL SCHOLARSHIP
• *See page 586*

AMERICAN LEGION AUXILIARY DEPARTMENT OF MAINE

http://www.mainelegion.org/

AMERICAN LEGION AUXILIARY DEPARTMENT OF MAINE DANIEL E. LAMBERT MEMORIAL SCHOLARSHIP
• *See page 592*

AMERICAN LEGION AUXILIARY DEPARTMENT OF MAINE NATIONAL PRESIDENT'S SCHOLARSHIP
• *See page 550*

AMERICAN LEGION AUXILIARY DEPARTMENT OF MARYLAND

http://www.alamd.org/

AMERICAN LEGION AUXILIARY DEPARTMENT OF MARYLAND CHILDREN AND YOUTH SCHOLARSHIPS
• *See page 592*

AMERICAN LEGION AUXILIARY DEPARTMENT OF MASSACHUSETTS

http://www.masslegion-aux.org/

AMERICAN LEGION AUXILIARY DEPARTMENT OF MASSACHUSETTS DEPARTMENT PRESIDENT'S SCHOLARSHIP
• *See page 550*

AMERICAN LEGION AUXILIARY DEPARTMENT OF MASSACHUSETTS PAST PRESIDENTS' PARLEY SCHOLARSHIP
• *See page 592*

AMERICAN LEGION AUXILIARY DEPARTMENT OF MICHIGAN

http://www.michalaux.org/

AMERICAN LEGION AUXILIARY DEPARTMENT OF MICHIGAN MEMORIAL SCHOLARSHIP
• *See page 592*

AMERICAN LEGION AUXILIARY DEPARTMENT OF MICHIGAN SCHOLARSHIP FOR NON-TRADITIONAL STUDENT
• *See page 593*

AMERICAN LEGION AUXILIARY DEPARTMENT OF MINNESOTA

http://www.mnlegion.org/

AMERICAN LEGION AUXILIARY DEPARTMENT OF MINNESOTA SCHOLARSHIPS
• *See page 593*

AMERICAN LEGION AUXILIARY DEPARTMENT OF MISSOURI

http://www.missourilegion.org/

AMERICAN LEGION AUXILIARY DEPARTMENT OF MISSOURI LELA MURPHY SCHOLARSHIP
• *See page 504*

AMERICAN LEGION AUXILIARY DEPARTMENT OF MISSOURI NATIONAL PRESIDENT'S SCHOLARSHIP
• *See page 505*

AMERICAN LEGION AUXILIARY DEPARTMENT OF NEBRASKA

http://www.nebraskalegionaux.net/

AMERICAN LEGION AUXILIARY DEPARTMENT OF NEBRASKA RUBY PAUL CAMPAIGN FUND SCHOLARSHIP
• *See page 505*

AMERICAN LEGION AUXILIARY DEPARTMENT OF NORTH DAKOTA

http://www.ndlegion.org/

AMERICAN LEGION AUXILIARY DEPARTMENT OF NORTH DAKOTA NATIONAL PRESIDENT'S SCHOLARSHIP
• *See page 550*

AMERICAN LEGION AUXILIARY DEPARTMENT OF NORTH DAKOTA SCHOLARSHIPS
One-time award for North Dakota residents who are already attending a North Dakota institution of higher learning. Contact local or nearest American Legion Auxiliary Unit for more information. Must be a U.S. citizen.

Award: Scholarship for use in sophomore, junior, senior, or graduate years; not renewable. *Number:* 3. *Amount:* $400.

Eligibility Requirements: Applicant must be enrolled or expecting to enroll full-time at a two-year or four-year or technical institution or university; resident of North Dakota and studying in North Dakota. Available to U.S. citizens.

Application Requirements: Application form, driver's license, essay, financial need analysis, recommendations or references, self-addressed stamped envelope with application, test scores, transcript. *Deadline:* January 15.

Contact: Myrna Runholm, Department Secretary
American Legion Auxiliary Department of North Dakota
PO Box 1060
Jamestown, ND 58402-1060
Phone: 701-253-5992
E-mail: ala-hq@ndlegion.org

AMERICAN LEGION AUXILIARY DEPARTMENT OF OHIO

http://www.alaohio.org/

AMERICAN LEGION AUXILIARY DEPARTMENT OF OHIO CONTINUING EDUCATION FUND
• *See page 594*

AMERICAN LEGION AUXILIARY DEPARTMENT OF OHIO DEPARTMENT PRESIDENT'S SCHOLARSHIP
• *See page 594*

AMERICAN LEGION AUXILIARY DEPARTMENT OF OREGON

http://www.alaoregon.org/

AMERICAN LEGION AUXILIARY DEPARTMENT OF OREGON DEPARTMENT GRANTS
• *See page 594*

AMERICAN LEGION AUXILIARY DEPARTMENT OF OREGON NATIONAL PRESIDENT'S SCHOLARSHIP
• *See page 594*

AMERICAN LEGION AUXILIARY DEPARTMENT OF OREGON SPIRIT OF YOUTH SCHOLARSHIP
• *See page 505*

AMERICAN LEGION AUXILIARY DEPARTMENT OF PENNSYLVANIA

http://www.pa-legion.com/

AMERICAN LEGION AUXILIARY DEPARTMENT OF PENNSYLVANIA PAST DEPARTMENT PRESIDENTS' MEMORIAL SCHOLARSHIP

Renewable award of $400 given each year to high school seniors. Must be residents of Pennsylvania.

Award: Scholarship for use in freshman year; renewable. *Number:* 1. *Amount:* $400.

Eligibility Requirements: Applicant must be high school student; planning to enroll or expecting to enroll full-time at a four-year institution or university and resident of Pennsylvania. Available to U.S. citizens.

Application Requirements: Application form. *Deadline:* March 15.

Contact: Colleen Watson, Executive Secretary and Treasurer
    Phone: 717-763-7545
    Fax: 717-763-0617
    E-mail: paalad@hotmail.com

AMERICAN LEGION AUXILIARY DEPARTMENT OF PENNSYLVANIA SCHOLARSHIP FOR DEPENDENTS OF DISABLED OR DECEASED VETERANS

Renewable award of $600 to high school seniors who are residents of Pennsylvania. Applicants must enroll in full-time studies.

Award: Scholarship for use in freshman year; renewable. *Number:* 1. *Amount:* $600.

Eligibility Requirements: Applicant must be high school student; planning to enroll or expecting to enroll full-time at a four-year institution or university and resident of Pennsylvania. Available to U.S. citizens.

Application Requirements: Application form. *Deadline:* March 15.

Contact: Colleen Watson, Executive Secretary and Treasurer
    Phone: 717-763-7545
    Fax: 717-763-0617
    E-mail: paalad@hotmail.com

AMERICAN LEGION AUXILIARY DEPARTMENT OF PENNSYLVANIA SCHOLARSHIP FOR DEPENDENTS OF LIVING VETERANS

Renewable award of $600 for high school seniors who are residents of Pennsylvania. Applicants must enroll in a program of full-time study.

Award: Scholarship for use in freshman year; renewable. *Number:* 1. *Amount:* $600.

Eligibility Requirements: Applicant must be high school student; planning to enroll or expecting to enroll full-time at a four-year institution or university and resident of Pennsylvania. Available to U.S. citizens.

Application Requirements: Application form. *Deadline:* March 15.

Contact: Colleen Watson, Executive Secretary and Treasurer
    Phone: 717-763-7545
    Fax: 717-763-0617
    E-mail: paalad@hotmail.com

AMERICAN LEGION AUXILIARY DEPARTMENT OF SOUTH DAKOTA

http://www.sdlegion-aux.org/

AMERICAN LEGION AUXILIARY DEPARTMENT OF SOUTH DAKOTA COLLEGE SCHOLARSHIPS
• See page 505

AMERICAN LEGION AUXILIARY DEPARTMENT OF SOUTH DAKOTA SENIOR SCHOLARSHIP
• See page 505

AMERICAN LEGION AUXILIARY DEPARTMENT OF SOUTH DAKOTA VOCATIONAL SCHOLARSHIP
• See page 506

AMERICAN LEGION AUXILIARY DEPARTMENT OF TENNESSEE

http://www.legion-aux.org/

AMERICAN LEGION AUXILIARY DEPARTMENT OF TENNESSEE VARA GRAY SCHOLARSHIP-GENERAL
• See page 594

AMERICAN LEGION AUXILIARY DEPARTMENT OF TEXAS

http://www.alatexas.org/

AMERICAN LEGION AUXILIARY DEPARTMENT OF TEXAS GENERAL EDUCATION SCHOLARSHIP
• See page 595

AMERICAN LEGION AUXILIARY DEPARTMENT OF UTAH

http://www.legion-aux.org/

AMERICAN LEGION AUXILIARY DEPARTMENT OF UTAH NATIONAL PRESIDENT'S SCHOLARSHIP
• See page 506

AMERICAN LEGION AUXILIARY DEPARTMENT OF WISCONSIN

http://www.amlegionauxwi.org/

AMERICAN LEGION AUXILIARY DEPARTMENT OF WISCONSIN DELLA VAN DEUREN MEMORIAL SCHOLARSHIP
• See page 506

AMERICAN LEGION AUXILIARY DEPARTMENT OF WISCONSIN H.S. AND ANGELINE LEWIS SCHOLARSHIPS
• See page 506

AMERICAN LEGION AUXILIARY DEPARTMENT OF WISCONSIN MERIT AND MEMORIAL SCHOLARSHIPS
• See page 507

AMERICAN LEGION AUXILIARY DEPARTMENT OF WISCONSIN PAST PRESIDENTS' PARLEY HEALTH CAREER SCHOLARSHIPS
• See page 507

AMERICAN LEGION AUXILIARY DEPARTMENT OF WISCONSIN PRESIDENT'S SCHOLARSHIPS
• See page 507

AMERICAN LEGION DEPARTMENT OF ARIZONA

http://www.azlegion.org/

AMERICAN LEGION DEPARTMENT OF ARIZONA HIGH SCHOOL ORATORICAL CONTEST

Each student must present an 8 to 10 minute prepared oration on any part of the U.S. Constitution without any notes, podiums, or coaching. The student will then be asked to do a 3 to 5 minute oration on one of four possible topics. Which one of the four topics will not be known in advance, so students must be prepared to respond to any of the four. Open to students in grades 9 to 12.

Award: Scholarship for use in freshman year; not renewable. *Number:* 10–20. *Amount:* $50–$1500.

Eligibility Requirements: Applicant must be high school student; planning to enroll or expecting to enroll full-time at a two-year or four-

year institution or university; resident of Arizona and must have an interest in public speaking. Available to U.S. citizens.

Application Requirements: Application form, entry in a contest. *Deadline:* January 15.

Contact: Roger Munchbach, Department Oratorical Chairman
American Legion Department of Arizona
4701 North 19th Avenue, Suite 200
Phoenix, AZ 85015-3799
Phone: 602-264-7706
Fax: 602-264-0029
E-mail: legionoratoricalcontest@msn.com

AMERICAN LEGION DEPARTMENT OF ARKANSAS

http://www.arklegion.homestead.com/

AMERICAN LEGION DEPARTMENT OF ARKANSAS COUDRET SCHOLARSHIP AWARD

• *See page 508*

AMERICAN LEGION DEPARTMENT OF ARKANSAS HIGH SCHOOL ORATORICAL CONTEST

Oratorical contest open to students in ninth to twelfth grades of any accredited Arkansas high school. Begins with finalists at the post level and proceeds through area and district levels to national contest.

Award: Prize for use in freshman year; not renewable. *Number:* 4. *Amount:* $1250–$3500.

Eligibility Requirements: Applicant must be high school student; planning to enroll or expecting to enroll full-time at a four-year institution or university; resident of Arkansas and must have an interest in public speaking. Applicant must have 2.5 GPA or higher. Available to U.S. citizens.

Application Requirements: Application form, entry in a contest, personal photograph, recommendations or references. *Deadline:* December 15.

Contact: William Winchell, Department Adjutant
American Legion Department of Arkansas
PO Box 3280
Little Rock, AR 72203-3280
Phone: 501-375-1104
Fax: 501-375-4236
E-mail: alegion@swbell.net

AMERICAN LEGION DEPARTMENT OF HAWAII

http://www.legion.org/

AMERICAN LEGION DEPARTMENT OF HAWAII HIGH SCHOOL ORATORICAL CONTEST

Oratorical contest open to students in ninth to twelfth grades of any accredited Hawaii high school. Must be under 20 years of age. Speech contests begin in January at post level and continue on to the national competition. Contact local American Legion Post or department for deadlines and application details.

Award: Prize for use in freshman year; not renewable. *Number:* 1–3. *Amount:* $50–$1500.

Eligibility Requirements: Applicant must be high school student; age 14-20; planning to enroll or expecting to enroll full-time at a four-year institution or university and resident of Hawaii. Available to U.S. citizens.

Application Requirements: Application form, entry in a contest. *Deadline:* January 1.

Contact: Adm. Bernard Lee, Department Adjutant
American Legion Department of Hawaii
612 McCully Street
Honolulu, HI 96826-3935
Phone: 808-946-6383
Fax: 808-947-3957
E-mail: aldepthi@hawaii.rr.com

AMERICAN LEGION DEPARTMENT OF IDAHO

http://www.idlegion.home.mindspring.com/

AMERICAN LEGION DEPARTMENT OF IDAHO SCHOLARSHIP

• *See page 508*

AMERICAN LEGION DEPARTMENT OF ILLINOIS

http://www.illegion.org/

AMERICAN ESSAY CONTEST SCHOLARSHIP

• *See page 508*

AMERICAN LEGION DEPARTMENT OF ILLINOIS BOY SCOUT/EXPLORER SCHOLARSHIP

• *See page 508*

AMERICAN LEGION DEPARTMENT OF ILLINOIS HIGH SCHOOL ORATORICAL CONTEST

Single oratorical contest with winners advancing to the next level. Open to students in 9th to 12th grades of any accredited Illinois high school. Seniors must be in attendance as of January 1. Must contact local American Legion post or department headquarters for complete information and applications, which will be available in the fall.

Award: Scholarship for use in freshman year; not renewable. *Number:* 1–30. *Amount:* $100–$2000.

Eligibility Requirements: Applicant must be high school student; planning to enroll or expecting to enroll full- or part-time at a four-year institution or university; resident of Illinois and must have an interest in English language or public speaking. Available to U.S. citizens.

Application Requirements: Application form, entry in a contest. *Fee:* $125. *Deadline:* varies.

Contact: Mr. Gary Jenson, American Legion Department Assistant Adjutant
American Legion Department of Illinois
2720 East Lincoln Street
Bloomington, IL 61704
Phone: 309-663-0361
Fax: 309-663-5783
E-mail: gjenson@illegion.org

AMERICAN LEGION DEPARTMENT OF ILLINOIS SCHOLARSHIPS

• *See page 508*

AMERICAN LEGION DEPARTMENT OF INDIANA

http://www.hoosierlegionnaire.org

AMERICAN LEGION DEPARTMENT OF INDIANA, AMERICANISM AND GOVERNMENT TEST

Study guides are provided to high schools. Students take a test and write an essay. One male and one female student from each grade (10 to 12) are selected as state winners.

Award: Scholarship for use in freshman, sophomore, junior, or senior years; not renewable. *Number:* 6. *Amount:* $1000.

Eligibility Requirements: Applicant must be high school student; planning to enroll or expecting to enroll full- or part-time at a two-year or four-year or technical institution or university and resident of Indiana. Available to U.S. citizens.

Application Requirements: Entry in a contest, essay, test scores. *Deadline:* December 1.

Contact: Susan Long, Program Coordinator
Phone: 317-630-1264
Fax: 317-237-9891
E-mail: slong@indlegion.org

AMERICAN LEGION DEPARTMENT OF INDIANA HIGH SCHOOL ORATORICAL CONTEST

Oratorical contest open to students in grades nine to twelve of any accredited Indiana high school or home schooled students in an equivalent grade. Speech contests begin in November at post level and continue on to national competition. Contact local American Legion post for application details or visit our website at http://www.hoosierlegionnaire.org.

Award: Scholarship for use in freshman, sophomore, junior, or senior years; not renewable. *Number:* 4–8. *Amount:* $200–$4200.

Eligibility Requirements: Applicant must be high school student; planning to enroll or expecting to enroll full- or part-time at a two-year or four-year or technical institution or university; resident of Indiana and must have an interest in public speaking. Available to U.S. citizens.

Application Requirements: Application form, assigned and prepared speech contest, entry in a contest. *Deadline:* December 15.

Contact: Susan Long, Program Coordinator
Phone: 317-630-1264
Fax: 317-237-9891
E-mail: slong@indlegion.org

AMERICAN LEGION FAMILY SCHOLARSHIP
• *See page 508*

FRANK W. MCHALE MEMORIAL SCHOLARSHIPS

One-time award for Indiana high school junior boys who participated in The American Legion Hoosier Boys State Program. Must be nominated by Boys State official while in attendance at Hoosier Boys State. Write for more information and deadline.

Award: Scholarship for use in freshman, sophomore, junior, or senior years; not renewable. *Number:* 3. *Amount:* $1000–$1500.

Eligibility Requirements: Applicant must be high school student; planning to enroll or expecting to enroll full- or part-time at a two-year or four-year or technical institution or university; male; resident of Indiana and must have an interest in leadership. Available to U.S. citizens.

Application Requirements: Application form, essay, participation in the Boys State Program, nomination from Boys State official. *Deadline:* June 16.

Contact: Susan Long, Program Coordinator
American Legion Department of Indiana
777 North Meridan Street, Room 104
Indianapolis, IN 46204-1189
Phone: 317-630-1264
Fax: 317-237-9891
E-mail: slong@indlegion.org

AMERICAN LEGION DEPARTMENT OF IOWA

http://www.ialegion.org/

AMERICAN LEGION DEPARTMENT OF IOWA EAGLE SCOUT OF THE YEAR SCHOLARSHIP
• *See page 509*

AMERICAN LEGION DEPARTMENT OF IOWA HIGH SCHOOL ORATORICAL CONTEST

All contestants in the department of Iowa American Legion High School Oratorical Contest shall be citizens or lawful permanent residents of the United States. The department of Iowa American Legion High School Oratorical Contest shall consist of one contestant from each of the three area contests. The area contest shall consist of one contestant from each district in the designated Area.

Award: Prize for use in freshman year; not renewable. *Number:* up to 3. *Amount:* $1000–$2000.

Eligibility Requirements: Applicant must be high school student; planning to enroll or expecting to enroll full-time at a two-year or four-year institution or university; resident of Iowa and must have an interest in public speaking. Available to U.S. citizens.

Application Requirements: Application form, entry in a contest. *Deadline:* varies.

Contact: Kathy Nees, Program Director, Youth Programs
Phone: 515-282-5068
Fax: 515-282-7583
E-mail: knees@ialegion.org

AMERICAN LEGION DEPARTMENT OF IOWA OUTSTANDING SENIOR BASEBALL PLAYER

One-time award for Iowa residents who participated in the American Legion Senior Baseball Program and display outstanding sportsmanship, athletic ability, and proven academic achievements. Must be recommended by Baseball Committee.

Award: Scholarship for use in freshman year; not renewable. *Number:* 1. *Amount:* $750–$1500.

Eligibility Requirements: Applicant must be high school student; age 15-18; planning to enroll or expecting to enroll full-time at a two-year or four-year institution or university; resident of Iowa and must have an interest in athletics/sports. Available to U.S. citizens.

Application Requirements: Application form, entry in a contest, recommendations or references. *Deadline:* July 15.

Contact: Kathy Nees, Program Director, Youth Programs
Phone: 515-282-5068
Fax: 515-282-7583
E-mail: knees@ialegion.org

AMERICAN LEGION DEPARTMENT OF KANSAS

http://www.ksamlegion.org/

CHARLES W. AND ANNETTE HILL SCHOLARSHIP
• *See page 509*

DR. CLICK COWGER BASEBALL SCHOLARSHIP

Scholarship available to a high school senior or college freshman or sophomore enrolled in a Kansas institution. Applicant may intend to enroll in a junior college, university or trade school in Kansas only. Must be a male and should play or has played Kansas American Legion baseball. Must be an average or a better student scholastically.

Award: Scholarship for use in freshman or sophomore years; not renewable. *Number:* 1. *Amount:* $500.

Eligibility Requirements: Applicant must be enrolled or expecting to enroll full-time at a two-year or four-year or technical institution or university; male; resident of Kansas; studying in Kansas and must have an interest in athletics/sports. Available to U.S. citizens.

Application Requirements: Application form, financial need analysis, personal photograph, recommendations or references, transcript. *Deadline:* July 15.

Contact: Jim Gravenstein, Chairman, Scholarship Committee
American Legion Department of Kansas
1314 Topeka Boulevard, SW
Topeka, KS 66612
Phone: 785-232-9315
Fax: 785-232-1399

HUGH A. SMITH SCHOLARSHIP FUND
• *See page 509*

ROSEDALE POST 346 SCHOLARSHIP
• *See page 509*

TED AND NORA ANDERSON SCHOLARSHIPS
• *See page 510*

AMERICAN LEGION DEPARTMENT OF MAINE

http://www.mainelegion.org/

AMERICAN LEGION DEPARTMENT OF MAINE CHILDREN AND YOUTH SCHOLARSHIP
• *See page 596*

DANIEL E. LAMBERT MEMORIAL SCHOLARSHIP
• *See page 596*

JAMES V. DAY SCHOLARSHIP
• *See page 510*

AMERICAN LEGION DEPARTMENT OF MARYLAND

http://www.mdlegion.org/

AMERICAN LEGION DEPARTMENT OF MARYLAND GENERAL SCHOLARSHIP FUND

• *See page 596*

MARYLAND BOYS STATE SCHOLARSHIP

Scholarship awarded from applicants that have graduated from Maryland Boys State program. Applications must be received by May 1st of the Boys State graduate's SR year in High School. Application available at http://www.mdlegion.org/Forms/bsschol.pdf.

Award: Scholarship for use in freshman, sophomore, junior, or senior years; not renewable. *Number:* 1–10. *Amount:* up to $500.

Eligibility Requirements: Applicant must be high school student; planning to enroll or expecting to enroll full-time at a two-year or four-year institution or university; male and resident of Maryland. Available to U.S. citizens.

Application Requirements: Application form, test scores, transcript. *Deadline:* May 1.

Contact: Russell Myers, Department Adjutant
American Legion Department of Maryland
101 North Gay Street
Room E
Baltimore, MD 21202
Phone: 410-752-1405
Fax: 410-752-3822
E-mail: russell@mdlegion.org

AMERICAN LEGION DEPARTMENT OF MICHIGAN

http://www.michiganlegion.org/

AMERICAN LEGION DEPARTMENT OF MICHIGAN ORATORICAL SCHOLARSHIP PROGRAM

Oratorical contest open to students in ninth to twelfth grades of any accredited Michigan high school or state accredited home school. Five one-time awards of varying amounts. State winner advances to National Competition for scholarship money ranging from $14,000 to $18,000.

Award: Scholarship for use in freshman year; not renewable. *Number:* 5. *Amount:* $800–$1500.

Eligibility Requirements: Applicant must be high school student; planning to enroll or expecting to enroll full- or part-time at a two-year or four-year institution or university; resident of Michigan and must have an interest in public speaking. Available to U.S. citizens.

Application Requirements: Application form, entry in a contest, essay. *Deadline:* January 2.

Contact: Deanna Clark, Department Administrative Assistant for Programs
American Legion Department of Michigan
212 North Verlinden Avenue, Suite A
Lansing, MI 48915
Phone: 517-371-4720 Ext. 11
Fax: 517-371-2401
E-mail: programs@michiganlegion.org

GUY M. WILSON SCHOLARSHIPS

• *See page 596*

WILLIAM D. AND JEWELL W. BREWER SCHOLARSHIP TRUSTS

• *See page 596*

AMERICAN LEGION DEPARTMENT OF MINNESOTA

http://www.mnlegion.org/

AMERICAN LEGION DEPARTMENT OF MINNESOTA HIGH SCHOOL ORATORICAL CONTEST

Oratorical contest open to students in ninth to twelfth grades of any accredited Minnesota high school or home-schooled students. Must be Minnesota resident. Speech must be student's original work on the general subject of the Constitution. Speech contests begin in December at local Legion post level and continue on to the national competition. See website for specific topic and application details http://www.mnlegion.org.

Award: Prize for use in freshman year; not renewable. *Number:* 4. *Amount:* $500–$1500.

Eligibility Requirements: Applicant must be high school student; planning to enroll or expecting to enroll full- or part-time at a two-year or four-year or technical institution or university; resident of Minnesota and must have an interest in public speaking. Available to U.S. citizens.

Application Requirements: Application form, entry in a contest. *Deadline:* November 30.

Contact: Jennifer Kelley, Program Coordinator
American Legion Department of Minnesota
20 West 12th Street, Room 300-A
St. Paul, MN 55155
Phone: 651-291-1800
Fax: 651-291-1057
E-mail: department@mnlegion.org

AMERICAN LEGION DEPARTMENT OF MINNESOTA MEMORIAL SCHOLARSHIP

• *See page 510*

MINNESOTA LEGIONNAIRES INSURANCE TRUST SCHOLARSHIP

• *See page 510*

AMERICAN LEGION DEPARTMENT OF MISSOURI

http://www.missourilegion.org/

CHARLES L. BACON MEMORIAL SCHOLARSHIP

• *See page 510*

LILLIE LOIS FORD SCHOLARSHIP FUND

• *See page 597*

AMERICAN LEGION DEPARTMENT OF MONTANA

http://mtlegion.org/

AMERICAN LEGION DEPARTMENT OF MONTANA HIGH SCHOOL ORATORICAL CONTEST

Applicants participate in a statewide memorized oratorical contest on the U.S. Constitution. Four places are awarded. Must be a Montana high school student. Contact state adjutant American Legion Department of Montana for further details. Each state winner who competes in the first round of the national contest will receive a $1000 scholarship. Participants in the second round who do not advance to the national final round will receive an additional $1000 scholarship.

Award: Scholarship for use in freshman year; not renewable. *Number:* 1–4. *Amount:* $300–$2000.

Eligibility Requirements: Applicant must be high school student; planning to enroll or expecting to enroll full-time at a two-year or four-year or technical institution or university; resident of Montana and must have an interest in public speaking. Available to U.S. citizens.

Application Requirements: Application form, entry in a contest. *Deadline:* continuous.

Contact: Gary White, State Adjutant
Phone: 406-324-3989
Fax: 406-324-3991
E-mail: amlegmt@in-tch.com

AMERICAN LEGION DEPARTMENT OF NEBRASKA

http://www.nebraskalegion.net/

AMERICAN LEGION BASEBALL SCHOLARSHIP-NEBRASKA AMERICAN LEGION BASEBALL PLAYER OF THE YEAR

Any Team Manager or Head Coach of an American Legion Post-affiliated team may nominate one player for consideration for this award. Application, letters of recommendation, and certification form must be completed, postmarked, and mailed to the state's Department Headquarters no later than July 15. Three letters of testimony must be attached to the nomination form.

Award: Scholarship for use in freshman year; not renewable. *Number:* 1. *Amount:* $600–$750.

Eligibility Requirements: Applicant must be high school student; planning to enroll or expecting to enroll full- or part-time at a two-year or four-year or technical institution or university; resident of Nebraska and must have an interest in athletics/sports. Available to U.S. citizens.

Application Requirements: Application form, community service, personal photograph, recommendations or references. *Deadline:* July 15.

Contact: Brent Hagel-Pitt, Activities Director
American Legion Department of Nebraska
PO Box 5205
Lincoln, NE 68505-0205
Phone: 402-464-6338
Fax: 402-464-6330
E-mail: actdirlegion@windstream.net

AMERICAN LEGION DEPARTMENT OF NEBRASKA HIGH SCHOOL ORATORICAL CONTEST

Local high school winners advance to District. Fifteen District Winners advance to Area contest. Area contestants awarded $100. Four Area winners advance to State contest. State prizes range from $200 to $1000. State winner advances to National contest. National prizes range from $14,000 to $18,000.

Award: Prize for use in freshman year; not renewable. *Number:* 4–19. *Amount:* $100–$1000.

Eligibility Requirements: Applicant must be high school student; planning to enroll or expecting to enroll full- or part-time at a two-year or four-year or technical institution or university; resident of Nebraska and must have an interest in public speaking. Available to U.S. citizens.

Application Requirements: 8- to 10-minute prepared oration on some aspect the U.S. Constitution, a discourse on an assigned topic lasting 3 to 5 minutes, entry in a contest. *Deadline:* varies.

Contact: Brent Hagel-Pitt, Activities Director
American Legion Department of Nebraska
PO Box 5205
Lincoln, NE 68505-0205
Phone: 402-464-6338
Fax: 402-464-6880
E-mail: actdirlegion@windstream.net

AMERICAN LEGION DEPARTMENT OF NEBRASKA JIM HURLBERT MEMORIAL BASEBALL SCHOLARSHIP

Award to a Nebraska American Legion Baseball player in last year of eligibility and/or graduating senior. One applicant nominated by each Senior American Legion Baseball team. Student must attend a postsecondary educational institution within the state of Nebraska, and must have maintained a GPA in the upper half of his/her graduating class.

Award: Scholarship for use in freshman year; not renewable. *Number:* up to 4. *Amount:* up to $500.

Eligibility Requirements: Applicant must be high school student; planning to enroll or expecting to enroll full- or part-time at a two-year or four-year or technical institution or university; resident of Nebraska;

studying in Nebraska and must have an interest in athletics/sports. Applicant must have 2.5 GPA or higher. Available to U.S. citizens.

Application Requirements: Application form, community service, financial need analysis, recommendations or references, transcript. *Deadline:* June 15.

Contact: Brent Hagel-Pitt, Activities Director
American Legion Department of Nebraska
PO Box 5205
Lincoln, NE 68505-0205
Phone: 402-464-6338
Fax: 402-464-6330
E-mail: actdirlegion@windstream.net

EAGLE SCOUT OF THE YEAR SCHOLARSHIP
• *See page 511*

MAYNARD JENSEN AMERICAN LEGION MEMORIAL SCHOLARSHIP
• *See page 511*

AMERICAN LEGION DEPARTMENT OF NEW YORK

http://www.ny.legion.org/

AMERICAN LEGION DEPARTMENT OF NEW YORK HIGH SCHOOL ORATORICAL CONTEST

Oratorical contest open to students under 20 years in 9th-12th grades of any accredited New York high school. Speech contests begin in November at post levels and continue to national competition. Must be U.S. citizen or permanent resident. Payments are made directly to college and are awarded over a four-year period. Deadline varies.

Award: Scholarship for use in freshman year; not renewable. *Amount:* $2000–$6000.

Eligibility Requirements: Applicant must be high school student; planning to enroll or expecting to enroll full-time at a four-year institution or university; resident of New York and must have an interest in public speaking. Available to U.S. citizens.

Application Requirements: Application form, entry in a contest. *Deadline:* varies.

Contact: Richard Pedro, Department Adjutant
American Legion Department of New York
112 State Street, Suite 400
Albany, NY 12207
Phone: 518-463-2215
Fax: 518-427-8443
E-mail: newyork@legion.org

AMERICAN LEGION DEPARTMENT OF NORTH CAROLINA

http://www.nclegion.org/

AMERICAN LEGION DEPARTMENT OF NORTH CAROLINA HIGH SCHOOL ORATORICAL CONTEST

Objective of the contest is to develop a deeper knowledge and appreciation of the U.S. Constitution, develop leadership qualities, the ability to think and speak clearly and intelligently, and prepare for acceptance of duties, responsibilities, rights, and privileges of American citizenship. Open to North Carolina high school students. Must be U.S. citizen or lawful permanent resident. The contestant must have a prepared eight to ten minute oration on some aspect of the Constitution of the United States, as well as 4 three to five minute discourses on specific assigned topics to test the speaker's knowledge of the subject.

Award: Scholarship for use in freshman year; not renewable. *Number:* 5. *Amount:* $500–$2000.

Eligibility Requirements: Applicant must be high school student; planning to enroll or expecting to enroll full- or part-time at a two-year or four-year or technical institution or university; resident of North Carolina and must have an interest in public speaking. Available to U.S. citizens.

Application Requirements: Entry in a contest,. *Deadline:* January 5.

Contact: Deborah Rose, Department Executive Secretary
American Legion Department of North Carolina
4 North Blount Street, PO Box 26657
Raleigh, NC 27611-6657
Phone: 919-832-7506
Fax: 919-832-6428
E-mail: drose-nclegion@nc.rr.com

AMERICAN LEGION DEPARTMENT OF NORTH DAKOTA

http://www.ndlegion.org/

AMERICAN LEGION DEPARTMENT OF NORTH DAKOTA NATIONAL HIGH SCHOOL ORATORICAL CONTEST

Oratorical contest for high school students in grades nine to twelve. Contestants must prepare to speak on the topic of the U.S. Constitution. Must graduate from an accredited North Dakota high school. Contest begins at the local level and continues to the national level. Several one-time awards of $100 to $2000.

Award: Prize for use in freshman, sophomore, junior, or senior years; not renewable. *Number:* 38. *Amount:* $100–$2000.

Eligibility Requirements: Applicant must be high school student; planning to enroll or expecting to enroll full-time at a four-year institution or university; resident of North Dakota and must have an interest in public speaking. Available to U.S. citizens.

Application Requirements: Application form, entry in a contest. *Deadline:* November 30.

Contact: Teri Bryant, Programs/Membership Coordinator
Phone: 701-293-3120
Fax: 701-293-9951
E-mail: programs@ndlegion.org

HATTIE TEDROW MEMORIAL FUND SCHOLARSHIP

• *See page 597*

NORTH DAKOTA CARING CITIZEN SCHOLARSHIP

One-time award for North Dakota high school juniors who participated in the Boys State Program. Must be nominated by Boys State official. Must demonstrate care and concern for fellow students.

Award: Scholarship for use in freshman year; not renewable.

Eligibility Requirements: Applicant must be high school student; planning to enroll or expecting to enroll full-time at a two-year or four-year or technical institution or university; male and resident of North Dakota. Available to U.S. citizens.

Application Requirements: Application form, nomination, recommendations or references. *Deadline:* varies.

Contact: Teri Bryant, Programs/Membership Coordinator
Phone: 701-293-3120
Fax: 701-293-9951
E-mail: programs@ndlegion.org

AMERICAN LEGION DEPARTMENT OF OREGON

http://www.orlegion.org/

AMERICAN LEGION DEPARTMENT OF OREGON HIGH SCHOOL ORATORICAL CONTEST

Students give two orations, one prepared and one extemporaneous on an assigned topic pertaining to the Constitution of the United States of America. Awards are given at Post, District, and State level with the state winner advancing to the National level contest. Open to students enrolled in high schools within the state of Oregon.

Award: Scholarship for use in freshman year; not renewable. *Number:* up to 4. *Amount:* $200–$500.

Eligibility Requirements: Applicant must be high school student; planning to enroll or expecting to enroll full-time at a four-year institution or university; resident of Oregon and must have an interest in public speaking. Available to U.S. citizens.

Application Requirements: Application form, entry in a contest. *Deadline:* December 1.

Contact: Barry Snyder, Adjutant
Phone: 503-685-5006
Fax: 503-968-5432
E-mail: orlegion@aol.com

AMERICAN LEGION DEPARTMENT OF PENNSYLVANIA

http://www.pa-legion.com/

AMERICAN LEGION DEPARTMENT OF PENNSYLVANIA HIGH SCHOOL ORATORICAL CONTEST

Oratorical contest open to students in 9th-12th grades of any accredited Pennsylvania high school. Speech contests begin in January at post level and continue on to national competition. Contact local American Legion post for deadlines and application details. Three one-time awards ranging from $7500 for first place, second place $5000, and third place $4000.

Award: Prize for use in freshman year; not renewable. *Number:* 3. *Amount:* $4000–$7500.

Eligibility Requirements: Applicant must be high school student; planning to enroll or expecting to enroll full-time at a two-year or four-year or technical institution or university; resident of Pennsylvania and must have an interest in public speaking. Available to U.S. citizens.

Application Requirements: Application form, entry in a contest. *Deadline:* varies.

Contact: Colleen Washinger, Executive Secretary
American Legion Department of Pennsylvania
PO Box 2324
Harrisburg, PA 17105-2324
Phone: 717-730-9100
Fax: 717-975-2836
E-mail: hq@pa-legion.com

JOSEPH P. GAVENONIS COLLEGE SCHOLARSHIP (PLAN I)

• *See page 511*

AMERICAN LEGION DEPARTMENT OF SOUTH DAKOTA

http://www.sdlegion.org/

AMERICAN LEGION DEPARTMENT OF SOUTH DAKOTA HIGH SCHOOL ORATORICAL CONTEST

Provide an 8 to 10 minute oration on some phase of the U.S. Constitution. Be prepared to speak extemporaneously for 3 to 5 minutes on specified articles or amendments. Compete at Local, District, and State levels. State winner goes on to National Contest and opportunity to win $18,000 in scholarships. Contact local American Legion post for contest dates.

Award: Prize for use in freshman, sophomore, junior, or senior years; not renewable. *Number:* 1–4. *Amount:* $200–$1000.

Eligibility Requirements: Applicant must be enrolled or expecting to enroll full-time at a two-year or four-year or technical institution or university; resident of South Dakota and must have an interest in public speaking. Available to U.S. citizens.

Application Requirements: Entry in a contest, oration. *Deadline:* varies.

Contact: Dennis Brendan, Department Adjutant
American Legion Department of South Dakota
PO Box 67
Watertown, SD 57201-0067
Phone: 605-886-3604
Fax: 605-886-2870
E-mail: sdlegion@dailypost.com

AMERICAN LEGION DEPARTMENT OF TENNESSEE

http://www.tennesseelegion.org/

AMERICAN LEGION DEPARTMENT OF TENNESSEE EAGLE SCOUT OF THE YEAR

• *See page 512*

AMERICAN LEGION DEPARTMENT OF TENNESSEE HIGH SCHOOL ORATORICAL CONTEST

Scholarship for graduating Tennessee high school seniors enrolled either part-time or full-time in accredited colleges or universities.

Award: Scholarship for use in freshman, sophomore, junior, or senior years; not renewable. *Number:* up to 3. *Amount:* $1000–$3000.

Eligibility Requirements: Applicant must be high school student; planning to enroll or expecting to enroll full- or part-time at a two-year or four-year institution or university; resident of Tennessee and must have an interest in public speaking. Available to U.S. citizens.

Application Requirements: 3-5 oration and 8-10 oration on the Constitution, application form, entry in a contest, essay. *Deadline:* varies.

Contact: Darlene Burgess, Executive Secretary
  Phone: 615-391-5088
  E-mail: taltnadj@bellsouth.net

JROTC SCHOLARSHIP
• *See page 582*

AMERICAN LEGION DEPARTMENT OF TEXAS

http://www.txlegion.org/

AMERICAN LEGION DEPARTMENT OF TEXAS HIGH SCHOOL ORATORICAL CONTEST

Scholarships will be given to the winners of oratorical contests. Contestants must be in high school with plans to further their education in a postsecondary institution. The winner of first place will be certified to national headquarters as the Texas representative in the quarter finals and the department will award a $2000 scholarship to the college of the applicant's choice. The department champion will receive additional scholarships each time he/she advances to the next level.

Award: Prize for use in freshman year; not renewable. *Number:* up to 20. *Amount:* $500–$2000.

Eligibility Requirements: Applicant must be high school student; planning to enroll or expecting to enroll full-time at a two-year or four-year or technical institution or university; resident of Texas and must have an interest in public speaking. Available to U.S. citizens.

Application Requirements: Application form, copy of prepared oration, entry in a contest, essay, interview. *Deadline:* varies.

Contact: Robert Squyres, Director of Internal Affairs
  American Legion Department of Texas
  3401 Ed Bluestein Boulevard
  Austin, TX 78721-2902
  Phone: 512-472-4138
  Fax: 512-472-0603
  E-mail: programs@txlegion.org

AMERICAN LEGION DEPARTMENT OF VERMONT

http://www.vtlegion.org

AMERICAN LEGION DEPARTMENT OF VERMONT DEPARTMENT SCHOLARSHIPS

Awards for high school seniors who attend a Vermont high school or similar school in an adjoining state whose parents are legal residents of Vermont, or reside in an adjoining state and attend a Vermont secondary school.

Award: Scholarship for use in freshman year; not renewable. *Number:* up to 12. *Amount:* $500–$1500.

Eligibility Requirements: Applicant must be high school student; planning to enroll or expecting to enroll full- or part-time at a two-year or four-year or technical institution or university and resident of New Hampshire, New York, Vermont. Available to U.S. citizens.

Application Requirements: Application form, essay, financial need analysis, recommendations or references, transcript. *Deadline:* April 1.

Contact: Huzon "Jerry" Stewart, Chairman
  American Legion Department of Vermont
  PO Box 396
  Montpelier, VT 05601-0396
  Phone: 802-223-7131
  Fax: 802-223-0318
  E-mail: alvthq@myfairpoint.net

AMERICAN LEGION DEPARTMENT OF VERMONT HIGH SCHOOL ORATORICAL CONTEST

Students in grades 9 to 12 are eligible to compete. Must attend an accredited Vermont high school. Must be a U.S. citizen. Selection based on oration.

Award: Prize for use in freshman year; not renewable. *Number:* 1. *Amount:* $1500–$200.

Eligibility Requirements: Applicant must be high school student; planning to enroll or expecting to enroll full- or part-time at a two-year or four-year or technical institution or university; resident of Vermont and must have an interest in public speaking. Available to U.S. citizens.

Application Requirements: Application form, entry in a contest. *Deadline:* January 1.

Contact: Karlene DeVine, Chairman
  American Legion Department of Vermont
  126 State Street
  Montpelier, VT 05601
  Phone: 802-223-7131
  Fax: 802-223-0318
  E-mail: alvthq@myfairpoint.net

AMERICAN LEGION EAGLE SCOUT OF THE YEAR
• *See page 512*

AMERICAN LEGION DEPARTMENT OF VIRGINIA

http://www.valegion.org/

AMERICAN LEGION DEPARTMENT OF VIRGINIA HIGH SCHOOL ORATORICAL CONTEST

Three one-time awards of up to $1100. Oratorical contest open to applicants who are winners of the Virginia department oratorical contest and who attend high school in Virginia. Competitors must demonstrate their knowledge of the U.S. Constitution. Must be students in ninth to twelfth grades at accredited Virginia high schools.

Award: Prize for use in freshman year; not renewable. *Number:* 3. *Amount:* $600–$1100.

Eligibility Requirements: Applicant must be high school student; planning to enroll or expecting to enroll full-time at a four-year institution or university and resident of Virginia. Available to U.S. citizens.

Application Requirements: Application form, entry in a contest. *Deadline:* December 1.

Contact: Dale Chapman, Adjutant
  American Legion Department of Virginia
  1708 Commonwealth Avenue
  Richmond, VA 23230
  Phone: 804-353-6606
  Fax: 804-358-1940
  E-mail: eeccleston@valegion.org

AMERICAN LEGION DEPARTMENT OF WASHINGTON

http://www.walegion.org/

AMERICAN LEGION DEPARTMENT OF WASHINGTON CHILDREN AND YOUTH SCHOLARSHIPS
• *See page 512*

AMERICAN LEGION DEPARTMENT OF WEST VIRGINIA

http://www.wvlegion.org/

AMERICAN LEGION DEPARTMENT OF WEST VIRGINIA BOARD OF REGENTS SCHOLARSHIP

One-time prize awarded annually to the winner of the West Virginia American Legion State Oratorical Scholarship Program Contest. Must be in ninth to twelfth grade of an accredited West Virginia high school to compete. For use at a West Virginia institution only.

Award: Scholarship for use in freshman year; not renewable. *Number:* 1. *Amount:* up to $1500.

Eligibility Requirements: Applicant must be high school student; planning to enroll or expecting to enroll full-time at a four-year institution or university; resident of West Virginia; studying in West Virginia and must have an interest in public speaking. Available to U.S. citizens.

Application Requirements: Application form, entry in a contest. *Deadline:* January 1.

Contact: Mr. Miles Epling, State Adjutant
American Legion Department of West Virginia
2016 Kanawha Boulevard East, PO Box 3191
Charleston, WV 25332-3191
Phone: 304-343-7591
Fax: 304-343-7592
E-mail: wvlegion@suddenlinkmail.com

AMERICAN LEGION DEPARTMENT OF WEST VIRGINIA HIGH SCHOOL ORATORICAL CONTEST

Oratorical Scholarship Program Contest open to students in ninth to twelfth grades of any accredited West Virginia high school. Speech contests begin in January at post level and continue on to national competition. Contact local American Legion Post for deadlines and application details, or American Legion State Headquarters 304-343-7591.

Award: Scholarship for use in freshman year; not renewable. *Number:* 25–39. *Amount:* $150–$500.

Eligibility Requirements: Applicant must be high school student; planning to enroll or expecting to enroll full-time at a four-year institution or university; resident of West Virginia and must have an interest in public speaking. Available to U.S. citizens.

Application Requirements: Application form, entry in a contest. *Deadline:* January 1.

Contact: Ms. Lois Moles, State Adjutant
American Legion Department of West Virginia
2016 Kanawha Boulevard East, PO Box 3191
Charleston, WV 25332-3191
Phone: 304-343-7591
Fax: 304-343-7592
E-mail: wvlegion@suddenlinkmail.com

SONS OF THE AMERICAN LEGION WILLIAM F. "BILL" JOHNSON MEMORIAL SCHOLARSHIP

• See page 512

AMERICAN QUARTER HORSE FOUNDATION (AQHF)

http://www.aqha.com/foundation

ARIZONA QUARTER HORSE YOUTH SCHOLARSHIP
• See page 513

ARIZONA QUARTER RACING SCHOLARSHIP
• See page 513

CHRISTOPHER LAWRENCE JUNKER NEBRASKA SCHOLARSHIP
• See page 513

DR. GERALD O'CONNOR MICHIGAN QHY SCHOLARSHIP
• See page 513

INDIANA QUARTER HORSE YOUTH SCHOLARSHIP
• See page 514

JAMES F. AND DORIS M. BARTON SCHOLARSHIP
• See page 514

JOAN CAIN FLORIDA QUARTER HORSE YOUTH SCHOLARSHIP
• See page 514

JOYCE WYATT PENNSYLVANIA QUARTER HORSE YOUTH SCHOLARSHIP
• See page 514

NEBRASKA QUARTER HORSE YOUTH SCHOLARSHIP
• See page 514

OKLAHOMA QUARTER HORSE YOUTH SCHOLARSHIP
• See page 514

SWAYZE WOODRUFF MEMORIAL MID-SOUTH SCHOLARSHIP
• See page 514

AMERICAN SAVINGS FOUNDATION

http://www.asfdn.org/

AMERICAN SAVINGS FOUNDATION SCHOLARSHIPS

Scholarship awards range from $500 to $3000 for students entering any year of a two- or four-year undergraduate program or technical/vocational program at an accredited institution. Applicant must be a Connecticut resident. Minimum 2.5 GPA required.

Award: Scholarship for use in freshman, sophomore, junior, or senior years; renewable. *Amount:* $500–$3000.

Eligibility Requirements: Applicant must be enrolled or expecting to enroll full- or part-time at a two-year or four-year or technical institution or university and resident of Connecticut. Applicant must have 2.5 GPA or higher. Available to U.S. citizens.

Application Requirements: Application form, financial need analysis, recommendations or references, transcript. *Deadline:* March 31.

Contact: Maria Falvo, Senior Program Officer, Scholarships
Phone: 860-827-2572
Fax: 860-832-4582
E-mail: mfalvo@asfdn.org

AMERICAN SWEDISH INSTITUTE

http://www.ASImn.org

LILLY LORENZEN SCHOLARSHIP

One-time award for a Minnesota resident, or a student attending a school in Minnesota. Must have working knowledge of Swedish and present a creditable plan for study in Sweden. Must be a U.S. citizen.

Award: Scholarship for use in freshman, sophomore, junior, senior, graduate, or postgraduate years; not renewable. *Number:* 1. *Amount:* $1000.

Eligibility Requirements: Applicant must be enrolled or expecting to enroll full- or part-time at a two-year or four-year or technical institution or university; resident of Minnesota and must have an interest in Scandinavian language. Available to U.S. citizens.

Application Requirements: Application form, interview, transcript. *Deadline:* May 1.

Contact: Karin Krull, Adult Programs Coordinator
American Swedish Institute
2600 Park Avenue
Minneapolis, MN 55407-1090
Phone: 612-870-3355
Fax: 612-871-8682
E-mail: karink@ASImn.org

ARIZONA COMMISSION FOR POSTSECONDARY EDUCATION

http://www.azhighered.gov/

LEVERAGING EDUCATIONAL ASSISTANCE PARTNERSHIP

Grants to financially needy students, who enroll in and attend postsecondary education or training in Arizona schools. Program was formerly known as the State Student Incentive Grant or SSIG Program.

Award: Grant for use in freshman, sophomore, junior, senior, or graduate years; not renewable. *Amount:* $100–$2500.

Eligibility Requirements: Applicant must be enrolled or expecting to enroll full- or part-time at a two-year or four-year or technical institution or university; resident of Arizona and studying in Arizona. Available to U.S. citizens.

Application Requirements: Application form, financial need analysis, transcript. *Deadline:* April 30.

Contact: Mila Zaporteza, Business Manager and LEAP Financial Aid Manager
Arizona Commission for Postsecondary Education
2020 North Central Avenue, Suite 650
Phoenix, AZ 85004-4503
Phone: 602-258-2435 Ext. 102
Fax: 602-258-2483
E-mail: mila@azhighered.gov

ARIZONA PRIVATE SCHOOL ASSOCIATION

http://www.arizonapsa.org/

ARIZONA PRIVATE SCHOOL ASSOCIATION SCHOLARSHIP

Scholarships are for graduating students from Arizona and the high school determines the recipients of the awards. Each spring the Arizona Private School Association awards two $1000 scholarships to every private high school in Arizona.

Award: Scholarship for use in freshman year; not renewable. *Number:* 600. *Amount:* $1000.

Eligibility Requirements: Applicant must be high school student; planning to enroll or expecting to enroll full-time at a four-year institution or university and resident of Arizona. Available to U.S. citizens.

Application Requirements: Application form, essay. *Deadline:* April 30.

Contact: Fred Lockhart, Executive Director
Arizona Private School Association
202 East McDowell Road, Suite 273
Phoenix, AZ 85004
Phone: 602-254-5199
Fax: 602-254-5073
E-mail: apsa@eschelon.com

ARKANSAS DEPARTMENT OF HIGHER EDUCATION

http://www.adhe.edu/

ARKANSAS ACADEMIC CHALLENGE SCHOLARSHIP PROGRAM

Awards for Arkansas residents who are graduating high school seniors, currently enrolled college students and nontraditional students to study at an approved Arkansas institution. Must have at least a 2.5 GPA or 19 ACT composite score (or the equivalent). Renewable up to three additional years.

Award: Scholarship for use in freshman, sophomore, junior, or senior years; renewable. *Number:* 30,000–35,000. *Amount:* $1250–$4500.

Eligibility Requirements: Applicant must be enrolled or expecting to enroll full- or part-time at a two-year or four-year institution or university; resident of Arkansas and studying in Arkansas. Applicant must have 2.5 GPA or higher. Available to U.S. citizens.

Application Requirements: Application form, application form may be submitted online (http://www.adhe.edu), financial need analysis, test scores, transcript. *Deadline:* June 1.

Contact: Philip Axelroth, Financial Aid Program Coordinator
Phone: 501-371-2000

ARKANSAS GOVERNOR'S SCHOLARS PROGRAM

Awards for outstanding Arkansas high school seniors. Must be an Arkansas resident and have a high school GPA of at least 3.5 or have scored at least 27 on the ACT. Award is $4000 per year for four years of full-time undergraduate study. Applicants who attain 32 or above on ACT, 1410 or above on SAT and have an academic 3.5 GPA, or are selected as National Merit or National Achievement finalists may receive an award equal to tuition, mandatory fees, room, and board up to $10,000 per year at any Arkansas institution.

Award: Scholarship for use in freshman, sophomore, junior, senior, or graduate years; renewable. *Number:* 75–375. *Amount:* $4000–$10,000.

Eligibility Requirements: Applicant must be high school student; planning to enroll or expecting to enroll full-time at a two-year or four-year institution or university; resident of Arkansas and studying in Arkansas. Applicant must have 3.5 GPA or higher. Available to U.S. citizens.

Application Requirements: Application form, application form may be submitted online (http://www.adhe.edu), community service, test scores, transcript. *Deadline:* February 1.

Contact: Philip Axelroth, Financial Aid Program Coordinator
Phone: 501-371-2000

LAW ENFORCEMENT OFFICERS' DEPENDENTS SCHOLARSHIP–ARKANSAS

Scholarship for dependents, under 23 years old, of Arkansas law-enforcement officers killed or permanently disabled in the line of duty. Renewable award is a waiver of tuition, fees, and room at two- or four-year Arkansas institution. Submit birth certificate, death certificate, and claims commission report of findings of fact. Proof of disability from State Claims Commission may also be submitted.

Award: Scholarship for use in freshman, sophomore, junior, or senior years; renewable. *Number:* 27–32.

Eligibility Requirements: Applicant must be enrolled or expecting to enroll full- or part-time at a two-year or four-year or technical institution or university; resident of Arkansas and studying in Arkansas. Available to U.S. citizens.

Application Requirements: Application form. *Deadline:* continuous.

Contact: Tara Smith, Director of Financial Aid
Arkansas Department of Higher Education
114 East Capitol Avenue
Little Rock, AR 72201-3818
Phone: 501-371-2000
Fax: 501-371-2001
E-mail: taras@adhe.edu

MILITARY DEPENDENT'S SCHOLARSHIP PROGRAM
• *See page 598*

SECOND EFFORT SCHOLARSHIP

Awarded to those scholars who achieved one of the 10 highest scores on the Arkansas High School Diploma Test (GED). Must be at least age 18 and not have graduated from high school. Students do not apply for this award, they are contacted by the Arkansas Department of Higher Education.

Award: Scholarship for use in freshman, sophomore, junior, or senior years; renewable. *Number:* 10. *Amount:* up to $1000.

Eligibility Requirements: Applicant must be enrolled or expecting to enroll full- or part-time at a two-year or four-year institution or university; resident of Arkansas and studying in Arkansas. Available to U.S. citizens.

Application Requirements: Application form, application form may be submitted online (http://www.adhe.edu). *Deadline:* varies.

Contact: Philip Axelroth, Financial Aid Program Coordinator
Phone: 501-371-2000

ARKANSAS SINGLE PARENT SCHOLARSHIP FUND

http://www.aspsf.org/

ARKANSAS SINGLE PARENT SCHOLARSHIP

Scholarships are awarded to economically disadvantaged single parents who reside in Arkansas. Applicants must have custodial care of at least one minor child and have not already received a 4-year degree. Some scholarships may be awarded to single parents enrolled in a Masters of Arts in Teaching program. Application forms, award values, deadlines, and other requirements vary by county. Visit http://www.aspsf.org for more information.

Award: Scholarship for use in freshman, sophomore, junior, senior, or graduate years; not renewable. *Number:* up to 2600. *Amount:* $200–$1800.

Eligibility Requirements: Applicant must be enrolled or expecting to enroll full- or part-time at a two-year or four-year or technical institution or university; single and resident of Arkansas. Available to U.S. and non-U.S. citizens.

Application Requirements: Application form, application form may be submitted online (http://www.aspsf.org), essay, FAFSA Student Aid Report (SAR), financial need analysis, interview, recommendations or references, transcript. *Deadline:* varies.

Contact: Ruthanne Hill, Executive Director
Phone: 479-927-1402 Ext. 11
E-mail: rhill@aspsf.org

ARKANSAS STUDENT LOAN AUTHORITY

http://www.asla.info/

R. PRESTON WOODRUFF JR. SCHOLARSHIP

Twenty $1000 scholarships awarded annually. Online entries only and only one entry per applicant. Eligible entries will be drawn at random to select the scholarship winners. Winners must submit a 500-word essay. One renewable scholarship (up to 4 years) will be awarded to the student with the most outstanding essay.

Award: Scholarship for use in freshman, sophomore, junior, senior, or graduate years; renewable. *Number:* 20. *Amount:* $1000.

Eligibility Requirements: Applicant must be enrolled or expecting to enroll full- or part-time at a two-year or four-year or technical institution or university and resident of Arkansas. Available to U.S. citizens.

Application Requirements: Application form, application form may be submitted online (http://www.asla.info). *Deadline:* April 1.

Contact: Nancy Smith, Federal Contracts and Compliance Manager
Phone: 800-443-6030
E-mail: nsmith@asla.info

ARRL FOUNDATION INC.

http://www.arrl.org/

ALBERT H. HIX, W8AH, MEMORIAL SCHOLARSHIP

One-time $500 award available to general class or higher class amateur radio operators. Preference is given to the residents of the West Virginia section who are attending postsecondary school in the West Virginia section. Minimum GPA of 3.0 or higher required.

Award: Scholarship for use in freshman, sophomore, junior, or senior years; not renewable. *Number:* 1. *Amount:* $500.

Eligibility Requirements: Applicant must be enrolled or expecting to enroll full-time at a two-year or four-year or technical institution or university; resident of West Virginia; studying in West Virginia and must have an interest in amateur radio. Applicant must have 3.0 GPA or higher. Available to U.S. citizens.

Application Requirements: Application form, test scores, transcript. *Deadline:* February 1.

Contact: Ms. Mary Hobart, Secretary
Phone: 860-594-0397
E-mail: k1mmh@arrl.org

ARRL ROCKY MOUNTAIN DIVISION SCHOLARSHIP

One $500 award to a student with an active amateur radio license attending an accredited two- or four-year college or university. Preference given to residents of the ARRL Rocky Mountain Division (Colorado, New Mexico, Utah or Wyoming). Must be a US citizen, and a graduating high school senior or undergraduate student. Must submit a letter of recommendation from a sitting officer of an ARRL-affiliated club attesting to regular activity on the amateur radio spectrum and within the Amateur Radio community.

Award: Scholarship for use in freshman, sophomore, junior, or senior years; not renewable. *Number:* 1. *Amount:* $500.

Eligibility Requirements: Applicant must be enrolled or expecting to enroll full- or part-time at a two-year or four-year institution or university; resident of Colorado, New Mexico, Utah, Wyoming and must have an interest in amateur radio. Available to U.S. citizens.

Application Requirements: Application form, recommendations or references, transcript. *Deadline:* February 1.

Contact: Ms. Mary Hobart, Secretary
Phone: 860-594-0397
E-mail: k1mmh@arrl.org

BYRON BLANCHARD, N1EKV, MEMORIAL SCHOLARSHIP FUND

One $500 scholarship for a student in residence in ARRL New England Division (Massachusetts, New Hampshire, Connecticut, Rhode Island, Vermont and Maine). Must have an active Amateur Radio License Class license.

Award: Scholarship for use in freshman, sophomore, junior, or senior years; not renewable. *Number:* 1. *Amount:* $500.

Eligibility Requirements: Applicant must be enrolled or expecting to enroll full- or part-time at a two-year or four-year or technical institution or university; resident of Connecticut, Maine, Massachusetts, New Hampshire, Rhode Island, Vermont and must have an interest in amateur radio. Available to U.S. citizens.

Application Requirements: Application form, transcript. *Deadline:* February 1.

Contact: Ms. Mary Hobart, Secretary
Phone: 860-594-0397
E-mail: k1mmh@arrl.org

CENTRAL ARIZONA DX ASSOCIATION SCHOLARSHIP

One $1000 award is a available to a student who is an Arizona resident and who a possesses a Technician class or higher radio license. Must have cumulative GPA of 3.2 or above. Graduating high school students will be considered before current college students.

Award: Scholarship for use in freshman, sophomore, junior, or senior years; not renewable. *Number:* 1. *Amount:* $1000.

Eligibility Requirements: Applicant must be enrolled or expecting to enroll full- or part-time at a two-year or four-year institution or university; resident of Arizona and must have an interest in amateur radio. Available to U.S. citizens.

Application Requirements: Application form, transcript. *Deadline:* February 1.

Contact: Ms. Mary Hobart, Secretary
Phone: 860-594-0397
E-mail: k1mmh@arrl.org

CHICAGO FM CLUB SCHOLARSHIP FUND

Multiple awards available to amateur radio operators with technician license who are U.S. citizens or within 3 months of citizenship. Preference given to residents of FCC Ninth Call District (Indiana, Illinois, Wisconsin) pursuing post-secondary course of study at accredited 2- or 4-year college or trade school.

Award: Scholarship for use in freshman, sophomore, junior, or senior years; not renewable. *Amount:* $500.

Eligibility Requirements: Applicant must be enrolled or expecting to enroll full-time at a two-year or four-year or technical institution or university; resident of Illinois, Indiana, Wisconsin and must have an interest in amateur radio. Available to U.S. citizens.

Application Requirements: Application form, transcript. *Deadline:* February 1.

Contact: Ms. Mary Hobart, Secretary
Phone: 860-594-0397
E-mail: k1mmh@arrl.org

DAVID KNAUS MEMORIAL SCHOLARSHIP

One $1500 award for a student with an active amateur radio license pursuing a bachelor's degree or a 2-year associate's degree. Preference given to a resident of Wisconsin or, if no qualified applicant from Wisconsin, to applicant from the ARRL Central Division (Illinois, Indiana, Wisconsin).

Award: Scholarship for use in freshman, sophomore, junior, or senior years; not renewable. *Number:* 1. *Amount:* $1500.

Eligibility Requirements: Applicant must be enrolled or expecting to enroll full- or part-time at a two-year or four-year or technical institution; resident of Illinois, Indiana, Wisconsin and must have an interest in amateur radio. Available to U.S. citizens.

Application Requirements: Application form, transcript. *Deadline:* February 1.

Contact: Ms. Mary Hobart, Secretary
Phone: 860-594-0397
E-mail: k1mmh@arrl.org

GWINNETT AMATEUR RADIO SOCIETY SCHOLARSHIP

One $500 award available to a Georgia resident possessing an active amateur radio license. Preference is given to students from Gwinnett County, GA studying at four-year colleges or universities.

Award: Scholarship for use in freshman, sophomore, junior, senior, or graduate years; not renewable. *Number:* 1. *Amount:* $500.

Eligibility Requirements: Applicant must be enrolled or expecting to enroll full- or part-time at a four-year institution or university; resident of Georgia and must have an interest in amateur radio. Available to U.S. citizens.

Application Requirements: Application form, transcript. *Deadline:* February 1.

Contact: Ms. Mary Hobart, Secretary
Phone: 860-594-0397
E-mail: k1mmh@arrl.org

JACKSON COUNTY ARA SCHOLARSHIP

One $500 award for a student with an active amateur radio license. Preference given to students from Mississippi. If no applicant is identified, preference will be given to a student from the ARRL Delta Division (Arkansas, Louisiana, Mississippi, and Tennessee).

Award: Scholarship for use in freshman, sophomore, junior, or senior years; not renewable. *Number:* 1. *Amount:* $500.

Eligibility Requirements: Applicant must be enrolled or expecting to enroll full- or part-time at a two-year or four-year or technical institution or university; resident of Arkansas, Louisiana, Mississippi, Tennessee and must have an interest in amateur radio. Available to U.S. citizens.

Application Requirements: Application form, transcript. *Deadline:* February 1.

Contact: Ms. Mary Hobart, Secretary
Phone: 860-594-0397
E-mail: k1mmh@arrl.org

LOUISIANA MEMORIAL SCHOLARSHIP

One $750 award is available to a resident of Louisiana or a student studying in Louisiana who possesses a technician class or higher amateur radio license. Must be studying at a four-year college or university and maintain a minimum 3.0 GPA.

Award: Scholarship for use in freshman, sophomore, junior, or senior years; not renewable. *Number:* 1. *Amount:* $750.

Eligibility Requirements: Applicant must be enrolled or expecting to enroll full- or part-time at a four-year institution or university; resident of Louisiana; studying in Louisiana and must have an interest in amateur radio. Applicant must have 3.0 GPA or higher. Available to U.S. citizens.

Application Requirements: Application form, transcript. *Deadline:* February 1.

Contact: Ms. Mary Hobart, Secretary
Phone: 860-594-0397
E-mail: k1mmh@arrl.org

MARY LOU BROWN SCHOLARSHIP

Multiple awards available to amateur radio operators with general license. Preference given to residents of Alaska, Idaho, Montana, Oregon, and Washington pursuing baccalaureate or higher course of study. GPA of 3.0 or higher required. Must demonstrate interest in promoting Amateur Radio Service.

Award: Scholarship for use in freshman, sophomore, junior, senior, or graduate years; not renewable. *Amount:* $2500.

Eligibility Requirements: Applicant must be enrolled or expecting to enroll full-time at a four-year institution or university; resident of Alaska, Idaho, Montana, Oregon, Washington and must have an interest in amateur radio. Applicant must have 3.0 GPA or higher. Available to U.S. citizens.

Application Requirements: Application form, transcript. *Deadline:* February 1.

Contact: Ms. Mary Hobart, Secretary
Phone: 860-594-0397
E-mail: k1mmh@arrl.org

NEW ENGLAND FEMARA SCHOLARSHIPS

One-time award of $1000 available to students licensed as amateur radio operator technicians. Multiple awards per year. Preference is given to the residents of Vermont, Maine, New Hampshire, Rhode Island, Massachusetts, or Connecticut.

Award: Scholarship for use in freshman, sophomore, junior, or senior years; not renewable. *Amount:* $1000.

Eligibility Requirements: Applicant must be enrolled or expecting to enroll full-time at a four-year institution or university; resident of Connecticut, Maine, Massachusetts, New Hampshire, Rhode Island, Vermont and must have an interest in amateur radio. Available to U.S. citizens.

Application Requirements: Application form, transcript. *Deadline:* February 1.

Contact: Ms. Mary Hobart, Secretary
Phone: 860-594-0397
E-mail: k1mmh@arrl.org

NORMAN E. STROHMEIER, W2VRS, MEMORIAL SCHOLARSHIP

One $500 award is available to students who are residents of western New York and who possess technician class or higher amateur radio licenses. Preference is given to graduating high school seniors with a 3.2 GPA. Must provide documentation of Amateur Radio activities and achievements and any honor from community service.

Award: Scholarship for use in freshman, sophomore, junior, senior, or graduate years; not renewable. *Number:* 1. *Amount:* $500.

Eligibility Requirements: Applicant must be enrolled or expecting to enroll full- or part-time at a two-year or four-year or technical institution or university; resident of New York and must have an interest in amateur radio. Available to U.S. citizens.

Application Requirements: Application form, community service, documentation of amateur radio activities or achievements, transcript. *Deadline:* February 1.

Contact: Ms. Mary Hobart, Secretary
Phone: 860-594-0397
E-mail: k1mmh@arrl.org

OUTDOOR HAMS SCHOLARSHIP

Scholarship for a North Carolina resident who has an active Amateur Radio license of any class. Preference given to Amateur Radio operators that incorporate Amateur Radio into outdoor activities. One $1000 award per year for 4-year college student or two $500 awards for 2-year college students.

Award: Scholarship for use in freshman, sophomore, junior, or senior years; not renewable. *Number:* 1–2. *Amount:* $500–$1000.

Eligibility Requirements: Applicant must be enrolled or expecting to enroll full- or part-time at a two-year or four-year or technical institution or university; resident of North Carolina and must have an interest in amateur radio. Available to U.S. citizens.

Application Requirements: Application form, transcript. *Deadline:* February 1.

Contact: Ms. Mary Hobart, Secretary
Phone: 860-594-0397
E-mail: k1mmh@arrl.org

PEORIA AREA AMATEUR RADIO CLUB SCHOLARSHIP

One $500 award is available to residents of the Central Illinois counties of Peoria, Tazewell, Woodford, Knox, McLean, Fulton, Logan, Marshall, and Stark. Applicants must possess a technician class or higher amateur radio license and attend an accredited two- or four-year college or university.

Award: Scholarship for use in freshman, sophomore, junior, or senior years; not renewable. *Number:* 1. *Amount:* $500.

Eligibility Requirements: Applicant must be enrolled or expecting to enroll full- or part-time at a two-year or four-year institution or university; resident of Illinois and must have an interest in amateur radio. Available to U.S. citizens.

Application Requirements: Application form, transcript. *Deadline:* February 1.

Contact: Ms. Mary Hobart, Secretary
Phone: 860-594-0397
E-mail: k1mmh@arrl.org

SIX METER CLUB OF CHICAGO SCHOLARSHIP

One-time $500 award for licensed amateur radio operators. Preference given to students with grade point average of 2.5 or better and in good academic standing. Must be a resident of Illinois, or resident of ARRL Central Division (Indiana, Wisconsin) attending school part-time or full-time at a regionally accredited technical school, community college, college, or university and pursuing an undergraduate degree.

Award: Scholarship for use in freshman, sophomore, junior, or senior years; not renewable. *Number:* 1. *Amount:* $500.

Eligibility Requirements: Applicant must be enrolled or expecting to enroll full- or part-time at a two-year or four-year or technical institution or university; resident of Illinois, Indiana, Wisconsin and must have an interest in amateur radio. Applicant must have 2.5 GPA or higher. Available to U.S. citizens.

Application Requirements: Application form, transcript. *Deadline:* February 1.

Contact: Ms. Mary Hobart, Secretary
Phone: 860-594-0397
E-mail: k1mmh@arrl.org

THOMAS W. PORTER, W8KYZ, SCHOLARSHIP HONORING MICHAEL DAUGHERTY, W8LSE

One $1000 award available to a student with a technician class or higher amateur radio license. Preference given to students from Ohio or West Virginia at accredited 2- or 4-year colleges/universities or technical schools.

Award: Scholarship for use in freshman, sophomore, junior, or senior years; not renewable. *Number:* 1. *Amount:* $1000.

Eligibility Requirements: Applicant must be enrolled or expecting to enroll full- or part-time at a two-year or four-year or technical institution or university; resident of Ohio, West Virginia and must have an interest in amateur radio. Available to U.S. citizens.

Application Requirements: Application form, transcript. *Deadline:* February 1.

Contact: Ms. Mary Hobart, Secretary
Phone: 860-594-0397
E-mail: k1mmh@arrl.org

TOM AND JUDITH COMSTOCK SCHOLARSHIP

One-time award of $2000 for high school seniors. Preference given to residents of Texas and Oklahoma. Must be licensed amateur radio operator and be accepted at a two- or four-year institution.

Award: Scholarship for use in freshman year; not renewable. *Number:* 1. *Amount:* $2000.

Eligibility Requirements: Applicant must be high school student; planning to enroll or expecting to enroll full-time at a two-year or four-year institution or university; resident of Oklahoma, Texas and must have an interest in amateur radio. Available to U.S. citizens.

Application Requirements: Application form, transcript. *Deadline:* February 1.

Contact: Ms. Mary Hobart, Secretary
Phone: 860-594-0397
E-mail: k1mmh@arrl.org

WILLIAM BENNETT, W7PHO, MEMORIAL SCHOLARSHIP

One $500 award is available to residents of ARRL's Northwest, Pacific, and Southwest divisions. Must have a general class or higher amateur radio license, attend a four-year college or university, and have a minimum 3.0 GPA.

Award: Scholarship for use in freshman, sophomore, junior, or senior years; not renewable. *Number:* 1. *Amount:* $500.

Eligibility Requirements: Applicant must be enrolled or expecting to enroll full- or part-time at a four-year institution or university; resident of Arizona, California, Colorado, Idaho, Montana, Nevada, New Mexico, Oregon, Utah, Washington, Wyoming and must have an interest in amateur radio. Applicant must have 3.0 GPA or higher. Available to U.S. citizens.

Application Requirements: Application form, transcript. *Deadline:* February 1.

Contact: Ms. Mary Hobart, Secretary
Phone: 860-594-0397
E-mail: k1mmh@arrl.org

YANKEE CLIPPER CONTEST CLUB INC. YOUTH SCHOLARSHIP

One-time award available to general class or higher licensed amateur radio operators. Must reside or attend an accredited college or university within a175-mile radius of YCCC Center in Erving, MA.

Award: Scholarship for use in freshman, sophomore, junior, or senior years; not renewable. *Number:* 1. *Amount:* $1200.

Eligibility Requirements: Applicant must be enrolled or expecting to enroll full-time at a two-year or four-year institution or university; resident of Connecticut, Maine, Massachusetts, New Hampshire, New Jersey, New York, Pennsylvania, Rhode Island, Vermont and must have an interest in amateur radio. Available to U.S. citizens.

Application Requirements: Application form, transcript. *Deadline:* February 1.

Contact: Ms. Mary Hobart, Secretary
Phone: 860-594-0397
E-mail: k1mmh@arrl.org

YOU'VE GOT A FRIEND IN PENNSYLVANIA SCHOLARSHIP

• See page 515

ZACHARY TAYLOR STEVENS SCHOLARSHIP

One $750 award is available to students who possess a technician class or higher amateur radio license. Preference will be given to residents of Michigan, Ohio, and West Virginia. Must attend an accredited 2-year or 4-year college, university, or technical school.

Award: Scholarship for use in freshman, sophomore, junior, or senior years; not renewable. *Number:* 1. *Amount:* $750.

Eligibility Requirements: Applicant must be enrolled or expecting to enroll full- or part-time at a two-year or four-year or technical institution or university; resident of Michigan, Ohio, West Virginia and must have an interest in amateur radio. Available to U.S. citizens.

Application Requirements: Application form, transcript. *Deadline:* February 1.

Contact: Ms. Mary Hobart, Secretary
Phone: 860-594-0397
E-mail: k1mmh@arrl.org

ASIAN PACIFIC COMMUNITY FUND

http://www.apcf.org/

ASIAN PACIFIC COMMUNITY FUND - VERIZON SCHOLARSHIP AWARDS PROGRAM (HIGH SCHOOL SENIORS)

Applicants must be high school seniors planning to enter his or her freshman year of college during Fall 2013. He or she must be planning to major in math, engineering, or any science field.

Award: Scholarship for use in freshman year; not renewable. *Number:* 10. *Amount:* $1000.

Eligibility Requirements: Applicant must be high school student; planning to enroll or expecting to enroll full-time at a four-year institution or university; resident of California, Oregon, Washington and studying in California, Oregon, Washington. Applicant must have 3.0 GPA or higher. Available to U.S. and non-U.S. citizens.

Application Requirements: Application form, application form may be submitted online (http://apcf.wufoo.com/forms/scholarship-application-form/), essay, recommendations or references, transcript. *Deadline:* April 30.

Contact: Mr. Martin Mai, Marketing and Program Manager
Asian Pacific Community Fund
1145 Wilshire Boulevard
Suite 105
Los Angeles, CA 90017
Phone: 213-624-6400 Ext. 4
Fax: 213-624-6406
E-mail: mmai@apcf.org

CHEN FOUNDATION 2013 SCHOLARSHIP PROGRAM

The Chen Foundation is focused on helping economically-challenged youth fulfill their dreams of obtaining a higher education. The scholarship is renewable, allowing scholarship recipients to receive an additional $2000 award after their first quarter/semester of college if they maintain a 3.0 GPA or higher and active involvement in community service. Eligibility: high school seniors who reside in California; plan to attend a California State University as a 1st year college student in the Fall of 2013; plan to major in math, engineering, or a science; have a minimum cumulative unweighted high school GPA of 3.0; and have a household income at or below "Low Income" based on the California Low Income Level.

Award: Scholarship for use in freshman year; renewable. *Number:* 5. *Amount:* $2000.

Eligibility Requirements: Applicant must be high school student; planning to enroll or expecting to enroll full-time at a four-year institution; resident of California and studying in California. Applicant must have 3.0 GPA or higher. Available to U.S. and non-U.S. citizens.

Application Requirements: Application form, application form may be submitted online (http://apcf.org/what-we-do/197-chen-foundation-scholarship), essay, recommendations or references, transcript. *Deadline:* April 30.

Contact: Mr. Martin Mai, Marketing and Program Manager
Asian Pacific Community Fund
1145 Wilshire Boulevard, Suite 105
Los Angeles, CA 90017
Phone: 213-624-6400 Ext. 4
Fax: 213-624-6406
E-mail: mmai@apcf.org

ASIAN REPORTER

http://www.arfoundation.net/

ASIAN REPORTER SCHOLARSHIP
• *See page 617*

ASSOCIATION OF BLIND CITIZENS

http://www.blindcitizens.org/

REGGIE JOHNSON MEMORIAL SCHOLARSHIP
• *See page 567*

A.W. BODINE-SUNKIST GROWERS INC.

http://www.sunkist.com/

A.W. BODINE-SUNKIST MEMORIAL SCHOLARSHIP
• *See page 551*

BARKING FOUNDATION

BARKING FOUNDATION GRANTS

One-time award of $3000 available to Maine residents. Minimum GPA of 3.5 is desirable. Only first 300 completed applications will be accepted. Essay, financial information, and transcripts required. Available to full- and part-time students. Scholarships vary in number from year to year.

Award: Grant for use in freshman, sophomore, junior, senior, graduate, or postgraduate years; not renewable. *Number:* up to 25. *Amount:* $3000.

Eligibility Requirements: Applicant must be enrolled or expecting to enroll full- or part-time at a four-year institution or university and resident of Maine. Applicant must have 3.5 GPA or higher. Available to U.S. citizens.

Application Requirements: Application form, copy of SAR, essay, financial need analysis, recommendations or references, transcript. *Deadline:* February 15.

Contact: Stephanie Leonard, Administrator
Barking Foundation
PO Box 855
Bangor, ME 04402
Phone: 207-990-2910
Fax: 207-990-2975
E-mail: info@barkingfoundation.org

BIG Y FOODS INC.

http://www.bigy.com/

BIG Y SCHOLARSHIPS

Awards for customers or dependents of customers of Big Y Foods. Big Y trade area covers Norfolk county, western and central Massachusetts, and Connecticut. Also awards for Big Y employees and dependents of employees. Awards are based on academic excellence. Grades, board scores and two letters of recommendation required.

Award: Scholarship for use in freshman, sophomore, junior, senior, or graduate years; not renewable. *Number:* 300–350. *Amount:* $500–$2000.

Eligibility Requirements: Applicant must be enrolled or expecting to enroll full- or part-time at a two-year or four-year or technical institution or university; resident of Connecticut, Massachusetts and studying in Connecticut, Massachusetts. Available to U.S. and non-U.S. citizens.

Application Requirements: Application form, recommendations or references, resume, test scores, transcript. *Deadline:* February 1.

Contact: Missy Lajoie, Scholarship Committee
Big Y Foods Inc.
PO Box 7840
Springfield, MA 01102-7840
Phone: 413-504-4047
Fax: 413-504-6509
E-mail: wecare@bigy.com

BLUE GRASS ENERGY

http://www.bgenergy.com/

BLUE GRASS ENERGY ACADEMIC SCHOLARSHIP

Scholarships for Kentucky high school seniors living with parents or guardians who are members of Blue Grass Energy. Must have minimum GPA of 3.0 and have demonstrated academic achievement, extracurricular involvement and financial need. For application and information, visit website http://www.bgenergy.com/forStudents.aspx.

Award: Scholarship for use in freshman year; not renewable. *Number:* 10. *Amount:* $1000.

Eligibility Requirements: Applicant must be high school student; planning to enroll or expecting to enroll full-time at a two-year or four-year or technical institution or university and resident of Kentucky. Applicant must have 3.0 GPA or higher. Available to U.S. citizens.

Application Requirements: Application form, essay, explanation of how scholarship is necessary to further education, financial need analysis, resume, test scores, transcript. *Deadline:* April 1.

Contact: Ms. Magen Howard, Communications Adviser
Phone: 859-885-2104
E-mail: magenh@bgenergy.com

BNY MELLON, N.A.

http://www.bnymellon.com/

CHARLES C. ELY EDUCATIONAL FUND

Award for men who are residents of Massachusetts. Academic performance, character and financial need will be considered. Eligible applicant must be recommended by educational institution. Not for graduate study programs.

Award: Scholarship for use in freshman, sophomore, junior, or senior years; not renewable. *Amount:* up to $2000.

Eligibility Requirements: Applicant must be enrolled or expecting to enroll full-time at a two-year or four-year or technical institution or university; male and resident of Massachusetts. Available to U.S. citizens.

Application Requirements: Application form, essay, transcript. *Deadline:* April 15.

Contact: June Kfoury McNeil, Vice President
BNY Mellon, N.A.
201 Washington Street, 024-0092
Boston, MA 02108
Phone: 617-722-3891
E-mail: brown-mcmullen.s@mellon.com

HENRY FRANCIS BARROWS SCHOLARSHIP
• *See page 650*

BOETTCHER FOUNDATION
http://www.boettcherfoundation.org/

BOETTCHER FOUNDATION SCHOLARSHIPS
Merit-based scholarship available to graduating seniors in the state of Colorado. Selection based on class rank (top 5 percent), test scores, leadership, service and character. Renewable for four years and can be used at any Colorado university or college. Includes full tuition and fees, living stipend of $2800 per year, and a stipend for books.

Award: Scholarship for use in freshman, sophomore, junior, or senior years; renewable. *Number:* 40. *Amount:* $13,000–$40,000.

Eligibility Requirements: Applicant must be high school student; planning to enroll or expecting to enroll full-time at a four-year institution or university; resident of Colorado; studying in Colorado and must have an interest in leadership. Applicant must have 3.5 GPA or higher. Available to U.S. citizens.

Application Requirements: Application form, essay, interview, recommendations or references, test scores, transcript. *Deadline:* November 1.

Contact: Ms. Stephanie Panion, Scholarship Program Coordinator
Boettcher Foundation
600 17th Street, Suite 2210 S
Denver, CO 80202-5422
Phone: 303-285-6207
Fax: 303-534-1943
E-mail: scholarships@boettcherfoundation.org

BOYS AND GIRLS CLUBS OF CHICAGO
http://www.bgcc.org/

BOYS AND GIRLS CLUBS OF CHICAGO SCHOLARSHIPS
• *See page 515*

BUFFALO AFL-CIO COUNCIL
http://www.wnyalf.org/

AFL-CIO COUNCIL OF BUFFALO SCHOLARSHIP WNY ALF SCHOLARSHIP
• *See page 516*

CABRILLO CIVIC CLUBS OF CALIFORNIA INC.
http://www.cabrillocivicclubs.org/

CABRILLO CIVIC CLUBS OF CALIFORNIA SCHOLARSHIP
• *See page 618*

CALIFORNIA COMMUNITY COLLEGES
http://www.cccco.edu/

COOPERATIVE AGENCIES RESOURCES FOR EDUCATION PROGRAM
Renewable award available to California resident enrolled as a full-time student at a two-year California community college. Must currently receive CalWORKs/TANF and have at least one child under fourteen years of age at time of acceptance into CARE program. Must be in EOPS, a single head of household, and age 18 or older. Contact local college EOPS-CARE office for application and more information. To locate nearest campus, see http://www.icanaffordcollege.com/applications/homepage2.cfm.

Award: Grant for use in freshman or sophomore years; renewable. *Number:* 10,000–11,000.

Eligibility Requirements: Applicant must be enrolled or expecting to enroll full-time at a two-year institution; single; resident of California and studying in California. Available to U.S. citizens.

Application Requirements: Application form, financial need analysis, test scores, transcript. *Deadline:* continuous.

CALIFORNIA CORRECTIONAL PEACE OFFICERS ASSOCIATION
http://www.ccpoa.org/

CALIFORNIA CORRECTIONAL PEACE OFFICERS ASSOCIATION JOE HARPER SCHOLARSHIP
• *See page 552*

CALIFORNIA COUNCIL OF THE BLIND
http://www.ccbnet.org/

CALIFORNIA COUNCIL OF THE BLIND SCHOLARSHIPS
• *See page 567*

CALIFORNIA GRANGE FOUNDATION
http://www.californiagrange.org/

CALIFORNIA GRANGE FOUNDATION SCHOLARSHIP
• *See page 516*

CALIFORNIA JUNIOR MISS SCHOLARSHIP PROGRAM
http://www.ajm.org/

CALIFORNIA JUNIOR MISS SCHOLARSHIP PROGRAM
Scholarship program to recognize and reward outstanding high school junior females in the areas of academics, leadership, athletics, public speaking, and the performing arts. Must be single, U.S. citizen, and resident of California. Minimum 3.0 GPA required.

Award: Scholarship for use in freshman year; not renewable. *Number:* 25. *Amount:* $500–$10,000.

Eligibility Requirements: Applicant must be high school student; age 15-17; planning to enroll or expecting to enroll full-time at a four-year institution or university; single female; resident of California and must have an interest in beauty pageant, leadership, or public speaking. Applicant must have 3.0 GPA or higher. Available to U.S. citizens.

Application Requirements: Application form, essay, interview, test scores, transcript. *Deadline:* varies.

Contact: Joan McDonald, Chairman
California Junior Miss Scholarship Program
385 Via Montanosa
Encinitas, CA 92024
Phone: 760-420-4177
E-mail: jmcdonald@bellmicro.com

CALIFORNIA STATE PARENT-TEACHER ASSOCIATION
http://www.capta.org/

CONTINUING EDUCATION-PTA VOLUNTEERS SCHOLARSHIP
• *See page 516*

GRADUATING HIGH SCHOOL SENIOR SCHOLARSHIP
• *See page 552*

CALIFORNIA STUDENT AID COMMISSION
http://www.csac.ca.gov/

CAL GRANT C
Award for California residents who are enrolled in a short-term vocational training program. Program must lead to a recognized degree or certificate. Course length must be a minimum of 4 months and no longer than 24 months. Students must be attending an approved California institution and show financial need.

Award: Grant for use in freshman or sophomore years; renewable. *Number:* up to 7761. *Amount:* $576–$3168.

Eligibility Requirements: Applicant must be enrolled or expecting to enroll full- or part-time at a two-year or technical institution; resident of California and studying in California. Available to U.S. citizens.

Application Requirements: Application form, financial need analysis, GPA verification. *Deadline:* March 2.

Contact: Catalina Mistler, Chief, Program Administration and Services Division
California Student Aid Commission
PO Box 419026
Rancho Cordova, CA 95741-9026
Phone: 916-526-7268
Fax: 916-526-8002
E-mail: studentsupport@csac.ca.gov

COMPETITIVE CAL GRANT A
Award for California residents who are not recent high school graduates attending an approved college or university within the state. Must show financial need and meet minimum 3.00 GPA requirement.

Award: Grant for use in freshman, sophomore, junior, or senior years; renewable. *Number:* 1000–2000. *Amount:* $5472–$12,192.

Eligibility Requirements: Applicant must be enrolled or expecting to enroll full- or part-time at a two-year or four-year institution or university; resident of California and studying in California. Applicant must have 3.0 GPA or higher. Available to U.S. citizens.

Application Requirements: Application form, financial need analysis, GPA verification. *Deadline:* March 2.

Contact: Catalina Mistler, Chief, Program Administration and Services Division
California Student Aid Commission
PO Box 419026
Rancho Cordova, CA 95741-9026
Phone: 916-526-7268
Fax: 916-526-8002
E-mail: studentsupport@csac.ca.gov

ENTITLEMENT CAL GRANT B
Provide grant funds for access costs for low-income students in an amount not to exceed $1473 and tuition/fee expenses of up to $12192. Must be California residents and enroll in an undergraduate academic program of not less than one academic year at a qualifying postsecondary institution. Must show financial need and meet the minimum 2.00 GPA requirement.

Award: Grant for use in freshman, sophomore, junior, or senior years; renewable. *Number:* 56,200. *Amount:* $700–$13,665.

Eligibility Requirements: Applicant must be enrolled or expecting to enroll full- or part-time at a two-year or four-year or technical institution or university; resident of California and studying in California. Available to U.S. citizens.

Application Requirements: Application form, financial need analysis. *Deadline:* March 2.

Contact: Catalina Mistler, Chief, Program Administration and Services Division
California Student Aid Commission
PO Box 419026
Rancho Cordova, CA 95741-9026
Phone: 916-526-7268
Fax: 916-526-8002
E-mail: studentsupport@csac.ca.gov

LAW ENFORCEMENT PERSONNEL DEPENDENTS SCHOLARSHIP
• *See page 552*

CALIFORNIA TEACHERS ASSOCIATION (CTA)
http://www.cta.org/

CALIFORNIA TEACHERS ASSOCIATION SCHOLARSHIP FOR MEMBERS
• *See page 516*

CALIFORNIA WINE GRAPE GROWERS FOUNDATION
http://www.cwggf.org/

CALIFORNIA WINE GRAPE GROWERS FOUNDATION SCHOLARSHIP
Scholarship for high school seniors whose parents or legal guardians are vineyard employees of wine grape growers. Recipients may study the subject of their choice at any campus of the University of California system, the California State University system, or the California Community College system.

Award: Scholarship for use in freshman year; renewable. *Number:* 6–6. *Amount:* $2000–$8000.

Eligibility Requirements: Applicant must be high school student; planning to enroll or expecting to enroll full-time at a two-year or four-year institution or university; resident of California and studying in California. Available to U.S. citizens.

Application Requirements: Application form, community service, essay, financial need analysis, recommendations or references, test scores, transcript. *Deadline:* April 2.

Contact: Carolee Williams, Assistant Executive Director
California Wine Grape Growers Foundation
1325 J Street, #1560
Sacramento, CA 95814
Phone: 800-241-1800
Fax: 916-379-8999
E-mail: carolee@cawg.org

CAREER COLLEGES AND SCHOOLS OF TEXAS
http://www.ccst.org/

CAREER COLLEGES AND SCHOOLS OF TEXAS SCHOLARSHIP PROGRAM
One-time award available to graduating high school seniors who plan to attend a Texas trade or technical institution. Must be a Texas resident. Criteria selection, which is determined independently by each school's guidance counselors, may be based on academic excellence, financial need, or student leadership. Must be U.S. citizen. Deadline: continuous.

Award: Scholarship for use in freshman year; not renewable. *Number:* up to 27,770. *Amount:* $1000.

Eligibility Requirements: Applicant must be high school student; planning to enroll or expecting to enroll full- or part-time at a technical institution; resident of Texas and studying in Texas. Available to U.S. citizens.

Application Requirements: Application form, recommendations or references. *Deadline:* continuous.

Contact: Jennifer George, Association Manager
Career Colleges and Schools of Texas
823 Congress Avenue, Suite 230
Austin, TX 78701
Phone: 512-479-0425 Ext. 17
Fax: 512-495-9031
E-mail: jgeorge@eami.com

CENTRAL SCHOLARSHIP

http://www.central-scholarship.org

CENTRAL SCHOLARSHIP BUREAU GRANTS

A limited number of grants are available each year on a competitive basis. Selection criteria is a combination of merit and demonstrated need.

Award: Grant for use in freshman, sophomore, junior, senior, or graduate years; renewable. *Number:* 20–30. *Amount:* $1000–$5000.

Eligibility Requirements: Applicant must be enrolled or expecting to enroll full-time at a two-year or four-year or technical institution or university and resident of Maryland. Applicant must have 3.0 GPA or higher. Available to U.S. citizens.

Application Requirements: Application form, CSB online application, essay, financial need analysis, interview, resume, transcript. *Deadline:* May 1.

Contact: Roberta Goldman, Program Director
Phone: 410-415-5558
Fax: 410-415-5501
E-mail: rgoldman@centralsb.org

LESSANS FAMILY SCHOLARSHIP

• See page 619

MARY RUBIN AND BENJAMIN M. RUBIN SCHOLARSHIP FUND

Renewable scholarship for tuition only to women who are attending a college, university, or other institution of higher learning. Must be a resident of Maryland. Have a GPA of 3.0 or better and meet the financial requirements. Contact for application or download from website http://www.centralsb.org.

Award: Scholarship for use in sophomore, junior, senior, or graduate years; renewable. *Number:* 20–35. *Amount:* $1000–$2500.

Eligibility Requirements: Applicant must be enrolled or expecting to enroll full- or part-time at a two-year or four-year or technical institution or university; female and resident of Maryland. Applicant must have 3.0 GPA or higher. Available to U.S. citizens.

Application Requirements: Application form, essay, financial need analysis, recommendations or references, transcript. *Deadline:* May 1.

Contact: Roberta Goldman, Program Director
Phone: 410-415-5558
Fax: 410-415-5501
E-mail: rgoldman@centralsb.org

SHOE CITY-WB54/WB50 SCHOLARSHIP

Scholarship for high school seniors who are permanent residents of Maryland or Washington D.C. Four $1500 awards are granted annually. For more information, visit website http://www.centralsb.org.

Award: Scholarship for use in freshman year; not renewable. *Number:* 4. *Amount:* up to $1500.

Eligibility Requirements: Applicant must be high school student; planning to enroll or expecting to enroll full-time at a four-year institution or university and resident of District of Columbia, Maryland. Available to U.S. citizens.

Application Requirements: Application form, community service, essay, financial need analysis, interview, recommendations or references, resume, test scores, transcript. *Deadline:* May 1.

Contact: Roberta Goldman, Program Director
Phone: 410-415-5558
Fax: 410-415-5501
E-mail: rgoldman@centralsb.org

STRAUS SCHOLARSHIP PROGRAM FOR UNDERGRADUATE EDUCATION

Scholarship provides assistance to Maryland residents who are full-time undergraduate students in their sophomore, junior, or senior years at an accredited college or university. Renewable grants of up to $5000 each per year will be awarded. If the recipient graduates within four years with a cumulative GPA of 3.0 or higher, an additional $5000 grant will be awarded to apply toward student loan debt.

Award: Scholarship for use in sophomore, junior, or senior years; renewable. *Number:* 5–8. *Amount:* up to $5000.

Eligibility Requirements: Applicant must be enrolled or expecting to enroll full-time at a four-year institution or university and resident of Maryland. Applicant must have 3.0 GPA or higher. Available to U.S. citizens.

Application Requirements: Application form, CSB online application, essay, financial need analysis, interview, resume, transcript. *Deadline:* May 1.

Contact: Roberta Goldman, Program Director
Phone: 410-415-5558
Fax: 410-415-5501
E-mail: rgoldman@centralsb.org

CHICANA/LATINA FOUNDATION

http://www.chicanalatina.org/

SCHOLARSHIPS FOR LATINA STUDENTS ENROLLED IN COLLEGES/UNIVERSITIES IN NORTHERN CALIFORNIA

• See page 619

CHINESE AMERICAN ASSOCIATION OF MINNESOTA

http://www.caam.org/

CHINESE AMERICAN ASSOCIATION OF MINNESOTA (CAAM) SCHOLARSHIPS

• See page 619

CIVIL SERVICE EMPLOYEES INSURANCE COMPANY

http://www.cseinsurance.com

YOUTH AUTOMOBILE SAFETY SCHOLARSHIP ESSAY COMPETITION FOR CHILDREN OF PUBLIC EMPLOYEES

Students must compose an essay (500 words or less) about automobile safety related topics they feel are important to their peers. Applicants must be children of civil service employees. Additional requirements may be found on CSE's website: www.cseinsurance.com.

Award: Scholarship for use in freshman year; not renewable. *Number:* 12. *Amount:* $250–$1500.

Eligibility Requirements: Applicant must be high school student; planning to enroll or expecting to enroll full-time at a two-year or four-year institution or university and resident of Arizona, California, Nevada, Utah. Applicant must have 3.0 GPA or higher. Available to U.S. citizens.

Application Requirements: Application form, entry in a contest, essay, recommendations or references, transcript. *Deadline:* May 3.

Contact: Mrs. Cynthia Diaz, Marketing Program Manager
Civil Service Employees Insurance Company
2121 North California Boulevard, Suite 555
PO Box 8041
Walnut Creek, CA 94956-8041
Phone: 925-817-6434
E-mail: cdiaz@cseinsurance.com

COALITION OF TEXANS WITH DISABILITIES

http://www.cotwd.org/

KENNY MURGIA MEMORIAL SCHOLARSHIP

• See page 568

COLLEGEBOUND FOUNDATION

http://www.collegeboundfoundation.org/

AENZI INVESTMENTS SCHOLARSHIP

AENZI Investments was created in 2001 to stimulate and educate its members in investments in NYSE and NASDAQ exchanges. Our mission is to be a comprehensive source of investment information and strategies aimed at teaching the principles of collective investment by taking advantage of the global economy and empowering our communities.

Award: Scholarship for use in freshman year; not renewable. *Number:* up to 1. *Amount:* $500.

Eligibility Requirements: Applicant must be high school student; planning to enroll or expecting to enroll full-time at a two-year or four-year institution or university and resident of Maryland. Applicant must have 3.0 GPA or higher. Available to U.S. citizens.

Application Requirements: *Deadline:* March 1.

Contact: Michael Thornton, Associate Program Director, Scholarship Programs
Phone: 410-783-2905 Ext. 207
Fax: 410-727-5786
E-mail: mthornton@collegeboundfoundation.org

ANNA AND ELI BERKENFELD MEMORIAL SCHOLARSHIP

This scholarship honors the memory of Anna and Eli Berkenfeld by supporting the efforts of students who have demonstrated financial need to attend college. You must have verifiable community service; have a cumulative 3.0 GPA or better; and demonstrate financial need.

Award: Scholarship for use in freshman year; not renewable. *Number:* up to 4. *Amount:* $1000.

Eligibility Requirements: Applicant must be high school student; planning to enroll or expecting to enroll full-time at a two-year or four-year institution or university and resident of Maryland. Applicant must have 3.0 GPA or higher. Available to U.S. citizens.

Application Requirements: *Deadline:* March 1.

Contact: Michael Thornton, Associate Program Director, Scholarship Programs
Phone: 410-783-2905 Ext. 207
Fax: 410-727-5786
E-mail: mthornton@collegeboundfoundation.org

ANNABELLE L. JOHNSON SCHOLARSHIP FUND

Devoted to a true everyday hero that is gone but certainly not forgotten, the Annabelle L. Johnson Scholarship Fund has been established in memory of the mother of Dominic L. and Adrian S. Johnson. She was a down-to-earth mom who loved her boys unconditionally and who generously gave of herself to her family, friends and her community. She was a lifelong resident of Baltimore City. You must: have a cumulative 2.0 GPA or better; submit an essay (500-1,000 words) describing/honoring a family member who gives of themselves to their family and community; and must be accepted to and attend a 2- or 4- year college or university.

Award: Scholarship for use in freshman year; not renewable. *Number:* up to 1. *Amount:* $500.

Eligibility Requirements: Applicant must be high school student; planning to enroll or expecting to enroll full-time at a two-year or four-year institution or university and resident of Maryland. Applicant must have 2.5 GPA or higher. Available to U.S. citizens.

Application Requirements: *Deadline:* March 1.

Contact: Michael Thornton, Associate Program Director, Scholarship Programs
Phone: 410-783-2905 Ext. 207
Fax: 410-727-5786
E-mail: mthornton@collegeboundfoundation.org

BALTIMORE RAVENS SCHOLARSHIP PROGRAM

The Baltimore Ravens established this scholarship program to enable local youth to continue their education on a collegiate level. The team has a long-standing history of service to local communities, and this fund will support those who do the same. In addition, this renewable scholarship will be based on financial need and academic achievement. You must: have a cumulative 3.0 GPA or better; demonstrate financial need (include a SAR if available); be accepted to and attend a 4-year college or university; have verifiable community service; submit one (1) reference from an individual who can attest to your commitment to helping others; submit one (1) reference from a teacher, school counselor or administrator; and submit a 1-2 page essay describing the environment in which you live (household, neighborhood, etc.), a personal challenge you faced and how you overcame it, and the most meaningful contribution you have made as a volunteer to the betterment of your community.

Award: Scholarship for use in freshman, sophomore, junior, or senior years; renewable. *Number:* up to 5. *Amount:* $5000.

Eligibility Requirements: Applicant must be high school student; planning to enroll or expecting to enroll full-time at a four-year institution or university and resident of Maryland. Applicant must have 3.0 GPA or higher. Available to U.S. citizens.

Application Requirements: Application form, application form may be submitted online (http://www.scholarships.mycbf.net/STARS), community service, essay, interview, recommendations or references, resume, transcript. *Deadline:* March 1.

Contact: Deana Carr-Davis, Associate Program Director, Scholarship Programs
CollegeBound Foundation
300 Water Street, Suite 300
Baltimore, MD 21202
E-mail: dcarr-davis@collegeboundfoundation.org

CARMEN V. D'ANNA MEMORIAL SCHOLARSHIP OF THE MARS SUPERMARKET EDUCATIONAL FUND

Must be a senior in a Baltimore City public high school entering a Maryland college or university for the first time. Must demonstrate financial need and exhibit a strong desire to achieve. Submit a typed one-page essay describing why a college education is important to you.

Award: Scholarship for use in freshman, sophomore, junior, or senior years; renewable. *Number:* 1. *Amount:* up to $10,000.

Eligibility Requirements: Applicant must be high school student; planning to enroll or expecting to enroll full-time at a two-year or four-year institution or university; resident of Maryland and studying in Maryland. Available to U.S. citizens.

Application Requirements: Application form, application form may be submitted online (http://www.scholarships.mycbf.net/STARS), essay, financial need analysis, recommendations or references, resume, transcript. *Deadline:* March 1.

Contact: Michael Thornton, Associate Program Director, Scholarship Programs
Phone: 410-783-2905 Ext. 207
Fax: 410-727-5786
E-mail: mthornton@collegeboundfoundation.org

COLLEGEBOUND FOUNDATION LAST DOLLAR GRANT

A need-based award for Baltimore City public high school graduates whose expected family contribution and financial aid package total less than the cost to attend college. Grant value is up to $3000 per year, renewable for up to five years of college or the maximum amount of $15,000.

Award: Grant for use in freshman, sophomore, junior, or senior years; renewable. *Number:* 45–60. *Amount:* $500–$3000.

Eligibility Requirements: Applicant must be high school student; planning to enroll or expecting to enroll full-time at a four-year institution or university; resident of Maryland and studying in Maryland. Available to U.S. citizens.

Application Requirements: Acceptance letter, application form, application form may be submitted online (http://www.scholarships.mycbf.net/STARS/), financial need analysis, transcript. *Deadline:* March 1.

Contact: Ms. Deana Carr-Davis, Associate Program Director, Scholarship Programs
CollegeBound Foundation
300 Water Street, Suite 300
Baltimore, MD 21202
Phone: 410-783-2905 Ext. 207

DUNBAR CLASS OF 1958 SCHOLARSHIP

The Dunbar Class of 1958 established this scholarship with the intention to give back to the community in which they were raised and went to school. The Class of 1958 views Dunbar as the source of their many successes, and hopes to provide financial assistance so that current graduates have the same opportunities to succeed. You must: be a senior at Paul Laurence Dunbar High School; have a cumulative high school GPA between a 2.0 and a 3.0; and demonstrate financial need.

Award: Scholarship for use in freshman, sophomore, junior, or senior years; not renewable. *Number:* up to 3. *Amount:* $1000.

Eligibility Requirements: Applicant must be high school student; planning to enroll or expecting to enroll full-time at a two-year or four-year institution or university and resident of Maryland. Applicant must have 2.5 GPA or higher. Available to U.S. citizens.

Application Requirements: *Deadline:* March 1.

Contact: Michael Thornton, Associate Program Director, Scholarship Programs
Phone: 410-783-2905 Ext. 207
Fax: 410-727-5786
E-mail: mthornton@collegeboundfoundation.org

EXCHANGE CLUB OF BALTIMORE SCHOLARSHIP

Award for Baltimore City public high school graduates. Minimum GPA of 3.0 and SAT score of 1000 is required. Must have verifiable community service. Submit a typed one-page essay describing your personal and professional goals and your expectations for college.

Award: Scholarship for use in freshman year; not renewable. *Number:* 1–5. *Amount:* $1000–$2000.

Eligibility Requirements: Applicant must be high school student; planning to enroll or expecting to enroll full-time at a two-year or four-year institution or university and resident of Maryland. Applicant must have 3.0 GPA or higher. Available to U.S. citizens.

Application Requirements: Application form, application form may be submitted online (http://www.scholarships.mycbf.net/STARS), community service, essay, financial aid award letters, Student Aid Report (SAR), financial need analysis, recommendations or references, test scores, transcript. *Deadline:* March 1.

Contact: Michael Thornton, Associate Program Director, Scholarship Programs
Phone: 410-783-2905 Ext. 207
Fax: 410-727-5786
E-mail: mthornton@collegeboundfoundation.org

GEORGINE NEWMAN EDGERTON SCHOLARSHIP

This award has been created by the family of Georgine Newman Edgerton in recognition of her many accomplishments as a community activist, volunteer and advocate for the citizens of Baltimore. You must be a senior at Frederick Douglass High School, Institute of Business and Entrepreneurship, or Maritime Industries Academy High School and demonstrate financial need.

Award: Scholarship for use in freshman year; not renewable. *Number:* up to 1. *Amount:* $500.

Eligibility Requirements: Applicant must be high school student; planning to enroll or expecting to enroll full-time at a two-year or four-year institution or university and resident of Maryland. Available to U.S. citizens.

Application Requirements: *Deadline:* March 1.

Contact: Michael Thornton, Associate Program Director, Scholarship Programs
Phone: 410-783-2905 Ext. 207
Fax: 410-727-5786
E-mail: mthornton@collegeboundfoundation.org

GREEN FAMILY BOOK AWARD

One-time award of $800 for a high school graduate who possess a minimum GPA of 3.0. Must have verifiable community service and demonstrate financial need. Must submit an essay (250-500 words) describing a significant experience, achievement or risk that you have taken and its impact on you.

Award: Scholarship for use in freshman year; not renewable. *Number:* 1. *Amount:* $800.

Eligibility Requirements: Applicant must be high school student; planning to enroll or expecting to enroll full-time at a two-year or four-year institution or university and resident of Maryland. Applicant must have 3.0 GPA or higher. Available to U.S. citizens.

Application Requirements: Application form, application form may be submitted online (http://www.scholarships.mycbf.net/STARS), community service, essay, financial need analysis, recommendations or references, resume, transcript. *Deadline:* March 1.

Contact: Michael Thornton, Associate Program Director, Scholarship Programs
Phone: 410-783-2905 Ext. 207
Fax: 410-727-5786
E-mail: mthornton@collegeboundfoundation.org

HY ZOLET STUDENT ATHLETE SCHOLARSHIP

Scholarship available to a high school athlete with a minimum cumulative GPA of 2.5. Must furnish at least two letters verifying participation in high school athletics. Must submit SAT (critical reading

and math) scores, and a one-page essay indicating why you should receive this award.

Award: Scholarship for use in freshman, sophomore, junior, or senior years; renewable. *Number:* 4. *Amount:* $1000.

Eligibility Requirements: Applicant must be high school student; planning to enroll or expecting to enroll full-time at a four-year institution or university; resident of Maryland and must have an interest in athletics/sports. Applicant must have 2.5 GPA or higher. Available to U.S. citizens.

Application Requirements: Application form, application form may be submitted online (http://www.scholarships.mycbf.net/STARS/), essay, recommendations or references, test scores, transcript. *Deadline:* March 1.

Contact: Michael Thornton, Associate Program Director, Scholarship Programs
Phone: 410-783-2905 Ext. 207
Fax: 410-727-5786
E-mail: mthornton@collegeboundfoundation.org

JANE AND CLARENCE SPILMAN SCHOLARSHIP

You must: have a cumulative 3.0 GPA or better; verifiable community service; and an SAT (CR+M) score of at least 1000.

Award: Scholarship for use in freshman, sophomore, junior, or senior years; renewable. *Number:* 1. *Amount:* $1500.

Eligibility Requirements: Applicant must be high school student; planning to enroll or expecting to enroll full-time at a two-year or four-year institution or university; resident of Maryland and studying in Maryland. Applicant must have 3.0 GPA or higher. Available to U.S. citizens.

Application Requirements: Application form, application form may be submitted online (http://www.scholarships.mycbf.net/STARS), community service, financial need analysis, recommendations or references, resume, test scores, transcript. *Deadline:* March 1.

Contact: Michael Thornton, Associate Program Director, Scholarship Programs
Phone: 410-783-2905 Ext. 207
Fax: 410-727-5786
E-mail: mthornton@collegeboundfoundation.org

JOSEPH AND REBECCA MEYERHOFF SCHOLARSHIP

This scholarship honors Joseph and Rebecca Meyerhoff and their long-time philanthropic efforts both in Baltimore and around the globe. This scholarship supports the efforts of Baltimore City public high school students to attend college. You must have a cumulative 3.0 GPA or better, an SAT (CR+M) score of at least 1000, demonstrate financial need, and be accepted to and attend Bowie State University, Coppin State University, Frostburg State University, Morgan State University, St. Mary's College of Maryland, Stevenson University, Towson University, University of Maryland College Park, or University of Maryland Eastern Shore.

Award: Scholarship for use in freshman, sophomore, junior, or senior years; renewable. *Number:* 3–5. *Amount:* $1000–$3000.

Eligibility Requirements: Applicant must be high school student; planning to enroll or expecting to enroll full-time at a four-year institution or university; resident of Maryland and studying in Maryland. Applicant must have 3.0 GPA or higher. Available to U.S. citizens.

Application Requirements: *Deadline:* March 1.

Contact: Michael Thornton, Associate Program Director, Scholarship Programs
Phone: 410-783-2905 Ext. 207
Fax: 410-727-5786
E-mail: mthornton@collegeboundfoundation.org

THE JOYCE A. KROELLER MEMORIAL SCHOLARSHIP

You must have verifiable community service; have a cumulative 2.5 GPA or better; demonstrate financial need; submit at least one (1) reference from an individual who can attest to your commitment to helping others; submit an essay (minimum of 500 words) about one of the following topics: 1) describe an individual who has had an impact on you and why or 2) describe the volunteer activities in which you have been involved and how you plan to continue to give back to your community; and be accepted to and attend Bowie State University, Coppin State University, Frostburg State University, Morgan State University, St. Mary's College of Maryland, Stevenson University, Towson University, University of Maryland College Park, or University of Maryland Eastern Shore.

Award: Scholarship for use in freshman, sophomore, junior, or senior years; renewable. *Number:* up to 1. *Amount:* $1500.

Eligibility Requirements: Applicant must be high school student; planning to enroll or expecting to enroll full-time at a two-year or four-year institution or university; resident of Maryland and studying in Maryland. Applicant must have 2.5 GPA or higher. Available to U.S. citizens.

Application Requirements: *Deadline:* March 1.

Contact: Michael Thornton, Associate Program Director, Scholarship Programs
Phone: 410-783-2905 Ext. 207
Fax: 410-727-5786
E-mail: mthornton@collegeboundfoundation.org

KENNETH HOFFMAN SCHOLARSHIP

You must: have a cumulative 3.0 GPA or better; verifiable community service; and an SAT (CR+M) score of at least 1000.

Award: Scholarship for use in freshman, sophomore, junior, or senior years; renewable. *Number:* 1. *Amount:* $1500.

Eligibility Requirements: Applicant must be high school student; planning to enroll or expecting to enroll full-time at a four-year institution or university; resident of Maryland and studying in Maryland. Applicant must have 3.0 GPA or higher. Available to U.S. citizens.

Application Requirements: Application form, application form may be submitted online (http://www.scholarships.mycbf.net/STARS), community service, financial need analysis, recommendations or references, resume, test scores, transcript. *Deadline:* March 1.

Contact: Michael Thornton, Associate Program Director, Scholarship Programs
Phone: 410-783-2905 Ext. 207
Fax: 410-727-5786
E-mail: mthornton@collegeboundfoundation.org

KHIA "DJ K-SWIFT" MEMORIAL SCHOLARSHIP

You must have a cumulative 2.5 GPA or better; submit SAT (CR+M) scores, demonstrate financial need, and submit an essay (500 words) describing the importance of a college education and why you should receive this award.

Award: Scholarship for use in freshman year; not renewable. *Number:* up to 2. *Amount:* $1000.

Eligibility Requirements: Applicant must be high school student; planning to enroll or expecting to enroll full-time at a two-year or four-year institution and resident of Maryland. Applicant must have 2.5 GPA or higher. Available to U.S. citizens.

Application Requirements: *Deadline:* March 1.

Contact: Michael Thornton, Associate Program Director, Scholarship Programs
Phone: 410-783-2905 Ext. 207
Fax: 410-727-5786
E-mail: mthornton@collegeboundfoundation.org

THE KIDS FUND, INC. SCHOLARSHIP

KIDS Fund, Inc. supports the efforts of Baltimore City public school students to attend college. You must: have a cumulative 2.0 GPA or better; have verifiable community service; and demonstrate need. Preference given to a resident of Govans or a senior at W.E.B. DuBois High School or Reginald F. Lewis High School.

Award: Scholarship for use in freshman year; not renewable. *Number:* up to 2. *Amount:* $1000.

Eligibility Requirements: Applicant must be high school student; planning to enroll or expecting to enroll full-time at a two-year or four-year institution or university and resident of Maryland. Applicant must have 2.5 GPA or higher. Available to U.S. citizens.

Application Requirements: *Deadline:* March 1.

Contact: Michael Thornton, Associate Program Director, Scholarship Programs
Phone: 410-783-2905 Ext. 207
Fax: 410-727-5786
E-mail: mthornton@collegeboundfoundation.org

LESLIE MOORE FOUNDATION SCHOLARSHIP

Three awards for students from Baltimore City public high schools and two from other county schools. Must have GPA of at least 2.0 and verifiable community service. See website for application, http://www.collegeboundfoundation.org.

Award: Scholarship for use in freshman, sophomore, junior, or senior years; renewable. *Number:* 5. *Amount:* $2500.

Eligibility Requirements: Applicant must be high school student; planning to enroll or expecting to enroll full-time at a two-year or four-year institution and resident of Maryland. Available to U.S. citizens.

Application Requirements: Application form, application form may be submitted online (http://www.scholarships.mycbf.net/STARS/), community service, essay, financial need analysis, interview, recommendations or references, transcript. *Deadline:* March 1.

Contact: Michael Thornton, Associate Program Director, Scholarship Programs
Phone: 410-783-2905 Ext. 207
Fax: 410-727-5786
E-mail: mthornton@collegeboundfoundation.org

LORENZO FELDER SCHOLARSHIP

• *See page 620*

MAGALINE THOMPSON BOOK SCHOLARSHIP

This award was created by Randolph Thompson, a former Assistant Principal at Paul Laurence Dunbar High School, in memory of his mother, Magaline Thompson, in recognition of her sacrifices and dedication as a single mother. You must be a senior at Paul Laurence Dunbar High School; be a teenage mother; and demonstrate financial need.

Award: Scholarship for use in freshman year; not renewable. *Number:* up to 1. *Amount:* $210.

Eligibility Requirements: Applicant must be high school student; planning to enroll or expecting to enroll full-time at a two-year or four-year institution; female and resident of Maryland. Available to U.S. citizens.

Application Requirements: *Deadline:* March 1.

Contact: Michael Thornton, Associate Program Director, Scholarship Programs
Phone: 410-783-2905 Ext. 207
Fax: 410-727-5786
E-mail: mthornton@collegeboundfoundation.org

MANAGERIAL AND PROFESSIONAL SOCIETY (MAPS) OF BALTIMORE MERIT SCHOLARSHIP

You must have a cumulative 3.0 GPA or better; an SAT (CR+M) score of at least 950; verifiable community service; and submit an essay (500-1000 words) describing the importance of a college education and community service you have been involved in. Only dues-paying MAPS members and their immediate family members are eligible to apply. Winners must attend a MAPS quarterly meeting held in September.

Award: Scholarship for use in freshman year; not renewable. *Number:* up to 3. *Amount:* $1000.

Eligibility Requirements: Applicant must be high school student; planning to enroll or expecting to enroll full-time at a two-year or four-year institution and resident of Maryland. Applicant must have 3.0 GPA or higher. Available to U.S. citizens.

Application Requirements: *Deadline:* March 1.

Contact: Michael Thornton, Associate Program Director, Scholarship Programs
Phone: 410-783-2905 Ext. 207
Fax: 410-727-5786
E-mail: mthornton@collegeboundfoundation.org

MANAGERIAL AND PROFESSIONAL SOCIETY (MAPS) OF BALTIMORE SERVICE AWARD SCHOLARSHIP

You must have verifiable community service; have a cumulative 2.5 GPA or better; and submit an essay (500-1000 words) describing the importance of a college education and community service you have been involved in. Only dues-paying MAPS members and their immediate family members are eligible to apply. Winners must attend a MAPS quarterly meeting held in September.

Award: Scholarship for use in freshman year; not renewable. *Number:* up to 2. *Amount:* $1000.

Eligibility Requirements: Applicant must be high school student; planning to enroll or expecting to enroll full-time at a two-year or four-year institution or university and resident of Maryland. Applicant must have 2.5 GPA or higher. Available to U.S. citizens.

Application Requirements: *Deadline:* March 1.

Contact: Michael Thornton, Associate Program Director, Scholarship
Programs
Phone: 410-783-2905 Ext. 207
Fax: 410-727-5786
E-mail: mthornton@collegeboundfoundation.org

MARK & PATRICIA ROTHLEITNER NAF HIGH SCHOOL SCHOLARSHIP

You must have a cumulative 2.5 or better; be accepted to and attend a 4-year college or university; graduate from NAF with a certificate in chosen field (Finance, Travel & Tourism, IT, etc.); preference will be given to Academy of Finance graduates and to students who are active in their communities or working part-time.

Award: Scholarship for use in freshman, sophomore, junior, or senior years; renewable. *Number:* up to 1. *Amount:* $3000.

Eligibility Requirements: Applicant must be high school student; planning to enroll or expecting to enroll full-time at a four-year institution or university and resident of Maryland. Applicant must have 2.5 GPA or higher. Available to U.S. and non-Canadian citizens.

Application Requirements: *Deadline:* March 1.

Contact: Michael Thornton, Associate Program Director, Scholarship
Programs
Phone: 410-783-2905 Ext. 207
Fax: 410-727-5786
E-mail: mthornton@collegeboundfoundation.org

MECU, BALTIMORE'S CREDIT UNION, SERVICE AWARD SCHOLARSHIP

You must have a cumulative 2.5 GPA or better; verifiable community service; and submit an essay (500-1000 words) describing the importance of a college education and community service in which you have been involved. Winners must attend a MECU reception and will receive a complimentary credit union membership.

Award: Scholarship for use in freshman year; not renewable. *Number:* up to 5. *Amount:* $1000.

Eligibility Requirements: Applicant must be high school student; planning to enroll or expecting to enroll full-time at a four-year institution or university and resident of Maryland. Applicant must have 2.5 GPA or higher. Available to U.S. citizens.

Application Requirements: *Deadline:* March 1.

Contact: Michael Thornton, Associate Program Director, Scholarship
Programs
Phone: 410-783-2905 Ext. 207
Fax: 410-727-5786
E-mail: mthornton@collegeboundfoundation.org

THE RICHARD E. DUNNE, III SCHOLARSHIP

Richard E. Dunne, a partner with the law firm of Hogan and Hartson, tragically died in an airplane crash on Thanksgiving Day, 1997. An active supporter and volunteer for the CollegeBound Foundation, learning and doing were key to Rich's approach to life. His good humor and commitment challenged and inspired his family, his friends, and his colleagues alike to make the most of every opportunity. This scholarship honors that commitment by helping to provide students with an opportunity that they might otherwise not have to attend college. You must: have a cumulative 3.0 GPA or better; have verifiable community service and must attend a Maryland college or university.

Award: Scholarship for use in freshman, sophomore, junior, or senior years; renewable. *Number:* up to 1. *Amount:* $1000.

Eligibility Requirements: Applicant must be high school student; planning to enroll or expecting to enroll full-time at a two-year or four-year institution or university; resident of Maryland and studying in Maryland. Applicant must have 3.0 GPA or higher. Available to U.S. citizens.

Application Requirements: *Deadline:* March 1.

Contact: Michael Thornton, Associate Program Director, Scholarship
Programs
Phone: 410-783-2905 Ext. 207
Fax: 410-727-5786
E-mail: mthornton@collegeboundfoundation.org

SCARBOROUGH-SCHEELER SCHOLARSHIP

Scholarship for students with a cumulative high school GPA of at least 2.5. Must demonstrate financial need. Submit an essay (500¿1000 words) describing your college expectations. Must plan on attending Goucher College, McDaniel College, Towson University or University of Maryland College Park.

Award: Scholarship for use in freshman, sophomore, junior, or senior years; renewable. *Number:* 1. *Amount:* $1000.

Eligibility Requirements: Applicant must be high school student; planning to enroll or expecting to enroll full-time at a four-year institution or university; resident of Maryland and studying in Maryland. Applicant must have 2.5 GPA or higher. Available to U.S. citizens.

Application Requirements: Application form, application form may be submitted online (http://www.scholarships.mycbf.net/STARS), essay, financial need analysis, recommendations or references, transcript. *Deadline:* March 1.

Contact: Michael Thornton, Associate Program Director, Scholarship
Programs
Phone: 410-783-2905 Ext. 207
Fax: 410-727-5786
E-mail: mthornton@collegeboundfoundation.org

SHONDA DENISE GREEN MEMORIAL SCHOLARSHIP

Shonda Denise Green was a senior at Western High School (Class of 1998). The Sylvan Learning Foundation has established this scholarship to encourage other Western High School students to strive for a college education and fulfill their dreams. You must: be a senior at Western High School; and have a cumulative 3.0 GPA or better.

Award: Scholarship for use in freshman, sophomore, junior, or senior years; renewable. *Number:* up to 1. *Amount:* $1000.

Eligibility Requirements: Applicant must be high school student; planning to enroll or expecting to enroll full-time at a two-year or four-year institution or university and resident of Maryland. Applicant must have 3.0 GPA or higher. Available to U.S. citizens.

Application Requirements: *Deadline:* March 1.

Contact: Michael Thornton, Associate Program Director, Scholarship
Programs
Phone: 410-783-2905 Ext. 207
Fax: 410-727-5786
E-mail: mthornton@collegeboundfoundation.org

WALTER G. AMPREY SCHOLARSHIP

Walter G. Amprey, former Superintendent of Baltimore City Public Schools, dedicated his career to educating children. This scholarship honors him and supports the efforts of Baltimore City public school students to attend college. You must: have a cumulative 3.0 GPA or better; and demonstrate financial need.

Award: Scholarship for use in freshman year; not renewable. *Number:* up to 1. *Amount:* $1000.

Eligibility Requirements: Applicant must be high school student; planning to enroll or expecting to enroll full-time at a four-year institution or university and resident of Maryland. Applicant must have 3.0 GPA or higher. Available to U.S. citizens.

Application Requirements: *Deadline:* March 1.

Contact: Michael Thornton, Associate Program Director, Scholarship
Programs
Phone: 410-783-2905 Ext. 207
Fax: 410-727-5786
E-mail: mthornton@collegeboundfoundation.org

COLLEGE FOUNDATION OF NORTH CAROLINA

http://www.cfnc.org/

GOLDEN LEAF SCHOLARSHIP (PUBLIC UNIVERSITY AND PRIVATE COLLEGE AND UNIVERSITY PROGRAM)

Scholarship for current high school seniors and current community college students planning to enter a North Carolina public or private college or university. Must be a permanent resident of a qualifying rural NC county that is economically distressed and/or tobacco crop-dependent. Must demonstrate financial need. For this program, the real value of farm property is not considered when determining need. (See complete listing of participating campuses and qualifying counties at www.CFNC.org/goldenleaf.)

Award: Grant for use in freshman, sophomore, junior, or senior years; renewable. *Number:* 215. *Amount:* $3000.

Eligibility Requirements: Applicant must be enrolled or expecting to enroll full-time at a two-year or four-year institution or university; resident of North Carolina and studying in North Carolina. Available to U.S. citizens.

Application Requirements: Application form, essay, financial need analysis, transcript. *Deadline:* March 1.

Contact: Edna Williams, Grant Manager, North Carolina State
        Education Assistance Authority
    College Foundation of North Carolina
    PO Box 13663
    RTP, NC 27709-3663
    Phone: 866-866-CFNC
    Fax: 919-248-6632
    E-mail: programinformation@cfnc.org

UNIVERSITY OF NORTH CAROLINA NEED-BASED GRANT

Grants available for eligible students attending one of the 16 campuses of the University of North Carolina. Students must be enrolled in at least 6 credit hours at one of the 16 constituent institutions of The University of North Carolina. Award amounts vary based on legislative appropriations.

Award: Grant for use in freshman, sophomore, junior, or senior years; not renewable.

Eligibility Requirements: Applicant must be enrolled or expecting to enroll full- or part-time at a four-year institution or university; resident of North Carolina and studying in North Carolina. Available to U.S. citizens.

Application Requirements: Financial need analysis. *Deadline:* continuous.

COLLEGE NOW GREATER CLEVELAND, INC.

http://www.collegenowgc.org/

COLLEGE NOW GREATER CLEVELAND ADULT LEARNER PROGRAM SCHOLARSHIP

Scholarship for students pursuing first associate or bachelor's degree in an eligible two- or four-year program. Individuals already having a bachelor's degree are not eligible. Students must be 19 years old or older and must have interrupted the education for at least one year. Applicants must be a resident of Ashtabula, Cuyahoga, Geauga, Lake, Lorain, Mahoning, Medina, Portage, Stark, Summit or Trumbull County. Student must meet income guidelines and maintain a 2.5 GPA. Student must be attending a public or private not for profit institution.

Award: Scholarship for use in freshman, sophomore, junior, or senior years; renewable. *Number:* 250–450. *Amount:* $500–$4000.

Eligibility Requirements: Applicant must be enrolled or expecting to enroll full- or part-time at a two-year or four-year or technical institution or university and resident of Ohio. Applicant must have 2.5 GPA or higher. Available to U.S. citizens.

Application Requirements: Application form, essay, financial need analysis, transcript. *Deadline:* April 15.

Contact: Mr. Robert Durham, Director of Scholarship Services and
        Financial Aid
    College Now Greater Cleveland, Inc.
    50Public Square, Suite 1800
    Cleveland, OH 44113
    Phone: 216-635-0450
    Fax: 216-241-6184
    E-mail: rdurham@collegenowgc.org

COLLEGE SUCCESS FOUNDATION

http://www.collegesuccessfoundation.org/

GOVERNORS SCHOLARSHIP PROGRAM

Scholarship award amounts range from $1000 to $5000 depending on each student's financial need. Scholarships can be used up to five years until completion of the student's program of study. Students must be enroll full time and maintain satisfactory academic progress in order to renew scholarships each year. Minimum 2.0 GPA required.

Award: Scholarship for use in freshman year; renewable. *Number:* 30. *Amount:* $1000–$5000.

Eligibility Requirements: Applicant must be high school student; planning to enroll or expecting to enroll full-time at a four-year institution or university; resident of Washington and studying in Washington. Available to U.S. citizens.

Application Requirements: Application form, FAFSA, recommendations or references. *Deadline:* March 4.

Contact: Erica Meier, Director, Human Resources and Operations
    Phone: 425-416-2000
    Fax: 425-416-2001
    E-mail: info@collegesuccessfoundation.org

WASHINGTON STATE ACHIEVERS PROGRAM SCHOLARSHIP

Scholarship amounts will be established annually for students attending public community colleges, public four-year and independent institutions. Scholarships averages approximately between $5000 to $10,000.

Award: Scholarship for use in freshman year; not renewable. *Number:* 600. *Amount:* $5000–$10,000.

Eligibility Requirements: Applicant must be high school student; planning to enroll or expecting to enroll full-time at a two-year or four-year or technical institution or university; resident of Washington and studying in Washington. Available to U.S. citizens.

Application Requirements: Application form, financial need analysis. *Deadline:* varies.

Contact: Erica Meier, Director, Human Resources and Operations
    Phone: 425-416-2000
    Fax: 425-416-2001
    E-mail: info@collegesuccessfoundation.org

COLLEGE SUCCESS NETWORK

http://www.collegesuccessnetwork.org/

NEW MEXICO FINISH LINE SCHOLARSHIP

Awards range from $300 to $1000. Scholarship is for the academically proven New Mexico college student who has completed at least one semester of undergraduate coursework. Must have at least 3.0 GPA.

Award: Scholarship for use in freshman, sophomore, junior, or senior years; renewable. *Number:* 1. *Amount:* $300–$1000.

Eligibility Requirements: Applicant must be enrolled or expecting to enroll full- or part-time at a four-year institution or university; resident of New Mexico and studying in New Mexico. Applicant must have 3.0 GPA or higher. Available to U.S. citizens.

Application Requirements: Application form, essay, financial aid award letter, self-addressed stamped envelope with application, transcript. *Deadline:* October 15.

Contact: Robert Paton, Business Development and Outreach Director
    College Success Network
    414 Alvarado Square, SW
    Albuquerque, NM 87158
    Phone: 505-241-4483
    Fax: 505-241-4484
    E-mail: bpaton@collegesuccessnetwork.org

COLORADO COMMISSION ON HIGHER EDUCATION

http://www.highered.colorado.gov/dhedefault.html

COLORADO STUDENT GRANT

Grants for Colorado residents attending eligible public, private, or vocational institutions within the state. Students must complete a Free Application for Federal Student Aid (FAFSA) and qualify at 150% of Pell eligibility. Application deadlines vary by institution. Renewable award for undergraduates. Contact the financial aid office at the college/institution for application and more information.

Award: Grant for use in freshman, sophomore, junior, or senior years; not renewable. *Number:* up to 69,602. *Amount:* $850–$5000.

Eligibility Requirements: Applicant must be enrolled or expecting to enroll full- or part-time at a two-year or four-year or technical institution or university; resident of Colorado and studying in Colorado. Available to U.S. citizens.

Application Requirements: Application form, financial need analysis, student must have an active FAFSA on file at the institution. *Deadline:* continuous.

Contact: Celina Duran, Financial Aid Administrator
Colorado Commission on Higher Education
1560 Broadway
Suite 1600
Denver, CO 80202
Phone: 303-866-2723
E-mail: celina.duran@dhe.state.co.us

COLORADO EDUCATIONAL SERVICES AND DEVELOPMENT ASSOCIATION

http://www.cesda.org

CESDA DIVERSITY SCHOLARSHIPS

Award for underrepresented, economically, and disadvantaged high school seniors planning to pursue undergraduate studies at a Colorado college or university. Must be Colorado resident. Applicant must be a first generation student, or member of an underrepresented ethnic or racial minority, and/or show financial need. Minimum 2.8 GPA required.

Award: Scholarship for use in freshman, sophomore, junior, or senior years; not renewable. *Number:* 6. *Amount:* $1000.

Eligibility Requirements: Applicant must be high school student; planning to enroll or expecting to enroll full- or part-time at a two-year or four-year or technical institution or university; resident of Colorado and studying in Colorado. Applicant must have 2.5 GPA or higher. Available to U.S. and non-Canadian citizens.

Application Requirements: Application form, application form may be submitted online (http://www.cesda.org/scholarships.html), essay, financial need analysis, resume, transcript. *Deadline:* April 9.

Contact: Hannah Brown, CESDA Scholarship Chair
Colorado Educational Services and Development Association
3645 West 112th Avenue
Westminster, CO 80031
Phone: 303-404-5234
Fax: 303-466-1623
E-mail: hannah.brown@frontrange.edu

COLORADO MASONS BENEVOLENT FUND ASSOCIATION

http://www.coloradofreemasons.org/

COLORADO MASONS BENEVOLENT FUND SCHOLARSHIPS

Applicants must be graduating seniors from a Colorado public high school accepted at a Colorado postsecondary institution. The maximum grant is $7000 renewable over four years. Obtain scholarship materials and specific requirements from high school counselor.

Award: Scholarship for use in freshman, sophomore, junior, or senior years; renewable. *Number:* 10–14. *Amount:* up to $7000.

Eligibility Requirements: Applicant must be high school student; planning to enroll or expecting to enroll full-time at a two-year or four-year or technical institution or university; resident of Colorado and studying in Colorado. Available to U.S. citizens.

Application Requirements: Application form, essay, financial need analysis, interview, recommendations or references, test scores, transcript. *Deadline:* March 7.

Contact: Ron Kadera, Scholarship Administrator
Colorado Masons Benevolent Fund Association
1130 Panorama Drive
Colorado Springs, CO 80904
Phone: 719-471-9587
Fax: 719-471-9157
E-mail: scholarships@coloradofreemasons.org

COMMUNITY BANKERS ASSOCIATION OF GEORGIA

http://www.cbaofga.com/

JULIAN AND JAN HESTER MEMORIAL SCHOLARSHIP

Scholarship available to Georgia high school seniors who will be entering a Georgia two- or four-year college or university, or a program at a technical institution. Recipients will be named on the basis of merit, and family financial need is not considered. Application must be sponsored by a local community bank, and must include an essay on community banking and what it represents.

Award: Scholarship for use in freshman year; not renewable. *Number:* 4. *Amount:* $1000.

Eligibility Requirements: Applicant must be high school student; planning to enroll or expecting to enroll full-time at a two-year or four-year or technical institution or university; resident of Georgia and studying in Georgia. Available to U.S. citizens.

Application Requirements: Application form, community service, recommendations or references, test scores, transcript. *Deadline:* March 30.

Contact: Lauren Dismuke, Public Relations and Marketing Coordinator
Phone: 770-541-4490
Fax: 770-541-4496
E-mail: lauren@cbaofga.com

COMMUNITY BANKERS ASSOCIATION OF ILLINOIS

http://www.cbai.com/

COMMUNITY BANKERS ASSOC. OF IL ANNUAL SCHOLARSHIP PROGRAM

Open to Illinois high school seniors who are sponsored by a CBAI member bank. Student bank employees, immediate families of bank employees, board members, stockholders, CBAI employees, and judges are ineligible. For more details see website http://www.cbai.com.

Award: Scholarship for use in freshman year; not renewable. *Number:* up to 16. *Amount:* $500–$4000.

Eligibility Requirements: Applicant must be high school student; planning to enroll or expecting to enroll full-time at a two-year or four-year or technical institution or university and resident of Illinois. Available to U.S. citizens.

Application Requirements: Application form, entry in a contest, essay. *Deadline:* February 10.

Contact: Ms. Andrea Cusick, Senior Vice President of Communications
Community Bankers Association of Illinois
901 Community Drive
Springfield, IL 62703
Phone: 217-529-2265
Fax: 217-585-8738
E-mail: cbaicom@cbai.com

COMMUNITY BANKERS ASSOC OF IL CHILD OF A BANKER SCHOLARSHIP

• See page 517

THE COMMUNITY FOUNDATION FOR GREATER ATLANTA, INC.

http://cfgreateratlanta.org/

GEORGE AND PEARL STRICKLAND SCHOLARSHIP

For undergraduate or graduate students with financial need pursuing degrees at Atlanta University Center Colleges. For complete eligibility requirements and for an application, please visit http://www.cfgreateratlanta.org.

Award: Scholarship for use in freshman, sophomore, junior, senior, or graduate years; not renewable. *Number:* 1–25. *Amount:* $1000–$3000.

Eligibility Requirements: Applicant must be enrolled or expecting to enroll full- or part-time at a four-year institution or university; resident of Georgia and studying in Georgia. Available to U.S. citizens.

Application Requirements: Application form, application form may be submitted online (http://www.cfgreateratlanta.org/Grants-Support/Scholarships.aspx), community service, driver's license, essay, financial need analysis, recommendations or references, transcript. *Deadline:* March 1.

Contact: Kristina Morris, Program Associate
The Community Foundation for Greater Atlanta, Inc.
50 Hurt Plaza
Suite 449
Atlanta, GA 30303
Phone: 404-688-5525
E-mail: scholarships@cfgreateratlanta.org

NANCY PENN LYONS SCHOLARSHIP FUND

Award for graduating high school seniors with financial need living in Georgia who have been accepted for enrollment at prestigious or out-of-state universities. (Due to the timing of application, college acceptance will be verified before scholarships are awarded but are not necessary at time of application). Please visit the website (www.cfgreateratlanta.org) for complete eligibility requirements and link to the application.

Award: Scholarship for use in freshman, sophomore, junior, or senior years; renewable. *Number:* 1–5. *Amount:* $5000.

Eligibility Requirements: Applicant must be high school student; planning to enroll or expecting to enroll full-time at a four-year institution or university and resident of Georgia. Applicant must have 3.0 GPA or higher. Available to U.S. citizens.

Application Requirements: Application form, application form may be submitted online (http://www.cfgreateratlanta.org/Grants-Support/Scholarships.aspx), community service, driver's license, essay, financial need analysis, interview, recommendations or references, test scores, transcript. *Deadline:* March 1.

Contact: Kristina Morris, Program Associate
The Community Foundation for Greater Atlanta, Inc.
50 Hurt Plaza
Suite 449
Atlanta, GA 30303
Phone: 404-688-5525
E-mail: scholarships@cfgreateratlanta.org

COMMUNITY FOUNDATION FOR PALM BEACH AND MARTIN COUNTIES

http://www.yourcommunityfoundation.org/

COMMUNITY FOUNDATION SCHOLARSHIP PROGRAM

Awards range between $1000 and $15,000 per year. Applicant must be a full-time student and graduating high school senior from a public or independent high school located in Palm Beach County or Martin County, Florida.

Award: Scholarship for use in freshman, sophomore, junior, senior, or graduate years; renewable. *Number:* 100–150. *Amount:* $1000–$15,000.

Eligibility Requirements: Applicant must be high school student; planning to enroll or expecting to enroll full-time at a two-year or four-year or technical institution or university and resident of Florida. Applicant must have 2.5 GPA or higher. Available to U.S. citizens.

Application Requirements: Application form, application form may be submitted online (http://www.yourcommunityfoundation.org), community service, essay, financial need analysis, interview, proof of citizenship/legal resident, recommendations or references, test scores, transcript. *Deadline:* February 1.

Contact: Ms. Patricia Rowan, Fund Distributions Manager
Community Foundation for Palm Beach and Martin Counties
700 South Dixie Highway, Suite 200
West Palm Beach, FL 33401
Phone: 561-659-6800
Fax: 561-832-6542
E-mail: prowan@cfpbmc.org

COMMUNITY FOUNDATION OF WESTERN MASSACHUSETTS

http://www.communityfoundation.org/

DEERFIELD PLASTICS/BARKER FAMILY SCHOLARSHIP
• See page 545

MASSMUTUAL CAREER PATHWAYS SCHOLARS PROGRAM

Graduating high school seniors from Hartford County, CT and Hampden County, MA with a strong interest in pursuing careers in business, financial services, or information technology.

Award: Scholarship for use in freshman year; not renewable. *Number:* 40. *Amount:* $5000.

Eligibility Requirements: Applicant must be high school student; planning to enroll or expecting to enroll full-time at a two-year or four-year institution or university and resident of Connecticut, Massachusetts. Applicant must have 3.0 GPA or higher. Available to U.S. citizens.

Application Requirements: Application form, application form may be submitted online (http://www.communityfoundation.org), essay, financial need analysis, transcript. *Deadline:* March 29.

Contact: Dorothy Theriaque, Education Office Associate
Community Foundation of Western Massachusetts
1500 Main Street
Suite 2300
Springfield, MA 01115
Phone: 413-732-2858
Fax: 413-733-8565
E-mail: scholar@communityfoundation.org

CONNECTICUT ARMY NATIONAL GUARD

http://www.ct.ngb.army.mil/

CONNECTICUT ARMY NATIONAL GUARD 100% TUITION WAIVER
• See page 588

CONNECTICUT ASSOCIATION OF LATINOS IN HIGHER EDUCATION (CALAHE)

http://www.calahe.org/

CONNECTICUT ASSOCIATION OF LATINOS IN HIGHER EDUCATION SCHOLARSHIPS
• See page 621

CONNECTICUT COMMUNITY FOUNDATION

http://www.conncf.org/

REGIONAL AND RESTRICTED SCHOLARSHIP AWARD PROGRAM

Supports accredited college or university study for residents of the Connecticut community twenty-one town service area. In addition, a variety of restricted award programs are based on specific fund criteria (residency, school, course of study, etc). Scholarships are awarded on a competitive basis with consideration given to academic record, extracurricular activities, work experience, financial need, reference letter, and an essay.

Award: Scholarship for use in freshman, sophomore, junior, or senior years; renewable. *Number:* 200–300. *Amount:* $250–$5000.

Eligibility Requirements: Applicant must be enrolled or expecting to enroll full-time at a two-year or four-year institution or university and resident of Connecticut. Applicant must have 3.0 GPA or higher.

Application Requirements: Application form, community service, essay, financial need analysis, recommendations or references, transcript. *Deadline:* March 15.

Contact: Josh Carey, Director of Grants Management
Connecticut Community Foundation
43 Field Street
Waterbury, CT 06702
Phone: 203-753-1315
E-mail: jcarey@conncf.org

CONNECTICUT OFFICE OF HIGHER EDUCATION

http://www.ctohe.org

CAPITOL SCHOLARSHIP PROGRAM

Award for Connecticut residents attending eligible institutions in Connecticut or in a state with reciprocity with Connecticut (Massachusetts, Pennsylvania, Rhode Island, Vermont, or Washington, D.C). Must be U.S. citizen or permanent resident alien who is a high school senior or graduate. Must rank in top 20% of class or score at least 1800 on SAT or score at least 27 on the ACT. Students must also demonstrate financial need as a result of filing the FAFSA.

Award: Scholarship for use in freshman, sophomore, junior, or senior years; renewable. *Number:* 2500–3500. *Amount:* $350–$2000.

Eligibility Requirements: Applicant must be enrolled or expecting to enroll full- or part-time at a two-year or four-year or technical institution or university; resident of Connecticut and studying in Connecticut, District of Columbia, Massachusetts, Pennsylvania, Rhode Island, Vermont. Available to U.S. citizens.

Application Requirements: Application form, FAFSA, financial need analysis, test scores. *Deadline:* February 15.

Contact: Mrs. Linda Diamond, Senior Associate
Connecticut Office of Higher Education
61 Woodland Street
Hartford, CT 06105
Phone: 860-947-1855
Fax: 860-947-1313
E-mail: csp@ctohe.org

CONNECTICUT AID TO PUBLIC COLLEGE STUDENTS GRANT

Award for Connecticut residents attending public colleges or universities within the state. Renewable awards based on financial need. Application deadline varies by institution. Apply at college financial aid office.

Award: Grant for use in freshman, sophomore, junior, or senior years; renewable.

Eligibility Requirements: Applicant must be enrolled or expecting to enroll full- or part-time at a two-year or four-year institution or university; resident of Connecticut and studying in Connecticut. Available to U.S. citizens.

Application Requirements: FAFSA, financial need analysis. *Deadline:* continuous.

Contact: Ms. Lynne Little, Executive Assistant
Connecticut Office of Higher Education
61 Woodland Street
Hartford, CT 06105
Phone: 860-947-1855
Fax: 860-947-1838
E-mail: caps@ctohe.org

CONNECTICUT INDEPENDENT COLLEGE STUDENT GRANTS

Award for Connecticut residents attending a not for profit independent college or university within the state on at least a half-time basis. Renewable awards based on financial need. Application deadline varies by institution. Apply at college financial aid office.

Award: Grant for use in freshman, sophomore, junior, or senior years; renewable. *Amount:* $250–$8166.

Eligibility Requirements: Applicant must be enrolled or expecting to enroll full- or part-time at a two-year or four-year institution or university; resident of Connecticut and studying in Connecticut. Available to U.S. citizens.

Application Requirements: FAFSA, financial need analysis. *Deadline:* continuous.

Contact: Ms. Lynne Little, Executive Assistant
Connecticut Office of Higher Education
61 Woodland Street
Hartford, CT 06105
Phone: 860-947-1855
Fax: 860-947-1838
E-mail: cics@ctohe.org

CORPORATION FOR OHIO APPALACHIAN DEVELOPMENT (COAD)

http://www.coadinc.org/

DAVID V. STIVISON APPALACHIAN SCHOLARSHIP FUND

Provides financial assistance to students who are residents in the Corporation for Ohio Appalachian Development's (COAD) service area and want to attend college but lack the required resources. Individual income must not exceed 200 percent of Federal Poverty Level. See website for application information http://www.coadinc.org/Main.php?page=scholarships-info.

Award: Scholarship for use in freshman, sophomore, junior, or senior years; not renewable. *Number:* 17. *Amount:* $500–$1500.

Eligibility Requirements: Applicant must be enrolled or expecting to enroll full-time at a two-year or four-year institution or university and resident of Ohio. Available to U.S. citizens.

Application Requirements: Application form, financial need analysis, personal photograph, transcript. *Deadline:* March 1.

Contact: Allyssa Mefford, Operations Manager
Phone: 740-594-8499 Ext. 213
E-mail: amefford@coadinc.org

COURAGE CENTER, VOCATIONAL SERVICES DEPARTMENT

http://www.couragecenter.org/

SCHOLARSHIP FOR PEOPLE WITH DISABILITIES

Award provides financial assistance to students with sensory or physical disabilities. May reapply each year. Applicant must be pursuing educational goals or technical expertise beyond high school. Must be U.S. citizen and resident of Minnesota, or participate in Courage Center Services. Indication of extracurricular work and volunteer history must be submitted along with application form.

Award: Scholarship for use in freshman, sophomore, junior, or senior years; not renewable. *Number:* 15–19. *Amount:* $500–$1000.

Eligibility Requirements: Applicant must be enrolled or expecting to enroll full-time at a two-year or four-year or technical institution or university and resident of Minnesota. Available to U.S. citizens.

Application Requirements: Application form, essay, financial need analysis, interview. *Deadline:* May 31.

Contact: Ms. Nancy Robinow, Administrative Assistant
Courage Center, Vocational Services Department
3915 Golden Valley Road
Minneapolis, MN 55422
Phone: 763-520-0553
Fax: 763-520-0861
E-mail: nrobiow@couragecenter.org

DADE COMMUNITY FOUNDATION

http://www.jackituckfield.org/

ALAN R. EPSTEIN SCHOLARSHIP

Award available for a high school senior who is a Dade county resident. Must have a 3.0 GPA and attach a copy of acceptance letter to two- or four-year college or university. For additional information and application, visit website at http://www.dadecommunityfoundation.org.

Award: Scholarship for use in freshman year; not renewable.

Eligibility Requirements: Applicant must be high school student; planning to enroll or expecting to enroll full-time at a two-year or four-year institution or university and resident of Florida. Applicant must have 3.0 GPA or higher. Available to U.S. citizens.

Application Requirements: Acceptance letter, personal statement, application form, financial need analysis, recommendations or references, transcript. *Deadline:* April 10.

Contact: Ted Seijo, Scholarship Coordinator
Phone: 305-371-2711
E-mail: ted.seijo@dadecommunityfoundation.org

CONTINENTAL GROUP SCHOLARSHIP

Renewable award for the children of current full-time employees of Continental Group and its subsidiaries. Must be a high school senior planning to enroll in a college or university in the U.S. Minimum 3.0 GPA required. Award may be available up to four years. For additional information and application, visit website http:// www.dadecommunityfoundation.org.

Award: Scholarship for use in freshman, sophomore, junior, or senior years; renewable. *Number:* 4. *Amount:* $1000.

Eligibility Requirements: Applicant must be high school student; planning to enroll or expecting to enroll full-time at a four-year institution or university and resident of Florida. Applicant must have 3.0 GPA or higher. Available to U.S. citizens.

Application Requirements: Application form, recommendations or references, transcript. *Deadline:* March 27.

Contact: Ted Seijo, Scholarship Coordinator
Phone: 305-371-2711
E-mail: ted.seijo@dadecommunityfoundation.org

RODNEY THAXTON/MARTIN E. SEGAL SCHOLARSHIP
• See page 621

SIDNEY M. ARONOVITZ SCHOLARSHIP
• See page 621

THE DALLAS FOUNDATION

http://www.dallasfoundation.org/

THE AKIN AYODELE SCHOLARSHIP IN MEMORY OF MICHAEL TILMON

Michael Tilmon was a best friend and teammate of Dallas Cowboy Akin Ayodele while at MacArthur High School. Sadly, he passed away in a car accident in March of 1997. This scholarship program is intended to honor those who demonstrate the type of character and integrity that Michael possessed.

Award: Scholarship for use in freshman year; not renewable. *Amount:* $10,000.

Eligibility Requirements: Applicant must be high school student; planning to enroll or expecting to enroll full-time at a two-year or four-year institution or university and resident of Texas.

Application Requirements: Application form, transcript. *Deadline:* April 15.

Contact: Rachel Lasseter, Program Associate
Phone: 214-741-9898
E-mail: scholarships@dallasfoundation.org

DR. DAN J. AND PATRICIA S. PICKARD SCHOLARSHIP
• See page 622

DR. DON AND ROSE MARIE BENTON SCHOLARSHIP

Award is available to students, parents of students and volunteers who have been affiliated with Trinity River Mission in Dallas, Texas. Must be enrolled in a graduate or undergraduate program in a regionally accredited college or university. Scholarship is renewable for two years if the student maintains a specified grade point average and fulfills all reporting requirements as determined by the Scholarship Committee.

Award: Scholarship for use in freshman, sophomore, junior, senior, graduate, or postgraduate years; renewable. *Number:* 1–3. *Amount:* $1500.

Eligibility Requirements: Applicant must be enrolled or expecting to enroll full-time at a two-year or four-year institution or university and resident of Texas.

Application Requirements: Application form, transcript. *Deadline:* April 1.

Contact: Ms. Dolores Sosa Green, Trinity River Mission
The Dallas Foundation
2060 Singleton Boulevard, Suite 104
Dallas, TX 75212
Phone: 214-744-5648

THE LANDON RUSNAK SCHOLARSHIP

The Landon Rusnak Scholarship Fund was established at The Dallas Foundation in 2007. This scholarship is established by the employees of LEAM Drilling Systems, Inc. and Conroe Machine, LLC in memory of Landon Rusnak, son of David and Janet Rusnak and brother of Cady Rusnak. Landon's sister Cady is an active member of the Mexia High School Black Cat Band.

Award: Scholarship for use in freshman year; not renewable. *Number:* 1. *Amount:* $3000.

Eligibility Requirements: Applicant must be high school student; planning to enroll or expecting to enroll full-time at a two-year or four-year institution or university; resident of Texas and must have an interest in music.

Application Requirements: Application form, financial need analysis, transcript. *Deadline:* February 28.

Contact: Rachel Lasseter, Program Associate
Phone: 214-741-9898
E-mail: scholarships@dallasfoundation.org

THE MAYOR'S CHESAPEAKE ENERGY SCHOLARSHIP

The Mayor's Chesapeake Energy Scholarship was established at The Dallas Foundation by Chesapeake Energy Corporation. The goal of the Fund is to make a college degree or vocational certification possible for minority and socially disadvantaged youth. Graduating students in the Dallas ISD are eligible to apply. Applicants should be female or a member of a minority group. Applicants must have participated in the Education is Freedom program.

Award: Scholarship for use in freshman, sophomore, junior, or senior years; renewable. *Amount:* $20,000.

Eligibility Requirements: Applicant must be high school student; planning to enroll or expecting to enroll full-time at a two-year or four-year or technical institution or university and resident of Texas. Applicant must have 3.0 GPA or higher. Available to U.S. citizens.

Application Requirements: Application form, financial need analysis, test scores, transcript. *Deadline:* April 15.

Contact: Rachel Lasseter, Program Associate
Phone: 214-741-9898
E-mail: scholarships@dallasfoundation.org

TOMMY TRANCHIN AWARD

Established at The Dallas Foundation to support students with physical, emotional or intellectual disabilities who have excelled or shown promise in a chosen field of interest. Tommy's family wants to recognize his creativity and his refusal to allow his disability to limit his personal growth by helping others to develop their own talents. Applicants should be residents of North Texas.

Award: Scholarship for use in freshman year; not renewable. *Amount:* $1500.

Eligibility Requirements: Applicant must be high school student; planning to enroll or expecting to enroll full-time at a two-year or four-year or technical institution or university and resident of Texas.

Application Requirements: Application form, physical, proof of physical, emotional or intellectual disability. *Deadline:* March 5.

Contact: Rachel Lasseter, Program Associate
Phone: 214-741-9898
E-mail: scholarships@dallasfoundation.org

DELAWARE HIGHER EDUCATION OFFICE

http://www.doe.k12.de.us

AGENDA FOR DELAWARE WOMEN TRAILBLAZER SCHOLARSHIP
• See page 553

DIAMOND STATE SCHOLARSHIP

Award for legal residents of Delaware who are U.S. citizens or eligible non-citizens. Must be enrolled as a full-time student in a degree program at a nonprofit, regionally accredited institution. Minimum 3.0 GPA required. High school seniors should rank in upper quarter of class and have a combined score of at least 1800 on the SAT.

Award: Scholarship for use in freshman year; renewable. *Number:* 50. *Amount:* $1250.

Eligibility Requirements: Applicant must be high school student; planning to enroll or expecting to enroll full-time at a four-year institution or university and resident of Delaware. Applicant must have 3.0 GPA or higher. Available to U.S. citizens.

Application Requirements: Application form, application form may be submitted online (http://www.doe.k12.de.us/infosuites/

students_family/dheo/how_to_apply/financial_aid/FA_webpages/
diamond_scholarship.shtml), essay, test scores, transcript. *Deadline:*
March 22.

Contact: Carylin Brinkley, Program Administrator
> *Phone:* 302-735-4120
> *Fax:* 302-739-5894
> *E-mail:* cbrinkley@doe.k12.de.us

EDUCATIONAL BENEFITS FOR CHILDREN OF DECEASED VETERANS
• *See page 553*

FIRST STATE MANUFACTURED HOUSING ASSOCIATION SCHOLARSHIP

Award for legal residents of Delaware who are high school seniors or former graduates seeking to further their education. Must have been a resident of a manufactured home for at least one year prior to the application. Evaluated on scholastic record, financial need, essay, and recommendations. Award for any type of accredited two- or four-year degree program, or for any accredited training, licensing, or certification program.

Award: Scholarship for use in freshman, sophomore, junior, or senior years; renewable. *Number:* up to 2. *Amount:* up to $2000.

Eligibility Requirements: Applicant must be enrolled or expecting to enroll full- or part-time at a two-year or four-year or technical institution or university and resident of Delaware. Available to U.S. citizens.

Application Requirements: Application form, essay, FAFSA, financial need analysis, recommendations or references, transcript. *Deadline:* March 7.

Contact: Carylin Brinkley, Program Administrator
> *Phone:* 302-735-4120
> *Fax:* 302-739-5894
> *E-mail:* cbrinkley@doe.k12.de.us

GOVERNOR'S WORKFORCE DEVELOPMENT GRANT

Grants for part-time undergraduate students attending Delaware College of Art and Design, Delaware State University, Delaware Technical and Community College, Goldey-Beacom College, University of Delaware, Wesley College, Widener University (Delaware Campus), or Wilmington College. Must be at least 18 years old, a resident of Delaware, and employed by a company in Delaware that contributes to the Blue Collar Training Fund Program.

Award: Grant for use in freshman, sophomore, junior, or senior years; renewable. *Number:* 40. *Amount:* $2000.

Eligibility Requirements: Applicant must be enrolled or expecting to enroll full- or part-time at a two-year or four-year institution or university; resident of Delaware and studying in Delaware. Available to U.S. and non-U.S. citizens.

Application Requirements: Application form. *Deadline:* varies.

Contact: Carylin Brinkley, Program Administrator
> *Phone:* 302-735-4120
> *Fax:* 302-739-5894
> *E-mail:* cbrinkley@doe.k12.de.us

LEGISLATIVE ESSAY SCHOLARSHIP

Award for legal residents of Delaware who are U.S. citizens or eligible non-citizens. Must be high school seniors in public or private schools or in home school programs who plans to enroll full-time at a nonprofit, regionally accredited college. Must submit an essay on topic: "Pluribus Unum: Is this motto adopted in 1782 relevant to our country today?"

Award: Prize for use in freshman year; not renewable. *Number:* up to 62. *Amount:* $1000–$10,000.

Eligibility Requirements: Applicant must be high school student; planning to enroll or expecting to enroll full- or part-time at a two-year or four-year or technical institution or university and resident of Delaware. Available to U.S. citizens.

Application Requirements: Application form, entry in a contest, essay. *Deadline:* November 30.

Contact: Carylin Brinkley, Program Administrator
> *Phone:* 302-735-4120
> *Fax:* 302-739-5894
> *E-mail:* cbrinkley@doe.k12.de.us

SCHOLARSHIP INCENTIVE PROGRAM (SCIP)

Award for legal residents of Delaware who are U.S. citizens or eligible non-citizens. Must demonstrate substantial financial need and enroll full-time in an undergraduate degree program at a nonprofit, regionally accredited institution in Delaware or Pennsylvania. Minimum 2.5 GPA required.

Award: Grant for use in freshman, sophomore, junior, senior, or graduate years; not renewable. *Number:* 1000–1253. *Amount:* $700–$2200.

Eligibility Requirements: Applicant must be enrolled or expecting to enroll full-time at a two-year or four-year institution or university; resident of Delaware and studying in Delaware, Pennsylvania. Applicant must have 2.5 GPA or higher. Available to U.S. citizens.

Application Requirements: Application form, FAFSA, financial need analysis, transcript. *Deadline:* April 15.

Contact: Carylin Brinkley, Program Administrator
> *Phone:* 302-735-4120
> *Fax:* 302-739-5894
> *E-mail:* cbrinkley@doe.k12.de.us

DENVER FOUNDATION

http://www.denverfoundation.org/

REISHER FAMILY SCHOLARSHIP FUND

Scholarships awarded to Colorado residents who attend Metropolitan State College, the University of Northern Colorado, and the University of Colorado at Denver. Sophomores or transferring juniors who do not have sufficient funding to otherwise complete their degrees are eligible to apply. Must have at least a 3.0 GPA.

Award: Scholarship for use in sophomore or junior years; not renewable.

Eligibility Requirements: Applicant must be enrolled or expecting to enroll full-time at a four-year institution or university; resident of Colorado and studying in Colorado. Applicant must have 3.0 GPA or higher. Available to U.S. citizens.

Application Requirements: Application form. *Deadline:* varies.

Contact: Karla Bieniulis, Scholarship Committee
> *Phone:* 303-300-1790 Ext. 103
> *Fax:* 303-300-6547
> *E-mail:* info@denverfoundation.org

DEPARTMENT OF EDUCATION, DIVISION OF HIGHER LEARNING, HIGHER EDUCATION COMMISSION

http://www.nh.gov/postsecondary

SCHOLARSHIPS FOR ORPHANS OF VETERANS-NEW HAMPSHIRE
• *See page 599*

DIAMANTE, INC.

http://www.diamanteinc.org/

LATINO DIAMANTE SCHOLARSHIP FUND
• *See page 553*

DISTRICT OF COLUMBIA OFFICE OF THE STATE SUPERINTENDENT OF EDUCATION

http://www.osse.dc.gov/

DC TUITION ASSISTANCE GRANT PROGRAM (DCTAG)

Grant pays the difference between in-state and out-of-state tuition and fees at any public college or university in the United States, Guam, Puerto Rico or U.S. Virgin Islands, up to $10,000 per year. It also pays up to $2500 per year of tuition and fees at private colleges and universities in the Washington metropolitan area and at historically black colleges and universities throughout the United States. Students must be enrolled in a degree-granting program at an eligible institution, and be domiciled in the District of Columbia.

Award: Grant for use in freshman, sophomore, junior, or senior years; not renewable. *Number:* up to 6000. *Amount:* $2500–$10,000.

Eligibility Requirements: Applicant must be enrolled or expecting to enroll full- or part-time at a two-year or four-year institution or university and resident of District of Columbia. Available to U.S. citizens.

Application Requirements: Application form, application form may be submitted online(dconeapp.dc.gov), Student Aid Report (SAR), current utility bill, D-40 tax return. *Deadline:* May 31.

Contact: Mr. Gregory Meeropol, Deputy Assistant Superintendent, Postsecondary and Career Education
District of Columbia Office of the State Superintendent of Education
810 First Street, NE, 3rd Floor
Washington, DC 20002
Phone: 202-727-2824
Fax: 202-281-3947
E-mail: gregory.meeropol@dc.gov

DIXIE BOYS BASEBALL

http://www.dixie.org/boys

DIXIE BOYS BASEBALL BERNIE VARNADORE SCHOLARSHIP PROGRAM

Eleven scholarships presented annually to deserving high school seniors who have participated in the Dixie Boys Baseball Program. Citizenship, scholarship, residency in a state with Dixie Baseball Programs and financial need are considered in determining the awards.

Award: Scholarship for use in freshman year; not renewable. *Number:* 11. *Amount:* $1250.

Eligibility Requirements: Applicant must be high school student; planning to enroll or expecting to enroll full-time at a two-year or four-year institution or university; resident of Alabama, Arkansas, Florida, Georgia, Louisiana, Mississippi, North Carolina, South Carolina, Tennessee, Texas, Virginia and must have an interest in athletics/sports. Available to U.S. citizens.

Application Requirements: Application form, financial need analysis, personal photograph, recommendations or references. *Deadline:* April 1.

Contact: Mr. James Jones, Commissioner/CEO
Phone: 334-793-3331
E-mail: jjones29@sw.rr.com

DIXIE YOUTH SCHOLARSHIP PROGRAM

Scholarships are presented annually to deserving high school seniors who participated in the Dixie Youth Baseball program while age 12 and under. Financial need is considered. Scholarship value is $2000.

Award: Scholarship for use in freshman year; not renewable. *Number:* up to 70. *Amount:* $2000.

Eligibility Requirements: Applicant must be high school student; planning to enroll or expecting to enroll full-time at a two-year or four-year or technical institution or university; resident of Alabama, Arkansas, Florida, Georgia, Louisiana, Mississippi, North Carolina, South Carolina, Tennessee, Texas, Virginia and must have an interest in athletics/sports. Available to U.S. citizens.

Application Requirements: 1040 form, application form, essay, financial need analysis, personal photograph, recommendations or references, transcript. *Deadline:* March 1.

DON'T MESS WITH TEXAS

http://www.dontmesswithtexas.org/

DON'T MESS WITH TEXAS SCHOLARSHIP PROGRAM

Scholarship for Texas graduating high school seniors who plan to attend accredited two- or four-year colleges or public or private universities in Texas.

Award: Scholarship for use in freshman year; not renewable. *Number:* 2–3. *Amount:* $1000–$3000.

Eligibility Requirements: Applicant must be high school student; planning to enroll or expecting to enroll full- or part-time at a two-year or four-year institution or university; resident of Texas and studying in Texas. Available to U.S. and non-U.S. citizens.

Application Requirements: Application form, essay, recommendations or references. *Deadline:* April 4.

Contact: Michael Roberts, Scholarship Committee
Phone: 512-476-4368
Fax: 512-476-4392
E-mail: scholarship@dontmesswithtexas.org

EAST BAY COLLEGE FUND

http://www.eastbaycollegefund.org/

GREAT EXPECTATIONS AWARD

Program provides renewable scholarships, mentoring, college counseling, and life skills training. Must have at least 3.0 cumulative GPA. Restricted to graduating seniors of Oakland, California public high schools.

Award: Scholarship for use in freshman, sophomore, junior, or senior years; renewable. *Number:* 20. *Amount:* $16,000.

Eligibility Requirements: Applicant must be enrolled or expecting to enroll full-time at a four-year institution or university and resident of California. Applicant must have 3.0 GPA or higher. Available to U.S. and non-U.S. citizens.

Application Requirements: Application form, essay, financial need analysis, interview, recommendations or references, transcript.

EAST BAY FOOTBALL OFFICIALS ASSOCIATION

http://www.ebfoa.org/

EAST BAY FOOTBALL OFFICIALS ASSOCIATION COLLEGE SCHOLARSHIP

Scholarship for high school seniors who currently participate in one of the football programs served by the East Bay Football Officials Association. Must be a resident of California, achieve at least a 3.0 GPA and have plans to attend any accredited two- or four-year institution.

Award: Scholarship for use in freshman year; renewable. *Number:* 3–4. *Amount:* up to $1000.

Eligibility Requirements: Applicant must be high school student; planning to enroll or expecting to enroll full-time at a two-year or four-year institution or university; resident of California and must have an interest in athletics/sports. Applicant must have 3.0 GPA or higher. Available to U.S. citizens.

Application Requirements: Application form, essay, recommendations or references, transcript. *Deadline:* October 31.

Contact: Sam Moriana, Program Coordinator
East Bay Football Officials Association
21 Chatham Pointe
Alameda, CA 94502
Phone: 510-521-4121
E-mail: smoriana@comcast.net

EAST LOS ANGELES COMMUNITY UNION (TELACU) SCHOLARSHIP PROGRAM

http://www.telacu.com/

TELACU EDUCATION FOUNDATION

Applicant must be a first-generation college student from a low-income family and have a minimum GPA of 2.5. Must attend partnering colleges and universities and be enrolled full-time for the entire academic year. California applicants: Must be permanent resident of unincorporated East Los Angeles, Bell Gardens, Commerce, Huntington Park, City of Los Angeles, Montebello, Monterey Park, Pico Rivera, Pomona and the Inland Empire, Santa Ana, South Gate, or other communities selected by foundation. Texas applicants: Must be permanent resident of San Antonio or Austin. Illinois Applicants: Must be permanent resident of Greater Chicagoland Area. New York applicants: Must be permanent resident of the state of New York.

Award: Scholarship for use in freshman, sophomore, junior, or senior years; not renewable. *Number:* 350–600. *Amount:* $500–$7500.

Eligibility Requirements: Applicant must be enrolled or expecting to enroll full-time at a two-year or four-year institution or university and resident of California, Illinois, New York, Texas. Applicant must have 2.5 GPA or higher. Available to U.S. citizens.

Application Requirements: Application form, essay, financial need analysis, interview, recommendations or references, resume, test scores, transcript. *Deadline:* March 14.

Contact: Mr. Daniel Garcia, Associate Director
East Los Angeles Community Union (TELACU) Scholarship Program
5400 East Olympic Boulevard
Los Angeles, CA 90022
Phone: 323-721-1655 Ext. 486
E-mail: dgarcia@TELACU.com

EDMONTON COMMUNITY FOUNDATION
http://www.DollarsForLearners.com/

YOUTH FORMERLY IN CARE BURSARY
• *See page 622*

EDMUND F. MAXWELL FOUNDATION
http://www.maxwell.org/

EDMUND F. MAXWELL FOUNDATION SCHOLARSHIP
Scholarships awarded to residents of Western Washington to attend accredited independent colleges or universities. Awards up to $5000 per year based on need, merit, citizenship, and activities. Renewable for up to four years if academic progress is suitable and financial need is unchanged.

Award: Scholarship for use in freshman year; renewable. *Number:* 110. *Amount:* up to $5000.

Eligibility Requirements: Applicant must be enrolled or expecting to enroll full-time at a four-year institution or university and resident of Washington. Available to U.S. citizens.

Application Requirements: Application form, employment history, essay, financial need analysis, test scores, transcript. *Deadline:* April 30.

Contact: Jane Thomas, Administrator
Edmund F. Maxwell Foundation
PO Box 22537
Seattle, WA 98122
Phone: 206-303-4402
Fax: 206-303-4419
E-mail: admin@maxwell.org

EDUCATION FOUNDATION. INC. NATIONAL GUARD ASSOCIATION OF COLORADO
http://www.ngaco.org/

EDUCATION FOUNDATION, INC. NATIONAL GUARD ASSOCIATION OF COLORADO SCHOLARSHIPS
• *See page 583*

ENLISTED ASSOCIATION OF THE NATIONAL GUARD OF NEW JERSEY
http://www.eang-nj.org/

CSM VINCENT BALDASSARI MEMORIAL SCHOLARSHIP PROGRAM
• *See page 583*

EPILEPSY FOUNDATION OF IDAHO
http://www.epilepsyidaho.org/

MARK MUSIC MEMORIAL SCHOLARSHIP
• *See page 570*

EQUALITYMAINE FOUNDATION
http://www.equalitymaine.org/

JOEL ABROMSON MEMORIAL FOUNDATION
One-time award for full-time postsecondary study available to winner of essay contest. Open to Maine residents only. Contact for essay topic and complete information.

Award: Scholarship for use in freshman year; not renewable. *Number:* 3. *Amount:* $500–$1000.

Eligibility Requirements: Applicant must be high school student; planning to enroll or expecting to enroll full-time at a two-year or four-year or technical institution or university and resident of Maine. Available to U.S. citizens.

Application Requirements: Application form, copy of acceptance letter to institution of higher learning, entry in a contest, essay, recommendations or references, self-addressed stamped envelope with application. *Deadline:* April 15.

Contact: Betsy Smith, Executive Director
Phone: 207-761-3732
Fax: 207-761-3752
E-mail: info@equalitymaine.org

EQUALITY SCHOLARSHIP COLLABORATIVE
http://www.equalityscholarship.org

SCHOLARSHIPS FOR HIGH SCHOOL GRADUATES
• *See page 554*

ESSAYJOLT.COM
http://www.essayjolt.com/

ESSAYJOLT SCHOLARSHIP
Essay contest open to high school juniors and seniors who may be citizens of any country, but must live in New Jersey. Essays are judged on originality, insight, and quality of writing by an independent panel of writers and editors. Only one winner is selected. See website for current essay question and guidelines http://www.essayjolt.com.

Award: Prize for use in freshman year; not renewable. *Number:* 1. *Amount:* $500.

Eligibility Requirements: Applicant must be high school student; planning to enroll or expecting to enroll full- or part-time at a two-year or four-year or technical institution or university; resident of New Jersey and must have an interest in writing. Available to U.S. and non-U.S. citizens.

Application Requirements: Entry in a contest, essay. *Deadline:* varies.

Contact: Meg Hartmann, Director
Phone: 917-575-3165
E-mail: scholarship@essayjolt.com

EVERLY SCHOLARSHIP FUND INC.

EVERLY SCHOLARSHIP
Renewable award for undergraduates attending an accredited institution full-time. Must be New Jersey residents. Minimum 3.0 GPA required and minimum SAT score of 1100.

Award: Scholarship for use in senior year; renewable. *Amount:* $2500.

Eligibility Requirements: Applicant must be enrolled or expecting to enroll full-time at a four-year institution or university and resident of New Jersey. Applicant must have 3.0 GPA or higher. Available to U.S. citizens.

Application Requirements: Application form, driver's license, essay, financial need analysis, interview, recommendations or references, test scores, transcript. *Deadline:* May 1.

Contact: John Lolio, President
Everly Scholarship Fund Inc.
4300 Haddonfield Road, Suite 311
Pennsauken, NJ 08109
Phone: 856-661-2094
Fax: 856-662-0165
E-mail: jlolio@sskrplaw.com

FINANCE AUTHORITY OF MAINE

http://www.famemaine.com/

STATE OF MAINE GRANT PROGRAM

Scholarship for residents of Maine, attending an eligible school in Connecticut, Maine, Massachusetts, New Hampshire, Pennsylvania, Rhode Island, Washington, D.C., or Vermont. Award based on need. Must apply annually. Complete free application for Federal Student Aid to apply. One-time award for undergraduate study. For further information see website http://www.famemaine.com.

Award: Grant for use in freshman, sophomore, junior, or senior years; not renewable. *Number:* up to 32,295. *Amount:* $250–$1250.

Eligibility Requirements: Applicant must be enrolled or expecting to enroll full- or part-time at a two-year or four-year or technical institution or university; resident of Maine and studying in Connecticut, District of Columbia, Maine, Massachusetts, New Hampshire, Pennsylvania, Rhode Island, Vermont. Available to U.S. citizens.

Application Requirements: Application form, FAFSA, financial need analysis. *Deadline:* May 1.

Contact: Claude Roy, Education Services Officer
Phone: 207-620-3507
E-mail: education@famemaine.com

TUITION WAIVER PROGRAMS
• *See page 554*

FLORIDA ASSOCIATION FOR MEDIA IN EDUCATION

http://www.floridamedia.org/

INTELLECTUAL FREEDOM STUDENT SCHOLARSHIP

Scholarship in the amount of $1000 is awarded annually to a graduating senior from a high school in Florida. Only students whose library media specialists are members of FAME are eligible. Essays written by senior students will be submitted to the FAME Intellectual Freedom Committee.

Award: Scholarship for use in freshman year; not renewable. *Number:* 1. *Amount:* $1000.

Eligibility Requirements: Applicant must be high school student; planning to enroll or expecting to enroll full-time at a two-year or four-year or technical institution or university and resident of Florida. Available to U.S. citizens.

Application Requirements: Application form, essay. *Deadline:* March 15.

Contact: Larry Bodkin, Executive Director
Phone: 850-531-8350
Fax: 850-531-8344
E-mail: lbodkin@floridamedia.org

FLORIDA PTA/PTSA

http://www.floridapta.org/

FLORIDA PTA/PTSA ANNUAL SCHOLARSHIP

Renewable scholarship of $1000 awarded to students enrolled full-time in their undergraduate study. Must maintain minimum 3.0 GPA.

Award: Scholarship for use in freshman, sophomore, junior, or senior years; renewable. *Number:* 2–3. *Amount:* $1000.

Eligibility Requirements: Applicant must be enrolled or expecting to enroll full-time at a four-year institution or university and resident of Florida. Applicant must have 3.0 GPA or higher. Available to U.S. citizens.

Application Requirements: Application form, essay, recommendations or references. *Deadline:* March 1.

Contact: Janice Bailey, Executive Director
Phone: 407-855-7604
Fax: 407-240-9577
E-mail: janice@floridapta.org

FLORIDA PTA/PTSA COMMUNITY/JUNIOR COLLEGE SCHOLARSHIP

One time award of $1000 to high school students who enrolled in a community or junior college. Must be a resident of Florida for at least 2 years. Must be a U.S. citizen and have at least a two-year attendance in a Florida PTA/PTSA high school. Minimum 2.5 GPA or higher.

Award: Scholarship for use in freshman year; not renewable. *Number:* 1–2. *Amount:* $1000.

Eligibility Requirements: Applicant must be enrolled or expecting to enroll full-time at a two-year institution and resident of Florida. Applicant must have 2.5 GPA or higher. Available to U.S. citizens.

Application Requirements: Application form, essay, proof of enrollment, recommendations or references. *Deadline:* March 1.

Contact: Janice Bailey, Executive Director
Phone: 407-855-7604
Fax: 407-240-9577
E-mail: janice@floridapta.org

FLORIDA PTA/PTSA VOCATIONAL/TECHNICAL SCHOLARSHIP

Scholarship of $1000 is awarded to graduating senior enrolled full time in a vocational/technical institution within the state of Florida. Must have at least a two-year attendance in a Florida PTA/PTSA high school. Minimum GPA is 2.0.

Award: Scholarship for use in freshman year; not renewable. *Number:* 3. *Amount:* $1000.

Eligibility Requirements: Applicant must be high school student; planning to enroll or expecting to enroll full-time at a two-year or technical institution; resident of Florida and studying in Florida. Available to U.S. citizens.

Application Requirements: Application form, essay, proof of enrollment, recommendations or references. *Deadline:* March 1.

Contact: Janice Bailey, Executive Director
Phone: 407-855-7604
Fax: 407-240-9577
E-mail: janice@floridapta.org

FLORIDA SOCIETY, SONS OF THE AMERICAN REVOLUTION

http://www.flssar.org/

GEORGE S. AND STELLA M. KNIGHT ESSAY CONTEST

Award for the best essay about an event, person, philosophy, or ideal associated with the American Revolution, the Declaration of Independence, or the framing of the U.S. Constitution. Must be a resident of Florida and U.S. citizen or legal resident. State winner may enter the national contest. For more information, see website http://www.patriot-web.com/essay/.

Award: Prize for use in sophomore, junior, or senior years; not renewable. *Number:* up to 3. *Amount:* up to $500.

Eligibility Requirements: Applicant must be high school student; planning to enroll or expecting to enroll full- or part-time at a two-year or four-year or technical institution or university and resident of Florida. Available to U.S. citizens.

Application Requirements: Entry in a contest, essay. *Deadline:* January 31.

FLORIDA STATE DEPARTMENT OF EDUCATION

http://www.floridastudentfinancialaid.org/

ACCESS TO BETTER LEARNING AND EDUCATION GRANT

Grant program provides tuition assistance to Florida undergraduate students enrolled in degree programs at eligible private Florida colleges or universities. Must be a U.S. citizen or eligible non-citizen and must meet Florida residency requirements. The participating institution determines application procedures, deadlines, and student eligibility. An eligible student must complete and submit the FAFSA in order to receive program funding. For more details, visit the website at http://www.FloridaStudentFinancialAid.org/SSFAD/home/uamain.htm.

Award: Grant for use in freshman, sophomore, junior, or senior years; renewable. *Amount:* up to $803.

Eligibility Requirements: Applicant must be enrolled or expecting to enroll full-time at a four-year institution or university; resident of Florida and studying in Florida. Available to U.S. citizens.

FIRST GENERATION MATCHING GRANT PROGRAM

Need-based grants to Florida resident undergraduate students who are enrolled in state universities and community colleges in Florida and whose parents have not earned baccalaureate degrees. Available state funds are contingent upon matching contributions from private sources on a dollar-for-dollar basis. Institutions determine application procedures, deadlines, and student eligibility. For more details, visit the website at http://www.FloridaStudentFinancialAid.org/SSFAD/home/uamain.htm.

Award: Grant for use in freshman, sophomore, junior, or senior years; renewable.

Eligibility Requirements: Applicant must be enrolled or expecting to enroll full- or part-time at a two-year or four-year institution or university; resident of Florida and studying in Florida. Available to U.S. citizens.

Application Requirements: Application form, financial need analysis.

FLORIDA BRIGHT FUTURES SCHOLARSHIP PROGRAM

Three lottery-funded scholarships reward Florida high school graduates for high academic achievement. Program is comprised of the following three awards: Florida Academic Scholars Award, Florida Medallion Scholars Award and Florida Gold Seal Vocational Scholars Award. An eligible student must complete and submit the FAFSA in order to receive program funding. For more details, visit the website at http://www.FloridaStudentFinancialAid.org/SSFAD/home/uamain.htm.

Award: Scholarship for use in freshman, sophomore, junior, or senior years; renewable.

Eligibility Requirements: Applicant must be high school student; planning to enroll or expecting to enroll full- or part-time at a two-year or four-year or technical institution or university; resident of Florida and studying in Florida. Applicant must have 3.0 GPA or higher. Available to U.S. citizens.

Application Requirements: Application form, community service, test scores, transcript.

FLORIDA POSTSECONDARY STUDENT ASSISTANCE GRANT

Scholarships to degree-seeking, resident, undergraduate students who demonstrate substantial financial need and are enrolled in eligible degree-granting private colleges and universities not eligible under the Florida Private Student Assistance Grant. FSAG is a decentralized program, and each participating institution determines application procedures, deadlines and student eligibility. Number of awards varies. For more details, visit the website at http://www.FloridaStudentFinancialAid.org/SSFAD/home/uamain.htm.

Award: Grant for use in freshman, sophomore, junior, or senior years; renewable. *Amount:* $200–$2534.

Eligibility Requirements: Applicant must be enrolled or expecting to enroll full-time at a two-year or four-year institution or university; resident of Florida and studying in Florida. Available to U.S. citizens.

Application Requirements: Application form, financial need analysis.

FLORIDA PRIVATE STUDENT ASSISTANCE GRANT

Grants for Florida residents who are U.S. citizens or eligible non-citizens attending eligible private, nonprofit, four-year colleges and universities in Florida. Must be a full-time student and demonstrate substantial financial need. For renewal, must have earned a minimum cumulative GPA of 2.0 at the last institution attended. For more details, visit the website at http://www.FloridaStudentFinancialAid.org/SSFAD/home/uamain.htm.

Award: Grant for use in freshman, sophomore, junior, or senior years; renewable. *Amount:* $200–$2534.

Eligibility Requirements: Applicant must be enrolled or expecting to enroll full-time at a four-year institution or university; resident of Florida and studying in Florida. Available to U.S. citizens.

Application Requirements: Application form, financial need analysis.

FLORIDA PUBLIC STUDENT ASSISTANCE GRANT

Grants for Florida residents, U.S. citizens or eligible non-citizens who attend state universities and public community colleges and demonstrate substantial financial need. For renewal, must have earned a minimum cumulative GPA of 2.0 at the last institution attended. For more details, visit the website at http://www.FloridaStudentFinancialAid.org/SSFAD/home/uamain.htm.

Award: Grant for use in freshman, sophomore, junior, or senior years; renewable. *Amount:* $200–$2534.

Eligibility Requirements: Applicant must be enrolled or expecting to enroll full- or part-time at a two-year or four-year institution or university; resident of Florida and studying in Florida. Available to U.S. citizens.

Application Requirements: Application form, financial need analysis.

FLORIDA STUDENT ASSISTANCE GRANT-CAREER EDUCATION

Need-based grant program available to Florida residents enrolled in certificate programs of 450 or more clock hours at participating community colleges or career centers operated by district school boards. FSAG-CE is a decentralized state of Florida program, which means that each participating institution determines application procedures, deadlines, student eligibility, and award amounts. For more details, visit the website at http://www.FloridaStudentFinancialAid.org/SSFAD/home/uamain.htm.

Award: Grant for use in freshman, sophomore, junior, or senior years; renewable. *Amount:* $200–$2534.

Eligibility Requirements: Applicant must be enrolled or expecting to enroll full- or part-time at a two-year or technical institution; resident of Florida and studying in Florida. Available to U.S. citizens.

Application Requirements: Application form, financial need analysis.

FLORIDA WORK EXPERIENCE PROGRAM

Need-based program providing eligible Florida residents work experiences that will complement and reinforce their educational and career goals. Must maintain GPA of 2.0. Postsecondary institution will determine applicant's eligibility, number of hours to be worked per week, and the award amount. For more details, visit the website at http://www.FloridaStudentFinancialAid.org/SSFAD/home/uamain.htm.

Award: Grant for use in freshman, sophomore, junior, or senior years; renewable.

Eligibility Requirements: Applicant must be enrolled or expecting to enroll full- or part-time at a two-year or four-year institution or university; resident of Florida and studying in Florida. Available to U.S. citizens.

Application Requirements: Application form, financial need analysis.

JOSE MARTI SCHOLARSHIP CHALLENGE GRANT FUND

• *See page 623*

MARY MCLEOD BETHUNE SCHOLARSHIP

Renewable award to Florida residents with a GPA of 3.0 or above, who will attend Bethune-Cookman University, Edward Waters College, Florida A&M University, or Florida Memorial University. Must not have previously received a baccalaureate degree. Must demonstrate financial need as specified by the institution. For more details, visit the website at http://www.FloridaStudentFinancialAid.org/SSFAD/home/uamain.htm.

Award: Scholarship for use in freshman, sophomore, junior, or senior years; renewable. *Amount:* $3000.

Eligibility Requirements: Applicant must be enrolled or expecting to enroll full-time at a four-year institution or university; resident of Florida and studying in Florida. Applicant must have 3.0 GPA or higher. Available to U.S. citizens.

Application Requirements: Application form, financial need analysis.

SCHOLARSHIPS FOR CHILDREN & SPOUSES OF DECEASED OR DISABLED VETERANS
• *See page 600*

WILLIAM L. BOYD IV FLORIDA RESIDENT ACCESS GRANT

Renewable awards to Florida undergraduate residents attending an eligible private, nonprofit Florida college or university. Postsecondary institution will determine applicant's eligibility. Renewal applicant must have earned a minimum institutional GPA of 2.0. An eligible student must complete and submit the FAFSA in order to receive program funding. For more details, visit the website at http://www.FloridaStudentFinancialAid.org/SSFAD/home/uamain.htm.

Award: Grant for use in freshman, sophomore, junior, or senior years; renewable. *Amount:* up to $2150.

Eligibility Requirements: Applicant must be enrolled or expecting to enroll full-time at a four-year institution or university; resident of Florida and studying in Florida. Available to U.S. citizens.

Application Requirements: Application form.

THE FORD FAMILY FOUNDATION SCHOLARSHIP OFFICE

http://www.tfff.org

FORD OPPORTUNITY PROGRAM

Hallie E. Ford and The Ford Family Foundation established the Ford Opportunity Scholarship Program to provide scholarships to college students who are single parents with custody of dependent children (18 years of age or younger) and be the head of household as defined by IRS regulations. The intention of this scholarship is to assist single parents who do not have the support of a domestic partner. Recipients must attend college in their home start of Oregon or California and plan to pursue a bachelor's degree.

Award: Scholarship for use in freshman, sophomore, junior, senior, graduate, or postgraduate years; renewable. *Number:* up to 36. *Amount:* $1000–$25,000.

Eligibility Requirements: Applicant must be enrolled or expecting to enroll full-time at a two-year or four-year institution or university; single; resident of California, Oregon and studying in California, Oregon. Applicant must have 3.0 GPA or higher. Available to U.S. citizens.

Application Requirements: Application form, application form may be submitted online (http://www.oregonstudentaid.gov), essay, financial need analysis, interview, transcript. *Deadline:* March 1.

Contact: Tricia Tate, Scholarship Programs Manager
The Ford Family Foundation Scholarship Office
440 E Broadway, Suite 200
Eugene, OR 97401
Phone: 541-485-6211 Ext. 2513
Fax: 541-485-6223
E-mail: fordscholarships@tfff.org

FORD RESTART PROGRAM

The Ford Family Foundation established the Ford ReStart Scholarship Program to encourage adults, age 25 or older, to begin or return to full-time, post-secondary education. Each year, up to 46 applicants are selected from Oregon and Siskiyou County, California to receive a Ford ReStart scholarship. An applicant must be at least 25 years old by March 1 of the application year and seek a certificate, a 2-year associate's degree, or a bachelor's degree at an eligible institution (and not previously have earned a bachelor's degree).

Award: Scholarship for use in freshman, sophomore, junior, senior, graduate, or postgraduate years; renewable. *Number:* up to 46. *Amount:* $1000–$25,000.

Eligibility Requirements: Applicant must be enrolled or expecting to enroll full-time at a two-year or four-year or technical institution or university; resident of California, Oregon and studying in California, Oregon. Available to U.S. citizens.

Application Requirements: Application form, application form may be submitted online (http://www.OregonStudentAid.gov), essay, financial need analysis, interview, recommendations or references, transcript. *Deadline:* March 1.

Contact: Tricia Tate, Scholarship Programs Manager
The Ford Family Foundation Scholarship Office
440 E Broadway, Suite 200
Eugene, OR 97401
Phone: 541-485-6211 Ext. 2513
Fax: 541-485-6223
E-mail: fordscholarships@tfff.org

FORD SCHOLARS PROGRAM

The Ford Family Foundation established the Ford ReStart Scholarship Program to encourage adults, age 25 or older, to begin or return to full-time, post-secondary education. Each year, up to 46 applicants are selected from Oregon and Siskiyou County, California to receive a Ford ReStart scholarship. An applicant must be at least 25 years old by March 1 of the application year and seek a certificate, a 2-year associate's degree, or a bachelor's degree at an eligible institution (and not previously have earned a bachelor's degree).

Award: Scholarship for use in freshman, sophomore, junior, senior, graduate, or postgraduate years; renewable. *Number:* up to 46. *Amount:* $1000–$25,000.

Eligibility Requirements: Applicant must be enrolled or expecting to enroll full-time at a two-year or four-year or technical institution or university; resident of California, Oregon and studying in California, Oregon. Available to U.S. citizens.

Application Requirements: Application form, application form may be submitted online (http://www.oregonstudentaid.gov), essay, financial need analysis, interview, recommendations or references, transcript. *Deadline:* March 1.

Contact: Tricia Tate, Scholarship Programs Manager
The Ford Family Foundation Scholarship Office
440 E Broadway, Suite 200
Eugene, OR 97401
Phone: 541-485-6211 Ext. 2513
Fax: 541-485-6223
E-mail: fordscholarships@tfff.org

FRATERNAL ORDER OF POLICE ASSOCIATES OF OHIO INC.

http://www.fopaohio.org/

FRATERNAL ORDER OF POLICE ASSOCIATES, STATE LODGE OF OHIO INC., SCHOLARSHIP FUND
• *See page 554*

FRIENDS OF 440 SCHOLARSHIP FUND INC.

http://www.440scholarship.org/

FRIENDS OF 440 SCHOLARSHIP FUND, INC.

Scholarships to students who are dependents of workers who were injured or killed in the course and scope of their employment and who are eligible to receive benefits under the Florida Workers' Compensation system, or are dependents of those primarily engaged in the administration of the Florida Workers' Compensation Law.

Award: Scholarship for use in freshman, sophomore, junior, or senior years; renewable. *Number:* 1–60. *Amount:* $500–$6000.

Eligibility Requirements: Applicant must be enrolled or expecting to enroll full-time at a two-year or four-year or technical institution or university and resident of Florida. Available to U.S. and non-U.S. citizens.

Application Requirements: Application form, copy of tax return, transcript. *Deadline:* February 28.

Contact: Ms. Sharon McMorris, Executive Director
Phone: 305-423-8710
Fax: 305-670-0716
E-mail: info@440scholarship.org

FULFILLMENT FUND

http://www.fulfillment.org/

FULFILLMENT FUND SCHOLARSHIPS

Award is for undergraduates. Serving students in seven partner high schools, Fremont, Hamilton, Locke, Los Angeles, Manual Arts,

Crenshaw and Wilson. Only students who participated in the Fulfillment Fund High School Program for at least two years are eligible to apply for the scholarship.

Award: Scholarship for use in freshman, sophomore, junior, or senior years; not renewable. *Amount:* $1000–$1500.

Eligibility Requirements: Applicant must be enrolled or expecting to enroll full- or part-time at a four-year institution or university and resident of California. Available to U.S. citizens.

Application Requirements: Application form. *Deadline:* varies.

Contact: Darcine Thomas, Community Outreach Manager
Phone: 323-900-8753
Fax: 525-3095

GENERAL FEDERATION OF WOMEN'S CLUBS OF MASSACHUSETTS

http://www.gfwcma.org/

GENERAL FEDERATION OF WOMEN'S CLUBS OF MASSACHUSETTS STUDY ABROAD SCHOLARSHIP

Scholarship for undergraduate or graduate students to study abroad. Applicant must submit personal statement and letter of endorsement from the president of the sponsoring General Federation of Women's Clubs of Massachusetts. Must be resident of Massachusetts.

Award: Scholarship for use in freshman, sophomore, junior, senior, or graduate years; not renewable. *Number:* 1. *Amount:* $800.

Eligibility Requirements: Applicant must be enrolled or expecting to enroll full-time at a four-year institution or university and resident of Massachusetts. Available to U.S. citizens.

Application Requirements: Application form, essay, interview, recommendations or references, self-addressed stamped envelope with application, transcript. *Deadline:* March 1.

Contact: Marta DiBenedetto, Scholarship Chairperson
General Federation of Women's Clubs of Massachusetts
PO Box 679, 245 Dutton Road
Sudbury, MA 01776-0679
Phone: 978-444-9105
E-mail: marta_dibenedetto@nylim.com

GENERAL FEDERATION OF WOMEN'S CLUBS OF VERMONT

BARBARA JEAN BARKER MEMORIAL SCHOLARSHIP FOR A DISPLACED HOMEMAKER

Applicants must be Vermont residents who have been homemakers (primarily) for at least fifteen years and have lost their main means of support through death, divorce, separation, spouse's long-time illness, or spouse's long-time unemployment. Provides one to three scholarships ranging from $500 to $1500.

Award: Grant for use in freshman, sophomore, junior, senior, or graduate years; not renewable. *Number:* 1–3. *Amount:* $500–$1500.

Eligibility Requirements: Applicant must be enrolled or expecting to enroll full- or part-time at a two-year or four-year or technical institution or university; female and resident of Vermont. Available to U.S. citizens.

Application Requirements: Application form, driver's license, financial need analysis, interview, recommendations or references. *Deadline:* March 15.

Contact: Betty Haggerty, Chairman
Phone: 802-463-4159
E-mail: hubett@hotmail.com

GEORGE SNOW SCHOLARSHIP FUND

http://www.scholarship.org/

GEORGE SNOW SCHOLARSHIP FUND/FEMINIST SCHOLARSHIP

Scholarships available to graduating Florida high school seniors entering their first year of college. Students applying for this scholarship can attend any accredited college, university, vocational/technical school they wish, anywhere in the country and major in any subject.

Award: Scholarship for use in freshman year; not renewable.

Eligibility Requirements: Applicant must be high school student; planning to enroll or expecting to enroll full- or part-time at a two-year or four-year or technical institution or university and resident of Florida. Available to U.S. and non-U.S. citizens.

Application Requirements: Application form, interview, IRS 1040 forms, FAFSA, transcript. *Deadline:* February 1.

GEORGIA STUDENT FINANCE COMMISSION

http://www.GAcollege411.org/

GEORGIA HOPE SCHOLARSHIP PROGRAM

Scholarship and Grant program for Georgia residents who are college undergraduates to attend an accredited two or four-year Georgia institution. Pays a percentage of actual undergraduate tuition charged at public postsecondary institutions. Percentage paid will vary from year to year. At private postsecondary institutions in Georgia, students may receive up to $3600 per year for full-time study or $1800 per year for part-time. Minimum 3.0 GPA required. Renewable if student maintains grades. See www.GAcollege411.org for full details.

Award: Scholarship for use in freshman, sophomore, junior, or senior years; renewable. *Number:* 200,000–230,000. *Amount:* up to $6000.

Eligibility Requirements: Applicant must be enrolled or expecting to enroll full- or part-time at a two-year or four-year institution or university; resident of Georgia and studying in Georgia. Applicant must have 3.0 GPA or higher. Available to U.S. citizens.

Application Requirements: Application form, high schools must report transcripts to GSFC. *Deadline:* continuous.

Contact: Tracy Ireland, Vice President
Georgia Student Finance Commission
2082 East Exchange Place, Suite 100
Tucker, GA 30084
Phone: 800-505-4732
E-mail: tracyi@gsfc.org

GEORGIA PUBLIC SAFETY MEMORIAL GRANT

Award for children of Georgia Public Safety Officers, prison guards, fire fighters, law enforcement officers or emergency medical technicians killed or permanently disabled in the line of duty. Must attend an accredited postsecondary Georgia school. Complete the Public Safety Memorial Grant application.

Award: Grant for use in freshman, sophomore, junior, or senior years; not renewable. *Number:* 20–40. *Amount:* $2000.

Eligibility Requirements: Applicant must be enrolled or expecting to enroll full-time at a two-year or four-year or technical institution or university; resident of Georgia and studying in Georgia. Available to U.S. citizens.

Application Requirements: Application form, selective service registration. *Deadline:* continuous.

Contact: Caylee French, Division Director
Georgia Student Finance Commission
2082 East Exchange Place, Suite 100
Tucker, GA 30084
Phone: 770-724-9244
E-mail: cayleef@gsfc.org

GEORGIA TUITION EQUALIZATION GRANT (GTEG)
• *See page 570*

GIRL SCOUTS OF CONNECTICUT

http://www.gsofct.org/

EMILY CHAISON GOLD AWARD SCHOLARSHIP
• *See page 520*

GRANGE INSURANCE ASSOCIATION

http://www.grange.com/

GRANGE INSURANCE GROUP SCHOLARSHIP

Scholarships to current GIG policyholder/ member (or children or grandchildren of GIG policyholder) in California, Colorado, Idaho,

Oregon, Washington or Wyoming. See website at http://www.grange.com for further details.

Award: Scholarship for use in freshman, sophomore, junior, senior, graduate, or postgraduate years; renewable. *Number:* 25–28. *Amount:* $1000–$1500.

Eligibility Requirements: Applicant must be enrolled or expecting to enroll full- or part-time at a two-year or four-year or technical institution or university and resident of California, Colorado, Idaho, Oregon, Washington, Wyoming. Available to U.S. citizens.

Application Requirements: Application form, driver's license, essay, financial need analysis, recommendations or references, transcript. *Deadline:* April 15.

GREATER KANAWHA VALLEY FOUNDATION

http://www.tgkvf.org/

C. RAYMOND & DELSIA R. COLLINS SCHOLARSHIP

Renewable award for a full-time student who is a resident of West Virginia pursing postsecondary studies. Must demonstrate academic excellence.

Award: Scholarship for use in freshman, sophomore, junior, or senior years; renewable. *Amount:* $1000.

Eligibility Requirements: Applicant must be enrolled or expecting to enroll full-time at a four-year institution or university and resident of West Virginia. Available to U.S. citizens.

Application Requirements: Application form, financial need analysis, recommendations or references, test scores, transcript. *Deadline:* January 15.

Contact: Susan Hoover, Scholarship Program Officer
Greater Kanawha Valley Foundation
900 Lee Street East, 16th Floor
Charleston, WV 25301
Phone: 304-346-3620
E-mail: tgkvf@tgkvf.org

DRS. CHARLENE & CHARLES BYRD SCHOLARSHIP

Renewable award for a West Virginia resident pursuing full-time postsecondary studies. Minimum 2.5 GPA required.

Award: Scholarship for use in freshman, sophomore, junior, or senior years; renewable.

Eligibility Requirements: Applicant must be enrolled or expecting to enroll full-time at a four-year institution or university and resident of West Virginia. Applicant must have 2.5 GPA or higher. Available to U.S. citizens.

Application Requirements: Application form, recommendations or references, transcript. *Deadline:* January 15.

Contact: Susan Hoover, Scholarship Program Officer
Greater Kanawha Valley Foundation
900 Lee Street East, 16th Floor
Charleston, WV 25301
Phone: 304-346-3620
E-mail: tgkvf@tgkvf.org

EVANS MEMORIAL SCHOLARSHIP

Renewable award available to West Virginia resident who is enrolling or has enrolled in a two-year or four-year college/university in West Virginia. Must demonstrate financial need.

Award: Scholarship for use in freshman, sophomore, junior, or senior years; renewable. *Number:* up to 24. *Amount:* $1000.

Eligibility Requirements: Applicant must be enrolled or expecting to enroll full-time at a two-year or four-year institution or university; resident of West Virginia and studying in West Virginia. Available to U.S. citizens.

Application Requirements: Application form, financial need analysis, test scores, transcript. *Deadline:* January 15.

Contact: Susan Hoover, Scholarship Program Officer
Greater Kanawha Valley Foundation
900 Lee Street East, 16th Floor
Charleston, WV 25301
Phone: 304-346-3620
E-mail: tgkvf@tgkvf.org

HENRY E. KING SCHOLARSHIP FUND

Award available for immediate family members of owners, or employees, of companies that are current members of, and have been members of, the Home Builders Association of Greater Charleston, West Virginia. Award to be used for full-time study in a two- or four-year college/university. Must be a resident of West Virginia and demonstrate financial need. Renewable only for current members.

Award: Scholarship for use in freshman, sophomore, junior, or senior years; not renewable. *Number:* 1. *Amount:* $1000.

Eligibility Requirements: Applicant must be enrolled or expecting to enroll full-time at a two-year or four-year institution or university and resident of West Virginia. Available to U.S. citizens.

Application Requirements: Application form, financial need analysis, transcript. *Deadline:* January 15.

Contact: Susan Hoover, Scholarship Program Officer
Greater Kanawha Valley Foundation
900 Lee Street East, 16th Floor
Charleston, WV 25301
Phone: 304-346-3620
E-mail: tgkvf@tgkvf.org

JAMES & MARIANNE LANE SCHOLARSHIP

Renewable award for a West Virginia resident pursuing postsecondary studies. Minimum 2.5 GPA required. Preference given to students attending Washington & Jefferson College.

Award: Scholarship for use in freshman, sophomore, junior, or senior years; renewable.

Eligibility Requirements: Applicant must be enrolled or expecting to enroll full-time at a four-year institution or university and resident of West Virginia. Applicant must have 2.5 GPA or higher. Available to U.S. citizens.

Application Requirements: Application form, financial need analysis, recommendations or references, test scores, transcript. *Deadline:* January 15.

Contact: Susan Hoover, Scholarship Program Officer
Greater Kanawha Valley Foundation
900 Lee Street East, 16th Floor
Charleston, WV 25301
Phone: 304-346-3620
E-mail: tgkvf@tgkvf.org

KID'S CHANCE OF WEST VIRGINIA SCHOLARSHIP

Award for children (between the ages of 16 and 25) of a parent injured in a WV work-related accident. Preference shall be given to students with financial need, academic performance, leadership abilities, demonstrated and potential contributions to school and community who are pursuing any field of study in any accredited trade, vocational school, college, or university. Must attach a copy of the order or letter from the worker's compensation carrier granting a permanent total disability award or dependent's benefits.

Award: Scholarship for use in freshman, sophomore, junior, or senior years; renewable. *Number:* up to 8. *Amount:* $1500.

Eligibility Requirements: Applicant must be age 16-25; enrolled or expecting to enroll full-time at a two-year or four-year or technical institution or university; resident of West Virginia and must have an interest in leadership. Available to U.S. citizens.

Application Requirements: Application form, essay, financial need analysis, recommendations or references, transcript, workers compensation order/letter. *Deadline:* January 15.

Contact: Susan Hoover, Scholarship Program Officer
Greater Kanawha Valley Foundation
900 Lee Street East, 16th Floor
Charleston, WV 25301
Phone: 304-346-3620
E-mail: tgkvf@tgkvf.org

LAWRENCE C. YEARDLEY SCHOLARSHIP

Renewable award for resident of West Virginia pursuing postsecondary studies. Must demonstrate academic excellence and have a minimum 2.5 GPA.

Award: Scholarship for use in freshman, sophomore, junior, or senior years; renewable.

Eligibility Requirements: Applicant must be enrolled or expecting to enroll full-time at a four-year institution or university and resident of

West Virginia. Applicant must have 2.5 GPA or higher. Available to U.S. citizens.

Application Requirements: Application form, financial need analysis, recommendations or references, test scores, transcript. *Deadline:* January 15.

Contact: Susan Hoover, Scholarship Program Officer
Greater Kanawha Valley Foundation
900 Lee Street East, 16th Floor
Charleston, WV 25301
Phone: 304-346-3620
E-mail: tgkvf@tgkvf.org

MABEL W. WALKER SCHOLARSHIP

Renewable award for West Virginia residents pursuing full-time postsecondary studies. Minimum 2.5 GPA required. Preference given to residents of Campbell Creek and then Upper Kanawha.

Award: Scholarship for use in freshman, sophomore, junior, or senior years; renewable. *Amount:* $1000.

Eligibility Requirements: Applicant must be enrolled or expecting to enroll full-time at a four-year institution or university and resident of West Virginia. Applicant must have 2.5 GPA or higher. Available to U.S. citizens.

Application Requirements: Application form, financial need analysis, recommendations or references, test scores, transcript. *Deadline:* January 15.

Contact: Susan Hoover, Scholarship Program Officer
Greater Kanawha Valley Foundation
900 Lee Street East, 16th Floor
Charleston, WV 25301
Phone: 304-346-3620
E-mail: tgkvf@tgkvf.org

MILLIE SNYDER SCHOLARSHIP

Renewable award for a West Virginia resident pursuing full-time postsecondary studies. Must be a member of Weight Watchers. Minimum 2.5 GPA required.

Award: Scholarship for use in freshman, sophomore, junior, or senior years; renewable.

Eligibility Requirements: Applicant must be enrolled or expecting to enroll full-time at a four-year institution or university and resident of West Virginia. Applicant must have 2.5 GPA or higher. Available to U.S. citizens.

Application Requirements: Application form, recommendations or references, transcript. *Deadline:* January 15.

Contact: Susan Hoover, Scholarship Program Officer
Greater Kanawha Valley Foundation
900 Lee Street East, 16th Floor
Charleston, WV 25301
Phone: 304-346-3620
E-mail: tgkvf@tgkvf.org

NORMAN S. AND BETTY M. FITZHUGH FUND

Award available to West Virginia residents who demonstrate academic excellence and financial need to attend any accredited college or university. Scholarships are awarded for full-time study for one or more years.

Award: Scholarship for use in freshman, sophomore, junior, or senior years; renewable. *Number:* 1.

Eligibility Requirements: Applicant must be enrolled or expecting to enroll full-time at a two-year or four-year or technical institution or university and resident of West Virginia. Available to U.S. citizens.

Application Requirements: Application form, essay, financial need analysis, recommendations or references, transcript. *Deadline:* January 15.

Contact: Susan Hoover, Scholarship Program Officer
Greater Kanawha Valley Foundation
900 Lee Street East, 16th Floor
Charleston, WV 25301
Phone: 304-346-3620
E-mail: tgkvf@tgkvf.org

O'HAIR SCHOLARSHIP

Renewable award for West Virginia residents pursuing full-time postsecondary studies. Must demonstrate academic ability. Minimum 2.5 GPA required.

Award: Scholarship for use in freshman, sophomore, junior, or senior years; renewable. *Amount:* $1000.

Eligibility Requirements: Applicant must be enrolled or expecting to enroll full-time at a four-year institution or university and resident of West Virginia. Applicant must have 2.5 GPA or higher. Available to U.S. citizens.

Application Requirements: Application form, financial need analysis, recommendations or references, test scores, transcript. *Deadline:* January 15.

Contact: Susan Hoover, Scholarship Program Officer
Greater Kanawha Valley Foundation
900 Lee Street East, 16th Floor
Charleston, WV 25301
Phone: 304-346-3620
E-mail: tgkvf@tgkvf.org

RHUDY SCHOLARSHIP

Renewable award for a West Virginia resident pursuing full-time postsecondary studies. Minimum 2.5 GPA required. Must demonstrate academic ability and financial need.

Award: Scholarship for use in freshman, sophomore, junior, or senior years; renewable. *Amount:* $1000.

Eligibility Requirements: Applicant must be enrolled or expecting to enroll full-time at a four-year institution or university and resident of West Virginia. Applicant must have 2.5 GPA or higher. Available to U.S. citizens.

Application Requirements: Application form, financial need analysis, recommendations or references, test scores, transcript. *Deadline:* January 15.

Contact: Susan Hoover, Scholarship Program Officer
Greater Kanawha Valley Foundation
900 Lee Street East, 16th Floor
Charleston, WV 25301
Phone: 304-346-3620
E-mail: tgkvf@tgkvf.org

R. RAY SINGLETON FUND

Renewable award available for undergraduate or graduate study in a West Virginia two- or four-year college/university. Applicant must be resident of Kanawha, Boone, Clay, Putnam, Lincoln, or Fayette counties, and demonstrate financial need and academic excellence.

Award: Scholarship for use in freshman, sophomore, junior, or senior years; renewable. *Amount:* $1000.

Eligibility Requirements: Applicant must be enrolled or expecting to enroll full-time at a four-year institution or university; resident of West Virginia and studying in West Virginia. Available to U.S. citizens.

Application Requirements: Application form, financial need analysis, transcript. *Deadline:* January 15.

Contact: Susan Hoover, Scholarship Program Officer
Greater Kanawha Valley Foundation
900 Lee Street East, 16th Floor
Charleston, WV 25301
Phone: 304-346-3620
E-mail: tgkvf@tgkvf.org

RUTH ANN JOHNSON SCHOLARSHIP

Renewable award for a full-time postsecondary student who is a resident of West Virginia. Must demonstrate academic excellence. Minimum 2.5 GPA required.

Award: Scholarship for use in freshman, sophomore, junior, or senior years; renewable. *Amount:* $1000.

Eligibility Requirements: Applicant must be enrolled or expecting to enroll full-time at a four-year institution or university and resident of West Virginia. Applicant must have 2.5 GPA or higher. Available to U.S. citizens.

Application Requirements: Application form, financial need analysis, recommendations or references, test scores, transcript. *Deadline:* January 15.

Contact: Susan Hoover, Scholarship Program Officer
Greater Kanawha Valley Foundation
900 Lee Street East, 16th Floor
Charleston, WV 25301
Phone: 304-346-3620
E-mail: tgkvf@tgkvf.org

STUART & LUCILLE ARMSTRONG SCHOLARSHIP

• *See page 651*

THALHEIMER FAMILY SUPPLEMENTAL SCHOLARSHIP

Award available to West Virginia students who are current scholarship winners to provide supplemental funds for goods and services necessary for the student to attend college. Must be a resident of Kanawha, Putnam, Boone, Clay, Fayette, or Lincoln counties and submit a written request for additional aid, listing all financial aid that has been awarded and reason for request.

Award: Scholarship for use in freshman, sophomore, junior, or senior years; not renewable. *Number:* 1. *Amount:* $1000.

Eligibility Requirements: Applicant must be enrolled or expecting to enroll full-time at a two-year or four-year institution or university and resident of West Virginia. Available to U.S. citizens.

Application Requirements: Application form, financial need analysis, letter requesting aid, transcript. *Deadline:* January 15.

Contact: Susan Hoover, Scholarship Program Officer
Greater Kanawha Valley Foundation
900 Lee Street East, 16th Floor
Charleston, WV 25301
Phone: 304-346-3620
E-mail: tgkvf@tgkvf.org

WEST VIRGINIA GOLF ASSOCIATION FUND

Award of $1000 available to students at any accredited West Virginia college or university. This fund is open to individuals who (1) have played golf in WV as an amateur for recreation or competition or (2) have been or are presently employed in WV as a caddie, groundskeeper, bag boy, etc. Must also include a reference by a coach, golf professional, or employer and an essay explaining how the game of golf has made an impact in applicant's life.

Award: Scholarship for use in freshman, sophomore, junior, or senior years; not renewable. *Number:* 2. *Amount:* $1000.

Eligibility Requirements: Applicant must be enrolled or expecting to enroll full-time at a two-year or four-year or technical institution or university; resident of West Virginia; studying in West Virginia and must have an interest in golf. Available to U.S. citizens.

Application Requirements: Application form, essay, recommendations or references, transcript. *Deadline:* January 15.

Contact: Susan Hoover, Scholarship Program Officer
Greater Kanawha Valley Foundation
900 Lee Street East, 16th Floor
Charleston, WV 25301
Phone: 304-346-3620
E-mail: tgkvf@tgkvf.org

WILLIAM GIACOMO FIREFIGHTER SCHOLARSHIP

Scholarship for an active firefighter, or a spouse, child, or grandchild of an active firefighter on a department that is a member of and in good standing with Fayette County Firefighters Association and pursing a postsecondary degree. Student must have completed one year of college (minimum 24 credit hours) and have a minimum of a 2.75 GPA. May attend school anywhere in WV, unless pursing a Fire Safety degree (in which case, the student must be a WV resident). Applicants must submit a notarized statement from the Fayette County Fire Service Coordinator with the original application.

Award: Scholarship for use in sophomore, junior, or senior years; not renewable.

Eligibility Requirements: Applicant must be enrolled or expecting to enroll full-time at a two-year or four-year institution or university and resident of West Virginia. Available to U.S. citizens.

Application Requirements: Application form, notarized statement of firefighter status, transcript. *Deadline:* January 15.

Contact: Susan Hover, Scholarship Program Officer
Greater Kanawha Valley Foundation
900 Lee Street East, 16th Floor
Charleston, WV 25301
Phone: 304-346-3620
E-mail: tgkvf@tgkvf.org

W. P. BLACK SCHOLARSHIP FUND

Renewable award for West Virginia residents who demonstrate academic excellence and financial need and who are enrolled in an undergraduate program in any accredited college or university.

Award: Scholarship for use in freshman, sophomore, junior, or senior years; renewable. *Amount:* $1000.

Eligibility Requirements: Applicant must be enrolled or expecting to enroll full-time at a four-year institution or university and resident of West Virginia. Available to U.S. citizens.

Application Requirements: Application form, essay, financial need analysis, recommendations or references, self-addressed stamped envelope with application, test scores, transcript. *Deadline:* January 15.

Contact: Susan Hoover, Scholarship Coordinator
Greater Kanawha Valley Foundation
900 Lee Street East, 16th Floor
Charleston, WV 25301
Phone: 304-346-3620
E-mail: tgkvf@tgkvf.org

GREATER WASHINGTON URBAN LEAGUE

http://www.gwul.org/

SAFEWAY/GREATER WASHINGTON URBAN LEAGUE SCHOLARSHIP

• *See page 555*

GREAT LAKES HEMOPHILIA FOUNDATION

http://www.glhf.org/

GLHF INDIVIDUAL CLASS SCHOLARSHIP

• *See page 571*

GREAT LAKES HEMOPHILIA FOUNDATION EDUCATION SCHOLARSHIP

• *See page 571*

GREENHOUSE SCHOLARS

http://www.greenhousescholars.org/

GREENHOUSE SCHOLARS

• *See page 555*

HARTFORD WHALERS BOOSTER CLUB

http://www.whalerwatch.com/

HARTFORD WHALERS BOOSTER CLUB SCHOLARSHIP

Scholarship for graduating high-school seniors who have played high school hockey and intend to play collegiate hockey. Must be a Connecticut resident.

Award: Scholarship for use in freshman year; not renewable. *Number:* 1. *Amount:* up to $1000.

Eligibility Requirements: Applicant must be high school student; planning to enroll or expecting to enroll full- or part-time at a four-year institution or university; resident of Connecticut and must have an interest in athletics/sports. Available to U.S. citizens.

Application Requirements: Application form, brief description of career goals, recommendations or references, resume, transcript. *Deadline:* March 20.

Contact: Alan Victor, President
Phone: 860-225-0265
Fax: 860-257-8331
E-mail: alan_m_victor@sbcglobal.net

HAWAII EDUCATION ASSOCIATION

http://www.heaed.com/

HAWAII EDUCATION ASSOCIATION HIGH SCHOOL STUDENT SCHOLARSHIP

• *See page 521*

HAWAII SCHOOLS FEDERAL CREDIT UNION

http://www.hawaiischoolsfcu.org/home/

EDWIN KUNIYUKI MEMORIAL SCHOLARSHIP

Annual scholarship for an incoming college freshman in recognition of academic excellence. Applicant must be Hawaii Schools Federal Credit Union member for one year prior to scholarship application.

Award: Scholarship for use in freshman year; not renewable. *Number:* 1. *Amount:* $1000.

Eligibility Requirements: Applicant must be high school student; planning to enroll or expecting to enroll full-time at a two-year or four-year or technical institution or university and resident of Hawaii. Applicant must have 3.0 GPA or higher. Available to U.S. citizens.

Application Requirements: Application form, essay, recommendations or references, transcript. *Deadline:* February 28.

Contact: Kristy Garan, Administrative Assistant
Phone: 808-521-0302
Fax: 808-791-6229
E-mail: kgaran@hawaiischoolsfcu.org

HAWAII STATE POSTSECONDARY EDUCATION COMMISSION

HAWAII STATE STUDENT INCENTIVE GRANT

Grants are given to residents of Hawaii who are enrolled in a participating Hawaiian state school. Funds are for undergraduate tuition only. Applicants must submit a financial need analysis.

Award: Grant for use in freshman, sophomore, junior, or senior years; renewable. *Number:* 470. *Amount:* $200–$2000.

Eligibility Requirements: Applicant must be enrolled or expecting to enroll full- or part-time at a two-year or four-year or technical institution or university; resident of Hawaii and studying in Hawaii. Available to U.S. citizens.

Application Requirements: Application form, financial need analysis. *Deadline:* continuous.

Contact: Janine Oyama, Financial Aid Specialist
Hawaii State Postsecondary Education Commission
University of Hawaii
Honolulu, HI 96822
Phone: 808-956-6066

HEARING BRIDGES (FORMERLY LEAGUE FOR THE DEAF AND HARD OF HEARING AND EAR FOUNDATION)

http://www.hearingbridges.org/

LINDA COWDEN MEMORIAL SCHOLARSHIP
* See page 571

HELLENIC UNIVERSITY CLUB OF PHILADELPHIA

http://www.hucphila.org/

CHRISTOPHER DEMETRIS SCHOLARSHIP
* See page 624

DR. NICHOLAS PADIS MEMORIAL GRADUATE SCHOLARSHIP
* See page 624

DORIZAS MEMORIAL SCHOLARSHIP
* See page 624

FOUNDERS SCHOLARSHIP
* See page 624

JAMES COSMOS MEMORIAL SCHOLARSHIP
* See page 625

PAIDEIA SCHOLARSHIP
* See page 521

HENRY SACHS FOUNDATION

http://www.sachsfoundation.org/

SACHS FOUNDATION SCHOLARSHIPS
* See page 625

HERBERT HOOVER PRESIDENTIAL LIBRARY ASSOCIATION

http://www.hooverassociation.org/

HERBERT HOOVER UNCOMMON STUDENT AWARD

Award for juniors attending an Iowa high school or home school program only. Grades and test scores are not evaluated. Applicants are chosen on the basis of submitted project proposals. Those chosen to complete their project and make a presentation receive $1000. Three are chosen for $5000 award.

Award: Scholarship for use in junior year; not renewable. *Number:* 15. *Amount:* $1000–$5000.

Eligibility Requirements: Applicant must be high school student; planning to enroll or expecting to enroll full-time at a two-year or four-year or technical institution or university and resident of Iowa. Available to U.S. citizens.

Application Requirements: Application form, application form may be submitted online (http://www.hooverassociation.org/cms/?q=grantsawards/uncommon_student/application), project proposal, recommendations or references. *Deadline:* March 31.

Contact: Ms. Delene McConnaha, Academic Programs Manager
Herbert Hoover Presidential Library Association
PO Box 696
302 Parkside Drive
West Branch, IA 52358-0696
Phone: 319-643-5327
Fax: 319-643-2391
E-mail: scholarship@hooverassociation.org

HERB KOHL EDUCATIONAL FOUNDATION INC.

http://www.kohleducation.org/

HERB KOHL EXCELLENCE SCHOLARSHIP PROGRAM
* See page 556

HISPANIC METROPOLITAN CHAMBER SCHOLARSHIPS

http://www.hmccoregon.com/

HISPANIC METROPOLITAN CHAMBER SCHOLARSHIPS
* See page 625

HOUSTON COMMUNITY SERVICES

AZTECA SCHOLARSHIP
* See page 626

HUMANE SOCIETY OF THE UNITED STATES

http://www.hsus.org/

SHAW-WORTH MEMORIAL SCHOLARSHIP

Scholarship for a New England high school senior, who has made a meaningful contribution to animal protection over a significant amount of time. Passive liking of animals or the desire to enter an animal care field does not justify the award.

Award: Scholarship for use in freshman year; not renewable. *Number:* 1. *Amount:* $2000.

Eligibility Requirements: Applicant must be high school student; planning to enroll or expecting to enroll full-time at a four-year institution or university and resident of Connecticut, Maine, Massachusetts, New Hampshire, Rhode Island, Vermont. Available to U.S. citizens.

Application Requirements: Essay, recommendations or references. *Deadline:* March 17.

IDAHO POWER COMPANY

http://www.idahopower.com/

IDAHO POWER SCHOLARSHIP FOR ACADEMIC EXCELLENCE

Scholarship of $1000 for graduating high school students of Idaho. Applicants must have a minimum 3.75 unweighted GPA. Must be enrolled at an accredited Idaho or Oregon college, university or vocational-technical school. Recipients may renew their scholarship annually, up to three times.

Award: Scholarship for use in freshman year; renewable. *Number:* 5. *Amount:* $1000.

Eligibility Requirements: Applicant must be high school student; planning to enroll or expecting to enroll full-time at a two-year or four-year or technical institution or university; resident of Idaho and studying in Idaho, Oregon. Available to U.S. citizens.

Application Requirements: Application form, essay, recommendations or references, resume, test scores, transcript. *Deadline:* June 15.

IDAHO STATE BOARD OF EDUCATION

http://www.boardofed.idaho.gov/

FREEDOM SCHOLARSHIP
• *See page 600*

IDAHO GOVERNOR'S CUP SCHOLARSHIP
• *See page 556*

IDAHO OPPORTUNITY SCHOLARSHIP

Scholarship for Idaho residents who are full-time students at colleges and universities in Idaho. Award is meant as a last dollar scholarship, so a student must apply for federal financial aid and have a self or family contribution element before they would be eligible. Must be a graduate of an Idaho high school and maintain satisfactory academic progress for financial aid purposes at their college/university.

Award: Scholarship for use in freshman, sophomore, junior, or senior years; not renewable.

Eligibility Requirements: Applicant must be enrolled or expecting to enroll full-time at a four-year institution or university; resident of Idaho and studying in Idaho. Available to U.S. citizens.

Application Requirements: Application form, financial need analysis. *Deadline:* February 15.

PUBLIC SAFETY OFFICER DEPENDENT SCHOLARSHIP
• *See page 556*

ROBERT R. LEE PROMISE CATEGORY A SCHOLARSHIP

One-time $3000 awards for Idaho residents who are graduating seniors at Idaho high schools enrolling as full-time students in an academic or professional-technical program. Academic applicants must have a cumulative GPA of 3.5 or above and an ACT score of 28 or above; professional-technical applicants must have a cumulative GPA of 2.8 or

above and take the COMPASS test (reading, writing and algebra scores required).

Award: Scholarship for use in freshman year; not renewable. *Number:* up to 25. *Amount:* $3000.

Eligibility Requirements: Applicant must be high school student; planning to enroll or expecting to enroll full-time at a two-year or four-year institution or university and resident of Idaho. Available to U.S. citizens.

Application Requirements: Application form. *Deadline:* February 15.

Contact: Dana Kelly, Program Manager, Student Affairs
    Phone: 208-332-1574
    E-mail: dana.kelly@osbe.idaho.gov

ILLINOIS AMVETS

http://www.ilamvets.org/

ILLINOIS AMVETS JUNIOR ROTC SCHOLARSHIPS

One year non-renewal $1000 per year for students who have taken the ACT or SAT tests. Preference will be given to children or grandchildren of veterans.

Award: Scholarship for use in freshman, sophomore, junior, or senior years; not renewable. *Amount:* $1000.

Eligibility Requirements: Applicant must be high school student; age 17-19; planning to enroll or expecting to enroll full-time at a four-year institution or university and resident of Illinois. Available to U.S. citizens.

Application Requirements: Application form, test scores. *Deadline:* March 1.

Contact: Britton Czmyr, Executive Assistant
    Phone: 217-528-4713 Ext. 207
    E-mail: britton@ilamvets.org

ILLINOIS AMVETS LADIES AUXILIARY MEMORIAL SCHOLARSHIP
• *See page 600*

ILLINOIS AMVETS LADIES AUXILIARY WORCHID SCHOLARSHIPS
• *See page 601*

ILLINOIS AMVETS SERVICE FOUNDATION
• *See page 601*

ILLINOIS AMVETS TRADE SCHOOL SCHOLARSHIP
• *See page 601*

ILLINOIS COUNCIL OF THE BLIND

http://www.icbonline.org/

FLOYD R. CARGILL SCHOLARSHIP
• *See page 572*

ILLINOIS COUNTIES ASSOCIATION

http://www.illinoiscountiesassociation.org/

ILLINOIS COUNTIES ASSOCIATION SCHOLARSHIP

Preferential consideration will be given to individuals demonstrating a dedicated pursuit toward a career in governmental, public service or public administration, as evidenced by involvement in course of study, work and volunteer service or internships in public, governmental, community and/or legislative environments.

Award: Scholarship for use in freshman year; not renewable. *Number:* up to 15. *Amount:* $3000.

Eligibility Requirements: Applicant must be high school student; planning to enroll or expecting to enroll full-time at a four-year institution or university and resident of Illinois. Applicant must have 3.0 GPA or higher. Available to U.S. citizens.

Application Requirements: Application form, application form may be submitted online, essay, financial need analysis, transcript. *Deadline:* March 15.

Contact: Nicole Palmisano, Scholarship Coordinator
Illinois Counties Association
100 East Washington
Springfield, IL 62701
Phone: 217-528-3434
E-mail: nicolepalmisano@frontline-online.net

ILLINOIS DEPARTMENT OF VETERANS' AFFAIRS

http://www.state.il.us/agency/dva

MIA/POW SCHOLARSHIPS
• *See page 601*

VETERANS' CHILDREN EDUCATIONAL OPPORTUNITIES
• *See page 601*

ONE MILLION DEGREES

http://www.onemilliondegrees.org

ONE MILLION DEGREES SIGNATURE FUND SCHOLARSHIP

The One Million Degrees Signature Scholarship Program offers groundbreaking, whole-student programming to low-income, highly motivated community college students.

Award: Scholarship for use in freshman, sophomore, junior, or senior years; renewable. *Number:* 1–80. *Amount:* $500–$3000.

Eligibility Requirements: Applicant must be enrolled or expecting to enroll full-time at a two-year institution; resident of Illinois and studying in Illinois. Available to U.S. citizens.

Application Requirements: Application form, community service, completion of FAFSA, essay, financial need analysis, interview, recommendations or references, test scores, transcript. *Deadline:* June 1.

Contact: Ms. Nina Sanchez, Director, Scholarship and Academics
Phone: 312-920-9605
E-mail: apply@onemilliondegrees.org

ILLINOIS STUDENT ASSISTANCE COMMISSION (ISAC)

http://www.collegezone.org/

GRANT PROGRAM FOR DEPENDENTS OF POLICE, FIRE, OR CORRECTIONAL OFFICERS

Awards available to Illinois residents who are dependents of police, fire, and correctional officers killed or disabled in line of duty. Provides for tuition and fees at approved Illinois institutions. Number of grants and individual dollar amount awarded vary.

Award: Grant for use in freshman, sophomore, junior, senior, graduate, or postgraduate years; renewable.

Eligibility Requirements: Applicant must be enrolled or expecting to enroll full- or part-time at a two-year or four-year or technical institution or university; resident of Illinois and studying in Illinois. Available to U.S. citizens.

Application Requirements: Application form, proof of status. *Deadline:* varies.

HIGHER EDUCATION LICENSE PLATE PROGRAM-HELP

Grants for students who attend Illinois colleges for which the special collegiate license plates are available. The Illinois Secretary of State issues the license plates, and part of the proceeds are used for grants for undergraduate students attending these colleges, to pay tuition and mandatory fees.

Award: Grant for use in freshman, sophomore, junior, or senior years; not renewable.

Eligibility Requirements: Applicant must be enrolled or expecting to enroll full- or part-time at a two-year or four-year institution or university; resident of Illinois and studying in Illinois. Available to U.S. citizens.

Application Requirements: Application form, financial need analysis. *Deadline:* varies.

ILLINOIS MONETARY AWARD PROGRAM

Awards to Illinois residents enrolled in a minimum of 3 hours per term in a degree program at an approved Illinois institution. See website for complete list of participating schools. Must demonstrate financial need, based on the information provided on the Free Application for Federal Student Aid. Number of grants and the individual dollar amount awarded vary. Deadline: As soon as possible after January 1 of the year in which the student will enter college.

Award: Grant for use in freshman, sophomore, junior, or senior years; renewable. *Amount:* $2599.

Eligibility Requirements: Applicant must be enrolled or expecting to enroll full- or part-time at a two-year or four-year or technical institution or university; resident of Illinois and studying in Illinois. Available to U.S. citizens.

Application Requirements: FAFSA online, financial need analysis. *Deadline:* varies.

ILLINOIS NATIONAL GUARD GRANT PROGRAM
• *See page 583*

ILLINOIS STUDENT-TO-STUDENT PROGRAM OF MATCHING GRANTS

Matching grant is available to undergraduates at participating state-supported colleges. Number of grants and the individual dollar amount awarded vary. Contact financial aid office at institution.

Award: Grant for use in freshman, sophomore, junior, or senior years; not renewable. *Amount:* $300–$1000.

Eligibility Requirements: Applicant must be enrolled or expecting to enroll full- or part-time at a two-year or four-year institution or university; resident of Illinois and studying in Illinois. Available to U.S. citizens.

Application Requirements: Application form, financial need analysis. *Deadline:* varies.

ILLINOIS VETERAN GRANT PROGRAM-IVG
• *See page 601*

INDIANA DEPARTMENT OF VETERANS AFFAIRS

http://www.in.gov/dva

CHILD OF DISABLED VETERAN GRANT OR PURPLE HEART RECIPIENT GRANT
• *See page 602*

DEPARTMENT OF VETERANS AFFAIRS FREE TUITION FOR CHILDREN OF POW/MIA'S IN VIETNAM
• *See page 602*

INDIAN AMERICAN CULTURAL ASSOCIATION

http://www.iasf.org/

INDIAN AMERICAN SCHOLARSHIP FUND
• *See page 626*

INTER-COUNTY ENERGY

http://www.intercountyenergy.net/

INTER-COUNTY ENERGY SCHOLARSHIP

One $1000 scholarship given to a high school senior in each of Inter-County Energy's six directorial districts: Boyle, Lincoln, Mercer, Garrard, Casey and Marion. Applicant's parent or legal guardian must be a member of Inter-County Energy with the primary residence being on the cooperative lines.

Award: Scholarship for use in freshman year; not renewable. *Number:* 6. *Amount:* up to $1000.

Eligibility Requirements: Applicant must be high school student; planning to enroll or expecting to enroll full-time at a four-year institution or university and resident of Kentucky. Available to U.S. citizens.

Application Requirements: Application form, autobiography, community service, financial need analysis, recommendations or references, transcript. *Deadline:* March 22.

Contact: Farrah Coleman, Communications Specialist
Phone: 859-236-4561 Ext. 7821
Fax: 859-236-5012
E-mail: farrah@intercountyenergy.net

IOWA COLLEGE STUDENT AID COMMISSION

http://www.iowacollegeaid.gov/

ALL IOWA OPPORTUNITY SCHOLARSHIP

Students attending eligible Iowa colleges and universities may receive awards of up to $6420. Minimum 2.5 GPA. Priority will be given to students who participated in the Federal TRIO Programs or graduated from alternative high schools or alternative high school programs. Applicant must enroll within two academic years of graduating from high school. Maximum individual awards cannot exceed more than the resident tuition and fee rate at Iowa Regent Universities.

Award: Scholarship for use in freshman or sophomore years; not renewable. *Number:* 200–800.

Eligibility Requirements: Applicant must be enrolled or expecting to enroll full- or part-time at a two-year or four-year or technical institution or university; resident of Iowa and studying in Iowa. Applicant must have 2.5 GPA or higher. Available to U.S. citizens.

Application Requirements: Application form, application form may be submitted online (http://www.iowacollegeaid.gov), financial need analysis. *Deadline:* March 1.

Contact: Todd Brown, Director, Scholarships, Grants, and Loan Forgiveness
Iowa College Student Aid Commission
603 East 12th Street, 5th Floor
Des Moines, IA 50319
Phone: 877-272-4456
Fax: 515-725-3401
E-mail: grants@iowacollegeaid.gov

IOWA GRANTS

Statewide need-based program to assist high-need Iowa residents. Recipients must demonstrate a high level of financial need to receive awards ranging from $100 to $1000. Awards are prorated for students enrolled for less than full-time. Awards must be used at Iowa postsecondary institutions.

Award: Grant for use in freshman, sophomore, junior, or senior years; not renewable. *Number:* 1000–3000. *Amount:* $100–$1000.

Eligibility Requirements: Applicant must be enrolled or expecting to enroll full- or part-time at a two-year or four-year or technical institution or university; resident of Iowa and studying in Iowa. Available to U.S. citizens.

Application Requirements: Application form, application form may be submitted online (http://www.fafsa.gov), financial need analysis. *Deadline:* continuous.

Contact: Todd Brown, Director, Scholarships, Grants, and Loan Forgiveness
Iowa College Student Aid Commission
603 East 12th Street, 5th Floor
Des Moines, IA 50319
Phone: 877-272-4456
Fax: 515-725-3401
E-mail: grants@iowacollegeaid.gov

IOWA NATIONAL GUARD EDUCATION ASSISTANCE PROGRAM
• *See page 584*

IOWA TUITION GRANT PROGRAM

Program assists students who attend independent postsecondary institutions in Iowa. Iowa residents currently enrolled, or planning to enroll, for at least 3 semester hours at one of the eligible Iowa postsecondary institutions may apply. Awards currently range from $100 to $4000. Grants may not exceed the difference between independent college and university tuition fees and the average tuition fees at the three public Regent universities.

Award: Grant for use in freshman, sophomore, junior, or senior years; not renewable. *Number:* 16,500–19,000. *Amount:* $100–$4000.

Eligibility Requirements: Applicant must be enrolled or expecting to enroll full- or part-time at a two-year or four-year institution or university; resident of Iowa and studying in Iowa. Available to U.S. citizens.

Application Requirements: Application form, application form may be submitted online (http://www.fafsa.gov), financial need analysis. *Deadline:* July 1.

Contact: Todd Brown, Director, Scholarships, Grants, and Loan Forgiveness
Iowa College Student Aid Commission
603 East 12th Street, 5th Floor
Des Moines, IA 50319
Phone: 877-272-4456
Fax: 515-725-3401
E-mail: todd.brown@iowa.gov

IOWA VOCATIONAL-TECHNICAL TUITION GRANT PROGRAM

Program provides need-based financial assistance to Iowa residents enrolled in career education (vocational-technical), and career option programs at Iowa area community colleges. Grants range from $150 to $1200, depending on the length of the program, financial need, and available funds.

Award: Grant for use in freshman or sophomore years; not renewable. *Number:* 2500–3500. *Amount:* $150–$1200.

Eligibility Requirements: Applicant must be enrolled or expecting to enroll full- or part-time at a two-year or technical institution; resident of Iowa and studying in Iowa. Available to U.S. citizens.

Application Requirements: Application form, application form may be submitted online (http://www.fafsa.gov), financial need analysis. *Deadline:* July 1.

Contact: Todd Brown, Director, Program Administration
Iowa College Student Aid Commission
603 East 12th Street, 5th Floor
Des Moines, IA 50319
Phone: 515-725-3405
Fax: 515-725-3401
E-mail: todd.brown@iowa.gov

ITALIAN-AMERICAN CHAMBER OF COMMERCE OF CHICAGO

http://www.iacc-chicago.com/

ITALIAN-AMERICAN CHAMBER OF COMMERCE OF CHICAGO SCHOLARSHIP
• *See page 626*

ITALIAN CATHOLIC FEDERATION INC.

http://www.icf.org/

ITALIAN CATHOLIC FEDERATION FIRST YEAR SCHOLARSHIP
• *See page 523*

JACKSON ENERGY COOPERATIVE

http://www.jacksonenergy.com/

JACKSON ENERGY SCHOLARSHIP ESSAY CONTEST

Scholarships are awarded to winners in an essay contest. Applicants, their parents, or legal guardians must be members of Jackson Energy Cooperative; may not be a spouse or an employee or director of Jackson Energy. Scholarships are paid directly to winner's college, university, or institution of higher education.

Award: Scholarship for use in freshman, sophomore, junior, or senior years; not renewable. *Number:* 8. *Amount:* $1200.

Eligibility Requirements: Applicant must be enrolled or expecting to enroll full-time at a two-year or four-year or technical institution or university and resident of Kentucky. Available to U.S. citizens.

Application Requirements: Application form, entry in a contest, essay. *Deadline:* March 1.

Contact: Karen Combs, Director of Public Relations
Jackson Energy Cooperative
115 Jackson Energy Lane
McKee, KY 40447
Phone: 606-364-9223
Fax: 606-364-1011
E-mail: karencombs@jacksonenergy.com

JAMES F. BYRNES FOUNDATION

http://www.byrnesscholars.org/

JAMES F. BYRNES SCHOLARSHIP

Renewable award for residents of South Carolina ages 17-22 with one or both parents deceased. Must show financial need; a satisfactory scholastic record; and qualities of character, ability, and enterprise. Award is for undergraduate study. Results of SAT must be provided. Information available on website http://www.byrnesscholars.org.

Award: Scholarship for use in freshman year; renewable. *Number:* 6–10. *Amount:* up to $13,000.

Eligibility Requirements: Applicant must be high school student; age 17-19; planning to enroll or expecting to enroll full-time at a four-year institution and resident of South Carolina. Available to U.S. citizens.

Application Requirements: Application form, essay, financial need analysis, interview, personal photograph, recommendations or references, test scores, transcript. *Deadline:* February 15.

Contact: Kenya White, Executive Secretary
James F. Byrnes Foundation
PO Box 6781
Columbia, SC 29260-6781
Phone: 803-254-9325
Fax: 803-254-9354
E-mail: info@byrnesscholars.org

J. CRAIG AND PAGE T. SMITH SCHOLARSHIP FOUNDATION

http://www.smithscholarships.com/

FIRST IN FAMILY SCHOLARSHIP

Scholarships are available for graduating Alabama high school seniors. Must be planning to enroll in an Alabama institution in fall and pursue a four-year degree. Students who apply must want to give back to their community by volunteer and civic work. Special consideration will be given to applicants who would be the first in either their mother's or father's family (or both) to attend college.

Award: Scholarship for use in freshman year; renewable. *Number:* 10. *Amount:* $12,500–$15,000.

Eligibility Requirements: Applicant must be high school student; planning to enroll or expecting to enroll full-time at a four-year institution or university; resident of Alabama and studying in Alabama. Applicant must have 2.5 GPA or higher. Available to U.S. citizens.

Application Requirements: Application form, community service, essay, financial need analysis, recommendations or references, test scores, transcript. *Deadline:* January 15.

Contact: Ahrian Tyler, Administrator/Chairman of the Board
Phone: 205-250-6669
Fax: 205-328-7234
E-mail: ahrian@jcraigsmithfoundation.org

JEWISH VOCATIONAL SERVICE LOS ANGELES

http://www.jvsla.org/

JEWISH VOCATIONAL SERVICE SCHOLARSHIP FUND
• *See page 627*

KANSAS BOARD OF REGENTS

http://www.kansasregents.org/

KANSAS ETHNIC MINORITY SCHOLARSHIP
• *See page 627*

KE ALI'I PAUAHI FOUNDATION

http://www.pauahi.org/

DANIEL KAHIKINA AND MILLIE AKAKA SCHOLARSHIP
• *See page 559*

JALENE KANANI BELL 'OHANA SCHOLARSHIP

Scholarship open to part-time or full-time undergraduate or graduate students who is a Hawaii residents with a GPA of 2.5 or above. Demonstrate characteristics of a well-rounded, community minded student of good moral character with a "can-do" attitude. Submit two letters of recommendation one from a teacher or counselor and one from a community organization. Submit essay that explains where you draw inspiration and strength from.

Award: Scholarship for use in freshman, sophomore, junior, senior, or graduate years; not renewable. *Number:* 1. *Amount:* $700.

Eligibility Requirements: Applicant must be enrolled or expecting to enroll full- or part-time at a two-year or four-year institution or university and resident of Hawaii. Applicant must have 2.5 GPA or higher. Available to U.S. citizens.

Application Requirements: Application form, application form may be submitted online (http://www.pauahi.org/scholarships), essay, recommendations or references, Student Aid Report (SAR), college acceptance letter, transcript. *Deadline:* April 1.

Contact: Mavis Shiraishi-Nagao, Scholarship Administrator
Phone: 808-534-3966
E-mail: scholarships@pauahi.org

KAMEHAMEHA SCHOOLS ALUMNI ASSOCIATION-MAUI REGION SCHOLARSHIP
• *See page 559*

KAMEHAMEHA SCHOOLS CLASS OF 1956 GRANT

Grant to assist at least one male and one female student who demonstrate financial need and have a minimum 2.5 GPA. Applicants must show an interest in Hawaiian language, culture and history, and demonstrate a commitment to contribute to the greater community. Submit two letters of recommendation from a teacher, counselor, employer or community organization.

Award: Grant for use in freshman, sophomore, junior, senior, or graduate years; not renewable. *Number:* 2. *Amount:* $500.

Eligibility Requirements: Applicant must be enrolled or expecting to enroll full-time at a four-year institution or university; resident of Hawaii and must have an interest in Hawaiian language/culture. Applicant must have 2.5 GPA or higher. Available to U.S. citizens.

Application Requirements: Application form, application form may be submitted online (http://www.pauahi.org/scholarships), financial need analysis, recommendations or references, Student Aid Report (SAR), college acceptance letter, transcript. *Deadline:* April 1.

Contact: Mavis Shiraishi-Nagao, Scholarship Administrator
Phone: 808-534-3966
E-mail: scholarships@pauahi.org

KAMEHAMEHA SCHOOLS CLASS OF 1972 SCHOLARSHIP

Scholarship to assist Kamehameha Schools Class of 1972 graduates, and their children and grandchildren with a minimum GPA of 2.8, to earn an undergraduate or graduate degree. May also be awarded to assist individuals whose lives have been impacted by challenging circumstances, such as death of a significant family member, domestic violence, sexual abuse, poverty, or major illness.

Award: Scholarship for use in freshman, sophomore, junior, senior, or graduate years; not renewable. *Amount:* $1100.

Eligibility Requirements: Applicant must be enrolled or expecting to enroll full-time at a four-year institution or university and resident of Hawaii. Available to U.S. citizens.

Application Requirements: Application form, financial need analysis, recommendations or references, Student Aid Report (SAR), college acceptance letter, transcript. *Deadline:* May 2.

Contact: Mavis Shiraishi-Nagao, Scholarship Administrator
Ke Ali'i Pauahi Foundation
567 South King Street, Suite 160
Honolulu, HI 96813
Phone: 808-534-3966
E-mail: scholarships@pauahi.org

KAMEHAMEHA SCHOOLS CLASS OF 1973 "PROUD TO BE 73" SCHOLARSHIP

Provides scholarships to students who graduated from a Hawaiian Focused Charter School in the state of Hawaii. Part-time students is acceptable.

Award: Scholarship for use in freshman, sophomore, junior, senior, or graduate years; not renewable. *Number:* 2. *Amount:* $700.

Eligibility Requirements: Applicant must be enrolled or expecting to enroll full- or part-time at a two-year or four-year or technical institution or university and resident of Hawaii. Available to U.S. citizens.

Application Requirements: Application form, application form may be submitted online (http://www.pauahi.org/scholarships), Student Aid Report (SAR), college acceptance letter, transcript. *Deadline:* April 1.

Contact: Mavis Shiraishi-Nagao, Scholarship Administrator
Phone: 808-534-3966
E-mail: scholarships@pauahi.org

KAMEHAMEHA SCHOOLS CLASS OF 1974 SCHOLARSHIP

Scholarship will provide support to students enrolled at a postsecondary institution, including non-traditional programs such as Hawaiian culture or self-improvement seminars. Applicants must have a minimum GPA of 2.8 and demonstrate financial need. Preference will be given to family members of Kamehameha Schools Class of 1974.

Award: Scholarship for use in freshman, sophomore, junior, senior, or graduate years; not renewable. *Amount:* $1200.

Eligibility Requirements: Applicant must be enrolled or expecting to enroll full-time at a two-year or four-year institution or university; resident of Hawaii and must have an interest in Hawaiian language/culture. Available to U.S. citizens.

Application Requirements: Application form, financial need analysis, recommendations or references, Student Aid Report (SAR), college acceptance letter, transcript. *Deadline:* May 2.

Contact: Mavis Shiraishi-Nagao, Scholarship Administrator
Ke Ali'i Pauahi Foundation
567 South King Street, Suite 160
Honolulu, HI 96813
Phone: 808-534-3966
E-mail: scholarships@pauahi.org

KENERGY CORPORATION

http://www.kenergycorp.com/

KENERGY SCHOLARSHIP

Student must be a member owner of Kenergy, or must have his/her primary residence with a parent or legal guardian who receives electric service from Kenergy. Must be accompanied by his/her parent(s) or legal guardians to the Kenergy Annual Membership Meeting in Henderson, Kentucky where the student may register for scholarship drawings.

Award: Scholarship for use in freshman, sophomore, junior, senior, or graduate years; not renewable. *Number:* up to 20. *Amount:* $500.

Eligibility Requirements: Applicant must be enrolled or expecting to enroll full-time at a two-year or four-year or technical institution or university and resident of Kentucky. Available to U.S. and non-U.S. citizens.

Application Requirements: Application form, transcript. *Deadline:* varies.

Contact: Beverly Hooper, Scholarship Coordinator
Phone: 270-826-3991 Ext. 3811
Fax: 270-826-3999
E-mail: bhooper@kenergycorp.com

KENTUCKY ASSOCIATION OF ELECTRIC COOPERATIVES, INC.

http://www.kaec.com/

WIRE SCHOLARSHIPS

Scholarship available to Kentucky students who are juniors or seniors in a Kentucky college or university and have 60 credit hours by the fall semester. Immediate family of student must be served by one of the state's 24 rural electric distribution cooperatives. Awards based on academic achievement, extracurricular activities, career goals, recommendations.

Award: Scholarship for use in junior or senior years; not renewable. *Number:* 3–5. *Amount:* $1000.

Eligibility Requirements: Applicant must be enrolled or expecting to enroll full-time at a two-year or four-year or technical institution or university; resident of Kentucky and studying in Kentucky. Available to U.S. citizens.

Application Requirements: Application form, letter explaining how this scholarship would enhance your academic goals, transcript. *Deadline:* May 10.

Contact: Mary Beth Dennis, Meeting Coordinator
Kentucky Association of Electric Cooperatives, Inc.
PO Box 32170
Louisville, KY 40232
Phone: 502-815-6302
E-mail: mbdennis@kaec. org

KENTUCKY DEPARTMENT OF VETERANS AFFAIRS

http://www.veterans.ky.gov/

DEPARTMENT OF VETERANS AFFAIRS TUITION WAIVER-KY KRS 164-507

Scholarship available to college students who are residents of Kentucky under the age of 26.

Award: Scholarship for use in freshman, sophomore, junior, or senior years; not renewable. *Number:* 400.

Eligibility Requirements: Applicant must be enrolled or expecting to enroll full- or part-time at a two-year or four-year institution or university and resident of Kentucky. Available to U.S. citizens.

Application Requirements: Application form. *Deadline:* varies.

Contact: Barbara Sipek, Tuition Waiver Coordinator
Phone: 502-595-4447
E-mail: barbaraa.sipek@ky.gov

KENTUCKY HIGHER EDUCATION ASSISTANCE AUTHORITY (KHEAA)

http://www.kheaa.com/

COLLEGE ACCESS PROGRAM (CAP) GRANT

Award for U.S. citizens and Kentucky residents seeking their first undergraduate degree. Applicants enrolled in sectarian institutions are not eligible. Must submit Free Application for Federal Student Aid to demonstrate financial need. Funding is limited. Awards are made on a first-come, first-serve basis.

Award: Grant for use in freshman, sophomore, junior, or senior years; not renewable. *Number:* 35,000–45,000. *Amount:* up to $1900.

Eligibility Requirements: Applicant must be enrolled or expecting to enroll full- or part-time at a two-year or four-year or technical institution or university; resident of Kentucky and studying in Kentucky. Available to U.S. citizens.

Application Requirements: Application form may be submitted online (http://www.fafsa.ed.gov), FAFSA. *Deadline:* continuous.

Contact: Sheila Roe, Program Coordinator
Kentucky Higher Education Assistance Authority (KHEAA)
PO Box 798
Frankfort, KY 40602-0798
Phone: 800-928-8926 Ext. 67393
Fax: 502-696-7373
E-mail: sroe@kheaa.com

GO HIGHER GRANT

Need-based grant for adult students pursuing their first undergraduate degree. Completion of the FAFSA is required.

Award: Grant for use in freshman, sophomore, junior, or senior years; not renewable. *Number:* 100–300. *Amount:* up to $1000.

Eligibility Requirements: Applicant must be enrolled or expecting to enroll full- or part-time at a two-year or four-year or technical institution or university; resident of Kentucky and studying in Kentucky. Available to U.S. citizens.

Application Requirements: Application form, application form may be submitted online (http://www.fafsa.ed.gov), FAFSA. *Deadline:* continuous.

Contact: Sheila Roe, Grant Program Coordinator
Kentucky Higher Education Assistance Authority (KHEAA)
PO Box 798
Frankfort, KY 40206-0798
Phone: 800-928-8926 Ext. 67393
E-mail: sroe@kheaa.com

KENTUCKY EDUCATIONAL EXCELLENCE SCHOLARSHIP (KEES)

Annual award based on yearly high school GPA and highest ACT or SAT score received by high school graduation. Awards are renewable, if required cumulative GPA is maintained at a Kentucky postsecondary school. Must be a Kentucky resident, and a graduate of a Kentucky high school.

Award: Scholarship for use in freshman, sophomore, junior, or senior years; renewable. *Number:* 65,000–70,000. *Amount:* $125–$2500.

Eligibility Requirements: Applicant must be enrolled or expecting to enroll full- or part-time at a two-year or four-year or technical institution or university; resident of Kentucky and studying in Kentucky. Available to U.S. citizens.

Application Requirements: Data submitted by KY high schools, test scores. *Deadline:* continuous.

Contact: Megan Cummins, KEES Coordinator
Kentucky Higher Education Assistance Authority (KHEAA)
PO Box 798
Frankfort, KY 40602
Phone: 800-928-8926 Ext. 67397
Fax: 502-696-7373
E-mail: mcummins@kheaa.com

KENTUCKY TUITION GRANT (KTG)

Grants available to Kentucky residents who are full-time undergraduates at an independent college within the state. Based on financial need. Must submit FAFSA.

Award: Grant for use in freshman, sophomore, junior, or senior years; not renewable. *Number:* 11,500–12,500. *Amount:* $200–$3000.

Eligibility Requirements: Applicant must be enrolled or expecting to enroll full-time at a two-year or four-year institution or university; resident of Kentucky and studying in Kentucky. Available to U.S. citizens.

Application Requirements: Application form may be submitted online (http://www.fafsa.ed.gov), FAFSA. *Deadline:* continuous.

Contact: Sheila Roe, Grant Program Coordinator
Kentucky Higher Education Assistance Authority (KHEAA)
PO Box 798
Frankfort, KY 40602-0798
Phone: 800-928-8926 Ext. 67393
Fax: 502-696-7373
E-mail: sroe@kheaa.com

KENTUCKY TOUCHSTONE ENERGY COOPERATIVES

http://www.ekpc.coop

TOUCHSTONE ENERGY ALL "A" CLASSIC SCHOLARSHIP

Award of $1000 for senior student in good standing at a Kentucky high school which is a member of the All Classic. Applicant must be a U.S. citizen and must plan to attend a postsecondary institution in Kentucky in the upcoming year as a full-time student and be drug free.

Award: Scholarship for use in freshman year; not renewable. *Number:* 12. *Amount:* $1000.

Eligibility Requirements: Applicant must be high school student; planning to enroll or expecting to enroll full-time at a two-year or four-year or technical institution or university; resident of Kentucky and studying in Kentucky. Available to U.S. citizens.

Application Requirements: Application form, essay, personal photograph, recommendations or references, transcript. *Deadline:* December 3.

Contact: David Cowden, Chairperson, Scholarship Committee
Kentucky Touchstone Energy Cooperatives
1320 Lincoln Road
Lewisport, KY 42351
Phone: 859-744-4812
E-mail: allaclassic@alltel.net

KOSCIUSZKO FOUNDATION

http://www.thekf.org

MASSACHUSETTS FEDERATION OF POLISH WOMEN'S CLUBS SCHOLARSHIPS

• See page 629

POLISH AMERICAN CLUB OF NORTH JERSEY SCHOLARSHIPS

• See page 629

POLISH NATIONAL ALLIANCE OF BROOKLYN USA INC. SCHOLARSHIPS

• See page 629

LEE-JACKSON EDUCATIONAL FOUNDATION

http://www.lee-jackson.org/

LEE-JACKSON EDUCATIONAL FOUNDATION SCHOLARSHIP COMPETITION

Essay contest for junior and senior Virginia high school students. Must demonstrate appreciation for the exemplary character and soldierly virtues of Generals Robert E. Lee and Thomas J. "Stonewall" Jackson. Three one-time awards of $1000 in each of Virginia's eight regions. A bonus scholarship of $1000 will be awarded to the author of the best essay in each of the eight regions. An additional award of $8000 will go to the essay judged the best in the state.

Award: Scholarship for use in freshman, sophomore, junior, or senior years; not renewable. *Number:* 27. *Amount:* $1000–$10,000.

Eligibility Requirements: Applicant must be high school student; planning to enroll or expecting to enroll full-time at a four-year institution or university; resident of Virginia and must have an interest in writing. Available to U.S. citizens.

Application Requirements: Application form, entry in a contest, essay, transcript. *Deadline:* December 21.

Contact: Stephanie Leech, Administrator
Lee-Jackson Educational Foundation
PO Box 8121
Charlottesville, VA 22906
Phone: 434-977-1861
E-mail: salp_leech@yahoo.com

LIBERTY GRAPHICS INC.

http://www.lgtees.com/

ANNUAL LIBERTY GRAPHICS ART CONTEST

One-time scholarship to the successful student who submits the winning artwork depicting appreciation of the natural environment of Maine. Applicants must be residents of Maine and be a high school senior. Original works in traditional flat media are the required format. Photography, sculpture and computer-generated work will not be considered. Multiple submissions are allowed.

Award: Prize for use in freshman year; not renewable. *Number:* 1. *Amount:* $1000.

Eligibility Requirements: Applicant must be high school student; planning to enroll or expecting to enroll full- or part-time at a two-year or four-year or technical institution or university and resident of Maine. Available to U.S. citizens.

Application Requirements: Application form, artwork in keeping with the contest theme, entry in a contest, self-addressed stamped envelope with application. *Deadline:* March 21.

Contact: Mr. Jay Sproul, Scholarship Coordinator
Liberty Graphics Inc.
44 Main Street, PO Box 5
Liberty, ME 04949
Phone: 207-589-4596
Fax: 207-589-4415
E-mail: jay@lgtees.com

LOS ALAMOS NATIONAL LABORATORY FOUNDATION

http://www.lanlfoundation.org/

LOS ALAMOS EMPLOYEES' SCHOLARSHIP

Scholarship supports students in Northern New Mexico who are pursuing undergraduate degrees in fields that will serve the region. Financial need, diversity, and regional representation are integral components of the selections process. Applicant should be a permanent resident of Northern New Mexico with at least a 3.25 cumulative GPA and 19 ACT or 930 SAT score.

Award: Scholarship for use in freshman, sophomore, junior, or senior years; renewable. *Number:* 50. *Amount:* $1000–$30,000.

Eligibility Requirements: Applicant must be enrolled or expecting to enroll full- or part-time at a two-year or four-year institution or university and resident of New Mexico. Available to U.S. and non-U.S. citizens.

Application Requirements: Application form, essay, personal photograph, recommendations or references, test scores, transcript. *Deadline:* January 22.

Contact: Tony Fox, Program Officer
Phone: 505-753-8890 Ext. 16
Fax: 505-753-8915
E-mail: tfox@lanlfoundation.org

LOS PADRES FOUNDATION

http://www.lospadresfoundation.com/

COLLEGE TUITION ASSISTANCE PROGRAM
• *See page 630*

SECOND CHANCE SCHOLARSHIPS
• *See page 630*

LOUISIANA DEPARTMENT OF VETERAN AFFAIRS

http://www.vetaffairs.la.gov

LOUISIANA DEPARTMENT OF VETERANS AFFAIRS STATE EDUCATIONAL AID PROGRAM
• *See page 602*

LOUISIANA NATIONAL GUARD, JOINT TASK FORCE LA

http://geauxguard.com/

LOUISIANA NATIONAL GUARD STATE TUITION EXEMPTION PROGRAM
• *See page 584*

LOUISIANA OFFICE OF STUDENT FINANCIAL ASSISTANCE

http://www.osfa.la.gov/

TAYLOR OPPORTUNITY PROGRAM FOR STUDENTS HONORS LEVEL

Program awards 8 semesters or 12 terms of tuition to any Louisiana State postsecondary institution plus $400 stipend per semester. Program awards 8 semesters or 12 terms of an amount equal to the weighted average public tuition to students attending a LAICU (Louisiana Association of Independent Colleges and Universities) institution plus $400 stipend per semester. Program awards 8 semesters or 12 terms of an amount equal to the weighted average public tuition to two out-of-state Institutions for Hearing Impaired Students: Gallaudet University and Rochester Institute of Technology plus $400 stipend per semester. Program awards $1520 per year to Approved Proprietary and Cosmetology schools plus a stipend of $800 per year. When you submit the FAFSA, you have automatically applied for all four levels of TOPS, for Federal Pell Grants and Go Grants and for Federal Student Loans. Please do not send separate letters of application to the TOPS office.

Award: Scholarship for use in freshman, sophomore, junior, or senior years; renewable. *Number:* 8781. *Amount:* $780–$6131.

Eligibility Requirements: Applicant must be enrolled or expecting to enroll full-time at a two-year or four-year or technical institution or university; resident of Louisiana and studying in Louisiana. Applicant must have 3.0 GPA or higher. Available to U.S. citizens.

Application Requirements: Application form, application form may be submitted online (http://www.fafsa.ed.gov), FAFSA, test scores, transcript. *Deadline:* July 1.

TAYLOR OPPORTUNITY PROGRAM FOR STUDENTS OPPORTUNITY LEVEL

Program awards 8 semesters or 12 terms of tuition to any Louisiana State postsecondary institution. Program awards 8 semesters or 12 terms of an amount equal to the weighted average public tuition to students attending a LAICU (Louisiana Association of Independent Colleges and Universities) institution. Program awards 8 semesters or 12 terms of an amount equal to the weighted average public tuition to two out-of-state Institutions for Hearing Impaired Students: Gallaudet University and Rochester Institute of Technology. Program awards $1520 per year to Approved Proprietary and Cosmetology schools. When you submit the FAFSA, you have automatically applied for all four levels of TOPS, and for Federal Pell Grants and Go Grants. Please do not send separate letters of application to the TOPS office.

Award: Scholarship for use in freshman, sophomore, junior, or senior years; renewable. *Number:* 23,870. *Amount:* $380–$5331.

Eligibility Requirements: Applicant must be enrolled or expecting to enroll full-time at a two-year or four-year or technical institution or university; resident of Louisiana and studying in Louisiana. Applicant must have 2.5 GPA or higher. Available to U.S. citizens.

Application Requirements: Application form, application form may be submitted online (http://www.fafsa.ed.gov), FAFSA, test scores, transcript. *Deadline:* July 1.

TAYLOR OPPORTUNITY PROGRAM FOR STUDENTS PERFORMANCE LEVEL

Program awards 8 semesters or 12 terms of tuition to any Louisiana State postsecondary institution plus $200 stipend per semester. Program awards 8 semesters or 12 terms of an amount equal to the weighted average public tuition to students attending a LAICU (Louisiana Association of Independent Colleges and Universities) institution plus $200 stipend per semester. Program awards 8 semesters or 12 terms of an amount equal to the weighted average public tuition to two out-of-state Institutions for Hearing Impaired Students: Gallaudet University and Rochester Institute of Technology plus $200 stipend per semester. Program awards $1520 plus $400 per year to Approved Proprietary and Cosmetology schools. When you submit the FAFSA, you have automatically applied for all four levels of TOPS, for Federal Pell Grants and Go Grants and for Federal Student Loans. Please do not send separate letters of application to the TOPS office.

Award: Scholarship for use in freshman, sophomore, junior, or senior years; renewable. *Number:* 10,938. *Amount:* $580–$5731.

Eligibility Requirements: Applicant must be enrolled or expecting to enroll full-time at a two-year or four-year or technical institution or university; resident of Louisiana and studying in Louisiana. Applicant must have 3.0 GPA or higher. Available to U.S. citizens.

Application Requirements: Application form, application form may be submitted online (http://www.fafsa.ed.gov), FAFSA, test scores, transcript. *Deadline:* July 1.

TAYLOR OPPORTUNITY PROGRAM FOR STUDENTS TECH LEVEL

Program awards an amount equal to tuition for up to 4 semesters and two summers of technical training at a Louisiana postsecondary institution that offers a vocational or technical education certificate or diploma program, or a non-academic degree program; or up to $1520 to an approved Proprietary or Cosmetology school. Must have completed the TOPS Opportunity core curriculum or the TOPS Tech core curriculum, must have achieved a 2.50 grade point average over the core curriculum only, and must have achieved an ACT score of 17 or an SAT score of 810. Program awards an amount equal to the weighted average public tuition for technical programs to students attending a LAICU private institution for technical training. When you submit the FAFSA, you have automatically applied for all four levels of TOPS, for Federal Pell Grants and Go Grants and Federal Student Loans. Please do not send separate letters of application to the TOPS office.

Award: Scholarship for use in freshman or sophomore years; renewable. *Number:* 1242. *Amount:* $380–$3556.

Eligibility Requirements: Applicant must be enrolled or expecting to enroll full-time at a technical institution; resident of Louisiana and studying in Louisiana. Applicant must have 2.5 GPA or higher. Available to U.S. citizens.

Application Requirements: Application form, application form may be submitted online (http://www.fafsa.ed.gov), FAFSA, test scores, transcript. *Deadline:* July 1.

MAINE COMMUNITY COLLEGE SYSTEM

http://www.mccs.me.edu/

EARLY COLLEGE FOR ME

Scholarship for high school students who in their junior year have not made plans for college but are academically capable of success in college. Recipients are selected by their school principal or Guidance Director. Students must be entering a Maine Community College. Refer to website http://www.mccs.me.edu/scholarships.html.

Award: Scholarship for use in freshman or sophomore years; renewable. *Number:* 250–500. *Amount:* $2000.

Eligibility Requirements: Applicant must be high school student; planning to enroll or expecting to enroll full-time at a two-year institution; resident of Maine and studying in Maine. Available to U.S. citizens.

Application Requirements: Application form, financial need analysis, recommendations or references, transcript. *Deadline:* varies.

Contact: Charles Collins, State Director, Center for Career
Development
Maine Community College System
6 Fundy Road
Falmouth, ME 04105
Phone: 207-767-5210 Ext. 4897
Fax: 207-781-0986
E-mail: ccollins@mccs.me.edu

MAINE COMMUNITY FOUNDATION, INC.

http://www.mainecf.org/

MAINE COMMUNITY FOUNDATION SCHOLARSHIP PROGRAMS

Various scholarships available for Maine residents attending secondary, post-secondary, and graduate programs. Restrictions and application requirements vary based on specific scholarship. See website for details, http://www.mainecf.org. Deadline varies.

Award: Scholarship for use in freshman, sophomore, junior, or senior years; not renewable. *Number:* 150–700. *Amount:* $500–$5000.

Eligibility Requirements: Applicant must be enrolled or expecting to enroll full- or part-time at a two-year or four-year or technical institution or university and resident of Maine. Available to U.S. citizens.

Application Requirements: Application form,. *Deadline:* continuous.

Contact: Ms. Amy Pollien, Grants Administration
Maine Community Foundation, Inc.
245 Main Street
Ellsworth, ME 04605
Phone: 207-667-9735
Fax: 207-667-0447
E-mail: apollien@mainecf.org

MAINE DIVISION OF VETERANS SERVICES

http://www.maine.gov/dvem/bvs

VETERANS DEPENDENTS EDUCATIONAL BENEFITS-MAINE

• *See page 602*

MAINE EDUCATION SERVICES

http://www.mesfoundation.com/

MAINE LEGISLATIVE MEMORIAL SCHOLARSHIP

One-time awards for students going to a two- or four-year degree-granting Maine school. Scholarships are available to graduating high school seniors or full/part-time postsecondary students accepted or enrolled in a Maine college. Graduate students are also eligible.

Award: Scholarship for use in freshman, sophomore, junior, senior, graduate, or postgraduate years; not renewable. *Number:* up to 16. *Amount:* up to $1000.

Eligibility Requirements: Applicant must be enrolled or expecting to enroll full- or part-time at a two-year or four-year or technical institution or university; resident of Maine and studying in Maine. Available to U.S. citizens.

Application Requirements: Application form, community service, essay, financial need analysis, recommendations or references, transcript. *Deadline:* April 16.

Contact: Kim Benjamin, Vice President of Operations
Phone: 207-791-3600

MAINE STATE CHAMBER OF COMMERCE SCHOLARSHIP-ADULT LEARNER

One $1500 scholarship is given to an adult learner planning to pursue an education at a two-year, four-year degree granting college. Preference may be to a student attending a Maine college and seeking a degree in a business- or education-related field. Awards are based on an adult being 23 years or older and having legal dependents other than a spouse.

Award: Scholarship for use in freshman, sophomore, junior, or senior years; not renewable. *Number:* up to 1. *Amount:* up to $1500.

Eligibility Requirements: Applicant must be enrolled or expecting to enroll full- or part-time at a two-year or four-year or technical institution or university and resident of Maine. Available to U.S. citizens.

Application Requirements: Application form, community service, essay, financial need analysis, recommendations or references, transcript. *Deadline:* April 18.

Contact: Kim Benjamin, Vice President of Operations
Phone: 207-791-3600

MAINE STATE SOCIETY FOUNDATION OF WASHINGTON, DC INC.

http://www.mainestatesociety.org/

MAINE STATE SOCIETY FOUNDATION SCHOLARSHIP

Scholarship(s) awarded to full-time students enrolled in undergraduate courses at a four-year degree-granting, nonprofit institution in Maine. Must be Maine resident. All inquiries must be accompanied by a self-addressed stamped envelope. Applicant must be 25 or younger.

Award: Scholarship for use in sophomore, junior, or senior years; not renewable. *Number:* 5–10. *Amount:* $1000–$2500.

Eligibility Requirements: Applicant must be enrolled or expecting to enroll full-time at a four-year institution; resident of Maine and studying in Maine. Applicant must have 3.0 GPA or higher. Available to U.S. citizens.

Application Requirements: Application form, essay, self-addressed stamped envelope with application, transcript. *Deadline:* April 15.

Contact: Hugh Dwelley, Director
Maine State Society Foundation of Washington, DC Inc.
3508 Wilson Street
Fairfax, VA 22030
Phone: 703-352-0846
E-mail: hldwelley@aol.com

MANA DE SAN DIEGO

http://www.manasd.org/

MANA DE SAN DIEGO SYLVIA CHAVEZ MEMORIAL SCHOLARSHIP

• *See page 559*

MARYLAND STATE HIGHER EDUCATION COMMISSION

http://www.mhec.state.md.us/

DELEGATE SCHOLARSHIP PROGRAM-MARYLAND

Delegate scholarships help Maryland residents attending Maryland degree-granting institutions, certain career schools, or nursing diploma schools. May attend out-of-state institution if Maryland Higher Education Commission deems major to be unique and not offered at a Maryland institution. Free Application for Federal Student Aid may be required. Students interested in this program should apply by contacting their legislative district delegate.

Award: Scholarship for use in freshman, sophomore, junior, or senior years; not renewable. *Number:* up to 3500. *Amount:* $200–$8650.

Eligibility Requirements: Applicant must be enrolled or expecting to enroll full- or part-time at a two-year or four-year or technical institution or university; resident of Maryland and studying in Maryland. Available to U.S. citizens.

Application Requirements: Application form, FAFSA. *Deadline:* continuous.

Contact: Monica Wheatley, Office of Student Financial Assistance
Maryland State Higher Education Commission
839 Bestgate Road, Suite 400
Annapolis, MD 21401-3013
Phone: 800-974-1024
Fax: 410-260-3200
E-mail: osfamail@mhec.state.md.us

DISTINGUISHED SCHOLAR AWARD-MARYLAND

Renewable award for Maryland students enrolled full-time at Maryland institutions. National Merit Scholar Finalists automatically offered award. Others may qualify for the award in satisfying criteria of a minimum 3.7 GPA or in combination with high test scores, or for Talent in Arts competition in categories of music, drama, dance, or visual arts. Must maintain annual 3.0 GPA in college for award to be renewed.

Award: Scholarship for use in freshman, sophomore, junior, or senior years; renewable. *Number:* up to 1400. *Amount:* up to $3000.

Eligibility Requirements: Applicant must be high school student; planning to enroll or expecting to enroll full-time at a two-year or four-year institution or university; resident of Maryland and studying in Maryland. Available to U.S. citizens.

Application Requirements: Application form, test scores, transcript.

Contact: Tamika McKelvin, Program Administrator
Maryland State Higher Education Commission
839 Bestgate Road, Suite 400
Annapolis, MD 21401-3013
Phone: 410-260-4546
Fax: 410-260-3200
E-mail: tmckelvi@mhec.state.md.us

DISTINGUISHED SCHOLAR COMMUNITY COLLEGE TRANSFER PROGRAM

Scholarship available for Maryland residents who have completed 60 credit hours or an associate degree at a Maryland community college and are transferring to a Maryland four-year institution.

Award: Scholarship for use in freshman or sophomore years; renewable. *Number:* 127. *Amount:* $3000.

Eligibility Requirements: Applicant must be enrolled or expecting to enroll full-time at a two-year institution; resident of Maryland and studying in Maryland. Available to U.S. citizens.

Application Requirements: Application form, transcript. *Deadline:* March 1.

Contact: Maura Sappington, Program Manager
Maryland State Higher Education Commission
839 Bestgate Road, Suite 400
Annapolis, MD 21401-3013
Phone: 410-260-4569
Fax: 410-260-3203
E-mail: msapping@mhec.state.md.us

EDWARD T. CONROY MEMORIAL SCHOLARSHIP PROGRAM

• *See page 560*

HOWARD P. RAWLINGS EDUCATIONAL EXCELLENCE AWARDS EDUCATIONAL ASSISTANCE GRANT

Award for Maryland residents accepted or enrolled in a full-time undergraduate degree or certificate program at a Maryland institution or hospital nursing school. Must submit financial aid form by March 1. Must earn 2.0 GPA in college to maintain award.

Award: Grant for use in freshman, sophomore, junior, or senior years; renewable. *Number:* 15,000–30,000. *Amount:* $400–$2700.

Eligibility Requirements: Applicant must be enrolled or expecting to enroll full-time at a two-year or four-year institution or university; resident of Maryland and studying in Maryland. Available to U.S. citizens.

Application Requirements: Application form, financial need analysis. *Deadline:* March 1.

HOWARD P. RAWLINGS EDUCATIONAL EXCELLENCE AWARDS GUARANTEED ACCESS GRANT

Award for Maryland resident enrolling full-time in an undergraduate program at a Maryland institution. Must be under 21 at time of first award and begin college within one year of completing high school in Maryland with a minimum 2.5 GPA. Must have an annual family income less than 130 percent of the federal poverty level guideline.

Award: Grant for use in freshman, sophomore, junior, or senior years; renewable. *Number:* up to 1000. *Amount:* $400–$14,800.

Eligibility Requirements: Applicant must be enrolled or expecting to enroll full-time at a two-year or four-year institution or university; resident of Maryland and studying in Maryland. Applicant must have 3.5 GPA or higher. Available to U.S. citizens.

Application Requirements: Application form, financial need analysis, transcript. *Deadline:* March 1.

Contact: Theresa Lowe, Office of Student Financial Assistance
Maryland State Higher Education Commission
839 Bestgate Road, Suite 400
Annapolis, MD 21401-3013
Phone: 410-260-4555
Fax: 410-260-3200
E-mail: osfamail@mhec.state.md.us

J.F. TOLBERT MEMORIAL STUDENT GRANT PROGRAM

Awards of $500 granted to Maryland residents attending a private career school in Maryland. The scholarship deadline continues.

Award: Grant for use in freshman or sophomore years; not renewable. *Number:* 522. *Amount:* $500.

Eligibility Requirements: Applicant must be enrolled or expecting to enroll full-time at a technical institution; resident of Maryland and studying in Maryland. Available to U.S. citizens.

Application Requirements: Application form, financial need analysis. *Deadline:* continuous.

Contact: Glenda Hamlet, Office of Student Financial Assistance
Maryland State Higher Education Commission
839 Bestgate Road, Suite 400
Annapolis, MD 21401-3013
Phone: 800-974-1024
Fax: 410-260-3200
E-mail: osfamail@mhec.state.md.us

PART-TIME GRANT PROGRAM-MARYLAND

Funds provided to Maryland colleges and universities. Eligible students must be enrolled on a part-time basis (6 to 11 credits) in an undergraduate degree program. Must demonstrate financial need and also be Maryland resident. Contact financial aid office at institution for more information.

Award: Grant for use in freshman, sophomore, junior, or senior years; renewable. *Number:* 1800–9000. *Amount:* $200–$1500.

Eligibility Requirements: Applicant must be enrolled or expecting to enroll part-time at a two-year or four-year institution or university; resident of Maryland and studying in Maryland. Available to U.S. citizens.

Application Requirements: Application form, financial need analysis. *Deadline:* March 1.

Contact: Monica Wheatley, Program Manager
Maryland State Higher Education Commission
839 Bestgate Road, Suite 400
Annapolis, MD 21401
Phone: 410-260-4560
Fax: 410-260-3202
E-mail: mwheatle@mhec.state.md.us

SENATORIAL SCHOLARSHIPS-MARYLAND

Renewable award for Maryland residents attending a Maryland degree-granting institution, nursing diploma school, or certain private career schools. May be used out-of-state only if Maryland Higher Education Commission deems major to be unique and not offered at Maryland institution. The scholarship value is $400 to $7000.

Award: Scholarship for use in freshman, sophomore, junior, or senior years; renewable. *Number:* up to 7000. *Amount:* $400–$7000.

Eligibility Requirements: Applicant must be enrolled or expecting to enroll full- or part-time at a two-year or four-year or technical institution or university; resident of Maryland and studying in Maryland. Available to U.S. citizens.

Application Requirements: Application form, financial need analysis, test scores. *Deadline:* March 1.

Contact: Monica Wheatley, Office of Student Financial Assistance
Maryland State Higher Education Commission
839 Bestgate Road, Suite 400
Annapolis, MD 21401-3013
Phone: 800-974-1024
Fax: 410-260-3200
E-mail: osfamail@mhec.state.md.us

TUITION WAIVER FOR FOSTER CARE RECIPIENTS

Applicant must be a high school graduate or GED recipient and under the age of 21. Must either have resided in a foster care home in Maryland at the time of high school graduation or GED reception, or until 14th birthday, and been adopted after 14th birthday. Applicant, if status approved, will be exempt from paying tuition and mandatory fees at a public college in Maryland.

Award: Grant for use in freshman, sophomore, junior, senior, or graduate years; renewable.

Eligibility Requirements: Applicant must be enrolled or expecting to enroll full- or part-time at a two-year or four-year institution or university; resident of Maryland and studying in Maryland. Available to U.S. citizens.

Application Requirements: Application form, financial need analysis, must inquire at financial aid office of schools. *Deadline:* March 1.

Contact: Robert Parker, Director
Phone: 410-260-4558
E-mail: rparker@mhec.state.md.us

VETERANS OF THE AFGHANISTAN AND IRAQ CONFLICTS SCHOLARSHIP PROGRAM

• See page 603

WORKFORCE SHORTAGE STUDENT ASSISTANCE GRANT PROGRAM

Scholarship of $4000 available to students who will be required to major in specific areas and will be obligated to serve in the state of Maryland after completion of degree.

Award: Scholarship for use in freshman, sophomore, junior, or senior years; renewable. *Number:* 1300. *Amount:* $4000.

Eligibility Requirements: Applicant must be enrolled or expecting to enroll full- or part-time at a two-year or four-year institution or university; resident of Maryland and studying in Maryland. Available to U.S. citizens.

Application Requirements: Application form, certain majors require additional documentation, essay, financial need analysis, recommendations or references, resume, transcript. *Deadline:* July 1.

Contact: Maura Sappington, Program Manager
Maryland State Higher Education Commission
839 Bestgate Road, Suite 400
Annapolis, MD 21401-3013
Phone: 410-260-4569
Fax: 410-260-3203
E-mail: msapping@mhec.state.md.us

MASSACHUSETTS AFL-CIO

http://www.massaflcio.org/

MASSACHUSETTS AFL-CIO SCHOLARSHIP

Scholarships to union members, their children/stepchildren, grandchildren, nieces, nephews, and non-union Massachusetts high school seniors.

Award: Scholarship for use in freshman year; not renewable. *Number:* 100–150. *Amount:* $250–$12,000.

Eligibility Requirements: Applicant must be high school student; planning to enroll or expecting to enroll full-time at a four-year institution or university; resident of Massachusetts and studying in Massachusetts. Available to U.S. citizens.

Application Requirements: Application form. *Deadline:* December 21.

Contact: Jackie Bergantino, Scholarship Administrator
Phone: 781-324-8230
Fax: 781-324-8225
E-mail: jbergantino@massaflcio.org

MASSACHUSETTS OFFICE OF STUDENT FINANCIAL ASSISTANCE

http://www.osfa.mass.edu/

AGNES M. LINDSAY SCHOLARSHIP

Scholarships for students with demonstrated financial need who are from rural areas of Massachusetts and attend public institutions of higher education in Massachusetts. Deadline varies.

Award: Scholarship for use in freshman, sophomore, junior, or senior years; not renewable.

Eligibility Requirements: Applicant must be enrolled or expecting to enroll full-time at a two-year or four-year institution or university; resident of Massachusetts and studying in Massachusetts. Available to U.S. citizens.

Application Requirements: Application form, financial need analysis. *Deadline:* varies.

Contact: Robert Brun, Director of Scholarships and Grants
Phone: 617-727-9420
Fax: 617-727-0667
E-mail: osfa@osfa.mass.edu

CHRISTIAN A. HERTER MEMORIAL SCHOLARSHIP

Renewable award for Massachusetts residents who are in the tenth and eleventh grades, and whose socio-economic backgrounds and environment may inhibit their ability to attain educational goals. Must exhibit severe personal or family-related difficulties, medical problems, or have overcome a personal obstacle. Provides up to 50 percent of the student's calculated need, as determined by federal methodology, at the college of their choice within the continental United States.

Award: Scholarship for use in freshman, sophomore, junior, or senior years; renewable. *Number:* 25. *Amount:* up to $15,000.

Eligibility Requirements: Applicant must be high school student; planning to enroll or expecting to enroll full-time at a two-year or four-year or technical institution or university and resident of Massachusetts. Applicant must have 2.5 GPA or higher. Available to U.S. citizens.

Application Requirements: Application form, community service, financial need analysis, interview, recommendations or references. *Deadline:* February 1.

Contact: Robert Brun, Director of Scholarships and Grants
Phone: 617-727-9420
Fax: 617-727-0667
E-mail: osfa@osfa.mass.edu

DSS ADOPTED CHILDREN TUITION WAIVER

Need-based tuition waiver for Massachusetts residents who are full-time undergraduate students. Must attend a Massachusetts public institution of higher education and be under 24 years of age. File the FAFSA after January 1. Contact school financial aid office for more information.

Award: Scholarship for use in freshman, sophomore, junior, or senior years; renewable.

Eligibility Requirements: Applicant must be enrolled or expecting to enroll full-time at a two-year or four-year institution and resident of Massachusetts. Available to U.S. and non-Canadian citizens.

Application Requirements: Application form, FAFSA, financial need analysis. *Deadline:* varies.

Contact: Robert Brun, Director of Scholarships and Grants
Phone: 617-727-9420
Fax: 617-727-0667
E-mail: osfa@osfa.mass.edu

JOHN AND ABIGAIL ADAMS SCHOLARSHIP

Scholarship to reward and inspire student achievement, attract more high-performing students to Massachusetts public higher education, and provide families of college-bound students with financial assistance. Must be a U.S. citizen or an eligible non-citizen. There is no application process for the scholarship. Students who are eligible will be notified in the fall of their senior year in high school.

Award: Scholarship for use in freshman year; not renewable.

Eligibility Requirements: Applicant must be high school student; planning to enroll or expecting to enroll full-time at a two-year or four-year institution or university; resident of Massachusetts and studying in Massachusetts. Applicant must have 3.0 GPA or higher. Available to U.S. citizens.

Application Requirements: *Deadline:* varies.

Contact: Robert Brun, Director of Scholarships and Grants
Phone: 617-727-9420
Fax: 617-727-0667
E-mail: osfa@osfa.mass.edu

MASSACHUSETTS ASSISTANCE FOR STUDENT SUCCESS PROGRAM

Provides need-based financial assistance to Massachusetts residents to attend undergraduate postsecondary institutions in Connecticut, Maine, Massachusetts, New Hampshire, Pennsylvania, Rhode Island, Vermont, and District of Columbia. High school seniors may apply. Expected Family Contribution (EFC) should be $3850. Timely filing of FAFSA required.

Award: Grant for use in freshman, sophomore, junior, or senior years; not renewable. *Number:* 50,000–57,000. *Amount:* $300–$1600.

Eligibility Requirements: Applicant must be enrolled or expecting to enroll full-time at a two-year or four-year or technical institution or university; resident of Massachusetts and studying in Connecticut, District of Columbia, Maine, Massachusetts, New Hampshire, Pennsylvania, Rhode Island, Vermont. Available to U.S. citizens.

Application Requirements: FAFSA, financial need analysis. *Deadline:* May 1.

Contact: Robert Brun, Director of Scholarships and Grants
Phone: 617-727-9420
Fax: 617-727-0667
E-mail: osfa@osfa.mass.edu

MASSACHUSETTS CASH GRANT PROGRAM

A need-based grant to assist with mandatory fees and non-state supported tuition. This supplemental award is available to Massachusetts residents, who are undergraduates at public two-year, four-year colleges and universities in Massachusetts. Must file FAFSA before May 1. Contact college financial aid office for information.

Award: Grant for use in freshman, sophomore, junior, or senior years; not renewable.

Eligibility Requirements: Applicant must be enrolled or expecting to enroll full-time at a two-year or four-year institution or university and resident of Massachusetts. Available to U.S. citizens.

Application Requirements: Application form, FAFSA, financial need analysis. *Deadline:* continuous.

Contact: Robert Brun, Director of Scholarships and Grants
Phone: 617-727-9420
Fax: 617-727-0667
E-mail: osfa@osfa.mass.edu

MASSACHUSETTS GILBERT MATCHING STUDENT GRANT PROGRAM

Grants for permanent Massachusetts residents attending an independent, regionally accredited Massachusetts school or school of nursing full time. Must be U.S. citizen and permanent legal resident of Massachusetts. File the Free Application for Federal Student Aid after January 1. Contact college financial aid office for complete details and deadlines.

Award: Grant for use in freshman, sophomore, junior, or senior years; not renewable. *Amount:* $200–$2500.

Eligibility Requirements: Applicant must be enrolled or expecting to enroll full-time at a four-year institution or university; resident of Massachusetts and studying in Massachusetts. Available to U.S. citizens.

Application Requirements: FAFSA, financial need analysis. *Deadline:* varies.

Contact: Robert Brun, Director of Scholarships and Grants
Massachusetts Office of Student Financial Assistance
454 Broadway, Suite 200
Revere, MA 02151
Phone: 617-727-9420
Fax: 617-727-0667
E-mail: rbrun@osfa.mass.edu

MASSACHUSETTS PART-TIME GRANT PROGRAM

Award for permanent Massachusetts residents who have enrolled part-time for at least one year in a state-approved postsecondary school. The recipient must not have a bachelor's degree. FAFSA must be filed before May 1. Contact college financial aid office for further information.

Award: Grant for use in freshman, sophomore, junior, or senior years; not renewable. *Number:* 200. *Amount:* $200–$1150.

Eligibility Requirements: Applicant must be enrolled or expecting to enroll part-time at a two-year or four-year or technical institution or university and resident of Massachusetts. Available to U.S. citizens.

Application Requirements: Application form, FAFSA, financial need analysis. *Deadline:* varies.

Contact: Robert Brun, Director of Scholarships and Grants
Phone: 617-727-9420
Fax: 617-727-0667
E-mail: osfa@osfa.mass.edu

MASSACHUSETTS PUBLIC SERVICE GRANT PROGRAM
• *See page 560*

PAUL TSONGAS SCHOLARSHIP PROGRAM

Scholarship to recognize achievement and reward Massachusetts students, who have graduated from high school within three years with a GPA of 3.75 and a SAT score of at least 1200, and who also meet the one year residency requirement for tuition classification at the state colleges.

Award: Scholarship for use in freshman, sophomore, junior, or senior years; renewable.

Eligibility Requirements: Applicant must be enrolled or expecting to enroll full-time at a two-year or four-year institution or university; resident of Massachusetts and studying in Massachusetts. Available to U.S. citizens.

Application Requirements: Application form, test scores. *Deadline:* varies.

Contact: Robert Brun, Director of Scholarships and Grants
Phone: 617-727-9420
Fax: 617-727-0667
E-mail: osfa@osfa.mass.edu

MCCURRY FOUNDATION INC.

http://www.mccurryfoundation.org/

MCCURRY FOUNDATION SCHOLARSHIP

Scholarship open to all public high school seniors, with preference given to applicants from Clay, Duval, Nassau, and St. Johns Counties, Florida and from Glynn County, Georgia. Scholarship emphasizes leadership, work ethic, and academic excellence. A minimum GPA of 3.0 is required and family income cannot exceed a maximum of $75,000 (AGI).

Award: Scholarship for use in freshman, sophomore, junior, or senior years; renewable. *Number:* 1–10. *Amount:* $750–$1250.

Eligibility Requirements: Applicant must be high school student; planning to enroll or expecting to enroll full-time at a two-year or four-year or technical institution or university; resident of Florida, Georgia and must have an interest in leadership. Applicant must have 3.0 GPA or higher. Available to U.S. and non-U.S. citizens.

Application Requirements: Application form, essay, financial need analysis, interview, recommendations or references, report card, tax return, resume, transcript. *Deadline:* February 15.

MICHIGAN DEPARTMENT OF TREASURY - BUREAU OF STATE AND AUTHORITY FINANCE

http://www.michigan.gov/ssg

MICHIGAN COMPETITIVE SCHOLARSHIP

Renewable awards for Michigan resident to pursue undergraduate study at a Michigan institution. Awards limited to tuition. Must maintain at least a 2.0 grade point average and meet the college's academic progress requirements. Must file Free Application for Federal Student Aid.

Award: Scholarship for use in freshman, sophomore, junior, or senior years; renewable. *Amount:* $575–$575.

Eligibility Requirements: Applicant must be enrolled or expecting to enroll full- or part-time at a two-year or four-year institution or university; resident of Michigan and studying in Michigan. Available to U.S. citizens.

Application Requirements: Application form, financial need analysis, test scores. *Deadline:* March 1.

MICHIGAN TUITION GRANT

Need-based program. Students must be Michigan residents and attend a Michigan private, nonprofit, degree-granting college. Must file the Free Application for Federal Student Aid and meet the college's academic progress requirements.

Award: Grant for use in freshman, sophomore, junior, or senior years; renewable. *Amount:* $1512–$1512.

Eligibility Requirements: Applicant must be enrolled or expecting to enroll full- or part-time at a four-year institution or university; resident of Michigan and studying in Michigan. Available to U.S. citizens.

Application Requirements: Financial need analysis. *Deadline:* July 1.

TUITION INCENTIVE PROGRAM

Award for Michigan residents who receive or have received Michigan Medicaid for required period of time through the Department of Human Services. Scholarship provides two years tuition towards an associate degree at a Michigan college or university and $2000 total assistance for third and fourth years. Must apply before graduating from high school or earning a general education development diploma and before age 20.

Award: Grant for use in freshman, sophomore, junior, or senior years; renewable.

Eligibility Requirements: Applicant must be enrolled or expecting to enroll full- or part-time at a two-year or four-year institution or university; resident of Michigan and studying in Michigan. Available to U.S. citizens.

Application Requirements: Application form, Medicaid eligibility for specified period of time. *Deadline:* continuous.

MIDWESTERN HIGHER EDUCATION COMPACT

http://www.mhec.org/

MIDWEST STUDENT EXCHANGE PROGRAM

Over 140 colleges and universities in Illinois, Indiana, Kansas, Michigan, Minnesota, Missouri, Nebraska, North Dakota, and Wisconsin participate in the MSEP tuition reciprocity program. It is not a scholarship, but for qualified students, provides a discount on out-of-state tuition. Requirements vary by institution. See website for details http://msep.mhec.org.

Award: Grant for use in freshman, sophomore, junior, senior, graduate, or postgraduate years; renewable.

Eligibility Requirements: Applicant must be enrolled or expecting to enroll full- or part-time at a two-year or four-year or technical institution or university; resident of Illinois, Indiana, Kansas, Michigan, Minnesota, Missouri, Nebraska, North Dakota, Wisconsin and studying in Illinois, Indiana, Kansas, Michigan, Minnesota, Missouri, Nebraska, North Dakota, Wisconsin. Available to U.S. citizens.

Application Requirements: Application form,.

Contact: Ms. Amber Cameron, Research Associate
Midwestern Higher Education Compact
1300 South Second Street, Suite 130
Minneapolis, MN 55454-1079
Phone: 612-625-4368
Fax: 612-626-8290
E-mail: amberc@mhec.org

MINNESOTA AFL-CIO

http://www.mnaflcio.org/

BILL PETERSON SCHOLARSHIP
• See page 525

MARTIN DUFFY ADULT LEARNER SCHOLARSHIP AWARD
• See page 525

MINNESOTA DEPARTMENT OF MILITARY AFFAIRS

http://www.minnesotanationalguard.org/

LEADERSHIP, EXCELLENCE, AND DEDICATED SERVICE SCHOLARSHIP
• See page 560

MINNESOTA OFFICE OF HIGHER EDUCATION

http://www.getreadyforcollege.org/

MINNESOTA GI BILL PROGRAM
• See page 604

MINNESOTA INDIAN SCHOLARSHIP
• See page 631

MINNESOTA RECIPROCAL AGREEMENT

Renewable tuition waiver for Minnesota residents. Waives all or part of non-resident tuition surcharge at public institutions in Illinois, Indiana, Iowa, Kansas, Michigan, Missouri, Nebraska, North Dakota, South Dakota, Wisconsin and Manitoba. Deadline: last day of academic term.

Award: Scholarship for use in freshman, sophomore, junior, senior, graduate, or postgraduate years; renewable. *Amount:* up to $10,000.

Eligibility Requirements: Applicant must be enrolled or expecting to enroll full- or part-time at a two-year or four-year or technical institution or university; resident of Minnesota and studying in Illinois, Indiana, Iowa, Kansas, Manitoba, Michigan, Missouri, Nebraska, North Dakota, South Dakota, Wisconsin. Available to U.S. citizens.

Application Requirements: Application form, application form may be submitted online (http://www.getreadyforcollege.org). *Deadline:* continuous.

Contact: Jodi Rouland, Program Assistant
Phone: 651-355-0614
Fax: 651-642-0675
E-mail: jodi.rouland@state.mn.us

MINNESOTA STATE GRANT PROGRAM

Need-based grant program available for Minnesota residents attending Minnesota colleges. Student covers 46% of cost with remainder covered by Pell Grant, parent contribution and state grant. Students apply with FAFSA and colleges administer the program on campus.

Award: Grant for use in freshman, sophomore, junior, or senior years; not renewable. *Number:* 71,000–105,000. *Amount:* $100–$9620.

Eligibility Requirements: Applicant must be enrolled or expecting to enroll full- or part-time at a two-year or four-year or technical institution or university; resident of Minnesota and studying in Minnesota. Available to U.S. citizens.

Application Requirements: Application form, application form may be submitted online (http://www.fafsa.gov), financial need analysis. *Deadline:* continuous.

MINNESOTA STATE VETERANS' DEPENDENTS ASSISTANCE PROGRAM

• *See page 604*

POSTSECONDARY CHILD CARE GRANT PROGRAM-MINNESOTA

Grant available for students not receiving MFIP. Based on financial need. Cannot exceed actual child care costs or maximum award chart (based on income). Must be Minnesota resident. For use at Minnesota two- or four-year school, including public technical colleges. Available until student has attended college for the equivalent of four full-time academic years.

Award: Grant for use in freshman, sophomore, junior, or senior years; not renewable. *Number:* 2500–3000. *Amount:* $100–$2800.

Eligibility Requirements: Applicant must be enrolled or expecting to enroll full- or part-time at a two-year or four-year or technical institution or university; resident of Minnesota and studying in Minnesota. Available to U.S. citizens.

Application Requirements: Application form, financial need analysis. *Deadline:* continuous.

Contact: Brenda Larter, Program Administrator
Minnesota Office of Higher Education
1450 Energy Park Drive, Suite 350
St. Paul, MN 55108-5227
Phone: 651-355-0612
Fax: 651-642-0675
E-mail: brenda.larter@state.mn.us

SAFETY OFFICERS' SURVIVOR GRANT PROGRAM

• *See page 560*

MISSISSIPPI OFFICE OF STUDENT FINANCIAL AID

http://www.mississippi.edu/financialaid

HIGHER EDUCATION LEGISLATIVE PLAN (HELP)

Eligible applicant must be resident of Mississippi and apply for the first time as a freshman and/or sophomore student who graduated from high school within the immediate past two years. Must demonstrate need as determined by the results of the FAFSA, documenting an average family adjusted gross income of $36,500 or less over the prior two years. Must be enrolled full-time at a Mississippi college or university, have a GPA of 2.5, have completed a specific high school core curriculum, and have scored 20 on the ACT.

Award: Scholarship for use in freshman, sophomore, junior, or senior years; not renewable. *Amount:* $721–$5835.

Eligibility Requirements: Applicant must be enrolled or expecting to enroll full-time at a two-year or four-year institution or university; resident of Mississippi and studying in Mississippi. Applicant must have 2.5 GPA or higher. Available to U.S. citizens.

Application Requirements: Application form, application form may be submitted online (http://www.mississippi.edu/financialaid), FAFSA,

specific high school curriculum, residency documentation, financial need analysis, test scores, transcript. *Deadline:* March 31.

Contact: Mrs. Jennifer Rogers, Director of Student Financial Aid
Phone: 601-432-6997
E-mail: sfa@mississippi.edu

LAW ENFORCEMENT OFFICERS/FIREMEN SCHOLARSHIP

• *See page 560*

MISSISSIPPI EMINENT SCHOLARS GRANT

Award for an entering freshmen or as a renewal for sophomore, junior or senior, who are residents of Mississippi. Applicants must achieve a GPA of 3.5 and must have scored 29 on the ACT. Must enroll full-time at an eligible Mississippi college or university.

Award: Grant for use in freshman, sophomore, junior, or senior years; not renewable. *Amount:* $392–$2500.

Eligibility Requirements: Applicant must be enrolled or expecting to enroll full-time at a two-year or four-year institution or university; resident of Mississippi and studying in Mississippi. Applicant must have 3.5 GPA or higher. Available to U.S. citizens.

Application Requirements: Application form, application form may be submitted online (http://www.mississippi.edu/financialaid), residency documentation, test scores, transcript. *Deadline:* September 15.

Contact: Mrs. Jennifer Rogers, Director of Student Financial Aid
Phone: 601-432-6997
E-mail: sfa@mississippi.edu

MISSISSIPPI RESIDENT TUITION ASSISTANCE GRANT

Must be a resident of Mississippi enrolled full-time at an eligible Mississippi college or university. Must maintain a minimum 2.5 GPA each semester. MTAG awards may be up to $500 per academic year for freshman and sophomores and $1000 per academic year for juniors and seniors.

Award: Grant for use in freshman, sophomore, junior, or senior years; not renewable. *Amount:* $17–$1000.

Eligibility Requirements: Applicant must be enrolled or expecting to enroll full-time at a two-year or four-year institution or university; resident of Mississippi and studying in Mississippi. Applicant must have 2.5 GPA or higher. Available to U.S. citizens.

Application Requirements: Application form, application form may be submitted online (http://www.mississippi.edu/financialaid), residency documentation, test scores, transcript. *Deadline:* September 15.

Contact: Mrs. Jennifer Rogers, Director of Student Financial Aid
Phone: 601-432-6997
E-mail: sfa@mississippi.edu

NISSAN SCHOLARSHIP

Renewable award for Mississippi residents attending a Mississippi institution. Must be graduating from a Mississippi high school in the current year. The scholarship will pay full tuition and a book allowance. Minimum GPA of 2.0 as well as an ACT composite of at least 20 or combined SAT scores of 940 or better. Must demonstrate financial need and leadership abilities.

Award: Scholarship for use in freshman, sophomore, junior, or senior years; renewable. *Amount:* $6292–$6306.

Eligibility Requirements: Applicant must be high school student; planning to enroll or expecting to enroll full-time at a two-year or four-year institution or university; resident of Mississippi and studying in Mississippi. Applicant must have 2.5 GPA or higher. Available to U.S. citizens.

Application Requirements: Application form, application form may be submitted online (http://www.mississippi.edu/financialaid), essay, financial need analysis, recommendations or references, residency documentation, resume, test scores, transcript. *Deadline:* March 1.

Contact: Mrs. Jennifer Rogers, Director of Student Financial Aid
Phone: 601-432-6997
E-mail: sfa@mississippi.edu

SUMMER DEVELOPMENTAL PROGRAM GRANT

The Summer Developmental Program Grant was designed to assist students who do not meet the criteria for admission to one of the Mississippi's public universities. Grants are available to assist Mississippi residents participating in the Summer Developmental Program who demonstrate financial need. Awards are dependent upon demonstrated remaining financial need; however, no award will exceed financial need or the total cost of attendance. Grants are funded by the state through money awarded by the Ayers settlement.

Award: Grant for use in freshman year; not renewable. *Amount:* $656–$6280.

Eligibility Requirements: Applicant must be high school student; planning to enroll or expecting to enroll full-time at an institution or university; resident of Mississippi and studying in Mississippi. Available to U.S. citizens.

Application Requirements: Application form, application form may be submitted online (http://www.mississippi.edu/financialaid), financial need analysis, residency documentation. *Deadline:* July 21.

Contact: Mrs. Jennifer Rogers, Director of Student Financial Aid
> *Phone:* 601-432-6997
> *E-mail:* sfa@mississippi.edu

MISSOURI CONSERVATION AGENTS ASSOCIATION SCHOLARSHIP

http://www.moagent.com/

MISSOURI CONSERVATION AGENTS ASSOCIATION SCHOLARSHIP

Scholarship of up to $500 per student per year for full-time undergraduate students who reside in the state of Missouri. The applicant must be a U.S. citizen.

Award: Scholarship for use in freshman, sophomore, junior, or senior years; not renewable. *Amount:* up to $500.

Eligibility Requirements: Applicant must be enrolled or expecting to enroll full-time at a four-year or technical institution or university and resident of Missouri. Applicant must have 2.5 GPA or higher. Available to U.S. citizens.

Application Requirements: Essay, transcript. *Deadline:* February 1.

Contact: Brian Ham, Scholarship Committee
> *Phone:* 573-896-8628

MISSOURI DEPARTMENT OF HIGHER EDUCATION

http://www.dhe.mo.gov/

ACCESS MISSOURI FINANCIAL ASSISTANCE PROGRAM

Need-based program that provides awards to students who are enrolled full time and have an expected family contribution (EFC) of $12,000 or less based on their Free Application for Federal Student Aid (FAFSA). Awards vary depending on EFC and the type of postsecondary school.

Award: Grant for use in freshman, sophomore, junior, or senior years; not renewable.

Eligibility Requirements: Applicant must be enrolled or expecting to enroll full-time at a two-year or technical institution or university; resident of Missouri and studying in Missouri. Applicant must have 2.5 GPA or higher. Available to U.S. citizens.

Application Requirements: FAFSA on file by April 1.

MARGUERITE ROSS BARNETT MEMORIAL SCHOLARSHIP

Scholarship was established for students who are employed while attending school part-time. Must be enrolled at least half-time but less than full-time at a participating Missouri postsecondary school, be employed and compensated for at least 20 hours per week, be 18 years of age, be a Missouri resident and a U.S. citizen or a permanent resident.

Award: Scholarship for use in freshman, sophomore, junior, or senior years; renewable.

Eligibility Requirements: Applicant must be enrolled or expecting to enroll part-time at a two-year or four-year or technical institution or university; resident of Missouri and studying in Missouri. Applicant must have 2.5 GPA or higher. Available to U.S. citizens.

Application Requirements: FAFSA on file by August 1. *Deadline:* August 1.

MISSOURI HIGHER EDUCATION ACADEMIC SCHOLARSHIP (BRIGHT FLIGHT)

Program encourages top-ranked high school seniors to attend approved Missouri postsecondary schools. Must be a Missouri resident and a U.S. citizen or permanent resident. Must have a composite score on the ACT or SAT in the top 5 percent of all Missouri students taking those tests. Students with scores in the top 3 percent are eligible for an annual award of up to $3000 (up to $1500 each semester). Students with scores in the top 4% and 5% are eligible for an annual award of up to $1000 (up to $500 each semester). Award amounts, and the availability of the award for students in the 4% and 5%, are subject to change based on the amount of funding allocated for the program in the legislative session.

Award: Scholarship for use in freshman, sophomore, junior, or senior years; renewable. *Amount:* $1000–$3000.

Eligibility Requirements: Applicant must be enrolled or expecting to enroll full-time at a two-year or four-year or technical institution or university; resident of Missouri and studying in Missouri. Applicant must have 2.5 GPA or higher. Available to U.S. citizens.

Application Requirements: Test scores.

MITCHELL INSTITUTE

http://www.mitchellinstitute.org/

THE SENATOR GEORGE J. MITCHELL SCHOLARSHIP RESEARCH INSTITUTE

The Mitchell Institute awards scholarship to graduating senior from every public high school in Maine each year. The scholarship award is in the amount of $6000 broken down into $1500 awards per year for up to four years.

Award: Scholarship for use in freshman, sophomore, junior, or senior years; renewable. *Number:* 129. *Amount:* $1500.

Eligibility Requirements: Applicant must be high school student; planning to enroll or expecting to enroll full- or part-time at a two-year or four-year or technical institution or university and resident of Maine. Available to U.S. citizens.

Application Requirements: Application form, community service, essay, financial need analysis, recommendations or references, transcript. *Deadline:* April 1.

Contact: Jared Cash, Scholarship Director
> Mitchell Institute
> 22 Monument Square, Suite 200
> Portland, ME 04101
> *Phone:* 207-773-7700
> *Fax:* 207-773-1133
> *E-mail:* jcash@mitchellinstitute.org

MONTANA UNIVERSITY SYSTEM, OFFICE OF COMMISSIONER OF HIGHER EDUCATION

http://www.scholarship.mt.gov/

MONTANA HIGHER EDUCATION OPPORTUNITY GRANT

This grant is awarded based on need to undergraduate students attending either part-time or full-time who are residents of Montana and attending participating Montana schools. Awards are limited to the most needy students. A specific major or program of study is not required. This grant does not need to be repaid, and students may apply each year. Apply by filing FAFSA by March 1 and contacting the financial aid office at the admitting college.

Award: Grant for use in freshman, sophomore, junior, or senior years; not renewable. *Number:* up to 800. *Amount:* $400–$600.

Eligibility Requirements: Applicant must be enrolled or expecting to enroll full- or part-time at a two-year or four-year institution or university; resident of Montana and studying in Montana. Available to U.S. citizens.

Application Requirements: Application form, FAFSA, financial need analysis, resume. *Deadline:* March 1.

Contact: Jamie Dushin, Budget Analyst
Montana University System, Office of Commissioner of
Higher Education
PO Box 203101
Helena, MT 59620-3101
Phone: 406-444-0638
Fax: 406-444-1869
E-mail: jdushin@mgslp.state.mt.us

MONTANA TUITION ASSISTANCE PROGRAM-BAKER GRANT

Need-based grant for Montana residents attending participating Montana schools who have earned at least $2575 during the previous calendar year. Must be enrolled full time. Grant does not need to be repaid. Award covers the first undergraduate degree or certificate. Apply by filing FAFSA by March 1 and contacting the financial aid office at the admitting college.

Award: Grant for use in freshman, sophomore, junior, or senior years; not renewable. *Number:* 1000–3000. *Amount:* $100–$1000.

Eligibility Requirements: Applicant must be enrolled or expecting to enroll full-time at a two-year or four-year institution or university; resident of Montana and studying in Montana. Available to U.S. citizens.

Application Requirements: Application form, FAFSA, financial need analysis, resume. *Deadline:* March 1.

Contact: Jamie Dushin, Budget Analyst
Montana University System, Office of Commissioner of
Higher Education
PO Box 203101
Helena, MT 59620-3101
Phone: 406-444-0638
Fax: 406-444-1869
E-mail: jdushin@mgslp.state.mt.us

MONTANA UNIVERSITY SYSTEM HONOR SCHOLARSHIP

Scholarship will be awarded annually to high school seniors graduating from accredited Montana high schools. The MUS Honor Scholarship is a four year renewable scholarship that waives the tuition and registration fee at one of the Montana University System campuses or one of the three community colleges (Flathead Valley in Kalispell, Miles in Miles City or Dawson in Glendive). The scholarship must be used within 9 months after high school graduation. Applicant must have a minimum GPA of 3.4.

Award: Scholarship for use in freshman, sophomore, junior, or senior years; renewable. *Number:* up to 200. *Amount:* $4000–$6000.

Eligibility Requirements: Applicant must be high school student; planning to enroll or expecting to enroll full-time at a two-year or four-year institution or university; resident of Montana and studying in Montana. Applicant must have 3.5 GPA or higher. Available to U.S. citizens.

Application Requirements: Application form, college acceptance letter, test scores, transcript. *Deadline:* March 15.

Contact: Sheila Newlun, Grants and Scholarship Coordinator
Phone: 406-444-0638
Fax: 406-444-1869
E-mail: snewlun@montana.edu

MOUNT VERNON URBAN RENEWAL AGENCY

http://www.ci.mount-vernon.ny.us/

THOMAS E. SHARPE MEMORIAL EDUCATIONAL ASSISTANCE PROGRAM

Awards offered only to the low and moderate income residents of the city of Mount Vernon for the purpose of pursuing higher education at a vocational/technical school or college.

Award: Grant for use in freshman, sophomore, junior, or senior years; renewable. *Number:* up to 150.

Eligibility Requirements: Applicant must be enrolled or expecting to enroll full-time at a two-year or four-year or technical institution or university and resident of New York. Applicant must have 2.5 GPA or higher. Available to U.S. citizens.

Application Requirements: Application form, essay, financial need analysis, proof of residence, transcript. *Deadline:* July 1.

Contact: Mary Fleming, Director, Scholarship Programs
Mount Vernon Urban Renewal Agency
Department of Planning, One Roosevelt Square, City Hall
Mount Vernon, NY 10550
Phone: 914-699-7230 Ext. 110
Fax: 914-699-1435
E-mail: mfleming@ci.mount-vernon.ny.us

NATIONAL BURGLAR AND FIRE ALARM ASSOCIATION

http://www.alarm.org/

NBFAA YOUTH SCHOLARSHIP PROGRAM
• *See page 562*

NATIONAL COUNCIL OF JEWISH WOMEN NEW YORK SECTION

http://www.ncjwny.org/

JACKSON-STRICKS SCHOLARSHIP
• *See page 573*

NATIONAL DEFENSE TRANSPORTATION ASSOCIATION-SCOTT ST. LOUIS CHAPTER

http://www.ndtascottstlouis.org/

NATIONAL DEFENSE TRANSPORTATION ASSOCIATION, SCOTT AIR FORCE BASE-ST. LOUIS AREA CHAPTER SCHOLARSHIP

The Scott/St. Louis Chapter of the NDTA intends to award a minimum of two (2) scholarships of $3500 each and four (4) scholarships of $2000 each. Additional awards may be granted pending availability of funds. Scholarships are open to any high school student that meets the eligibility criteria. High school students must be reside and go to school in Illinois or Missouri. College applicants must be a full-time student in the following states: CO, IA, IL, IN, KS, MI, MN, MO, MT, ND, NE, SD, WI, or WY.

Award: Scholarship for use in freshman, sophomore, junior, or senior years; not renewable. *Number:* 6. *Amount:* $2000–$3500.

Eligibility Requirements: Applicant must be enrolled or expecting to enroll full-time at a two-year or four-year institution or university; resident of Illinois, Missouri and studying in Colorado, Illinois, Indiana, Iowa, Kansas, Michigan, Minnesota, Missouri, Montana, Nebraska, North Dakota, South Dakota, Wisconsin, Wyoming. Applicant must have 3.0 GPA or higher. Available to U.S. citizens.

Application Requirements: Application form, community service, essay, recommendations or references, test scores, transcript. *Deadline:* March 1.

Contact: Mr. Michael Carnes, Chairman, Professional Development
Committee
National Defense Transportation Association-Scott St. Louis
Chapter
PO Box 25486
Scott AFB, IL 62225
Phone: 618-229-4756
E-mail: michael.carnes.ctr@ustranscom.mil

NATIONAL FEDERATION OF BLIND OF MISSOURI

http://www.nfbmo.org/

NATIONAL FEDERATION OF THE BLIND OF MISSOURI SCHOLARSHIPS TO LEGALLY BLIND STUDENTS
• *See page 573*

NATIONAL FEDERATION OF THE BLIND OF CALIFORNIA

http://www.nfbcal.org/

GERALD DRAKE MEMORIAL SCHOLARSHIP
• See page 575

JULIE LANDUCCI SCHOLARSHIP
• See page 575

LA VYRL "PINKY" JOHNSON MEMORIAL SCHOLARSHIP
• See page 575

LAWRENCE "MUZZY" MARCELINO MEMORIAL SCHOLARSHIP
• See page 575

NATIONAL FEDERATION OF THE BLIND OF CALIFORNIA MERIT SCHOLARSHIPS
• See page 575

NATIONAL KIDNEY FOUNDATION OF INDIANA INC.

http://www.kidneyindiana.org/

LARRY SMOCK SCHOLARSHIP
• See page 575

NEBRASKA'S COORDINATING COMMISSION FOR POSTSECONDARY EDUCATION

http://www.ccpe.state.ne.us/

NEBRASKA OPPORTUNITY GRANT

Available to undergraduates attending a participating postsecondary institution in Nebraska. Must demonstrate financial need. Nebraska residency required. Awards determined by each participating institution. Student must complete the Free Application for Federal Student Aid (FAFSA) to apply. Contact financial aid office at institution for additional information.

Award: Grant for use in freshman, sophomore, junior, or senior years; not renewable. *Amount:* $100–$3600.

Eligibility Requirements: Applicant must be enrolled or expecting to enroll full- or part-time at a two-year or four-year or technical institution or university; resident of Nebraska and studying in Nebraska. Available to U.S. citizens.

Application Requirements: Application form, application form may be submitted online (http://www.fafsa.ed.gov), financial need analysis. *Deadline:* continuous.

Contact: Mr. J. Ritchie Morrow, Financial Aid Coordinator
Nebraska's Coordinating Commission for Postsecondary
Education
140 North 8th Street, Suite 300
PO Box 95005
Lincoln, NE 68509-5005
Phone: 402-471-2847
Fax: 402-471-2886
E-mail: Ritchie.Morrow@nebraska.gov

NEBRASKA SPORTS COUNCIL/THE GALLUP ORGANIZATION

http://www.cornhuskerstategames.com/

NEBRASKA SPORTS COUNCIL/GALLUP ORGANIZATION CORNHUSKER STATE GAMES SCHOLARSHIP PROGRAM

One-time award for Nebraska students who are participants in the Cornhusker State Games. For use at a Nebraska postsecondary institution.

Award: Scholarship for use in freshman, sophomore, junior, or senior years; not renewable. *Number:* 5. *Amount:* $1000.

Eligibility Requirements: Applicant must be enrolled or expecting to enroll full- or part-time at a two-year or four-year or technical institution or university; resident of Nebraska; studying in Nebraska and must have an interest in athletics/sports. Available to U.S. citizens.

Application Requirements: Application form, essay, transcript. *Deadline:* June 1.

Contact: Dave Mlnarik, Executive Director
Phone: 402-471-2544
E-mail: info@nebraskasportscouncil.com

NEED

http://www.needld.org/

UNMET NEED GRANT PROGRAM
• See page 633

NEVADA OFFICE OF THE STATE TREASURER

http://www.nevadatreasurer.gov/

GOVERNOR GUINN MILLENNIUM SCHOLARSHIP

Scholarship for Nevada residents. Student must graduate from a public or private high school within Nevada with a minimum GPA of 3.25. Must complete core curriculum. Maximum award is $10,000. Student must acknowledge award and use it within 6 years of high school graduation.

Award: Scholarship for use in freshman, sophomore, junior, or senior years; renewable. *Number:* 1. *Amount:* $1–$10,000.

Eligibility Requirements: Applicant must be enrolled or expecting to enroll full-time at a two-year or four-year institution or university; resident of Nevada and studying in Nevada. Available to U.S. citizens.

Application Requirements: Application form may be submitted online (http://nevadatreasurer.gov), High schools determine eligibility. Student must accept award. *Deadline:* varies.

Contact: Linda English, Executive Director
Phone: 702-486-3889
Fax: 702-486-3246
E-mail: info@nevadatreasurer.gov

NEW ENGLAND BOARD OF HIGHER EDUCATION

http://www.nebhe.org/

NEW ENGLAND REGIONAL STUDENT PROGRAM-TUITION BREAK

Tuition discount for residents of six New England states (Connecticut, Maine, Massachusetts, New Hampshire, Rhode Island, Vermont). Students pay reduced out-of-state tuition at public colleges or universities in other New England states when enrolling in certain majors not offered at public institutions in home state. Details are available at http://www.nebhe.org/tuitionbreak.

Award: Scholarship for use in freshman, sophomore, junior, senior, or graduate years; renewable.

Eligibility Requirements: Applicant must be enrolled or expecting to enroll full- or part-time at a two-year or four-year institution or university; resident of Connecticut, Maine, Massachusetts, New Hampshire, Rhode Island, Vermont and studying in Connecticut, Maine,

Massachusetts, New Hampshire, Rhode Island, Vermont. Available to U.S. citizens.

Application Requirements: College application for admission. *Deadline:* continuous.

Contact: Wendy Lindsay, Senior Director of Regional Student Program
New England Board of Higher Education
45 Temple Place
Boston, MA 02111
Phone: 617-357-9620 Ext. 111
Fax: 617-338-1577
E-mail: tuitionbreak@nebhe.org

NEW HAMPSHIRE FOOD INDUSTRIES EDUCATION FOUNDATION

http://www.grocers.org/

NEW HAMPSHIRE FOOD INDUSTRY SCHOLARSHIPS
• *See page 547*

NEW JERSEY DEPARTMENT OF MILITARY AND VETERANS AFFAIRS

http://www.state.nj.us/military

NEW JERSEY WAR ORPHANS TUITION ASSISTANCE
• *See page 604*

POW-MIA TUITION BENEFIT PROGRAM
• *See page 604*

VETERANS TUITION CREDIT PROGRAM-NEW JERSEY
• *See page 604*

NEW JERSEY HIGHER EDUCATION STUDENT ASSISTANCE AUTHORITY

http://www.hesaa.org/

DANA CHRISTMAS SCHOLARSHIP FOR HEROISM

Honors young New Jersey residents for acts of heroism. Scholarship is a nonrenewable award of up to $10,000 for 5 students. This scholarship may be used for undergraduate or graduate study. Deadline varies.

Award: Scholarship for use in freshman, sophomore, junior, or senior years; not renewable. *Number:* up to 5. *Amount:* up to $10,000.

Eligibility Requirements: Applicant must be enrolled or expecting to enroll full- or part-time at a two-year or four-year or technical institution or university and resident of New Jersey. Available to U.S. citizens.

Application Requirements: Application form. *Deadline:* varies.

Contact: Gisele Joachim, Director, Financial Aid Services
New Jersey Higher Education Student Assistance Authority
4 Quakerbridge Plaza, PO Box 540
Trenton, NJ 08625
Phone: 800-792-8670 Ext. 2349
Fax: 609-588-7389
E-mail: gjoachim@hesaa.org

LAW ENFORCEMENT OFFICER MEMORIAL SCHOLARSHIP
• *See page 562*

NEW JERSEY STUDENT TUITION ASSISTANCE REWARD SCHOLARSHIP II

Earn an associate degree from the home New Jersey county college as an NJ STARS recipient and graduate with a cumulative GPA of 3.25 or higher. Family income (taxable and untaxed income) must be less than $250,000 as derived from the FAFSA. NJ STARS II students may receive up to $1,250 per semester, paid completely by the State, after all other sources of federal and State grants and scholarships are applied to tuition charges.

Award: Scholarship for use in freshman year; renewable. *Number:* 2500–2500. *Amount:* up to $2500.

Eligibility Requirements: Applicant must be enrolled or expecting to enroll full-time at a four-year institution or university; resident of New Jersey and studying in New Jersey. Applicant must have 3.0 GPA or higher. Available to U.S. citizens.

Application Requirements: Application form, FAFSA. *Deadline:* varies.

Contact: Mr. Andre Maglione, Acting Director of Client Services and Marketing
New Jersey Higher Education Student Assistance Authority
PO Box 071
Trenton, NJ 08625
Phone: 609-584-4486
Fax: 609-588-7389
E-mail: amaglione@hesaa.org

NEW JERSEY WORLD TRADE CENTER SCHOLARSHIP

Scholarship was established by the legislature to aid the dependent children and surviving spouses of New Jersey residents who were killed in the terrorist attacks, or who are missing and officially presumed dead as a direct result of the attacks; applies to instate and out-of-state institutions for students seeking undergraduate degrees. Deadlines: March 1 for fall, October 1 for spring.

Award: Scholarship for use in freshman, sophomore, junior, or senior years; renewable. *Amount:* up to $6500.

Eligibility Requirements: Applicant must be enrolled or expecting to enroll full-time at a four-year institution or university and resident of New Jersey. Available to U.S. citizens.

Application Requirements: Application form. *Deadline:* varies.

Contact: Giselle Joachim, Director of Financial Aid Services
New Jersey Higher Education Student Assistance Authority
PO Box 540
Trenton, NJ 08625
Phone: 800-792-8670 Ext. 2349
Fax: 609-588-7389
E-mail: gjoachim@hesaa.org

NJ STUDENT TUITION ASSISTANCE REWARD SCHOLARSHIP

Scholarship for students who graduate in the top 15 percent of their high school class. Recipients may be awarded up to five semesters of tuition (up to 15 credits per term) at one of New Jersey's nineteen county colleges.

Award: Scholarship for use in freshman, sophomore, junior, or senior years; renewable. *Amount:* $500–$2600.

Eligibility Requirements: Applicant must be enrolled or expecting to enroll full-time at a two-year or four-year institution or university; resident of New Jersey and studying in New Jersey. Applicant must have 3.0 GPA or higher. Available to U.S. citizens.

Application Requirements: Application form, transcript. *Deadline:* varies.

Contact: Carol Muka, Assistant Director of Grants and Scholarships
New Jersey Higher Education Student Assistance Authority
PO Box 540
Trenton, NJ 08625
Phone: 800-792-8670 Ext. 3266
Fax: 609-588-2228
E-mail: cmuka@hessa.org

PART-TIME TUITION AID GRANT (TAG) FOR COUNTY COLLEGES

Provides financial aid to eligible part-time undergraduate students enrolled for 9 to 11 credits at participating New Jersey community colleges. Deadlines are March 1 for spring and October 1 for fall.

Award: Grant for use in freshman, sophomore, junior, or senior years; not renewable. *Amount:* $419–$628.

Eligibility Requirements: Applicant must be enrolled or expecting to enroll part-time at a two-year or four-year institution or university; resident of New Jersey and studying in New Jersey. Available to U.S. citizens.

Application Requirements: Application form, financial need analysis. *Deadline:* varies.

Contact: Sherri Fox, Acting Director of Grants and Scholarships
New Jersey Higher Education Student Assistance Authority
PO Box 540
Trenton, NJ 08625
Phone: 800-792-8670
Fax: 609-588-2228

SURVIVOR TUITION BENEFITS PROGRAM
• *See page 562*

TUITION AID GRANT

The program provides tuition fees to eligible undergraduate students attending participating in-state institutions. Deadlines are March 1 for fall and October 1 for spring.

Award: Grant for use in freshman, sophomore, junior, or senior years; not renewable. *Amount:* $868–$7272.

Eligibility Requirements: Applicant must be enrolled or expecting to enroll full-time at a two-year or four-year institution or university; resident of New Jersey and studying in New Jersey. Available to U.S. citizens.

Application Requirements: Application form, financial need analysis. *Deadline:* varies.

Contact: Sherri Fox, Acting Director of Grants and Scholarships
New Jersey Higher Education Student Assistance Authority
PO Box 540
Trenton, NJ 08625
Phone: 800-792-8670
Fax: 609-588-2228

NEW JERSEY VIETNAM VETERANS' MEMORIAL FOUNDATION

http://www.njvvmf.org/

NEW JERSEY VIETNAM VETERANS' MEMORIAL FOUNDATION SCHOLARSHIP

One-time scholarship for graduating high school seniors of New Jersey. For full-time study only.

Award: Scholarship for use in freshman year; not renewable. *Number:* 2. *Amount:* $2500.

Eligibility Requirements: Applicant must be high school student; planning to enroll or expecting to enroll full-time at a two-year or four-year or technical institution or university and resident of New Jersey. Available to U.S. citizens.

Application Requirements: Application form, college acceptance letter, essay. *Deadline:* April 19.

Contact: Lynn Duane, Administrator
New Jersey Vietnam Veterans' Memorial Foundation
One Memorial Lane, PO Box 648
Holmdel, NJ 07733
Phone: 732-335-0033 Ext. 100
Fax: 732-335-1107
E-mail: lduane@njvvmf.org

NEW MEXICO COMMISSION ON HIGHER EDUCATION

http://www.hed.state.nm.us/

COLLEGE AFFORDABILITY GRANT

Grant available to New Mexico students with financial need who do not qualify for other state grants and scholarships to attend and complete educational programs at a New Mexico public college or university. Student must have unmet need after all other financial aid has been awarded. Student may not be receiving any other state grants or scholarships. Renewable upon satisfactory academic progress.

Award: Grant for use in freshman, sophomore, junior, or senior years; renewable. *Number:* 1. *Amount:* up to $1000.

Eligibility Requirements: Applicant must be enrolled or expecting to enroll full- or part-time at a two-year or four-year institution or university; resident of New Mexico and studying in New Mexico. Available to U.S. citizens.

Application Requirements: Application form, FAFSA, financial need analysis. *Deadline:* continuous.

Contact: Tashina Acker, Director of Financial Aid
New Mexico Commission on Higher Education
1068 Cerrillos Road
Santa Fe, NM 87505-1650
Phone: 505-476-6549
Fax: 505-476-6511
E-mail: tashina.banks-moore@state.nm.us

LEGISLATIVE ENDOWMENT SCHOLARSHIPS

Renewable scholarships to provide aid for undergraduate students with substantial financial need who are attending public postsecondary institutions in New Mexico. Four-year schools may award up to $2500 per academic year, two-year schools may award up to $1000 per academic year. Deadlines varies.

Award: Scholarship for use in freshman, sophomore, junior, or senior years; renewable. *Number:* 1. *Amount:* $1000–$2500.

Eligibility Requirements: Applicant must be enrolled or expecting to enroll full- or part-time at a two-year or four-year institution or university; resident of New Mexico and studying in New Mexico. Available to U.S. citizens.

Application Requirements: Application form, FAFSA, financial need analysis. *Deadline:* varies.

Contact: Tashina Moore, Director of Financial Aid
New Mexico Commission on Higher Education
1068 Cerrillos Road
Santa Fe, NM 87505-1650
Phone: 505-475-6549
Fax: 505-476-6511
E-mail: tashina.banks-moore@state.nm.us

LEGISLATIVE LOTTERY SCHOLARSHIP

Renewable Scholarship for New Mexico high school graduates or GED recipients who plan to attend an eligible New Mexico public college or university. Must be enrolled full-time and maintain 2.5 GPA.

Award: Scholarship for use in freshman year; renewable. *Number:* 1.

Eligibility Requirements: Applicant must be high school student; planning to enroll or expecting to enroll full-time at a four-year institution or university; resident of New Mexico and studying in New Mexico. Applicant must have 3.5 GPA or higher. Available to U.S. citizens.

Application Requirements: Application form, FAFSA. *Deadline:* varies.

Contact: Tashina Moore, Director of Financial Aid
New Mexico Commission on Higher Education
1068 Cerrillos Road
Santa Fe, NM 87505
Phone: 505-476-6549
Fax: 505-476-6511
E-mail: tashina.banks-moore@state.nm.us

NEW MEXICO SCHOLARS' PROGRAM

Renewable award program created to encourage New Mexico high school students to attend public postsecondary institutions or the following private colleges in New Mexico: College of Santa Fe, St. John's College, College of the Southwest. For details visit http://fin.hed.state.nm.us.

Award: Scholarship for use in freshman year; renewable. *Number:* 1.

Eligibility Requirements: Applicant must be high school student; planning to enroll or expecting to enroll full-time at a two-year or four-year institution; resident of New Mexico and studying in New Mexico. Available to U.S. citizens.

Application Requirements: Application form, FAFSA, financial need analysis, test scores. *Deadline:* varies.

Contact: Tashina Moore, Director of Financial Aid
New Mexico Commission on Higher Education
1068 Cerrillos Road
Santa Fe, NM 87505-1650
Phone: 505-476-6549
Fax: 505-476-6511
E-mail: tashina.banks-moore@state.nm.us

NEW MEXICO STUDENT INCENTIVE GRANT

Grant created to provide aid for undergraduate students with substantial financial need who are attending public colleges or universities or the following eligible colleges in New Mexico: College of Santa Fe, St.

John's College, College of the Southwest, Institute of American Indian Art, Crownpoint Institute of Technology, Dine College and Southwestern Indian Polytechnic Institute. Part-time students are eligible for pro-rated awards.

Award: Grant for use in freshman, sophomore, junior, or senior years; not renewable. *Number:* 1. *Amount:* $200–$2500.

Eligibility Requirements: Applicant must be enrolled or expecting to enroll full- or part-time at a two-year or four-year or technical institution or university; resident of New Mexico and studying in New Mexico. Available to U.S. citizens.

Application Requirements: Application form, FAFSA, financial need analysis. *Deadline:* varies.

Contact: Tashina Moore, Director of Financial Aid
New Mexico Commission on Higher Education
1068 Cerrillos Road
Santa Fe, NM 87505-1650
Phone: 505-476-6549
Fax: 505-476-6511
E-mail: tashina.banks-moore@state.nm.us

VIETNAM VETERANS' SCHOLARSHIP PROGRAM
• *See page 605*

NEW MEXICO DEPARTMENT OF VETERANS' SERVICES
http://www.dvs.state.nm.us/

CHILDREN OF DECEASED VETERANS SCHOLARSHIP-NEW MEXICO
• *See page 605*

NEW MEXICO VIETNAM VETERAN SCHOLARSHIP
• *See page 605*

NEW YORK STATE EDUCATION DEPARTMENT
http://www.highered.nysed.gov/

SCHOLARSHIP FOR ACADEMIC EXCELLENCE
Renewable award for New York residents. Scholarship winners must attend a college or university in New York. 2000 scholarships are for $1500 and 6000 are for $500. The selection criteria used are based on Regents test scores or rank in class or local exam. Must be U.S. citizen or permanent resident.

Award: Scholarship for use in freshman year; renewable. *Number:* up to 8000. *Amount:* $500–$1500.

Eligibility Requirements: Applicant must be high school student; planning to enroll or expecting to enroll full-time at a two-year or four-year institution or university; resident of New York and studying in New York. Available to U.S. citizens.

Application Requirements: Application form. *Deadline:* December 19.

Contact: Lewis Hall, Supervisor
Phone: 518-486-1319
Fax: 518-486-5346
E-mail: scholar@mail.nysed.gov

NEW YORK STATE GRANGE
http://www.nysgrange.org/

CAROLINE KARK AWARD
• *See page 530*

SUSAN W. FREESTONE EDUCATION AWARD
• *See page 530*

NEW YORK STATE HIGHER EDUCATION SERVICES CORPORATION
http://www.hesc.com/

NEW YORK AID FOR PART-TIME STUDY (APTS)
Renewable scholarship provides tuition assistance to part-time undergraduate students who are New York residents, meet income eligibility requirements and are attending New York accredited institutions. Deadline varies. Must be U.S. citizen.

Award: Grant for use in freshman, sophomore, junior, or senior years; renewable. *Amount:* up to $2000.

Eligibility Requirements: Applicant must be enrolled or expecting to enroll part-time at a two-year or four-year institution or university; resident of New York and studying in New York. Available to U.S. citizens.

Application Requirements: Application form, financial need analysis. *Deadline:* varies.

NEW YORK MEMORIAL SCHOLARSHIPS FOR FAMILIES OF DECEASED POLICE OFFICERS, FIRE FIGHTERS, AND PEACE OFFICERS
Renewable scholarship for children, spouses and financial dependents of deceased fire fighters, volunteer firefighters, police officers, peace officers and emergency medical service workers who died in the line of duty. Provides up to the cost of SUNY educational expenses.

Award: Scholarship for use in freshman, sophomore, junior, or senior years; renewable.

Eligibility Requirements: Applicant must be enrolled or expecting to enroll full-time at a four-year institution or university; resident of New York and studying in New York. Available to U.S. citizens.

Application Requirements: Application form, financial need analysis, transcript. *Deadline:* May 1.

NEW YORK STATE AID TO NATIVE AMERICANS
• *See page 633*

NEW YORK STATE TUITION ASSISTANCE PROGRAM
Award for New York state residents attending a New York postsecondary institution. Must be full-time student in approved program with tuition over $200 per year. Must show financial need and not be in default in any other state program. Renewable award of $500 to $5000 dependent on family income and tuition charged.

Award: Grant for use in freshman, sophomore, junior, or senior years; renewable. *Number:* 350,000–360,000. *Amount:* $500–$5000.

Eligibility Requirements: Applicant must be enrolled or expecting to enroll full-time at a two-year or four-year institution or university; resident of New York and studying in New York. Available to U.S. citizens.

Application Requirements: Application form, financial need analysis. *Deadline:* May 1.

NEW YORK VIETNAM/PERSIAN GULF/AFGHANISTAN VETERANS TUITION AWARDS
• *See page 605*

REGENTS AWARD FOR CHILD OF VETERAN
• *See page 605*

SCHOLARSHIPS FOR ACADEMIC EXCELLENCE
Renewable awards of up to $1500 for academically outstanding New York State high school graduates planning to attend an approved postsecondary institution in New York State. For full-time study only. Contact high school guidance counselor to apply.

Award: Scholarship for use in freshman, sophomore, junior, or senior years; renewable. *Number:* up to 8000. *Amount:* $500–$1500.

Eligibility Requirements: Applicant must be high school student; planning to enroll or expecting to enroll full-time at a four-year institution or university; resident of New York and studying in New York. Available to U.S. citizens.

Application Requirements: Application form. *Deadline:* varies.

Contact: Rita McGivern, Student Information
New York State Higher Education Services Corporation
99 Washington Avenue, Room 1320
Albany, NY 12255
E-mail: scholarship@hesc.com

NORTH CAROLINA 4-H

http://www.nc4h.org/

NORTH CAROLINA 4-H DEVELOPMENT FUND SCHOLARSHIPS

Scholarship for a resident of North Carolina, enrolling as an undergraduate in a four-year accredited North Carolina college or university or a junior or community college in the state, provided the program of study selected is transferable to a four-year college. Must demonstrate an aptitude for college work through SAT scores. For some of the awards, financial need is a prerequisite. Some awards have geographic restrictions to regions of the state. Some scholarships are renewable.

Award: Scholarship for use in freshman, sophomore, junior, or senior years; renewable. *Amount:* $500–$2500.

Eligibility Requirements: Applicant must be enrolled or expecting to enroll full-time at a two-year or four-year institution or university; resident of North Carolina and studying in North Carolina. Available to U.S. citizens.

Application Requirements: Application form, financial need analysis, test scores, transcript. *Deadline:* January 15.

Contact: Shannon McCollum, Extension 4-H Associate
E-mail: shannon_mccollum@ncsu.edu

NORTH CAROLINA ASSOCIATION OF EDUCATORS

http://www.ncae.org/

NORTH CAROLINA ASSOCIATION OF EDUCATORS MARTIN LUTHER KING JR. SCHOLARSHIP

One-time award for high school seniors who are North Carolina residents to attend a postsecondary institution. Must be a U.S. citizen. Based upon financial need, GPA, and essay. Must have a GPA of at least 3.5 on a 5.0 scale or a 2.5 on a 4.0 scale.

Award: Scholarship for use in freshman year; not renewable. *Number:* 3–4. *Amount:* $500–$1000.

Eligibility Requirements: Applicant must be high school student; planning to enroll or expecting to enroll full-time at a four-year institution or university and resident of North Carolina. Available to U.S. citizens.

Application Requirements: Application form, community service, essay, financial need analysis, recommendations or references, test scores, transcript. *Deadline:* February 1.

Contact: Derevana Leach, Scholarship Coordinator
North Carolina Association of Educators
PO Box 27347
Raleigh, NC 27611
Phone: 800-662-7924 Ext. 205
E-mail: derevana.leach@ncae.org

NORTH CAROLINA BAR ASSOCIATION

http://www.ncbar.org/

NORTH CAROLINA BAR ASSOCIATION YOUNG LAWYERS DIVISION SCHOLARSHIP

Renewable award for children of North Carolina Law Enforcement Officers killed or permanently disabled in the line of duty, studying full-time in accredited colleges or universities. Must be resident of North Carolina and under 26 years of age for first time application. The number of awards and the dollar value of the award varies annually.

Award: Scholarship for use in freshman, sophomore, junior, senior, graduate, or postgraduate years; renewable.

Eligibility Requirements: Applicant must be enrolled or expecting to enroll full-time at a two-year or four-year or technical institution or university and resident of North Carolina. Available to U.S. citizens.

Application Requirements: Application form, essay, financial need analysis, personal photograph, test scores, transcript, verification letter from law enforcement agency. *Deadline:* April 1.

Contact: Ms. Jacquelyn Terrell, Director of Sections/Divisions
Activities, YLD Staff Liaison
North Carolina Bar Association
PO Box 3688
Cary, NC 27519
Phone: 919-677-0561 Ext. 331
Fax: 919-677-0761
E-mail: jterrell@ncbar.org

NORTH CAROLINA DIVISION OF SERVICES FOR THE BLIND

http://www.ncdhhs.gov/

NORTH CAROLINA DIVISION OF SERVICES FOR THE BLIND REHABILITATION SERVICES

• *See page 576*

NORTH CAROLINA DIVISION OF VETERANS AFFAIRS

http://www.doa.state.nc.us/vets/va.htm

NORTH CAROLINA VETERANS SCHOLARSHIPS CLASS I-A

• *See page 605*

NORTH CAROLINA VETERANS SCHOLARSHIPS CLASS I-B

• *See page 606*

NORTH CAROLINA VETERANS SCHOLARSHIPS CLASS II

• *See page 606*

NORTH CAROLINA VETERANS SCHOLARSHIPS CLASS III

• *See page 606*

NORTH CAROLINA VETERANS SCHOLARSHIPS CLASS IV

• *See page 606*

NORTH CAROLINA DIVISION OF VOCATIONAL REHABILITATION SERVICES

http://www.dhhs.state.nc.us/

TRAINING SUPPORT FOR YOUTH WITH DISABILITIES

• *See page 576*

NORTH CAROLINA NATIONAL GUARD

http://www.nc.ngb.army.mil/

NORTH CAROLINA NATIONAL GUARD TUITION ASSISTANCE PROGRAM

• *See page 585*

NORTH CAROLINA SOCIETY OF HISPANIC PROFESSIONALS

http://www.thencshp.org/

NORTH CAROLINA HISPANIC COLLEGE FUND SCHOLARSHIP

• *See page 633*

NORTH CAROLINA STATE EDUCATION ASSISTANCE AUTHORITY

http://www.ncseaa.edu/

AUBREY LEE BROOKS SCHOLARSHIPS

A renewable scholarship for graduating high school seniors who are residents of designated North Carolina counties: Alamance, Bertie, Caswell, Durham. Forsyth, Granville, Guilford, Orange, Person, Rockingham, Stokes, Surry, Swain and Warren counties. The scholarship may be used at North Carolina State University, the University of North Carolina at Chapel Hill or the University of North Carolina at Greensboro. Scholarship is renewable, provided the recipient has continued financial need, remains enrolled full-time at an eligible institution and maintains specified academic standards. Additional details and application at http://www.CFNC.org/Brooks

Award: Scholarship for use in freshman, sophomore, junior, or senior years; renewable. *Number:* 17–17. *Amount:* up to $11,100.

Eligibility Requirements: Applicant must be high school student; planning to enroll or expecting to enroll full-time at a four-year institution or university; resident of North Carolina and studying in North Carolina. Available to U.S. and non-Canadian citizens.

Application Requirements: Application form, application form may be submitted online (http://www.CFNC.org/Brooks), essay, financial need analysis, interview, recommendations or references, test scores, transcript. *Deadline:* January 31.

Contact: Mr. Trae Brookins, Scholarship and Grant Manager
North Carolina State Education Assistance Authority
PO Box 13663
Research Triangle Park, NC 27709-3663
Phone: 919-248-4650
Fax: 919-248-6650
E-mail: tbrookins@ncseaa.edu

JAGANNATHAN SCHOLARSHIP

Available to graduating high school seniors who plan to enroll as college freshmen in a full-time degree program at one of the constituent institutions of The University of North Carolina. Applicant must be resident of North Carolina. Applicant must document financial need.

Award: Scholarship for use in freshman year; renewable. *Amount:* up to $3500.

Eligibility Requirements: Applicant must be enrolled or expecting to enroll full-time at a four-year institution or university; resident of North Carolina and studying in North Carolina. Applicant must have 3.0 GPA or higher. Available to U.S. citizens.

Application Requirements: Application form, financial need analysis. *Deadline:* February 15.

Contact: Bill Carswell, Manager of Scholarship and Grant Division
North Carolina State Education Assistance Authority
PO Box 13663
Research Triangle Park, NC 27709
Phone: 919-549-8614
Fax: 919-248-4687
E-mail: carswellb@ncseaa.edu

NORTH CAROLINA COMMUNITY COLLEGE GRANT PROGRAM

Grants are available to North Carolina residents who demonstrate financial need and are enrolled at NC community colleges. The applicant must be a NC resident for tuition purposes, enroll for at least six credit hours per semester in a curriculum program, and meet the Satisfactory Academic Progress requirements of the institution. Eligibility is determined based on the same criteria as the Federal Pell Grant; students not eligible for the Federal Pell Grant may be considered for the grant based on the expected family contribution (EFC). Student who have earned a bachelor's (four-year) degree already are ineligible. Applicants must complete the Free Application for Federal Student Aid (FAFSA). Consideration is AUTOMATIC once the FAFSA is filed. Please contact the financial aid office at the local community college for more specific information regarding institutional processes.

Award: Grant for use in freshman or sophomore years; not renewable. *Number:* 25,000. *Amount:* $150–$950.

Eligibility Requirements: Applicant must be enrolled or expecting to enroll full- or part-time at a two-year or technical institution; resident of North Carolina and studying in North Carolina. Available to U.S. citizens.

Application Requirements: Application form may be submitted online (http://www.CFNC.org/NCCCG), FAFSA, financial need analysis. *Deadline:* varies.

Contact: Trae Brookins, Scholarship and Grant Manager
North Carolina State Education Assistance Authority
PO Box 13663
Research Triangle Park, NC 27709-3663
Phone: 919-248-4650
Fax: 919-248-6650
E-mail: tbrookins@ncseaa.edu

UNIVERSITY OF NORTH CAROLINA NEED-BASED GRANT

Applicants must be enrolled in at least 6 credit hours at one of sixteen UNC system universities. Eligibility based on need; award varies, consideration for grant automatic when FAFSA is filed. Late applications may be denied due to insufficient funds.

Award: Grant for use in freshman, sophomore, junior, or senior years; renewable.

Eligibility Requirements: Applicant must be enrolled or expecting to enroll full- or part-time at an institution or university; resident of North Carolina and studying in North Carolina. Available to U.S. citizens.

Application Requirements: Application form, FAFSA, financial need analysis. *Deadline:* varies.

Contact: Bill Carswell, Manager of Scholarship and Grant Division
North Carolina State Education Assistance Authority
PO Box 13663
Research Triangle Park, NC 27709
Phone: 919-549-8614
Fax: 919-248-4687
E-mail: carswellb@ncseaa.edu

NORTH DAKOTA UNIVERSITY SYSTEM

http://www.ndus.edu/

NORTH DAKOTA ACADEMIC SCHOLARSHIP

The ND Academic Scholarships goal is to reward students for taking rigorous high school courses and to retain students in ND. The scholarship has an ACT test score and GPA requirement, and requires students to complete specific high school courses. The scholarship is jointly administered with the Department of Public Instruction (DPI). DPI verifies eligibility, and the ND University System disburses funds and verifies continued eligibility. Students must be enrolled full-time and must maintain a cumulative GPA of 2.75 or higher.

Award: Scholarship for use in freshman, sophomore, junior, or senior years; renewable. *Number:* up to 10,000. *Amount:* $6000.

Eligibility Requirements: Applicant must be high school student; planning to enroll or expecting to enroll full-time at a two-year or four-year institution or university; resident of North Dakota and studying in North Dakota. Applicant must have 3.0 GPA or higher. Available to U.S. citizens.

Application Requirements: Application form, application form may be submitted online (https://www.dpi.state.nd.us/DPI/Scholarship/Login.aspx?ReturnUrl=%2fdpi%2fScholarship%2flogin.aspx%2f), test scores, transcript. *Deadline:* June 7.

Contact: Gina Padilla, Assistant Director of Financial Aid
North Dakota University System
1815 Schafer Street, Suite 202
Bismarck, ND 58501
Phone: 701-224-2647
E-mail: ndfinaid@ndus.edu

NORTH DAKOTA CAREER AND TECHNICAL EDUCATION SCHOLARSHIP

The ND Career and Technical Education Scholarship's goal is to reward students taking rigorous courses in high school, to increase awareness of career and technical programs, and to retain students in ND. The scholarship has an ACT or WorkKeys exam score requirement, a GPA requirement, and a specific high school course list that must be completed to qualify. The scholarships are jointly administered with the Department of Public Instruction (DPI). DPI verifies eligibility requirements, and the ND University System disburses funds and verifies continued eligibility. Students must be enrolled full-time and cumulative GPA must be 2.75 or higher.

Award: Scholarship for use in freshman, sophomore, junior, or senior years; renewable. *Number:* up to 10,000. *Amount:* $6000.

Eligibility Requirements: Applicant must be high school student; planning to enroll or expecting to enroll full-time at a two-year or four-year institution or university; resident of North Dakota and studying in North Dakota. Applicant must have 3.0 GPA or higher. Available to U.S. citizens.

Application Requirements: Application form, application form may be submitted online (https://www.dpi.state.nd.us/DPI/Scholarship/Login.aspx?ReturnUrl=%2fdpi%2fScholarship%2flogin.aspx%2f), test scores, transcript. *Deadline:* June 7.

Contact: Gina Padilla, Assistant Director of Financial Aid
North Dakota University System
1815 Schafer Street, Suite 202
Bismarck, ND 58501
Phone: 701-224-2647
E-mail: ndfinaid@ndus.edu

NORTH DAKOTA INDIAN SCHOLARSHIP PROGRAM
• See page 634

NORTH DAKOTA SCHOLARS PROGRAM
Provides scholarships equal to cost of tuition at the public colleges in North Dakota for North Dakota residents. To be eligible for consideration for a ND Scholars scholarship, a high school junior must take the ACT Assessment between October and June of their junior year and score in the upper five percentile of all ND ACT test takers. The numeric sum of the English, Math, reading and science reasoning scores will be used as a second selection criteria. The numeric sum of a student's English and mathematics scores will be used as selection criteria if a tie-breaker is needed.

Award: Scholarship for use in freshman, sophomore, junior, or senior years; renewable. *Number:* 45–50. *Amount:* $4588–$8135.

Eligibility Requirements: Applicant must be high school student; planning to enroll or expecting to enroll full-time at a two-year or four-year institution or university; resident of North Dakota and studying in North Dakota. Available to U.S. citizens.

Application Requirements: No application required, test scores.

NORTH DAKOTA STATE STUDENT INCENTIVE GRANT PROGRAM
The North Dakota State Grant supports North Dakota residents attending an approved college or university in North Dakota. Must be enrolled in a program of at least nine months in length. Must be a U.S. citizen. Completing the FAFSA is the only application required.

Award: Grant for use in freshman, sophomore, junior, or senior years; not renewable. *Number:* 7500–8500. *Amount:* $750–$1500.

Eligibility Requirements: Applicant must be enrolled or expecting to enroll full-time at a two-year or four-year institution or university; resident of North Dakota and studying in North Dakota. Available to U.S. citizens.

Application Requirements: Financial need analysis, submit a FAFSA. *Deadline:* April 15.

OHIO ASSOCIATION FOR ADULT AND CONTINUING EDUCATION
http://www.oaace.org/

LIFELONG LEARNING SCHOLARSHIP
Scholarship available for a Ohio resident student with Ohio high school equivalence diploma or high school diploma, who is currently enrolled in any adult education program or has been enrolled within the last twelve months. Must enroll in postsecondary education or training within six months of receiving scholarship. Number of awards granted varies.

Award: Scholarship for use in freshman year; not renewable. *Amount:* $1500.

Eligibility Requirements: Applicant must be high school student; planning to enroll or expecting to enroll full-time at a four-year institution or university and resident of Ohio. Available to U.S. citizens.

Application Requirements: Application form, recommendations or references. *Deadline:* March 1.

LINDA LUCA MEMORIAL GED SCHOLARSHIP
$1500 scholarship available for a Ohio resident student who scored in the top 100 of GED scores for the year. Must enroll in postsecondary education or training within six months of receiving scholarship.

Award: Scholarship for use in freshman year; not renewable. *Amount:* $1500.

Eligibility Requirements: Applicant must be high school student; planning to enroll or expecting to enroll full-time at a four-year institution or university and resident of Ohio. Available to U.S. citizens.

Application Requirements: Application form, recommendations or references. *Deadline:* varies.

OAACE MEMBER SCHOLARSHIP
Scholarship for Ohio resident and member of OAACE. Should enroll in postsecondary education or professional development training within six months of receiving scholarship.

Award: Scholarship for use in freshman year; not renewable. *Amount:* $2000.

Eligibility Requirements: Applicant must be high school student; planning to enroll or expecting to enroll full-time at a four-year institution or university and resident of Ohio. Available to U.S. citizens.

Application Requirements: Application form, recommendations or references. *Deadline:* March 1.

OHIO ASSOCIATION OF CAREER COLLEGES AND SCHOOLS
http://www.ohiocareercolleges.org/

LEGISLATIVE SCHOLARSHIP
One-time scholarship for graduating high school seniors enrolling in a career college or school that is a participating member of OACCS. The applicant must be an Ohio high school student with a 2.0 GPA or better and does not have to demonstrate a financial need. The scholarship amount and the number of scholarships granted varies.

Award: Scholarship for use in freshman or sophomore years; not renewable. *Number:* 300–350. *Amount:* $2000–$12,995.

Eligibility Requirements: Applicant must be high school student; planning to enroll or expecting to enroll full-time at a two-year or four-year or technical institution or university; resident of Ohio and studying in Ohio. Available to U.S. and non-U.S. citizens.

Application Requirements: Application form, essay, recommendations or references, transcript. *Deadline:* April 1.

Contact: R. Rankin, Executive Director
Phone: 614-487-8180
Fax: 614-487-8190
E-mail: oaccs1@aol.com

OHIO BOARD OF REGENTS
http://www.ohiohighered.org

OHIO COLLEGE OPPORTUNITY GRANT
OCOG provides grant money to Ohio residents who demonstrate the highest levels of financial need (as determined by the results of the FAFSA) who are enrolled at Ohio public university main campuses (not regional campuses or community colleges), Ohio private, non-profit colleges or universities, Ohio private, for-profit institutions or eligible Pennsylvania institutions.

Award: Grant for use in freshman, sophomore, junior, or senior years; not renewable. *Amount:* up to $2280.

Eligibility Requirements: Applicant must be enrolled or expecting to enroll full- or part-time at a two-year or four-year institution or university; resident of Ohio and studying in Ohio, Pennsylvania. Available to U.S. citizens.

Application Requirements: Application form may be submitted online (http://www.fafsa.ed.gov/), FAFSA. *Deadline:* October 1.

Contact: Tamika Braswell, Program Manager
Ohio Board of Regents
25 South Front Street
Columbus, OH 43215
Phone: 614-728-8862
Fax: 614-752-5903
E-mail: ocog_admin@regents.state.oh.us

OHIO SAFETY OFFICERS COLLEGE MEMORIAL FUND

Renewable award covering up to full tuition is available to children and surviving spouses of peace officers, other safety officers and fire fighters killed in the line of duty in any state. Children must be under 26 years of age. Dollar value of each award varies. Must be an Ohio resident and enroll full-time or part-time at an Ohio college or university. Any spouse/child of a member of the armed services of the U.S., who has been killed in the line duty during Operation Enduring Freedom, Operation Iraqi Freedom or a combat zone designated by the President of the United States. Dollar value of each award varies.

Award: Scholarship for use in freshman, sophomore, junior, or senior years; renewable.

Eligibility Requirements: Applicant must be enrolled or expecting to enroll full- or part-time at a two-year or four-year institution or university; resident of Ohio and studying in Ohio. Available to U.S. citizens.

Application Requirements: *Deadline:* continuous.

Contact: Barbara Thoma, Assistant Director
Ohio Board of Regents
30 East Broad Street, 36th Floor
Columbus, OH 43215
Phone: 614-752-9535
Fax: 614-752-5903
E-mail: osom_admin@regents.state.oh.us

OHIO WAR ORPHANS SCHOLARSHIP
• *See page 606*

OHIO CIVIL SERVICE EMPLOYEES ASSOCIATION

http://www.ocsea.org/

LES BEST SCHOLARSHIP
• *See page 531*

OHIO NATIONAL GUARD

http://www.ongsp.org/

OHIO NATIONAL GUARD SCHOLARSHIP PROGRAM
• *See page 585*

OKLAHOMA ALUMNI & ASSOCIATES OF FHA, HERO AND FCCLA INC.

http://www.okfccla.net/

OKLAHOMA ALUMNI & ASSOCIATES OF FHA, HERO, AND FCCLA INC. SCHOLARSHIP
• *See page 531*

OKLAHOMA STATE REGENTS FOR HIGHER EDUCATION

http://www.okhighered.org/

OKLAHOMA TUITION AID GRANT

Award for Oklahoma residents enrolled at an Oklahoma institution at least part time each semester in a degree program. May be enrolled in two- or four-year or approved vocational-technical institution. Award for students attending public institutions or private colleges. Application is made through FAFSA.

Award: Grant for use in freshman, sophomore, junior, or senior years; not renewable. *Amount:* $1000–$1300.

Eligibility Requirements: Applicant must be enrolled or expecting to enroll full- or part-time at a two-year or four-year or technical institution or university; resident of Oklahoma and studying in Oklahoma. Available to U.S. citizens.

Application Requirements: Application form, FAFSA, financial need analysis. *Deadline:* varies.

Contact: Mr. Chris Wadsworth, Scholarship Programs Coordinator
Phone: 405-225-9131
E-mail: cwadsworth@osrhe.edu

REGIONAL UNIVERSITY BACCALAUREATE SCHOLARSHIP

Renewable award for Oklahoma residents attending one of 11 participating Oklahoma public universities. Must have an ACT composite score of at least 30 or be a National Merit semifinalist or commended student. In addition to the award amount, each recipient will receive a resident tuition waiver from the institution. Must maintain a 3.25 GPA. Deadlines vary depending upon the institution attended.

Award: Scholarship for use in freshman, sophomore, junior, or senior years; renewable. *Amount:* $3000.

Eligibility Requirements: Applicant must be enrolled or expecting to enroll full-time at an institution or university; resident of Oklahoma and studying in Oklahoma. Available to U.S. citizens.

Application Requirements: Application form. *Deadline:* varies.

WILLIAM P. WILLIS SCHOLARSHIP

Renewable award for low-income Oklahoma residents attending an Oklahoma institution. Must be a full-time undergraduate. Deadline varies.

Award: Scholarship for use in freshman, sophomore, junior, or senior years; renewable. *Amount:* $2000–$3000.

Eligibility Requirements: Applicant must be enrolled or expecting to enroll full-time at a two-year or four-year institution or university; resident of Oklahoma and studying in Oklahoma. Available to U.S. citizens.

Application Requirements: Application form. *Deadline:* varies.

OREGON COMMUNITY FOUNDATION

http://www.oregoncf.org/

ERNEST ALAN AND BARBARA PARK MEYER SCHOLARSHIP FUND

Scholarship for Oregon high school graduates for use in the pursuit of a postsecondary education (undergraduate or graduate) at a nonprofit two- or four-year college or university.

Award: Scholarship for use in freshman, sophomore, junior, or senior years; renewable. *Number:* up to 5. *Amount:* $1000–$4500.

Eligibility Requirements: Applicant must be enrolled or expecting to enroll full-time at a two-year or four-year or technical institution or university and resident of Oregon. Available to U.S. citizens.

Application Requirements: Application form, recommendations or references. *Deadline:* March 1.

Contact: Dianne Causey, Program Associate for Scholarships and Grants
Phone: 503-227-6846 Ext. 1418
E-mail: dcausey@oregoncf.org

FRIENDS OF BILL RUTHERFORD EDUCATION FUND

Scholarship for Oregon high school graduates or GED recipients who are dependent children of individuals holding statewide elected office or currently serving in the Oregon State Legislature. Students must be enrolled full time in a two- or four-year college or university. For more information, see web http://www.getcollegefunds.org.

Award: Scholarship for use in freshman, sophomore, junior, or senior years; renewable. *Number:* 1–2. *Amount:* $1000–$2500.

Eligibility Requirements: Applicant must be enrolled or expecting to enroll full-time at a two-year or four-year institution or university and resident of Oregon. Available to U.S. citizens.

Application Requirements: Application form, recommendations or references. *Deadline:* March 1.

Contact: Dianne Causey, Program Associate for Scholarships and Grants
> *Phone:* 503-227-6846 Ext. 1418
> *E-mail:* dcausey@oregoncf.org

MARY E. HORSTKOTTE SCHOLARSHIP FUND

Award available for academically talented and financially needy students for use in the pursuit of a postsecondary education. Must be an Oregon resident. For full-time study only.

Award: Scholarship for use in freshman, sophomore, junior, or senior years; not renewable. *Number:* 1–10. *Amount:* $2000.

Eligibility Requirements: Applicant must be enrolled or expecting to enroll full-time at a two-year or four-year or technical institution or university and resident of Oregon. Available to U.S. citizens.

Application Requirements: Application form, recommendations or references. *Deadline:* March 1.

Contact: Dianne Causey, Program Associate for Scholarships and Grants
> *Phone:* 503-227-6846 Ext. 1418
> *E-mail:* dcausey@oregoncf.org

RUBE AND MINAH LESLIE EDUCATIONAL FUND

Scholarship for Oregon residents for the pursuit of a postsecondary education. Selection is based on financial need.

Award: Scholarship for use in freshman, sophomore, junior, or senior years; renewable. *Number:* up to 50. *Amount:* $2000.

Eligibility Requirements: Applicant must be enrolled or expecting to enroll full-time at a two-year or four-year institution or university and resident of Oregon. Available to U.S. citizens.

Application Requirements: Application form, financial need analysis. *Deadline:* March 1.

Contact: Dianne Causey, Program Associate for Scholarships and Grants
> *Phone:* 503-227-6846 Ext. 1418
> *E-mail:* dcausey@oregoncf.org

WILLIAM L. AND DELLA WAGGONER SCHOLARSHIP FUND

Scholarship for undergraduates of any Oregon high school who show academic potential and financial need for use in the pursuit of a postsecondary education. For more information, see website at http://www.getcollegefunds.org.

Award: Scholarship for use in freshman, sophomore, junior, or senior years; renewable. *Number:* up to 30. *Amount:* $2000.

Eligibility Requirements: Applicant must be enrolled or expecting to enroll full-time at a two-year or four-year institution or university and resident of Oregon. Available to U.S. citizens.

Application Requirements: Application form. *Deadline:* March 1.

Contact: Dianne Causey, Program Associate for Scholarships and Grants
> *Phone:* 503-227-6846 Ext. 1418
> *E-mail:* dcausey@oregoncf.org

OREGON DEPARTMENT OF VETERANS' AFFAIRS

http://www.oregon.gov/odva

OREGON VETERANS' EDUCATION AID
• *See page 606*

OREGON STUDENT ASSISTANCE COMMISSION

http://www.GetCollegeFunds.org/

AFSCME: AMERICAN FEDERATION OF STATE, COUNTY, AND MUNICIPAL EMPLOYEES LOCAL 2067 SCHOLARSHIP
• *See page 531*

ANDEO SCHOLARSHIP

One-time award for graduating seniors (including GED recipients and home-schooled seniors) of Oregon or Washington high schools. Must have hosted an international student through ANDEO International Homestays in 2011, 2012, or 2013 and taken 3+ years of a foreign language by the end of the current academic year. Minimum 3.5 GPA preferred. Must enroll at least half time at any U.S. college or university.

Award: Scholarship for use in freshman year; not renewable.

Eligibility Requirements: Applicant must be high school student; planning to enroll or expecting to enroll full- or part-time at a four-year institution or university and resident of Oregon, Washington. Available to U.S. citizens.

Application Requirements: Application form, FAFSA. *Deadline:* March 1.

A. VICTOR ROSENFELD SCHOLARSHIP
• *See page 547*

BANDON SUBMARINE CABLE COUNCIL'S LENNY MONTALBANO MEMORIAL SCHOLARSHIP

Award for members or dependent children of members of the Bandon Submarine Cable Council; any commercial fisherman who resides in Coos County or family member; any postsecondary student residing in Clatsop, Coos, Curry, Lane, Lincoln, or Tillamook County; or any postsecondary student in Oregon. Essay must be submitted. Award is automatically renewable if criteria is met.

Award: Scholarship for use in freshman, sophomore, junior, senior, or graduate years; renewable.

Eligibility Requirements: Applicant must be enrolled or expecting to enroll full-time at a four-year institution and resident of Oregon. Available to U.S. citizens.

Application Requirements: Activities chart, FAFSA, application form, essay, financial need analysis, transcript. *Deadline:* March 1.

BENJAMIN FRANKLIN/EDITH GREEN SCHOLARSHIP

One-time award for graduating Oregon high school seniors to attend four-year public Oregon colleges. Minimum GPA of 3.45 to 3.55 required. Award is based on financial need.

Award: Scholarship for use in freshman year; not renewable.

Eligibility Requirements: Applicant must be high school student; planning to enroll or expecting to enroll full- or part-time at a four-year institution; resident of Oregon and studying in Oregon. Available to U.S. citizens.

Application Requirements: Activity chart, FAFSA, application form, essay, financial need analysis, transcript. *Deadline:* March 1.

BEN SELLING SCHOLARSHIP

Award for Oregon residents enrolling as undergraduate sophomores, juniors, or seniors. College GPA 3.5 or higher required. Apply/compete annually.

Award: Scholarship for use in sophomore, junior, or senior years; not renewable.

Eligibility Requirements: Applicant must be enrolled or expecting to enroll full-time at a two-year or four-year institution and resident of Oregon. Applicant must have 3.5 GPA or higher. Available to U.S. citizens.

Application Requirements: Activity chart, application form, essay, financial need analysis, recommendations or references, transcript. *Deadline:* March 1.

CONGRESSMAN PETER DEFAZIO SCHOLARSHIP

Award is available to dislocated workers residing in Oregon's Fourth Congressional District, which includes parts of Benton, Coos, Curry, Douglas, Josephine, Lane, and Linn counties. Recipients must attend one of Lane, Linn-Benton, Rogue, Southwestern Oregon or Umpqua Community Colleges and enroll at least half-time. If selected as a semi-finalist for the scholarship, verification of status as a dislocated worker is required.

Award: Scholarship for use in freshman, sophomore, junior, or senior years; not renewable.

Eligibility Requirements: Applicant must be enrolled or expecting to enroll full- or part-time at a two-year institution; resident of Oregon and studying in Oregon. Available to U.S. citizens.

Application Requirements: Application form, proof of unemployment, FAFSA. *Deadline:* March 1.

DOROTHY CAMPBELL MEMORIAL SCHOLARSHIP

Renewable award for female Oregon high school graduates with a minimum 2.75 GPA. Must submit essay describing strong, continuing interest in golf and the contribution that sport has made to applicant's development. Must have played on high school golf team (including intramural), if available.

Award: Scholarship for use in freshman, sophomore, junior, or senior years; renewable.

Eligibility Requirements: Applicant must be enrolled or expecting to enroll full-time at a four-year institution; female; resident of Oregon; studying in Oregon and must have an interest in golf. Available to U.S. citizens.

Application Requirements: Application form, essay, financial need analysis, transcript. *Deadline:* March 1.

ESSEX GENERAL CONSTRUCTION SCHOLARSHIP

• See page 547

FORD OPPORTUNITY PROGRAM

Renewable award for Oregon residents who are single heads of household with custody of a dependent child or children and without the support of a domestic partner. Must be planning to earn a bachelor's degree and study full-time at an Oregon college or university. Minimum cumulative GPA of 3.0 required. If minimum requirements are not met, special recommendation form required (see high school counselor or contact OSAC).

Award: Scholarship for use in freshman, sophomore, junior, or senior years; renewable.

Eligibility Requirements: Applicant must be enrolled or expecting to enroll full-time at a four-year institution or university; single; resident of Oregon and studying in Oregon. Applicant must have 3.0 GPA or higher. Available to U.S. citizens.

Application Requirements: Activities chart, application form, essay, financial need analysis, interview, transcript. *Deadline:* March 1.

FORD RESTART PROGRAM

Award to support nontraditional, full-time adult students who wish to begin or continue education at the postsecondary level in Oregon. Must be an Oregon resident and at least 25 years of age by March 1 of the application year. Must have a high school diploma or GED certificate and must not have previously earned a bachelors degree. A Restart Reference Form is required and must be submitted with the application. Strong preference given to applicants with little or no recent college experience.

Award: Scholarship for use in freshman, sophomore, junior, or senior years; renewable.

Eligibility Requirements: Applicant must be enrolled or expecting to enroll full-time at a two-year or four-year or technical institution or university; resident of Oregon and studying in Oregon. Available to U.S. citizens.

Application Requirements: Activity chart, reference form, FAFSA, application form, essay, financial need analysis, interview, transcript. *Deadline:* March 1.

FORD SCHOLARS PROGRAM

Renewable award for Oregon residents who are graduating high school seniors or students at the point of transferring from a community college to a four-year college. Must have minimum cumulative GPA of 3.0, be planning to earn a bachelor's degree, and be enrolled as a full-time student. If minimum requirements are not met, special recommendation form required (see high school counselor or contact OSAC).

Award: Scholarship for use in freshman, sophomore, junior, or senior years; renewable.

Eligibility Requirements: Applicant must be enrolled or expecting to enroll full-time at a four-year institution or university; resident of Oregon and studying in Oregon. Applicant must have 3.0 GPA or higher. Available to U.S. citizens.

Application Requirements: Application form, essay, financial need analysis, interview, test scores, transcript. *Deadline:* March 1.

GLENN JACKSON SCHOLARS SCHOLARSHIPS

• See page 547

HARRY LUDWIG MEMORIAL SCHOLARSHIP

• See page 577

IDA M. CRAWFORD SCHOLARSHIP

Scholarship available to graduates of accredited Oregon high schools. Minimum GPA of 3.5 required. Not available to applicants majoring in law, medicine, theology, teaching, or music. U.S. Bank employees, their children or near relatives, are not eligible. Reapply annually for award renewal.

Award: Scholarship for use in freshman year; not renewable.

Eligibility Requirements: Applicant must be enrolled or expecting to enroll full-time at a four-year institution and resident of Oregon. Applicant must have 3.5 GPA or higher. Available to U.S. citizens.

Application Requirements: Activities chart, copy of birth certificate, application form, essay, financial need analysis, transcript. *Deadline:* March 1.

JEROME B. STEINBACH SCHOLARSHIP

Award for Oregon residents enrolled in Oregon institution as sophomore or above with minimum 3.5 GPA. Award for undergraduate study only. U.S. Bank employees, their children, or near relatives are not eligible. Must submit proof of U.S. birth.

Award: Scholarship for use in sophomore, junior, or senior years; renewable.

Eligibility Requirements: Applicant must be enrolled or expecting to enroll full-time at a four-year institution or university and resident of Oregon. Applicant must have 3.5 GPA or higher. Available to U.S. citizens.

Application Requirements: Application form, essay, financial need analysis, proof of U.S. birth, transcript. *Deadline:* March 1.

KONNIE MEMORIAL DEPENDENTS SCHOLARSHIP

• See page 547

MARIA C. JACKSON/GENERAL GEORGE A. WHITE SCHOLARSHIP

• See page 607

OREGON DUNGENESS CRAB COMMISSION SCHOLARSHIP

One-time scholarship available to children, stepchildren, or legal dependents of licensed Oregon Dungeness Crab fishermen or crew. If a high school senior, may be enrolled in any major; other students must be enrolled in marine biology, environmental science, wildlife science, or related major. Must be 23 years of age or under as of the March scholarship deadline.

Award: Scholarship for use in freshman, sophomore, junior, or senior years; not renewable.

Eligibility Requirements: Applicant must be enrolled or expecting to enroll full-time at a four-year institution and resident of Oregon. Available to U.S. citizens.

Application Requirements: Activity chart, name of vessel in place of work-site in membership section, application form, essay, financial need analysis, transcript. *Deadline:* March 1.

OREGON OCCUPATIONAL SAFETY AND HEALTH DIVISION WORKERS MEMORIAL SCHOLARSHIP

One-time award for Oregon high school graduates or GED recipients who are either dependents or spouses of an Oregon worker who has incurred permanent total disability or was fatally injured on the job while working for an Oregon employer. Must submit essay on how the injury or death of your parent or spouse affected or influenced your decision to further your education.

Award: Scholarship for use in freshman, sophomore, junior, or senior years; not renewable.

Eligibility Requirements: Applicant must be enrolled or expecting to enroll full- or part-time at a four-year institution or university and resident of Oregon. Available to U.S. citizens.

Application Requirements: Activity chart, proof of death or disability , application form, essay, financial need analysis, test scores, transcript. *Deadline:* March 1.

OREGON SALMON COMMISSION SCOTT BOLEY MEMORIAL SCHOLARSHIP

Award for dependents of licensed Oregon troll salmon permit fishermen. Preference given to graduating high school seniors. To be used for full-time study at any U.S. college or university. FAFSA is required.

Award: Scholarship for use in freshman year; not renewable.

Eligibility Requirements: Applicant must be enrolled or expecting to enroll full-time at a four-year institution or university and resident of Oregon. Available to U.S. citizens.

Application Requirements: Activity chart, FAFSA, application form, essay, financial need analysis, transcript. *Deadline:* March 1.

OREGON SCHOLARSHIP FUND TRANSFER STUDENT AWARD

Award open to Oregon residents who are currently enrolled in their second year at an Oregon community college and are planning to transfer to a four-year college in Oregon. Prior recipients may apply for one additional year. Must enroll at least half-time. FAFSA is required.

Award: Scholarship for use in junior or senior years; not renewable.

Eligibility Requirements: Applicant must be enrolled or expecting to enroll full- or part-time at a four-year institution or university; resident of Oregon and studying in Oregon. Available to U.S. citizens.

Application Requirements: Activity chart, FAFSA, application form, essay, financial need analysis, transcript. *Deadline:* March 1.

OREGON STATE FISCAL ASSOCIATION SCHOLARSHIP

• *See page 532*

OREGON TRAWL COMMISSION JOE EASLEY MEMORIAL SCHOLARSHIP

Award for graduating Oregon high school seniors and college students in any accredited U.S. college or university who are dependents of licensed Oregon Trawl fishermen or crew. Must reapply annually for renewal.

Award: Scholarship for use in freshman, sophomore, junior, or senior years; not renewable.

Eligibility Requirements: Applicant must be enrolled or expecting to enroll full-time at a four-year institution or university and resident of Oregon. Available to U.S. citizens.

Application Requirements: Activity chart, application form, essay, financial need analysis, recommendations or references, transcript. *Deadline:* March 1.

PACIFIC NW FEDERAL CREDIT UNION SCHOLARSHIP

Scholarship available to graduating high school senior who is a member of Pacific North West Federal Credit Union. Must submit an essay on "Why My Credit Union is an Important Consumer Choice." Immediate family members of Pacific NW Federal Credit Union employees and credit union elected or appointed officials are not eligible. Oregon and Washington state residents eligible.

Award: Scholarship for use in freshman year; not renewable.

Eligibility Requirements: Applicant must be high school student; planning to enroll or expecting to enroll full-time at a four-year institution or university and resident of Oregon, Washington. Available to U.S. citizens.

Application Requirements: Application form, essay, recommendations or references, transcript. *Deadline:* March 1.

P.E.O. JEAN FISH GIBBONS SCHOLARSHIP

Award is available to female graduates of high schools in Jackson, Josephine, or Klamath County who will be college juniors or seniors in the upcoming academic year. For use at four-year public or nonprofit colleges and universities. Minimum GPA of 3.5 is required to apply. Recipients may reapply for one additional year of funding.

Award: Scholarship for use in junior or senior years; not renewable.

Eligibility Requirements: Applicant must be enrolled or expecting to enroll full-time at a four-year institution or university; female and resident of Oregon. Applicant must have 3.5 GPA or higher. Available to U.S. citizens.

Application Requirements: Application form, FAFSA, financial need analysis, transcript. *Deadline:* March 1.

PETER CROSSLEY MEMORIAL SCHOLARSHIP

Renewable award for graduating seniors of Oregon public alternative high schools. Must be highly motivated to succeed despite overcoming a severe personal obstacle or challenge during high school career. Must submit essay and plan to enroll at least half-time in an Oregon college or university.

Award: Scholarship for use in freshman, sophomore, junior, or senior years; renewable.

Eligibility Requirements: Applicant must be high school student; planning to enroll or expecting to enroll full- or part-time at a four-year institution or university; resident of Oregon and studying in Oregon. Available to U.S. citizens.

Application Requirements: Activity chart, FAFSA, application form, essay, financial need analysis, transcript. *Deadline:* March 1.

RAY'S CHARITABLE FOUNDATION SCHOLARSHIP

One-time award for eligible employees and dependents of eligible employees of C&K Market, Inc. and C&K Express. Must be a resident of Oregon or California and studying at a U.S. college. Preference given to high school seniors with a minimum GPA of 3.0 or college students with a GPA of 2.5.

Award: Scholarship for use in freshman, sophomore, junior, or senior years; not renewable.

Eligibility Requirements: Applicant must be enrolled or expecting to enroll full-time at a four-year institution or university and resident of California, Oregon. Available to U.S. citizens.

Application Requirements: Application form, FAFSA. *Deadline:* March 1.

SALEM FOUNDATION ANSEL & MARIE SOLIE SCHOLARSHIP

• *See page 577*

TEAMSTERS CLYDE C. CROSBY/JOSEPH M. EDGAR MEMORIAL SCHOLARSHIP

• *See page 532*

WILLETT AND MARGUERITE LAKE SCHOLARSHIP

• *See page 548*

WOODARD FAMILY SCHOLARSHIP

• *See page 548*

OWEN ELECTRIC COOPERATIVE

http://www.owenelectric.com/

OWEN ELECTRIC COOPERATIVE SCHOLARSHIP PROGRAM

Scholarships available to college juniors and seniors who are enrolled full-time at a four-year college or university. Parents of applicant must have an active Owen Electric account in good standing. If applicant has not earned 60 hours at time of application, must provide additional transcript upon completion of 60 hours. Must submit 400- to 700-word essay. For essay topics, application, and additional information visit website http://www.owenelectric.com.

Award: Scholarship for use in junior or senior years; not renewable. *Number:* 12. *Amount:* $2000.

Eligibility Requirements: Applicant must be enrolled or expecting to enroll full-time at a four-year institution or university and resident of Kentucky. Applicant must have 3.0 GPA or higher. Available to U.S. citizens.

Application Requirements: Application form, community service, entry in a contest, essay, recommendations or references, transcript. *Deadline:* February 1.

Contact: Brian Linder, Manager of Key Accounts
Phone: 502-484-3471 Ext. 3542
Fax: 502-484-2661
E-mail: blinder@owenelectric.com

PACERS FOUNDATION INC.

http://www.pacersfoundation.org/

PACERS TEAMUP SCHOLARSHIP
• See page 563

PACIFIC AND ASIAN AFFAIRS COUNCIL

http://www.paachawaii.org/

PAAC ACADEMIC SCHOLARSHIPS

PAAC's academic scholarships are available to college-bound seniors and underclassmen attending Hawaii public or private high school. Applicants must be active in PAAC's high school program.

Award: Scholarship for use in freshman year; not renewable. *Number:* 5. *Amount:* $300–$1000.

Eligibility Requirements: Applicant must be high school student; planning to enroll or expecting to enroll full-time at a two-year or four-year or technical institution or university and resident of Hawaii. Available to U.S. and non-U.S. citizens.

Application Requirements: Application form, essay, recommendations or references, transcript. *Deadline:* April 2.

Contact: Natasha Schultz, High School Program Director
Pacific and Asian Affairs Council
1601 East-West Road, 4th Floor
Honolulu, HI 96848
Phone: 808-944-7759

PENNSYLVANIA BURGLAR AND FIRE ALARM ASSOCIATION

http://www.pbfaa.com/

PENNSYLVANIA BURGLAR AND FIRE ALARM ASSOCIATION YOUTH SCHOLARSHIP PROGRAM
• See page 563

PENNSYLVANIA FEDERATION OF DEMOCRATIC WOMEN INC.

http://www.pfdw.org/

PENNSYLVANIA FEDERATION OF DEMOCRATIC WOMEN INC. ANNUAL SCHOLARSHIP AWARDS
• See page 532

PENNSYLVANIA HIGHER EDUCATION ASSISTANCE AGENCY

http://www.pheaa.org/

PENNSYLVANIA STATE GRANT

Award for Pennsylvania residents attending an approved postsecondary institution as undergraduates in a program of at least two years duration. Renewable for up to eight semesters if applicants show continued need and academic progress. Must submit FAFSA. Number of awards granted varies annually. Scholarship value is $200 to $4348. Deadlines: May 1 and August 1.

Award: Grant for use in freshman, sophomore, junior, or senior years; renewable. *Amount:* $200–$4348.

Eligibility Requirements: Applicant must be enrolled or expecting to enroll full- or part-time at a two-year or four-year or technical institution or university and resident of Pennsylvania. Available to U.S. citizens.

Application Requirements: Application form, application form may be submitted online (http://pheaa.org/funding-opportunities/state-grant-program/index.shtml), FAFSA, financial need analysis. *Deadline:* varies.

Contact: Keith New, Director of Public Relations
Pennsylvania Higher Education Assistance Agency
1200 North Seventh Street
Harrisburg, PA 17102-1444
Phone: 717-720-2509
Fax: 717-720-3903

POSTSECONDARY EDUCATION GRATUITY PROGRAM
• See page 585

PETER DOCTOR MEMORIAL INDIAN SCHOLARSHIP FOUNDATION INC.

PETER DOCTOR MEMORIAL IROQUOIS SCHOLARSHIP
• See page 635

PFUND FOUNDATION

http://www.pfundonline.org/

PFUND SCHOLARSHIP AWARD PROGRAM

PFund Foundation's Scholarship Award Program is available for gay, lesbian, bisexual, transgender and allied student leaders. Applicants must be a resident of Minnesota or attending a qualifying Minnesota academic institution. For more details, visit http://www.pfundonline.org/scholarships.html.

Award: Scholarship for use in freshman, sophomore, junior, senior, or graduate years; not renewable. *Number:* 18–20. *Amount:* $2000–$5000.

Eligibility Requirements: Applicant must be enrolled or expecting to enroll full- or part-time at a two-year or four-year or technical institution or university; resident of Minnesota; studying in Minnesota and must have an interest in LGBT issues. Available to U.S. and non-U.S. citizens.

Application Requirements: Application form, confidentiality statement, essay, personal photograph, recommendations or references, transcript. *Deadline:* February 1.

Contact: Ms. Kayva Yang, Program Officer
PFund Foundation
1409 Willow Street
Suite 109
Minneapolis, MN 55403
Phone: 612-870-1806
E-mail: kyang@PFundOnline.org

PHILIPINO-AMERICAN ASSOCIATION OF NEW ENGLAND

http://www.pamas.org/

BLESSED LEON OF OUR LADY OF THE ROSARY AWARD
• See page 636

PAMAS RESTRICTED SCHOLARSHIP AWARD
• See page 533

RAVENSCROFT FAMILY AWARD
• See page 636

PHOENIX SUNS CHARITIES/SUN STUDENTS SCHOLARSHIP

http://www.suns.com/

SUN STUDENT COLLEGE SCHOLARSHIP PROGRAM
• See page 563

PINE TREE STATE 4-H CLUB FOUNDATION/ 4-H POSTSECONDARY SCHOLARSHIP

http://www.umaine.edu/

PARKER-LOVEJOY SCHOLARSHIP

One-time scholarship of $1000 is available to a graduating high school senior. Applicants must be residents of Maine.

Award: Scholarship for use in freshman year; not renewable. *Number:* 1. *Amount:* $1000.

Eligibility Requirements: Applicant must be high school student; planning to enroll or expecting to enroll full-time at a two-year or four-

year institution or university and resident of Maine. Available to U.S. citizens.

Application Requirements: Application form. *Deadline:* March 14.

Contact: Angela Martin, Administrative Assistant
Phone: 207-581-3739
Fax: 207-581-1387
E-mail: amartin@umext.maine.edu

WAYNE S. RICH SCHOLARSHIP

Scholarship for an outstanding Maine or New Hampshire 4-H member for postsecondary study. Awarded to a Maine student in odd numbered years and a New Hampshire student in even numbered years.

Award: Scholarship for use in freshman year; not renewable. *Number:* 1. *Amount:* up to $1000.

Eligibility Requirements: Applicant must be high school student; planning to enroll or expecting to enroll full-time at a two-year or four-year institution or university and resident of Maine, New Hampshire. Available to U.S. citizens.

Application Requirements: Application form. *Deadline:* March 14.

Contact: Angela Martin, Administrative Assistant
Phone: 207-581-3739
Fax: 207-581-1387
E-mail: amartin@umext.maine.edu

POLISH HERITAGE ASSOCIATION OF MARYLAND

http://www.pha-md.org/

POLISH HERITAGE SCHOLARSHIP
• *See page 636*

PORTUGUESE FOUNDATION INC.

http://www.pfict.org/

PORTUGUESE FOUNDATION SCHOLARSHIP PROGRAM
• *See page 636*

PRIDE FOUNDATION

http://www.PrideFoundation.org/

PRIDE FOUNDATION SCHOLARSHIP PROGRAM

Pride Foundation provides scholarships to current and future lesbian, gay, bisexual, transgender and straight-ally student leaders from Alaska, Idaho, Montana, Oregon, and Washington. Our scholarships cover most accredited post-secondary schools, including community colleges; 4-year public or private colleges and universities; trade or certificate programs; and graduate, medical, or law school.

Award: Scholarship for use in freshman, sophomore, junior, senior, graduate, or postgraduate years; not renewable. *Number:* 85–125. *Amount:* $1000–$20,000.

Eligibility Requirements: Applicant must be enrolled or expecting to enroll full- or part-time at a two-year or four-year or technical institution or university; resident of Alaska, Idaho, Montana, Oregon, Washington and must have an interest in LGBT issues. Available to U.S. and non-U.S. citizens.

Application Requirements: Application form, application form may be submitted online (http://www.PrideFoundationScholar.org), community service, essay, interview, recommendations or references, transcript. *Deadline:* January 31.

Contact: Anthony Papini, Director of Educational Leadership
Pride Foundation
1122 East Pike Street
PMB 1001
Seattle, WA 98122
Phone: 206-323-3318 Ext. 110
Fax: 206-323-1017
E-mail: scholarships@pridefoundation.org

PROJECT BEST SCHOLARSHIP FUND

http://www.projectbest.com/

PROJECT BEST SCHOLARSHIP
• *See page 534*

PUEBLO OF SAN JUAN, DEPARTMENT OF EDUCATION

http://www.sanjuaned.org/

OHKAY OWINGEH TRIBAL SCHOLARSHIP OF THE PUEBLO OF SAN JUAN
• *See page 563*

POP'AY SCHOLARSHIP
• *See page 563*

RHODE ISLAND FOUNDATION

http://www.rifoundation.org/

ALDO FREDA LEGISLATIVE PAGES SCHOLARSHIP

Awarded to support Rhode Island Legislative Pages enrolled in a college or university. Must show scholastic achievement and good citizenship. Must be accepted into a full-time accredited postsecondary institution or graduate program. Must be a Rhode Island resident and a citizen of the United States.

Award: Scholarship for use in freshman, sophomore, junior, senior, or graduate years; not renewable. *Number:* 2–3. *Amount:* $1000–$1500.

Eligibility Requirements: Applicant must be enrolled or expecting to enroll full- or part-time at a two-year or four-year institution or university and resident of Rhode Island. Available to U.S. citizens.

Application Requirements: Application form, essay, financial need analysis, recommendations or references, transcript. *Deadline:* June 3.

Contact: Libby Monahan, Funds Administrator
Phone: 401-274-4564 Ext. 3117
E-mail: libbym@rifoundation.org

ANDREW BELL SCHOLARSHIP

Scholarships to high school graduates pursuing a post-secondary education. Must demonstrate financial need.

Award: Scholarship for use in freshman, sophomore, junior, or senior years; not renewable.

Eligibility Requirements: Applicant must be enrolled or expecting to enroll full-time at a two-year or four-year or technical institution or university and resident of Rhode Island. Available to U.S. citizens.

Application Requirements: Application form, financial need analysis. *Deadline:* continuous.

A.T. CROSS SCHOLARSHIP
• *See page 549*

BRUCE AND MARJORIE SUNDLUN SCHOLARSHIP

Scholarships for low-income single parents seeking to upgrade their career skills. Preference given to single parents previously receiving state support, and also for those previously incarcerated. Must be a Rhode Island resident and must attend school in the state.

Award: Scholarship for use in freshman, sophomore, junior, or senior years; not renewable. *Amount:* up to $1500.

Eligibility Requirements: Applicant must be enrolled or expecting to enroll full- or part-time at a two-year or four-year or technical institution or university; resident of Rhode Island and studying in Rhode Island. Available to U.S. and non-U.S. citizens.

Application Requirements: Application form, essay, financial need analysis, recommendations or references, self-addressed stamped envelope with application, transcript. *Deadline:* June 14.

Contact: Libby Monahan, Funds Administrator
Phone: 401-274-4564 Ext. 3117
E-mail: libbym@rifoundation.org

LILY AND CATELLO SORRENTINO MEMORIAL SCHOLARSHIP

Scholarships for Rhode Island residents. Applicant must be 25 years or older wishing to attend college or university in Rhode Island (only students attending non-parochial schools). Must demonstrate financial need. Preference given to first-time applicants. Financial need must be demonstrated.

Award: Scholarship for use in freshman, sophomore, junior, or senior years; not renewable. *Amount:* $500–$1000.

Eligibility Requirements: Applicant must be enrolled or expecting to enroll full- or part-time at a four-year institution or university; resident of Rhode Island and studying in Rhode Island. Available to U.S. citizens.

Application Requirements: Application form, financial need analysis, self-addressed stamped envelope with application, transcript. *Deadline:* May 1.

Contact: Libby Monahan, Funds Administrator
Phone: 401-274-4564 Ext. 3117
E-mail: libbym@rifoundation.org

NONDRAS HURST VOLL SCHOLARSHIP

Scholarship for single mothers transitioning off public assistance who are enrolled or planning to enroll in college certificate or degree program. Must be a Rhode Island resident and demonstrate financial need.

Award: Scholarship for use in freshman, sophomore, junior, or senior years; not renewable.

Eligibility Requirements: Applicant must be enrolled or expecting to enroll full- or part-time at a two-year or four-year institution or university; single female and resident of Rhode Island. Available to U.S. citizens.

Application Requirements: Application form, copy of US income tax return; list of dependent children; copy of financial aid award letter if applicable, essay, financial need analysis, transcript. *Deadline:* April 19.

PATTY & MELVIN ALPERIN FIRST GENERATION SCHOLARSHIP

Renewable scholarship for Rhode Island high school seniors whose parents did not graduate from college. Must be accepted or enrolled in an accredited two- or four-year college and demonstrate financial need.

Award: Scholarship for use in freshman year; renewable. *Amount:* $1000.

Eligibility Requirements: Applicant must be high school student; planning to enroll or expecting to enroll at a two-year or four-year institution or university and resident of Rhode Island. Available to U.S. citizens.

Application Requirements: Application form, financial need analysis, transcript. *Deadline:* May 1.

Contact: Libby Monahan, Funds Administrator
Phone: 401-274-4564 Ext. 3117
E-mail: libbym@rifoundation.org

RHODE ISLAND ASSOCIATION OF FORMER LEGISLATORS SCHOLARSHIP

One-time award of $1500 for graduating high school seniors who are Rhode Island residents. Must have a history of substantial voluntary involvement in community service. Must be accepted into an accredited post-secondary institution and should be able to demonstrate financial need.

Award: Scholarship for use in freshman year; not renewable. *Number:* 4–5. *Amount:* $1500.

Eligibility Requirements: Applicant must be high school student; planning to enroll or expecting to enroll full-time at a four-year institution or university and resident of Rhode Island. Available to U.S. citizens.

Application Requirements: Application form, essay, financial need analysis, recommendations or references, self-addressed stamped envelope with application, test scores, transcript. *Deadline:* May 1.

Contact: Libby Monahan, Funds Administrator
Phone: 401-274-4564 Ext. 3117
E-mail: libbym@rifoundation.org

RHODE ISLAND COMMISSION ON WOMEN/FREDA GOLDMAN EDUCATION AWARD

Scholarship to assist women with transportation, child-care, tutoring, educational materials, and/or other support services. Must be pursuing education or job training beyond high school. Preference given to highly motivated, self-supporting, low-income women completing a first undergraduate degree or certificate program.

Award: Scholarship for use in freshman, sophomore, junior, or senior years; not renewable. *Amount:* $500–$1000.

Eligibility Requirements: Applicant must be enrolled or expecting to enroll full- or part-time at a four-year institution or university; female and resident of Rhode Island. Available to U.S. citizens.

Application Requirements: Application form, essay, recommendations or references, self-addressed stamped envelope with application, transcript. *Deadline:* June 14.

Contact: Libby Monahan, Funds Administrator
Phone: 401-274-4564 Ext. 3117
E-mail: libbym@rifoundation.org

UNITED ITALIAN AMERICAN INC. SCHOLARSHIP

For Rhode Island residents with financial need who wish to attend a two- or four-year college or university. Scholarship is based on merit as evidenced by superior achievement and leadership in school and/or community.

Award: Scholarship for use in freshman, sophomore, junior, or senior years; not renewable.

Eligibility Requirements: Applicant must be enrolled or expecting to enroll full-time at a two-year or four-year institution or university; resident of Rhode Island and must have an interest in leadership. Available to U.S. citizens.

Application Requirements: Application form, community service, financial need analysis, transcript. *Deadline:* June 3.

Contact: Libby Monahan, Funds Administrator
Phone: 401-274-4564 Ext. 3117
E-mail: libbym@rifoundation.org

RHODE ISLAND HIGHER EDUCATION ASSISTANCE AUTHORITY

http://www.riheaa.org/

COLLEGE BOUND FUND ACADEMIC PROMISE SCHOLARSHIP

Award to graduating high school seniors. Eligibility based on financial need and SAT/ACT scores. Must maintain specified GPA each year for renewal. Must be Rhode Island resident and attend college full-time. Must complete the FAFSA. Must maintain an escalating college GPA to remain eligible—2.5 at the end of the freshman year, 2.62 at the end of the sophomore year, and 2.75 at the end of the junior year.

Award: Scholarship for use in freshman, sophomore, junior, or senior years; renewable. *Number:* 100. *Amount:* $2500.

Eligibility Requirements: Applicant must be high school student; planning to enroll or expecting to enroll full-time at a two-year or four-year or technical institution or university and resident of Rhode Island. Available to U.S. citizens.

Application Requirements: Application form, application form may be submitted online (http://www.fafsa.edu.gov), financial need analysis, test scores. *Deadline:* March 1.

Contact: Mr. Michael Joyce, Director of Program Administration
Rhode Island Higher Education Assistance Authority
560 Jefferson Boulevard, Suite 100
Warwick, RI 02886
Phone: 401-736-1170
Fax: 401-736-1178
E-mail: grants@riheaa.org

RHODE ISLAND STATE GRANT PROGRAM

Grants for residents of Rhode Island attending an accredited, Title-IV approved post secondary undergraduate program in the United States, Canada, or Mexico. Based on need as reported by the student and his or her family on the Free Application for Federal Student Aid (FAFSA). Renewable for up to four years if in good academic standing and student continues to meet financial need requirements.

Award: Grant for use in freshman, sophomore, junior, or senior years; not renewable. *Number:* 10,000–20,000. *Amount:* $250–$700.

Eligibility Requirements: Applicant must be enrolled or expecting to enroll full- or part-time at a two-year or four-year or technical institution or university and resident of Rhode Island. Available to U.S. citizens.

Application Requirements: Application form, application form may be submitted online (http://www.fafsa.edu.gov), financial need analysis. *Deadline:* March 1.

Contact: Mr. Michael Joyce, Director of Program Administration
Rhode Island Higher Education Assistance Authority
560 Jefferson Boulevard, Suite 100
Warwick, RI 02886
Phone: 401-736-1170
Fax: 401-736-1178
E-mail: grants@riheaa.org

ROBERT H. MOLLOHAN FAMILY CHARITABLE FOUNDATION, INC.

http://www.mollohanfoundation.org/

CARL R. MORRIS MEMORIAL SCHOLARSHIP

The Carl. R. Morris Memorial Scholarship is a $1000 scholarship that will be awarded to a resident of Calhoun County that best emulates Mr. Morris' commitment to community and education. The student must be enrolled, or planning to enroll, at Alderson-Broaddus College, Glenville State College, or West Virginia University, must have at least a 3.0 GPA, and must have demonstrated financial need.

Award: Scholarship for use in freshman, sophomore, junior, or senior years; not renewable. *Number:* 1–60. *Amount:* $1000.

Eligibility Requirements: Applicant must be enrolled or expecting to enroll full-time at a four-year institution or university; resident of West Virginia and studying in West Virginia. Applicant must have 3.0 GPA or higher. Available to U.S. citizens.

Application Requirements: Application form, essay, recommendations or references, resume, test scores, transcript.

Contact: Aime Shaffer, Program Manager
Phone: 304-333-6783
E-mail: ashaffer@wvhtf.org

DR. ROBERTO F. CUNANAN MEMORIAL SCHOLARSHIP

The Dr. Roberto F. Cunanan Memorial Scholarship was created to honor Dr. Cunanan's energetic spirit and loving heart. This $1,000 scholarship is awarded to a Bridgeport High School student who is enrolled or planning to enroll at a West Virginia college or university, and who is an active participant in both academics and athletics.

Award: Scholarship for use in freshman, sophomore, junior, or senior years; not renewable. *Number:* 1–60. *Amount:* $1000.

Eligibility Requirements: Applicant must be high school student; planning to enroll or expecting to enroll full-time at a four-year institution or university; resident of West Virginia and must have an interest in athletics/sports. Available to U.S. citizens.

Application Requirements: Application form, essay, recommendations or references, resume, test scores, transcript.

Contact: Aime Shaffer, Program Manager
Phone: 304-333-6783
E-mail: ashaffer@wvhtf.org

HELEN HOLT MOLLOHAN SCHOLARSHIP

The Helen Holt Mollohan Scholarship is a $1000 scholarship that is awarded to a West Virginia female who is enrolled, or planning to enroll, at Glenville State College. This young woman should exhibit strong character, integrity, service to community, concern for others, and high standards of scholarship, like the late Mrs. Mollohan herself.

Award: Scholarship for use in freshman, sophomore, junior, or senior years; renewable. *Amount:* $1000.

Eligibility Requirements: Applicant must be high school student; planning to enroll or expecting to enroll full-time at a four-year institution or university; female; resident of West Virginia and studying in West Virginia. Available to U.S. citizens.

Application Requirements: Application form, essay, recommendations or references, resume, transcript.

Contact: Aime Shaffer, Program Manager
Phone: 304-333-6783
E-mail: ashaffer@wvhtf.org

RYU FAMILY FOUNDATION, INC.

http://www.seolbong.org/

SEOL BONG SCHOLARSHIP
• See page 577

ST. ANDREW'S SOCIETY OF WASHINGTON, DC

http://www.saintandrewsociety.org/

DONALD MALCOLM MACARTHUR SCHOLARSHIP
• See page 637

ST. CLAIRE REGIONAL MEDICAL CENTER

http://www.st-claire.org/

SR. MARY JEANNETTE WESS, S.N.D. SCHOLARSHIP
• See page 563

ST. PETERSBURG TIMES FUND INC.

http://www.sptimes.com/

ST. PETERSBURG TIMES BARNES SCHOLARSHIP

Four high school seniors from the St. Petersburg Times' audience area are selected each year and each are awarded up to $15,000 annually for four years to attend any nationally accredited college or university. Criteria for scholarship include high academic achievement, financial need, evidence of having overcome significant obstacles in life, and community service.

Award: Scholarship for use in freshman year; renewable. *Number:* 4. *Amount:* up to $15,000.

Eligibility Requirements: Applicant must be high school student; planning to enroll or expecting to enroll full- or part-time at a four-year institution or university and resident of Florida. Available to U.S. citizens.

Application Requirements: Application form, community service, entry in a contest, financial need analysis. *Deadline:* October 15.

Contact: Nancy Waclawek, Director
Phone: 727-893-8780
Fax: 727-892-2257
E-mail: waclawek@sptimes.com

SALT RIVER ELECTRIC COOPERATIVE CORPORATION

http://www.srelectric.com/

SALT RIVER ELECTRIC SCHOLARSHIP PROGRAM

Scholarships available to Kentucky high school seniors who reside in Salt River Electric Service area or the primary residence of their parents/guardian is in the service area. Must be enrolled or plan to enroll in a postsecondary institution. Minimum GPA of 2.5 required. Must demonstrate financial need. Must submit a 500-word essay on a topic chosen from the list on the website. Application and additional information available on website http://www.srelectric.com.

Award: Scholarship for use in freshman year; not renewable. *Number:* 4. *Amount:* $1000.

Eligibility Requirements: Applicant must be high school student; planning to enroll or expecting to enroll full- or part-time at a two-year or four-year or technical institution or university and resident of Kentucky. Applicant must have 2.5 GPA or higher. Available to U.S. citizens.

Application Requirements: Application form, community service, essay, financial need analysis, personal photograph, transcript. *Deadline:* April 4.

Contact: Nicky Rapier, Scholarship Coordinator
Phone: 502-348-3931
Fax: 502-348-1993
E-mail: nickyr@srelectric.com

SALVADORAN AMERICAN LEADERSHIP AND EDUCATIONAL FUND

http://www.salef.org/

FULFILLING OUR DREAMS SCHOLARSHIP FUND
• *See page 637*

SAN FRANCISCO FOUNDATION

http://www.sff.org/

JOSEPH HENRY JACKSON LITERARY AWARD

Award presented annually to an author of an unpublished work in progress: fiction, nonfiction, prose, or poetry. Must be residents of and currently living in northern California or the state of Nevada for three consecutive years and be between 20 to 35 years of age. Award values from $2000 to $3000. Submit manuscript.

Award: Prize for use in freshman, sophomore, junior, senior, graduate, or postgraduate years; not renewable. *Number:* 3. *Amount:* $2000–$3000.

Eligibility Requirements: Applicant must be age 20-35; enrolled or expecting to enroll full- or part-time at a two-year or four-year institution or university; resident of California, Nevada and must have an interest in writing. Available to U.S. citizens.

Application Requirements: Application form, entry in a contest, manuscript, self-addressed stamped envelope with application. *Deadline:* March 31.

SHELBY ENERGY COOPERATIVE

http://www.shelbyenergy.com/

SHELBY ENERGY COOPERATIVE SCHOLARSHIPS

Scholarships for high school seniors in Kentucky, whose parents or guardians are Shelby Energy members. Award based on financial need, academic excellence, community and school involvement, and essay.

Award: Scholarship for use in freshman year; not renewable. *Number:* 6. *Amount:* $1000.

Eligibility Requirements: Applicant must be high school student; planning to enroll or expecting to enroll full-time at a four-year institution or university and resident of Kentucky. Available to U.S. citizens.

Application Requirements: Application form, community service, financial need analysis. *Deadline:* April 5.

Contact: Teresa Atha, Marketing Department
Phone: 502-633-4420
Fax: 502-633-2387
E-mail: shelbyenergy@shelbyenergy.com

SIMON FOUNDATION FOR EDUCATION AND HOUSING

http://www.sfeh.org/

SIMON SCHOLARS PROGRAM

Scholarships are given to high school seniors at qualified high schools in Atlanta, GA, Santa Fe and Albuquerque, NM, and Anaheim, Santa Ana, Oceanside, or Garden Grove, CA. Deadlines vary for each region. For more details visit website http://www.simonscholars.org.

Award: Scholarship for use in freshman year; not renewable. *Number:* 100. *Amount:* $16,000.

Eligibility Requirements: Applicant must be high school student; planning to enroll or expecting to enroll full-time at a two-year or four-year institution or university and resident of California, Georgia, New Mexico. Applicant must have 3.0 GPA or higher. Available to U.S. citizens.

Application Requirements: Application form, community service, essay, financial need analysis, interview, recommendations or references, test scores, transcript. *Deadline:* varies.

Contact: Dr. Heather Huntley, Director of Partnerships and Development
Phone: 949-270-3622
Fax: 949-729-8072
E-mail: heatherh@simonscholars.org

SONS OF NORWAY FOUNDATION

http://www.sonsofnorway.com/

ASTRID G. CATES AND MYRTLE BEINHAUER SCHOLARSHIP FUNDS
• *See page 537*

SOUTH CAROLINA COMMISSION ON HIGHER EDUCATION

http://www.che.sc.gov/

PALMETTO FELLOWS SCHOLARSHIP PROGRAM

Renewable award for qualified high school seniors in South Carolina to attend a four-year South Carolina institution. The scholarship must be applied directly towards the cost of attendance, less any other gift aid received.

Award: Scholarship for use in freshman year; renewable. *Number:* 4846. *Amount:* $6700–$7500.

Eligibility Requirements: Applicant must be high school student; planning to enroll or expecting to enroll full-time at a four-year institution or university; resident of South Carolina and studying in South Carolina. Applicant must have 3.5 GPA or higher. Available to U.S. citizens.

Application Requirements: Application form, test scores, transcript. *Deadline:* December 15.

Contact: Dr. Karen Woodfaulk, Director of Student Services
South Carolina Commission on Higher Education
1333 Main Street, Suite 200
Columbia, SC 29201
Phone: 803-737-2244
Fax: 803-737-3610
E-mail: kwoodfaulk@che.sc.gov

SOUTH CAROLINA HOPE SCHOLARSHIP

A merit-based scholarship for eligible first-time entering freshman attending a four-year South Carolina institution. Minimum GPA of 3.0 required. Must be a resident of South Carolina.

Award: Scholarship for use in freshman year; not renewable. *Number:* 2605. *Amount:* $2800.

Eligibility Requirements: Applicant must be high school student; planning to enroll or expecting to enroll full-time at a four-year institution or university; resident of South Carolina and studying in South Carolina. Applicant must have 3.0 GPA or higher. Available to U.S. citizens.

Application Requirements: Transcript. *Deadline:* continuous.

Contact: Gerrick Hampton, Scholarship Coordinator
South Carolina Commission on Higher Education
1333 Main Street, Suite 200
Columbia, SC 29201
Phone: 803-737-4544
Fax: 803-737-3610
E-mail: ghampton@che.sc.gov

SOUTH CAROLINA NEED-BASED GRANTS PROGRAM

Award based on FAFSA. A student may receive up to $2500 annually for full-time and up to $1250 annually for part-time study. The grant must be applied directly towards the cost of college attendance for a maximum of eight full-time equivalent terms.

Award: Grant for use in freshman, sophomore, junior, senior, or graduate years; renewable. *Number:* 1–26,730. *Amount:* $1250–$2500.

Eligibility Requirements: Applicant must be enrolled or expecting to enroll full- or part-time at a two-year or four-year or technical institution or university; resident of South Carolina and studying in South Carolina. Available to U.S. citizens.

Application Requirements: Application form, financial need analysis. *Deadline:* continuous.

Contact: Dr. Karen Woodfaulk, Director of Student Service
South Carolina Commission on Higher Education
1333 Main Street, Suite 200
Columbia, SC 29201
Phone: 803-737-2244
Fax: 803-737-2297
E-mail: kwoodfaulk@che.sc.gov

SOUTH CAROLINA DEPARTMENT OF EDUCATION

http://www.ed.sc.gov/

ROBERT C. BYRD HONORS SCHOLARSHIP-SOUTH CAROLINA

Renewable award for a graduating high school senior from South Carolina, who will be attending a two- or four-year institution. Applicants should be superior students who demonstrate academic achievement and show promise of continued success at a postsecondary institution. Interested applicants should contact their high school counselors after the first week of December for an application.

Award: Scholarship for use in freshman year; renewable.

Eligibility Requirements: Applicant must be high school student; planning to enroll or expecting to enroll full-time at a two-year or four-year institution or university and resident of South Carolina. Available to U.S. citizens.

Application Requirements: ACT or SAT scores, application form, test scores. *Deadline:* varies.

Contact: Beth Cope, Program Coordinator
South Carolina Department of Education
1424 Senate Street
Columbia, SC 29201
Phone: 803-734-8116
Fax: 803-734-4387
E-mail: bcope@sde.state.sc.us

SOUTH CAROLINA DIVISION OF VETERANS AFFAIRS

http://www.govoepp.state.sc.us/vetaff.htm

EDUCATIONAL ASSISTANCE FOR CERTAIN WAR VETERANS DEPENDENTS SCHOLARSHIP-SOUTH CAROLINA

• *See page 608*

SOUTH CAROLINA STATE EMPLOYEES ASSOCIATION

http://www.scsea.com/

ANNE A. AGNEW SCHOLARSHIP

• *See page 537*

RICHLAND/LEXINGTON SCSEA SCHOLARSHIP

• *See page 537*

SOUTH CAROLINA TUITION GRANTS COMMISSION

http://www.sctuitiongrants.com/

SOUTH CAROLINA TUITION GRANTS PROGRAM

Need-based grant set aside for 21 eligible independent colleges in South Carolina. Student must be a South Carolina resident. Must apply annually by submitting the Free Application for Federal Student Aid (FAFSA). Freshmen must graduate in top 75% of high school class OR score 900 on SAT/19 on ACT OR graduate with at least 2.0 on SC Uniform Grading Scale. Upperclassmen must pass a minimum of 24 credit hours annually.

Award: Grant for use in freshman, sophomore, junior, or senior years; not renewable. *Amount:* $100–$2600.

Eligibility Requirements: Applicant must be enrolled or expecting to enroll full-time at a two-year or four-year institution or university; resident of South Carolina and studying in South Carolina. Available to U.S. citizens.

Application Requirements: Application form, FAFSA. *Deadline:* June 30.

Contact: Toni Cave, Financial Aid Counselor
South Carolina Tuition Grants Commission
800 Dutch Square Boulevard, Suite 260A
Columbia, SC 29210
Phone: 803-896-1120
Fax: 803-896-1126
E-mail: toni@sctuitiongrants.org

SOUTH DAKOTA BOARD OF REGENTS

http://www.sdbor.edu/

SOUTH DAKOTA BOARD OF REGENTS MARLIN R. SCARBOROUGH MEMORIAL SCHOLARSHIP

One-time merit-based award for a student who is a junior at a South Dakota university. Must be nominated by the university and must have community service and leadership experience. Minimum 3.5 GPA required. Application deadline varies.

Award: Scholarship for use in junior year; not renewable. *Number:* 1. *Amount:* $1000.

Eligibility Requirements: Applicant must be enrolled or expecting to enroll full-time at an institution or university; resident of South Dakota; studying in South Dakota and must have an interest in leadership. Applicant must have 3.5 GPA or higher. Available to U.S. citizens.

Application Requirements: Application form, essay. *Deadline:* varies.

Contact: Dr. Paul Turman, System Vice President for Research and Economic Development
South Dakota Board of Regents
301 East Capital Avenue, Suite 200
Pierre, SD 57501
Phone: 605-773-3455
Fax: 605-773-2422
E-mail: paul.turman@sdbor.edu

SOUTH DAKOTA OPPORTUNITY SCHOLARSHIP

Renewable scholarship may be worth up to $5000 over four years to students who take a rigorous college-prep curriculum while in high school and stay in the state for their postsecondary education.

Award: Scholarship for use in freshman, sophomore, junior, or senior years; renewable. *Number:* 1000. *Amount:* $1000.

Eligibility Requirements: Applicant must be high school student; planning to enroll or expecting to enroll full-time at a two-year or four-year or technical institution or university; resident of South Dakota and studying in South Dakota. Applicant must have 3.0 GPA or higher. Available to U.S. citizens.

Application Requirements: Application form, test scores, transcript. *Deadline:* September 1.

Contact: Janelle Toman, Scholarship Committee
South Dakota Board of Regents
306 East Capitol, Suite 200
Pierre, SD 57501-2545
Phone: 605-773-3455
Fax: 605-773-2422
E-mail: info@sdbor.edu

SOUTH FLORIDA FAIR AND PALM BEACH COUNTY EXPOSITIONS INC.

http://www.southfloridafair.com/

SOUTH FLORIDA FAIR COLLEGE SCHOLARSHIP

Renewable award of up to $4000 for students who might not otherwise have an opportunity to pursue a college education. Must be a permanent resident of Florida.

Award: Scholarship for use in freshman, sophomore, junior, or senior years; renewable. *Number:* 10. *Amount:* $1000–$4000.

Eligibility Requirements: Applicant must be enrolled or expecting to enroll full- or part-time at a four-year institution or university and resident of Florida. Available to U.S. and non-U.S. citizens.

Application Requirements: Application form, community service, essay, recommendations or references, self-addressed stamped envelope with application, test scores, transcript. *Deadline:* October 15.

STATE EMPLOYEES ASSOCIATION OF NORTH CAROLINA (SEANC)

http://www.seanc.org/

STATE EMPLOYEES ASSOCIATION OF NORTH CAROLINA (SEANC) SCHOLARSHIPS

Scholarships available to SEANC members, their spouses and dependents seeking postsecondary education. Awarded in three categories: based on academic merit, financial need, and awards for SEANC members only. For application and more information visit http://www.seanc.org/.

Award: Scholarship for use in freshman, sophomore, junior, or senior years; not renewable. *Number:* 2. *Amount:* $500–$1000.

Eligibility Requirements: Applicant must be enrolled or expecting to enroll full-time at a two-year or four-year or technical institution or university and resident of North Carolina. Available to U.S. citizens.

Application Requirements: Application form, financial need analysis, test scores, transcript. *Deadline:* April 15.

STATE OF WYOMING, ADMINISTERED BY UNIVERSITY OF WYOMING

http://www.uwyo.edu/scholarships

VIETNAM VETERANS AWARD-WYOMING
• See page 608

STATE STUDENT ASSISTANCE COMMISSION OF INDIANA (SSACI)

http://www.in.gov/ssaci

FRANK O'BANNON GRANT PROGRAM

A need-based, tuition-restricted program for students attending Indiana public, private, or proprietary institutions seeking a first undergraduate degree. Students (and parents of dependent students) who are U.S. citizens and Indiana residents must file the FAFSA yearly by the March 10 deadline.

Award: Grant for use in freshman, sophomore, junior, or senior years; not renewable. *Number:* 48,408–70,239. *Amount:* $200–$10,992.

Eligibility Requirements: Applicant must be enrolled or expecting to enroll full-time at a two-year or four-year or technical institution or university; resident of Indiana and studying in Indiana. Available to U.S. citizens.

Application Requirements: Application form, FAFSA, financial need analysis. *Deadline:* March 10.

HOOSIER SCHOLAR AWARD

A $500 nonrenewable award. Based on the size of the senior class, one to three scholars are selected by the guidance counselors of each accredited high school in Indiana. The award is based on academic merit and may be used for any educational expense at an eligible Indiana institution of higher education.

Award: Scholarship for use in freshman year; not renewable. *Number:* 666–840. *Amount:* $500.

Eligibility Requirements: Applicant must be high school student; planning to enroll or expecting to enroll full-time at a two-year or four-year institution or university; resident of Indiana and studying in Indiana. Applicant must have 3.5 GPA or higher. Available to U.S. citizens.

Application Requirements: Application form, recommendations or references. *Deadline:* March 10.

Contact: Ada Sparkman, Program Coordinator
State Student Assistance Commission of Indiana (SSACI)
150 West Market Street, Suite 500
Indianapolis, IN 46204-2805
Phone: 317-232-2350
Fax: 317-232-3260

INDIANA NATIONAL GUARD SUPPLEMENTAL GRANT
• See page 585

PART-TIME GRANT PROGRAM

Program is designed to encourage part-time undergraduates to start and complete their associate or baccalaureate degrees or certificates by subsidizing part-time tuition costs. It is a term-based award that is based on need. State residency requirements must be met and a FAFSA must be filed. Eligibility is determined at the institutional level subject to approval by SSACI.

Award: Grant for use in freshman, sophomore, junior, or senior years; not renewable. *Number:* 4680–6700. *Amount:* $20–$4000.

Eligibility Requirements: Applicant must be enrolled or expecting to enroll part-time at a two-year or four-year or technical institution or university; resident of Indiana and studying in Indiana. Available to U.S. citizens.

Application Requirements: Application form, financial need analysis. *Deadline:* continuous.

TWENTY-FIRST CENTURY SCHOLARS GEAR UP SUMMER SCHOLARSHIP

Grant of up to $3000 that pays for summer school tuition and regularly assessed course fees (does not cover other costs such as textbooks or room and board).

Award: Scholarship for use in freshman, sophomore, junior, or senior years; not renewable. *Number:* 1. *Amount:* up to $3000.

Eligibility Requirements: Applicant must be enrolled or expecting to enroll full-time at a two-year or four-year institution or university; resident of Indiana and studying in Indiana. Available to U.S. citizens.

Application Requirements: Application form, must be in twenty-first century scholars program, high school diploma. *Deadline:* varies.

STEPHEN PHILLIPS MEMORIAL SCHOLARSHIP FUND

http://www.phillips-scholarship.org/

STEPHEN PHILLIPS MEMORIAL SCHOLARSHIP FUND

Award open to full-time undergraduate students with financial need who display academic excellence, strong citizenship and character, and a desire to make a meaningful contribution to society. Only to students who are permanent residents of a New England state are eligible. Qualifying students may attend college anywhere in the U.S. For more details see website http://www.phillips-scholarship.org.

Award: Scholarship for use in freshman, sophomore, junior, or senior years; renewable. *Number:* 150–200. *Amount:* $3000–$10,000.

Eligibility Requirements: Applicant must be enrolled or expecting to enroll full-time at a two-year or four-year institution or university and resident of Connecticut, Maine, Massachusetts, New Hampshire, Rhode Island, Vermont. Applicant must have 3.0 GPA or higher. Available to U.S. citizens.

Application Requirements: Application form, community service, essay, financial need analysis, recommendations or references, test scores, transcript. *Deadline:* May 1.

Contact: Karen Emery, Program Director
Stephen Phillips Memorial Scholarship Fund
PO Box 870
Salem, MA 01970
Phone: 978-744-2111
Fax: 978-744-0456
E-mail: kemery@spscholars.org

STEPHEN T. MARCHELLO SCHOLARSHIP FOUNDATION

http://www.stmfoundation.org/

A LEGACY OF HOPE SCHOLARSHIPS FOR SURVIVORS OF CHILDHOOD CANCER

Scholarship of up to $10,000 per year for four years of postsecondary undergraduate education. Applicant must be a survivor of childhood cancer. Must submit a letter from doctor, clinic, or hospital where cancer treatment was received. Residents of CO and MT are eligible. Must be U.S. citizen. Minimum 2.5 GPA required.

Award: Scholarship for use in freshman year; not renewable. *Number:* 1–6. *Amount:* $500–$10,000.

Eligibility Requirements: Applicant must be high school student; age 17-20; planning to enroll or expecting to enroll full- or part-time at a two-year or four-year or technical institution or university and resident of Colorado, Montana. Applicant must have 2.5 GPA or higher. Available to U.S. citizens.

Application Requirements: Application form, essay, recommendations or references, self-addressed stamped envelope with application, test scores, transcript. *Deadline:* March 15.

Contact: Mr. Mario Marchello, Secretary
Stephen T. Marchello Scholarship Foundation
1170 East Long Place
Centennial, CO 80122
Phone: 303-886-5018

SWISS BENEVOLENT SOCIETY OF CHICAGO

http://www.sbschicago.org/

SWISS BENEVOLENT SOCIETY OF CHICAGO SCHOLARSHIPS
• *See page 639*

SWISS BENEVOLENT SOCIETY OF NEW YORK

http://www.sbsny.org/

PELLEGRINI SCHOLARSHIP GRANTS
• *See page 639*

SYNOD OF THE COVENANT

http://www.synodofthecovenant.org/

RACIAL ETHNIC SCHOLARSHIP
• *See page 564*

TENNESSEE EDUCATION ASSOCIATION

http://www.teateachers.org/

TEA DON SAHLI-KATHY WOODALL SONS AND DAUGHTERS SCHOLARSHIP
• *See page 537*

TENNESSEE STUDENT ASSISTANCE CORPORATION

http://www.tn.gov/collegepays

DEPENDENT CHILDREN SCHOLARSHIP PROGRAM

Scholarship for Tennessee residents who are dependent children of a Tennessee law enforcement officer, fireman, or an emergency medical service technician who have been killed or totally and permanently disabled while performing duties within the scope of such employment. The scholarship is awarded to full-time undergraduate students for a maximum of four academic years or the period required for the completion of the program of study.

Award: Scholarship for use in freshman, sophomore, junior, or senior years; renewable.

Eligibility Requirements: Applicant must be enrolled or expecting to enroll full-time at a two-year or four-year institution or university; resident of Tennessee and studying in Tennessee. Available to U.S. citizens.

Application Requirements: Application form, application form may be submitted online (http://www.tn.gov/collegepays), FAFSA. *Deadline:* July 15.

Contact: Ms. Naomi Derryberry, Director of Grant and Scholarship Programs
Tennessee Student Assistance Corporation
Parkway Towers, 404 James Robertson Parkway, Suite 1510
Nashville, TN 37243-0820
Phone: 615-253-7478
Fax: 615-741-6101
E-mail: naomi.derryberry@tn.gov

HOPE WITH ASPIRE

HOPE Scholarship of $2000 per semester (four-year institution) or $1000 per semester (two-year institution) with $750 supplement per semester. Must meet Tennessee HOPE Scholarship requirements and Adjusted Gross Income (AGI) attributable to the student must be $36,000 or less.

Award: Scholarship for use in freshman, sophomore, junior, or senior years; renewable. *Amount:* up to $5500.

Eligibility Requirements: Applicant must be enrolled or expecting to enroll full- or part-time at a two-year or four-year institution or university; resident of Tennessee and studying in Tennessee. Applicant must have 3.0 GPA or higher. Available to U.S. citizens.

Application Requirements: Application form, application form may be submitted online (http://www.fafsa.gov), financial need analysis. *Deadline:* September 1.

Contact: Mr. Robert Biggers, Director of Lottery Scholarship Programs
Tennessee Student Assistance Corporation
Parkway Towers, 404 James Robertson Parkway, Suite 1510
Nashville, TN 37243-0820
Phone: 615-253-7453
Fax: 615-741-6101
E-mail: robert.biggers@tn.gov

NED MCWHERTER SCHOLARS PROGRAM

Award for Tennessee high school seniors with high academic ability. Must have minimum high school GPA of 3.5 and a score of 29 on the ACT or SAT equivalent. Must attend a college or university in Tennessee and be a permanent U.S. citizen. For more information, visit website http://tn.gov/collegepays.

Award: Scholarship for use in freshman, sophomore, junior, or senior years; renewable. *Number:* up to 200. *Amount:* up to $3000.

Eligibility Requirements: Applicant must be enrolled or expecting to enroll full-time at a two-year or four-year or technical institution or university; resident of Tennessee and studying in Tennessee. Applicant must have 3.5 GPA or higher. Available to U.S. citizens.

Application Requirements: Application form, application form may be submitted online (http://www.tn.gov/collegepays), test scores, transcript. *Deadline:* February 15.

Contact: Mrs. Kathy Stripling, Scholarship Administrator
Tennessee Student Assistance Corporation
404 James Robertson Parkway, Suite 1510, Parkway Towers
Nashville, TN 37243-0820
Phone: 615-253-7480
Fax: 615-741-6101
E-mail: kathy.stripling@tn.gov

TENNESSEE DUAL ENROLLMENT GRANT

Grant for study at an eligible Tennessee postsecondary institution awarded to juniors and seniors in a Tennessee high school who have been admitted to undergraduate study while still pursuing a high school diploma. For more information, visit website http://www.tn.gov/collegepays.

Award: Grant for use in freshman year; renewable. *Amount:* up to $1200.

Eligibility Requirements: Applicant must be high school student; planning to enroll or expecting to enroll part-time at a two-year or four-year or technical institution or university; resident of Tennessee and studying in Tennessee. Available to U.S. citizens.

Application Requirements: Application form, application form may be submitted online (http://www.tn.gov/collegepays). *Deadline:* September 1.

Contact: Mr. Robert Biggers, Director of Lottery Scholarship Program
Tennessee Student Assistance Corporation
Parkway Towers, 404 James Robertson Parkway, Suite 1510
Nashville, TN 37243-0820
Phone: 615-253-7453
Fax: 615-741-1601
E-mail: robert.biggers@tn.gov

TENNESSEE EDUCATION LOTTERY SCHOLARSHIP PROGRAM HOPE ACCESS GRANT

Non-renewable award of $2750 for students at four-year colleges or $1750 for students at two-year colleges. Entering freshmen must have a minimum GPA of 2.75, ACT score of 18-20 (or SAT equivalent), and adjusted gross income attributable to the student must be $36,000 or less. Recipients will become eligible for Tennessee HOPE Scholarship by meeting HOPE Scholarship renewal criteria.

Award: Scholarship for use in freshman, sophomore, junior, or senior years; not renewable. *Amount:* up to $2750.

Eligibility Requirements: Applicant must be enrolled or expecting to enroll full- or part-time at a two-year or four-year institution or university; resident of Tennessee and studying in Tennessee. Available to U.S. citizens.

Application Requirements: Application form, application form may be submitted online (http://www.fafsa.gov), financial need analysis. *Deadline:* September 1.

Contact: Mr. Robert Biggers, Director of Lottery Scholarship Programs
Tennessee Student Assistance Corporation
Parkway Towers, 404 James Robertson Parkway, Suite 1510
Nashville, TN 37243-0820
Phone: 615-253-7453
Fax: 615-741-6101
E-mail: robert.biggers@tn.gov

TENNESSEE EDUCATION LOTTERY SCHOLARSHIP PROGRAM-HOPE WITH GENERAL ASSEMBLY MERIT SCHOLARSHIP (GAMS)

HOPE Scholarship of $2000 per semester (four-year institution) or $1000 per semester (two-year institution) with supplemental award of $500 per semester. Entering freshmen must have 3.75 GPA and 29 ACT (1280 SAT). Must be a U.S. citizen and a resident of Tennessee.

Award: Scholarship for use in freshman, sophomore, junior, or senior years; renewable. *Amount:* up to $5000.

Eligibility Requirements: Applicant must be enrolled or expecting to enroll full- or part-time at a two-year or four-year institution or university; resident of Tennessee and studying in Tennessee. Available to U.S. citizens.

Application Requirements: Application form, application form may be submitted online (http://www.fafsa.gov). *Deadline:* September 1.

Contact: Mr. Robert Biggers, Director of Lottery Scholarship Programs
Tennessee Student Assistance Corporation
Parkway Towers, 404 James Robertson Parkway, Suite 1510
Nashville, TN 37243-0820
Phone: 615-253-7453
Fax: 615-741-6101
E-mail: robert.biggers@tn.gov

TENNESSEE EDUCATION LOTTERY SCHOLARSHIP PROGRAM TENNESSEE HOPE SCHOLARSHIP

Award amount is $2000 for per semester at four-year institutions and $1000 per semester at two-year institutions. Must be a Tennessee resident attending an eligible postsecondary institution in Tennessee. For more information, visit http://www.TN.gov/CollegePays.

Award: Scholarship for use in freshman, sophomore, junior, or senior years; renewable. *Amount:* $2000-$6000.

Eligibility Requirements: Applicant must be enrolled or expecting to enroll full- or part-time at a two-year or four-year institution or university; resident of Tennessee and studying in Tennessee. Applicant must have 3.0 GPA or higher. Available to U.S. citizens.

Application Requirements: Application form, application form may be submitted online (http://www.fafsa.gov). *Deadline:* September 1.

TENNESSEE EDUCATION LOTTERY SCHOLARSHIP PROGRAM WILDER-NAIFEH TECHNICAL SKILLS GRANT

Award up to $2000 for students enrolled in a certificate or diploma program at a Tennessee Technology Center. Cannot be prior recipient of Tennessee HOPE Scholarship. For more information, visit http://www.TN.gov/CollegePays.

Award: Grant for use in freshman or sophomore years; renewable. *Amount:* up to $2000.

Eligibility Requirements: Applicant must be enrolled or expecting to enroll full- or part-time at a technical institution; resident of Tennessee and studying in Tennessee. Available to U.S. citizens.

Application Requirements: Application form, application form may be submitted online (http://www.fafsa.gov). *Deadline:* November 1.

Contact: Mr. Robert Biggers, Director of Lottery Scholarship Programs
Tennessee Student Assistance Corporation
Parkway Towers, 404 James Robertson Parkway, Suite 1510
Nashville, TN 37243-0820
Phone: 615-253-7453
Fax: 615-741-6101
E-mail: robert.biggers@tn.gov

TENNESSEE HOPE FOSTER CHILD TUITION GRANT

Renewable tuition award available for recipients of the HOPE Scholarship or HOPE Access Grant. Student must have been in Tennessee state custody as a foster child for at least one year after reaching age 14. Award amount varies and shall not exceed the tuition and mandatory fees at an eligible Tennessee public postsecondary institution. For additional information, visit website http://www.tn.gov/collegepays.

Award: Scholarship for use in freshman, sophomore, junior, or senior years; renewable.

Eligibility Requirements: Applicant must be enrolled or expecting to enroll full- or part-time at a two-year or four-year institution or university; resident of Tennessee and studying in Tennessee. Applicant must have 3.0 GPA or higher. Available to U.S. citizens.

Application Requirements: Application form, application form may be submitted online (http://www.fafsa.gov). *Deadline:* September 1.

Contact: Mr. Robert Biggers, Director of Lottery Scholarship Programs
Tennessee Student Assistance Corporation
Parkway Towers, 404 James Robertson Parkway, Suite 1510
Nashville, TN 37243-0820
Phone: 615-253-7453
Fax: 615-741-6101
E-mail: robert.biggers@tn.gov

TENNESSEE STUDENT ASSISTANCE AWARD

Award to assist financially-needy Tennessee residents attending an approved college or university within the state. Complete a Free Application for Federal Student Aid form. FAFSA must be processed as soon as possible after January 1 for priority consideration. To apply, go to http://www.fafsa.gov. For more information, go to www.tn.gov/collegepays

Award: Grant for use in freshman, sophomore, junior, or senior years; not renewable. *Number:* 30,000–35,000. *Amount:* $100–$4000.

Eligibility Requirements: Applicant must be enrolled or expecting to enroll full- or part-time at a two-year or four-year or technical institution or university; resident of Tennessee and studying in Tennessee. Available to U.S. citizens.

Application Requirements: Application form, application form may be submitted online (http://www.fafsa.gov), financial need analysis.

Contact: Ms. Naomi Derryberry, Director of Grants and Scholarship
Programs
Tennessee Student Assistance Corporation
Parkway Towers, 404 James Robertson Parkway, Suite 1510
Nashville, TN 37243-0820
Phone: 615-253-7478
Fax: 615-741-6101
E-mail: naomi.derryberry@tn.gov

TERRY FOUNDATION

http://www.terryfoundation.org/

TERRY FOUNDATION SCHOLARSHIP

Scholarships to Texas high school seniors who have been admitted to the universities affiliated with the foundation: University of Texas at Austin, Texas A&M University at College Station, University of Houston, Texas State University San Marcos, University of Texas at San Antonio and University of Texas at Dallas. Minimum 2.5 GPA required. Scholarship is based upon leadership potential and character; scholastic record and ability; and financial need.

Award: Scholarship for use in freshman year; renewable. *Number:* 208–650. *Amount:* $19,000–$76,000.

Eligibility Requirements: Applicant must be high school student; planning to enroll or expecting to enroll full-time at a four-year institution or university; resident of Texas; studying in Texas and must have an interest in leadership. Applicant must have 2.5 GPA or higher. Available to U.S. citizens.

Application Requirements: Application form, essay, financial need analysis, interview, recommendations or references, transcript. *Deadline:* varies.

Contact: Ms. Beth Freeman, Scholarship Committee
Phone: 713-552-0002
Fax: 713-650-8729
E-mail: beth.freeman@terryfoundation.org

TEXAS 4-H YOUTH DEVELOPMENT FOUNDATION

http://texas4hfoundation.org/

TEXAS 4-H OPPORTUNITY SCHOLARSHIP

Renewable award for Texas 4-H members to attend a Texas college or university. Minimum GPA of 2.5 required. Must attend full-time.

Award: Scholarship for use in freshman, sophomore, junior, or senior years; renewable. *Number:* 225. *Amount:* $1500–$15,000.

Eligibility Requirements: Applicant must be enrolled or expecting to enroll full-time at a two-year or four-year or technical institution; resident of Texas; studying in Texas and must have an interest in animal/agricultural competition. Applicant must have 2.5 GPA or higher. Available to U.S. citizens.

Application Requirements: Application form, essay, financial need analysis, interview, recommendations or references, test scores, transcript. *Deadline:* varies.

Contact: Jim Reeves, Executive Director
Phone: 979-845-1213
Fax: 979-845-6495
E-mail: jereeves@ag.tamu.edu

TEXAS AFL-CIO

http://www.texasaflcio.org/

TEXAS AFL-CIO SCHOLARSHIP PROGRAM
• *See page 538*

TEXAS BLACK BAPTIST SCHOLARSHIP COMMITTEE

TEXAS BLACK BAPTIST SCHOLARSHIP
• *See page 639*

TEXAS HIGHER EDUCATION COORDINATING BOARD

http://www.collegefortexans.com/

TEXAS NATIONAL GUARD TUITION ASSISTANCE PROGRAM
• *See page 585*

TOWARD EXCELLENCE ACCESS AND SUCCESS (TEXAS GRANT)

Renewable aid for students enrolled in public colleges or universities in Texas. Must be a resident of Texas and have completed the Recommended High School Curriculum or Distinguished Achievement Curriculum in high school. For renewal awards, must maintain a minimum GPA of 2.5. Based on need. Amount of award is determined by the financial aid office of each school. Deadlines vary. Contact the college/university financial aid office for application information.

Award: Grant for use in freshman, sophomore, junior, or senior years; renewable. *Amount:* $2680–$6080.

Eligibility Requirements: Applicant must be enrolled or expecting to enroll full- or part-time at a two-year or four-year or technical institution or university; resident of Texas and studying in Texas. Available to U.S. citizens.

Application Requirements: Financial need analysis, transcript.

TUITION EQUALIZATION GRANT (TEG) PROGRAM

Renewable award for Texas residents enrolled full-time at an independent college or university within the state. Based on financial need. Renewal awards require the student to maintain an overall college GPA of at least 2.5. Deadlines vary by institution. Must not be receiving athletic scholarship. Contact college/university financial aid office for application information. Nonresidents who are National Merit Finalists may also receive awards.

Award: Grant for use in freshman, sophomore, junior, or senior years; renewable. *Amount:* $3808–$5712.

Eligibility Requirements: Applicant must be enrolled or expecting to enroll full-time at a two-year or four-year institution or university; resident of Texas and studying in Texas. Available to U.S. citizens.

Application Requirements: FAFSA, financial need analysis.

TEXAS TENNIS FOUNDATION

http://www.texastennisfoundation.com/

TEXAS TENNIS FOUNDATION SCHOLARSHIPS AND ENDOWMENTS

College scholarships for highly recommended students residing in Texas, with an interest in tennis. Financial need is considered. Must be between the ages of 17 and 19. Refer to website for details, http://www.texastennisfoundation.com/web90/scholarships/tenniscampsscholarships.asp.

Award: Scholarship for use in freshman, sophomore, junior, or senior years; not renewable. *Number:* 10. *Amount:* $1000.

Eligibility Requirements: Applicant must be age 17-19; enrolled or expecting to enroll full-time at a two-year or four-year or technical institution or university; resident of Texas and must have an interest in athletics/sports. Available to U.S. citizens.

Application Requirements: Application form, copy of parent or guardian's federal tax return, essay, financial need analysis, personal photograph, recommendations or references, test scores, transcript. *Deadline:* April 15.

Contact: Ken McAllister, Executive Director
Phone: 512-443-1334 Ext. 201
Fax: 512-443-4748
E-mail: kmcallister@texas.usta.com

THEODORE R. AND VIVIAN M. JOHNSON SCHOLARSHIP FOUNDATION INC.

http://www.jsf.bz/

THEODORE R. AND VIVIAN M. JOHNSON SCHOLARSHIP PROGRAM FOR CHILDREN OF UPS EMPLOYEES OR UPS RETIREES

• See page 549

TIDEWATER SCHOLARSHIP FOUNDATION

http://www.accesscollege.org/

ACCESS SCHOLARSHIP/LAST DOLLAR AWARD

A renewable scholarship of $500 to $1000 for the undergraduates participating in Norfolk, Portsmouth, and Virginia Beach, Virginia secure scholarships and financial aid for college.

Award: Scholarship for use in freshman year; renewable. *Amount:* $500–$1000.

Eligibility Requirements: Applicant must be high school student; planning to enroll or expecting to enroll full-time at a two-year or four-year institution or university and resident of Virginia. Applicant must have 2.5 GPA or higher. Available to U.S. citizens.

Application Requirements: Application form, financial need analysis. *Deadline:* May 1.

Contact: Bonnie Sutton, President and Chief Executive Officer
Phone: 757-962-6113
Fax: 757-962-7314
E-mail: bsutton@accesscollege.org

TIGER WOODS FOUNDATION

http://www.tigerwoodsfoundation.org/

ALFRED "TUP" HOLMES MEMORIAL SCHOLARSHIP

Given yearly to one worthy Atlanta metropolitan area graduating high school senior who has displayed high moral character while demonstrating leadership potential and academic excellence. Must be U.S. citizen. Minimum 3.0 GPA required.

Award: Scholarship for use in freshman year; not renewable. *Number:* 1. *Amount:* $2500.

Eligibility Requirements: Applicant must be high school student; planning to enroll or expecting to enroll full-time at a two-year or four-year institution or university and resident of Georgia. Applicant must have 3.0 GPA or higher. Available to U.S. citizens.

Application Requirements: Application form, community service, essay, recommendations or references, test scores, transcript. *Deadline:* April 1.

Contact: Michelle Kim, Scholarship and Grant Coordinator
Phone: 949-725-3003
Fax: 949-725-3002
E-mail: grants@tigerwoodsfoundation.org

TKE EDUCATIONAL FOUNDATION

http://www.tke.org/

ELMER AND DORIS SCHMITZ SR. MEMORIAL SCHOLARSHIP

• See page 539

TORTOISE CAPITAL ADVISORS, LLC

http://www.tortoiseadvisors.com

TORTOISE YOUNG ENTREPRENEURS SCHOLARSHIP

The program is designed to give deserving students a leg up in their academic endeavors. In turn, we hope their educational experience will help them mold an entrepreneurial mindset that helps them conceive or support firms that create innovative products, processes and solutions. To be eligible, applicants must be a permanent resident of Kansas or Missouri who is enrolled or plans to enroll in a full-time undergraduate course of study towards a bachelor's degree, or be a non-resident of either state who is enrolled or plans to enroll as a full-time student in a four-year bachelor's program at a Kansas or Missouri accredited university or college, and have a minimum 3.3 grade-point average (on a 4.0 scale or equivalent) and a minimum ACT score of 24 or minimum SAT score of 1680 (includes writing section).

Award: Scholarship for use in freshman, sophomore, junior, or senior years; not renewable. *Number:* 3–3. *Amount:* $1000–$2500.

Eligibility Requirements: Applicant must be enrolled or expecting to enroll full-time at a four-year institution or university; resident of Kansas, Missouri and studying in Kansas, Missouri. Applicant must have 3.0 GPA or higher. Available to U.S. citizens.

Application Requirements: Application form, application form may be submitted online (http://www.tortoiseadvisors.com/scholarship/), community service, essay, recommendations or references, test scores, transcript. *Deadline:* April 1.

Contact: Ben Fraser, Institutional Client Relations Coordinator
Phone: 913-890-2118
E-mail: bfraser@tortoiseadvisors.com

TOWNSHIP OFFICIALS OF ILLINOIS

http://www.toi.org/

TOWNSHIP OFFICIALS OF ILLINOIS SCHOLARSHIP FUND

The scholarships are awarded to graduating Illinois high school seniors who have a B average or above, have demonstrated an active interest in school activities, who have submitted an essay on "The Importance of Township Government," high school transcript, and letters of recommendation. Students must attend Illinois institutions, either four-year or junior colleges. Must be full-time student. Must complete an interview with a current township official.

Award: Scholarship for use in freshman year; not renewable. *Number:* 7. *Amount:* $2000.

Eligibility Requirements: Applicant must be high school student; planning to enroll or expecting to enroll full-time at a two-year or four-year institution or university; resident of Illinois and studying in Illinois. Applicant must have 3.0 GPA or higher. Available to U.S. citizens.

Application Requirements: Application form, essay, interview, recommendations or references, test scores, transcript. *Deadline:* March 1.

Contact: Bryan Smith, Editor and Executive Director
Township Officials of Illinois
408 South Fifth Street
Springfield, IL 62701-1804
Phone: 217-744-2212
Fax: 217-744-7419
E-mail: bryan@toi.org

TRIANGLE COMMUNITY FOUNDATION

http://www.trianglecf.org/

GLAXOSMITHKLINE OPPORTUNITY SCHOLARSHIP

Scholarship available to U.S. citizens who are residents of Orange, Durham, and Wake counties who have overcome significant adversity. Must be used for a public higher education institute in North Carolina. No income limitations. Must demonstrate the potential to succeed despite adversity as well as an exceptional desire to improve himself or herself through further education. For further information, see website at http://www.tranglecf.org.

Award: Scholarship for use in freshman, sophomore, junior, senior, or graduate years; renewable. *Number:* 1–10. *Amount:* $5000–$20,000.

Eligibility Requirements: Applicant must be enrolled or expecting to enroll full- or part-time at a two-year or four-year institution or university; resident of North Carolina and studying in North Carolina. Available to U.S. citizens.

Application Requirements: Application form, application form may be submitted online (http://www.trianglecf.org/grants_support/view_scholarships/glaxosmithkline_opportunity_scholarship/), essay, financial need analysis, proof of U.S. citizenship, recommendations or references, test scores, transcript. *Deadline:* March 15.

Contact: Ms. Gina Andersen, Scholarships and Community Outreach
Coordinator
Triangle Community Foundation
324 Blackwell Street, Suite 1220
Durham, NC 27701
Phone: 919-474-8370 Ext. 145
Fax: 919-941-9208
E-mail: Scholarships@trianglecf.org

ULMAN CANCER FUND FOR YOUNG ADULTS

http://www.ulmanfund.org/

MARILYN YETSO MEMORIAL SCHOLARSHIP

Provides support for the financial needs of college students who have a
parent with cancer or who have lost a parent to cancer. Currently
attending, or accepted to, a two- or four-year college, university or
vocational program (including graduate and professional schools). Must
be a resident of, or attending or planning to attend an educational
institution in: Maryland, Virginia, or Washington, D.C.

Award: Scholarship for use in freshman, sophomore, junior, or senior
years; not renewable. *Number:* 1–2. *Amount:* $1000.

Eligibility Requirements: Applicant must be age 15-35; enrolled or
expecting to enroll full- or part-time at a two-year or four-year or
technical institution or university; resident of District of Columbia,
Maryland, Virginia and studying in District of Columbia, Maryland,
Virginia. Available to U.S. and non-U.S. citizens.

Application Requirements: Application form, essay, financial need
analysis, parent's medical history, recommendations or references, self-
addressed stamped envelope with application. *Deadline:* May 10.

Contact: Fay Baker, Scholarship Coordinator
Phone: 410-964-0202
E-mail: scholarship@ulmanfund.org

VERA YIP MEMORIAL SCHOLARSHIP

• *See page 579*

UNITED DAUGHTERS OF THE CONFEDERACY

http://www.hqudc.org/

CHARLOTTE M. F. BENTLEY/NEW YORK CHAPTER 103 SCHOLARSHIP

• *See page 540*

GERTRUDE BOTTS-SAUCIER SCHOLARSHIP

• *See page 541*

LOLA B. CURRY SCHOLARSHIP

• *See page 541*

UNITED METHODIST CHURCH

http://www.gbhem.org/

J. A. KNOWLES MEMORIAL SCHOLARSHIP

• *See page 652*

UNITED NEGRO COLLEGE FUND

http://www.uncf.org/

ALASKA SCHOLARSHIP PROGRAM

• *See page 641*

ALLEN AND JOAN BILDNER SCHOLARSHIP

• *See page 641*

BRISTOL-MYERS SQUIBB SCHOLARSHIP

• *See page 641*

CHARLES & ELLORA ALLIS FOUNDATION SCHOLARSHIP

• *See page 641*

CHICAGO PUBLIC SCHOOLS UNCF CAMPAIGN

• *See page 642*

CITY OF CLEVELAND: MAYOR JACKSON SCHOLARSHIP FOR CLEVELAND METROPOLITAN SCHOOL DISTRICT

• *See page 642*

CITY OF CLEVELAND: MAYOR JACKSON SCHOLARSHIP FOR HISTORICALLY BLACK COLLEGES AND UNIVERSITIES

• *See page 642*

DALLAS INDEPENDENT SCHOOL DISTRICT SCHOLARSHIP

• *See page 642*

DAVENPORT FORTE PEDESTAL FUND

• *See page 642*

DAVID GEFFEN FOUNDATION SCHOLARSHIP

• *See page 642*

DEBORAH L. VINCENT FAHRO EDUCATION SCHOLARSHIP AWARD

• *See page 642*

DOMINIQUE AND JACQUES CASIMIR SCHOLARSHIP

• *See page 642*

EDNA F. BLUM FOUNDATION SCHOLARSHIP

• *See page 643*

EDWARD FITTERMAN FOUNDATION SCHOLARSHIP

• *See page 643*

ELMER ROE DEAVER FOUNDATION SCHOLARSHIP

• *See page 643*

EVELYN LEVINA WRIGHT SCHOLARSHIP

• *See page 643*

FEDERAL EXPRESS/UNCF SCHOLARSHIP INITIATIVE

• *See page 643*

FORT WORTH INDEPENDENT SCHOOL DISTRICT SCHOLARSHIP

• *See page 643*

HARRY PINKERTON SCHOLARSHIP

• *See page 644*

IOWA STUDENT AID SCHOLARSHIP

• *See page 644*

JAY CHARLES LEVINE SCHOLARSHIP

• *See page 644*

JOHN W. ANDERSON FOUNDATION SCHOLARSHIP

• *See page 644*

LOUISVILLE GALA SCHOLARSHIP

• *See page 645*

MAYA ANGELOU/VIVIAN BAXTER SCHOLARSHIP

• *See page 565*

MAYOR DOUGLAS PALMER TRENTON/UNCF SCHOLARSHIP
• *See page 645*

MINNESOTA STUDENT AID SCHOLARSHIP
• *See page 645*

NEBRASKA STUDENT AID SCHOLARSHIP
• *See page 646*

OKLAHOMA GOVERNOR'S LUNCHEON SCHOLARSHIP
• *See page 646*

ORACLE COMMUNITY IMPACT SCHOLARSHIP
• *See page 646*

PENNSYLVANIA STATE EMPLOYEES SCHOLARSHIP (SECA)
• *See page 646*

RONALD MCDONALD'S CHICAGOLAND AND NORTHWEST INDIANA SCHOLARSHIP
• *See page 646*

RYAN HOWARD FAMILY FOUNDATION SCHOLARSHIP-ST. LOUIS/PHILADELPHIA
• *See page 565*

ST. PETERSBURG GOLF CLASSIC SCHOLARSHIP
• *See page 646*

VALLANTEEN ABBINGTON SCHOLARSHIP
• *See page 647*

WHIRLPOOL FOUNDATION SCHOLARSHIP
• *See page 647*

YOUTH EMPOWERMENT SCHOLARSHIP
• *See page 647*

UNIVERSITY OF NEW MEXICO
http://www.unm.edu/

BRIDGE TO SUCCESS SCHOLARSHIP
Scholarship to the students who reside in New Mexico and are U.S. citizens. Applicant must be a graduate from a New Mexico public (or accredited private) high school or be a GED recipient. Must have a minimum high school GPA of 2.5 or GED score 530. Deadline varies for fall it is June 30 and for spring it is November 30.

Award: Scholarship for use in freshman year; not renewable.

Eligibility Requirements: Applicant must be high school student; planning to enroll or expecting to enroll full-time at a four-year institution or university and resident of New Mexico. Applicant must have 2.5 GPA or higher. Available to U.S. citizens.

Application Requirements: Application form, proof of enrollment, transcript. *Deadline:* continuous.

Contact: Robert Romero, Financial Aid Adviser
    Phone: 505-277-6090
    Fax: 505-277-5275
    E-mail: schol@unm.edu

NM LOTTERY SUCCESS SCHOLARSHIP
Scholarship to the residents of New Mexico. Applicant must be graduate from a New Mexico public (or accredited private) high school or receive a GED. Must enroll full-time in a baccalaureate degree program.

Award: Scholarship for use in freshman year; renewable.

Eligibility Requirements: Applicant must be enrolled or expecting to enroll full-time at a four-year institution or university and resident of New Mexico. Applicant must have 2.5 GPA or higher. Available to U.S. citizens.

Application Requirements: Application form, resume, transcript. *Deadline:* varies.

Contact: Robert Romero, Financial Aid Adviser
    Phone: 505-277-6090
    Fax: 505-277-5275
    E-mail: schol@unm.edu

URBAN LEAGUE OF RHODE ISLAND INC.
http://www.ulri.org/

URBAN LEAGUE OF RHODE ISLAND SCHOLARSHIP
• *See page 648*

UTAH HIGHER EDUCATION ASSISTANCE AUTHORITY
http://www.uheaa.org/

HIGHER EDUCATION SUCCESS STIPEND PROGRAM
Award available to students with substantial financial need for use at any of the participating Utah institutions. The student must be a Utah resident. Contact the financial aid office of the participating institution for requirements and deadlines.

Award: Grant for use in freshman, sophomore, junior, or senior years; not renewable. *Number:* 422–7028. *Amount:* $300–$5000.

Eligibility Requirements: Applicant must be enrolled or expecting to enroll full- or part-time at a two-year or four-year or technical institution or university; resident of Utah and studying in Utah. Available to U.S. citizens.

Application Requirements: FAFSA, financial need analysis. *Deadline:* continuous.

Contact: Mr. David Hughes, Manager of Student Aid Partnerships
    Phone: 801-321-7220
    Fax: 801-321-7168
    E-mail: dhughes@utahsbr.edu

UTAH LEVERAGING EDUCATIONAL ASSISTANCE PARTNERSHIP
Award available to Utah resident students with substantial financial need for use at any of the participating Utah institutions. Contact the financial aid office of the participating institution for requirements and deadlines. This is a State Federal matching program. All State funds were rolled into the Higher Education Success Stipend Program (HESSP).

Award: Grant for use in freshman, sophomore, junior, or senior years; not renewable. *Amount:* $300–$2500.

Eligibility Requirements: Applicant must be enrolled or expecting to enroll full- or part-time at a two-year or four-year or technical institution or university; resident of Utah and studying in Utah. Available to U.S. citizens.

Application Requirements: FAFSA, financial need analysis. *Deadline:* continuous.

Contact: Mr. David Hughes, Manager of Student Aid Partnerships
    Phone: 801-321-7220
    Fax: 801-321-7168
    E-mail: dhughes@utahsbr.edu

UTAH STATE BOARD OF REGENTS
http://www.higheredutah.org

NEW CENTURY SCHOLARSHIP PROGRAM
The New Century Scholarship is for Utah high school students who complete the requirements for an Associate's Degree by the date they graduate from high school with a minimum cumulative GPA of 3.5. Recipients receive an award of $1250 per eligible semester at eligible institutions in Utah for up to the shortest of 4 terms, 60 credit hours or completion of a bachelors degree. recipients must complete a minimum of 12 credit hours for each semester of payment with a minimum 3.0 semester GPA.

Award: Scholarship for use in junior or senior years; renewable. *Number:* 2300. *Amount:* $1250.

Eligibility Requirements: Applicant must be enrolled or expecting to enroll full-time at a four-year institution or university; resident of Utah and studying in Utah. Applicant must have 3.0 GPA or higher. Available to U.S. citizens.

Application Requirements: Application form, GPA/copy of enrollment verification from an eligible Utah 4-year institution, verification from registrar of completion of requirements for associate's degree, transcript. *Deadline:* February 1.

Contact: David Hughes, Manager of Student Aid Partnerships
Utah State Board of Regents
Board of Regents Building, The Gateway
60 South 400 West
Salt Lake City, UT 84101-1284
Phone: 801-321-7220
Fax: 801-321-7168
E-mail: dhughes@utahsbr.edu

VERMONT STUDENT ASSISTANCE CORPORATION

http://www.vsac.org/

VERMONT INCENTIVE GRANTS

Renewable grants for Vermont residents based on financial need. Must meet needs test. Must be college undergraduate or graduate student enrolled full-time at an approved post secondary institution. Only available to Vermont residents.

Award: Grant for use in freshman, sophomore, junior, or senior years; renewable. *Amount:* $500–$10,800.

Eligibility Requirements: Applicant must be enrolled or expecting to enroll full-time at a two-year or four-year or technical institution or university and resident of Vermont. Available to U.S. citizens.

Application Requirements: Application form, FAFSA, financial need analysis. *Deadline:* continuous.

VERMONT NON-DEGREE STUDENT GRANT PROGRAM

Need-based, renewable grants for Vermont residents enrolled in non-degree programs in a college, vocational school, or high school adult program, that will improve employability or encourage further study. Award amounts vary.

Award: Grant for use in freshman, sophomore, junior, or senior years; renewable.

Eligibility Requirements: Applicant must be enrolled or expecting to enroll full- or part-time at a two-year or four-year or technical institution or university and resident of Vermont. Available to U.S. citizens.

Application Requirements: Application form, financial need analysis. *Deadline:* continuous.

VERMONT PART-TIME STUDENT GRANTS

For undergraduates carrying less than twelve credits per semester who have not received a bachelor's degree. Must be Vermont resident. Based on financial need. Complete Vermont Financial Aid Packet to apply. May be used at any approved post-secondary institution.

Award: Grant for use in freshman, sophomore, junior, or senior years; renewable. *Amount:* $250–$8100.

Eligibility Requirements: Applicant must be enrolled or expecting to enroll part-time at a four-year institution or university and resident of Vermont. Available to U.S. citizens.

Application Requirements: Application form, financial need analysis. *Deadline:* continuous.

VIKKI CARR SCHOLARSHIP FOUNDATION

http://vikkicarr.com

VIKKI CARR SCHOLARSHIPS
• *See page 649*

VINCENT L. HAWKINSON FOUNDATION FOR PEACE AND JUSTICE

http://www.hawkinsonfoundation.org

VINCENT L. HAWKINSON SCHOLARSHIP FOR PEACE AND JUSTICE

Scholarships are awarded to students who demonstrate a deep commitment to peace and justice and are residents of or attend school in Minnesota, Iowa, Wisconsin, North or South Dakota. Awarded without regard to financial need or religious affiliation. Finalists are personally interviewed in Minneapolis.

Award: Scholarship for use in freshman, sophomore, junior, senior, graduate, or postgraduate years; not renewable. *Number:* 1–6. *Amount:* $4000–$5000.

Eligibility Requirements: Applicant must be enrolled or expecting to enroll full- or part-time at a two-year or four-year or technical institution or university; resident of Iowa, Minnesota, North Dakota, South Dakota, Wisconsin; studying in Iowa, Minnesota, North Dakota, South Dakota, Wisconsin and must have an interest in leadership. Available to U.S. and non-U.S. citizens.

Application Requirements: Application form, essay, interview, recommendations or references, transcript. *Deadline:* March 15.

Contact: Jill Abenth, Administrative Assistant
Vincent L. Hawkinson Foundation for Peace and Justice
324 Harvard Street, SE
Minneapolis, MN 55414
Phone: 612-331-8125
E-mail: info@graceattheu.org

VIRGINIA DEPARTMENT OF EDUCATION

http://www.pen.k12.va.us/

GRANVILLE P. MEADE SCHOLARSHIP

High school seniors only are eligible to apply for scholarship. Students are selected based upon GPA, standardized test scores, letters of recommendations, extra curricular activities, and financial need.

Award: Scholarship for use in freshman year; renewable. *Number:* 5. *Amount:* $2000.

Eligibility Requirements: Applicant must be high school student; planning to enroll or expecting to enroll full-time at a two-year or four-year institution or university and resident of Virginia. Available to U.S. citizens.

Application Requirements: Application form, essay, financial need analysis, recommendations or references, test scores, transcript. *Deadline:* March 16.

Contact: Joseph Wharff, School Counseling Connections Specialist
Phone: 804-225-3370
E-mail: joseph.wharff@doe.virginia.gov

VIRGINIA DEPARTMENT OF VETERANS SERVICES

http://www.dvs.virginia.gov/

VIRGINIA MILITARY SURVIVORS AND DEPENDENTS EDUCATION PROGRAM
• *See page 608*

VIRGINIA STATE COUNCIL OF HIGHER EDUCATION

http://www.schev.edu/

VIRGINIA COMMONWEALTH AWARD

Need-based award for undergraduate or graduate study at a Virginia public two- or four-year college, or university. Undergraduates must be Virginia residents. The application and awards process are administered by the financial aid office at the Virginia public institution where student is enrolled. Dollar value of each award varies. Contact financial aid office for application and deadlines.

Award: Grant for use in freshman, sophomore, junior, or senior years; not renewable.

Eligibility Requirements: Applicant must be enrolled or expecting to enroll full- or part-time at a two-year or four-year institution or university; resident of Virginia and studying in Virginia. Available to U.S. citizens.

Application Requirements: Financial need analysis.

VIRGINIA GUARANTEED ASSISTANCE PROGRAM

Awards to undergraduate students proportional to their need, up to full tuition, fees and book allowance. Must be a graduate of a Virginia high school. High school GPA of 2.5 required. Must be enrolled full-time in a public Virginia two- or four-year institution and demonstrate financial need. Must maintain minimum college GPA of 2.0 for renewal awards.

Award: Grant for use in freshman, sophomore, junior, or senior years; not renewable.

Eligibility Requirements: Applicant must be enrolled or expecting to enroll full-time at a two-year or four-year institution or university; resident of Virginia and studying in Virginia. Available to U.S. citizens.

Application Requirements: Financial need analysis, transcript.

VIRGINIA TUITION ASSISTANCE GRANT PROGRAM (PRIVATE INSTITUTIONS)

Awards for undergraduate students. Also available to graduate and first professional degree students pursuing a health-related degree program. Not to be used for religious study. Must be US citizen or eligible non-citizen, Virginia domiciled, and enrolled full-time at an approved private, nonprofit college within Virginia. Information and application available from participating Virginia colleges financial aid office. Visit http://www.schev.edu and click on Financial Aid.

Award: Grant for use in freshman, sophomore, junior, senior, or graduate years; renewable. *Number:* 22,000. *Amount:* up to $2850.

Eligibility Requirements: Applicant must be enrolled or expecting to enroll full-time at a four-year institution or university; resident of Virginia and studying in Virginia. Available to U.S. citizens.

Application Requirements: Application form. *Deadline:* July 31.

WALLACE S. AND WILMA K. LAUGHLIN FOUNDATION TRUST

http://www.nefda.org/

SWANSON SCHOLARSHIP

Scholarship for a Nebraska student entering the mortuary science program at a Kansas City community college. Must be a US citizen, a high school graduate and have completed Nebraska pre-mortuary science hours. Scholarship value and number of awards varies annually.

Award: Scholarship for use in junior or senior years; not renewable. *Number:* 1–10. *Amount:* $1000–$10,000.

Eligibility Requirements: Applicant must be enrolled or expecting to enroll full-time at a two-year institution and resident of Nebraska. Available to U.S. citizens.

Application Requirements: Application form, financial need analysis, interview, recommendations or references, transcript. *Deadline:* June 30.

Contact: Craig Draucker, Chairman
Wallace S. and Wilma K. Laughlin Foundation Trust
1633 Normandy Court, Suite A
Lincoln, NE 68516
Phone: 402-423-8900
Fax: 402-476-6547

WASHINGTON HOSPITAL HEALTHCARE SYSTEM

http://www.whhs.com/

WASHINGTON HOSPITAL EMPLOYEE ASSOCIATION SCHOLARSHIP

Scholarship for a dependent of a Washington Hospital Employee. Must be a graduating senior, community college student, transferring community college student, or a student attending a four-year institution.

Award: Scholarship for use in freshman, sophomore, junior, or senior years; not renewable. *Number:* 1. *Amount:* $2000.

Eligibility Requirements: Applicant must be enrolled or expecting to enroll full- or part-time at a two-year or four-year or technical institution or university and resident of California. Available to U.S. citizens.

Application Requirements: Application form, driver's license, essay, recommendations or references, test scores, transcript. *Deadline:* March 5.

WASHINGTON STATE HIGHER EDUCATION COORDINATING BOARD

http://www.hecb.wa.gov/

AMERICAN INDIAN ENDOWED SCHOLARSHIP

• See page 649

PASSPORT TO COLLEGE PROMISE SCHOLARSHIP

Scholarship to encourage Washington residents to prepare for and succeed in college. Recipients must have spent at least one year in foster care after their 16th birthday and emancipated from care in Washington state.

Award: Scholarship for use in freshman, sophomore, junior, or senior years; renewable. *Number:* 1–400. *Amount:* $1–$4500.

Eligibility Requirements: Applicant must be age 18-26; enrolled or expecting to enroll full- or part-time at a two-year or four-year or technical institution or university; resident of Washington and studying in Washington. Available to U.S. citizens.

Application Requirements: Application form, application form may be submitted online (http://www.wsac.wa.gov/sites/default/files/PassportConsentForm-2012.pdf), consent form, financial need analysis. *Deadline:* continuous.

Contact: Ms. Dawn Cypriano-McAferty, Program Manager
Washington State Higher Education Coordinating Board
917 Lakeridge Way SW, PO Box 43430
Olympia, WA 98504-3430
Phone: 888-535-0747 Ext. 5
Fax: 360-704-6246
E-mail: passporttocollege@hecb.wa.gov

WASHINGTON AWARD FOR VOCATIONAL EXCELLENCE (WAVE)

Award to honor vocational students from the legislative districts of Washington. Grants for up to two years of undergraduate resident tuition. Must be enrolled in Washington high school, skills center, or community or technical college at time of application. To be eligible to apply student must complete 360 hours in single vocational program in high school or one year at technical college. Contact principal, guidance counselor, or on-campus WAVE coordinator for more information. No new monetary scholarships awarded for 2011 and 2012 cohorts due to state budget cuts. Payments made during current fiscal year fulfill monetary commitments to cohorts awarded in 2010 and prior.

Award: Scholarship for use in freshman, sophomore, junior, or senior years; renewable. *Number:* 147.

Eligibility Requirements: Applicant must be enrolled or expecting to enroll full- or part-time at a two-year or four-year or technical institution or university; resident of Washington and studying in Washington. Available to U.S. citizens.

Application Requirements: Application form, recommendations or references.

Contact: Terri Colbert, Program Specialist
Washington State Higher Education Coordinating Board
Workforce Training and Education Coordinating Board, PO Box 43105
Olympia, WA 98504-3105
Phone: 360-709-4623
Fax: 360-586-5862
E-mail: tcolbert@wtb.wa.gov

WASHINGTON SCHOLARS PROGRAM

Awards high school students from the legislative districts of Washington. Must enroll in college or university in Washington. Scholarships up to four years of full-time resident undergraduate tuition and fees. Student must not pursue a degree in theology. Contact principal or guidance counselor for more information. Requires nomination by high school principal and rank within the top 1 percent of his or her graduating senior class. Awards for new recipients selected for the 2011-2013 biennium are honorary recognition-only certificates. The monetary scholarship benefit has been suspended for new Washington Scholars during those years due to state budget cuts. Available funding is obligated to honoring residual, pre-existing monetary benefits awarded to scholarship-eligible recipients selected in 2010 and earlier.

Award: Scholarship for use in freshman, sophomore, junior, or senior years; renewable. *Number:* 147.

Eligibility Requirements: Applicant must be high school student; planning to enroll or expecting to enroll full- or part-time at a two-year or four-year institution or university; resident of Washington and studying in Washington. Available to U.S. citizens.

Application Requirements: Application form, community service, leadership activities, test scores, transcript. *Deadline:* January 22.

Contact: Ann Voyles, Program Manager
Washington State Higher Education Coordinating Board
917 Lakeridge Way, PO Box 43430
Olympia, WA 98504-3430
Phone: 360-753-7843
Fax: 360-704-6243
E-mail: annv@wsac.wa.gov

WASHINGTON STATE NEED GRANT PROGRAM

The program helps Washington's lowest-income undergraduate students to pursue degrees, hone skills, or retrain for new careers. Students with family incomes equal to or less than 50 percent of the state median are eligible for up to 100 percent of the maximum grant. Students with incomes between 51-70% of the state median are prorated dependent on income. All grants are subject to funding.

Award: Grant for use in freshman, sophomore, junior, or senior years; not renewable. *Number:* 74,000. *Amount:* $176–$10,868,

Eligibility Requirements: Applicant must be enrolled or expecting to enroll full- or part-time at a two-year or four-year or technical institution or university; resident of Washington and studying in Washington. Available to U.S. citizens.

Application Requirements: Application form, FAFSA, financial need analysis. *Deadline:* continuous.

WASHINGTON STATE PARENT TEACHER ASSOCIATION SCHOLARSHIP PROGRAM

http://www.wastatepta.org/

WASHINGTON STATE PARENT TEACHER ASSOCIATION SCHOLARSHIPS FOUNDATION

One-time scholarships for students who have graduated from a public high school in the state of Washington, and who greatly need financial help to begin full-time postsecondary education.

Award: Scholarship for use in freshman year; not renewable. *Number:* 60–80. *Amount:* $1000–$2000.

Eligibility Requirements: Applicant must be high school student; planning to enroll or expecting to enroll full-time at a four-year institution or university and resident of Washington. Available to U.S. citizens.

Application Requirements: Application form, community service, essay, financial need analysis, recommendations or references, transcript. *Deadline:* March 31.

Contact: Mr. Bill Williams, Executive Director
Phone: 253-565-2153
Fax: 253-565-7753
E-mail: jcarpenter@wastatepta.org

WATSON-BROWN FOUNDATION INC.

http://www.watson-brown.org/

WATSON-BROWN FOUNDATION SCHOLARSHIP

Scholarships are awarded based on academic merit and financial need. Students must be from designated counties in Georgia or South Carolina and may attend any four- year, accredited, non-profit U.S. college or university. Renewable scholarships are awarded on two levels: $3000 and $5000.

Award: Scholarship for use in freshman, sophomore, junior, or senior years; renewable. *Number:* 200–200. *Amount:* $3000–$5000.

Eligibility Requirements: Applicant must be enrolled or expecting to enroll full-time at a four-year institution or university and resident of Georgia, South Carolina. Applicant must have 3.0 GPA or higher. Available to U.S. citizens.

Application Requirements: Application form, essay, financial need analysis, IRS Form 1040, recommendations or references, test scores, transcript. *Deadline:* February 15.

Contact: Sarah Drury, Director, Scholarships and Alumni Relations
Watson-Brown Foundation Inc.
310 Tom Watson Way
Thomson, GA 30824
Phone: 706-595-8886
E-mail: skdrury@watson-brown.org

WESTERN INTERSTATE COMMISSION FOR HIGHER EDUCATION

http://www.wiche.edu/

WICHE'S WESTERN UNDERGRADUATE EXCHANGE (WUE)

Students from designated states can enroll in two- and four-year undergraduate programs at some 150 public institutions in participating Western states and pay 150 percent of resident tuition. Applicants apply directly to the admissions office at participating institution. Applicants must indicate that they want to be considered for the WUE tuition discount. Participating institutions and the majors available at the WUE rate are listed at http://wiche.edu/wue.

Award: Scholarship for use in freshman, sophomore, junior, or senior years; renewable.

Eligibility Requirements: Applicant must be enrolled or expecting to enroll full-time at a two-year or four-year institution or university; resident of Alaska, Arizona, California, Colorado, Hawaii, Idaho, Montana, Nevada, New Mexico, North Dakota, Oregon, South Dakota, Utah, Washington, Wyoming and studying in Alaska, Arizona, California, Colorado, Hawaii, Idaho, Montana, Nevada, New Mexico, North Dakota, Oregon, South Dakota, Utah, Washington, Wyoming. Available to U.S. citizens.

Application Requirements: Application form, must demonstrate residency of a WICHE member states (western U.S.), test scores, transcript.

Contact: Ms. Laura Ewing, Administrative Assistant, Student Exchange
Western Interstate Commission for Higher Education
3035 Center Green Drive
Boulder, CO 80301
Phone: 303-541-0270
E-mail: info-sep@wiche.edu

WEST VIRGINIA HIGHER EDUCATION POLICY COMMISSION-STUDENT SERVICES

http://wvhepcnew.wvnet.edu/

WEST VIRGINIA HIGHER EDUCATION GRANT PROGRAM

Award available for West Virginia resident for one year immediately preceding the date of application, high school graduate or the equivalent, demonstrate financial need, and enroll as a full-time undergraduate at an approved university or college located in West Virginia or Pennsylvania.

Award: Grant for use in freshman, sophomore, junior, or senior years; not renewable. *Number:* 19,000–21,152. *Amount:* $300–$2500.

Eligibility Requirements: Applicant must be enrolled or expecting to enroll full-time at a two-year or four-year institution or university; resident of West Virginia and studying in Pennsylvania, West Virginia. Available to U.S. citizens.

Application Requirements: FAFSA, financial need analysis. *Deadline:* April 15.

Contact: Judy Smith, Senior Project Coordinator
West Virginia Higher Education Policy Commission-Student Services
1018 Kanawha Boulevard East, Suite 700
Charleston, WV 25301-2827
Phone: 304-558-4618
Fax: 304-558-4622
E-mail: kee@hepc.wvnet.edu

WILLIAM D. SQUIRES EDUCATIONAL FOUNDATION INC.

http://www.wmdsquiresfoundation.org/

WILLIAM D. SQUIRES SCHOLARSHIP

Applicants must be graduating high school seniors from Ohio that are planning to pursue a four year program. The William D. Squires Scholarship is primarily financial need based but students must also have a clear career goal and be highly motivated. Minimum 3.2 GPA is required.

Award: Scholarship for use in freshman, sophomore, junior, or senior years; renewable. *Number:* 12. *Amount:* $12,000.

Eligibility Requirements: Applicant must be high school student; planning to enroll or expecting to enroll full-time at a four-year institution or university and resident of Ohio. Available to U.S. citizens.

Application Requirements: Application form, essay, financial need analysis, recommendations or references, test scores, transcript. *Deadline:* April 5.

Contact: Cynthia Gross, Scholarship Director
William D. Squires Educational Foundation Inc.
PO Box 2940
Jupiter, FL 33468
Phone: 561-741-7751
E-mail: info@wmdsquiresfoundation.org

WILLIAM F. COOPER SCHOLARSHIP TRUST

http://www.wachoviascholars.com/

WILLIAM F. COOPER SCHOLARSHIP

Scholarship to provide financial assistance to women living within the state of Georgia for undergraduate studies. Cannot be used for law, theology or medicine fields of study. Nursing is an approved area of study. For more details visit website http://www.wachoviascholars.com.

Award: Scholarship for use in freshman, sophomore, junior, or senior years; renewable. *Amount:* $1000.

Eligibility Requirements: Applicant must be enrolled or expecting to enroll full- or part-time at a four-year institution or university; female and resident of Georgia. Available to U.S. citizens.

Application Requirements: Application form, federal tax form 1040, W-2 forms, financial need analysis, recommendations or references, test scores, transcript. *Deadline:* April 1.

Contact: Sally King, Program Coordinator
Phone: 800-576-5135
Fax: 864-268-7160
E-mail: sallyking@bellsouth.net

WILLIAM G. AND MARIE SELBY FOUNDATION

http://www.selbyfdn.org/

SELBY SCHOLAR PROGRAM

Must be a resident of Sarasota, Manatee, Charlotte, or Desoto counties in Florida. Scholarships awarded up to $7000 annually, not to exceed 1/3 of individual's financial need. Renewable for four years if student is full-time undergraduate at accredited college or university and maintains 3.0 GPA. Must demonstrate financial need and values of leadership and service to the community.

Award: Scholarship for use in freshman, sophomore, junior, or senior years; renewable. *Number:* 40. *Amount:* $1000–$7000.

Eligibility Requirements: Applicant must be enrolled or expecting to enroll full-time at a four-year institution or university; resident of Florida and must have an interest in leadership. Applicant must have 3.0 GPA or higher. Available to U.S. citizens.

Application Requirements: Application form, essay, financial need analysis, interview, recommendations or references, resume, test scores, transcript. *Deadline:* April 1.

Contact: Evan Jones, Grants Manager
William G. and Marie Selby Foundation
1800 Second Street, Suite 954
Sarasota, FL 34236
Phone: 941-957-0442
Fax: 941-957-3135
E-mail: ejones@selbyfdn.org

FRESH START SCHOLARSHIP FOUNDATION

http://www.wwb.org/fresh-start-scholarship

FRESH START SCHOLARSHIP

Must be entering an undergraduate program at a college or university in Delaware. Scholarship offering a fresh start to women who are returning to school after a hiatus of two years to better their life and opportunities. Applicants must be Delaware residents or employed in Delaware for at least 12 months.

Award: Scholarship for use in freshman, sophomore, junior, or senior years; not renewable. *Number:* 10–15. *Amount:* $1000–$3000.

Eligibility Requirements: Applicant must be enrolled or expecting to enroll full- or part-time at a two-year or four-year institution or university; female; resident of Delaware and studying in Delaware. Applicant must have 2.5 GPA or higher. Available to U.S. citizens.

Application Requirements: Application form, essay, financial need analysis, recommendations or references, transcript. *Deadline:* May 31.

WISCONSIN DEPARTMENT OF VETERANS AFFAIRS (WDVA)

http://www.dva.state.wi.us/

VETERANS EDUCATION (VETED) REIMBURSEMENT GRANT

• See page 582

WISCONSIN HIGHER EDUCATIONAL AID BOARD

http://www.heab.wi.gov/

HANDICAPPED STUDENT GRANT-WISCONSIN

• See page 579

MINORITY UNDERGRADUATE RETENTION GRANT-WISCONSIN

• See page 649

TALENT INCENTIVE PROGRAM GRANT

Grant assists residents of Wisconsin who are attending a nonprofit institution in Wisconsin, and who have substantial financial need. Must meet income criteria, be considered economically and educationally disadvantaged, and be enrolled at least half-time. Refer to website for further details http://www.heab.state.wi.us.

Award: Grant for use in freshman, sophomore, junior, or senior years; renewable. *Amount:* $250–$1800.

Eligibility Requirements: Applicant must be enrolled or expecting to enroll full- or part-time at a two-year or four-year or technical institution or university; resident of Wisconsin and studying in Wisconsin. Available to U.S. citizens.

Application Requirements: Application form, financial need analysis, nomination by financial aid office. *Deadline:* continuous.

Contact: Colette Brown, Program Coordinator
Wisconsin Higher Educational Aid Board
PO Box 7885
Madison, WI 53707-7885
Phone: 608-266-1665
Fax: 608-267-2808
E-mail: colette.brown@wi.gov

WISCONSIN ACADEMIC EXCELLENCE SCHOLARSHIP

Renewable award for high school seniors with the highest GPA in graduating class. Must be a Wisconsin resident attending a nonprofit

Wisconsin institution full-time. Scholarship value is $2250 toward tuition each year for up to four years. Must maintain 3.0 GPA for renewal. Refer to your high school counselor for more details.

Award: Scholarship for use in freshman year; renewable. *Amount:* up to $2250.

Eligibility Requirements: Applicant must be high school student; planning to enroll or expecting to enroll full-time at a two-year or four-year or technical institution or university; resident of Wisconsin and studying in Wisconsin. Applicant must have 3.0 GPA or higher. Available to U.S. citizens.

Application Requirements: Application form, test scores, transcript. *Deadline:* continuous.

Contact: Nancy Wilkison, Program Coordinator
Wisconsin Higher Educational Aid Board
PO Box 7885
Madison, WI 53707-7885
Phone: 608-267-2213
Fax: 608-267-2808
E-mail: nancy.wilkison@wi.gov

WISCONSIN HIGHER EDUCATION GRANTS (WHEG)

Grants for residents of Wisconsin enrolled at least half-time in degree or certificate programs at a University of Wisconsin Institution, Wisconsin Technical College or an approved Tribal College. Must show financial need. Refer to website for further details http://www.heab.wi.gov.

Award: Grant for use in freshman, sophomore, junior, or senior years; not renewable. *Amount:* $250–$3000.

Eligibility Requirements: Applicant must be enrolled or expecting to enroll full- or part-time at a two-year or four-year or technical institution or university; resident of Wisconsin and studying in Wisconsin. Available to U.S. citizens.

Application Requirements: Application form, financial need analysis. *Deadline:* continuous.

Contact: Sandra Thomas, Program Coordinator
Wisconsin Higher Educational Aid Board
PO Box 7885
Madison, WI 53707-7885
Phone: 608-266-0888
Fax: 608-267-2808
E-mail: sandy.thomas@heab.state.wi.us

WISCONSIN NATIVE AMERICAN/INDIAN STUDENT ASSISTANCE GRANT

• See page 649

WISCONSIN SCHOOL COUNSELOR ASSOCIATION

http://www.wscaweb.org/

WISCONSIN SCHOOL COUNSELOR ASSOCIATION HIGH SCHOOL SCHOLARSHIP

Scholarship is available to high school seniors in Wisconsin who plan to attend a two-year or four-year postsecondary institution in the fall. Students are asked to submit an essay that describes how a school counselor or school counseling program has impacted their life.

Award: Scholarship for use in freshman year; not renewable. *Number:* 2–4. *Amount:* $1000.

Eligibility Requirements: Applicant must be high school student; planning to enroll or expecting to enroll full-time at a two-year or four-year institution or university and resident of Wisconsin. Available to U.S. citizens.

Application Requirements: Application form, entry in a contest, essay. *Deadline:* December 1.

Contact: Andrew Stendahl, Professional Recognition and Scholarship
Committee
Phone: 608-695-5786
E-mail: andrewstendahl@gmail.com

WYOMING DEPARTMENT OF EDUCATION

http://edu.wyoming.gov/

DOUVAS MEMORIAL SCHOLARSHIP

Available to Wyoming residents who are first-generation Americans. Must be between 18 and 22 years old. Must be used at any Wyoming public institution of higher education for study in freshman year.

Award: Scholarship for use in freshman year; not renewable. *Number:* 2. *Amount:* $500.

Eligibility Requirements: Applicant must be age 18-22; enrolled or expecting to enroll full- or part-time at a two-year or four-year institution or university; resident of Wyoming and studying in Wyoming. Available to U.S. citizens.

Application Requirements: Application form. *Deadline:* April 30.

Contact: Stephanie Brady, Social Studies Consultant
Wyoming Department of Education
2300 Capitol Avenue
Hathaway Building, 2nd Floor
Cheyenne, WY 82002
Phone: 307-777-3793
Fax: 307-777-6234
E-mail: stephanie.brady@wyo.gov

HATHAWAY SCHOLARSHIP

Scholarship for Wyoming students to pursue postsecondary education within the state. Award ranges from $800 to $1600 per semester. Deadline varies.

Award: Scholarship for use in freshman, sophomore, junior, senior, or graduate years; renewable. *Amount:* $800–$1600.

Eligibility Requirements: Applicant must be enrolled or expecting to enroll full- or part-time at a two-year or four-year institution or university; resident of Wyoming and studying in Wyoming. Applicant must have 2.5 GPA or higher. Available to U.S. citizens.

Application Requirements: Application form, test scores, transcript. *Deadline:* varies.

Contact: Lori Kimbrough, Hathaway Scholarship Consultant
Wyoming Department of Education
2300 Capitol Avenue
Hathaway Building, 2nd Floor
Cheyenne, WY 82002
Phone: 307-777-8979
Fax: 307-777-6234
E-mail: lori.kimbrough@wyo.gov

WYOMING FARM BUREAU FEDERATION

http://www.wyfb.org/

KING-LIVINGSTON SCHOLARSHIP

• See page 544

WYOMING FARM BUREAU CONTINUING EDUCATION SCHOLARSHIPS

• See page 544

WYOMING FARM BUREAU FEDERATION SCHOLARSHIPS

• See page 544

TALENT/INTEREST AREA

ACTORS THEATRE OF LOUISVILLE

http://www.actorstheatre.org/

NATIONAL TEN-MINUTE PLAY CONTEST

Writers submit short plays (10 pages or less) that have not received an equity production, which are considered for the annual Apprentice Showcase (to be eligible, characters in the play must be appropriate for actors aged 20 to 30), the Humana Festival of new American plays, and the $1000 Heideman Award. Must be U.S. citizen.

Award: Prize for use in freshman, sophomore, junior, senior, graduate, or postgraduate years; not renewable. *Number:* 1. *Amount:* $1000.

Eligibility Requirements: Applicant must be enrolled or expecting to enroll full- or part-time at a two-year or four-year or technical institution or university and must have an interest in theater or writing. Available to U.S. citizens.

Application Requirements: 10-page play, application form, entry in a contest. *Deadline:* November 1.

Contact: Ms. Amy Wegener, Literary Manager
Actors Theatre of Louisville
316 West Main Street
Louisville, KY 40202-4218
Phone: 502-584-1265 Ext. 3031
Fax: 502-561-3300
E-mail: awegener@actorstheatre.org

ADELANTE! U.S. EDUCATION LEADERSHIP FUND

http://www.adelantefund.org/

ADELANTE FUND SCHOLARSHIPS
• *See page 613*

ALBERTA HERITAGE SCHOLARSHIP FUND

http://www.alis.alberta.ca/

CHARLES S. NOBLE JUNIOR A HOCKEY SCHOLARSHIPS
• *See page 614*

CHARLES S. NOBLE JUNIOR FOOTBALL SCHOLARSHIPS
• *See page 614*

EARL AND COUNTESS OF WESSEX-WORLD CHAMPIONSHIPS IN ATHLETICS SCHOLARSHIPS
• *See page 614*

JIMMIE CONDON ATHLETIC SCHOLARSHIPS
• *See page 614*

LAURENCE DECORE AWARDS FOR STUDENT LEADERSHIP
• *See page 615*

PRAIRIE BASEBALL ACADEMY SCHOLARSHIPS
• *See page 655*

ALERT SCHOLARSHIP

http://www.alertmagazine.org/

ALERT SCHOLARSHIP
• *See page 655*

THE ALEXANDER FOUNDATION

http://www.thealexanderfoundation.org/

THE ALEXANDER FOUNDATION SCHOLARSHIP PROGRAM
• *See page 655*

AMERICAN BOWLING CONGRESS

http://www.bowl.com/

CHUCK HALL STAR OF TOMORROW SCHOLARSHIP
• *See page 503*

AMERICAN CANCER SOCIETY

http://www.cancer.org/

AMERICAN CANCER SOCIETY, FLORIDA DIVISION R.O.C.K. COLLEGE SCHOLARSHIP PROGRAM
• *See page 566*

AMERICAN INDIAN GRADUATE CENTER

http://www.aigcs.org/

GATES MILLENNIUM SCHOLARS PROGRAM
• *See page 616*

AMERICAN INSTITUTE FOR FOREIGN STUDY

http://www.aifsabroad.com/

AIFS AFFILIATE SCHOLARSHIPS

Students from colleges and universities that participate in the AIFS Affiliates program are eligible. Application fee: $95. For more details, visit http://www.aifsabroad.com/scholarships.asp.

Award: Scholarship for use in freshman, sophomore, junior, or senior years; not renewable.

Eligibility Requirements: Applicant must be enrolled or expecting to enroll full-time at a two-year or four-year institution or university and must have an interest in international exchange. Available to U.S. and non-U.S. citizens.

Application Requirements: Application form, essay, personal photograph, recommendations or references, transcript. *Fee:* $95. *Deadline:* varies.

Contact: David Mauro, Admissions Counselor
American Institute for Foreign Study
River Plaza, 9 West Broad Street
Stamford, CT 06902-3788
Phone: 800-727-2437 Ext. 5163
Fax: 203-399-5463
E-mail: dmauro@aifs.com

AIFS DIVERSITYABROAD.COM SCHOLARSHIP
• *See page 616*

AIFS GILMAN SCHOLARSHIP BONUS-$500 SCHOLARSHIPS

Award of $500 available to each undergraduate recipient for use toward an AIFS program. More information is available at http://www.iie.org/gilman.

Award: Scholarship for use in freshman, sophomore, junior, or senior years; not renewable. *Amount:* $500.

Eligibility Requirements: Applicant must be enrolled or expecting to enroll full-time at a four-year institution or university and must have an interest in international exchange. Available to U.S. and non-U.S. citizens.

Application Requirements: Application form, essay, personal photograph, recommendations or references, transcript. *Fee:* $95. *Deadline:* varies.

Contact: David Mauro, Admissions Counselor
American Institute for Foreign Study
River Plaza, 9 West Broad Street
Stamford, CT 06902-3788
Phone: 800-727-2437 Ext. 5163
Fax: 203-399-5463
E-mail: dmauro@aifs.com

AIFS-HACU SCHOLARSHIPS
• *See page 616*

AIFS INTERNATIONAL SCHOLARSHIPS

Awards available to undergraduates on an AIFS study abroad program. Applicants must demonstrate leadership potential, have a minimum 3.0 cumulative GPA, and meet program requirements. The program application fee is $95. Deadlines: April 15 for fall, October 1 for spring, and March 1 for summer.

Award: Scholarship for use in freshman, sophomore, junior, or senior years; not renewable. *Number:* up to 130. *Amount:* $500–$1000.

Eligibility Requirements: Applicant must be enrolled or expecting to enroll full-time at a two-year or four-year institution or university and must have an interest in international exchange or leadership. Applicant must have 3.0 GPA or higher. Available to U.S. and non-U.S. citizens.

Application Requirements: Application form, essay, personal photograph, recommendations or references, transcript. *Fee:* $95. *Deadline:* varies.

Contact: David Mauro, Admissions Counselor
American Institute for Foreign Study
River Plaza, 9 West Broad Street
Stamford, CT 06902-3788
Phone: 800-727-2437 Ext. 5163
Fax: 203-399-5463
E-mail: dmauro@aifs.com

AIFS STUDY AGAIN SCHOLARSHIPS

Students who studied abroad on an AIFS summer program will receive a $1000 scholarship to study abroad on an AIFS semester or academic year catalog program or a $500 scholarship toward a summer catalog program. Students who studied abroad on an AIFS semester or academic year program will receive a $500 scholarship toward a summer catalog program or a $1000 scholarship toward a semester program in a different academic year. Deadlines: April 15 for fall, October 15 for spring, and March 1 for summer.

Award: Scholarship for use in freshman, sophomore, junior, or senior years; not renewable. *Amount:* $500–$1000.

Eligibility Requirements: Applicant must be enrolled or expecting to enroll full-time at a two-year or four-year institution or university and must have an interest in international exchange. Applicant must have 2.5 GPA or higher. Available to U.S. and non-U.S. citizens.

Application Requirements: Application form, essay, personal photograph, recommendations or references, transcript. *Fee:* $95. *Deadline:* varies.

Contact: David Mauro, Admissions Counselor
American Institute for Foreign Study
River Plaza, 9 West Broad Street
Stamford, CT 06902-3788
Phone: 800-727-2437 Ext. 5163
Fax: 203-399-5463
E-mail: dmauro@aifs.com

AMERICAN JEWISH LEAGUE FOR ISRAEL

http://www.americanjewishleague.org/

AMERICAN JEWISH LEAGUE FOR ISRAEL SCHOLARSHIP PROGRAM

Scholarship provides support with tuition for a full year of study (September to May) at one of seven Israeli universities, Bar Ilan, Ben Gurion, Haifa, Hebrew, Tel Aviv, Technion, and Weizmann, Interdisciplinary Center at Herzliya. Additional information is available on website http://www.americanjewishleague.org/ScholarshipInformation.html.

Award: Scholarship for use in freshman, sophomore, junior, or senior years; not renewable. *Number:* 3–15. *Amount:* $2000.

Eligibility Requirements: Applicant must be enrolled or expecting to enroll full-time at a four-year institution or university and must have an interest in Jewish culture. Available to U.S. citizens.

Application Requirements: Application form, essay, personal and academic aspirations, recommendations or references, transcript. *Deadline:* May 1.

Contact: Mr. Karl Zukerman, University Scholarship Fund
American Jewish League for Israel
4485 Hazleton Lane
Wellington, FL 33449
Fax: 561-963-2923
E-mail: kdzwork@aol.com

AMERICAN LEGION BASEBALL

http://www.legion.org/baseball

AMERICAN LEGION BASEBALL SCHOLARSHIP

Awarded to graduated seniors who were nominated by American Legion Baseball coach who demonstrate outstanding academics, citizenship, community spirit, leadership and financial need.

Award: Scholarship for use in freshman, sophomore, junior, senior, graduate, or postgraduate years; not renewable. *Number:* 1–51. *Amount:* $500–$1000.

Eligibility Requirements: Applicant must be high school student; planning to enroll or expecting to enroll full-time at a two-year or four-year or technical institution or university and must have an interest in athletics/sports. Applicant must have 2.5 GPA or higher. Available to U.S. and non-Canadian citizens.

Application Requirements: Application form, personal photograph, transcript. *Deadline:* June 15.

Contact: Mr. Steve Cloud, Assistant National Program Coordinator
American Legion Baseball
PO Box 1055
Indianapolis, IN 46206
Phone: 317-630-1213
Fax: 317-360-1369
E-mail: baseball@legion.org

AMERICAN LEGION DEPARTMENT OF ARIZONA

http://www.azlegion.org/

AMERICAN LEGION DEPARTMENT OF ARIZONA HIGH SCHOOL ORATORICAL CONTEST

• *See page 658*

AMERICAN LEGION DEPARTMENT OF ARKANSAS

http://www.arklegion.homestead.com/

AMERICAN LEGION DEPARTMENT OF ARKANSAS HIGH SCHOOL ORATORICAL CONTEST

• *See page 659*

AMERICAN LEGION DEPARTMENT OF ILLINOIS

http://www.illegion.org/

AMERICAN ESSAY CONTEST SCHOLARSHIP

• *See page 508*

AMERICAN LEGION DEPARTMENT OF ILLINOIS HIGH SCHOOL ORATORICAL CONTEST

• *See page 659*

AMERICAN LEGION DEPARTMENT OF INDIANA

http://www.hoosierlegionnaire.org

AMERICAN LEGION DEPARTMENT OF INDIANA HIGH SCHOOL ORATORICAL CONTEST

• *See page 660*

FRANK W. MCHALE MEMORIAL SCHOLARSHIPS

• *See page 660*

AMERICAN LEGION DEPARTMENT OF IOWA

http://www.ialegion.org/

AMERICAN LEGION DEPARTMENT OF IOWA HIGH SCHOOL ORATORICAL CONTEST
• See page 660

AMERICAN LEGION DEPARTMENT OF IOWA OUTSTANDING SENIOR BASEBALL PLAYER
• See page 660

AMERICAN LEGION DEPARTMENT OF KANSAS

http://www.ksamlegion.org/

AMERICAN LEGION DEPARTMENT OF KANSAS HIGH SCHOOL ORATORICAL CONTEST

Awards a total of $2400 ($1500, $500, $250, and $150) in scholarships to the top four winners in each state. The state winner's school receives $500. The top three contestants in the nation are awarded scholarships totaling $48,000 ($18,000, $16,000, and $14,000).

Award: Prize for use in freshman year; not renewable. *Number:* 4. *Amount:* $150–$18,000.

Eligibility Requirements: Applicant must be high school student; planning to enroll or expecting to enroll full-time at a four-year institution or university and must have an interest in public speaking. Available to U.S. citizens.

Application Requirements: Application form, entry in a contest. *Deadline:* varies.

Contact: Ralph Snyder, Oratorical Contest Committee
American Legion Department of Kansas
1314 Topeka Boulevard, SW
Topeka, KS 66612
Phone: 785-232-9315
Fax: 785-232-1399

DR. CLICK COWGER BASEBALL SCHOLARSHIP
• See page 660

PAUL FLAHERTY ATHLETIC SCHOLARSHIP

Scholarship available to high school seniors, college level freshmen or sophomores enrolled or intending to enroll in an approved junior college, college, university, or trade school. Must have participated in any form of high school athletics. Must be an average or a better student scholastically.

Award: Scholarship for use in freshman or sophomore years; not renewable. *Number:* 1. *Amount:* $250.

Eligibility Requirements: Applicant must be enrolled or expecting to enroll full-time at a two-year or four-year or technical institution or university; studying in Kansas and must have an interest in athletics/sports. Available to U.S. citizens.

Application Requirements: Application form, financial need analysis, latest 1040 income statement of supporting parents, personal photograph, recommendations or references, transcript. *Deadline:* July 15.

Contact: Jim Gravenstein, Chairman, Scholarship Committee
American Legion Department of Kansas
1314 Topeka Boulevard, SW
Topeka, KS 66612
Phone: 785-232-9513
Fax: 785-232-1399

AMERICAN LEGION DEPARTMENT OF MICHIGAN

http://www.michiganlegion.org/

AMERICAN LEGION DEPARTMENT OF MICHIGAN ORATORICAL SCHOLARSHIP PROGRAM
• See page 661

AMERICAN LEGION DEPARTMENT OF MINNESOTA

http://www.mnlegion.org/

AMERICAN LEGION DEPARTMENT OF MINNESOTA HIGH SCHOOL ORATORICAL CONTEST
• See page 661

AMERICAN LEGION DEPARTMENT OF MONTANA

http://mtlegion.org/

AMERICAN LEGION DEPARTMENT OF MONTANA HIGH SCHOOL ORATORICAL CONTEST
• See page 661

AMERICAN LEGION DEPARTMENT OF NEBRASKA

http://www.nebraskalegion.net/

AMERICAN LEGION BASEBALL SCHOLARSHIP-NEBRASKA AMERICAN LEGION BASEBALL PLAYER OF THE YEAR
• See page 662

AMERICAN LEGION DEPARTMENT OF NEBRASKA HIGH SCHOOL ORATORICAL CONTEST
• See page 662

AMERICAN LEGION DEPARTMENT OF NEBRASKA JIM HURLBERT MEMORIAL BASEBALL SCHOLARSHIP
• See page 662

AMERICAN LEGION DEPARTMENT OF NEW JERSEY

http://www.njamericanlegion.org/

AMERICAN LEGION DEPARTMENT OF NEW JERSEY HIGH SCHOOL ORATORICAL CONTEST

Award to promote and coordinate the Oratorical Contest Program at the Department, District, County and Post Levels. High School Oratorical Contest is to develop a deeper knowledge and understanding of the constitution of the United States.

Award: Prize for use in freshman year; not renewable. *Number:* 5. *Amount:* $1000–$4000.

Eligibility Requirements: Applicant must be high school student; planning to enroll or expecting to enroll full-time at a four-year institution or university and must have an interest in public speaking. Available to U.S. citizens.

Application Requirements: Application form, entry in a contest. *Deadline:* March 8.

Contact: John Baker, Department Adjutant
Phone: 609-695-5418
Fax: 609-394-1532
E-mail: adjutant@njamericanlegion.org

AMERICAN LEGION DEPARTMENT OF NEW YORK

http://www.ny.legion.org/

AMERICAN LEGION DEPARTMENT OF NEW YORK HIGH SCHOOL ORATORICAL CONTEST
• See page 662

AMERICAN LEGION DEPARTMENT OF NORTH CAROLINA

http://www.nclegion.org/

AMERICAN LEGION DEPARTMENT OF NORTH CAROLINA HIGH SCHOOL ORATORICAL CONTEST
• *See page 662*

AMERICAN LEGION DEPARTMENT OF NORTH DAKOTA

http://www.ndlegion.org/

AMERICAN LEGION DEPARTMENT OF NORTH DAKOTA NATIONAL HIGH SCHOOL ORATORICAL CONTEST
• *See page 663*

AMERICAN LEGION DEPARTMENT OF OREGON

http://www.orlegion.org/

AMERICAN LEGION DEPARTMENT OF OREGON HIGH SCHOOL ORATORICAL CONTEST
• *See page 663*

AMERICAN LEGION DEPARTMENT OF PENNSYLVANIA

http://www.pa-legion.com/

AMERICAN LEGION DEPARTMENT OF PENNSYLVANIA HIGH SCHOOL ORATORICAL CONTEST
• *See page 663*

AMERICAN LEGION DEPARTMENT OF SOUTH DAKOTA

http://www.sdlegion.org/

AMERICAN LEGION DEPARTMENT OF SOUTH DAKOTA HIGH SCHOOL ORATORICAL CONTEST
• *See page 663*

AMERICAN LEGION DEPARTMENT OF TENNESSEE

http://www.tennesseelegion.org/

AMERICAN LEGION DEPARTMENT OF TENNESSEE HIGH SCHOOL ORATORICAL CONTEST
• *See page 664*

AMERICAN LEGION DEPARTMENT OF TEXAS

http://www.txlegion.org/

AMERICAN LEGION DEPARTMENT OF TEXAS HIGH SCHOOL ORATORICAL CONTEST
• *See page 664*

AMERICAN LEGION DEPARTMENT OF VERMONT

http://www.vtlegion.org

AMERICAN LEGION DEPARTMENT OF VERMONT HIGH SCHOOL ORATORICAL CONTEST
• *See page 664*

AMERICAN LEGION DEPARTMENT OF WEST VIRGINIA

http://www.wvlegion.org/

AMERICAN LEGION DEPARTMENT OF WEST VIRGINIA BOARD OF REGENTS SCHOLARSHIP
• *See page 665*

AMERICAN LEGION DEPARTMENT OF WEST VIRGINIA HIGH SCHOOL ORATORICAL CONTEST
• *See page 665*

AMERICAN LEGION NATIONAL HEADQUARTERS

http://www.legion.org/

AMERICAN LEGION NATIONAL HIGH SCHOOL ORATORICAL CONTEST
Scholarship up to $18,000 will be presented to the 3 finalists in the final round of the national contest. Students currently in high school are eligible to apply for this contest.

Award: Scholarship for use in freshman, sophomore, junior, or senior years; not renewable. *Number:* 54. *Amount:* $1500–$18,000.

Eligibility Requirements: Applicant must be high school student; planning to enroll or expecting to enroll full-time at a two-year or four-year institution or university and must have an interest in public speaking. Available to U.S. citizens.

Application Requirements: Application form, entry in a contest. *Deadline:* December 1.

Contact: Mrs. Sandy Wong, Program Administrator
American Legion National Headquarters
PO Box 2788
Honolulu, HI 96803
Phone: 808-564-1386
Fax: 808-523-3937
E-mail: sandyw@servco.com

AMERICAN MORGAN HORSE INSTITUTE

http://www.morganhorse.com/

AMERICAN MORGAN HORSE INSTITUTE EDUCATIONAL SCHOLARSHIPS
Selection is based on the ability and aptitude for serious study, community service, leadership, and financial need. Must be actively involved with registered Morgan Horses Association. Application deadline varies every year. For information and application go to http://www.morganhorse.com.

Award: Scholarship for use in freshman year; not renewable. *Number:* 5. *Amount:* $3000.

Eligibility Requirements: Applicant must be enrolled or expecting to enroll full- or part-time at a two-year or four-year or technical institution or university and must have an interest in animal/agricultural competition. Available to U.S. and non-U.S. citizens.

Application Requirements: Application form, essay, personal photograph, recommendations or references, transcript. *Deadline:* varies.

Contact: Sally Wadhams, Development Officer
Phone: 802-985-8477
Fax: 802-985-8430
E-mail: amhioffice@aol.com

AMERICAN MORGAN HORSE INSTITUTE GRAND PRIX DRESSAGE AWARD

Award available to riders of registered Morgan horses who reach a certain proficiency at the Grand Prix dressage level. For information and application go to http://www.morganhorse.com. The application deadline varies every year.

Award: Scholarship for use in freshman, sophomore, junior, senior, graduate, or postgraduate years; not renewable. *Number:* 1. *Amount:* $2500.

Eligibility Requirements: Applicant must be enrolled or expecting to enroll full- or part-time at a two-year or four-year or technical institution or university and must have an interest in animal/agricultural competition. Available to U.S. and non-U.S. citizens.

Application Requirements: Application form, copy of horse's USDF report, essay, personal photograph, recommendations or references, transcript. *Deadline:* varies.

Contact: Sally Wadhams, Development Officer
    Phone: 802-985-8477
    Fax: 802-985-8430
    E-mail: amhioffice@aol.com

AMERICAN MORGAN HORSE INSTITUTE GRAYWOOD YOUTH HORSEMANSHIP GRANT

Provides a youth who is an active member of the American Morgan Horse Association (AMHA) or an AMHA youth group with the opportunity to further his/her practical study of Morgan horses. For information and application go to http://www.morganhorse.com.

Award: Grant for use in freshman year; not renewable. *Number:* up to 2. *Amount:* $250–$500.

Eligibility Requirements: Applicant must be age 13-21; enrolled or expecting to enroll full- or part-time at a two-year or four-year or technical institution or university and must have an interest in animal/agricultural competition. Available to U.S. and non-U.S. citizens.

Application Requirements: Application form, essay, personal photograph, recommendations or references, transcript. *Deadline:* February 1.

Contact: Sally Wadhams, Development Officer
    Phone: 802-985-8477
    Fax: 802-985-8430
    E-mail: amhioffice@aol.com

AMERICAN MORGAN HORSE INSTITUTE VAN SCHAIK DRESSAGE SCHOLARSHIP

Awarded to an individual wishing to further their proficiency in classically ridden dressage on a registered Morgan horse. For information and application go to http://www.morganhorse.com.

Award: Scholarship for use in freshman, sophomore, junior, senior, graduate, or postgraduate years; not renewable. *Number:* 1. *Amount:* $1000.

Eligibility Requirements: Applicant must be enrolled or expecting to enroll full- or part-time at a two-year or four-year or technical institution or university and must have an interest in animal/agricultural competition. Available to U.S. and non-U.S. citizens.

Application Requirements: Application form, essay, narrative, personal photograph, recommendations or references. *Deadline:* February 1.

Contact: Sally Wadhams, Development Officer
    Phone: 802-985-8477
    Fax: 802-985-8430
    E-mail: amhioffice@aol.com

AMERICAN MUSEUM OF NATURAL HISTORY

http://www.amnh.org/

YOUNG NATURALIST AWARDS

Essay contest open to students in grades 7-12 who are currently enrolled in a public, private, parochial, or home school in the United States, Canada, the U.S. territories, or a U.S.-sponsored school abroad. Essays must be based on an original scientific investigation conducted by the student. See website for guidelines http://www.amnh.org/nationalcenter/youngnaturalistawards/read.html.

Award: Prize for use in freshman year; not renewable. *Number:* 1.

Eligibility Requirements: Applicant must be high school student; planning to enroll or expecting to enroll part-time at a four-year institution or university and must have an interest in writing. Available to Canadian citizens.

Application Requirements: Application form, essay, personal photograph. *Deadline:* March 1.

Contact: Maria Rios-Dickson, Assistant Director, Fellowships and Student Affairs
    Phone: 212-769-5017
    E-mail: fellowships-rggs@amnh.org

AMERICAN QUARTER HORSE FOUNDATION (AQHF)

http://www.aqha.com/foundation

DR. GERALD O'CONNOR MICHIGAN QHY SCHOLARSHIP
• See page 513

SWAYZE WOODRUFF MEMORIAL MID-SOUTH SCHOLARSHIP
• See page 514

AMERICAN SHEEP INDUSTRY ASSOCIATION

http://www.sheepusa.org/

NATIONAL MAKE IT WITH WOOL COMPETITION

Awards available for entrants ages 13 years & older. Must enter at state level with home-constructed garment of at least 60 percent wool. Applicant must model garment. Entry fee is $10.

Award: Prize for use in freshman, sophomore, junior, senior, or graduate years; not renewable. *Number:* 2–26. *Amount:* $25–$1500.

Eligibility Requirements: Applicant must be enrolled or expecting to enroll full- or part-time at a two-year or four-year or technical institution or university and must have an interest in sewing. Available to U.S. citizens.

Application Requirements: Application form, entry in a contest, sample of fabric (5x5), entry fee. *Fee:* $10. *Deadline:* continuous.

Contact: Marie Lehfeldt, National Coordinator
    American Sheep Industry Association
    PO Box 175
    Lavina, MT 59046
    Phone: 406-636-2731
    Fax: 406-636-2731
    E-mail: levi@midrivers.com

AMERICAN STRING TEACHERS ASSOCIATION

http://www.astaweb.com/

NATIONAL SOLO COMPETITION

Twenty-six individual awards. Instrument categories are violin, viola, cello, double bass, classical guitar, and harp. Applicants competing in Junior Division must be under age 19. Senior Division competitors must be ages 19 to 25. Application fee is $75. Visit website for application forms. Applicant must be a member of ASTA.

Award: Prize for use in freshman, sophomore, junior, senior, or graduate years; not renewable. *Number:* 26.

Eligibility Requirements: Applicant must be age 19-25; enrolled or expecting to enroll full- or part-time at a two-year or four-year or technical institution or university and must have an interest in music. Available to U.S. and Canadian citizens.

Application Requirements: Application form, entry in a contest, proof of age, proof of membership. *Fee:* $75. *Deadline:* varies.

Contact: Laura Kobayashi, Committee Chair
American String Teachers Association
4153 Chain Bridge Road
Fairfax, VA 22030
Phone: 703-279-2113
Fax: 703-279-2114
E-mail: lkobayas@myway.com

AMERICAN SWEDISH INSTITUTE

http://www.ASImn.org

LILLY LORENZEN SCHOLARSHIP

• *See page 665*

AMERICAN THEATRE ORGAN SOCIETY INC.

http://www.atos.org/

AMERICAN THEATRE ORGAN SOCIETY ORGAN PERFORMANCE SCHOLARSHIP

Renewable awards available to students between the ages of 13 to 27. Must have a talent in music and have an interest in theater organ performance studies (not for general music studies). There are two categories for this scholarship Category A: Organ students studying with professional theatre organ instructors. Category B: Theatre organ students furthering their musical education by working toward a college organ performance degree.

Award: Scholarship for use in freshman, sophomore, junior, or senior years; renewable. *Number:* 11. *Amount:* $500–$1000.

Eligibility Requirements: Applicant must be age 13-27; enrolled or expecting to enroll full- or part-time at a four-year institution or university and must have an interest in music. Available to U.S. and non-U.S. citizens.

Application Requirements: Application form, essay. *Deadline:* April 15.

Contact: Carlton Smith, Chairperson, Scholarship Program
American Theatre Organ Society Inc.
2175 North Irwin Street
Indianapolis, IN 46219-2220
Phone: 317-356-1270
Fax: 317-322-9379
E-mail: smith@atos.org

AMERICA'S JUNIOR MISS SCHOLARSHIP PROGRAM, INC. D/B/A DISTINGUISHED YOUNG WOMEN

http://www.distinguishedyw.org

AMERICA'S JUNIOR MISS SCHOLARSHIP PROGRAM, INC. D/B/A DISTINGUISHED YOUNG WOMEN

Awards are given to contestants in local, regional, and national levels of competition. Must be female, high school juniors or seniors, U.S. citizens, and legal residents of the county and state of competition. Contestants are evaluated on scholastic, interview, talent, fitness, and poise. The number of awards and their amount vary from year to year.

Award: Scholarship for use in freshman year; not renewable.

Eligibility Requirements: Applicant must be high school student; age 16-18; planning to enroll or expecting to enroll full-time at a two-year or four-year institution or university; single female and must have an interest in beauty pageant. Available to U.S. citizens.

Application Requirements: Application form, birth certificate, certificate of health, entry in a contest, test scores, transcript. *Deadline:* varies.

Contact: Jennifer Tolbert, National Field Director
America's Junior Miss Scholarship Program, Inc. d/b/a
Distinguished Young Women
751 Government Street
Mobile, AL 36602
Phone: 251-438-3621
Fax: 251-431-0063
E-mail: jennifer@distinguishedyw.org

APPALACHIAN STUDIES ASSOCIATION, INC.

http://www.appalachianstudies.org/

WEATHERFORD AWARD

One-time award given to the best work of fiction, non-fiction, book, poetry, or short piece about the Appalachian South published in the most recent calendar year. Two awards will be given: one for non-fiction, one for fiction, and one for poetry. Seven copies of the nominated work must be sent to the chair of the award committee.

Award: Prize for use in freshman, sophomore, junior, or senior years; not renewable. *Number:* 3. *Amount:* up to $500.

Eligibility Requirements: Applicant must be enrolled or expecting to enroll full- or part-time at a two-year or four-year or technical institution or university and must have an interest in writing. Available to U.S. and non-U.S. citizens.

Application Requirements: Application form, nomination, 7 copies of the book. *Deadline:* December 31.

Contact: Chad Berry, Chair, Award Committee
Appalachian Studies Association, Inc.
Loyal Jones Appalachian Center, Berea College
205 North Main Street, CPO 2166
Berea, KY 40404

APPALOOSA HORSE CLUB-APPALOOSA YOUTH PROGRAM

http://www.appaloosayouth.com/

APPALOOSA YOUTH EDUCATIONAL SCHOLARSHIPS

• *See page 515*

ARRL FOUNDATION INC.

http://www.arrl.org/

ALBERT H. HIX, W8AH, MEMORIAL SCHOLARSHIP

• *See page 667*

ARRL ROCKY MOUNTAIN DIVISION SCHOLARSHIP

• *See page 667*

ARRL SCHOLARSHIP TO HONOR BARRY GOLDWATER, K7UGA

One $5000 award is available to an undergraduate or graduate student with a Novice class or higher radio operator license. Must attend a regionally accredited institution.

Award: Scholarship for use in freshman, sophomore, junior, senior, or graduate years; not renewable. *Number:* 1. *Amount:* $5000.

Eligibility Requirements: Applicant must be enrolled or expecting to enroll full-time at a four-year institution or university and must have an interest in amateur radio. Available to U.S. citizens.

Application Requirements: Application form, transcript. *Deadline:* February 1.

Contact: Ms. Mary Hobart, Secretary
Phone: 860-594-0397
E-mail: k1mmh@arrl.org

BILL, W2ONV, AND ANN SALERNO MEMORIAL SCHOLARSHIP

Two one-time $1000 awards are available to students who possess any amateur radio license. Must have a 3.7 GPA or higher. Aggregate annual income of the family household should not exceed $100,000. Must attend an accredited four year college or university.

Award: Scholarship for use in freshman, sophomore, junior, senior, or graduate years; not renewable. *Number:* 2. *Amount:* $1000.

Eligibility Requirements: Applicant must be enrolled or expecting to enroll full-time at a four-year institution or university and must have an interest in amateur radio. Applicant must have 3.5 GPA or higher. Available to U.S. citizens.

Application Requirements: Application form, transcript. *Deadline:* February 1.

Contact: Ms. Mary Hobart, Secretary
Phone: 860-594-0397
E-mail: k1mmh@arrl.org

BYRON BLANCHARD, N1EKV, MEMORIAL SCHOLARSHIP FUND
• *See page 667*

CENTRAL ARIZONA DX ASSOCIATION SCHOLARSHIP
• *See page 667*

CHALLENGE MET SCHOLARSHIP
• *See page 567*

CHICAGO FM CLUB SCHOLARSHIP FUND
• *See page 667*

DAVID KNAUS MEMORIAL SCHOLARSHIP
• *See page 668*

DAYTON AMATEUR RADIO ASSOCIATION SCHOLARSHIPS
Four $1000 awards are available to students with any active amateur radio license. Must attend an accredited four-year college or university.

Award: Scholarship for use in freshman, sophomore, junior, or senior years; not renewable. *Number:* 4. *Amount:* $1000.

Eligibility Requirements: Applicant must be enrolled or expecting to enroll full- or part-time at a four-year institution or university and must have an interest in amateur radio. Available to U.S. citizens.

Application Requirements: Application form, transcript. *Deadline:* February 1.

Contact: Ms. Mary Hobart, Secretary
Phone: 860-594-0397
E-mail: k1mmh@arrl.org

GENERAL FUND SCHOLARSHIPS
Available to students who are amateur radio operators. Students can be licensed in any class of operators. Nonrenewable award for use in undergraduate years. Multiple awards per year.

Award: Scholarship for use in freshman, sophomore, junior, or senior years; not renewable. *Amount:* $2000.

Eligibility Requirements: Applicant must be enrolled or expecting to enroll full-time at a four-year institution or university and must have an interest in amateur radio. Available to U.S. citizens.

Application Requirements: Application form, transcript. *Deadline:* February 1.

Contact: Ms. Mary Hobart, Secretary
Phone: 860-594-0397
E-mail: k1mmh@arrl.org

GWINNETT AMATEUR RADIO SOCIETY SCHOLARSHIP
• *See page 668*

JACKSON COUNTY ARA SCHOLARSHIP
• *See page 668*

K2TEO MARTIN J. GREEN SR. MEMORIAL SCHOLARSHIP
Available to students with a general amateur license for radio operation. Preference given to students from a ham family. Nonrenewable award for use in undergraduate years.

Award: Scholarship for use in freshman, sophomore, junior, or senior years; not renewable. *Number:* 1. *Amount:* $1000.

Eligibility Requirements: Applicant must be enrolled or expecting to enroll full-time at a four-year institution or university and must have an interest in amateur radio. Available to U.S. citizens.

Application Requirements: Application form, transcript. *Deadline:* February 1.

Contact: Ms. Mary Hobart, Secretary
Phone: 860-594-0397
E-mail: k1mmh@arrl.org

L.B. CEBIK, W4RNL, AND JEAN CEBIK, N4TZP, MEMORIAL SCHOLARSHIP
One $1000 award is available to a student with a Technician class or higher radio license. Must attend a four-year college or university.

Award: Scholarship for use in freshman, sophomore, junior, or senior years; not renewable. *Number:* 1. *Amount:* $1000.

Eligibility Requirements: Applicant must be enrolled or expecting to enroll full- or part-time at a four-year institution or university and must have an interest in amateur radio. Available to U.S. citizens.

Application Requirements: Application form, transcript. *Deadline:* February 1.

Contact: Ms. Mary Hobart, Secretary
Phone: 860-594-0397
E-mail: k1mmh@arrl.org

LOUISIANA MEMORIAL SCHOLARSHIP
• *See page 668*

MARY LOU BROWN SCHOLARSHIP
• *See page 668*

NEW ENGLAND FEMARA SCHOLARSHIPS
• *See page 668*

NORMAN E. STROHMEIER, W2VRS, MEMORIAL SCHOLARSHIP
• *See page 668*

OUTDOOR HAMS SCHOLARSHIP
• *See page 668*

PEORIA AREA AMATEUR RADIO CLUB SCHOLARSHIP
• *See page 668*

RICHARD W. BENDICKSEN, N7ZL, MEMORIAL SCHOLARSHIP
One $2000 award available to a student with any active amateur radio license attending a four-year college or university.

Award: Scholarship for use in freshman, sophomore, junior, or senior years; not renewable. *Number:* 1. *Amount:* $2000.

Eligibility Requirements: Applicant must be enrolled or expecting to enroll full- or part-time at a four-year institution or university and must have an interest in amateur radio. Available to U.S. citizens.

Application Requirements: Application form, transcript. *Deadline:* February 1.

Contact: Ms. Mary Hobart, Secretary
Phone: 860-594-0397
E-mail: k1mmh@arrl.org

SCHOLARSHIP OF THE MORRIS RADIO CLUB OF NEW JERSEY
One $1000 award available to a student who possesses a technician class or higher amateur radio license and attends a four-year college or university.

Award: Scholarship for use in freshman, sophomore, junior, or senior years; not renewable. *Number:* 1. *Amount:* $1000.

Eligibility Requirements: Applicant must be enrolled or expecting to enroll full- or part-time at a four-year institution or university and must have an interest in amateur radio. Available to U.S. citizens.

Application Requirements: Application form, transcript. *Deadline:* February 1.

Contact: Ms. Mary Hobart, Secretary
Phone: 860-594-0397
E-mail: k1mmh@arrl.org

SIX METER CLUB OF CHICAGO SCHOLARSHIP
• *See page 669*

TED, W4VHF, AND ITICE, K4LVV, GOLDTHORPE SCHOLARSHIP
One $500 scholarship to a student attending a four-year college or university and possessing an active amateur radio license. Financial need and active volunteer service in the community will be taken into consideration.

Award: Scholarship for use in freshman, sophomore, junior, or senior years; not renewable. *Number:* 1. *Amount:* $500.

Eligibility Requirements: Applicant must be enrolled or expecting to enroll full- or part-time at a four-year institution or university and must have an interest in amateur radio. Available to U.S. citizens.

Application Requirements: Application form, community service, financial need analysis, transcript. *Deadline:* February 1.

Contact: Ms. Mary Hobart, Secretary
Phone: 860-594-0397
E-mail: k1mmh@arrl.org

THOMAS W. PORTER, W8KYZ, SCHOLARSHIP HONORING MICHAEL DAUGHERTY, W8LSE
• *See page 669*

TOM AND JUDITH COMSTOCK SCHOLARSHIP
• *See page 669*

WILLIAM BENNETT, W7PHO, MEMORIAL SCHOLARSHIP
• *See page 669*

YANKEE CLIPPER CONTEST CLUB INC. YOUTH SCHOLARSHIP
• *See page 669*

YOU'VE GOT A FRIEND IN PENNSYLVANIA SCHOLARSHIP
• *See page 515*

ZACHARY TAYLOR STEVENS SCHOLARSHIP
• *See page 669*

AUTHOR SERVICES, INC.
http://www.writersofthefuture.com/

L. RON HUBBARD'S ILLUSTRATORS OF THE FUTURE CONTEST
An ongoing competition for new and amateur artists judged by professional artists. Eligible submissions consist of three science fiction or fantasy illustrations. Prize amount ranges from $500 to $5000. Quarterly deadlines are December 31, March 31, June 30, and September 30. All entrants retain rights to artwork.

Award: Prize for use in freshman, sophomore, junior, senior, graduate, or postgraduate years; not renewable. *Number:* up to 12. *Amount:* $500–$5000.

Eligibility Requirements: Applicant must be enrolled or expecting to enroll full- or part-time at a two-year or four-year or technical institution or university and must have an interest in art. Available to U.S. and non-U.S. citizens.

Application Requirements: 3 illustrations, entry in a contest, self-addressed stamped envelope with application. *Deadline:* continuous.

Contact: Joni Labaqui, Contest Administrator
Author Services, Inc.
PO Box 3190
Los Angeles, CA 90078
Phone: 323-466-3310
Fax: 323-466-6474
E-mail: contests@authorservicesinc.com

L. RON HUBBARD'S WRITERS OF THE FUTURE CONTEST
An ongoing competition for new and amateur writers judged by professional writers. Eligible submissions are short stories and novelettes of science fiction or fantasy. Deadline varies and prize amount ranges from $500 to $5000.

Award: Prize for use in freshman, sophomore, junior, senior, graduate, or postgraduate years; not renewable. *Number:* up to 12. *Amount:* $500–$5000.

Eligibility Requirements: Applicant must be enrolled or expecting to enroll full- or part-time at a two-year or four-year or technical institution or university and must have an interest in writing. Available to U.S. and non-U.S. citizens.

Application Requirements: Copy of the manuscript, entry in a contest, self-addressed stamped envelope with application. *Deadline:* continuous.

Contact: Joni Labaqui, Contest Administrator
Author Services, Inc.
PO Box 1630
Los Angeles, CA 90078
Phone: 323-466-3310
Fax: 323-466-6474
E-mail: contests@authorservicesinc.com

AUTOMOTIVE HALL OF FAME
http://www.automotivehalloffame.org/

AUTOMOTIVE HALL OF FAME EDUCATIONAL FUNDS
Award for full-time undergraduate and graduate students pursuing studies in automotive and related technologies. Must submit two letters of recommendation supporting automotive interests. Minimum 3.0 cumulative GPA required. Student must study in the United States and either be a United States Citizen or on a Student Visa.

Award: Scholarship for use in freshman, sophomore, junior, senior, or graduate years; renewable. *Number:* 20. *Amount:* $500–$2000.

Eligibility Requirements: Applicant must be enrolled or expecting to enroll full-time at a two-year or four-year or technical institution or university and must have an interest in automotive. Applicant must have 3.0 GPA or higher. Available to U.S. and non-U.S. citizens.

Application Requirements: Application form, application form may be submitted online (http://www.automotivehalloffame.org), essay, financial need analysis, recommendations or references, self-addressed stamped envelope with application, transcript. *Deadline:* June 1.

AYN RAND INSTITUTE
http://www.aynrandnovels.org

ANTHEM ESSAY CONTEST
Entrant must be in the 8th, 9th, or 10th grade. Essays will be judged on both style and content. Winning essays must demonstrate an outstanding grasp of the philosophical meaning of Ayn Rand's novelette, "Anthem." For complete rules and guidelines visit website http://www.aynrand.org/contests.

Award: Prize for use in freshman, sophomore, junior, graduate, or postgraduate years; not renewable. *Number:* 236. *Amount:* $30–$2000.

Eligibility Requirements: Applicant must be high school student; planning to enroll or expecting to enroll full- or part-time at a two-year or four-year or technical institution or university and must have an interest in writing. Available to U.S. and non-U.S. citizens.

Application Requirements: Entry in a contest, essay. *Deadline:* March 20.

Contact: Jason Eriksen, Essay Contest Coordinator
Ayn Rand Institute
2121 Alton Parkway, Suite 250
Irvine, CA 92606
Phone: 949-222-6550 Ext. 247
Fax: 949-222-6558
E-mail: essay@aynrand.org

BABE RUTH LEAGUE INC.
http://www.baberuthleague.org/

BABE RUTH SCHOLARSHIP PROGRAM
Program to provide assistance to individuals (former Babe Ruth Baseball, Cal Ripken Baseball or Babe Ruth Softball players) who plan on furthering their education beyond high school. Outstanding student athletes will receive $1000 each towards their college tuition.

Award: Scholarship for use in freshman year; not renewable. *Number:* 1–10. *Amount:* $1000.

Eligibility Requirements: Applicant must be high school student; planning to enroll or expecting to enroll full- or part-time at a two-year or four-year institution or university and must have an interest in athletics/sports. Available to U.S. citizens.

Application Requirements: Application form, application form may be submitted online (http://www.baberuthleague.org), recommendations or references, transcript. *Deadline:* September 1.

Contact: Mr. Joseph Smiegocki, Scholarship Committee
    Phone: 800-880-3142
    Fax: 609-695-2505
    E-mail: info@baberuthleague.org

BILL DICKEY SCHOLARSHIP ASSOCIATION

http://www.nmjgsa.org/

BDSA SCHOLARSHIPS

One-time and renewable awards available. Awards are based on academic achievement, entrance exam scores, financial need, references, evidence of community service, and golfing ability. High school seniors or younger who are not already in the association's database may see website to enter profile for eligibility and for application.

Award: Scholarship for use in freshman year; renewable. *Amount:* $1000–$3500.

Eligibility Requirements: Applicant must be high school student; planning to enroll or expecting to enroll full-time at a four-year institution or university and must have an interest in golf. Available to U.S. citizens.

Application Requirements: Application form, community service, financial need analysis, recommendations or references. *Deadline:* April 20.

Contact: Andrea Bourdeaux, Executive Director
    Phone: 602-258-7851
    E-mail: andrea@bdscholar.org

BOETTCHER FOUNDATION

http://www.boettcherfoundation.org/

BOETTCHER FOUNDATION SCHOLARSHIPS
• *See page 671*

CALIFORNIA JUNIOR MISS SCHOLARSHIP PROGRAM

http://www.ajm.org/

CALIFORNIA JUNIOR MISS SCHOLARSHIP PROGRAM
• *See page 671*

CANADA ICELAND FOUNDATION INC. SCHOLARSHIPS

http://logberg.com/scholarship.asp

CANADA ICELAND FOUNDATION SCHOLARSHIP PROGRAM

One scholarship of $500, to be awarded annually. To be offered to a university student studying towards a degree in any Canadian university.

Award: Scholarship for use in freshman, sophomore, junior, senior, or graduate years; not renewable. *Number:* 1. *Amount:* $500.

Eligibility Requirements: Applicant must be enrolled or expecting to enroll full-time at an institution or university; studying in Alberta, British Columbia, Manitoba, New Brunswick, Newfoundland, Nova Scotia, Ontario, Quebec, Saskatchewan and must have an interest in leadership. Available to Canadian citizens.

Application Requirements: Application form, community service, recommendations or references, test scores, transcript. *Deadline:* varies.

Contact: Karen Bowman, Administrative Assistant
    Phone: 204-284-5686
    Fax: 204-284-7099
    E-mail: karen@lh-inc.ca

CENTER FOR LESBIAN AND GAY STUDIES (C.L.A.G.S.)

http://www.clags.org/

CENTER FOR GAY AND LESBIAN STUDIES UNDERGRADUATE PAPER AWARDS

A cash prize of $250 awarded to the best paper written in a City University of New York or State University of New York undergraduate class on a topic related to gay, lesbian, bisexual, queer, or transgender experiences. Essays should be between 12 and 30 pages.

Award: Prize for use in freshman, sophomore, junior, or senior years; not renewable. *Number:* 1. *Amount:* $250.

Eligibility Requirements: Applicant must be enrolled or expecting to enroll full- or part-time at a four-year institution or university and must have an interest in LGBT issues. Available to U.S. and non-U.S. citizens.

Application Requirements: Application form may be submitted online (http://clags.org/?p=undergraduate_paper), essay. *Deadline:* June 15.

Contact: Noam Parness, Membership and Fellowships Coordinator
    Phone: 212-817-1958
    E-mail: clagsfellowships@gmail.com

SYLVIA RIVERA AWARD IN TRANSGENDER STUDIES

Award given for the best book or article to appear on transgender studies during the current year. Applications may be submitted by the author or by nomination.

Award: Prize for use in freshman, sophomore, junior, senior, graduate, or postgraduate years; not renewable. *Number:* 1. *Amount:* $1000.

Eligibility Requirements: Applicant must be enrolled or expecting to enroll full- or part-time at a two-year or four-year institution or university and must have an interest in LGBT issues or writing. Available to U.S. and non-U.S. citizens.

Application Requirements: 6 copies of the article or 6 copies of the first chapter or first 20 pages for books, cover sheet, details about the publication, contact details, application form, application form may be submitted online (http://clags.org/?p=rivera). *Deadline:* June 1.

Contact: Noam Parness, Membership and Fellowships Coordinator
    Phone: 212-817-1958
    E-mail: clagsfellowships@gmail.com

CHRISTOPHERS

http://www.christophers.org/

POSTER CONTEST FOR HIGH SCHOOL STUDENTS

Contest invites students in grades nine through twelve to interpret the theme "You can make a difference." Posters must include this statement and illustrate the idea that one person can change the world for the better. Judging is based on overall impact, content, originality, and artistic merit. More information can be found at http://www.christophers.org.

Award: Prize for use in freshman, sophomore, junior, or senior years; not renewable. *Number:* up to 8. *Amount:* $100–$1000.

Eligibility Requirements: Applicant must be high school student; planning to enroll or expecting to enroll full-time at a four-year institution or university and must have an interest in art. Available to U.S. citizens.

Application Requirements: Application form, entry in a contest, poster. *Deadline:* February 13.

Contact: Sarah Holinski, Youth Coordinator
    Christophers
    5 Hanover Square, 22nd Floor
    New York, NY 10004
    Phone: 212-759-4050 Ext. 240
    Fax: 212-838-5073
    E-mail: youth@christophers.org

VIDEO CONTEST FOR COLLEGE STUDENTS

Contest requires college students to use any style or format to express the following theme "One person can make a difference." Entries can be up to 5 minutes in length and must be submitted in standard, full-sized DVD format. Entries will be judged on content, artistic and technical proficiency, and adherence to contest rules. More information is available at http://www.christophers.org.

Award: Prize for use in freshman, sophomore, junior, senior, graduate, or postgraduate years; not renewable. *Number:* 2–6. *Amount:* $1000–$2000.

Eligibility Requirements: Applicant must be enrolled or expecting to enroll full- or part-time at a two-year or four-year or technical institution or university and must have an interest in art. Available to U.S. citizens.

Application Requirements: Application form, DVD, entry in a contest. *Deadline:* February 13.

Contact: Sarah Holinski, Youth Coordinator
Christophers
5 Hanover Square, 22nd Floor
New York, NY 10004
Phone: 212-759-4050 Ext. 240
Fax: 212-838-5073
E-mail: s.holinski@christophers.org

COCA-COLA SCHOLARS FOUNDATION INC.

http://www.coca-colascholars.org/

COCA-COLA TWO-YEAR COLLEGES SCHOLARSHIP
• *See page 552*

COLAGE: PEOPLE WITH A LESBIAN, GAY, BISEXUAL, TRANSGENDER OR QUEER PARENT

http://www.colage.org/

COLAGE SCHOLARSHIP PROGRAM FOR STUDENTS WITH LESBIAN, GAY, BISEXUAL, TRANSGENDER AND/OR QUEER (LGBTQ) PARENT(S)

COLAGE will award four scholarships to children of LGBTQ parents. Each scholarship will provide $1,000 to post-secondary students who have one or more LGBTQ parent(s)/guardian(s) and have demonstrated ability and commitment to effecting change in the LGBTQ community and the community at large.

Award: Scholarship for use in freshman, sophomore, junior, or senior years; not renewable. *Number:* 3–5. *Amount:* $500–$1000.

Eligibility Requirements: Applicant must be enrolled or expecting to enroll full- or part-time at a two-year or four-year or technical institution or university and must have an interest in leadership or LGBT issues. Available to U.S. citizens.

Application Requirements: Application form, essay, financial need analysis, proof of enrollment, transcript. *Deadline:* April 30.

COLLEGEBOUND FOUNDATION

http://www.collegeboundfoundation.org/

HY ZOLET STUDENT ATHLETE SCHOLARSHIP
• *See page 675*

COLLEGEFINANCIALAIDINFORMATION.COM

http://www.easyaid.com/

FRANK O'NEILL MEMORIAL SCHOLARSHIP

One-time award available to applicants attending or aspiring to attend a university, college, trade school, technical institute, vocational training, or other postsecondary education program. Must submit essay explaining educational goals and financial need.

Award: Scholarship for use in freshman, sophomore, junior, senior, or graduate years; not renewable. *Number:* 2. *Amount:* $1000.

Eligibility Requirements: Applicant must be enrolled or expecting to enroll full- or part-time at a two-year or four-year or technical institution or university and must have an interest in writing. Available to U.S. and non-U.S. citizens.

Application Requirements: Application form, essay. *Deadline:* December 31.

Contact: Geoff Anderla, Owner
Phone: 623-972-4282
E-mail: questions@easyaid.com

COLLEGEWEEKLIVE.COM

http://www.collegeweeklive.com/

COLLEGEWEEKLIVE.COM SCHOLARSHIP

$2500 scholarship to high school students demonstrating excellence in writing ability, creativity and originality. Students must submit an online application and participate in an online virtual college fair. For more information, see website at http://www.collegeweeklive.com/register.php?code=SE_D.

Award: Scholarship for use in freshman year; not renewable. *Number:* 1. *Amount:* $2500.

Eligibility Requirements: Applicant must be high school student; planning to enroll or expecting to enroll full- or part-time at a two-year or four-year or technical institution or university and must have an interest in writing. Available to U.S. citizens.

Application Requirements: Application form, essay. *Deadline:* varies.

Contact: Lori Grandstaff, Scholarship Management Coordinator
CollegeWeekLive.com
3020 Hartley Road, Suite 220
Jacksonville, FL 32257
Phone: 904-854-6750 Ext. 11
Fax: 904-483-2934
E-mail: lori@scholarshipexperts.com

COLUMBIA 300

http://www.columbia300.com/

COLUMBIA 300 JOHN JOWDY SCHOLARSHIP

Renewable scholarship for graduating high school seniors who are actively involved in the sport of bowling. Must have minimum GPA of 3.0.

Award: Scholarship for use in freshman year; renewable. *Number:* 1. *Amount:* $500.

Eligibility Requirements: Applicant must be high school student; planning to enroll or expecting to enroll full- or part-time at a four-year institution or university and must have an interest in bowling. Applicant must have 3.0 GPA or higher. Available to U.S. citizens.

Application Requirements: Application form. *Deadline:* April 1.

Contact: Dale Garner, Scholarship Committee
Columbia 300
PO Box 13430
San Antonio, TX 78213
Phone: 800-531-5920

COLUMBIA UNIVERSITY, DEPARTMENT OF MUSIC

http://www.music.columbia.edu/

JOSEPH H. BEARNS PRIZE IN MUSIC

This prize is open to U.S. citizens between 18 and 25 years of age on January 1st of the competition year, and offers prizes for both short form and long form works of music in order to encourage talented young composers.

Award: Prize for use in freshman, sophomore, junior, or senior years; renewable. *Number:* 2. *Amount:* $2000–$3000.

Eligibility Requirements: Applicant must be age 18-25; enrolled or expecting to enroll full- or part-time at a two-year or four-year or technical institution or university and must have an interest in music. Available to U.S. citizens.

Application Requirements: Entry in a contest, music score, information regarding prior studies, social security number, self-addressed stamped envelope with application. *Deadline:* March 17.

CONTEMPORARY RECORD SOCIETY

http://www.crsnews.org/

CONTEMPORARY RECORD SOCIETY NATIONAL COMPETITION FOR PERFORMING ARTISTS

There are no age restrictions to participate. Applicant may submit one performance tape of varied length including music of any period of music with each application. The applicant may use any number of instrumentalists and voices. First prize is a commercial distribution of the winner's recording. Application fee is $50 for each recording submitted. Submit self-addressed stamped envelope with the application. The winning applicant will participate in a CD recording released by CRS. (This prize is not applicable toward tuition.)

Award: Prize for use in freshman, sophomore, junior, senior, graduate, or postgraduate years; not renewable. *Number:* 1. *Amount:* $2000–$6000.

Eligibility Requirements: Applicant must be enrolled or expecting to enroll full- or part-time at a two-year or four-year or technical institution or university and must have an interest in music/singing. Available to U.S. and non-U.S. citizens.

Application Requirements: Application form, entry in a contest, recommendations or references, resume, self-addressed stamped envelope with application. *Fee:* $50. *Deadline:* March 30.

Contact: Mr. Jack Shusterman, Artist Representative
Contemporary Record Society
724 Winchester Road
Broomall, PA 19008
Phone: 610-544-5920
Fax: 915-808-4232
E-mail: crsnews@verizon.net

NATIONAL COMPETITION FOR COMPOSERS' RECORDINGS

First prize is a CD recording grant (not tuition). Limited to nine performers and twenty-five minutes duration. Works with additional performers will be accepted provided there is a release of the original recorded master for CD reproduction. Must submit a musical composition that is non-published and not commercially recorded. Limit of 5 works per applicant.

Award: Prize for use in freshman, sophomore, junior, senior, graduate, or postgraduate years; not renewable. *Number:* 1. *Amount:* $2000–$6000.

Eligibility Requirements: Applicant must be enrolled or expecting to enroll full- or part-time at a two-year or four-year or technical institution or university and must have an interest in music/singing. Available to U.S. and non-U.S. citizens.

Application Requirements: Application form, entry in a contest, recommendations or references, resume, self-addressed stamped envelope with application. *Fee:* $50. *Deadline:* March 30.

Contact: Mr. Jack Shusterman, Artist Representative
Contemporary Record Society
724 Winchester Road
Broomall, PA 19008
Phone: 610-544-5920
Fax: 915-808-4232
E-mail: crsnews@verizon.net

CROSSLITES

http://www.crosslites.com/

CROSSLITES SCHOLARSHIP AWARD

Scholarship contest is open to high school, college and graduate school students. There are no minimum GPA, SAT, ACT, GMAT, GRE, or any other test score requirements.

Award: Prize for use in freshman, sophomore, junior, senior, or graduate years; not renewable. *Number:* 33. *Amount:* $100–$2500.

Eligibility Requirements: Applicant must be enrolled or expecting to enroll full- or part-time at a two-year or four-year or technical institution or university and must have an interest in writing. Available to U.S. and non-U.S. citizens.

Application Requirements: Application form, entry in a contest, essay. *Deadline:* December 15.

Contact: Samuel Certo, Scholarship Committee
CrossLites
1000 Holt Avenue
Winter Park, FL 32789

THE DALLAS FOUNDATION

http://www.dallasfoundation.org/

THE LANDON RUSNAK SCHOLARSHIP

• *See page 682*

DELAWARE HIGHER EDUCATION OFFICE

http://www.doe.k12.de.us

AGENDA FOR DELAWARE WOMEN TRAILBLAZER SCHOLARSHIP

• *See page 553*

DEVRY, INC.

http://www.devry.edu/

DEVRY UNIVERSITY FIRST SCHOLAR AWARD

Award to high school graduates and GED recipients. Must be a registered participant in any regional FIRST Robotics Competition. Must have an ACT composite score of 19 or SAT combined math and verbal/critical reading score of at least 900. Must submit letter of recommendation from FIRST team advisor. Deadline: one year from high school graduation to apply and start.

Award: Scholarship for use in freshman year; renewable. *Amount:* $3000–$9000.

Eligibility Requirements: Applicant must be high school student; planning to enroll or expecting to enroll full-time at an institution or university and must have an interest in science. Available to U.S. and Canadian citizens.

Application Requirements: Application form, essay, recommendations or references, test scores, transcript.

Contact: Thonie Simpson, National High School Program Manager
Phone: 630-706-3122
E-mail: scholarships@devry.edu

DIAMANTE, INC.

http://www.diamanteinc.org/

LATINO DIAMANTE SCHOLARSHIP FUND

• *See page 553*

DIVERSITY CITY MEDIA

http://www.blacknews.com/

BLACKNEWS.COM SCHOLARSHIP ESSAY CONTEST

• *See page 622*

DIXIE BOYS BASEBALL

http://www.dixie.org/boys

DIXIE BOYS BASEBALL BERNIE VARNADORE SCHOLARSHIP PROGRAM

• *See page 684*

DIXIE YOUTH SCHOLARSHIP PROGRAM

• *See page 684*

DUPONT IN COOPERATION WITH GENERAL LEARNING COMMUNICATIONS

http://www.thechallenge.dupont.com/

DUPONT CHALLENGE SCIENCE ESSAY AWARDS PROGRAM

Student science and technology prize program in the United States and Canada. Students must submit an essay of 700 to 1000 words discussing a scientific or technological development, event, or theory that has captured their interest. For students in grades 7¿12. Must mail all entries in a 9x12 inch envelope. For more details go to website http://www.thechallenge.dupont.com.

Award: Prize for use in freshman year; not renewable. *Number:* 100. *Amount:* $100–$3000.

Eligibility Requirements: Applicant must be high school student; age 12-19; planning to enroll or expecting to enroll full- or part-time at a four-year institution or university and must have an interest in writing. Available to U.S. and Canadian citizens.

Application Requirements: Entry in a contest, essay, official entry form. *Deadline:* January 31.

Contact: Carole Rubenstein, Editorial Director
DuPont in Cooperation with General Learning
Communications
900 Skokie Boulevard, Suite 200
Northbrook, IL 60062-4028
Phone: 847-205-3000
Fax: 847-564-8197
E-mail: c.rubenstein@glcomm.com

EAST BAY FOOTBALL OFFICIALS ASSOCIATION

http://www.ebfoa.org/

EAST BAY FOOTBALL OFFICIALS ASSOCIATION COLLEGE SCHOLARSHIP
• *See page 684*

ELDER & LEEMAUR PUBLISHERS

http://www.elpublishers.com/

AUTHORS OF TOMORROW SCHOLARSHIP

Scholarship is available to current undergraduate students in any field of study and any student in either junior or senior high school.

Award: Scholarship for use in freshman, sophomore, junior, or senior years; not renewable. *Amount:* up to $10,000.

Eligibility Requirements: Applicant must be enrolled or expecting to enroll full- or part-time at a four-year institution or university and must have an interest in writing. Available to U.S. citizens.

Application Requirements: Application form, essay. *Deadline:* December 1.

Contact: Joni Hara, Public Relations Assistant
Phone: 604-263-3540
E-mail: joni@elpublishers.com

ELIE WIESEL FOUNDATION FOR HUMANITY

http://www.eliewieselfoundation.org/

ELIE WIESEL PRIZE IN ETHICS ESSAY CONTEST

Scholarship for full-time junior or senior at a four-year accredited college or university in the United States. Up to five awards are granted.

Award: Prize for use in junior or senior years; not renewable. *Number:* up to 5. *Amount:* $500–$5000.

Eligibility Requirements: Applicant must be enrolled or expecting to enroll full-time at a four-year institution or university and must have an interest in writing. Available to U.S. and non-U.S. citizens.

Application Requirements: Application form, entry in a contest, essay, self-addressed stamped envelope with application, student entry form, faculty sponsor form. *Deadline:* December 3.

Contact: Ms. Chelsea Friedman, Essay Contest Coordinator
Elie Wiesel Foundation for Humanity
555 Madison Avenue, 20th Floor
New York, NY 10022
Phone: 212-490-7788
Fax: 212-490-6006
E-mail: chelsea@eliewieselfoundation.org

ELKS NATIONAL FOUNDATION

http://www.elks.org/enf

ELKS NATIONAL FOUNDATION MOST VALUABLE STUDENT SCHOLARSHIP CONTEST

Five hundred awards ranging from $1000 to $15,000 per year, renewable for four years, are allocated nationally by state quota for graduating high school seniors. Based on scholarship, leadership, and financial need. Must be a U.S. citizen pursuing a 4-year degree full-time at a U.S. college or university. For more information, visit http://www.elks.org/enf/scholars.

Award: Scholarship for use in freshman, sophomore, junior, or senior years; renewable. *Number:* 500. *Amount:* $4000–$60,000.

Eligibility Requirements: Applicant must be high school student; planning to enroll or expecting to enroll full-time at a four-year institution or university and must have an interest in leadership. Available to U.S. citizens.

Application Requirements: Application form, community service, entry in a contest, essay, financial need analysis, self-addressed stamped envelope with application, test scores, transcript. *Deadline:* December 7.

EQUALITY SCHOLARSHIP COLLABORATIVE

http://www.equalityscholarship.org

SCHOLARSHIPS FOR HIGH SCHOOL GRADUATES
• *See page 554*

ESSAYJOLT.COM

http://www.essayjolt.com/

ESSAYJOLT SCHOLARSHIP
• *See page 685*

FINANCIAL SERVICE CENTERS OF AMERICA INC.

http://www.fisca.org/

FINANCIAL SERVICE CENTERS OF AMERICA SCHOLARSHIP FUND

Cash grants of at least $2000 to two students from each of the 5 geographic regions across the country. Criteria is based on academic achievement, financial need, leadership skills in schools and the community, and an essay written expressly for the competition. Applicant must be single.

Award: Grant for use in freshman year; not renewable. *Number:* 10–22. *Amount:* $2000.

Eligibility Requirements: Applicant must be high school student; planning to enroll or expecting to enroll full-time at a two-year or four-year institution or university; single and must have an interest in leadership. Available to U.S. citizens.

Application Requirements: Application form, community service, entry in a contest, essay, financial need analysis, personal photograph, recommendations or references, transcript. *Deadline:* April 8.

Contact: Henry Shyne, Executive Director
Phone: 201-487-0412
E-mail: hshyne@fisca.org

FOREST ROBERTS THEATRE

http://www.nmu.edu/

MILDRED AND ALBERT PANOWSKI PLAYWRITING AWARD

Prize designed to encourage and stimulate artistic growth among playwrights. Winner receives a cash prize and a world premiere of their play.

Award: Prize for use in freshman, sophomore, junior, senior, graduate, or postgraduate years; not renewable. *Number:* 1. *Amount:* $2000.

Eligibility Requirements: Applicant must be enrolled or expecting to enroll full- or part-time at a two-year or four-year or technical institution or university and must have an interest in theater or writing. Available to U.S. and non-U.S. citizens.

Application Requirements: Application form, entry in a contest, manuscript in English, self-addressed stamped envelope with application. *Deadline:* October 31.

Contact: Matt Hudson, Playwriting Award Coordinator
Forest Roberts Theatre
Northern Michigan University, 1401 Presque Isle Avenue
Marquette, MI 49855-5364
Phone: 906-227-2559
Fax: 906-227-2567

FOUNDATION FOR CHRISTIAN COLLEGE LEADERS

http://www.collegechristianleader.com/

FOUNDATION FOR COLLEGE CHRISTIAN LEADERS SCHOLARSHIP

• *See page 651*

FREEDOM FROM RELIGION FOUNDATION

http://www.ffrf.org/

FREEDOM FROM RELIGION FOUNDATION COLLEGE ESSAY COMPETITION

Any currently enrolled college student may submit essay. Essays should be typed, double-spaced 4¿5 pages with standard margins. Contestants must choose an original title for essay. 2010 topic: "Why I Reject Religion," "Why I am an Atheist/Agnostic/Unbeliever," or "Growing Up a Freethinker." Each contestant must include a paragraph biography giving campus and permanent addresses, phone numbers, and emails. The scholarship value varies. The essay topic and specific guidelines are posted in February.

Award: Scholarship for use in freshman, sophomore, junior, or senior years; not renewable. *Number:* 5–10. *Amount:* $200–$2000.

Eligibility Requirements: Applicant must be enrolled or expecting to enroll full-time at a four-year institution or university and must have an interest in writing. Available to U.S. and Canadian citizens.

Application Requirements: Entry in a contest, essay, one-paragraph biography. *Deadline:* July 1.

FREEDOM FROM RELIGION FOUNDATION HIGH SCHOOL SENIOR ESSAY COMPETITION

High-school essay submitted must have an original title. 2010 topic: "The Harm of Religion" or "The Harm of Religion to Women." Each entrant must include a paragraph biography giving campus and permanent addresses, phone numbers and emails. First prize winner will receive $2000, second place $1000, third place $500, honorable mentions $200. The essay topic and specific guidelines are posted in February. For more information visit http://www.ffrf.org/.

Award: Scholarship for use in freshman year; not renewable. *Number:* 5–10. *Amount:* $200–$2000.

Eligibility Requirements: Applicant must be high school student; planning to enroll or expecting to enroll full-time at a two-year or four-year or technical institution or university and must have an interest in writing. Available to U.S. and Canadian citizens.

Application Requirements: Entry in a contest, essay, one-paragraph biography. *Deadline:* June 1.

GENERAL BOARD OF HIGHER EDUCATION AND MINISTRY

http://www.gbhem.org

HANA SCHOLARSHIP

• *See page 623*

THE REV. DR. KAREN LAYMAN GIFT OF HOPE: 21ST CENTURY SCHOLARS PROGRAM

• *See page 651*

GEORGE T. WELCH TRUST

http://www.bakerboyer.com/

EDUCATION EXCHANGE COLLEGE GRANT PROGRAM

Awards range from four $1000 to thirty $5000 scholarships. Must be U.S. citizens and provide written acceptance to an accredited four-year college by May 15 of the award year.

Award: Grant for use in freshman year; not renewable. *Number:* 34. *Amount:* $1000–$5000.

Eligibility Requirements: Applicant must be high school student; planning to enroll or expecting to enroll full-time at a four-year institution or university and must have an interest in leadership. Available to U.S. citizens.

Application Requirements: Acceptance letter to a four-year institution, copy of first two pages of parent or guardian's federal income tax return, application form, essay, recommendations or references, transcript. *Deadline:* March 15.

GLAMOUR

http://www.glamour.com/

TOP 10 COLLEGE WOMEN COMPETITION

Female students with leadership experience on and off campus, excellence in field of study, and inspiring goals can apply for this competition. Winners will be awarded $3000 along with a trip to New York City. Must be a junior studying full-time with a minimum GPA of 3.0. in either the United States or Canada. Non-U.S. citizens may apply if attending U.S. postsecondary institutions.

Award: Prize for use in junior year; not renewable. *Number:* 10. *Amount:* $3000.

Eligibility Requirements: Applicant must be enrolled or expecting to enroll full-time at a four-year institution or university; female and must have an interest in leadership. Applicant must have 3.0 GPA or higher. Available to U.S. and non-U.S. citizens.

Application Requirements: Application form, essay, personal photograph, recommendations or references, transcript. *Deadline:* February 2.

Contact: Lynda Laux-Bachand, Reader Services Editor
Glamour
Four Times Square, 16th Floor
New York, NY 10036-6593
Phone: 212-286-6667
Fax: 212-286-6922

GLENN MILLER BIRTHPLACE SOCIETY

http://www.glennmiller.org/

GLENN MILLER INSTRUMENTAL SCHOLARSHIP

One-time awards for high school seniors and college freshmen. Scholarships are awarded as competition prizes and must be used for any education-related expenses. Must submit 10-minute, high-quality audio tape of pieces selected for competition or those of similar style. Applicant is responsible for travel to and lodging during the competition.

Award: Scholarship for use in freshman year; not renewable. *Number:* 3. *Amount:* $1000–$4500.

Eligibility Requirements: Applicant must be high school student; planning to enroll or expecting to enroll full-time at a four-year institution or university and must have an interest in music/singing. Available to U.S. and non-U.S. citizens.

Application Requirements: Application form, entry in a contest, essay, performance tape or CD. *Deadline:* March 15.

Contact: Arlene Leonard, Secretary
Glenn Miller Birthplace Society
107 East Main Street, PO Box 61
Clarinda, IA 51632-0061
Phone: 712-542-2461
Fax: 712-542-2461
E-mail: gmbs@heartland.net

JACK PULLAN MEMORIAL SCHOLARSHIP

One scholarship for a male or female vocalist, awarded as competition prize and, to be used for any education-related expenses. Must submit 10 minute, high-quality audio tape of pieces selected for competition or those of similar style. Applicant is responsible for travel to and lodging during the competition. One-time award for high school seniors and college freshmen. More information on http://www.glennmiller.org/scholar.htm.

Award: Scholarship for use in freshman year; not renewable. *Number:* 1. *Amount:* $1000.

Eligibility Requirements: Applicant must be high school student; planning to enroll or expecting to enroll full-time at a four-year institution or university and must have an interest in music/singing. Available to U.S. and non-U.S. citizens.

Application Requirements: Application form, entry in a contest, essay, performance tape or CD. *Deadline:* March 15.

Contact: Arlene Leonard, Secretary
Glenn Miller Birthplace Society
107 East Main Street, PO Box 61
Clarinda, IA 51632-0061
Phone: 712-542-2461
Fax: 712-542-2461
E-mail: gmbs@heartland.net

RALPH BREWSTER VOCAL SCHOLARSHIP

One scholarship for a male or female vocalist, awarded as competition prize and, to be used for any education-related expenses. Must submit 10 minute, high-quality audio tape of pieces selected for competition or those of similar style. Applicant is responsible for travel to and lodging during the competition. One-time award for high school seniors and college freshmen.

Award: Scholarship for use in freshman year; not renewable. *Number:* 1. *Amount:* $2000.

Eligibility Requirements: Applicant must be high school student; planning to enroll or expecting to enroll full-time at a four-year institution or university and must have an interest in music/singing. Available to U.S. and non-U.S. citizens.

Application Requirements: Application form, entry in a contest, essay, performance tape of competition or concert quality (up to 5 minutes duration). *Deadline:* March 15.

Contact: Arlene Leonard, Secretary
Glenn Miller Birthplace Society
107 East Main Street, PO Box 61
Clarinda, IA 51632-0061
Phone: 712-542-2461
Fax: 712-542-2461
E-mail: gmbs@heartland.net

GLORIA BARRON PRIZE FOR YOUNG HEROES

http://www.barronprize.org/

GLORIA BARRON PRIZE FOR YOUNG HEROES

Award honors young people ages 8 to 18 who have shown leadership and courage in public service to people or to the planet. Must be nominated by a responsible adult who is not a relative. Award is to be applied to higher education or a service project. For further information and nomination forms, see website at http://www.barronprize.org.

Award: Prize for use in freshman year; not renewable. *Number:* 1–10. *Amount:* up to $2000.

Eligibility Requirements: Applicant must be age 8-18; enrolled or expecting to enroll full- or part-time at a two-year or four-year or technical institution or university and must have an interest in leadership. Available to U.S. and Canadian citizens.

Application Requirements: Application form, community service, essay, nomination form, references form, personal photograph. *Deadline:* April 30.

Contact: Barbara Ann Richman, Executive Director
Gloria Barron Prize for Young Heroes
545 Pearl Street
Boulder, CO 80302
E-mail: ba_richman@barronprize.org

GRACO INC.

http://www.graco.com/

GRACO EXCELLENCE SCHOLARSHIP
• *See page 546*

GREATER KANAWHA VALLEY FOUNDATION

http://www.tgkvf.org/

KID'S CHANCE OF WEST VIRGINIA SCHOLARSHIP
• *See page 690*

WEST VIRGINIA GOLF ASSOCIATION FUND
• *See page 692*

GREENHOUSE SCHOLARS

http://www.greenhousescholars.org/

GREENHOUSE SCHOLARS
• *See page 555*

HARNESS HORSE YOUTH FOUNDATION

http://www.hhyf.org/

CURT GREENE MEMORIAL SCHOLARSHIP
• *See page 555*

HARTFORD WHALERS BOOSTER CLUB

http://www.whalerwatch.com/

HARTFORD WHALERS BOOSTER CLUB SCHOLARSHIP
• *See page 692*

HEMOPHILIA FEDERATION OF AMERICA

ARTISTIC ENCOURAGEMENT GRANT
• *See page 571*

HERB KOHL EDUCATIONAL FOUNDATION INC.

http://www.kohleducation.org/

HERB KOHL EXCELLENCE SCHOLARSHIP PROGRAM
• *See page 556*

HOLLAND & KNIGHT CHARITABLE FOUNDATION HOLOCAUST REMEMBRANCE PROJECT

http://www.foundation.hklaw.com/

HOLOCAUST REMEMBRANCE PROJECT ESSAY CONTEST

Contest open to all students age 19 and under who are currently enrolled as high school students, and are residents of either the United States or Mexico, or who are United States citizens living abroad. Submit essay on any aspect of the Holocaust using relevant research sources and addressing key points indicated in the instructions. Prizes for winning essays include scholarships. Essay must be submitted online. For information see website http://holocaust.hklaw.com.

Award: Prize for use in freshman year; not renewable. *Number:* 30. *Amount:* $300–$10,000.

Eligibility Requirements: Applicant must be high school student; planning to enroll or expecting to enroll full- or part-time at a four-year institution or university and must have an interest in writing. Available to U.S. citizens.

Application Requirements: Application form, essay. *Deadline:* April 30.

HORIZONS FOUNDATION

http://www.horizonsfoundation.org/

MARKOWSKI-LEACH SCHOLARSHIP

Scholarship of $1250 awarded to a student who attends San Francisco State University, Stanford University, or University of California, and self-identifies as lesbian, gay, bisexual, transgender, or queer. Recipient is chosen based on demonstrated promise for becoming a positive role model for other LGBTQ people. All prospective undergraduate and graduate students may apply. Students transferring to one of these universities are also encouraged to apply.

Award: Scholarship for use in freshman, sophomore, junior, or senior years; renewable. *Number:* 1. *Amount:* $1250.

Eligibility Requirements: Applicant must be enrolled or expecting to enroll full-time at a two-year or four-year or technical institution or university; studying in California and must have an interest in LGBT issues. Applicant must have 2.5 GPA or higher. Available to U.S. and Canadian citizens.

Application Requirements: Application form, essay, recommendations or references. *Deadline:* April 1.

HOSTESS COMMITTEE SCHOLARSHIPS/ MISS AMERICA PAGEANT

http://www.missamerica.org/

MISS AMERICA COMMUNITY SERVICE SCHOLARSHIPS
• *See page 556*

MISS AMERICA ORGANIZATION COMPETITION SCHOLARSHIPS

Scholarship competition open to 70 contestants, each serving as state representative. Women will be judged in Private Interview, Swimsuit, Evening Wear and Talent competition. Other awards may be based on points assessed by judges during competitions. Upon reaching the National level, award values range from $2000 to $50,000. Additional awards not affecting the competition can be won with values from $1000 to $10,000.

Award: Prize for use in freshman, sophomore, junior, senior, or graduate years; not renewable. *Number:* 70. *Amount:* $2000–$50,000.

Eligibility Requirements: Applicant must be age 17-24; enrolled or expecting to enroll full- or part-time at a two-year or four-year or technical institution or university; female and must have an interest in beauty pageant. Available to U.S. citizens.

Application Requirements: Application form, entry in a contest. *Deadline:* varies.

Contact: Doreen Lindell Gordon, Controller and Scholarship Administrator
Phone: 609-345-7571 Ext. 27
Fax: 609-347-6079
E-mail: doreen@missamerica.org

MISS AMERICA SCHOLAR AWARD

$1000 award offered to one woman in each state, District of Columbia and U.S. Virgin Islands, competing at the state level, for academic excellence. Competition is opened only to those competing at the state level. Must submit official transcripts of the immediate prior two years (4 semesters) of academic study, along with application.

Award: Scholarship for use in freshman, sophomore, junior, senior, graduate, or postgraduate years; not renewable.

Eligibility Requirements: Applicant must be enrolled or expecting to enroll full- or part-time at a four-year institution or university; female and must have an interest in beauty pageant. Available to U.S. citizens.

Application Requirements: Application form, transcript. *Deadline:* varies.

Contact: Doreen Lindell Gordon, Controller and Scholarship Administrator
Phone: 609-345-7571 Ext. 27
Fax: 609-347-6079
E-mail: doreen@missamerica.org

HUMANIST MAGAZINE

http://www.thehumanist.org/

HUMANIST ESSAY CONTEST

Contest is open to students residing in the United States or Canada who are enrolled in grades 9¿12. Essays should be 1500 to 2500 words, written in English, single-spaced, on a topic relevant to humanists.

Award: Prize for use in freshman year; not renewable. *Number:* 3. *Amount:* up to $1000.

Eligibility Requirements: Applicant must be high school student; planning to enroll or expecting to enroll full- or part-time at a two-year or four-year or technical institution or university and must have an interest in writing. Available to U.S. and Canadian citizens.

Application Requirements: Application form, entry in a contest, essay. *Deadline:* March 3.

JACKIE ROBINSON FOUNDATION

http://www.jackierobinson.org/

JACKIE ROBINSON SCHOLARSHIP
• *See page 558*

JUNIOR ACHIEVEMENT

http://www.ja.org/

JOE FRANCOMANO SCHOLARSHIP
• *See page 523*

KE ALI'I PAUAHI FOUNDATION

http://www.pauahi.org/

DWAYNE "NAKILA" STEELE SCHOLARSHIP

Scholarship supports students who demonstrate a desire to work in the area of perpetuating the Hawaiian language upon graduation. Requirements include demonstrated interest in the Hawaiian language, culture, and history, in addition to a commitment to contribute to the greater community and demonstrated financial need. Submit two letters of recommendation; one from a teacher or counselor and one from a community organization or other citing how the applicant is working toward perpetuating the Hawaiian Language.

Award: Scholarship for use in freshman, sophomore, junior, senior, or graduate years; not renewable. *Number:* 1. *Amount:* $800.

Eligibility Requirements: Applicant must be enrolled or expecting to enroll full-time at a two-year or four-year institution or university and must have an interest in Hawaiian language/culture. Available to U.S. citizens.

Application Requirements: Application form, application form may be submitted online (http://www.pauahi.org/scholarships), financial need analysis, recommendations or references, Student Aid Report (SAR), college acceptance letter, transcript. *Deadline:* April 1.

Contact: Mavis Shiraishi-Nagao, Scholarship Administrator
Phone: 808-534-3966
E-mail: scholarships@pauahi.org

KAMEHAMEHA SCHOOLS CLASS OF 1956 GRANT
• *See page 697*

KAMEHAMEHA SCHOOLS CLASS OF 1974 SCHOLARSHIP
• *See page 698*

KNIGHTS OF PYTHIAS

http://www.pythias.org/

KNIGHTS OF PYTHIAS POSTER CONTEST

Poster contest open to all high school students in the U.S. and Canada. Contestants must submit an original drawing. Eight winners are chosen. The winners are not required to attend institution of higher education.

Award: Prize for use in freshman year; not renewable. *Number:* 8. *Amount:* $100–$1000.

Eligibility Requirements: Applicant must be high school student; planning to enroll or expecting to enroll full- or part-time at a four-year institution or university and must have an interest in art. Available to U.S. and Canadian citizens.

Application Requirements: Entry in a contest. *Deadline:* April 30.

Contact: Alfred Saltzman, Supreme Secretary
    Phone: 617-472-8800
    Fax: 617-376-0363
    E-mail: kop@earthlink.net

KOSCIUSZKO FOUNDATION

http://www.thekf.org

MARCELLA SEMBRICH VOICE COMPETITION

The competition encourages young singers to study the repertoire of Polish composers. Three prizes awarded: $2000, $1250 and $750. Open to all singers who are at least 18 years old and preparing for professional careers. Must be U.S. citizens or international full-time students with a valid student visa.

Award: Prize for use in freshman, sophomore, junior, senior, or graduate years; not renewable. *Number:* 3. *Amount:* $750–$2000.

Eligibility Requirements: Applicant must be enrolled or expecting to enroll full- or part-time at a four-year institution or university and must have an interest in music/singing. Available to U.S. and non-Canadian citizens.

Application Requirements: 2 cassette tapes, application form, entry in a contest, personal photograph, recommendations or references. *Fee:* $35. *Deadline:* January 18.

Contact: Mr. Thomas Pniewski, Director of Cultural Programs
    Kosciuszko Foundation
    15 East 65th Street
    New York, NY 10021-6595
    Phone: 212-734-2130
    Fax: 212-628-4552
    E-mail: tompkf@aol.com

KURT WEILL FOUNDATION FOR MUSIC

http://www.kwf.org/

LOTTE LENYA COMPETITION FOR SINGERS

The competition recognizes excellence in the performance of music for the theater, including opera, operetta, and American musical theater. Applicants should contact the foundation for more information.

Award: Prize for use in freshman, sophomore, junior, senior, or graduate years; not renewable.

Eligibility Requirements: Applicant must be age 19-32; enrolled or expecting to enroll full- or part-time at a two-year or four-year institution or university and must have an interest in music/singing or theater. Available to U.S. and non-U.S. citizens.

Application Requirements: Application form, audition, entry in a contest.

Contact: Carolyn Weber, Director
    Phone: 212-505-5240
    E-mail: cweber@kwf.org

LADIES AUXILIARY TO THE VETERANS OF FOREIGN WARS

http://www.ladiesauxvfw.org/

JUNIOR GIRLS SCHOLARSHIP PROGRAM

• *See page 525*

YOUNG AMERICAN CREATIVE PATRIOTIC ART AWARDS PROGRAM

One-time awards for high school students in grades 9 through 12. Must submit an original work of art expressing their patriotism. First place state-level winners go on to national competition. Eight awards of varying amounts. Must reside in same state as sponsoring organization.

Award: Scholarship for use in freshman year; not renewable. *Number:* up to 8. *Amount:* $500–$10,000.

Eligibility Requirements: Applicant must be high school student; planning to enroll or expecting to enroll full-time at a two-year or four-year or technical institution; single and must have an interest in art. Available to U.S. citizens.

Application Requirements: Application form, entry in a contest, recommendations or references. *Deadline:* March 31.

Contact: Judith Millick, Administrator of Programs
    Phone: 816-561-8655
    E-mail: jmillick@ladiesauxvfw.org

LEAGUE FOUNDATION

http://www.leaguefoundation.org/

LEAGUE FOUNDATION ACADEMIC SCHOLARSHIP

Every student has the right and the potential to excel. The LEAGUE Foundation provides financial resources for America's Gay, Lesbian, Bisexual, Transgender youth to attend institutions of higher learning to meet this mission. More information can be found on the LEAGUE Foundation website: http://www.LEAGUEFoundation.org.

Award: Scholarship for use in freshman year; not renewable. *Number:* 4–8. *Amount:* $1500–$2500.

Eligibility Requirements: Applicant must be high school student; planning to enroll or expecting to enroll full-time at a two-year or four-year or technical institution or university and must have an interest in LGBT issues. Applicant must have 3.0 GPA or higher. Available to U.S. and Canadian citizens.

Application Requirements: Application form, college or university acceptance letter, community service, essay, recommendations or references, test scores, transcript. *Deadline:* April 30.

Contact: Charles Eader, Executive Director
    LEAGUE Foundation
    One AT&T Way, Room 5C215R
    Bedminster, NJ 07921
    Phone: 571-354-4525
    E-mail: info@leaguefoundation.org

LEARNING ALLY

http://www.learningally.org/

MARION HUBER LEARNING THROUGH LISTENING AWARDS

• *See page 525*

MARY P. OENSLAGER SCHOLASTIC ACHIEVEMENT AWARDS

• *See page 525*

LEE-JACKSON EDUCATIONAL FOUNDATION

http://www.lee-jackson.org/

LEE-JACKSON EDUCATIONAL FOUNDATION SCHOLARSHIP COMPETITION

• *See page 699*

LIEDERKRANZ FOUNDATION

http://www.liederkranznycity.org/

LIEDERKRANZ FOUNDATION SCHOLARSHIP AWARD FOR VOICE

Nonrenewable awards for voice for both full-and part-time study. Those studying general voice must be between ages 18 to 45 years old while those studying Wagnerian voice must be between ages 25 to 45 years old. Application fee of $50. Applications not available before August and September.

Award: Prize for use in freshman, sophomore, junior, senior, or graduate years; not renewable. *Number:* 14–18. *Amount:* $1000–$8000.

Eligibility Requirements: Applicant must be age 18-45; enrolled or expecting to enroll full- or part-time at a four-year institution or university and must have an interest in music/singing. Available to U.S. and non-U.S. citizens.

Application Requirements: Application form, entry in a contest, proof of age, self-addressed stamped envelope with application. *Fee:* $50. *Deadline:* November 15.

THE LINCOLN FORUM

http://www.thelincolnforum.org/

PLATT FAMILY SCHOLARSHIP PRIZE ESSAY CONTEST

Scholarship essay contest is designed for students who are full-time students in an American college or university. For details, refer to website at http://www.thelincolnforum.org/essayContest.html.

Award: Prize for use in freshman, sophomore, junior, or senior years; not renewable. *Number:* 3. *Amount:* $250–$1000.

Eligibility Requirements: Applicant must be enrolled or expecting to enroll full-time at a two-year or four-year institution or university and must have an interest in writing. Available to U.S. citizens.

Application Requirements: Entry in a contest, essay. *Deadline:* July 31.

Contact: Don McCue, Curator
    Phone: 909-798-7632
    E-mail: archives@akspl.org

LIVE POETS SOCIETY OF NJ AND JUST POETRY!!! MAGAZINE

http://www.highschoolpoetrycontest.com/

NATIONAL HIGH SCHOOL POETRY CONTEST

Award to encourage the youth of America in the pursuit of literary exploration and excellence, and to help provide a venue in which American High School students may share their poetic works. All U.S. high school students are eligible to enter this contest by submitting an original poem of 20 lines or less according to the Official Rules and Entry Procedures on our website, www.highschoolpoetrycontest.com , under the 'To Enter' tab.

Award: Scholarship for use in freshman year; not renewable. *Number:* 1–9. *Amount:* $100–$1000.

Eligibility Requirements: Applicant must be high school student; planning to enroll or expecting to enroll full-time at a two-year or four-year institution or university and must have an interest in English language or writing. Available to U.S. citizens.

Application Requirements: Application form may be submitted online (http://www.highschoolpoetrycontest.com/to_enter), entry in a contest, poem of 20 lines or less, self-addressed stamped envelope with application. *Deadline:* continuous.

Contact: Mr. D. Edwards, Editor
    E-mail: lpsnj@comcast.net

LOWE'S COMPANIES INC.

http://www.lowes.com/

LOWE'S EDUCATIONAL SCHOLARSHIP
• *See page 559*

MANA DE SAN DIEGO

http://www.manasd.org/

MANA DE SAN DIEGO SYLVIA CHAVEZ MEMORIAL SCHOLARSHIP
• *See page 559*

MARTIN D. ANDREWS SCHOLARSHIP

http://mdascholarship.tripod.com/

MARTIN D. ANDREWS MEMORIAL SCHOLARSHIP FUND

One-time award for student seeking undergraduate or graduate degree. Recipient must have been in a Drum Corp for at least three years. Must submit essay and two recommendations. Must be U.S. citizen.

Award: Scholarship for use in freshman, sophomore, junior, senior, or graduate years; not renewable. *Number:* 2–5. *Amount:* $300–$1000.

Eligibility Requirements: Applicant must be enrolled or expecting to enroll full- or part-time at a two-year or four-year institution or university and must have an interest in drum corps. Available to U.S. citizens.

Application Requirements: Application form, essay, recommendations or references. *Deadline:* April 1.

Contact: Peter Andrews, Scholarship Committee
    Martin D. Andrews Scholarship
    2069 Perkins Street
    Bristol, CT 06010
    Phone: 860-673-2929
    E-mail: mdascholarship@musician.org

MCCURRY FOUNDATION INC.

http://www.mccurryfoundation.org/

MCCURRY FOUNDATION SCHOLARSHIP
• *See page 705*

MINNESOTA AFL-CIO

http://www.mnaflcio.org/

BILL PETERSON SCHOLARSHIP
• *See page 525*

MINNESOTA DEPARTMENT OF MILITARY AFFAIRS

http://www.minnesotanationalguard.org/

LEADERSHIP, EXCELLENCE, AND DEDICATED SERVICE SCHOLARSHIP
• *See page 560*

MISS AMERICAN COED PAGEANTS INC.

http://www.gocoed.com/

MISS AMERICAN COED PAGEANT

Awards available for girls aged 3 to 22. Must be single and maintain a 3.0 GPA where applicable. Prizes are awarded by age groups. Winners of state competitions may compete at the national level. Application fee would vary for each state between $25 to $35 and will be refunded if not accepted into competition. Deadline varies each year.

Award: Prize for use in freshman year; not renewable. *Number:* up to 52. *Amount:* $150–$3000.

Eligibility Requirements: Applicant must be age 3-22; enrolled or expecting to enroll full- or part-time at a two-year or four-year institution; single female and must have an interest in beauty pageant. Applicant must have 3.0 GPA or higher. Available to U.S. citizens.

Application Requirements: Application form, entry in a contest, transcript. *Deadline:* varies.

Contact: George Scarborough, National Director
Miss American Coed Pageants Inc.
3695 Wimbledon Drive
Pensacola, FL 32504-4555
Phone: 850-432-0069
Fax: 850-469-8841
E-mail: amerteen@aol.com

NATIONAL AMATEUR BASEBALL FEDERATION (NABF)

http://www.nabf.com/

NATIONAL AMATEUR BASEBALL FEDERATION SCHOLARSHIP FUND

Scholarships are awarded to candidates who are enrolled in an accredited college or university. Applicant must be a bona fide participant in a federation event and be sponsored by an NABF-franchised member association. Self-nominated candidates are not eligible for this scholarship award.

Award: Scholarship for use in freshman, sophomore, junior, or senior years; not renewable.

Eligibility Requirements: Applicant must be enrolled or expecting to enroll full-time at a two-year or four-year or technical institution or university and must have an interest in athletics/sports. Available to U.S. citizens.

Application Requirements: Application form, community service, essay, letter of acceptance, recommendations or references, transcript. *Deadline:* November 15.

NATIONAL ASSOCIATION FOR CAMPUS ACTIVITIES

http://www.naca.org/

LORI RHETT MEMORIAL SCHOLARSHIP
• *See page 561*

MULTICULTURAL SCHOLARSHIP PROGRAM
• *See page 631*

NATIONAL ASSOCIATION FOR CAMPUS ACTIVITIES EAST COAST UNDERGRADUATE SCHOLARSHIP FOR STUDENT LEADERS
• *See page 561*

NATIONAL ASSOCIATION FOR CAMPUS ACTIVITIES REGIONAL COUNCIL STUDENT LEADER SCHOLARSHIPS

Scholarships will be given to undergraduate students in good standing at the time of the application and during the academic term in which the scholarship is awarded. Must demonstrate significant leadership skill and ability while holding a significant leadership position on campus. The scholarship value and the number of awards granted varies.

Award: Scholarship for use in freshman, sophomore, junior, or senior years; not renewable. *Number:* up to 7. *Amount:* $250–$300.

Eligibility Requirements: Applicant must be enrolled or expecting to enroll full- or part-time at a four-year institution or university and must have an interest in leadership. Available to U.S. and non-U.S. citizens.

Application Requirements: Application form, essay, recommendations or references, resume, transcript. *Deadline:* May 1.

Contact: Dionne Ellison, Administrative Assistant
Phone: 803-732-6222 Ext. 131
Fax: 803-749-1047
E-mail: dionnee@naca.org

NATIONAL ASSOCIATION FOR CAMPUS ACTIVITIES SOUTHEAST REGION STUDENT LEADERSHIP SCHOLARSHIP
• *See page 561*

NATIONAL ASSOCIATION FOR CAMPUS ACTIVITIES WISCONSIN REGION STUDENT LEADERSHIP SCHOLARSHIP
• *See page 561*

SCHOLARSHIPS FOR STUDENT LEADERS
• *See page 561*

TESS CALDARELLI MEMORIAL SCHOLARSHIP

Scholarship available to undergraduate or graduate students with a minimum 3.0 GPA. Must demonstrate significant leadership skills and hold a significant position on campus. Must attend school in the NACA Great Lakes Region. The scholarship is to be used for educational purposes, such as tuition, fees and books or for professional development purposes.

Award: Scholarship for use in freshman, sophomore, junior, senior, or graduate years; not renewable. *Amount:* $250–$300.

Eligibility Requirements: Applicant must be enrolled or expecting to enroll full- or part-time at a two-year or four-year institution or university; studying in Kentucky, Michigan, Ohio, Pennsylvania, West Virginia and must have an interest in leadership. Applicant must have 3.0 GPA or higher. Available to U.S. citizens.

Application Requirements: Application form, recommendations or references, resume, transcript. *Deadline:* November 1.

Contact: Dionne Ellison, Administrative Assistant
Phone: 803-732-6222 Ext. 131
Fax: 803-749-1047
E-mail: dionnee@naca.org

ZAGUNIS STUDENT LEADERS SCHOLARSHIP

Scholarships will be awarded to undergraduate or graduate students maintaining a cumulative GPA of 3.0 or better at the time of the application and during the academic term in which the scholarship is awarded. Applicants should demonstrate leadership skills and abilities while holding a significant leadership position on campus. Applicants must submit two letters of recommendation and a description of the applicant's leadership activities, skills, abilities and accomplishments. Must be enrolled in a college/university in the NACA Great Lakes Region.

Award: Scholarship for use in freshman, sophomore, junior, senior, or graduate years; not renewable. *Number:* 1. *Amount:* $300.

Eligibility Requirements: Applicant must be enrolled or expecting to enroll full- or part-time at a two-year or four-year institution or university; studying in Kentucky, Michigan, Ohio, Pennsylvania, West Virginia and must have an interest in leadership. Applicant must have 3.0 GPA or higher. Available to U.S. citizens.

Application Requirements: Application form, current enrollment form, recommendations or references, resume, transcript. *Deadline:* November 1.

Contact: Dionne Ellison, Administrative Assistant
Phone: 803-732-6222 Ext. 131
Fax: 803-749-1047
E-mail: dionnee@naca.org

NATIONAL ASSOCIATION FOR THE SELF-EMPLOYED

http://www.NASE.org/

NASE FUTURE ENTREPRENEUR SCHOLARSHIP
• *See page 526*

NASE SCHOLARSHIPS
• *See page 526*

NATIONAL ASSOCIATION OF SECONDARY SCHOOL PRINCIPALS

http://www.nhs.us/

PRINCIPAL'S LEADERSHIP AWARD

One-time award available only to high school seniors for use at an accredited two- or four-year college or university. Selection based on leadership and school or community involvement. Contact school counselor or principal. Citizens of countries other than the U.S. may only apply if attending a United States overseas institution. Minimum 3.0 GPA. Application fee: $6.

Award: Scholarship for use in freshman year; not renewable. *Number:* 100. *Amount:* $1000–$12,000.

Eligibility Requirements: Applicant must be high school student; planning to enroll or expecting to enroll full-time at a two-year or four-year institution or university and must have an interest in leadership. Applicant must have 3.0 GPA or higher. Available to U.S. and non-U.S. citizens.

Application Requirements: Application form, essay, recommendations or references, test scores, transcript. *Fee:* $6. *Deadline:* December 5.

Contact: Wanda Carroll, Program Manager
    Phone: 703-860-0200
    E-mail: carrollw@principals.org

NATIONAL FEDERATION OF STATE POETRY SOCIETIES (NFSPS)

http://www.nfsps.com/

NATIONAL FEDERATION OF STATE POETRY SOCIETIES SCHOLARSHIP AWARDS-COLLEGE/UNIVERSITY LEVEL POETRY COMPETITION

Must submit application and ten original poems, forty-line per-poem limit. Manuscript must be titled. For more information, visit the website.

Award: Scholarship for use in freshman, sophomore, junior, or senior years; not renewable. *Number:* 2. *Amount:* $500.

Eligibility Requirements: Applicant must be enrolled or expecting to enroll full-time at a two-year or four-year institution or university and must have an interest in writing. Available to U.S. citizens.

Application Requirements: Application form, entry in a contest, must be notarized. *Deadline:* February 1.

Contact: Colwell Snell, Chairman
    National Federation of State Poetry Societies (NFSPS)
    3444 South Dover Terrace, PO Box 520698
    Salt Lake City, UT 84152-0698
    Phone: 801-484-3113
    E-mail: sbsenior@juno.com

NATIONAL ORDER OF OMEGA

http://www.orderofomega.org/

FOUNDERS SCHOLARSHIP
• *See page 528*

NATIONAL SOCIETY OF COLLEGIATE SCHOLARS (NSCS)

http://www.nscs.org/

NSCS EXEMPLARY SCHOLAR AWARD
• *See page 529*

NATIONAL SOCIETY OF HIGH SCHOOL SCHOLARS

http://www.nshss.org/

CLAES NOBEL ACADEMIC SCHOLARSHIPS FOR NSHSS MEMBERS
• *See page 530*

NATIONAL SOCIETY OF THE SONS OF THE AMERICAN REVOLUTION

http://www.sar.org/

JOSEPH S. RUMBAUGH HISTORICAL ORATION CONTEST

Prize ranging from $1000 to $3000 is awarded to a sophomore, junior, or senior. The oration must be original and not less than five minutes or more than six minutes in length.

Award: Prize for use in sophomore, junior, or senior years; not renewable. *Number:* 1–3. *Amount:* $1000–$3000.

Eligibility Requirements: Applicant must be enrolled or expecting to enroll full-time at a two-year or four-year or technical institution or university and must have an interest in public speaking. Available to U.S. and non-U.S. citizens.

Application Requirements: Application form, entry in a contest. *Deadline:* June 15.

Contact: Lawrence Mckinley, National Chairman
    National Society of the Sons of the American Revolution
    12158 Holly Knoll Circle
    Great Fall, VA 22066
    E-mail: dustoff@bellatlantic.net

NEBRASKA SPORTS COUNCIL/THE GALLUP ORGANIZATION

http://www.cornhuskerstategames.com/

NEBRASKA SPORTS COUNCIL/GALLUP ORGANIZATION CORNHUSKER STATE GAMES SCHOLARSHIP PROGRAM
• *See page 709*

NETAID FOUNDATION/MERCY CORPS

GLOBAL ACTION AWARDS
• *See page 562*

NEXTGEN NETWORK INC.

http://www.nextgennetwork.com/

DONNA JAMISON LAGO MEMORIAL SCHOLARSHIP
• *See page 633*

NIMROD INTERNATIONAL JOURNAL

http://www.utulsa.edu/nimrod

THE KATHERINE ANNE PORTER PRIZE FOR FICTION

The Katherine Ann Porter Prize is given for a single extraordinary short story of less than 7,500 words.

Award: Prize for use in freshman, sophomore, junior, senior, or postgraduate years; not renewable. *Number:* 2. *Amount:* $1000–$2000.

Eligibility Requirements: Applicant must be enrolled or expecting to enroll full- or part-time at a two-year or four-year or technical institution or university and must have an interest in writing. Available to U.S. citizens.

Application Requirements: Application form, entry in a contest, essay, short story. *Fee:* $20. *Deadline:* April 30.

Contact: Ellis O'Neal, Managing Editor
    Nimrod International Journal
    The University of Tulsa, 800 South Tucker Drive
    Tulsa, OK 74112
    Phone: 918-631-3080
    Fax: 918-631-3033
    E-mail: nimrod@utulsa.edu

THE PABLO NERUDA PRIZE FOR POETRY

The Pablo Neruda Prize is given for an extraordinary single long poem or group of poems.

Award: Prize for use in freshman, sophomore, junior, senior, graduate, or postgraduate years; not renewable. *Number:* 2. *Amount:* $1000–$2000.

Eligibility Requirements: Applicant must be enrolled or expecting to enroll full- or part-time at a two-year or four-year or technical institution or university and must have an interest in writing. Available to U.S. citizens.

Application Requirements: Application form, entry in a contest, essay, single long poem or group of poems. *Fee:* $20. *Deadline:* April 30.

Contact: Ellis O'Neal, Managing Editor
Nimrod International Journal
The University of Tulsa, 800 South Tucker Drive
Tulsa, OK 74104
Phone: 918-631-3080
Fax: 918-631-3033
E-mail: nimrod@utulsa.edu

OPTIMIST INTERNATIONAL FOUNDATION

http://www.optimist.org/

OPTIMIST INTERNATIONAL ESSAY CONTEST

Essay contest for youth under the age of 19 who have not graduated high school or its equivalent. US students attending school on a military installation outside the United States are eligible to enter in their last US home of record. Club winners advance to the District contest to compete for a college scholarship. District winners are entered into the International essay contest where one first place winner is awarded a plaque and recognition in "The Optimist" magazine.

Award: Scholarship for use in freshman, sophomore, junior, or senior years; not renewable. *Number:* 40–49. *Amount:* up to $2500.

Eligibility Requirements: Applicant must be enrolled or expecting to enroll full- or part-time at a two-year or four-year or technical institution or university and must have an interest in writing. Available to U.S. and Canadian citizens.

Application Requirements: Application form, birth certificate, entry in a contest, essay, self-addressed stamped envelope with application. *Deadline:* varies.

Contact: Danielle Baugher, Director of International Programs
Optimist International Foundation
4494 Lindell Boulevard
St. Louis, MO 63108
Phone: 800-500-8130
Fax: 314-371-6006
E-mail: programs@optimist.org

OPTIMIST INTERNATIONAL ORATORICAL CONTEST

Contest for youth to gain experience in public speaking and to provide them with the opportunity to compete for college scholarships. The contest is open to youth under the age of 18 as of December 31 of the current school year, who have not yet graduated from high school or the equivalent. Students must first compete at the Club level. Club winners are then entered into the Zone/Regional contest and those winners compete in the District contest. District winners are awarded scholarships.

Award: Scholarship for use in freshman, sophomore, junior, or senior years; not renewable. *Number:* 90–115. *Amount:* $1000–$2500.

Eligibility Requirements: Applicant must be enrolled or expecting to enroll full- or part-time at a two-year or four-year or technical institution or university and must have an interest in public speaking. Available to U.S. and Canadian citizens.

Application Requirements: Application form, birth certificate, speech, entry in a contest, self-addressed stamped envelope with application. *Deadline:* varies.

Contact: Danielle Baugher, Director of International Programs
Optimist International Foundation
4494 Lindell Boulevard
St. Louis, MO 63108
Phone: 800-500-8130
Fax: 314-371-6006
E-mail: programs@optimist.org

OREGON COMMUNITY FOUNDATION

http://www.oregoncf.org/

DOROTHY S. CAMPBELL MEMORIAL SCHOLARSHIP FUND

Scholarship for female graduates of Oregon high schools with a strong and continuing interest in the game of golf. For use in the pursuit of a postsecondary education at a four-year college or university in Oregon.

Award: Scholarship for use in freshman, sophomore, junior, or senior years; renewable. *Number:* 9. *Amount:* $1000.

Eligibility Requirements: Applicant must be enrolled or expecting to enroll full-time at a four-year institution or university; female and must have an interest in golf. Available to U.S. citizens.

Application Requirements: Application form, recommendations or references. *Deadline:* March 1.

Contact: Dianne Causey, Program Associate for Scholarships and Grants
Phone: 503-227-6846 Ext. 1418
E-mail: dcausey@oregoncf.org

OREGON STUDENT ASSISTANCE COMMISSION

http://www.GetCollegeFunds.org/

DOROTHY CAMPBELL MEMORIAL SCHOLARSHIP
• *See page 718*

OUR WORLD UNDERWATER SCHOLARSHIP SOCIETY

http://www.owuscholarship.org/

OUR WORLD UNDERWATER SCHOLARSHIPS

Annual award for individual planning to pursue a career in a water-related discipline through practical exposure to various fields and leaders of underwater endeavors. Scuba experience required. Must be at least 21 but not yet 26. Scholarship value is $20,000 for the North American Rolex Scholar, open to North American citizens only. The European Rolex Scholarship is open to European citizens and the Australasian Rolex Scholarship is open to citizens of the Australasian region.

Award: Scholarship for use in freshman, sophomore, junior, or senior years; not renewable. *Number:* 3. *Amount:* $20,000.

Eligibility Requirements: Applicant must be age 21-26; enrolled or expecting to enroll full- or part-time at a two-year or four-year or technical institution or university and must have an interest in scuba diving. Available to U.S. and non-U.S. citizens.

Application Requirements: Application form, community service, driver's license, essay, interview, recommendations or references, resume, scuba diver certification, transcript. *Fee:* $25. *Deadline:* December 31.

Contact: Roberta Flanders, Scholarship Application Coordinator
Our World Underwater Scholarship Society
PO Box 4428
Chicago, IL 60680-4428
Phone: 800-969-6690
Fax: 630-969-6690
E-mail: info@owuscholarship.org

PENGUIN GROUP

http://www.us.penguingroup.com/static/pages/services-academic/essayhome.html

SIGNET CLASSIC SCHOLARSHIP ESSAY CONTEST

Open to 11th and 12th grade full-time matriculated students who are attending high schools located in the fifty United States and the District of Columbia, or home-schooled students between the ages of 16¿18 who are residents of the fifty United States and the District of Columbia. Students should submit four copies of a two- to three-page double-spaced essay answering one of three possible questions on a designated novel. Entries must be submitted by a high school English teacher.

Award: Scholarship for use in freshman year; not renewable. *Number:* 5. *Amount:* $1000.

Eligibility Requirements: Applicant must be high school student; planning to enroll or expecting to enroll full-time at a four-year institution or university and must have an interest in writing. Available to U.S. citizens.

Application Requirements: Entry in a contest, essay, recommendations or references. *Deadline:* April 15.

Contact: Kym Giacoppe, Academic Marketing Assistant
Phone: 212-366-2377
E-mail: academic@penguin.com

PFUND FOUNDATION

http://www.pfundonline.org/

PFUND SCHOLARSHIP AWARD PROGRAM
• *See page 720*

PHI SIGMA PI NATIONAL HONOR FRATERNITY

http://www.phisigmapi.org/

RICHARD CECIL TODD AND CLAUDA PENNOCK TODD TRIPOD SCHOLARSHIP
• *See page 533*

PIRATE'S ALLEY FAULKNER SOCIETY

http://www.wordsandmusic.org/

WILLIAM FAULKNER-WILLIAM WISDOM CREATIVE WRITING COMPETITION

Prizes for unpublished manuscripts written in English. One prize awarded in each category: $7500, novel; $2500, novella; $2000, book-length narrative non-fiction; $1500, novel-in-progress; $1500, short story; $750, essay; $750, poem; $750 high school short story-student author, $250 sponsoring teacher. Manuscripts must be submitted by e-mail; entry forms and accompanying entry fee ranging from $10 for high school category to $40 for novel must be submitted hard copy by snail mail.

Award: Prize for use in freshman, sophomore, junior, senior, graduate, or postgraduate years; not renewable. *Number:* 8. *Amount:* $250–$7500.

Eligibility Requirements: Applicant must be age 15-75; enrolled or expecting to enroll full- or part-time at a two-year or four-year or technical institution or university and must have an interest in English language or writing. Available to U.S. and non-U.S. citizens.

Application Requirements: Application form, application form may be submitted online, entry in a contest,. *Deadline:* May 1.

Contact: Ms. Rosemary James, Director
Pirate's Alley Faulkner Society
624 PiratesAlley'
New Orleans, LA 70116
Phone: 504-586-1609
E-mail: faulkhouse@aol.com

PONY OF THE AMERICAS CLUB

http://www.poac.org/

PONY OF THE AMERICAS SCHOLARSHIP
• *See page 533*

PRIDE FOUNDATION

http://www.PrideFoundation.org/

PRIDE FOUNDATION SCHOLARSHIP PROGRAM
• *See page 721*

PRO BOWLERS ASSOCIATION

http://www.pba.com/

BILLY WELU BOWLING SCHOLARSHIP

Scholarship awarded annually, recognizing exemplary qualities in male and female college students who compete in the sport of bowling. Winner will receive $1000. Candidates must be amateur bowlers who are currently in college (preceding the application deadline) and maintain at least a 2.5 GPA or equivalent.

Award: Scholarship for use in freshman, sophomore, junior, or senior years; not renewable. *Number:* 1. *Amount:* $1000.

Eligibility Requirements: Applicant must be enrolled or expecting to enroll full-time at a two-year or four-year institution or university and must have an interest in bowling. Applicant must have 2.5 GPA or higher. Available to U.S. citizens.

Application Requirements: Application form, essay, transcript. *Deadline:* May 31.

Contact: Karen Day, Controller
Phone: 206-332-9688
Fax: 206-332-9722
E-mail: karen.day@pba.com

THE RESERVE OFFICERS ASSOCIATION

http://www.roa.org/

HENRY J. REILLY MEMORIAL SCHOLARSHIP-HIGH SCHOOL SENIORS AND FIRST YEAR FRESHMEN
• *See page 535*

RHODE ISLAND FOUNDATION

http://www.rifoundation.org/

UNITED ITALIAN AMERICAN INC. SCHOLARSHIP
• *See page 722*

ROBERT H. MOLLOHAN FAMILY CHARITABLE FOUNDATION, INC.

http://www.mollohanfoundation.org/

DR. ROBERTO F. CUNANAN MEMORIAL SCHOLARSHIP
• *See page 723*

RON BROWN SCHOLAR FUND

http://www.ronbrown.org/

RON BROWN SCHOLAR PROGRAM
• *See page 637*

ST. CLAIRE REGIONAL MEDICAL CENTER

http://www.st-claire.org/

SR. MARY JEANNETTE WESS, S.N.D. SCHOLARSHIP
• *See page 563*

SAN FRANCISCO FOUNDATION

http://www.sff.org/

JAMES DUVAL PHELAN LITERARY AWARD

Award presented annually to an author of an unpublished work in progress: fiction, nonfiction, prose, poetry, or drama. Must have been born in California, but need not be a current resident. Must be between 20 to 35 years of age. Submit manuscript.

Award: Prize for use in freshman, sophomore, junior, senior, graduate, or postgraduate years; not renewable. *Number:* 3. *Amount:* $2000–$3000.

Eligibility Requirements: Applicant must be age 20-35; enrolled or expecting to enroll full- or part-time at a two-year or four-year institution or university and must have an interest in writing. Available to U.S. citizens.

Application Requirements: Application form, entry in a contest, manuscript, self-addressed stamped envelope with application. *Deadline:* March 31.

JOSEPH HENRY JACKSON LITERARY AWARD
• *See page 724*

SCHOLARSHIP WORKSHOP LLC

http://www.scholarshipworkshop.com/

LEADING THE FUTURE II SCHOLARSHIP

Scholarship designed to elevate students' consciousness about their future and their role in helping others once they receive a college degree and become established in a community. It is open to U.S. residents who are high school seniors or college undergraduates at any level. Students must visit http://www.scholarshipworkshop.com to get additional information and to download an application.

Award: Scholarship for use in freshman, sophomore, junior, or senior years; not renewable. *Number:* 1–3. *Amount:* $100–$300.

Eligibility Requirements: Applicant must be enrolled or expecting to enroll full-time at a four-year institution or university and must have an interest in leadership. Available to U.S. citizens.

Application Requirements: Application form, essay. *Deadline:* March 1.

SEVENTEEN MAGAZINE

http://www.seventeen.com/

SEVENTEEN MAGAZINE FICTION CONTEST

Enter by submitting an original short story of no longer than 2000 words. Submissions must be typed, double-spaced, on one side of each sheet of paper, and must not have been previously published in any form, with the exception of school publications. All entries must include the full name, age, home and e-mail addresses, telephone number, date of birth, and signature in the top right hand corner of each page of every story you send. Multiple entries are permitted.

Award: Prize for use in freshman, sophomore, junior, senior, graduate, or postgraduate years; not renewable. *Number:* 8. *Amount:* $100–$2500.

Eligibility Requirements: Applicant must be age 13-21; enrolled or expecting to enroll full- or part-time at a two-year or four-year or technical institution or university and must have an interest in writing. Available to U.S. citizens.

Application Requirements: Copy of story, entry in a contest, essay, personal photograph. *Deadline:* December 31.

SISTER KENNY REHABILITATION INSTITUTE

http://www.allina.com/ahs/ski.nsf

INTERNATIONAL ART SHOW FOR ARTISTS WITH DISABILITIES
• *See page 577*

SKILLSUSA

http://www.skillsusa.org/

INTERNATIONAL SKILLSUSA DEGREE SCHOLARSHIP

Scholarship for students who successfully receive their degree. To qualify, all candidates must submit a letter of application for the scholarship within 45 days of receipt of the degree. The scholarship candidate must include with the application copies of receipts for lodging, meals, travel, and preparation of the presentation.

Award: Scholarship for use in senior year; not renewable. *Number:* 1. *Amount:* up to $1000.

Eligibility Requirements: Applicant must be enrolled or expecting to enroll full-time at a four-year institution or university and must have an interest in leadership. Available to U.S. citizens.

Application Requirements: Application form, copies of receipts for lodging, meals, travel, and preparation of the presentation, recommendations or references. *Deadline:* May 1.

Contact: Karen Perrino, Associate Director
    Phone: 703-737-0610
    Fax: 703-777-8999
    E-mail: kperrino@skillsusa.org

NTHS SKILLSUSA SCHOLARSHIP

NTHS will award two $1000 scholarships to SkillsUSA members at the SkillsUSA national leadership conference. One scholarship will be awarded to a high school member, and one scholarship will be awarded to a college/postsecondary member. Students must be active, dues-paying members of both SkillsUSA and NTHS.

Award: Scholarship for use in freshman, sophomore, junior, or senior years; not renewable. *Number:* 2. *Amount:* $1000.

Eligibility Requirements: Applicant must be enrolled or expecting to enroll full-time at a two-year or four-year or technical institution or university and must have an interest in leadership. Available to U.S. citizens.

Application Requirements: Application form, community service, recommendations or references. *Deadline:* March 1.

Contact: Karen Perrino, Associate Director
    Phone: 703-737-0610
    Fax: 703-777-8999
    E-mail: kperrino@skillsusa.org

SKILLSUSA ALUMNI AND FRIENDS MERIT SCHOLARSHIP
• *See page 564*

SOCIETY OF DAUGHTERS OF THE UNITED STATES ARMY

SOCIETY OF DAUGHTERS OF THE UNITED STATES ARMY SCHOLARSHIPS
• *See page 587*

SOUTH DAKOTA BOARD OF REGENTS

http://www.sdbor.edu/

SOUTH DAKOTA BOARD OF REGENTS MARLIN R. SCARBOROUGH MEMORIAL SCHOLARSHIP
• *See page 725*

SOUTHERN TEXAS PGA

http://www.stpga.com/

DICK FORESTER COLLEGE SCHOLARSHIP

One-time award of $4000 to promote the attainment of higher education goals of youth who have demonstrated a high level of achievement during high school or college. Must demonstrate financial need, and have shown an interest in the game of golf.

Award: Scholarship for use in freshman, sophomore, junior, senior, graduate, or postgraduate years; not renewable. *Number:* 1. *Amount:* $4000.

Eligibility Requirements: Applicant must be enrolled or expecting to enroll full-time at a two-year or four-year institution or university and must have an interest in golf. Available to U.S. citizens.

Application Requirements: Application form, financial need analysis, test scores, transcript. *Deadline:* April 4.

Contact: Steve Termeer, Scholarship Committee Chairperson
    Phone: 832-442-2404
    Fax: 832-442-2403
    E-mail: stexas@pgahq.com

STONEWALL COMMUNITY FOUNDATION

http://www.stonewallfoundation.org/

GENE AND JOHN ATHLETIC FUND SCHOLARSHIP

Scholarship of $2500 to $5000 for LGBT student athletes looking to continue their education while pursuing athletics.

Award: Scholarship for use in freshman, sophomore, junior, senior, graduate, or postgraduate years; not renewable. *Number:* 1–3. *Amount:* $2500–$5000.

Eligibility Requirements: Applicant must be enrolled or expecting to enroll full-time at a two-year or four-year or technical institution or university and must have an interest in athletics/sports or LGBT issues. Available to U.S. and Canadian citizens.

Application Requirements: Application form, application form may be submitted online (http://www.stonewallfoundation.org), essay, recommendations or references. *Deadline:* July 31.

Contact: Mr. Jarrett Lucas, Program Manager
Stonewall Community Foundation
c/o Stonewall Community Foundation
446 West 33rd Street, Sixth Floor
New York, NY 10001
Phone: 212-367-1156
Fax: 212-367-1157
E-mail: grants@stonewallfoundation.org

HARRY BARTEL MEMORIAL SCHOLARSHIP

• *See page 564*

TRAUB-DICKER RAINBOW SCHOLARSHIP

Non-renewable scholarships available to lesbian-identified students who are involved in LGBTQ activism. Must be graduating high school seniors planning to attend a recognized college, or already matriculated college students in any year of study, including graduate school.

Award: Scholarship for use in freshman, sophomore, junior, senior, or graduate years; not renewable. *Number:* 3–9. *Amount:* $1000–$3000.

Eligibility Requirements: Applicant must be enrolled or expecting to enroll full- or part-time at a four-year institution or university; female and must have an interest in LGBT issues. Available to U.S. citizens.

Application Requirements: Application form, application form may be submitted online (http://www.stonewallfoundation.org), essay, letter of acceptance may be substituted for transcript, recommendations or references, transcript. *Deadline:* April 15.

Contact: Mr. Jarrett Lucas, Program Manager
Stonewall Community Foundation
446 West 33rd Street, Sixth Floor
New York, NY 10001
Phone: 212-367-1156
Fax: 212-367-1157
E-mail: grants@stonewallfoundation.org

SUPERCOLLEGE.COM

http://www.supercollege.com/

$1,500 SUPERCOLLEGE.COM SCHOLARSHIP

An award for outstanding high school, college or graduate students. Based on academic and extracurricular achievement, leadership, and integrity. May study any major and attend or plan to attend any accredited college or university in the United States. No paper applications accepted. Applications are only available online at http://www.supercollege.com/scholarship/.

Award: Scholarship for use in freshman, sophomore, junior, senior, or graduate years; not renewable. *Number:* 1–5. *Amount:* $500–$1500.

Eligibility Requirements: Applicant must be enrolled or expecting to enroll full-time at a two-year or four-year or technical institution or university and must have an interest in leadership. Available to U.S. citizens.

Application Requirements: Application form, application form may be submitted online (http://www.supercollege.com/scholarship/). *Deadline:* continuous.

SWISS BENEVOLENT SOCIETY OF NEW YORK

http://www.sbsny.org/

MEDICUS STUDENT EXCHANGE

• *See page 639*

TAG AND LABEL MANUFACTURERS INSTITUTE, INC.

http://www.tlmi.com/

TLMI 2 YEAR COLLEGE DEGREE SCHOLARSHIP PROGRAM

Scholarship program for students enrolled at a two-year college or in a degree technical program whose major course work includes courses appropriate for future work in the tag and label manufacturing industry. Must submit statements including personal information, financial circumstances, career and/or educational goals, employment experience, and reasons applicant should be selected for this award.

Award: Scholarship for use in sophomore year; not renewable. *Number:* up to 4. *Amount:* $1000.

Eligibility Requirements: Applicant must be enrolled or expecting to enroll full- or part-time at a two-year or technical institution and must have an interest in designated field specified by sponsor. Applicant must have 3.0 GPA or higher. Available to U.S. and Canadian citizens.

Application Requirements: Application form, portfolio, recommendations or references, transcript. *Deadline:* March 31.

TERRY FOUNDATION

http://www.terryfoundation.org/

TERRY FOUNDATION SCHOLARSHIP

• *See page 729*

TERRY FOX HUMANITARIAN AWARD PROGRAM

http://www.terryfox.org/

TERRY FOX HUMANITARIAN AWARD

• *See page 564*

TEXAS 4-H YOUTH DEVELOPMENT FOUNDATION

http://texas4hfoundation.org/

TEXAS 4-H OPPORTUNITY SCHOLARSHIP

• *See page 729*

TEXAS TENNIS FOUNDATION

http://www.texastennisfoundation.com/

TEXAS TENNIS FOUNDATION SCHOLARSHIPS AND ENDOWMENTS

• *See page 729*

TKE EDUCATIONAL FOUNDATION

http://www.tke.org/

ALL-TKE ACADEMIC TEAM RECOGNITION AND JOHN A. COURSON TOP SCHOLAR AWARD

• *See page 538*

CANADIAN TKE SCHOLARSHIP

• *See page 538*

CHARLES WALGREEN JR. SCHOLARSHIP
• *See page 538*

DONALD A. AND JOHN R. FISHER MEMORIAL SCHOLARSHIP
• *See page 538*

DWAYNE R. WOERPEL MEMORIAL LEADERSHIP AWARD
• *See page 538*

ELMER AND DORIS SCHMITZ SR. MEMORIAL SCHOLARSHIP
• *See page 539*

EUGENE C. BEACH MEMORIAL SCHOLARSHIP
• *See page 539*

J. RUSSEL SALSBURY MEMORIAL SCHOLARSHIP
• *See page 539*

MICHAEL J. MORIN MEMORIAL SCHOLARSHIP
• *See page 539*

MILES GRAY MEMORIAL SCHOLARSHIP
• *See page 539*

RONALD REAGAN LEADERSHIP AWARD
• *See page 539*

T.J. SCHMITZ SCHOLARSHIP
• *See page 539*

WALLACE MCCAULEY MEMORIAL SCHOLARSHIP
• *See page 540*

WILLIAM V. MUSE SCHOLARSHIP
• *See page 540*

WILLIAM WILSON MEMORIAL SCHOLARSHIP
• *See page 540*

TOSHIBA/NSTA
http://www.exploravision.org/

EXPLORAVISION SCIENCE COMPETITION
Competition for students in grades K-12 who enter as small teams by grade level and work on a science project. In each group, first place team members are each awarded a savings bond worth $10,000 at maturity, second place, a $5000 savings bond. Deadline varies.

Award: Prize for use in freshman year; not renewable. *Amount:* $5000–$10,000.

Eligibility Requirements: Applicant must be enrolled or expecting to enroll full- or part-time at a four-year institution or university and must have an interest in science. Available to U.S. citizens.

Application Requirements: Application form, entry in a contest. *Deadline:* varies.

Contact: Paloma Olbes, Media Contact
Phone: 212-388-1400
E-mail: polbes@dba-pr.com

TOURO SYNAGOGUE FOUNDATION
http://www.tourosynagogue.org/

AARON AND RITA SLOM SCHOLARSHIP FUND FOR FREEDOM AND DIVERSITY
Scholarship available for high school seniors who plan to enroll in an institute of higher learning for a minimum of 6 credits. Entries should include an interpretative work focusing on the historic "George Washington Letter to the Congregation" in context with the present time.

Text of the letter is available on the website. Submissions may be in the form of an essay, story, poem, film, video, or computer presentation. Applications, guidelines, resource materials are available on website http://www.touro

Award: Scholarship for use in freshman year; not renewable. *Number:* 2–4. *Amount:* $500–$1000.

Eligibility Requirements: Applicant must be high school student; planning to enroll or expecting to enroll full- or part-time at a two-year or four-year institution or university and must have an interest in writing. Available to U.S. citizens.

Application Requirements: Application form, interpretative work based on historic George Washington letter. *Deadline:* April 22.

UNITED NATIONS ASSOCIATION OF THE UNITED STATES OF AMERICA
http://www.unausa.org/

NATIONAL HIGH SCHOOL ESSAY CONTEST
Essay contest is open to all US students in grades 9-12. Essays should be no longer than 1500 words, typed and double-spaced.

Award: Prize for use in freshman year; not renewable. *Number:* 3. *Amount:* $750–$3000.

Eligibility Requirements: Applicant must be high school student; planning to enroll or expecting to enroll full- or part-time at a four-year institution or university and must have an interest in writing. Available to U.S. citizens.

Application Requirements: Application form, entry in a contest, essay. *Deadline:* January 3.

UNITED NEGRO COLLEGE FUND
http://www.uncf.org/

ANHEUSER-BUSCH LEGENDS OF THE CROWN SCHOLARSHIP PROGRAM
• *See page 641*

MALCOLM X SCHOLARSHIP FOR EXCEPTIONAL COURAGE
• *See page 645*

MASSMUTUAL SCHOLARS PROGRAM
• *See page 645*

SAFE PASSAGE FOUNDATION EDUCATIONAL AND SCHOLARSHIP FUND
• *See page 646*

UNITED STATES JUNIOR CHAMBER OF COMMERCE
http://www.usjaycees.org/

JAYCEE WAR MEMORIAL FUND SCHOLARSHIP
$1000 scholarship for students who are U.S. citizens, possess academic potential and leadership qualities, and show financial need. Minimum 2.5 GPA required. To receive an application, send $10 application fee and stamped, self-addressed envelope by February 1.

Award: Scholarship for use in freshman, sophomore, junior, or senior years; not renewable. *Number:* 10. *Amount:* $1000.

Eligibility Requirements: Applicant must be enrolled or expecting to enroll full-time at a two-year or four-year or technical institution or university and must have an interest in leadership. Applicant must have 2.5 GPA or higher. Available to U.S. citizens.

Application Requirements: Application form, financial need analysis, self-addressed stamped envelope with application, transcript. *Fee:* $10. *Deadline:* February 1.

Contact: Karen Fitzgerald, Customer Service and Data Processing
Phone: 918-584-2481
E-mail: customerservice@usjaycees.org

USA BADMINTON REGION 1

http://www.northeastbadminton.net/

BADMINTON SCHOLARSHIP PROGRAM

Scholarship awarded to a collegiate varsity badminton player exhibiting outstanding achievement, participation, and performance during the badminton playing season. Award is restricted to residents of the northeast region of the United States.

Award: Scholarship for use in freshman, sophomore, junior, or senior years; renewable. *Number:* 1. *Amount:* $1000.

Eligibility Requirements: Applicant must be enrolled or expecting to enroll full-time at a four-year institution or university and must have an interest in athletics/sports. Available to U.S. citizens.

Application Requirements: Application form, coaches letter, NCAA team verification, entry in a contest, recommendations or references. *Deadline:* continuous.

Contact: Eric Miller, Scholarship Program Coordinator
USA Badminton Region 1
125 Prospect Street
Phoenixville, PA 19460
Phone: 610-999-5960
E-mail: eric@usbadminton.net

USA TODAY/MILKPEP—GOT MILK?

http://www.bodybymilk.com/

SAMMY AWARDS (SCHOLAR ATHLETE MILK MUSTACHE OF THE YEAR)

One-time award for senior high school athletes who also achieve in academics, community service, and leadership. Open to legal residents of the 48 contiguous United States and District of Columbia. Residents of Hawaii, Alaska, and Puerto Rico are not eligible. Must submit essay of 75 words or less on how drinking milk has been a part of their life and training regimen. Application only through website http://www.bodybymilk.com.

Award: Scholarship for use in freshman year; not renewable. *Number:* 25. *Amount:* $7500.

Eligibility Requirements: Applicant must be high school student; planning to enroll or expecting to enroll full-time at a four-year institution or university and must have an interest in athletics/sports. Available to U.S. citizens.

Application Requirements: Application form, application form may be submitted online (https://www.sammyapplication.com), community service, essay, personal photograph, recommendations or references, transcript. *Deadline:* March 9.

Contact: Debbie McMahon, Director, Marketing Programs
USA TODAY/MilkPEP—Got Milk?
USA TODAY
7950 Jones Branch Drive
McLean, VA 22108
Phone: 703-854-5418
E-mail: dmcmahon@usatoday.com

VETERANS OF FOREIGN WARS OF THE UNITED STATES

http://www.vfw.org/

PATRIOT'S PEN

Nationwide essay contest that gives middle school students in grades 6, 7, and 8 the opportunity to write essays expressing their views on democracy and win monies to be used towards paying for their education. Participants must be permanent U.S. residents; U.S. Citizenship is not required.

Award: Prize for use in freshman, sophomore, junior, senior, graduate, or postgraduate years; not renewable. *Number:* up to 46. *Amount:* $500–$5000.

Eligibility Requirements: Applicant must be enrolled or expecting to enroll full- or part-time at a two-year or four-year or technical institution or university and must have an interest in writing. Available to U.S. citizens.

Application Requirements: Application form, entry in a contest, essay. *Deadline:* November 1.

Contact: Kris Harmer, Program Coordinator
Veterans of Foreign Wars of the United States
406 West 34th Street
Kansas City, MO 64111
Phone: 816-968-1117
Fax: 816-968-1149
E-mail: kharmer@vfw.org

VOICE OF DEMOCRACY PROGRAM

Student must be sponsored by a local VFW Post. Student submits a three to five minute audio essay on a contest theme (changes each year). Open to high school students (9th to 12th grade). Award available for all levels of postsecondary study in an American institution. Open to permanent U.S. residents only. Competition starts at local level. No entries are to be submitted to the National Headquarters. Visit website http://www.vfw.org for more information.

Award: Scholarship for use in freshman, sophomore, junior, senior, graduate, or postgraduate years; not renewable. *Number:* 54. *Amount:* $1000–$30,000.

Eligibility Requirements: Applicant must be high school student; age 14-19; planning to enroll or expecting to enroll full- or part-time at a two-year or four-year or technical institution or university and must have an interest in public speaking or writing. Available to U.S. citizens.

Application Requirements: Application form, audio cassette tape or CD of essay, entry in a contest, essay. *Deadline:* November 1.

Contact: Kris Harmer, Program Coordinator
Veterans of Foreign Wars of the United States
406 West 34th Street
Kansas City, MO 64111
Phone: 816-968-1117
Fax: 816-968-1149
E-mail: kharmer@vfw.org

VINCENT L. HAWKINSON FOUNDATION FOR PEACE AND JUSTICE

http://www.hawkinsonfoundation.org

VINCENT L. HAWKINSON SCHOLARSHIP FOR PEACE AND JUSTICE

• See page 733

VSA

http://www.kennedy-center.org/education/vsa/

VSA PLAYWRIGHT DISCOVERY AWARD

One-time award for students in grades 6 to 12, with and without disabilities. One-act script must explore the experience of living with a disability. One script is selected for production at the John F. Kennedy Center for the Performing Arts. A jury of theater professionals selects the winning script, and award recipients receive monetary awards and a trip to Washington, D.C. to view the production.

Award: Prize for use in freshman year; not renewable. *Number:* 1. *Amount:* $2000.

Eligibility Requirements: Applicant must be high school student; age 12-18; planning to enroll or expecting to enroll full- or part-time at a four-year institution or university and must have an interest in theater or writing. Available to U.S. citizens.

Application Requirements: 2 copies of typed script, application form, driver's license, entry in a contest. *Deadline:* April 11.

Contact: Sonja Cendak, VSA Programs Manager
Phone: 800-416-8898
Fax: 202-429-0868
E-mail: scendak@kennedy-center.org

THE WALTER J. TRAVIS SOCIETY

http://www.travissociety.com

THE WALTER J. TRAVIS MEMORIAL SCHOLARSHIP

This scholarship is awarded to students who are pursuing a career in one of the following professions: golf course architecture, golf course superintendent/turfgrass manager, sports journalism, or professional golf management. Also, any college student who is an outstanding amateur golfer is eligible. Awards based on academic record, extracurricular activities including volunteer service, work experience, and golf-related interests and accomplishments. Award may be used for any educational expenses.

Award: Scholarship for use in freshman, sophomore, junior, senior, or graduate years; not renewable. *Number:* 4–5. *Amount:* $700.

Eligibility Requirements: Applicant must be enrolled or expecting to enroll full-time at a two-year or four-year or technical institution or university and must have an interest in golf. Applicant must have 2.5 GPA or higher. Available to U.S. and non-U.S. citizens.

Application Requirements: Application form, application form may be submitted online (http://www.travissociety.com/scholarship), community service, recommendations or references, transcript. *Deadline:* June 1.

Contact: Mr. Edward Homsey, Scholarship Chairman
The Walter J. Travis Society
24 Sandstone Drive
Rochester, NY 14616
Phone: 585-663-6120
E-mail: TravisSociety@yahoo.com

WALTER W. NAUMBURG FOUNDATION
http://www.naumburg.org/

INTERNATIONAL VIOLONCELLO COMPETITION
Prizes of $2500 to $7500 awarded to violoncellists between the ages of 17 and 31. Application fee is $125.

Award: Prize for use in freshman, sophomore, junior, senior, graduate, or postgraduate years; not renewable. *Number:* 3. *Amount:* $2500–$7500.

Eligibility Requirements: Applicant must be age 17–31; enrolled or expecting to enroll full- or part-time at a two-year or four-year or technical institution or university and must have an interest in music. Available to U.S. and non-U.S. citizens.

Application Requirements: Applicant's audio track (CD) of no less than 30 minutes, application form, entry in a contest, recommendations or references, self-addressed stamped envelope with application. *Fee:* $125. *Deadline:* March 1.

Contact: Lucy Mann, Executive Director
Phone: 212-362-9877
Fax: 212-362-9877
E-mail: luciamann@aol.com

WILLIAM G. AND MARIE SELBY FOUNDATION
http://www.selbyfdn.org/

SELBY SCHOLAR PROGRAM
• *See page 736*

WILLIAM RANDOLPH HEARST FOUNDATION
http://www.hearstfdn.org/

UNITED STATES SENATE YOUTH PROGRAM
Scholarship for high school juniors and seniors holding elected student offices. Two students selected from each state. Selection process will vary by state. Contact school principal or state department of education for information. Deadlines: early fall of each year for most states, but specific date will vary by state (see website www.ussenateyouth.org). Program is open to citizens and permanent residents of the United States Department of Defense schools overseas and the District of Columbia (not the territories).

Award: Scholarship for use in freshman, sophomore, junior, or senior years; not renewable. *Number:* 104. *Amount:* $5000.

Eligibility Requirements: Applicant must be high school student; planning to enroll or expecting to enroll full-time at a two-year or four-year institution or university; single and must have an interest in leadership or public speaking. Applicant must have 3.5 GPA or higher. Available to U.S. citizens.

Application Requirements: Application form, application procedures will vary by state, essay, interview. *Deadline:* varies.

Contact: Lynn DeSmet, Deputy Program Director
William Randolph Hearst Foundation
90 New Montgomery Street
Suite 1212
San Francisco, CA 94105
Phone: 412-908-4540
Fax: 412-243-0760
E-mail: ussyp@hearstfdn.org

WOMEN'S BASKETBALL COACHES ASSOCIATION
http://www.wbca.org/

WBCA SCHOLARSHIP AWARD
One-time award for two women's basketball players who have demonstrated outstanding commitment to the sport of women's basketball and to academic excellence. Minimum 3.5 GPA required. Must be nominated by the head coach of women's basketball who is WBCA member.

Award: Scholarship for use in freshman, sophomore, junior, senior, or graduate years; not renewable. *Number:* up to 2. *Amount:* up to $1000.

Eligibility Requirements: Applicant must be enrolled or expecting to enroll full- or part-time at a four-year institution or university; female and must have an interest in athletics/sports. Applicant must have 3.5 GPA or higher. Available to U.S. and non-U.S. citizens.

Application Requirements: Application form, recommendations or references, statistics. *Deadline:* February 15.

Contact: Betty Jaynes, Consultant
Phone: 770-279-8027 Ext. 102
Fax: 770-279-6290
E-mail: bettyj@wbca.org

WOMEN'S INTERNATIONAL BOWLING CONGRESS
http://www.bowl.com/

ALBERTA E. CROWE STAR OF TOMORROW AWARD
Nonrenewable award for a U.S. or Canadian female college student who competes in the sport of bowling. Must be a current USBC member in good standing, and under 21 years of age. Minimum 2.5 GPA required.

Award: Scholarship for use in sophomore, junior, or senior years; not renewable. *Number:* 1. *Amount:* $6000.

Eligibility Requirements: Applicant must be enrolled or expecting to enroll full-time at a four-year institution or university; female and must have an interest in bowling. Applicant must have 2.5 GPA or higher. Available to U.S. and non-U.S. citizens.

Application Requirements: Application form, essay, recommendations or references, transcript. *Deadline:* October 1.

Contact: Ed Gocha, Manager
Phone: 800-514-2695 Ext. 3343
Fax: 414-423-3014
E-mail: readsmart@bowl.com

WOMEN'S WESTERN GOLF FOUNDATION
http://www.wwga.org/WWGA.org/
Scholarship_Information.html

WOMEN'S WESTERN GOLF FOUNDATION SCHOLARSHIP
Scholarships for female high school seniors for use at a four-year college or university. Based on academic record, financial need, character, and involvement in golf. Golf skill not a criteria. Must continue to have financial need. Award is $2000 per student per year. Must be 17 to 18 years of age.

Award: Scholarship for use in freshman year; renewable. *Number:* up to 70. *Amount:* $2000.

Eligibility Requirements: Applicant must be high school student; age 17-18; planning to enroll or expecting to enroll full-time at a four-year institution or university; female and must have an interest in golf. Applicant must have 3.0 GPA or higher. Available to U.S. citizens.

Application Requirements: Application form, self-addressed stamped envelope with application. *Deadline:* March 1.

Contact: David Grady, President
Phone: 817-265-4074
E-mail: grady@orderofomega.org

WRITER'S DIGEST

http://www.writersdigest.com/

WRITER'S DIGEST ANNUAL WRITING COMPETITION

Annual writing competition. Only original, unpublished entries in any of the ten categories accepted. Send self-addressed stamped envelope for guidelines and entry form. Application fee: $15.

Award: Prize for use in freshman, sophomore, junior, senior, or graduate years; not renewable. *Number:* 100. *Amount:* $25–$3000.

Eligibility Requirements: Applicant must be enrolled or expecting to enroll full- or part-time at a two-year or four-year or technical institution or university and must have an interest in writing. Available to U.S. and non-U.S. citizens.

Application Requirements: Application form, entry in a contest, self-addressed stamped envelope with application. *Fee:* $15. *Deadline:* May 1.

Contact: Joan Gay, Customer Service Representative
Phone: 513-531-2690
Fax: 513-531-0798
E-mail: competitions@fwpubs.com

WRITER'S DIGEST POPULAR FICTION AWARDS

Writing contest accepts as many manuscripts as the applicant likes in each of the following categories: romance, mystery/crime fiction, sci-fi/fantasy, thriller/suspense and horror. Manuscripts must not be more than 4000 words.

Award: Prize for use in freshman, sophomore, junior, senior, graduate, or postgraduate years; not renewable. *Number:* 6. *Amount:* $500–$2500.

Eligibility Requirements: Applicant must be enrolled or expecting to enroll full- or part-time at a two-year or four-year or technical institution or university and must have an interest in writing. Available to U.S. and non-U.S. citizens.

Application Requirements: Application form, entry in a contest, manuscript, self-addressed stamped envelope with application. *Fee:* $12. *Deadline:* November 1.

Contact: Terri Boes, Customer Service Representative
Writer's Digest
4700 East Galbraith Road
Cincinnati, OH 45236
Phone: 513-531-2690 Ext. 1328
Fax: 513-531-0798
E-mail: competitions@fwpubs.com

WRITER'S DIGEST SELF-PUBLISHED BOOK AWARDS

Awards open to self-published books for which the author has paid full cost. Send self-addressed stamped envelope for guidelines and entry form. Application fee: $100.

Award: Prize for use in freshman, sophomore, junior, senior, graduate, or postgraduate years; not renewable. *Number:* 10. *Amount:* $1000–$3000.

Eligibility Requirements: Applicant must be enrolled or expecting to enroll full- or part-time at a two-year or four-year or technical institution or university and must have an interest in writing. Available to U.S. and non-U.S. citizens.

Application Requirements: Application form, entry in a contest, self-addressed stamped envelope with application. *Fee:* $100. *Deadline:* May 1.

Contact: Joan Gay, Customer Service Representative
Writer's Digest
4700 East Galbraith Road
Cincinnati, OH 45236
Phone: 513-531-2690 Ext. 1328
Fax: 513-531-0798
E-mail: competitions@fwpubs.com

UNITED STATES BOWLING CONGRESS (USBC)

http://www.bowl.com/

GIFT FOR LIFE SCHOLARSHIP
• See page 544

USBC ALBERTA E. CROWE STAR OF TOMORROW AWARD

Award annually recognizes star qualities in a female USBC Youth member who competes in the sport of bowling. Star qualities include distinguished certified bowling performances on the local, state and national level, academic achievement and extra-curricular activities.

Award: Scholarship for use in freshman, sophomore, junior, or senior years; not renewable. *Number:* 1. *Amount:* $6000.

Eligibility Requirements: Applicant must be enrolled or expecting to enroll full-time at a two-year or four-year institution or university; female and must have an interest in bowling. Applicant must have 3.0 GPA or higher. Available to U.S. citizens.

Application Requirements: Application form, entry in a contest, recommendations or references, transcript. *Deadline:* December 1.

Contact: Denise Lish, SMART Program Administrator
Phone: 800-514-2695
E-mail: smart@bowl.com

USBC ANNUAL ZEB SCHOLARSHIP
• See page 566

USBC CHUCK HALL STAR OF TOMORROW SCHOLARSHIP

Scholarship annually recognizes star qualities in a male USBC Youth member who competes in the sport of bowling. Award is given to a male high school senior or college student and must be a current USBC Youth or USBC member in good standing.

Award: Scholarship for use in freshman, sophomore, junior, or senior years; renewable. *Number:* 1. *Amount:* $6000.

Eligibility Requirements: Applicant must be enrolled or expecting to enroll full-time at a two-year or four-year institution or university; male and must have an interest in bowling. Applicant must have 3.0 GPA or higher. Available to U.S. citizens.

Application Requirements: Application form, recommendations or references, transcript. *Deadline:* December 1.

Contact: Denise Lish, SMART Program Administrator
Phone: 800-514-2695
E-mail: smart@bowl.com

USBC EARL ANTHONY MEMORIAL SCHOLARSHIP
• See page 544

USBC EARL ANTHONY MEMORIAL SCHOLARSHIPS

Scholarship given to recognize male and/or female bowlers for their community involvement and academic achievements, both in high school and college. Candidates must be enrolled in their senior year of high school or presently attending college and be current members of USBC in good standing.

Award: Scholarship for use in freshman, sophomore, junior, or senior years; not renewable. *Number:* 5. *Amount:* $5000.

Eligibility Requirements: Applicant must be enrolled or expecting to enroll full- or part-time at a two-year or four-year institution or university and must have an interest in bowling. Applicant must have 2.5 GPA or higher. Available to U.S. citizens.

Application Requirements: Application form, recommendations or references, transcript. *Deadline:* May 1.

Contact: Denise Lish, SMART Program Administrator
Phone: 800-514-2695
E-mail: smart@bowl.com

USBC YOUTH AMBASSADOR OF THE YEAR (M/F)

Annually recognizes one male and one female USBC Youth bowler for his/her exemplary contributions to the sport of bowling, academic accomplishments and community involvement.

Award: Scholarship for use in freshman year; not renewable. *Number:* 2. *Amount:* $1500.

Contact: Denise Lish, SMART Program Administrator
Phone: 800-514-2695
E-mail: smart@bowl.com

USBC YOUTH AMBASSADOR OF THE YEAR (M/F)

Annually recognizes one male and one female USBC Youth bowler for his/her exemplary contributions to the sport of bowling, academic accomplishments and community involvement.

Award: Scholarship for use in freshman year; not renewable. *Number:* 2. *Amount:* $1500.

Eligibility Requirements: Applicant must be high school student; planning to enroll or expecting to enroll full- or part-time at a four-year institution or university and must have an interest in bowling. Available to U.S. citizens.

Application Requirements: Application form, recommendations or references, transcript. *Deadline:* December 1.

Contact: Denise Lish, SMART Program Administrator
Phone: 800-514-2695
E-mail: smart@bowl.com

YOUNGARTS, NATIONAL FOUNDATION FOR ADVANCEMENT IN THE ARTS

http://www.youngarts.org

YOUNGARTS, NATIONAL FOUNDATION FOR ADVANCEMENT IN THE ARTS

One-time award for high school students ages 15 to 18 years old who show talent in dance, film and video, jazz, music, photography, theater, visual arts, voice, and/or writing. Must submit on-line media of portfolio, or audition materials along with on-line application and application fee (fee waivers available). Must be citizens or permanent residents of the U.S.

Award: Prize for use in freshman year; not renewable. *Number:* up to 700. *Amount:* $100–$10,000.

Eligibility Requirements: Applicant must be age 15-18; enrolled or expecting to enroll full- or part-time at a two-year or four-year or technical institution or university and must have an interest in art, music/singing, photography/photogrammetry/filmmaking, theater, or writing. Available to U.S. citizens.

Application Requirements: Application form, application form may be submitted online (http://youngarts.org), Audition (in performing arts areas), portfolio. *Fee:* $35. *Deadline:* October 18.

Contact: Allison Ball, Director of Education
YoungArts, National Foundation for Advancement in the Arts
2100 Biscayne Boulevard
Miami, FL 33137
Phone: 305-377-1140 Ext. 1702
E-mail: aball@youngarts.org

Miscellaneous Criteria

101ST AIRBORNE DIVISION ASSOCIATION

http://www.screamingeagle.org/

101ST AIRBORNE DIVISION ASSOCIATION CHAPPIE HALL SCHOLARSHIP PROGRAM

Scholarship to provide financial assistance to students who have the potential to become assets to our nation. The major factors to be considered in the evaluation and rating of applicants are eligibility, career objectives, academic record, financial need, and insight gained from the letter and/or essay requesting consideration, and letters of recommendation. Applicant's parents, grandparents, or spouse, living or deceased must have/had regular membership with 101st Airborne Division. Dollar amount and total number of awards varies.

Award: Scholarship for use in freshman, sophomore, junior, or senior years; not renewable. *Number:* 15–25. *Amount:* $1000–$2000.

Eligibility Requirements: Applicant must be enrolled or expecting to enroll full-time at a two-year or four-year or technical institution or university. Available to U.S. and non-U.S. citizens.

Application Requirements: Application form, community service, essay, personal photograph, proof of regular membership in 101st Airborne Division Association, recommendations or references, test scores, transcript. *Deadline:* May 10.

Contact: Sam Bass, Executive Secretary-Treasurer
101st Airborne Division Association
PO Box 929
Fort Campbell, KY 42223-0929
Phone: 931-431-0199 Ext. 35
Fax: 931-431-0195
E-mail: 101exec@comcast.net

ACADEMY OF TELEVISION ARTS AND SCIENCES FOUNDATION

http://www.emmysfoundation.org/

ACADEMY OF TELEVISION ARTS AND SCIENCES COLLEGE TELEVISION AWARDS

A competition for excellence in college student video, digital, and film productions. Rules and guidelines are updated annually in the fall at emmysfoundation.org. Awards of up to $4000. Open to those students who have produced their video while enrolled in a community college, college, or university in the United States.

Award: Prize for use in freshman, sophomore, junior, or senior years; not renewable. *Number:* 20–25. *Amount:* $500–$10,000.

Eligibility Requirements: Applicant must be enrolled or expecting to enroll full- or part-time at a two-year or four-year or technical institution or university. Available to U.S. and non-U.S. citizens.

Application Requirements: Application form, online application and video submission. *Fee:* $25.

Contact: Debbie Slavkin, Program Manager
Academy of Television Arts and Sciences Foundation
5220 Lankershim Boulevard
North Hollywood, CA 91601
Phone: 818-754-2820
Fax: 818-761-2827
E-mail: ctasupport@ermmys.org

ALFRED G. AND ELMA M. MILOTTE SCHOLARSHIP FUND

http://www.milotte.org/

ALFRED G. AND ELMA M. MILOTTE SCHOLARSHIP

Grant of up to $4000 to high school graduate or students holding the GED. Applicants must have been accepted at a trade school, art school, two-year or four-year college or university for undergraduate or graduate studies.

Award: Scholarship for use in freshman, sophomore, junior, senior, or graduate years; not renewable. *Amount:* up to $4000.

Eligibility Requirements: Applicant must be enrolled or expecting to enroll full- or part-time at a two-year or four-year or technical institution or university. Applicant must have 3.0 GPA or higher. Available to U.S. citizens.

Application Requirements: Application form, recommendations or references, samples of work expressing applicant's observations of the natural world, transcript. *Deadline:* March 1.

Contact: Sean Ferguson, Assistant Vice President
Phone: 800-832-9071
Fax: 800-552-3182
E-mail: info@milotte.org

ALL-INK.COM PRINTER SUPPLIES ONLINE

http://www.all-ink.com/

ALL-INK.COM COLLEGE SCHOLARSHIP PROGRAM

One-time award for any level of postsecondary education. Minimum 2.5 GPA. Must apply online only at website http://www.all-ink.com. Recipients selected annually.

Award: Scholarship for use in freshman, sophomore, junior, senior, graduate, or postgraduate years; not renewable. *Number:* 5–10. *Amount:* $1000–$5000.

Eligibility Requirements: Applicant must be enrolled or expecting to enroll full-time at a two-year or four-year or technical institution or university. Applicant must have 2.5 GPA or higher. Available to U.S. and non-U.S. citizens.

Application Requirements: Application form, entry in a contest, essay. *Deadline:* December 31.

Contact: Aaron Gale, President
All-Ink.com Printer Supplies Online
1460 North Main Street, Suite 2
Spanish Fork, UT 84660
Phone: 801-794-0123
Fax: 801-794-0124
E-mail: scholarship@all-ink.com

ALPHA KAPPA ALPHA EDUCATIONAL ADVANCEMENT FOUNDATION, INC.

http://www.akaeaf.org

AKA EDUCATIONAL ADVANCEMENT FOUNDATION, INC. FINANCIAL NEEDS SCHOLARSHIP

Scholarship for students who have completed a minimum of one year in a degree-granting institution and need financial aid to continue their studies in such an institution. May also be a student in a non-institutional based program that may or may not grant degrees, and must submit a course of study outline. Must have a minimum GPA of 2.5.

Award: Scholarship for use in sophomore, junior, senior, or graduate years; not renewable.

Eligibility Requirements: Applicant must be enrolled or expecting to enroll full-time at a four-year institution or university. Applicant must have 2.5 GPA or higher. Available to U.S. and non-U.S. citizens.

Application Requirements: Application form, essay, financial need analysis, recommendations or references, resume, transcript. *Deadline:* varies.

Contact: Barbara Sutton, Executive Director
Phone: 773-947-0026
E-mail: akaeaf@akaeaf.net

AKA EDUCATIONAL ADVANCEMENT FOUNDATION, INC. MERIT SCHOLARSHIP

Scholarships for students demonstrating exceptional academic achievements. Applicant must have completed a minimum of one year in a degree-granting institution and be continuing their program in that institution. Must have GPA of 3.0 or higher and show evidence of leadership by participating in community or campus activities.

Award: Scholarship for use in sophomore, junior, senior, or graduate years; not renewable. *Amount:* $1000–$2000.

Eligibility Requirements: Applicant must be enrolled or expecting to enroll full-time at a four-year institution or university. Applicant must have 3.0 GPA or higher. Available to U.S. and non-U.S. citizens.

Application Requirements: Application form, essay, recommendations or references, resume, transcript. *Deadline:* varies.

Contact: Barbara Sutton, Executive Director
Phone: 773-947-0026
E-mail: akaeaf@akaeaf.net

AKA EDUCATIONAL ADVANCEMENT FOUNDATION, INC. YOUTH PARTNERS ACCESSING CAPITAL SCHOLARSHIP

Scholarship for a member of the society. Must be an undergraduate of at least sophomore status. Must have a minimum GPA of 3.0 and participate in leadership, volunteer, civic, or campus activities. Must demonstrate academic achievement or financial need.

Award: Scholarship for use in sophomore, junior, or senior years; not renewable.

Eligibility Requirements: Applicant must be enrolled or expecting to enroll full-time at a four-year institution or university. Applicant must have 3.0 GPA or higher. Available to U.S. and non-U.S. citizens.

Application Requirements: Application form, essay, recommendations or references, transcript. *Deadline:* April 15.

Contact: Barbara Sutton, Executive Director
Phone: 773-947-0026
E-mail: akaeaf@akaeaf.net

ALPHA LAMBDA DELTA

http://www.nationalald.org/

JO ANNE J. TROW SCHOLARSHIPS

One-time award for initiated members of Alpha Lambda Delta. Minimum 3.5 GPA required. Must be nominated by chapter.

Award: Scholarship for use in junior year; not renewable. *Number:* up to 35. *Amount:* $1000–$6000.

Eligibility Requirements: Applicant must be enrolled or expecting to enroll full-time at a four-year institution or university. Applicant must have 3.5 GPA or higher. Available to U.S. and non-U.S. citizens.

Application Requirements: Application form, essay, recommendations or references, transcript. *Deadline:* April 1.

Contact: Dr. Glenda Earwood, Executive Director
Alpha Lambda Delta
PO Box 4403
Macon, GA 31208
Phone: 478-744-9595
E-mail: glenda@nationalald.org

AMERICAN ATHEISTS

http://www.atheists.org/

FOUNDERS' SCHOLARSHIP

The grant can be used for current college students or for high school students entering college next year. Applicants must be Atheists.

Award: Scholarship for use in freshman, sophomore, junior, or senior years; not renewable. *Number:* 3. *Amount:* $1000–$2000.

Eligibility Requirements: Applicant must be enrolled or expecting to enroll at a four-year institution or university. Applicant must have 2.5 GPA or higher. Available to U.S. citizens.

Application Requirements: *Deadline:* January 31.

AMERICAN FIRE SPRINKLER ASSOCIATION

http://www.afsascholarship.org/

AFSA HIGH SCHOOL SCHOLARSHIP CONTEST

One-time award for high school seniors. This scholarship essay contest requires applicants to go online to http://www.afsascholarship.org, and read a short essay about sprinklers and fire safety. After finishing, they complete a ten-question quiz on what they just read. Each correct answer gives the student a chance at winning one of ten $2,000 scholarships (maximum 10 chances per entrant).

Award: Scholarship for use in freshman year; not renewable. *Number:* 10. *Amount:* $2000.

Eligibility Requirements: Applicant must be high school student and planning to enroll or expecting to enroll full-time at a two-year or four-year or technical institution or university. Available to U.S. citizens.

Application Requirements: Application form may be submitted online (http://www.afsascholarship.org), entry in a contest. *Deadline:* April 3.

Contact: D'Arcy Montalvo, Public Relations Manager
American Fire Sprinkler Association
12750 Merit Drive, Suite 350
Dallas, TX 75251
Phone: 214-349-5965
Fax: 214-343-8898
E-mail: dmontalvo@firesprinkler.org

AFSA SECOND CHANCE SCHOLARSHIP CONTEST

Online entries only. Enter at http://www.afsascholarship.org/ and click on Second Chance Contest; U.S. citizens or legal residents who graduated from U.S. high school may enter. University/trade school/college must be accredited using link provided on website. No phone calls or emails. Entrants read an online essay and then take online quiz for up to 10 chances to win.

Award: Scholarship for use in freshman, sophomore, junior, senior, graduate, or postgraduate years; not renewable. *Number:* 5–5. *Amount:* $1000–$1000.

Eligibility Requirements: Applicant must be enrolled or expecting to enroll full-time at a two-year or four-year or technical institution or university. Available to U.S. citizens.

Application Requirements: Application form may be submitted online (http://www.afsascholarship.org), entry in a contest. *Deadline:* August 27.

Contact: Mrs. D'Arcy Montalvo, PR Manager
American Fire Sprinkler Association
12750 Merit Drive, Suite 350
Dallas, TX 75251
Phone: 214-349-5965 Ext. 115
Fax: 214-343-8898
E-mail: dmontalvo@firesprinkler.org

AMERICAN INSTITUTE FOR FOREIGN STUDY

http://www.aifsabroad.com/

STUDY AGAIN SCHOLARSHIPS

Scholarships for AIFS alumni. AIFS summer program students will receive a $1000 scholarship to study abroad on an AIFS semester or academic year program. AIFS semester or academic year program students will receive a $500 scholarship toward a summer program.

Award: Scholarship for use in freshman, sophomore, junior, or senior years; not renewable. *Amount:* $500–$1000.

Eligibility Requirements: Applicant must be enrolled or expecting to enroll full-time at a two-year or four-year institution or university. Applicant must have 2.5 GPA or higher. Available to U.S. and non-U.S. citizens.

Application Requirements: Application form, essay, personal photograph, recommendations or references, transcript. *Fee:* $95. *Deadline:* varies.

Contact: David Mauro, Admissions Counselor
American Institute for Foreign Study
9 West Broad Street, River Plaza
Stamford, CT 06902
Phone: 800-727-2437 Ext. 5163
Fax: 203-399-5597
E-mail: info@aifs.com

AMERICAN LEGION DEPARTMENT OF MARYLAND

http://www.mdlegion.org/

AMERICAN LEGION, DEPARTMENT OF MARYLAND, HIGH SCHOOL ORATORICAL SCHOLARSHIP CONTEST

Scholarship awarded to winner of the Department of MD High School Oratorical Contest. Applicants must apply at their local Posts and compete in and win their Post, County, and District level competitions for eligibility. The winner of this contest goes on to compete at Nationals for a chance at $18,000 first prize scholarship. For details http://www.legion.org/oratorical

Award: Scholarship for use in freshman, sophomore, junior, or senior years; not renewable. *Number:* 1–7. *Amount:* $500–$2000.

Eligibility Requirements: Applicant must be high school student and planning to enroll or expecting to enroll full-time at a two-year or four-year institution or university. Available to U.S. citizens.

Application Requirements: Entry in a contest, must win post, county, and district contests. *Deadline:* varies.

Contact: Russell Myers, Department Adjutant
American Legion Department of Maryland
101 North Gay Street
Room E
Baltimore, MD 21202
Phone: 410-752-1405
Fax: 410-752-3822
E-mail: russell@mdlegion.org

AMERICAN NATIONAL CATTLE WOMEN INC.

http://www.nationalbeefambassador.org/

NATIONAL BEEF AMBASSADOR PROGRAM

Award's purpose is to train young spokespersons in the beef industry. Applicant must be fully prepared to answer questions and debate focusing on topic related to beef consumption and distribution, as well as social factors related to the industry. The prize value is $1,000. Details and tools for preparation are available on the website http://www.nationalbeefambassador.org.

Award: Scholarship for use in freshman, sophomore, junior, or senior years; not renewable. *Number:* 5. *Amount:* $1000.

Eligibility Requirements: Applicant must be age 17-20; enrolled or expecting to enroll full-time at a two-year or four-year institution or university and single. Applicant must have 2.5 GPA or higher. Available to U.S. citizens.

Application Requirements: Applicants must compete in and win their state beef ambassador competition, entry in a contest. *Deadline:* varies.

AMERICAN OCCUPATIONAL THERAPY FOUNDATION INC.

http://www.aotf.org/

AOTA'S ASSEMBLY OF STUDENT DELEGATES AWARD

Award for study leading to a degree as an occupational therapy assistant or a Master's in occupational therapy. Must be a member of the American Occupational Therapy Association.

Award: Scholarship for use in sophomore, junior, senior, or graduate years; not renewable. *Number:* 2. *Amount:* $600.

Eligibility Requirements: Applicant must be enrolled or expecting to enroll full-time at a two-year or four-year institution or university. Available to U.S. citizens.

Application Requirements: Application form, Curriculum Director's statement, essay, recommendations or references. *Deadline:* varies.

Contact: Jeanne Cooper, Scholarship Coordinator
    Phone: 301-652-6611 Ext. 2550
    Fax: 301-656-3620
    E-mail: jcooper@aotf.org

AMERICAN SWEDISH INSTITUTE

http://www.ASImn.org

MALMBERG SCHOLARSHIP FOR STUDY IN SWEDEN

Award for a U.S. resident interested in Sweden and Swedish America. Applicant must be either a student enrolled in a degree-granting program at an accredited college or university or a qualified scholar engaged in study or research whose work can be enhanced by study in Sweden. Scholarships are usually granted for a full academic year term (nine months) but can be for study periods of shorter duration.

Award: Scholarship for use in junior, senior, graduate, or postgraduate years; not renewable. *Number:* up to 1. *Amount:* up to $10,000.

Eligibility Requirements: Applicant must be enrolled or expecting to enroll full- or part-time at a four-year institution or university. Available to U.S. citizens.

Application Requirements: Application form, essay, letter of invitation from host institution, recommendations or references, resume, transcript. *Deadline:* November 15.

Contact: Karin Krull, Adult Programs Coordinator
    American Swedish Institute
    2600 Park Avenue
    Minneapolis, MN 55407
    Phone: 612-870-3355
    Fax: 612-871-8682
    E-mail: karink@ASImn.org

AMERICAN TRAFFIC SAFETY SERVICES FOUNDATION

http://www.atssa.com/cs/roadway-worker-scholarship

ROADWAY WORKER MEMORIAL SCHOLARSHIP PROGRAM

Scholarship will provide financial assistance for post-high school education to the children of roadway workers killed or permanently disabled in work zone accidents, including mobile operations and the installation of roadway safety features are eligible for the Foundation's annual scholarships in support of higher education (college or vocational). Parents with custody or legal guardianship of surviving children are also eligible.

Award: Scholarship for use in freshman, sophomore, junior, senior, graduate, or postgraduate years; not renewable. *Number:* 2–5. *Amount:* $2000–$3000.

Eligibility Requirements: Applicant must be enrolled or expecting to enroll full- or part-time at a two-year or four-year or technical institution or university. Available to U.S. citizens.

Application Requirements: 200-word statement, application form, community service, essay, financial need analysis, recommendations or references, resume, test scores, transcript. *Deadline:* February 15.

Contact: Melanie McKee, Foundation Director
    American Traffic Safety Services Foundation
    15 Riverside Parkway, Suite 100
    Fredericksburg, VA 22406
    Phone: 540-368-1701 Ext. 112
    Fax: 540-368-1717
    E-mail: melanie.mckee@atssa.com

ANYCOLLEGE.COM

http://www.anycollege.com/

ANYCOLLEGE.COM SCHOLARSHIP

Four $2000 scholarships awarded annually by random drawing. All students planning to attend an accredited college or university that they had not previously attended are eligible to apply. Deadlines are March 31, June 30, September 30, and December 31.

Award: Scholarship for use in freshman, sophomore, junior, or senior years; not renewable. *Number:* 4. *Amount:* $2000.

Eligibility Requirements: Applicant must be enrolled or expecting to enroll full-time at a two-year or four-year or technical institution or university. Available to U.S. and non-U.S. citizens.

Application Requirements: Application form. *Deadline:* continuous.

Contact: Mr. Cory Klinnert, Director of Marketing
    AnyCollege.com
    403 Center Avenue, Seventh Floor
    Moorhead, MN 56560
    Phone: 218-284-9933
    Fax: 218-284-3394
    E-mail: cklinnert@anycollege.com

APPALACHIAN STUDIES ASSOCIATION, INC.

http://www.appalachianstudies.org/

CARL A. ROSS STUDENT PAPER AWARD

Middle/high school students should submit papers of 12-15 pages in length and undergraduate/graduate students should submit papers of 20-30 pages in length. Winners receive $100 each. Costs of attending the conference are the winners' responsibility. All papers must adhere to the guidelines for scholarly research. Must be enrolled in courses at the time of the conference. To verify their student status, students can submit one of the following: a copy of a schedule of classes for the term, transcripts, or letter from a faculty advisor stating their current student status.

Award: Prize for use in freshman, sophomore, junior, senior, or graduate years; not renewable. *Number:* 2. *Amount:* $100.

Eligibility Requirements: Applicant must be enrolled or expecting to enroll full- or part-time at a two-year or four-year or technical institution or university. Available to U.S. and non-U.S. citizens.

Application Requirements: Application form may be submitted online, essay, resume, to verify student status, submit a copy of a schedule of classes or transcripts indicating enrollment for spring 2013 to kywoman102950@gmail.com by December 15, 2013 or a letter from a faculty advisor verifying student status for spring 2013 including the faculty member's email, phone, and mailing address. *Deadline:* December 15.

ARMED FORCES COMMUNICATIONS AND ELECTRONICS ASSOCIATION, EDUCATIONAL FOUNDATION

http://www.afcea.org/scholarships

AFCEA CYBER STUDIES SCHOLARSHIP

$5000 scholarships will be awarded to undergraduate students majoring in a field directly related to the support of U.S. cyber enterprises with relevance to the mission of AFCEA such as cyber security, cyber attack, computer science, information technology, or electronic engineering.

Award: Scholarship for use in sophomore, junior, or senior years; not renewable. *Number:* 3–4. *Amount:* $5000.

Eligibility Requirements: Applicant must be enrolled or expecting to enroll full-time at a two-year or four-year institution or university. Applicant must have 3.0 GPA or higher. Available to U.S. citizens.

Application Requirements: Application form, application form may be submitted online, recommendations or references, transcript. *Deadline:* November 15.

Contact: Miss. Norma Corrales, Senior Director of AFCEA Educational
    Foundation Scholarship Program
    Armed Forces Communications and Electronics Association,
    Educational Foundation
    4400 Fair Lakes Court
    Fairfax, VA 22033
    Phone: 703-631-6149
    E-mail: ncorrales@afcea.org

INTELLIGENCE UNDERGRADUATE SCHOLARSHIPS

Intelligence Scholarships of $2250 (undergraduate) will be awarded to students enrolled full-time in degree-granting programs in fields directly related to the support of U.S. intelligence or homeland security enterprises, and/or foreign languages.

Award: Scholarship for use in sophomore or junior years; not renewable. *Number:* 2–3. *Amount:* $2500.

Eligibility Requirements: Applicant must be enrolled or expecting to enroll full-time at a four-year institution or university. Applicant must have 3.0 GPA or higher. Available to U.S. citizens.

Application Requirements: Application form, application form may be submitted online (http://www.afcea.org/scholarships), recommendations or references, transcript. *Deadline:* November 15.

Contact: Ms. Norma Corrales, Senior Director, Scholarships and Awards
Armed Forces Communications and Electronics Association, Educational Foundation
4400 Fair Lakes Court
Fairfax, VA 22033
Phone: 703-631-6149
E-mail: scholarships@afcea.org

MILITARY PERSONNEL/DEPENDENTS SCHOLARSHIP (GENERAL EMMETT PAIGE)

Candidate must be ajoring in the following or C4I-related fields of electrical, chemical, systems or aerospace engineering; mathematics; physics; science or mathematics education; technology management; management information systems; or computer science. Majors directly related to the support of U.S. intelligence enterprises or national security with relevance to the mission of AFCEA will also be eligible.

Award: Scholarship for use in sophomore or junior years; not renewable. *Number:* 3–3. *Amount:* $2000.

Eligibility Requirements: Applicant must be enrolled or expecting to enroll full-time at a four-year institution or university. Applicant must have 3.0 GPA or higher. Available to U.S. citizens.

Application Requirements: Application form, application form may be submitted online (http://www.afcea.org/scholarships), Military ID/ DD214, recommendations or references, transcript. *Deadline:* November 1.

Contact: Mrs. Norma Corrales, Senior Director, Scholarships and Awards
Armed Forces Communications and Electronics Association, Educational Foundation
4400 Fair Lakes Court
Fairfax, VA 22033
Phone: 703-631-6141
E-mail: scholarships@afcea.org

SCIENCE TECHNOLOGY, ENGINEERING AND MATH (STEM) MAJORS SCHOLARSHIP UNDERGRADUATE AND GRADUATE STUDENTS

The AFCEA Educational Foundation is offering at least 50 scholarships of $5,000 each to students actively pursuing an undergraduate degree, graduate degree or credential/licensure for the purpose of teaching STEM (science, technology, engineering or math) subjects at a U.S. middle or secondary school. The scholarships are made possible by generous contributions from Booz Allen Hamilton, Terremark Worldwide, AFCEA International and several of AFCEA's regional chapters. To be eligible, students must be U.S. citizens with a minimum overall GPA of 3.0 (or equivalent). Undergraduate candidates must be attending an accredited U.S. college or university on-campus and majoring in secondary education or a STEM field for the purpose of teaching STEM subjects in a U.S. middle or secondary school. Undergraduate applications will be accepted from current sophomores, juniors, and seniors. Graduate-level candidates must be currently enrolled in at least two semester-equivalent classes at an accredited U.S. college or university. Credential and licensure students must have completed a bachelor's degree in a STEM major.

Award: Scholarship for use in sophomore, junior, senior, or graduate years; not renewable. *Number:* 50–55. *Amount:* $5000.

Eligibility Requirements: Applicant must be enrolled or expecting to enroll full- or part-time at a four-year institution or university. Applicant must have 3.0 GPA or higher. Available to U.S. citizens.

Application Requirements: Application form, recommendations or references, transcript. *Deadline:* April 1.

Contact: Ms. Norma Corrales, Senior Director, Scholarships and Awards
Armed Forces Communications and Electronics Association, Educational Foundation
4400 Fair Lakes Court
Fairfax, VA 22033
Phone: 703-631-6141
E-mail: scholarships@afcea.org

STEM TEACHERS SCHOLARSHIP

The AFCEA Educational Foundation will offer scholarships of $5000 to students actively pursuing an undergraduate degree, graduate degree or credential/licensure for the purpose of teaching STEM (Science, Technology, Engineering or Mathematics) subjects at a U.S. middle or secondary school.

Award: Scholarship for use in junior, senior, or postgraduate years; not renewable. *Number:* 38. *Amount:* $5000.

Eligibility Requirements: Applicant must be enrolled or expecting to enroll full-time at a four-year institution or university. Applicant must have 3.0 GPA or higher. Available to U.S. citizens.

Application Requirements: Application form, application form may be submitted online (http://www.afcea.org/education/scholarships/ undergraduate/TeachersScholarship.asp), recommendations or references, transcript. *Deadline:* May 1.

Contact: Miss. Norma Corrrales, Director of AFCEA Educational Scholarship Program
Armed Forces Communications and Electronics Association, Educational Foundation
4400 Fair Lakes Court
Fairfax, VA 22033
Phone: 703-631-7149
E-mail: ncorrales@afcea.org

ARMY EMERGENCY RELIEF (AER)

http://www.aerhq.org/

OVERSEAS SPOUSE EDUCATION ASSISTANCE PROGRAM

The Overseas Spouse Education Assistance Program (OSEAP) is a need-based education assistance program designed to provide spouses with financial assistance to pursue educational goals. Spouses must physically reside at overseas residence, and be enrolled, accepted, or pending acceptance as students for the entire term in postsecondary or vocational institutions under contract at the education office and approved by the U.S. Department of Education.

Award: Scholarship for use in freshman, sophomore, or junior years; renewable. *Amount:* $500–$2500.

Eligibility Requirements: Applicant must be enrolled or expecting to enroll full- or part-time at an institution or university and married. Available to U.S. citizens.

Application Requirements: *Deadline:* continuous.

ASIAN PACIFIC COMMUNITY FUND

http://www.apcf.org/

ASIAN PACIFIC COMMUNITY FUND - VERIZON SCHOLARSHIP AWARDS PROGRAM (2ND YEAR COLLEGE STUDENTS)

Currently a 2nd year college student in California, Oregon or Washington OR attending college in one of those states. Plan to enroll as a third year college student in a U.S. accredited 4-year college or university as a full-time, degree-seeking student majoring in math, engineering, or a science in the Fall of 2013. Transfer students are eligible. Have a minimum cumulative unweighted GPA of 3.0. Awardees will be selected based on the following criteria: Essay questions; GPA; community involvement; leadership.

Award: Scholarship for use in junior year; not renewable. *Number:* 10. *Amount:* $1000.

Eligibility Requirements: Applicant must be enrolled or expecting to enroll full-time at a four-year institution or university. Applicant must have 3.0 GPA or higher.

Application Requirements: Application form, application form may be submitted online (http://apcf.wufoo.com/forms/scholarship-application-form/), essay, recommendations or references, transcript. *Deadline:* April 30.

Contact: Mr. Martin Mai, Marketing and Program Manager
Asian Pacific Community Fund
1145 Wilshire Boulevard, Suite 105
Los Angeles, CA 90017
Phone: 213-624-6400 Ext. 4
Fax: 213-624-6406
E-mail: mmai@apcf.org

ASSOCIATION OF SIKH PROFESSIONALS

http://www.sikhprofessionals.org/

SIKH EDUCATION AID FUND

This fund has been set up to support financially deserving Sikh students, to recognize Sikh students of outstanding academic abilities, and to support those individuals doing research in the Sikh religion or engaged in Sikh studies. Awards are in the form of scholarships, grants through endowments, and interest-free loans for which repayment is expected after graduation.

Award: Scholarship for use in freshman, sophomore, junior, or senior years. *Amount:* $400–$4000.

Eligibility Requirements: Applicant must be enrolled or expecting to enroll at an institution or university. Available to U.S. citizens.

Application Requirements: *Deadline:* June 1.

AMERICAN ASSOCIATION OF TEACHERS OF JAPANESE BRIDGING CLEARINGHOUSE FOR STUDY ABROAD IN JAPAN

http://www.aatj.org

BRIDGING SCHOLARSHIP FOR STUDY ABROAD IN JAPAN

Scholarships for U.S. students studying in Japan on semester or year-long programs. Deadlines: April 8 and October 8.

Award: Scholarship for use in junior or senior years; not renewable. *Number:* 40–80. *Amount:* $2500–$4000.

Eligibility Requirements: Applicant must be enrolled or expecting to enroll full-time at a two-year or four-year institution or university. Available to U.S. citizens.

Application Requirements: Application form, essay, financial need analysis, recommendations or references, transcript. *Deadline:* April 6.

Contact: Ms. Susan Schmidt, Executive Director, Bridging Project
Phone: 303-492-5487
E-mail: susan.schmidt@colorado.edu

AVERMEDIA INFORMATION, INC.

http://www.averusa.com/

AVERVISION SCHOLARSHIP PROGRAM

The AVerMedia scholarship will be awarded to two 2011 graduating High School Seniors entering an accredited four year college. Applicants must submit a one-page essay answering: Explain how classroom technology has changed throughout your educational path. How has classroom technology impacted your learning?

Award: Scholarship for use in freshman year. *Number:* 2. *Amount:* $2500.

Eligibility Requirements: Applicant must be high school student and planning to enroll or expecting to enroll full-time at a four-year institution or university. Applicant must have 2.5 GPA or higher. Available to U.S. and Canadian citizens.

Application Requirements: *Deadline:* May 31.

AYN RAND INSTITUTE

http://www.aynrandnovels.org

ATLAS SHRUGGED ESSAY CONTEST

Annual Essay Contest on Ayn Rand's novel, Atlas Shrugged, for college/university and 12th grade students. Essays will be judged on both style and content. Judges will look for writing that is clear, articulate and logically organized. Winning essays must demonstrate an outstanding grasp of the philosophic and psychological meaning of Atlas Shrugged. For complete rules and guidelines, visit website http://www.aynrand.org/contests.

Award: Prize for use in freshman, sophomore, junior, senior, graduate, or postgraduate years; not renewable. *Number:* 84. *Amount:* $50–$10,000.

Eligibility Requirements: Applicant must be enrolled or expecting to enroll full- or part-time at a two-year or four-year or technical institution or university. Available to U.S. and non-U.S. citizens.

Application Requirements: Entry in a contest, essay. *Deadline:* September 17.

Contact: Jason Eriksen, Essay Contest Coordinator
Ayn Rand Institute
2121 Alton Parkway, Suite 250
Irvine, CA 92606
Phone: 949-222-6550 Ext. 247
Fax: 949-222-6558
E-mail: essay@aynrand.org

THE FOUNTAINHEAD ESSAY CONTEST

Annual Essay Contest on Ayn Rand's novel, The Fountainhead, for 11th and 12th graders. Essays will be judged on both style and content. Judges will look for writing that is clear, articulate and logically organized. Winning essays must demonstrate an outstanding grasp of the philosophic and psychological meaning of The Fountainhead. Essays should be between 800 and 1600 words. For complete rules and guidelines, refer to website http://www.aynrand.org/contests.

Award: Prize for use in freshman, sophomore, junior, senior, graduate, or postgraduate years; not renewable. *Number:* 236. *Amount:* $50–$10,000.

Eligibility Requirements: Applicant must be high school student and planning to enroll or expecting to enroll full- or part-time at a two-year or four-year or technical institution or university. Available to U.S. and non-U.S. citizens.

Application Requirements: Entry in a contest, essay. *Deadline:* April 26.

Contact: Jason Eriksen, Essay Contest Coordinator
Ayn Rand Institute
2121 Alton Parkway, Suite 250
Irvine, CA 92606
Phone: 949-222-6550 Ext. 247
Fax: 949-222-6558
E-mail: essay@aynrand.org

WE THE LIVING ESSAY CONTEST

Open to students in grades 10-12. Submit an essay on one of three topics. See www.aynrandnovels.org/essay-contests.html for complete details.

Award: Scholarship for use in freshman, sophomore, junior, senior, graduate, or postgraduate years; not renewable. *Number:* 116. *Amount:* $25–$3000.

Eligibility Requirements: Applicant must be high school student and planning to enroll or expecting to enroll full- or part-time at a two-year or four-year or technical institution or university. Available to U.S. and non-U.S. citizens.

Application Requirements: Entry in a contest, essay. *Deadline:* May 6.

Contact: Jason Eriksen, Essay Contest Coordinator
Ayn Rand Institute
2121 Alton Parkway, Suite 250
Irvine, CA 92606
Phone: 949-222-6550 Ext. 247
Fax: 949-222-6558
E-mail: essay@aynrand.org

BAPTIST JOINT COMMITTEE FOR RELIGIOUS LIBERTY

http://www.BJConline.org/

RELIGIOUS LIBERTY ESSAY SCHOLARSHIP CONTEST

To enter, students submit an essay based on the year's topic. All high school juniors and seniors are eligible, and they must have an essay adviser (a teacher or church staff member) to verify that the student's work is his or her own.

Award: Scholarship for use in freshman year; not renewable. *Number:* up to 3. *Amount:* $250–$2000.

Eligibility Requirements: Applicant must be high school student and planning to enroll or expecting to enroll full- or part-time at a two-year or four-year or technical institution or university. Available to U.S. citizens.

Application Requirements: Application form, entry in a contest, essay, essay adviser form. *Deadline:* March 1.

Contact: Cherilyn Crowe, Associate Director of Communications
  Phone: 202-544-4226
  Fax: 202-544-2094
  E-mail: ccrowe@BJConline.org

BARBIZON INTERNATIONAL LLC

http://www.barbizonscholarship.com/

BARBIZON COLLEGE TUITION SCHOLARSHIP

Scholarship for full college tuition is awarded every other year by random drawing. Entry forms are available at high schools throughout the United States. For more details, visit website at http://www.barbizonscholarship.com.

Award: Scholarship for use in freshman, sophomore, junior, or senior years; not renewable. *Number:* 1. *Amount:* up to $100,000.

Eligibility Requirements: Applicant must be enrolled or expecting to enroll full-time at a four-year institution or university. Available to U.S. citizens.

Application Requirements: Application form, entry in a contest. *Deadline:* December 1.

Contact: Wendy Cleveland, Vice President of Marketing
  Phone: 954-345-4140
  Fax: 954-345-8055
  E-mail: wendy@barbizonmodeling.com

BG SCHOLARSHIP.COM

http://www.bgscholarship.com

BG SCHOLARSHIP

The scholarship is available to students in currently enrolled in high school and in college. You must have a minimum 2.0 GPA to be eligible for this award and you must submit an essay about your academic goals and your contributions to your school and/or community. The essays are judged two ways: need-based - financial need of the student; and or merit-based - how the student has affected his/her community for the better.

Award: Scholarship for use in freshman, sophomore, junior, senior, graduate, or postgraduate years; not renewable. *Number:* 1–12. *Amount:* $300–$300.

Eligibility Requirements: Applicant must be enrolled or expecting to enroll full- or part-time at a two-year or four-year or technical institution or university. Available to U.S. and non-U.S. citizens.

Application Requirements: Application form, application form may be submitted online (http://www.bgscholarship.com/scholarship.html), essay. *Deadline:* continuous.

Contact: Virginia Pijlman, Founder, BG scholarship
  BG Scholarship.com
  2751 Cridge Street
  Riverside, CA 92507
  Phone: 949-547-9427
  Fax: 951-289-9905
  E-mail: virginiapijlman@bgscholarship.com

BRIDGESTONE FIRESTONE

http://www.bfor.com/

SAFETY SCHOLARS VIDEO CONTEST SCHOLARSHIP

Three $5000 college scholarships for the most compelling and effective videos that drive home life-saving messages on auto and tire safety. Must be between the ages of 16 and 21, possess a valid driver's license, and be enrolled as a full-time student in an accredited secondary, college level, or trade school.

Award: Scholarship for use in freshman, sophomore, junior, or senior years; not renewable. *Number:* 3. *Amount:* $10,000–$25,000.

Eligibility Requirements: Applicant must be age 16-21 and enrolled or expecting to enroll full-time at a four-year institution. Available to U.S. citizens.

Application Requirements: 25- or 55-second video about auto safety, entry in a contest. *Deadline:* June 22.

Contact: Miss. Ashley Charlton, Assistant Account Executive
  Bridgestone Firestone
  209 Seventh Avenue, North
  Nashville, TN 37219
  Phone: 615-780-3383
  E-mail: ashley.charlton@dvl.com

BRITISH COLUMBIA MINISTRY OF ADVANCED EDUCATION

http://www.studentaidbc.ca/

IRVING K. BARBER BRITISH COLUMBIA SCHOLARSHIP PROGRAM (FOR STUDY IN BRITISH COLUMBIA)

Scholarship to students who, after completing two years at a British Columbia public community college, university college or institute, must transfer to another public postsecondary institution in British Columbia to complete their degree. Students must demonstrate merit as well as exceptional involvement in their institution and community. Must have a GPA of at least 3.5. For more details, visit http://www.aved.gov.bc.ca/studentaidbc/specialprograms/irvingkbarber/bc_scholarship.htm.

Award: Scholarship for use in junior or senior years; not renewable. *Number:* up to 150. *Amount:* up to $5000.

Eligibility Requirements: Applicant must be enrolled or expecting to enroll full-time at a four-year institution or university and studying in British Columbia. Applicant must have 3.5 GPA or higher. Available to Canadian citizens.

Application Requirements: Application form, community service, essay, recommendations or references, test scores, transcript. *Deadline:* March 31.

Contact: Victoria Thibeau, Loan Remission and Management Unit
  Phone: 250-387-6100
  E-mail: victoria.thibeau@gov.bc.ca

BWDVM SCHOLARSHIP FOUNDATION

http://www.peacescholarships.org/

BARBARA WIEDNER AND DOROTHY VANDERCOOK MEMORIAL PEACE SCHOLARSHIP

Scholarships given to high school seniors or college freshmen with demonstrated leadership and personal initiative involving peace and social justice, nuclear disarmament issues, or conflict resolution. There are no GPA or age requirements, and students from any country may apply. Application and references required. Download application PDF from http://www.peacescholarships.org/ and follow the instructions for applying.

Award: Scholarship for use in freshman or sophomore years; not renewable. *Number:* 1–10. *Amount:* $250–$500.

Eligibility Requirements: Applicant must be enrolled or expecting to enroll full- or part-time at a two-year or four-year institution or university. Available to U.S. and non-U.S. citizens.

Application Requirements: Application form, essay, recommendations or references, self-addressed stamped envelope with application. *Deadline:* March 1.

Contact: Mrs. Leal Portis, President, BWDVM Scholarship Foundation
Phone: 530-265-3887
E-mail: portis.leal@gmail.com

CALIFORNIA INTERSCHOLASTIC FEDERATION

http://www.cifstate.org/

CIF/FARMERS SCHOLAR-ATHLETE OF THE YEAR

Honors one male and one female statewide and is based on excellence in athletics, academics and character. An additional male and female student-athlete from each CIF Section (20 section winners total) also will be recognized.

Award: Scholarship for use in freshman year. *Number:* 22. *Amount:* $2000–$5000.

Eligibility Requirements: Applicant must be high school student and planning to enroll or expecting to enroll at an institution or university. Applicant must have 3.5 GPA or higher. Available to U.S. citizens.

Application Requirements: *Deadline:* February 11.

CARPE DIEM FOUNDATION OF ILLINOIS

http://www.carpediemfoundation.org/

CARPE DIEM FOUNDATION OF ILLINOIS SCHOLARSHIP COMPETITION

The Carpe Diem Foundation of IL is not able to offer new scholarships for the Fall 2013 Term. We will continue to fully fund all scholarships that have previously been granted, pursuant to our existing criteria. We will re-evaluate whether we are in a position to fund new grants from time to time. Please check our website about 1/01/2014 to determine whether applications will be accepted for a 2014 scholarship competition. Renewable awards for U.S. citizens studying full-time at accredited U.S. educational institutions, including music conservatories, schools of design, and academies of the arts. For undergraduate study only. Merit based. Priority is given to students whose parents are or have been employed in education; local, state, or federal government; social service or public health; the administration of justice; or the fine arts.

Award: Scholarship for use in freshman, sophomore, junior, or senior years; not renewable. *Number:* 15–20. *Amount:* $1500–$2500.

Eligibility Requirements: Applicant must be enrolled or expecting to enroll full-time at a four-year institution or university. Available to U.S. citizens.

Application Requirements: Application form, community service, essay, portfolio, CD, website (if arts or music candidate), recommendations or references, self-addressed stamped envelope with application, test scores, transcript. *Fee:* $10.

Contact: Mr. Gordon Levine, Executive Director
Carpe Diem Foundation of Illinois
PO Box 3194A
Chicago, IL 60690-3194
E-mail: glevine@carpediemfoundation.org

CASUALTY ACTUARIES OF THE SOUTHEAST

http://www.casact.org/community/affiliates/case/

CASUALTY ACTUARIES OF THE SOUTHEAST SCHOLARSHIP PROGRAM

Scholarships available for undergraduate students in the southeastern states for the study of actuarial science. Must be studying in: Alabama, Arkansas, Florida, Georgia, Kentucky, Louisiana, Mississippi, North Carolina, South Carolina, Tennessee, or Virginia. Incoming freshmen/first-year students are not eligible for the scholarship.Demonstated strong interest in mathematics or mathematics-related field.High scholastic achievement.Applicants should demonstrate interest in the actuarial profession, mathematical aptitude and communication skills.

Award: Scholarship for use in sophomore, junior, or senior years; not renewable. *Number:* 2. *Amount:* $1500.

Eligibility Requirements: Applicant must be enrolled or expecting to enroll full-time at a four-year institution or university and studying in Alabama, Arkansas, Florida, Georgia, Kentucky, Louisiana, Mississippi, North Carolina, South Carolina, Tennessee, Virginia. Available to U.S. and Canadian citizens.

Application Requirements: Application form, essay, recommendations or references, transcript. *Deadline:* May 1.

Contact: Zachery Ziegler, Vice President of College Relations
Casualty Actuaries of the Southeast
4505 Country Club Road
Suite 200
Winston-Salem, NC 27104
Phone: 336-768-8217
Fax: 336-768-2185
E-mail: Zachery.Ziegler@FTIConsulting.com

CENTRAL NATIONAL BANK & TRUST COMPANY OF ENID TRUSTEE

http://www.onecentralsource.us

May T. HENRY SCHOLARSHIP FOUNDATION

A $1000 scholarship renewed annually for four years. Awarded to any student enrolled in an Oklahoma state-supported college, university or tech school. Based on need, scholastic performance and personal traits valued by May T. Henry. Minimum 3.0 GPA required.

Award: Scholarship for use in freshman, sophomore, junior, senior, graduate, or postgraduate years; renewable. *Amount:* $1000.

Eligibility Requirements: Applicant must be enrolled or expecting to enroll full-time at a two-year or four-year or technical institution or university and studying in Oklahoma. Applicant must have 3.0 GPA or higher. Available to U.S. and non-U.S. citizens.

Application Requirements: Application form, essay, financial need analysis, recommendations or references, test scores, transcript. *Deadline:* April 1.

CHURCH HILL CLASSICS

http://www.diplomaframe.com/

"FRAME MY FUTURE" SCHOLARSHIP CONTEST

Students submit an original creation within a digital image (ex. photo, collage, art piece, poem, etc.), that expresses what they hope to achieve in their personal and professional life after college. 24 Finalists will be selected by Church Hill Classics & the public will vote to select 5 $1,000 scholarship winners. The recipient with the most votes will also receive a bonus matching $1,000 donation for their college or university's scholarship endowment fund. Full scholarship details & rules are available at http://www.framemyfuture.com.

Award: Scholarship for use in freshman, sophomore, junior, senior, or graduate years; not renewable. *Number:* 6. *Amount:* $1000.

Eligibility Requirements: Applicant must be enrolled or expecting to enroll full-time at a two-year or four-year institution or university. Available to U.S. citizens.

Application Requirements: Application form may be submitted online (http://www.framemyfuture.com), submission of original creation in an image format. *Deadline:* March 6.

CIEE: COUNCIL ON INTERNATIONAL EDUCATIONAL EXCHANGE

http://www.ciee.org/

JOHN E. BOWMAN TRAVEL GRANT

The applicant must attend a CIEE Member or CIEE Academic Consortium member institution, and must have applied and been accepted to study at a CIEE Study Center in a non-traditional destination. Regions currently eligible include: Africa, Asia, Eastern Europe, and Latin America. Recipients receive awards to be used as partial reimbursement for travel costs to program destination. Deadlines: April 1 and November 1. Students may ONLY apply for this award as part of their CIEE Study Abroad on-line program application. Written/mailed applications are not accepted.

Award: Grant for use in freshman, sophomore, junior, or senior years; not renewable. *Number:* 50–60. *Amount:* $1000–$1000.

Eligibility Requirements: Applicant must be enrolled or expecting to enroll full-time at a two-year or four-year institution or university. Available to U.S. and non-U.S. citizens.

Application Requirements: Application form, application form may be submitted online (http://www.ciee.org), CIEE Study Abroad program application, essay, financial need analysis, personal photograph, recommendations or references, transcript. *Deadline:* varies.

CLARICODE

http://www.claricode.com/

CLARICODE MEDICAL SOFTWARE SCHOLARSHIP ESSAY

One awards of $1250 available to full-time undergraduate or graduate students attending a U.S. accredited college or university. Must be at least 18 years old at time of entry and submit a 500 to 1000-word essay on the topic chosen by Claricode (and listed on the website). All majors/concentrations are welcome to apply. For additional information visit website http://www.claricode.com/scholarship.

Award: Scholarship for use in freshman, sophomore, junior, senior, graduate, or postgraduate years; not renewable. *Number:* 1. *Amount:* $1250–$1250.

Eligibility Requirements: Applicant must be enrolled or expecting to enroll full-time at a two-year or four-year or technical institution or university. Available to U.S. citizens.

Application Requirements: Application form, application form may be submitted online (http://www.claricode.com/scholarship/), essay. *Deadline:* October 31.

COCA-COLA SCHOLARS FOUNDATION INC.

http://www.coca-colascholars.org/

COCA-COLA SCHOLARS PROGRAM

Renewable scholarship for graduating high school seniors enrolled either full-time or part-time in accredited colleges or universities. Minimum 3.0 GPA required. 252 awards are granted annually.

Award: Scholarship for use in freshman, sophomore, junior, senior, or graduate years; renewable. *Number:* 250. *Amount:* $10,000–$20,000.

Eligibility Requirements: Applicant must be high school student and planning to enroll or expecting to enroll full- or part-time at a two-year or four-year or technical institution or university. Applicant must have 3.0 GPA or higher. Available to U.S. citizens.

Application Requirements: Application form, application form may be submitted online (http://www.coca-colascholars.org), community service, essay, interview, recommendations or references, test scores, transcript. *Deadline:* October 31.

Contact: Mark Davis, President
Coca-Cola Scholars Foundation Inc.
PO Box 442
Atlanta, GA 30301-0442
Phone: 800-306-2653
Fax: 404-733-5439
E-mail: scholars@na.ko.com

CODA INTERNATIONAL

http://coda-international.org/blog/

MILLIE BROTHER SCHOLARSHIP FOR CHILDREN OF DEAF ADULTS

Scholarship awarded to any higher education student who is the hearing child of deaf parents. One-time award based on transcripts, letters of reference, and an essay.

Award: Scholarship for use in freshman, sophomore, junior, senior, or graduate years; not renewable. *Number:* 2–5. *Amount:* $1000–$3000.

Eligibility Requirements: Applicant must be enrolled or expecting to enroll full- or part-time at a two-year or four-year institution or university. Available to U.S. and non-U.S. citizens.

Application Requirements: Application form, application form may be submitted online (http://coda-international.org/blog/scholarship/), essay, letter of agreement to publish essay, recommendations or references, transcript. *Deadline:* April 4.

Contact: Dr. Jennie Pyers, Chair, CODA Scholarship Committee
CODA International
Wellesley College, 106 Central Street
Wellesley, MA 02481
Phone: 413-650-2632
Fax: 781-283-3730
E-mail: coda.scholarship@gmail.com

COLLEGE IN COLORADO

http://www.collegeincolorado.org/

GET SCHOOLED! SCHOLARSHIP

Entrants must be legal residents of the United States and a student between the ages of 13-18 residing in Colorado. Residency is subject to verification under Colorado law. One entry per student. Amount ranges from $400 to $850.

Award: Scholarship for use in freshman year; not renewable. *Amount:* $400–$850.

Eligibility Requirements: Applicant must be age 13-18 and enrolled or expecting to enroll full- or part-time at a four-year institution or university. Available to U.S. citizens.

Application Requirements: Application form, essay. *Deadline:* varies.

COLLEGE INSIDER RESOURCES

http://www.ezcir.com/

COLLEGE INSIDER RADIO SCHOLARSHIP

Scholarship for both high school and college students in the U.S. as well as international students. High school students must have a 2.0 GPA, and college students must have 2.5 GPA. This is a need/merit based scholarship awarded monthly.

Award: Scholarship for use in freshman, sophomore, junior, senior, graduate, or postgraduate years; renewable. *Number:* 1–3. *Amount:* $500–$1000.

Eligibility Requirements: Applicant must be enrolled or expecting to enroll full-time at a two-year or four-year institution or university. Available to U.S. and non-U.S. citizens.

Application Requirements: Application form, community service, essay, financial need analysis. *Deadline:* continuous.

Contact: Mr. Cliff deQuilettes, CEO
Phone: 406-670-3866
E-mail: cliff@ezcir.com

COLLEGE INSIDER SCHOLARSHIP PROGRAM

Scholarship offered to undergraduate students with a minimum GPA of 2.5. International students attending college in the United States are also eligible. Refer to website for additional information, http://www.ezcir.com/college_request.asp.

Award: Scholarship for use in freshman, sophomore, junior, or senior years; renewable. *Number:* 1. *Amount:* $1000.

Eligibility Requirements: Applicant must be enrolled or expecting to enroll full-time at a two-year or four-year or technical institution or university. Available to U.S. and non-U.S. citizens.

Application Requirements: Application form. *Deadline:* varies.

Contact: Mr. Cliff deQuilettes, CEO
Phone: 406-652-8900
E-mail: cliff@ezcir.com

COLLEGE JUMPSTART SCHOLARSHIP FUND

http://www.jumpstart-scholarship.net

COLLEGE JUMPSTART SCHOLARSHIP

Annual, merit-based competition (financial need is not considered) that is open to 10th-12th graders, college students, and non-traditional students. Must be committed to going to school and able to express your goals for getting a higher education.

Award: Scholarship for use in freshman, sophomore, junior, senior, or graduate years; not renewable. *Number:* 6. *Amount:* $750–$1500.

Eligibility Requirements: Applicant must be high school student and planning to enroll or expecting to enroll full- or part-time at a two-year or four-year or technical institution or university. Available to U.S. citizens.

Application Requirements: Application form, application form may be submitted online (http://www.jumpstart-scholarship.net/application-us), essay. *Deadline:* October 17.

COLLEGE PROWLER INC.

http://www.collegeprowler.com/

$2,000 "NO ESSAY" SCHOLARSHIP

We know you're busy and we know that times are tough. That's why we decided to create the easiest possible scholarship to give something back to students. Students can use the money to help cover tuition, housing, meal plans, books, computers, or any education-related expenses.

Award: Scholarship for use in freshman, sophomore, junior, senior, graduate, or postgraduate years; not renewable. *Number:* 12. *Amount:* $2000.

Eligibility Requirements: Applicant must be enrolled or expecting to enroll full- or part-time at a two-year or four-year or technical institution or university. Available to U.S. citizens.

Application Requirements: Application form. *Deadline:* continuous.

Contact: Omid Gahari, Chief Operating Officer
College Prowler Inc.
5830 Ellsworth Avenue
Suite 101
Pittsburgh, PA 15232
Phone: 800-290-2682
Fax: 412-361-5086
E-mail: scholarship@collegeprowler.com

COLLEGETOOLKIT.COM

http://www.collegetoolkit.com/

COLLEGE TOOLKIT SCHOLARSHIP CONTEST FOR COLLEGE STUDENTS

College Toolkit is giving away a $1000 scholarship to a college student. We want you to hear your thoughts about the college you attend. The award is open to anyone who will be an undergraduate college student this upcoming fall. You must be attending an accredited 2-year or 4-year college and a U.S. resident to enter.

Award: Scholarship for use in sophomore, junior, or senior years; not renewable. *Number:* 1. *Amount:* $1000.

Eligibility Requirements: Applicant must be enrolled or expecting to enroll full- or part-time at a two-year or four-year institution or university. Available to U.S. citizens.

Application Requirements: Application form. *Deadline:* September 30.

COLLEGE TOOLKIT SCHOLARSHIP CONTEST FOR HIGH SCHOOL STUDENTS

College Toolkit is giving away a $1000 scholarship to a high school student. We want you to share with us what colleges you are most interested in. The award is open to anyone who will be a high school student this upcoming fall. You must be 14 years of age or older and a U.S. resident to enter.

Award: Scholarship for use in freshman year; not renewable. *Number:* 1. *Amount:* $1000.

Eligibility Requirements: Applicant must be high school student and planning to enroll or expecting to enroll full- or part-time at a two-year or four-year institution. Available to U.S. citizens.

Application Requirements: Application form.

COMMON KNOWLEDGE SCHOLARSHIP FOUNDATION

http://www.cksf.org/

COMMON KNOWLEDGE SCHOLARSHIPS

The Common Knowledge Scholarship Foundation awards scholarships to students who score the highest on internet-based quizzes. Winners are determined by time and accuracy while taking the quizzes with no essays required. Register once at http://www.cksf.org and all of the scholarship quizzes for which you are eligible will appear in y our account. A student may use the same CKSF account from 9th grade through graduate school.

Award: Scholarship for use in freshman, sophomore, junior, senior, graduate, or postgraduate years; not renewable. *Number:* 20–50. *Amount:* $250–$1000.

Eligibility Requirements: Applicant must be enrolled or expecting to enroll full- or part-time at a two-year or four-year or technical institution or university. Available to U.S. and non-U.S. citizens.

Application Requirements: Application form may be submitted online (http://www.cksf.org), CKSF account and online quizzes, entry in a contest. *Deadline:* continuous.

Contact: Mr. Daryl Hulce, President
Phone: 954-262-8553
E-mail: Daryl.hulce@cksf.org

THE COMMUNITY FOUNDATION FOR GREATER ATLANTA, INC.

http://cfgreateratlanta.org/

DREAMS SQUARED SCHOLARSHIP

Scholarship designed to provide scholarship opportunities for deserving students who want to pursue their education. Minimum 2.0 GPA, maximum 3.0 GPA required. For complete eligibility requirements or to submit an application, please visit http://www.cfgreateratlanta.org.

Award: Scholarship for use in freshman, sophomore, junior, or senior years; not renewable. *Number:* up to 6. *Amount:* $2000.

Eligibility Requirements: Applicant must be enrolled or expecting to enroll full-time at a two-year or four-year or technical institution or university. Available to U.S. citizens.

Application Requirements: Application form, application form may be submitted online (http://www.cfgreateratlanta.org/Grants-Support/Scholarships.aspx), community service, driver's license, essay, financial need analysis, recommendations or references, transcript. *Deadline:* March 1.

Contact: Kristina Morris, Program Associate
The Community Foundation for Greater Atlanta, Inc.
50 Hurt Plaza
Suite 449
Atlanta, GA 30303
Phone: 404-688-5525
E-mail: scholarships@cfgreateratlanta.org

CONGRESSIONAL BLACK CAUCUS FOUNDATION, INC.

http://www.cbcfinc.org/

CONGRESSIONAL BLACK CAUCUS SPOUSES EDUCATION SCHOLARSHIP

Program that awards scholarships to academically talented and highly motivated students who intend to pursue full-time undergraduate, graduate, or doctoral degrees. Awards are made to students who reside or attend school in a congressional district represented by a member of the Congressional Black Caucus. Minimum 2.5 GPA required.

Award: Scholarship for use in freshman, sophomore, junior, senior, or graduate years; not renewable. *Number:* 250–400. *Amount:* $500–$5000.

Eligibility Requirements: Applicant must be enrolled or expecting to enroll full-time at a two-year or four-year or technical institution or university. Applicant must have 2.5 GPA or higher. Available to U.S. citizens.

Application Requirements: Application form, application form may be submitted online (http://www.cbcfinc.org/scholarships), essay, financial need analysis, personal photograph, recommendations or references, resume, transcript. *Deadline:* May 31.

Contact: Ms. Janet Carter, Program Administrator
Congressional Black Caucus Foundation, Inc.
1720 Massachusetts Avenue, NW
Washington, DC 20036
Phone: 202-263-2800
Fax: 202-263-0845
E-mail: scholarships@cbcfinc.org

COURAGE TO GROW SCHOLARSHIP PROGRAM

http://couragetogrowscholarship.com/

COURAGE TO GROW SCHOLARSHIP

High school seniors or college students with a minimum GPA of 2.5 or better are eligible. U.S. citizens only please. An essay of 250 words or less is required. One award of $500 will be given out per month. Applicants can reapply each month throughout the year.

Award: Scholarship for use in freshman, sophomore, junior, senior, graduate, or postgraduate years; not renewable. *Number:* 1–12. *Amount:* up to $500.

Eligibility Requirements: Applicant must be enrolled or expecting to enroll full- or part-time at a two-year or four-year or technical institution or university. Applicant must have 2.5 GPA or higher. Available to U.S. citizens.

Application Requirements: Application form, application form may be submitted online (http://www.couragetogrowscholarship.com), essay. *Deadline:* continuous.

Contact: Kimberly Johnson, Founder
Courage to Grow Scholarship Program
PO Box 2507
Chelan, WA 98816
Phone: 509-731-3056
E-mail: support@couragetogrowscholarship.com

THE DALLAS FOUNDATION

http://www.dallasfoundation.org/

BROOK HOLLOW GOLF CLUB SCHOLARSHIP

Established in 2007 to benefit children or grandchildren of full- or part-time employees of Brook Hollow Golf Club. Applicants must be a child or grandchild of an active employee in good standing of Brook Hollow Golf Club and a graduating high school senior who has been accepted in, or a student already enrolled in, an undergraduate program of study in pursuit of a degree from a public or private, regionally accredited community college, college, university, or vocational or trade institute. Applicants must demonstrate financial need.

Award: Scholarship for use in freshman or sophomore years; renewable. *Amount:* $2000–$4500.

Eligibility Requirements: Applicant must be high school student and planning to enroll or expecting to enroll full-time at a two-year or four-year or technical institution or university.

Application Requirements: Application form, financial need analysis, transcript. *Deadline:* April 1.

Contact: Rachel Lasseter, Program Associate
Phone: 214-741-9898
E-mail: scholarships@dallasfoundation.org

THE HIRSCH FAMILY SCHOLARSHIP

The Hirsch Family Scholarship was established as a scholarship fund in 2009 to benefit dependent children of active employees of Eagle Materials, Performance Chemicals and Ingredients, Martin Fletcher, Hadlock Plastics, Highlander Partners and any of their majority-owned subsidiaries.

Award: Scholarship for use in freshman, sophomore, junior, or senior years; not renewable. *Amount:* $2000–$10,000.

Eligibility Requirements: Applicant must be enrolled or expecting to enroll full-time at a two-year or four-year or technical institution or university.

Application Requirements: Application form, transcript. *Deadline:* March 15.

Contact: Rachel Lasseter, Program Associate
Phone: 214-741-9898
E-mail: scholarships@dallasfoundation.org

KRISTOPHER KASPER MEMORIAL SCHOLARSHIP

Award for a child of a Centex Homes Texas Region employee. Based on the eligibility criteria, one scholarship of at least $1000 will be awarded annually. The scholarship may be used for tuition, fees, or books, and will be paid directly to the school. There will be an opportunity for renewal if renewal requirements are met.

Award: Scholarship for use in freshman, sophomore, junior, or senior years; renewable. *Number:* 1. *Amount:* $1000.

Eligibility Requirements: Applicant must be high school student and planning to enroll or expecting to enroll full-time at a two-year or four-year or technical institution or university. Applicant must have 2.5 GPA or higher.

Application Requirements: Application form, community service, recommendations or references, resume, transcript. *Deadline:* April 15.

Contact: Rachel Lasseter, Program Associate
Phone: 214-741-9898
E-mail: scholarships@dallasfoundation.org

THE DAVID & DOVETTA WILSON SCHOLARSHIP FUND

http://www.wilsonfund.org/

THE DAVID & DOVETTA WILSON SCHOLARSHIP FUND

The purpose of The David and Dovetta Wilson Scholarship Fund (DDWSF) is to provide deserving high school seniors across the nation with financial assistance to pursue their academic goals.

Award: Scholarship for use in freshman year; not renewable. *Number:* up to 9. *Amount:* $300–$1000.

Eligibility Requirements: Applicant must be high school student and planning to enroll or expecting to enroll full-time at a two-year or four-year institution or university. Available to U.S. citizens.

Application Requirements: Application form, community service, financial need analysis, recommendations or references, religious involvement, transcript. *Fee:* $20. *Deadline:* March 31.

Contact: Timothy Wilson, Treasurer
The David & Dovetta Wilson Scholarship Fund
115-67 237th Street
Elmont, NY 11003
Phone: 516-643-5762
E-mail: ddwsf4@aol.com

DELETE CYBERBULLYING

http://www.deletecyberbullying.org

DELETE CYBERBULLYING SCHOLARSHIP

Two $1500 scholarship available for undergraduate and graduate students. Must submit an essay on one of these two topics: 1. "Why is it important to work to delete cyberbullying?" Essay topic option 2: "How has cyberbullying personally affected you?" Application only available online.

Award: Scholarship for use in freshman, sophomore, junior, senior, or graduate years; not renewable. *Number:* 2. *Amount:* $1500.

Eligibility Requirements: Applicant must be enrolled or expecting to enroll full- or part-time at a two-year or four-year or technical institution or university. Available to U.S. citizens.

Application Requirements: Application form, application form may be submitted online (http://www.deletecyberbullying.org/scholarship), essay. *Deadline:* June 30.

DEVRY, INC.

http://www.devry.edu/

DEVRY DEAN'S SCHOLARSHIPS

Awards to high school seniors or GED recipients who have SAT scores of 1100 or higher, or ACT scores of 24 or higher; Canada-Composite CPT of 430 or higher for Canadians. There is no separate scholarship application.

Award: Scholarship for use in freshman year; renewable. *Amount:* $1500–$13,500.

Eligibility Requirements: Applicant must be high school student and planning to enroll or expecting to enroll full-time at a four-year institution or university. Available to U.S. and Canadian citizens.

Application Requirements: Application form, interview, test scores, transcript. *Deadline:* varies.

Contact: Thonie Simpson, National High School Program Manager
Phone: 630-706-3122
E-mail: scholarships@devry.edu

DEVRY HIGH SCHOOL SCHOLARSHIP

Award to high school graduates. Amount of $1000 per semester to students, valued up to $9000. Must be in top 50 percent of class or have a GPA of 2.7. Nominations must be received by July 1 and students have one year from high school graduation to apply and start.

Award: Scholarship for use in freshman year; renewable. *Amount:* $2000–$9000.

Eligibility Requirements: Applicant must be high school student and planning to enroll or expecting to enroll full-time at an institution or university. Available to U.S. and Canadian citizens.

Application Requirements: Application form, interview, recommendations or references, test scores, transcript. *Deadline:* July 1.

Contact: Thonie Simpson, National High School Program Manager
Phone: 630-706-3122
E-mail: scholarships@devry.edu

DIRECTTEXTBOOK.COM

http://www.DirectTextbook.com

2013 SCHOLARSHIP ESSAY CONTEST

Non-renewable essay contest. Awards are $2500 for first place, $1000 for second place, and $250 for third place. Must complete a 500-word essay that answers a specific question given on the application. Open to current U.S. citizens, enrolled in an accredited 2- or 4-year college or university for fall of 2012, and have a most recent GPA of 2.0 or higher. Applicant must not be currently incarcerated. Applications are accepted only through the online form and will not be accepted after final deadline.

Award: Prize for use in freshman, sophomore, junior, or senior years; not renewable. *Number:* 3. *Amount:* $250–$2500.

Eligibility Requirements: Applicant must be enrolled or expecting to enroll full-time at a two-year or four-year institution or university. Available to U.S. citizens.

Application Requirements: Application form may be submitted online (http://www.directtextbook.com/scholarship.php), entry in a contest, essay. *Deadline:* continuous.

Contact: Megan Lindgren, Controller
DirectTextbook.com
1525 Chemeketa Street, NE
Salem, OR 97301
Phone: 503-779-4056
Fax: 503-210-0716
E-mail: megan@directtextbook.com

E-COLLEGEDEGREE.COM

http://www.e-collegedegree.com/

E-COLLEGEDEGREE.COM ONLINE EDUCATION SCHOLARSHIP AWARD

The award is to be used for online education. Application must be submitted online. Visit website for more information and application, http://www.e-collegedegree.com.

Award: Scholarship for use in freshman, sophomore, junior, senior, graduate, or postgraduate years; renewable. *Number:* 1. *Amount:* $1000.

Eligibility Requirements: Applicant must be enrolled or expecting to enroll full- or part-time at a two-year or four-year or technical institution or university. Available to U.S. citizens.

Application Requirements: Application form, entry in a contest, essay. *Deadline:* December 31.

Contact: Chris Lee, Site Manager
e-CollegeDegree.com
9109 West 101st Terrace
Overland Park, KS 66212
Phone: 913-341-6949
E-mail: scholarship@e-collegedegree.com

EXECUTIVE WOMEN INTERNATIONAL

http://www.ewiconnect.com/

ADULT STUDENTS IN SCHOLASTIC TRANSITION

Scholarship for adult students at transitional points in their lives. Applicants may be single parents, individuals just entering the workforce, or displaced homemakers. Applications are available on the organization's website, http://www.ewiconnect.com.

Award: Scholarship for use in freshman, sophomore, junior, or senior years; not renewable. *Number:* 100–150. *Amount:* $250–$2500.

Eligibility Requirements: Applicant must be enrolled or expecting to enroll full-time at a two-year or four-year or technical institution or university. Available to U.S. and non-U.S. citizens.

Application Requirements: Application form, essay, financial need analysis, interview, personal photograph, recommendations or references, self-addressed stamped envelope with application, tax information, transcript.

EXECUTIVE WOMEN INTERNATIONAL SCHOLARSHIP PROGRAM

Competitive award to high school juniors planning careers in any business or professional field of study which requires a four-year college degree. Award is renewable based on continuing eligibility. All awards are given through local Chapters of the EWI. Applicant must apply through nearest Chapter and live within the Chapter's boundaries. Student must have a sponsoring teacher and school to be considered, and only one applicant per school. For more details visit http://www.ewiconnect.com.

Award: Scholarship for use in freshman, sophomore, junior, or senior years; renewable. *Number:* 75–100. *Amount:* $1000–$10,000.

Eligibility Requirements: Applicant must be high school student; age 15–17 and planning to enroll or expecting to enroll full-time at a four-year institution or university. Available to U.S. and non-U.S. citizens.

Application Requirements: Application form, community service, essay, interview, personal photograph, recommendations or references, self-addressed stamped envelope with application, transcript.

Contact: Mr. James Pollan, Executive Director and Trustee
E-mail: stuhrstudents@earthlink.net

FEDERAL EMPLOYEE EDUCATION AND ASSISTANCE FUND

http://www.feea.org/

FEDERAL EMPLOYEE EDUCATION AND ASSISTANCE FUND SCHOLARSHIP PROGRAM

The FEEA Scholarship Program is for current civilian federal employees and their dependent family members (spouse/child). The applicant or the applicant's sponsoring federal employee must have at least three (3) years of civilian federal service by August 31. The applicant must be at least a college freshman by the fall semester. All applicants must have at least a 3.0 cumulative grade point average (CGPA) unweighted on a 4.0 scale. Current college freshman must have a minimum 3.0 GPA for the fall semester. All applicants must be current high school seniors or college students working towards an accredited degree or enrolled in a two- or four-year undergraduate, graduate or postgraduate program.

Award: Scholarship for use in freshman, sophomore, junior, senior, graduate, or postgraduate years; not renewable. *Number:* 350–450. *Amount:* $500–$2000.

Eligibility Requirements: Applicant must be enrolled or expecting to enroll full- or part-time at a two-year or four-year institution or university. Applicant must have 3.0 GPA or higher. Available to U.S. citizens.

Application Requirements: Application form, community service, essay, recommendations or references, self-addressed stamped envelope with application, transcript. *Deadline:* March 28.

Contact: Niki Gleason, Office Manager/Scholarship Coordinator
Phone: 303-933-7580
E-mail: ngleason@feea.org

NATIONAL ACTIVE AND RETIRED FEDERAL EMPLOYEE SCHOLARSHIP PROGRAM

Children, grandchildren, great-grandchildren and step-children of all current NARFE members are eligible. Applicant must be a high school senior planning to attend college full time in the fall of the application year. Must have a GPA of at least 3.0 on an unweighted 4.0 scale.

Award: Scholarship for use in freshman year; not renewable. *Number:* 60. *Amount:* $1000.

Eligibility Requirements: Applicant must be high school student and planning to enroll or expecting to enroll full-time at a two-year or four-year institution or university. Applicant must have 3.0 GPA or higher. Available to U.S. citizens.

Application Requirements: Application form, community service, essay, recommendations or references, self-addressed stamped envelope with application, test scores, transcript. *Deadline:* April 30.

Contact: Niki Gleason, Office Manager/Scholarship Coordinator
Phone: 303-933-7580
E-mail: ngleason@feea.org

FEDERATION OF AMERICAN CONSUMERS AND TRAVELERS

http://www.usafact.org/

FEDERATION OF AMERICAN CONSUMERS AND TRAVELERS IN-SCHOOL SCHOLARSHIP

FACT scholarships are offered in four categories for current high school seniors, persons who graduated from high school, four or more years ago and now plan to go to a university or college, for students currently enrolled in a college or university, and for trade or technical school aspirants. Scholarships range in amount from $2500 to $10,000. Members of FACT, their children and grandchildren are eligible to apply.

Award: Scholarship for use in freshman, sophomore, junior, or senior years; not renewable. *Number:* 2. *Amount:* $2500–$10,000.

Eligibility Requirements: Applicant must be enrolled or expecting to enroll full-time at a two-year or four-year institution or university. Available to U.S. citizens.

Application Requirements: Application form, essay, recommendations or references, resume, test scores, transcript. *Deadline:* January 15.

Contact: Vicki Rolens, Managing Director
Phone: 800-872-3228
E-mail: vrolens@usafact.org

FEDERATION OF AMERICAN CONSUMERS AND TRAVELERS SECOND CHANCE SCHOLARSHIP

FACT scholarships are offered in four categories: (1) for current high school seniors: (2) for persons who graduated from high school four or more years ago and now plan to go to a university or college; (3) for students currently enrolled in a college or university, and (4) for trade or technical school aspirants. Scholarships range in size from $2500 to $10,000. Members of FACT, their children and grandchildren are eligible to apply.

Award: Scholarship for use in freshman, sophomore, junior, or senior years; not renewable. *Number:* 2. *Amount:* $2500–$10,000.

Eligibility Requirements: Applicant must be enrolled or expecting to enroll full- or part-time at a two-year or four-year or technical institution or university. Available to U.S. citizens.

Application Requirements: Application form, community service, essay, recommendations or references, resume, test scores, transcript. *Deadline:* January 15.

Contact: Vicki Rolens, Managing Director
Federation of American Consumers and Travelers
PO Box 104
Edwardsville, IL 62025
Phone: 800-872-3228
Fax: 618-656-5369
E-mail: vrolens@usafact.org

FIRST COMMAND EDUCATIONAL FOUNDATION

http://www.fcef.com/

DONALDSON D. FRIZZELL SCHOLARSHIP

Scholarship awarded to students seeking associate, undergraduate, or graduate degrees. Also available to those seeking professional

certification or attending vocational school. Details announced in February of each year.

Award: Scholarship for use in freshman, sophomore, junior, senior, or graduate years; not renewable. *Number:* up to 6. *Amount:* $2500–$5000.

Eligibility Requirements: Applicant must be enrolled or expecting to enroll full-time at a four-year or technical institution or university. Available to U.S. and non-U.S. citizens.

Application Requirements: Application form, application form may be submitted online (http://www.fcef.com/direct-apply-scholarship.php), community service, essay, recommendations or references, resume, transcript. *Deadline:* March 31.

Contact: Sandra King, Scholarship Programs Manager
E-mail: Scholarships@fcef.com

FLORIDA STATE DEPARTMENT OF EDUCATION

http://www.floridastudentfinancialaid.org/

ROSEWOOD FAMILY SCHOLARSHIP FUND

Renewable award for eligible direct descendants of African-American Rosewood families affected by the incident of January 1923. Must not have previously received a baccalaureate degree. For more details, visit the website at http://www.FloridaStudentFinancialAid.org/SSFAD/home/uamain.htm.

Award: Scholarship for use in freshman, sophomore, junior, or senior years; renewable. *Number:* up to 25. *Amount:* up to $4000.

Eligibility Requirements: Applicant must be enrolled or expecting to enroll full-time at a two-year or four-year or technical institution or university and studying in Florida. Available to U.S. citizens.

Application Requirements: Application form, documentation of Rosewood ancestry, financial need analysis. *Deadline:* April 1.

THE FORD FAMILY FOUNDATION SCHOLARSHIP OFFICE

http://www.tfff.org

SCHOLARSHIP PROGRAM FOR SONS & DAUGHTERS OF EMPLOYEES OF ROSEBURG FOREST PRODUCTS CO.

Kenneth W. Ford and The Ford Family Foundation established the Ford Sons & Daughters Program to provide scholarships to sons and daughters of Roseburg Forest Products Co. employees as they pursue education beyond high school. Each year, up to 10% of all eligible applicants are selected to receive the Ford Sons & Daughters Scholarship. An applicant must be a dependent child or stepchild (age 21 or younger) of an employee of Roseburg Forest Products Co. The employee must be full time and have been employed by Roseburg Forest Products Co. for a minimum of 18 months as of March 1 of the application year.

Award: Scholarship for use in freshman, sophomore, junior, or senior years; renewable. *Number:* up to 100. *Amount:* $3000–$5000.

Eligibility Requirements: Applicant must be age 21 or under and enrolled or expecting to enroll full-time at a two-year or four-year institution or university. Available to U.S. citizens.

Application Requirements: Application form, application form may be submitted online (http://www.oregonstudentaid.gov), essay, interview, transcript. *Deadline:* March 1.

Contact: Tricia Tate, Scholarship Programs Manager
The Ford Family Foundation Scholarship Office
440 E Broadway, Suite 200
Eugene, OR 97401
Phone: 541-485-6211 Ext. 2513
Fax: 541-485-6223
E-mail: fordscholarships@tfff.org

FORECLOSURE.COM

http://www.foreclosure.com/

FORECLOSURE.COM SCHOLARSHIP PROGRAM

The Foreclosure.com Scholarship Program encourages students to offer innovative ideas and solutions to 'solve the foreclosure crisis' in the form of an essay. Essay submissions must be between 1000 and 2500 words and all accepted freshman and enrolled under-graduate and graduate-students are eligible to apply. First place prize is $5,000 and second through fifth place will be awarded $1,000 each. Checks will be made out to the college or university attended in the form of a non-renewable scholarship grant. The best five plans will be sent to Congress and to President Barack Obama.

Award: Grant for use in freshman, sophomore, junior, senior, graduate, or postgraduate years; not renewable. *Number:* 5. *Amount:* $1000–$5000.

Eligibility Requirements: Applicant must be enrolled or expecting to enroll full- or part-time at a two-year or four-year or technical institution or university. Available to U.S. citizens.

Application Requirements: Application form, entry in a contest, essay. *Deadline:* continuous.

Contact: Mrs. Linda Yates, Director of Education
  Phone: 561-988-9669 Ext. 7383
  E-mail: lyates@foreclosure.com

FOSTER CARE TO SUCCESS (FORMERLY ORPHAN FOUNDATION OF AMERICA)

http://www.fc2success.org/

FOSTER CARE TO SUCCESS/CASEY FAMILY SCHOLARS SCHOLARSHIP PROGRAM

Award of up to $6000 to young people under the age of 25 who spent the 12 consecutive months prior to their 18th birthday in foster care or who were adopted or placed into legal guardianship from foster care after their 16th birthday. Scholarships are awarded for the pursuit of postsecondary education, including vocational/technical training, and are renewable for up to five years based on satisfactory progress and financial need.

Award: Scholarship for use in freshman, sophomore, junior, or senior years; not renewable. *Number:* 100. *Amount:* $1000–$6000.

Eligibility Requirements: Applicant must be enrolled or expecting to enroll full- or part-time at a two-year or four-year or technical institution or university. Available to U.S. citizens.

Application Requirements: Application form, essay, financial need analysis, foster care verification, parent's death certificates, recommendations or references, transcript. *Deadline:* March 31.

Contact: Ms. Tina Raheem, Scholarship Director
  Phone: 571-203-0270 Ext. 102
  Fax: 571-203-0273
  E-mail: tinar@fc2success.org

FOUNDATION FOR INDEPENDENT HIGHER EDUCATION

http://www.fihe.org/

HSBC FIRST OPPORTUNITY PARTNERS SCHOLARSHIPS

Award targets the students with multiple at-risk factors as identified by financial aid officers in FIHE colleges. For undergraduate students with at least 2.4 GPA after the first semester of the freshman year. Deadline varies.

Award: Scholarship for use in sophomore or junior years; renewable. *Amount:* $5000.

Eligibility Requirements: Applicant must be enrolled or expecting to enroll full-time at a four-year institution or university. Available to U.S. citizens.

Application Requirements: Application form, essay, financial need analysis, transcript. *Deadline:* varies.

Contact: Ms. Jacalyn Cox, Program Manager
  E-mail: jcox@fihe.org

UPS SCHOLARSHIP PROGRAM

Scholarship program for undergraduate students attending FIHE-affiliated colleges. Deadline varies.

Award: Scholarship for use in freshman, sophomore, junior, or senior years; not renewable. *Amount:* $2700.

Eligibility Requirements: Applicant must be enrolled or expecting to enroll full- or part-time at a four-year institution or university. Available to U.S. and non-U.S. citizens.

Application Requirements: *Deadline:* varies.

Contact: Dr. Myrvin Christopherson, Acting President
  Phone: 202-367-0333
  E-mail: info@fihe.org

FOUNDATION FOR OUTDOOR ADVERTISING RESEARCH AND EDUCATION (FOARE)

http://www.oaaa.org/

FOARE SCHOLARSHIP PROGRAM

One-time award of $2000 for 6 students. High school seniors, undergraduates, and graduate students enrolled in or accepted to an accredited institution are eligible to apply. Selections are based on financial need, academic performance, and career goals.

Award: Scholarship for use in freshman, sophomore, junior, senior, or graduate years; not renewable. *Number:* 6. *Amount:* $2000.

Eligibility Requirements: Applicant must be enrolled or expecting to enroll full-time at a four-year institution or university. Available to U.S. citizens.

Application Requirements: Application form, essay, financial need analysis, transcript. *Deadline:* June 15.

THE FRANK M. AND GERTRUDE R. DOYLE FOUNDATION INC.

http://www.frankmdoyle.org/

THE FRANK M. AND GERTRUDE R. DOYLE FOUNDATION, INC.

Eligible applicants for this scholarship must be: Graduating seniors or graduates, (G.E.D. is acceptable), of the Huntington Beach Union High School District, Huntington Beach, California; Washoe County Unified High School District, Reno, Nevada; students or graduates of the Huntington Beach Adult High School; students or graduates of the Washoe County Adult High School; graduates or current/previous students of the following community colleges in Southern California: Orange Coast, Golden West, Coastline, Irvine Valley, Fullerton, Cypress, Santa Ana, Saddleback, or Santiago Canyon. Age is not a factor. Applications may be downloaded from the foundations website, http://www.frankmdoyle.org anytime after 1 December. See website for details.

Award: Scholarship for use in freshman, sophomore, junior, senior, graduate, or postgraduate years; not renewable. *Amount:* $500–$30,000.

Eligibility Requirements: Applicant must be age 17-99 and enrolled or expecting to enroll full- or part-time at a two-year or four-year or technical institution or university. Available to U.S. citizens.

Application Requirements: Application form, essay, recommendations or references, Student Aid Report (SAR), transcript. *Deadline:* March 1.

FREETESTPREP.COM

http://www.freetestprep.com

FREETESTPREP.COM SCHOLARSHIP CONTEST

Scholarship of up to $10,000 for undergraduate students. Students can submit the essay that got them in to the school they now attend; these essays are then shared with other students as examples. Freetestprep.com will have the right to publish them on their website.

Award: Scholarship for use in freshman, sophomore, junior, or senior years; not renewable. *Number:* 1. *Amount:* $1000–$10,000.

Eligibility Requirements: Applicant must be enrolled or expecting to enroll full-time at a four-year institution or university. Available to U.S. citizens.

Application Requirements: Application form may be submitted online (http://www.freetestprep.com), entry in a contest, essay. *Deadline:* July 1.

GEN AND KELLY TANABE FOUNDATION

http://www.gkscholarship.com/

GEN AND KELLY TANABE SCHOLARSHIP

The scholarship is open to 9th-12th grade high school students, college students, or graduate students who are legal residents of the U.S. Applicants may study any major and attend any college in the U.S. Only online applications are accepted.

Award: Scholarship for use in freshman, sophomore, junior, senior, or graduate years; not renewable. *Number:* 2–8. *Amount:* $1000–$1000.

Eligibility Requirements: Applicant must be enrolled or expecting to enroll full- or part-time at a two-year or four-year or technical institution or university. Available to U.S. citizens.

Application Requirements: Application form, application form may be submitted online (http://www.gkscholarship.com), essay. *Deadline:* July 31.

GEORGE T. WELCH TRUST

http://www.bakerboyer.com/

JOHN O. HENDRICKS MEMORIAL SCHOLARSHIP

Grants payable to students after completion of first quarter or semester. Must be enrolled full-time. Must maintain a minimum GPA of 2.0. Must reapply. The budget form must be completed and cover the entire school year.

Award: Scholarship for use in freshman, sophomore, junior, or senior years; not renewable.

Eligibility Requirements: Applicant must be enrolled or expecting to enroll full-time at a four-year institution or university. Available to U.S. citizens.

Application Requirements: Application form, responsibility shown in one or more of the following areas: community, school, home, church. *Deadline:* April 13.

Contact: Ted Cohan, Trust Portfolio Manager
    Phone: 509-526-1204
    Fax: 509-522-3136
    E-mail: cohant@bakerboyer.com

MILTON-FREEWATER AREA FOUNDATION SCHOLARSHIPS

Grants for all four years of undergraduate work. Entering freshman must maintain a GPA of 2.5, and all students must maintain a minimum GPA of 2.0. Must reapply. The budget form must be completed and cover the entire school year.

Award: Scholarship for use in freshman, sophomore, junior, senior, or graduate years; not renewable.

Eligibility Requirements: Applicant must be enrolled or expecting to enroll full-time at a two-year or four-year institution or university. Available to U.S. citizens.

Application Requirements: Application form. *Deadline:* April 13.

GERMAN ACADEMIC EXCHANGE SERVICE (DAAD)

http://www.daad.org/

DAAD GROUP STUDY VISITS

Grants are available for an information visit of seven to twelve days to groups of 10 to 15 students, accompanied by a faculty member. They are intended to encourage contact with academic institutions, groups and individuals in Germany, and offer insight into current issues in the academic, scientific, economic, political and cultural realms. All departments/disciplines are eligible, preference is given to groups with a homogeneous academic background and may be drawn from more than one institution. Applications must reach DAAD New York at least six months before the beginning date of the planned visit. DAAD awards a subsidy of €50 per participant per day, up to €9600 toward costs of room and board. Groups will not be eligible for funding in successive years.

Award: Grant for use in junior, senior, or graduate years; not renewable.

Eligibility Requirements: Applicant must be enrolled or expecting to enroll full-time at a four-year institution or university. Available to U.S. and non-U.S. citizens.

Application Requirements: Application form, application form may be submitted online (http://www.daad.org/?p=groupvisits). *Deadline:* varies.

Contact: Jane Fu, Information Officer
    Phone: 212-758-3223
    E-mail: daadny@daad.org

DAAD STUDY SCHOLARSHIP

Scholarship awarded for study at all public universities in Germany. Study scholarships are granted for one academic year (10 months) with the possibility of a one-year extension for students completing a full degree program in Germany. Scholarship award includes monthly stipend, health insurance, and some international travel reimbursement.

Award: Scholarship for use in senior, graduate, or postgraduate years; renewable.

Eligibility Requirements: Applicant must be enrolled or expecting to enroll full-time at a four-year institution or university. Available to U.S. and non-U.S. citizens.

Application Requirements: Application form, application form may be submitted online (http://daad.org/?p=gradstudy), proposal, DAAD German language certificate, recommendations or references, resume, transcript. *Deadline:* November 15.

Contact: Jane Fu, Information Officer
    Phone: 212-758-3223
    E-mail: daadny@daad.org

DAAD UNDERGRADUATE SCHOLARSHIP

Highly qualified undergraduate students are invited to apply for scholarships to fund study, senior thesis research and/or internships in Germany. Preference is given to students whose enroll independently at German universities or participate in a project or program based at and organized by a German university. Scholarships may also be applied toward participation in an organized study abroad program, such as study abroad semester or year. It must take place during the German academic year, from October to July, either one semester (four months) or an academic year (10 months) in duration. Award package includes a monthly stipend (~ €650/month), health insurance, and some reimbursement for international travel.

Award: Scholarship for use in sophomore or junior years; not renewable.

Eligibility Requirements: Applicant must be enrolled or expecting to enroll full-time at a four-year institution or university. Available to U.S. and non-U.S. citizens.

Application Requirements: Application form, application form may be submitted online (http://www.daad.org/?p=undergrad), recommendations or references, resume, transcript. *Deadline:* January 31.

Contact: Jane Fu, Information Officer
    Phone: 212-758-3223
    E-mail: daadny@daad.org

GETEDUCATED.COM

http://www.geteducated.com/

$1,000 EXCELLENCE IN ONLINE EDUCATION SCHOLARSHIP

Scholarships for distance education available only to U.S. citizens enrolled in a CHEA-accredited online degree program located in the USA with a minimum cumulative GPA of 3.0. Provide a copy of your most recent grade transcripts, completed application, a copy of your most recent FAFSA or 1040 tax return, and submit a 500-word essay: "What a College Degree Means to Me."

Award: Scholarship for use in freshman, sophomore, junior, senior, or graduate years; not renewable. *Number:* 3–7. *Amount:* $1000.

Eligibility Requirements: Applicant must be enrolled or expecting to enroll full- or part-time at a two-year or four-year institution or university. Applicant must have 3.0 GPA or higher. Available to U.S. citizens.

Application Requirements: Application form, essay, financial need analysis, transcript. *Deadline:* March 15.

GOLDEN KEY INTERNATIONAL HONOUR SOCIETY

http://www.goldenkey.org/

GOLDEN KEY SERVICE AWARD

One award totaling $500, disbursed as $250 to the recipient and $250 to the charity of the recipient's choice. Undergraduate and graduate members who were enrolled as students during the previous academic year are eligible.

Award: Scholarship for use in sophomore, junior, senior, or graduate years; not renewable. *Number:* 1. *Amount:* $500.

Eligibility Requirements: Applicant must be enrolled or expecting to enroll full- or part-time at a four-year institution or university. Available to Canadian and non-U.S. citizens.

Application Requirements: Application form, community service, cover page from the online registration, statement of project, essay, recommendations or references. *Deadline:* March 3.

Contact: Crystal Hunter, Program Manager
    Phone: 800-377-2401
    E-mail: awards@goldenkey.org

GUERNSEY-MUSKINGUM ELECTRIC COOPERATIVE INC.

http://www.gmenergy.com/

HIGH SCHOOL SENIOR SCHOLARSHIP

Two $1000 scholarships, two $500 scholarships, two $300 scholarships, and two $200 scholarships are available to a student graduating from high school whose parent or legal guardian receives electric service from Guernsey-Muskingum Electric Cooperative.

Award: Scholarship for use in freshman year; not renewable. *Number:* 8. *Amount:* $200–$1000.

Eligibility Requirements: Applicant must be high school student and planning to enroll or expecting to enroll full-time at a two-year or four-year institution or university. Applicant must have 3.0 GPA or higher. Available to U.S. citizens.

Application Requirements: Application form, interview, recommendations or references, transcript. *Deadline:* February 1.

Contact: Brian Bennett, Manager, Member Services
    Phone: 740-826-7661
    Fax: 740-826-7171
    E-mail: mailbox@gmenergy.com

HELPING HANDS FOUNDATION

http://www.helpinghandsbookscholarship.com/

HELPING HANDS BOOK SCHOLARSHIP PROGRAM

The grant assists students with the high cost of textbooks and study materials. Awards are open to individuals of ages 16 and up, planning to attend or currently attending a two- or four-year college or university or a technical/vocational institution. Application fee is $5. Scholarship value is from $100 to $1000. Deadline varies.

Award: Grant for use in freshman, sophomore, junior, senior, or graduate years; not renewable. *Number:* 20–50. *Amount:* $100–$1000.

Eligibility Requirements: Applicant must be enrolled or expecting to enroll full- or part-time at a two-year or four-year or technical institution or university. Available to U.S. and non-U.S. citizens.

Application Requirements: Application form, essay, self-addressed stamped envelope with application, transcript. *Fee:* $5. *Deadline:* varies.

HEMOPHILIA FEDERATION OF AMERICA

PARENT CONTINUING EDUCATION SCHOLARSHIP

Scholarship for a parent of a school-age child with a blood clotting disorder. For use in furthering the parent's own education. Previous scholarship recipients are encouraged to reapply.

Award: Scholarship for use in freshman or sophomore years; not renewable. *Number:* 2. *Amount:* $1500.

Eligibility Requirements: Applicant must be enrolled or expecting to enroll full- or part-time at a technical institution. Available to U.S. citizens.

Application Requirements: Application form, essay, financial need analysis, recommendations or references. *Deadline:* April 30.

Contact: Sandy Aultman, Scholarship Coordinator
    Hemophilia Federation of America
    1045 West Pinhook Road, Suite 101
    Lafayette, LA 70503
    Phone: 337-261-9787
    Fax: 337-261-1787

SIBLING CONTINUING EDUCATION SCHOLARSHIP

Scholarship for the sibling of a school-age child with a blood clotting disorder. For use in furthering the sibling's own education. Previous scholarship recipients may reapply.

Award: Scholarship for use in freshman year; not renewable. *Number:* 3. *Amount:* $1500.

Eligibility Requirements: Applicant must be high school student and planning to enroll or expecting to enroll full- or part-time at a four-year institution or university. Available to U.S. citizens.

Application Requirements: Application form, essay, financial need analysis, recommendations or references. *Deadline:* April 30.

HENKEL CONSUMER ADHESIVES INC.

http://www.ducktapeclub.com/

DUCK BRAND DUCT TAPE "STUCK AT PROM" SCHOLARSHIP CONTEST

Contest is open to residents of the United States and Canada. Must be 14 years or older. First place winners receive a $3000 college scholarship each and $3000 for the high school hosting the winning couple's prom. The second place winners will each receive a $2000 college scholarship, with the high school receiving $2000. The third place couple will each win a $1000 college scholarship and the high school will receive $1000.

Award: Prize for use in freshman, sophomore, junior, or senior years; not renewable. *Number:* 3. *Amount:* $1000–$3000.

Eligibility Requirements: Applicant must be enrolled or expecting to enroll full- or part-time at a two-year or four-year or technical institution or university. Available to U.S. and Canadian citizens.

Application Requirements: Application form, entry form, release form, entry in a contest, personal photograph. *Deadline:* June 11.

Contact: Michelle Heffner, Digital Marketing Communications
    Manager
    Henkel Consumer Adhesives Inc.
    32150 Just Imagine Drive
    Avon, OH 44011-1355
    Phone: 440-937-7000

HISPANIC ASSOCIATION OF COLLEGES AND UNIVERSITIES (HACU)

http://www.hacu.net/

HISPANIC ASSOCIATION OF COLLEGES AND UNIVERSITIES SCHOLARSHIP PROGRAMS

The scholarship programs are sponsored by corporate organizations. To be eligible, students must attend a HACU member college or university and meet all additional criteria. Visit website, http://www.hacu.net, for details.

Award: Scholarship for use in freshman, sophomore, junior, senior, or graduate years; not renewable. *Number:* up to 200. *Amount:* up to $2000.

Eligibility Requirements: Applicant must be enrolled or expecting to enroll full- or part-time at a two-year or four-year institution or university. Applicant must have 3.0 GPA or higher. Available to U.S. citizens.

Application Requirements: Application form, enrollment certification form, essay, financial need analysis, resume, transcript. *Deadline:* May 27.

HONOR SOCIETY OF PHI KAPPA PHI

http://www.PhiKappaPhi.org/

STUDY ABROAD GRANT COMPETITION

Grants up to $1000 awarded to undergraduates as support for seeking knowledge and experience by studying abroad. Must have 3.75+ cumulative GPA and attend a school with an Active Phi Kappa Phi chapter. Travel cannot begin prior to May 1.

Award: Grant for use in freshman, sophomore, junior, or senior years; not renewable. *Number:* 50. *Amount:* $1000.

Eligibility Requirements: Applicant must be enrolled or expecting to enroll full-time at a four-year institution or university. Available to U.S. and non-U.S. citizens.

Application Requirements: Application form, community service, essay, letter of acceptance into a study abroad program, recommendations or references, transcript. *Deadline:* April 1.

Contact: Mrs. Maria Davis, Awards and Benefits Manager
Honor Society of Phi Kappa Phi
7576 Goodwood Boulevard
Baton Rouge, LA 70806
Phone: 225-388-4917 Ext. 35
Fax: 225-388-4900
E-mail: mdavis@phikappaphi.org

HORATIO ALGER ASSOCIATION OF DISTINGUISHED AMERICANS, INC.

http://www.horatioalger.org

HORATIO ALGER ASSOCIATION SCHOLARSHIP PROGRAMS

The Association provides financial assistance to high school seniors (U.S citizens only) who have faced adversity, have financial need, and are pursuing higher education. Recipients must pursue a bachelor's degree however they may start their studies at a 2 year school and then transfer to a 4 year university. Minimum 2.0 GPA required.

Award: Scholarship for use in freshman, sophomore, junior, or senior years; renewable. *Number:* 965. *Amount:* $5000–$20,000.

Eligibility Requirements: Applicant must be high school student and planning to enroll or expecting to enroll full-time at a four-year institution or university. Available to U.S. and Canadian citizens.

Application Requirements: Application form, application form may be submitted online (https://www.horatioalger.org/scholarships/apply.cfm), essay, financial need analysis, recommendations or references, test scores, transcript. *Deadline:* October 25.

Contact: Ms. Lindsay Paul, Educational Programs Coordinator
Horatio Alger Association of Distinguished Americans, Inc.
99 Canal Center Plaza, Suite 320
Alexandria, VA 22314
Phone: 703-684-9444
Fax: 703-684-9445
E-mail: lpaul@horatioalger.com

HUMANA FOUNDATION

http://www.humanafoundation.org/

HUMANA FOUNDATION SCHOLARSHIP PROGRAM

Applicants must be under 25 years of age and a United States citizen. Must be a dependent of a Humana Inc. employee. For more information, visit website http://www.humanafoundation.org.

Award: Scholarship for use in freshman, sophomore, junior, or senior years; renewable. *Number:* up to 75. *Amount:* $1500–$3000.

Eligibility Requirements: Applicant must be enrolled or expecting to enroll full-time at a two-year or four-year institution or university. Available to U.S. citizens.

Application Requirements: Application form, recommendations or references, transcript. *Deadline:* January 15.

Contact: Charles Jackson, Program Manager
Humana Foundation
500 West Main Street, Room 208
Louisville, KY 40202
Phone: 502-580-1245
Fax: 502-580-1256
E-mail: cjackson@humana.com

ILLINOIS STUDENT ASSISTANCE COMMISSION (ISAC)

http://www.collegezone.org/

ILLINOIS COLLEGE SAVINGS BOND BONUS INCENTIVE GRANT PROGRAM

Program offers Illinois college savings bond holders a grant for each year of bond maturity payable upon bond redemption if at least 70 percent of proceeds are used to attend college in Illinois. The amount of grant will depend on the amount of the bond, ranging from a $40 to $440 grant per $5000 of the bond. Applications are accepted between August 1 and May 30 of the academic year in which the bonds matured, or in the academic year immediately following maturity.

Award: Grant for use in freshman, sophomore, junior, senior, graduate, or postgraduate years; not renewable.

Eligibility Requirements: Applicant must be enrolled or expecting to enroll full- or part-time at a two-year or four-year or technical institution or university and studying in Illinois. Available to U.S. citizens.

Application Requirements: Application form. *Deadline:* varies.

IMAGINE AMERICA FOUNDATION

http://www.imagine-america.org

ADULT SKILLS EDUCATION PROGRAM (ASEP)

The Adult Skills Education Program (ASEP) offers scholarships to non-traditional students who decide to pursue career college training. This $1000 award is available to any qualified adult student for attendance at a participating career college.

Award: Scholarship for use in freshman, sophomore, junior, or senior years; not renewable. *Number:* up to 10,000. *Amount:* $1000.

Eligibility Requirements: Applicant must be enrolled or expecting to enroll full-time at a two-year or four-year or technical institution. Available to U.S. citizens.

Application Requirements: Application form, application form may be submitted online (http://www.imagine-america.org/scholarshipsforadults), complete the NCCT Educational Success Potential Assessment. *Deadline:* continuous.

Contact: Lee Doubleday, Student Services Representative
Imagine America Foundation
12001 Sunrise Valley Drive, Suite 203
Reston, VA 20191
Phone: 571-267-3015
Fax: 866-734-5812
E-mail: leed@imagine-america.org

IMAGINE AMERICA HIGH SCHOOL SCHOLARSHIP

Imagine America, sponsored by the Imagine America Foundation (IAF), is a $1000 career education award that is available to recent high school graduates who are pursuing postsecondary education at participating career colleges across the United States. Only recent high school graduates who meet the following recommended guidelines should apply: likelihood of successful completion of postsecondary education; high school grade point average of 2.5 or greater; financial need; demonstrated voluntary community service during senior year.

Award: Scholarship for use in freshman year; not renewable. *Number:* up to 15,000. *Amount:* $1000.

Eligibility Requirements: Applicant must be age 16-19 and enrolled or expecting to enroll full- or part-time at a two-year or four-year or technical institution. Applicant must have 2.5 GPA or higher. Available to U.S. citizens.

Application Requirements: Application form, application form may be submitted online (http://www.imagine-america.org/highschoolscholarships). *Deadline:* December 31.

Contact: Lee Doubleday, Student Services Representative
Imagine America Foundation
12001 Sunrise Valley Drive, Suite 203
Reston, VA 20191
Phone: 571-267-3015
Fax: 866-734-5812
E-mail: leed@imagine-america.org

INDEPENDENT INSTITUTE

http://www.independent.org/

SIR JOHN M. TEMPLETON FELLOWSHIPS ESSAY CONTEST

Essay contest for junior higher education faculty and students. Student applicants must be born on or after May 2, 1972. Student applicants may be pursuing any degree including associates, undergraduate, postgraduate or doctoral.

Award: Prize for use in freshman, sophomore, junior, senior, graduate, or postgraduate years; not renewable. *Number:* 6. *Amount:* $1000–$10,000.

Eligibility Requirements: Applicant must be enrolled or expecting to enroll full- or part-time at a two-year or four-year institution or university. Available to U.S. and non-U.S. citizens.

Application Requirements: Application form, entry in a contest, essay. *Deadline:* May 1.

Contact: Carl Close, Academic Affairs Director
Phone: 510-632-1366
Fax: 510-568-6040
E-mail: cclose@independent.org

INTEREXCHANGE FOUNDATION

http://www.interexchange.org/foundation/grant-funding/making-global-difference

CHRISTIANSON GRANT

The Christianson Grant is awarded to individuals who have arranged their own work abroad programs. Proposed programs must be at least six months in length and emphasize a work component. The grant program does not support independent research projects or academic study abroad programs.Application Deadlines: March 15, July 15, & October 15

Award: Grant for use in freshman, sophomore, junior, senior, graduate, or postgraduate years; not renewable. *Number:* 8. *Amount:* $2500–$10,000.

Eligibility Requirements: Applicant must be age 18-28 and enrolled or expecting to enroll full- or part-time at a four-year institution or university. Available to U.S. citizens.

Application Requirements: Application form, essay, interview, recommendations or references, resume. *Fee:* $50.

Contact: Myisha Battle, Director of Organizational Development
InterExchange Foundation
161 Sixth Avenue
New York, NY 10013
Phone: 917-305-5400
E-mail: grants@interexchange.org

WORKING ABROAD GRANT

The Working Abroad Grant is available to certain participants who have been accepted into InterExchange's respected Working Abroad program. The grants are awarded to applicants who show a high level of commitment to their chosen Working Abroad program. Preference is given toward applicants with limited or no previous international travel experience.

Award: Grant for use in freshman, sophomore, junior, senior, graduate, or postgraduate years; not renewable. *Number:* 5–8. *Amount:* $1500.

Eligibility Requirements: Applicant must be age 18-28 and enrolled or expecting to enroll full- or part-time at a four-year institution or university. Available to U.S. citizens.

Application Requirements: Application form, essay, interview, recommendations or references, resume. *Deadline:* continuous.

Contact: Myisha Battle, Director of Organizational Development
InterExchange Foundation
161 Sixth Avenue
New York, NY 11206
Phone: 917-305-5400
E-mail: grants@interexchange.org

INTERNATIONAL FLIGHT SERVICES ASSOCIATION

http://www.ifsanet.com

GOURMET FOODS SCHOLARSHIP AWARD

Individuals are selected to receive the award based on scholastic merit and dedication to an advanced education. Must be an employee of a current IFSA member company in good standing, or a relative of an employee of a current IFSA member company. Please address financial need within essay.

Award: Scholarship for use in freshman, sophomore, junior, or senior years; not renewable. *Number:* 1. *Amount:* $5000.

Eligibility Requirements: Applicant must be enrolled or expecting to enroll full- or part-time at an institution or university. Applicant must have 3.0 GPA or higher. Available to U.S. and non-U.S. citizens.

Application Requirements: Application form, essay, recommendations or references, transcript. *Deadline:* May 14.

Contact: Jacqueline Petty, Communications Manager
International Flight Services Association
1100 Johnson Ferry Road NE
Suite 300
Atlanta, GA 30342
Phone: 404-252-3663 Ext. 2969
Fax: 404-252-0774
E-mail: jpetty@kellencompany.com

HARVEY & LAURA ALPERT SCHOLARSHIP AWARD

Individuals are selected to receive this award based on scholastic merit and dedication to pursuing a career in onboard services operations. Must be an employee of a current IFSA member company in good standing, or a relative of an IFSA member company employee.

Award: Scholarship for use in freshman, sophomore, junior, or senior years; not renewable. *Number:* 1. *Amount:* $5000.

Eligibility Requirements: Applicant must be enrolled or expecting to enroll full-time at an institution or university. Available to U.S. and non-U.S. citizens.

Application Requirements: Application form, essay, recommendations or references, transcript. *Deadline:* May 14.

Contact: Jacqueline Petty, Communications Manager
International Flight Services Association
1100 Johnson Ferry Road NE
Suite 300
Atlanta, GA 30342
Phone: 404-252-3663 Ext. 2969
Fax: 404-252-0774
E-mail: jpetty@kellencompany.com

JACK KENT COOKE FOUNDATION

http://www.jackkentcookefoundation.org/

JACK KENT COOKE FOUNDATION UNDERGRADUATE TRANSFER SCHOLARSHIP PROGRAM

Scholarships to students and recent alumni from community college to complete their bachelor's degrees at accredited four-year colleges or universities in the United States or abroad. Candidates must be nominated by a faculty representative from their community college.

Award: Scholarship for use in freshman, sophomore, junior, or senior years; renewable. *Number:* 50. *Amount:* $30,000.

Eligibility Requirements: Applicant must be enrolled or expecting to enroll full-time at a four-year institution or university. Applicant must have 3.5 GPA or higher. Available to U.S. and non-U.S. citizens.

Application Requirements: Application form, essay, financial need analysis, recommendations or references, transcript. *Deadline:* February 1.

Contact: Myisha Battle, Director of Organizational Development
InterExchange Foundation
161 Sixth Avenue
New York, NY 11206
Phone: 917-305-5400
E-mail: grants@interexchange.org

Contact: Gaby Ruess, Scholarship Committee
Jack Kent Cooke Foundation
44325 Woodridge Parkway
Lansdowne, VA 20176
Phone: 800-498-6478
E-mail: jkc-u@act.org

JEANNETTE RANKIN WOMEN'S SCHOLARSHIP FUND

http://www.rankinfoundation.org/

JEANNETTE RANKIN WOMEN'S SCHOLARSHIP FUND

Applicants must be low-income women, age 35 or older, who are U.S. citizens or permanent residents of the U.S. pursuing a technical/vocational education, an associate degree, or a first bachelor's degree at a regionally or ACICS accredited college. Applications are available on our website from November through February.

Award: Scholarship for use in freshman, sophomore, junior, or senior years; renewable. *Number:* 87. *Amount:* $2000.

Eligibility Requirements: Applicant must be enrolled or expecting to enroll full- or part-time at a two-year or four-year or technical institution or university and female. Available to U.S. citizens.

Application Requirements: Application form, application form may be submitted online (http://www.rankinfoundation.org/students/application/), essay, financial need analysis, recommendations or references, transcript. *Deadline:* March 1.

Contact: April Greene, Program Coordinator
Jeannette Rankin Women's Scholarship Fund
1 Huntington Road, #701
Athens, GA 30606
Phone: 706-208-1211
E-mail: info@rankinfoundation.org

JOURNALISM EDUCATION ASSOCIATION

http://www.jea.org/

NATIONAL HIGH SCHOOL JOURNALIST OF THE YEAR/SISTER RITA JEANNE SCHOLARSHIPS

One-time award recognizes the nation's top high school journalists. Open to graduating high school seniors who have worked at least two years on school media. Applicants must have JEA member as adviser. Minimum 3.0 GPA required. Submit portfolio to state contest coordinator by March 1 or by the deadline set by the state organization.

Award: Scholarship for use in freshman year; not renewable. *Number:* 1–7. *Amount:* $1000–$3000.

Eligibility Requirements: Applicant must be high school student; age 17-19 and planning to enroll or expecting to enroll full-time at a four-year institution or university. Applicant must have 3.0 GPA or higher. Available to U.S. citizens.

Application Requirements: Application form, application form may be submitted online (http://jea.org/home/awards-honors/journalist-of-the-year/), entry in a contest, essay, personal photograph, portfolio, recommendations or references, samples of work, self-addressed stamped envelope with application, transcript. *Deadline:* March 1.

Contact: Connie Fulkerson, Administrative Assistant
Journalism Education Association
Kansas State University, 103 Kedzie Hall
Manhattan, KS 66506-1505
Phone: 785-532-5532
Fax: 785-532-5563
E-mail: jea@spub.ksu.edu

J. WOOD PLATT CADDIE SCHOLARSHIP TRUST

http://www.plattcaddiescholarship.org/

J. WOOD PLATT CADDIE SCHOLARSHIP TRUST

The Platt Caddie Scholarship is available to individuals who caddie at Golf Association of Philadelphia Member Clubs and is solely based on financial need, as a result of submitting the FAFSA application and other financial documents. This is not an athletic or golf scholarship.

Award: Scholarship for use in freshman, sophomore, junior, senior, graduate, or postgraduate years; renewable. *Amount:* $1000–$100,000.

Eligibility Requirements: Applicant must be enrolled or expecting to enroll full-time at a two-year or four-year institution or university. Available to U.S. and non-U.S. citizens.

Application Requirements: Application form, application form may be submitted online (http://www.plattcaddiescholarship.org), essay, financial need analysis, interview, recommendations or references, test scores, transcript. *Deadline:* April 25.

Contact: Bradley Kane, Director, Platt Caddie Scholarship
J. Wood Platt Caddie Scholarship Trust
1974 Sproul Road
Suite 400
Broomall, PA 19008
Phone: 610-687-2340 Ext. 21
Fax: 610-687-2082
E-mail: bkane@gapgolf.org

K2 PROGRESSIVE, LLC

http://www.admissionscholarship.com/aboutus/

ADMISSIONSCHOLARSHIP.COM SCHOLARSHIP

Two $1000 scholarships per year to students who are currently enrolled or are planning on enrolling in a college or university. Scholarships are awarded through random drawings to give each student an equal chance of winning. Deadlines are June 30 and December 31 of each year.

Award: Scholarship for use in freshman, sophomore, junior, senior, graduate, or postgraduate years; not renewable. *Number:* 2. *Amount:* $1000.

Eligibility Requirements: Applicant must be enrolled or expecting to enroll full- or part-time at a two-year or four-year or technical institution or university. Available to U.S. and non-U.S. citizens.

Application Requirements: Application form. *Deadline:* continuous.

Contact: Mr. Cory Klinnert, President
K2 Progressive, LLC
PO Box 23
Moorhead, MN 56561
Phone: 218-329-1308
E-mail: info@admissionscholarship.com

KE ALI'I PAUAHI FOUNDATION

http://www.pauahi.org/

CHOY-KEE 'OHANA SCHOLARSHIP

Scholarship recognizes the academic achievements and efforts of worthy students with a minimum GPA of 3.0 who are pursuing a postsecondary education. Must submit essay addressing what the biggest problem in Hawaii is and potential solutions. Submit two letters of recommendation; one from teacher or counselor and one from a community organization.

Award: Scholarship for use in freshman, sophomore, junior, senior, or graduate years; not renewable. *Number:* 2. *Amount:* $500.

Eligibility Requirements: Applicant must be enrolled or expecting to enroll full-time at a two-year or four-year institution or university. Applicant must have 3.0 GPA or higher. Available to U.S. citizens.

Application Requirements: Application form, application form may be submitted online (http://www.pauahi.org/scholarships), essay, recommendations or references, Student Aid Report (SAR), college acceptance letter, transcript. *Deadline:* April 1.

Contact: Mavis Shiraishi-Nagao, Scholarship Administrator
Phone: 808-534-3966
E-mail: scholarships@pauahi.org

DENIS WONG & ASSOCIATES SCHOLARSHIP

Scholarship to recognize an outstanding student pursuing an undergraduate degree in liberal arts or science, or a graduate degree in a professional field from an accredited university. Recipient must have a well-rounded and balanced record of achievement in preparation for career objectives, demonstrate a commitment to contribute to the greater community. Minimum GPA of 3.5 required. Submit two letters of recommendation from teacher, counselors, coaches or employers citing applicant's credentials and potential for success.

Award: Scholarship for use in freshman, sophomore, junior, senior, or graduate years; not renewable. *Number:* up to 3. *Amount:* up to $1000.

Eligibility Requirements: Applicant must be enrolled or expecting to enroll full-time at a four-year institution or university. Applicant must have 3.5 GPA or higher. Available to U.S. citizens.

Application Requirements: Application form, application form may be submitted online (http://www.pauahi.org/scholarships), college acceptance letter, copy of SAR, essay, recommendations or references, transcript. *Deadline:* April 1.

Contact: Mavis Shiraishi-Nagao, Scholarship Administrator
  Phone: 808-534-3966
  E-mail: scholarships@pauahi.org

KAMEHAMEHA SCHOOLS CLASS OF 1952 "NA HOALOHA O KAMEHAMEHA" SCHOLARSHIP

Scholarship to assist students pursuing a certificate or degree from an accredited vocational/business school or a two- or four-year post-secondary institution. Must demonstrate financial need. Minimum 2.0 GPA required.

Award: Scholarship for use in freshman, sophomore, junior, or senior years; not renewable. *Number:* 1–2. *Amount:* $1000.

Eligibility Requirements: Applicant must be enrolled or expecting to enroll full-time at a two-year or four-year or technical institution or university. Available to U.S. citizens.

Application Requirements: Application form, application form may be submitted online (http://www.pauahi.org/scholarships), financial need analysis, Student Aid Report (SAR), college acceptance letter, transcript. *Deadline:* April 1.

Contact: Mavis Shiraishi-Nagao, Scholarship Administrator
  Phone: 808-534-3966
  E-mail: scholarships@pauahi.org

KAMEHAMEHA SCHOOLS CLASS OF 1968 "KA POLI O KAIONA" SCHOLARSHIP

Scholarships for students pursuing a two-year, four-year, or graduate degree from an accredited post-secondary institution. Minimum 2.8 GPA required. Must demonstrate financial need. Submit two letters of recommendation from educator, employer or community organization. Submit essay on how this award would support and extend the legacy of Ke Ali`i Bernice Pauahi Bishop.

Award: Scholarship for use in freshman, sophomore, junior, senior, or graduate years; not renewable. *Number:* up to 2. *Amount:* up to $700.

Eligibility Requirements: Applicant must be enrolled or expecting to enroll full-time at a two-year or four-year institution or university. Applicant must have 2.5 GPA or higher. Available to U.S. citizens.

Application Requirements: Application form, application form may be submitted online (http://www.pauahi.org/scholarships), essay, financial need analysis, recommendations or references, Student Aid Report (SAR), college acceptance letter, transcript. *Deadline:* April 1.

Contact: Mavis Shiraishi-Nagao, Scholarship Administrator
  Phone: 808-534-3966
  E-mail: scholarships@pauahi.org

KENNEDY FOUNDATION

http://www.columbinecorp.com/kennedyfoundation

KENNEDY FOUNDATION SCHOLARSHIPS

Renewable scholarships for current high school students for up to four years of undergraduate study. Renewal contingent upon academic performance. Must maintain a GPA of 2.5. Send self-addressed stamped envelope for application. See website for details http://www.columbinecorp.com/kennedyfoundation to download an application.

Award: Scholarship for use in freshman year; renewable. *Number:* 8–14. *Amount:* $2000.

Eligibility Requirements: Applicant must be high school student and planning to enroll or expecting to enroll full-time at a two-year or four-year institution or university. Applicant must have 2.5 GPA or higher. Available to U.S. citizens.

Application Requirements: Application form, self-addressed stamped envelope with application, test scores, transcript. *Deadline:* June 30.

Contact: Jonathan Kennedy, Vice President

KENTUCKY OFFICE OF VOCATIONAL REHABILITATION

http://www.ovr.ky.gov/

KENTUCKY OFFICE OF VOCATIONAL REHABILITATION

Grant provides services necessary to secure employment. Eligible individual must possess physical or mental impairment that results in a substantial impediment to employment; benefit from vocational rehabilitation services in terms of an employment outcome; and require vocational rehabilitation services to prepare for, enter, or retain employment.

Award: Grant for use in freshman, sophomore, junior, senior, graduate, or postgraduate years; renewable.

Eligibility Requirements: Applicant must be enrolled or expecting to enroll full- or part-time at a two-year or four-year or technical institution or university.

Application Requirements: Application form, eligibility for OVR services and in proper priority category, financial need analysis, interview, transcript. *Deadline:* continuous.

Contact: Charles Puckett, Program Administrator
  Kentucky Office of Vocational Rehabilitation
  600 West Cedar Street, Suite 2E
  Louisville, KY 40202
  Phone: 502-595-4173
  Fax: 502-564-2358
  E-mail: marianu.spencer@mail.state.ky.us

LEOPOLD SCHEPP FOUNDATION

http://www.scheppfoundation.org/

LEOPOLD SCHEPP SCHOLARSHIP

Scholarship for undergraduates under 30 years of age and graduate students under 40 years of age at the time of application. Applicants must have a minimum GPA of 3.0. High school seniors are not eligible. All applicants must either be enrolled in college or have completed at least one year of college at the time of issuing the application. Must be citizens or permanent residents of the United States. Deadline varies.

Award: Scholarship for use in sophomore, junior, senior, or graduate years; renewable. *Number:* 1–30. *Amount:* up to $8500.

Eligibility Requirements: Applicant must be enrolled or expecting to enroll full-time at a four-year institution or university. Applicant must have 3.0 GPA or higher. Available to U.S. citizens.

Application Requirements: Application form, financial need analysis, interview, recommendations or references, transcript. *Deadline:* varies.

LIFE AND HEALTH INSURANCE FOUNDATION FOR EDUCATION

http://www.lifehappens.org

LIFE LESSONS SCHOLARSHIP PROGRAM

The LIFE Lessons Scholarship Program is for college students and college-bound high school seniors who have experienced the death of a parent or legal guardian. To apply students must complete and submit an application, including an essay of no more than 500 words or a 3 minutes video discussing how the death of a parent or guardian affected his or her life financially and emotionally. Applicants must explain how the lack of adequate life insurance coverage (or no coverage at all) impacted their family's financial situation. Please make sure to review the Scholarship Program rules at www.lifehappens.org/scholarship-program-rules.

Award: Scholarship for use in freshman, sophomore, junior, senior, or graduate years; not renewable. *Number:* up to 60. *Amount:* $2000–$15,000.

Eligibility Requirements: Applicant must be age 17-24 and enrolled or expecting to enroll full- or part-time at a two-year or four-year or technical institution or university. Available to U.S. citizens.

Application Requirements: Application form, application form may be submitted online (http://www.lifehappens.org/scholarship), entry in a contest, essay or video. *Deadline:* March 31.

Contact: Julie Holsinger, Manager of Consumer Education Programs
Life and Health Insurance Foundation for Education
1655 North Fort Myer Drive
Suite 610
Arlington, VA 22209
Phone: 202-464-5000 Ext. 4446
Fax: 202-464-5011
E-mail: scholarship@lifehappens.org

MARGARET MCNAMARA MEMORIAL FUND

http://www.wbfn.org/

MARGARET MCNAMARA MEMORIAL FUND FELLOWSHIPS

One-time award for female students from developing countries enrolled in accredited graduate programs relating to women and children. Must be attending an accredited institution in the United States. Candidates must plan to return to their countries or a developing country within two years. Must be over 25 years of age. U.S. citizens are not eligible.

Award: Grant for use in sophomore, junior, senior, graduate, or postgraduate years; not renewable. *Number:* 6–12. *Amount:* $12,000–$12,000.

Eligibility Requirements: Applicant must be enrolled or expecting to enroll full-time at a four-year institution or university and female. Available to citizens of countries other than the U.S. or Canada.

Application Requirements: Application form, application form may be submitted online (http://www.mmmf-grants.org/grants-us-application-process.html), autobiography, copy of visa, I20 and DS2019, essay, financial need analysis, interview, personal photograph, recommendations or references, transcript. *Deadline:* January 15.

MENNONITE WOMEN

http://www.mennonitewomenusa.org/

INTERNATIONAL WOMEN'S FUND

Scholarship for women from developing countries for postsecondary studies. Must submit letter of recommendations or reference from the church.

Award: Scholarship for use in freshman, sophomore, junior, senior, graduate, or postgraduate years; renewable. *Number:* 12. *Amount:* $500–$1000.

Eligibility Requirements: Applicant must be enrolled or expecting to enroll full- or part-time at a two-year or four-year institution or university and female. Available to citizens of countries other than the U.S. or Canada.

Application Requirements: Application form, recommendations or references. *Deadline:* September 1.

Contact: Rhoda Keener, Program Director
Phone: 717-532-9723
Fax: 316-283-0454
E-mail: office@mennonitewomenusa.org

MICHAEL AND SUSAN DELL FOUNDATION

http://www.msdf.org/

DELL SCHOLARS PROGRAM

250 scholarships offered annually to high school students participating in approved college readiness programs. Must have a minimum 2.4 GPA and should be participating in a MSDF-approved college readiness program for a minimum of two years prior to application.

Award: Scholarship for use in freshman year; not renewable. *Number:* 250.

Eligibility Requirements: Applicant must be high school student and planning to enroll or expecting to enroll full- or part-time at a two-year or four-year or technical institution or university. Available to U.S. citizens.

Application Requirements: Application form, recommendations or references, transcript. *Deadline:* January 15.

MILITARY ORDER OF THE STARS AND BARS

http://www.militaryorderofthestarsandbars.org/

MILITARY ORDER OF THE STARS AND BARS SCHOLARSHIPS

Applicants must be accepted to a degree-granting junior college or four-year college or university or already enrolled in such a facility. Awards shall be made annually, and the total amount of the scholarship money to be awarded each year to each recipient shall not exceed $1000. Applicants must be sponsored by a local MOS&B Chapter or MOS&B State Society. Applicants must be able to prove they are a descendant of a commissioned officer or civil servant of the Confederate States of America. Preference is given to relatives of currently active MOS&B members. All application information is found on the MOS&B website.

Award: Scholarship for use in freshman, sophomore, junior, senior, graduate, or postgraduate years; not renewable. *Number:* 5–6. *Amount:* $1000.

Eligibility Requirements: Applicant must be enrolled or expecting to enroll full-time at a two-year or four-year institution or university. Applicant must have 3.0 GPA or higher. Available to U.S. and non-U.S. citizens.

Application Requirements: Application form, autobiography, personal photograph, recommendations or references, resume, sponsor's letter and descendant proof, transcript. *Deadline:* March 1.

Contact: Dr. Gary Loudermilk, Scholarship Chairman
Military Order of the Stars and Bars
2801 14th Street
Brownwood, TX 76801
E-mail: gmldhl@harrisbb.com

MORRIS J. AND BETTY KAPLUN FOUNDATION

http://www.kaplunfoundation.org/

MORRIS J. AND BETTY KAPLUN FOUNDATION ANNUAL ESSAY CONTEST

Prize up to $1800 will be awarded to the first place contest winner for essay on a topic related to Jewish heritage, culture, or values. One need not be Jewish to enter. Additional awards for five finalists. Essay must be between 250 and 1000 words. Open to middle and high school students in grades 7-12. See website for specific essay questions and additional details at www.kaplunfoundation.org

Award: Prize for use in freshman, sophomore, junior, or senior years; not renewable. *Number:* 12. *Amount:* $750–$1800.

Eligibility Requirements: Applicant must be high school student; age 12-18 and planning to enroll or expecting to enroll full-time at a four-year institution or university. Available to U.S. and non-U.S. citizens.

Application Requirements: Application form may be submitted online, entry in a contest, essay. *Deadline:* March 17.

Contact: Eve Seligson-Mor, Essay Contest Committee
Phone: 212-966-5020
Fax: 212-966-6205

NAAS-USA FUND, INC.

http://www.naas.org/

NAAS II NATIONAL AWARDS

One renewable scholarship of $500 to $3000 available for tuition, room, board, books, and academic supplies. Applicant must be college freshman or sophomore attending an American college/university. U.S. citizenship is not required. Must be under the age of 25. Applicants that request an application by mail must enclose a $3 handling fee and a self-addressed stamped envelope. Electronic applications are available to NAAS Subscribers at http://www.naas.org; no fees for NAAS subscribers.

Award: Scholarship for use in freshman or sophomore years; renewable. *Number:* 1–5. *Amount:* $500–$3000.

Eligibility Requirements: Applicant must be enrolled or expecting to enroll full-time at a four-year institution or university. Available to U.S. and non-U.S. citizens.

Application Requirements: Application form. *Deadline:* May 1.

NATIONAL ASSOCIATION OF RAILWAY BUSINESS WOMEN

http://www.narbw.org/

NARBW SCHOLARSHIP

Scholarship awarded to the members of NARBW and their relatives. The number of awards varies every year. Applications are judged on scholastic ability, ambition and potential, and financial need.

Award: Scholarship for use in freshman, sophomore, junior, or senior years; not renewable. *Amount:* $500–$1000.

Eligibility Requirements: Applicant must be enrolled or expecting to enroll full-time at a two-year or four-year or technical institution or university and female. Available to U.S. citizens.

Application Requirements: Application form, financial need analysis. *Deadline:* varies.

NATIONAL BLACK MBA ASSOCIATION

http://www.nbmbaa.org/

NATIONAL BLACK MBA ASSOCIATION GRADUATE SCHOLARSHIP PROGRAM

Program's mission is to identify and increase the pool of Black talent for business, public, private and non-profit sectors.

Award: Scholarship for use in freshman, sophomore, junior, or senior years; not renewable. *Number:* 10–25. *Amount:* $2500–$15,000.

Eligibility Requirements: Applicant must be enrolled or expecting to enroll full-time at a four-year institution or university. Available to U.S. and non-U.S. citizens.

Application Requirements: Application form, community service, essay, interview, resume, transcript. *Deadline:* April 17.

Contact: Ms. Lori Johnson, Program Administrator, University Relations
National Black MBA Association
180 North Michigan Avenue, Suite 1400
Chicago, IL 60601
Phone: 312-580-8086
E-mail: scholarship@nbmbaa.org

NATIONAL HEMOPHILIA FOUNDATION

http://www.hemophilia.org/

KEVIN CHILD SCHOLARSHIP

Scholarship applicants must be individuals diagnosed with either hemophilia A or B, and a high school senior with aspirations of attending an institute of higher education (college, university or vocational-technical school), a college student already pursuing a post-secondary education, or a student in a graduate-level program. Interested students need to submit an application along with a current official transcript of their grades and one letter of recommendation from a person familiar with their personal and academic achievements (ex. teacher, mentor). The Kevin Child Scholarship recipient will be chosen on the basis of their academic performance, participation in school or community activities and the personal application essay detailing their educational and career goals.

Award: Scholarship for use in freshman, sophomore, junior, senior, or graduate years; not renewable. *Number:* 1. *Amount:* up to $1000.

Eligibility Requirements: Applicant must be enrolled or expecting to enroll full- or part-time at a two-year or four-year or technical institution or university. Available to U.S. citizens.

Application Requirements: Application form, community service, essay, recommendations or references, transcript. *Deadline:* June 3.

NATIONAL JUNIOR ANGUS ASSOCIATION

http://www.angus.org/njaa/

AMERICAN ANGUS AUXILIARY SCHOLARSHIP

Scholarship available to graduating high school senior. Can apply only in one state. Any unmarried girl or unmarried boy recommended by a state or regional Auxiliary is eligible.

Award: Scholarship for use in freshman year; not renewable. *Number:* 10. *Amount:* $1000–$14,000.

Eligibility Requirements: Applicant must be high school student; planning to enroll or expecting to enroll full-time at a two-year or four-year or technical institution or university and single. Available to U.S. and Canadian citizens.

Application Requirements: Application form, entry in a contest, personal photograph, recommendations or references, test scores, transcript. *Deadline:* May 1.

Contact: Mrs. Anne Lampe, American Angus Auxiliary Scholarship Chairman
National Junior Angus Association
5201 East Road 110
Scott City, KS 67871
Phone: 620-872-3915

NATIONAL RIFLE ASSOCIATION

http://www.friendsofnra.org/yes

NRA YOUTH EDUCATIONAL SUMMIT (YES) SCHOLARSHIPS

Awards for Youth Educational Summit participants based on the initial application, on-site debate, and degree of participation during the week-long event. Must be graduating high school seniors enrolled in undergraduate program. Must have a minimum GPA of 3.0.

Award: Scholarship for use in freshman, sophomore, or junior years; not renewable. *Number:* 1–6. *Amount:* $1000–$10,000.

Eligibility Requirements: Applicant must be high school student and planning to enroll or expecting to enroll full- or part-time at a two-year or four-year or technical institution or university. Applicant must have 3.0 GPA or higher. Available to U.S. citizens.

Application Requirements: Application form, entry in a contest, essay, recommendations or references, transcript. *Deadline:* February 1.

NATIONAL SOCIETY OF HIGH SCHOOL SCHOLARS

http://www.nshss.org/

ROBERT P. SHEPPARD LEADERSHIP AWARD FOR NSHSS MEMBERS

Scholarship of $1000 awarded to an NSHSS member demonstrating outstanding dedication to community service and initiative in volunteer activities. Runner up awards of $250 are given as well.

Award: Scholarship for use in freshman year; not renewable. *Number:* 1–5. *Amount:* $250–$1000.

Eligibility Requirements: Applicant must be high school student and planning to enroll or expecting to enroll full- or part-time at a four-year institution or university. Applicant must have 3.5 GPA or higher. Available to U.S. and non-U.S. citizens.

Application Requirements: Application form, essay, personal photograph, recommendations or references, transcript. *Deadline:* February 15.

Contact: Dr. Susan Thurman, Scholarship Director
National Society of High School Scholars
1936 North Druid Hills Road
Atlanta, GA 30319
Phone: 404-235-5500
Fax: 404-235-5510
E-mail: information@nshss.org

NATIONAL SPEAKERS ASSOCIATION

http://www.nsaspeaker.org/

NATIONAL SPEAKERS ASSOCIATION SCHOLARSHIP

One-time award for junior, senior, or graduate students who have a burning desire to pursue professional speaking as a career. Must be full-time student at accredited four-year institution with above average academic record. Submit 500 word essay on goals. Application available only on website http://www.nsafoundation.org.

Award: Scholarship for use in junior, senior, or graduate years; not renewable. *Number:* 4. *Amount:* $5000.

Eligibility Requirements: Applicant must be enrolled or expecting to enroll full-time at a four-year institution or university. Available to U.S. and non-U.S. citizens.

Application Requirements: Application form, essay, link to URL of applicant speaking, recommendations or references, transcript. *Deadline:* June 1.

Contact: Andrea DiMickele, Foundation Specialist
National Speakers Association
1500 South Priest Drive
Tempe, AZ 85281
Phone: 480-968-2552
Fax: 480-968-0911
E-mail: andrea@nsaspeaker.org

NAVAL SERVICE TRAINING COMMAND/ NROTC

https://www.nrotc.navy.mil/

NROTC SCHOLARSHIP PROGRAM

Scholarships are based on merit and are awarded through a highly competitive national selection process. NROTC scholarships pay for college tuition, fees, uniforms, a book stipend, a monthly allowance and other financial benefits. Room and board expenses are not covered. Scholarship nominees must be medically qualified. Upon graduation scholarship recipients have an obligation of eight years commissioned service, five of which must be active duty. For more information, visit our website at https://www.nrotc.navy.mil.

Award: Scholarship for use in freshman, sophomore, junior, or senior years; renewable. *Number:* 2400–2900.

Eligibility Requirements: Applicant must be age 17-23 and enrolled or expecting to enroll full-time at a four-year institution or university. Available to U.S. citizens.

Application Requirements: Application form, essay, interview, recommendations or references, test scores, transcript. *Deadline:* January 31.

NAVY COUNSELORS ASSOCIATION

http://www.usnca.org/

NAVY COUNSELORS ASSOCIATION EDUCATIONAL SCHOLARSHIP

The program awards at least one scholarship to a deserving student who is currently enrolled in, or accepted to, an undergraduate-level college, university or vocational tech program. Scholarship nominations must be from immediate family members of NCA members.

Award: Scholarship for use in freshman, sophomore, junior, or senior years; not renewable. *Number:* 1–4.

Eligibility Requirements: Applicant must be enrolled or expecting to enroll full- or part-time at a four-year institution or university. Applicant must have 3.0 GPA or higher. Available to U.S. citizens.

Application Requirements: Application form, essay, recommendations or references, transcript. *Deadline:* April 30.

Contact: Joseph Mack, President
Phone: 901-874-3194
Fax: 901-874-2055
E-mail: president@usnca.org

NEEDHAM AND COMPANY WTC SCHOLARSHIP FUND

http://www.needhamco.com/

NEEDHAM AND COMPANY SEPTEMBER 11TH SCHOLARSHIP FUND

Scholarship going to those individuals who had a pre-September 11th gross income of less than $125,000. Must be currently accepted or attending an accredited university or college. Recipients decided on a case-by-case basis. Fund designed to benefit the children of the victims who lost their lives at the World Trade Center.

Award: Scholarship for use in freshman, sophomore, junior, or senior years; not renewable. *Number:* 8–15. *Amount:* $7000–$10,000.

Eligibility Requirements: Applicant must be enrolled or expecting to enroll full-time at a four-year institution or university. Available to U.S. citizens.

Application Requirements: Application form, financial need analysis. *Deadline:* continuous.

Contact: Joseph Turano, Secretary and Treasurer
Needham and Company WTC Scholarship Fund
445 Park Avenue
New York, NY 10022
Phone: 212-705-0314
E-mail: jturano@needhamco.com

NEW MEXICO COMMISSION ON HIGHER EDUCATION

http://www.hed.state.nm.us/

NEW MEXICO COMPETITIVE SCHOLARSHIP

Scholarships for non-residents or non-citizens of the United States to encourage out-of-state students who have demonstrated high academic achievement in high school to enroll in public four-year universities in New Mexico. Renewable for up to four years. For details visit http://fin.hed.state.nm.us.

Award: Scholarship for use in freshman year; renewable.

Eligibility Requirements: Applicant must be high school student; planning to enroll or expecting to enroll full-time at a four-year institution or university and studying in New Mexico. Available to Canadian and non-U.S. citizens.

Application Requirements: Application form, essay, recommendations or references, test scores. *Deadline:* varies.

Contact: Tashina Moore, Director of Financial Aid
New Mexico Commission on Higher Education
1068 Cerrillos Road
Santa Fe, NM 87505
Phone: 505-476-6549
Fax: 505-476-6511
E-mail: tashina.banks-moore@state.nm.us

NEW YORK STATE HIGHER EDUCATION SERVICES CORPORATION

http://www.hesc.com/

WORLD TRADE CENTER MEMORIAL SCHOLARSHIP

Renewable awards of up to the cost of educational expenses at a State University of New York four-year college. Available to the children, spouses and financial dependents of victims who died or were severely disabled as a result of the September 11, 2001 terrorist attacks on the U.S. and the rescue and recovery efforts.

Award: Scholarship for use in freshman, sophomore, junior, or senior years; renewable.

Eligibility Requirements: Applicant must be enrolled or expecting to enroll full-time at a four-year institution or university and studying in New York. Available to U.S. and non-U.S. citizens.

Application Requirements: Application form, financial need analysis, recommendations or references, transcript. *Deadline:* May 1.

NEXTSTEPU

http://www.nextstepu.com/

WIN FREE COLLEGE TUITION GIVEAWAY

NextStepU will award a year of free tuition, up to $10,000, to one randomly selected winner. Applicants must enter online at http://www.nextstepu.com/winfreetuition or see official rules for alternate method of entry. Winner must be enrolled in college within 3 years of when prize is awarded.

Award: Scholarship for use in freshman, sophomore, junior, or senior years; not renewable. *Number:* 1. *Amount:* $500–$10,000.

Eligibility Requirements: Applicant must be enrolled or expecting to enroll full- or part-time at a two-year or four-year or technical institution or university. Available to U.S. and Canadian citizens.

Application Requirements: Application form, application form may be submitted online (http://www.nextstepu.com/winfreetuition). *Deadline:* June 30.

NICODEMUS WILDERNESS PROJECT

http://www.wildernessproject.org/

APPRENTICE ECOLOGIST SCHOLARSHIP

The Apprentice Ecologist Scholarship is open to students interested in protecting wildlife and the environment. This program elevates young people into leadership roles by engaging them in environmental stewardship and conservation projects that benefit native ecosystems and local communities. Applicants should demonstrate personal initiative, leadership, and dedication in their projects.

Award: Scholarship for use in freshman, sophomore, junior, or senior years; not renewable. *Number:* 3. *Amount:* $100–$500.

Eligibility Requirements: Applicant must be age 13-21 and enrolled or expecting to enroll full- or part-time at a two-year or four-year or technical institution or university. Available to U.S. and non-U.S. citizens.

Application Requirements: Essay. *Deadline:* December 31.

Contact: Dr. Robert Dudley, Director
Nicodemus Wilderness Project
PO Box 40712
Albuquerque, NM 87196-0712
E-mail: mail@wildernessproject.org

NORTH CAROLINA STATE DEPARTMENT OF HEALTH AND HUMAN SERVICES/ DIVISION OF SOCIAL SERVICES

http://www.dhhs.state.nc.us/dss/

NORTH CAROLINA EDUCATION AND TRAINING VOUCHER PROGRAM

Four-year scholarship for foster youth and former foster youth. Must have been accepted into or be enrolled in a degree, certificate or other accredited program at a college, university, technical or vocational school and show progress towards a degree or certificate. Must be a U.S. citizen or qualified non-citizen. Applications available at: nc@statevoucher.org.

Award: Grant for use in freshman, sophomore, junior, or senior years; renewable. *Amount:* up to $5000.

Eligibility Requirements: Applicant must be age 18-23 and enrolled or expecting to enroll full- or part-time at a two-year or four-year or technical institution or university. Available to U.S. citizens.

Application Requirements: Application form, application form may be submitted online (http://www.statevoucher.org), essay. *Deadline:* continuous.

Contact: Mrs. Danielle McConaga, NCDSS LINKS Independent Living Coordinator
North Carolina State Department of Health and Human Services/Division of Social Services
325 North Salisbury Street
Raleigh, NC 27699
Phone: 919-334-1110
E-mail: Danielle.McConaga@dhhs.nc.gov

OKLAHOMA STATE REGENTS FOR HIGHER EDUCATION

http://www.okhighered.org/

ACADEMIC SCHOLARS PROGRAM

Awards for students of high academic ability to attend institutions in Oklahoma. Renewable up to four years. ACT or SAT scores must fall between 99.5 and 100th percentiles, or applicant must be designated as a National Merit scholar or finalist. Oklahoma public institutions can also select institutional nominees.

Award: Scholarship for use in freshman, sophomore, junior, senior, or graduate years; renewable. *Amount:* $1800–$5500.

Eligibility Requirements: Applicant must be high school student; planning to enroll or expecting to enroll full-time at a two-year or four-year institution or university and studying in Oklahoma. Available to U.S. citizens.

Application Requirements: Application form, test scores, transcript. *Deadline:* continuous.

OP LOFTBED COMPANY

http://www.oploftbed.com/

OP LOFTBED $500 SCHOLARSHIP AWARD

Scholarship is awarded to the student whose answers to the application questions on the OP Loftbed website are the most creative and interesting. Must be a U.S. citizen who is enrolled in a college or university in the U.S. Deadline for summer award: 7/31. Deadline for winter award: 1/31. Submit entry on website http://www.oploftbed.com.

Award: Scholarship for use in freshman, sophomore, junior, senior, graduate, or postgraduate years; not renewable. *Number:* 2. *Amount:* $500.

Eligibility Requirements: Applicant must be enrolled or expecting to enroll full- or part-time at a two-year or four-year or technical institution or university. Available to U.S. citizens.

Application Requirements: Application form, application form may be submitted online (http://www.oploftbed.com/), essay.

OREGON POLICE CORPS

http://www.portlandonline.com/

OREGON POLICE CORPS SCHOLARSHIP

Scholarships available for undergraduate juniors and seniors and graduate students, or for reimbursement of educational expenses for college graduates. Must agree to commit to four years of employment at a participating law enforcement agency. Check website for details http://www.oregonpolicecorps.com.

Award: Scholarship for use in junior, senior, or graduate years; not renewable. *Number:* 10. *Amount:* up to $30,000.

Eligibility Requirements: Applicant must be enrolled or expecting to enroll full-time at a four-year institution or university. Available to U.S. citizens.

Application Requirements: Application form, essay, interview, recommendations or references, resume. *Deadline:* continuous.

Contact: Tim Evans, Scholarship Coordinator
Oregon Police Corps
1120 Fifth Avenue, SW, Room 404
Portland, OR 97204
Phone: 888-735-4259
E-mail: tevans@police.ci.portland.or.us

OREGON STUDENT ASSISTANCE COMMISSION

http://www.GetCollegeFunds.org/

ALLCOTT/HUNT SHARE IT NOW II SCHOLARSHIP, HONORING EMORY S. AND ELIZABETH BURKETT HUNT

Award for first or second generation immigrants to the United States. Eligible applicants must provide an answer to the citizenship status question in Item 4 of the Scholarship Application. Recipients must enroll at least half-time in college in the United States. FAFSA filing is strongly recommended. Essay and references are required.

Award: Scholarship for use in freshman, sophomore, junior, or senior years; not renewable.

Eligibility Requirements: Applicant must be enrolled or expecting to enroll full- or part-time at a two-year or four-year institution or university. Available to U.S. and non-U.S. citizens.

Application Requirements: Application form, essay, recommendations or references. *Deadline:* March 1.

BARTOO/MOSHINSKY SCHOLARSHIP

Award is available to first-time freshmen and undergraduates who are dependents of eligible employees of credit unions affiliated with, current clients of, or past clients of Merger Solution Group, The Watch Reports, and any other division of Bartoo Associates, LLC. Oregon residency is not required. Recipient must enroll at least half-time in a college or university in the United States.

Award: Scholarship for use in freshman, sophomore, junior, or senior years; not renewable.

Eligibility Requirements: Applicant must be enrolled or expecting to enroll full- or part-time at a two-year or four-year institution or university. Available to U.S. citizens.

Application Requirements: Application form. *Deadline:* March 1.

BETTER A LIFE SCHOLARSHIP

Scholarship award available to single parents age 17-25. High schools seniors must have at least 3.0 GPA and college students must have at least a 2.5 GPA. For use at Oregon public and nonprofit colleges and universities. Applicants may not already possess a bachelor's degree. May reapply for one additional year of funding.

Award: Scholarship for use in freshman, sophomore, junior, or senior years; not renewable.

Eligibility Requirements: Applicant must be age 17-25; enrolled or expecting to enroll full- or part-time at a two-year or four-year institution or university; single and studying in Oregon. Available to U.S. citizens.

Application Requirements: Application form, FAFSA, transcript. *Deadline:* March 1.

BRUCE AND KARIN BAILEY SCHOLARSHIP

Award is for dependents of eligible employees of Bend Garbage & Recycling, Deschutes Recycling, Deschutes Transfer, High Country Disposal, and Mid Oregon Recycling. Eligible employees must have been employed by one of these companies two or more years as of the March scholarship deadline. High school seniors must have at least a 3.25 GPA.

Award: Scholarship for use in freshman year; not renewable.

Eligibility Requirements: Applicant must be enrolled or expecting to enroll full-time at a two-year or four-year institution or university. Available to U.S. citizens.

Application Requirements: Application form, transcript. *Deadline:* March 1.

CHILDREN OF INSITU SCHOLARSHIP

Award available to dependents of eligible employees or former employees of Insitu, Inc. Oregon residency is not required. Recipients must enroll at least half-time in a college or university in the United States. FAFSA is required.

Award: Scholarship for use in freshman, sophomore, junior, or senior years; not renewable.

Eligibility Requirements: Applicant must be enrolled or expecting to enroll full- or part-time at a four-year institution or university. Available to U.S. citizens.

Application Requirements: Application form, FAFSA, transcript. *Deadline:* March 1.

CLYDE C. CROSBY/JOSEPH M. EDGAR AND THOMAS J. MALLOY MEMORIAL SCHOLARSHIP

Renewable award for graduating high school seniors who are children or dependent stepchildren of active, retired, disabled, or deceased members of local unions affiliated with Joint Council of Teamsters #37. Qualifying members must have been active 1+ year as of February 1 immediately preceding the March scholarship deadline. Minimum 3.0 GPA and FAFSA are required.

Award: Scholarship for use in freshman year; renewable.

Eligibility Requirements: Applicant must be high school student and planning to enroll or expecting to enroll full-time at a two-year or four-year or technical institution or university. Applicant must have 3.0 GPA or higher. Available to U.S. citizens.

Application Requirements: Application form, FAFSA. *Deadline:* March 1.

CORNELIA VALENTINE MURPHY SCHOLARSHIP

Award for undergraduate study to Oregon AFSCME Council #75 members (active, laid-off, retired, or disabled) in good standing, or spouses (including life partners and their children), children, or grandchildren of members (active, laid-off, retired, disabled, or deceased) in good standing. Member must have been active in the Oregon Council 1+ year as of the March scholarship deadline or have been a member 1+ year preceding the date of layoff, death, disability, or retirement. Part-time enrollment (minimum six credit hours) will be considered for active members, their spouses (or life partners), or laid-off members. Essay required.

Award: Scholarship for use in freshman, sophomore, junior, or senior years; not renewable.

Eligibility Requirements: Applicant must be enrolled or expecting to enroll full- or part-time at a four-year institution or university. Available to U.S. citizens.

Application Requirements: Application form, essay, FAFSA, financial need analysis. *Deadline:* March 1.

DR. GENE AND MONICA VANG SCHOLARSHIP

Award for students who have a strong familiarity with the Hmong language and/or culture. Preference given to graduating high school seniors. Minimum 3.0 GPA and essay required.

Award: Scholarship for use in freshman, sophomore, junior, senior, or graduate years; not renewable.

Eligibility Requirements: Applicant must be enrolled or expecting to enroll full-time at a four-year institution or university. Applicant must have 3.0 GPA or higher. Available to U.S. citizens.

Application Requirements: Application form, essay, FAFSA. *Deadline:* March 1.

DREAM FOR FOSTER YOUTH SCHOLARSHIP

Award for first-time freshman, undergraduate, or graduate student who meets one of the following criteria: applies for and qualifies for the Chafee Education and Training Grant, was adopted from foster care between the ages of 14 and 16, is a former Chafee awardee now over age 23 and currently enrolled in a degree-seeking program, or is a Chafee-eligible youth who did not receive Chafee funds before age 21. Apply/ compete annually.

Award: Scholarship for use in freshman, sophomore, junior, senior, or graduate years; not renewable.

Eligibility Requirements: Applicant must be enrolled or expecting to enroll full-time at a four-year institution or university. Available to U.S. citizens.

Application Requirements: Application form, FAFSA. *Deadline:* March 1.

ERIK NIELSEN SCHOLARSHIP

Award for at least half time study at Oregon public and nonprofit colleges. Applicants must have or recently had at least a three-year gap in their education. First preference given to GED recipients, then those with a high school diploma, then undergraduates who have been out of college for at least three years. Not for applicants with existing bachelor's degree. FAFSA is required.

Award: Scholarship for use in freshman, sophomore, junior, or senior years; not renewable.

Eligibility Requirements: Applicant must be enrolled or expecting to enroll full- or part-time at a two-year or four-year institution or university and studying in Oregon. Available to U.S. citizens.

Application Requirements: Application form, FAFSA. *Deadline:* March 1.

ERNEST ALAN AND BARBARA PARK MEYER SCHOLARSHIP

Award for graduates of Oregon high schools who are first-generation college attendees and have transferred (or will be transferring during the same calendar year as the application year) from a community college to a four-year college in Oregon. Minimum 3.5 GPA required.

Award: Scholarship for use in freshman, sophomore, junior, or senior years; not renewable.

Eligibility Requirements: Applicant must be enrolled or expecting to enroll full-time at a four-year institution or university and studying in Oregon. Applicant must have 3.5 GPA or higher. Available to U.S. citizens.

Application Requirements: Application form, FAFSA. *Deadline:* March 1.

Contact: Mike McNickle, Director of Scholarships and Access
Programs
Phone: 541-687-7385
E-mail: mike.d.mcnickle@state.or.us

FORD SONS AND DAUGHTERS OF EMPLOYEES OF ROSEBURG FOREST PRODUCTS COMPANY SCHOLARSHIP

Renewable award for dependents of eligible employees of Roseburg Forest Products Company. Parent must have been a full-time employee a minimum of 18 months prior to the March scholarship application deadline. Must enroll full time, on campus, in the fall of the application year and be under 21 years of age. Not for applicants with existing bachelors degrees. May attend any eligible U.S. technical, 2- or 4-year school or college. Interview required.

Award: Scholarship for use in freshman, sophomore, junior, or senior years; renewable.

Eligibility Requirements: Applicant must be enrolled or expecting to enroll full-time at a two-year or four-year or technical institution. Available to U.S. citizens.

Application Requirements: Application form, interview. *Deadline:* March 1.

FRANZ STENZEL M.D. AND KATHRYN STENZEL SCHOLARSHIP

One award for graduates (including GED recipients and home-schooled graduates) of Oregon high schools and one award for nontraditional students, first-generation college students, and students approaching the final year of their programs. Students applying for first award must be majoring in medicine (pre-med and graduate-level), nursing, or physician assistant studies. Second award is not open to medical, nursing, or physician assistant students. For both awards, high school seniors must have minimum 2.75 GPA and college students a minimum 2.5 GPA. Both awards are automatically renewable if renewal criteria is met.

Award: Scholarship for use in freshman, sophomore, junior, senior, or graduate years; renewable.

Eligibility Requirements: Applicant must be enrolled or expecting to enroll full- or part-time at a four-year institution or university. Available to U.S. citizens.

Application Requirements: Application form, FAFSA. *Deadline:* March 1.

FRIENDS OF BILL RUTHERFORD EDUCATION SCHOLARSHIP

Award for children of individuals serving in the Oregon State Legislature or holding statewide elected office (Governor, Treasurer, Attorney General, Secretary of State, Commissioner of Labor, or Superintendent of Public Instruction); this does not include judicial positions. For use at public and nonprofit colleges in the U.S.

Award: Scholarship for use in freshman, sophomore, junior, or senior years; not renewable.

Eligibility Requirements: Applicant must be enrolled or expecting to enroll full-time at a four-year institution or university. Available to U.S. citizens.

Application Requirements: Application form, FAFSA. *Deadline:* March 1.

GEORGIA HARRIS MEMORIAL SCHOLARSHIP

Award for employees and dependents of eligible employees of Papa's Pizza. Eligible employees must have been employed by Papa's Pizza 1+ year as of the March scholarship deadline. Oregon residency is not required. Must submit essay and apply/compete annually.

Award: Scholarship for use in freshman, sophomore, junior, or senior, or graduate years; not renewable.

Eligibility Requirements: Applicant must be enrolled or expecting to enroll full-time at a two-year or four-year or technical institution or university. Available to U.S. citizens.

Application Requirements: Application form, essay, FAFSA. *Deadline:* March 1.

LYNDA PILGER MEMORIAL SCHOLARSHIP

One-time award available to graduating seniors (including home-schooled seniors) of Clackamas, Multnomah, or Washington County high schools. Minimum GPA of 2.75 required. Award must be used at a four-year public college or university in the United States. Must submit an essay describing work in the area of animal rights or animal welfare and how a college education will enhance efforts in these areas.

Award: Scholarship for use in freshman year; not renewable.

Eligibility Requirements: Applicant must be high school student and planning to enroll or expecting to enroll full-time at a four-year institution or university. Available to U.S. citizens.

Application Requirements: Application form, essay, FAFSA. *Deadline:* March 1.

MULTNOMAH COUNTY DEPUTY SHERIFFS' ASSOCIATION DEPENDENTS SCHOLARSHIP

Award for children (including stepchildren) of active or deceased Multnomah County Deputy Sheriffs' Association members (preference to active members). For undergraduate and graduate studies at any U.S. college. Apply/compete annually.

Award: Scholarship for use in freshman, sophomore, junior, senior, or graduate years; not renewable.

Eligibility Requirements: Applicant must be enrolled or expecting to enroll full-time at a four-year institution or university. Available to U.S. citizens.

Application Requirements: Application form. *Deadline:* March 1.

NECA OREGON-COLUMBIA CHAPTER SCHOLARSHIP

Award for graduating high school seniors who are either children of members of NECA Oregon-Columbia Chapter, children of employees of members of NECA Oregon-Columbia Chapter, or grandchildren of retired members of NECA Oregon-Columbia Chapter. Oregon state residency is not required. Automatically renewable if renewal criteria met.

Award: Scholarship for use in freshman year; renewable.

Eligibility Requirements: Applicant must be high school student and planning to enroll or expecting to enroll full-time at a two-year or four-year or technical institution or university. Available to U.S. citizens.

Application Requirements: Application form. *Deadline:* March 1.

ONE WORLD SCHOLARSHIP ESSAY

One-time award for the best essay analyzing the inter-relationships of policy, programs, and personal responsibility on hunger and the stability of the food supply. Must be 21 or under as of the March scholarship deadline and pursuing undergraduate work at any public and nonprofit U.S. college.

Award: Scholarship for use in freshman, sophomore, junior, or senior years; not renewable.

Eligibility Requirements: Applicant must be enrolled or expecting to enroll full-time at a four-year institution or university. Available to U.S. citizens.

Application Requirements: Essay. *Deadline:* March 1.

OREGON ALBACORE COMMISSION SCHOLARSHIP

One-time award for first-time freshmen or undergraduates enrolled at least part time at any college or university in the U.S. Open to Oregon commercially licensed albacore tuna landing permit holders, their captains, and their children and dependents who have paid assessments to the Oregon Albacore Commission within the past year; and processors, employees and their children and dependents where the business has purchased Oregon albacore tuna and paid assessments to the Oregon Albacore Commission within the past year. FAFSA required. Apply/compete for additional year of funding.

Award: Scholarship for use in freshman, sophomore, junior, or senior years; not renewable.

Eligibility Requirements: Applicant must be enrolled or expecting to enroll full- or part-time at a two-year or four-year institution or university. Available to U.S. citizens.

Application Requirements: Application form. *Deadline:* March 1.

OREGON MOVING AND STORAGE ASSOCIATION JACK L. STEWART SCHOLARSHIP

Award for dependents of Oregon Moving and Storage Association (OMSA) members or dependents of employees 1+ year) of OMSA members. For undergraduate study at any Oregon college. Apply/compete annually.

Award: Scholarship for use in freshman, sophomore, junior, or senior years; not renewable.

Eligibility Requirements: Applicant must be enrolled or expecting to enroll full-time at a four-year institution or university and studying in Oregon. Available to U.S. citizens.

Application Requirements: Application form. *Deadline:* March 1.

OREGON SCHOLARSHIP FUND COMMUNITY COLLEGE STUDENT AWARD

Scholarship open to students enrolled or planning to enroll at least half time in Oregon community college programs. Recipients may reapply for one additional year. FAFSA is required.

Award: Scholarship for use in freshman or sophomore years; not renewable.

Eligibility Requirements: Applicant must be enrolled or expecting to enroll full- or part-time at a two-year institution and studying in Oregon. Available to U.S. citizens.

Application Requirements: Activity chart, FAFSA, application form, essay, financial need analysis, transcript. *Deadline:* March 1.

OREGON STUDENT ACCESS COMMISSION EMPLOYEE AND DEPENDENTS SCHOLARSHIP

Award for current permanent employees of OSAC who are past initial trial service as of the March scholarship deadline; or children, stepchildren, or legal dependents of either a current permanent employee of OSAC at the time of the March scholarship deadline; a former OSAC employee who retires, is permanently disabled, or is deceased directly from employment at OSAC, or a former permanent OSAC employee who was past initial trial service who was laid off within one year of the March scholarship deadline. Children and dependents must enroll full time and be 23 or under as of the March scholarship deadline. Employees must enroll at least half time.

Award: Scholarship for use in freshman, sophomore, junior, or senior years; not renewable.

Eligibility Requirements: Applicant must be enrolled or expecting to enroll full- or part-time at a four-year institution or university. Available to U.S. citizens.

Application Requirements: Application form. *Deadline:* March 1.

REGISTER-GUARD FEDERAL CREDIT UNION SCHOLARSHIP

Award is available to first-time freshmen, undergraduate, and graduate students who are current members of the Register-Guard Federal Credit Union, or those eligible for membership, with preference in the following order: (1) current employees, independent contractors of The Register-Guard including members of their immediate families or households, (2) retired persons as pensioners or annuitants, (3) spouses of persons who died within membership, (4) organizations of such persons, (5) members of the Confederated Tribes of Grande Ronde or their immediate family members, and (6) employees or contracted employees of the law office of Donald Slayton and Alan Seglison or their immediate family members. Oregon residency is not required. Minimum 2.5 GPA and essay required.

Award: Scholarship for use in freshman, sophomore, junior, senior, or graduate years; not renewable.

Eligibility Requirements: Applicant must be enrolled or expecting to enroll full-time at a two-year or four-year institution or university. Applicant must have 2.5 GPA or higher. Available to U.S. citizens.

Application Requirements: Application form, essay, FAFSA, transcript. *Deadline:* March 1.

SALEM ELECTRIC COOPERATIVE SCHOLARSHIP

Award for a high school graduate who is or whose parents/legal guardians are receiving service from Salem Electric at their primary residence. Salem Electric staff, board members, and immediate family are not eligible.

Award: Scholarship for use in freshman, sophomore, junior, or senior years; not renewable.

Eligibility Requirements: Applicant must be enrolled or expecting to enroll full-time at a four-year institution or university. Available to U.S. citizens.

Application Requirements: Application form. *Deadline:* March 1.

SEIU LOCAL 503/OPEU STUDENT FINANCIAL AID SCHOLARSHIP

Award for students who are SEIU Local 503/OPEU active members, laid-off members; children, grandchildren, spouses, or domestic partners of active or retired members in good standing; or dependents of deceased members who were active members at time of death. Qualifying members must have been active (full membership dues payer) 1+ year as of the March scholarship deadline. Children, grandchildren, or dependents of qualifying members must be 24 or younger as of the March scholarship deadline, must enroll full time, and will be considered only for undergraduate programs. Part-time enrollment (minimum six credit hours) or graduate program enrollment will be considered only for active members, spouses, domestic partners, or laid-off members. FAFSA is required.

Award: Scholarship for use in freshman, sophomore, junior, senior, or graduate years; not renewable.

Eligibility Requirements: Applicant must be enrolled or expecting to enroll full- or part-time at a four-year institution or university. Available to U.S. citizens.

Application Requirements: Application form, FAFSA. *Deadline:* March 1.

SP FIBER TECHNOLOGIES DEPENDENTS SCHOLARSHIP

Award for dependents of eligible employees of SP Fiber Technologies. Eligible employees must have been employed by SP Fiber Technologies 1+ year as of the March scholarship deadline. Oregon residency is not required.

Award: Scholarship for use in freshman, sophomore, junior, or senior years; not renewable.

Eligibility Requirements: Applicant must be enrolled or expecting to enroll full-time at a two-year or four-year institution or university. Available to U.S. citizens.

Application Requirements: Application form. *Deadline:* March 1.

TECHNICAL TRAINING FUND SCHOLARSHIP

Award is available to graduates (including GED recipients and home-schooled graduates) of Oregon high schools. Preference will be given to students who will enroll as a junior, senior, or graduate-level student for fall term/semester at a traditional four-year institution; then applicants at any class level enrolled at a special vocational/trade school. Applicants must demonstrate extraordinary technical or artistic potential in areas such as craftsmanship, manual skills, art, music, or culinary arts. Recipient must enroll at least half-time.

Award: Scholarship for use in freshman, sophomore, junior, senior, or graduate years; not renewable.

Eligibility Requirements: Applicant must be enrolled or expecting to enroll full- or part-time at a four-year or technical institution or university. Available to U.S. citizens.

Application Requirements: Application form, essay, FAFSA, recommendations or references. *Deadline:* March 1.

TYKESON FAMILY CHARITABLE TRUST SCHOLARSHIP

Renewable award available to dependents of full-time employees of Bend Cable Communications; Bend Broadband, Central Oregon Cable Advertising; Tykeson/Associates Enterprises; or ZoloMedia, Bend Broadband Vault. Eligible employees must have been employed by one of these companies two or more years as of the March scholarship deadline. Applicants must be enrolled or planning to enroll in an undergraduate program at an Oregon public college or university. College students applying must have minimum 2.5 GPA.

Award: Scholarship for use in freshman, sophomore, junior, or senior years; renewable.

Eligibility Requirements: Applicant must be enrolled or expecting to enroll full-time at a four-year institution or university and studying in Oregon. Available to U.S. citizens.

Application Requirements: Activity chart, application form, essay, financial need analysis, recommendations or references, transcript. *Deadline:* March 1.

UMATILLA ELECTRIC COOPERATIVE SCHOLARSHIP

Award for a high school graduate of high schools in Morrow or Umatilla County (including home-school graduate) or GED recipient enrolled or planning to enroll at a U.S. college or university. Applicant or applicant's parents/legal guardians must be active members of the Umatilla Electric Cooperative (UEC) and be receiving service from UEC at their primary residence. Must reapply for award annually.

Award: Scholarship for use in freshman, sophomore, junior, or senior years; not renewable.

Eligibility Requirements: Applicant must be enrolled or expecting to enroll full- or part-time at a four-year institution or university. Available to U.S. citizens.

Application Requirements: Activity chart, application form, essay, financial need analysis, recommendations or references, transcript. *Deadline:* March 1.

UNIVERSITY CLUB OF PORTLAND SCHOLARSHIP

Award available to eligible employees and dependents of eligible employees of the University Club of Portland. Eligible employees must be in good standing and must have been employed by University Club of Portland one or more years as of the March scholarship deadline. Oregon residency is not required. College applicants must have a minimum 2.5 GPA. Apply/compete annually; prior recipients must be currently enrolled to reapply.

Award: Scholarship for use in freshman, sophomore, junior, senior, or graduate years; not renewable.

Eligibility Requirements: Applicant must be enrolled or expecting to enroll full- or part-time at a four-year institution or university. Available to U.S. citizens.

Application Requirements: Application form, FAFSA, transcript. *Deadline:* March 1.

WAYNE MORSE LEGACY SCHOLARSHIP

Award for graduates (including GED recipients and home-schooled graduates) of Oregon high schools who are enrolled or planning to enroll at least half time at Oregon public and nonprofit institutions. Must be a U.S. citizen and have a minimum 2.8 GPA. Essay and FAFSA required.

Award: Scholarship for use in freshman, sophomore, junior, senior, or graduate years; not renewable.

Eligibility Requirements: Applicant must be enrolled or expecting to enroll full- or part-time at a two-year or four-year institution or university and studying in Oregon. Available to U.S. citizens.

Application Requirements: Application form, essay, FAFSA. *Deadline:* March 1.

W.C. AND PEARL CAMPBELL SCHOLARSHIP

One-time award for graduating seniors of Oregon high schools. 1220+ combined math and critical reading SAT scores or ACT composite of 27+ required. Minimum GPA of 3.85 required. Must be planning to attend an Oregon college or university.

Award: Scholarship for use in freshman year; not renewable.

Eligibility Requirements: Applicant must be high school student; planning to enroll or expecting to enroll full-time at a four-year institution or university and studying in Oregon. Available to U.S. citizens.

Application Requirements: Application form, FAFSA. *Deadline:* March 1.

OUTSTANDING STUDENTS OF AMERICA

http://www.outstandingstudentsofamerica.com/

OUTSTANDING STUDENTS OF AMERICA SCHOLARSHIP

Awards of $1000 each are payable to the college of the recipient's choice. Students must be high school seniors, participate in community/school activities, and maintain a minimum GPA of 3.0. For details refer to website, http://www.outstandingstudentsofamerica.com/.

Award: Scholarship for use in freshman year; not renewable. *Amount:* $1000.

Eligibility Requirements: Applicant must be high school student and planning to enroll or expecting to enroll full- or part-time at a four-year institution or university. Applicant must have 3.0 GPA or higher. Available to U.S. citizens.

Application Requirements: Application form, community service, self-addressed stamped envelope with application. *Deadline:* October 1.

Contact: Michael Layson, President
Phone: 205-344-6322
Fax: 205-344-6322
E-mail: info@outstandingstudentsofamerica.com

PADGETT BUSINESS SERVICES FOUNDATION

http://www.smallbizpros.com/

PADGETT BUSINESS SERVICES FOUNDATION SCHOLARSHIP PROGRAM

Scholarship awards to the dependents of small business owners throughout the United States and Canada. Must be a dependent of a business owner who employs fewer than 20 people, owns at least 10 percent of the stock or capital in the business, and is active in the day-to-day operations of the business. For more details, visit the website http://www.smallbizpros.com.

Award: Scholarship for use in freshman year; not renewable. *Number:* 65–75. *Amount:* $500.

Eligibility Requirements: Applicant must be high school student and planning to enroll or expecting to enroll full-time at a two-year or four-year or technical institution or university. Available to U.S. and Canadian citizens.

Application Requirements: Application form, community service, essay, school activities, test scores, transcript. *Deadline:* March 1.

Contact: Heather Stokley, Administrator
Padgett Business Services Foundation
160 Hawthorne Park
Athens, GA 30606
Phone: 800-723-4388
Fax: 800-548-1040
E-mail: hstokley@smallbizpros.com

PAPERCHECK

http://www.papercheck.com/

PAPERCHECK, LLC—CHARLES SHAFAE' SCHOLARSHIP FUND

Awards two $500 scholarships each year to winners of the Papercheck essay contest. Must be enrolled at an accredited four-year college or university. Must maintain a cumulative GPA of at least 3.2. Scholarship guidelines available at http://http://www.papercheck.com/scholarship.asp.

Award: Scholarship for use in freshman, sophomore, junior, or senior years; not renewable. *Number:* 2. *Amount:* $500–$500.

Eligibility Requirements: Applicant must be enrolled or expecting to enroll full-time at a four-year institution or university. Applicant must have 3.0 GPA or higher. Available to U.S. citizens.

Application Requirements: Application form, application form may be submitted online (http://www.papercheck.com/scholarship.asp), entry in a contest, essay, transcript. *Deadline:* continuous.

Contact: Mr. Darren Shafae, Scholarship Coordinator
Papercheck
12 Geary Street
Suite 808
San Francisco, CA 94108
Phone: 866-693-3348
E-mail: scholarships@papercheck.com

PATIENT ADVOCATE FOUNDATION

http://www.patientadvocate.org/

SCHOLARSHIPS FOR SURVIVORS

Scholarships to provide support to patients seeking to initiate or complete a course of study that has been interrupted or delayed by a diagnosis of cancer or another critical or life threatening illness. Up to ten awards of $3000 available to U.S. citizens. Minimum 3.0 GPA required.

Award: Scholarship for use in freshman, sophomore, junior, or senior years; renewable. *Number:* up to 10. *Amount:* up to $3000.

Eligibility Requirements: Applicant must be enrolled or expecting to enroll full-time at a two-year or four-year institution or university. Applicant must have 3.0 GPA or higher. Available to U.S. citizens.

Application Requirements: Application form, essay, financial need analysis, physician letter, recommendations or references, transcript. *Deadline:* April 14.

Contact: Ruth Anne Reed, Vice President of Human Resource Programs
Patient Advocate Foundation
700 Thimble Shoals Boulevard, Suite 200
Newport News, VA 23606
Phone: 800-532-5274
Fax: 757-952-2475
E-mail: scholarship@patientadvocate.org

PATRICK KERR SKATEBOARD SCHOLARSHIP FUND

PATRICK KERR SKATEBOARD SCHOLARSHIP

Scholarship for high school senior accepted in a full-time undergraduate course of study at an accredited two- or four-year college/university. One individual will receive a $5000 scholarship and three individuals will receive a $1000 scholarship. Applicant must be a skateboarder and U.S. citizen. Minimum 2.5 GPA required.

Award: Scholarship for use in freshman year; not renewable. *Number:* 4. *Amount:* $1000–$5000.

Eligibility Requirements: Applicant must be high school student and planning to enroll or expecting to enroll full-time at a two-year or four-year institution or university. Applicant must have 2.5 GPA or higher. Available to U.S. citizens.

Application Requirements: Application form, essay, recommendations or references, transcript. *Deadline:* April 20.

Contact: Patrick Kerr, Scholarship Committee
Phone: 215-663-9329
Fax: 215-663-5897
E-mail: info@skateboardscholarship.org

PHI BETA SIGMA FRATERNITY INC.

http://www.pbs1914.org/

PHI BETA SIGMA FRATERNITY NATIONAL PROGRAM OF EDUCATION

Scholarships are awarded to both graduate and undergraduate students. Applicants must have minimum 3.0 GPA.

Award: Scholarship for use in freshman, sophomore, junior, senior, or graduate years; not renewable.

Eligibility Requirements: Applicant must be enrolled or expecting to enroll full-time at a four-year institution or university and male. Applicant must have 3.0 GPA or higher. Available to U.S. citizens.

Application Requirements: Application form, essay, personal photograph, recommendations or references, resume, transcript. *Deadline:* June 15.

Contact: Emile Pitre, Chairman
Phi Beta Sigma Fraternity Inc.
2 Belmonte Circle, SW
Atlanta, GA 30311
Phone: 404-759-6827
E-mail: mikewhines@aol.com

PROOF READING, LLC

http://www.proof-reading.com/

PROOF READING, LLC SCHOLARSHIP PROGRAM

Applicants must write an essay that satisfies the question found on the organization website. The minimum word count is 1,500 words. Focus will be on grammar and ability to present ideas clearly. Include a Works Cited page, with a minimum of three sources. The essay must follow MLA writing guidelines. For more information, visit website http://www.proof-reading.com/proof-reading_scholarship_program.asp.

Award: Scholarship for use in freshman, sophomore, junior, or senior years; not renewable. *Number:* 1. *Amount:* $1500–$1500.

Eligibility Requirements: Applicant must be enrolled or expecting to enroll full-time at a four-year institution or university. Applicant must have 3.5 GPA or higher. Available to U.S. citizens.

Application Requirements: Application form, entry in a contest, essay, transcript. *Deadline:* continuous.

Contact: Mr. Mike Williams, Scholarship Coordinator
Proof Reading, LLC
12 Geary Street
Suite 806
San Francisco, CA 94108
Phone: 866-433-4867
E-mail: scholarships@proof-reading.com

PRUDENT PUBLISHING COMPANY INC.

http://www.gallerycollection.com/

4TH ANNUAL CREATE-A-GREETING-CARD $10,000 SCHOLARSHIP CONTEST

Students must submit an original photo, piece of artwork, or computer graphic for the front of a greeting card. The student with the best design will win a $10,000 scholarship and have his or her entry made into an actual greeting card to be sold in The Gallery Collection's line. The winning student's school will also receive a $1,000 prize for helping to promote the contest. For complete details visit http://www.gallerycollection.com/greeting-cards-scholarship.htm.

Award: Scholarship for use in freshman, sophomore, junior, senior, or graduate years; not renewable. *Number:* 1. *Amount:* $10,000.

Eligibility Requirements: Applicant must be enrolled or expecting to enroll full- or part-time at a two-year or four-year or technical institution or university. Available to U.S. citizens.

Application Requirements: Application form, entry in a contest, greeting card design. *Deadline:* December 31.

PUSH FOR EXCELLENCE

http://www.pushexcel.org/

ORA LEE SANDERS SCHOLARSHIP

U.S. Citizens who will be freshmen, sophomore, juniors or seniors are eligible. The scholarship is renewable up to 4 years based upon GPA. Full time study with minimum 2.5 GPA.

Award: Scholarship for use in freshman, sophomore, junior, or senior years; renewable. *Amount:* $1000.

Eligibility Requirements: Applicant must be enrolled or expecting to enroll full-time at a four-year institution or university. Applicant must have 2.5 GPA or higher. Available to U.S. citizens.

Application Requirements: Application form, essay, proof of current enrollment or acceptance in a college or university, recommendations or references, self-addressed stamped envelope with application, transcript. *Deadline:* April 30.

RENEE B. FISHER FOUNDATION

http://www.rbffoundation.org/

MILTON FISHER SCHOLARSHIP FOR INNOVATION AND CREATIVITY

The Milton Fisher Scholarship is a four-year scholarship of up to $20,000 awarded to exceptionally innovative and creative high school juniors, seniors, and college freshmen from the Connecticut and New York City Metropolitan Area, or those who plan to attend university in this area.

Award: Scholarship for use in freshman, sophomore, junior, or senior years; renewable. *Number:* 5–8. *Amount:* $1000–$20,000.

Eligibility Requirements: Applicant must be enrolled or expecting to enroll full-time at a four-year institution or university. Available to U.S. citizens.

Application Requirements: Application form, essay, IRS forms, letter of admission to college, recommendations or references, transcript. *Deadline:* April 30.

Contact: Ms. Emily Casaretto, Associate Philanthropic Officer
Renee B. Fisher Foundation
77 Audubon Street
New Haven, CT 06510
Phone: 203-777-2386
Fax: 203-787-6584

RHODE ISLAND FOUNDATION

http://www.rifoundation.org/

BEACON BRIGHTER TOMORROWS SCHOLARSHIP

Scholarship for a dependent child whose parent sustained a work related injury with an employer who had workers compensation insurance with Beacon Mutual Insurance Company. Must have been accepted into an accredited post-secondary institution (including an academic, trade, or vocational program) on a full-time or part-time basis. Must have maintained a grade point average of C or better for the past two year, be a U.S. citizen or legal resident, and demonstrate financial need.

Award: Scholarship for use in freshman, sophomore, junior, or senior years; renewable.

Eligibility Requirements: Applicant must be high school student and planning to enroll or expecting to enroll full- or part-time at a two-year or four-year or technical institution or university. Available to U.S. citizens.

Application Requirements: Application form, copy of your student aid report calculated upon completion of the FAFSA , proof of acceptance to an accredited institution, financial need analysis, recommendations or references, transcript. *Deadline:* June 15.

Contact: Libby Monahan, Funds Administrator
Phone: 401-274-4564 Ext. 3117
E-mail: libbym@rifoundation.org

ROOTHBERT FUND INC.

http://www.roothbertfund.org/

ROOTHBERT FUND INC. SCHOLARSHIP

Scholarships are open to all in the United States regardless of sex, age, color, nationality or religious background. Provide SASE when requesting an application.

Award: Scholarship for use in freshman, sophomore, junior, senior, or graduate years; renewable. *Number:* 20. *Amount:* $2000–$3000.

Eligibility Requirements: Applicant must be enrolled or expecting to enroll full-time at a two-year or four-year or technical institution or university and studying in Connecticut, Delaware, District of Columbia, Maryland, Massachusetts, New Hampshire, New Jersey, New York, Ohio, Pennsylvania, Rhode Island, Vermont, Virginia, West Virginia. Available to U.S. citizens.

Application Requirements: Application form, driver's license, essay, financial need analysis, interview, personal photograph, recommendations or references, self-addressed stamped envelope with application, test scores, transcript. *Deadline:* February 1.

Contact: Percy Preston, Office Manager
Roothbert Fund Inc.
475 Riverside Drive, Room 252
New York, NY 10115
Phone: 212-870-3116

ROPAGE GROUP LLC

http://www.patricias-scholarship.org/

PATRICIA M. MCNAMARA MEMORIAL SCHOLARSHIP

Scholarship open to students who are already attending college or will be attending college within a year of the deadline. Students must utilize the online form to submit the scholarship application and essay. For more details, see website at http://www.patricias-scholarship.org.

Award: Scholarship for use in freshman, sophomore, junior, or senior years; not renewable. *Number:* 1. *Amount:* $1000.

Eligibility Requirements: Applicant must be enrolled or expecting to enroll full- or part-time at a two-year or four-year or technical institution or university. Available to U.S. and non-U.S. citizens.

Application Requirements: Application form, essay. *Deadline:* varies.

SABERTEC LLC/BLADE YOUR RIDE

http://www.bladeyourride.com/

BLADE YOUR RIDE SCHOLARSHIP PROGRAM

Scholarship for students enrolled in a full-time bachelor's degree program or master's degree program. Applicant should maintain a GPA of 3.0.

Award: Scholarship for use in freshman, sophomore, junior, senior, or graduate years; not renewable. *Number:* 3–5. *Amount:* $5000–$15,000.

Eligibility Requirements: Applicant must be enrolled or expecting to enroll full-time at a four-year institution or university. Applicant must have 3.0 GPA or higher. Available to U.S. and non-U.S. citizens.

Application Requirements: Application form, recommendations or references, resume, short video/webcast, transcript. *Deadline:* June 30.

Contact: Ashley Fontaine, Scholarship Committee
Phone: 512-358-6219
E-mail: ashley@bladeyourride.com

SALLIE MAE FUND

http://www.thesalliemaefund.org/

SALLIE MAE 911 EDUCATION FUND SCHOLARSHIP PROGRAM

Scholarship program open to children of those who were killed or permanently disabled as a result of the 9/11 terrorist attacks who are enrolled as full-time undergraduate students at approved accredited institutions. May be renewed on an annual academic basis subject to satisfactory academic progress. Applications available at the following website http://www.thesalliemaefund.org/smfnew/pdf/911application.pdf.

Award: Scholarship for use in freshman, sophomore, junior, or senior years; renewable. *Number:* up to 335. *Amount:* up to $2500.

Eligibility Requirements: Applicant must be enrolled or expecting to enroll full-time at a two-year or four-year institution or university. Available to U.S. citizens.

Application Requirements: Application form, financial need analysis, proof of death or disability of parent. *Deadline:* May 15.

Contact: Laura Gemery, Scholarship Committee
Phone: 703-810-3000
Fax: 703-984-5042

SALLIE MAE FUND UNMET NEED SCHOLARSHIP PROGRAM

Open to families with a combined income of $30,000 or less, this program is intended to supplement financial aid packages that fall more than $1000 short of students' financial need. Open to U.S. citizens and permanent residents who are accepted or enrolled as full-time undergraduate students. Students must have minimum 2.5 GPA.

Award: Scholarship for use in freshman, sophomore, junior, or senior years; not renewable. *Amount:* $1000–$3800.

Eligibility Requirements: Applicant must be enrolled or expecting to enroll full-time at a four-year institution or university. Applicant must have 2.5 GPA or higher. Available to U.S. citizens.

Application Requirements: Application form, test scores, transcript. *Deadline:* May 31.

SAMUEL HUNTINGTON FUND

http://www.nationalgridus.com/huntington.asp

SAMUEL HUNTINGTON PUBLIC SERVICE AWARD

Award provides a $10,000 stipend to a graduating college senior to perform a one-year public service project anywhere in the world immediately following graduation. Written proposals of 1000 words or less are required with application. Project may encompass any activity that furthers the public good. Awards will be based on quality of proposal, academic record, and other personal achievements. Semi-finalists will be interviewed.

Award: Grant for use in senior year; not renewable. *Number:* 1–3. *Amount:* $10,000.

Eligibility Requirements: Applicant must be enrolled or expecting to enroll full-time at a four-year institution or university. Available to U.S. and non-U.S. citizens.

Application Requirements: Application form, application form may be submitted online (http://www.nationalgridus.com/huntington.asp), essay, financial need analysis, recommendations or references, resume, transcript. *Deadline:* January 18.

Contact: Amy Stacy, Executive Assistant
Samuel Huntington Fund
National Grid
40 Sylvan Road
Waltham, MA 02451
Phone: 781-907-3358
Fax: 781-907-5705
E-mail: amy.stacy@us.ngrid.com

THE SAN DIEGO FOUNDATION

http://www.sdfoundation.org/

COMMON SCHOLARSHIP APPLICATION

The Common Scholarship Application uses one online form to access more than 100 scholarships. Scholarships are available for graduating high school seniors, undergraduates, graduate students and adult re-entry students who are attending 2-year colleges, 4-year universities, trade/vocational schools, graduate, medical and professional schools and teaching credential programs. Scholarships range from $500 to more than $5,000 and - depending on the scholarship - can pay for tuition, room and board, books, fees and other related expenses. Note that almost all of our scholarships require San Diego County residency.

Award: Scholarship for use in freshman, sophomore, junior, senior, or graduate years; renewable. *Number:* 95–110. *Amount:* $500–$15,000.

Eligibility Requirements: Applicant must be enrolled or expecting to enroll full- or part-time at a two-year or four-year or technical institution or university. Available to U.S. citizens.

Application Requirements: Application form, application form may be submitted online (http://www.sdfoundation.org/GrantsScholarships/Scholarships/ForStudents/CommonScholarshipApplication.aspx), essay.

SCHOLARSHIPEXPERTS.COM

http://www.scholarshipexperts.com/apply.htx

ALL ABOUT EDUCATION SCHOLARSHIP

Applicants must: Complete a profile on the scholarshipexperts.com website. Be thirteen years of age or older at the time of application. Be legal residents of the fifty United States or the District of Columbia. Be currently enrolled (or enroll no later than the fall of 2017) in an accredited post-secondary institution of higher education. Submit an online short written response (250 words or less) for the topic: "How will a $3,000 scholarship for education make a difference in your life?"

Award: Scholarship for use in freshman, sophomore, junior, senior, graduate, or postgraduate years; not renewable. *Number:* 1. *Amount:* $3000.

Eligibility Requirements: Applicant must be enrolled or expecting to enroll full- or part-time at a two-year or four-year or technical institution or university. Available to U.S. citizens.

Application Requirements: Application form, application form may be submitted online (http://www.scholarshipexperts.com/apply.htx), essay. *Deadline:* April 30.

DO-OVER SCHOLARSHIP

Applicants must: Be thirteen years of age or older at the time of application. Be legal residents of the fifty United States or the District of Columbia. Be currently enrolled (or enroll no later than the fall of 2017) in an accredited post-secondary institution of higher education. Submit an online short written response (250 words or less) for the question: "If you could get one 'do over' in life, what would it be and why?"

Award: Scholarship for use in freshman, sophomore, junior, senior, graduate, or postgraduate years; not renewable. *Number:* 1. *Amount:* $1500.

Eligibility Requirements: Applicant must be enrolled or expecting to enroll full- or part-time at a two-year or four-year or technical institution or university. Available to U.S. citizens.

Application Requirements: Application form, application form may be submitted online (http://www.scholarshipexperts.com/apply.htx), essay. *Deadline:* June 30.

EDUCATION MATTERS SCHOLARSHIP

Applicants must: Complete a profile on the ScholarshipExperts.com website. Be thirteen years of age or older at the time of application. Be legal residents of the fifty United States or the District of Columbia. Be currently enrolled (or enroll no later than the fall of 2018) in an accredited post-secondary institution of higher education. Submit an online short written response (250 words or less) for the question: "What would you say to someone who thinks education doesn't matter, or that college is a waste of time and money?"

Award: Scholarship for use in freshman, sophomore, junior, senior, graduate, or postgraduate years; not renewable. *Number:* 1. *Amount:* $5000.

Eligibility Requirements: Applicant must be enrolled or expecting to enroll full- or part-time at a two-year or four-year or technical institution or university. Available to U.S. citizens.

Application Requirements: Application form, application form may be submitted online (http://www.scholarshipexperts.com/apply.htx), essay. *Deadline:* October 31.

FIFTH MONTH SCHOLARSHIP

Applicants must: Be thirteen years of age or older at the time of application. Be legal residents of the fifty United States or the District of Columbia. Be currently enrolled (or enroll no later than the fall of 2018) in an accredited post-secondary institution of higher education and submit an online short written response (250 words or less) for the topic: "May is the fifth month of the year. Write a letter to the number five explaining why five is important. Be serious or be funny. Either way, here's a high five to you just for being original."

Award: Scholarship for use in freshman, sophomore, junior, senior, graduate, or postgraduate years; not renewable. *Number:* 1. *Amount:* $1500.

Eligibility Requirements: Applicant must be enrolled or expecting to enroll full- or part-time at a two-year or four-year or technical institution or university. Available to U.S. citizens.

Application Requirements: Application form, application form may be submitted online (http://www.scholarshipexperts.com/apply.htx), essay. *Deadline:* May 31.

GOOD DEEDS SCHOLARSHIP

Applicants must: Be thirteen years of age or older at the time of application. Be legal residents of the fifty United States or the District of Columbia. Be currently enrolled (or enroll no later than the fall of 2018) in an accredited post-secondary institution of higher education and submit an online short written response (250 words or less) for the topic: "Have you ever volunteered, done community service, or helped others in a way that changed the world for the better? If not, what would you do in the future to make a difference? Explain how your good deed positively contributed (or will contribute) to society."

Award: Scholarship for use in freshman year; not renewable. *Number:* 1. *Amount:* $1000.

Eligibility Requirements: Applicant must be high school student; age 13-19 and planning to enroll or expecting to enroll full- or part-time at a two-year or four-year or technical institution or university. Available to U.S. citizens.

Application Requirements: Application form, application form may be submitted online (http://www.scholarshipexperts.com/apply.htx), essay. *Deadline:* December 31.

I HAVE A DREAM SCHOLARSHIP

Applicants must: Be thirteen years of age or older at the time of application. Be legal residents of the fifty United States or the District of Columbia. Be currently enrolled (or enroll no later than the fall of 2018) in an accredited post-secondary institution of higher education and submit an online short written response (250 words or less) for the topic: "We want to know—what do you dream about? Whether it's some bizarre dream from last week, or your hopes for the future, share your dreams with us for a chance to win $1,000 for college."

Award: Scholarship for use in freshman, sophomore, junior, senior, graduate, or postgraduate years; not renewable. *Number:* 1. *Amount:* $1000.

Eligibility Requirements: Applicant must be enrolled or expecting to enroll full- or part-time at a two-year or four-year or technical institution or university. Available to U.S. citizens.

Application Requirements: Application form, application form may be submitted online (http://www.scholarshipexperts.com/apply.htx), essay. *Deadline:* January 31.

NEXT BIG THING SCHOLARSHIP

Applicants must: Be thirteen years of age or older at the time of application. Be legal residents of the fifty United States or the District of Columbia. Be currently enrolled (or enroll no later than the fall of 2018) in an accredited post-secondary institution of higher education and submit an online short written response (250 words or less) for the topic: "If you could create the 'next big thing,' what would it be, what would it do, and why is it needed?"

Award: Scholarship for use in freshman, sophomore, junior, senior, graduate, or postgraduate years; not renewable. *Number:* 1. *Amount:* $1500.

Eligibility Requirements: Applicant must be enrolled or expecting to enroll full- or part-time at a two-year or four-year or technical institution or university. Available to U.S. citizens.

Application Requirements: Application form, application form may be submitted online (http://www.scholarshipexperts.com/apply.htx), essay. *Deadline:* February 28.

SHOUT IT OUT SCHOLARSHIP

Applicants must: Be thirteen years of age or older at the time of application. Be legal residents of the fifty United States or the District of Columbia. Be currently enrolled (or enroll no later than the fall of 2018) in an accredited post-secondary institution of higher education and submit an online short written response (250 words or less) for the topic: "If you could say one thing to the entire world at once, what would it be and why?"

Award: Scholarship for use in freshman, sophomore, junior, senior, graduate, or postgraduate years; not renewable. *Number:* 1. *Amount:* $1500.

Eligibility Requirements: Applicant must be enrolled or expecting to enroll full- or part-time at a two-year or four-year or technical institution or university. Available to U.S. citizens.

Application Requirements: Application form, application form may be submitted online (http://www.scholarshipexperts.com/apply.htx), essay. *Deadline:* September 30.

SUPERPOWER SCHOLARSHIP

Applicants must: Be thirteen years of age or older at the time of application. Be legal residents of the fifty United States or the District of Columbia. Be currently enrolled (or enroll no later than the fall of 2018) in an accredited post-secondary institution of higher education. Submit an online short written response (250 words or less) for the question: "Which superhero or villain would you want to changes places with for a day and why?"

Award: Scholarship for use in freshman, sophomore, junior, or senior years; not renewable. *Number:* 1. *Amount:* $2500.

Eligibility Requirements: Applicant must be enrolled or expecting to enroll full- or part-time at a two-year or four-year or technical institution or university. Available to U.S. citizens.

Application Requirements: Application form, application form may be submitted online (http://www.scholarshipexperts.com/apply.htx), essay. *Deadline:* March 31.

TOP TEN LIST SCHOLARSHIP

Applicants must: Be thirteen years of age or older at the time of application. Be legal residents of the fifty United States or the District of Columbia. Be currently enrolled (or enroll no later than the fall of 2018) in an accredited post-secondary institution of higher education. Submit an online short written response (250 words or less) for the topic: "Create a Top Ten List of the top ten reasons you should get this scholarship."

Award: Scholarship for use in freshman, sophomore, junior, senior, graduate, or postgraduate years; not renewable. *Number:* 1. *Amount:* $1500.

Eligibility Requirements: Applicant must be enrolled or expecting to enroll full- or part-time at a two-year or four-year or technical institution or university. Available to U.S. citizens.

Application Requirements: Application form, application form may be submitted online (http://www.scholarshipexperts.com/apply.htx), essay. *Deadline:* December 31.

SCHOLARSHIP WORKSHOP LLC

http://www.scholarshipworkshop.com/

RAGINS/BRASWELL NATIONAL SCHOLARSHIP

Scholarship available to high school seniors, undergraduate, and graduate students who attend The Scholarship Workshop presentation or an online class given by Marianne Ragins. Award is based on application, essay, leadership, extracurricular activities, achievements, and community responsibility. See website http://www.scholarshipworkshop.com. Scholarship amounts vary.

Award: Scholarship for use in freshman, sophomore, junior, or senior years; not renewable. *Number:* 1–3. *Amount:* $100–$500.

Eligibility Requirements: Applicant must be enrolled or expecting to enroll full-time at a four-year institution or university. Available to U.S. citizens.

Application Requirements: Application form, essay. *Deadline:* April 30.

SCREEN ACTORS' GUILD FOUNDATION

http://www.sagfoundation.org/

JOHN L. DALES SCHOLARSHIP PROGRAM

Applicant must have ten vested years of pension credits with the SAG AFTRA union or lifetime earnings of $150,000. Must be U.S. citizen. Scholarship amount ranges between $1000 and $5000. Consult office or website for more information.

Award: Scholarship for use in freshman, sophomore, junior, senior, graduate, or postgraduate years; not renewable. *Number:* 1–16. *Amount:* $1000–$5000.

Eligibility Requirements: Applicant must be high school student and planning to enroll or expecting to enroll full- or part-time at a two-year or four-year institution or university. Available to U.S. citizens.

Application Requirements: Application form, community service, essay, financial need analysis, recommendations or references, resume, test scores, transcript. *Deadline:* March 15.

Contact: Davidson Lloyd, Director of Assistance Programs
Screen Actors' Guild Foundation
5757 Wilshire Boulevard
Suite 124
Los Angeles, CA 90036
Phone: 323-549-6649
Fax: 323-549-6710
E-mail: dlloyd@sagfoundation.org

SCREEN ACTORS GUILD FOUNDATION/JOHN L. DALES SCHOLARSHIP FUND (STANDARD)

Applicant must be a member of SAG AFTRA Union or the child of a member of SAG AFTRA Union. Member under the age of twenty-one must have been a member of AFTRA SAG Union for five years and have a lifetime earnings of $30,000. Parent of an applicant must have ten vested years of pension credits OR lifetime earnings of $150,000. Consult office or website for more information. Number and amount of awards vary.

Award: Scholarship for use in freshman, sophomore, junior, senior, graduate, or postgraduate years; not renewable. *Number:* 100–135. *Amount:* $1000–$5000.

Eligibility Requirements: Applicant must be enrolled or expecting to enroll full-time at a two-year or four-year or technical institution or university. Available to U.S. citizens.

Application Requirements: Application form, community service, essay, financial need analysis, recommendations or references, resume, test scores, transcript. *Deadline:* March 15.

Contact: Davidson Lloyd, Director of Assistance Programs
Screen Actors' Guild Foundation
5757 Wilshire Boulevard
Suite 124
Los Angeles, CA 90036
Phone: 323-549-6649
Fax: 323-549-6710
E-mail: dlloyd@sagfoundation.org

SEVENSECURE

http://www.changingpossibilities-us.com/
SupportPrograms/SevenSecure.aspx

SEVENSECURE ADULT EDUCATION GRANT

Provides grants to adults aged 23 and over with either hemophilia with inhibitors or FVII deficiency who would are continuing their education in pursuit of a degree/certificate, either to improve their career or transition to a new one, as well as primary caregivers of minor enrollees. Applications are accepted throughout the year. One award per eligible patient per year (up to four awards lifetime).

Award: Grant for use in freshman, sophomore, junior, senior, graduate, or postgraduate years; not renewable. *Amount:* up to $2500.

Eligibility Requirements: Applicant must be enrolled or expecting to enroll full- or part-time at a two-year or four-year or technical institution or university. Available to U.S. citizens.

Application Requirements: Application form.

SIMON YOUTH FOUNDATION

http://www.sms.scholarshipamerica.org/simonyouth

SIMON YOUTH FOUNDATION COMMUNITY SCHOLARSHIP PROGRAM

Scholarships available to high school seniors attending school and living in close proximity of a Simon Property Mall or Community Center. Recipients should reside within 50 miles of a Simon Mall. Must be planning to enroll in a full-time undergraduate course of study at an accredited two- or four-year college, university, or vocational/technical school.

Award: Scholarship for use in freshman year; not renewable. *Number:* 100–200. *Amount:* $1400–$2500.

Eligibility Requirements: Applicant must be high school student and planning to enroll or expecting to enroll full-time at a two-year or four-year or technical institution or university. Available to U.S. citizens.

Application Requirements: Application form, community service, copy of page 1 of parent's tax Form 1040, financial need analysis, test scores, transcript. *Deadline:* March 1.

Contact: Casey Rubischko, Program Manager
Phone: 507-931-1682

SOCIETY FOR SCIENCE & THE PUBLIC

http://www.societyforscience.org/

INTEL INTERNATIONAL SCIENCE AND ENGINEERING FAIR

Culminating event in a series of local, regional, and state science fairs. Students in ninth through twelfth grades must compete at local fairs and win the right to attend Intel ISEF. Awards include scholarships. Visit website for more information http://www.societyforscience.org/isef.

Award: Prize for use in freshman year; not renewable. *Number:* 1–600. *Amount:* $500–$75,000.

Eligibility Requirements: Applicant must be high school student and planning to enroll or expecting to enroll full- or part-time at a two-year or four-year institution or university. Available to U.S. and non-U.S. citizens.

Application Requirements: Application form, entry in a contest, essay, interview. *Deadline:* varies.

Contact: Ms. Michele Glidden, Director, Science Education Programs
Phone: 202-785-2255
E-mail: mglidden@societyforscience.org

INTEL SCIENCE TALENT SEARCH

Science competition for high school seniors. Students must submit an independent research project. Forty finalists will be chosen to attend Intel Science Talent Institute in Washington, D.C. to exhibit their project and compete for $100,000 award. For more information, visit website http://www.societyforscience.org/sts.

Award: Prize for use in freshman year; not renewable. *Number:* 40. *Amount:* $7500–$100,000.

Eligibility Requirements: Applicant must be high school student and planning to enroll or expecting to enroll full-time at a two-year or four-year institution or university. Available to U.S. citizens.

Application Requirements: Application form, application form may be submitted online (http://www.societyforscience.org/sts), entry in a contest, essay, recommendations or references, resume, test scores, transcript. *Deadline:* November 12.

Contact: Ms. Caitlin Sullivan, Intel Science Talent Search Program Manager

SPENDONLIFE.COM

SPENDONLIFE COLLEGE SCHOLARSHIP

$500 to $5000 scholarship program offers financial assistance for college students who are unable to obtain student loans due to a negative credit history. Awards are based on financial need and participation in the application process.

Award: Scholarship for use in freshman, sophomore, junior, senior, graduate, or postgraduate years; not renewable. *Number:* 2–10. *Amount:* $500–$5000.

Eligibility Requirements: Applicant must be enrolled or expecting to enroll full-time at a two-year or four-year institution or university. Available to U.S. citizens.

Application Requirements: Application form, essay. *Deadline:* May 15.

Contact: Keith Lauren, Scholarship Administrator
Phone: 469-916-1700 Ext. 269
E-mail: scholarship@spendonlife.com

STATE DEPARTMENT FEDERAL CREDIT UNION ANNUAL SCHOLARSHIP PROGRAM

http://www.sdfcu.org/

STATE DEPARTMENT FEDERAL CREDIT UNION ANNUAL SCHOLARSHIP PROGRAM

Scholarships available to members who are currently enrolled in a degree program and have completed 12 credit hours of coursework at an accredited college or university. Must have own account in good standing with SDFCU, have a minimum 2.5 GPA, submit official cumulative transcripts, and describe need for financial assistance to continue their education. Scholarship only open to members of State Department Federal Credit Union.

Award: Scholarship for use in sophomore, junior, senior, or graduate years; not renewable. *Amount:* $2500.

Eligibility Requirements: Applicant must be enrolled or expecting to enroll full-time at a four-year institution or university. Applicant must have 2.5 GPA or higher. Available to U.S. and non-U.S. citizens.

Application Requirements: Application form, entry in a contest, financial need analysis, personal statement, transcript. *Deadline:* April 29.

STEPHEN K. FISCHEL MEMORIAL SCHOLARSHIP

Scholarships available to members who are currently enrolled in a degree program and have completed 12 credit hours of coursework at an accredited college or university. Must have own account in good standing with SDFCU. Must include a one (1) page essay answering, "How do Credit Unions reflect a commitment to community service?"

Award: Scholarship for use in sophomore, junior, senior, or graduate years; not renewable. *Number:* 1. *Amount:* $5000.

Eligibility Requirements: Applicant must be enrolled or expecting to enroll full-time at a four-year institution or university. Applicant must have 2.5 GPA or higher. Available to U.S. citizens.

Application Requirements: *Deadline:* April 29.

STRAIGHTFORWARD MEDIA

http://www.straightforwardmedia.com/

DALE E. FRIDELL MEMORIAL SCHOLARSHIP

Scholarships are open to anyone aspiring to attend a university, college, trade school, technical institute, vocational training, or other postsecondary education program. Eligible students may not have already been awarded a full tuition scholarship or waiver from another source. International students are welcome to apply. For more information, visit website http://www.straightforwardmedia.com/fridell/form.php.

Award: Scholarship for use in freshman, sophomore, junior, or senior years; not renewable. *Number:* 2. *Amount:* $1000.

Eligibility Requirements: Applicant must be enrolled or expecting to enroll full- or part-time at a two-year or four-year or technical institution or university. Available to U.S. and non-U.S. citizens.

Application Requirements: Essay. *Deadline:* varies.

HELPING HAND SCHOLARSHIP

Annual award to help students hampered by debt to continue their studies. Must be attending or planning to attend a college, trade school, technical institute, vocational program or other postsecondary education program. For more information, see web http://www.straightforwardmedia.com/debt2/debt-apply.html.

Award: Scholarship for use in freshman, sophomore, junior, or senior years; not renewable. *Number:* 4. *Amount:* $500.

Eligibility Requirements: Applicant must be enrolled or expecting to enroll full- or part-time at a two-year or four-year or technical institution or university. Available to U.S. and non-U.S. citizens.

Application Requirements: Essay. *Deadline:* varies.

MESOTHELIOMA MEMORIAL SCHOLARSHIP

Open to all students attending or planning to attend a postsecondary educational program, including 2- or 4-year college or university, vocational school, continuing education, ministry training, and job skills training. Refer to website for details http://www.straightforwardmedia.com/meso/.

Award: Scholarship for use in freshman, sophomore, junior, or senior years; not renewable. *Number:* 4. *Amount:* $500.

Eligibility Requirements: Applicant must be enrolled or expecting to enroll full- or part-time at a two-year or four-year or technical institution or university. Available to U.S. and non-U.S. citizens.

Application Requirements: Essay. *Deadline:* varies.

STUDENT INSIGHTS

http://www.student-view.com/

STUDENT-VIEW SCHOLARSHIP PROGRAM

Scholarship available by random drawing from the pool of entrants who respond to an online survey from Student Insights marketing organization. Parental permission to participate required for applicants under age 18.

Award: Scholarship for use in freshman year; not renewable. *Number:* 11. *Amount:* $500–$4000.

Eligibility Requirements: Applicant must be high school student and planning to enroll or expecting to enroll full-time at a two-year or four-year or technical institution or university. Available to U.S. citizens.

Application Requirements: Application form. *Deadline:* April 22.

Contact: Mr. John Becker, Program Coordinator
Student Insights
136 Justice Drive
Valencia, PA 16059
Phone: 724-612-3685
E-mail: contact@studentinsights.com

SUNTRUST BANK

http://www.suntrusteducation.com/

OFF TO COLLEGE SCHOLARSHIP SWEEPSTAKES AWARD

Award of $1000 to a high school senior planning to attend college in the fall. Must complete an online entry form by accessing the website http://www.offtocollege.info. Scholarship sweepstakes drawings are random and occur every other week from October 31 to May 15.

Award: Scholarship for use in freshman year; not renewable. *Number:* 15. *Amount:* $1000.

Eligibility Requirements: Applicant must be high school student and planning to enroll or expecting to enroll full- or part-time at a two-year or four-year or technical institution or university. Available to U.S. citizens.

Application Requirements: Application form. *Deadline:* continuous.

Contact: Joy Blauvelt, Scholarship Coordinator
Phone: 800-552-3006

TALBOTS CHARITABLE FOUNDATION

http://www.talbots.com/

TALBOTS WOMEN'S SCHOLARSHIP FUND

One-time scholarship for women who earned their high school diploma or GED at least 10 years ago, and who are now seeking an undergraduate college degree.

Award: Scholarship for use in freshman, sophomore, junior, or senior years; not renewable. *Number:* 5–50. *Amount:* $1000–$10,000.

Eligibility Requirements: Applicant must be enrolled or expecting to enroll full- or part-time at a two-year or four-year or technical institution or university and female. Available to U.S. citizens.

Application Requirements: Application form, essay, financial need analysis, recommendations or references, transcript. *Deadline:* January 3.

Contact: Genny Miller, Program Manager, Scholarship America
Talbots Charitable Foundation
1 Scholarship Way, PO Box 297
Saint Peter, MN 56082
Phone: 507-931-0452
Fax: 507-931-9278
E-mail: gmiller@scholarshipamerica.org

TALL CLUBS INTERNATIONAL FOUNDATION, INC.

http://www.tall.org

KAE SUMNER EINFELDT SCHOLARSHIP

Females 5'10", or males 6'2" (minimum heights), are eligible to apply for the scholarship. Interested individuals should contact their local Tall Clubs Chapter. Canadian and U.S. winners are selected from finalists submitted by each local chapter.

Award: Scholarship for use in freshman year; not renewable. *Number:* 2–6. *Amount:* $1000.

Eligibility Requirements: Applicant must be age 17-21 and enrolled or expecting to enroll full- or part-time at a four-year institution or university. Available to U.S. and Canadian citizens.

Application Requirements: Application form, essay, personal photograph, recommendations or references, transcript, verification of height. *Deadline:* March 1.

Contact: Sheila Koster, TCI Foundation Scholarship Contact
E-mail: bskoster@aol.com

TEXAS FEDERATION OF BUSINESS AND PROFESSIONAL WOMEN'S FOUNDATION

http://www.texasbpwfoundation.org/scholarships.php

GILDA MURRAY SCHOLARSHIP

Scholarship of $500 awarded to members of BPW/Texas, age 25 or older, to obtain education or training at an accredited college or university, technology institution, or training center. The number of awards varies.

Award: Scholarship for use in freshman, sophomore, junior, or senior years; not renewable. *Amount:* $500.

Eligibility Requirements: Applicant must be enrolled or expecting to enroll full- or part-time at a four-year or technical institution or university. Available to U.S. citizens.

Application Requirements: Application form, essay, recommendations or references, regular attendance at LO meetings, active participation on at least one BPW committee. *Deadline:* May 1.

Contact: Nancy Jackson, Chair
Phone: 817-283-0862
E-mail: bpwtx@sbcglobal.net

TEXAS GUARANTEED STUDENT LOAN CORPORATION

http://www.tgslc.org/

CHARLEY WOOTAN GRANT PROGRAM

Provides assistance to students who have difficulties pursuing their higher education dreams because of financial need. Deadline for Texas residents, 4-year school-May 15; Deadline for Texas residents, 2-year school-May 2; Deadline for non-Texas residents-April 29.

Award: Scholarship for use in freshman, sophomore, junior, or senior years; not renewable. *Amount:* $1000–$4394.

Eligibility Requirements: Applicant must be enrolled or expecting to enroll full- or part-time at a two-year or four-year or technical institution or university. Available to U.S. citizens.

TEXAS MUTUAL INSURANCE COMPANY

http://www.texasmutual.com/

TEXAS MUTUAL INSURANCE COMPANY SCHOLARSHIP PROGRAM

A scholarship program open to qualified family members of policyholder employees who died from on-the-job injuries or accidents, policyholder employees who qualify for lifetime income benefits pursuant to the Texas Workers Compensation Act, and family members of injured employees who qualify for lifetime income benefits.

Award: Scholarship for use in freshman, sophomore, junior, or senior years; not renewable. *Number:* 1–10. *Amount:* $500–$4000.

Eligibility Requirements: Applicant must be enrolled or expecting to enroll full-time at a two-year or four-year or technical institution or university. Applicant must have 2.5 GPA or higher. Available to U.S. and non-U.S. citizens.

Application Requirements: Application form, fee bill, death certificate of family member, acceptance letter for freshmen, financial need analysis, recommendations or references, test scores, transcript. *Deadline:* continuous.

Contact: Lynda House, Administrative Assistant
Phone: 800-859-5995 Ext. 3820
E-mail: lhouse@texasmutual.com

THETA DELTA CHI EDUCATIONAL FOUNDATION INC.

http://www.tdx.org/

THETA DELTA CHI EDUCATIONAL FOUNDATION INC. SCHOLARSHIP

Scholarships for undergraduate or graduate students enrolled in an accredited institution. Awards are based on candidate's history of service to the fraternity, scholastic achievement, and need. See website for application and additional information http://www.tdx.org/scholarship/scholarship.html.

Award: Scholarship for use in freshman, sophomore, junior, senior, or graduate years; renewable. *Number:* 15. *Amount:* $1000–$5000.

Eligibility Requirements: Applicant must be enrolled or expecting to enroll full-time at a four-year institution or university. Available to U.S. and non-U.S. citizens.

Application Requirements: Application form, financial need analysis, recommendations or references, transcript. *Deadline:* May 15.

Contact: William McClung, Executive Director
Phone: 617-742-8886
Fax: 617-742-8868
E-mail: execdir@tdx.org

THURGOOD MARSHALL SCHOLARSHIP FUND

http://www.thurgoodmarshallfund.org/

THURGOOD MARSHALL SCHOLARSHIP

Merit scholarships for students attending one of 45 member HBCUs (historically black colleges, universities) including 5 member law schools. Must maintain an average GPA of 3.0 to renew, demonstrate financial need, and be a U.S. citizen. Apply through member HBCU's campus scholarship coordinator. For further details refer to website http://www.thurgoodmarshallfund.org.

Award: Scholarship for use in freshman, sophomore, junior, senior, or graduate years; renewable. *Amount:* up to $4400.

Eligibility Requirements: Applicant must be enrolled or expecting to enroll full-time at a four-year institution or university. Applicant must have 3.0 GPA or higher. Available to U.S. citizens.

Application Requirements: Application form, essay, financial need analysis, interview, personal photograph, recommendations or references, resume, test scores, transcript. *Deadline:* July 15.

Contact: Sophia Rogers, Scholarship Manager
Phone: 212-573-8888
E-mail: srogers@tmcfund.org

TRIANGLE EDUCATION FOUNDATION

http://www.triangle.org/

MORTIN SCHOLARSHIP

One-time award of $2500 annually for an active member of the Triangle Fraternity. Awarded based on a combination of need, grades and participation in campus and Triangle Activities. Minimum 3.0 GPA. Further information available at website http://www.triangle.org.

Award: Scholarship for use in freshman, sophomore, junior, or senior years; not renewable. *Number:* 1. *Amount:* up to $2500.

Eligibility Requirements: Applicant must be enrolled or expecting to enroll full-time at a four-year institution or university and male. Applicant must have 3.0 GPA or higher. Available to U.S. and non-U.S. citizens.

Application Requirements: Application form, essay, financial need analysis, recommendations or references, self-addressed stamped envelope with application, transcript. *Deadline:* February 15.

Contact: Scott Bova, President
Phone: 317-705-9803
Fax: 317-837-9642
E-mail: sbova@triangle.org

PETER AND BARBARA BYE SCHOLARSHIP

Scholarship for a Triangle Fraternity member for undergraduate study. Preference given to applicants from Cornell University Triangle chapter. Applicant must have a minimum GPA of 2.7. Additional information on website http://www.triangle.org.

Award: Scholarship for use in freshman, sophomore, junior, or senior years; not renewable. *Number:* 1. *Amount:* up to $2000.

Eligibility Requirements: Applicant must be enrolled or expecting to enroll full- or part-time at a four-year institution or university and male. Available to U.S. and non-U.S. citizens.

Application Requirements: Application form, financial need analysis, recommendations or references, transcript. *Deadline:* February 15.

Contact: Scott Bova, President
Phone: 317-705-9803
Fax: 317-837-9642
E-mail: sbova@triangle.org

TWIN TOWERS ORPHAN FUND

http://www.ttof.org/

TWIN TOWERS ORPHAN FUND

Fund offers assistance to children who lost one or both parents in the terrorist attacks on September 11, 2001. Long-term education program established to provide higher education needs to children until they complete their uninterrupted studies, or reach age of majority. Visit website for additional information http://www.ttof.org.

Award: Scholarship for use in freshman, sophomore, junior, senior, or graduate years; not renewable. *Amount:* $5000–$7000.

Eligibility Requirements: Applicant must be enrolled or expecting to enroll full- or part-time at a two-year or four-year or technical institution or university. Available to U.S. and non-U.S. citizens.

Application Requirements: Application form, birth certificate, parent's death certificate, marriage license, financial need analysis. *Deadline:* varies.

Contact: Karlene Boss, Case Manager
  Phone: 661-633-9076
  E-mail: ttof2@ttof.org

THE MORRIS K. UDALL AND STEWART L. UDALL FOUNDATION

http://www.udall.gov/

UDALL UNDERGRADUATE SCHOLARSHIP

Fifty one-time scholarships and fifty one-time honorable mention awards to full-time college sophomores or juniors with demonstrated commitment to careers related to the environment, tribal public policy (Native American/Alaska Native students only), or Native American health care (Native American/Alaska Native students only). Students from all fields and disciplines are encouraged to apply. Students must be nominated by their college or university. Visit http://www.udall.gov for additional information.

Award: Scholarship for use in junior or senior years; not renewable. *Number:* 50. *Amount:* up to $5000.

Eligibility Requirements: Applicant must be enrolled or expecting to enroll full-time at a two-year or four-year institution or university. Applicant must have 3.0 GPA or higher. Available to U.S. citizens.

Application Requirements: Application form, application form may be submitted online(www.udall.gov), essay, nomination by campus faculty representative, recommendations or references, transcript. *Deadline:* March 1.

Contact: Paula Randler, Scholarship Program Manager
  The Morris K. Udall and Stewart L. Udall Foundation
  130 South Scott Avenue
  Tucson, AZ 85701
  Phone: 520-901-8564
  Fax: 520-901-8570
  E-mail: randler@udall.gov

UNITED NEGRO COLLEGE FUND

http://www.uncf.org/

AMERICAN AIRLINES SCHOLARSHIP

20 scholarships available to full-time undergraduate students enrolled at an UNCF institution. Students must have a financial need due to the negative impact from Hurricane Katrina. Minimum 2.5 GPA required.

Award: Scholarship for use in freshman, sophomore, junior, or senior years; not renewable. *Number:* 20. *Amount:* $1677.

Eligibility Requirements: Applicant must be enrolled or expecting to enroll full-time at a four-year institution. Applicant must have 2.5 GPA or higher. Available to U.S. citizens.

Application Requirements: Application form. *Deadline:* continuous.

UNITED REALTY PARTNERS, LLC

http://www.urpa.com

UNITED REALTY STUDENTS SCHOLARSHIP PROGRAM

United Realty Students is a scholarship program intended to provide students with $100,000 per year in Educational Scholarships. United Realty Partners, LLC is dedicated to investing in our future by investing in student education. For this reason, we've created United Realty Students—a scholarship program with multiple prizes awarded to students who best answer the question "How Do I Invest In My Future?"

Award: Scholarship for use in freshman, sophomore, junior, senior, or graduate years; renewable. *Number:* 14–14. *Amount:* $5000–$10,000.

Eligibility Requirements: Applicant must be age 16-22 and enrolled or expecting to enroll full- or part-time at a two-year or four-year or technical institution or university. Available to U.S. citizens.

Application Requirements: Application form, application form may be submitted online (http://www.urpa.com/scholarship.html), entry in a contest, essay. *Deadline:* continuous.

Contact: Mr. Eric Fischgrund, Vice President of Marketing
  United Realty Partners, LLC
  44 Wall Street, 2nd Floor
  New York, NY 10005
  Phone: 212-388-6800
  E-mail: scholarship@urpa.com

UNITED STATES ACHIEVEMENT ACADEMY

http://www.usaa-academy.com/

DR. GEORGE A. STEVENS FOUNDER'S AWARD

One $10,000 scholarship cash grant to enhance the intellectual and personal growth of students who demonstrate a genuine interest in learning. Award must be used for educational purposes. Must maintain a minimum GPA of 3.0.

Award: Grant for use in freshman year; not renewable. *Number:* 1. *Amount:* $10,000.

Eligibility Requirements: Applicant must be high school student and planning to enroll or expecting to enroll full-time at a four-year institution or university. Applicant must have 3.0 GPA or higher. Available to U.S. and non-U.S. citizens.

Application Requirements: Application form.

NATIONAL SCHOLARSHIP CASH GRANT

The Foundation awards 400 national scholarship cash grants of $1500. All scholarship winners are determined by an independent selection committee. Winners are selected based on GPA, school activities, SAT scores (if applicable), honors and awards. All students in grades 6¿12 are eligible.

Award: Grant for use in freshman year; not renewable. *Number:* 400. *Amount:* $1500.

Eligibility Requirements: Applicant must be high school student and planning to enroll or expecting to enroll full-time at a four-year institution or university. Applicant must have 3.0 GPA or higher. Available to U.S. and non-U.S. citizens.

Application Requirements: Application form, application form may be submitted online (http://www.fs22.formsite.com/USAA/form23/index.html). *Deadline:* June 1.

UNITED STATES-INDONESIA SOCIETY

http://www.usindo.org/

UNITED STATES-INDONESIA SOCIETY TRAVEL GRANTS

Grants are provided to fund travel to Indonesia or the United States for American and Indonesian students and professors to conduct research, language training or other independent study/research. Must have a minimum 3.0 GPA.

Award: Grant for use in freshman, sophomore, junior, senior, graduate, or postgraduate years; not renewable. *Number:* 1–15. *Amount:* $1000–$2000.

Eligibility Requirements: Applicant must be enrolled or expecting to enroll full- or part-time at a four-year institution or university. Applicant must have 3.0 GPA or higher. Available to U.S. and non-Canadian citizens.

Application Requirements: Application form, basic budget, recommendations or references, resume, transcript. *Deadline:* continuous.

Contact: Thomas Spooner, Educational Officer
  Phone: 202-232-1400
  Fax: 202-232-7300
  E-mail: tspooner@usindo.org

UNITED TRANSPORTATION UNION INSURANCE ASSOCIATION

http://www.utuia.org/

UTUIA SCHOLARSHIP

Scholarships of $500 awarded to undergraduate students. Applicant must be at least a high school senior or equivalent, age 25 or under, be a UTU or UTUIA insured member, the child or grandchild of a UTU or UTUIA insured member, or the child of a deceased UTU or UTUIA-insured member.

Award: Scholarship for use in freshman, sophomore, junior, or senior years; renewable. *Number:* 50. *Amount:* $500.

Eligibility Requirements: Applicant must be enrolled or expecting to enroll full-time at a four-year institution or university. Available to U.S. citizens.

Application Requirements: Application form. *Deadline:* March 31.

U.S. BANK INTERNET SCHOLARSHIP PROGRAM

http://www.usbank.com/

U.S. BANK INTERNET SCHOLARSHIP PROGRAM

A high school senior planning to enroll or a current college freshmen, sophomore or junior at an eligible four-year college or university participating in the U.S. Bank No Fee Education Loan Program. Apply online at usbank.com/studentbanking from October through March. No paper applications accepted.

Award: Scholarship for use in freshman, sophomore, or junior years; not renewable. *Number:* up to 40. *Amount:* up to $1000.

Eligibility Requirements: Applicant must be enrolled or expecting to enroll full- or part-time at a four-year institution or university. Available to U.S. and non-U.S. citizens.

Application Requirements: Application form. *Deadline:* March 31.

Contact: Mary Ennis, Scholarship Coordinator
Phone: 800-242-1200
E-mail: mary.ennis@usbank.com

US PAN ASIAN AMERICAN CHAMBER OF COMMERCE EDUCATION FOUNDATION

http://www.uspaacc.com/

BRUCE LEE SCHOLARSHIP

The applicant should demonstrate: academic achievement of 3.3 GPA or higher; leadership in extracurricular activities; involvement in community service; financial need. The amount of the scholarship depends on the sponsors' contributions and varies between $2,000 and $5,000.

Award: Scholarship for use in freshman year; renewable. *Number:* 1. *Amount:* $2000–$5000.

Eligibility Requirements: Applicant must be high school student and planning to enroll or expecting to enroll full-time at an institution or university. Available to U.S. citizens.

Application Requirements: *Deadline:* March 18.

THE VEGETARIAN RESOURCE GROUP

http://www.vrg.org/

THE VEGETARIAN RESOURCE GROUP SCHOLARSHIP

Two scholarships will be awarded to graduating U.S. high school students who have promoted vegetarianism in their schools and/or communities. Vegetarians do not eat meat, fish, or fowl. Applicants will be judged on having shown compassion, courage, and a strong commitment to promoting a peaceful world through a vegetarian diet/lifestyle.

Award: Scholarship for use in freshman year; not renewable. *Number:* up to 2. *Amount:* up to $5000.

Eligibility Requirements: Applicant must be high school student and planning to enroll or expecting to enroll full- or part-time at a two-year or four-year or technical institution or university. Available to U.S. citizens.

Application Requirements: Application form, application form may be submitted online (http://www.vrg.org/student/scholar.htm), essay, recommendations or references, transcript. *Deadline:* February 20.

Contact: Sonja Helman, Scholarship Coordinator
Phone: 410-366-8343
Fax: 410-366-8804
E-mail: sonjah@vrg.org

VHMNETWORK LLC

http://www.vhmnetwork.com/

SCHOLARSHIPCOIN

Advertising-based scholarship available twice a year to students age 18 and older for tuition, books, rent, or additional expenses. See website for details http://www.ScholarshipCoin.com.

Award: Scholarship for use in freshman, sophomore, junior, or senior years; not renewable. *Number:* 2. *Amount:* $2000.

Eligibility Requirements: Applicant must be enrolled or expecting to enroll full- or part-time at a two-year or four-year or technical institution or university. Available to U.S. citizens.

Application Requirements: Application form, application form may be submitted online (http://www.ScholarshipCoin.com).

Contact: Michael Derikrava, President
Phone: 800-299-7326
E-mail: michael@vhmnetwork.com

WAL-MART FOUNDATION

http://www.walmartfoundation.org/

SAM WALTON COMMUNITY SCHOLARSHIP

Award for high school seniors not affiliated with Wal-Mart stores. Based on financial need, academic merit, and school or community work activities. Must be a permanent legal resident of the United States. For use at an accredited two- or four-year U.S. institution. Applications available online at https://www.applyists.net, Access key: SWCS. Applicants may apply beginning November 1.

Award: Scholarship for use in freshman year; not renewable. *Number:* 2695. *Amount:* $3000.

Eligibility Requirements: Applicant must be high school student and planning to enroll or expecting to enroll full-time at a two-year or four-year institution or university. Applicant must have 2.5 GPA or higher. Available to U.S. citizens.

Application Requirements: Application form, financial need analysis, test scores, transcript. *Deadline:* January 31.

WELLS FARGO

http://www.wellsfargo.com/

EDUCAID GIMME FIVE SCHOLARSHIP SWEEPSTAKES

Awards twelve high school seniors for their first year at an accredited college or trade school. The scholarships are not based on grades or financial need, so every eligible high school senior who enters has an equal chance of winning. Apply online at the following website http://www.educaid.com.

Award: Prize for use in freshman year; not renewable. *Number:* 12. *Amount:* $5000.

Eligibility Requirements: Applicant must be enrolled or expecting to enroll full-time at a two-year or four-year or technical institution or university. Available to U.S. citizens.

Application Requirements: Application form, self-addressed stamped envelope with application. *Deadline:* March 31.

WISECHOICE BRANDS, LLC

http://www.wisechoice.com/

$2500 'ADVICE TO YOUR HIGH SCHOOL SELF' SCHOLARSHIP

Students must apply online. Students will submit a complete survey about their college campus. Limit one survey per person. The online form includes, at the very end, a place for applicants to type (or paste) a short original, previously unpublished written response to the scholarship topic, 'Assume you could go back in time and talk to yourself as a high school senior. Knowing what you know now about college life and making the transition, what advice would you give yourself?' All U.S. students enrolled at a college or university* (as well as recent college graduates who finished with an Associate's or Bachelor's degree in 2011, 2012 or 2013) are eligible to apply.

Award: Scholarship for use in sophomore, junior, senior, graduate, or postgraduate years; not renewable. *Number:* 1. *Amount:* $2500.

Eligibility Requirements: Applicant must be enrolled or expecting to enroll full- or part-time at a two-year or four-year or technical institution or university. Available to U.S. citizens.

Application Requirements: Application form, application form may be submitted online (http://www.campusdiscovery.com/college-scholarships), essay, survey. *Deadline:* January 31.

WISECHOICE $2,500 'FIND THE RIGHT COLLEGE' SCHOLARSHIP

This scholarship program was designed to assist students in the college planning process, and to help them to really investigate their options when it comes to choosing a college for the right reasons. Applicants must register at WiseChoice.com.

Award: Scholarship for use in freshman year; not renewable. *Number:* 1. *Amount:* $2500.

Eligibility Requirements: Applicant must be high school student and planning to enroll or expecting to enroll full- or part-time at a two-year or four-year or technical institution or university. Available to U.S. citizens.

Application Requirements: Application form, application form may be submitted online (http://www.wisechoice.com/scholarship?sid=ssl), essay, free registration with WiseChoice.com. *Deadline:* May 31.

WOMEN'S INDEPENDENCE SCHOLARSHIP PROGRAM, INC.

http://www.wispinc.org/

WOMEN'S INDEPENDENCE SCHOLARSHIP PROGRAM

Scholarship of $250 to $5000 to enable female survivors of domestic violence (partner abuse) to return to school to gain skills necessary to become independent and self-sufficient. Requires sponsorship by nonprofit domestic violence service agency. First priority candidates are single mothers with young children. Must be U.S. citizens or permanent legal residents with critical financial need. Deadline varies.

Award: Scholarship for use in freshman, sophomore, junior, senior, or graduate years; renewable. *Number:* 500–600. *Amount:* $250–$5000.

Eligibility Requirements: Applicant must be enrolled or expecting to enroll full- or part-time at a two-year or four-year or technical institution or university and female. Available to U.S. citizens.

Application Requirements: Application form, essay, financial need analysis, recommendations or references,. *Deadline:* continuous.

Contact: Nancy Soward, Executive Director
Women's Independence Scholarship Program, Inc.
4900 Randall Parkway, Suite H
Wilmington, NC 28403
Phone: 910-397-7742 Ext. 101
Fax: 910-397-0023
E-mail: nancy@wispinc.org

WOMEN'S JEWELRY ASSOCIATION

http://www.womensjewelry.org/

WJA MEMBER GRANT

Grants are generally up to $500 and can be used by members to pay for any aspect of further education during the year. For more information please visit website http://www.womensjewelry.org/.

Award: Grant for use in freshman, sophomore, junior, senior, graduate, or postgraduate years; not renewable. *Number:* 1. *Amount:* up to $500.

Eligibility Requirements: Applicant must be enrolled or expecting to enroll full- or part-time at a two-year or four-year or technical institution or university and female. Available to U.S. and non-U.S. citizens.

Application Requirements: Application form, essay. *Deadline:* January 1.

WOMEN'S OVERSEAS SERVICE LEAGUE

http://www.wosl.org/

WOMEN'S OVERSEAS SERVICE LEAGUE SCHOLARSHIPS FOR WOMEN

Awarded to women committed to careers in public service who have completed 12 semester or 18 quarter units in any higher education institution with a 2.5 GPA, are admitted to an institution in a program leading to an Associate's Degree or higher and enrolled for a minimum of 6 semester or 9 quarter hours.

Award: Scholarship for use in sophomore, junior, senior, graduate, or postgraduate years; renewable. *Number:* 10–20. *Amount:* $1000–$2000.

Eligibility Requirements: Applicant must be enrolled or expecting to enroll full- or part-time at a two-year or four-year or technical institution or university and female. Applicant must have 2.5 GPA or higher. Available to U.S. citizens.

Application Requirements: Application form, community service, essay, financial need analysis, recommendations or references, resume, transcript. *Deadline:* March 1.

Contact: Ms. Ann Kelsey, Scholarship Committee Chair
Fax: 973-887-7644
E-mail: kelsey@openix.com

WOMEN'S SPORTS FOUNDATION

http://www.womenssportsfoundation.org/

LINDA RIDDLE/SGMA ENDOWED SCHOLARSHIP

Two $3000 awards to provide young female athletes of limited financial means the opportunity to continue to pursue their sport in addition to their college studies. If you plan to participate in intercollegiate sports at a Division I school, consult with your college compliance office to determine whether this scholarship will affect your eligibility. Please check website for application procedures.

Award: Scholarship for use in freshman year; not renewable. *Number:* 2. *Amount:* $3000.

Eligibility Requirements: Applicant must be high school student; planning to enroll or expecting to enroll full-time at a two-year or four-year institution and female. Applicant must have 3.5 GPA or higher. Available to U.S. citizens.

Application Requirements: Application form, application form may be submitted online (http://www.womenssportsfoundation.org/sitecore/content/home/programs/grants/linda-riddle-sgma-endowed-scholarship.aspx), recommendations or references, transcript, transcript outlining athletic and leadership activities freshman through senior year. *Deadline:* May 10.

ZETA PHI BETA SORORITY INC. NATIONAL EDUCATIONAL FOUNDATION

http://www.zpbnef1975.org/

GENERAL UNDERGRADUATE SCHOLARSHIP

$500-$1000 scholarships available for female undergraduate students. Awarded for full-time study for one academic year. See website for information and application, http://www.zpbnef1975.org/.

Award: Scholarship for use in freshman, sophomore, junior, or senior years; not renewable. *Number:* 1. *Amount:* $500–$1000.

Eligibility Requirements: Applicant must be enrolled or expecting to enroll full-time at a four-year institution or university. Available to U.S. citizens.

Application Requirements: Application form, essay, proof of enrollment, recommendations or references, transcript. *Deadline:* February 1.

Contact: Cheryl Williams, National Second Vice President
Fax: 318-232-4593
E-mail: 2ndanti@zphib1920.org

ZINCH

http://www.zinch.com/

SWEET DIGGITY DAWG SCHOLARSHIP

Scholarships available to students based on their Zinch profile. Fellow Zinch users vote to advance the best profile until only one student remains to claim the scholarship. Must be a high school student with a minimum 2.0 GPA. See website for details www.zinch.com/scholarships/sweet-diggity-dawg.

Award: Scholarship for use in freshman, sophomore, junior, or senior years; not renewable. *Number:* 30–41. *Amount:* $500–$20,000.

Eligibility Requirements: Applicant must be high school student and planning to enroll or expecting to enroll full-time at a two-year or four-year institution or university. Available to U.S. citizens.

Application Requirements: Application form may be submitted online (http://www.zinch.com/scholarships/sweet-diggity-dawg), entry in a contest, Zinch profile. *Deadline:* January 15.

Contact: Sean Castillo, Community Strategist
    Zinch
    185 Berry Street
    Suite 4807
    San Francisco, CA 94107
    Phone: 888-226-9636
    E-mail: scastillo@chegg.com

ZONTA INTERNATIONAL FOUNDATION

http://www.zonta.org/

YOUNG WOMEN IN PUBLIC AFFAIRS AWARD

One-time award for pre-college women with a commitment to the volunteer sector and evidence of volunteer leadership achievements. Must be 16 to 19 years of age with a career interest in public affairs, public policy and community organizations. Further information and application available at website http://www.zonta.org.

Award: Scholarship for use in freshman, sophomore, or junior years; not renewable. *Number:* up to 5. *Amount:* $1000–$4000.

Eligibility Requirements: Applicant must be high school student; age 16-19; planning to enroll or expecting to enroll full-time at a four-year institution and female. Available to U.S. and non-U.S. citizens.

Application Requirements: Application form, recommendations or references. *Deadline:* varies.

Contact: Ana Ubides, Programs Manager
    Fax: 630-928-1559
    E-mail: progrmas@zonta.org

INDEXES

Award Name

American Morgan Horse Institute Grand Prix Dressage Award 742

American Morgan Horse Institute Graywood Youth Horsemanship Grant 742

American Morgan Horse Institute van Schaik Dressage Scholarship 742

American Nephrology Nurses' Association Career Mobility Scholarship 428

American Nephrology Nurses' Association NNCC Career Mobility Scholarship 428

American Nephrology Nurses' Association Watson Pharma Inc. Career Mobility Scholarship 429

American Nuclear Society Operations and Power Scholarship 422

American Nuclear Society Undergraduate Scholarships 423

American Nuclear Society Vogt Radiochemistry Scholarship 273

American Occupational Therapy Foundation State Association Scholarships 330

American Physical Society Corporate-Sponsored Scholarship for Minority Undergraduate Students Who Major in Physics 462

American Physical Society Scholarship for Minority Undergraduate Physics Majors 460

American Restaurant Scholarship 215

American Savings Foundation Scholarships 665

American-Scandinavian Foundation Translation Prize 385

American Society for Enology and Viticulture Scholarships 90

American Society of Civil Engineers-Maine High School Scholarship 180

American Society of Criminology Gene Carte Student Paper Competition 211

American Society of Naval Engineers Scholarship 103

American Society of Women Accountants Two-Year College Scholarship 70

American Society of Women Accountants Undergraduate Scholarship 70

American Theatre Organ Society Organ Performance Scholarship 743

American Water Ski Educational Foundation Scholarship 515

American Welding Society District Scholarship Program 261

American Welding Society International Scholarship 262

America Responds Memorial Scholarship 444

America's Intercultural Magazine (AIM) Short Story Contest 385

America's Junior Miss Scholarship Program, Inc. d/b/a Distinguished Young Women 743

AMI Group Scholarship Award 557

AMS Freshman Undergraduate Scholarship 301

AMVETS National Ladies Auxiliary Scholarship 515

Amy Lowell Poetry Traveling Scholarship 385

Anchor Scholarship Foundation Program 610

ANDEO Scholarship 717

Andrew Bell Scholarship 721

Androscoggin Amateur Radio Club Scholarship 200

Angus Foundation Scholarships 528

Anheuser-Busch Legends of the Crown Scholarship Program 641

Anna and Eli Berkenfeld Memorial Scholarship 674

Anna and John Kolesar Memorial Scholarships 231

Annabelle L. Johnson Scholarship Fund 674

Anna May Rolando Scholarship Award 430

Anne A. Agnew Scholarship 537

Anne and Matt Harbison Scholarship 577

Anne Ford & Allegra Ford Scholarship 573

Anne Maureen Whitney Barrow Memorial Scholarship 172

Anne Seaman Professional Grounds Management Society Memorial Scholarship 95

Annual Award Program 650

Annual Liberty Graphics Art Contest 699

Annual Scholarship Grant Program 213

Annual SfAA Student Endowed Award 100

ANS Incoming Freshman Scholarship 423

Anthem Essay Contest 745

AnyCollege.com Scholarship 768

AOCS Analytical Division Student Award 165

AOCS Biotechnology Student Excellence Award 90

AOCS Health and Nutrition Division Student Excellence Award 313

AOCS Processing Division Awards 166

A.O. Putnam Memorial Scholarship 282

AOTA'S Assembly of Student Delegates Award 767

APEX Scholarship 617

Appaloosa Youth Educational Scholarships 515

Applegate/Jackson/Parks Future Teacher Scholarship 241

Applications International Corporation Scholarship 444

Applied Computer Security Association Cybersecurity Scholarship 204

Appraisal Institute Education Trust Education Scholarships 469

Apprentice Ecologist Scholarship 788

AQHF General Scholarship 513

AQHF Journalism or Communications Scholarship 188

AQHF Racing Scholarships 98

AQHF Youth Scholarships 513

ARC of Washington Trust Fund Stipend Program 480

AREMA Michael R. Garcia Scholarship 179

AREMA Presidential Spouse Scholarship 180

AREMA Undergraduate Scholarships 180

Arizona Chapter Dependent/Employee Membership Scholarship 492

Arizona Chapter Gold Scholarship 493

Arizona Hydrological Society Scholarship 226

Arizona Nursery Association Foundation Scholarship 347

Arizona Private School Association Scholarship 666

Arizona Professional Chapter of AISES Scholarship 276

Arizona Quarter Horse Youth Scholarship 513

Arizona Quarter Racing Scholarship 513

Arkansas Academic Challenge Scholarship Program 666

Arkansas Governor's Scholars Program 666

Arkansas Single Parent Scholarship 667

Armed Forces Communications and Electronics Association General Emmett Paige Scholarship 127

Armed Forces Communications and Electronics Association ROTC Scholarship Program 127

Armenian Relief Society Undergraduate Scholarship 617

Armenian Students Association of America Inc. Scholarships 617

Army Officers Wives Club of the Greater Washington Area Scholarship 586

Army ROTC Green to Gold Scholarship Program for Two-Year, Three-Year and Four-Year Scholarships, Active Duty Enlisted Personnel 586

Army (ROTC) Reserve Officers Training Corps Two-, Three-, Four-Year Campus-Based Scholarships 569

Arne Engebretsen Wisconsin Mathematics Council Scholarship 246

ARRL Northwestern Division Scholarship Fund 150

ARRL Rocky Mountain Division Scholarship 667

ARRL Scholarship To Honor Barry Goldwater, K7UGA 743

Arsham Amirikian Engineering Scholarship 181

ARTBA-TDF Lanford Family Highway Workers Memorial Scholarship Program 551

ARTC Glen Moon Scholarship 234

Art Directors Club National Scholarships 117

Arthur and Gladys Cervenka Scholarship Award 289

Arthur E. and Helen Copeland Scholarships 579

Arthur J. Packard Memorial Scholarship 213

Arthur Ross Foundation Scholarship 641

Artistic Encouragement Grant 571

ASCPA Educational Foundation Scholarship 69

ASCSA Summer Sessions Scholarships 100

Ashby B. Carter Memorial Scholarship Fund Founders Award 526

ASHRAE General Scholarships 260

ASHRAE Memorial Scholarship 249

ASHRAE Region III Boggarm Setty Scholarship 166

ASHRAE Region IV Benny Bootle Scholarship 109

ASHRAE Region VIII Scholarship 261

ASHS Scholars Award 347

Asian-American Journalists Association Scholarship 189

Asian Pacific Community Fund - Verizon Scholarship Awards Program (2nd Year College Students) 769

Asian Pacific Community Fund - Verizon Scholarship Awards Program (High School Seniors) 669

Asian Reporter Scholarship 617

ASID Foundation Legacy Scholarship for Undergraduates 360

ASLA Council of Fellows Scholarship 376

ASME Auxiliary Undergraduate Scholarship Charles B. Sharp 401

ASM Outstanding Scholars Awards 277

ASSE Construction Safety Scholarship 444

ASSED Foundation Military Service Scholarship 444

ASSE Diversity Committee Scholarship 444

ASSE-Gulf Coast Past Presidents Scholarship 445

ASSE-Marsh Risk Consulting Scholarship 445

ASSE-United Parcel Service Scholarship 445

Associate Degree Nursing Scholarship Program 434

Associated General Contractors NYS Scholarship Program 181

Associated Press Television/Radio Association-Clete Roberts Journalism Scholarship Awards 364

Association for Food and Drug Officials Scholarship Fund 150

Sponsor

101st Airborne Division Association   *328, 459, 765*

1st Infantry Division Foundation   *586*

37th Division Veterans Association   *590*

AACE International   *108, 124, 149, 162, 179, 207, 248, 259, 271, 400*

Abbie Sargent Memorial Scholarship Inc.   *84, 89, 98, 300, 346*

Academy Foundation of the Academy of Motion Picture Arts and Sciences   *308*

Academy of Television Arts and Sciences Foundation   *765*

ACL/NJCL National Latin Exam   *186, 319*

Actors Theatre of Louisville   *737*

The Actuarial Foundation   *359, 396*

ADC Research Institute   *187, 308, 363, 496*

Adelante! U.S. Education Leadership Fund   *613, 738*

AEG Foundation   *225, 271, 474*

Agriliance, Land O' Lakes, and Croplan Genetics   *89*

AHIMA Foundation   *340*

AHS International—The Vertical Flight Technical Society   *124, 248, 259, 271, 400*

AIA New Jersey Scholarship Foundation, Inc.   *109*

Aiken Electric Cooperative Inc.   *653*

Aim Magazine Short Story Contest   *385*

Air & Waste Management Association–Allegheny Mountain Section   *300*

Air & Waste Management Association–Coastal Plains Chapter   *300, 459*

Aircraft Electronics Association Educational Foundation   *125, 486*

Air Force Aid Society   *579, 582*

Air Force Reserve Officer Training Corps   *424, 580, 582*

Air Line Pilots Association, International   *502*

Airmen Memorial Foundation/Air Force Sergeants Association   *580, 582*

Airport Minority Advisory Council Educational and Scholarship Program   *126*

Air Traffic Control Association Inc.   *126, 271, 550*

AIST Foundation   *142, 162, 179, 199, 248, 259, 271, 300, 358, 392, 400, 459*

Alabama Broadcasters Association   *496*

Alabama Commission on Higher Education   *582, 588, 653*

Alabama Department of Veterans Affairs   *590, 654*

Alabama Funeral Directors Association Inc.   *322*

Alabama Golf Course Superintendents Association   *89, 347*

Alabama Indian Affairs Commission   *613, 654*

Alabama Society of Certified Public Accountants   *69*

Alaska Geological Society Inc.   *226*

Alaskan Aviation Safety Foundation   *127*

Alaska Society of Certified Public Accountants   *69*

Alaska Commission on Postsecondary Education   *654*

Alberta Agriculture Food and Rural Development 4-H Branch   *502, 654*

Alberta Heritage Scholarship Fund   *89, 142, 210, 218, 231, 273, 319, 326, 328, 354, 378, 379, 424, 456, 476, 478, 479, 484, 486, 496, 613, 654, 738*

Albuquerque Community Foundation   *655*

Alert Scholarship   *655, 738*

The Alexander Foundation   *655, 738*

Alexander Graham Bell Association for the Deaf and Hard of Hearing   *566*

Alfred G. and Elma M. Milotte Scholarship Fund   *766*

Alice L. Haltom Educational Fund   *341, 383*

Alliance for Young Artists and Writers Inc.   *117, 385*

All-Ink.com Printer Supplies Online   *766*

Alpena Regional Medical Center   *328*

Alpha Kappa Alpha Educational Advancement Foundation, Inc.   *766*

Alpha Lambda Delta   *766*

Alpha Mu Gamma, The National Collegiate Foreign Language Society   *319*

Alpha Omega Alpha   *328*

Amarillo Area Foundation   *424*

American Academy of Oral and Maxillofacial Radiology   *219*

American Academy of Religion   *472*

American Alliance for Health, Physical Education, Recreation and Dance   *470, 480*

American Association for Health Education   *231*

American Association of Airport Executives-Southwest Chapter   *127*

American Association of Blood Banks-SBB Scholarship Awards   *142*

American Association of Family & Consumer Services   *346*

American Association of Hispanic Certified Public Accountants (AAHCPA)   *69, 149*

American Association of Neuroscience Nurses   *425*

American Atheists   *766*

American Baptist Financial Aid Program   *615, 650*

American Board of Funeral Service Education   *322*

American Bowling Congress   *503, 738*

American Cancer Society   *566, 656, 738*

American Chemical Society   *162, 301, 392, 419, 452*

American Chemical Society, Rubber Division   *163, 273, 392, 400, 474*

American Classical League/National Junior Classical League   *187, 320, 354*

American College of Musicians/National Guild of Piano Teachers   *408*

American Congress on Surveying and Mapping   *149, 481*

American Copy Editors Society   *363*

American Council for Polish Culture   *113, 320, 408*

American Council of Engineering Companies of Pennsylvania (ACEC/PA)   *163, 179, 249, 259, 273, 392, 400*

American Council of the Blind   *566*

American Criminal Justice Association-Lambda Alpha Epsilon   *211, 379, 476*

American Culinary Federation   *212, 316*

American Dental Assistants Association   *219*

American Dental Association (ADA) Foundation   *219*

American Dental Hygienists' Association (ADHA) Institute For Oral Health   *220*

American Dietetic Association   *312*

American Federation of State, County, and Municipal Employees   *97, 100, 343, 464, 466, 476, 478, 502, 503*

American Federation of Teachers   *231, 503, 550*

American Fire Sprinkler Association   *767*

American Foreign Service Association   *503, 615*

American Foundation for Pharmaceutical Education   *456*

American Foundation for the Blind   *199, 232, 249, 273, 385, 409, 419, 460, 484, 566*

American Foundation for Translation and Interpretation   *320*

American Ground Water Trust   *179, 355, 416*

American Health and Beauty Aids Institute   *210*

American Hotel and Lodging Educational Foundation   *212, 316, 351, 471, 492*

American Indian Education Foundation   *615*

American Indian Graduate Center   *616, 738*

American Indian Science and Engineering Society   *102, 142, 149, 226, 232, 273, 326, 329, 392, 406, 416, 419, 422, 460*

American Institute for Foreign Study   *616, 738, 767*

American Institute of Aeronautics and Astronautics   *102, 127, 249, 259, 273, 392, 400, 460, 474*

American Institute of Architects   *109*

American Institute of Architects West Virginia Chapter   *109*

American Institute of Certified Public Accountants   *69*

American Institute of Chemical Engineers   *163, 301, 358*

American Institute of Polish Culture Inc.   *117, 187, 232, 320, 363, 468*

American Institute of Wine and Food-Pacific Northwest Chapter   *312, 316, 352*

American Jewish League for Israel   *739*

American Legion Auxiliary Department of Alabama   *591, 656*

American Legion Auxiliary Department of Arizona   *329, 425, 465, 468, 478, 480*

American Legion Auxiliary Department of California   *425, 503, 586, 656*

American Legion Auxiliary Department of Colorado   *425, 591, 656*

American Legion Auxiliary Department of Connecticut   *504, 591, 656*

American Legion Auxiliary Department of Florida   *504, 591, 656*

American Legion Auxiliary Department of Idaho   *425*

American Legion Auxiliary Department of Indiana   *591, 656*

American Legion Auxiliary Department of Iowa   *232, 426, 591, 656*

American Legion Auxiliary Department of Kentucky   *586, 592, 656*

American Legion Auxiliary Department of Maine   *329, 426, 550, 592, 656*

American Legion Auxiliary Department of Maryland   *426, 504, 592, 657*

American Legion Auxiliary Department of Massachusetts   *550, 592, 657*

American Legion Auxiliary Department of Michigan   *329, 426, 484, 592, 657*

American Legion Auxiliary Department of Minnesota   *329, 593, 657*

American Legion Auxiliary Department of Missouri   *426, 504, 593, 657*

American Legion Auxiliary Department of Nebraska   *505, 593, 657*

American Legion Auxiliary Department of North Dakota *426, 550, 593, 657*

American Legion Auxiliary Department of Ohio *427, 594, 657*

American Legion Auxiliary Department of Oregon *427, 505, 594, 657*

American Legion Auxiliary Department of Pennsylvania *658*

American Legion Auxiliary Department of South Dakota *505, 594, 658*

American Legion Auxiliary Department of Tennessee *594, 658*

American Legion Auxiliary Department of Texas *329, 595, 658*

American Legion Auxiliary Department of Utah *506, 595, 658*

American Legion Auxiliary Department of Wisconsin *427, 506, 595, 658*

American Legion Auxiliary Department of Wyoming *222, 330, 427, 484*

American Legion Auxiliary National Headquarters *507, 595*

American Legion Baseball *739*

American Legion Department of Arizona *658, 739*

American Legion Department of Arkansas *508, 595, 659, 739*

American Legion Department of Hawaii *659*

American Legion Department of Idaho *508, 595, 659*

American Legion Department of Illinois *508, 595, 659, 739*

American Legion Department of Indiana *508, 659, 739*

American Legion Department of Iowa *509, 660, 740*

American Legion Department of Kansas *409, 427, 454, 509, 595, 660, 740*

American Legion Department of Maine *510, 596, 660*

American Legion Department of Maryland *396, 460, 596, 661, 767*

American Legion Department of Michigan *596, 661, 740*

American Legion Department of Minnesota *510, 597, 661, 740*

American Legion Department of Missouri *232, 427, 510, 597, 661*

American Legion Department of Montana *661, 740*

American Legion Department of Nebraska *511, 597, 662, 740*

American Legion Department of New Jersey *511, 586, 740*

American Legion Department of New York *187, 662, 740*

American Legion Department of North Carolina *662, 741*

American Legion Department of North Dakota *90, 222, 312, 456, 597, 617, 663, 741*

American Legion Department of Ohio *511, 597*

American Legion Department of Oregon *663, 741*

American Legion Department of Pennsylvania *486, 511, 663, 741*

American Legion Department of South Dakota *663, 741*

American Legion Department of Tennessee *512, 582, 588, 663, 741*

American Legion Department of Texas *664, 741*

American Legion Department of Vermont *512, 551, 664, 741*

American Legion Department of Virginia *664*

American Legion Department of Washington *512, 597, 664*

American Legion Department of West Virginia *512, 597, 665, 741*

American Legion National Headquarters *428, 551, 597, 741*

American Legion Press Club of New Jersey *187, 363, 457, 496*

American Mathematical Association of Two Year Colleges *396*

American Medical Association Foundation *330*

American Medical Technologists *222, 330*

American Meteorological Society *301, 356, 389, 406, 450*

American Military Retirees Association *598*

American Mobile Healthcare *428*

American Montessori Society *233*

American Morgan Horse Institute *741*

American Museum of Natural History *742*

American National Cattle Women Inc. *767*

American Nephrology Nurses' Association *428*

American Nuclear Society *257, 273, 422*

American Occupational Therapy Foundation Inc. *330, 484, 767*

American Oil Chemists' Society *90, 165, 313*

American Optometric Foundation *452*

American Philological Association *108, 117, 187, 320, 343*

American Physical Society *460*

American Physical Therapy Association *233, 330, 484*

American Physiological Society *98, 143, 301, 331, 387, 419, 422, 481*

American Planning Association *501*

American Postal Workers Union *512, 551*

American Public Transportation Foundation *150, 179, 249, 259, 273, 400, 490*

American Quarter Horse Foundation (AQHF) *98, 188, 363, 457, 484, 513, 551, 665, 742*

American Railway Engineering and Maintenance of Way Association *179, 207, 249, 259, 274, 297, 400, 490*

American Research Institute in Turkey (ARIT) *320*

American Respiratory Care Foundation *331, 484*

American Road & Transportation Builders Association-Transportation Development Foundation (ARTBA-TDF) *551*

American Savings Foundation *665*

American-Scandinavian Foundation *385*

American School of Classical Studies at Athens *100, 108, 109, 116, 117, 187, 342, 343, 354, 408, 457, 472*

American Sephardi Foundation *650*

American Sheep Industry Association *742*

American Society for Engineering Education *102, 260, 274, 397, 460*

American Society for Enology and Viticulture *90, 166, 313, 347*

American Society for Horticultural Science *347*

American Society for Information Science and Technology *199, 383*

American Society of Agronomy, Crop Science Society of America, Soil Science Society of America *90, 226, 297, 301, 416, 419*

American Society of Certified Engineering Technicians *274*

American Society of Civil Engineers *180, 207*

American Society of Civil Engineers-Maine Section *180*

American Society of Criminology *211, 378, 379, 476*

American Society of Heating, Refrigerating, and Air Conditioning Engineers, Inc. *109, 166, 207, 249, 257, 260, 274, 341, 400, 452, 486*

American Society of Ichthyologists and Herpetologists *143*

American Society of Interior Designers (ASID) Education Foundation Inc. *360*

American Society of Mechanical Engineers (ASME) *400*

American Society of Mechanical Engineers Auxiliary Inc. *401*

American Society of Naval Engineers *103, 127, 180, 251, 257, 275, 389, 393, 401, 460*

American Society of Plumbing Engineers *275, 358*

American Society of Safety Engineers (ASSE) Foundation *444*

American Society of Travel Agents (ASTA) Foundation *492*

American Society of Women Accountants *70*

American String Teachers Association *742*

American Swedish Institute *665, 743, 768*

American Theatre Organ Society Inc. *743*

American Traffic Safety Services Foundation *768*

American Water Resources Association *416*

American Water Ski Educational Foundation *515*

American Welding Society *150, 181, 261, 275, 393, 401, 487*

American Wholesale Marketers Association *150*

America's Junior Miss Scholarship Program, Inc. d/b/a Distinguished Young Women *743*

AMVETS Auxiliary *515, 598*

Amy Lowell Poetry Travelling Scholarship Trust *385*

Anchor Scholarship Foundation *610*

AnyCollege.com *768*

Appalachian Studies Association, Inc. *743, 768*

Appaloosa Horse Club-Appaloosa Youth Program *99, 515, 743*

Appraisal Institute Education Trust *469*

Arab American Scholarship Foundation *188, 465*

Archaeological Institute of America *108*

ARC of Washington Trust Fund *480*

Arctic Institute of North America *233, 301, 416, 420*

Arizona Business Education Association *233*

Arizona Commission for Postsecondary Education *666*

Arizona Hydrological Society *226, 357, 416, 424, 474*

Arizona Nursery Association *347*

Arizona Private School Association *666*

Arizona Professional Chapter of AISES *276, 332, 416, 460*

Arkansas Department of Higher Education *598, 666*

Arkansas Single Parent Scholarship Fund *667*

Arkansas Student Loan Authority *667*

Armed Forces Communications and Electronics Association, Educational Foundation *127, 166, 188, 200, 234, 251, 263, 276, 320, 362, 397, 460, 598, 768*

Armenian Relief Society of Eastern USA Inc.-Regional Office *617*

Armenian Students Association of America Inc. *617*

Army Emergency Relief (AER) *769*

Army Officers' Wives Club of Greater Washington Area *586*

Arnold and Mabel Beckman Foundation *143, 332, 422, 460*

ARRL Foundation Inc. *91, 103, 143, 150, 166, 181, 188, 200, 207, 222, 251, 257, 263, 276, 332, 343, 362, 363, 379, 389, 393, 401, 420, 429, 451, 452, 460, 474, 484, 496, 515, 567, 667, 743*

Art Directors Club *117*

Asian American Journalists Association *189, 363, 457, 496*

Marine Corps Tankers Association Inc. *609*

Marine Technology Society *285, 388, 390, 451*

Marion D. and Eva S. Peeples Foundation Trust Scholarship Program *240, 285, 315, 436, 488*

Marsha's Angels Scholarship Fund *436*

Martin D. Andrews Scholarship *754*

Maryland Association of Certified Public Accountants Educational Foundation *75*

Maryland Association of Private Colleges and Career Schools *157, 202, 224, 285, 315, 346, 488, 498*

Maryland/Delaware/District of Columbia Press Foundation *368*

Maryland State Higher Education Commission *224, 240, 311, 337, 381, 436, 479, 485, 488, 560, 603, 702*

Massachusetts AFL-CIO *703*

Massachusetts Broadcasters Association *498*

Massachusetts Office of Student Financial Assistance *240, 560, 603, 703*

McCurry Foundation Inc. *705, 754*

Media Action Network for Asian Americans *120, 308, 498*

Memorial Foundation for Jewish Culture *241, 473, 479*

Mennonite Women *785*

Menominee Indian Tribe of Wisconsin *630*

Michael and Susan Dell Foundation *785*

Michigan Association of Broadcasters Foundation *498*

Michigan Association of CPAs *75*

Michigan Council of Teachers of Mathematics *398*

Michigan Department of Treasury - Bureau of State and Authority Finance *705*

Michigan League for Nursing *436*

Michigan Society of Professional Engineers *169, 183, 208, 253, 285, 403*

Microsoft Corporation *202*

Midwestern Higher Education Compact *705*

Midwest Roofing Contractors Association *112, 183, 209, 225, 285, 359, 394, 488*

Military Officers Association of America (MOAA) Scholarship Fund *603*

Military Order of the Purple Heart *603*

Military Order of the Stars and Bars *785*

Minerals, Metals, and Materials Society (TMS) *266, 285, 394*

Minnesota AFL-CIO *525, 705, 754*

Minnesota Broadcasters Association *498*

Minnesota Department of Military Affairs *560, 585, 589, 705, 754*

Minnesota Office of Higher Education *120, 321, 387, 398, 475, 477, 560, 604, 631, 705*

Minnesota Society of Certified Public Accountants *75*

Minnesota Soybean Research and Promotion Council *86, 92, 315*

Minority Nurse Magazine *437*

Miss American Coed Pageants Inc. *754*

Mississippi Association of Broadcasters *368, 498*

Mississippi Nurses' Association (MNA) *437*

Mississippi Office of Student Financial Aid *560, 706*

Mississippi Press Association Education Foundation *368*

Missouri Broadcasters Association Scholarship Program *499*

Missouri Conservation Agents Association Scholarship *707*

Missouri Department of Higher Education *707*

Missouri Department of Natural Resources *304*

Missouri Funeral Directors & Embalmers Association *323*

Missouri Insurance Education Foundation *360*

Missouri Sheriffs' Association *211*

Missouri Travel Council *318, 353, 495*

Mitchell Institute *707*

Mongolia Society, Inc. *631*

Monsanto Agribusiness Scholarship *86, 93, 475*

Montana Broadcasters Association *499*

Montana Federation of Garden Clubs *228, 350, 377, 418*

Montana Society of Certified Public Accountants *76*

Montana University System, Office of Commissioner of Higher Education *707*

Morris J. and Betty Kaplun Foundation *785*

Mount Sinai Hospital Department of Nursing *437*

Mount Vernon Urban Renewal Agency *708*

NAACP Legal Defense and Educational Fund Inc. *631*

NAAS-USA FUND, INC. *526, 785*

NANA (Northwest Alaska Native Association) Regional Corporation *631*

NASA Florida Space Grant Consortium *132, 228, 394, 398, 403*

NASA Idaho Space Grant Consortium *146, 169, 183, 202, 228, 254, 324, 394, 398, 403, 421, 462*

NASA/Maryland Space Grant Consortium *132, 146, 169, 202, 228, 285, 305, 394, 398, 462*

NASA Minnesota Space Grant Consortium *132, 228, 285, 398, 462*

NASA Mississippi Space Grant Consortium *132, 267, 285, 398, 462*

NASA Montana Space Grant Consortium *133, 146, 169, 183, 203, 254, 286, 398, 403*

NASA Rhode Island Space Grant Consortium *133, 241, 267, 286, 398, 407, 475*

NASA South Carolina Space Grant Consortium *133, 146, 228, 267, 286*

NASA South Dakota Space Grant Consortium *134, 228, 258, 267, 286, 305, 394, 399, 421, 462, 475*

NASA's Virginia Space Grant Consortium *105, 134, 146, 169, 203, 209, 225, 254, 267, 286, 305, 359, 394, 399, 403, 462, 476*

NASA West Virginia Space Grant Consortium *134, 203, 258, 268, 286, 305, 407, 421, 424, 462*

NASA Wisconsin Space Grant Consortium *134*

National Academy of Television Arts and Sciences *192, 499*

National Academy of Television Arts and Sciences-National Capital/Chesapeake Bay Chapter *368, 499*

National Action Council for Minorities in Engineering-NACME Inc. *286*

National Agricultural Aviation Association *526*

National Air Transportation Foundation *134*

National Alliance of Postal and Federal Employees (NAPFE) *526*

National Amateur Baseball Federation (NABF) *755*

National AMBUCS Inc. *124, 485*

National Arab American Medical Association *224, 337, 452*

National Asphalt Pavement Association Research and Education Foundation *183, 209*

National Association Directors of Nursing Administration *437*

National Association for Campus Activities *161, 561, 631, 755*

National Association for the Advancement of Colored People *169, 268, 286, 462, 526, 631*

National Association for the Self-Employed *526, 755*

National Association of Black Journalists *192, 368, 458, 499*

National Association of Broadcasters *192, 369, 499*

National Association of Colored Women's Clubs *632*

National Association of Energy Service Companies *527*

National Association of Geoscience Teachers & Far Western Section *228*

National Association of Hispanic Journalists (NAHJ) *192, 321, 325, 369, 459, 499*

National Association of Hispanic Nurses *437*

National Association of Letter Carriers *527*

National Association of Negro Business and Professional Women's Clubs Inc. *230, 369, 632*

National Association of Pastoral Musicians *413, 473*

National Association of Railway Business Women *786*

National Association of Secondary School Principals *527, 755*

National Association of Water Companies-New Jersey Chapter *146, 157, 192, 203, 228, 230, 286, 381, 418, 462, 488*

National Association of Women in Construction *112, 184, 225, 254, 268, 286, 361, 377, 403, 488*

National Association to Advance Fat Acceptance *307*

National Athletic Trainers' Association Research and Education Foundation *337, 341, 481, 485*

National Beta Club *527*

National Bicycle League (NBL) *528*

National Black MBA Association *786*

National Black MBA Association-Twin Cities Chapter *76, 157*

National Black Nurses Association Inc. *437*

National Black Police Association *212, 379, 381, 477, 479*

National Board of Boiler and Pressure Vessel Inspectors *169, 254, 403*

National Burglar and Fire Alarm Association *562, 708*

National Business Aviation Association Inc. *135*

National Cattlemen's Foundation *87, 93, 192*

National Center for Learning Disabilities, Inc. *573*

National Community Pharmacist Association (NCPA) Foundation *457*

National Construction Education Foundation *209*

National Council of Jewish Women New York Section *573, 708*

National Council of State Garden Clubs Inc. Scholarship *93, 147, 305, 351*

National Council of Teachers of Mathematics *241, 399*

National Court Reporters Association *381*

National Customs Brokers and Forwarders Association of America *491*

National Dairy Shrine *87, 93, 99, 315, 370, 391, 499*

National Defense Transportation Association-Scott St. Louis Chapter *708*

National Dental Association Foundation *224*

National Environmental Health Association/ American Academy of Sanitarians *299, 467*

National Federation of Blind of Missouri *573, 708*

National Federation of Paralegal Associations Inc. (NFPA) *381*

Society of Plastics Engineers (SPE)
Foundation *171, 255, 293, 359, 395, 489*

Society of Professional Journalists, Los Angeles
Chapter *374, 500*

Society of Professional Journalists Maryland Pro
Chapter *374*

Society of Satellite Professionals
International *138, 196, 382, 407, 408*

Society of Women Engineers *172, 185, 204, 209, 255, 258, 270, 293, 390, 395, 404, 453*

Society of Women Engineers-Dallas
Section *205, 295*

Society of Women Engineers-Rocky Mountain
Section *176, 186, 205, 210, 256, 259, 270, 295, 390, 396, 405*

Society of Women Engineers-Twin Tiers
Section *205, 295*

Soil and Water Conservation Society *88, 95, 229, 299, 306, 418, 422*

Soil and Water Conservation Society-New Jersey
Chapter *88, 95, 99, 148, 229, 306, 351, 418, 422*

Sons of Italy Foundation *322, 638*

Sons of Norway Foundation *115, 176, 256, 405, 537, 724*

Sons of the Republic of Texas *98, 345*

South Asian Journalists Association (SAJA) *374*

South Carolina Association of Certified Public
Accountants *80*

South Carolina Association of Heating and Air
Conditioning Contractors *342*

South Carolina Commission on Higher
Education *724*

South Carolina Department of Education *725*

South Carolina Division of Veterans Affairs *608, 725*

South Carolina Police Corps *379*

South Carolina Press Association
Foundation *375*

South Carolina Public Health Association *468*

South Carolina State Employees
Association *537, 725*

South Carolina Tuition Grants Commission *725*

South Dakota Board of Regents *89, 95, 244, 419, 725, 759*

South Dakota CPA Society *80*

South Dakota Retailers Association *80, 159, 205, 210, 218, 256, 326, 342, 354, 361, 378, 457*

Southern Nursery Association *351*

Southern Texas PGA *759*

South Florida Fair and Palm Beach County
Expositions Inc. *95, 725*

Specialty Equipment Market Association *80, 84, 159, 196, 206, 256, 295, 310, 391, 405, 489, 491*

Spencer Educational Foundation Inc. *360*

SPENDonLIFE.com *797*

Spina Bifida Association of America *578*

State Department Federal Credit Union Annual
Scholarship Program *797*

State Employees Association of North Carolina
(SEANC) *726*

State Farm Companies/Youth Service
America *564*

State of Wyoming, Administered by University of
Wyoming *244, 608, 726*

State Student Assistance Commission of Indiana
(SSACI) *441, 585, 589, 726*

Stephen Phillips Memorial Scholarship Fund *726*

Stephen T. Marchello Scholarship
Foundation *726*

Steven Knezevich Trust *638*

Stonewall Community Foundation *564, 760*

StraightForward Media *84, 99, 116, 122, 159, 176, 186, 187, 196, 210, 218, 224, 231, 244, 256, 259, 270, 295, 299, 310, 312, 322, 328,*

339, 341, 342, 345, 355, 375, 387, 391, 396, 405, 442, 450, 451, 452, 453, 457, 459, 466, 467, 470, 478, 480, 481, 486, 489, 500, 638, 797

Student Insights *798*

Student Pilot Network *138*

SunTrust Bank *798*

SuperCollege.com *760*

Supreme Guardian Council, International Order of
Job's Daughters *224, 537*

Swiss Benevolent Society of Chicago *639, 727*

Swiss Benevolent Society of New York *639, 727, 760*

Synod of the Covenant *564, 639, 652, 727*

Tafford Uniforms *442*

Tag and Label Manufacturers Institute, Inc. *270, 312, 326, 760*

Tailhook Educational Foundation *590, 610, 612*

Talbots Charitable Foundation *798*

Tall Clubs International Foundation, Inc. *798*

Tau Beta Pi Association *295*

Technical Association of the Pulp & Paper
Industry (TAPPI) *270, 295, 306, 326, 419, 453*

Teletoon *122, 309*

Tennessee Education Association *244, 537, 727*

Tennessee Society of CPAs *81*

Tennessee Student Assistance Corporation *245, 608, 727*

Terry Foundation *729, 760*

Terry Fox Humanitarian Award Program *564, 639, 760*

Texas 4-H Youth Development Foundation *729, 760*

Texas AFL-CIO *538, 729*

Texas Arts and Crafts Educational
Foundation *122*

Texas Association of Broadcasters *196, 500*

Texas Black Baptist Scholarship Committee *639, 652, 729*

Texas Department of Transportation *186, 206, 450*

Texas Family Business Association and
Scholarship Foundation *159*

Texas Federation of Business and Professional
Women's Foundation *798*

Texas Gridiron Club Inc. *197, 375, 459, 501*

Texas Guaranteed Student Loan Corporation *799*

Texas Higher Education Coordinating
Board *442, 585, 589, 729*

Texas Mutual Insurance Company *799*

Texas Outdoor Writers Association *197, 306, 419*

Texas Restaurant Association *564*

Texas Tennis Foundation *729, 760*

Texas Women in Law Enforcement *538*

Theodore R. and Vivian M. Johnson Scholarship
Foundation Inc. *549, 730*

Theta Delta Chi Educational Foundation Inc. *799*

Third Marine Division Association, Inc. *610, 612*

Thurgood Marshall Scholarship Fund *799*

Tidewater Scholarship Foundation *730*

Tiger Woods Foundation *730*

TKE Educational Foundation *81, 107, 148, 159, 197, 229, 245, 306, 382, 399, 407, 419, 464, 466, 538, 730, 760*

Tlicho Government *639*

Topsfield Historical Society *345*

Tortoise Capital Advisors, LLC *730*

Toshiba/NSTA *761*

Touchmark Foundation *442*

Touro Synagogue Foundation *761*

Township Officials of Illinois *730*

TPA Scholarship Trust for the Deaf and Near
Deaf *578*

Transportation Clubs International *270, 491*

Triangle Community Foundation *730*

Triangle Education Foundation *296, 799*

Truckload Carriers Association *159, 492*

Tuition Exchange Inc. *565*

Turf and Ornamental Communicators
Association *96, 197, 351*

Turner Construction Company *113, 186, 210, 256, 270, 296, 362, 378, 396, 405*

Tuskegee Airmen Scholarship Foundation *640*

Twin Towers Orphan Fund *799*

Two Ten Footwear Foundation *565*

UCB, Inc. *578*

The Morris K. Udall and Stewart L. Udall
Foundation *800*

UDT-Seal Association *612*

Ulman Cancer Fund for Young Adults *579, 731*

UNICO Foundation Inc. *442, 640*

Union Plus Scholarship Program *540*

Unitarian Universalist Association *123, 382, 459, 474, 652*

United Community Services for Working
Families *479, 489*

United Daughters of the Confederacy *160, 206, 315, 345, 346, 387, 442, 540, 731*

United Food and Commercial Workers
International Union *541*

United Methodist Church *640, 652, 731*

United Methodist Communications *197, 375, 459, 474, 501*

United Methodist Youth Organization *641, 653*

United Nations Association of the United States of
America *761*

United Negro College Fund *81, 89, 96, 98, 100, 102, 113, 116, 123, 148, 160, 176, 186, 198, 206, 210, 231, 245, 256, 271, 296, 306, 310, 316, 324, 339, 345, 354, 375, 382, 387, 390, 391, 399, 406, 415, 422, 454, 455, 457, 464, 466, 469, 474, 476, 478, 479, 502, 565, 579, 641, 731, 761, 800*

United Realty Partners, LLC *800*

United South and Eastern Tribes Inc. *647*

United States Achievement Academy *800*

United States Association for Blind Athletes *579*

United States Department of Agriculture *96, 100, 149, 316, 419, 647*

United States Environmental Protection
Agency *307, 419*

United States Hispanic Leadership Institute *648*

United States-Indonesia Society *800*

United States Institute of Peace *362, 454*

United States Junior Chamber of Commerce *542, 761*

United States Marine Corps Scholarship
Foundation, Inc. *542, 610*

United States Naval Sea Cadet Corps *542*

United States Submarine Veterans *543, 565, 612*

United Transportation Union Insurance
Association *800*

Universities Space Research Association *107, 138, 177, 186, 229, 257, 297, 396, 406, 424, 464, 476*

University Aviation Association *138*

University Film and Video Association *309*

University of New Mexico *732*

Urban League of Rhode Island Inc. *648, 732*

USA Badminton Region 1 *762*

USA TODAY/MilkPEP—Got Milk? *762*

U.S. Bank Internet Scholarship Program *801*

U. S. Department of Health and Human
Services *225, 340, 443, 486*

U.S. Fish and Wildlife Service *123*

US Pan Asian American Chamber of Commerce
Education Foundation *648, 801*

Academic Fields/Career Goals

Accounting

5th Year Full Tuition Scholarship *80*
AICPA/Accountemps Student Scholarship *69*
Alfred Chisholm/BASF Memorial Scholarship
    Fund *81*
ALPFA Annual Scholarship Program *69*
American Society of Women Accountants Two-
    Year College Scholarship *70*
American Society of Women Accountants
    Undergraduate Scholarship *70*
ASCPA Educational Foundation Scholarship *69*
Avis Budget Group Scholarship *81*
AXA Achievement Scholarship Program *81*
Carl W. Christiansen Scholarship *79*
Central Intelligence Agency Undergraduate
    Scholarship Program *70*
Charles Earp Memorial Scholarship *76*
Cheryl A. Ruggiero Scholarship *79*
Cohen and Company CPAs Scholarship *71*
Colorado College and University
    Scholarships *71*
Comerica Charitable Foundation Scholarship *81*
CSCPA Candidate's Award *71*
Edward M. Nagel Foundation Scholarship *82*
Esther R. Sawyer Research Award *74*
Excellence in Accounting Scholarship *80*
F. Grant Waite, CPA, Memorial Scholarship *72*
FICPA Educational Foundation Scholarships *73*
Fifth/Graduate Year Student Scholarship *75*
Fifth-Year Scholarship Awards *77*
Ford/UNCF Corporate Scholars Program *82*
Foundation for Accounting Education
    Scholarship *78*
GGFOA Scholarship *73*
Greater Springfield Accountants Scholarship *71*
Greater Washington Society of CPAs
    Scholarship *73*
Harry J. Donnelly Memorial Scholarship *81*
HSCPA Scholarship Program for Accounting
    Students *74*
Illinois CPA Society Accounting Scholarship
    Program *74*
Institute of Management Accountants Memorial
    Education Fund Scholarships *74*
Kathleen M. Peabody, CPA, Memorial
    Scholarship *72*
Kentucky Society of Certified Public Accountants
    College Scholarship *75*
Lawrence P. Doss Scholarship Foundation *75*
Lockheed Martin/UNCF Scholarship *82*
Michele L. McDonald Scholarship *71*
Minorities in Government Finance
    Scholarship *73*
MNCPA Scholarship Program *75*
Money Run formerly 1040K Run/Walk
    Scholarships *73*
Montana Society of Certified Public Accountants
    Scholarship *76*
MSCPA Firm Scholarship *72*
NASCAR/Wendell Scott, Sr. Scholarship *82*
National Society of Accountants Scholarship *76*
Nebraska Society of CPAs Scholarship *77*
Nevada Society of CPAs Scholarship *77*
New England Employee Benefits Council
    Scholarship Program *77*
New Hampshire Society of Certified Public
    Accountants Scholarship Fund *77*
New Jersey Society of Certified Public
    Accountants College Scholarship
    Program *78*

New Jersey Society of Certified Public
    Accountants High School Scholarship
    Program *78*
North Carolina Association of CPAs Foundation
    Scholarships *77*
NSA Louis and Fannie Sager Memorial
    Scholarship Award *76*
OAIA Scholarship *78*
Oregon Association of Certified Fraud Examiners
    Scholarship *78*
OSCPA Educational Foundation Scholarship
    Program *79*
Pacific Gas and Electric Company
    Scholarship *82*
Paul Hagelbarger Memorial Fund
    Scholarship *69*
Paychex Inc. Entrepreneur Scholarship *72*
Pennsylvania Institute of Certified Public
    Accountants Sophomore Scholarship *79*
PSE&G Scholarship *82*
Rhode Island Society of Certified Public
    Accountants Scholarship *79*
Ritchie-Jennings Memorial Scholarship *70*
Robert Half International Scholarship *82*
Rolf S. Jaehnigen Family Scholarship *74*
Rowling, Dold & Associates LLP
    Scholarship *71*
SCACPA Educational Fund Scholarships *80*
Scholarship for Minority Accounting
    Students *69*
Seattle American Society of Women Accountants
    Chapter Scholarship *72*
Society of Automotive Analysts Scholarship *79*
Society of Louisiana CPAs Scholarships *79*
South Dakota Retailers Association Scholarship
    Program *80*
Specialty Equipment Market Association
    Memorial Scholarship Fund *80*
Stanley H. Stearman Scholarship *76*
Stuart Cameron and Margaret McLeod Memorial
    Scholarship *74*
Student Scholarship in Accounting MD
    Association of CPAs *75*
Tennessee Society of CPA Scholarship *81*
Tribal Business Management Program
    (TBM) *70*
Twin Cities Chapter Undergraduate
    Scholarship *76*
UBS/PaineWebber Scholarship *82*
Virchow, Krause and Company Scholarship *82*
W. Allan Herzog Scholarship *81*
Women In Need scholarship *72*
Women In Transition Scholarship *72*
Wyoming Trucking Association Scholarship Trust
    Fund *83*

Advertising/Public Relations

Great Falls Advertising Federation College
    Scholarship *83*
High School Marketing/Communications
    Scholarship *83*
International Foodservice Editorial Council
    Communications Scholarship *83*
J. D. Edsal Scholarship *84*
Public Relations Society of America Multicultural
    Affairs Scholarship *83*
Specialty Equipment Market Association
    Memorial Scholarship Fund *80*
StraightForward Media Business School
    Scholarship *84*

StraightForward Media Media &
    Communications Scholarship *84*

Agribusiness

Abbie Sargent Memorial Scholarship *84*
Bryan A. Champion Memorial Scholarship *85*
CHS Foundation High School Scholarships *84*
CHS Foundation Two-Year College
    Scholarships *85*
CHS Foundation University Scholarships *85*
CME Beef Industry Scholarship *87*
Donald A. Williams Scholarship Soil
    Conservation Scholarship *88*
Edward R. Hall Scholarship *88*
Golf Course Superintendents Association of
    America Student Essay Contest *85*
Maine Rural Rehabilitation Fund Scholarship
    Program *86*
Masonic Range Science Scholarship *88*
Melville H. Cohee Student Leader Conservation
    Scholarship *88*
Minnesota Soybean Research and Promotion
    Council Youth Soybean Scholarship *86*
Monsanto Canada Opportunity Scholarship
    Program *86*
Monsanto/UNCF 1890's Scholarship
    Program *89*
National Poultry and Food Distributors
    Association Scholarship Foundation *87*
NDS Student Recognition Contest *87*
New York State Association of Agricultural Fairs
    and New York State Showpeople's
    Association Annual Scholarship *87*
Potato Industry Scholarship *87*
Robert H. Rumler Scholarship *85*
South Dakota Board of Regents Bjugstad
    Scholarship *89*
Timothy and Palmer W. Bigelow Jr.,
    Scholarship *86*
Truman D. Picard Scholarship *86*
Virgil Thompson Memorial Scholarship
    Contest *87*
Willamette Valley Agricultural Association
    Scholarship *88*

Agriculture

Abbie Sargent Memorial Scholarship *84*
Alabama Golf Course Superintendent's
    Association's Donnie Arthur Memorial
    Scholarship *89*
Alberta Barley Commission-Eugene Boyko
    Memorial Scholarship *89*
American Society for Enology and Viticulture
    Scholarships *90*
Anne Seaman Professional Grounds Management
    Society Memorial Scholarship *95*
AOCS Biotechnology Student Excellence
    Award *90*
Bernice and Pat Murphy Scholarship Fund *92*
Calcot-Seitz Scholarship *91*
California Cattlemen's Association
    Scholarship *91*
Careers in Agriculture Scholarship Program *89*
CHS Foundation High School Scholarships *84*
CHS Foundation Two-Year College
    Scholarships *85*
CHS Foundation University Scholarships *85*
CME Beef Industry Scholarship *87*
College Soybean Scholarship *92*
Donald A. Williams Scholarship Soil
    Conservation Scholarship *88*

Child and Family Studies

Civil Engineering

Lillian Moller Gilbreth Memorial Scholarship 174

Lockheed Martin Aeronautics Corporation Scholarships 205

Lockheed Martin/UNCF Scholarship 82

LTG Douglas D. Buchholz Memorial Scholarship 128

Lynda Baboyian Memorial Scholarship 153

Magnolia DX Association Scholarship 189

Maryland Association of Private Colleges and Career Schools Scholarship 157

Master's Scholarship Program 171

Math, Engineering, Science, Business, Education, Computers Scholarships 151

Monsanto/UNCF 1890's Scholarship Program 89

Montana Space Grant Scholarship Program 133

NASA Idaho Space Grant Consortium Scholarship Program 146

NASA Maryland Space Grant Consortium Undergraduate Scholarships 132

NASCAR/Wendell Scott, Sr. Scholarship 82

National Association of Water Companies-New Jersey Chapter Scholarship 146

National Security Agency Stokes Educational Scholarship Program 203

National Society of Women Engineers Scholarships 205

National Space Grant College and Fellowship Program 106

North Fulton Amateur Radio League Scholarship Fund 200

Pacific Gas and Electric Company Scholarship 82

Paul and Helen Trussell Science and Technology Scholarship 104

Paul W. Ruckes Scholarship 199

PHD Scholarship 201

PSE&G Scholarship 82

Ray, N0RP, & Katie, W0KTE, Pautz Scholarship 201

Rockwell Collins Scholarship 205

Rolf S. Jaehnigen Family Scholarship 74

SanDisk Corporation Scholarship 206

Scott Tarbell Scholarship 202

Social Entrepreneurship Scholarship 203

Society of Women Engineers-Rocky Mountain Section Scholarship Program 176

Society of Women Engineers-Twin Tiers Section Scholarship 205

South Dakota Retailers Association Scholarship Program 80

Southeastern DX Club Scholarship Fund 201

Specialty Equipment Market Association Memorial Scholarship Fund 80

Sprint Scholars Program for Sophomores, Juniors, and Seniors 100

Technical Minority Scholarship 177

Toshiba/NSTA ExploraVision Awards Program 203

Tribal Business Management Program (TBM) 70

Undergraduate STEM Research Scholarships 106

Verizon Scholarship 205

Vermont Space Grant Consortium Scholarship Program 107

Veterans of Enduring Freedom (Afghanistan) and Iraqi Freedom Scholarship 200

ViaSat Software Engineering Scholarship 205

Walter Reed Smith Scholarship 160

West Virginia Space Grant Consortium Undergraduate Fellowship Program 134

WIFLE Scholarship Program 207

William R. Goldfarb Memorial Scholarship 150

Wyoming Trucking Association Scholarship Trust Fund 83

You Can Make a Difference Scholarship 202

Construction Engineering/Management

AACE International Competitive Scholarship 108

Ada I. Pressman Memorial Scholarship 172

AGC Education and Research Foundation Graduate Scholarships 207

AGC Education and Research Foundation Undergraduate Scholarships 181

Alfred Chisholm/BASF Memorial Scholarship Fund 81

Alfred E. Friend Jr., W4CF, Memorial Scholarship 166

Anne Maureen Whitney Barrow Memorial Scholarship 172

AREMA Michael R. Garcia Scholarship 179

AREMA Presidential Spouse Scholarship 180

AREMA Undergraduate Scholarships 180

ASHRAE Region III Boggarm Setty Scholarship 166

Associated General Contractors NYS Scholarship Program 181

Betty Lou Bailey SWE Region F Scholarship 172

BK Krenzer Memorial Reentry Scholarship 172

Carol Stephens Region F Scholarship 172

Colorado Contractors Association Scholarship Program 208

Community College STEM Scholarships 105

Construction Engineering Scholarship 207

David F. Ludovici Scholarship 182

Dr. Ivy M. Parker Memorial Scholarship 173

Dorothy P. Morris Scholarship 173

FECON Scholarship 182

FEFPA Assistantship 110

Gary Wagner, K3OMI, Scholarship 166

IFMA Foundation Scholarships 112

Indian Health Service Health Professions Scholarship Program 208

Lillian Moller Gilbreth Memorial Scholarship 174

Mary V. Munger Scholarship 174

MASWE Memorial Scholarship 174

Meridith Thoms Memorial Scholarships 174

Michigan Society of Professional Engineers Harry R. Ball, P.E. Grant 169

Michigan Society of Professional Engineers Kenneth B. Fishbeck, P.E. Memorial Grant 169

MRCA Foundation Scholarship Program 112

National Asphalt Pavement Association Research and Education Foundation Scholarship Program 183

Odebrecht Award for Sustainable Development 110

Olive Lynn Salembier Memorial Reentry Scholarship 174

Samuel Fletcher Tapman ASCE Student Chapter Scholarship 180

Society of Women Engineers-Rocky Mountain Section Scholarship Program 176

Steven Engineering Scholarship 167

Susan Miszkowicz Memorial Scholarship 175

SWE Baltimore-Washington Section Scholarship 175

SWE Central New Mexico Pioneers Scholarship 175

SWE Central New Mexico Reentry Scholarship 175

SWE Mid-Hudson Section Scholarship 175

SWE Past Presidents Scholarship 175

SWE Phoenix Section Scholarship 175

SWE Region H Scholarships 176

Ted G. Wilson Memorial Scholarship Foundation 184

Trimmer Education Foundation Scholarships for Construction Management 209

Utah Society of Professional Engineers Joe Rhoads Scholarship 177

Wanda Munn Scholarship 176

WRI College Scholarship Program 186

YouthForce 2020 Scholarship Program 113

Cosmetology

Fred Luster, Sr. Education Foundation Scholarship Fund 210

Joe Francis Haircare Scholarship Program 210

South Dakota Retailers Association Scholarship Program 80

StraightForward Media Vocational-Technical School Scholarship 99

Criminal Justice/Criminology

Alphonso Deal Scholarship Award 212

American Criminal Justice Association-Lambda Alpha Epsilon National Scholarship 211

American Society of Criminology Gene Carte Student Paper Competition 211

CIA Undergraduate Scholarships 97

Connecticut Association of Women Police Scholarship 211

Indiana Sheriffs' Association Scholarship Program 211

John Dennis Scholarship 211

North Carolina Sheriffs' Association Undergraduate Criminal Justice Scholarships 212

Oregon Association of Certified Fraud Examiners Scholarship 78

Ritchie-Jennings Memorial Scholarship 70

Robert C. Carson Memorial Bursary 210

Culinary Arts

Allen Susser Scholarship 215

American Academy of Chefs College Scholarship 212

American Academy of Chefs High School Scholarship 212

American Hotel & Lodging Educational Foundation Pepsi Scholarship 212

American Restaurant Scholarship 215

Annual Scholarship Grant Program 213

Arthur J. Packard Memorial Scholarship 213

Azurea at One Ocean Resort Hotel & Spa Scholarship 215

Bern Laxer Memorial Scholarship 215

Bill Ramsey/Craig Noone Memorial Scholarship 215

Bob Zappatelli Memorial Scholarship 215

CANFIT Nutrition, Physical Education and Culinary Arts Scholarship 214

Careers Through Culinary Arts Program Cooking Competition for Scholarships 214

The Chefs for Louisiana Cookery Scholarship 216

Christian Wolffer Scholarship 216

Clay Triplette Scholarship 216

Culinary Trust Scholarship Program for Culinary Study and Research 214

Ecolab Scholarship Program 213

The Elkes Family Culinary Scholarship 216

Food Network Scholarship for Immigrants in the Kitchen 216

French Culinary Institute/Italian Culinary Experience Scholarship 218

Golden Gate Restaurant Association Scholarship Foundation 214

Hyatt Hotels Fund for Minority Lodging Management 213

American Legion Auxiliary Department of Iowa Harriet Hoffman Memorial Merit Award for Teacher Training 232

American Montessori Society Teacher Education Scholarship Fund 233

Anna and John Kolesar Memorial Scholarships 231

Applegate/Jackson/Parks Future Teacher Scholarship 241

Arne Engebretsen Wisconsin Mathematics Council Scholarship 246

ARTC Glen Moon Scholarship 234

Bank of America Scholarship 160

Bill Kane Scholarship 231

Bill Mason Scholarship Fund 235

Black Executive Exchange Program Jerry Bartow Scholarship Fund 157

Brookmire-Hastings Scholarships 246

Burlington Northern Santa Fe Foundation Scholarship 102

Carrol C. Hall Memorial Scholarship 107

Charles Cockett 'Ohana Scholarship 115

Charlotte Plummer Owen Memorial Scholarship 247

Child Development Teacher and Supervisor Grant Program 177

Christa McAuliffe Scholarship Program 245

Continental Society, Daughters of Indian Wars Scholarship 236

Dan and Rachel Mahi Educational Scholarship 239

Delta Gamma Foundation Florence Margaret Harvey Memorial Scholarship 232

Developmental Disabilities Scholastic Achievement Scholarship for College Students who are Lutheran 222

Disabled War Veterans Scholarship 128

Distinguished Student Scholar Award 243

Earl C. Sams Foundation Scholarship 245

Early Childhood Development Scholarship 178

Early Childhood Educators Scholarship Program 240

Edith M. Allen Scholarship 237

Education Achievement Awards 237

Erman W. Taylor Memorial Scholarship 232

Ethel A. Neijahr Wisconsin Mathematics Council Scholarship 247

Francis J. Flynn Memorial Scholarship 245

Frieda L. Koontz Scholarship 246

Future Teacher Scholarship-Oklahoma 242

GAE GFIE Scholarship for Aspiring Teachers 237

General Scholarships 246

Gladys Kamakakuokalani Ainoa Brandt Scholarship 239

Golden Apple Scholars of Illinois 237

Graduate Student Scholar Award 243

Haines Memorial Scholarship 244

Harriet A. Simmons Scholarship 242

Harriet Irsay Scholarship Grant 117

Harry A. Applegate Scholarship 153

Hawaiian Lodge Scholarships 114

Hawaii Education Association Student Teacher Scholarship 238

Hiroshi Barbara Kim Yamashita HEA Scholarship 238

Hispanic Heritage Youth Awards 155

Illinois Future Teachers Corps Program 238

Illinois PTA Lillian E. Glover Scholarship 238

Indiana Retired Teachers Association Foundation Scholarship 239

Inspirational Educator Scholarship 240

International Technology Education Association Undergraduate Scholarship in Technology Education 239

Isabel M. Herson Scholarship in Education 247

Jack J. Isgur Foundation Scholarship 119

James Carlson Memorial Scholarship 242

Janet B. Sondheim Scholarship 117

Janet L. Hoffmann Loan Assistance Repayment Program 240

Jewish Federation Academic Scholarship Program 120

Jim Bourque Scholarship 233

John L. Bates Scholarship 234

Joseph C. Basile, II Memorial Scholarship Fund 238

Kansas Teacher Service Scholarship 239

Languages in Teacher Education Scholarships 231

Leo J. Krysa Undergraduate Scholarship 114

L. Gordon Bittle Memorial Scholarship 234

Marion A. and Eva S. Peeples Scholarships 240

Martha Ann Stark Memorial Scholarship 247

Martin Luther King, Jr. Memorial Scholarship 234

Mary McMillan Scholarship Award 233

Mary Morrow-Edna Richards Scholarship 241

Math, Engineering, Science, Business, Education, Computers Scholarships 151

Medical Imaging Educators Scholarship 234

Memorial Foundation for Jewish Culture, Scholarships for Post-Rabbinical Students 241

Minority Teacher Incentive Grant Program 236

Minority Teachers of Illinois Scholarship Program 238

Myron & Laura Thompson Scholarship 178

Nadeen Burkeholder Williams Music Scholarship 243

NASA RISGC Summer Scholarship for Undergraduate Students 133

Native American Leadership in Education (NALE) 151

Nettie Hanselman Jaynes Scholarship 242

Newtonville Woman's Club Scholarships 237

Northern Alberta Development Council Bursary 219

Oregon Alpha Delta Kappa Scholarship 242

Oregon College Savings Plan Education Celebration Scholarship 242

Paraprofessional Teacher Preparation Grant 240

Paul W. Rodgers Scholarship 227

Penelope Hanshaw Scholarship 226

Prospective Secondary Teacher Course Work Scholarships 241

Reverend Nate Brooks Scholarship 235

Robert G. Porter Scholars Program-AFT Members 231

Rudolph Dillman Memorial Scholarship 232

Sara Carlson Memorial Fund 237

Sarah Elizabeth Klenke Memorial Teaching Scholarship 243

Scholarship for Minority College Students 236

Scholarship for Minority High School Students 236

Scholarships for Education, Business and Religion 153

Sheila Z. Kolman Memorial Scholarship 235

Sister Mary Petronia Van Straten Wisconsin Mathematics Council Scholarship 247

S. John Davis Scholarship 246

Society for the Scientific Study of Sexuality Student Research Grant 102

South Dakota Board of Regents Annis I. Fowler/ Kaden Scholarship 244

StraightForward Media Teacher Scholarship 244

Student Opportunity Scholarship 243

Student Support Scholarship 243

Superior Student in Education Scholarship-Wyoming 244

T.E.A.C.H. Early Childhood OHIO Scholarships 178

Teacher Assistant Scholarship Fund 241

Teacher Education Scholarship 242

Teaching Assistant Program in France 97

TEA Don Sahli-Kathy Woodall Future Teachers of America Scholarship 244

TEA Don Sahli-Kathy Woodall Minority Scholarship 244

TEA Don Sahli-Kathy Woodall Undergraduate Scholarship 245

Tobin Sorenson Physical Education Scholarship 243

Underwood-Smith Teacher Scholarship Program 246

Vermont-NEA/Maida F. Townsend Scholarship 245

Volkwein Memorial Scholarship 247

William Rucker Greenwood Scholarship 227

Electrical Engineering/Electronics

AACE International Competitive Scholarship 108

Accenture Scholarship 172

Ada I. Pressman Memorial Scholarship 172

AIAA Foundation Undergraduate Scholarship 102

AISI/AIST Foundation Premier Scholarship 248

AIST William E. Schwabe Memorial Scholarship 248

Alan Lucas Memorial Educational Scholarship 111

Al-Ben Scholarship for Academic Incentive 168

Al-Ben Scholarship for Professional Merit 168

Al-Ben Scholarship for Scholastic Achievement 168

Alfred Chisholm/BASF Memorial Scholarship Fund 81

Alfred E. Friend Jr., W4CF, Memorial Scholarship 166

Alwin B. Newton Scholarship 249

American Society of Naval Engineers Scholarship 103

Androscoggin Amateur Radio Club Scholarship 200

Anne Maureen Whitney Barrow Memorial Scholarship 172

AREMA Michael R. Garcia Scholarship 179

AREMA Presidential Spouse Scholarship 180

AREMA Undergraduate Scholarships 180

Armed Forces Communications and Electronics Association General Emmett Paige Scholarship 127

Armed Forces Communications and Electronics Association ROTC Scholarship Program 127

ASHRAE Memorial Scholarship 249

ASHRAE Region III Boggarm Setty Scholarship 166

Association for Iron and Steel Technology Benjamin F. Fairless Scholarship (AIME) 162

Association for Iron and Steel Technology David H. Samson Canadian Scholarship 162

Association for Iron and Steel Technology Ohio Valley Chapter Scholarship 142

Association for Iron and Steel Technology Ronald E. Lincoln Scholarship 248

Association for Iron and Steel Technology Willy Korf Memorial Scholarship 162

Astronaut Scholarship Foundation 104

Bertha Lamme Memorial Scholarship 255

Betty Lou Bailey SWE Region F Scholarship 172

Betty Weatherford, KQ6RE, Memorial Scholarship 251

BK Krenzer Memorial Reentry Scholarship 172

Energy and Power Engineering

Hospitality Management

Humanities

Human Resources

Hydrology

Industrial Design

Insurance and Actuarial Science

Interior Design

Landscape Forms Design for People
Scholarship *377*
Life Member Montana Federation of Garden Clubs
Scholarship *228*
Muggets Scholarship *349*
National Garden Clubs Inc. Scholarship
Program *94*
NAWIC Undergraduate Scholarships *112*
Peridian International, Inc./Rae L. Price, FASLA
Scholarship *377*
Rain Bird Intelligent Use of Water
Scholarship *377*
Robert Lewis Baker Scholarship *347*
Russell W. Myers Scholarship *304*
South Dakota Retailers Association Scholarship
Program *80*
Spring Meadow Nursery Scholarship *350*
Steven G. King Play Environments
Scholarship *377*
Ted G. Wilson Memorial Scholarship
Foundation *184*
Timothy and Palmer W. Bigelow Jr.,
Scholarship *86*
Usrey Family Scholarship *298*
Western Reserve Herb Society Scholarship *349*
Whitley Place Scholarship *110*
YouthForce 2020 Scholarship Program *113*

Law Enforcement/Police Administration
Alphonso Deal Scholarship Award *212*
American Society of Criminology Gene Carte
Student Paper Competition *211*
Captain James J. Regan Scholarship *378*
CIA Undergraduate Scholarships *97*
Connecticut Association of Women Police
Scholarship *211*
DEA Drug Abuse Prevention Service
Awards *379*
Federal Criminal Investigators Service
Award *379*
Indiana Sheriffs' Association Scholarship
Program *211*
John Charles Wilson Scholarship & Robert Doran
Scholarship *311*
North Carolina Sheriffs' Association
Undergraduate Criminal Justice
Scholarships *212*
Robert C. Carson Memorial Bursary *210*
Sheryl A. Horak Memorial Scholarship *378, 379*
South Carolina Police Corps Scholarship *379*
WIFLE Scholarship Program *207*

Law/Legal Services
Alfred Chisholm/BASF Memorial Scholarship
Fund *81*
Alphonso Deal Scholarship Award *212*
American Criminal Justice Association-Lambda
Alpha Epsilon National Scholarship *211*
American Society of Criminology Gene Carte
Student Paper Competition *211*
Bernice Pickins Parsons Fund *380*
BESLA Scholarship Legal Writing
Competition *380*
Council on Approved Student Education's
Scholarship Fund *381*
Decatur H. Miller Scholarship *343*
Francis Walton Memorial Scholarship *91*
Frank Sarli Memorial Scholarship *381*
Graduate and Professional Scholarship Program-
Maryland *224*
Harry J. Donnelly Memorial Scholarship *81*
Humane Studies Fellowships *190*
Jamie Bowie Memorial Scholarship *381*
Janet L. Hoffmann Loan Assistance Repayment
Program *240*
Jason Lang Scholarship *218*

Jeanette R. Wolman Scholarship *178*
Law in Society Award Competition *382*
MCCA Lloyd M. Johnson Jr. Scholarship *382*
MCCA Lloyd M. Johnson Jr. Scholarship
Program *382*
National Association of Water Companies-New
Jersey Chapter Scholarship *146*
National Federation of Paralegal Associates Inc.
Thomson Reuters Scholarship *381*
National JACL Headquarters Scholarship *92*
New England Employee Benefits Council
Scholarship Program *77*
Oregon Association of Certified Fraud Examiners
Scholarship *78*
Raymond W. Cannon Memorial Scholarship *382*
Richard V. Cruz Memorial Foundation
Scholarship *382*
Robert C. Carson Memorial Bursary *210*
The Robert Spar Memorial Scholarship *343*
Spence Reese Scholarship *279*
SSPI International Scholarships *138*
Stanfield and D'Orlando Art Scholarship *123*
Student Member Tuition Grant *381*
Warner Norcross and Judd LLP Scholarship for
Minority Students *380*
William S. Richardson Commemorative
Scholarship *380*
WSTLA American Justice Essay Scholarship
Contest *383*

Library and Information Sciences
AISLE Scholarship Fund *384*
Alice L. Haltom Educational Fund *341*
Bernice Pickins Parsons Fund *380*
FAME/Sandy Ulm Scholarship *383*
Florida Library Association-Associate's Degree
Scholarship *383*
Florida Library Association-Bachelor's Degree
Scholarship *384*
Idaho Library Association Gardner Hanks
Scholarship *384*
John Blanchard Memorial Fund Scholarship *383*
John Wiley & Sons Best JASIST Paper
Award *199*
Justin G. Schiller Prize for Bibliographical Work in
Pre-20th-Century Children's Books *383*
Nebraska Library Association Duane Munson
Scholarship *384*
Scholarship for the Education of Rural Librarians
Gloria Hoegh Memorial Fund *384*
WLA Continuing Education Scholarship *384*

Literature/English/Writing
AFSCME/UNCF/Harvard University LWP Union
Scholars Program *98*
American-Scandinavian Foundation Translation
Prize *385*
America's Intercultural Magazine (AIM) Short
Story Contest *385*
Amy Lowell Poetry Traveling Scholarship *385*
Buerkle Scholarship *372*
Davidson Fellows Scholarship Program *386*
Evert Clark/Seth Payne Award *370*
Helen James Brewer Scholarship *345*
Humane Studies Fellowships *190*
International Foodservice Editorial Council
Communications Scholarship *83*
Jack J. Isgur Foundation Scholarship *119*
Janet Jackson/Rhythm Nation Scholarship *123*
Justin G. Schiller Prize for Bibliographical Work in
Pre-20th-Century Children's Books *383*
Lambda Iota Tau Literature Scholarship *386*
Literary Achievement Awards *386*
Mae Maxey Memorial Scholarship *123*
Michael Jackson Scholarship *198*

Minnesota Academic Excellence
Scholarship *120*
National JACL Headquarters Scholarship *92*
National Writers Association Foundation
Scholarships *370*
Norma Ross Walter Scholarship *387*
Outdoor Writers Association of America - Bodie
McDowell Scholarship Award *193*
Profile in Courage Essay Contest *386*
Reader's Digest Foundation Scholarship *198*
R.L. Gillette Scholarship *385*
Scholastic Art and Writing Awards-Art
Section *117*
Scholastic Art and Writing Awards-Writing
Section Scholarship *117*
Sehar Saleha Ahmad and Abrahim Ekramullah
Zafar Foundation Scholarship *387*
StraightForward Media Liberal Arts
Scholarship *116*
Teaching Assistant Program in France *97*

Marine Biology
Charles H. Bussman Undergraduate
Scholarship *388*
David S. Bruce Awards for Excellence in
Undergraduate Research *98*
Elizabeth and Sherman Asche Memorial
Scholarship Fund *91*
Financial Support for Marine or Maritime
Studies *389*
John C. Bajus Scholarship *388*
Libbie H. Hyman Memorial Scholarship *148*
Loeblich and Tappan Student Research
Award *144*
MTS Student Scholarship *388*
MTS Student Scholarship for Graduate and
Undergraduate Students *388*
MTS Student Scholarship for Two-Year Technical,
Engineering and Community College
Students *388*
Norm Manly—YMTA Maritime Educational
Scholarships *389*
Paros-Digiquartz Scholarship *388*
Paul W. Rodgers Scholarship *227*
Rockefeller State Wildlife Scholarship *146*
ROV Scholarship *389*

Marine/Ocean Engineering
Ada I. Pressman Memorial Scholarship *172*
Alfred E. Friend Jr., W4CF, Memorial
Scholarship *166*
American Society of Naval Engineers
Scholarship *103*
AMS Freshman Undergraduate Scholarship *301*
Anne Maureen Whitney Barrow Memorial
Scholarship *172*
Betty Lou Bailey SWE Region F
Scholarship *172*
BK Krenzer Memorial Reentry Scholarship *172*
Carol Stephens Region F Scholarship *172*
CDM Scholarship/Internship *176*
Charles H. Bussman Undergraduate
Scholarship *388*
Dr. Ivy M. Parker Memorial Scholarship *173*
Dorothy Lemke Howarth Memorial
Scholarship *173*
Dorothy P. Morris Scholarship *173*
Jill S. Tietjen P.E. Scholarship *173*
John C. Bajus Scholarship *388*
Lillian Moller Gilbreth Memorial
Scholarship *174*
Maine Metal Products Education Fund Scholarship
Program *132*
Mary V. Munger Scholarship *174*
MASWE Memorial Scholarship *174*
Meridith Thoms Memorial Scholarships *174*

Meteorology/Atmospheric Science

Military and Defense Studies

Museum Studies

Music

Natural Resources

Natural Sciences

Near and Middle East Studies

Neurobiology

Nuclear Science

Nursing

American Legion Auxiliary Department of Oregon Nurses Scholarship 427

American Legion Auxiliary Department of Wisconsin Past Presidents' Parley Registered Nurse Scholarship 427

American Legion Auxiliary Department of Wyoming Past Presidents' Parley Health Care Scholarship 222

American Mobile Healthcare Annual Scholarship 428

American Nephrology Nurses' Association Career Mobility Scholarship 428

American Nephrology Nurses' Association NNCC Career Mobility Scholarship 428

American Nephrology Nurses' Association Watson Pharma Inc. Career Mobility Scholarship 429

Anna May Rolando Scholarship Award 430

Associate Degree Nursing Scholarship Program 434

Bernard and Carolyn Torraco Memorial Nursing Scholarship Program 442

Bernice Pickins Parsons Fund 380

Bertha P. Singer Nurses Scholarship 440

Breakthrough to Nursing Scholarships for Racial/Ethnic Minorities 432

Bruno Rolando Scholarship Award 431

BSN Student Scholarship/Work Repayment Program 437

Cambridge Home Health Care Nursing Excellence Scholarships 429

Canadian Nurses Foundation Scholarships 429

Career Mobility Scholarship 430

Carole J. Streeter, KB9JBR, Scholarship 222

Caroline Simpson Maheady Scholarship Award 431

Chesapeake Urology Associates Scholarship 334

Chester and Helen Luther Scholarship 338

Clark-Phelps Scholarship 224

C.R. Bard Foundation, Inc. Nursing Scholarship 435

Cynthia E. Morgan Memorial Scholarship Fund, Inc. 298

Deloras Jones RN Excellence in Bachelor's Degree Nursing Scholarship 435

Deloras Jones RN Nursing as a Second Career Scholarship 435

Deloras Jones RN Scholarship Program 435

Deloras Jones RN Underrepresented Groups in Nursing Scholarship 436

Developmental Disabilities Awareness Awards for High School Students who are Lutheran 333

Dr. Hilda Richards Scholarship 437

Dr. Lauranne Sams Scholarship 438

Edna Hicks Fund Scholarship 432

Edward J. and Virginia M. Routhier Nursing Scholarship 441

E. Eugene Waide, MD Memorial Scholarship 424

Eight and Forty Lung and Respiratory Nursing Scholarship Fund 428

Eleanora G. Wylie Scholarship 433

Elizabeth and Sherman Asche Memorial Scholarship Fund 91

Foundation of the National Student Nurses' Association Career Mobility Scholarship 432

Foundation of the National Student Nurses' Association General Scholarships 432

Foundation of the National Student Nurses' Association Specialty Scholarship 433

Frances L. Booth Medical Scholarship sponsored by LAVFW Department of Maine 336

Franks Foundation Scholarship 440

Franz Stenzel M.D. and Kathryn Stenzel Scholarship Fund 338

Gala Nursing Scholarships 433

Genevieve Saran Richmond Award 431

Good Samaritan Foundation Scholarship 433

Graduate and Professional Scholarship Program-Maryland 224

Gustavus B. Capito Fund 433

Health Careers Scholarship 223

Health Professions Education Foundation Bachelor of Science Nursing Scholarship Program 434

Health Professions Preparatory Scholarship Program 141

Helen Hall and John Seely Memorial Scholarship 338

Hobble (LPN) Nursing Scholarship 427

Indiana Health Care Policy Institute Nursing Scholarship 435

Indiana Nursing Scholarship Fund 441

Indian Health Service Health Professions Scholarship Program 208

Institute for Nursing Scholarship 439

Janel Parker Career Mobility Scholarship 429

Janet L. Hoffmann Loan Assistance Repayment Program 240

Jennet Colliflower Scholarship 430

Jewish Federation Academic Scholarship Program 120

Jill Laura Creedon Scholarship Award 431

June Gill Nursing Scholarship 439

Kaiser Permanente School of Anesthesia Scholarship 438

Kansas Nursing Service Scholarship Program 436

The Louis Stokes Health Scholars Program 144

Marion A. and Eva S. Peeples Scholarships 240

Marion A. Lindeman Scholarship 338

Marsha's Angels Scholarship Fund 436

Martha R. Dudley LVN/LPN Scholarship 438

Mary Marshall Practical Nursing Scholarship (LPN) 443

Mary Marshall Registered Nursing Scholarships 443

Mary Serra Gili Scholarship Award 431

Mary York Scholarship Fund 432

Mayo Foundations Scholarship 438

M.D. "Jack" Murphy Memorial Scholarship 427

Minority Nurse Magazine Scholarship Program 437

Mississippi Nurses' Association Foundation Scholarship 437

NADONA/LTC Stephanie Carroll Memorial Scholarship 437

NAHN Scholarships 437

Nancy Gerald Memorial Nursing Scholarship 424

National Society Daughters of the American Revolution Caroline E. Holt Nursing Scholarships 438

National Society Daughters of the American Revolution Madeline Pickett (Halbert) Cogswell Nursing Scholarship 438

National Society Daughters of the American Revolution Mildred Nutting Nursing Scholarship 439

NBNA Board of Directors Scholarship 438

Neuroscience Nursing Foundation Scholarship 425

New York State ENA September 11 Scholarship Fund 439

Nightingale Awards of Pennsylvania Nursing Scholarship 439

NLN Ella McKinney Scholarship Fund 440

Nursing Scholarship 430

Nursing Scholarship for High School Seniors 443

Nursing Spectrum Scholarship 438

Nursing Student Scholarship 436

Odd Fellows and Rebekahs Ellen F. Washburn Nurses Training Award 440

ONS Foundation Josh Gottheil Memorial Bone Marrow Transplant Career Development Awards 440

ONS Foundation/Oncology Nursing Certification Corporation Bachelor's Scholarships 440

ONS Foundation/Pearl Moore Career Development Awards 440

Overlook Hospital Foundation Professional Development Program 333

Pacific Health Workforce Award 327

Pacific Mental Health Work Force Award 327

Peter Gili Scholarship Award 431

Phoebe Pember Memorial Scholarship 442

Pilot International Foundation Ruby Newhall Memorial Scholarship 339

Pilot International Foundation Scholarship Program 339

Promise of Nursing Scholarship 433

Registered Nurse Education Loan Repayment Program 434

RN Education Scholarship Program 434

Ruth Finamore Scholarship Fund 432

Ruth Shaw Junior Board Scholarship 334

Society for the Scientific Study of Sexuality Student Research Grant 102

Society of Pediatric Nurses Educational Scholarship 178

Sonne Scholarship 434

StraightForward Media Medical Professions Scholarship 224

StraightForward Media Nursing School Scholarship 442

Tafford Uniforms Nursing Scholarship Program 442

Texas Professional Nursing Scholarships 442

Texas Vocational Nursing Scholarships 442

Touchmark Foundation Nursing Scholarship 442

Tuition Reduction for Non-Resident Nursing Students 436

Undine Sams and Friends Scholarship Fund 432

U.S. Army ROTC Four-Year Nursing Scholarship 430

U. S. Public Health Service-Health Resources and Services Administration, Bureau of Health Professions Scholarships for Disadvantaged Students 225

Vocational Nurse Scholarship Program 434

Walter C. and Marie C. Schmidt Scholarship 441

Walter Reed Smith Scholarship 160

Willard & Marjorie Scheibe Nursing Scholarship 441

William R. Goldfarb Memorial Scholarship 150

Wisconsin League for Nursing, Inc. Scholarship 443

WOCN Accredited Nursing Education Program Scholarship 444

Occupational Safety and Health

America Responds Memorial Scholarship 444

Applications International Corporation Scholarship 444

ASSE Construction Safety Scholarship 444

ASSED Foundation Military Service Scholarship 444

ASSE Diversity Committee Scholarship 444

ASSE-Gulf Coast Past Presidents Scholarship 445

ASSE-Marsh Risk Consulting Scholarship 445

ASSE-United Parcel Service Scholarship 445

BCSP Fred A. Manuele Professional Scholarship 445

BCSP Kevin Moorhead Technician/Technologist, Supervisory Scholarship 445

Bervin Hall Memorial Scholarship 445

Civic, Professional, Social, or Union Affiliation

AFL-CIO
AFL-CIO Council of Buffalo Scholarship WNY ALF Scholarship *516*
Bill Peterson Scholarship *525*
Martin Duffy Adult Learner Scholarship Award *525*
Minnesota AFL-CIO Scholarships *525*
PA AFL-CIO Unionism in America Essay Contest *532*
Project BEST Scholarship *534*
Ronald Lorah Memorial Scholarship *489*
Ted Bricker Scholarship *479*
Texas AFL-CIO Scholarship Program *538*
Union Plus Education Foundation Scholarship Program *540*

Airline Pilots Association
Airline Pilots Association Scholarship Program *502*

Alpha Mu Gamma
National Alpha Mu Gamma Scholarships *319*

American Academy of Physicians Assistants
Physician Assistant Foundation Annual Scholarship *338*

American Angus Association
Angus Foundation Scholarships *528*

American College of Musicians
American College of Musicians/National Guild of Piano Teachers $200 Scholarships *408*

American Congress on Surveying and Mapping
ACSM Fellows Scholarship *481*
ACSM Lowell H. and Dorothy Loving Undergraduate Scholarship *481*
American Association for Geodetic Surveying Joseph F. Dracup Scholarship Award *481*
Berntsen International Scholarship in Surveying *482*
Berntsen International Scholarship in Surveying Technology *482*
Cady McDonnell Memorial Scholarship *482*
National Society of Professional Surveyors Board of Governors Scholarship *482*
National Society of Professional Surveyors Scholarships *482*
Nettie Dracup Memorial Scholarship *482*
Schonstedt Scholarship in Surveying *483*
Tri-State Surveying and Photogrammetry Kris M. Kunze Memorial Scholarship *149*

American Criminal Justice Association
American Criminal Justice Association-Lambda Alpha Epsilon National Scholarship *211*

American Dental Assistants Association
Juliette A. Southard/Oral B Laboratories Scholarship *219*

American Dental Hygienist's Association
Colgate "Bright Smiles, Bright Futures" Minority Scholarship *220*

Crest Oral-B Laboratories Dental Hygiene Scholarship *220*
Sigma Phi Alpha Undergraduate Scholarship *221*
Wilma Motley California Merit Scholarship *221*

American Dietetic Association
American Dietetic Association Foundation Scholarship Program *312*

American Federation of State, County, and Municipal Employees
AFSCME: American Federation of State, County, and Municipal Employees Council # 75 Scholarship *531*
AFSCME: American Federation of State, County, and Municipal Employees Local 2067 Scholarship *531*
AFSCME/UNCF/Harvard University LWP Union Scholars Program *98*
American Federation of State, County, and Municipal Employees Scholarship Program *503*
Jerry Clark Memorial Scholarship *464*
Union Plus Credit Card Scholarship Program *503*

American Federation of Teachers
Robert G. Porter Scholars Program-American Federation of Teachers Dependents *503*

American Foreign Service Association
American Foreign Service Association (AFSA) Financial Aid Award Program *503*

American Health Information Management Association
AHIMA Foundation Student Merit Scholarship *340*

American Institute of Aeronautics and Astronautics
AIAA Foundation Undergraduate Scholarship *102*

American Legion or Auxiliary
Albert M. Lappin Scholarship *509*
American Essay Contest Scholarship *508*
American Legion Auxiliary Department of California Junior Scholarship *503*
American Legion Auxiliary Department of Colorado Past Presidents' Parley Nurses Scholarship *425*
American Legion Auxiliary Department of Connecticut Memorial Educational Grant *504*
American Legion Auxiliary Department of Connecticut Past Presidents' Parley Memorial Education Grant *504*
American Legion Auxiliary Department of Florida Memorial Scholarship *504*
American Legion Auxiliary Department of Iowa M.V. McCrae Memorial Nurses Merit Award *426*
American Legion Auxiliary Department of Minnesota Past Presidents' Parley Health Care Scholarship *329*

American Legion Auxiliary Department of Missouri Lela Murphy Scholarship *504*
American Legion Auxiliary Department of Missouri National President's Scholarship *505*
American Legion Auxiliary Department of Missouri Past Presidents' Parley Scholarship *426*
American Legion Auxiliary Department of Nebraska Ruby Paul Campaign Fund Scholarship *505*
American Legion Auxiliary Department of North Dakota Past Presidents' Parley Nurses Scholarship *426*
American Legion Auxiliary Department of Oregon Spirit of Youth Scholarship *505*
American Legion Auxiliary Department of South Dakota College Scholarships *505*
American Legion Auxiliary Department of South Dakota Senior Scholarship *505*
American Legion Auxiliary Department of South Dakota Thelma Foster Scholarship for Senior Auxiliary Members *505*
American Legion Auxiliary Department of South Dakota Thelma Foster Scholarships for Junior Auxiliary Members *506*
American Legion Auxiliary Department of South Dakota Vocational Scholarship *506*
American Legion Auxiliary Department of Utah National President's Scholarship *506*
American Legion Auxiliary Department of Wisconsin Della Van Deuren Memorial Scholarship *506*
American Legion Auxiliary Department of Wisconsin H.S. and Angeline Lewis Scholarships *506*
American Legion Auxiliary Department of Wisconsin Merit and Memorial Scholarships *507*
American Legion Auxiliary Department of Wisconsin Past Presidents' Parley Health Career Scholarships *507*
American Legion Auxiliary Department of Wisconsin Past Presidents' Parley Registered Nurse Scholarship *427*
American Legion Auxiliary Department of Wisconsin President's Scholarships *507*
American Legion Auxiliary Non-Traditional Students Scholarships *507*
American Legion Auxiliary Spirit of Youth Scholarships for Junior Members *507*
American Legion Department of Arkansas Coudret Scholarship Award *508*
American Legion Department of Idaho Scholarship *508*
American Legion Department of Illinois Scholarships *508*
American Legion Department of Minnesota Memorial Scholarship *510*
American Legion Department of New Jersey Scholarship *511*
American Legion Department of New York Press Association Scholarship *187*
American Legion Department of Washington Children and Youth Scholarships *512*

Corporate Affiliation

Employment/Volunteer Experience

Impairment

IMPAIRMENT

Military Service

American Legion Auxiliary Department of Idaho
Nursing Scholarship *425*

American Legion Auxiliary Department of Indiana
Edna M. Burcus/Hoosier Schoolhouse
Memorial Scholarship *591*

American Legion Auxiliary Department of Iowa
Children of Veterans Merit Award *591*

American Legion Auxiliary Department of Iowa
Harriet Hoffman Memorial Merit Award for
Teacher Training *232*

American Legion Auxiliary Department of Iowa
M.V. McCrae Memorial Nurses Merit
Award *426*

American Legion Auxiliary Department of
Kentucky Mary Barrett Marshall
Scholarship *592*

American Legion Auxiliary Department of Maine
Daniel E. Lambert Memorial
Scholarship *592*

American Legion Auxiliary Department of Maine
National President's Scholarship *550*

American Legion Auxiliary Department of Maine
Past Presidents' Parley Nurses
Scholarship *329*

American Legion Auxiliary Department of
Maryland Children and Youth
Scholarships *592*

American Legion Auxiliary Department of
Maryland Past Presidents' Parley Nurses
Scholarship *426*

American Legion Auxiliary Department of
Massachusetts Department President's
Scholarship *550*

American Legion Auxiliary Department of
Massachusetts Past Presidents' Parley
Scholarship *592*

American Legion Auxiliary Department of
Michigan Medical Career Scholarship *329*

American Legion Auxiliary Department of
Michigan Memorial Scholarship *592*

American Legion Auxiliary Department of
Michigan Scholarship for Non-Traditional
Student *593*

American Legion Auxiliary Department of
Minnesota Scholarships *593*

American Legion Auxiliary Department of
Missouri Lela Murphy Scholarship *504*

American Legion Auxiliary Department of
Missouri National President's
Scholarship *505*

American Legion Auxiliary Department of
Missouri Past Presidents' Parley
Scholarship *426*

American Legion Auxiliary Department of
Nebraska Ruby Paul Campaign Fund
Scholarship *505*

American Legion Auxiliary Department of North
Dakota National President's Scholarship *550*

American Legion Auxiliary Department of North
Dakota Past Presidents' Parley Nurses
Scholarship *426*

American Legion Auxiliary Department of Ohio
Continuing Education Fund *594*

American Legion Auxiliary Department of Ohio
Department President's Scholarship *594*

American Legion Auxiliary Department of Ohio
Past Presidents' Parley Nurses
Scholarship *427*

American Legion Auxiliary Department of Oregon
Department Grants *594*

American Legion Auxiliary Department of Oregon
National President's Scholarship *594*

American Legion Auxiliary Department of Oregon
Nurses Scholarship *427*

American Legion Auxiliary Department of Oregon
Spirit of Youth Scholarship *505*

American Legion Auxiliary Department of South
Dakota College Scholarships *505*

American Legion Auxiliary Department of South
Dakota Senior Scholarship *505*

American Legion Auxiliary Department of South
Dakota Thelma Foster Scholarship for Senior
Auxiliary Members *505*

American Legion Auxiliary Department of South
Dakota Thelma Foster Scholarships for Junior
Auxiliary Members *506*

American Legion Auxiliary Department of South
Dakota Vocational Scholarship *506*

American Legion Auxiliary Department of
Tennessee Vara Gray Scholarship-
General *594*

American Legion Auxiliary Department of Texas
General Education Scholarship *595*

American Legion Auxiliary Department of Texas
Past Presidents' Parley Medical
Scholarship *329*

American Legion Auxiliary Department of Utah
National President's Scholarship *506*

American Legion Auxiliary Department of
Wisconsin Della Van Deuren Memorial
Scholarship *506*

American Legion Auxiliary Department of
Wisconsin H.S. and Angeline Lewis
Scholarships *506*

American Legion Auxiliary Department of
Wisconsin Merit and Memorial
Scholarships *507*

American Legion Auxiliary Department of
Wisconsin Past Presidents' Parley Health
Career Scholarships *507*

American Legion Auxiliary Department of
Wisconsin Past Presidents' Parley Registered
Nurse Scholarship *427*

American Legion Auxiliary Department of
Wisconsin President's Scholarships *507*

American Legion Auxiliary National President's
Scholarship *593*

American Legion Auxiliary National President's
Scholarships *595*

American Legion Auxiliary Spirit of Youth
Scholarship *593*

American Legion Department of Arkansas Coudret
Scholarship Award *508*

American Legion Department of Idaho
Scholarship *508*

American Legion Department of Illinois
Scholarships *508*

American Legion Department of Maine Children
and Youth Scholarship *596*

American Legion Department of Maryland
General Scholarship Fund *596*

American Legion Department of Maryland Math-
Science Scholarship *396*

American Legion Department of Minnesota
Memorial Scholarship *510*

American Legion Department of New York Press
Association Scholarship *187*

American Legion Department of Washington
Children and Youth Scholarships *512*

American Legion Legacy Scholarship *597*

American Legion Press Club of New Jersey and
Post 170 Arthur Dehardt Memorial
Scholarship *187*

AMVETS National Ladies Auxiliary
Scholarship *515*

Armed Forces Communications and Electronics
Association General Emmett Paige
Scholarship *127*

Charles L. Bacon Memorial Scholarship *510*

Charles W. and Annette Hill Scholarship *509*

Child of Disabled Veteran Grant or Purple Heart
Recipient Grant *602*

Children of Deceased Veterans Scholarship-New
Mexico *605*

Daniel E. Lambert Memorial Scholarship *596*

Darlene Hooley for Oregon Veterans
Scholarship *607*

Department of Veterans Affairs Free Tuition for
Children of POW/MIA's in Vietnam *602*

DeVry/Keller Military Service Grant *600*

Disabled War Veterans Scholarship *128*

Disabled War Veterans Scholarship (Afghanistan
& Iraq) *598*

Educational Assistance for Certain War Veterans
Dependents Scholarship-South Carolina *608*

Educational Benefits for Children of Deceased
Veterans *553*

Edward T. Conroy Memorial Scholarship
Program *560*

Erman W. Taylor Memorial Scholarship *232*

Explosive Ordnance Disposal Memorial
Scholarship *554*

Foundation of the 1st Cavalry Division Association
Scholarship *600*

Frances L. Booth Medical Scholarship sponsored
by LAVFW Department of Maine *336*

Francis P. Matthews and John E. Swift Educational
Trust Scholarships *524*

Freedom Scholarship *600*

General John Ratay Educational Fund
Grants *603*

Guy M. Wilson Scholarships *596*

Hattie Tedrow Memorial Fund Scholarship *597*

Helping Heroes Grant *608*

Henry J. Reilly Memorial Scholarship-High
School Seniors and First Year Freshmen *535*

Henry J. Reilly Memorial Undergraduate
Scholarship Program for College
Attendees *535*

Hugh A. Smith Scholarship Fund *509*

Illinois AMVETS Ladies Auxiliary Memorial
Scholarship *600*

Illinois AMVETS Ladies Auxiliary Worchid
Scholarships *601*

Illinois AMVETS Service Foundation *601*

Illinois AMVETS Trade School Scholarship *601*

Illinois Veteran Grant Program-IVG *601*

James V. Day Scholarship *510*

Kansas Educational Benefits for Children of MIA,
POW, and Deceased Veterans of the Vietnam
War *602*

Kathern F. Gruber Scholarship *599*

Lillie Lois Ford Scholarship Fund *597*

Louisiana Department of Veterans Affairs State
Educational Aid Program *602*

LTG Douglas D. Buchholz Memorial
Scholarship *128*

Maria C. Jackson/General George A. White
Scholarship *607*

Massachusetts Public Service Grant
Program *560*

Maynard Jensen American Legion Memorial
Scholarship *511*

M.D. "Jack" Murphy Memorial Scholarship *427*

MIA/POW Scholarships *601*

Military Award Program (MAP) *581*

Military Dependent's Scholarship Program *598*

Military Education Scholarship *608*

Military Order of the Purple Heart
Scholarship *603*

Minnesota GI Bill Program *604*

Minnesota Legionnaires Insurance Trust
Scholarship *510*

Minnesota State Veterans' Dependents Assistance
Program *604*

MOAA American Patriot Scholarship *603*

Montgomery GI Bill (Active Duty) Chapter
30 *599*

Nationality or Ethnic Heritage

Religious Affiliation

Baptist

American Baptist Financial Aid Program Native
American Grants *615*

American Baptist Scholarships *650*

Texas Black Baptist Scholarship *639*

Woman's Missionary Union Scholarship
Program *653*

Christian

Foundation For College Christian Leaders
Scholarship *651*

Disciple of Christ

David Tamotsu Kagiwada Memorial
Scholarship *472*

Disciple Chaplains Scholarship *472*

Edwin G. and Lauretta M. Michael
Scholarship *472*

Katherine J. Shutze Memorial Scholarship *473*

Rowley/Ministerial Education Scholarship *473*

Eastern Orthodox

Eastern Orthodox Committee on Scouting
Scholarships *518*

Episcopalian

Stuart & Lucille Armstrong Scholarship *651*

Jewish

Broome and Allen Boys Camp and Scholarship
Fund *650*

Jewish Vocational Service Scholarship
Fund *627*

Lessans Family Scholarship *619*

Memorial Foundation for Jewish Culture,
Scholarships for Post-Rabbinical
Students *241*

Lutheran

Amelia Kemp Scholarship *650*

Belmer/Flora Prince Scholarship *653*

Developmental Disabilities Awareness Awards
for High School Students who are
Lutheran *333*

Developmental Disabilities Scholastic
Achievement Scholarship for College
Students who are Lutheran *222*

Methodist

Bishop Joseph B. Bethea Scholarship *623*

David W. Self Scholarship *653*

E. Craig Brandenburg Graduate Award *651*

Edith M. Allen Scholarship *237*

Ethnic Minority Scholarship *623*

HANA Scholarship *623*

Helen and Allen Brown Scholarship *651*

J. A. Knowles Memorial Scholarship *652*

Leonard M. Perryman Communications
Scholarship for Ethnic Minority
Students *197*

The Rev. Dr. Karen Layman Gift of Hope: 21st
Century Scholars Program *651*

Richard S. Smith Scholarship *641*

United Methodist Church Ethnic
Scholarship *640*

United Methodist Church Hispanic, Asian, and
Native American Scholarship *640*

Muslim Faith

Annual Award Program *650*

Presbyterian

National Presbyterian College Scholarship *652*

Racial Ethnic Scholarship *564*

Samuel Robinson Award *652*

Student Opportunity Scholarship *243*

Ullery Charitable Trust Fund *473*

Protestant

Ed E. and Gladys Hurley Foundation
Scholarship *473*

Henry Francis Barrows Scholarship *650*

Roman Catholic

Fourth Degree Pro Deo and Pro Patria
(Canada) *523*

Fourth Degree Pro Deo and Pro Patria
Scholarships *523*

Francis P. Matthews and John E. Swift
Educational Trust Scholarships *524*

Italian Catholic Federation First Year
Scholarship *523*

John W. McDevitt (Fourth Degree)
Scholarships *524*

Mae Lassley Osage Scholarship *637*

Percy J. Johnson Endowed Scholarships *524*

Unitarian Universalist

Children of Unitarian Universalist Ministers *652*

Joseph Sumner Smith Scholarship *652*

Marion Barr Stanfield Art Scholarship *123*

Pauly D'Orlando Memorial Art Scholarship *123*

Roy H. Pollack Scholarship *474*

Stanfield and D'Orlando Art Scholarship *123*

Residence

North Carolina Hispanic College Fund
Scholarship 633
North Carolina National Guard Tuition Assistance
Program 585
North Carolina Sheriffs' Association
Undergraduate Criminal Justice
Scholarships 212
North Carolina Veterans Scholarships Class I-
A 605
North Carolina Veterans Scholarships Class I-
B 606
North Carolina Veterans Scholarships Class
II 606
North Carolina Veterans Scholarships Class
III 606
North Carolina Veterans Scholarships Class
IV 606
Outdoor Hams Scholarship 668
Sidney B. Meadows Scholarship 351
Southeast American Society of Travel Agents
Chapter Scholarship 495
State Employees Association of North Carolina
(SEANC) Scholarships 726
Teacher Assistant Scholarship Fund 241
Ted G. Wilson Memorial Scholarship
Foundation 184
Training Support for Youth with Disabilities 576
University of North Carolina Need-Based
Grant 678, 714
Wachovia Technical Scholarship Program 488

North Dakota
Alert Scholarship 655
American Legion Auxiliary Department of North
Dakota National President's Scholarship 550
American Legion Auxiliary Department of North
Dakota Past Presidents' Parley Nurses
Scholarship 426
American Legion Auxiliary Department of North
Dakota Scholarships 657
American Legion Department of North Dakota
National High School Oratorical Contest 663
Burlington Northern Santa Fe Foundation
Scholarship 102
Carol Bauhs Benson Scholarship 220
Hattie Tedrow Memorial Fund Scholarship 597
Midwest Student Exchange Program 705
North Dakota Academic Scholarship 714
North Dakota Career and Technical Education
Scholarship 714
North Dakota Caring Citizen Scholarship 663
North Dakota Indian Scholarship Program 634
North Dakota Scholars Program 715
North Dakota State Student Incentive Grant
Program 715
O. Nesheim Memorial Scholarship 90
Printing Industry Midwest Education Foundation
Scholarship Fund 194
Rocky Mountain Coal Mining Institute
Scholarship 185
Rocky Mountain Coal Mining Institute Technical
Scholarship 489
South Dakota Board of Regents Bjugstad
Scholarship 89
Vincent L. Hawkinson Scholarship for Peace and
Justice 733
WICHE's Western Undergraduate Exchange
(WUE) 735
Young Artist Competition 455

Ohio
American Legion Auxiliary Department of Ohio
Continuing Education Fund 594
American Legion Auxiliary Department of Ohio
Department President's Scholarship 594

American Legion Auxiliary Department of Ohio
Past Presidents' Parley Nurses
Scholarship 427
Bill Schwartz Memorial Scholarship 353
Carol A. Ratza Memorial Scholarship 190
City of Cleveland: Mayor Jackson Scholarship for
Cleveland Metropolitan School District 642
City of Cleveland: Mayor Jackson Scholarship for
Historically Black Colleges and
Universities 642
College Now Greater Cleveland Adult Learner
Program Scholarship 678
David V. Stivison Appalachian Scholarship
Fund 681
Engineers Foundation of Ohio General Fund
Scholarship 264
Fraternal Order of Police Associates, State Lodge
of Ohio Inc., Scholarship Fund 554
Joseph Fitcher Scholarship Contest 94
Katharine M. Grosscup Scholarships in
Horticulture 348
Larry Fullerton Photojournalism
Scholarship 458
Legislative Scholarship 715
Les Best Scholarship 531
Lifelong Learning Scholarship 715
Linda Luca Memorial GED Scholarship 715
Lloyd A. Chacey, PE-Ohio Society of Professional
Engineers Memorial Scholarship 264
OAACE Member Scholarship 715
Ohio College Opportunity Grant 715
Ohio Forestry Association Memorial
Scholarship 418
Ohio National Guard Scholarship Program 585
Ohio Newspapers Foundation Minority
Scholarship 371
Ohio Newspapers Foundation University
Journalism Scholarship 371
Ohio Safety Officers College Memorial
Fund 716
Ohio War Orphans Scholarship 606
Project BEST Scholarship 534
Racial Ethnic Scholarship 564
Raymond H. Fuller, PE Memorial
Scholarship 264
T.E.A.C.H. Early Childhood OHIO
Scholarships 178
Thomas W. Porter, W8KYZ, Scholarship
Honoring Michael Daugherty, W8LSE 669
Virgil Thompson Memorial Scholarship
Contest 87
Western Reserve Herb Society Scholarship 349
William B. Howell Memorial Scholarship 263
William D. Squires Scholarship 736
Zachary Taylor Stevens Scholarship 669

Oklahoma
Burlington Northern Santa Fe Foundation
Scholarship 102
Fred R. McDaniel Memorial Scholarship 188
Future Teacher Scholarship-Oklahoma 242
ISNetworld Scholarship 447
Lone Star Community Scholarships 195
Oklahoma Alumni & Associates of FHA, HERO,
and FCCLA Inc. Scholarship 531
Oklahoma Governor's Luncheon
Scholarship 646
Oklahoma Quarter Horse Youth Scholarship 514
Oklahoma Tuition Aid Grant 716
Regional University Baccalaureate
Scholarship 716
Sidney B. Meadows Scholarship 351
Tom and Judith Comstock Scholarship 669
William P. Willis Scholarship 716

Oregon
AFSCME: American Federation of State, County,
and Municipal Employees Local 2067
Scholarship 531
Alert Scholarship 655
American Legion Auxiliary Department of Oregon
Department Grants 594
American Legion Auxiliary Department of Oregon
National President's Scholarship 594
American Legion Auxiliary Department of Oregon
Nurses Scholarship 427
American Legion Auxiliary Department of Oregon
Spirit of Youth Scholarship 505
American Legion Department of Oregon High
School Oratorical Contest 663
ANDEO Scholarship 717
ARRL Northwestern Division Scholarship
Fund 150
Asian Pacific Community Fund - Verizon
Scholarship Awards Program (High School
Seniors) 669
Asian Reporter Scholarship 617
A. Victor Rosenfeld Scholarship 547
Bandon Submarine Cable Council's Lenny
Montalbano Memorial Scholarship 717
Benjamin Franklin/Edith Green Scholarship 717
Ben Selling Scholarship 717
Bertha P. Singer Nurses Scholarship 440
Burlington Northern Santa Fe Foundation
Scholarship 102
Cady McDonnell Memorial Scholarship 482
Chapter 63-Portland James E. Morrow
Scholarship 290
Chapter 63-Portland Uncle Bud Smith
Scholarship 290
Chester and Helen Luther Scholarship 338
Clark-Phelps Scholarship 224
Congressman Peter DeFazio Scholarship 717
Dorothy Campbell Memorial Scholarship 718
Ernest Alan and Barbara Park Meyer Scholarship
Fund 716
Essex General Construction Scholarship 547
Ford Opportunity Program 688, 718
Ford ReStart Program 688
Ford Restart Program 718
Ford Scholars Program 688, 718
Franks Foundation Scholarship 440
Franz Stenzel M.D. and Kathryn Stenzel
Scholarship Fund 338
Friends of Bill Rutherford Education Fund 716
Glenn Jackson Scholars Scholarships 547
Grange Insurance Group Scholarship 689
Harriet A. Simmons Scholarship 242
Harry Ludwig Memorial Scholarship 577
Helen Hall and John Seely Memorial
Scholarship 338
Hispanic Metropolitan Chamber
Scholarships 625
Ida M. Crawford Scholarship 718
Jackson Foundation Journalism Scholarship 372
Jackson Foundation Journalism Scholarship
Fund 371
James Carlson Memorial Scholarship 242
Jerome B. Steinbach Scholarship 718
Konnie Memorial Dependents Scholarship 547
Maria C. Jackson/General George A. White
Scholarship 607
Mary E. Horstkotte Scholarship Fund 717
Mary Lou Brown Scholarship 668
Nettie Hanselman Jaynes Scholarship 242
NLN Ella McKinney Scholarship Fund 440
OAB Foundation Scholarship 193
OAIA Scholarship 78
Oregon Dungeness Crab Commission
Scholarship 718

Virginia

Washington

West Virginia

Wisconsin

Location of Study

RBC Dain Rauscher Colorado Scholarship
Fund *280*
Reisher Family Scholarship Fund *683*
Sales Professionals-USA Scholarship *159*
WICHE's Western Undergraduate Exchange
(WUE) *735*

Connecticut
Big Y Scholarships *670*
Capitol Scholarship Program *681*
Connecticut Aid to Public College Students
Grant *681*
Connecticut Army National Guard 100% Tuition
Waiver *588*
Connecticut Association of Latinos in Higher
Education Scholarships *621*
Connecticut Association of Women Police
Scholarship *211*
Connecticut Independent College Student
Grants *681*
Connecticut SPJ Bob Eddy Scholarship
Program *190*
CSCPA Candidate's Award *71*
Diana Donald Scholarship *502*
Dr. James L. Lawson Memorial Scholarship *188*
Federated Garden Clubs of Connecticut Inc.
Scholarships *144*
Korean-American Scholarship Foundation
Northeastern Region Scholarships *628*
Malcolm Baldrige Scholarship *152*
Massachusetts Assistance for Student Success
Program *704*
Minority Teacher Incentive Grant Program *236*
New England Employee Benefits Council
Scholarship Program *77*
New England Regional Student Program-Tuition
Break *709*
Roothbert Fund Inc. Scholarship *794*
Scholarship for Minority College Students *236*
Scholarship for Minority High School
Students *236*
Seol Bong Scholarship *577*
State of Maine Grant Program *686*

Delaware
Agenda For Delaware Women Trailblazer
Scholarship *553*
ASHRAE Region III Boggarm Setty
Scholarship *166*
Delaware Solid Waste Authority John P. "Pat"
Healy Scholarship *264*
Fresh Start Scholarship *736*
Governor's Workforce Development Grant *683*
Korean-American Scholarship Foundation Eastern
Region Scholarships *628*
National Association for Campus Activities East
Coast Undergraduate Scholarship for Student
Leaders *561*
Penelope Hanshaw Scholarship *226*
Roothbert Fund Inc. Scholarship *794*
Scholarship Incentive Program (ScIP) *683*
Seol Bong Scholarship *577*
State Tuition Assistance *582*
William Rucker Greenwood Scholarship *227*

District of Columbia
ASHRAE Region III Boggarm Setty
Scholarship *166*
Betty Endicott/NTA-NCCB Student
Scholarship *368*
Capitol Scholarship Program *681*
Greater Washington Society of CPAs
Scholarship *73*
Korean-American Scholarship Foundation Eastern
Region Scholarships *628*
Marilyn Yetso Memorial Scholarship *731*

Maryland SPJ Pro Chapter College
Scholarship *374*
Massachusetts Assistance for Student Success
Program *704*
National Association for Campus Activities East
Coast Undergraduate Scholarship for Student
Leaders *561*
Penelope Hanshaw Scholarship *226*
Roothbert Fund Inc. Scholarship *794*
Sigma Delta Chi Scholarships *373*
State of Maine Grant Program *686*
SWE Baltimore-Washington Section
Scholarship *175*
Thrysa Frazier Svager Scholarship *397*
Vera Yip Memorial Scholarship *579*
William Rucker Greenwood Scholarship *227*

Florida
Access to Better Learning and Education
Grant *686*
Adelante Fund Scholarships *613*
Agnes Naughton RN-BSN Fund *431*
American Cancer Society, Florida Division
R.O.C.K. College Scholarship Program *566*
American Legion Auxiliary Department of Florida
Department Scholarships *591*
American Legion Auxiliary Department of Florida
Memorial Scholarship *504*
Azurea at One Ocean Resort Hotel & Spa
Scholarship *215*
Bank of America Scholarship *160*
Casualty Actuaries of the Southeast Scholarship
Program *772*
Costas G. Lemonopoulos Scholarship *527*
David F. Ludovici Scholarship *182*
Dr. Felix H. Reyler (FIBA) Scholarship *152*
Earl I. Anderson Scholarship *251*
Edna Hicks Fund Scholarship *432*
Edward S. Roth Manufacturing Engineering
Scholarship *291*
Eric Primavera Memorial Scholarship *280*
FAME/Sandy Ulm Scholarship *383*
FECON Scholarship *182*
FEFPA Assistantship *110*
FICPA Educational Foundation Scholarships *73*
First Generation Matching Grant Program *687*
Florida Bright Futures Scholarship Program *687*
Florida Library Association-Associate's Degree
Scholarship *383*
Florida Library Association-Bachelor's Degree
Scholarship *384*
Florida Postsecondary Student Assistance
Grant *687*
Florida Private Student Assistance Grant *687*
Florida PTA/PTSA Fine Arts Scholarship *118*
Florida PTA/PTSA Vocational/Technical
Scholarship *686*
Florida Public Student Assistance Grant *687*
Florida Space Research Program *132*
Florida Student Assistance Grant-Career
Education *687*
Florida Work Experience Program *687*
Jennet Colliflower Scholarship *430*
Jose Marti Scholarship Challenge Grant
Fund *623*
Korean-American Scholarship Foundation
Southern Region Scholarships *628*
Mary McLeod Bethune Scholarship *687*
Mary York Scholarship Fund *432*
Money Run formerly 1040K Run/Walk
Scholarships *73*
National Association for Campus Activities
Southeast Region Student Leadership
Scholarship *561*
Promise of Nursing Scholarship *433*
Raymond W. Miller, PE Scholarship *280*

Richard B. Gassett, PE Scholarship *280*
Rosewood Family Scholarship Fund *777*
Ruth Finamore Scholarship Fund *432*
Scholarships for Children & Spouses of Deceased
or Disabled Veterans *600*
Ted G. Wilson Memorial Scholarship
Foundation *184*
Theodore R. and Vivian M. Johnson Scholarship
Program for Children of UPS Employees or
UPS Retirees *549*
Undine Sams and Friends Scholarship Fund *432*
William B. Howell Memorial Scholarship *263*
William L. Boyd IV Florida Resident Access
Grant *688*

Georgia
ASHRAE Region IV Benny Bootle
Scholarship *109*
Atlanta Press Club Journalism Scholarship
Program *365*
Bank of America Scholarship *160*
B. Phinizy Spalding, Hubert B. Owens, and The
National Society of the Colonial Dames of
America in the State of Georgia Academic
Scholarships *97*
Casualty Actuaries of the Southeast Scholarship
Program *772*
Charles Clarke Cordle Memorial
Scholarship *188*
Connie and Robert T. Gunter Scholarship *291*
GAE GFIE Scholarship for Aspiring
Teachers *237*
George and Pearl Strickland Scholarship *679*
Georgia HOPE Scholarship Program *689*
Georgia Press Educational Foundation
Scholarships *366*
Georgia Public Safety Memorial Grant *689*
Georgia Tuition Equalization Grant (GTEG) *570*
GGFOA Scholarship *73*
Julian and Jan Hester Memorial Scholarship *679*
Korean-American Scholarship Foundation
Southern Region Scholarships *628*
National Association for Campus Activities
Southeast Region Student Leadership
Scholarship *561*
Promise of Nursing Scholarship *433*
Southeast American Society of Travel Agents
Chapter Scholarship *495*
Ted G. Wilson Memorial Scholarship
Foundation *184*
Thrysa Frazier Svager Scholarship *397*

Hawaii
Associated Press Television/Radio Association-
Clete Roberts Journalism Scholarship
Awards *364*
Hawaii State Student Incentive Grant *693*
HSCPA Scholarship Program for Accounting
Students *74*
Kathryn Dettman Memorial Journalism
Scholarship *364*
Korean-American Scholarship Foundation
Western Region Scholarships *629*
National Association of Geoscience Teachers-Far
Western Section scholarship *228*
Native Hawaiian Visual Arts Scholarship *120*
Sarah Keli'ilolena Lum Konia Nakoa
Scholarship *321*
SWAAAE Academic Scholarships *127*
WICHE's Western Undergraduate Exchange
(WUE) *735*

Idaho
American Legion Department of Idaho
Scholarship *508*
ARC of Washington Trust Fund Stipend
Program *480*

The Chefs for Louisiana Cookery
Scholarship *216*
Korean-American Scholarship Foundation
Southern Region Scholarships *628*
Louisiana Department of Veterans Affairs State
Educational Aid Program *602*
Louisiana Memorial Scholarship *668*
Louisiana National Guard State Tuition Exemption
Program *584*
Markley Scholarship *161*
Rockefeller State Wildlife Scholarship *146*
Society of Louisiana CPAs Scholarships *79*
Southeast American Society of Travel Agents
Chapter Scholarship *495*
Taylor Opportunity Program for Students Honors
Level *700*
Taylor Opportunity Program for Students
Opportunity Level *700*
Taylor Opportunity Program for Students
Performance Level *700*
Taylor Opportunity Program for Students Tech
Level *701*

Maine

Dr. James L. Lawson Memorial Scholarship *188*
Early College for ME *701*
Korean-American Scholarship Foundation
Northeastern Region Scholarships *628*
Maine Legislative Memorial Scholarship *701*
Maine Metal Products Association
Scholarship *403*
Maine Metal Products Education Fund Scholarship
Program *132*
Maine School Food Service Association
Continuing Education Scholarship *218*
Maine Society of Professional Engineers Vernon
T. Swaine-Robert E. Chute Scholarship *266*
Maine State Society Foundation Scholarship *701*
Massachusetts Assistance for Student Success
Program *704*
New England Employee Benefits Council
Scholarship Program *77*
New England Regional Student Program-Tuition
Break *709*
Odd Fellows and Rebekahs Ellen F. Washburn
Nurses Training Award *440*
Seol Bong Scholarship *577*
State of Maine Grant Program *686*
Tuition Waiver Programs *554*
Veterans Dependents Educational Benefits-
Maine *602*

Maryland

ASHRAE Region III Boggarm Setty
Scholarship *166*
Betty Endicott/NTA-NCCB Student
Scholarship *368*
Carmen V. D'Anna Memorial Scholarship of the
Mars Supermarket Educational Fund *674*
Charles W. Riley Fire and Emergency Medical
Services Tuition Reimbursement
Program *311*
CollegeBound Foundation Last Dollar Grant *674*
Cynthia E. Morgan Memorial Scholarship Fund,
Inc. *298*
Decatur H. Miller Scholarship *343*
Delegate Scholarship Program-Maryland *702*
Distinguished Scholar Award-Maryland *702*
Distinguished Scholar Community College
Transfer Program *702*
Dr. Freeman A. Hrabowski, III Scholarship *279*
Edward T. Conroy Memorial Scholarship
Program *560*
George V. McGowan Scholarship *279*
Graduate and Professional Scholarship Program-
Maryland *224*

Howard P. Rawlings Educational Excellence
Awards Educational Assistance Grant *702*
Howard P. Rawlings Educational Excellence
Awards Guaranteed Access Grant *702*
Jane and Clarence Spilman Scholarship *675*
Janet L. Hoffmann Loan Assistance Repayment
Program *240*
J.F. Tolbert Memorial Student Grant
Program *702*
Joseph and Rebecca Meyerhoff Scholarship *675*
The Joyce A. Kroeller Memorial Scholarship *675*
Kenneth Hoffman Scholarship *676*
Korean-American Scholarship Foundation Eastern
Region Scholarships *628*
Marilyn Yetso Memorial Scholarship *731*
Maryland Association of Private Colleges and
Career Schools Scholarship *157*
Maryland SPJ Pro Chapter College
Scholarship *374*
NASA Maryland Space Grant Consortium
Undergraduate Scholarships *132*
National Association for Campus Activities East
Coast Undergraduate Scholarship for Student
Leaders *561*
Part-Time Grant Program-Maryland *703*
Penelope Hanshaw Scholarship *226*
The Richard E. Dunne, III Scholarship *677*
The Robert Spar Memorial Scholarship *343*
Roothbert Fund Inc. Scholarship *794*
SAE Baltimore Section Bill Brubaker
Scholarship *288*
Scarborough-Scheeler Scholarship *677*
Senatorial Scholarships-Maryland *703*
Sigma Delta Chi Scholarships *373*
Student Scholarship in Accounting MD
Association of CPAs *75*
SWE Baltimore-Washington Section
Scholarship *175*
Tuition Reduction for Non-Resident Nursing
Students *436*
Tuition Waiver for Foster Care Recipients *703*
Vera Yip Memorial Scholarship *579*
Veterans of the Afghanistan and Iraq Conflicts
Scholarship Program *603*
William Rucker Greenwood Scholarship *227*
Workforce Shortage Student Assistance Grant
Program *703*

Massachusetts

Agnes M. Lindsay Scholarship *703*
American Legion Auxiliary Department of
Massachusetts Department President's
Scholarship *550*
American Legion Auxiliary Department of
Massachusetts Past Presidents' Parley
Scholarship *592*
Big Y Scholarships *670*
Capitol Scholarship Program *681*
Dr. James L. Lawson Memorial Scholarship *188*
Edward S. Roth Manufacturing Engineering
Scholarship *291*
John and Abigail Adams Scholarship *704*
Korean-American Scholarship Foundation
Northeastern Region Scholarships *628*
Massachusetts AFL-CIO Scholarship *703*
Massachusetts Assistance for Student Success
Program *704*
Massachusetts Gilbert Matching Student Grant
Program *704*
Massachusetts Public Service Grant
Program *560*
New England Employee Benefits Council
Scholarship Program *77*
New England Regional Student Program-Tuition
Break *709*
Paul Tsongas Scholarship Program *704*

Paychex Inc. Entrepreneur Scholarship *72*
Promise of Nursing Scholarship *433*
Roothbert Fund Inc. Scholarship *794*
Seol Bong Scholarship *577*
State of Maine Grant Program *686*

Michigan

American Legion Auxiliary Department of
Michigan Medical Career Scholarship *329*
American Legion Auxiliary Department of
Michigan Memorial Scholarship *592*
American Legion Auxiliary Department of
Michigan Scholarship for Non-Traditional
Student *593*
Carol A. Ratza Memorial Scholarship *190*
Chapter 198-Downriver Detroit Scholarship *290*
Chapter 31-Tri City Scholarship *290*
Chick Evans Caddie Scholarship *565*
Detroit Chapter One-Founding Chapter
Scholarship *291*
Earl I. Anderson Scholarship *251*
Fifth/Graduate Year Student Scholarship *75*
Guy M. Wilson Scholarships *596*
Indiana Health Care Policy Institute Nursing
Scholarship *435*
Michigan Competitive Scholarship *705*
Michigan Society of Professional Engineers Harry
R. Ball, P.E. Grant *169*
Michigan Society of Professional Engineers
Kenneth B. Fishbeck, P.E. Memorial
Grant *169*
Michigan Tuition Grant *705*
Midwest Student Exchange Program *705*
Minnesota Reciprocal Agreement *705*
National Association for Campus Activities
Wisconsin Region Student Leadership
Scholarship *561*
National Defense Transportation Association,
Scott Air Force Base-St. Louis Area Chapter
Scholarship *708*
North Central Region 9 Scholarship *292*
Nursing Student Scholarship *436*
Promise of Nursing Scholarship *433*
SWE Region H Scholarships *176*
Tess Caldarelli Memorial Scholarship *755*
Thelma Orr Memorial Scholarship *328*
Tuition Incentive Program *705*
Warner Norcross and Judd LLP Scholarship for
Minority Students *380*
William B. Howell Memorial Scholarship *263*
WXYZ-TV Broadcasting Scholarship *498*
Zagunis Student Leaders Scholarship *755*

Minnesota

American Legion Auxiliary Department of
Minnesota Past Presidents' Parley Health Care
Scholarship *329*
American Legion Auxiliary Department of
Minnesota Scholarships *593*
American Legion Department of Minnesota
Memorial Scholarship *510*
Bill Peterson Scholarship *525*
Carol A. Ratza Memorial Scholarship *190*
Chick Evans Caddie Scholarship *565*
Edward S. Roth Manufacturing Engineering
Scholarship *291*
Martin Duffy Adult Learner Scholarship
Award *525*
Midwest Student Exchange Program *705*
Minnesota Academic Excellence
Scholarship *120*
Minnesota AFL-CIO Scholarships *525*
Minnesota GI Bill Program *604*
Minnesota Indian Scholarship *631*
Minnesota Legionnaires Insurance Trust
Scholarship *510*

Talent/Interest Area

Amateur Radio

Albert H. Hix, W8AH, Memorial Scholarship 667

Alfred E. Friend Jr., W4CF, Memorial Scholarship 166

Allen and Bertha Watson Memorial Scholarship 276

Androscoggin Amateur Radio Club Scholarship 200

ARRL Northwestern Division Scholarship Fund 150

ARRL Rocky Mountain Division Scholarship 667

ARRL Scholarship To Honor Barry Goldwater, K7UGA 743

Betty Weatherford, KQ6RE, Memorial Scholarship 251

Bill, W2ONV, and Ann Salerno Memorial Scholarship 743

Byron Blanchard, N1EKV, Memorial Scholarship Fund 667

Carole J. Streeter, KB9JBR, Scholarship 222

Central Arizona DX Association Scholarship 667

Challenge Met Scholarship 567

Charles Clarke Cordle Memorial Scholarship 188

Charles N. Fisher Memorial Scholarship 103

Chicago FM Club Scholarship Fund 667

David Knaus Memorial Scholarship 668

Dayton Amateur Radio Association Scholarships 744

Dr. James L. Lawson Memorial Scholarship 188

Don Riebhoff Memorial Scholarship 362

Earl I. Anderson Scholarship 251

Edmond A. Metzger Scholarship 251

Eugene "Gene" Sallee, W4YFR, Memorial Scholarship 188

Francis Walton Memorial Scholarship 91

Fred R. McDaniel Memorial Scholarship 188

Gary Wagner, K3OMI, Scholarship 166

General Fund Scholarships 744

Gwinnett Amateur Radio Society Scholarship 668

Henry Broughton, K2AE, Memorial Scholarship 263

Indianapolis Amateur Radio Association Scholarship Fund 200

IRARC Memorial, Joseph P. Rubino, WA4MMD, Scholarship 252

Irving W. Cook, WA0CGS, Scholarship 189

Jackson County ARA Scholarship 668

K2TEO Martin J. Green Sr. Memorial Scholarship 744

L.B. Cebik, W4RNL, and Jean Cebik, N4TZP, Memorial Scholarship 744

Louisiana Memorial Scholarship 668

L. Phil and Alice J. Wicker Scholarship 189

Magnolia DX Association Scholarship 189

Mary Lou Brown Scholarship 668

Mississippi Scholarship 103

New England FEMARA Scholarships 668

Norman E. Strohmeier, W2VRS, Memorial Scholarship 668

North Fulton Amateur Radio League Scholarship Fund 200

Outdoor Hams Scholarship 668

Outdoor Writers Association of America - Bodie McDowell Scholarship Award 193

Paul and Helen L. Grauer Scholarship 103

Peoria Area Amateur Radio Club Scholarship 668

PHD Scholarship 201

Ray, N0RP, & Katie, W0KTE, Pautz Scholarship 201

Richard W. Bendicksen, N7ZL, Memorial Scholarship 744

Scholarship of the Morris Radio Club of New Jersey 744

Six Meter Club of Chicago Scholarship 669

Southeastern DX Club Scholarship Fund 201

Ted, W4VHF, and Itice, K4LVV, Goldthorpe Scholarship 744

Thomas W. Porter, W8KYZ, Scholarship Honoring Michael Daugherty, W8LSE 669

Tom and Judith Comstock Scholarship 669

Victor Poor, W5SMM, Memorial Scholarship Fund 252

William Bennett, W7PHO, Memorial Scholarship 669

William R. Goldfarb Memorial Scholarship 150

Yankee Clipper Contest Club Inc. Youth Scholarship 669

YASME Foundation Scholarship 143

You've Got a Friend in Pennsylvania Scholarship 515

Zachary Taylor Stevens Scholarship 669

Animal/Agricultural Competition

American Morgan Horse Institute Educational Scholarships 741

American Morgan Horse Institute Grand Prix Dressage Award 742

American Morgan Horse Institute Graywood Youth Horsemanship Grant 742

American Morgan Horse Institute van Schaik Dressage Scholarship 742

Appaloosa Youth Educational Scholarships 515

AQHF Journalism or Communications Scholarship 188

Curt Greene Memorial Scholarship 555

Dr. Gerald O'Connor Michigan QHY Scholarship 513

Pony of the Americas Scholarship 533

Swayze Woodruff Memorial Mid-South Scholarship 514

Texas 4-H Opportunity Scholarship 729

Art

AIA New Jersey Scholarship Program 109

Artistic Encouragement Grant 571

Elizabeth Greenshields Award/Grant 118

Emerging Texas Artist Scholarship 122

Federal Junior Duck Stamp Conservation and Design Competition 123

General Federation of Women's Clubs of Massachusetts Pennies For Art Scholarship 119

International Art Show for Artists with Disabilities 577

John F. and Anna Lee Stacey Scholarship Fund 120

Knights of Pythias Poster Contest 753

Library Research Grants 116

Lois McMillen Memorial Scholarship Fund 118

L. Ron Hubbard's Illustrators of the Future Contest 745

Minnesota Academic Excellence Scholarship 120

MJSA Education Foundation Jewelry Scholarship 122

Native Hawaiian Visual Arts Scholarship 120

NSS Educational Scholarships 121

Outdoor Writers Association of America - Bodie McDowell Scholarship Award 193

P. Buckley Moss Endowed Scholarship 121

Poster Contest for High School Students 746

Scholastic Art and Writing Awards-Art Section 117

Student Research Scholarship 340

Video Contest for College Students 746

Visual and Performing Arts Achievement Awards 119

WJA Scholarship Program 124

Young American Creative Patriotic Art Awards Program 753

YoungArts, National Foundation for Advancement in the Arts 765

Asian Language

1B USD Worldwide Venture Capital 107

Athletics/Sports

American Legion Baseball Scholarship 739

American Legion Baseball Scholarship-Nebraska American Legion Baseball Player of the Year 662

American Legion Department of Iowa Outstanding Senior Baseball Player 660

American Legion Department of Nebraska Jim Hurlbert Memorial Baseball Scholarship 662

Babe Ruth Scholarship Program 745

Badminton Scholarship Program 762

Charles S. Noble Junior A Hockey Scholarships 614

Charles S. Noble Junior Football Scholarships 614

Dixie Boys Baseball Bernie Varnadore Scholarship Program 684

Dixie Youth Scholarship Program 684

Dr. Click Cowger Baseball Scholarship 660

Dr. Roberto F. Cunanan Memorial Scholarship 723

Earl and Countess of Wessex-World Championships in Athletics Scholarships 614

East Bay Football Officials Association College Scholarship 684

Gene and John Athletic Fund Scholarship 760

Graco Excellence Scholarship 546

Hartford Whalers Booster Club Scholarship 692

Hy Zolet Student Athlete Scholarship 675

Jimmie Condon Athletic Scholarships 614

National Amateur Baseball Federation Scholarship Fund 755

Nebraska Sports Council/Gallup Organization Cornhusker State Games Scholarship Program 709

LGBT Issues

Music

Music/Singing